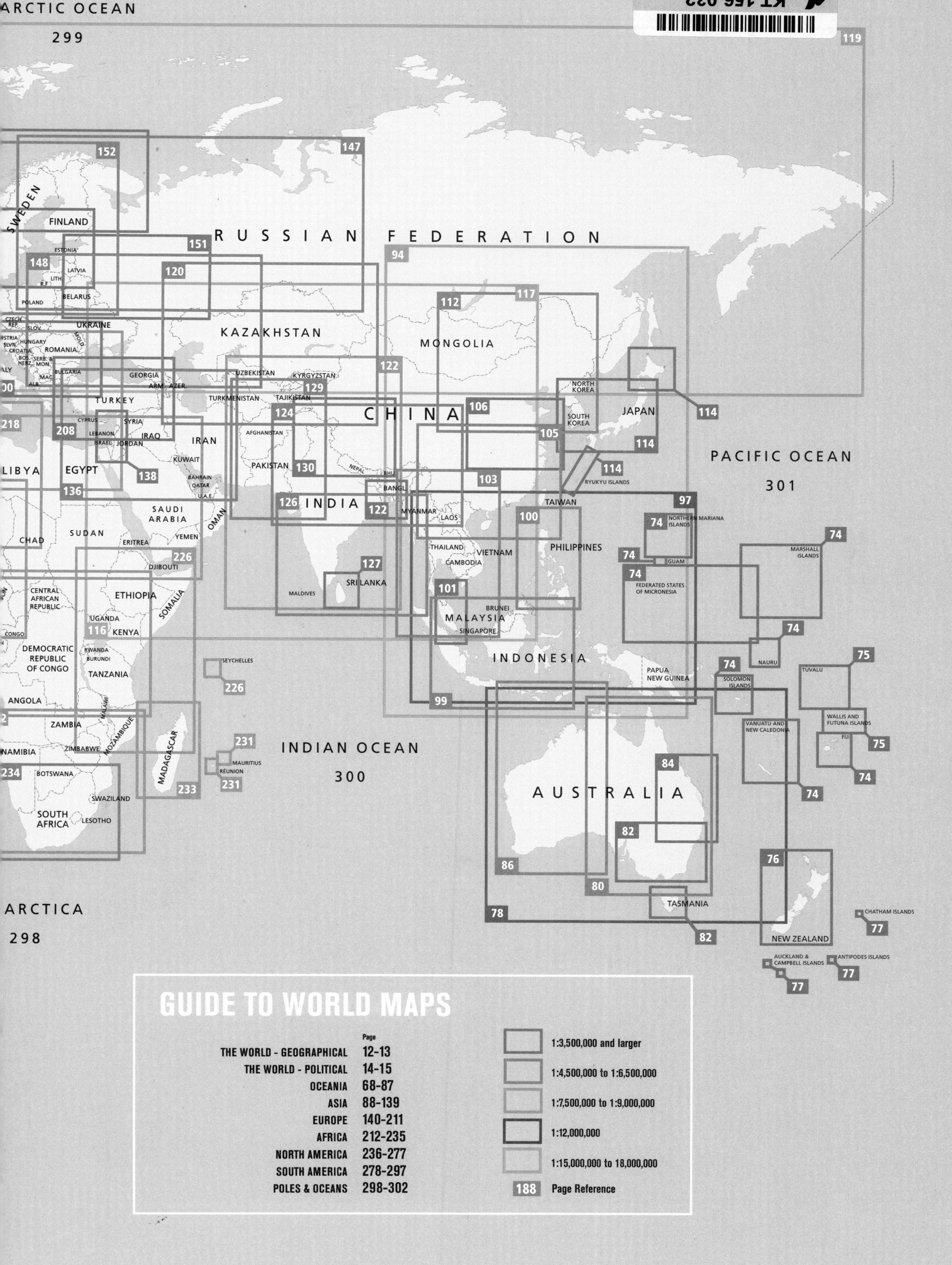

ARCTIC OCEAN
299

119

SWEDEN
FINLAND
152
147
ESTONIA
148
LATVIA
151
120
LITH
R.F.
BELARUS
POLAND
CZECH
REP.
SLOV.
AUSTRIA
HUNGARY
SLVN.
UKRAINE
CROATIA
ROMANIA
BOS. SERB. &
HERZ. MON.
MOLD
RUSSIAN FEDERATION
94
KAZAKHSTAN
ALB.
MAC
BULGARIA
112
117
MONGOLIA
GEORGIA
122
218
208
TURKEY
ARM. AZER.
UZBEKISTAN
KYRGYZSTAN
129
NORTH
KOREA
JAPAN
114
CYPRUS
SYRIA
TURKMENISTAN
TAJIKISTAN
124
CHINA
106
SOUTH
KOREA
LEBANON
105
114
ISRAEL
JORDAN
IRAQ
IRAN
AFGHANISTAN
114
PACIFIC OCEAN
LIBYA
EGYPT
KUWAIT
138
BAHRAIN
PAKISTAN
130
NEPAL
BHU
103
RYUKYU ISLANDS
301
136
QATAR
U.A.E.
BANGL
TAIWAN
97
SAUDI
ARABIA
126
INDIA
122
MYANMAR
100
74
NORTHERN MARIANA
ISLANDS
CHAD
SUDAN
OMAN
LAOS
PHILIPPINES
74
MARSHALL
ISLANDS
74
YEMEN
THAILAND
VIETNAM
74
GUAM
ERITREA
226
CAMBODIA
127
FEDERATED STATES
OF MICRONESIA
DJIBOUTI
MALDIVES
SRI LANKA
101
CENTRAL
AFRICAN
REPUBLIC
ETHIOPIA
SOMALIA
BRUNEI
74
UGANDA
MALAYSIA
NAURU
CONGO
116
KENYA
SINGAPORE
74
75
RWANDA
BURUNDI
DEMOCRATIC
REPUBLIC
OF CONGO
TANZANIA
INDONESIA
74
TUVALU
SEYCHELLES
PAPUA
NEW GUINEA
SOLOMON
ISLANDS
ANGOLA
226
99
WALLIS AND
FUTUNA ISLANDS
2
ZAMBIA
VANUATU AND
NEW CALEDONIA
75
FIJI
NAMIBIA
ZIMBABWE
MADAGASCAR
231
INDIAN OCEAN
74
MAURITIUS
234
BOTSWANA
233
RÉUNION
231
300
84
AUSTRALIA
74
SWAZILAND
82
SOUTH
AFRICA
LESOTHO
86
76
80
82
ARCTICA
78
TASMANIA
CHATHAM ISLANDS
77
298
82
NEW ZEALAND
AUCKLAND &
CAMPBELL ISLANDS
ANTIPODES ISLANDS
77
77

	1:3,500,000 and larger
	1:4,500,000 to 1:6,500,000
	1:7,500,000 to 1:9,000,000
	1:12,000,000
	1:15,000,000 to 18,000,000
188	Page Reference

BRAZIL Settlement and
the need for agricultural
land has entirely cleared
the north bank of the river
of its rain forest. The other
bank remains intact.

READER'S
DIGEST
WORLD
ATLAS

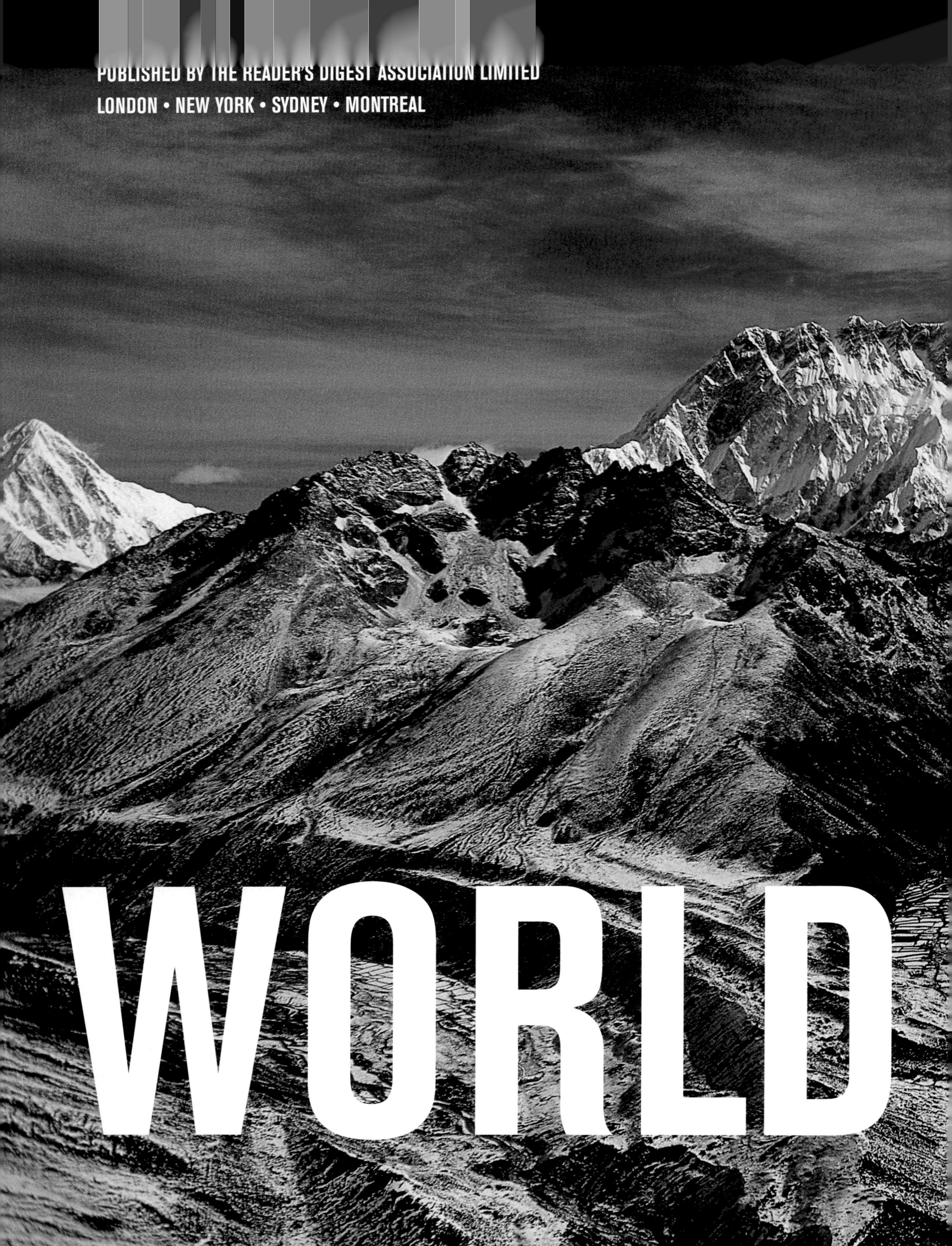

PUBLISHED BY THE READER'S DIGEST ASSOCIATION LIMITED

LONDON • NEW YORK • SYDNEY • MONTREAL

WORLD

MOUNT EVEREST Named 'she whose head touches the sky' by the Nepalese, the world's tallest mountain is still growing at a rate of 4mm (1/16 in) a year.

READER'S DIGEST
ATLAS

INTRODUCTION

An atlas is a picture of the world at a moment in its history. The populations of towns and cities, the course of a river, the shape of a lake or coastline and the boundaries indicating the relationships between nations all reflect that point in time, and events and processes both recent and historic.

In this book you will take a journey from the farthest reaches of space, through the creation of the Earth and its landscape and oceans, to experience the diversity of life on every continent. You will explore how humans live in the world, from the cities we create to how we work, consume the world's resources and communicate with one another. A startling set of statistics illuminates the similarities and differences between members of the global community.

At the heart of the atlas are 200 pages of entirely new mapping, which take you from an overview of the whole world, through portraits of the continents to a detailed picture of all the world's countries and regions. The maps have been designed to do full justice to the sheer variety of the Earth's landscape, with detailed terrain modelling and colouring. They also show how humans have moulded the land for their own needs, built towns and cities, and the highways, roads and railways that link them.

All the information in the maps can be simply reached through a detailed Index-Gazetteer, with more than 80,000 places named and referenced, and brief statistical profiles of all the world's countries.

This is the latest and best in a distinguished line of Reader's Digest World Atlases. We hope you enjoy the book for many years to come.

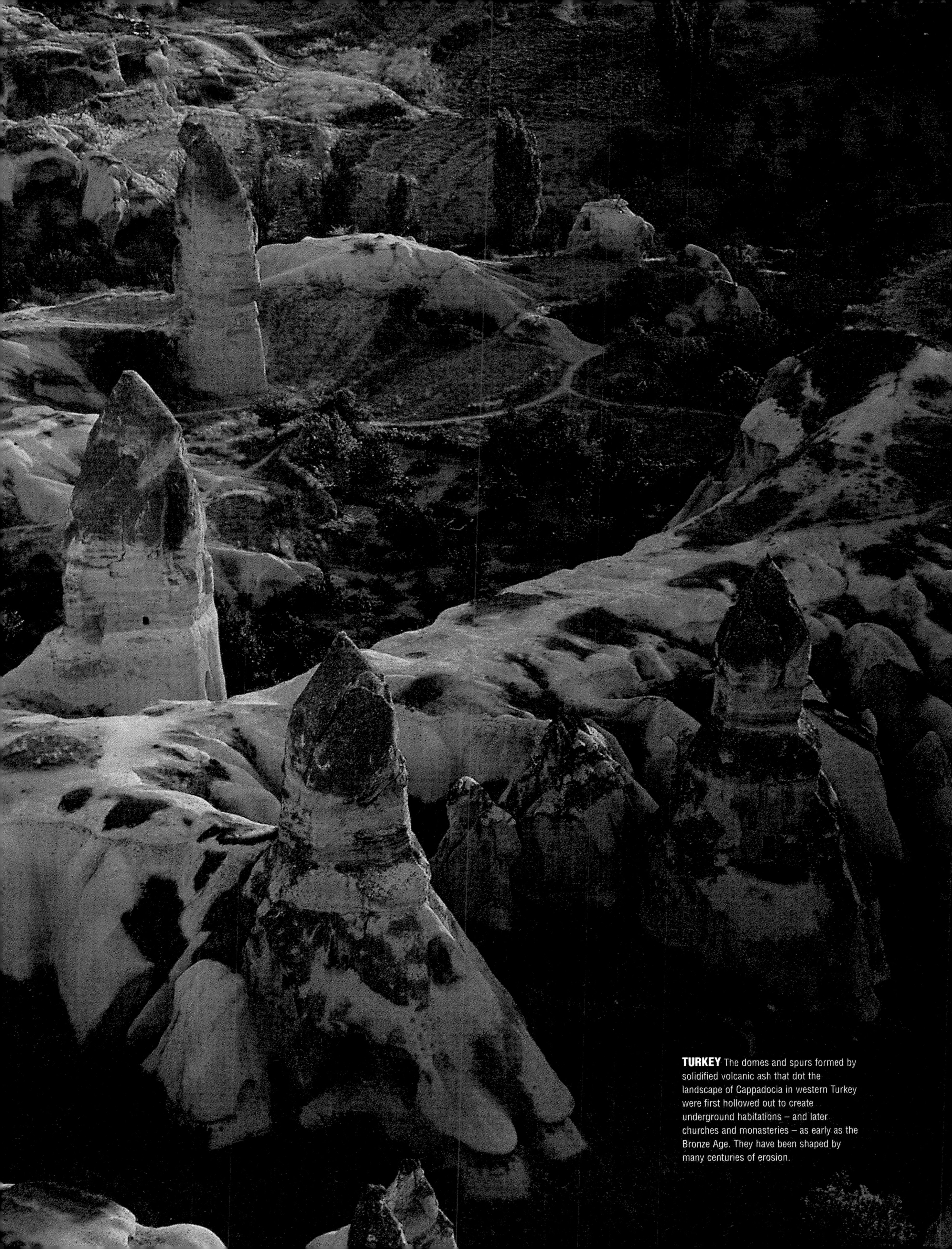

TURKEY The domes and spurs formed by
solidified volcanic ash that dot the
landscape of Cappadocia in western Turkey
were first hollowed out to create
underground habitations – and later
churches and monasteries – as early as the
Bronze Age. They have been shaped by
many centuries of erosion.

CONTENTS

QUICKFIND MAP LOCATORS

ASIA
pages 88–139

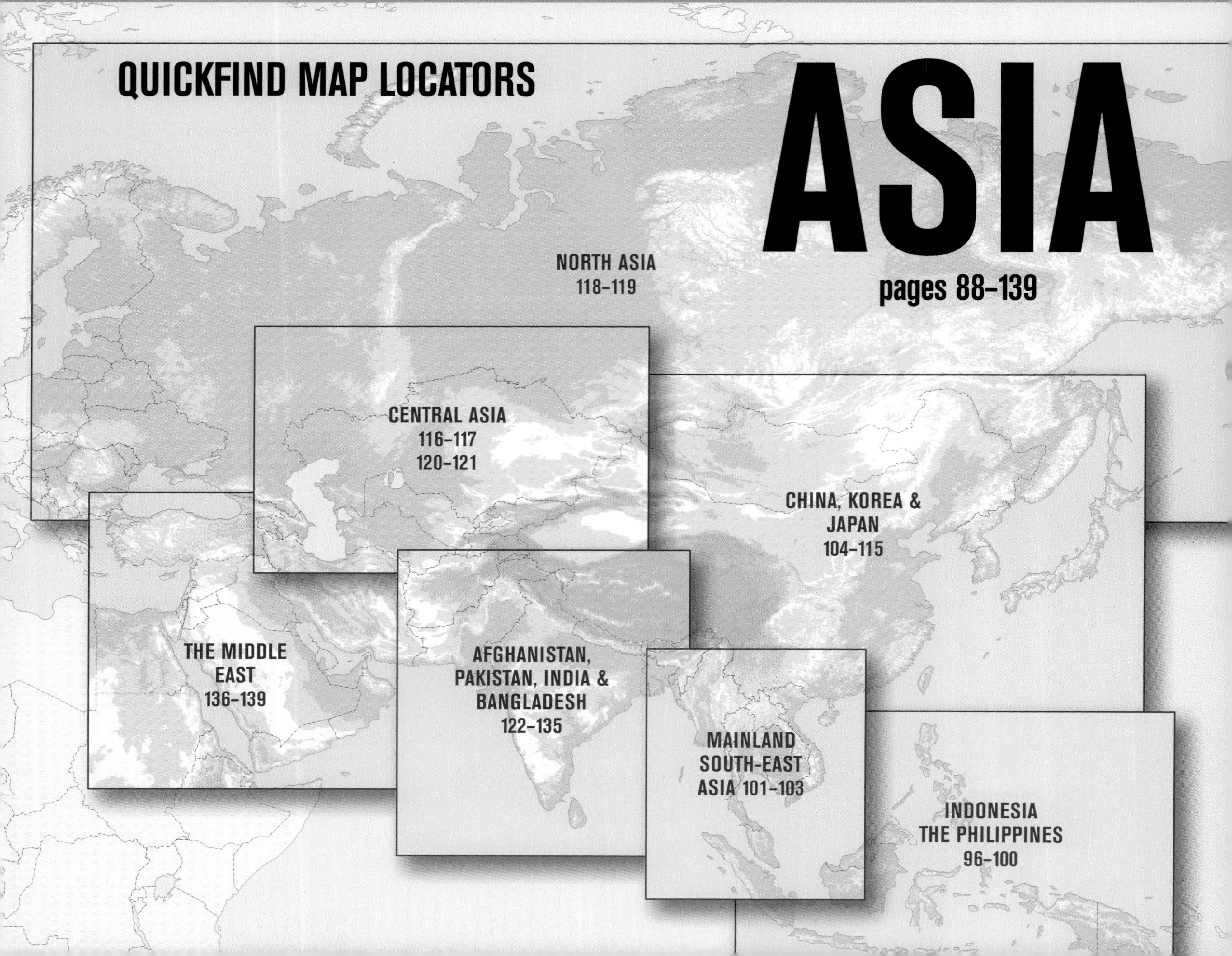

NORTH ASIA
118–119

CENTRAL ASIA
116–117
120–121

CHINA, KOREA &
JAPAN
104–115

THE MIDDLE
EAST
136–139

AFGHANISTAN,
PAKISTAN, INDIA &
BANGLADESH
122–135

MAINLAND
SOUTH-EAST
ASIA 101–103

INDONESIA
THE PHILIPPINES
96–100

AUSTRALASIA & OCEANIA pages 68–87

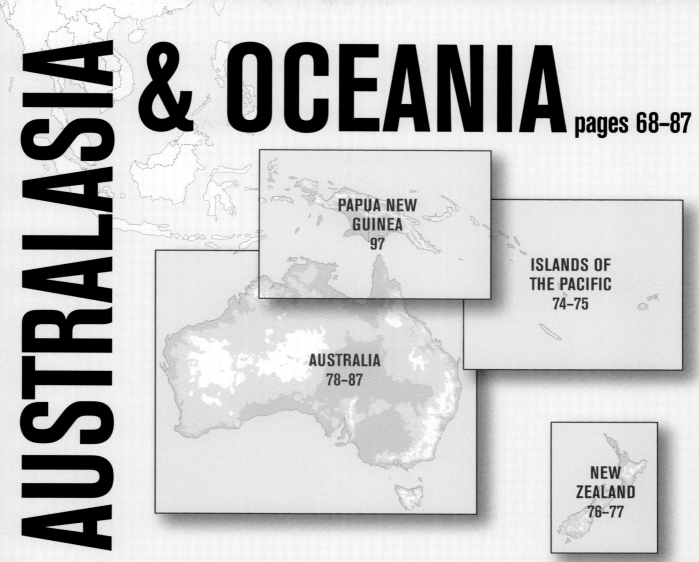

EUROPE pages 140–211

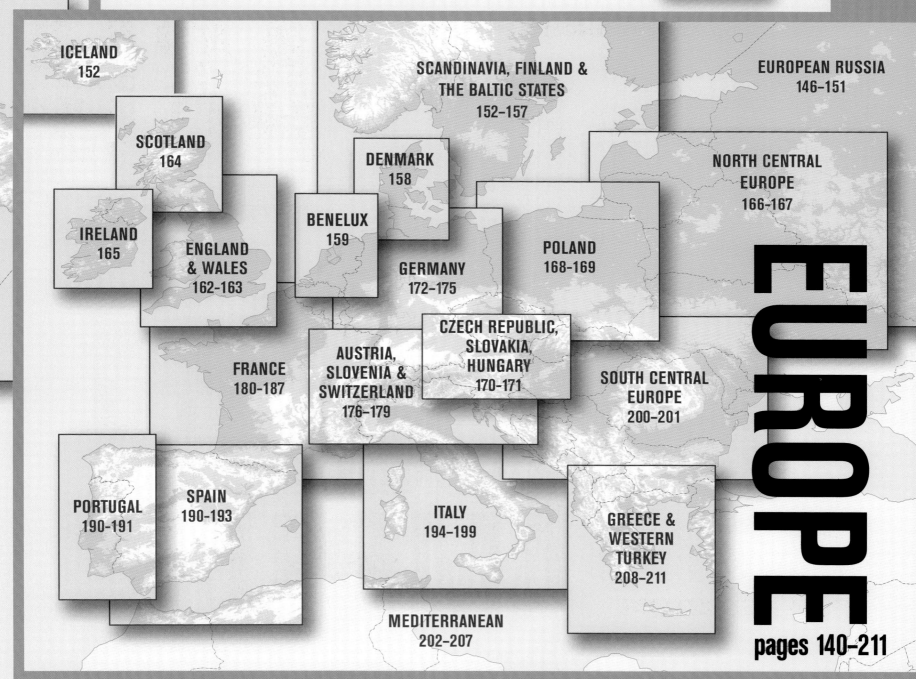

ALASKA & THE YUKON
246–247

CENTRAL CANADA
242–243
246–251

UNITED STATES
244–245
246, 254–265

MEXICO
244–245
272–275

CENTRAL
AMERICA
276–277

NORTHERN
SOUTH
AMERICA
284–285

WESTERN
SOUTH AMERICA
292–293

BRAZIL
284–291

SOUTHERN
SOUTH AMERICA
294–297

SOUTH AMERICA

pages 278–297

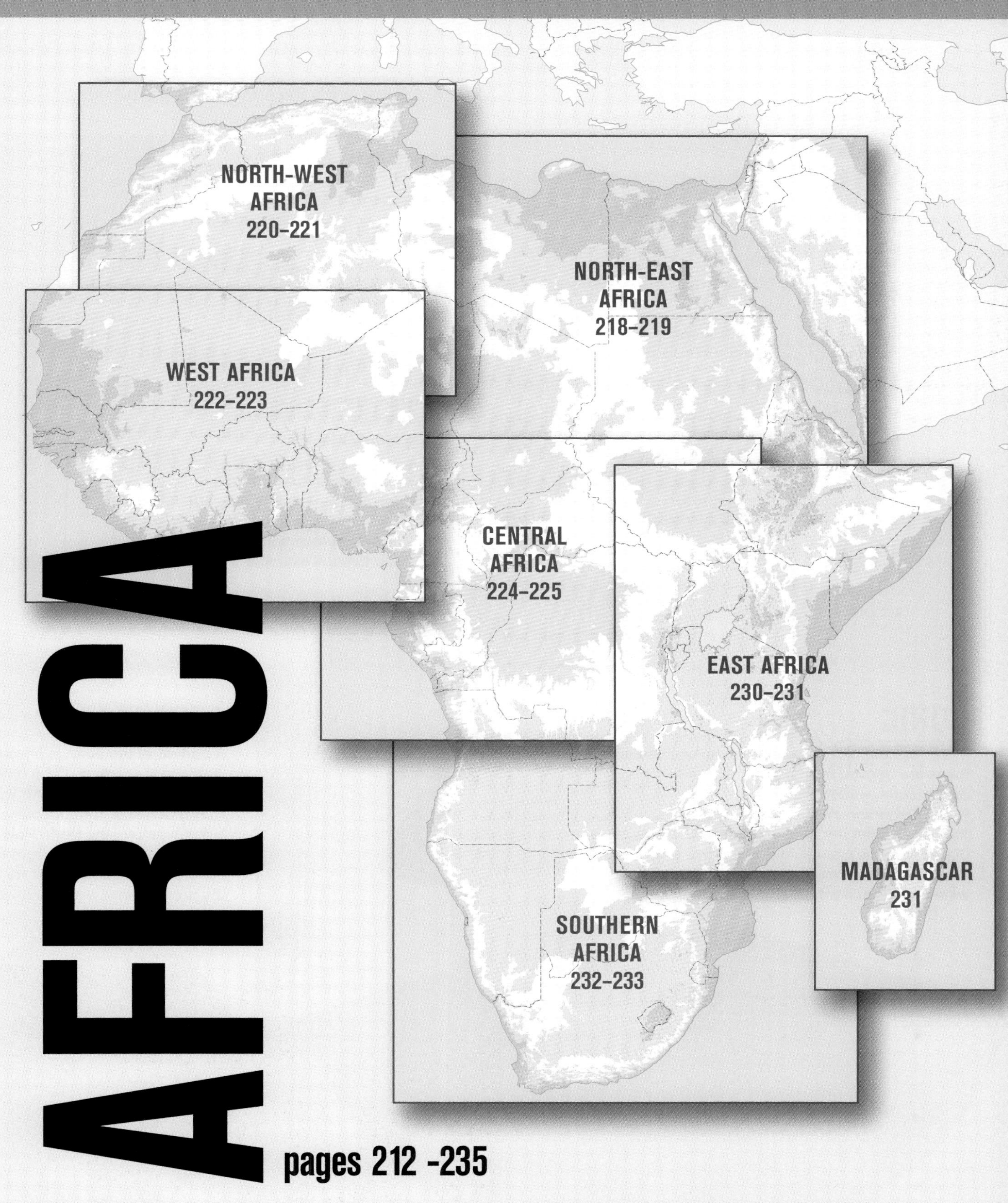

NORTH & CENTRAL AMERICA pages 236–277

AFRICA
pages 212 –235

POLES & OCEANS pages 298–302

MAKING MAPS

For over 4000 years cartographers have tried to find ways of representing the shape, terrain and features of our three-dimensional planet on a flat plane. In doing so, they have made use of increasingly sophisticated surveys of the land surface, and have exploited successive innovations in technology, from theodolites to computers, laser beams and satellites. Maps are devised to give an objective picture of reality; cartographers must assess the purpose and function of the map and select, generalize and categorize information accordingly.

What is a projection?

A projection is the representation of the spherical surface of the Earth on a flat surface. Parallel circles – lines of latitude – are drawn around the Earth to express distances north or south from the Equator. Lines of longitude run north-south through the poles to express east-west distances.

Why is there more than one?

Since the Earth is a globe, all flat maps involve distortion of its true geometry. So cartographers must select a projection that will minimize distortion of the main features on a map. Conformal projections, which seek to preserve true angles and shapes, are ideal for topographical maps. Azimuthal projections retain relative sizes of land masses more accurately, so are better for maps showing political or economic data.

CYLINDRICAL

The sphere of the Earth is 'unwrapped' onto a surrounding cylinder, which is 'rolled out' to form a flat map. All the compass directions are shown as straight lines. Places of similar latitudes appear at the same height. Distortion is greatest around the Poles. Cylindrical projections are often used for world maps and for almost all navigational charts. The Mercator projection of 1569 is a famous example.

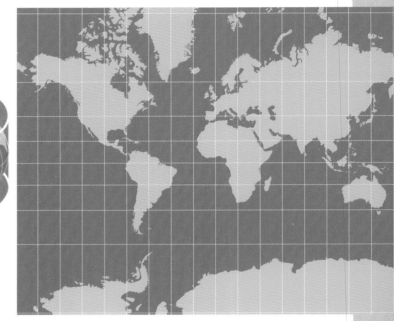

Mercator projection

CONIC

In this system, developed by the Ancient Greeks, maps are derived from a projection of the globe onto a cone, with its point above one of the Poles. Distortion increases between the parallels that are nearest the tip of the cone, so this type of projection is most suited to the mapping of mid-latitude regions that are larger from east to west than from north to south, such as Canada.

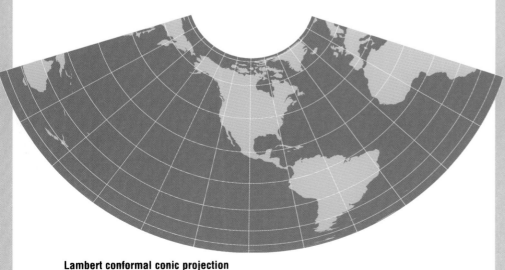

Lambert conformal conic projection

AZIMUTHAL

A portion of the Earth is shown as a flattened disc, placed at a tangent to the globe, with latitude and longitude lines extending from the point of tangency – for example, the North Pole. As distortion increases with distance from this point, these projections are best for maps of the polar regions and whole continents.

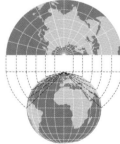

Azimuthal equal area projections

Making relief maps

The representation of relief on maps has challenged cartographers for centuries. Hachuring – fine parallel or crossed lines – gave a good idea of relief, but not of height. Contour lines, first used in the 19th century, represented height well, but not relief. Today, computers can produce accurate, life-like images of the landscape, as in the fold-out maps of this atlas. Data on the elevation of the Earth's surface – collected by satellite – is used to create a framework, on which hypsometric bands of colour (see Mountains and colour scales, right) are applied. Contours are then suitably enhanced and highlighted with simulated 'sunlight'.

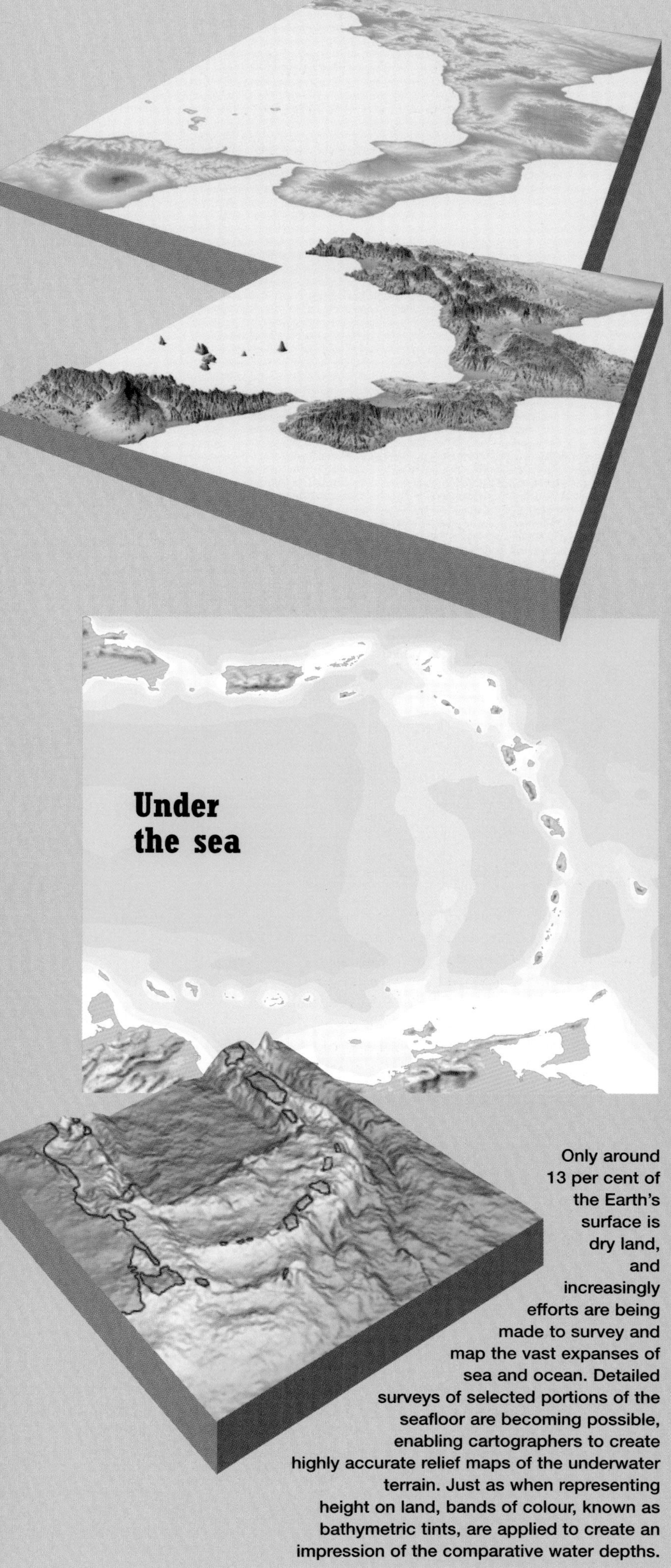

Under the sea

Only around 13 per cent of the Earth's surface is dry land, and increasingly efforts are being made to survey and map the vast expanses of sea and ocean. Detailed surveys of selected portions of the seafloor are becoming possible, enabling cartographers to create highly accurate relief maps of the underwater terrain. Just as when representing height on land, bands of colour, known as bathymetric tints, are applied to create an impression of the comparative water depths.

The Reader's Digest World Atlas was made using digital cartography combined with hand-rendered hill-shading. Map data, including land heights, place names, roads, rivers and borders, was gathered to create a huge database for the whole world. Detail was then extracted from this to create individual maps, with the underlying relief drawn in by hand.

Hill-shading

The topography or 'lie of the land' is represented using hand-rendered shading, working from detailed aerial photographs and satellite data. It creates a base on which the land height colour (see below) is then 'draped' to create a realistic impression of how the landscape actually appears.

Mountains and colour

scales Heights of surface features above sea level are determined by trigonometric surveys, by measuring differences in atmospheric pressure and using three-dimensional satellite or inertial systems. On maps, the height of land is shown by a scale, in which different colours – hypsometric tints – are used to represent various elevation ranges.

Rivers, roads, borders

Rivers, transport infrastructure and enclosed areas, such as countries and administrative districts, are shown using lines. While rivers are invariably depicted by blue lines, roads, railways, canals and air routes are indicated by a wide range of line conventions and colours. The weight of a line and prominence of its colour indicate the comparative importance of terrain divisions.

Names and symbols

All possible places and features are labelled to maximize the usefulness of the map. The size and weight of the typography used for place names represents their importance. Some names must be omitted to avoid overcrowding and poor legibility. Symbols are widely used to denote specific places, such as airports. Although many have become standardized, it is customary to clarify all symbols in a key accompanying the map.

At least 20 layers of data are integrated to create the finished map (bottom right)

165°W 150° 135° 120° 105° 90° 75° 60° 45° 30° 15°W 0°

ARCTIC OCEAN

Queen Elizabeth Islands

Ellesmere Island

Greenland Sea

Greenland

Banks Island

Baffin Bay

Jan Mayen

75°N

Wrangel Island

Chukchi Sea

Beaufort Sea

Victoria Island

Gulf of Boothia

Baffin Island

Denmark Strait

Norwegian Sea

Arctic Circle

Brooks Range

Great Bear Lake

Foxe Basin

Davis Strait

Cape Chidley

Iceland

Faroe Islands

Shetland Islands

Yukon

Mt. McKinley 6194

Mackenzie Mountains

Great Slave Lake

Hudson Strait

Cape Farewell

60°

Bering Sea

Mt Logan 5959

Gulf of Alaska

Peace

Reindeer Lake

Hudson Bay

Peninsula d'Ungava

Labrador

Labrador Sea

North Se

Aleutian Range

Queen Charlotte Islands

N. Saskatchewan

Nelson

Newfoundland

British Isles

Bering Strait

Coast Mountains

Lake Athabasca

NORTH

Canadian Shield

English Channel

45°

Aleutian Islands

Vancouver Island

Fraser

Rocky Mountains

AMERICA

Lake Winnipeg

Lake Nipigon

Lake Superior

St Lawrence

Gulf of St Lawrence

Nova Scotia

Bay of Biscay

Cape Finisterre

Massif Central

NORTH

Columbia

Snake

Great Plains

Lake Michigan

Lake Huron

Lake Ontario

Lake Erie

Cape Cod

ATLANTIC

Azores

Iberian Peninsula

Pyrenees

NORTH

Great Salt Lake

Coast Ranges

Colorado

Missouri

Ohio

Appalachian Mountains

Cape Hatteras

OCEAN

Cabo de São Vicente

Strait of Gibraltar

Jbel Toubkal 4165

Atlas Mountains

PACIFIC

30°

Sierra Nevada

Edwards Plateau

Mississippi

Coastal Plain

Bermuda

Madeira

Canary Islands

Grand Erg Occidental

Erg Chech

S a

Hogg

Tropic of Cancer

Rio Grande

Gulf of Mexico

Sargasso Sea

OCEAN

Midway Islands

Baja California

Sierra Madre Occidental

Bahía de Campeche

West Indies

Greater Antilles

Cape Verde Islands

S a h

15°N

Hawaiian Islands

Yucatán

Sierra Madre del Sur

Caribbean Sea

Lesser Antilles

Cap Vert

Senegal

Niger

International Date Line

Lake Nicaragua

Cap Palmas

Lake Volta

Gulf of Guine

Île Clipperton

Llanos

Orinoco

Guiana Highlands

Fouta Djallon

0°

Equator

Islas Galápagos

Andes

Negro

Amazon

Xingu

Fernando de Noronha

Cabo de São Roque

Ascension

Phoenix Islands

Ucayali

Amazon Rain Forest

Madeira

São Francisco

International Date Line

Polynesia

Îles Marquises

SOUTH

15°S

Vanua Levu

Cook Islands

Lake Titicaca

Planalto do Mato Grosso

AMERICA

Brazilian Highlands

St Helena

Niue

Tahiti

Ilha da Trindade

Ilhas Martin Vas

SOUTH

Viti Levu

Gran Chaco

Serra do Mar

Tropic of Capricorn

Rarotonga

Paraná

ATLANTIC

30°

Pitcairn Island

Isla Sala y Gómez

Isla San Ambrosio

Cerro Aconcagua 6960

Colorado

Pampas

Río de la Plata

OCEAN

Tristan da Cunha

Isla de Pascua (Easter Island)

Archipiélago Juan Fernández

Bahía Blanca

Gough Island

North Island

Bahía Grande

Golfo de San Jorge

New Zealand

Patagonia

Falkland Islands

South Georgia

45°

Chatham Islands

SOUTH

Peninsula Valdés

PACIFIC

Bahía Grande

Tierra del Fuego

Cabo de Hornos (Cape Horn)

South Sandwich Islands

Bouvet Island

OCEAN

Drake Passage

60°

International Date Line

South Shetland Islands

South Orkney Islands

Antarctic Circle

Antarctic Peninsula

Bellingshausen Sea

A N T A R

75°S

Amundsen Sea

Weddell Sea

Queen Mau

Marie Byrd Land

Ellsworth Land

Ross Sea

180° 165°W 150° 135° 120° 105° 90° 75° 60° 45° 30° 15°W 0°

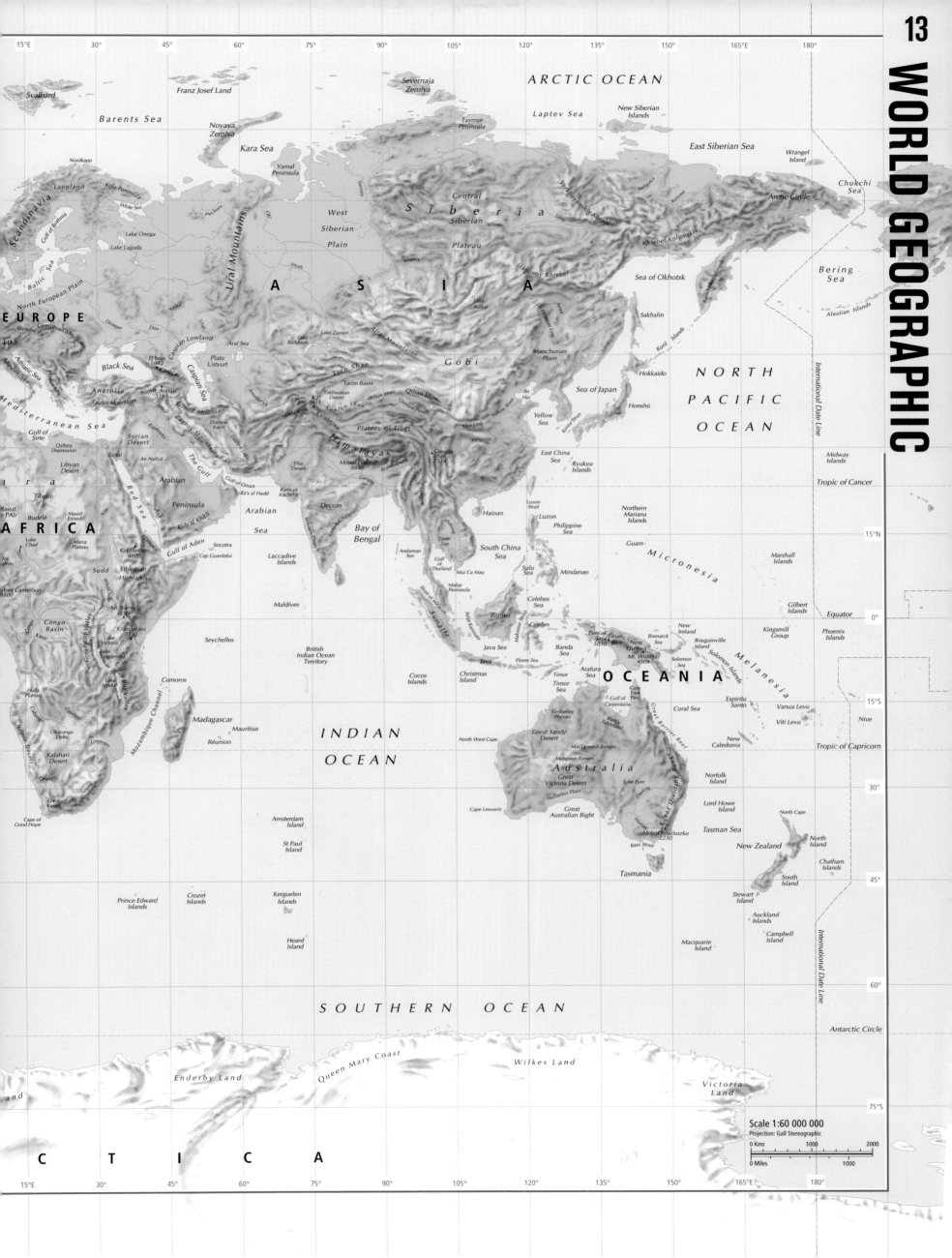

15°E   30°   45°   60°   75°   90°   105°   120°   135°   150°   165°E   180°

ARCTIC OCEAN

Svalbard

Franz Josef Land

Severnaja Zemlya

New Siberian Islands

Barents Sea

Laptev Sea

East Siberian Sea

Wrangel Island

Novaya Zemlya

Taymyr Peninsula

Arctic Circle

Chukchi Sea

Nordkapp

Kara Sea

Lappland

Yamal Peninsula

Kola Peninsula

White Sea

Pechora

West Siberian Plain

Central Siberian Plateau

S i b e r i a

Verkhoyanskiy Khrebet

Indigirka

Kolyma

Khrebet Kolymskiy

Bering Sea

Scandinavia

Gulf of Bothnia

Lake Onega

Ob'

Yenisey

Vilyuy

Lena

Sea of Okhotsk

Aleutian Islands

Lake Lagoda

Ural Mountains

Irtysh

A S I A

Angara

Lake Baikal

Stanovoy Khrebet

Amur

Sakhalin

Baltic Sea

North European Plain

EUROPE

Volga

Don

Caspian Lowland

Aral Sea

Lake Balkhash

Lake Zaysan

Altai Mountains

Gobi

Manchurian Plain

Bo Hai

Hokkaido

NORTH PACIFIC OCEAN

Carpathian Mountains

Dnieper

Caspian Sea

Plato Ustyurt

Amudar'ya

Tien Shan

Tarim Basin

Kunlun Shan

Altun Shan

Qilian Shan

Qaidam Pendi

Yellow River

Sea of Japan

Honshū

Black Sea

El'brus 5642

Caucasus

Taklimakan Desert

K2 8611

Hindu Kush

Karakorum

Plateau of Tibet

Qin Ling

Yellow Sea

Korea Strait

International Date Line

Alps

Anatolia

Mt. Ararat 5165

Elburz Mountains

Dashte Kavir

Pamir

Yangtze

East China Sea

Ryukyu Islands

Midway Islands

Apennines

Adriatic Sea

Pindus Mts.

Taurus Mountains

Zagros Mountains

Dasht-e Lut

H i m a l a y a s

Mount Everest 8848

Brahmaputra

Gongga Shan 7514

Tropic of Cancer

Mediterranean Sea

Syrian Desert

Euphrates

Tigris

Indus

Ganges

Irrawaddy

Salween

Hainan

Luzon Strait

Northern Mariana Islands

Gulf of Sirte

Qattara Depression

Sinai

The Gulf

Gulf of Oman

Ra's al Hadd

Thar Desert

Rann of Kachchh

Deccan

Luzon

Philippine Sea

Guam

Marshall Islands

15°N

Libyan Desert

An Nafūd

Arabian Peninsula

Mekong

South China Sea

Micronesia

Sahara

Tibesti

Red Sea

Arabian Sea

Tonle Sap

Mui Ca Mau

Gilbert Islands

Equator

Massif du l'Aïr

Bodélé

Gulf of Aden

Socotra

Cap Guardafui

Laccadive Islands

Andaman Sea

Gulf of Thailand

Sulu Sea

Mindanao

AFRICA

Massif de l'Ennedi

Marra Plateau

Ras Dashen 4620

Malay Peninsula

Celebes Sea

Kingsmill Group

Phoenix Islands

Lake Chad

Sudd

Ethiopian Highlands

Maldives

Borneo

Celebes

Mont Cameroun 4100

Mt. Kenya

White Nile

Seychelles

British Indian Ocean Territory

Sumatra

Strait of Malacca

Java Sea

Banda Sea

New Ireland

Bougainville Island

Solomon Islands

Congo

Kasai

Great Rift Valley

Lake Victoria

Kilimanjaro 5892

Makassar Strait

Puncak Jaya 5030

I-rian Jaya

New Guinea

Mt. Wilhelm 4509

Bismarck Sea

Solomon Sea

Melanesia

Congo Basin

Lake Tanganyika

Java

Flores Sea

Arafura Sea

OCEANIA

Espiritu Santo

Vanua Levu

Huíla Plateau

Lake Nyasa

Comoros

Cocos Islands

Christmas Island

Timor

Timor Sea

Cape York Pen.

Gulf of Carpentaria

Coral Sea

Niue

Viti Levu

15°S

Cubango

Zambezi

Mozambique Channel

Madagascar

Mauritius

Réunion

INDIAN OCEAN

North West Cape

Kimberley Plateau

Barkly Tableland

Great Barrier Reef

New Caledonia

Limpopo

Great Sandy Desert

MacDonnell Ranges

Norfolk Island

Tropic of Capricorn

Namib Desert

Okavango Delta

Kalahari Desert

Musgrave Ranges

A u s t r a l i a

Lake Eyre

Darling

Great Dividing Range

Lord Howe Island

North Cape

30°

Orange

Great Victoria Desert

Nullarbor Plain

Great Australian Bight

Murray

Mount Kosciuszko 2230

Tasman Sea

New Zealand

North Island

Great Karoo

Cape Leeuwin

Bass Strait

Chatham Islands

Cape of Good Hope

Amsterdam Island

Tasmania

South Island

Prince Edward Islands

Crozet Islands

Kerguelen Islands

St Paul Island

Stewart Island

45°

Auckland Islands

Heard Island

Campbell Island

Macquarie Island

60°

International Date Line

SOUTHERN OCEAN

Antarctic Circle

ANTARCTICA

Enderby Land

Queen Mary Coast

Wilkes Land

Victoria Land

75°S

Scale 1:60 000 000
Projection: Gall Stereographic

0 Kms   1000   2000

0 Miles   1000

15°E   30°   45°   60°   75°   90°   105°   120°   135°   150°   165°E   180°

ARCTIC OCEAN

Ellesmere Island

Greenland Sea

Queen Elizabeth Islands

GREENLAND
(Denmark)

Beaufort Sea

Baffin Bay

Jan Mayen (Norway)

75°N

Victoria Island

Denmark Strait

Norwegian Sea

RUSSIAN FEDERATION

Arctic Circle

ALASKA
(U.S.A.)

Baffin Island

ICELAND

Reykjavik

Faroe Islands (Denmark)

Yukon

Mackenzie

Nuuk

Davis Strait

Bering Sea

60°

Anchorage

Great Bear Lake

North Sea

Juneau

CANADA

Glasgow

UNITED KINGDOM

Gulf of Alaska

Rocky Mountains

Great Slave Lake

Hudson Bay

Dublin

REPUBLIC OF IRELAND

London

Vancouver

NORTH

Newfoundland

St Lawrence

Paris

FRANC

Aleutian Islands

NORTH PACIFIC OCEAN

Seattle

Portland

AMERICA

Lake Winnipeg

Minneapolis

Lake Superior

Lake Michigan

Ottawa

Toronto

St Pierre et Miquelon (France)

St John's

Lake Huron

Boston

NORTH

Barcelona

AND.

45°

San Francisco

Denver

Chicago

Detroit

Lake Ontario

New York

Azores (Portugal)

PORTUGAL

Madrid

Lake Erie

ATLANTIC

Lisbon

SPAIN

UNITED STATES

St Louis

Philadelphia

Washington D.C.

GIBRALTAR (U.K.)

Los Angeles

OF AMERICA

Appalachian Mountains

Casablanca

Rabat

Algie

30°

Tropic of Cancer

San Diego

Phoenix

Dallas

Atlanta

OCEAN

Madeira (Portugal)

MOROCCO

Midway Islands (U.S.A.)

El Paso

Rio Grande

Bermuda (U.K.)

Canary Islands (Spain)

ALGERI

Houston

Mississippi

WESTERN SAHARA

Sa

Hawaiian Islands (U.S.A.)

MEXICO

Monterrey

Gulf of Mexico

Miami

THE BAHAMAS

Nouakchott

MAURITANIA

MALI

15°N

Guadalajara

México City

Havana

CUBA

Caribbean Sea

DOMINICAN REP.

Santo Domingo

CAPE VERDE

Dakar

SENEGAL

Ouagadougou

Niame

GUATEMALA

BELIZE

JAMAICA

HAITI

Kingston

Port-

ANTIGUA AND BARBUDA

Puerto Rico (U.S.A.)

Guadeloupe (France)

THE GAMBIA

Bamako

BURKINA

Île Clipperton (France)

Guatemala

HONDURAS

Tegucigalpa

au-Prince

DOMINICA

Martinique (France)

GUINEA-BISSAU

Conakry

GUINEA

CÔTE

GHANA

San Salvador

EL SALVADOR

NICARAGUA

Managua

San José

Caracas

ST VINCENT GRENADA

ST LUCIA

BARBADOS

Freetown

SIERRA LEONE LIBERIA

D'IVOIRE

Lagos

COSTA RICA

Panamá

Port of Spain

TRINIDAD AND TOBAGO

Monrovia

Abidjan

Accra

PANAMA

VENEZUELA

Medellín

Georgetown

GUYANA

Paramaribo

SÃO TOM AND PRINCI

Cali

Bogotá

SUR.

FRENCH GUIANA

0°

Equator

Quito

ECUADOR

COLOMBIA

Islas Galápagos (Ecuador)

Guayaquil

Manaus

Amazon

Belém

Fortaleza

Fernando de Noronha (Brazil)

Cabo de São Roque

Ascension (U.K.)

Phoenix Islands

KIRIBATI

Polynesia

Madeira

Recife

TUVALU

Tokelau (N.Z.)

BRAZIL

SOUTH

Lima

PERU

AMERICA

Salvador

St Helena (U.K.)

SAMOA

American Samoa (U.S.A.)

Íles Marquises

15°S

Suva

FIJI

TONGA

Cook Islands (N.Z.)

Niue (N.Z.)

Tahiti

BOLIVIA

La Paz

Sucre

Brasília

Santa Cruz

Belo Horizonte

Ilhas Martin Vas (Brazil)

SOUTH

Tropic of Capricorn

French Polynesia (France)

Pitcairn Island (U.K.)

Campinas

PARAGUAY

Ilha da Trindade (Brazil)

Rio de Janeiro

ATLANTIC

Isla Sala y Gómez (Chile)

Isla San Ambrosio (Chile)

Asunción

São Paulo

Curitiba

30°

Isla de Pascua (Easter Island) (Chile)

Archipiélago Juan Fernández (Chile)

ARGENTINA

Córdoba

URUGUAY

Porto Alegre

OCEAN

NEW ZEALAND

Santiago

Rosario

Montevideo

Tristan da Cunha (U.K.)

Buenos Aires

Gough Island (U.K.)

North Island

Wellington

45°

Chatham Islands (N.Z.)

SOUTH

PACIFIC

Bounty Islands (N.Z.)

OCEAN

Falkland Islands (U.K.)

South Georgia (U.K.)

Punta Arenas

Cabo de Hornos (Cape Horn)

South Sandwich Islands (U.K.)

Bouvet Island (Norway)

Drake Passage

60°

Antarctic Circle

International Date Line

South Shetland Islands (U.K.)

South Orkney Islands (U.K.)

Antarctic Peninsula

Amundsen Sea

Bellingshausen Sea

Weddell Sea

Queen Maud Lan

75°S

Ross Sea

Marie Byrd Land

Ellsworth Land

A N T A R R

ARCTIC OCEAN

Franz Josef Land
Svalbard (Norway)
Barents Sea
Novaya Zemlya
Kara Sea
Severnaja Zemlya
Laptev Sea
New Siberian Islands
East Siberian Sea
Arctic Circle
Bering Strait

NORWAY
SWEDEN
FINLAND
Oslo
Stockholm
Helsinki
St. Petersburg
ESTONIA
LATVIA
Copenhagen
DENMARK
Berlin
GERMANY
POLAND
LITH.
RUS.
BELARUS
Minsk
Moscow
Nizhniy Novgorod
Perm'
Ekaterinburg
Omsk
Novosibirsk

RUSSIAN FEDERATION

Siberia
Ural Mountains
Ob'
Yenisey
Lena

Sea of Okhotsk
Bering Sea
Kuril Islands
Aleutian Islands

EUROPE
Kiev
UKRAINE
CZECH REP.
SLOV.
Budapest
HUNGARY
SWITZ.
SLVN.
ROMANIA
Samara
Volgograd
Volga
ASIA
Astana
KAZAKHSTAN
Aral Sea
Lake Balkhash
Lake Baikal
MONGOLIA
Ulaanbaatar
Gobi
Altai Mountains
Harbin

Milan
ITALY
Rome
BOS.-HERZ.
SERB. & MON.
Sofia
BULGARIA
CROATIA
MAC.
Ankara
Istanbul
TURKEY
GREECE
Athens
Izmir
Black Sea
GEORGIA
ARM.
AZER.
Caspian Sea
UZBEKISTAN
Bishkek
Almaty
KYRGYZSTAN
Tashkent
TURKMENISTAN
Ashgabat
TAJIKISTAN
Dushanbe
Tien Shan
Ürümqi
Shenyang
Beijing
Taiyuan
Tianjin
NORTH KOREA
Sea of Japan
Sapporo
Hokkaidō

NORTH PACIFIC OCEAN

Tunis
TUNISIA
Tripoli
Mediterranean Sea
CYPRUS
LEBANON
SYRIA
Baghdād
IRAQ
Tehrān
IRAN
Eşfahān
Ābādān
KUWAIT
Kābul
AFGHANISTAN
Islamabad
Rawalpindi
Lahore
CHINA
Xi'an
Chengdu
Chongqing
Nanjing
Wuhan
Changsha
Shanghai
Seoul
SOUTH KOREA
Pusan
Fukuoka
JAPAN
Tōkyō
Ōsaka
Kyūshū
Yellow River
Yangtze

Alexandria
Cairo
ISRAEL
JORDAN
Amman
SAUDI ARABIA
Riyadh
BAHRAIN
QATAR
U.A.E.
Masqat
OMAN
Karachi
PAKISTAN
Delhi
New Delhi
NEPAL
Kathmandu
BHUTAN
Himalayas
Ganges
BANGL.
Dhaka
MYANMAR (BURMA)
Guangzhou
Hong Kong
TAIWAN
T'aipei
Ryukyu Islands
Midway Islands (U.S.A.)
Tropic of Cancer

LIBYA
EGYPT
Red Sea
YEMEN
Şan'ā'
Socotra (Yemen)
Ahmadabad
Mumbai (Bombay)
Pune
INDIA
Hyderabad
Bangalore
Chennai (Madras)
Kolkata (Calcutta)
Rangoon
Bay of Bengal
Bangkok
THAILAND
LAOS
Viangchan
Ha Nôi
Hainan
South China Sea
VIETNAM
CAMBODIA
Phnom Pénh
Hô Chi Minh
Manila
PHILIPPINES
Luzon
Philippine Sea
Northern Mariana Islands (U.S.A.)
Guam (U.S.A)
MARSHALL ISLANDS
International Date Line
15°N

AFRICA
NIGER
CHAD
Kano
NIGERIA
Khartoum
SUDAN
ERITREA
DJIBOUTI
Djibouti
Ādīs Ābeba
ETHIOPIA
SOMALIA
Ndjamena
Lake Chad
CENTRAL AFRICAN REPUBLIC
Bangui
CAMEROON
Yaoundé
Laccadive Islands (India)
MALDIVES
Colombo
SRI LANKA
Sri Jayewardenepura Kotte
Medan
MALAYSIA
Kuala Lumpur
Singapore
SINGAPORE
BRUNEI
Borneo
Sulawesi
INDONESIA
Mindanao
FEDERATED STATES OF MICRONESIA
PALAU
Micronesia
Equator
0°

E.G.
Libreville
GABON
Brazzaville
DEMOCRATIC REPUBLIC OF CONGO
Kinshasa
UGANDA
KENYA
Nairobi
RWANDA
BURUNDI
Bujumbura
Lake Victoria
TANZANIA
Dodoma
Dar es Salaam
Mogadishu
SEYCHELLES
British Indian Ocean Territory (U.K.)
Sumatra
Java
Jakarta
Surabaya
Dili
EAST TIMOR
Christmas Island (Australia)
Cocos Islands (Australia)
Irian Jaya
PAPUA NEW GUINEA
Port Moresby
OCEANIA
SOLOMON ISLANDS
NAURU
Kingsmill Group
KIRIBATI
Gilbert Islands
Phoenix Islands
TUVALU
Tokelau (N.Z.)
American Samoa (U.S.A.)
15°S

Luanda
ANGOLA
Lubumbashi
ZAMBIA
Lusaka
Lake Tanganyika
MALAWI
Lilongwe
MOZAMBIQUE
Harare
ZIMBABWE
Antananarivo
MADAGASCAR
Mozambique Channel
COMOROS
Mayotte (France)
Réunion (France)
MAURITIUS
INDIAN OCEAN
Melanesia
Coral Sea
New Caledonia (France)
VANUATU
Wallis and Futuna Islands (France)
SAMOA
FIJI
Suva
Niue (N.Z.)
TONGA

NAMIBIA
Windhoek
BOTSWANA
Gaborone
Pretoria
Johannesburg
Maputo
SWAZILAND
SOUTH AFRICA
LESOTHO
Durban
Cape Town
Cape of Good Hope
Amsterdam Island (France)
St Paul Island (France)
AUSTRALIA
Darling
Brisbane
Norfolk Island (Australia)
Tropic of Capricorn
30°

Perth
Adelaide
Canberra
Sydney
Melbourne
Tasman Sea
Tasmania
Wellington
North Island
Chatham Islands (N.Z.)
NEW ZEALAND
South Island
45°

Prince Edward Islands (South Africa)
Crozet Islands (France)
Kerguelen Islands (France)
Heard Island (Australia)
Auckland Islands (N.Z.)
Bounty Islands (N.Z.)
Campbell Island (N.Z.)
Macquarie Island (Australia)
60°

SOUTHERN OCEAN
Antarctic Circle
Wilkes Land
Enderby Land
75°S

ANTARCTICA

Scale 1:60 000 000
Projection: Gall Stereographic
0 Kms 1000 2000
0 Miles 1000

ABBREVIATED COUNTRY NAMES

ALB.	ALBANIA
AND.	ANDORRA
ARM.	ARMENIA
AZER.	AZERBAIJAN
BANGL.	BANGLADESH
BEL.	BELGIUM
BOS.-HERZ.	BOSNIA-HERZEGOVINA
CZECH REP.	CZECH REPUBLIC
E.G.	EQUATORIAL GUINEA
LITH.	LITHUANIA
LUX.	LUXEMBOURG
MAC.	MACEDONIA
MOLD.	MOLDOVA
NETH.	NETHERLANDS
RUS.	RUSSIAN FEDERATION
SERB. & MON.	SERBIA & MONTENEGRO
SLOV.	SLOVAKIA
SLVN.	SLOVENIA
SUR.	SURINAME
SWITZ.	SWITZERLAND
U.A.E.	UNITED ARAB EMIRATES

SPACE

Space is the final frontier, the prime target for exploration in the third millennium and beyond. But we already know a great deal about the Universe, thanks to technological advances that began 400 years ago with Galileo's telescope. By tuning into all kinds of radiation from space, astronomers have tracked down black holes, planets orbiting other stars and even radiation from the afterglow of the Big Bang. Yet many questions remain unanswered: in particular, whether there is any form of life out there.

1 KNOWN UNIVERSE In the Universe, there are billions of galaxies, each containing a vast number of stars, all similar to our Sun. But we only see as far into the Universe as light – which travels at 300,000 km (186,000 miles) per second – has come since the Big Bang. At present, the most distant galaxies perceivable from Earth lie 13 billion light years away. Space may be infinite. Evidence suggests that over 90 per cent of the Universe is invisible. The presence of this mysterious 'dark matter' is inferred by the gravitational force it exerts.

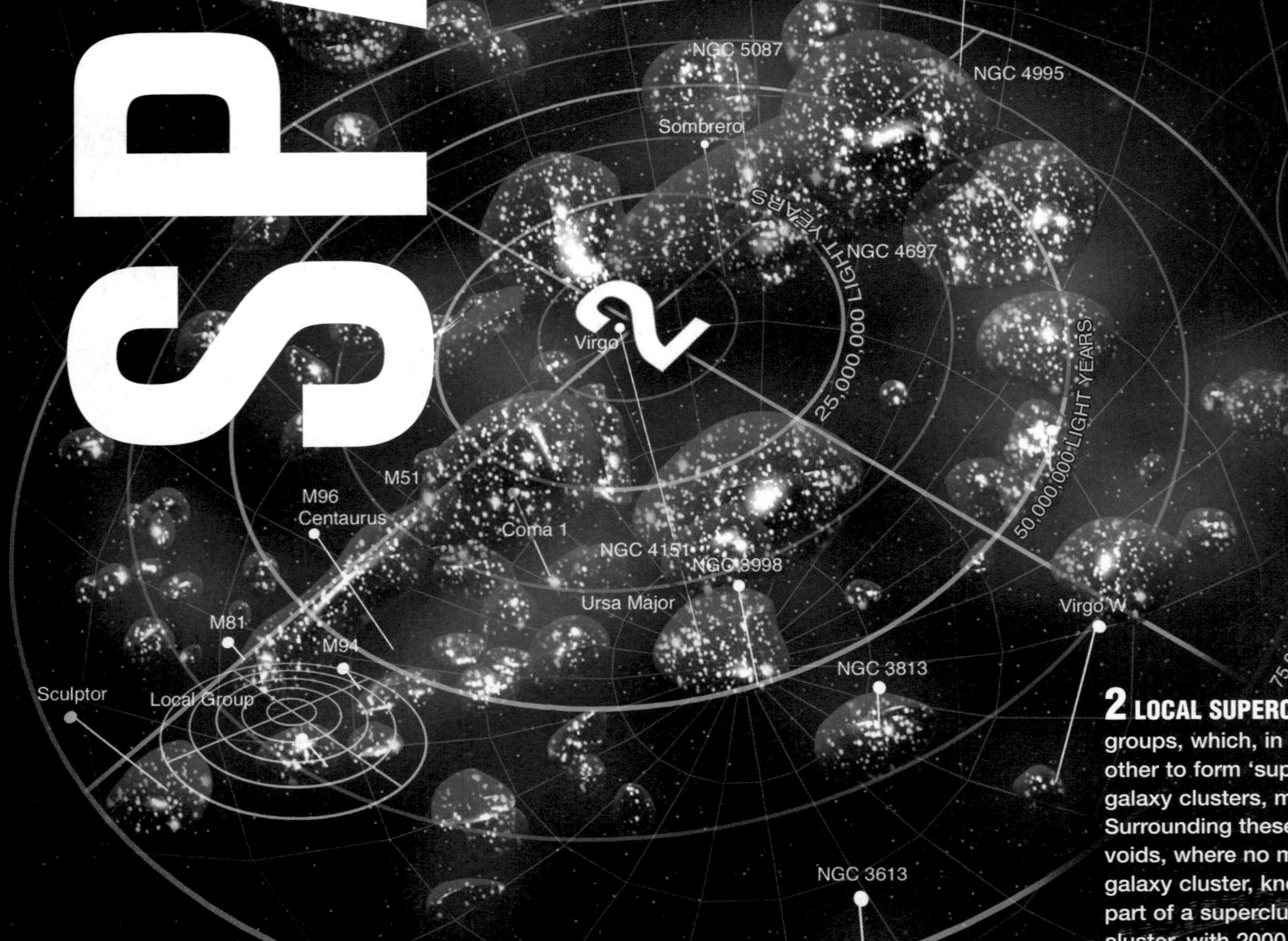

2 LOCAL SUPERCLUSTER Galaxies exist in groups, which, in turn, are attracted to each other to form 'superclusters' – vast strings of galaxy clusters, millions of light years across. Surrounding these, there appear to be huge voids, where no matter is detectable. Our own galaxy cluster, known as the Local Group, is part of a supercluster, in which the Virgo galaxy cluster, with 2000 members, is by far the biggest.

The Big Bang and the fate of the Universe
Around 13-14 billion years ago, the Universe was created in a vast explosion – the Big Bang. And because both time and space were born from this colossal detonation, there was never a 'before the Big Bang'. In less than a second, the infant Universe had expanded trillions of times. This rapid 'cosmic inflation' explains why space is so smooth and empty. Within less than three minutes of the initial explosion, the first atoms – hydrogen and helium – formed, as the fireball cooled. But it was another half a billion years before these combined to form matter, then stars, then galaxies. The Universe is still expanding, at an ever growing rate, becoming colder and emptier.

KUIPER BELT

PLUTO
(5870 million km/
3647 million miles
from Sun)

NEPTUNE
(4495 million km/
2793 million miles
from Sun)

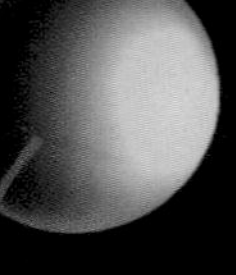

URANUS
(2872 million km/
1785 million miles
from Sun)

SATURN
(1427 million km/
887 million miles
from Sun)

A light year is the distance that light travels in one year.
1 light year = 9,460,700 million km (5,878,600 million miles)

3 LOCAL GROUP Our own galaxy, the Milky Way, and the nearby Andromeda Galaxy are the biggest members of their galaxy cluster, or Local Group. Andromeda, with 400,000 million stars, is twice the size of the Milky Way, and – at 2.9 million light years away – the most distant object visible to the naked eye. Most of the other 30 Group members are small and faint.

4 MILKY WAY GALAXY The Milky Way's name comes from the misty appearance of its 200 billion distant stars, that form a band across our sky. But If you could fly over it, the Galaxy's spiral shape, with young stars and interstellar gas marking out the arms, would be clearly visible. The Sun and its associated planets sit in the Orion Arm of the spiral, about halfway out from the centre – the site of a massive black hole.

5 LOCAL STARS All stars, including our Sun, are natural nuclear reactors, formed from swirling clouds of gas and dust drawn together by gravity. Stars differ in their mass, luminosity and temperature. The twin Alpha Centauri stars, just over 4 light years from Earth, are similar in size and brightness to our Sun. Sirius, the brightest star in the sky lies 8.6 light years away and shines 23 times more brilliantly, burning out much faster than our Sun, which is halfway through its 10,000-million-year lifespan. Most stars, however, are 'red dwarfs' – small and relatively cool, glowing feebly but for considerably longer.

Globular clusters
Sagittarius Arm
Perseus Arm
Carina
Draco
Leo II
Small Magellanic Cloud
Large Magellanic Cloud
Sagdig
Orion Arm
Sculptor
Leo I
Central bar
4
Sun
10,000 LIGHT YEARS
LGS 3
20,000 LIGHT YEARS
Outer Arm
30,000 LIGHT YEARS
Cygnus Arm
Fornax
40,000 LIGHT YEARS

Struve 2398
Groombridge 34
Giclas 51-5
Lalande 21185
61 Cygni
Wolf 359
Epsilon
Eridani
Ross 128
Procyon
5
Barnard's
Star
Luyten 726-8
Sirius
Tau
Ceti
Luyten 725-32
10 LIGHT YEARS
Sun
15 LIGHT YEARS
Ross 154
Luyten 789-6
Alpha Centauri
Lacaille 9352
20 LIGHT YEARS
Epsilon Indi

6 THE SOLAR SYSTEM Our Sun dominates its family of planets, moons, asteroids and comets, which are essentially the debris left over from its formation. The small rocky planets that lie close to the Sun – Mercury, Venus, Earth and Mars – were created in an environment that was too hot to hold on to a dense atmosphere. Jupiter, Saturn, Uranus and Neptune, however, are almost all atmosphere – they were sufficiently far away from the forming Sun to hang onto gases from the collapsing cloud of matter. Pluto is almost certainly the largest member of an outer zone of orbiting debris, the Kuiper Belt.

MARS
(228 million km/
142million miles
from Sun)

EARTH
(150 million km/
93 million miles
from Sun)

VENUS
(108 million km/
67 million miles
from Sun)

MERCURY
(58 million km/
36 million miles
from Sun)

SUN

JUPITER
(778 million km/
484 million miles
from Sun)

6

**ASTEROID
BELT**

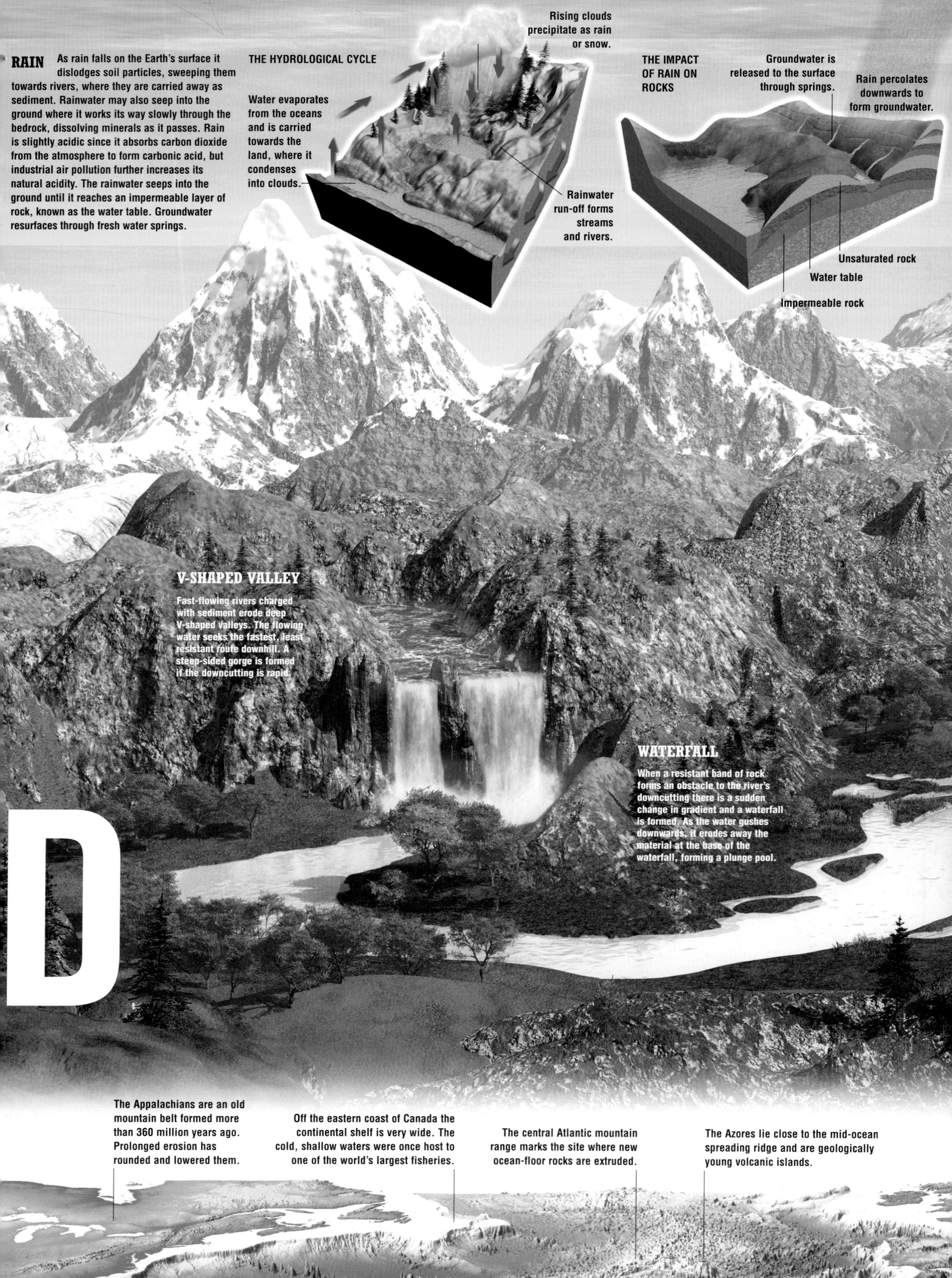

RAIN As rain falls on the Earth's surface it dislodges soil particles, sweeping them towards rivers, where they are carried away as sediment. Rainwater may also seep into the ground where it works its way slowly through the bedrock, dissolving minerals as it passes. Rain is slightly acidic since it absorbs carbon dioxide from the atmosphere to form carbonic acid, but industrial air pollution further increases its natural acidity. The rainwater seeps into the ground until it reaches an impermeable layer of rock, known as the water table. Groundwater resurfaces through fresh water springs.

THE HYDROLOGICAL CYCLE

Rising clouds precipitate as rain or snow.

Water evaporates from the oceans and is carried towards the land, where it condenses into clouds.

Rainwater run-off forms streams and rivers.

THE IMPACT OF RAIN ON ROCKS

Groundwater is released to the surface through springs.

Rain percolates downwards to form groundwater.

Unsaturated rock

Water table

Impermeable rock

V-SHAPED VALLEY

Fast-flowing rivers charged with sediment erode deep V-shaped valleys. The flowing water seeks the fastest, least resistant route downhill. A steep-sided gorge is formed if the downcutting is rapid.

WATERFALL

When a resistant band of rock forms an obstacle to the river's downcutting there is a sudden change in gradient and a waterfall is formed. As the water gushes downwards, it erodes away the material at the base of the waterfall, forming a plunge pool.

D

The Appalachians are an old mountain belt formed more than 360 million years ago. Prolonged erosion has rounded and lowered them.

Off the eastern coast of Canada the continental shelf is very wide. The cold, shallow waters were once host to one of the world's largest fisheries.

The central Atlantic mountain range marks the site where new ocean-floor rocks are extruded.

The Azores lie close to the mid-ocean spreading ridge and are geologically young volcanic islands.

GLACIERS

Formed of compacted snow and ice, glaciers are dramatic sculptors of landscapes, grinding away uplands and moulding lowlands with rocky debris as they move seawards. Glaciers such as the Turner glacier in Alaska (left) move at rates of up to 55m (180ft) a day.

Wind and weather

In drier parts of the world, where there is little moisture or vegetation to bind together loose sediment, the wind lifts and carries sand and dust. Charged with particles, winds attack soils or rock, sandblasting and polishing softer rock surfaces. But rocks are also subject to other forces. Frost and temperature change can cause them to split and fissure, while roots of plants and trees can crack them apart. Soluble minerals such as limestone, marble and sandstone react to chemicals in rainwater, causing the rocks to dissolve.

Ice

Over the past few million years the Earth has been in the grip of an Ice Age, with alternating glacial and interglacial periods. During glacial periods, which last up to 100,000 years, large polar and alpine parts of the continents are shrouded in ice sheets up to 3km (1¾ miles) thick. With so much water locked up in ice, sea levels drop, exposing land-bridges. In the last Ice Age, which ended 10,000 years ago, ice sheets and glaciers were three times more extensive than today, and Britain was joined to Europe and Alaska to Siberia.

Rounded hills
V-shaped valleys

LANDSCAPE BEFORE GLACIATION

Before the onset of glaciation, mountain valleys are sculpted by rivers and by weathering. They create a distinctive landscape with rounded hills and V-shaped valleys. Glaciation begins when snow persists and accumulates on the coldest slopes, gradually hollowing out a basin called a cirque.

LANDSCAPE DURING GLACIATION

As snow accumulates in the cirque it is compacted into glacial ice, which spills over the cirque into the valley. Neighbouring cirques may intersect, producing a sharp rock ridge, known as an arête. The valley glacier, impelled by the force of gravity, begins to move downwards.

Arête
Horn peak
Cirque

Over many millennia the action of water, ice, wind and weather has transformed the Earth's surface. These natural agents have moulded the landscape through processes of weathering and erosion, but have also transported rock and sediment, creating new landforms.

Horn peak
Arête

LANDSCAPE AFTER GLACIATION

The moving ice gathers rock debris which grinds and sculpts the valley, creating a steep-walled U-shaped trough. As the ice melts, rock debris is deposited in ridges, mounds and sheets known as moraine. Streams and lakes are formed by meltwater gushing from the glacier.

Cirque with lake
Hanging valley
U-shaped valley

LAN

The Earth's surface

A slice from around the Earth's northern latitudes reveals a striking range of topography, from jagged mountains on land and on the ocean bed to flat plains extending for thousands of kilometres.

The cross-section (right) runs along latitude 30°N from 180°E to 180°W.

The Rocky Mountains were uplifted about 70–100 million years ago, and have an elevation ranging from 1500m (5000ft) to 4399m (14,433ft) at Mt Elbert in Colorado.

The tributaries of the Missouri river rise in the Great Plains of America's Midwest.

Six billion years ago Within our local galaxy, a rotating cloud of gases from earlier super-novae (exploded stars) was contracted by gravitational forces. This clump of denser material, known as a nebula, condensed to form the Solar System.

Five billion years ago Small amounts of heavier elements in the nebula began to collapse inwards. It became hotter and denser until nuclear reactions occurred and a star – our Sun – was formed. The planets were formed from the remaining gas and dust. The dense rocky planets were created near to the Sun; farther away they tended to be gaseous and icy.

EARTH

The Big Bang, the formation of the Universe about 13.7 billion years ago, was an event of incredible magnitude. Compressed into a single point of unimaginable intensity, all the Universe's matter exploded as a rapidly expanding fireball of subatomic particles. Hydrogen and other elements were created, ultimately building the galaxies and stars, including the Sun, its Solar System and planet Earth.

The still-moving Earth

The configuration of the continents is far from static; for billions of years the rigid plates that make up the crust have been moving across the surface of the planet, carried by currents deep within the mantle. New ocean-floor crust is formed by the extrusion of magma at plate boundaries located at central oceanic ridges, and destroyed at subduction zones.

WITHIN THE EARTH

The movement of the Earth's plates is powered by forces deep within its interior. As hot, molten magma rises towards the surface it encounters cooler material, forming convection currents that mobilize the continental plates. Currents in the liquid outer core drive the Earth's magnetic field.

The upper 700km (435 miles) of the mantle is relatively cool and rigid.

2200km (1367 miles) Rock in the lower mantle, subject to high pressures and temperatures (up to 3500°C), flows plastically.

2885km (1800 miles) Outer core is liquid made up of iron and iron sulphide.

5145km (3170 miles) The inner core is solid iron-nickel alloy, probably crystallized from the liquid outer core. Temperatures may reach 4700°C.

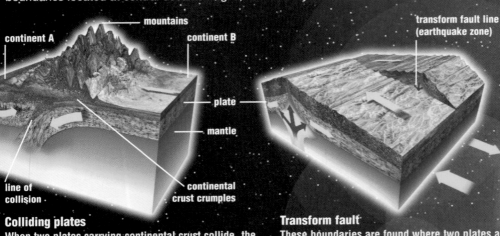

continent A — mountains — continent B

transform fault line (earthquake zone)

plate

mantle

line of collision

continental crust crumples

Colliding plates
When two plates carrying continental crust collide, the crust is thickened and crumpled by the plate movements, forming mountains. Eventually, when movement ceases, the boundary becomes tectonically inactive.

Transform fault
These boundaries are found where two plates are simply sliding past each other, without creating or destroying any crust. A notable example is the San Andreas fault in California, USA.

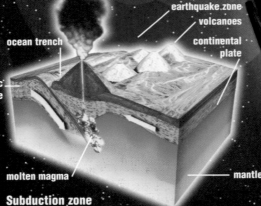

oceanic ridge — molten magma forced to surface

ocean trench

earthquake zone
volcanoes
continental plate

oceanic plate

mantle

molten magma

mantle

Oceanic ridge
Where two oceanic plates pull apart, the upper mantle melts to form magma erupting onto the surface as lavas. As the lavas cool they solidify to form new ocean crust. The mid-ocean ridge's central zone is marked by a rift valley.

Subduction zone
Where an oceanic plate collides with another plate, it is pushed down into the mantle. A deep ocean trench and subduction zone is formed with high pressures generating earthquakes, magma and volcanoes.

About 4.6 billion years ago The Earth started life as a ball of hot rock, with an atmosphere of hydrogen. The Earth was heated to 5000∞C (9000∞F). As the surface began to cool, material from the hot interior of the planet was released in gaseous form to create the atmosphere.

The formation of the Moon

Around 4.5 billion years ago, the Earth collided with a planetary body the size of Mars. The impact flung out huge chunks of matter, which coalesced within the Earth's gravitational field to form the Moon. The young Moon seethed with volcanoes: its thick mantle melted and erupted to form plains of basaltic lava. Volcanic activity ceased about 3 billion years ago. Ever since the surface has been bombarded with meteorites, which easily penetrate the thin atmosphere.

From 4.5 billion years ago
Continual volcanic eruptions produced an atmosphere of carbon dioxide and water vapour. As temperatures fell, water vapour condensed to create the first oceans about 3.8 billion years ago. Oxygen released by the evaporation of water vapour and sea-dwelling micro-organisms built up in the atmosphere.

Vendian
620 million years ago

Late Cambrian
500 million years ago

3.65 billion years ago Oxygen was slowly building up in the oceans and atmosphere. Permanent continental crust started to form and clouds of water vapour reflected some of the Sun's radiation back into space, lowering temperatures. Fluctuations in the Earth's atmospheric temperature produced occasional widespread glaciation.

Triassic
240 million years ago

The continents take shape

When the Earth first formed, some 4.5 billion years ago, there was no differentiation between continents and oceans. Pieces of crust formed as the surface cooled, but were reworked into the mantle beneath. Some 3.8 billion years ago, the surface of the Earth was cool enough for crust to mostly resist reworking. The crust became a thin skin, composed of a few major rigid plates and several smaller platelets, all moving relative to one another.

The Earth today
Even now the Earth is not a static body. The tectonic forces that shaped the continents and oceans continue to move and rework them. Volcanoes and earth-quakes are evidence of this constant process.

Late Cretaceous
95 million years ago

The coast

Coastlines are transient environments, eroded by the constant battering of waves or built up by the deposition of marine sediments. Over tens of thousands of years changes can be profound. The last Ice Age caused a dramatic fall in sea level, revealing new land, while subsequent global warming has melted ice sheets and rising sea levels have inundated low-lying areas.

The Mississippi delta today

THE CHANGING SHAPE OF THE MISSISSIPPI DELTA

2500 BC

1500 BC

500 BC

AD 1000

AD 1500

The Old Man of Hoy (above), a 137m (450ft) sandstone sea stack on Hoy in the Orkney Islands, was formed by gradual erosion of the headland.

CREATION OF A HEADLAND

Coastlines consist of bands of rocks that have different resistances to erosion from waves. Rock material is removed from the base of cliffs made up of softer, less resistant rock. The undercut cliffs collapse creating bays, while the more resistant rock is left intact to form headlands. Debris at the cliff base is eventually washed away. As the process is repeated, bays deepen and headlands are exposed to further wave attack.

Soft rock is eroded first, creating deep bays in the cliff face.

Hard rocks form headland

Sea breaks through hard rock to create cove

EROSION OF A HEADLAND

Cave

Waves hurl water and rocks at headlands, exploiting any weakness in the cliff base to excavate caves. Deepened caves on both sides of a headland may eventually join to form a tunnel and rock arch above. Stacks are formed when the roof of an arch collapses, leaving an isolated column of rock.

Arch

Roof of arch collapses to form stack

WAVE ACTION

Powerful waves attack coasts with huge force. Pressure from collapsing waves exploits any natural weaknesses. Even apparently solid rocks and concrete sea defences can eventually be destroyed. Rock debris carried by strong waves further batters exposed surfaces, breaking off pieces which in turn promote erosion.

Cliff debris and river sediments are carried along the shore by the sea and deposited to form beaches, spits and bars. The largest beaches, such as Ninety Mile Beach in Victoria, Australia, are found in the calmest waters. Spits and bars are ridges of sand deposited at the mouth of a bay or river.

COASTAL DEPOSITION

Western China and Tibet form the world's largest plateau above 5500m (16,650ft).

Japan's main islands form an active volcanic arc stretching for 2400km (1500 miles)

East of the volcanic Aleutian Islands lies the Kuril ocean trench, 34,587m (10,542ft) deep.

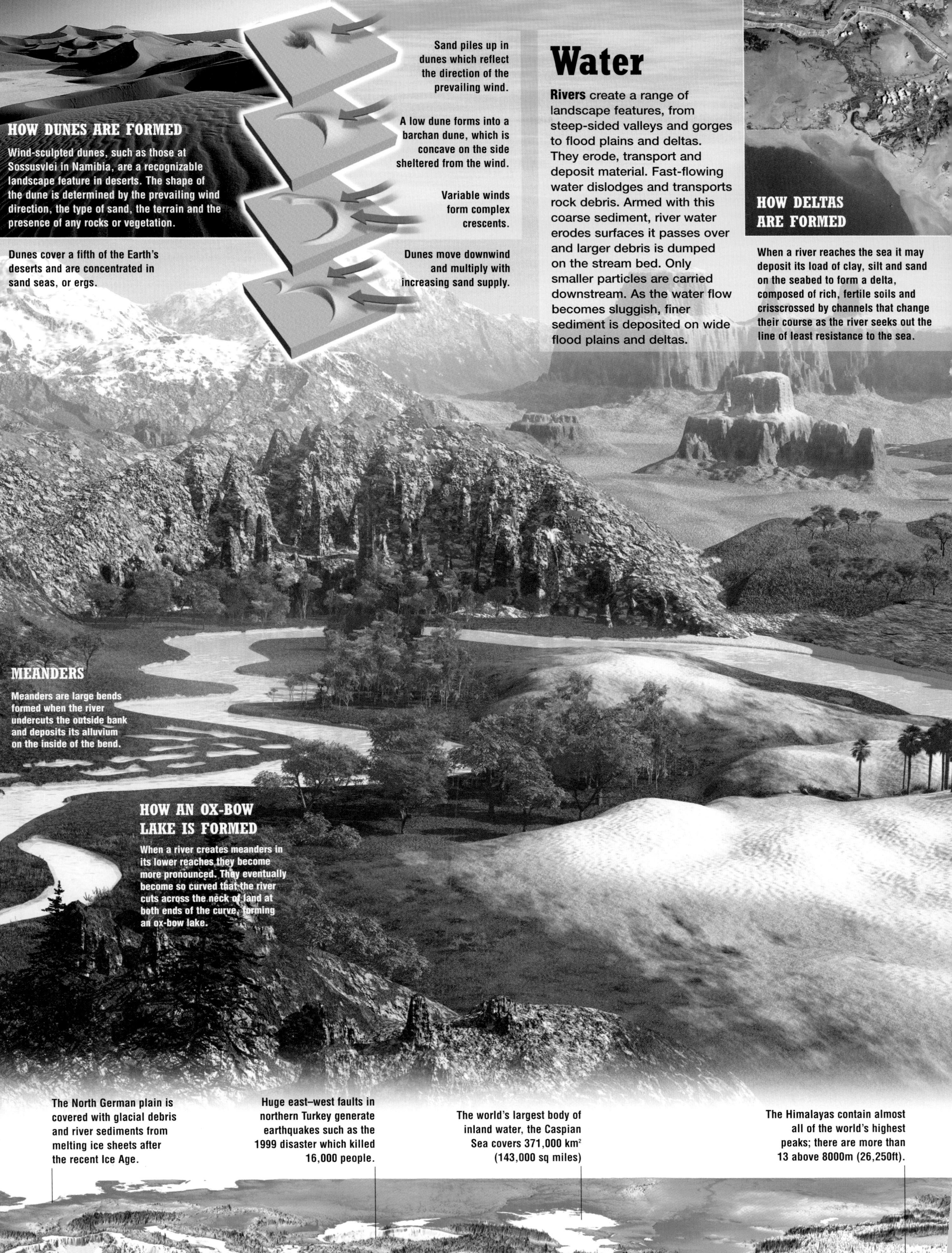

HOW DUNES ARE FORMED

Wind-sculpted dunes, such as those at Sossusvlei in Namibia, are a recognizable landscape feature in deserts. The shape of the dune is determined by the prevailing wind direction, the type of sand, the terrain and the presence of any rocks or vegetation.

Dunes cover a fifth of the Earth's deserts and are concentrated in sand seas, or ergs.

Sand piles up in dunes which reflect the direction of the prevailing wind.

A low dune forms into a barchan dune, which is concave on the side sheltered from the wind.

Variable winds form complex crescents.

Dunes move downwind and multiply with increasing sand supply.

Water

Rivers create a range of landscape features, from steep-sided valleys and gorges to flood plains and deltas. They erode, transport and deposit material. Fast-flowing water dislodges and transports rock debris. Armed with this coarse sediment, river water erodes surfaces it passes over and larger debris is dumped on the stream bed. Only smaller particles are carried downstream. As the water flow becomes sluggish, finer sediment is deposited on wide flood plains and deltas.

HOW DELTAS ARE FORMED

When a river reaches the sea it may deposit its load of clay, silt and sand on the seabed to form a delta, composed of rich, fertile soils and crisscrossed by channels that change their course as the river seeks out the line of least resistance to the sea.

MEANDERS

Meanders are large bends formed when the river undercuts the outside bank and deposits its alluvium on the inside of the bend.

HOW AN OX-BOW LAKE IS FORMED

When a river creates meanders in its lower reaches they become more pronounced. They eventually become so curved that the river cuts across the neck of land at both ends of the curve, forming an ox-bow lake.

The North German plain is covered with glacial debris and river sediments from melting ice sheets after the recent Ice Age.

Huge east–west faults in northern Turkey generate earthquakes such as the 1999 disaster which killed 16,000 people.

The world's largest body of inland water, the Caspian Sea covers 371,000 km² (143,000 sq miles)

The Himalayas contain almost all of the world's highest peaks; there are more than 13 above 8000m (26,250ft).

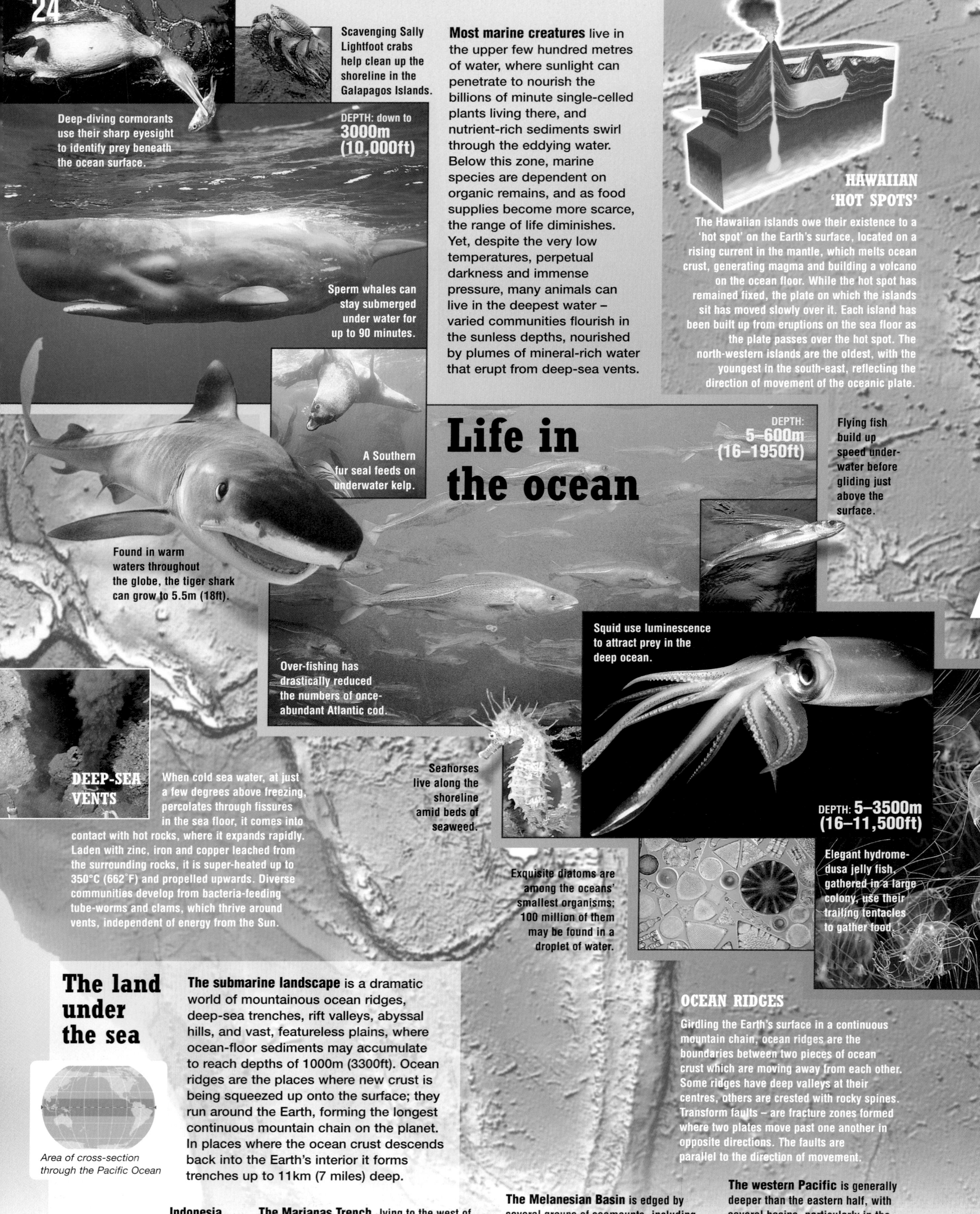

Deep-diving cormorants use their sharp eyesight to identify prey beneath the ocean surface.

Scavenging Sally Lightfoot crabs help clean up the shoreline in the Galapagos Islands.

Most marine creatures live in the upper few hundred metres of water, where sunlight can penetrate to nourish the billions of minute single-celled plants living there, and nutrient-rich sediments swirl through the eddying water. Below this zone, marine species are dependent on organic remains, and as food supplies become more scarce, the range of life diminishes. Yet, despite the very low temperatures, perpetual darkness and immense pressure, many animals can live in the deepest water – varied communities flourish in the sunless depths, nourished by plumes of mineral-rich water that erupt from deep-sea vents.

DEPTH: down to **3000m (10,000ft)**

Sperm whales can stay submerged under water for up to 90 minutes.

HAWAIIAN 'HOT SPOTS'

The Hawaiian islands owe their existence to a 'hot spot' on the Earth's surface, located on a rising current in the mantle, which melts ocean crust, generating magma and building a volcano on the ocean floor. While the hot spot has remained fixed, the plate on which the islands sit has moved slowly over it. Each island has been built up from eruptions on the sea floor as the plate passes over the hot spot. The north-western islands are the oldest, with the youngest in the south-east, reflecting the direction of movement of the oceanic plate.

Life in the ocean

A Southern fur seal feeds on underwater kelp.

DEPTH: **5–600m (16–1950ft)**

Flying fish build up speed under-water before gliding just above the surface.

Found in warm waters throughout the globe, the tiger shark can grow to 5.5m (18ft).

Squid use luminescence to attract prey in the deep ocean.

Over-fishing has drastically reduced the numbers of once-abundant Atlantic cod.

DEEP-SEA VENTS

When cold sea water, at just a few degrees above freezing, percolates through fissures in the sea floor, it comes into contact with hot rocks, where it expands rapidly. Laden with zinc, iron and copper leached from the surrounding rocks, it is super-heated up to 350°C (662°F) and propelled upwards. Diverse communities develop from bacteria-feeding tube-worms and clams, which thrive around vents, independent of energy from the Sun.

Seahorses live along the shoreline amid beds of seaweed.

Exquisite diatoms are among the oceans' smallest organisms; 100 million of them may be found in a droplet of water.

DEPTH: **5–3500m (16–11,500ft)**

Elegant hydrome-dusa jelly fish, gathered in a large colony, use their trailing tentacles to gather food.

The land under the sea

Area of cross-section through the Pacific Ocean

The submarine landscape is a dramatic world of mountainous ocean ridges, deep-sea trenches, rift valleys, abyssal hills, and vast, featureless plains, where ocean-floor sediments may accumulate to reach depths of 1000m (3300ft). Ocean ridges are the places where new crust is being squeezed up onto the surface; they run around the Earth, forming the longest continuous mountain chain on the planet. In places where the ocean crust descends back into the Earth's interior it forms trenches up to 11km (7 miles) deep.

OCEAN RIDGES

Girdling the Earth's surface in a continuous mountain chain, ocean ridges are the boundaries between two pieces of ocean crust which are moving away from each other. Some ridges have deep valleys at their centres, others are crested with rocky spines. Transform faults – are fracture zones formed where two plates move past one another in opposite directions. The faults are parallel to the direction of movement.

Indonesia

The Marianas Trench, lying to the west of the Philippines, is the oceans' deepest point, reaching down to 10,911m (35,800ft) in places.

The Melanesian Basin is edged by several groups of seamounts, including the Marshalls in the north and the Gilbert seamounts to the east.

The western Pacific is generally deeper than the eastern half, with several basins, particularly in the north, reaching depths of more than 6000m (19,685ft).

OCEAN

ATLANTIC OCEAN
Covering a fifth of the Earth's surface, the Atlantic Ocean has an area of 82,439,700km² (31,830,000 sq miles), with an average depth of 3329m (10,925ft).

PACIFIC OCEAN
The largest of the oceans, the Pacific covers a third of the Earth's surface: 165,250,000km² (63,800,000 sq miles), and has an average depth of 4280m (10,040ft).

INDIAN OCEAN
With an area of 73,550,000km² (28,360,000 sq miles), the Indian Ocean covers a seventh of the Earth at an average depth of 3890m (12,760ft).

ANTARCTIC OCEAN
The ocean that surrounds the Antarctic continent forms the southern portion of the Atlantic, Pacific and Indian Oceans; its maximum depth is 4500m (14,705ft).

ARCTIC OCEAN
The world's smallest ocean, the Arctic Ocean is 14,000,000km² (5,500,000 sq miles). Much of it is covered by pack ice throughout the year.

The age of the ocean floor

Oceanic crust, formed at the spreading centres of ocean ridges, is up to 7km (4½ miles) thick, and is thinner, denser and considerably younger than continental crust – no oceanic crust is more than 200 million years old. Maps of sea-floor topography show how rocks increase in age in regular parallel bands as they move away from ocean ridges. The rocks have been shunted away by the formation of new crust at the ocean ridge.

NORTH ATLANTIC OCEAN

Mid-Atlantic Ridge

PACIFIC OCEAN

INDIAN OCEAN

SOUTH ATLANTIC OCEAN

- 0.5 million years
- 5-21 million years
- 21-38 million years
- 38-65 million years
- 65-140 million years
- 140-180 million years

The oceans cover three-quarters of the Earth's surface and contain 97 per cent of its surface water. They are the largest of the world's habitable environments and teem with life. Sonar, satellite and electromagnetic surveys have recently revealed mountain ridges, plunging trenches, volcanoes, deep canyons, plains and plateaus beneath the oceans.

DEPTH: some species down to **2500m (8200ft)**

Colourful red and orange starfish feed on algae and sponges in the coastal waters of the Indian and Pacific Oceans.

Feather duster tube worms live in tubes of sand, held together with a glue secreted by their bodies.

Giant kelp is a type of brown algae. It is found in extensive underwater 'forests'.

A Spanish shawl sea slug cruises the ocean floor off California.

Giant clams can reach up to 1m (3ft) in width and weigh 300kg (660lb).

DEPTH: **50–2500m (165–8200ft)**

The deep sea hatchet fish and anglerfish can survive under extreme pressure.

Large reserves of nickel and copper have been found close to the Clipperton Fracture zone.

The Atacama Trench runs for 5900km (3666 miles) 160km (100 miles) off the western coasts of Chile and Peru. Its maximum depth is 8065m (26,460ft) in Richard Deep.

South America

Communications and some astronomical satellites (above) orbit the Earth in the exosphere. Space shuttles 'fly' mostly in the thermosphere, but can reach 600km (370 miles).

EXOSPHERE 500–2000km (310–1240 miles), the outer limit of Earth's atmosphere. Mostly composed of helium and hydrogen. The boundary between the exosphere and the thermosphere below it is indistinct.

THERMOSPHERE 80–500km (50–310 miles). Composed mainly of nitrogen molecules to 200km (150 miles); above this height, oxygen is the dominant constituent. Temperature rises with height to 1650°C. Overlapping the mesosphere and thermosphere is the **ionosphere** (50–500km/31–310 miles), in which layers of ionized helium, oxygen and nitrogen reflect radio waves back around the Earth – important for long-distance communications.

The atmosphere

The Earth is surrounded by layers of gases, each with a different composition but mainly composed of nitrogen and oxygen, held in place by gravitational attraction. This atmosphere protects the planet from harmful radiation and absorbs energy from the Sun, maintaining an average surface temperature of around 14°C (57°F). The presence of certain 'greenhouse' gases, which include carbon dioxide and water vapour, traps some of the heat radiating back from the Earth's surface – without this barrier heat loss would be far too drastic for any life to survive on land.

Every part of the world experiences a yearly cycle of temperature and precipitation, which is termed its climate. Latitude will influence this, determining whether a region is basically hot (nearer the Equator) or cold, and whether it has pronounced seasonal changes. Climate is also influenced by the prevailing winds and ocean currents, by altitude, and by the nature of the terrain. Although there are exceptions and extremes, there is enough similarity between the climates of different regions to group them together and classify them as climate zones. Such zones can be widely dispersed across the Earth's surface; the Mediterranean climate is, of course, typical of the region from which it takes its name, but it is also found in California, Australia and South Africa.

The Earth's climate

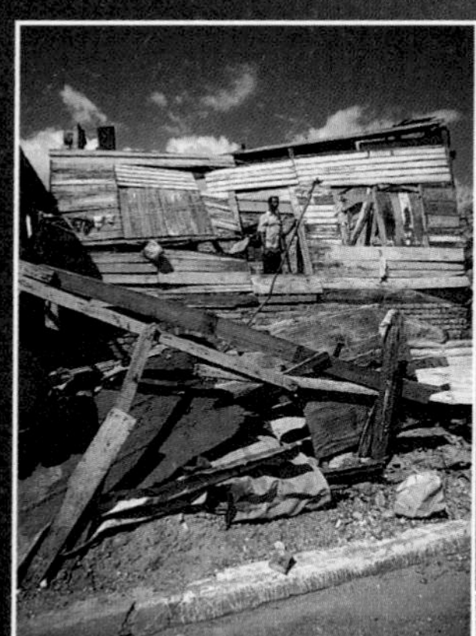

Hurricanes occur when air rises rapidly above hot tropical ocean waters. As humid air cools it forms spiral storm clouds and torrential rains. Winds rotate at speeds of 118km/h (73mph).

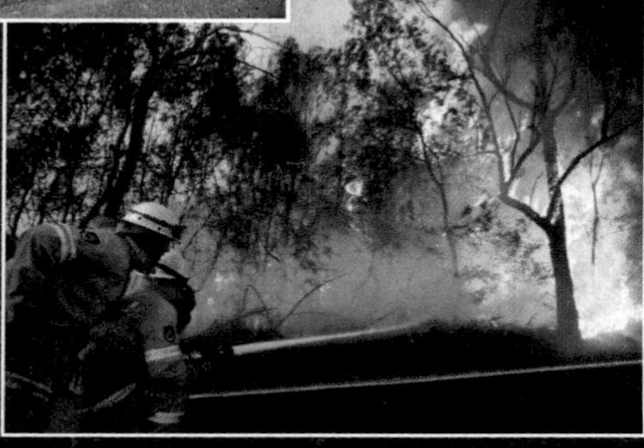

Forests are both important stores of carbon and inflammable ecosystems in which wildfire is common. While fire is part of a natural process of clearance and regeneration, it is also potentially devastating, turning forests into blazing infernos and causing severe air pollution.

Snow is a solid form of water that crystallizes in the atmosphere. A blizzard is an intense snowstorm with winds of more than 50km/h (31mph), and very limited visibility. During freak freezes, for example in Canada in 1998, giant accumulations of ice crushed power lines, causing chaos.

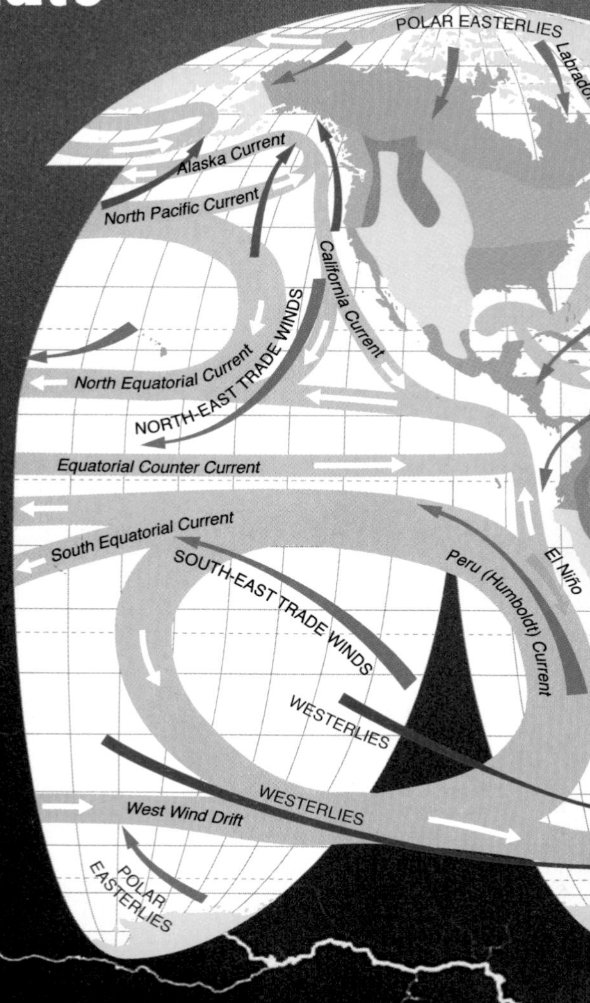

POLAR EASTERLIES
Labrador Current
Alaska Current
North Pacific Current
California Current
North Equatorial Current
NORTH-EAST TRADE WINDS
Equatorial Counter Current
South Equatorial Current
SOUTH-EAST TRADE WINDS
Peru (Humboldt) Current
El Niño
WESTERLIES
West Wind Drift
WESTERLIES
POLAR EASTERLIES

Weather balloons gather meteorological data at up to 50km (31 miles).

MESOSPHERE 50–80km (31–50 miles). Lowest atmospheric temperature: -93°C (-135°F).

STRATOSPHERE 15–50km (9–31 miles). Composed mainly of nitrogen (78 per cent) and oxygen (20 per cent). Carbon dioxide (0.0003 per cent) absorbs heat. In the lower part of the stratosphere lies the **ozone layer** (15–30km/9–18 miles), which filters out ultraviolet radiation from the Sun.

TROPOSPHERE Ground level–15km (9 miles). Most weather phenomena occur within this zone.

WEATHER

Storm clouds, torrential rainfall, calm blue skies, high winds and swirling eddies of water are all features of a dynamic global system that ensures that heat is transferred, by the turbulent motion of the Earth's atmosphere, from the Equator towards the poles. Huge moving masses of air are warm or cold, moist or dry, depending on the land or water surfaces over which they have passed. The most changeable weather occurs at the fronts between these different air masses.

EL NIÑO Up to 30 times in a century, the El Niño effect occurs, when east-to-west trade winds sweeping over the Pacific Ocean become unusually weak, allowing warm water, normally held back by the winds, to flow eastwards along the Equator. The current creates a warm band of water and an area of low atmospheric pressure with violent storms right across the eastern Pacific. The global weather machine is thrown into chaos; random and unusual weather events, such as hurricanes, heatwaves, freak floods and droughts, occur around the globe, bringing devastation in their wake. The graph on the right shows the effect of El Niño on the temperature of water in the central Pacific region.

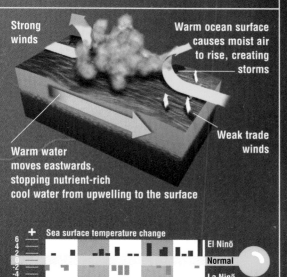

Strong winds

Warm ocean surface causes moist air to rise, creating storms

Warm water moves eastwards, stopping nutrient-rich cool water from upwelling to the surface

Weak trade winds

Sea surface temperature change

El Niño
Normal
La Niña

1950 1960 1970 1980 1990 2000

THE SHRINKING OZONE LAYER

Ozone gas is concentrated in the stratosphere and helps to protect life on Earth from solar ultraviolet radiation, which is a major cause of skin cancer. But the ozone layer is currently being depleted by man-made chemicals, known as chlorofluorocarbons (CFCs), which have been used in aerosols and refrigerating systems. Once they are released into the atmosphere, CFCs interact with sunlight to produce chlorine, which in turn reacts with ozone and reduces its effectiveness in screening out ultraviolet radiation. The maps below show the changing size of the ozone hole around the south pole in September of various years; orange, red, purple and blue mark areas of greatest loss.

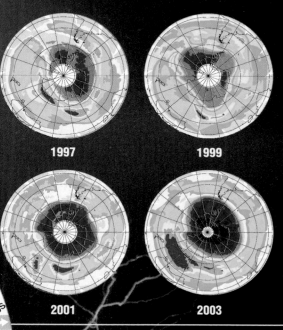

1997   1999

2001   2003

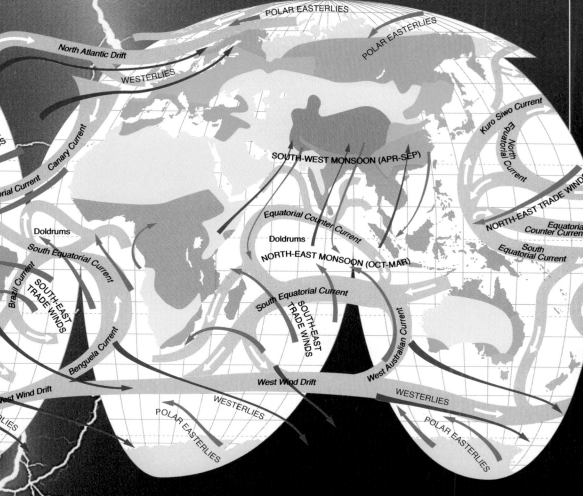

POLAR EASTERLIES
North Atlantic Drift
WESTERLIES
POLAR EASTERLIES
NORTH-EAST TRADE WINDS
Canary Current
th Equatorial Current
Doldrums
South Equatorial Current
SOUTH-EAST TRADE WINDS
Brazil Current
Benguela Current
Falkland Current
West Wind Drift
WESTERLIES
POLAR EASTERLIES
WESTERLIES
POLAR
ERLIES
SOUTH-WEST MONSOON (APR-SEP)
Equatorial Counter Current
Doldrums
NORTH-EAST MONSOON (OCT-MAR)
South Equatorial Current
SOUTH-EAST TRADE WINDS
West Australian Current
West Wind Drift
WESTERLIES
POLAR EASTERLIES
Kuro Siwo Current
North Equatorial Current
NORTH-EAST TRADE WINDS
Equatorial Counter Current
South Equatorial Current

The middle latitudes of the Earth are dominated by swirling storms, which link together across oceans and continents. They occur at the boundary between cold polar air and warm air masses. If the temperature contrast accelerates the jet stream winds, storms can escalate, with winds reaching speeds of 193km/h (120mph).

A tornado is a localized, violently rotating wind. It begins as a funnel-shaped cloud within a thunderstorm, that eventually bursts out of the main cloud mass. It swoops along the ground, travelling at speeds of up to 500km/h (300mph), its pent-up energy vacuuming up everything that lies in its path. The central states of the USA experience up to around 1200 tornadoes every year.

TYPES OF CLIMATE
- Polar
- Subarctic
- Cool temperature
- Warm temperature
- Arid
- Tropical
- High altitude

Winds and currents

The winds and currents that circulate across the surface of the planet act as a global heat exchange mechanism, transferring warmth from the tropics, which receive the most heat from the Sun, towards the cold polar regions. If air in one region of the globe is heated above the temperature of the surrounding air, it becomes less dense and rises. Cooler, denser air in another part of the atmosphere sinks – a constant cycle of heat exchange and air circulation, known as the prevailing winds. The surface currents of the ocean, which extend to depths of several hundred metres, are influenced by global wind patterns. The transfer of warm water polewards can have a strong influence on neighbouring continents – the warm Gulf Stream in the Atlantic, for example, keeps north-west Europe free of ice.

In South-east Asia, six months of drought alternates with a season of torrential rainfall. The cause of the monsoon circulation lies in the unequal heating of the tropical continents and oceans as the Sun swings back and forth in its annual cycle between the two hemispheres. Monsoon rains are intense – the Western Ghats in India are deluged with between 2–5m (6½–16ft) of rain during the monsoon season.

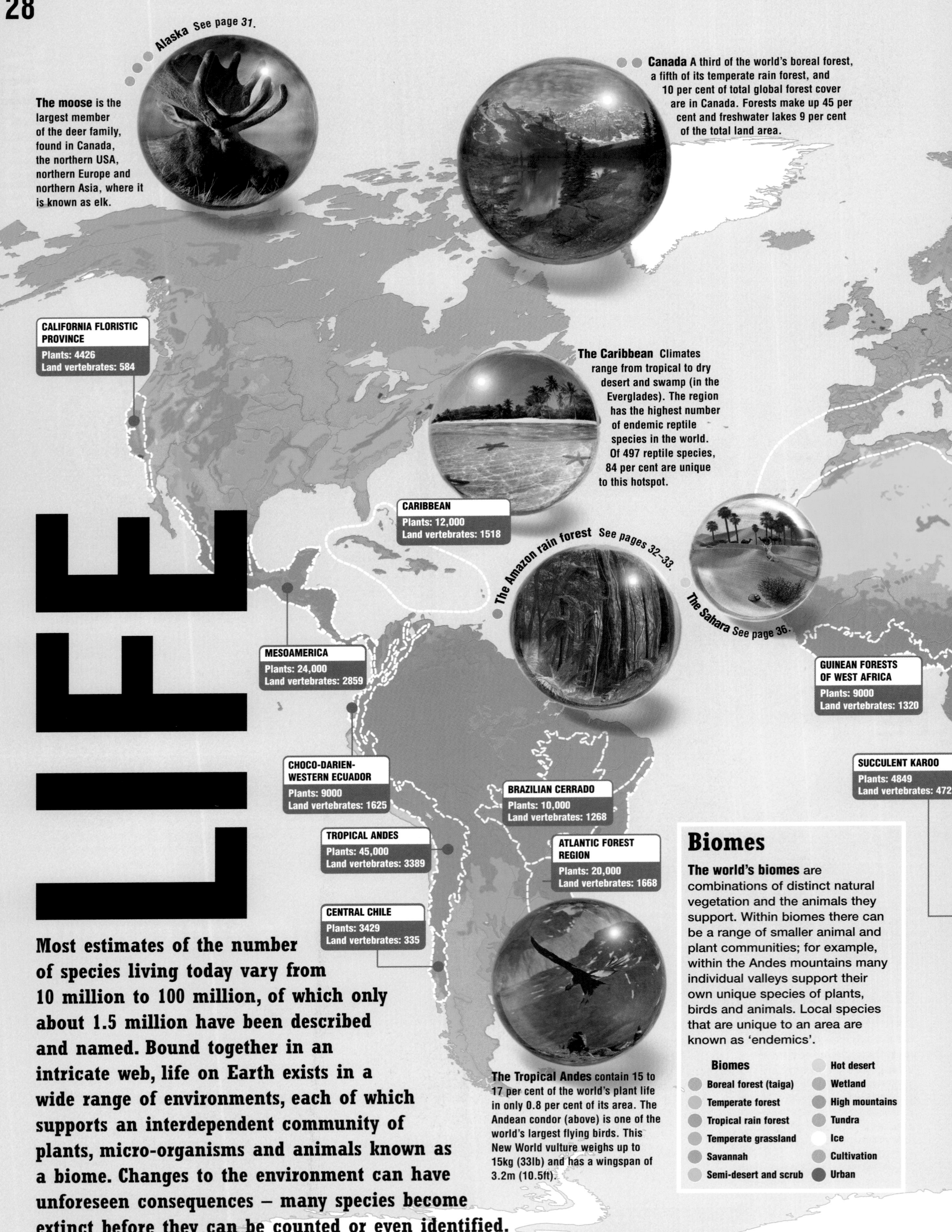

Alaska See page 31.

The moose is the largest member of the deer family, found in Canada, the northern USA, northern Europe and northern Asia, where it is known as elk.

Canada A third of the world's boreal forest, a fifth of its temperate rain forest, and 10 per cent of total global forest cover are in Canada. Forests make up 45 per cent and freshwater lakes 9 per cent of the total land area.

CALIFORNIA FLORISTIC PROVINCE
Plants: 4426
Land vertebrates: 584

The Caribbean Climates range from tropical to dry desert and swamp (in the Everglades). The region has the highest number of endemic reptile species in the world. Of 497 reptile species, 84 per cent are unique to this hotspot.

CARIBBEAN
Plants: 12,000
Land vertebrates: 1518

The Amazon rain forest See pages 32–33.

The Sahara See page 36.

GUINEAN FORESTS OF WEST AFRICA
Plants: 9000
Land vertebrates: 1320

MESOAMERICA
Plants: 24,000
Land vertebrates: 2859

SUCCULENT KAROO
Plants: 4849
Land vertebrates: 472

CHOCO-DARIEN-WESTERN ECUADOR
Plants: 9000
Land vertebrates: 1625

BRAZILIAN CERRADO
Plants: 10,000
Land vertebrates: 1268

LIFE

TROPICAL ANDES
Plants: 45,000
Land vertebrates: 3389

ATLANTIC FOREST REGION
Plants: 20,000
Land vertebrates: 1668

Biomes

The world's biomes are combinations of distinct natural vegetation and the animals they support. Within biomes there can be a range of smaller animal and plant communities; for example, within the Andes mountains many individual valleys support their own unique species of plants, birds and animals. Local species that are unique to an area are known as 'endemics'.

CENTRAL CHILE
Plants: 3429
Land vertebrates: 335

Most estimates of the number of species living today vary from 10 million to 100 million, of which only about 1.5 million have been described and named. Bound together in an intricate web, life on Earth exists in a wide range of environments, each of which supports an interdependent community of plants, micro-organisms and animals known as a biome. Changes to the environment can have unforeseen consequences – many species become extinct before they can be counted or even identified.

The Tropical Andes contain 15 to 17 per cent of the world's plant life in only 0.8 per cent of its area. The Andean condor (above) is one of the world's largest flying birds. This New World vulture weighs up to 15kg (33lb) and has a wingspan of 3.2m (10.5ft).

Biomes

- Boreal forest (taiga)
- Temperate forest
- Tropical rain forest
- Temperate grassland
- Savannah
- Semi-desert and scrub
- Hot desert
- Wetland
- High mountains
- Tundra
- Ice
- Cultivation
- Urban

Estonia The flower meadows, forests and coastal regions of Estonia contain some of Europe's most varied ecosystems. Many rare plant species flourish, including a large number of orchids (left).

Siberia *See page 38.*

Siberia's taiga or boreal forest contains 54 per cent of the world's coniferous forests.

China's South-west Mountains *See page 38.*

The Caucasus The Western tur (left), a species of wild goat, is native to the Caucasus, where deserts, savannahs, swamp forests and dry woodlands contain more than twice the animal diversity found in adjacent regions of Europe and Asia.

CAUCASUS
Plants: 6300
Land vertebrates: 632

MOUNTAINS OF SOUTH-WEST CHINA
Plants: 12,000
Land vertebrates: 1141

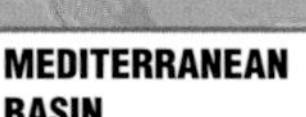

MEDITERRANEAN BASIN
Plants: 25,000
Land vertebrates: 770
See page 34

PHILIPPINES
Plants: 7620
Land vertebrates: 1114

The Philippines Today, only 7 per cent of the original rain forest remains but the islands are still among the world's most biodiverse. Rare birds and animals such as the Philippine tarsier (above) survive in forest fragments.

WESTERN GHATS AND SRI LANKA
Plants: 4780
Land vertebrates: 1073
See page 38

INDO-BURMA
Plants: 13,500
Land vertebrates: 2185

Lion numbers have fallen throughout Africa but Serengeti maintains a population of around 1500 individuals.

POLYNESIA AND MICRONESIA
Plants: 6557
Land vertebrates: 342

EASTERN ARC MOUNTAINS AND COASTAL FORESTS
Plants: 4000
Land vertebrates: 1019

The Serengeti *See page 36.*

SUNDALAND
Plants: 25,000
Land vertebrates: 1800

WALLACEA
Plants: 10,000
Land vertebrates: 1142

The Great Barrier Reef *See page 41.*

Madagascar *See page 37.*

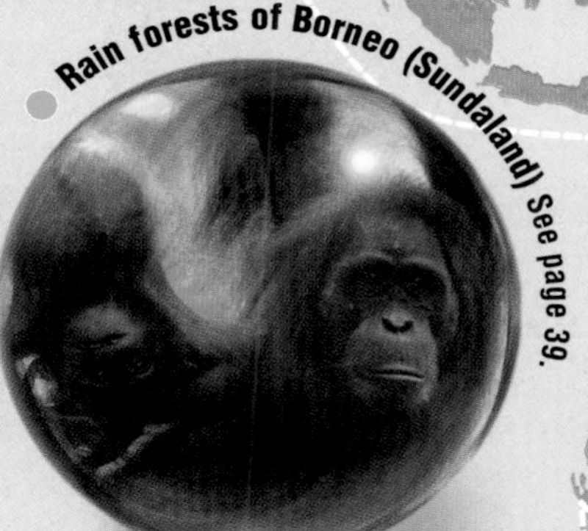

Rain forests of Borneo (Sundaland) *See page 39.*

CAPE FLORISTIC PROVINCE
Plants: 8200
Land vertebrates: 562

MADAGASCAR AND INDIAN OCEAN ISLANDS
Plants: 12,000
Land vertebrates: 987

NEW CALEDONIA
Plants: 3332
Land vertebrates: 190

NEW ZEALAND
Plants: 2300
Land vertebrates: 217

SOUTH-WEST AUSTRALIA
Plants: 5469
Land vertebrates: 456
Australia *See page 40*

Biodiversity hotspots

Over a third of the world's terrestrial plants and animals live in regions amounting to less than 2 per cent of the land area. Christened 'hotspots' by ecologist Norman Myers, they are remarkable for the sheer variety of the plants they support, and the biological diversity – biodiversity – which follows the richness of plant life.

Biodiversity hotspot information panel

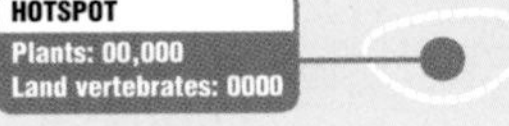

HOTSPOT
Plants: 00,000
Land vertebrates: 0000

Biodiversity hotspot perimeters

The Antarctic *See page 41.*

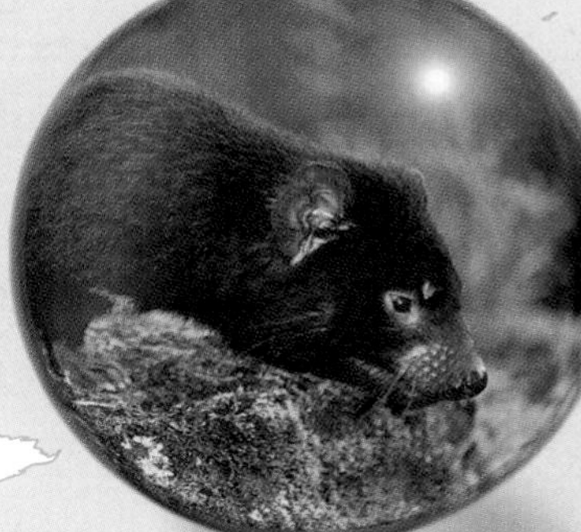

The Tasmanian devil, a small, fiercely carnivorous marsupial, survives in parts of Tasmania, though it is extinct in mainland Australia.

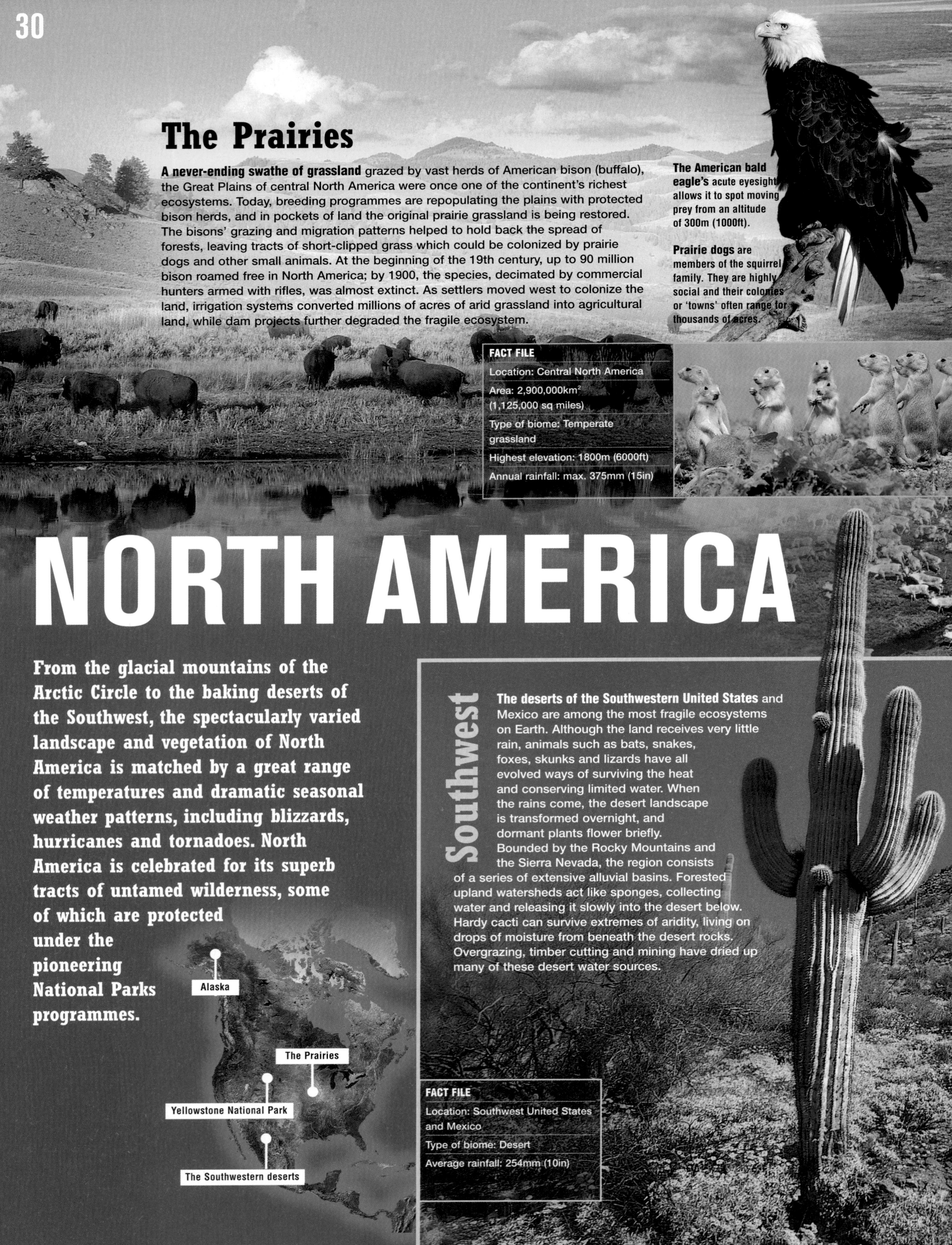

The Prairies

A never-ending swathe of grassland grazed by vast herds of American bison (buffalo), the Great Plains of central North America were once one of the continent's richest ecosystems. Today, breeding programmes are repopulating the plains with protected bison herds, and in pockets of land the original prairie grassland is being restored. The bisons' grazing and migration patterns helped to hold back the spread of forests, leaving tracts of short-clipped grass which could be colonized by prairie dogs and other small animals. At the beginning of the 19th century, up to 90 million bison roamed free in North America; by 1900, the species, decimated by commercial hunters armed with rifles, was almost extinct. As settlers moved west to colonize the land, irrigation systems converted millions of acres of arid grassland into agricultural land, while dam projects further degraded the fragile ecosystem.

The American bald eagle's acute eyesight allows it to spot moving prey from an altitude of 300m (1000ft).

Prairie dogs are members of the squirrel family. They are highly social and their colonies or 'towns' often range for thousands of acres.

FACT FILE

Location: Central North America

Area: 2,900,000km² (1,125,000 sq miles)

Type of biome: Temperate grassland

Highest elevation: 1800m (6000ft)

Annual rainfall: max. 375mm (15in)

NORTH AMERICA

From the glacial mountains of the Arctic Circle to the baking deserts of the Southwest, the spectacularly varied landscape and vegetation of North America is matched by a great range of temperatures and dramatic seasonal weather patterns, including blizzards, hurricanes and tornadoes. North America is celebrated for its superb tracts of untamed wilderness, some of which are protected under the pioneering National Parks programmes.

Alaska

The Prairies

Yellowstone National Park

The Southwestern deserts

Southwest

The deserts of the Southwestern United States and Mexico are among the most fragile ecosystems on Earth. Although the land receives very little rain, animals such as bats, snakes, foxes, skunks and lizards have all evolved ways of surviving the heat and conserving limited water. When the rains come, the desert landscape is transformed overnight, and dormant plants flower briefly. Bounded by the Rocky Mountains and the Sierra Nevada, the region consists of a series of extensive alluvial basins. Forested upland watersheds act like sponges, collecting water and releasing it slowly into the desert below. Hardy cacti can survive extremes of aridity, living on drops of moisture from beneath the desert rocks. Overgrazing, timber cutting and mining have dried up many of these desert water sources.

FACT FILE

Location: Southwest United States and Mexico

Type of biome: Desert

Average rainfall: 254mm (10in)

About 70 per cent of North America's 58,000 grizzly bears live in Alaska. The bears at Kodiak Island, almost 3m (9ft) high, are the largest brown bears in the world, thriving on rich supplies of migrating salmon.

Between 4000–7000 grey wolves live in Alaska. Over most of the region, they travel in packs, with territories as large as 13,000km² (5000 sq miles), and hunt animals such as Arctic goats and caribou.

Much of Alaska is a wilderness of ice and snow. It has the highest mountain in the United States, Denali (Mt McKinley) 6194m (20,321ft) and North America's largest piedmont glacier, Malaspina, which spreads out from high ground to extend 65km (40 miles) long and 55km (34 miles) wide across a broad plain. Moist maritime air collides with towering mountain ranges, producing thick snow to nourish the glaciers. The landscape is scoured by ice, wind and blizzards. Much of the region is tundra; the ground is permanently frozen up to a metre below the surface. Water saturates the peaty top soil and creates an intricate network of lakes, interspersed with sedges, grasses and dwarf trees. Thick-furred, sturdy-limbed mammals such as grey wolves, Arctic foxes, moose and snowshoe hares have evolved to live with the cold. Up to a million caribou, in about 32 herds, migrate across the sodden land.

Alaska

FACT FILE

Location: Northwest North America and north Pacific

Area: 1,530,700km² (591,005sq miles)

Type of biome: Tundra, mountains and forest

Highest elevation: Denali (Mt McKinley) 6194m (20,321ft)

Saguaro cacti are perfectly developed for desert life. Their pleated stems can expand like an accordion to absorb and store enormous quantities of water whenever it becomes available.

The adaptable coyote is found throughout the United States and much of Canada. Slim, hardy desert coyotes may be only about half the weight of their northern mountain-dwelling relations.

Collared lizards live mainly in dry gullies and canyons. Even when basking they stay alert for predators.

The world's oldest national park, Yellowstone was established in 1872, the brainchild of President Theodore Roosevelt. It consists mainly of volcanic plateaus, with thousands of fumaroles, hot springs and boiling mud pools, and 200 geysers. Yellowstone preserves an area of outstanding mountain wilderness. The foundation of Yellowstone pioneered a robust land conservation movement in the 20th century. Today, there are over 54 million acres of government-protected land in the United States, and a total of 51 National Parks.

FACT FILE

Location: Western United States

Area: 8984km² (3469 sq miles)

Type of biome: Temperate deciduous forest, grassland, wetland

Yellowstone National Park

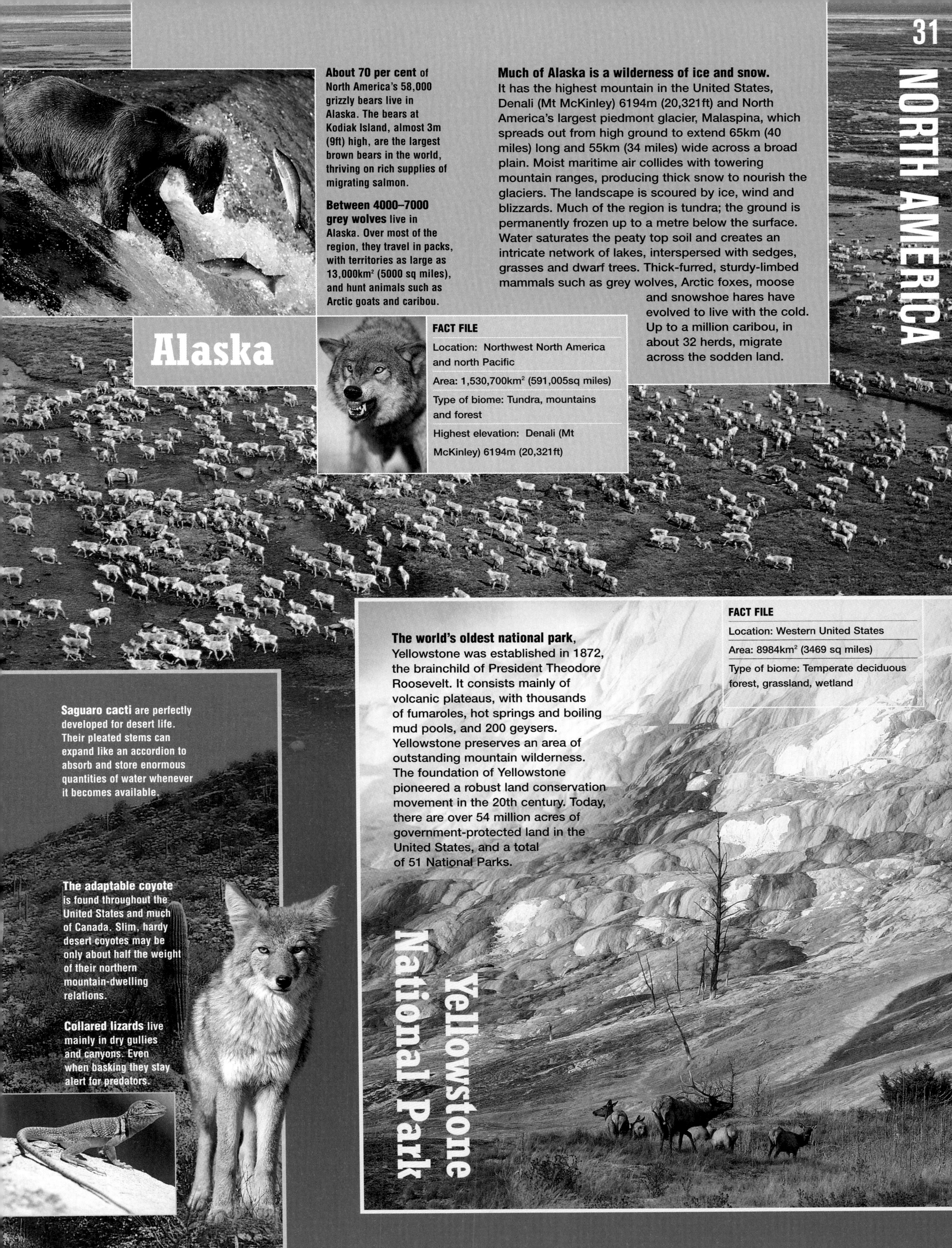

The wetlands, tropical rain forests and Andean cloud forests of South America form a region of unparalleled biodiversity, home to many thousands of unique species. They are among the Earth's most productive environments, supporting huge concentrations of mammals, birds, reptiles, fish, insects and plants. The River Amazon runs 6400km (4000 miles) across the continent, its volume swelled by seasonal rains that can exceed 3m (10ft) a year. Its vast river basin covers nearly 40 per cent of the total area of South America, and contains more than half of the world's remaining tropical rain forest.

Amazon rain forest

alapagos

The Pantanal

SOUTH AMERICA

The Pantanal

Hyacinth macaws have glossy deep violet feathers and measure about 1m (3ft) from beak to tail. Probably fewer than 7500 birds remain in the wild.

Capybaras, found only in South America, are the world's largest rodents. These semi-aquatic creatures are 1.2m (4ft) long and weigh 45kg (100lb).

The Pantanal, a sprawling expanse of lagoons and pastures lying in southern Brazil, Bolivia and Paraguay, is the largest freshwater wetland on Earth. During the rainy season, the River Paraguay and its tributaries flood the plains with water more than 3m (10ft) deep, marooning small islands as far as the eye can see. The rains recede in April, creating a rich grassland, plentifully supplied with pools and waterholes – a perfect breeding ground for birds and mammals. This watery paradise contains the most intense concentration of animal species per square kilometre outside Africa and is particularly rich in water birds such as the huge jabiru stork, graceful egrets and the roseate spoonbill.

The extraordinary leaf-eating hoatzin has a digestive system unlike that of all other birds except for the unrelated kakapo: like ruminant mammals, it ferments tough plant food with the aid of bacteria.

During flood season pink river dolphins move out of the main river into flooded forests and grasslands.

The Amazon rain forest

The Amazon rain forest is the largest in the world, with a value to the planet that goes far beyond its immediate environment. Over 20 per cent of the world's oxygen is produced here. If Amazonia were a country it would be the ninth largest on Earth. On its 6400-km (4000-mile) journey across the continent, from high in the Peruvian Andes to the Atlantic Ocean, the River Amazon drains a low-lying basin covering 6.5 million km² (2.5 million sq miles) with a fifth of the world's river water. Fed by rainfall and melted snow from the Andes, the Amazon floods regularly. Of the total area, about 100,000km² (39,000sq miles) lie under up to 9m (30ft) of water for months, and some parts are continuously submerged, forming swamps. Average daily temperatures of around 33°C (91°F), combined with high humidity, make for an exceptionally fertile environment.

The quantity and diversity of life in the forest is truly astonishing. Estimates of the total number of insect species range between 5 million and 30 million though only a fraction have been classified: a single tree may contain as many as 95 species of ants, only 10 fewer than in the whole of Germany.

Golden-eyed tree frogs make their homes in water-filled tree holes, from which they call to other frogs as night falls.

FACT FILE

Location: Northern South America

Area: 5.2 million km² (2–3 million sq miles)

Type of biome: Tropical rain forest

Unique plant species: 30,000+

Unique tree species: 2500

Native animal species: 2500 fish species, 1600 bird species

Average annual rainfall: 1945mm (77in); varies between 613–3309mm (12–130in)

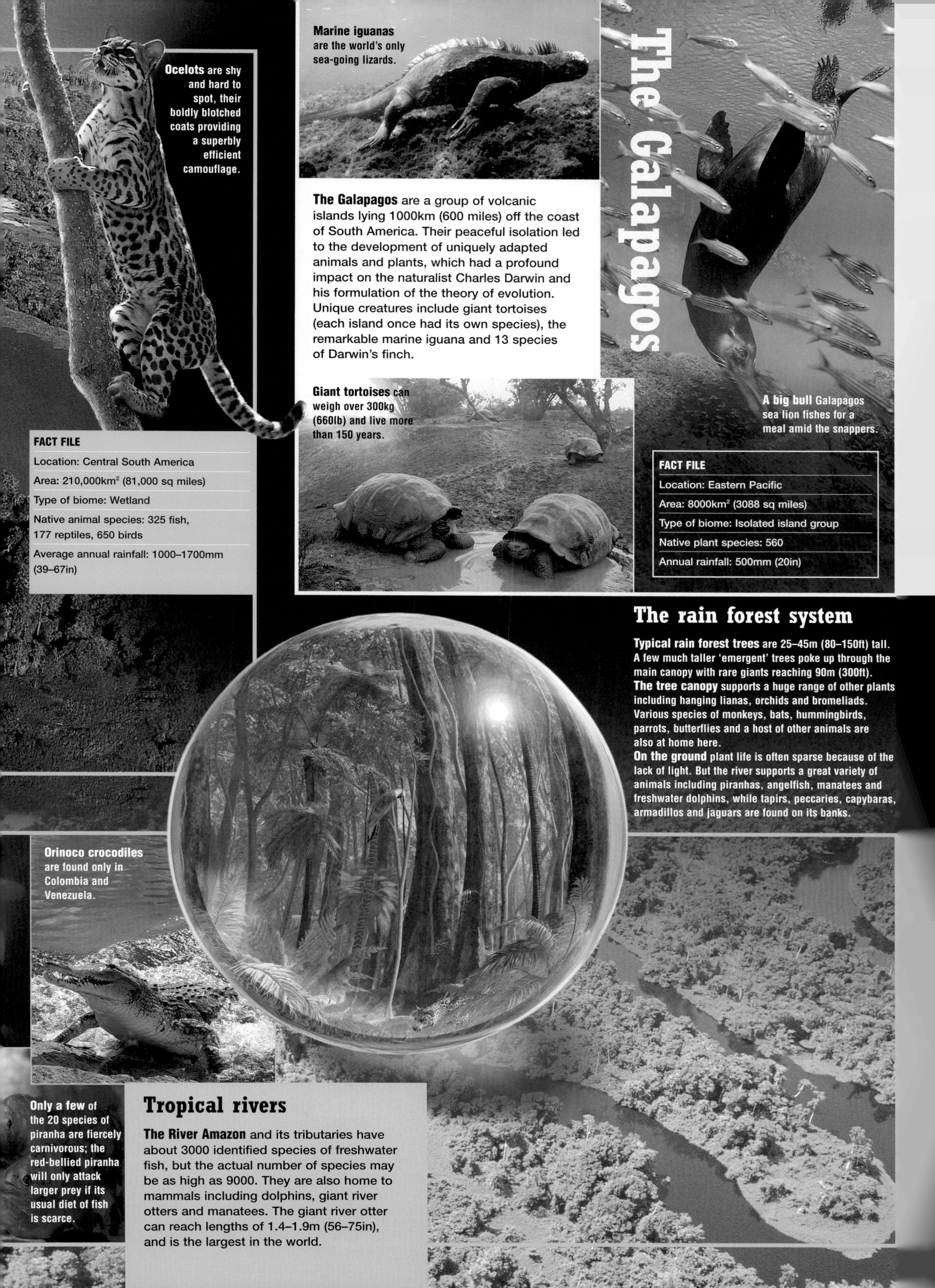

Ocelots are shy and hard to spot, their boldly blotched coats providing a superbly efficient camouflage.

Marine iguanas are the world's only sea-going lizards.

The Galapagos are a group of volcanic islands lying 1000km (600 miles) off the coast of South America. Their peaceful isolation led to the development of uniquely adapted animals and plants, which had a profound impact on the naturalist Charles Darwin and his formulation of the theory of evolution. Unique creatures include giant tortoises (each island once had its own species), the remarkable marine iguana and 13 species of Darwin's finch.

Giant tortoises can weigh over 300kg (660lb) and live more than 150 years.

A big bull Galapagos sea lion fishes for a meal amid the snappers.

FACT FILE

Location: Central South America

Area: 210,000km² (81,000 sq miles)

Type of biome: Wetland

Native animal species: 325 fish, 177 reptiles, 650 birds

Average annual rainfall: 1000–1700mm (39–67in)

FACT FILE

Location: Eastern Pacific

Area: 8000km² (3088 sq miles)

Type of biome: Isolated island group

Native plant species: 560

Annual rainfall: 500mm (20in)

The rain forest system

Typical rain forest trees are 25–45m (80–150ft) tall. A few much taller 'emergent' trees poke up through the main canopy with rare giants reaching 90m (300ft).
The tree canopy supports a huge range of other plants including hanging lianas, orchids and bromeliads. Various species of monkeys, bats, hummingbirds, parrots, butterflies and a host of other animals are also at home here.
On the ground plant life is often sparse because of the lack of light. But the river supports a great variety of animals including piranhas, angelfish, manatees and freshwater dolphins, while tapirs, peccaries, capybaras, armadillos and jaguars are found on its banks.

Orinoco crocodiles are found only in Colombia and Venezuela.

Only a few of the 20 species of piranha are fiercely carnivorous; the red-bellied piranha will only attack larger prey if its usual diet of fish is scarce.

Tropical rivers

The River Amazon and its tributaries have about 3000 identified species of freshwater fish, but the actual number of species may be as high as 9000. They are also home to mammals including dolphins, giant river otters and manatees. The giant river otter can reach lengths of 1.4–1.9m (56–75in), and is the largest in the world.

The Southern European wetlands

Wildernesses of dunes, sandbars, marshes and lagoons, fertilized by rich, alluvial river water, the wetlands of southern Europe are formed by the deltas of rivers such as the Guadalquivir and the Rhône. They are a magnet for breeding birds such as herons, spoonbills, storks, vultures, ducks, egrets and flamingoes. As well as plentiful deer and wild boar, the Spanish wetlands also attract the rare Iberian lynx, while in the Camargue region of southern France white horses run wild.

FACT FILE

Location: Coto Doñana, southern Spain

Area: 771km² (298 sq miles)

Type of biome: Wetland

Average rainfall: 525mm (20in)

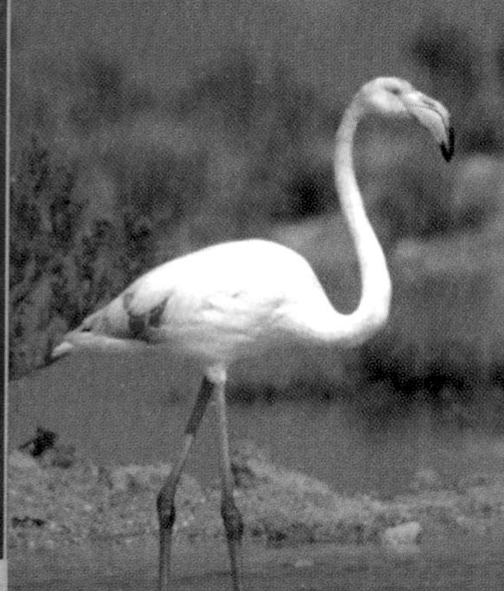

The Spanish imperial eagle is one of the world's rarest birds of prey. There are fewer than 130 breeding pairs now left in the wild.

In spring, up to 10,000 greater flamingo feed in the shallow lagoons of Coto Doñana. During wet spells the birds nest in the area.

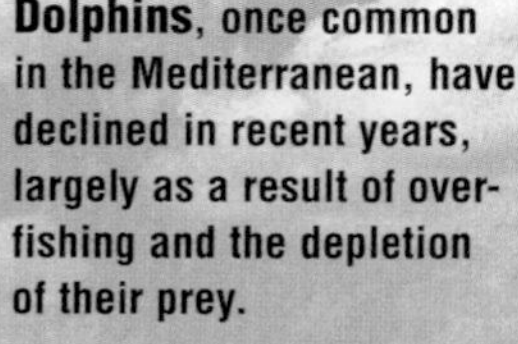

Dolphins, once common in the Mediterranean, have declined in recent years, largely as a result of over-fishing and the depletion of their prey.

FACT FILE

Location: Southern Europe, west Asia and north Africa

Type of biome: Chaparral/ temperate deciduous forest

Remaining intact vegetation: 110,000km² (38,610 sq miles), 4.7 per cent of the original extent

Plant species: 25,000

Land vertebrates: 770 species

The Mediterranean region contains a wide range of endemic plant species, supporting about 80 per cent of the European total. Species are often highly localized, for instance restricted to small mountain ranges or islands. The characteristic vegetation of the region is the *maquis*, a mixed scrubland of evergreen shrubs, including mints, laurels and myrtles, and small trees such as olives and figs. These hardy, drought-resistant plants are perfectly suited to long, hot, dry summers and warm, moist winters. Centuries of farming and grazing by goats have impoverished the soil and depleted the *maquis*.

The Mediterranean

At the end of the last Ice Age much of the European continent was blanketed with dense, primeval forest. Pockets of forest survive in isolated areas, such as the Bialowieza National Park in Poland and the Czech Republic's Bohemian forest. Winters are long, with snow from October to April. The remains of these forests support mixed broadleaved and coniferous trees including beech, oak, alder, maple, elm, ash and pine and spruce. The forests are also a refuge for larger European mammals, including brown bears, deer, wild boar, lynx, wolves and beavers.

The forests of Central and Eastern Europe

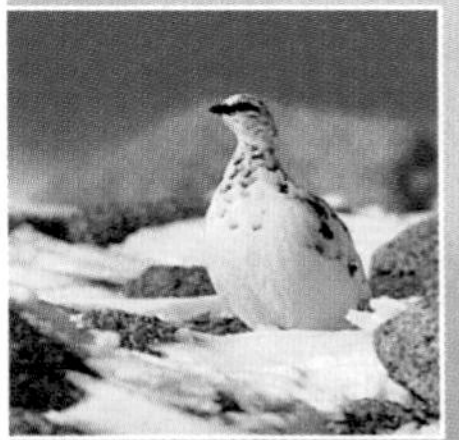

The snow-capped peaks, deep mountain valleys, fast-flowing streams and flowering meadows of the European Alps have been shaped by millennia of glacial erosion. Vegetation and local climate are influenced by elevation. Deciduous trees such as beech and birch are found on the lower slopes. Coniferous trees and meadows, rich in grasses, flowers and shrubs, flourish between 1600–2400m (5000–8000ft). At higher elevations the stony peaks are permanently capped with snow. National parks protect native animals such as the ibex, chamois, marmot and mountain hare.

The Alps

Ptarmigan (above) have feathered feet which enable them to walk on snowy ground. They are superbly camouflaged throughout the year, their plumage changing with each season.

Alpine ibex (right) live at altitudes above 2000–3500m (6500–11,500ft). Strongly muscled and sure-footed, they move with ease in the rocky terrain.

FACT FILE

Length of mountain chain: 1050km (650 miles)

Type of biome: Temperate deciduous forest, alpine grassland

Highest elevation: Mont Blanc 4807m (15,771ft)

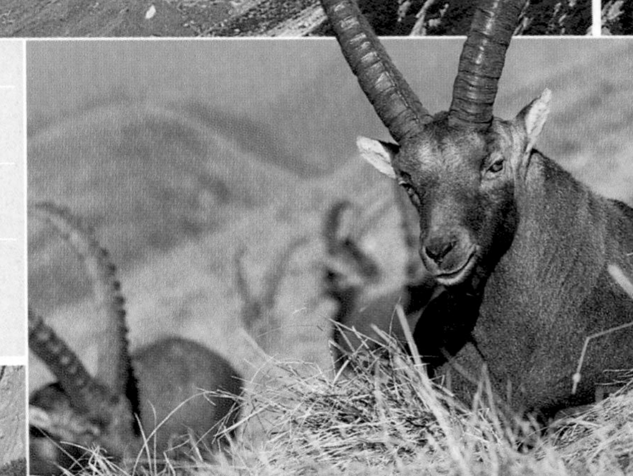

Eagle owls prey on anything from small birds and mice to roe deer fawns.

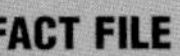

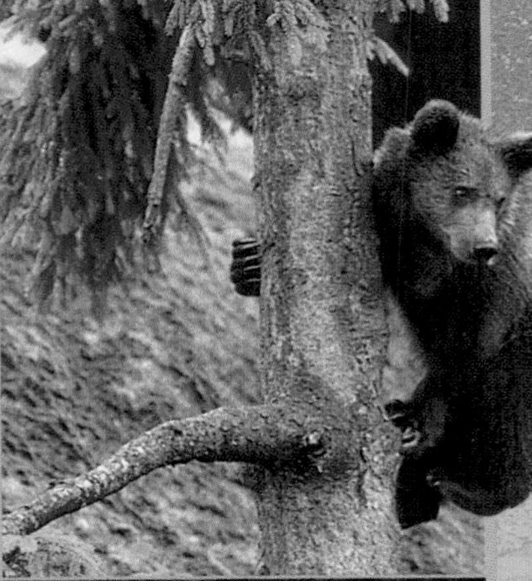

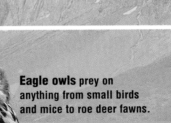

FACT FILE

Location: Central and Eastern Europe

Type of biome: Temperate deciduous forest

Average annual rainfall: 640mm (25in)

Grey wolves once roamed all over Europe, adapting to every habitat. They now remain mainly in isolated pockets.

European brown bears are solitary animals, which feed on small mammals, fish, wild plants and honey.

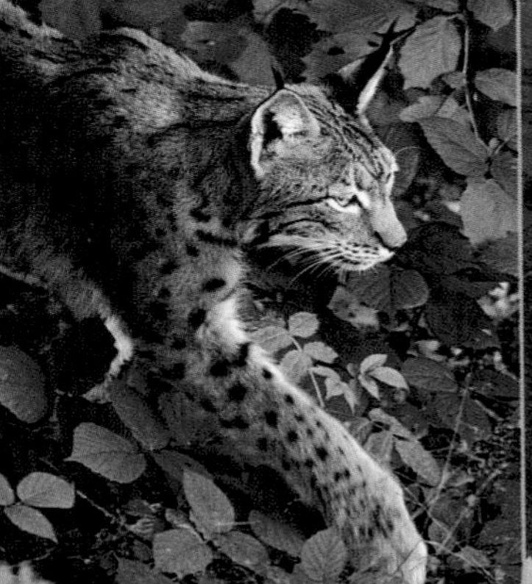

European lynx are still found in mountain and forest regions of Central and Northern Europe. The most abundant populations are in Scandinavia, Finland, the Baltic states, Belarus and Russia.

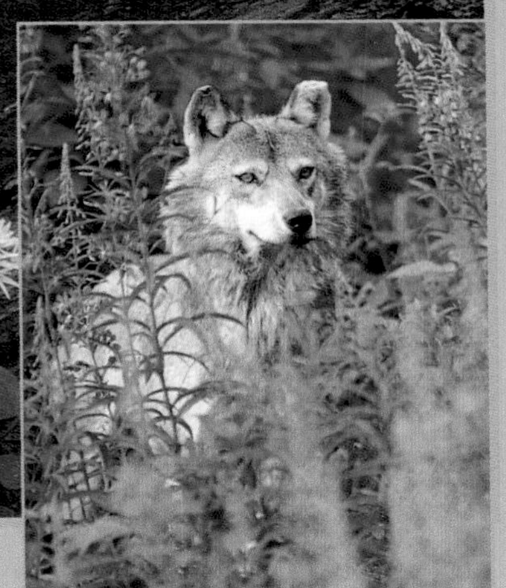

EUROPE

Despite centuries of human influence and a population now standing at more than 500 million, Europe's landscape still contains a tapestry of forests, mountains, lakes, arid plateaus and wetlands. Much of the temperate forest that once covered the continent has been cleared, but pockets of true wilderness remain, particularly in the north, including Scandinavia, Finland and the Baltic states, and in central Europe.

Forests of Central and Eastern Europe

Alps

Coto Doñana

Carmargue

Mediterranean

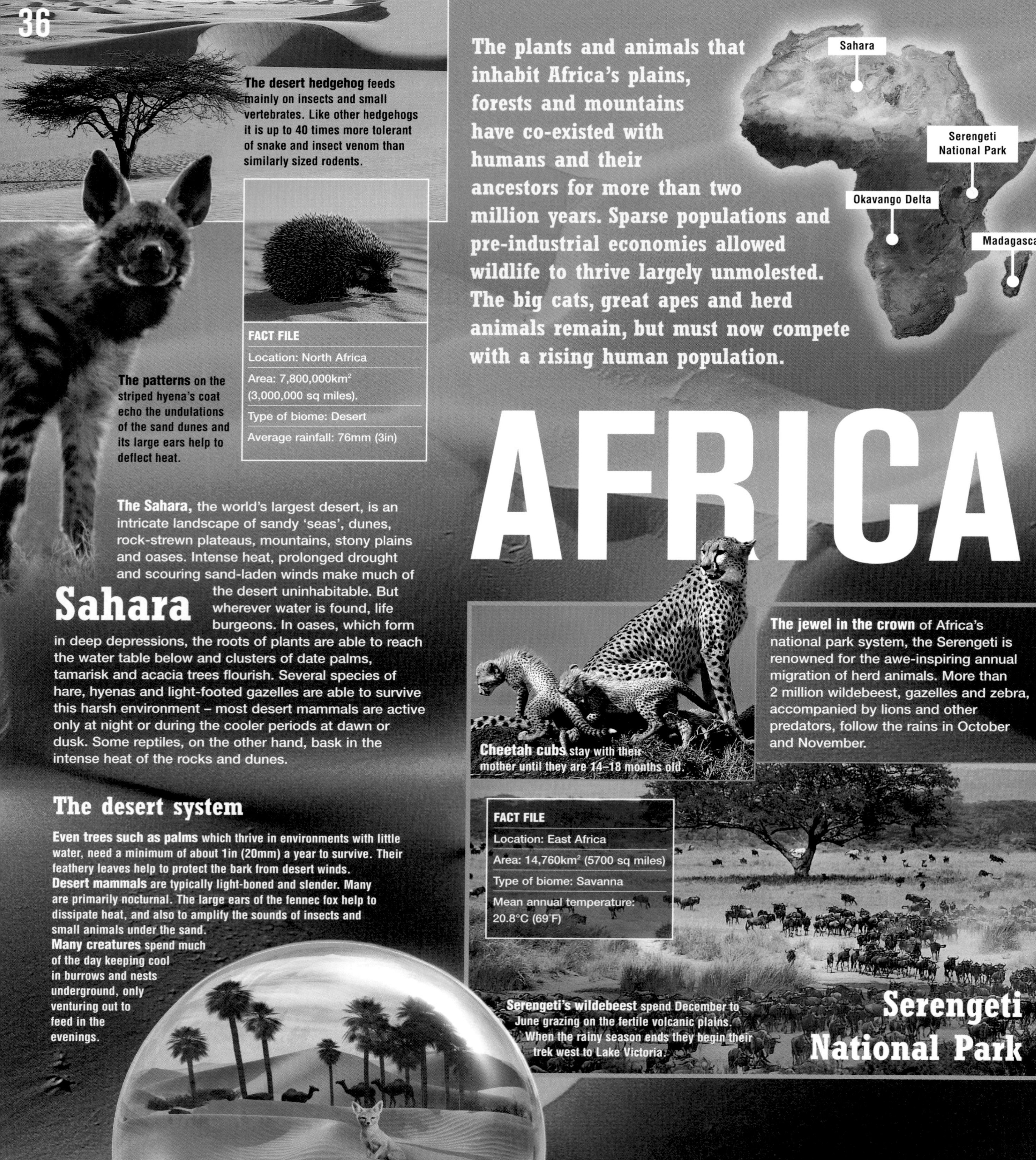

The desert hedgehog feeds mainly on insects and small vertebrates. Like other hedgehogs it is up to 40 times more tolerant of snake and insect venom than similarly sized rodents.

The patterns on the striped hyena's coat echo the undulations of the sand dunes and its large ears help to deflect heat.

FACT FILE

Location: North Africa

Area: 7,800,000km² (3,000,000 sq miles).

Type of biome: Desert

Average rainfall: 76mm (3in)

The plants and animals that inhabit Africa's plains, forests and mountains have co-existed with humans and their ancestors for more than two million years. Sparse populations and pre-industrial economies allowed wildlife to thrive largely unmolested. The big cats, great apes and herd animals remain, but must now compete with a rising human population.

Sahara

Serengeti National Park

Okavango Delta

Madagascar

AFRICA

Sahara

The Sahara, the world's largest desert, is an intricate landscape of sandy 'seas', dunes, rock-strewn plateaus, mountains, stony plains and oases. Intense heat, prolonged drought and scouring sand-laden winds make much of the desert uninhabitable. But wherever water is found, life burgeons. In oases, which form in deep depressions, the roots of plants are able to reach the water table below and clusters of date palms, tamarisk and acacia trees flourish. Several species of hare, hyenas and light-footed gazelles are able to survive this harsh environment – most desert mammals are active only at night or during the cooler periods at dawn or dusk. Some reptiles, on the other hand, bask in the intense heat of the rocks and dunes.

The desert system

Even trees such as palms which thrive in environments with little water, need a minimum of about 1in (20mm) a year to survive. Their feathery leaves help to protect the bark from desert winds.
Desert mammals are typically light-boned and slender. Many are primarily nocturnal. The large ears of the fennec fox help to dissipate heat, and also to amplify the sounds of insects and small animals under the sand.
Many creatures spend much of the day keeping cool in burrows and nests underground, only venturing out to feed in the evenings.

Cheetah cubs stay with their mother until they are 14–18 months old.

The jewel in the crown of Africa's national park system, the Serengeti is renowned for the awe-inspiring annual migration of herd animals. More than 2 million wildebeest, gazelles and zebra, accompanied by lions and other predators, follow the rains in October and November.

FACT FILE

Location: East Africa

Area: 14,760km² (5700 sq miles)

Type of biome: Savanna

Mean annual temperature: 20.8°C (69°F)

Serengeti's wildebeest spend December to June grazing on the fertile volcanic plains. When the rainy season ends they begin their trek west to Lake Victoria.

Serengeti National Park

Madagascar

Madagascar is the only place in the world where lemurs occur as native mammals. It is the world's fourth largest island, located 400km (250 miles) off the south-eastern coast of Africa. The terrain ranges from beaches and mangrove-fringed lagoons to mountains, rain forests, grasslands and deserts. Many of Madagascar's plants and animals are unique – a legacy of the island's separation from the Indian continent about 95 million years ago – which encouraged the development of special adaptations. On Madagascar, lemurs could flourish, completely free from competition from monkeys.

A leaf-tailed gecko (far left) opens its mouth wide in a threat display to deter potential predators.

In the hierarchical lemur society, this mother ring-tailed lemur's status in the group will be critical to her infant's survival.

MOUNTAIN GORILLAS OF THE VIRUNGA

The Virunga volcanoes straddle the borders of Rwanda, Zaire and Uganda. The last of Africa's rare mountain gorillas live on their forested slopes – probably no more than 600 survive. In 1925, Africa's first national park was established to protect them. Gorillas are highly social animals, usually living in groups of five to ten, headed by a male and several females, which start to breed from about ten years of age.

A mature male, or silverback, gorilla.

Able to survive long periods without water – they can travel 1000km (620 miles) in eight days without drinking – camels are perfectly developed to cope with the extreme aridity of the Sahara.

Marabou storks get much of their food from scavenging – from victims of scrub fires, from lion kills and even piles of rubbish.

Okavango Delta

One of the world's largest inland water systems, the Okavango Delta is the junction of a complex system of waterways that flow through Angola, Namibia and Botswana. It is a vibrant island of life in the dry Kalahari savanna.

During the rainy season from November to April, migrant birds return to a delta now alive with luxuriant growth.

The Angolan rains, between November and April, cause floods that meander slowly through the flat lands, eventually reaching Okavango in July. As water flows into the delta, large congregations of wildlife, including elephants, buffalos, crocodiles and hippopotamuses, begin to gather around the edge of the newly flooded areas, and the dried-out vegetation breaks into flower.

The hippopotamus spends much of the day in the water and can remain completely submerged for more than five minutes at a time.

A green-carpeted spine of mountains that runs for almost 1600km (1000 miles) down south-west India, the Western Ghats are the principal watershed for all India, their summits trapping moisture-laden monsoon clouds. This fertile landscape of rivers, rain forests and grasslands is a unique ecosystem, supporting tigers, lion-tailed macaques, leopards, gaur (wild cattle), the Nilghiri tahr, a goat-antelope, and elephants – and many other species found nowhere else on Earth. A number of wildlife sanctuaries, including tiger reserves, have been established to protect the plant and animal life of the Ghats.

The Western Ghats

FACT FILE

Area: 160,000km² (62,000 sq miles)

Type of biome: Savanna, fragmented rain forest

Remaining intact vegetation: 12,450km² (4806 sq miles), 6.8 per cent of original extent

Hanuman langurs are sociable monkeys, equally at home in trees or on the ground, where they spend much of their time.

One function of the large 'casque' atop the great Indian hornbill's mighty beak is thought to be to amplify the bird's calls.

The Himalayan griffon vulture is found in parts of central Asia, living mainly at altitudes of 1200–4500ft (4000–14,800ft) and feeding on animal carcasses at up to 6000m (20,000ft) or more.

The slow loris is a carnivorous primate, feeding on snails, birds, insects, lizards and small mammals as well as fruit.

China's south-west mountains

An area no more than a tenth of all China, the lush mountains of the southwest contain 50 per cent of the country's birds and mammals. Sharp increases in elevation between ridge tops and river valleys support a wide spectrum of vegetation, from tropical forest to alpine meadows. In summer, the high Tibetan plateau traps monsoon rains, and the region becomes moist and lush. More than 12,000 species of plants are found, including hundreds of species of rhododendron. Animal life is equally plentiful. The beloved but endangered panda lives here along with golden monkeys, snow leopards, sika deer, musk deer and many species of pheasant.

Giant pandas are gentle, bamboo-eating members of the bear family. Numbers are dwindling, as their habitat is reduced by forest clearance.

FACT FILE

Location: Western China, bordering India and Myanmar

Area: 800,000km² (308,880 sq miles)

Type of biome: Temperate or deciduous forest

Remaining intact vegetation: 64,000km² (24,710 sq miles), 8 per cent of original extent

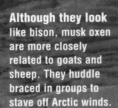

Although they look like bison, musk oxen are more closely related to goats and sheep. They huddle braced in groups to stave off Arctic winds.

FACT FILE

Area: 13,487,400km² (5,207,900 sq miles)

Type of biome: Boreal forest/tundra

Minimum temperature: –68°C (–90°F)

Snowy owls are native to the Arctic tundra. They use their excellent vision to spot their prey, hares and lemmings, and often hunt by day.

Siberia

The sweeping northern land of Siberia is notorious for the severity of its winters, with temperatures as low as –68°C (–90°F). A land of bleak, windswept plains, drained by great rivers, much of Siberia is covered by coniferous forest known as taiga, around 25 per cent of the world's total forest. Much of the wilderness of Russian birch, firs, spruce and pine has been virtually untouched by humans. Great brown bears hibernate in the winter, while Siberian lynx, wolves and the rare Amur tiger roam the forests. Birds include goshawks, grouse, nutcrackers, crossbills, thrushes and owls.

TIGERS

Well over half the world's wild tigers live in India, Nepal and Bangladesh. A network of 23 national parks in India are now dedicated to their conservation. But rising human populations are encroaching on tiger territories, and the poaching of tigers for the illegal trade in body parts for Chinese traditional medicines is increasing. Tigers need huge supplies of meat; a tigress with two cubs requires 3090kg (6800lb) of meat annually, an exhausting annual total of 40–70 kills.

Siberia

Mountains of south-west China

Western Ghats

Rain forests of Borneo

Asia, the world's greatest landmass, encompasses frozen tundra and wind-whipped pine forests as well as the world's highest mountain range and dry plateau. Further south are tropical rain forests and mangrove swamps, the source of some of the most numerous and important communities of plants and animals on Earth.

ASIA

Only 5000 to 7000 tigers remain in the wild. There may have been more than 100,000 at the start of the 20th century.

The rain forests of Borneo

Cloaked in dense, tropical rain forest, its coastline and rivers fringed with mangrove swamps, the island of Borneo is home to some fast-disappearing species. Solitary orang-utans are increasingly held in breeding sanctuaries. Proboscis monkeys live exclusively in Borneo's coastal forests and swamps. Fewer than 8000 of these distinctive, large-nosed, leaf-eating monkeys remain. With partially webbed feet, they are excellent swimmers, escaping from predators by diving into the water. Felling of mangrove forests, swamp drainage and forest fires all threaten the habitat of these unique primates.

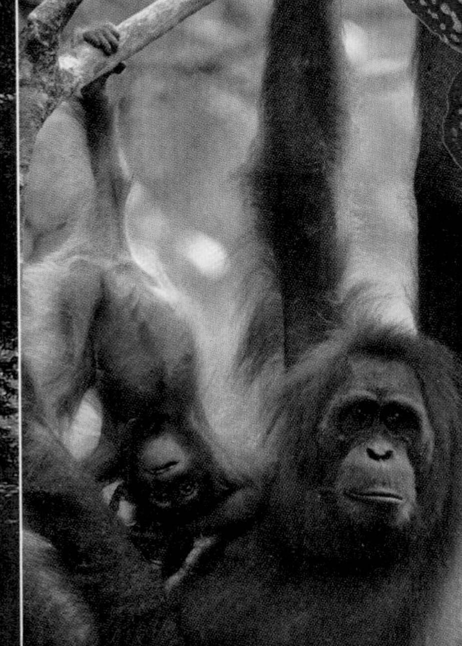

Orang-utans have a close bond with their young, which stay with the mothers for up to six years.

Rafflesias produce the world's largest flower with a diameter of 90cm (3ft).

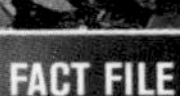

FACT FILE

Location: Island, South-east Asia

Area: 755,000km^2 (292,000 sq miles)

Type of biome: Rain forest

Highest elevation: Mount Kinabalu, 4101m (13,455ft)

Average annual rainfall: 3800mm (150in)

Endangered species: Orang-utan, clouded leopard

AUSTRALASIA & THE PACIFIC

Encompassing a huge range of climatic and topographical extremes, Australasia and the Pacific preserve a unique ecology. Millennia of relative isolation have encouraged the development of specially adapted plants and animals – found nowhere else on Earth.

Gregarious kangaroos live in large groups or 'mobs'. Males range widely looking for females to mate with.

The Great Barrier Reef

New Zealand

Antarctica

Koalas (above) have a very specialized diet, feeding on about 500g (1lb) of eucalyptus each night.

Wombats (left) forage for food mainly at night. Their young are held in a rear-facing pouch.

THE MARSUPIALS OF AUSTRALIA

Marsupials are mammals with external pouches in which their young develop. They may have originated in North America and are thought to have crossed to Australia by an early land bridge some 65 to 60 million years ago. Today, all except one group – the 55 species of opossum – are limited to Australasia, with about 155 species native to Australia. The best-known marsupials are the three species of large kangaroo, which live on the plains of central Australia. Smaller rat kangaroos, tree kangaroos and others thrive in habitats from subtropical forests to rocky outcrops.

New Zealand

Some 80 to 100 million years ago, New Zealand drifted away from the supercontinent of Gondwanaland into the South Pacific and became a storehouse of evolution, rich in unique species of flora and fauna. Before humans arrived, New Zealand's native birds had no predators, so several species – most notably the kiwis – became flightless, a development which left them vulnerable to introduced mammal predators. Others, such as the kakapo and takahe, have become endangered because of loss of habitat and hunting. Other relics of the past include the two species of lizard-like tuataras, the only members of their group left in the world, now found only on protected offshore islands.

The jewelled gecko is a tree-dwelling New Zealand native. Most are brilliant green with long prehensile tails which they use to aid climbing.

The plankton-rich waters of the Antarctic Ocean are a magnet for whales, including the minke, the smallest of the baleen, or whalebone, whales.

The takahe, with its indigo plumage and red beak, was believed to be extinct, until it was 'rediscovered' in 1948.

A kiwi is about the size of a chicken yet produces an egg twice as large.

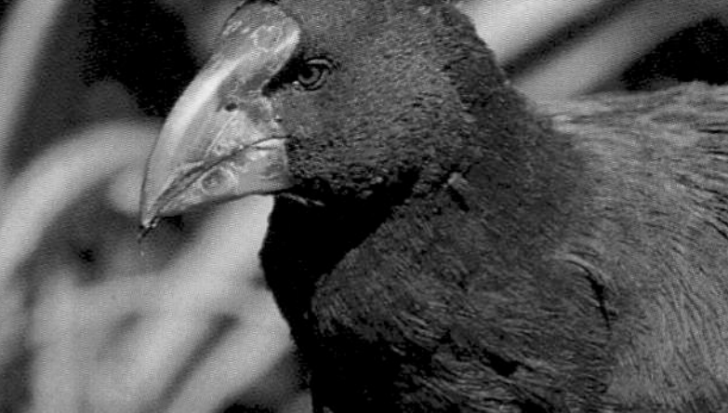

FACT FILE

Type of biome: Temperate deciduous forest

Plant species: 2300

Land vertebrates: 217 species

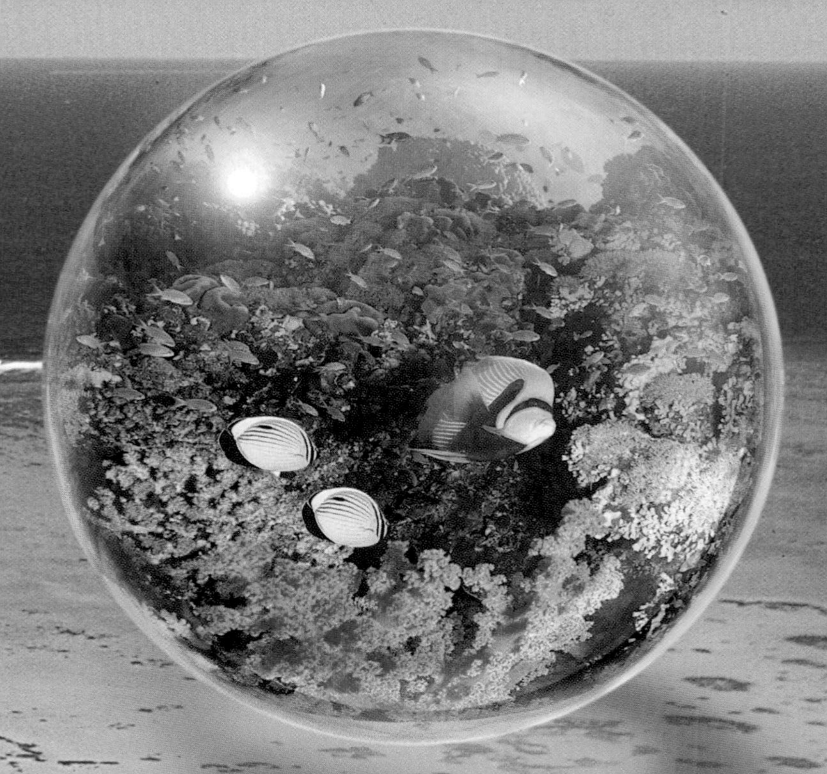

The reef system

An estimated 300 species of hard, reef-building corals support about 1500 species of fish.
As many as 150 species of coral have been found on a single atoll or reef. Some corals are delicately branched, others are flat, while some form massive boulders. Coral growth is sensitive to temperature and is most prolific at dusk.

FACT FILE

Location: Off east coast of Australia

Area: About 300,000km^2 (116,000 sq miles)

Type of biome: Coral reef system

The crown of thorns starfish, its numerous arms ridged with venomous spines, can devastate coral reefs when present in large numbers or 'outbreaks'.

The Great Barrier Reef

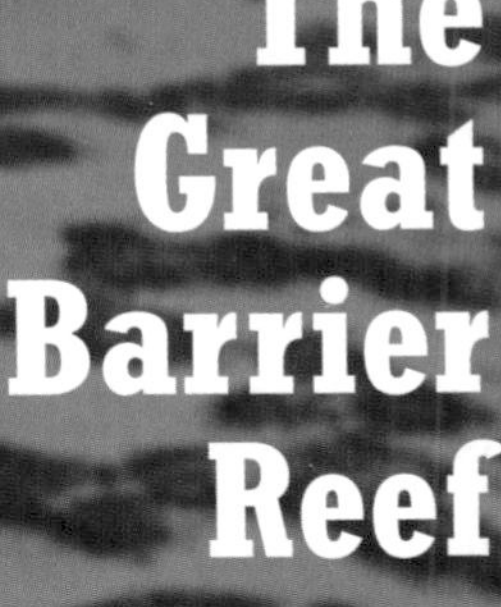

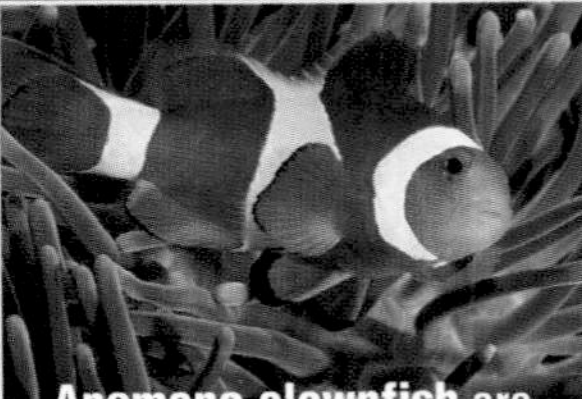

Anemone clownfish are one of the reef's colourful inhabitants.

The reef contains nesting grounds of world significance for six of the world's seven species of sea turtle, including the green turtle.

The largest structure on Earth built by living organisms, the Great Barrier Reef is, in fact, a broken maze of coral reefs and coral cays larger than the entire area of the British Isles. It includes about 3000 individual reefs, which provide a habitat for an amazing variety of marine life – more than 1500 species of fish, over 4000 mollusc species and 400 of sponges. Cays and islands support hundreds of bird species, including herons, osprey and pelicans.

Antarctica

The world's coldest continent with winter temperatures of about –60˚C (–76˚F), Antarctica is totally dark for six months a year. It is entirely blanketed by ice sheets, yet 800 species of lichens, fungi and algae (but only two kinds of flowering plant) are able to survive the cold. The absence of land mammal predators creates a haven for about 45 species of seabird. The 18 Antarctic mammal species are all marine, and include whales, seals and dolphins.

FACT FILE

Area: 13.9 million km^2 (5.36 million sq miles)

Typical temperatures on land:
Summer –20 to –35˚C (–5 to –31˚F)
Winter –40 to –70˚C (–40 to –94˚F)

The largest colony of Adélie penguins at Cape Adare contains an estimated 220,000 breeding pairs.

Male southern elephant seals may weigh almost 4 tons and can barely move on land. They take their name from the trunk-like proboscis.

Population density

Number of inhabitants
per km²   per sq mile
Over 200   Over 500
40-200   50-500
10-40   25-50
below 10   below 25

Number of inhabitants
per km²   per sq mile
Over 200   Over 500
40-200   50-500
10-40   25-50
below 10   below 25

Overall population density
in the USA is low, with
29 people per km². Around
23 per cent of the population
live in rural districts.

The average European
birth rate is 1.8 per
woman, leading to a
gradually ageing
population.

The US birth rate of
2.08 per woman is
the highest in the
developed world.

The population of central
Africa is expected to
increase by 193 per cent
between 2003 and 2050;
that of southern Africa is
projected to fall by 22 per
cent, mainly because of
the impact of AIDS.

About 90 per cent of the Earth's people live on
just 10 per cent of the land. Additionally, about
90 per cent of the people live north of the Equator.
Global population densities peak in the eastern USA,
Europe, India and East Asia. But densely populated areas
are not necessarily over-populated, as long as they have
sufficient resources – food, energy and water. The region
with the fastest growing population, Africa, faces the most
serious shortages of these essentials.

PEOPLE

There are almost 6 billion people in the world, and 99 per cent of
population growth – a total of nearly 80 million people a year – is
in the developing world. Globally, the average birth rate per woman
has fallen from six to three over the past 30 years, the result of
education programmes, improved healthcare and access
to contraception. But the poorer
developing countries are unable to
provide these services to dispersed
rural populations, and as a result
disparities in standards of living
are exacerbated.

A village of traditional African houses
made of mud-brick and roofed with straw.
In much of Africa small-scale subsistence
farming is the main way of life.

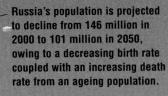

Russia's population is projected to decline from 146 million in 2000 to 101 million in 2050, owing to a decreasing birth rate coupled with an increasing death rate from an ageing population.

Mongolia is the world's least densely populated country, with less than two people per km².

To check population growth in China, a one-child policy was adopted in 1979. Despite increasing industrial growth, almost 70 per cent of the population live in rural districts.

Bangladesh is one of the world's most densely populated countries, with about 835 people per km².

In Australia, over 80 per cent of the population live in two coastal areas, which together cover only about 1 per cent of the country.

A disappearing lifestyle

Hunter-gatherers live by hunting, fishing in rivers or the sea, and collecting wild plant resources. Hunter-gathering sustained the human population for most of its history, but today it supports only 0.001 per cent of the world's people. These groups can be found in Africa, Asia, Australia, the Americas, and the Arctic and sub-Arctic. Some groups interact with surrounding societies, by selling goods and services, others exist entirely in isolation. Many groups are threatened by disease or by eviction from their lands.

The Lapps were once a mostly nomadic people, herding reindeer along migration routes spanning vast arctic regions of Europe (in modern-day Norway, Sweden, Finland and Russia). Only about 10 per cent of the Lapp population are now nomads, and migration routes are controlled by national governments.

The traditional way of life of the Penan tribespeople of Borneo has been affected by intensive commercial logging in the island's rain forests, driving them towards government settlements.

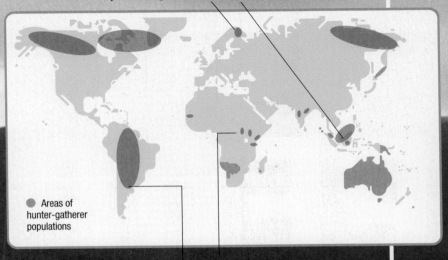

● Areas of hunter-gatherer populations

Following the discovery of gold in the Amazonian region of Brazil in the 1980s, and an influx of miners to the area, thousands of previously isolated Yanomami people died of diseases such as influenza, measles and tuberculosis.

The Mbuti of the Ituri rain forest, in the north-east of the Democratic Republic of Congo, are pygmy hunters and gatherers. They exchange forest goods for metal and cloth from surrounding villages.

Most urban
Monaco
100%

Least urban
Nauru
0%

Urban population

● under 20% urban
● 20 - 50%
● 50 - 80%
● over 80%
○ none

DEGREES OF URBANIZATION

Where people live

Urbanization – the move to towns and cities, away from smaller rural communities – is an increasing trend: 47 per cent of the world's population is now urban. While cities are expanding in the developing nations of South America and Asia, Europe still heads the urbanization league, with a continuous influx into historic urban centres, especially of young people in search of employment. Rural areas and the traditional farming economy are being abandoned. The countries of sub-Saharan Africa, however, remain overwhelmingly rural, with large numbers of people relying on subsistence farming.

Teeming urban populations place huge pressure on housing, sanitation and transport in developing countries such as India. Today 32 cities in India have more than a million residents.

Much of sparsely populated Mongolia consists of a high plateau given over to pasture land. The seminomadic herdsmen move over vast expanses with herds of horse, sheep, cattle and goat. They live in felt-covered tents, or yurts.

Quality of life

The Human Development Index measures a nation's socio-economic development by combining information on life expectancy, educational attainment and income. The HDI shows that the disparity between the world's richest and its poorest nations continues to widen. In some countries population growth is outstripping economic expansion and hence the provision of government services such as healthcare and education. Life expectancy is also very disparate; while the average globally is 67 years, Japan has the highest at nearly 80 years, and Sierra Leone the lowest at 38 years. Disease – in particular HIV/AIDS – wars and poverty are all factors in diminishing life expectancy in some regions of the world, especially in large areas of Africa. The panel on the right shows a sample of the HDI rankings that have been calculated for 175 countries.

The Human Development Index			
High	0	0.5	1
Norway 0.944			
Japan 0.932			
New Zealand 0.917			
Czech Republic 0.861			
Cuba 0.806			
Medium			
Bulgaria 0.795			
Philippines 0.751			
China 0.721			
Tajikistan 0.677			
India 0.590			
Low			
Pakistan 0.499			
Kenya 0.489			
Gambia 0.463			
Mozambique 0.356			
Sierra Leone 0.275			

● 0.1, one-tenth of a maximum HDI ranking of 1

Stretching 800km (500 miles) from Boston to Washington DC is the USA's largest megalopolis, or urban complex, taking in several large cities and their surrounding areas (visible as a thick band of light within the square outline below). It emerged in the 1960s when people living in east coast cities began to migrate to the suburbs, attracted by cheaper housing and a better lifestyle. Over the next 30 years the ribbons of suburban development multiplied and entwined. The suburbs themselves became commercial and employment focuses, agglomerating into one giant, urbanized area with a total population of approaching 44 million people.

Megalopolis

In some cities the physical environment sets limits on expansion, so housing moves upwards as high-rise blocks or former industrial sites are transformed into residential areas. But many cities continue to expand outwards, with semi-urban development stretching far out into the neighbouring countryside. In less

Pushing the city boundaries

developed countries, growth fuelled by the arrival of migrant workers has led to the creation of informal 'shantytowns' on the edge of the city. In industrialized nations, the search for better housing, more space and tranquillity has led to the proliferation of suburbs and an increasing dependence on cars. In the USA, urban sprawl, such as the estate (above) built for golfing enthusiasts near Palm Springs in California, is claiming farmland at the rate of 1.2 million acres a year.

Largest cities

WORLD'S TOP 25 CITIES: 2000, 1975, 1950

As the 21st century turned, most of the largest were now in Asia. China has the most cities with a population of at least 5 million people.

By 1975, there had been a huge expansion in the number and size of the major cities: Tokyo more than quadrupled in size.

In 1950, the largest were in the west, with the great European cities still among the most populous.

By 2030, more than half the world's population will be living in cities. The five largest are Tokyo, Mexico City, São Paulo, New York City and Mumbai (Bombay). As the population expands in developing countries, increasing numbers of people will live in cities with more than 5 million people – in 2000 41 cities had reached this size. In 1950 only New York City was a 'megacity', with a population of more than 10 million; by 2015 there will be 23 megacities, with Lagos in Nigeria and Dhaka in Bangladesh joining the top five.

2000: 26.4 TOKYO · 18.1 MEXICO CITY · 18.1 SÃO PAULO · 16.6 NEW YORK · 18.1 MUMBAI · 12.8 LAGOS · 13.1 LOS ANGELES · 12.3 DHAKA · 12.0 BEIJING · 14.2 SHANGHAI · 10.2 TIANJIN · 12.2 SEOUL · 10.6 OSAKA · 9.5 LONDON · 9.7 PARIS · 8.8 ISTANBUL · 10.7 CAIRO · 8.3 MOSCOW · 11.8 KARACHI · 11.7 DELHI · 12.9 CALCUTTA · 17.3 RIO DE JANEIRO · 10.6 RIO DE JANEIRO · 7.4 LIMA · 9.9 BUENOS AIRES · 15.9 NEW YORK · 10.6 JAKARTA · 10.8 MANILA

1975: 19.8 TOKYO · 8.9 LOS ANGELES · 8.9 MEXICO CITY · 8.2 LONDON · 8.9 PARIS · 6.4 RHEIN-RUHR N · 4.3 ST PETERSBURG · 7.6 MOSCOW · 5.5 MILAN · 6.1 CAIRO · 4.4 DELHI · 7.3 MUMBAI · 7.9 CALCUTTA · 8.5 BEIJING · 6.2 TIANJIN · 11.4 SHANGHAI · 6.8 SEOUL · 9.8 OSAKA · 10.3 SÃO PAULO · 7.9 RIO DE JANEIRO · 9.2 BUENOS AIRES · 4.8 JAKARTA · 5.0 MANILA

1950: 6.9 TOKYO · 4.0 LOS ANGELES · 3.1 MEXICO CITY · 3.5 SÃO PAULO · 2.9 RIO DE JANEIRO · 5.0 BUENOS AIRES · 12.3 NEW YORK · 6.1 CHICAGO · 2.7 DETROIT · 2.9 PHILADELPHIA · 8.7 LONDON · 5.4 PARIS · 2.3 MANCHESTER · 3.6 MILAN · 5.3 RHEIN-RUHR N · 3.3 BERLIN · 2.9 ST PETERSBURG · 5.3 MOSCOW · 2.8 NAPLES · 2.4 CAIRO · 3.0 MUMBAI · 4.4 CALCUTTA · 3.9 BEIJING · 5.5 SHANGHAI · 4.2 OSAKA

PARIS: A PLANNED CITY

In the mid 19th century, Paris was transformed by Baron Haussmann, who razed much of the labyrinthine medieval city with its twisting, narrow streets, and built a grandiose capital in its stead. Four new bridges were constructed to span the Seine, and working-class neighbourhoods were destroyed to make way for wide, sweeping boulevards, displacing many people to the suburbs. Haussmann also planned railway links between the centre of Paris and its outlying regions.

A dramatic satellite image of the Earth at night, highlights the distribution of cities along the rims of the continents.

CAIRO: CITY WITH AN ANCIENT HEART

Although there was a settlement on the River Nile in Roman times, the foundations of the modern city of Cairo were laid in AD 969. The 10th-century mosque and university of Al-Azhar are the most important in Egypt, and three great medieval gates still dominate the city. In the 19th century, the expanding medieval capital was modernized and transformed by European architects. In the 20th century, there has been a spectacular explosion in population – the city has quadrupled in size since 1950 – leading to the construction of many outlying satellite towns.

CITY

The mass industrialization of the 19th century transformed the way people lived, drawing them into expanding urban centres in search of jobs. By 1900, 14 per cent of the global population lived in cities. In the 20th century, the rate of urbanization escalated; in 2000, about 47 per cent of the world's population – some 2.8 billion people – lived in urban areas. Many cities are notorious for their problems: overcrowding, crime, slums and congestion. But with their wide range of employment and educational opportunities, and often better health and social services, they can act as dynamic engines for cultural and technical innovation, as well as social change.

Building upwards is often the best way to accommodate the expanding population of many modern cities, such as Tokyo (above).

MIGRATION

International migration has reached unprecedented levels, with 150 million people – just over 2 per cent of the global population – living outside their countries of birth or nationality. Many migrants seek homes in new countries for economic reasons; they can sell their labour more dearly and achieve a higher standard of living. But war, human rights abuses, repression and environmental degradation also compel people to leave their homeland.

Home to an estimated 150,000 ethnic Chinese, New York's Chinatown is also the focus of a thriving business community.

In search of a better life

In the past 40 years, the number of international migrants has doubled. Population pressures can be a major contributing factor, since many societies with a rapidly increasing population are unable to generate sufficient opportunities for employment. Just 15 per cent of the world's 6 billion people live in the 22 richest countries. It is these flourishing economies – often with not enough people to do the necessary jobs – that tend to attract most migrants.

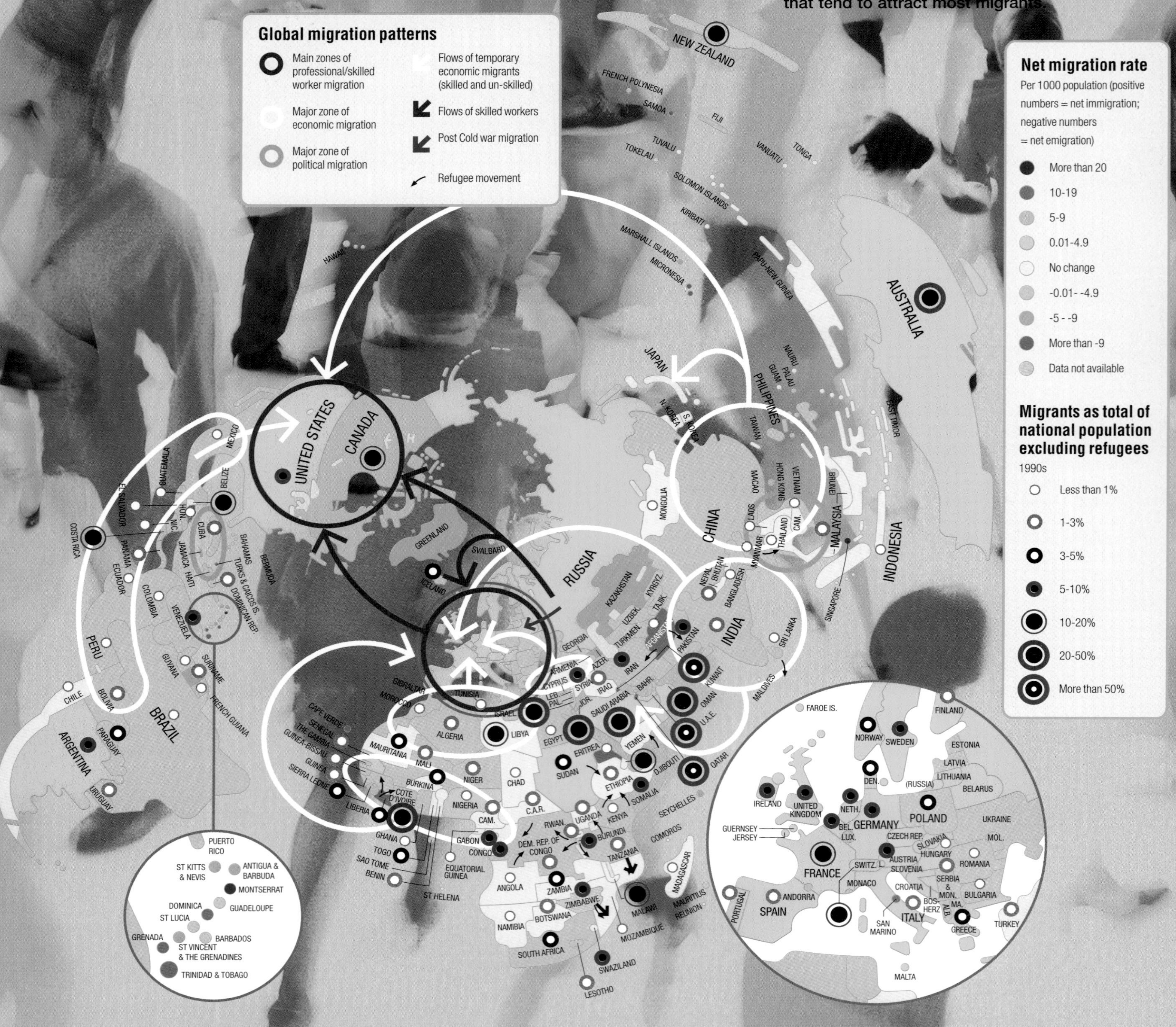

Global migration patterns

- ○ Main zones of professional/skilled worker migration
- ○ Major zone of economic migration
- ○ Major zone of political migration
- Flows of temporary economic migrants (skilled and un-skilled)
- ↙ Flows of skilled workers
- ↙ Post Cold war migration
- ↘ Refugee movement

Net migration rate

Per 1000 population (positive numbers = net immigration; negative numbers = net emigration)

- More than 20
- 10-19
- 5-9
- 0.01-4.9
- No change
- -0.01- -4.9
- -5 - -9
- More than -9
- Data not available

Migrants as total of national population excluding refugees

1990s

- Less than 1%
- 1-3%
- 3-5%
- 5-10%
- 10-20%
- 20-50%
- More than 50%

Tourism

Increased affluence, improvements in mass transport and sophisticated global infrastructures have made tourism the world's biggest industry; international tourist arrivals exceeded 700 million in 2002. Europe – in particular France and the Mediterranean countries of Spain and Italy – is the most popular tourist destination, with North America in second place. While concerns about terrorism have lead to localized slumps in the industry, the health of the global economy generally has a far more direct – and widespread – impact.

Top ten tourist destinations
Tourists arriving (millions)

France 77
Spain 51.7
USA 41.9
Italy 39.8
China 36.8
UK 24.2
Canada 20.1
Mexico 19.7
Austria 18.6
Germany 18

Top ten spenders on tourism
Spending ($US billions)

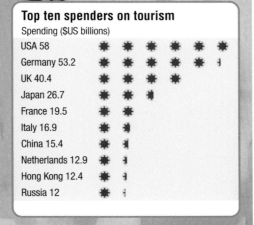

USA 58
Germany 53.2
UK 40.4
Japan 26.7
France 19.5
Italy 16.9
China 15.4
Netherlands 12.9
Hong Kong 12.4
Russia 12

Economic migration

Many of today's well-established patterns of migration began, decades ago, with the active recruitment of foreign workers. From the 1940s to 60s, the USA operated a guest worker programme with Mexico. In the 1960s and 70s, many European countries brought in labour from Turkey, north Africa and southern Europe. Oil-rich Libya and the Persian Gulf recruited workers from other Muslim countries and south, east, and South-east Asia.

Working abroad
Migrant workers as a % of total population

Germany 9%	Côte d'Ivoire 30%
USA 9%	Hong Kong 40%
Canada 16%	Qatar 64%
Australia 22%	Kuwait 72%
Saudi Arabia 26%	United Arab Emirates 90%

LANGUAGE

More than 6000 languages are in daily use across the world, but their distribution is very uneven. Mandarin Chinese is spoken by a billion people across a huge area of Asia, while the part of the world with most linguistic diversity is tiny New Guinea, where around 1000 languages are spoken by a population of just 5 million.

Speaking the language

Twelve of the world's top 20 languages, spoken by half of the world's population, belong to the Indo-European family. English, Spanish and Portuguese were spread by colonial expansion. As governments become more centralized, and economies more internationally integrated, the languages with wide currency, such as English and Mandarin Chinese, become dominant. Many of the world's rarer languages are under threat.

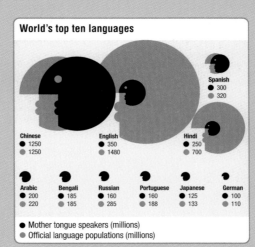

World's top ten languages

Chinese ● 1250 ● 1250
English ● 350 ● 1480
Spanish ● 300 ● 320
Hindi ● 250 ● 700
Arabic ● 200 ● 220
Bengali ● 185 ● 185
Russian ● 160 ● 285
Portuguese ● 160 ● 188
Japanese ● 125 ● 133
German ● 100 ● 110

● Mother tongue speakers (millions)
● Official language populations (millions)

The Hispanicization of the USA

The Hispanic population of the USA is 35 million strong, and has risen in tandem with high levels of immigration from neighbouring Spanish-speaking countries. Some 20 major languages – other than English – are spoken at home in the US. After Spanish (28.1 million), Chinese is the most widely spoken (2 million). Many linguistic experts argue that this is only a temporary phenomenon; second generation immigrants generally prefer to speak English, and by the third generation it tends to predominate.

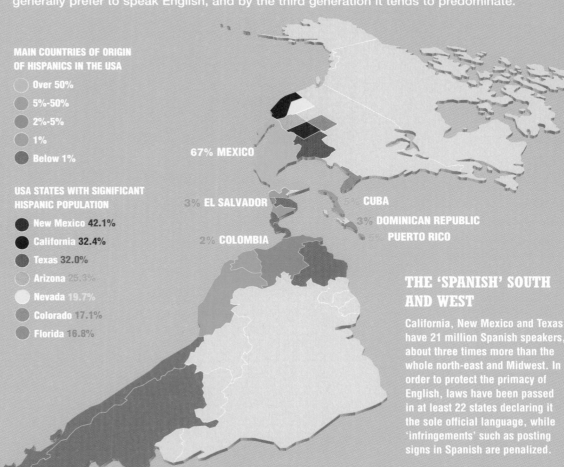

MAIN COUNTRIES OF ORIGIN OF HISPANICS IN THE USA

○ Over 50%
○ 5%-50%
○ 2%-5%
○ 1%
○ Below 1%

USA STATES WITH SIGNIFICANT HISPANIC POPULATION

● New Mexico 42.1%
● California 32.4%
● Texas 32.0%
● Arizona 25.3%
● Nevada 19.7%
● Colorado 17.1%
● Florida 16.8%

67% MEXICO
3% EL SALVADOR
2% COLOMBIA
CUBA
3% DOMINICAN REPUBLIC
PUERTO RICO

THE 'SPANISH' SOUTH AND WEST

California, New Mexico and Texas have 21 million Spanish speakers, about three times more than the whole north-east and Midwest. In order to protect the primacy of English, laws have been passed in at least 22 states declaring it the sole official language, while 'infringements' such as posting signs in Spanish are penalized.

North America
The United States and Canada, with fertile soils, favourable climatic conditions and advanced technology, produce most of the world's corn, wheat and soybeans. Service industry is the fastest growing sector, with manufacturing in decline. Many factories have moved to Mexico, which has a large and inexpensive workforce, and enjoys a close trading relationship with Canada and the USA.

Who controls the economy?
The top twelve global economies dominate world trade; the USA alone accounts for nearly a third of the world's GDP. China is the fastest growing economy. With a large industrial sector, it has become the workshop of the world, and its abundant cheap labour attracts investment from a growing number of multinational corporations. If China continues to expand at its present pace, it will outgrow Britain and France to become the fourth largest economy by the end of 2005.

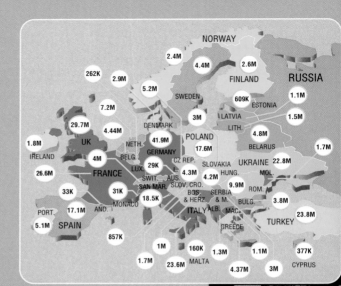

Financial traders analyse market data at the Börse, Frankfurt's stock exchange.

Robots weld car bodies on a production line in Detroit, USA.

'Maquiladora' factories in Mexico and central America employ millions of workers. Textiles and consumer goods are partly assembled in these factories and then trucked over the border into the United States to exploit a unique duty-free arrangement.

Bundles of hemp are hung out to dry in the sun before being woven into rope. Sisal, from which hemp is taken, is grown mainly in Africa, as here in Madagascar, and South America.

Beef farming on expansive cattle ranches remains one of South America's leading export industries, though the land required for pasture is often obtained at the expense of rain forest.

The world economy
GDP in $US million
- More than 1,000,000
- 200,000 – 999,999
- 100,000 – 199,999
- 20,000 – 99,999
- 10,000 – 19,999
- 5000 – 9999
- 1000 – 4999
- Less than 1000

2M — Number of people in the work force (if available)

000 — Top 5 economies by continent (GDP)

South America
Resources including oil, natural gas, hydroelectricity and mineral reserves have enabled heavy industry to develop in several countries. Subsistence farming is widespread, with about 30 per cent of the population working 15 per cent of the land. Meat (particularly beef, above), coffee (Brazil is a major world producer), bananas, sugarcane and soybeans are exported world wide. Many countries remain heavily indebted to the World Bank.

Africa
Three-quarters of the world's cocoa beans and about a third of its peanuts are grown in Africa, but many people still farm primarily for subsistence. Manufacturing is concentrated in South Africa and North African countries such as Egypt and Algeria. Tourism is particularly important in Mediterranean North Africa, Kenya, Tanzania and South Africa.

Women on a beach in Senegal sell freshly landed fish to local customers.

Map labels

North America
- CANADA 730,100 — 16.4M
- UNITED STATES 10,456,000
- UNITED STATES 637,200
- MEXICO 637,200 — 39.8M
- GUATEMALA 23,800 — 4.2M
- CUBA 26,652 — 141.8M
- CUBA 84,600
- COLOMBIA 81,500
- VENEZUELA 84,600

- BAHAMAS 156K — 3.6M
- HAITI
- DOM. REP. 2.3M
- DOMINICA 25K
- ST KITTS & NEVIS 18K
- ANTIGUA & BARBUDA 30K
- BARBADOS 129K
- ST LUCIA 44K
- GRENADA 67K
- ST VINCENT & THE GRENADINES 42K
- TRINIDAD & TOBAGO 564K
- BELIZE 90K
- JAM. 1.1M
- HONDURAS 2.4M
- GUATEMALA 2.3M
- NICARAGUA 1.7M
- EL SALV.
- PANAMA 1.9M 1.1M
- COSTA RICA
- VENEZ. 9.9M
- COLOMBIA 18.3M
- ECUADOR 3.7M
- GUY.
- SUR.
- FRENCH GUIANA

South America
- PERU 7.5M
- BRAZIL 430,600 — 79M
- BOLIVIA 2.5M
- PARAGUAY 2M
- ARGENTINA 104,600 — 15M
- CHILE 62,200
- URUGUAY 1.2M
- 5.9M

Europe
- NORWAY 2.4M
- 262K
- 2.9M
- FINLAND 2.6M
- RUSSIA 1.1M
- SWEDEN 5.2M
- 4.4M
- 7.2M
- 3M
- ESTONIA 609K
- LATVIA 1.5M
- DENMARK
- LITH. 4.8M
- UK 29.7M
- NETH. 4.44M
- BELARUS 1.7M
- IRELAND 1.8M
- GERMANY 41.9M
- POLAND 17.6M
- UKRAINE 22.8M
- FRANCE 26.6M
- LUX. BELG.
- CZ REP. 4.3M
- SLOVAKIA 4.2M HUNG.
- MOL.
- 4M
- SWIT. AUS. 29K
- SLOV. BOS. & HERZ. SERBIA & M. ROM.
- SAN MAR. 33K
- MONACO 31K
- 18.5M
- 9.9M
- BULG. 3.8M
- AND.
- ITALY ALB. MAC.
- PORT. 17.1M
- GREECE
- TURKEY 23.8M
- SPAIN 5.1M
- 857K
- MALTA 1.3M
- CYPRUS 377K

Africa
- MOROCCO 40,045 — 11M
- ALGERIA 54,924 — 9.4M
- NIGERIA 40,700
- SOUTH AFRICA 102,635 — 17M
- EGYPT 77,504
- GEORGIA 2.1M
- TUNISIA 2.69M
- LIBYA 1.5M
- MOROCCO
- ALGERIA
- W.SAHARA
- MAURITANIA 786K
- MALI 3.9M
- NIGER 70K
- CHAD 1.5M
- SUDAN 11M
- ERITREA
- SEN. 400K
- THE GAMB. 480K
- GUINEA BISSAU 3M
- GUINEA 1.4M
- BURK. 5M
- BEN.
- NIGERIA 66M
- C.A.R.
- ETHIOPIA
- CÔTE D'IV. 9M
- GHANA.
- TOGO 1.74M
- SIERRA LEONE LIBERIA
- CAM.
- UGANDA
- KENYA 12M
- 10M
- SÃO TOMÉ & PRÍNCIPE
- EQ. GUINEA 600K
- GABON
- CONGO NA
- CONGO, DEM. REP 14.5M
- RWANDA 4.6M
- BURUNDI 3.7M
- TANZANIA 13.5M
- ANGOLA 5M
- ZAMBIA 4.29M
- MALAWI 4.5M
- ZIMBABWE 5.8M
- MOZAMBIQUE 9.2M
- NAMIBIA 725K
- BOTSWANA 264K
- SWAZILAND 383K
- LESOTHO 838K

Asia/Middle East
- TURKEY 23.8M
- LEB. 5.2M
- SYRIA 1.5M
- ISRAEL 2.5M
- EGYPT 20.6M
- JORDAN 1.4M

Top economies (cylinder labels)
- CANADA 730,100
- UNITED STATES 10,456,000
- UNITED STATES 637,200
- MEXICO 637,200
- GUATEMALA 23,800
- CUBA 26,652
- VENEZUELA 84,600
- COLOMBIA 81,500
- BRAZIL 430,600
- ARGENTINA 104,600
- CHILE 62,200
- MOROCCO 40,045
- ALGERIA 54,924
- NIGERIA 40,700
- EGYPT 77,504
- SOUTH AFRICA 102,635
- SPAIN 648,800
- UNITED KINGDOM 1,545,000
- FRANCE 1,433,000
- GERMANY 1,993,000
- ITALY 1,184,000
- ICELAND 159K

Europe
Heavy industry is now in decline, only playing a significant role in eastern Europe. Fewer and fewer people work on the land, though in the EU countries farming is heavily subsidized, to the tune of £23 billion a year. Most leading European economies have service industries at their heart, with global financial centres in Frankfurt and London.

GLOBALISATION: THE STORY OF THE TRAINER
The production of sports shoes is a truly global operation. They are usually designed in the USA, manufactured in China, Thailand, Indonesia and Vietnam using raw materials from several countries, under the control of contractors from Taiwan and South Korea, and marketed around the world.

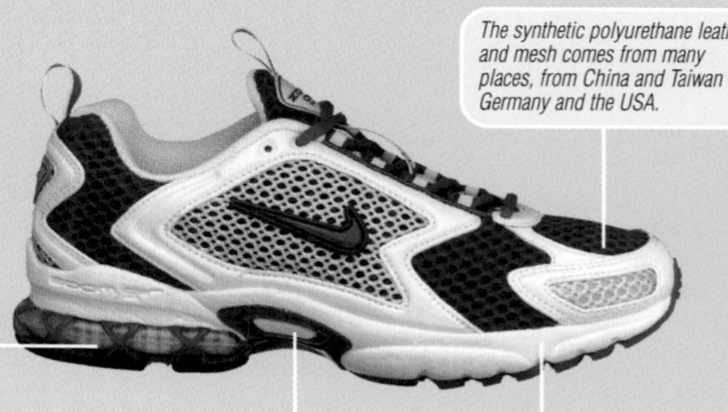

Below the heel is a concealed polyurethane bag filled with pressurized gas, produced in the USA.

The synthetic polyurethane leather and mesh comes from many places, from China and Taiwan to Germany and the USA.

The foam midsole is made from a polymer called Phylon, sourced from China, Taiwan or South Korea.

The outer sole is of synthetic rubber, made from Saudi Arabian petroleum and benzene, produced locally in Asia.

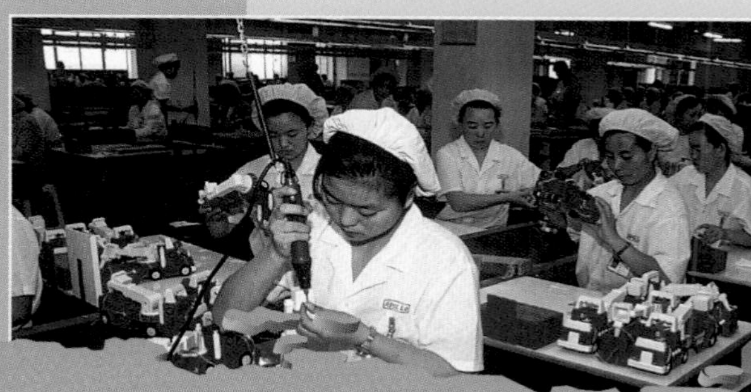

Asia
Nearly 60 per cent of the world's labour force will be in Asia by 2010. Agriculture, such as the tea plantation in Sri Lanka (below left) still employs more than half the total workforce. But in China, Russian Asia, South Korea and Taiwan, industrialization is increasing rapidly. Skilled workers (left) produce goods such as toys and clothing for the western market. Japan is the dominant economy in the region and the second largest in the world.

A giant ore shovel cuts into a wall of rock at Port Hedland, Western Australia, a leading mining centre.

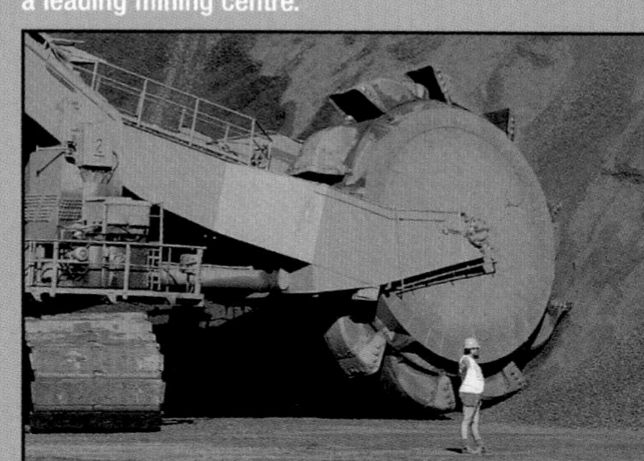

Australasia
Arable farming employs just 3 per cent of Australia's population but the wheat crop is sufficiently abundant for most to be exported. Today service is the leading economic sector but primary industries such as mining (right) remain important. New Zealand has started to industrialize its economy over the past 20 years. The Pacific Islands remain remote, dependent on aid to prop up their economies.

RUSSIA 71.8M

ARMENIA 1.4M

KAZAKHSTAN 8.4M

MONGOLIA 1.4M

CHINA 1,259,400

SOUTH KOREA 470,600

JAPAN 3,933,000

AZER. 3.7M

UZBEKISTAN 11.9M

KYRGYZSTAN 2.7M

INDIA 496,800

NORTH KOREA 9.6M

TAIWAN 278,200

TURKMEN. 2.34M

TAJIKISTAN 3.2M

CHINA

SOUTH KOREA 22M

JAPAN 68M

IRAQ 295K

BAHRAIN

IRAN 21M

AFGHANISTAN 10M

PAKISTAN 40.4M

NEPAL 10M

BHUTAN

KUWAIT 280K

QATAR 1.6M

SAUDI ARABIA 7M

UAE

OMAN 920K

INDIA 406M

BANGL. 64.1M

MYANMAR (BURMA) 23.7M

LAOS 2.4M

TAIWAN 10M

VIETNAM 38.2M

PHILIPPINES 33.7M

YEMEN

SRI LANKA 6.6M

THAILAND 33.4M

CAMB. 6M

DJIBOUTI 282K

SOMALIA 3.7M

MALAYSIA 9.9M

BRUNEI

PALAU 10K

PAPUA NEW GUINEA 2771

MARSHALL ISLANDS 29K

SEYCHELLES 31K

SINGAPORE 2.2M

INDONESIA 99M

MICRONESIA NA

SOLOMON ISLANDS 27K

SOLOMON ISLANDS 264

KIRIBATI 8K

COMOROS 145K

EAST TIMOR

PAPUA NEW GUINEA 2.3M

NAURU

TUVALU 7K

FIJI 1,463

7.3M

MADAGASCAR

SAMOA 90K

VANUATU

FIJI 137K

TONGA 34K

AUSTRALIA

AUSTRALIA 400,000

9.2M

NEW CALEDONIA

NEW ZEALAND 57,241

NEW ZEALAND 1.9M

Tea picking in Sri Lanka is an intensive form of cultivation; most of the harvesting is done by hand.

Developed countries increasingly look to the rest of the world for cheaper labour and raw materials. In contrast, developing countries are more dependent than they used to be on foreign trade and investment, calling on richer nations to remove trade barriers, and reduce protective subsidies that restrict exports.

WORK

A thirsty world

Accessible fresh water, which accounts for less than 1 per cent of the planet's total water, has long been over-exploited, polluted and fought over. The Earth's growing population is now putting this vital resource under increasing pressure; the United Nations estimates that by 2025 2.7 billion people will face severe water shortages if current rates of consumption continue. One-third of the world's people live in countries where water supplies cannot meet demand, while 2.5 billion people lack proper sanitation and sewerage.

Use of available water supply

- 100 per cent and above
- 50–99
- 10–49
- Less than 10

The Ataturk Dam (top left) is the largest of a series of 22 dams and 19 hydroelectric power stations built on the Tigris and Euphrates to provide water to south-eastern Turkey.

ALTERNATIVE ENERGY

Increasing demands on diminishing supplies of coal, gas and oil have prompted greater use of renewable energy sources, such as sunlight, water and wind, which now supply about 10 per cent of the world's total energy. Hydroelectricity is the most commonly used form. In areas of volcanic activity, geothermal sources can provide renewable energy from superheated rocks and water deep beneath the Earth's crust.

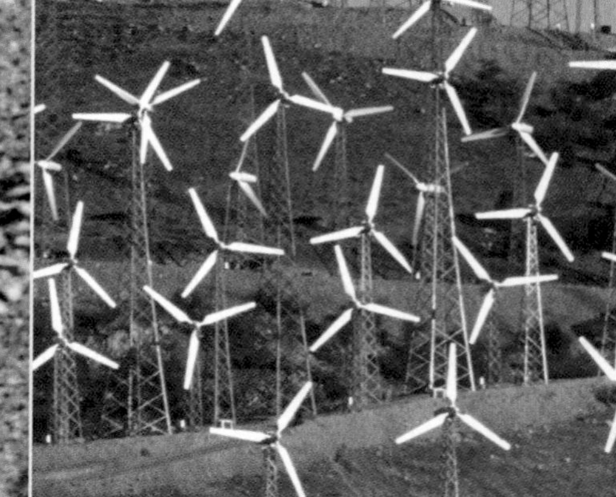

Hi-tech wind farms are becoming a common sight across the European Union. Those already installed generate 24,626 MW of energy.

Food

Each of us eats an average of 2740 calories a day. Intensive farming, agrochemicals and biologically engineered plant varieties have all helped to increase food yields. Yet about 20 per cent of the world's population are undernourished. The poorest countries cannot afford to invest in these new developments or to supplement shortages in domestic production with foreign exports.

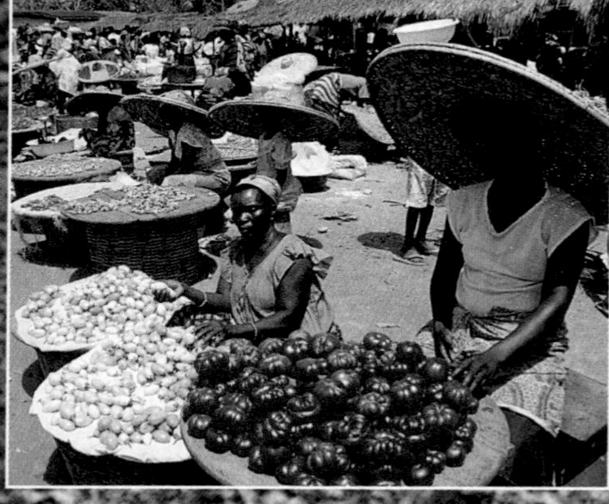

Many people still grow food for themselves and their families. Any excess can be sold for cash – as at this market in Ghana.

Fruit	Total in metric tonnes
China 68,941,170	
India 46,221,300	
Brazil 32,746,521	
USA 30,016,190	
Italy 18,275,670	

Cereals	Total in metric tonnes
China 398,395,135	
USA 325,480,116	
India 243,375,204	
Russia 83,262,600	
France 60,264,485	

Vegetables	Total in metric tonnes
China 356,511,784	
India 78,047,300	
USA 36,181,212	
Turkey 24,165,062	
Italy 15,370,414	

Meat	Total in metric tonnes
China 65,263,996	
USA 37,810,800	
Brazil 15,166,625	
France 6,534,300	
Germany 6,470,378	

Pulses	Total in metric tonnes
India 10,655,200	
China 5,121,527	
Australia 2,507,000	
Brazil 2,465,931	
Nigeria 2,222,000	

The politics of oil

The oil industry is dominated by a trading cartel, the Organization of the Petroleum Exporting Countries (OPEC) – Algeria, Indonesia, Iran, Iraq, Kuwait, Libya, Nigeria, Qatar, Saudi Arabia, the United Arab Emirates and Venezuela. This OPEC domination of the world's oil supplies during the 1970s galvanized many non-OPEC countries into exploring new sources and investing in new oil fields. This was seen as the most effective method of releasing the economic stranglehold that OPEC had on the industry.

OIL CONSUMPTION

Worldwide oil consumption is projected to increase by about 2.2 per cent annually over the next 20 years, with much of the growth in the developing regions of Asia and Central and South America, where lifestyles increasingly resemble those of the older industrialized world. The USA, home to just 5 per cent of the world's population, is currently the top consumer: it has only 2 per cent of the world's oil reserves yet consumes 25 per cent of the world's oil. In 2000, it alone consumed just over 75 per cent of all the oil used by the next nine top consumer countries together.

The top ten oil consumers (millions of barrels per day)

1 USA
19,708
25.4% of world total

2 China
5362
7% of world total

3 Japan
5337
6.9% of world total

4 Germany
2709
3.6% of world total

5 Russia
2469
3.5% of world total

6 South Korea
2288
3% of world total

7 India
2090
2.8% of world total

8 Canada
1988
2.5% of world total

9 France
1967
2.6% of world total

10 Italy
1943
2.6% of world total

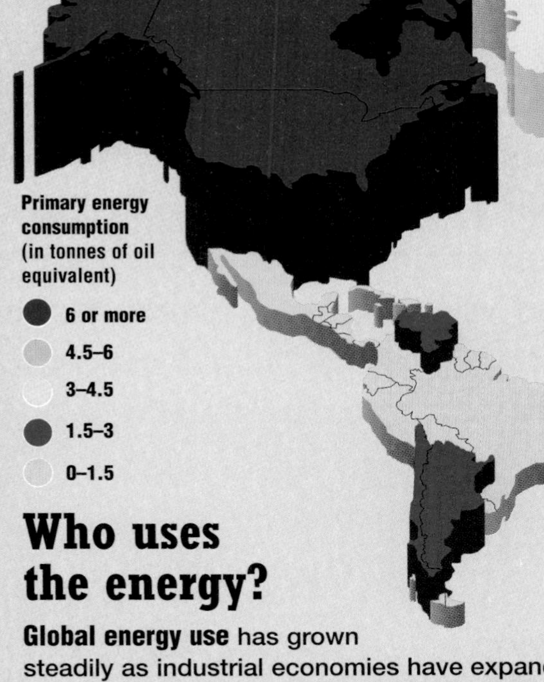

Primary energy consumption (in tonnes of oil equivalent)

- 6 or more
- 4.5–6
- 3–4.5
- 1.5–3
- 0–1.5

Who uses the energy?

Global energy use has grown steadily as industrial economies have expanded. Today, developed nations consume nearly three-quarters of all commercial energy. But developing nations, especially in East and South Asia, are expected to increase their share of world energy use to almost 40 per cent by 2010. This change reflects high population growth and rapid economic expansion in the area, along with the substitution of fossil fuels for traditional biomass fuels, such as wood, dung, methane gas and grain alcohol.

Leading energy users   Per cent

Rest of the World 34

- United States 25
- China 10
- Russia 7
- Japan 6
- Germany 4
- India 3
- France 3
- UK 3
- Canada 3
- South Korea 2

RESOURCES

Fossil fuels still provide 85 per cent of the world's commercial energy, but will not last indefinitely. Energy demand has nearly doubled in the past 30 years and cleaner, renewable sources, such as hydropower, solar cells and wind turbines, are becoming a global priority, both for industry and the environment. Access to water is equally critical for many nations and its distribution and control is of international importance.

Oil reserves

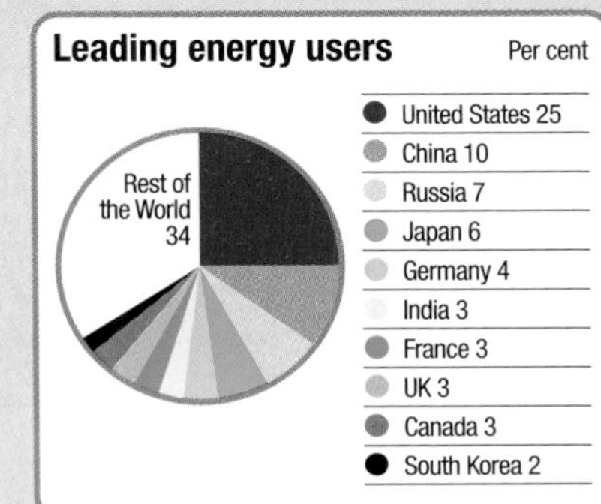

- USA
- S & Central America
- Europe & Eurasia
- Middle East
- Africa
- Asia Pacific

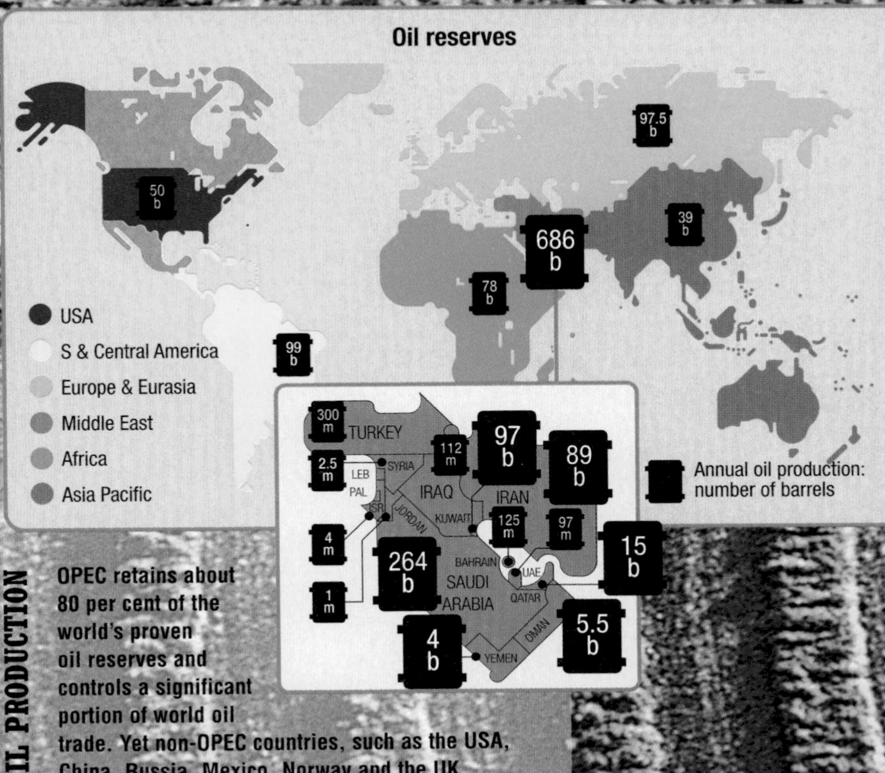

Annual oil production: number of barrels

OIL PRODUCTION

OPEC retains about 80 per cent of the world's proven oil reserves and controls a significant portion of world oil trade. Yet non-OPEC countries, such as the USA, China, Russia, Mexico, Norway and the UK, produced 60 per cent of the world's oil in 2000. Non-OPEC production is expected to rise in the years ahead, with the greatest increases in the area around the Caspian Sea in Russia and in Mexico.

WIRED WORLD

Connected by a vast array of telephone lines, fibre-optic cables and satellites, the world is communicating at an unprecedented speed. Use of the Internet is doubling annually, television programmes are beamed by satellite into even the remotest homes, and mobile phones are found in almost all corners of the globe. In some parts of the developing world, particularly in Africa, the use of wireless mobile technology is rapidly supplanting that of indequate, and generally unreliable, telecommunications infrastructures.

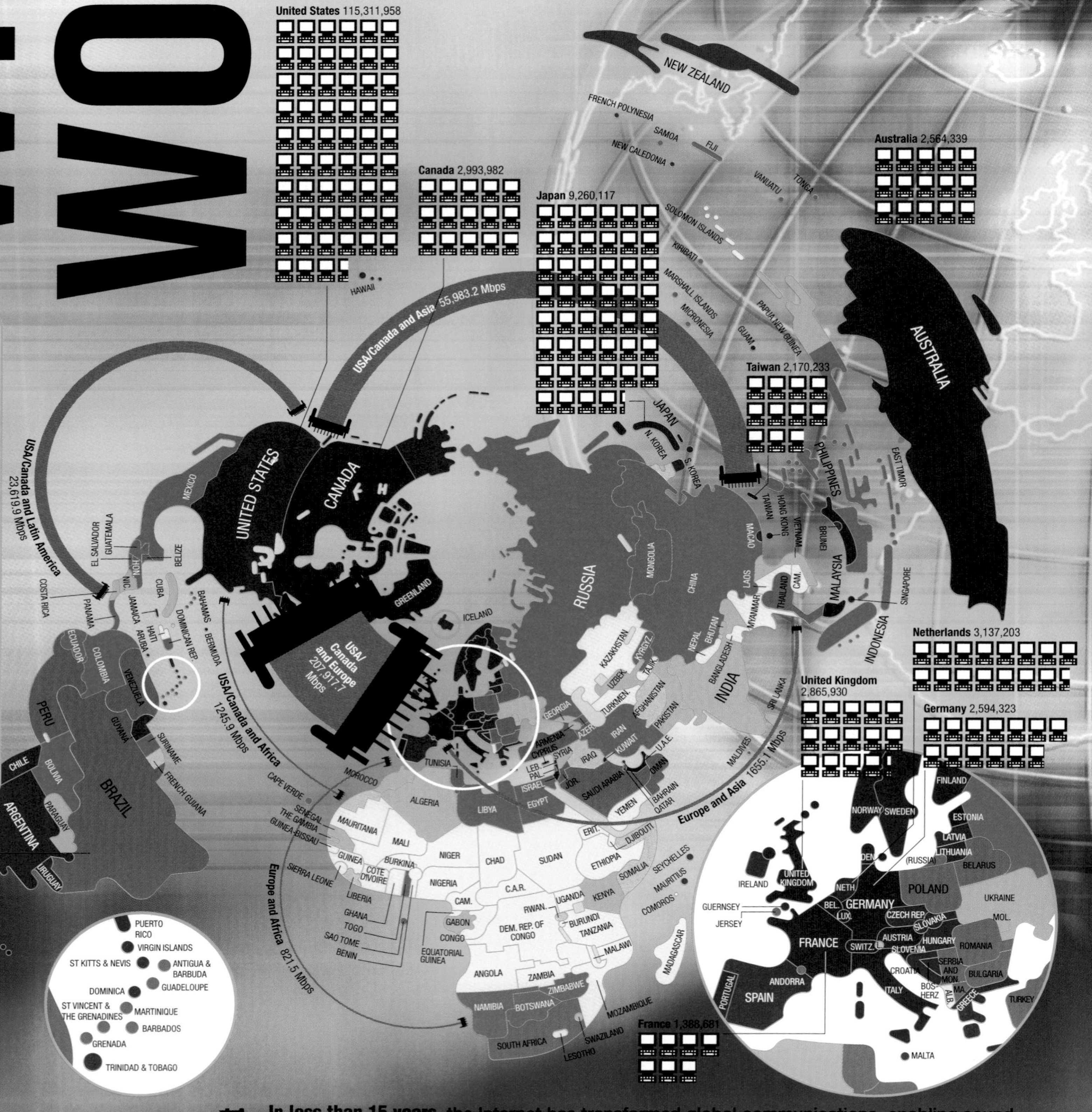

The Internet

Users per 10,000 inhabitants 2002

- More than 5000
- 3001–5000
- 1001–3000
- 501–1000
- 200–500
- 101–200
- Fewer than 100
- Data not available

Web site hosts 2002

Bandwidth 2002

Rate of data transmission in Mbps (megabits per second)

United States 115,311,958
Canada 2,993,982
Japan 9,260,117
Australia 2,564,339
Taiwan 2,170,233
Netherlands 3,137,203
United Kingdom 2,865,930
Germany 2,594,323
France 1,388,681
Brazil 2,237,527

USA/Canada and Asia 55,983.2 Mbps
USA/Canada and Latin America 23,619.9 Mbps
USA/Canada and Europe 207,917.7 Mbps
USA/Canada and Africa 1245.9 Mbps
Europe and Africa 821.5 Mbps
Europe and Asia 1655.1 Mbps

The Internet

In less than 15 years, the Internet has transformed global communications, enabling sound, graphics and moving images to be piped into home computers. In Scandinavia and the USA, more than 50 per cent of the population are now connected to the net. In most of Africa, Asia, eastern Europe and South America, the connection rate is still less than 3 per cent. By the end of 2005, the number of worldwide Internet users is expected to double to around 1.12 billion. Currently, inadequate telephone infrastructures are restricting Internet access – Norway, for example, has more phone lines than Bangladesh, a country with 30 times the number of inhabitants. But in the future, it is likely that devices such as web-enabled mobile phones will allow a growing number of people to view the Internet.

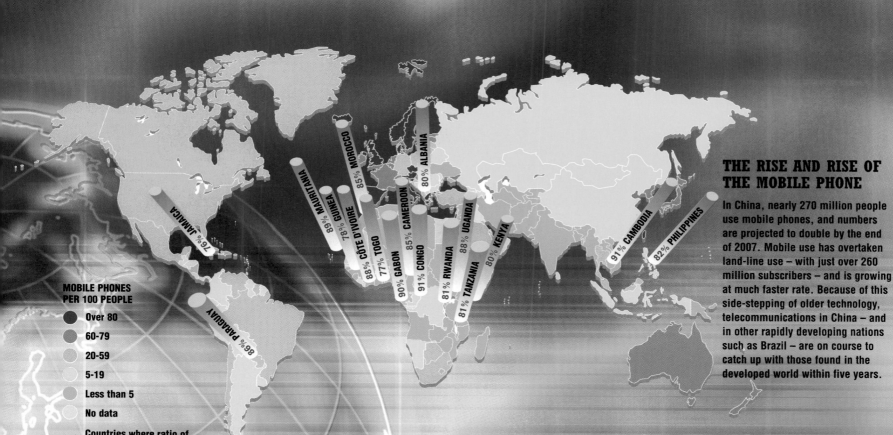

MOBILE PHONES PER 100 PEOPLE

- Over 80
- 60-79
- 20-59
- 5-19
- Less than 5
- No data
- Countries where ratio of mobile phones to land lines exceeds 75 per cent

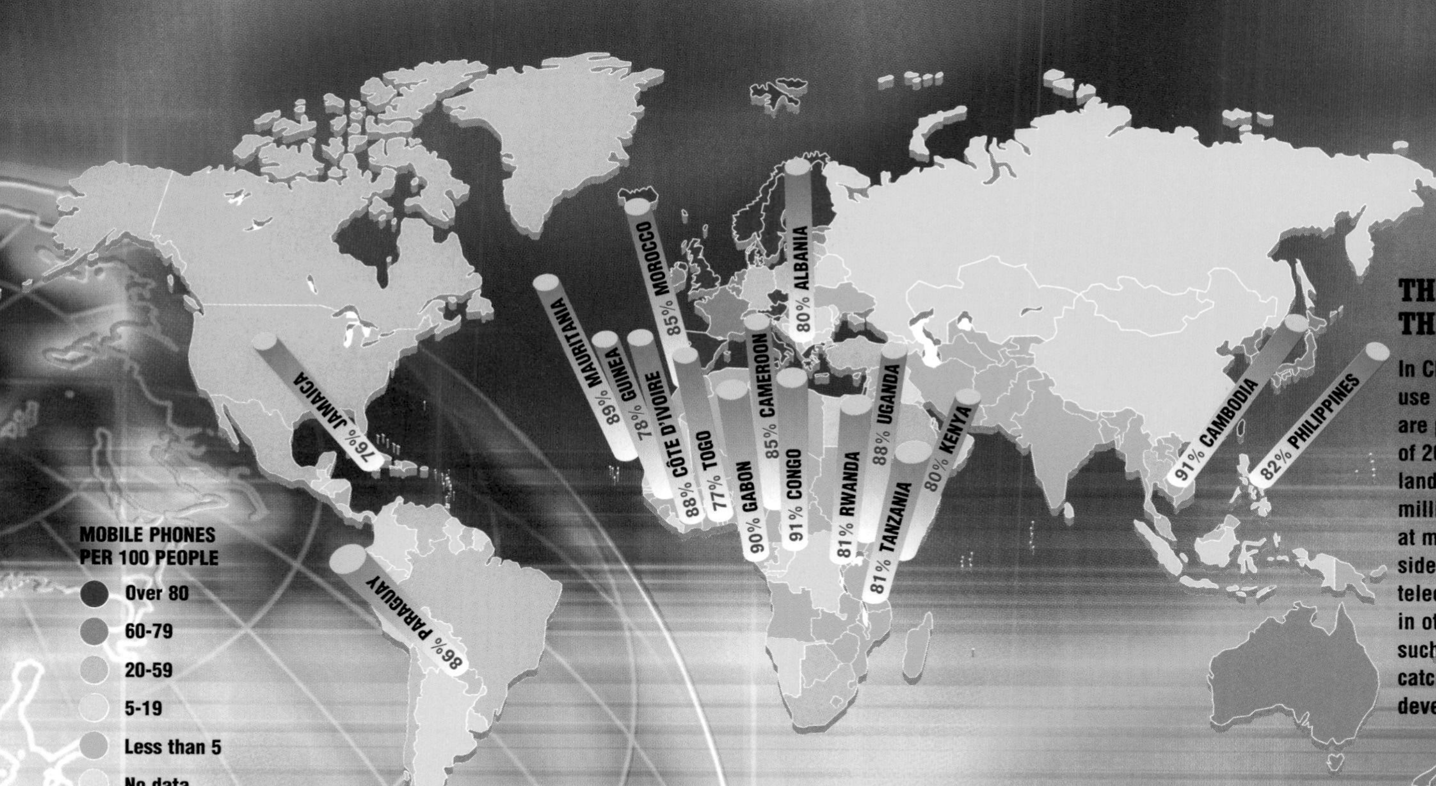

THE RISE AND RISE OF THE MOBILE PHONE

In China, nearly 270 million people use mobile phones, and numbers are projected to double by the end of 2007. Mobile use has overtaken land-line use – with just over 260 million subscribers – and is growing at much faster rate. Because of this side-stepping of older technology, telecommunications in China – and in other rapidly developing nations such as Brazil – are on course to catch up with those found in the developed world within five years.

Talking to each other

The number of telephone connections indicates not only a country's level of participation in the information economy; it is also a measure of its ability to adapt to new technologies and to take full advantage of innovation. Estonia, for example, is starting to reap the benefits of its close proximity to well-wired Finland – it has roughly as many mobile connections per person as France or Germany, despite the current wide disparity in wealth. At the other end of the scale, mobile phones, which have cheaper network costs, outnumber fixed-line connections across most of Africa to a much greater degree than in any other continent, and are helping many of the businesses there to completely transform their systems of communication.

Telecommunications
Worldwide subscribers (millions)

1999
Land lines 1400 Mobile subscribers 500

2002
Land lines 2400 Mobile subscribers 1300

2005
Land lines 4200 Mobile subscribers 2500

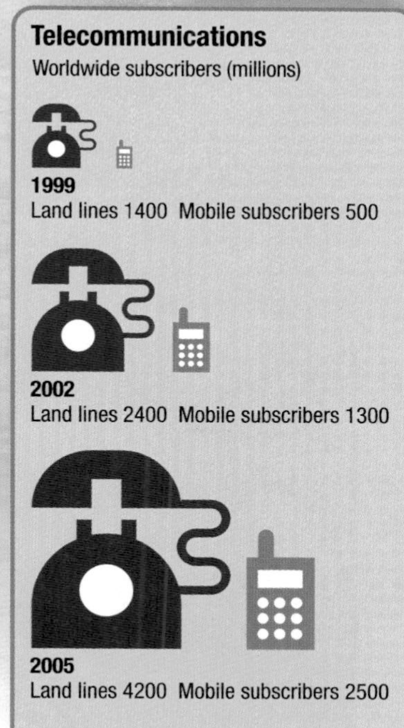

Television

Recent developments in satellite and cable television have included a huge expansion in the number of television channels for both international and local coverage. There are around 9000 cable television systems in the USA alone, and over 1500 channels are broadcast worldwide by satellite. Asia has proved a very fertile ground for satellite television. In 2002, nearly 7 million households were being served by 17 satellite TV platforms, generating over $2 billion in revenue. Some governments fear the impact of this: in Iran, satellite dishes are officially banned, although most households own one.

The biggest creator of television content in the world is the USA. American television programmes are beamed to all parts of the globe, with revenue from such exports playing a major role in the national economy.

The computer age

Computers have revolutionized society. They are used to educate, entertain, organize, and communicate. Linked to the Internet, they have broken down traditional barriers in both time and space. The USA leads the world in computer ownership, with more than 60 machines for every one hundred people. At the other end of the scale, many of the countries in Asia and Africa have less than one computer for every hundred people, although – as is the case in India – this may belie the many advances in communications technology that have occurred in both continents in recent years.

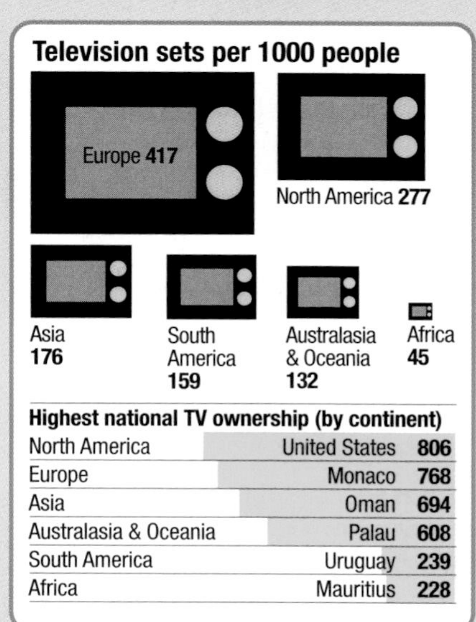

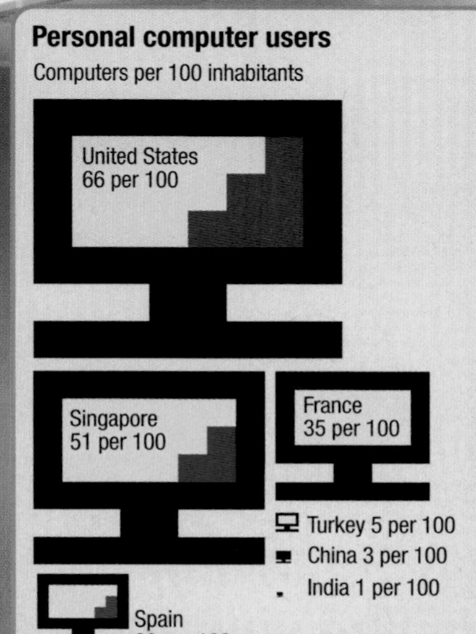

THE HOME COMPUTER

Developing countries will have to be the major source of sales growth for the computer industry as markets in North America, Europe and Japan reach saturation point. It has been estimated that emerging markets will account for approximately half of global sales by 2005, more than doubling the figure for 1999. The emphasis is on sales through government projects, aimed at promotion of computer use in schools and institutions.

Personal computer users
Computers per 100 inhabitants

- United States 66 per 100
- Singapore 51 per 100
- France 35 per 100
- Turkey 5 per 100
- China 3 per 100
- India 1 per 100
- Spain 20 per 100

Television sets per 1000 people

- Europe 417
- North America 277
- Asia 176
- South America 159
- Australasia & Oceania 132
- Africa 45

Highest national TV ownership (by continent)		
North America	United States	806
Europe	Monaco	768
Asia	Oman	694
Australasia & Oceania	Palau	608
South America	Uruguay	239
Africa	Mauritius	228

POPULATION

Nearly 6 billion people are alive today, most of them in the developing world, and despite a rapid decline in fertility rates, the world's population is expected to increase by 2 billion over the first quarter of the century. Most of the growth will occur in developing countries, while developed populations will remain static or even fall. An ageing population in Europe and East Asia is a growing concern.

Birth rate
Annual number of births per 1000 total population

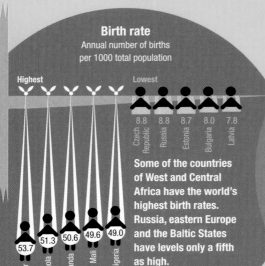

Highest
Niger 53.7
Angola 51.3
Uganda 50.6
Mali 49.6
Nigeria 49.0

Lowest
Czech Republic 8.8
Russia 8.8
Estonia 8.7
Bulgaria 8.0
Latvia 7.8

Some of the countries of West and Central Africa have the world's highest birth rates. Russia, eastern Europe and the Baltic States have levels only a fifth as high.

Death rate
Annual number of deaths per 1000 total population

Highest		Lowest	
Sierra Leone	27.7	Oman, Saudi Arabia	4.1
Botswana	24.5	Marshall Islands	4.0
Niger	24.0	Syria	4.0
Mozambique	23.9	Tajikistan	4.0
Swaziland	23.0	Andorra	3.9
Malawi	22.6	Bahrain	3.7
Lesotho	21.9	United Arab Emirates	3.0
Afghanistan	21.4	Brunei	2.6
Burundi	20.8	Kuwait	2.0
Rwanda	20.6	Qatar	1.9

High death rates in Africa are largely due to the AIDS epidemic. In contrast, oil-rich Arab countries have very low rates thanks to high standards of living and large expatriate communities.

Population growth and density Even an apparently modest annual rate can yield a startling growth in population. Africa, with a rate of less than 3 per cent, will almost triple its population in 30 years, while Asia, with 1.5 per cent, will add 2 billion people over the same period. Singapore is the most crowded larger nation in the world, but Bangladesh, with 130 million people and fewer resources, has more than 800 people per km². The Netherlands and Belgium are the most densely packed countries in Europe.

Population aged under 15 (%)
Selected countries

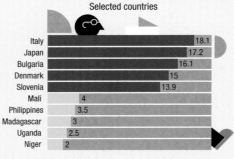

Micronesia 54.9
Uganda 49.2
Solomon Islands 44.8
Nepal 41.1
Uzbekistan 36.3
Latvia 18.1
Belgium 17.3
Czech Republic 16.4
Greece 15.1
San Marino 14.1

The world's youngest populations are all in the developing world, with up to half the population aged under 15. Low numbers of young people indicate a falling birth rate.

Population aged over 65 (%)
Selected countries

Italy 18.1
Japan 17.2
Bulgaria 16.1
Denmark 15
Slovenia 13.9
Mali 4
Philippines 3.5
Madagascar 3
Uganda 2.5
Niger 2

In many European nations, nearly a fifth of the population is aged 65 or over; in some nations this is likely to grow to a quarter in the next 25 years.

Contraceptive use
by married women aged 15-49 (%)

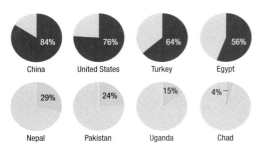

China 84%
United States 76%
Turkey 64%
Egypt 56%
Nepal 29%
Pakistan 24%
Uganda 15%
Chad 4%

Although on the increase, use of contraception varies widely: lack of education and money results in its use by only 25 per cent of women in sub-Saharan Africa.

Infant mortality rate
(Infant deaths per 1000 live births)

Highest countries		Selection of lowest countries	
Sierra Leone	182	United States	7
Niger	156	Cuba	7
Angola	154	New Zealand	6
Mali	141	Brunei	6
Guinea-Bissau	130	Netherlands	5
Congo, Dem. Rep.	129	Austria	5
Mozambique	125	Denmark	4
Mauritania	120	France	4
Chad	117	Sweden	3
Ethiopia	116	Japan	3

Africa's poorest countries have the world's highest infant mortality rates. The situation has been exacerbated in some African countries by the impact of AIDS.

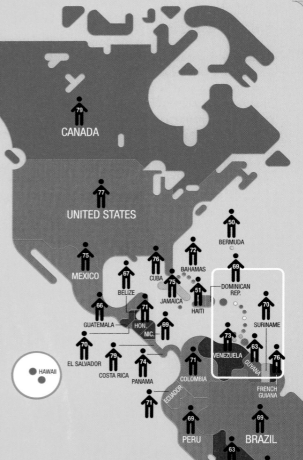

CANADA 79
UNITED STATES 77
BERMUDA 50
MEXICO 75
BELIZE 67
CUBA 76
BAHAMAS 72
JAMAICA 75
HAITI 51
DOMINICAN REP. 69
SURINAME 70
GUATEMALA 66
HON. 71
NIC. 69
VENEZUELA 73
GUYANA 63
FRENCH GUIANA 76
EL SALVADOR 70
COSTA RICA 79
PANAMA
COLOMBIA 71
ECUADOR 74
HAWAII
PERU 69
BRAZIL 69
BOLIVIA 63
PARAGUAY 71
CHILE 76
URUGUAY 75
ARGENTINA 74

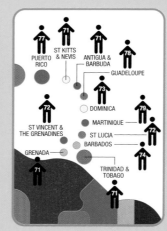

PUERTO RICO
ST KITTS & NEVIS
ANTIGUA & BARBUDA 71
GUADELOUPE 76
DOMINICA
ST VINCENT & THE GRENADINES
MARTINIQUE 79
ST LUCIA
BARBADOS
GRENADA 71
TRINIDAD & TOBAGO 74 71

Population pyramids

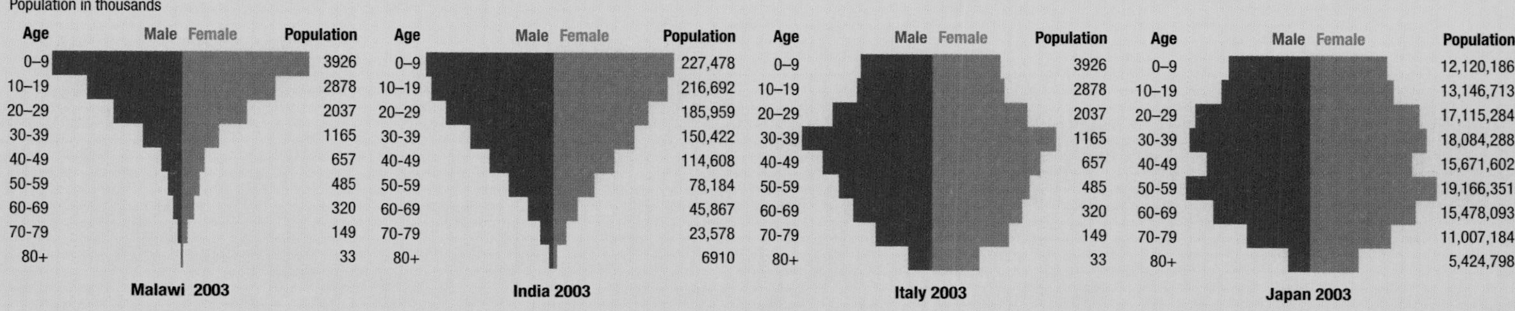

Population in thousands

Age	Male Female	Population	Age	Male Female	Population	Age	Male Female	Population	Age	Male Female	Population
0–9		3926	0–9		227,478	0–9		3926	0–9		12,120,186
10–19		2878	10–19		216,692	10–19		2878	10–19		13,146,713
20–29		2037	20–29		185,959	20–29		2037	20–29		17,115,284
30–39		1165	30–39		150,422	30–39		1165	30–39		18,084,288
40–49		657	40–49		114,608	40–49		657	40–49		15,671,602
50–59		485	50–59		78,184	50–59		485	50–59		19,166,351
60–69		320	60–69		45,867	60–69		320	60–69		15,478,093
70–79		149	70–79		23,578	70–79		149	70–79		11,007,184
80+		33	80+		6910	80+		33	80+		5,424,798

Malawi 2003 | **India 2003** | **Italy 2003** | **Japan 2003**

Population pyramids show the age structure of a nation. Countries with a fast-growing population have pyramids like those of India and Malawi, with a wide base of youth and relatively few older people. Static or ageing populations, such as Japan or Italy, have a more rounded shape. Pyramids can also reflect the impact of war (fewer younger men) or disease – as in the case of AIDS-hit Malawi.

Children born to each woman

High fertility rate		Congo	6.3	United Kingdom	1.6
Niger	8.0	Ethiopia	6.1	Cuba	1.6
Angola	7.2	Equatorial Guinea	5.9	Barbados	1.5
Uganda	7.1	Mauritania	5.8	Canada	1.5
Yemen	7.0	Rwanda	5.7	Germany	1.4
Mali	7.0	Low fertility rate		Japan	1.3
Burundi	6.8	Norway	1.8	Greece	1.3
Burkina	6.7	China	1.8	Czech Republic	1.2
Chad	6.7	Croatia	1.7	Italy	1.2
Sierra Leone	6.5	Australia	1.7	Russia	1.1

Eight children are born on average to every mother in Niger. In contrast, many families in Europe are having only one child; in China parents with more than one child are subject to government-imposed penalties.

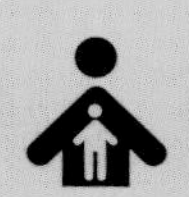

The population of Chad, with a growth rate of 3.4 per cent, will double in 25 years.

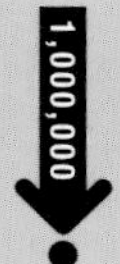

Ukraine, with a growth rate of –0.6 per cent, will lose a million people over five years.

%

Nearly 90 per cent of the world's people live in the Northern Hemisphere.

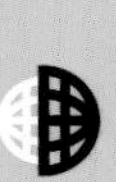

More people live in China and India than in the next 22 most populous nations combined.

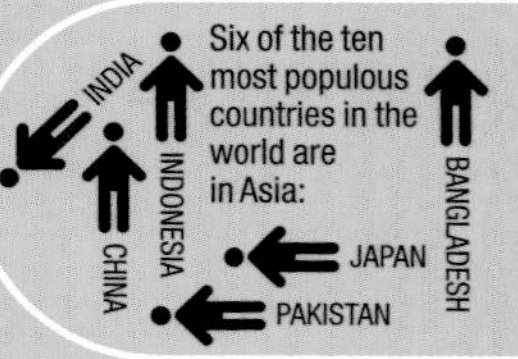

Six of the ten most populous countries in the world are in Asia: INDIA, INDONESIA, CHINA, JAPAN, PAKISTAN, BANGLADESH

10m x21

There are now 21 cities with populations of more than 10 million people.

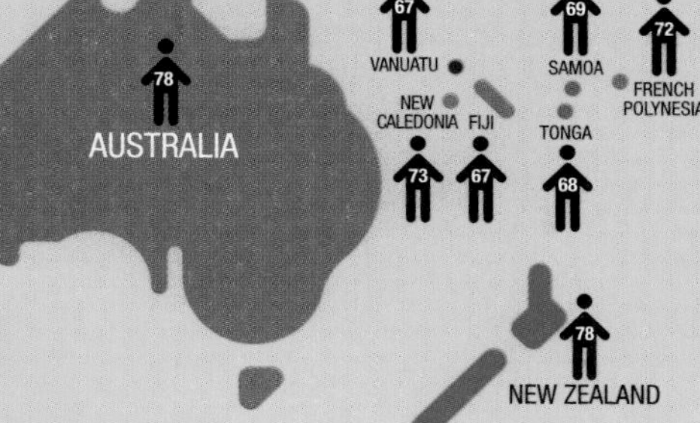

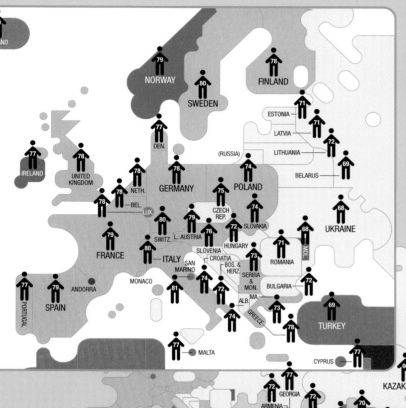

Population annual growth rate (%)

- Less than 0
- 0 – 0.4
- 0.5 – 0.9
- 1 – 1.4
- 1.5 – 1.9
- 2 – 2.4
- 2.5 – 2.9
- 3 and over
- Data not available

Average life expectancy at birth

75

Number of doctors per 100,000 people

Selected countries

Country	Value
India	48
Peru	93.2
United Kingdom	164
United States	279
France	303
Germany	350
Greece	392
Monaco	664

In the wealthy principality of Monaco, there is a doctor for every 150 people. In Liberia and Eritrea there is only one for every 30,000 to 40,000 people.

Improved drinking water

World 81%

Good access to improved water sources

| Canada 100% | Hungary 99% | Costa Rica 98% | Bangladesh 97% | Jordan 96% |
| Egypt 95% | Algeria 94% | Guatemala 92% | Colombia 91% | Honduras 90% |

Poor access to improved water sources

| Guinea 48% | Fiji 47% | Eritrea 46% | Congo, Dem. Rep. 45% | Papua New Guinea 42% |
| Rwanda 41% | Angola 38% | Cambodia 30% | Sierra Leone 28% | Chad 27% |

Bangladesh has good access to drinking water because of geography and climate. In sub-Saharan Africa, the supply is much more limited.

Number of dentists per 100,000 people

Selected countries

Country	Value
Mali	0.1
Nigeria	2.6
Russia	32.2
United Kingdom	39.8
United States	59.8
Japan	68.6
Sweden	152

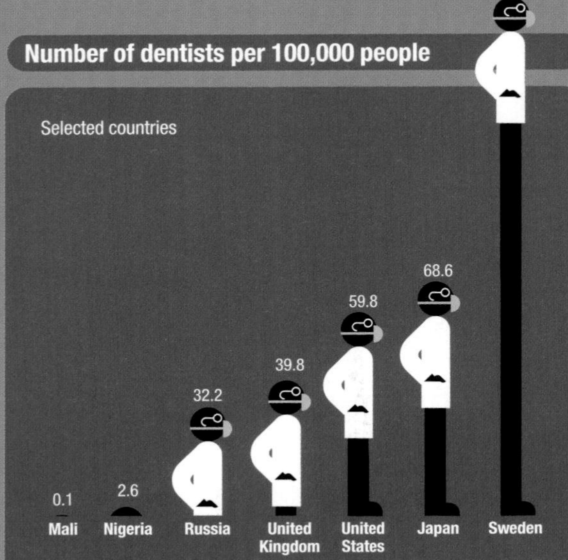

Sweden has nearly three times as many dentists as the USA, in proportion to the size of the population. In Mali and Nigeria, most people will never see a dentist – extraction is the only solution for dental problems.

LIFESTYLE

Wealth and health are inextricably intertwined: inhabitants of the richest countries, with their advanced health services, have the longest life expectancy. But lifestyles in the developed world pose different threats. Lack of exercise, heavy television viewing, car-driving, smoking and excess alcohol consumption all take their toll.

Quality of life The link between high GDP and the expectation of a long and healthy life is all too apparent. Increases in life expectancy are due to three factors: better nutrition, a clean water supply and access to health services. People of the poorest countries, especially those of sub-Saharan Africa, have the shortest healthy life. Even in wealthy countries, it is the richest people who live longest.

Leading causes of death in 2001

Developing countries	Number of deaths	Developed countries	Number of deaths
1 HIV/AIDS	2,678,000	1 Ischaemic heart disease	3,512,000
2 Lower respiratory infections	2,643,000	2 Cerebrovascular disease	3,346,000
3 Ischaemic heart disease	2,484,000	3 Chronic obstructive pulmonary disease	1,829,000
4 Diarrhoeal diseases	1 793 000	4 Lower respiratory infections	1,180,000
5 Cerebrovascular disease	1,381,000	5 Trachea/bronchus/lung cancers	938,000
6 Childhood diseases	1,217,000	6 Road traffic accidents	669,000
7 Malaria	1,103,000	7 Stomach cancer	657,000
8 Tuberculosis	1,021,000	8 Hypertensive heart disease	635,000
9 Chronic obstructive pulmonary disease	748,000	9 Tuberculosis	571,000
10 Measles	674,000	10 Self-inflicted	499,000

Many diseases of the developed world are linked to a sedentary lifestyle, over-eating, alcohol and smoking. In developing countries, HIV/AIDS is the main killer, but infectious diseases, such as malaria, measles and other childhood ailments, are frequently fatal.

Alcohol consumption per person (litres)

Selected countries

Country	Value
Mauritania	0.02
India	1.01
Ukraine	3.79
China	5.17
United States	9.08
United Kingdom	10.02
France	13.31
Portugal	16.59

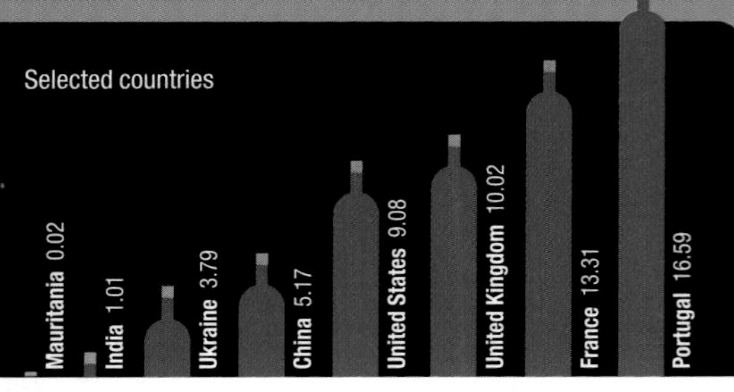

Many western European cultures have a strong tradition of social drinking. A high alcohol intake among certain groups can be a sign of social or economic malaise.

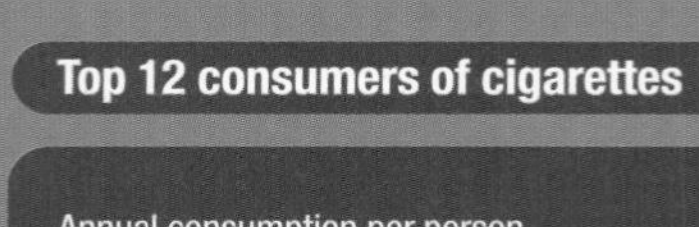

Top 12 consumers of cigarettes

Annual consumption per person

Country	Value
Spain	2670
United States	2670
Australia	2710
Serbia & Montenegro	2800
Netherlands	2820
Iceland	2860
Switzerland	2910
South Korea	3010
Japan	3240
Hungary	3260
Greece	3590
Poland	3620

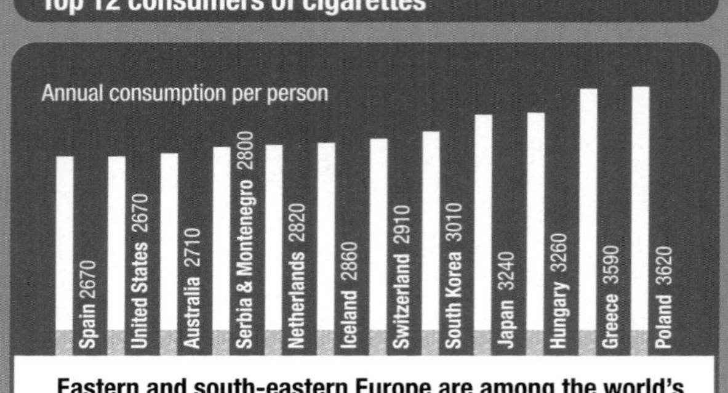

Eastern and south-eastern Europe are among the world's leading smokers, with cheap cigarettes and ineffectual government campaigns to warn of smoking's dangers.

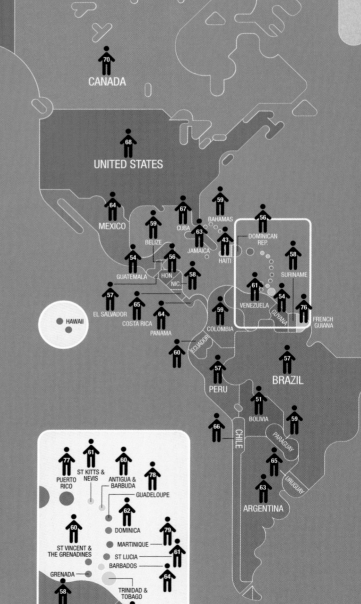

CANADA 70
UNITED STATES 68
MEXICO 64
HAWAII
GUATEMALA 54
EL SALVADOR 57
COSTA RICA 64
PANAMA
BELIZE 59
HON 56
NIC 58
CUBA 67
JAMAICA 63
HAITI 43
BAHAMAS 59
DOMINICAN REP. 56
PUERTO RICO 77
ST KITTS & NEVIS 61
ANTIGUA & BARBUDA 60
GUADELOUPE 78
DOMINICA 62
MARTINIQUE 79
ST LUCIA 61
BARBADOS 64
ST VINCENT & THE GRENADINES 60
GRENADA 58
TRINIDAD & TOBAGO 60
COLOMBIA 59
VENEZUELA 61
GUYANA 54
SURINAME 58
FRENCH GUIANA 76
ECUADOR 60
PERU 57
BRAZIL 57
BOLIVIA 51
CHILE 66
PARAGUAY 65
URUGUAY 63
ARGENTINA 59

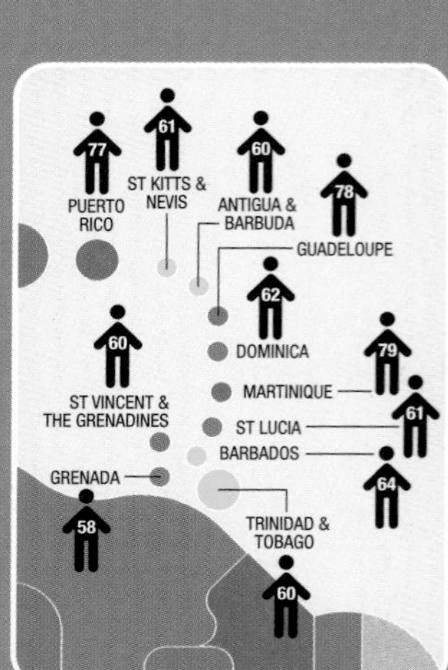

Number of television sets per 1000 population

806	United States
768	Monaco
710	Canada
686	Japan
595	France
567	Germany
554	Australia
521	United Kingdom
337	Poland
4	The Gambia
3	Tajikstan
1	Chad

The United States is the main global consumer and purveyor of television programmes, with viewing figures of over 30 hours per week. In sub-Saharan Africa and other developing nations, television viewing is a communal activity.

Number of radio sets per 1000 population

The United States leads the world in radio ownership, followed by many European countries. Radio provides poorer, sometimes isolated nations with news of the wider world. The remote Himalayan kingdom of Bhutan until recently banned all forms of mass media in an attempt to preserve the integrity of a centuries-old Buddhist heritage.

United States	2116
Finland	1498
United Kingdom	1443
Australia	1391
Nepal	38
Burkina	34
Azerbaijan	23
Bhutan	19

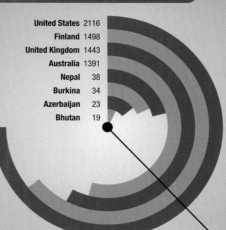

Number of cars per 1000 people

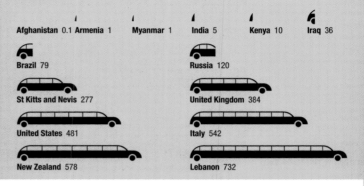

Afghanistan 0.1	Armenia 1	Myanmar 1	India 5	Kenya 10	Iraq 36

Brazil 79	Russia 120
St Kitts and Nevis 277	United Kingdom 384
United States 481	Italy 542
New Zealand 578	Lebanon 732

Tiny Monaco and Liechtenstein, with the largest number of cars in the world as a proportion of population, have the fewest roads. Cars have become a necessity in some developed countries where there is little public transport and people live far apart. But for many, they are an extreme luxury.

The Japanese are the world's longest-lived people with a life expectancy of twice that of someone born in Angola.

Cardio-vascular diseases kill two and half times as many people world wide as cancer.

x56 Norway has 56 times more doctors per person than Mozambique.

One billion (16 per cent) of the world's people are overweight; 300 million (5 per cent) are obese.

800m According to the WHO, 800 million people worldwide have an inadequate diet.

The rate of car ownership in Lebanon (732 per 1000) is 195 times that of Niger (4 per 1000).

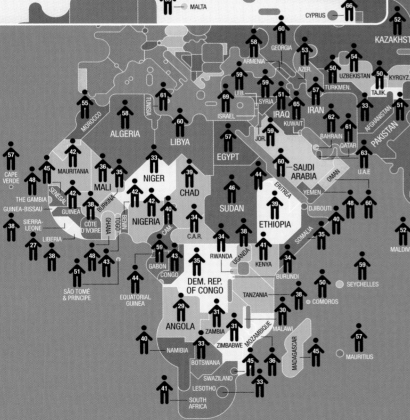

Wealth: GDP per person (in $US)

- 0 – 199
- 200 – 399
- 400 – 799
- 800 – 1599
- 1600 – 3199
- 3200 – 6399
- 6400 – 12,799
- 12,800 – 25,599
- 25,600 +

Expectation of years of healthy life at birth, 2001

 69

Major world religions (% of world population)

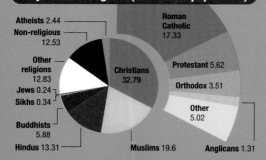

- Atheists 2.44
- Non-religious 12.53
- Other religions 12.83
- Jews 0.24
- Sikhs 0.34
- Buddhists 5.88
- Hindus 13.31
- Muslims 19.6
- Christians 32.79
- Roman Catholic 17.33
- Protestant 5.62
- Orthodox 3.51
- Other 5.02
- Anglicans 1.31

Christianity is the dominant world religion, with Islam in second place. A small but increasing proportion of the world's population, 12.5 per cent, is non-religious, reflecting the diminishing role of religion in many developed countries.

Households headed by women (%)

Top				Bottom			
Botswana	47	New Zealand	37	Nigeria	14	Niger	10
Slovenia	44	Bahamas	36	Sudan	13	Turkey	10
Denmark	42	United States	36	Egypt	13	Bangladesh	9
Finland	42	Hungary	35	Indonesia	13	India	9
Swaziland	40	Norway	34	Nepal	13	Mali	8
Haiti	39	Kenya	33	Fiji	12	Papua New Guinea	8
Namibia	39	Zimbabwe	33	Yemen	2	Burkina	7
Cape Verde	38	Vietnam	32	Algeria	11	Guinea	7
Jamaica	38	Poland	31	Philippines	11	Pakistan	7
Sweden	37	Eritrea	31	Sierra Leone	11	Iran	6
Ghana	37	Canada	30	Tunisia	11	Kuwait	5

In the West, high divorce rates contribute to comparatively high proportions of households headed by women. Elsewhere, for example in certain Caribbean and West African nations, the figure reflects a society where women are economically dominant, or where many men work away from home.

Average age at first marriage
Men and women

	Oldest Men		Oldest Women	
	Sweden	33	Sweden	31
	Denmark	32	Denmark	30
	Finland	32	Iceland	30
	Guyana	32	Finland	29
	Iceland	32	Guyana	29
	Youngest		**Youngest**	
	Niger	23	Uganda	19
	São Tomé and Príncipe	23	Bangladesh	18
	Tajikistan	23	São Tomé and Príncipe	18
	Yemen	23	Sierra Leone	18
	Solomon Is.	21	Niger	17

In wealthy nations, the age of marriage is rising as the young concentrate on careers before starting family life. Poorer nations may defer marriage to build up capital to start a family.

Teenage marriage
Currently married men and women, ages 15-19 (%)

Women

Niger	Eritrea	Paraguay	Portugal	Norway
62%	38%	17%	6%	1%

Men

Niger	Eritrea	Paraguay	Portugal	Norway
4%	2%	3%	1%	1%

In some countries, extremely youthful marriages are customary; families act as the main provider of social welfare. Generations live together, sharing the care of older family members.

Use of the death penalty
Selected countries

Used		Not used in practice		Not used	
Barbados	✓	Argentina	✓	Australia	✗
China	✓	Greece	✓	Cambodia	✗
Egypt	✓	Israel	✓	Canada	✗
India	✓	Latvia	✓	Colombia	✗
Indonesia	✓	Mexico	✓	France	✗
Iran	✓	Peru	✓	Germany	✗
Malaysia	✓	Russia	✓	Hungary	✗
Nigeria	✓	Serbia & Mon.	✓	Nepal	✗
Pakistan	✓	Sri Lanka	✓	Poland	✗
Singapore	✓	Togo	✓	South Africa	✗
United States	✓	Turkey	✓	United Kingdom	✗

The USA leads the world in judicial execution, but capital punishment is legal in much of Asia and Africa. Islamic nations with Sharia law, China and Russia also have a high use of capital punishment.

Participation in the labour force
Ages 15-64 (%)

Highest	Female	Male	Highest
Burundi	86	94	Burundi
Rwanda	86	94	Rwanda
Cambodia	85	93	Niger
Mozambique	84	91	Switzerland
China	80	91	Uganda
Lowest			**Lowest**
Iran, Syria	30	76	France
Jordan	28	76	Luxembourg
Libya	26	76	Slovenia
Saudi Arabia	23	75	Croatia
Oman	20	73	Belgium

Almost three-quarters of the world's male population is employed at any given time. Rates of female employment are more variable and reflect economic necessity and the status of women.

CANADA 100 58
UNITED STATES 97 77
MEXICO 71 18
CUBA 79 19
BAHAMAS 88 25
DOMINICAN REP. 66 22
SURINAME 7
BELIZE 54 1
JAMAICA 90 9
HAITI 29 1
GUATEMALA 34 8
HON. 32 13
NIC. 49 11
EL SALVADOR 50 18
VENEZUELA 35 29 / 78 10
COSTA RICA 48 31
PANAMA 68 30
COLOMBIA 53 15
ECUADOR 56 18
BRAZIL 83 14
PERU 81 29
BOLIVIA 39 24
CHILE 85 34
PARAGUAY 51 10
URUGUAY 88 35
ARGENTINA 89 47
PUERTO RICO 65 41
ST KITTS & NEVIS 100 29
TRINIDAD & TOBAGO 80 6

Countries with highest numbers of prisoners (top 20)

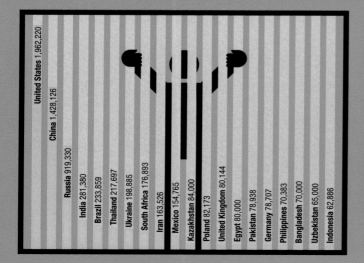

- United States 1,962,220
- China 1,428,126
- Russia 919,330
- India 281,380
- Brazil 233,859
- Thailand 217,697
- Ukraine 198,885
- South Africa 176,893
- Iran 163,526
- Mexico 154,765
- Kazakhstan 84,000
- Poland 82,173
- United Kingdom 80,144
- Egypt 80,000
- Pakistan 78,938
- Germany 78,707
- Philippines 70,383
- Bangladesh 70,000
- Uzbekistan 65,000
- Indonesia 62,886

Countries with highest rates of imprisonment, per 100,000 of the national population (top 20)

- United States 686
- Russia 638
- Belarus 554
- Kazakhstan 522
- Turkmenistan 489
- Belize 459
- Suriname 437
- Dominica 420
- Bahamas 416
- Maldives 414
- South Africa 404
- Kyrgyzstan 390
- Botswana 381
- Swaziland 362
- Latvia 361
- Singapore 359
- Trinidad & Tobago 351
- Thailand 342
- St. Kitts & Nevis 338
- Estonia 337

Both the United States and China have high prison populations, a reflection of their large populations as well as their strict penal systems, but the USA imprisons its citizens at a significantly higher rate – about six times as high as China's. The Caribbean nations also have strict penalties and large numbers of prisoners relative to their populations. Prisons are expensive to maintain; many developing countries are exploring non-custodial sentences, such as community service, as an alternative form of punishment.

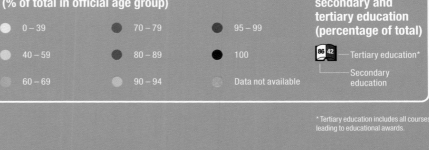

Net primary school enrolment/attendance (% of total in official age group)

- 0 – 39
- 40 – 59
- 60 – 69
- 70 – 79
- 80 – 89
- 90 – 94
- 95 – 99
- 100
- Data not available

Enrolment in secondary and tertiary education (percentage of total)

 86 42 — Tertiary education*
— Secondary education

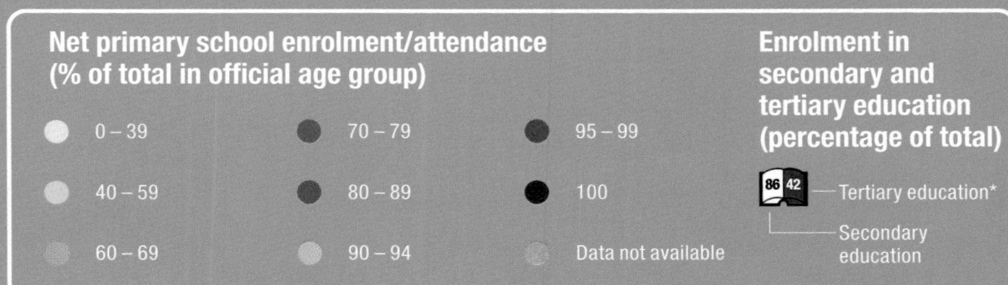

* Tertiary education includes all courses leading to educational awards.

100	40 ICELAND
100	65 NORWAY
100	83 FINLAND
100	63 SWEDEN
100	48 ESTONIA
87	51 LATVIA
90	41 LITHUANIA
100	55 DEN.
100	45 IRELAND
100	58 UNITED KINGDOM
100	49 NETH.
98	46 GERMANY
96	35 POLAND
93	42 BELARUS
100	56 BEL.
97	10 LUX.
82	26 CZECH REP.
86	27 SLOVAKIA
93	42 UKRAINE
94	36 SWITZ.
96	50 AUSTRIA
99	53 SLOVENIA
98	34 HUNGARY
81	25 MOLD.
95	47 ITALY
96	38 CROATIA
64 BOS. & HERZ.
80	13 ROMANIA
100	51 FRANCE
82	100
87	43 SERBIA AND MON.
86	42 RUSSIA
68	16 BULGARIA
38	11 ALB.
83	22 GREECE
70	14 TURKEY
99	45 PORTUGAL
100	56 SPAIN
92	20 MALTA
96	50 MA...
83	19 CYPRUS

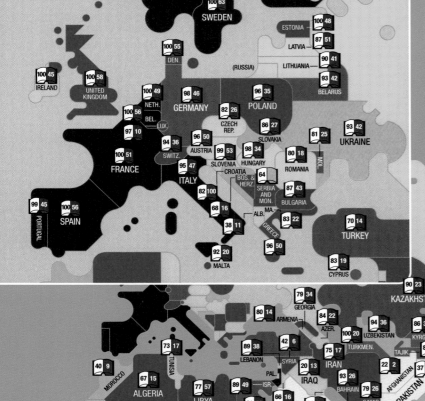

Swedes wait the longest to get married; their average age at first marriage is 32.

Fifty per cent of brides in Mali are in their teens; in Poland only 2 per cent are.

90% More than half the world's nations have a 90 per cent opportunity to go to primary school.

90	23 KAZAKHSTAN
79	34 GEORGIA
80	14 ARMENIA
84	22 AZER.
100	20 UZBEKISTAN
94	36 KYRGYZ.
86	30
59	25 MONGOLIA
89	38 LEBANON
42	6 SYRIA
75	17 TURKMEN.
81	20 TAJIK.
62	6 CHINA
100	52 S. KOREA
100	44 JAPAN
20	13 PAL.
93	26 IRAQ
89	49 ISR.
64	19 JOR.
37	3 IRAN
20	2 AFGHANISTAN
81	20
73	17 TUNISIA
67	15 ALGERIA
77	57 LIBYA
7	1 NIGER
100	20 BAHRAIN
79	26 QATAR
66	11 PAKISTAN
48	3 NEPAL
10	BHUTAN
40	9 MOROCCO
18	6 MAURITANIA
14	2 MALI
11	1
66	19 SAUDI ARABIA
64	19 KUWAIT
47	5 BANGLADESH
36	5 MYANMAR (BURMA)
33	3 LAOS
61	11 VIETNAM
69	20 CAPE VERDE
20	4
31	2 THE GAMBIA
15	1 SENEGAL
21 BURKINA
3	2 BENIN
20	5 TOGO
81	39 EGYPT
66	OMAN
24	1 ERITREA
45	10 YEMEN
67	5
49	7 INDIA
88	30 THAILAND
22	1 CAM.
11	SIERRA LEONE
17	1 LIBERIA
24	7 CÔTE D'IVOIRE
23	7 GHANA
34	1
33	4
55	8 EQUATORIAL GUINEA
53	8 GABON
32 CAMEROON
10	2 C.A.R.
16	2
18	2 CONGO
9	1 RWANDA
31	1 UGANDA
6	3 SOMALIA
56 MALDIVES
71	5 SRI LANKA
98	12 MALAYSIA
100	11 BRUNEI
77	28 GUAM
67	34 SINGAPORE
22	1 PHILIPPINES
51	11 INDONESIA
29	7 SUDAN
17	1
17	1 ETHIOPIA
30	1 KENYA
25	1 COMOROS
SEYCHELLES
5	1 TANZANIA
47	6 DEM. REP. OF CONGO
BURUNDI
16	1 ANGOLA
27	3 ZAMBIA
17	<1 MALAWI
59	7 NAMIBIA
77	4 ZIMBABWE
9	1 MOZAMBIQUE
16	2 MADAGASCAR
71	7 MAURITIUS
100	73 AUSTRALIA
22	1 PAPUA NEW GUINEA
18 SOLOMON ISLANDS
23	<1 VANUATU
73	8 SAMOA
69	13 FIJI
56	3 BOTSWANA
47	6 SWAZILAND
56	5 LESOTHO
32	2
100	17 SOUTH AFRICA
100	60 NEW ZEALAND

N. KOREA
TAIWAN
MICRONESIA
PALAU
MARSHALL ISLANDS
NAURU KIRIBATI
EAST TIMOR
TUVALU
TONGA NIUE COOK ISLANDS

The educational lottery Literacy is an essential tool for life in modern societies. The industrially advanced countries of the developed world have been developing their education systems over the past century with the goal of achieving universal literacy. Increasingly large proportions of their populations are moving into tertiary education (university and further education) – Finland, the United States and Australia lead the world, with more than 70 per cent. The developing countries of Asia are making great strides in their provision of primary education but parts of sub-Saharan Africa lag behind.

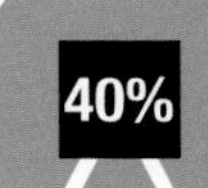

SOCIETY

The welfare of the world's citizens can be measured in many ways. Access to education is the cornerstone of social advantage, and many developing countries are still struggling to reach even basic standards. Attitudes to marriage reflect economic confidence; in the developed world, reproduction is no longer an imperative but a choice.

40% Nearly half the world's countries have a less than 40 per cent chance to go to secondary school.

 More than 80 countries use the death penalty.

 The United States imprisons seven times as many people per 100,000 of the population as Germany.

276,700

Female representation in parliament

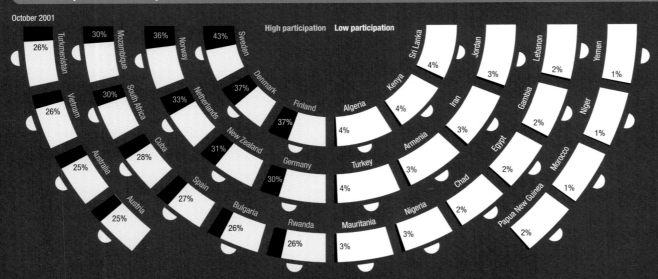

October 2001

High participation   Low participation

Turkmenistan 26%
Mozambique 30%
Norway 36%
Sweden 43%
Vietnam 26%
South Africa 30%
Netherlands 33%
Denmark 37%
Australia 25%
Cuba 28%
New Zealand 31%
Finland 37%
Austria 25%
Spain 27%
Germany 30%
Bulgaria 26%
Rwanda 26%
Sri Lanka 4%
Kenya 4%
Algeria 4%
Turkey 4%
Mauritania 3%
Jordan 3%
Iran 3%
Armenia 3%
Nigeria 3%
Lebanon 2%
Gambia 2%
Egypt 2%
Chad 2%
Yemen 1%
Niger 1%
Morocco 1%
Papua New Guinea 2%

The countries of Scandinavia consistently show the most positive attitude to gender equality, and this is reflected in the number of seats allocated to women in parliament. Among the world's leading economies, the United States and the United Kingdom have low rates of female governance at 14 and 17 per cent respectively. Female parliamentarians are exceptionally rare in some Islamic countries.

Military spending ($US million)

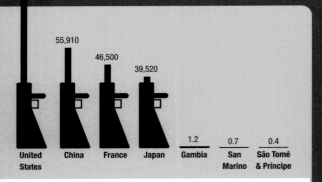

United States 55,910
China 46,500
France 39,520
Japan
Gambia 1.2
San Marino 0.7
São Tomé & Príncipe 0.4

The USA, the remaining global superpower, has the largest military budget. Russia no longer ranks among the top five, but Japan, despite its post-Second World War withdrawal from militarism, is a major spender. The UK, though ranking sixth, only spends 2.5 per cent of GDP on defence.

The nuclear power club

While the main nuclear powers claim their arsenal constitutes an effective deterrent, there is anxiety about countries with nuclear arms and a history of conflict, such as Israel, Pakistan, India and especially North Korea, which will not divulge its nuclear secrets.

Countries which admit having nuclear weapons and have signed the CTBT (Comprehensive Test Ban Treaty) and the NPT (Non-Proliferation Treaty)

United States	First nuclear blast 1945. Conducted 1030 tests. Nuclear arsenal: 10,000+. Signed NPT: 1970
Russia	First nuclear test 1949. Conducted 715 tests. Nuclear arsenal: 20,000+. Signed NPT: 1970
UK	First nuclear test 1952. Conducted 45 tests. Nuclear arsenal: 185. Signed NPT: 1968
France	First nuclear test 1960. Conducted 200 tests. Nuclear arsenal: 350. Signed NPT: 1992
China	First nuclear test 1964. Conducted 46 tests. Nuclear arsenal: 400 (est.). Signed NPT: 1992

Non-NPT members

Israel	Thought to have started nuclear programme in 1950s and produced first bomb in 1967. Nuclear arsenal: believed to be 100-200.
India	First nuclear test 1974. Conducted 4 tests to date. Nuclear arsenal: estimated 45-95.
Pakistan	First nuclear test 1998. Conducted 5 tests to date Nuclear arsenal: estimated 30-55.

Suspected nuclear aspirants

? Iran	Nuclear arsenal: 0. Signed NPT: 1970 Iran has agreed to a regime of tough United Nations inspections of its facilities in the light of growing international concern over its nuclear plans.
? North Korea	Nuclear arsenal: thought to have enough fissile material for one or two warheads. Signed NPT: 1985 but has refused to let the International Atomic Energy Agency inspect its facilities and pulled out of NPT in 2002.

Countries which formerly had nuclear weapons/programmes
Algeria, Argentina, Belarus, Brazil, Kazakhstan, Iraq, Libya, Romania, South Africa, Ukraine

Top spenders on defence (% of GDP)

		As % of GDP			As % of GDP
1.	Eritrea	20.9	18.	Algeria	6.3
2.	Angola	17.0		Serbia & Mont.	6.3
3.	Oman	14.4	20.	Cambodia	5.8
4.	Saudi Arabia	14.1		Iran	5.8
5.	Afghanistan	12.2		Rwanda	5.8
6.	Kuwait	12.1	23.	Liberia	5.6
7.	North Korea	11.6	24.	Brunei	5.5
8.	Syria	10.9		Burundi	5.5
9.	Ethiopia	9.8	26.	Suriname	5.3
10.	Israel	9.5	27.	Singapore	5.1
11.	Iraq	9.3		Sri Lanka	5.1
12.	Congo	8.9	29.	Turkey	5.0
13.	Jordan	8.5	30.	Bahrain	4.8
14.	Yemen	8.1		Greece	4.8
15.	Vietnam	7.2	32.	Egypt	4.7
16.	Qatar	7.1	33.	United Arab Emirates	4.6
17.	Armenia	6.5	34.	Chile, Pakistan, Somalia	4.4

The nations that spend the greatest proportion of their GDP on defence are locked in conflict. North Korea, the most militarized country in the world, is effectively an armed camp, braced against invasion from the South.

Aid donors and recipients

While Japan and the USA top the world league tables in absolute aid donations, only a small number of countries (the Netherlands, Denmark, Norway and Sweden) exceed the United Nation's recommendation of a donation of 7 per cent of GDP.

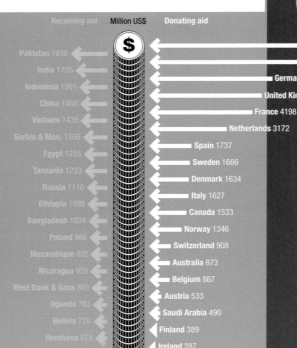

Receiving aid   Million US$ Donating aid

Pakistan 1938
India 1705
Indonesia 1501
China 1460
Vietnam 1435
Serbia & Mon. 1306
Egypt 1255
Tanzania 1233
Russia 1110
Ethiopia 1080
Bangladesh 1024
Poland 966
Mozambique 935
Nicaragua 928
West Bank & Gaza 865
Uganda 783
Bolivia 729
Honduras 678
Ghana 652

United States 11,429
Japan 9847
Germany 4990
United Kingdom 4579
France 4198
Netherlands 3172
Spain 1737
Sweden 1666
Denmark 1634
Italy 1627
Canada 1533
Norway 1346
Switzerland 908
Australia 873
Belgium 867
Austria 533
Saudi Arabia 490
Finland 389
Ireland 287

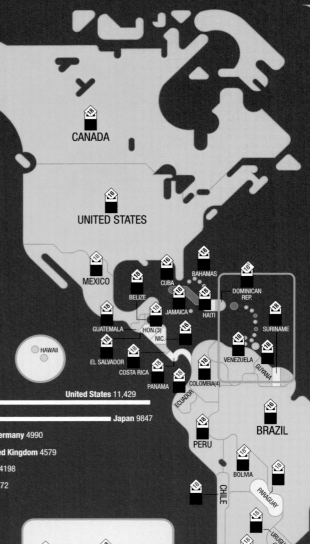

CANADA

UNITED STATES

MEXICO
CUBA
BAHAMAS
BELIZE
DOMINICAN REP.
JAMAICA
HAITI
GUATEMALA
HON. (3)
NIC.
SURINAME
EL SALVADOR
COSTA RICA
VENEZUELA
GUYANA
PANAMA
COLOMBIA(4)
HAWAII
ECUADOR
PERU
BRAZIL
BOLIVIA
CHILE
PARAGUAY
URUGUAY
ARGENTINA

PUERTO RICO
ST KITTS & NEVIS
ANTIGUA & BARBUDA
GUADELOUPE
DOMINICA
MARTINIQUE
ST VINCENT & THE GRENADINES
ST LUCIA
BARBADOS
GRENADA
TRINIDAD & TOBAGO

The European Union and NATO

European Union	Sweden	Slovenia	Greece
Member states	The Netherlands	**Applicant countries**	Hungary
Austria	United Kingdom	Bulgaria	Iceland
Belgium	**New member states**	Romania	Italy
Denmark	**(joining in 2004)**	Turkey	Luxembourg
Finland	Cyprus		Netherlands
France	Czech Republic	**NATO**	Norway
Germany	Estonia	**Member countries**	Poland
Greece	Hungary	Belgium	Portugal
Ireland	Latvia	Canada	Spain
Italy	Lithuania	Czech Republic	Turkey
Luxembourg	Malta	Denmark	United Kingdom
Portugal	Poland	France	United States
Spain	Slovakia	Germany	

The EU seeks to integrate European policies to ensure peace and prosperity.
NATO aims to unite its member states in a mutual defence cooperation treaty.

There are currently 193 independent nations. Over the past 15 years a proliferation of new states has appeared, as a result of the break-up of the Soviet Union and the Eastern bloc. Smaller countries such as Palau and East Timor have recently won the right to self-determination. Only a few territories, mainly in the western Pacific and the Caribbean, still have links to former colonial powers.

Changing governments The world political map has undergone a striking change since the 1990s, when many countries in sub-Saharan Africa and the nations of the former Soviet Union and Communist Eastern Europe became multiparty democracies. But the prerequisites of democracy – free and fair elections, with equal access to the public media – are not always upheld in these transitional democracies.

Political system (type of government)

- Multiparty democracy
- Multiparty democracy adopted 1990s
- One-party regime
- Rule by monarch
- Military rule
- Transitional regime (or recently occupied territory)
- Other

The right to vote

- Age of voting (universal)
- Age of voting (compulsory)
- ✕ No voting

Notes 1 Military rule in fact. 2 Widespread disorder. 3 Allegations of ballot rigging in recent elections. 4 Recent disorder. 5 Partly occupied territory. 6 Recent period of military rule. 7 One party regime in fact. A 18 if married, 21 if single. B 16 if employed. C Married people can vote regardless of age. D Adult males who have been naturalized for 30 years or more or have resided in Kuwait since before 1920 and their male descendants at age 21. E In 2000 elections, limited to c.175,000 Omanis chosen by the government to vote in elections for the Majlis al-Shura.

Oceans and seas

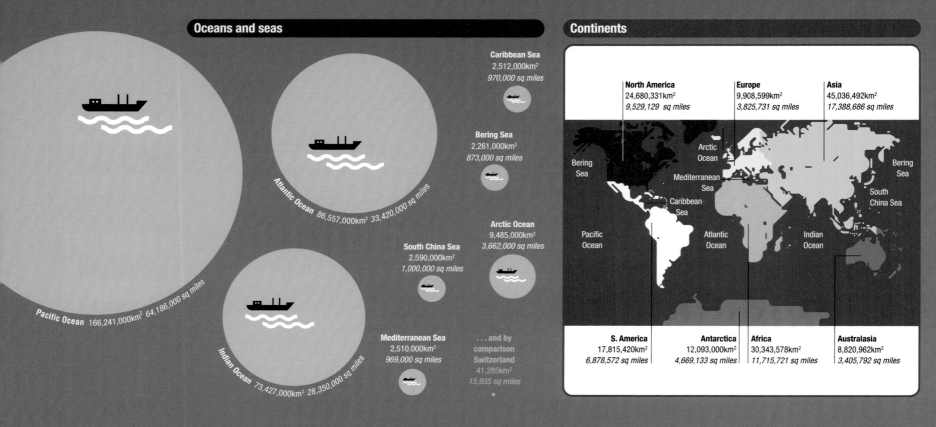

Caribbean Sea
2,512,000km²
970,000 sq miles

Bering Sea
2,261,000km²
873,000 sq miles

Atlantic Ocean 86,557,000km² *33,420,000 sq miles*

Arctic Ocean
9,485,000km²
3,662,000 sq miles

South China Sea
2,590,000km²
1,000,000 sq miles

Pacific Ocean 166,241,000km² *64,186,000 sq miles*

Indian Ocean 73,427,000km² *28,350,000 sq miles*

Mediterranean Sea
2,510,000km²
969,000 sq miles

...and by
comparison
Switzerland
41,285km²
15,935 sq miles

Continents

North America 24,680,331km² *9,529,129 sq miles*	Europe 9,908,599km² *3,825,731 sq miles*	Asia 45,036,492km² *17,388,686 sq miles*

Bering Sea

Arctic Ocean

Mediterranean Sea

Bering Sea

Caribbean Sea

South China Sea

Pacific Ocean

Atlantic Ocean

Indian Ocean

S. America 17,815,420km² *6,878,572 sq miles*	**Antarctica** 12,093,000km² *4,669,133 sq miles*	**Africa** 30,343,578km² *11,715,721 sq miles*	**Australasia** 8,820,962km² *3,405,792 sq miles*

EXTREMES

Our world is full of extraordinary natural features: towering peaks and plunging ocean depths, endless rivers and islands bigger than many nations, baking deserts and flooded forests. Find the wettest places on Earth — and those that see no rain for decades. Wastes so cold that they will extinguish most life in moments — or so hot you can fry food on a rock. Rivers that traverse the breadth of a continent and water several countries, and freshwater lakes greater than a sea. Here are the vital statistics of every continent, along with some of the world's most extraordinary places and phenomena.

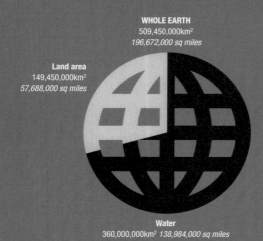

WHOLE EARTH
509,450,000km²
196,672,000 sq miles

Land area
149,450,000km²
57,688,000 sq miles

Water
360,000,000km² *138,984,000 sq miles*

Comparative mountains

Highest mountain on land:
Everest 8848m *(29,028ft)*

Mt Chimborazo is 2150m farther from the centre of the Earth than Everest

Lowest point on land:
Dead Sea shoreline 400m
(1360ft)

Highest active volcano:
Volcán Cotopaxi, Mexico 5896m
(19,343ft)

Tallest mountain
(but undersea):
Mauna Kea, Hawaii 10,206m
(33,484ft) from seabed

Deepest sea trench:
Challenger Deep, Mariana Trench (Pacific Ocean) 10,020m
(35,826ft) deep

Mt Chimborazo is 2150m farther from the centre of the Earth than Everest, at 6310m *(20,700ft)*, because of a bulge in the Earth's crust.

Mountains - the highest by continent

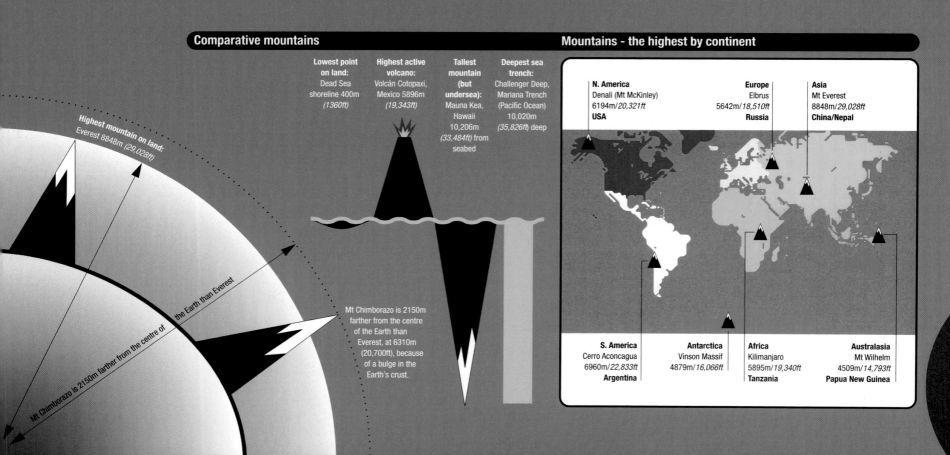

N. America Denali (Mt McKinley) 6194m/*20,321ft* USA	Europe Elbrus 5642m/*18,510ft* Russia	Asia Mt Everest 8848m/*29,028ft* China/Nepal

S. America Cerro Aconcagua 6960m/*22,833ft* Argentina	Antarctica Vinson Massif 4879m/*16,066ft*	Africa Kilimanjaro 5895m/*19,340ft* Tanzania	Australasia Mt Wilhelm 4509m/*14,793ft* Papua New Guinea

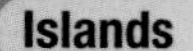

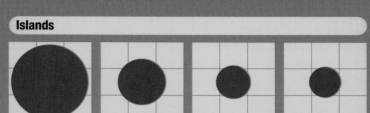

Islands

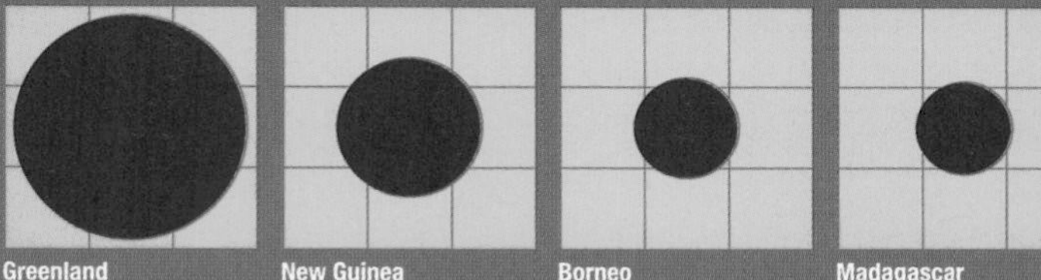

Greenland
1,175,600km²
840,004 sq miles

New Guinea
808,510km²
312,167 sq miles

Borneo
745,561km²
287,863 sq miles

Madagascar
587,040km²
226,657 sq miles

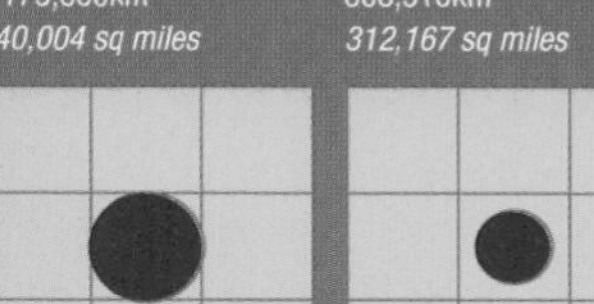

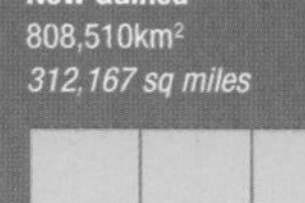

Baffin Island
507,451km²
195,927 sq miles

Sumatra
473,606km²
182,860 sq miles

Honshu
227,414km²
87,805 sq miles

Great Britain
218,476km²
84,354 sq miles

Largest islands

Baffin Island | Greenland | Great Britain | Borneo | Honshu

Madagascar | Sumatra | New Guinea

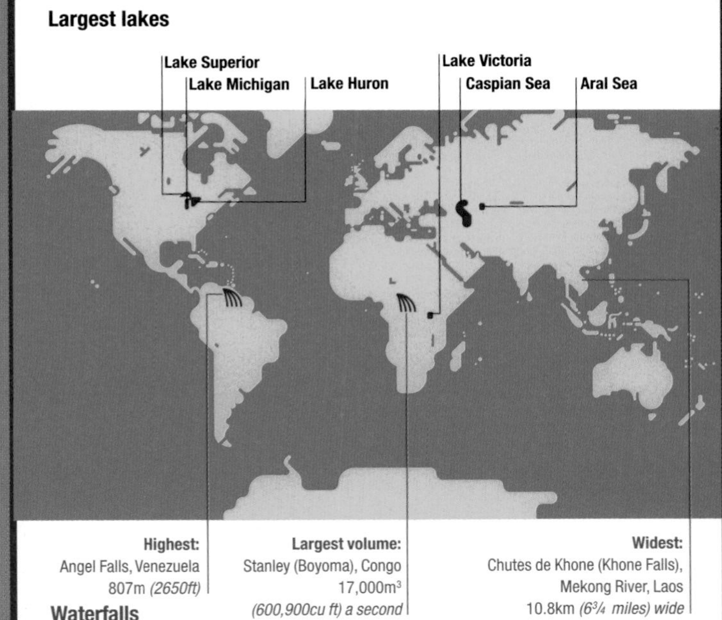

Climate extremes

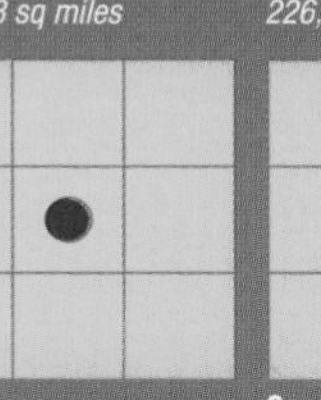

Hottest place:
El Azizia, Libya 58°C (136°F)

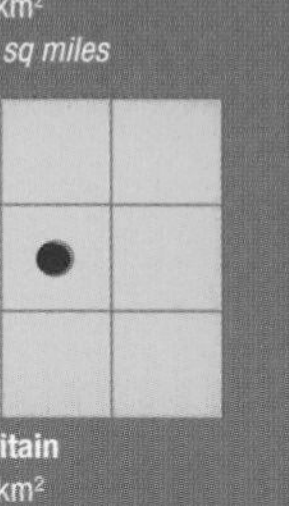

Wettest year: The most rainfall ever recorded in one year was 1041.78 inches (about 2646cm). It fell on Cherrapunji, India, from August 1860 to July 1861.

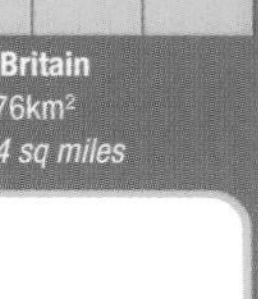

Coldest place:
Vostok Station, Antarctica
-89.4°C (-129°F)

Wettest place:
Mawsynram, India: annual average rainfall 1143cm (467in)

Driest place:
Aswân, Egypt: average annual rainfall 0.5mm (0.02in)

Hottest | Driest | Wettest

Coldest

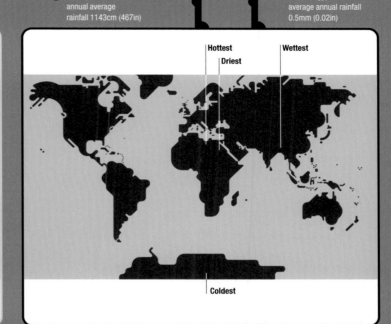

Lakes and waterfalls

Largest lakes

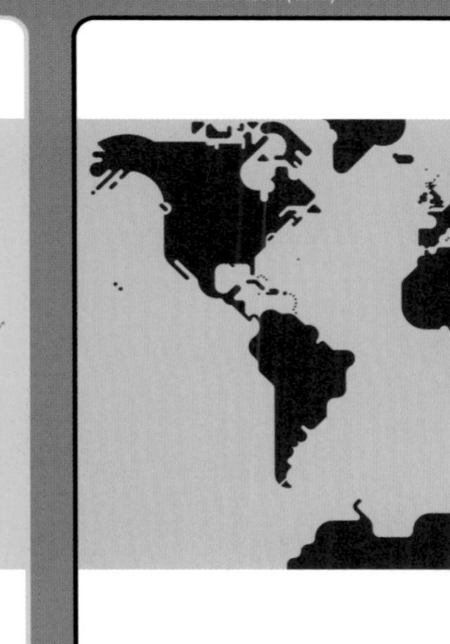

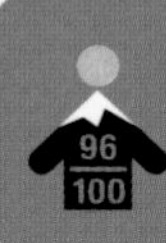

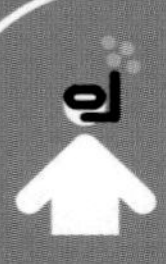

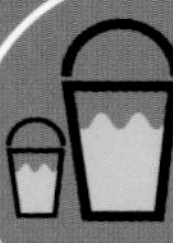

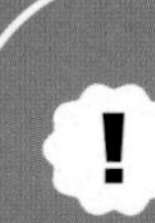

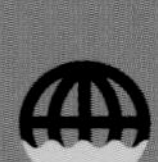

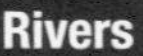

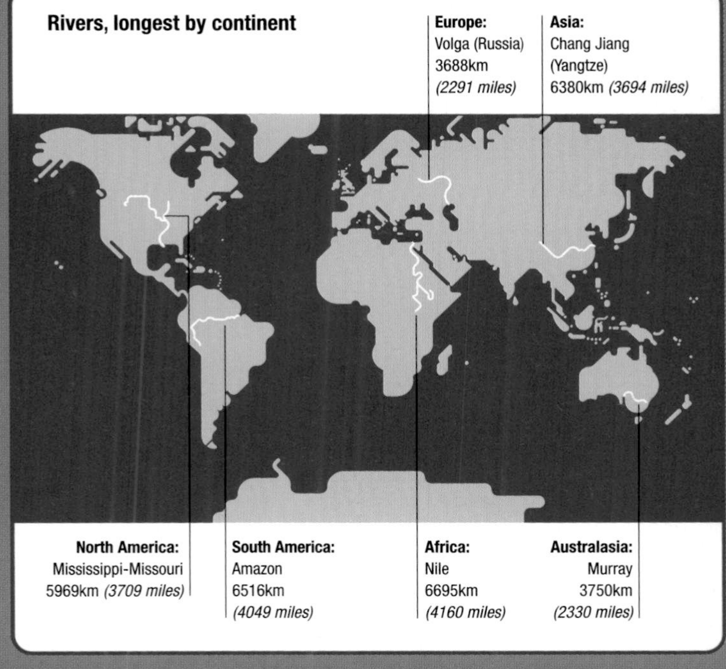

Lake Superior | Lake Michigan | Lake Huron | Lake Victoria | Caspian Sea | Aral Sea

Highest:
Angel Falls, Venezuela
807m (2650ft)

Largest volume:
Stanley (Boyoma), Congo
17,000m³
(600,900cu ft) a second

Widest:
Chutes de Khone (Khone Falls),
Mekong River, Laos
10.8km (6¾ miles) wide

Waterfalls

Rivers

Rivers, longest by continent

Europe:
Volga (Russia)
3688km
(2291 miles)

Asia:
Chang Jiang (Yangtze)
6380km *(3694 miles)*

North America:
Mississippi-Missouri
5969km *(3709 miles)*

South America:
Amazon
6516km *(4049 miles)*

Africa:
Nile
6695km *(4160 miles)*

Australasia:
Murray
3750km *(2330 miles)*

Aral Sea 33,640km² *12,988 sq miles*

Lake Michigan 57,800km² *22,316 sq miles*

Lake Superior 83,270km² *31,696 sq miles*

Caspian Sea 371,000km² *143,243 sq miles*

...and by comparison Switzerland 41,285km² 15,935 sq miles

Lake Victoria 68,800km² *26,563 sq miles*

Lake Huron 59,600km² *23,011 sq miles*

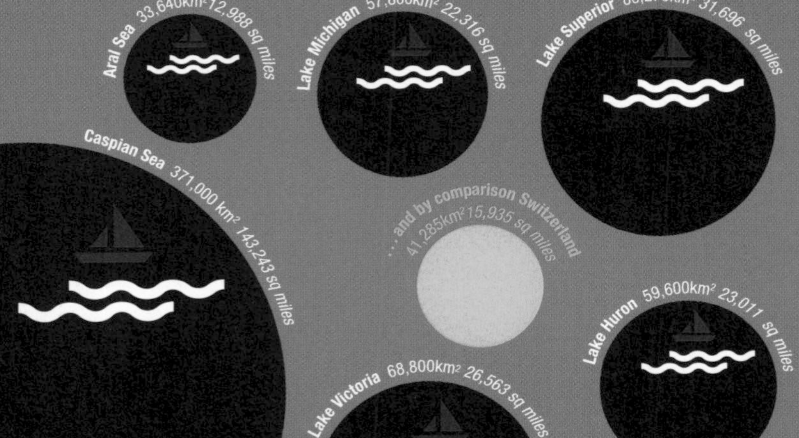

The world's longest rivers

Nile 6695km *4160 miles*

Amazon 6516km *4049 miles*

Chang Jiang (Yangtze) 6380km *3964 miles*

Mississippi-Missouri 5969km *3709 miles*

Ob'-Irtysh 5568km *3459 miles*

Yenisey-Angara-Selenga 5550km *3448 miles*

Huang He (Yellow River) 5464km *3395 miles*

...and by comparison...

River Thames 330km 205 miles

28 Empire State Buildings 381m (125ft) high would fit into the Mariana Trench in the Pacific Ocean.

The Himalayas (including the Karakoram range) contains 96 of the world's 100 tallest mountains.

The longest mountain range in the world is the Mid-Atlantic Ridge which lies under the Atlantic Ocean.

The Amazon River's drainage basin at 7,050,000km² (2,722,000 sq miles), is nearly twice the size of its closest rival.

The world's largest river delta is the Ganges–Brahmaputra; 75,000km² (28,957 sq miles).

The Pacific Ocean contains more than half of the world's salt water.

FLAGS

Flags were probably invented by the ancient Indians or Chinese to identify opposing sides in battle. Their use spread to the Islamic world, and they were introduced to Europeans by the Saracens. The colours and designs of modern national flags can give a vivid insight into the history, culture, or religion of different countries. Many flags display a common origin, linked by traditions and by geography.

Americas

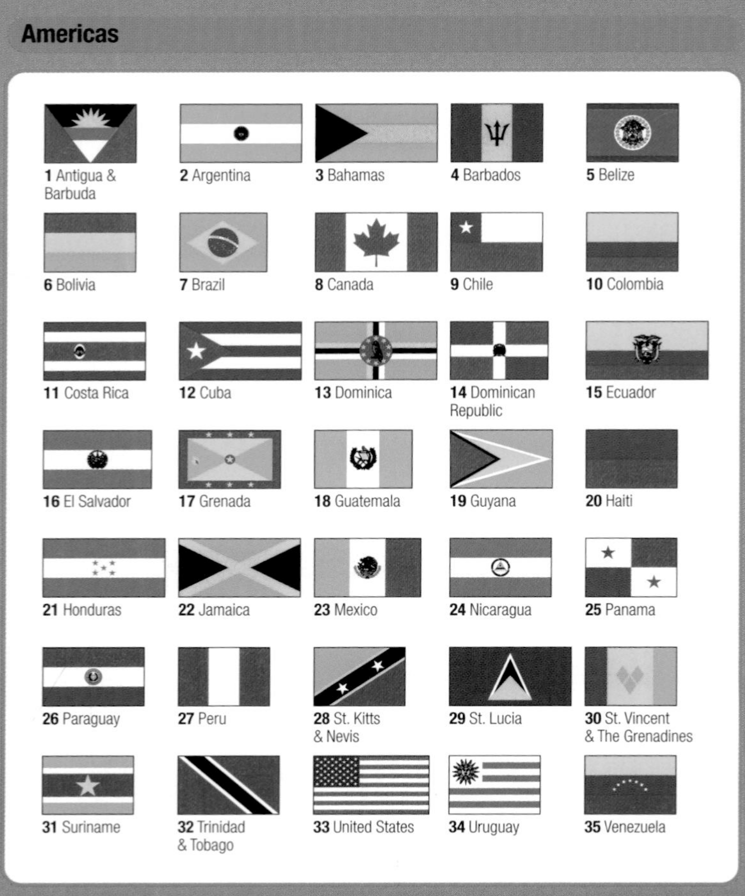

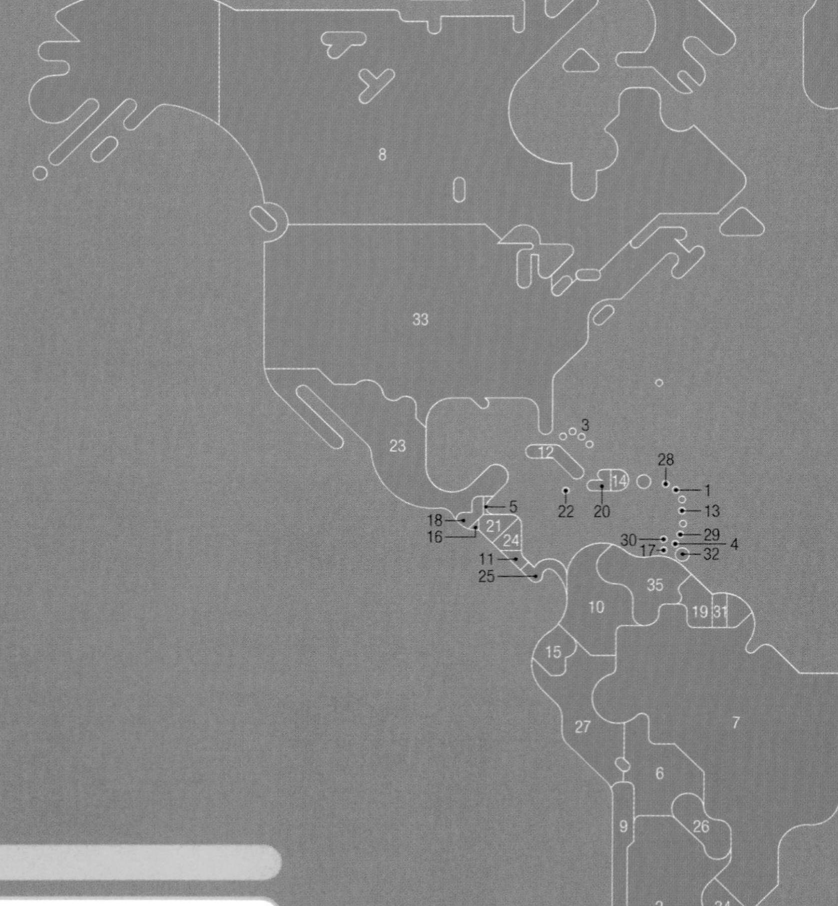

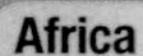

1 Antigua & Barbuda
2 Argentina
3 Bahamas
4 Barbados
5 Belize
6 Bolivia
7 Brazil
8 Canada
9 Chile
10 Colombia
11 Costa Rica
12 Cuba
13 Dominica
14 Dominican Republic
15 Ecuador
16 El Salvador
17 Grenada
18 Guatemala
19 Guyana
20 Haiti
21 Honduras
22 Jamaica
23 Mexico
24 Nicaragua
25 Panama
26 Paraguay
27 Peru
28 St. Kitts & Nevis
29 St. Lucia
30 St. Vincent & The Grenadines
31 Suriname
32 Trinidad & Tobago
33 United States
34 Uruguay
35 Venezuela

Africa

80 Algeria
81 Angola
82 Benin
83 Botswana
84 Burkina
85 Burundi
86 Cameroon
87 Cape Verde
88 Central African Republic
89 Chad
90 Comoros
91 Congo, Dem. Rep.
92 Congo
93 Côte d'Ivoire
94 Djibouti
95 Egypt
96 Equatorial Guinea
97 Eritrea
98 Ethiopia
99 Gabon
100 The Gambia
101 Ghana
102 Guinea
103 Guinea-Bissau
104 Kenya
105 Lesotho
106 Liberia
107 Libya
108 Madagascar
109 Malawi
110 Mali
111 Mauritania
112 Mauritius
113 Morocco
114 Mozambique
115 Namibia
116 Niger
117 Nigeria
118 Rwanda
119 São Tomé & Príncipe
120 Senegal
121 Seychelles
122 Sierra Leone
123 Somalia
124 South Africa
125 Sudan
126 Swaziland
127 Tanzania
128 Togo
129 Tunisia
130 Uganda
131 Zambia
132 Zimbabwe

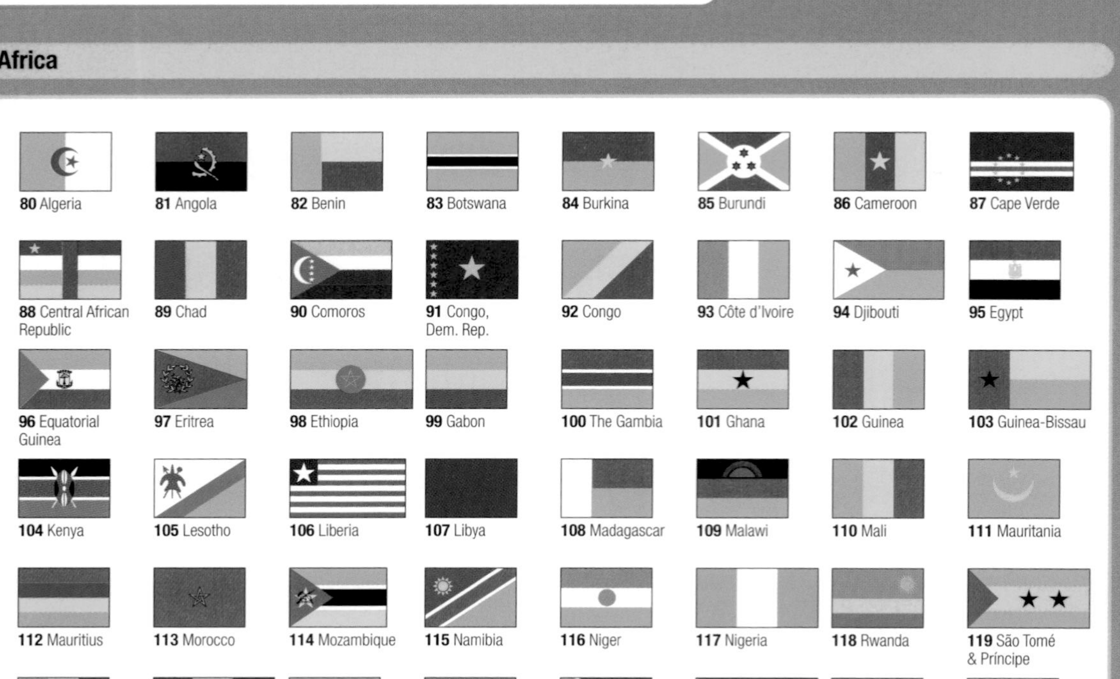

Western flags The oldest European flags display the Christian cross, first widely seen in the Crusades. The heraldic devices of European royal families appeared on some later flags. Red, white and blue, associated with the pursuit of liberty, was adopted by the French following the Revolution, and by the newly independent USA.

Eastern flags In the Middle East flag colours have been based on the Muslim red, white, green and black. Most Arab states use one or several of these colours in a tricolour format. Others, such as Turkey, Algeria and Pakistan, use the star and crescent motif as a sign of their Islamic faith.

Europe and Russia

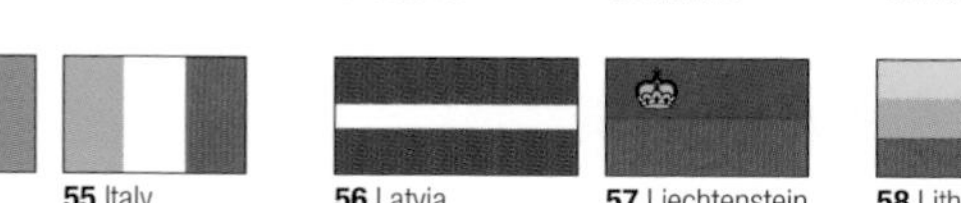

 36 Albania
 37 Andorra
 38 Austria
 39 Belarus
40 Belgium
41 Bosnia & Herzegovina
42 Bulgaria
 43 Croatia
 44 Cyprus

 45 Czech Republic
 46 Denmark
 47 Estonia
 48 Finland
 49 France
 50 Germany
51 Greece
52 Hungary
53 Iceland

54 Ireland
55 Italy
56 Latvia
57 Liechtenstein
58 Lithuania
59 Luxembourg
60 Macedonia
61 Malta
62 Moldova

63 Monaco
64 Netherlands
65 Norway
66 Poland
67 Portugal
68 Romania
69 Russia
70 San Marino
71 Serbia & Montenegro

72 Slovakia
73 Slovenia
74 Spain
75 Sweden
76 Switzerland
77 Ukraine
78 United Kingdom
79 Vatican City

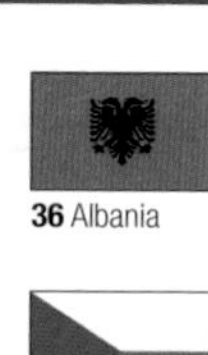

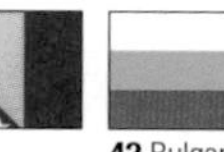

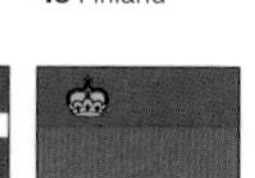

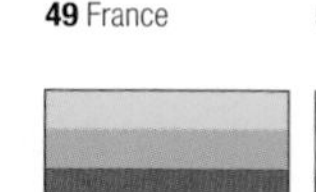

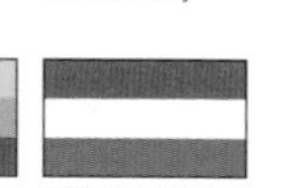

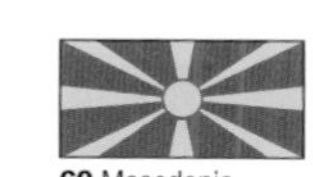

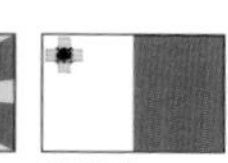

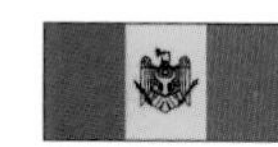

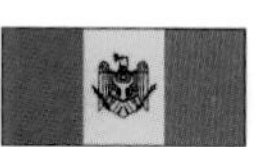

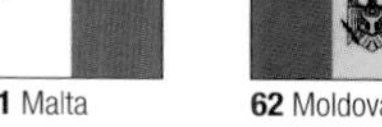

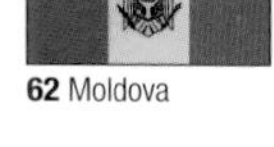

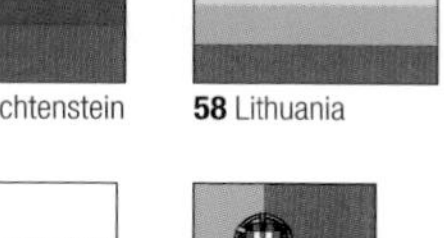

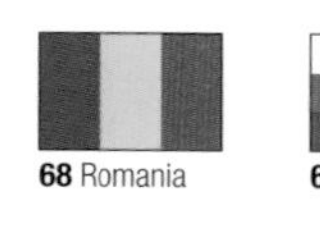

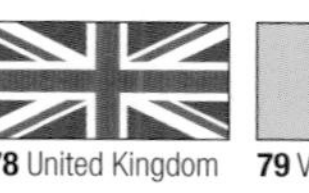

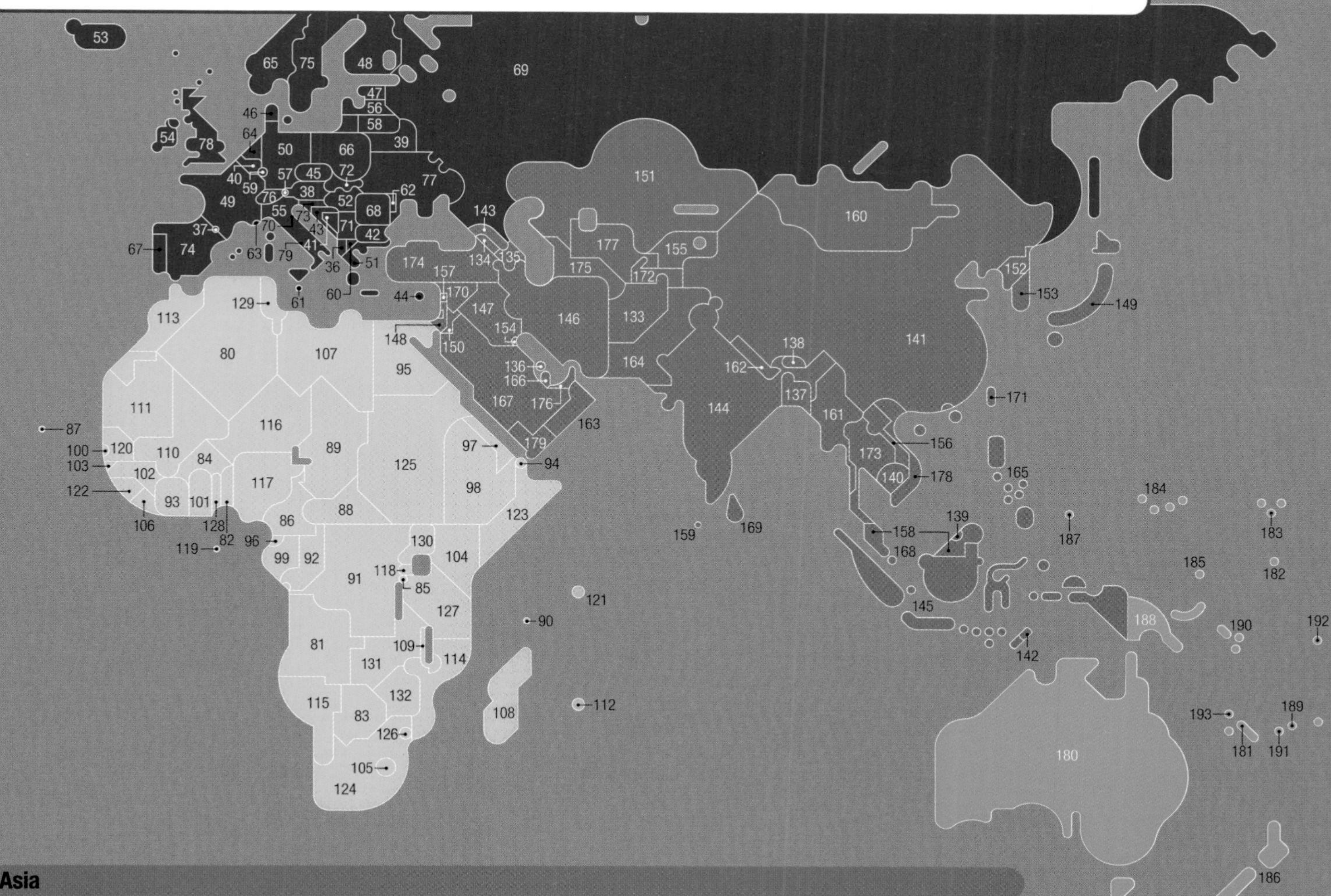

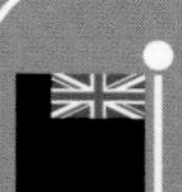

 Afghanistan has had more flags in recent history than any other country.

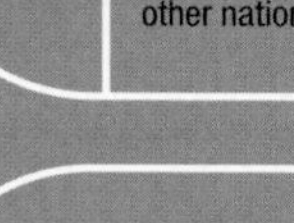

 The Union Flag of the United Kingdom appears on the flags of four other nations.

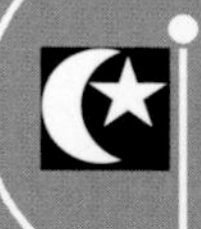

 Eight countries use the Islamic crescent moon and star on their national flag.

 139 national flags contain the colour red.

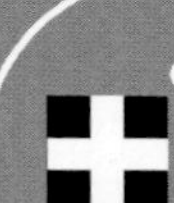

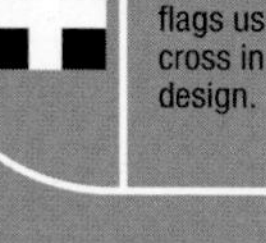

 Thirteen national flags use a cross in their design.

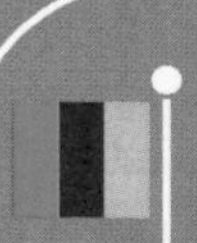

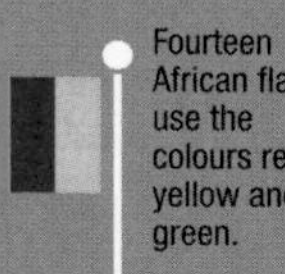

Fourteen African flags use the colours red, yellow and green.

Asia

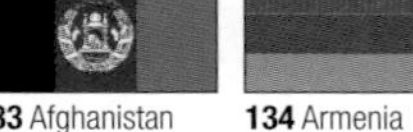

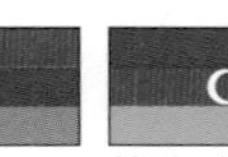

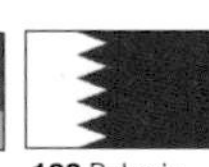

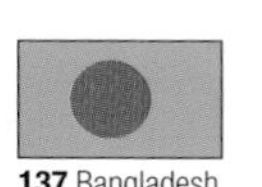

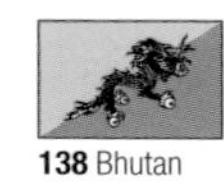

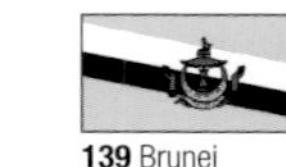

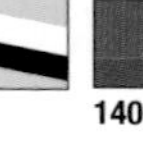

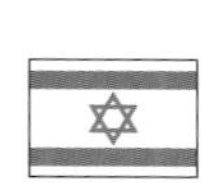

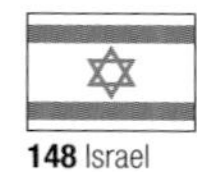

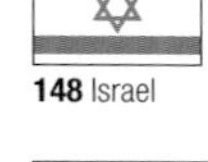

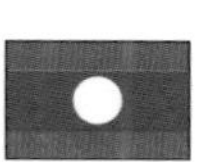

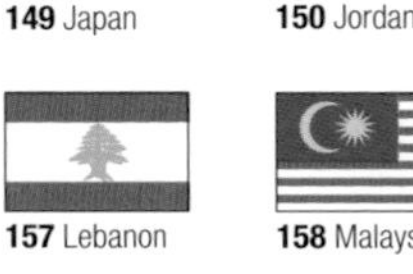

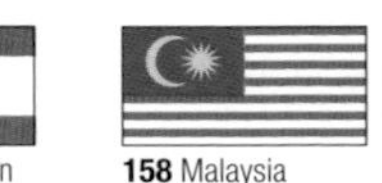

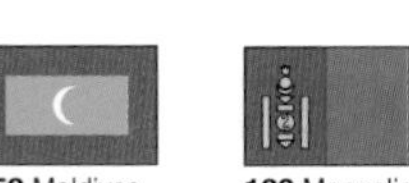

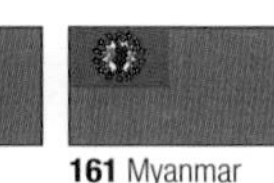

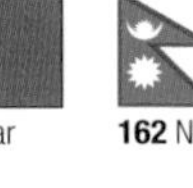

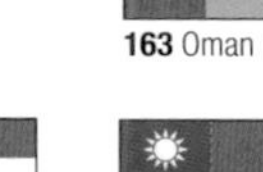

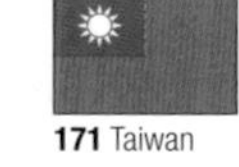

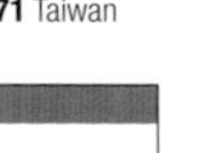

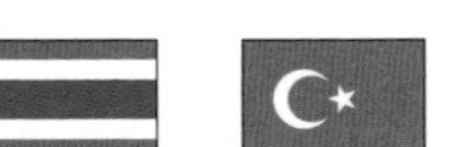

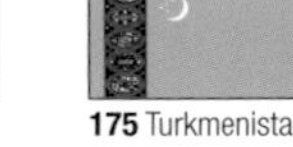

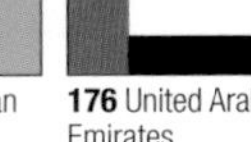

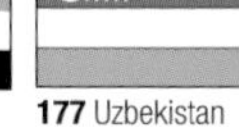

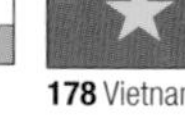

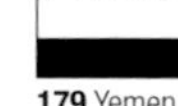

 133 Afghanistan
 134 Armenia
 135 Azerbaijan
 136 Bahrain
 137 Bangladesh
 138 Bhutan
 139 Brunei
 140 Cambodia

141 China
142 East Timor
143 Georgia
144 India
145 Indonesia
146 Iran
147 Iraq
148 Israel

149 Japan
150 Jordan
151 Kazakhstan
152 Korea, North
153 Korea, South
154 Kuwait
155 Kyrgyzstan
156 Laos

157 Lebanon
158 Malaysia
159 Maldives
160 Mongolia
161 Myanmar (Burma)
162 Nepal
163 Oman
164 Pakistan

165 Philippines
166 Qatar
167 Saudi Arabia
168 Singapore
169 Sri Lanka
170 Syria
171 Taiwan
172 Tajikistan

173 Thailand
174 Turkey
175 Turkmenistan
176 United Arab Emirates
177 Uzbekistan
178 Vietnam
179 Yemen

Australasia

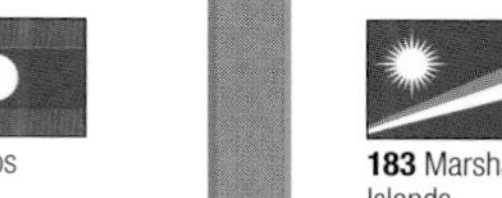

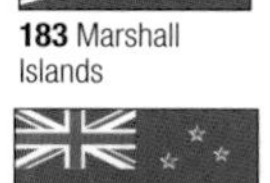

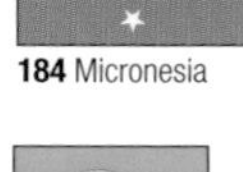

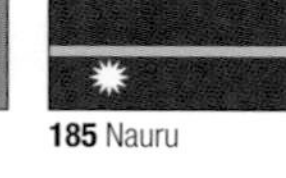

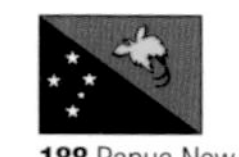

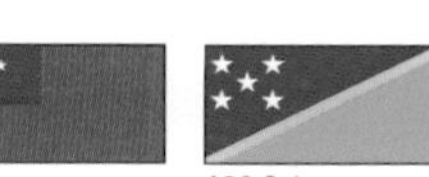

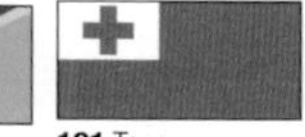

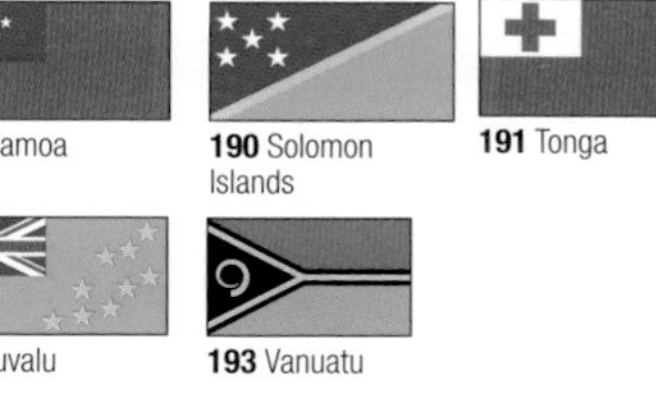

180 Australia
181 Fiji
182 Kiribati

183 Marshall Islands
184 Micronesia
185 Nauru

186 New Zealand
187 Palau
188 Papua New Guinea

189 Samoa
190 Solomon Islands
191 Tonga

192 Tuvalu
193 Vanuatu

WORLD ATLAS

Beginning with Oceania, the atlas moves westwards through Asia, Europe and Africa before crossing the Atlantic to the Americas on a grand tour of the continents. The maps give a vivid picture of the Earth's varied topography while conveying all the fine detail of human habitation, from cities that are home to millions to small towns, major highways and railways to dams and canals. Interspersed with the main mapping are fold-out spreads showing an eagle's eye view of five remarkable places: the Yangtze River, the Himalayas, Africa's Great Rift Valley, the Mediterranean Sea and the islands of the Caribbean.

USING THE MAPS

❶ Grid reference All place names in the Atlas are referenced using an alphanumeric grid. Read across and then down to find the place you are looking for.

❷ Page continuation arrows These take the reader to the next part of the area shown. There may be more than one page reference given.

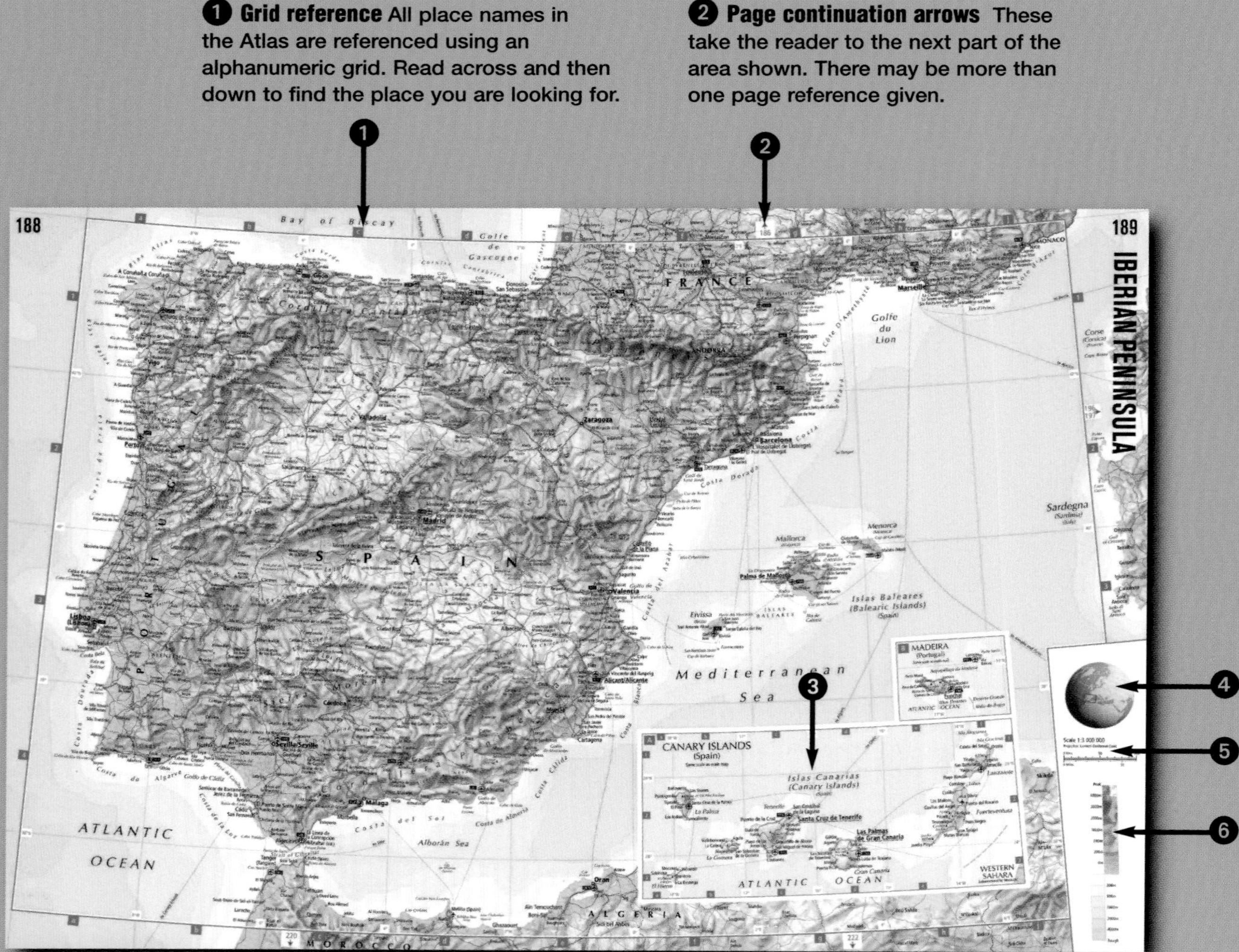

❸ Map insets Islands which fall in sea areas off the map are often shown as insets. The scale may be different to that on the main map.

❹ Map locator The locator shows the position of the country or region in relation to the rest of the world.

❺ Scale and projection The scale at which the area is mapped and the projection chosen are given here.

❻ Elevation and depth The scale gives the height of the land and the depth below sea level. Each level is distinguished by a different colour.

CITIES AND TOWNS

Scale 1:500 000 – 1:7 500 000   **1:8 000 000 – 1:16 000 000**

Over 5 million	▣ **MEXICO**	▣ **MEXICO**
1 – 5 million	▣ **Puebla**	▣ **Puebla**
500 000 – 1 million	▫ Guerrero	▫ Guerrero
250 000 – 500 000	⊙ Tucson	⊙ Tucson
100 000 – 250 000	◎ Orizaba	◎ Orizaba
50 000 – 100 000	○ Cuautla	○ Cuautla
10 000 – 50 000	○ Chignahuapan	○ Chignahuapan
Under 10 000	○ Mariscala	

Scale 1:24 000 000 – 1:60 000 000

Over 5 million	▣ **MEXICO**
1 – 5 million	▣ **Puebla**
250,000 – 1 million	⊙ Guerrero
100,000 – 250,000	○ Cuautla
Under 100,000	○ Chignahuapan

POLITICAL BOUNDARIES

	international (definite)
	international (scales 1:24 000 000 – 1:60 000 000)
	international (undefined, indefinite or disputed)
	international through water
Line of Control	**other (eg a ceasefire line)**
	administrative: state, province or county NB. Where map scales allow, the primary administrative area is indicated by a thicker line and the secondary level by a thinner line.
	administrative through water
	**urban area**
GUATEMALA	**independent country name**
CHIAPAS	**dependent territory or state name (admin level 1)**
PERNAMBUCO	**administrative area (admin level 2)**
DELTA	**cultural or historic area**

TRANSPORTATION

	motorway, highway
	motorway, highway in tunnel
	main road
	main road in tunnel
	other road
	track (sparse areas)
	main railway
	main railway in tunnel
to Kingston upon Hull	**car ferry**
✈ CEN	**international airport with IATA code**
✈	**regional airport (selected)**

CULTURAL FEATURES

• ⬚ Saguaro N.P. (West)	**national park, reserve or reservation**
★ Lubaantun	**World Heritage Site**
⸪ Barranca del Cobre	**ruin**
⌂⌂⌂⌂⌂	**ancient wall**

HYDROGRAPHIC FEATURES

	intra-coastal waterway
	aqueduct
	lake, reservoir
	intermittent lake, reservoir
	salt lake
	intermittent salt lake
	dry lake bed, salt pan
	river, stream
	intermittent river
	waterfall
	canal
	dam
	oasis
	reef
	marsh, swamp area
	desert area
	glacier, ice cap
ATLANTIC	**ocean name**
Gulf	**large gulf or sea name**
Laguna Santiaguillo	**river, lake or canal name**
Badia de Palma	**bay name**

CAPITALS OF POLITICAL UNITS

	independent country capital underline
	state province (admin level 1) underline
	state province (admin level 2) underline
(U.K.)	**administering country**
(Temporarily administered by the United Nations)	**political notes**

ELEVATIONS AND DEPTH SCALES

Peak
5000m
4000m
3000m
2000m
1000m
500m
200m
100m
0m — sea level
below sea level

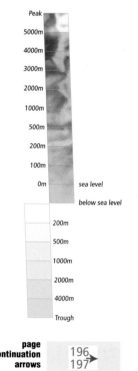

200m
500m
1000m
2000m
4000m
Trough

page continuation arrows 196 197 →

TOPOGRAPHIC FEATURES

▲ *Mount Lemmon* 2791	**elevation above sea level in metres**
▲ *Mount Fuji* 3776	**volcano**
▽ 65	**elevation below sea level**
⊐⊏	**mountain pass**
Sierra Madre	**mountain range, plain etc**
Mallorca	**island**
Cap de Fomenter	**cape, point**
Sahara	**physical region, desert, forest**

AUSTRALASIA & OCEANIA

Lying between the Indian and Pacific Oceans is Australia, the world's smallest continent. To the north and east, stretching across a vast swathe of the Pacific, are thousands of volcanic and coral islands. Most of these are tiny: Papua New Guinea and New Zealand together account for almost 90 per cent of the total land area across the Pacific. These remote islands were the last places on Earth to be settled by humankind – humans did not reach them until the first millennium AD.

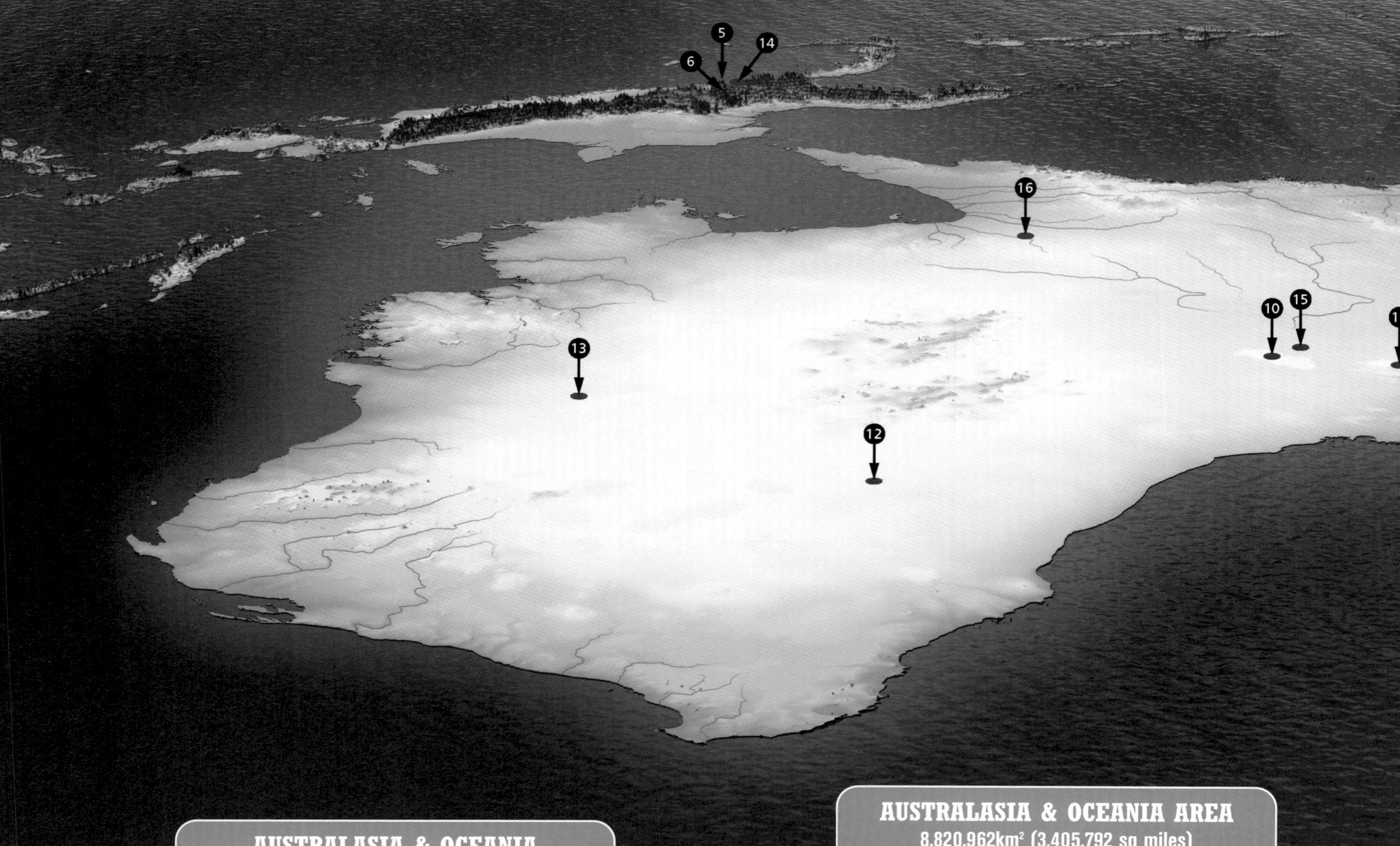

AUSTRALASIA & OCEANIA POPULATION
30,215,000

AUSTRALASIA & OCEANIA AREA
8,820,962km² (3,405,792 sq miles)

LARGEST COUNTRY
Australia 7,682,300km² (2,966,153 sq miles)

SMALLEST COUNTRY
Nauru 21km² (8 sq miles)

LONGEST RIVERS
(all Australia)
1 Murray-Darling 3750km (2330 miles)
2 Murrumbidgee 1690km (1050 miles)
3 Lachlan 1480km (919 miles)
4 Maquarie 950km (590 miles)

HIGHEST PEAKS
5 Mt Wilhelm, Papua New Guinea 4509m (14,793ft)
6 Mt Kubor, Papua New Guinea 4359m (14,301ft)
7 Aoraki (Mt Cook), New Zealand 3754m (12,316ft)
8 Mt Tasman, New Zealand 3498m (11,476ft)
9 Mt Kosciusko, Australia 2228m (7309ft)

LARGEST LAKES
10 Lake Eyre, Australia 0-8900km² (0-3436 sq miles)
11 Lake Torrens, Australia 0-5780km² (0-2232 sq miles)
(Both lakes are normally dry salt pans,
but occasionally fill during heavy rains)

LOWEST POINT
10 Lake Eyre, Australia 15m (49ft) below sea level

LARGEST DESERTS
12 Great Victorian, Australia 647,000km² (249,742 sq miles)
13 Great Sandy, Australia 400,000km² (154,400 sq miles)

WETTEST PLACE
14 Madang, Papua New Guinea 3344mm (132in) annual rainfall

DRIEST PLACE
15 Mulka (Troudaninna), Australia 103mm (4.05in)
annual rainfall

HIGHEST RECORDED TEMPERATURE
16 Cloncurry, Australia 53.1°C (127.5°F), Jan 16 1889

LOWEST RECORDED TEMPERATURE
17 Charlotte Pass, Australia -23°C (-9.4°F), June 18 1994

Age

Under 15	%	Over 65	%
Micronesia		Australia	12.3
Marshall Islands		New Zealand	11.7
Solomon Islands		Fiji	5.7
Vanuatu		Palau	5.6
Samoa		Tonga	5.4
Tuvalu	34.4	Papua New Guinea	4.1
Fiji	33.4	Micronesia	3.5
Palau	28	Vanuatu	3.2
New Zealand	23	Solomon Islands	2.6
Australia	20.5	Marshall Islands	2.5

Birth rate

Births per 1000 population

Country	Value
Solomon Islands	
Papua New Guinea	
Vanuatu	
Samoa	
Micronesia	
Palau	21.6
Tuvalu	21
Nauru	20.3
New Zealand	15
Australia	13

Adult literacy

%

Country	Value
Nauru	99
New Zealand	99
Samoa	
Australia	
Tuvalu	
Tonga	93
Marshall Islands	91
Papua New Guinea	66
Solomon Islands	60
Vanuatu	53

Wealth

GDP per head $US

Country	Value
Australia	
New Zealand	
Nauru	
Palau	5450
Micronesia	2055
Vanuatu	1042
Tuvalu	900
Solomon Islands	570
Kiribati	566
Papua New Guinea	495

■ Top five   ■ Bottom five

Health, wealth and education

Both Australia and New Zealand have some of the highest standards of living in the world, and 30-40 per cent of school leavers go on to further education. The story is very different on some of the remoter Pacific islands, where poor sanitation and hygiene commonly lead to high rates of malaria and other tropical diseases. In a number of the Pacific states, obesity and its related ailments have become serious problems. A high birth rate is generally coupled with significant infant mortality, but educational improvements have increased literacy levels in recent years.

Climate of Australia

The interior of Australia is arid with less than 250mm (10in) of rain annually. By contrast, the coast is well-watered and the north-east and south-east have tropical climates. Australia is generally warm year-round, and has frequent heat waves, when the temperature exceeds 100°F (38°C).

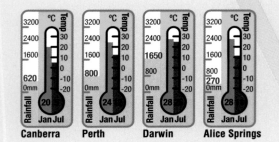

Canberra   Perth   Darwin   Alice Springs

Population

Australia is the least peopled continent in the world, with a total population of just over 19 million (Australasia & Oceania have a combined population of 30 million). More than 80 per cent of Australians live in coastal areas and the interior is sparsely populated. In New Zealand, 75 per cent of the population live on the North Island. The Pacific islands are densely populated, though many outlying islets are uninhabited.

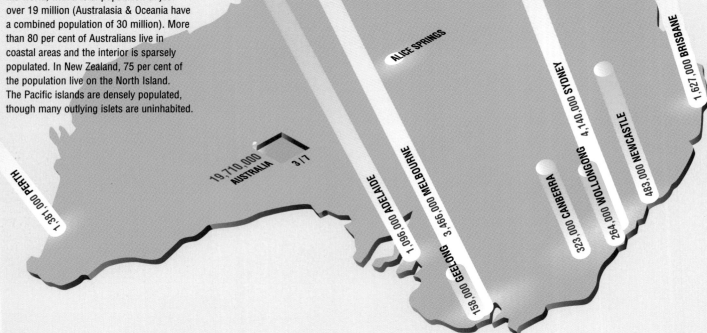

Employment

Service industries are the main employers in Australia and New Zealand, with tourism of particular importance to the ecomony of both countries, as well as that of many Pacific islands, such as Fiji. Agriculture and rearing livestock now employ fewer people in Australia and New Zealand, but are still a significant source of revenue. On a number of Pacific islands, isolation and limited natural resources have prevented industrial development, and their economies remain primarily at a subsistence level.

Australasia & Oceania: employment by sector

Country top ten	Primary (inc. Agriculture) %	Industry %	Service %	GDP $US million
Australia	3	26	71	400,000
New Zealand	8	23	69	57,241
Papua New Guinea	32	36	32	2771
Fiji	17	25	58	1463
Solomon Islands	42	11	47	264
Micronesia	50	4	46	259
Samoa	14	23	63	245
Vanuata	65	30	5	219
Tonga	26	12	62	130
Nauru				94

■ Primary (inc. Agriculture) %   ■ Industry %   ■ Service %

Climate of New Zealand

New Zealand has a temperate climate with abundant rainfall, ranging from 635–1525mm (25–60in) annually. Summers are warm, especially on the more tropical North Island, but cold Antarctic winds bring snow to the South Island in winter.

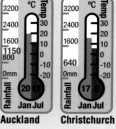

Auckland   Christchurch

Fiji
°C Temp
30
20
10
0
-10
-20
2970
2400
1600
800
0mm
Rainfall
26
Jan Jul

Solomon Islands
°C Temp
30
20
10
0
-10
-20
3200
2170
1600
800
0mm
Rainfall
27 29
Jan Jul

Climate of the Pacific islands

The Pacific islands are generally hot and humid, with an average annual rainfall of 2000mm (78in). Seasonal changes in temperature, humidity and rainfall are usually moderate.

57,000 MARSHALL ISLANDS
316 / 814

13,000 NAURU
610 / 1585

90,000 KIRIBATI
103 / 268

10,000 TUVALU
384 / 1000

463,000 SOLOMON ISLANDS
16 / 43

210,000 VANUATU
16 / 57

830,000 FIJI
44 / 116

180,000 SAMOA
56 / 145

135 / 349 101,000 TONGA

KEY

Country population 2003

101,000 TONGA
135 / 349

Country density: People per square mile/km

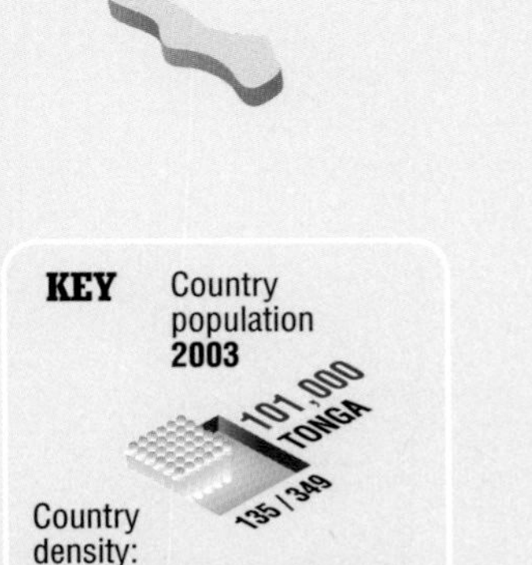

1,075,000 AUCKLAND
166,000 HAMILTON
96,000 TAURANGA
340,000 WELLINGTON
73,000 PALMERSTON NORTH
114,000 NAPIER HASTINGS
53,000 ROTORUA
334,000 CHRISTCHURCH
107,000 DUNEDIN

3,850,000 NEW ZEALAND
14 / 36

Legend (farming/land use)

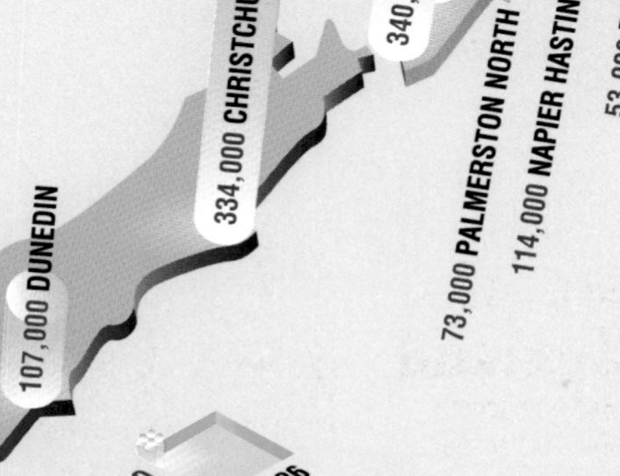

- Cereals, livestock
- Cash crops, mixed farming
- Dairy, livestock
- General and mixed farming
- Special crops
- Livestock ranching and herding
- Diversified tropical and subtropical crops
- Forests
- Nonproductive land

How the land is used

Australia has an urban population of 91 per cent, housed mainly along the coast because of the inhospitable nature of the interior. Although arable land accounts for just 6 per cent of its total area, Australia supports the world's largest sheep herd – around 100 million animals. Much of New Zealand is given over to pastures for grazing sheep and cattle, and a large swathe of the South Island is both mountainous and forested. The islands of the Pacific are predominantly rural, with most of the land, on all but the largest islands, being used for subsistence farming. Much of Papua New Guinea is covered by rain forest and several other islands, such as Vanuatu, are also very heavily forested.

The lie of the land

Australia, the smallest, flattest and most arid of the continents, is the heart of the Pacific region. To the south-east is New Zealand, a temperate and volcanic island, and to the north, Papua New Guinea, blanketed by tropical rain forest. Scattered across the Pacific Ocean lie thousands of coral atolls and volcanic islands. While a few islands such as Papua New Guinea have mountains, others such as Tuvalu and Nauru are so low-lying that they are under threat from rising sea levels.

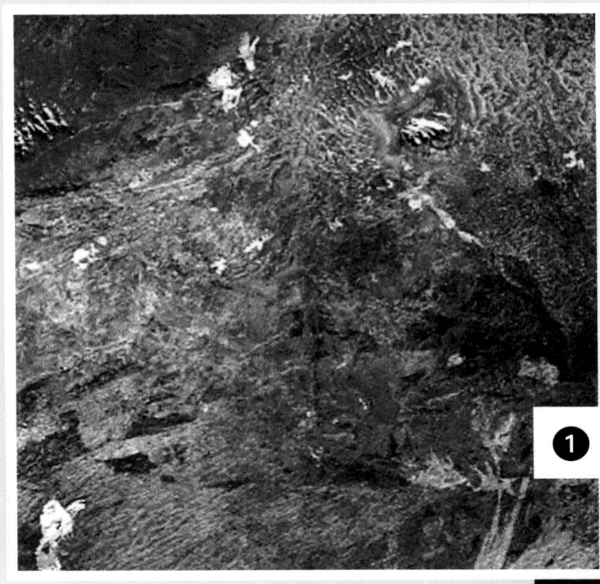

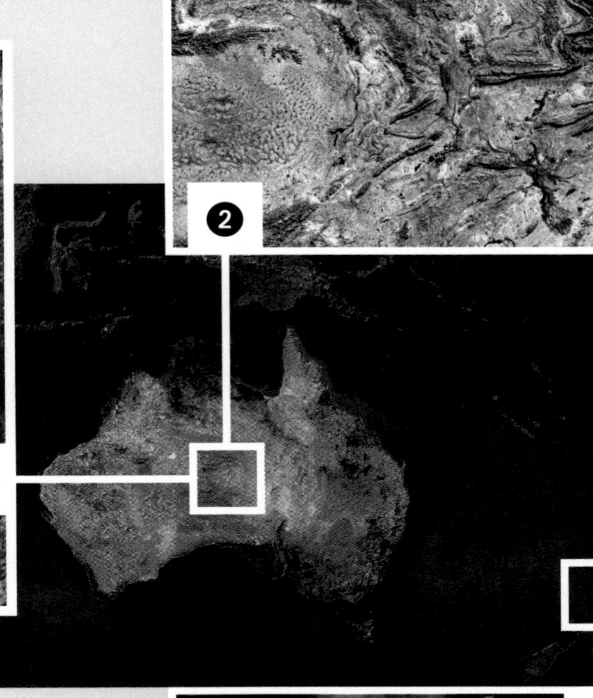

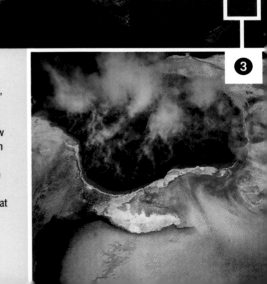

❶ Uluru (Ayers Rock) Uluru (in the top right corner) is a sandstone monolith 863m (2831ft) high and 9km (5½ miles) across. Vegetation is shown in red with the desert a grey-brown. **❷ MacDonnell Range** Tectonic forces crumpled layers of rock upwards to form these mountains, which rise 1000–1500m (3300–4921ft) from Australia's dry interior. They have since been heavily eroded to reveal their underlying structure. Loops and swirls in the image show valleys lining the mountain ridges and yellow areas show the surrounding sand dunes. **❸ Champagne Pool** The 60m (200ft) deep geothermal pool is located at Waiotapu on New Zealand's North Island, in a crater formed by a volcanic eruption 900 years ago. The 74°C (165°F) water contains silicate of lime (sinter), which has created a huge geothermal terrace surrounding the pool (shown in yellow and grey at the bottom of the image).

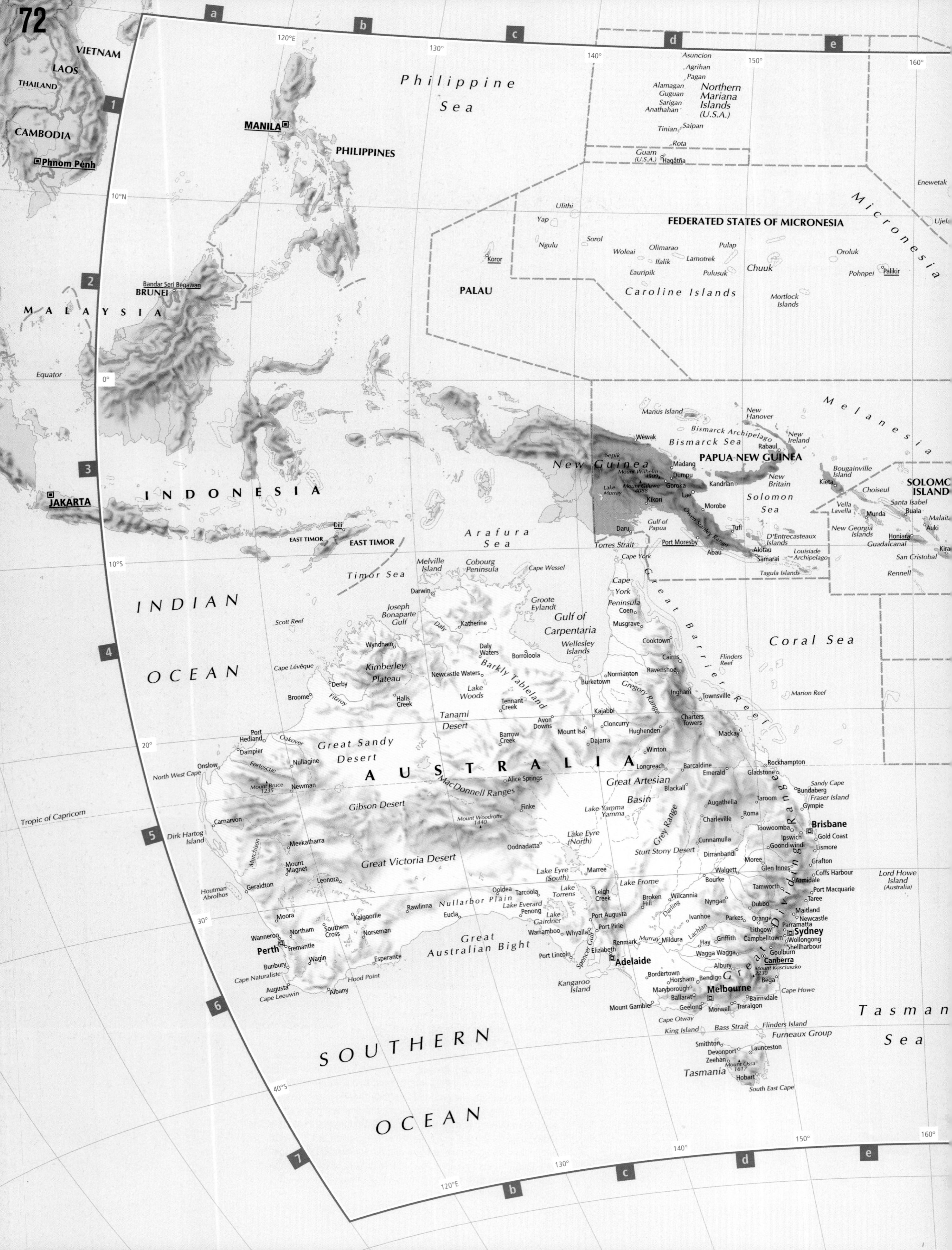

VIETNAM
LAOS
THAILAND
CAMBODIA
Phnom Penh
MANILA
PHILIPPINES
Philippine Sea
Northern Mariana Islands (U.S.A.)
Asuncion
Agrihan
Pagan
Alamagan
Guguan
Sarigan
Anathahan
Saipan
Tinian
Rota
Guam (U.S.A.)
Hagåtña
FEDERATED STATES OF MICRONESIA
Micronesia
Ulithi
Yap
Ngulu
Sorol
Woleai
Olimarao
Ifalik
Lamotrek
Pulap
Eauripik
Pulusuk
Chuuk
Oroluk
Pohnpei
Palikir
Koror
PALAU
Caroline Islands
Mortlock Islands
Enewetak
BRUNEI
Bandar Seri Begawan
MALAYSIA
Equator
INDONESIA
JAKARTA
Dili
EAST TIMOR
Timor Sea
Arafura Sea
Manus Island
New Hanover
New Ireland
Bismarck Archipelago
Bismarck Sea
Wewak
Rabaul
PAPUA NEW GUINEA
New Guinea
Sepik
Mount Wilhelm 4509
Madang
Dumpu
Goroka
Lae
Kikori
Lake Murray
Mount Giluwe 4088
Kandrian
New Britain
Bougainville Island
Kieta
Melanesia
Solomon Sea
Morobe
Gulf of Papua
Daru
Owen Stanley Range
Tufi
Port Moresby
Abau
Alotau
Samarai
D'Entrecasteaux Islands
Louisiade Archipelago
Tagula Islands
Torres Strait
SOLOMON ISLANDS
Choiseul
Santa Isabel
Vella Lavella
Munda
Buala
New Georgia Islands
Honiara
Guadalcanal
Auki
Malaita
San Cristobal
Rennell
INDIAN OCEAN
Scott Reef
Melville Island
Cobourg Peninsula
Cape Wessel
Darwin
Joseph Bonaparte Gulf
Daly
Katherine
Groote Eylandt
Gulf of Carpentaria
Wellesley Islands
Cape York
Cape York Peninsula
Coen
Musgrave
Cooktown
Great Barrier Reef
Coral Sea
Flinders Reef
Cairns
Wyndham
Kimberley Plateau
Daly Waters
Borroloola
Barkly Tableland
Cape Lévêque
Derby
Newcastle Waters
Lake Woods
Burketown
Normanton
Ravenshoe
Gregory Range
Ingham
Townsville
Marion Reef
Broome
Fitzroy
Halls Creek
Tennant Creek
Tanami Desert
Kajabbi
Charters Towers
Avon Downs
Cloncurry
Mount Isa
Hughenden
Mackay
Port Hedland
Oakover
Great Sandy Desert
Barrow Creek
Dajarra
Winton
Dampier
Nullagine
AUSTRALIA
Rockhampton
Onslow
North West Cape
Fortescue
Mount Bruce 1235
Newman
Alice Springs
MacDonnell Ranges
Longreach
Barcaldine
Emerald
Gladstone
Great Artesian Basin
Blackall
Sandy Cape
Bundaberg
Fraser Island
Gympie
Taroom
Gibson Desert
Finke
Lake Yamma Yamma
Augathella
Roma
Tropic of Capricorn
Carnarvon
Mount Woodroffe 1440
Charleville
Grey Range
Brisbane
Toowoomba
Ipswich
Gold Coast
Dirk Hartog Island
Meekatharra
Lake Eyre (North)
Oodnadatta
Cunnamulla
Goondiwindi
Lismore
Murchison
Great Victoria Desert
Sturt Stony Desert
Dirranbandi
Moree
Grafton
Mount Magnet
Leonora
Lake Eyre (South)
Marree
Walgett
Glen Innes
Coffs Harbour
Lord Howe Island (Australia)
Armidale
Houtman Abrolhos
Geraldton
Ooldea
Tarcoola
Lake Torrens
Leigh Creek
Lake Frome
Bourke
Tamworth
Port Macquarie
Taree
Nullarbor Plain
Lake Everard
Broken Hill
Wilcannia
Nyngan
Dubbo
Maitland
Rawlinna
Penong
Darling
Newcastle
Moora
Kalgoorlie
Eucla
Lake Gairdner
Port Augusta
Ivanhoe
Parkes
Orange
Parramatta
Southern Cross
Norseman
Great Australian Bight
Warramboo
Whyalla
Port Pirie
Lithgow
Sydney
Northam
Spencer Gulf
Murray
Mildura
Lachlan
Hay
Griffith
Campbelltown
Wollongong
Wanneroo
Perth
Fremantle
Renmark
Shellharbour
Wagin
Esperance
Port Lincoln
Elizabeth
Adelaide
Wagga Wagga
Goulburn
Canberra
Bunbury
Albury
Mount Kosciuszko 2230
Cape Naturaliste
Hood Point
Kangaroo Island
Bordertown
Horsham
Bendigo
Great Dividing Range
Bega
Augusta
Albany
Cape Leeuwin
Maryborough
Ballarat
Melbourne
Cape Howe
Bairnsdale
Mount Gambier
Geelong
Morwell
Traralgon
Tasman Sea
Cape Otway
King Island
Bass Strait
Flinders Island
Furneaux Group
SOUTHERN OCEAN
Smithton
Devonport
Launceston
Zeehan
Mount Ossa 1617
Tasmania
Hobart
South East Cape
120°E
130°
140°
150°
160°
10°N
0°
10°S
20°
30°
40°S
a
b
c
d
e
1
2
3
4
5
6
7

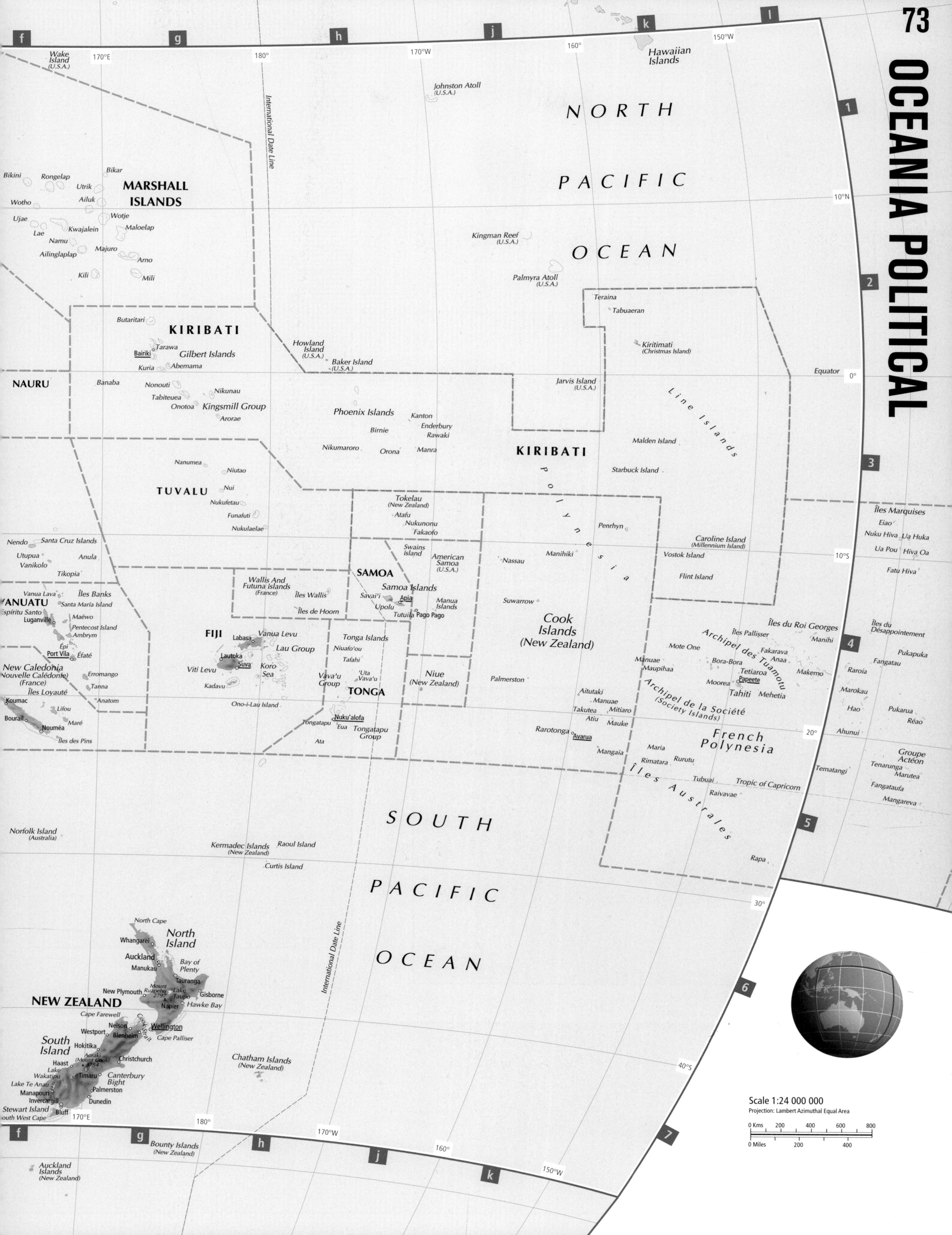

OCEANIA POLITICAL

NORTH PACIFIC OCEAN
SOUTH PACIFIC OCEAN
MARSHALL ISLANDS
KIRIBATI
NAURU
TUVALU
SAMOA
FIJI
TONGA
NEW ZEALAND
Cook Islands (New Zealand)
French Polynesia
New Caledonia Nouvelle Calédonie (France)
Hawaiian Islands
Johnston Atoll (U.S.A.)
Kingman Reef (U.S.A.)
Palmyra Atoll (U.S.A.)
Howland Island (U.S.A.)
Baker Island (U.S.A.)
Jarvis Island (U.S.A.)
Kiritimati (Christmas Island)
Phoenix Islands
Gilbert Islands
Kingsmill Group
Line Islands
Polynesia
Tokelau (New Zealand)
American Samoa (U.S.A.)
Wallis And Futuna Islands (France)
Niue (New Zealand)
Kermadec Islands (New Zealand)
Chatham Islands (New Zealand)
Bounty Islands (New Zealand)
Auckland Islands (New Zealand)
Norfolk Island (Australia)
Wake Island (U.S.A.)
International Date Line
Equator
Tropic of Capricorn
Archipel des Tuamotu
Archipel de la Société (Society Islands)
Îles Australes
Îles Marquises
North Island
South Island
Wellington
Auckland
Christchurch
Scale 1:24 000 000
Projection: Lambert Azimuthal Equal Area

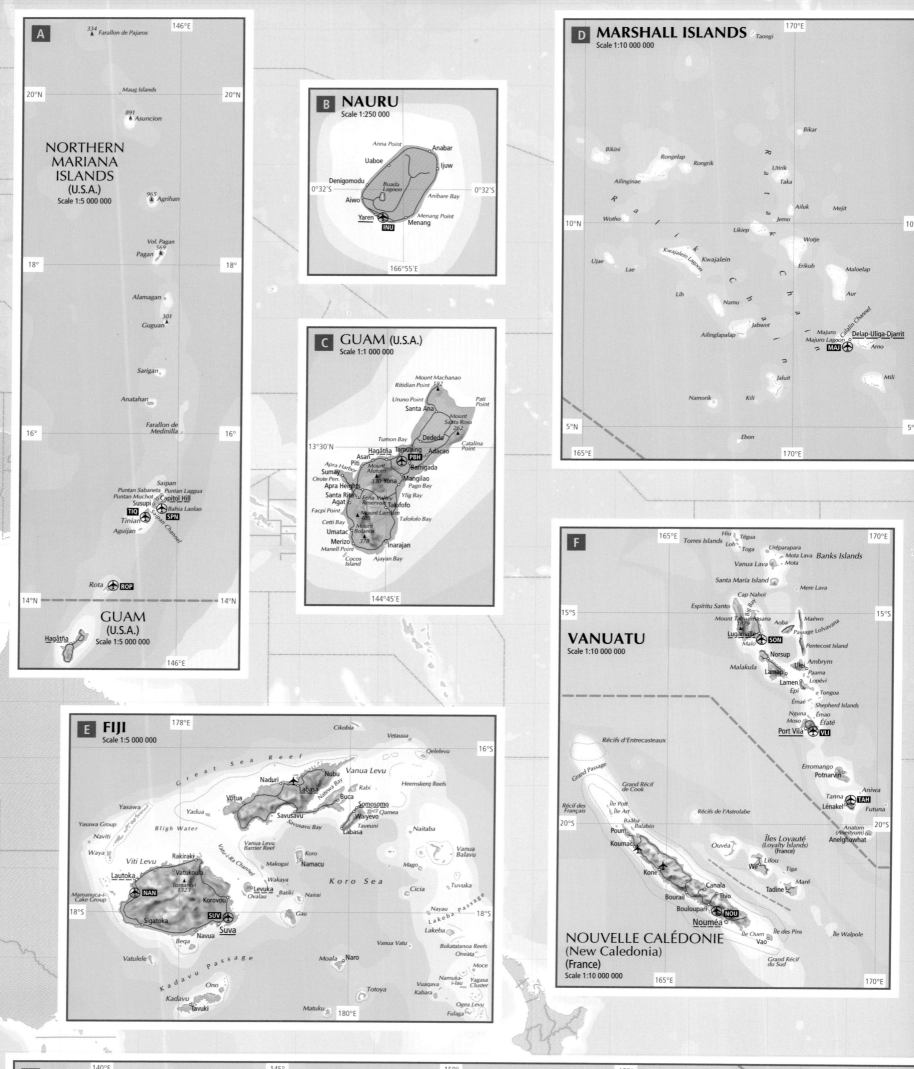

A 334 ▲ Farallon de Pajaros 146°E

20°N Maug Islands 20°N

891 ▲ Asuncion

NORTHERN MARIANA ISLANDS (U.S.A.)
Scale 1:5 000 000

965 ▲ Agrihan

18° Vol. Pagan 569 ▲ Pagan 18°

Alamagan

Guguan 301 ▲

Sarigan

Anatahan

16° Farallon de Medinilla 16°

Saipan
Puntan Sabaneta Puntan Laggua
Puntan Muchot Capitol Hill
Susupi Bahia Laolao
TIQ SPN
Tinian
Aguijan

14°N Rota ✈ ROP 14°N

GUAM (U.S.A.)
Scale 1:5 000 000

Hagåtña

146°E

B NAURU
Scale 1:250 000

0°32'S Anna Point Anabar
Uaboe Ijuw
Denigomodu 0°32'S
Buada Lagoon
Aiwo Anibare Bay
Yaren Menang Point
INU Menang

166°55'E

C GUAM (U.S.A.)
Scale 1:1 000 000

Mount Machanao
Ritidian Point 192 ▲
Uruno Point Pati Point
Santa Ana
Mount Santa Rosa 262 ▲
13°30'N Tumon Bay Catalina Point
Hagåtña Tamuning Dededo
PBH Adacao
Asan Barrigada
Apra Harbor Piti
Sumay Mount Alutom
Orote Pen. 330 ▲ Yona
Apra Heights Mangilao
Santa Rita Pago Bay
Agat Ylig Bay
Fena Valley Reservoir Talofofo
Facpi Point Mount Lamlam ▲
Cetti Bay Talofofo Bay
Umatac Mount Bolanos
Merizo 370 ▲ Inarajan
Manell Point
Cocos Island Ajayan Bay

144°45'E

D MARSHALL ISLANDS
Scale 1:10 000 000 170°E

Taongi

Bikar

Bikini Rongelap Rongrik Utirik Taka
Ailinginae Mejit
10°N Wotho Ailuk 10°N
Jemo
Likiep Wotje
Ujae Lae Erikub
Lib Namu Aur
Ailinglapalap Jabwot
Majuro Calalin Channel
Majuro Lagoon Delap-Uliga-Djarrit
MAJ ✈ Arno
5°N Namorik Kili 5°N
165°E Jaluit Mili
Ebon 170°E

E FIJI
Scale 1:5 000 000 178°E

Cikobia
Vetauua
16°S
Great Sea Reef Qelelevu
Naduri ✈ Nubu Vanua Levu
Votua Labasa Natewa Bay Rabi
Yasawa Yadua Buca Heemskerq Reefs
Yasawa Group Savusavu Somosomo
Naviti Savusavu Bay Waiyevo Qamea
Waya Bligh Water Labasa Taveuni Naitaba
Vanua Levu Barrier Reef Vanua Balavu
Viti Levu Rakiraki Makogai Koro Mago
Lautoka Vatukoula Wakaya
NAN Tomanivi 1323 ▲ Levuka Cicia Tuvuca
Mamanuca-i-Cake Group Korovou Ovalau Batiki Nairai
Koro Sea Nayau
Sigatoka SUV Suva Gau Lakeba Passage Lakeba 18°S
Navua Bukatatanoa Reefs
Beqa Moala Naro Oneata Moce
Vatulele Vanua Vatu Namuka-i-lau Yagasa Cluster
Kadavu Passage Moala Kabara
Ono Totoya Ogea Levu
Kadavu Tavuki Matuku Fulaga
180°E

F 165°E Hiu ● Tégua 170°E
Torres Islands Loh Toga
Uréparapara
Vanua Lava ▲ Mota Banks Islands
Mota Lava
Santa María Island Mere Lava
Cap Nahoï
15°S Espíritu Santo Maéwo 15°S
Mount Tabwemasana 1879 ▲ Aoba
Luganville Passage Lolvavana
SON Malo Pentecost Island
VANUATU Norsup
Scale 1:10 000 000 Ulei Ambrym
Malakula Lamap Lamen Lopévi
Epi Tongoa
Émaé Shepherd Islands
Nguna Émao
Moso Étaté
Port Vila ✈ VLI

Erromango
Potnarvin
Récifs d'Entrecasteaux
Tanna Aniwa
Grand Passage Lénakel TAH Futuna
Grand Récif de Cook
Récif des Français Île Pott Récifs de l'Astrolabe
Anatom (Aneityum) 20°S
20°S Balabio Poum Anelghowhat
Koumac ✈ Ouvéa Îles Loyauté (Loyalty Islands) (France)
Lifou Tiga
Kone We Maré
Bourail Canala Tadine
Boulouparis Thio
Nouméa NOU
Île Ouen Île des Pins
Vao Île Walpole
NOUVELLE CALÉDONIE (New Caledonia) (France)
Scale 1:10 000 000
Grand Récif du Sud
165°E 170°E

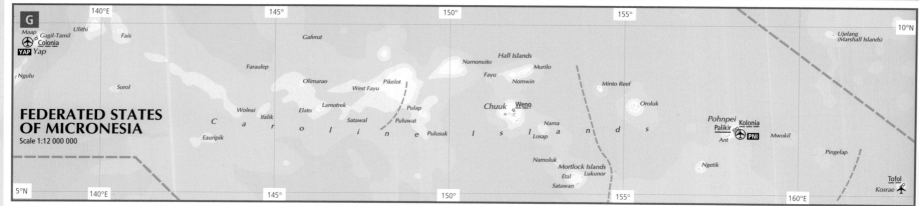

G 140°E 145° 150° 155° 10°N
Maap Gagil-Tamil Ulithi
Fais Gaferut Ujelang (Marshall Islands)
Colonia Sorol West Fayu Hall Islands
YAP ✈ Yap Namonuito Murilo
Ngulu Faraulep Olimarao Pikelot Fayu Minto Reef Oroluk
Sorol Elato Lamotrek Satawal Pulap Chuuk Weno Nomwin
Ifalik West Fayu Puluwat Nama Losap
Eauripik Woleai Satawal Pulusuk Pohnpei Kolonia
FEDERATED STATES OF MICRONESIA Caroline Islands Palikir PNI
Scale 1:12 000 000 Ant Mwokil
Namoluk Pingelap
Mortlock Islands
Lukunor Ngetik
Etal Satawan Tofol
5°N 140°E 145° 150° 155° Kosrae 160°E

H KIRIBATI
Scale 1:20 000 000

Makin Meang
Butaritari
Abaiang
Marakei
Bingham Channel Tarawa
Bairiki TRW
Maiana
Kuria Abemama
Banaba Aranuka
(Ocean Island) Nonouti
Beru Nikunau
Tabiteuea
Onotoa Kingsmill Group
Tamana
Arorae

Gilbert Islands
(Tungaru)

Teraina
Tabuaeran
(Fanning Island)
Kiritimati
(Christmas Island)
London Cape Manning
South-West Aeon Point
Point

Howland Island
(U.S.A.)
Baker Island
(U.S.A.)

Jarvis Island
(U.S.A.)

Malden Island

Kanton
McKean Enderbury
Birnie
Rawaki
Nikumaroro Orona
Manra

Phoenix Islands

Starbuck Island

Equator Equator

Nanumea
Nanumanga
Niutao
Nui
Vaitupu
Nukufetau

TUVALU Funafuti FUN
Nukulaelae

Atafu
Tokelau
(New Zealand)
Nukunono
Fakaofo

Cook Islands
(New Zealand)
Rakahanga

Penrhyn

Manihiki
Pukapuka
Nassau

Vostok Island

Niulakita

Swains Island

Cherry
Island
Tikopia
Mitre
Island
Rotuma (Fiji)

Wallis And Futuna Islands
(France)
Îles Wallis

SAMOA

American Samoa
(U.S.A.)

Suwarrow

Flint Island

Savai'i APW
Upolu Tutuila

Îles de Hoorn

J TONGA
Scale 1:5 000 000

Fonualei Tokū
Vava'u
Vava'u Group Neiafu
Late
Kotu Group Kao Ha'ano
Tofua Lifuka Foa
Nomuka Group 'Uiha Pangai Ha'apai Group
Nomuka
Falcon Island

Nuku'alofa
Tongatapu Mu'a
TBU 'Eua
Tongatapu Group

K FRENCH POLYNESIA
(France)
Scale 1:20 000 000

Motu One
Eiao
Motu Iti Ua Huka
Nuku Hiva NHV Îles Marquises
Caroline Island Ua Pu Fatu Huku
(Millennium Island) HIX Hiva Oa
(Kiribati) Tahuata Motane
Vostok Island Fatu Hiva
(Kiribati)
Flint Island
(Kiribati)

Îles du Désappointement
Napuka Tepoto
Manihi Pukapuka
Mataiva Takaroa
Rangiroa Ahé
Apataki Tikéi
Motu One Tupai Kaukura Toau Fangatau
Manuae Maupiti Tahaa Huahine Niau Kauehi Kahahina
Maupihaa Bora-Bora Raiatea Faaite Katiu Raroia
Moorea Haraiki Tahanea Marutea Tauere Tatakoto
Papeete Anaa Motutunga Tekokota Amanu
PPT Tahiti Marokau Hao Akiaki Pukarua
Mehetia Ravahere Vahitahi Reao
Nengonengo Paraoa Nukutavaké
Manuhangi Pinaki
Héréhérétué Ahunui

Archipel des Tuamotu
Îles du Vent
Archipel de la Société

Anuanuraro Îles du Duc
Anuanurunga de Gloucester Vanavana
Nukutepipi Tureia
Maria Tenaruga Vahanga
Rimatara Tematangi Mururoa
Rurutu Fangataufa Maria Marutea
Tubuai
Tropic of Capricorn Îles Gambier
Raivavae Mangareva
Îles Australes

Rapa
Marotiri

L FUTUNA ISLANDS
(France)
Scale 1:1 000 000

Pointe Fatua Pointe Matapu
Pointe Matagalua
Mont Puke Utu Magalua
524
Nuku Île Futuna
Poi FTA
Alo Pointe Vele
Anse de Sigave Alofitai Pointe Sauma
Pointe Mafa'a Mont Kolofau
417
Îles de Hoorn Île Alofi
Pointe Afaga

WALLIS ISLANDS
(France)
Scale 1:1 000 000

Nukuloa Îles Wallis
Passe Fatumanini Vailala Nukuteatea
Passe Fuga'uvea Nukutapu
Île Uvea Lano
WLS Mata'utu
Pointe Vaha'a'utu Lac Kikila
Lac Lalolalo Baie de
Mata'otu
Halalo Mala'efo'ou
Nukuatea Pointe Matala'a
Île Faioa
Passe Honikulu

M SAMOA
Scale 1:7 500 000

AMERICAN SAMOA
(U.S.A.)
Scale 1:7 500 000

Cape
Mulinu'u Cape
Savai'i
Falealupo Pu'apu'a
Mauga Silisili Apia
1858 APW Mount Fito
Savai'i Salani
Taga Cape
Tapaga
Upolu

Manua
Islands
Pago Pago Maia
Olosega
Tutuila Ofu
PPG Tau

N TUVALU
Scale 1:7 500 000

Nanumea Lolua
Niutao
Kulia
Nanumanga

Nui
Vaitupu
Asau

Nukufetau

Vaiaku Funafuti
FUN

Nukulaelae

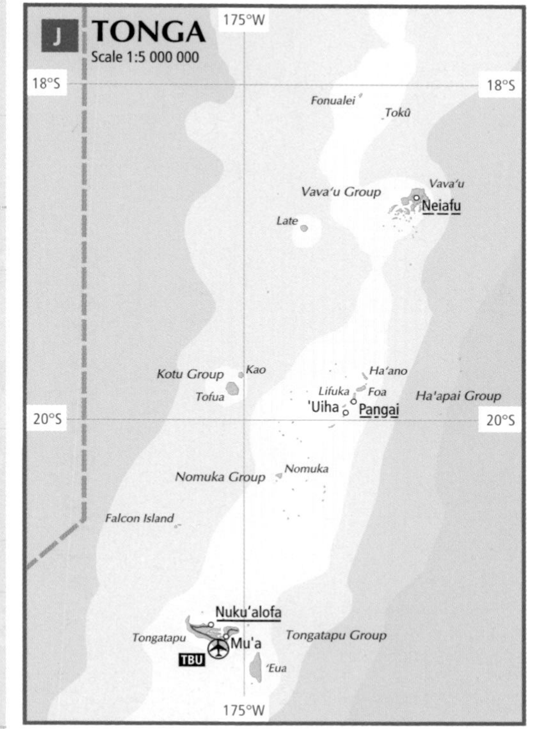

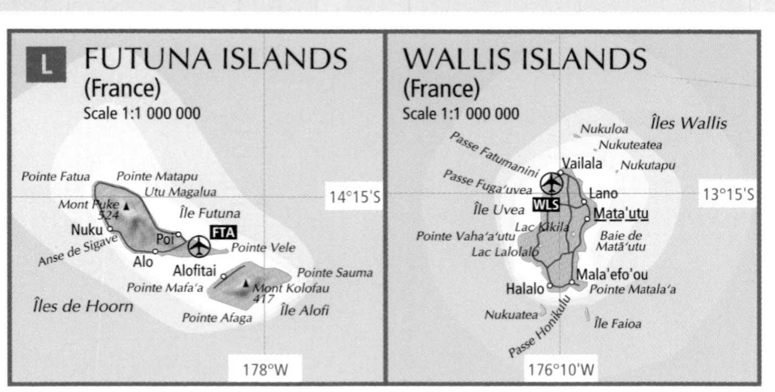

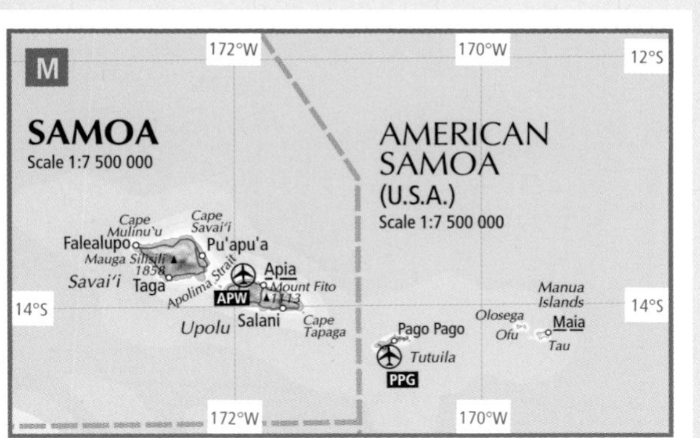

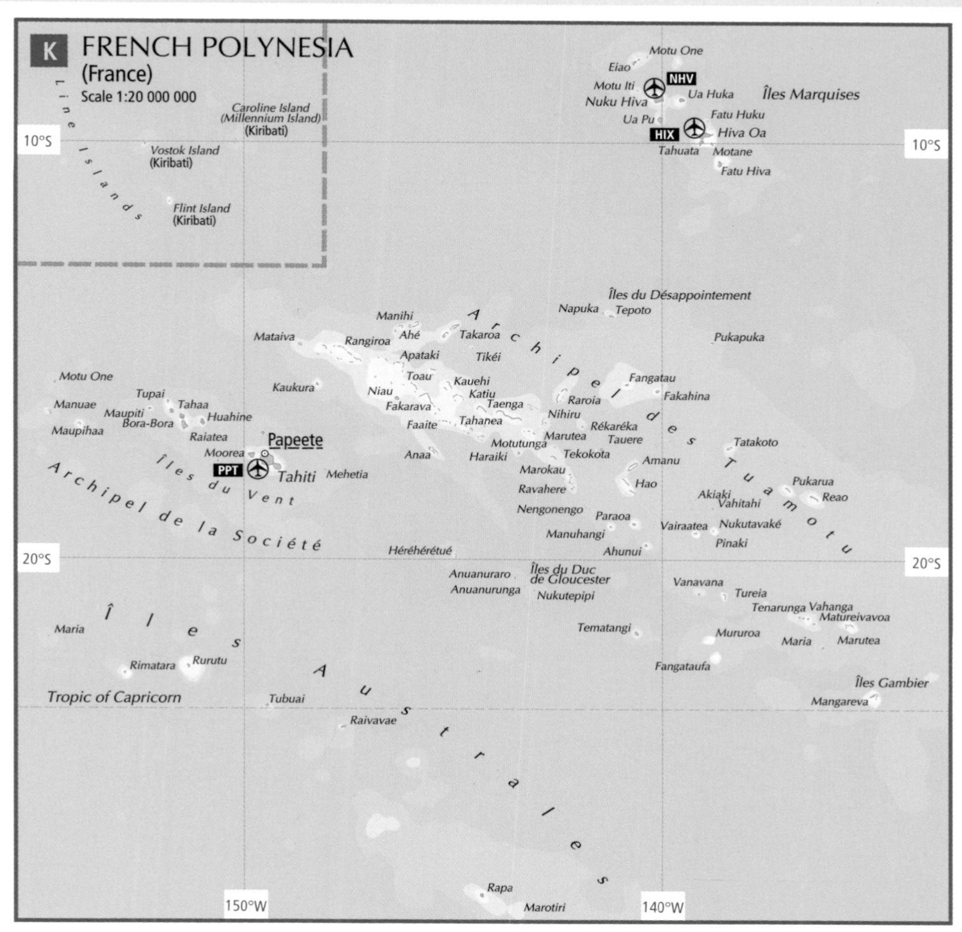

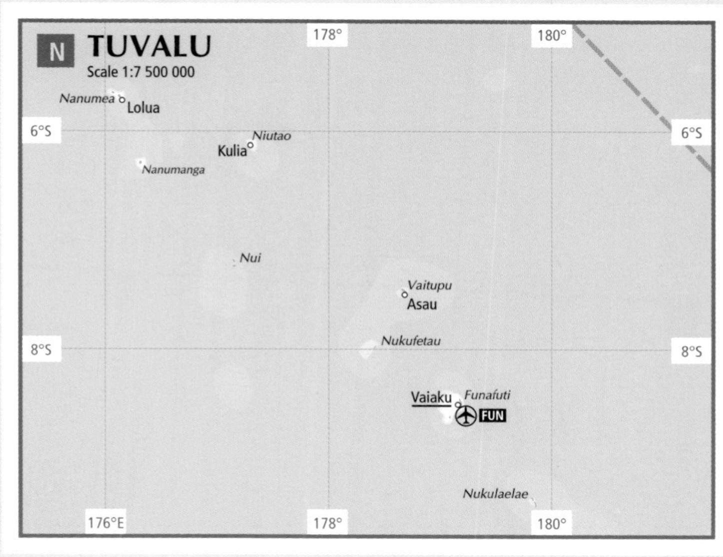

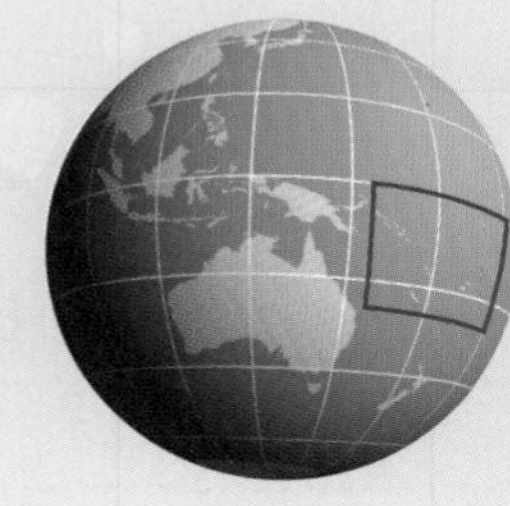

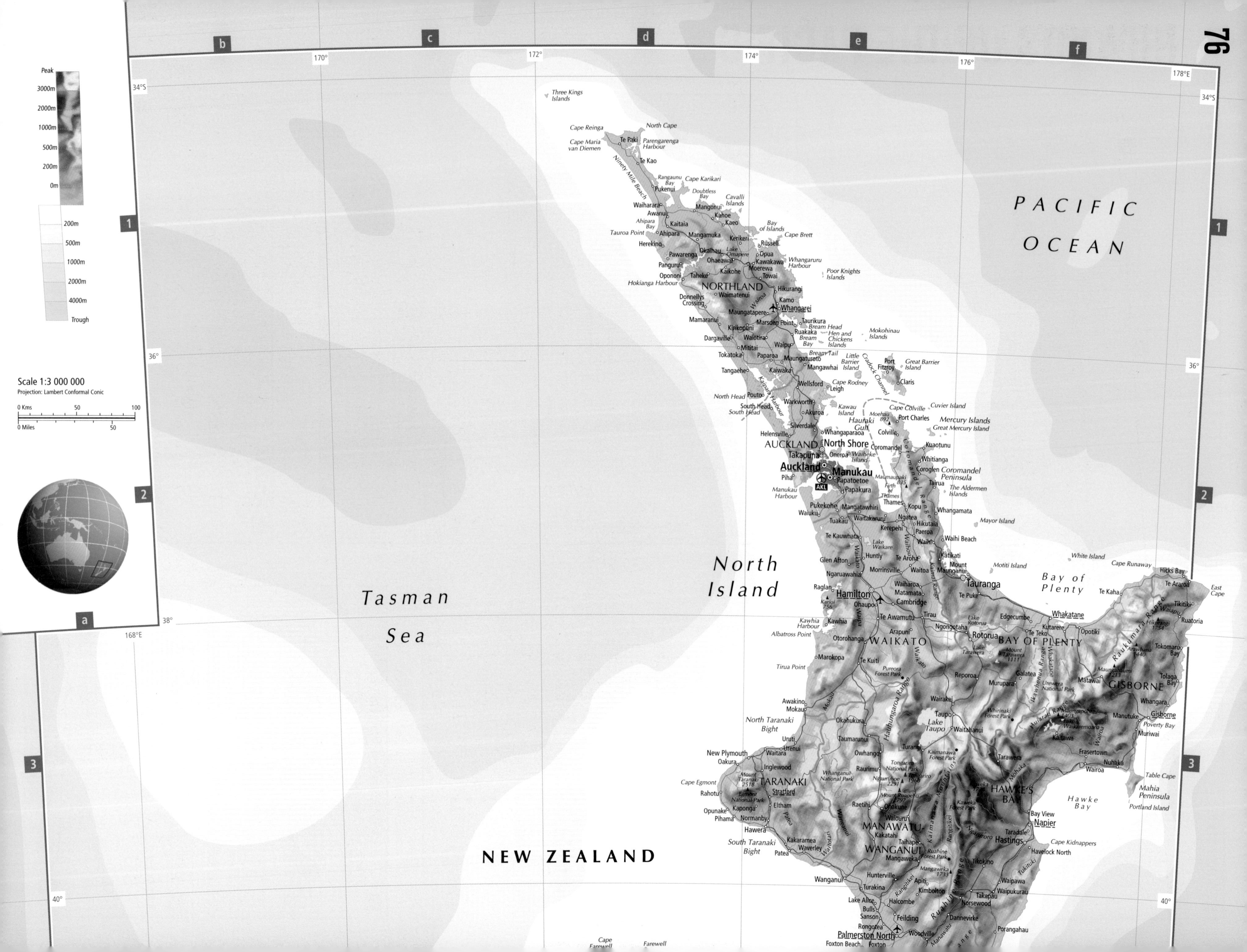

PACIFIC

OCEAN

NORTHLAND

North Cape
Cape Reinga
Cape Maria
van Diemen
Three Kings
Islands

Te Paki
Parengarenga
Harbour
Rangaunu
Bay
Cape Karikari
Pukenui
Awanui
Kaitaia
Ahipara
Bay
Tauroa Point
Ninety Mile Beach
Herekino
Panguru
Hokianga Harbour
Opononi
Donnelly's
Crossing
Dargaville
Kaihu

Cavalli
Islands
Doubtless
Bay
Mangonui
Kaeo
Kerikeri
Bay
of Islands
Opua
Russell
Okaihau
Kawakawa
Kaikohe
Waimatenui
Waipoua
Kaikohe
Tokatoka
Tangaehu

Whangaroa
Harbour
Cape Brett
Whangaruru
Harbour
Hikurangi
Kamo
Whangarei
Waiotira
Maungatapere
Maungaturoto
Ruakaka
Bream
Bay
Bream Head
Poor Knights
Islands
Hen and
Chickens
Islands
Waipu
Mangawhai
Kaiwaka
Wellsford
Cape Rodney
Leigh

Kaipara Harbour
North Head
South Head
Helensville
Silverdale
Waiwera
Waitoki
Paparoa
Warkworth

Kawau
Island
Whangaparaoa
Takapuna
North Shore
AUCKLAND
Manukau
Papatoetoe
Manukau
Harbour
Waiuku
Pukekohe
Tuakau
Pokeno
Piha

Great Barrier
Island
Port
Fitzroy
Claris
Cradock Channel
Little
Barrier
Island
Mokohinau
Islands

Mercury Islands
Great Mercury Island
Cuvier Island
Cape Colville
Port Charles
Colville
Coromandel
Coromandel
Peninsula
The Aldermen
Islands
Whitianga
Kuaotunu
Mayor Island
Whangamata
Waihi Beach
Waihi
Katikati
Waihou
Te Aroha
Paeroa
Ngatea
Thames
Kerepehi
Firth of
Thames
Miranda
Hauraki
Gulf
Whangapoua

White Island

Bay of
Plenty
BAY OF PLENTY
Whakatane
Opotiki
Te Kaha
Cape Runaway
Hicks Bay
Te Araroa
East Cape
Tokomaru
Bay
Tolaga Bay
GISBORNE
Gisborne
Poverty Bay
Muriwai
Table Cape
Mahia
Peninsula
Portland Island

Tauranga
Mount
Maunganui
Te Puke
Kaimai Range
Matamata
Morrinsville
Cambridge
Hamilton
Ohaupo
Te Awamutu
Kihikihi
Pirongia
Te Kuiti
Otorohanga

WAIKATO
Waikato
Ngaruawahia
Huntly
Glen Afton
Raglan
Waingaro
Kawhia
Harbour
Kawhia
Albatross Point

Rotorua
Lake
Rotorua
Lake
Taupo
Lake
Taupo
Reporoa
Taupo
Mangakino

Edgecumbe
Kawerau
Murupara

HAWKE'S
BAY
Hawke
Bay
Napier
Hastings
Havelock North
Cape Kidnappers
Bay View

MANAWATU
WANGANUI
Palmerston North
Foxton
Foxton Beach

NORTH
TARANAKI
BIGHT
Cape Egmont
New Plymouth
Oakura
Opunake
Pihama
STRATFORD
Stratford
Eltham
Normanby
Hawera
Patea
Waverley

SOUTH TARANAKI
BIGHT

North Island

NEW ZEALAND

Tasman Sea

Cape
Farewell

Scale 1:3 000 000
Projection: Lambert Conformal Conic

Peak
3000m
2000m
1000m
500m
200m
0m
200m
500m
1000m
2000m
4000m
Trough

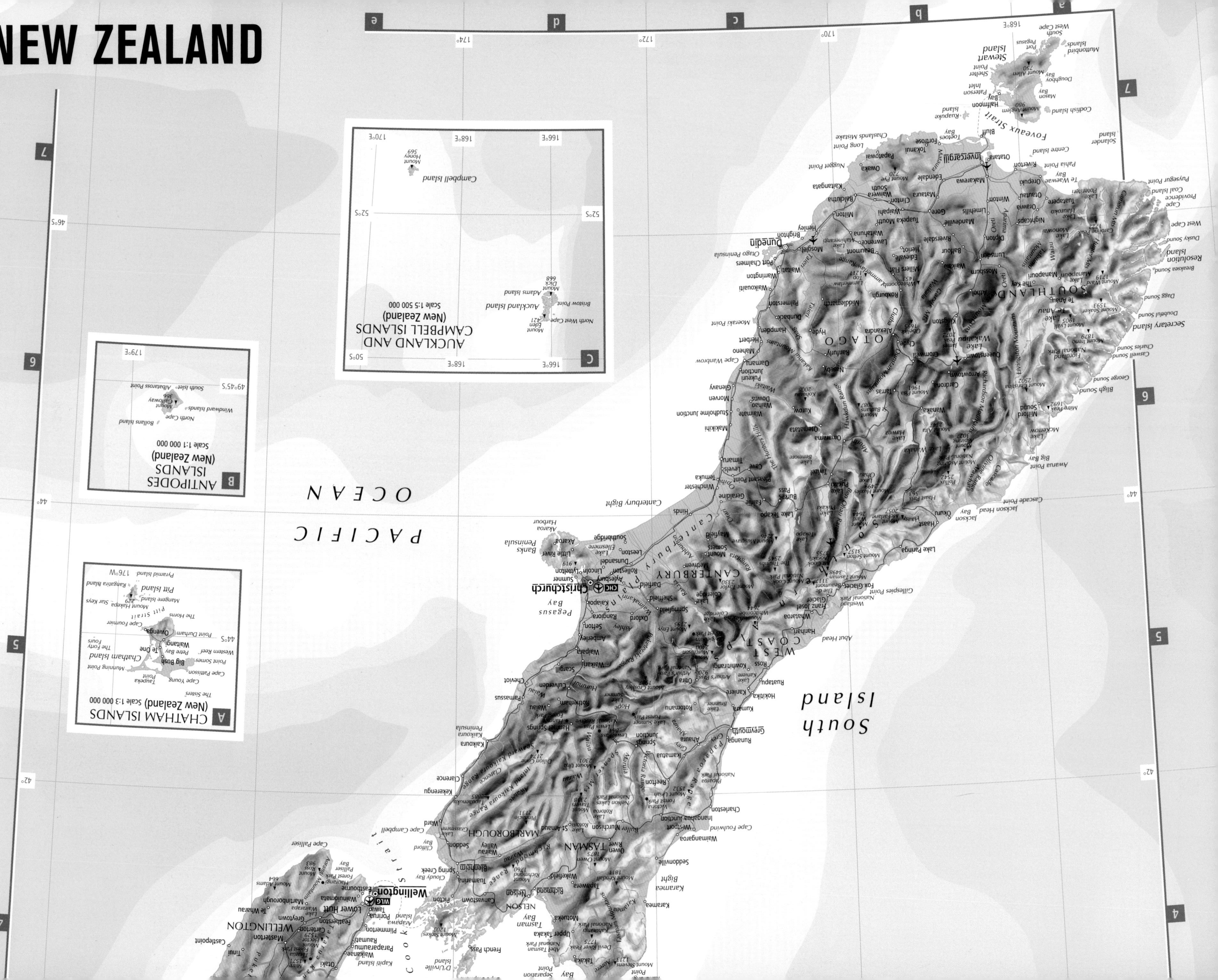

A CHATHAM ISLANDS
(New Zealand) Scale 1:3 000 000

The Sisters
Cape Young
Cape Pattisson
Point Somes   Morning Point
Western Reef   Big Bush   Chatham Island
44°S   Petre Bay Te One   The Forty
Waitangi   Owenga   Fours
Point Durham   Pitt Strait
The Horns   Mount Hakepa   Star Keys
429
Mangere Island
Pitt Island   Rangatira Island
Pyramid Island   176°W

B ANTIPODES ISLANDS
(New Zealand)
Scale 1:1 000 000

Bollans Island
North Cape
Mount
Galloway
Windward Islands   366
South Islet Albatross Point
49°45'S   179°E

C AUCKLAND AND CAMPBELL ISLANDS
(New Zealand)
Scale 1:5 500 000

50°S   52°S
168°E
Mount
Eden
North West Cape   321
Mount Auckland Island
Bristow Point Dick Adams Island
668
52°S   166°E   168°E   170°E
Campbell Island
Mount
Honey
569

PACIFIC OCEAN

Cook Strait

WELLINGTON
Wellington

South Island

WEST COAST

TASMAN

NELSON

MARLBOROUGH

CANTERBURY

Christchurch

Banks Peninsula
Pegasus Bay

Canterbury Bight

OTAGO

SOUTHLAND

Dunedin

Invercargill
Bluff
Foveaux Strait
Stewart Island

Greymouth
Hokitika
Westport

Southern Alps

Lake Te Anau
Lake Wakatipu
Lake Wanaka
Lake Hawea

Fiordland National Park

Milford Sound

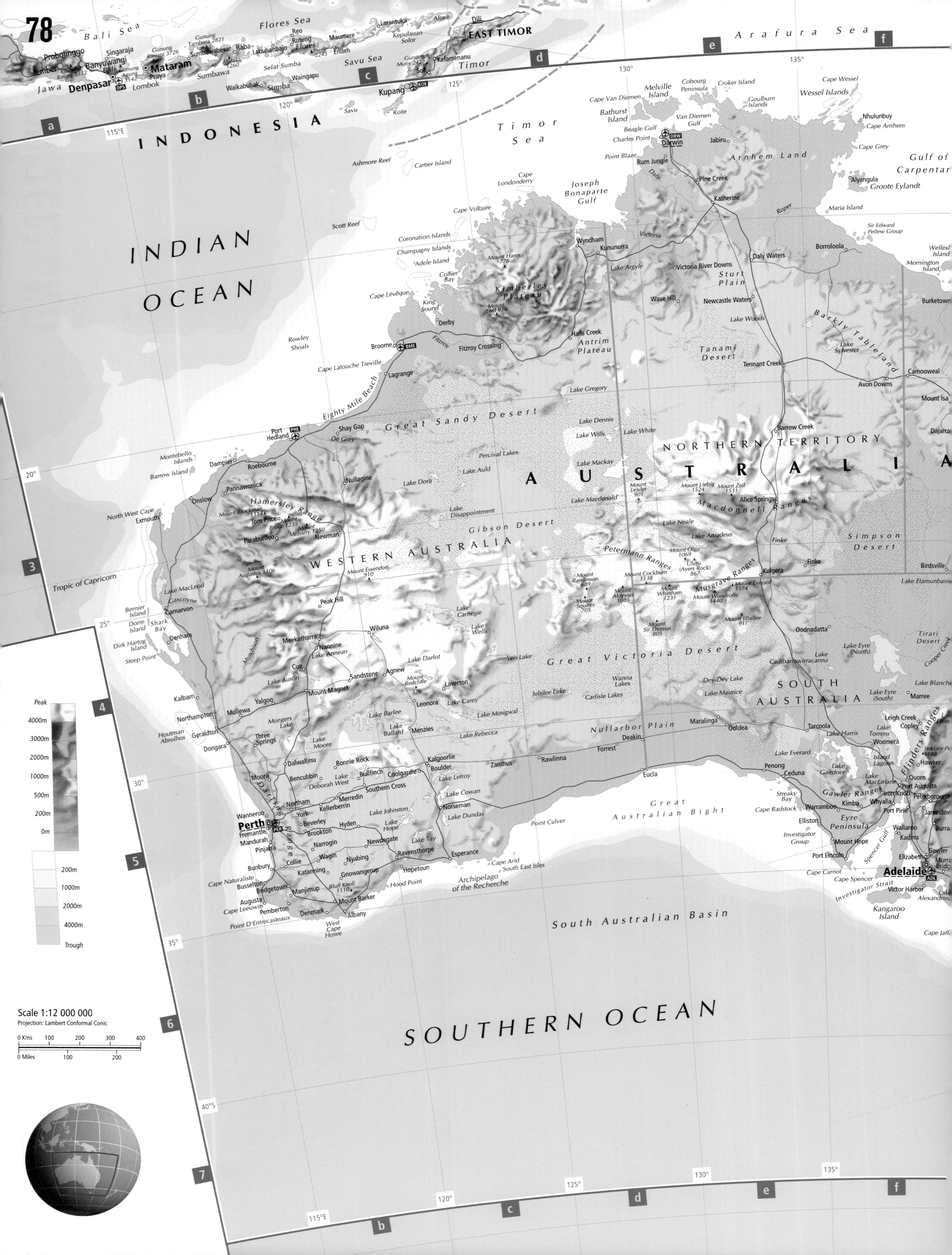
Bali Sea
Flores Sea
Arafura Sea
Timor Sea
Savu Sea
Selat Sumba
INDONESIA
EAST TIMOR
Probolinggo
Jember
Banyuwangi
Singaraja
Bali
Denpasar
Jawa
Lombok
Mataram
Praya
Sumbawa
Sumbawabesar
Raba
Labuhanbajo
Reo
Ruteng
Flores
Maumere
Ende
Larantuka
Alor
Kepulauan Solor
Waingapu
Waikabubak
Sumba
Savu
Rote
Kupang
Soe
Kefamenanu
Timor
Dili
INDIAN OCEAN
SOUTHERN OCEAN
AUSTRALIA
NORTHERN TERRITORY
WESTERN AUSTRALIA
SOUTH AUSTRALIA
Ashmore Reef
Cartier Island
Scott Reef
Rowley Shoals
Melville Island
Bathurst Island
Cape Van Diemen
Cobourg Peninsula
Croker Island
Goulburn Islands
Van Diemen Gulf
Beagle Gulf
Charles Point
Darwin
Point Blaze
Rum Jungle
Daly
Jabiru
Arnhem Land
Cape Wessel
Wessel Islands
Nhulunbuy
Cape Arnhem
Cape Grey
Gulf of Carpentaria
Alyangula
Groote Eylandt
Maria Island
Sir Edward Pellew Group
Borroloola
Wellesley Island
Mornington Island
Burketown
Pine Creek
Katherine
Roper
Cape Londonderry
Joseph Bonaparte Gulf
Cape Voltaire
Coronation Islands
Champagny Islands
Adele Island
Collier Bay
Cape Lévêque
King Sound
Derby
Wyndham
Kununurra
Lake Argyle
Victoria
Victoria River Downs
Daly Waters
Sturt Plain
Wave Hill
Newcastle Waters
Lake Woods
Barkly Tableland
Lake Sylvester
Mount Hann 776
Kimberley Plateau
Mount Ord 936
Broome
Fitzroy
Fitzroy Crossing
Halls Creek
Antrim Plateau
Tanami Desert
Tennant Creek
Camooweal
Avon Downs
Mount Isa
Cape Latouche Treville
Lagrange
Eighty Mile Beach
Lake Gregory
Great Sandy Desert
Port Hedland
Shay Gap
De Grey
Lake Dennis
Lake Wills
Lake White
Barrow Creek
Dajarra
Montebello Islands
Barrow Island
Dampier
Roebourne
Percival Lakes
Lake Auld
Lake Mackay
Pannawonica
Nullagine
Lake Dora
Mount Liebig 1524
Mount Zeil 1531
Mount Leisler 901
Lake Macdonald
Alice Springs
Macdonnell Ranges
Onslow
Hamersley Range
Mount Brockman 1114
Tom Price
Mount Bruce 1235
Mount Meharry 1250
Newman
North West Cape
Exmouth
Lake Disappointment
Gibson Desert
Lake Neale
Lake Amadeus
Simpson Desert
Finke
Paraburdoo
Mount Olga 1069
Uluru (Ayers Rock) 867
Petermann Ranges
Mount Augustus 1106
Mount Essendon 910
Mount Rawlinson 689
Mount Cockburn 1138
Musgrave Ranges
Mount Everard 1174
Kulgera
Birdsville
Tropic of Capricorn
Lake MacLeod
Gascoyne
Mount Aloysius 1085
Mount Whinham 1231
Mount Woodroffe 1440
Lake Eyre
Lake Etamunbanie
Peak Hill
Mount Squires 705
Bernier Island
Carnarvon
Lake Carnegie
Mount Illbillee 917
Dorre Island
Shark Bay
Lake Wells
Mount Sir Thomas 805
Oodnadatta
Denham
Wiluna
Tirari Desert
Dirk Hartog Island
Steep Point
Murchison
Meekatharra
Nannine
Lake Annean
Lake Darlot
Yeo Lake
Great Victoria Desert
Lake Eyre (North)
Cadibarrawirracanna
Cooper Creek
Cue
Lake Austin
Sandstone
Agnew
Mount Redcliffe 576
Laverton
Wanna Lakes
Dey-Dey Lake
Lake Blanche
Kalbarri
Mount Magnet
Yalgoo
Leonora
Lake Carey
Jubilee Lake
Carlisle Lakes
Lake Maurice
Lake Eyre (South)
Marree
Northampton
Mullewa
Mongers Lake
Lake Barlee
Lake Minigwal
Leigh Creek
Copley
Houtman Abrolhos
Geraldton
Lake Ballard
Menzies
Nullarbor Plain
Maralinga
Ooldea
Tarcoola
Lake Torrens
Flinders Ranges
Dongara
Three Springs
Lake Moore
Lake Rebecca
Deakin
Lake Harris
Woomera
Forrest
Dalwallinu
Bonnie Rock
Kalgoorlie
Boulder
Zanthus
Rawlinna
Lake Everard
Island Lagoon
Hawker
St Mary Peak 1188
Moora
Bencubbin
Lake Deborah West
Bullfinch
Coolgardie
Lake Lefroy
Eucla
Penong
Ceduna
Lake Gairdner
Lake Macfarlane
Quorn
Port Augusta
Darling Range
Northam
Southern Cross
Merredin
Kellerberrin
Lake Cowan
Norseman
Great Australian Bight
Streaky Bay
Gawler Ranges
Iron Knob
Peterborough
Wanneroo
Perth
Fremantle
York
Beverley
Hyden
Lake Johnston
Lake Hope
Lake Dundas
Cape Radstock
Wirramboo
Kimba
Whyalla
Port Pirie
Jamestown
Mandurah
Pinjarra
Brookton
Narrogin
Newdegate
Lake Tay
Point Culver
Elliston
Eyre Peninsula
Wallaroo
Kadina
Investigator Group
Mount Hope
Spencer Gulf
Burra
Wagin
Nyabing
Ravensthorpe
Esperance
Cape Arid
South East Isles
Port Lincoln
Gawler
Elizabeth
Murray Bridge
Bunbury
Collie
Katanning
Gnowangerup
Hopetoun
Archipelago of the Recherche
Cape Carnot
Cape Spencer
Adelaide
Cape Naturaliste
Busselton
Bridgetown
Manjimup
Bluff Knoll 1110
Hood Point
Investigator Strait
Victor Harbor
Alexandrina
Augusta
Cape Leeuwin
Pemberton
Mount Barker
Denmark
Albany
Kangaroo Island
Point D'Entrecasteaux
West Cape Howe
South Australian Basin
Cape Jaffa
Peak
4000m
3000m
2000m
1000m
500m
200m
0m
200m
1000m
2000m
4000m
Trough
Scale 1:12 000 000
Projection: Lambert Conformal Conic
0 Kms 100 200 300 400
0 Miles 100 200
115°E
120°
125°
130°
135°
20°
25°
30°
35°
40°S
a
b
c
d
e
f
3
4
5
6
7

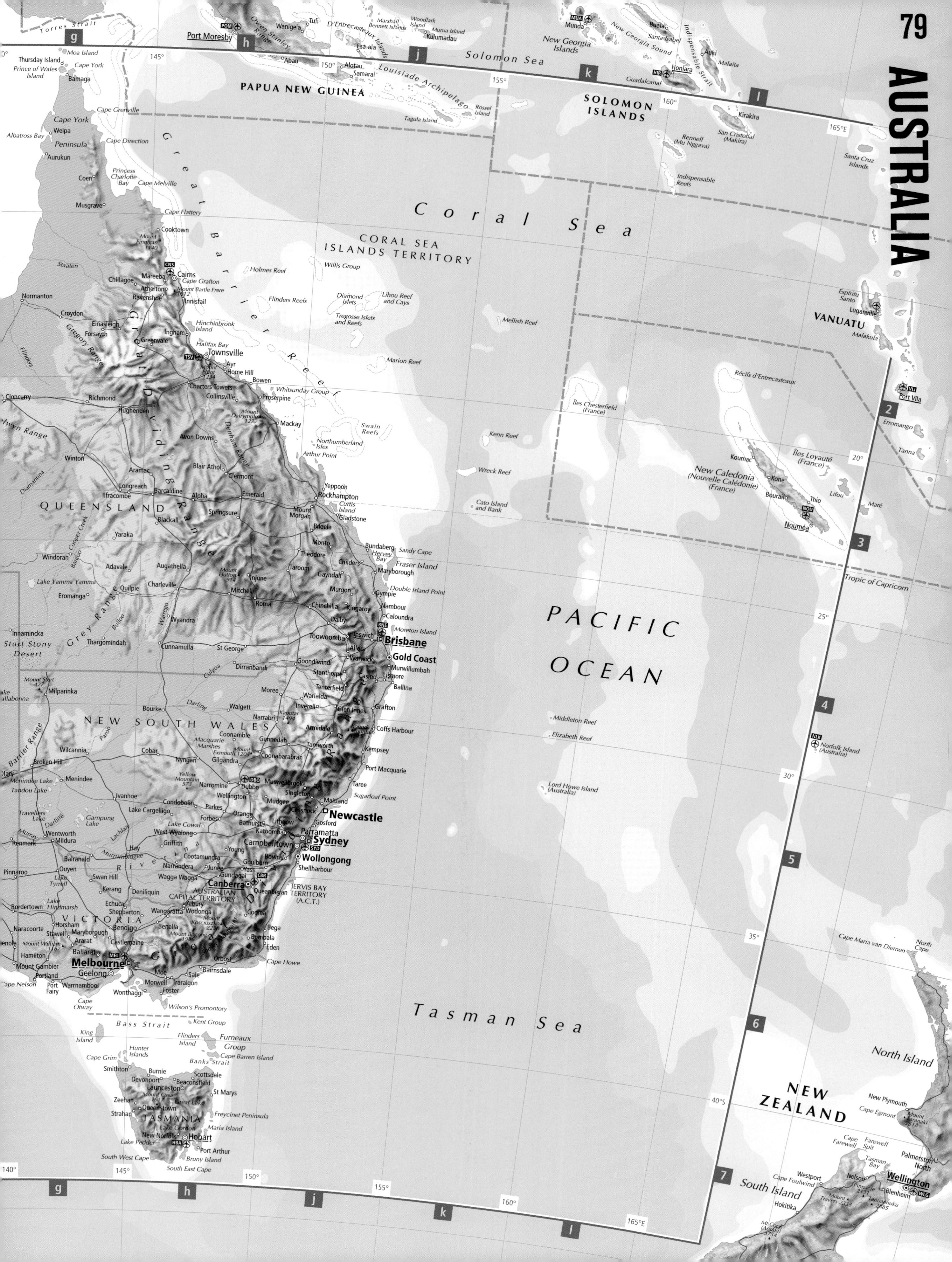
Torres Strait
Port Moresby
Owen Stanley Range
Wanigela
Tufi
D'Entrecasteaux Islands
Marshall Bennett Islands
Woodlark Island
Murua Island
Kulumadau
Esa-ala
Abau
Alotau
Samarai
Louisiade Archipelago
Rossel Island
Tagula Island
PAPUA NEW GUINEA
Solomon Sea
Munda
New Georgia Islands
New Georgia Sound
Buala
Santa Isabel
Indispensable Strait
Auki
Malaita
Honiara
Guadalcanal
SOLOMON ISLANDS
Kirakira
San Cristobal (Makira)
Rennell (Mu Nggava)
Indispensable Reefs
Santa Cruz Islands
Moa Island
Thursday Island
Prince of Wales Island
Cape York
Bamaga
Cape Grenville
Cape York Peninsula
Weipa
Albatross Bay
Cape Direction
Aurukun
Coen
Princess Charlotte Bay
Cape Melville
Musgrave
Cape Flattery
Cooktown
Mount Finnigan 1140
Great Barrier Reef
Coral Sea
CORAL SEA ISLANDS TERRITORY
Willis Group
Holmes Reef
Flinders Reefs
Diamond Islets
Lihou Reef and Cays
Tregosse Islets and Reefs
Mellish Reef
Marion Reef
Staaten
Chillagoe
Mareeba
Cairns
Cape Grafton
Atherton
Mount Bartle Frere 1612
Innisfail
Ravenshoe
Normanton
Croydon
Einasleigh
Forsayth
Gregory Range
Hinchinbrook Island
Ingham
Greenvale
Halifax Bay
Townsville
Ayr
Home Hill
Mount Elliot 1234
Bowen
Whitsunday Group
Proserpine
Charters Towers
Collinsville
Flinders
Cloncurry
Richmond
Hughenden
Mount Dalrymple 1227
Mackay
Denham Range
Swain Reefs
Northumberland Isles
Arthur Point
Avon Downs
Winton
Blair Athol
Clermont
Great Dividing Range
Aramac
Longreach
Barcaldine
Alpha
Emerald
Yeppoon
Rockhampton
Curtis Island
Gladstone
Mount Morgan
Ilfracombe
QUEENSLAND
Springsure
Blackall
Biloela
Diamantina
Cooper Creek
Yaraka
Monto
Theodore
Bundaberg
Hervey Bay
Sandy Cape
Fraser Island
Childers
Maryborough
Windorah
Barcoo
Adavale
Augathella
Mount Hutton 914
Taroom
Gayndah
Injune
Lake Yamma Yamma
Quilpie
Charleville
Mitchell
Murgon
Gympie
Double Island Point
Eromanga
Roma
Chinchilla
Kingaroy
Nambour
Caloundra
Grey Range
Bulloo
Warrego
Wyandra
Dalby
Moreton Island
Innamincka
Sturt Stony Desert
Thargomindah
Cunnamulla
St George
Toowoomba
Ipswich
Brisbane
Allora
Warwick
Gold Coast
Murwillumbah
Goondiwindi
Dirranbandi
Culgoa
Stanthorpe
Casino
Lismore
Ballina
Mount Sturt 427
Milparinka
Moree
Tenterfield
Warialda
Darling
Bourke
Walgett
Inverell
Glen Innes
Grafton
Narrabri
Kaputar 1494
NEW SOUTH WALES
Armidale
Coffs Harbour
Barrier Range
Paroo
Coonamble
Macquarie Marshes
Gunnedah
Mount Exmouth 1206
Tamworth
Kempsey
Wilcannia
Cobar
Nyngan
Coonabarabran
Gilgandra
Broken Hill
Port Macquarie
Menindee
Menindee Lake
Yellow Mountain 573
Narromine
Dubbo
Muswellbrook
Taree
Tandou Lake
Wellington
Singleton
Sugarloaf Point
Ivanhoe
Condobolin
Mudgee
Maitland
Lake Cargelligo
Parkes
Cessnock
Newcastle
Travellers Lake
Garnpung Lake
Forbes
Orange
Bathurst
Lithgow
Gosford
Lake Cowal
Katoomba
Parramatta
Wentworth
Mildura
Lachlan
West Wyalong
Sydney
Renmark
Hay
Griffith
Campbelltown
Murrumbidgee
Young
Wollongong
Balranald
Cootamundra
Goulburn
Bowral
Riverina
Narrandera
Yass
Shellharbour
Pinnaroo
Ouyen
Junee
Gundagai
Swan Hill
Wagga Wagga
Lake Tyrrell
Kerang
Deniliquin
Canberra
Queanbeyan
JERVIS BAY TERRITORY (A.C.T.)
AUSTRALIAN CAPITAL TERRITORY
Echuca
Albury
Bordertown
Lake Hindmarsh
Shepparton
Wangaratta
Wodonga
Mount Kosciuszko 2228
Naracoorte
Horsham
VICTORIA
Benalla
Cooma
Bega
Stawell
Maryborough
Bendigo
Ararat
Castlemaine
Mount Bogong 1986
Bombala
Mount William 1167
Eden
Hamilton
Ballarat
Melbourne
Orbost
Cape Howe
Mount Gambier
Geelong
Moe
Sale
Bairnsdale
Portland
Cape Nelson
Port Fairy
Warrnambool
Morwell
Traralgon
Wonthaggi
Foster
Cape Otway
Wilson's Promontory
Bass Strait
Kent Group
King Island
Flinders Island
Furneaux Group
Cape Barren Island
Hunter Islands
Cape Grim
Banks Strait
Smithton
Burnie
Scottsdale
Devonport
Beaconsfield
Launceston
St Marys
Zeehan
Cradle Mountain
Great Lake
Strahan
Queenstown
TASMANIA
Freycinet Peninsula
Lake Gordon
Maria Island
New Norfolk
Hobart
Lake Pedder
Port Arthur
South West Cape
Bruny Island
South East Cape
Espíritu Santo
Luganville
VANUATU
Malakula
Port Vila
Erromango
Tanna
Récifs d'Entrecasteaux
Îles Chesterfield (France)
Kenn Reef
Wreck Reef
Cato Island and Bank
Koumac
Îles Loyauté (France)
New Caledonia (Nouvelle Calédonie) (France)
Kone
Bourail
Thio
Lifou
Maré
Nouméa
Tropic of Capricorn
PACIFIC OCEAN
Middleton Reef
Elizabeth Reef
Norfolk Island (Australia)
Lord Howe Island (Australia)
Tasman Sea
Cape Maria van Diemen
North Cape
North Island
NEW ZEALAND
New Plymouth
Cape Egmont
Mount Taranaki 2518
Cape Farewell
Farewell Spit
Tasman Bay
Palmerston North
Westport
Cape Foulwind
Nelson
Wellington
Blenheim
South Island
Hokitika
Mount Travers 2338
Tapuaenuku 2885
Mt Cook (Aoraki) 3754
145°
150°
155°
160°
165°E
140°
20°
25°
30°
35°
40°S
g
h
j
k
l
2
3
4
5
6
7

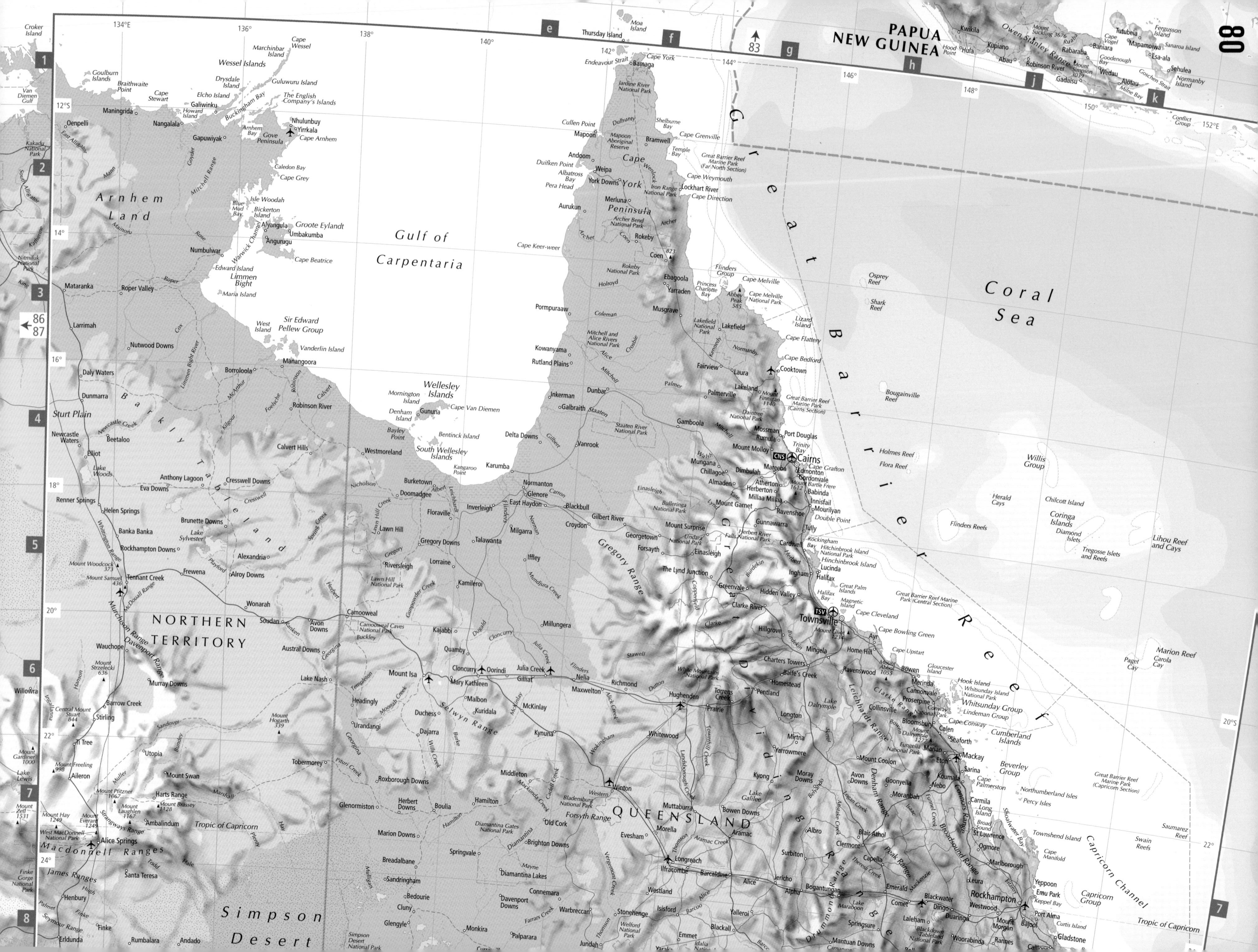
PAPUA NEW GUINEA
Coral Sea
Great Barrier Reef
Gulf of Carpentaria
QUEENSLAND
NORTHERN TERRITORY
Great Dividing Range
Barkly Tableland
Arnhem Land
Simpson Desert
Cape York Peninsula
Wellesley Islands
Sir Edward Pellew Group
Groote Eylandt
Wessel Islands
Capricorn Channel
Tropic of Capricorn
Thursday Island
Cooktown
Cairns
Townsville
Mackay
Rockhampton
Gladstone
Mount Isa
Cloncurry
Longreach
Winton
Hughenden
Charters Towers
Normanton
Karumba
Weipa
Tennant Creek
Alice Springs
Mataranka
Borroloola
Nhulunbuy
Emerald
Barcaldine
Bowen
Proserpine
Ingham
Innisfail
Camooweal
Boulia
Macdonnell Ranges
Selwyn Range
Gregory Range
Leichhardt Range
Whitsunday Group
Cumberland Islands
Willis Group
Lihou Reef and Cays
Marion Reef
Flinders Reefs
Herald Cays
Osprey Reef
Bougainville Reef
Holmes Reef
Flora Reef
Coringa Islands
Owen Stanley Range
12°S
14°
16°
18°
20°
22°
24°
134°E
136°
138°
140°
142°
144°
146°
148°
150°
152°E
20°S
83
86
87

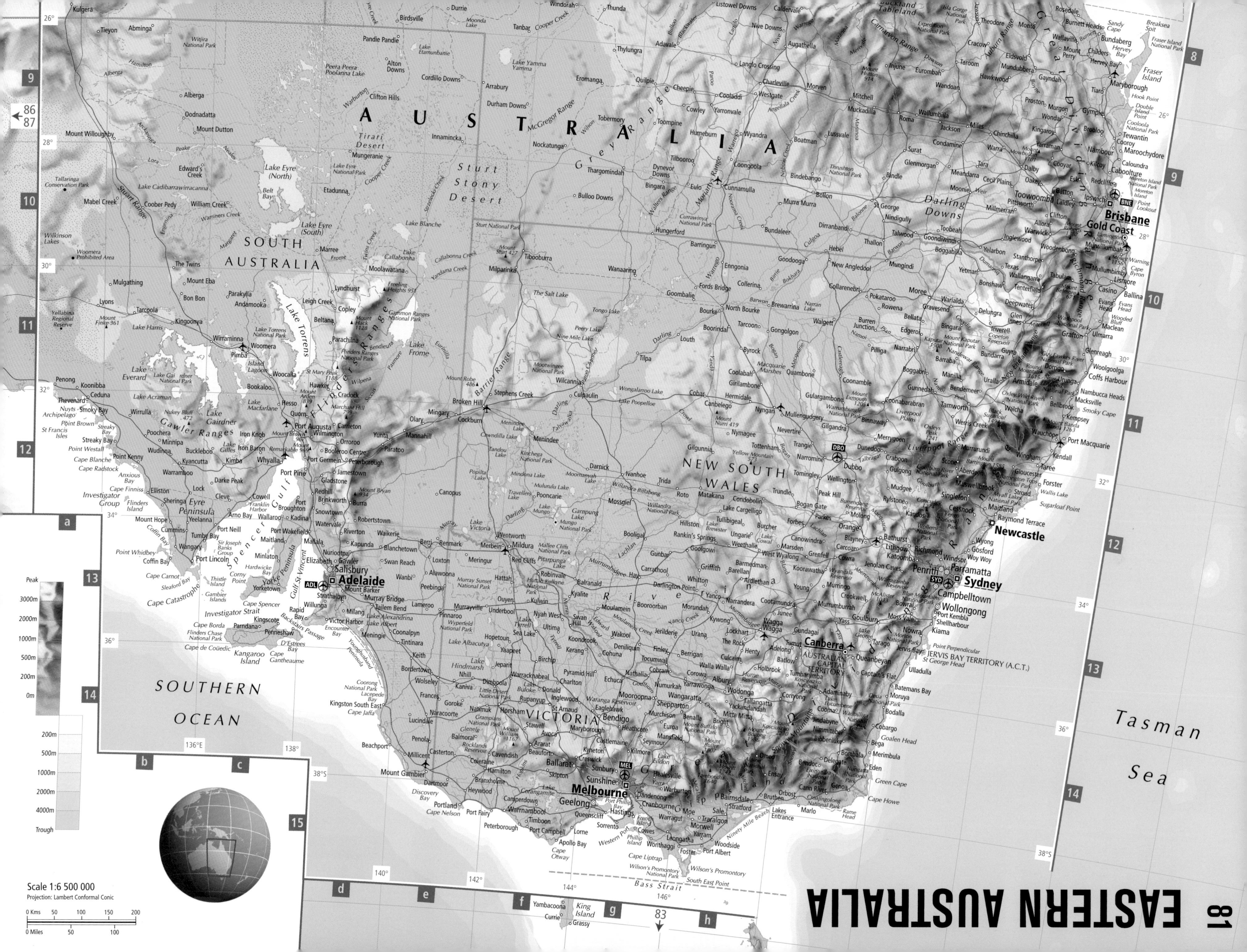

Tasman Sea

SOUTHERN OCEAN

Great Dividing Range

QUEENSLAND

NEW SOUTH WALES

SOUTH AUSTRALIA

VICTORIA

Brisbane
Gold Coast
Newcastle
Sydney
Wollongong
Canberra
AUSTRALIAN CAPITAL TERRITORY (A.C.T.)
Melbourne
Geelong
Ballarat
Bendigo
Adelaide
Salisbury

Bass Strait
King Island
Currie
Grassy

Scale 1:6 500 000
Projection: Lambert Conformal Conic

Peak
3000m
2000m
1000m
500m
200m
0m

4000m
2000m
1000m
500m
200m
0m
Trough

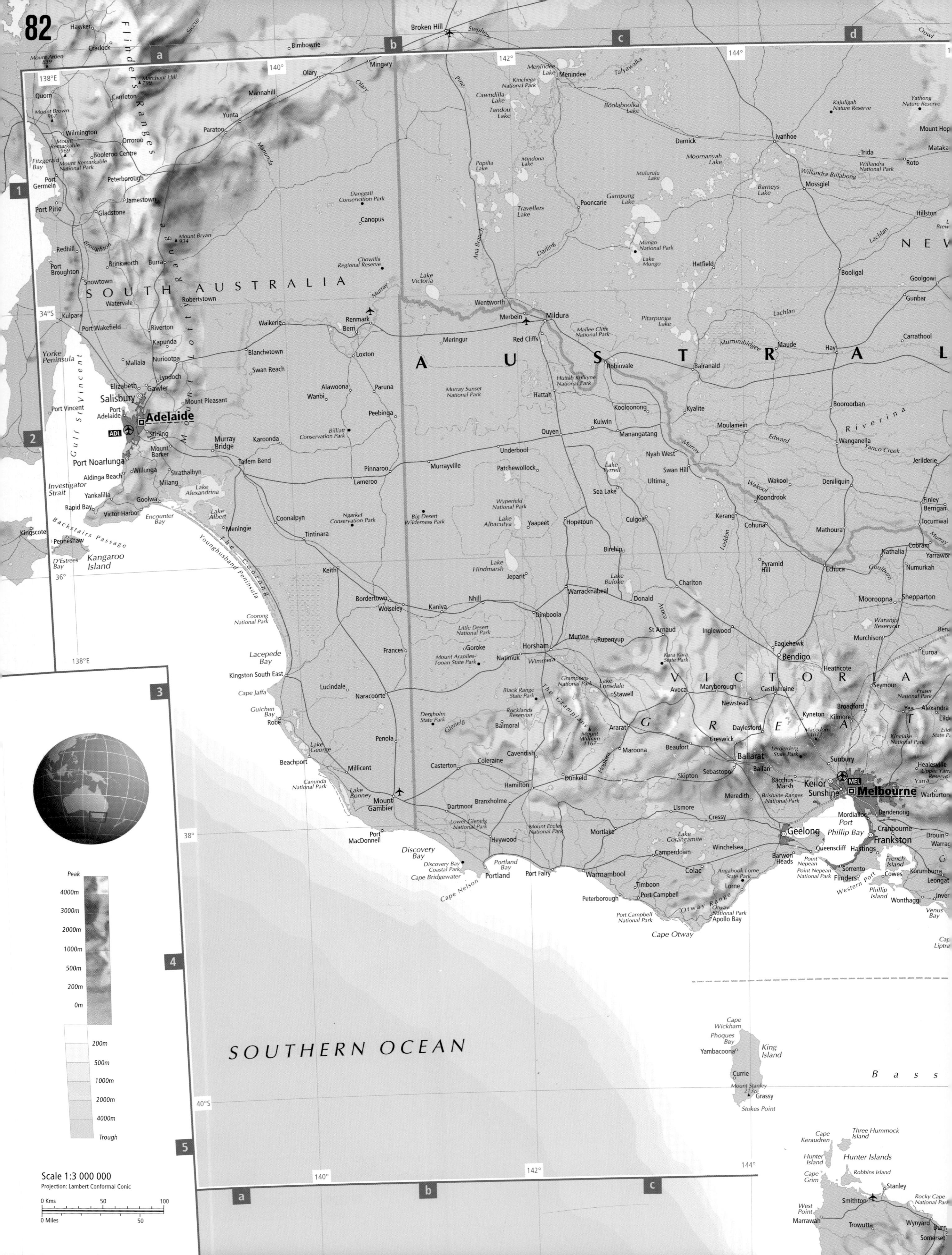
SOUTH AUSTRALIA
AUSTRALIA
VICTORIA
GREAT
SOUTHERN OCEAN
Bass
Adelaide
Melbourne
Geelong
Ballarat
Bendigo
Mildura
Broken Hill
Port Pirie
Port Augusta
Salisbury
Port Noarlunga
Mount Gambier
Warrnambool
Portland
Horsham
Shepparton
Frankston
Swan Hill
Echuca
Hamilton
Kangaroo Island
Yorke Peninsula
Gulf St Vincent
Investigator Strait
Backstairs Passage
Encounter Bay
Lake Alexandrina
Lake Albert
The Coorong
Younghusband Peninsula
Lacepede Bay
Discovery Bay
Portland Bay
Port Phillip Bay
Western Port
Cape Otway
Cape Nelson
King Island
Hunter Islands
Murray
Darling
Murrumbidgee
Lachlan
Riverina
Flinders Ranges
Mount Lofty Ranges
The Grampians
Otway Range
Scale 1:3 000 000
Projection: Lambert Conformal Conic
0 Kms
50
100
0 Miles
50
Peak
4000m
3000m
2000m
1000m
500m
200m
0m
200m
500m
1000m
2000m
4000m
Trough
138°E
140°
142°
144°
34°S
36°
38°
40°S
a
b
c
d
1
2
3
4
5

SOUTH-EAST AUSTRALIA

magee
Tottenham
Tomingley
Trangie
Dunedoo
Craboon
Scone
Glenbawn Reservoir
Aberdeen
Muswellbrook
Wingham
Taree
Crowdy Bay National Park
Gloucester
Forster
Wallis Lake
Dubbo
DBO
Narromine
Ulan
Goulburn River National Park
Denman
Singleton
Dungog
Stroud
Myall Lake
Sugarloaf Point
Myall Lakes National Park
Port Stephens
Broughton Islands

Yellow Mountain 573
Geurie
Wellington
Gulgong
Mudgee
Rylstone
Coricudgy
Wollemi National Park
Branxton
Maitland
Kurri Kurri
Cessnock
Raymond Terrace
Newcastle
Lake Macquarie
Morisset
Swansea

Round Hill ture Reserve
Condobolin
Peak Hill
Molong
Orange
Kandos
Yengo National Park
Wyong
The Entrance
Brisbane Water National Park

Euabalong
Parkes
Forbes
Bathurst
Lithgow
Richmond
Windsor
Marra Marra National Park
Gosford
Woy Woy
Broken Bay
Ku-Ring-Gai Chase National Park

SOUTH WALES
Burcher
Lake Cowal
Bogan Gate
Trundle
Wallerawang
Blayney
Tarana
Katoomba
Blue Mountains National Park
Penrith
Parramatta
SYD
Sydney
Port Jackson

Ungarie
Marsden
Caragabal
Grenfell
Cowra
Canowindra
Carcoar
Kanangra-Boyd National Park
Jenolan Caves
Camden
Picton
Campbelltown
Botany Bay

West Wyalong
Weethalle
Barmedman
Weddin Mountains National Park
Koorawatha
Wyangala Reservoir
Nattai National Park
Bargo
Wollongong
Port Kembla
Shellharbour

Barellan
Young
Murringo
Crookwell
McAlister 1033
Mittagong
Bowral
Moss Vale
Kiama

Riverina
Narrandera
Grong Grong
Cootamundra
Murrumburrah
Tarlo River National Park
Marulan
Nowra
Point Perpendicular

Yanco
Junee
Yass
Goulburn
Morton National Park
Beecroft Peninsula
Jervis Bay
St George Head

Wagga Wagga
Gundagai
Yass
Lake George
Lake Bathurst
Tarago
JERVIS BAY TERRITORY (A.C.T)
Ulladulla

Canberra
AUSTRALIAN CAPITAL TERRITORY
Queanbeyan
Bungendore
Braidwood
Budawang National Park
Shoalhaven

The Rock
Tarcutta
Adelong
Tumut
Tharwa
Namadgi National Park
Captain's Flat

Henty
Kyeamba
Batlow
Cooma
Michelago
Batemans Bay
Deua National Park

Culcairn
Holbrook
Tumbarumba
Kiandra
Mount Bimberi 1912
Bredbo
Moruya

Albury
Hume Reservoir
Burrowa Pine Mountain National Park
Corryong
Kosciuszko National Park
Lake Eucumbene
Bodalla

Wodonga
Corryong
Mount Townsend 2209
Mount Kosciuszko 2228
Jindabyne
Narooma
Cape Dromedary

Yackandandah
Tallangatta
Dartmouth Reservoir
Nimmitabel
Wadbilliga National Park
Cobargo
Goalen Head

Wangaratta
Myrtleford
Mitta Mitta
Mount Bogong 1986
The Pilot 1836
Bombala
Merimbula
Mimosa Rocks National Park

Mount Buffalo National Park
Bright
Mount Feathertop 1922
Alpine National Park
Mount Cobberas 1836
Delegate
Bega
Tantawanglo

Mount Hotham 1860
Mount Buller 1804
Omeo
Bendoc
Errinundra National Park
Eden
Twofold Bay
Ben Boyd National Park

Tamboritha 1640
Mount Howitt 1742
Ensay
Mount Ellery 1296
Cann River
Nungatta National Park
Green Cape

Bruthen
Orbost
Marlo
Alfred National Park
Genoa
Disaster Bay
Nadgee Nature Reserve
Cape Howe

Baw Baw National Park
Bairnsdale
Stratford
The Lakes National Park
Lakes Entrance
Croajingolong National Park
Mallacoota Inlet
Cape Gabo Island
Rame Head

Sale
Lake Wellington
Gippsland Lakes Coastal Park
Ninety Mile Beach

Moe
Morwell
Traralgon

Yarram
Port Welshpool
Woodside
Port Albert

Corner Inlet
Snake Island

Mount La Trobe 755
Wilson's Promontory National Park
South East Point

Tasman Sea

Hogan Group

Curtis Group
Kent Group
Deal Island
South West Island

West Sister Island
Palana
North Point
Cape Frankland
Marshall Bay
Emita
Flinders Island
Babel Island
Furneaux
Group

Prime Seal Island
Whitemark
Strzelecki Peak 756
Lady Barron

Chappell Islands
Franklin Sound
Mount Munro 1836
Cape Barren Island
Clarke Island

Banks Strait
Ringarooma Bay
Cape Portland
Mount William National Park
Tomahawk
Eddystone Point

Anderson Bay
Asbestos Range National Park
George Town
Bridport
Gladstone
Scottsdale
Derby

TASMANIA

TASMANIA (Australia)

Same scale as main map

West Sister Island
Palana
North Point
Cape Frankland
Marshall Bay
Emita
Flinders Island
Babel Island
Furneaux

Three Hummock Island
Hunter Islands
Prime Seal Island
Whitemark
Strzelecki Peak 756
Lady Barron
Group

Hunter Island
Cape Grim
Robbins Island
Perkins Bay
Stanley
Chappell Islands
Franklin Sound
Cape Barren Island
Mount Munro 1836

West Point
Smithton
Rocky Cape National Park
Cape Portland
Banks Strait
Clarke Island

Marrawah
Wynyard
Burnie
Penguin
Ulverstone
Asbestos Range National Park
Bridport
Scottsdale
Gladstone
Eddystone Point

Trowutta
Somerset
Devonport
Beaconsfield
George Town
Derby
St Helens Point

Temma
Latrobe
Lilydale
Ringarooma
St Helens

Sandy Cape
Waratah
Deloraine
Westbury
Ben Lomond National Park
Legges Tor 1572
St Marys

Corinna
Cradle Mountain 1545
Launceston
Fingal
Avoca
Douglas Apsley National Park

Rosebery
Southwest Conservation Area
Longford
Conara Junction
Bicheno

Zeehan
Cradle Mountain Lake St Clair National Park
Mount Ossi 1617
Walls of Jerusalem National Park
Miena
Great Lake
Arthur Lakes
Campbell Town

Queenstown
Strahan
Lake Echo
Sorell Lake
Swansea

Cape Sorell
Frenchman's Cap 1444
Tarraleah
Freycinet National Park
Coles Bay

Macquarie Harbour
Franklin-Gordon National Park
Bothwell
Oatlands
Schouten Island
Great Oyster Bay
Freycinet Peninsula

Point Hibbs
Mount Field National Park
Kempton
Triabunna
Orford
Maria Island National Park

Strathgordon
Lake Gordon
Mount Field National Park
Mount Anne 1426
Bridgewater
Richmond
Sorell
Maria Island

High Rocky Point
Lake Pedder
New Norfolk
Maydena
HBA
Hobart
Rokeby
Dunalley
Forestier Peninsula

Low Rocky Point
South West National Park
Kingston
Huonville
Cygnet
Storm Bay
Port Arthur
Tasman Peninsula

Cape Davey
Port Davey
Hartz Mountains National Park
Dover
Bruny Island
Cape Pillar

SOUTHERN OCEAN
South West Cape
Catamaran
South East Cape
Maatsuyker Group
Tasman Head
South East Cape

Tasman Sea

Tasman Sea

T A S M A N I A

Bass Strait

Southern Ocean

148°E 150° 152°E
34°S 36° 40°S 42°S
146°E 148°E

extension north
Same scale as main map

Great Barrier Reef

Daintree National Park · Mossman · Port Douglas · Rumula · Mount Molloy · Mareeba · Mitchell · Lake Mitchell · Dimbulah · Atherton · Herberton · Mount Garnet · Gunnawarra · Greenvale · Maryvale

Cape Grafton · Green Island · Grafton Passage · Flora Passage · Trinity Bay · Cairns · Edmonton · Gordonvale · Babinda · Innisfail · Mourilyan · Double Point · Dunk Island · Ravenshoe · Millaa Millaa · Tully Falls · Tully · Mount Bartle Frere 1612 · Edmund Kennedy National Park · Yamanie Falls National Park · Herbert · Hidden Valley · Clarke River · Clarke

Great Barrier Reef Marine Park (Cairns Section) · Hinchinbrook Island · Hitchinbrook Island National Park · Great Palm Island · Orpheus Island · Rockingham Bay · Cardwell · Lucinda · Halifax · Ingham · Halifax Bay · Magnetic Island · Cleveland Bay · Townsville · Mount Elliot 1234 · Mount Spec National Park · Seaview Range · Gorge Range

Great Dividing Range

Coral Sea

Great Barrier Reef (Central Section) · Hook Reef · Hook Island · Hayman Island · Holbourne Island · Gloucester Island

Great Barrier Reef (Capricorn Section) · Percy Isles · Northumberland Islands · Prudhoe Island · Beverley Group · Cumberland Islands · Whitsunday Group · Whitsunday Island · Whitsunday Island National Park · Lindeman Group · Cape Conway · Repulse Bay · Long Island · Broad Sound · Arthur Point · Shoalwater Bay · Townshend Island · Broad Sound Channel · Cape Palmerston · Cape Palmerston National Park · Cape Clinton · Cape Manifold · Keppel Bay · Great Keppel Island · Keppel Island · Emu Park · Yeppoon

Capricorn Channel · Heron Island · Bunker Group · Capricorn Group · Curtis Channel · Cape Capricorn · Curtis Island · Facing Island · Gladstone · Port Alma · Rockhampton · Bajool · Mount Morgan · Mount Larcom · Calliope · Boyne · Tannum Sands · Bustard Head · Round Hill Head · Boyne · Agnes · Miriam Vale · Bororen · Rosedale · Bundaberg · Gin Gin · Wallaville · Mount Perry

Breaksea Spit · Sandy Cape · Fraser Island · Fraser Island National Park · Waddy Point · Woodgate National Park · Burrum River National Park · Burnett Heads · Burrum Heads · Hervey Bay · Hervey Bay · Childers · Biggenden · Maryborough · Mary · Tiaro · Hook Point · Wide Bay · Double Island Point · Rainbow Beach · Cooloola National Park · Gayndah · Barandum · Proston

Normanby Range · Maryborough · Yaamba · Byfield · Byfield National Park · Westwood · Marlborough · Ogmore · St Lawrence · Carmila · Fitzroy · Dawson · Banana · Theodore · Goovigen · Woorabinda · Baralaba · Moura · Dingo · Blackdown Tableland National Park · Jambin · Biloela · Thangool · Monto · Eidsvold · Nogo · Burnett · Abercorn · Hawkwood · Brovinia

Coast Range · *Auburn Range*

Cape Hillsborough · Cape Hillsborough National Park · Seaforth · Calen · Mackay · Sarina · Koumala · Connors Range · Broadsound Range · Leura · Isaac · Middlemount · Funnel Creek · Ropee Creek · Dysart · Nebo · Eton · Marian · Mirani · Eungella · Eungella National Park · Mount Dalrymple · Dingo · Bluff · Blackwater · Comet · Rolleston · Meteor Creek · Consuelo · Springsure · Emerald · Comet · Lake Maraboon · Capella · Lake Nuga Nuga · Expedition National Park · Carnarvon National Park · Carnarvon Range · Isla Gorge National Park · Cracow · Precipice National Park · Taroom · Glenden · Moranbah · Goonyella · Denham Range · Peak Range · Clermont · Anakie · Rubyvale · Blair Athol · Logan Creek · Bogantungan · Mantuan Downs · Buckland Tableland · Buckland Tableland · Mount Hutton 914 · Injune · Expedition Range

Coral Sea · *Great Barrier Reef (Central Section)*

Bowen · Merinda · Binbee · Collinsville · Mount Abbot 1055 · Bogie · Clarke Range · Don · Bowen · Gregory Range · Leichhardt Range · Burdekin Falls · Lake Dalrymple · Suttor · Cape · Mistake Creek · Fox Creek · Belyando · Avon Downs · Moray Downs · Abro · Alpha · Alpha Creek · Surbiton · Epping Forest National Park · Theresa Creek · Belyando

Airlie Beach · Cannonvale · Proserpine · Bloomsbury · Calen

Cape Upstart · Cape Upstart National Park · Abbot Bay · Ayr · Home Hill · Dalbeg · Millaroo · Mirna · Campaspe · Blackwood National Park

Warrego Range

Bowling Green Bay · Bowling Green Bay National Park · Woodstock · Mingela · Ravenswood · Balfe's Creek · Burdekin · Charters Towers · Homestead · Cape

Hervey Range · White Mountains National Park · Pentland · Torrens Creek · Torrens Creek · Prairie · Towerhill Creek · Flinders

Hillgrove · Maryvale · Basalt · Great Basalt Wall National Park · Porcupine Gorge National Park · Porcupine Creek · Hughenden

Kyong · Lake Buchanan · Lake Galilee · Aramac · Muttaburra · Cornish · Tangorin · Landsborough Creek · Aramac Creek · Kyabra · Reedy Creek · Patrick Creek · Yalleroi · Blackall · Jericho · Alice · Jordan Creek · Barcaldine · Barcoo · Lake

Bowen Downs · Thomson · Ilfracombe · Longreach · Tambo · Barcoo · Ravensbourne Creek · Lorne · Listowel Downs · Forest Hill · Augathella · Nive Downs · Nive · Ward · Warrego · Carwell · Caldervale · Westland · Bisford · Emmet · Windorah · Yaraka · Barcoo · Gowan Range · Tambo · Powell Creek · Hellhole Gorge National Park · Idalia National Park · Ambathala · Mariala National Park · Blackwater · Adavale · Langlo Crossing · Langlo · Bullo

Tropic of Capricorn

Great Dividing Range

20°S · 22°S · 24°S · 26°S · 18°S
146°E · 148°E · 150°E · 20° · 22° · 24°

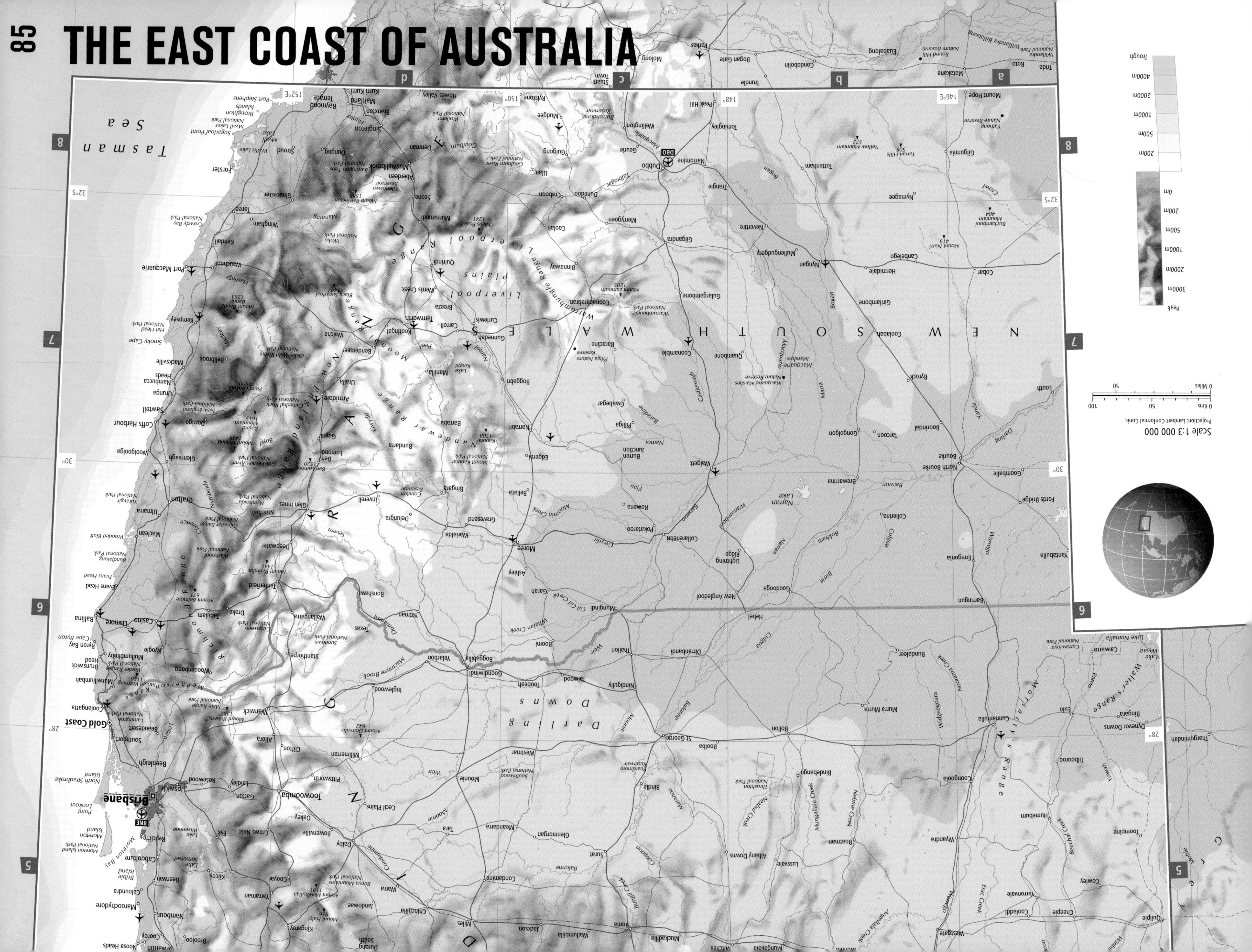

T a s m a n   S e a

Scale 1:3 000 000
Projection: Lambert Conformal Conic

Peak
3000m
2000m
1000m
500m
200m
0m

200m
500m
1000m
2000m
4000m
Trough

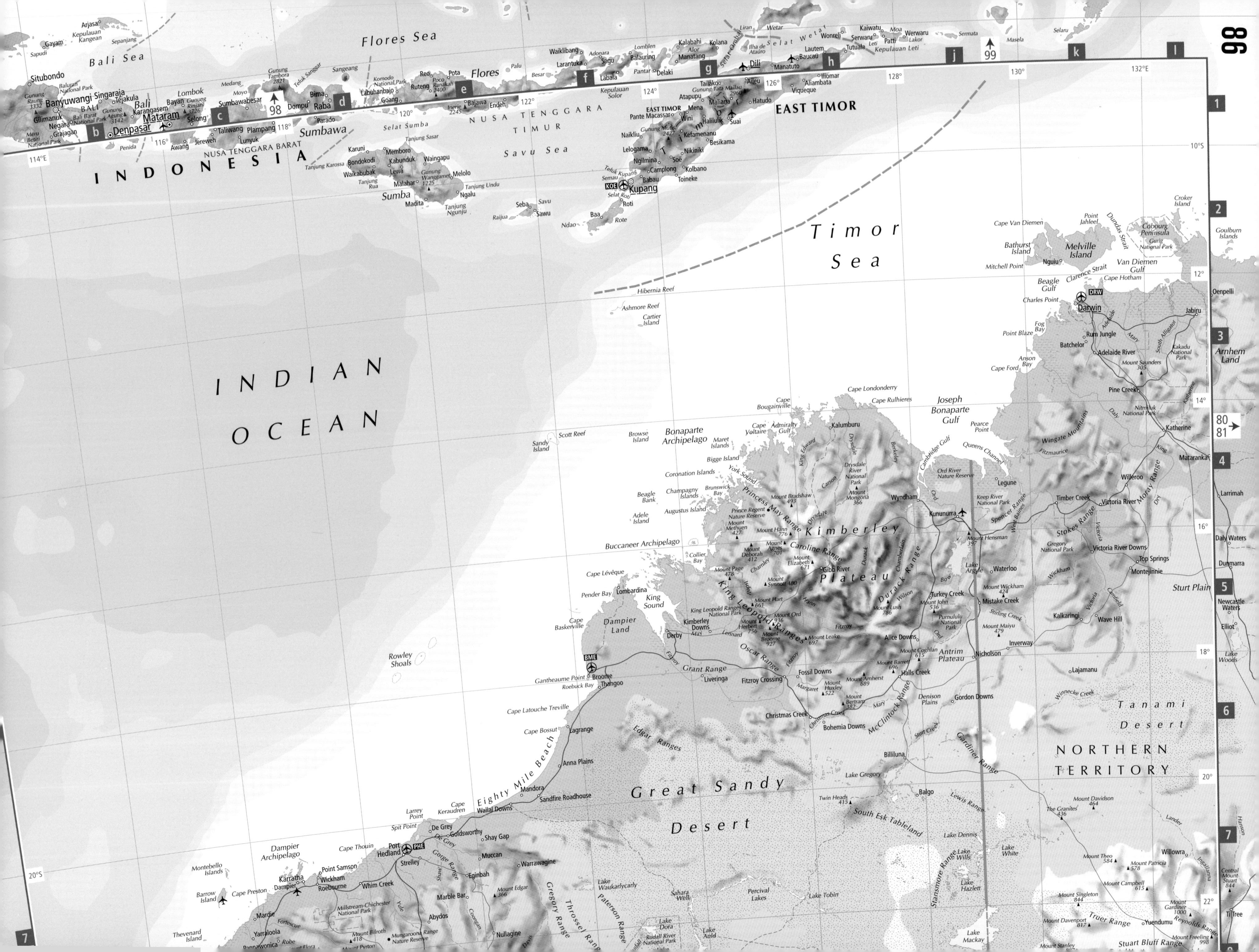

INDIAN OCEAN
Timor Sea
Savu Sea
Flores Sea
Bali Sea
INDONESIA
EAST TIMOR
NUSA TENGGARA TIMUR
NUSA TENGGARA BARAT
NORTHERN TERRITORY
Great Sandy Desert
Tanami Desert
Kimberley Plateau
Joseph Bonaparte Gulf
Bonaparte Archipelago
Buccaneer Archipelago
Dampier Land
Eighty Mile Beach
Arnhem Land
Van Diemen Gulf
Melville Island
Bathurst Island
Beagle Gulf
Darwin
Katherine
Kununurra
Wyndham
Derby
Broome
Port Hedland
Karratha
Dampier
Halls Creek
Fitzroy Crossing
Kupang
Dili
Denpasar
Mataram
Lombok
Bali
Sumbawa
Flores
Sumba
Timor
Wetar
Alor
Rote
Sawu
King Leopold Ranges
Durack Range
Oscar Range
Grant Range
Edgar Ranges
Gregory Range
Throssel Range
Paterson Range
McClintock Range
Gardiner Range
Stansmore Range
South Esk Tableland
Antrim Plateau
Stokes Range
Wingate Mountains
Moray Range
Sturt Plain
Rowley Shoals
Scott Reef
Ashmore Reef
Cartier Island
Hibernia Reef
Browse Island

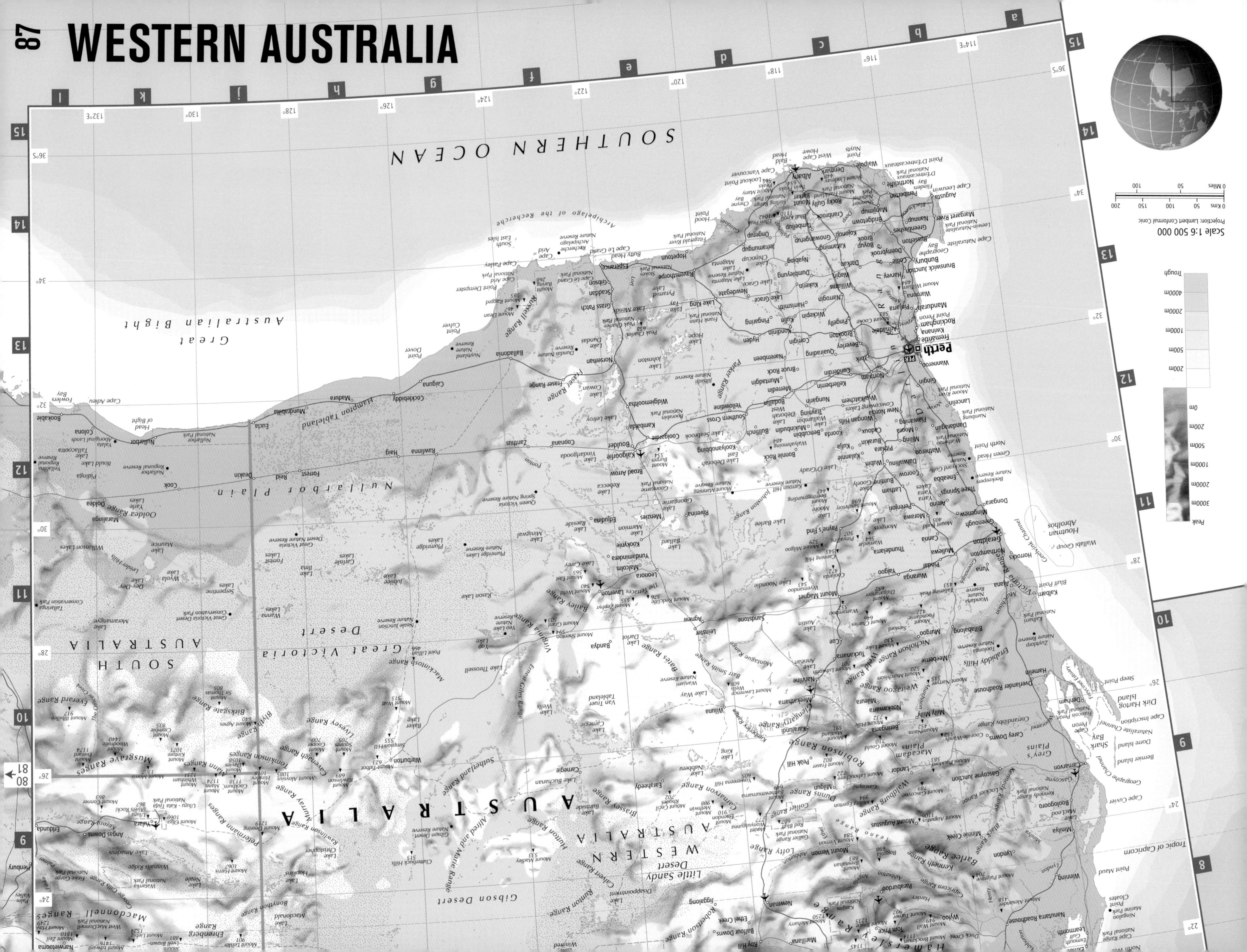

Scale 1:6 500 000
Projection: Lambert Conformal Conic

ASIA POPULATION
3,680,942,526

ASIA AREA
45,036,492km² (17,388,686 sq miles)

LARGEST COUNTRY
Asiatic Russia 13,119,582km² (5,065,471 sq miles)

SMALLEST COUNTRY
Maldives 298km² (115 sq miles)

LONGEST RIVERS
1 Yangtze (Chang Jiang), China 6380km (3964 miles)
2 Ob'-Irtysh, Kazakhstan/Russia 5568km (3459 miles)
3 Yenisey-Angara-Selenga, Russia 5550km (3448 miles)
4 Huang He (Yellow River), China 5464km (3395 miles)
5 Mekong, China/Myanmar/Laos/Thailand/Cambodia 4425km (2749 miles)
6 Heilong Hiang-Argun' (Amur), China/Russia 4416km (2744 miles)
7 Indus, Pakistan 3180km (1976 miles)

LOWEST POINT
8 Dead Sea, Israel/Jordan 400m (1312ft) below sea level

HIGHEST PEAKS
9 Mt Everest, China/Nepal 8848m (29,028ft)
10 K2 (Godwin Austen), India/Pakistan 8611m (28,251ft)
11 Kangchenjunga, India/Nepal 8586m (28,169ft)
12 Lhotse, China/Nepal 8516m (27,939ft)
13 Makalu, China/Nepal 8463m (27,765ft)
14 Cho Oyu, China/Nepal 8201m (26,906ft)

LARGEST DESERTS
20 Arabian 2,300,000km² (887,800 sq miles)
21 Gobi, China/Mongolia 1,166,000km² (450,076 sq miles)
22 Kyzylkum, Uzbekistan/Kazakhstan 300,000km² (115,800 sq miles)

WETTEST PLACE
23 Mawsynram, India 11,872mm (467in) average annual rainfall

DRIEST PLACE
24 Aden, Yemen 46mm (1.8in) average annual rainfall

LARGEST LAKES
15 Caspian Sea 371,000km² (143,243 sq miles)
16 Aral Sea 33,640km² (12,988 sq miles)
17 Lake Baikal, Asiatic Russia 30,500km² (11,776 sq miles)
18 Lake Balkhash, Kazakhstan 17,400km² (6718 sq miles)
19 Tônlé Sap, Cambodia 2850km² (1000 sq miles)

HIGHEST RECORDED TEMPERATURE
25 Tirat Zevi, Israel 53.9C° (129°F), June 21 1942

LOWEST RECORDED TEMPERATURE
26 Oymyakon, Russia -67.7C° (-89.9°F), Feb 6 1933

ASIA

The Earth's largest continent, Asia stretches from the Arctic Ocean to the equatorial rain forests of Borneo. Mountains and high plateaus dominate: two-thirds of the land is over 500m (1600ft) above sea level, and all the world's highest peaks are found in the Himalayas. In contrast to the high, cold deserts of Tibet and Mongolia, much of the south and east of the continent is drained by some of the longest rivers in the world. To the west, the Ural Mountains mark the boundary between European and Asiatic Russia, while to the south-west the narrow strip of the Red Sea and the Sinai Peninsula separates Asia and Africa.

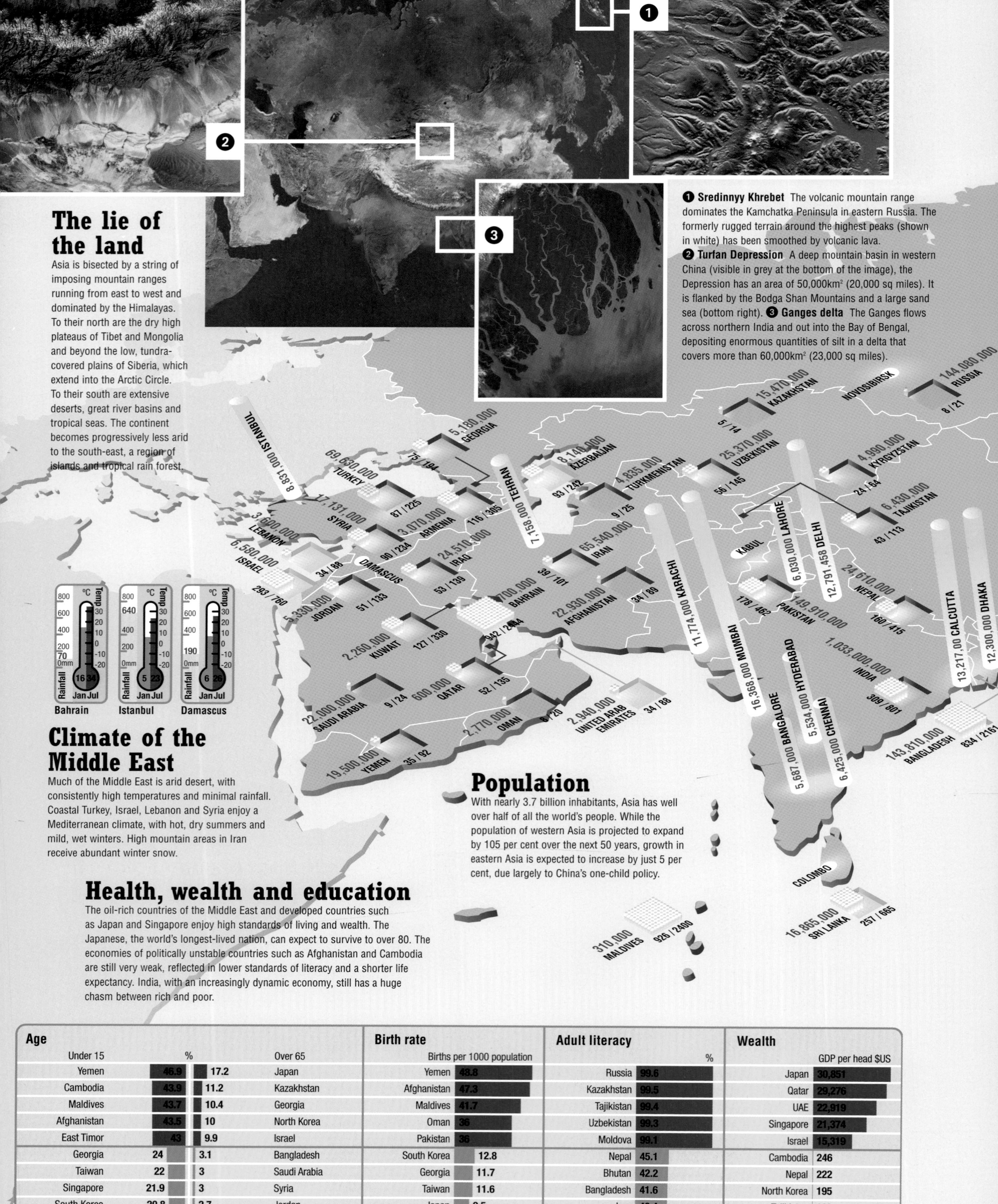

The lie of the land

Asia is bisected by a string of imposing mountain ranges running from east to west and dominated by the Himalayas. To their north are the dry high plateaus of Tibet and Mongolia and beyond the low, tundra-covered plains of Siberia, which extend into the Arctic Circle. To their south are extensive deserts, great river basins and tropical seas. The continent becomes progressively less arid to the south-east, a region of islands and tropical rain forest.

❶ Sredinnyy Khrebet The volcanic mountain range dominates the Kamchatka Peninsula in eastern Russia. The formerly rugged terrain around the highest peaks (shown in white) has been smoothed by volcanic lava.
❷ Turfan Depression A deep mountain basin in western China (visible in grey at the bottom of the image), the Depression has an area of 50,000km² (20,000 sq miles). It is flanked by the Bodga Shan Mountains and a large sand sea (bottom right). **❸ Ganges delta** The Ganges flows across northern India and out into the Bay of Bengal, depositing enormous quantities of silt in a delta that covers more than 60,000km² (23,000 sq miles).

Climate of the Middle East

Much of the Middle East is arid desert, with consistently high temperatures and minimal rainfall. Coastal Turkey, Israel, Lebanon and Syria enjoy a Mediterranean climate, with hot, dry summers and mild, wet winters. High mountain areas in Iran receive abundant winter snow.

Bahrain · **Istanbul** · **Damascus**

Population

With nearly 3.7 billion inhabitants, Asia has well over half of all the world's people. While the population of western Asia is projected to expand by 105 per cent over the next 50 years, growth in eastern Asia is expected to increase by just 5 per cent, due largely to China's one-child policy.

Health, wealth and education

The oil-rich countries of the Middle East and developed countries such as Japan and Singapore enjoy high standards of living and wealth. The Japanese, the world's longest-lived nation, can expect to survive to over 80. The economies of politically unstable countries such as Afghanistan and Cambodia are still very weak, reflected in lower standards of literacy and a shorter life expectancy. India, with an increasingly dynamic economy, still has a huge chasm between rich and poor.

Age				Birth rate		Adult literacy		Wealth	
Under 15	%	Over 65		Births per 1000 population		%		GDP per head $US	
Yemen	46.9	17.2	Japan	Yemen	48.8	Russia	99.6	Japan	30,851
Cambodia	43.9	11.2	Kazakhstan	Afghanistan	47.3	Kazakhstan	99.5	Qatar	29,276
Maldives	43.7	10.4	Georgia	Maldives	41.7	Tajikistan	99.4	UAE	22,919
Afghanistan	43.5	10	North Korea	Oman	36	Uzbekistan	99.3	Singapore	21,374
East Timor	43	9.9	Israel	Pakistan	36	Moldova	99.1	Israel	15,319
Georgia	24	3.1	Bangladesh	South Korea	12.8	Nepal	45.1	Cambodia	246
Taiwan	22	3	Saudi Arabia	Georgia	11.7	Bhutan	42.2	Nepal	222
Singapore	21.9	3	Syria	Taiwan	11.6	Bangladesh	41.6	North Korea	195
South Korea	20.8	2.7	Jordan	Japan	9.5	Iraq	40.4	Tajikistan	169
Japan	14.7	2.1	Bahrain	Armenia	9	Afghanistan	31.5	Myanmar (Burma)	97

Top five · Bottom five

Climate of Central and North Asia

Much of Central Asia has an extreme continental climate with huge seasonal variations in temperature: in the Gobi it falls to −40°C in winter, and climbs to 45°C in summer. Northern Russia has arctic winters, while the Caucasian nations have an almost Mediterranean climate.

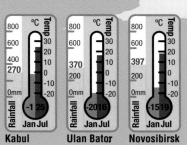

	Kabul	Ulan Bator	Novosibirsk

Asia: employment by sector

Country top ten	%			GDP $US million
Japan	1	31	68	3,933,000
China	15	51	34	1,259,400
India	25	25	50	496,800
South Korea	4	42	54	470,600
Taiwan	2	31	67	278,200
Saudi Arabia	5	51	44	185,632
Indonesia	17	41	42	180,000
Thailand	11	40	49	120,200
Iran	19	26	55	114,375
Israel	3	30	67	100,800

Primary (inc. Agriculture) %   ▪ Industry %   ▪ Service %

Employment

Japan, China and India are Asia's biggest economies. Japan leads the world market in high-tech goods and cars and India's broad industrial base is attracting foreign investment, with strong growth in high-tech support and development. Low labour costs have encouraged European and North America firms to transfer manufacture of textiles and other goods to China and south-east Asian nations, including Thailand, Vietnam and the Philippines. The oil industry and spin-off services are major employers in the Middle East. South and south-east Asia are important rice producers exporting internationally, but many other crops are still produced at subsistence level.

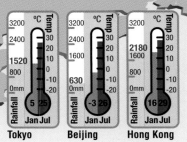

	Tokyo	Beijing	Hong Kong

Climate of East Asia

East Asia has great extremes, with monsoon rains and tropical temperatures in southern China and Japan, an arid climate in parts of northern China, and continental temperatures in Korea and northern Japan with cold winters and warm summers.

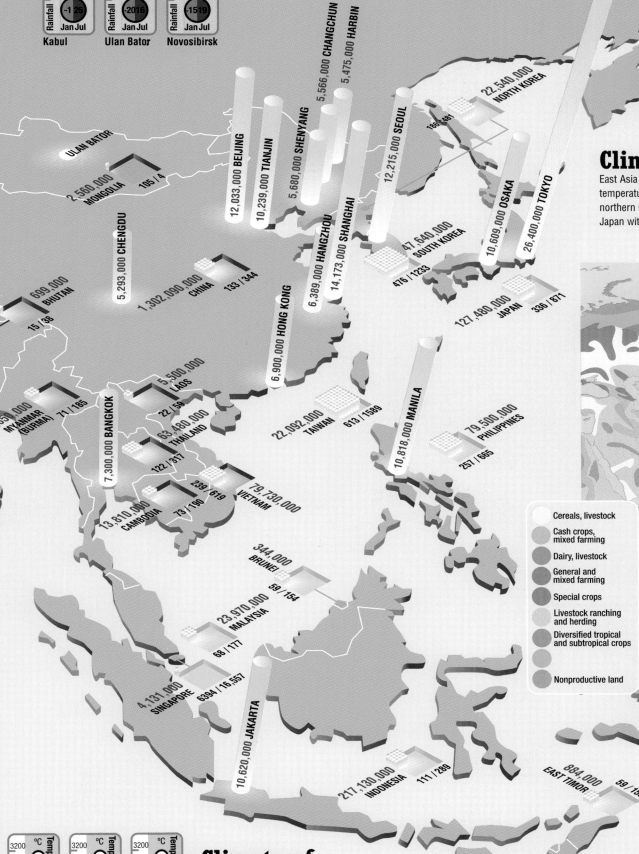

Cereals, livestock
Cash crops, mixed farming
Dairy, livestock
General and mixed farming
Special crops
Livestock ranching and herding
Diversified tropical and subtropical crops
Nonproductive land

How the land is used

Asia is still one of the least urbanized continents although development is progressing rapidly – particularly in the south and east, which have some of the world's largest and fastest-growing cities. The Middle East and Central Asia are mainly desert and the far north forest and tundra. In the south and south-east, particularly in India and eastern China, there is intensive farming of rice and other crops on the fertile river plains. The grasslands of Central Asia are grazed by herds of sheep and goats and are separated from the north by imposing mountain ranges. Large parts of the south-east are covered in rain forest.

	Delhi	Colombo	Bangkok

Climate of South and South-east Asia

Asiatic monsoon winds produce wet and dry seasons. The summer monsoon brings three to six months of heavy rainfall – up to 2000–3000mm (80–120in) of rain a year. The winds then reverse, creating drier winters. South-east Asia is hot and humid all year while eastern India is arid.

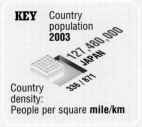

KEY Country population **2003**

127,480,000
JAPAN
336 / 871

Country density:
People per square **mile/km**

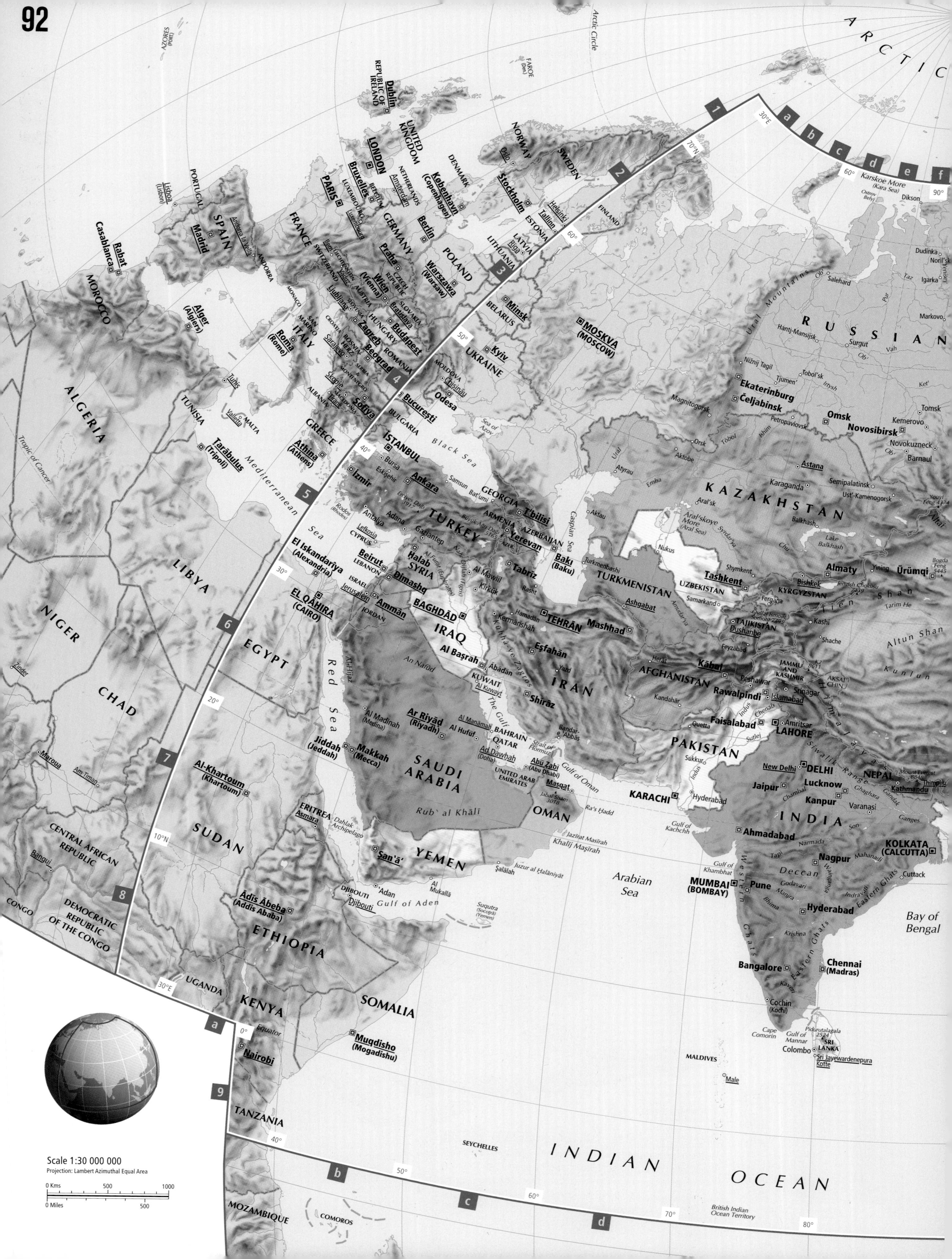
ARCTIC
Arctic Circle
AZORES (Port.)
FAROE (Den.)
REPUBLIC OF IRELAND
Dublin
UNITED KINGDOM
LONDON
NORWAY
Oslo
SWEDEN
Stockholm
DENMARK
København (Copenhagen)
NETHERLANDS
Amsterdam
BELGIUM
Bruxelles
LUXEMBOURG
PARIS
FRANCE
GERMANY
Berlin
POLAND
Warszawa (Warsaw)
PORTUGAL
Lisboa (Lisbon)
SPAIN
Madrid
ANDORRA
MOROCCO
Rabat
Casablanca
ALGERIA
Alger (Algiers)
TUNISIA
Tunis
MALTA
Valletta
ITALY
Roma (Rome)
SAN MARINO
MONACO
SWITZERLAND
AUSTRIA
Wien (Vienna)
CZECH REPUBLIC
Praha
SLOVAKIA
HUNGARY
Budapest
SLOVENIA
Ljubljana
CROATIA
Zagreb
BOSNIA HERZ.
Sarajevo
SERBIA
Beograd
MONTENEGRO
ALBANIA
MACEDONIA
Skopje
BULGARIA
Sofiya
GREECE
Athina (Athens)
ROMANIA
Bucureşti
MOLDOVA
Chişinău
UKRAINE
Kyiv
Odesa
BELARUS
Minsk
LITHUANIA
LATVIA
Riga
ESTONIA
Tallinn
Helsinki
FINLAND
MOSKVA (MOSCOW)
RUSSIAN
Karskoe More (Kara Sea)
Ostrov Belyi
Dikson
Dudinka
Noril'sk
Igarka
Salehard
Ural Mountains
Ob'
Markovo
Hanti-Mansijsk
Surgut
Nižnij Tagil
Tobol'sk
Ekaterinburg
Čeljabinsk
Tjumen'
Magnitogorsk
Omsk
Novosibirsk
Tomsk
Kemerovo
Novokuznetsk
Barnaul
Petropavlovsk
Orsk
Aktobe
Astana
Karaganda
Semipalatinsk
Ust'-Kamenogorsk
KAZAKHSTAN
Aral'sk
Aral'skoye More (Aral Sea)
Balkhash
Lake Balkhash
Atyrau
Aktau
Caspian Sea
Black Sea
Sea of Azov
İSTANBUL
Bursa
Eskişehir
İzmir
Ankara
Samsun
TURKEY
Antalya
Adana
Gaziantep
Rodos (Rhodes)
CYPRUS
Lefkosia
GEORGIA
T'bilisi
ARMENIA
Yerevan
AZERBAIJAN
Bakı (Baku)
Mediterranean Sea
Tarābulus (Tripoli)
LIBYA
El Iskandarîya (Alexandria)
EL QÂHIRA (CAIRO)
EGYPT
LEBANON
Beirut
SYRIA
Halab
Dimashq
ISRAEL
Jerusalem
JORDAN
'Ammān
IRAQ
BAGHDĀD
Al Mawşil
Al Başrah
KUWAIT
Al Kuwayt
Tabrīz
Rasht
TEHRĀN
Hamadān
Kermānshāh
Eşfahān
Yazd
Shīrāz
IRAN
Mashhad
Bandar-e 'Abbās
TURKMENISTAN
Turkmenbashi
Ashgabat
UZBEKISTAN
Nukus
Tashkent
Samarkand
KYRGYZSTAN
Bishkek
TAJIKISTAN
Dushanbe
Almaty
Ürümqi
Kashi
Shache
Tarim He
Altun Shan
Kunlun
AFGHANISTAN
Herāt
Kābul
Kandahār
Peshawar
Rawalpindi
Islamabad
JAMMU AND KASHMIR
Srinagar
AKSAI CHIN
PAKISTAN
Quetta
Faisalabad
LAHORE
Amritsar
Sukkur
KARACHI
Hyderabad
NIGER
Zinder
CHAD
SUDAN
Al-Khartoum (Khartoum)
Red Sea
An Nafūd
SAUDI ARABIA
Al Madīnah (Medina)
Ar Riyāḑ (Riyadh)
Al Hufūf
Jiddah (Jeddah)
Makkah (Mecca)
Rub' al Khālī
BAHRAIN
Al Manāmah
QATAR
Ad Dawḩah (Doha)
UNITED ARAB EMIRATES
Abū Zabī (Abu Dhabi)
The Gulf
Strait of Hormuz
Gulf of Oman
Masqaţ
OMAN
Ra's al Hadd
ERITREA
Asmara
Dahlak Archipelago
YEMEN
Şan'ā'
'Adan
Al Mukallā
Şalālah
DJIBOUTI
Djibouti
Gulf of Aden
Suquţrā (Socotra) (Yemen)
ETHIOPIA
Ādīs Ābeba (Addis Ababa)
SOMALIA
Muqdisho (Mogadishu)
CENTRAL AFRICAN REPUBLIC
Bangui
DEMOCRATIC REPUBLIC OF THE CONGO
CONGO
Maroua
UGANDA
KENYA
Nairobi
Equator
TANZANIA
MOZAMBIQUE
COMOROS
SEYCHELLES
Arabian Sea
INDIAN OCEAN
MALDIVES
Male
British Indian Ocean Territory
Gulf of Kachchh
Gulf of Khambhat
Ahmadabad
MUMBAI (BOMBAY)
Pune
INDIA
New Delhi
DELHI
Jaipur
Lucknow
Kanpur
Varanasi
NEPAL
Kathmandu
Thimphu
Nagpur
KOLKATA (CALCUTTA)
Cuttack
Deccan
Hyderabad
Bangalore
Chennai (Madras)
Cochin (Kochi)
Bay of Bengal
Eastern Ghats
Western Ghats
Gulf of Mannar
Cape Comorin
SRI LANKA
Colombo
Sri Jayewardenepura Kotte
Tropic of Cancer
Scale 1:30 000 000
Projection: Lambert Azimuthal Equal Area
0 Kms 500 1000
0 Miles 500

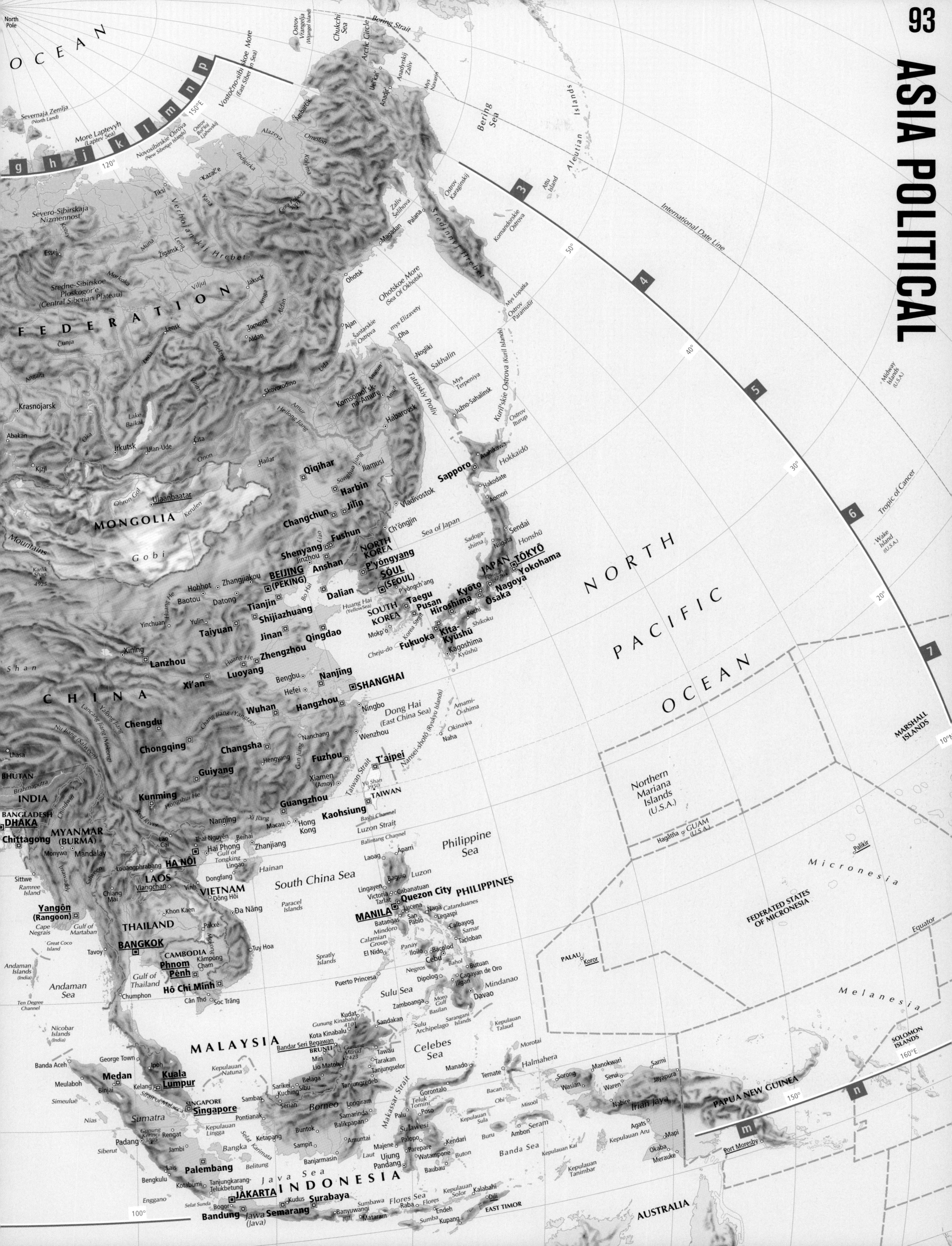

OCEAN

North Pole

Severnaja Zemlja (North Land)

More Laptevyh (Laptev Sea)

Vostočno-sibirskoe More (East Siberian Sea)

Ostrov Vrangelja (Wrangel Island)

Chukchi Sea

Bering Strait

Arctic Circle

Severo-Sibirskaja Nizmennost'

Novosibirskie Ostrova (New Siberian Islands)

Tiksi

Kotel'nyj

Anabarskij Zaliv

Aleutian Islands

Bering Sea

Atka Island

International Date Line

Midway Islands (U.S.A.)

Srednij Hrebet

Wake Island (U.S.A.)

Tropic of Cancer

NORTH

PACIFIC

OCEAN

MARSHALL ISLANDS

Northern Mariana Islands (U.S.A.)

GUAM (U.S.A.)

Hagåtña

Palikir

Micronesia

FEDERATED STATES OF MICRONESIA

PALAU

Koror

Melanesia

SOLOMON ISLANDS

FEDERATION

MONGOLIA

Ulaanbaatar

Gobi

CHINA

Lanzhou

Xi'an

Chengdu

Chongqing

Guiyang

Kunming

Beijing (Peking)

Tianjin

Shijiazhuang

Taiyuan

Jinan

Zhengzhou

Luoyang

Wuhan

Changsha

Hengyang

Nanchang

Fuzhou

Xiamen (Amoy)

Guangzhou

Kaohsiung

Hangzhou

Nanjing

SHANGHAI

Hefei

Ningbo

Wenzhou

Qiqihar

Harbin

Jilin

Changchun

Fushun

Shenyang

Anshan

Dalian

Qingdao

NORTH KOREA

P'yŏngyang

SŎUL (SEOUL)

SOUTH KOREA

Taegu

Pusan

Sapporo

Hokkaidō

JAPAN

TŌKYŌ

Yokohama

Kyōto

Nagoya

Ōsaka

Hiroshima

Fukuoka

Kita-Kyūshū

Kagoshima

Kyūshū

Sea of Japan

Vladivostok

Sakhalin

Kuril'skie Ostrova (Kuril Islands)

Ohotskoe More (Sea Of Okhotsk)

Huang Hai (Yellow Sea)

Dong Hai (East China Sea)

T'aipei

TAIWAN

Hong Kong

Macau

Hainan

South China Sea

Philippine Sea

Luzon

Manila

Quezon City

PHILIPPINES

Mindanao

Davao

BHUTAN

INDIA

BANGLADESH

DHAKA

Chittagong

MYANMAR (BURMA)

Mandalay

Yangôn (Rangoon)

THAILAND

BANGKOK

LAOS

Viangchan

HÀ NỘI

VIETNAM

CAMBODIA

Phnom Pênh

Hồ Chi Minh

MALAYSIA

BRUNEI

Bandar Seri Begawan

Borneo

SINGAPORE

Singapore

Kuala Lumpur

Medan

Sumatra

Palembang

JAKARTA

INDONESIA

Bandung

Semarang

Surabaya

Jawa (Java)

Celebes Sea

Sulawesi

Banda Sea

Irian Jaya

PAPUA NEW GUINEA

Port Moresby

AUSTRALIA

EAST TIMOR

RUSSIAN FEDERATION

RESPUBLIKA SAKHA

KAMCHATSKIJ KRAJ (Kamchatka Peninsula)

Poluostrov Kamčatskij

Sea of Okhotsk

Kuril'skie Ostrova (Kuril Islands)

HABAROVSKII KRAJ

Komsomol'sk-na-Amure

Habarovsk

PRIMORSKII KRAJ

Vladivostok

Nahodka

Sakhalin (Sakhalin)

SAKHALINSKAJA OBLAST'

Južno-Sahalinsk

Hokkaidō

Sapporo

Asahikawa

Otaru

Hakodate

Kuširo

JAPAN

Honshū

Sendai

TOKYO

Yokohama

Kyoto

Osaka

Kōbe

Nagoya

Sea of Japan

Izu-Shotō

Ogasawara-shotō (Bonin Islands)

Ryukyu Islands (Nansei-shotō)

Naha

Okinawa

East China Sea

NORTH KOREA

Pyongyang

Hamhung

SOUTH KOREA

SŎUL (Seoul)

Inch'ŏn

Taejŏn

Taegu

Pusan

Kwangju

Kagoshima

Kyūshū

Fukuoka

Hiroshima

MONGOLIA

Ulaanbaatar (Ulan Bator)

Gobi

RESPUBLIKA BURJATIJA

Ulan-Ude

Ozero Bajkal (Lake Baikal)

Irkutsk

IRKUTSKAJA OBLAST'

Bratsk

RESPUBLIKA TUVA

RESPUBLIKA ALTAI

Krasnojarsk

KRASNOJARSKII KRAJ

Tomsk

Kemerovo

Novosibirsk

Barnaul

Novokuzneck

Prokop'evsk

ALTAJSKII KRAJ

KAZACHSTAN

Omsk

CHITINSKAJA OBLAST'

Čita

AMURSKAJA OBLAST'

Blagoveščensk

EVREJSKAJA AVTONOMNAJA OBLAST'

HEILONGJIANG

Harbin

Qiqihar

Suihua

Yichun

Hegang

Jiamusi

Shuangyashan

Jixi

Mudanjiang

NEI MONGOL ZIZHIQU

Hailar

Manzhouli

Hohhot

Baotou

Wuhai

JILIN

Changchun

Jilin

Siping

LIAONING

Shenyang

Fushun

Benxi

Anshan

Dalian

Jinzhou

BEIJING (Peking)

TIANJIN

HEBEI

Tangshan

Baoding

Shijiazhuang

Zhangjiakou

Datong

SHANXI

Taiyuan

Linfen

SHANDONG

Jinan

Qingdao

Yantai

Weifang

Zibo

Yellow Sea

Bo Hai

NINGXIA

Yinchuan

GANSU

Lanzhou

QINGHAI

Xining

XINJIANG UYGUR ZIZHIQU

Ürümqi

Tarim Pendi

Taklimakan Shamo

Kunlun Shan

XIZANG ZIZHIQU

Lhasa

Altun Shan

Qilian Shan

Qaidam Pendi

SHAANXI

Xi'an

Baoji

Xianyang

Yan'an

HENAN

Zhengzhou

Luoyang

Kaifeng

Anyang

Xinxiang

Pingdingshan

ANHUI

Hefei

Bengbu

Huainan

JIANGSU

Nanjing

Wuxi

Suzhou

Xuzhou

Changzhou

SHANGHAI

ZHEJIANG

Hangzhou

Ningbo

Wenzhou

Shaoxing

Jinhua

Quzhou

HUBEI

Wuhan

Yichang

Xiangfan

Jingzhou

SICHUAN

Chengdu

Mianyang

Leshan

Yibin

Zigong

CHONGQING

Chongqing

GUIZHOU

Guiyang

Zunyi

YUNNAN

Kunming

Qujing

Zhaotong

Chuxiong

HUNAN

Changsha

Zhuzhou

Hengyang

Yueyang

Changde

JIANGXI

Nanchang

JIANGXI

FUJIAN

Fuzhou

Xiamen

Quanzhou

GUANGXI ZHUANGZU ZIZHIQU

Guilin

Liuzhou

Hechi

TAIWAN

Taipei

Kaohsiung

T'aichung

Taizhong

Chilung

MYANMAR (BURMA)

BHUTAN

INDIA

BANGLADESH

DHAKA

Guwahati

Tropic of Cancer

Kazan-rettō (Volcano Islands)

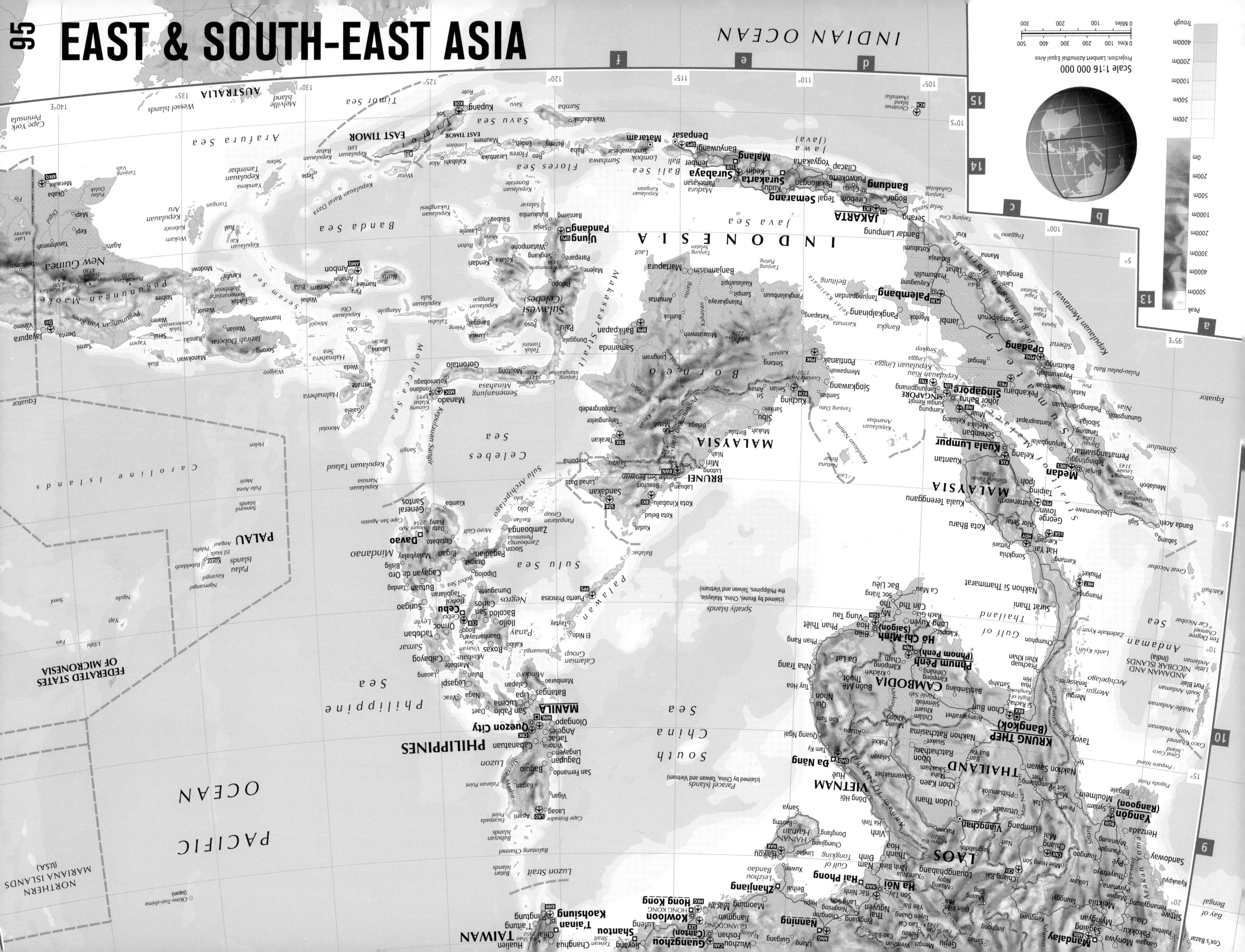

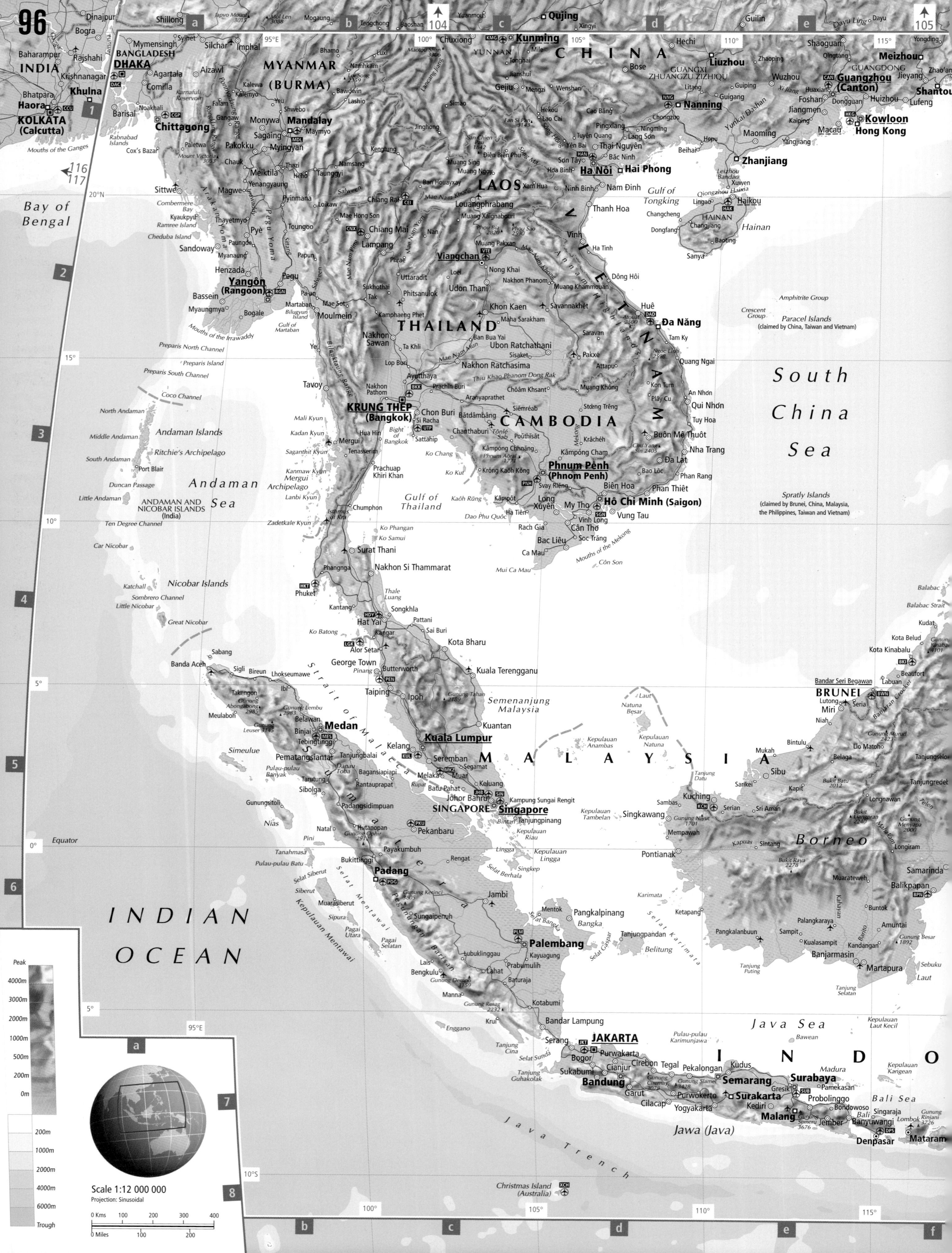
104
105
116
117
95°E
100°
105°
110°
115°
20°N
15°
10°
5°
0°
5°
10°S
a
b
c
d
e
f
1
2
3
4
5
6
7
8
INDIA
BANGLADESH
DHAKA
Khulna
Haora
KOLKATA
(Calcutta)
Dinajpur
Bogra
Shillong
Baharampur
Rajshahi
Krishnanagar
Bhatpara
Mymensingh
Sylhet
Silchar
Imphal
Agartala
Aizawl
Comilla
Barisal
Noakhali
Chittagong
Cox's Bazar
Mouths of the Ganges
MYANMAR
(BURMA)
Mandalay
Maymyo
Monywa
Sagaing
Myingyan
Pakokku
Meiktila
Taunggyi
Magwe
Sittwe
Bhamo
Lashio
Kengtung
Yenangyaung
Pyinmana
Loikaw
Thayetmyo
Pyè
Toungoo
Sandoway
Henzada
Yangôn
(Rangoon)
Bassein
Myaungmya
Pegu
Bogale
Moulmein
Martaban
Mouths of the Irrawaddy
Gulf of Martaban
Ye
Tavoy
Mergui
Mergui Archipelago
Bay of Bengal
Preparis North Channel
Preparis Island
Preparis South Channel
Coco Channel
North Andaman
Middle Andaman
Andaman Islands
Ritchie's Archipelago
South Andaman
Port Blair
Duncan Passage
Little Andaman
Andaman Sea
ANDAMAN AND NICOBAR ISLANDS
(India)
Ten Degree Channel
Car Nicobar
Nicobar Islands
Katchall
Sombrero Channel
Little Nicobar
Great Nicobar
CHINA
YUNNAN
Kunming
Qujing
Chuxiong
Gejiu
Mengzi
Bose
GUANGXI
ZHUANGZU ZIZHIQU
Liuzhou
Nanning
Guilin
Hechi
Wuzhou
Guangzhou
(Canton)
Foshan
Dongguan
Huizhou
Jiangmen
Macau
Kowloon
Hong Kong
Shaoguan
Meizhou
Shantou
GUANGDONG
Zhanjiang
Beihai
Maoming
Haikou
HAINAN
Hainan
Sanya
Gulf of Tongking
LAOS
Louangphrabang
Viangchan
Savannakhet
Pakxé
Attapu
VIETNAM
Ha Nôi
Hai Phong
Nam Đinh
Thanh Hoa
Vinh
Ha Tinh
Dông Hôi
Huê
Đa Năng
Quang Ngai
Qui Nhơn
Kon Tum
Plây Cu
Buôn Mê Thuôt
Nha Trang
Đa Lat
Phan Rang
Phan Thiêt
Biên Hoa
Hô Chi Minh (Saigon)
Vung Tau
My Tho
Vinh Long
Cân Thơ
Soc Trăng
Rach Gia
Bac Liêu
Ca Mau
Mouths of the Mekong
Côn Son
THAILAND
Chiang Mai
Chiang Rai
Lampang
Phrae
Nan
Uttaradit
Phitsanulok
Sukhothai
Tak
Mae Sot
Kamphaeng Phet
Nakhon Sawan
Udon Thani
Khon Kaen
Nong Khai
Nakhon Phanom
Maha Sarakham
Ubon Ratchathani
Nakhon Ratchasima
Lop Buri
Ayutthaya
KRUNG THEP
(Bangkok)
Nakhon Pathom
Chon Buri
Si Racha
Sattahip
Hua Hin
Prachuap Khiri Khan
Chumphon
Surat Thani
Nakhon Si Thammarat
Phuket
Songkhla
Hat Yai
Gulf of Thailand
Ko Samui
Ko Phangan
CAMBODIA
Phnum Pénh
(Phnom Penh)
Bătdâmbâng
Siĕmréab
Kâmpóng Cham
Kâmpôt
Krâchéh
Stœng Trêng
Tônlé Sab
MALAYSIA
Semenanjung Malaysia
Alor Setar
George Town
Butterworth
Taiping
Ipoh
Kota Bharu
Kuala Terengganu
Kuantan
Kuala Lumpur
Kelang
Seremban
Melaka
Muar
Batu Pahat
Keluang
Johor Bahru
SINGAPORE
Singapore
Kuching
Sibu
Bintulu
Miri
Kota Kinabalu
Kudat
Labuan
BRUNEI
Bandar Seri Begawan
Borneo
South China Sea
Paracel Islands
(claimed by China, Taiwan and Vietnam)
Spratly Islands
(claimed by Brunei, China, Malaysia, the Philippines, Taiwan and Vietnam)
Strait of Malacca
Sumatera
Banda Aceh
Sabang
Lhokseumawe
Medan
Binjai
Tebingtinggi
Pematangsiantar
Tanjungbalai
Sibolga
Padangsidimpuan
Pekanbaru
Bukittinggi
Padang
Jambi
Palembang
Bengkulu
Lahat
Bandar Lampung
Simeulue
Nias
Kepulauan Mentawai
Bangka
Pangkalpinang
Belitung
Tanjungpandan
Pontianak
Singkawang
Ketapang
Palangkaraya
Banjarmasin
Balikpapan
Samarinda
INDO
Java Sea
Jawa (Java)
JAKARTA
Bogor
Sukabumi
Bandung
Cirebon
Tegal
Pekalongan
Semarang
Surakarta
Yogyakarta
Surabaya
Malang
Madura
Bali Sea
Denpasar
Mataram
Java Trench
Christmas Island
(Australia)
Equator
INDIAN OCEAN
Peak
4000m
3000m
2000m
1000m
500m
200m
0m
200m
1000m
2000m
4000m
6000m
Trough
Scale 1:12 000 000
Projection: Sinusoidal
0 Kms
100
200
300
400
0 Miles
100
200

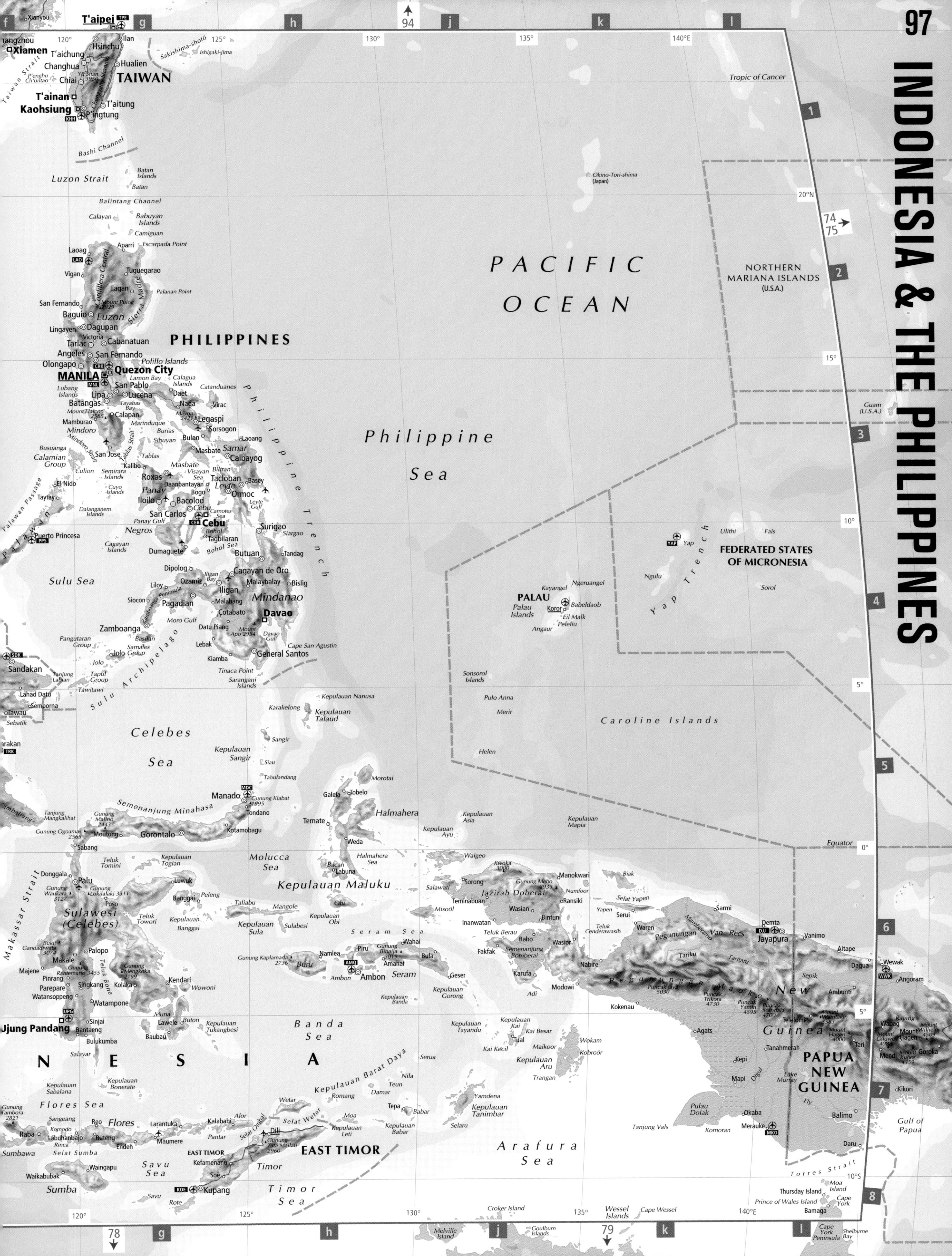

T'aipei g h j 94 j k l

Xiamen
Changzhou
T'aichung
Changhua
Chiai
T'ainan
Kaohsiung
P'ingtung

TAIWAN

Hsinchu
Hualien
Ilan
Sakishima-shotō
Ishigaki-jima

Bashi Channel

Luzon Strait

Batan Islands
Batan

Balintang Channel

Calayan
Babuyan Islands
Camiguan

Laoag
Aparri
Escarpada Point
Vigan
Tuguegarao

Cordillera Central
Ilagan
Palanan Point

San Fernando
Mount Pulog 2922
Baguio
Luzon
Sierra Madre
Lingayen
Dagupan
Tarlac
Victoria
Cabanatuan

PHILIPPINES

Angeles
San Fernando
Olongapo
CRK
Polillo Islands
MANILA
Quezon City
MNL
Lamon Bay
Calagua Islands
San Pablo
Catanduanes
Lubang Islands
Lipa
Lucena
Daet
Mamburao
Batangas
Tayabas Bay
Naga
Virac
Calapan
Marinduque
Legaspi
Mount Halcon 2585
Mayon 2421
Sorsogon

PACIFIC
OCEAN

Okino-Tori-shima
(Japan)

Tropic of Cancer

1

20°N

74
75

**NORTHERN
MARIANA ISLANDS**
(U.S.A.)

2

15°

Guam
(U.S.A.)

3

Mindoro
Mindoro Strait
San Jose
Busuanga
Calamian Group
Culion
Semirara Islands
El Nido
Cuyo Islands
Taytay
Dalanganem Islands

Tablas
Burias
Bulan
Laoang
Masbate
Samar
Calbayog
Visayan Sea
Biliran
Tacloban
Leyte
Ormoc
Basey

*Philippine
Sea*

10°

Roxas
Panay
Iloilo
Bacolod
San Carlos
Cebu
Bohol
CEB
Negros
Dumaguete
Bohol Sea
Tagbilaran
Butuan
Surigao
Siargao
Tandag

Camotes
Leyte Gulf

Yap
YAP
Ulithi
Fais

**FEDERATED STATES
OF MICRONESIA**

Palawan
Puerto Princesa
PPS

Sulu Sea

Cagayan Islands

Dipolog
Iligan Bay
Cagayan de Oro
Malaybalay
Bislig

Liloy
Ozamiz
Iligan
Mindanao
Siocon
Pagadian
Malabang
Cotabato
Zamboanga
Datu Piang
Davao

Kayangel
Ngeruangel
Ngulu

PALAU
Palau Islands
Koror
Babeldaob
Eil Malk
Peleliu
Angaur

Sorol

4

Sandakan
SDK
Basilan
Samales Group
Jolo
Lebak
Mount Apo 2954
Davao Gulf
Cape San Agustin
Kiamba
General Santos

Pangutaran Group
Sulu Archipelago
Tinaca Point
Sarangani Islands

Sonsorol Islands

Pulo Anna
Merir

Caroline Islands

5°

Tawitawi
Tapul Group

Kepulauan Nanusa
Karakelong
Kepulauan Talaud

Helen

Lahad Datu
Semporna
Tawau
Sebatik

Sangir

*Celebes
Sea*

Kepulauan Sangir
Siau
Tahulandang

Morotai

5

TRK

Sarakan

Tanjung Labian

Semenanjung Minahasa
Manado
MDC
Gunung Klabat 1995
Tondano

Galela
Tobelo

Equator
0°

Tanjung Mangkalihat

Kotamobagu

Ternate
Weda

Halmahera

Kepulauan Asia
Kepulauan Mapia

Gunung Waukara 4127

Gorontalo

*Molucca
Sea*

Halmahera Sea
Bacan
Labuna

Kepulauan Ayu

Waigeo
Kwoka 3000

Biak
Manokwari
Numfoor

Sarmi

6

Donggala
Palu
Gunung Lokilalaki 3311
Poso

Luwuk
Banggai

Peleng

Taliabu
Mangole

Obi

Sorong
Jazirah Doberai
Salawati
Misoöl
Gunung Mibo 2939
Ransiki
Teminabuan
Wasian
Bintuni

Selat Yapen
Yapen
Serui
Teluk Cenderawasih
Waren

Demta
Jayapura
Yanimo

5°

Makassar Strait

Gunung Waluka

**Sulawesi
(Celebes)**

Bukit Gandadiwata 3074

Makale
Rantemario 3455
Gunung Mengkoka 2790

Palopo

Teluk Tomini
Kepulauan Togian

Teluk Tolo

Kepulauan Banggai

Kepulauan Sula

Kepulauan Obi

Seram Sea
Gunung Binaia 3027
Piru
Wahai
Bula

Namlea
Baru
AMQ
Amahai
Ambon
Seram

Teluk Berau
Fakfak
Babo
Semenanjung Bomberai
Geser

Karufa
Kepulauan Gorong
Adi

Inanwatan

Nabire
Modowi

Mamberamo
Pegunungan Van Rees
Tariku
Taritatu

New

Wewak
WWK

Parepare
Sinkang
Kolaka
Kendari
Wowoni

Watansoppeng
Watampone

Teluk Bone

Majene

Pinrang

*Banda
Sea*

Kepulauan Banda

Kepulauan Tanimbar
Kepulauan Kai
Kai Besar

Agats

Puncak Jaya 5030
Puncak Trikora 4730
Pegunungan Maoke
Puncak Mandala 4760
Puncak Yamin 4595

Guinea

Angoram

Mount Wilhelm

7

Ujung Pandang
UPG

Bantaeng
Bulukumba

Sinjai

Muna
Lawele
Buton

Kepulauan Tukangbesi

Kokenau
Kepi
Tual
Kai Kecil
Maikoor
Kobroör
Wokam
Kepulauan Aru
Trangan

Teluk Maro

Kepulauan Tayandu

Mapi

**PAPUA
NEW
GUINEA**

Lake Murray

Kikori

Kepulauan Sabalana
Kepulauan Bonerate

Salayar

Flores Sea

Kepulauan Barat Daya

Wetar
Nila
Teun
Damar
Serua
Babar

Yamdena

Selaru

Tanjung Vals
Komoran

Okaba
Merauke
MKQ

Balimo

Fly

Gulf of
Papua

Gunung Tambora 2821

Sangeang
Reo
Flores
Ruteng
Komodo
Rinca

Larantuka
Pantar
Alor
Kalabahi

Moa
Romang

Selat Wetar

Tepa
Kepulauan Babar

East Timor

Daru

10°S

N   E   S   I   A

Sumbawa
Raba

Labuhanbajo
Endeh
Maumere
Sumba
Waingapu

*Savu
Sea*

Dili
Gunung Tata Mailau 2960
EAST TIMOR
Kefamenanu
Soë
Timor
KOE
Kupang

*Timor
Sea*

Wetar

Selat Ombai

*Arafura
Sea*

Kroker Island
Wessel Islands
Cape Wessel

Pulau Dolak

Thursday Island
Prince of Wales Island

Cape York

Moa Island

8

Waikabubak
Rote
Savu

Melville Island
Goulburn Islands

78 g 120° h 125° j 79 130° k 135° l 140°E
Cape York Peninsula
Shelburne Bay
Bamaga

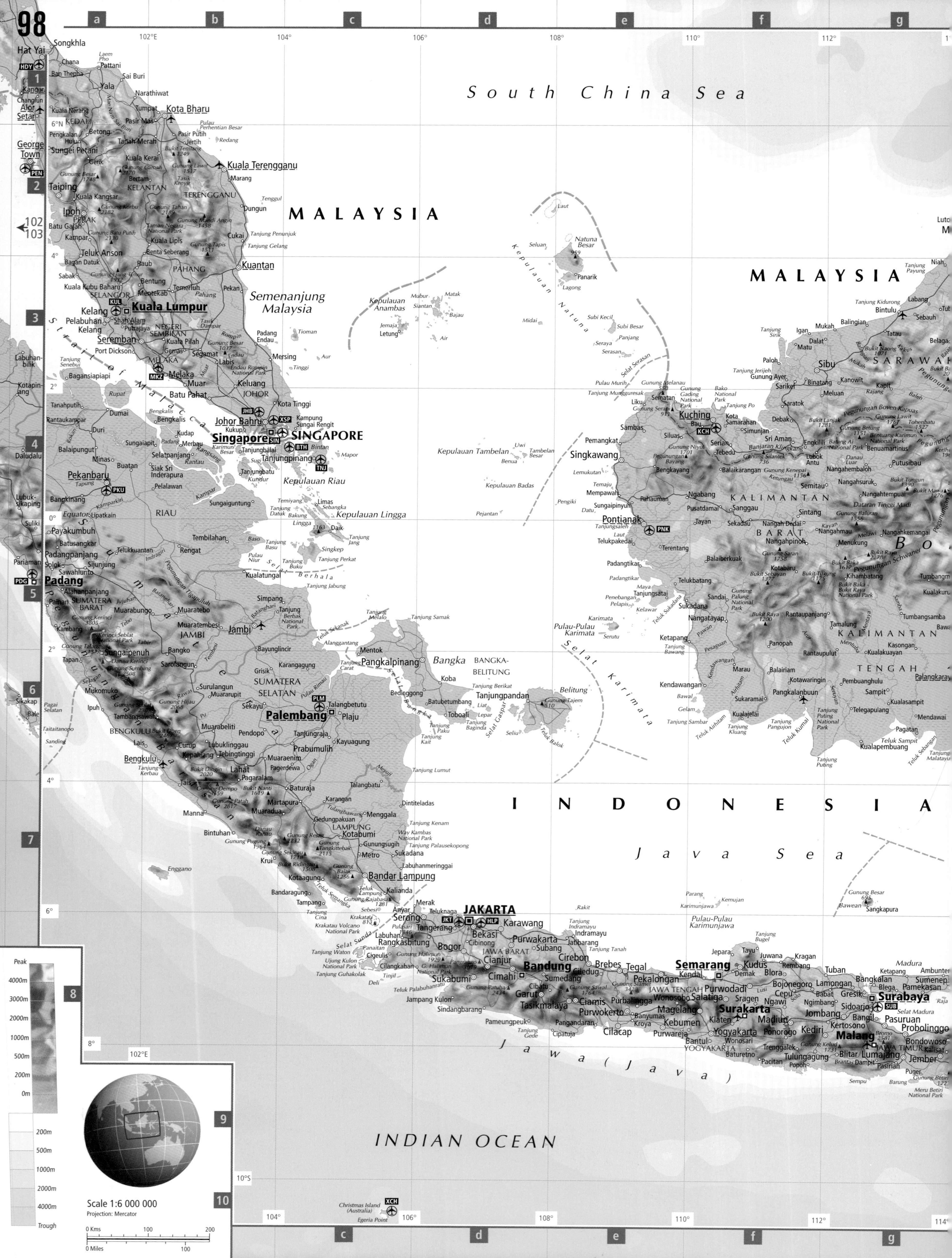

South China Sea

MALAYSIA

MALAYSIA

Semenanjung
Malaysia

Kepulauan
Anambas

Kepulauan Natuna

Natuna
Besar

Kuala Lumpur

Kuala Terengganu

KELANTAN
TERENGGANU

PAHANG

Kuantan

SELANGOR
NEGERI
SEMBILAN

Melaka

JOHOR

Johor Bahru

Singapore **SINGAPORE**

Kepulauan Riau

Kepulauan Tambelan

Kepulauan Lingga

RIAU

Kepulauan Badas

Pekanbaru

SARAWAK

Kuching

Singkawang

Pontianak

KALIMANTAN
BARAT

Padang

SUMATERA
BARAT

JAMBI

Jambi

Bangka

BANGKA-
BELITUNG

Tanjungpandan

Belitung

KALIMANTAN
TENGAH

SUMATERA
SELATAN

Palembang

Pangkalpinang

Selat Karimata

Bengkulu

BENGKULU

LAMPUNG

Bandar Lampung

INDONESIA

Java Sea

JAKARTA

JAWA BARAT

Bandung

Semarang

JAWA TENGAH

Surakarta

Surabaya

Madura

Yogyakarta

YOGYAKARTA

JAWA TIMUR

Malang

Jawa (Java)

INDIAN OCEAN

Peak
4000m
3000m
2000m
1000m
500m
200m
0m

200m
500m
1000m
2000m
4000m
Trough

Scale 1:6 000 000
Projection: Mercator

0 Kms   100   200
0 Miles   100

Christmas Island
(Australia)
Egeria Point

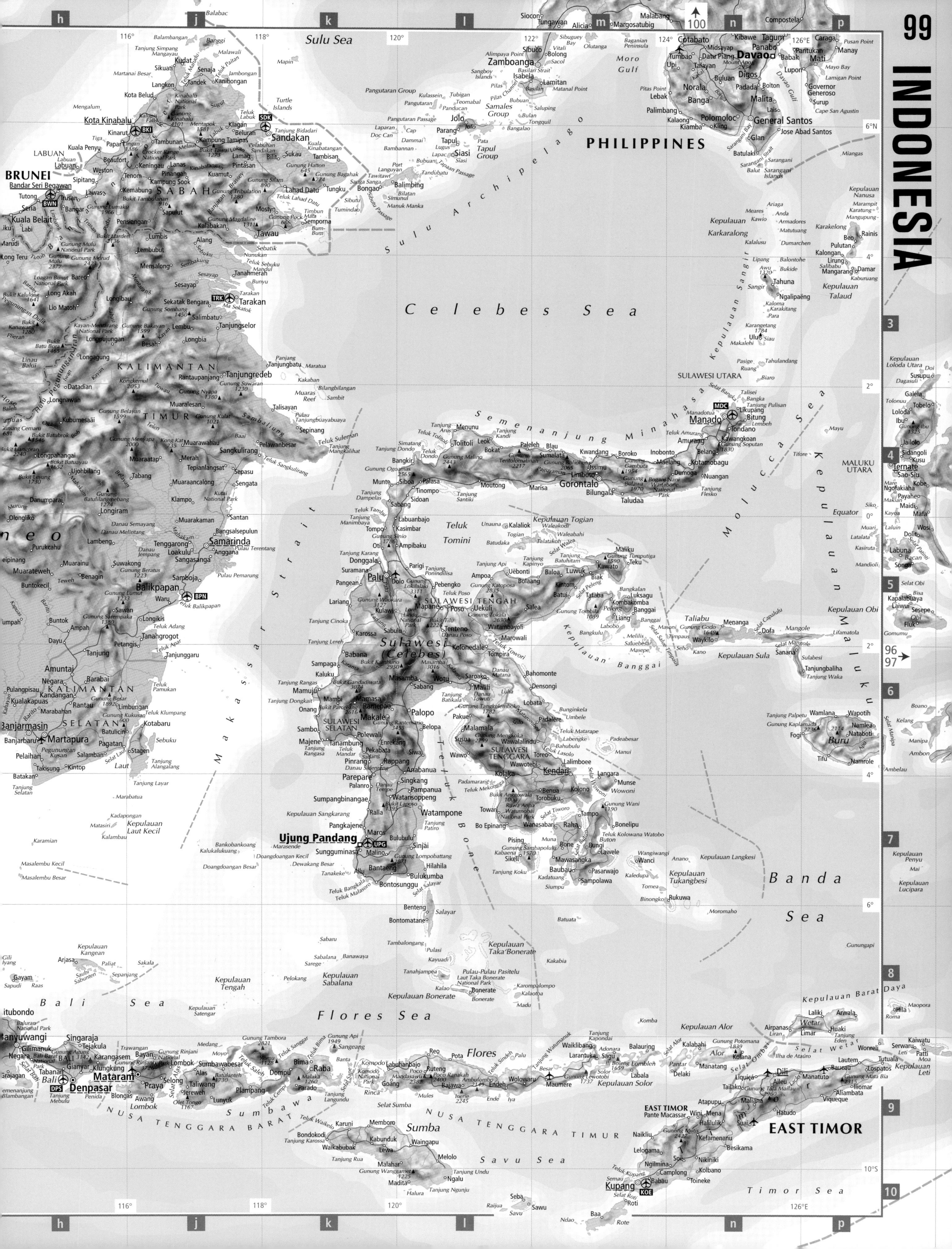

h
j
k
l
m
n
p
100
Sulu Sea
PHILIPPINES
Sulu Archipelago
Celebes Sea
BRUNEI
Bandar Seri Begawan
LABUAN
SABAH
Kota Kinabalu
Sandakan
Tawau
Kudat
Zamboanga
Jolo
Cotabato
Davao
General Santos
Moro Gulf
Davao Gulf
Kepulauan Sangir
Kepulauan Talaud
Kepulauan Karkaralong
Tarakan
KALIMANTAN TIMUR
Tanjungredeb
Samarinda
Balikpapan
Borneo
KALIMANTAN SELATAN
Banjarmasin
Martapura
Makassar Strait
SULAWESI UTARA
Manado
Gorontalo
Semenanjung Minahasa
Molucca Sea
Teluk Tomini
Kepulauan Togian
SULAWESI TENGAH
Palu
Poso
Sulawesi (Celebes)
Kepulauan Banggai
Kepulauan Sula
Kepulauan Obi
MALUKU UTARA
Ternate
Kepulauan Maluku
Buru
SULAWESI SELATAN
SULAWESI TENGGARA
Kendari
Teluk Bone
Ujung Pandang
Kepulauan Tukangbesi
Banda Sea
Kepulauan Sabalana
Kepulauan Bonerate
Flores Sea
Bali Sea
Kepulauan Alor
Kepulauan Barat Daya
Wetar
BALI
Denpasar
Lombok
Mataram
Sumbawa
Flores
Sumba
Savu Sea
NUSA TENGGARA BARAT
NUSA TENGGARA TIMUR
EAST TIMOR
Dili
Timor
Kupang
Timor Sea
Sawu
Rote
Equator
116°
118°
120°
122°
124°
126°E

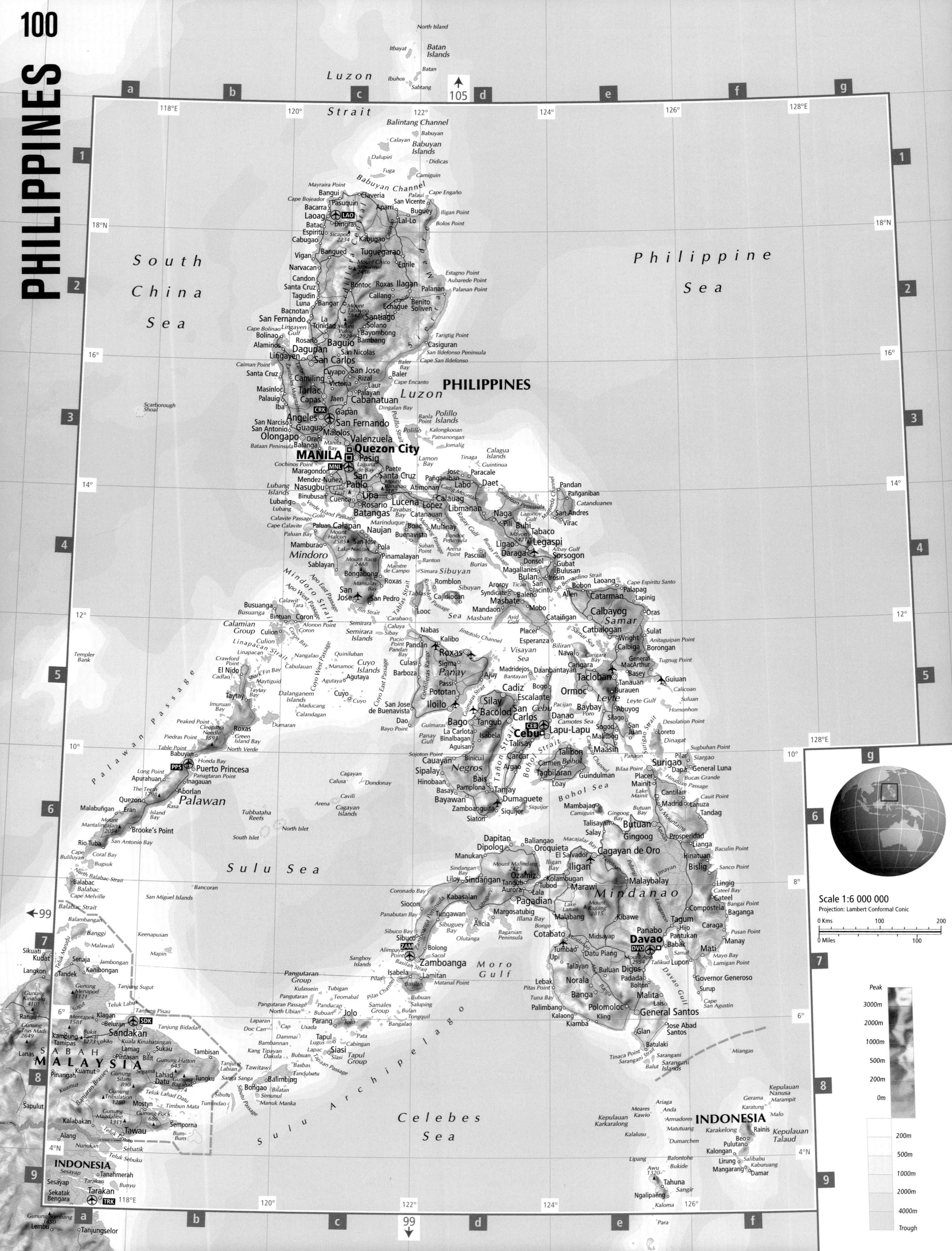
North Island
Batan Islands
Itbayat
Batan
Sabtang
Luzon Strait
Balintang Channel
Babuyan Islands
Calayan
Dalupiri
Fuga
Camiguin
Babuyan Channel
Cape Engaño
Cape Bojeador
Bangui
Pasuquin
Claveria
Aparri
Laoag
Batac
Dingras
Lal-Lo
Vigan
Bangued
Tuguegarao
Candon
Santa Cruz
Tagudin
Bontoc
Roxas
Ilagan
Palanan
San Fernando
Baguio
Santiago
Dagupan
San Carlos
Lingayen
Lingayen Gulf
Bolinao
Alaminos
Casiguran
South China Sea
Philippine Sea
PHILIPPINES
Luzon
Tarlac
Cabanatuan
Angeles
San Fernando
Olongapo
Malolos
Valenzuela
MANILA
Quezon City
Pasig
Manila Bay
Laguna de Bay
Polillo Islands
Lamon Bay
Nasugbu
Lipa
Batangas
Lucena
Calauag
Daet
Naga
Legaspi
Sorsogon
Catanduanes
Virac
Tabaco
Calapan
Mindoro
San Jose
Sibuyan Sea
Romblon
Masbate
Busuanga
Calamian Group
Coron
Mindoro Strait
Tablas Strait
Samar
Calbayog
Catbalogan
Borongan
Tacloban
Leyte
Ormoc
Leyte Gulf
Visayan Sea
Panay
Roxas
Iloilo
Kalibo
Negros
Bacolod
Cebu
Lapu-Lapu
Bohol
Tagbilaran
Bohol Sea
Dumaguete
Siquijor
Cuyo Islands
Cuyo
El Nido
Taytay
Palawan
Puerto Princesa
Palawan Passage
Brooke's Point
Scarborough Shoal
Sulu Sea
Tubbataha Reefs
Cagayan Islands
Surigao
Dinagat
Siargao
Butuan
Cagayan de Oro
Iligan
Dipolog
Dapitan
Ozamiz
Pagadian
Mindanao
Malaybalay
Bislig
Tagum
Davao
Davao Gulf
Cotabato
Moro Gulf
Zamboanga
Basilan
Isabela
Digos
General Santos
Sarangani Islands
Sulu Archipelago
Jolo
Siasi
Tawitawi
Bongao
Celebes Sea
Sabah
MALAYSIA
Sandakan
Lahad Datu
Tawau
Semporna
Kudat
Gunung Kinabalu 4101
INDONESIA
Tarakan
Talaud
Kepulauan Sangihe
Tahuna
Miangas
Scale 1:6 000 000
Projection: Lambert Conformal Conic
0 Kms 100 200
0 Miles 100
Peak
3000m
2000m
1000m
500m
200m
0m
200m
500m
1000m
2000m
4000m
Trough
105
99

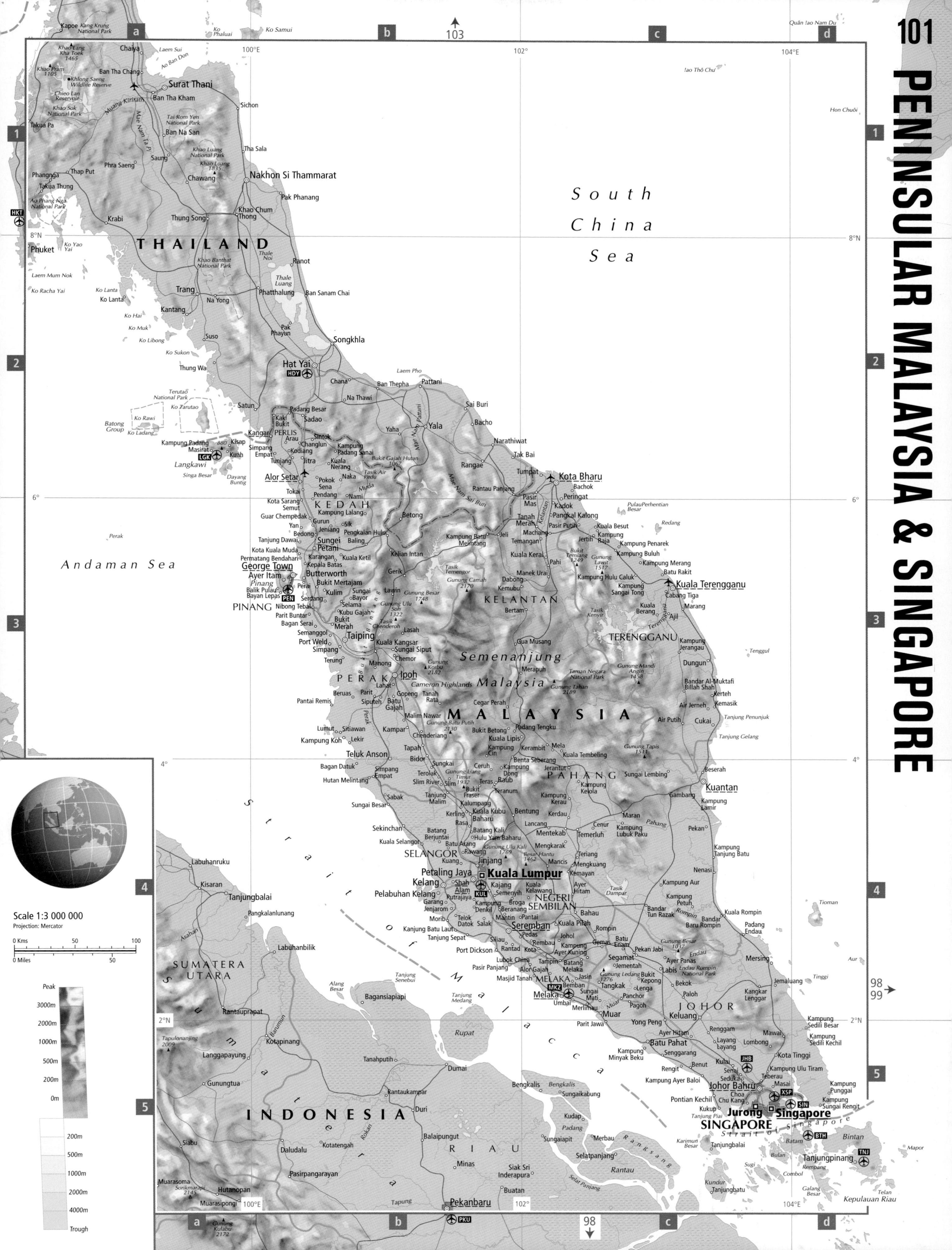

South
China
Sea

Andaman Sea

THAILAND

Phuket

Hat Yai

Songkhla

Surat Thani

Nakhon Si Thammarat

PERLIS

KEDAH

Alor Setar

George Town
Butterworth
PINANG
Taiping

PERAK

Ipoh

Cameron Highlands

KELANTAN

Kota Bharu

Kuala Terengganu

TERENGGANU

Semenanjung
Malaysia

MALAYSIA

PAHANG

Kuantan

SELANGOR

Petaling Jaya
Kelang
Shah
Alam

Kuala Lumpur

NEGERI
SEMBILAN

Seremban

MELAKA

Melaka

Muar

Batu Pahat

JOHOR

Kluang

Mersing

Tioman

Johor Bahru

Jurong Singapore
SINGAPORE

Strait of Singapore

Tanjungpinang

SUMATERA
UTARA

INDONESIA

RIAU

Pekanbaru

Scale 1:3 000 000
Projection: Mercator

0 Kms   50   100
0 Miles   50

Peak
3000m
2000m
1000m
500m
200m
0m

200m
500m
1000m
2000m
4000m
Trough

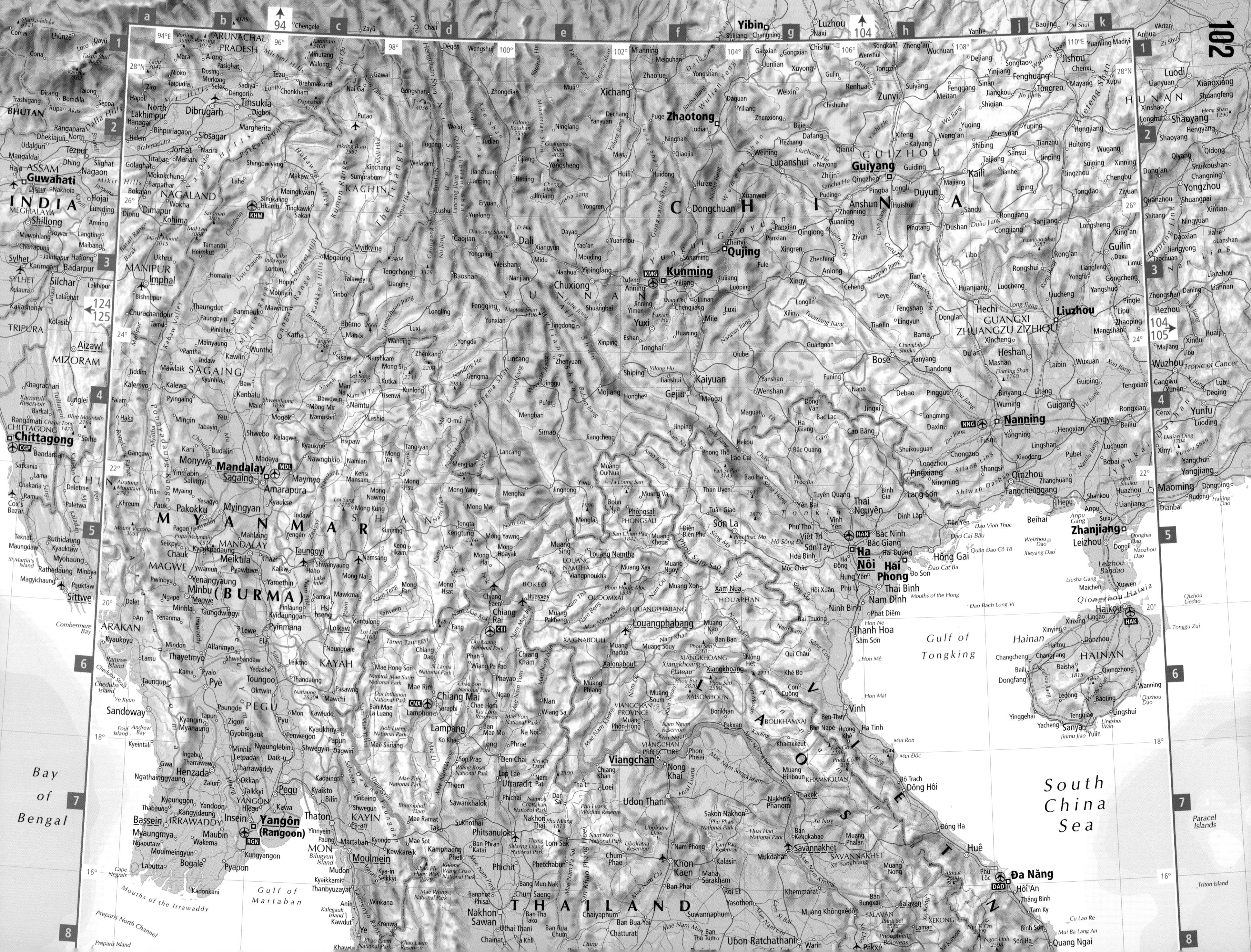

CHINA
GUIZHOU
YUNNAN
GUANGXI ZHUANGZU ZIZHIQU
HUNAN
MYANMAR (BURMA)
THAILAND
LAOS
VIETNAM
INDIA
BHUTAN
ARUNACHAL PRADESH
NAGALAND
MANIPUR
MIZORAM
TRIPURA
MEGHALAYA
ASSAM
CHITTAGONG
SAGAING
MANDALAY
MAGWE
KACHIN
SHAN
KAYAH
KAYIN
MON
PEGU
YANGON
IRRAWADDY
ARAKAN
CHIN
HAINAN
South China Sea
Gulf of Tongking
Gulf of Martaban
Bay of Bengal
Mouths of the Irrawaddy
Kunming
Guiyang
Nanning
Liuzhou
Zhanjiang
Haikou
Zhaotong
Qujing
Gejiu
Kaiyuan
Dali
Hà Nội
Hai Phong
Đà Nẵng
Vinh
Viangchan
Louangphabang
Mandalay
Yangôn (Rangoon)
Pegu
Moulmein
Chiang Mai
Chiang Rai
Udon Thani
Khon Kaen
Ubon Ratchathani
Nakhon Sawan
Chittagong
Guwahati
Imphal
Dibrugarh
Sittwe
Aizawl
Silchar

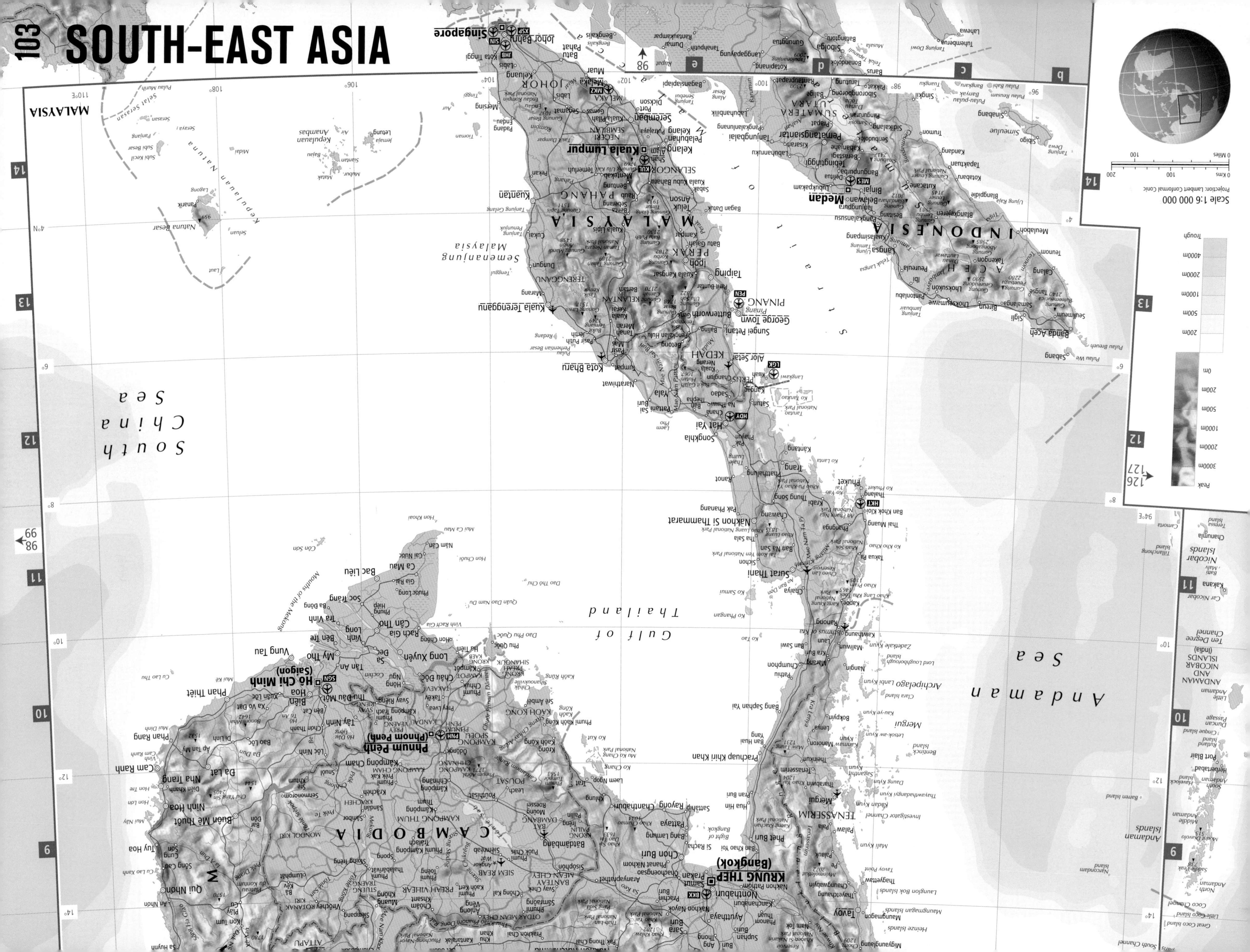

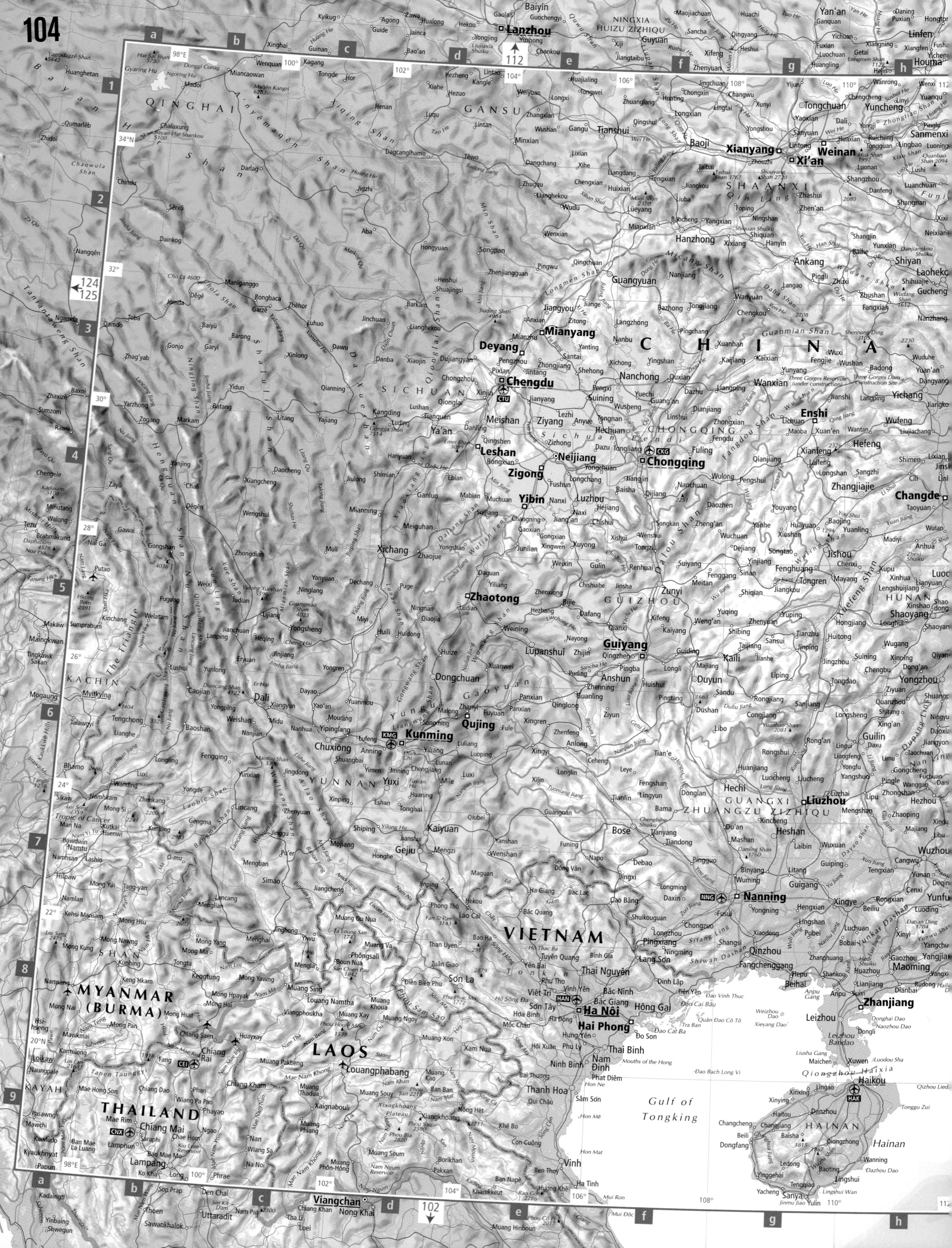

Lanzhou
112
124
125
102
QINGHAI
GANSU
NINGXIA HUIZU ZIZHIQU
SHAANXI
SICHUAN
CHONGQING
GUIZHOU
HUNAN
YUNNAN
GUANGXI ZHUANGZU ZIZHIQU
HAINAN
KACHIN
SHAN
KAYAH
C H I N A
VIETNAM
LAOS
THAILAND
MYANMAR (BURMA)
Gulf of Tongking
Hainan
Qiongzhou Haixia
Tropic of Cancer
Xianyang
Xi'an
Weinan
Baoji
Tianshui
Hanzhong
Ankang
Shiyan
Guangyuan
Mianyang
Deyang
Chengdu
Ya'an
Leshan
Neijiang
Zigong
Yibin
Chongqing
Nanchong
Wanxian
Enshi
Yichang
Changde
Zhangjiajie
Jishou
Zhaotong
Guiyang
Zunyi
Kaili
Anshun
Duyun
Qujing
Kunming
Dali
Chuxiong
Yuxi
Gejiu
Kaiyuan
Dongchuan
Xichang
Liuzhou
Guilin
Nanning
Bose
Hechi
Qinzhou
Beihai
Zhanjiang
Haikou
Sanya
Wuzhou
Yulin
Shaoyang
Yongzhou
Ha Nôi
Hai Phong
Hông Gai
Nam Đinh
Thanh Hoa
Vinh
Lao Cai
Điên Biên Phu
Luang Prabang
Louangphabang
Viangchan
Nong Khai
Chiang Rai
Chiang Mai
Lampang
Myitkyina
Bhamo
Lashio
Kengtung
Dêqên
Gonjo
Qamdo
Yushu
Xiangcheng
Mianning
Shiwan Dashan
Qin Ling
Daba Shan
Min Shan
Micang Shan
Longmen Shan
Hengduan Shan
Nu Shan
Yun Ling
Shaluli Shan
Daxue Shan
Qionglai Shan
Wuling Shan
Xuefeng Shan
Dalou Shan
Ailao Shan
Wuliang Shan
Gongga Shan 7514
Emei Shan 3099
Sichuan Pendi
Yunnan Gaoyuan
Tonkin
98°E
100°
102°
104°
106°
108°
110°
34°N
32°
30°
28°
26°
24°
22°
20°N
CTU
CKG
KMG
NNG
HAN
HAK
CNX
CEI

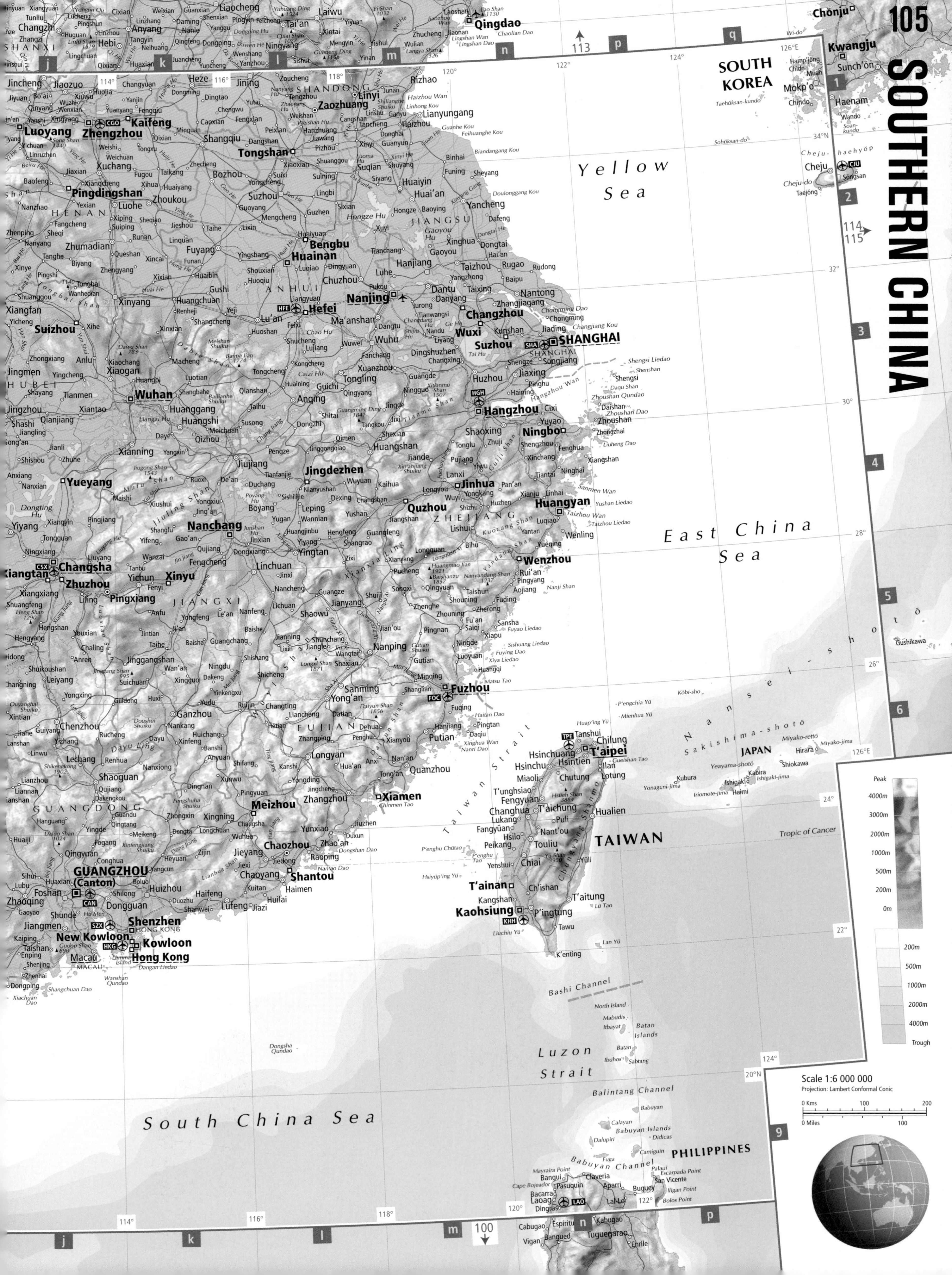
SOUTH KOREA
Yellow Sea
East China Sea
South China Sea
Taiwan Strait
Luzon Strait
Bashi Channel
Balintang Channel
Babuyan Channel
TAIWAN
JAPAN
PHILIPPINES
Nansei-shotō
Sakishima-shotō
Tropic of Cancer
SHANDONG
JIANGSU
ANHUI
HENAN
HUBEI
ZHEJIANG
JIANGXI
FUJIAN
GUANGDONG
SHANXI
SHANGHAI
Nanjing
Hefei
Hangzhou
Ningbo
Wuhan
Nanchang
Changsha
Fuzhou
Xiamen
Shantou
GUANGZHOU (Canton)
Shenzhen
Kowloon
New Kowloon
Hong Kong
Macau
T'aipei
Kaohsiung
T'ainan
Qingdao
Zhengzhou
Kaifeng
Luoyang
Pingdingshan
Bengbu
Huainan
Wuxi
Suzhou
Changzhou
Wenzhou
Huangyan
Jinhua
Quzhou
Jingdezhen
Yueyang
Xinyu
Zhuzhou
Pingxiang
Meizhou
Zhangzhou
Quanzhou
Putian
Nanping
Sanming
Longyan
Shaoguan
Chenzhou
Ganzhou
Zhanjiang
Xuzhou
Lianyungang
Tongshan
Linyi
Zaozhuang
Kwangju
Cheju
Chŏnju
Scale 1:6 000 000
Projection: Lambert Conformal Conic
0 Kms 100 200
0 Miles 100
Peak
4000m
3000m
2000m
1000m
500m
200m
0m
200m
500m
1000m
2000m
4000m
Trough

The Yangtze, or Chang Jiang, is 6380km (3964 miles) long, the third-longest river in the world, with more than 700 tributaries. It is also the deepest and in places floods have caused the river to rise by up to 50m (170ft). It rises in the Kunlun Mountains on the Tibetan border and, fed by summer snowmelt, flows through high mountains for 3790km (2355 miles). On its highland journey, the Yangtze has carved out a dramatic landscape of overhanging precipices, sheer cliffs and craggy gorges. The river then runs through a vast alluvial plain, before discharging into the East China Sea at Shanghai.

Gobi Desert The Gobi is the largest desert in Asia, covering an area of 1,166,000km² (450,076 sq miles), and has temperatures ranging from 45°C (113°F) to -40°C (-40°F). It is mostly stony with little sand and sparse vegetation due to a rainfall of less than 250mm (10in) a year.

❶ Mekong The 4425km (2749 mile) long Mekong is the longest river in south-east China. It rises high on the Plateau of Tibet and has a total fall of 5000m (16,3000ft) along its course before it flows into the South China Sea.

❷ Yunnan-Guizhou Plateau Over 300,000km² (115,900 sq miles) of limestone raised 1–2km (½–1¼ miles) above sea level form the distinctive Guizhou Plateau. To the north, towers of limestone with rounded 'sugar-loaf' hills rise abruptly from the cultivated plains.

Sichuan Pendi Covering 229,500km² (88,600 sq miles) of red sandstone, the basin's mild climate and fertile soils, watered by the Yangtze, have enabled the development of a wide range of agriculture. The main crops are rice, sweet potatoes and rapeseed.

Chongqing At this river port, upriver of the Three Gorges, the Yangtze is between 305–488m (1000–1600ft) wide, and more than 9m (30ft) deep in places.

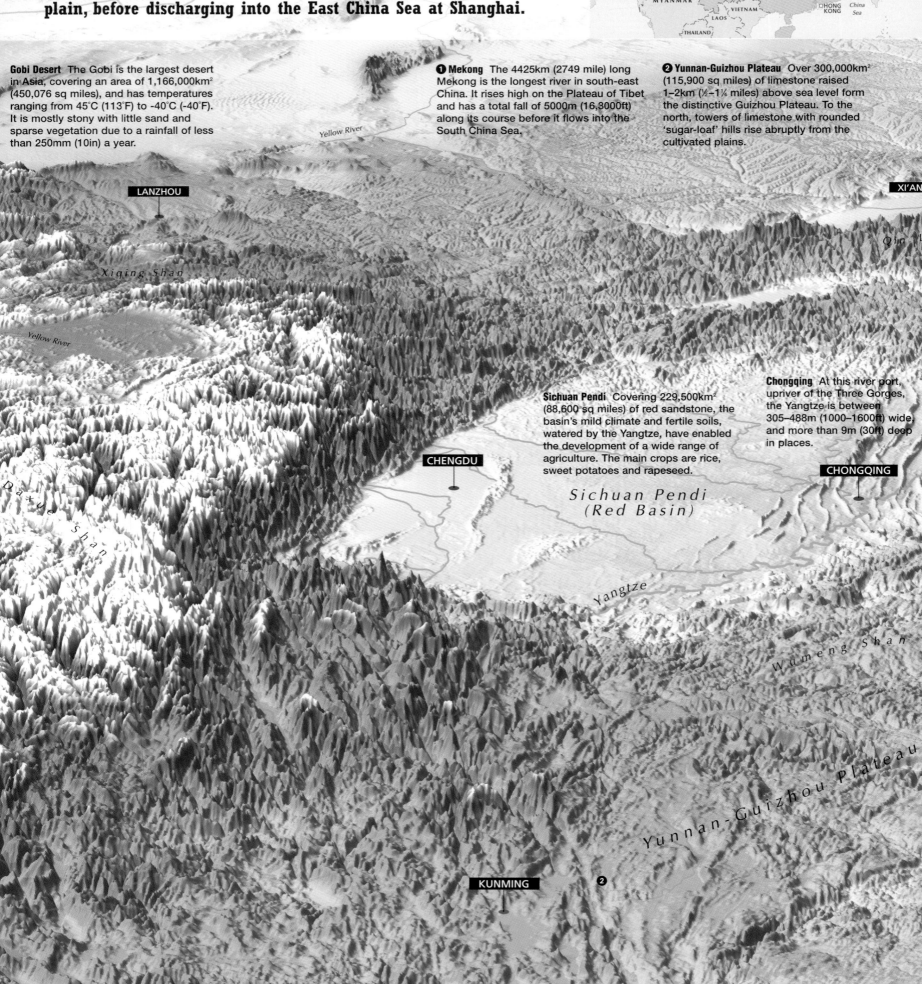

MONGOLIA

G o b i   D e s e r t

Qinghai Hu At 3200m above sea level, the lake covers an area of 4400km² (1700 sq miles) and has internal drainage with no river flowing from it, although the Huang He (Yellow River) passes only 100km (62 miles) to the east.

Altun Shan

Qilian Shan

N

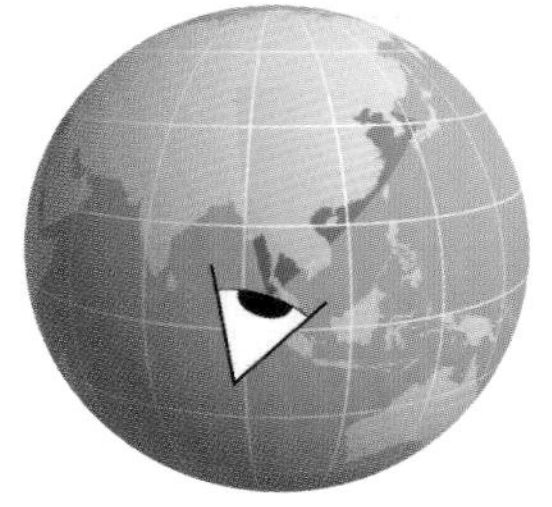

The map follows the course of the Yangtze from its mountain source on the border with Tibet down into the Yangtze river valley and finally to its mouth in the East China Sea.

Qinghai Hu

Kunlun Shan

B a y a n   H a r   S h a n

Source of the Yangtze

Jinsha Jiang The river is the westernmost of the major headwater streams of the Yangtze.

Source of the Yangtze The Wu-lan-mu-lun (Ulan Muren) river originates in glacial meltwaters on the slopes of the T'ang-ku-la Mountains in southern Tsinghai province, on the border with Tibet.

Jinsha Jiang (Yangtze)

Shaluli Shan

P l a t e a u   o f   T i b e t

Hengduan Shan

Tanjantaweng Shan

Himalayas

Jinsha Jiang (Yangtze)

1

Nu Jiang (Salween)

Lancang Jiang (Mekong)

Brahmaputra

INDIA

MYANMAR (BURMA)

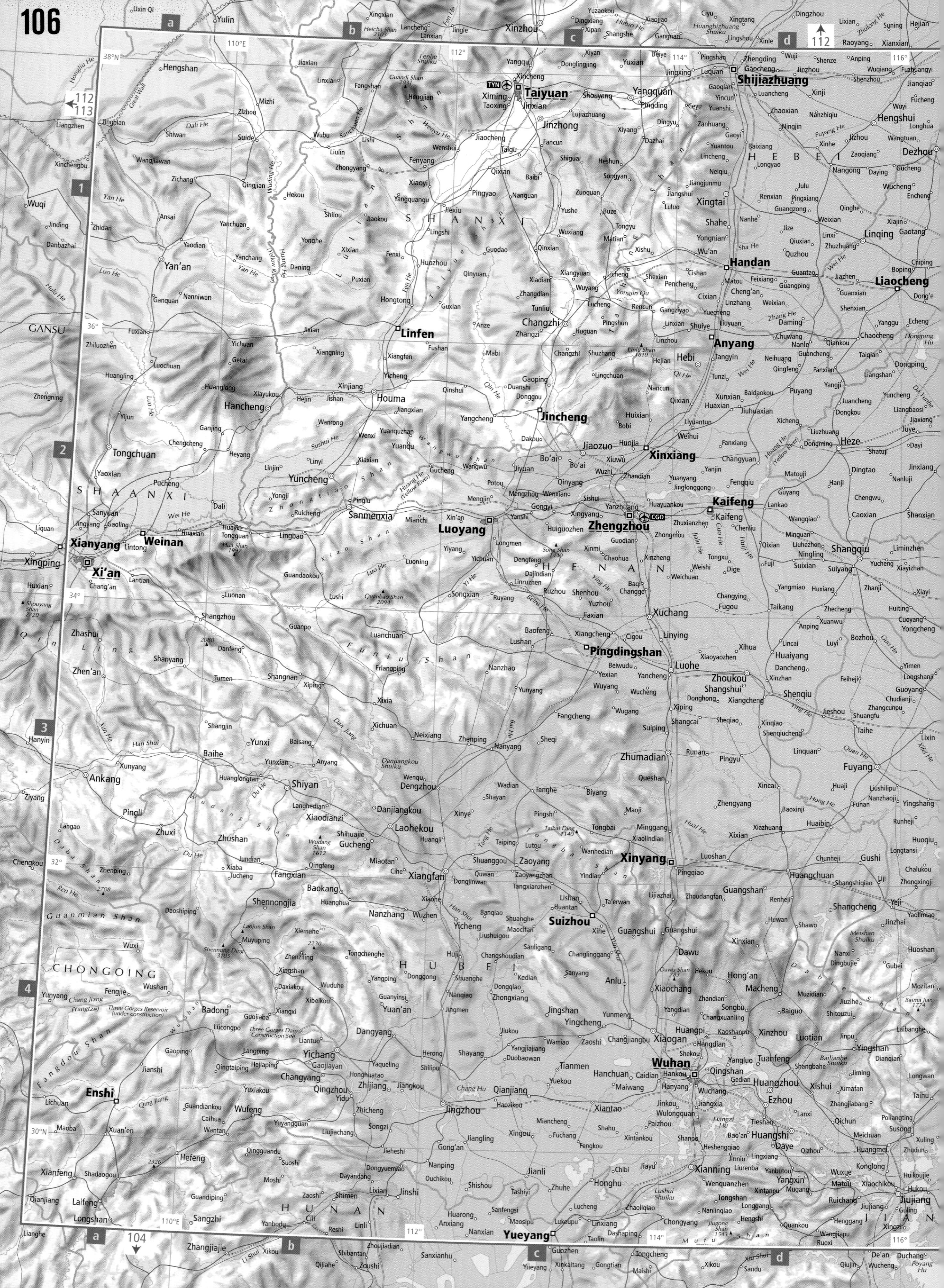
112
113
112
104
a
b
c
d
1
2
3
4
110°E
112°
114°
116°
38°N
36°
34°
32°
30°N
Uxin Qi
Yulin
Xingxian
Heicha Shan 2203
Lancheng
Lanxian
Jingle
Fen He
Xinzhou
Yuzaokou
Dingxiang
Xipan
Shangshe
Hutuo He
Xiaojiao
Gangnan
Ciyu
Xingtang
Huangbizhuang Shuiku
Lingshou
Xinle
Dingzhou
Lixian
Zhulong He
Suning
Hejian
Raoyang
Xianxian
Hengshan
Jiaxian
Fenhe Shuiku
Yangqu
Donglingjing
Xiyan
Yuxian
Beiye
Jingxing
Luquan
Pingshan
Zhengding
Gaocheng
Shijiazhuang
Wuji
Jinzhou
Shenze
Anping
Wuqiang
Fuzhuangyi
Shenzhou
Jianqiao
Hongliu He
Great Wall
Linxian
Fangshan
Guandi Shan 2831
Hengjian
Xincheng
TYN
Taiyuan
Ximing
Taoxing
Jinxian
Shouyang
Yangquan
Pingding
Ceyu
Gaoqian
Yincun
Yuanshi
Luancheng
Xinji
Fucheng
Mizhi
Zizhou
Jingbian
Liangzhen
Dali He
Shiwan
Suide
Wubu
Sanchuan He
Lishi
Wenyu He
Jiaocheng
Lujiazhuang
Jinzhong
Xiyang
Dazhai
Dingyu
Zanhuang
Gaoyi
Zhaoxian
Ningjin
Nanzhiqiu
Hengshui
Wuyi
Longhua
Wangjiawan
Xinchengbu
Liulin
Wenshui
Taigu
Fancun
Yuantou
Fuyang He
Jizhou
Xinhe
Wangtuan
Dezhou
Zhongyang
Fenyang
Shiguai
Heshun
Lincheng
Baixiang
Zaoqiang
H E B E I
Longyao
Nangong
Daying
Gucheng
Zichang
Qingjian
Wuding He
Qixian
Songyan
Neiqiu
Hekou
Xiaoyi
Pingyao
Baibi
Jiangjunmu
Julu
Wucheng
Wuqi
Yan He
Yangquangu
Nanguan
Zuoquan
Jiangshui
Renxian
Pingxiang
Encheng
Ansai
Shilou
Jiexiu
Yushe
Buze
Xingtai
Guangzong
Qinghe
Zhidan
Jinding
Yanchuan
Jiaokou
S H A N X I
Lingshi
Wuxiang
Tongyu
Luluo
Shahe
Nanhe
Weixian
Xiajin
Danbazhai
Yaodian
Yonghe
Xixian
Fenxi
Guodao
Qinxian
Matian
Xishu
Yongnian
Jize
Linxi
Qiuxian
Linqing
Gaotang
Yan'an
Yanchang
Huang He (Yellow River)
Huozhou
Wu'an
Sha He
Zhuzhuang
Quzhou
Handan
Chiping
Luo He
Yan He
Daning
Puxian
Qinyuan
Xiadian
Xiangyuan
Licheng
Shexian
Cishan
Wei He
Boping
Liaocheng
Zhangdian
Wuyang
Yongjin Qu
Pencheng
Matou
Feixiang
Guantao
Jiazhen
Nanniwan
Hongtong
Guxian
Tunliu
Lucheng
Rencun
Gangziyao
Cixian
Cheng'an
Guangping
Guanxian
Dong'e
Hulu He
Ganquan
Linzhang
Weixian
Zhang He
Shenxian
GANSU
Fuxian
Jixian
Linfen
Anze
Changzhi
Pingshun
Linxian
Yuecheng
Daming
Yanggu
Echeng
Zhangzi
Huguan
Shuiye
Liuyuan
Chuwang
Chaocheng
Dongping Hu
Zhiluozhen
Yichuan
Fushan
Linzhou
Anyang
Nanle
Qiankou
Getai
Xiangning
Mabi
Changzhi
Shuzhang
Linlu Shan 1619
Hejian
Hebi
Tangyin
Neihuang
Guancheng
Taiqian
Luochuan
Xiangfen
Lingchuan
Qi He
Qingfeng
Fanxian
Liangshan
Dongping
Huangling
Yicheng
Gaoping
Tunzi
Wei He
Yangji
Huanglong
Xinjiang
Qinshui
Duanshi
Nancun
Baidaokou
Puyang
Juancheng
Yuncheng
Da Yunhe
Zhengning
Xiayukou
Hejin
Jishan
Houma
Qin He
Donggou
Qixian
Xunxian
Dongkou
Liangbaosi
Hancheng
Jiangxian
Jincheng
Huaxian
Jiuhuaxian
Luo He
Yijun
Yangcheng
Huixian
Liyuantun
Xicheng
Jiaxiang
Ganjing
Wanrong
Yuanquzhan
Bobi
Liuzhuang
Juye
Wenxi
Yuanqu
Dakou
Weihui
Fanxiang
Dongming
Heze
Dayi
Chengcheng
Heyang
Sushui He
Jiaozuo
Huojia
Xinxiang
Changyuan
Huang He (Yellow River)
Shatuji
Tongchuan
Xiaxian
Wangwu Shan
Bo'ai
Xiuwu
Linyi
Gucheng
Wangwu
Jiyuan
Wuzhi
Zhandian
Yanjin
Dingtao
Jinxiang
Yaoxian
Linjin
Yuncheng
Zhongtiao Shan
Huang He (Yellow River)
Potou
Qinyang
Yuanyang
Jinglonggong
Fengqiu
Matouji
Nanluji
Pucheng
Yongji
Mengjin
Mengzhou
Wenxian
Hanji
Chengwu
S H A A N X I
Pinglu
Gongyi
Sishui
Yanzhuang
Huayuankou
Kaifeng
Lankao
Dali
Sanyuan
Ruicheng
Sanmenxia
Mianchi
Xin'an
Yanshi
Xingyang
CGO
Zhengzhou
Kaifeng
Wangqiao
Caoxian
Shanxian
Jingyang
Gaoling
Wei He
Huayin
Luoyang
Huiguozhen
Zhuxianzhen
Chenliu
Liquan
Xianyang
Weinan
Huaxian
Tongguan
Lingbao
Longmen
Guodian
Zhongmou
Jialu He
Guo He
Huiji He
Minquan
Xingping
Lintong
Hua Shan 1997
Xiao Shan
Yiyang
Song Shan 1440
Xinmi
Qixian
Liuhezhen
Ningling
Shangqiu
Liminzhen
Xi'an
Lantian
Yichuan
Dengfeng
Chaohua
Xinzheng
Tongxu
Fuji
Suixian
Suiyang
Yucheng
Xiayizhan
Chang'an
Luoning
Dajindian
H E N A N
Weishi
Dige
Huxian
Guandaokou
Luo He
Linruzhen
Weichuan
Shouyang Shan 2720
Yi He
Ruzhou
Shenhou
Ying He
Baqi
Changge
Yangmiao
Huxiang
Zhanji
Xiayi
Luonan
Lushi
Quanbao Shan 2094
Songxian
Ruyang
Beiru He
Yuzhou
Changying
Fugou
Taikang
Shangzhou
Jiaxian
Xuchang
Zhecheng
Huiting
Cuoyang
Qin Ling
Guanpo
Luanchuan
Baofeng
Xiangcheng
Cigou
Linying
Anping
Xuanwu
Yongcheng
Zhashui
Danfeng
Funiu Shan
Lushan
Pingdingshan
Xihua
Lincai
Luyi
Bozhou
Guo He
2080
Xiaoyaozhen
Huaiyang
Shanyang
Nanzhao
Beiwudu
Luohe
Dancheng
Yimen
Zhen'an
Erlangping
Yexian
Yancheng
Zhoukou
Feiheji
Longshanji
Tumen
Shangnan
Xiping
Yunyang
Wuyang
Wucheng
Shangshui
Xinzhan
Guoyang
Donghong
Xiangcheng
Shenqiu
Chudianji
Xixia
Wugang
Xiping
Jieshou
Zhangcunpu
Shuangfu
Shangjin
Xichuan
Fangcheng
Suiping
Shangcai
Sheqiao
Xinqiao
Shenqiucheng
Taihe
Xun He
Neixiang
Zhenping
Bai He
Sheqi
Lixin
Hanyin
Han Shui
Yunxi
Baisang
Dan Jiang
Nanyang
Zhumadian
Runan
Pingyu
Linquan
Quan He
Xifei He
Baihe
Xunyang
Yunxian
Anyang
Danjiangkou Shuiku
Queshan
Fuyang
Ankang
Huanglongtan
Du He
Shiyan
Wenqu
Dengzhou
Wadian
Tanghe
Biyang
Xincai
Huaji
Liushilipu
Nanzhaoji
Ziyang
Shayan
Funan
Yingshang
Pingli
Langhedian
Xiaodianzi
Danjiangkou
Xinye
Pingshi
Maoji
Zhengyang
Baoxinji
Hong He
Runheji
Langao
Zhuxi
Wudang Shan
Shihuajie
Laohekou
Taibai Ding 1140
Tongbai
Minggang
Huai He
Xiazhuang
Huaibin
Huoqiu
Zhushan
Wudang Shan 1612
Gucheng
Huangji
Tang He
Taiping
Lutou
Tongbai Shan
Wanhedian
Xiaolindian
Xixian
Longtansi
Daba Shan
Jundian
Miaotan
Xinyang
Luoshan
Chunheji
Gushi
Chalukou
Chengkou
Xiaba
Qingfeng
Cihe
Xiangfan
Shuanggou
Zaoyang
Yindian
Pingqiao
Huangchuan
Liji
Zhongxingji
Zhenping
Tucheng
Fangxian
Quwan
Zaoyangzhan
Dongjinwan
Tangxianzhen
Shangshiqiao
Ren He
2708
Baokang
Lijiazhai
Zhoudangfan
Guangshan
Renheji
Yeji
Huanghua
Xiaohe
Lishan
Huantan
Ta'erwan
Shangcheng
Guanmian Shan
Daoshiping
Shennongjia
Nanzhang
Wuzhen
Han Shui
Banqiao
Suizhou
Shuanghe
Maocifan
Xihe
Guangshui
Huwan
Shawo
Jinzhai
Yaolinhao
Laojun Shan
Xiemahe
Yicheng
Liushuigou
Xinxian
Meishan Shuiku
Wuxi
2230
Hujia
Changshoudian
Sanligang
Changlinggang
Dawu
Nanxi
Huoshan
Muyuping
Shennong Ding 3105
Zhenziling
Tongchenghe
H U B E I
Yun Shui
Dingbujie
Gubei
CHONGQING
Xingshan
Yangping
Donggong
Shuanghe
Kedian
Dawu Shan 793
Hekou
Hong'an
Fengjie
Wushan
Daxiakou
Wuduhe
Dongqiao
Sanyang
Anlu
Macheng
Mozitan
Yunyang
Chang Jiang (Yangtze)
Three Gorges Reservoir (under construction)
Badong
Xibeikou
Guanyinsi
Nanqiao
Zhongxiang
Xiaochang
Zhandian
Muzidian
Dabie Shan
Baima Jian 1774
Xiangxi
Yuan'an
Jingmen
Jingshan
Yangdian
Songbu
Baiguo
Jiuzihe
Guojiaba
Changxuanling
Shitouzui
Lucongpo
Three Gorges Dam Construction Site
Dangyang
Yingcheng
Yunmeng
Huangpi
Kaoshanpu
Xinzhou
Luotian
Jinpu
Laibanghe
Wushan
Fangdou Shan
Liantuo
Jiukou
Wamiao
Zaoshi
Changjiangbu
Xiaogan
Hengdian
Yingshan
Gaoping
Langping
Yichang
Herong
Shayang
Yangjiajiang
Shekou
Yangluo
Tuanfeng
Bailianhe Shuiku
Jianshi
Qingtaiping
Hejiaping
Gaojiayan
Yaqueling
Shilipu
Duobaowan
Tianmen
Hanchuan
Caidian
Wuhan
Hankou
Qingshan
Shangbahe
Jiming
Changyang
Honghuatao
Hanyang
Gedian
Huangzhou
Xishui
Longwan
Enshi
Yuxiakou
Qingzhou
Zhijiang
Jiangkou
Chang Hu
Qianjiang
Yuekou
Maiwang
Wuchang
Ximafan
Lichuan
Qing Jiang
Yidu
Haozikou
Jinkou
Jiangxia
Ezhou
Taihu
Guandiankou
Wufeng
Jingzhou
Xiantao
Wulongquan
Zhangjiabang
Caihua
Zhicheng
Miancheng
Liangzi Hu
Lanxi
Qichun
Poliangting
Maoba
Xuan'en
Wantan
Yuyangguan
Liujiachang
Songzi
Xingou
Fuchang
Shahu
Xintankou
Paizhou
Tieshan
Huangshi
Meichuan
Susong
Jiangling
Fengkou
Shanpo
Bao'an
Daye
Huangmei
Xuling
Zhudun
Qingguandu
Gong'an
Heshengqiao
Qizhou
Hefeng
2326
Suoshi
Jieheshi
Chibi
Jiayu
Xianning
Lingxiang
Kuokou
Konglong
Huikoujie
Xianfeng
Shadaogou
Dongyuemiao
Nanping
Jianli
Liurenba
Yanbutou
Yangxin
Wuxue
Matou
Xiaochikou
Hukou
Moshi
Dayandang
Ouchikou
Shishou
Zhuhe
Honghu
Jinniu
Wenquanzhen
Xintanpu
Mugang
Qianjiang
Zaoshi
Shimen
Lixian
Jinshi
Tashiyi
Lushui Shuiku
Tongshan
Ruichang
Jiujiang
Laifeng
Guandiping
H U N A N
Lucheng
Zhaoliqiao
Nanlinqiao
Longgang
Hengshi
Henggang
Jiujiang
Guling
Longshan
Sangzhi
Cili
Huarong
Sanfengsi
Linxiang
Chongyang
Jiugong Shan 1543
Quankou
J I A N
Lianghe
Yanbodu
Reshi
Linli
Anxiang
Nanxian
Maosipu
Yueyang
Dashaping
Mufu Shan
Wangjiaqiao
Xingzi
Zhangjiajie
Li Shui
Xikou
Zhoujiadian
Lukeopu
Taolin
Ruoxi
Shibantan
Sanxianhu
Guozhen
Tongcheng
Xiu Shui
De'an
Duchang
Qijiahe
Zoushi
Yueyang
Xinkaitang
Gongtian
Maishi
Xikou
Sandu
Qiujin
Wucheng
Poyang Hu

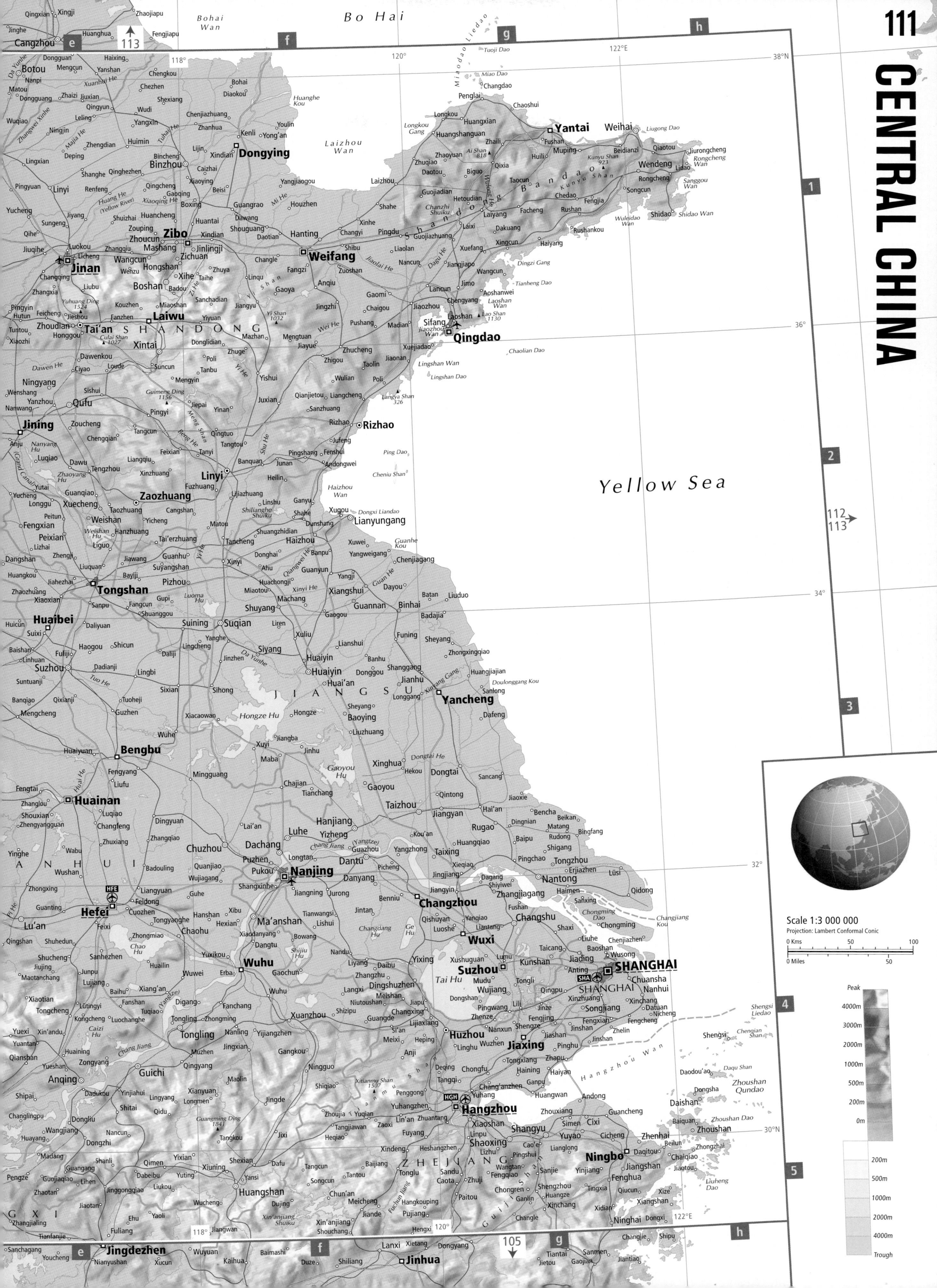

Bo Hai

Bohai Wan

Laizhou Wan

Yellow Sea

SHANDONG

JIANGSU

ANHUI

ZHEJIANG

Jinan
Zibo
Dongying
Binzhou
Yantai
Weihai
Weifang
Laiwu
Tai'an
Xintai
Qingdao
Qufu
Jining
Linyi
Zaozhuang
Rizhao
Tongshan
Huaibei
Lianyungang
Suzhou
Bengbu
Huainan
Yancheng
Hefei
Huaiyin
Huai'an
Nanjing
Changzhou
Wuxi
Suzhou
SHANGHAI
Ma'anshan
Wuhu
Tongling
Huzhou
Jiaxing
Anqing
Hangzhou
Ningbo
Shaoxing
Huangshan
Jingdezhen
Jinhua

Chang Jiang (Yangtze)

Tai Hu

Hangzhou Wan

Zhoushan Qundao

Zhoushan Dao

Shengsi Liedao

Scale 1:3 000 000
Projection: Lambert Conformal Conic

0 Kms   50   100
0 Miles   50

Peak
4000m
3000m
2000m
1000m
500m
200m
0m

200m
500m
1000m
2000m
4000m
Trough

The flooding of the Yangtze During the monsoon season, between June and September, the Yangtze floods regularly. Intensity of settlement and loss of vegetation have increased the danger that these floods pose. Over centuries the Yangtze basin has lost 85 per cent of the forests that once held much of the monsoon rain, enabling it to percolate slowly into the ground and drain away. Global warming may also be a contributing factor as higher temperatures aid evaporation, leading to heavier rainfall, and greater snowmelt in the mountains that feed the Yangtze. More intense monsoon storms also occur – as temperatures heat up over the land, the warm air rises, drawing moisture-laden air from the oceans inland. The 1998 floods – shown left – were the worst for 44 years; more than 2000 people died and 13.8 million were made homeless.

The Three Gorges The gorges are 201km (125 miles) in length with water depths between 152–183m (500–600ft), making the Yangtze at this point the deepest river in the world.

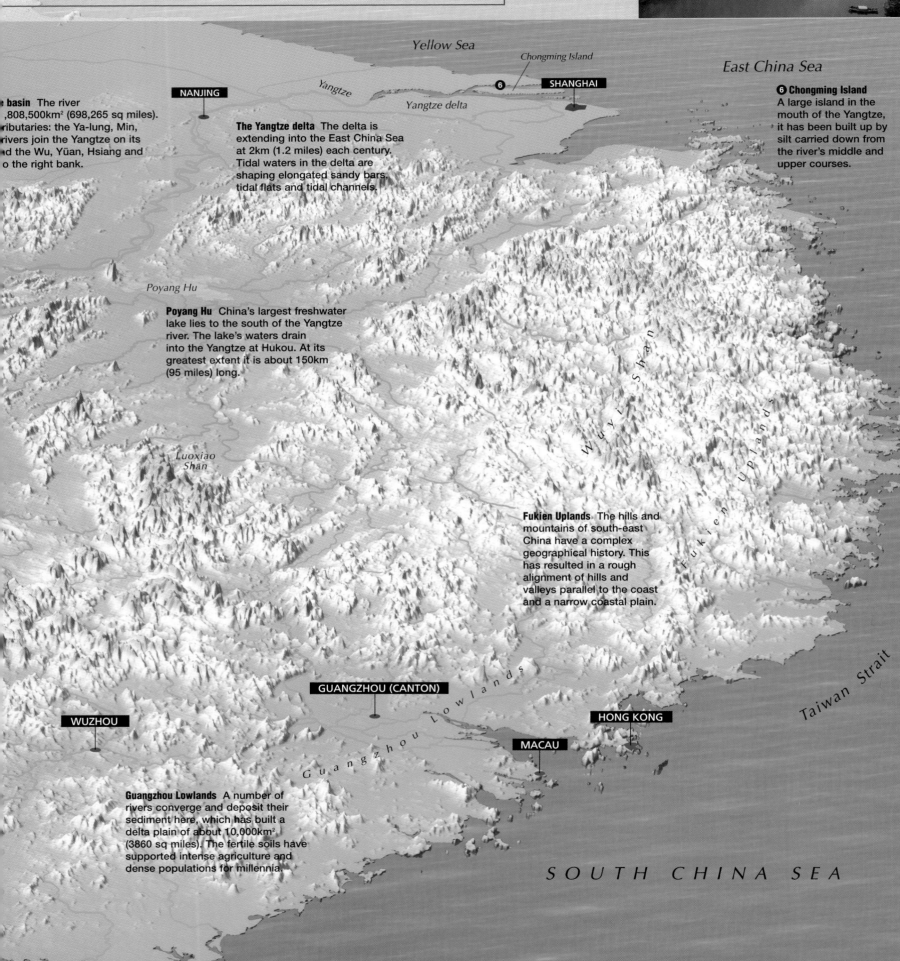

e basin The river ,808,500km² (698,265 sq miles). ributaries: the Ya-lung, Min, rivers join the Yangtze on its d the Wu, Yüan, Hsiang and o the right bank.

Yellow Sea

Yangtze

Chongming Island

6 **SHANGHAI**

NANJING

Yangtze delta

East China Sea

6 Chongming Island A large island in the mouth of the Yangtze, it has been built up by silt carried down from the river's middle and upper courses.

The Yangtze delta The delta is extending into the East China Sea at 2km (1.2 miles) each century. Tidal waters in the delta are shaping elongated sandy bars, tidal flats and tidal channels.

Poyang Hu

Poyang Hu China's largest freshwater lake lies to the south of the Yangtze river. The lake's waters drain into the Yangtze at Hukou. At its greatest extent it is about 150km (95 miles) long.

Wu yi Shan

Luoxiao Shan

Fukien Uplands

Fukien Uplands The hills and mountains of south-east China have a complex geographical history. This has resulted in a rough alignment of hills and valleys parallel to the coast and a narrow coastal plain.

Taiwan Strait

GUANGZHOU (CANTON)

Guangzhou Lowlands

HONG KONG

WUZHOU

MACAU

Guangzhou Lowlands A number of rivers converge and deposit their sediment here, which has built a delta plain of about 10,000km² (3860 sq miles). The fertile soils have supported intense agriculture and dense populations for millennia.

SOUTH CHINA SEA

Leizhou Bandao

Hainan

How the Yangtze was formed The original Yangtze river, formed 180 million years ago, flowed west towards an ancient ocean called Tethys, of which the Mediterranean is a remnant. Around 40 million years later, geological upheavals created a series of fold mountains along the borders of Sichuan and Hubei provinces, while eastward-flowing rivers formed along their slopes.

When the Indo-Australian plate began to collide with the Asian plate between 30 and 40 million years ago, the western end of the present river's course was raised, reversing its flow. Over thousands of years the 'western river' cut deep gorges through layers of geological strata, penetrating through rocks to join up with the 'eastern river'. Once the rivers had joined, the waters broke through the mountains to reach the plains of central China.

The Three Gorges

YUEYANG

SUIZHOU

Yangtze

WUHAN

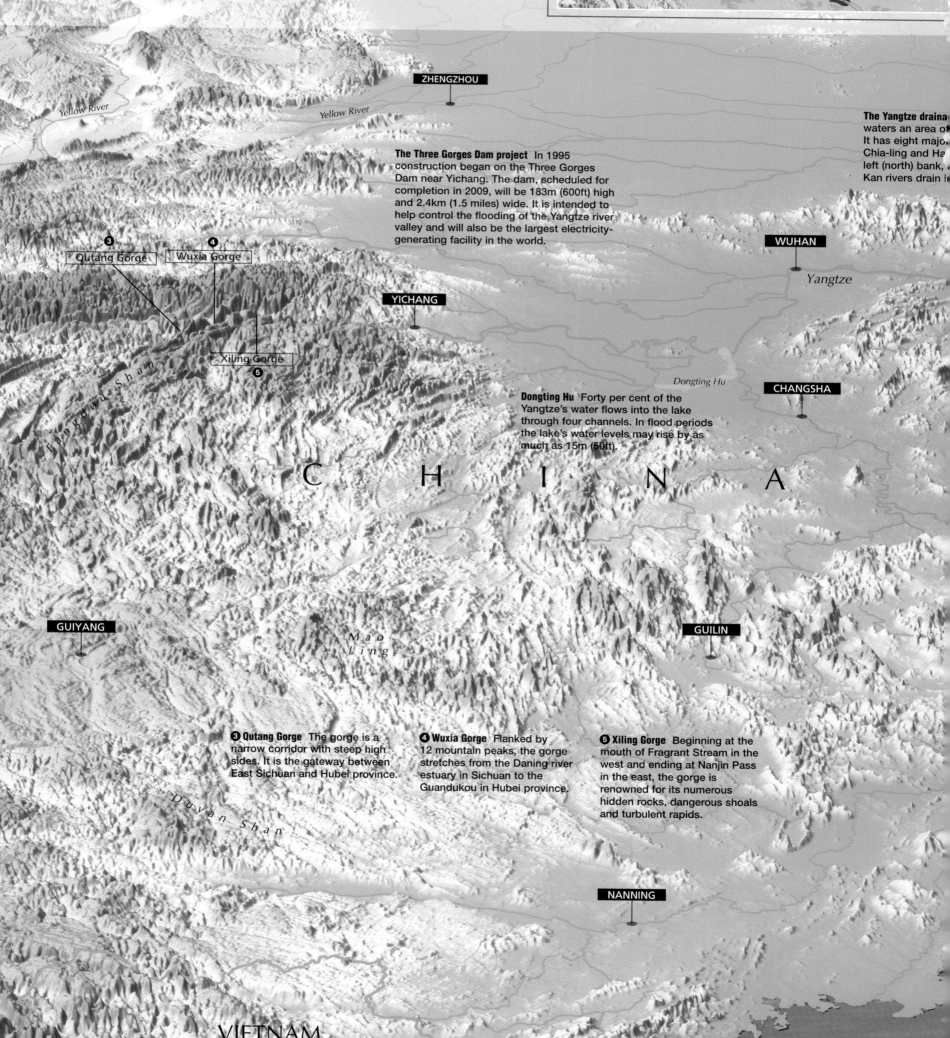

ZHENGZHOU

Yellow River

Yellow River

The Yangtze draina waters an area of It has eight majo Chia-ling and Ha left (north) bank, Kan rivers drain i

The Three Gorges Dam project In 1995 construction began on the Three Gorges Dam near Yichang. The dam, scheduled for completion in 2009, will be 183m (600ft) high and 2.4km (1.5 miles) wide. It is intended to help control the flooding of the Yangtze river valley and will also be the largest electricity-generating facility in the world.

WUHAN

❸ Qutang Gorge ❹ Wuxia Gorge

Yangtze

YICHANG

Xiling Gorge

❺

Dongting Hu

CHANGSHA

Dongting Hu Forty per cent of the Yangtze's water flows into the lake through four channels. In flood periods the lake's water levels may rise by as much as 15m (50ft).

Fangdiou Shan

C H I N A

GUIYANG

Mao Ling

GUILIN

Duyan Shan

❸ Qutang Gorge The gorge is a narrow corridor with steep high sides. It is the gateway between East Sichuan and Hubei province.

❹ Wuxia Gorge Flanked by 12 mountain peaks, the gorge stretches from the Daning river estuary in Sichuan to the Guandukou in Hubei province.

❺ Xiling Gorge Beginning at the mouth of Fragrant Stream in the west and ending at Nanjin Pass in the east, the gorge is renowned for its numerous hidden rocks, dangerous shoals and turbulent rapids.

NANNING

VIETNAM

Gulf of Tongking

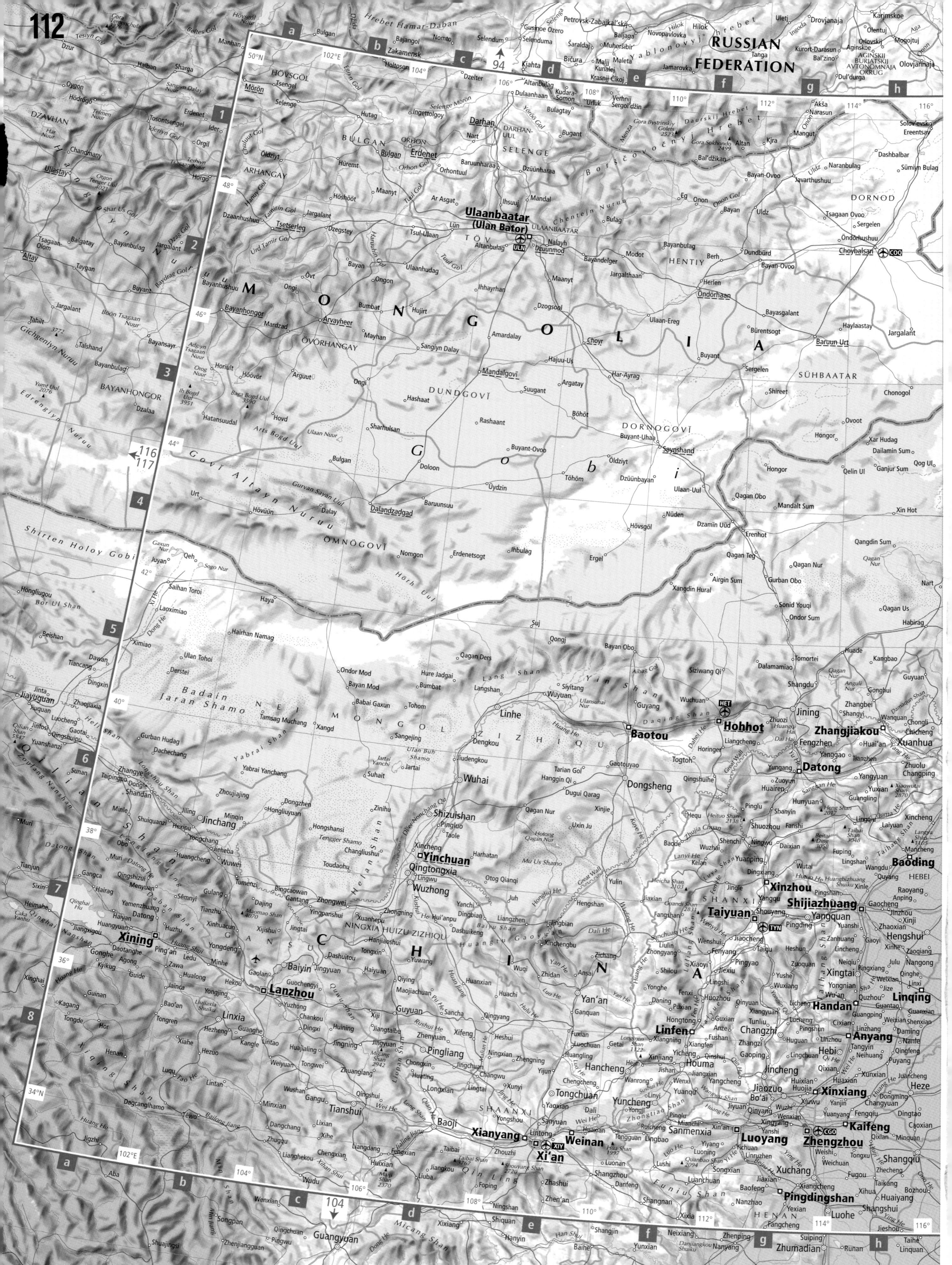
RUSSIAN FEDERATION
MONGOLIA
CHINA
Gobi
NEI MONGOL ZIZHIQU
NINGXIA HUIZU ZIZHIQU
GANSU
SHAANXI
SHANXI
HEBEI
HENAN
HÖVSGÖL
DZAVHAN
BULGAN
ORHON
ARHANGAY
SELENGE
DARHAN-UUL
TÖV
HENTIY
DORNOD
SÜHBAATAR
BAYANHONGOR
ÖVÖRHANGAY
DUNDGOVĬ
DORNOGOVĬ
ÖMNÖGOVĬ
Ulaanbaatar (Ulan Bator)
Darhan
Erdenet
Bulgan
Mörön
Uliastay
Tsetserleg
Bayanhongor
Arvayheer
Mandalgovĭ
Dalandzadgad
Saynshand
Choybalsan
Öndörhaan
Baruun Urt
Choyr
Altay
Kjahta
Hrebet Hamar-Daban
Jablonovyj hrebet
Hangayn Nuruu
Govĭ Altayn Nuruu
Shirten Holoy Gobi
Badain Jaran Shamo
Tengger Shamo
Mu Us Shamo
Yin Shan
Lang Shan
Qilian Shan
Helan Shan
Huang He
Wei He
Great Wall
Hohhot
Baotou
Jining
Zhangjiakou
Datong
Xuanhua
Baoding
Shijiazhuang
Taiyuan
Xinzhou
Yinchuan
Wuhai
Shizuishan
Linhe
Dongsheng
Xining
Lanzhou
Jinchang
Jiayuguan
Baiyin
Wuzhong
Linxia
Guyuan
Pingliang
Tianshui
Baoji
Xianyang
Xi'an
Weinan
Tongchuan
Yan'an
Linfen
Changzhi
Handan
Linqing
Xingtai
Anyang
Hebi
Xinxiang
Jiaozuo
Luoyang
Zhengzhou
Kaifeng
Pingdingshan
Sanmenxia
Yuncheng
Hancheng
Zhumadian
Guangyuan
Qin Ling
Funiu Shan
94
104
116
117
50°N
48°
46°
44°
42°
40°
38°
36°
34°N
102°E
104°
106°
108°
110°
112°
114°
116°
a
b
c
d
e
f
g
h
1
2
3
4
5
6
7
8

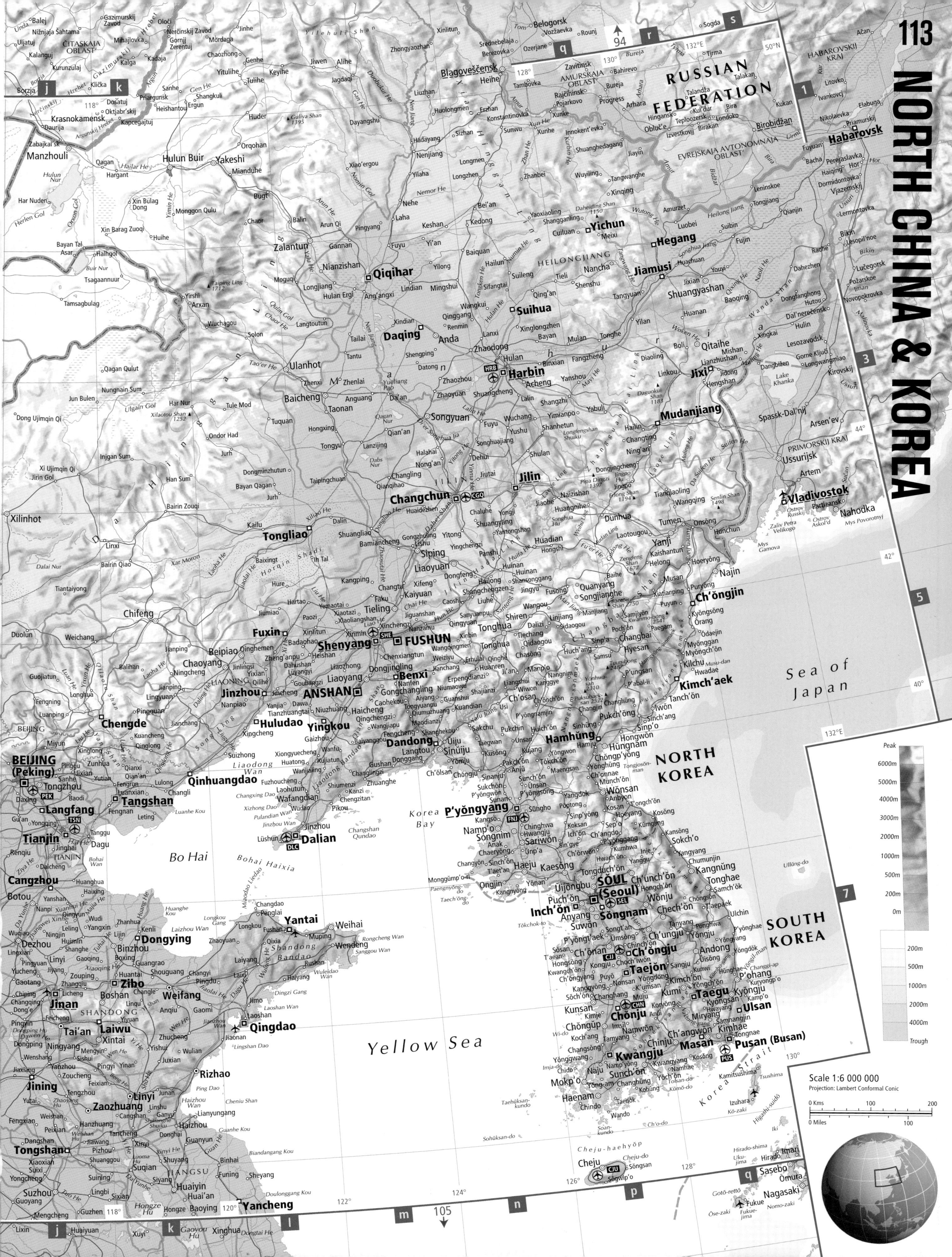

Scale 1:6 000 000
Projection: Lambert Conformal Conic

| 0 Kms | 100 | 200 |
| 0 Miles | 100 | |

Peak
6000m
5000m
4000m
3000m
2000m
1000m
500m
200m
0m

200m
500m
1000m
2000m
4000m
Trough

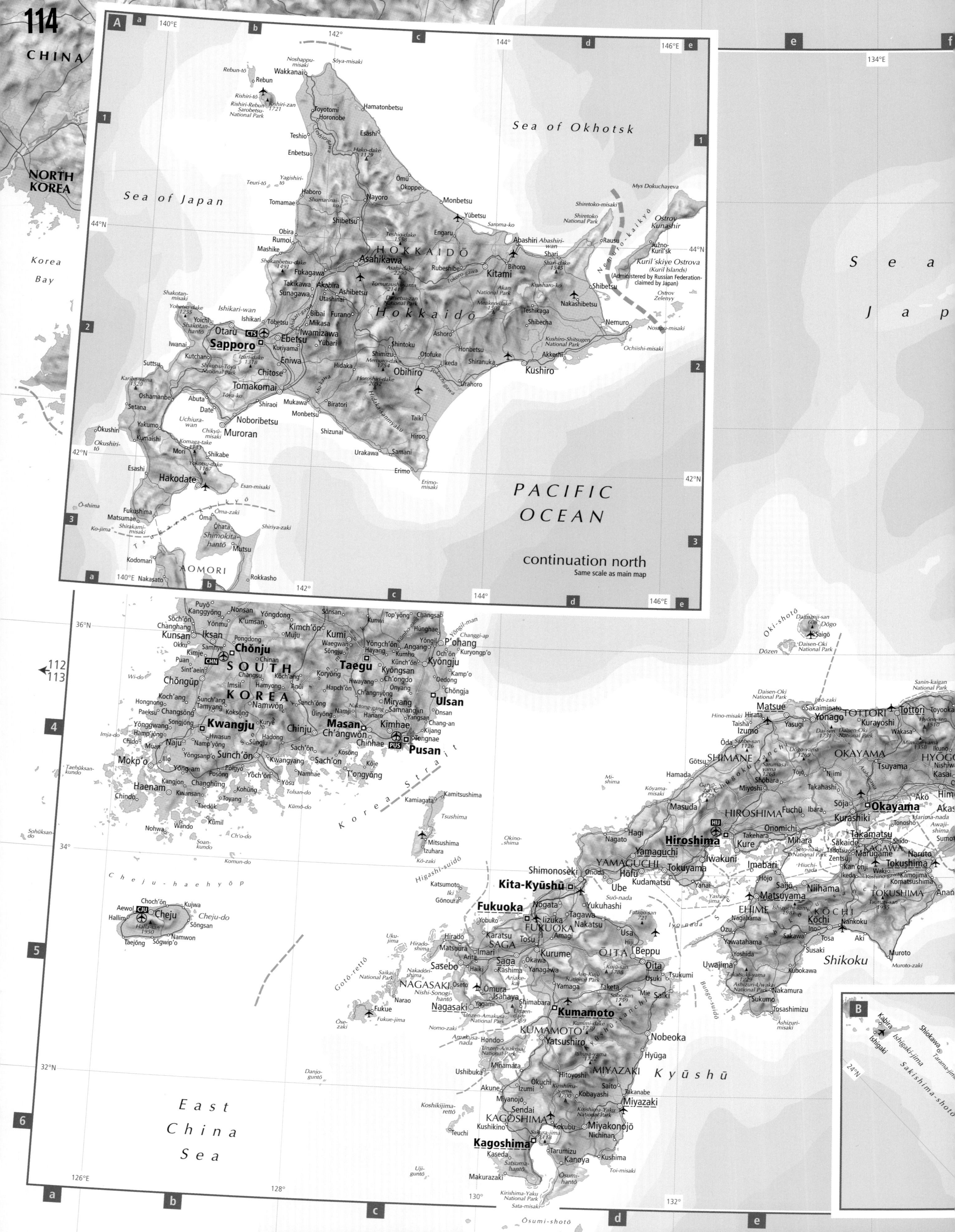
CHINA
NORTH KOREA
Korea Bay
Sea of Japan
Sea of Okhotsk
PACIFIC OCEAN
continuation north
Same scale as main map
Wakkanai
Rebun
Rishiri-tō
Rishiri-zan 1721
Rishiri-Rebun-Sarobetsu National Park
Sōya-misaki
Toyotomi
Horonobe
Hamatonbetsu
Esashi
Teshio
Enbetsu
Teuri-tō
Yagishiri-tō
Haboro
Omu
Okoppe
Tomamae
Nayoro
Monbetsu
Yūbetsu
Saroma-ko
Shibetsu
Obira
Rumoi
Mashike
Engaru
Abashiri
HOKKAIDŌ
Hokkaidō
Asahikawa
Fukagawa
Takikawa
Akabira
Ashibetsu
Sunagawa
Utashinai
Rubeshibe
Kitami
Bihoro
Shari
Shiretoko-misaki
Shiretoko National Park
Rausu
Shibetsu
Nakashibetsu
Teshikaga
Shibecha
Nemuro
Nosappu-misaki
Ochiishi-misaki
Akkeshi
Kushiro
Kushiro-Shitsugen National Park
Mys Dokuchayeva
Ostrov Kunashir
Južno-Kuril'sk
Kuril'skiye Ostrova (Kuril Islands)
(Administered by Russian Federation, claimed by Japan)
Ostrov Zelenyy
Nemuro-kaikyō
Ishikari-wan
Shakotan-misaki
Shakotan-hantō
Yoichi
Ishikari
Tōbetsu
Otaru
CTS
Sapporo
Ebetsu
Iwamizawa
Bibai
Mikasa
Furano
Yūbari
Kuriyama
Eniwa
Chitose
Tomakomai
Iwanai
Kutchan
Suttsu
Shikotsu-Tōya National Park
Shintoku
Otofuke
Shimizu
Obihiro
Ikeda
Honbetsu
Shiranuka
Ashoro
Hidaka
Oshamanbe
Setana
Abuta
Date
Shiraoi
Noboribetsu
Muroran
Uchiura-wan
Mukawa
Monbetsu
Biratori
Taiki
Hiroo
Shizunai
Urakawa
Samani
Erimo
Erimo-misaki
Okushiri
Okushiri-tō
Yakumo
Kumaishi
Mori
Shikabe
Esashi
Hakodate
Esan-misaki
Ō-shima
Fukushima
Matsumae
Ko-jima
Shirakami-misaki
Tsugaru-kaikyō
Ōma-zaki
Ōma
Ohata
Shimokita-hantō
Shiriya-zaki
Mutsu
Kodomari
AOMORI
Nakasato
Rokkasho
Sea of Japan
Oki-shotō
Dōgo
Saigō
Dōzen
Daisen-Oki National Park
Puyō
Nonsan
Kanggyŏng
Yŏngdong
Kimch'ŏn
Kunsan
Iksan
Chŏnju
CHN
SOUTH KOREA
Kumi
P'ohang
Taegu
Kyŏngju
Chŏngŭp
Kwangju
Namwŏn
Ulsan
Masan
Ch'angwŏn
Chinju
Kimhae
PUS
Pusan
Mokp'o
Sunch'ŏn
Yŏsu
Haenam
Wando
T'ongyŏng
Korea Strait
Tsushima
Kamitsushima
Mitsushima
Izuhara
Cheju-haehyŏp
Cheju
CJU
Cheju-do
Halla-san 1950
Sŏgwip'o
Hallim
Aewol
Namwon
East China Sea
Gotō-rettō
Fukue
Danjo-guntō
Koshikijima-rettō
Uji-guntō
Matsue
Yonago
Tottori
Izumo
SHIMANE
OKAYAMA
Okayama
Kurashiki
Hamada
HIROSHIMA
HIJ
Hiroshima
Kure
Iwakuni
Onomichi
Fukuyama
Takamatsu
KAGAWA
Tokushima
TOKUSHIMA
Naruto
Imabari
Matsuyama
EHIME
KŌCHI
Kōchi
Shikoku
Muroto
Muroto-zaki
Uwajima
Sukumo
Ashizuri-misaki
Hagi
Yamaguchi
YAMAGUCHI
Tokuyama
Hōfu
Ube
Shimonoseki
Kita-Kyūshū
Fukuoka
FUKUOKA
SAGA
Saga
Karatsu
Sasebo
Hirado
NAGASAKI
Nagasaki
Isahaya
Omura
Shimabara
Kurume
ŌITA
Ōita
Beppu
Usuki
Saiki
Kumamoto
KUMAMOTO
Yatsushiro
Nobeoka
Hyūga
MIYAZAKI
Miyazaki
Kyūshū
Hitoyoshi
Kobayashi
Miyakonojō
Nichinan
Sendai
KAGOSHIMA
Kagoshima
Kanoya
Makurazaki
Ōsumi-hantō
Satsuma-hantō
Ōsumi-shotō
Sata-misaki
Bungo-suidō
B
Ishigaki
Ishigaki-jima
Sakishima-shotō
Shiokawa
Kabira
112
113

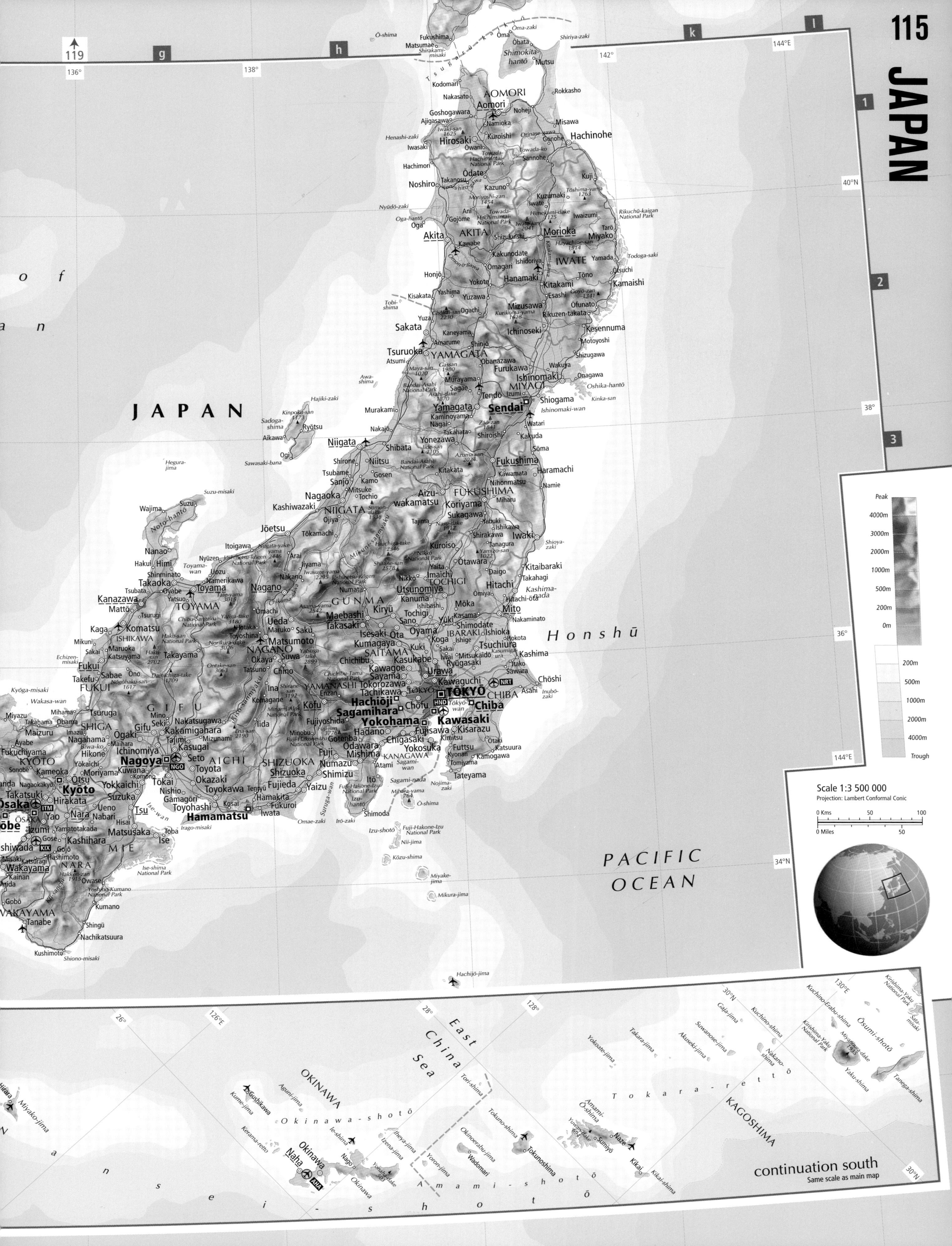
JAPAN
Honshū
PACIFIC OCEAN
AOMORI
Aomori
Hirosaki
Hachinohe
Shimokita-hantō
Mutsu
Ōdate
Noshiro
Akita
AKITA
Morioka
IWATE
Miyako
Kamaishi
Hanamaki
Kitakami
Mizusawa
Ichinoseki
Kesennuma
Sakata
Tsuruoka
YAMAGATA
Yamagata
Ishinomaki
MIYAGI
Sendai
Shiogama
Niigata
NIIGATA
Nagaoka
Kashiwazaki
Jōetsu
Sado-shima
Fukushima
FUKUSHIMA
Kōriyama
Aizu-wakamatsu
Iwaki
Hitachi
Mito
IBARAKI
Utsunomiya
TOCHIGI
GUNMA
Maebashi
Takasaki
Nagano
NAGANO
Matsumoto
Toyama
TOYAMA
Kanazawa
ISHIKAWA
Fukui
FUKUI
SAITAMA
Urawa
Tōkyō
TŌKYŌ
Chiba
CHIBA
Kawasaki
Yokohama
KANAGAWA
Sagamihara
Hachiōji
Yokosuka
Kōfu
YAMANASHI
Shizuoka
SHIZUOKA
Hamamatsu
Numazu
Gifu
GIFU
Nagoya
AICHI
Toyohashi
Okazaki
Tsu
MIE
Kyōto
KYOTO
Ōsaka
Nara
NARA
Wakayama
SHIGA
Ōtsu
Izu-shotō
Ōshima
Miyake-jima
Hachijō-jima
Scale 1:3 500 000
Projection: Lambert Conformal Conic
0 Kms 50 100
0 Miles 50
Peak
4000m
3000m
2000m
1000m
500m
200m
0m
200m
500m
1000m
2000m
4000m
Trough
East China Sea
OKINAWA
Okinawa-shotō
Naha
Okinawa
KAGOSHIMA
Tokara-rettō
Amami-shotō
Nansei-shotō
Ōsumi-shotō
Yaku-shima
Tanega-shima
Tokuno-shima
continuation south
Same scale as main map

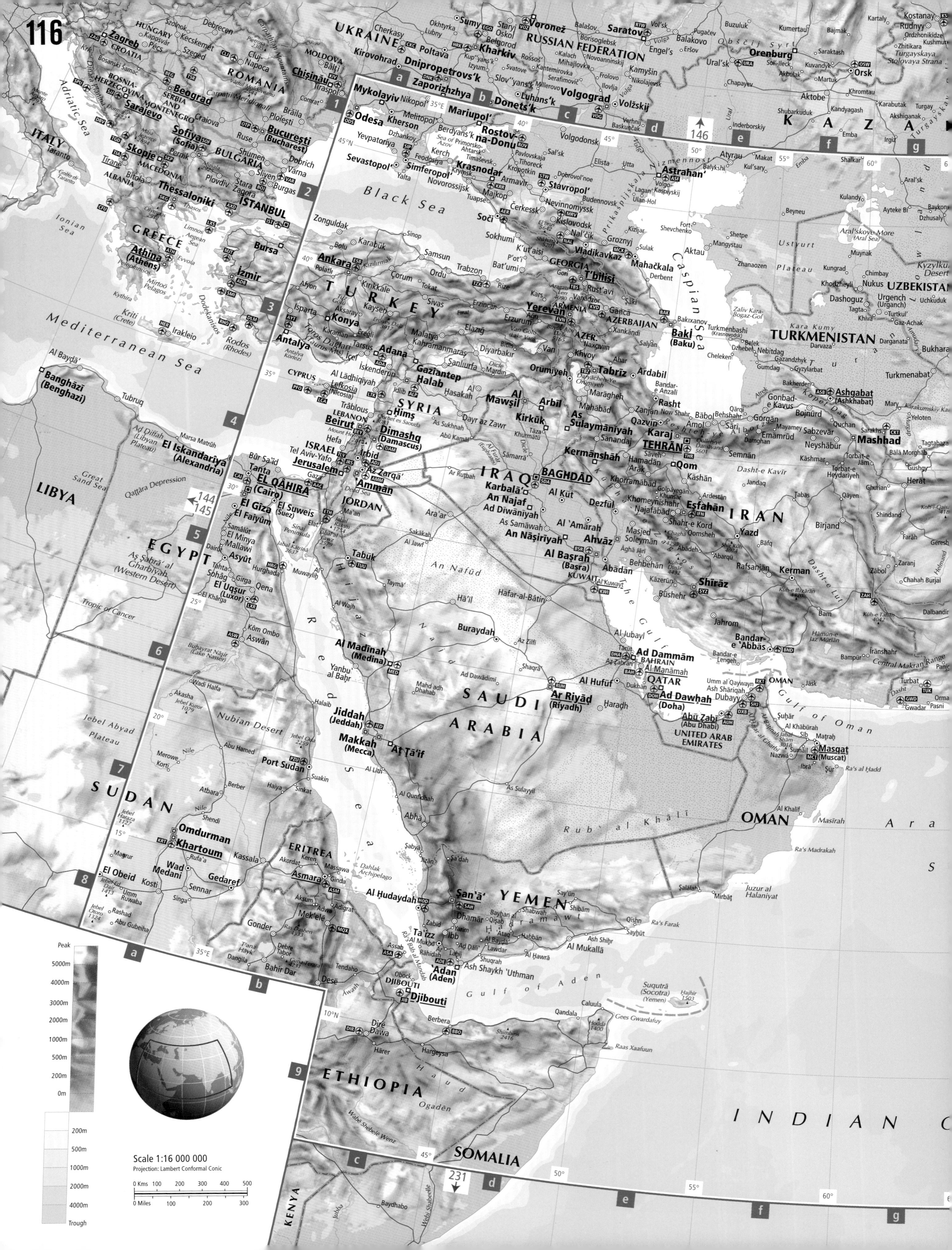
UKRAINE
RUSSIAN FEDERATION
KAZA
HUNGARY
CROATIA
Zagreb
Debrecen
Szolnok
Kecskemét
Szeged
Pécs
ROMANIA
Cluj-Napoca
MOLDOVA
Chişinău
Tiraspol
Cherkasy
Kirovohrad
Dnipropetrovs'k
Poltava
Okhtyrka
Lubny
Sumy
Kharkiv
Belgorod
Stary Oskol
Voronež
Balašov
Saratov
Vol'sk
Pugačev
Balakovo
Engel's
Borisoglebsk
Novoanninskij
Mihajlovka
Kalach
Kamyšin
Frolovo
Ilovlja
Nikolajevsk
Buzuluk
Kumertau
Bajmak
Obščij Syrt
Orenburg
Ural'sk
Sol'-Ileck
Kuvandyk
Orsk
Akbulak
Martuk
Chapayev
Aktobe
Khromtau
Kartaly
Kostanay
Rudnyy
Turgayskaya Stolovaya Strana
BOSNIA-HERZEGOVINA
SERBIA AND MONTENEGRO
Beograd
Sarajevo
Adriatic Sea
Craiova
Bucureşti (Bucharest)
Ploieşti
Brăila
Zaporizhzhya
Mykolayiv
Nikopol'
Melitopol'
Kherson
Odesa
Mariupol'
Rostov-na-Donu
Donets'k
Luhans'k
Volgograd
Volžskij
Berdyans'k
Dzhankoy
Yevpatoriya
Sevastopol'
Simferopol'
Yalta
Feodosiya
Kerch
Sea of Azov
Krasnodar
Novorossijsk
Tuapse
Majkop
Armavir
Stavropol'
Elista
Volgodonsk
Sal'sk
Astrahan'
Atyrau
Makat
Kul'sary
Emba
Shalkar
Aral'sk
ITALY
Taranto
Sofiya (Sofia)
BULGARIA
Skopje
MACEDONIA
Tirane
ALBANIA
Varna
Burgas
Dobrich
Plovdiv
Thessaloniki
ISTANBUL
Ionian Sea
GREECE
Athina (Athens)
Bursa
İzmir
Black Sea
Zonguldak
Sinop
Samsun
Trabzon
Soči
Sokhumi
K'ut'aisi
Bat'umi
GEORGIA
T'bilisi
Vladikavkaz
Groznyj
Nal'čik
Kislovodsk
Nevinnomyssk
Mahačkala
Derbent
Caspian Sea
Aktau
Ustyurt Plateau
Aral'skoye More (Aral Sea)
UZBEKISTAN
Kyzylkum Desert
Nukus
Urgench
Dashoguz
Khiva
Ankara
TURKEY
Kayseri
Sivas
Erzurum
Yerevan
ARMENIA
AZERBAIJAN
Bakı (Baku)
Konya
Antalya
Adana
Malatya
Diyarbakır
Van
Tabrīz
Ardabil
Turkmenbashi
TURKMENISTAN
Ashgabat (Ashkhabat)
Mary
Turkmenabat
Bukhara
Mediterranean Sea
Kriti (Crete)
Irakleio
Rodos (Rhodes)
CYPRUS
Lefkosia (Nicosia)
Gaziantep
Halab
SYRIA
Hims
Al Mawşil
Arbīl
Kirkūk
Orūmīyeh
Rasht
Qazvīn
Karaj
TEHRĀN
Mashhad
Banghāzī (Benghazi)
Tubruq
LEBANON
Beirut
Dimashq (Damascus)
ISRAEL
Tel Aviv-Yafo
Jerusalem
'Ammān
Az Zarqā'
JORDAN
IRAQ
BAGHDĀD
Karbalā'
An Najaf
Kermānshāh
Hamadān
Qom
Kāshān
Eşfahān
IRAN
Yazd
Herat
El Iskandarîya (Alexandria)
El Qâhira (Cairo)
El Giza
El Suweis (Suez)
Qattara Depression
LIBYA
EGYPT
Great Sand Sea
Aş Şahrā' al Gharbīyah (Western Desert)
Asyût
Luxor
Aswân
Tropic of Cancer
Tabūk
An Nafūd
Ḩā'il
Al Başrah (Basra)
KUWAIT
Al Kuwayt
Ahvāz
Shīrāz
Kerman
Bandar-e 'Abbās
Al Madīnah (Medina)
Buraydah
Ad Dammām
BAHRAIN
Al Manāmah
QATAR
Ad Dawḩah (Doha)
Dubayy
Abū Zabī (Abu Dhabi)
UNITED ARAB EMIRATES
OMAN
Masqaţ (Muscat)
Gulf of Oman
Ar Riyāḍ (Riyadh)
SAUDI ARABIA
Jiddah (Jeddah)
Makkah (Mecca)
Aţ Ţā'if
Red Sea
Nubian Desert
Jebel Abyad Plateau
Port Sudan
SUDAN
Omdurman
Khartoum
Kassala
ERITREA
Asmara
Rub' al Khālī
OMAN
Arabian Sea
Ṣan'ā'
YEMEN
Al Ḩudaydah
Ta'izz
'Adan (Aden)
Al Mukallā
Gulf of Aden
Suquţrā (Socotra) (Yemen)
DJIBOUTI
Djibouti
ETHIOPIA
Ogadēn
SOMALIA
KENYA
INDIAN OCEAN
146
144
145
231
Peak
5000m
4000m
3000m
2000m
1000m
500m
0m
200m
500m
1000m
2000m
4000m
Trough
Scale 1:16 000 000
Projection: Lambert Conformal Conic
0 Kms 100 200 300 400 500
0 Miles 100 200 300

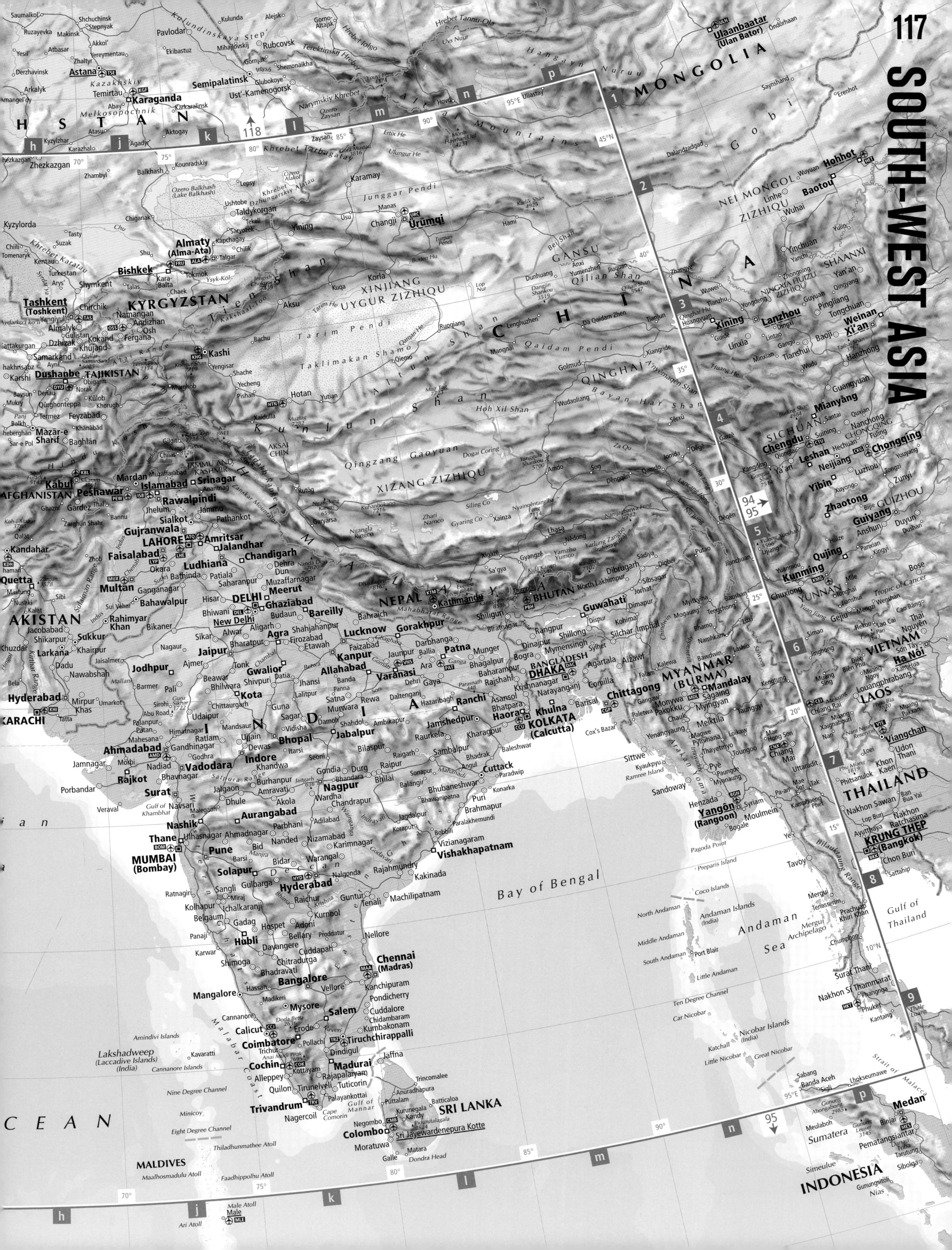
MONGOLIA
Ulaanbaatar (Ulan Bator)
Gobi
NEI MONGOL ZIZHIQU
Hohhot
Baotou
Astana
Karaganda
Semipalatinsk
Pavlodar
Almaty (Alma-Ata)
Bishkek
KYRGYZSTAN
Tashkent (Toshkent)
TAJIKISTAN
Dushanbe
Ürümqi
XINJIANG UYGUR ZIZHIQU
Tarim Pendi
Taklimakan Shamo
Kashi
Kunlun Shan
CHINA
QINGHAI
GANSU
Xining
Lanzhou
Xi'an
SICHUAN
Chengdu
Chongqing
GUIZHOU
Guiyang
YUNNAN
Kunming
XIZANG ZIZHIQU
Qingzang Gaoyuan
Lhasa
AFGHANISTAN
Kābul
Peshawar
Islamabad
Rawalpindi
Srinagar
Lahore
Faisalabad
Multan
Quetta
PAKISTAN
Hyderabad
KARACHI
Amritsar
Chandigarh
Ludhiana
DELHI
New Delhi
NEPAL
Kathmandu
BHUTAN
Guwahati
Agra
Lucknow
Kanpur
Jaipur
Jodhpur
Gwalior
Allahabad
Varanasi
Patna
INDIA
BANGLADESH
DHAKA
KOLKATA (Calcutta)
Chittagong
MYANMAR (BURMA)
Mandalay
Yangon (Rangoon)
Ahmadabad
Vadodara
Surat
Rajkot
Indore
Bhopal
Jabalpur
Nagpur
Cuttack
Nashik
Thane
MUMBAI (Bombay)
Pune
Solapur
Aurangabad
Hyderabad
Vishakhapatnam
Bay of Bengal
Hubli
Bangalore
Chennai (Madras)
Mangalore
Mysore
Salem
Coimbatore
Madurai
Cochin
Trivandrum
Tiruchchirappalli
SRI LANKA
Colombo
Sri Jayewardenepura Kotte
MALDIVES
Male
Lakshadweep (Laccadive Islands) (India)
Andaman Islands (India)
Andaman Sea
Nicobar Islands (India)
VIETNAM
Ha Nôi
LAOS
Viangchan
THAILAND
KRUNG THEP (Bangkok)
Gulf of Thailand
INDONESIA
Medan
Sumatera
OCEAN

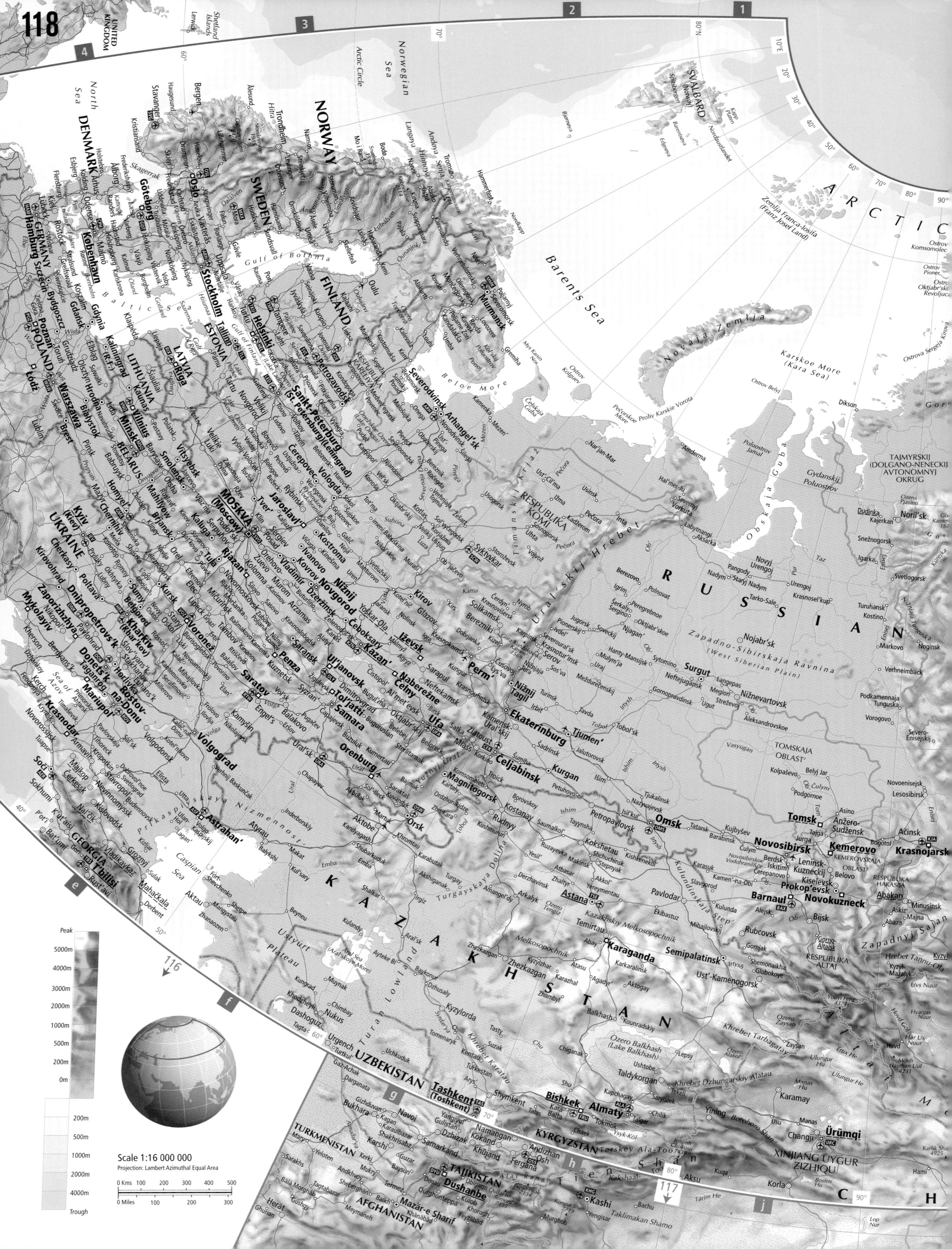

UNITED KINGDOM
Shetland Islands
Lerwick
Norwegian Sea
Arctic Circle
North Sea
SVALBARD (Norway)
Spitsbergen
Nordaustlandet
Barentsøya
Edgeøya
Bjørnøya
Kong Karls Land
NORWAY
SWEDEN
FINLAND
DENMARK
ESTONIA
LATVIA
LITHUANIA
BELARUS
POLAND
GERMANY
UKRAINE
RUSSIA
KAZAKHSTAN
UZBEKISTAN
TURKMENISTAN
TAJIKISTAN
KYRGYZSTAN
AFGHANISTAN
GEORGIA
XINJIANG UYGUR ZIZHIQU
ARCTIC
Zemlja Franca-Iosifa (Franz Josef Land)
Barents Sea
Novaja Zemlja
Karskoe More (Kara Sea)
Beloe More
Gulf of Bothnia
Baltic Sea
Gulf of Finland
Skagerrak
Caspian Sea
Sea of Azov
Aral Sea (Aral'skoye More)
Ozero Balkhash (Lake Balkhash)
Ural'skij Hrebet
Zapadno-Sibirskaja Ravnina (West Siberian Plain)
Turan Lowland
Kazakhskiy Melkosopochnik
Prikaspijskaja Nizmennost'
Ustyurt Plateau
Tien Shan
Taklimakan Shamo
Obskaja Guba
Gydanskij Poluostrov
Poluostrov Jamal
TAJMYRSKIJ (DOLGANO-NENECKIJ AVTONOMNYJ) OKRUG
RESPUBLIKA KOMI
RESPUBLIKA KARELIYA
TOMSKAJA OBLAST'
KEMEROVSKAJA OBLAST'
RESPUBLIKA HAKASIJA
RESPUBLIKA ALTAJ
Oslo
Stockholm
Helsinki
Tallinn
Riga
Vilnius
Minsk
København
Hamburg
Warszawa
Gdańsk
Kaliningrad (R.F.)
Göteborg
Bergen
Stavanger
Trondheim
Oulu
Murmansk
Arkhangel'sk
Severodvinsk
Petrozavodsk
Sankt-Peterburg (St Petersburg/Leningrad)
Novgorod
Vologda
Čerepovec
Jaroslavl'
Tver'
MOSKVA (Moscow)
Kyiv (Kiev)
Smolensk
Vitsyebsk
Homyel'
Kharkiv
Dnipropetrovs'k
Zaporizhzhya
Mykolayiv
Donets'k
Rostov-na-Donu
Krasnodar
Voronež
Kursk
Tula
Rjazan'
Ivanovo
Kostroma
Kirov
Nižnij Novgorod
Kazan'
Iževsk
Perm'
Ufa
Samara
Saratov
Penza
Volgograd
Astrakhan'
Orenburg
Čeljabinsk
Ekaterinburg
Nižnij Tagil
Tjumen'
Kurgan
Magnitogorsk
Omsk
Novosibirsk
Tomsk
Kemerovo
Krasnojarsk
Barnaul
Novokuzneck
Noril'sk
Vorkuta
Syktyvkar
Surgut
Astana
Karaganda
Semipalatinsk
Pavlodar
Aktobe
Atyrau
Almaty
Bishkek
Tashkent (Toshkent)
Dushanbe
Samarkand
Bukhara
Kashi
Ürümqi
Tbilisi
Groznyj
Mahačkala
Soči
Scale 1:16 000 000
Projection: Lambert Azimuthal Equal Area
0 Kms 100 200 300 400 500
0 Miles 100 200 300
Peak
5000m
4000m
3000m
2000m
1000m
500m
200m
0m
200m
500m
1000m
2000m
4000m
Trough
116
117

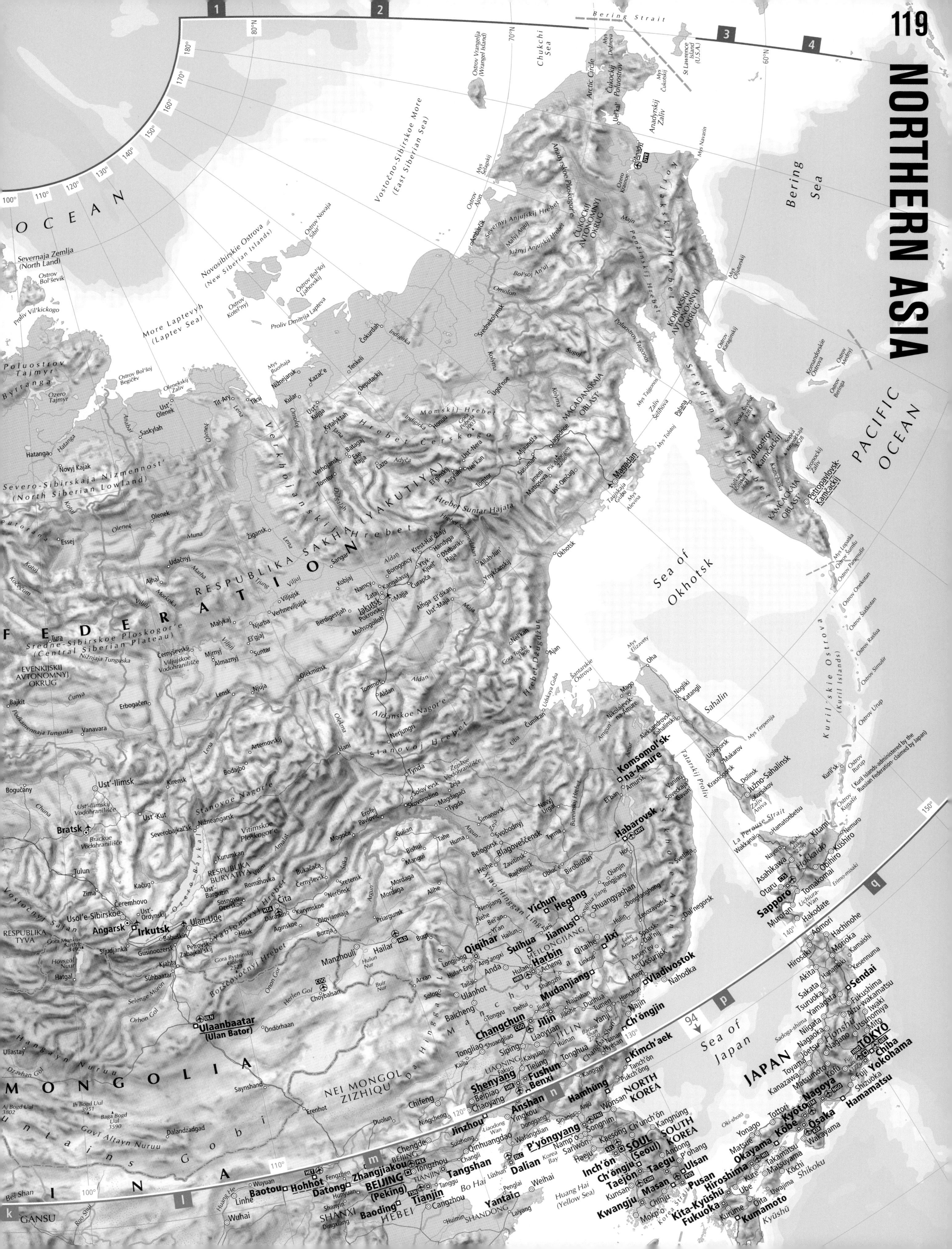
Bering Strait
Chukchi Sea
Bering Sea
PACIFIC OCEAN
Sea of Okhotsk
Sea of Japan
OCEAN
Vostočno-Sibirskoe More
(East Siberian Sea)
More Laptevyh
(Laptev Sea)
Novosibirskie Ostrova
(New Siberian Islands)
Severnaja Zemlja
(North Land)
Poluostrov Tajmyr
Severo-Sibirskaja Nizmennost'
(North Siberian Lowland)
Sredne-Sibirskoe Ploskogor'e
(Central Siberian Plateau)
RESPUBLIKA SAKHA (YAKUTIYA)
FEDERATION
ČUKOTSKIJ AVTONOMNYJ OKRUG
KORJAKSKIJ AVTONOMNYJ OKRUG
MAGADANSKAJA OBLAST'
KAMČATSKAJA OBLAST'
EVENKIJSKIJ AVTONOMNYJ OKRUG
RESPUBLIKA BURYATIYA
RESPUBLIKA TYVA
Verhojanskij Hrebet
Hrebet Čerskogo
Stanovoj Hrebet
Sredinnyj Hrebet
Poluostrov Kamčatka
Petropavlovsk-Kamčatskij
Magadan
Jakutsk
Komsomol'sk-na-Amure
Habarovsk
Vladivostok
Sahalin
Kuril'skie Ostrova
(Kuril Islands)
Ozero Bajkal
Irkutsk
Ulan-Ude
Bratsk
Ulaanbaatar
(Ulan Bator)
MONGOLIA
Gobi
NEI MONGOL ZIZHIQU
HEILONGJIANG
JILIN
LIAONING
Harbin
Changchun
Shenyang
BEIJING
(Peking)
Tianjin
NORTH KOREA
P'yŏngyang
SOUTH KOREA
SOUL
(Seoul)
Pusan
JAPAN
Hokkaidō
Sapporo
Honshū
TŌKYŌ
Yokohama
Nagoya
Ōsaka
Kyōto
Kōbe
Hiroshima
Fukuoka
Kyūshū
Shikoku
Huang Hai
(Yellow Sea)
Bo Hai

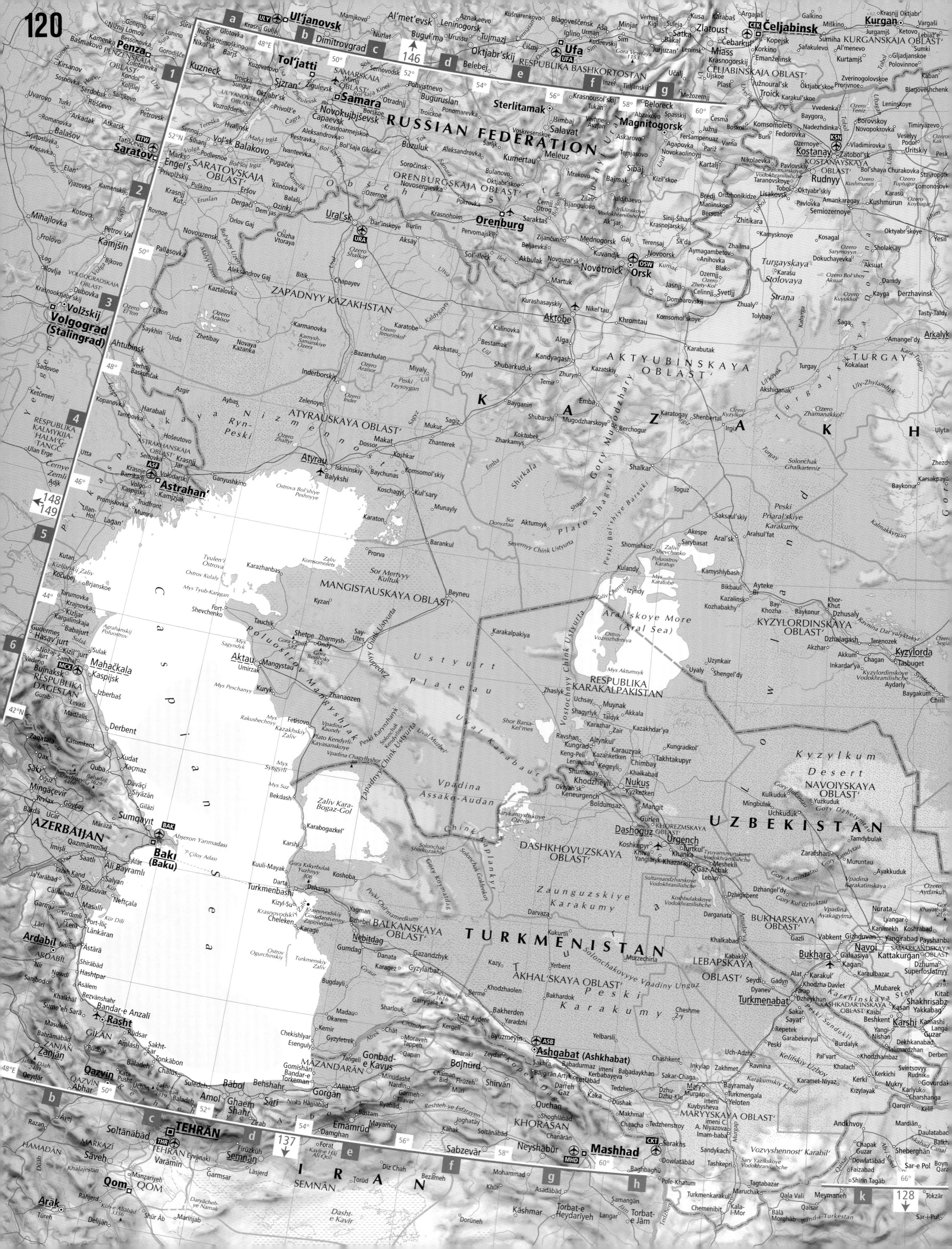
RUSSIAN FEDERATION
KAZAKH
UZBEKISTAN
TURKMENISTAN
AZERBAIJAN
IRAN
Caspian Sea
Aral'skoye More (Aral Sea)
Ul'janovsk
Dimitrovgrad
Tol'jatti
Samara
Novokujbyševsk
Syzran'
Penza
Saratov
Engel's
Volžskij
Volgograd (Stalingrad)
Astrahan'
Mahačkala
Kaspijsk
Derbent
Sumqayit
Bakı (Baku)
Ufa
Sterlitamak
Salavat
Magnitogorsk
Beloreck
Zlatoust
Miass
Čeljabinsk
Kurgan
Kostanay
Rudnyy
Orenburg
Orsk
Novotroick
Ural'sk
Aktobe
Atyrau
Aktau
Beyneu
Kyzylorda
Nukus
Urgench
Dashoguz
Bukhara
Navoi
Karshi
Turkmenabat
Ashgabat (Ashkhabat)
Mary
Turkmenbashi
Nebitdag
Mashhad
Tehrān
Qazvin
Zanjān
Ardabil
Rasht
Semnān
Qom
Arāk
Gorgān
Sāri
Bābol
SARATOVSKAJA OBLAST'
SAMARSKAJA OBLAST'
ORENBURGSKAJA OBLAST'
RESPUBLIKA BASHKORTOSTAN
ČELJABINSKAJA OBLAST'
KURGANSKAJA OBLAST'
KOSTANAYSKAYA OBLAST'
ZAPADNYY KAZAKHSTAN
AKTYUBINSKAYA OBLAST'
ATYRAUSKAYA OBLAST'
MANGISTAUSKAYA OBLAST'
KYZYLORDINSKAYA OBLAST'
RESPUBLIKA KARAKALPAKISTAN
NAVOIYSKAYA OBLAST'
BUKHARSKAYA OBLAST'
KHOREZMSKAYA OBLAST'
DASHKHOVUZSKAYA OBLAST'
BALKANSKAYA OBLAST'
AKHAL'SKAYA OBLAST'
LEBAPSKAYA OBLAST'
MARYYSKAYA OBLAST'
RESPUBLIKA DAGESTAN
RESPUBLIKA KALMYKIJA-HALMG' TANGC
ASTRAHANSKAJA OBLAST'
VOLGOGRADSKAJA OBLAST'
KHORASAN
MĀZANDARĀN
GĪLĀN
SEMNĀN
Ustyurt Plateau
Kyzylkum Desert
Zaunguzskiye Karakumy
Peski Karakumy
Zaliv Kara-Bogaz-Gol
Poluostrov Mangyshlak
Prikaspiyskaya Nizmennost'
Obščij Syrt
Turgayskaya Stolovaya Strana
148 149
146
137
128

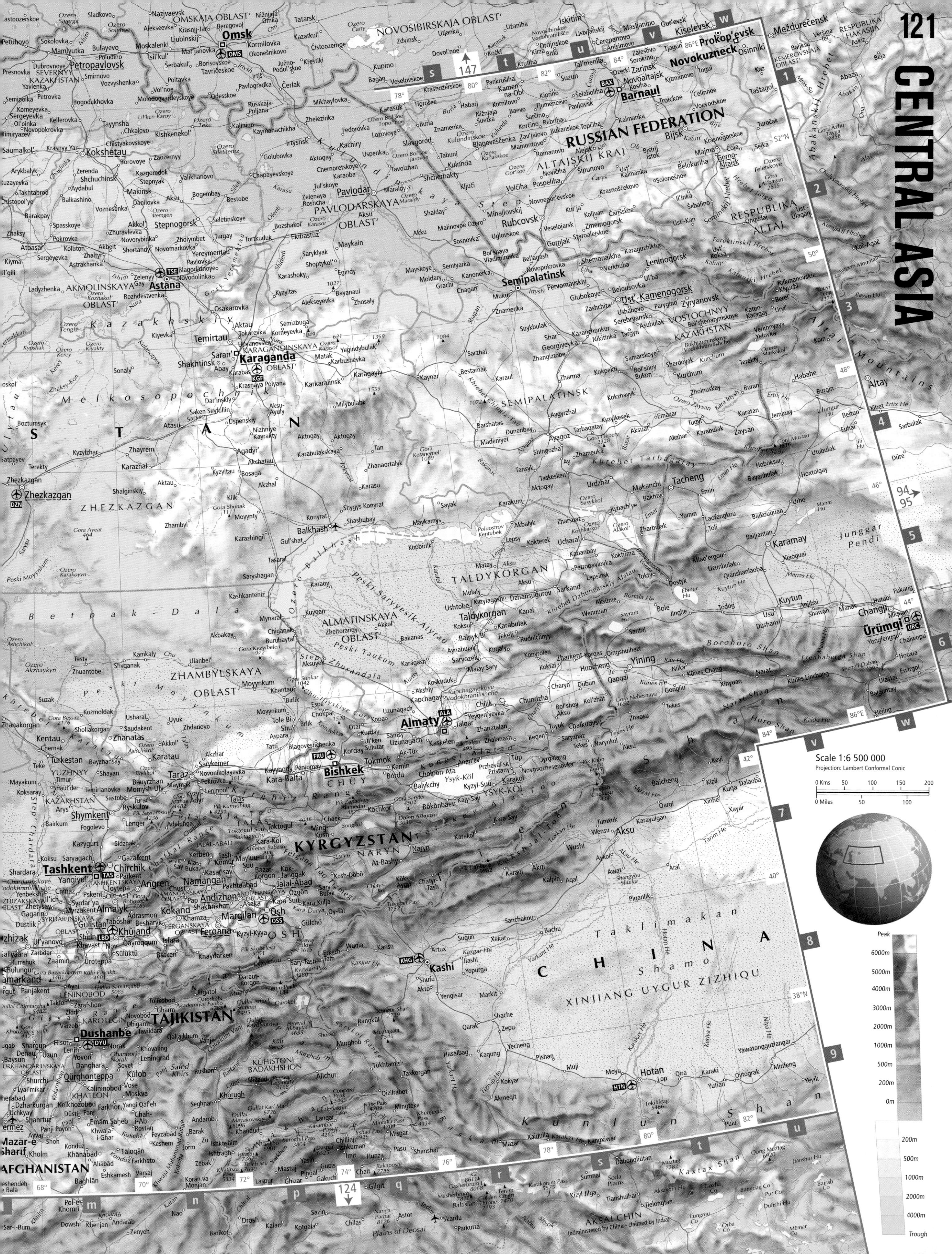

RUSSIAN FEDERATION

Omsk
OMS

NOVOSIBIRSKAJA OBLAST'

Iskitim

Kiselevsk w

Prokop'evsk

Novokuzneck

Mezdurečensk

REPUBLIKA HAKASIA

Barnaul
BAX

Novoaltajsk

Bijsk

ALTAJSKIJ KRAJ

Gorno-Altajsk

KEMEROVSKAJA OBLAST'

Abakan

Abaza

Taštagol

Petropavlovsk

SEVERNYY KAZAKHSTAN

Kokshetau

RESPUBLIKA ALTAJ

Altaj Mountains

Pavlodar

PAVLODARSKAYA OBLAST'

Semipalatinsk

Ust'-Kamenogorsk

Zyryanovsk

AKMOLINSKAYA OBLAST'

Astana
TSB

VOSTOCHNYY KAZAKHSTAN

K a z a k h s k i y   STAN

Temirtau
Karaganda
KGF

KARAGANDINSKAYA OBLAST'

Shakhtinsk

SEMIPALATINSK

Khrebet Tarbagatay

Tacheng

Zhezkazgan
DZN

ZHEZKAZGAN

Melkosopochnik

Junggar Pendi

Karamay

Balkhash

TALDYKORGAN

Ürümqi
URC

ALMATINSKAYA OBLAST'

Taldykorgan

Borohoro Shan

ZHAMBYLSKAYA OBLAST'

Yining

Almaty
ALA

Bishkek
FRU

CHÜY

Taras

Tashkent
TAS

KYRGYZSTAN

Bishkek

Naryn

YSYK-KÖL

Shymkent

Namangan

Andizhan

Osh
OSS

Margilan

Fergana

Khüjand
LBD

TAJIKISTAN

Dushanbe
DYU

Kashi
KHG

C H I N A   S h a m o

XINJIANG UYGUR ZIZHIQU

Hotan
HTN

KÜHISTONI BADAKHSHON

Kunlun Shan

AFGHANISTAN

Mazar-e Sharif

147
124
94/95

Scale 1:6 500 000
Projection: Lambert Conformal Conic

0 Kms   50   100   150   200
0 Miles   50   100

Peak
6000m
5000m
4000m
3000m
2000m
1000m
500m
200m
0m

200m
500m
1000m
2000m
4000m
Trough

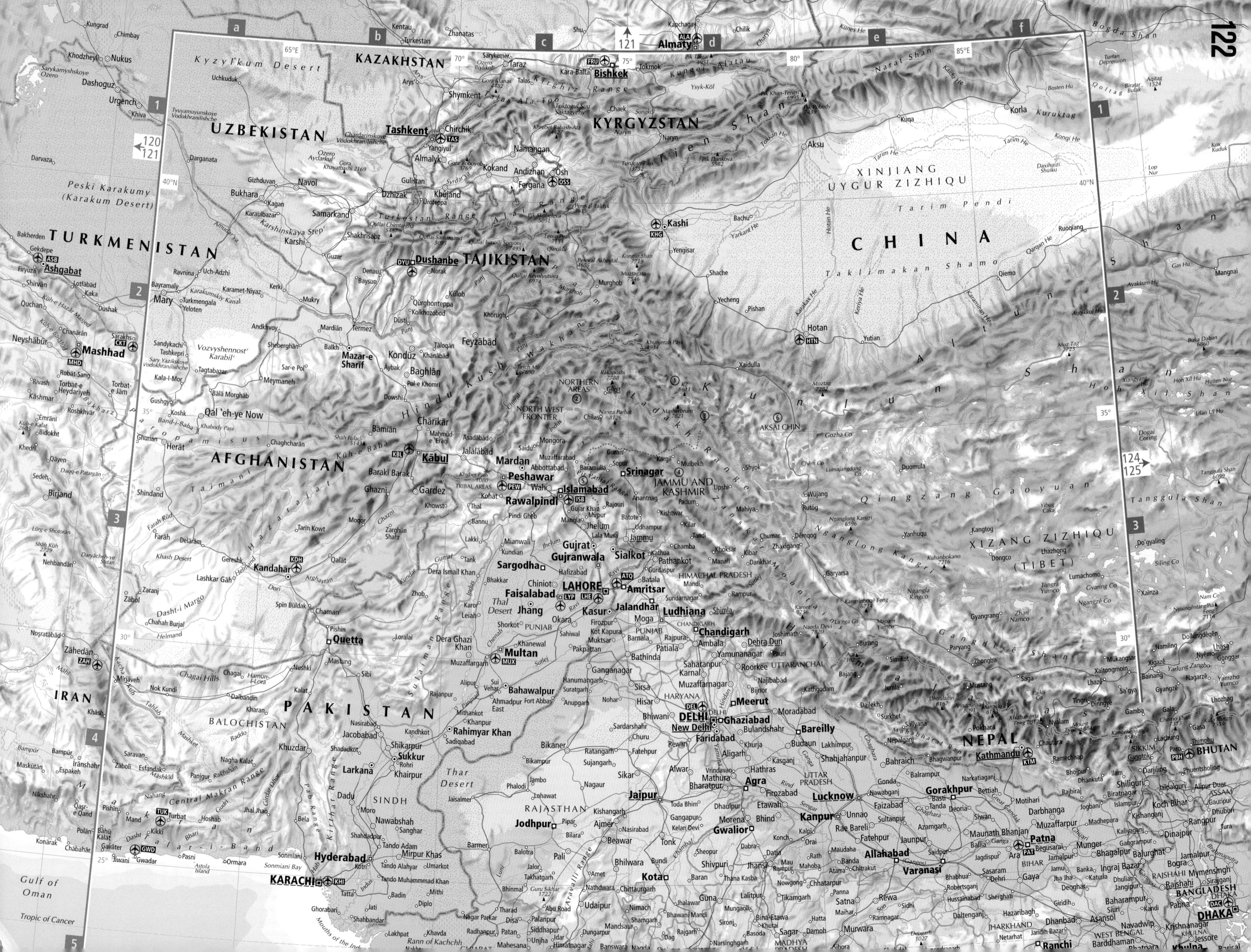
KAZAKHSTAN
UZBEKISTAN
TURKMENISTAN
KYRGYZSTAN
TAJIKISTAN
AFGHANISTAN
PAKISTAN
IRAN
CHINA
NEPAL
BHUTAN
BANGLADESH
XINJIANG UYGUR ZIZHIQU
XIZANG ZIZHIQU (TIBET)
Taklimakan Shamo
Tarim Pendi
Kyzyl'kum Desert
Peski Karakumy (Karakum Desert)
Thar Desert
Tien Shan
Hindu Kush
Kunlun Shan
Qingzang Gaoyuan
BALOCHISTAN
SINDH
PUNJAB
RAJASTHAN
UTTAR PRADESH
HIMACHAL PRADESH
JAMMU AND KASHMIR
NORTH WEST FRONTIER
NORTHERN AREAS
AKSAI CHIN
BIHAR
JHARKHAND
HARYANA
UTTARANCHAL
Almaty
Bishkek
Tashkent
Dushanbe
Kābul
Islamabad
Rawalpindi
Peshawar
LAHORE
Faisalabad
Multan
Quetta
Hyderabad
KARACHI
DELHI
New Delhi
Kathmandu
DHAKA
Ashgabat
Mashhad
Herāt
Kandahār
Kashi
Hotan
Srinagar
Amritsar
Jaipur
Agra
Lucknow
Kanpur
Varanasi
Patna
Allahabad
Gwalior
Jodhpur
Samarkand
Bukhara
Mazār-e Sharīf
Gulf of Oman
Tropic of Cancer
120
121
124
125

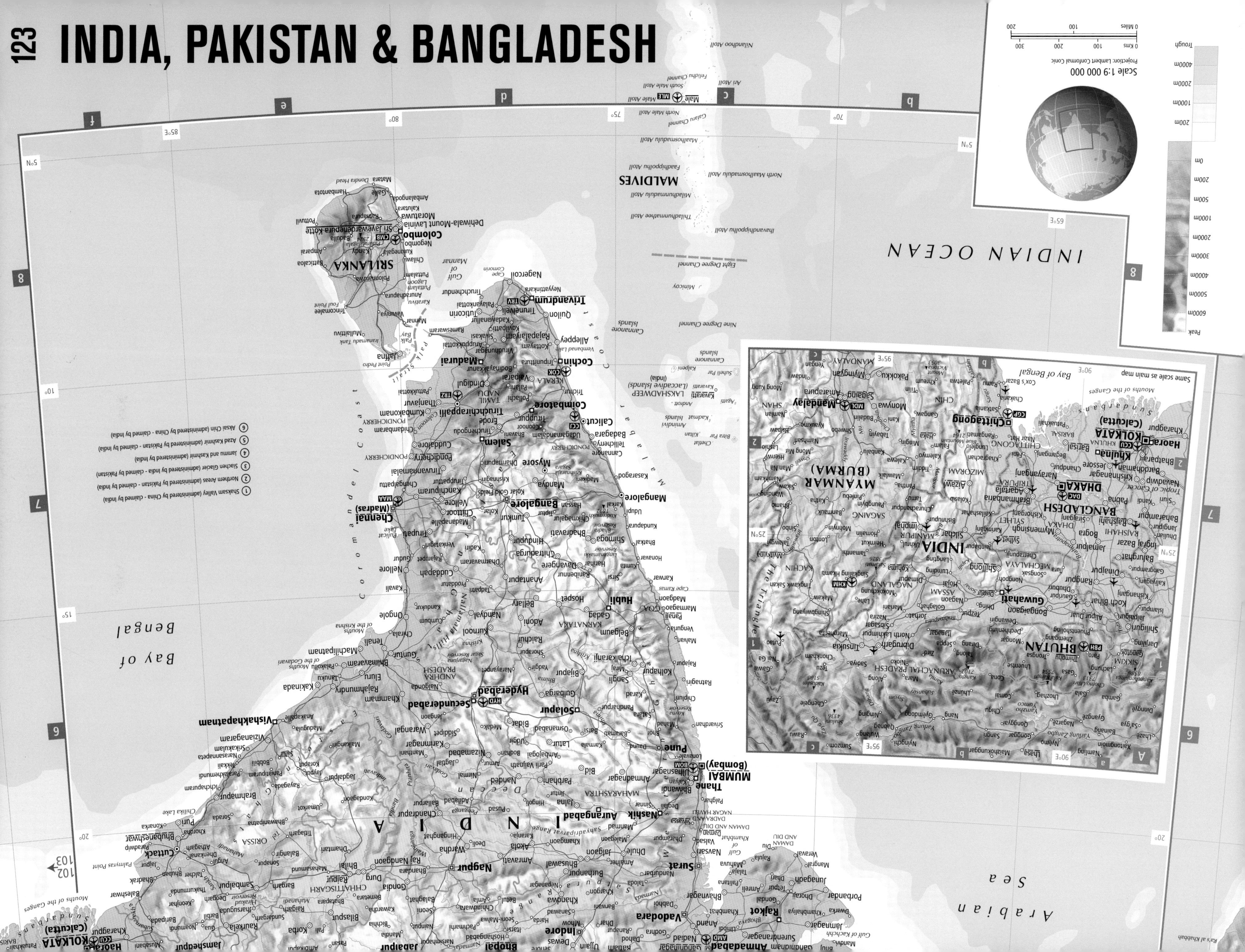

① Shaksam Valley (administered by China - claimed by India)
② Northern Areas (administered by India - claimed by Pakistan)
③ Siachen Glacier (administered by India - claimed by Pakistan)
④ Jammu and Kashmir (administered by Pakistan - claimed by India)
⑤ Azad Kashmir (administered by Pakistan - claimed by India)
⑥ Aksai Chin (administered by China - claimed by India)

Bay of Bengal

Coromandel Coast

Arabian Sea

INDIAN OCEAN

I N D I A

PAKISTAN

SRI LANKA

MALDIVES

MYANMAR (BURMA)

BANGLADESH

BHUTAN

The Triangle

Mouths of the Ganges

Same scale as main map

Scale 1:9 000 000
Projection: Lambert Conformal Conic

0 Kms   100   200   300
0 Miles   100   200

Peak
6000m
5000m
4000m
3000m
2000m
1000m
500m
200m
0m
200m
1000m
2000m
4000m
Trough

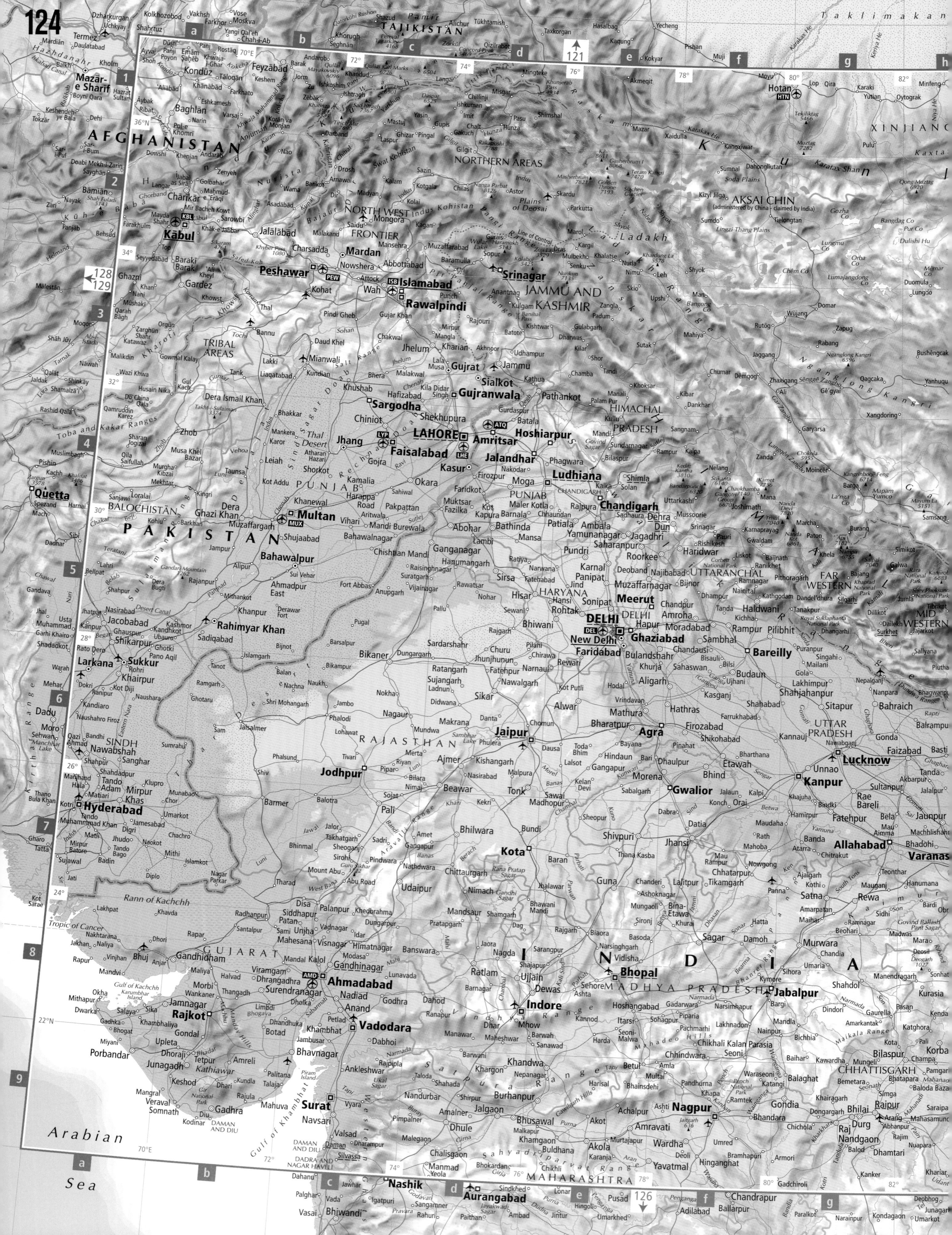
AFGHANISTAN
PAKISTAN
INDIA
TAJIKISTAN
XINJIANG
AKSAI CHIN
(administered by China - claimed by India)
NORTHERN AREAS
NORTH WEST FRONTIER
TRIBAL AREAS
JAMMU AND KASHMIR
BALOCHISTĀN
PUNJAB
SINDH
HIMACHAL PRADESH
HARYANA
DELHI
UTTARANCHAL
UTTAR PRADESH
RAJASTHAN
GUJARAT
MADHYA PRADESH
CHHATTISGARH
MAHARASHTRA
FAR WESTERN
MID WESTERN
DAMAN AND DIU
DADRA AND NAGAR HAVELI
CHANDIGARH
Arabian Sea
Taklimakan
Ladakh
Thar Desert
Rann of Kachchh
Gulf of Kachchh
Gulf of Khambhat
Tropic of Cancer
Kābul
Mazār-e Sharīf
Jalālābād
Peshawar
Islamabad
Rawalpindi
Mardan
Srinagar
Quetta
Multan
Faisalabad
LAHORE
Amritsar
Gujranwala
Sargodha
Jhang
Bahawalpur
Rahimyar Khan
Sukkur
Larkana
Hyderabad
Ludhiana
Jalandhar
Chandigarh
Shimla
Dehra Dun
Meerut
DELHI
New Delhi
Ghaziabad
Faridabad
Bareilly
Lucknow
Kanpur
Agra
Jaipur
Jodhpur
Bikaner
Ajmer
Kota
Gwalior
Allahabad
Varanasi
Bhopal
Jabalpur
Indore
Ujjain
Ahmadabad
Gandhinagar
Vadodara
Rajkot
Surat
Bhavnagar
Nagpur
Nashik
Aurangabad
Hotan
121
126
128
129
a
b
c
d
e
f
g
h
1
2
3
4
5
6
7
8
9

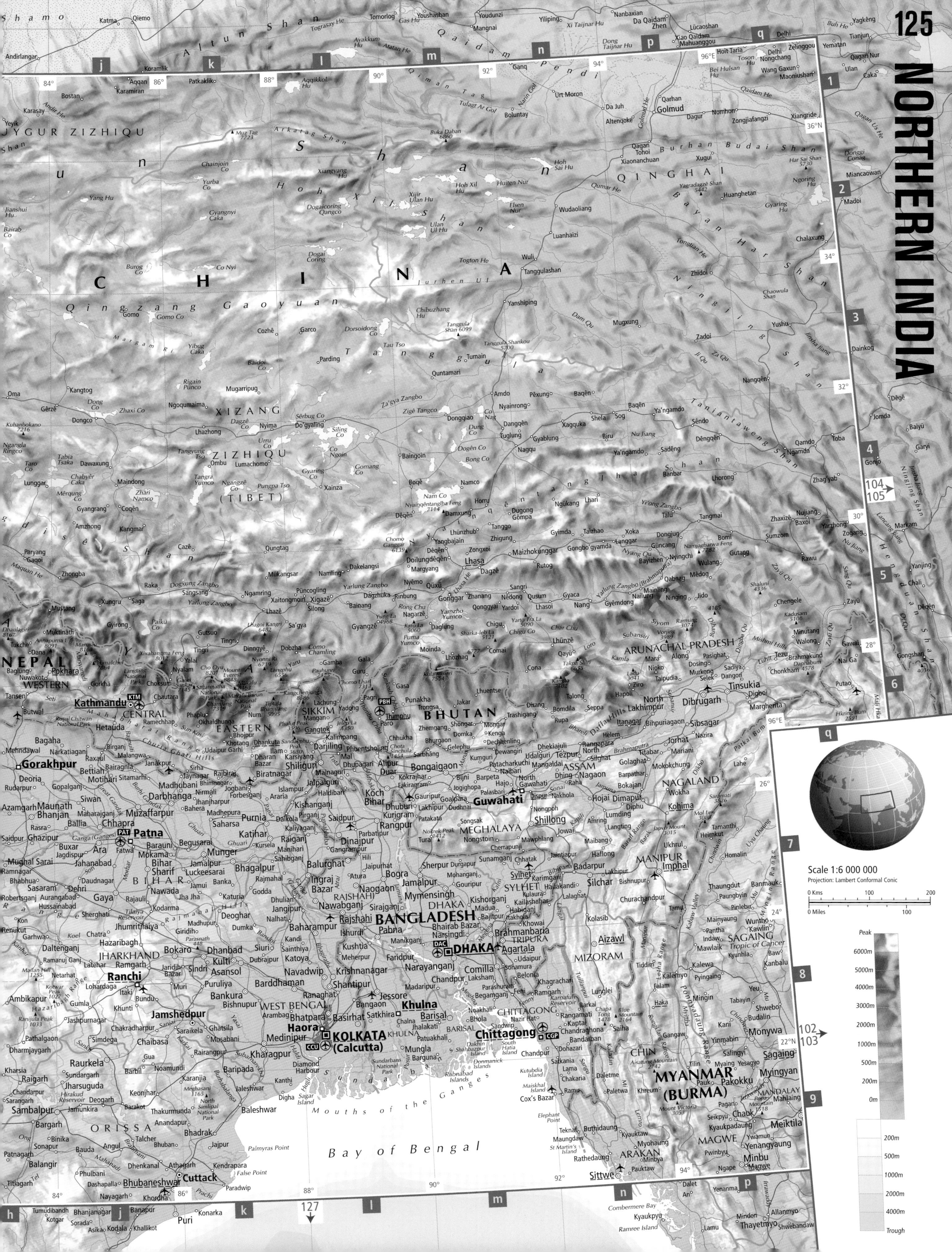
CHINA
Qingzang Gaoyuan
XIZANG ZIZHIQU (TIBET)
QINGHAI
Qaidam Pendi
Altun Shan
Hoh Xil Shan
Tanggula Shan
Bayan Har Shan
Nyainqêntanglha Shan
Golmud
Lhasa
Xigazê
Nagqu
NEPAL
Kathmandu
BHUTAN
Thimphu
SIKKIM
ARUNACHAL PRADESH
ASSAM
MEGHALAYA
NAGALAND
MANIPUR
MIZORAM
TRIPURA
BANGLADESH
DHAKA
Chittagong
Khulna
Rajshahi
MYANMAR (BURMA)
WEST BENGAL
KOLKATA (Calcutta)
Haora
BIHAR
Patna
JHARKHAND
Ranchi
Jamshedpur
ORISSA
Cuttack
Bhubaneshwar
Puri
Gorakhpur
Guwahati
Shillong
Imphal
Aizawl
Agartala
Dibrugarh
Sittwe
Sagaing
Mandalay
Mouths of the Ganges
Bay of Bengal
Sundarbans National Park
Tropic of Cancer
Scale 1:6 000 000
Projection: Lambert Conformal Conic
0 Kms 100 200
0 Miles 100
Peak
6000m
5000m
4000m
3000m
2000m
1000m
500m
200m
0m
200m
500m
1000m
2000m
4000m
Trough
104 105
102 103
127

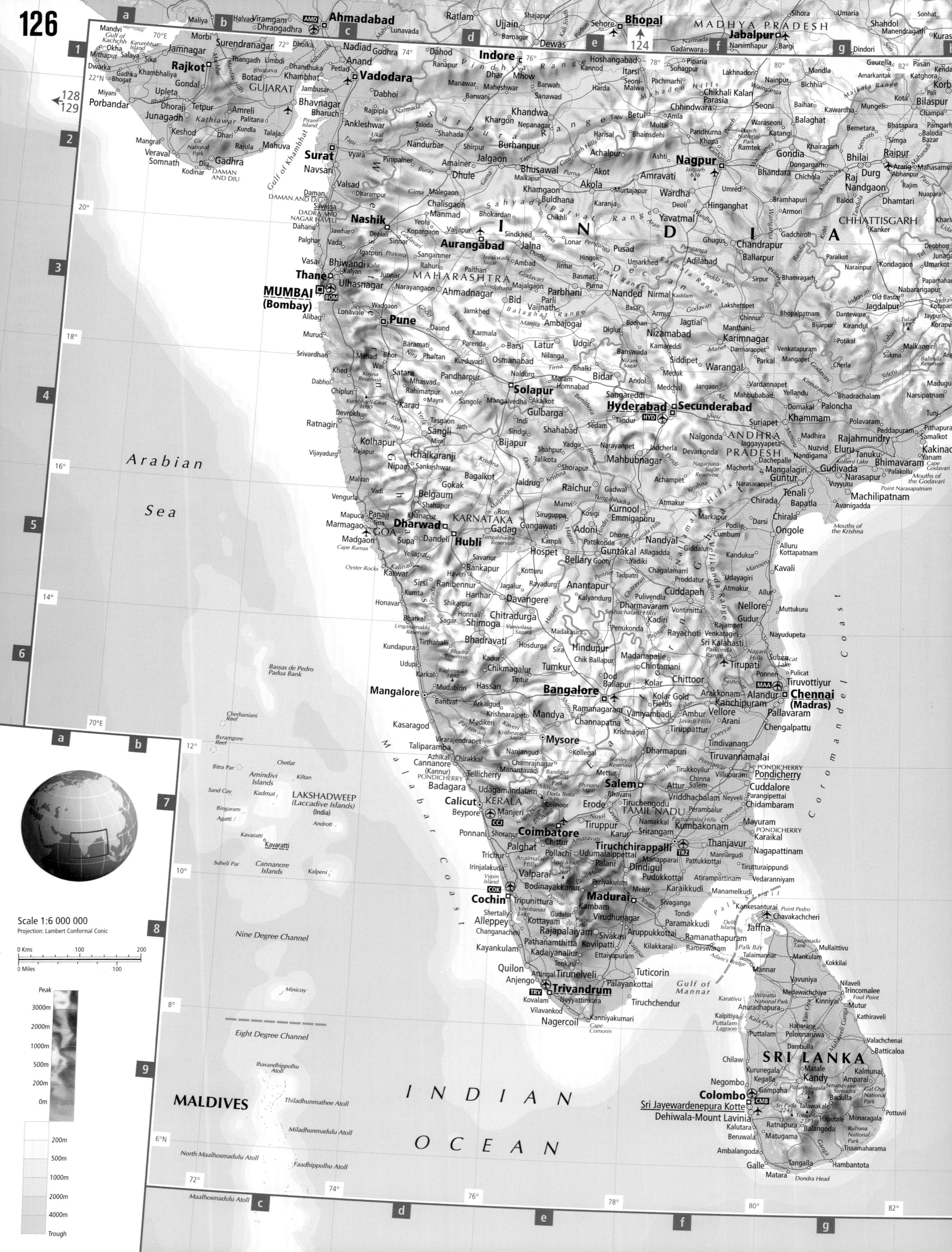

INDIA
MAHARASHTRA
KARNATAKA
ANDHRA PRADESH
TAMIL NADU
KERALA
GOA
GUJARAT
MADHYA PRADESH
CHHATTISGARH
DAMAN AND DIU
DADRA AND NAGAR HAVELI
PONDICHERRY
LAKSHADWEEP (Laccadive Islands) (India)
MALDIVES
SRI LANKA
Arabian Sea
INDIAN OCEAN
Gulf of Mannar
Palk Strait
Palk Bay
Gulf of Khambhat
Malabar Coast
Coromandel Coast
Nine Degree Channel
Eight Degree Channel
Ahmadabad
Bhopal
Jabalpur
Indore
Rajkot
Vadodara
Surat
Nagpur
Nashik
Aurangabad
MUMBAI (Bombay)
Thane
Pune
Solapur
Hyderabad
Secunderabad
Dharwad
Hubli
Bangalore
Chennai (Madras)
Mysore
Salem
Calicut
Coimbatore
Tiruchchirappalli
Madurai
Cochin
Trivandrum
Jaffna
Colombo
Sri Jayewardenepura Kotte
Kandy
128
129
124
Scale 1:6 000 000
Projection: Lambert Conformal Conic
0 Kms 100 200
0 Miles 100
Peak
3000m
2000m
1000m
500m
200m
0m
200m
500m
1000m
2000m
4000m
Trough

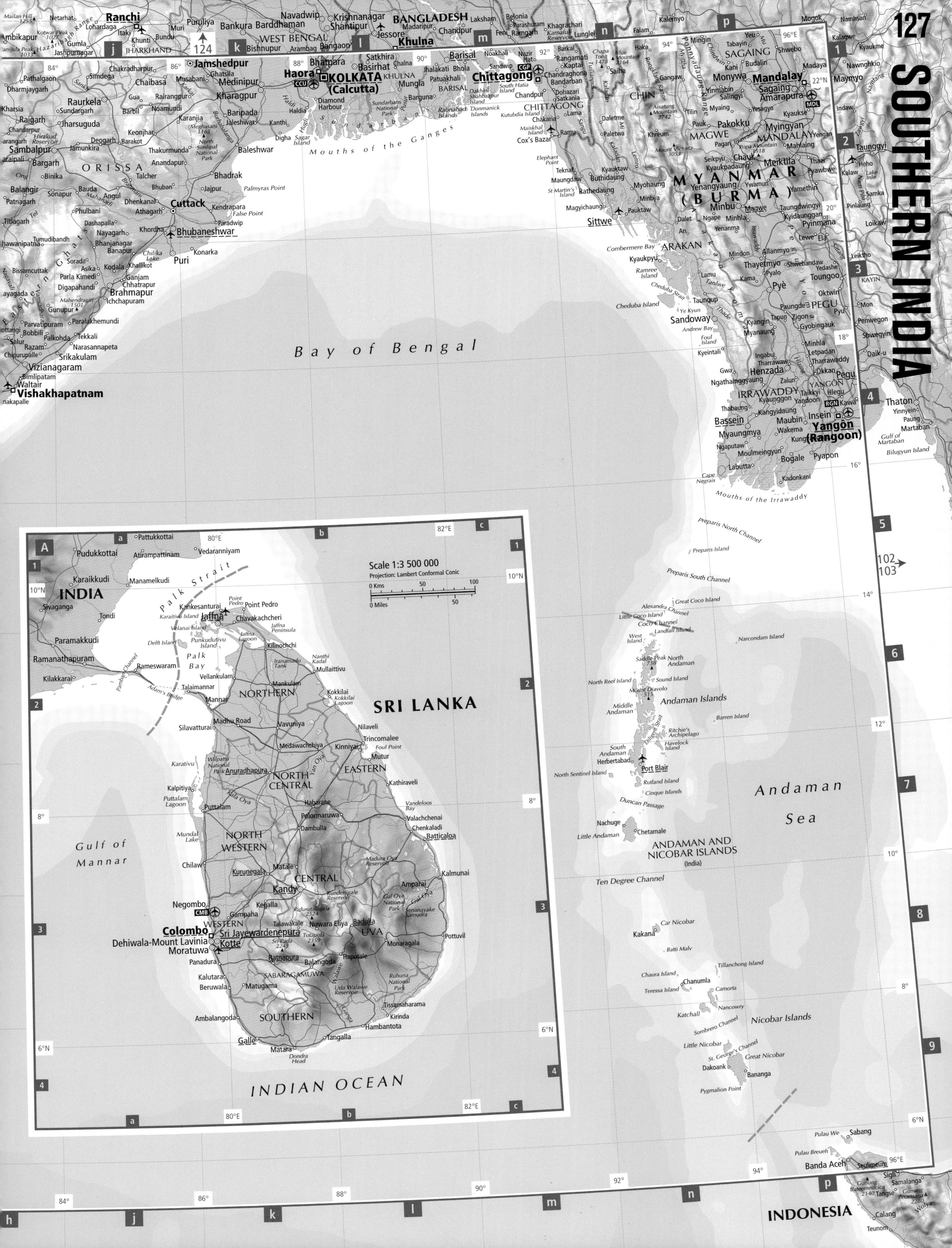
Ranchi
Purulia
Bankura
Barddhaman
Navadwip
Krishnanagar
Shantipur
BANGLADESH
Jessore
Khulna
WEST BENGAL
JHARKHAND
124
Jamshedpur
Chaibasa
Medinipur
Kharagpur
Haora
KOLKATA
(Calcutta)
Basirhat
Satkhira
Bhatpara
Diamond Harbour
Haldia
Barisal
Bhola
Patuakhali
Mungla
BARISAL
Barguna
Chandpur
Chittagong
CHITTAGONG
Cox's Bazar
Mouths of the Ganges
Raurkela
Sundargarh
Raigarh
Jharsuguda
Sambalpur
Bargarh
ORISSA
Baripada
Jaleshwar
Baleshwar
Keonjhar
Bhadrak
Palmyras Point
Jajpur
Cuttack
Kendrapara
False Point
Paradwip
Bhubaneshwar
Puri
Konarka
Khordha
Chilika Lake
Berhampur
Brahmapur
Ichchapuram
Gunupur
Parvatipuram
Bobbili
Palkohda
Tekkali
Narasannapeta
Srikakulam
Vizianagaram
Bimlipatam
Waltair
Vishakhapatnam
Eastern Ghats
Bay of Bengal
Mandalay
Sagaing
Amarapura
Monywa
SAGAING
CHIN
MAGWE
Pakokku
Myingyan
MANDALAY
Meiktila
Taunggyi
MYANMAR
(BURMA)
Minbu
Magwe
Sittwe
Kyaukpyu
ARAKAN
Ramree Island
Cheduba Island
Thayetmyo
Pyè
Toungoo
Taungup
Sandoway
PEGU
Henzada
IRRAWADDY
Bassein
Myaungmya
Maubin
Insein
Yangôn
(Rangoon)
Pegu
Thaton
Martaban
Gulf of Martaban
Bogale
Pyapon
Labutta
Mouths of the Irrawaddy
Preparis North Channel
Preparis Island
Preparis South Channel
Great Coco Island
Little Coco Island
Coco Channel
North Andaman
Andaman Islands
Middle Andaman
South Andaman
Port Blair
Rutland Island
Duncan Passage
Little Andaman
ANDAMAN AND NICOBAR ISLANDS
(India)
Andaman Sea
Ten Degree Channel
Car Nicobar
Nicobar Islands
Great Nicobar
Pygmalion Point
Sabang
Banda Aceh
INDONESIA
102
103
Scale 1:3 500 000
Projection: Lambert Conformal Conic
0 Kms
50
100
0 Miles
50
Pudukkottai
Karaikkudi
INDIA
Sivaganga
Paramakkudi
Ramanathapuram
Rameswaram
Palk Strait
Palk Bay
Point Pedro
Jaffna
Kankesanturai
Chavakachcheri
Kilinochchi
Mullaittivu
Mannar
Adam's Bridge
NORTHERN
SRI LANKA
Vavuniya
Trincomalee
Anuradhapura
NORTH CENTRAL
EASTERN
Kalpitiya
Puttalam
NORTH WESTERN
Gulf of Mannar
Batticaloa
Kurunegala
Matale
CENTRAL
Kandy
Kalmunai
Negombo
Gampaha
WESTERN
Colombo
Sri Jayewardenepura
Kotte
Dehiwala-Mount Lavinia
Moratuwa
Nuwara Eliya
Badulla
UVA
Monaragala
Pottuvil
Ratnapura
SABARAGAMUWA
Kalutara
Beruwala
Ambalangoda
SOUTHERN
Galle
Matara
Tangalla
Hambantota
INDIAN OCEAN

CHINA

KYRGYZSTAN

UZBEKISTAN

TAJIKISTAN

TURKMENISTAN

AFGHANISTAN

JAMMU AND KASHMIR

NORTHERN AREAS

NORTH WEST FRONTIER

HIMACHAL PRADESH

PUNJAB

Kabul
KABUL
Dushanbe
Peshawar
Islamabad
Rawalpindi
Srinagar
Lahore
Amritsar
Jalandhar
Ludhiana
Chandigarh
Faisalabad
Gujranwala
Sargodha
Kandahar
Herat
Mazar-e Sharif
Kunduz
Samarkand
Bukhara
Khujand
Fergana
Kashi
Ghazni
Jalalabad

120 121 130 135

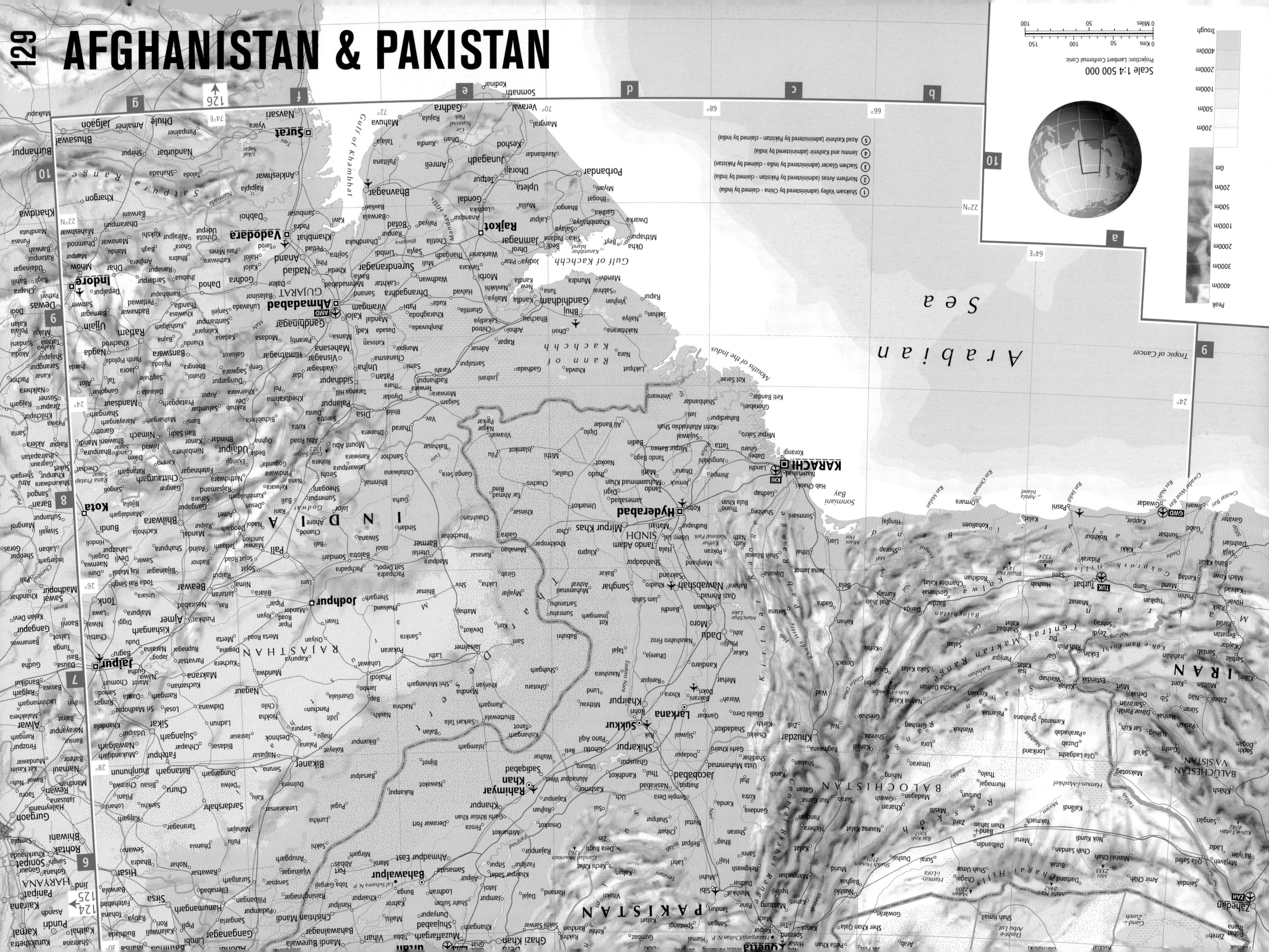

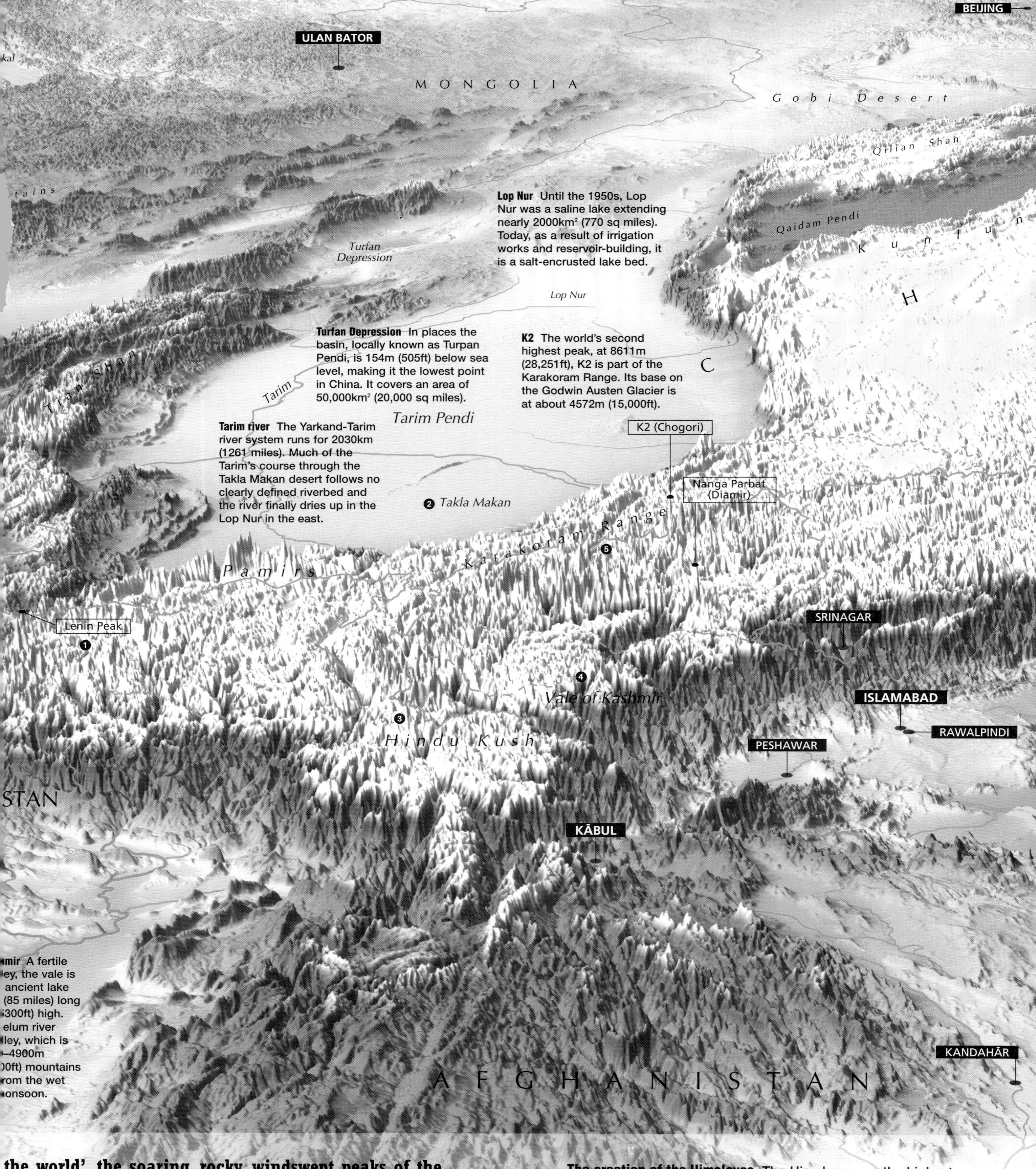

BEIJING

ULAN BATOR

M O N G O L I A

Gobi Desert

Qilian Shan

Turfan Depression

Qaidam Pendi

Lop Nur Until the 1950s, Lop Nur was a saline lake extending nearly 2000km² (770 sq miles). Today, as a result of irrigation works and reservoir-building, it is a salt-encrusted lake bed.

Lop Nur

K u n l u n

H

C

Tarim

Turfan Depression In places the basin, locally known as Turpan Pendi, is 154m (505ft) below sea level, making it the lowest point in China. It covers an area of 50,000km² (20,000 sq miles).

K2 The world's second highest peak, at 8611m (28,251ft), K2 is part of the Karakoram Range. Its base on the Godwin Austen Glacier is at about 4572m (15,000ft).

Tarim Pendi

K2 (Chogori)

Tarim river The Yarkand-Tarim river system runs for 2030km (1261 miles). Much of the Tarim's course through the Takla Makan desert follows no clearly defined riverbed and the river finally dries up in the Lop Nur in the east.

❷ *Takla Makan*

Nanga Parbat (Diamir)

Karakoram Range

❺

Pamirs

SRINAGAR

Lenin Peak **❶**

❹

Vale of Kashmir

ISLAMABAD

❸

Hindu Kush

RAWALPINDI

PESHAWAR

STAN

KĀBUL

mir A fertile ley, the vale is ancient lake (85 miles) long 300ft) high. elum river ley, which is —4900m 00ft) mountains rom the wet onsoon.

KANDAHĀR

A F G H A N I S T A N

the world', the soaring, rocky, windswept peaks of the orm a 2400km (1500 mile) arc, from Kashmir in the west the east, rising to nearly 9000m (29,500ft) above sea level. egetation and permanently snow-covered, they are cut leep river gorges. To the south, the huge expanse of the ying Ganges plain is crisscrossed by alluvium-heavy north, the dramatic mountain barrier gives way to nd-scoured desert Plateau of Tibet, a desolate wilderness m (1250 miles) wide and 5000m (16,000ft) above sea level.

The creation of the Himalayas The Himalayas are the highest and one of the youngest mountain chains in the world, formed between 10 and 20 million years ago when the Indo-Australian continental plate collided with the continent of Asia. As the Indo-Australian plate converged on the Asian plate, the intervening rock strata were hugely compressed and intensely crumpled to form the Himalayas. The height and angularity of the peaks is due to processes of glaciation and rapid erosion, as well as their continuing uplift at a rate of about 5mm (¼in) a year.

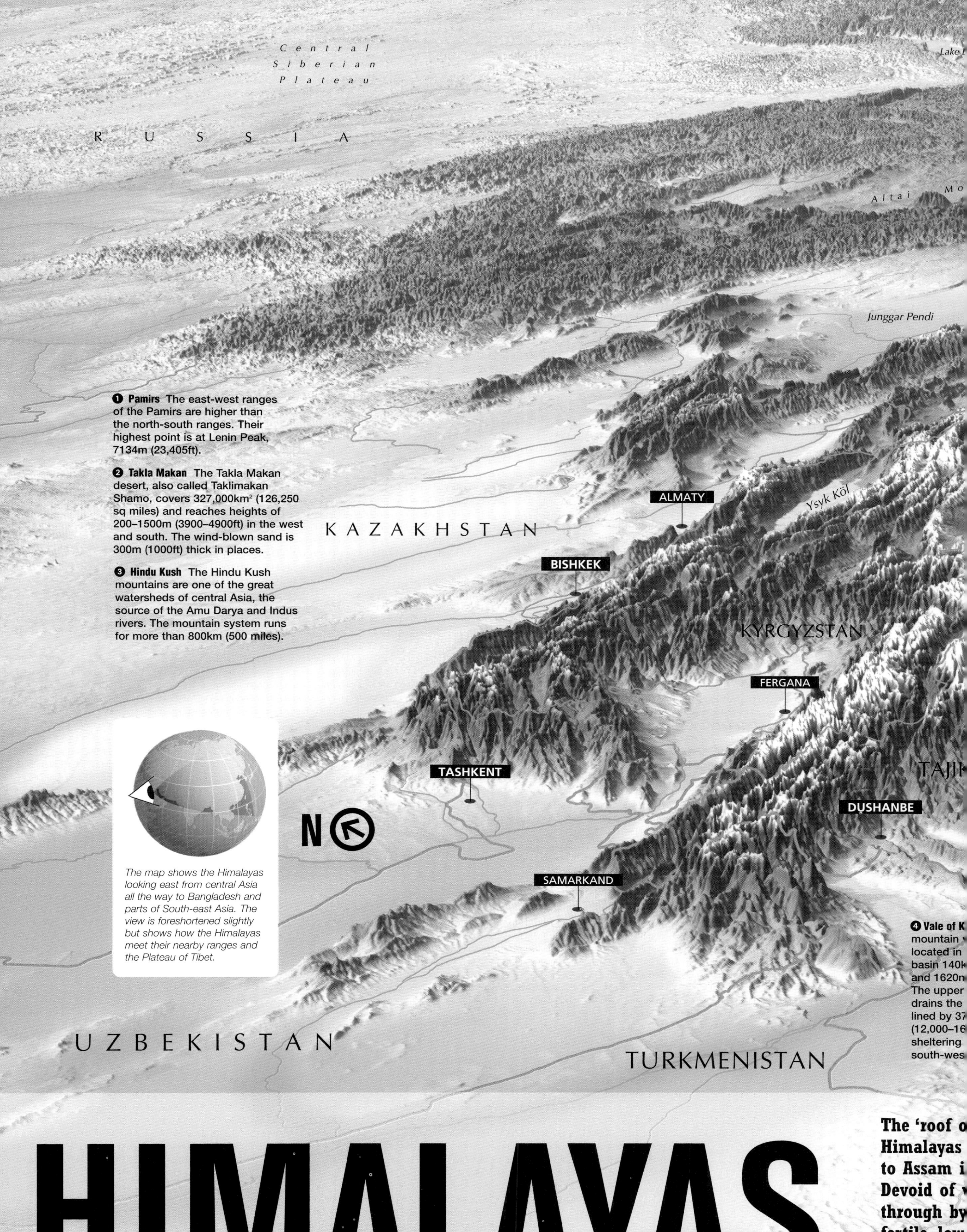

Central
Siberian
Plateau

Lake

R U S S I A

Altai Mo

Junggar Pendi

❶ Pamirs The east-west ranges
of the Pamirs are higher than
the north-south ranges. Their
highest point is at Lenin Peak,
7134m (23,405ft).

❷ Takla Makan The Takla Makan
desert, also called Taklimakan
Shamo, covers 327,000km² (126,250
sq miles) and reaches heights of
200–1500m (3900–4900ft) in the west
and south. The wind-blown sand is
300m (1000ft) thick in places.

❸ Hindu Kush The Hindu Kush
mountains are one of the great
watersheds of central Asia, the
source of the Amu Darya and Indus
rivers. The mountain system runs
for more than 800km (500 miles).

ALMATY

Ysyk Köl

K A Z A K H S T A N

BISHKEK

KYRGYZSTAN

FERGANA

TAJI

DUSHANBE

TASHKENT

N

SAMARKAND

The map shows the Himalayas
looking east from central Asia
all the way to Bangladesh and
parts of South-east Asia. The
view is foreshortened slightly
but shows how the Himalayas
meet their nearby ranges and
the Plateau of Tibet.

❹ Vale of K
mountain
located in
basin 140k
and 1620n
The upper
drains the
lined by 37
(12,000–16
sheltering
south-wes

U Z B E K I S T A N

TURKMENISTAN

HIMALAYAS

The 'roof o
Himalayas
to Assam i
Devoid of v
through by
fertile, low
rivers. To t
the high, v
nearly 2000

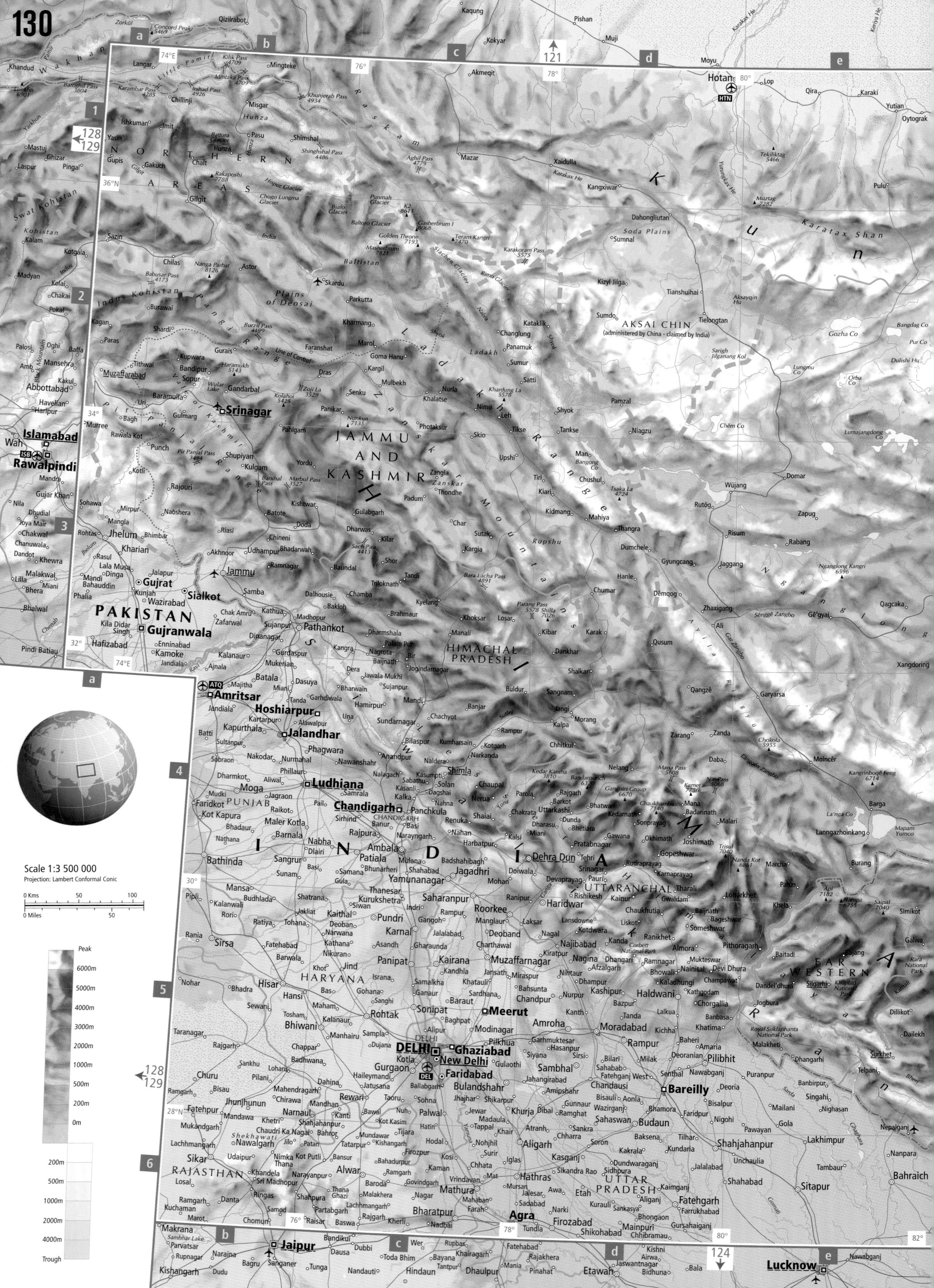
a
b
c
d
e
1
2
3
4
5
6
121
124
128
129
74°E
76°
78°
80°
82°
36°N
34°
32°
30°
28°N
Wakhan
Little Pamir
Zorkŭl
Concord Peak 5469
Qizilrabot
Kaqung
Pishan
Muji
Kokyar
Moyu
Hotan
HTN
Lop
Qira
Karaki
Yutian
Oytograk
Karakax He
Keriya He
Khandud
Langar
Kilik Pass 4709
Mintaka Pass 4709
Irshad Pass 4926
Karambar Pass 4285
Baroghil Pass 3804
Chillinji
Mingteke
Khunjerab Pass 4934
Akmeqit
Raskam
Misgar
Hunza
Ishkuman
Imit
Yasin
Pasu
Shimshal
Shingshal Pass 4486
Batura Glacier
Mastuj
Ghizar
Laspur
Pingal
Gupis
Gakuch
Gilgit
Chalt
NORTHERN AREAS
Rakaposhi 7788
Hispar Glacier
Chogo Lungma Glacier
Biafo Glacier
Punmah Glacier
Baltoro Glacier
K2 8611
Gasherbrum I 8068
Aghil Pass 4779
Mazar
Xaidulla
Kangxiwar
Dahongliutan
Soda Plains
Sumnal
Karatax Shan
Kunlun
Tekiliktag 5466
Muztag 7282
Pulu
Yurungkax He
Swat Kohistan
Kohistan
Kalam
Sazin
Kotgala
Indus
Chilas
Nanga Parbat 8126
Astor
Golden Throne 7193
Masherbrum 7821
Teram Kangri 7470
Siachen Glacier
Karakoram Pass 5575
Rimo Glacier
Baltistan
Skardu
Madyan
Kolai
Chakai
Babusar Pass 4173
Indus Kohistan
Pokal
Plains of Deosai
Parkutta
Kizyl Jilga
Tianshuihai
Aksayqin Hu
Burawai
Kagan
Shardi
Paras
Burzil Pass 4100
Kharmang
Sumdo
Tielongtan
AKSAI CHIN
(administered by China - claimed by India)
Bangdag Co
Gozha Co
Pur Co
Dulishi Hu
Palosi
Oghi
Baffa
Mansehra
Amb
Black Mountain
Gurais
Faranshat
Line of Control
Marol
Chanlung
Panamuk
Kataklik
Shyok
Ladakh
Goma Hanu
Sumur
Sarigh Jilganang Kol
Lungmu Co
Orba Co
Kakul
Abbottabad
Havelian
Haripur
Muzaffarabad
Tithwal
Kupwara
Haramukh 5143
Bandipur
Sopur
Wular Lake
Gandarbal
Baramulla
Dras
Kargil
Mulbekh
Satti
Khardung La 5578
Nurla
Khalatse
Nimu
Leh
Senku
Zoji La 3529
Kolahoi 5425
Uri
Srinagar
Panikar
Pamzal
Chêm Co
Lumajangdong Co
Murree
Bagh
Gulmarg
Nunkun 7135
Photaksur
Skio
Tikse
Tankse
Niagzu
Islamabad
Wah
ISB
Rawalpindi
Rawala Kot
Punch
Pir Panjal Pass 3494
Shupiyan
Pahlgam
JAMMU AND KASHMIR
Upshi
Man
Bangong Co
Chushul
Domar
Kotli
Kulgam
Banihal Pass
Marbul Pass 3527
Yordu
Zangla
Zanskar
Thondhe
Tiri
Kiari
Tsaka La 4724
Wüjang
Mandra
Gujar Khan
Rajouri
Padum
Nila
Dhudial
Joya Mair
Sohawa
Mirpur
Naoshera
Kishtwar
Batote
Gulabgarh
Kidmang
Mahiya
Rutög
Zapug
Mangla
Chakwal
Rohtas
Jhelum
Bhimbar
Riasi
Doda
Char
Dharwas
Sutak
Thangra
Risum
Rabang
Chanuwala
Dandot
Khewra
Kharian
Akhnoor
Chineni
Udhampur
Bhadarwah
Kilar
Sach Pass 4413
Kargia
Rupshu
Dumchele
Gyungcang
Jaggang
Nganglong Kangri 6596
Rasul
Lala Musa
Dinga
Mandi Bahauddin
Jammu
Ramnagar
Baundal
Shor
Tandi
Malakwal
Lilla
Bhera
Miani
Jalapur
Gujrat
Sialkot
Kunjah
Wazirabad
Phalia
Samba
Triloknath
Bara Lacha Pass 4891
Hanle
Chumar
Dêmqog
Qagcaka
Zhaxigang
Sênggê Zangbo
Gê'gyai
Dalhousie
Chamba
Bakloh
Kyelang
Parang Pass 5578
Shilla 7026
PAKISTAN
Chak Amru
Zafarwal
Kathua
Sujanpur
Madhopur
Pathankot
Brahmaur
Khoksar
Losar
Kibar
Karak
Bhalwal
Kila Didar Singh
Gujranwala
Chenab
Hafizabad
Enninabad
Kamoke
Jandiala
Dinanagar
Gurdaspur
Dharmshala
Manali
Kangra
Nagrota
Palam Pur
Bir
Baijnath
Jogindarnagar
HIMACHAL PRADESH
Dankhar
Qusum
Gar Zangbo
Pindi Batiau
Kalanaur
Mukerian
Ravi
Ajnala
Dera
Jawala Mukhi
Shalkar
Xangdoring
ATQ
Majitha
Batala
Dasuya
Amritsar
Miani
Bharwain
Sujanpur
Buldur
Qangzê
Garyarsa
Jandiala
Tanda
Garhdiwala
Hamirpur
Mandi
Banjar
Sangnam
Hoshiarpur
Alawalpur
Una
Sundarnagar
Chachyot
Jangi
Morang
Kartarpur
Kapurthala
Jalandhar
Batti
Sultanpur
Sutlej
Rampur
Kalpa
Zarang
Zanda
Chokola 5955
Bilaspur
Kumharsain
Kotgarh
Chhitkul
Phagwara
Sobraon
Nakodar
Nurmahal
Nawanshahr
Anandpur
Narkanda
Nelang
Daba
Moincêr
Langqên Zangbo
Dharmkot
Aliwal
Phillaur
Nalagach
Kasumpti
Shimla
Naldera
Mana Pass 5608
Kamet 7756
Niti Pass 5068
Kedar Kantha 3810
Bandarpunch 6316
Kangrinboqê Feng 6714
Ludhiana
Moga
Mudki
Jagraon
Sabathu
Kasanli
Solan
Chaupal
Gangotri Group 6670
Mana
Badarinath
Faridkot
Kot Kapura
PUNJAB
Raikot
Samrala
Pail
Kalka
Dagshai
Nahna
Nerua
Parola
Rajgarh
Barkot
Chaukhamba 7140
Chandigarh
Panchkula
CHANDIGARH
Sirhind
Banur
Basi
Renuka
Shaiai
Chakrata
Uttarkashi
Dunda
Bhatwari
Kedarnath
Sonprayag
Malari
Barga
La'nga Co
Bhadaur
Maler Kotla
Nathana
Barnala
Nabha
Rajpura
Narayangarh
Nahan
Harbatpur
Dharasu
Bhetiara
Miani
Okhimath
Joshimath
Lanngazhoinkang
Mapam Yumco
Bathinda
Sangrur
Dlairi
Patiala
Ambala
Mulana
Badshahibagh
Dehra Dun
Tehri
Pratabnagar
Gawana
Trisul 7040
Gopeshwar
Nanda Kot 6861
Burang
INDIA
Basi
Samana
Bhunarheri
Shahabad
Yamunanagar
Jagadhri
Doiwala
Devaprayag
Pauri
Rudraprayag
Karnaprayag
Marcha
Sunam
Mohan
Mansa
Gula
Thanesar
Saharanpur
Raniput
Rishikesh
UTTARANCHAL
Tharali
Patan
Scale 1:3 500 000
Projection: Lambert Conformal Conic
0 Kms
50
100
0 Miles
50
Pipli
Budhlada
Shatrana
Kurukshetra
Siwan
Indri
Rampur
Roorkee
Haridwar
Kainur
Gwaldam
Lohaghat
Khela
Api 7182
Nampa 6755
Saipal 7040
Kalanwali
Rorio
Jakliat
Kaithal
Deoban
Pundri
Gangoh
Manglaur
Laksar
Lansdowne
Chaukhutia
Liskot
Baijnath
Bageshwar
Someshwar
Simikot
Ratiya
Tohana
Narwana
Karnal
Jalalabad
Deoband
Nagal
Kotdwara
Ranikhet
Almora
Pithoragarh
Galwa
Rania
Sirsa
Fatehabad
Kathana
Asandh
Gharaunda
Charthawal
Najibabad
Kanda
Corbett National Park
Baitadi
Peak
6000m
5000m
4000m
3000m
2000m
1000m
500m
200m
0m
Barwala
Nikuran
Panipat
Kairana
Muzaffarnagar
Kiratpur
Nagina
Dhangari
Ramnagar
Mukteswar
Nainital
Devi Dhura
Bajang
FAR WESTERN
Rara National Park
Khot
Jind
Kandhla
Jansath
Miraspur
Nihtaur
Afzalgarh
Bhowali
Champawat
Dandel'dhura
Silgarhi
Khaptad National Park
Nohar
Bhadra
Hisar
HARYANA
Israna
Samalkha
Khatauli
Dhampur
Kashipur
Kaladhungi
Haldwani
Kathgodam
Bas
Gohana
Ganaur
Sardhana
Bahsunta
Chandpur
Nurpur
Bazpur
Chorgallia
Jogbura
Dillikot
Sewani
Hansi
Maham
Sanghi
Baraut
Meerut
Tosham
Kalanaur
Rohtak
Sonipat
Baghpat
Amroha
Kanth
Tanda
Lalkua
Banbasa
Bhiwani
Manhairu
Sampla
Alipur
Modinagar
Moradabad
Kichha
Khatima
Royal Suklaphanta National Park
Dailekh
Taranagar
Rajgarh
Chappar
Dujana
DELHI
Pilkhua
Garhmuktesar
Hasanpur
Siyana
Rampur
Baheri
Amaria
Malakheti
Badhwana
Ghaziabad
New Delhi
Gulaothi
Sirsi
Bilari
Milak
Deoranian
Pilibhit
Surkhet
Dhangarhi
Churu
Sankhu
Loharu
Pilani
Kotla
Gurgaon
Faridabad
DEL
Sambhal
Sahabab
Fatehganj West
Senthal
Nawabganj
Puranpur
Telpani
Bisau
Dahina
Haileymandi
Jatusana
Ballabgarh
Bulandshahr
Jahangirabad
Chandausi
Bareilly
Deoria
Banbirpur
Ramgarh
Jhunjhunun
Mahendragarh
Chirawa
Mandhan
Rewari
Taoru
Sohna
Jhajhar
Shikarpur
Amipshahr
Bisauli
Aonla
Bisalpur
Singahi
Fatehpur
Mandawa
Khetri
Narnaul
Kanti
Bawal
Palwal
Jewar
Khurja
Dibai
Gunnaur
Ramghat
Wazirganj
Faridpur
Bhamora
Mailani
Nighasan
Mukandgarh
Shekhawati
Chaudri Ka Nagal
Shajahanpur
Bahror
Kot Kasim
Nuh
Hatin
Madaula
Tappal
Atrauli
Sahaswan
Budaun
Nigohi
Pawayan
Gola
Nepalganj
Lachhmangarh
Nawalgarh
Jilo
Patan
Mundawar
Tijara
Kishangarh
Tatarpur
Hodal
Khair
Nohjhil
Aligarh
Chharra
Sankra
Soron
Baksena
Tilhar
Shahjahanpur
Lakhimpur
Sikar
Udaipur
Nimka Thana
Kot Putli
Bansur
Firozpur
Kosi
Surir
Iglas
Kasganj
Kakrala
Kundaria
Unchaulia
Nanpara
RAJASTHAN
Khandela
Sri Madhopur
Narayanpur
Alwar
Bahadurpur
Kaman
Chhata
Sikandra Rao
Sidhpura
Dundwaraganj
Jalalabad
Tambaur
Losal
Ringas
Thana Ghazi
Baroda
Ramgarh
Govindgarh
Vrindavan
Mat
Hathras
Mursan
Jalesar
Awa
Etah
UTTAR PRADESH
Kaimganj
Shahabad
Sitapur
Bahraich
Ramgarh
Danta
Kuchaman
Marot
Samod
Shahpura
Partabgarh
Malakhera
Lachhmangarh
Nagar
Mathura
Mahaban
Farah
Sadabad
Narki
Kurauli
Sankasya
Aliganj
Fatehgarh
Farrukhabad
Bhongaon
Chomun
Raisar
Baswa
Rajgarh
Kherli
Bharatpur
Nadbai
Agra
Tundla
Firozabad
Shikohabad
Mainpuri
Chhibramau
Gursahaiganj
Makrana
Sambhar Lake
Parvatsar
Rupnagar
Narajna
Kishangarh
Bagru
Dudu
Jaipur
Sanganer
Bandikui
Dausa
Dubbi
Tunga
Toda Bhim
Nandauti
Wer
Rupbas
Bayana
Hindaun
Khairagarh
Tantpur
Dhaulpur
Fatehabad
Rajakhera
Mania
Pinahat
Kishni
Airwa
Jaswantnagar
Etawah
Bidhuna
Bala
Lucknow
Nawabganj
200m
500m
1000m
2000m
4000m
Trough

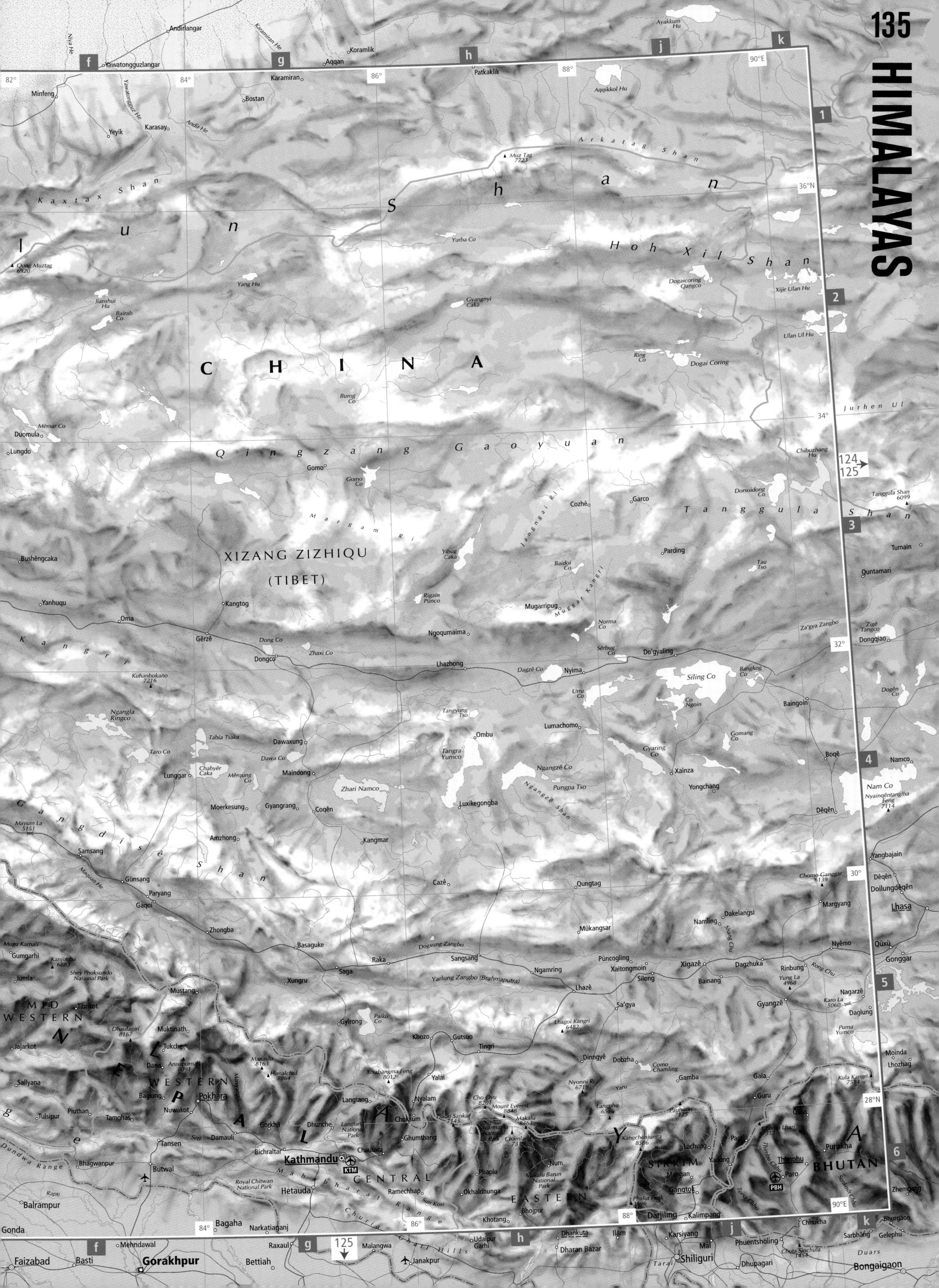
CHINA
XIZANG ZIZHIQU
(TIBET)
Kunlun Shan
Qingzang Gaoyuan
Arkatag Shan
Hoh Xil Shan
Kaxtax Shan
Tanggula Shan
Kangri
Gangdisê Shan
NEPAL
BHUTAN
SIKKIM
HIMALAYA
Muz Tag 7723
Qong Muztag 6920
Lhasa
Xigazê
Kathmandu
Pokhara
Thimphu
Gangtok
Darjiling
Shiliguri
Gorakhpur
Mount Everest 8848
Kangchenjunga 8586
Makalu 8463
Cho Oyu 8201
Dhaulagiri 8167
Manaslu 8163
Annapurna 8091
Xixabangma Feng 8012
Nyainqêntanglha Feng 7114
Yarlung Zangbo (Brahmaputra)
Siling Co
Nam Co
Zhari Namco
Tangra Yumco
Dogai Coring
Mahabharat Range
Churia Ghati Hills
Dundwa Range
Duars
Tarai
Chomo Ganggar 6139
Tanggula Shan 6099
Kula Kangri 7554
Lhagoi Kangri 6482
Kuhanbokano 7216
Mayum La 5151
Yung La 4968
Karo La 5060
124
125
125
82°
84°
86°
88°
90°E
36°N
34°
32°
30°
28°N
f
g
h
j
k
1
2
3
4
5
6

TAIWAN

P H I L I P P I N E S

East China Sea

Hainan

HA NÔI

V I E T N A M

L A O S

CAMBODIA

T H A I L A N D

MANDALAY

YANGÔN (RANGOON)

M Y A N M A R   (B U R M A)

CHITTAGONG

DHAKA

BANGLADESH

Ganges Delta

CALCUTTA

Bay of Bengal

INDIAN OCEAN

source in the
ier in the Tibetan
maputra flows
to its confluence

Ganges delta The Ganges and Brahmaputra
rivers dump over 2 billion tonnes of sediment
each year into the Bay of Bengal, creating a
vast delta that covers 60,000km² (23,000 sq
miles) and is highly prone to flooding.

RANASI

Eastern Ghats

Ganges The Ganges, the holy river of
Hindus, has a drainage area of 10 million
km² (3.9 million sq miles). It rises at
Gaumukh in the Himalayas and flows
2510km (1560 miles) across the Gangetic
plain, home to successive Indian
civilizations, to the Bay of Bengal.

V i n d h y a   R a n g e

NAGPUR

I N D I A

n²
e Thar
ravel
unes,

ds.

Western Ghats

AHMADABAD

SURAT

*Gulf of
Khambhat*

HYDERABAD

*Gulf of
Kachchh*

KARACHI

ARABIAN SEA

Himalayas

India

Continental crust is
pushed up under Asia
at 5cm (2in) a year

*Plateau
of Tibet*

ction of India under Asia
es the Plateau of Tibet

Himalayas override Indian
plate along a fault line

High mountains and the climate

The foothills of the Himalayas are
thickly forested with sub-tropical
vegetation and have an annual rainfall
of several metres. Monsoon rains fall
on the fertile land, running off the
hillsides in torrents. The moisture does
not reach north beyond the Himalayas.
The mountains form a climatic barrier,
trapping rain-laden clouds from the Indian
Ocean. To the north, the high Plateau of
Tibet is a cold desert, and rainfall is rare.

*Warm and dry
air rises*

*Mountains block cold
continental air from
moving south*

*Heavy rains
on slopes of
Himalayas:
1520–3040mm
(60–120in) in
a year*

*Moisture-laden
winds and
monsoon rains
from the Indian
Ocean*

*Average
annual rainfall
in the Plateau of
Tibet: 457mm
(18in) in a year*

*Perpetual
snowline:
4877m (16,000ft)*

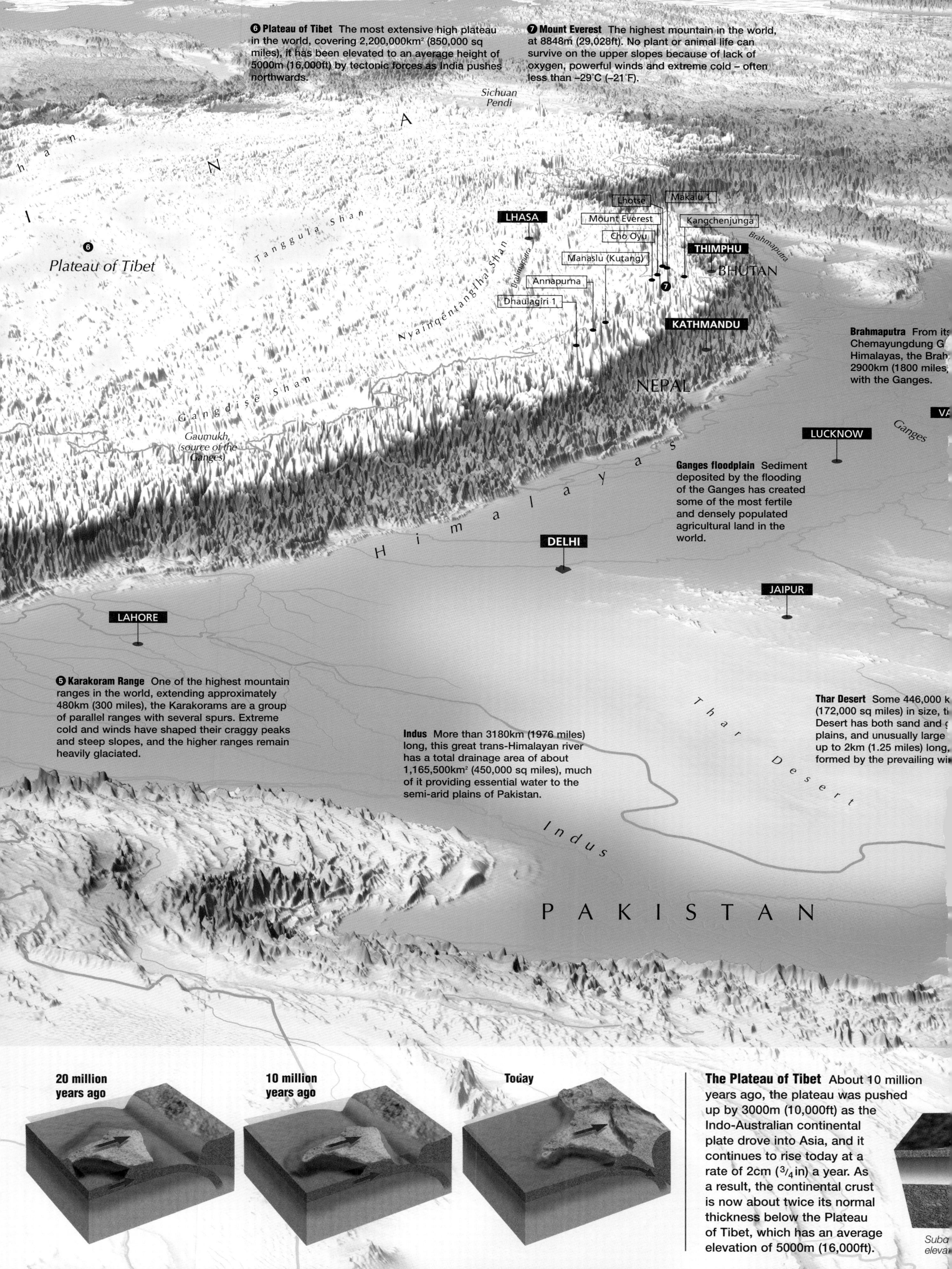

❻ Plateau of Tibet The most extensive high plateau in the world, covering 2,200,000km² (850,000 sq miles), it has been elevated to an average height of 5000m (16,000ft) by tectonic forces as India pushes northwards.

❼ Mount Everest The highest mountain in the world, at 8848m (29,028ft). No plant or animal life can survive on the upper slopes because of lack of oxygen, powerful winds and extreme cold – often less than –29°C (–21°F).

Sichuan Pendi

N

A

A

h a n

h

Tanggula Shan

❻
Plateau of Tibet

Nyainqêntanglha Shan

Gangdisê Shan

Gaumukh, (source of the Ganges)

LHASA

Brahmaputra

Lhotse
Makalu
Mount Everest
Kangchenjunga
Cho Oyu
Manaslu (Kutang)
Annapurna
Dhaulagiri 1

❼

THIMPHU
BHUTAN

Brahmaputra

KATHMANDU

NEPAL

Brahmaputra From its Chemayungdung G┃ Himalayas, the Brah┃ 2900km (1800 miles┃ with the Ganges.

LUCKNOW

Ganges

VA┃

Ganges floodplain Sediment deposited by the flooding of the Ganges has created some of the most fertile and densely populated agricultural land in the world.

Himalayas

DELHI

JAIPUR

LAHORE

❺ Karakoram Range One of the highest mountain ranges in the world, extending approximately 480km (300 miles), the Karakorams are a group of parallel ranges with several spurs. Extreme cold and winds have shaped their craggy peaks and steep slopes, and the higher ranges remain heavily glaciated.

Thar Desert Some 446,000 k┃ (172,000 sq miles) in size, t┃ Desert has both sand and ┃ plains, and unusually large ┃ up to 2km (1.25 miles) long, ┃ formed by the prevailing wi┃

Thar Desert

Indus More than 3180km (1976 miles) long, this great trans-Himalayan river has a total drainage area of about 1,165,500km² (450,000 sq miles), much of it providing essential water to the semi-arid plains of Pakistan.

Indus

P A K I S T A N

20 million years ago

10 million years ago

Today

The Plateau of Tibet About 10 million years ago, the plateau was pushed up by 3000m (10,000ft) as the Indo-Australian continental plate drove into Asia, and it continues to rise today at a rate of 2cm (³/₄ in) a year. As a result, the continental crust is now about twice its normal thickness below the Plateau of Tibet, which has an average elevation of 5000m (16,000ft).

Suba┃
eleva┃

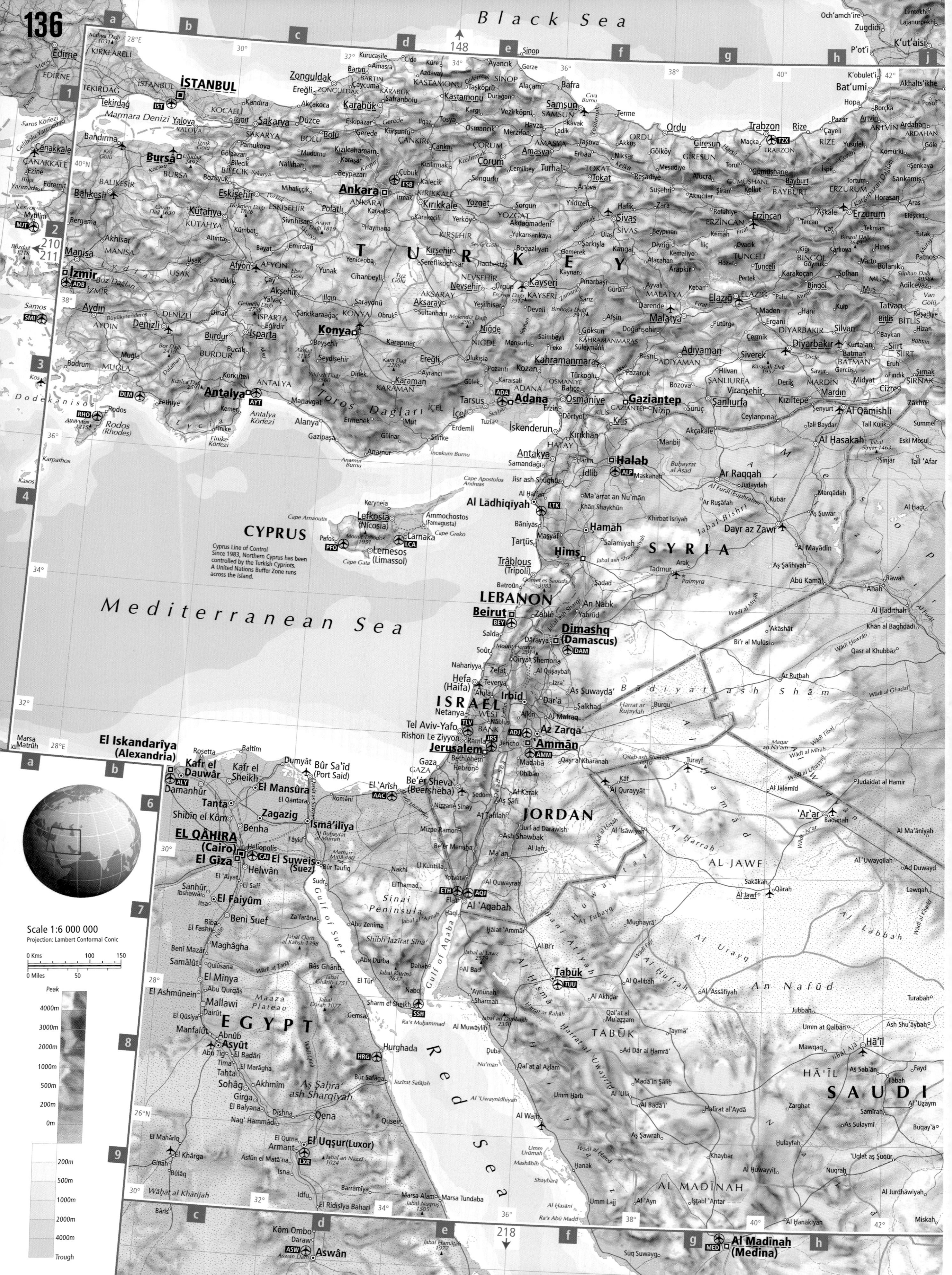

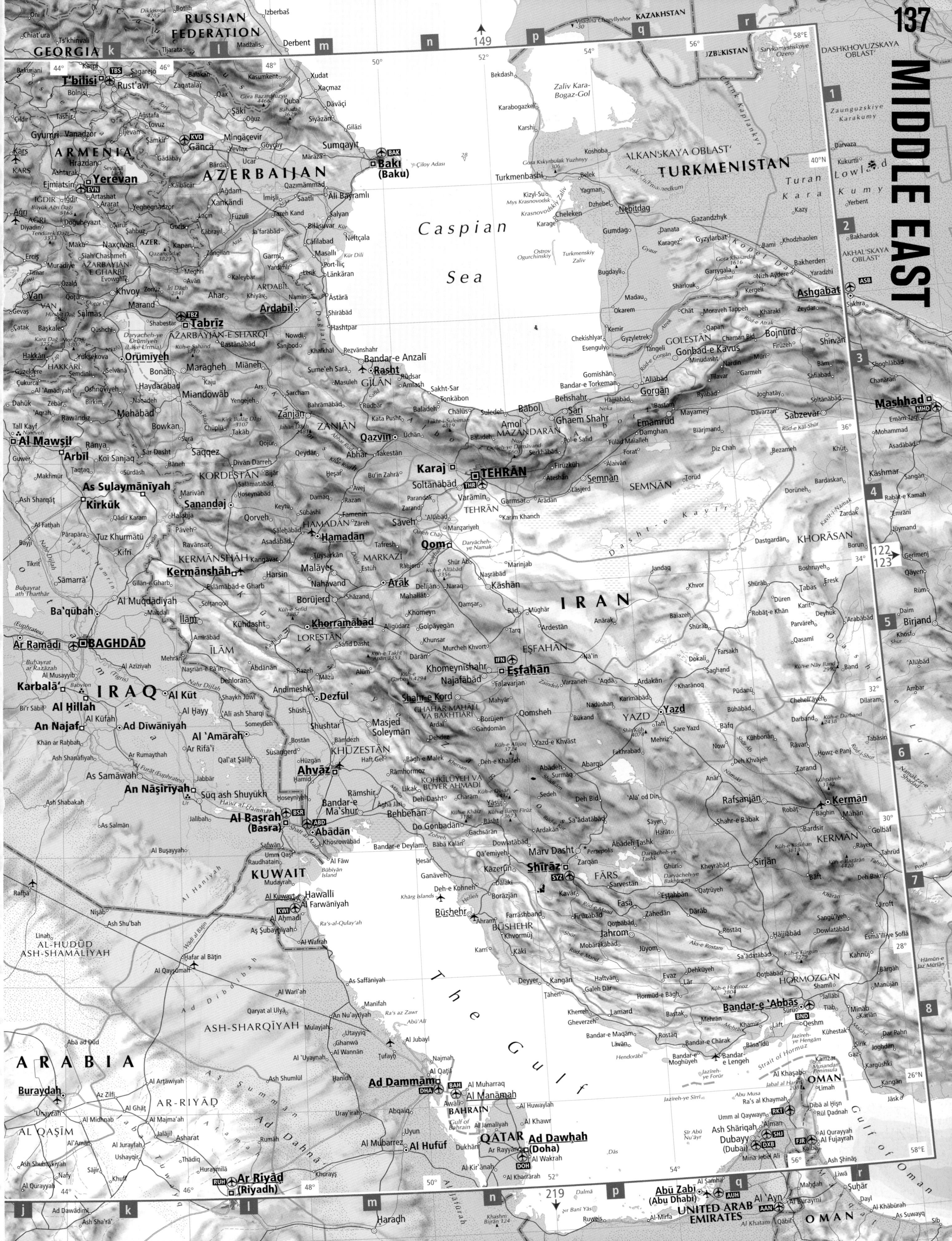

RUSSIAN FEDERATION
GEORGIA
KAZAKHSTAN
UZBEKISTAN
TURKMENISTAN

T'bilisi
Rust'avi
Bolnisi

ARMENIA
Gyumri
Vanadzor
Yerevan
KARS
Kars

AZERBAIJAN
AZER.
Naxçıvan
Gäncä
Baki
(Baku)
Sumqayıt

Caspian
Sea

Turkmenbashi
Ashgabat
Nebitdag
Bojnurd

Van
VAN
Orümiyeh
Tabriz
Ardabil
Rasht
GILAN
MAZANDARAN
Gorgan
GOLESTAN
Mashhad
KHORASAN

Al Mawsil
Arbil
As Sulaymaniyah
Kirkük
Sanandaj
KORDESTAN
Hamadan
HAMADAN
Zanjan
ZANJAN
Qazvin
Karaj
TEHRAN
TEHRAN
Qom
Semnan
SEMNAN

IRAQ
BAGHDAD
Ar Ramadi
Karbala'
An Najaf
Khorramabad
LORESTAN
ILAM
KERMANSHAH
Kermanshah
MARKAZI
Arak
Kashan
ESFAHAN
Esfahan
YAZD
Yazd
IRAN

Dezful
Ahvaz
KHUZESTAN
Shahr-e Kord
CHAHAR MAHALL VA BAKHTIARI
KOHKILUYEH VA BUYER AHMADI
FARS
Shiraz
Kerman
KERMAN

An Nasiriyah
Al Basrah
(Basra)
Abadan

KUWAIT
Al Kuwayt
Hawalli
BUSHEHR
Büshehr

ARABIA

Buraydah
AL QASIM
AR-RIYAD
ASH-SHARQIYAH
AL-HUDUD ASH-SHAMALIYAH

HORMOZGAN
Bandar-e 'Abbas
OMAN

The Gulf

Ad Dammam
BAHRAIN
Al Manamah
QATAR
Ad Dawhah
(Doha)
Dubayy
(Dubai)
Ash Shariqah
UNITED ARAB EMIRATES
Abu Zabi
(Abu Dhabi)
Ar Riyad
(Riyadh)

Gulf of Oman
Strait of Hormuz

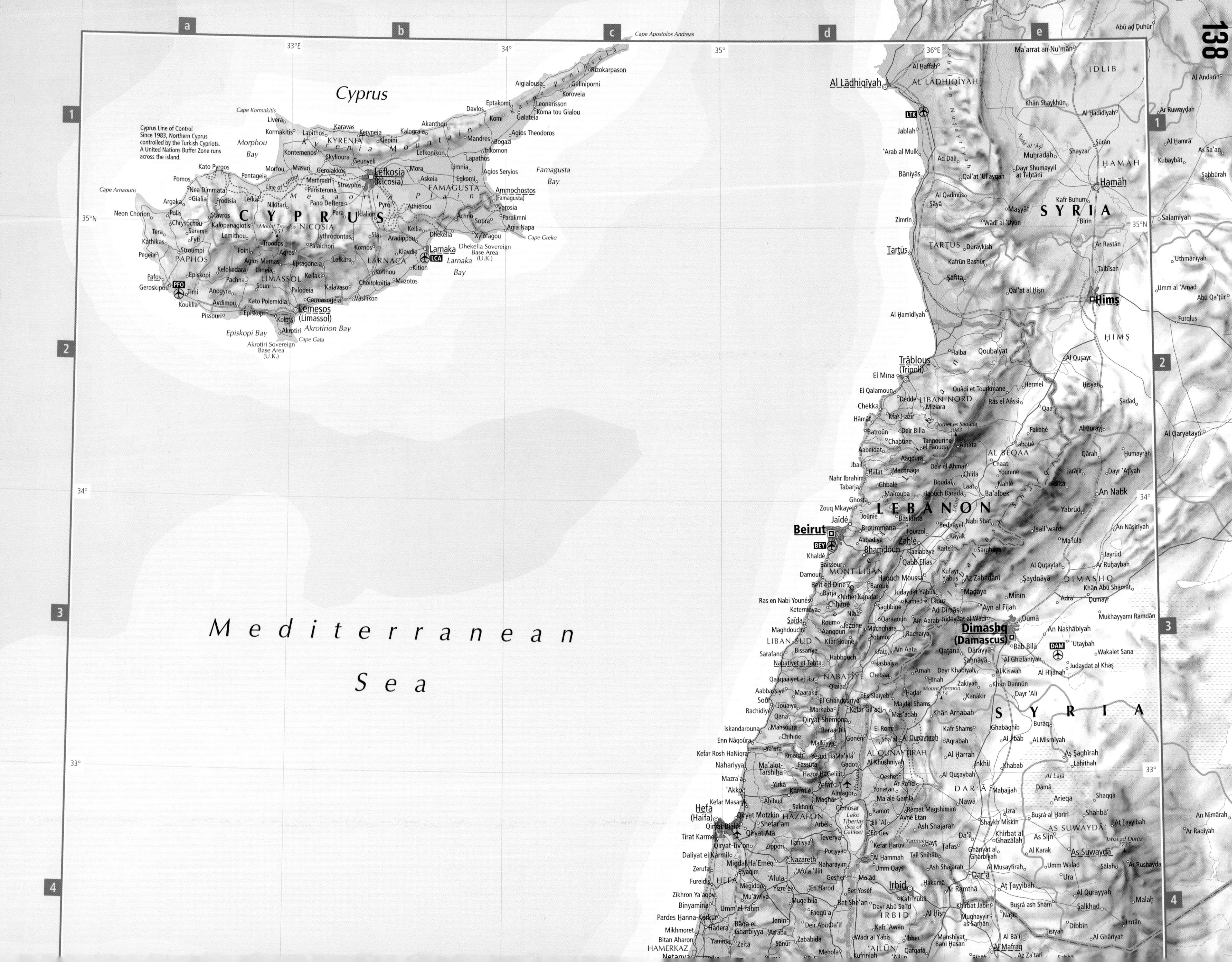
Cyprus
Cyprus Line of Control Since 1983, Northern Cyprus controlled by the Turkish Cypriots. A United Nations Buffer Zone runs across the island.
Mediterranean Sea
CYPRUS
LEBANON
SYRIA
Lefkosia (Nicosia)
Lemesos (Limassol)
Larnaka
Pafos
Ammochostos (Famagusta)
Famagusta Bay
Larnaka Bay
Morphou Bay
Episkopi Bay
Akrotirion Bay
Cape Apostolos Andreas
Cape Greko
Cape Gata
Cape Kormakitis
Cape Arnaoutis
Dhekelia Sovereign Base Area (U.K.)
Akrotiri Sovereign Base Area (U.K.)
KYRENIA
NICOSIA
FAMAGUSTA
LARNACA
LIMASSOL
PAPHOS
Beirut
Trâblous (Tripoli)
Zahlé
Saïda
Ba'albek
Dimashq (Damascus)
Ḩimş
Ḩamāh
Al Lādhiqīyah
Ţarţūs
Irbid
Dar'ā
As Suwaydā'
Hefa (Haifa)
Nazareth
Lake Tiberias (Sea of Galilee)
Mount Hermon 2814
IDLIB
ḨAMĀH
AL LĀDHIQĪYAH
ŢARŢŪS
ḨIMŞ
DIMASHQ
AL QUNAYŢIRAH
DAR'Ā
AS SUWAYDĀ'
IRBID
'AJLŪN
HEFA
HAZAFON
HAMERKAZ
LIBAN-NORD
MONT-LIBAN
LIBAN-SUD
NABATIYÉ
AL BEQAA
33°E
34°
35°
36°E
35°N
34°
33°

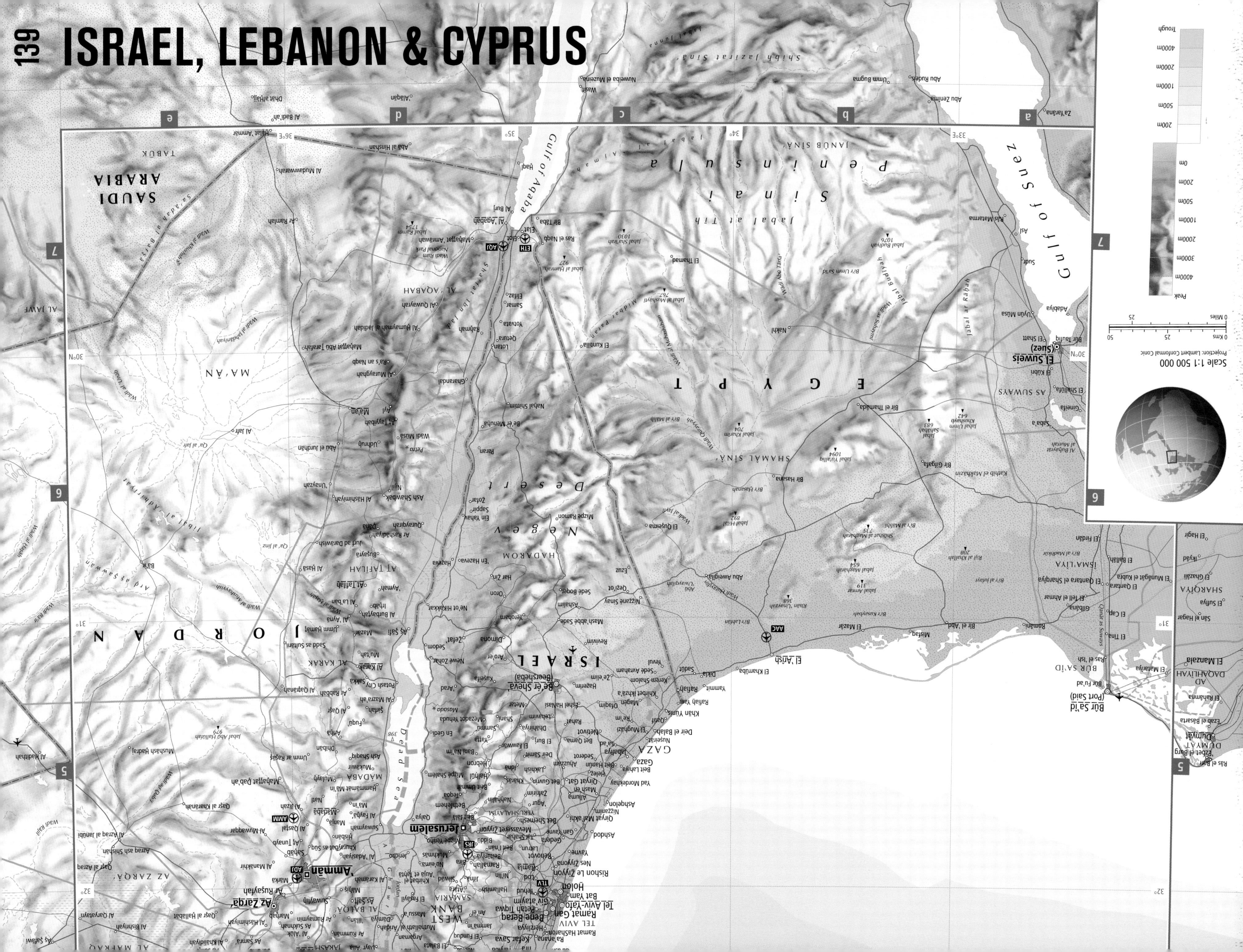

ISRAEL, LEBANON & CYPRUS

SAUDI
ARABIA

TABŪK

MA'ĀN

J O R D A N

Al JAWF

'Ammān

AL BALQĀ'

MADABA

AL KARAK

AT TAFĪLAH

Az Zarqā'

AL MAFRAQ

AZ ZARQĀ'

Dead Sea

Jerusalem

Bethlehem

Hebron

WEST
BANK

SAMARIA

JUDAEA

TEL AVIV

Tel Aviv-Yafo

Holon

Bat Yam

Rishon Le Ziyyon

Ashdod

Ashqelon

Gaza

GAZA

Khān Yūnis

Rafiah Yam

I S R A E L

Be'er Sheva
(Beersheba)

Dimona

N e g e v

HADAROM

HADAROM

D e s e r t

Al 'Aqabah

Gulf of Aqaba

Elat

E G Y P T

SHAMĀL SĪNĀ'

S i n a i   P e n i n s u l a

JANŪB SĪNĀ'

AS SUWAYS

El Suweis
(Suez)

Būr Sa'īd
(Port Said)

DUMYĀT

AD
DAQAHLĪYA

SHARQĪYA

ISMĀ'ĪLĪYA

Gulf of Suez

El Mazâr

El 'Arîsh

Scale 1:1 500 000
Projection: Lambert Conformal Conic

0 Kms   25   50
0 Miles 25

Peak
4000m
3000m
2000m
1000m
500m
200m
0m

4000m
2000m
1000m
500m
200m
0m
Trough

EUROPE POPULATION
725,136,000

EUROPE AREA
9,908,599km² (3,825,731 sq miles)

HIGHEST PEAKS
1 Elbrus, European Russia 5642m (18,510ft)
2 Gora Dykh-Tau, European Russia 5204m (17,073ft)
3 Shkhara, European Russia/Georgia 5201m (17,063ft)
4 Kazbek, European Russia/Georgia 5047m (16,558ft)
5 Mont Blanc, France/Italy 4808m (15,774ft)

LARGEST DESERTS
Europe is the only continent with no desert

LARGEST COUNTRY
European Russia 3,955,818km² (1,527,341 sq miles)

SMALLEST COUNTRY
Vatican 44ha (108.7 acres)

WETTEST PLACE
13 Crkvica, Bosnia-Herzegovina 4648.2mm (183in)
average annual rainfall

DRIEST PLACE
14 Astrahan, European Russia 162.5mm (6.4in) average annual rainfall

HIGHEST RECORDED TEMPERATURE
15 Seville, Spain 50°C (122°F), Aug 4 1881

LOWEST RECORDED TEMPERATURE
16 Ust-Shchugor, European Russia -55°C (-67°F)

LOWEST POINT
⑥ Caspian Sea, 29m (94ft) below sea level

LARGEST LAKES
⑩ Lake Ladoga (Ladozhskoye Ozero), European Russia 18,390km² (7100 sq miles)
⑪ Lake Onega (Onezhskoye Ozero), European Russia 9600km² (3706 sq miles)
⑫ Vänern, Sweden 5585km² (2156 sq miles)

LONGEST RIVERS
⑦ Volga, European Russia 3688km (2291 miles)
⑧ Danube, Germany/Austria/Bulgaria/Romania/Croatia/
Slovakia/Hungary 2850km (1770 miles)
⑨ Dnieper, Belarus/Ukraine 2285km (1149 miles)

EUROPE

Europe – the second smallest continent after Australia – accounts for only 7 per cent of the Earth's land. Despite its small size, its jigsaw of different terrain encompasses the intricately indented Atlantic coast, the forested central plains, the steppe grasslands of the Ukraine and the coastal scrub of the Mediterranean region. To the south-east, Turkey and the Anatolian plateau link Europe with western Asia; to the north-west, the volcanic island of Iceland sits on the ocean ridge separating Europe and North America.

Health, wealth and education

The larger countries of western Europe have some of the world's highest average yearly incomes, and health, educational and welfare services are correspondingly sophisticated, with average life expectancy in the high 70s. The former Eastern bloc countries are still significantly poorer as they strive to overcome decades of state planning, with fewer health and wealth provisions. In some cases, life expectancy is much lower. Literacy rates are high throughout Europe, reaching at least 80 per cent in every country.

Age					Birth rate		Adult literacy			Wealth	
Under 15		%		Over 65		Births per 1000 population			%		GDP per head $US
Albania	30		18.1	Italy	Albania	16.2	Vatican City	100		Luxembourg	48,072
Croatia	26.5		17.6	Greece	Ireland	15.1	Latvia	99.8		Norway	42,224
Luxembourg	24.3		17.4	Sweden	Macedonia	14.5	Estonia	99.8		Liechtenstein	39,848
Bosnia & Herz.	23.5		17	Belgium	Iceland	14.3	Poland	99.8		Switzerland	37,407
Iceland	23.3		17	Spain	Cyprus	13.9	Belarus	99.7		Denmark	33,607
Andorra	15.5		9.6	Serbia & Montenegro	Czech Republic	8.8	Slovakia	93		Belarus	1431
Germany	15.5		9.5	Liechtenstein	Russia	8.8	Bosnia & Herz.	93		Serbia & Montenegro	1299
Spain	14.7		9.3	Moldova	Estonia	8.7	Malta	92.8		Bosnia & Herz.	1183
Italy	14.3		7.1	Bosnia & Herz.	Bulgaria	8.0	Serbia & Montenegro	89		Ukraine	842
San Marino	14.1		5.9	Albania	Latvia	7.8	Albania	86.5		Moldova	366

■ Top five ■ Bottom five

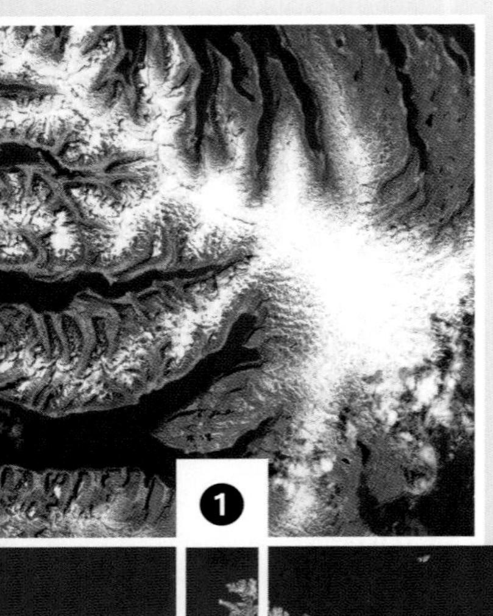

The lie of the land

More than half of Europe consists of lowlands, including the sweeping plains of northern and eastern Europe. To the south lies a belt of mountains running from the Pyrenees in the west to the Balkans in the east. They incorporate Europe's highest peaks – in the Alps. The Mediterranean Sea, North Sea and Atlantic Ocean have rugged, fragmented coastlines, with numerous peninsulas, inlets and islands.

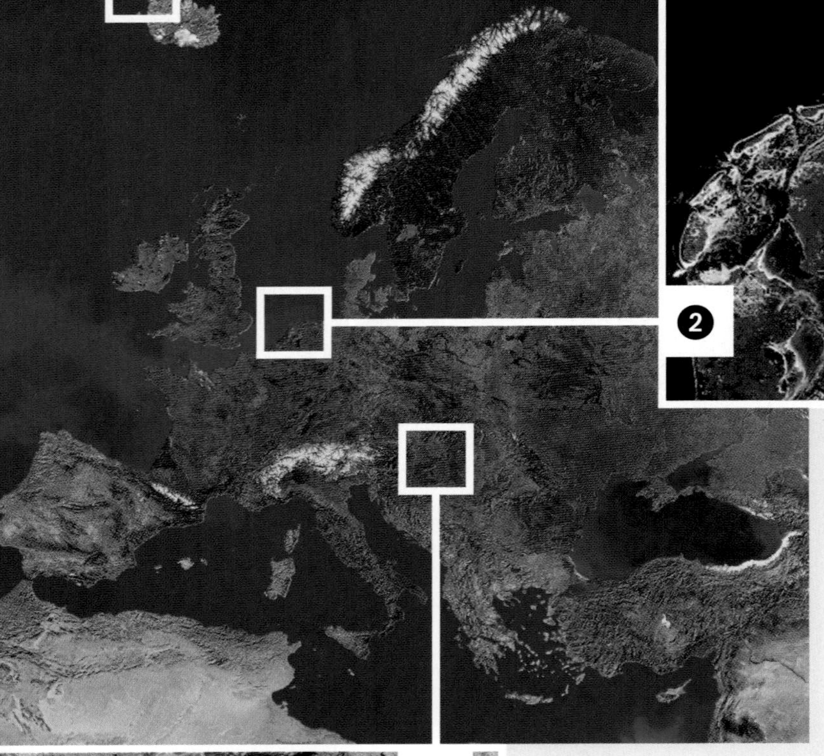

Population

More than 80 per cent of Europeans live in towns or cities in the world's second most densely populated continent. Across the countries of the European Union there are on average nearly 120 people per square kilometre. Europe's population is ageing: most nations have birth rates below replacement level, that is, lower than 2.1 children per woman.

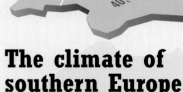

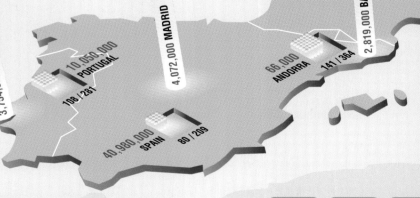

❶ **West Fjords (Vestfirdir) peninsula** The fjords – long narrow inlets (dark blue) – along the jagged coastline of north-west Iceland (orange) were flooded following periods of glaciation, which hollowed out deep, broad and high-sided valleys. ❷ **Ijsselmeer** Once a shallow inlet of the North Sea, parts of the Ijsselmeer in Holland have been dammed off and drained, creating new areas of fertile land (blue), known as polders. ❸ **Baja wetlands** The town of Baja in southern Hungary sits to the east of the River Danube (thick black line). Oxbow lakes can be seen along the course of the Danube. They formed where old meanders were cut off as the river silted up, and became small crescent-shaped lakes.

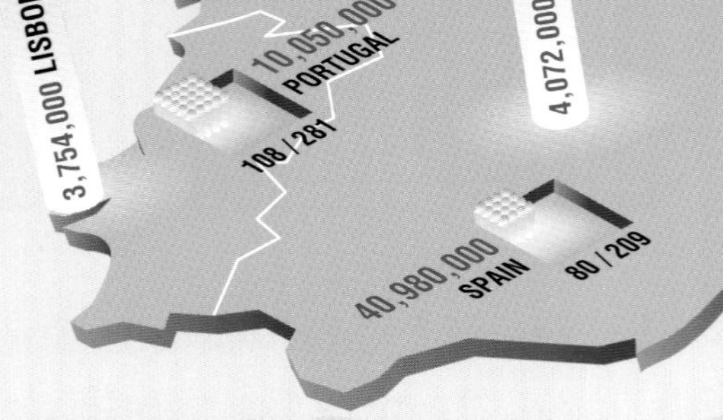

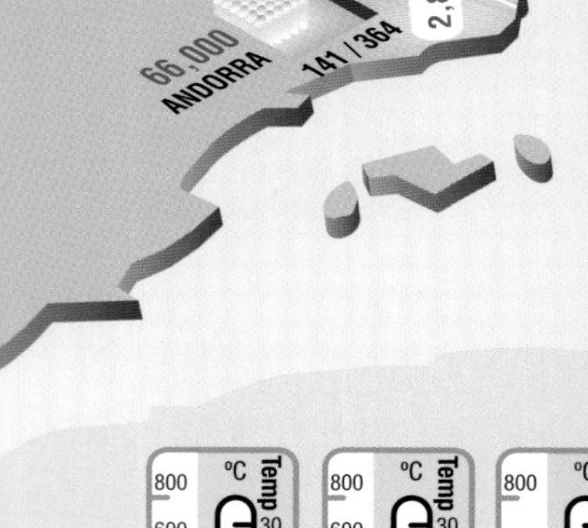

The climate of southern Europe

In the west, the Atlantic Ocean brings heavy rainfall and cool summers, though the warming Gulf Stream ensures mild winters. The Mediterranean lands have hot summers, but lack of rain often creates near-desert conditions. Winters are wetter and generally mild, thanks to the protective barrier of the Pyrenees and Alps.

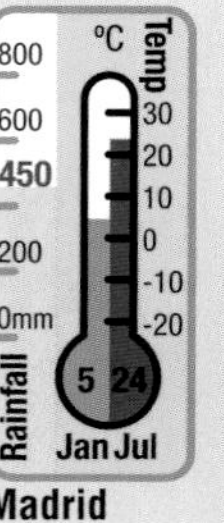

Madrid   Athens   Malta

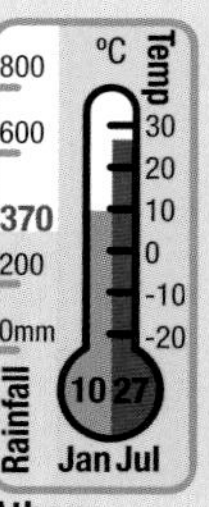

143

EUROPE

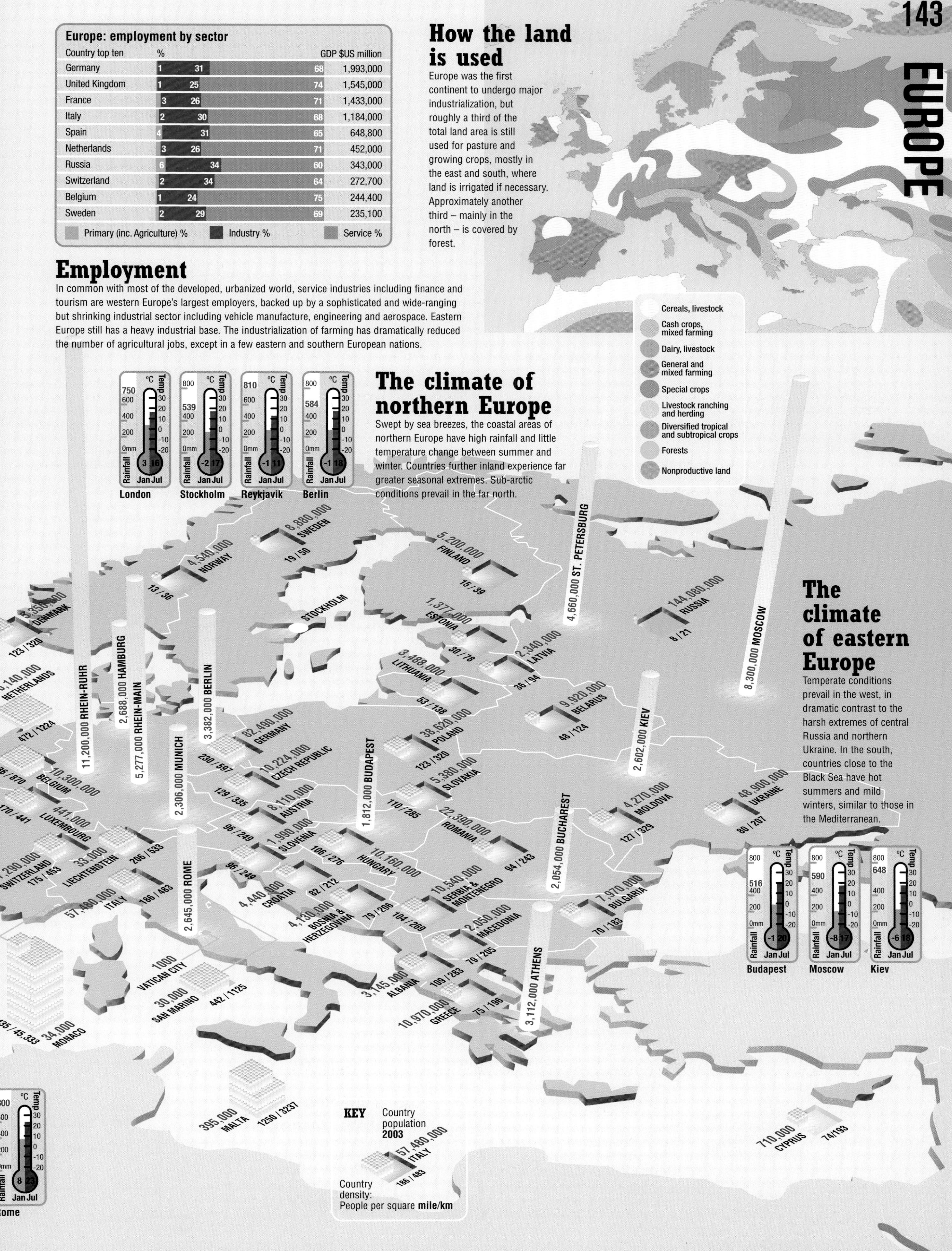

Europe: employment by sector

Country top ten	%		GDP $US million
Germany	1	31	68	1,993,000
United Kingdom	1	25	74	1,545,000
France	3	26	71	1,433,000
Italy	2	30	68	1,184,000
Spain	4	31	65	648,800
Netherlands	3	26	71	452,000
Russia	6	34	60	343,000
Switzerland	2	34	64	272,700
Belgium	1	24	75	244,400
Sweden	2	29	69	235,100

Primary (inc. Agriculture) %   Industry %   Service %

How the land is used

Europe was the first continent to undergo major industrialization, but roughly a third of the total land area is still used for pasture and growing crops, mostly in the east and south, where land is irrigated if necessary. Approximately another third – mainly in the north – is covered by forest.

Employment

In common with most of the developed, urbanized world, service industries including finance and tourism are western Europe's largest employers, backed up by a sophisticated and wide-ranging but shrinking industrial sector including vehicle manufacture, engineering and aerospace. Eastern Europe still has a heavy industrial base. The industrialization of farming has dramatically reduced the number of agricultural jobs, except in a few eastern and southern European nations.

Cereals, livestock
Cash crops, mixed farming
Dairy, livestock
General and mixed farming
Special crops
Livestock ranching and herding
Diversified tropical and subtropical crops
Forests
Nonproductive land

Climate graphs — northern Europe

London — 750 / 600 / 400 / 200 / 0mm Rainfall — °C Temp 30/20/10/0/-10/-20 — 3 16 Jan Jul

Stockholm — 800 / 539 / 400 / 200 / 0mm Rainfall — °C Temp — -2 17 Jan Jul

Reykjavik — 810 / 600 / 400 / 200 / 0mm Rainfall — °C Temp — -1 11 Jan Jul

Berlin — 800 / 584 / 400 / 200 / 0mm Rainfall — °C Temp — -1 18 Jan Jul

The climate of northern Europe

Swept by sea breezes, the coastal areas of northern Europe have high rainfall and little temperature change between summer and winter. Countries further inland experience far greater seasonal extremes. Sub-arctic conditions prevail in the far north.

The climate of eastern Europe

Temperate conditions prevail in the west, in dramatic contrast to the harsh extremes of central Russia and northern Ukraine. In the south, countries close to the Black Sea have hot summers and mild winters, similar to those in the Mediterranean.

Budapest — 800 / 516 / 400 / 200 / 0mm Rainfall — °C Temp — -1 20 Jan Jul

Moscow — 800 / 590 / 400 / 200 / 0mm Rainfall — °C Temp — -8 17 Jan Jul

Kiev — 800 / 648 / 400 / 200 / 0mm Rainfall — °C Temp — -6 18 Jan Jul

Rome — 800 / 600 / 400 / 200 / 0mm Rainfall — °C Temp — 8 23 Jan Jul

Map labels (population / density people per square mile/km)

8,880,000 SWEDEN 19 / 50
4,540,000 NORWAY 13 / 36
5,200,000 FINLAND 15 / 39
4,660,000 ST. PETERSBURG
144,080,000 RUSSIA 8 / 21
8,300,000 MOSCOW
1,377,000 ESTONIA 30 / 78
2,340,000 LATVIA 36 / 94
3,488,000 LITHUANIA 53 / 138
9,920,000 BELARUS 48 / 124
2,602,000 KIEV
48,900,000 UKRAINE 80 / 207
3,350,000 DENMARK 123 / 320
11,200,000 RHEIN-RUHR
2,688,000 HAMBURG
5,277,000 RHEIN-MAIN
3,382,000 BERLIN
82,490,000 GERMANY 230 / 597
38,520,000 POLAND 123 / 320
5,380,000 SLOVAKIA 110 / 285
4,270,000 MOLDOVA 127 / 329
16,140,000 NETHERLANDS 472 / 1224
10,300,000 BELGIUM 336 / 870
441,000 LUXEMBOURG 170 / 441
2,306,000 MUNICH
10,224,000 CZECH REPUBLIC 129 / 335
8,110,000 AUSTRIA 96 / 249
38,520,000 BUDAPEST
1,812,000 BUDAPEST
10,160,000 HUNGARY 110 / 285
22,390,000 ROMANIA 94 / 243
2,054,000 BUCHAREST
7,290,000 SWITZERLAND 175 / 453
33,000 LIECHTENSTEIN 206 / 533
1,990,000 SLOVENIA 96 / 249
4,440,000 CROATIA 82 / 212
4,130,000 BOSNIA & HERZEGOVINA 79 / 206
10,540,000 SERBIA & MONTENEGRO 104 / 269
7,970,000 BULGARIA 70 / 183
2,050,000 MACEDONIA 79 / 205
2,645,000 ROME
57,480,000 ITALY 196 / 483
1000 VATICAN CITY
30,000 SAN MARINO 442 / 1125
34,000 MONACO 17,435 / 45,333
3,145,000 ALBANIA 109 / 283
3,112,000 ATHENS
10,970,000 GREECE 75 / 196
395,000 MALTA 1250 / 3237
710,000 CYPRUS 74 / 193

KEY
Country population **2003**
57,480,000 ITALY
Country density: People per square **mile/km**
196 / 483

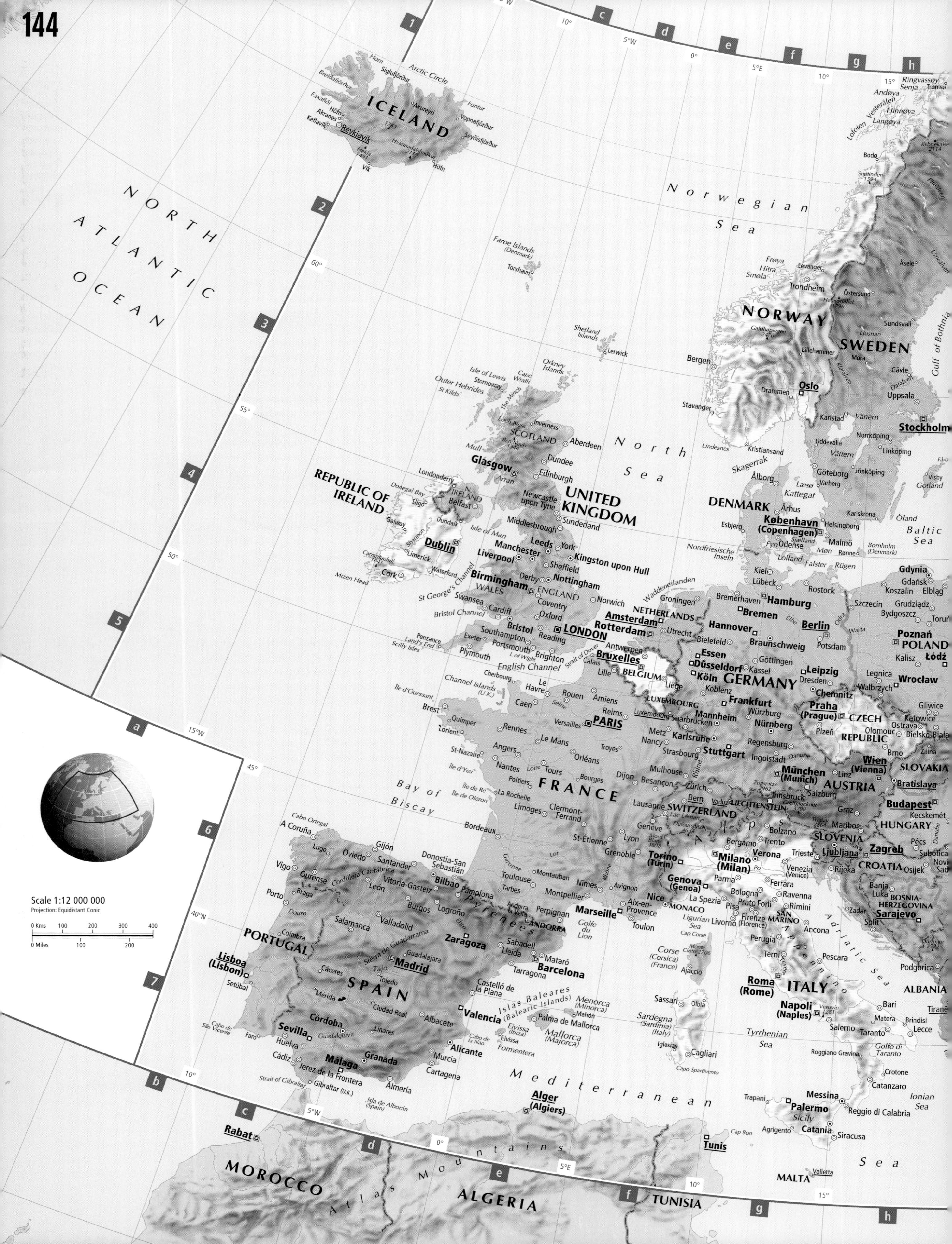

NORTH ATLANTIC OCEAN

ICELAND

Horn
Siglufjörður
Breiðafjörður
Akureyri
Faxaflói Hófn
Akranes
Keflavík
Reykjavík
Hella
Vík
Vopnafjörður
Fontur
Seyðisfjörður
Hvannadalshnúkur
Höfn

Arctic Circle

NORWAY

Norwegian Sea

Ringvassøy
Andøya Senja Tromsø
Vesterålen
Lofoten Hinnøya
Langøya
Bodø
Kebnekaise 2114
Snøtinden 1594

Faroe Islands (Denmark)
Torshavn

Frøya
Hitra
Smøla
Trondheim
Levanger
Åsele
Østersund

Galdhøpiggen 2469
Helligskogen 2286
Lillehammer
Ljusnan
Sundsvall

SWEDEN

Shetland Islands
Lerwick

Bergen
Stavanger
Drammen
Oslo
Mora
Gävle
Dalälven
Uppsala

Isle of Lewis
Stornoway
Orkney Islands
Cape Wrath
St Kilda
Outer Hebrides
The Minch

Lindesnes
Kristiansand
Skagerrak

Karlstad
Vänern
Norrköping
Linköping

Stockholm

Uddevalla
Vättern
Göteborg
Jönköping

Visby
Gotland
Öland

SCOTLAND
Inverness
Loch Ness
Ben Nevis 1344
Aberdeen
Dundee
Glasgow
Arran
Edinburgh

North Sea

Ålborg
Läsø
Varberg
Halmstad
Helsingborg
Malmö
Bornholm (Denmark)

DENMARK

København (Copenhagen)
Odense
Møn
Rønne

Gdynia
Gdańsk
Koszalin
Elbląg
Szczecin
Bydgoszcz
Grudziądz
Toruń

REPUBLIC OF IRELAND
Londonderry
N. IRELAND
Belfast
Donegal Bay
Sligo
Galway
Shannon
Dundalk
Isle of Man
Dublin
Limerick
Carrauntoohil 1041
Waterford
Cork
Mizen Head

Newcastle upon Tyne
Middlesbrough
Sunderland
Kingston upon Hull
York
Leeds
Manchester
Liverpool
Sheffield
Nottingham
Derby
Birmingham
WALES
ENGLAND

UNITED KINGDOM

Esbjerg
Kiel
Lübeck
Rostock

Nordfriesische Inseln
Fyn
Sjælland
Lolland
Falster
Rügen

Berlin

Poznań
POLAND
Kalisz
Łódź

Swansea
Cardiff
Bristol Channel
Bristol
Reading
LONDON
Brighton
Portsmouth
Southampton
Exeter
Plymouth

St George's Channel
Land's End
Scilly Isles
Penzance

Coventry
Oxford
Norwich

Groningen
NETHERLANDS
Amsterdam
Rotterdam
Utrecht
Antwerpen
Bruxelles
BELGIUM
Lille
Calais
Liège

Waddeneilanden
Bremerhaven
Bremen
Hamburg
Hannover
Braunschweig
Bielefeld
Göttingen
Kassel
Essen
Düsseldorf
Köln
GERMANY

Elbe
Potsdam
Leipzig
Dresden
Chemnitz

Praha (Prague)
CZECH REPUBLIC
Plzeň

Legnica
Wrocław
Walbrzych
Gliwice
Katowice
Ostrava
Olomouc
Bielsko-Biała

L. of Wight
English Channel
Strait of Dover
Cherbourg
Le Havre

Koblenz
Frankfurt
Würzburg
Mannheim
Nürnberg

Brno
Zlina

Channel Islands (U.K.)
Île d'Ouessant
Brest
Rouen
Amiens
Reims
LUXEMBOURG
Saarbrücken
Metz
Nancy
Karlsruhe
Stuttgart
Ingolstadt

Regensburg
Danube
München (Munich)
Linz
Wien (Vienna)
AUSTRIA
SLOVAKIA
Bratislava

Quimper
Lorient
St-Nazaire
Île d'Yeu
Rennes
Le Mans
Angers
Nantes
Loire
Tours
Orléans
Versailles
PARIS
Troyes
Dijon
Bourges
Poitiers
FRANCE

Besançon
Zürich
Bern
SWITZERLAND
Vaduz
LIECHTENSTEIN 1998
Zugspitze 2962
Innsbruck
Salzburg
Graz
Budapest
Kecskemét
HUNGARY
Pécs

Mulhouse
Strasbourg
Nancy
Lausanne
Lac Léman
Genève

Bolzano
Trento
Maribor
SLOVENIA
Ljubljana
Zagreb
CROATIA
Subotica
Novi Sad
Osijek

Bay of Biscay
Île de Ré
Île d'Oléron
La Rochelle

Limoges
Clermont-Ferrand
St-Étienne
Lyon
Grenoble

Bergamo
Torino (Turin)
Milano (Milan)
Verona
Venezia (Venice)
Trieste
Rijeka
Banja Luka
BOSNIA-HERZEGOVINA
Sarajevo

Cabo Ortegal
A Coruña
Lugo
Oviedo
Gijón
Santander
Donostia-San Sebastián
Vigo
Ourense
Porto
Braga
Douro
Vitoria-Gasteiz
León
Burgos
Logroño
Pamplona
Bilbao

Cordillera Cantábrica
Sierra de Guadarrama

Toulouse
Montauban
Tarbes
ANDORRA
Andorra la Vella
Perpignan
Pyrenees

Nîmes
Avignon
Montpellier
Marseille
Aix-en-Provence
Toulon
Golfe du Lion

Nice
MONACO
Genova (Genoa)
La Spezia
Pisa
Parma
Ferrara
Bologna
Prato
Firenze (Florence)
Livorno
Ligurian Sea
Rimini
Ravenna
Forlì
SAN MARINO
Ancona
Zadar
Split
Adriatic Sea

PORTUGAL
Coimbra
Salamanca
Valladolid
Zaragoza
Sabadell
Lleida
Mataró
Barcelona
Tarragona

Lisboa (Lisbon)
Setúbal
Cáceres
Tajo
Mérida
Madrid
SPAIN
Toledo
Guadalajara
Ciudad Real
Linares

Castelló de la Plana
Valencia
Islas Baleares (Balearic Islands)
Menorca (Minorca)
Eivissa (Ibiza)
Palma de Mallorca
Mallorca (Majorca)
Formentera

Perugia
Terni
Pescara
Roma (Rome)
ITALY
Napoli (Naples)
Vesuvio 1281
Salerno

Monte Cinto 2706
Corse (Corsica) (France)
Ajaccio
Cap Corse
Sassari
Olbia
Sardegna (Sardinia) (Italy)
Cagliari
Iglesias

Podgorica
ALBANIA
Tirane
Bari
Matera
Brindisi
Lecce
Taranto
Golfo di Taranto

Cabo de São Vicente
Faro
Huelva
Sevilla
Córdoba
Guadalquivir
Cádiz
Jerez de la Frontera
Gibraltar (U.K.)
Strait of Gibraltar
Isla de Alborán (Spain)

Málaga
Granada
Murcia
Cartagena
Almería
Albacete
Alicante
Cabo de la Nao

Mediterranean Sea

Trapani
Messina
Palermo
Reggio di Calabria
Sicily
Agrigento
Catania
Siracusa
Ionian Sea
Crotone
Catanzaro
Roggiano Gravina
Capo Spartivento
MALTA
Valletta

Rabat
MOROCCO
Atlas Mountains
ALGERIA
Alger (Algiers)
Cap Bon
Tunis
TUNISIA

Scale 1:12 000 000
Projection: Equidistant Conic

0 Kms 100 200 300 400
0 Miles 100 200

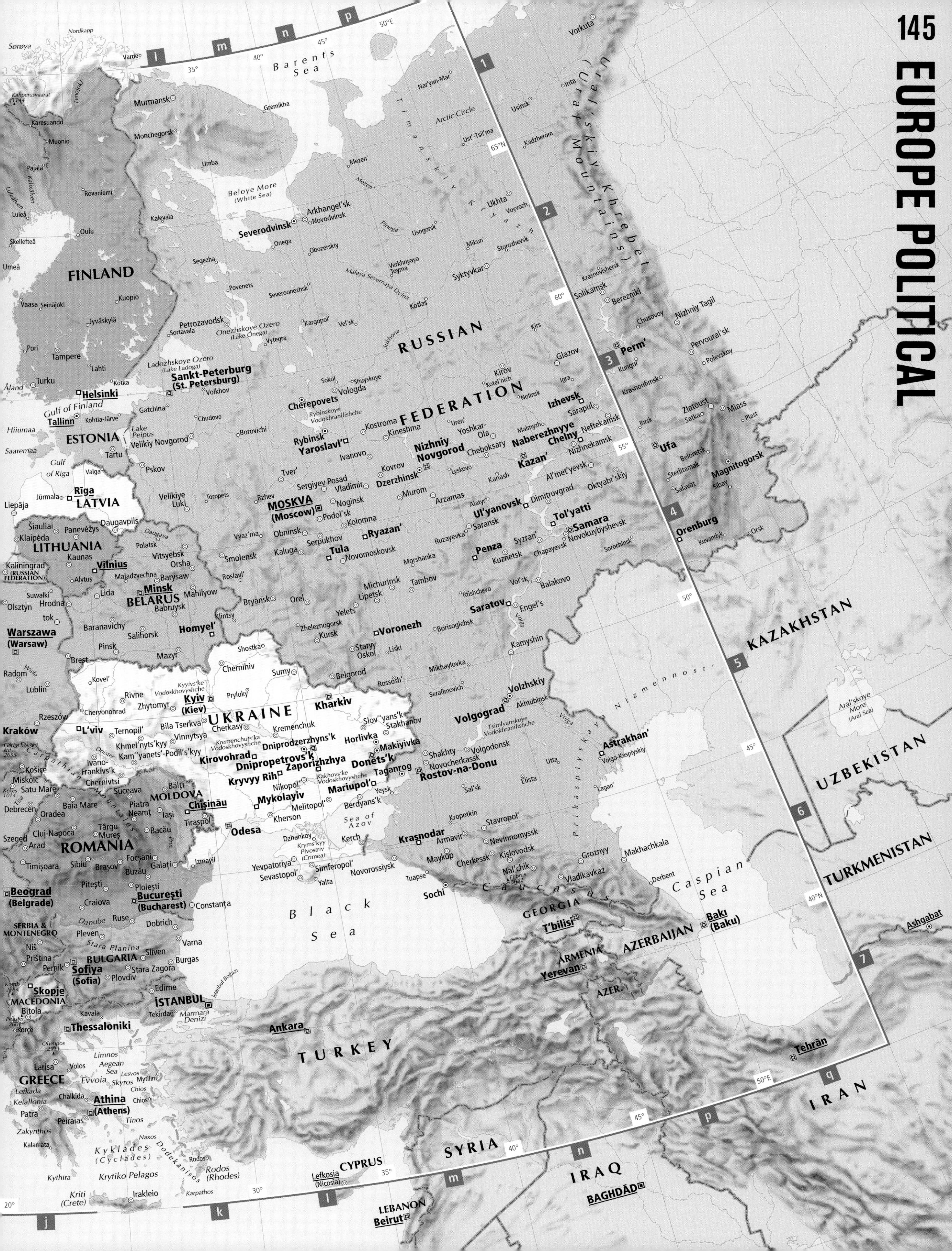

Nordkapp
Søroya
Vardø
Barents Sea
Vorkuta
Inta
Kaljerusvaara (774)
Teriberka
Usinsk
Karesuando
Murmansk
Nar'yan-Mar
Gremikha
Usogorsk
Arctic Circle
Kadzherom
Muonio
Monchegorsk
65°N
Pajala
Rovaniemi
Umba
Mezen'
Ust'-Tsil'ma
Voyvozh
Skellefteå
Onega
Beloye More (White Sea)
Usogorsk
Ukhta
Kalevala
Arkhangel'sk
Mezen
Mikun'
Stogrozhevsk
Vorozhsk
Luleå
Oulu
Severodvinsk
Novodvinsk
Pinega
Krasnovishersk
Umeå
Segezha
Syktyvkar
Solikamsk
Bereziki
Severoonezhsk
Obozerskiy
Verkhnyaya Toyma
60°
Vaasa
Seinäjoki
FINLAND
Povenets
Malaya Severnaya Dvina
Nizhniy Tagil
Chusovoy
Kuopio
Vel'sk
Kargopol
Pervoural'sk
Polevskoy
Kotlas
Åland
Pori
Tampere
Lahti
Petrozavodsk
Onezhskoye Ozero (Lake Onega)
Kirs
Perm'
Kungur
Turku
Sortavala
Vytegra
Sukhona
Glazov
3
Krasnoufimsk
Ladozhskoye Ozero (Lake Ladoga)
Sokol
Shuyskaya
RUSSIAN
Igra
Zlatoust
Miass
Helsinki
Kotka
Sankt-Peterburg (St. Petersburg)
Volkhov
Vologda
Rybinskoye Vodokhranilishche
Kirov
Kotel'nich
Nolinsk
Izhevsk
Sarapul
Satka
Plast
Gulf of Finland
Gatchina
Chudovo
Chérepovets
FEDERATION
55°
Ufa
Birsk
Tallinn
Hiiumaa
Lake Peipus
Velikiy Novgorod
Borovichi
Rybinsk
Yaroslavl'
Kostroma
Kineshma
Yoshkar-Ola
Naberezhnyye Chelny
Neftekamsk
Beloretsk
ESTONIA
Tartu
Pskov
Nizhniy Novgorod
Cheboksary
Kazan'
Nizhnekamsk
Saaremaa
Toropets
Ivanovo
Uren'
Malmyzh
Gulf of Riga
Valga
Tver'
Kovrov
Lyskovo
Al'met'yevsk
Sterlitamak
Magnitogorsk
Rīga
Velikiye Luki
Jūrmala
Sergiyev Posad
Vladimir
Dzerzhinsk
Murom
Arzamas
Alatyr'
Ul'yanovsk
Dimitrovgrad
Oktyabr'skiy
Salavat
Sibay
Liepāja
LATVIA
Rzhev
Noginsk
Saransk
Tol'yatti
4
Orsk
Šiauliai
Daugavpils
Daugava
MOSKVA (Moscow)
Podol'sk
Kolomna
Ruzayevka
Samara
Novokuybyshevsk
Kuvandyk
Panevėžys
Polatsk
Vyaz'ma
Obninsk
Serpukhov
Ryazan'
Penza
Syzran'
Chapayevsk
Orenburg
Klaipėda
LITHUANIA
Vitsyebsk
Smolensk
Kaluga
Tula
Novomoskovsk
Morshanka
Kuznetsk
Sorochinsk
Kaliningrad (RUSSIAN FEDERATION)
Kaunas
Vilnius
Orsha
Roslavl'
Michurinsk
Tambov
Vol'sk
Balakovo
Alytus
Maladzyechna
Minsk
Mahilyow
Bryansk
Orel
Yelets
Lipetsk
Rtishchevo
Suwałki
Hrodna
BELARUS
Babruysk
Klintsy
Kursk
Zheleznogorsk
Voronezh
Borisoglebsk
Saratov
Engel's
Kamyshin
Olsztyn
tok
Lida
Baranavichy
Salihorsk
Homyel'
Shostka
Staryy Oskol
Mikhaylovka
50°
Warszawa (Warsaw)
Pinsk
Mazyr
Chernihiv
Sumy
Belgorod
Rossosh'
Serafimovich
Volzhskiy
Radom
Brest
Kovel'
Kyyiv's'ke Vodoskhovyshche
Pryluky
Liski
Akhtubinsk
Lublin
Rivne
Zhytomyr
Kyiv (Kiev)
Kharkiv
Slov''yans'k
Stakhanov
Tsimlyanskoye Vodokhranilishche
Rzeszów
Chervonohrad
Bila Tserkva
Cherkasy
Kremenchuk
UKRAINE
Horlivka
Volgograd
Utta
Volgodonsk
Kraków
L'viv
Ternopil'
Khmel'nyts'kyy
Vinnytsya
Kremenchuts'ke Vodoskhovyshche
Dniprodzerzhyns'k
Makiyivka
Shakhty
Astrakhan'
Košice
Ivano-Frankivs'k
Kam''yanets'-Podil's'kyy
Kirovohrad
Dnipropetrovs'k
Zaporizhzhya
Donets'k
Novocherkassk
Volgo-Kaspiyskiy
Miskolc
Chernivtsi
Kryvyy Rih
Nikopol
Kakhovs'ke Vodoskhovyshche
Taganrog
Rostov-na-Donu
Yeysk
Sal'sk
Elista
Lagan'
Satu Mare
Bălți
MOLDOVA
Mykolayiv
Melitopol
Berdyans'k
Kropotkin
Debrecen
Oradea
Baia Mare
Piatra Neamţ
Iaşi
Chişinău
Odesa
Kherson
Sea of Azov
Stavropol'
Nevinnomyssk
Szeged
Cluj-Napoca
Târgu Mureş
Bacău
Tiraspol
Dzhankoy
Kerch
Krasnodar
Armavir
Groznyy
Makhachkala
Arad
Suceava
Izmayil
Kryms'kyy Pivostriv (Crimea)
Krasnodar
Maykop
Cherkessk
Kislovodsk
Derbent
Timişoara
Sibiu
Braşov
Buzău
Galaţi
Yevpatoriya
Simferopol'
Novorossiysk
Nal'chik
Vladikavkaz
ROMANIA
Focşani
Sevastopol'
Yalta
Tuapse
Caucasus
Beograd (Belgrade)
Pitești
Ploiești
Constanţa
Sochi
GEORGIA
Caspian Sea
Craiova
Bucureşti (Bucharest)
Black Sea
T'bilisi
Bakı (Baku)
SERBIA & MONTENEGRO
Pleven
Danube
Ruse
Dobrich
ARMENIA
AZERBAIJAN
Niš
Pernik
Stara Planina
Sliven
Varna
Yerevan
Priština
Sofiya (Sofia)
Stara Zagora
Burgas
AZER.
Skopje
BULGARIA
Plovdiv
Edirne
MACEDONIA
Bitola
İstanbul Boğazı
İSTANBUL
Tekirdağ
Marmara Denizi
Kavala
Thessaloniki
Larisa
Volos
Aegean Sea
Lesvos
Mytilini
Chios
Ankara
Tehrān
Leftkada
Kefallonia
Evvoia
Skyros
Chios
TURKEY
Patra
Peiraias
Athina (Athens)
Tinos
Kalamata
Kyklades (Cyclades)
Naxos
Dodekanisos
SYRIA
Kythira
Kriti (Crete)
Krytiko Pelagos
Rodos (Rhodes)
Karpathos
Irakleio
CYPRUS
Lefkosia (Nicosia)
IRAQ
LEBANON
Beirut
BAGHDĀD
IRAN
Ashgabat
TURKMENISTAN
KAZAKHSTAN
Aral'skoye More (Aral Sea)
UZBEKISTAN
Ural'skiy Khrebet (Ural Mountains)

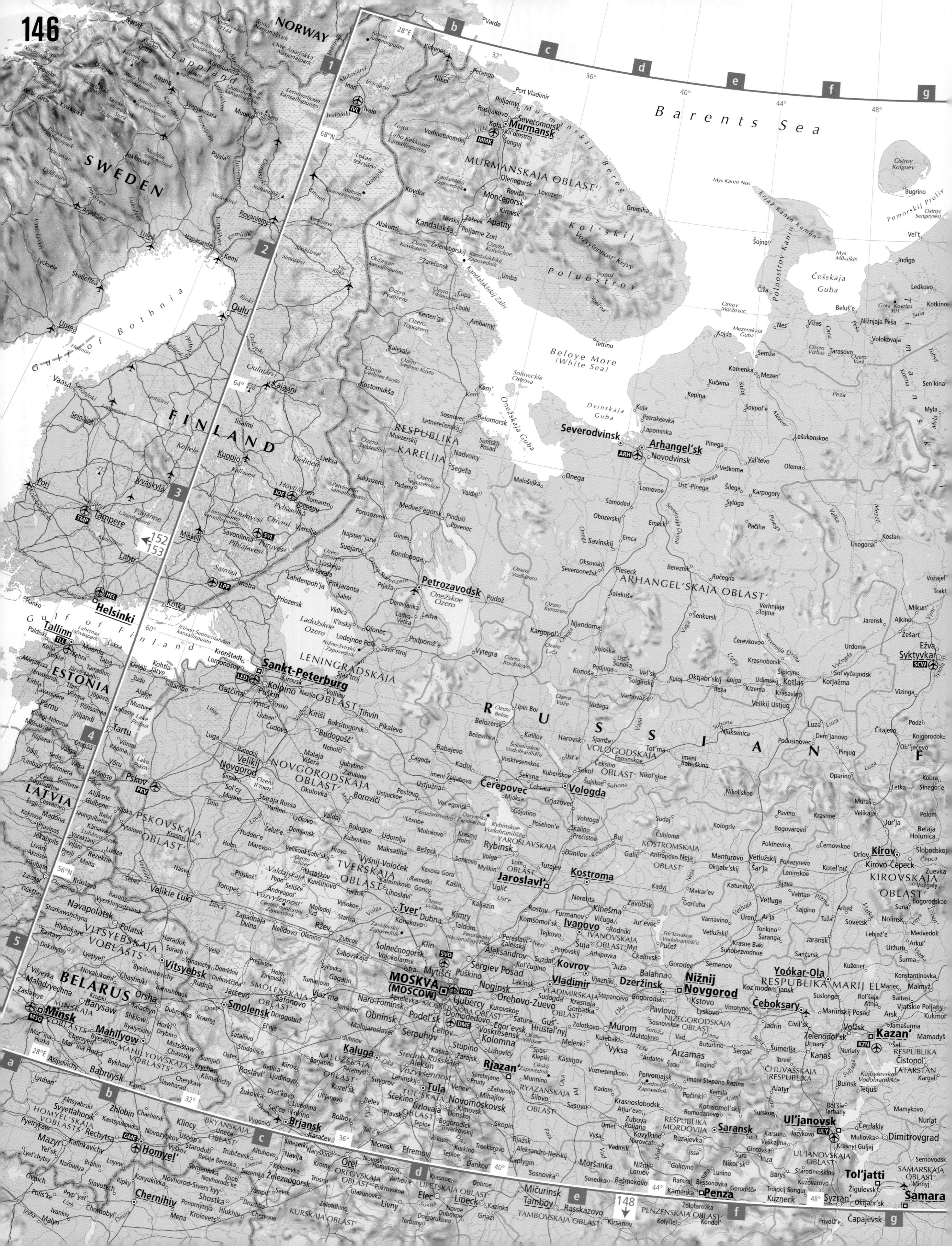

NORWAY
SWEDEN
FINLAND
ESTONIA
LATVIA
BELARUS
RUSSIAN F
Barents Sea
Gulf of Bothnia
Gulf of Finland
Beloye More (White Sea)
Dvinskaja Guba
Onežskaja Guba
Kandalakšskij Zaliv
Češskaja Guba
Kol'skij Poluostrov
Murmanskij Bereg
Poluostrov Kanin
Ostrov Kolguev
Mys Kanin Nos
MURMANSKAJA OBLAST'
RESPUBLIKA KARELIJA
ARHANGEL'SKAJA OBLAST'
LENINGRADSKAJA OBLAST'
NOVGORODSKAJA OBLAST'
PSKOVSKAJA OBLAST'
TVERSKAJA OBLAST'
VOLOGODSKAJA OBLAST'
YAROSLAVSKAJA OBLAST'
KOSTROMSKAJA OBLAST'
KIROVSKAJA OBLAST'
IVANOVSKAJA OBLAST'
VLADIMIRSKAJA OBLAST'
NIZEGORODSKAJA OBLAST'
MOSKOVSKAJA OBLAST'
SMOLENSKAJA OBLAST'
KALUŽSKAJA OBLAST'
TUL'SKAJA OBLAST'
RJAZANSKAJA OBLAST'
BRJANSKAJA OBLAST'
ORLOVSKAJA OBLAST'
LIPECKAJA OBLAST'
KURSKAJA OBLAST'
TAMBOVSKAJA OBLAST'
PENZENSKAJA OBLAST'
RESPUBLIKA MORDOVIJA
ČUVAŠSKAJA RESPUBLIKA
RESPUBLIKA TATARSTAN
RESPUBLIKA MARIJ EL
UL'JANOVSKAJA OBLAST'
SAMARSKAJA OBLAST'
VITSYEBSKAJA VOBLASTS'
MINSKAJA VOBLASTS'
MAHILYOWSKAJA VOBLASTS'
HOMYEL'SKAJA VOBLASTS'
Ladožskoe Ozero
Onežskoe Ozero
Rybinskoe Vodohranilišče
Murmansk
Arhangel'sk
Severodvinsk
Petrozavodsk
Sankt-Peterburg
Helsinki
Tallinn
Tampere
Oulu
Kajaani
Kuopio
Rovaniemi
Velikij Novgorod
Pskov
Vologda
Čerepovec
Jaroslavl'
Kostroma
Ivanovo
Vladimir
Tver'
MOSKVA (MOSCOW)
Smolensk
Vitsyebsk
Minsk
Mahilyow
Homyel'
Kaluga
Tula
Rjazan'
Brjansk
Orel
Lipeck
Tambov
Penza
Saransk
Nižnij Novgorod
Dzeržinsk
Kovrov
Čeboksary
Yoškar-Ola
Kazan'
Ul'janovsk
Tol'jatti
Samara
Kirov
Syktyvkar
Kotlas
Novomoskovsk
Kolomna
Mytišči
Ljubercy
Podol'sk
Obninsk
Serpuhov
Arzamas
Murom
Dimitrovgrad
Mičurinsk
Chernihiv
Velikie Luki
Kirkenes
Vardø
Kiruna
Luleå
Umeå
Vaasa
Pori
Jyväskylä
Joensuu
Tartu
Pärnu
Narva
28°E
32°
36°
40°
44°
48°
56°N
60°
64°
68°N

152
153

148

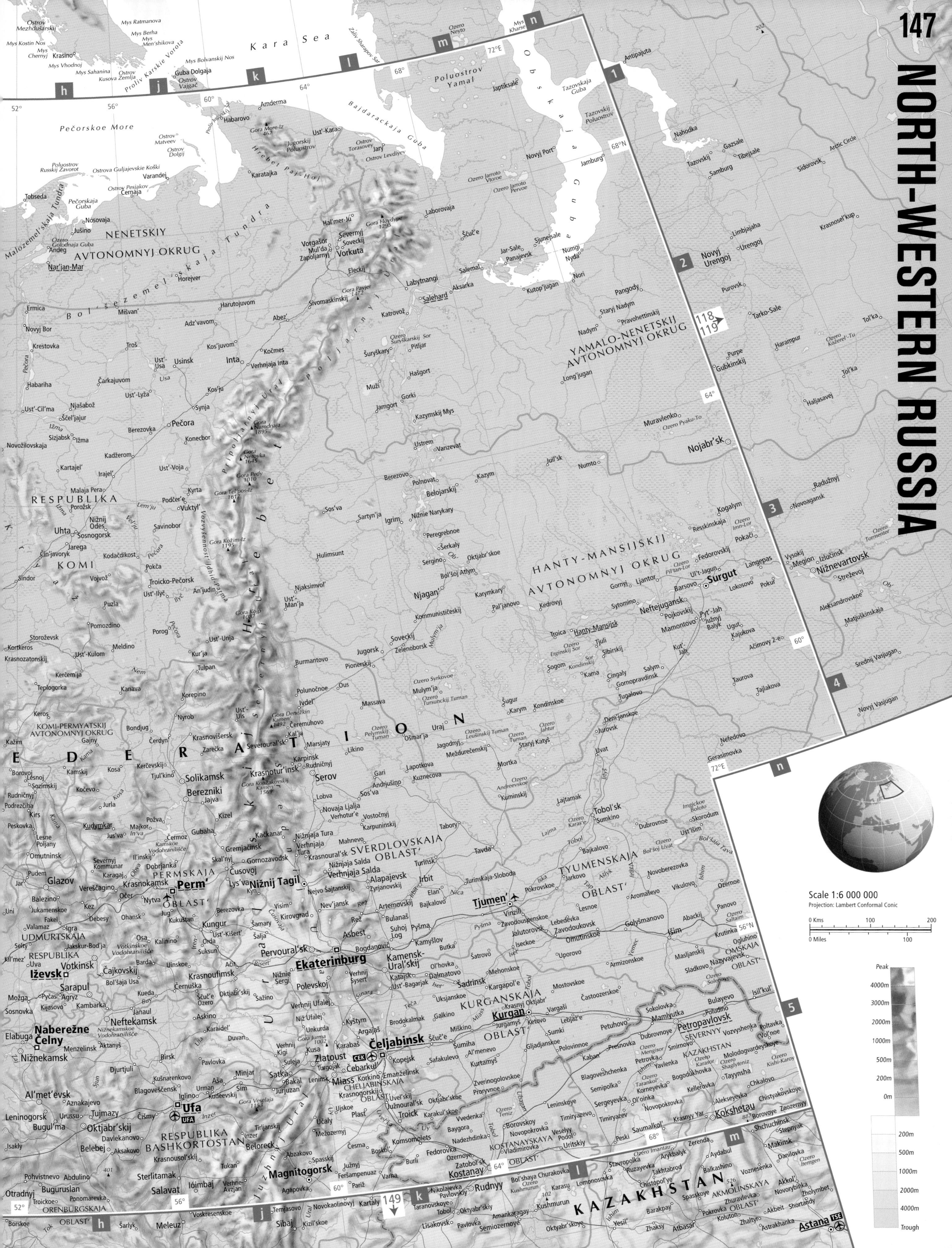
Kara Sea
Ostrov Mezhdušarskij
Mys Ratmanova
Mys Kostin Nos
Mys Cherny
Krasino
Mys Vhodnoj
Mys Sahanina
Kusova Zemlja
Proliv Karskie Vorota
Guba Dolgaja
Ostrov Vajgač
Mys Bolvanskij Nos
Zaliv Sharapov Sar
Ozero Neyto
Mys Kharse
Poluostrov Yamal
Japtiksalé
Obskaja Guba
Tazovskaja Guba
Tazovskij Poluostrov
Bajdarackaja Guba
Pečorskoe More
Amderma
Habarovo
Gora Narodnaja
Ust'-Kara
Jugorskij Poluostrov
Ostrov Torasovey
Jary
Ostrov Matveev
Ostrov Dolgij
Poluostrov Russkij Zavorot
Ostrova Guljajevskie Koški
Varandej
Ostrov Pesjakov
Černaja
Karatajka
Hrebet Paj-Hoj
Novyj Port
Jamburg
Ozero Jarroto
Tobseda
Pečorskaja Guba
Nosovaja
Jušino
NENETSKIY AVTONOMNYJ OKRUG
Malozemel'skaja Tundra
Bol'šezemel'skaja Tundra
Nar'jan-Mar
Andeg
Horejver
Vorgašor
Mul'da
Zapoljarnyj
Severnyj
Sovetskij
Vorkuta
Hal'mer-Ju
Gora Pajer
Laborovaja
Ščuč'e
Jar-Sale
Panajevsk
Sjunejsale
Numgi
Nyda
Nori
Eleckij
Labytnangi
Salemal
Aksarka
Salehard
Kutop'jugan
Sivomaskinskij
Harutojuvom
Abez'
Katrovož
Ermica
Mišvan'
Novyj Bor
Adz'vavom
Krestovka
Troš
Kos'juvom
Kočmes
Ust'-Usa
Usinsk
Inta
Verhnjaja Inta
Šuryškary
Pitljar
Habariha
Čarkajuvom
Ust'-Lyža
Kos'ju
Synja
Muži
Hašgort
Gorki
Jamgort
Kazymskij Mys
Ust'-Cil'ma
Njašabož
Ščel'jajur
Izma
Sizjabsk
Novožilovskaja
Berezovka
Pečora
Konecbor
Ustrem
Vanzevat
Kadžerom
Kartajel'
Irajel'
Ust'-Voja
Malaja Pera
RESPUBLIKA KOMI
Porožsk
Uhta
Sosnogorsk
Nižnij Odes
Podčer'e
Vuktyl'
Kyrta
Savinobor
Jarega
Čin'javoryk
Kodačdikost
Sindor
Vojvož
Pokča
Troicko-Pečorsk
Ust'-Ilyč
An'judin
Puzla
Pomozdino
Porog
Storoževsk
Kortkeros
Krasnozatonskij
Ust'-Kulom
Meldino
Ust'-Unja
Kur'ja
Tulpan
Kerčem'ja
Teplogorka
Kanava
Korepino
Keros
KOMI-PERMYATSKIJ AVTONOMNYJ OKRUG
Kažim
Gajny
Bondjug
Čerdyn'
Nyrob
Krasnovišersk
Zarečka
Severoural'sk
Ust'-Uls
Kal'ja
Karpinsk
Krasnotur'insk
Rudničnyj
Serov
Solikamsk
Berezniki
Jajva
Kizel
Kočevo
Kosa
Kamskij
Tjul'kino
Jurla
Kudymkar
Majkor
Požva
Jus'va
Gubaha
Kačkanar
Čermoz
Gremjačinsk
Gornozavodsk
Il'inskij
Dobrjanka
Čusovoj
PERMSKAJA OBLAST'
Perm'
Krasnokamsk
Lys'va
Nižnij Tagil
Nytva
Kungur
Kukuštan
Ohansk
Kirovgrad
Nev'jansk
Pervoural'sk
Ekaterinburg
Asbest
Bogdanovič
Kamensk-Ural'skij
Polevskoj
Sysert
Revda
Krasnoufimsk
Nižnie Sergi
Verhnij Ufalej
Kyštym
Argajaš
Čeljabinsk
Kopejsk
Zlatoust
Miass
Čebarkul'
Satka
Bakal
Juržan'
Ufa
Ižhevsk
Votkinsk
Glazov
Sarapul
UDMURTSKAJA RESPUBLIKA
Neftekamsk
Naberežne Čelny
Elabuga
Nižnekamsk
Al'met'evsk
Bugul'ma
Leninogorsk
Tujmazy
Oktjabr'skij
Belebej
Davlekanovo
RESPUBLIKA BASHKORTOSTAN
Sterlitamak
Salavat
Ishimbaj
Beloreck
Magnitogorsk
Sibaj
Meleuz
Buguruslan
Otradnyj
Abdulino
ORENBURGSKAJA OBLAST'
Orsk
Kostanay
Rudnyy
KOSTANAYSKAYA OBLAST'
Troick
Južnoural'sk
Plast
Uvel'skij
Korkino
Emanželinsk
CHELJABINSKAJA OBLAST'
Šadrinsk
Dalmatovo
Kataisk
KURGANSKAJA OBLAST'
Kurgan
Šumiha
Petropavlovsk
SEVERNYY KAZAKHSTAN
Mamlyutka
Bulayevo
Kokshetau
Shchuchinsk
AKMOLINSKAYA OBLAST'
Astana
KAZAKHSTAN
Yesil'
Atbasar
Tjumen'
TYUMENSKAJA OBLAST'
Jalutorovsk
Zavodoukovsk
Išim
Omutinskoe
Tobol'sk
Vagaj
Uvat
Tavda
Turinsk
Irbit
Alapajevsk
Artemovskij
SVERDLOVSKAJA OBLAST'
Verhnjaja Salda
Nižnjaja Salda
Nižnjaja Tura
Verhotur'e
Novaja Ljalja
Karpuninskij
Tabory
Sos'va
Lobva
Gari
Ivdel'
Pelym
Polunočnoe
Ous
Massava
Burmantovo
Pionerskij
Jugorsk
Sovetskij
Zelenoborsk
Kommunističeskij
Njagan'
Nyaksimvol'
Hulimsunt
Sergino
Oktjabr'skoe
Igrim
Nižnie Narykary
Sartyn'ja
Sos'va
Berezovo
Polnovat
Belojarskij
Kazym
HANTY-MANSIJSKIJ AVTONOMNYJ OKRUG
Hanty-Mansijsk
Surgut
Neftejugansk
Pyt'-Jah
Nižnevartovsk
Megion
Langepas
Pokači
Kogalym
Raduznyj
Fedorovskij
Ljantor
Uray
Mežduréčenskij
Kondinskoe
YAMALO-NENETSKIJ AVTONOMNYJ OKRUG
Nadym
Staryj Nadym
Pangody
Novyj Urengoj
Urengoj
Tarko-Sale
Purovsk
Gubkinskij
Muravlenko
Nojabr'sk
Numto
Nahodka
Tazovskij
Gazsale
Samburg
Tibejsale
Sidorovsk
Krasnosel'kup
Limbjajaha
Purpe
Harampur
Tol'ka
Haljasavej
Novoagansk
Vysokij
Izlučinsk
Streževoj
Aleksandrovskoe
Matjuškinskaja
Kajukova
Ačimovy 2-e
Srednij Vasjugan
Tajlakova
Novyj Vasjugan
Nefedovo
Gerasimovka
Ural Mountains
Severnyj Ural
Pripoljarnyj Ural
Poljarnyj Ural
Južnyj Ural
Arctic Circle
R U S S I A N F E D E R A T I O N
Scale 1:6 000 000
Projection: Lambert Conformal Conic
0 Kms 100 200
0 Miles 100
Peak
4000m
3000m
2000m
1000m
500m
200m
0m
200m
500m
1000m
2000m
4000m
Trough
118 119
149

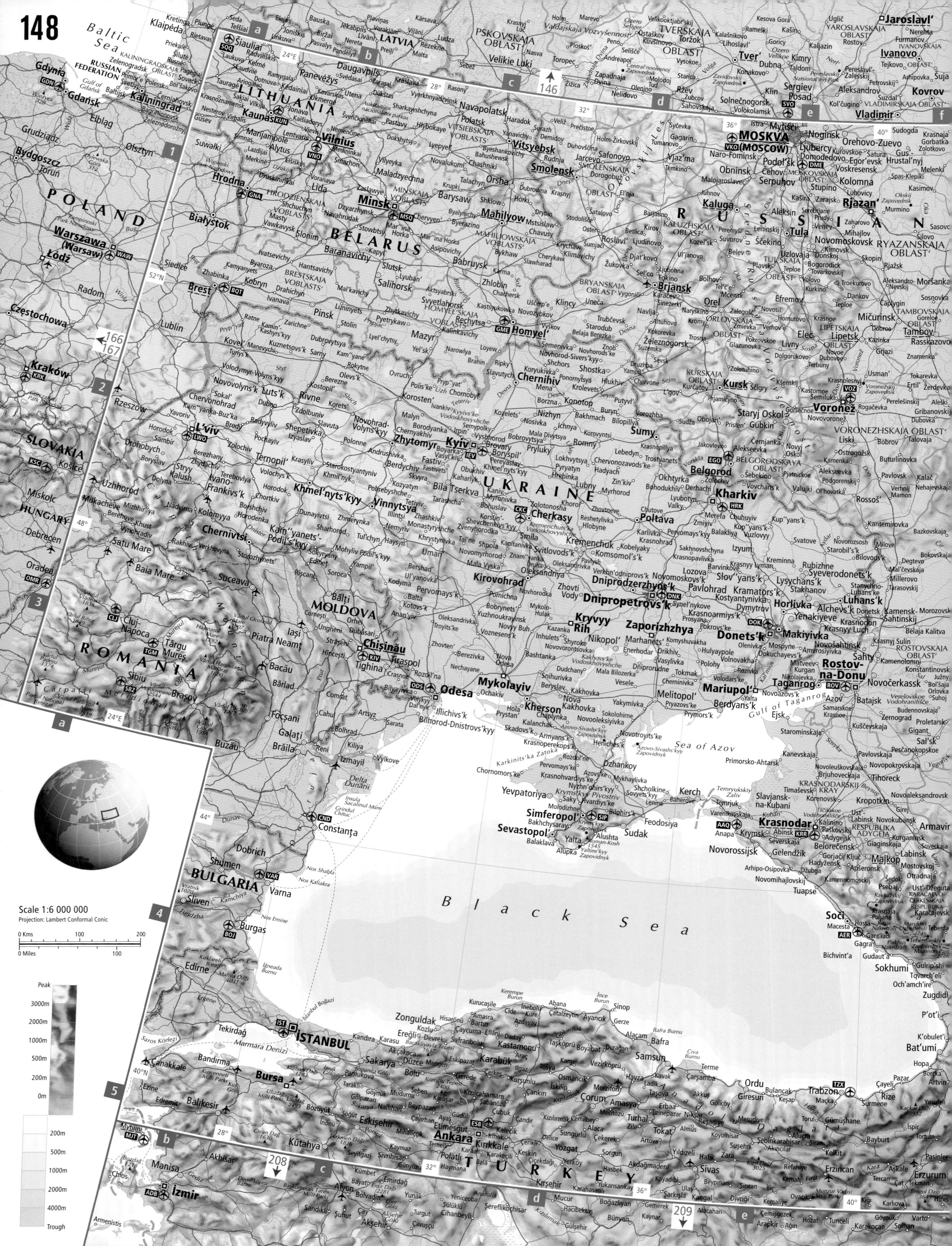
Baltic Sea
LATVIA
LITHUANIA
BELARUS
POLAND
RUSSIAN FEDERATION
RUSSIAN
SLOVAKIA
HUNGARY
UKRAINE
MOLDOVA
ROMANIA
BULGARIA
TURKEY
Black Sea
Sea of Azov
Gulf of Taganrog
Gulf of Gdańsk
Klaipėda
Šiauliai
Daugavpils
Kaliningrad
Gdynia
Gdańsk
Elbląg
Olsztyn
Bydgoszcz
Toruń
Grudziądz
Kaunas
Vilnius
Hrodna
Białystok
Warszawa (Warsaw)
Łódź
Radom
Częstochowa
Lublin
Kraków
Rzeszów
Košice
Miskolc
Debrecen
Oradea
Satu Mare
Baia Mare
Cluj-Napoca
Târgu Mureș
Sibiu
Brașov
Bacău
Piatra Neamț
Iași
Suceava
Focșani
Galați
Brăila
Buzău
Constanța
Dobrich
Shumen
Varna
Sliven
Burgas
Edirne
Tekirdağ
İSTANBUL
Çanakkale
Bandırma
Bursa
Balıkesir
Manisa
İzmir
Kütahya
Eskişehir
Afyon
Ankara
Kırıkkale
Zonguldak
Karabük
Kastamonu
Sinop
Samsun
Bafra
Çorum
Amasya
Tokat
Sivas
Yozgat
Ordu
Giresun
Trabzon
Rize
Erzincan
Erzurum
Bat'umi
Sokhumi
Soči
Tuapse
Novorossijsk
Krasnodar
Anapa
Kerch
Feodosiya
Simferopol'
Sevastopol'
Yalta
Yevpatoriya
Kherson
Mykolayiv
Odesa
Chișinău
Tiraspol
Bălți
Kirovohrad
Kryvyy Rih
Zaporizhzhya
Dnipropetrovs'k
Dniprodzerzhyns'k
Donets'k
Makiyivka
Luhans'k
Horlivka
Mariupol'
Melitopol'
Berdyans'k
Taganrog
Rostov-na-Donu
Novočerkassk
Kharkiv
Poltava
Kremenchuk
Cherkasy
Sumy
Belgorod
Kursk
Voronež
Staryj Oskol
Lipetsk
Tambov
Orel
Brjansk
Kaluga
Tula
Rjazan'
MOSKVA (MOSCOW)
Tver'
Jaroslavl'
Ivanovo
Vladimir
Kovrov
Smolensk
Vitsyebsk
Mahilyow
Homyel'
Minsk
Brest
Baranavichy
Babruysk
Navapolatsk
Chernihiv
Kyiv
Zhytomyr
Vinnytsya
Khmel'nyts'kyy
Ternopil'
L'viv
Ivano-Frankivs'k
Chernivtsi
Rivne
Luts'k
Uzhhorod
Scale 1:6 000 000
Projection: Lambert Conformal Conic
0 Kms 100 200
0 Miles 100
Peak
3000m
2000m
1000m
500m
200m
0m
200m
500m
1000m
2000m
4000m
Trough
146
166
167
208
209

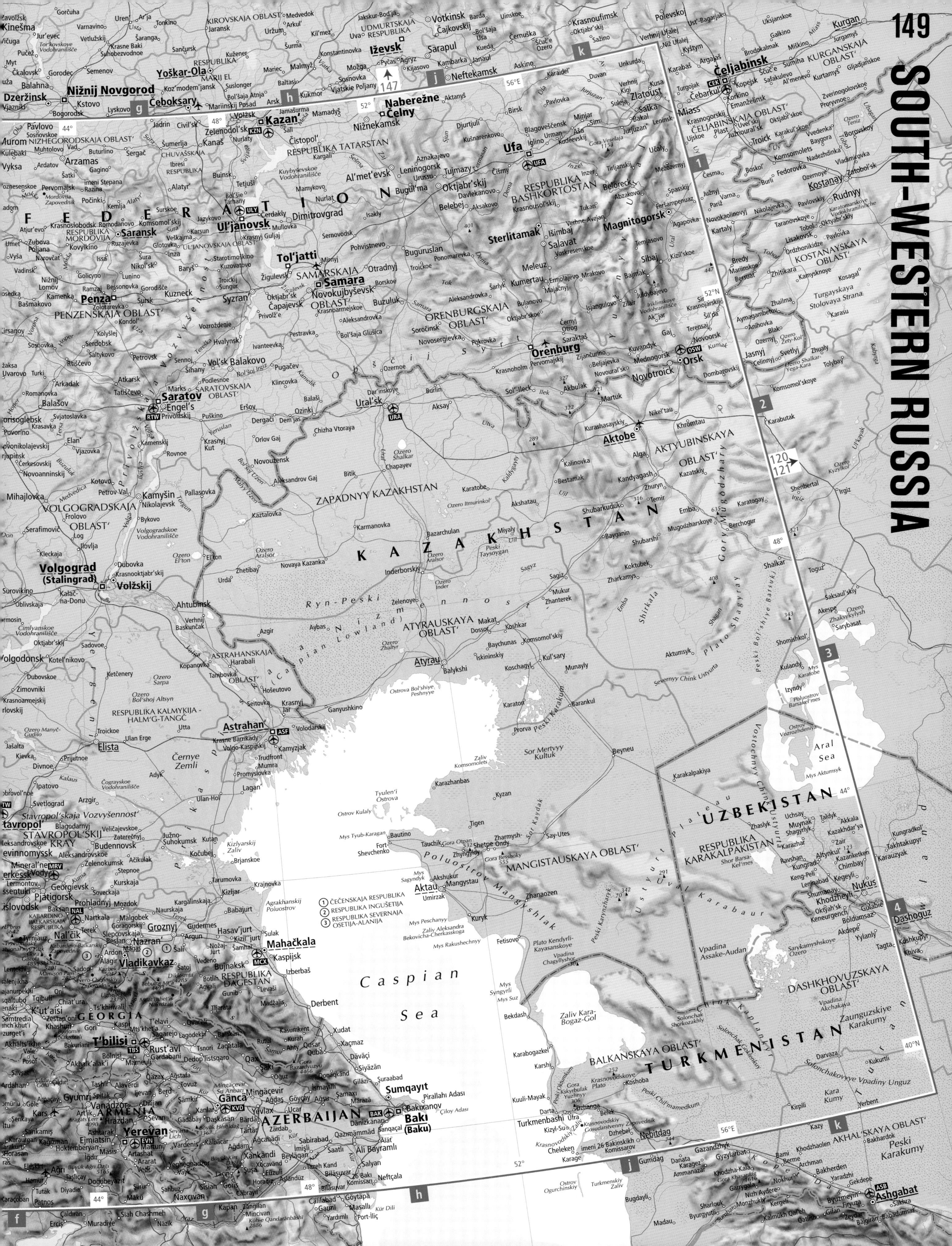
FEDERATION
KAZAKHSTAN
UZBEKISTAN
TURKMENISTAN
GEORGIA
ARMENIA
AZERBAIJAN
Caspian Sea
Aral Sea
Nižnij Novgorod
Kazan'
Samara
Saratov
Volgograd (Stalingrad)
Astrahan'
Orenburg
Ufa
Čeljabinsk
Magnitogorsk
Ul'janovsk
Penza
Saransk
Tol'jatti
Uralsk
Aktobe
Atyrau
Aktau
Mahačkala
Groznyj
Vladikavkaz
Nal'čik
Stavropol'
Elista
T'bilisi
Yerevan
Bakı (Baku)
Sumqayıt
Gəncə
Ashgabat
Turkmenbashi
Nukus
Dashoguz
Kostanay
Orsk
Izhevsk
Naberežnye Čelny
Čeboksary
Joškar-Ola
ZAPADNYY KAZAKHSTAN
ATYRAUSKAYA OBLAST'
MANGISTAUSKAYA OBLAST'
AKTYUBINSKAYA OBLAST'
KOSTANAYSKAYA OBLAST'
ORENBURGSKAJA OBLAST'
SAMARSKAJA OBLAST'
SARATOVSKAJA OBLAST'
VOLGOGRADSKAJA OBLAST'
ASTRAHANSKAJA OBLAST'
PENZENSKAJA OBLAST'
RESPUBLIKA BASHKORTOSTAN
RESPUBLIKA TATARSTAN
RESPUBLIKA KALMYKIJA - HALM'G-TANGČ
RESPUBLIKA DAGESTAN
STAVROPOL'SKIJ KRAY
RESPUBLIKA KARAKALPAKISTAN
DASHKHOVUZSKAYA OBLAST'
BALKANSKAYA OBLAST'
AKHAL'SKAYA OBLAST'
ČELJABINSKAJA OBLAST'
KURGANSKAJA OBLAST'
1 ČEČENSKAJA RESPUBLIKA
2 RESPUBLIKA INGUŠETIJA
3 RESPUBLIKA SEVERNAJA OSETIJA-ALANIJA
Zaliv Kara-Bogaz-Gol
Poluostrov Mangyshlak
Ryn-Peski
Prikaspiyskaya Nizmennost (Caspian Lowland)
Zaunguzskiye Karakumy
Obščij Syrt
147
120 121

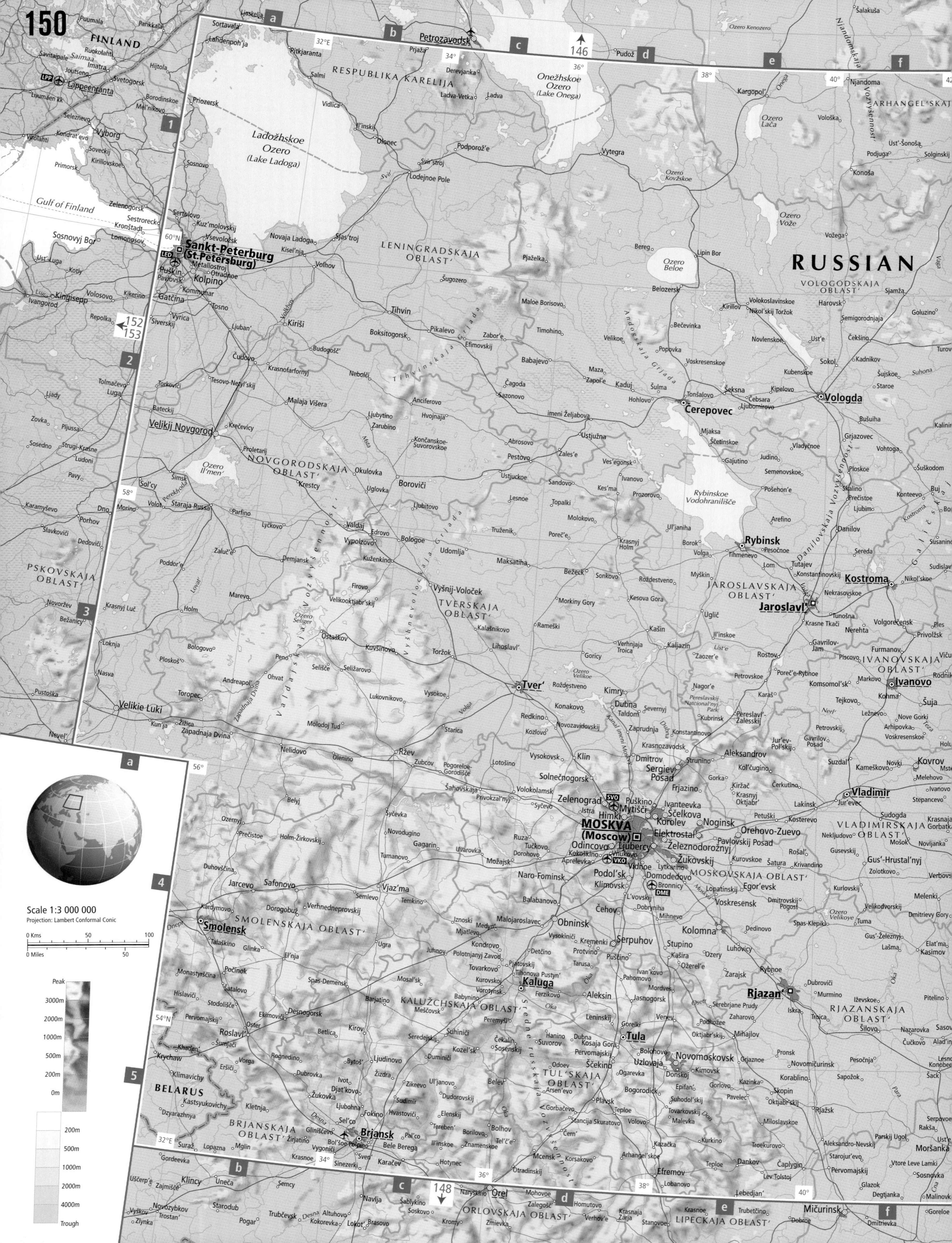
FINLAND
RUSSIAN
BELARUS
Gulf of Finland
Ladožhskoe Ozero (Lake Ladoga)
Onežhskoe Ozero (Lake Onega)
Ozero Beloe
Rybinskoe Vodohranilišče
Ozero Il'men'
RESPUBLIKA KARELIJA
LENINGRADSKAJA OBLAST'
VOLOGODSKAJA OBLAST'
NOVGORODSKAJA OBLAST'
PSKOVSKAJA OBLAST'
TVERSKAJA OBLAST'
JAROSLAVSKAJA OBLAST'
IVANOVSKAJA OBLAST'
VLADIMIRSKAJA OBLAST'
MOSKOVSKAJA OBLAST'
SMOLENSKAJA OBLAST'
KALUŽCHSKAJA OBLAST'
TUL'SKAJA OBLAST'
RJAZANSKAJA OBLAST'
BRJANSKAJA OBLAST'
ORLOVSKAJA OBLAST'
LIPECKAJA OBLAST'
Sankt-Peterburg (St.Petersburg)
MOSKVA (Moscow)
Petrozavodsk
Vologda
Čerepovec
Rybinsk
Jaroslavl'
Kostroma
Ivanovo
Vladimir
Tver'
Velikij Novgorod
Velikie Luki
Smolensk
Kaluga
Tula
Rjazan'
Brjansk
Orel
Mičurinsk
Lappeenranta
Vyborg
Kolpino
Tihvin
Kiriši
Borovići
Vyšnij-Voloček
Rževa
Obninsk
Serpuhov
Kolomna
Sergiev Posad
Noginsk
Elektrostal'
Podol'sk
Novomoskovsk
Orehovo-Zuevo
Kovrov
146
148
152
153
Scale 1:3 000 000
Projection: Lambert Conformal Conic
0 Kms 50 100
0 Miles 50
Peak
3000m
2000m
1000m
500m
200m
0m
200m
500m
1000m
2000m
4000m
Trough

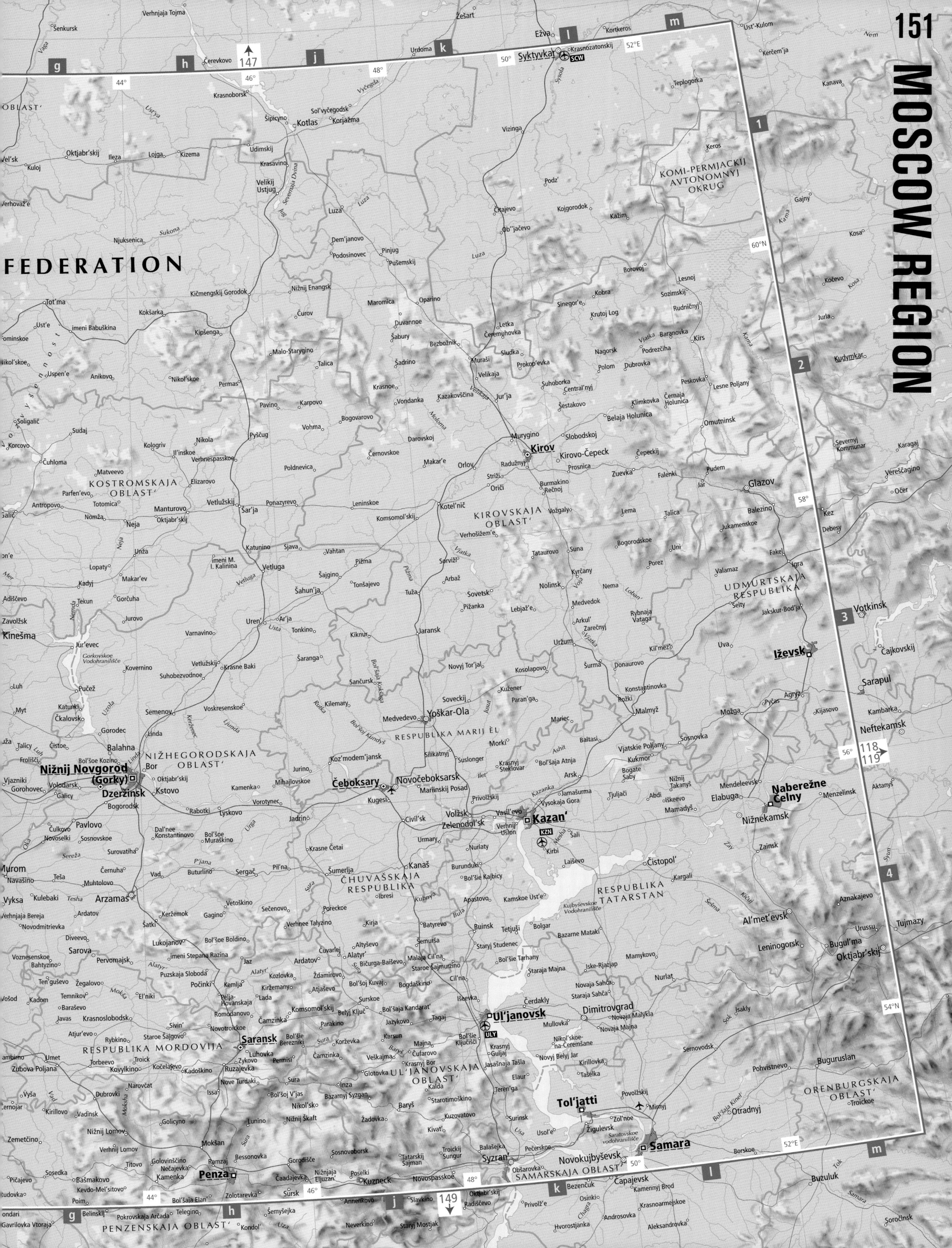
FEDERATION
KOMI-PERMJACKIJ AVTONOMNYJ OKRUG
KOSTROMSKAJA OBLAST'
KIROVSKAJA OBLAST'
UDMURTSKAJA RESPUBLIKA
NIŽHEGORODSKAJA OBLAST'
RESPUBLIKA MARIJ ÈL
ČHUVAŠSKAJA RESPUBLIKA
RESPUBLIKA TATARSTAN
RESPUBLIKA MORDOVIJA
UL'JANOVSKAJA OBLAST'
ORENBURGSKAJA OBLAST'
SAMARSKAJA OBLAST'
PENZENSKAJA OBLAST'
147
149
118
119
Syktyvkar
SCW
Kotlas
Velikij Ustjug
Kirov
Kirovo-Čepeck
Glazov
Votkinsk
Iževsk
Sarapul
Neftekamsk
Naberežne Čelny
Nižnekamsk
Elabuga
Kazan'
KZN
Čistopol'
Al'met'evsk
Bugul'ma
Oktjabr'skij
Leningorsk
Dimitrovgrad
Ul'janovsk
ULY
Tol'jatti
Samara
Novokujbyševsk
Syzran'
Čapajevsk
Buzuluk
Bugurusian
Otradnyj
Penza
Saransk
Kuzneck
Čeboksary
Novočeboksarsk
Yoškar-Ola
Nižnij Novgorod (Gorky)
Dzeržinsk
Kstovo
Bor
Balahna
Gorodec
Arzamas
Murom
Pavlovo
Kinešma
Kudymkar
Kujbyševskoe Vodohranilišče
Gorkovskoe Vodohranilišče
Saratovskoe vodohranilišče
44°
46°
48°
50°
52°E
54°N
56°
58°
60°N
g
h
j
k
l
m
1
2
3
4

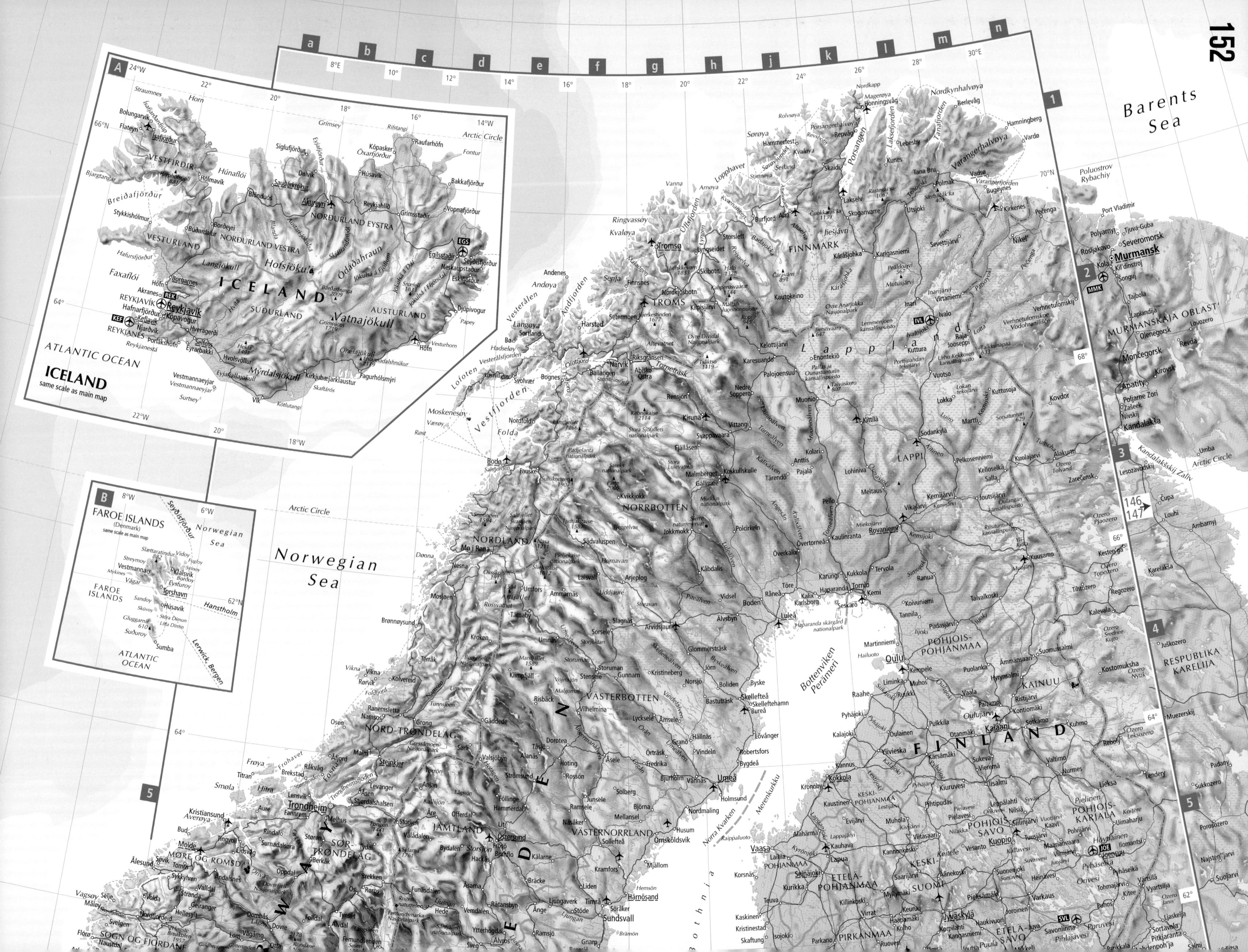
Barents Sea
Norwegian Sea
Arctic Circle
FINLAND
Lappland
LAPPI
FINNMARK
TROMS
NORRBOTTEN
VÄSTERBOTTEN
NORDLAND
NORD-TRØNDELAG
SØR-TRØNDELAG
JÄMTLAND
VÄSTERNORRLAND
MØRE OG ROMSDAL
SOGN OG FJORDANE
POHJOIS-POHJANMAA
KAINUU
PIRKANMAA
MURMANSKAJA OBLAST'
RESPUBLIKA KARELIJA
Bottenviken
Perämeri
Lofoten
Vesterålen
Vestfjorden
Murmansk
Tromsø
Trondheim
Oulu
Luleå
Umeå
Bodø
Narvik
Kiruna
Rovaniemi
Östersund
Kajaani
Kuopio
Vaasa
Sundsvall
Molde
Kristiansund
Ålesund
A
ICELAND
same scale as main map
ATLANTIC OCEAN
Vatnajökull
Hofsjökull
Langjökull
Mýrdalsjökull
Reykjavík
Akureyri
Ísafjörður
Egilsstaðir
Höfn
VESTFIRÐIR
VESTURLAND
NORÐURLAND VESTRA
NORÐURLAND EYSTRA
AUSTURLAND
SUÐURLAND
REYKJANES
Vestmannaeyjar
Breiðafjörður
Faxaflói
B
FAROE ISLANDS
(Denmark)
same scale as main map
Tórshavn
Norwegian Sea
ATLANTIC OCEAN
Lerwick, Bergen
146
147

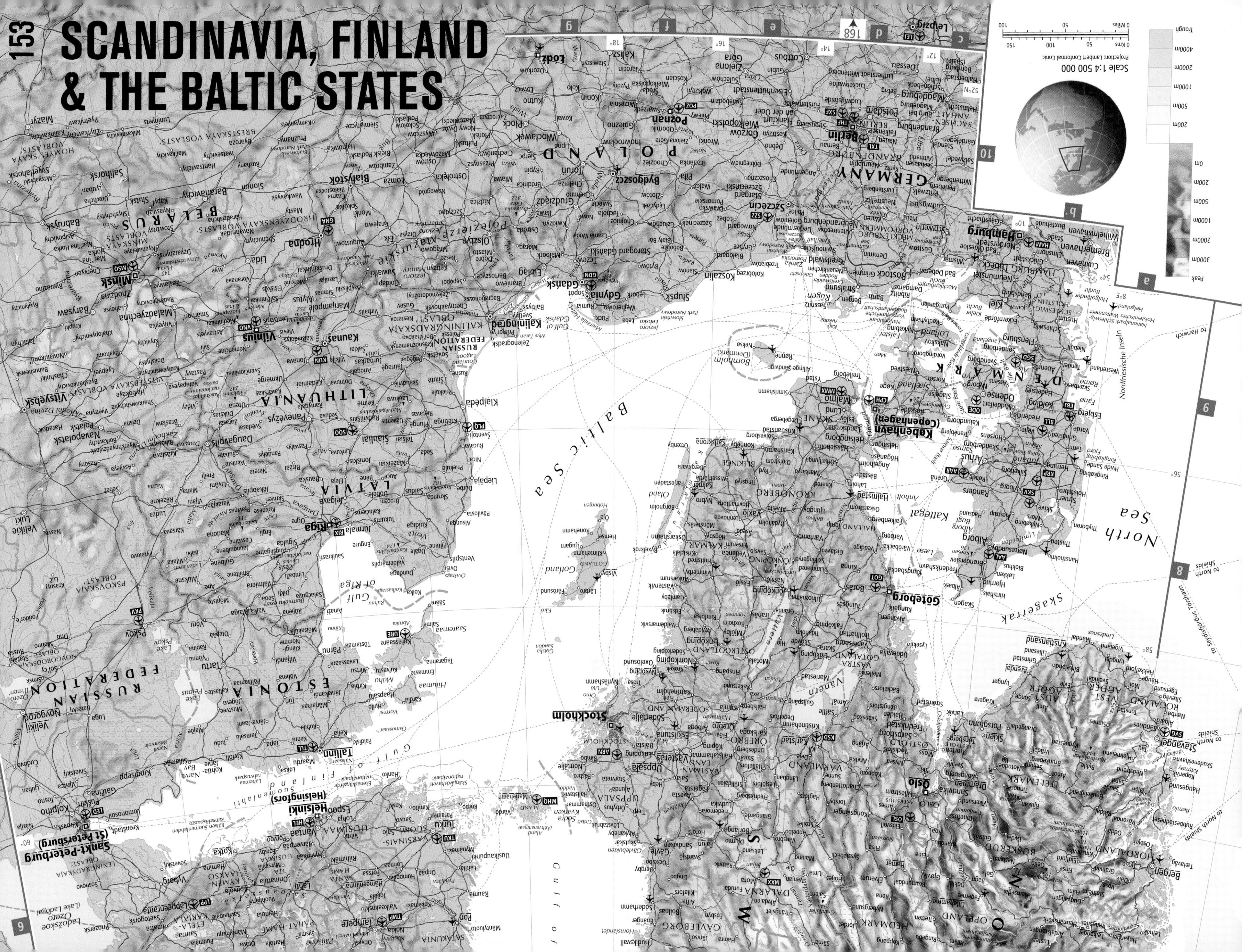

Scale 1:4 500 000

Projection: Lambert Conformal Conic

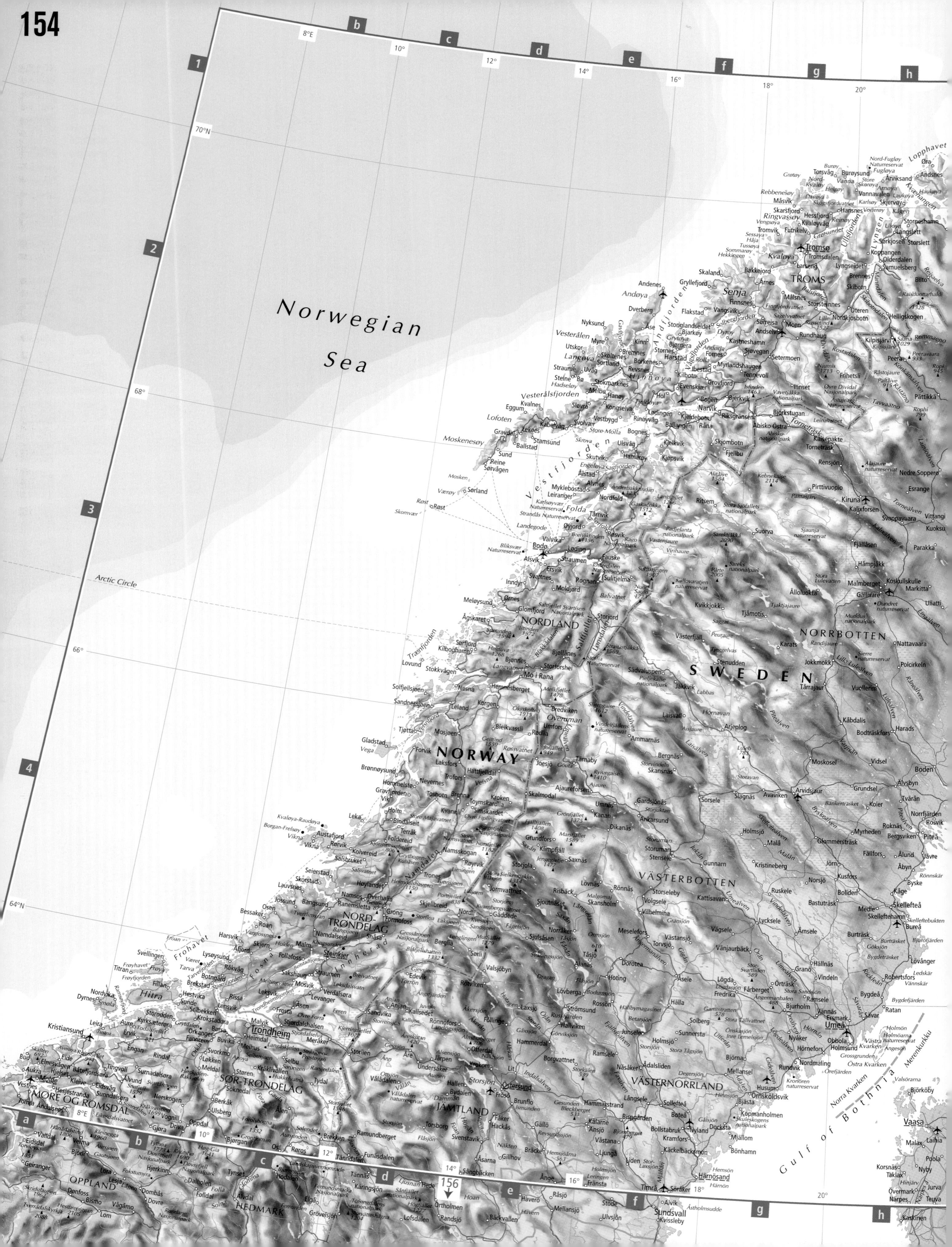

Norwegian

Sea

TROMS

Senja

Vesterålen

Lofoten

Moskenesøy

NORDLAND

NORWAY

NORD-
TRØNDELAG

SØR-TRØNDELAG

MØRE OG ROMSDAL

OPPLAND

HEDMARK

Trondheim

Tromsø

Bodø

Narvik

NORRBOTTEN

SWEDEN

VÄSTERBOTTEN

VÄSTERNORRLAND

JÄMTLAND

Kiruna

Gällivare

Jokkmokk

Boden

Piteå

Skellefteå

Umeå

Vaasa

Vaasa

Östersund

Sundsvall

Härnösand

Gulf of Bothnia

Arctic Circle

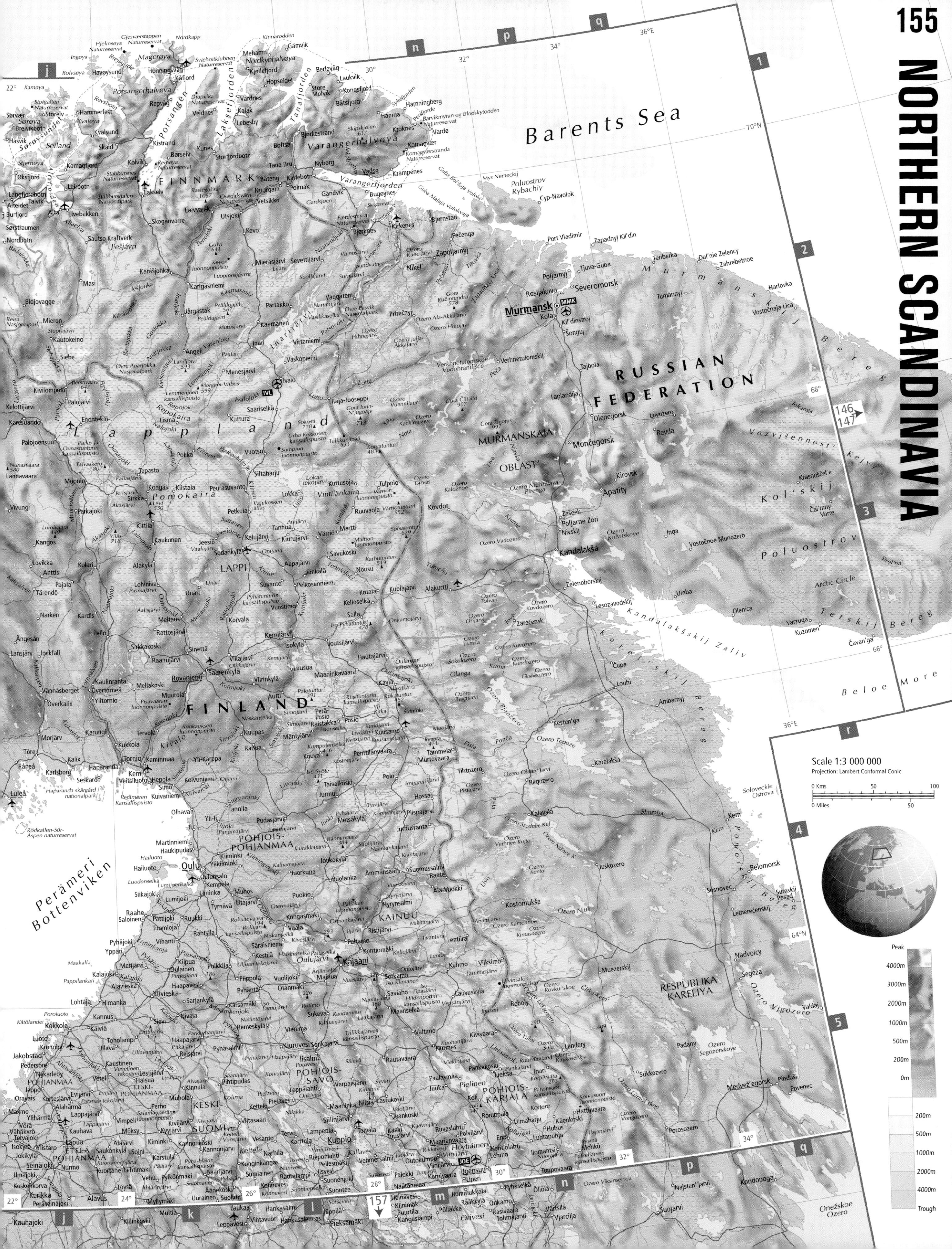
Barents Sea
RUSSIAN FEDERATION
FINLAND
FINNMARK
Lappland
LAPPI
MURMANSKAJA OBLAST'
RESPUBLIKA KARELIYA
POHJOIS-POHJANMAA
KAINUU
POHJOIS-SAVO
POHJOIS-KARJALA
KESKI-SUOMI
ETELÄ-POHJANMAA
POHJANMAA
Perämeri Bottenviken
Kandalakšskij Zaliv
Beloe More
Onežskoe Ozero
Kol'skij Poluostrov
Murmansk
Kola
Severomorsk
Kandalakša
Apatity
Kirovsk
Mončegorsk
Olenegorsk
Kirkenes
Vadsø
Vardø
Hammerfest
Alta
Honningsvåg
Magerøya
Nordkapp
Ivalo
Inari
Sodankylä
Rovaniemi
Kemijärvi
Tornio
Kemi
Oulu
Kajaani
Kuopio
Joensuu
Luleå
Kostomukša
Kem'
Belomorsk
Segeža
Medvez'egorsk
Kondopoga
Scale 1:3 000 000
Projection: Lambert Conformal Conic
0 Kms 50 100
0 Miles 50
Peak
4000m
3000m
2000m
1000m
500m
200m
0m
200m
500m
1000m
2000m
4000m
Trough
146
147
157

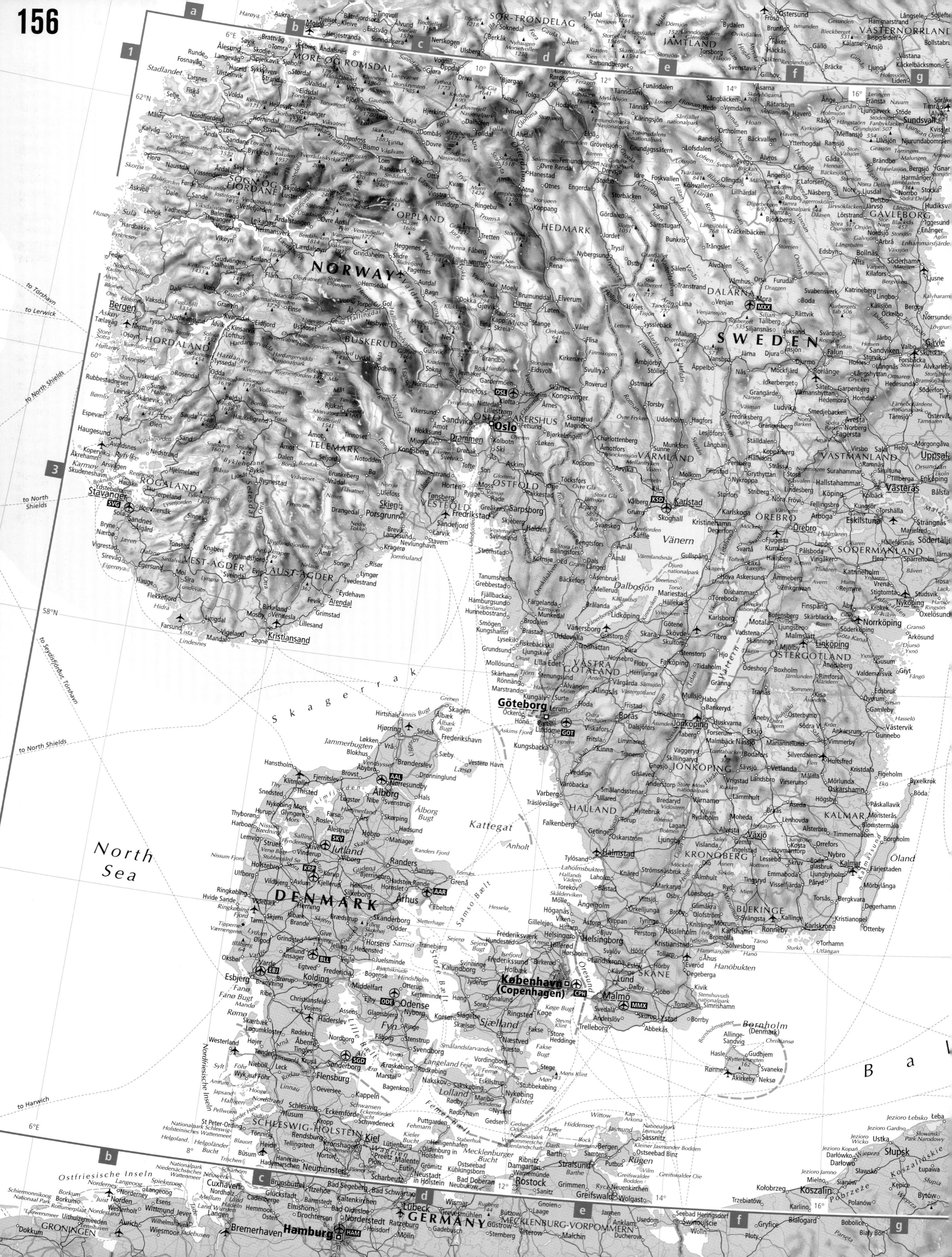
NORWAY
SWEDEN
DENMARK
GERMANY
North Sea
Skagerrak
Kattegat
MØRE OG ROMSDAL
SØR-TRØNDELAG
JÄMTLAND
VÄSTERNORRLAND
SOGN OG FJORDANE
OPPLAND
HEDMARK
GÄVLEBORG
DALARNA
HORDALAND
BUSKERUD
AKERSHUS
ROGALAND
TELEMARK
ØSTFOLD
VESTFOLD
VÄRMLAND
VÄSTMANLAND
ÖREBRO
SÖDERMANLAND
VEST-AGDER
AUST-AGDER
ÖSTERGÖTLAND
VÄSTRA GÖTALAND
JÖNKÖPING
HALLAND
KALMAR
KRONOBERG
BLEKINGE
SKÅNE
SCHLESWIG-HOLSTEIN
MECKLENBURG-VORPOMMERN
Oslo
Bergen
Stavanger
Kristiansand
Göteborg
København (Copenhagen)
Malmö
Hamburg
Kiel
Lübeck
Rostock
Ålborg
Århus
Odense
Karlstad
Västerås
Uppsala
Gävle
Norrköping
Linköping
Jönköping
Växjö
Kalmar
Halmstad
Helsingborg
Öland
Bornholm (Denmark)
Rügen
Vänern
Vättern
to Tórshavn
to Lerwick
to North Shields
to Harwich
to Seyðisfjörður, Tórshavn

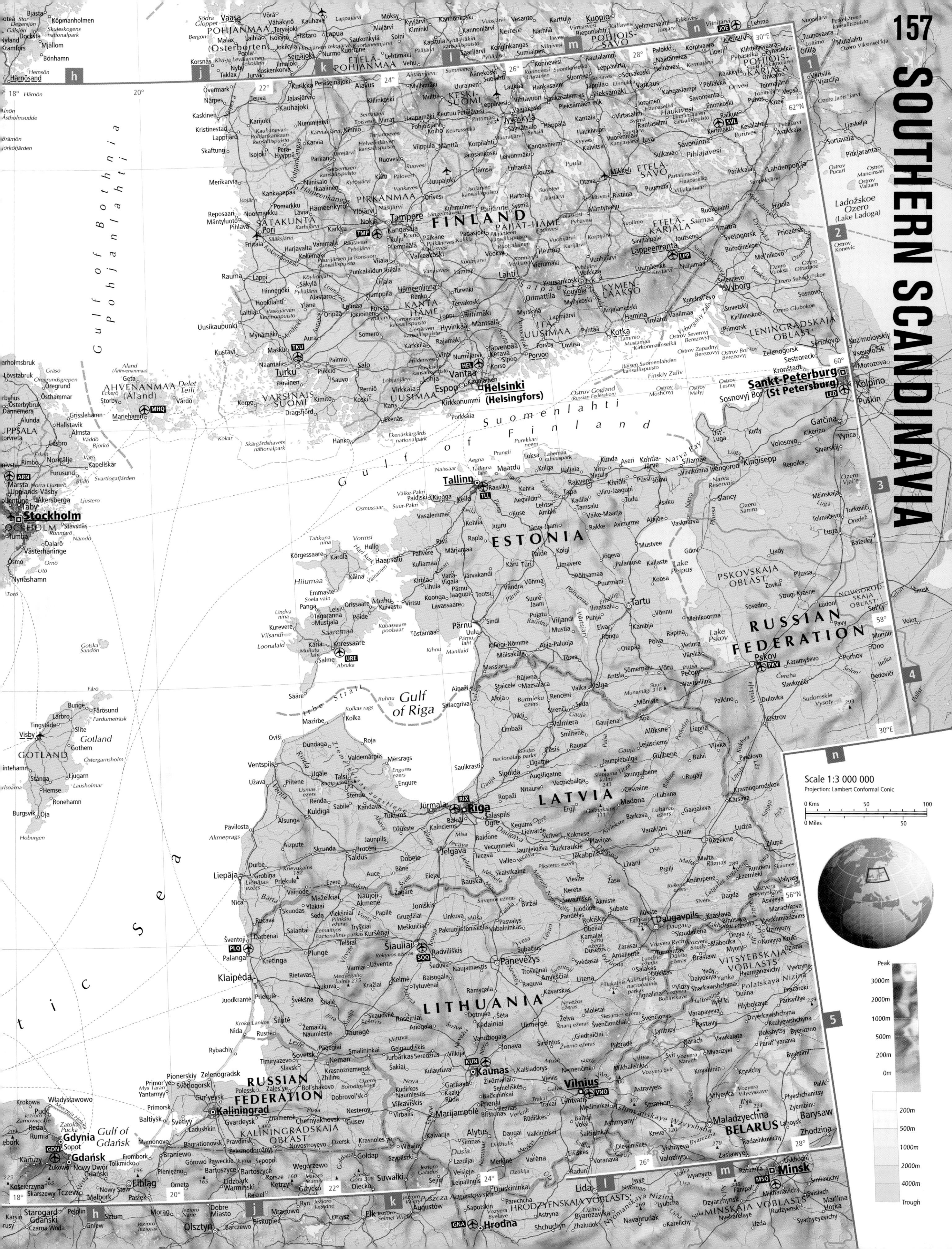
FINLAND
ESTONIA
LATVIA
LITHUANIA
RUSSIAN FEDERATION
BELARUS
Gulf of Bothnia
Pohjanlahti
Gulf of Finland
Suomenlahti
Gulf of Riga
Baltic Sea
Gulf of Gdańsk
Irbe Strait
Narva Bay
Ladožskoe Ozero (Lake Ladoga)
Lake Peipus
Lake Pskov
Hiiumaa
Saaremaa
Gotland
AHVENANMAA (Åland)
Helsinki (Helsingfors)
Tallinn
Riga
Vilnius
Minsk
Stockholm
Sankt-Peterburg (St Petersburg)
Kaliningrad
Gdańsk
Gdynia
Tampere
Turku
Kaunas
Tartu
Pärnu
Daugavpils
Klaipėda
Šiauliai
Liepāja
Jūrmala
Jelgava
Ventspils
Vyborg
Pskov
Hrodna
Elbląg
Espoo
Vantaa
Lahti
Kotka
Kouvola
Lappeenranta
Mikkeli
Jyväskylä
Kuopio
Vaasa
Pori
Rauma
Porvoo
Hämeenlinna
Narva
Panevėžys
Alytus
Marijampolė
Sovetsk
Maladzyechna
Scale 1:3 000 000
Projection: Lambert Conformal Conic
0 Kms 50 100
0 Miles 50
Peak
3000m
2000m
1000m
500m
200m
0m
200m
500m
1000m
2000m
4000m
Trough

DENMARK

BORNHOLM (DENMARK)
1:1 500 000

BORNHOLM

Allinge-Sandvig
Hasle
Gudhjem
Svaneke
Rønne
Rytterknægten 162
Åkirkeby
Nexø
Dueodde

Scale 1:1 500 000
Projection: Lambert Conformal Conic

0 Kms 25 50
0 Miles 25

Peak
3000m
2000m
1000m
500m
200m
100m
0m

200m
500m
1000m
2000m
4000m
Trough

Skagerrak

North Sea

Kattegat

① FREDERIKSBERG
② KØBENHAVN (CITY DISTRICT)
③ KØBENHAVN

Göteborg (Gothenburg)

SWEDEN

Limfjorden

Ålborg

Viborg

Randers

ÅRHUS

Århus

Jylland

RINGKØBING

Esbjerg

VEJLE

Vejle

Kolding

Odense

Fyn

Svendborg

Åbenrå

Sønderborg

SØNDERJYLLAND

DENMARK

København (Copenhagen)

Frederiksberg

Roskilde

Malmö

Sjælland

VESTSJÆLLAND

Møn

Lolland

Falster

Nykøbing

Baltic Sea

Flensburg

Kiel

SCHLESWIG-HOLSTEIN

Neumünster

Lübeck

Rostock

Hamburg

GERMANY

NIEDERSACHSEN

MECKLENBURG-VORPOMMERN

Schwerin

Bremerhaven

Wilhelmshaven

Cuxhaven

North Frisian Islands / Nordfriesische Inseln

156 157
172 173
172 173

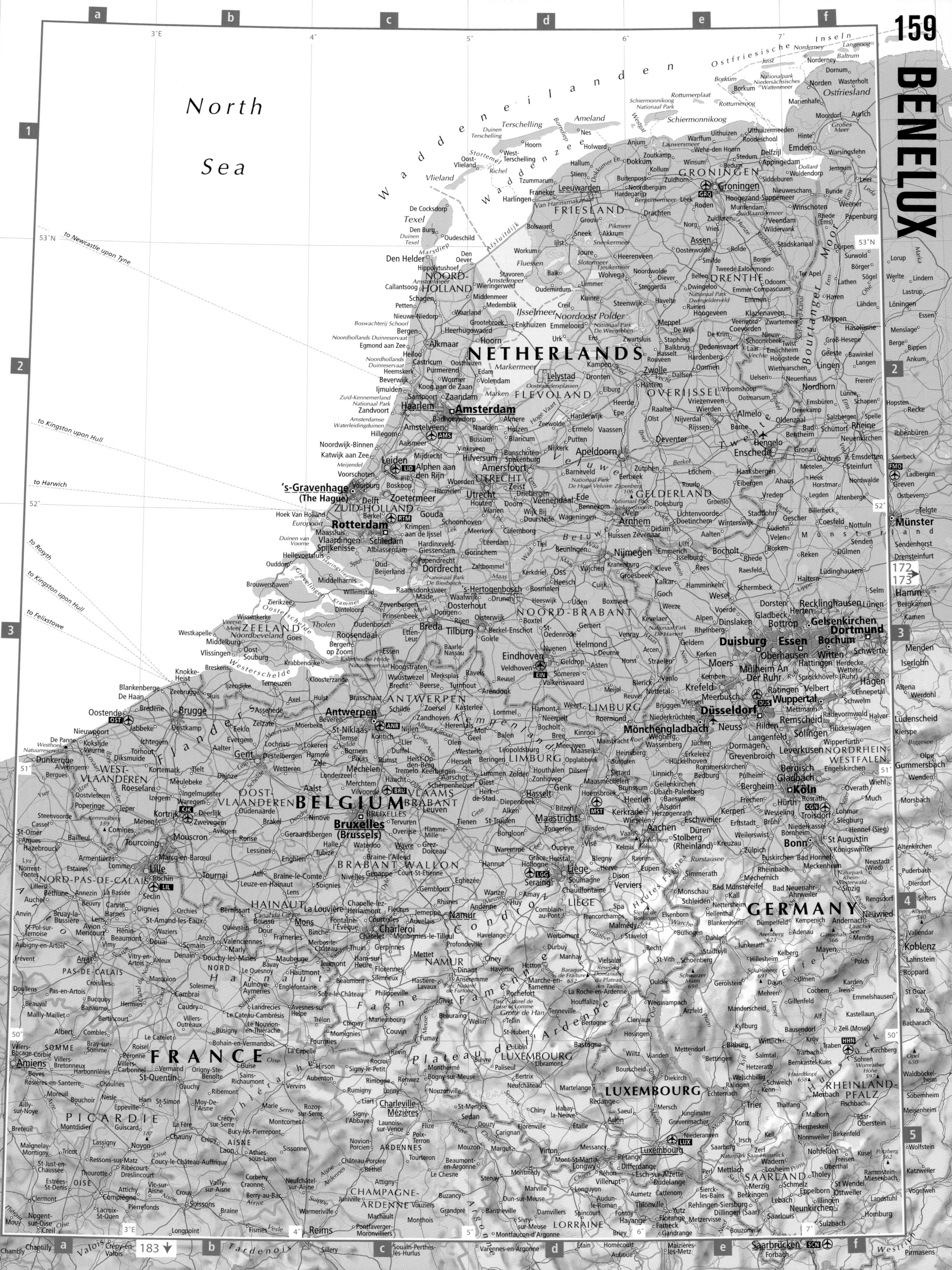
North Sea
Waddeneilanden
Waddenzee
Ostfriesische Inseln
NETHERLANDS
BELGIUM
LUXEMBOURG
GERMANY
FRANCE
Amsterdam
Rotterdam
's-Gravenhage (The Hague)
Utrecht
Groningen
Leeuwarden
Zwolle
Apeldoorn
Arnhem
Nijmegen
Eindhoven
Tilburg
Breda
Haarlem
Leiden
Dordrecht
Enschede
Maastricht
Bruxelles (Brussels)
Antwerpen
Gent
Brugge
Oostende
Liège
Namur
Charleroi
Mons
Leuven
Hasselt
Lille
Amiens
Reims
Saint-Quentin
Luxembourg
Trier
Aachen
Köln
Bonn
Düsseldorf
Duisburg
Essen
Dortmund
Münster
Koblenz
Saarbrücken
FRIESLAND
GRONINGEN
DRENTHE
NOORD-HOLLAND
ZUID-HOLLAND
UTRECHT
FLEVOLAND
OVERIJSSEL
GELDERLAND
NOORD-BRABANT
ZEELAND
LIMBURG
WEST-VLAANDEREN
OOST-VLAANDEREN
ANTWERPEN
VLAAMS BRABANT
BRABANT WALLON
HAINAUT
NAMUR
LIÈGE
LUXEMBOURG
NORDRHEIN-WESTFALEN
RHEINLAND-PFALZ
SAARLAND
NORD-PAS-DE-CALAIS
PICARDIE
CHAMPAGNE-ARDENNE
LORRAINE
IJsselmeer
Markermeer
Noordoost Polder
Plateau de l'Ardenne
Eifel
Hunsrück
to Newcastle upon Tyne
to Kingston upon Hull
to Harwich
to Rosyth
to Felixstowe
53°N
52°
51°
50°
3°E
4°
5°
6°
7°
172
173
183

NORWAY

to Bergen

60°N

2°E

0°

North Sea

UNITED
KINGDOM

Haroldswick
Baltasound
Unst
Fetlar
Out Skerries
Isbister
Hillswick
Ulsta
Yell Sound
Whalsay
Ronas Hill 450
Toft
Bressay
Mainland
Lerwick
St Magnus Bay
Muckle Roe
Walls
Sumburgh
Foula
Sumburgh Head
Fair Isle

Shetland Islands

Papa Westray
Sanday
Stronsay
North Ronaldsay
Westray
Rousay
Eday
Shapinsay
Birsay
Mainland
Gairsay
Stromness
Kirkwall
St Margaret's Hope
South Ronaldsay
Burwick
Linksness
Ward Hill 479
Longhope
Island of Stroma
Duncansby Head

Orkney Islands

Rattray Head
Fraserburgh
Rosehearty
Macduff
Banff
Peterhead
Turriff
Ellon
Newburgh
Buckie
Keith
Inverurie
Aberdeen
Dyce
Elgin
Dufftown
Oldmeldrum
Insch
Stonehaven
Lossiemouth
Forres
Rothes
Inverbervie
Nairn
Grantown-on-Spey
Ballater
Montrose
Braemar
Banchory
Brechin
Forfar
Arbroath
Glamis
Carnoustie
Blairgowrie
Broughty Ferry
Dundee
St Andrews
Crail
Anstruther
Firth of Forth
North Berwick
St Abb's Head
Eyemouth
Berwick-upon-Tweed
Haddington
East Linton
Coldstream
Kelso
Jedburgh
Duns

SCOTLAND

Thurso
Halkirk
Wick
Lybster
Dunbeath
Helmsdale
Brora
Golspie
Dornoch
Tain
Cromarty
Invergordon
Alness
Dingwall
Muir of Ord
Beauly
Inverness
Aviemore
Kingussie
Newtonmore
Dalwhinnie
Pitlochry
Blair Atholl
Aberfeldy
Crieff
Comrie
Callander
Dunblane
Stirling
Falkirk
Linlithgow
Livingston
Bathgate
Edinburgh
Penicuik
Peebles
Galashiels
Selkirk
Hawick
Melrose
Moffat
Lockerbie
Lauder

Dunnet Head
Cape Wrath
Durness
Tongue
Melvich
Bettyhill
Strathy Point
Point of Stoer
Scourie
Lochinver
Ullapool
Gairloch
Achnasheen
Kinlochewe
Strathcarron
Applecross
Kyle of Lochalsh
Mallaig
Arisaig
Glenfinnan
Fort William
Ballachulish
Glencoe
Dalmally
Tyndrum
Crianlarich
Inveraray
Lochgilphead
Tarbert
Ardrishaig
Oban
Tobermory
Craignure
Salen

Moray Firth
Pentland Firth
Pentland Hills
Grampian Mountains

Butt of Lewis
Port Ness
Stornoway
Carloway
Harris
Tarbert
Leverburgh
Uig
Portree
Dunvegan
Broadford
Sligachan
Skye
Armadale
Ardvasar
Sound of Sleat
Inner Sound
Rùm
Eigg
Muck
Canna
Coll
Tiree
Arinagour
Scarinish
Colonsay
Port Askaig
Port Ellen
Islay
Jura
Sound of Jura

Isle of Lewis
Scarp
Taransay
Clisham 799
Sound of Harris
Lochmaddy
North Uist
Benbecula
South Uist
Lochboisdale
Barra
Vatersay

Outer Hebrides
Sea of the Hebrides
The Minch
Little Minch

Sula Sgeir
Rona
Sule Skerry
Sule Stack

St Kilda

Glasgow
Paisley
Motherwell
Hamilton
East Kilbride
Kilmarnock
Ayr
Prestwick
Troon
Irvine
Kilbirnie
Largs
Greenock
Port Glasgow
Helensburgh
Dumbarton
Alexandria
Kilsyth
Airdrie
Cumbernauld
Dunfermline
Kirkcaldy
Glenrothes
Alloa
Stonehouse
Strathaven
Lanark
Biggar
Sanquhar
New Galloway
Castle Douglas
Kirkcudbright
Dalbeattie
Dumfries
Gatehouse of Fleet
Newton Stewart
Wigtown
Whithorn
Stranraer
Girvan
Maybole
Dalmellington
Cumnock
Muirkirk
Firth of Clyde
Mull of Kintyre
Campbeltown
Brodick
Arran
Bute
Rothesay
Tarbert
Lochranza
Millport

Firth of Lorn
Sound of Mull

to Bergen
to Bergen, Haugesund, Stavanger
to Göteborg, Kristiansand

to Zeebrugge

South Shields
Newcastle upon Tyne
Gateshead
Sunderland
Washington
Consett
Durham
Bishop Auckland
Hartlepool
Redcar
Houghton le Spring
Amble
North Sunderland
Holy Island
Alnwick
Wooler
Rothbury
Morpeth
Blyth
Bedlington
Ashington
Cramlington
Ponteland
Corbridge
Prudhoe
Hexham
Haltwhistle
Brampton
Carlisle
Wigton
Maryport
Workington
Cheviot Hills
The Cheviot 815

Berwickshire

North Channel

NORTHERN
IRELAND

Belfast
Bangor
Newtownabbey
Carrickfergus
Larne
Ballymena
Antrim
Lisburn
Ballyclare
Ballymoney
Coleraine
Portrush
Portstewart
Londonderry
Limavady
Magherafelt
Cookstown
Strabane
Omagh
Dungannon
Rathlin Island
Fair Head
Giant's Causeway
Antrim Hills
Garron Point
Cushendun
Ballycastle

Malin Head
Horn Head
Bloody Foreland
Aran Island
Gweedore
Glenties
Killybegs
Donegal
Ballybofey
Letterkenny
Lifford
Stranorlar
Raphoe
Buncrana
Moville
Carndonagh
Lough Swilly
Lough Foyle
Inishowen
Derryveagh Mountains
Errigal 752

ATLANTIC
OCEAN

to Tórshavn

Faroe Islands
Suðuroy
Sandoy
Skúvoy
Spaðafjall 459

10°W
8°
6°
4°
2°
58°
56°
60°N

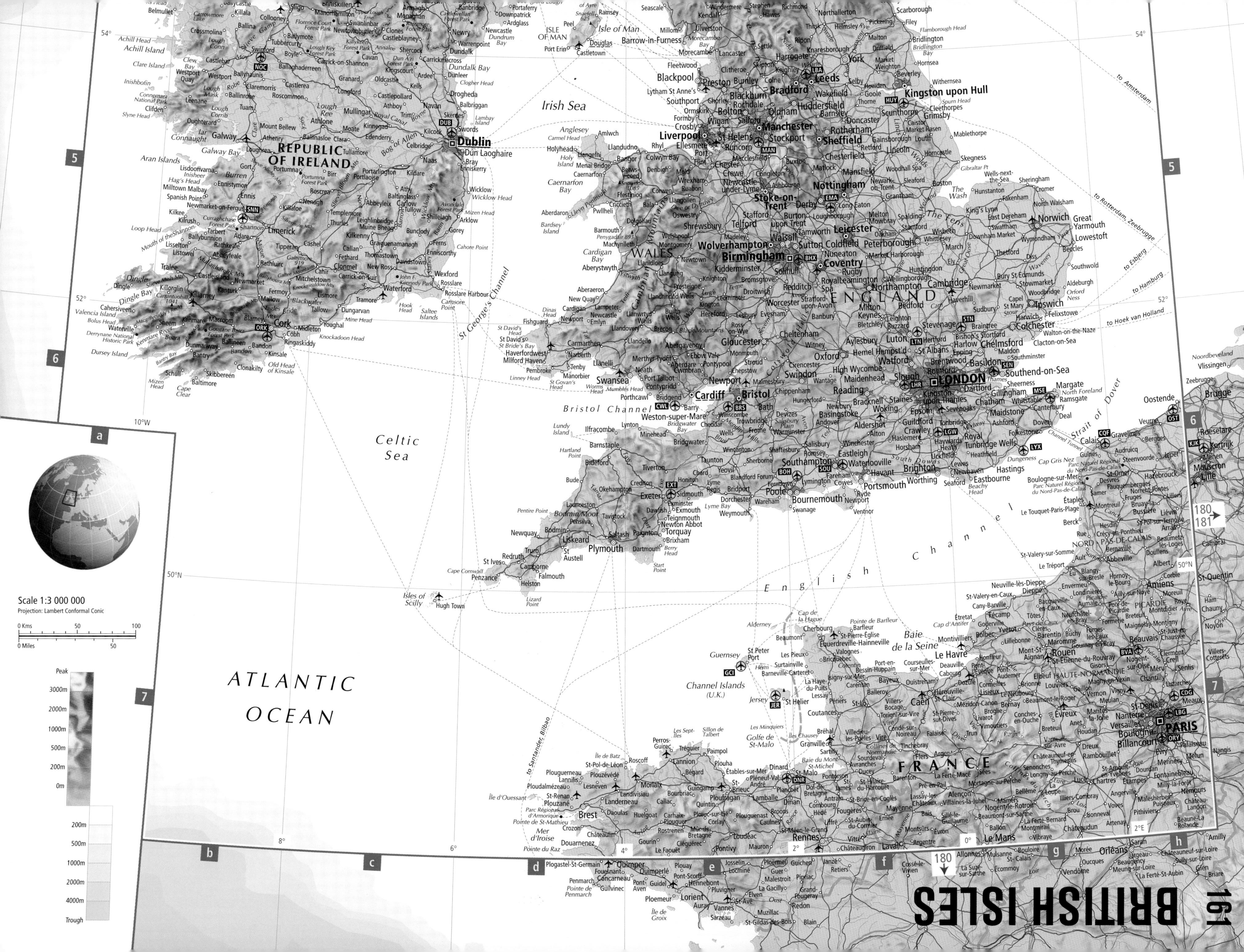

ATLANTIC OCEAN

Celtic Sea

Irish Sea

REPUBLIC OF IRELAND

Dublin
Dún Laoghaire

ENGLAND

WALES

LONDON

FRANCE

PARIS

English Channel

Bristol Channel

St George's Channel

Strait of Dover

Scale 1:3 000 000
Projection: Lambert Conformal Conic

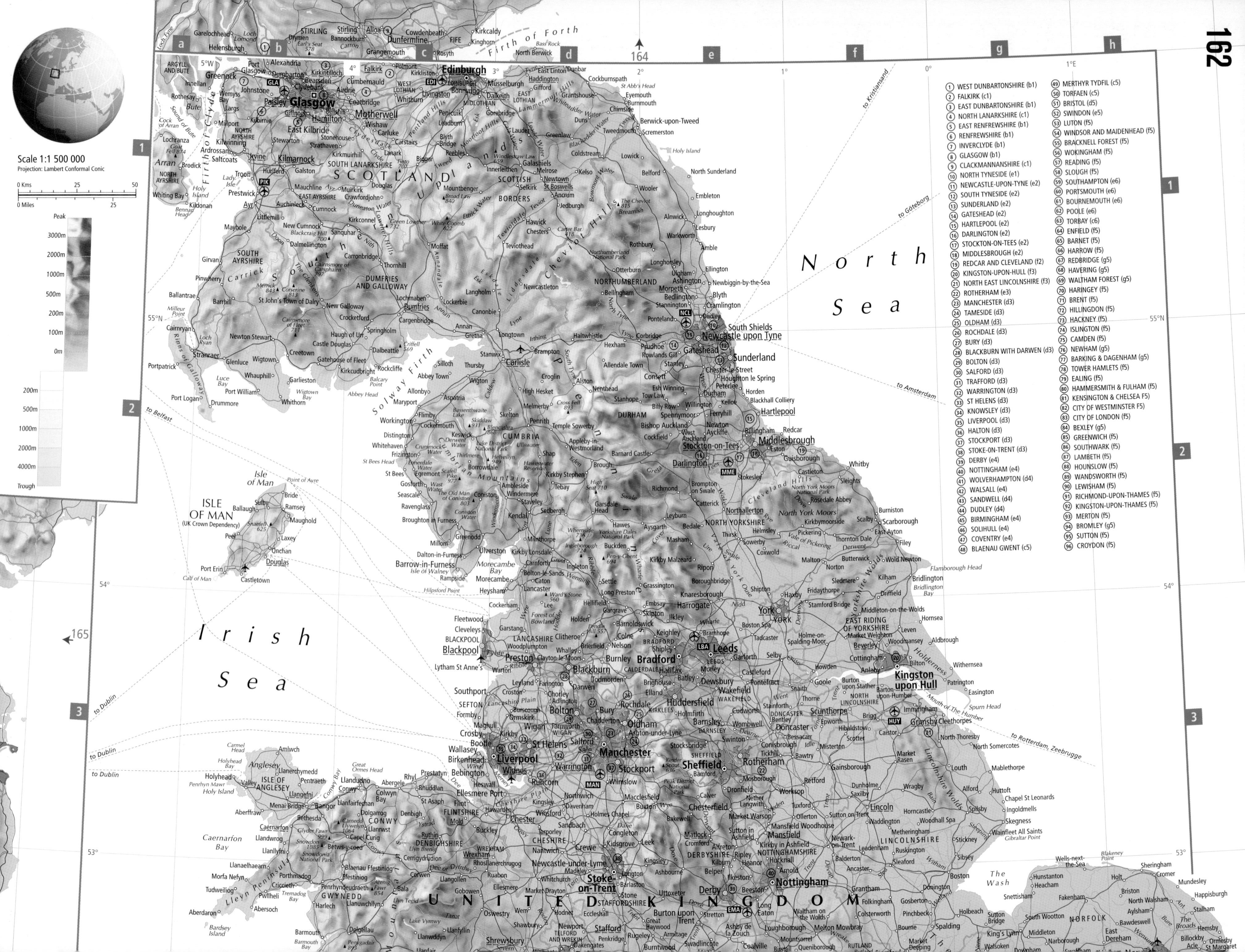

1 WEST DUNBARTONSHIRE (b1)
2 FALKIRK (c1)
3 EAST DUNBARTONSHIRE (b1)
4 NORTH LANARKSHIRE (c1)
5 EAST RENFREWSHIRE (b1)
6 RENFREWSHIRE (b1)
7 INVERCLYDE (b1)
8 GLASGOW (b1)
9 CLACKMANNANSHIRE (c1)
10 NORTH TYNESIDE (e1)
11 NEWCASTLE-UPON-TYNE (e2)
12 SOUTH TYNESIDE (e2)
13 SUNDERLAND (e2)
14 GATESHEAD (e2)
15 HARTLEPOOL (e2)
16 DARLINGTON (e2)
17 STOCKTON-ON-TEES (e2)
18 MIDDLESBROUGH (e2)
19 REDCAR AND CLEVELAND (f2)
20 KINGSTON-UPON-HULL (f3)
21 NORTH EAST LINCOLNSHIRE (f3)
22 ROTHERHAM (e3)
23 MANCHESTER (d3)
24 TAMESIDE (d3)
25 OLDHAM (d3)
26 ROCHDALE (d3)
27 BURY (d3)
28 BLACKBURN WITH DARWEN (d3)
29 BOLTON (d3)
30 SALFORD (d3)
31 TRAFFORD (d3)
32 WARRINGTON (d3)
33 ST HELENS (d3)
34 KNOWSLEY (d3)
35 LIVERPOOL (d3)
36 HALTON (d3)
37 STOCKPORT (d3)
38 STOKE-ON-TRENT (d3)
39 DERBY (e4)
40 NOTTINGHAM (e4)
41 WOLVERHAMPTON (d4)
42 WALSALL (e4)
43 SANDWELL (d4)
44 DUDLEY (d4)
45 BIRMINGHAM (e4)
46 SOLIHULL (e4)
47 COVENTRY (e4)
48 BLAENAU GWENT (c5)
49 MERTHYR TYDFIL (c5)
50 TORFAEN (c5)
51 BRISTOL (d5)
52 SWINDON (e5)
53 LUTON (f5)
54 WINDSOR AND MAIDENHEAD (f5)
55 BRACKNELL FOREST (f5)
56 WOKINGHAM (f5)
57 READING (f5)
58 SLOUGH (f5)
59 SOUTHAMPTON (e6)
60 PORTSMOUTH (e6)
61 BOURNEMOUTH (e6)
62 POOLE (e6)
63 TORBAY (c6)
64 ENFIELD (f5)
65 BARNET (f5)
66 HARROW (f5)
67 REDBRIDGE (g5)
68 HAVERING (g5)
69 WALTHAM FOREST (g5)
70 HARINGEY (f5)
71 BRENT (f5)
72 HILLINGDON (f5)
73 HACKNEY (f5)
74 ISLINGTON (f5)
75 CAMDEN (f5)
76 NEWHAM (g5)
77 BARKING & DAGENHAM (g5)
78 TOWER HAMLETS (f5)
79 EALING (f5)
80 HAMMERSMITH & FULHAM (f5)
81 KENSINGTON & CHELSEA F5)
82 CITY OF WESTMINSTER F5)
83 CITY OF LONDON (f5)
84 BEXLEY (g5)
85 GREENWICH (f5)
86 SOUTHWARK (f5)
87 LAMBETH (f5)
88 HOUNSLOW (f5)
89 WANDSWORTH (f5)
90 LEWISHAM (f5)
91 RICHMOND-UPON-THAMES (f5)
92 KINGSTON-UPON-THAMES (f5)
93 MERTON (f5)
94 BROMLEY (g5)
95 SUTTON (f5)
96 CROYDON (f5)
North Sea
Irish Sea
UNITED KINGDOM
SCOTLAND
ISLE OF MAN (UK Crown Dependency)
164
165
Scale 1:1 500 000
Projection: Lambert Conformal Conic
0 Kms 25 50
0 Miles 25
Peak
3000m
2000m
1000m
500m
200m
100m
0m
200m
500m
1000m
2000m
4000m
Trough

ENGLAND & WALES

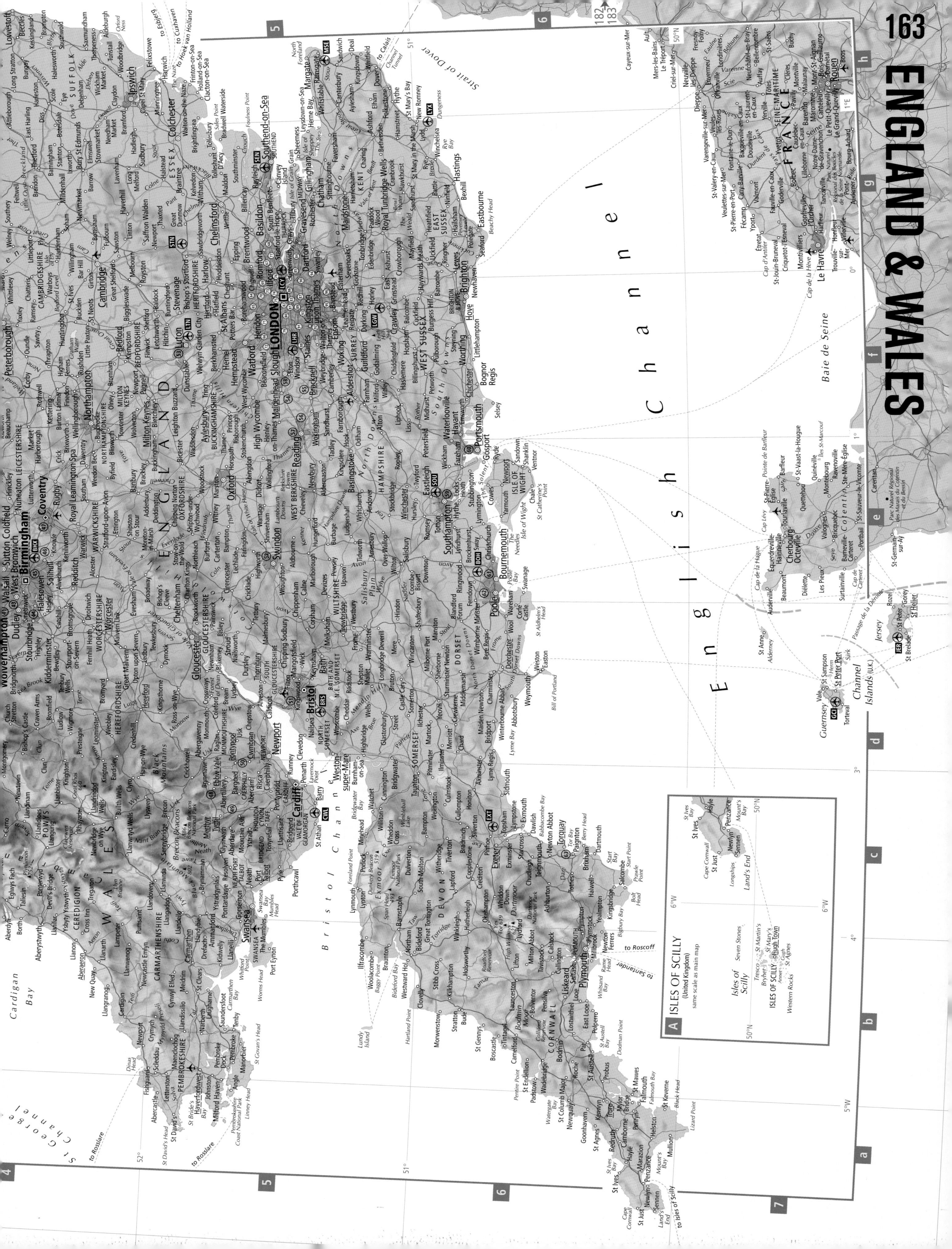

182
183

A ISLES OF SCILLY
(United Kingdom)
same scale as main map

Isles of Scilly

ISLES OF SCILLY · Hugh Town

St Martin's
Tresco
St Mary's
Bryher
St Agnes
Annet
Gugh
Western Rocks
Seven Stones

English Channel

Bristol Channel

Cardigan Bay

Baie de Seine

Channel Islands (U.K.)

Guernsey · St Peter Port
Jersey · St Helier
Alderney

FRANCE

WALES

ENGLAND

LONDON

Cardiff

Bristol

Birmingham

Plymouth

Strait of Dover

St George's Channel

SCOTLAND

1. WEST DUNBARTONSHIRE (d3)
2. EAST DUNBARTONSHIRE (d4)
3. NORTH LANARKSHIRE (d4)
4. FALKIRK (e4)
5. WEST LOTHIAN (e4)
6. EDINBURGH (e4)
7. MIDLOTHIAN (e4)
8. INVERCLYDE (d4)
9. RENFREWSHIRE (d4)
10. GLASGOW (d4)
11. EAST RENFREWSHIRE (d4)
12. CLACKMANNANSHIRE (e3)

IRELAND

1. BELFAST (e2)
2. CARRICKFERGUS (f2)
3. NEWTOWNABBEY (e2)
4. ANTRIM (e2)
5. LISBURN (e2)
6. CASTLEREAGH (f2)
7. ARDS (f2)
8. DOWN (f2)
9. BANBRIDGE (e2)
10. CRAIGAVON (e2)
11. COOKSTOWN (e2)
12. MAGHERAFELT (e2)
13. BALLYMENA (e2)
14. LARNE (f2)
15. MOYLE (e1)
16. BALLYMONEY (e1)
17. COLERAINE (e1)
18. LIMAVADY (e2)
19. DERRY CITY (d2)
20. STRABANE (d2)
21. OMAGH (d2)
22. FERMANAGH (d2)
23. DUNGANNON (e2)
24. ARMAGH (e2)
25. NEWRY & MOURNE (e2)

ATLANTIC OCEAN

Irish Sea

Celtic Sea

NORTHERN IRELAND

REPUBLIC OF IRELAND

162 163 →

Peak
3000m
2000m
1000m
500m
200m
100m
0m
200m
500m
1000m
2000m
4000m
Trough

Scale 1:1 500 000
Projection: Lambert Conformal Conic

0 Kms 25 50
0 Miles 25

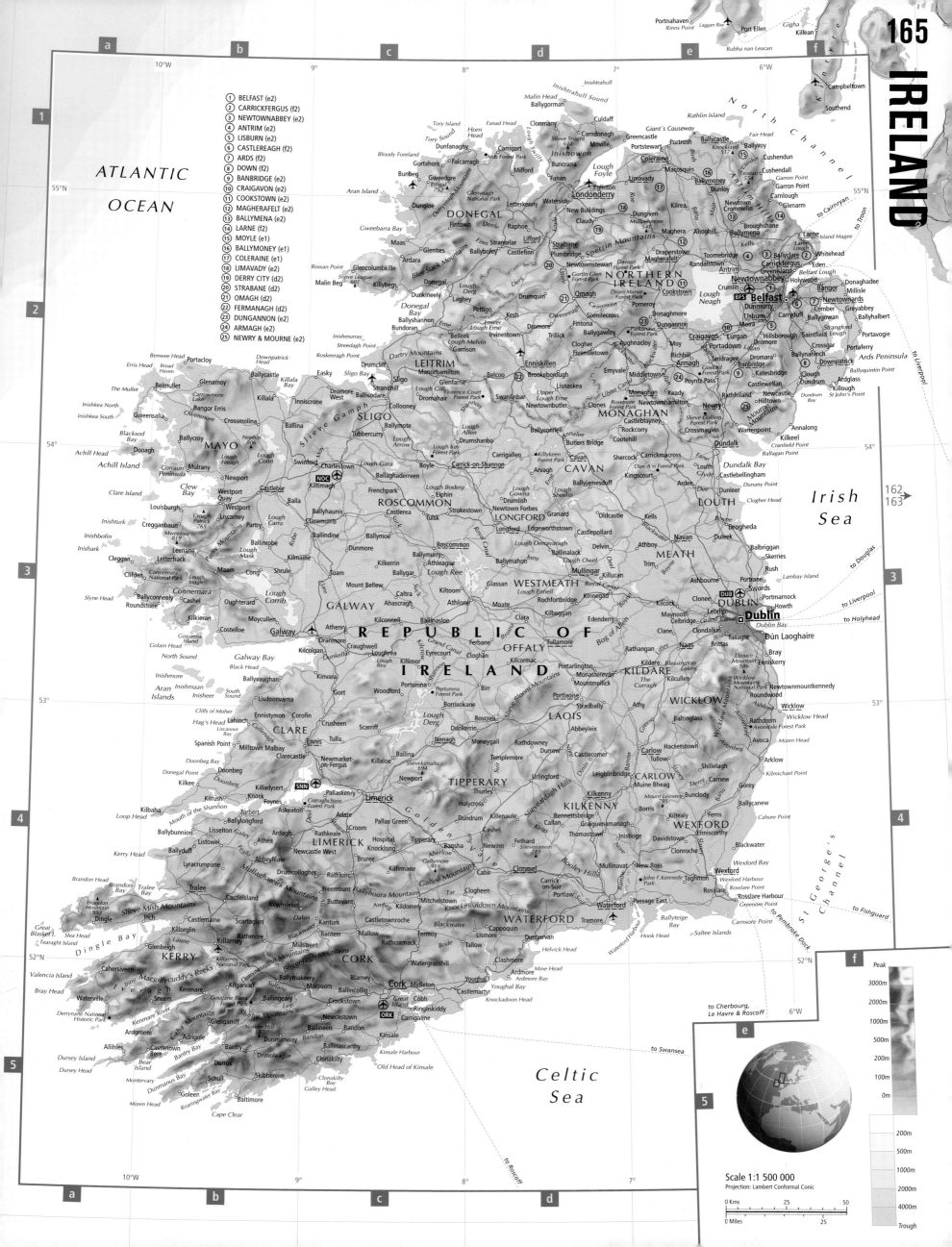

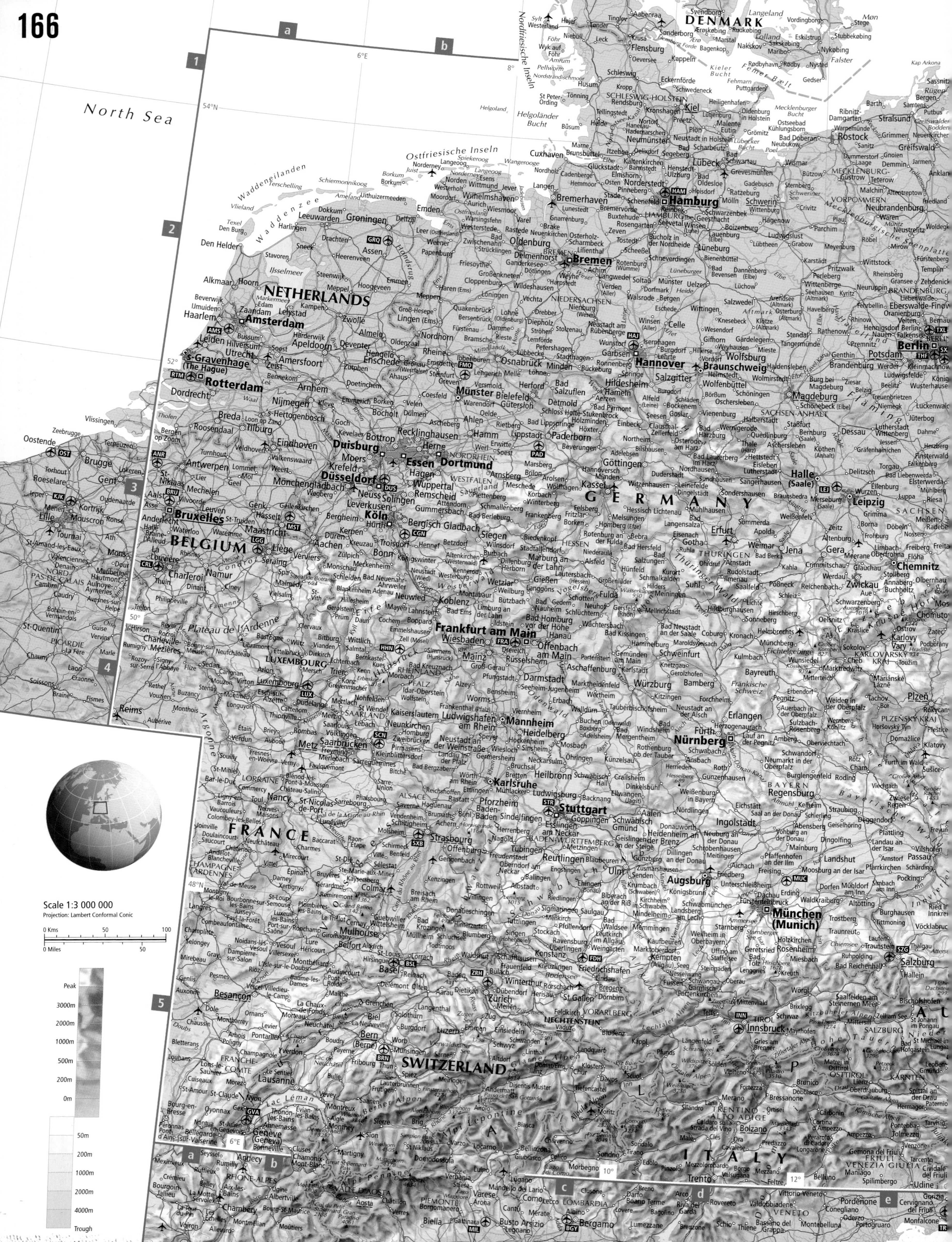

North Sea

DENMARK

NETHERLANDS

Amsterdam

's-Gravenhage
(The Hague)

Rotterdam

BELGIUM

Bruxelles

GERMANY

Hamburg

Bremen

Hannover

Braunschweig

Berlin

Magdeburg

Halle
(Saale)

Leipzig

Chemnitz

Essen Dortmund

Duisburg

Düsseldorf

Köln

Frankfurt am Main

Wiesbaden

Offenbach
am Main

Mainz

Erfurt

Jena

Gera

LUXEMBOURG

Luxembourg

Mannheim

Nürnberg

Fürth

Saarbrücken

FRANCE

Karlsruhe

Stuttgart

Erlangen

Augsburg

München
(Munich)

Strasbourg

Ulm

Salzburg

Scale 1:3 000 000
Projection: Lambert Conformal Conic

0 Kms   50   100

0 Miles   50

Peak
3000m
2000m
1000m
500m
200m
0m

50m
200m
1000m
2000m
4000m
Trough

Basel

Zürich

Bern
(Berne)

Innsbruck

SWITZERLAND

Genève
Geneva

Lausanne

ITALY

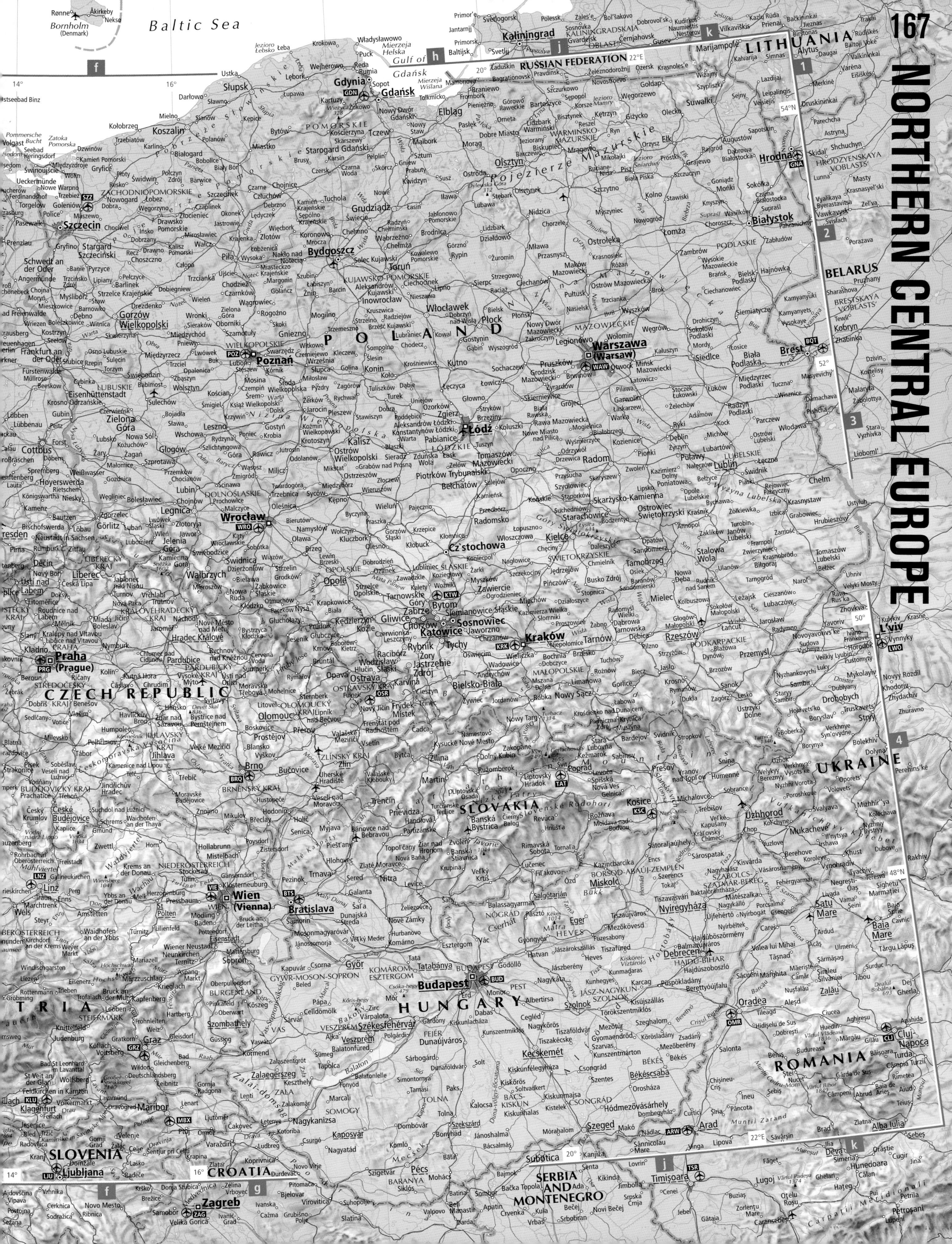

167
NORTHERN CENTRAL EUROPE
Baltic Sea
Bornholm (Denmark)
Gulf of Gdańsk
RUSSIAN FEDERATION
Kaliningrad
LITHUANIA
BELARUS
POLAND
Warszawa (Warsaw)
Gdańsk
Gdynia
Szczecin
Bydgoszcz
Toruń
Olsztyn
Białystok
Poznań
Łódź
Wrocław
Kraków
Lublin
Katowice
CZECH REPUBLIC
Praha (Prague)
Brno
Ostrava
SLOVAKIA
Bratislava
Košice
UKRAINE
L'viv
HUNGARY
Budapest
Debrecen
Szeged
Wien (Vienna)
Graz
Linz
ROMANIA
Cluj-Napoca
Oradea
Arad
Timișoara
SLOVENIA
Ljubljana
CROATIA
Zagreb
SERBIA AND MONTENEGRO

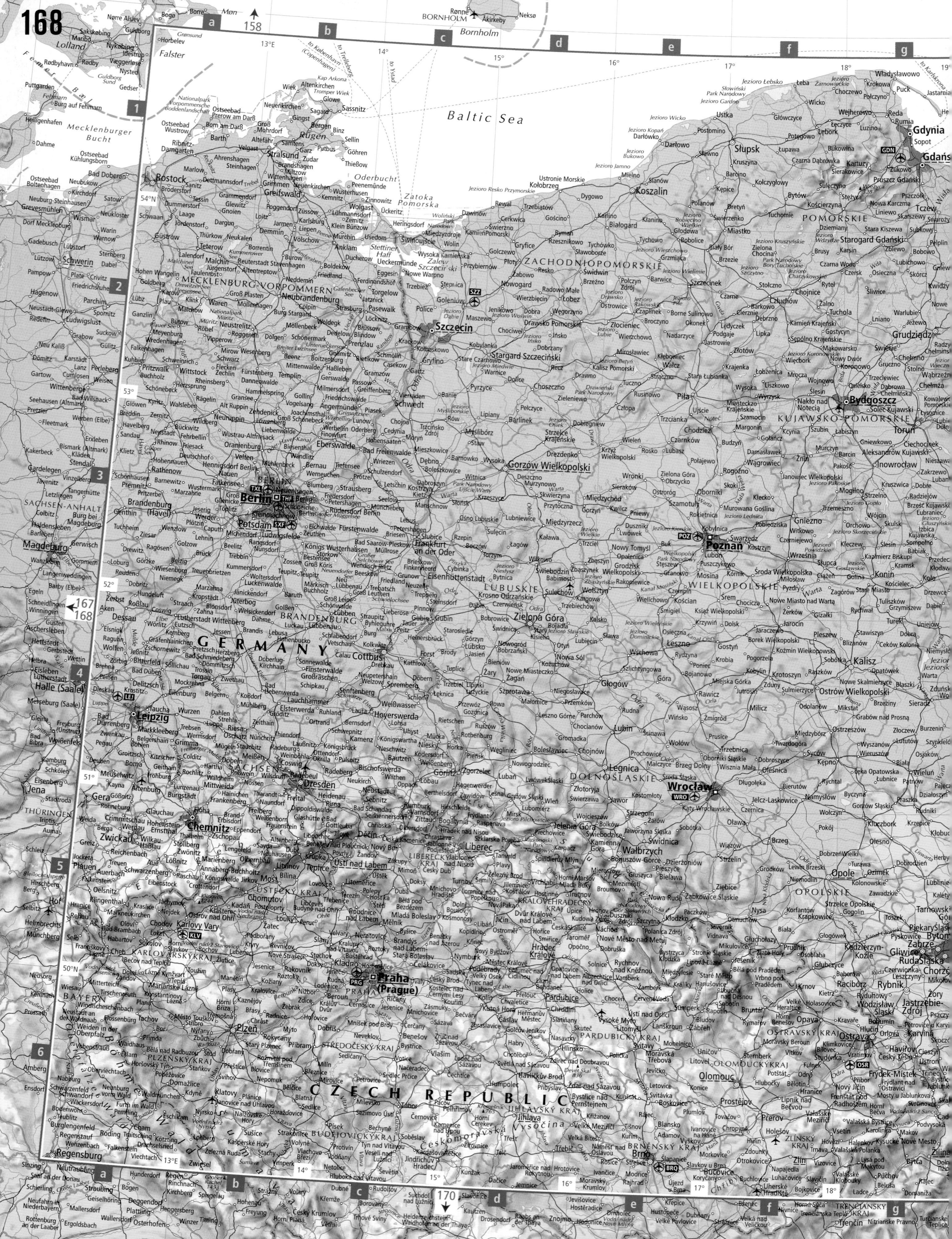
Baltic Sea
GERMANY
CZECH REPUBLIC
MECKLENBURG-VORPOMMERN
BRANDENBURG
SACHSEN-ANHALT
SACHSEN
THÜRINGEN
BAYERN
ZACHODNIOPOMORSKIE
POMORSKIE
KUJAWSKO-POMORSKIE
LUBUSKIE
WIELKOPOLSKIE
DOLNOŚLĄSKIE
OPOLSKIE
ÚSTECKÝ KRAJ
LIBERECKÝ KRAJ
KRÁLOVÉHRADECKÝ KRAJ
KARLOVARSKÝ KRAJ
PLZEŇSKÝ KRAJ
STŘEDOČESKÝ KRAJ
PARDUBICKÝ KRAJ
OLOMOUCKÝ KRAJ
MORAVSKOSLEZSKÝ KRAJ
ZLÍNSKÝ KRAJ
JIHOMORAVSKÝ KRAJ
JIHOČESKÝ KRAJ
KRAJ VYSOČINA
Mecklenburger Bucht
Pomorska Zatoka
Stettiner Haff
Oderbucht
Rügen
Bornholm
Falster
Lolland
Møn
Fehmarn
Fehmarn Belt
Berlin
Potsdam
Rostock
Stralsund
Greifswald
Schwerin
Neubrandenburg
Magdeburg
Halle (Saale)
Leipzig
Dresden
Chemnitz
Cottbus
Frankfurt an der Oder
Szczecin
Koszalin
Słupsk
Gdynia
Gdańsk
Sopot
Bydgoszcz
Toruń
Grudziądz
Piła
Poznań
Gorzów Wielkopolski
Zielona Góra
Legnica
Wrocław
Wałbrzych
Opole
Kalisz
Gniezno
Konin
Liberec
Ústí nad Labem
Praha (Prague)
Plzeň
Karlovy Vary
Hradec Králové
Pardubice
Jihlava
Olomouc
Ostrava
Brno
Zlín
Regensburg
Jena
Gera
Zwickau
Plauen
Hof
Weiden in der Oberpfalz
Amberg
Český Krumlov
Znojmo
Trenčín
Českomoravská Vysočina
Šumava
Böhmerwald
Bayerischer Wald
1
2
3
4
5
6
a
b
c
d
e
f
g
158
170
167
168
13°E
14°
15°
16°
17°
18°
54°N
53°
52°
51°
50°N

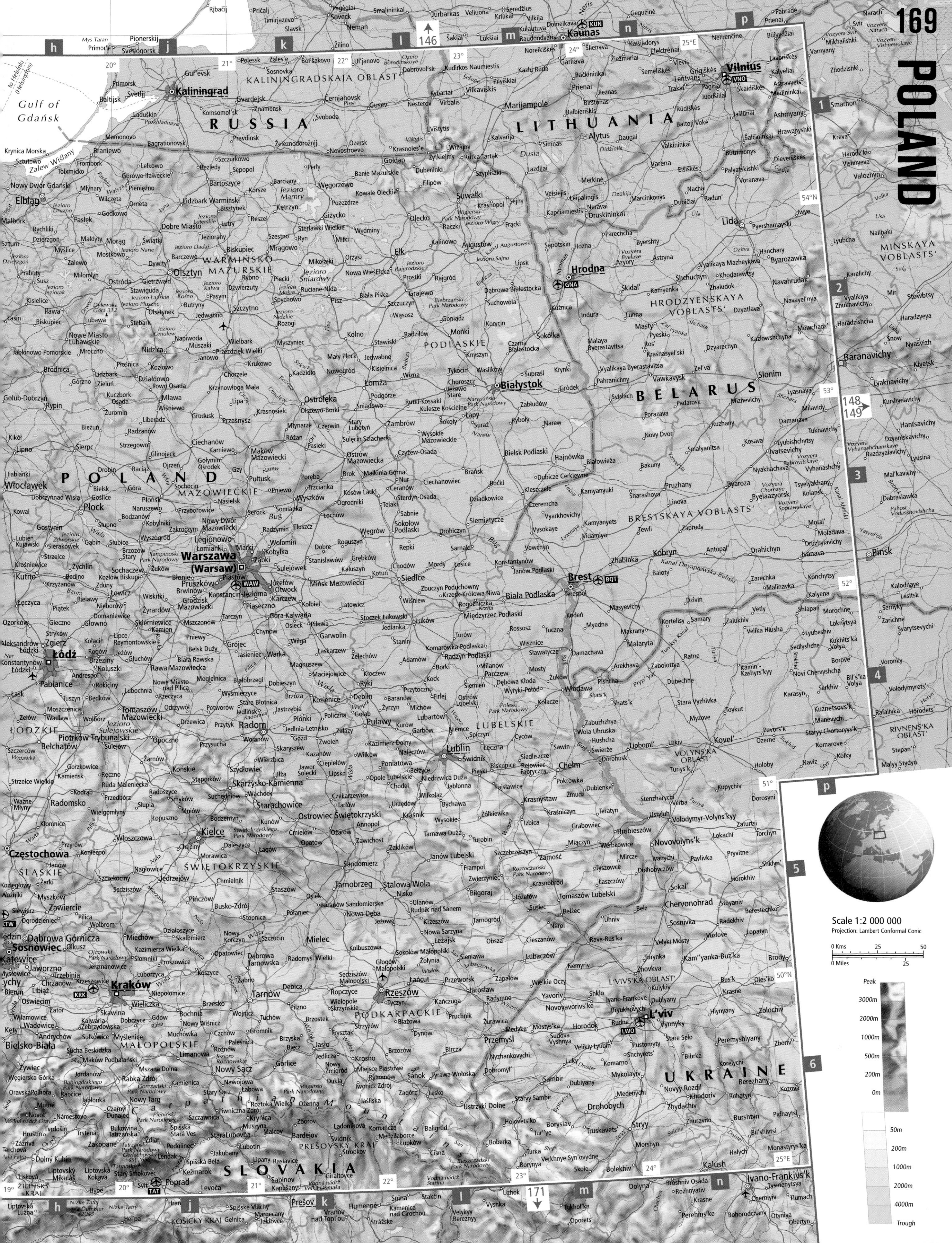
RUSSIA
KALININGRADSKAJA OBLAST'
LITHUANIA
BELARUS
POLAND
UKRAINE
SLOVAKIA
Gulf of Gdańsk
Kaliningrad
Kaunas
Vilnius
Hrodna
Białystok
Brest
Warszawa (Warsaw)
Łódź
Lublin
Kielce
Częstochowa
Kraków
Rzeszów
L'viv
Przemyśl
Tarnów
Nowy Sącz
Olsztyn
Elbląg
Płock
Radom
Lida
Pinsk
Kovel'
Slonim
Baranavichy
Suwałki
Poprad
Katowice
Sosnowiec
Bielsko-Biała
WARMIŃSKO-MAZURSKIE
PODLASKIE
MAZOWIECKIE
ŁÓDZKIE
LUBELSKIE
ŚWIĘTOKRZYSKIE
ŚLĄSKIE
MAŁOPOLSKIE
PODKARPACKIE
MINSKAYA VOBLASTS'
HRODZYENSKAYA VOBLASTS'
BRESTSKAYA VOBLASTS'
VOLYNS'KA OBLAST'
RIVNENS'KA OBLAST'
L'VIVS'KA OBLAST'
PREŠOVSKÝ KRAJ
KOŠICKÝ KRAJ
Carpathian Mountains
146
148
149
171
Scale 1:2 000 000
Projection: Lambert Conformal Conic
0 Kms 25 50
0 Miles 25
Peak
3000m
2000m
1000m
500m
200m
0m
50m
200m
1000m
2000m
4000m
Trough

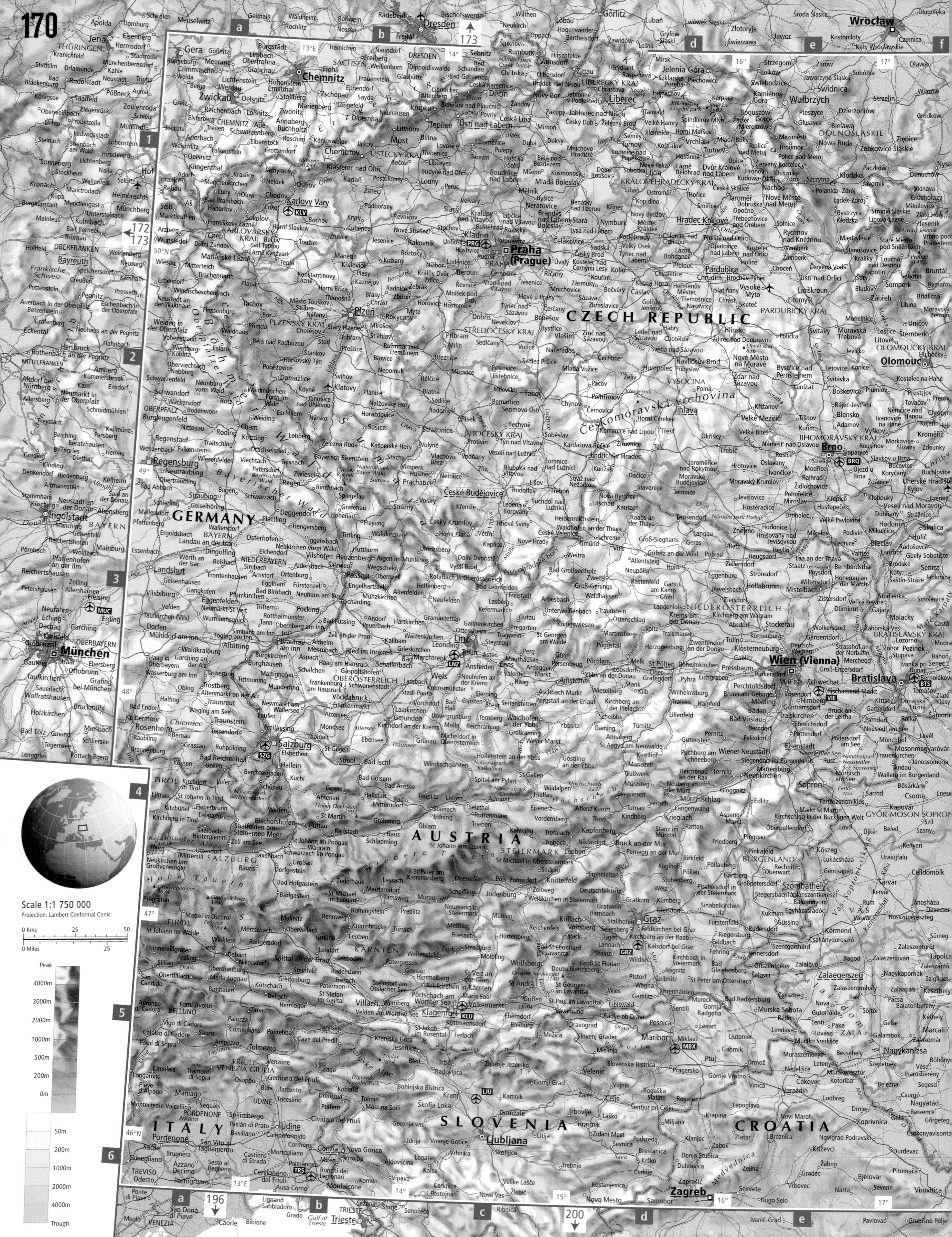
CZECH REPUBLIC
GERMANY
AUSTRIA
SLOVENIA
CROATIA
ITALY
Praha (Prague)
Wien (Vienna)
Bratislava
München
Ljubljana
Zagreb
Dresden
Wrocław
Chemnitz
Plzeň
Brno
Olomouc
Linz
Salzburg
Graz
Klagenfurt
Maribor
Regensburg
Ingolstadt
Passau
Liberec
Hradec Králové
Pardubice
České Budějovice
Jihlava
Karlovy Vary
Ústí nad Labem
Trieste
Udine
Zwickau
Bayreuth
Landshut
Innsbruck
Villach
Sopron
Szombathely
Zalaegerszeg
Nagykanizsa
Pordenone
Českomoravská vrchovina
Böhmerwald
Bayerischer Wald
Hohe Tauern
Niedere Tauern
Erzgebirge
173
172
173
196
200
a
b
c
d
e
f
1
2
3
4
5
6
13°E
14°
15°
16°
17°
50°N
49°
48°
47°
46°N
Scale 1:1 750 000
Projection: Lambert Conformal Conic
0 Kms 25 50
0 Miles 25
Peak
4000m
3000m
2000m
1000m
500m
200m
0m
50m
200m
1000m
2000m
4000m
Trough

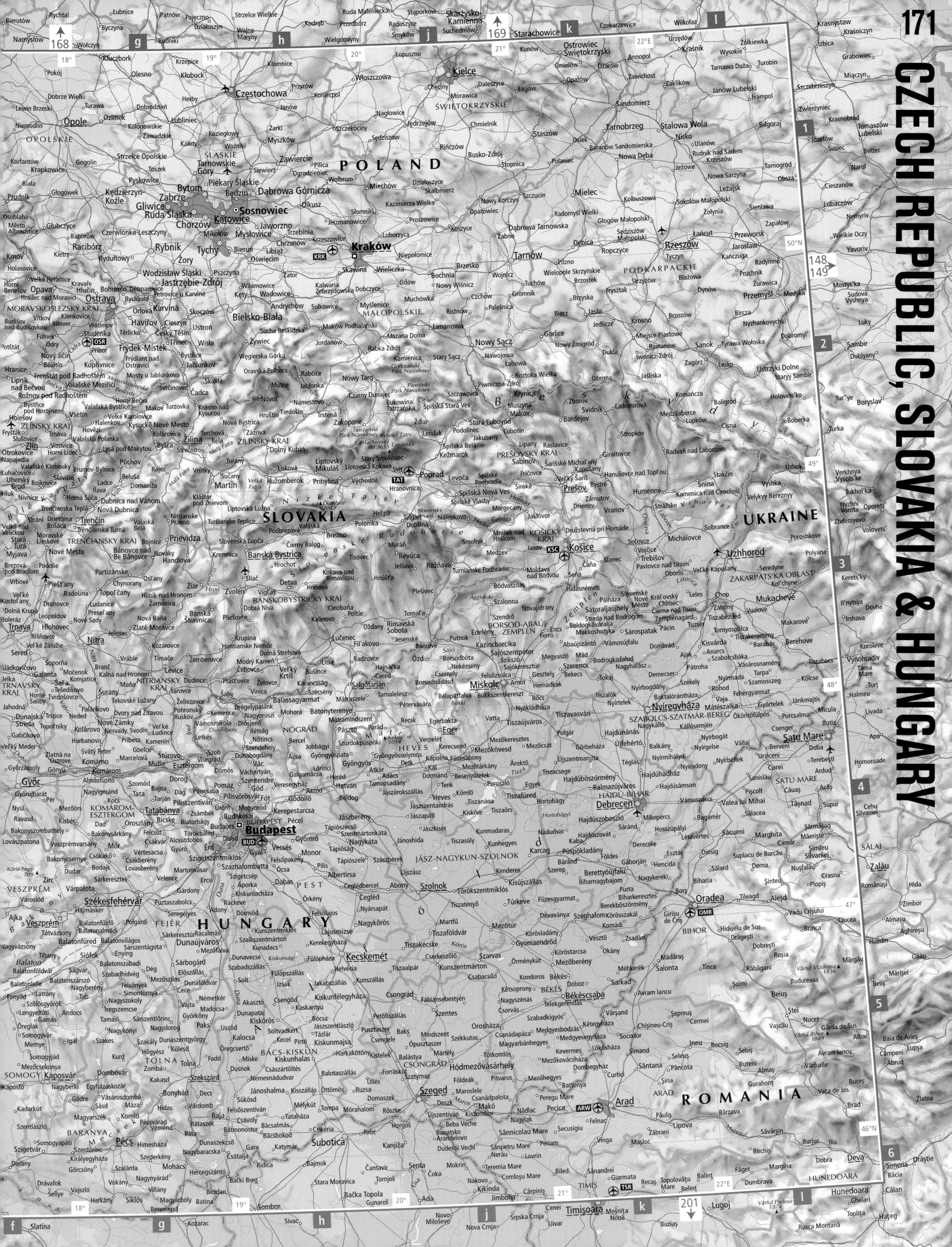

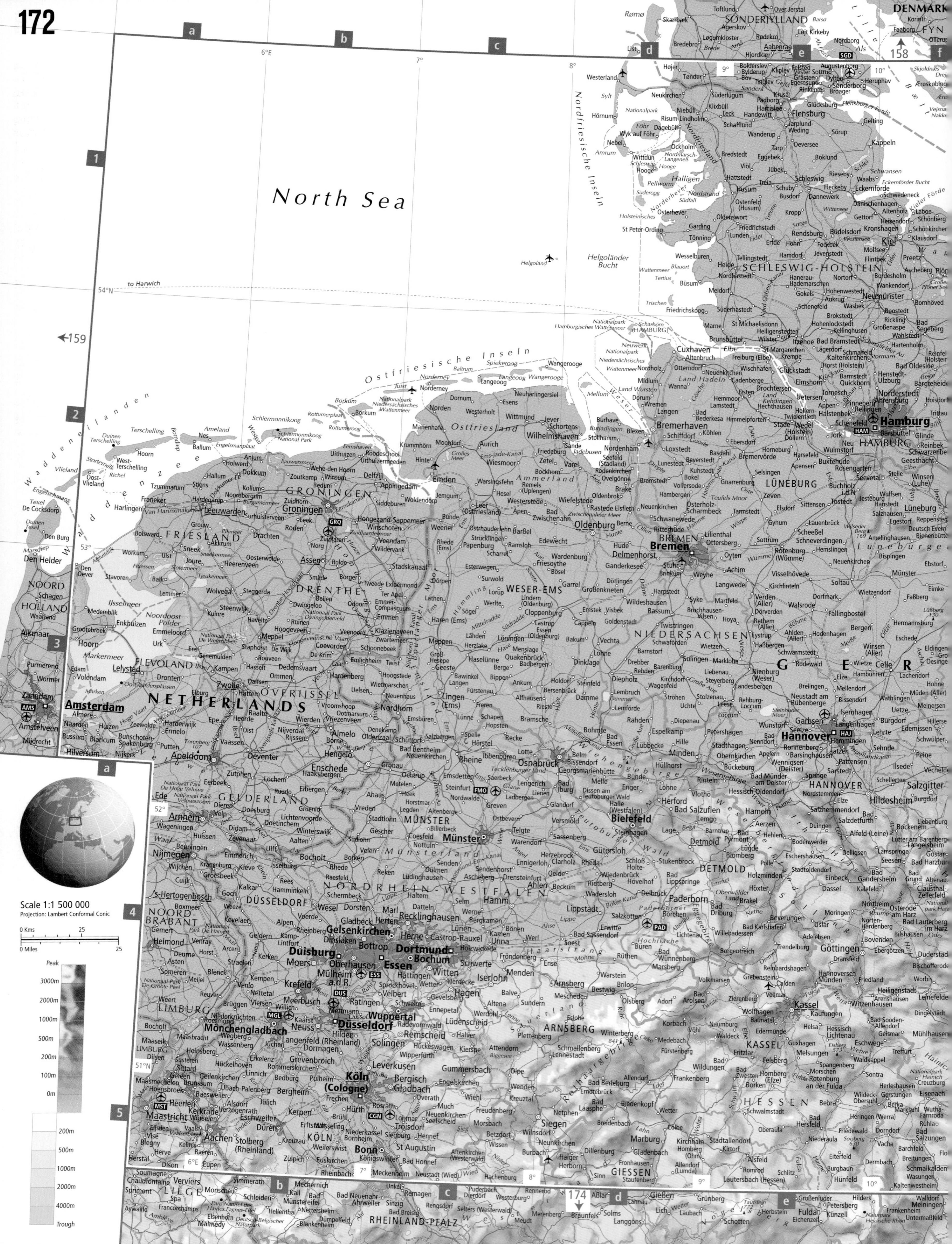
DENMARK
SØNDERJYLLAND
FYN
North Sea
Nordfriesische Inseln
Helgoländer Bucht
Ostfriesische Inseln
Waddeneilanden
Waddenzee
to Harwich
SCHLESWIG-HOLSTEIN
Kiel
Flensburg
Hamburg
HAMBURG
Bremen
BREMEN
Bremerhaven
Oldenburg
WESER-EMS
NIEDERSACHSEN
Hannover
HANNOVER
LÜNEBURG
Osnabrück
Bielefeld
DETMOLD
Münster
MÜNSTER
NORDRHEIN-WESTFALEN
Dortmund
Essen
Duisburg
Gelsenkirchen
Bochum
Düsseldorf
DÜSSELDORF
Wuppertal
Mönchengladbach
Köln (Cologne)
KÖLN
Bonn
ARNSBERG
Kassel
KASSEL
Göttingen
Paderborn
Siegen
Marburg
Gießen
GIESSEN
HESSEN
RHEINLAND-PFALZ
Aachen
Maastricht
LIÈGE
LIMBURG
NOORD-BRABANT
GELDERLAND
OVERIJSSEL
DRENTHE
GRONINGEN
Groningen
FRIESLAND
Leeuwarden
FLEVOLAND
Lelystad
NETHERLANDS
Amsterdam
NOORD-HOLLAND
Den Helder
Alkmaar
Zaandam
Zwolle
Apeldoorn
Arnhem
Nijmegen
Enschede
Emden
Wilhelmshaven
Cuxhaven
Ostfriesland
GERMANY
Scale 1:1 500 000
Projection: Lambert Conformal Conic
0 Kms 25
0 Miles 25
Peak
3000m
2000m
1000m
500m
200m
100m
0m
200m
500m
1000m
2000m
4000m
Trough
158
159
174

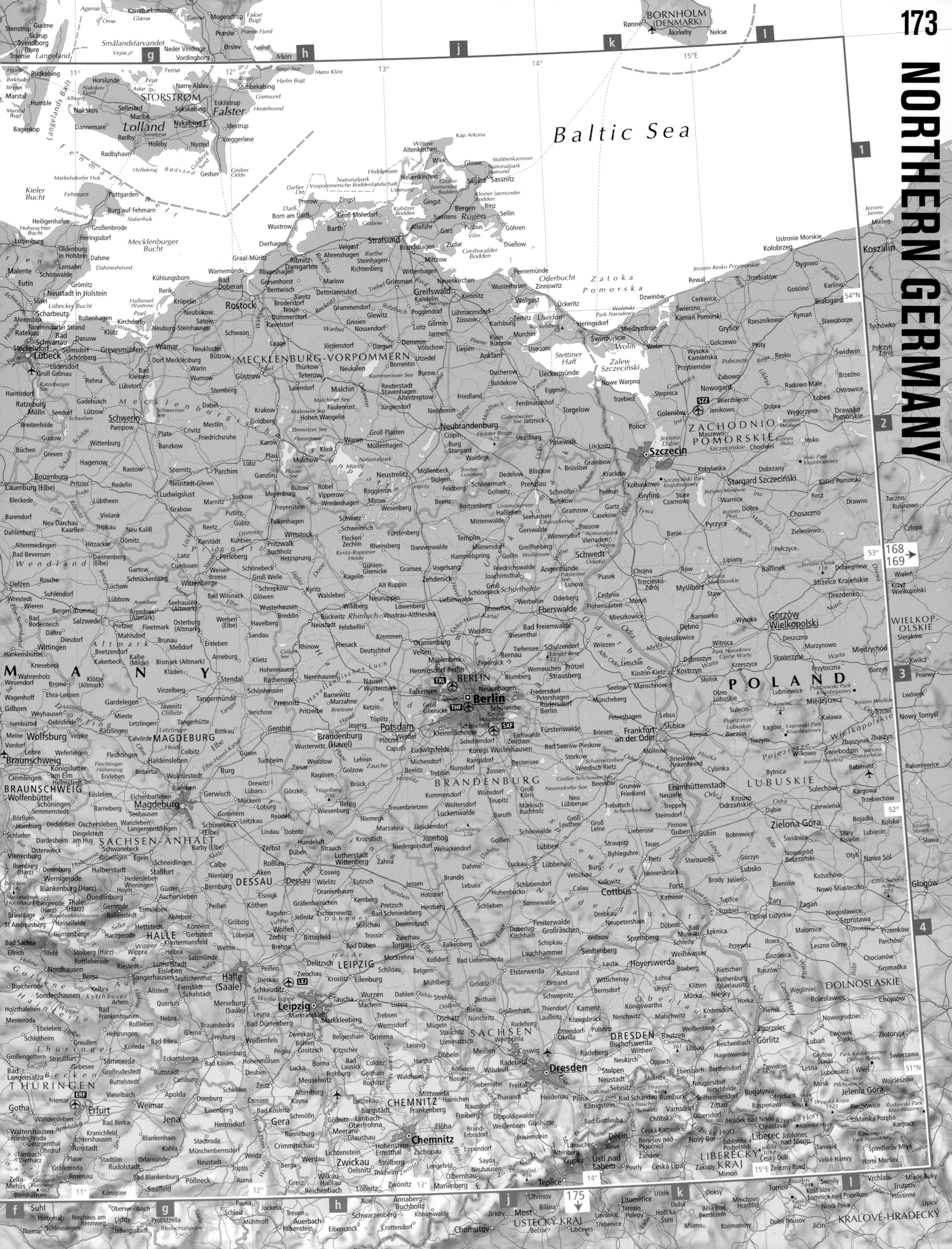

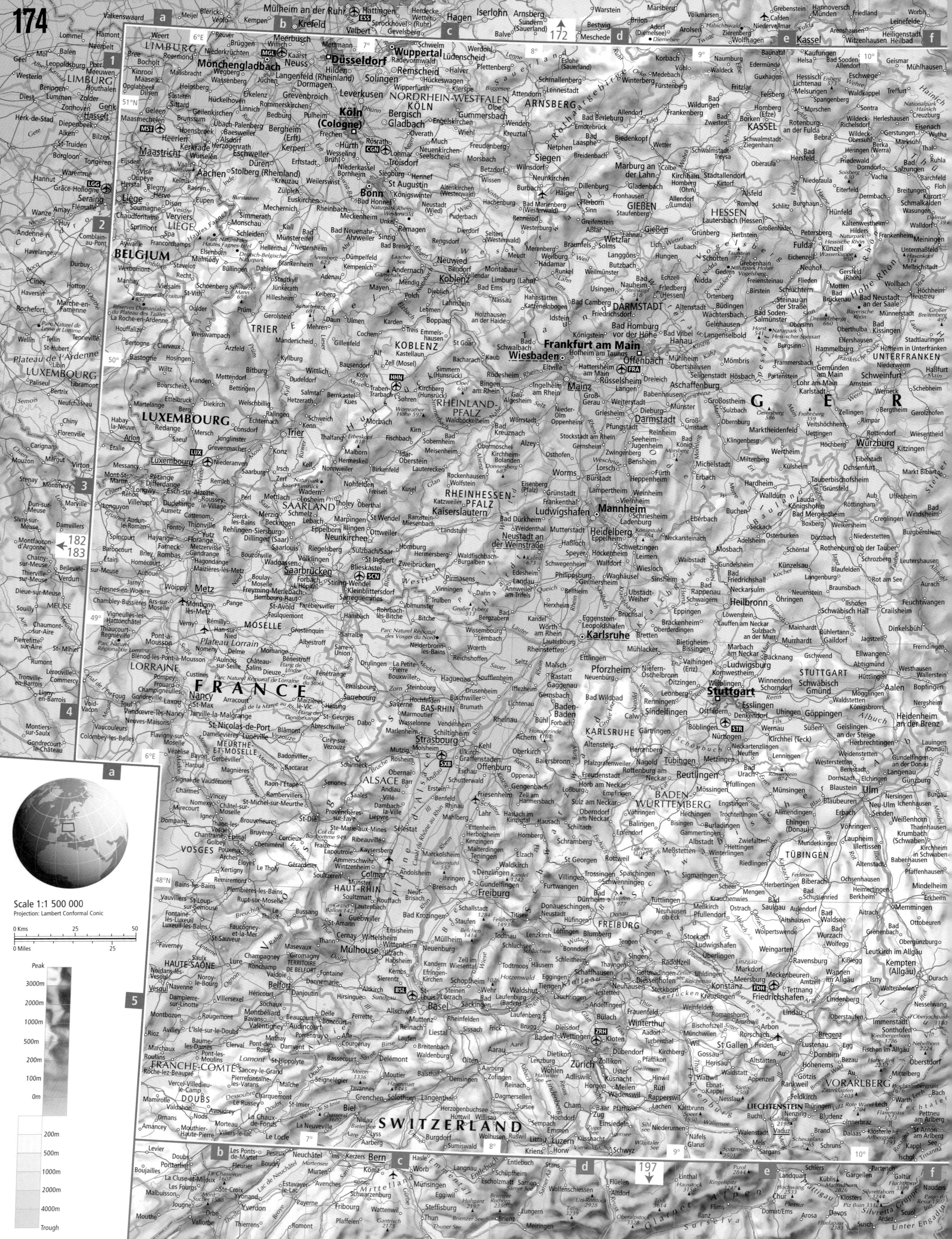
BELGIUM
LUXEMBOURG
FRANCE
SWITZERLAND
LIECHTENSTEIN
NORDRHEIN-WESTFALEN
RHEINLAND-PFALZ
SAARLAND
HESSEN
BADEN-WÜRTTEMBERG
ALSACE
LORRAINE
FRANCHE-COMTÉ
Köln (Cologne)
Düsseldorf
Frankfurt am Main
Stuttgart
Strasbourg
Zürich
Bern
Basel
Mannheim
Karlsruhe
Wiesbaden
Mainz
Saarbrücken
Metz
Nancy
Luxembourg
Liège
Scale 1:1 500 000
Projection: Lambert Conformal Conic
0 Kms 25 50
0 Miles 25
Peak
3000m
2000m
1000m
500m
200m
0m
200m
500m
1000m
2000m
4000m
Trough

173
168
169
176
177
176
POLAND
CZECH REPUBLIC
AUSTRIA
SACHSEN
THÜRINGEN
OBERFRANKEN
MITTELFRANKEN
OBERPFALZ
NIEDERBAYERN
OBERBAYERN
SCHWABEN
BAYERN
TIROL
SALZBURG
OBERÖSTERREICH
NIEDERÖSTERREICH
STEIERMARK
KÄRNTEN
KARLOVARSKÝ KRAJ
ÚSTECKÝ KRAJ
LIBERECKÝ KRAJ
STŘEDOČESKÝ KRAJ
PLZEŇSKÝ KRAJ
JIHOČESKÝ KRAJ
VYSOČINA KRAJ
PRAHA
Praha (Prague)
Dresden
Leipzig
Chemnitz
Zwickau
Erfurt
Nürnberg
Regensburg
Ingolstadt
Augsburg
München (Munich)
Salzburg
Linz
Innsbruck
Plzeň
České Budějovice
Graz
Passau
Landshut
11°
12°
13°
14°
15°E
51°N
50°
49°
48°N

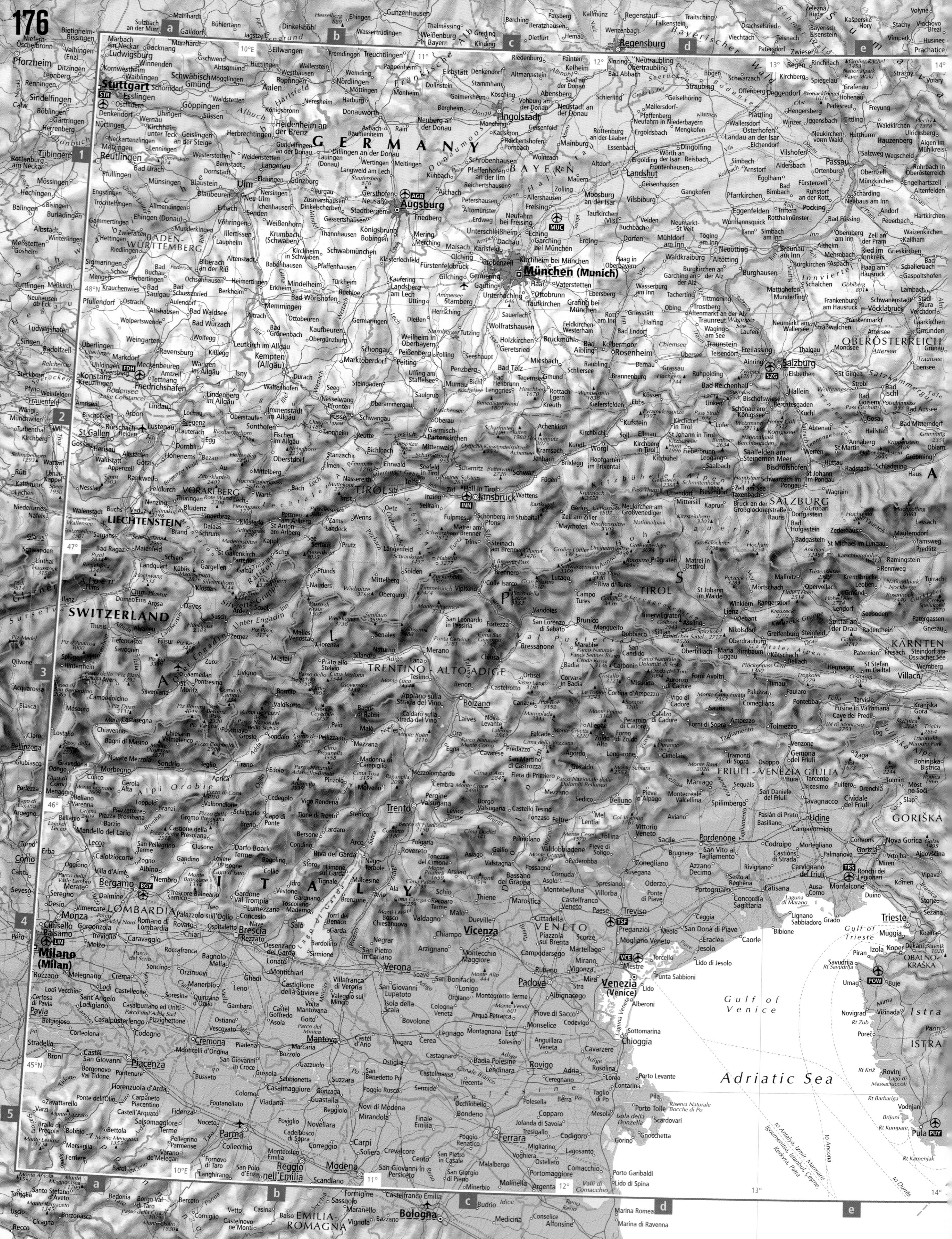
GERMANY
BAYERN
BADEN-WÜRTTEMBERG
Stuttgart
Augsburg
München (Munich)
Ingolstadt
Regensburg
Ulm
Salzburg
Innsbruck
OBERÖSTERREICH
SALZBURG
TIROL
VORARLBERG
KÄRNTEN
LIECHTENSTEIN
SWITZERLAND
ITALY
LOMBARDIA
TRENTINO - ALTO ADIGE
VENETO
FRIULI - VENEZIA GIULIA
EMILIA-ROMAGNA
ISTRA
GORIŠKA
OBALNO-KRAŠKA
Milano (Milan)
Bergamo
Brescia
Verona
Vicenza
Padova
Venezia (Venice)
Trento
Bolzano
Udine
Trieste
Mantova
Cremona
Parma
Modena
Ferrara
Bologna
Gulf of Venice
Gulf of Trieste
Adriatic Sea
Lago di Garda
Bodensee (Lake Constance)
10°E
11°
12°
13°
14°
45°N
46°
47°
48°N
a
b
c
d
e
1
2
3
4
5

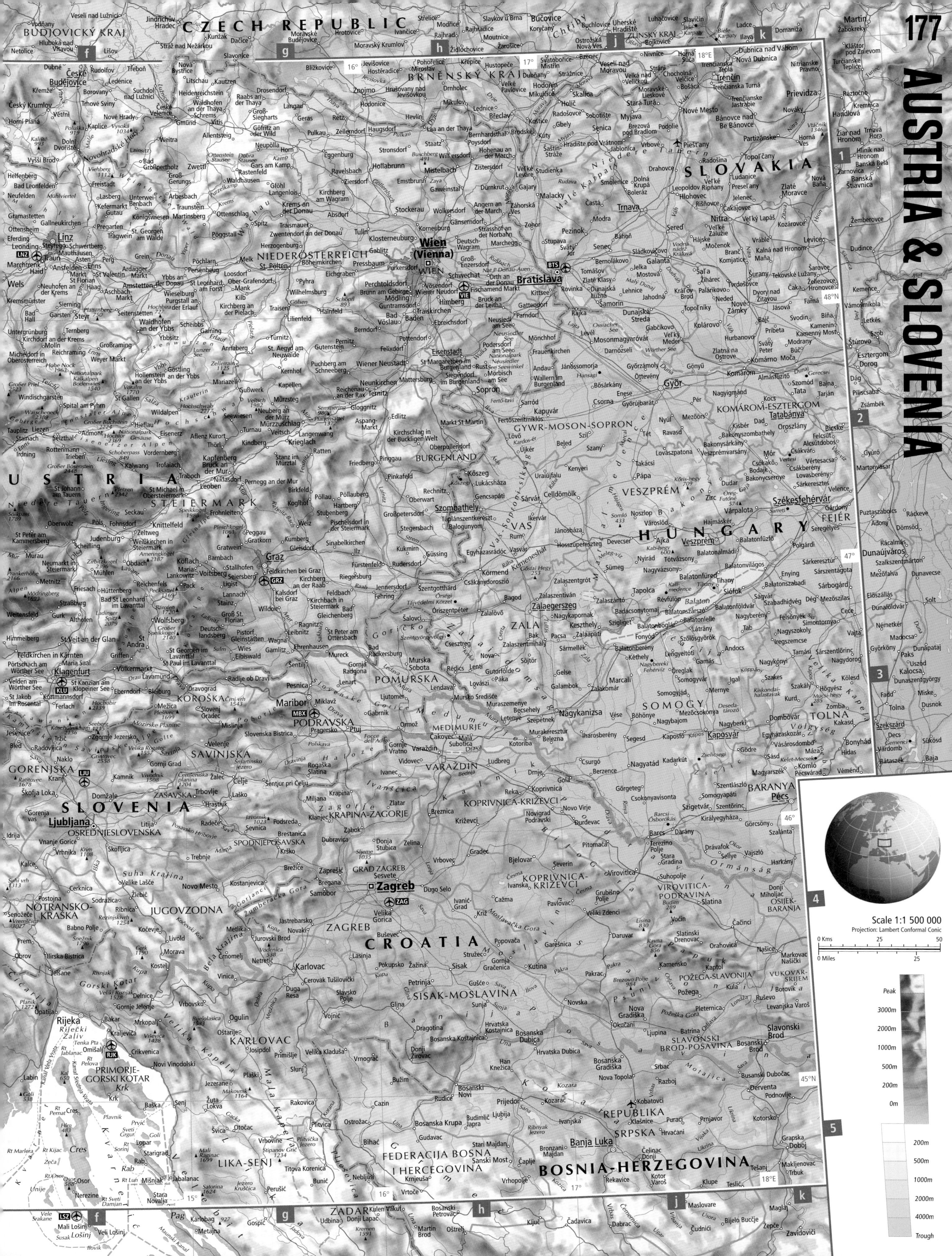

CZECH REPUBLIC

SLOVAKIA

Wien
(Vienna)

WIEN

Bratislava

NIEDERÖSTERREICH

AUSTRIA

STEIERMARK

BURGENLAND

HUNGARY

Graz

Klagenfurt

Maribor

PODRAVSKA

KOROŠKA

SAVINJSKA

POMURSKA

VAS

VESZPRÉM

KOMÁROM-ESZTERGOM

Győr

ZALA

SOMOGY

TOLNA

BARANYA
Pécs

GORENJSKA

SLOVENIA

Ljubljana

OSREDNJESLOVENSKA

ZASAVSKA

SPODNJEPOSAVSKA

KRAPINA-ZAGORJE

KOPRIVNICA-KRIZEVCI

NOTRANSKO-
KRAŠKA

JUGOVZODNA

ZAGREB

Zagreb

GRAD ZAGREB

CROATIA

VARAZDIN

MEDIMURJE

VIROVITICA-
PODRAVINA

OSIJEK-
BARANJA

Rijeka

PRIMORJE-
GORSKI KOTAR

KARLOVAC

SISAK-MOSLAVINA

POŽEGA-SLAVONIJA

SLAVONSKI
BROD-POSAVINA

REPUBLIKA
SRPSKA

Banja Luka

FEDERACIJA BOSNA
I HERCEGOVINA

LIKA-SENJ

BOSNIA-HERZEGOVINA

Scale 1:1 500 000
Projection: Lambert Conformal Conic

0 Kms   25   50

0 Miles   25

Peak
3000m
2000m
1000m
500m
200m
0m

200m
500m
1000m
2000m
4000m
Trough

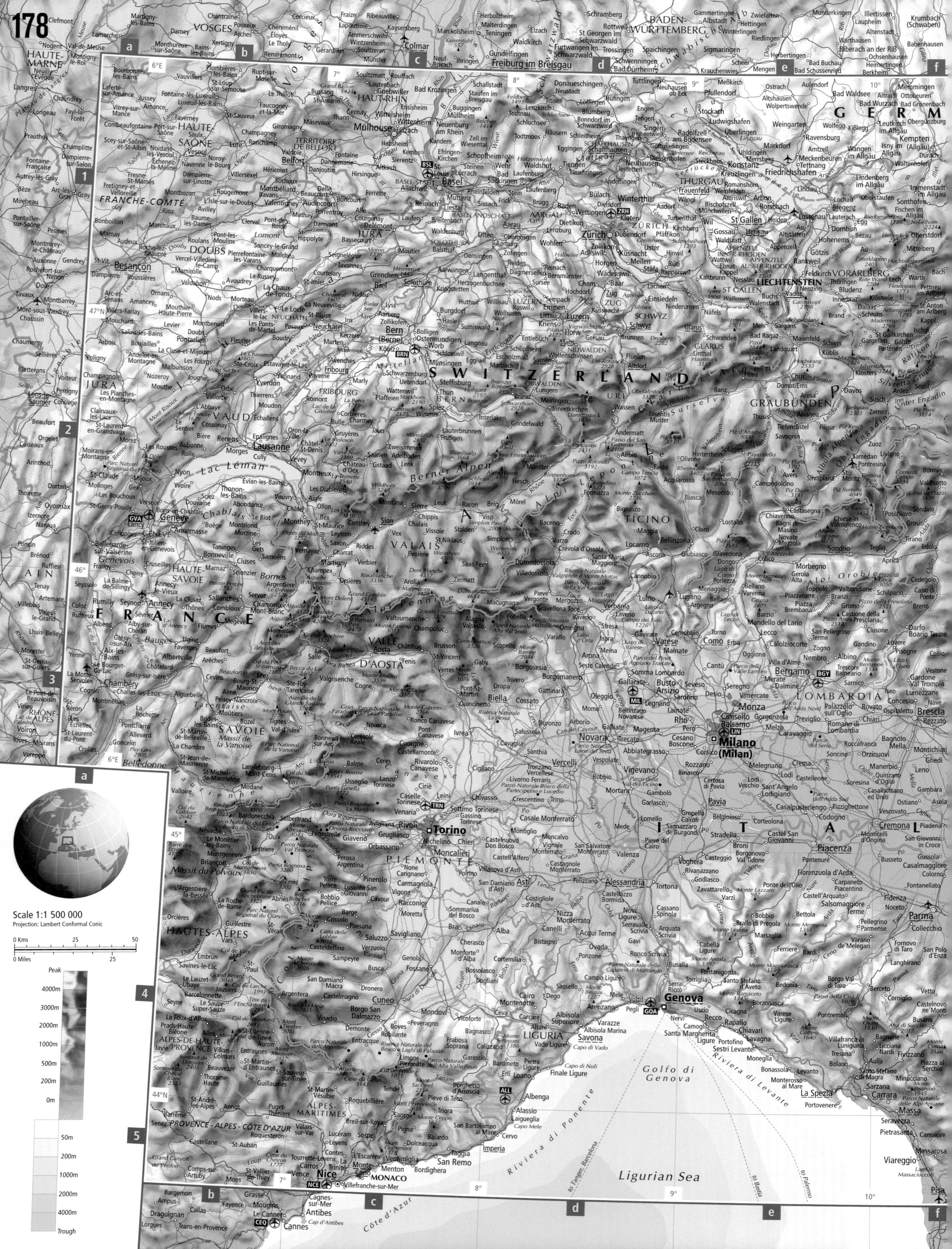
SWITZERLAND
FRANCE
ITALY
GERMANY
LIECHTENSTEIN
MONACO
BADEN-WÜRTTEMBERG
HAUTE-MARNE
VOSGES
HAUT-RHIN
HAUTE-SAÔNE
TERRITOIRE DE BELFORT
FRANCHE-COMTÉ
JURA
DOUBS
VAUD
VALAIS
FRIBOURG
BERN
NEUCHÂTEL
GENÈVE
LUZERN
ZUG
SCHWYZ
URI
GLARUS
AARGAU
ZÜRICH
THURGAU
ST GALLEN
APPENZELL INNER-RHODEN
APPENZELL AUSSER-RHODEN
GRAUBÜNDEN
TICINO
VORARLBERG
HAUTE-SAVOIE
SAVOIE
AIN
RHÔNE-ALPES
HAUTES-ALPES
ALPES-DE-HAUTE-PROVENCE
ALPES-MARITIMES
PROVENCE-ALPES-CÔTE D'AZUR
VALLE D'AOSTA
PIEMONTE
LOMBARDIA
LIGURIA
Lac Léman
Berner Alpen
Alpi Pennine
Alpi Lepontine
Golfo di Genova
Riviera di Ponente
Riviera di Levante
Ligurian Sea
Côte d'Azur
Besançon
Bern (Berne)
Zürich
Basel
Lausanne
Genève
Torino
Milano (Milan)
Genova
Nice
Scale 1:1 500 000
Projection: Lambert Conformal Conic
0 Kms 25 50
0 Miles 25
Peak
4000m
3000m
2000m
1000m
500m
200m
0m
50m
200m
1000m
2000m
4000m
Trough

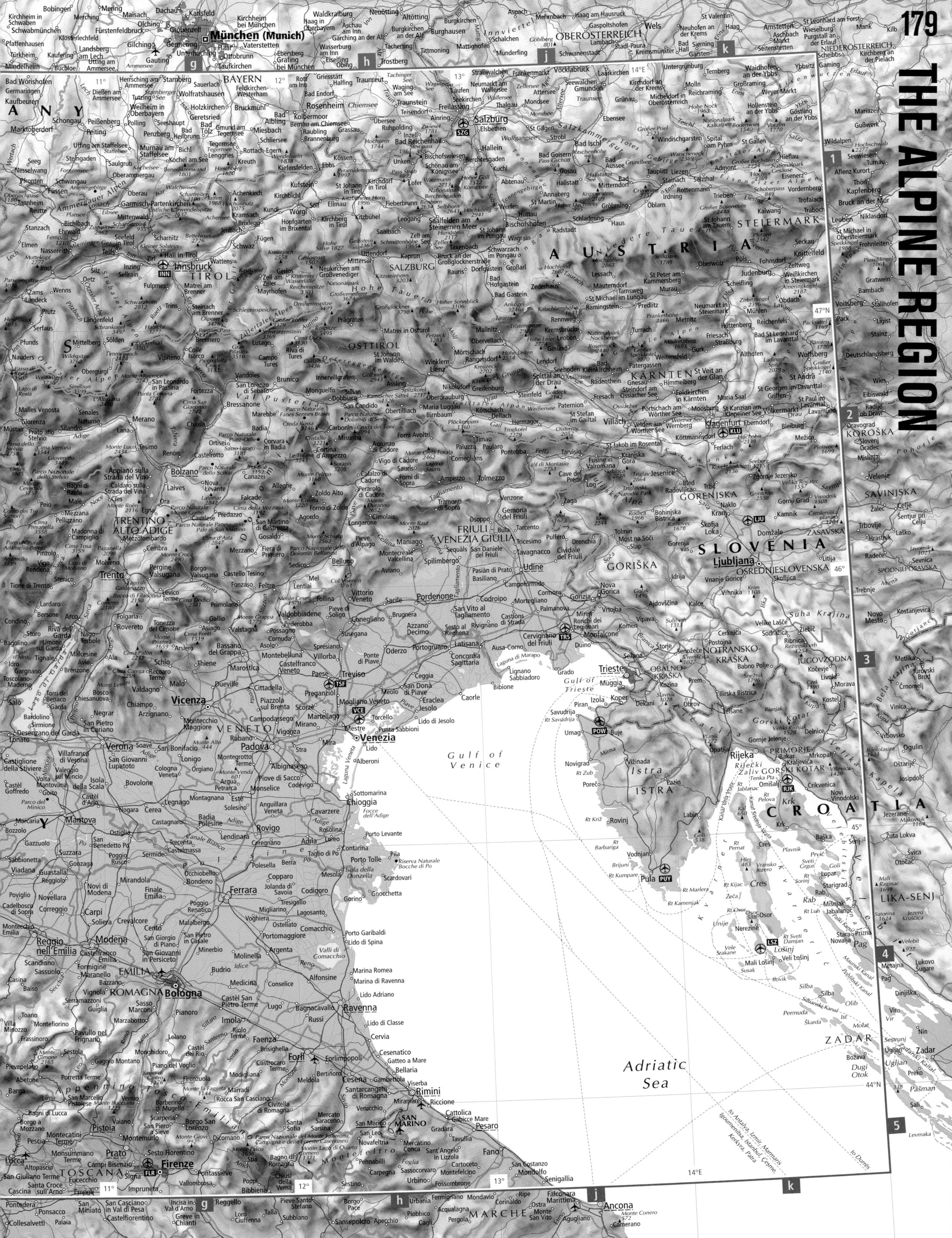
München (Munich)
BAYERN
OBERÖSTERREICH
NIEDERÖSTERREICH
Salzburg
SALZBURG
STEIERMARK
A U S T R I A
Innsbruck
TIROL
OSTTIROL
KÄRNTEN
Klagenfurt
Villach
Graz
SLOVENIA
Ljubljana
GORENJSKA
GORIŠKA
OSREDNJESLOVENSKA
NOTRANJSKO-KRAŠKA
OBALNO-KRAŠKA
KOROŠKA
SAVINJSKA
JUGOVZODNA
C R O A T I A
PRIMORJE-GORSKI KOTAR
LIKA-SENJ
ISTRA
Rijeka
Pula
Trieste
Gulf of Trieste
Gulf of Venice
Adriatic Sea
Venezia
Padova
Verona
Vicenza
Treviso
Udine
Bolzano
Trento
TRENTINO ALTO ADIGE
FRIULI-VENEZIA GIULIA
VENETO
EMILIA-ROMAGNA
Bologna
Ferrara
Modena
Reggio nell'Emilia
Ravenna
Rimini
SAN MARINO
Firenze
TOSCANA
MARCHE
Ancona
Pesaro
ZADAR
Zadar
11°
12°
13°
14°E
47°N
46°
45°
44°N
g
h
j
k
1
2
3
4
5

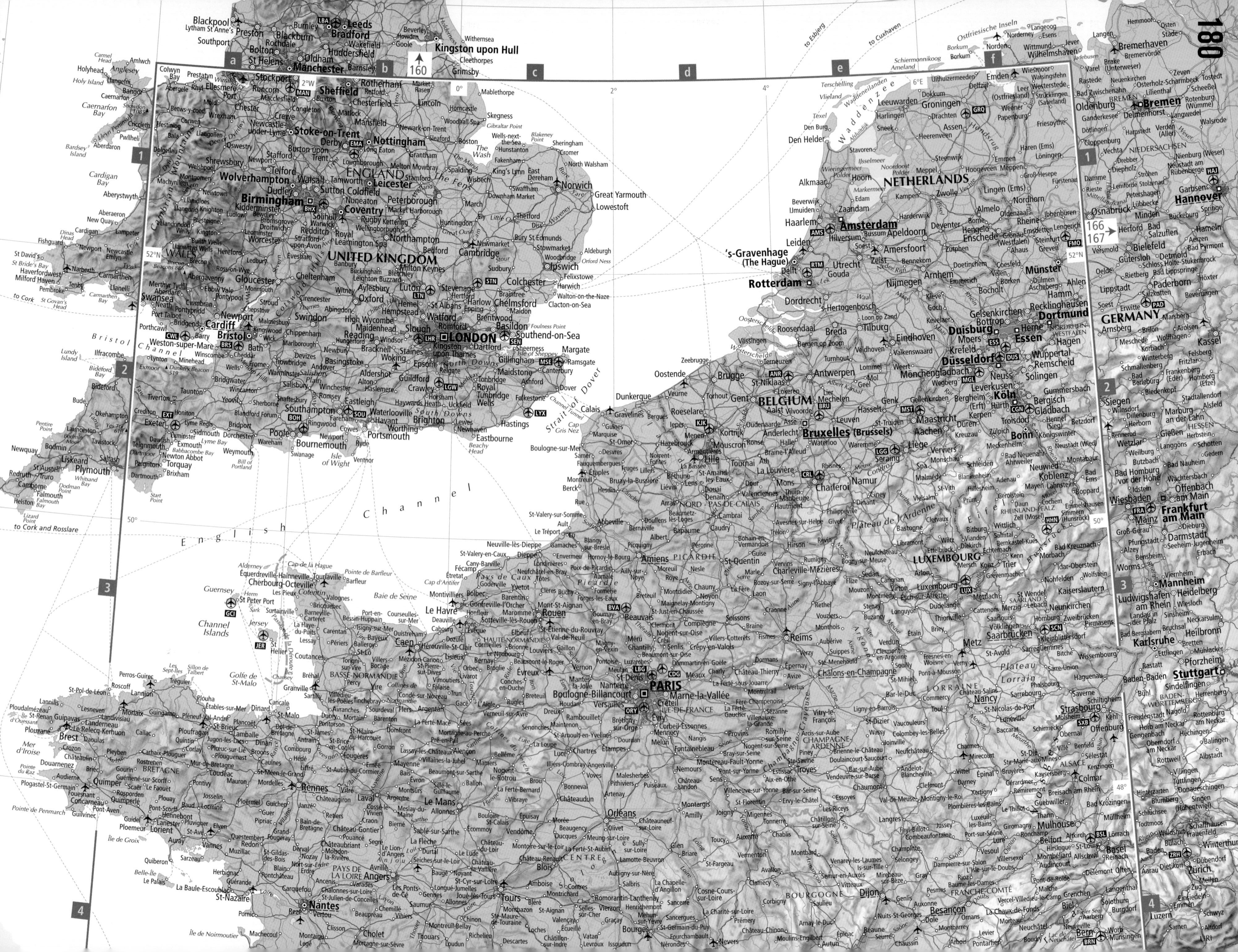

UNITED KINGDOM
ENGLAND
WALES
NETHERLANDS
BELGIUM
LUXEMBOURG
GERMANY
LONDON
PARIS
Amsterdam
Rotterdam
's-Gravenhage (The Hague)
Bruxelles (Brussels)
Köln
Düsseldorf
Essen
Dortmund
Duisburg
Frankfurt am Main
Mannheim
Stuttgart
Hannover
Bremen
Bremerhaven
Birmingham
Manchester
Leeds
Sheffield
Kingston upon Hull
Nottingham
Leicester
Coventry
Bristol
Cardiff
Plymouth
Southampton
Portsmouth
Brighton
Norwich
Rennes
Nantes
Le Havre
Rouen
Caen
Lille
Reims
Le Mans
Tours
Orléans
Dijon
Strasbourg
Metz
Nancy
English Channel
Bristol Channel
Strait of Dover
Channel Islands
to Cork and Rosslare
to Cork
to Esbjerg
to Cuxhaven
160
166
167

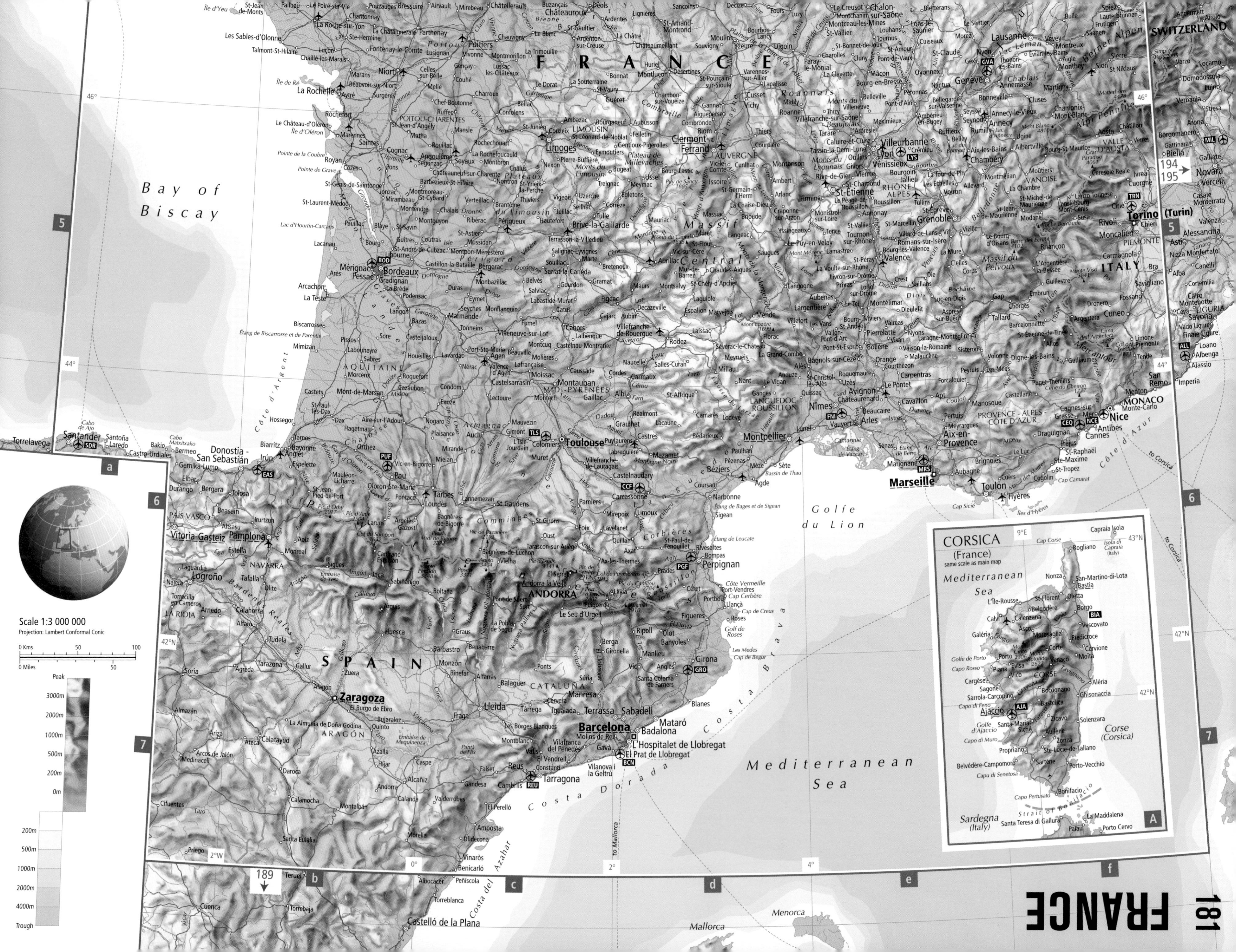

181
FRANCE
FRANCE
SWITZERLAND
ITALY
SPAIN
ANDORRA
MONACO
Bay of Biscay
Golfe du Lion
Mediterranean Sea
Côte d'Argent
Côte d'Azur
Costa Brava
Costa Dorada
Costa del Azahar
Massif Central
Bordeaux
Toulouse
Montpellier
Marseille
Nice
Lyon
Villeurbanne
Grenoble
St-Étienne
Clermont-Ferrand
Limoges
Poitiers
La Rochelle
Genève
Lausanne
Torino (Turin)
Barcelona
Zaragoza
Perpignan
Pamplona
Vitoria-Gasteiz
Donostia - San Sebastián
Santander
Logroño
Lleida
Tarragona
Girona
Mallorca
Menorca
CORSICA
(France)
same scale as main map
Mediterranean Sea
Corse (Corsica)
Ajaccio
Bastia
Sardegna (Italy)
Strait of Bonifacio
A
Scale 1:3 000 000
Projection: Lambert Conformal Conic
0 Kms
50
100
0 Miles
50
Peak
3000m
2000m
1000m
500m
200m
0m
200m
500m
1000m
2000m
4000m
Trough
194
195
189

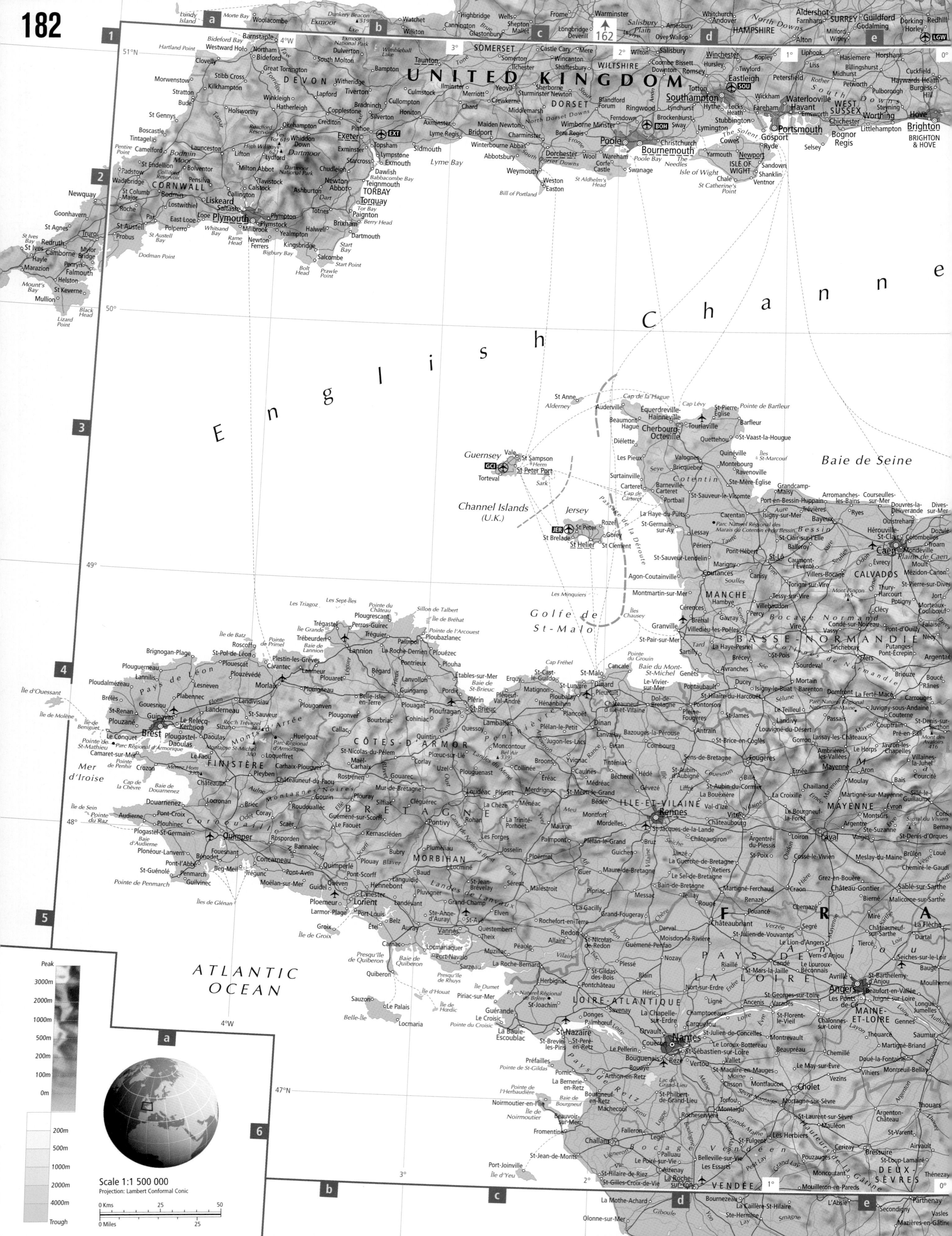
UNITED KINGDOM
English Channel
FRANCE
ATLANTIC OCEAN
Channel Islands (U.K.)
Guernsey
Jersey
Alderney
Sark
Golfe de St-Malo
Baie de Seine
Lyme Bay
Mer d'Iroise
DEVON
CORNWALL
DORSET
SOMERSET
WILTSHIRE
HAMPSHIRE
SURREY
WEST SUSSEX
ISLE OF WIGHT
TORBAY
FINISTÈRE
CÔTES-D'ARMOR
MORBIHAN
BRETAGNE
ILLE-ET-VILAINE
LOIRE-ATLANTIQUE
MAYENNE
MAINE-ET-LOIRE
VENDÉE
DEUX-SÈVRES
MANCHE
CALVADOS
BASSE-NORMANDIE
PAYS DE LA LOIRE
Plymouth
Exeter
Torquay
Bournemouth
Poole
Southampton
Portsmouth
Brighton
Weymouth
Cherbourg-Octeville
St Peter Port
St Helier
Caen
Brest
Quimper
Lorient
Vannes
St-Brieuc
St-Malo
Rennes
Laval
Nantes
St-Nazaire
Angers
Cholet
Belle-Île
Île d'Ouessant
Île d'Yeu
51°N
50°
49°
48°
47°N
4°W
3°
2°
1°
0°
162
Peak
3000m
2000m
1000m
500m
200m
0m
200m
500m
1000m
2000m
4000m
Trough
Scale 1:1 500 000
Projection: Lambert Conformal Conic
0 Kms 25 50
0 Miles 25

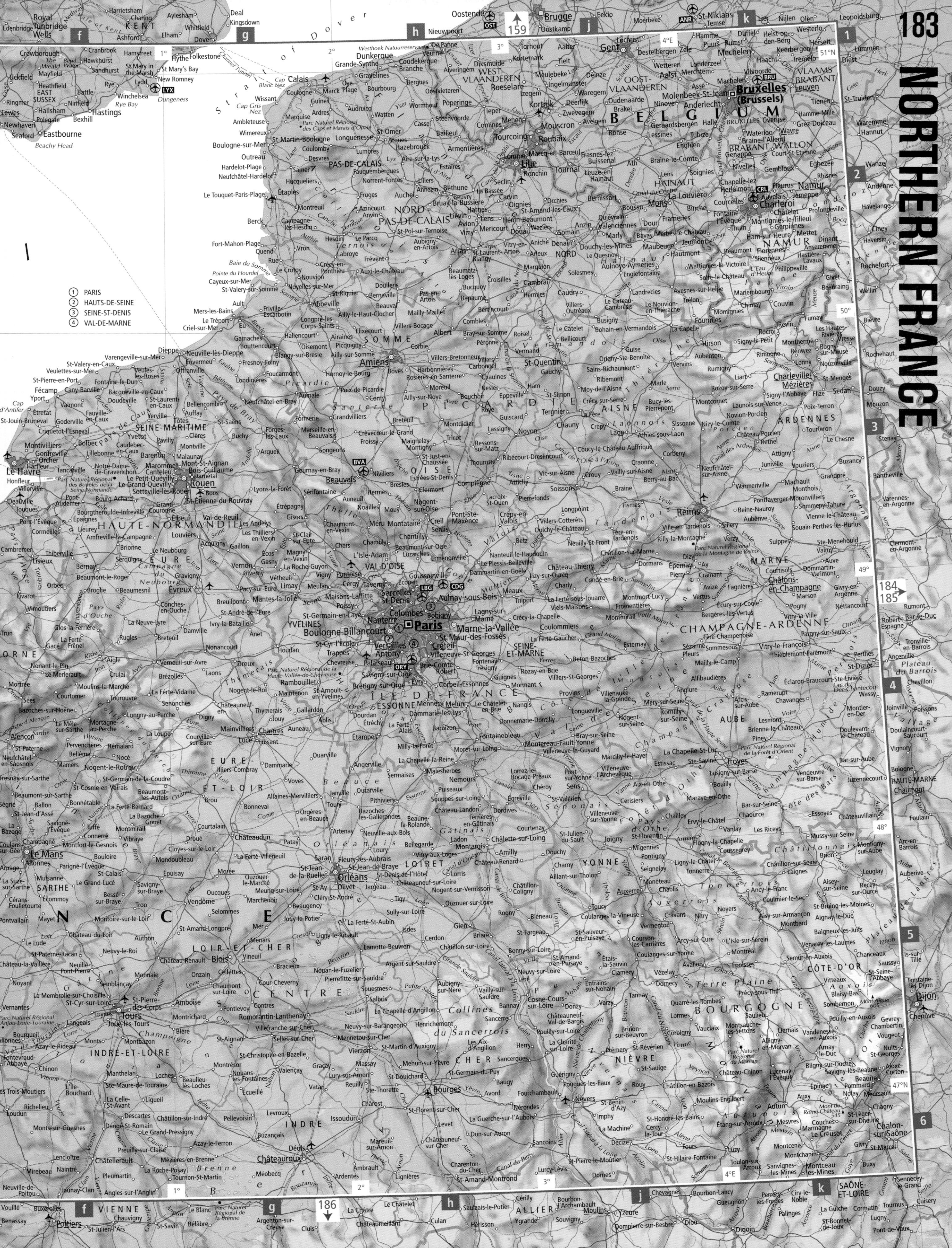
① PARIS
② HAUTS-DE-SEINE
③ SEINE-ST-DENIS
④ VAL-DE-MARNE
159
184
185
186
f
g
h
j
k
1
2
3
4
5
6
1°
2°
3°
4°E
51°N
50°
49°
48°
47°N
Strait of Dover
KENT
EAST SUSSEX
Hastings
Eastbourne
Folkestone
Dover
Oostende
Brugge
Gent
Bruxelles (Brussels)
BELGIUM
OOST-VLAANDEREN
WEST-VLAANDEREN
VLAAMS BRABANT
BRABANT WALLON
HAINAUT
NAMUR
Charleroi
Namur
Mons
Calais
Dunkerque
Boulogne-sur-Mer
Lille
Roubaix
Tourcoing
PAS-DE-CALAIS
NORD
NORD-PAS-DE-CALAIS
Arras
Amiens
SOMME
PICARDIE
AISNE
OISE
Beauvais
Compiègne
St-Quentin
Reims
ARDENNES
Charleville-Mézières
MARNE
Châlons-en-Champagne
CHAMPAGNE-ARDENNE
Troyes
AUBE
HAUTE-MARNE
Chaumont
Le Havre
Rouen
SEINE-MARITIME
HAUTE-NORMANDIE
EURE
Évreux
VAL-D'OISE
YVELINES
Paris
ÎLE-DE-FRANCE
ESSONNE
SEINE-ET-MARNE
Versailles
Melun
Chartres
EURE-ET-LOIR
ORNE
Alençon
Le Mans
SARTHE
LOIRET
Orléans
LOIR-ET-CHER
Blois
Tours
INDRE-ET-LOIRE
CENTRE
CHER
Bourges
INDRE
Châteauroux
VIENNE
Poitiers
NIÈVRE
Nevers
YONNE
Auxerre
BOURGOGNE
CÔTE-D'OR
Dijon
SAÔNE-ET-LOIRE
ALLIER
Moulins

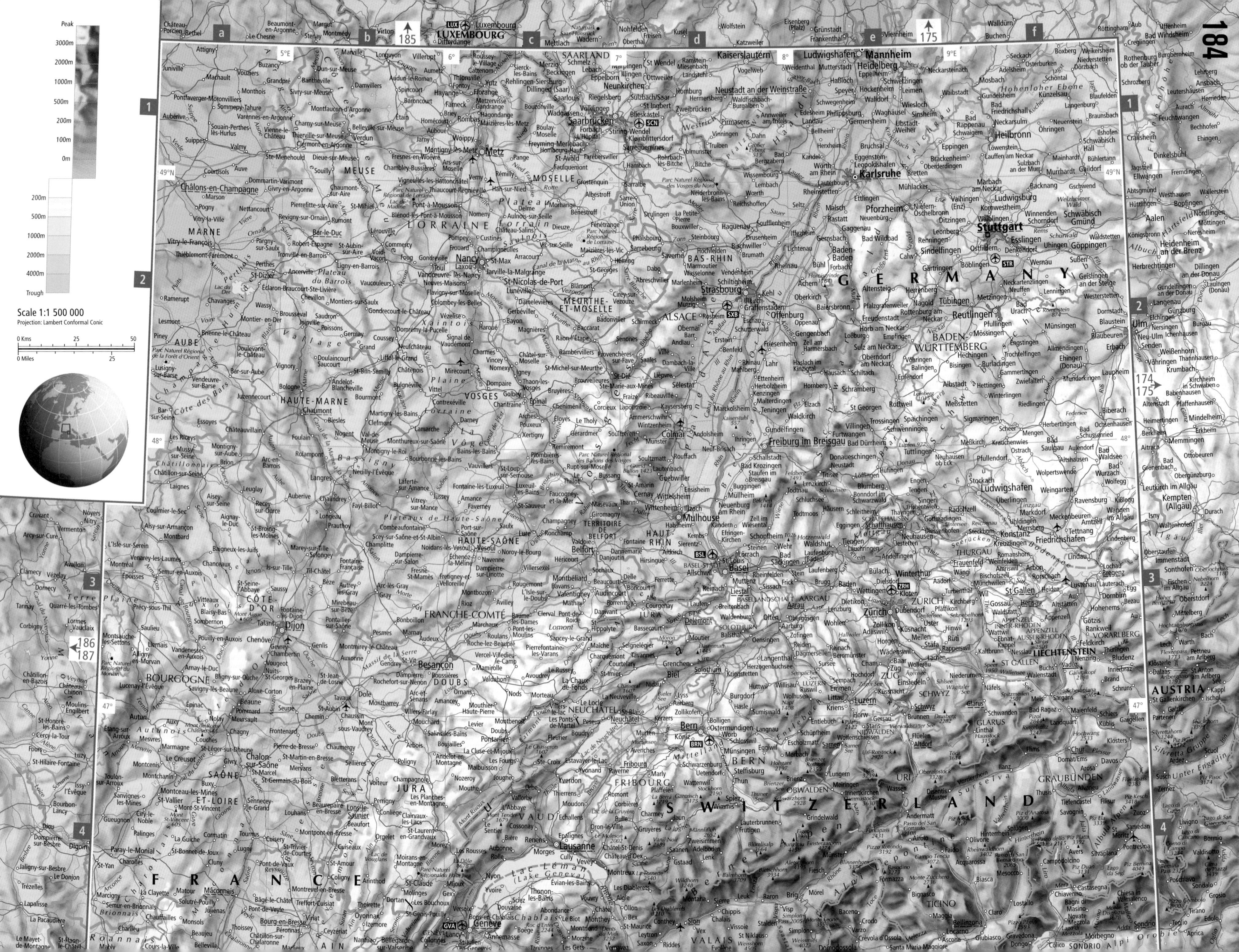

GERMANY
FRANCE
SWITZERLAND
AUSTRIA
LUXEMBOURG
LIECHTENSTEIN
SAARLAND
LORRAINE
ALSACE
BADEN-WÜRTTEMBERG
FRANCHE-COMTÉ
BOURGOGNE
Luxembourg
Saarbrücken
Metz
Nancy
Strasbourg
Karlsruhe
Mannheim
Heidelberg
Stuttgart
Mulhouse
Basel
Zürich
Bern
Lausanne
Genève
Besançon
Dijon
Freiburg im Breisgau
Lac Léman (Lake Geneva)
Peak
3000m
2000m
1000m
500m
200m
100m
0m
200m
500m
1000m
2000m
4000m
Trough
Scale 1:1 500 000
Projection: Lambert Conformal Conic
0 Kms
25
50
0 Miles
25

SOUTH-EAST FRANCE

196→197

186→187

CORSICA (France)

Corse (Corsica)

Same scale as main map

Mediterranean Sea

Ligurian Sea

Golfe du Lion

Sardegna (Italy)

ITALY

LOMBARDIA

PIEMONTE

VALLE D'AOSTA

HAUTE-SAVOIE

SAVOIE

ISÈRE

DRÔME

ARDÈCHE

RHÔNE

LOIRE

HAUTE-LOIRE

GARD

VAUCLUSE

BOUCHES-DU-RHÔNE

VAR

ALPES-MARITIMES

ALPES-DE-HAUTE-PROVENCE

HAUTES-ALPES

PROVENCE-ALPES-CÔTE D'AZUR

HAUTE-CORSE

CORSE-DU-SUD

Milano (Milan)

Torino (Turin)

Genève

Lyon

Grenoble

Chambéry

Annecy

Valence

St-Étienne

Marseille

Toulon

Nice

Cannes

Antibes

Monaco

Monte-Carlo

MONACO

Aix-en-Provence

Avignon

Nîmes

Arles

Montpellier

Cuneo

IMPERIA

San Remo

Bastia

Ajaccio

Calvi

Bonifacio

Porto-Vecchio

L'Île-Rousse

Bergamo

Brescia

Cremona

PARMA

MASSA-CARRARA

Novara

VERCELLI

BIELLA

Côte d'Azur

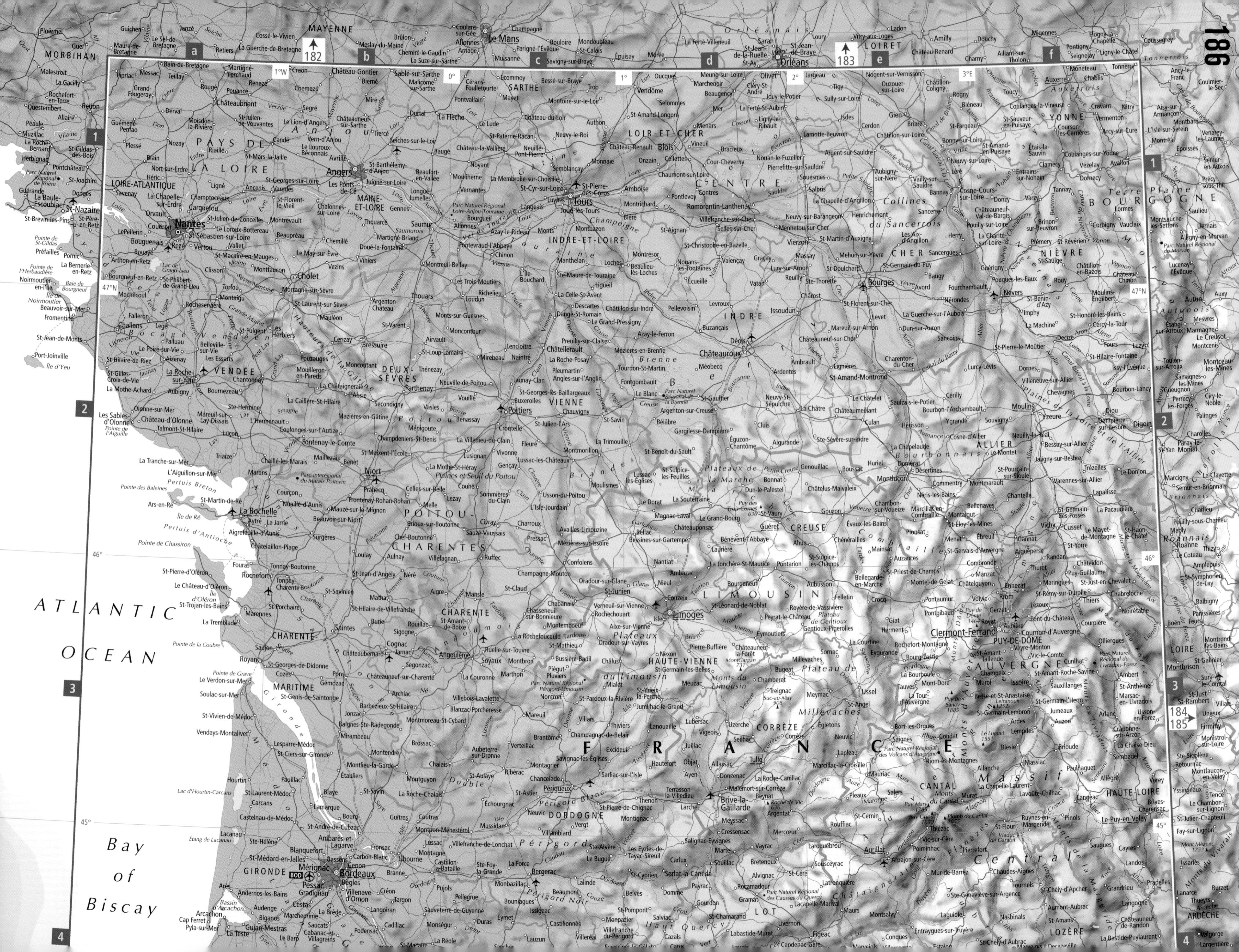
ATLANTIC OCEAN
Bay of Biscay
FRANCE
PAYS DE LA LOIRE
CENTRE
LIMOUSIN
AUVERGNE
POITOU-CHARENTES
Massif Central
BOURGOGNE
LOIRE-ATLANTIQUE
MAINE-ET-LOIRE
INDRE-ET-LOIRE
LOIR-ET-CHER
LOIRET
CHER
INDRE
NIÈVRE
ALLIER
CREUSE
HAUTE-VIENNE
CORRÈZE
PUY-DE-DÔME
CANTAL
HAUTE-LOIRE
LOZÈRE
VENDÉE
DEUX-SÈVRES
VIENNE
CHARENTE
CHARENTE-MARITIME
DORDOGNE
GIRONDE
LOT
SARTHE
MAYENNE
YONNE
MORBIHAN
LOIRE
ARDÈCHE
Nantes
Angers
Le Mans
Tours
Orléans
Blois
Bourges
Châteauroux
Poitiers
Limoges
Clermont-Ferrand
La Rochelle
Niort
Angoulême
Périgueux
Bordeaux
Nevers
Cholet
St-Nazaire
Brive-la-Gaillarde
Aurillac
Le Puy-en-Velay
182
183
184
185
47°N
46°
45°
1°W
0°
1°
2°
3°E
a
b
c
d
e
f
1
2
3
4

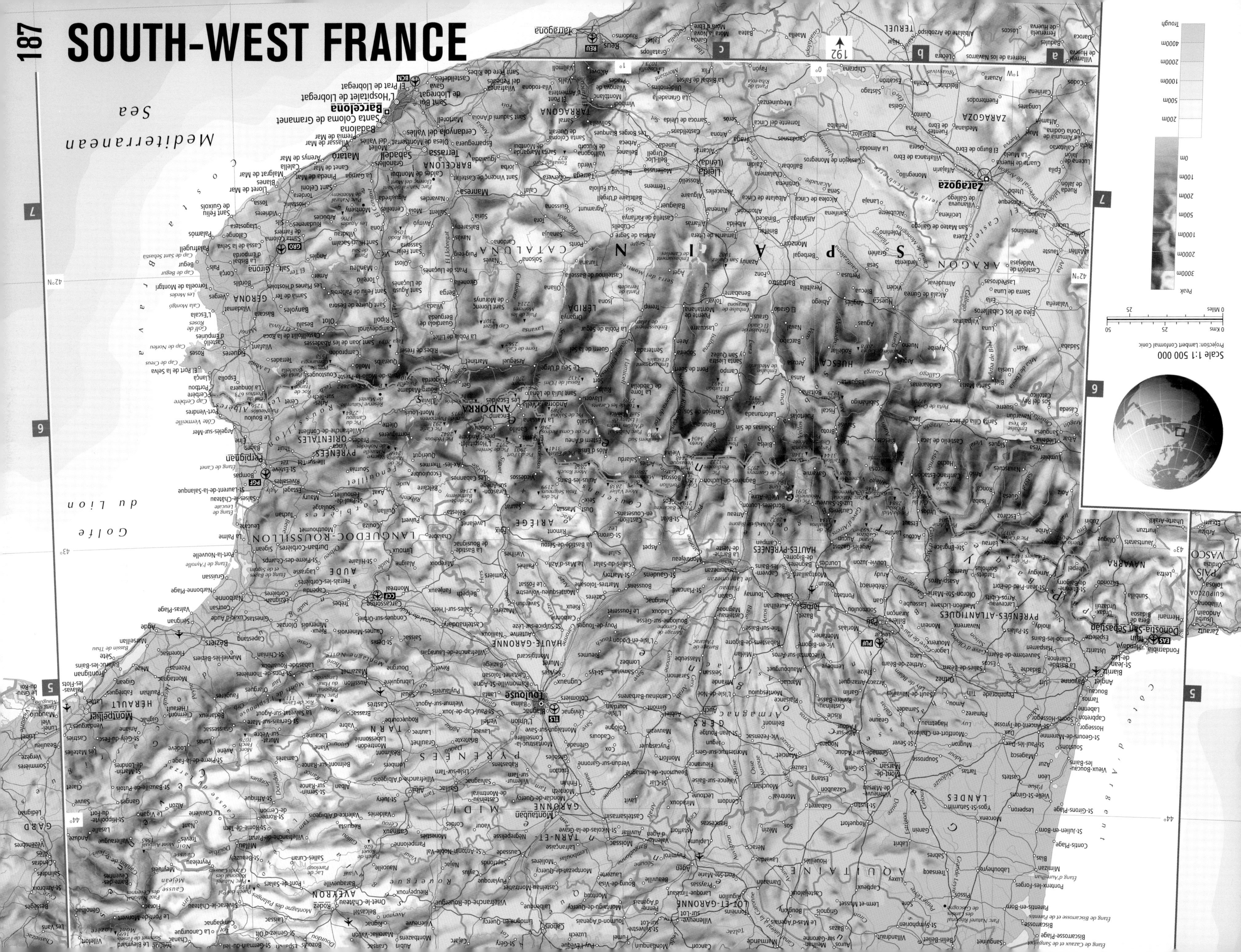

SOUTH-WEST FRANCE

Mediterranean Sea

Golfe du Lion

Scale 1:1 500 000
Projection: Lambert Conformal Conic

Bay of Biscay

Golfe de Gascogne

Costa Verde • Cornisa Cantabrica • Côte d'Argent

Rías Altas

Cabo Ortegal • Punta da Estaca de Bares • Cervo • Viveiro • Ribadeo • Navia • Luarca • Cudillero • Avilés • Candás • Villaviciosa • Ribadesella • Llanes • San Vicente de la Barquera • Santander • Cabo de Ajo • Santoña • Cabo Machichaco • Castro Urdiales • Donostia-San Sebastián • Bayonne • Biarritz • St-Jean-de-Luz • Hendaye

Cabo Prior • Cedeira • Ortigueira • Ferrol • Pontedeume • As Pontes de García Rodríguez • Mondoñedo • Embalse de Doiras • Pravia • Grado • OVD • Oviedo • Pola de Siero • Gijón • Luanco • Laredo • El Astillero • Portugalete • BIO • Bilbao • Barakaldo • Arizgoiti • Elgoibar • Azpeitia • Zarautz • Renteria • Irún

A Coruña/La Coruña • Cabo de San Adrián • Laxe • Camariñas • Betanzos • Ría de Betanzos • Lugo • Guitiriz • Belmonte • Mieres • Pola de Lena • Cangas del Narcea • Cabrales • Picos de Europa • Potes • Reinosa • Villasana de Mena • Llodio • Vitoria-Gasteiz • PAÍS VASCO • Zumarraga • Roncesvalles • Pamplona • NAVARRA • Estella

ATLANTIC OCEAN

PORTUGAL • SPAIN • Madrid • MAD

Vigo • Pontevedra • Ourense • Porto • OPO • Vila Nova de Gaia • Braga • Guimarães • Vila Real • Viseu • Coimbra • Aveiro • Leiria • Lisboa (Lisbon) • LIS • Setúbal • Évora • Badajoz • Mérida • Cáceres • Salamanca • Ávila • Segovia • Valladolid • Zamora • León • Burgos • Logroño • Palencia • Soria

Sevilla/Seville • SVQ • Córdoba • Jaén • Granada • GRX • Málaga • AGP • Cádiz • Huelva • Faro • FAO • Algeciras • Gibraltar (U.K.) • GIB • Almería • LEI • Murcia • Albacete • Ciudad Real • Toledo • Cuenca

Sierra Nevada • Mulhacén 3482m • Cordillera Penibética • Costa del Sol • Alborán Sea

Strait of Gibraltar • Ceuta (Spain) • Tánger (Tangiers) • TNG • Tétouan • Melilla (Spain) • Nador

MOROCCO

220

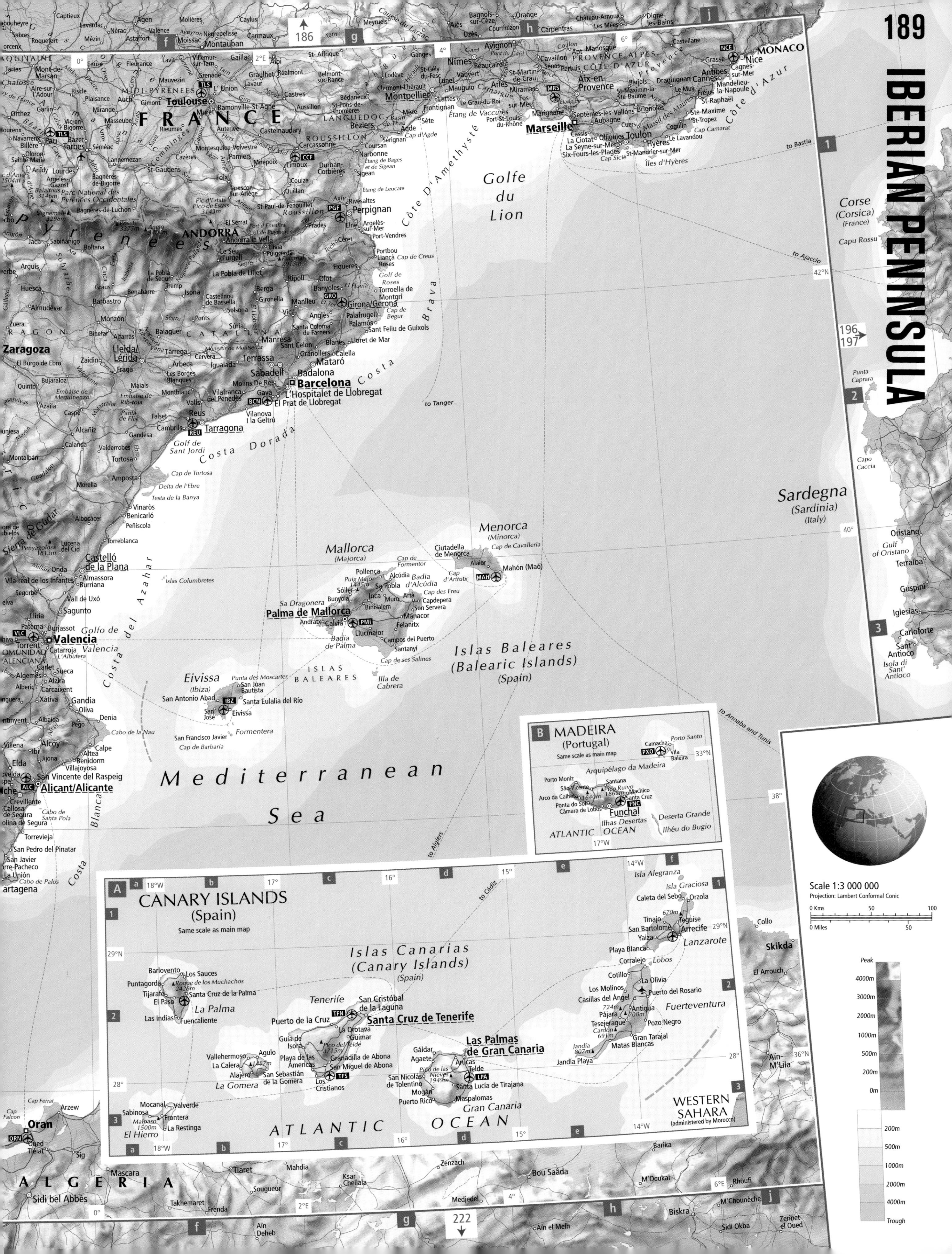

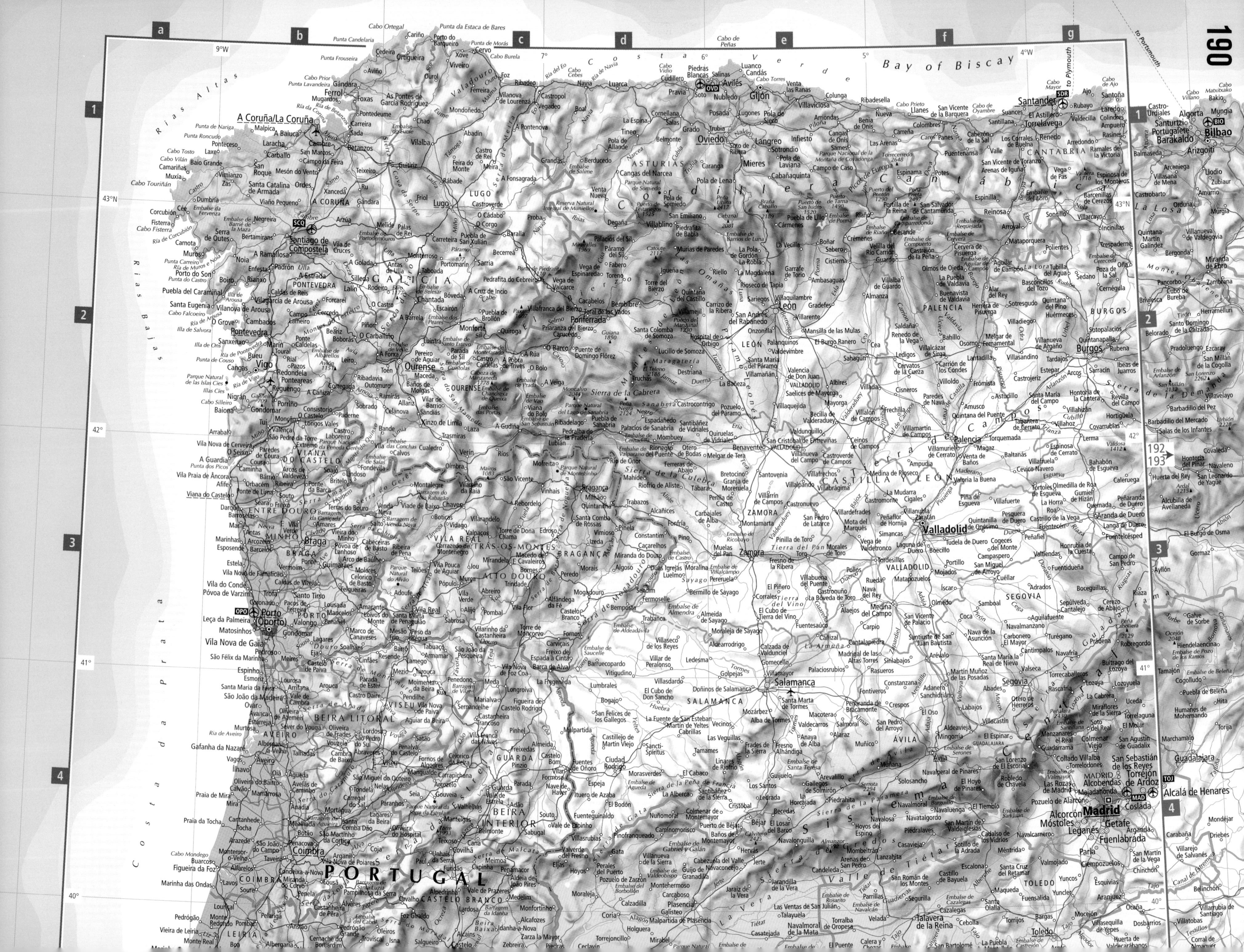

Bay of Biscay
Costa Verde
Cordillera Cantábrica
PORTUGAL
Rias Altas
Rias Bajas
Costa da Prata
to Portsmouth
to Plymouth
192
193
A Coruña/La Coruña
Santiago de Compostela
Oviedo
Gijón
Santander
Bilbao
León
Burgos
Palencia
Valladolid
Zamora
Salamanca
Segovia
Ávila
Madrid
Porto (Oporto)
Braga
Coimbra
Vigo
Ourense
Lugo
Pontevedra
Bragança
Viseu
Guadalajara
Alcalá de Henares
Toledo
Talavera de la Reina

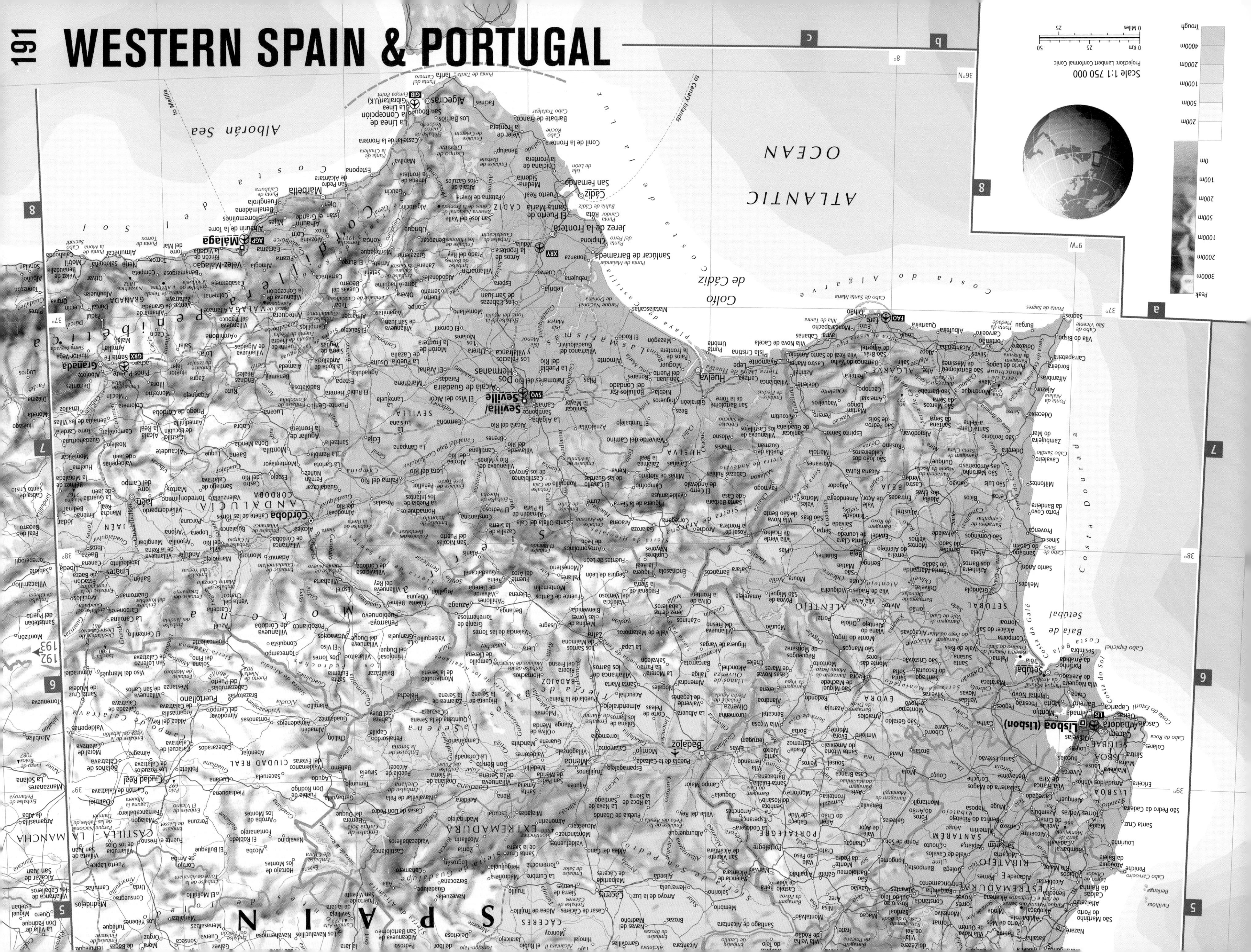

WESTERN SPAIN & PORTUGAL

Scale 1:1 750 000

Projection: Lambert Conformal Conic

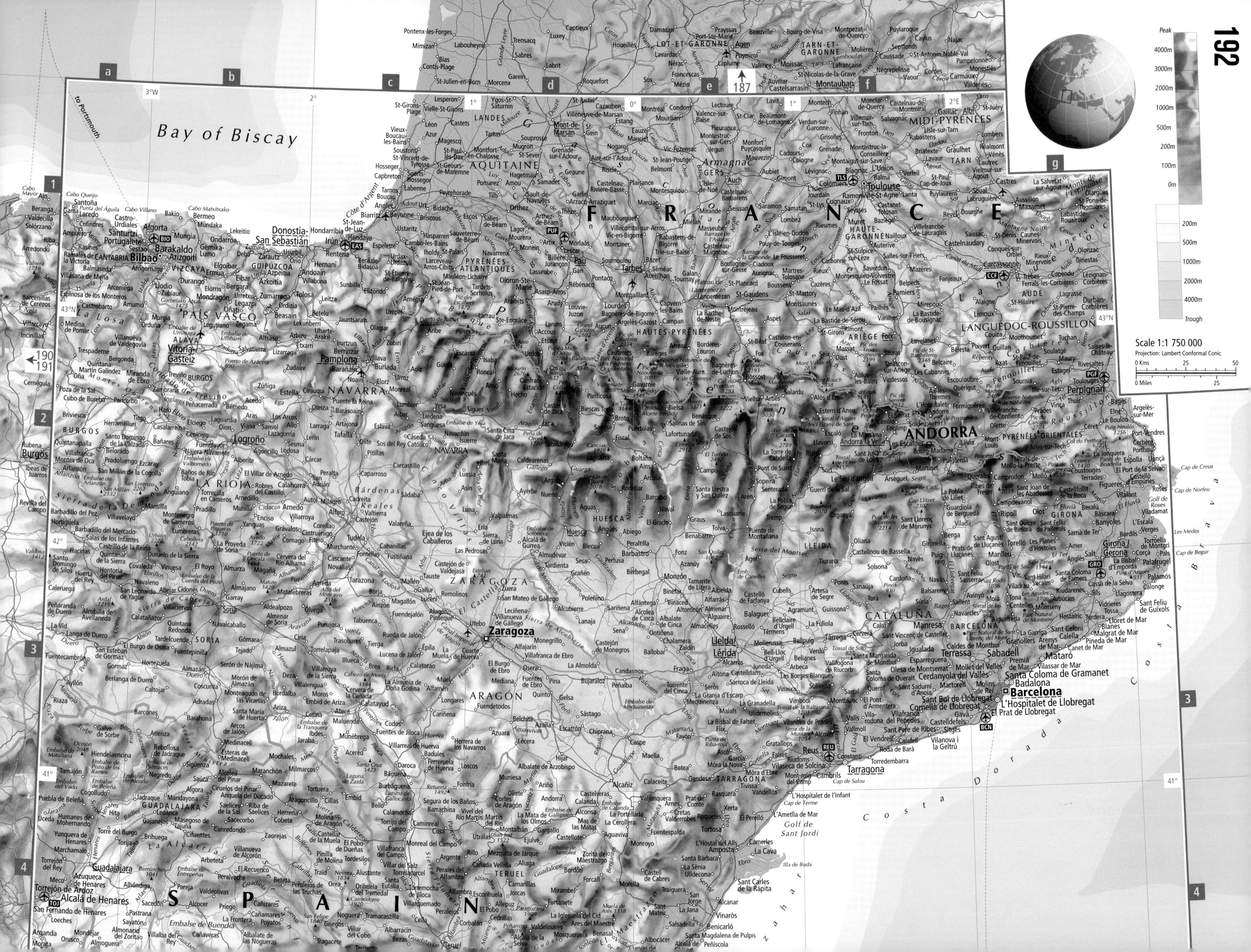
Peak
4000m
3000m
2000m
1000m
500m
200m
100m
0m
200m
500m
1000m
2000m
4000m
Trough
Scale 1:1 750 000
Projection: Lambert Conformal Conic
0 Kms 25 50
0 Miles 25
Bay of Biscay
to Portsmouth
F R A N C E
S P A I N
ANDORRA
AQUITAINE
MIDI-PYRÉNÉES
LANGUEDOC-ROUSSILLON
PYRÉNÉES-ORIENTALES
PYRÉNÉES-ATLANTIQUES
HAUTES-PYRÉNÉES
HAUTE-GARONNE
ARIÈGE
AUDE
TARN
GERS
LANDES
LOT-ET-GARONNE
TARN-ET-GARONNE
NAVARRA
PAÍS VASCO
LA RIOJA
ARAGÓN
CATALUÑA
HUESCA
ZARAGOZA
TERUEL
LLEIDA
GIRONA
BARCELONA
TARRAGONA
SORIA
BURGOS
GUADALAJARA
CANTABRIA
VIZCAYA
GUIPÚZCOA
ÁLAVA
Toulouse
Perpignan
Montauban
Carcassonne
Pau
Tarbes
Bayonne
Biarritz
Donostia-San Sebastián
Bilbao
Barakaldo
Vitoria-Gasteiz
Pamplona
Logroño
Zaragoza
Huesca
Lleida/Lérida
Girona/Gerona
Barcelona
Badalona
Santa Coloma de Gramanet
L'Hospitalet de Llobregat
El Prat de Llobregat
Tarragona
Reus
Mataró
Sabadell
Terrassa
Manresa
Burgos
Soria
Guadalajara
Alcalá de Henares
Torrejón de Ardoz
Andorra la Vella
Costa Brava
Costa Dorada
Golf de Sant Jordi
187
190
191

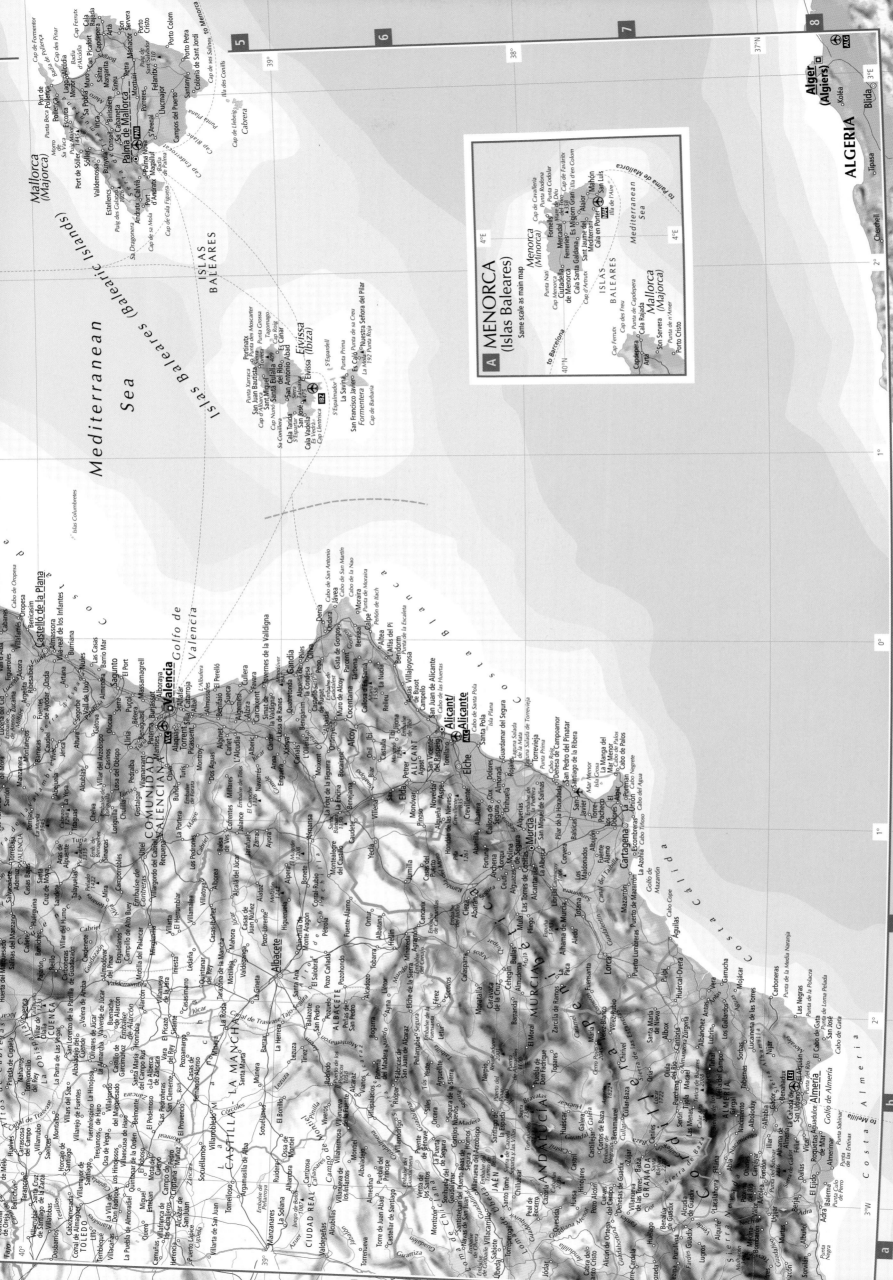

EASTERN SPAIN & THE BALEARICS

ALGERIA

Alger (Algiers)
Tipasa
Chechell
Kolëa
Blida
Cherchell

MENORCA (Islas Baleares)
Same scale as main map

Menorca (Minorca)

Cap de Cavalleria
Punta Nati
Cap Menorca
Ciutadella de Menorca
Ferreries
Cala Santa Galdana
Cap d'Artrutx
ISLAS BALEARES
Punta Prima
Cala en Porter
Maó
Mahón
San Luís
Illa de l'Aire
Punta Codolar
Cap de Favàritx
Illa d'en Colom
Es Migjorn Gran
Alaior
Mercadal
Monte Toro 358
Cap de Bajoli

Mallorca (Majorca)
Cap Ferrutx
Capdepera
Artá
Cala Rajada
Son Servera
Porto Cristo
Punta de Capdepera

Mediterranean Sea

Mallorca (Majorca)

Palma de Mallorca
Palma
Inca
Sóller
Manacor
Felanitx
Santanyí
Llucmajor
Campos del Puerto
Cabrera
Cap de ses Salines
Illa de Cabrera

ISLAS BALEARES

Islas Baleares (Balearic Islands)

Eivissa (Ibiza)
Sant Antoni de Portmany
Santa Eulària del Río
Eivissa (Ibiza)
Formentera
San Francisco Javier
Cap de Barbaria

Mediterranean Sea

COMUNIDAD VALENCIANA

Castelló de la Plana
Benicàssim
Borriana
Sagunto
Valencia
Gandía
Dénia
Xàbia
Calpe
Benidorm
Villajoyosa
Alicante
Elche
Santa Pola
Torrevieja

MURCIA

Murcia
Cartagena
Mazarrón
Águilas
Lorca

ALBACETE
Albacete

CASTILLA-LA MANCHA

ANDALUCÍA

Almería

188
189

200
201

CZECH REPUBLIC
SLOVAKIA
GERMANY
FRANCE
SWITZERLAND
LIECHTENSTEIN
AUSTRIA
HUNGARY
SLOVENIA
CROATIA
BOSNIA HERZEGOVINA
CRNA GORA
ITALY
SAN MARINO
MONACO
Corse (Corsica) (France)
Ligurian Sea
Adriatic Sea
Gulf of Venice
Gulf of Trieste

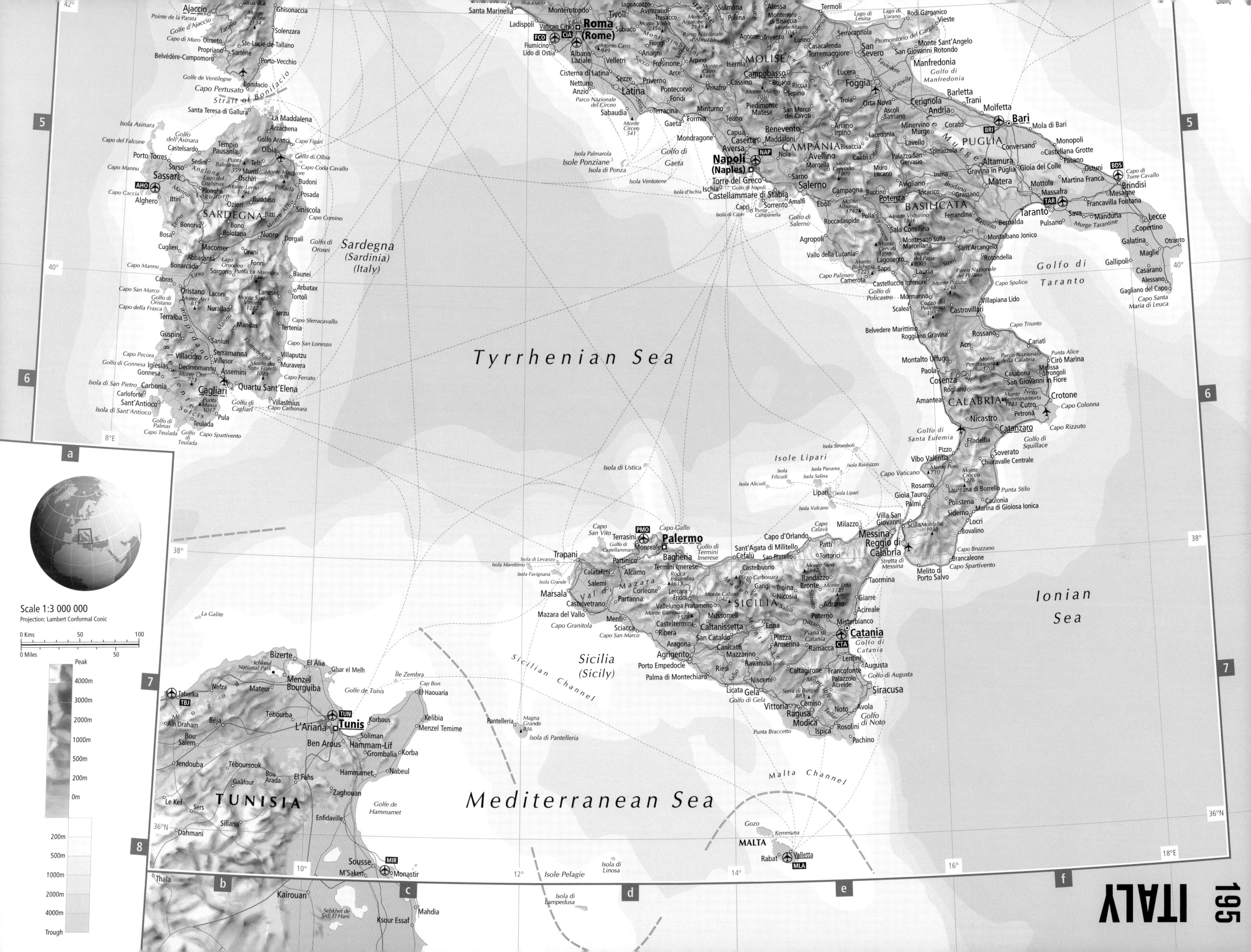

18°E

38°

f

16°

Ionian

Sea

e

14°

MALTA
Valletta
Rabat
Kemmuna
Gozo

d

Isola di
Linosa

Isole Pelagie

Isola di
Lampedusa

c

Mediterranean Sea

12°

b

36°N

a

8

7

Scale 1:3 000 000
Projection: Lambert Conformal Conic

0 Kms   100

0 Miles   50

Peak
4000m
3000m
2000m
1000m
500m
200m
0m

200m
500m
1000m
2000m
4000m
Trough

5

7

6

Roma
(Rome)

Vatican City

Napoli
(Naples)

Tyrrhenian Sea

Sardegna
(Sardinia) (Italy)

SARDEGNA

Cagliari

Sassari

Bari

PUGLIA

BASILICATA

CAMPANIA

MOLISE

Brindisi

Lecce

Golfo di
Taranto

Taranto

Potenza

Salerno

CALABRIA

Catanzaro

Crotone

Reggio di
Calabria

Messina

Palermo

Catania

Siracusa

SICILIA
(Sicily)

Sicilian Channel

Malta Channel

TUNISIA

Tunis

Sousse

Monastir

Bizerte

40°

38°

10°

36°N

5

6

7

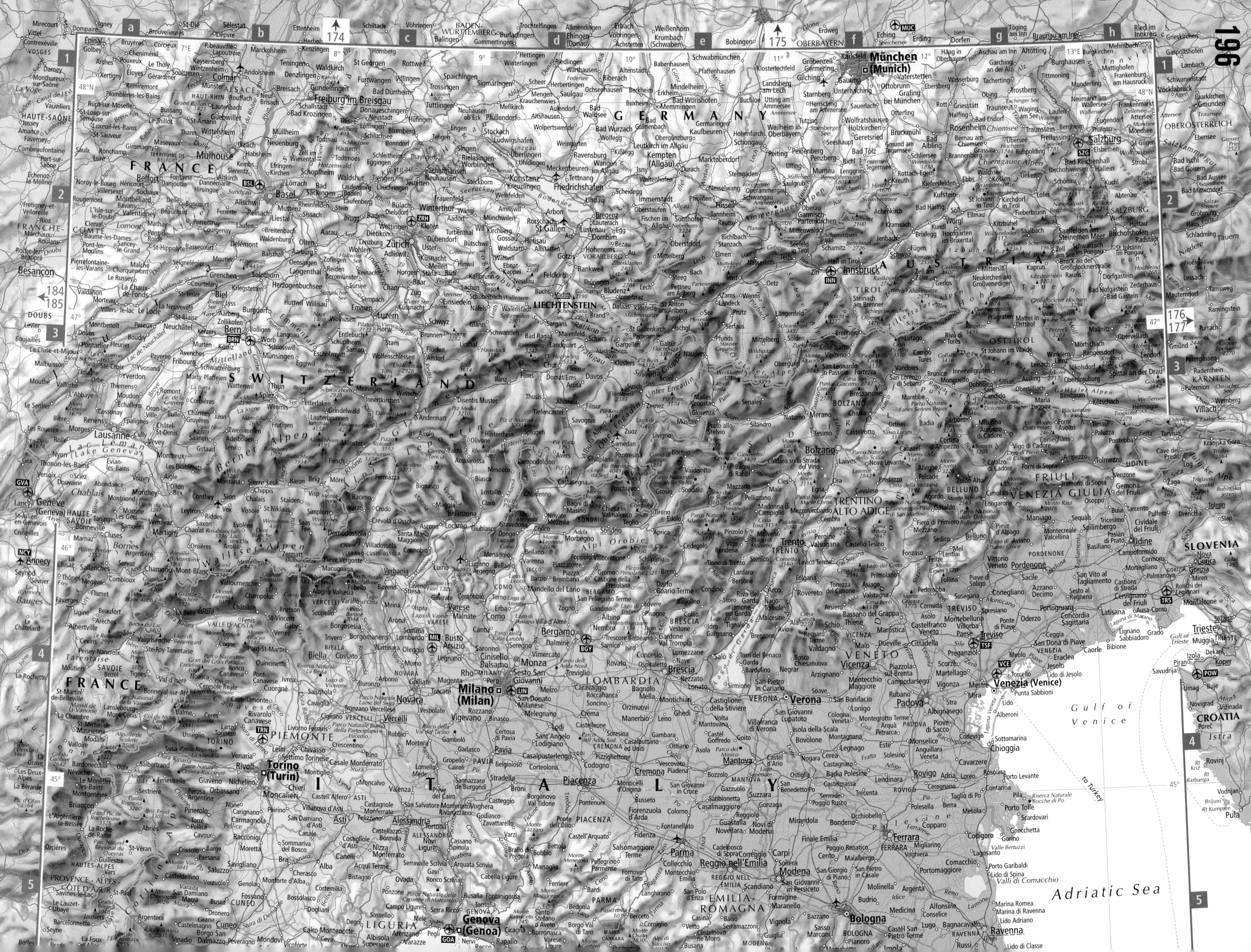
GERMANY
FRANCE
SWITZERLAND
AUSTRIA
LIECHTENSTEIN
ITALY
SLOVENIA
CROATIA
Adriatic Sea
Gulf of Venice
Gulf of Trieste
München (Munich)
Zürich
Basel
Bern
Luzern
Lausanne
Genève (Geneva)
Innsbruck
Salzburg
Bolzano
Trento
Verona
Vicenza
Padova
Venezia (Venice)
Treviso
Trieste
Udine
Milano (Milan)
Bergamo
Brescia
Torino (Turin)
Genova (Genoa)
Bologna
Modena
Parma
Piacenza
Cremona
Mantova
Ferrara
Ravenna
Novara
Pavia
Alessandria
Mulhouse
Besançon
Freiburg im Breisgau
Kempten (Allgäu)
Rosenheim
Annecy
TRENTINO ALTO ADIGE
VENETO
LOMBARDIA
PIEMONTE
EMILIA-ROMAGNA
LIGURIA
FRIULI-VENEZIA GIULIA
TIROL
VORARLBERG
OBERBAYERN
BADEN WÜRTTEMBERG
to Turkey
174
175
176
177
184
185

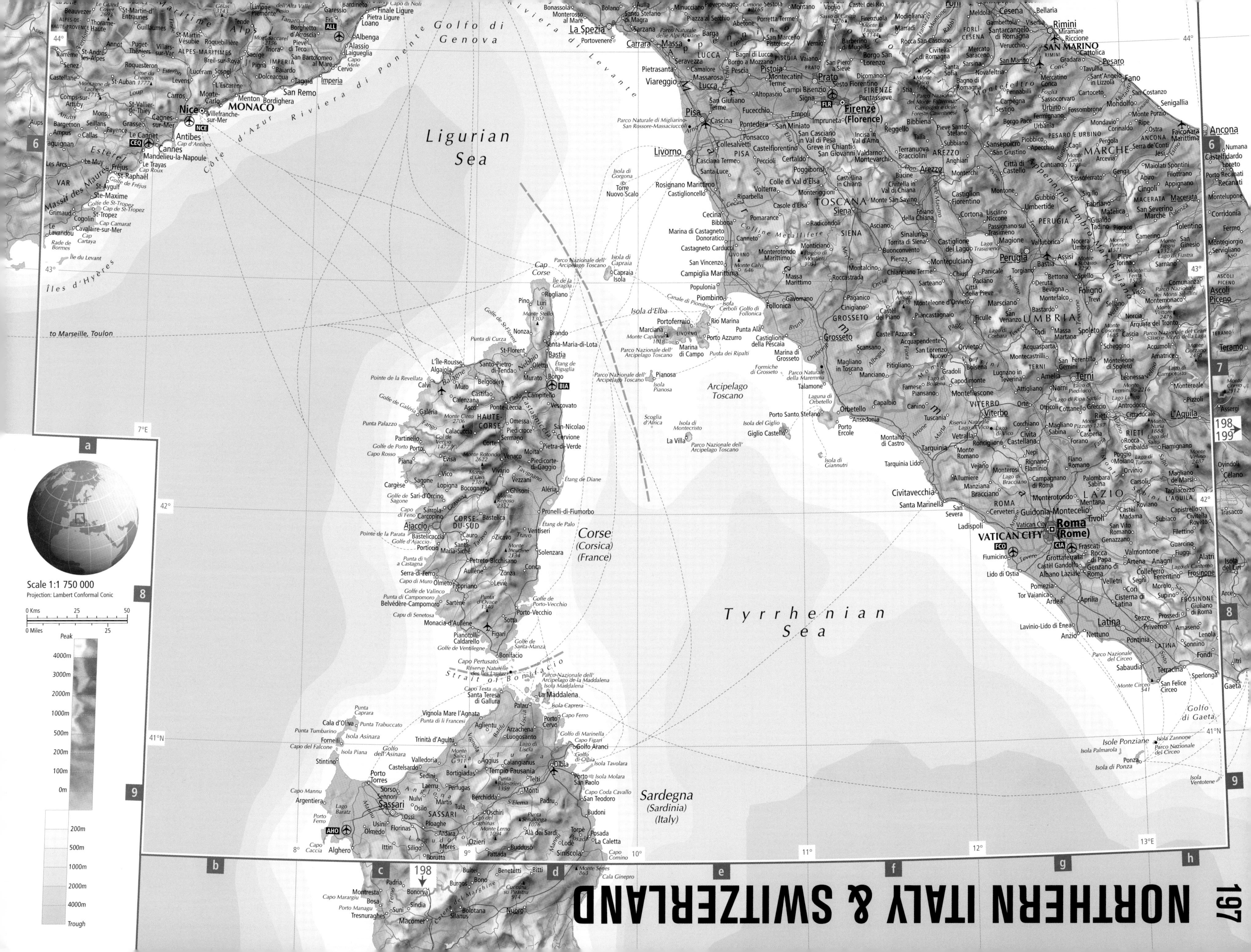

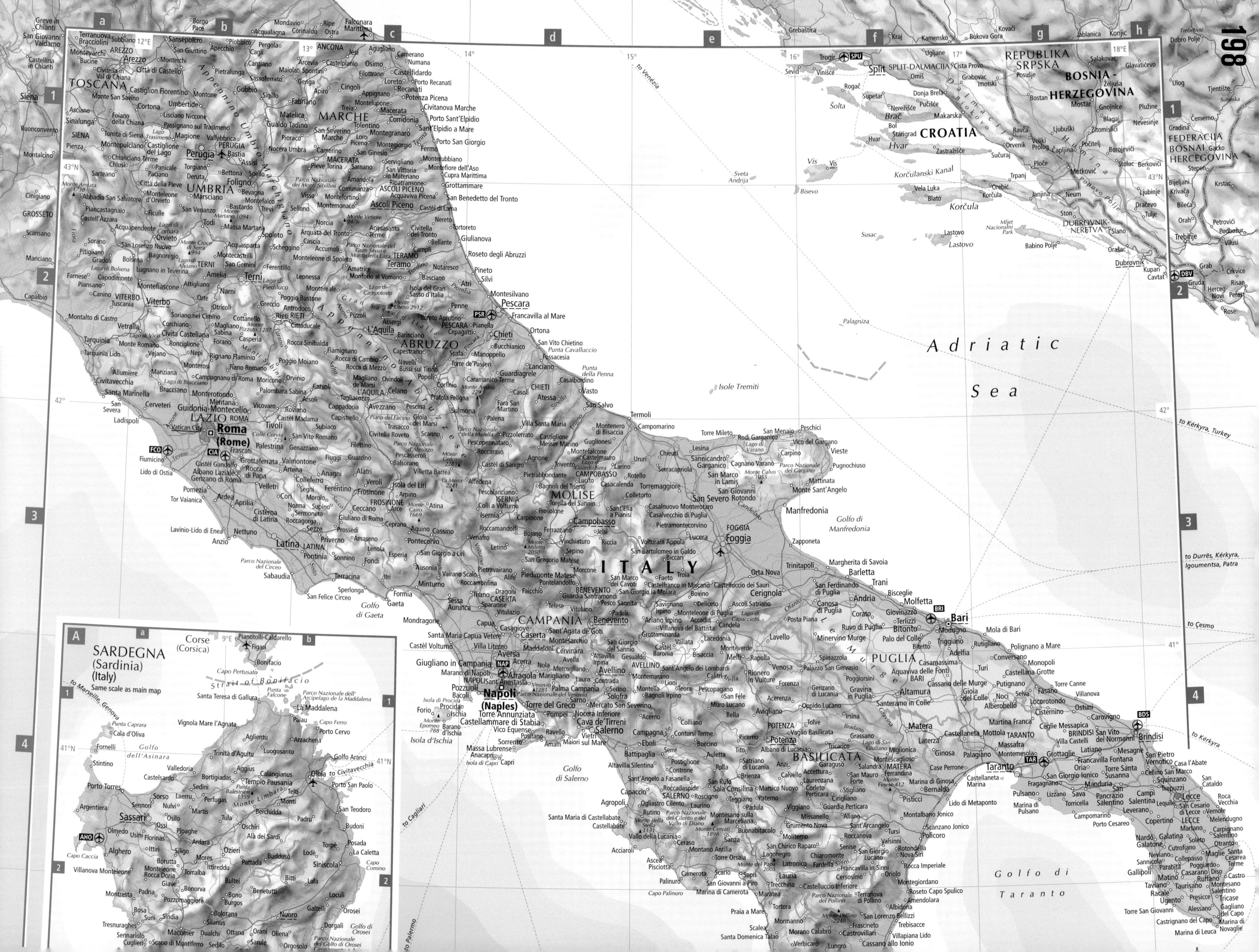

Adriatic Sea
ITALY
CROATIA
BOSNIA-HERZEGOVINA
REPUBLIKA SRPSKA
FEDERACIJA BOSNAI HERCEGOVINA
HERZEGOVINA
SPLIT-DALMACIJA
DUBROVNIK-NERETVA
TOSCANA
UMBRIA
MARCHE
LAZIO
ABRUZZO
MOLISE
CAMPANIA
PUGLIA
BASILICATA
Roma (Rome)
Napoli (Naples)
Bari
Pescara
Foggia
Taranto
Brindisi
Lecce
Ancona
Perugia
Split
Dubrovnik
Golfo di Manfredonia
Golfo di Gaeta
Golfo di Salerno
Golfo di Taranto
Isole Tremiti
to Venézia
to Durrës, Kérkyra, Igoumentsa, Patra
to Çesmo
to Kérkyra, Turkey
to Kérkyra
to Cagliari
to Palermo
SARDEGNA (Sardinia) (Italy)
Same scale as main map
Corse (Corsica)
Strait of Bonifacio
to Marseille, Genova
Golfo dell'Asinara

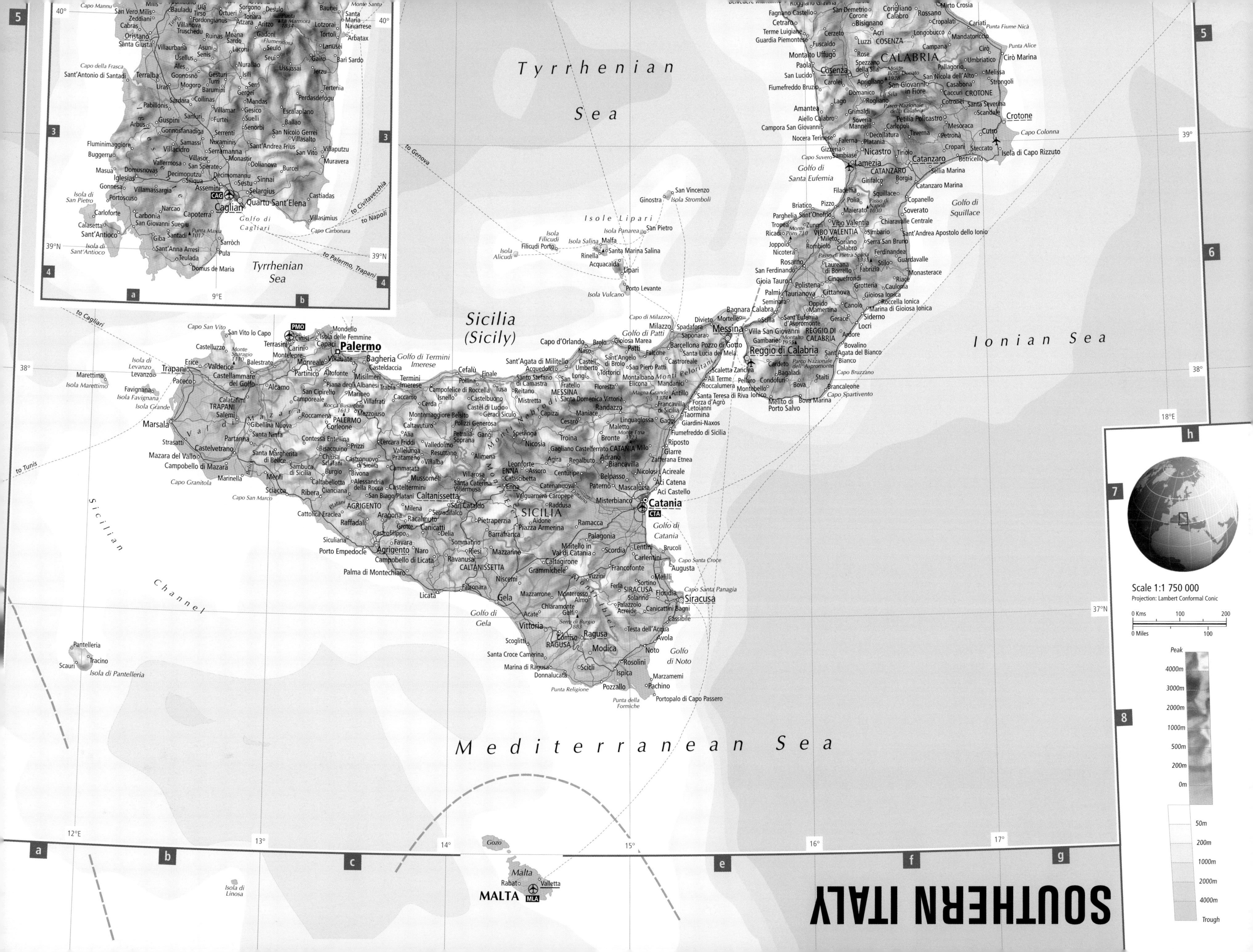

SOUTHERN ITALY

Scale 1:1 750 000
Projection: Lambert Conformal Conic

Tyrrhenian Sea

Ionian Sea

Mediterranean Sea

Sicilian Channel

Sicilia (Sicily)

Isole Lipari

CALABRIA

Catanzaro

Cosenza

Crotone

Reggio di Calabria

Messina

Catania

Siracusa

RAGUSA

PALERMO

Trapani

Marsala

AGRIGENTO

CALTANISSETTA

ENNA

MALTA
Valletta

Cagliari

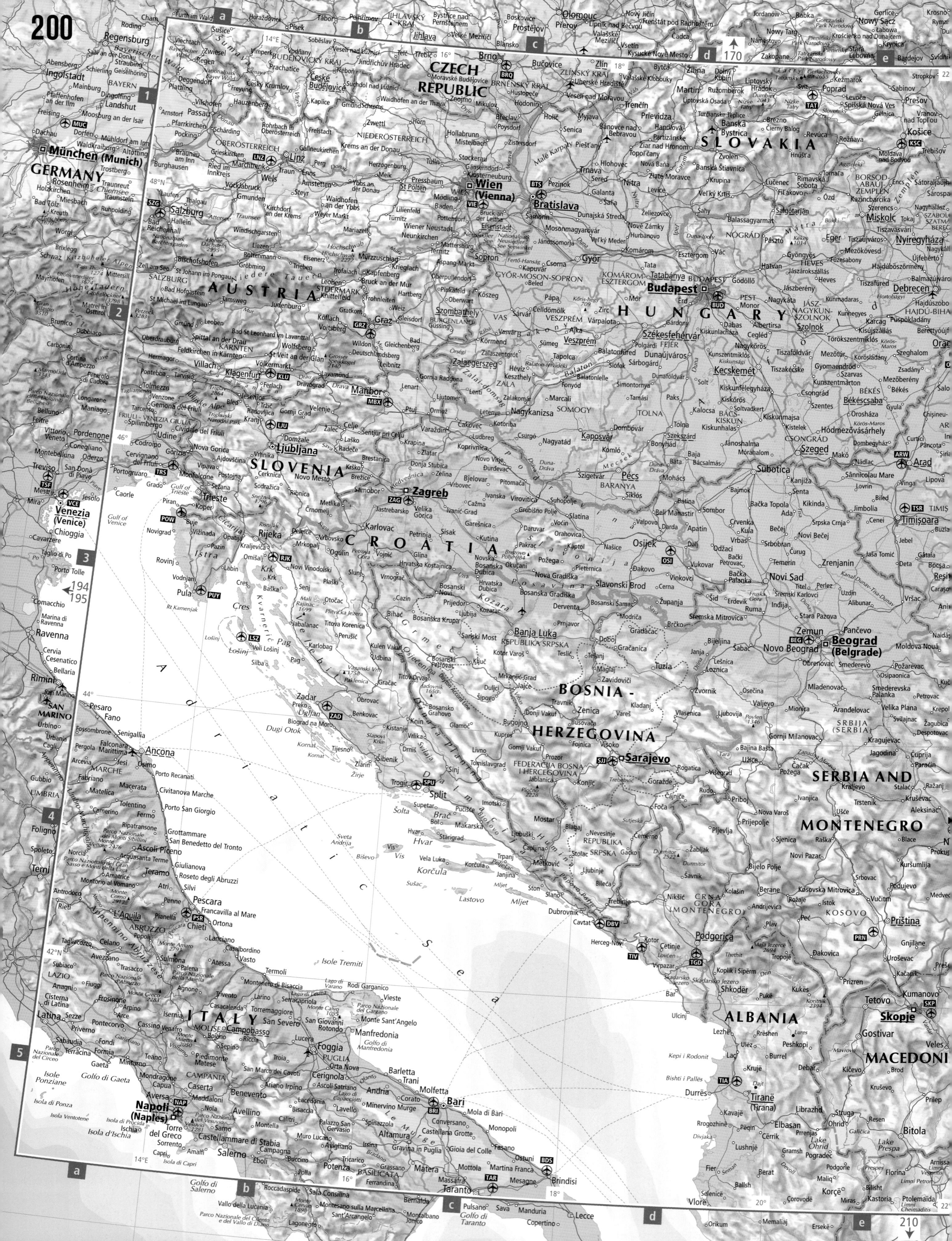

a
b
c
d
e
170
1
2
3
4
5
194
195
210
CZECH REPUBLIC
SLOVAKIA
AUSTRIA
GERMANY
HUNGARY
SLOVENIA
CROATIA
BOSNIA - HERZEGOVINA
SERBIA AND MONTENEGRO
ALBANIA
MACEDONI
ITALY
SAN MARINO
Adriatic Sea
München (Munich)
Regensburg
Ingolstadt
Landshut
Passau
Salzburg
Linz
Wien (Vienna)
Bratislava
Brno
Olomouc
Budapest
Graz
Klagenfurt
Ljubljana
Maribor
Zagreb
Rijeka
Trieste
Venezia (Venice)
Pula
Zadar
Split
Banja Luka
Sarajevo
Dubrovnik
Podgorica
Beograd (Belgrade)
Novi Sad
Osijek
Szeged
Pécs
Debrecen
Miskolc
Košice
Nyíregyháza
Timişoara
Arad
Subotica
Priština
Skopje
Tiranë (Tirana)
Durrës
Shkodër
Bitola
Ohrid
Bari
Brindisi
Taranto
Foggia
Napoli (Naples)
Pescara
Ancona
Rimini
Ravenna
Kecskemét
Győr
Székesfehérvár
Veszprém
Szombathely
Nitra
Trnava
Žilina
Poprad
Zlín
Prešov

SOUTHERN CENTRAL EUROPE

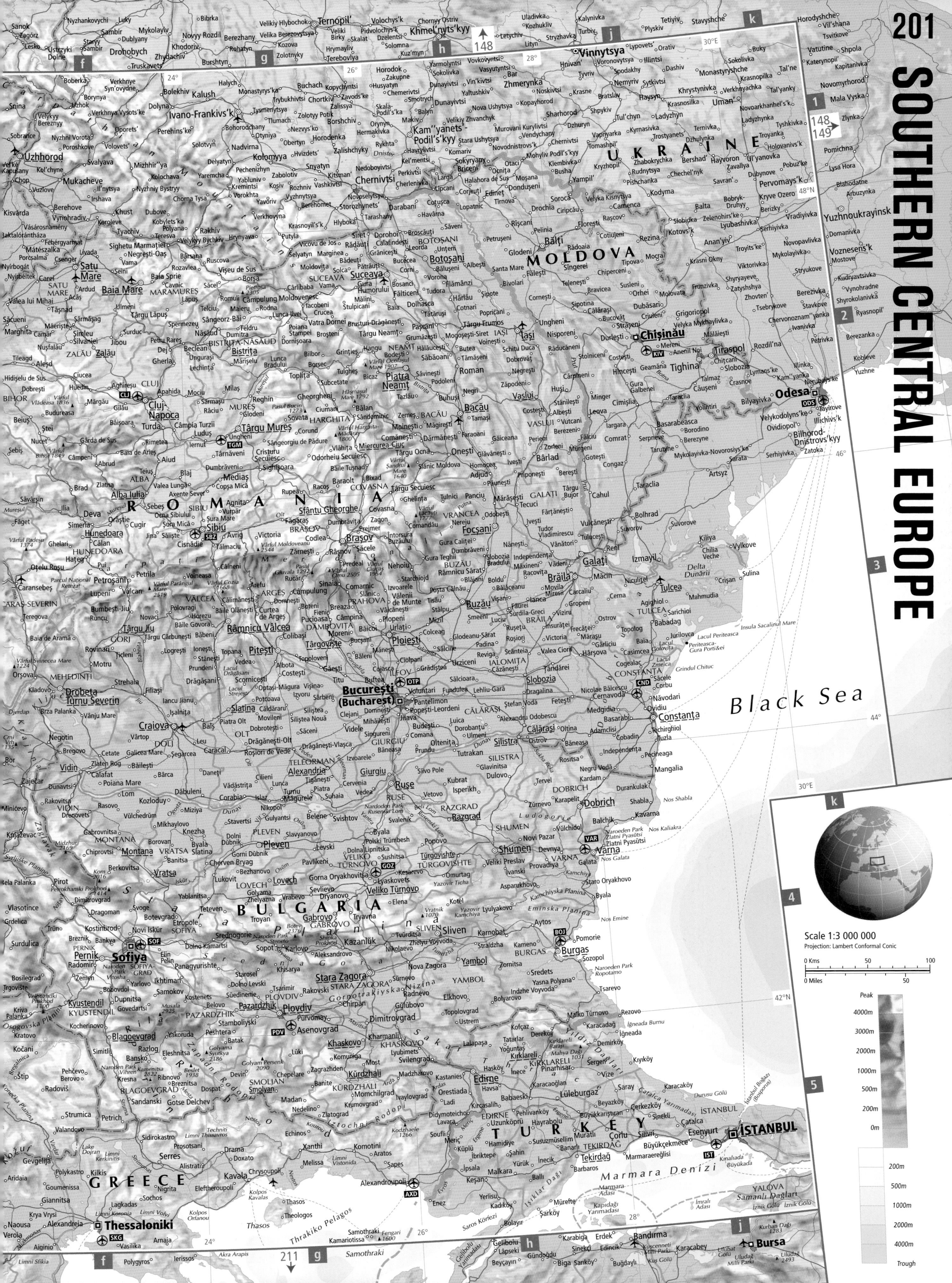

148
148 149
211

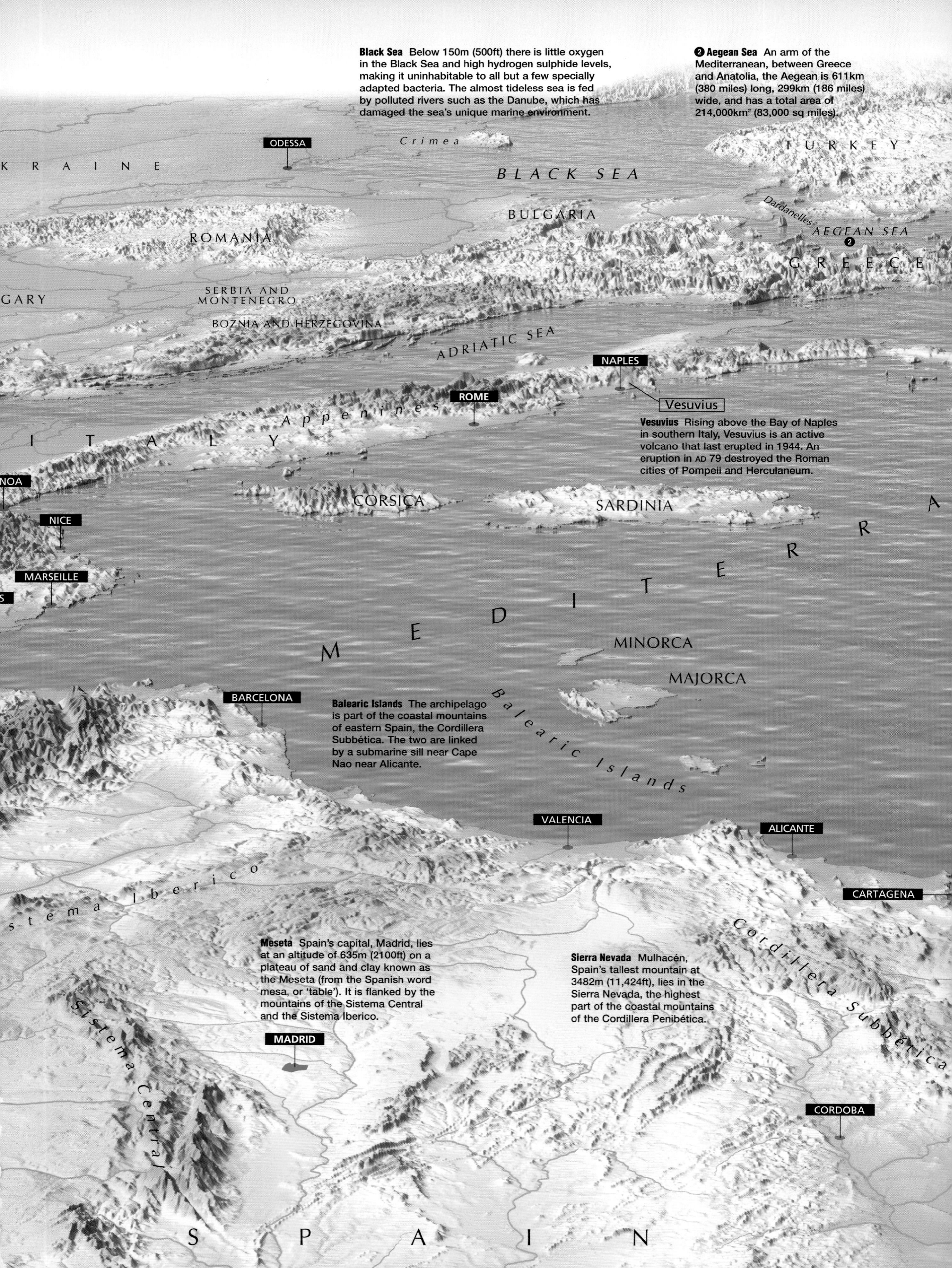

Black Sea Below 150m (500ft) there is little oxygen in the Black Sea and high hydrogen sulphide levels, making it uninhabitable to all but a few specially adapted bacteria. The almost tideless sea is fed by polluted rivers such as the Danube, which has damaged the sea's unique marine environment.

② Aegean Sea An arm of the Mediterranean, between Greece and Anatolia, the Aegean is 611km (380 miles) long, 299km (186 miles) wide, and has a total area of 214,000km² (83,000 sq miles).

ODESSA

Crimea

BLACK SEA

K R A I N E

ROMANIA

BULGARIA

T U R K E Y

Dardanelles

AEGEAN SEA
②

SERBIA AND MONTENEGRO

GARY

BOZNIA AND HERZEGOVINA

G R E E C E

ADRIATIC SEA

NAPLES

ROME

Vesuvius

Vesuvius Rising above the Bay of Naples in southern Italy, Vesuvius is an active volcano that last erupted in 1944. An eruption in AD 79 destroyed the Roman cities of Pompeii and Herculaneum.

I T A L Y

Appenines

NOA

CORSICA

SARDINIA

M E D I T E R R A

NICE

MARSEILLE

M E D I T E R R A

MINORCA

MAJORCA

BARCELONA

Balearic Islands The archipelago is part of the coastal mountains of eastern Spain, the Cordillera Subbética. The two are linked by a submarine sill near Cape Nao near Alicante.

Balearic Islands

Sistema Iberico

VALENCIA

ALICANTE

CARTAGENA

Cordillera Subbética

Meseta Spain's capital, Madrid, lies at an altitude of 635m (2100ft) on a plateau of sand and clay known as the Meseta (from the Spanish word mesa, or 'table'). It is flanked by the mountains of the Sistema Central and the Sistema Iberico.

Sierra Nevada Mulhacén, Spain's tallest mountain at 3482m (11,424ft), lies in the Sierra Nevada, the highest part of the coastal mountains of the Cordillera Penibética.

Sistema Central

MADRID

CORDOBA

S P A I N

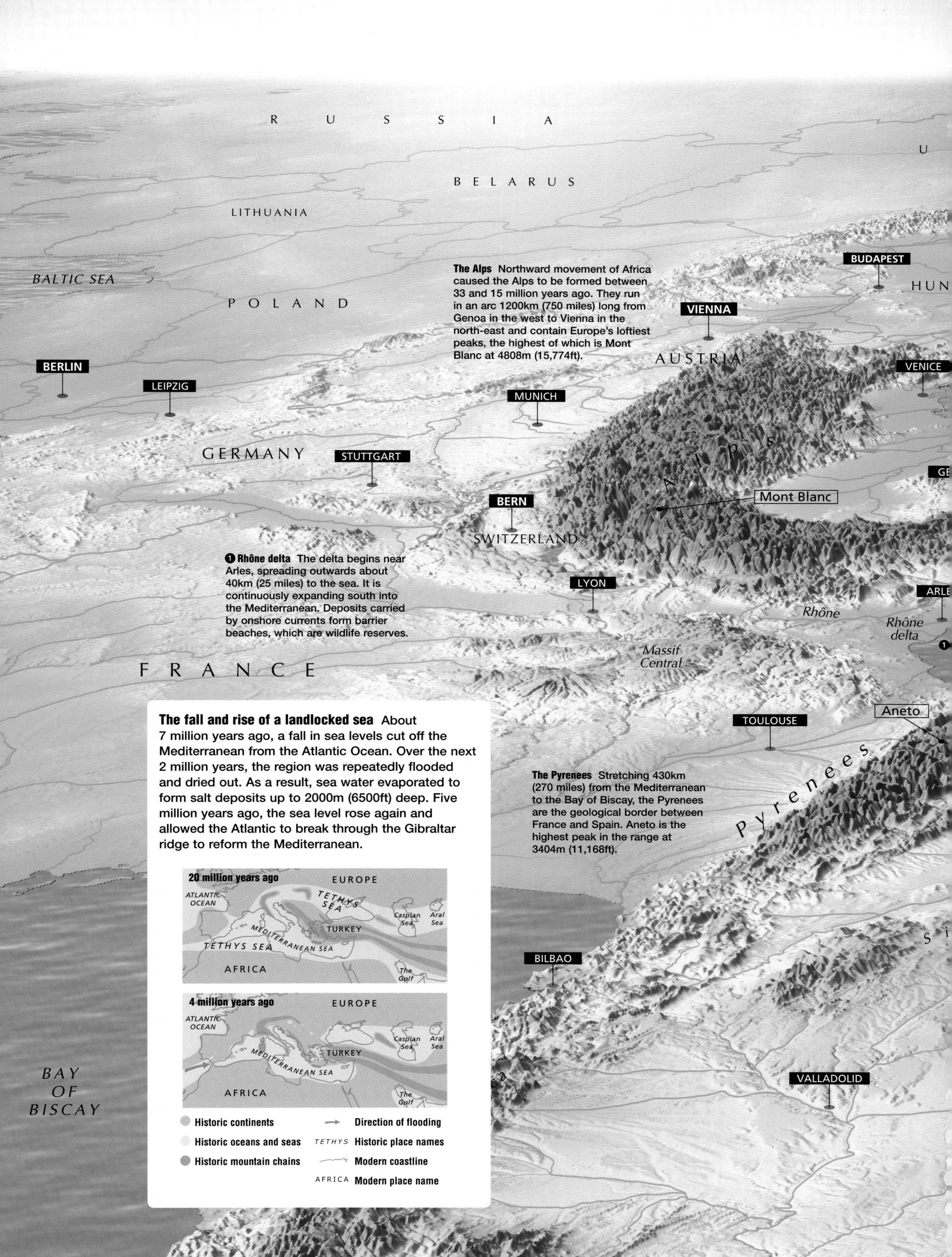

R U S S I A

U

B E L A R U S

LITHUANIA

BALTIC SEA

P O L A N D

The Alps Northward movement of Africa caused the Alps to be formed between 33 and 15 million years ago. They run in an arc 1200km (750 miles) long from Genoa in the west to Vienna in the north-east and contain Europe's loftiest peaks, the highest of which is Mont Blanc at 4808m (15,774ft).

BUDAPEST

HUN

VIENNA

A U S T R I A

VENICE

BERLIN

LEIPZIG

MUNICH

GERMANY

STUTTGART

A l p s

GE

BERN

Mont Blanc

SWITZERLAND

❶ **Rhône delta** The delta begins near Arles, spreading outwards about 40km (25 miles) to the sea. It is continuously expanding into the Mediterranean. Deposits carried by onshore currents form barrier beaches, which are wildlife reserves.

LYON

ARLE

Rhône

Rhône delta

F R A N C E

Massif Central

❶

TOULOUSE

Aneto

The fall and rise of a landlocked sea About 7 million years ago, a fall in sea levels cut off the Mediterranean from the Atlantic Ocean. Over the next 2 million years, the region was repeatedly flooded and dried out. As a result, sea water evaporated to form salt deposits up to 2000m (6500ft) deep. Five million years ago, the sea level rose again and allowed the Atlantic to break through the Gibraltar ridge to reform the Mediterranean.

The Pyrenees Stretching 430km (270 miles) from the Mediterranean to the Bay of Biscay, the Pyrenees are the geological border between France and Spain. Aneto is the highest peak in the range at 3404m (11,168ft).

P y r e n e e s

20 million years ago   EUROPE

ATLANTIC OCEAN

T E T H Y S SEA

Caspian Sea   Aral Sea

TURKEY

MEDITERRANEAN SEA

T E T H Y S   S E A

AFRICA

The Gulf

4 million years ago   EUROPE

ATLANTIC OCEAN

Caspian Sea   Aral Sea

TURKEY

MEDITERRANEAN SEA

AFRICA

The Gulf

BILBAO

S

● Historic continents   → Direction of flooding

○ Historic oceans and seas   *TETHYS* Historic place names

● Historic mountain chains   ⌒ Modern coastline

                                          AFRICA Modern place name

BAY OF BISCAY

VALLADOLID

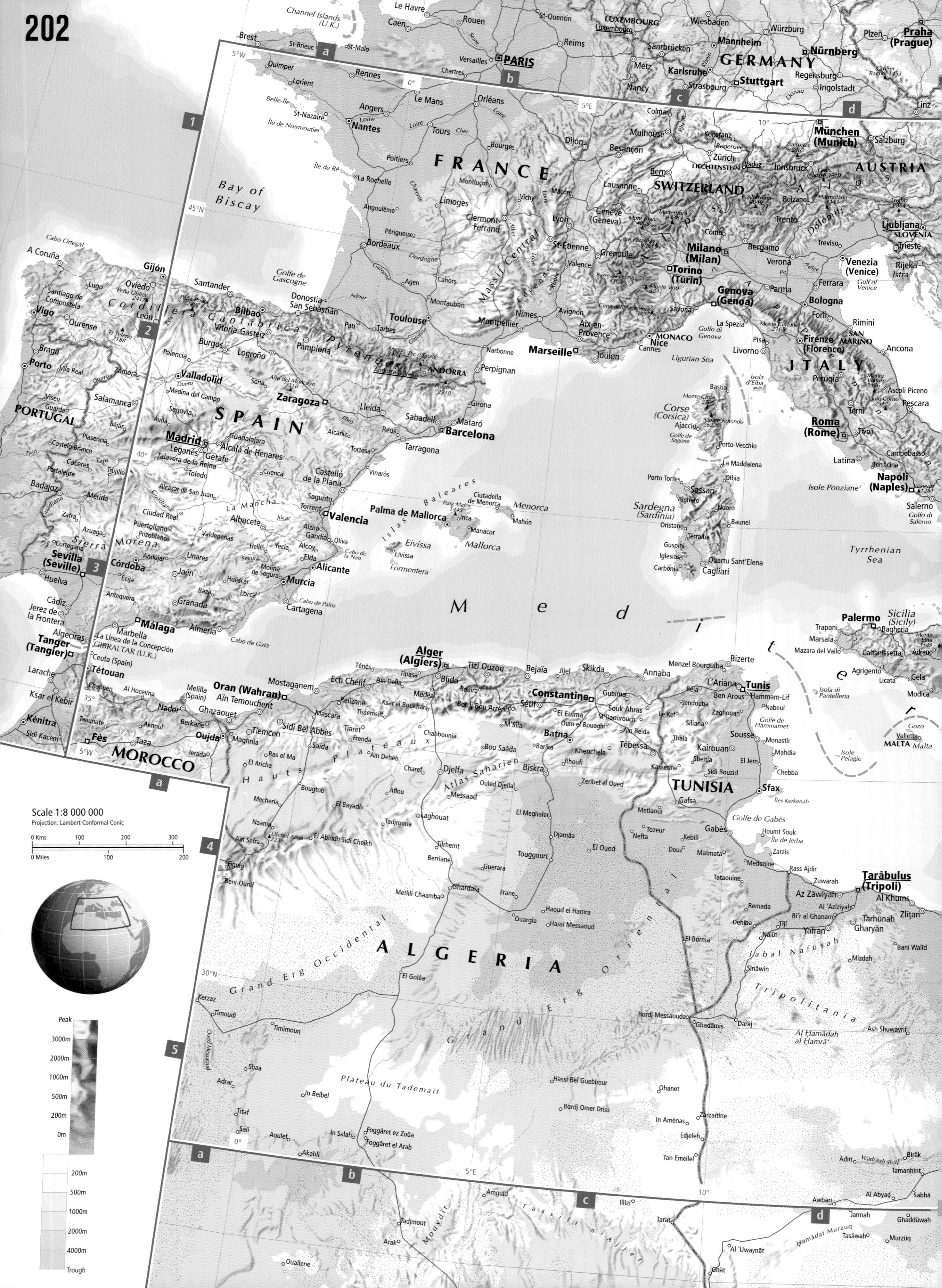

Channel Islands (U.K.)
Le Havre
LUXEMBOURG
Wiesbaden
Würzburg
Plzeň
Praha (Prague)
Brest
St-Brieuc
St-Malo
Caen
Rouen
St-Quentin
Luxembourg
Mannheim
Nürnberg
GERMANY
Linz
Quimper
Rennes
Versailles
PARIS
Reims
Metz
Saarbrücken
Karlsruhe
Stuttgart
Regensburg
Ingolstadt
Lorient
Le Mans
Chartres
Nancy
Strasbourg
Großer
Rachel 1453
Belle-Île
Angers
Orléans
Colmar
Rhein
Donau
München (Munich)
Salzburg
Nantes
Tours
Loire
Mulhouse
Konstanz
Bodensee
Zugspitze
2962
AUSTRIA
Île de Noirmoutier
Poitiers
Cher
Bourges
Dijon
Besançon
Zürich
Innsbruck
Bolzano
Ljubljana
SLOVENIA
La Rochelle
Île de Ré
Limoges
Vichy
Allier
LIECHTENSTEIN
Vaduz
Dolomiti
Treviso
Rijeka
Istria
Trieste
Bay of Biscay
Angoulême
Clermont-Ferrand
St-Étienne
Lausanne
SWITZERLAND
Bern
Bergamo
Verona
Venezia (Venice)
Gulf of Venice
Bordeaux
Périgueux
Lyon
Genève (Geneva)
Mont Blanc
Milano (Milan)
Parma
Ferrara
Bologna
Forlì
Rimini
A Coruña
Cabo Ortegal
Gijón
Santander
Golfe de Gascogne
Agen
Montauban
Valence
Grenoble
Torino (Turin)
Genova (Genoa)
La Spezia
Savona
Firenze (Florence)
SAN MARINO
Ancona
Vigo
Oviedo
Peña Ubiña
2417
Cordillera Cantábrica
Donostia-San Sebastián
Pau
Tarbes
Nîmes
Avignon
MONACO
Nice
Cannes
Golfo di Genova
Livorno
Perugia
Ascoli Piceno
Ourense
León
Bilbao
Vitoria-Gasteiz
Pamplona
Montpellier
Aix-en-Provence
Ligurian Sea
Bastia
ITALY
Braga
Porto
Burgos
Logroño
Pyrenees
Narbonne
Marseille
Toulon
Corse (Corsica)
Ajaccio
Isola d'Elba
Monte Cimone 2165
Terni
Pescara
Vila Real
Zamora
Palencia
Soria
Zaragoza
Lleida
Perpignan
ANDORRA
Andorra la Vella
Girona
Golfe de Sagone
Porto-Vecchio
Roma (Rome)
Tivoli
Viseu
Salamanca
Valladolid
Medina del Campo
Duero
SPAIN
Sabadell
Mataró
Barcelona
Porto Torres
Sassari
La Maddalena
Latina
PORTUGAL
Guarda
Ávila
Madrid
Alcalá de Henares
Castelló de la Plana
Tarragona
Olbia
Campobasso
Castelo Branco
Plasencia
Trujillo
Leganés
Getafe
Cuenca
Sagunto
Vinaròs
Reus
Sardegna (Sardinia)
Nuoro
Napoli (Naples)
Isole Ponziane
Cáceres
Portalegre
Toledo
Talavera de la Reina
Albacete
Valencia
Torrent
Baleares
Ciutadella de Menorca
Menorca
Oristano
Baunei
Badajoz
Mérida
Guadiana
Ciudad Real
Júcar
Alzira
Gandía
Palma de Mallorca
Inca
Manacor
Mahón
Terralba
Salerno
Golfo di Salerno
Zafra
Azuaga
Pozoblanco
Andújar
Linares
Alcoy
Elda
Eivissa
Mallorca
Guspini
Iglesias
Carbonia
Sevilla (Seville)
Córdoba
Jaén
Hellín
Yecla
Alicante
Islas
Eivissa
Formentera
Quartu Sant'Elena
Cagliari
Tyrrhenian Sea
Huelva
Sierra Morena
Baza
Huéscar
Murcia
Palermo
Sicilia (Sicily)
Bagheria
Cádiz
Jerez de la Frontera
Granada
Lorca
Cartagena
Cabo de Palos
Trapani
Marsala
Caltanissetta
Adrano
Algeciras
GIBRALTAR (U.K.)
Málaga
Almería
Cabo de Gata
Mediterranean
Mazara del Vallo
Agrigento
Licata
Gela
Modica
Tanger (Tangier)
Ceuta (Spain)
Melilla (Spain)
Alger (Algiers)
Tizi Ouzou
Bejaïa
Jijel
Skikda
Annaba
Bizerte
Gozo
Valletta
MALTA Malta
Tétouan
Al Hoceima
Oran (Wahran)
Aïn Temouchent
Mostaganem
Ech Chélif
Aïn Defla
Blida
Bouira
Sétif
Constantine
Guelma
Tunis
Fès
Tlemcen
Sidi Bel Abbès
Mascara
Relizane
Médéa
Batna
Tébessa
Kairouan
Sousse
MOROCCO
Oujda
Saïda
Tiaret
Djelfa
Biskra
TUNISIA
Sfax
ALGERIA
Grand Erg Occidental
El Goléa
Grand Erg Oriental
Ghadamès
Tarābulus (Tripoli)
Tripolitania

Scale 1:8 000 000
Projection: Lambert Conformal Conic

0 Kms   100   200   300
0 Miles   100   200

Peak
3000m
2000m
1000m
500m
200m
0m
200m
500m
1000m
2000m
4000m
Trough

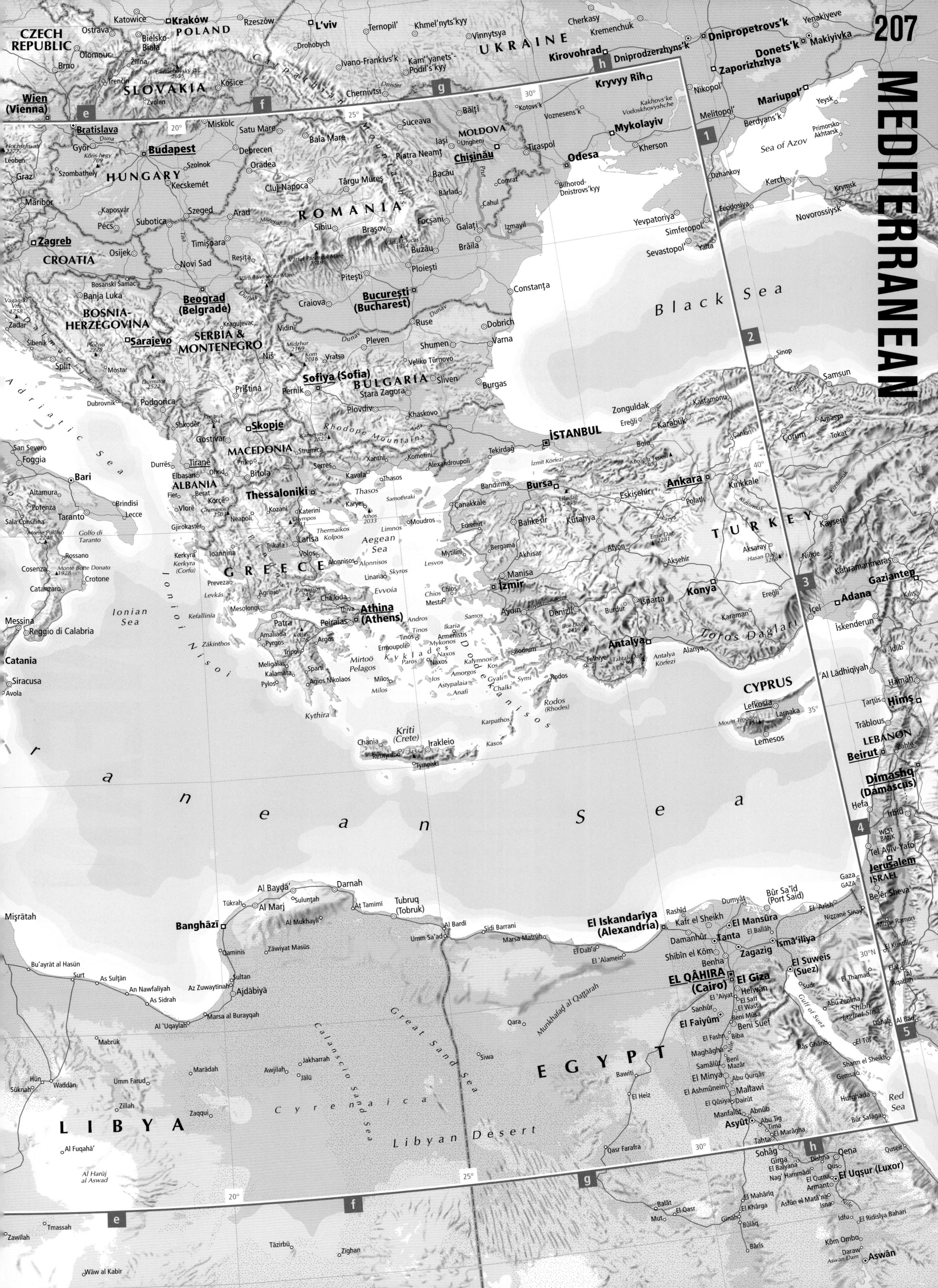
CZECH REPUBLIC
POLAND
UKRAINE
SLOVAKIA
HUNGARY
MOLDOVA
ROMANIA
CROATIA
BOSNIA-HERZEGOVINA
SERBIA & MONTENEGRO
BULGARIA
MACEDONIA
ALBANIA
GREECE
TURKEY
CYPRUS
LEBANON
ISRAEL
WEST BANK
GAZA
EGYPT
LIBYA
Katowice
Kraków
Rzeszów
L'viv
Ternopil'
Khmel'nyts'kyy
Cherkasy
Kremenchuk
Dnipropetrovs'k
Yenakiyeve
Ostrava
Bielsko-Biała
Drohobych
Vinnytsya
Kirovohrad
Dniprodzerzhyns'k
Donets'k
Makiyivka
Olomouc
Žilina
Ivano-Frankivs'k
Kam''yanets'-Podil's'kyy
Kryvyy Rih
Zaporizhzhya
Brno
Trenčín
Košice
Chernivtsi
Nikopol'
Mariupol'
Wien (Vienna)
Zvolen
Kotovs'k
Voznesens'k
Kakhovs'ke Vodoskhovyshche
Melitopol'
Yeysk
Bratislava
Miskolc
Satu Mare
Suceava
Bălţi
Mykolayiv
Berdyans'k
Primorsko-Akhtarsk
Győr
Budapest
Debrecen
Baia Mare
Iaşi
Ungheni
Chişinău
Tiraspol
Kherson
Sea of Azov
Leoben
Szombathely
Szolnok
Oradea
Piatra Neamţ
Odesa
Graz
Kecskemét
Cluj-Napoca
Târgu Mureş
Bacău
Comrat
Bilhorod-Dnistrovs'kyy
Dzhankoy
Kerch
Krymsk
Maribor
Bârlad
Cahul
Kaposvár
Szeged
Arad
Subotica
Sibiu
Braşov
Focşani
Galaţi
Izmayil
Feodosiya
Novorossiysk
Pécs
Yevpatoriya
Simferopol'
Zagreb
Osijek
Timişoara
Reşiţa
Buzău
Brăila
Sevastopol'
Yalta
Novi Sad
Ploieşti
Bosanski Šamac
Piteşti
Constanţa
Banja Luka
Beograd (Belgrade)
Craiova
Bucureşti (Bucharest)
Black Sea
Zadar
Kragujevac
Vidin
Ruse
Dobrich
Šibenik
Sarajevo
Pleven
Shumen
Varna
Split
Niš
Vratsa
Veliko Tŭrnovo
Mostar
Sofiya (Sofia)
Sliven
Sinop
Samsun
Priština
Pernik
Stara Zagora
Burgas
Dubrovnik
Podgorica
Plovdiv
Zonguldak
Kastamonu
Shkodër
Skopje
Khaskovo
Ereğli
Karabük
Amasya
Gostivar
Rhodope Mountains
İSTANBUL
Çankırı
Çorum
Tokat
San Severo
Foggia
Strumica
Xanthi
Komotini
Tekirdağ
Bolu
Durrës
Tiranë
Prilep
Ohrid
Serres
Kavala
Alexandroupoli
İzmit Körfezi
Bari
Elbasan
Bitola
Thasos
Bandırma
Bursa
Ankara
Kırıkkale
Altamura
Fier
Berat
Thessaloniki
Samothraki
Eskişehir
Potenza
Brindisi
Vlorë
Korçë
Karyes
Çanakkale
Polatlı
Taranto
Lecce
Katerini
Neapoli
Kozani
Moudros
Sala Consilina
Gjirokastër
Olympos
Edremit
Balıkesir
Kütahya
Kayseri
Golfo di Taranto
Thermaikos Kolpos
Limnos
Aegean Sea
Ioannina
Trikala
Larisa
Volos
Mytilini
Bergama
Akhisar
Afyon
Aksaray
Niğde
Rossano
Kerkyra (Corfu)
Alonnisos
Lesvos
Hasan Dağı
Akşehir
Cosenza
Crotone
Skyros
Manisa
Kahramanmaraş
Gaziantep
Catanzaro
Preveza
Linaria
Evvoia
İzmir
Konya
Kilis
Levkás
Agrinio
Chalkida
Chios
Adana
Ionian Sea
Mesolongi
Thiva
Athina (Athens)
Mesta
Aydın
Denizli
Isparta
Ereğli
İçel
Messina
Reggio di Calabria
Kefallinía
Patra
Peiraias
Andros
Samos
Burdur
Karaman
İskenderun
Amaliada
Tinos
Ikaria
Armenistis
Toros Dağları
Pyrgos
Argos
Mykonos
Antalya
Antalya Körfezi
Alanya
Idlib
Catania
Zákinthos
Tripoli
Ermoupoli
Kyklades
Bodrum
Naxos
Paros
Kalymnos
Kos
Fethiye
Meligalas
Sparti
Mirtoö Pelagos
Amorgos
Al Lādhiqīyah
Siracusa
Kalamata
Agios Nikolaos
Milos
Ios
Astypalaia
Gyali
Chalki
Symi
Rodos
Hamāh
Avola
Pylos
Anafi
Rodos (Rhodes)
Ḥimş
Dodekanisos
Lefkosia
Larnaka
Kythira
Karpathos
Mount Troodos
Ţarţūs
Trāblous
Lemesos
Kriti (Crete)
Chania
Irakleio
Kasos
Rethymno
Tympaki
Beirut
Zahle
Dimashq (Damascus)
Mediterranean Sea
Hefa
Irbid
Tel Aviv-Yafo
Jerusalem
Be'er Sheva'
Gaza
Al Bayḑā'
Darnah
Ţūkrah
Al Marj
Suluntah
At Tamimi
Tubruq (Tobruk)
Bûr Sa'îd (Port Said)
Rashîd
Dumyât
El 'Arîsh
Nizzane Sinay
Mişrātah
Banghāzī
Al Mukhaylī
Al Burdī
Sīdī Barrānī
El Iskandarîya (Alexandria)
Kafr el Sheikh
El Mansûra
Umm Sa'ad
Marsa Maţrūḩ
Damanhûr
Tanta
El Ballâh
Ismâ'ilîya
Mizpe Ramon
Qaminis
Zāwiyat Masūs
El Dab'a
Zagazig
Shibîn el Kôm
El Kuntilla
El 'Alamein
Benha
El Suweis (Suez)
Bu'ayrāt al Hasūn
Sirt
As Sulţān
Sultan
Az Zuwaytīnah
Ajdābiyā
EL QÂHIRA (Cairo)
El Giza
Eilat
Al 'Aqabah
An Nawfalīyah
As Sidrah
Munkhafaḑ al Qaţţārah
Helwân
El 'Aiyat
El Saff
El Wasta
Sudr
El Thamad
Marsa al Burayqah
Sanhûr
Abu Zenîma
Shibh Jazīrat Sīnā'
Al 'Uqaylah
Qara
Beni Mûsa
El Faiyûm
Beni Suef
Gulf of Suez
Dahab
Al Bad'
Mabrūk
Great Sand Sea
El Fashn
Biba
Râs Ghârib
El Tûr
Calanscio Sand Sea
Siwa
Maghâgha
Beni Mazâr
Sharm el Sheikh
Marādah
Jakharrah
Awjilah
Jālū
Samâlût
Bawiti
El Minya
Abu Qurqâs
Gemsa
Hūn
Waddān
Umm Farud
El Ashmûnein
Mallawi
Sūknah
El Heiz
El Qûsîya
Dairût
Hurghada
Red Sea
Zillah
Cyrenaica
Manfalût
Abnûb
Zaqqui
Asyût
Abu Tig
Tima
Bûr Safâga
El Marâgha
Libyan Desert
Tahta
Al Fuqahā'
Qasr Farafra
Sohâg
Dishna
Qena
Quseir
Girga
El Balyana
Qus
Nag' Hammâdi
El Qurna
El Uqsur (Luxor)
Armant
Al Harūj al Aswad
El Mahâriq
El Khârga
Balât
Asfûn el Matâ'na
Isna
El Qasr
Mut
Ginah
Bûlâq
Idfu
El Ridîsîya Bahari
Tmassah
Zawīlah
Kôm Ombo
Bârîs
Tāzirbū
Zighan
Daraw
Aswan Dam
Aswân
Wāw al Kabīr

...ean via the Suez
...odies of water in the
...ae *Trichodesmium*
...reddish brown tint.

D SEA

E G Y P T

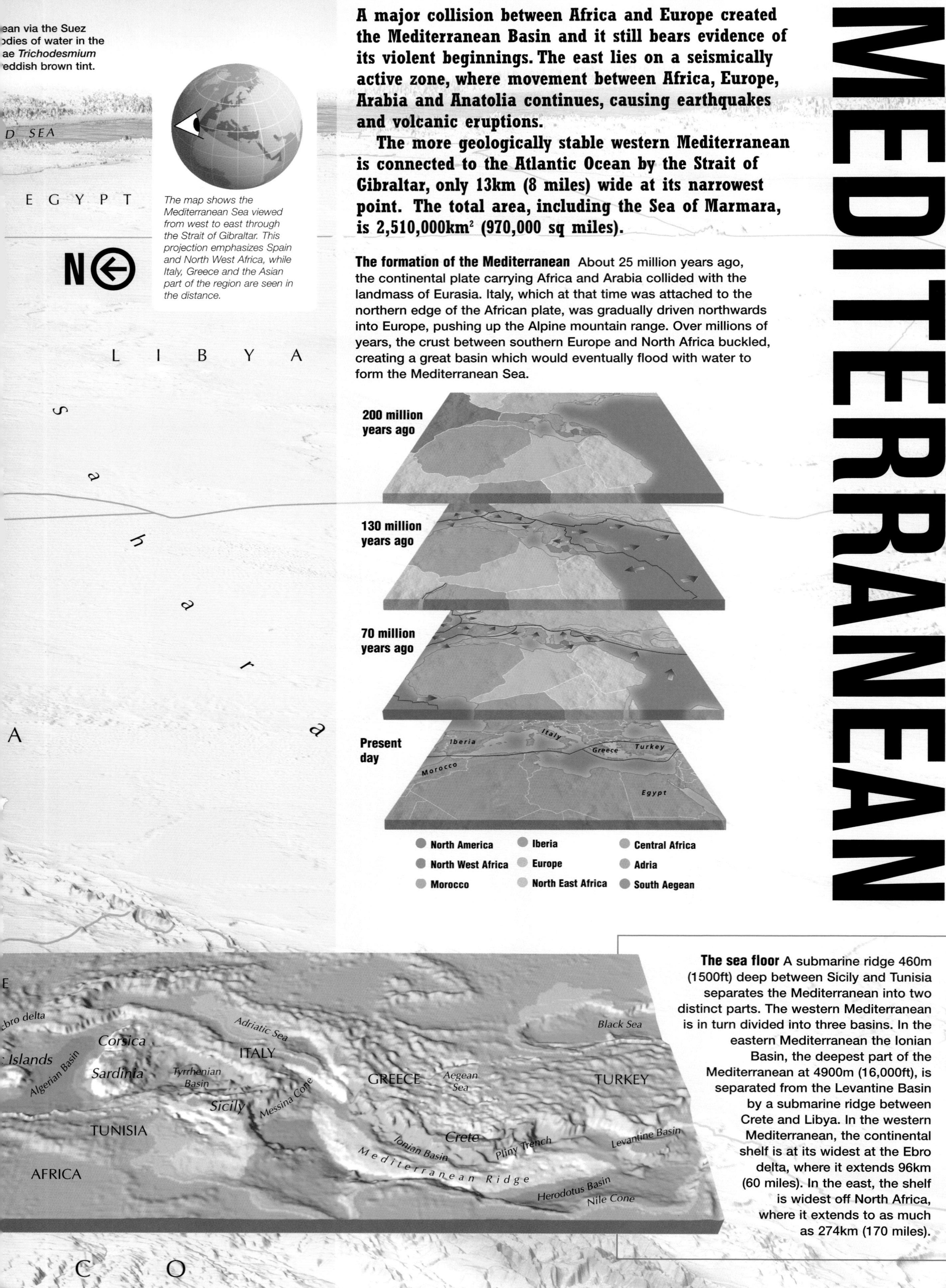

The map shows the Mediterranean Sea viewed from west to east through the Strait of Gibraltar. This projection emphasizes Spain and North West Africa, while Italy, Greece and the Asian part of the region are seen in the distance.

N ⊖

L I B Y A

S a h a r a

A

A major collision between Africa and Europe created the Mediterranean Basin and it still bears evidence of its violent beginnings. The east lies on a seismically active zone, where movement between Africa, Europe, Arabia and Anatolia continues, causing earthquakes and volcanic eruptions.

The more geologically stable western Mediterranean is connected to the Atlantic Ocean by the Strait of Gibraltar, only 13km (8 miles) wide at its narrowest point. The total area, including the Sea of Marmara, is 2,510,000km² (970,000 sq miles).

The formation of the Mediterranean About 25 million years ago, the continental plate carrying Africa and Arabia collided with the landmass of Eurasia. Italy, which at that time was attached to the northern edge of the African plate, was gradually driven northwards into Europe, pushing up the Alpine mountain range. Over millions of years, the crust between southern Europe and North Africa buckled, creating a great basin which would eventually flood with water to form the Mediterranean Sea.

200 million years ago

130 million years ago

70 million years ago

Present day

Iberia — Italy — Turkey
Morocco — Greece
Egypt

- North America
- North West Africa
- Morocco
- Iberia
- Europe
- North East Africa
- Central Africa
- Adria
- South Aegean

The sea floor A submarine ridge 460m (1500ft) deep between Sicily and Tunisia separates the Mediterranean into two distinct parts. The western Mediterranean is in turn divided into three basins. In the eastern Mediterranean the Ionian Basin, the deepest part of the Mediterranean at 4900m (16,000ft), is separated from the Levantine Basin by a submarine ridge between Crete and Libya. In the western Mediterranean, the continental shelf is at its widest at the Ebro delta, where it extends 96km (60 miles). In the east, the shelf is widest off North Africa, where it extends to as much as 274km (170 miles).

E

Ebro delta

Corsica — Adriatic Sea — Black Sea

Islands — Sardinia — ITALY

Algerian Basin — Tyrrhenian Basin — GREECE — Aegean Sea — TURKEY

Sicily — Messina Cone

TUNISIA — Crete — Levantine Basin

AFRICA — Ionian Basin — Pliny Trench

Mediterranean Ridge

Herodotus Basin — Nile Cone

C O

Red Sea Artificially connected to the Mediterra[nean] Canal, this is one of the warmest and saltiest b[odies of] world. The Red Sea takes its name from the al[gae] *erythraeum*, which gives the sea its distinctive [colour]

Nile delta The fertile sediments of the 180km (110 mile) wide delta at the mouth of the Nile have been cultivated by farmers for thousands of years. Modern irrigation has depleted the supply of sediment and the delta is now shrinking.

❸ **Mount Etna** At 3323m (10,906ft) high, Etna is the highest active volcano in Europe and has erupted about 90 times over the past 4000 years. The last major eruption was in 1983. Relative motion between the African continent and Italy causes volcanic activity.

❹ **Santorini** The southernmost of the Cyclades Islands, Santorini is the remaining half of an exploded volcano. The massive eruption took place in 1640 BC, scattering ash and pumice as far as Egypt and Israel.

Atlas Mountains The Tell (northern) Atlas is a young, folded mountain range created by the same movements that formed the Alps. But the southern Saharan Atlas belong to the ancient plateaus of the African continent.

Strait of Gibraltar The strait is a narrow gap in an arc formed by the Atlas Mountains and the high plateau of Spain. A surface current flows eastward through the 365m (1200ft) deep channel, counteracting a westward flow of deeper, colder, more saline water, and preventing the Mediterranean from becoming a shrinking salt lake.

SYRIA

SAUDI ARABIA

JERUSALEM

ISRAEL

ALEXANDRIA

CAIRO

CYPRUS

Nile delta

Nile

ATHENS

SANTORINI ❹

BENGHAZI

CRETE

SEA

Mt Etna

❸

SICILY

MALTA

MEDITERRANEAN

TRIPOLI

TUNIS

TUNISIA

ALGIERS

ALGERIA

OUJDA

Atlas Mountains

Sierra Nevada

Mulhacén

GRANADA

Cordillera Penibética

SPAIN

Balear[ic]

Rif

MALAGA

Strait of Gibraltar

Alborán Basin

FRANC[E]

GIBRALTAR

Strait of Gibraltar

TANGIER

MORO[CCO]

Guadalquivir

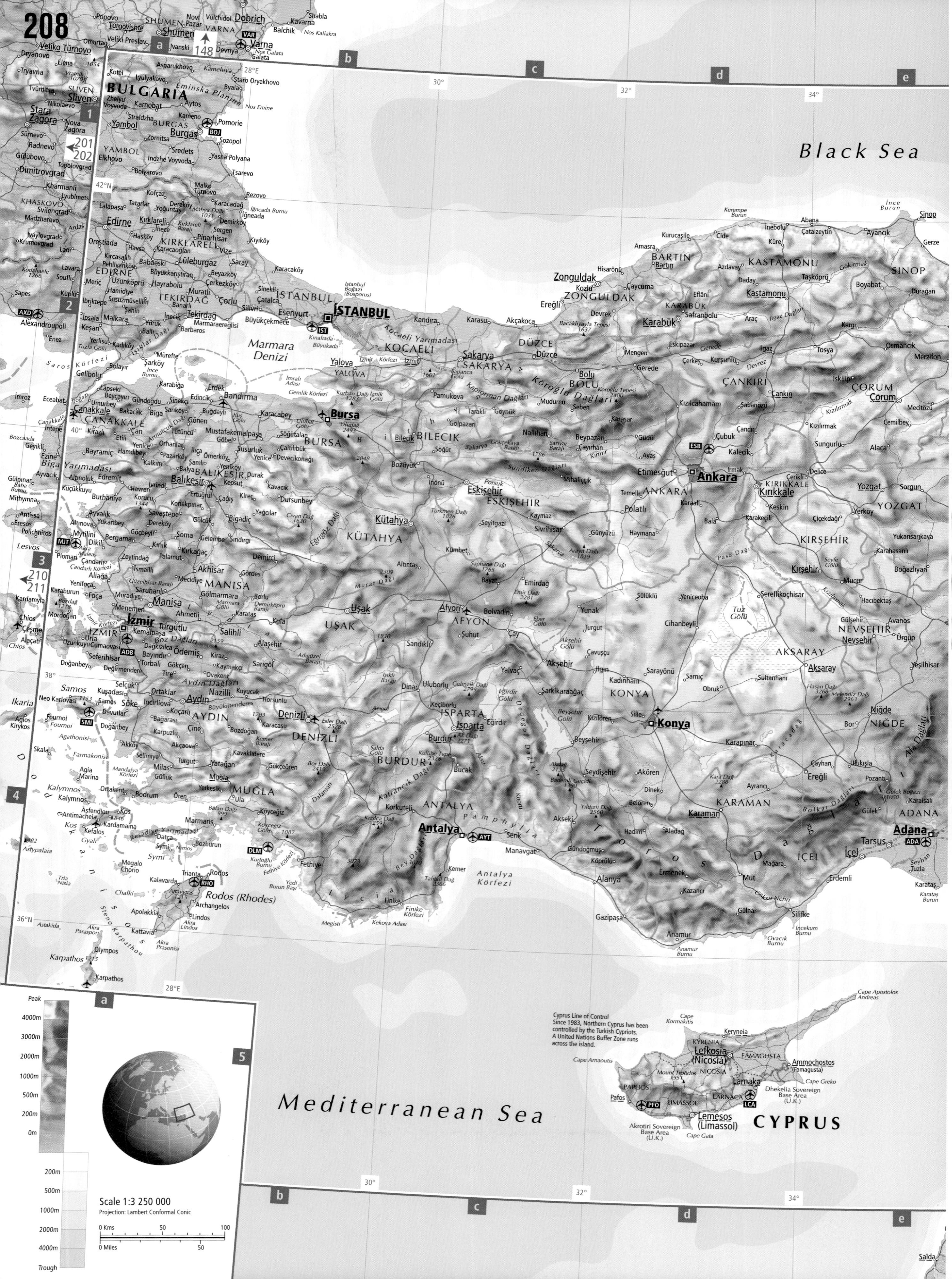
Black Sea
Mediterranean Sea
BULGARIA
CYPRUS
Marmara Denizi
Antalya Körfezi
Sinop
Samsun
Kastamonu
Zonguldak
Bartın
Karabük
Düzce
Bolu
Çankırı
Çorum
İstanbul
Kocaeli
Sakarya
Yalova
Bursa
Bilecik
Eskişehir
Ankara
Kırıkkale
Yozgat
Kırşehir
Nevşehir
Aksaray
Niğde
Konya
Karaman
Adana
İçel
Tarsus
Edirne
Kırklareli
Tekirdağ
Çanakkale
Balıkesir
Manisa
İzmir
Aydın
Muğla
Denizli
Uşak
Kütahya
Afyon
Isparta
Burdur
Antalya
Alanya
Lesvos
Chios
Samos
Ikaria
Rodos (Rhodes)
Karpathos
Lefkosia (Nicosia)
Lemesos (Limassol)
Larnaka
Ammochostos (Famagusta)
Pafos
Keryneia
Varna
Burgas
Shumen
Dobrich
Sliven
Stara Zagora
Dimitrovgrad
Veliko Tŭrnovo
Alexandroupoli
Tuz Gölü
Toros Dağları
Cyprus Line of Control
Since 1983, Northern Cyprus has been controlled by the Turkish Cypriots. A United Nations Buffer Zone runs across the island.
Akrotiri Sovereign Base Area (U.K.)
Dhekelia Sovereign Base Area (U.K.)
148
201
202
210
211
Peak
4000m
3000m
2000m
1000m
500m
200m
0m
200m
500m
1000m
2000m
4000m
Trough
Scale 1:3 250 000
Projection: Lambert Conformal Conic
0 Kms 50 100
0 Miles 50

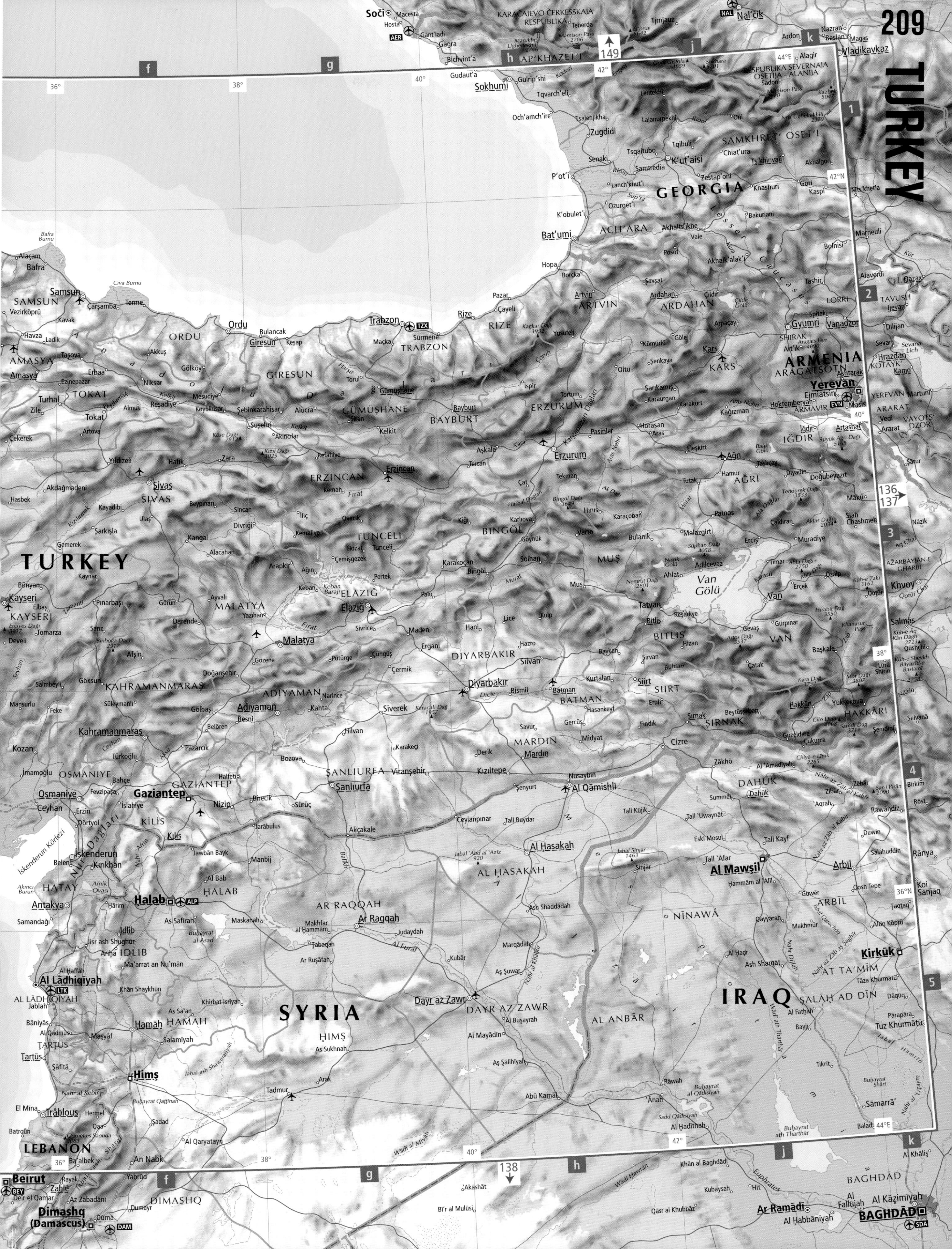
149
136
137
138
TURKEY
GEORGIA
ARMENIA
SYRIA
IRAQ
LEBANON
Soči
Sokhumi
Kut'aisi
Bat'umi
P'ot'i
Zugdidi
Samtredia
Akhalts'ikhe
Vladikavkaz
Nal'čik
Yerevan
Gyumri
Vanadzor
Hrazdan
Ashtarak
SAMSUN
Samsun
Bafra
Çarşamba
Terme
Ordu
Giresun
Trabzon
Rize
Hopa
Artvin
Ardahan
Kars
Erzurum
Bayburt
Gümüşhane
Erzincan
Sivas
Tokat
Amasya
Turhal
Zile
Kayseri
Malatya
Elazığ
Tunceli
Bingöl
Muş
Ağrı
Iğdır
Doğubeyazıt
Van
Van Gölü
Tatvan
Bitlis
Siirt
Batman
Diyarbakır
Mardin
Şırnak
Cizre
Hakkâri
Yüksekova
Adıyaman
Kahramanmaraş
Gaziantep
Kilis
Osmaniye
Şanlıurfa
Birecik
Nizip
İskenderun
Antakya
HATAY
Halab
Idlib
Al Lādhiqīyah
Ḩamāh
Ḩimş
Tarţūs
Ţarābulus
Tadmur
Dayr az Zawr
Ar Raqqah
Al Ḩasakah
Al Qāmishlī
Al Mawşil
Arbīl
Kirkūk
Dahūk
Zākhō
Tikrīt
Sāmarrā'
Ar Ramādī
Al Fallūjah
Al Kāzimīyah
BAGHDĀD
Beirut
Dimashq
(Damascus)
Zahlé
Khvoy
Salmās
Mākū
Anadolu Dağları
Lesser Caucasus
Nur Dağları
Euphrates
Al Furāt
Dicle
Fırat
Murat
Nahr Dijlah
Buḩayrat ath Tharthār
Buḩayrat al Qādisīyah
Ağrı Dağı 5165
Kaçkar Dağı 3932
Nemrut Dağı 2801
Süphan Dağı 4058
36°
38°
40°
42°
44°E
36°N
38°
40°
42°N
1
2
3
4
5
f
g
h
j
k

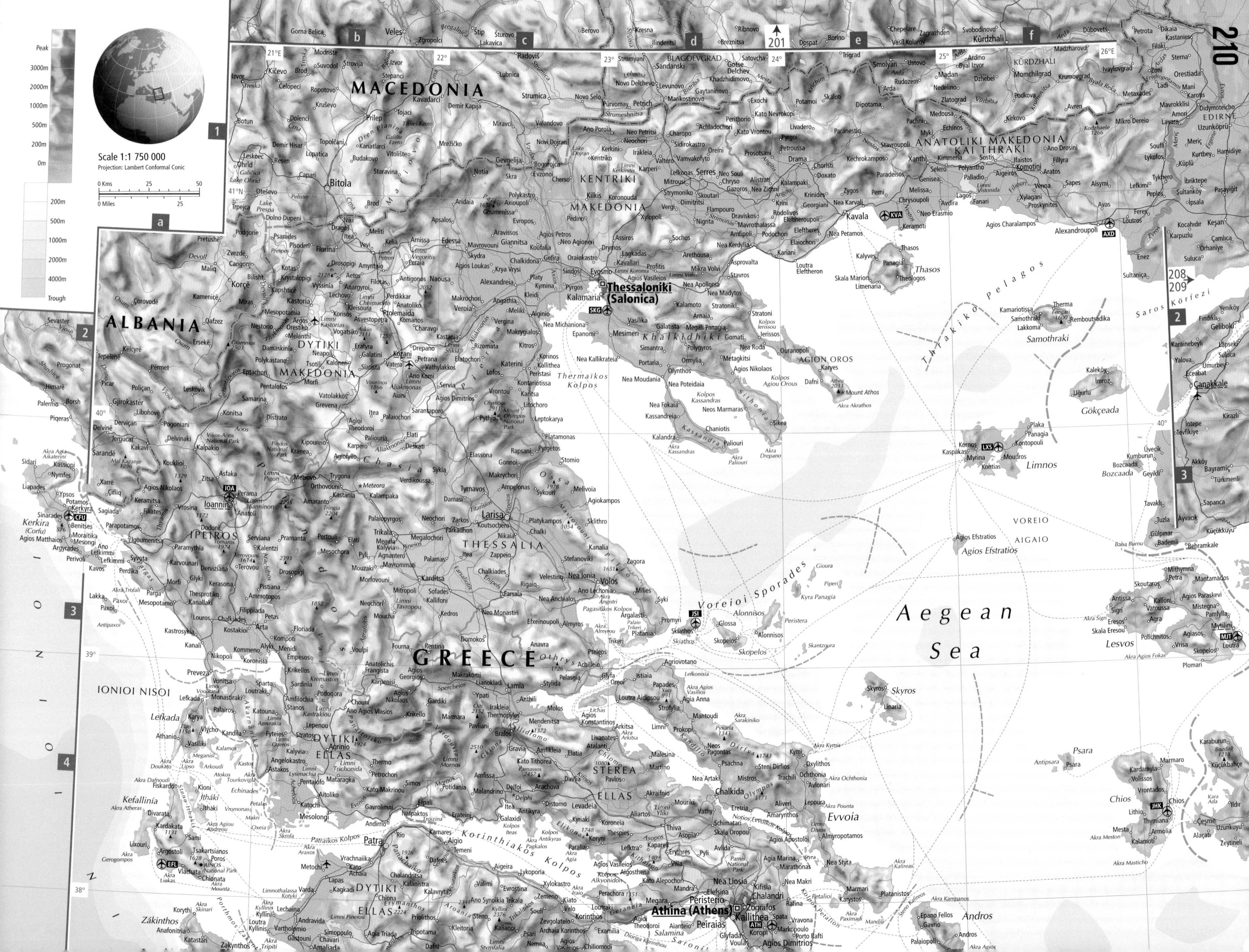

Aegean Sea

GREECE

MACEDONIA

ALBANIA

THESSALIA

STEREA ELLAS

Athina (Athens)

Thessaloniki (Salonica)

Larisa

Volos

Voreioi Sporades

Evvoia

Lesvos

Chios

Limnos

Samothraki

Thasos

Kavala

Skyros

Andros

AGION OROS

ANATOLIKI MAKEDONIA KAI THRAKI

KENTRIKI MAKEDONIA

DYTIKI MAKEDONIA

DYTIKI ELLAS

IPEIROS

IONIOI NISOI

Kerkira (Corfu)

Kefallinia

Zakinthos

Lefkada

Ioannina

Patra

Ioulis

Korinthiakos Kolpos

Thermaikos Kolpos

Kassandra

Sithonia

Thraikiko Pelagos

VOREIO AIGAIO

EDIRNE

KURDZHALI

MACEDONIA

Bitola

Veles

Skopje

Gökçeada

Limnos

208 209 2
201

Scale 1:1 750 000

Projection: Lambert Conformal Conic

0 Kms 50

0 Miles 25

Peak 3000m 2000m 1000m 500m 200m 0m 200m 500m 1000m 2000m 4000m Trough

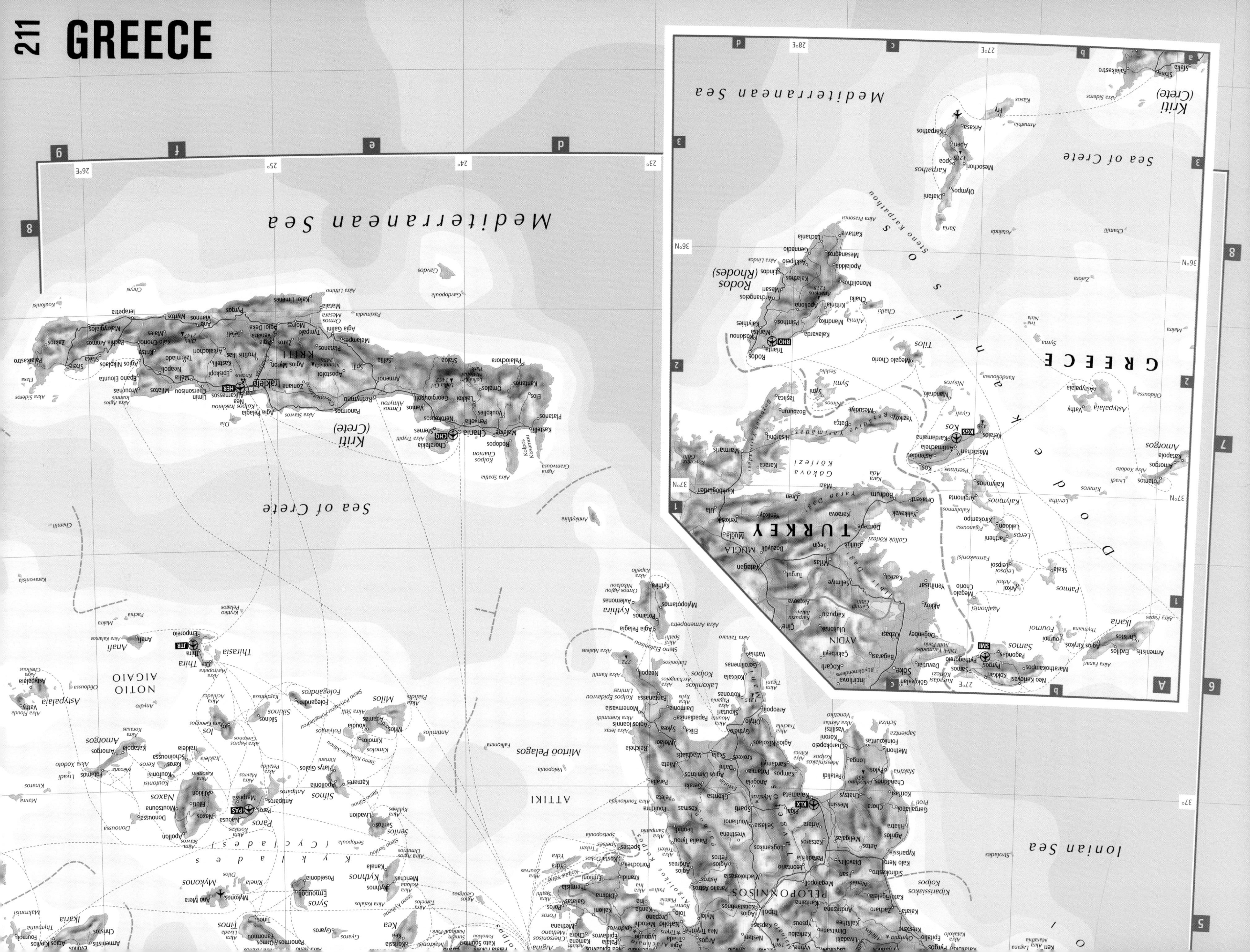
Mediterranean Sea
Sea of Crete
Kriti (Crete)
KRITI
Iraklejo
Chania
Rethymno
Ionian Sea
Mirtoö Pelagos
ATTIKI
PELOPONNISOS
NOTIO AIGAIO
Kyklades (Cyclades)
Naxos
Paros
Milos
Thira
Kythira
TURKEY
GREECE
Dodekanisos
Rodos (Rhodes)
Kos
Samos
Karpathos
Gökova Körfezi
Steno Karpathou

AFRICA

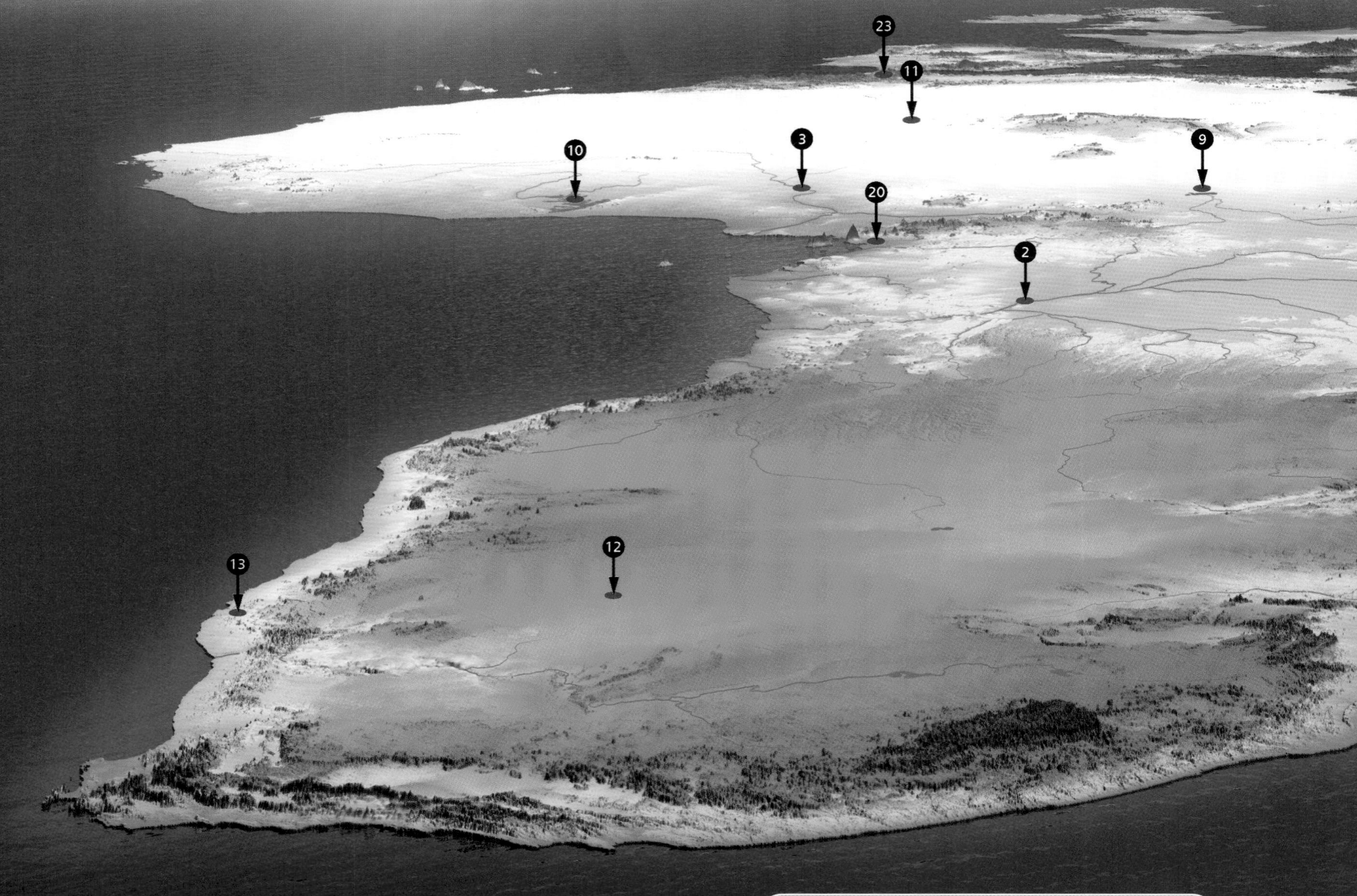

AFRICA AREA
30,343,578km² (11,715,721 sq miles)

AFRICA POPULATION
804,955,560

LARGEST COUNTRY
Sudan 2,505,814km² (967,500 sq miles)

SMALLEST COUNTRY
Seychelles 454km² (176 sq miles)

LARGEST LAKES
❻ Lake Victoria, Uganda/Kenya/Tanzania 68,800km² (26,563 sq miles)
❼ Lake Tanganyika, Tanzania/Zimbabwe/Dem Rep of Congo/Burundi
32,900km² (12,702 sq miles)
❽ Lake Malawi (Lake Nyasa), Malawi/Mozambique
30,044km² (11,600 sq miles)
❾ Lake Chad, Chad/Cameroon/Nigeria/Niger
10,000–26,000km² (3861–10,039 sq miles)
❿ Lake Volta, Ghana 8485km² (3276 sq miles)

LONGEST RIVERS
❶ Nile, Uganda/Sudan/Egypt 6695km (4160 miles)
❷ Congo, Dem Rep of Congo/Congo/Angola 4667km (2900 miles)
❸ Niger, Guinea/Mali/Niger/Benin/Nigeria 4184km (2599 miles)
❹ Zambezi, Angola/Zambia/Namibia/Zimbabwe/Mozambique
2736km (1700 miles)
❺ Wabe Shebele Wenz (Webi Shabeelle), Ethiopia/Somalia
2490km (1547 miles)

The second largest continent after Asia, covering a fifth of the Earth's land area, Africa is bisected by the Equator, an area of high rainfall and lush rain forests. Its interior is characterized by extensive high plateaus covered by undulating savannah grasslands, which drop dramatically to narrow coastal plains. The world's largest desert, the Sahara, occupies a quarter of Africa's land area. On the eastern side of the continent is the Great Rift Valley, formed 10–20 million years ago by a crack in the Earth's crust and marked by a series of lakes and volcanoes.

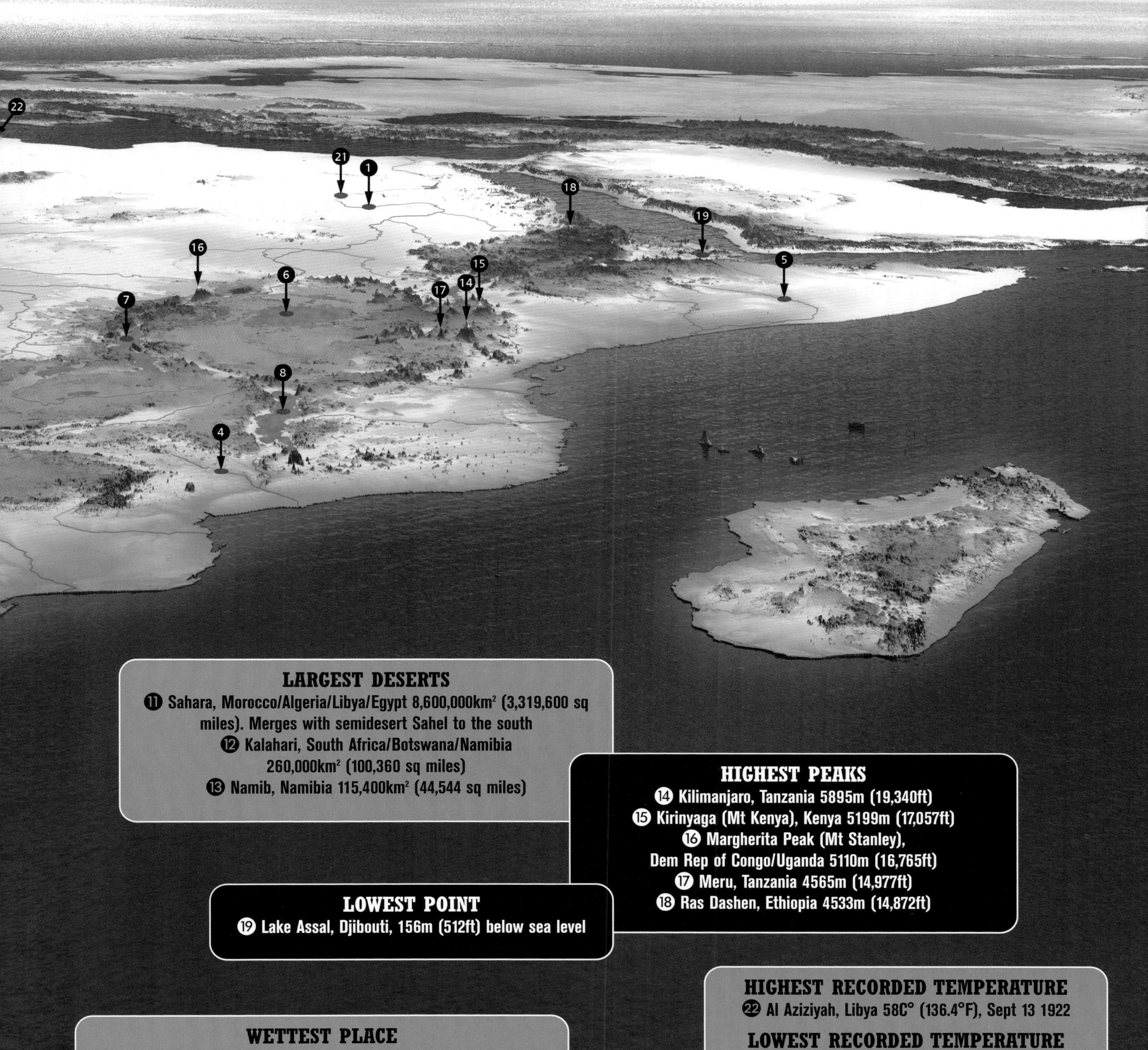

LARGEST DESERTS
⓫ Sahara, Morocco/Algeria/Libya/Egypt 8,600,000km² (3,319,600 sq miles). Merges with semidesert Sahel to the south
⓬ Kalahari, South Africa/Botswana/Namibia 260,000km² (100,360 sq miles)
⓭ Namib, Namibia 115,400km² (44,544 sq miles)

HIGHEST PEAKS
⓮ Kilimanjaro, Tanzania 5895m (19,340ft)
⓯ Kirinyaga (Mt Kenya), Kenya 5199m (17,057ft)
⓰ Margherita Peak (Mt Stanley), Dem Rep of Congo/Uganda 5110m (16,765ft)
⓱ Meru, Tanzania 4565m (14,977ft)
⓲ Ras Dashen, Ethiopia 4533m (14,872ft)

LOWEST POINT
⓳ Lake Assal, Djibouti, 156m (512ft) below sea level

HIGHEST RECORDED TEMPERATURE
㉒ Al Aziziyah, Libya 58C° (136.4°F), Sept 13 1922

LOWEST RECORDED TEMPERATURE
㉓ Ifrane, Morocco -23.9C° (-11°F), Feb 11 1935

WETTEST PLACE
⓴ Debundscha, Cameroon 10,287mm (405in) average annual rainfall

DRIEST PLACE
㉑ Wadi Halfa, Sudan 2.5mm (0.01in) average annual rainfall

Employment

Almost two-thirds of Africans work the land – many as subsistence farmers, others growing cash crops for export. Although Africa has a wealth of mineral and energy resources, only a few countries, such as South Africa, have been able to exploit them successfully. Tourism is a growing sector throughout the continent, taking advantage of spectacular scenery and wildlife, although threatened in places by political instability. South Africa and Egypt are the leading economies; both have a significant service sector, while Nigeria is able to exploit its oil reserves. Many nations, especially in the Horn of Africa, cannot support their populations and rely on foreign aid for survival.

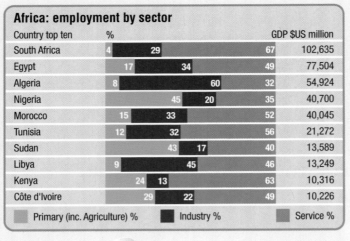

Africa: employment by sector

Country top ten	%			GDP $US million
South Africa	4	29	67	102,635
Egypt	17	34	49	77,504
Algeria	8	60	32	54,924
Nigeria		45	20	35	40,700
Morocco	15	33	52	40,045
Tunisia	12	32	56	21,272
Sudan		43	17	40	13,589
Libya	9	45	46	13,249
Kenya		24	13	63	10,316
Côte d'Ivoire		29	22	49	10,226

Primary (inc. Agriculture) %   Industry %   Service %

Climate of North and West Africa

The Sahara desert has intense sun, little rainfall and extremely high daytime temperatures, which plummet at night. In contrast, the Atlas Mountains and the Ethiopean Plateau receive plentiful rainfall and snow on the highest peaks in winter. The coastal countries of Morocco, Algeria and Tunisia enjoy a Mediterranean climate. The northern reaches of West Africa that border the Sahara are hot and arid but farther south the savannah has rainy seasons that can last as long as six months, becoming more prolonged near the Equator.

Khartoum   Lagos   Nouakchott

Climate of Central and southern Africa

Temperatures are high for most of the year, although they are moderated by elevation and the influence of ocean currents. There are several different climatic zones: a pocket of Mediterranean climate in South Africa; the arid deserts of the Namib and Kalahari; humid heat in the equatorial rain forests of Congo; mists and even snow in the mountains of Rwanda; and tropical dry and rainy seasons in the savannah. Madagascar has a subtropical climate with monsoon rains and cooler temperatures in the mountains.

Kigali   Nairobi   Cape Town   Antananarivo

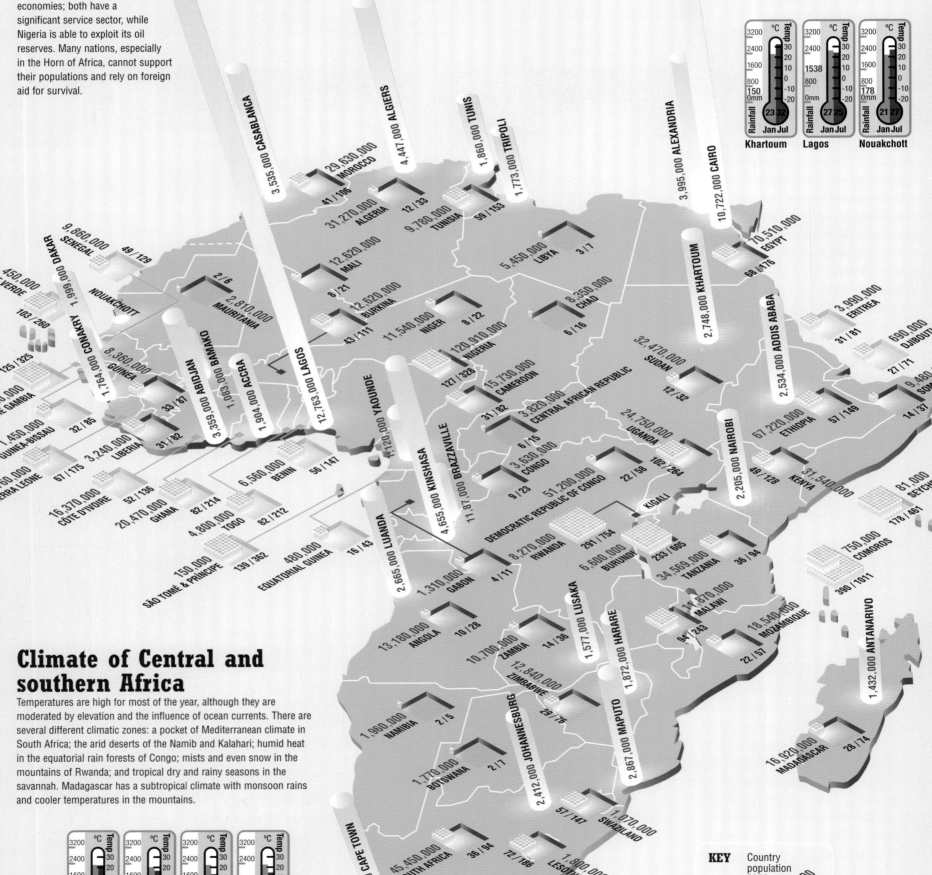

KEY
Country population 2003
11,870,000 MALAWI

Country density: People per square mile/km
94/243 MALAWI

The lie of the land

Although a rain forest belt girdles the middle of the continent, Africa as a whole is an exceptionally arid region. Its northern half is dominated by the great expanses of the Sahara desert and the Sahel to the south – an area which is vulnerable to increasing desertification. Great rivers, such as the Nile, Congo and Niger, carve epic journeys across the continent, while the great lakes of East Africa's rift valley teem with life.

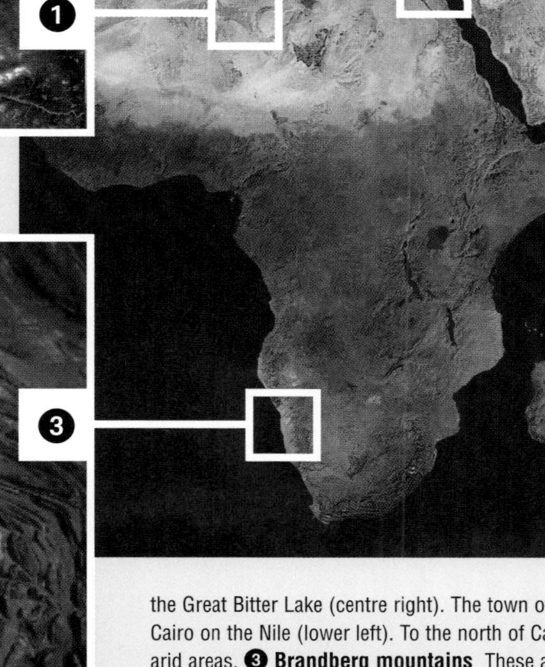

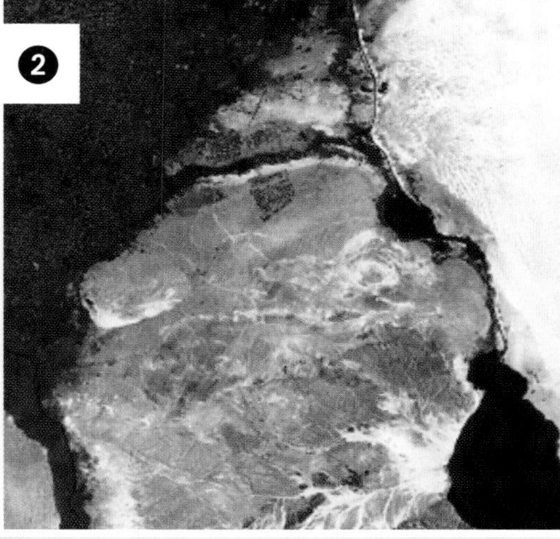

❶ Ghadamis River The dry riverbed of the Ghadamis scars the arid landscape of the Sahara Desert in the Tinrhert Hamada Mountains in Libya.
❷ Suez Canal The image shows the canal as it passes from the Gulf of Suez (lower right) into the Great Bitter Lake (centre right). The town of Suez is visible in grey at the south end of the canal, and Cairo on the Nile (lower left). To the north of Cairo, the Nile delta stands out in green against the surrounding arid areas. **❸ Brandberg mountains** These ancient mountains in Damaraland, Namibia, were formed between 400 and 600 million years ago. The striated, multicoloured patterns of the different rock strata were created by continual weathering and erosion by wind and rain.

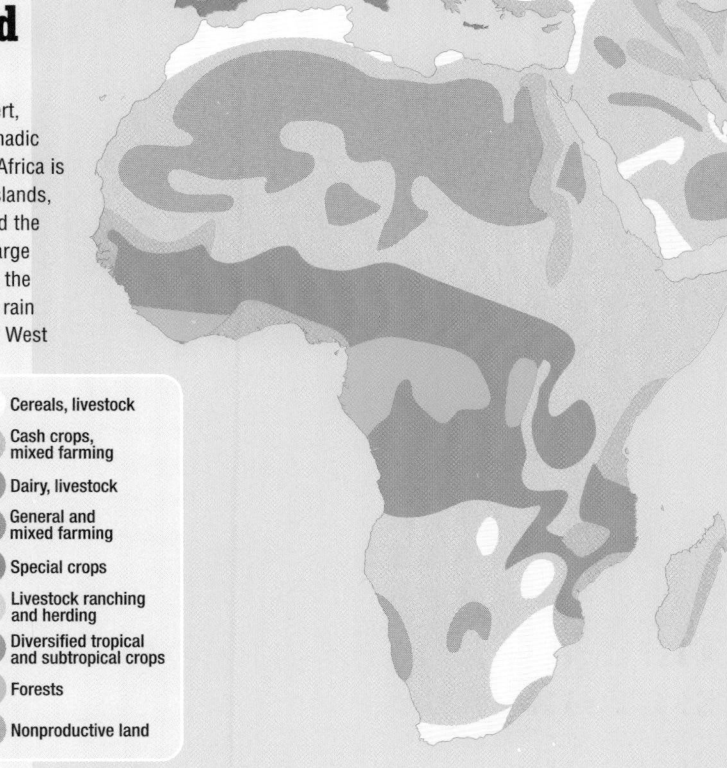

Population

Despite rapid growth in the past century, Africa remains sparsely populated. Most people live near the coasts and rivers, around the great lakes in the east African highlands, and in South Africa. The population is predominantly rural although in South Africa and the oil-rich countries of Libya and Nigeria, 40 per cent of people live in cities. Central Africa is expected to almost double its population between 2003 and 2050, while the population of sub-Saharan Africa is predicted to fall by 22 per cent due to HIV and AIDS.

Health, wealth and education

Continental Africa has the world's lowest per capita GDP. Despite its natural riches, half the people live on 65 cents a day or less. Most African countries do not have compulsory education, and supplies of teachers and resources are limited. Healthcare services in Africa tend to be basic and strain to cope with malnutrition and infectious diseases such as malaria, typhoid and dysentery. HIV/AIDS is cutting a terrible swathe through the population of sub-Saharan Africa; 26 million people are already dead, 25 million more are infected with HIV.

How the land is used

Roughly a third of Africa is desert, able to support only limited nomadic pastoral herding. Nearly half of Africa is covered in open savannah grasslands, grazed by herds of livestock, and the world's greatest abundance of large mammals. Close to the Equator, the wetter climate supports belts of rain forest in the Congo and parts of West Africa. Rich soils on river deltas and along the banks of rivers and lakes make fertile croplands, notably the Nile Valley and Lake Victoria basin. The coastal plains are also crop-growing areas, especially the Mediterranean coast and southern coast of South Africa where citrus fruits thrive.

- Cereals, livestock
- Cash crops, mixed farming
- Dairy, livestock
- General and mixed farming
- Special crops
- Livestock ranching and herding
- Diversified tropical and subtropical crops
- Forests
- Nonproductive land

Age				Birth rate		Adult literacy		Wealth	
Under 15		%	Over 65	Births per 1000 population			%		GDP per head $US
Uganda	49.2	6.2	Mauritius	Niger	53.7	Zimbabwe	90.7	Seychelles	8641
Congo, Dem. Rep.	48.8	5.9	Tunisia	Angola	51.3	South Africa	86.4	Equatorial Guinea	5191
Burkina	48.7	5.8	Gabon	Uganda	50.6	Equatorial Guinea	85.7	Mauritius	4025
Angola	48.2	4.6	Cape Verde	Mali	49.6	Mauritius	85.6	Botswana	3368
Burundi	47.6	4.2	Lesotho	Nigeria	49	Kenya	85.1	Gabon	3157
Algeria	34.8	2.6	Rwanda	Morocco	24.8	Mali	27.9	Mozambique	151
South Africa	34	2.5	Senegal	South Africa	24.6	Burkina	26.6	Sierra Leone	151
Libya	33.9	2.5	Uganda	Seychelles	18.2	São Tomé & Príncipe	25	Congo, Dem. Rep.	146
Tunisia	29.7	2.4	Tanzania	Tunisia	17.9	Somalia	24.1	Burundi	100
Mauritius	25.6	2	Niger	Mauritius	17.3	Niger	17.6	Ethiopia	84

■ Top five ■ Bottom five

1 210 000
MAURITIUS
508 / 1522

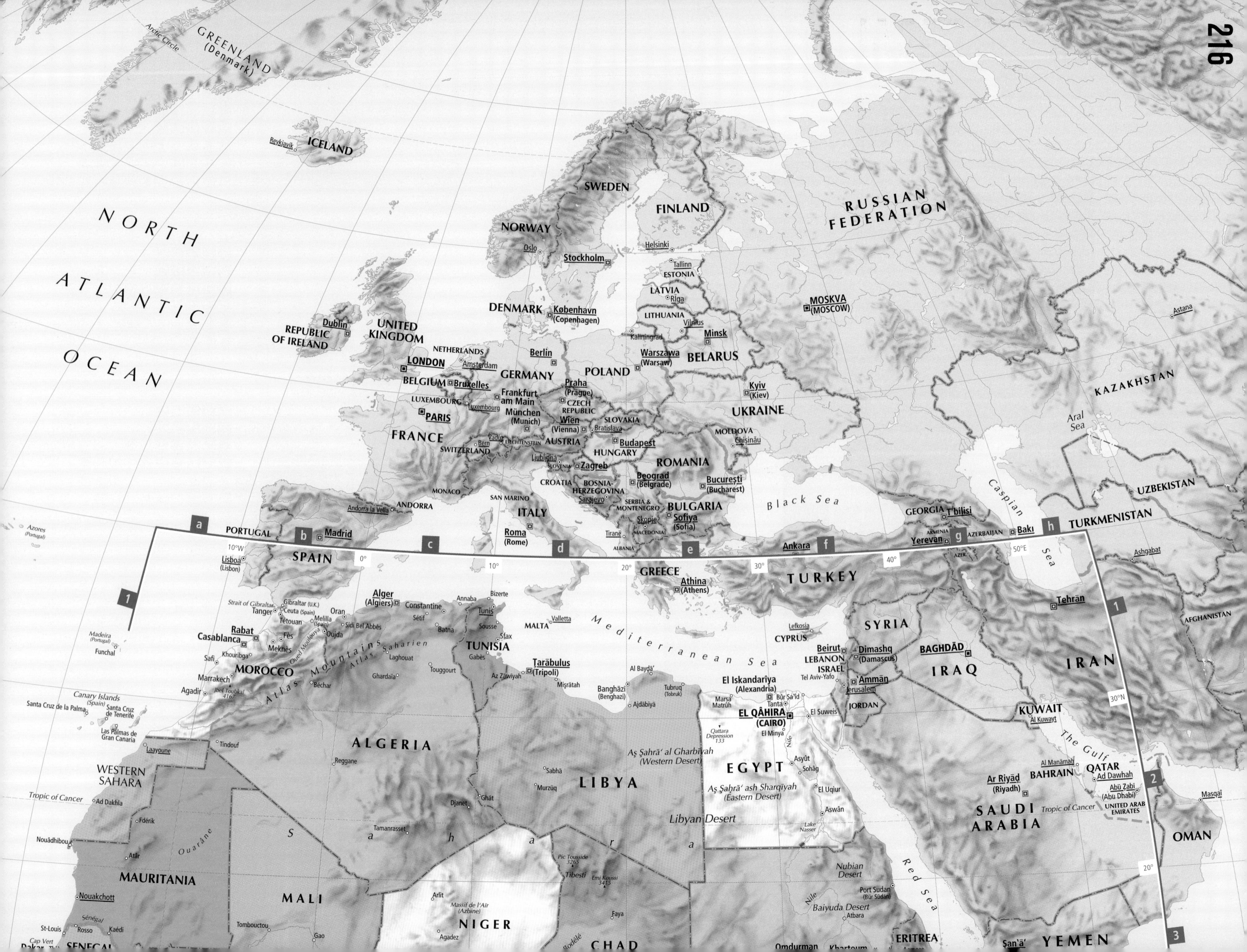
GREENLAND
(Denmark)
Arctic Circle
ICELAND
Reykjavík
NORTH
ATLANTIC
OCEAN
REPUBLIC OF IRELAND
Dublin
UNITED KINGDOM
LONDON
NORWAY
Oslo
SWEDEN
Stockholm
FINLAND
Helsinki
RUSSIAN
FEDERATION
MOSKVA
(MOSCOW)
DENMARK
København
(Copenhagen)
ESTONIA
Tallinn
LATVIA
Riga
LITHUANIA
Vilnius
Kaliningrad
BELARUS
Minsk
NETHERLANDS
Amsterdam
BELGIUM
Bruxelles
LUXEMBOURG
Luxembourg
GERMANY
Berlin
Frankfurt am Main
München
(Munich)
POLAND
Warszawa
(Warsaw)
Praha
(Prague)
CZECH REPUBLIC
SLOVAKIA
Bratislava
Wien
(Vienna)
AUSTRIA
HUNGARY
Budapest
FRANCE
PARIS
SWITZERLAND
Bern
Vaduz
LIECHTENSTEIN
MONACO
ANDORRA
Andorra la Vella
PORTUGAL
Lisboa
(Lisbon)
SPAIN
Madrid
ITALY
Roma
(Rome)
SAN MARINO
SLOVENIA
Ljubljana
CROATIA
Zagreb
BOSNIA-HERZEGOVINA
Sarajevo
SERBIA & MONTENEGRO
Beograd
(Belgrade)
MACEDONIA
Skopje
ALBANIA
Tiranë
GREECE
Athina
(Athens)
BULGARIA
Sofiya
(Sofia)
ROMANIA
Bucureşti
(Bucharest)
MOLDOVA
Chişinău
UKRAINE
Kyiv
(Kiev)
Black Sea
KAZAKHSTAN
Astana
Aral Sea
UZBEKISTAN
TURKMENISTAN
Ashgabat
AFGHANISTAN
Caspian Sea
GEORGIA
T'bilisi
ARMENIA
Yerevan
AZERBAIJAN
Bakı
TURKEY
Ankara
CYPRUS
Lefkosia
SYRIA
Dimashq
(Damascus)
LEBANON
Beirut
ISRAEL
Tel Aviv-Yafo
Jerusalem
JORDAN
'Ammān
IRAQ
BAGHDĀD
IRAN
Tehrān
KUWAIT
Al Kuwayt
The Gulf
BAHRAIN
Al Manāmah
QATAR
Ad Dawhah
UNITED ARAB EMIRATES
Abū Ẓabī
(Abu Dhabi)
OMAN
Masqaṭ
SAUDI ARABIA
Ar Riyāḍ
(Riyadh)
Tropic of Cancer
YEMEN
Ṣan'ā'
Red Sea
ERITREA
Mediterranean Sea
MALTA
Valletta
EGYPT
EL QÂHIRA
(CAIRO)
El Iskandarîya
(Alexandria)
Libyan Desert
Nubian Desert
Nile
LIBYA
Ṭarābulus
(Tripoli)
Banghāzī
(Benghazi)
TUNISIA
Tunis
ALGERIA
Alger
(Algiers)
MOROCCO
Rabat
Casablanca
Strait of Gibraltar
Atlas Mountains
Sahara
WESTERN SAHARA
Laayoune
MAURITANIA
Nouakchott
MALI
NIGER
CHAD
Canary Islands
(Spain)
Madeira
(Portugal)
Azores
(Portugal)
SENEGAL
10°W
0°
10°
20°
30°
40°
50°E
30°N
20°

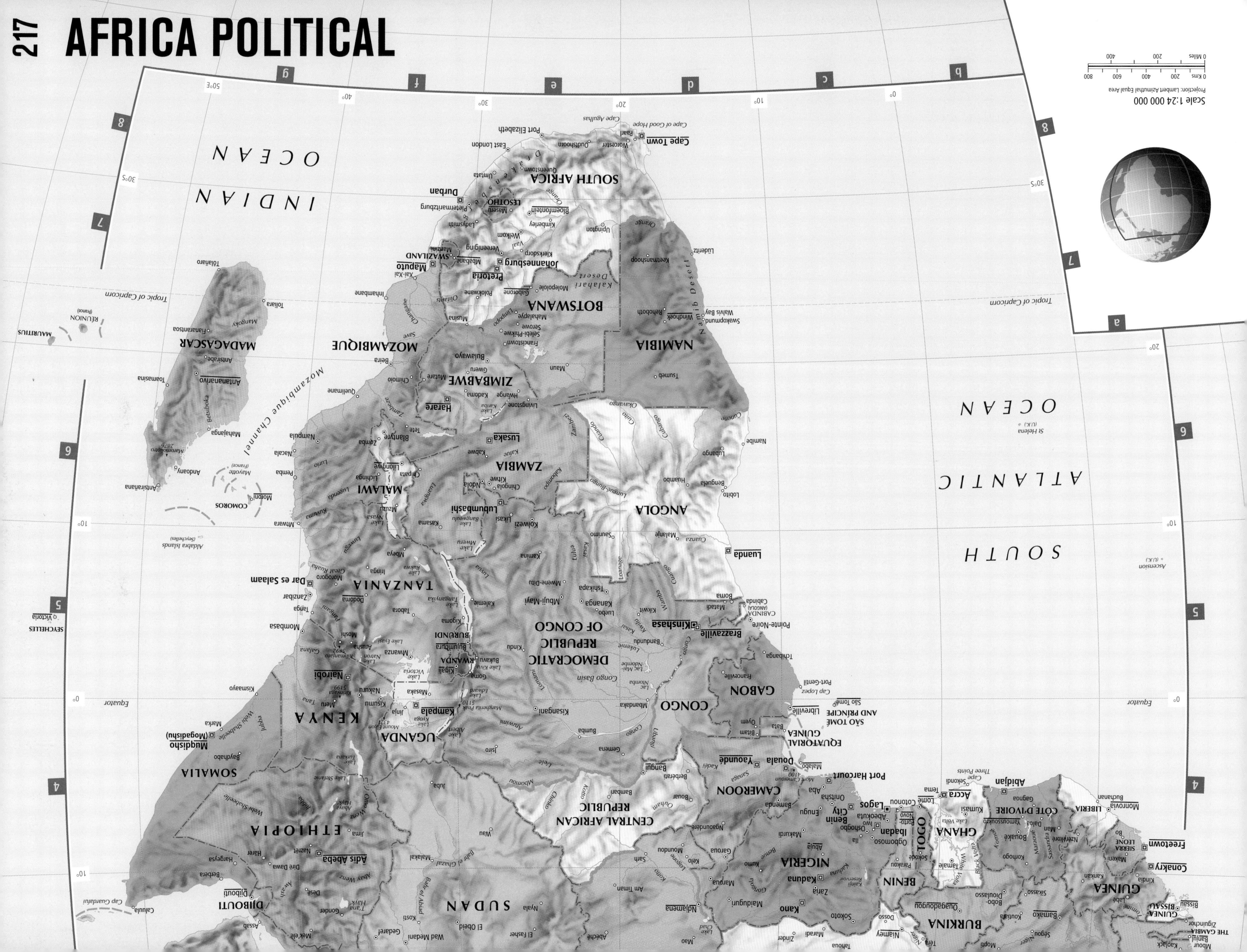

SEYCHELLES
○ Victoria
MAURITIUS
RÉUNION
(France)

Cap Guardafui
10°
0°
Equator

DJIBOUTI
○ Djibouti
Assab
Berbera
Hargeysa
Bayhabo
Marka
Muqdisho
(Mogadishu)
SOMALIA
Kismaayo

ETHIOPIA
Ādīs Ābeba
Harēr
Dīre Dawa
Nazrēt
Desē
Gonder
Gedaref
Mek'elē
New Wenz
Tana Hāyk'
Jīma
Lake Stefanie
Lake Turkana
Wabi Shebelē
Web Shebelē
Jubba
Ganale

SUDAN
El Fasher
Nyala
El Obeid
Wad Medani
Kosti
Malakal
Bahr el Ghazal
Wau
Juba
Abéché
Am Timan
Sarh

COMOROS
Mayotte (France)
Moroni

MADAGASCAR
Antsirañana
Andoany
Mahajanga
Antananarivo
Antsirabe
Fianarantsoa
Betsiboka
Toamasina
Toliara
Tôlañaro
Mangoky

Aldabra Islands (Seychelles)

UGANDA
Kampala
Masaka
Jinja
KENYA
Nairobi
Mombasa
Nakuru
Kisumu
Meru
Mount Kenya 5199
Mount Elgon
Lake Victoria
Lake Kyoga
Galana
Tana
Malindi

RWANDA
Kigali
Margherita Pk 5110
BURUNDI
Bujumbura
Gitega
Kigoma
Tabora

TANZANIA
Dodoma
Dar es Salaam
Zanzibar
Tanga
Arusha
Moshi
Mwanza
Singida
Iringa
Mbeya
Mtwara
Lake Eyasi
Lake Natron
Pangani
Ruvuma

MALAWI
Lilongwe
Mzuzu
Blantyre
Zomba
Lake Nyasa
Lichinga

MOZAMBIQUE
Nampula
Nacala
Pemba
Quelimane
Beira
Chimoio
Tete
Chipata
Changane
Xai-Xai
Inhambane
Maputo
Save
Zambeze

ZAMBIA
Lusaka
Lubumbashi
Ndola
Kitwe
Kabwe
Chingola
Kasama
Mansa
Kolwezi
Likasi
Lake Mweru
Lake Bangweulu
Lake Kariba

DEMOCRATIC REPUBLIC OF CONGO
Kinshasa
Kisangani
Mbuji-Mayi
Kananga
Kolwezi
Lubumbashi
Kindu
Bukavu
Goma
Bumba
Mbandaka
Bandundu
Kikwit
Kamina
Tshikapa
Bunia
Isiro
Gemena
Kwilu
Lomami
Congo Basin
Lulua
Kasai
Lopori
Tshuapa

CENTRAL AFRICAN REPUBLIC
Bangui
Bambari
Bouar
Berbérati
Bossangoa
Ndélé

CAMEROON
Yaoundé
Douala
Bamenda
Garoua
Maroua
Ngaoundéré
Mont Cameroun 4100

NIGERIA
Lagos
Abuja
Kano
Kaduna
Ibadan
Benin City
Port Harcourt
Enugu
Onitsha
Aba
Makurdi
Zaria
Maiduguri
Sokoto
Ilorin
Oshogbo
Ogbomoso
Abeokuta
Ado

GABON
Libreville
Port-Gentil
Franceville
Cap Lopez

EQUATORIAL GUINEA
Malabo
Bata

SÃO TOMÉ AND PRÍNCIPE
São Tomé

CONGO
Brazzaville
Pointe-Noire
Tchibanga

ANGOLA
Luanda
Huambo
Lobito
Benguela
Lubango
Malanje
Cuito
Namibe
Saurimo
CABINDA (ANGOLA)
Cabinda
Cuanza
Cuango
Cunene

NAMIBIA
Windhoek
Rehoboth
Swakopmund
Walvis Bay
Lüderitz
Tsumeb
Namib Desert
Okavango

BOTSWANA
Gaborone
Francistown
Maun
Serowe
Molepolole
Mahalapye
Selebi-Phikwe
Kalahari Desert

ZIMBABWE
Harare
Bulawayo
Gweru
Mutare
Kwekwe
Kadoma
Hwange
Masvingo

SOUTH AFRICA
Pretoria
Johannesburg
Bloemfontein
Durban
Cape Town
Port Elizabeth
East London
Kimberley
Welkom
Klerksdorp
Vereeniging
Pietermaritzburg
Ladysmith
Upington
Worcester
Queenstown
Umtata
Mossel Bay
Oudtshoorn
Springbok
Paarl
Cape of Good Hope
Cape Agulhas

LESOTHO
Maseru

SWAZILAND
Mbabane
Manzini

Vaal
Orange

GUINEA
Conakry
Kankan
Kindia
GUINEA-BISSAU
Bissau
THE GAMBIA
Banjul
SIERRA LEONE
Freetown
Makeni
Bo
LIBERIA
Monrovia
Buchanan

BURKINA
Ouagadougou
Bobo-Dioulasso
MALI
Bamako
Ségou
Sikasso
Mopti
Kayes

NIGER
Niamey
Maradi
Zinder
Tahoua

BENIN
Porto-Novo
Cotonou
Parakou

TOGO
Lomé

GHANA
Accra
Kumasi
Tamale
Sekondi
Tema
Lake Volta
White Volta
Black Volta
Cape Three Points

CÔTE D'IVOIRE
Yamoussoukro
Abidjan
Bouaké
Daloa
Korhogo
Man
Gagnoa

Niger
Lake Chad
Ndjamena
Mao
Maroua

SOUTH ATLANTIC OCEAN
St Helena (U.K.)
Ascension (U.K.)

INDIAN OCEAN

Tropic of Capricorn

Equator

30°S

20°S

10°N
0°
10°
20°
30°
40°
50°E

Mozambique Channel

Scale 1:24 000 000
Projection: Lambert Azimuthal Equal Area
0 Kms   200   400   600   800
0 Miles   200   400

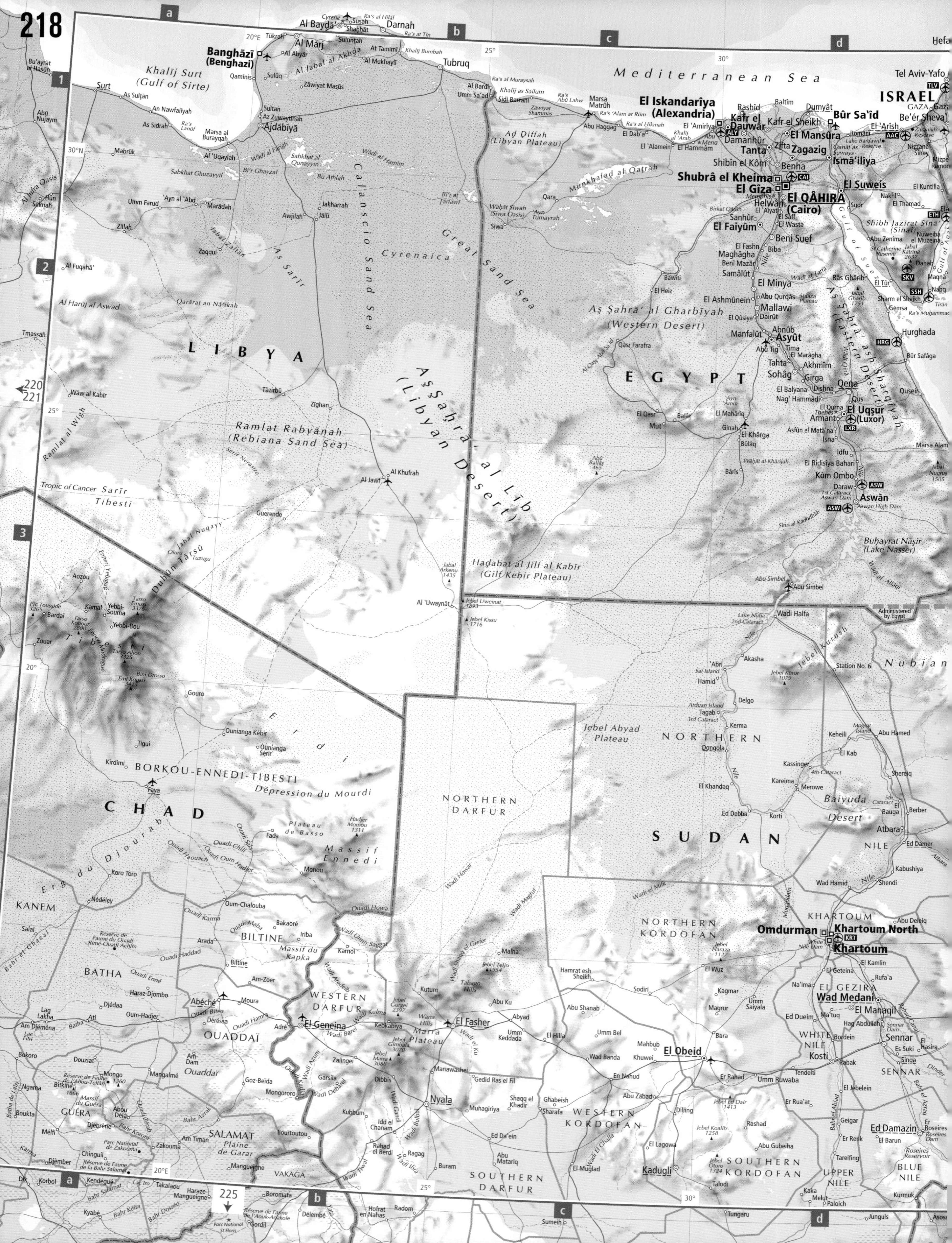
Mediterranean Sea
Khalīj Surt
(Gulf of Sirte)
Banghāzī
(Benghazi)
Al Bayḍā'
Darnah
Cyrene
Al Marj
Tubruq
Ajdābiyā
Al Jabal al Akhḍar
LIBYA
Cyrenaica
Calanscio Sand Sea
As Sarīr
Great Sand Sea
Aṣ Ṣaḥrā' al Lībīyah
(Libyan Desert)
Ramlat Rabyānah
(Rebiana Sand Sea)
Al Kufrah
Al Jawf
Tazirbū
Zighan
Jalū
Awjilah
Marādah
Zillah
Zaqqui
Al Fuqahā'
Waw al Kabīr
Ramlat al Wigh
Tropic of Cancer
Sarīr Tibesti
Al Harūj al Aswad
Tmassah
Al 'Uwaynāt
Jebel Uweinat
1893
Jebel Kissu
1716
Jabal Arkenu
1435
EGYPT
El Iskandarîya
(Alexandria)
Marsa Matrûh
Sidi Barrani
As Sallum
Aḍ Ḍiffah
(Libyan Plateau)
Munkhafaḍ al Qaṭṭārah
Wāḥāt Siwah
(Siwa Oasis)
Siwa
Qara
Rashîd
Baltîm
Dumyât
Bûr Sa'îd
Kafr el Dauwâr
Damanhûr
Tanta
El Mansûra
Zagazig
Ismâ'ilîya
Benha
Shubrâ el Kheima
El Gîza
EL QÂHIRA
(Cairo)
Helwân
El Suweis
El Faiyûm
Beni Suef
Maghâgha
Samâlût
El Minya
Mallawi
Manfalût
Asyût
Tahta
Sohâg
Girga
Qena
El Uqṣur
(Luxor)
Armant
Isna
Idfu
Kôm Ombo
Aswân
Aswan High Dam
Buḥayrat Nāṣir
(Lake Nasser)
Abu Simbel
Aṣ Ṣaḥrā' al Gharbīyah
(Western Desert)
Aṣ Ṣaḥrā' ash Sharqīyah
(Eastern Desert)
El Khârga
El Qasr
Mut
Balât
Bawîti
Qasr Farafra
Ḥaḍabat al Jilf al Kabīr
(Gilf Kebir Plateau)
Gulf of Suez
Shibh Jazîrat Sînâ
(Sinai)
Sharm el Sheikh
Hurghada
Bûr Safâga
Quseir
Marsa Alam
El 'Arîsh
ISRAEL
Tel Aviv-Yafo
GAZA
Be'ér Sheva
Gulf of Aqaba
Dahab
Nuweiba
Tirân
Ra's Muhammad
SUDAN
Wadi Halfa
2nd Cataract
3rd Cataract
4th Cataract
5th Cataract
Nubian
Station No. 6
Jebel Kurush
Akasha
Delgo
Kerma
Dongola
NORTHERN
Jebel Abyad Plateau
Kareima
Merowe
Abu Hamed
Bayuda Desert
Atbara
Ed Damer
Berber
Shendi
NILE
KHARTOUM
Omdurman
Khartoum North
Khartoum
NORTHERN KORDOFAN
NORTHERN DARFUR
El Obeid
El Fasher
Nyala
El Geneina
Marra Plateau
Jebel Marra
3088
WESTERN DARFUR
SOUTHERN DARFUR
WESTERN KORDOFAN
SOUTHERN KORDOFAN
Kadugli
Kosti
WHITE NILE
Wad Medani
EL GEZIRA
Sennar
SENNAR
Ed Damazin
BLUE NILE
UPPER NILE
CHAD
Tibesti
Emi Koussi
3415
Bardai
Zouar
Faya
BORKOU-ENNEDI-TIBESTI
Dépression du Mourdi
Erdi
Massif Ennedi
Plateau de Basso
Fada
Erg du Djourab
Koro Toro
KANEM
BILTINE
BATHA
OUADDAÏ
Abéché
Biltine
Am Djéména
SALAMAT
GUÉRA
Mongo
Am Timan
Plaine de Garar
Aozou
Ounianga Kébir
Kirdimi
VAKAGA
Birao

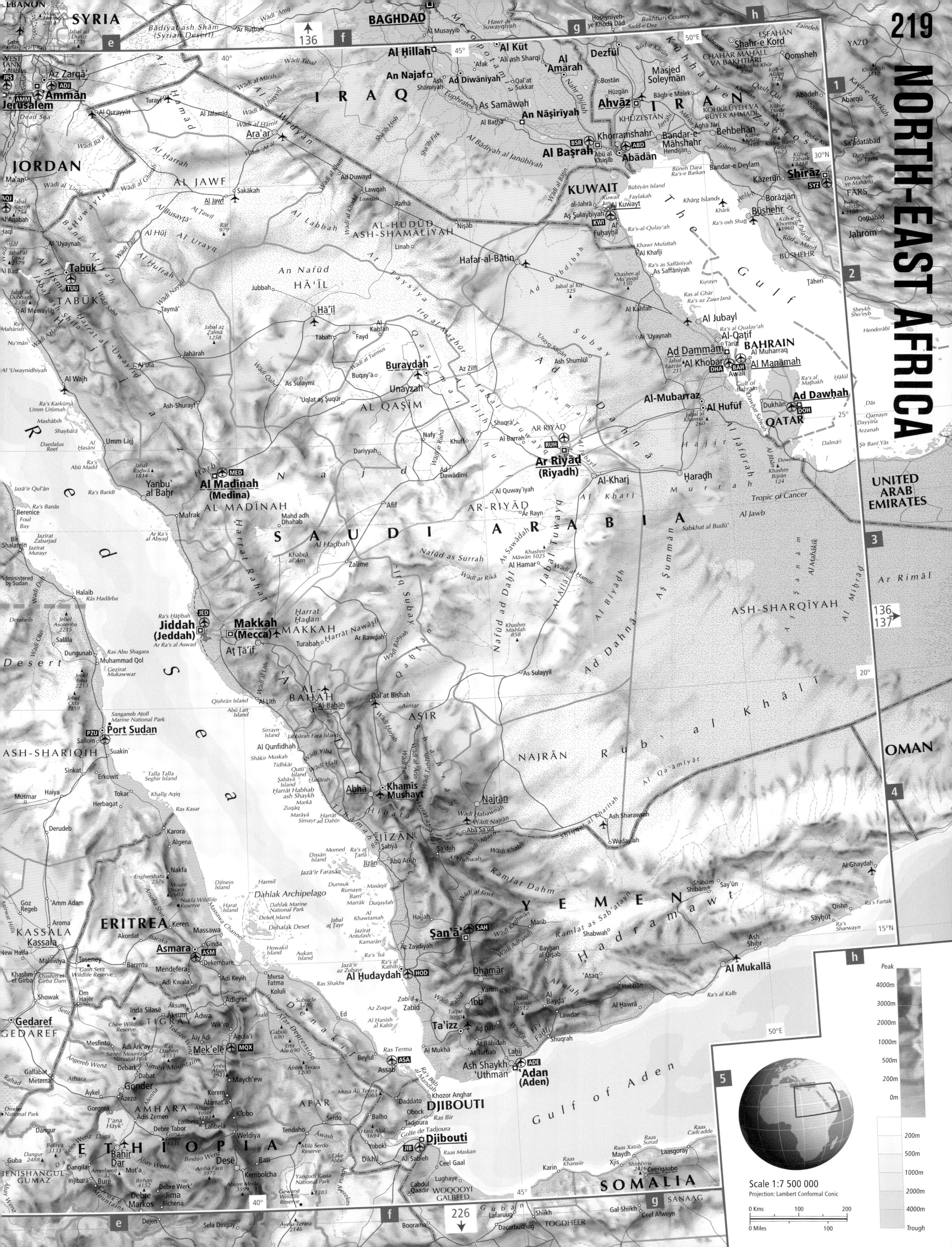

SYRIA

BAGHDAD

IRAQ

JORDAN

SAUDI ARABIA

IRAN

KUWAIT

Ar Riyād
(Riyadh)

BAHRAIN

QATAR

Ad Dawḥah

UNITED ARAB EMIRATES

OMAN

Al Madīnah
(Medina)

Makkah
(Mecca)

Jiddah
(Jeddah)

Port Sudan

Rub al Khālī

ERITREA

YEMEN

Ṣanʿāʾ

Al Mukallā

Asmara

Al Ḥudaydah

Aden
(Adan)

DJIBOUTI

Djibouti

ETHIOPIA

SOMALIA

Gulf of Aden

Red Sea

The Gulf

Scale 1:7 500 000
Projection: Lambert Conformal Conic

Peak
4000m
3000m
2000m
1000m
500m
200m
0m
Trough

AZORES
(Açores)
(Portugal)
Same scale as main map

Corvo
Flores
Graciosa
Serra de Santa Barbara
Pico Gorda 1043
1053
Terceira
Faial 1021
São Jorge
Pico 2351
Angra do Heroísmo
Pico

ATLANTIC OCEAN

São Miguel
ARQUIPÉLAGO DOS AÇORES
Ponta Delgada
1103

Santa Maria

PORTUGAL
Santarém
Portalegre
Alcázar de San Juan
Tomelloso
La Roda
Valencia
Lisboa (Lisbon)
Almada
Badajoz
Mérida
Don Benito
Ciudad Real
Valdepeñas
Albacete
Alzira
Barreiro
Cabeza del Buey
Almadén
Gandía
Setúbal
Torrão
Cabo Espichel
Zafra
Andújar
Pozoblanco
Hellín
Alcoy
Sines
Beja
Serpa
Córdoba
Úbeda
Alicante
Évora
Aljustrel
Cortegana
Jaén
Baza
Lorca
Morena
SPAIN
Odemira
Guadalquivir
Écija
Lucena
Granada
Mulhacén 3482
Almería
Murcia
Cartagena
Sevilla
Huelva
Loja
Vélez-Rubio
Portimão
Lagos
Faro
Cádiz
Málaga
Motril
Cabo de Gata
Golfo de Cádiz
Jerez de la Frontera
Estepona
Ronda
Marbella
Málaga
Alboran Sea
Cabo de São Vicente
Algeciras
La Línea de la Concepción
Gibraltar (U.K.)
Isla de Alboran (Spain)
Cabo Trafalgar
Strait of Gibraltar
Ceuta (Spain)
Cap des Trois Fourches
Oran
Aïn Temouchent
Tanger (Tangier)
Tétouan
Melilla (Spain)
Beni-Saf
Larache
Al Hoceima
Nador
Ghazaouet
Asilah
Chaouèn
Réserve de Merdja Zerga
Berkane
Maghnia
Ksar el Kebir
Taounate
Akhoul
Oujda
Souk el Arbaâ du Rharb
Ouezzane
Taourirt
Sidi Bel Abbès
Kénitra
Sidi Kacem
Fès
Taza
Guercif
El Aricha
Rabat
Sefrou
Mechena
Casablanca
Khemisset
Meknès
Aïn Beni Mathar
El Jadida
Ben Slimane
Ifrane
Azrou
Boulemane
Sebkha en Naama
Berrechid
Benahmed
Azemmour
Oued Zem
Missour
Settat
Khenifra
Tendrara
Safi
Sidi Bennour
Benguerir
Fkih Ben Salah
Boudenib
Bou Arfa
Youssoufia
Kasba Tadla
Figuig
Chemaia
El Kelaâ des Srarhna
Beni Mellal
Er Rachidia
Béchar
Essaouira
Marrakech
Ibel Toubkal 4167
Ouarzazate
Ounara
Tahanaoute
Imi-n-Tanoute
Amizmiz
Taghit
Tamanar
Ibel Aoulime 3555
MOROCCO
Agadir
Taroudant
Tinerhir
Abadla
Parc National Souss-Massa
Oulad Teima
Oued Sous
Tazenakht
Hamaguir
Tiznit
Tafraoute
Tata
Ibel Bani
Zagora
Cap Rhir
Assa
Akka
Er Raoui
Sidi Ifni
Goulimine
Bou Izakarn
Ouarkziz
Hamada du Drâa
Tabelbala
Guerzim
Kerzaz
Cap Drâa
Tan-Tan
Oued Tigzerte
Zag
Hamada Tounassine
Timoudi
Tinfouchy
Adrar
Cap Juby
Tarfaya
Laâyoune
Sabkhat Tah
Sabkhat Oum Dba
Dawra
Al Haggounia
Al Mahbas
Tindouf
Bordj Flye Ste-Marie
El Mannsour
Cap Bojador
El Cabiño
As Saquia al Hamra
Haguza
Idiniya
Boujdour
Es Semara
Bir Lahmar
Tfaritiy
Mcherrah
El Eglab
Sabkhat Aridal
Amasing
Boukrâ
Aïn Ben Tili
El Hank
Chenachane
Sabkhat Arridi
Galat Zemmour
Zemmour
Bir Bel Guerdane
Sebkhet Iguetti
Chegga
Skaymat
WESTERN SAHARA
(Administered by Morocco)
Bir Mogrein
TIRIS ZEMMOUR
Sebkha Oumm ed Droûs Telli
El Kâghet
Et H
Erg Chech
Ad Dakhla
Al Argoub
Bir Anzarane
Sabkhat Aghzoumal
Sebkha Oumm ed Droûs Guebli
Bahía de Río de Oro
Imlili
La Raygaa
Sabkhat Tamwakka
Zouérat
Golfo de Cintra
Sabkhat Tidsit
Awserd
Federik
Sebkhet ej Jill
MAURITANIA
Cap Corbeiro
Sabkhet Lamhar Touil
TOMBOUCTOU
Nouâdhibou
Bir Gandouz
Tichla
Atoui
Taoudenni
Hamâda El Haricha
DAKHLET NOUÂDHIBOU
Tmeimichât
Choûm
Ras Nouâdhibou
Ras Cansado
Dakhlet Nouâdhibou
Ouadâne
Chami
INCHIRI
Atâr
Parc National du Banc d'Arguin
Chinguetti
ADRAR
Et Tidra
Oujeft
Dhar
S a h a r a
Akjoujt
Elbel Fçâl
Erg Atouila
TAGANT
Moudjéria
Tidjikja
Tichit
Dhar Tichit
Dhar Oualâta
TRARZA
BRÂKNA
Magta-Lahjar
Aleg
Boutilimit
HODH ECH CHARGUI
Oualâta
Bogué
Bababé
Guérou
ASSABA
Kiffa
Aïoun el 'Atroûs
HODH EL GHARBI
MALI
Araouane
El Khnâchîch
Nioro
Kaédi
Tâmchekket
Timbedgha
Tintâne
Dendâra
Timbouctou
Tombouctou

Peak
4000m
3000m
2000m
1000m
500m
200m
0m

Scale 1:7 500 000
Projection: Lambert Conformal Conic

0 Kms 100 200
0 Miles 100

200m
500m
1000m
2000m
4000m
Trough

Madeira (Portugal)
Ilha de Porto Santo
Funchal
Machico
Ilhas Desertas

ATLANTIC OCEAN

Islas Canarias (Canary Islands) (Spain)
La Palma
Santa Cruz de la Palma
Lanzarote
Arrecife
Tenerife
Santa Cruz de Tenerife
La Orotava
Pico del Teide 3718
La Gomera
San Sebastián de la Gomera
Las Palmas de Gran Canaria
Puerto del Rosario
Fuerteventura
El Hierro
Valverde
Telde
Gran Canaria

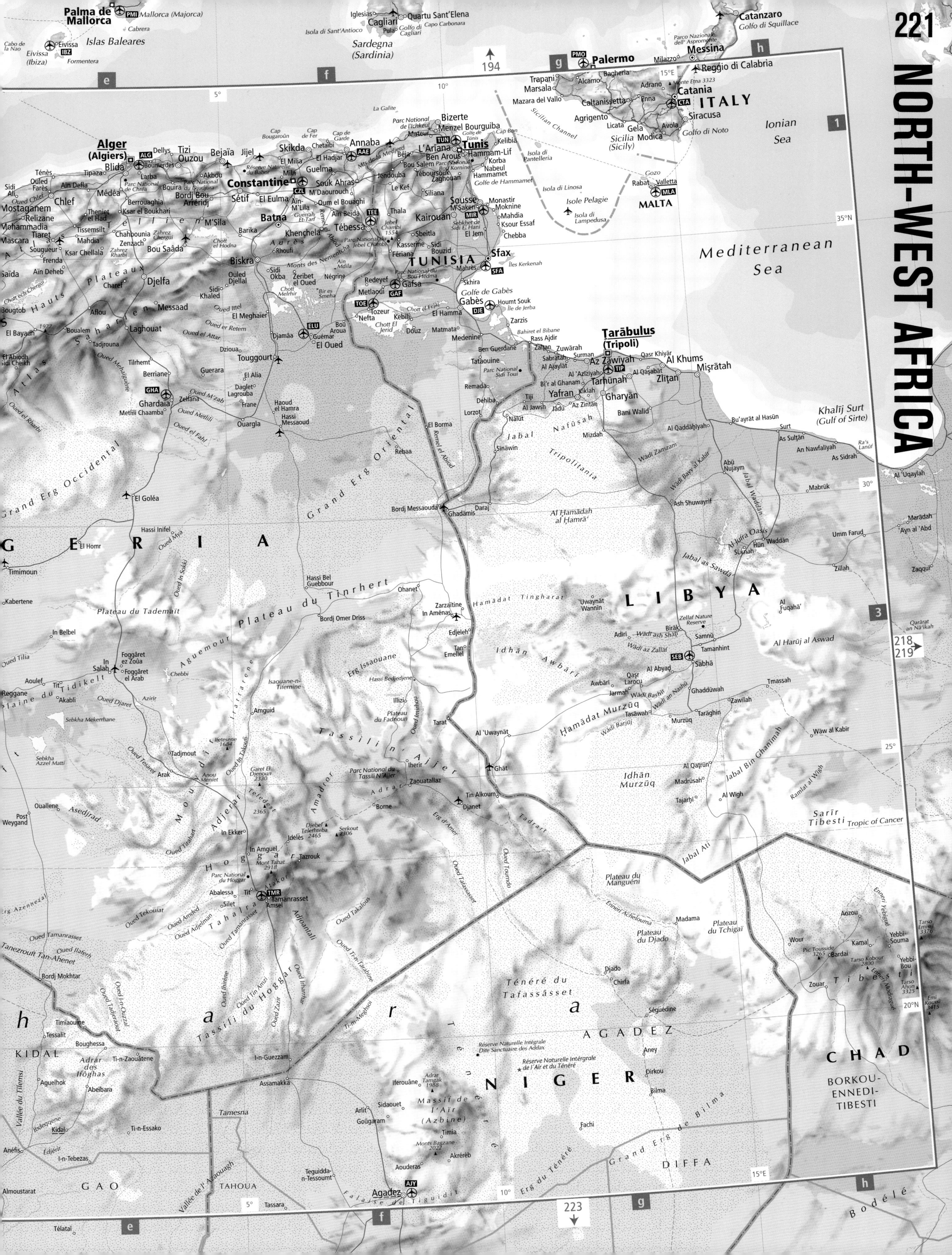

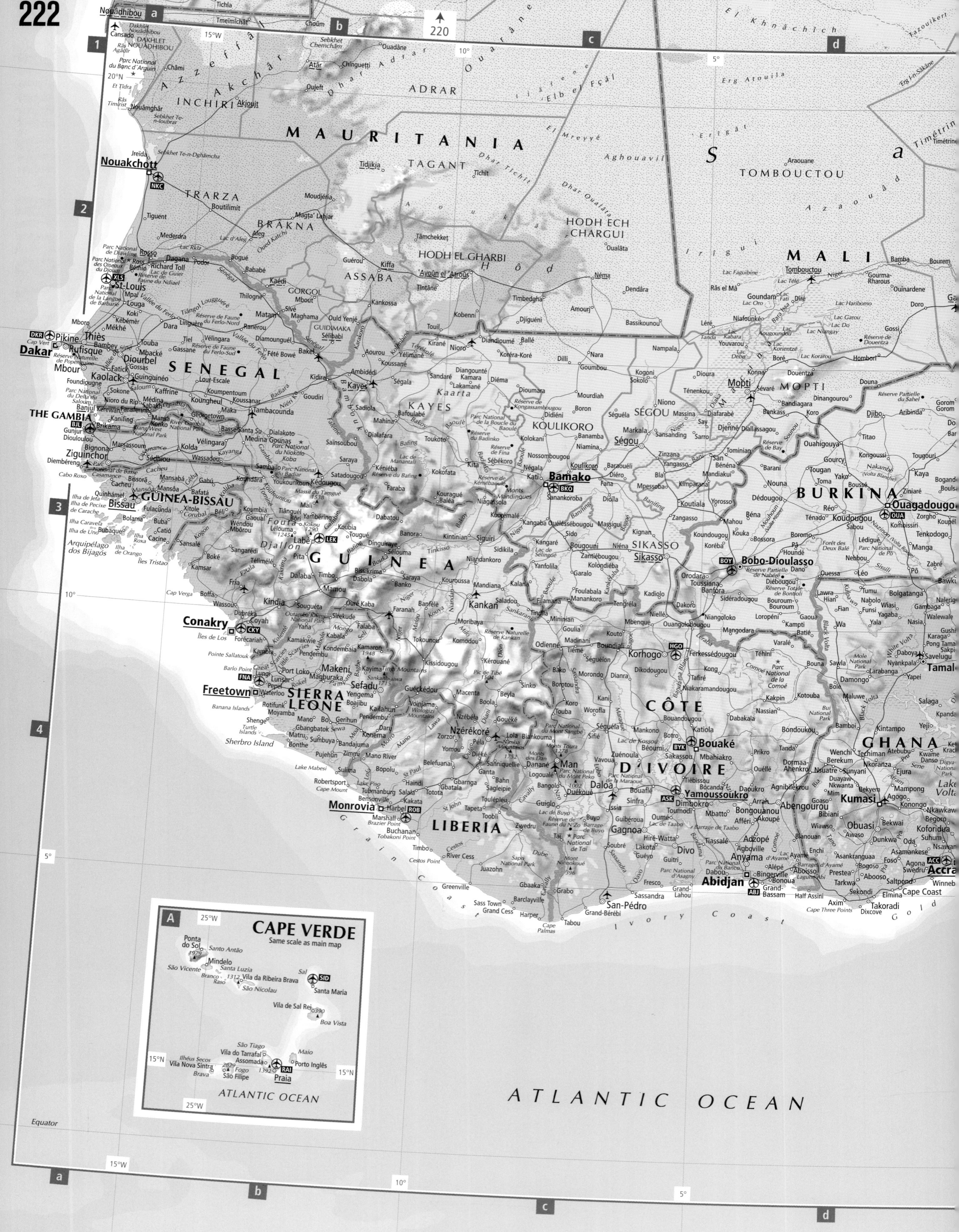
220
MAURITANIA
ADRAR
INCHIRI
TAGANT
TRARZA
BRAKNA
GORGOL
ASSABA
GUIDIMAKA
HODH EL GHARBI
HODH ECH CHARGUI
TOMBOUCTOU
MALI
MOPTI
SÉGOU
KOULIKORO
KAYES
SIKASSO
SENEGAL
THE GAMBIA
GUINEA-BISSAU
GUINEA
SIERRA LEONE
LIBERIA
CÔTE D'IVOIRE
BURKINA
GHANA
Nouâdhibou
Nouakchott
Dakar
St-Louis
Thiès
Rufisque
Diourbel
Kaolack
Tambacounda
Ziguinchor
Banjul
Bissau
Conakry
Freetown
Monrovia
Bamako
Ségou
Mopti
Tombouctou
Kayes
Kankan
Sikasso
Bobo-Dioulasso
Ouagadougou
Korhogo
Bouaké
Yamoussoukro
Abidjan
San-Pédro
Man
Daloa
Kumasi
Accra
Tamale
Cape Coast
Takoradi
Buchanan
Harper
Makeni
Bo
Kenema
Labé
Kindia
Nzérékoré
Grain Coast
Ivory Coast
ATLANTIC OCEAN
Equator
15°W
10°
5°
20°N
CAPE VERDE
Same scale as main map
Santo Antão
São Vicente
Mindelo
Santa Luzia
São Nicolau
Vila da Ribeira Brava
Sal
Santa Maria
Vila de Sal Rei
Boa Vista
Maio
Porto Inglês
São Tiago
Vila do Tarrafal
Assomada
Praia
Fogo
São Filipe
Brava
Vila Nova Sintra
ATLANTIC OCEAN
25°W
15°N

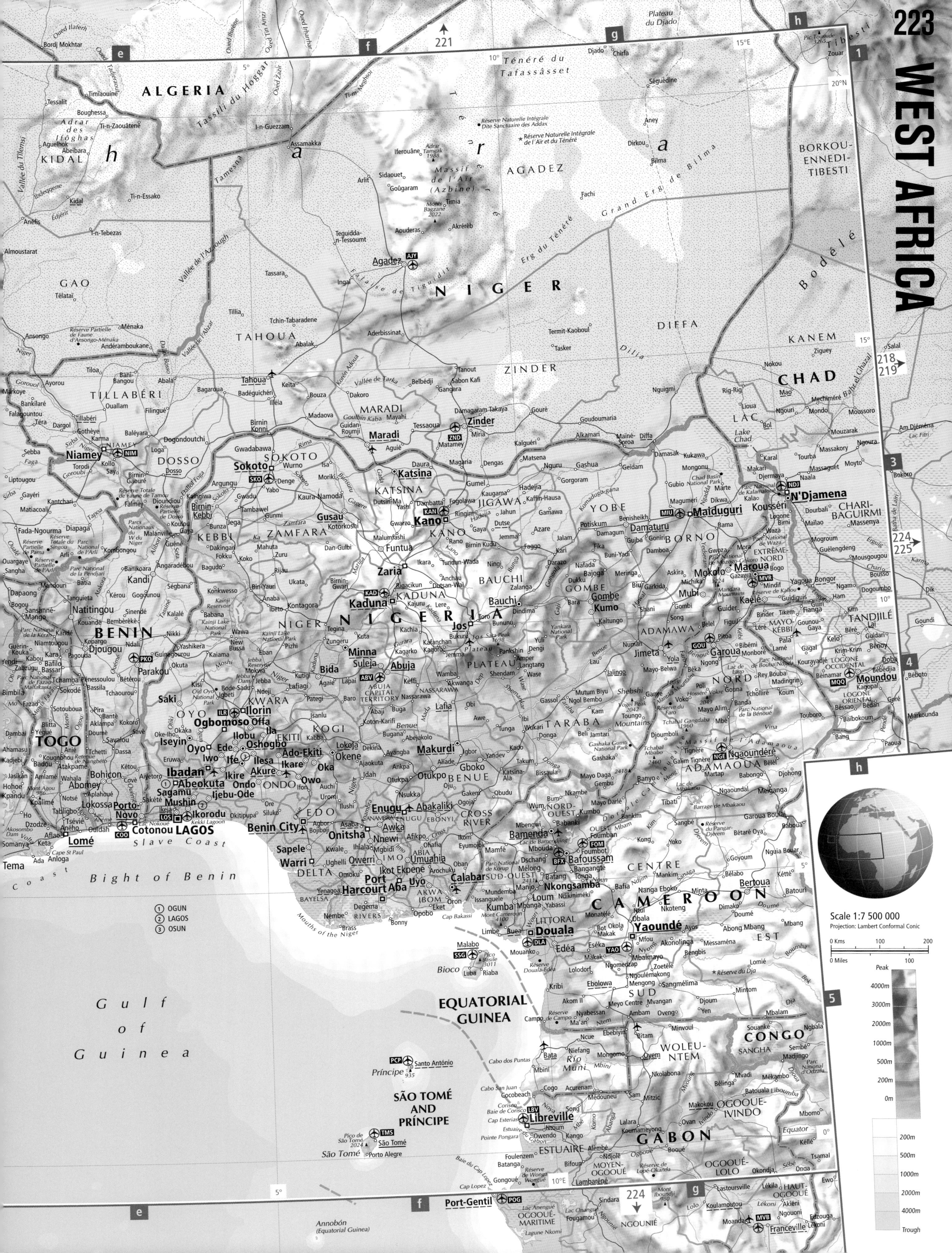

ALGERIA
NIGER
NIGERIA
BENIN
TOGO
CHAD
CAMEROON
EQUATORIAL GUINEA
SÃO TOMÉ AND PRÍNCIPE
GABON
CONGO
Gulf of Guinea
Bight of Benin
Slave Coast
Mouths of the Niger
Ténéré du Tafassâsset
Ténéré
Grand Erg de Bilma
Erg du Ténéré
Massif de l'Aïr (Azbine)
Adrar des Ifôghas
Tassili du Hoggar
Plateau du Djado
Tibesti
Bodélé
Falaise de Tiguidit
Vallée de l'Azaouagh
Dallol Bosso
Massif de l'Adamaoua
Lake Chad
KIDAL
GAO
TAHOUA
TILLABÉRI
DOSSO
MARADI
ZINDER
AGADEZ
DIFFA
KANEM
LAC
BORKOU-ENNEDI-TIBESTI
CHARI-BAGUIRMI
SOKOTO
KATSINA
JIGAWA
YOBE
BORNO
ZAMFARA
KEBBI
KANO
KADUNA
BAUCHI
GOMBE
ADAMAWA
PLATEAU
NIGER
KWARA
OYO
KOGI
BENUE
TARABA
EKITI
OSUN
ONDO
EDO
DELTA
ENUGU
EBONYI
CROSS RIVER
AKWA IBOM
RIVERS
BAYELSA
ABUJA CAPITAL TERRITORY
IMO
ABIA
ANAMBRA
EXTRÊME-NORD
NORD
ADAMAOUA
NORD-OUEST
OUEST
SUD-OUEST
LITTORAL
CENTRE
EST
SUD
LOGONE OCCIDENTAL
LOGONE ORIENTAL
MAYO-KÉBBI
TANDJILÉ
WOLEU-NTEM
ESTUAIRE
MOYEN-OGOOUÉ
OGOOUÉ-IVINDO
OGOOUÉ-LOLO
OGOOUÉ-MARITIME
NGOUNIÉ
HAUT-OGOOUÉ
SANGHA
Agadez
Niamey
Zinder
Maradi
Tahoua
Sokoto
Katsina
Kano
Maiduguri
N'Djamena
Kousséri
Zaria
Kaduna
Jos
Bauchi
Abuja
Minna
Ilorin
Ogbomoso
Oshogbo
Ibadan
Abeokuta
LAGOS
Porto Novo
Cotonou
Lomé
Benin City
Onitsha
Enugu
Port Harcourt
Calabar
Makurdi
Garoua
Maroua
Ngaoundéré
Bamenda
Bafoussam
Douala
Yaoundé
Malabo
Bata
Libreville
Port-Gentil
Lambaréné
Franceville
Moundou
São Tomé
Santo António
Príncipe
Bioco
Annobón (Equatorial Guinea)
Equator
① OGUN
② LAGOS
③ OSUN
Scale 1:7 500 000
Projection: Lambert Conformal Conic
0 Kms 100 200
0 Miles 100
Peak
4000m
3000m
2000m
1000m
500m
200m
0m
200m
500m
1000m
2000m
4000m
Trough
221
218
219
224
225
224

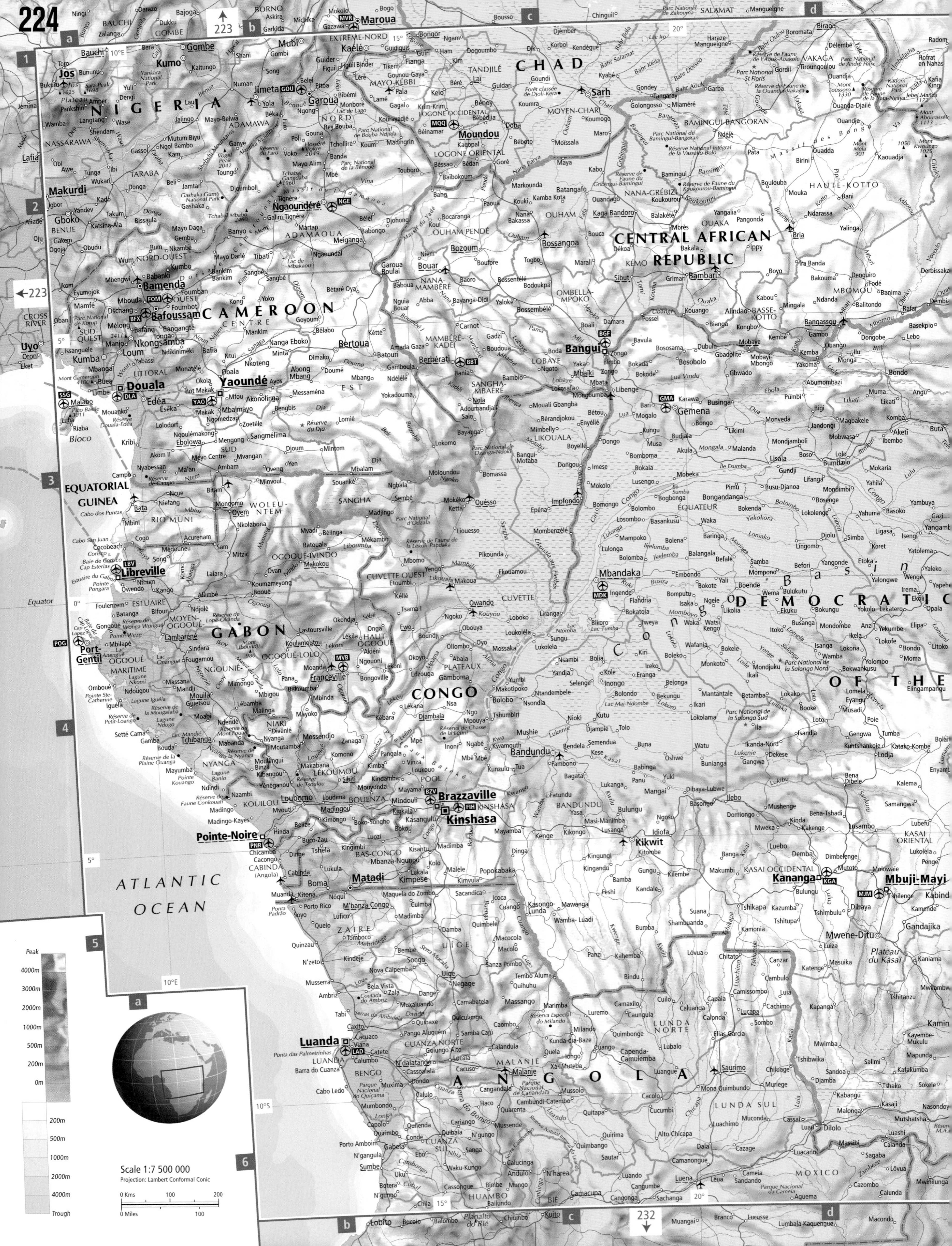

NIGERIA
CAMEROON
CHAD
CENTRAL AFRICAN REPUBLIC
EQUATORIAL GUINEA
GABON
CONGO
DEMOCRATIC
OF THE
ANGOLA
ATLANTIC OCEAN
Congo Basin
Equator
Jos
Makurdi
Uyo
Garoua
Maroua
Moundou
Sarh
Ngaoundéré
Bamenda
Bafoussam
Douala
Yaoundé
Malabo
Bata
Libreville
Port-Gentil
Franceville
Bangui
Bambari
Bossangoa
Berbérati
Gemena
Mbandaka
Bandundu
Brazzaville
Kinshasa
Pointe-Noire
Matadi
Kikwit
Kananga
Mbuji-Mayi
Luanda
Malanje
Saurimo
Luena
Peak
4000m
3000m
2000m
1000m
500m
200m
0m
200m
500m
1000m
2000m
4000m
Trough
Scale 1:7 500 000
Projection: Lambert Conformal Conic
0 Kms 100 200
0 Miles 100

223
232

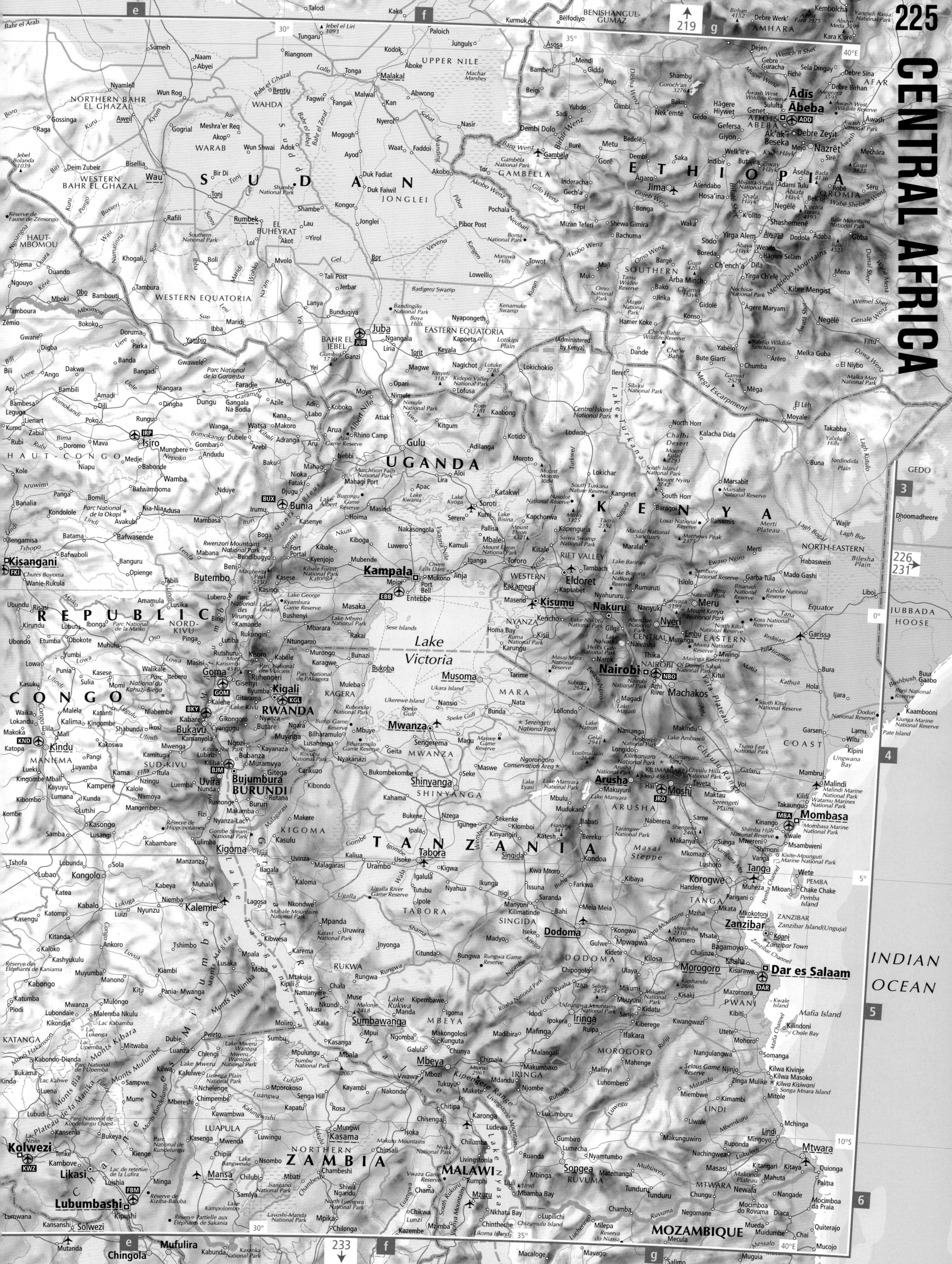
SUDAN
ETHIOPIA
UGANDA
KENYA
REPUBLIC
CONGO
RWANDA
BURUNDI
TANZANIA
ZAMBIA
MALAWI
MOZAMBIQUE
INDIAN
OCEAN
Lake
Victoria
Ādīs
Ābeba
Juba
Kampala
Nairobi
Kigali
Bujumbura
Dodoma
Dar es Salaam
Mombasa
Zanzibar
Kisangani
Lubumbashi
Kolwezi
Mbeya
Iringa
Morogoro
Arusha
Moshi
Nakuru
Eldoret
Kisumu
Nyeri
Meru
Machakos
Malindi
Tanga
Mwanza
Tabora
Kigoma
Shinyanga
Musoma
Bukoba
Goma
Bukavu
Uvira
Kindu
Kalemie
Sumbawanga
Songea
Lindi
Mtwara
Gulu
Bunia
Isiro
Wau
Malakal
Jimma
Nazrēt
Gambela
UPPER NILE
JONGLEI
WESTERN EQUATORIA
EASTERN EQUATORIA
BAHR EL JEBEL
NORTHERN BAHR EL GHAZAL
WESTERN BAHR EL GHAZAL
EL BUHEYRAT
WAHDA
WARAB
GAMBELLA
OROMIA
SOUTHERN
AMHARA
AFAR
BENISHANGUL-GUMAZ
HAUT-CONGO
NORD-KIVU
SUD-KIVU
MANIEMA
KATANGA
HAUT-MBOMOU
NYANZA
WESTERN
RIFT VALLEY
CENTRAL
EASTERN
NORTH-EASTERN
COAST
JUBBADA HOOSE
GEDO
KAGERA
MARA
MWANZA
KIGOMA
TABORA
SINGIDA
DODOMA
RUKWA
MBEYA
IRINGA
MOROGORO
LINDI
MTWARA
RUVUMA
PWANI
TANGA
ARUSHA
KILIMANJARO
SHINYANGA
LUAPULA
NORTHERN
ZANZIBAR
PEMBA
Lake Turkana
Lake Tanganyika
Lake Malawi
Lake Rukwa
Lake Mweru
Lake Kivu
Lake Albert
Lake Edward
Lake Kyoga
Sese Islands
Masai Steppe
Serengeti National Park
Mafia Island
Equator
0°
5°
10°S
30°
35°
40°E
e
f
g
3
4
5
6
219
226
231
233

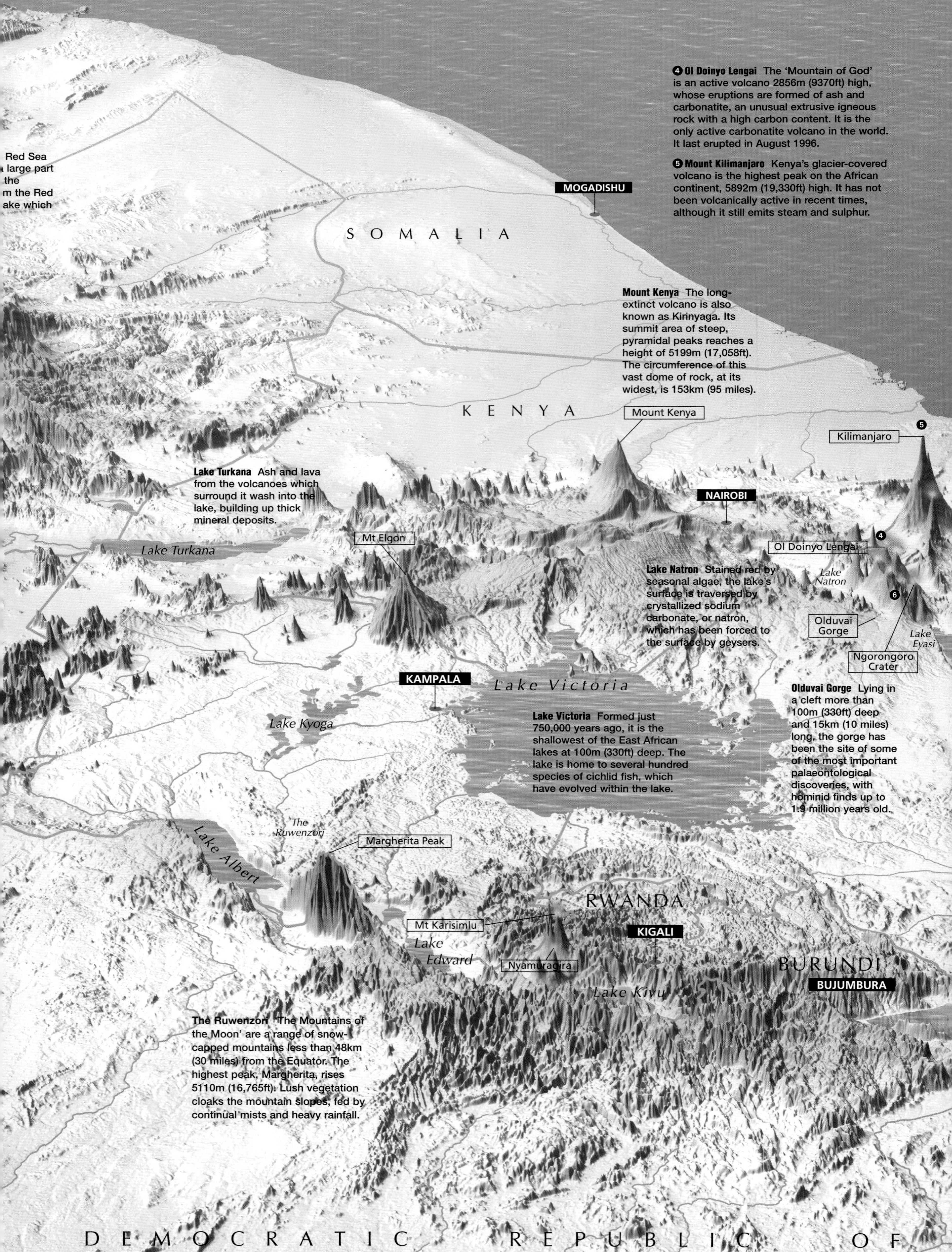

Red Sea
large part
the
m the Red
ake which

SOMALIA

MOGADISHU

④ **Ol Doinyo Lengai** The 'Mountain of God' is an active volcano 2856m (9370ft) high, whose eruptions are formed of ash and carbonatite, an unusual extrusive igneous rock with a high carbon content. It is the only active carbonatite volcano in the world. It last erupted in August 1996.

⑤ **Mount Kilimanjaro** Kenya's glacier-covered volcano is the highest peak on the African continent, 5892m (19,330ft) high. It has not been volcanically active in recent times, although it still emits steam and sulphur.

Mount Kenya The long-extinct volcano is also known as Kirinyaga. Its summit area of steep, pyramidal peaks reaches a height of 5199m (17,058ft). The circumference of this vast dome of rock, at its widest, is 153km (95 miles).

K E N Y A

Mount Kenya

Kilimanjaro ⑤

NAIROBI

Lake Turkana Ash and lava from the volcanoes which surround it wash into the lake, building up thick mineral deposits.

Lake Turkana

Mt Elgon

Ol Doinyo Lengai ④

Lake Natron

Lake Natron Stained red by seasonal algae, the lake's surface is traversed by crystallized sodium carbonate, or natron, which has been forced to the surface by geysers.

⑥

Olduvai Gorge

Lake Eyasi

Ngorongoro Crater

KAMPALA

Lake Victoria

Lake Kyoga

Lake Victoria Formed just 750,000 years ago, it is the shallowest of the East African lakes at 100m (330ft) deep. The lake is home to several hundred species of cichlid fish, which have evolved within the lake.

Olduvai Gorge Lying in a cleft more than 100m (330ft) deep and 15km (10 miles) long, the gorge has been the site of some of the most important palaeontological discoveries, with hominid finds up to 1.9 million years old.

The Ruwenzori

Margherita Peak

Lake Albert

RWANDA

KIGALI

Mt Karisimlu

Lake Edward

Nyamuragira

Lake Kivu

BURUNDI

BUJUMBURA

The Ruwenzori 'The Mountains of the Moon' are a range of snow-capped mountains less than 48km (30 miles) from the Equator. The highest peak, Margherita, rises 5110m (16,765ft). Lush vegetation cloaks the mountain slopes, fed by continual mists and heavy rainfall.

D E M O C R A T I C   R E P U B L I C   O F

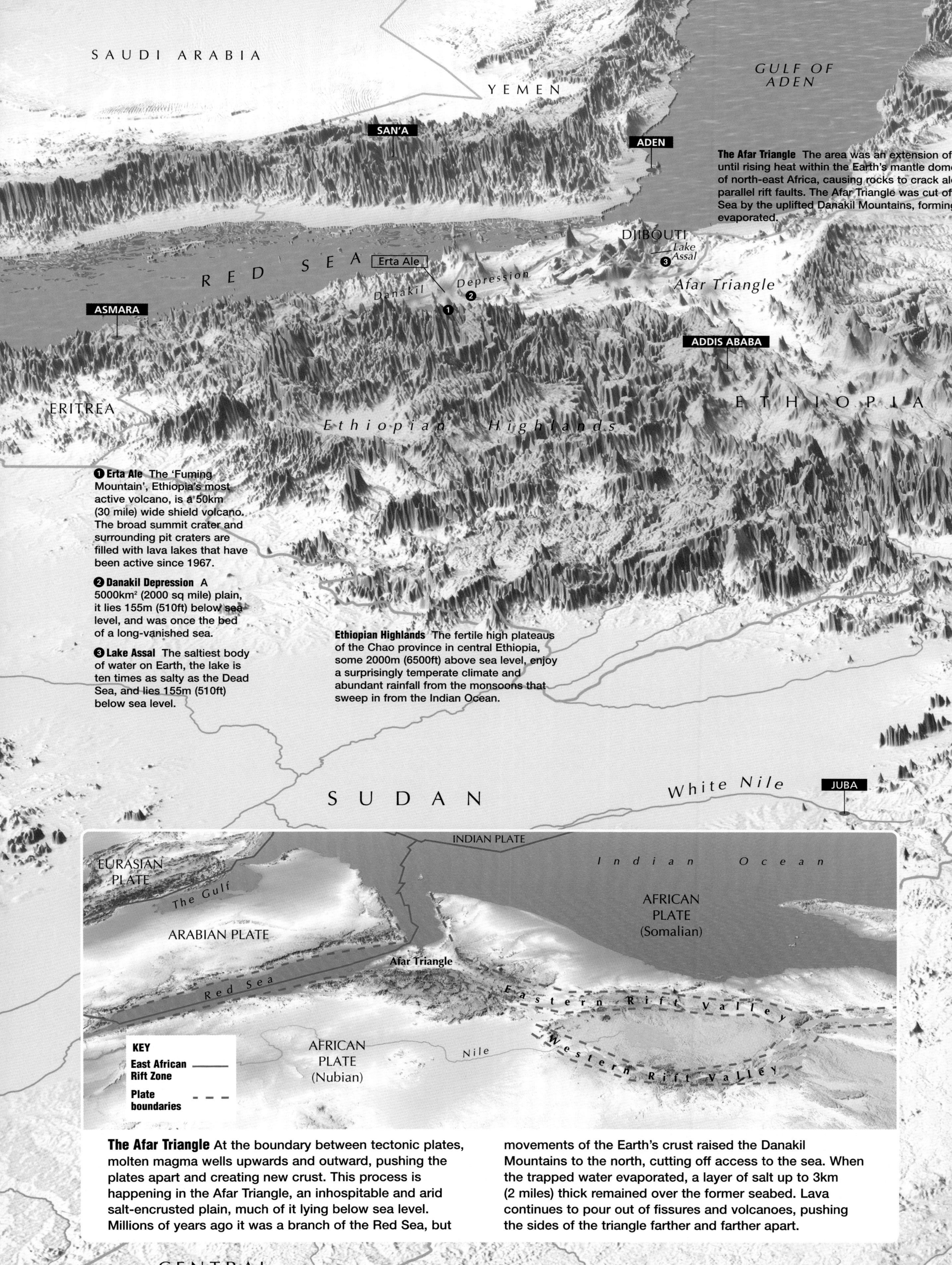

SAUDI ARABIA

YEMEN

GULF OF ADEN

SAN'A

ADEN

The Afar Triangle The area was an extension of the
until rising heat within the Earth's mantle domed
of north-east Africa, causing rocks to crack along
parallel rift faults. The Afar Triangle was cut off fr
Sea by the uplifted Danakil Mountains, forming a
evaporated.

RED SEA

Erta Ale

Danakil   Depression

DJIBOUTI   Lake Assal   ❸

Afar Triangle

❶

❷

ASMARA

ADDIS ABABA

ERITREA

ETHIOPIA

Ethiopian   Highlands

❶ **Erta Ale** The 'Fuming
Mountain', Ethiopia's most
active volcano, is a 50km
(30 mile) wide shield volcano.
The broad summit crater and
surrounding pit craters are
filled with lava lakes that have
been active since 1967.

❷ **Danakil Depression** A
5000km² (2000 sq mile) plain,
it lies 155m (510ft) below sea
level, and was once the bed
of a long-vanished sea.

❸ **Lake Assal** The saltiest body
of water on Earth, the lake is
ten times as salty as the Dead
Sea, and lies 155m (510ft)
below sea level.

Ethiopian Highlands The fertile high plateaus
of the Chao province in central Ethiopia,
some 2000m (6500ft) above sea level, enjoy
a surprisingly temperate climate and
abundant rainfall from the monsoons that
sweep in from the Indian Ocean.

SUDAN

White Nile

JUBA

INDIAN PLATE

EURASIAN PLATE

Indian   Ocean

The Gulf

AFRICAN PLATE
(Somalian)

ARABIAN PLATE

Afar Triangle

Red Sea

Eastern   Rift   Valley

KEY
East African
Rift Zone ———

Plate
boundaries − − −

AFRICAN PLATE
(Nubian)

Nile

Western   Rift   Valley

The Afar Triangle At the boundary between tectonic plates,
molten magma wells upwards and outward, pushing the
plates apart and creating new crust. This process is
happening in the Afar Triangle, an inhospitable and arid
salt-encrusted plain, much of it lying below sea level.
Millions of years ago it was a branch of the Red Sea, but

movements of the Earth's crust raised the Danakil
Mountains to the north, cutting off access to the sea. When
the trapped water evaporated, a layer of salt up to 3km
(2 miles) thick remained over the former seabed. Lava
continues to pour out of fissures and volcanoes, pushing
the sides of the triangle farther and farther apart.

CENTRAL
AFRICAN REPUBLIC

219
218
224 225

SEYCHELLES
Scale 1:1 600 000

Mahé

North Point · Île du Nord · Île Moyenne · Île au Cerf · Cascade · Victoria · Beau Vallon · Baie Beau Vallon · Morne Seychellois · Anse Boileau · Anse à la Mouche · Anse Royal · Takamaka · Pointe du Sud · Île Thérèse · Île Conception

INDIAN OCEAN

SUDAN

SOUTHERN KORDOFAN · BLUE NILE · UPPER NILE · JONGLEI · EASTERN EQUATORIA · WAHDA

Ed Damazin · El Renk · Malakal · Juba · Bor

ETHIOPIA

AMHARA · OROMIA · BENISHANGUL-GUMAZ · GAMBELLA · AFAR · SOMALI

Adis Abeba · Bahir Dar · Debre Markos · Dire Dawa · Harer · Nazrēt · Jima · Desē

DJIBOUTI

Djibouti · Tadjoura

SOMALIA

BARI · NUGAAL · SOOL · SANAAG · TOGDHEER · MUDUG · GALGUDUUD · HIIRAAN · BAKOOL · GEDO · JUBBADA DHEXE · JUBBADA HOOSE · SHABEELLAHA DHEXE · SHABEELLAHA HOOSE

Muqdisho (Mogadishu) · Hargeysa · Berbera · Boosaaso · Marka · Kismaayo · Baydhabo

Gulf of Aden · Indian Ocean · Ogaden

KENYA

RIFT VALLEY · EASTERN · NORTH-EASTERN · COAST · WESTERN · NYANZA · MARA

Nairobi · Nakuru · Eldoret · Kisumu · Nyeri · Meru · Embu · Garissa

Lake Turkana · Lake Victoria

UGANDA

Kampala · Gulu · Jinja · Entebbe

RWANDA

TANZANIA

MARA · MWANZA · KAGERA

Mwanza · Musoma · Arusha

Lake Victoria

EAST AFRICA

INDIAN OCEAN

MAURITIUS
Scale 1:2 000 000

Goodlands • Rivière du Rempart • Pointe Lafayette • Centre de Flacq • Grande Rivière Sud-Est • Mahébourg
Triolet • Pointe aux Canonniers • Beau Bassin • Rose Hill • Phoenix • Rose Belle
Port Louis • Quatre Bornes • Vacoas • Curepipe • Surinam
Pointe aux Sables • Tamarin • Mount Coode 828 • Bel Ombre • Pointe Sud Ouest
57°30'E 20°S INDIAN OCEAN

RÉUNION (France)
Scale 1:2 000 000

Sainte-Marie • Saint-André • Saint-Benoît • Sainte-Rose • Bois-Blanc
Saint-Denis • Le Port • Saint-Paul • Le Brûlé • Cilaos • Piton des Neiges 3069 • La Plaine-des-Palmistes • Piton de la Fournaise 2632 • Saint-Philippe
La Saline • Saint-Leu • Les Avirons • La Plaine-des-Cafres • Le Tampon • Saint-Joseph • Saint-Pierre • Saint-Louis
55°30'E 21°S INDIAN OCEAN

COMOROS
Pointe Nord • Nzuwani (Anjouan) 1595 • Mwali (Mohéli)
Nazidja/Grande Comore • Kartala 2361 • **Moroni** • Pointe Sud

Aldabra Islands (Seychelles) • Cosmoledo Atoll • Aldabra Atoll • Îles Glorieuses (France) • Geyser Reef • Mayotte (France) • St-Pierre • Farquhar Group (Seychelles)

MADAGASCAR
Antsiranana • Mahajanga • Antananarivo • Toamasina • Antsirabe
Mahajanga • Antananarivo

Mozambique Channel

MOZAMBIQUE
Nacala • Mossuril • Nampula • Quelimane • Beira • Mocuba • Blantyre
CABO DELGADO • NIASSA • NAMPULA • ZAMBEZIA • SOFALA • TETE
Mtwara • Lindi • Pemba • Mocímboa da Praia

TANZANIA
Dar es Salaam • Mombasa • Tanga • Zanzibar • Morogoro • Dodoma • Iringa • Mbeya • Tabora • Songea
ARUSHA • DODOMA • MOROGORO • IRINGA • MBEYA • TABORA • SHINYANGA • SINGIDA • RUVUMA • LINDI • MTWARA • PWANI
Serengeti Plains • Masai Steppe • Masai Steppe

MALAWI
Lilongwe • Blantyre • Mzuzu
NORTHERN • CENTRAL • SOUTHERN

ZAMBIA
Chipata • Kasama
EASTERN • NORTHERN

Lake Tanganyika • Lake Nyasa/Lake Malawi • Lake Rukwa • Lake Eyasi

KIGOMA • SHINYANGA • RUKWA

INDIAN OCEAN

Scale 1:7 500 000
Projection: Lambert Conformal Conic

0 Kms 100 200
0 Miles 100

Peak • 4000m • 3000m • 2000m • 1000m • 500m • 200m • 0m • 200m • 500m • 1000m • 2000m • 4000m • Trough

232 233
233

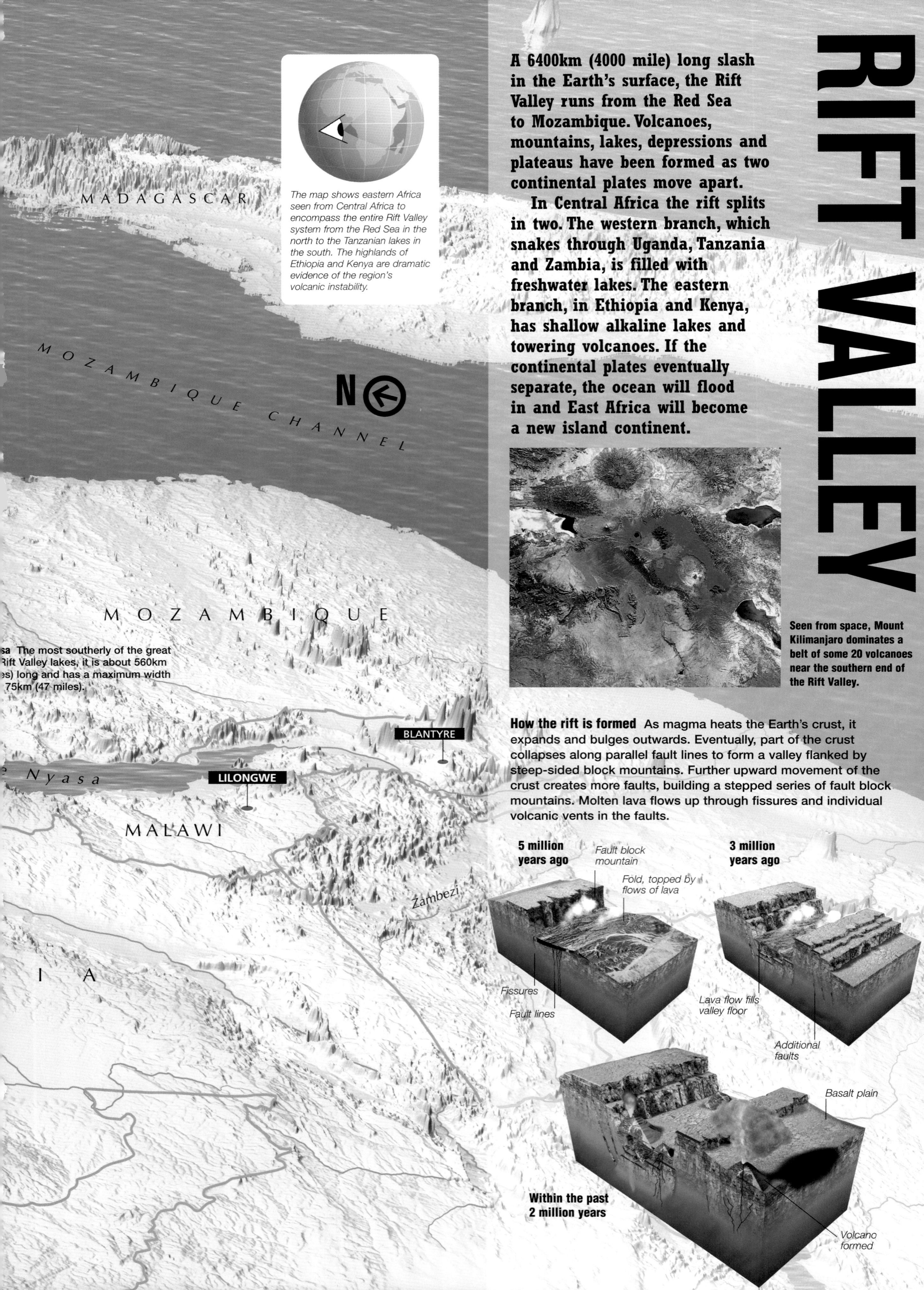

A 6400km (4000 mile) long slash in the Earth's surface, the Rift Valley runs from the Red Sea to Mozambique. Volcanoes, mountains, lakes, depressions and plateaus have been formed as two continental plates move apart.

In Central Africa the rift splits in two. The western branch, which snakes through Uganda, Tanzania and Zambia, is filled with freshwater lakes. The eastern branch, in Ethiopia and Kenya, has shallow alkaline lakes and towering volcanoes. If the continental plates eventually separate, the ocean will flood in and East Africa will become a new island continent.

The map shows eastern Africa seen from Central Africa to encompass the entire Rift Valley system from the Red Sea in the north to the Tanzanian lakes in the south. The highlands of Ethiopia and Kenya are dramatic evidence of the region's volcanic instability.

MADAGASCAR

M O Z A M B I Q U E   C H A N N E L

N

M O Z A M B I Q U E

...sa The most southerly of the great
...Rift Valley lakes, it is about 560km
...es) long and has a maximum width
...75km (47 miles).

BLANTYRE

LILONGWE

...e N y a s a

MALAWI

Zambezi

I A

Seen from space, Mount Kilimanjaro dominates a belt of some 20 volcanoes near the southern end of the Rift Valley.

How the rift is formed As magma heats the Earth's crust, it expands and bulges outwards. Eventually, part of the crust collapses along parallel fault lines to form a valley flanked by steep-sided block mountains. Further upward movement of the crust creates more faults, building a stepped series of fault block mountains. Molten lava flows up through fissures and individual volcanic vents in the faults.

5 million years ago

Fault block mountain

Fold, topped by flows of lava

Fissures

Fault lines

3 million years ago

Lava flow fills valley floor

Additional faults

Basalt plain

Within the past 2 million years

Volcano formed

INDIAN OCEAN

6 Ngorongoro Once volcanic, this peak is now a crater 20km (12 miles) wide with a saltwater lake and springs that make the crater a fertile haven for wildlife.

COMOROS

MOMBASA

DAR ES SALAAM

DODOMA

Lake Ny
African
(348 mi
of abou

T A N Z A N I A

Lak

Lake Tanganyika With a length of 670km (416 miles), Tanganyika is the longest lake in the world and the second deepest, at 1470m (4822ft), after Lake Baikal in Siberia. It is estimated that 90 per cent of the water in the lake evaporates each year, causing the water level to drop by 45cm (18in) a year.

Lake Rukwa

Z A M B

Lake Tanganyika

Lake Bangweulu

Lake Mweru

C O N G O

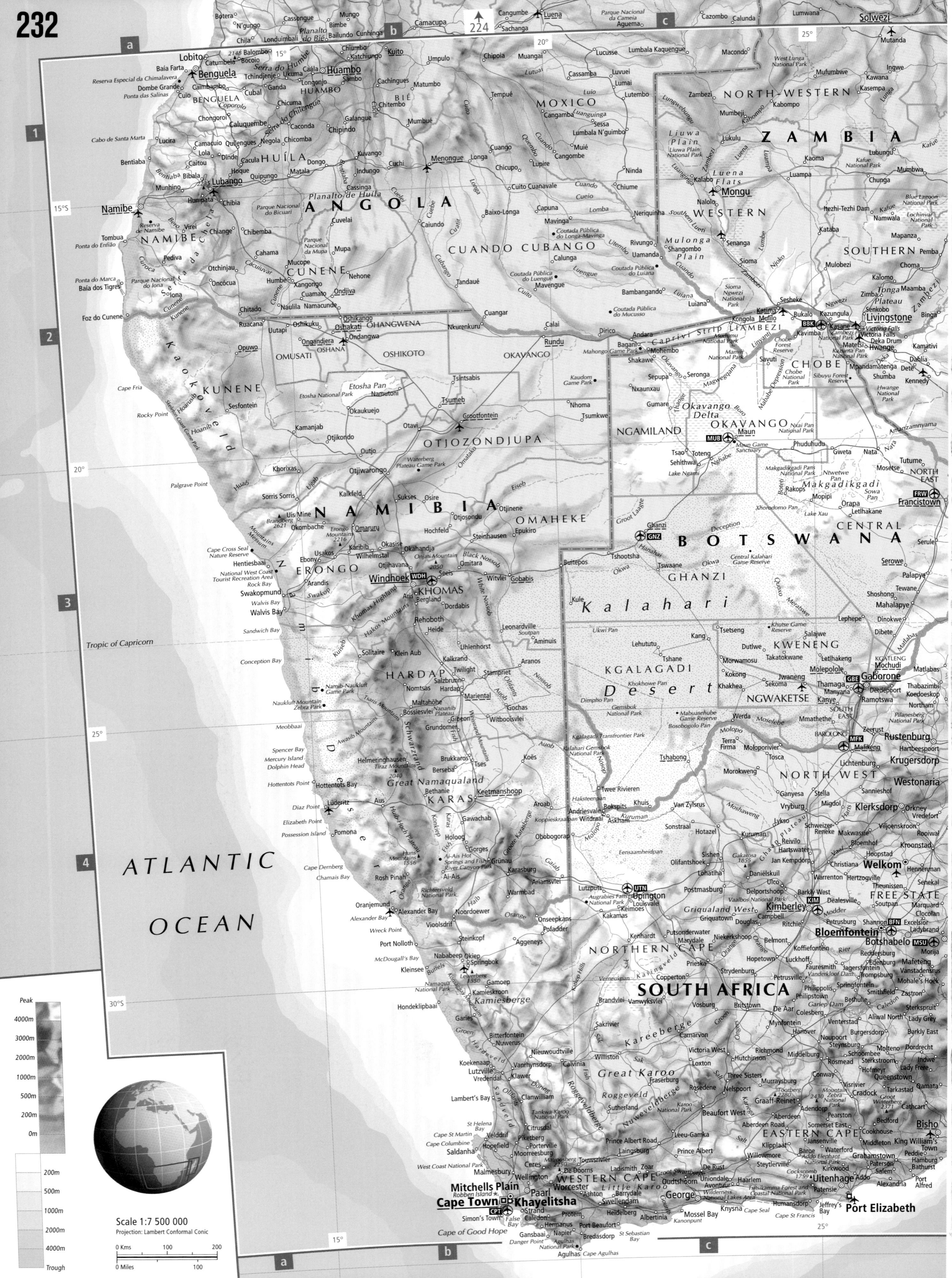
224
ANGOLA
NAMIBIA
BOTSWANA
ZAMBIA
SOUTH AFRICA
ATLANTIC
OCEAN
BENGUELA
HUAMBO
BIÉ
MOXICO
HUÍLA
NAMIBE
CUNENE
CUANDO CUBANGO
NORTH-WESTERN
WESTERN
SOUTHERN
OHANGWENA
OMUSATI
OSHANA
OSHIKOTO
OKAVANGO
KUNENE
OTJOZONDJUPA
OMAHEKE
ERONGO
KHOMAS
HARDAP
KARAS
CHOBE
NGAMILAND
CENTRAL
NORTH EAST
GHANZI
KWENENG
KGALAGADI
SOUTH EAST
NGWAKETSE
NORTH WEST
FREE STATE
NORTHERN CAPE
EASTERN CAPE
WESTERN CAPE
Kalahari
Desert
Namib Desert
Kaokoveld
Great Karoo
Little Karoo
Great Namaqualand
Caprivi Strip
Okavango Delta
Makgadikgadi
Etosha Pan
Tropic of Capricorn
Lobito
Benguela
Huambo
Kuito
Lubango
Namibe
Menongue
Luena
Solwezi
Mongu
Livingstone
Windhoek
Walvis Bay
Swakopmund
Lüderitz
Keetmanshoop
Rundu
Tsumeb
Grootfontein
Maun
Ghanzi
Francistown
Serowe
Gaborone
Molepolole
Kanye
Mafikeng
Rustenburg
Krugersdorp
Westonaria
Klerksdorp
Welkom
Kimberley
Bloemfontein
Botshabelo
Upington
Bisho
Uitenhage
Port Elizabeth
George
Mitchells Plain
Cape Town
Khayelitsha
Cape of Good Hope
Cape Agulhas
Peak
4000m
3000m
2000m
1000m
500m
200m
0m
200m
500m
1000m
2000m
4000m
Trough
Scale 1:7 500 000
Projection: Lambert Conformal Conic
0 Kms 100 200
0 Miles 100

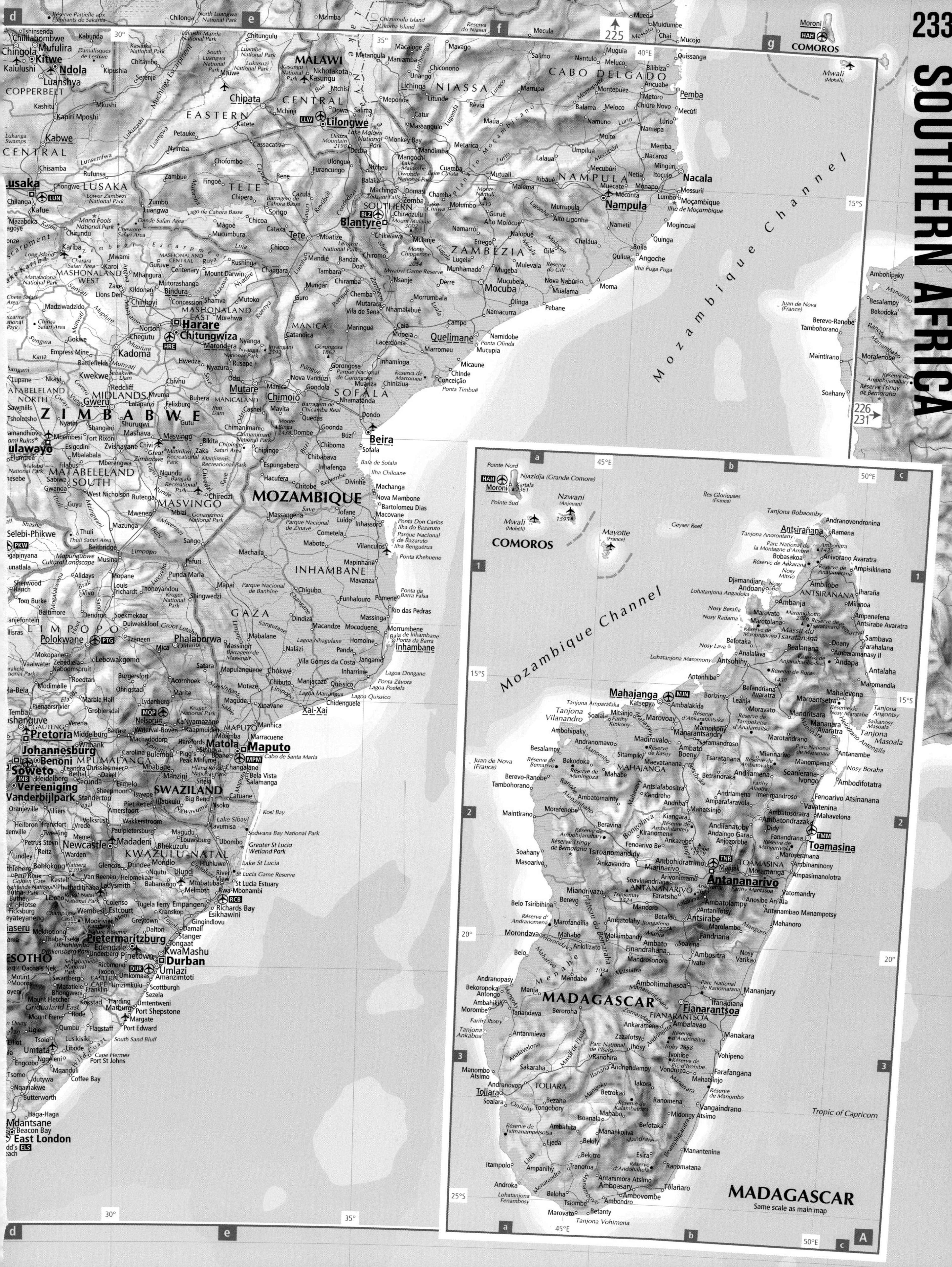
MALAWI
MOZAMBIQUE
ZIMBABWE
SWAZILAND
LESOTHO
COMOROS
MADAGASCAR
Mozambique Channel
CABO DELGADO
NIASSA
NAMPULA
ZAMBEZIA
TETE
MANICA
SOFALA
INHAMBANE
GAZA
MAPUTO
EASTERN
CENTRAL
LUSAKA
COPPERBELT
SOUTHERN
MASHONALAND WEST
MASHONALAND CENTRAL
MASHONALAND EAST
MIDLANDS
MANICALAND
MASVINGO
MATABELELAND NORTH
MATABELELAND SOUTH
LIMPOPO
MPUMALANGA
GAUTENG
KWAZULU-NATAL
EASTERN CAPE
Lusaka
Ndola
Kitwe
Kabwe
Lilongwe
Blantyre
Zomba
Chipata
Harare
Chitungwiza
Bulawayo
Gweru
Mutare
Masvingo
Tete
Quelimane
Nampula
Nacala
Pemba
Beira
Chimoio
Inhambane
Xai-Xai
Maputo
Matola
Pretoria
Johannesburg
Soweto
Benoni
Vereeniging
Vanderbijlpark
Polokwane
Phalaborwa
Mbabane
Manzini
Newcastle
Pietermaritzburg
Durban
Umlazi
KwaMashu
Richards Bay
East London
Umtata
Port Shepstone
Moroni
Mwali
Nzwani
Njazidja (Grande Comore)
Mayotte (France)
Juan de Nova (France)
Antsiranana
Mahajanga
Toamasina
Antananarivo
Antsirabe
Fianarantsoa
Toliara
Tôlañaro
Morondava
ANTSIRANANA
MAHAJANGA
TOAMASINA
ANTANANARIVO
FIANARANTSOA
TOLIARA
Tropic of Capricorn
MADAGASCAR
Same scale as main map
225
226
231

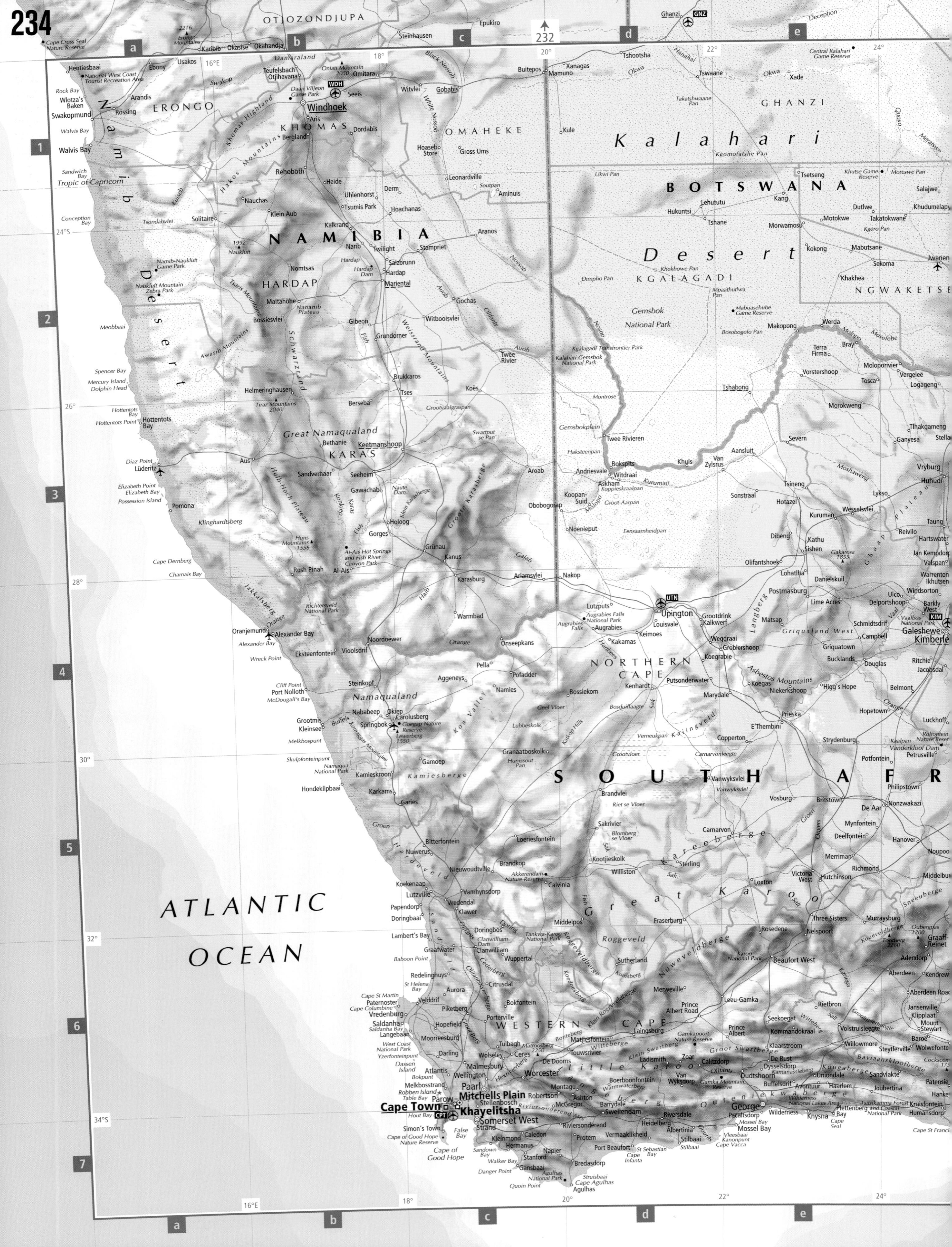

OTJOZONDJUPA
232
ATLANTIC
OCEAN
NAMIBIA
BOTSWANA
SOUTH AFR
Kalahari
Desert
Namib
Desert
ERONGO
KHOMAS
HARDAP
KARAS
OMAHEKE
GHANZI
KGALAGADI
NGWAKETSE
NORTHERN CAPE
WESTERN CAPE
Great Karoo
Little Karoo
Great Namaqualand
Namaqualand
Windhoek
Rehoboth
Mariental
Keetmanshoop
Lüderitz
Walvis Bay
Swakopmund
Tropic of Capricorn
Gobabis
Upington
Kimberley
Galeshewe
Cape Town
Mitchells Plain
Khayelitsha
Paarl
Stellenbosch
Somerset West
Worcester
George
Mossel Bay
Beaufort West
Graaff-Reinet
Springbok
Port Nolloth
Alexander Bay
Oranjemund
Karasburg
Aus
Maltahöhe
Gibeon
Ghanzi
Tshabong
Werda
Kuruman
Vryburg
Postmasburg
Prieska
Calvinia
Carnarvon
Victoria West
Oudtshoorn
Knysna
Plettenberg Bay
Cape of Good Hope
Cape Agulhas
Agulhas
Saldanha
Vredenburg
Langebaan
Clanwilliam
Vanrhynsdorp
Vredendal
Lutzville
Kenhardt
Pofadder
Aggeneys
Sutherland
Laingsburg
Prince Albert
Ladismith
Calitzdorp
Swellendam
Bredasdorp
Hermanus
Caledon
Robertson
Montagu
Ceres
Tulbagh
Malmesbury
Wellington
Parow
Atlantis
Robben Island
Simon's Town
False Bay
Walker Bay
Kalahari Gemsbok National Park
Gemsbok National Park
Kgalagadi Transfrontier Park
Augrabies Falls National Park
Richtersveld National Park
Namaqua National Park
Karoo National Park
Namib-Naukluft Game Park
Fish River Canyon Park
Orange
Nossob
Molopo
Fish
Auob
Kuruman
Hartbees
Sak
Olifants
Kamiesberge
Cederberg
Nuweveldberge
Roggeveld
Swartberge
Langeberg
Outeniekwaberge
Kouga berge
Karas
Klein Karasberge
Groot Karasberge
Schwarzrand
Huib-Hoch Plateau
Koa Valley
a
b
c
d
e
1
2
3
4
5
6
7
16°E
18°
20°
22°
24°
24°S
26°
28°
30°
32°
34°S
WDH
GNZ
UTN
KIM
CPT

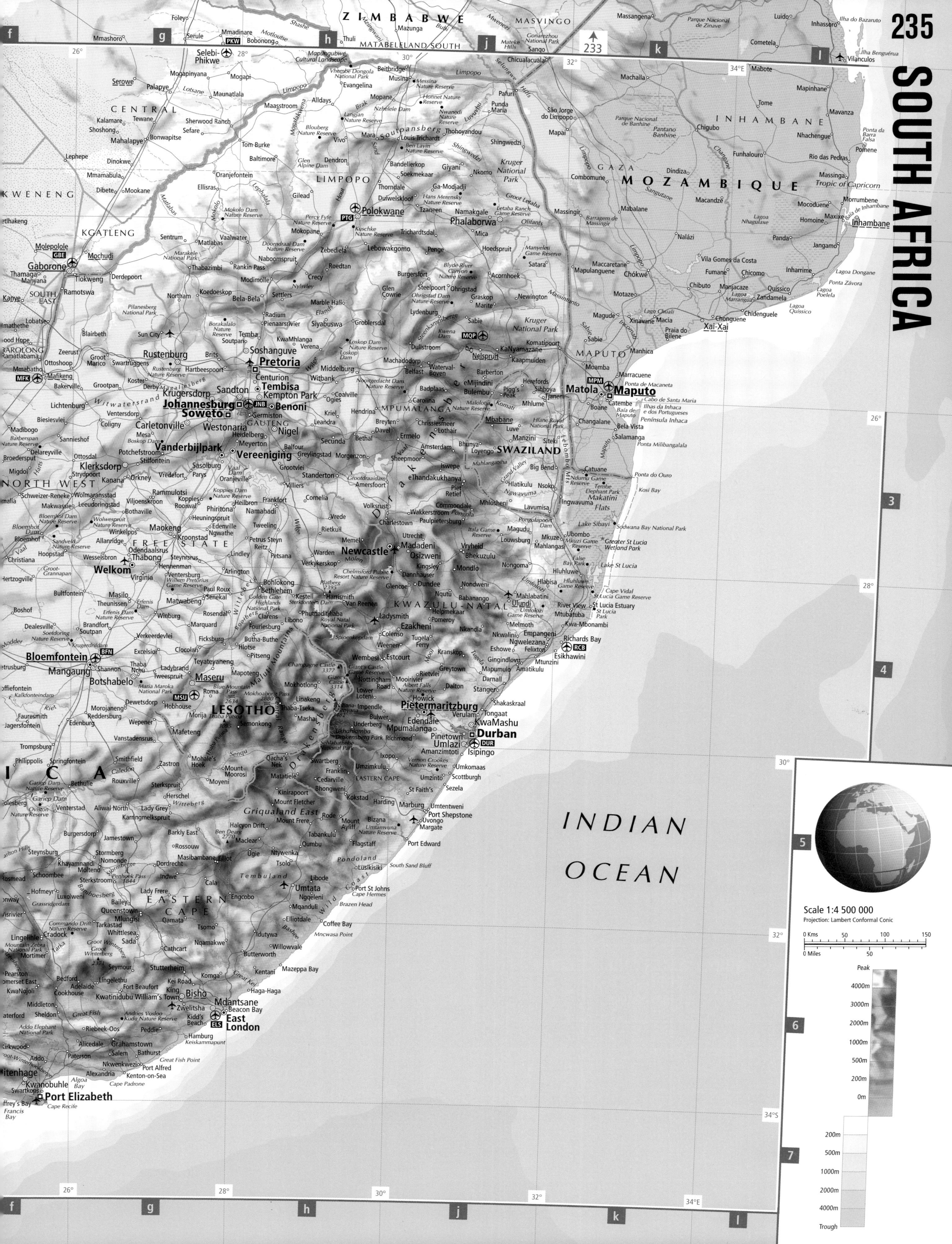

ZIMBABWE

MASVINGO

MATABELELAND SOUTH

MOZAMBIQUE

INHAMBANE

GAZA

CENTRAL

KWENENG

KGATLENG

LIMPOPO

SOUTH EAST

NORTH WEST

FREE STATE

MPUMALANGA

SWAZILAND

KWAZULU-NATAL

LESOTHO

EASTERN CAPE

Griqualand East

Pondoland

Tembuland

EASTERN CAPE

Gaborone

Pretoria

Johannesburg

Soweto

Vanderbijlpark

Vereeniging

Klerksdorp

Welkom

Bloemfontein

Mangaung

Maseru

Botshabelo

Maputo

Matola

Mbabane

Manzini

Newcastle

Pietermaritzburg

Durban

Umlazi

Pinetown

KwaMashu

Edendale

Richards Bay

Esikhawini

Port Elizabeth

Kwanobuhle

East London

Mdantsane

Bisho

Umtata

Grahamstown

Polokwane

Phalaborwa

Nelspruit

Rustenburg

Kruger National Park

INDIAN OCEAN

Scale 1:4 500 000
Projection: Lambert Conformal Conic

0 Kms   50   100   150

0 Miles   50

Peak

4000m
3000m
2000m
1000m
500m
200m
0m

200m
500m
1000m
2000m
4000m

Trough

NORTH & CENT

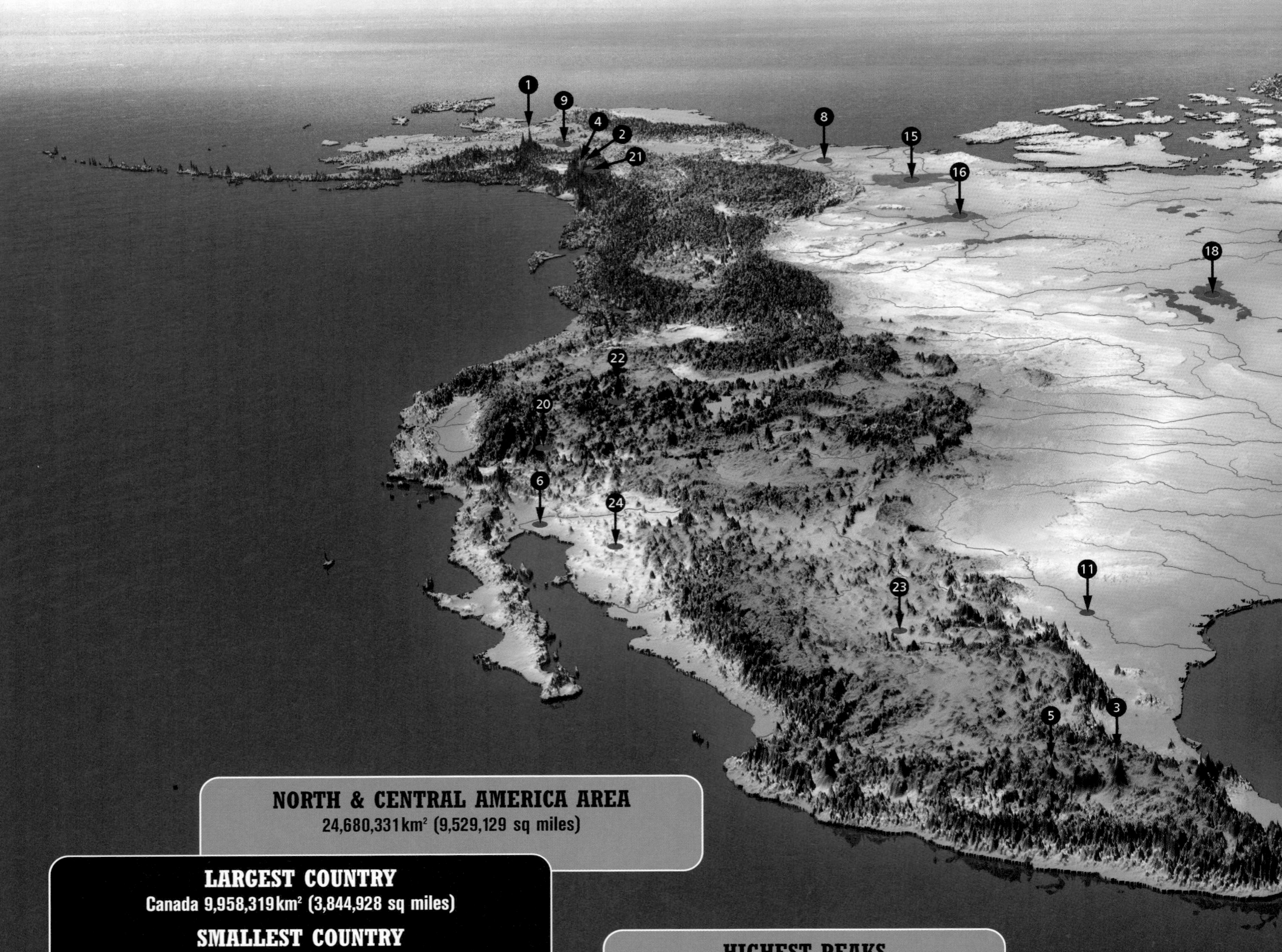

NORTH & CENTRAL AMERICA AREA
24,680,331km² (9,529,129 sq miles)

LARGEST COUNTRY
Canada 9,958,319km² (3,844,928 sq miles)

SMALLEST COUNTRY
Grenada 344km² (133 sq miles)

NORTH & CENTRAL AMERICA POPULATION
487,494,000

HIGHEST PEAKS
1 Denali (Mt McKinley), USA 6194m (20,321ft)
2 Mt Logan, Canada 5959m (19,550ft)
3 Pico de Orizaba, Mexico 5610m (18,405ft)
4 Mt St Elias, USA 5489m (18,008ft)
5 Popocatépetl, Mexico 5452m (17,887ft)

WETTEST AREA
Mt Waialeale, Kauai, Hawaii 11,684mm (460in)
annual rainfall (see page 263, map 263A b1)

DRIEST AREA
6 Batagues, Mexico 30.5mm (1.2in) annual rainfall

LONGEST RIVERS
7 Mississippi–Missouri, USA 5969km (3709 miles)
8 Mackenzie–Peace–Finlay, USA/Canada 4241km (2635 miles)
9 Yukon, Canada/USA 3185km (1979 miles)
St Lawrence, USA/Canada 3058km (1900 miles)
Rio Grande (Rio Bravo del Norte), USA/Mexico 3057km (1899 miles)

RAL AMERICA

The North American continent covers about 13 per cent of the world's land surface. Its terrain ranges from the rugged snow-capped peaks of Alaska and the northern Pacific coast to the deserts and canyons of the south-west and the humid tropical forests of Central America. In the continental interior is a vast belt of fertile lowlands, one of the most productive agricultural regions in the world. To the south-east, a string of islands separates the Atlantic Ocean from the Caribbean Sea and the Gulf of Mexico.

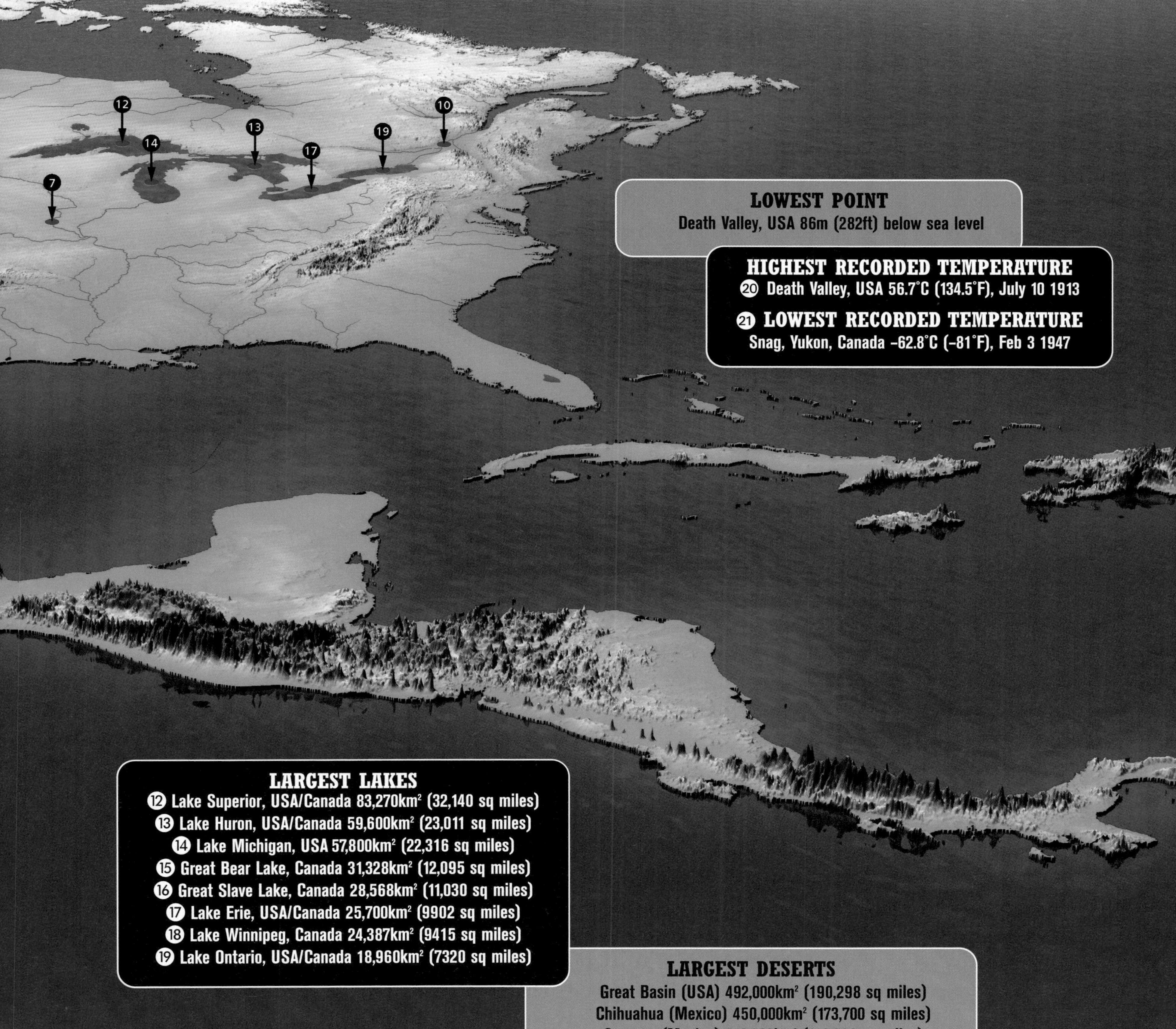

LOWEST POINT
Death Valley, USA 86m (282ft) below sea level

HIGHEST RECORDED TEMPERATURE
⓴ Death Valley, USA 56.7°C (134.5°F), July 10 1913

㉑ **LOWEST RECORDED TEMPERATURE**
Snag, Yukon, Canada –62.8°C (–81°F), Feb 3 1947

LARGEST LAKES
⑫ Lake Superior, USA/Canada 83,270km² (32,140 sq miles)
⑬ Lake Huron, USA/Canada 59,600km² (23,011 sq miles)
⑭ Lake Michigan, USA 57,800km² (22,316 sq miles)
⑮ Great Bear Lake, Canada 31,328km² (12,095 sq miles)
⑯ Great Slave Lake, Canada 28,568km² (11,030 sq miles)
⑰ Lake Erie, USA/Canada 25,700km² (9902 sq miles)
⑱ Lake Winnipeg, Canada 24,387km² (9415 sq miles)
⑲ Lake Ontario, USA/Canada 18,960km² (7320 sq miles)

LARGEST DESERTS
Great Basin (USA) 492,000km² (190,298 sq miles)
Chihuahua (Mexico) 450,000km² (173,700 sq miles)
Sonoran (Mexico) 310,000km² (119,660 sq miles)

Age				Birth rate		Adult literacy		Wealth	
Under 15	%		Over 65	Births per 1000 population		%		GDP per head $US	
Guatemala	43.5	12.6	Canada	Guatemala	36.2	Barbados	99.7	United States	35,926
Nicaragua	42.5	12.3	United States	Honduras	32.6	Canada	99	Canada	23,244
Honduras	41.8	10.4	Barbados	Nicaragua	32.2	Trinidad & Tobago	98.6	The Bahamas	16,645
Belize	41	9.6	Cuba	Haiti	30.6	St Kitts & Nevis	97.3	Barbados	9611
Haiti	39.9	8.9	Costa Rica	El Salvador	28.9	Cuba	97	Antigua & Barbuda	7788
Antigua & Barbuda	27.6	3.8	Dominican Republic	Barbados	15	El Salvador	80.1	El Salvador	2227
Trinidad & Tobago	26.9	3.8	Haiti	Trinidad & Tobago	14.5	Honduras	76.8	Guatemala	1984
Cuba	21.9	3.5	Guatemala	United States	14.5	Guatemala	70.5	Honduras	974
Barbados	20.7	3.4	Honduras	Cuba	13.5	Nicaragua	67.5	Nicaragua	468
Canada	19.1	3	Nicaragua	Canada	10.7	Haiti	52.9	Haiti	386

■ Top five ■ Bottom five

Health, wealth and education

The United States and Canada are among the world's richest nations, although high average income masks sometimes wide disparities between rich and poor in the USA. Central America and the Caribbean are much less developed and Haiti, the region's poorest country, has an average personal income of just $US1700 a year. These inequalities are matched in healthcare, welfare and education. Average life expectancy in Canada is nearly 80 years, and just 51 years in Haiti. Lack of educational opportunities limits the economic potential of the youthful population found in many of the poorer countries.

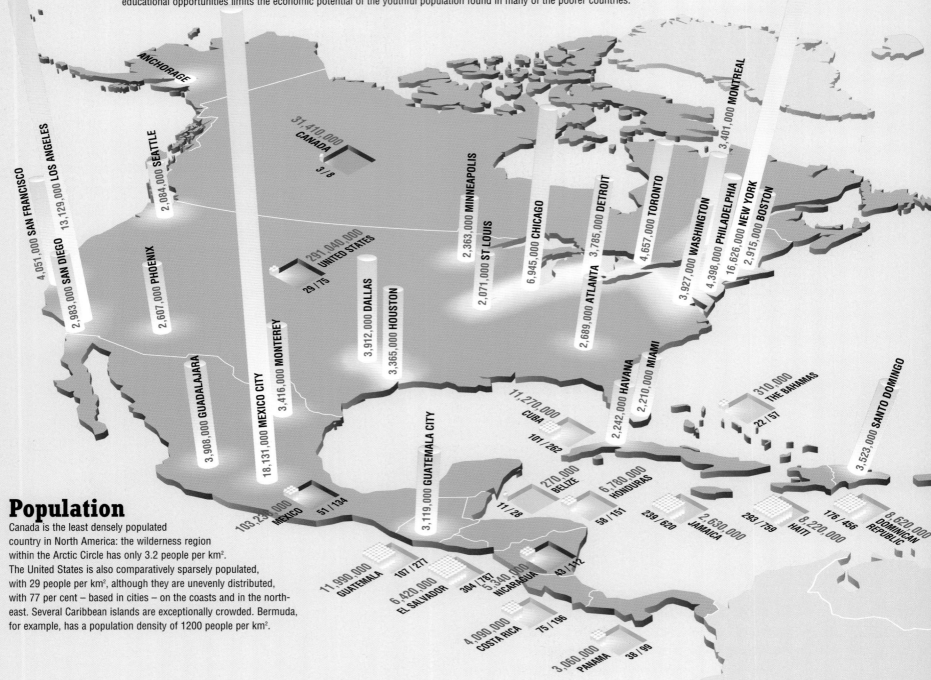

Population

Canada is the least densely populated country in North America: the wilderness region within the Arctic Circle has only 3.2 people per km². The United States is also comparatively sparsely populated, with 29 people per km², although they are unevenly distributed, with 77 per cent – based in cities – on the coasts and in the north-east. Several Caribbean islands are exceptionally crowded. Bermuda, for example, has a population density of 1200 people per km².

Climate of North America

Much of North America is temperate, though extreme cold prevails in the Arctic Circle, while parts of the south have a tropical or sub-tropical climate. The north-west Pacific coast is the wettest region, with 1000mm (65in) of rain per year. Large areas of the south-west are arid, with less than 250mm (10in) rainfall per year.

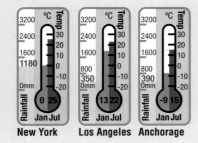

New York   Los Angeles   Anchorage

Climate of Central America and the Caribbean

Southern Mexico, Central America and the Caribbean are hot and humid. The wettest months are June to early October, with a dry season from late October to May. Hurricanes are common in the Gulf of Mexico and the Caribbean from early August to late October.

Havana   Jamaica   Guatemala City

The lie of the land

The wall of mountains which traces the entire western coast, and the immense watery expanse of Hudson Bay in the north-east, are North America's most dramatic geographical features. The Great Lakes, remnants of the last Ice Age, contain 20 per cent of the world's fresh water. To the south, centuries of silt and sediment deposited by the huge Mississippi-Missouri river system have created fertile floodplains.

❶ **San Andreas Fault** California is at serious risk from earthquakes, because of fault lines crossing it. Along the San Andreas Fault, two of the Earth's tectonic plates rub against each other constantly, making land above extremely unstable.

❷ **Appalachian Mountains** The red colouring of dense wooded areas reveals the pattern of rock folding that created the Appalachians about 400-500 million years ago. Agricultural land is pale blue.

❸ **Sierra Madre Oriental** Heavy erosion has etched deep valleys into the sides of the mountain spurs (grey).The twisting of the rocky ridges (green) is the result of the Earth's crust buckling as the mountains were formed.

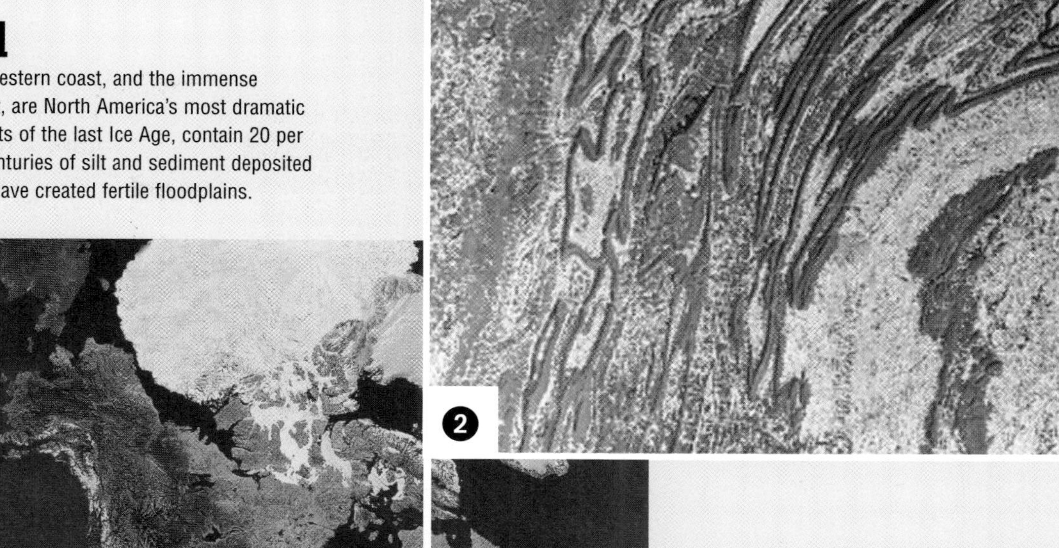

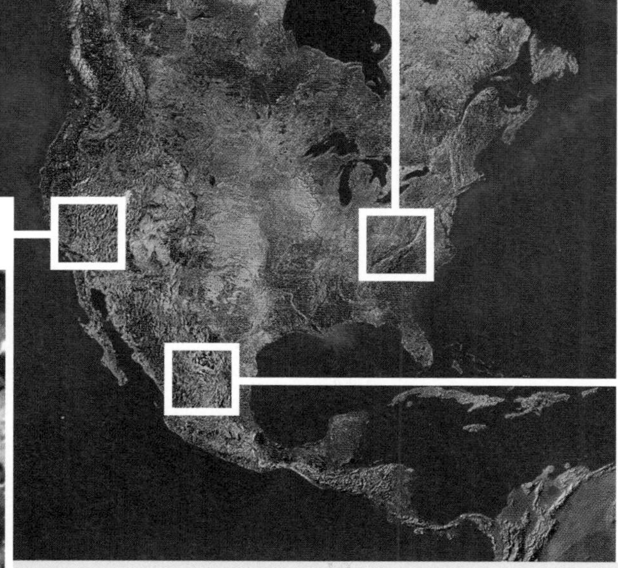

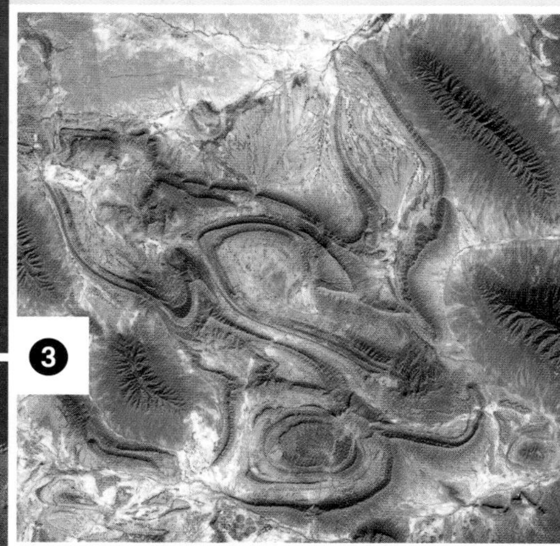

Employment

Service industries supply most jobs in North and Central America and the Caribbean Islands, where tourism is often central to the economy. About 25 per cent of North American workers are still active in various sectors of industry, although many assembly plants have drifted from the USA to Mexico and Central America, where costs are lower. Few Americans and Canadians work in agriculture, although the sector still employs over half the workforce in parts of Central America and the Caribbean, where some islands are dependent on a single cash crop, such as bananas.

North & Central America: employment by sector

Country top ten	Primary (inc. Agriculture) %	Industry %	Service %	GDP $US million
United States	2	18	80	10,456,000
Canada	2	27	71	730,100
Mexico	5	26	69	632,100
Cuba	8	34	58	26,052
Guatemala	23	20	57	22,046
Dominican Republic	11	34	55	20,928
Costa Rica	9	30	61	16,368
El Salvador	10	30	60	14,141
Panama	7	17	76	10,499
Trinidad & Tobago	2	43	55	8893

■ Primary (inc. Agriculture) %   ■ Industry %   ■ Service %

How the land is used

Although North America is one of the most urbanized continents in the world, many parts of Central America and the Caribbean remain predominantly rural. The tiny island of Montserrat, for example, has an urban population of just 13 per cent. Arable land accounts for about an eighth of the total land area in North America and is among the world's most productive. A third of the continent is covered by forests, mostly across northern Canada.

ANTIGUA & BARBUDA 77,000 — 175 / 455
ST KITTS & NEVIS 40,000 — 145 / 376
DOMINICA 72,000 — 95 / 247
BARBADOS 270,000 — 623 / 1614
ST LUCIA 160,000 — 256 / 663
ST VINCENT & THE GRENADINES 120,000 — 280 / 726
GRENADA 101,000 — 294 / 759
TRINIDAD & TOBAGO 1,280,000 — 253 / 656

KEY   Country population **2003**

JAMAICA 2,630,000 — 239 / 620

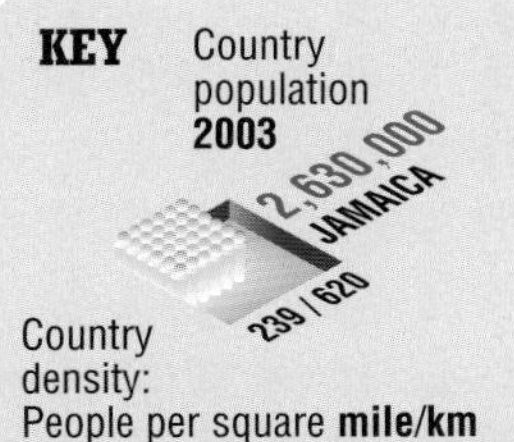

Country density: People per square **mile/km**

Cereals, livestock
Cash crops, mixed farming
Dairy, livestock
General and mixed farming
Special crops
Livestock ranching and herding
Diversified tropical and subtropical crops
Forests
Nonproductive land

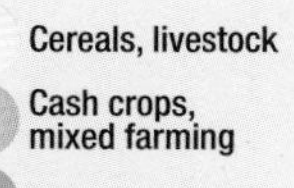

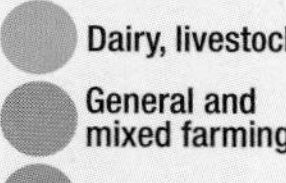

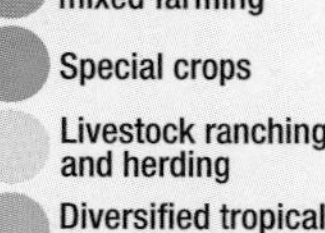

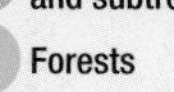

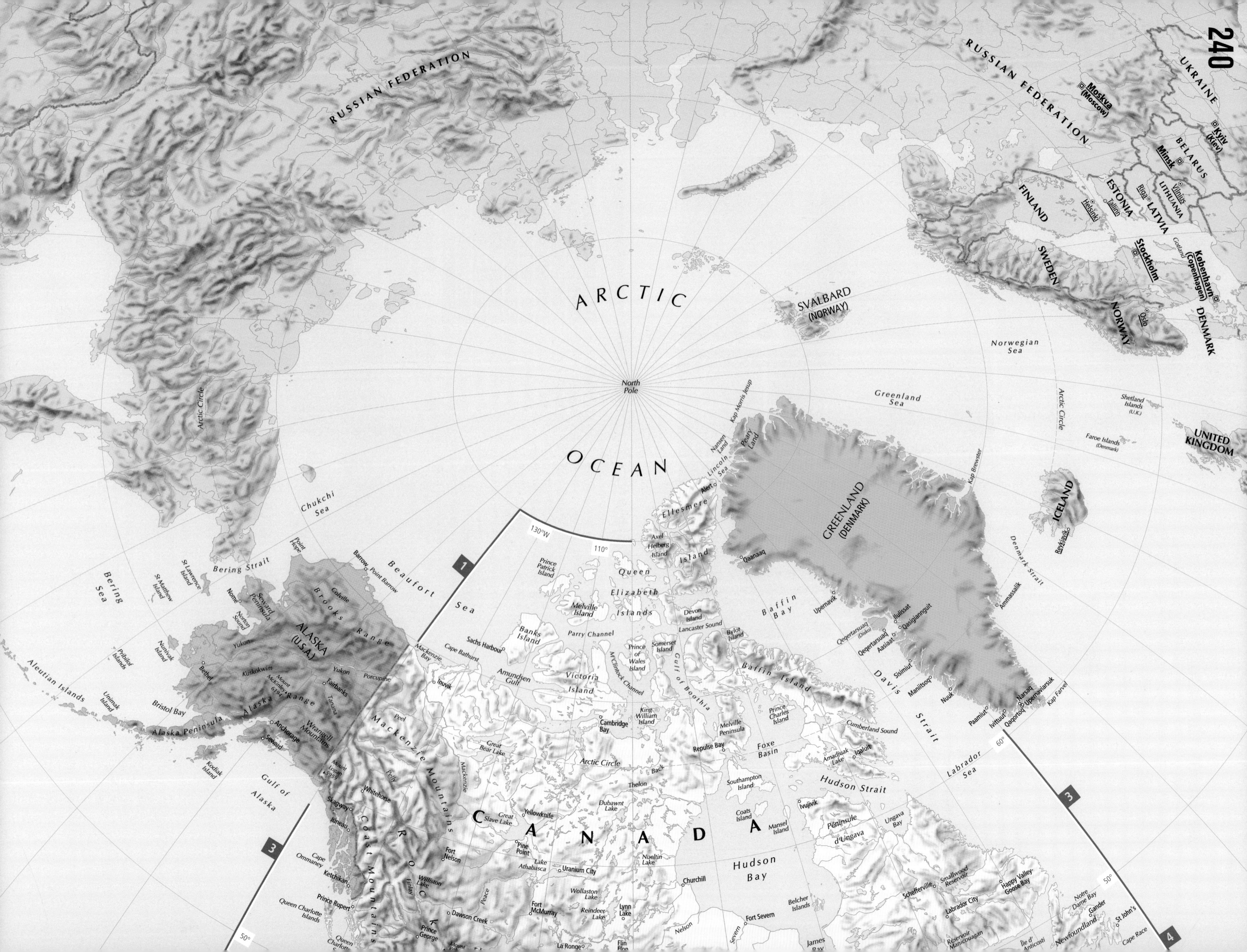

UKRAINE

BELARUS

Kyiv
(Kiev)

Minsk

Vilnius
LITHUANIA

Riga LATVIA

ESTONIA

Tallinn

Mockba
(Moscow)

RUSSIAN FEDERATION

København
(Copenhagen)

DENMARK

Gotland

Stockholm

Oslo

NORWAY

SWEDEN

FINLAND

Helsinki

United
Kingdom

Shetland
Islands
(U.K.)

Faeroe Islands
(Denmark)

Arctic Circle

Norwegian
Sea

ICELAND

Reykjavik

Denmark Strait

Kap Brewster

Ammassalik

Greenland
Sea

SVALBARD
(NORWAY)

Nansen
Land

Kap Morris Jesup

Peary
Land

Lincoln
Sea

GREENLAND
(DENMARK)

Kap Farvel

Nassa

Qaqortoq

Ivittuut

Narsaq

Nuuk

Maniitsoq

Sisimiut

Kangerlussuaq

Aasiaat

Ilulissat

Qasigiannguit

Qeqertarsuaq

Uummannaq

Upernavik

Qaanaaq

Davis
Strait

Labrador Sea

Baffin
Bay

RUSSIAN FEDERATION

ARCTIC

North
Pole

OCEAN

Ellesmere
Island

Axel
Heiberg
Island

Queen
Elizabeth
Islands

110°

Devon
Island

Lancaster Sound

Somerset
Island

Prince
of
Wales
Island

Gulf of Boothia

Melville
Peninsula

Foxe
Basin

Repulse Bay

Southampton
Island

Coats
Island

Mansel
Island

Belcher
Islands

Hudson Strait

Ungava
Bay

Peninsula
d'Ungava

Iqaluit

Amadjuak
Lake

Nettilling
Lake

Baffin
Island

Bylot
Island

CANADA

Hudson
Bay

Churchill

Fort Severn

Nelson

Severn

James
Bay

130°W

Prince
Patrick
Island

Melville
Island

Parry Channel

Banks
Island

Victoria
Island

King
William
Island

M'Clintock Channel

Cambridge
Bay

Arctic Circle

Dubawnt
Lake

Thelon

Baker
Lake

Elk
Flon

Lynn
Lake

Reindeer
Lake

Nueltin
Lake

Sachs Harbour

Amundsen
Gulf

Cape Bathurst

Mackenzie
Bay

Beaufort
Sea

Inuvik

Mackenzie

Great
Bear Lake

Great
Slave Lake

Yellowknife

Uranium City

Wollaston
Lake

Lake
Athabasca

Fort
McMurray

Pine
Point

La Ronge

Chukchi
Sea

Point Barrow

Barrow

Colville

Brooks Range

ALASKA
(U.S.A.)

Porcupine

Yukon

Fairbanks

Tanana

Mackenzie Mountains

Fort
Nelson

Peace

R
O
C
K

Williston
Lake

Finlay

Peace

Dawson Creek

Bering Strait

Point
Hope

Seward
Peninsula

Nome

Norton
Sound

Koyukuk

Bethel

Kuskokwim

Yukon

Alaska Range

Mount
McKinley
6194

Wrangell
Mountains

Anchorage

Seward

Whitehorse

Pelly

Skagway

Juneau

Coast Mountains

Mount
Logan

Gulf of
Alaska

Cape
Ommaney

Ketchikan

Prince Rupert

Cape
St James

Queen Charlotte
Islands

St Lawrence
Island

St Matthew
Island

Nunivak
Island

Bristol Bay

Alaska Peninsula

Kodiak
Island

Pribilof
Islands

Bering
Sea

Unimak
Island

Aleutian Islands

Newfoundland

Île
d

Strait
of

Gander

St John's

Avalon
Peninsula

Placentia Bay

Notre
Dame Bay

White Bay

Labrador City

Schefferville

Smallwood
Reservoir

1

3

4

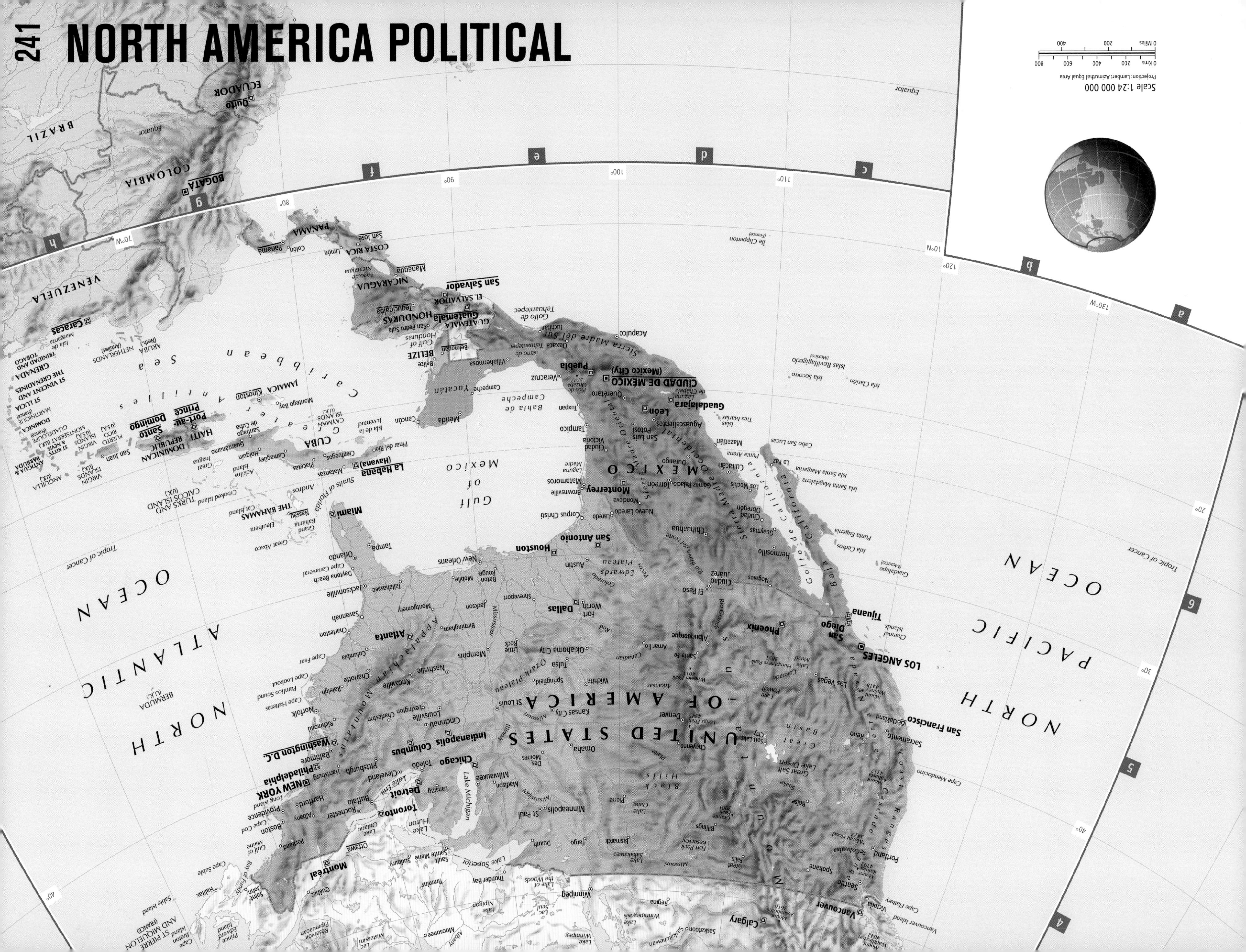

NORTH AMERICA POLITICAL

Scale 1:24 000 000
Projection: Lambert Azimuthal Equal Area

0 Kms   200   400   600   800
0 Miles   200   400

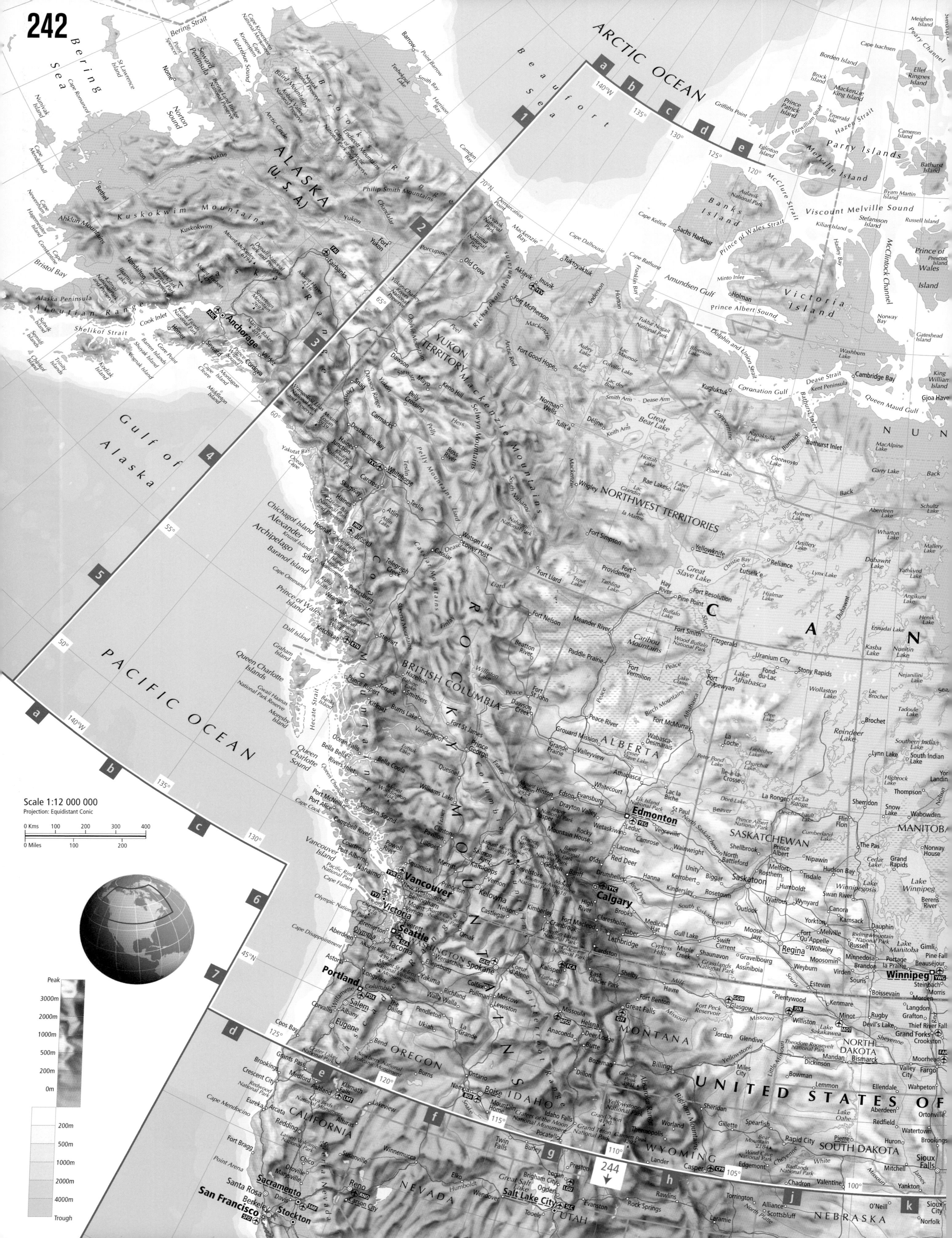
ARCTIC OCEAN
Beaufort Sea
Bering Sea
Bering Strait
ALASKA (U.S.A.)
Brooks Range
Alaska Range
Kuskokwim Mountains
Aleutian Range
Alaska Peninsula
Gulf of Alaska
PACIFIC OCEAN
YUKON TERRITORY
NORTHWEST TERRITORIES
BRITISH COLUMBIA
ALBERTA
SASKATCHEWAN
MANITOBA
CANADA
ROCKY MOUNTAINS
Mackenzie Mountains
Coast Mountains
Cascade Range
Sierra Nevada
Great Bear Lake
Great Slave Lake
Lake Athabasca
Lake Winnipeg
Victoria Island
Banks Island
Parry Islands
Melville Island
Amundsen Gulf
Queen Charlotte Islands
Vancouver Island
Alexander Archipelago
UNITED STATES OF
WASHINGTON
OREGON
CALIFORNIA
NEVADA
IDAHO
MONTANA
WYOMING
UTAH
NORTH DAKOTA
SOUTH DAKOTA
NEBRASKA
Anchorage
Fairbanks
Whitehorse
Yellowknife
Edmonton
Calgary
Vancouver
Victoria
Seattle
Portland
Regina
Winnipeg
Saskatoon
Spokane
Boise
Salt Lake City
Sacramento
San Francisco
Scale 1:12 000 000
Projection: Equidistant Conic
0 Kms 100 200 300 400
0 Miles 100 200
Peak
3000m
2000m
1000m
500m
200m
0m
200m
500m
1000m
2000m
4000m
Trough
244

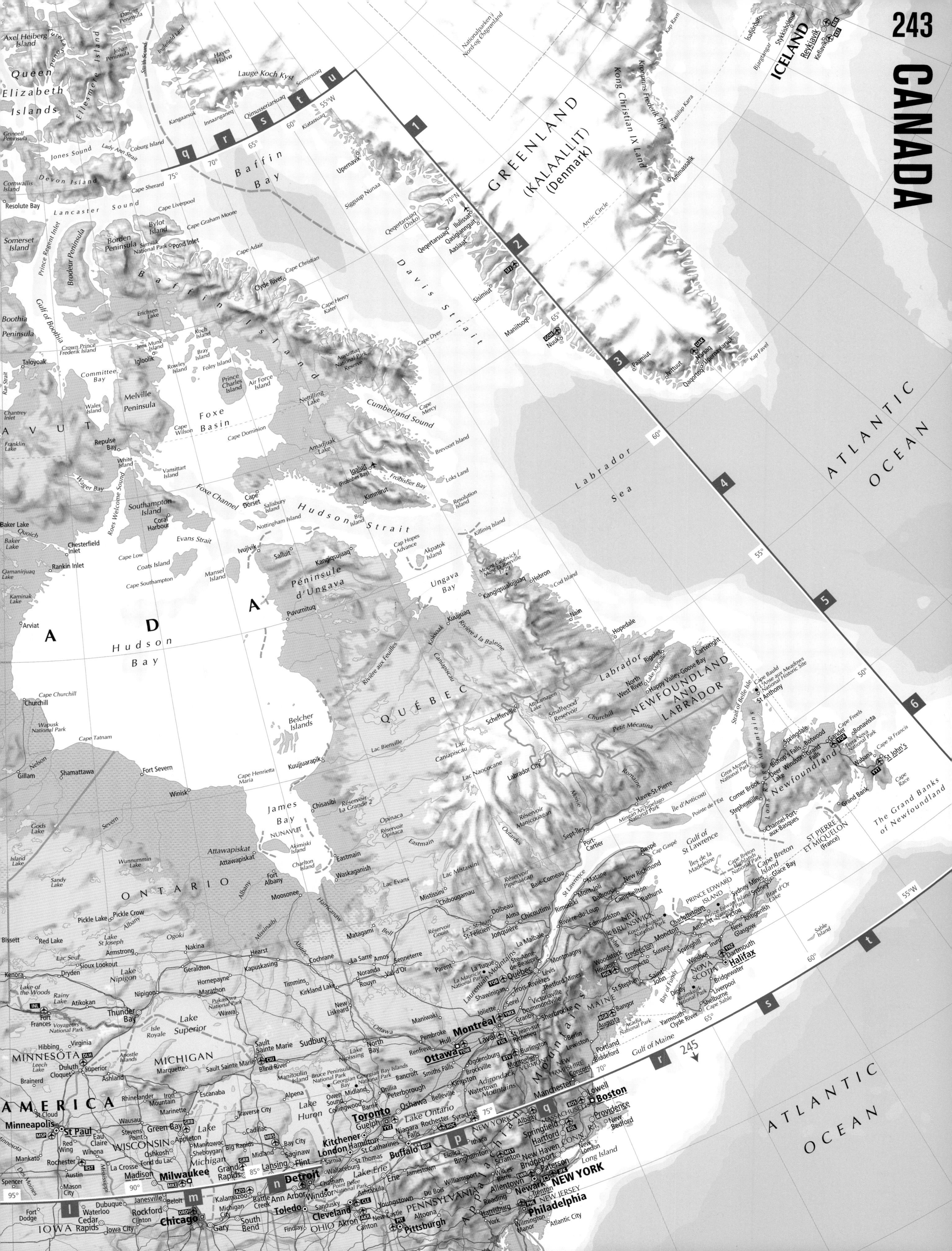

GREENLAND
(KALAALLIT)
(Denmark)

ICELAND

ATLANTIC
OCEAN

Davis Strait

Labrador
Sea

Baffin
Bay

Queen
Elizabeth
Islands

Axel Heiberg
Island

Ellesmere Island

Baffin Island

Foxe
Basin

Hudson Strait

Péninsule
d'Ungava

Ungava
Bay

Labrador

NEWFOUNDLAND
AND
LABRADOR

Hudson
Bay

QUÉBEC

Newfoundland

The Grand Banks
of Newfoundland

James
Bay

NUNAVUT

ONTARIO

Lake
Superior

Lake
Michigan

Lake
Huron

Lake Ontario

Lake Erie

Gulf of
St Lawrence

PRINCE EDWARD
ISLAND

NOVA
SCOTIA

NEW
BRUNSWICK

MAINE

ST PIERRE
ET MIQUELON
(France)

AMERICA

MINNESOTA

WISCONSIN

MICHIGAN

IOWA

OHIO

PENNSYLVANIA

NEW YORK

NEW
JERSEY

Minneapolis

St Paul

Milwaukee

Chicago

Detroit

Toronto

Ottawa

Montréal

Québec

Halifax

Boston

NEW YORK

Newark

Philadelphia

Cleveland

Pittsburgh

Buffalo

ATLANTIC
OCEAN

245

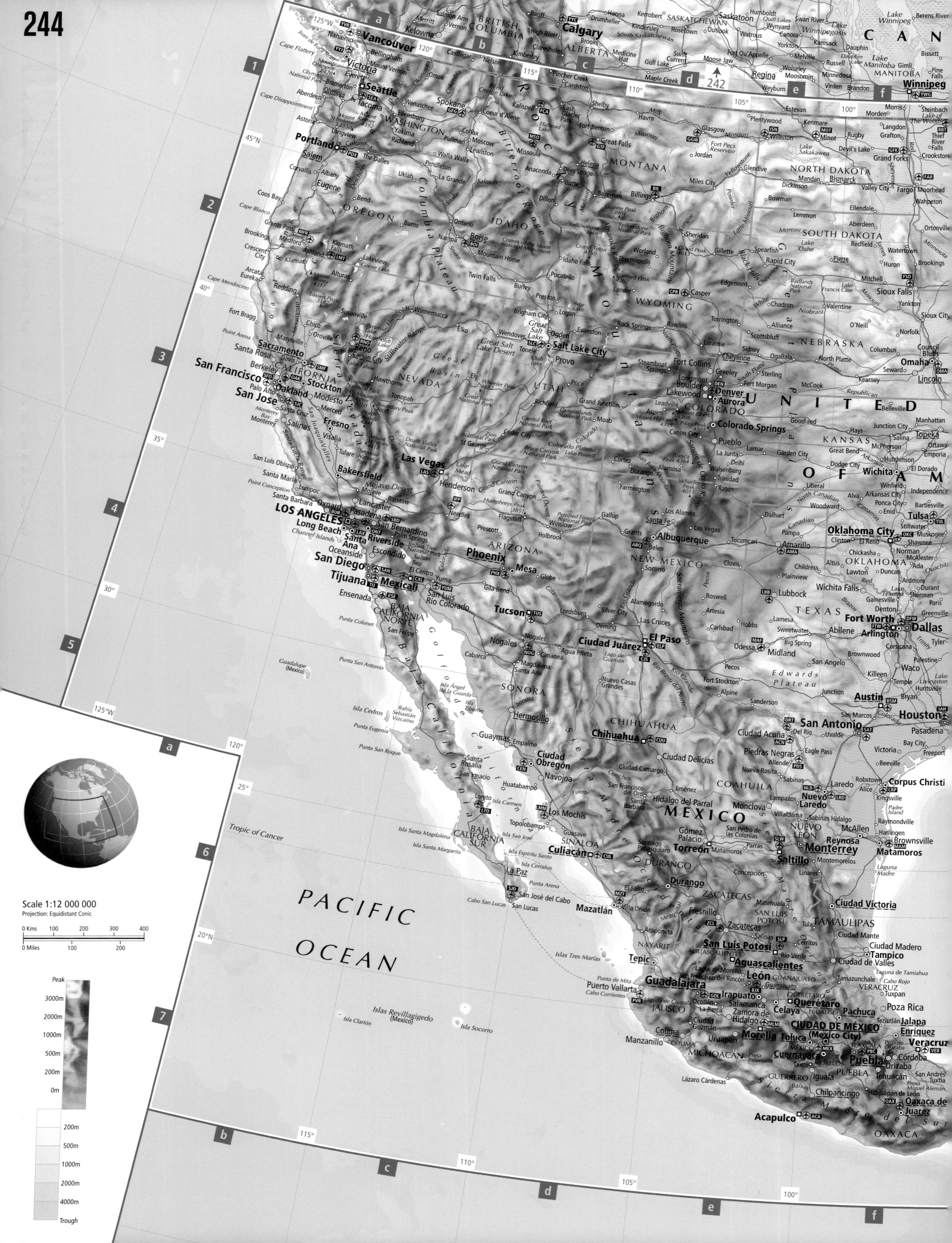
PACIFIC
OCEAN
UNITED
OF AM
CAN
MEXICO
BRITISH COLUMBIA
ALBERTA
SASKATCHEWAN
MANITOBA
WASHINGTON
OREGON
IDAHO
MONTANA
NORTH DAKOTA
SOUTH DAKOTA
WYOMING
NEBRASKA
CALIFORNIA
NEVADA
UTAH
COLORADO
KANSAS
ARIZONA
NEW MEXICO
OKLAHOMA
TEXAS
BAJA CALIFORNIA NORTE
BAJA CALIFORNIA SUR
SONORA
CHIHUAHUA
COAHUILA
NUEVO LEÓN
SINALOA
DURANGO
ZACATECAS
TAMAULIPAS
NAYARIT
JALISCO
MICHOACÁN
GUERRERO
PUEBLA
VERACRUZ
OAXACA
Vancouver
Victoria
Seattle
Tacoma
Portland
Salem
Eugene
Spokane
Boise
Calgary
Regina
Winnipeg
Helena
Billings
Bismarck
Pierre
Cheyenne
Casper
Salt Lake City
Denver
Aurora
Colorado Springs
Pueblo
Sacramento
San Francisco
Oakland
Stockton
San Jose
Fresno
Bakersfield
Las Vegas
LOS ANGELES
Long Beach
Santa Ana
Riverside
San Bernardino
San Diego
Tijuana
Mexicali
Phoenix
Mesa
Tucson
Albuquerque
Santa Fe
El Paso
Ciudad Juárez
Lubbock
Amarillo
Oklahoma City
Tulsa
Wichita
Topeka
Lincoln
Omaha
Fort Worth
Dallas
Arlington
Austin
San Antonio
Houston
Corpus Christi
Chihuahua
Hermosillo
Culiacán
La Paz
Mazatlán
Durango
Torreón
Monterrey
Saltillo
Matamoros
Ciudad Victoria
Tampico
Zacatecas
San Luis Potosí
Aguascalientes
Tepic
Guadalajara
León
Querétaro
Pachuca
Morelia
Toluca
CIUDAD DE MÉXICO
(Mexico City)
Puebla
Jalapa Enríquez
Veracruz
Cuernavaca
Oaxaca de Juarez
Acapulco
Rocky Mountains
Great Basin
Sierra Madre Occidental
Golfo de California
Tropic of Cancer
Islas Revillagigedo (Mexico)
Scale 1:12 000 000
Projection: Equidistant Conic
0 Kms 100 200 300 400
0 Miles 100 200
Peak
3000m
2000m
1000m
500m
200m
0m
200m
500m
1000m
2000m
4000m
Trough
242

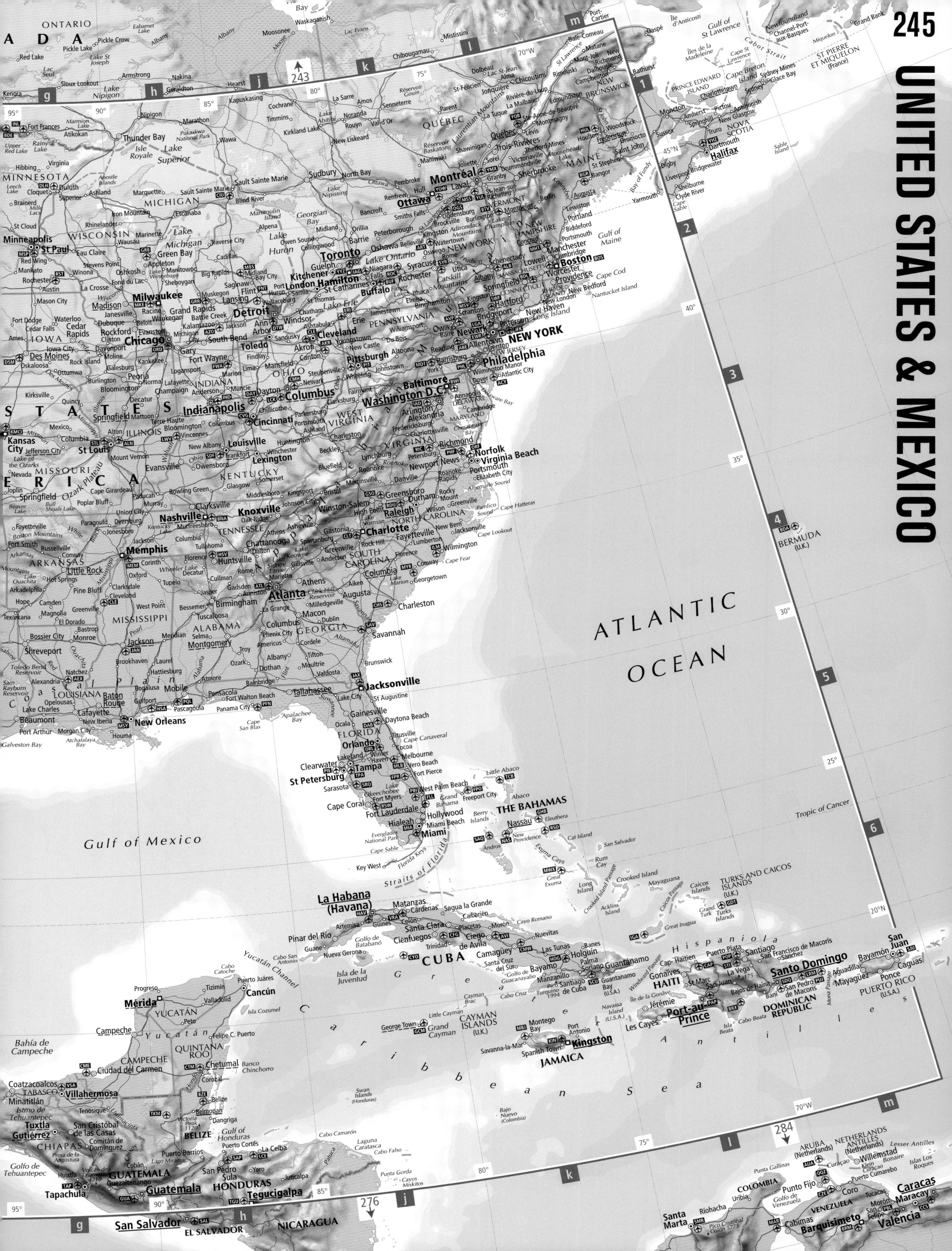
ATLANTIC
OCEAN
Gulf of Mexico
Caribbean Sea
Greater Antilles
ONTARIO
QUÉBEC
NEW BRUNSWICK
NOVA SCOTIA
PRINCE EDWARD ISLAND
ST PIERRE ET MIQUELON (France)
Gulf of St Lawrence
Bay of Fundy
MINNESOTA
WISCONSIN
MICHIGAN
IOWA
ILLINOIS
INDIANA
OHIO
PENNSYLVANIA
NEW YORK
VERMONT
NEW HAMPSHIRE
MAINE
MASSACHUSETTS
CONNECTICUT
RHODE ISLAND
NEW JERSEY
DELAWARE
MARYLAND
WEST VIRGINIA
VIRGINIA
KENTUCKY
TENNESSEE
NORTH CAROLINA
SOUTH CAROLINA
GEORGIA
ALABAMA
MISSISSIPPI
LOUISIANA
ARKANSAS
MISSOURI
FLORIDA
Lake Superior
Lake Michigan
Lake Huron
Lake Erie
Lake Ontario
Appalachian Mountains
Montréal
Ottawa
Toronto
Québec
Halifax
Chicago
Detroit
Milwaukee
Minneapolis
St Paul
Indianapolis
Columbus
Cincinnati
Cleveland
Pittsburgh
Buffalo
Boston
NEW YORK
Philadelphia
Baltimore
Washington D.C.
Richmond
Norfolk
Virginia Beach
Raleigh
Charlotte
Atlanta
Nashville
Memphis
Knoxville
Louisville
St Louis
Kansas City
Birmingham
Jacksonville
Orlando
Tampa
St Petersburg
Miami
New Orleans
Baton Rouge
Charleston
Savannah
BERMUDA (U.K.)
THE BAHAMAS
Nassau
Tropic of Cancer
CUBA
La Habana (Havana)
TURKS AND CAICOS ISLANDS (U.K.)
HAITI
Port-au-Prince
DOMINICAN REPUBLIC
Santo Domingo
PUERTO RICO (U.S.A.)
San Juan
JAMAICA
Kingston
CAYMAN ISLANDS (U.K.)
Hispaniola
YUCATÁN
CAMPECHE
QUINTANA ROO
Mérida
Cancún
BELIZE
GUATEMALA
Guatemala
HONDURAS
Tegucigalpa
EL SALVADOR
San Salvador
NICARAGUA
COLOMBIA
VENEZUELA
Caracas
ARUBA (Netherlands)
NETHERLANDS ANTILLES (Netherlands)
243
276
284

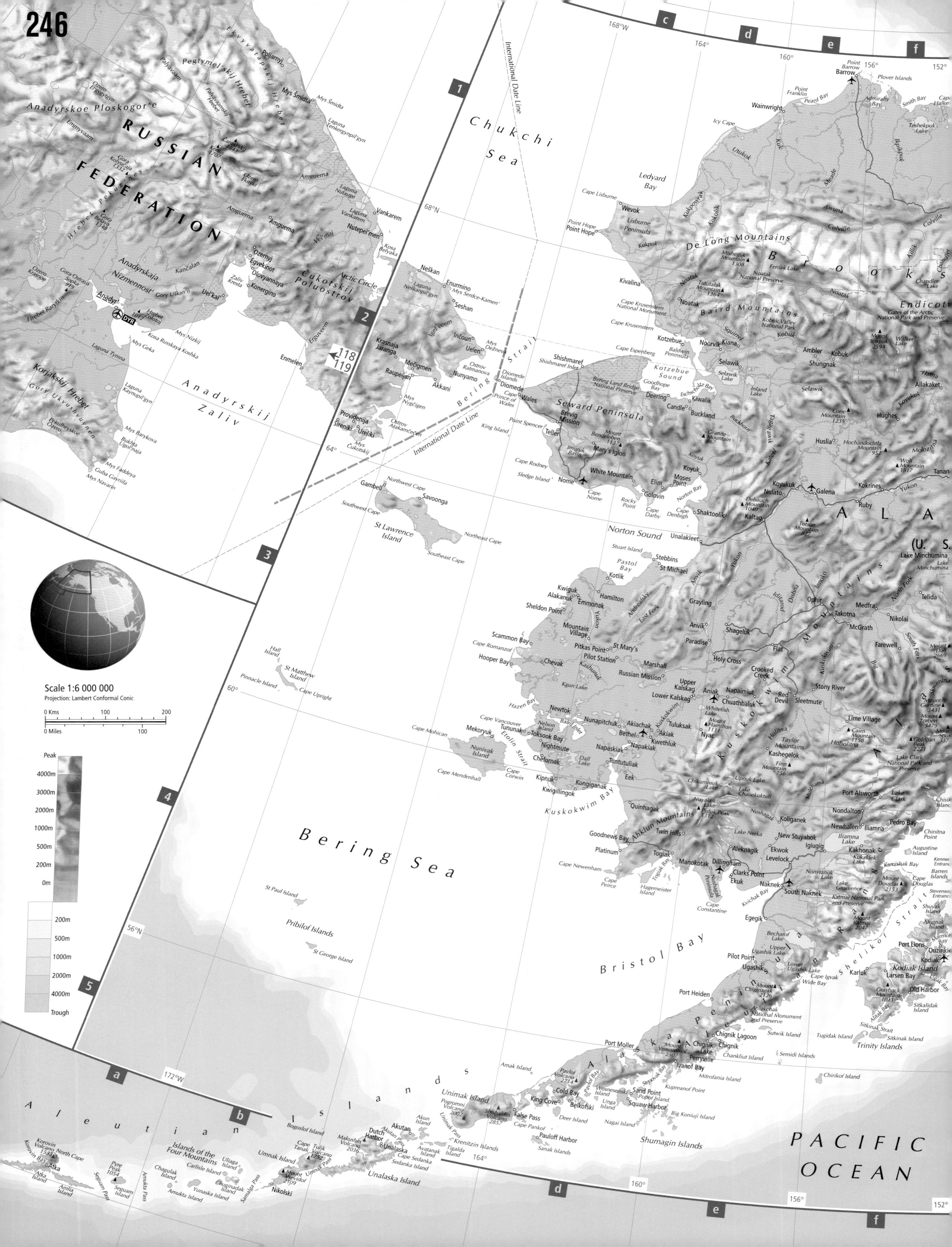

RUSSIAN

FEDERATION

Anadyrskoe Ploskogor'e

Hrebet Pekul'nej

Korjakskij Hrebet

Gory Ukvusvujngm

Chukchi

Sea

International Date Line

Arctic Circle

Cukotskij
Poluostrov

Bering Strait

Anadyrskij
Zaliv

International Date Line

Bering Sea

Scale 1:6 000 000
Projection: Lambert Conformal Conic

0 Kms   100   200

0 Miles   100

Peak

4000m
3000m
2000m
1000m
500m
200m
0m

200m
500m
1000m
2000m
4000m

Trough

Chukchi
Sea

Point
Barrow
Barrow

Wainwright

Icy Cape

Ledyard
Bay

Cape Lisburne

Point Hope
Point Hope

De Long Mountains

Brooks

Baird Mountains

Endicott

Kotzebue

Seward Peninsula

Nome
Cape
Nome

Norton Sound

Unalakleet

ALA

(U. S.

Bethel

Kuskokwim
Mountains

Bering Sea

Bristol Bay

Pribilof Islands

St Paul Island

St George Island

Aleutian

Islands

Unimak Island

Unalaska Island

PACIFIC

OCEAN

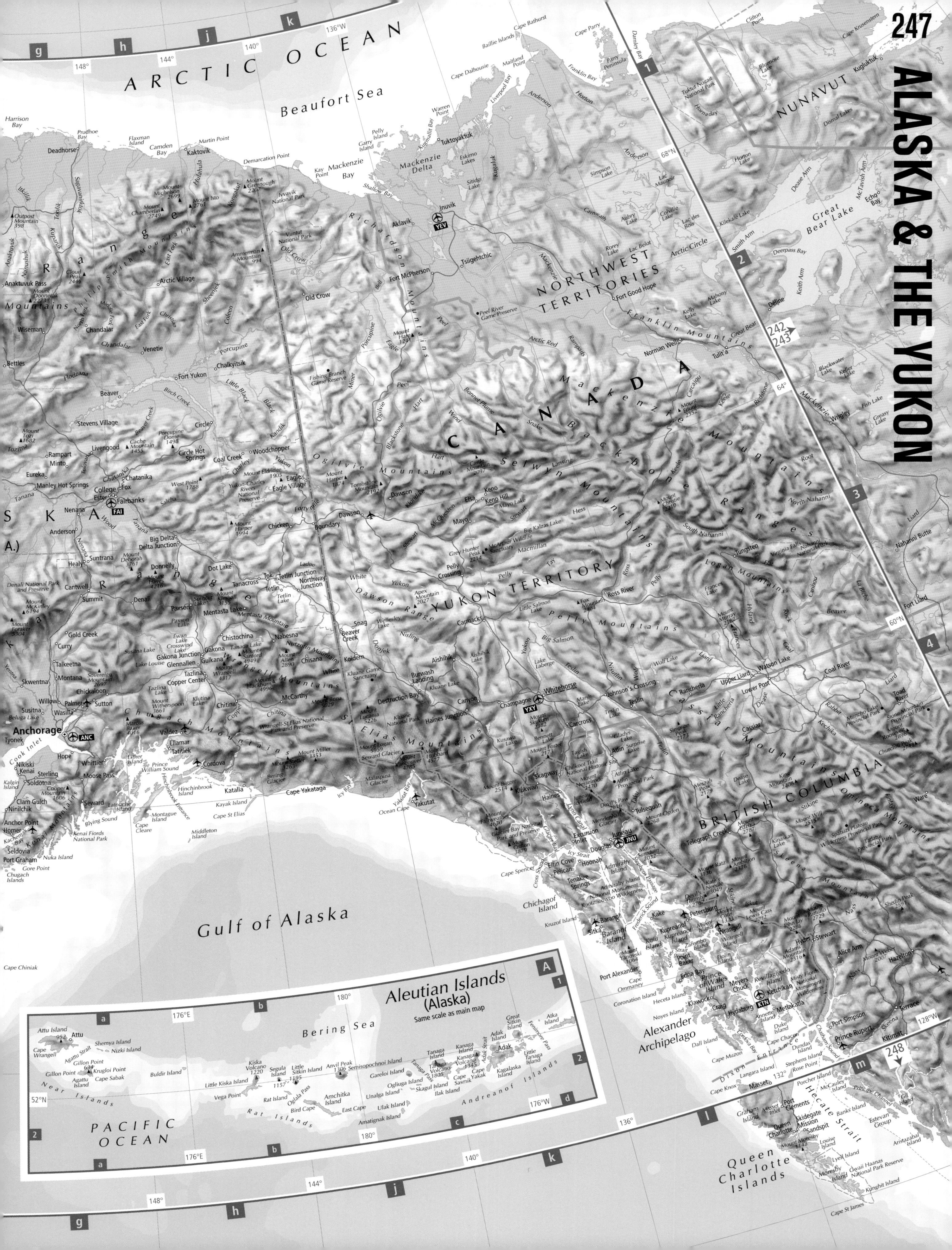

ARCTIC OCEAN

Beaufort Sea

NUNAVUT

NORTHWEST
TERRITORIES

CANADA

YUKON TERRITORY

BRITISH COLUMBIA

Gulf of Alaska

Pacific Ocean

Aleutian Islands
(Alaska)
Same scale as main map

Bering Sea

PACIFIC
OCEAN

Alexander
Archipelago

Queen
Charlotte
Islands

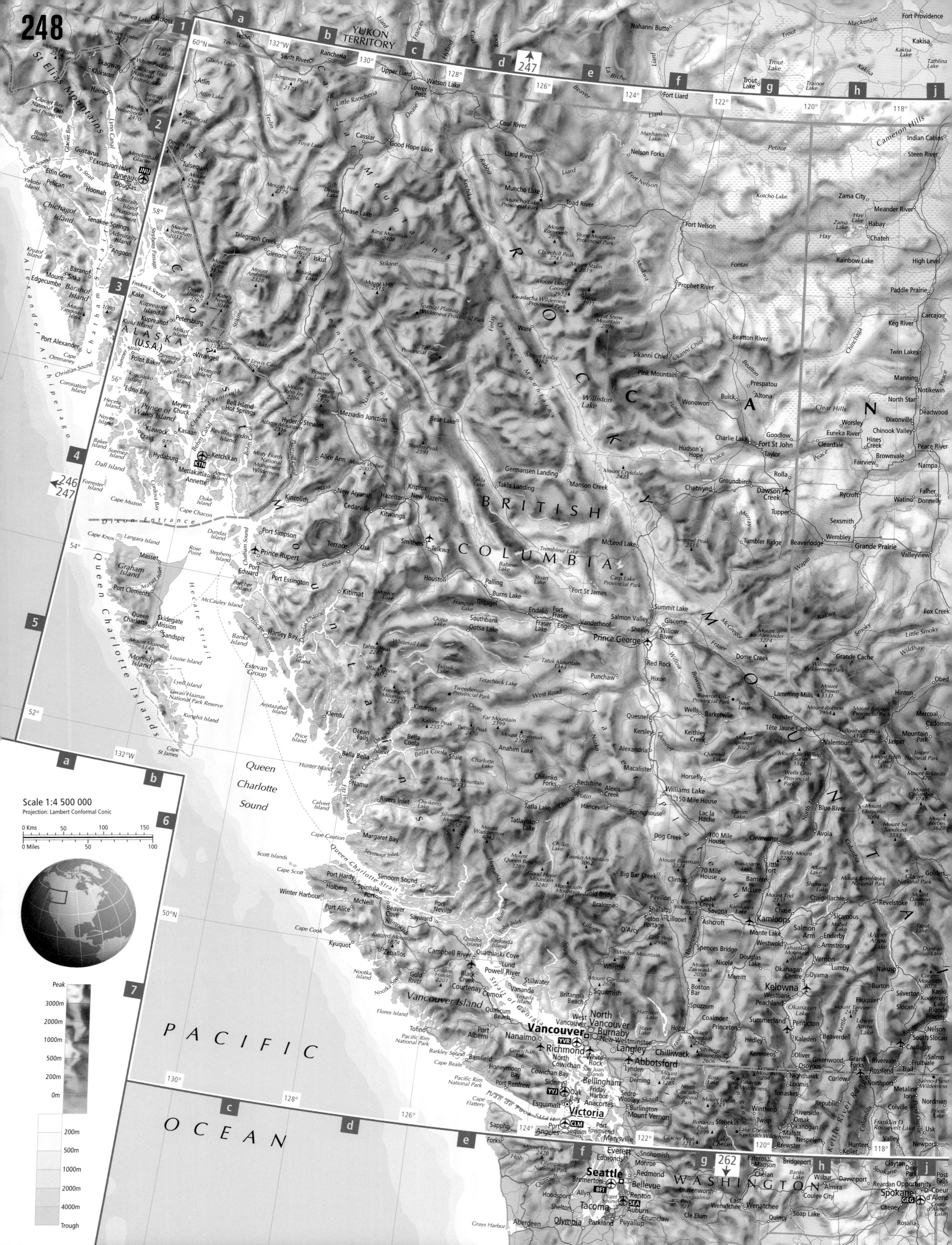
YUKON TERRITORY
BRITISH COLUMBIA
ALASKA (U.S.A.)
WASHINGTON
PACIFIC OCEAN
Queen Charlotte Sound
Queen Charlotte Islands
Alexander Archipelago
St Elias Mountains
Coast Mountains
Cassiar Mountains
Skeena Mountains
Omineca Mountains
ROCKY MOUNTAINS
CANADA
Dixon Entrance
Hecate Strait
Queen Charlotte Strait
Strait of Georgia
Juan de Fuca Strait
Vancouver Island
Graham Island
Moresby Island
Prince of Wales Island
Chichagof Island
Baranof Island
Whitehorse
Juneau
Sitka
Ketchikan
Prince Rupert
Terrace
Kitimat
Smithers
Prince George
Fort Nelson
Fort St John
Dawson Creek
Grande Prairie
Quesnel
Williams Lake
Kamloops
Kelowna
Penticton
Vancouver
North Vancouver
Burnaby
New Westminster
Richmond
Abbotsford
Chilliwack
Nanaimo
Victoria
Seattle
Tacoma
Olympia
Bellingham
Everett
Spokane
Wenatchee
Port Angeles
Campbell River
Courtenay
Port Hardy
Bella Coola
Watson Lake
Lower Post
Liard River
Toad River
Valemount
Jasper
Revelstoke
Nelson
Trail
Scale 1:4 500 000
Projection: Lambert Conformal Conic
0 Kms 50 100 150
0 Miles 50 100
Peak
3000m
2000m
1000m
500m
200m
0m
200m
500m
1000m
2000m
4000m
Trough
246
247
262

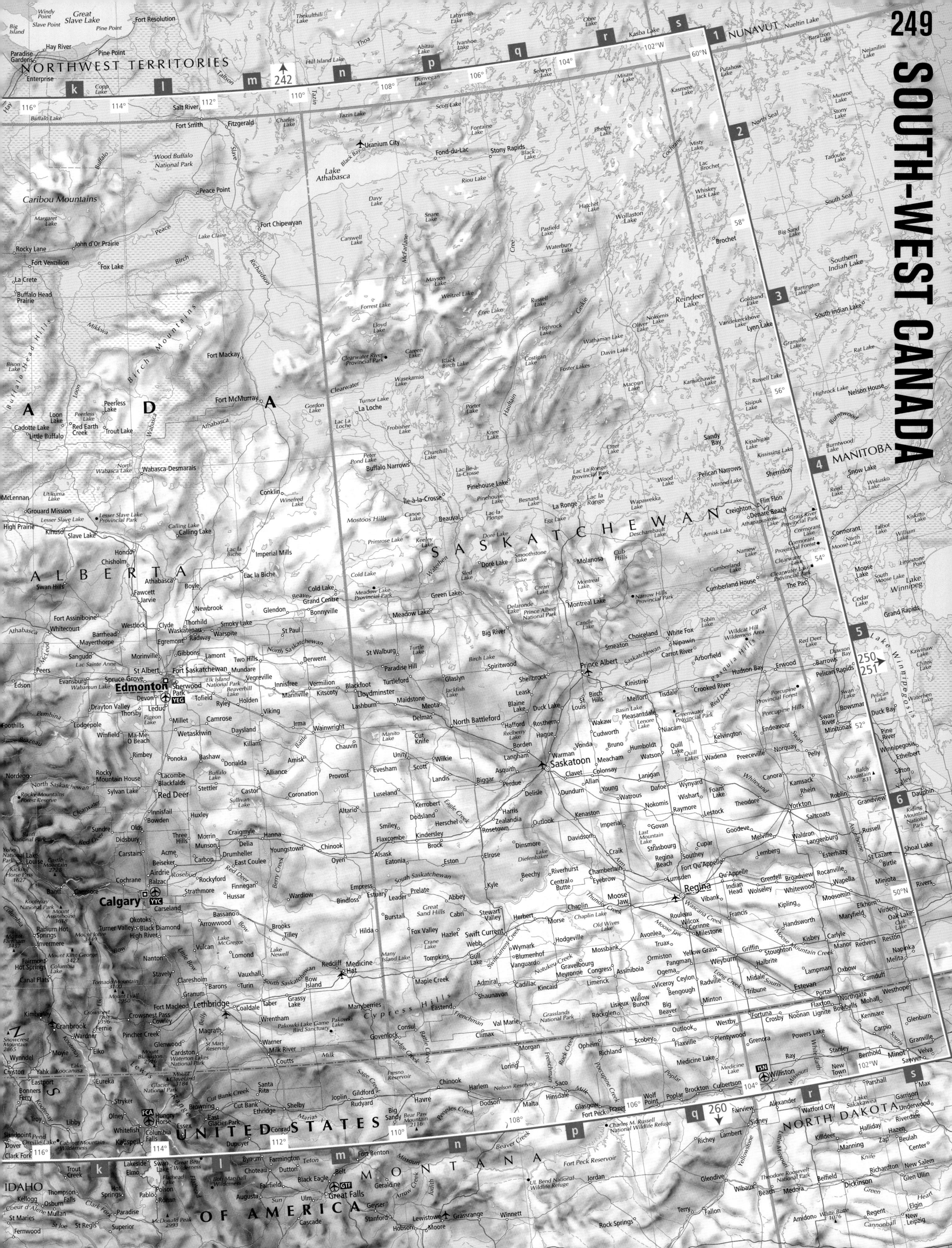

SOUTH-WEST CANADA

NORTHWEST TERRITORIES
NUNAVUT
MANITOBA
SASKATCHEWAN
ALBERTA
UNITED STATES
OF AMERICA
MONTANA
NORTH DAKOTA
IDAHO
Great Slave Lake
Fort Resolution
Hay River
Pine Point
Enterprise
Salt River
Fort Smith
Fitzgerald
Wood Buffalo National Park
Uranium City
Fond-du-Lac
Stony Rapids
Lake Athabasca
Caribou Mountains
Peace Point
Fort Chipewyan
Rocky Lane
John d'Or Prairie
Fort Vermilion
Fox Lake
La Crete
Buffalo Head Prairie
Birch Mountains
Fort Mackay
Fort McMurray
Clearwater River Provincial Park
Reindeer Lake
Wollaston Lake
Brochet
Southern Indian Lake
South Indian Lake
Lynn Lake
La Loche
Buffalo Narrows
Wabasca-Desmarais
Red Earth Creek
Trout Lake
Loon Lake
Peerless Lake
Cadotte Lake
Little Buffalo
McLennan
Grouard Mission
High Prairie
Kinuso
Slave Lake
Lesser Slave Lake Provincial Park
Calling Lake
Conklin
Pinehouse Lake
Ile-à-la-Crosse
Beauval
La Ronge
Lac La Ronge Provincial Park
Pelican Narrows
Sandy Bay
Sherridon
Flin Flon
Creighton
Denare Beach
Cormorant
Snow Lake
Grand Rapids
Lake Winnipeg
Lake Winnipegosis
Hondo
Chisholm
Imperial Mills
Swan Hills
Athabasca
Boyle
Lac la Biche
Cold Lake
Grand Centre
Bonnyville
Glendon
Meadow Lake
Green Lake
Doré Lake
Molanosa
Cumberland House
The Pas
Montreal Lake
Prince Albert National Park
Narrow Hills Provincial Park
Fawcett
Jarvie
Newbrook
Smoky Lake
Fort Assiniboine
Whitecourt
Barrhead
Westlock
Clyde
Mayerthorpe
Waskatenau
Thorhild
Warspite
Radway
Egremont
St Paul
Big River
Choiceland
White Fox
Nipawin
Carrot River
Arborfield
Hudson Bay
Erwood
Barrows
Pelican Rapids
Smeaton
Prince Albert
Shellbrook
Spiritwood
Glaslyn
St Walburg
Turtleford
Paradise Hill
Lloydminster
Maidstone
Meota
North Battleford
Kinistino
Melfort
Tisdale
Crooked River
Porcupine Provincial Forest
Porcupine Hills
Swan River
Minitonas
Bowsmar
Duck Bay
Edson
Evansburg
Spruce Grove
Edmonton
Sherwood Park
St Albert
Fort Saskatchewan
Morinville
Gibbons
Lamont
Two Hills
Mundare
Vegreville
Innisfree
Vermilion
Mannville
Kitscoty
Blackfoot
Derwent
Devon
Leduc
Tofield
Ryley
Holden
Viking
Drayton Valley
Thorsby
Lodgepole
Winfield
Millet
Camrose
Wetaskiwin
Daysland
Irma
Wainwright
Killam
Chauvin
Unity
Wilkie
Cut Knife
Delmas
Hafford
Blaine Lake
Duck Lake
Rosthern
Hague
Borden
Langham
Saskatoon
Warman
Wakaw
Cudworth
Humboldt
Watson
Quill Lake
Wadena
Kelvington
Preeceville
Norquay
Pelly
Rimbey
Ponoka
Bashaw
Donalda
Alliance
Provost
Evesham
Scott
Landis
Biggar
Asquith
Perdue
Delisle
Clavet
Colonsay
Allan
Lanigan
Young
Watrous
Dafoe
Wynyard
Wishart
Foam Lake
Theodore
Canora
Kamsack
Yorkton
Roblin
Grandview
Dauphin
Nordegg
Rocky Mountain House
Sylvan Lake
Red Deer
Lacombe
Blackfalds
Stettler
Castor
Coronation
Luseland
Kerrobert
Dodsland
Herschel
Harris
Zealandia
Rosetown
Outlook
Kenaston
Imperial
Nokomis
Raymore
Lestock
Saltcoats
Melville
Russell
Innisfail
Bowden
Olds
Sundre
Didsbury
Carstairs
Three Hills
Morrin
Munson
Craigmyle
Delia
Hanna
Drumheller
Youngstown
Chinook
Oyen
Smiley
Flaxcombe
Kindersley
Brock
Eston
Elrose
Dinsmore
Davidson
Craik
Strasbourg
Cupar
Southey
Fort Qu'Appelle
Esterhazy
Langenburg
Birtle
Banff National Park
Banff
Canmore
Lake Louise
Airdrie
Cochrane
Calgary
Beiseker
Acme
Carbon
East Coulee
Rockyford
Strathmore
Finnegan
Hussar
Empress
Bindloss
Leader
Prelate
Abbey
Kyle
Beechy
Riverhurst
Central Butte
Eyebrow
Chamberlain
Lumsden
Regina
Qu'Appelle
Indian Head
Grenfell
Broadview
Wolseley
Whitewood
Moosomin
Rocanville
Wapella
Kipling
Okotoks
Carseland
Bassano
Arrowwood
Turner Valley
Black Diamond
High River
Vulcan
Brooks
Tilley
Burstall
Great Sand Hills
Cabri
Stewart Valley
Herbert
Morse
Chaplin
Moose Jaw
Vibank
Francis
Rouleau
Wilcox
Corinne
Milestone
Avonlea
Handsworth
Maryfield
Kisbey
Carlyle
Redvers
Reston
Manor
Melita
Stavely
Nanton
Lomond
Hilda
Fox Valley
Hazlet
Swift Current
Webb
Gull Lake
Tompkins
Wymark
Blumenhof
Vanguard
Hodgeville
Mossbank
Gravelbourg
Congress
Assiniboia
Ormiston
Pangman
Yellow Grass
Weyburn
Griffin
Stoughton
Halbrite
Lampman
Oxbow
Carnduff
Claresholm
Barrons
Vauxhall
Turin
Redcliff
Medicine Hat
Bow Island
Maple Creek
Admiral
Cadillac
Kincaid
Limerick
Viceroy
Ceylon
Radville
Midale
Estevan
Tribune
Bengough
Minton
Fort Macleod
Lethbridge
Coaldale
Taber
Grassy Lake
Granum
Crowsnest Pass
Coleman
Pincher Creek
Magrath
Cardston
Glenwood
Warner
Milk River
Manyberries
Cypress Hills
Eastend
Shaunavon
Consul
Climax
Val Marie
Grasslands National Park
Rockglen
Willow Bunch
Big Beaver
Fortuna
Crosby
Noonan
Lignite
Bowbells
Kenmare
Mohall
Westhope
Cranbrook
Fernie
Kimberley
Wardner
Elko
Moyie
Yahk
Creston
Eastport
Bonners Ferry
Eureka
Waterton Lakes National Park
Glacier National Park
Coutts
Sweetgrass
Cut Bank
Shelby
Chester
Havre
Chinook
Harlem
Malta
Hinsdale
Glasgow
Fort Peck
Frazer
Wolf Point
Poplar
Culbertson
Williston
Plentywood
Medicine Lake
Scobey
Flaxville
Opheim
Richland
Morgan
Loring
Saco
Joplin
Rudyard
Gildford
Big Sandy
Conrad
Dupuyer
Valier
Browning
East Glacier Park
Essex
Columbia Falls
Hungry Horse
Whitefish
Kalispell
Libby
Troy
Olney
Stryker
Sandpoint
Dover
Clark Fork
Fort Benton
Great Falls
Choteau
Augusta
Fairfield
Geraldine
Stanford
Lewistown
Grassrange
Winnett
Jordan
Fort Peck Reservoir
Charles M. Russell National Wildlife Refuge
UL Bend National Wildlife Refuge
Glendive
Sidney
Fairview
Richey
Lambert
Wibaux
Beach
Medora
Belfield
Dickinson
Richardton
Glen Ullin
New Salem
Beulah
Hazen
Zap
Halliday
Killdeer
Manning
Theodore Roosevelt National Park
Watford City
Alexander
Garrison
Underwood
Riverdale
Parshall
Max
New Town
Stanley
Berthold
Minot
Sawyer
Velva
Granville
Carpio
Glenburn
Ray
Tioga
Powers Lake
Polson
Ronan
Pablo
Hot Springs
Paradise
Superior
St Regis
Mullan
Kellogg
Osburn
Thompson Falls
Trout Creek
St Maries
Fernwood
Coeur d'Alene
Rock Springs
Terry
Fallon
Amidon
Elgin
Heart
New Leipzig
Cannonball
242
250
251
260

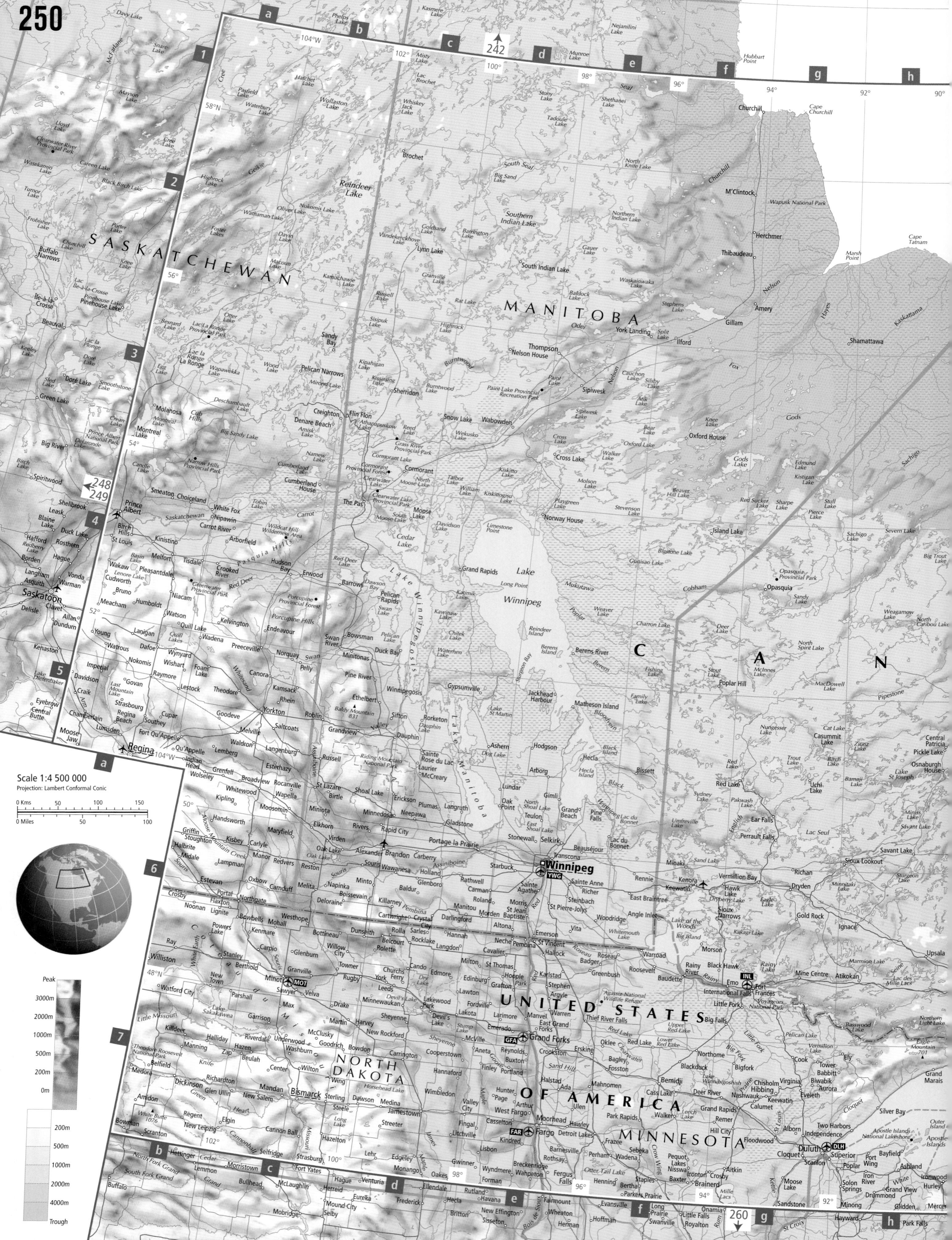

SASKATCHEWAN

MANITOBA

CANADA

UNITED STATES OF AMERICA

NORTH DAKOTA

MINNESOTA

Scale 1:4 500 000
Projection: Lambert Conformal Conic

0 Kms   50   100   150
0 Miles   50   100

Peak
3000m
2000m
1000m
500m
200m
0m

200m
500m
1000m
2000m
4000m
Trough

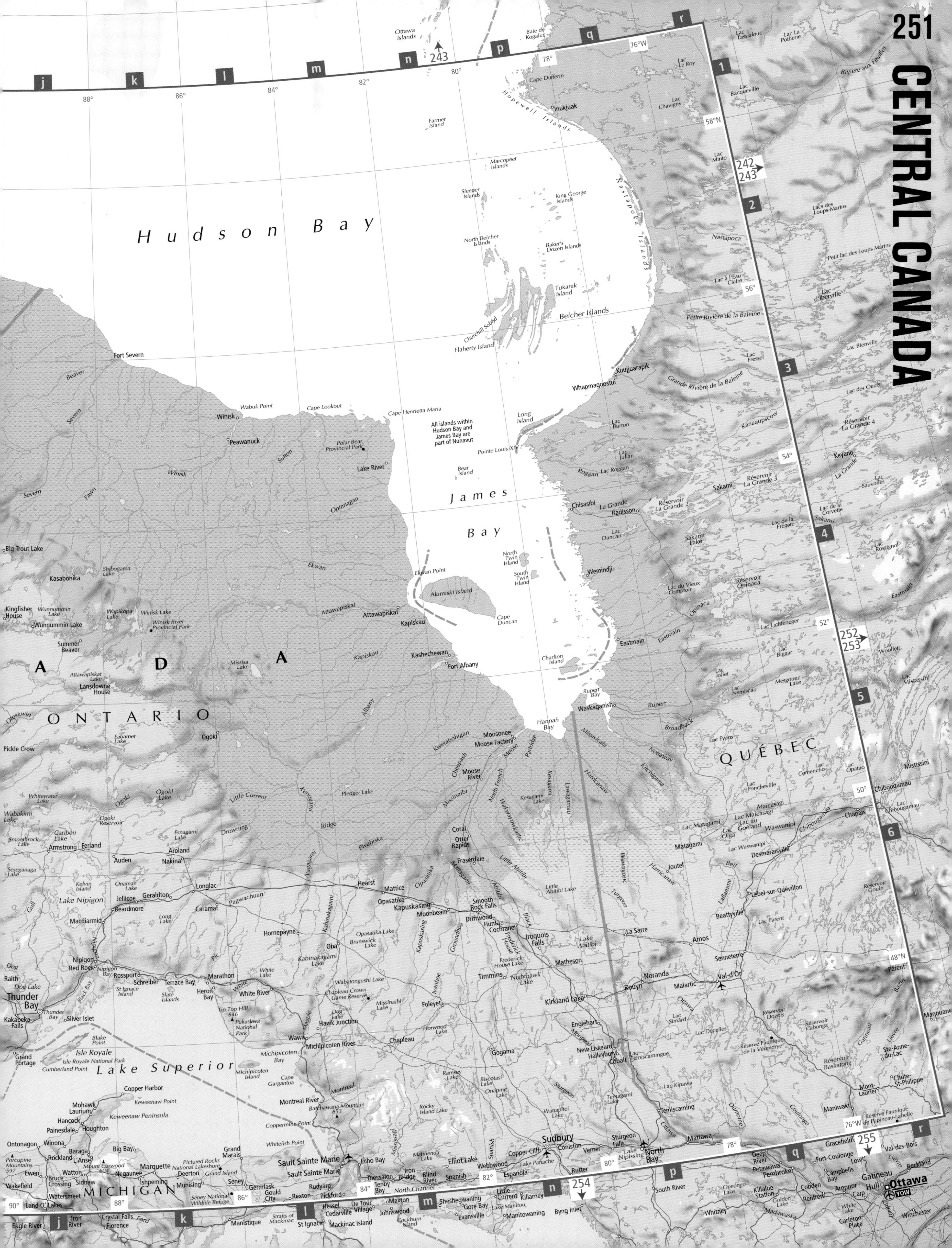
Hudson Bay
James Bay
Lake Superior
Lake Nipigon
ONTARIO
QUÉBEC
MICHIGAN
All islands within Hudson Bay and James Bay are part of Nunavut
Ottawa Islands
Baie de Kogaluc
Cape Dufferin
Inukjuak
Hopewell Islands
Farmer Island
Marcopeet Islands
Sleeper Islands
King George Islands
Nastapoka Islands
North Belcher Islands
Baker's Dozen Islands
Tukarak Island
Belcher Islands
Churchill Sound
Flaherty Island
Kuujjuarapik
Whapmagoostui
Long Island
Pointe Louis-XIV
Bear Island
Cape Henrietta Maria
Cape Lookout
Wabuk Point
Fort Severn
Winisk
Peawanuck
Polar Bear Provincial Park
Lake River
North Twin Island
South Twin Island
Ekwan Point
Akimiski Island
Cape Duncan
Charlton Island
Attawapiskat
Kapiskau
Kashechewan
Fort Albany
Rupert Bay
Hannah Bay
Waskaganish
Moosonee
Moose Factory
Chisasibi
Radisson
Wemindji
Eastmain
Big Trout Lake
Kasabonika
Kingfisher House
Wunnummin Lake
Summer Beaver
Lansdowne House
Winisk River Provincial Park
Pickle Crow
Ogoki
Armstrong
Aroland
Nakina
Longlac
Geraldton
Jellicoe
Beardmore
Macdiarmid
Nipigon
Red Rock
Rossport
Schreiber
Terrace Bay
Marathon
Heron Bay
White River
Thunder Bay
Kakabeka Falls
Silver Islet
Isle Royale
Isle Royale National Park
Grand Portage
Wawa
Michipicoten River
Hawk Junction
Chapleau
Foleyet
Timmins
Hearst
Mattice
Opasatika
Kapuskasing
Moonbeam
Smooth Rock Falls
Cochrane
Iroquois Falls
Matheson
Kirkland Lake
Englehart
New Liskeard
Haileybury
Cobalt
Temiscaming
Mattawa
North Bay
Sudbury
Copper Cliff
Espanola
Sault Sainte Marie
Echo Bay
Blind River
Elliot Lake
Manitowaning
Byng Inlet
Rouyn
Noranda
Malartic
Val-d'Or
Amos
La Sarre
Senneterre
Matagami
Joutel
Chibougamau
Chapais
Mistissini
Lebel-sur-Quévillon
Desmaraisville
Maniwaki
Mont-Laurier
Gracefield
Ottawa
Gatineau
Hull
Pembroke
Petawawa
Deep River
Renfrew
Arnprior
Carleton Place
Marquette
Munising
Houghton
Hancock
Copper Harbor
Keweenaw Peninsula
Ontonagon
Iron River
Escanaba
Manistique
St Ignace
Mackinac Island
Lac Bienville
Réservoir La Grande 4
Réservoir La Grande 3
Réservoir La Grande 2
Réservoir Opinaca
Lac Mistassini
Réservoir Gouin
Réservoir Cabonga
Réservoir Baskatong
Lac Abitibi
Lac Témiscamingue
Lake Nipissing
North Channel
Grande Rivière de la Baleine
Petite Rivière de la Baleine
Albany
Severn
Ekwan
Kenogami
Missinaibi
Harricanaw
Nottaway
Broadback
Rupert
243
242 243
252 253
254
255
76°W
78°
80°
82°
84°
86°
88°
90°
58°N
56°
54°
52°
50°
48°N

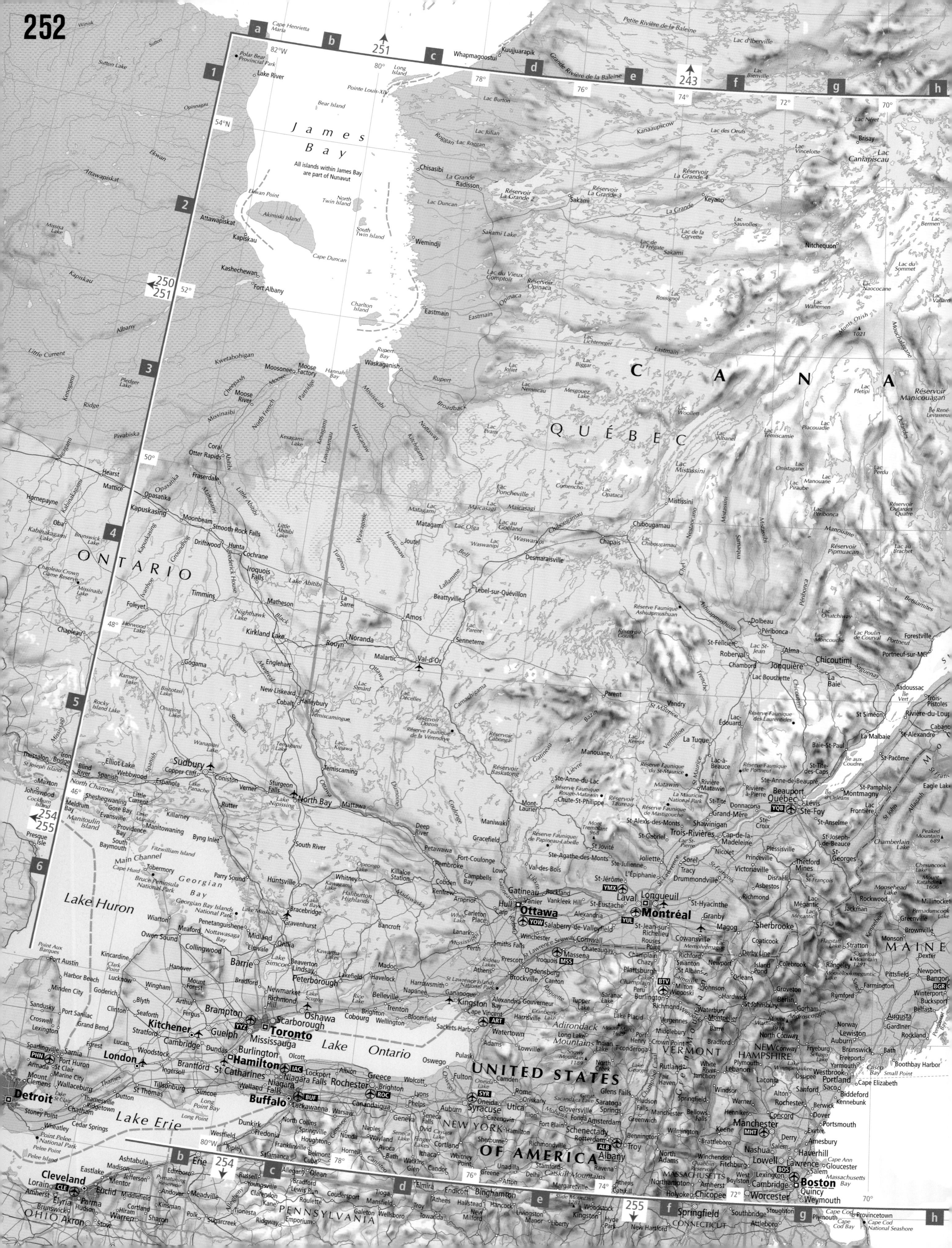

James Bay
All islands within James Bay are part of Nunavut
Akimiski Island
North Twin Island
South Twin Island
Charlton Island
Cape Henrietta Maria
Polar Bear Provincial Park
Lake River
Attawapiskat
Kapiskau
Kashechewan
Fort Albany
Moosonee
Moose Factory
Rupert Bay
Hannah Bay
Waskaganish
Eastmain
Wemindji
Chisasibi
Radisson
Whapmagoostui
Kuujjuarapik
Grande Rivière de la Baleine
Petite Rivière de la Baleine
Lac d'Iberville
Lac Bienville
Réservoir La Grande 2
Réservoir La Grande 3
Réservoir La Grande 4
Sakami
Lac Caniapiscau
Nitchequon
Monts Otish
Réservoir Manicouagan
CANADA
QUÉBEC
ONTARIO
Lac Mistassini
Mistissini
Chibougamau
Chapais
Matagami
Lebel-sur-Quévillon
Amos
Val-d'Or
Senneterre
Rouyn
Noranda
Kirkland Lake
Timmins
Cochrane
Hearst
Kapuskasing
Iroquois Falls
Lake Abitibi
New Liskeard
Haileybury
Cobalt
Lac Témiscamingue
Réserve Faunique de la Vérendrye
Lac St-Jean
Roberval
Alma
Jonquière
Chicoutimi
Dolbeau
Péribonca
Tadoussac
La Malbaie
Baie-St-Paul
La Tuque
Trois-Rivières
Shawinigan
Québec
Ste-Foy
Lévis
Sudbury
Elliot Lake
Espanola
North Bay
Mattawa
Temiscaming
Manitoulin Island
Lake Huron
Georgian Bay
Parry Sound
Huntsville
Pembroke
Ottawa
Hull
Gatineau
Montréal
Laval
Longueuil
Sherbrooke
Granby
Kingston
Belleville
Peterborough
Barrie
Orillia
Owen Sound
Toronto
Mississauga
Scarborough
Hamilton
Brampton
Kitchener
Guelph
Cambridge
London
Lake Ontario
Lake Erie
St Catharines
Niagara Falls
Buffalo
Rochester
Syracuse
Utica
Albany
Troy
Schenectady
Binghamton
Detroit
Windsor
Cleveland
Erie
Akron
UNITED STATES OF AMERICA
NEW YORK
PENNSYLVANIA
OHIO
VERMONT
NEW HAMPSHIRE
MAINE
MASSACHUSETTS
CONNECTICUT
Adirondack Mountains
Lake Champlain
Burlington
Plattsburgh
Montpelier
Manchester
Concord
Portland
Augusta
Bangor
Lewiston
Nashua
Lowell
Lawrence
Boston
Worcester
Springfield
Cape Cod
Provincetown
Lake Placid
Watertown
Oswego
Ithaca
Elmira
Jamestown

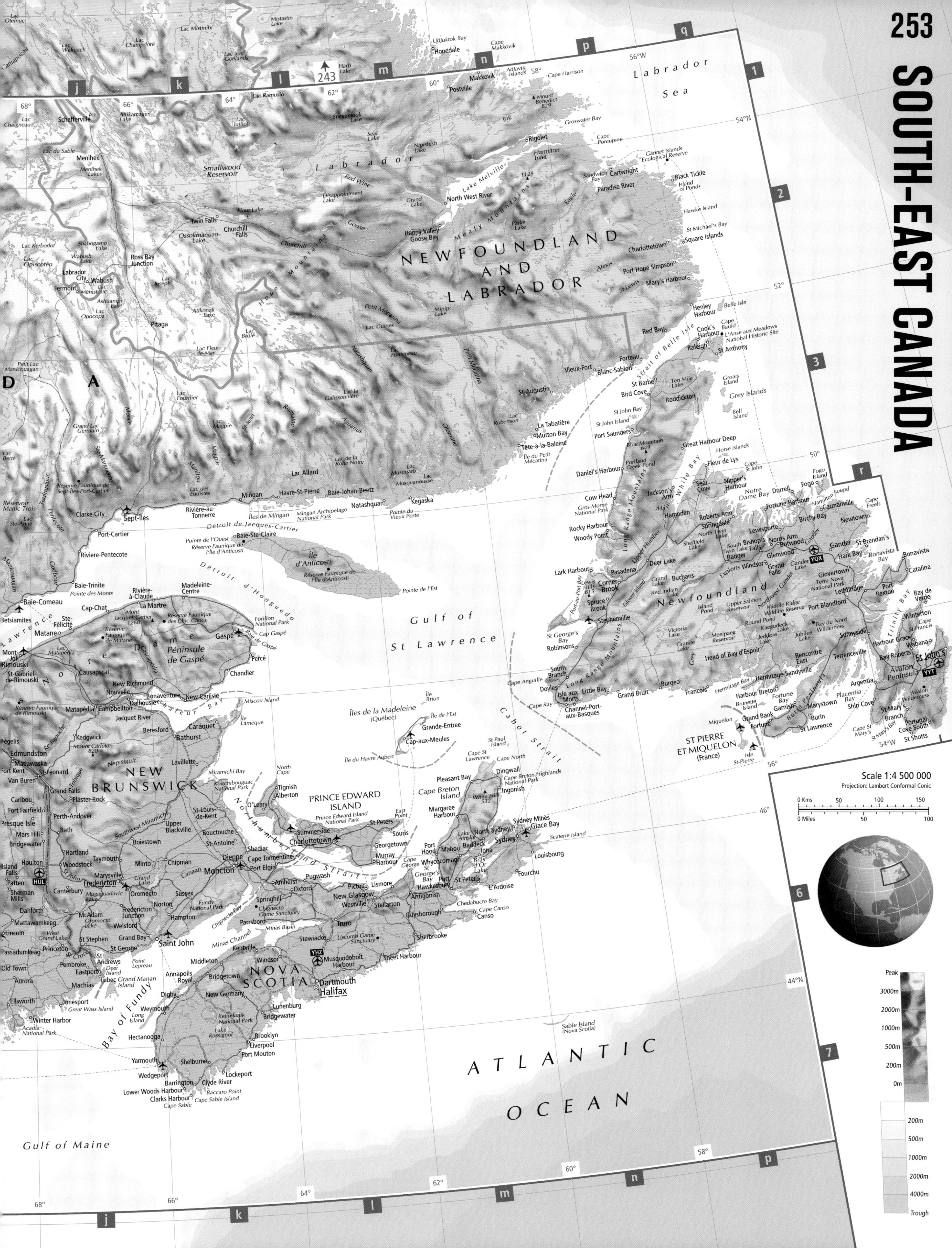
253
SOUTH-EAST CANADA
Scale 1:4 500 000
Projection: Lambert Conformal Conic
0 Kms 50 100 150
0 Miles 50 100
Peak
3000m
2000m
1000m
500m
200m
0m
200m
500m
1000m
2000m
4000m
Trough
Labrador Sea
Labrador
NEWFOUNDLAND AND LABRADOR
Newfoundland
Gulf of St Lawrence
ATLANTIC OCEAN
Gulf of Maine
Bay of Fundy
Cabot Strait
Strait of Belle Isle
Northumberland Strait
Détroit de Jacques-Cartier
Détroit d'Honguedo
Chaleur Bay
NEW BRUNSWICK
NOVA SCOTIA
PRINCE EDWARD ISLAND
Prince Edward Island National Park
ST PIERRE ET MIQUELON (France)
Île d'Anticosti
Îles de la Madeleine (Québec)
Péninsule de Gaspé
Cape Breton Island
Avalon Peninsula
Burin Peninsula
Long Range Mountains
Mealy Mountains
Smallwood Reservoir
Lake Melville
Churchill Falls
Happy Valley-Goose Bay
North West River
Cartwright
Hopedale
Makkovik
Postville
Rigolet
Labrador City
Wabush
Fermont
Schefferville
Menihek
Sept-Îles
Port-Cartier
Baie-Comeau
Havre-St-Pierre
Natashquan
Kegaska
Blanc-Sablon
Forteau
Red Bay
St Anthony
Corner Brook
Stephenville
Deer Lake
Gander
Grand Falls
Windsor
Botwood
Lewisporte
Clarenville
Port Blandford
Channel-Port-aux-Basques
St John's
Placentia
Marystown
Burin
Grand Bank
Fortune
Miquelon
St-Pierre
Gaspé
Matane
Rimouski
Campbellton
Bathurst
Miramichi Bay
Moncton
Fredericton
Saint John
St Stephen
Charlottetown
Summerside
Souris
Georgetown
Sydney
Glace Bay
Louisbourg
Truro
New Glasgow
Antigonish
Halifax
Dartmouth
Windsor
Kentville
Digby
Yarmouth
Lunenburg
Bridgewater
Liverpool
Shelburne
Sable Island (Nova Scotia)
Cape Sable
Grand Manan Island
YHZ
YQX
YYT
HUL
243
j k l m n p q r
1 2 3 6 7
68° 66° 64° 62° 60° 58° 56°W 54°W
54°N 52° 50° 46° 44°N

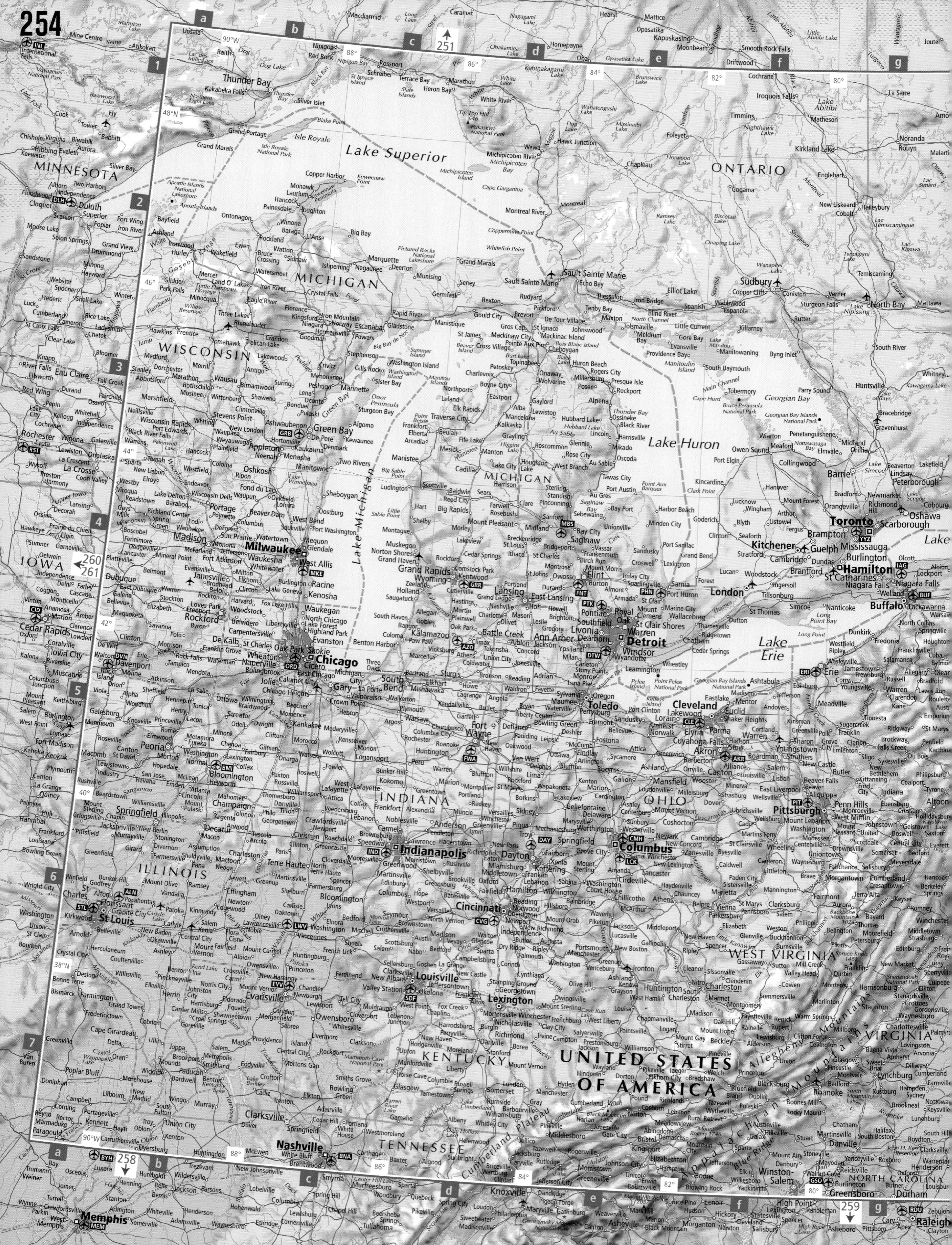

251
258
259
260
261
a
b
c
d
e
f
g
1
2
3
4
5
6
7
90°W
88°
86°
84°
82°
80°
48°N
46°
44°
42°
40°
38°N
Lake Superior
Lake Michigan
Lake Huron
Lake Erie
Georgian Bay
Lake
MINNESOTA
WISCONSIN
MICHIGAN
IOWA
ILLINOIS
INDIANA
OHIO
KENTUCKY
TENNESSEE
WEST VIRGINIA
VIRGINIA
NORTH CAROLINA
ONTARIO
UNITED STATES
OF AMERICA
Appalachian Mountains
Allegheny Mountains
Cumberland Plateau
Thunder Bay
Duluth
Sault Sainte Marie
Sudbury
North Bay
Green Bay
Milwaukee
Madison
Chicago
Rockford
Peoria
Springfield
St Louis
Grand Rapids
Lansing
Flint
Saginaw
Detroit
Ann Arbor
Toledo
Cleveland
Akron
Columbus
Dayton
Cincinnati
Indianapolis
Fort Wayne
South Bend
Louisville
Lexington
Evansville
Nashville
Knoxville
Memphis
Pittsburgh
Toronto
Hamilton
Kitchener
London
Buffalo
Erie
Cedar Rapids
Davenport
Raleigh

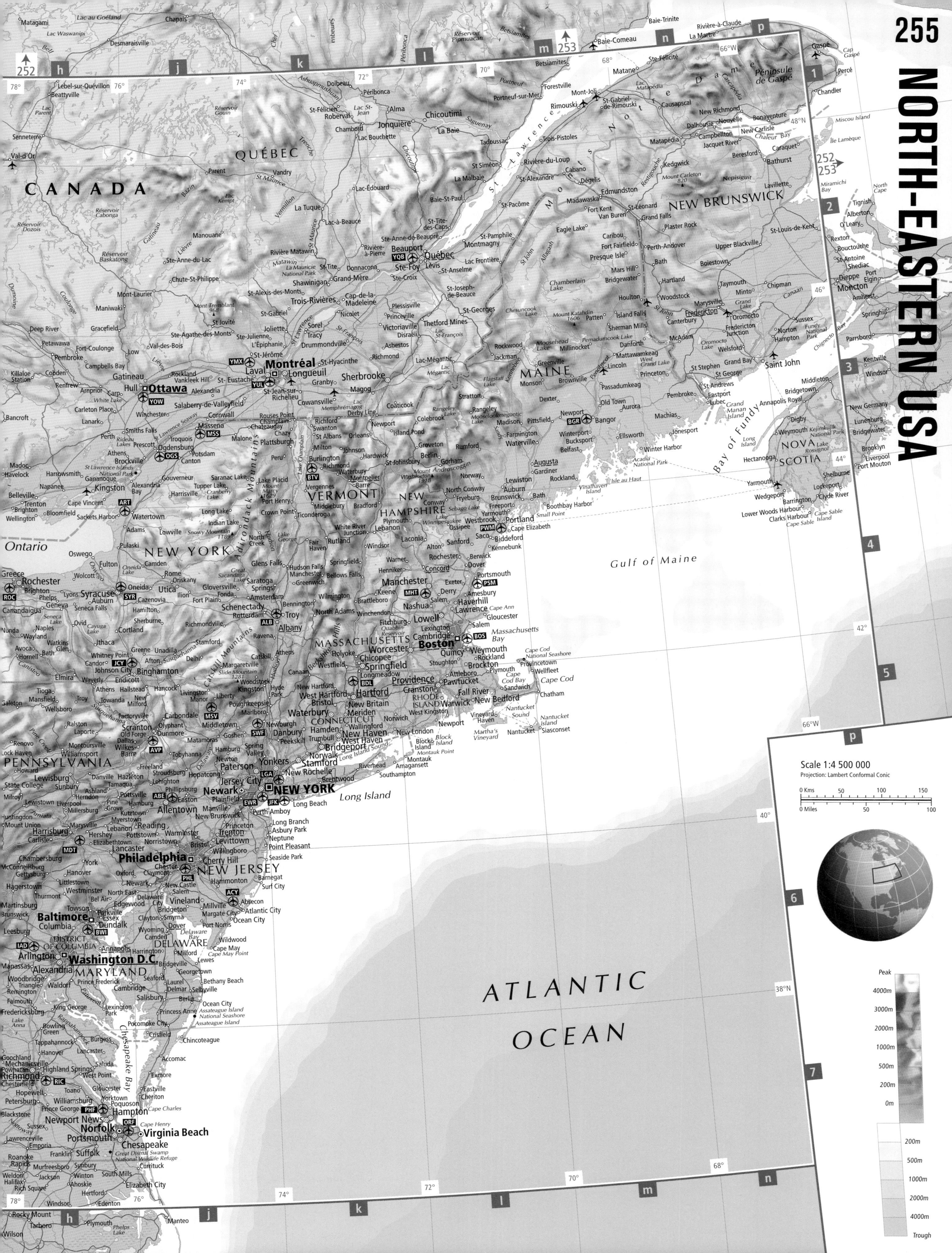

CANADA

QUÉBEC

NEW BRUNSWICK

NOVA SCOTIA

Ontario

NEW YORK

VERMONT

NEW HAMPSHIRE

MAINE

MASSACHUSETTS

Boston

RHODE ISLAND

CONNECTICUT

PENNSYLVANIA

NEW YORK

Long Island

NEW JERSEY

Philadelphia

DELAWARE

Baltimore

DISTRICT OF COLUMBIA

Washington D.C.

MARYLAND

Gulf of Maine

Massachusetts Bay

Cape Cod

ATLANTIC

OCEAN

Scale 1:4 500 000
Projection: Lambert Conformal Conic

0 Kms   50   100   150
0 Miles   50   100

Peak
4000m
3000m
2000m
1000m
500m
200m
0m

200m
500m
1000m
2000m
4000m
Trough

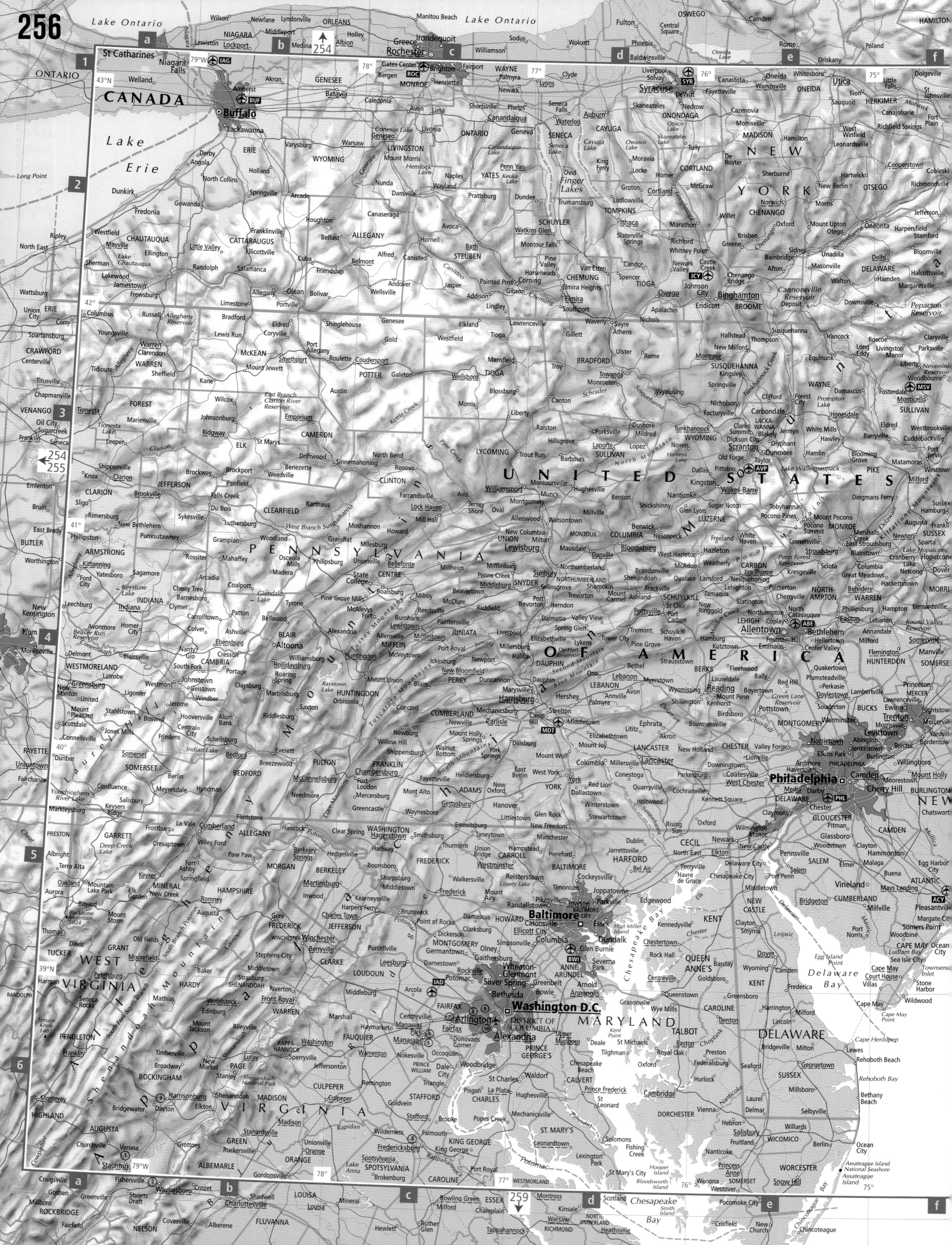
Lake Ontario
CANADA
ONTARIO
St Catharines
Niagara Falls
Buffalo
Lake Erie
Rochester
Syracuse
Utica
Binghamton
NEW YORK
Finger Lakes
UNITED STATES OF AMERICA
PENNSYLVANIA
Williamsport
Scranton
Wilkes-Barre
Allentown
Bethlehem
Reading
Harrisburg
Lancaster
Altoona
Philadelphia
Camden
Trenton
Wilmington
Baltimore
Washington D.C.
DISTRICT OF COLUMBIA
Arlington
Alexandria
MARYLAND
DELAWARE
Dover
Chesapeake Bay
Delaware Bay
WEST VIRGINIA
VIRGINIA
Charlottesville
Appalachian Mountains
Allegheny Mountains
Potomac
Susquehanna
254
255
259
79°W
78°
77°
76°
75°
43°N
42°
41°
40°
39°N
a
b
c
d
e
f
1
2
3
4
5
6

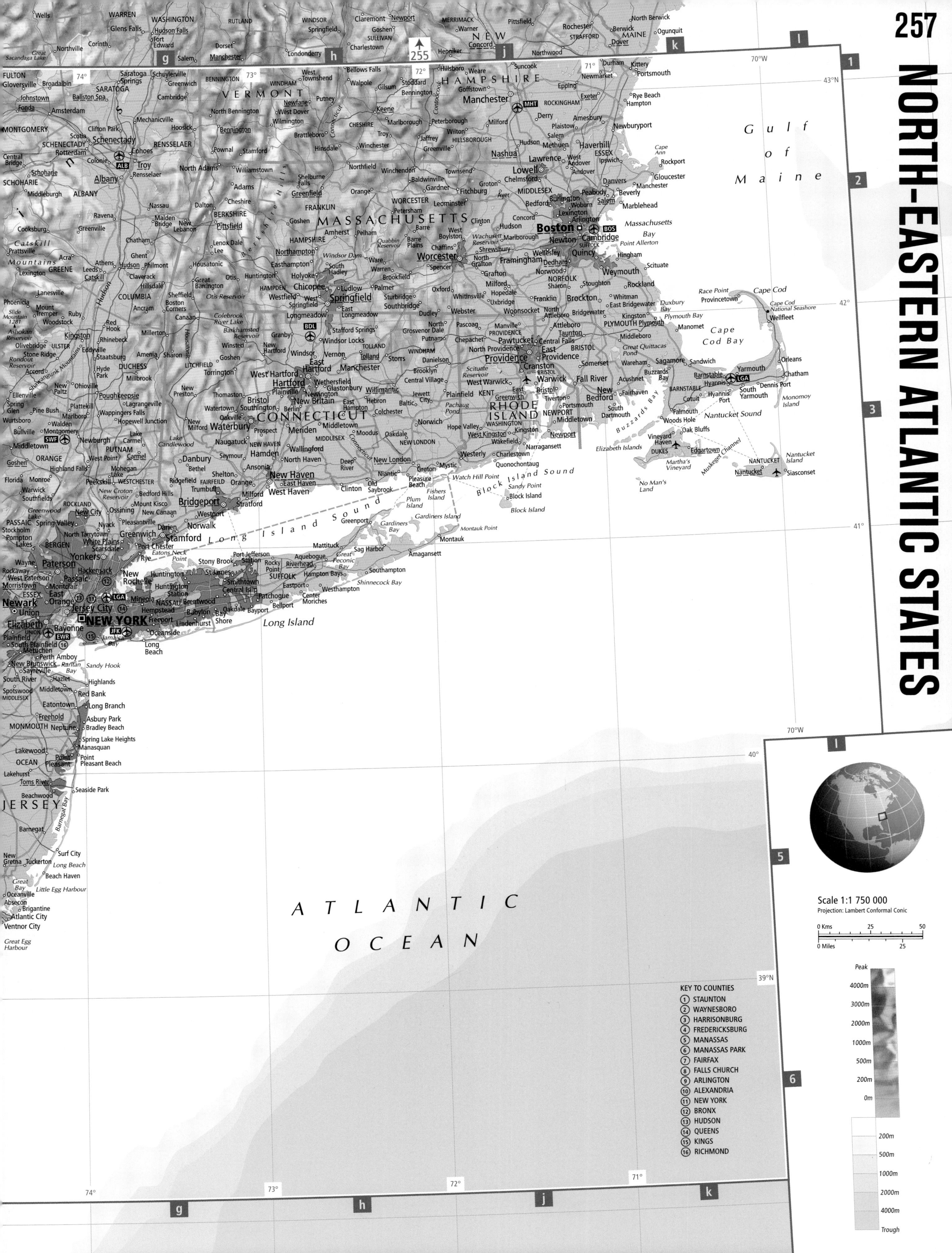
255
VERMONT
NEW HAMPSHIRE
MAINE
MASSACHUSETTS
CONNECTICUT
RHODE ISLAND
JERSEY
Gulf of Maine
Massachusetts Bay
Cape Cod Bay
Cape Cod
Nantucket Sound
Buzzards Bay
Block Island Sound
Long Island Sound
Long Island
ATLANTIC OCEAN
Boston
Cambridge
Worcester
Springfield
Providence
Hartford
New Haven
Bridgeport
Stamford
Manchester
Albany
Schenectady
Troy
Lowell
Lawrence
Brockton
Waterbury
Yonkers
Paterson
Newark
Jersey City
NEW YORK
Elizabeth
Catskill Mountains
Martha's Vineyard
Nantucket
Block Island
43°N
42°
41°
40°
39°N
70°W
71°
72°
73°
74°
Scale 1:1 750 000
Projection: Lambert Conformal Conic
0 Kms 25 50
0 Miles 25
Peak
4000m
3000m
2000m
1000m
500m
200m
0m
200m
500m
1000m
2000m
4000m
Trough
KEY TO COUNTIES
1 STAUNTON
2 WAYNESBORO
3 HARRISONBURG
4 FREDERICKSBURG
5 MANASSAS
6 MANASSAS PARK
7 FAIRFAX
8 FALLS CHURCH
9 ARLINGTON
10 ALEXANDRIA
11 NEW YORK
12 BRONX
13 HUDSON
14 QUEENS
15 KINGS
16 RICHMOND

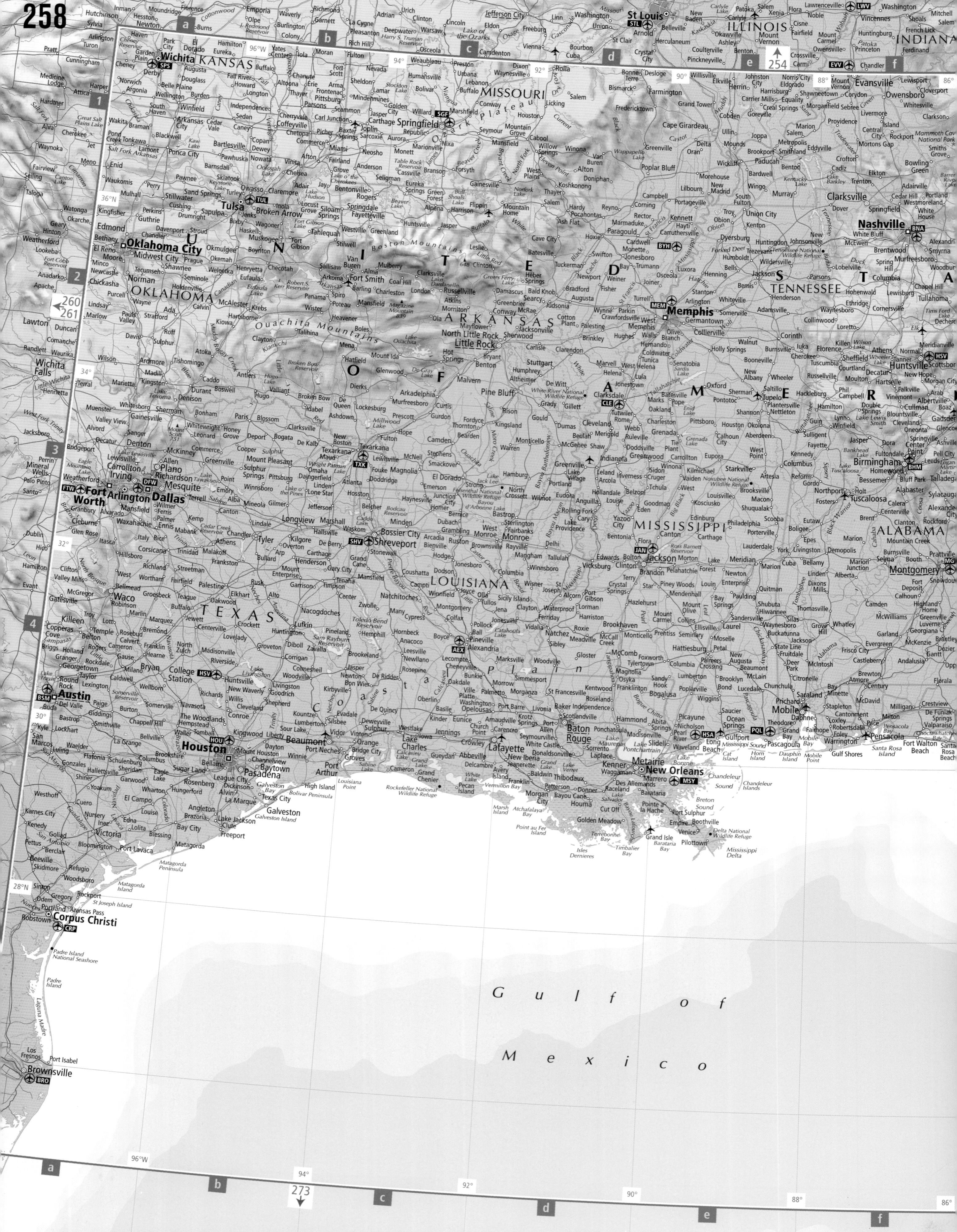

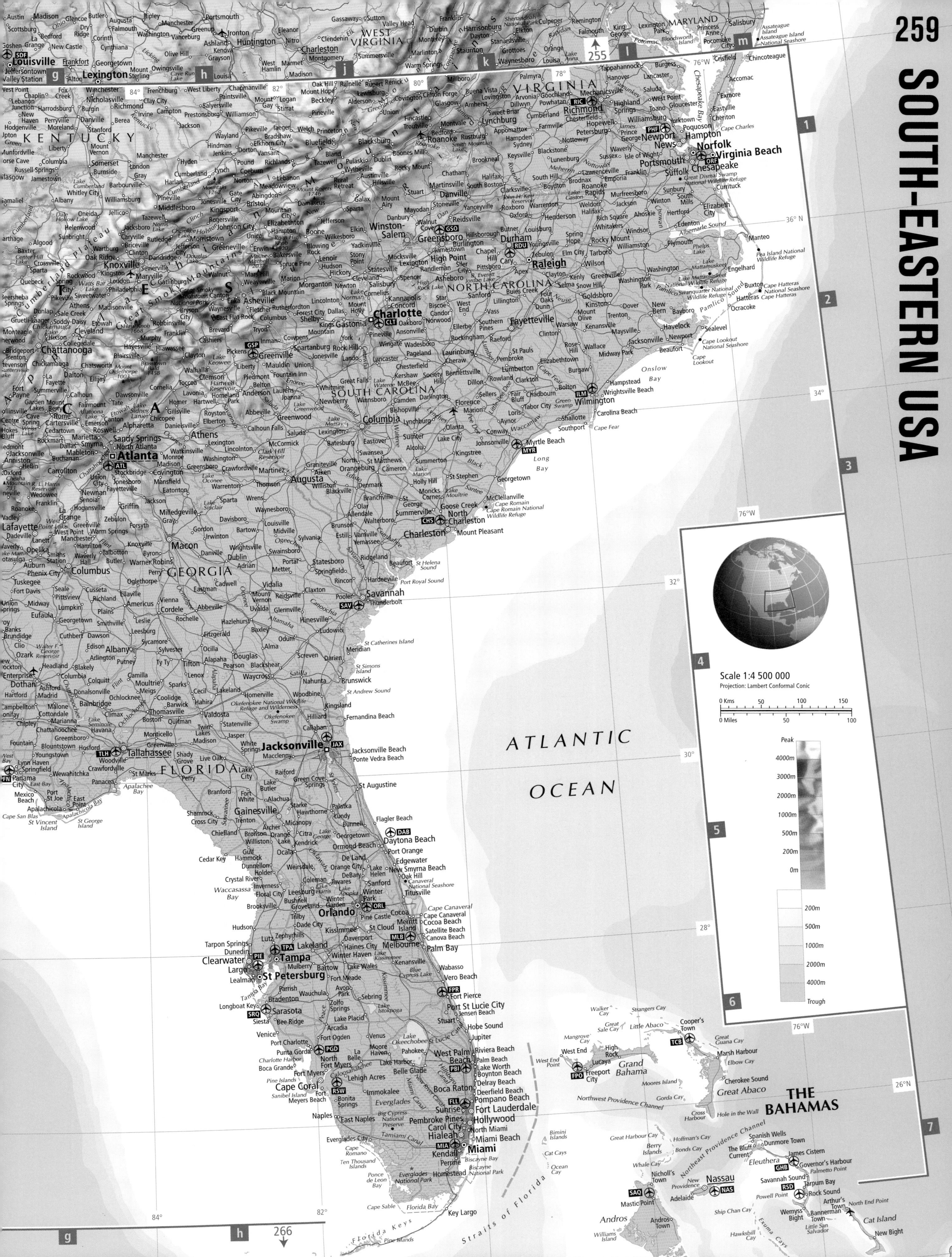

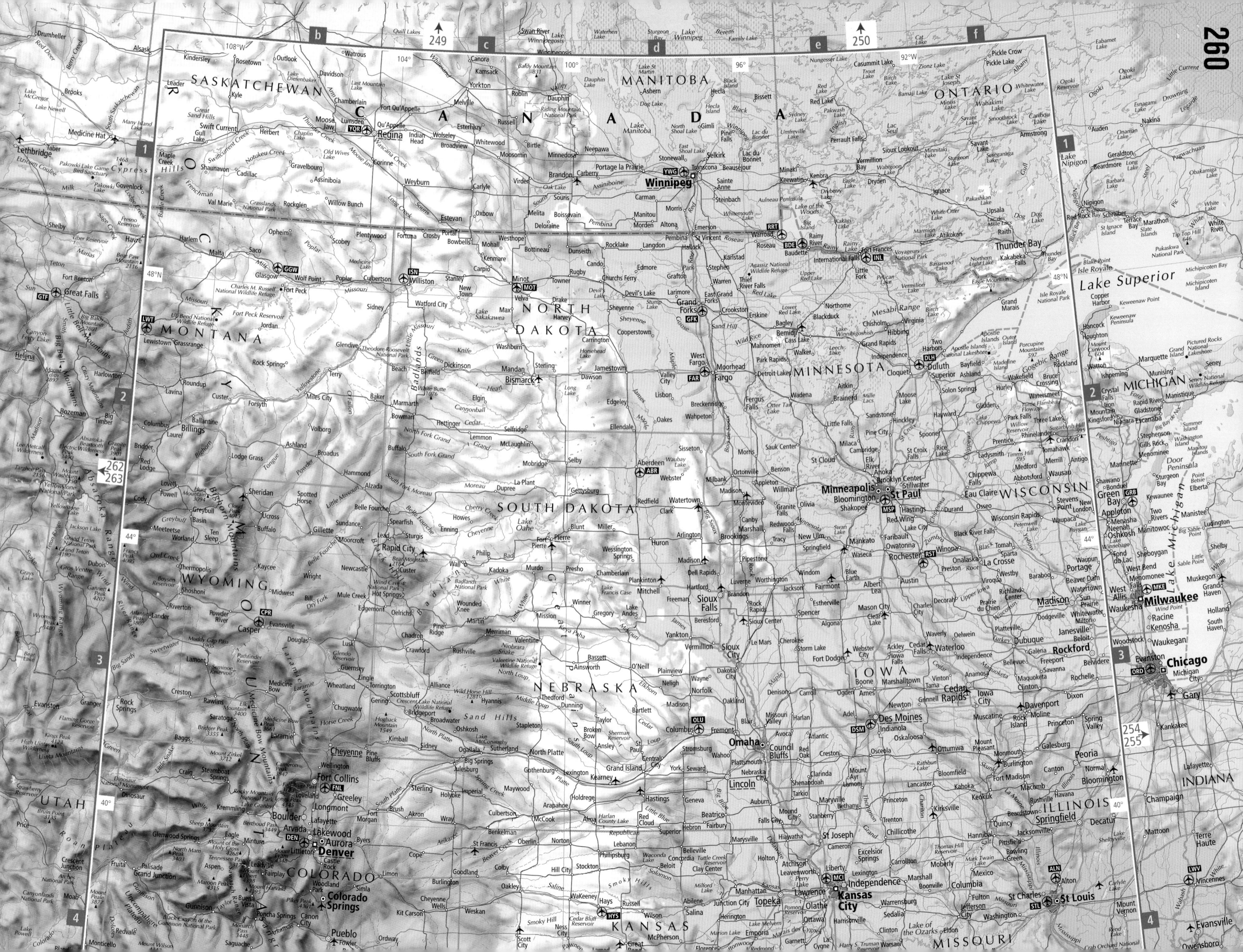
SASKATCHEWAN
MANITOBA
ONTARIO
CANADA
MONTANA
NORTH DAKOTA
SOUTH DAKOTA
MINNESOTA
WISCONSIN
MICHIGAN
IOWA
ILLINOIS
INDIANA
MISSOURI
NEBRASKA
KANSAS
WYOMING
COLORADO
UTAH
Lake Superior
Lake Michigan
Lake Winnipeg
Regina
Winnipeg
Thunder Bay
Minneapolis
St Paul
Milwaukee
Chicago
Des Moines
Omaha
Kansas City
St Louis
Denver
Colorado Springs
Bismarck
Pierre
Cheyenne
Billings
Great Falls
Lethbridge
Medicine Hat
Sioux Falls
Fargo
Duluth
Madison
Springfield
Topeka
Lincoln
Rapid City
Casper
Bighorn Mountains
Medicine Bow Mountains
Laramie Mountains
Absaroka Range
Black Hills
Badlands
Sand Hills
48°N
44°
40°
249
250
254
255
262
263

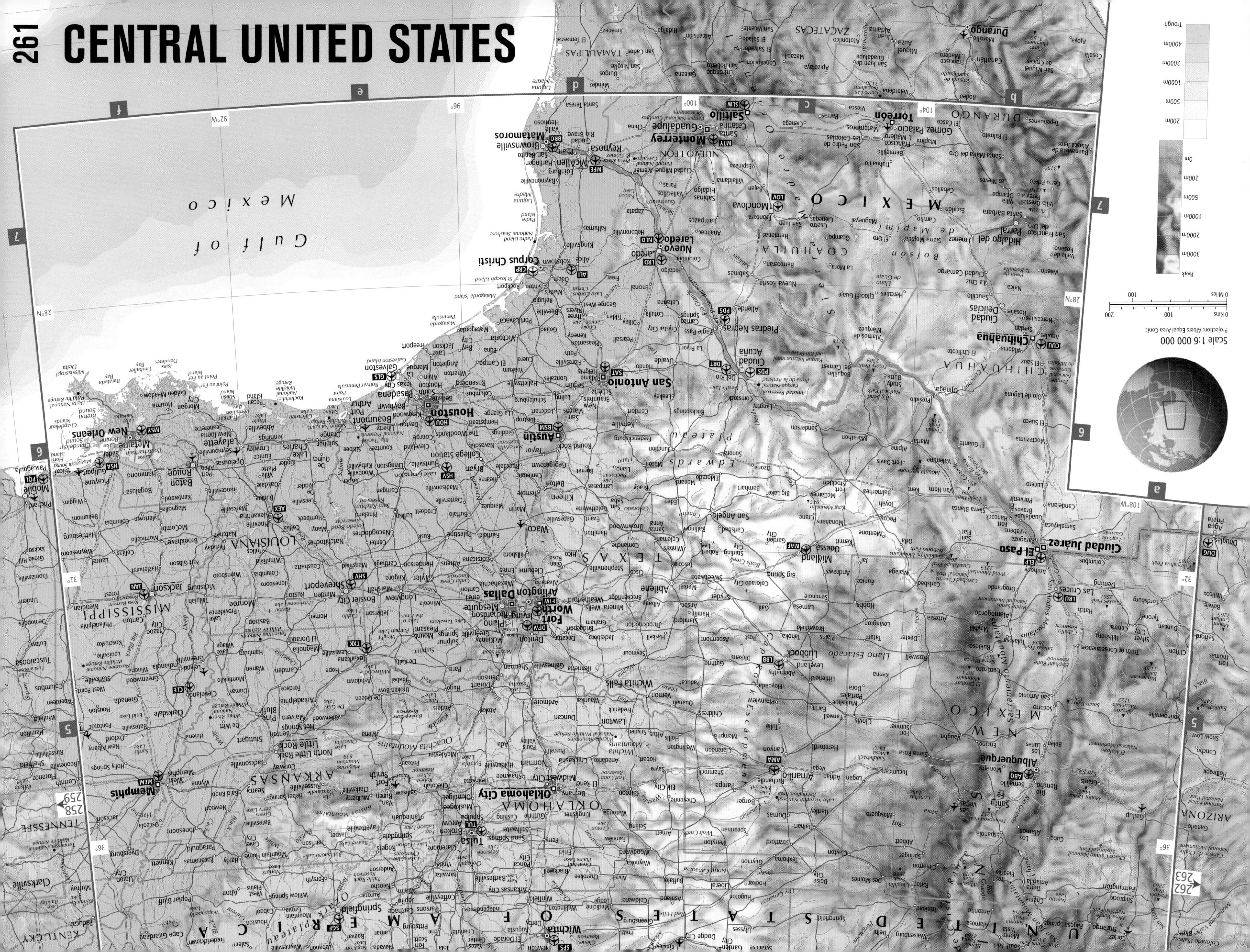

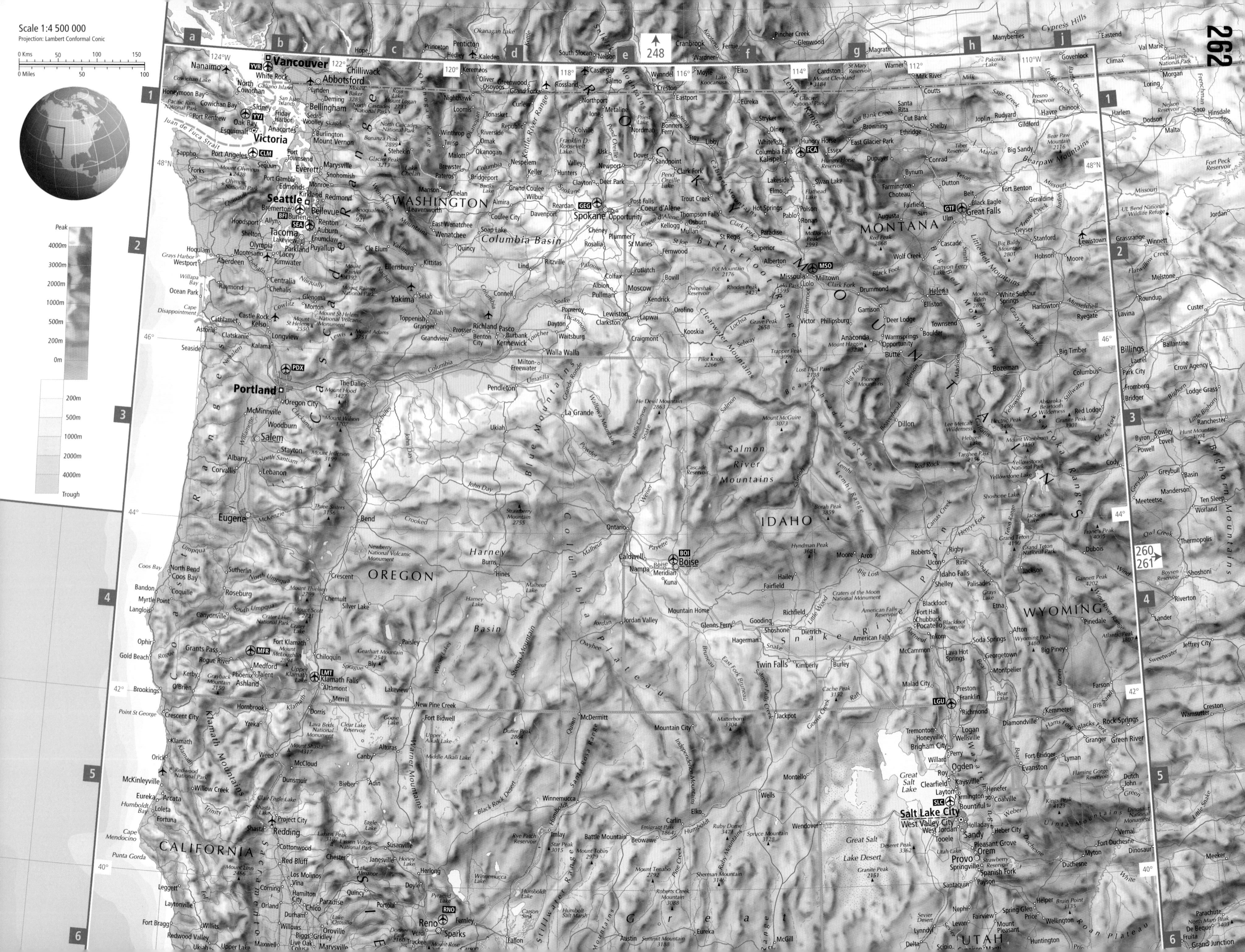

Scale 1:4 500 000
Projection: Lambert Conformal Conic
0 Kms 50 100 150
0 Miles 50 100
Peak
4000m
3000m
2000m
1000m
500m
200m
0m
200m
500m
1000m
2000m
4000m
Trough
248
260
261
WASHINGTON
OREGON
IDAHO
MONTANA
WYOMING
UTAH
CALIFORNIA
Vancouver
Victoria
Seattle
Tacoma
Portland
Salem
Eugene
Spokane
Boise
Salt Lake City
Reno
Great Falls
Helena
Missoula
Billings
Columbia Basin
Columbia Plateau
Blue Mountains
Salmon River Mountains
Klamath Mountains
Bighorn Mountains
Great Salt Lake

States & Regions

NEVADA · CALIFORNIA · ARIZONA · MEXICO · SONORA · BAJA CALIFORNIA NORTE

PACIFIC OCEAN

Golfo de California

HAWAII (U.S.A)
Same scale as main map

Major cities and places

San Francisco · Oakland · Berkeley · Sacramento · San Jose · Stockton · Modesto · Fresno · Bakersfield · Las Vegas · Henderson · Los Angeles · Long Beach · Santa Ana · Riverside · San Bernardino · Pasadena · Glendale · Santa Monica · Huntington Beach · Oxnard · Ventura · Santa Barbara · Lancaster · Palmdale · San Diego · Chula Vista · Escondido · Oceanside · Tijuana · Mexicali · Phoenix · Tempe · Mesa · Glendale · Peoria · Sun City · Tucson · Nogales · Yuma · San Luis Río Colorado

Honolulu · Hilo · Kailua · Kaneohe

Death Valley · Mojave Desert · Sierra Nevada · Grand Canyon · Monument Valley · Painted Desert · Colorado Plateau · Lake Mead · Lake Havasu · Salton Sea

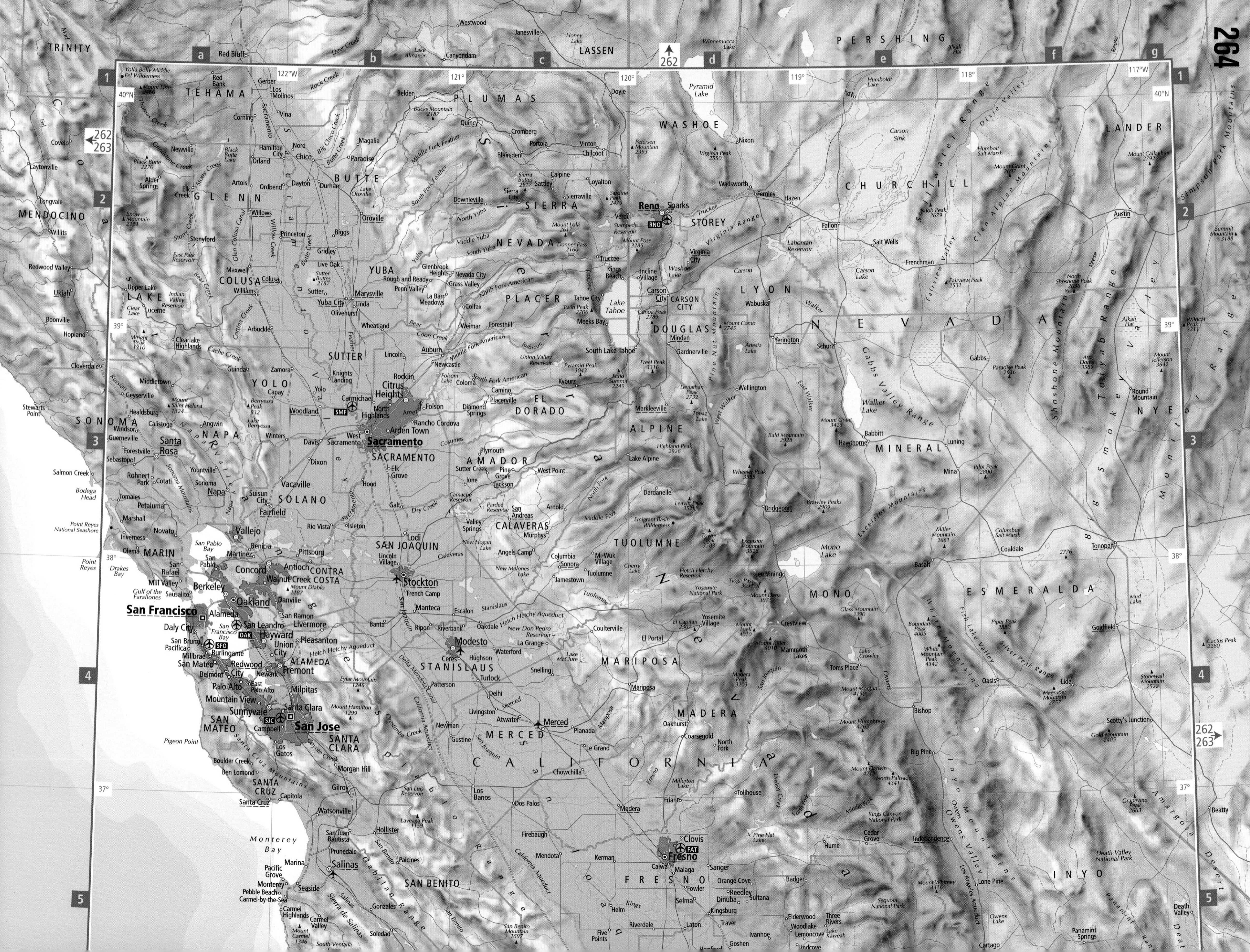

CALIFORNIA
NEVADA
Diablo Range
Gabilan Range
Santa Cruz Mountains
Sonoma Mountains
White Mountains
Inyo Mountains
Owens Valley
Fish Lake Valley
Silver Peak Range
Excelsior Mountains
Gabbs Valley Range
Pine Nut Mountains
Virginia Range
Shoshone Mountains
Toiyabe Range
Big Smoky Valley
Monitor Range
Clan Alpine Mountains
Stillwater Range
Dixie Valley
Fairview Valley
Simpson Park Mountains
Amargosa Desert
Panamint Range
Sierra de Salinas
Death Valley National Park
Kings Canyon National Park
Sequoia National Park
Yosemite National Park
Emigrant Basin Wilderness
Yolla Bolly Middle Eel Wilderness
Point Reyes National Seashore
Monterey Bay
San Pablo Bay
San Francisco Bay
Gulf of the Farallones
Drakes Bay
Point Reyes
Bodega Head
Pigeon Point
Lake Tahoe
Mono Lake
Walker Lake
Pyramid Lake
Honey Lake
Carson Lake
Carson Sink
Humboldt Salt Marsh
Columbus Salt Marsh
Lake Almanor
Clear Lake
Lake Berryessa
Folsom Lake
New Melones Lake
New Don Pedro Reservoir
Lake McClure
Millerton Lake
Pine Flat Lake
Lahontan Reservoir
Los Angeles Aqueduct
California Aqueduct
Delta Mendota Canal
Hetch Hetchy Aqueduct
Glen-Colusa Canal
TRINITY
TEHAMA
PLUMAS
LASSEN
BUTTE
GLENN
COLUSA
SUTTER
YUBA
SIERRA
NEVADA
PLACER
EL DORADO
AMADOR
CALAVERAS
ALPINE
TUOLUMNE
MARIPOSA
MADERA
FRESNO
MERCED
STANISLAUS
SAN JOAQUIN
SACRAMENTO
YOLO
SOLANO
NAPA
LAKE
SONOMA
MARIN
CONTRA COSTA
ALAMEDA
SANTA CLARA
SAN MATEO
SANTA CRUZ
SAN BENITO
MENDOCINO
MONO
INYO
PERSHING
CHURCHILL
LANDER
NYE
MINERAL
ESMERALDA
WASHOE
STOREY
LYON
DOUGLAS
CARSON CITY
San Francisco
Sacramento
San Jose
Oakland
Stockton
Modesto
Fresno
Reno
Sparks
Carson City
Santa Rosa
Salinas
Merced
Berkeley
Vallejo
Fairfield
Napa
Concord
Hayward
Fremont
Sunnyvale
Mountain View
Palo Alto
Redwood City
San Mateo
Daly City
Pacifica
Alameda
Walnut Creek
Pleasanton
Livermore
Lodi
Manteca
Turlock
Ceres
Atwater
Los Banos
Gilroy
Hollister
Watsonville
Santa Cruz
Capitola
Los Gatos
Monterey
Pacific Grove
Carmel-by-the-Sea
Marina
Seaside
Davis
Woodland
Vacaville
Dixon
Yuba City
Marysville
Chico
Oroville
Paradise
Orland
Willows
Colusa
Red Bluff
Auburn
Placerville
Folsom
Citrus Heights
Rancho Cordova
Arden Town
Grass Valley
Nevada City
Truckee
South Lake Tahoe
Jackson
Sonora
Mariposa
Madera
Clovis
Bishop
Independence
Lone Pine
Bridgeport
Lee Vining
Mammoth Lakes
Hawthorne
Tonopah
Goldfield
Fallon
Fernley
Yerington
Minden
Gardnerville
Austin
Beatty
Ukiah
Willits
Mount Diablo
Mount Whitney 4418
Mount Lola 2617
Mount Rose 3285
Freel Peak 3316
Boundary Peak 4005
White Mountain Peak 4342
Mount Humphreys 4263
Mount Dana 3979
Mount Lyell 4010
Mount Hamilton 1299
Mount Saint Helena 1324
Mount Jefferson 3642
Mount Callaghan 2792
262
263

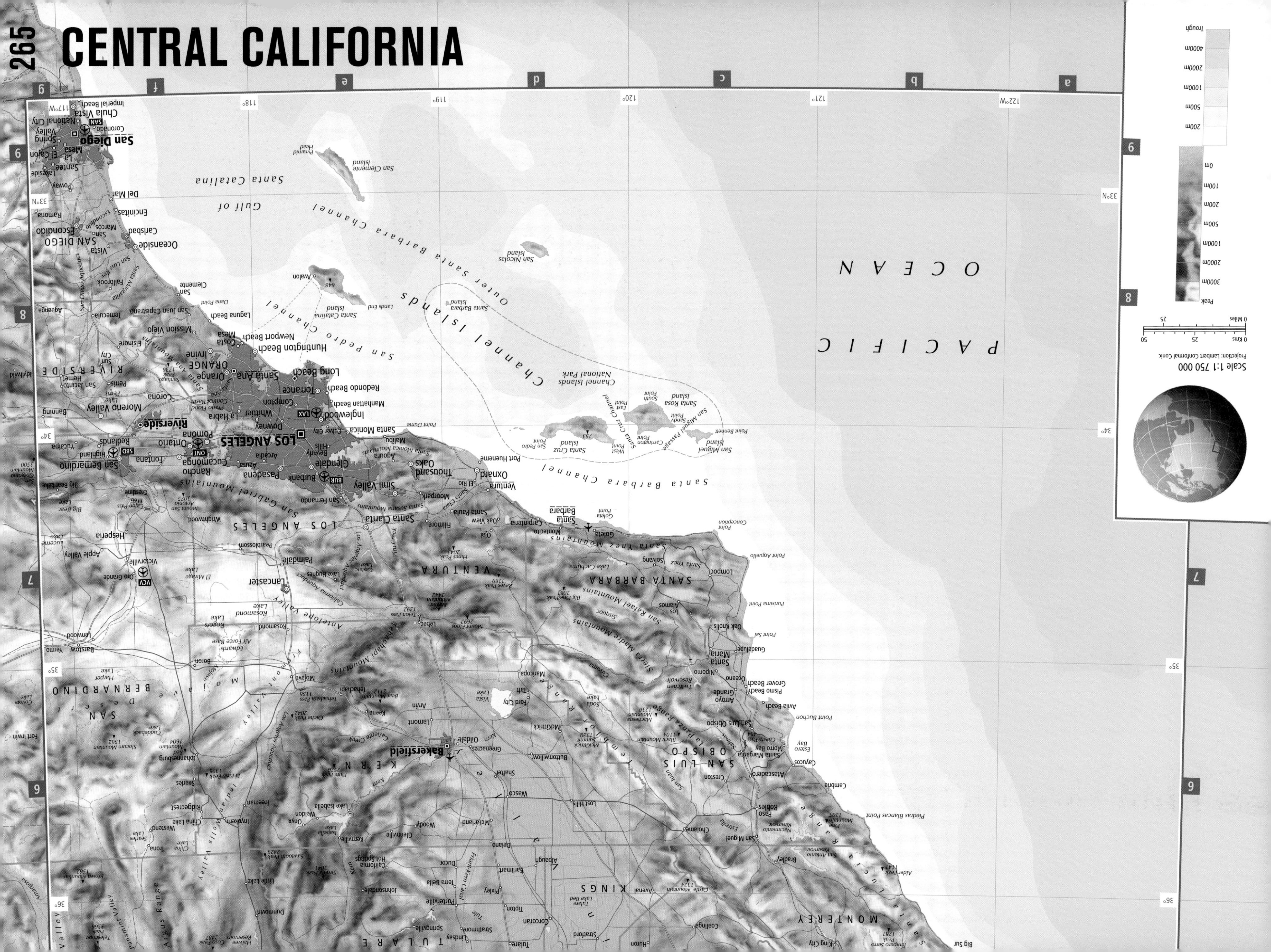

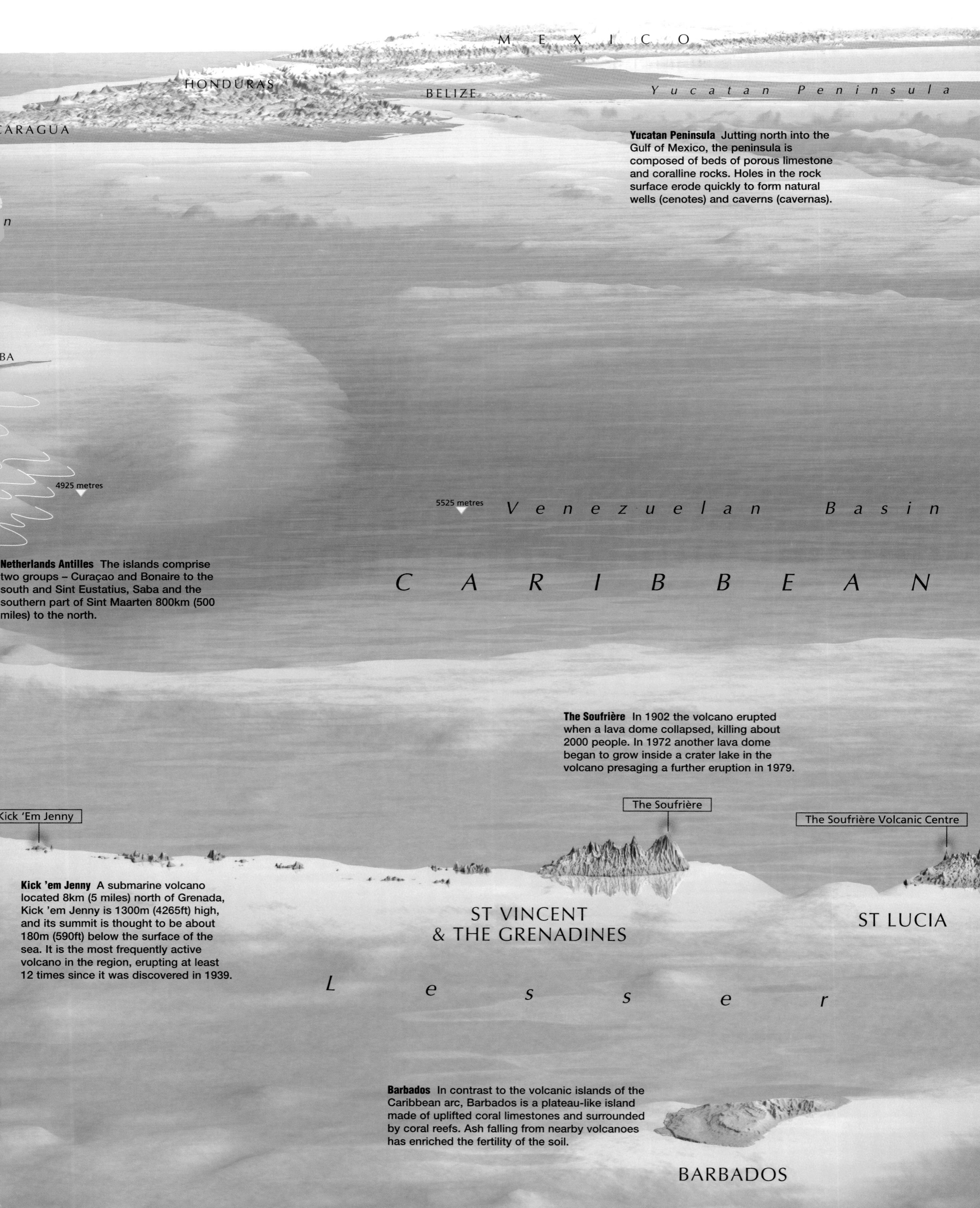

MEXICO

HONDURAS

BELIZE

Yucatan Peninsula

CARAGUA

n

Yucatan Peninsula Jutting north into the Gulf of Mexico, the peninsula is composed of beds of porous limestone and coralline rocks. Holes in the rock surface erode quickly to form natural wells (cenotes) and caverns (cavernas).

BA

4925 metres

5525 metres   *V e n e z u e l a n   B a s i n*

Netherlands Antilles The islands comprise two groups – Curaçao and Bonaire to the south and Sint Eustatius, Saba and the southern part of Sint Maarten 800km (500 miles) to the north.

C A R I B B E A N

The Soufrière In 1902 the volcano erupted when a lava dome collapsed, killing about 2000 people. In 1972 another lava dome began to grow inside a crater lake in the volcano presaging a further eruption in 1979.

Kick 'Em Jenny

The Soufrière

The Soufrière Volcanic Centre

Kick 'em Jenny A submarine volcano located 8km (5 miles) north of Grenada, Kick 'em Jenny is 1300m (4265ft) high, and its summit is thought to be about 180m (590ft) below the surface of the sea. It is the most frequently active volcano in the region, erupting at least 12 times since it was discovered in 1939.

ST VINCENT & THE GRENADINES

ST LUCIA

L   e   s   s   e   r

Barbados In contrast to the volcanic islands of the Caribbean arc, Barbados is a plateau-like island made of uplifted coral limestones and surrounded by coral reefs. Ash falling from nearby volcanoes has enriched the fertility of the soil.

BARBADOS

PACIFIC OCEAN

COSTA RICA

PANAMA

Colombian   Basi

COLOMBIA

NI

*Gulf of
Venezuela*

Lake Maracaibo ❶

ARU

CURAÇAO

*Netherlands
Antilles*

BONAIRE

VENEZUELA

CARACAS

❶ **Lake Maracaibo** Located on the
southern shores of the Caribbean,
Lake Maracaibo has accumulated
large deposits of organic sediments,
which form some of the largest
oilfields in the world.

500 metres

2000 metres

4000 metres

Mt St Catherine

PORT OF SPAIN

Gulf of Paria

Trinidad and Tobago The two most southerly islands
in the Caribbean have a total area of 5123km²
(1978 sq miles). Trinidad is separated from
Venezuela by the Gulf of Paria and two narrow
channels and is only 11km (7 miles) from the South
American coast at its nearest point.

GRENADA

TRINIDAD

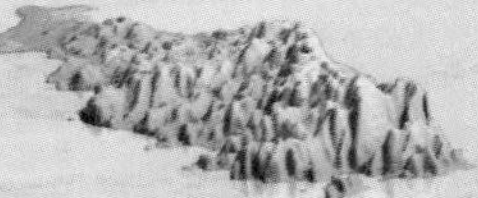

TOBAGO

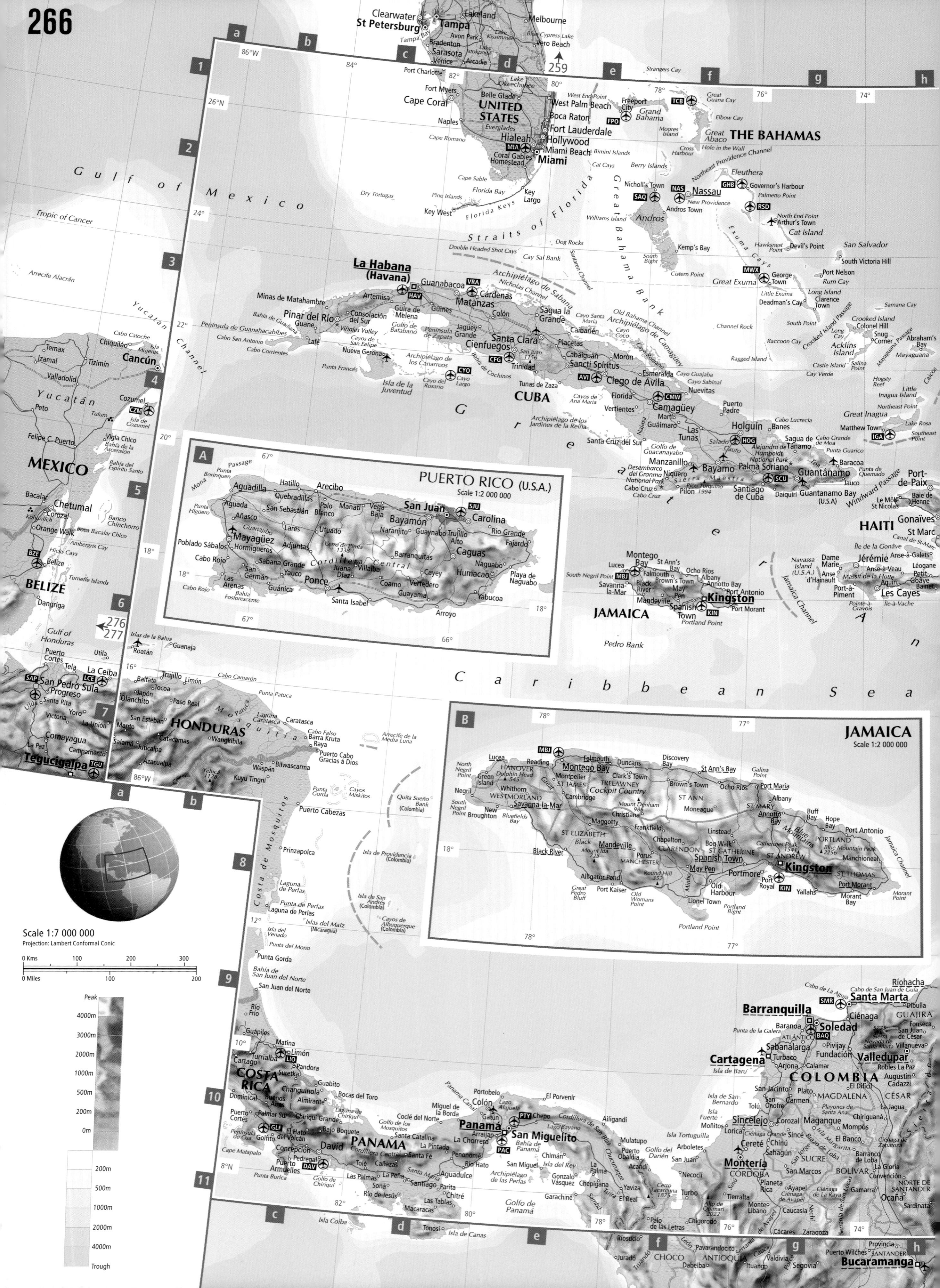

Scale 1:7 000 000
Projection: Lambert Conformal Conic

| 0 Kms | 100 | 200 | 300 |
| 0 Miles | | 100 | 200 |

PUERTO RICO (U.S.A.)
Scale 1:2 000 000

JAMAICA
Scale 1:2 000 000

Peak
4000m
3000m
2000m
1000m
500m
200m
0m

200m
500m
1000m
2000m
4000m
Trough

ISLANDS OF THE CARIBBEAN

GUADELOUPE (France)
Scale 1:2 000 000

Guadeloupe Passage · Pointe d'Antigues · Port Louis · Pointe Allègre · Grand Cul-de-Sac Marin · Grande-Terre · Moule · La Désirade · Pointe Ferry · Ste-Rose · Les Abymes · Morne-à-l'Eau · Pointe Noire · Petit-Bourg · Pointe-à-Pitre · St-François · Basse-Terre · Goyave · Îles de la Petite Terre · Bouillante · Soufrière 1467 · Capesterre · BBR · Basse-Terre · Trois-Rivières · St-Louis · Marie-Galante · Pointe du Vieux-Fort · Îles des Saintes · Grand Bourg · Pointe de Tali · Terre-de-Bas · Terre-de-Haut · Pointe des Basses · Dominica Passage

ANTIGUA & BARBUDA
Scale 1:2 000 000

Cedar Tree Point · Goat Point · Codrington · Barbuda · Palmetto Point · Spanish Point · Boon Point · St John's · ANU · Parham · Indian Town Point · Jennings · All Saints · Johnsons Point · Old Road · Falmouth · Antigua

TRINIDAD & TOBAGO
Scale 1:2 000 000

Tobago · Charlotteville · Plymouth · Roxborough · Little Tobago · Canaan · Scarborough · Crown Point · Columbus Point · Chupara Point · ARIMA-TUNAPUNA-PIARCO · Toco · Galera Point · Diego Martin · Blanchisseuse · Redhead · Punta Piedras · San Juan · Tunapuna · Valencia · Saline Bay · Port of Spain · POS · Arima · Sangre Grande · Manzanilla Point · Chaguanas · COUVA-TABAQUITE-TALPARO · Cocos Bay · Gulf of Paria · Mount Tamana 308 · Nariva Swamp · Trinidad · San Fernando · Rio Claro · Guataro Point · La Brea · Oropuche · Pierreville · Guapo Bay · POINT FORTIN · Prince's Town · PENAL DEBE · Ortoire · Mayaro Bay · Point Fortin · Siparia · Penal · Basse Terre · Guayaguayare · Galeota Point · Bonasse · Moruga · Fullarton · Icacos Point · Serpent's Mouth

ST KITTS & NEVIS
Scale 1:2 000 000

St Eustatius (Neth. Antilles) · Oranjestad · Mount Liamuiga · Sadlers · Bello Tete · SKB · Mansion · Basseterre · Sandy Point Town · Old Road Town · St.Kitts · Nag's Head · The Narrows · Newcastle · Nevis Peak 1096 · Nevis · New River · Charlestown

GRENADA
Scale 1:2 000 000

Ronde · London Bridge · Bedford Point · Sauteurs · Victoria · Telescope Point · Mount Sinai 767 · Grenville · St George's · GND · Marquis · Point Salines · Prickly Point

BARBADOS
Scale 1:2 000 000

North Point · Speightstown · St Andrew · Bathsheba · Holetown · Mount Hillaby 336 · The Crane · Bridgetown · BGI · Needhams Point · Six Cross Roads · Hastings · Oistins · South Point

MARTINIQUE (France)
Scale 1:2 000 000

Cap St-Martin · Basse-Pointe · Montagne Pelée 1397 · Le Lorrain · Ste-Marie · St-Pierre · La Trinité · Pointe du Diable · Case-Pilote · St-Joseph · Presqu'île de la Caravelle · Schœlcher · Le Robert · Fort-de-France · FDF · Le Lamentin · Le François · Cap Salomon · Rivière-Pilote · Le Marin · Pointe du Diamant · Ste-Luce · Le Ferré · Pointe des Salines · St Lucia Channel

ST LUCIA
Scale 1:2 000 000

Pointe du Cap · Pigeon Point · Gros Islet · Cap Marquis · Choc Bay · Castries · Pitou Flou 570 · Cul de Sac Bay · Praslin Bay · Soufrière · Mount Gimie 950 · Grand Caille Point · Micoud · Gros Piton 798 · QSL · Vieux Fort · Cape Moule à Chique · St. Vincent Passage

Main map

TURKS & CAICOS ISLANDS (U.K.) · North Caicos · Middle Caicos · East Caicos · Caicos Islands · West Caicos · Cockburn Harbour · GDT · Grand Turk · Turks Islands · Silver Bank Passage · Silver Bank · Navidad Bank · HISPANIOLA · CAP · Cap-Haïtien · Monte Cristi · Luperón · Puerto Plata · POP · Cabo Francés Viejo · Limbé · Fort Liberté · Mao · Santiago · STI · Cabrera · Cabo Samaná · Plaisance · Ennery · Sabaneta · La Vega · San Francisco de Macorís · Samaná · Sabana de la Mar · Hinche · Jarabacoa · Otui · Yuna · Miches · El Macao · PUERTO RICO (U.S.A.) · VIRGIN ISLANDS (U.K.) · Anegada · ANGUILLA (U.K.) · Port-au-Prince · San Juan · El Seibo · Hato Mayor · Aguadilla · Arecibo · San Juan · SJU · Charlotte Amalie · Road Town · The Valley · St Martin (Neth.) · PAP · Santo Domingo · SDQ · LRM · La Romana · Mayagüez · Bayamón · Caguas · STT · EIS · Marigot · Philipsburg · St Barthélemy · Pétionville · Jimaní · Neiba · Azua · Bajos de Barrollo · Yauco · Ponce · Humacao · VQS · St Croix · STX · St Eustatius (Neth. Antilles) · Oranjestad · Jacmel · Duvergé · San Juan · Haina · San Pedro de Macorís · Guánica · Guayama · SBH · Gustavia · Anse-à-Pitre · Cabral · Barahona · BRX · Bani · Isla Saona · Basseterre · SKB · ANTIGUA AND BARBUDA · Pedernales · Enriquillo · DOMINICAN REPUBLIC · Isla Mona · VIRGIN ISLANDS (U.S.A.) · ST KITTS AND NEVIS · St John's · Falmouth · Isla Beata · Cabo Beata · MONTSERRAT (U.K.) · Plymouth · GUADELOUPE (France) · Port Louis · PTP · Pointe-à-Pitre · Ste-Rose · Pointe Noire · BBR · Basse-Terre · Capesterre · Grand Bourg · Portsmouth · Marigot · Morne Diablotins 1447 · DOMINICA · Roseau · Martinique Passage · Fort-de-France · FDF · Ste-Marie · Le Robert · Rivière-Pilote · MARTINIQUE (France) · Gros Islet · ST LUCIA · Castries · QSL · Micoud · Vieux Fort · Soufrière 1234 · St Vincent Passage · Speightstown · BARBADOS · Kingstown · Bequia · Bridgetown · BGI · Six Cross Roads · ST VINCENT & THE GRENADINES · Mustique · Balliceaux · Canouan · The Grenadines · Union Island · Hillsborough · Carriacou · Grenville · GRENADA · St George's · GND · Point Salines

VENEZUELA

ARUBA (Netherlands) · Kudarebe · Oranjestad · AUA · NETHERLANDS ANTILLES · St Christoffelberg 372 · Bonaire · Kralendijk · Curaçao · Willemstad · Islas Las Aves · Islas Los Roques · Los Testigos · Tobago · Little Tobago · Crown Point · Scarborough · TRINIDAD & TOBAGO · Port of Spain · POS · Trinidad · San Fernando · Punta Gallinas · Cabo de la Vela · Peninsula de la Guajira · Punta de Calaboza · Isla de Margarita · NUEVA ESPARTA · Juangriego · La Asunción · Rio Caribe · Punta Peñas · Península de Paria · Güiria · Punta Araguapiche · Inosu · Castilletes · Puerto Estrella · Espada Península de Paraguaná · QQZ · Adicora · Isla La Tortuga · Pampatar · PMV · Porlamar · Carúpano · El Pilar · Río Caribe · Carrizal · Maicao · Golfo de Venezuela · Golfete de Coro · CZE · Punto Fijo · Puerto Cumarebo · Isla Coche · SUCRE · Point Fortin · Maracaibo · MAR · Coro · FALCÓN · CCS · DISTRITO FEDERAL · Cumaná · BLA · Pedernales · Puerto La Cruz · Guanta · Cumanacoa · Caripe · San Juan · Caripito · Orinoco Delta · Barquisimeto · BRM · Valencia · Maracay · PBL · Caracas · Petare · Turiamo · Puerto Cabello · Maiquetía · Barcelona · Guatire · Maturín · MUN · Isla Mariusa · San Cristóbal · Valera · Barinas · SVZ · STD · Mérida · CUC · Cúcuta · Ciudad Guayana · CGU · Ciudad Bolívar · BARINAS · BOLÍVAR · DELTA AMACURO · GUYANA · Pomeroon-Supenaam · CUYUNI-MAZARUNI · El Dorado · Tumeremo · Matthews Ridge · Kartuni

Tropic of Cancer

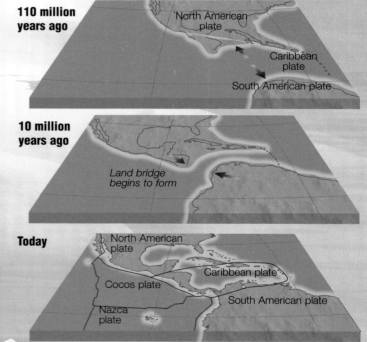

CARIBBEAN

The Caribbean islands extend in a broad arc of more than 4000km (2485 miles) from the Bahamas in the north to Guyana and Surinam in the south. The tranquillity of the islands is deceptive: the region was forged on a boundary between tectonic plates, creating an area of intense seismic activity, where earthquakes and volcanic eruptions are common.

The formation of the Caribbean About 90 million years ago, the North and South American continental plates began to converge. The North American plate dived under the Caribbean plate, creating an arc of volcanic islands along the north-east and eastern margin of the Caribbean plate. As the Pacific and Atlantic seafloors spread outwards, North and South America were compressed from east and west, leading to mountain-building along the edges of the continents. Eventually, about 10 million years ago, the continents joined together and a land bridge was formed. The bridge area is still unstable, with frequent earthquakes.

110 million years ago
North American plate
Caribbean plate
South American plate

10 million years ago
Land bridge begins to form

Today
North American plate
Cocos plate
Nazca plate
Caribbean plate
South American plate

Seismic forces No Caribbean island is completely free of the threat of earthquakes, although the deepest tremors, at more than 200km (125 miles), occur on the west of the island arc where the Atlantic plate is pushed below the Caribbean plate. There are also 19 live volcanoes in the east Caribbean. In the past 300 years, more than 30,000 lives have been lost because of volcanic eruptions, and 15,000 as a result of earthquakes.

The map focuses on the south-east part of the Caribbean island chain with the volcanic islands of the eastern Antilles highlighted in the foreground. Larger islands such as Cuba and the islets of the Bahamas appear farther away.

UNITED STATES

0m (100ft)
h occupy
wamp. The
grass
with mangrove
n² (2354 sq
onal Park.

❻ Florida

verglades

➤N

THE BAHAMAS

The Bahamas More than 700 islands and cays and more than 2000 low-lying rocky islets make up the Bahamas. The archipelago sprawls across 233,000km² (90,000 sq miles) of ocean in the western Atlantic to the south-east of Florida.

depths in
400m
deepest
n. It is
lary, where
ch other,
to
ic activity.

200 metres
1000 metres
2000 metres
4000 metres
6000 metres

Sargasso Sea

Puerto Rico Trench
8605 metres

Anegada Passage

VIRGIN ISLANDS

volcanic eruption
1997 destroyed
outh, and caused
uption. Smoke and
volcano has made
nd uninhabitable.

Mt Scenery
Mt Liamuiga
The Quill
Nevis Peak
Soufrière Hills

ST KITTS
NEVIS
MONTSERRAT

BARBUDA

ANTIGUA

ADELOUPE

e-Terre island,
ctive volcano 1467m
ufrière erupted in
ckily 72,000 people
ated from the area
asualties were avoided.

Montserrat
Trinidad
Guadeloupe
Dominica
Martinique

The areas with the greatest incidence of seismic activity are shown in yellow

4 Cuba The main island and more than 1600 islets cover more than half the land area of the Caribbean, a total of 110,861km² (42,804 sq miles). Cuba's 5745km (3570 mile) coastline is fringed by bays, sandy beaches, mangrove plantations, swamps, coral reefs and rugged cliffs.

5 Blue holes in the Bahamas Beneath the Bahamian island of Andros are subterranean caves and canyons, formed when sea levels were up to 120m (400ft) lower. Open shafts between the caves and the surface then filled with water, creating the 'blue holes'. At high tide sea levels rise above the island's water table.

The pressure of the sea forces water into the caves, creating whirlpools so strong that small boats can be sucked into their vortex. At low tide, the process reverses and the holes spew out domes of water.

6 Florida Almost all of Florida is less tha above sea level. The coastal lowlands w three-quarters of the land are covered by Everglades at the southern tip contain sa marshlands watered by Lake Okeechobe swamps along the coast. More than 609 miles) of the region is designated as a N

Gulf of Mexico

Cayman Trench A submarine trench with a maximum depth of 7686m (25,216ft), it is the deepest point in the Caribbean Sea.

Archipiélago de Sabana

4 CUBA

5 Andros

Cayman Trench

7535 metres ▽

JAMAICA

Windward Passage

2

Duarte Peak

3

Jamaica The island is surrounded by coral reefs. More hard corals are found near Jamaica than anywhere else in the Caribbean. Over the past two decades the reefs have been damaged by frequent hurricanes, coral-smothering algae and disease.

HAITI

DOMINICAN REPUBLIC

Puerto Rico Trench Wa the trench can excee (25,600ft), making it th part of the Atlantic O located at a plate bou two plates slide past making the region pro earthquakes and volc

Moria Passage

2 Windward Passage The strait, which lies between Cuba and Hispaniola, connects the Atlantic Ocean with the Caribbean Sea. It is 80km (50 miles) wide and has a threshold depth of 1700m (5500ft).

5750 metres ▽

Dominican Republic Rock strata between 40 and 15 million years old on the island are one of the richest sources of amber in the world. Amber has been used in jewellery for centuries and is of scientific interest because of the fossils it sometimes contains.

PUERTO RICO

3 Duarte Peak At 3175m (10,400ft), this is the highest point in the Caribbean.

Boiling Lake Not a lake but a large geyser, it lies 700m (2300ft) above sea level in the Morne Trois Pitons National Park. The waters are often forced 1m (3ft) above normal levels by the pressure of escaping volcanic gases.

Soufrière Hills on Montserra the capital, P widespread d debris from th much of the i

S E A

Watt Mt / Valley Of Desolation

Morne Trois Pitons / Micotin

Morne Anglais

Morne Diabolains

La Soufrière

Grand Soufrière Hills

Morne Aux Diables

Martinique In 1902, a day after La Soufrière on St Vincent erupted, the volcano of Mt Pelée sent a cloud of incandescent volcanic ash and gas over the town of St Pierre, killing most of its inhabitants – around 20,000 people.

Plat Pays Volcanic Complex

Montagne Pelée

Martinique Passage

DOMINICA

G

La Soufrière (Ba Guadeloupe) A (4813ft) high, August 1976. had been eva beforehand s

MARTINIQUE

Antilles

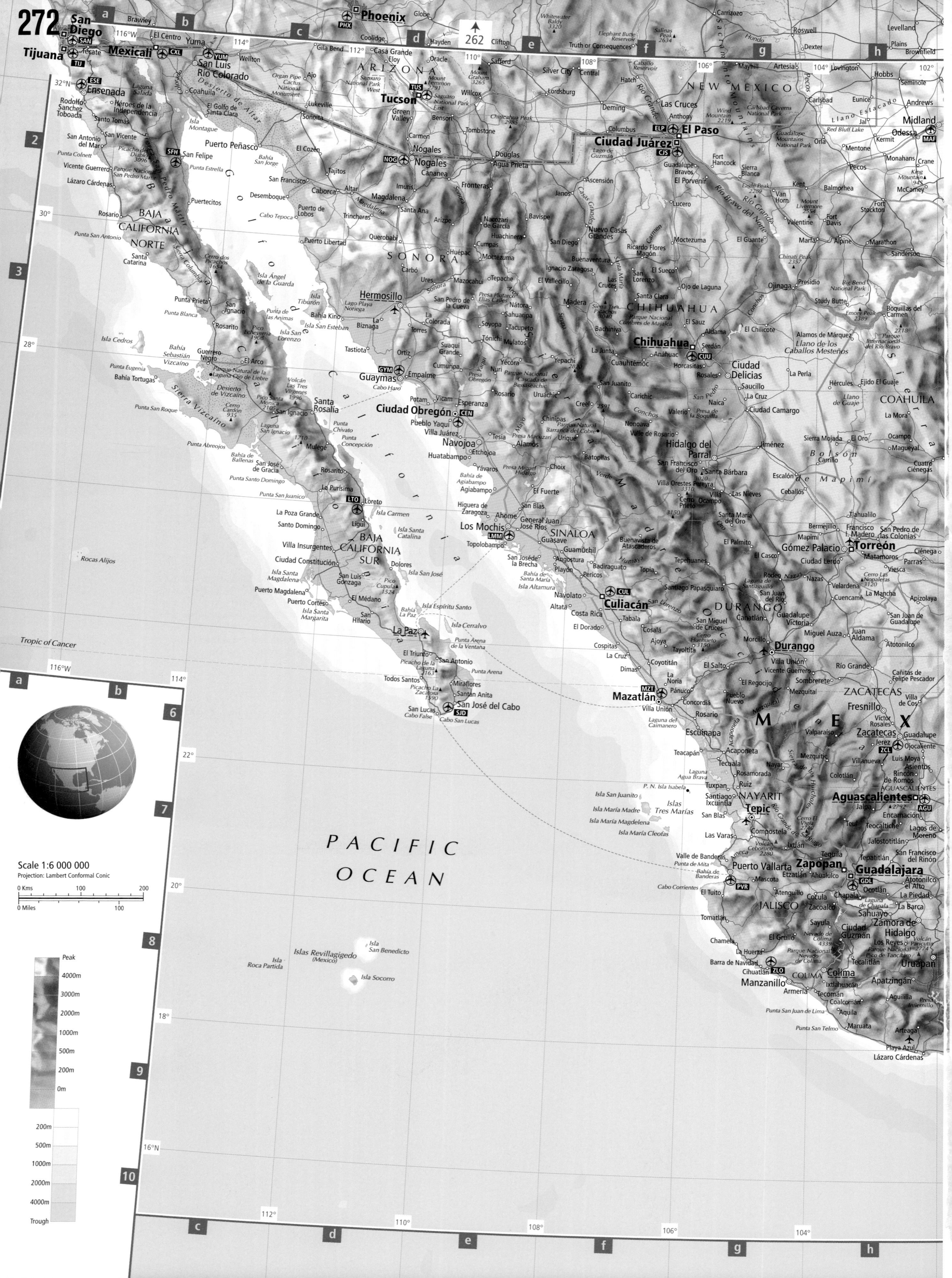

262
San Diego
Tijuana
Mexicali
El Centro
Yuma
San Luis Río Colorado
Brawley
Phoenix
Globe
Coolidge
Casa Grande
Gila Bend
Eloy
Hayden
Oracle
Clifton
Safford
Truth or Consequences
Elephant Butte Reservoir
Salinas Peak 2634
Carrizozo
Roswell
Dexter
Levelland
Plains
Brownfield
Welton
Ajo
Organ Pipe Cactus National Monument
ARIZONA
Saguaro National Park West
Mount Lemmon 2791
Mount Graham 3265
Tucson
Willcox
Saguaro National Park East
Silver City
Central
Caballo Reservoir
Hatch
Rio Grande
Mayhill
Artesia
Lovington
Hobbs
Seminole
NEW MEXICO
Las Cruces
Deming
Lordsburg
Anthony
Carlsbad
Eunice
Andrews
Carlsbad Caverns National Park
Wind Mountain 2219
Llano Estacado
Jal
Midland
Odessa
Red Bluff Lake
Kermit
Sacramento Mountains
Guadalupe Mountains National Park
Orla
Columbus
El Paso
Ciudad Juárez
Lago de Guzmán
Mentone
Monahans
Crane
Pecos
Fort Hancock
Sierra Blanca
Guadalupe Bravos
El Porvenir
Ascensión
King Mountain 945
McCamey
Kent
Balmorhea
Eagle Peak 2289
Van Horn
Mount Livermore 2554
Fort Stockton
Fort Davis
Valentine
Marfa
Alpine
Marathon
Sanderson
Chinati Peak 2357
Presidio
Ojinaga
Big Bend National Park
Study Butte
Emory Peak 2389
Boquillas del Carmen
Coahuila
Lukeville
Sonoita
Bensori
Green Valley
Tombstone
Chiricahua Peak 2985
Carmen
Nogales
Douglas
Agua Prieta
Cananea
Fronteras
Janos
Casas Grandes
Nuevo Casas Grandes
Lucero
Moctezuma
El Guante
Río Bravo del Norte
Desierto de Altar
El Golfo de Santa Clara
Coahuila
Laguna Salada
32°N
Ensenada
Rodolfo Sanchez Toboada
Héroes de la Independencia
Santo Tomás
San Antonio del Mar
San Vicente
Punta Colnett
Picacho del Diablo 3096
San Felipe
Punta Estrella
Isla Montague
Puerto Peñasco
Bahía San Jorge
El Cozón
Tajitos
San Francisco
Vicente Guerrero
Parque Nacional San Pedro Mártir
Lázaro Cárdenas
Puertecitos
Desemboque
Caborca
Altar
Imuris
Magdalena
Santa Ana
Arizpe
Nacozari de García
Bavispe
Huachinera
Cumpas
Moctezuma
Ricardo Flores Magón
Buenaventura
Ignacio Zaragoza
El Sueco
San Diego
30°
Rosario
BAJA CALIFORNIA NORTE
Cabo Tepoca
Puerto de Lobos
Trincheras
Querobabi
Puerto Libertad
SONORA
Huépac
Punta San Antonio
Santa Catarina
Cerro dos Picachos 1654
Isla Ángel de la Guarda
Carbó
Ures
Mazocahui
Tepache
El Vallecillo
Las Cruces
San Lorenzo
Ojo de Laguna
Santa Clara
CHIHUAHUA
Parque Nacional Cumbres de Majalca
Punta Prieta
San Ignacio
Isla Tiburón
Hermosillo
Lago Playa Noriega
San Pedro de la Cueva
Presa Plutarco Elías Calles
Nátora
Sahuaripa
Madera
Bachíniva
Sierra Tres Picachos 3040
El Sauz
Aldama
El Chilicote
Alamos de Márquez
Llano de los Caballos Mesteños
Parque Internacional del Río Bravo
Punta Blanca
Punta de las Animas
Bahía Kino
Isla San Esteban
La Colorada
Soyopa
Tacupeto
Tónichi
Mulatos
Chihuahua
Sierra Madre
Rosarito
Pico Echeverría 1908
Isla San Lorenzo
Bíznaga
Torres
Tastiota
Isla Cedros
28°
Bahía Sebastián Vizcaíno
Guerrero Negro
El Arco
Ortiz
Suaqui Grande
Cumunpa
Yécora
Nuri
Yepachi
La Junta
Cuauhtémoc
Anáhuac
Sérdan
Horcasitas
Ciudad Delicias
Rosales
Saucillo
La Perla
Hércules
Ejido El Guaje
Punta Eugenia
Bahía Tortugas
Parque Natural de la Laguna Ojo de Liebre
Volcán Las Tres Virgenes 1996
Guaymas
Empalme
Cabo Haro
Presa Obregón
Parque Nacional Cascada de Basaseachic
Rosario
Uruáchic
San Juanito
Carichic
La Cruz
Ciudad Camargo
Llano de Guaje
COAHUILA
Sierra Vizcaíno
Desierto de Vizcaíno
Pico Santa Monica 2105
Cerro Cardón 935
San Ignacio
Santa Rosalía
Potam
Vicam
Esperanza
Ciudad Obregón
Creel
Nonoava
Valle de Rosario
Valerio
Presa de la Boquilla
Naica
La Mora
Punta San Roque
Laguna San Ignacio
Punta Chivato
Punta Concepción
Pueblo Yaqui
Villa Juárez
Navojoa
Tesia
Álamos
Presa Mocúzari
Chínipas
Parque Natural Barranca del Cobre
Urique
Hidalgo del Parral
Jiménez
Sierra Mojada
El Oro
Ocampo
Magueyal
Mulegé
Punta Abreojos
Bahía de Ballenas
San José de Gracia
Huatabampo
Etchojoa
Yávaros
Presa Miguel Hidalgo
Choix
Batopilas
San Francisco del Oro
Santa Bárbara
Bolsón de Mapimí
Carrillo
Escalón
Cuatro Ciénegas
Punta Santo Domingo
Rosarito
Bahía de Agiabampo
Agiabampo
El Fuerte
Villa Orestes Pereyra
Cerro Prieto
Villa Ocampo
Las Nieves
Ceballos
Punta San Juanico
La Purísima
Loreto
Higuera de Zaragoza
San Blas
Ahome
La Poza Grande
Isla Carmen
Santo Domingo
Ligüí
Isla Santa Catalina
Los Mochis
General Juan José Ríos
Santa María del Oro
Tlahualilo
Bermejillo
Francisco I. Madero
San Pedro de las Colonias
Villa Insurgentes
BAJA CALIFORNIA SUR
Topolobampo
SINALOA
Guasave
Guamúchil
Buenavista de Atascaderos
El Palmito
Mapimí
Gómez Palacio
Torreón
Ciénega
Matamoros
Parras
Ciudad Constitución
Dolores
Isla San José
San José de la Brecha
Angostura
Badiraguato
Tepehuanes
El Casco
Ciudad Lerdo
Viesca
Rocas Alijos
Isla Santa Magdalena
San Luis Gonzaga
Pico Cupula 1324
Bahía de Santa María
Isla Altamura
Playón
Pericos
Topia
Rodeo
Nazas
Cerro Las Noparleras 3120
Velardena
La Mancha
Puerto Magdalena
Navolato
Culiacán
Santiago Papasquiaro
Laguna de Santiaguillo
San Juan del Río
Cuencamé
Apizolaya
Puerto Cortés
Isla Santa Margarita
El Médano
San Hilario
Bahía La Paz
Isla Espíritu Santo
Altata
Costa Rica
Tabala
DURANGO
Canatlán
Guadalupe Victoria
San Juan de Guadalupe
La Paz
Isla Cerralvo
El Dorado
Cosalá
San Miguel de Cruces
Miguel Auza
Juan Aldama
Tropic of Cancer
Punta Arena de la Ventana
Ajoya
Cerro Huehueto 3150
Tayoltita
Morcillo
Durango
Atotonilco
Cospitas
La Cruz
116°W
El Triunfo
Picacho de la Laguna 2163
San Antonio
Dimas
Coyotitán
El Salto
Villa Unión
Vicente Guerrero
Río Grande
Cañitas de Felipe Pescador
Punta Arena
Todos Santos
Miraflores
Picacho La Zacatosa 1590
Santa Anita
San José del Cabo
San Lucas
Cabo False
Cabo San Lucas
Mazatlán
La Noria
Pánuco
El Regocijo
Sombrerete
ZACATECAS
Pueblo Nuevo
Mezquital
Concordia
Villa Unión
Fresnillo
Villa de Cos
Laguna del Caimanero
Rosario
Escuinapa
Valparaíso
MEXICO
Victor Rosales
Zacatecas
Guadalupe
Jerez
Ojocaliente
22°
Teacapán
Acaponeta
Mezquitic
Villanueva
Luis Moya
Asientos
Tecuala
Rosamorada
Nayar
Colotlán
Rincón de Romos
AGUASCALIENTES
Laguna Agua Brava
P. N. Isla Isabela
Tuxpan
Ruiz
Santiago Ixcuintla
NAYARIT
Aguascalientes
Isla San Juanito
Islas Tres Marías
Isla María Madre
Isla María Magdelena
Isla María Cleofas
San Blas
Tepic
Jalpa
Encarnación
Teul
Teocaltiche
Lagos de Moreno
Las Varas
Compostela
Ixtlán
Jalostotitlán
PACIFIC OCEAN
Volcán Ceboruco 2280
Valle de Banderas
Punta de Mita
Tequila
Tepatitlán
San Francisco del Rincón
Puerto Vallarta
Zapopan
Guadalajara
Bahía de Banderas
Mascota
Etzatlán
Ahualulco
Atotonilco el Alto
Cabo Corrientes
El Tuito
Atenguillo
Ocotlán
Cocula
Chapala
La Piedad
JALISCO
Zacoalco
Laguna de Chapala
La Barca
Sahuayo
Tomatlán
Sayula
Zamora de Hidalgo
Ciudad Guzmán
Chamela
El Grullo
Nevado de Colima 4339
Los Reyes
Volcán Paricutín 2774
La Huerta
Parque Nacional Nevado de Colima
Tecalitlán
Uruapan
Barra de Navidad
Cihuatlán
COLIMA
Colima
Apatzingán
Manzanillo
Ixtlahuacán
Armería
Tecomán
Aguililla
Coalcomán
Aquila
Punta San Juan de Lima
Punta San Telmo
Maruata
Arteaga
Playa Azul
Lázaro Cárdenas
Isla San Benedicto
Islas Revillagigedo (Mexico)
Isla Roca Partida
Isla Socorro
Scale 1:6 000 000
Projection: Lambert Conformal Conic
0 Kms 100 200
0 Miles 100
Peak
4000m
3000m
2000m
1000m
500m
200m
0m
200m
500m
1000m
2000m
4000m
Trough
20°
18°
16°N
112°
110°
108°
106°
104°
102°
114°

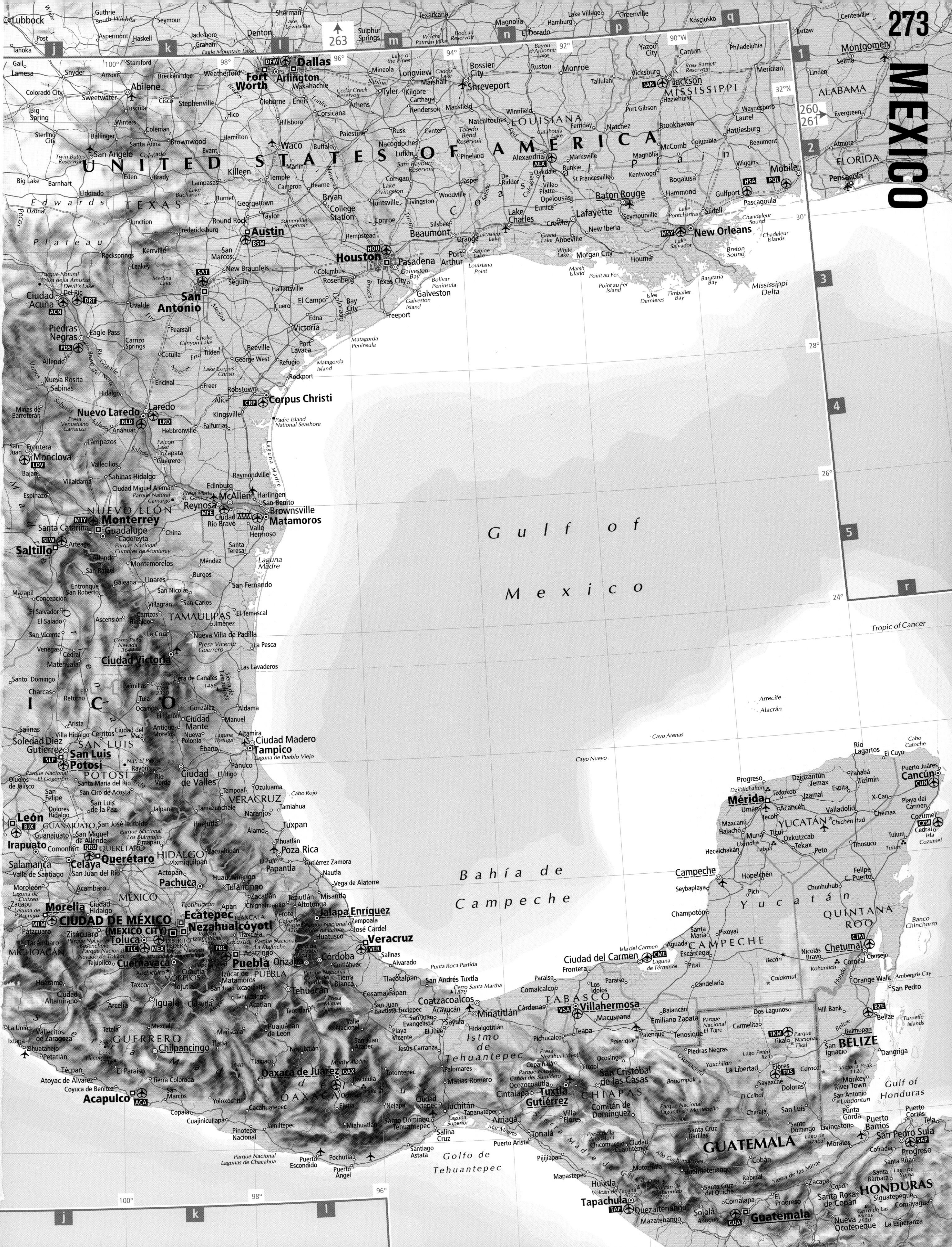
UNITED STATES OF AMERICA
TEXAS
LOUISIANA
MISSISSIPPI
ALABAMA
FLORIDA
Edwards Plateau
Coastal Plain
Lubbock
Abilene
Dallas
Fort Worth
Arlington
Waco
Shreveport
Jackson
Montgomery
Mobile
Pensacola
Baton Rouge
New Orleans
Lafayette
Lake Charles
Beaumont
Houston
Pasadena
Galveston
Austin
San Antonio
Corpus Christi
Laredo
Nuevo Laredo
Brownsville
Matamoros
McAllen
Reynosa
Ciudad Acuña
Piedras Negras
Monclova
Monterrey
Guadalupe
Saltillo
NUEVO LEÓN
TAMAULIPAS
Ciudad Victoria
Ciudad Madero
Tampico
SAN LUIS POTOSÍ
San Luis Potosí
Ciudad de Valles
VERACRUZ
Tuxpan
Poza Rica
Papantla
León
Irapuato
Celaya
Querétaro
QUERÉTARO
GUANAJUATO
HIDALGO
Pachuca
Morelia
CIUDAD DE MÉXICO
(MEXICO CITY)
Ecatepec
Nezahualcóyotl
Toluca
Cuernavaca
Puebla
Xalapa Enríquez
Veracruz
Córdoba
Orizaba
Tehuacán
Iguala
Chilpancingo
Acapulco
GUERRERO
MICHOACÁN
MÉXICO
PUEBLA
OAXACA
Oaxaca de Juárez
Coatzacoalcos
Minatitlán
Villahermosa
TABASCO
Ciudad del Carmen
Campeche
CAMPECHE
Mérida
YUCATÁN
Cancún
Chetumal
QUINTANA ROO
CHIAPAS
Tuxtla Gutiérrez
San Cristóbal de las Casas
Tapachula
Istmo de Tehuantepec
Golfo de Tehuantepec
Sierra Madre de Chiapas
Sierra Madre del Sur
Sierra Madre Oriental
MEXICO
Gulf of Mexico
Bahía de Campeche
Yucatán
Tropic of Cancer
Gulf of Honduras
BELIZE
Belmopan
Belize
GUATEMALA
Guatemala
Quetzaltenango
HONDURAS
San Pedro Sula
263
260
261
1
2
3
4
5
j
k
l
m
n
p
q
r
100°
98°
96°
94°
92°
90°W
32°N
30°
28°
26°
24°

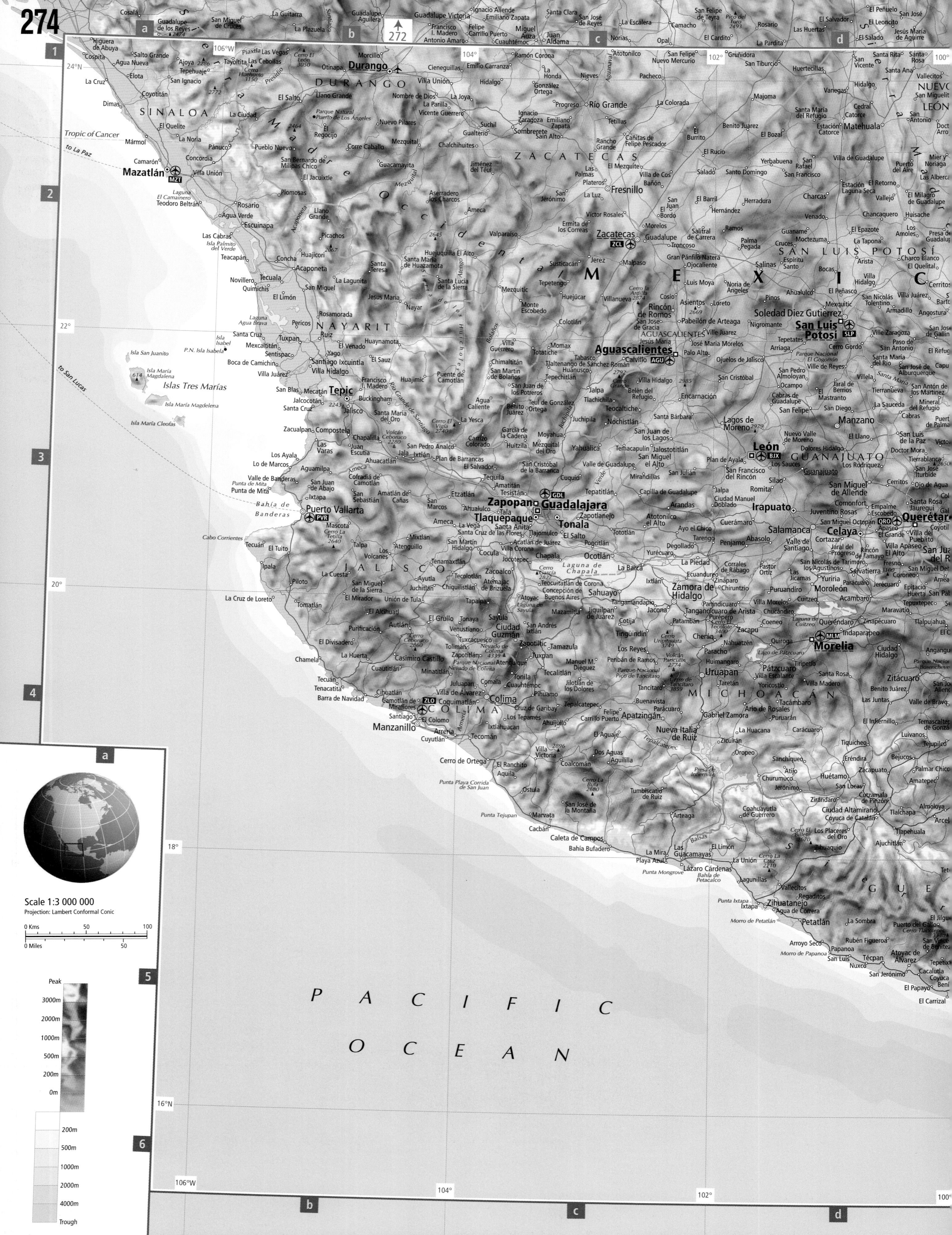

272
MEXICO
SINALOA
DURANGO
ZACATECAS
NAYARIT
JALISCO
COLIMA
MICHOACÁN
GUANAJUATO
SAN LUIS POTOSÍ
AGUASCALIENTES
Sierra Madre Occidental
Tropic of Cancer
to La Paz
to San Lucas
Islas Tres Marías
Isla María Madre
Isla María Magdalena
Isla María Cleofas
Isla San Juanito
Mazatlán
Durango
Zacatecas
Fresnillo
Aguascalientes
San Luis Potosí
Soledad Díez Gutiérrez
León
Irapuato
Salamanca
Celaya
Querétaro
Tepic
Puerto Vallarta
Bahía de Banderas
Cabo Corrientes
Zapopan
Guadalajara
Tlaquepaque
Tonala
Laguna de Chapala
Zamora de Hidalgo
Uruapan
Morelia
Colima
Manzanillo
Apatzingán
Lázaro Cárdenas
Zihuatanejo
Petatlán
PACIFIC OCEAN
106°W
104°
102°
100°
24°N
22°
20°
18°
16°N
Scale 1:3 000 000
Projection: Lambert Conformal Conic
0 Kms 50 100
0 Miles 50
Peak
3000m
2000m
1000m
500m
200m
0m
200m
500m
1000m
2000m
4000m
Trough

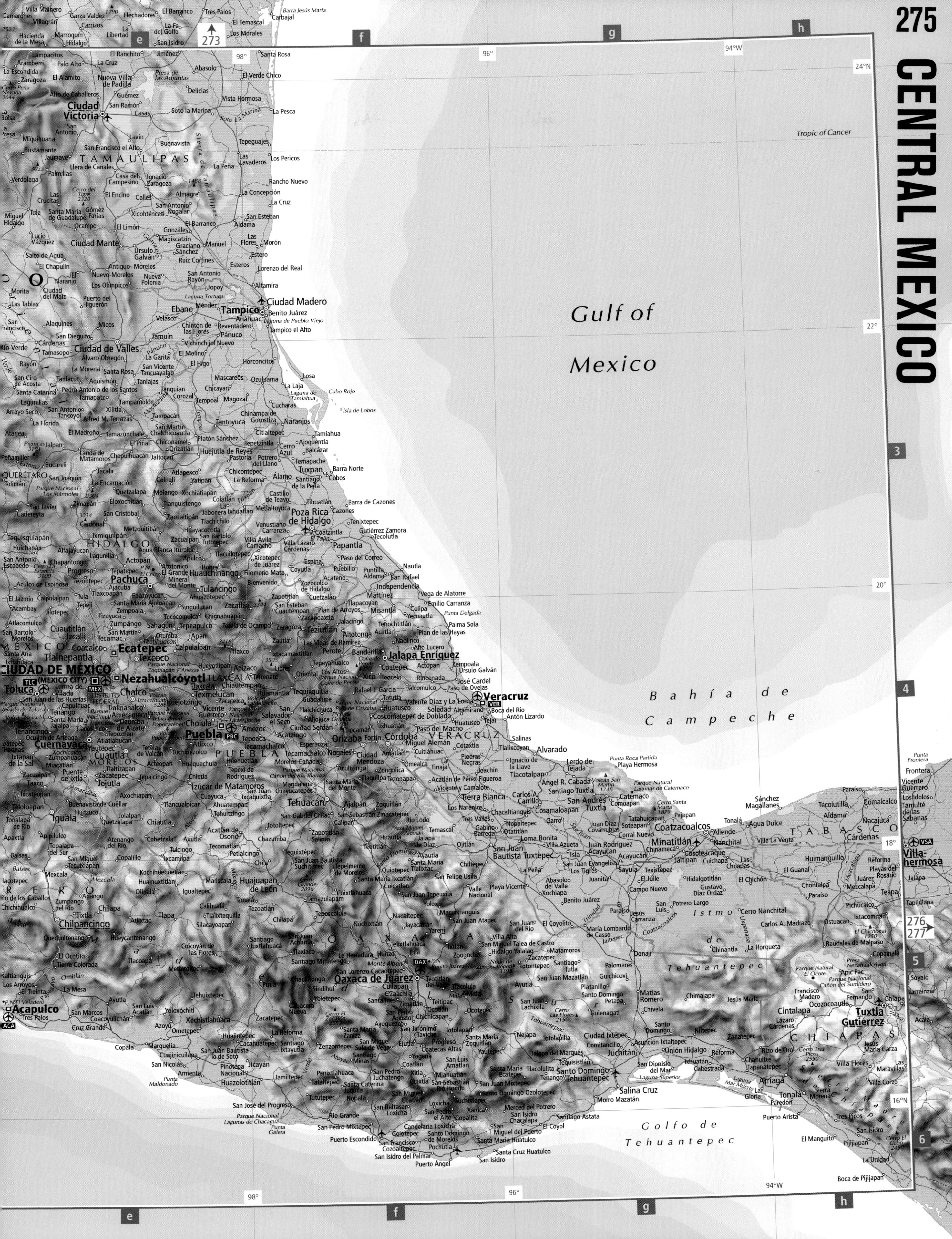
Gulf of Mexico
Bahía de Campeche
Golfo de Tehuantepec
Tropic of Cancer
Istmo de Tehuantepec
TAMAULIPAS
HIDALGO
MÉXICO
TLAXCALA
PUEBLA
VERACRUZ
OAXACA
TABASCO
CHIAPAS
Ciudad Victoria
Ciudad Mante
Ciudad Madero
Tampico
Ciudad de Valles
Tuxpan
Poza Rica de Hidalgo
Pachuca
Ecatepec
Nezahualcóyotl
CIUDAD DE MÉXICO (MEXICO CITY)
Toluca
Chalco
Cuernavaca
Cuautla
Puebla
Jalapa Enríquez
Veracruz
Orizaba
Córdoba
Tehuacán
Iguala
Chilpancingo
Acapulco
Oaxaca de Juárez
Huajuapan de León
Coatzacoalcos
Minatitlán
San Andrés Tuxtla
Tierra Blanca
Villahermosa
Juchitán
Salina Cruz
Santo Domingo Tehuantepec
Tuxtla Gutiérrez
Arriaga
Tonalá
Puerto Escondido
Puerto Ángel
24°N
22°
20°
18°
16°N
98°
96°
94°W
273
276
277

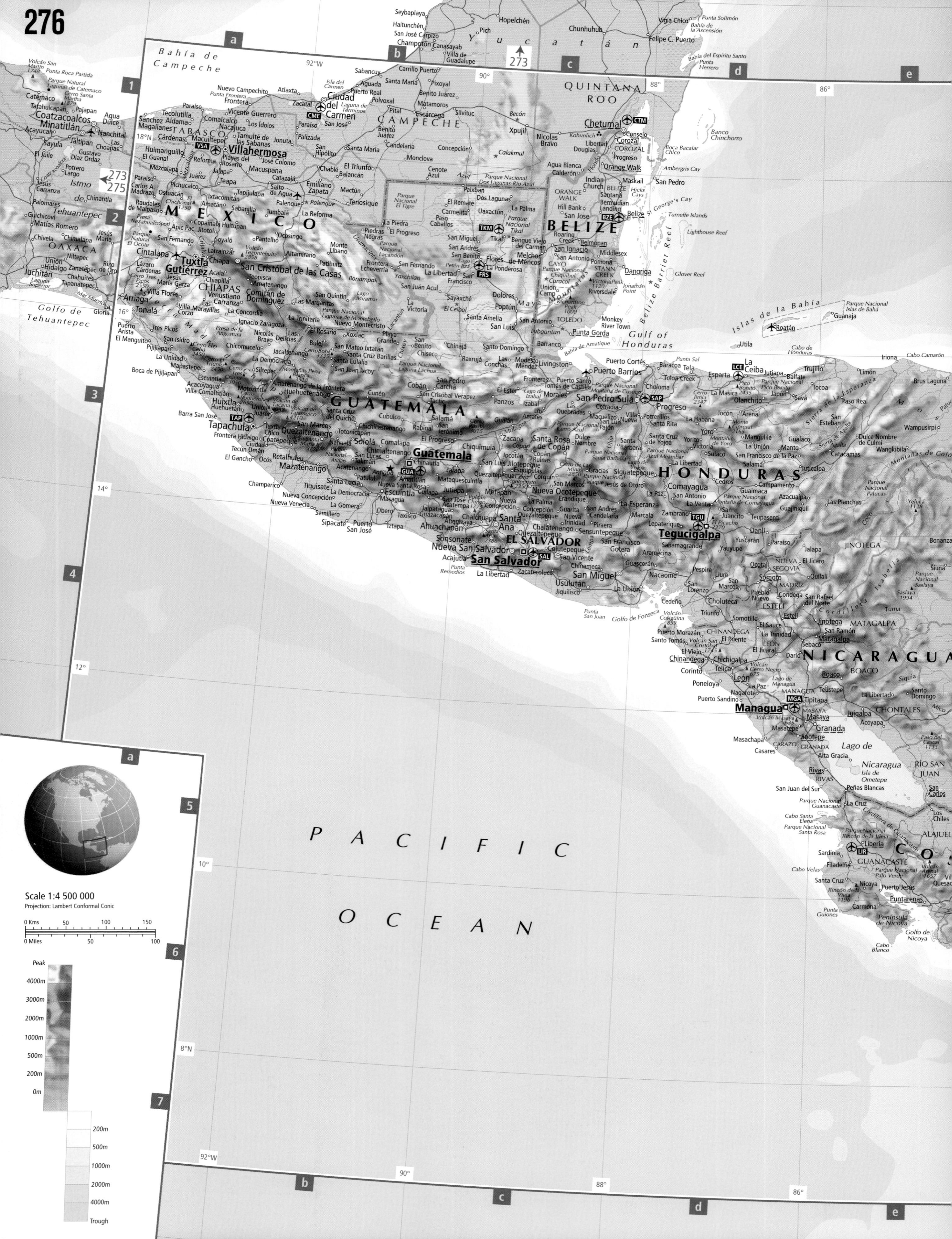

Bahía de Campeche
Yucatán
273
QUINTANA ROO
CAMPECHE
TABASCO
Ciudad del Carmen
Villahermosa
Chetumal
Coatzacoalcos
Minatitlán
Istmo de Tehuantepec
273
275
OAXACA
CHIAPAS
MEXICO
Tuxtla Gutiérrez
San Cristóbal de las Casas
Comitán de Domínguez
Tapachula
Golfo de Tehuantepec
BELIZE
Belize
Belmopan
Orange Walk
Dangriga
Punta Gorda
Belize Barrier Reef
Gulf of Honduras
Islas de la Bahía
Roatán
Guanaja
GUATEMALA
Guatemala
Quezaltenango
Escuintla
Flores
Puerto Barrios
EL SALVADOR
San Salvador
Santa Ana
San Miguel
HONDURAS
Tegucigalpa
San Pedro Sula
La Ceiba
Choluteca
Golfo de Fonseca
NICARAGUA
Managua
León
Granada
Lago de Nicaragua
CO
Liberia
Puntarenas
Península de Nicoya
Golfo de Nicoya
PACIFIC OCEAN
92°W
90°
88°
86°
18°N
16°
14°
12°
10°
8°N
Scale 1:4 500 000
Projection: Lambert Conformal Conic
0 Kms 50 100 150
0 Miles 50 100
Peak
4000m
3000m
2000m
1000m
500m
200m
0m
200m
500m
1000m
2000m
4000m
Trough

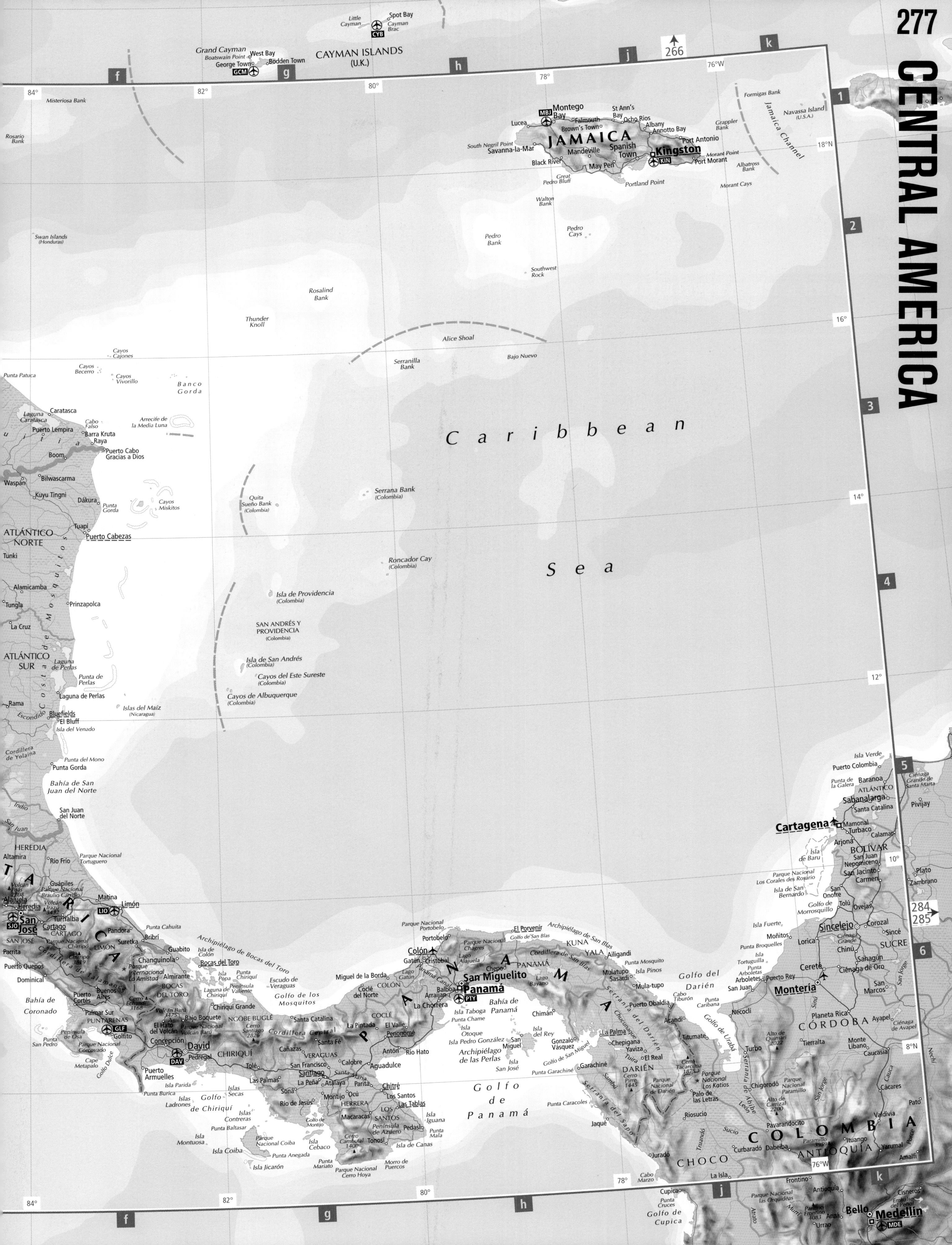
Little Cayman
Spot Bay
Cayman Brac
CYB
Grand Cayman
Boatswain Point
West Bay
George Town
Bodden Town
GCM
CAYMAN ISLANDS
(U.K.)
266
f
g
h
j
k
76°W
84°
82°
80°
78°
Misteriosa Bank
Rosario Bank
Montego Bay
MBJ
Lucea
Falmouth
Brown's Town
St Ann's Bay
Ocho Rios
Albany
Annotto Bay
Port Antonio
JAMAICA
South Negril Point
Savanna-la-Mar
Mandeville
Spanish Town
Kingston
KIN
Black River
May Pen
Morant Point
Port Morant
Great Pedro Bluff
Portland Point
Formigas Bank
Navassa Island (U.S.A.)
Grappler Bank
Jamaica Channel
Albatross Bank
Morant Cays
18°N
Walton Bank
Pedro Bank
Pedro Cays
Southwest Rock
Swan Islands (Honduras)
Rosalind Bank
Thunder Knoll
16°
Alice Shoal
Bajo Nuevo
Serranilla Bank
Cayos Cajones
Punta Patuca
Cayos Becerro
Cayos Vivorillo
Banco Gorda
Caratasca
Laguna Caratasca
Cabo Falso
Arrecife de la Media Luna
Puerto Lempira
Barra Kruta
Raya
Boom
Puerto Cabo Gracias a Dios
Caribbean
Waspán
Bilwascarma
Kuyu Tingni
Dákura
Punta Gorda
Cayos Miskitos
Serrana Bank (Colombia)
Quita Sueño Bank (Colombia)
14°
ATLÁNTICO NORTE
Tuapi
Puerto Cabezas
Tunki
Roncador Cay (Colombia)
Sea
Alamicamba
Tungla
Prinzapolca
Isla de Providencia (Colombia)
La Cruz
SAN ANDRÉS Y PROVIDENCIA (Colombia)
ATLÁNTICO SUR
Laguna de Perlas
Punta de Perlas
Isla de San Andrés (Colombia)
Cayos del Este Sureste (Colombia)
Cayos de Albuquerque (Colombia)
12°
Rama
Islas del Maíz (Nicaragua)
Bluefields
El Bluff
Isla del Venado
Cordillera de Yolaina
Punta del Mono
Punta Gorda
Bahía de San Juan del Norte
San Juan del Norte
HEREDIA
Altamira
Río Frío
Parque Nacional Tortuguero
Guápiles
Alajuela
Heredia
Matina
Limón
LIO
San José
SJO
Turrialba
Cartago
CARTAGO
SAN JOSÉ
Parrita
Puerto Quepos
Dominical
Bahía de Coronado
Punta Cahuita
Pandora
Bribrí
Suretka
LIMÓN
Guabito
Changuinola
Almirante
Bocas del Toro
BOCAS DEL TORO
Archipiélago de Bocas del Toro
Isla de Colón
Isla Popa
Punta Chiriquí
Península Valiente
Laguna de Chiriquí
Escudo de Veraguas
Golfo de los Mosquitos
Chiriquí Grande
Puerto Cortés
Buenos Aires
Palmar Sur
PUNTARENAS
GLF
Golfito
Península de Osa
Punta San Pedro
Parque Nacional Corcovado
Cape Metapalo
Golfo Dulce
Bajo Boquete
El Hato del Volcán
Concepción
David
DAV
Pedregal
CHIRIQUÍ
NGOBE BUGLÉ
Puerto Armuelles
Punta Burica
Isla Parida
Islas Secas
Golfo de Chiriquí
Islas Ladrones
Islas Contreras
Punta Baltasar
Isla Montuosa
Isla Coiba
Parque Nacional Coiba
Isla Jicarón
Punta Anegada
Isla Cebaco
Punta Mariato
Parque Nacional Cerro Hoya
Morro de Puercos
Santa Catalina
Cordillera Central
Santa Fé
Cañazas
VERAGUAS
San Francisco
Santiago
Calobre
Aguadulce
Tolé
Las Palmas
Soná
La Peña
Atalaya
Parita
Chitré
Río de Jesús
Montijo
Ocú
Los Santos
Las Tablas
HERRERA
Macaracas
LOS SANTOS
Península de Azuero
Pedasí
Isla Iguana
Punta Mala
Tonosí
Isla de Cañas
Cerro Cambutal 1400
Golfo de Montijo
Parque Nacional Portobelo
Portobelo
Colón
Cristóbal
Gatún
Lago Gatún
Miguel de la Borda
Coclé del Norte
COLÓN
Panama Canal
Lago Alajuela
Parque Nacional Chagres
Chepo
El Porvenir
Golfo de San Blas
Archipiélago de San Blas
KUNA YALA
Ailigandi
Cordillera de San Blas
PANAMÁ
San Miguelito
Panamá
PTY
Balboa
Arraiján
La Chorrera
Lago Bayano
COCLÉ
La Pintada
El Valle
Penonomé
Antón
Río Hato
Isla Taboga
Punta Chame
Isla Otoque
Isla Pedro González
Bahía de Panamá
Archipiélago de las Perlas
San Miguel
Isla del Rey
Isla San José
Chimán
Golfo de Panamá
Punta Garachiné
Garachiné
Punta Caracoles
Jaqué
Gonzalo Vásquez
Golfo de San Miguel
Chepigana
La Palma
Yaviza
Tuira
El Real
DARIÉN
Cerro Pirre 1445
Parque Nacional de Darién
Puerto Obaldía
Mulatupo Sasardí
Punta Mosquito
Mula-tupo
Isla Pinos
Golfo del Darién
Cabo Tiburón
Punta Caribana
Acandí
Serranía del Darién
Serranía de Sapo
Golfo de Urabá
Titumate
Cerro Tacarcuna 1875
Parque Nacional Los Katios
Palo de las Letras
Riosucio
Turbo
Necoclí
Serranía de Abibe
Sucio
Jurado
CHOCO
La Isla
Cabo Marzo
Cupica
Punta Cruces
Golfo de Cupica
Isla Verde
Puerto Colombia
Barranoa
Punta de la Galera
ATLÁNTICO
Sabanalarga
Santa Catalina
Ciénaga Grande de Santa Marta
Pivijay
Cartagena
Mamonal
Turbaco
Calamar
Arjona
Isla de Baru
BOLÍVAR
San Juan Nepomuceno
San Jacinto
Carmen
10°
Plato
Zambrano
Parque Nacional Los Corales des Rosario
Isla de San Bernardo
San Onofre
Tolú
Ovejas
Golfo de Morrosquillo
284
285
Isla Fuerte
Moñitos
Sincelejo
Corozal
Sincé
Punta Broquelles
Lorica
Chinú
SUCRE
Isla Tortuguilla
Punta Arboletes
Arboletes
Puerto Rey
Cereté
Sahagún
Ciénaga de Oro
San Juan
Montería
San Marcos
Planeta Rica
Ayapel
CÓRDOBA
Tierralta
Monte Líbano
Caucasia
8°N
Alto de Quimari 2022
Chigorodó
Parque Nacional Paramillo
Alto de Carrizal 2200
Cáceres
Valdivia
Pavarandocito
COLOMBIA
Curbaradó
Dabeiba
Ituango
Yarumal
ANTIOQUIA
Amalfi
Frontino
Antioquia
Parque Nacional las Orquídeas
Anzá
Bello
Medellín
MDE
Urrao
Cisneros
1
2
3
4
5
6
78°
80°
82°
84°

SOUTH

SOUTH AMERICA POPULATION
348,671,880

SOUTH AMERICA AREA
17,815,420km² (6,878,572 sq miles)

LARGEST COUNTRY
Brazil 8,511,996km² (3,286,500 sq miles)

SMALLEST COUNTRY
Suriname 163,265km² (63,037 sq miles)

LOWEST POINT
3 Peninsula Valdés, Argentina 40m (131ft) below sea level

HIGHEST RECORDED TEMPERATURE
1 Rivadavia, Argentina 48.9°C (120°F), Dec 11 1905

LOWEST RECORDED TEMPERATURE
2 Sarmiento, Argentina –33°C (–27°F), June 1 1907

WETTEST PLACE
4 Quibdo, Colombia 8991mm (354in) average annual rainfall

DRIEST PLACE
5 Arica, Chile 0.7mm (0.03in) average annual rainfall

AMERICA

Four-fifths of the South American continent lies within the tropics. Almost the whole of its Pacific coast is edged by the Andes Mountains, which extend for a distance of some 8800km (5500 miles). In the interior is the mighty river basin of the Amazon, which drains more than a third of the continent's land area, and the Amazon rain forest, the largest area of tropical rain forest in the world. To the south are the pampas of central Argentina, South America's most fertile area, formed by the accumulation of loose sediment from the Andes.

HIGHEST PEAKS
⑪ Cerro Aconcagua, Argentina 6960m (22,833ft)
⑫ Nevado Ojos del Salado, Argentina/Chile 6908m (22,664ft)
⑬ Cerro Bonete, Argentina 6872m (22,456ft)
⑭ Cerro Pissis, Argentina 6858m (22,500ft)
⑮ Cerro Tupungato, Argentina/Chile 6800m (22,309ft)
⑯ Cerro Mercedario, Argentina 6770m (22,211ft)

LONGEST RIVERS
⑥ Amazon, Peru/Brazil 6516m (4049 miles)
⑦ Rio de la Plata–Paraná, Argentina 4500m (2796 miles)
⑧ Purus, Brazil 3218km (1999 miles)
⑨ Madeira, Brazil 3218km (1988 miles)
⑩ São Francisco, Brazil 2900km (1802 miles)

LARGEST LAKES
⑰ Lago Titicaco (Lake Titicaca), Bolivia/Peru 8300km² (3200 sq miles)
⑱ Lagoa Mirim, Brazil/Uruguay 3000km² (1158 sq miles)
⑲ Lago de Poopó, Bolivia 2530km² (977 sq miles)

LARGEST DESERTS
Patagonian Desert, Argentina 673,000km² (259,778 sq miles)
Atacama Desert, Chile 80,000km² (31,000 sq miles)

The lie of the land

South America has the world's largest area of tropical rain forest, watered by the mighty Amazon and its many tributaries. In the east lie the Brazilian Highlands and Guiana Highlands, the oldest rocks in South America. The centre consists of a series of lowlands and river basins. To the west are the Andes, where the highest peaks are permanently snow-capped.

❶ **Iguaçu Falls and Itaipu Dam** The Falls (lower right) lie on the River Iguaçu, and the Dam (upper centre) on the River Paraná. Iguaçu Falls lie in a 3km (2 mile) crescent-shaped rim and the waters plunge the height of a 24-storey building into the gorge below. Areas of water appear dark green; they are lighter in tone where they are rich in sediment. ❷ **Gran Chaco Desert and the Pantanal** The Gran Chaco (left), the biggest semi-arid area in South America, spreads across three countries – Argentina, Paraguay and Bolivia – while the Pantanal (dark area, right) is the Earth's largest area of tropical wetland. ❸ **Lago Argentina** is fringed by glaciers of the southern Patagonian ice fields. Meltwater from the Perrito Moreno glacier (centre left) and Upsala glacier (centre right) feed the lake with sediment-laden waters.

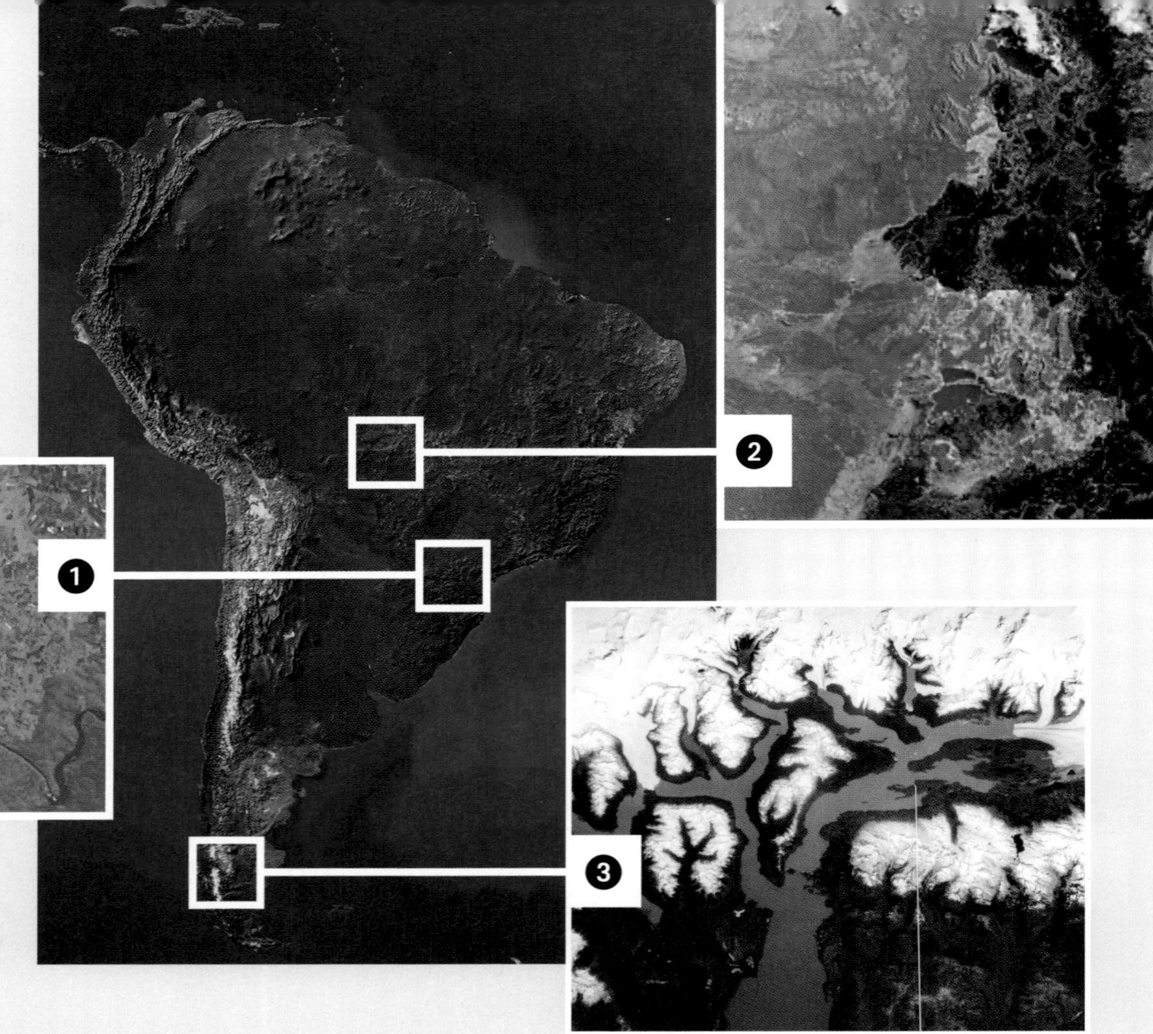

Age						Birth rate		Adult literacy		Wealth	
Under 15		%		Over 65		Births per 1000 population		%		GDP per head $US	
Paraguay		41.5	12.7	Uruguay		Bolivia	30.5	Guyana	98.8	Chile	3989
Bolivia		39.9	9.7	Argentina		Paraguay	30.5	Uruguay	97.8	Uruguay	3518
Venezuela		34	7.2	Chile		Suriname	23.6	Argentina	97.1	Venezuela	3353
Peru		33.4	5.1	Brazil		Ecuador	23.2	Chile	96.2	Argentina	2754
Colombia		32.8	5	Guyana		Peru	22.6	Paraguay	93.9	Brazil	2465
Brazil	28.8		4.7	Colombia		Venezuela	21.6	Colombia	92.4	Suriname	1834
Chile	28.5		4.6	Ecuador		Brazil	19.2	Ecuador	92.4	Ecuador	1711
Argentina	27.7		4.4	Venezuela		Argentina	18.8	Peru	90.9	Guyana	979
Uruguay	24.8		3.9	Bolivia		Chile	17.2	Brazil	88.1	Paraguay	962
Ecuador	22.9		3.5	Paraguay		Uruguay	16.6	Bolivia	87.2	Bolivia	871

■ Top five ■ Bottom five

Health, wealth and education

The development of manufacturing industries and growth of agricultural exports are helping to boost the economy of countries such as Chile and Argentina. But wealth in South America is unevenly distributed. There is a small elite of industrialists and rich landowners, a diminishing middle class and vast numbers of people living in poverty. In Brazil, 10 per cent of the population owns 60 per cent of the wealth, and similar inequalities exist in most other Latin American states. Many social benefits, such as healthcare, education and pensions are being privatized, leaving fewer people with ready access to schools, hospitals and medicines.

Employment

In South America's urbanized society, service industries now offer most employment opportunities, drawing many away from their traditional life in small rural communities. But without qualifications, and often even a basic education, most simply swell the growing ranks of the unemployed, feeding the growth of urban shantytowns all over the continent. The linked rise in crime and corruption is creating widespread political and economic instability.

How the land is used

Nearly half of South America is still covered by dense rain forest, although it is disappearing all too quickly. A quarter of the continent is used for agriculture, most of it permanent pasture, primarily for beef cattle, with only about 7 per cent of the total land mass being arable. In fact, nearly all South Americans – just over 80 per cent – are city dwellers. Urban areas are growing rapidly, as more people are drawn to them by the prospect of a better life. The most urbanized country is Argentina, with 90 per cent of its citizens living in towns and cities.

- Cereals, livestock
- Cash crops, mixed farming
- Dairy, livestock
- General and mixed farming
- Special crops
- Livestock ranching and herding
- Diversified tropical and subtropical crops
- Forests
- Nonproductive land

South America: employment by sector

Country top ten	%			GDP $US million
Brazil	8	36	56	430,600
Argentina	5	28	67	104,600
Venezuela	5	50	45	84,600
Colombia	13	30	57	81,500
Chile	11	34	55	62,200
Peru	10	27	63	55,700
Ecuador	11	33	56	20,800
Uruguay	6	27	67	11,824
Bolivia	20	20	60	7533
Paraguay	27	27	46	5525

■ Primary (inc. Agriculture) %   ■ Industry %   ■ Service %

Population

South America's inhospitable interior is sparsely settled. Most of the continent's 330 million people live in coastal regions, in rapidly expanding towns and cities. Population is projected to grow by 40 per cent in the first 50 years of the 21st century. With the exception of Argentina, Chile and Uruguay, children younger than 15 years constitute more than a third of the continent's population, with just 6 per cent over the age of 64. This youthful population helps to keep fertility rates high, although in poorer countries, such as Bolivia, infant mortality is generally high too – 7 per cent of its children die before their first birthday.

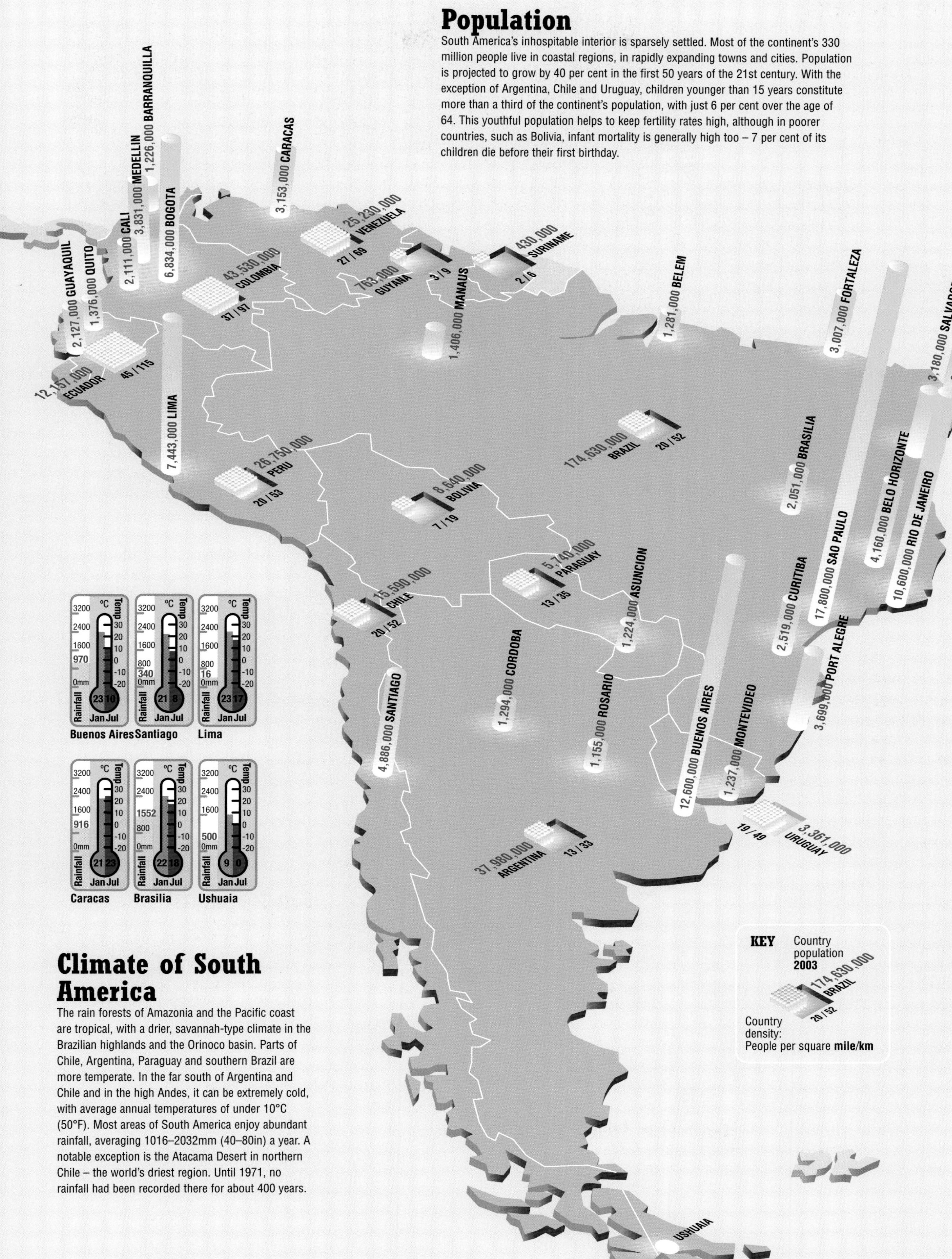

1,226,000 BARRANQUILLA
2,111,000 MEDELLIN
3,831,000 CALI
6,834,000 BOGOTA
3,153,000 CARACAS
25,230,000 VENEZUELA 27 / 69
430,000 SURINAME 2 / 6
763,000 GUYANA 3 / 9
1,406,000 MANAUS
1,261,000 BELEM
1,376,000 QUITO
2,127,000 GUAYAQUIL
12,157,000 ECUADOR 45 / 115
43,530,000 COLOMBIA 37 / 97
7,443,000 LIMA
26,750,000 PERU 20 / 53
8,640,000 BOLIVIA 7 / 19
174,630,000 BRAZIL 20 / 52
2,051,000 BRASILIA
3,007,000 FORTALEZA
3,180,000 SALVADOR
3,307,000 RECIFE
4,160,000 BELO HORIZONTE
10,600,000 RIO DE JANEIRO
2,519,000 CURITIBA
17,800,000 SAO PAULO
3,699,000 PORT ALEGRE
15,590,000 CHILE 20 / 52
5,740,000 PARAGUAY 13 / 35
1,224,000 ASUNCION
1,294,000 CORDOBA
1,155,000 ROSARIO
4,886,000 SANTIAGO
12,600,000 BUENOS AIRES
1,237,000 MONTEVIDEO
3,361,000 URUGUAY 19 / 49
37,980,000 ARGENTINA 13 / 33
USHUAIA

Thermometers (left group):

Buenos Aires — °C Temp: Jan 23, Jul 10; Rainfall 970mm
Santiago — °C Temp: Jan 21, Jul 8; Rainfall 340mm, 800mm
Lima — °C Temp: Jan 23, Jul 17; Rainfall 16mm, 800mm

Caracas — °C Temp: Jan 21, Jul 23; Rainfall 916mm
Brasilia — °C Temp: Jan 22, Jul 18; Rainfall 800mm, 1552mm
Ushuaia — °C Temp: Jan 9, Jul 0; Rainfall 500mm

KEY
Country population 2003
174,630,000 BRAZIL
Country density: People per square mile/km
20 / 52

Climate of South America

The rain forests of Amazonia and the Pacific coast are tropical, with a drier, savannah-type climate in the Brazilian highlands and the Orinoco basin. Parts of Chile, Argentina, Paraguay and southern Brazil are more temperate. In the far south of Argentina and Chile and in the high Andes, it can be extremely cold, with average annual temperatures of under 10°C (50°F). Most areas of South America enjoy abundant rainfall, averaging 1016–2032mm (40–80in) a year. A notable exception is the Atacama Desert in northern Chile – the world's driest region. Until 1971, no rainfall had been recorded there for about 400 years.

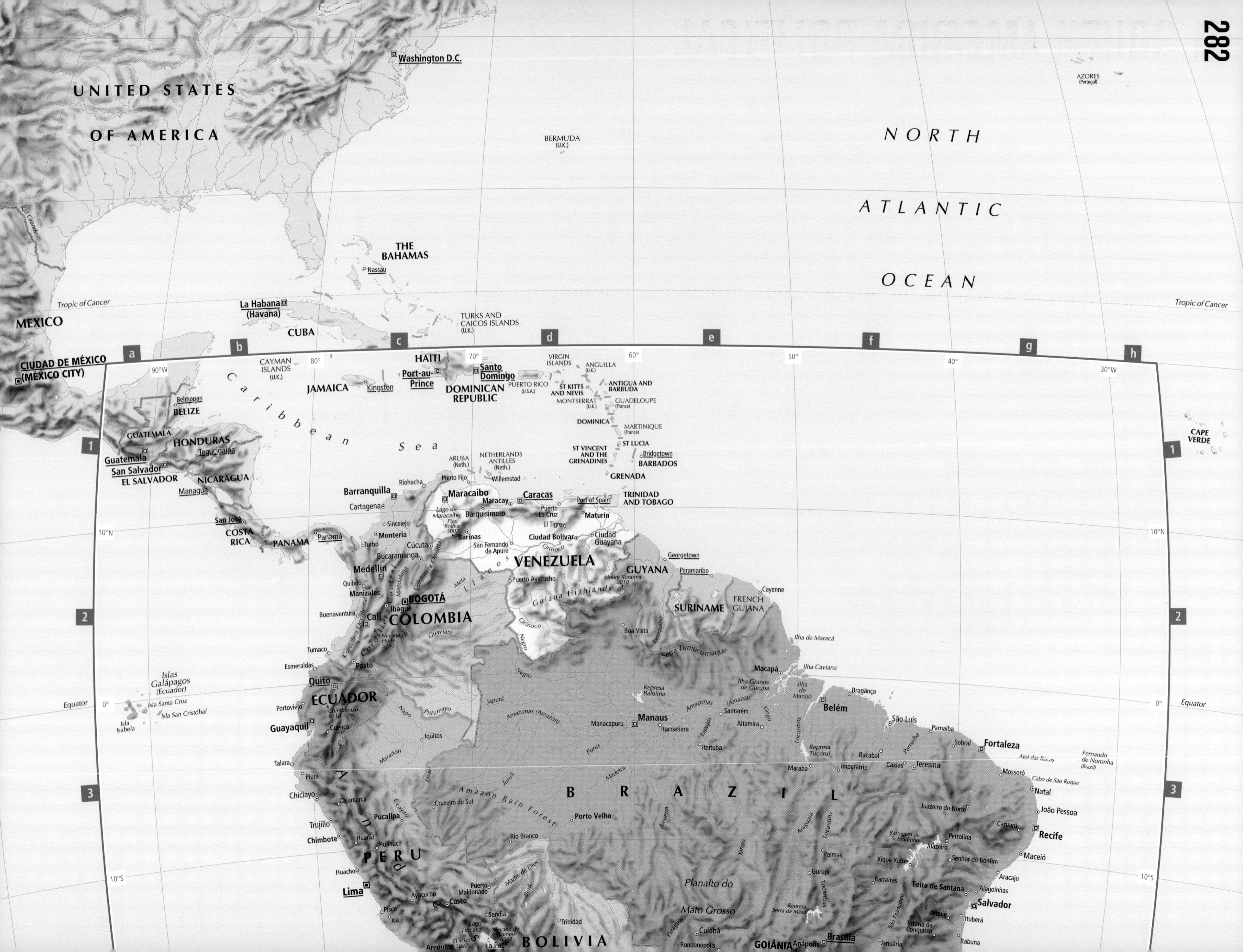

UNITED STATES

OF AMERICA

N O R T H

A T L A N T I C

O C E A N

Tropic of Cancer

AZORES
(Portugal)

CAPE
VERDE

□ Washington D.C.

MEXICO

CIUDAD DE MÉXICO
(MÉXICO CITY)

BERMUDA
(U.K.)

THE
BAHAMAS

Nassau □

La Habana □
(Havana)

CUBA

CAYMAN
ISLANDS
(U.K.)

TURKS AND
CAICOS ISLANDS
(U.K.)

C a r i b b e a n   S e a

JAMAICA

Kingston

HAITI

Port-au-
Prince

Santo
Domingo

DOMINICAN
REPUBLIC

PUERTO RICO
(U.S.A.)

VIRGIN
ISLANDS

ANGUILLA
(U.K.)

ST KITTS
AND NEVIS

MONTSERRAT
(U.K.)

ANTIGUA AND
BARBUDA

GUADELOUPE
(France)

DOMINICA

MARTINIQUE
(France)

ST LUCIA

BARBADOS

ST VINCENT
AND THE
GRENADINES

GRENADA

Bridgetown

TRINIDAD
AND TOBAGO

Port of Spain

NETHERLANDS
ANTILLES
(Neth.)

ARUBA
(Neth.)

Willemstad

Maracaibo

Barquisimeto

Caracas

Maracay

Puerto
La Cruz

Maturín

Ciudad
Guayana

Ciudad Bolívar

El Tigre

VENEZUELA

San Fernando
de Apure

Barinas

GEORGETOWN

GUYANA

Paramaribo

SURINAME

FRENCH
GUIANA

Cayenne

Guiana Highlands

Puerto Ayacucho

Negro

Boa Vista

Mitu

Manacapuru

Orinoco

Riohacha

Barranquilla

Cartagena

Sincelejo

Montería

Cúcuta

Bucaramanga

Medellín

Manizales

Quibdó

Cali

Ibagué

BOGOTÁ

COLOMBIA

Pasto

Buenaventura

Tumaco

Esmeraldas

Quito

ECUADOR

Portoviejo

Guayaquil

Cuenca

Iquitos

PERU

Pucallpa

BELIZE

Belmopan □

GUATEMALA

Guatemala □

San Salvador □
EL SALVADOR

HONDURAS

Tegucigalpa □

NICARAGUA

Managua □

COSTA
RICA

San José □

PANAMA

Panamá □

Islas
Galápagos
(Ecuador)

Isla Santa Cruz

Isla San Cristóbal

Isla
Isabela

B R A Z I L

Manaus

Amazon Rain Forest

Amazonas (Amazon)

Porto Velho

Rio Branco

Cruzeiro do Sul

Madeira

Santarém

Altamira

Macapá

Belém

São Luís

Imperatriz

Marabá

Bragança

Fortaleza

Sobral

Teresina

Caxias

Bacabal

Natal

João Pessoa

Recife

Maceió

Salvador

GOIÂNIA

Brasília

BOLIVIA

La Paz

Planalto do

Mato Grosso

Cuiabá

Tropic of Cancer

Rio Grande

Equator

Equator

10°N

10°N

10°S

10°S

0°

0°

30°W

40°

50°

60°

70°

80°

90°W

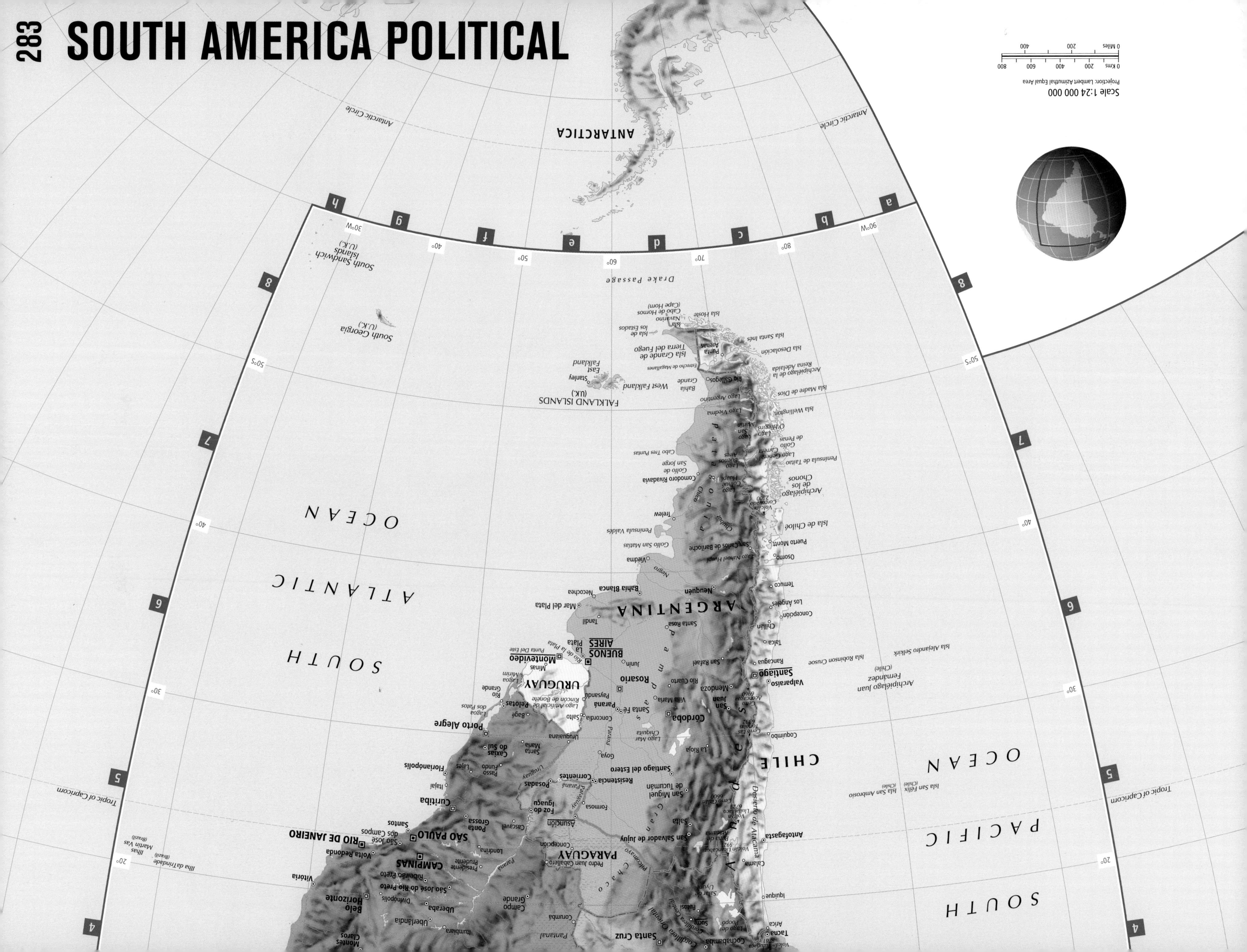

Ilha da Trindade *(Brazil)*
Ilhas Martin Vaz *(Brazil)*

Tropic of Capricorn

20°
30°
40°
50°S

4
5
6
7
8

S O U T H   A T L A N T I C   O C E A N

Montes Claros
Belo Horizonte
Vitória
Divinópolis
Uberaba
Uberlândia
Ribeirão Preto
São José do Rio Preto
Volta Redonda
RIO DE JANEIRO
Campinas
CAMPINAS
SÃO PAULO
São José dos Campos
Santos
Presidente Prudente
Londrina
Curitiba
Ponta Grossa
Itajaí
Florianópolis
Cascavel
Lajes
Caxias do Sul
Passo Fundo
Porto Alegre
Foz do Iguaçu
Posadas
Santa Maria
Bagé
Rio Grande
Pelotas
Lagoa dos Patos
Lagoa Mirim
Minas
Punta Del Este
Montevideo
Concepción
Corumbá
Pantanal
Campo Grande
Asunción
Pedro Juan Caballero
PARAGUAY
Formosa
Corrientes
Resistencia
Posadas
Paraná
Goya
Uruguaiana
Salto
Paysandú
Concordia
Santa Fé
URUGUAY
Río de la Plata
La Plata
BUENOS AIRES
Santa Cruz
Cordillera Oriental
Cochabamba
Tarija
Cordillera Central
San Salvador de Jujuy
Salta
San Miguel de Tucumán
Santiago del Estero
Lago Mar Chiquita
Córdoba
La Rioja
Villa María
Rosario
Junín
Tandil
Necochea
Bahía Blanca
Mar del Plata
Tacna
Arica
Iquique
Calama
Volcán Ojos del Salado
Antofagasta
Desierto de Atacama
Cerro las Tórtolas
Coquimbo
La Serena
Aconcagua
San Juan
Mendoza
San Rafael
Río Cuarto
San Luis
CHILE
Valparaíso
Santiago
Rancagua
Talca
Chillán
Concepción
Los Ángeles
Temuco
Santa Rosa
Neuquén
Negro
A R G E N T I N A
Viedma
Golfo San Matías
Península Valdés
Puerto Montt
Osorno
Isla de Chiloé
Chubut
San Carlos de Bariloche
Trelew
Comodoro Rivadavia
Golfo de San Jorge
P a t a g o n i a
Archipiélago de los Chonos
Península de Taitao
Golfo de Penas
Lago Buenos Aires
Cabo Tres Puntas
Isla Wellington
Isla Madre de Dios
Archipiélago de la Reina Adelaida
Isla Desolación
Isla Santa Inés
Estrecho de Magallanes
Bahía Grande
Río Gallegos
Punta Arenas
FALKLAND ISLANDS (U.K.)
West Falkland
Stanley
East Falkland
Isla Grande de Tierra del Fuego
Cabo de Hornos (Cape Horn)
Isla de los Estados
Isla Navarino
Isla Hoste
Drake Passage

South Georgia *(U.K.)*
South Sandwich Islands *(U.K.)*

Antarctic Circle

ANTARCTICA

30°W
40°
50°
60°
70°
80°
90°W

a
b
c
d
e
f
g
h

S O U T H   P A C I F I C   O C E A N

Isla San Ambrosio *(Chile)*
Isla San Félix *(Chile)*
Archipiélago Juan Fernández *(Chile)*
Isla Robinson Crusoe
Isla Alejandro Selkirk

Tropic of Capricorn

20°
30°
40°
50°S

4
5
6
7
8

Scale 1:24 000 000
Projection: Lambert Azimuthal Equal Area

0 Kms   200   400   600   800
0 Miles   200   400

266

75° 70° Lesser Antilles d

a b c

80°W

Caribbean Sea

Roncador Cay

Punta Gallinas Kudarebe ARUBA (Netherlands) Oranjestad St Christoffelberg 372 NETHERLANDS ANTILLES Bonaire Islas Las Aves Isla La Tortuga Isla Orchila

Punta Estrella Cabo de la Vela Castilletes Puerto López Willemstad Curaçao Kralendijk Islas Los Roques

Peninsula de la Guajira Puerto Cumarebo

Santa Marta SMR Riohacha GUAJIRA Maicao Coro CRZ Puerto Fijo QQZ Piritu FALCON Puerto Cabello **Caracas** CCS DISTRITO FEDERAL MIRANDA

Barranquilla BAQ **Maracaibo** MAR **Morón** PBL **Maracay** **Petare** **Valencia** **Turiamo** **Cabimas** **Barquisimeto** BRM Ocumare del Tuy

Soledad **Cartagena** **Valledupar** ZULIA CESAR Ciudad Ojeda LARA Puente Torres **Teques** San Juan de los Morros GUÁRICO

Lago de Maracaibo **Mérida** MRD Valera TRUJILLO PORTUGUESA **Barinas** Calabozo Valle de la Pascua

Montería SUCRE BOLÍVAR NORTE DE SANTANDER BARINAS Guanare El Baúl Las Mercedes Embalse del Guárico

Sincelejo Corozal Magangué El Banco **Cúcuta** CUC SVZ TÁCHIRA **San Cristóbal** SID APURE San Fernando de Apure

Caucasia **Bucaramanga** Pamplona ARAUCA Arauca **Puerto Ayacucho** GUAINÍA

Bello **Medellín** MDE **Envigado** ANTIOQUIA SANTANDER Barrancabermeja CASANARE Puerto Carreño

Quibdó CHOCÓ CALDAS BOYACÁ Yopal VICHADA Puerto Inírida

Manizales **Pereira** PEI Tunja Sogamoso Puerto Inírida

Armenia **BOGOTÁ** BOG CUNDINAMARCA **Villavicencio** META AMAZONAS

Ibagué TOLIMA Puerto López

Buenaventura VALLE **Cali** Neiva HUILA GUAVIARE San José del Guaviare GUAINÍA

Popayán CAUCA COLOMBIA Florencia CAQUETÁ Mitú VAUPÉS

Pasto NARIÑO PUTUMAYO Mocoa Leticia LET TBT Tabatinga

Tumaco Ipiales Loja SUCUMBÍOS AMAZONAS Benjamin Constant

Esmeraldas ESMERALDAS Ibarra Nueva Loja NAPO Santo Domingo de los Colorados **Quito** UIO PICHINCHA

Equator 0° **ECUADOR** PASTAZA

Manta MEC MANABÍ Ambato BOLÍVAR Puyo MORONA-SANTIAGO Iquitos IQT LORETO

Portoviejo LOS RÍOS Riobamba Macas

Guayaquil GYE GUAYAS Cuenca AZUAY ZAMORA-CHINCHIPE Amazonas

Machala Loja LOJA **PERÚ** SAN MARTÍN

Tumbes TUMBES CAJAMARCA Moyobamba Tarapoto

PIURA AMAZONAS Chachapoyas LAMBAYEQUE

Chiclayo CIX Cajamarca Pucallpa PCL

La Libertad **Trujillo** Cruzeiro do Sul CZS

80°W 75° 70°

PACIFIC OCEAN

10°N

5°

292

NORTHERN SOUTH AMERICA

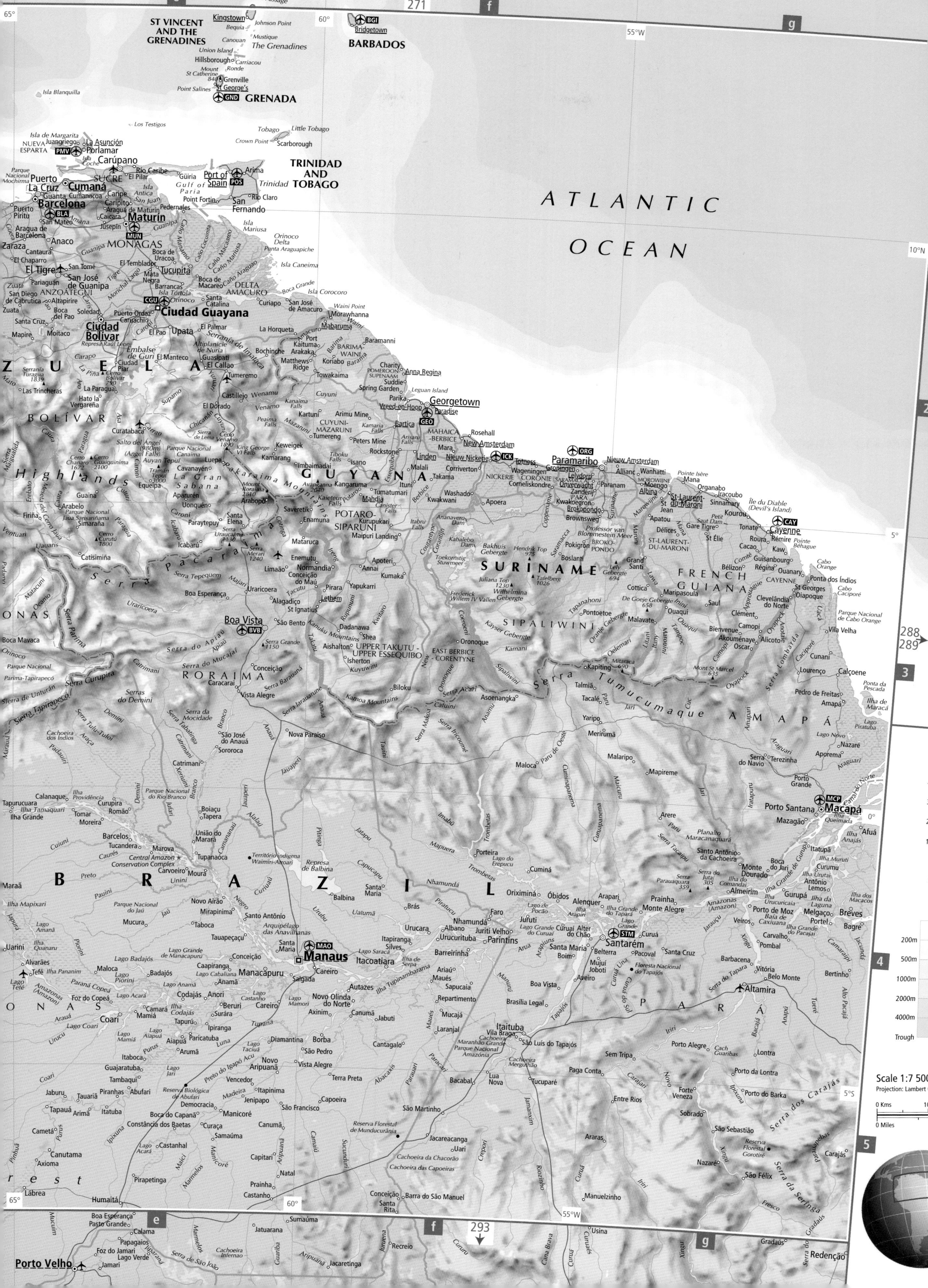

ATLANTIC OCEAN

TRINIDAD AND TOBAGO

BARBADOS

GRENADA

ST VINCENT AND THE GRENADINES

VENEZUELA

GUYANA

SURINAME

FRENCH GUIANA

BRAZIL

Georgetown

Paramaribo

Cayenne

Manaus

Macapá

Boa Vista

Santarém

Scale 1:7 500 000
Projection: Lambert Conformal Conic

0 Kms	100	200
0 Miles	100	

Peak
4000m
3000m
2000m
1000m
500m
200m
0m

200m
500m
1000m
2000m
4000m
Trough

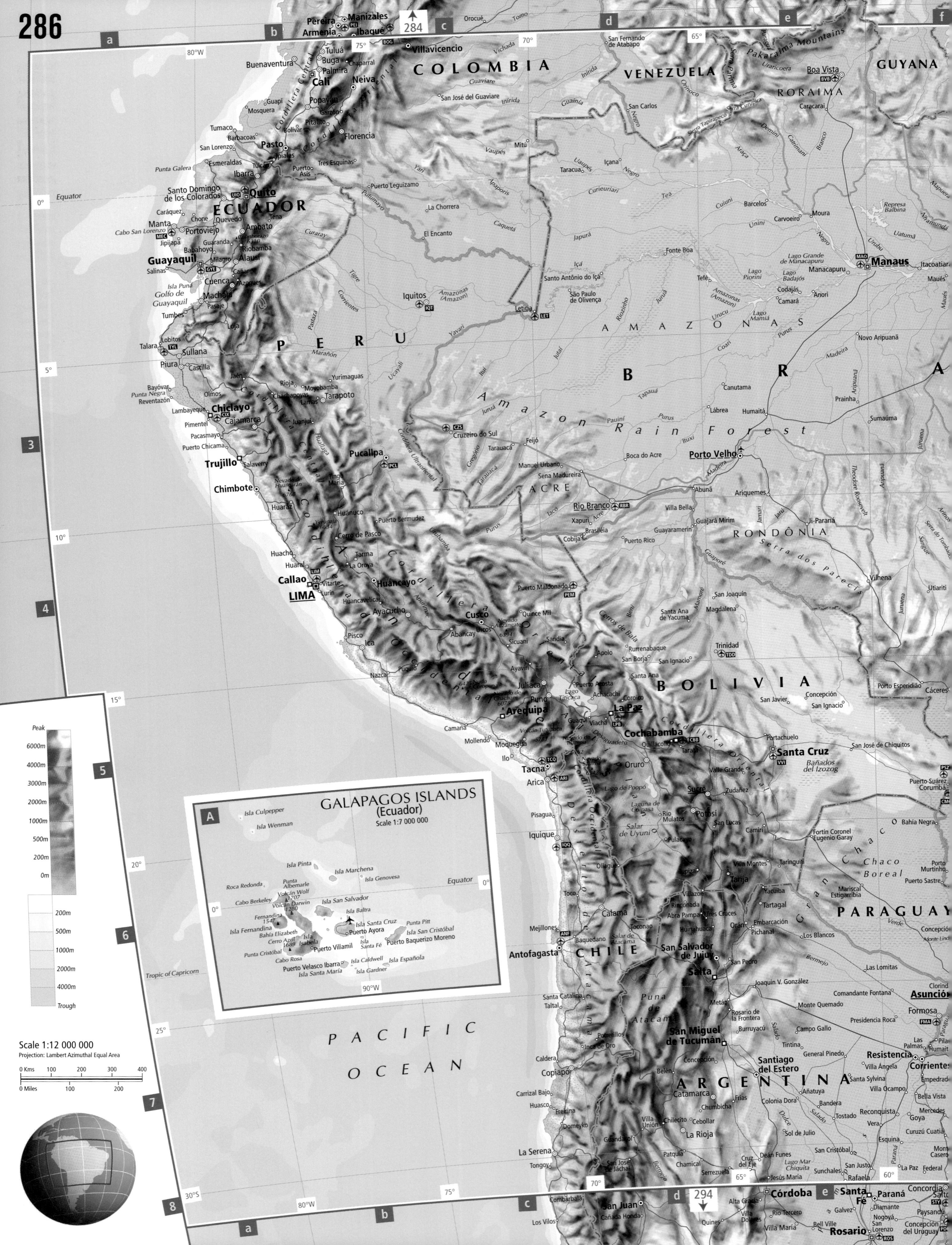

284
294
COLOMBIA
VENEZUELA
GUYANA
ECUADOR
PERU
BOLIVIA
CHILE
ARGENTINA
PARAGUAY
B R A
A M A Z O N A S
RORAIMA
RONDÔNIA
ACRE
Amazon Rain Forest
Pakaraima Mountains
Serra dos Parecis
Gran Chaco
Chaco Boreal
Puna de Atacama
Salar de Uyuni
Lago Titicaca
Lago de Poopó
Cordillera Occidental
Cordillera Oriental
Cordillera Central
Cordillera Blanca
Desierto de Atacama
PACIFIC OCEAN
Equator
Tropic of Capricorn
Golfo de Guayaquil
Bogotá
Manizales
Pereira
Armenia
Ibagué
Villavicencio
Cali
Neiva
Popayán
Pasto
Florencia
Buenaventura
Tumaco
Quito
Guayaquil
Cuenca
Machala
Manta
Portoviejo
Esmeraldas
Santo Domingo de los Colorados
Ambato
Riobamba
Iquitos
Leticia
Manaus
Boa Vista
Porto Velho
Rio Branco
Piura
Talara
Sullana
Tumbes
Chiclayo
Trujillo
Chimbote
Cajamarca
Tarapoto
Pucallpa
Huánuco
Huancayo
Callao
LIMA
Ayacucho
Cusco
Arequipa
Juliaca
Puno
Tacna
Arica
Iquique
Antofagasta
Calama
Copiapó
La Serena
La Paz
Cochabamba
Oruro
Sucre
Potosí
Santa Cruz
Trinidad
Tarija
San Salvador de Jujuy
Salta
San Miguel de Tucumán
Santiago del Estero
Catamarca
La Rioja
San Juan
Córdoba
Santa Fé
Paraná
Rosario
Asunción
Resistencia
Corrientes
Formosa
GALAPAGOS ISLANDS
(Ecuador)
Scale 1:7 000 000
Isla Culpepper
Isla Wenman
Isla Pinta
Isla Marchena
Isla Genovesa
Isla San Salvador
Isla Fernandina
Isla Isabela
Isla Santa Cruz
Isla San Cristóbal
Isla Española
Isla Santa María
Puerto Ayora
Puerto Baquerizo Moreno
Puerto Villamil
Peak
6000m
4000m
3000m
2000m
1000m
500m
200m
0m
200m
500m
1000m
2000m
4000m
Trough
Scale 1:12 000 000
Projection: Lambert Azimuthal Equal Area
0 Kms 100 200 300 400
0 Miles 100 200

SURINAME
FRENCH GUIANA
St Georges
Oiapoque
Saul
Cunani
Amapá
Lago Novo
Ilha de Maracá
Serra Tumucumaque
AMAPÁ
Serra do Navio
Macapá
Mazagão
Ilha Mexiana
Mouths of the Amazon
Equator 0°

Oriximiná
Óbidos
Alenquer
Monte Alegre
Santarém
Almeirim
Porto de Moz
Portel
Cametá
Gurupá
Breves
Ilha de Marajó
Belém
Abaetetuba
Bragança
Carutapera
Cururupu
ATLANTIC OCEAN

Faro
Parintins
Itaituba
Tapajós

PARÁ
Altamira
Tucuruí
Represa Tucuruí
Marabá
Araguatins
Imperatriz
São João do Araguaia

BRAZIL
Xingu
Conceição do Araguaia
Gradaús
Araguaína
Araguacema

São Luís
Rosário
Parnaíba
Camocim
Acaraú
Sobral
Baturité
Fortaleza
Pacajus
Canoa Quebrada
Areia Branca
Macau
Atol das Rocas

Teresina
Caxias
Codó
União
Campo Maior
Crateús
Quixadá
Mossoró
Ceará Mirim
Natal

MARANHÃO
Bacabal
Grajaú
Colinas
Floriano
Picos
Oeiras
CEARÁ
Iguatu
Juazeiro do Norte
Crato
Sousa
Calçó
Currais Novos
Rio Tinto
RIO GRANDE DO NORTE
Guarabira
João Pessoa

PIAUÍ
Alto Parnaíba
São Raimundo Nonato
Paulistana
Salgueiro
Patos
PARAÍBA
Campina Grande
Itabaiana
PERNAMBUCO
Caruaru
Arcoverde
Jaboatão
Olinda
Recife
Palmares

TOCANTINS
Palmas
Porto Nacional
Dianópolis
Gurupi
Natividade
Paranã
Arraias
Barreiras
Petrolina
Paulo Afonso
Garanhuns
ALAGOAS
Arapiraca
Rio Largo
Maceió
SERGIPE
Aracaju
Estância

MATO GROSSO
Diamantino
Rosário Oeste
Barão de Melgaço
Cuiabá
Planalto do Mato Grosso
BAHIA
Ibotirama
Xique Xique
Jacobina
Morro do Chapéu
Feira de Santana
Alagoinhas
Salvador
Ilha de Itaparica

Pantanal
Porto Esperança
Coxim
Barragem de São Simão
Posse
Bom Jesus da Lapa
Paramirim
Guanambi
Itaberaba
Santo Antônio de Jesus
Valença

GOIÁS
Aruanã
Taguatinga
Ceilândia
Brasília
DISTRITO FEDERAL
Gama
Luziânia
Formosa
São Francisco
Januária
Monte Azul
Vitória da Conquista
Jequié
Itabuna
Ilhéus

Goiânia
Anápolis
Pires do Rio
Montes Clares
Pirapora
Bocaiúva
Araçuaí
Canavieiras
Belmonte
Santa Cruz Cabrália
Porto Seguro

MINAS GERAIS
Uberlândia
Uberaba
Sete Lagoas
Teófilo Otôni
Governador Valadares
Diamantina
Caravelas
Arquipélago dos Abrolhos

CAMPO GRANDE
MATO GROSSO DO SUL
Três Lagoas
Paranaíba
Franca
Barretos
Belo Horizonte
Conselheiro Lafaiete
ESPÍRITO SANTO
Colatina
Vitória
Vila Velha
Cachoeiro de Itapemirim

SÃO PAULO
Ribeirão Preto
São José do Rio Preto
Araraquara
Bauru
Marília
Presidente Prudente
Campinas
Juiz de Fora
RIO DE JANEIRO
Campos dos Goitacazes
Macaé
Cabo Frio

Dourados
Maringá
Londrina
Sorocaba
SÃO PAULO
Santo André
São José dos Campos
Volta Redonda
Petrópolis
Nova Friburgo
Niterói
RIO DE JANEIRO

PARANÁ
Curitiba
Ponta Grossa
Guarapuava
Foz do Iguaçu
Paranaguá
Santos
São Vicente

URUGUAY
Pelotas
Rio Grande
SANTA CATARINA
Blumenau
Joinville
Florianópolis
Criciúma

RIO GRANDE DO SUL
Passo Fundo
Santa Maria
Caxias do Sul
Novo Hamburgo
São Leopoldo
Porto Alegre
Lagoa dos Patos

Tropic of Capricorn

ATLANTIC OCEAN

ATLANTIC OCEAN

SURINAME
FRENCH GUIANA

Mouths of the Amazon

Belém
São Luís
Fortaleza
Teresina
Natal
João Pessoa
Recife
Olinda
Cabo de Santo Agostinho
Maceió
Salvador
Macapá
Santarém
Altamira
Marabá
Imperatriz
Araguaína
Palmas
Parnaíba
Sobral
Caucaia
Mossoró
Campina Grande
Feira de Santana
Aracaju

CEARÁ
PIAUÍ
MARANHÃO
PARÁ
TOCANTINS
PERNAMBUCO
PARAÍBA
RIO GRANDE DO NORTE
ALAGOAS
SERGIPE
BAHIA
MATO GROSSO

Serra do Tiracambu
Serra da Ibiapaba
Chapada Diamantina
Serra dos Xavantes
Serra do Cachimbo

Equator

EASTERN SOUTH AMERICA

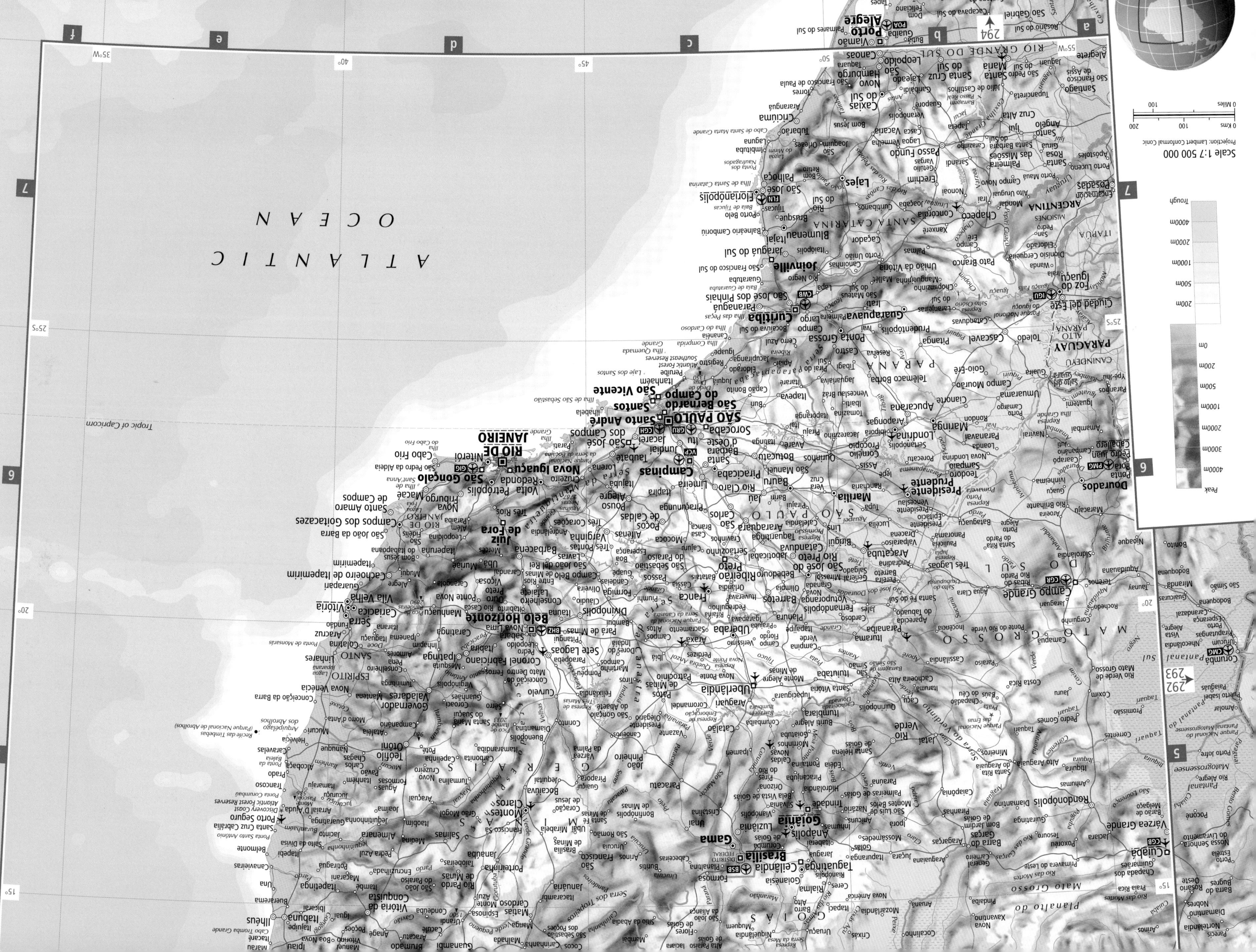
ATLANTIC OCEAN
Tropic of Capricorn
SÃO PAULO
RIO DE JANEIRO
Belo Horizonte
Brasília
Goiânia
Curitiba
Porto Alegre
Florianópolis
Campo Grande
Vitória
Campinas
Santos
Juiz de Fora
Uberlândia
Londrina
Joinville
MATO GROSSO DO SUL
SÃO PAULO
MINAS GERAIS
GOIÁS
PARANÁ
SANTA CATARINA
RIO GRANDE DO SUL
ESPÍRITO SANTO
RIO DE JANEIRO
PARAGUAY
ARGENTINA
URUGUAY
292
293
294
Peak
4000m
3000m
2000m
1000m
500m
200m
0m
200m
500m
1000m
2000m
4000m
Trough
Scale 1:7 500 000
Projection: Lambert Conformal Conic
0 Kms
100
200
0 Miles
100

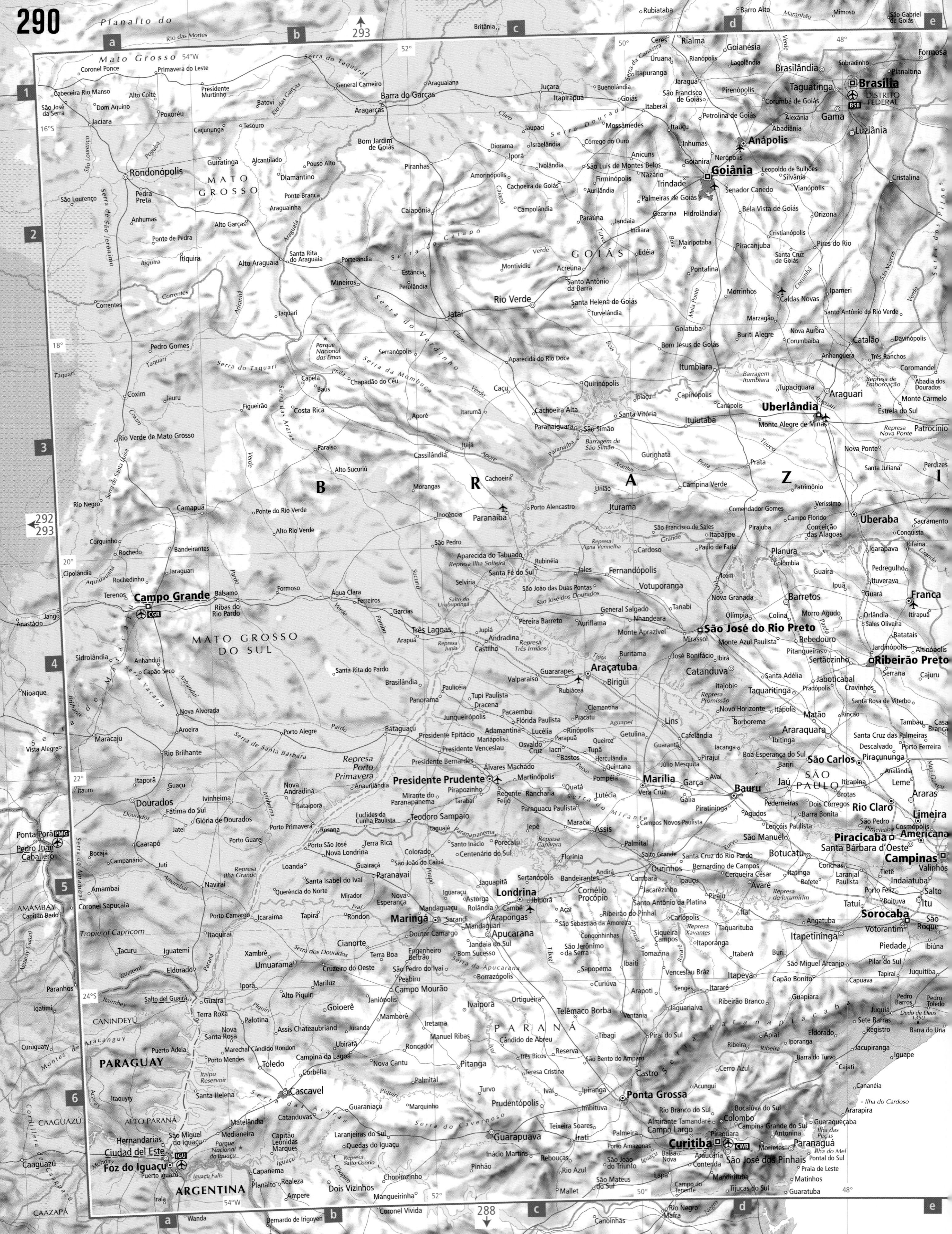

293
292
293
288
a
b
c
d
e
1
2
3
4
5
6
Planalto do
Mato Grosso
Rio das Mortes
54°W
52°
50°
48°
16°S
18°
20°
22°
24°S
Rubiataba
Barro Alto
Mimoso
São Gabriel de Goiás
Britânia
Formosa
Coronel Ponce
Primavera do Leste
Serra do Taquaral
General Carneiro
Araguaiana
Cabeceira Rio Manso
São José da Serra
Dom Aquino
Alto Coité
Presidente Murtinho
Batovi
Poxoréu
Jaciara
Barra do Garças
Aragarças
Juçara
Itapirapuã
Buenolândia
Goiás
Ceres
Rialma
Uruana
Goianésia
Rianópolis
Lagolândia
Itapuranga
Brasilândia
Sobradinho
Planaltina
Brasília
DISTRITO FEDERAL
Taguatinga
BSB
Jaraguá
Pirenópolis
São Francisco de Goiás
Itaberaí
Corumbá de Goiás
Petrolina de Goiás
Alexânia
Gama
Abadiânia
Luziânia
Serra Dourada
Mossâmedes
Itauçu
Inhumas
Anápolis
Nerópolis
Goianira
Goiânia
Trindade
Senador Canedo
Leopoldo de Bulhões
Silvânia
Vianópolis
Cristalina
Caçununga
Tesouro
Jaupaci
Israelândia
Córrego do Ouro
Bom Jardim de Goiás
Diorama
Iporá
Ivolândia
São Luís de Montes Belos
Anicuns
Nazário
Firminópolis
Aurilândia
Palmeiras de Goiás
Hidrolândia
Bela Vista de Goiás
Orizona
Guiratinga
Alcantilado
Pouso Alto
Rondonópolis
MATO GROSSO
Diamantino
Piranhas
Amorinópolis
Cachoeira de Goiás
Campolândia
Pedra Preta
São Lourenço
Ponte Branca
Araguainha
Caiapônia
Anhumas
Alto Garças
Ponte de Pedra
Itiquira
Alto Araguaia
Santa Rita do Araguaia
Portelândia
Serra do Caiapó
Paraúna
Jandaia
Indiara
Gezarina
Mairipotaba
Piracanjuba
Cristianópolis
Pires do Rio
Santa Cruz de Goiás
GOIÁS
Edéia
Acreúna
Montividiu
Santo Antônio da Barra
Pontalina
Correntes
Mineiros
Estância
Perolândia
Rio Verde
Santa Helena de Goiás
Turvelândia
Morrinhos
Caldas Novas
Ipameri
Santo Antônio do Rio Verde
Taquari
Jataí
Serra do Verdinho
Marzagão
Goiatuba
Buriti Alegre
Nova Aurora
Corumbaíba
Catalão
Davinópolis
Bom Jesus de Goiás
Pedro Gomes
Parque Nacional das Emas
Serranópolis
Serra da Mombuca
Serra do Taquari
Aparecida do Rio Doce
Itumbiara
Barragem Itumbiara
Anhanguera
Três Ranchos
Coromandel
Capela
Baús
Chapadão do Céu
Caçu
Quirinópolis
Tupaciguara
Araguari
Abadia dos Dourados
Coxim
Jauru
Figueirão
Serra das Araras
Costa Rica
Aporé
Itarumã
Cachoeira Alta
Ipiaçu
Capinópolis
Canápolis
Uberlândia
Monte Carmelo
Estrela do Sul
Paranaiguara
São Simão
Santa Vitória
Ituiutaba
Monte Alegre de Minas
Patrocínio
Rio Verde de Mato Grosso
Paraíso
Cassilândia
Itajá
Barragem de São Simão
Gurinhatã
Prata
Nova Ponte
Santa Juliana
Perdizes
Alto Sucuriú
Cachoeira
B
R
A
Z
I
Morangas
Campina Verde
Patrimônio
Rio Negro
Camapuã
Paranaíba
Porto Alencastro
União
Iturama
Comendador Gomes
Veríssimo
Uberaba
Sacramento
Ponte do Rio Verde
Inocência
Campo Florido
Pirajuba
Conceição das Alagoas
Conquista
Alto Rio Verde
São Francisco de Sales
Itapajipe
Corguinho
Rochedo
Bandeirantes
São Pedro
Aparecida do Tabuado
Represa Água Vermelha
Cardoso
Paulo de Faria
Planura
Colômbia
Igarapava
Rifaina
Pedregulho
Cipolândia
Rochedinho
Jaraguari
Represa Ilha Solteira
Rubinéia
Santa Fé do Sul
Jales
Fernandópolis
Guaíra
Ituverava
Terenos
Campo Grande
Bálsamo
Formoso
Água Clara
Ferreiros
Selvíria
São João das Duas Pontes
Votuporanga
Ipuã
Guará
Franca
Jango
Anastácio
CGR
Ribas do Rio Pardo
Salto do Urubupungá
São José dos Dourados
Nova Granada
Barretos
Garcias
General Salgado
Tanabi
Olímpia
Colina
Morro Agudo
Orlândia
Itirapuã
Três Lagoas
Jupiá
Andradina
Pereira Barreto
Auriflama
Nhandeara
São José do Rio Preto
Sales Oliveira
MATO GROSSO DO SUL
Arapuã
Represa Jupiá
Castilho
Represa Três Irmãos
Monte Aprazível
Mirassol
Monte Azul Paulista
Bebedouro
Batatais
Sidrolândia
Anhanduí
Capão Seco
Serra Vacaria
Buritama
José Bonifácio
Ibirá
Pitangueiras
Jardinópolis
Altinópolis
Sertãozinho
Ribeirão Preto
Santa Rita do Pardo
Guararapes
Araçatuba
Catanduva
Serrana
Cajuru
Nioaque
Brasilândia
Valparaíso
Rubiácea
Birigüi
Itajobi
Santa Adélia
Jaboticabal
Paulicéia
Tupi Paulista
Represa Promissão
Taquaritinga
Pradópolis
Cravinhos
Nova Alvorada
Panorama
Dracena
Pacaembu
Clementina
Novo Horizonte
Itápolis
Santa Rosa de Viterbo
Maracaju
Aroeira
Junqueirópolis
Flórida Paulista
Piacatu
Lins
Borborema
Matão
Rincão
Tambaú
Casa Branca
Porto Alegre
Bataguaçu
Presidente Epitácio
Adamantina
Lucélia
Rinópolis
Getulina
Cafelândia
Araraquara
Vista Alegre
Rio Brilhante
Serra de Santa Bárbara
Mariápolis
Osvaldo Cruz
Parapuã
Queiroz
Guarantã
Ibitinga
Santa Cruz das Palmeiras
Descalvado
Porto Ferreira
Presidente Venceslau
Iacri
Tupã
Represa Porto Primavera
Bastos
Herculândia
Pirajuí
Boa Esperança do Sul
São Carlos
Pirassununga
Quintana
Presidente Bernardes
Álvares Machado
Júlio Mesquita
Bariri
SÃO PAULO
Analândia
Itaum
Itaporã
Guaçu
Nova Andradina
Anaurilândia
Presidente Prudente
Martinópolis
Quatá
Pompéia
Marília
Garça
Bauru
Jaú
Itirapina
Leme
Araras
Dourados
Ivinheima
Pirapozinho
Mirante do Paranapanema
Tarabai
Regente Feijó
Rancharia
Vera Cruz
Gália
Pederneiras
Dois Córregos
Brotas
Rio Claro
Fátima do Sul
Bataiporã
Paraguaçu Paulista
Lutécia
Piratininga
Barra Bonita
Limeira
Ponta Porã
PMG
Pedro Juan Caballero
Jateí
Glória de Dourados
Euclides da Cunha Paulista
Teodoro Sampaio
Maracaí
Serra do Mirante
Campos Novos Paulista
Agudos
Lençóis Paulista
São Pedro
Cosmópolis
Americana
Porto Primavera
Rosana
Itaguajé
Paranapanema
Iepê
Assis
São Manuel
Piracicaba
Santa Bárbara d'Oeste
Caarapó
Porto Guarei
Porto São José
Terra Rica
Santo Inácio
Porecatu
Represa Capivara
Palmital
Botucatu
Bocajá
Nova Londrina
Colorado
Centenário do Sul
Salto Grande
Santa Cruz do Rio Pardo
Campinas
Campanário
Juti
Represa Ilha Grande
Loanda
São João do Caiuá
Florínia
Ourinhos
Bernardino de Campos
Conchas
Valinhos
Amambai
Naviraí
Guairaçá
Paranavaí
Jaguapitã
Sertanópolis
Bandeirantes
Andirá
Cambará
Cerqueira César
Itatinga
Laranjal Paulista
Tietê
Indaiatuba
Santa Isabel do Ivaí
Querência do Norte
Mirador
Nova Esperança
Iguaraçu
Astorga
Londrina
Cornélio Procópio
Jacarezinho
Ipauçu
Avaré
Bofete
Porto Feliz
Itu
AMAMBAY
Capitán Bado
Coronel Sapucaia
Ivaí
Mandaguaçu
Rolândia
Cambé
Ibiporã
Santo Antônio da Platina
Represa de Jurumirim
Piraju
Tatuí
Boituva
Porto Camargo
Icaraíma
Tapira
Rondon
Maringá
Sarandi
Mandaguari
Arapongas
Açaí
Ribeirão do Pinhal
Carlópolis
Fartura
Angatuba
Sorocaba
Salto
Tropic of Capricorn
Itaquiraí
Doutor Camargo
Apucarana
São Sebastião da Amoreira
Congonhinhas
Siqueira Campos
Represa Xavantes
Taquarituba
Itapetininga
Votorantim
São Roque
Tacuru
Iguatemi
Xambrê
Cianorte
Engenheiro Beltrão
Jandaia do Sul
São Jerônimo da Serra
Tomazina
Itaporanga
Buri
Piedade
Ibiúna
Serra dos Dourados
Terra Boa
Bom Sucesso
Serra da Apucarana
Itaberá
São Miguel Arcanjo
Pilar do Sul
Umuarama
Cruzeiro do Oeste
São Pedro do Ivaí
Borrazópolis
Ibaiti
Eldorado
Peabiru
Sapopema
Wenceslau Braz
Itapeva
Capão Bonito
Tapiraí
Juquitiba
Paranhos
Iporã
Mariluz
Campo Mourão
Curiúva
Arapoti
Sengés
Itararé
Capivari
Guapiara
Igatimi
Salto del Guairá
Guaíra
Terra Roxa
Alto Piquiri
Janiópolis
Ivaiporã
Ortigueira
Telêmaco Borba
Jaguariaíva
Ribeirão Branco
Juquiá
Pedro Barros
Pedro de Toledo
CANINDEYÚ
Palotina
Goioerê
Mamborê
Ventania
Dedo de Deus
Sete Barras
Registro
Barra do Una
Nova Santa Rosa
Assis Chateaubriand
Juranda
Iretama
PARANÁ
Apiaí
Eldorado
Curuguaty
Montes de Aracanguy
Puerto Adela
Marechal Cândido Rondon
Ubiratã
Manuel Ribas
Cândido de Abreu
Tibagi
Piraí do Sul
Ribeira
Iporanga
Jacupiranga
PARAGUAY
Pato Bragado
Puerto Mendes
Roncador
Reserva
Serra Paranapiacaba
Barra do Turvo
Iguape
Itaipu Reservoir
Toledo
Campina da Lagoa
Nova Cantu
Pitanga
Três Bicos
São Bento do Amparo
Castro
Cerro Azul
Cajati
Corbélia
Teresa Cristina
Acaray
Itaquyry
Cascavel
Palmital
Turvo
Ivaí
Ipiranga
Ponta Grossa
Acungui
Cananéia
Santa Helena
Serra das Araras
Guaraniaçu
Marquinho
Prudentópolis
Imbituva
Rio Branco do Sul
Bocaiúva do Sul
Ilha do Cardoso
Ararapira
CAAGUAZÚ
ALTO PARANÁ
Catanduvas
Serra do Cavernoso
Teixeira Soares
Almirante Tamandaré
Colombo
Campina Grande do Sul
Guaraqueçaba
Matelândia
Medianeira
Capitão Leônidas Marques
Laranjeiras do Sul
Guarapuava
Irati
Palmeira
Campo Largo
Piraquara
Antonina
Ilha das Peças
Hernandarias
São Miguel do Iguaçu
Parque Nacional do Iguaçu
Quedas do Iguaçu
Represa Salto Osório
Inácio Martins
Porto Amazonas
Curitiba
CWB
Morretes
Paranaguá
Ilha do Mel
Ciudad del Este
IGU
Monday
Foz do Iguaçu
Caaguazú
Puerto Iguazú
Iguaçu Falls
Capanema
Chopim
Pinhão
Rebouças
São João do Triunfo
Balsa Nova
Araucária
Contenda
São José dos Pinhais
Pontal do Sul
Praia de Leste
Matinhos
Guaratuba
Cordillera de Caaguazú
Planalto
Realeza
Chopinzinho
Dois Vizinhos
Rio Azul
São Mateus do Sul
Lapa
Mandirituba
Campo do Tenente
Tijucas do Sul
ARGENTINA
Irala
Ampere
Mangueirinha
Mallet
Rio Negro
Mafra
CAAZAPÁ
Wanda
Bernardo de Irigoyen
Coronel Vivida
Canoinhas
Negro

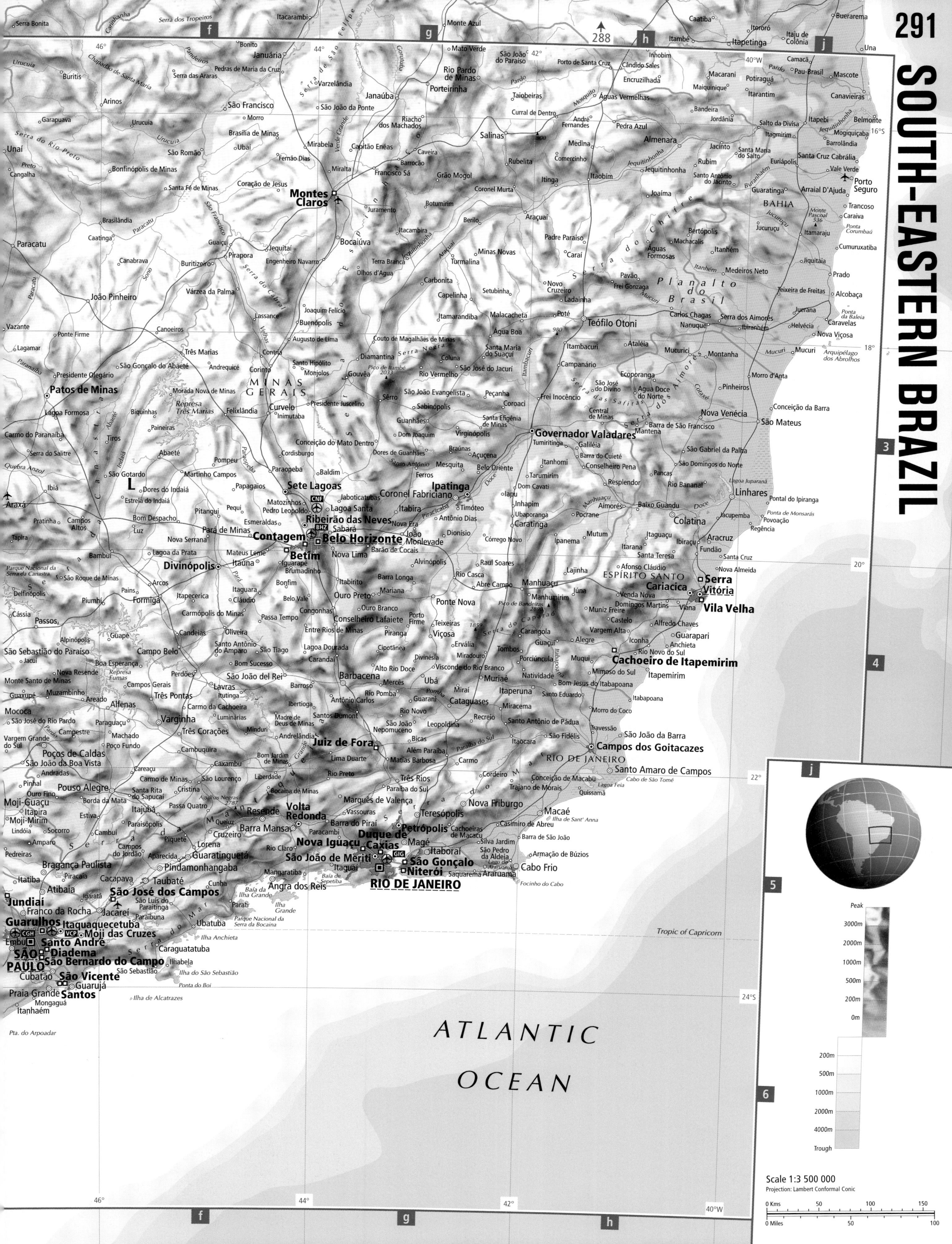

ATLANTIC

OCEAN

Scale 1:3 500 000
Projection: Lambert Conformal Conic

Peak
3000m
2000m
1000m
500m
200m
0m

200m
500m
1000m
2000m
4000m
Trough

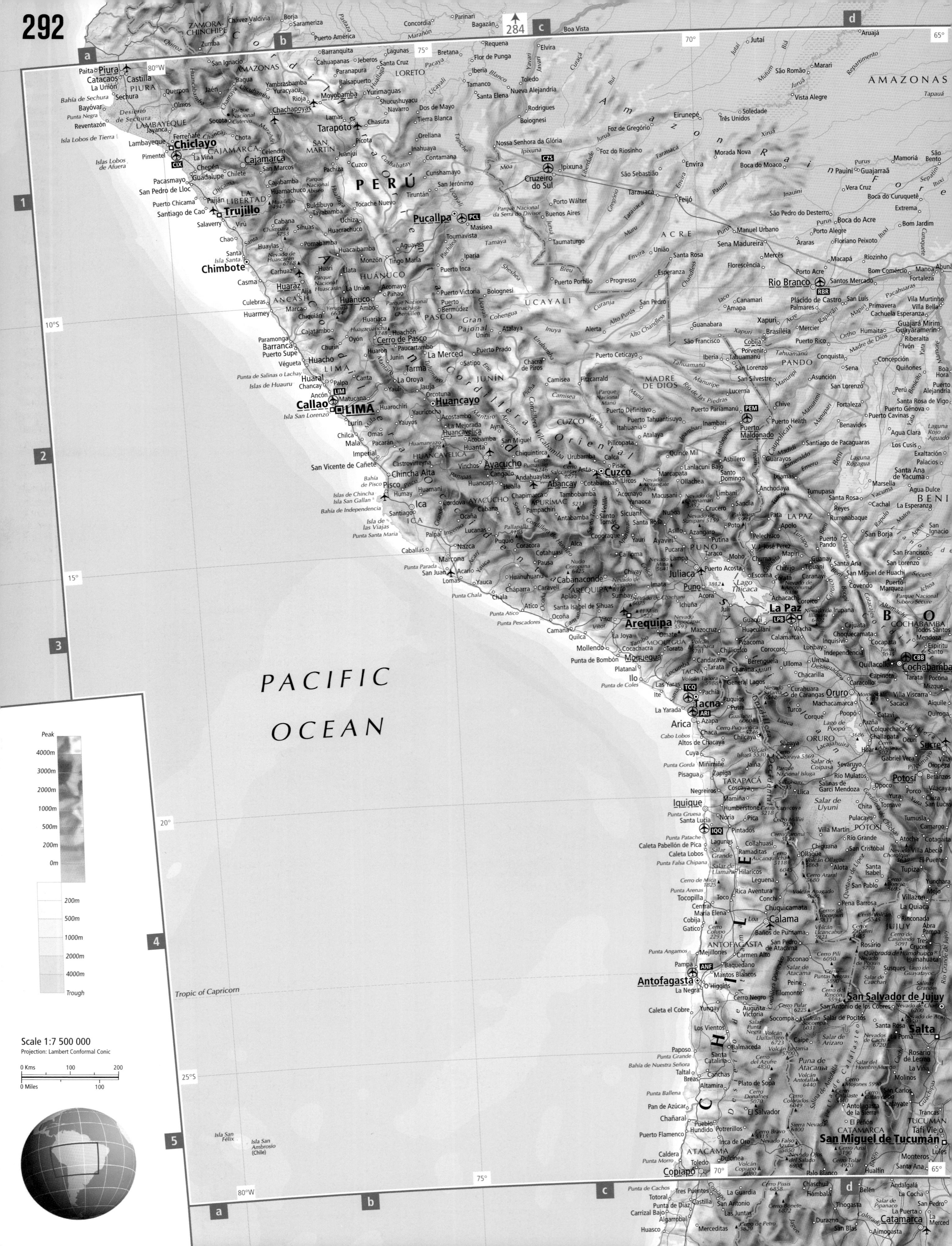
284
PACIFIC
OCEAN
PERÚ
AMAZONAS
LORETO
PIURA
LAMBAYEQUE
CAJAMARCA
LA LIBERTAD
SAN MARTÍN
ANCASH
HUÁNUCO
UCAYALI
PASCO
JUNÍN
LIMA
HUANCAVELICA
AYACUCHO
APURÍMAC
CUZCO
MADRE DE DIOS
ICA
AREQUIPA
PUNO
MOQUEGUA
TACNA
ACRE
PANDO
BENI
COCHABAMBA
ORURO
POTOSÍ
TARAPACÁ
ANTOFAGASTA
ATACAMA
JUJUY
SALTA
CATAMARCA
TUCUMÁN
CHILE
Piura
Chiclayo
Cajamarca
Trujillo
Chimbote
Huaraz
Huánuco
Cerro de Pasco
Callao
LIMA
Huancayo
Huancavelica
Ayacucho
Abancay
Cuzco
Ica
Pisco
Nazca
Arequipa
Moquegua
Tacna
Arica
Iquique
Calama
Antofagasta
Copiapó
Juliaca
Puno
La Paz
Oruro
Cochabamba
Sucre
Potosí
San Salvador de Jujuy
Salta
San Miguel de Tucumán
Catamarca
Pucallpa
Tarapoto
Moyobamba
Chachapoyas
Puerto Maldonado
Rio Branco
Cruzeiro do Sul
Lago Titicaca
Salar de Uyuni
Salar de Atacama
Tropic of Capricorn
10°S
15°
20°
25°S
80°W
75°
70°
65°
Peak
4000m
3000m
2000m
1000m
500m
200m
0m
200m
500m
1000m
2000m
4000m
Trough
Scale 1:7 500 000
Projection: Lambert Conformal Conic
0 Kms 100 200
0 Miles 100

B R A Z I L

Countries / Regions:
RONDÔNIA · MATO GROSSO · TOCANTINS · GOIÁS · DISTRITO FEDERAL · MATO GROSSO DO SUL · SÃO PAULO · PARANÁ · SANTA CATARINA · CHUQUISACA · SANTA CRUZ · TARIJA · SALTA · BOLIVIA · PARAGUAY · ARGENTINA

Major cities:
Porto Velho · Ji-Paraná · Vilhena · Cuiabá · Várzea Grande · Santa Cruz · Corumbá · Campo Grande · Dourados · Ponta Porã · Pedro Juan Caballero · Asunción · Resistencia · Corrientes · Posadas · Foz do Iguaçu · Ciudad del Este · Guarapuava · Curitiba · Paranaguá · Joinville · Blumenau · Florianópolis · Uberlândia · Uberaba · Franca · Ribeirão Preto · São José do Rio Preto · Araçatuba · Marília · Presidente Prudente · Bauru · Londrina · Maringá · SÃO PAULO · Campinas · Sorocaba · Piracicaba · Limeira · Rio Claro · São Carlos · São José dos Campos · Santos · Santo André · São Bernardo do Campo · São Vicente · Jundiaí · Santiago del Estero · La Banda · Anápolis · Goiânia · Brasília · Rio Verde · Jataí · Paranaíba · Três Lagoas

PARÁ · Marabá · Itacaiuna · Redenção · Conceição do Araguaia

Planalto do Mato Grosso · Ilha do Bananal · Pantanal Matogrossense · Chaco Boreal · Alto Paraguay · Presidente Hayes · Chaco Central

ATLANTIC OCEAN

294 · 288 · 289 · 285 · 288

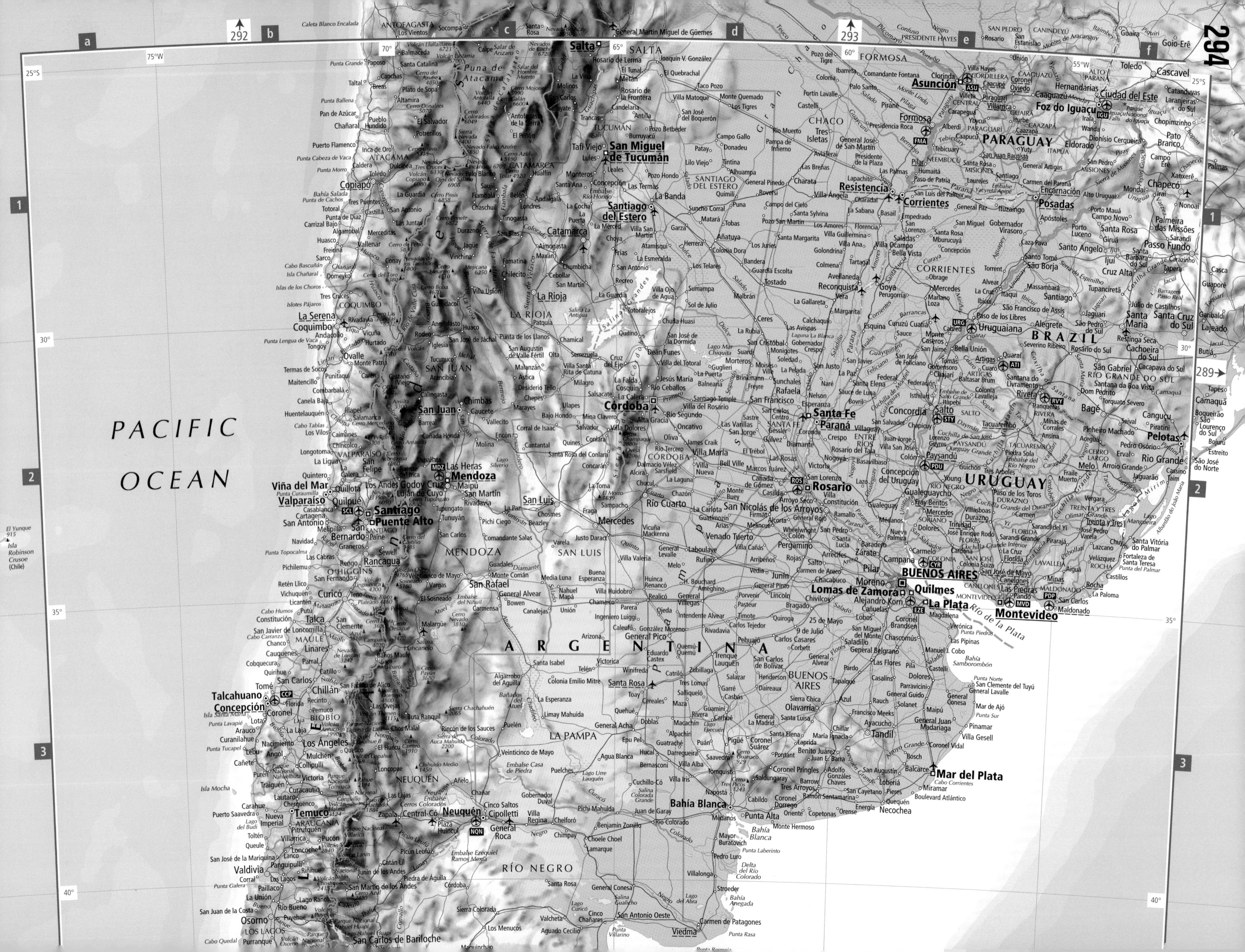
PACIFIC
OCEAN
A R G E N T I N A
URUGUAY
PARAGUAY
BRAZIL
BUENOS AIRES
Montevideo
Asunción
Santiago
Puente Alto
Valparaíso
Viña del Mar
Mendoza
San Juan
Córdoba
Rosario
Santa Fe
Paraná
San Miguel de Tucumán
Santiago del Estero
Salta
Catamarca
La Rioja
Resistencia
Corrientes
Posadas
Foz do Iguaçu
Ciudad del Este
Formosa
Pelotas
Quilmes
Lomas de Zamora
La Plata
Mar del Plata
Bahía Blanca
Neuquén
Temuco
Concepción
Talcahuano
Chillán
Los Ángeles
Rancagua
Talca
Coquimbo
La Serena
Copiapó
San Luis
San Nicolás de los Arroyos
Río Cuarto
Tandil
Santa Rosa
Viedma
Osorno
Valdivia
San Carlos de Bariloche
Río de la Plata
292
293
289

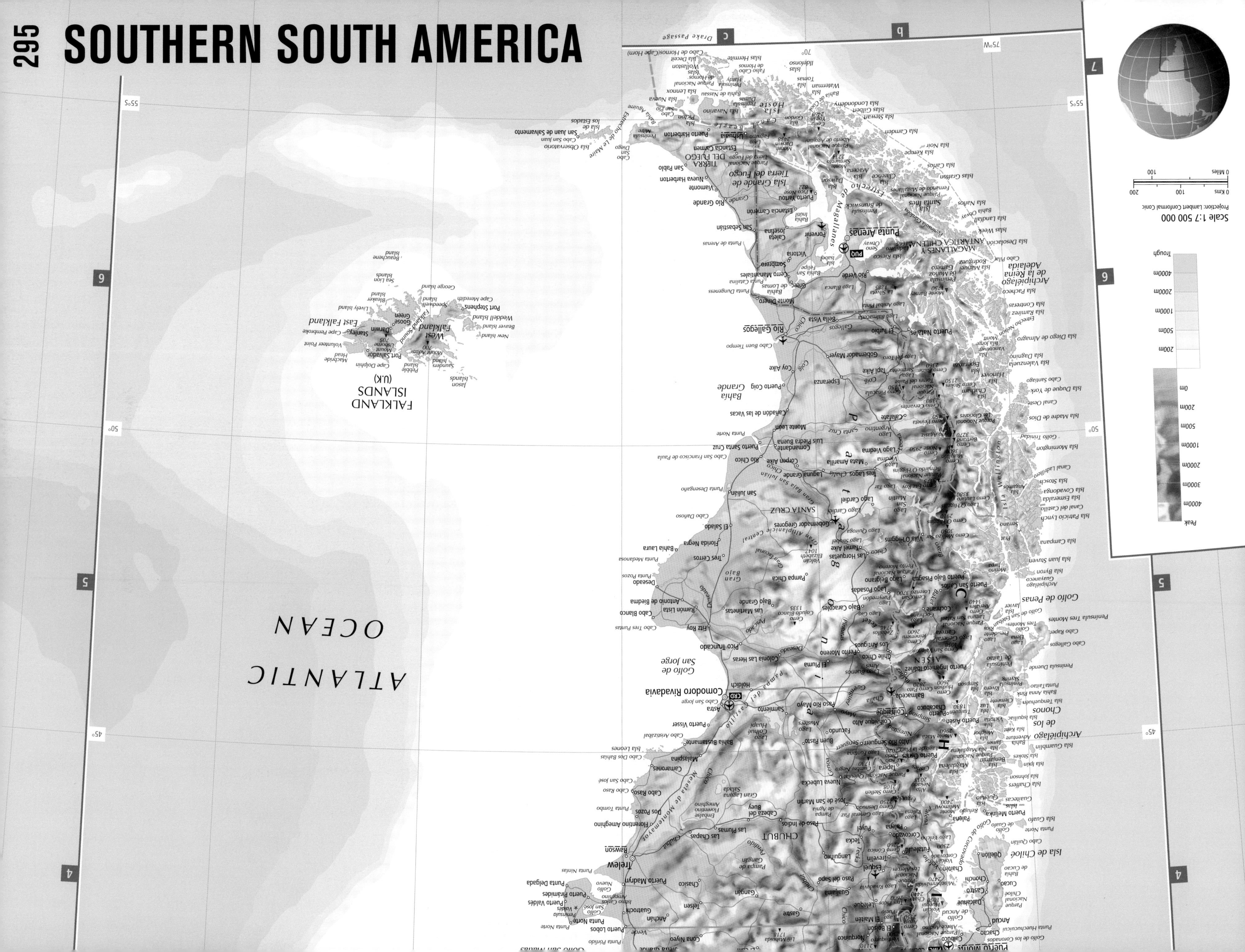

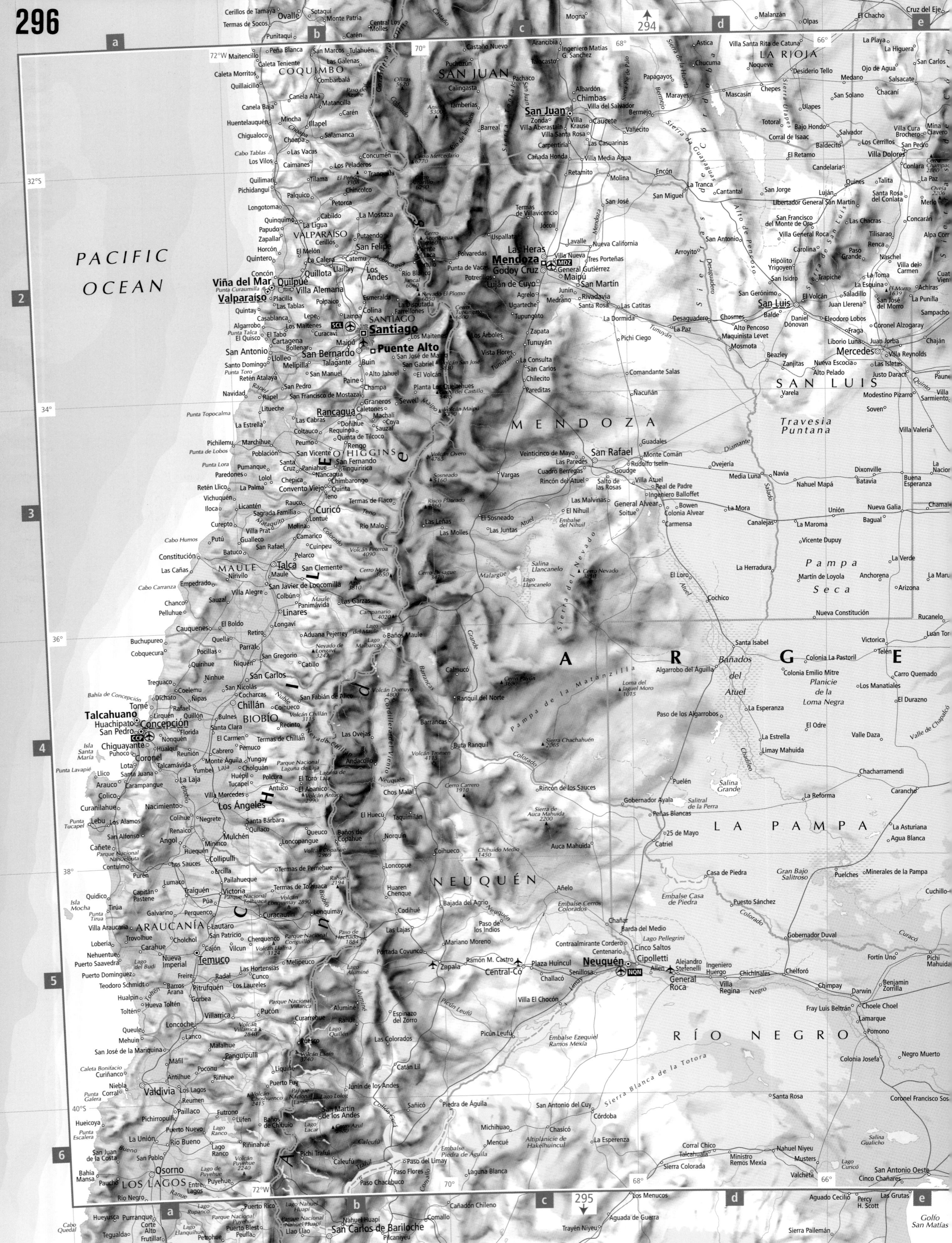
PACIFIC OCEAN
294
295
a
b
c
d
e
2
3
4
5
6
32°S
34°
36°
38°
40°S
72°W
70°
68°
66°
COQUIMBO
VALPARAÍSO
SANTIAGO
O'HIGGINS
MAULE
BIOBÍO
ARAUCANÍA
LOS LAGOS
SAN JUAN
LA RIOJA
SAN LUIS
MENDOZA
NEUQUÉN
LA PAMPA
RÍO NEGRO
C H I L E
A R G E
A n d e s
Travesia Puntana
Pampa Seca
Bañados del Atuel
Planicie de la Loma Negra
Pampa de la Matanzilla
Sierra Blanca de la Totora
Sierra del Nevado
Cordillera del Viento
Cerillos de Tamaya
Termas de Socos
Ovalle
Sotaqui
Monte Patria
Punitaqui
Carén
Maitencillo
Peña Blanca
Caleta Teniente
Caleta Morritos
Quillaicillo
Combarbalá
Canela Baja
Canela Alta
Matancilla
Huentelauquén
Mincha
Illapel
Chigualoco
Choapa
Salamanca
Cabo Tablas
Los Vilos
Las Vacas
Caimanes
Los Peladeros
Concumén
Quilimari
Pichidangui
Tilama
Chincolco
Longotoma
Petorca
Quinquimo
Cabildo
La Ligua
La Mostaza
Papudo
Zapallar
Horcón
Quintero
Concón
Putaendo
Cerrillos
San Felipe
El Melón
La Calera
Catemu
Llaillay
Los Andes
Quillota
Viña del Mar
Quilpué
Valparaíso
Villa Alemana
Placilla
Las Tablas
Quintay
Casablanca
Lepe
Lampa
Colina
Curacaví
Algarrobo
El Quisco
El Tabo
Cartagena
San Antonio
Santo Domingo
Punta Toro
Llolleo
Bollenar
Melipilla
San Bernardo
Maipú
Santiago
Puente Alto
Talagante
San Manuel
Buin
Alto Jahuel
Paine
Champa
Retén Atalaya
Rapel
Navidad
San Pedro
San Francisco de Mostazal
Punta Topocalma
Litueche
Graneros
Caletones
Sewell
Rancagua
La Estrella
Las Cabras
Doñihue
Machalí
Coya
Coltauco
Requínoa
Sauzal
Pichilemu
Marchihue
Peumo
Quinta de Tilcoco
Rengo
Punta de Lobos
Población
San Vicente
San Fernando
Tinguiririca
Pumanque
Santa Cruz
Paniahue
Nancagua
Paredones
Lolol
Chépica
Chimbarongo
Retén Llico
La Palma
Convento Viejo
Quinta
Teno
Vichuquén
Iloca
Licantén
Rauco
Curicó
Termas de Flaco
Sagrada Familia
Lontué
Curepto
Villa Prat
Molina
Río Malo
Cabo Humos
Putú
Gualleco
Camarico
San Rafael
Cuinpeu
Constitución
Batuco
Pelarco
Talca
San Clemente
Las Cañas
Maule
Nirivilo
San Javier de Loncomilla
Empedrado
Cabo Carranza
Villa Alegre
Colbún
Las Garzas
Chanco
Sauzal
Panimávida
Pelluhue
Linares
Cauquenes
El Boldo
Longaví
Retiro
Aduana Pejerrey
Baños Maule
Buchupureo
Quella
Cobquecura
Pocillas
Parral
San Gregorio
Quirihue
Niquén
Catillo
Ninhue
San Carlos
Treguaco
Coelemu
San Nicolás
Dichato
Nipas
Cocharcas
San Fabián de Alico
Tomé
Rafael
Chillán
Coihueco
Talcahuano
Lirquén
Quillón
Huachipato
Concepción
Bulnes
San Pedro
Florida
Santa Clara
Chiguayante
Nonquén
El Carmen
Termas de Chillán
Hualqui
Cabrero
Pemuco
Isla Santa María
Puhoco
Coronel
Reunión
Monte Águila
Yungay
Lota
Talcamávida
Santa Juana
Chol Chol
Punta Lavapié
Llico
Laja
Huépil
Polcura
Arauco
Carampangue
La Laja
Tucapel
Antuco
El Abanico
Colico
Curanilahue
Villa Mercedes
Los Ángeles
Nacimiento
Punta Tucapel
Lebu
Los Alamos
Coihue
Negrete
Renaico
Santa Bárbara
Quilaco
San Alfonso
Angol
Mininco
Mulchén
Cañete
Huequén
Collipulli
Contulmo
Los Sauces
Purén
Lumaco
Ercilla
Pailahueque
Termas de Pemehue
Quidico
Capitán Pastene
Traiguén
Victoria
Isla Mocha
Tirúa
Púa
Punta Tirúa
Galvarino
Perquenco
Curacautín
Lonquimay
Villa Araucanía
Lautaro
Lobería
Cholchol
San Patricio
Cherquenco
Nehuentue
Trovolhue
Carahue
Cajón
Vilcun
Puerto Saavedra
Nueva Imperial
Temuco
Melipeuco
Puerto Domínguez
Freire
Las Hortensias
Teodoro Schmidt
Barros Arana
Radal
Cunco
Los Laureles
Hualpín
Gorbea
Pitrufquén
Hueva Toltén
Toltén
Villarrica
Pucón
Loncoche
Queule
Curarrehue
Mehuín
Lanco
San José de la Mariquina
Malalhue
Panguipulli
Caleta Bonifacio
Curiñanco
Máfil
Poconu
Riñihue
Liquiñe
Niebla
Corral
Antilhue
Los Lagos
Puerto Fuy
Punta Galera
Valdivia
Reumén
Paillaco
Futrono
Llifén
Pichirropulli
Hueicoya
Punta Escalera
Puerto Nuevo
La Unión
Río Bueno
San Juan de la Costa
San Pablo
Riñinahue
Lago Ranco
Osorno
Bahía Mansa
Pauchó
Entre Lagos
Puyehue
Río Negro
Ranue
Hueyusca
Purranque
Corte Alto
Frutillar
Cabo Quedal
Tegualdao
Petrohue
Puerto Rico
Puerto Blest
Peulla
Llao Llao
San Carlos de Bariloche
Comallo
Cañadón Chileno
Pilcaniyeu
Los Menucos
Aguada de Guerra
Trayén Niyeu
Sierra Pailemán
Golfo San Matías
Las Grutas
Percy H. Scott
Aguada Cecilio
Mogna
Malanzán
Olpas
El Chacho
Cruz del Eje
Arancibia
Ingeniero Matías G. Sánchez
Castaño Nuevo
Pachaco
Talacasto
Calingasta
Tamberías
Barreal
Albardón
Chimbas
Villa del Salvador
San Juan
Zonda
Villa Krause
Caucete
Villa Aberastain
Villa Santa Rosa
Carpintería
Las Casuarinas
Cañada Honda
Villa Media Agua
Retamito
Molina
Vallecito
Bermejo
Papagayos
Marayes
Astica
Chucuma
Villa Santa Rita de Catuna
Noqueve
Desiderio Tello
Mascasín
Chepes
Ulapes
La Playa
La Higuera
San Carlos
Ojo de Agua
Medano
Salsacate
Chacaní
San Solano
Totoral
Bajo Hondo
Corral de Isaac
Salvador
Baldecito
Los Cerrillos
Villa Cura Brochero
Mina Clavero
San Pedro
Villa Dolores
Conlara
El Retamo
Candelaria
Encón
La Tranca
Cantantal
San Miguel
San Jorge
Quines
Talita
La Paz
Luján
Libertador General San Martín
Santa Rosa del Conlara
Merlo
San Francisco del Monte de Oro
Las Chacras
Concarán
Villa General Roca
Tilisarao
Renca
Alpa Corral
Carolina
Paso Grande
Naschel
Hipólito Yrigoyen
Villa del Carmen
San Isidro
Trapiche
La Toma
La Esquina
El Morro
San Gerónimo
El Volcán
Saladillo
La Punilla
San Luis
Juan Llerena
San José del Morro
Sampacho
Balde
Daniel Donovan
Eleodoro Lobos
Coronel Alzogaray
Fraga
Chajan
Liborio Luna
Juan Jorba
Mercedes
Villa Reynolds
Beazley
Zanjitas
Nueva Escocia
Las Isletas
Alto Pelado
Justo Daract
Varela
Modestino Pizarro
Villa Sarmiento
Soven
Villa Valeria
Termas de Villavicencio
Jocolí
Uspallata
Lavalle
Nueva California
Las Heras
Mendoza
Villa Nueva
Tres Porteñas
Godoy Cruz
General Gutiérrez
Maipú
Polvaredas
Punta de Vacas
Potrerillos
Luján de Cuyo
San Martín
Agrelo
Junín
Rivadavia
Ugarteche
Medrano
Santa Rosa
Las Catitas
Tupungato
La Dormida
Zapata
Tunuyán
Pichi Ciego
Vista Flores
La Consulta
San Carlos
Chilecito
Pareditas
Comandante Salas
Ñacuñán
Desaguadero
La Paz
Chosmes
Alto Pencoso
Maquinista Levet
Mosmota
San Antonio
Arroyito
San José
Los Árboles
Los Maitenes
San José de Maipo
San Gabriel
El Volcán
Planta Los Queltehues
Guadales
Monte Comán
Veinticinco de Mayo
San Rafael
Las Paredes
Rodolfo Iselin
Cuadro Benegas
Goudge
Rincón del Atuel
Salto de las Rosas
Villa Atuel
Real de Padre
Ingeniero Balloffet
Vargas
Ovejería
Media Luna
Navia
Nahuel Mapá
Dixonville
Batavia
Buena Esperanza
Las Malvinas
General Alvear
Soitue
Bowen
Colonia Alvear
Carmensa
El Nihuil
Embalse del Nihuil
El Sosneado
Las Juntas
La Mora
Unión
Nueva Galia
Canalejas
La Maroma
Bagual
Vicente Dupuy
Las Leñas
Las Molles
Malargüe
Salina Llancanelo
Lago Llancanelo
El Loro
Cochico
La Herradura
La Verde
Martín de Loyola
Anchorena
Arizona
Nueva Constitución
Rucanelo
Luan Toro
Santa Isabel
Victorica
Telén
Colonia La Pastoril
Algarrobo del Águila
Colonia Emilio Mitre
Carro Quemado
Los Manatiales
El Durazno
La Esperanza
Paso de los Algarrobos
El Odre
La Estrella
Valle Daza
Limay Mahuida
Chacharramendi
Puelén
Salina Grande
Carancho
La Reforma
Gobernador Ayala
Peñas Blancas
Salitral de la Perra
La Asturiana
Agua Blanca
25 de Mayo
Catriel
Calmucó
Ranquil del Norte
Barrancas
Buta Ranquil
Las Ovejas
Andacollo
Chos Malal
Rincón de los Sauces
El Huecú
Taquimilán
Norquín
Auca Mahuida
Loncopangue
Coihueco
Loncopue
Huaren Chenque
Codihué
Bajada del Agrio
Paso de los Indios
Añelo
Casa de Piedra
Gran Bajo Salitroso
Puelches
Minerales de la Pampa
Cuchillo-Có
Embalse Casa de Piedra
Puesto Sánchez
Embalse Cerros Colorados
Chañar
Barda del Medio
Lago Pellegrini
Contraalmirante Cordero
Cinco Saltos
Centenario
Cipolletti
Gobernador Duval
Las Lajas
Mariano Moreno
Portada Covunco
Zapala
Ramón M. Castro
Central-Có
Plaza Huincul
Neuquén
Alejandro Stefenelli
Ingeniero Huergo
Senillosa
Allen
Chichinales
Chelforó
Fortín Uno
Pichi Mahuida
Challacó
General Roca
Villa Regina
Chimpay
Darwin
Benjamín Zorrilla
Villa El Chocón
Fray Luis Beltrán
Choele Choel
Lamarque
Pomona
Aluminé
Rahue
Espinazo del Zorro
Picún Leufú
Embalse Ezequiel Ramos Mexía
Las Colorados
Catán Lil
Colonia Josefa
Negro Muerto
Junín de los Andes
Santa Rosa
Coronel Francisco Sosa
Sañicó
Piedra de Águila
San Antonio del Cuy
Córdoba
San Martín de los Andes
Michihuao
Chasicó
Altiplanicie de Hakelhuincul
La Esperanza
Mencué
Salina Gualicho
Pichi Traful
Embalse Piedra de Águila
Corral Chico
Talcahuano
Nahuel Niyeu
Caleufú
Paso del Limay
Ministro Remos Mexía
Sierra Colorada
Musters
Paso Flores
Laguna Blanca
Valcheta
Lago Curicó
San Antonio Oeste
Cinco Chañares
Paso Chacabuco
Limay
Collón Curá
Atuel
Colorado
Neuquén
Tunuyán
Diamante
Salado
Desaguadero
Sierra de la Huerta
Sierra de Valle Fértil
Sierra de Guayaguas
Sierra de Ulapes
Sierra de San Luis
Sierra de Pie de Palo
Sierra de Auca Mahuida
Sierra Chachahuén
Cerro Nevado
Cerro Payún
Loma del Jagüel Moro
Chihuido Medio
Cerro Mercedario
Cerro Aconcagua
Volcán Tupungato
Volcán Maipo
Volcán San José
Volcán Overo
Sosneado
Risco Plateado
Volcán Peteroa
Cerro Mora
Cerro Campanario
Nevado de Longaví
Volcán Domuyo
Volcán Chillán
Volcán Tromen
Cerro Carrero
Volcán Antuco
Volcán Copahue
Volcán Llaima
Volcán Lonquimay
Volcán Villarrica
Volcán Lanín
Volcán Choshuenco
Volcán Puyehue
Cerro Azul
Ollitas
El Peñón
Juncal
Nevado El Plomo
Cerro Tupungato
Paso de Agua Negra
Lago del Maule
Laguna de Laja
Lago Malbarco
Lago Aluminé
Lago Quillén
Lago Lácar
Lago Ranco
Lago de Puyehue
Lago Rupanco
Lago Llanquihue
Lago Nahuel Huapi
Lago Budi
Lago Calafquén
Lago Villarrica
Parque Nacional Laguna de Laja
Parque Nacional Conguillío
Parque Nacional Villarrica
Parque Nacional Puyehue
Parque Nacional Lanín
Parque Nacional Nahuel Huapi
Parque Nacional Nahuelbuta
Parque Nacional Tolhuaca
Bahía de Concepción
SCL
MDZ
CCP
NQN
Gran Bajo Salitroso

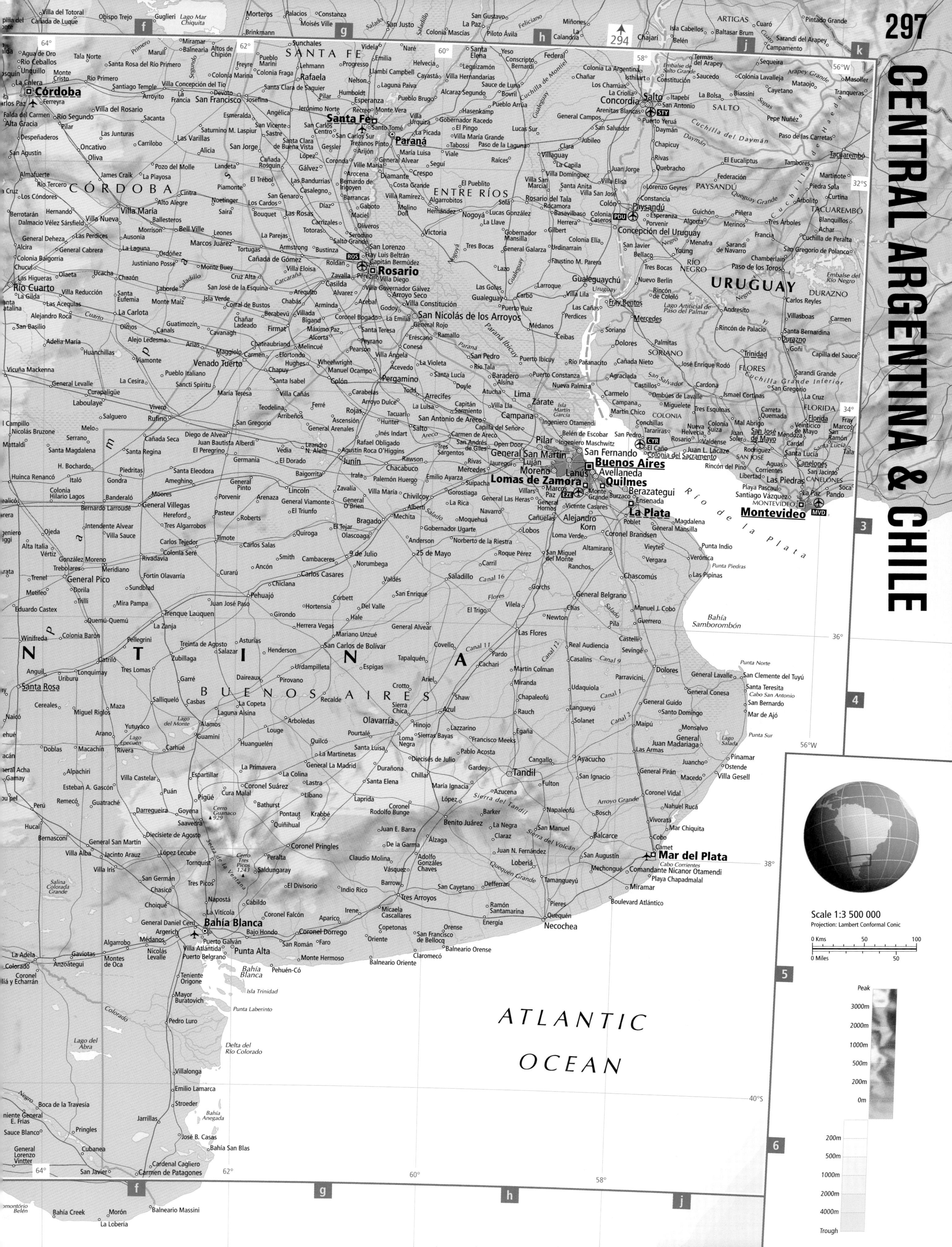
294
SANTA FE
CÓRDOBA
ENTRE RÍOS
BUENOS AIRES
URUGUAY
PAYSANDÚ
SALTO
RÍO NEGRO
SORIANO
COLONIA
FLORES
FLORIDA
DURAZNO
TACUAREMBÓ
ARTIGAS
CANELONES
MONTEVIDEO
SAN JOSÉ
Córdoba
Río Cuarto
Villa María
Santa Fe
Paraná
Rosario
San Nicolás de los Arroyos
Venado Tuerto
Pergamino
Junín
Concordia
Salto
Paysandú
Concepción del Uruguay
Gualeguaychú
Fray Bentos
Mercedes
Colonia del Sacramento
Buenos Aires
Lomas de Zamora
Quilmes
La Plata
Montevideo
General Pico
Santa Rosa
Trenque Lauquen
Olavarría
Tandil
Mar del Plata
Necochea
Tres Arroyos
Bahía Blanca
Punta Alta
Río de la Plata
Bahía Samborombón
ATLANTIC
OCEAN
Delta del Río Colorado
Bahía Blanca
Bahía Anegada
Colorado
Negro
Sierra del Tandil
Sierra de la Ventana
Carmen de Patagones
San Javier
64°
62°
60°
58°
56°W
32°S
34°
36°
38°
40°S
f
g
h
j
k
3
4
5
6
Scale 1:3 500 000
Projection: Lambert Conformal Conic
0 Kms
50
100
0 Miles
50
Peak
3000m
2000m
1000m
500m
200m
0m
200m
500m
1000m
2000m
4000m
Trough

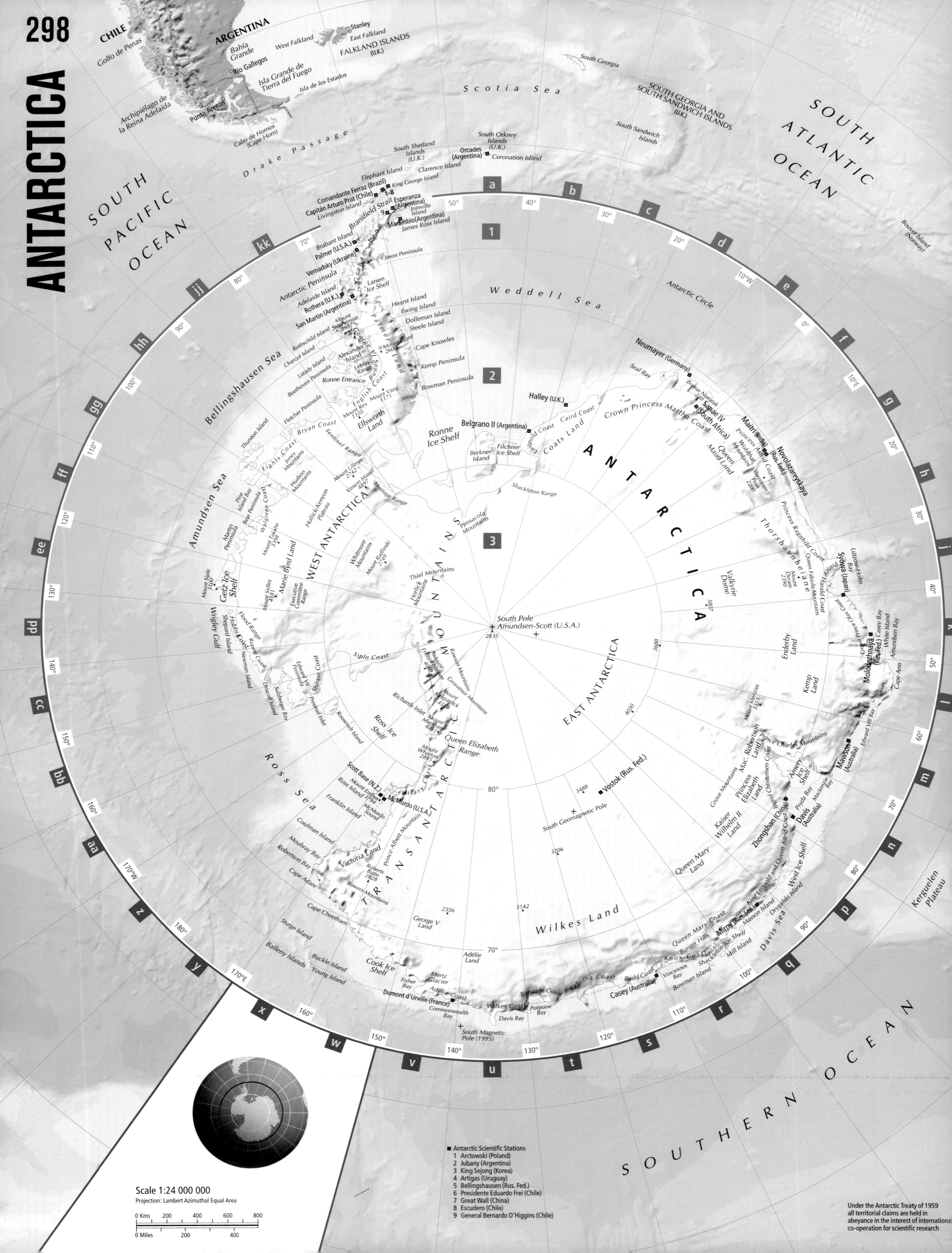

ANTARCTICA

CHILE
ARGENTINA
Golfo de Penas
Bahía Grande
Río Gallegos
West Falkland
Stanley
East Falkland
FALKLAND ISLANDS
(U.K.)
Isla Grande de Tierra del Fuego
Isla de los Estados
Archipiélago de la Reina Adelaida
Punta Arenas
Cabo de Hornos (Cape Horn)

SOUTH GEORGIA
SOUTH GEORGIA AND SOUTH SANDWICH ISLANDS
(U.K.)
South Sandwich Islands

SOUTH ATLANTIC OCEAN

Bouvet Island (Norway)

SOUTH PACIFIC OCEAN

Scotia Sea

Drake Passage

South Orkney Islands
Orcades (Argentina)
(U.K.)
Coronation Island

South Shetland Islands (U.K.)
Clarence Island

Elephant Island
King George Island
Comandante Ferraz (Brazil)
Capitán Arturo Prat (Chile)
1-8
Livingston Island
Bransfield Strait Esperanza
9 (Argentina)
Joinville
Marambio(Argentina)
James Ross Island

Brabant Island
Palmer (U.S.A.)
Vernadsky (Ukraine)
Antarctic Peninsula
Adelaide Island
Rothera (U.K.)
San Martín (Argentina)

Jason Peninsula
Larsen Ice Shelf
Hearst Island

Antarctic Circle

Weddell Sea

Neumayer (Germany)

Seal Bay
Maitri (India)
Sanae IV (South Africa)
Novolazarevskaya (Rus. Fed.)

Crown Princess Martha Coast
Queen Maud Land

Syowa (Japan)

Bellingshausen Sea

Rothschild Island
Charcot Island
Alexander Island
Latady Island
Beethoven Peninsula

Ewing Island
Dolleman Island
Steele Island
Cape Knowles
Kemp Peninsula
Bowman Peninsula

Halley (U.K.)
Belgrano II (Argentina)

Berkner Island

Ronne Ice Shelf
Filchner Ice Shelf

Coats Land
Shackleton Range

ANTARCTICA

Thorshavnheiane
Princess Ragnhild Coast
Princess Astrid Coast
Prince Harald Coast

Enderby Land

Lützow-Holm Bay
Prince Olav Coast
Casey Bay
White Island
Amundsen Bay
Cape Ann

Molodezhnaya (Rus. Fed.)

Amundsen Sea

Thurston Island
Fletcher Peninsula
Bryan Coast
Eights Coast
Jones Mountains
Hudson Mountains

Ellsworth Land

English Coast

Pensacola Mountains

WEST ANTARCTICA

Hollick-Kenyon Plateau
Vinson Massif 4897
Sentinel Range

Whitmore Mountains
Thiel Mountains
Hoodick Mountains

EAST ANTARCTICA

Kemp Land

Mawson (Australia)

Mac. Robertson Land
Prince Charles Mountains

Pine Island Bay
Bear Peninsula
Martin Peninsula
Walgreen Coast
Marie Byrd Land

Mount Takahe
Executive Committee Range

South Pole
Amundsen-Scott (U.S.A.)
2835

Lambert Glacier
Amery Ice Shelf

Grove Mountains

Mount Siple 3110
Getz Ice Shelf
Mount Sidley 4181

Wrigley Gulf
Shepard Island
Hobbs Coast
Ruppert Coast
Hull Bay
Newman Island

Siple Coast

Ross Ice Shelf

Queen Elizabeth Range

South Geomagnetic Pole

Vostok (Rus. Fed.)
3488

Kaiser Wilhelm II Land

Zhongshan (China)
Davis (Australia)
Prydz Bay

Princess Elizabeth Land

Roosevelt Island

Mount Whitney
Scott Base (N.Z.)
McMurdo (U.S.A.)

TRANSANTARCTIC MOUNTAINS

Queen Mary Land
3206

Wilkes Land

Mirny (Rus. Fed.)
Shackleton Ice Shelf

Ross Sea

Coulman Island
Franklin Island
Moubray Bay
Robertson Bay
Cape Adare

Victoria Land

Prince Albert Mountains

3142

Queen Mary Coast
Knox Coast
Bunger Hills
Vincennes Bay

Davis Sea

Mill Island

Cape Cheetham
George V Land
2356

Adélie Land

Budd Coast
Casey (Australia)
Bowman Island

Kerguelen Plateau

Sturge Island
Balleny Islands
Buckle Island
Young Island
Cook Ice Shelf

Mertz Glacier
Fisher Bay

Dumont d'Urville (France)
Commonwealth Bay
Davis Bay
Adélie Coast
Wilkes Coast
Porpoise Bay

South Magnetic Pole (1995)

SOUTHERN OCEAN

Scale 1:24 000 000
Projection: Lambert Azimuthal Equal Area

0 Kms 200 400 600 800
0 Miles 200 400

Antarctic Scientific Stations
1 Arctowski (Poland)
2 Jubany (Argentina)
3 King Sejong (Korea)
4 Artigas (Uruguay)
5 Bellingshausen (Rus. Fed.)
6 Presidente Eduardo Frei (Chile)
7 Great Wall (China)
8 Escudero (Chile)
9 General Bernardo O'Higgins (Chile)

Under the Antarctic Treaty of 1959 all territorial claims are held in abeyance in the interest of international co-operation for scientific research

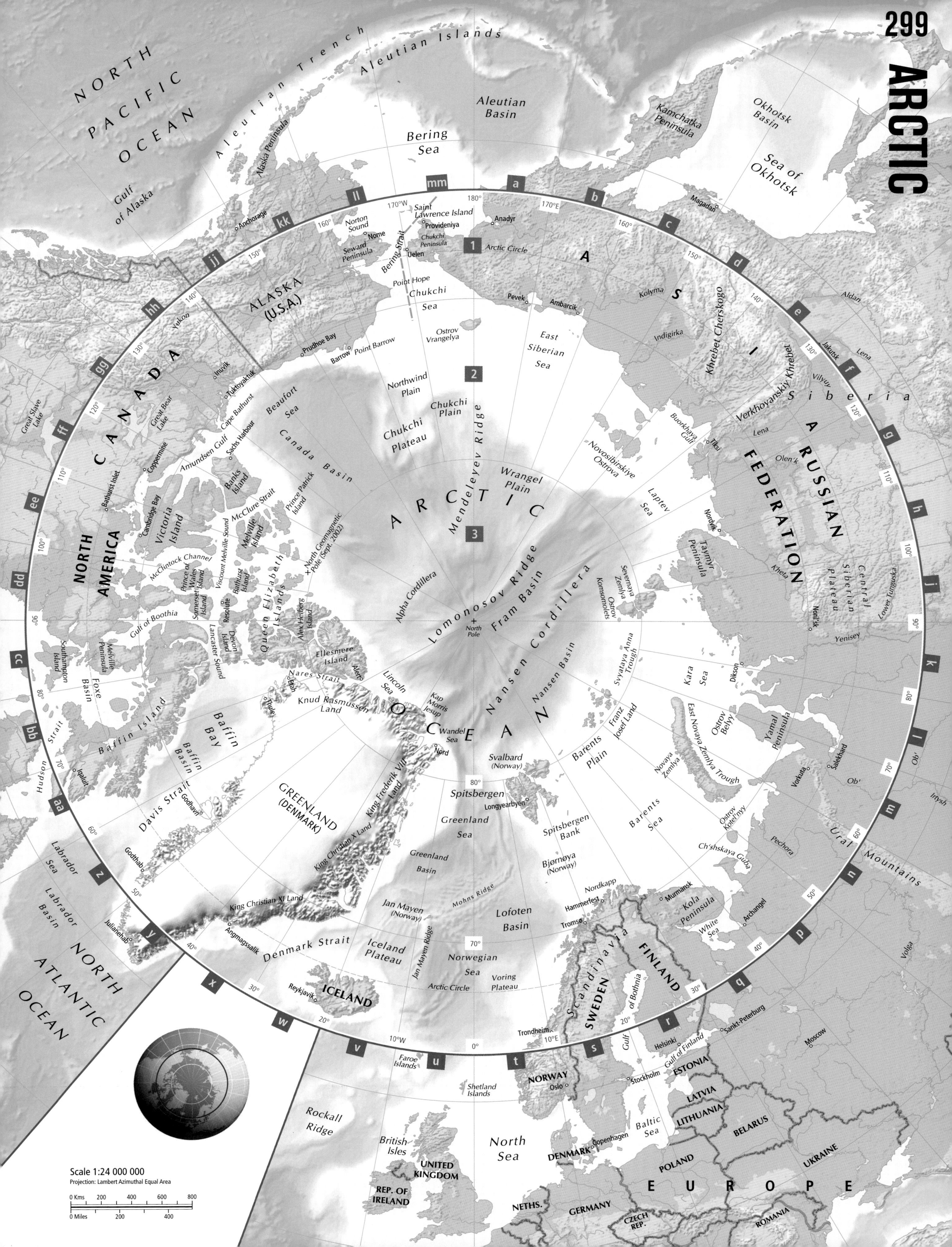

NORTH PACIFIC OCEAN

Gulf of Alaska

Aleutian Trench

Aleutian Islands

Aleutian Basin

Bering Sea

Kamchatka Peninsula

Okhotsk Basin

Sea of Okhotsk

Magadan

ll

mm

a

b

c

Anchorage

kk

Alaska Peninsula

Saint Lawrence Island

Providyeniya

Anadyr

Chukchi Peninsula

Uelen

Arctic Circle

Kolyma

d

jj

Norton Sound

Nome

Bering Strait

1

Pevek

Ambarcik

Khrebet Cherskogo

Aldan

hh

Seward Peninsula

Point Hope

Chukchi Sea

Indigirka

e

ALASKA (U.S.A.)

Barrow

Point Barrow

Ostrov Vrangelya

East Siberian Sea

Verkhoyanskiy Khrebet

Jakutsk

Lena

f

gg

Inuvik

Yukon

Prudhoe Bay

Northwind Plain

A   S   I   A

Vilyuy

Tiksi

Buorkhaya Gulf

Siberia

120°

g

Tuktoyaktuk

Cape Bathurst

Beaufort Sea

Chukchi Plain

Mendeleyev Ridge

Wrangel Plain

Novosibirskiye Ostrova

Laptev Sea

Lena

Olen'k

ff

C   A   N   A   D   A

Great Slave Lake

Great Bear Lake

Coppermine

Amundsen Gulf

Sachs Harbour

Canada Basin

Chukchi Plateau

A   R   C   T   I   C

RUSSIAN FEDERATION

Nordvik

110°

h

ee

Bathurst Inlet

Banks Island

McClure Strait

Prince Patrick Island

3

Fram Basin

Severnaya Zemlya

Taymyr Peninsula

Central Siberian Plateau

Nor11sk

NORTH AMERICA

Cambridge Bay

Victoria Island

Melville Island

North Geomagnetic Pole Sept. 2003

Alpha Cordillera

Lomonosov Ridge

North Pole

Nansen Cordillera

Ostrov Komsomolets

Kheta

Yenisey

Lower Tunguska

j

dd

McClintock Channel

Prince of Wales Island

Viscount Melville Sound

Resolute

Bathurst Island

Queen Elizabeth Islands

Ellef Ringnes Island

Nansen Basin

Svyataya Anna Trough

Kara Sea

Dikson

Ob'

cc

Gulf of Boothia

Melville Peninsula

Somerset Island

Devon Island

Ellesmere Island

Lancaster Sound

Nares Strait

Lincoln Sea

Kap Morris Jesup

Franz Josef Land

East Novaya Zemlya Trough

Ostrov Belyy

Yamal Peninsula

Vorkuta

Salekhard

k

Southampton Island

Foxe Basin

Baffin Island

Baffin Bay

Alert

Knud Rasmussen Land

Nord

Wandel Sea

Barents Plain

Novaya Zemlya

Ostrov Kotel'nyy

Ch'shskaya Guba

Pechora

l

bb

Hudson Strait

Iqaluit

Baffin Basin

Thule

King Frederik VIII Land

Svalbard (Norway)

Barents Sea

Ural Mountains

m

aa

Davis Strait

Godhavn

GREENLAND (DENMARK)

King Christian X Land

Spitsbergen

Longyearbyen

Spitsbergen Bank

Ostrov Kolguyev

Irtysh

z

Labrador Sea

Godthåb

Greenland Sea

Barents Sea

Nordkapp

Murmansk

Kola Peninsula

Archangel

n

50°

y

Labrador Basin

Julianehåb

King Christian XI Land

Greenland Basin

Bjørnøya (Norway)

Hammerfest

Tromsø

White Sea

Volga

p

Angmagssalik

Denmark Strait

Jan Mayen (Norway)

Mohns Ridge

Lofoten Basin

Nordkapp

FINLAND

40°

x

NORTH ATLANTIC OCEAN

Reykjavik

ICELAND

Iceland Plateau

Jan Mayen Ridge

Norwegian Sea

Voring Plateau

Trondheim

S C a n d i n a v i a

SWEDEN

Gulf of Bothnia

Sankt-Peterburg

Moscow

q

w

30°

Arctic Circle

r

v

u

t

Faroe Islands

Rockall Ridge

Shetland Islands

NORWAY

Oslo

Helsinki

Stockholm

Gulf of Finland

ESTONIA

s

British Isles

North Sea

DENMARK

Copenhagen

Baltic Sea

LATVIA

LITHUANIA

BELARUS

UKRAINE

UNITED KINGDOM

REP. OF IRELAND

NETHS.

GERMANY

POLAND

CZECH REP.

ROMANIA

E   U   R   O   P   E

Scale 1:24 000 000
Projection: Lambert Azimuthal Equal Area

0 Kms   200   400   600   800
0 Miles   200   400

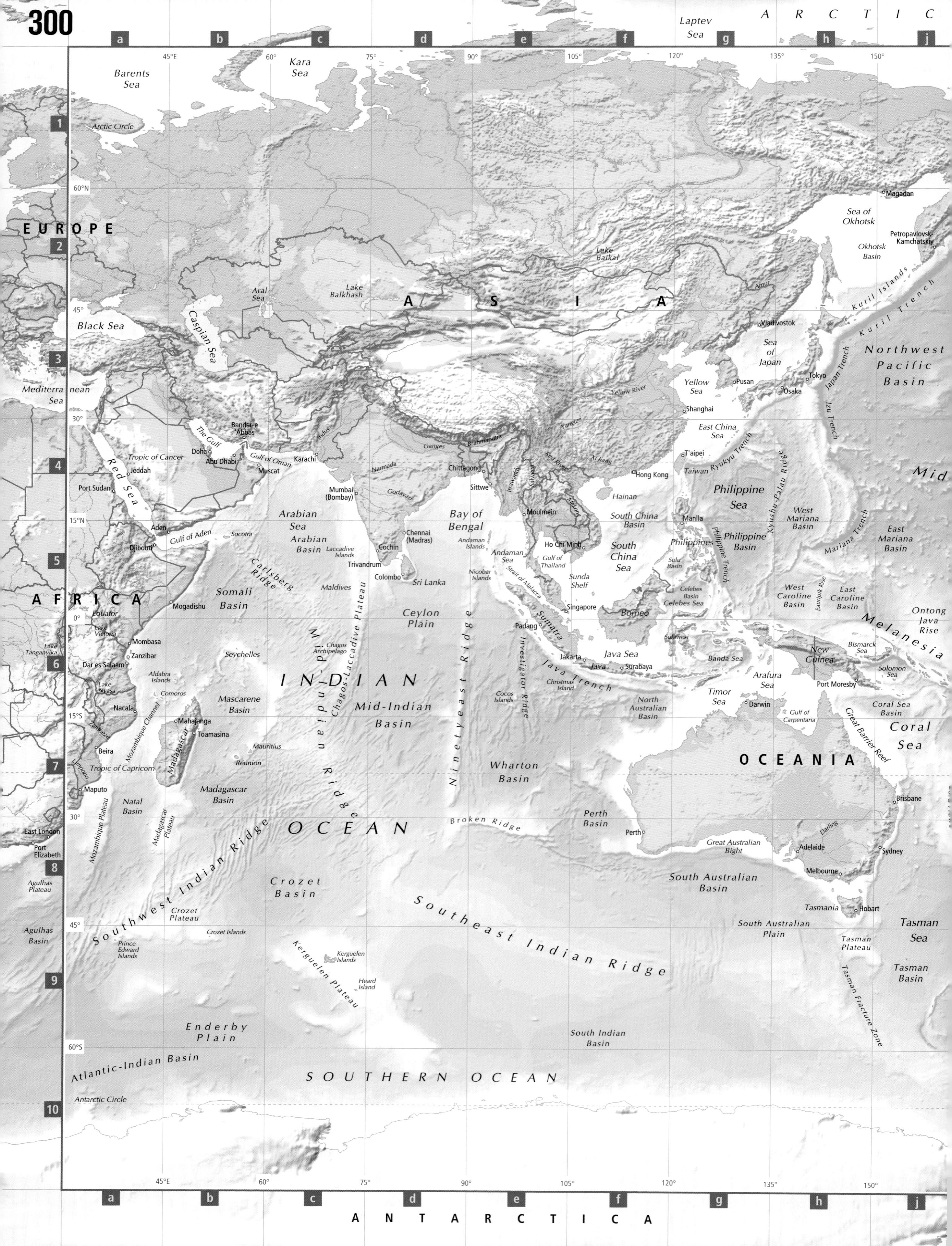

ARCTIC

Laptev Sea

Barents Sea

Kara Sea

Arctic Circle

60°N

EUROPE

Black Sea

Mediterranean Sea

Caspian Sea

Aral Sea

Lake Balkhash

A S I A

Lake Baikal

Sea of Okhotsk

Magadan

Petropavlovsk-Kamchatskiy

Okhotsk Basin

Vladivostok

Sea of Japan

Kuril Islands

Kuril Trench

Northwest Pacific Basin

30°

The Gulf

Bandar-e Abbas

Doha

Abu Dhabi

Gulf of Oman

Muscat

Karachi

Indus

Tropic of Cancer

Jeddah

Red Sea

Port Sudan

Aden

Gulf of Aden

Djibouti

AFRICA

Mogadishu

Somali Basin

Mombasa

Zanzibar

Dar es Salaam

Lake Nyasa

Lake Tanganyika

Lake Victoria

Equator

Narmada

Godavari

Mumbai (Bombay)

Arabian Sea

Arabian Basin

Laccadive Islands

Chennai (Madras)

Cochin

Trivandrum

Colombo

Sri Lanka

Maldives

Catlsberg Ridge

Chagos Archipelago

Chagos-Laccadive Plateau

Ceylon Plain

Mid-Indian Basin

I N D I A N

15°N

Ganges

Brahmaputra

Chittagong

Sittwe

Moulmein

Bay of Bengal

Andaman Islands

Andaman Sea

Nicobar Islands

Irrawaddy

Salween

Mekong

Ho Chi Minh

Gulf of Thailand

Strait of Malacca

Singapore

Sunda Shelf

Padang

Sumatra

Jakarta

Java

Surabaya

Java Sea

Christmas Island

Cocos Islands

Investigator Ridge

Ninetyeast Ridge

Java Trench

Wharton Basin

Yellow River

Yellow Sea

Pusan

Xi Jiang

Yangtze

Red River

Shanghai

Hong Kong

T'aipei

East China Sea

Hainan

South China Sea

South China Basin

Manila

Philippines

Philippine Sea

Philippine Basin

Philippine Trench

Taiwan

Ryukyu Trench

Kyushu-Palau Ridge

Izu Trench

Japan Trench

Tokyo

Osaka

Mid

West Mariana Basin

Mariana Trench

East Mariana Basin

Sulu Basin

Celebes Basin

Celebes Sea

Sulawesi

Borneo

Eauripik Rise

West Caroline Basin

East Caroline Basin

Ontong Java Rise

Melanesia

Banda Sea

Timor Sea

Darwin

Arafura Sea

Gulf of Carpentaria

New Guinea

Bismarck Sea

Solomon Sea

Port Moresby

Coral Sea Basin

Coral Sea

Great Barrier Reef

OCEANIA

Brisbane

North Australian Basin

Mascarene Basin

Seychelles

Aldabra Islands

Comoros

Mahajanga

Toamasina

Madagascar

Mozambique Channel

Nacala

Beira

Quelimane

Mozambique Plateau

Natal Basin

Maputo

East London

Port Elizabeth

Agulhas Plateau

Agulhas Basin

I N - D I A N   R i d g e

Mid-Indian Ridge

Madagascar Plateau

Madagascar Basin

Mauritius

Réunion

Tropic of Capricorn

15°S

O C E A N

Southwest Indian Ridge

Crozet Plateau

Crozet Basin

Crozet Islands

Prince Edward Islands

Kerguelen Plateau

Kerguelen Islands

Heard Island

Broken Ridge

Southeast Indian Ridge

Perth Basin

Perth

Great Australian Bight

South Australian Basin

Adelaide

Melbourne

Sydney

Darling

Tasmania

Hobart

South Australian Plain

Tasman Plateau

Tasman Sea

Tasman Basin

Tasman Fracture Zone

30°

45°

Enderby Plain

South Indian Basin

Atlantic-Indian Basin

60°S

S O U T H E R N   O C E A N

Antarctic Circle

A N T A R C T I C A

45°E   60°   75°   90°   105°   120°   135°   150°

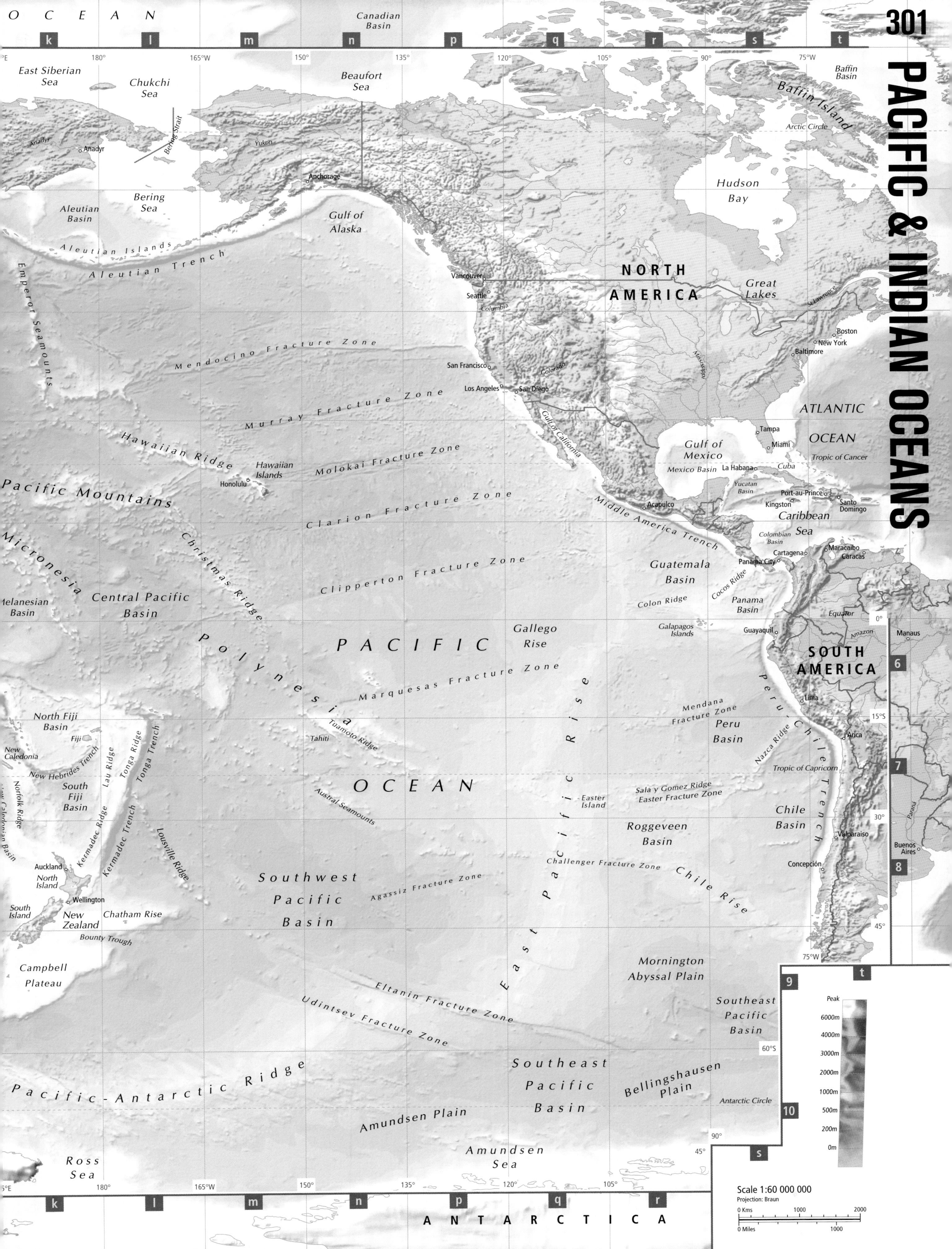
O C E A N
Canadian Basin
East Siberian Sea
Chukchi Sea
Beaufort Sea
Baffin Basin
Baffin Island
Arctic Circle
Anadyr
Bering Strait
Yukon
Anchorage
Hudson Bay
Aleutian Basin
Bering Sea
Gulf of Alaska
Aleutian Islands
Aleutian Trench
Emperor Seamounts
NORTH AMERICA
Vancouver
Seattle
Columbia
Great Lakes
St Lawrence
Boston
New York
Baltimore
Mendocino Fracture Zone
San Francisco
Colorado
Mississippi
Los Angeles
San Diego
Murray Fracture Zone
ATLANTIC OCEAN
Gulf of California
Tampa
Miami
Hawaiian Ridge
Hawaiian Islands
Honolulu
Molokai Fracture Zone
Gulf of Mexico
Mexico Basin
La Habana
Cuba
Tropic of Cancer
Yucatan Basin
Port-au-Prince
Kingston
Santo Domingo
Pacific Mountains
Clarion Fracture Zone
Acapulco
Middle America Trench
Caribbean Sea
Colombian Basin
Cartagena
Maracaibo
Caracas
Micronesia
Christmas Ridge
Clipperton Fracture Zone
Guatemala Basin
Panama City
Cocos Ridge
Melanesian Basin
Central Pacific Basin
Colon Ridge
Panama Basin
Equator
Gallego Rise
Galapagos Islands
Guayaquil
Amazon
Manaus
PACIFIC
Polynesia
SOUTH AMERICA
Marquesas Fracture Zone
Lima
Mendana Fracture Zone
North Fiji Basin
Fiji
Tahiti
Tuamoto Ridge
Peru Basin
Peru-Chile Trench
Arica
New Caledonia
New Hebrides Trench
Lau Ridge
Tonga Ridge
Tonga Trench
Nazca Ridge
Tropic of Capricorn
South Fiji Basin
OCEAN
Norfolk Ridge
Easter Island
Sala y Gomez Ridge
Easter Fracture Zone
Austral Seamounts
Chile Basin
Kermadec Ridge
Kermadec Trench
Lousville Ridge
Roggeveen Basin
Parana
Valparaiso
Buenos Aires
Auckland
North Island
Challenger Fracture Zone
Concepción
Southwest Pacific Basin
Agassiz Fracture Zone
East Pacific Rise
Chile Rise
Wellington
South Island
New Zealand
Chatham Rise
Bounty Trough
Campbell Plateau
Mornington Abyssal Plain
Eltanin Fracture Zone
Udintsev Fracture Zone
Southeast Pacific Basin
Pacific-Antarctic Ridge
Southeast Pacific Basin
Bellingshausen Plain
Antarctic Circle
Amundsen Plain
Amundsen Sea
Ross Sea
ANTARCTICA
180°
165°W
150°
135°
120°
105°
90°
75°W
0°
15°S
30°
45°
60°S
k l m n p q r s t
6 7 8 9 10
Peak
6000m
4000m
3000m
2000m
1000m
500m
200m
0m
Scale 1:60 000 000
Projection: Braun
0 Kms 1000 2000
0 Miles 1000

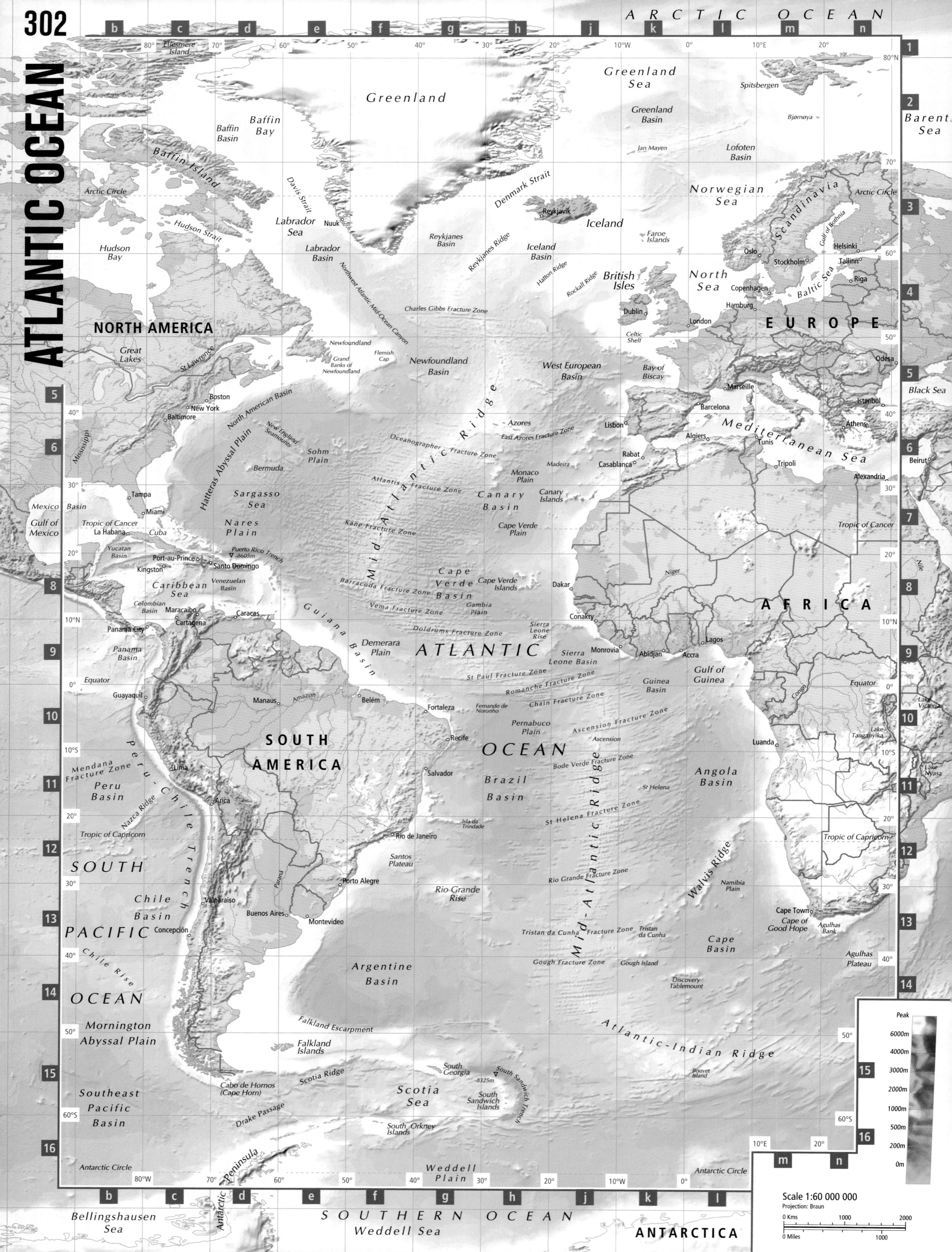

ATLANTIC OCEAN

ARCTIC OCEAN

NORTH AMERICA

EUROPE

AFRICA

SOUTH AMERICA

ATLANTIC

OCEAN

SOUTH

PACIFIC

OCEAN

ANTARCTICA

SOUTHERN OCEAN

Greenland

Greenland Sea

Spitsbergen

Bjørnøya

Barents Sea

Baffin Island

Baffin Basin

Baffin Bay

Greenland Basin

Jan Mayen

Lofoten Basin

Ellesmere Island

Norwegian Sea

Scandinavia

Arctic Circle

Hudson Bay

Hudson Strait

Davis Strait

Labrador Sea

Nuuk

Denmark Strait

Reykjavik

Iceland

Faroe Islands

Oslo

Stockholm

Helsinki

Gulf of Bothnia

Tallinn

Riga

Labrador Basin

Reykjanes Basin

Reykjanes Ridge

Iceland Basin

Hatton Ridge

Rockall Ridge

British Isles

North Sea

Copenhagen

Hamburg

Baltic Sea

Great Lakes

St Lawrence

Newfoundland

Grand Banks of Newfoundland

Flemish Cap

Newfoundland Basin

Charles Gibbs Fracture Zone

Celtic Shelf

Dublin

London

West European Basin

Bay of Biscay

Odesa

Boston

New York

Baltimore

North American Basin

New England Seamounts

Sohm Plain

Azores

East Azores Fracture Zone

Lisbon

Marseille

Barcelona

Istanbul

Athens

Black Sea

Mississippi

Hatteras Abyssal Plain

Bermuda

Sargasso Sea

Oceanographer Fracture Zone

Atlantis Fracture Zone

Monaco Plain

Madeira

Algiers

Rabat

Casablanca

Tunis

Tripoli

Mediterranean Sea

Beirut

Alexandria

Mexico Basin

Gulf of Mexico

Tampa

Miami

Tropic of Cancer

La Habana

Cuba

Nares Plain

Kane Fracture Zone

Canary Basin

Canary Islands

Cape Verde Plain

Tropic of Cancer

Nile

Yucatan Basin

Kingston

Port-au-Prince

Santo Domingo

Puerto Rico Trench ▽ -8605m

Cape Verde Basin

Cape Verde Islands

Dakar

Colombian Basin

Caribbean Sea

Maracaibo

Venezuelan Basin

Caracas

Cartagena

Barracuda Fracture Zone

Vema Fracture Zone

Gambia Plain

Conakry

Panama City

Panama Basin

Guiana Basin

Doldrums Fracture Zone

Sierra Leone Rise

Monrovia

Abidjan

Accra

Lagos

Equator

Guayaquil

Manaus

Amazon

Belém

Demerara Plain

St Paul Fracture Zone

Sierra Leone Basin

Gulf of Guinea

Guinea Basin

Equator

Lake Victoria

Fortaleza

Fernando de Noronha

Romanche Fracture Zone

Chain Fracture Zone

Recife

Pernabuco Plain

Ascension Fracture Zone

Ascension

Luanda

Lake Tanganyika

Mendana Fracture Zone

Peru Basin

Lima

Arica

Salvador

Brazil Basin

Bode Verde Fracture Zone

St Helena

Angola Basin

Lake Nyasa

Nazca Ridge

Peru-Chile Trench

Isla da Trindade

St Helena Fracture Zone

Tropic of Capricorn

Rio de Janeiro

Santos Plateau

Parana

Porto Alegre

Rio Grande Fracture Zone

Namibia Plain

Walvis Ridge

Tropic of Capricorn

Chile Basin

Valparaiso

Concepción

Buenos Aires

Montevideo

Rio Grande Rise

Cape Town

Cape of Good Hope

Agulhas Bank

Cape Basin

Chile Rise

Tristan da Cunha Fracture Zone

Tristan da Cunha

Agulhas Plateau

Argentine Basin

Gough Fracture Zone

Gough Island

Discovery Tablemount

Mornington Abyssal Plain

Falkland Escarpment

Falkland Islands

Scotia Ridge

South Georgia ▽ -8325m

Mid-Atlantic Ridge

Bouvet Island

Atlantic-Indian Ridge

Southeast Pacific Basin

Cabo de Hornos (Cape Horn)

Scotia Sea

South Sandwich Islands

South Sandwich Trench

Drake Passage

South Orkney Islands

Antarctic Peninsula

Bellingshausen Sea

Weddell Plain

Weddell Sea

Antarctic Circle

Antarctic Circle

Peak

6000m

4000m

3000m

2000m

1000m

500m

200m

0m

Scale 1:60 000 000

Projection: Braun

0 Kms 1000 2000

0 Miles 1000

The gazetteer, containing more than 80,000 names, lists all the countries, internal divisions, towns and cities, lakes and rivers, mountains and deserts, seas and oceans that appear in the World Atlas. Each place is listed using a page number and an alphanumeric grid reference. Also included is its status – whether it is a political or physical feature – and the country or region to which it belongs. Short statistical profiles of every one of the world's nation states appear in alphabetical order throughout the gazetteer. They give data on the population, economy and social make-up of each country.

GAZETTEER

The index includes in a single alphabetical list more than 80,000 names of towns or features that appear on the maps. Each name is followed by a map reference and page reference.

Names Local official names are used on the maps and in the index. The names are shown in full, including diacritical marks. Features that extend beyond the boundaries of one country and have no single official name are usually named in English.

Transliteration For names in languages not written in the Roman alphabet, the locally official system has been used where one exists. Thus, the transliteration for mainland Chinese names follows the Pinyin system which has been officially adopted in mainland China and that for the Russian Federation follows the GOST 1983 system. For languages with no one locally accepted system, transliteration closely follows a system adopted by the United Kingdom Permanent Committee on Geographical Names (PCGN) and the United States Board on Geographic Names (BGN).

Abbreviation and capitalization Abbreviations of names on the maps have been standardized as much as possible. Names that are abbreviated on the maps are generally spelled out in full in the index. The abbreviation 'St' is used only for 'Saint'. The German 'Sankt' and other forms of this term are spelled out.

Most initial letters of names are capitalized except for generic terms in Russia and a number of other countries in eastern Europe and central Asia, and a few Dutch names such as ''s-Gravenhage'. Capitalization of non-initial words in a name generally follows local practice.

Alphabetization Names are alphabetized in the order of the letters of the English alphabet. *ñ*, for example, is not treated as a distinct letter. Furthermore, diacritical marks are disregarded in alphabetization – German or Scandinavian *ä* or *ö* are treated as *a* or *o*.

The names of physical features may appear inverted, since they are always alphabetized under the proper, not the generic, part of the name as in 'Gibraltar, Strait of'. Otherwise, every entry, whether consisting of one word or more, is alphabetized as a single continuous entity. 'Lakeland', for example, appears after 'La Crosse' and before 'La Salle'. Names beginning with articles other than 'The' (Le Havre, Den Helder, Al-Qahirah, As-Suways) are not inverted. Names beginning 'St' and 'Sainte' are alphabetized as though spelled 'Saint'.

In the case of identical names, towns are listed first, then political divisions, then physical features. Entries that are completely identical (including symbols, explained below) are distinguished by abbreviations of their country names. The abbreviations used for places in the United States and Canada indicate the state or province in which the feature is located. (See List of Abbreviations right.)

Symbols The names of cities and towns are not followed by symbols. The names of all other features are followed by symbols that graphically represent broad categories of features, for example △ for mountain (Everest, Mount △). A complete list of symbols, including those with superior numbers, follows the List of Abbreviations.

Map references and page references The map references and page references are found in the last two columns of each entry. Each map reference consists of a letter followed by a number. The letters to which they refer appear along the top and bottom of the maps and numbers appear down the sides of the maps. Map references for point features, such as towns, cities and mountain peaks, indicate the locations of the symbols. For extensive features, such as countries, mountain ranges and rivers, locations are given for the centre of the name.

The page number generally refers to the map that shows the feature at the most appropriate scale. Countries, mountain ranges and other extensive features are usually indexed to maps that not only show the features completely but also show them in their relationship to broader areas. If a page contains several maps or insets, an upper case letter identifies the specific map or inset.

LIST OF ABBREVIATIONS

Afg.	Afghanistan	**Gren.**	Grenada	**Russ. Fed.**	Russian Federation
Afr.	Africa	**Guad.**	Guadeloupe	**Rw.**	Rwanda
Alb.	Albania	**Guat.**	Guatemala	**San Mar.**	San Marino
Alg.	Algeria	**Gui.**	Guinea	**Sau. Ar.**	Saudi Arabia
Am. Sam.	American Samoa	**Gui.-B.**	Guinea-Bissau	**Sen.**	Senegal
And.	Andorra	**Guy.**	Guyana	**Serbia/Mont.**	Serbia and
Ang.	Angola	**Hond.**	Honduras		Montenegro
Antig.	Antigua and Barbuda	**Hung.**	Hungary	**Sey.**	Seychelles
Arg.	Argentina	**Ice.**	Iceland	**Sing.**	Singapore
Arm.	Armenia	**Indon.**	Indonesia	**S. Kor.**	South Korea
Aus.	Austria	**I.O.M.**	Isle of Man	**S.L.**	Sierra Leone
Aust.	Australia	**Ire.**	Republic of Ireland	**Slvk.**	Slovakia
Azer.	Azerbaijan	**Isr.**	Israel	**Slvn.**	Slovenia
Bah.	The Bahamas	**Jam.**	Jamaica	**Sol. Is.**	Solomon Islands
Bahr.	Bahrain	**Kaz.**	Kazakhstan	**Som.**	Somalia
Bang.	Bangladesh	**Kir.**	Kiribati	**Sri L.**	Sri Lanka
Barb.	Barbados	**Kuw.**	Kuwait	**St K./N.**	St Kitts and Nevis
Bel.	Belgium	**Kyrg.**	Kyrgyzstan	**St Luc.**	St Lucia
Bela.	Belarus	**Lat.**	Latvia	**S. Tom./P.**	São Tomé & Príncipe
Ber.	Bermuda	**Leb.**	Lebanon	**St P./M.**	St Pierre et Miquelon
Bhu.	Bhutan	**Leso.**	Lesotho	**St Vin.**	St Vincent and the
Bol.	Bolivia	**Lib.**	Liberia		Grenadines
Bos.	Bosnia-Herzegovina	**Liech.**	Liechtenstein	**Sur.**	Suriname
Bots.	Botswana	**Lith.**	Lithuania	**Swaz.**	Swaziland
Braz.	Brazil	**Lux.**	Luxembourg	**Swe.**	Sweden
Bru.	Brunei	**Mac.**	Macedonia	**Switz.**	Switzerland
Bul.	Bulgaria	**Mad.**	Madeira	**Tai.**	Taiwan
Bur.	Burundi	**Madag.**	Madagascar	**Taj.**	Tajikistan
Cam.	Cameroon	**Mal.**	Malawi	**Tan.**	Tanzania
Camb.	Cambodia	**Malay.**	Malaysia	**Thai.**	Thailand
Can.	Canada	**Mald.**	Maldives	**Tok.**	Tokelau
Can. Is.	Canary Islands	**Marsh. Is.**	Marshall Islands	**Trin.**	Trinidad and Tobago
Cape. V.	Cape Verde	**Mart.**	Martinique	**Tun.**	Tunisia
C.A.R.	Central African Republic	**Maur.**	Mauritius	**Tur.**	Turkey
C.I.	Côte d'Ivoire	**Maurit.**	Mauritania	**Turk.**	Turkmenistan
Col.	Colombia	**May.**	Mayotte	**U.A.E.**	United Arab Emirates
Com.	Comoros	**Mex.**	Mexico	**Ug.**	Uganda
C.R.	Costa Rica	**Mol.**	Moldova	**U.K.**	United Kingdom
Cro.	Croatia	**Mong.**	Mongolia	**Ukr.**	Ukraine
Cyp.	Cyprus	**Mor.**	Morocco	**Ur.**	Uruguay
Czech Rep.	Czech Republic	**Moz.**	Mozambique	**U.S.A.**	United States of America
Den.	Denmark	**Myan.**	Myanmar	**Uzb.**	Uzbekistan
Dji.	Djibouti	**Nam.**	Namibia	**Ven.**	Venezuela
Dom.	Dominica	**Neth.**	Netherlands	**Viet.**	Vietnam
Dom. Rep.	Dominican Republic	**Neth. Ant.**	Netherlands Antilles	**V.I. (UK)**	Virgin Islands (U.K.)
D.R.C.	Democratic Republic	**New Cal.**	New Caledonia	**V.I. (USA)**	Virgin Islands
	of Congo	**Nic.**	Nicaragua		(U.S.A.)
Ec.	Ecuador	**Nig.**	Nigeria	**Wake I.**	Wake Island
El Sal.	El Salvador	**N. Mar. Is.**	Northern Mariana	**W. Sah.**	Western Sahara
Eq. Gui.	Equatorial Guinea		Islands	**Zam.**	Zambia
Erit.	Eritrea	**Nor.**	Norway	**Zimb.**	Zimbabwe
Est.	Estonia	**N.Z.**	New Zealand		
Eth.	Ethiopia	**Pak.**	Pakistan		
Fin.	Finland	**Pan.**	Panama		
Fr.	France	**Para.**	Paraguay		
Fr. Gu.	French Guiana	**Phil.**	Philippines		
F.S.M.	Federated States	**P.N.G.**	Papua New Guinea		
	of Micronesia	**Pol.**	Poland		
Gam.	The Gambia	**Port.**	Portugal		
Geor.	Georgia	**P.R.**	Puerto Rico		
Ger.	Germany	**Reu.**	Réunion		
G.land	Greenland	**Rom.**	Romania		
Grc.	Greece	**R.S.A.**	Republic of South Africa		

KEY TO SYMBOLS

POLITICAL UNIT
Independent nation (followed by country fact box)

X Dependency

1 Admin 1 division

2 Admin 2 division

CULTURAL MISC

◆ Region

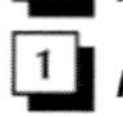

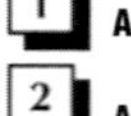

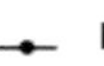

⊸ Dam

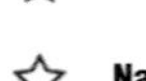

★ World Heritage site

☆ National Park, regional park

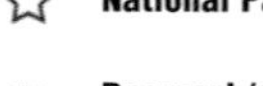

■ Research/scientific station

∴ Archeological site

HYDROGRAPHIC FEATURES

〰 River

⊔ Canal

≏ Marsh, bog

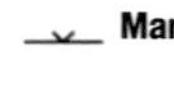

〜 River mouth

〜 Sea, ocean

〜 Sea feature

═ Strait, channel

⊶ Glacier

⊸ Ice cap

═ Ice shelf

◯ Reef

〜 Sea basin

◀ Gulf, bay

◯ Lake, loch

① Reservoir

⊙ Salt lake

⊂⊃ Dry intermittent lake

⌣ Well, oasis

 Waterfall

TOPOGRAPHIC FEATURES

⊨ Fiord

▶ Peninsula, cape

≍ Pass

△ Peak

◬ Mountain range

▲ Volcano

〰 Valley

⌄ Desert

⌐ Pan, depression, lowland

⌐ Plateau, plain, moor

⊏⊐ Island, island group

Aa → Aiello 305

16 de Julio g4 297
17 de Agosto f4 297
1st Cataract d3 218
25 de Mayo, Buenos Aires, Arg. g3 297
25 de Mayo, La Pampa, Arg. d4 296
25 de Mayo, Arg. c3 296
25 de Mayo, Ur. j3 297
26 Bakı Komissarı m2 137
2nd Cataract d3 218
30 de Agosto f4 297
3rd Cataract d4 218
4th Cataract d4 218
5th Cataract d4 218
9 de Julio g3 297

A

Aa, Fr. h2 183
Aa, Münster, Ger. c3 172
Aa, Detmold, Ger. d3 172
Aabadiyé d3 138
Aabbassiyé d3 138
Aabeïdat d2 138
Aach e5 174
Aachen e4 159
Aadloun d3 138
Aadorf c2 196
Aajaltoun d3 138
Aalen d2 174
Aali en Nahri e3 138
Aalisjärvi k3 155
Aalma ech Chaab d3 138
Aalsmeer c2 159
Aalst c4 159
Aalten e3 159
Aalter b3 159
Äänekoski k5 155
Aanqoun d3 138
Aansluit e3 234
Aapajärvi l3 155
Aaqoura d2 138
Aar d2 174
Aarau c2 196
Aarberg b2 196
Aarburg b2 196
Aare c2 196
Aarsal e2 138
Aarschot c4 159
Aarwangen b2 196
Aasiaat u2 243
Aba, China c2 104
Aba, D.R.C. f3 225
Aba, Nig. f4 223
Abā ad Dūd k8 137
Abā al Hinshan d7 139
Abacaxis f5 285
Abackij m4 147
Ābādān m6 137
Ābādeh p6 137
Ābādeh Ţashk p7 137
Abades f4 190
Abadia dos Dourados e3 290
Abadiânia d2 290
Abadín c1 190
Abadla d2 220
Abaeté, Braz. f3 291
Abaeté, Minas Gerais, Braz. f3 291
Abaetetuba c2 288
Abaiang H 75
A Baiuca b1 190
Abaji f4 223
Abakaliki f4 223
Abakan k4 118
Abala, Congo c4 224
Abala, Niger e3 223
Abalak f2 223
Abalessa e4 221
Abana e2 208
Ābana Merekes f5 219
Abancay c2 292
Abanga b3 224
Abanilla c6 193
Abapó e3 293
Abarán c6 193
Abarqū p6 137
A Barrela c2 190
Abashiri Ad1 114
Abashiri-wan Ad1 114
Abasolo, Guanajuato, Mex. d3 274
Abasolo, Tamaulipas, Mex. e1 275
Abasolo del Valle g5 275
Abaújszántó k3 171
Abava k4 157
Abay p3 121
Ābaya Hāyk' b2 226
Ābay Wenz e5 219
Abaza k4 118
Abba c2 224
Abbadia San Salvatore f7 197
Abbasanta Aa2 198
Abbekås e5 156
Abbe, Lake c1 226
Abbeville, Fr. g2 183
Abbeville, Georgia, U.S.A. h4 259
Abbeville, Louisiana, U.S.A. c5 258
Abbeville, South Carolina, U.S.A. h2 259
Abbeyfeale b4 165
Abbey Head e5 164
Abbeyleix d4 165
Abbey Peak g3 80
Abbey Town e5 164
Abbiategrasso c4 196
Abbot Bay b1 84
Abbot, Mount b2 85
Abbotsbury d6 163
Abbotsford, Can. b1 262
Abbotsford, U.S.A. a3 254
Abbott b4 261
Abbottabad f3 128
'Abd al 'Azīz, Jabal h4 209
Ābdānān l5 137
Abdi l4 151
Abdollāhābād r3 137
Abéché b5 218
Abeïbara e5 221
Abejar b3 192
Abejuela d5 193
Abejukolo f4 223
Abela b6 191
Abel Tasman National Park d4 77
Abemama H 75
Abengourou d4 222
Abenójar f6 191
Åbenrå c3 158
Abens g4 175
Abensberg f4 175
Abeokuta e4 223
Aberaeron b4 163
Abercarn c5 163
Abercastle a5 163
Aberchirder f2 164
Abercrombie f1 83
Aberdare c5 163
Aberdare National Park b4 226
Aberdaron b4 162
Aberdeen, Aust. k12 81
Aberdeen, R.S.A. f6 234
Aberdeen, Scotland, U.K. g2 164
Aberdeen, U.K. f2 164
Aberdeen, Mississippi, U.S.A. e3 258
Aberdeen, South Dakota, U.S.A. d2 260
Aberdeen, Washington, U.S.A. b2 262
Aberdeen Road f6 234
Aberdeenshire f2 164
Aberdovey b4 163
Aberfeldy e3 164
Aberffraw b3 162
Aberfoyle d3 164
Abergavenny c5 163
Abergele c3 162
Abergynolwyn c4 162
Abernathy c5 261
Abernethy e3 164
Abersoch b4 162
Abertillery c5 163
Aberystwyth b4 163
Abetone e5 197
Abez' k2 147
Abhā f4 219
Abhanpur g9 124
Abhar m3 137
Abhar Rūd m3 137
Abia f4 223
Abiad, Bahr el d5 218
Ābīata Hāyk' b2 226
Abibe, Serranía de b2 284
Abidjan d4 222
Abiego d2 192
Abijatta-Shalla National Park b2 226
Abi, Lagune d4 222
Abilene, Kansas, U.S.A. d4 260
Abilene, Texas, U.S.A. d5 261
Abingdon, U.K. e5 163
Abingdon, U.S.A. h1 259
Abington e4 256
Abinsk e3 148
Abión b3 192
Ab-i-Safed k9 120
Abiseo, Parque Nacional b5 284
Abisko nationalpark g2 154
Abisko Östra g2 154
Abita Springs d4 258
Abitibi n6 251
Abitibi, Lake p6 251
Abja-Paluoja l3 157
Abla b7 193
Ablach e5 174
Ablah d3 138
Ablis g4 183
Abminga b9 81
Abnûb c8 136
Abohar g5 128
Aboisso d4 222
Aboke f2 225
Abomey e4 223
Abondance c4 184
Abongabong, Gunung c13 103
Abong Mbang b3 224
Abony j4 171
Abooso d4 222
Aborigen, Pik q3 119
Aborlan b6 100
Abou Déia a5 218
Abourasséin, Mont d2 224
Aboyne f2 164
Abqaiq m9 137
Abra, Canal b6 295
Abraham's Bay h3 271
Abra, Lago del f5 297
Abrantes b5 191
Abra Pampa d4 292
Abrau l6 97
Abraveses c4 190
Abre Campo g4 291
Abreiro c3 190
Abreschviller d2 184
'Abri d3 218
Abriès c6 185
Abrolhos, Arquipélago dos j3 291
Abrosovo c2 150
Abrud f2 201
Abruka k3 157
Abruzzo c2 198
Abruzzo, Parco Nazionale d' c3 198
Absaroka Range h3 262
Absdorf g1 177
Absecon f5 257
Abşeron Yarımadası c7 120
Abtenau e2 176
Abtsgmünd e4 174
Abū al Khaşīb m6 137
Abū 'Arīsh f4 219
Abu Aweigîla c6 139
Abū Ballāş c3 218
Abu Deleiq d4 218
Abu Durba d7 136
Ābū el Jurdhān d6 139
Abufari e5 285
Abu Gubeiha d5 218
Abu Haggag c1 218
Abū Ḩallūfah, Jabal e5 139
Abū Hallūfah, Jabal e5 139
Abu Hamed d4 218
Abuja f4 223
Abū Kamāl h5 209
Abu Kebîr c6 136
Abu Ku c5 218
Abū Lahw, Ra's c1 218
Abū Latt Island f4 219
Abū Madd, Ra's e3 219
Abu Matariq c5 218
Abu Mena c1 218
Abumombazi d3 224
Abu Musa q9 137
Abunã d1 292
Abunai d4 284
Ābune Yosēf e5 219
Abū Nujaym h2 221
Abu Qîr c6 137
Abu Qurqâs c8 136
Abu Road f8 129
Abu Shagara, Ras e3 219
Abu Shanab c5 218
Abu Simbel, Egypt d3 218
Abu Simbel, Aswân, Egypt d3 218
Abū Şukhayr k6 137
Abuta Ab2 114
Abū Ţarfā', Wādī b7 139
Abut Head c5 77
Abu Tig c8 136
Abū 'Uwayqilah RJ c6 139
Abuye Meda b1 226
Abuyog e5 100
Abu Zabad c5 218
Abū Ẓabī e6 116
Abu Zenîma d7 136
Abwong f2 225
Åby g3 156
Abyad c5 218
Åbybro c1 158
Abydos d7 86
Abyei e2 225
Åbyn h4 154
Abzakovo j5 147
Acacias c3 284
Acacoyagua a3 276
Acadia National Park m3 255
Açaí c5 290
Açailândia c3 288
Acajutiba e4 288
Acajutla c4 276
Acala a2 276
Acambaro d3 274
Acambay e4 275
Acancéh q7 273
Acandí j6 277
A Cañiza b2 190
Acaponeta, Mex. b2 274
Acaponeta, Nayarit, Mex. b2 274
Acapulco e5 275
Acará, Braz. c2 288
Acará, Pará, Braz. c2 288
Acará, Lago, Braz. e4 285
Acará, Lago, Braz. e5 285
Acará Miri c2 288
Acaraú, Braz. d2 288
Acaraú, Ceará, Braz. d2 288
Acaray a6 290
Acarí, Braz. e3 288
Acarí, Peru c3 292
Acarí, Arequipa, Peru c3 292
Acarigua d2 284
Acari, Serra f3 285
Acâş l4 171
Acate d7 199
Acatenango b3 276
Acateno f3 275
Acatlan e4 275
Acatlán f4 275
Acatlán de Juárez c3 274
Acatlán de Pérez Figueroa f4 275
Acatzingo f4 275
Acay, Nevado de d4 292
Acayucán g5 275
Accadia e3 198
Accettura f4 198
Acciaroli e4 198
Accomac j7 255
Accord f3 257
Accous b6 187
Accra d4 222
Accumoli h7 197
Aceba g2 297
Acedera e5 191
Acedo b2 192
Aceguá f2 294
Aceh c13 103
Acered c3 192
Acerenza e4 198
Acerno e4 198
Acerra d4 198
Aceuchal d6 191
Acevedo g2 297
Ach, Aus. j4 175
Ach, Ger. g5 175
Achacachi d3 292
Achaguas d2 284
Achalpur e9 124
Achampet f4 126
Achar j2 297
Acheleia a2 138
Acheloös b4 210
Acheng p3 113
Achenkirch c2 176
Achern g3 174
Achilleio c3 210
Achill Head a3 165
Achill Island a3 165
Achim e2 172
Achin e3 128
Achiras e2 296
Achisay m6 121
Achlades, Akra f6 211
Achladochori d1 210
Achnasheen c2 164
Achno b1 138
Ačhoj-Martan g4 149
A'Chralaig c2 164
Aci Castello e7 199
Aci Catena e7 199
Acıgöl b4 208
Ačikulak g3 149
Ačimovy 2-e n3 147
Ačinsk k4 118
Acireale e7 199
Ačit j4 147
Ackley e3 260
Acklins Island g3 266
Acle h4 162
Acobamba c2 292
Acolin j6 183
Acomayo, Cusco, Peru c2 292
Acomayo, Huánuco, Peru b1 292
Aconcagua b2 296
Aconcagua, Cerro c2 296
Aconquija, Nevado de c1 294
Acopiara e3 288
Acora d3 292
Açores, Arquipélago dos A 220
Acornhoek j2 235
A Coruña b1 190
A Coruña b1 190
Acostambo b2 292
Acoyapa e5 276
Acquacalda d6 199
Acqualagna g6 197
Acquapendente f7 197
Acquarossa c3 196
Acquasanta Terme h7 197
Acquasparta g7 197
Acquaviva Picena c2 198
Acquedolci d6 199
Acquigny g3 183
Acqui Terme c5 196
Acra f2 257
Acraman, Lake b12 81
Acre, Braz. c1 292
Acre, Braz. d2 292
Acre, HaZafon, Isr. d4 138
Acreúna c2 290
Acri f5 199
A Cruz de Incio c2 190
Acsa h4 171
Acteopan e4 275
Actopán e3 275
Actopan f4 275
Açuçena g3 291
Açu, Lago d2 288
Aculco de Espinosa e3 275
Acultzingo f4 275
Acungui d6 290
Acurenam g5 223
Acushnet k3 257
Ada, Ghana e4 223
Ada, Serbia/Mont. j6 171
Ada, Minnesota, U.S.A. e7 250
Ada, Oklahoma, U.S.A. a2 258
Ādaba b2 226
Adabîya a7 139
Adacao C 74
Adács h4 171
Adair b1 258
Adair, Cape q1 243
Adairville f1 258
Adaja f3 190
Adak Ac2 247
Adak Island Ac1 247
Adak Strait Ac2 247
Ådalen g5 154
Ådalsliden f5 154
Adamantina c4 290
Adamaoua b2 224
Adamaoua, Massif de l' b2 224
Adamas e6 211
Adamawa g4 223
Adamclisi h3 201
Adamello e3 196
Adamello-Brenta, Parco Naturale e3 196
Adaminaby j13 81
Ādamī Tulu b2 226
Adam, Mount e6 295
Adamov e2 170
Adamów l4 169
Adams, Massachusetts, U.S.A. g2 257
Adams, New York, U.S.A. h4 255
Adam's Bridge A 127
Adams Island C 77
Adams Lake h6 248
Adams, Mount c2 262
Adams Mountain m5 247
Adamsville e2 258
Adamuz f6 191
'Adan f5 219
Adana, Tur. e4 208
Adana, Adana, Tur. e4 208
Adanero f4 190
Adang, Teluk j5 99
Adão c4 190
Adare c4 165
Adare, Cape y2 298
Adavale g8 81
Adda, C.A.R. d2 224
Adda, Italy d3 196
Ad Daghghārah k5 137
Ad Dahnā' g3 219
Ad Dakhla a4 220
Ad Dālī e1 138
Aḑ Ḑāli' f5 219
Ad Dammām n8 136
Adda Nord, Parco dell' d4 196
Ad Dār al Ḩamrā' f8 137
Adda Sud, Parco dell' d4 196
Ad Dawādimī f3 219
Ad Dawḩah n9 137
Addax, Réserve Naturelle Intégrale dite Sanctuaire des f2 223
Adderbury e4 163
Ad Dibdibah g2 219
Aḑ Ḑiffah c1 218
Ad Dīmās e3 138
Addison c2 256
Ad Dīwānīyah k6 137
Addo f6 235
Addo Elephant National Park f6 235
Ad Duwayd j6 137
Ad Duwayḩirah k8 136
Adel e3 260
Adelaide, Northern Territory, Aust. k3 86
Adelaide, Aust. d13 81
Adelaide, Bah. l7 259
Adelaide, R.S.A. g6 235
Adelaide Island kk1 298
Adelaide River k3 86
Adelboden b3 196
Adelebsen e4 172
Adelfia f3 198
Adelia María e2 297
Adélie Coast v1 298
Adélie Land u1 298
Adelong j13 81
Adelsdorf e5 175
Adelsheim e2 174
Adelunga n6 121
Ademuz c4 193
Aden, 'Adan, Yemen c8 116
Aden, 'Adan, Yemen f5 219
Adenau e4 159
Adendorp f6 234
Aden, Gulf of d1 226
Aderbissinat f2 223
Adesar e9 129
Adgiyn Tsagaan Nuur a3 112
Adhanah, Wādī g4 219
Adh Dhayd q9 136
Adhi Kot e4 128
Adhoi e9 129
Adi f3 225
Ādī Ārk'ay e5 219
Adieu, Cape k13 87
Adige f4 196
Ādīgrat e5 219
Adıgüzel Barajı b3 208
Adi Keyih e5 219
Adi Kwala e5 219
Adilabad f3 126
Adilanga f3 225
Adilcevaz j3 209
Adin c5 262
Adīrī g3 221
Adirondack Mountains j3 255
Ādīs Ābeba, Eth. b2 226
Ādīs Ābeba, Ādīs Ābeba, Eth. b2 226
Adiščevo g3 151
Ādīs Zemen e5 219
Adıyaman, Tur. g4 209
Adıyaman, Adıyaman, Tur. g4 209
Adjelman, Oued e4 221
Adjerar e4 221
Adjoantali f4 221
Adjud h2 201
Adjuntas A 270
Adlington d3 162
Adliswil c2 196
Admiralty Bay k4 255
Admiralty Gulf g4 86
Admiralty Island l4 247
Admiralty Island National Monument - Kootznoowoo Wilderness l4 247
Admont f2 177
Ado-Ekiti f4 223
Adok f2 225
Adolfo Gonzáles Chaves g5 297
Adonara m9 99
Adoni e5 126
Adony g4 171
Adorf, Ger. h2 175
Adorf (Diemelsee) d4 172
Adoufe c3 190
Adoumandjali c3 224
Adour a5 187
Adra, Spain a8 193
Adra, Andalucía, Spain a8 193
'Adrā' e3 138
Adradas b3 192
Adrados f3 190
Adranga f3 225
Adrano d7 199
Adrar, Alg. f4 221
Adrar, Alg. d3 220
Adrar, Maurit. b4 220
Adrar des Ifôghas e2 223
Adrar, Ḑhar b4 220
Adrar Souttouf a4 220
Adrar Tamgak f2 223
Adrasmon m7 121
Adré b5 218
Adria g4 196
Adrian, Georgia, U.S.A. h3 259
Adrian, Michigan, U.S.A. d5 254
Adrian, Texas, U.S.A. c5 261
Adrigole b5 165
Aduana Pejerrey b4 296
Adusa e3 225
Adventure, Bahía b5 295
Ādwa e5 219
Adyča p3 119
Adygeja, Respublika f3 148
Adygejsk e3 148
Adyk g3 149
Adzaneta d4 193
Adzhiyan q3 136
Adzopé d4 222
Adz'vavom j2 147
Æbelø d3 158
Aegna l3 157
Aegviidu l3 157
Aeon Point H 75
Ærø d4 158
Aeron b4 163
Ærøskøbing d4 158
Aerzen e3 172
A Estrada b2 190
Aetos, Dytiki Makedonia, Grc. b2 210
Aetos, Peloponnisos, Grc. b5 211
Afaga, Pointe L 75
'Afak k5 137
Afar c1 226
Aff c5 182
Afféri d4 222
Afghanistan d5 92

AFGHANISTAN

THE ISLAMIC STATE OF AFGHANISTAN
Area 652,225km^2 (251,773sq miles)
Capital Kabul
Organizations ECO, IDB, OIC
Population 22,930,000
Pop. growth (%) -1
Life expectancy 42 (m); 42 (f)
Languages Pashto, Dari (dialect of Farsi or Iranian), many local languages
Literacy 31.5%
Currency new afghani (US $1 = 43 new afghani)
GDP (US million $) 21,000
GDP per head ($US) 915

Afgooye d3 226
Afife b3 190
Afikpo f4 223
Afiq d4 138
Åfjord c5 154
Aflao e4 223
Aflenz Kurort g2 177
Aflou e2 221
Afmadow c3 226
Afognak Island f4 246
A Fonsagrada c1 190
Afonso Cláudio h4 291
A Forxa c2 190
Afragola d4 198
Afram d4 222
Afrânio d3 288
Āfrēra Terara f5 219
'Afrīn, Nahr f4 209
Afşin f3 209
Afsluitdijk DK d1 159
Afton, New York, U.S.A. e2 256
Afton, Oklahoma, U.S.A. b1 258
Afton, Wyoming, U.S.A. h4 262
Afuá b2 288
'Afula d4 138
'Afula 'Illit d4 138
Afyon, Tur. c3 208
Afyon, Afyon, Tur. c3 208
Afzalgarh d5 130
Agadez, Niger g2 223
Agadez, Agadez, Niger f2 223
Agadir c2 220
Agâdîr, Râs a4 220
Agadyr' p3 121
Agaete Ad2 189
Agaie f4 223
Agalta, Sierra de e3 276
Agana, Agaña, Guam C 74
Agapovka j5 147
Āgaro b2 226
Agartala m8 125
Agasiz, Cerro b6 295
Agassiz Fracture Zone p8 301
Agassiz National Wildlife Refuge e1 260
Agathonisi Ab1 211
Agats k7 97
Agatti c7 126
Agattu Island Aa1 247
Agattu Strait Aa1 247
Agbor Bojiboji f4 223
Agboville d4 222
Ağcabädi g4 149
Ağdam g5 149
Ağdaş g4 149
Agde f5 187
Agen c4 187
Àger e2 192
Agerbæk b3 158
Āgere Maryam b2 226
Ägerisee c2 196
Agernæs d3 158
Agerskov c3 158
Agersø e3 158
Aggeneys c4 234
Agger c5 172
Aggersund c1 158
Aggius Ab2 198
Aggteleki j3 171
Āghā Jārī m6 137
Aghil Pass c1 130
Aghireşu f2 201
Aghzoumal, Sabkhat b4 220
Agia Aikaterini, Akra a3 210
Agia, Akra c4 210
Agia Anna d4 210
Agiabampo e4 272
Agia Galini e7 211
Agia Marina, Attiki, Grc. e4 210
Agia Marina, Notio Aigaio, Grc. Ab1 210
Agia Napa c2 138
Agia Pelagia, Attiki, Grc. c6 211
Agia Pelagia, Kriti, Grc. f7 211
Agiasos g3 210
Agia Triada, Dytiki Ellas, Grc. b5 211
Agia Triada, Peloponnisos, Grc. c5 211
Agia Vervara f7 211
Agighiol j3 201
Ağın g3 209
Aginskij Burjackij Avtonomnyj Okrug e2 94
Aginskoye e2 94
Agiofyllo b3 210
Agioi Apostoloi d4 210
Agioi Deka e7 211
Agioi Theodoroi, Dytiki Makedonia, Grc. b3 210
Agioi Theodoroi, Peloponnisos, Grc. d5 211
Agiokampos c3 210
Agion Oros e2 210
Agios Andreas c5 211
Agios Charalampos f2 210
Agios Dimitrios, Attiki, Grc. d5 211
Agios Dimitrios, Kentriki Makedonia, Grc. c2 210
Agios Dimitrios, Peloponnisos, Grc. c6 211
Agios Dimitrios, Akra e5 211
Agios Efstratios, Grc. f3 210
Agios Efstratios, Voreio Aigaio, Grc. e3 210
Agios Fokas, Akra g3 210
Agios Georgios, Grc. d5 211
Agios Georgios, Sterea Ellas, Grc. b4 210
Agios Ioannis c6 211
Agios Ioannis, Akra f7 211
Agios Kirykos Ab1 210
Agios Konstantinos, Peloponnisos, Grc. c5 211
Agios Konstantinos, Sterea Ellas, Grc. c4 210
Agios Kosmas, Akra f5 210
Agios Loukas c2 210
Agios Mamas a2 138
Agios Myron f7 211
Agios Nikolaos, Ionioi Nisoi, Grc. a5 211
Agios Nikolaos, Ipeiros, Grc. a3 210
Agios Nikolaos, Kentriki Makedonia, Grc. d2 210
Agios Nikolaos, Kriti, Grc. f7 211
Agios Nikolaos, Peloponnisos, Grc. c6 211
Agios Nikolaos, Sterea Ellas, Grc. b4 210
Agios Paraskevi g3 210
Agios Petros, Kentriki Makedonia, Grc. c2 210
Agios Petros, Peloponnisos, Grc. c5 211
Agios Seryios b1 138
Agios Theodoros c1 138
Agios Vasileios, Kentriki Makedonia, Grc. d2 210
Agios Vasileios, Peloponnisos, Grc. c5 211
Agios Vasileios, Sterea Ellas, Grc. d4 210
Agios Vasilios, Akra d4 210
Agiou Andreou, Akra a4 210
Agiou Orous, Kolpos d2 210
Agira d7 199
Agirwat Hills e4 219
Agkistri d5 211
Aglientu Ab1 198
Agly e6 187
Agnantero b3 210
Agna Vermelha, Represa c4 290
Agnes, Mount, South Australia, Aust. j10 87
Agnes, Mount, Western Australia, Aust. g5 86
Agnew e10 87
Agnia, Pampa de c4 295
Agnibilékrou d4 222
Agnita g3 201
Agno f4 196
Agnone d3 198
Agogna c4 196
Agogo d4 222
A Golada c2 190
Agön g2 156
Agona Swedru d4 222
Agoncillo b2 192
Agon-Coutainville d3 182
Agong a7 112
Agordo g3 196
Agost d6 193
Agou, Mont e4 223
Agoura e7 265
Agout d5 187
Agra, Grc. g3 210
Agra, India d6 130
Agraciada h2 297
Agrafiotis b3 210
Agrahanskij Poluostrov g4 149
Agramón c6 193
Agramunt f3 192
Agreda c3 192
Agrelo c2 296
Ağrı, Tur. j3 209
Ağrı, Ağrı, Tur. j3 209
Agria Gramvousa d7 211
Agrigento, Sicilia, Italy c7 199
Agrigento, Sicilia, Italy c7 199
Agrihan A 74
Agrilos b5 211
Agrinio b4 210
Agriovotano d3 210
Agropoli d4 198
Agros b2 138
Agryz m3 151
Ågskaret d3 154
Ağstafa g4 149
Ağsu h4 149
Agua Blanca, Arg. e4 296
Agua Blanca, Mex. c1 276
Agua Blanca Iturbide e3 275
Água Boa g2 291
Agua Brava, Laguna b2 274
Agua, Cabo del d7 193
Agua Caliente, Bol. e3 293
Agua Caliente, Mex. c3 274
Agua Clara d2 292
Água Clara b4 290
Aguaclara c3 284
Aguada, Mex. b1 276
Aguada, P.R. A 270
Agua de Correra d5 274
Agua de Oro e1 297
Aguadilla A 270
Aguado Cecilio c4 294
Agua Doce do Norte h3 291
Agua Dulce, Bol. d2 292
Agua Dulce, Mex. g4 275
Aguadulce, Pan. g6 277
Aguadulce, Andalucía, Spain f7 191
Aguadulce, Andalucía, Spain b8 193
Agua Dulce a6 258
Aguamilpa b3 274
Aguanaval c1 274
Aguanga g8 265
Agua Nueva a1 274
Aguanus l3 253
Aguapeí, Braz. c4 290
Aguapeí, Mato Grosso, Braz. f3 293
Aguapeí, Serra f3 293
Aguapey e1 294
Agua Prieta j10 263
Aguarague, Cordillera de e4 293
Aguaray e4 293
A Guardia b3 190
Aguarico b4 284
Aguaro-Guariquito, Parque Nacional d2 284
Aguaruto f5 272
Aguas, Spain c7 193
Aguas, Aragón, Spain d2 192
Águas Belas e3 288
Aguascalientes, Mex. c2 274
Aguascalientes, Aguascalientes, Mex. c3 274
Aguas Corrientes j3 297
Aguas de Busot d6 193
Águas Formosas h2 291
Águas Vermelhas h1 291
Agua Verde b2 274
Aguaviva d4 192
Aguaytia b1 292
Agua Zarca h10 263
A Gudiña c2 190
Agudo f6 191
Agudos d5 290
Águeda, Port d4 190
Águeda, Port b4 190
Agueda, Embalse de d4 190
Aguelhok e5 221
Aguema d6 224
Aguemour e3 221
Agüera a1 192
Agugliano h6 197
Aguiar da Beira c4 190
Aguié f3 223
Aguieira, Barragem da b4 190
Aguijan A 74
Aguila g9 263
Aguilafuente f3 190
Águila, Punta del a1 192
Aguilar de Campóo f2 190
Aguilar de Campóo, Embalse de f2 190
Aguilar de la Frontera f7 191
Águilas c7 193
Aguililla c4 274
Agüimes Ad3 189
Aguirre, Bahía c6 295
Aguisan d5 100
Aguisejo a3 192
Aguja, Cerro b4 295
Āgula'i e5 219
Agulhas d7 234
Agulhas Bank n13 302
Agulhas, Cape d7 234
Agulhas National Park c7 234
Agulhas Negras f5 291
Agulhas Plateau n13 302
Agulo Ab2 189
Agung, Gunung h9 99
'Agur c5 139
Agusan e6 100
Agustín Roca O'Higgins g3 297
Agutaya, Phil. c5 100
Agutaya, Phil. c5 100
Agvali g4 149
Ahamasu e4 223
Ahar, Rajasthan, India f8 129
Ahar, India d5 130
Ahar, Iran l2 137
Ahascragh c3 165
Ahaura c5 77
Ahaus f2 159
Ahé K 75
Ahémé, Lac e4 223
Aherlow c4 165
Aḩihud d4 138
Ahillones e6 191
Ahinski, Kanal p3 169
Ahipara d1 76
Ahipara Bay d1 76
Ahklun Mountains d4 246
Ahlat j3 209
Ahlden (Aller) e3 172
Ahlen c4 172
Ahmadabad f9 129
Ahmadnagar d3 126
Ahmadpur East e6 129
Ahmadpur Sial e5 128
Ahmetli a3 208
Ahoghill e2 165
Ahome e5 272
Ahore f8 129
Ahorn e3 175
Ahoskie h7 255
Ahr b2 174
Ahram n7 137
Ahrensbök d4 158
Ahrensburg d5 158
Ahrenshagen f4 158
Ahse d4 172
Ahta Dağı, Tur. j3 209
Ahta Dağı, Tur. j3 209
Ähtäri k5 155
Ähtärinjärvi l1 157
Ähtävänjoki j5 155
Ahtubinsk g2 149
Ahty g4 149
Ahu f2 111
Āhū m6 137
Ahuacatlán b3 274
Ahuachapán c4 276
Ahualulco, Jalisco, Mex. c3 274
Ahualulco, San Luis Potosí, Mex. d2 274
Ahuatempan e4 275
Ahuazotepec e3 275
Ahuijullo c4 274
Ahun e2 186
Ahunui K 75
Ahuriri b6 77
Åhus f5 156
Aḩuzzam c5 139
Ahvāz m6 137
Ahzar, Vallée de l' e2 223
Ai-Ais b3 234
Ai-Ais Hot Springs and Fish River Canyon Park b3 234
Aiani b2 210
Aianteio d5 211
Aiapuá e4 285
Aiapuá, Lago e4 285
Aibag Gol f5 112
Aibar c2 192
Aichach f2 175
Aichi g4 115
Aidanskoe Nagor'e n4 119
Aidone d7 199
Aiello Calabro f5 199

306 Aigeira → Al Ḩasā

Aigeira c4 210
Aigeiros f1 210
Aigen im Mühlkreis e1 176
Aigialousa c1 138
Aigina, Grc. ▭ d5 211
Aigina, Attiki, Grc. d5 211
Aiginio c2 210
Aigio c4 210
Aigle a3 195
Aignay-le-Duc a3 184
Aigosthena d4 210
Aigoual, Mont △ f4 187
Aigre c3 186
Aigrefeuille-d'Aunis b2 186
Aiguá f2 294
Aiguafreda g3 192
Aiguebelle c5 185
Aigue, Mont △ k5 182
Aigueperse f2 186
Aigues ≈ b6 185
Aigues-Mortes a7 184
'Aigües Tortes i Estany de Sant Maurici, Parc Nacional d ☆ f2 192
Aiguille du Midi △ c5 185
Aiguille, Pointe de l' ◄ a2 186
Aiguilles d'Arves △ c5 185
Aiguillon c4 187
Aigurande d2 186
Aija b1 292
Aikawa h2 115
Aiken j3 259
Ailao Shan ▣ c6 104
Aileron a7 80
Aileu n9 99
Ailigandi h6 277
Ailinginae ▭ D 74
Ailinglaplap ▭ D 74
Aillant-sur-Tholon j5 183
Aille ≈ c7 185
Ailly-le-Haut-Clocher g2 183
Ailly-sur-Noye h3 183
Ailly-sur-Somme h3 183
Ailsa Craig ▭ c4 164
Ailuk ▭ D 74
Aimargues a7 184
Aime c5 185
Aimogasta c1 294
Aimorés h3 291
Aimorés, Serra dos ▣ h3 291
Ain, Fr. ≈ b4 184
Ain, Rhône-Alpes, Fr. ▣ b4 184
Aïn Aarab d3 138
Aïn Aata d3 138
Ainata e2 138
Ainaži l4 157
Aïn Beïda f1 221
Aïn Beni Mathar d2 220
'Aïn Ben Tili c3 220
Aïn Defla e1 221
Aïn Deheb e2 221
Aïn Mdila ⊙ f2 221
Aïn-M'Lila f1 221
Ainos National Park ☆ a4 210
Ainsa e2 192
Aïn Sefra d2 220
Ainslie, Lake ○ m5 253
Ainsworth d3 260
Aïn Temouchent d1 220
Aïntoura d3 138
Aïn Zhalta d3 138
Ainzón c3 192
Aipe b3 284
Aiquile d3 292
Air ▭ d3 98
Airaines g3 183
Airdrie e4 164
Aire ≈ a1 184
Aire, Canal d' ═ h2 183
Aire, Illa de l' ▭ A 193
Aire, Serra de ▣ b5 191
Aire-sur-l'Adour b5 187
Aire-sur-la-Lys a4 159
Air et du Ténéré, Réserve Naturelle Intégrale de l' ★ g2 223
Air Force Island ▭ q2 243
Airgin Sum f4 112
Airhitam ≈ f6 98
Airhitam, Teluk ◄ f6 98
Air Jerneh c3 101
Aïr, Massif de l' ▣ f2 223
Airolo c3 196
Airpanas n8 99
Air Putih c3 101
Airvault e6 182
Aisatung Mountain △ a5 102
Aisau k6 97
Aisch ≈ f3 175
Aisén ▣ b5 295
Aisey-sur-Seine a3 184
Aishalton f3 285
Ai Shan △ g1 111
Aishihik k3 247
Aishihik Lake ○ k3 247
Aisjaure ○ f3 154
Aisne, Fr. ≈ h3 183
Aisne, Picardie, Fr. ▣ j3 183
Aissa, Djebel △ d2 220
Aisymi f1 210
Aisy-sur-Armançon a3 184
Aïta el Foukhar d3 138
Aitana △ d6 193
Aitape l6 97
Aiterach ≈ h4 175
Aitkin g7 250
Aitoliko b4 210
Aitona e3 192
Aitrach g4 174
Aiud f2 201
Aiviekste ≈ m3 157
Aiwo B 74
Aix ▭ f3 186
Aix-en-Othe j4 183
Aix-en-Provence b7 185
Aixe-sur-Vienne d3 186
Aix-les-Bains b5 185
Aiy Adi e5 219
Aiyang n5 113
Aiyetoro e4 223
Aizawl n8 125
Aizenay d6 182
Aizkraukle l4 157
Aizpute j4 157
Aizu-wakamatsu h3 115
Aj ≈ k1 149
Ajaccio A 185
Ajaccio, Golfe d' ◄ A 185
Ajacuba e3 275
Ajai Game Reserve ☆ f3 225
Ajaigarh g7 124
Ajajú ≈ c3 284
Ajak l3 171
Ajalpán f4 275
Ajana b10 87
Ajaokuta f4 223
Ajaureforsen e4 154
Ajayan Bay ◄ C 74
Ajdābiyā b1 218
Ajdovščina e4 176
Ajhal m3 119
Ajigasawa j1 115
Ajil c3 101
Ajka f4 171
Ajkino g3 146
'Ajlūn, Jordan ▣ d4 138
'Ajlūn, 'Ajlūn, Jordan d4 139
Ajmah, Jabal al ' ▣ c7 139
'Ajman q9 137
Ajmer g7 129
Ajnala b4 130
Ajo, Spain g1 190
Ajo, U.S.A. g9 263
Ajo, Cabo de ◄ g1 190
Ajofrín g5 191
Ajon, Ostrov ▭ s2 119
Ajoquentla f3 275
Ajoya a1 274
Ajrestan c4 128
Ajuchitlán d4 274
Ajuy d5 100
Akabira Ac2 114
Akabli e3 221
Akaki b1 138
Āk'ak'i Beseka b2 226
Akalkot e4 126
Akan National Park ☆ Ad2 114
Akanthou b1 138
Akarnanika ▣ a4 210
Akaroa d5 77
Akaroa Harbour ◄ d5 77
Akasha d3 218
'Akāshāt g5 136
Akashi f4 114
Äkäsjärvi ○ k3 155
Äkäsjoki ≈ j3 155
Akasztó h5 171
Akbakay p5 121
Akbalyk s4 121
Akbar d3 128
Akbarābād p7 137
Akbarpur h6 124
Akbeit n2 121
Akbou e1 221
Akbulak j2 149
Akçakale g4 209
Akçakoca c2 208
Akçaova a4 208
Akchakaya, Vpadina ⌒ g7 120
Akchār ≈ b4 220
Akchatau p4 121
Akdağ △ c4 208
Ak Dağı, Tur. △ c4 208
Ak Dağı, Tur. ▣ h3 209
Akdağmadeni e3 208
Akdepe k4 149
Akelamo h5 97
Aken h4 173
Åkerån ≈ e5 154
Åkersberga h3 157
Akershus ▣ d3 156
Åkersjön ○ f5 154
Akespe h4 120
Aketi d3 224
Akhalgori k1 209
Akhalk'alak'i j2 209
Akhal'skaya Oblast' ▣ g8 120
Akhalts'ikhe j2 209
Akhisar a3 208
Akhmīm c8 136
Akhnoor b3 130
Aki e5 114
Akiachak d3 246
Akiak d3 246
Akiaki ▭ K 75
Akiéni b4 224
Akıncı Burun ◄ e4 209
Akıncılar g2 209
Åkirkeby f5 156
Akita, Japan ▣ j2 115
Akita, Akita, Japan j2 115
Ak"jar k2 149
Akjoujt b5 220
Akka c3 220
Akkala k4 149
Akkani b2 246
Akkerendam Nature Reserve ☆ c5 234
Akkeshi Ad2 114
Akkol', Akmolinskaya Oblast', Kaz. n1 121
Akkol', Almatinskaya Oblast', Kaz. q5 121
Akkol', Zhambylskaya Oblast', Kaz. n6 121
Akköy a4 208
Akkrum d1 159
Akku r2 121
Akkum k5 120
Akkuş f2 209
Akkyr, Gory ▣ e7 120
Aklampa e4 223
Aklavik l1 247
Akmena ≈ k5 157
Akmeņrags ◄ j4 157
Akmeqit c1 130
Akmola, Akmolinskaya Oblast', Kaz. n2 121
Akmolinskaya Oblast' ▣ m2 121
Akniste l4 157
Aknoul d2 220
Aknysta ≈ l5 157
Akō f4 114
Akobo f2 225
Akobo Wenz ≈ f2 225
Akola e9 124
Akom II g5 223
Akonolinga b3 224
Akop e2 225
Akordat e4 219
Akören d4 208
Akosombo Dam ⌒ e4 223
Akot, India e9 124
Akot, Sudan f2 225
Akouménaye g3 285
Akoupé d4 222
Akpatok Island ▭ q3 243
Akqi s7 121
Akrafnio d4 210
Akranes A 152
Akrathos, Akra ◄ e2 210
Akrehamn a3 156
Akréréb f2 223
Akritas, Akra ◄ b6 211
Akron, Colorado, U.S.A. c3 260
Akron, New York, U.S.A. b1 256
Akron, Ohio, U.S.A. f5 254
Akron, Pennsylvania, U.S.A. d4 256
Akrotiri a2 138
Akrotirion Bay ◄ b2 138
Akša g1 112
Aksai Chin (China) ▣ e5 92
Aksakovo h5 147
Aksaray, Tur. ▣ d3 208
Aksaray, Aksaray, Tur. e3 208
Aksarka l2 147
Aksay j2 149
Aksayqin Hu ○ e2 130
Akşehir c3 208
Akşehir Gölü ○ c3 208
Akseki c4 208
Akselhovde △ d2 156
Aks-e Rostam ≈ q7 137
Akshatau j2 149
Akshiganak j3 120
Akshiy r6 121
Akshukur h4 149
Aksu, Xinjiang Uygur Zizhiqu, China t6 121
Aksu, China t7 121
Aksu, Kaz. ≈ s5 121
Aksu, Almatinskaya Oblast', Kaz. s5 121
Aksu, Pavlodarskaya Oblast', Kaz. r1 121
Aksu, Severnyy Kazakhstan, Kaz. n1 121
Aksu, Tur. ≈ c4 208
Aksuat, Kostanayskaya Oblast', Kaz. k2 120
Aksuat, Vostochnyy Kazakhstan, Kaz. u4 121
Aksu-Ayuly p3 121
Aksu He ≈ t7 121
Āksum e5 219
Aksüme t5 121
Aksuyek q5 121
Aktanyš h5 147
Aktas Dağı △ j3 209
Aktash b1 128
Aktau, Karagandinskaya Oblast', Kaz. p2 121
Aktau, Karagandinskaya Oblast', Kaz. n4 121
Aktau, Mangghystau Oblysy, Kaz. h4 149
Akto r8 121
Aktobe k2 149
Aktogay, Karagandinskaya Oblast', Kaz. q3 121
Aktogay, Karagandinskaya Oblast', Kaz. q3 121
Aktogay, Pavlodarskaya Oblast', Kaz. q1 121
Aktogay, Vostochnyy Kazakhstan, Kaz. s4 121
Aktsyabrski c1 148
Aktumsyk k3 149
Ak-Tüz q6 121
Aktyubinsk k2 149
Aktyubinskaya Oblast' ▣ j3 120
Akula d3 224
Akun Island ▭ c5 246
Akure f4 223
Akureyri A 152
Akuroa e2 76
Akutan c5 246
Akutan Pass ═ c5 246
Akwa Ibom ▣ f5 223
Akwanga f4 223
Akzhal p4 121
Akzhar, Kyzylordinskaya Oblast', Kaz. k5 120
Akzhar, Vostochnyy Kazakhstan, Kaz. u4 121
Akzhar, Zhambylskaya Oblast', Kaz. n6 121
Akzhaykyn, Ozero ○ m5 121
Ål c2 156
Ala f4 196
Alabama, U.S.A. ▣ f3 258
Alabama, Alabama, U.S.A. ≈ f4 258
Alabaster f3 258
Ala-Buka n7 121
Al Abyaḑ g3 221
Al Abyār b1 218
Alaca e2 208
Alacahan g3 209
Alaçam e2 208
Alacant, Valencia, Spain d6 193
Alachua h5 259
Aladağ d4 208
Ala Dağlar ▣ j3 209
Ala Dağları ▣ e4 208
Al 'Adasiyah d5 139
Alà dei Sardi Ab2 198
Alad'ino f4 150
Alaejos e3 190
Al Aflāj ⌄ g3 219
Alagadiço e3 285
Alagir k1 209
Alagna Valsesia b4 196
Alagnon ≈ e3 186
Alagoas ▣ e3 288
Alagoinhas e4 288
Alagón, Spain ≈ dd5 190
Alagón, Aragón, Spain c3 192
Alah ≈ e7 100
Alahanpanjang a5 98
Alahärmä j5 155
Al Aḩmadī m7 137
Alaigne e5 187
Alaior A 193
Ālaivān p4 137
Alajärvi j5 155
Alajaure naturreservat ☆ h2 154
Al Ajaylāt g2 221
Alajero Ab2 189
Al Ajfar j8 136
Alajõe m3 157
Alajuela, C.R. e5 276
Alajuela, Nic. ▣ e5 276
Alajuela, Lago ○ h6 277
Alakanuk c3 246
Al Akhḑar f7 136
Alakitka ○ m3 155
Alakol', Ozero ○ t4 121
Alakurtti n3 155
Alakylä k3 155
Al 'Āl d5 139
Alalaú ≈ e4 285
Al 'Ālūk d4 139
Alama c3 226
Al 'Amādīyah j4 209
Alamagan ▭ A 74
Al 'Amār k9 137
Al 'Amārah l6 137
'Alam ar Rūm, Ra's ◄ c1 218
'Alamat'ā e5 219
Alameda, Spain f7 191
Alameda, U.S.A. a4 264
Alamicamba e4 276
Alamillo f6 191
Alaminos b2 100
Alamito Creek ≈ b6 261
Álamo, Mex. f3 275
Álamo, Port ≈ c6 191
Alamo, Spain ≈ e8 191
Alamo, U.S.A. f7 263
Alamogordo b5 261
Alamo Heights k3 273
Alamos, Arg. f4 297
Alamos, Mex. ≈ j3 273
Alamos, Sonora, Mex. e4 272
Álamos, Sonora, Mex. d3 272
Alamosa b4 261
Alamos de Márquez h3 272
Alamos de Peña f2 272
Alanäs e4 154
Åland, Åland, Fin. ▭ h2 157
Åland, Ahvenanmaa, Fin. ▣ h2 157
Aland ≈ g3 173
Ålandern ○ f3 156
Alandroal c6 191
Alandur g6 126
Alang j2 99
Alangalang, Tanjung ◄ j6 99
Alang Besar ▭ b4 101
Alange d6 191
Alange, Embalse de ⊙ d6 191
Alanggantang ▭ c5 98
Alanís e6 191
Alanya d4 208
Al 'Anz e4 139
'Alā' od Din q6 137
Alaotra, Farihy ○ Ab2 233
Alapaha, Georgia, U.S.A. h4 259
Alapaha, Georgia, U.S.A. ≈ h4 259
Alapajevsk k4 147
Alapur d6 130
Al 'Aqabah, Jordan ▣ d7 139
Al 'Aqabah, Al 'Aqabah, Jordan e2 219
Alaquàs d5 193
Alaquines e2 275
Alaraz e4 190
Alarcón b5 193
Alarcón, Embalse de ⊙ b5 193
Alar del Rey f2 190
Al Argoub a4 220
Al Arṭāwīyah k8 137
Alas j9 99
Alaşehir b3 208
Alaska, U.S.A. ▣ g2 246
Alaska, Alaska, U.S.A. ≈ e1 246
Alaska, Gulf of ◄ n2 301
Alaska Peninsula ◄ e4 246
Alaska Range ▣ g3 247
Al 'Assāfiyah g7 136
Alas, Selat ═ j9 99
Alassio c5 197
Alastaro k2 157
Älät h5 149
Alat a1 128
Alatna ≈ f2 246
Alatoz c5 193
Alatri h8 197
Alatyr', Russ. Fed. ≈ h4 151
Alatyr', Čuvašskaja Respublika, Russ. Fed. j4 151
Alausí b4 284
Alava ▣ b2 192
Alaverdi g4 149
Alavieska k4 155
Ala-Vuokki m4 155
Alavus j5 155
Alawalpur b4 130
Al 'Awdah k9 137
Alawoona e13 81
Al Awshaziyah h8 137
Al 'Ayn g9 137
Al 'Aynā d6 139
Al 'Azīzīyah, Iraq k5 137
Al 'Azīzīyah, Libya g2 221
Al Azraq al Janūbī e5 139
Alba, Italy c5 196
Alba, Rom. ▣ f2 201
Alba, Michigan, U.S.A. d3 254
Alba, Texas, U.S.A. b3 258
Al Ba'ā'ith h8 137
Al Bāb f4 209
Albac l5 171
Albacete, Spain ▣ b6 193
Albacete, Castilla - La Mancha, Spain c6 193
Albacutya, Lake ○ b2 82
Al Bad' e7 136
Al Badā'i' g8 137
Alba de Tormes e4 190
Albæk d1 158
Ålbæk Bugt ◄ d1 158
Al'bagan, Gora △ w2 121
Al Bāḩah ▣ f3 219
Albaida d6 193
Al Bā'ij e4 139
Alba Iulia f2 201
Al Ba'jah j9 136
Albal d5 193
Albaladejo b6 193
Albaladejo del Cuende b5 193
Albalate de Arzobispo d3 192
Albalate de Cinca e3 192
Albalate de las Nogueras b4 192
Al Balqā' ▣ d4 139
Alban e5 187
Albánchez b7 193
Albanel, Lac ○ f3 252
Albania h6 144

ALBANIA

THE REPUBLIC OF ALBANIA
Area 28,748km² (11,100sq miles)
Capital Tirana
Organizations CE, EBRD, OIC
Population 3,145,000
Pop. growth (%) -3.1
Life expectancy 69 (m); 75 (f)
Languages Albanian (dialects: Gheg in the north, Tosk in the south)
Literacy 86.5%
Currency lek (US $1 = 109 lek)
GDP (US million $) 4700
GDP per head ($US) 1494

Alban, Monte ★ f5 275
Albano f4 285
Albano di Lucania f4 198
Albano Laziale g8 197
Albany, Aust. c14 87
Albany, Can. ≈ m5 251
Albany, Jam. B 270
Albany, Georgia, U.S.A. g4 259
Albany, Kentucky, U.S.A. g1 259
Albany, New York, U.S.A. g2 257
Albany, Oregon, U.S.A. b3 262
Albany, Texas, U.S.A. d5 261
Albany Downs c5 85
Albarca, Cap d' ◄ f5 193
Al Bardī c1 218
Albardón c1 296
Albarellos, Embalse de ⊙ b2 190
Albarine ≈ b5 185
Albaron a7 185
Albarracín c4 192
Albarragena ≈ d5 191
Al Barrah k9 137
Al Başrah l6 137
Albatana c6 193
Albatera d6 193
Al Baṭḩā' k6 137
Albatross Point ◄ B 77
Al Bayḑā' g5 219
Albay Gulf ◄ e4 100
Albe ≈ c2 184
Albegna ≈ f7 197
Albelda e3 192
Albemarle, Punta ◄ A 286
Albemarle Sound ◄ l1 259
Albenga c5 197
Albens b5 185
Al Beqaa ▣ e3 138
Alberche ≈ f4 190
Alberdi f5 293
Alberga, South Australia, Aust. b9 81
Alberga, South Australia, Aust. ≈ b9 81
Albergaria-a-Velha b4 190
Albergaria dos Doze b5 191
Albergian, Monte △ a4 196
Alberic d5 193
Alberite b2 192
Alberobello g4 198
Alberoni g4 196
Albersdorf c4 158
Albert, Aust. ≈ d4 80
Albert, Fr. a5 159
Alberta, Can. ▣ k4 249
Alberta, U.S.A. f3 258
Albert Falls Nature Reserve ☆ j4 235
Alberti g3 297
Albertinia d7 234
Albertirsa h4 171
Albert Kanaal ≈ c3 159
Albert, Lake, Aust. ○ a2 82
Albert, Lake, D.R.C. ○ f3 225
Albert Lea e3 260
Alberto de Agostini, Parque Nacional ☆ b6 295
Alberton, Can. k5 253
Alberton, U.S.A. f2 262
Albertville, Fr. c5 185
Albertville, U.S.A. f2 258
Albeşti, Botoşani, Rom. h2 201
Albeşti, Vaslui, Rom. h2 201
Albestroff c2 184
Albi e5 187
Albidona f5 198
Albignasego f4 196
Albina g2 285
Albino d4 196
Albion, Illinois, U.S.A. b6 254
Albion, Michigan, U.S.A. d4 254
Albion, New York, U.S.A. g4 254
Albion, Washington, U.S.A. e2 262
Al Bi'r f7 136
Albires e2 190
Al Bishriyah e4 139
Albisola Marina c5 197
Albisola Superiore c5 197
Al Biyāḑh ⌒ g3 219
Alblasserdam c3 159
Albocácer e4 192
Alboloduy b7 193
Albolote g7 191
Alboraän Sea ⌒ f8 191
Alboraya d5 193
Alborea c5 193
Ålborg c1 158
Ålborg Bugt ◄ d2 158
Alborn g7 250
Alborz, Reshteh-ye ▣ d9 137
Albota g3 201
Albox b7 193
Albrechtice nad Orlicí e1 170
Albro h7 80
Albstadt f5 174
Albuch ♦ f4 174
Al Budayyi n8 137
Albufeira b7 191
Al Buḩayrāt al Murrah ○ a6 139
Albujón c7 193
Al Bukayriyah j8 136
Albuñol a8 193
Albuñuelas g8 191
Albuquerque b5 261
Albuquerque, Cayos de ▭ g4 277
Al Burayj e2 138
Al Burbayṭah d6 139
Al Burj c7 139
Alburquerque d5 191
Albury h14 81
Al Buşayrah h5 209
Al Busayṭā' ⌒ e2 219
Al Buşayyah l6 137
Alby-sur-Chéran c5 185
Alca c3 292
Alcácer do Sal b6 191
Alcáçovas, Port b6 191
Alcáçovas, Évora, Port b6 191
Alcadozo c6 193
Alcafozes c5 191
Alcains c5 191
Alcalá de Chivert e4 192
Alcalá de Guadaira e7 191
Alcalá de Gurrea d2 192
Alcalá de Henares a4 192
Alcalá de la Selva d4 192
Alcalá del Júcar c5 193
Alcalá de los Gazules e8 191
Alcalá del Río e7 191
Alcalá la Real g7 191
Alcamo b7 199
Alcanadre ≈ d3 192
Alcanar e4 192
Alcanede b5 191
Alcanena b5 191
Alcañices d3 190
Alcañiz d3 192
Alcãntara d2 288
Alcántara d5 191
Alcántara, Embalse de ⊙ d5 191
Alcántara II, Embalse de ⊙ d5 191
Alcantarilha b7 191
Alcantarilla c7 193
Alcantilado b2 290
Alcaracejos f6 191
Alcaraz b6 193
Alcaraz Segundo h1 297
Alcaraz, Sierra de ▣ b6 193
Alcaria Ruiva c7 191
Alcarrache ≈ d6 191
Alcarràs e3 192
Alcatrazes, Ilha de ▭ f6 291
Alcaudete f7 191
Alcaudete de la Jara f5 191
Alcázar de San Juan a5 193
Alcester e4 163
Alchevs'k e2 148
Alcira e2 297
Alçıtepe g2 210
Alcoba f5 191
Alcobaça, Braz. j2 291
Alcobaça, Port b5 191
Alcobendas g4 190
Alcobertas b5 191
Alcocer b4 192
Alcoentre b5 191
Alcolea, Andalucia, Spain f7 191
Alcolea de Cinca e3 192
Alcolea del Pinar b3 192
Alcolea del Río e7 191
Alcollarín e5 191
Alcolu j3 259
Alconchel c6 191
Alcora d4 193
Alcorcón g4 190
Alcorisa d4 192
Alcorlo, Embalse de ⊙ b3 192
Alcorn d4 258
Alcorneo ≈ c5 191
Alcorta g2 297
Alcossebre e4 192
Alcoutim c7 191
Alcover f3 192
Alcoy d6 193
Alcsútdoboz g4 171
Alcubierre d3 192
Alcubierre, Sierra de ▣ d3 192
Alcubilla de Avellaneda a3 192
Alcubillas a6 193
Alcublas d5 193
Alcudia ≈ f6 191
Alcúdia h5 193
Alcúdia, Badia d' ◄ g5 193
Alcudia de Guadix a7 193
Alcudia, Sierra de ▣ f6 191
Alcuéscar d5 191
Aldabra Atoll ★ d5 231
Aldabra Islands ▭ d5 231
Aldama, Chihuahua, Mex. g3 272
Aldama, Tabasco, Mex. h4 275
Aldama, Tamaulipas, Mex. e2 275
Aldan, Russ. Fed. ≈ p3 119
Aldan, Respublika Saha (Jakutija), Russ. Fed. n4 119
Aldbourne e5 163
Aldbrough f3 162
Alde ≈ h4 163
Aldeadávila, Embalse de ⊙ d3 190
Aldea del Cano d5 191
Aldea del Rey g6 191
Aldea de Trujillo e5 191
Aldealpozo b3 192
Aldeanueva de San Bartolomé e5 191
Aldearrodrigo e3 190
Aldeavieja f4 190
Aldeburgh h4 163
Aldeia de João Pires c4 190
Aldeia dos Elvas b7 191
Aldeia Velha b3 288
Aldermaston e5 163
Aldermen Islands, The ▭ f2 76
Alderney ▭ c3 182
Alder Peak △ b6 265
Aldersbach e1 176
Aldershot f5 163
Alderson f7 254
Alder Springs a2 264
Aldinga Beach a2 82
à l'Eau Claire, Lac ○ r2 251
Aledo c7 193
Aleg b2 222
Aleg, Lac d' ○ b2 222
Alegranza, Isla ▭ Af1 189
Alegre, Braz. ≈ f3 293
Alegre, Espírito Santo, Braz. h4 291
Alegrete e1 294
Alegros Mountain △ a5 261
Alej ≈ u1 121
Alejandro de Humboldt National Park ★ g4 266
Alejandro Korn h3 297
Alejandro Roca f2 297
Alejandro Selkirk, Isla ▭ b6 283
Alejandro Stefenelli d5 296
Alejo Ledesma f2 297
Alejsk u1 121
Aleknagik e4 246
Aleksandra Bekovicha-Cherkasskoga, Zaliv ◄ c6 120
Aleksandro-Nevskij f5 150
Aleksandrov e3 150
Aleksandrov Gaj h2 149
Aleksandrovka, Orenburgskaja Oblast', Russ. Fed. j1 149
Aleksandrovka, Samarskaja Oblast', Russ. Fed. h1 149
Aleksandrovo g4 201
Aleksandrovskoe, Stavropol'skij Kraj, Russ. Fed. f3 149
Aleksandrovskoe, Stavropol'skij Kraj, Russ. Fed. g3 149
Aleksandrovskoe, Tomskaja Oblast', Russ. Fed. h3 118
Aleksandrovsk-Sakhalinskiy l2 94
Aleksandrów Kujawski g3 168
Aleksandrów Łódzki h4 169
Alekseevka, Belgorodskaja Oblast', Russ. Fed. e2 148
Alekseyevka, Pavlodarskaya Oblast', Kaz. q2 121
Alekseyevka, Severnyy Kazakhstan, Kaz. m5 147
Aleksin d4 150
Aleksinac e4 200
Alektora a2 138
Alèmbé b4 224
Além Paraíba g4 291
Ålen c5 154
Alençon f4 183
Alençon, Campagne d' ♦ f4 183
Alène ≈ j6 183
Alenquer, Braz. g4 285
Alenquer, Port b5 191
Alentejo, Port ▣ c6 191
Alentejo, Port ◄ c6 191
Alenuihaha Channel ═ Ac2 263
Alépé d4 222
Aleppo, Ḩalab, Syria f3 136
Aler ≈ f4 126
Alerce Andino, Parque Nacional ☆ b4 295
Aléria A 185
Alert aa3 298
Alerta c2 292
Alès a6 184
Ales Aa3 198
Alesd l4 171
Aleški f2 148
Alessandria, Italy ▣ c5 196
Alessandria, Piemonte, Italy c5 196
Alessandria della Rocca c7 199
Alessano c3 199
Ålestrup c2 158
Ålesund b1 156
Alethrikon b2 138
Aletschhorn △ b3 196
Aleutian Basin ⌒ k2 301
Aleutian Islands ▭ b5 246
Aleutian Range ▣ e4 246
Aleutian Trench ⌒ l2 301
Alevina, Mys ◄ r4 119
Alexander c6 250
Alexander Archipelago ▭ l5 247
Alexander Bay b4 234
Alexander City g3 259
Alexander Island ▭ kk2 298
Alexander, Mount △ b8 87
Alexandra, Aust. d3 82
Alexandra, N.Z. b6 77
Alexandreia c2 210
Alexandria, Aust. c5 80
Alexandria, British Columbia, Can. f5 248
Alexandria, Can. j3 255
Alexandria, El Iskandarîya, Egypt c1 218
Alexandria, Egypt c1 218
Alexandria, R.S.A. g6 235
Alexandria, Rom. g4 201
Alexandria, U.K. d4 164
Alexandria, U.S.A. ▣ k6 257
Alexandria, Indiana, U.S.A. d5 254
Alexandria, Louisiana, U.S.A. c4 258
Alexandria, Pennsylvania, U.S.A. b4 256
Alexandria, Tennessee, U.S.A. f1 258
Alexandria, Virginia, U.S.A. c6 256
Alexandria Bay j3 255
Alexandrina, Lake ○ a2 82
Alexandroupoli f2 210
Alexandru Odobescu h3 201
Alexânia d2 290
Alex Heiberg Island ▭ dd2 299
Alexis ≈ p2 253
'Āley d3 138
Aleyak r3 137
Alf f4 159
Alfafar d5 193
Alfajarín d3 192
Alfajayucan e3 275
Al Fallūjah j5 137
Alfambra, Spain ≈ c4 192
Alfambra, Aragón, Spain c4 192
Alfambras b7 191
Alfamén c3 192
Alfândega da Fé d3 190
Alfántega e3 192
Alfaraz b4 190
Alfarelos b4 190
Alfarnate f7 191
Alfaro c2 192
Alfarràs e3 192
Al Farwānīyah l7 137
Al Fatḩah j5 209
Al Fāw m7 137
Al Fayḩā' d5 139
Alfedena d3 198
Alfeios ≈ b5 211
Alfeizerão a5 191
Alfeld (Leine) e4 172
Alfenas f4 291
Alfhausen c3 172
Alföld ⌒ g5 171
Alfonsine g5 197
Alford, England, U.K. g3 162
Alford, Scotland, U.K. f2 164
Alfred c2 256
Alfred and Marie Range ▣ g9 87
Alfred M. Terrazas e3 275
Alfred National Park ☆ f3 83
Alfredo Chaves h4 291
Alfreton e3 162
Alfta g2 156
Álftanes A 152
Al Fuḩayḩīl m7 137
Al Fujayrah r9 137
Al Fuqahā' h3 221
Al Furāt ≈ g5 209
Alga k2 149
Algajola A 185
Algámitas e7 191
Ålgård a3 156
Algarinejo f7 191
Algarroba f5 297
Algarrobal b1 294
Algarrobitos g2 297
Algarrobo b2 296
Algarrobo del Aguilla d4 296
Algarve ▣ b7 191
Algatocín e8 191
Algeciras e8 191
Algemesí d5 193
Algena e4 219
Alger e1 221
Algeria c2 216

ALGERIA

THE PEOPLE'S DEMOCRATIC REPUBLIC OF ALGERIA
Area 2,381,741km² (919,595sq miles)
Capital Algiers
Organizations LAS, OPEC, OIC
Population 31,270,000
Pop. growth (%) 1.8
Life expectancy 67 (m); 70 (f)
Languages Arabic, French, Berber
Literacy 69.9%
Currency Algerian dinar (US $1 = 70 Algerian dinar)
GDP (US million $) 54,924
GDP per head ($US) 1756

Al Ghārīyah e4 139
Al Ghāţ k8 137
Al Ghayḑah h4 219
Alghero Aa2 198
Al Ghizlānīyah e3 138
Al Ghwaybiyah m9 136
Algibre ≈ b7 191
Algiers e1 221
Alginet d5 193
Algoa Bay ◄ g6 235
Algodón ≈ c4 284
Algodonales e8 191
Algodor, Port c7 191
Algodor, Spain ≈ g5 190
Algoma c3 254
Algona e3 260
Algood g1 259
Algora b4 192
Algorta, Spain b1 192
Algorta, Ur. j2 297
Algoso d3 190
Algoz b7 191
Alguaire e3 192
Alguazas c6 193
Algueña d6 193
Al Ḩabbānīyah j5 137
Alhabia b8 193
Al Ḩadbah ⌒ f3 219
Al Ḩadd n8 137
Al Ḩadīdīyah e1 138
Al Ḩadīthah j5 209
Al Ḩaḑr j5 209
Al Ḩaffah f5 209
Al Ḩafir al Fawqānī e3 138
Al Haggounia b3 220
Alhama ≈ g7 191
Al Ḩamād ⌒ e1 219
Alhama de Almería b8 193
Alhama de Granada g8 191
Alhama de Murcia c7 193
Alhambra a6 193
Al Ḩamīdīyah d2 138
Al Ḩammah d4 138
Al Ḩanākiyah h9 137
Al Ḩanīsh al Kabīr ▭ f5 219
Al Ḩanīyah ▣ l7 137
Al Ḩarrah ♦ e1 219
Al Ḩarrah e3 138
Al Ḩarūj al Aswad ♦ a2 218
Al Ḩasā d6 139

Al Ḩasakah → Amparo 307

Al Ḩasakah, Syria h4 209
Al Ḩasakah,
Al Ḩasakah, Syria h4 209
Al Ḩasānī e2 219
Al Hāshimīyah, Iraq k5 137
Al Hāshimīyah,
Az Zarqā', Jordan e4 139
Al Hāshimīyah,
Ma'an, Jordan d6 139
Alhaurín de la Torre f8 191
Alhaurín el Grande f8 191
Al Ḩawrā g5 219
Al Ḩayy l5 137
Al Ḩazm f7 136
Al Hijānah e3 138
Al Ḩillah k5 137
Al Hindīyah k5 137
Al Ḩinnāh m8 136
Al Ḩismā e2 219
Al Ḩişn d4 139
Al Hoceima d1 220
Alhóndiga b4 192
Alhuampa e5 293
Al Ḩudaydah f5 219
Al Ḩudūd ash
Shamālīyah f2 219
Al Ḩufrah e2 219
Al Hufūf m9 137
Al Hūj e2 219
Al Ḩumayḑah c7 139
Al Ḩumaymah al Jadīdah d7 139
Al Huwaylah n9 136
Al Ḩuwayyiţ h9 137
Ali d3 130
Alia c7 199
Alía e5 191
'Alīābād, Afg. d2 128
'Alīābād, Golestān, Iran q3 137
'Alīābād, Hormozgan, Iran q7 137
'Alīābād, Khorāsan, Iran r5 137
'Alīābād, Kordestān, Iran l4 137
'Alīābād, Qom, Iran n4 137
Alīābād, Kūh-e n4 137
Aliade f4 223
Aliaga d4 192
Aliağa a3 208
Aliakmonas c2 210
Aliakmonas, Limni b2 210
Aliambata p9 99
Aliano f4 198
Aliartos d4 210
'Alī ash Sharqī l5 137
Alibag c3 126
Ali Bandar d8 129
Äli Bayramlı h5 149
Alibori e3 223
Alibunar e3 200
Alicant d6 193
Alice, a3 84
Alice, Aust. g7 80
Alice, U.S.A. k4 273
Alice Arm c4 248
Alicedale g6 235
Alice Downs h5 86
Alice, Punta g5 199
Alice Shoal h2 277
Alice Springs a7 80
Alichur f2 128
Alicia, Arg. f1 297
Alicia, Phil. d7 100
Alick Creek f6 80
Alicoto g3 285
Alicún de Ortega a7 193
Alife d3 198
Alifuuto Nature Reserve d3 226
Aliganj d6 130
Aligarh d6 130
Alīgūdarz m5 137
Alihe g2 94
Alijó c3 190
Alījūq, Kūh-e n6 137
'Alī Kheyl d4 128
Alima c4 224
Alimena d7 199
Alimia Ac2 211
Alimpaya Point c7 100
Alindao d2 224
Alingsås e4 156
Alipur, India c5 130
Alipur, Pak. e6 129
Alipur Duar l6 125
Aliquippa f5 254
Alirajpur g9 129
Ali Sabieh c1 226
Al 'Īsāwīyah f6 136
Aliseda d5 191
Al Iskandarīyah k5 137
Aliste d3 190
Alistrati d1 210
Alitåive f3 154
Alitak Bay f4 246
Alì Terme e6 199
Aliveri e4 210
Aliwal b4 130
Aliwal North g5 235
Alizai e4 128
Al Jafr e6 139
Al Jāfūrah h3 219
Al Jahrah l7 137
Al Jālamīd h6 136
Al Jamalīyah n9 137
Al Jawb h3 219
Al Jawf, Libya b3 218
Al Jawf, Sau. Ar e1 219
Al Jawf, Al Jawf, Sau. Ar g7 137
Al Jawsh g2 221
Al Jazā'ir h4 136
Aljezur b7 191
Al Jibāb e3 138
Al Jībān h3 219
Al Jilh f2 219
Al Jithāmīyah h8 137
Al Jīzah d5 139
Aljojuca f4 275
Aljubarrota b5 191
Al Jubayl, Sau. Ar g3 219
Al Jubayl, Ash Sharqīyah,
Sau. Ar m8 136
Aljucén, Spain d5 191
Aljucén,
Extremadura, Spain d5 191
Al Jufra Oasis h3 221
Al Jurayfah k9 137
Al Jurdhāwīyah j9 137
Aljustrel b7 191
Al Kahfah,
Al Qaşīm, Sau. Ar j8 137
Al Kahfah,
Ash Sharqīyah, Sau. Ar m8 137
Alkali Flat, U.S.A. SN e1 264
Alkali Flat,
Nevada, U.S.A. f2 264
Alkamari g3 223
Al Karak, Jordan d5 139
Al Karak, Jordan d5 139
Al Karak, Syria e4 138
Al Karāmah d5 139
Al Kāẓimīyah k5 136
Alken d4 159
Al Khābūrah f6 116
Al Khalf h9 137
Al Khālidīyah e4 139
Al Khalīf f6 116
Al Khāliş k5 137
al Khārijah, Wāḩāt,
Egypt d3 218
Al Kharj g3 219
Al Kharrārah n9 137
Al Khaşab r8 137
Al Khawr n9 137
Al Khawtamah f4 219
Al Khobar n8 137
Al Khubrah m8 136
Al Khufrah b3 218
Al Khums g2 221
Al Khushnīyah d3 138
Al Khuwayr n8 137
Al Kifl k5 137
Al Kir'ānah n9 137
Al Kiswah e3 138
Alkmaar c2 159
Al Koiah d4 138
Al Kūfah k5 137
Al Kumayt l5 137
Al Kūt k5 137
Al Kuwayt l7 137
Alkyonidon, Kolpos c4 210
Al La'bān d6 139
Al Labbah e2 219
Al Lādhiqīyah, Syria e5 209
Al Lādhiqīyah,
Al Lādhiqīyah, Syria d1 138
Allagadda f5 126
Allahabad g7 124
Allah-Jun' p3 119
Allaines-Mervilliers g4 183
Allaire c5 182
Al Lajā e4 138
Allakaket f2 246
Allanche e3 186
Allanmyo b6 102
Allanridge g3 235
'Allāqī, Wādī al d3 218
Allariz c2 190
Allassac d3 186
Allatoona Lake g2 259
Allauch b7 185
Alldays h1 235
Allegan d4 254
Allegany, New York, U.S.A. b2 256
Alleghe g3 196
Allegheny a3 256
Allegheny Mountains f7 254
Allegheny Reservoir a3 256
Allègre f3 186
Allègre, Pointe C 271
Allemond c5 185
Allen, Arg. d5 296
Allen, Phil. e4 100
Allen, U.S.A. a3 258
Allendale j3 259
Allendale Town d2 162
Allende, Coahuila, Mex. j3 273
Allende, Nuevo León, Mex. j5 273
Allende, Veracruz, Mex. g4 275
Allendorf (Eder) c1 174
Allendorf (Lumda) c2 174
Allen, Lough d2 165
Allen, Mount, N.Z. a7 77
Allen, Mount, U.S.A. j3 247
Allensville c4 256
Allentown e4 256
Allentsteig g1 177
Allenwood d3 256
Alleppey e8 126
Allepuz d4 192
Allersberg d2 175
Allershausen g3 175
Allerton, Point k2 257
Allevard c5 185
Allgäu f5 174
Allianc g2 285
Alliance, Nebraska, U.S.A. c3 260
Alliance, Ohio, U.S.A. f5 254
Allibaudières k4 183
Allier, Fr. j6 183
Allier, Auvergne, Fr. f2 186
Alligator Pond B 266
Alligny-en-Morvan a3 184
Allihies a5 165
Allingåbro d2 158
Allinge-Sandvig f5 156
Al Līth f3 219
Allmendingen c2 174
Allo b2 192
Alloa e3 164
Ålloluokta g3 154
Allonby e5 164
Alloné HaBashan d3 138
Allonnes,
Pays de la Loire, Fr. f5 183
Allora l10 81
Allos c6 185
Allow c4 165
All Saints D 271
Allschwil b2 196
Allstedt g4 173
Allu k7 99
Alluma c5 139
Allumiere f7 197
Allur g5 126
Alluru Kottapatnam g5 126
Allyn b2 262
Alm e1 176
Alma, Can. g4 252
Alma, Arkansas, U.S.A. b2 258
Alma, Georgia, U.S.A. h4 259
Alma, Nebraska, U.S.A. d3 260
Al Ma'ānīyah j6 137
Alma-Ata,
Gorod Almaty, Kaz. r6 121
Almacelles e3 192
Almaciles, Puerto de b6 193
Almada a6 191
Almaden g4 80
Almadén f6 191
Almadén de la Plata d7 191
Almadenejos f6 191
Al Madīnah, Sau. Ar f3 219
Al Madīnah,
Al Madīnah, Sau. Ar e3 219
Al Madwar e4 139
Al Mafraq, Jordan e4 139
Al Mafraq,
Al Mafraq, Jordan e4 139
Almafuerte e2 297
Almagor d4 138
Almagre e2 275
Almagro g6 191
Al Mahākīk h3 219
Al Mahbas c3 220
Al Maḩmūdīyah k5 137
Almajano b3 192
Al Majdal d4 139
Al Majma'ah k9 137
Almalyk m7 121
Al Manākhir e5 139
Al Manāmah n8 137
Almanor, Lake c5 262
Almansa c6 193
Almanza e2 190
Almanzor e4 190
Almanzora b7 193
Al Ma'qil l6 137
Almār b3 128
Almar e4 190
Almaraz e5 191
Almargen e7 191
Al Marj b1 218
Almarza b3 192
Almaş l5 171
Almåsaberget e5 154
Almásfüzitő g4 171
Almas, Rio das c4 289
Almassora d5 193
Almatinskaya Oblast' q5 121
Al Mawşil j4 209
Al Mayādīn h5 209
Almazán b3 192
Almaznyj m3 119
Al Mazra'ah d5 139
Almazul b3 192
Alm Berg j4 175
Almedina b6 193
Almedinilla f7 191
Almeida d4 190
Almeida de Sayago d3 190
Almeirim, Braz. g4 285
Almeirim, Port b5 191
Almelo e2 159
Almenar e3 192
Almenara, Braz. h2 291
Almenara, Spain d5 193
Almenar de Soria b3 192
Almendra,
Embalse de d3 190
Almendral d6 191
Almendralejo d6 191
Al'menevo k5 147
Almere d2 159
Almería b8 193
Almería b7 193
Almería, Golfo de b8 193
Almerimar b8 193
Al'met'evsk m4 151
Älmhult f4 156
Al Midhnab k9 137
Al Miḩrāḑ h3 219
Almind c3 158
Almira d2 262
Almirantazgo, Seno del c6 295
Almirante f6 277
Almirante Tamandaré d6 290
Al Mish'āb m7 137
Al Mismīyah e3 138
Almodôvar b7 191
Almodóvar del Campo f6 191
Almodóvar del Pinar c5 193
Almodóvar del Río e7 191
Almogía f8 191
Almoguera b4 192
Almoharín d5 191
Almoloya d4 274
Almonacid del Zorita b4 192
Almond e3 164
Almondbank e3 164
Almont e4 254
Almonte, Spain e5 191
Almonte, Andalucía, Spain d7 191
Almora d5 130
Almoradí d6 193
Almoustarat e2 223
Älmsta h3 157
al Mu'ayqil,
Khashm g2 219
Al Mu'aḑḑamīyah e3 138
Al Mubarrez m9 137
Al Mudawwarah e7 139
Almudema c7 193
Almudévar d2 192
Al Muharraq n8 137
Al Mukallā g5 219
Al Mukhā f5 219
Al Mukhaylī b1 218
Almuñécar g8 191
Al Muqdādīyah k5 137
Álmuradiel g6 191
Al Murayghah d6 139
Almuro c6 191
Almus f2 209
Al Musayfirah e4 138
Al Musayyib k5 137
Al Mushannaf e4 138
Almussafes d5 193
Al Mutā'iyah e4 139
Al Muwaqqar e5 139
Al Muwayliḩ e8 137
Almyropotamos e4 210
Almyros c3 210
Almyrou, Akra c3 210
Alness d2 164
Alnön g1 157
Alnwick e1 162
Alo L 75
Alofi, Île L 75
Alofitai L 75
Aloi f3 225
Aloja l4 157
Along p5 125
Alonnisos, Grc. d3 210
Alonnisos, Thessalia, Grc. d3 210
Alonon Point c5 100
Alor n9 99
Alor Gajah c4 101
Alor, Kepulauan n8 99
Alor, Selat n9 99
Alor Setar b2 101
Alós d'Ensil f2 192
Alosno c7 191
Alot g9 129
Alota d4 292
Aloxe-Corton a3 184
Aloysius, Mount j9 87
Alozaina f8 191
Alp f2 192
Alpachiri f4 297
Alpa Corral e2 296
Alpalhão c5 191
Alpaugh d6 265
Alpedrinha c4 190
Alpen e3 159
Alpena, Arkansas, U.S.A. c1 258
Alpena, Michigan, U.S.A. e3 254
Alpera c6 193
Alpercatas c3 288
Alpercatas, Serra das d3 288
Alpes-de-Haute-
Provence c6 185
Alpes du Dauphiné b6 185
Alpes-Maritimes d7 185
Alpe Veglia, Parco
Naturale b4 196
Alpha, Aust. h7 80
Alpha, U.S.A. a5 254
Alpha Cordillera ff3 299
Alpha Creek b3 84
Alpharetta g2 259
Alphen aan den Rijn c2 159
Alpi Apuane,
Parco Naturale delle e5 197
Alpiarça b5 191
Alpi di Succiso e5 196
Alpi Lepontine c3 196
Alpine, Arizona, U.S.A. j9 263
Alpine, Texas, U.S.A. h2 272
Alpinópolis e4 291
Al Qa'āmīyāt g4 219
Al Qābūn e3 138
Al Qaddāḩīyah h2 221
Al Qadmūs e1 138
Al Qalībah f7 136
Al Qāmishlī h4 209
Al Qaryatayn, Jordan e4 139
Al Qaryatayn, Syria f5 209
Al Qaşabāt g2 221
Al Qaşīm f2 219
Al Qaşr, Jordan d5 139
Al Qaşr, Sau. Ar h8 136
Al Qasţal d5 139
Al Qaţīf n8 136
Al Qaţrānah e5 139
Al Qaţrūn g4 221
Al Qayşūmah l7 137
Alquería de la Condesa d6 193
Alquerías c6 193
Alquife a7 193
Al Qunayţirah, Syria d3 138
Al Qunayţirah,
Al Qunayţirah, Syria d3 138
Al Qunfidhah f4 219
Al Qurayn j9 137
Al Qurayyah, Sau. Ar j9 137
Al Qurayyah, Syria e4 138
Al Qurayyah, U.A.E. r9 137
Al Qurayyāt f6 136
Al Qurnah l6 137
Al Quşaybah d4 138
Al Quşayr e2 138
Al Quţayfah e3 138
Al Quwārah j8 137
Al Quwayrah d7 139
Alrø d3 158
Alroy Downs c5 80
Als, Den. c4 158
Als, Nordjylland, Den. d2 158
Alsace d2 184
Alsace, Plaine d' d2 184
Alsask n6 249
Alsdorf e4 159
Alsensjön d5 154
Alsenz c3 174
Alsfeld d4 174
Als Fjord c3 158
Alsína h2 297
Alslev b3 158
Alsónémedi h4 171
Ålsrode d2 158
Ålstad e3 154
Alster 2f 172
Alsterbro f4 156
Alston d2 162
Alsunga j4 157
Alsvik e3 154
Alta j2 155
Altacroce, Monte f3 196
Altaelva j2 155
Altafjorden j1 155
Alta Floresta f1 293
Alta Gracia, Arg. e1 297
Alta Gracia, Nic. e5 276
Altagracía c1 284
Altai Mountains n1 117
Alta Italia e3 297
Altaj, Respublika w2 121
Altajskij Kraj u1 121
Altamachi d3 292
Altamaha h4 259
Altamira, Amazonas, Braz. d3 284
Altamira, Braz. b2 288
Altamira, C.R. e5 276
Altamira, Chile d5 292
Altamira, Col. b3 284
Altamíra f2 275
Altamirano, Arg. h3 297
Altamirano, Chiapas, Mex. a2 276
Altamirano,
Veracruz, Mex. f4 275
Altamira, Sierra de e5 191
Altamont c4 262
Alta, Mount b6 77
Altamura f4 198
Altan f1 112
Altanbulag, Selenge, Mong. d1 112
Altanbulag, Töv, Mong. d2 112
Alta Paraiso de Goiás c4 289
Altapirire e2 285
Altar h10 263
Altar, Desierto de b1 272
Altare c5 197
Altata f5 272
Alta Valle Pesio,
Parco Naturale dell' b5 197
Alta Val Sesia,
Parco Naturale b4 196
Altavilla Irpina d4 198
Altavilla Silentina e4 198
Altdorf, Ger. h4 175
Altdorf, Switz. c3 196
Altdorf bei Nürnberg g4 175
Alte b7 191
Altea d6 193
Altefähr j1 173
Alteidet j1 155
Altena g1 174
Altenau, Ger. d4 172
Altenau,
Niedersachsen, Ger. f4 172
Altenberg j2 175
Altenberge f2 159
Altenbruch-Westerende b5 158
Altenburg h2 175
Altenfelden e1 176
Altenholz d4 158
Altenkirchen j1 173
Altenkirchen (Westerwald) c3 174
Altenmarkt an der Alz d1 176
Altenmarkt bei Sankt Gallen f2 177
Altenmedingen f2 173
Altenqoke p1 125
Altenstadt, Bayern, Ger. d2 174
Altenstadt, Hessen, Ger. c2 174
Altensteig f4 174
Altentreptow j2 173
Alte Oder k3 173
Alter do Chão, Braz. g4 285
Alter do Chão, Port c5 191
Altheim e1 176
Altheimer d2 258
Althofen f3 177
Altin Köprü k5 209
Altınoluk a3 208
Altinópolis e4 290
Altınova a3 208
Altıntaş c3 208
Altiplano d3 292
Altkirch d3 184
Altmannstein d4 175
Altmark g3 173
Altmühl f3 174
Altmühltal g4 175
Altnaharra d1 164
Alto b4 258
Alto Alegre f2 297
Alto Araguaia b2 290
Alto Chandless c2 292
Alto Chicapa c6 224
Alto Coité a1 290
Alto Cuchumatanes b3 276
Alto de Caballeros e2 275
Alto de Carrizal b2 284
Alto del Buey b2 284
Alto del Moncayo c3 192
Alto de Pencoso d2 296
Alto de Quimari b2 284
Alto de Tamar c2 284
Altofonte c6 199
Alto Garças b2 290
Alto Jahuel b2 296
Alto Ligonha f2 233
Alto Lucero f4 275
Alto Molócuè f2 233
Altomonte f5 198
Altomünster g4 175
Alton, U.K. f5 163
Alton, Illinois, U.S.A. a6 254
Alton, Kentucky, U.S.A. d6 254
Alton, Missouri, U.S.A. d1 258
Alton,
New Hampshire, U.S.A. g7 252
Altona e6 250
Alton Downs d9 81
Alto Nevado b4 295
Altoona, Kansas, U.S.A. b1 258
Altoona,
Pennsylvania, U.S.A. b4 256
Alto Pacajá b2 288
Alto Paraguay f4 293
Alto Paraná g4 293
Alto Parnaíba c3 288
Altopascio e6 197
Alto Pelado d2 296
Alto Pencoso d2 296
Alto Piquiri b6 290
Alto Purús c2 292
Alto Rabagão,
Barragem do c3 190
Alto Rio Doce g4 291
Alto Río Senguerr b5 295
Alto Rio Verde b3 290
Altorricón e3 192
Altos d3 288
Altos de Cabrejas b4 193
Altos de Chacaya d3 292
Altos de Chinchilla c6 193
Altos de Chipión f1 297
Alto Sucuriú b3 290
Altotonga f4 275
Altötting d1 176
Alto Uruguai g5 293
Alt Ruppin h3 173
Altsasu b2 192
Altshausen g4 174
Altstätten d2 196
Altuhovo d1 148
Altun Shan m3 117
Altura d5 193
Alturas c5 262
Altus d5 261
Altynkul' k4 149
Altyševo j4 151
Alucra g2 209
Al 'Uḑaylīyah m9 137
Alūksne m4 157
Al 'Ulā f8 137
Al'ulah g5 219
Alūm m5 137
Alum Bank b4 256
Aluminé, Arg. b5 296
Aluminé, Neuquén, Arg. b5 296
Aluminé, Lago b5 296
Alunadpur West e6 129
Ålund h4 154
Alunda h2 157
Alupka d3 148
Al 'Uqaylah a1 218
Al 'Uqayr n9 137
Al Urayq e2 219
Alushta d3 148
Alustante c4 192
Al Uthaylī f7 136
Alutom, Mount C 74
Al 'Uwaynāt,
Al Kufrah, Libya b3 218
Al 'Uwaynāt, Awbārī,
Libya g3 221
Al 'Uwaynidhiyah e2 219
Al 'Uwayqīlah j6 137
Al 'Uyaynah, Ash
Sharqīyah, Sau. Ar m8 137
Al 'Uyaynah,
Tabūk, Sau. Ar f7 136
Al 'Uẓaym j8 136
Al 'Uzayr l6 137
Alva, Port b4 190
Alva, U.S.A. d4 261
Alvaiázere b5 191
Alvajärvi k5 155
Alvalade b7 191
Alvaneu d3 196
Älvängen e4 156
Alvão,
Parque Natural do c3 190
Alvão, Serra de c3 190
Alvarado, Mex. g4 275
Alvarado, U.S.A. a3 258
Alvarães e4 285
Álvares b4 190
Álvares Machado c5 290
Alvarez g2 297
Álvaro Obregon e3 275
Alvdal d1 156
Älvdalen f2 156
Alvear e1 294
Alvechurch e4 163
Alverca a6 191
Alveringem a3 159
Alvesta f4 156
Alveston d5 163
Alvignac d4 186
Ålvik b2 156
Alvik g1 156
Alvin b5 258
Alvinópolis g4 291
Alvito c6 191
Älvkarleby g2 156
Alvnes e3 154
Alvord a3 258
Alvøy a2 156
Älvros f1 156
Älvsbyn h4 154
Ålvund b5 154
Al Wafrah l7 137
Al Wajh f8 137
Al Wakrah n9 137
Al Wannān m8 136
Alwar c6 130
Al Warī'ah l8 137
Al Wīgh g4 221
Al Wusayl n9 137
Al Yahūdīyah e4 138
Alyangula c2 80
Al Yarmūk d4 138
Alyki b3 210
Alyth e3 164
Alytus n1 169
Alz h4 175
Alzada b2 260
Alzaga h4 297
Alzette e5 159
Alzey e5 174
Alzira d5 193
Alzon f5 187
Amacayacu,
Parque Nacional c4 284
Amacuro e2 285
Amacuzac e4 275
Amada Gaza c3 224
Amadeus, Lake k9 87
Amadi e3 225
Amadjuak Lake q2 243
Amadora a6 191
Amadror f4 221
Amaga b2 284
Amagansett h4 257
Amager f3 158
Amahai h6 97
Amak Island d5 246
Åmål,
Västra Götaland, Swe. e3 156
Amalat e2 94
Amalfi, Col. k7 277
Amalfi, Italy d4 198
Amalia f3 235
Amaliada b5 211
Amalner g10 129
Amalvas k5 157
Amamapare k6 97
Amambaí, Braz. a5 290
Amambaí, Mato Grosso
do Sul, Braz. a5 290
Amambaí, Serra de a5 290
Amambay f4 293
Amami-Ō-shima B 115
Amami-shotō B 115
Amamula e4 225
Amån f2 156
Amana e2 285
Amanã, Lago e4 285
Amance b3 184
Amancey c3 184
Amanda e6 254
Amandola h7 197
Amangel'dy k2 120
Amankaragay k1 120
Amantea f5 199
Amanu K 75
Amanzamnyama d2 232
Amanzimtoti j5 235
Amapá g3 285
Amapa d2 292
Amapá g3 285
Amapari f3 285
Amar j6 97
Amarante, Braz. d3 288
Amarante, Port b3 190
Amarante do Maranhão c3 288
Amaranto b3 210
Amarapura c5 102
Amaravati e7 126
Amardalay d2 112
Amarela, Serra c3 190
Amareleja c6 191
Amares b3 190
Amargosa, Braz. e4 288
Amargosa, U.S.A. e8 263
Amargosa Desert g5 264
Amarguillo g5 191
Amaria d5 130
Amarillo c5 261
Amarillo, Cerro b2 296
Amarkantak g8 124
Amaro, Monte d2 198
Amarpatan g7 124
Amarume h2 115
Amarynthos d4 210
Amaseno c3 198
Amasine b3 220
Amasra d2 208
Amasya, Tur. e2 209
Amasya, Amasya, Tur. e2 208
Amatán a2 276
Amataurá d4 284
Amatenango a2 276
Amatenango de la
Frontera a3 276
Amatepec d4 274
Amatignak Island Ac2 247
Amatikulu j4 235
Amatique, Bahía de c2 276
Amatitán c3 274
Amatitlán b3 276
Amatlán f4 275
Amatlán de Cañas b3 274
Amatrice h7 197
Amay d4 159
Amazon g4 285
Amazonas, Braz. d4 285
Amazonas, Col. c4 284
Amazonas, Peru b5 284
Amazonas, Som. g4 285
Amazonas, Ven. d3 284
Amazónia,
Parque Nacional f4 285
Amazon,
Mouths of the c1 288
Amazon Rain Forest RT d3 286
Amaẕya c5 139
Amb f3 128
Āmba Ālagē e5 219
Ambad d3 126
Amba Farit b1 226
Ambahikily Aa3 233
Ambahita Ab3 233
Ambajogai e3 126
Ambala c4 130
Ambalakida Ab2 233
Ambalamanasy II Ab1 233
Ambalangoda g9 126
Ambalavao Ab3 233
Ambalindum b7 80
Ambam g5 223
Ambanja Ab1 233
Ambarčik s3 119
Ambarcik b1 298
Ambarès-et-Lagarve b4 186
Ambarnyj p4 155
Ambasaguas e2 190
Ambathala a4 84
Ambato b4 284
Ambato Boeny Ab2 233
Ambato Finandrahana Ab3 233
Ambatolahy Ab3 233
Ambatolampy Ab2 233
Ambatomainty Ab2 233
Ambatondrazaka Ab2 233
Ambatosoratra Ab2 233
Ambatovaky,
Réserve de Ab2 233
Ambazac d3 186
Ambela f3 128
Amberg d3 175
Ambergris Cay d1 276
Ambérieu-en-Bugey b5 185
Amberley d5 77
Ambert f3 186
Ambidédi b3 222
Ambikapur h8 125
Ambilobe Ab1 233
Ambinaninony Ab2 233
Ambition, Mount,
Can. b3 248
Ambition, Mount,
U.S.A. m4 247
Ambjörby e2 156
Ambla l3 157
Amble e1 162
Ambler e2 246
Ambleside d2 162
Ambleteuse g2 183
Amblève d4 159
Ambo b2 292
Amboasary Ab4 233
Ambodifotatra Ab2 233
Ambohidratrimo Ab2 233
Ambohijanahary,
Réserve de Ab2 233
Ambohimahasoa Ab3 233
Ambohipaky Aa2 233
Ambohitantely,
Réserve de Ab2 233
Ambohitra Ab1 233
Amboise f5 183
Ambon, Maluku, Indon. h6 97
Ambon, Maluku, Indon. h6 97
Ambondro Ab4 233
Amboseli, Lake b4 226
Amboseli National Park b4 226
Ambositra Ab3 233
Ambovombe Ab4 233
Ambrault d2 186
Ambrières-les-Vallées e4 182
Ambriz b5 224
Ambriz, Coutada do b5 224
Ambronay b4 185
Ambrosio d4 284
Ambrym F 74
Ambuleia, Serras da b5 224
Ambulombo l9 99
Ambunten g8 98
Ambunti l6 97
Ambur f6 126
Amchitka Island Ab2 247
Am-Dam b5 218
Amded, Oued e4 221
Amderma k1 147
Am Djéména h3 223
Amdo m3 125
Amealco d3 274
Ameca, Mex. b3 274
Ameca, Jalisco, Mex. b3 274
Ameca, Zacatecas, Mex. c2 274
Amecameca e4 275
Amedamit b1 226
Ameghino f3 297
Ameixial c7 191
Ameland d1 159
Amelia g7 197
Amelinghausen f2 172
Amendoeira c7 191
Amendolara f5 198
Amenia g3 257
Amer g2 192
Amer, Erg d' f4 221
American b3 264
Americana e5 290
American Falls g4 262
American Falls
Reservoir g4 262
American Samoa
(U.S.A.) j4 73
Americus g3 259
Ameringkogel f2 177
Amersfoort, Neth. d2 159
Amersfoort, R.S.A. h3 235
Amery f2 250
Amery Ice Shelf IH n1 298
Ames e3 260
Amesbury, U.K. e5 163
Amesbury, U.S.A. k2 257
Amet f8 129
Amfikleia c4 210
Amfilochia b4 210
Amfipoli d2 210
Amfissa c4 210
Amfreville-la-Campagne f3 183
Amga p3 119
Amguid f3 221
Amgun' k2 94
Amhara e5 219
Amherst, Can. k6 253
Amherst,
Massachusetts, U.S.A. h2 257
Amherst, New York, U.S.A. b2 256
Amherst, Ohio, U.S.A. e5 254
Amherst, Virginia, U.S.A. g7 254
Amherst, Mount h6 86
Amiata, Monte f7 197
Amidon b7 250
Amiens h3 183
Amik Ovası f4 209
Amilly h5 183
'Amīnābād p6 137
Amindivi Islands c7 126
Amino c3 226
Aminuis c1 234
Amipshahr d5 130
Amīrābād, Īlām, Iran l5 137
Amīrābād, Eşfahān, Iran n5 137
Amir Chah a6 129
Amisk Lake r4 249
Amistad Reservoir c6 261
Amizmiz c2 220
Amjhera g9 129
Amla f9 124
Amlamé e4 223
Amlash n3 137
Åmli c3 156
Amlia Island a5 246
Amlwch b3 162
'Amm Adam e4 219
'Ammān, Jordan e5 139
'Ammān,
'Ammān, Jordan d5 139
Ammanazar q2 137
Ammanford c5 163
Ämmänsaari m4 155
Ammarnäs f4 154
Ammassalik x2 243
Åmmeberg f3 156
Ammer g5 175
Ammergauer Alpen f5 175
Ammergebirge f5 175
Ammerland c2 172
Ammerman Mountain j1 247
Ammerschwihr d2 184
Ammochostos b1 138
Ammotopos a3 210
Amo Jiang d7 104
Amol p3 137
Amolar f3 293
Amontada e2 288
Amores e1 294
Amorgos Aa2 210
Amori g1 210
Amorinópolis c2 290
Amos g1 254
Åmose e3 158
Åmot, Buskerud, Nor. c3 156
Åmot, Telemark, Nor. b3 156
Åmot, Telemark, Nor. c3 156
Åmotfors e3 156
Amou b5 187
Amourj c2 222
Amozoc e4 275
Ampah h5 99
Ampanefena Ab1 233
Ampanihy Aa3 233
Amparafaka, Tanjona Ab1 233
Amparafaravola Ab2 233
Amparai g9 126
Amparo e5 291

308 Ampasimanolotra → Araguaiana

Ampasimanolotra Ab2 233
Ampato, Nevado de c3 292
Ampelonas c3 210
Ampenan j9 99
Amper, Ger. g4 175
Amper, Nig. f4 223
Ampere b6 290
Ampezzo g3 196
Ampibaku l5 99
Ampisikinana Ab1 233
Amplepuis a5 185
Ampoa l5 99
Amposta e4 192
Ampudia f3 190
Ampuero g1 190
Ampus c7 185
Amrar, Jabal b6 139
Amravati e9 124
Amreli e10 129
Amri d7 129
Amring n7 125
Amriswil d2 196
'Amrit d2 138
Amritsar b4 130
Amroha d5 130
Amrum d1 172
Amsel f4 221
Åmsele g4 154
Amstelmeer c2 159
Amstelveen c2 159
Amsterdam, Neth. c2 159
Amsterdam, R.S.A. j3 235
Amsterdam, U.S.A. f2 257
Amsterdamse Waterleidingduinen c2 159
Amstetten f1 177
Am Timan b5 218
Amtzell e5 174
Amudar'ya b1 128
Amu-Dar'ya b2 128
Amukta Island b5 246
Amukta Pass b5 246
Amulree e3 164
Amundsen Bay k1 298
Amundsen Gulf e1 242
Amundsen Plain p10 301
Amundsen-Scott (U.S.A.) k3 298
Amundsen Sea p10 301
Amungen f2 156
Amuntai h6 99
Amur r2 113
Amurang n4 99
Amurang, Teluk n4 99
Amurrio b1 192
Amursk k2 94
Amurskaja Oblast' h2 94
Amurzet r2 113
Amusco f2 190
Amvrakia, Limni b4 210
Amvrosiyivka e3 148
Amyntaio b2 210
Amzhong g4 135
Am-Zoer b5 218
An b6 102
Anaa K 75
Anaba e3 223
Anabanua l6 99
Anabar, Nauru B 74
Anabar, Russ. Fed. m2 119
Ana Branch b1 82
Anabtā d4 139
Anacapri d4 198
Anaco e2 285
Anacoco c4 258
Anaconda g2 262
Anacortes b1 262
Anadarko d5 261
Anadia b4 190
Anadolu Dağları g2 209
Anadyr' t3 119
Anadyrskoe Ploskogor'e t3 119
Anafi, Grc. f6 211
Anafi, Notio Aigaio, Grc. f6 211
Anafonitria a5 211
Anagé d4 289
Anagni h8 197
'Ānah h5 209
Anáhuac, Nuevo León, Mex. j4 273
Anáhuac, Veracruz, Mex. f2 275
Anaimalai Hills e7 126
Anai Mudi Peak e7 126
Anajás c2 288
Anajás, Ilha b2 288
Anajatuba d2 288
Anak n6 113
Anakapalle h4 127
Anakie b3 84
Anaktuvuk g1 247
Anaktuvuk Pass g1 246
Analalava Ab1 233
Analamerana, Réserve de Ab1 233
Analândia e5 290
Analavelona Aa3 233
Anamã e4 285
Anambas, Kepulauan c3 98
Anambra, Nig. f4 223
Anambra, Nig. f4 223
Anamosa f3 260
Anamu f3 285
Anamur d4 208
Anamur Burnu d4 208
Anan f5 114
Ananavero Dam f3 285
Anand f9 129
Anandapur k9 125
Anandpur, Gujarat, India e9 129
Anandpur, Punjab, India c4 130
Anan'ev r6 121
Anano n7 99
Anantapur e5 126
Anantnag b3 130
Anan'yiv j2 201
Anapa e3 148
Anápolis d2 290
Anapú b2 288
Anār q6 137
Anārak p5 137
Anarbar n4 137
Anarcs l3 171
Anargyroi b2 210
Anarjokka k2 155
Anarosa, Piz d' d3 196
Añasco A 270
'Anātā d5 139
Anatahan A 74
Anatoli a3 210
Anatolichis Frangista b4 210
Anatoliki Makedonia kai Thraki f1 210
Anatoliko b2 210
Anatom F 74
Añatuya d1 294
Anauá e3 285
Anaurilândia b5 290
Anavilhanas, Arquipélago das e4 285
Anavra c3 210
Anaya de Alba e4 190
Anayguiou, Sabkhat b3 220
'Anbarān m2 137
Anbyon p6 113
Ancash b1 292
Ancaster f4 162
Ancasti, Sierra c1 294
Ance f4 186
Ancenis d5 182
Ancerville b2 184
Anchán c4 294
Anchau f3 223
Anchieta h4 291
Anchieta, Ilha f5 291
Ancho, Canal b6 295
Anchodaya d2 292
Anchorage g3 247
Anchorena e3 296
Anchor Point g4 246
Ančia k5 157
Anciferovo b2 150
Ancohuma, Nevado de d3 292
Ancón, Arg. g3 297
Ancón, Peru b2 292
Ancona h6 197
Ancón de Sardinas, Bahía de b3 284
Ancram g2 257
Ancrum f4 164
Ancuabe b6 227
Ancud b4 294
Ancud, Golfo de b4 295
Ancy-le-Franc k5 183
Anda, China n2 113
Anda, Indon. n2 99
Anda, Nor. b2 156
Andacollo, Arg. b4 296
Andacollo, Chile b2 294
Andado b8 81
Andahuaylas c2 292
Andaingo Gara Ab2 233
Andalgalá c1 294
Åndalsnes b1 156
Andalucía f7 191
Andalusia f4 258
Andaman and Nicobar Islands n7 127
Andaman Islands n6 127
Andaman Sea e5 300
Andamooka c11 81
Andance a5 185
Andapa Ab1 233
Andara c2 232
Andarāb d3 128
Andarob e2 128
Andau j2 177
Andeg h2 147
Andelle g3 183
Andelot-Blancheville b2 184
Andelot-en-Montagne b4 184
Andenes f2 154
Andenne d4 159
Andéramboukane e2 223
Ånderbakktindan e3 154
Anderlecht c4 159
Andermatt c3 196
Andernach f4 159
Andernos-les-Bains a4 186
Anderslöv e5 156
Anderson, Arg. g3 297
Anderson, Can. d2 242
Anderson, Alaska, U.S.A. g2 247
Anderson, Indiana, U.S.A. d5 254
Anderson, Missouri, U.S.A. b1 258
Anderson, South Carolina, U.S.A. h2 259
Anderson Bay Ab2 83
Anderstorp e4 156
Andes, Col. b2 284
Andes, Som. c4 282
Andévalo, Sierra de c7 191
Andfjorden f2 154
Andhra Pradesh f4 126
Andilamena Ab2 233
Andilanatoby Ab2 233
Andimeshk m5 137
Andirá c5 290
Andir He g1 135
Andirrio b4 210
Andizhan p7 121
Andizhanskaya Oblast' p7 121
Andkhvoy b2 128
Andlau, Fr. d2 184
Andlau, Alsace, Fr. d2 184
Andoain b1 192
Andoany Ab1 233
Andoas b4 284
Andoas Nuevo b4 284
Andocs f5 171
Andogskaja Grjada d2 150
Andohahela, Réserve d' Ab3 233
Andol f4 126
Andolsheim d2 184
Andong, China g4 111
Andong, S. Kor. q7 113
Andongwei f2 111
Andoom e2 80
Andorf e1 176
Andørja f2 154
Andorra, Spain d4 192
Andorra e6 145

ANDORRA

THE PRINCIPALITY OF ANDORRA
Area 468km² (181sq miles)
Capital Andorra la Vella
Organizations CE
Population 66,000
Pop. growth (%) 3.3
Life expectancy 79 (m); 79 (f)
Languages Catalan, French, Spanish
Literacy 99%
Currency euro (US $1 = 0.81 euro)
GDP (US million $) 1040
GDP per head ($US) 15,757

Andorra la Vella d6 187
Andover, U.K. e5 163
Andover, Massachusetts, U.S.A. j2 257
Andover, New York, U.S.A. c2 256
Andover, Ohio, U.S.A. f5 254
Andøya e2 154
Andradas e5 291
Andradina c4 290
Andranomavo Ab2 233
Andranomena, Réserve d' Aa2 233
Andranopasy Aa3 233
Andranovondronina Ab1 233
Andranovory Aa3 233
Andratx g5 193
Andravida b5 211
Andreafsky d3 246
Andreanof Islands Ac2 247
Andreapol' b3 150
Andreevskoe, Ozero l4 147
André Félix, Parc National de d2 224
André Fernandes h1 291
Andrelândia f4 291
Andrequicé f3 291
Andresito j2 297
Andrespol h4 169
Andrew Bay b6 102
Andrews c5 261
Andrézieux-Bouthéon a5 185
Andria f3 198
Andriamena Ab2 233
Andriandampy Ab3 233
Andriba Ab2 233
Andriesvale d3 234
Andries Vosloo Kudu Nature Reserve g6 235
Andrijevica d4 200
Andringitra Ab3 233
Andringitra, Réserve d' Ab3 233
Andritsana b5 211
Andrijušino k4 147
Androka Aa4 233
Andros, Bah. k7 259
Andros, Notio Aigaio, Grc. e5 211
Andros, Notio Aigaio, Grc. e5 210
Androscoggin l3 255
Andros Town l7 259
Androtti c7 126
Andrupene m4 157
Andrushivka c2 148
Andrychów h6 169
Andselv g2 154
Andsnes h1 154
Andudu e3 225
Andújar f6 191
Andulo c6 224
Anduze f4 187
Aneby f4 156
Anéfis e2 223
Anegada, Bahía f6 297
Anegada Passage j5 271
Anegada, Punta g7 277
Aného e4 223
Anelghowhat F 74
Añelo c5 296
Anengué, Lac a4 224
Anenii Noi j2 201
Anet g4 183
Aneta e7 250
Aneto e2 192
Aney g5 221
Anfu k5 105
Angahook Lorne State Park c4 82
Angamos, Isla a5 295
Angamos, Punta c4 292
Angangueo d4 274
Ang'angxi m2 113
Angaradébou e3 223
Angarsk c2 94
Angas Downs l9 87
Angat c3 100
Angathia c2 210
Angatuba d5 290
Ånge f1 156
Angel c4 172
Ángel de la Guarda, Isla c3 272
Angeles c3 100
Angel Falls e2 285
Ängelholm e4 156
Angeli k2 155
Angelica g1 297
Angelina b4 258
Angellala Creek b5 85
Angelo d8 87
Angelokastro b4 210
Angel R. Cabada g4 275
Angels Camp c3 264
Ängereb Wenz e5 219
Ångermanälven g5 154
Ångermanbalen g5 154
Angermünde k2 173
Angern an der March h1 177
Angers e5 182
Ångersjö f2 156
Angerville h4 183
Ängesån j3 155
Angesön h5 154
Anggana j5 99
Anggowala, Bukit l7 99
Anggroto l6 97
Angguruk k6 97
Anghiari g6 197
Angical d4 288
Angicos e3 288
Angikuni Lake k3 242
Angistri, Akra c3 210
Angitis e1 210
Angkor Wat g9 103
Angle a5 163
Angle Inlet f6 250
Anglem, Mount a7 77
Anglès g3 192
Anglesey b3 162
Angles-sur-l'Anglin c2 186
Anglet a5 187
Angleton b5 258
Anglin c4 186
Anglure j4 183
Ango e3 225
Angoche f2 233
Angohrān r8 137
Angol a4 296
Angola, Indiana, U.S.A. d5 254
Angola, U.S.A. a2 256
Angola d6 217

ANGOLA

THE REPUBLIC OF ANGOLA
Area 1,246,700km² (481,354sq miles)
Capital Luanda
Organizations COMESA, SADC
Population 13,180,000
Pop. growth (%) 2.4
Life expectancy 43 (m); 46 (f)
Languages Portuguese, Umbundo, Kimbundo, Chokwe, Ganguela
Literacy 41.7%
Currency readjusted kwanza (US $1 = 77.86 readjusted kwanza)
GDP (US million $) 4522
GDP per head ($US) 343

Angola Basin l11 302
Angontsy, Tanjona Ac2 233
Angostura, San Luis Potosí, Mex. d2 274
Angostura, Sinaloa, Mex. e5 272
Angostura, Presa de la n9 273
Angoulême c3 186
Angoumois c3 186
Angra do Heroísmo A 220
Angra dos Reis f5 291
Angren n7 121
Ängsfjärden d5 154
Ang Thong e8 103
Angu d3 224
Angualasto c2 294
Anguang m3 113
Angüés d2 192
Anguiano b2 192
Anguil f4 297
Anguilla d3 258
Anguilla (U.K.) h7 241
Anguillara Veneta f4 196
Anguille, Cape n5 253
Angul j9 125
Anguli Nur h5 112
Angurugu c2 80
Angus f3 164
Angustura e1 293
Angwa e2 233
Angwin a3 264
Anhandui, Braz. a4 290
Anhanduí, Mato Grosso do Sul, Braz. a4 290
Anhanguera d3 290
Anholt e2 158
Anhua h4 104
Anhui e3 111
Anhumas a2 290
Ani j2 115
Aniak e3 246
Aniakchak National Monument and Preserve e4 246
Aniane f5 187
Anibal Pinta, Lago b6 295
Anibare Bay B 74
Aniche b4 159
Anicuns d2 290
Anié e3 223
Anie, Pic d' b6 187
Anihovka h2 120
Anikovo g2 151
Anin c8 102
Anina e3 200
Anitaguipan Point e5 100
Aniva, Mys l3 94
Aniva, Zaliv l3 94
Anivorano Avaratra Ab1 233
Aniwa F 74
Anjan, Swe. d5 154
Anjan, Jämtland, Swe. d5 154
Anjanaharibe-Sud, Réserve de Ab1 233
Anjar e9 129
'Anjarah d4 139
Anjengo e8 126
Anji f4 111
Anjihai v5 121
Anjir Avand q5 137
Anjoman r4 137
Anjou e5 182
Anjozorobe Ab2 233
Anju e2 111
Anjū n6 113
An'judin j3 147
Anjum e1 159
Ankaboa, Tanjona Aa3 233
Ankang a3 106
Ankara, Tur. d3 208
Ankara, Ankara, Tur. d3 208
Ankarafantsika, Réserve d' Ab2 233
Ankaramena Ab3 233
Ankarana, Réserve de Ab1 233
Ankaratra, Madag. Ab2 233
Ankaratra, Madag. Ab2 233
Ankarsrum g4 156
Ankarsund f4 154
Ankavandra Ab2 233
Ankazobe Ab2 233
Ankilizato Ab3 233
Anklam j2 173
Ankleshwar f10 129
Ankogel e2 176
Ankoro e5 225
Ankpa f4 223
Ankum c3 172
Anlaby f3 162
Anloga e4 223
Anlong e6 104
Ånlong Vêng g8 103
Anlu c4 106
Ånn d5 154
Anna d5 193
Annaba f1 221
Annaberg g2 177
Annaberg-Buchholtz j2 175
An Nabk e2 138
An Nafūd f2 219
Annai f3 285
An Najaf k6 137
Anna, Lake h6 255
Annalee d2 165
Annalong f2 165
An Nāmir e4 138
Annam Plateau g7 102
Annan, Scotland, U.K. e4 164
Annan, Scotland, U.K. e4 164
Annandale, U.K. e4 164
Annandale, U.S.A. f4 256
Anna Pink, Bahía b5 295
Anna Plains d6 86
Anna Point B 74
Annapolis d6 256
Annapolis Royal k6 253
Annapurna I g5 135
Ann Arbor e4 254
Anna Regina f2 285
An Nashābiyah e3 138
An Nāşiriyah, Iraq l6 137
An Nāşiriyah, Syria e3 138
An Nawfaliyah h2 221
Ann, Cape, Anguilla l1 298
Ann, Cape, U.S.A. k2 257
Annean, Lake d10 87
Anneberg f1 158
Annecy c5 185
Annecy, Lac d' c5 185
Annecy-le-Vieux c5 185
Annemasse c4 184
Annenkovo j5 151
Annet A 163
Annette Island m5 247
Annezin a4 159
An Nhơn j9 103
An Nimārah f5 136
Anning d6 104
Anning He d5 104
Anniston g3 259
Annobón f5 223
Annonay a5 185
Annone, Lago di d4 196
Annopol k5 169
Annot c7 185
Annotto Bay B 270
An Nu'ayriyah m8 137
An Nu'māniyah k5 137
An Nuqay'ah n9 137
Annville d4 256
Annweiler am Trifels g2 174
Ano Agios Vlasios b4 210
Ano Drosini f1 210
Anogeia c6 211
Anogyra a2 138
Anoka e2 260
Ano Komi b2 210
Ano Lechonia d3 210
Ano Lefkimmi a3 210
Ano Mera f5 211
Ano Poroïa d1 210
Anori e4 285
Anorontany, Tanjona Ab1 233
Anosibe An'Ala Ab2 233
Ano Synoikia Trikala c5 211
Anotaie f3 285
Anou Meniet e3 221
Ano Viannos f7 211
Anoya c5 154
Anping, Hebei, China d0 106
Anping, Henan, China d3 106
Anping, Liaoning, China m5 113
Anpu h8 104
Anqing e4 111
Anqiu f1 111
Anquela del Ducado b4 192
Anren j5 105
Ans c2 158
Ansager b3 158
Ansai a1 106
Ansas k6 97
Ansbach e4 175
Anse a5 185
Anse-à-Galets h5 271
Anse à la Mouche A 226
Anse-à-Pitre j5 271
Anse-à-Veau h5 266
Anseba Shet e4 219
Anse Boileau A 226
Anse d'Hainault g5 266
Ansedonia f7 197
Anseremme c4 159
Anserma b2 284
Anshan m5 113
Anshun e5 104
Ansião b5 191
Ansilta c1 296
Ansina e2 294
Ansjö f5 154
Ansley d3 260
Ansó d2 192
Anson d5 261
Anson Bay k3 86
Ansŏng p7 113
Ansongo e2 223
Ansonia g3 257
Ansonville j2 259
Anstruther f3 164
Ansudu k6 97
Ant, F. S. M. G 74
Ant, U.K. h4 162
Anta c2 292
Antabamba c2 292
Antakya f4 209
Antalaha Ac1 233
Antaliepté l5 157
Antalya, Tur. c4 208
Antalya, Antalya, Tur. c4 208
Antalya Körfezi c4 208
Antanambao Manampotsy Ab2 233
Antanambe Ab2 233
Antananarivo, Madag. Ab2 233
Antananarivo, Antananarivo, Madag. Ab2 233
Antanifotsy Ab2 233
Antanimora Atsimo Ab3 233
Antanmieva Aa3 233
Antarctica CT kk1 298
Antarctic Peninsula kk1 298
Antas, Braz. b7 289
Antas, Port b3 190
Antas, Spain c7 193
Antas, Andalucía, Spain c7 193
Antas de Ulla c2 190
An Teallach c2 164
Antelias d3 138
Antelope Valley e7 265
Anten e3 156
Antenne b3 186
Antequera f7 191
Anthili c4 210
Anthony f1 272
Anthony Lagoon b4 80
Anti Atlas c2 220
Antibes d7 185
Antibes, Cap d' c7 185
Antica, Isla e1 285
Anticosti, Île d' l4 253
Antifer, Cap d' f3 183
Antigo b3 254
Antigonish m6 253
Antigonos b2 210
Antigua, Guat. b3 276
Antigua, Iraq Ae2 189
Antigua and Barbuda h7 241

ANTIGUA & BARBUDA

ANTIGUA AND BARBUDA
Area 442km² (170sq miles)
Capital St John's, on Antigua
Organizations ACS, CARICOM, COMM, OECS
Population 77,426
Pop. growth (%) 0.5
Life expectancy 74 (m); 74 (f)
Languages English, English Patois
Literacy 90%
Currency East Caribbean dollar (US $1 = 2.67 East Caribbean dollar)
GDP (US million $) 603
GDP per head ($US) 7788

Antigues, Pointe d' C 271
Antiguo-Morelos e2 275
Antikyra c4 210
Antikyras, Kolpos c4 210
Antikythira d7 211
Antilhue b5 296
Antilla e5 293
Antillo e7 199
Antimacheia Ac2 211
Antimilos e6 211
Anting g4 111
Antioch b3 264
Antioquia b2 284
Antioquia b2 284
Antiparos, Grc. f5 211
Antiparos, Notio Aigaio, Grc. f5 211
Antipaxoi a3 210
Antipodes Islands B 77
Antipsara f4 210
Antisana, Cerro b4 284
Antissa f3 210
Antlers b2 258
Antofagasta, Antofagasta, Chile c4 292
Antofagasta, Región II, Chile d4 292
Antofagasta de la Sierra d5 292
Antofalla, Salina de d5 292
Antofalla, Volcán d5 292
Antón g6 277
Antonhibe Ab2 233
Antonina d6 290
Antônio Carlos g4 291
Antonio de Biedma c5 295
Antônio Dias g3 291
Antônio Lemos b2 288
Antonito b4 261
Antón Lizardo g4 275
Antony h4 183
Antopal' n3 169
Antrain d4 182
Antratsyt e2 148
Antrim, England, U.K. b1 165
Antrim, Northern Ireland, U.K. e2 165
Antrim Hills e2 164
Antrim Plateau j5 86
Antrodoco h7 197
Antropovo g2 151
Antsiafabositra Ab2 233
Antsirabe Ab2 233
Antsirabe Avaratra Ab1 233
Antsirañana, Madag. Ab1 233
Antsirañana, Antsirañana, Madag. Ab1 233
Antsla m4 157
Antsohihy Ab1 233
Anttis j3 155
Antuco b4 296
Antuco, Volcán b4 296
Antufash, Jazirat f4 219
Antwerpen, Bel. c3 159
Antwerpen, Antwerpen, Bel. c3 159
Anuanuraro K 75
Anuanurunga K 75
Anŭi p8 113
Anupgarh f6 129
Anuradhapura g8 126
Anvik, Alaska, U.S.A. d3 246
Anvik, Alaska, U.S.A. d3 246
Anvil Peak Ab1 247
Anvin h2 183
Anxi, Fujian, China m6 105
Anxi, Gansu, China b4 94
Anxian e3 104
Anxiang c5 106
Anxious Bay b12 81
Anyama d4 222
Anyang, Henan, China d1 106
Anyang, China b3 106
Anyang, S. Kor. p7 113
Anyar c8 98
Anydro f6 211
A'nyêmaqên Shan c1 104
Anykščiai l5 157
Anyuan k6 105
Anyue e3 104
Anze c1 106
Anzelberg g3 175
Anžero-Sudžensk j4 118
Anzi, D.R.C. d4 224
Anzi, Italy e4 198
Anzin b4 159
Anzio b3 198
Anzoátegui, Arg. f5 297
Anzoátegui, Ven. e2 285
Anzur f7 191
Aoba F 74
Ao Ban Don a1 101
Aob Luang National Park d6 102
Aoiz c2 192
Aojiang n5 105
Aomori, Japan j1 115
Aomori, Aomori, Japan j1 115
Aonla d5 130
Aoos a3 210
Ao Phang Nga National Park a1 101
Aorangi Mountains e4 77
Aorere d4 77
Aoshanwei g1 111
Aosta b4 196
Aosta, Valle d', Italy b4 196
Aosta, Valle d', Italy b4 196
Aoste b5 185
Aouderas f2 223
Aougoundou, Lac d2 222
Aoukâr c4 220
Aouk, Bahr d2 224
Aoulef e3 221
Aoulime, Jbel c2 220
Aourou b3 222
Aozou a3 218
Apac f3 225
Apache Junction h9 263
Apaga b4 284
Apagado, Volcán d4 292
Apahida f2 201
Apalachicola, Florida, U.S.A. g5 259
Apalachicola, Georgia, U.S.A. g4 259
Apalachin d2 256
Apan e4 275
Apango e5 275
Apaporis c4 284
Aparecida f5 291
Aparecida do Rio Doce c3 290
Aparecida do Tabuado c4 290
Aparico g5 297
Aparima b7 77
Aparri c1 100
Apar, Teluk j6 99
Aparurén e2 285
Apaseo El Grande d3 274
Apastovo k4 151
Apataki K 75
Apatin d3 200
Apatity p3 155
Apatou g2 285
Apatzingán c4 274
Apauwor k6 97
Apaxtla e4 275
Ape m4 157
Apecchio g6 197
Apediá e2 293
Apeldoorn d2 159
Apelern e3 172
Apen c2 172
Apensen c5 158
Apere d2 292
Aperi Ac3 211
Aper-Tief c2 172
Apex k2 259
Apex Mountain k3 247
Apfelstädt f5 173
Api, D.R.C. e3 225
Api, Nepal e4 130
Apia b2 284
Apiacá f2 293
Apiacas, Serra dos f2 293
Apiaí d6 290
Apiaú e3 285
Apiaú, Serra do e33 285
Apic Pac h5 275
Api, Gunung k9 99
Apipilulco e4 275
Apiro h6 197
Api, Tanjung l5 99
Apiti e3 76
Apizaco e4 275
Apizolaya h5 273
Aplahoué e4 223
Aplao c3 292
A Pobra de Trives c2 190
Apodi, Braz. e3 288
Apodi, Rio Grande do Norte, Braz. e3 288
Apo East Passage c4 100
Apoera f2 285
Apolakkia Ac2 211
Apolda c1 175
Apolima Strait M 75
Apollo Bay f15 81
Apollon f5 211
Apollona Ac2 211
Apollonia e6 211
Apolo d2 292
Apo, Mount e7 100
Aponguao e2 285
A Pontenova c1 190
Apopka, Lake j5 259
Aporé, Braz. c3 290
Aporé, Goiás, Braz. b3 290
Aporema g3 285
Äpörka h4 171
Apostle Islands a2 254
Apostle Islands National Lakeshore a2 254
Apóstoles e1 294
Apostoloi e7 211
Apostolos Andreas, Cape c1 138
Apoteri f3 285
Apo West Passage c4 100
Apozai d5 128
Appalachian Mountains f5 241
Äppelbo f2 156
Appen c5 158
Appennino Abruzzese c2 198
Appennino Tosco-Emiliano e5 197
Appennino Umbro-Marchigiano g6 197
Appenzell a2 176
Appiano sulla Strada del Vino f3 196
Appignano h6 197
Appingedam e1 159
Appleby-in-Westmorland d2 162
Applecross c2 164
Appleton, Minnesota, U.S.A. e2 260
Appleton, Wisconsin, U.S.A. b3 254
Apple Valley f7 265
Appomattox g7 254
Approuague f3 285
Apra Harbor C 74
Aprelevka d4 150
Aprica e3 196
Aprigliano f5 199
Aprilia g8 197
Apsalos c2 210
Apšeronsk e3 148
Apt b7 185
Ap Tan My j10 103
Apu p6 99
Apucarana c5 290
Apucarana, Serra da c5 290
Apulco e3 275
Apurahuan b6 100
Apure, Ven. d2 284
Apure, Ven. d2 284
Apurímac, Peru c2 292
Apurímac, Peru c2 292
Apurito d2 284
Aqaba, Gulf of e7 136
Aqal s7 121
Aqchah c2 128
'Aqdā p5 137
Āq Qal'eh q3 137
Aqqan j1 125
Aqqikkol Hu f2 122
'Aqrabah e3 138
'Aqrah j4 209
Aquaviva delle Fonti f4 198
Aquebogue h4 257
Aquidabán f4 293
Aquidauana, Braz. a4 290
Aquidauana, Mato Grosso do Sul, Braz. f4 293
Aquila c4 274
Aquiles f3 272
Aquin h5 266
Aquino c3 198
Aquio d3 284
Aquismón e3 275
Aquitaine b4 187
Ara, India j7 125
Ara, Spain d2 192
Āra Ārba c2 226
Arab, Afg. b5 128
Arab, U.S.A. f2 258
'Arabābād r5 137
'Arab al Mulk d1 138
Arab, Bahr el e1 225
Arabelo e3 285
Arabian Basin c5 300
Arabian Sea c4 300
Arabopó e2 285
Arac d6 187
Araç d2 208
Araça e3 285
Aracaju e4 288
Aracamuni, Cerro d3 284
Aracanguy, Montes de f4 293
Aracati e2 288
Aracatu d4 289
Araçatuba c4 290
Aracena d7 191
Aracena, Embalse de d7 191
Aracena, Isla b6 295
Aracena, Sierra de d7 191
Arachnaio, Grc. c5 211
Arachnaio, Peloponnisos, Grc. c5 211
Arachova c4 210
Arachthos b3 210
Aracruz h3 291
Araçuaí, Braz. g2 291
Araçuaí, Minas Gerais, Braz. g2 291
'Arad d5 139
Arad, Rom. e2 201
Arad, Arad, Rom. k5 171
Arada b5 218
Arādān p4 137
Arada, Serra de b4 190
Arade b7 191
Arade, Barragem de b7 191
Aradeib, Wadi b5 218
Aradippou b2 138
Arafura Sea g6 300
Aragarças b1 290
Aragats Lerr f4 148
Aragón, Spain d3 192
Aragón, Spain c2 192
Aragona c7 199
Aragoncillo b4 192
Aragua d2 284
Araguacema c3 288
Aragua de Barcelona e2 285
Aragua de Maturín e2 285
Araguaia c3 288
Araguaiana c1 290

Araguaia → Asind 309

Araguaia, Parque Nacional de ☆ c4 288
Araguaína c3 288
Araguainha b2 290
Araguana c3 288
Araguapiche, Punta ► e2 284
Araguari, Braz. ≈ d3 290
Araguari, Minas Gerais, Braz. d3 290
Araguatins c3 288
Aragvi ≈ g4 149
Arai h3 115
Araiosos d2 288
Arajärvi ○ l3 155
Arak, Alg. e3 221
Arak, Indon. k7 97
Arāk m4 137
Arak g5 209
Arakaka p11 271
Arakamčečen, Ostrov ▭ b2 246
Arakan [1] a6 102
Arakan Yoma ⛰ b6 102
Arakkonam f6 126
Araku h3 126
Aral t7 121
Aral Sea ⊙ g5 120
Aral'sk h4 120
Aral'skoye More ⊙ g5 120
Aralsor, Ozero, Kaz. ○ b3 120
Aralsor, Ozero, Kaz. ○ d3 120
Aralsul'fat h4 120
Aramac g7 80
Aramaçá, Ilha ▭ d4 284
Aramac Creek ≈ a3 84
Aramah ⌒ g2 219
A Ramallosa b2 190
Arambag k8 125
Aramberri e1 275
Arame c2 288
Aramecina d4 276
Aramits b5 187
Aramon a7 185
'Aramsha d3 138
Aran ≈ e9 124
Äran ≈ e2 156
Arancibia c1 296
Aranda ≈ c3 192
Aranda de Duero g3 190
Arandas c3 274
Aranđelovac e3 200
Arandis a1 234
Arang h9 124
Arani f6 126
Aran Island ▭ c1 165
Aran Islands ▭ b3 165
Aranjuez g4 190
Arano f4 297
Aranos c2 234
Aransas Pass a6 258
Arantes ≈ c3 290
Aranuka ▭ H 75
Aranyaprathet f9 103
Araouane d5 220
Arapahoe d3 260
Arapari g4 285
Arapawa Island ▭ e4 77
Arapey Grande ≈ j1 297
Arapicos b4 284
Arapiraca e3 288
Arapiri, Ilha ▭ b2 288
Arapiuns ≈ f4 285
Arapkir g3 209
Arapongas c5 290
Arapoti d6 290
Arapuá b4 290
Arapuni e3 76
'Ar'ar h6 137
Araracuara c4 284
Araral, Cerro △ d4 292
Araranguá c7 289
Ararapira d6 290
Araraquara d4 290
Araras, Amazonas, Braz. d1 292
Araras, Pará, Braz. b3 288
Araras, São Paulo, Braz. e5 290
Araras, Açude ⊙ d2 2880
Araras, Serra das, Braz. ⛰ b6 290
Ararat, Arm. g5 149
Ararat, Aust. f14 81
Arari d2 288
Araria k6 125
Arari, Lago ○ c2 288
Araripe d3 288
Araripina d3 288
Araruama g5 291
Araruama, Lago de ○ g5 291
'Ar'ar, Wādī ≈ f1 219
Aras, Spain b2 192
Aras, Tur. j3 209
Aras de Alpuente c5 193
Ar Asgat c1 112
Aras Nehri ≈ h3 209
Arata e3 297
Aratos f1 210
Arau b2 101
Arauá ≈ e4 285
Arauca, Col. [1] c2 284
Arauca, Col. c2 284
Arauca, Ven. ≈ d2 284
Araucanía [1] a5 296
Araucária d6 290
Arauco a4 296
Arauquita c2 284
Araure d2 284
Araviana ≈ c3 192
Aravissos c2 210
Arawhana △ f3 76
Araxá e3 291
Araxos, Akra ► b4 210
Araya, Península de ► e1 285
Araya, Punta de ► e1 284
Arayıt Dağı △ c3 208
Araz ≈ h5 149
Arazede b4 190
Arba ≈ c3 192
Arba de Biel ≈ d2 192
Arba de Luesia ≈ c2 192
Ārba Minch b2 226
Arbatax Ab3 198
Arbaž k3 151
Arbeca e3 192
Arbél d4 138
Arbesbach f1 177
Arbeteta b4 192
Arbia ≈ f6 197
Arbīl k4 209
Arbizu b2 192
Arboga f3 156
Arbois b4 184
Arboledas g4 297
Arboletas, Punta ► b2 284
Arboletes j6 277
Arbolito j2 297
Arbon d2 196
Arborfield b4 250
Arborg e5 250
Arborio c4 196
Arbrå g2 156
Arbroath f3 164
Arbúcies g3 192
Arbuckle a2 264
Arbu Lut, Dasht-e ≈ a6 129
Arbus Aa3 198
Arc ≈ b7 185
Arcachon a4 186
Arcachon, Bassin d' ◄ a4 186
Arcade b2 256
Arcadia, California, U.S.A. e7 265
Arcadia, Florida, U.S.A. j6 259
Arcadia, Louisiana, U.S.A. c3 258
Arcadia, Michigan, U.S.A. c3 254
Arcadia, Pennsylvania, U.S.A. b4 256
Arcata a5 262
Arc Dome △ f3 264
Arce c3 198
Arcelia d4 274
Arcen e3 159
Arc-en-Barrois b3 184
Arceniega a1 192
Arc-et-Senans b3 184
Arcevia g6 197
Archaia Korinthos c5 211
Archangelos Ad2 211
Archangelos, Akra ► c6 211
Archena c6 193
Archer, Aust. ≈ f2 80
Archer, U.S.A. h5 259
Archer Bend National Park ☆ f2 80
Arches c2 184
Arches National Park ☆ j6 263
Archiac b3 186
Archidona f7 191
Archipelago of the Recherche ▭ f14 87
Archipoli Ad2 211
Archman r2 137
Arcidosso f7 197
Arcipelago de la Maddalena, Parco Nazionale dell' ☆ Ab1 198
Arcipelago Toscano, Parco Nazionale dell' ☆ e7 197
Arcis-sur-Aube k4 183
Ärçivan m2 137
Arckaringa ≈ b9 81
Arc-lès-Gray b3 184
Arco, Italy e4 196
Arco, U.S.A. g4 262
Arco de Baúlhe c3 190
Arcola, Illinois, U.S.A. b6 254
Arcola, Mississippi, U.S.A. d3 258
Arcola, Virginia, U.S.A. c6 256
Arconce ≈ a4 184
Arcos, Braz. f4 291
Arcos, Spain g2 190
Arcos de Jalón b3 192
Arcos de la Frontera e8 191
Arcos de Valdevez b3 190
Arcouest, Pointe de l' ► c4 182
Arcoverde e3 288
Arcozelo, Braga, Port b3 190
Arcozelo, Guarda, Port c4 190
Arctic Ocean 〰 mm3 299
Arctic Red ≈ m2 247
Arctic Village h1 247
Arctowski (Poland) ▪ u1 298
Arcusa e2 192
Arcy-sur-Cure j5 183
Arda, Bul. ≈ f1 210
Arda, Bul. e1 210
Arda, Italy ≈ d5 196
Ardabīl, Iran [1] a8 120
Ardabīl, Ardabīl, Iran m2 137
Ardagger Markt f1 177
Ardagh b4 165
Ardahan, Tur. [1] j2 209
Ardahan, Ardahan, Tur. j2 209
Ardāk g9 120
Ardakān, Fārs, Iran p6 137
Ardakān, Yazd, Iran p5 137
Ardal n6 137
Årdal b2 156
Ardal △ a3 192
Ardalsknapen △ b3 156
Årdalstangen b2 156
Ardara, Ire. c2 165
Ardara, Italy Aa2 198
Ardas ≈ g1 210
Arḑ aş Şawwān ⌒ e6 139
Ardatov, Nižegorodskaja Oblast', Russ. Fed. g4 151
Ardatov, Respublika Mordovija, Russ. Fed. j4 151
Ardea g8 197
Ardèche, Fr. ≈ a6 185
Ardèche, Rhône-Alpes, Fr. [2] a6 185
Ardee e3 165
Arden c2 158
Arden, Mount △ c11 81
Ardennes [2] k3 183
Ardentes d2 186
Arden Town b3 264
Ardes f3 186
Ardestān p5 137
Ardez e3 196
Ardglass f2 165
Ardgroom b5 165
Ardila ≈ d6 191
Ardilla, Cerro la △ c2 274
Ardino f1 210
Ardivachar Point ► a2 164
Ardlethan h13 81
Ardlui d3 164
Ardlussa c3 164
Ardmolich c3 164
Ardmore, Ire. d5 165
Ardmore, Oklahoma, U.S.A. a2 258
Ardmore, Pennsylvania, U.S.A. e4 256
Ardmore Bay ◄ d5 165
Ardon g4 149
Ardore f6 199
Ardres g2 183
Ardrossan d4 164
Ards [2] b1 165
Ards Forest Park ☆ d1 165
Ards Peninsula ► f2 165
Arduan Island ▭ d3 218
Ardud l4 171
Ardvasar c2 164
Åre d5 154
Areado e4 291
Arebi e3 225
Arèches c5 185
Arecibo A 270
Areco ≈ g3 297
Arefino e2 150
Arefu g3 201
Areia Branca e2 288
Arekhava m4 169
Aremberg △ b2 174
Arén e2 192
Arena ▭ c6 100
Arenal d3 276
Arenales, Cerro △ b5 295
Arenal, Volcán △ e5 276
Arena Point ► d4 100
Arena, Point ► b6 263
Arenápolis f2 293
Arenas de Iguña f1 190
Arenas de San Pedro e4 190
Arenas, Punta ► c4 292
Arenaza g3 297
Arendal c3 156
Arendonk d3 159
Arendsee ○ g3 173
Arenitas Blancas j1 297
Arenos, Embalse de ⊙ d4 193
Arenshausen e4 172
Arenys de Mar g3 192
Arenzano c5 197
Areopoli c6 211
Areponapuchi f4 272
Arequipa, Peru [1] c3 292
Arequipa, Arequipa, Peru c3 292
Arequlto g2 297
Arere g4 285
Ārēro b3 226
Arès a4 186
Ares del Maestre d4 192
Åreskutan △ d5 154
Arethousa d2 210
Arevalillo, Spain ≈ f4 190
Arevalillo, Castilla y León, Spain e4 190
Arévalo f3 190
Arez c5 191
Arezzo, Italy [2] f6 197
Arezzo, Toscana, Italy f6 197
Arfara c5 211
Arga ≈ c2 192
Argajaš k5 147
Argaka a1 138
Argalasti d3 210
Argallanes, Sierra de los ⛰ e6 191
Argallón e6 191
Argaman d4 139
Argamasilla de Alba a5 193
Argamasilla de Calatrava f6 191
Arganda g4 190
Arganil b4 190
Argao d6 100
Argatay d3 112
Argegno d4 196
Argelès-Gazost b5 187
Argelès-sur-Mer f6 187
Argelita d4 193
Argens ≈ c7 185
Argenta, Italy f5 196
Argenta, U.S.A. b6 254
Argentan e4 182
Argentat d3 186
Argente c4 192
Argentera a5 197
Argentia q5 253
Argentiera Aa2 198
Argentière c5 185
Argentina d6 283

ARGENTINA

THE ARGENTINE REPUBLIC
Area 2,766,889km^2 (1,068,302sq miles)
Capital Buenos Aires
Organizations IADB, SELA, LAIA
Population 37,980,000
Pop. growth (%) 1
Life expectancy 69 (m); 76 (f)
Languages Spanish
Literacy 97.1%
Currency peso
(US $1 = 2.95 peso)
GDP (US million $) 104,600
GDP per head ($US) 2754

Argentine Basin ▦ f14 302
Argentino, Lago ○ b6 295
Argenton ≈ e5 182
Argenton-Château e6 182
Argenton-sur-Creuse d2 186
Argentre e4 182
Argentré-du-Plessis d4 182
Argent-sur-Sauldre h5 183
Argerich f5 297
Argerín △ b7 193
Argeș, Rom. [1] g3 201
Argeș, Rom. ≈ g3 201
Argés f5 191
Arghandab ≈ c4 128
Arghastan ≈ c5 128
Arginonta Ab1 210
Argolikos Kolpos ◄ c5 210
Argonia a1 258
Argonne ♦ k3 183
Argos, Grc. c5 211
Argos, Spain ≈ c6 193
Argos, U.S.A. c5 254
Argos Orestiko b2 210
Argostoli a4 210
Argueil g3 183
Arguellite b6 193
Arguello, Point ► c7 265
Arguenon ≈ c4 182
Arguís d2 192
Argun' ≈ k1 113
Argun g4 149
Argungu e3 223
Argunskij Hrebet △ j1 113
Argus Range ≋ f5 265
Arguut b3 112
Argyle e6 250
Argyle, Lake ○ j5 86
Argyll and Bute [2] c4 164
Arhangay [1] a1 112
Arhangel'sk e2 146
Arhangel'skaja Oblast' [1] e3 146
Arhangel'skoe d5 150
Arhara, Russ. Fed. ≈ r1 113
Arhara, Amurskaja Oblast', Russ. Fed. q1 113
Arhipo-Osipovka e3 148
Arhipovka f3 150
Århus, Den. [1] d2 158
Århus, Århus, Den. d2 158
Århus Bugt ◄ d2 158
Ariaga ▭ n2 99
Ariake-kai ◄ d5 114
Ariamsvlei c4 234
Ariano Irpino e3 198
Ariari ≈ c3 284
Arias f2 297
Ariaú f4 285
Aribe c2 192
Aribinda d3 222
Arica, Chile c3 292
Arica, Col. c4 284
Aricagua c2 284
Arida f4 115
Aridaia c2 210
Aridal, Sabkhat ⊙ b3 220
Arid, Cape ► f14 87
Ariège, Fr. ≈ d5 187
Ariège, Midi-Pyrénées, Fr. [2] d6 187
Ariel h4 297
Ari'él d4 139
Arieqa e4 138
Arīḩā, Jordan d5 139
Arīḩā, Syria f5 209
Arijón g1 297
Arikaree ≈ c4 260
Arimã e5 285
Arima E 271
Arima-Tunapuna-Piarco [1] 271 271
Arimu Mine f2 285
Arinaga Ad3 189
Arinagour b3 164
Ariño d3 192
Arinos, Braz. ≈ f2 293
Arinos, Mato Grosso, Braz. f2 293
Arinos, Minas Gerais, Braz. e1 291
Arinthod b4 184
'Arīn, Wādī al ≈ f4 219
Ario de Rosáles d4 274
Ariogala k5 157
Aripo, Mount △ E 271
Ariporo ≈ c2 284
Aripuanã, Braz. ≈ e5 285
Aripuanã, Mato Grosso, Braz. f2 293
Ariquemes e1 293
Ariranhá ≈ b2 290
Aris b1 234
Arisaig c3 164
Arisaru Falls ⌊ f2 285
Arismendi d2 284
Arista d2 274
Aristazabal Island ▭ c5 248
Aristizábal, Cabo ► c5 295
Aritwala f5 128
Aritzo Ab3 198
Arivonimamo Ab2 233
Ariza b3 192
Arizaro, Salar de ⌣ d4 292
Arize ≈ d5 187
Arizgoiti b1 192
Arizona, Arg. e3 296
Arizona, U.S.A. [1] h8 263
Arizpe h10 263
Ar'ja h3 151
Årjäng e3 156
Ärjänselkä ○ l4 155
Arjasa h8 99
Arjeplog f3 154
Arjona, Col. k5 277
Arjona, Spain f7 191
Arjonilla f7 191
Arkadak f2 149
Arkadelphia c2 258
Arkalgud e6 126
Arkalochori f7 211
Arkalyk l2 120
Arkansas, U.S.A. [1] c2 258
Arkansas, Arkansas, U.S.A. ≈ b2 258
Arkansas City a1 258
Arkasa Ac3 211
Arkatag Shan ⛰ j1 135
Arkenu, Jabal △ b3 218
Arkitsa d4 210
Arkitsa, Akra ► d4 210
Arklow e4 165
Arkoi, Grc. ▭ Ab1 211
Arkoi, Notio Aigaio, Grc. Ab1 210
Arkoma b2 258
Arkona, Kap ► j1 173
Arkösund g3 156
Arkoudi ▭ a4 210
Arkul' l3 151
Arlanc f3 186
Arlanza ≈ g2 190
Arlanzón ≈ g2 190
Arlas ≈ b4 192
Arlbergpass ≍ b2 176
Arles a7 185
Arles-sur-Tech e6 187
Arleux b4 159
Arli e3 223
Arlington, R.S.A. g4 235
Arlington, U.S.A. [2] k6 257
Arlington, Georgia, U.S.A. g4 259
Arlington, Massachusetts, U.S.A. j2 257
Arlington, Ohio, U.S.A. e5 254
Arlington, South Dakota, U.S.A. d2 260
Arlington, Tennessee, U.S.A. e2 258
Arlington, Texas, U.S.A. a3 258
Arlington, Virginia, U.S.A. c6 256
Arlit f2 223
Arlon d5 159
Arly ≈ c5 185
Arm ≈ q6 249
Arma b1 258
Armada e4 254
Armadale b13 87
Armadillo d2 274
Armadores IS▭ n2 99
Armagh, England, U.K. [2] b2 165
Armagh, Northern Ireland, U.K. e2 165
Armagnac ♦ c5 187
Armamar c3 190
Armance ≈ j4 183
Armançon ≈ k5 183
Armant d9 136
Armathia ▭ Ab3 211
Armavir f3 148
Armenia, Col. b3 284
Armenia b4 92

ARMENIA

THE REPUBLIC OF ARMENIA
Area 29,800km^2
(11,500sq miles)
Capital Yerevan
Organizations CIS, EBRD
Population 3,070,000
Pop. growth (%) 0.1
Life expectancy 69 (m); 75 (f)
Languages Armenian, Kurdish
Literacy 98.6%
Currency dram
(US $1 = 558.14 dram)
GDP (US million $) 2300
GDP per head ($US) 749

Armenistis Ab1 210
Armenoi e7 211
Armenopetra, Akra ► c6 211
Armenta e5 275
Armentières a4 159
Armeria c4 274
Armidale k11 81
Armilla g7 191
Arminda g2 297
Armitage e4 162
Armizonskoe l5 147
Armolia g4 210
Armona d5 265
Armopa k6 97
Armori g9 124
Armorique, Parc Régional d' ☆ a4 182
Armsjön ○ g1 156
Armstrong, Arg. g2 297
Armstrong, Can. j5 251
Armur f3 126
Armutçuk Dağı ⛰ a2 208
Armyans'k d3 148
Arnå ≈ c3 158
Arnage f5 183
'Arnah d3 138
Arnaia d2 210
Arnaoutis, Cape ► a1 138
Arnaudville d4 258
Arnawai e3 128
Arnay-le-Duc a3 184
Arnedillo b2 192
Arnedo b2 192
Arnéguy a5 187
Arneiroz d3 288
Årnes, Akershus, Nor. d2 156
Årnes, Troms, Nor. g2 154
Arnes e4 192
Arnett d4 261
Arnhem d3 159
Arnhem Bay ◄ c2 80
Arnhem, Cape ► c2 80
Arnhem Land ♦ b2 80
Arnissa b2 210
Arno, Italy ≈ f6 197
Arno, Marsh. Is. ▭ D 74
Arno Bay c12 81
Arnoia ≈ b2 190
Arnold, U.K. e3 162
Arnold, California, U.S.A. c3 264
Arnold, Maryland, U.S.A. d5 256
Arnold, Missouri, U.S.A. a6 254
Arnon ≈ h6 183
Arnót j3 171
Arnøya ▭ h1 154
Arnprior h3 255
Arnsberg, Ger. [2] d4 172
Arnsberg, Nordrhein-Westfalen, Ger. d4 172
Arnstadt f3 175
Arnstein f2 174
Arnstorf d1 176
Årø ▭ c3 158
Aro ≈ e2 285
Aroab c3 234
Aroania ⛰ c5 210
Arocena g2 297
Aroche d7 191
Arochuku f4 223
Aroeira a4 290
Aro'er d5 139
Ároktő j4 171
Aroland k5 251
Arolla b3 196
Arolsen e4 172
Aroma e4 219
Aromaševo m4 147
Aron, Fr. ≈ j6 183
Aron, Pays de la Loire, Fr. e4 182
Arona c4 196
Arorae ▭ H 75
Aroroy d4 100
Aros ≈ e3 272
Arosa d3 196
Arouca b4 190
Arousa, Illa de ▭ b2 190
Arousa, Ría de ◄ a2 190
Arp b3 258
Arpaçay j2 209
Arpajon-sur-Cère e4 186
Arpino c3 198
Arpoadar, Ponta do ► e6 291
Arquà Petrarca f4 196
Arquata del Tronto h7 197
Arquata Scrivia c5 196
Arques a4 159
Arques, Puig d' △ g3 192
Arquillos g6 191
Arra ≈ b7 129
'Arrāba d4 139
Arrabal b2 190
Ar Rabbah d5 139
Arrábida, Parque Natural da ☆ b6 191
Arrabury e9 81
Arracourt c2 184
Ar Rafīd d4 138
Arrah d4 222
Ar Raḩḩālīyah j5 137
Ar Rāhidah f5 219
Arraias, Braz. ≈ b4 288
Arraias, Tocantins, Braz. c4 288
Arraias, Serra de ⛰ c4 288
Arraijan h6 277
Arraiolos c6 191
Ar Ramādī j5 136
Ar Ramlah d7 139
Ar Ramthā e4 138
Arran ▭ c4 164
Ar Raqqah, Syria [1] g4 209
Ar Raqqah, Ar Raqqah, Syria g5 209
Arras a4 159
Ar Ra's al Abyaḑ ► e3 219
Ar Ra's al Aswad ► e3 219
Ar Rashādīyah d6 139
Ar-Rass j9 137
Ar Rastān e2 138
Arrats ≈ c5 187
Ar Rawḑah f3 219
Ar Rayyān n9 137
Arreau c6 187
Arrecifal d3 284
Arrecife Af2 189
Arrecife de la Media Luna ▭ f3 277
Arrecifes g3 297
Arredondo g1 190
Arrée, Monts d' ⛰ b4 182
Arresø ○ f3 158
Arriagá h5 275
Arriaga d3 274
Arriate e8 191
Arribeños g3 297
Arrieta Af1 189
Ar Rifā'ī l6 137
Arrifana b4 190
Arrigorriaga b1 192
Arrino b11 87
Arriondas e1 190
Ar Riyāḑ, Sau. Ar [1] g3 219
Ar Riyāḑ, Ar Riyāḑ, Sau. Ar g3 219
Arriyd, Sabkhat ⊙ b3 220
Arroba de los Montes f5 191
Arroio Grande f2 294
Arroios do Araguaia ≈ c3 288
Arromanches-les-Bains e3 182
Arronches c5 191
Arrone, Italy ≈ f7 197
Arrone, Italy ≈ g8 197
Arros ≈ c5 187
Arroux ≈ k6 183
Arrow ≈ d4 163
Arrow Creek ≈ h2 262
Arrow, Lough ○ c2 165
Arrowtown b6 77
Arroyal f2 190
Arroy Dulce g3 297
Arroyito, Córdoba, Arg. f1 297
Arroyito, Mendoza, Arg. d2 296
Arroyo A 270
Arroyo Baluarte ≈ d7 261
Arroyo de la Luz d5 191
Arroyo Grande, Arg. ≈ j4 297
Arroyo Grande, U.S.A. c6 265
Arroyomolinos de León d6 191
Arroyo Seco, Arg. g2 297
Arroyo Seco, Guerrero, Mex. d5 274
Arroyo Seco, Querétaro, Mex. e3 275
Ar Rubay'iyah k8 137
Arruda dos Vinhos a6 191
Ar Ruḩaybah e3 138
Ar Rumaymīn d4 139
Ar Rumaythā n9 137
Ar Rumaythah k6 137
Ar Rummān d4 139
Ar Ruşāfah g5 209
Ar Ruşayfah e4 139
Ar Rushaydah e4 138
Ar Ruţbah h5 137
Års c2 158
Ars l3 137
Arsèguel f2 192
Arsen'evo d5 150
Ars-en-Ré a2 186
Arsen'yev s3 113
Arsiero f4 196
Arsk k3 151
Årslev d3 158
Arso l6 97
Arsoli h7 197
Ars-sur-Formans a5 185
Ars-sur-Moselle c1 184
Arsvågen a3 156
Arta a3 210
Artà h5 193
Artajona c2 192
Artana d5 193
Artashat g5 149
Arteaga, Coahuila, Mex. j5 273
Arteaga, Michoacán, Mex. c4 274
Artem s4 113
Artemare b5 185
Artemisa c3 266
Artemivs'k e2 148
Artemovskij k4 147
Artemovskiy e1 94
Artena g8 197
Artenay g4 183
Artern (Unstrut) g4 173
Artesa de Segre f3 192
Artesia, Mississippi, U.S.A. e3 258
Artesia, New Mexico, U.S.A. b5 261
Artesia Lake ○ d3 264
Arthez-de-Béarn b5 187
Arthon-en-Retz d5 182
Arthur, Can. f4 254
Arthur, U.S.A. e7 250
Arthur Lake ○ Ab2 83
Arthur Pieman Protected Area ☆ Aa2 83
Arthur Point ► d3 84
Arthur's Pass △ c5 77
Arthur's Pass National Park ☆ c5 77
Arthur's Town m7 259
Arties e2 192
Artigas, Ur. [1] e2 294
Artigas, Artigas, Ur. e2 294
Artigas (Uruguay) ▪ u1 298
Art'ik j2 209
Art, Île ▭ F 74
Artillery Lake ○ h3 242
Artix b5 187
Artois, Fr. ♦ h2 183
Artois, U.S.A. a2 264
Artois, Collines de l' ⛰ h2 183
Artos Dağı △ j3 209
Artova f2 209
Artrutx, Cap d' ► A 193
Arts Bogd Uul ⛰ b3 112
Artsyz j3 201
Artuby ≈ c7 185
Artux r8 121
Artvin, Tur. [1] h2 209
Artvin, Artvin, Tur. h2 209
Artyk g9 120
Aru f3 225
Arua ≈ f4 285
A Rúa c2 190
Arua f3 225
Aruajá d5 284
Aruanã b4 289
Aruba (Netherlands) ❑ g7 241
Arucas Ad2 189
Arudy b5 187
Aru, Kepulauan ▭ j7 97
Arumã e4 285
Arunachal Pradesh [1] b1 102
Arun He ≈ m1 113
Årup d3 158
Aruppukkottai f8 126
Arurandéua ≈ c2 288
Arusha, Tan. [1] g4 225
Arusha, Arusha, Tan. b4 227
Arusha National Park ☆ g4 225
Arus, Tanjung ► l4 99
Arut ≈ f5 98
Aruti d4 284
Aruwimi ≈ e3 225
Arvada b4 260
Arvagh d3 165
Arvan ≈ c5 185
Arvayheer b2 112
Arve ≈ c5 185
Arviat l3 242
Arvidsjaur g4 154
Arvika e3 156
Årviksand h1 154
Arvin e6 265
Arvonia g7 254
Arwala p8 99
Arxan k2 113
Arykbalyk m1 121
Arys' m6 121
Arzachena Ab1 198
Arzacq-Arraziguet b5 187
Arzamas g4 151
Arzfeld e4 159
Arzgir g3 149
Arzignano, Veneto, Italy f4 196
Arzon ≈ f3 186
Arzúa b2 190
Aš a1 170
Ås d3 156
Aså d1 158
Aša j5 147
Åsa f1 158
Asa ≈ e2 285
Asaba f4 223
Asadābād, Afg. e3 128
Asadābād, Iran m4 137
Asad, Buḩayrat al ⊙ f5 209
Asagny, Parc National d' ☆ c4 222
Asahan ≈ a4 101
Asahi j4 115
Asahi-dake, Japan △ h2 115
Asahi-dake, Hokkaidō, Japan △ Ac2 114
Asahi-gawa ≈ e4 114
Asahikawa Ac2 114
Asaka p7 121
Āsalē ○ f5 219
Asālem m3 137
Asamankese d4 222
Asama-yama △ h3 115
Asandh c5 130
Asankranguaa d4 222
Asansol k8 125
Asar j2 113
Åsarna f1 156
Asasp-Arros b5 187
Asau N 75
Asbach-Bäumenheim e3 175
Asbest k4 147
Asbestos g6 252
Asbestos Mountains ⛰ e4 234
Asbestos Range National Park ☆ Ab2 83
Āsbe Teferi c2 226
Asbury Park f4 257
Ascea e4 198
Ascensión, Arg. g3 297
Ascensión, Bol. e3 293
Ascensión, Chihuahua, Mex. f2 272
Ascensión, Nuevo León, Mex. k5 273
Ascension Fracture Zone ▦ k10 302
Aschaffenburg f4 174
Aschau ≈ f3 172
Aschbach Markt f1 177
Ascheberg c4 172
Ascheberg (Holstein) d4 158
Aschersleben g4 173
Asciano f6 197
Asco A 185
Ascó e3 192
Ascochinga e1 297
Ascoli Piceno, Italy [2] c2 198
Ascoli Piceno, Marche, Italy c2 198
Ascoli Satriano e3 198
Ascona c3 196
Åse e2 154
Āsebot △ c2 226
Åseda f4 156
Asedjrad ⌒ e4 221
Āsela b2 226
Åsele f4 154
Åsen c5 154
Åsenbruk e3 156
Āsendabo b2 226
Asenovgrad g4 201
Aseri m3 157
Aserradero los Charcos b2 274
Aşfāk r4 137
Asfaka a3 210
Asfendiou Ac2 211
Asfûn el Matâ'na d9 136
Asgata b2 138
Ashalim c6 139
Asharat k9 137
Ashbourne, Ire. e3 165
Ashbourne, U.K. e3 162
Ashburton, Aust. ≈ c8 87
Ashburton, N.Z. ≈ c5 77
Ashburton, U.K. c6 163
Ashby de la Zouch e4 162
Ashchikol', Ozero, Kaz. ○ n6 121
Ashdod c5 139
Ashdown b3 258
Asheboro k2 259
Ashern d5 250
Asheville h2 259
Ash Flat d1 258
Ashford, Ire. ≈ e4 165
Ashford, U.K. g5 163
Ashford, U.S.A. g4 259
Ash Fork g8 263
Ashgabat g9 120
Ashibetsu Ac2 114
Ashington e1 162
Ashizuri-misaki ► e5 114
Ashizuri-Uwakai National Park ☆ e5 114
Ashkazar q6 137
Ashkhabad g9 120
Ashland, Illinois, U.S.A. a6 254
Ashland, Kansas, U.S.A. d4 261
Ashland, Kentucky, U.S.A. e6 254
Ashland, Montana, U.S.A. b2 260
Ashland, Ohio, U.S.A. e5 254
Ashland, Oregon, U.S.A. b4 262
Ashland, Pennsylvania, U.S.A. d4 256
Ashland, Wisconsin, U.S.A. h7 250
Ashley, Aust. c6 85
Ashley, N.Z. ≈ d5 77
Ashley, Illinois, U.S.A. b6 254
Ashley, Ohio, U.S.A. e5 254
Ashmore and Cartier Islands (Australia) ❑ c1 78
Ashmore Reef ○ f3 86
Ashmyanskaye Wzvyshsha ⛰ m5 157
Ashmyany p1 169
Ashoknagar e7 124
Ashoro Ac2 114
Ashqelon c5 139
Ash Shabakah j6 137
Ash Shaddādah h4 209
Ash Shajarah, Jordan d4 138
Ash Shajarah, Syria d4 138
Ash Sha'm r8 137
Ash Shāmīyah k6 137
Ash Shanāfīyah k6 137
Ash Shaqīq d5 139
Ash Shāriqah q9 137
Ash Sharqāţ j5 209
Ash Sharqīyah [1] h3 219
Ash Shaţrah l6 137
Ash Shawbak d6 139
Ash Shaykh 'Uthman f5 219
Ash Shiḩr g5 219
Ash Şhināş r9 137
Ash Shu'āybah j8 136
Ash Shu'bah k7 136
Ash Shubaykīyah j9 137
Ash Shumlūl l8 137
Ash Shūnah ash Shamālīyah d4 138
Ash Shuwayrif g3 221
Ashta e8 124
Ashtabula f5 254
Ashtarak k2 209
Ashti f9 124
Ashton d6 234
Ashton-under-Lyne d3 162
Ashuanipi Lake ○ j2 253
Ashuapmushuan ≈ f4 252
Ashurst g5 163
Ashville, Alabama, U.S.A. f3 258
Ashville, Pennsylvania, U.S.A. b4 256
Ashwaubenon b3 254
Asiago f4 196
Asia, Kepulauan ▭ j5 97
Asid Gulf ◄ d4 100
Asientos c2 274
Asika j3 127
Asilah c1 220
Asillo c2 292
Asín c2 192
'Āşī, Nahr al ≈ e1 138
Asinara, Golfo dell' ◄ Aa1 198
Asind g8 129

AUSTRALIA

THE COMMONWEALTH OF AUSTRALIA
Area 7,682,300km² (2,966,153sq miles)
Capital Canberra
Organizations APEC, COMM, OECD, SPC, PIF
Population 19,710,000
Pop. growth (%) 1
Life expectancy 75 (m); 81 (f)
Languages English, Aboriginal languages
Literacy 95%
Currency Australian dollar (US $1 = 1.34 Australian dollar)
GDP (US million $) 400,000
GDP per head ($US) 20,294

AUSTRIA

THE REPUBLIC OF AUSTRIA
Area 83,858km² (32,378sq miles)
Capital Vienna
Organizations CE, EBRD, EU, OECD
Population 8,110,000
Pop. growth (%) 0.3
Life expectancy 74 (m); 80 (f)
Languages German
Literacy 99%
Currency euro (US $1 = 0.81 euro)
GDP (US million $) 205,300
GDP per head ($US) 25,314

AZERBAIJAN

THE REPUBLIC OF AZERBAIJAN
Area 86,600km² (33,400sq miles)
Capital Baku
Organizations CIS, EBRD, ECO, IDB, OIC, CE
Population 8,140,000
Pop. growth (%) 1.1
Life expectancy 67 (m); 74 (f)
Languages Azeri (Latin script)
Literacy 97.3%
Currency Azerbaijani manat (US $1 = 4917 Azerbaijani manat)
GDP (US million $) 6113
GDP per head ($US) 750

Babbacombe Bay c6 163
Bāb Billā e3 138
Babbitt, Minnesota, U.S.A. h7 250
Babbitt, Nevada, U.S.A. e3 264
Babel Island Ac1 83
Babeljarum k6 97
Babenhausen, Bayern, Ger. d3 174
Babenhausen, Hessen, Ger. d3 174
Băbeni g3 201
Babiak g3 168
Babian Jiang c7 104
Babimost d3 168
Babín h2 171
Babinda g4 80
Babine Lake e4 248
Babinga c4 224
Babino Polje g2 198
Babi, Pulau c14 103
Babno Polje f4 177
Babo j6 97
Bābol p3 137
Bābol Sar p3 137
Babonde e3 225
Babongo b2 224
Baboon Point c6 234
Baborów f5 168
Babor, Réserve Naturelle du f1 221
Baboua b2 224
Babrovitskaye, Vozyera p3 169
Babruysk c1 148
Babuhri d7 129
Babuna b1 210
Babusar Pass b2 130
Babushkin d2 94
Babuyan, Phil. d1 100
Babuyan, Phil. b6 100
Babuyan Channel c1 100
Babuyan Islands d1 100
Babylon g4 257
Babynino c4 150
Bacaadweyn d2 226
Bacabáchi e4 272
Bacabal, Maranhão, Braz. d2 288
Bacabal, Pará, Braz. f5 285
Bacadéhuachi j11 263
Bacajá b2 288
Bacakliyayla Tepesi c2 208
Bacalar q8 273
Bacan h6 97
Bacanère, Pic de c6 187
Bacanora e3 272
Bacarra c1 100
Bacău, Rom. h2 201
Bacău, Bacău, Rom. h2 201
Baccarat c2 184
Baccaro Point k7 253
Bacchiglione g4 196
Bacchus Marsh d3 82
Baceno c3 196
Băc Giang h5 102
Bach b2 176
Bacha s1 113
Bachaquero c2 284
Bacharach f4 174
Bachhraon d5 130
Bachiniva f3 272
Bach Long Vi, Đao h6 104
Bacho b2 101
Bachok c2 101
Bachu s8 121
Bachuma b2 226
Back k2 242
Bačka Palanka d3 200
Bačka Topola h6 171
Backbone Mountain a5 256
Backbone Ranges m3 247
Bäckefors e3 156
Backesjön f2 156
Bačkininkai m1 169
Bački Petrovac d3 200
Backnang c2 174
Backstairs Passage a2 82
Bäckvallen f1 156
Bac Lac e7 104
Bac Liêu g11 103
Băc Ninh h5 102
Bacnotan c2 100
Bacoachi h10 263
Bacobampo e4 272
Bacoli d4 198
Bacolod d5 100
Baco, Mount c4 100
Băc Quang g4 102
Bacqueville-en-Caux f3 183
Bacqueville, Lac r1 251
Bácsalmás h5 171
Bácsbokod h5 171
Bács-Kiskun h5 171
Bacubirito f5 272
Baculin Bay f7 100
Baculin Point f6 100
Bacuri c2 288
Bacuri, Ilha do c2 285
Bād p5 137
Bad b3 260
Bada b2 226
Badacsonytomaj f5 171
Badagara d7 126
Bad Aibling h5 175
Badain Jaran Shamo a5 112
Badajia g3 111
Badajokka j2 155
Badajós, Amazonas, Braz. e4 285
Badajós, Pará, Braz. c2 288
Badajós, Lago e4 285
Badajoz, Spain d6 191
Badajoz, Extremadura, Spain d6 191
Badakhshān e2 128
Badalona g3 192
Badanah h6 137
Badaohao l5 113
Badarinath d4 130
Badarpur n7 125
Badas, Kepulauan d4 98
Bad Aussee e2 176
Bad Bentheim f2 159
Badbergen c3 172
Bad Bergzabern c3 174
Bad Berka f5 175
Bad Berleburg b3 174
Bad Berneck g2 175
Bad Bevensen f2 173
Bad Bibra k1 175
Bad Birnbach e1 176
Bad Blankenburg g2 175
Bad Brambach h2 175
Bad Bramstedt c5 158
Bad Breisig f4 159
Bad Brückenau g2 174
Bad Camberg d2 174
Baddeck m5 253
Baddo b6 129
Bad Doberan e4 158
Bad Driburg e4 172
Bad Düben h4 173
Bad Dürkheim c2 174
Bad Dürrenberg k1 175
Bad Dürrheim f3 174
Bade k7 97
Badéguichéri f3 223
Bademli g3 210
Bademli Geçidi c4 208
Bad Ems c2 174
Baden, Aus. h1 177
Baden, Switz. c2 196
Baden-Baden d3 174
Bad Endorf d2 176
Baden-Württemberg d4 174
Bad Essen d3 172
Bădeuți g2 201
Bad Frankenhausen (Kyffhäuser) g4 173
Bad Freienwalde k3 173
Bad Friedrichshall d4 174
Bad Füssing e1 176
Bad Gandersheim f4 172
Badgastein e2 176
Badger, Can. p4 253
Badger, California, U.S.A. d5 264
Badger, Minnesota, U.S.A. e6 250
Bādghīs a3 128
Bad Gleichenberg g3 177
Bad Goisern e2 176
Bad Grönenbach d2 174
Bad Großpertholz f1 177
Bad Grund (Harz) f4 172
Bad Hall f1 177
Bad Harzburg f4 173
Bad Heilbrunn e3 175
Bad Hersfeld g5 174
Badhoevedorp c2 159
Bad Hofgastein e2 176
Bad Homburg vor der Höhe c2 174
Bad Honnef f4 159
Badhwana c5 130
Badia f3 196
Badia Polesine f4 196
Badiara b3 222
Badiar, Parc National du b3 222
Bad Iburg d3 172
Badiel b4 192
Badigeru Swamp f2 225
Badin d8 129
Badin h3 171
Badinko c3 222
Badinko, Réserve du c3 222
Badiraguato f5 272
Bad Ischl e2 176
Bādiyat ash Shām g5 136
Bad Karlshafen e4 172
Bad Kissingen d2 174
Bad König e2 174
Bad Köstritz h2 175
Bad Kreuznach e4 174
Bad Krozingen e4 174
Bad Laasphe c5 174
Badlands c3 260
Badlands National Park c3 260
Bad Langensalza f5 175
Bad Lauterberg im Harz f4 172
Bad Leonfelden f1 177
Bad Liebenwerda j4 173
Bad Lippspringe d4 172
Bad Mergentheim e3 174
Bad Mitterndorf e2 176
Bad Münder am Deister c3 172
Bad Münstereifel e4 159
Bad Muskau k4 173
Bad Nauheim e3 174
Badnawar g9 129
Bad Nenndorf e3 172
Bad Neuenahr-Ahrweiler f4 159
Bad Neustadt an der Saale c2 174
Badnor g8 129
Badolatosa f7 191
Bad Oldesloe d5 158
Badong b4 106
Ba Đông h11 103
Badonviller c2 184
Badou, China e1 111
Badou, Togo e4 223
Badouling e3 111
Badplaas j2 235
Bad Pyrmont e4 172
Bad Radkersburg g3 177
Bad Ragaz d2 196
Bad Rappenau d2 174
Bad Reichenhall d2 176
Badr Ḩunayn e3 219
Bad Rodach f2 175
Bad Saarow-Pieskow k3 173
Bad Sachsa f4 173
Bad Säckingen e3 174
Bad Salzdetfurth f3 172
Bad Salzuflen d3 172
Bad Salzungen c5 174
Bad Sankt Leonhard im Lavanttal f3 177
Bad Sassendorf d4 172
Bad Saulgau e4 174
Bad Schallerbach e1 176
Bad Schandau k2 175
Bad Schmiedeberg h4 173
Bad Schussenried f2 174
Bad Schwalbach d2 174
Bad Schwartau d5 158
Bad Segeberg d5 158
Badshahibagh c4 130
Bad Sobernheim c3 174
Bad Soden-Salmünster f2 174
Bad Sooden-Allendorf e1 174
Bad Tölz e2 175
Badules c3 192
Badulla g9 126
Bad Urach g5 174
Bad Vilbel e4 174
Bad Vöslau h2 177
Bad Waldsee e4 174
Bad Wildbad e4 174
Bad Wildungen e3 174
Bad Wilsnack g3 173
Bad Windsheim e5 174
Bad Wörishofen g2 175
Bad Wurzach f3 174
Bad Zwesten b1 174
Bække d4 158
Bækmarksbro b2 158
Baena f7 191
Baesweiler e4 159
Baeza, Ec. b4 284
Baeza, Spain g7 191
Bafang g4 223
Bafatá b3 222
Baffa f3 128
Baffin Basin d2 302
Baffin Bay, Can. r1 243
Baffin Bay, Can. d1 302
Baffin Island q1 243
Bafia g5 223
Bafilo e4 223
Bafing b3 222
Bafing, Réserve du b3 222
Bafoulabé b3 222
Bafoussam g4 223
Bāfq q6 137
Bafra e2 208
Bafra Burnu e2 209
Bāft r7 137
Bafwaboli e3 225
Bafwamboma e3 225
Bafwasende e3 225
Baga Bogd Uul, Mong. a3 112
Baga Bogd Uul, Mong. a3 112
Bagaha g6 135
Bagahak, Gunung k2 99
Bagaladi e6 199
Bagalkot d4 126
Bagamér k4 171
Bagamoyo b5 227
Bagan Datuk b4 101
Baganga f7 100
Bagani c2 232
Bagan Serai b3 101
Bagansiapiapi b4 101
Baganza e5 196
Bagar u4 121
Bağarası a4 208
Bagaroua e3 223
Bagata c4 224
Bagazán c4 284
Bagbe b4 222
Bagé f2 294
Bâgé-le-Châtel a4 184
Bagenkop d4 158
Bages, Fr. e6 187
Bages, Spain f3 192
Bages et de Sigean, Étang de e5 187
Bageshwar d5 130
Baggs b3 260
Baggy Point b5 163
Bagh, India g9 129
Bagh, Pak. a3 130
Baghak b6 129
Baghbaghū h9 120
Baghdād k5 137
Bāgh-e Bābū'īyeh r7 137
Bāgh-e Malek m6 137
Bagheria c6 199
Bāghīn r6 137
Baghlān, Afg. d3 128
Baghlān, Baghlān, Afg. d2 128
Baghpat c5 130
Baghrān b4 128
Baghwana c7 129
Bagi c4 130
Baginda, Tanjung d6 98
Bagley f7 250
Baglung f5 135
Bagnacavallo c2 156
Bagnara Calabra f5 197
Bagnasco e6 199
Bagnères-de-Bigorre c5 197
Bagnères-de-Luchon c5 187
Bagni di Lucca c6 187
Bagni di Masino e5 197
Bagni di Rabbi d3 196
Bagno di Romagna e3 196
Bagnoli del Trigno f6 197
Bagnoli Irpino d3 198
Bagnolo Mella e4 198
Bagnols-sur-Cèze e4 196
Bagnone a6 185
Bagnoregio e5 197
Bagnuiti g7 197
Bāgō j6 125
Bago c3 158
Bagod d5 100
Bagodé e5 170
Bagolino c3 222
Bagor e6 196
Bagrame g8 129
Bagrationovsk d3 128
Bagre j1 169
Bagru b2 288
Bagua g7 129
Bagual b5 284
Bagudo e3 296
Baguena e3 223
Baguio c3 192
Baguio Point c2 100
Bagzane, Monts d2 100
Bahabón de Esgueva f2 223
Bahadurgarh g3 190
Bahadurgarh c5 130
Bahadur Khel e4 128
Bahadurpur c6 130
Bahamas, The g6 241

BAHAMAS, The

THE COMMONWEALTH OF THE BAHAMAS
Area 13,939km² (5382sq miles)
Capital Nassau, on New Providence Island
Organizations ACS, CARICOM, COMM, IADB, SELA
Population 310,000
Pop. growth (%) 1.7
Life expectancy 64 (m); 73 (f)
Languages English
Literacy 95.6%
Currency Bahamian dollar (US $1 = 1.00 Bahamian dollar)
GDP (US million $) 5160
GDP per head ($US) 16,645

Bahara c7 129
Baharampur l7 125
Bahardipur d8 129
Bahau, Indon. h3 99
Bahau, Malay. c4 101
Bahaur h6 99
Bahawalnagar f6 129
Bahawalpur e6 129
Bahçe f4 209
Ba He f3 104
Bahera k6 125
Baheri d5 130
Baherove e3 148
Bahi b5 227
Bahia d4 288
Bahía Blanca f5 297
Bahía Bufadero c4 274
Bahía Bustamante c5 295
Bahía de Coronado f6 277
Bahía, Islas de la d2 276
Bahía Kino d3 272
Bahía Laolao A 74
Bahía Laura c5 295
Bahía Mansa a6 296
Bahía Negra f4 293
Bahía San Blas f5 297
Bahía Tortugas b4 272
Bahíllo f2 190
Bahir Dar e5 219
Bahiret el Bibane g2 221
Bahirevo q1 113
Bahjoi d5 130
Bahn c4 222
Bahomonte l6 99
Bahraich e6 130
Bahrain c6 92

BAHRAIN

THE KINGDOM OF BAHRAIN
Area 695km² (268sq miles)
Capital Manama
Organizations CCASG, IDB, LAS, OAPEC, OIC
Population 700,000
Pop. growth (%) 3.1
Life expectancy 71 (m); 75 (f)
Languages Arabic, English
Literacy 89.1%
Currency Bahrain dinar (US $1 = 0.37 Bahrain dinar)
GDP (US million $) 8893
GDP per head ($US) 12,704

Bahrain, Gulf of h2 219
Bahrāmābād m3 137
Bahrāmjerd r7 137
Bahr el Nîl d2 218
Bahror c6 130
Bahsunta c5 130
Bahtyzino g4 151
Bahubulu m6 99
Bāhū Kālāt a4 122
Bahushewsk c1 148
Baia, Suceava, Rom. h2 201
Baia, Tulcea, Rom. j3 201
Baia de Aramă f3 201
Baia de Arieș f2 201
Baia dos Tigres a2 232
Baía Farta a1 232
Baia Mare f2 201
Baião c2 288
Baiardo b6 197
Baia Sprie f2 201
Baiazeh q5 137
Baibi c1 106
Baïbokoum c2 224
Baicheng, Jilin, China m3 113
Baicheng, Xinjiang Uygur Zizhiqu, China t7 121
Băicoi g3 201
Baidaokou d2 106
Baidoi Co h3 135
Baie-Comeau h4 253
Baie de Henne h5 266
Baie-Johan-Beetz l3 253
Baiersbronn g3 174
Baiersdorf d3 175
Baie-Ste-Claire k4 253
Baie-St-Paul g5 252
Baie-Trinite j4 253
Baignes-Ste-Radegonde b3 186
Baigneux-les-Juifs a3 184
Baigorrita g3 297
Baiguo d4 106
Baihar g8 124
Bai He c3 106
Baihe, Jilin, China q4 113
Baihe, Shaanxi, China b3 106
Baihu e4 111
Baijiang e3 111
Baijiantan v5 121
Baijnath, Himachal Pradesh, India c3 130
Baijnath, Uttaranchal, India d5 130
Baikouquan v5 121
Baile Átha Cliath, Dublin, Ire. e3 165
Baile Átha Cliath, Dublin, Ire. e3 165
Băile Govora g3 201
Băile Mhartainn a2 164
Băilen g6 191
Băile Olănești g3 201
Băilești f3 201
Băile Tușnad g2 201
Bailey g5 235
Bailey Range f11 87
Bailianhe Shuiku d4 106
Bailique, Ilha c1 288
Bailleul a4 159
Baillie Islands m1 247
Bailong Jiang d2 104
Bailundo c6 224
Baima Jian f4 111
Bain f3 162
Bainang j5 135
Bainbridge, Georgia, U.S.A. g4 259
Bainbridge, New York, U.S.A. e2 256
Bainbridge, Ohio, U.S.A. e6 254
Bain-de-Bretagne d5 182
Bainet h5 271
Baingoin k4 135
Bains-les-Bains c2 184
Baio Grande b1 190
Baiona b2 190
Baipu g3 111
Baiquan, Heilongjiang, China p2 113
Baiquan, Zhejiang, China h4 111
Ba'ir e6 139
Bairab Co f2 135
Bairagnia j6 125
Bairat c6 130
Baird Inlet c3 246
Baird Mountains d2 246
Bairiki H 75
Bairin Qiao k4 113
Bairkum m6 121
Bairnsdale h14 81
Bais, Fr. e4 182
Bais, Phil. d6 100
Baisang b3 106
Baïse c5 187
Baisha, Chongqing, China f4 104
Baisha, Hainan, China g9 104
Baisha, Jiangxi, China k5 105
Baishan e3 111
Baishanzu m5 105
Baishe l5 105
Baishui e5 197
Băișoara f2 201
Baisogala k5 157
Baissour, Al Janūb, Leb. d3 138
Baissour, Jabal Lubnān, Leb. d3 138
Baitadi e5 130
Bai Thưởng g6 102
Baixiang d1 106
Baixingt l4 113
Baixo Guandu h3 291
Baixo-Longa b2 232
Baiyanggou m5 113
Baiyin c7 112
Baiyü b3 104
Baiyuda Desert d4 218
Baiyu Shan d7 112
Baja g5 171
Baja California c5 241
Baja California Norte b3 272
Baja California Sur d5 272
Bajado del Agrio b5 296
Bajan j4 273
Bajang e5 130
Bajau d3 98
Bajawa l9 99
Bajč g4 171
Bajdarackaja Guba l1 147
Bajevo t1 121
Bājgīrān g9 120
Bajina Bašta d4 200
Bajitpur m7 125
Bajkalovo, Sverdlovskaja Oblast', Russ. Fed. k4 147
Bajkalovo, Tjumenskaja Oblast', Russ. Fed. l4 147
Bajkal, Ozero d2 94
Bajkit k3 119
Bajmak k1 149
Bajmok h6 171
Bajna, Hung. g4 171
Bajna, India g9 129
Bajo Baudó b2 284
Bajo Boquete f6 277
Bajo Caracoles b5 295
Bajoga g3 223
Bajo Grande c5 295
Bajo Guadalquivir, Canal del e7 191
Bajo Hondo, Buenos Aires, Arg. g5 297
Bajo Hondo, La Rioja, Arg. e1 296
Bajo Nuevo h3 277
Bajool k7 80
Bajos de Haina j5 271
Bajoz e3 190
Bak e5 170
Baka, Bukit g5 98
Baka - Bukit Raya National Park, Bukit g5 98
Bakacak a2 208
Bakal j5 147
Bakala d2 224
Bakanas, Kaz. s4 121
Bakanas, Almatinskaya Oblast', Kaz. r5 121
Bakaoré b4 218
Bakar, Cro. f4 177
Bakar, Pak. d7 129
Bakassi, Cap f5 223
Bakayan, Gunung j3 99
Bakel b3 222
Baker, Louisiana, U.S.A. d4 258
Baker, Montana, U.S.A. b2 260
Baker, West Virginia, U.S.A. b5 256
Baker, Canal l3 253
Baker Island (U.S.A.) h2 73
Baker Lake, Aust. h10 87
Baker Lake, Nunavut, Can. l3 243
Baker Lake, Nunavut, Can. k3 242
Baker, Mount c1 262
Baker's Dozen Islands p2 251
Bakersfield d6 265
Bakersville h1 259
Bakerville g2 235
Bå Kêv h9 103
Bakewell e3 162
Bakhā r8 137
Bakhaaoun e2 138
Bakhardok g8 120
Bakhasar e8 129
Bakhchysaray d3 148
Bakherden r2 137
Bakhmach d2 148
Bakhtegan, Daryācheh-ye q7 137
Bakhty u4 121
Bakhuis Gebergte f3 285
Bakı h4 149
Bakio b1 192
Bakixanov h4 149
Bakkafjörður A 152
Bakkejord g2 154
Bakloh b3 130
Bako, C.I. c4 222
Bako, Oromia, Eth. b2 226
Bako, Southern, Eth. b2 226
Bakony f4 170
Bakonycsernye g4 171
Bakonyszárkány g4 171
Bakonyszombathely f4 171
Bakool c3 226
Bakouma d2 224
Bakoumba b4 224
Bakoy b3 222
Bakrani d7 129
Baks j5 171
Baksan f4 149
Baksena d6 130
Baktalórántháza l4 171
Baku f3 225
Bakum d3 172
Bakung c4 98
Bakuny n3 169
Bakuriani j2 209
Bala d3 208
Balabac, Phil. c4 162
Balabac, Phil. a7 100
Balabac Strait a6 100
Balabanovo a7 100
Balabio d4 150
Bălă Bolūk F 74
Bălăceanu a4 128
Balad h3 201
Bala Deh k5 209
Baladeh, Māzandarān, Iran n7 137
Baladeh, Māzandarān, Iran n3 137
Balaghat g9 124
Balaghat Range e3 126
Balagna A 185
Balaguer e3 192
Balahna g3 151
Balaiberkuak f5 98
Balaikarangan f4 98
Balaipungut b5 101
Balairiam f6 98
Balaîtous d2 192
Balaka e1 233
Balakān g4 149
Balakété c2 224
Balak, Gunung c7 98
Balaklava d3 148
Balakliya e2 148
Balakovo g1 149
Balama b6 227
Bal'amā e4 139
Balambangan j1 99
Bālā Morghāb a3 128
Balan e7 129
Bălan g2 201
Balancán b2 276
Balan Dağı b4 208
Balanga c3 100
Balangala c3 224
Balangir h9 125
Balangoda g9 126
Balaruc-les-Bains f5 187
Balašejka k5 151
Balashov h2 149
Balasinor f9 129
Balassagyarmat h3 171
Balástya j5 171
Balát c2 218
Balaton f5 171
Balatonalmádi g4 171
Balatonberény f5 170
Balatonboglár f5 171
Balaton-felvidéki, Hung. c2 200
Balatonfőldvár f5 171
Balatonfüred f5 171
Balatonfűzfő g4 171
Balatonlelle f5 171
Balatonszabadi g5 171
Balatonszárszó f5 171
Balatonvilágos g5 171
Balauring m9 99
Balazote b6 193
Balbi, Mount m1 169
Balbigny a5 184
Balbina f4 285
Balbina, Represa de f4 285
Balboa h6 277
Balbriggan e3 165
Balcad d3 226
Balcarce h4 297
Balcary Point e5 164
Balcázar f3 275
Balchik j4 201
Balclutha b7 77
Balcombe f5 163
Balde d2 296
Baldecito e1 296
Balderton f3 162
Bald Head d14 87
Baldim g3 291
Bald Knob d2 258
Bald Mountain, Nevada, U.S.A. f7 263
Bald Mountain, Nevada, U.S.A. d3 264
Baldock f5 163
Baldock Lake e2 250
Baldone l4 157
Baldur d6 250
Baldwin, Louisiana, U.S.A. d5 258
Baldwin, Michigan, U.S.A. d4 254
Baldwin Peninsula d2 246
Baldwinville h2 257
Baldy Mount h6 248
Baldy Mountain c5 250
Baldy Peak j9 263
Bal'dzikan f1 112
Baléa b3 222
Baleares, Islas, Spain f5 193
Baleares, Islas, Spain f5 193
Baleh g4 98
Baleia, Ponta da j2 291
Baleines, Pointe des a2 186
Bale Mountains National Park b2 226
Balen d3 159
Băleni g3 201
Baleno d4 100
Baler c3 100
Baler Bay c3 100
Balerma b8 193
Baleshwar k9 125
Balestrand b2 156
Balestrate c6 199
Balestrieri, Punta Ab2 198
Baléyara e3 223
Balezino m3 151
Balfate d3 276
Balfe's Creek g6 80
Balfour, N.Z. b6 77
Balfour, R.S.A. h3 235
Balfour Downs e8 86
Balgo h7 86
Balguntay w6 121
Balho f5 219
Bali, Rajasthan, India f8 129
Bali, India f8 129
Bali, Indon. h9 99
Bali, Bali, Indon. h9 99
Baliangao d6 100
Bali Barat National Park h9 99
Balidianzi n5 113
Balige d14 103
Baligród l6 169
Balihan k5 113
Balıkesir, Tur. b3 208
Balıkesir, Balıkesir, Tur. a3 208
Balık Gölü j3 209
Balıkh g4 209
Balikpapan j5 99
Balikpapan, Teluk j5 99
Balik Pulau b3 101
Balimbing b3 100
Balimila Reservoir h3 126
Balimo l7 97
Balin m1 113
Balingen b3 101
Balingen g3 174
Balingian, Malay. g3 98
Balingian, Sarawak, Malay. g3 98
Balinţ k6 171
Balintang Channel c1 100
Bali Sea h8 99
Bali, Selat h9 99
Balitondo d2 224
Baljuvon d1 128
Balk d2 159
Balkanabat g2 137
Balkanskaya Oblast' d8 120
Balkány k4 171
Balkashino m1 121
Balkassar f4 128
Balkh, Afg. c2 128
Balkh, Balkh, Afg. c2 128
Balkhash q4 121
Balkhash, Ozero q4 121
Ball c4 258
Balla b3 165
Ballabgarh c5 130
Ballachulish c3 164
Balladonia f13 87
Ballagan Point e3 165
Ballaghaderreen c3 165
Ballan d3 82
Ballangen f2 154
Ballantine a2 260
Ballantrae c4 164
Ballao Ab3 198
Ballarat f14 81
Ballard, Lake e11 87
Ballarpur f3 126
Ballater e2 164
Ballaugh b2 162
Ballé c2 222
Ballena, Punta c5 292
Ballenero, Canal b6 295
Ballenstedt g4 173
Balleny Islands x1 298
Balleroy e3 182
Ballerup f3 158
Ballesteros f2 297
Balli h5 201
Ballia j7 125
Ballina, Aust. l10 81
Ballina, Mayo, Ire. b2 165
Ballina, Tipperary, Ire. c4 165
Ballinalack d3 165
Ballinascarthy c5 165
Ballinasloe c3 165
Ballincollig c5 165
Ballindine c3 165
Ballineen c5 165
Ballingeary b5 165
Ballinger d6 261
Ballinluig e3 164
Ballinrobe b3 165
Ballisodare c2 165
Ballobar e3 192
Balloch d2 164
Ballon f4 183
Ballsh d5 200
Ballstad d2 154
Ballston Spa g1 257
Ballum, Den. b3 158
Ballum, Neth. d1 159
Bally e4 256
Ballybofey d2 165
Ballybunnion b4 165
Ballycanew e4 165
Ballycastle, Ire. b2 165
Ballycastle, U.K. b4 164
Ballyclare b4 164
Ballyconneely a3 165
Ballyconnell d2 165
Ballycroy b2 165
Ballyduff b4 165
Ballygar c3 165
Ballygawley d2 165
Ballygorman d1 165
Ballygowan f2 165
Ballyhalbert f2 165
Ballyhaunis c3 165
Ballyhoura Mts c4 165
Ballyjamesduff d3 165
Ballylongford b4 165
Ballymahon d3 165
Ballymakeery b5 165
Ballymena, England, U.K. b2 165
Ballymena, Northern Ireland, U.K. e2 165
Ballymoe c3 165
Ballymoney, England, U.K. b2 165
Ballymoney, Northern Ireland, U.K. e1 165
Ballymote c2 165
Ballymurry c3 165
Ballynahinch f2 165
Ballyquintin Point f2 165
Ballyshannon c2 165
Ballyteige Bay e4 165
Ballyvaughan b3 165
Ballyvoy b4 164
Balma d5 187
Balmaceda, Aisén, Chile b5 295
Balmaceda, Antofagasta, Chile d4 292
Balmaceda, Lago b6 295
Balmaseda a1 192
Balmazújváros k4 171
Balme b4 196
Balmhorn b3 196
Balmoral e14 81
Balmorhea h2 272
Balnacra c2 164
Balnearia f1 297
Balneario Orense h5 297
Balneario Oriente g5 297
Baloa m5 99
Balochistan, Pak. b6 129
Balochistan, Pak. b7 129
Balod g9 124
Baloda Bazar h9 124
Balogunyom e4 170
Balok, Teluk d6 98
Balombo a1 232
Balonne c6 85
Balonтohe e9 100
Balotaszállás h5 171
Balotra f8 129
Baloty n3 169
Baloži l4 157
Balpyk Bi s5 121
Balrampur f6 135
Balranald f13 81
Balș g3 201
Balsa de Ves c5 193
Bálsamo b4 290
Balsa Nova d6 290
Balsapuerto b5 284
Balsareny f3 192
Balsas, Braz. c3 288
Balsas, Mex. c4 274
Balsas, Guerrero, Mex. e4 275
Balsas, Rio das, Braz. c3 288
Balsas, Rio das, Braz. c4 288
Balsfjorden g2 154
Balsicas d7 193
Balsorano c3 198
Bålsta g3 157
Balsthal b2 196
Balta j2 201
Baltanás f3 190
Baltasar Brum e2 294
Baltasar, Punta g7 277
Baltasi l3 151
Baltasound A 164
Bălți h2 201
Baltic b3 257
Baltijsk h1 169
Baltim c6 136
Baltimore, Ire. b5 165
Baltimore, R.S.A. h1 235
Baltimore, U.S.A. d5 256
Baltinglass e4 165
Baltistan c2 130
Baltoji Vokė p1 169
Baltoro Glacier c2 130
Baltra, Isla A 286
Baluarte d3 288
Balūchestān va Sīstān a6 129
Balupe m5 157
Baluran, Gunung g4 98
Balurghat l7 125
Bălușeni h2 201
Balut e8 100
Balvatnet e3 154
Balve c4 172
Balvi m4 157
Balya a3 208
Balykchy r6 121
Balykshi h3 149
Balyn h1 201
Balzar b4 284
Bam f5 116
Bām r3 137
Bama, China f6 104
Bama, Nig. g3 223
Bamaga f1 80
Bamaji Lake h5 250
Bamako c3 222
Bamba, D.R.C. c5 224
Bamba, Mali d2 222
Bambang c2 100
Bambangando c2 232
Bambannan c8 100
Bambari d2 224
Bamberg d4 175
Bambesa e3 225
Bambesi f2 225
Bambey a3 222
Bambili e3 225
Bambio c3 224

312 Bamboesberg → Baton Rouge

Bamboesberg g5 235
Bamboi d4 222
Bambouk b3 222
Bambou Mountains C 231
Bambouti e2 225
Bambudi d5 218
Bambuí f4 291
Bâmdezh m6 137
Bamenda g4 223
Bamford e3 162
Bami r2 137
Bāmiān, Afg. c3 128
Bāmiān, Bāmiān, Afg. c3 128
Bamiancheng n4 113
Bamingui, C.A.R. c2 224
Bamingui, Bamingui-Bangoran, C.A.R. d2 224
Bamingui-Bangoran d2 224
Bamingui-Bangoran, Parc National du c2 224
Bamoa e5 272
Bam Posht, Kūh-e a7 129
Bampton, England, U.K. c6 163
Bampton, England, U.K. e5 163
Bampūr g5 116
Banaadir d3 226
Banaba H 75
Banabuiu e3 288
Banabuiu, Açude e3 288
Bañados del Atuel d4 296
Bañados del Izozog e3 293
Banahao, Mount c3 100
Banalia e3 225
Banamba c3 222
Banámichi h11 263
Banana d4 84
Banana Islands b4 222
Bananal, Ilha do b4 288
Bananga n9 127
Banapur j3 127
Bañares b2 192
Banarlı h5 201
Banas e6 124
Banās, Ra's e3 219
Bana, Wādī g5 219
Banawaya k8 99
Ban Ban f6 102
Banbar p4 125
Banbasa e5 130
Banbirpur e5 130
Banbridge, England, U.K. b1 165
Banbridge, Northern Ireland, U.K. e2 165
Ban Bua Chum e8 102
Ban Bua Yai f8 102
Ban Bungxai h8 102
Banbury e4 163
Banc d'Arguin, Parc National du a4 220
Banchory f2 164
Banco Chinchorro p8 273
Banco Gorda f3 277
Banco, Parc National du d4 222
Bancoran b7 100
Bancroft h3 255
Band r5 137
Banda, Cam. g4 223
Banda, D.R.C. e3 225
Banda, India g7 124
Banda Aceh b13 103
Banda Banda, Mount e7 85
Banda Daud Shah e4 128
Bandahara, Gunung c14 103
Bandai-Asahi National Park h3 115
Bandajuma b4 222
Bandak c3 156
Banda, Kepulauan h6 97
Bandama Blanc c4 222
Bandaneira h6 97
Bandar e2 233
Bandaragung c7 98
Bandar Al-Muktafi Billah Shah c3 101
Bandarban n8 125
Bandar Baru Rompin c4 101
Bandar-e 'Abbās r8 137
Bandar-e Anzalī m3 137
Bandar-e Chārak q8 137
Bandar-e Deylam n6 137
Bandar-e Emām Khomeyni m6 137
Bandar-e Kong q8 137
Bandar-e Lengeh q8 137
Bandar-e Maqām p8 137
Bandar-e Ma'shur m6 137
Bandar-e Moghūyeh q8 137
Bandar-e Rīg n7 137
Bandar-e Torkeman p3 137
Bandar Lampung c7 98
Bandarpunch d4 130
Bandar Seri Begawan h2 99
Bandar Tun Razak c4 101
Bandar Wanaag c2 226
Banda Sea g6 300
Bande c2 190
Bandeira h1 291
Bandeirante b4 288
Bandeirantes, Mato Grosso do Sul, Braz. a3 290
Bandeirantes, Paraná, Braz. c5 290
Bandeiras, Pico de h4 291
Bandelierkop h1 235
Bandera d1 294
Banderaló f3 297
Banderas g2 272
Banderas, Bahía de b3 274
Banderilla f4 275
Bandhi d7 129
Bandholm e4 158
Bandia g3 126
Bandiagara d3 222
Band-i-Khan Jahan b6 129
Bandingilo National Park f2 225
Bandipur b2 130
Bandırma a2 208
Bandon, Ire. c5 165
Bandon, Ire. c5 165
Bandon, U.S.A. a4 262
Bāndovan Burnu b8 120
Band Qīr m6 137
Bandundu, D.R.C. c4 224
Bandundu, Bandundu, D.R.C. c4 224
Bandung d8 98
Bandya f10 87
Băneasa, Constanța, Rom. h3 201
Băneasa, Giurgiu, Rom. h3 201
Bāneh k4 137
Banemo h5 97
Banera g8 129
Banes g4 266
Banfèlè b3 222
Banff, Can. k6 249
Banff, U.K. f2 164
Banff National Park j6 249
Banfora d3 222
Bang c2 224
Banga, D.R.C. d5 224
Banga, Phil. e7 100
Banga, Phil. e7 100
Bangadi e3 225
Bangai Point f7 100
Bangalao c8 100
Bangala Recreational Park e3 233
Bangalore e6 126
Bangangté g4 223
Bangaon l8 125
Bangar, Bru. h2 99
Bangar, Phil. c2 100
Bangassou d3 224
Bangdag Co e2 130
Banggai, Indon. m5 99
Banggai, Sulawesi Tengah, Indon. m5 99
Banggai, Kepulauan m6 99
Banggi j1 99
Banghāzī b1 218
Bangil g8 98
Bangka, Indon. d6 98
Bangka, Indon. n4 99
Bangkalan, Indon. m5 99
Bangkalan, Jawa Timur, Indon. g8 98
Bangkala, Teluk k7 99
Bangkaru c15 103
Bangka, Selat, Indon. c6 98
Bangka, Selat, Indon. n4 99
Bangkinang a4 98
Bangkir l4 99
Bangko b6 98
Bangkog Co j4 135
Bangkok e9 103
Bangkok, Bight of e9 103
Bangkulu m5 99
Bangladesh c6 93

BANGLADESH

THE PEOPLE'S REPUBLIC OF BANGLADESH
Area 147,570km² (56,977sq miles)
Capital Dhaka
Organizations COMM, IDB, OIC, SAARC
Population 143,810,000
Pop. growth (%) 2.1
Life expectancy 58 (m); 58 (f)
Languages Bengali
Literacy 41.6%
Currency taka (US $1 = 58.47 taka)
GDP (US million $) 47,175
GDP per head ($US) 328

Bang Lamung e9 103
Bangma Shan b7 104
Bang Mun Nak e7 102
Bangolo c4 222
Bangong Co d3 130
Bangor, Northern Ireland, U.K. c5 164
Bangor, U.K. b3 162
Bangor, Maine, U.S.A. h6 253
Bangor, Michigan, U.S.A. c4 254
Bangoran c2 224
Bangor Erris b2 165
Bangsalsepulun j5 99
Bang Saphan Yai d10 103
Bangsjøen c4 154
Bangsund c4 154
Bangued c2 100
Bangui, C.A.R. c3 224
Bangui, Phil. c1 100
Bangui-Motaba c3 224
Bangunpurba d14 103
Banguru e3 225
Bangweulu, Lake e6 225
Banhine, Parque Nacional de k1 235
Ban Hin Heup f6 102
Banhu f3 111
Ban Huai Yang d10 103
Bani, Burkina d3 222
Bani, C.A.R. d2 224
Baní j5 271
Bani, Mali c3 222
Bani, Phil. b2 100
Bania c3 224
Bani Atiyah e2 219
Bani-Bangou e2 223
Banie c2 168
Banie Mazurskie l1 169
Banifing c3 222
Banija h4 177
Banī, Jbel c3 220
Banikoara e3 223
Banima d2 224
Bani Na'im d5 139
Banio, Lagune b4 224
Banite f1 210
Banitsa f4 201
Bani Walid g2 221
Bāniyās, Ţarţūs, Syria d1 138
Bāniyās, Al Qunayţirah, Syria d3 138
Banja Luka j5 177
Banjar c4 130
Banjarbaru h6 99
Banjarmasin h6 99
Banjul a3 222
Banka f5 124
Banka Banka b5 80
Bankapur d5 126
Bankass d3 222
Ban Kengkabao g7 102
Bänkerträsket h4 154
Bankeryd f4 156
Ban Khao Yoi d9 103
Bankhead Lake f3 258
Ban Khok Kloi d11 103
Bankilaré e3 223
Bankim g4 223
Banko b3 222
Banks g4 259
Banks Island, British Columbia, Can. e1 242
Banks Island, Northwest Territories, Can. e1 242
Banks Islands F 74
Banks Lake d2 262
Banks Peninsula d5 77
Banks Strait Ac2 83
Bankura k8 125
Bankya f4 201
Banla Point d3 100
Ban Mae La Luang c6 102
Ban Mae Mo d6 102
Banmauk b3 102
Bann, Ire. e4 165
Bann, U.K. e2 165
Bannalec b5 182
Ban Napè g6 102
Ban Na San a1 101
Bannay h5 183
Bannerman Town l7 259
Banning g8 265
Bannockburn e3 164
Bannu e4 128
Banon b6 185
Bañón c2 274
Banora b3 222
Baños b4 284
Baños de Chihuio b6 296
Baños de Copahue b4 296
Baños de Molgas c2 190
Baños de Montemayor e4 190
Baños de Puritama d4 292
Baños de Río Tobía b2 192
Baños Maule b4 296
Bánovce nad Bebravou g3 171
Ban Phai f7 102
Banphot Phisai d8 102
Ban Phran Katai d7 102
Banpu f2 111
Banqiao, Anhui, China e3 111
Banqiao, Hubei, China c4 106
Banquan f2 111
Bánréve j3 171
Ban Sanam Chai b2 101
Ban Sawi d10 103
Bansha c4 165
Banshi k6 105
Bansi g8 129
Banská Belá g3 171
Banská Bystrica h3 171
Banská Štiavnica g3 171
Bansko f5 201
Banskobystrický kraj h3 171
Bansloi k7 125
Banstead f5 163
Bansur c6 130
Banswada e3 126
Banswara g9 129
Banta, Indon. k9 99
Banta, U.S.A. b4 264
Bantaeng k7 99
Bantayan d5 100
Bantè e4 223
Banteer c4 165
Ban Tha Chang a1 101
Ban Tha Kham a1 101
Ban Tha Tako e8 102
Ban Tha Tum f8 102
Ban Thepha b2 101
Bantheville d5 159
Banton d4 100
Bantry b5 165
Bantry Bay b5 164
Bantul f8 98
Bantval d6 126
Banur c4 130
Banyak, Pulau-pulau c14 103
Banyo g4 223
Banyoles g2 192
Banyumas e8 98
Banyuwangi h9 99
Banzare Coast t1 298
Bao'an, Hubei, China d4 106
Bao'an, Qinghai, China d1 104
Baocheng f2 104
Baode f6 112
Baodi j6 113
Baoding h6 112
Baofeng c3 106
Bao Ha g4 102
Baoji f1 104
Baojing g4 104
Baokang b4 106
Bao Lôc h10 103
Baoqing s2 113
Baoro c2 224
Baoshan, Shanghai, China g4 111
Baoshan, Yunnan, China d3 102
Baoting j6 102
Baotou f5 112
Baotou Shan q5 113
Baoulé, Mali c3 222
Baoxinji d3 106
Baoying f3 111
Bap f7 129
Bapatla g5 126
Bapaume a4 159
Bāqa el Gharbiyya d4 139
Baqên, Xizang Zizhiqu, China n3 125
Baqên, Xizang Zizhiqu, China p4 125
Baqi c2 106
Ba'qūbah k5 136
Baquedano d4 292
Bar, Serbia/Mont. d4 200
Bar, Ukr. h1 201
Barú, Isla de b1 284
Bara, Nig. g3 223
Bara, Sudan d5 218
Baraachit d3 138
Baraawe c3 226
Barabai h6 99
Barabás l3 171
Barabinsk h4 118
Baraboo b4 254
Baracoa, Cuba g4 266
Baracoa, Hond. d3 276
Baradero h2 297
Baradine, New South Wales, Aust. c7 85
Baradine, New South Wales, Aust. c7 85
Baraga j7 251
Baragoi b3 226
Baragua d1 284
Baragua, Sierra de c1 284
Barahona, Dom. Rep. j5 271
Barahona, Spain b3 192
Barail Range a3 102
Bara Issa d2 222
Barajas de Melo b4 193
Barak, Afg. e2 128
Barak, India a3 102
Baraka e4 219
Barakaldo b1 192
Baraki Barak d4 128
Barakot j9 125
Barakpay l1 121
Bara Lacha Pass c3 130
Baralla c2 190
Baram h3 99
Baramanni q11 271
Baramati c3 126
Barambah b4 84
Baramulla b2 130
Baran e7 124
Barañain c2 192
Baranavichy b1 148
Bārānd k4 171
Barani d3 222
Barankul b3 149
Baranoa k5 277
Barano d'Ischia c4 198
Baranof l4 247
Baranof Island l4 247
Baranovka l2 151
Baranów l4 169
Baranów Sandomierska k5 169
Baranya g5 171
Barão de Cocais g3 291
Barão de Grajaú d3 288
Barão de Melgaço f3 293
Barão de Melgaço e2 293
Baraolt g2 201
Baraouéli c3 222
Baraque de Fraiture d4 159
Baraqueville e4 187
Baraševo g4 151
Barāsoain c2 192
Barataria d5 258
Barat Daya, Kepulauan p8 99
Barauaná, Serra e3 285
Barauni j7 125
Baraut c5 130
Baraya b3 284
Barbacena, Minas Gerais, Braz. g4 291
Barbacena, Braz. b2 288
Barbacena, Port c6 191
Barbacoas b3 284
Barbadillo del Mercado a2 192
Barbadillo del Pez a2 192
Barbado f3 293
Barbados q8 271

BARBADOS

BARBADOS
Area 430km² (166sq miles)
Capital Bridgetown
Organizations ACS, CARICOM, COMM, IADB, SELA
Population 270,000
Pop. growth (%) 0.3
Life expectancy 73 (m); 78 (f)
Languages English
Literacy 99.7%
Currency Barbados dollar (US $1 = 1.99 Barbados dollar)
GDP (US million $) 2595
GDP per head ($US) 9611

Barbaria, Cap de f6 193
Barbariga, Rt e5 176
Barbaros h5 201
Barbastro e2 192
Barbate de Franco e8 191
Barbate, Embalse de e8 191
Barbechitos f4 272
Barbentane a7 185
Barberino di Mugello f5 197
Barberspan Nature Reserve f3 235
Barberton, R.S.A. j2 235
Barberton, U.S.A. f5 254
Barbezieux-St-Hilaire b3 186
Barbil j8 125
Barbizon h4 183
Barbosa c2 284
Barbours d3 256
Barbourville h1 259
Barboza d5 100
Barby (Elbe) g4 173
Bârca f4 201
Barcabo d3 192
Barca de Alva d3 190
Barcaldine g7 80
Barcarrota d6 191
Barcellona Pozzo di Gotto e6 199
Barcelona, Spain g3 192
Barcelona, Spain g3 192
Barcelona, Ven. e1 285
Barcelonnette c6 185
Barcelos, Braz. e4 285
Barcelos, Port b3 190
Barcenillas de Cerezos g1 190
Barchfeld f3 174
Barciany k1 169
Barcillonnette b6 185
Barcin f3 168
Barcino e1 168
Barclay e5 256
Barclayville c5 222
Barcombe g6 163
Barcones b3 192
Barcoo a4 84
Barcs f6 170
Barczewo j2 169
Bärdä g4 149
Barda h4 147
Barda del Medio c5 296
Bardai h4 221
Bárðarbunga A 152
Bardaskan r4 137
Barddhaman k8 125
Bardejov k2 171
Bárdenas Reales c2 192
Bårdesø d3 158
Bardi, India h7 124
Bardi, Italy d5 196
Bardineto c5 197
Bardolino e4 196
Bar Đôn h9 103
Bardonecchia a4 196
Bardsey Island b4 162
Bard Shah n5 137
Bardsir r7 137
Bardwell e1 258
Barë c3 226
Barèges c6 187
Bareilly d5 130
Barei, Wadi b5 218
Barellan h13 81
Barenburg d3 172
Barendorf f2 173
Barendrecht c3 159
Barentin f3 183
Barenton e4 182
Barentsøya c2 118
Barents Sea e2 118
Barentu e4 219
Bareo h3 99
Barfleur d3 182
Barfleur, Pointe de d3 182
Barga, China e4 130
Barga, Italy e5 197
Bargaal e1 226
Bārgāh r8 137
Bargarh h9 125
Bargas f5 191
Bargë b2 226
Barge b5 196
Bargemon c7 185
Bargi f8 124
Bargo g2 83
Bargoed c5 163
Bargteheide d5 158
Barguelonne c4 187
Barguna m8 125
Barguzin e2 94
Bar Hill g4 163
Bari, D.R.C. c3 224
Bari, India e6 124
Bari, Italy f4 198
Bari, Italy f3 198
Bari, Som. d2 226
Barīdī, Ra's e3 219
Barika f1 221
Barikot e3 128
Barima f2 285
Barima-Waini f2 285
Barinas, Ven. c2 284
Barinas, Barinas, Ven. c2 284
Baringa d3 224
Baring, Mount f13 87
Baringo, Lake b3 226
Båring Vig c3 158
Baripada k9 125
Bariri d5 290
Bârîs d3 218
Bari Sadri g8 129
Barisal, Bang. m8 125
Barisal, Barisal, Bang. m8 125
Bari Sardo Ab3 198
Barisciano c2 198
Barito h5 99
Baritú, Parque Nacional e4 293
Barja d3 138
Barjac a6 185
Barjatino c4 150
Barjols c7 185
Barjūj, Wādī g3 221
Barkal n8 125
Barkam d3 104
Barkava m4 157
Barker h4 297
Barkerville g5 248
Barkhamsted Reservoir g3 257
Barkhan d6 129
Barking & Dagenham h3 162
Barkley, Lake c7 254
Barkley Sound e7 248
Barkly East g5 235
Barkly Tableland b4 80
Barkly West f4 234
Barkot d4 130
Barkowo f2 168
Bârlad h2 201
Barlaston d4 162
Barleben g3 173
Bar-le-Duc b2 184
Barlee, Lake d11 87
Barlee Range c8 87
Barles c6 185
Barletta f3 198
Barlinek c3 168
Barling b2 258
Barlo Point b4 222
Barmedman h13 81
Barmer e8 129
Barmouth b4 162
Barmstedt c5 158
Barnagar g9 129
Barnala b4 130
Barnard Castle e2 162
Barnaul u1 121
Barnbach g2 177
Barneberg g3 173
Barnegat f5 257
Barnegat Bay f5 257
Barnesboro b4 256
Barnesville e7 250
Barnet h2 162
Barneveld d2 159
Barneville-Carteret d3 182
Barnewitz h3 173
Barneys Lake d1 82
Barnhart c6 261
Barnim j3 173
Barningham g4 163
Barnoldswick d3 162
Barnowko c3 168
Barnsdall a1 258
Barnsley, England, U.K. e3 162
Barnsley, England, U.K. e3 162
Barnstable k3 257
Barnstaple b5 163
Barnstorf d3 172
Barntrup e4 172
Baro f4 223
Baroda c6 130
Baroe f6 234
Bärofen f3 177
Baroghil Pass f2 128
Baroncourt d5 159
Barone, Monte c4 196
Barong b3 104
Baronnies b6 185
Barouk d3 138
Baro Wenz a2 226
Barpathar n6 125
Barpeta m6 125
Barquinha b5 191
Barquisimeto d1 284
Barr d2 184
Barra, Braz. d4 288
Barra, U.K. a2 164
Barraba k11 81
Barra Bonita d5 290
Barracão do Barreto f1 293
Barracas d4 193
Barrachina c4 192
Barracuda Fracture Zone f8 302
Barra da Estiva d4 288
Barra de Cazones f3 275
Barra de Navidad b4 274
Barra de São Francisco h3 291
Barra de São João h5 291
Barra do Bugres f3 293
Barra do Corda c3 288
Barra do Cuanza b5 224
Barra do Cuieté h3 291
Barra do Garças b1 290
Barrado Mendes d4 288
Barra do Piraí g5 291
Barra do São Manuel f1 293
Barra do Turvo d6 290
Barra do Una e6 290
Barra Falsa, Ponta da l1 235
Barrafranca d7 199
Barrages d'Ayamé d4 222
Barra Kruta f3 277
Barra Longa g4 291
Barra Mansa f5 291
Barrāmīya d9 136
Barrana f5 128
Barranca, Peru b2 292
Barranca, Ven. c2 284
Barrancabermeja c2 284
Barranca del Cobre, Parque Natural f4 272
Barrancas, Arg. e1 294
Barrancas, Arg. b4 296
Barrancas, Neuquén, Arg. c4 296
Barrancas, Arg. g2 297
Barrancas, Barinas, Ven. c2 284
Barrancas, Monagas, Ven. e2 285
Barranco c2 276
Barranco de Loba c2 284
Barranco de Santiago Ab2 189
Barranco do Velho c7 191
Barrancos d6 191
Barranda c6 193
Barra Norte f3 275
Barranquilla, Atlántico, Col. k5 277
Barranquilla, Guaviare, Col. c3 284
Barranquita b5 284
Barranquitas A 270
Barras d2 288
Barra San José a3 276
Barrax b5 193
Barre, Massachusetts, U.S.A. h2 257
Barre, Vermont, U.S.A. k3 255
Barreal c1 296
Barre-des-Cévennes f4 187
Barre des Ecrins c6 185
Barreiras d4 288
Barreirinha f4 285
Barreirinhas d2 288
Barreiro a6 191
Barreiro do Nascimento b4 288
Barreiros e3 288
Barrême c7 185
Barren Island, Falk. Is e6 295
Barren Island, India p6 127
Barren Island, Cape Ab2 83
Barren Islands f4 246
Barren River Lake d7 254
Barre Plains h2 257
Barretos d4 290
Barrett, Mount h6 86
Barrhill d4 164
Barri f4 219
Barrie g3 254
Barrié de la Maza, Embalse de b2 190
Barrier Range e11 85
Barrington k7 253
Barrington Lake c2 250
Barrington, Mount d8 85
Barrington Tops National Park d8 85
Barringun g10 81
Bàrrio b3 190
Barrio Mar d5 193
Barrios de Luna, Embalse de e2 190
Barrit c3 158
Barrō c3 190
Barro Alto c5 289
Barrocão g2 291
Barrois, Plateau du b2 184
Barrolândia j2 291
Barros Arana a5 296
Barroselas b3 190
Barroso g4 291
Barros, Tierra de d6 191
Barroterán j4 273
Barrow, Arg. g5 297
Barrow, Ire. d4 165
Barrow, U.K. g4 163
Barrow, U.S.A. e1 246
Barrow Creek a6 80
Barrow-in-Furness c2 162
Barrow Island b7 86
Barrow, Point e1 246
Barrows c4 250
Barr Smith Range e10 87
Barruecopardo d3 190
Barry c5 163
Barrydale d6 234
Barryville f3 256
Barsalpur f6 129
Bârsana g2 201
Barsbüttel d5 158
Barshatas s3 121
Barsi d3 126
Barsinghausen e3 172
Barsø c3 158
Barsovo n3 147
Barßel c2 172
Barstow f7 265
Bar-sur-Aube a2 184
Bar-sur-Seine a2 184
Bārta j4 157
Barth f4 158
Barthe h1 173
Bartica f2 285
Bartın, Tur. d2 208
Bartın, Bartın, Tur. d2 208
Bartle Frere, Mount A 84
Bartlesville b1 258
Bartlett, Nebraska, U.S.A. d3 260
Bartlett, Tennessee, U.S.A. e2 258
Bartolomé, Isla A 286
Bartolomeu Dias f3 233
Barton-upon-Humber f3 162
Bartoszyce, Warmińsko-Mazurskie, Pol. j1 169
Bartow, Florida, U.S.A. j6 259
Bartow, Georgia, U.S.A. h3 259
Barumini Ab3 198
Barumun b5 101
Barung g9 98
Barus d14 103
Baruth j3 173
Baruunharaa d1 112
Baruunsuu c4 112
Baruun Urt g2 112
Barú, Volcán f6 277
Barvas b1 164
Barvikmyran og Blodskytodden Naturreservat n1 155
Barvinkove e2 148
Barwah e8 124
Barwala, Gujarat, India e9 129
Barwala, Haryana, India b5 130
Barwani g9 129
Barwice e2 168
Barwick h4 259
Barwon h10 81
Barwon Heads d4 82
Barycz e4 168
Baryš, Russ. Fed. j4 151
Baryš, Ul'janovskaja Oblast', Russ. Fed. j5 151
Barysaw c1 148
Bârzava l5 171
Barzio d4 196
Bas c5 130
Basaga b2 128
Basaguke g5 135
Bāsa'īdū q8 137
Basail e1 294
Basalt, Aust. a1 84
Basalt, U.S.A. e3 264
Basankusu c3 224
Basar e3 126
Basarabeasca j2 201
Basarabi j3 201
Basavilbaso h2 297
Basay d6 100
Basbas c8 100
Bàscara g2 192
Baščelakskij Hrebet v2 121
Basciano c2 198
Basconcillos del Tozo g2 190
Bas-Congo b5 224
Bascuñán, Cabo b1 294
Basdahl c5 158
Basekpio d3 224
Basel b2 196
Basey e5 100
Bashee h6 235
Bāshī n7 137
Bashi Channel g1 97
Bashir, Wādī g3 221
Basht n6 137
Bashtanka d3 148
Basi, Punjab, India c4 130
Basiad Bay d3 100
Basilan d7 100
Basilan Strait c7 100
Basildon g5 163
Basile c4 258
Basile, Pico f5 223
Basiliano h3 196
Basilicata f4 198
Basin a2 260
Basingstoke e5 163
Basin Lake q5 249
Başīr e3 138
Basirhat l8 125
Baška f5 177
Başkale k3 209
Baskatong, Réservoir r7 251
Baskerville, Cape f5 86
Baskinta d3 138
Baškortostan, Respublika k1 149
Basle b2 196
Bašmakovo g5 151
Basmat e3 126
Baso b5 98
Basoda e8 124
Basodino c3 196
Basoko d3 224
Basongo d4 224
Basque, Pays a5 187
Bas-Rhin d2 184
Bassano del Grappa f4 196
Bassar e4 223
Bassas de Pedro Padua Bank c6 126
Basse-Casamance, Parc National de a3 222
Bassecourt b2 196
Bassein b7 102
Basse-Kotto d2 224
Basse-Normandie e4 182
Bassens b4 186
Bassenthwaite Lake c2 162
Basse Santa Su b3 222
Basses, Pointe des C 271
Basse-Terre, Guad. C 271
Basse-Terre, Guad. C 271
Basseterre F 271
Bassett d3 260
Bassigny b3 184
Bassikounou c2 222
Bassila e4 223
Basso, Plateau de b4 218
Bass Strait d4 82
Bassum d3 172
Basswood Lake h6 250
Båstad e4 156
Bastak q8 137
Bastam q3 137
Bastānābād l3 137
Bastardo g7 197
Bastelica A 185
Bastelicaccia A 185
Basti h6 124
Bastia, Fr. A 185
Bastia, Italy g6 197
Bastogne d4 159
Bastos c4 290
Bastrop, Louisiana, U.S.A. d3 258
Bastrop, Texas, U.S.A. a4 258
Bastuträsk h4 154
Baswa c6 130
Bata f5 223
Báta g5 171
Bataan Peninsula b3 100
Batabanó, Golfo de c3 266
Batac c1 100
Batacosa e4 272
Batagaj p3 119
Bataguaçu b4 290
Bataiporã b5 290
Batajsk e3 148
Batak g5 201
Batakan h7 99
Batala b4 130
Batalha, Braz. d2 288
Batalha, Port b5 191
Batam d5 101
Batama e3 225
Batan, China g2 111
Batan, Phil. d1 100
Batang, China b3 104
Batang, Indon. e8 98
Batanga f6 223
Batangafo c2 224
Batangas c4 100
Batang Berjuntai b4 101
Batanghari b5 98
Batang Kali b4 101
Batang Melaka c4 101
Batangtoru d15 103
Bátaszék g5 171
Batatais e4 290
Batavia, Arg. e3 296
Batavia, U.S.A. b2 256
Batchawana Mountain l7 251
Batchelor k3 86
Bătdâmbâng f9 103
Batea e3 192
Bateckij a2 150
Bateemeucica, Gunung b13 103
Batéké, Plateaux b4 224
Batemans Bay, New South Wales, Aust. k13 81
Batemans Bay, New South Wales, Aust. g2 83
Båteng l1 155
Baterno f6 191
Batesburg j3 259
Bates Range e10 87
Batesville, Arkansas, U.S.A. d2 258
Batesville, Indiana, U.S.A. d6 254
Batesville, Mississippi, U.S.A. e2 258
Bath, Can. j5 253
Bath, St K./N. F 271
Bath, U.K. d5 163
Bath, Maine, U.S.A. h7 252
Bath, New York, U.S.A. c2 256
Batha, Chad a4 218
Batha, Chad a5 218
Batha de Laïri a5 218
Bath and N. E. Somerset d5 163
Bathinda b4 130
Bathsheba H 271
Bathurst, Arg. g4 297
Bathurst, Aust. j12 81
Bathurst, Can. k5 253
Bathurst, R.S.A. g6 235
Bathurst, Cape n1 247
Bathurst Inlet, Nunavut, Can. h2 242
Bathurst Inlet, Nunavut, Can. h2 242
Bathurst Island, Aust. k2 86
Bathurst Island, Can. k1 242
Bathurst, Lake f2 83
Bati f5 219
Batia e3 223
Batié d4 222
Batikala, Tanjung l6 99
Batiki E 74
Batina g6 177
Batista, Serra da, Braz. d3 288
Batken e1 128
Batley e3 162
Batlow j13 81
Batman h4 209
Bátmonostor g5 171
Batna f1 221
Båtnfjordsøra a5 154
Batong Group a2 101
Baton Rouge d4 258

Bátonyterenye → Beni Mellal 313

Bátonyterenye h4 171
Batopilas f4 272
Batote b3 130
Batouala b3 224
Batouri b3 224
Batovi b1 290
Batrina j4 177
Batroûn d2 138
Båtsfjord m1 155
Batthewmurnarna, Mount d9 87
Batti b4 130
Batticaloa g9 126
Battipaglia d4 198
Battle, Can. m5 249
Battle, U.K. g6 163
Battle Creek, Can. n7 249
Battle Creek, U.S.A. d4 254
Battlefields d2 233
Battle Mountain e5 262
Battonya k5 171
Battura Glacier b1 130
Batu b2 226
Batu Arang b4 101
Batuata m8 99
Batuayau, Bukit h4 99
Batubetumbang d6 98
Batu Bora, Bukit h3 99
Batubrok, Bukit h4 99
Batu, Bukit g3 98
Batuco b3 296
Batudaka l5 99
Batu Enam c4 101
Batu Gajah b3 101
Batuhitam, Tanjung m5 99
Batui m5 99
Batulaki e8 100
Batulanteh j9 99
Batulicin j6 99
Batulilangmebang, Gunung h4 99
Bat'umi h2 209
Batu Pahat c5 101
Batu, Pulau-pulau b6 96
Batu Putih, Gunung b3 101
Baturaja c7 98
Batu Rakit c3 101
Baturetno f9 98
Baturité e2 288
Baturité, Serra do e2 288
Batusangkar a5 98
Bat Yam c4 139
Batyrevo j4 151
Batz, Île de a4 182
Bau f4 98
Baubau m7 99
Baucau p9 99
Bauchi, Nig. f3 223
Bauchi, Bauchi, Nig. f3 223
Baud b5 182
Bauda j9 125
Baudette f6 250
Baudó b2 284
Baudo, Serranía de b2 284
Baugé e5 182
Bauges c5 185
Baugy e1 186
Bauhinia c4 84
Bauladu Aa2 198
Bauland e3 174
Bauld, Cape q3 253
Baume-les-Dames c3 184
Baunach f2 175
Baundal b3 130
Baunei Ab2 198
Bauru d5 290
Baús b3 290
Bausendorf e4 159
Bauska l4 157
Bautino h3 149
Bautzen e1 175
Bauyrzhan Momysh-Uly n6 121
Bavans c3 184
Bavay b4 159
Båven g3 156
Baveno c4 196
Baviaanskloofberge f6 234
Bavispe j10 263
Bavla f9 129
Bavliari f9 129
Bavtajokka k2 155
Bavula c3 224
Baw b4 102
Bawal, India c5 130
Bawal, Indon. e6 98
Bawan g5 98
Bawang, Tanjung e5 98
Baw Baw National Park e3 83
Bawdeswell h4 162
Bawdwin c4 102
Bawe j6 97
Bawean g7 98
Bawinkel f2 159
Bawiti c2 218
Bawku d3 222
Bawtry e3 162
Baxley h4 259
Baxoi q4 125
Baxter, Minnesota, U.S.A. f7 250
Baxter, Tennessee, U.S.A. g1 259
Baxter Springs b1 258
Bay, Som. c3 226
Bay, U.S.A. d2 258
Bayamo f4 266
Bayamón A 270
Bayan, China p2 113
Bayan, Indon. j9 99
Bayan, Arhangay, Mong. b2 112
Bayan, Hentiy, Mong. f1 112
Bayana e6 124
Bayanaul q2 121
Bayanbulag e2 112
Bayanbulak v4 121
Bayandelger e2 112
Bayanga c3 224
Bayanga-Didi c2 224
Bayang, Pegunungan e4 98
Bayan Har Shan q2 125
Bayan Har Shankou a1 104
Bayanhongor, Mong. b4 94
Bayanhongor, Bayanhongor, Mong. a2 112
Bayanhushuu a2 112
Bayan Lepas b3 101
Bayan Mod c5 112
Bayan Obo e5 112
Bayano, Lago h6 277
Bayan-Ölgiy a3 94
Bayan-Ovoo, Hentiy, Mong. f1 112
Bayan-Ovoo, Hentiy, Mong. g2 112
Bayan Qagan l3 113
Bayan Tal j1 113
Bayard a5 256
Bayas b2 192
Bayasgalant g2 112
Bayat c3 208
Bayawan d6 100
Bayāẑ q6 137
Baybay e5 100
Bayboro l2 259
Bayburt, Tur. h2 209
Bayburt, Bayburt, Tur. h2 209
Baychunas j3 149
Bay City, Michigan, U.S.A. e4 254
Bay City, Texas, U.S.A. b5 258
Bay de Verde r4 253
Baydhabo c3 226
Bay du Nord Wilderness q4 253
Bayelsa f5 223
Bayerisch Eisenstein j3 175
Bayerische Rhön e2 174
Bayerischer Spessart e3 174
Bayerischer Wald, Ger. h4 175
Bayerischer Wald, Ger. h3 175
Bayerische Wald, Nationalpark j3 174
Bayern g4 175
Bayer Wald, Nationalpark j4 175
Bayeux e3 182
Bayfield h7 250
Baygakum l5 120
Bayganin j2 149
Baygora k5 147
Bayḥan al Qiṣab g5 219
Bayiji e2 111
Bayındır a3 208
Bayizhen p5 125
Bayjī j5 209
Baykan h3 209
Bay-Khozha j5 120
Baykonur, Gorod Baykonur, Kaz. j5 120
Baykonur, Karagandinskaya Oblast', Kaz. l4 120
Bay, Laguna de c3 100
Bay Minette f4 258
Bay of Bengal d4 300
Bay of Biscay k5 302
Bay of Fundy j6 253
Bay of Harbours e6 295
Bay of Islands e1 76
Bay of Plenty, N.Z. f3 76
Bay of Plenty, N.Z. f2 76
Bayombong c2 100
Bayon b2 184
Bayonne, Fr. a5 187
Bayonne, U.S.A. f4 257
Bayo Point c5 100
Bayou Bartholomew d3 258
Bayou Cane d5 258
Bayou d'Arbonne Lake c3 258
Bayou Lafourche d5 258
Bayou Macon d3 258
Bayóvar a5 284
Bay Port e4 254
Bayport g4 257
Bayramaly a2 128
Bayramiç a3 208
Bay, Réserve de d3 222
Bayreuth f2 175
Bay Roberts r5 253
Bay Shore g4 257
Bays, Lake of c6 252
Bay Springs e4 258
Bayston Hill d4 162
Baysun c1 128
Baytown b5 258
Bayunglincir b5 98
Bay View f3 76
Bayy al Kabīr, Wādī g2 221
Bayzhansay m6 121
Baza, Spain b7 193
Baza, Andalucía, Spain b7 193
Bazarchulan h2 149
Bazardyuzyu, Gora h4 148
Bāzār-e Māsāl m3 137
Bazarkhanym, Gora d1 128
Bazar-Korgon p7 121
Bazarne Mataki k4 151
Bazarnyj Syzgan j5 151
Bazaruto, Ilha do f3 233
Bazaruto, Parque Nacional de f3 233
Bazas b4 187
Baza, Sierra de b7 193
Bazdar b7 129
Bazet c5 187
Bazhong f3 104
Baziège d5 187
Bazin r7 251
Bazkovskaja f2 148
Bazoches-les-Gallerandes h4 183
Bazoches-sur-Hoëne f4 183
Bazouges-la-Pérouse d4 182
Bazpur d5 130
Bazzano f5 197
Bchamoun d3 138
Be h10 103
Beach c2 260
Beach Haven f5 257
Beachport e14 81
Beachwood f5 257
Beachy Head g6 163
Beacon Bay g6 235
Beaconsfield, Aust. Ab2 83
Beaconsfield, U.K. f5 163
Beagle Bank f4 86
Beagle, Canal c6 295
Beagle Gulf k3 86
Bealanana Ab1 233
Beale, Cape e7 248
Beals Creek c5 261
Beampingaratra Ab3 233
Bear, California, U.S.A. b2 264
Bear, Idaho, U.S.A. h4 262
Bear Creek a2 264
Bearden c3 258
Beardmore k6 251
Beardmore Reservoir c5 85
Beardstown a5 254
Bear Island, Can. n3 251
Bear Island, Ire. b5 165
Beariz b2 190
Bear Lake, Can. e3 250
Bear Lake, U.S.A. h4 262
Bearma f8 124
Bear Mountain, California, U.S.A. e6 265
Bear Mountain, South Dakota, U.S.A. c3 260
Béarn b5 187
Bear Paw Mountain j1 262
Bearpaw Mountains j1 262
Bear Peninsula g2 298
Bearsden d4 164
Beas d7 191
Beasain b1 192
Beas de Segura b6 193
Beata, Cabo j6 267
Beata, Isla j6 267
Beatrice d3 260
Beatrice, Cape c3 80
Beatton g3 248
Beatton River g3 248
Beattyville h1 255
Beaucaire a7 185
Beauce g4 183
Beauchene Island e6 295
Beaucourt c3 184
Beaudesert e5 85
Beaufort, Aust. f14 81
Beaufort, Franche-Comté, Fr. b4 184
Beaufort, Fr. c5 185
Beaufort, Malay. h2 99
Beaufort, North Carolina, U.S.A. l2 259
Beaufort, South Carolina, U.S.A. j3 259
Beaufort-en-Vallée e5 182
Beaufortin c5 185
Beaufort Sea n1 301
Beaufort West e6 234
Beaugency g5 183
Beaujeu a4 184
Beaujolais, Monts du a4 185
Beaulieu, Languedoc-Roussillon, Fr. a7 184
Beaulieu-lès-Loches g5 183
Beauly, Scotland, U.K. d2 164
Beauly, Scotland, U.K. d2 164
Beaumes-de-Venise b6 185
Beaumesnil f3 183
Beaumetz-lès-Loges a4 159
Beaumont, Bel. c4 159
Beaumont, Aquitaine, Fr. c4 186
Beaumont, Fr. d3 182
Beaumont, N.Z. b6 77
Beaumont, Mississippi, U.S.A. e4 258
Beaumont, Texas, U.S.A. b4 258
Beaumont-de-Lomagne c5 187
Beaumont-en-Argonne d5 159
Beaumont-le-Roger f3 183
Beaumont-les-Autels f4 183
Beaumont-sur-Oise h3 183
Beaumont-sur-Sarthe f4 183
Beaune a3 184
Beaune-La Rolande h4 183
Beauport g5 252
Beaupréau e5 182
Beauraing c4 159
Beauregard, Lago di b4 196
Beaurepaire b5 185
Beaurepaire-en-Bresse b4 184
Beaurières b6 185
Beauséjour e5 250
Beauvais h3 183
Beauval h2 183
Beau Vallon A 226
Beauvezer c6 185
Beauville c4 187
Beauvoir-sur-Mer c6 182
Beauvoir-sur-Niort b2 186
Beaver, Alberta/Saskatchewan, Can. m4 249
Beaver, Ontario, Can. j3 251
Beaver, Alaska, U.S.A. h2 247
Beaver, Oklahoma, U.S.A. c4 261
Beaver, Pennsylvania, U.S.A. f5 254
Beaver, Utah, U.S.A. g6 263
Beaver, Yukon Territory, U.S.A. n3 247
Beaver Creek, Can. j3 247
Beaver Creek, Alaska, U.S.A. h2 247
Beaver Creek, Missouri, U.S.A. c1 258
Beaver Creek, Nebraska, U.S.A. c4 260
Beaver Dam b4 254
Beaver Falls f5 254
Beaverhead g3 262
Beaverhead Mountains g3 262
Beaverhill Lake f5 249
Beaverhill Lake f3 250
Beaver Island, Falk. Is d6 295
Beaver Island, U.S.A. d3 254
Beaver Lake c1 258
Beaver Run Reservoir a4 256
Beaverton g3 254
Beavertown c4 256
Beawar g7 129
Beazley d2 296
Beba Veche j5 171
Bebédjia c2 224
Bebedouro d4 290
Beberibe e2 288
Bebertal g3 173
Bebington c3 162
Bebóto c2 224
Bebra g3 174
Becán p8 273
Beca, Punta g5 193
Becca du Lac b4 196
Beccles h4 163
Becedas e4 190
Bečej e3 200
Becerreá c2 190
Becerro, Cayos f3 277
Bečevinka d2 150
Béchar d2 220
Becharof Lake e4 246
Bécherel d4 182
Bechhofen e2 175
Bechyně c2 170
Becilla de Valderaduey e2 190
Beckingen e5 159
Beckley f7 254
Beckov f3 171
Beckum d4 172
Beclean g2 201
Bečov b1 170
Bečov nad Teplou a1 170
Becsehely e5 170
Bečva f2 171
Bečváry d2 170
Bedadung g9 98
Bedale e2 162
Bedan c2 224
Bédarieux f5 187
Bédarrides a6 185
Bedburg e4 159
Bédée d4 182
Bedelē b2 226
Bedel Pass s7 121
Beder d2 158
Bederkesa b5 158
Bedēsa c2 226
Bedford, R.S.A. g6 235
Bedford, U.K. f4 163
Bedford, Indiana, U.S.A. c6 254
Bedford, Kentucky, U.S.A. d6 254
Bedford, Massachusetts, U.S.A. j2 257
Bedford, Pennsylvania, U.S.A. b4 256
Bedford, Virginia, U.S.A. g7 254
Bedford, Cape g3 80
Bedford Hills g3 257
Bedford Level f4 163
Bedford Point G 271
Bedfordshire f4 163
Bedi e9 129
Bedinggong d6 98
Będków h4 169
Bedla f8 129
Bedlington e1 162
Bedlno h3 169
Bedmar g7 191
Bednayel d3 138
Bednja h3 177
Bedong b3 101
Bedonia d5 196
Bedourie d8 80
Bedsted Stationsby b2 158
Bedum e1 159
Będzin h5 169
Beechal Creek a5 85
Beecher c5 254
Beech Grove c6 254
Beecroft Peninsula g2 83
Beekeepers Nature Reserve b11 87
Beelitz h3 173
Beenleigh e5 85
Beenz j2 173
Bee Ridge h6 259
Beeringgnurding, Mount c11 87
Be'ér Menuḥa d6 139
Beerse c3 159
Beersheba Springs g2 259
Be'ér Sheva' c5 139
Beerwah e5 85
Beeskow k3 173
Beeston e4 162
Beetaloo a4 80
Beethoven Peninsula jj2 298
Beetzendorf g3 173
Beetzsee h3 173
Beeville a5 258
Befale d3 224
Befandriana Avaratra Ab2 233
Befori d3 224
Befotaka, Fianarantsoa, Madag. Ab3 233
Befotaka, Mahajanga, Madag. Ab1 233
Bega, Aust. j14 81
Bega, Ger. d3 172
Begamganj m8 125
Bégard b4 182
Bègles b4 186
Beg-Meil b5 182
Begna d2 156
Begoro d4 222
Begun g8 129
Begur h3 192
Begusarai k7 125
Béhague, Pointe g3 285
Behbehān n6 137
Behshahr p3 137
Behsūd c3 128
Bei'an p1 113
Beidianzi g1 111
Beigi f2 225
Beihai g8 104
Bei Hulsan Hu q1 125
Bei Jiang j7 105
Beijing, Beijing, China j6 113
Beijing, Peking, China j5 113
Beikan g3 111
Beilen e2 159
Beili j6 102
Beilngries f3 175
Beinamar c2 224
Beine-Nauroy k3 183
Beinn an Oir b4 164
Beinn an Tuirc c4 164
Beinn Bheigeir b4 164
Beinn Bhreac c3 164
Beinn Dearg d2 164
Beinn Mhòr a2 164
Beinn Sgritheall c2 164
Beipan Jiang e6 104
Beipiao l5 113
Beira e2 233
Beirã c5 191
Beira Baixa c4 190
Beira Interior c4 190
Beira Litoral b4 190
Beiru He c2 106
Beirut d3 138
Bei Shan p2 117
Beisi f1 111
Beitai Ding, Shanxi, China g6 112
Beit Aulā d5 139
Beitbridge h1 235
Beit ed Dine d3 138
Beit Ḥanūn c5 139
Beit Ibā d4 139
Beit l'hān d5 139
Beit Jālā d5 139
Beit Lahiya c5 139
Beit Līd d4 139
Beit Meri d3 138
Beit Sāḥūr d5 139
Beit Ummar d5 139
Beitun w4 121
Beitūnīyā d5 139
Beiuş l5 171
Beiwudu c3 106
Beiye c0 106
Beja, Braz. c2 288
Beja, Port b7 191
Beja, Beja, Port c6 191
Béja f1 221
Bejaïa f1 221
Béjar e4 190
Bejestān s4 137
Bejsug f3 148
Bejucos d4 274
Bek d3 224
Beka g4 223
Bekasi d8 98
Bekdash j4 149
Bekecs k3 171
Békés, Hung. j5 171
Békés, Békés, Hung. k5 171
Békéscsaba k5 171
Bekily Ab3 233
Bekitro Ab3 233
Bekodoka Ab2 233
BeK'oji b2 226
Bekok c4 101
Bekoropoka-Antongo Aa3 233
Bekungu c4 224
Bekwai d4 222
Bekyem d4 222
Bela, India g7 124
Bela, Pak. c7 129
Belab d6 129
Bela-Bela, Limpopo, R.S.A. h2 235
Bélabo b3 224
Bélâbre d2 186
Belaga g3 98
Bel'agash t2 121
Bel Air, Fr. c4 182
Bel Air, U.S.A. d5 256
Belaja Berezka d1 148
Belaja Holunica l2 151
Belaja Kalitva f2 148
Bela Krajina g4 177
Belalcázar e6 191
Bělá nad Radbuzou a2 170
Belang n4 99
Bela Palanka f4 201
Bélapátfalva j3 171
Bělá pod Bezdězem c1 170
Bělá pod Pradědem f1 170
Belarus k4 145

BELARUS

THE REPUBLIC OF BELARUS
Area 207,595km² (80,153sq miles)
Capital Minsk
Organizations CIS, EBRD
Population 9,920,000
Pop. growth (%) -0.2
Life expectancy 62 (m); 74 (f)
Languages Belarussian, Russian
Literacy 99.7%
Currency Belarussian rouble (US $1 = 2156.5 Belarussian rouble)
GDP (US million $) 14,200
GDP per head ($US) 1431

Bela Vista, Ang. b5 224
Bela Vista, Amazonas, Braz. d3 284
Bela Vista, Braz. f4 293
Bela Vista, Moz. k3 235
Bela Vista de Goiás d2 290
Belawan d14 103
Belaya b1 226
Belayan h4 99
Belayan, Gunung h4 99
Belbédji f3 223
Belbo c5 196
Belcaire d6 187
Belcastel e4 187
Bełchatów h4 169
Belchen c5 174
Belcher c3 258
Belcher Islands p4 243
Belchiragh b3 128
Belchite d3 192
Bělčice b2 170
Belcoo d2 165
Belcourt d6 250
Belden b1 264
Belebej h5 147
Bele Berega c5 150
Beled f4 170
Beledweyne d3 226
Belefuanai c4 222
Belek j5 149
Bëlël b2 224
Belel g4 223
Belém c2 288
Belén, Arg. d5 292
Belén, Arg. c1 294
Belén, Para. f4 293
Belen, Tur. f4 209
Belen, U.S.A. b5 261
Beleña, Embalse de a4 192
Belén de Escobar h3 297
Belén del Refugio c3 274
Belene g4 201
Belesar, Embalse de c2 190
Bélesta d6 187
Beles Wenz b1 226
Belev d5 150
Belezna e5 170
Belfast, R.S.A. j2 235
Belfast, England, U.K. b1 165
Belfast, U.K. f2 165
Belfast, Maine, U.S.A. h6 252
Belfast, New York, U.S.A. b2 256
Belfast Lough f2 165
Belfield b7 250
Bélfodiyo d5 218
Belford g4 164
Belfort c3 184
Belgaum d5 126
Belgern j4 173
Belgershain c1 175
Belgioioso d4 196
Belgium e4 144

BELGIUM

THE KINGDOM OF BELGIUM
Area 30,528km² (11,787sq miles)
Capital Brussels
Organizations CE, EBRD, EU, NATO, OECD
Population 10,300,000
Pop. growth (%) 0.1
Life expectancy 74 (m); 81 (f)
Languages Flemish, French, German
Literacy 99%
Currency euro (US $1 = 0.81 euro)
GDP (US million $) 244,400
GDP per head ($US) 23,728

Belgodère A 185
Belgorod e2 148
Belgorodskaja Oblast' e2 148
Belgrade, Srbija, Serbia/Mont. e3 200
Belgrano II (Arg.) a2 298
Běli b3 222
Beli g4 223
Belianes f3 192
Belice b7 199
Beli Lom h4 201
Beli Manastir d3 200
Belimbing, Tanjung e4 98
Belin-Béliet b4 187
Belinchón a4 193
Bélinga b3 224
Belington g6 254
Belinskij g5 151
Belinţ k6 171
Belitung e6 98
Belize, Ang. b4 224
Belize, Belize c2 276
Belize, Belize c2 276
Belize f7 241

BELIZE

BELIZE
Area 22,965km² (8,867sq miles)
Capital Belmopan
Organizations ACS, CARICOM, COMM, IADB, SELA
Population 270,000
Pop. growth (%) 2.6
Life expectancy 72 (m); 75 (f)
Languages English, Spanish, Creole, Garifuna, Maya Ketchi, German dialect
Literacy 94.1%
Currency Belizean dollar (US $1 = 1.97 Belizean dollar)
GDP (US million $) 846
GDP per head ($US) 3133

Belize Barrier Reef d2 276
Bélizon g3 285
Beljajevka k2 149
Beljkofski d5 246
Bell, Aust. f1 83
Bell, Can. q6 251
Bell, U.S.A. k2 247
Bella e4 198
Bella Bella c5 248
Bellac d2 186
Bellaco j2 297
Bella Coola, British Columbia, Can. d5 248
Bella Coola, British Columbia, Can. d5 248
Bellagio d4 196
Bellaire b5 258
Bellamy e3 258
Bellano d3 196
Bellante c2 198
Bellaria g5 197
Bellary e5 126
Bellata j10 81
Bella Unión e2 294
Bella Vista, Corrientes, Arg. e1 294
Bella Vista, Arg. b6 295
Bella Vista, Bol. e3 293
Bella Vista, Para. f4 293
Bellavista b4 284
Bellbrook l11 81
Bellclaire d'Urgell e3 192
Belle-Anse h5 271
Belledonne c5 185
Belleek c2 165
Bellefontaine e5 254
Bellefonte c4 256
Belle Fourche, South Dakota, U.S.A. c2 260
Belle Fourche, South Dakota, U.S.A. c2 260
Bellegarde h5 183
Bellegarde-en-Marche e3 186
Bellegarde-sur-Valserine b4 184
Belle Glade j6 259
Belle-Île b5 182
Belle Isle q3 253
Belle-Isle-en-Terre b4 182
Belle Isle, Strait of p3 253
Bellême f4 183
Bellenaves f2 186
Bellencombre g3 183
Belle Ombre A 226
Belleplaine H 271
Belle Plaine a1 258
Belleville, Can. h3 255
Belleville, Fr. a4 184
Belleville, Illinois, U.S.A. b6 254
Belleville, Kansas, U.S.A. d4 260
Belleville-sur-Meuse b1 184
Belleville-sur-Vie d6 182
Bellevue, Iowa, U.S.A. a4 254
Bellevue, Ohio, U.S.A. e5 254
Bellevue, Washington, U.S.A. b2 262
Belley b5 185
Bellheim g3 174
Bellicourt b5 159
Bellinge d3 158
Bellingham, U.K. d1 162
Bellingham, U.S.A. f7 248
Bellingshausen Basin r10 301
Bellingshausen (Rus. Fed.) u1 298
Bellingshausen Sea hh2 298
Bellinzago Novarese c4 196
Bellinzona d3 196
Bell Island q3 253
Bell-Lloc d'Urgell e3 192
Bellmead a4 258
Bello, Col. b2 284
Bello, Spain c4 192
Bellows Falls k5 255
Bellpat d6 129
Bellport h4 257
Bellpuig f3 192
Bells e2 258
Bellshill d4 164
Belluno, Italy g3 196
Belluno, Veneto, Italy g3 196
Bell Ville f2 297
Bellville, R.S.A. c6 234
Bellville, U.S.A. a5 258
Bellwood b4 256
Belly l7 249
Belm d3 172
Bélmez e6 191
Bélmez de la Moraleda g7 191
Belmont, Fr. c5 187
Belmont, R.S.A. f4 234
Belmont, California, U.S.A. a4 264
Belmont, New York, U.S.A. b2 256
Belmont, Wisconsin, U.S.A. a4 254
Belmonte, Braz. j1 291
Belmonte, Port c4 190
Belmonte, Asturias, Spain d1 190
Belmonte, Castilla-La Mancha, Spain b5 193
Belmont-sur-Rance e5 187
Belmopan c2 276
Belmore, Mount e6 85
Belmullet b2 165
Belo Aa3 233
Beloe More d2 146
Beloe, Ozero d1 150
Belogorsk h2 94
Beloha Ab4 233
Belo Horizonte, Amazonas, Braz. d4 284
Belo Horizonte, Minas Gerais, Braz. g3 291
Beloit, Kansas, U.S.A. d4 260
Beloit, Wisconsin, U.S.A. b4 254
Belojarskij l3 147
Belokuriha v2 121
Belo Monte b2 288
Belomorsk q4 155
Belonga c4 224
Belonia m8 125
Belo Oriente g3 291
Belopa l6 99
Belorado a2 192
Belorečensk e3 148
Beloreck j5 147
Belören, Adıyaman, Tur. f4 209
Belören, Konya, Tur. d4 208
Bělotín f2 171
Belot, Lac d2 242
Belo Tsiribihina Aa2 233
Belousovka u2 121
Belo Vale f4 291
Belovo, Bul. g4 201
Belovo, Russ. Fed. j4 118
Belozersk d1 150
Belpasso d7 199
Belpech d5 187
Belper e3 162
Belpre f6 254
Belsk Duży j4 169
Belt h2 262
Beltana d11 81
Belt Bay c10 81
Belterra g4 285
Belton, U.K. h4 163
Belton, South Carolina, U.S.A. h2 259
Belton, Texas, U.S.A. a4 258
Beluga Lake g3 247
Beluran a8 100
Beluša g2 171
Beluš'e f2 147
Belvédère-Campomoro A 185
Belvedere Marittimo e5 198
Belvès d4 186
Belvidere, Illinois, U.S.A. b4 254
Belvidere, New Jersey, U.S.A. e4 256
Belvís de la Jara f5 191
Belyando b3 84
Belyj b4 150
Belyj Jar j4 118
Belyj Ključ j4 151
Belyj, Ostrov g2 118
Belz, Fr. b5 182
Belz, Ukr. n5 169
Bełżec m5 169
Belzig h3 173
Belzoni d3 258
Bełżyce l4 169
Bemaraha, Plateau du Ab2 233
Bemarivo Ab1 233
Bemarivo, Réserve de Aa2 233
Bemban c4 101
Bembe b5 224
Bembèrèkè e3 223
Bembézar e6 191
Bembézar, Embalse del e7 191
Bembibre d2 190
Bemetara g9 124
Bemidji f7 250
Bemis e2 258
Bemposta, Bragança, Port d3 190
Bemposta, Santarém, Port b5 191
Béna d3 222
Benabarre e2 192
Bena Dibele d4 224
Benagéber, Embalse de c5 193
Benagin h5 99
Benaguasil d5 193
Benahadux b8 193
Benahmed c2 220
Benalla g14 81
Benalmádena f8 191
Benalúa de Guadix a7 193
Benalúa de las Villas g7 191
Benalup de Sidonia e8 191
Benamargosa f8 191
Benamaurel b7 193
Benamejí f7 191
Benaocaz e8 191
Ben Arous g1 221
Benasal d4 192
Benasque e2 192
Benassay c2 186
Bénat, Cap c7 185
Benátky nad Jizerou c1 170
Bena-Tshadi d4 224
Benavente, Port b6 191
Benavente, Spain e3 190
Benavides d2 292
Benavila c5 191
Benbecula a2 164
Ben Boyd National Park g3 83
Bến Cat h10 103
Bencatel c6 191
Bencha g3 111
Ben Cleuch e3 164
Bencubbin c12 87
Bend c3 262
Bendearg g5 235
Bendela c4 224
Bendeleben, Mount c2 246
Bendemeer k11 81
Bender-Bayla e2 226
Bendieuta d11 81
Bendigo g14 81
Bendoc j14 81
Bendorf d3 174
Bene k4 157
Bene e2 233
Bene Beraq c4 139
Benedict, Mount n1 253
Benediktenwand g5 175
Benedita b5 191
Beneditinos d3 288
Benedito Leite d3 288
Benejama d6 193
Bénéna d3 222
Benešov c2 170
Benešov nad Ploučnicí c1 170
Bénestroff c2 184
Benet b2 186
Benetutti Ab2 198
Bénévent-l'Abbaye d2 186
Benevento, Italy d3 198
Benevento, Campania, Italy d3 198
Benezette b3 256
Benfeld d2 184
Benfica do Ribatejo b5 191
Bengamisa e3 225
Bengbis b3 224
Bengbu e3 111
Beng He f2 111
Bengkalis, Riau, Indon. b5 98
Bengkalis, Riau, Indon. c5 101
Bengkayang e4 98
Bengkulu, Indon. a6 98
Bengkulu, Bengkulu, Indon. b6 98
Bengo b5 224
Bengoi j6 97
Bengtsfors e3 156
Benguela, Ang. a1 232
Benguela, Benguela, Ang. a1 232
Ben Guerdane g2 221
Benguerir c2 220
Benguérua, Ilha f3 233
Benha c6 136
Ben Hope d1 164
Beni, Bol. d2 292
Beni, Bol. d3 292
Beni, D.R.C. e3 225
Beni-Abbès d2 220
Benia de Onís f1 190
Benicarló e4 192
Benicasim e4 193
Benicia a3 264
Benicito d2 292
Benidorm d6 193
Benifaió d5 193
Benigánim d6 193
Beniguet, Île de a4 182
Beni Guil d2 220
Beni Mazâr c7 136
Beni Mellal c2 220

Beni Mûsa c7 136
Benin c3 217

BENIN

THE REPUBLIC OF BENIN
Area 112,622km² (43,484sq miles)
Capital Porto-Novo
Organizations ECOWAS, FZ, OIC
Population 6,560,000
Pop. growth (%) 2.5
Life expectancy 51 (m); 55 (f)
Languages French, Bariba, Fulani, Fon and Yoruba
Literacy 40.9%
Currency CFA franc (US $1 = 534.95 CFA franc)
GDP (US million $) 2869
GDP per head ($US) 437

BHUTAN

THE KINGDOM OF BHUTAN
Area 46,500km² (17,954sq miles)
Capital Thimphu
Organizations SAARC
Population 699,000
Pop. growth (%) 2.2
Life expectancy 59 (m); 62 (f)
Languages Dzongkha
Literacy 42.2%
Currency ngultrum (US $1 = 45.52 ngultrum)
GDP (US million $) 527
GDP per head ($US) 753

316 Bolu → Breda

Bolu, Bolu, Tur. c2 208
Bolungarvík A 152
Boluntay n1 125
Bolvadin c3 208
Bolventor b6 163
Bolyarovo h4 201
Bolzano, Italy f3 196
Bolzano, Trentino - Alto Adige, Italy f3 196
Boma b5 224
Boma National Park f2 225
Bomassa c3 224
Bombala j14 81
Bombarral a5 191
Bombay, Maharashtra, India c3 126
Bomberai, Semenanjung j6 97
Bombo c4 224
Bomboma c3 224
Bom Comércio d1 292
Bom Despacho f3 291
Bomdila n6 125
Bomi p5 125
Bomili e3 225
Bom Jardim, Amazonas, Braz. d1 292
Bom Jardim, Pernambuco, Braz. e3 288
Bom Jardim de Goiás b2 290
Bom Jardim de Minas f4 291
Bom Jesus, Piauí, Braz. d3 288
Bom Jesus, Rio Grande do Sul, Braz. b7 289
Bom Jesus da Gurgueia, Serra do d3 288
Bom Jesus da Lapa d4 288
Bom Jesus de Goiás d3 290
Bom Jesus do Itabapoana h4 291
Bømlo a3 156
Bomokandi e3 225
Bomongo c3 224
Bompas e6 187
Bomputu d4 224
Bom Retiro c7 289
Bom Sucesso, Minas Gerais, Braz. f4 291
Bom Sucesso, Paraná, Braz. c5 290
Bonāb l3 137
Bonaire d1 284
Bona, Mount j3 247
Bonampak n9 273
Bonandolok d15 103
Bonanza, Nic. e4 276
Bonanza, Spain d8 191
Bonanza Peak c1 262
Bonaparte Archipelago g4 87
Bonaparte Lake g6 248
Boñar e2 190
Bonar Bridge d2 164
Bonarcado Aa2 198
Bonares d7 191
Bonasse E 271
Bonassola d5 197
Bonaventure k4 253
Bonavista r4 253
Bonavista Bay r4 253
Bonboillon b3 184
Bon Bon b11 81
Bon, Cap g1 221
Boncourt b2 196
Bond e4 258
Bondari g5 151
Bondeno f5 196
Bondjug h3 147
Bondo, Équateur, D.R.C. d4 224
Bondo, Orientale, D.R.C. d3 224
Bondoc Peninsula d4 100
Bondokodi k9 99
Bondoukou d4 222
Bondowoso g8 98
Bonds Cay l7 259
Bonduel b3 254
Bone m7 99
Bonelipu m7 99
Bönen c4 172
Bonerate, Indon. l8 99
Bonerate, Sulawesi Selatan, Indon. l8 99
Bonerate, Kepulauan l8 99
Bo'ness e3 164
Bonete c6 193
Bonete, Cerro, Arg. c1 294
Bonete, Cerro, Bol. d4 292
Bone, Teluk l7 99
Bonfim f4 291
Bonfinópolis de Minas f2 291
Bonga b2 226
Bongabong c4 100
Bongaigaon m6 125
Bongandanga d3 224
Bongao b8 100
Bong Co m4 125
Bongo, D.R.C. d3 224
Bongo, Phil. d7 100
Bongolava Ab2 233
Bongo, Massif des d2 224
Bongor c1 224
Bongo, Serra do c6 224
Bongouanou d4 222
Bongoville b4 224
Bonham a3 258
Bönhamn g5 154
Boniches c5 193
Bonifacio A 185
Bonifacio, Strait of A 185
Bonifay g4 259
Boni National Reserve c4 226
Bonita Springs j6 259
Bonito, Mato Grosso do Sul, Braz. f4 293
Bonito, Minas Gerais, Braz. f1 291
Bonito, Pico c3 276
Bonn f4 159
Bonnat d2 186
Bonndorf f4 174
Bonne b6 185
Bonners Ferry e1 262
Bønnerup Strand d2 158
Bonnétable f4 183
Bonne Terre d1 258
Bonnet, Lac du f5 250
Bonnet Plume l2 247
Bonneval g4 183
Bonneval-sur-Arc d5 185
Bonneville c4 184
Bonney, Lake b3 82
Bonnie Rock d12 87
Bonnieux b7 185
Bonny f5 223
Bonnyrigg e4 164
Bonny-sur-Loire h5 183
Bono Ab2 198
Bonoi k6 97
Bonom Mhai h10 103
Bonorva Aa2 198
Bonoua d4 222
Bons-en-Chablais c4 184
Bonshaw k10 81
Bonteberg d6 234
Bonthe b4 222
Bontioli, Réserve Totale de d3 222
Bontoc c2 100
Bontomatane l8 99
Bontosunggu k7 99
Bonwapitse g1 235
Bon Wier c4 258
Bonyhád g5 171
Bonython Range j8 87
Bookabie l12 87
Bookaloo c11 81
Booke d4 224
Boola c4 222
Boolaboolka Lake c1 82
Boolba c6 85
Booleroo Centre d12 81
Booley Hills d4 164
Booligal g12 81
Boologooro b9 87
Boom f3 277
Boomi c6 85
Boone, Iowa, U.S.A. e3 260
Boone, North Carolina, U.S.A. j1 259
Boones Mill g7 254
Booneville e2 258
Boon Point D 271
Boonsboro c5 256
Boonville e4 260
Boopi d3 292
Boorabin National Park e12 87
Boorama c2 226
Boorindal h11 81
Booroorban g13 81
Boos g3 183
Boosaaso d1 226
Boostedt d4 158
Booth f3 258
Boothbay Harbor h7 252
Boothia, Gulf of l1 243
Boothia Peninsula l1 243
Boothville e5 258
Bootle d3 162
Booué b4 224
Bopfingen d5 174
Boping e1 106
Bopolu b4 222
Boppard f4 174
Boqê k4 135
Boqueirão, Serra do d4 288
Boquerón e4 293
Boquerones, Cerro a3 276
Boquilla, Presa de la g4 272
Boquillas del Carmen h3 273
Boquillas del Refugio h5 273
Bor, Czech Rep. a2 170
Bor, Russ. Fed. h3 151
Bor, Serbia/Mont. f3 201
Bor, Sudan f2 225
Bor, Tur. e4 208
Bora-Bora K 75
Boraha, Nosy Ac2 233
Borah Peak g3 262
Borakalalo Nature Reserve g2 235
Bora, Réserve de Ab1 233
Borås e4 156
Borāzjān n7 137
Borba, Braz. f4 285
Borba, Port c6 191
Borbera c5 196
Borbollón, Embalse del d4 190
Borborema d4 290
Borborema, Planalto da e3 288
Borchen d4 172
Borçka h2 209
Borda, Cape c13 81
Borda da Mata e5 291
Bor Dağı b4 208
Bordalba b3 192
Bordalsvatnet b3 156
Bordeaux b4 186
Bordein d5 218
Bordeira b7 191
Borden Island g1 242
Borden Peninsula m1 243
Bordentown f4 256
Bordères-Louron c6 187
Border Ranges National Park e6 85
Bordertown e14 81
Bordesholm d4 158
Borðeyri A 152
Bordighera b6 197
Bordils g2 192
Bordj Bou Arréridj e1 221
Bordj Flye Ste-Marie d3 220
Bordj Messaouda f2 221
Bordj Mokhtar e4 221
Bordj Omer Driss f3 221
Bordón d4 192
Borðoy B 152
Bordu q6 121
Boré d2 222
Boreas Nunatak e2 298
Boreda b2 226
Borehamwood f5 163
Borek Wielkopolski f4 168
Borensberg f3 156
Borgan-Frelsøy c4 154
Borgarnes A 152
Børgefjell Nasjonalpark d4 154
Borgentreich e4 172
Börger f2 159
Borger, Neth. e2 159
Borger, U.S.A. c5 261
Borges f5 193
Borghetto d'Arroscia b5 197
Borgholm g4 156
Borgia f6 199
Borgie d1 164
Borgloon d4 159
Borgne, Lake e4 258
Borgo A 185
Borgo a Mozzano e6 197
Borgomanero c4 196
Borgonovo Val Tidone d4 196
Borgo Pace g6 197
Borgo San Dalmazzo b5 197
Borgo San Lorenzo f6 197
Borgosesia c4 196
Borgo Val di Taro d5 197
Borgo Valsugana f3 196
Borgvattnet e5 154
Bori g9 129
Borikhan f6 102
Borilovo c5 150
Borisoglebsk f2 149
Boriziny Ab2 233
Borja, Peru b4 284
Borja, Spain c3 192
Borjomis Nakrdzali f4 149
Borkavichy n5 157
Borkeh d2 128
Borken e3 159
Borken (Hessen) g1 174
Borkenes f2 154
Borki l4 169
Børkop c3 158
Borkou-Ennedi-Tibesti b4 218
Borkum, Ger. b2 172
Borkum, Niedersachsen, Ger. e1 159
Borlänge f2 156
Borlu b3 208
Bormes-les-Mimosas c7 185
Bormida c5 196
Bormio e3 196
Borna h1 175
Born am Darß f4 158
Borndiep d1 159
Borne, Fr. c4 185
Borne, Neth. e2 159
Borneo g5 98
Bornes, Fr. c5 185
Bornes, Port d3 190
Bornes, Serra de d3 190
Borne Sulinowo e2 168
Bornheim e4 159
Bornholm, Den. A 158
Bornholm, Bornholm, Den. f5 156
Bornholmsgattet f5 156
Bornhöved d4 158
Borno g3 223
Bornos, Embalse de e8 191
Bornova b3 192
Boro, Bots. c2 232
Boro, Sudan e2 225
Borodino j2 201
Borodinskoe n2 157
Borodyanka c2 148
Borogoncy p3 119
Borohoro Shan u6 121
Borok, Jaroslavskaja Oblast', Russ. Fed. e2 150
Borok, Kostromskaja Oblast', Russ. Fed. f2 150
Boroko m4 99
Boromata d1 224
Boromo d3 222
Boron, Mali c3 222
Boron, U.S.A. f7 265
Borongan e5 100
Bororen d4 84
Borotou c4 222
Boroughbridge e2 162
Borovan f4 201
Borovany f1 177
Borove p4 169
Boroviči b2 150
Borovik k4 177
Borovoj l2 151
Borovoye n1 121
Borovskoy l5 147
Borrazópolis c5 290
Borrby f5 156
Borre f4 158
Borrentin h2 173
Borris e4 165
Borrisokane c3 165
Borroloola c4 80
Borrowdale c2 162
Borş k4 171
Børsa c5 154
Borşa g2 201
Borša k3 171
Borsæ b3 156
Borščovočnyj Hrebet f1 112
Borsec g2 201
Børselv k1 155
Borshchiv h1 201
Borskoe l5 151
Borsod-Abaúj-Zemplén j3 171
Borsodbóta j3 171
Borsodnádasd j3 171
Börßum f3 173
Bortala He t5 121
Borth b4 163
Bortigiadas Ab2 198
Bort-les-Orgues e3 186
Borūjen n6 137
Borūjerd m5 137
Borun s4 137
Borup e3 158
Borutta Aa2 198
Borve b2 164
Borynya l6 169
Boryslav m6 169
Boryspil' c2 148
Borzja j1 113
Borzna d2 148
Borzonasca d5 197
Bosa Aa2 198
Bošáca f3 171
Bosaga p4 121
Bosanci h2 201
Bosanska Dubica h4 177
Bosanska Gradiška j4 177
Bosanska Kostajnica h4 177
Bosanska Krupa h5 177
Bosanski Brod k4 177
Bosanski Novi h4 177
Bosanski Petrovac c3 200
Bosanski Šamac d3 200
Bosansko Grahovo c3 200
Bősárkány f4 170
Bosberget f2 156
Boscastle b6 163
Bosch h4 297
Bosco Chiesanuova f4 196
Bosco della Partecipiano e Lucedio, Parco Naturale c4 196
Bosduiflaagte d4 234
Bose f7 104
Bösel c2 172
Bosencheve, Parque Nacional d4 274
Bosenge d3 224
Boshan e1 111
Boshof f4 235
Boshruyeh r5 137
Bosilegrad f4 201
Boskol' k5 147
Boskoop c2 159
Boskop Dam g3 235
Boskovice e2 170
Boslanti f3 285
Bosna d3 200
Bosnia-Herzegovina h6 144

BOSNIA & HERZEGOVINA

THE REPUBLIC OF BOSNIA AND HERZEGOVINA
Area 51,129km^2 (19,741sq miles)
Capital Sarajevo
Organizations EBRD, OIC
Population 4,130,000
Pop. growth (%) -2.3
Life expectancy 70 (m); 75 (f)
Languages Serbo-Croat (Muslims and Croats use Roman script, Serbs use Cyrillic)
Literacy 93%
Currency marka (US $1 = 1.6 marka)
GDP (US million $) 4889
GDP per head ($US) 1183

Bosnik k6 97
Boso d3 224
Bosobogolo Pan e2 234
Bosobolo c3 224
Bososama d3 224
Bossangoa c2 224
Bossembélé c2 224
Bossentélé c2 224
Bossiekom d4 234
Bossier City c3 258
Bossiesvlei b2 234
Bossolasco c5 196
Bossora d3 222
Bòssost e2 192
Bossut, Cape e6 86
Bostan g1 135
Bostān l6 137
Bosten Hu f1 122
Boston, U.K. f4 162
Boston, Georgia, U.S.A. h4 259
Boston, Massachusetts, U.S.A. j2 257
Boston Corners g2 257
Boston Mountains c2 258
Boston Spa e3 162
Boswachterij Schoorl c2 159
Boswell, Indiana, U.S.A. c5 254
Boswell, Oklahoma, U.S.A. b2 258
Boswell, Pennsylvania, U.S.A. a4 256
Botad e9 129
Botany Bay g2 83
Botão b4 190
Boteå f5 154
Boteni g3 201
Botera b6 224
Botesdale h4 163
Boteti c3 232
Botev g4 201
Botevgrad f4 201
Bothaville g3 235
Bothnia, Gulf of h2 157
Bothwell Ab3 83
Boticas c3 190
Botiz l4 171
Botkins d5 254
Botlih g4 149
Bot Makak g5 223
Botna j2 201
Botnafjellet b2 156
Botngård b5 154
Botolan Point b3 100
Botoşani, Rom. h2 201
Botoşani, Botoşani, Rom. h2 201
Botou e0 111
Bô Trach h7 102
Botricello f6 199
Botro c4 222
Botshabelo g4 235
Botswana e7 217

BOTSWANA

THE REPUBLIC OF BOTSWANA
Area 581,730km^2 (224,607sq miles)
Capital Gaborone
Organizations COMM, SADC
Population 1,770,000
Pop. growth (%) 2.1
Life expectancy 43 (m); 44 (f)
Languages English, Setswana
Literacy 79.8%
Currency pula (US $1 = 4.37 pula)
GDP (US million $) 5962
GDP per head ($US) 3368

Botte Donato, Monte f5 199
Bottenviken h2 157
Bottineau c6 250
Bottisham g4 163
Bottrop e3 159
Botucatu d5 290
Botumirim g2 291
Botun a1 210
Botwood q4 253
Bouaflé c4 222
Bouaké c4 222
Boualem e2 221
Bou Ali d3 220
Bouânane d2 220
Bouandougou c4 222
Bouar c2 224
Bouârfa d2 220
Bou Aroua f2 221
Bouaye d5 182
Bouba Ndjida, Parc National de b22 224
Bouca c2 224
Boucau a5 187
Boucé e4 182
Bouches-du-Rhône b7 185
Bouchoir h3 183
Boucle du Baoulé, Parc National de la c3 222
Bouctouche k5 253
Bouda b4 224
Boudaï e2 138
Boudenib d2 220
Boudoua c3 224
Boudry a3 196
Bouenza, Congo b4 224
Bouenza, Congo b4 224
Boufore c2 224
Bougainville, Cape g3 86
Bougainville Reef h3 80
Bougaroûn, Cap f1 221
Boughessa e5 221
Bouglon c4 187
Bougouni c3 222
Bougtob e2 221
Bouguenais d5 182
Bou-Hedma, Parc National du f2 221
Bouillante C 271
Bouillargues a7 185
Bouilly j4 183
Bouira e1 221
Bou Izakarn c3 220
Boujailles c4 184
Boujdour b3 220
Bouka b3 222
Bou Kornine, Parc National g1 221
Boukra b3 220
Boukta h3 223
Boulay-Moselle c1 184
Boulbon a7 185
Boulder, Aust. e12 87
Boulder, Colorado, U.S.A. b3 260
Boulder, Montana, U.S.A. g2 262
Boulder City f8 263
Boulder Creek a4 264
Boulemane d2 220
Boulevard Atlántico h5 297
Boulia d7 80
Boulogne d6 182
Boulogne-Billancourt h4 183
Boulogne-sur-Gesse c5 187
Boulogne-sur-Mer g2 183
Bouloire f5 183
Boulouba d2 224
Boulsa d3 222
Boumalne Dadès c2 220
Boumba b3 224
Boumbé I c2 224
Boumerdes e1 221
Boumort f2 192
Bouna d4 222
Bou Naceur, Jbel d2 220
Boundary j2 247
Boundiali c4 222
Boundji c4 224
Boungou d2 224
Bouniagues c4 186
Boun Nua e5 102
Bountiful h5 262
Bounty Trough l9 301
Bouquet g2 297
Bourail F 74
Bourbon-Lancy f2 186
Bourbon-l'Archambault f2 186
Bourbonnais e2 186
Bourbonne-les-Bains b3 184
Bourbourg h2 183
Bourbre b5 185
Bourbriac b4 182
Bourdeaux b6 185
Bourg b3 186
Bourg-Achard f3 183
Bourganeuf d3 186
Bourg-Argental a5 185
Bourg-de-Péage b5 185
Bourg-de-Visa c4 187
Bourg-en-Bresse b4 184
Bourges e1 186
Bourget, Lac du b5 185
Bourg-Lastic e3 186
Bourg-lès-Valence a6 185
Bourg-Madame d6 187
Bourgneuf, Baie de c6 182
Bourgneuf-en-Retz d5 182
Bourgogne k5 183
Bourgogne, Canal de k5 183
Bourgoin-Jallieu b5 185
Bourg-St-Andéol a6 185
Bourg-St-Maurice c5 185
Bourgtheroulde-Infreville f3 183
Bourgueil f5 183
Bourke g11 81
Bourmont b2 184
Bourne, Fr. b5 185
Bourne, U.K. f4 162
Bournemouth, England, U.K. h2 162
Bournemouth, England, U.K. e6 163
Bournezeau d6 182
Bou Rouhat, Oued d2 220
Bouroum-Bouroum d3 222
Bourscheid e5 159
Bourtanger Moor c3 172
Bourtoutou b5 218
Bou Saâda e1 221
Bou Salem f1 221
Bouse Wash f9 263
Boussac e2 186
Boussé d3 222
Boussens c5 187
Boussières b3 184
Bousso h3 223
Boussu b4 159
Boutilimit b2 222
Boutonne b3 186
Bouttencourt g3 183
Bouvet Island l15 302
Bouvetøya (Norway) l15 302
Bouvières b6 185
Bouxwiller d2 184
Bou Yala d2 220
Bouza f3 223
Bouzanne g6 183
Bouzonville e5 159
Bova e6 199
Bovalino f6 199
Bova Marina e7 199
Bóveda c2 190
Bovenden e4 172
Boven Kapuas, Pegunungan g4 98
Boves, Fr. h3 183
Boves, Italy b5 197
Bovill e2 262
Bovino e3 198
Bovolone f4 196
Bovril h1 297
Bow, Aust. j5 86
Bow, Can. l6 249
Bowang f4 111
Bowbells b6 250
Bowdon d7 250
Bowen, Arg. d3 296
Bowen, Queensland, Aust. j6 80
Bowen, Queensland, Aust. j6 80
Bowen Downs g7 80
Bowen, Mount f3 83
Bowen Mountains f3 83
Bowenville d5 85
Bowers Mountains w2 298
Bowie, Arizona, U.S.A. j9 263
Bowie, Maryland, U.S.A. d6 256
Bowkan l3 137
Bowling Green, Kentucky, U.S.A. f1 258
Bowling Green, Missouri, U.S.A. f4 260
Bowling Green, Ohio, U.S.A. e5 254
Bowling Green, Virginia, U.S.A. h6 255
Bowling Green Bay b1 84
Bowling Green Bay National Park A 84
Bowling Green, Cape h5 80
Bowman b7 250
Bowman Island r1 298
Bowman, Mount g6 248
Bowman Peninsula mm2 298
Bowmansville d4 256
Bowmont Water f4 164
Bowmore b4 164
Bowral k13 81
Bowron g5 248
Bowron Lake Provincial Park g5 248
Bowser Lake c3 248
Bowsman c4 250
Boxberg, Baden-Württemberg, Ger. c2 174
Boxberg, Sachsen, Ger. k4 173
Boxholm f3 156
Boxing f1 111
Boxmeer d3 159
Boxtel d3 159
Boyabat e2 208
Boyaca c2 284
Boyang l4 105
Boyarka c2 148
Boyce c4 258
Boyd e7 85
Boydton g7 254
Boyellé c3 224
Boyertown e4 256
Boyle c3 165
Boyne, Aust. d4 84
Boyne, Ire. e3 165
Boyne City d3 254
Boyni Qara c2 128
Boynton b2 258
Boynton Beach j6 259
Boyo d2 224
Boysen Reservoir b3 260
Boyuibe e4 293
Böyük Hinaldağ g4 148
Böyük Kirs Dağı g5 148
Boyup Brook c13 87
Bozburun b4 208
Bozburun Yarımadası Ac2 211
Bozcaada, Tur. f3 210
Bozcaada, Çanakkale, Tur. g3 210
Bozdağ a2 208
Boz Dağları a3 208
Bozdoğan b4 208
Bozel c5 185
Bozeman h3 262
Bozhou d3 111
Bozouls e4 187
Bozoum c2 224
Bozova g4 209
Bozovici f3 201
Bozshakol' q2 121
Boztumsyk l3 121
Bozüyük c3 208
Bozzolo e4 196
Bra b5 196
Braan e3 164
Braås f4 156
Brabant Island ll1 298
Brabant Wallon c4 159
Bracciano g7 197
Bracciano, Lago di g7 197
Bracebridge g3 254
Brachet, Lac au h4 252
Bracieux g5 183
Bräcke e5 154
Brackenheim d4 174
Brackley e4 163
Bracknell f5 163
Bracknell Forest h2 162
Brackoe Vodohranilišče, Russ. Fed. l4 119
Braço Menor do Rio Araguaia b4 288
Brad l5 171
Bradano f4 198
Bradenton h6 259
Bradford, Can. g3 254
Bradford, England, U.K. e3 162
Bradford, U.K. e3 162
Bradford, Arkansas, U.S.A. d2 258
Bradford, Pennsylvania, U.S.A. b3 256
Bradford, Vermont, U.S.A. f7 252
Bradley c6 265
Bradley Beach f4 257
Bradninch c6 163
Bradshaw f7 254
Bradshaw, Mount g4 86
Bradwell Waterside g5 163
Brady d6 261
Brædstrup c3 158
Braemar e2 164
Braga, Port b3 190
Braga, Braga, Port b3 190
Bragado g3 297
Bragança, Braz. c2 288
Bragança, Port d3 190
Bragança, Bragança, Port d3 190
Bragança Paulista e5 291
Brahin c2 148
Brahmakund q6 125
Brahmanbaria m8 125
Brahmani j9 125
Brahmapur j3 127
Brahmaputra Ab1 123
Brahmaputra j5 135
Brahmaur c3 130
Braidwood, Aust. f2 83
Braidwood, U.S.A. b5 254
Brăila, Rom. h3 201
Brăila, Brăila, Rom. h3 201
Braine b5 159
Braine-l'Alleud c4 159
Braine-le-Comte c4 159
Brainerd f7 250
Braintree g5 163
Braithwaite Point b1 80
Brak h1 235
Brake (Unterweser) b5 158
Brakel, Bel. b4 159
Brakel, Ger. e4 172
Brâkna b2 222
Brålanda e3 156
Brallo di Pregola d5 196
Bralos c4 210
Braman a1 258
Bramdrupdam c3 158
Bramford h4 163
Bramhapuri f9 124
Bramhope e3 162
Bramming b3 158
Brämön g1 157
Brampton, Can. g4 254
Brampton, England, U.K. h4 163
Brampton, England, U.K. f5 164
Bramsche d3 172
Bramsöfjärden g2 156
Bramstedt b5 158
Bramwell f2 80
Braña Caballo e1 190
Branč g3 171
Brancaleone f7 199
Branch r5 253
Branchville j3 259
Branco, Ang. c1 232
Branco, Braz. e3 285
Branco, Braz. e1 293
Branco, Cape. V. A 222
Brand a2 176
Brandaris d1 284
Brandberg a3 232
Brändbo g1 156
Brandbu d2 156
Brande c3 158
Brandenburg, Ger. j3 173
Brandenburg, Brandenburg, Ger. h3 173
Brand-Erbisdorf j2 175
Branderup c3 158
Brandes c2 186
Brandfort g4 235
Brandis j4 173
Brandkop c5 234
Brando A 185
Brandon, Can. d6 250
Brandon, U.K. g4 163
Brandon, Mississippi, U.S.A. e3 258
Brandon, South Dakota, U.S.A. d3 260
Brandon Bay a4 165
Brandon Head a4 165
Brandon Mountain a1 165
Brandonville d4 256
Brandshagen j1 173
Brandsø c3 158
Brandvlei d5 234
Brandýsek c1 170
Brandýs nad Labem-Stará Boleslav c1 170
Branford h5 259
Branica e4 176
Braniewo h1 169
Branlin j5 183
Branne b4 186
Brannenburg d2 176
Bransfield Strait ll1 298
Brańsk l3 169
Branson c1 258
Brantas g9 98
Brantford f4 254
Brantley f4 258
Brantôme c3 186
Branxholme e14 81
Branxton g1 83
Branzi d3 196
Brás f4 285
Bras d'Or Lake m6 253
Brasil c4 284
Brasilândia, Mato Grosso do Sul, Braz. b4 290
Brasilândia, Minas Gerais, Braz. d1 290
Brasilândia, Minas Gerais, Braz. e2 291
Brasiléia d2 292
Brasília e1 290
Brasília de Minas f2 291
Brasília Legal f4 285
Brasília, Parque Nacional de h3 293
Brasil, Planalto do h2 291
Braslaw m5 157
Braşov, Rom. g3 201
Braşov, Braşov, Rom. g3 201
Brass f5 223
Brassac e5 187
Brasschaat c3 159
Brassey, Banjaran j2 99
Brassey, Mount b7 80
Brassey Range f9 87
Brasstown Bald h2 259
Brastad d3 156
Břasy b2 170
Bratca l5 171
Bratislava f3 170
Bratislavský kraj f3 170
Bratsk c1 94
Bratslav j1 201
Brattefjell c3 156
Brattleboro h2 257
Brattvåg b1 156
Braulio Carrillo, Parque Nacional f5 277
Braúnas g3 291
Braunau am Inn e1 176
Braunfels e3 174
Braunlage f4 173
Braunsbach e3 174
Braunsbedra g1 175
Braunschweig, Ger. f3 173
Braunschweig, Niedersachsen, Ger. f3 173
Braunton b5 163
Brava A 222
Bravatas b7 193
Brave f6 254
Bravicea j2 201
Bravo b5 295
Bravo, Cerro, Bol. e3 293
Bravo, Cerro, Chile d5 292
Bravo del Norte, Río j3 273
Bravura, Barragem da b7 191
Brawley f9 263
Brawley Peaks e3 264
Bray, Ire. e3 165
Bray, R.S.A. e2 234
Braye f5 183
Bray Head a5 165
Bray Island p2 243
Bray, Pays de g3 183
Bray-sur-Seine j4 183
Bray-sur-Somme a5 159
Brazatortas f6 191
Brazeau j5 249
Brazeau, Mount j5 248
Brazey-en-Plaine b3 184
Brazier Point b4 222
Brazil e3 282

BRAZIL

THE FEDERATIVE REPUBLIC OF BRAZIL
Area 8,511,996km^2 (3,286,500sq miles)
Capital Brasília
Organizations IADB, MERCOSUR, SELA, LAIA
Population 174,630,000
Pop. growth (%) 1
Life expectancy 63 (m); 71 (f)
Languages Portuguese
Literacy 88.1%
Currency real, (plural reais) (US $1 = 2.94 reais)
GDP (US million $) 430,600
GDP per head ($US) 2465

Brazil Basin h11 302
Brazo de Loba c2 284
Brazoria b5 258
Brazos a5 258
Brazzaville c4 224
Brčko d3 200
Brda f2 168
Brdy b2 170
Brea c3 192
Breadalbane d7 80
Breaksea Sound a6 77
Breaksea Spit e4 84
Bream d5 163
Bream Bay e1 76
Bream Head e1 76
Breamish d1 162
Breanais a1 164
Breas c5 292
Breaza g3 201
Brebes e8 98
Brécey d4 182
Brêche h3 183
Brechin f3 164
Brecht c3 159
Breckenridge, Michigan, U.S.A. d4 254
Breckenridge, Minnesota, U.S.A. e7 250
Breckenridge, Texas, U.S.A. d5 261
Breckland g4 163
Břeclav h1 177
Brecon c5 163
Brecon Beacons c4 163
Brecon Beacons National Park c5 163
Breda c3 159

Bredaryd → Burgkirchen 317

Bredaryd e4 156
Bredasdorp d7 234
Bredbo f2 83
Breddin h3 173
Brede, Den. b3 158
Brede, U.K. g6 163
Bredebro b3 158
Bredene a3 159
Bredstedt b4 158
Bredsten c3 158
Bredviken e3 154
Bredy h1 120
Bree d3 159
Breeza d7 85
Breezewood b5 256
Bregalnica f5 201
Bregana g4 177
Bregenz a2 176
Bregenzer Wald a2 176
Bregninge d4 158
Bregovo f3 201
Bréhal d4 182
Bréhat, Île de c4 182
Brehna h4 173
Breiðafjörður A 152
Breidenbach d2 174
Breidfonn b3 156
Breil-sur-Roya d7 185
Breimsvatnet a2 156
Breisach d2 174
Breisgau c5 174
Breisundet k1 155
Breitenbach b2 196
Breitenfelde d5 158
Breitengüßbach c2 175
Breiter Luzinsee j2 173
Breitind b1 156
Breitungen e3 174
Breivatnet d5 154
Breivikbotn j1 155
Breiviktinden e3 154
Brejeira, Serra da b7 191
Brejinho de Nazaré c4 288
Brejning c3 158
Brejo, Braz. d3 288
Brejo, Maranhão, Braz. d2 288
Brejo da Porta c3 288
Brekken d1 156
Brekstad b5 154
Brèlès a4 182
Brelingen (Wedemark) e3 172
Brembo d4 196
Bremdal b2 158
Bremen, Ger. d2 172
Bremen, Bremen, Ger. d2 172
Bremerhaven b5 158
Bremerton b2 262
Bremervörde c5 158
Bremnes e2 154
Bremond a4 258
Breña, Embalse de la e7 191
Brenderup c3 158
Brenes e7 191
Brenna d4 154
Brenne, Fr. g6 183
Brenne, Indre-et-Loire, Fr. f5 183
Brenne, Jura, Fr. b4 184
Brenne, Parc Naturel Régional de la d2 186
Brennero f3 196
Brenner Pass c2 176
Brennes h2 154
Brenno c3 196
Breno e4 196
Brénod b4 184
Brent, U.K. h3 162
Brent, U.S.A. f3 258
Brenta f4 196
Brentwood, U.K. g5 163
Brentwood, New York, U.S.A. g4 257
Brentwood, Tennessee, U.S.A. f1 258
Brenzone e4 196
Brescia, Italy e4 196
Brescia, Lombardia, Italy e4 196
Breskens b3 159
Bresle g2 183
Bresles h3 183
Bresnahan, Mount d8 87
Bressanone f3 196
Bressay A 164
Bresse b4 184
Bressuire e6 182
Brest, Bela. m3 169
Brest, Fr. a4 182
Brestanica g4 177
Brestskaya Voblasts' b1 148
Bretagne b4 182
Bretana c5 284
Bretenoux d4 186
Breteuil, Haute-Normandie, Fr. f4 183
Breteuil, Picardie, Fr. h3 183
Brétigny-sur-Orge h4 183
Bretocino e3 190
Breton Sound e5 258
Brettach e3 174
Brett, Cape e1 76
Bretten f4 174
Breu c1 292
Breuchin c3 184
Breueh, Pulau b13 103
Breuilpont g4 183
Brevard h2 259
Breves b2 288
Brevig Mission c2 246
Brevik c3 156
Brevoort Island s3 243
Brevort d2 254
Brewarrina h10 81
Brewster d1 262
Brewster, Lake d1 82
Brewton f4 258
Breyten h3 235
Breza h2 171
Brežice g4 177
Breznica h3 177
Březnice b2 170
Breznik f4 201
Breznitsa f5 201
Brezno h3 171
Brézolles g4 183
Brezová pod Bradlom f3 171
Brezovo Polje j4 177
Bria d2 224
Briance d3 186
Briançon c6 185
Briare h5 183
Briare, Canal de h5 183
Briatexte d5 187
Briatico f6 199
Bribie Island e5 85
Bribrí f6 277
Briceni h1 201
Briceville g1 259
Brickan f2 156
Bricquebec d3 182
Bride, Ire. c4 165
Bride, U.K. b2 162
Brides-les-Bains c5 185
Bridge City c4 258
Bridgend, Scotland, U.K. b4 164
Bridgend, Wales, U.K. c5 163
Bridgend, Wales, U.K. c5 163
Bridge of Allan e3 164
Bridge of Orchy d3 164
Bridge of Walls A 164
Bridgeport, Alabama, U.S.A. g2 259
Bridgeport, California, U.S.A. d3 264
Bridgeport, Connecticut, U.S.A. g3 257
Bridgeport, Michigan, U.S.A. e4 254
Bridgeport, Nebraska, U.S.A. c3 260
Bridgeport, Texas, U.S.A. a3 258
Bridgeport, Washington, U.S.A. d2 262
Bridger j3 262
Bridger Peak b3 260
Bridgeton e5 256
Bridgetown, Aust. c13 87
Bridgetown, Barb. H 271
Bridgetown, Can. k6 253
Bridgeville e6 256
Bridgewater, Aust. Ab3 83
Bridgewater, Can. k6 253
Bridgewater, Maine, U.S.A. j5 253
Bridgewater, Massachusetts, U.S.A. k3 257
Bridgewater, Virginia, U.S.A. b6 256
Bridgewater, Cape b4 82
Bridgnorth d4 163
Bridgwater d5 163
Bridgwater Bay c5 163
Bridlington f2 162
Bridlington Bay f2 162
Bridport, Aust. Ab2 83
Bridport, U.K. d6 163
Brie j4 183
Briec b4 182
Brie-Comte-Robert h4 183
Brienne-le-Château a2 184
Brienza e4 198
Brienzer Rothorn c3 196
Brienzer See b3 196
Brière, Parc Naturel Régional de c5 182
Brierfield d3 162
Briesen k3 173
Brieskow-Finkenheerd k3 173
Briey b1 184
Brig b3 196
Brigantine f5 257
Brigg f3 162
Briggs a4 258
Brigham City g5 262
Brighouse e3 162
Bright h14 81
Brightlingsea h5 163
Brighton, Can. h3 255
Brighton, N.Z. c6 77
Brighton, U.K. f6 163
Brighton, Michigan, U.S.A. e4 254
Brighton, New York, U.S.A. h4 255
Brighton & Hove f6 163
Brighton Downs e7 80
Brigida, Rio da e3 288
Brignogan-Plage a4 182
Brignoles c7 185
Brihuega b4 192
Brijuni e5 176
Brikama a3 222
Brilhante a4 290
Brilon d4 172
Brinches c6 191
Brindisi, Italy g4 198
Brindisi, Puglia, Italy g4 198
Brinkley d2 258
Brinkmann d2 294
Brinkum d2 172
Brinkworth d12 81
Brinon-sur-Beuvron f1 186
Brion a3 184
Brion, Île m5 253
Brionnais a4 184
Brionne f3 183
Brioude f3 186
Brioux-sur-Boutonne b2 186
Briouze e4 182
Brisay g1 252
Brisbane l9 81
Brisbane Ranges National Park d3 82
Brisbane Water National Park g1 83
Brisben e2 256
Briscous a5 187
Brisighella f5 197
Bristol, England, U.K. h2 162
Bristol, U.K. d5 163
Bristol, Connecticut, U.S.A. h3 257
Bristol, Pennsylvania, U.S.A. f4 256
Bristol, Rhode Island, U.S.A. j3 257
Bristol, Tennessee, U.S.A. h1 259
Bristol Bay d4 246
Bristol Channel c5 163
Briston h4 162
Bristow Point C 77
Britel e3 138
Britelo b3 190
British Columbia, Can. e4 248
British Columbia, Can. l2 249
British Indian Ocean Territory (U.K.) e9 92
Brits g2 235
Britstown e5 234
Brittas e3 165
Brive-la-Gaillarde d3 186
Brives-Charensac f3 186
Briviesca a2 192
Brixham c6 163
Brixlegg c2 176
Brixworth f4 163
Brjansk c5 150
Brjanskaja Oblast' b5 150
Brjanskoe g3 149
Brjuhoveckaja e3 148
Brka p6 121
Brněnský kraj e2 170
Brno e2 170
Broad j2 259
Broadalbin f1 257
Broad Arrow e12 87
Broadback q5 251
Broadford, Aust. d3 82
Broadford, U.K. c2 164
Broad Haven b2 165
Broad Law e4 164
Broad Sound c3 84
Broad Sound Channel d3 84
Broadsound Range c3 84
Broads, The h4 162
Broadus b2 260
Broadview b5 250
Broadwater c3 260
Broadway, U.K. e4 163
Broadway, U.S.A. b6 256
Broadwood d1 76
Broager c4 158
Broby f4 156
Brobyværk d3 158
Brocēni k4 157
Brochel b2 164
Brochet c2 250
Brochet, Lac s2 249
Brocken f4 173
Brockenhurst e6 163
Brock Island g1 242
Brockport b3 256
Brockton j2 257
Brockville j3 255
Brockway b3 256
Brockworth d5 163
Broczyno e2 168
Brod, Mac. b1 210
Brod, Mac. b2 210
Brodalen d3 156
Broderstorf f4 158
Brodeur Peninsula m1 243
Brodhead b4 254
Brodick c4 164
Brodnax g7 254
Brodnica h2 169
Brodokalmak k5 147
Brodské f3 170
Brody, Pol. c4 168
Brody, Ukr. p5 169
Broedersput f3 235
Broga b4 101
Broglie f3 183
Brok k3 169
Broken Arrow b1 258
Broken Bay g1 83
Broken Bow, Nebraska, U.S.A. d3 260
Broken Bow, Oklahoma, U.S.A. b2 258
Broken Bow Reservoir b2 258
Brokenburg c6 256
Broken Hill e11 81
Broken Ridge e8 300
Brokopondo, Sur. f3 285
Brokopondo, Brokopondo, Sur. f2 285
Brokstedt c5 158
Brolo d6 199
Brombachsee f3 175
Brome f3 173
Bromfield d4 163
Bromham f4 163
Bromley h3 162
Brommö e3 156
Bromo g8 98
Bromölla f4 156
Brompton on Swale e2 162
Bromsgrove d4 163
Bromyard d4 163
Bron a5 185
Brønderslev c1 158
Broni d4 196
Bronnicy e4 150
Brønnøysund d4 154
Bronson, Florida, U.S.A. h5 259
Bronson, Michigan, U.S.A. d5 254
Bronte d7 199
Bronx k6 257
Bronzani Majdan h5 177
Bronzone, Monte d4 196
Brooke, U.K. h4 163
Brooke, U.S.A. c6 256
Brookeborough d2 165
Brookeland c4 258
Brooke's Point a6 100
Brookfield h2 257
Brookhaven d4 258
Brookings, Oregon, U.S.A. a4 262
Brookings, South Dakota, U.S.A. d2 260
Brooklyn, Can. k6 253
Brooklyn, Connecticut, U.S.A. j3 257
Brooklyn, Mississippi, U.S.A. e4 258
Brooklyn Center e2 260
Brookneal g7 254
Brookport e1 258
Brooks m6 249
Brookshire b5 258
Brooks Range g1 246
Brooksville, Florida, U.S.A. h5 259
Brooksville, Mississippi, U.S.A. e3 258
Brookton c13 87
Brookville, Indiana, U.S.A. d6 254
Brookville, Pennsylvania, U.S.A. a3 256
Brooloo l9 81
Broome f5 86
Broome, Mount g5 86
Broons c4 182
Broquelles, Punta b2 284
Brora, Scotland, U.K. d1 164
Brora, Scotland, U.K. e1 164
Brørup c3 158
Broscăuţi h2 201
Brosna d3 165
Brossac b3 186
Broşteni g2 201
Brotas, Braz. d5 290
Brotas, Port b6 191
Brotas de Macaúbas d4 288
Brotjacklriegel j3 175
Broto d2 192
Brotonne, Parc Naturel Régional de f3 183
Brou g4 183
Brough d2 162
Brough Ness f1 164
Broughshane e2 165
Broughton a1 82
Broughton in Furness c2 162
Broughton Islands e8 85
Broughty Ferry f3 164
Broummana d3 138
Broumov e1 170
Brousseval a2 184
Brouvelieures c2 184
Brouwershaven b3 159
Brovary c2 148
Brovinia d5 85
Brovst c1 158
Brownfield c5 261
Browning g1 262
Brown, Mount c12 81
Brown Mountain f6 265
Brown, Point a12 81
Brownsburg c6 254
Brown's Town B 270
Brownstown c6 254
Brownsville, Louisiana, U.S.A. c3 258
Brownsville, Pennsylvania, U.S.A. g5 254
Brownsville, Texas, U.S.A. a7 258
Brownsweg f2 285
Brownville h6 252
Brownwood d6 261
Browse Island f4 86
Broye a3 196
Brozas d5 191
Brozas, Embalse de d5 191
Bruay-la-Bussière a4 159
Bruce Crossing j7 251
Bruce, Mount c8 87
Bruce Rock d12 87
Bruche d2 184
Bruchhausen-Vilsen e3 172
Bruchsal e4 174
Brück h3 173
Bruck an der Großglocknerstraße d2 176
Bruck an der Leitha h1 177
Bruck an der Mur g2 177
Bruckmühl d3 175
Brucoli e7 199
Brue d5 163
Brugg c2 196
Brugge b3 159
Brüggen e3 159
Brugnera g4 196
Brühl e4 159
Bruin Point h6 262
Brukkaros c2 234
Brûlé, Lac l2 253
Brûlon e5 182
Brumadinho f4 291
Brumado d4 289
Brumath d2 184
Brumov-Bylnice g2 171
Brumunddal d2 156
Bruna e7 197
Brunau g3 173
Brundidge g4 259
Bruneau f4 262
Brunei j8 93

BRUNEI

THE STATE OF BRUNEI DARUSSALAM
Area 5,765km² (2,226sq miles)
Capital Bandar Seri Begawan
Organizations APEC, ASEAN, COMM, IDB, OIC
Population 344,000
Pop. growth (%) 3
Life expectancy 73 (m); 78 (f)
Languages Malay, Chinese, English
Literacy 91.8%
Currency Brunei dollar (US $1 = 1.71 Brunei dollar)
GDP (US million $) 4246
GDP per head ($US) 12,343

Bruny Bay h2 99
Brunette Downs b5 80
Brunette Island p5 253
Brunflo e5 154
Brunico f3 196
Brunkeberg c3 156
Brunn am Gebirge h1 177
Brunnen c2 196
Brunner, Lake c5 77
Bruno a4 250
Brunsbüttel c5 158
Brunson j3 259
Brunssum d4 159
Brunswick, Georgia, U.S.A. j4 259
Brunswick, Maine, U.S.A. h5 253
Brunswick, Maryland, U.S.A. c5 256
Brunswick, Ohio, U.S.A. f5 254
Brunswick Bay g4 86
Brunswick Head e6 85
Brunswick Junction b13 87
Brunswick Lake m6 251
Brunswick, Peninsula de b6 295
Bruntál f2 170
Bruny Island Ab3 83
Bruree c4 165
Brush c3 260
Brus Laguna e3 276
Brusque c7 289
Brussels, Bruxelles, Bel. c4 159
Brusson b4 196
Brüssow k2 173
Brusturi-Drăgănești h2 201
Brusy f2 168
Bruthen h14 81
Bruton d5 163
Bruxelles c4 159
Bruyères c2 184
Bruz d4 182
Bruzual d2 284
Bruzzano, Capo f6 199
Brwinów j3 169
Bryan, Ohio, U.S.A. d5 254
Bryan, Texas, U.S.A. a4 258
Bryan Coast jj2 298
Bryan, Mount a1 82
Bryant c2 258
Bryant Creek c1 258
Bryce Canyon National Park g7 263
Bryher A 163
Brynamman c5 163
Bryne a3 156
Brynmawr c5 163
Bryrup c2 158
Bryson City h2 259
Bryukhovychi m6 169
Brza Palanka f3 201
Brzeg f5 168
Brzeg Dolny e4 168
Brześć Kujawski g3 168
Brzesko j6 169
Brzezie e2 168
Brzeziny, Łódzkie, Pol. h4 169
Brzeziny, Wielkopolskie, Pol. g4 168
Brzeźno d2 168
Brzostek k6 169
Brzóza k4 169
Brzozów l6 169
Brzozów Stary j3 169
Brzyska k6 169
Btourram d2 138
Bua, Mal. a6 231
Bua, Swe. f1 158
Bu'aale c3 226
Buada Lagoon B 74
Buarcos b4 190
Buatan b5 101
Bū Athlah b2 218
Bu'ayrāt al Hasūn h2 221
Buba a3 222
Bubanza e4 225
Bubaque a3 222
Bubi e3 233
Būbiyān Island m7 137
Bubry b5 182
Bubuan, Phil. c7 100
Bubuan, Phil. c8 100
Búč g4 171
Buca E 74
Bucak c4 208
Bucaramanga c2 284
Bucareli e3 275
Bucas Grande f6 100
Buccaneer Archipelago f4 87
Bucchianico d2 198
Buccino e4 198
Bucecea h2 201
Bucelas a6 191
Buces l5 171
Buchach g1 201
Buchanan, Lib. b4 222
Buchanan, U.S.A. g3 259
Buchanan, Lake, Queensland, Aust. a2 84
Buchanan, Lake, Aust. f9 87
Buchanan, Lake, U.S.A. d6 261
Buchans p4 253
Bucharest, București, Rom. h3 201
Buchen g5 174
Büchen d5 158
Buchholz h2 173
Buchloe e3 175
Buchlovice f2 170
Bucholz in der Nordheide c5 158
Buchon, Point c6 265
Buchs d2 196
Buchupureo a4 296
Buchy g3 183
Bucine f6 197
Bucin, Pasul g2 201
Buckambool Mountain a7 85
Buckatunna e4 258
Buckden, England, U.K. d2 162
Buckden, England, U.K. f4 163
Bückeburg e3 172
Buckeye g9 263
Buckhannon, West Virginia, U.S.A. f6 254
Buckhannon, West Virginia, U.S.A. f6 254
Buckhaven e3 164
Buckhorn e2 246
Buckie f2 164
Buckingham, Mex. b3 274
Buckingham, U.K. f4 163
Buckingham Bay c1 80
Buckinghamshire f5 163
Buckland d2 246
Bucklands e4 234
Buckland Tableland c4 85
Buckleboo c12 81
Buckle Island x1 298
Buckley, Aust. d6 80
Buckley, U.K. c3 162
Bucks Mountain b2 264
Bucksport h6 253
Bückwitz h3 173
Bucovăţ j2 201
Bučovice f2 170
Buco-Zau b4 224
Bucquoy a4 159
Bucşani g3 201
Bucureşti h3 201
Bucy-lès-Pierrepont b5 159
Bucyrus e5 254
Bud a5 154
Buda a4 258
Buda, Illa de e4 192
Budakeszi g4 171
Budakovo b1 210
Budalin b4 102
Budaörs g4 171
Budapest, Hung. h4 171
Budapest, Budapest, Hung. h4 171
Búðardalur A 152
Budaun d5 130
Bud Bud d3 226
Budd Coast s1 298
Buddi c2 226
Budd, Mount b11 87
Buddusò Ab2 198
Bude b6 163
Budějovický kraj c2 170
Büdelsdorf c4 158
Budennovsk g3 149
Budennovskaja f3 148
Budeşti h3 201
Budhana c5 130
Budhapur d8 129
Budhlada b5 130
Budi, Lago del a5 296
Budim j4 177
Budimlić Japra h5 177
Büdingen d4 174
Budiyah, Jabal b7 139
Budjala c3 224
Budogošč' b2 150
Budoni Ab2 198
Budrio f5 196
Budū', Sabkhat al g3 219
Budureasa l5 171
Budyně nad Ohří c1 170
Budzyń e3 168
Buea f5 223
Buëch b6 185
Buena f5 256
Buenache de Alarcón b5 193
Buena Esperanza e3 296
Buenaventura, Col. b3 284
Buenaventura, Mex. f3 272
Buena Vista e3 293
Buenavista, Michoacán, Mex. c4 274
Buenavista, Mex. e2 275
Buenavista, Phil. c4 100
Buena Vista, Colorado, U.S.A. b4 260
Buena Vista, Virginia, U.S.A. g7 254
Buenavista de Atascaderos f5 272
Buenavista de Cuéllar e4 275
Buenavista del Norte Ac2 189
Buenavista de Valdavia f2 190
Buendia, Embalse de b4 192
Buenga c5 224
Bueno a6 296
Buenolândia c1 290
Buenópolis f2 291
Buenos Aires, Arg. g4 297
Buenos Aires, Arg. h3 297
Buenos Aires, Braz. c1 292
Buenos Aires, C.R. f6 277
Buenos Aires, Amazonas, Col. c4 284
Buenos Aires, Guaviare, Col. c3 284
Buenos Aires, Lago b5 295
Buen Pasto c5 295
Buen Tiempo, Cabo c6 295
Buerarema e4 289
Buesaco b3 284
Bueu b2 190
Bufareh k6 97
Buffalo, Can. k2 249
Buffalo, Arkansas, U.S.A. c1 258
Buffalo, Kansas, U.S.A. b1 258
Buffalo, Missouri, U.S.A. c1 258
Buffalo, New York, U.S.A. b2 256
Buffalo, Oklahoma, U.S.A. d4 261
Buffalo, South Dakota, U.S.A. c2 260
Buffalo, Tennessee, U.S.A. f2 258
Buffalo, Texas, U.S.A. a4 258
Buffalo, Wyoming, U.S.A. b2 260
Buffalo Head Hills j3 249
Buffalo Lake, Alberta, Can. k1 249
Buffalo Lake, Northwest Territories, Can. l5 249
Buff Bay B 270
Buffels b4 234
Buffelsdrif e6 234
Buftea g3 201
Bug m4 169
Buga, Col. b3 284
Buga, Nig. f4 223
Bugana f4 223
Bugant d1 112
Bugbrooke e4 163
Buğdaylı a2 208
Bugdayli q2 137
Bugeat d3 186
Bugel, Tanjung f8 98
Bugey b5 185
Buggerru Aa3 198
Bugojno c3 200
Bugøynes m2 155
Bugrino g1 147
Bugsuk a6 100
Bugt l1 113
Buguey c1 100
Bugul'ma m4 151
Bugungu Game Reserve f3 225
Buguruslan m5 151
Būhābād q6 137
Buhera e2 233
Buhi d4 100
Bühl e2 174
Bühler e3 174
Bühlertann d4 174
Buhu g5 225
Buhuşi h2 201
Buia h3 196
Buies Creek k2 259
Builth Wells c4 163
Buin b2 296
Bui National Park d4 222
Buin, Piz e3 196
Buinsk k4 151
Bu'in Zahrā n4 137
Buis-les-Baronnies b6 185
Buitepos c1 234
Buitrago del Lozoya g4 190
Būivydžiai p1 169
Buj, Russ. Fed. h4 147
Buj, Kostromskaja Oblast', Russ. Fed. f2 150
Bujalance f7 191
Bujaraloz d3 192
Buje e4 176
Bujnaksk g4 149
Bujumbura e4 225
Buk e3 168
Bukachacha f2 94
Buka Daban m1 125
Bukalo c2 232
Bukama e5 225
Bükand p6 137
Bukanskoe t1 121
Bukantau, Gory j6 120
Bukatatanoa Reefs E 74
Bukavu e4 225
Bukene f4 225
Bukeya e6 225
Bukhara b1 128
Bukharskaya Oblast' j7 120
Bukhtarminskoye Vodokhranilishche v3 121
Bukide e9 100
Bukit Betong b3 101
Bukit Fraser b4 101
Bukit Kepong c4 101
Bukit Merah b3 101
Bukit Mertajam b3 101
Bükki j3 171
Bükkszentkereszt j3 171
Bukoba f4 225
Bukombekombe f4 225
Bukowina f3 168
Bukowina Tatrzańska j6 169
Bukowo, Jezioro e1 168
Bukuru f4 223
Buku, Tanjung c5 98
Buky k1 201
Bula j6 97
Bülach c2 196
Bulacle d2 226
Bulag e1 112
Bulagtay d1 112
Bulan, Indon. c5 101
Bulan, Phil. c7 100
Bulan, Phil. d4 100
Bulanaš k4 147
Bulancak g2 209
Bulandshahr c5 130
Bulanık j3 209
Bulanovo j1 149
Būlāq c9 136
Bulawa, Gunung m4 99
Bulawayo d3 233
Bulayevo m5 147
Bulbul, Wadi b5 218
Buldhana e9 124
Buldibuyo b1 292
Buldir Island Aa1 247
Buldur c4 130
Bulej b3 276
Bulembu j2 235
Bulgan, Mong. b1 112
Bulgan, Ömnögovĭ, Mong. b3 112
Bulgan, Bulgan, Mong. b1 112
Bulgaria j6 145

BULGARIA

THE REPUBLIC OF BULGARIA
Area 110,994km² (42,855sq miles)
Capital Sofia
Organizations BSEC, CE, CEFTA, EBRD
Population 7,970,000
Pop. growth (%) -1.1
Life expectancy 67 (m); 74 (f)
Languages Bulgarian, Turkish
Literacy 98.6%
Currency lev (US $1 = 1.59 lev)
GDP (US million $) 18,822
GDP per head ($US) 2361

Bulghah h9 136
Bulgnéville b2 184
Buli h5 97
Bulilluyan, Cape a6 100
Bullaque f5 191
Bullard b3 258
Bullas c6 193
Bullaxaar c1 226
Bulle b3 196
Buller d4 77
Bulleringa National Park f4 80
Buller, Mount e3 83
Bullerup d3 158
Bullfinch d12 87
Bullhead City f8 263
Büllingen e4 159
Bullones c4 192
Bulloo a4 84
Bulloo Downs f10 81
Bulls e4 76
Bull Shoals Lake c1 258
Bullville f3 257
Bulnes a4 296
Buloke, Lake c3 82
Bultei Ab2 198
Bultfontein g4 235
Buluan e7 100
Bulubulu l7 99
Bulukumba l7 99
Bulukutu d4 224
Bulungu, Bandundu, D.R.C. c4 224
Bulungu, Kasai Occidental, D.R.C. d5 224
Bulungur c1 128
Bulusan e4 100
Bulwer h4 235
Bum g4 223
Bumba, Équateur, D.R.C. d3 224
Bumba, Bandundu, D.R.C. c5 224
Bumbat, China c5 112
Bumbat, Mong. c2 112
Bumbeşti-Jiu f3 201
Bum-Bum k2 99
Buna, D.R.C. c4 224
Buna, Kenya b3 226
Bunazi f4 225
Bunbeg c1 165
Bunbury b13 87
Bunclody e4 165
Buncrana d1 165
Bunda a4 226
Bundaberg l8 81
Bundaleer h10 81
Bundarra k11 81
Bunde f1 159
Bünde d3 172
Bundey b7 80
Bundi g8 129
Bundibugyo f3 225
Bundjalung National Park e6 85
Bundoran c2 165
Bundu j8 125
Bunduqiya f2 225
Bunga, Nig. f3 223
Bunga, Pak. f6 129
Bungay h4 163
Bunge h4 157
Bungendore f2 83
Bunger Hills r1 298
Bungi m7 99
Bungil Creek c5 85
Bunginkela m6 99
Bungo-suidō e5 114
Bunia f3 225
Bunianga d4 224
Bunić g5 177
Buni-Yadi g3 223
Bunker Group e3 84
Bunker Hill, Illinois, U.S.A. b6 254
Bunker Hill, Indiana, U.S.A. c5 254
Bunkie c4 258
Bunkris e2 156
Bunnell j5 259
Buñol d5 193
Bunschoten-Spakenburg d2 159
Bunsuru f3 223
Buntine c11 87
Buntingford f5 163
Buntok h5 99
Buntokecil h5 99
Bununu f4 223
Bunya Mountains National Park d5 85
Bünyan e3 208
Bunyola g5 193
Bunyu j3 99
Bunza e3 223
Buonabitacolo e4 198
Buonconvento f6 197
Buôn Mê Thuôt j9 103
Buorhaja, Mys p2 119
Bupul l7 97
Buq d2 226
Buq'ātā d3 138
Buqay'ā j8 137
Bura b4 226
Buraan d1 226
Burakin c12 87
Buram c5 218
Buran v3 121
Burang e4 130
Buranhaém j2 291
Burano g6 197
Burao d2 226
Burāq e3 138
Burauen e5 100
Burawai a2 130
Buraydah j8 137
Burbach f4 174
Burbage e5 163
Burbáguena c3 192
Burbank, California, U.S.A. e7 265
Burbank, Washington, U.S.A. d2 262
Burcei Ab3 198
Burcher h12 81
Burdalyk b1 128
Burdekin b2 84
Burdekin Falls b2 84
Burden a1 258
Burdur, Tur. c4 208
Burdur, Burdur, Tur. c4 208
Burē, Amhara, Eth. e5 219
Burē, Oromia, Eth. f2 225
Bure h4 162
Bureå h4 154
Bureinskij Hrebet j2 94
Bureja, Russ. Fed. j2 94
Bureja, Amurskaja Oblast', Russ. Fed. q1 113
Burejo f2 190
Burela, Cabo c1 190
Büren d4 172
Bürentsogt f2 112
Bure, Pic de b6 185
Burfjord j2 155
Burford e5 163
Burg k4 173
Burgas, Bul. h4 201
Burgas, Burgas, Bul. h4 201
Burgau, Ger. d2 174
Burgau, Port b7 191
Burg auf Fehmarn e4 158
Burgaw l2 259
Burg bei Magdeburg g3 173
Burgbernheim f4 174
Burgdorf, Niedersachsen, Ger. f3 172
Burgdorf, Ger. f3 172
Burgdorf, Switz. b2 196
Burgebrach f3 175
Burg el 'Arab c1 218
Burgenland h2 177
Burgeo p5 253
Burgersdorp g5 235
Burgersfort j2 235
Burges, Mount e12 87
Burgess h7 255
Burgess Hill f6 163
Burghaun f3 174
Burghausen d1 176
Burghead e2 164
Burgin g1 259
Burgio c7 199
Burgio, Serra di d8 199
Burgkirchen e1 176
Burgkirchen an der Alz d1 176

318 Burgkunstadt → Cambrai

Burgkunstadt e5 175
Burglengenfeld h3 175
Burgos, Italy Ab2 198
Burgos, Mex. k5 273
Burgos, Spain g2 190
Burgos,
Castilla y León, Spain g2 190
Burgsinn c3 174
Burgstädt h2 175
Burg Stargard j2 173
Burgsvik h4 157
Burguillo, Embalse de f4 190
Burhabalanga k9 125
Burhan Budai Shan q2 125
Burhaniye a3 208
Burhanpur e9 124
Burhave (Butjadingen) b5 158
Burhi Gandak j6 125
Buri d5 290
Buria c4 130
Burias d4 100
Burias Passage d4 100
Burica, Punta ► f6 277
Burie b3 186
Burien b2 262
Burigi Game Reserve ☆ f4 225
Burin q5 253
Burin Peninsula ► q5 253
Buriram f8 103
Buritama c4 290
Buriti d2 288
Buriti Alegre d3 290
Buriti Bravo d3 288
Buritirama d4 288
Buritis e1 291
Buritizeiro f2 291
Burj c5 128
Burjassot d5 193
Burjatija, Respublika e1 94
Burjuc l6 171
Burke e6 80
Burke Channel d5 248
Burkes Pass c6 77
Burketown d4 80
Burkina b3 217

BURKINA

THE DEMOCRATIC REPUBLIC OF BURKINA FASO
Area 274,200km² (105,870sq miles)
Capital Ouagadougou
Organizations ECOWAS, FZ, OIC
Population 12,620,000
Pop. growth (%) 2.8
Life expectancy 44 (m); 46 (f)
Languages French, Mossi, many local languages
Literacy 26.6%
Currency CFA franc (US $1 = 534.95 CFA franc)
GDP (US million $) 2667
GDP per head ($US) 211

Burla, Russ. Fed. s1 121
Burla, Altajskij Kraj,
Russ. Fed. s1 121
Burlada c2 192
Burladingen g3 174
Burleson a3 258
Burley g4 262
Burli k5 147
Burlin j2 149
Burlingame a4 264
Burlington, Can. g4 254
Burlington,
Colorado, U.S.A. c4 260
Burlington, Iowa, U.S.A. f3 260
Burlington,
Massachusetts, U.S.A. j2 257
Burlington,
New Jersey, U.S.A. f4 256
Burlington,
North Carolina, U.S.A. g7 254
Burlington, Vermont, U.S.A. k3 255
Burlington,
Washington, U.S.A. b1 262
Burlington,
Wisconsin, U.S.A. b4 254
Burma (see Myanmar) g6 93
Burmakino k2 151
Burmantovo k3 147
Burnaby b1 262
Burnet d6 261
Burnett e4 84
Burnett Heads l8 80
Burney, Monte △ b6 295
Burnham c4 256
Burnham-on-Sea d5 163
Burnie Aa2 83
Burniston f2 162
Burnley d3 162
Burnmouth f4 164
Burns d4 262
Burnside, Can. h2 242
Burnside, U.S.A. g1 259
Burnside, Lake ○ f9 87
Burns Lake e4 248
Burnsville, Alabama, U.S.A. f3 258
Burnsville,
Mississippi, U.S.A. e2 258
Burnsville,
West Virginia, U.S.A. f6 254
Burntwood, Can. d3 250
Burntwood, U.K. e4 162
Burntwood Lake ○ c3 250
Burog Co ○ g2 135
Buronzo c4 196
Burovoy j7 120
Burow j2 173
Burøy g1 154
Burøysund g1 154
Burqā d4 139
Burqin w4 121
Burqu' g5 136
Burra d12 81
Burray f1 164
Burrel e5 200
Burrendong Reservoir c8 85
Burren Junction j11 81
Burrewarra Point ► g2 83
Burriana d5 193
Burrinjuck Reservoir f2 83
Burrowa Pine Mountain
National Park ☆ e3 83
Burrum Heads e4 84
Burrum River
National Park ☆ e4 84
Burruyacú e5 293
Bursa, Tur. b2 208
Bursa, Bursa, Tur. b2 208
Bûr Safâga d8 136
Bûr Sa'îd d6 136
Burscough d3 162
Burshtyn n6 169
Bürstadt e3 174
Bûr Sudan b7 116
Bûr Taufiq a7 139
Burt Lake ○ d3 254
Burtnieku ezers l4 157
Burton, Michigan, U.S.A. e4 254
Burton, Texas, U.S.A. a4 258
Burton, Lac ○ q3 251
Burton Latimer f4 163
Burton upon Stather f3 162
Burton upon Trent e4 162
Burträsk h4 154
Burträsket ○ h4 154
Buru p6 99
Burubaytal p5 121
Burui l6 97
Burundi f5 217

BURUNDI

THE REPUBLIC OF BURUNDI
Area 27,834km² (10,747sq miles)
Capital Bujumbura
Organizations COMESA, CEEAC
Population 6,600,000
Pop. growth (%) 1.7
Life expectancy 39 (m); 41 (f)
Languages French, Kirundi, Swahili
Literacy 51.6%
Currency Burundian franc (US $1 = 1060 Burundian franc)
GDP (US million $) 660
GDP per head ($US) 100

Burunduki k4 151
Bururi e4 225
Burwash Landing k3 247
Burwick B 164
Bury, England, U.K. h1 162
Bury, England, U.K. d3 162
Buryn' d2 148
Bury St Edmunds g4 163
Burzaco h3 297
Burzenin g4 168
Burzet a6 185
Burzil Pass b2 130
Busalla c5 196
Busana e5 197
Busanga d4 224
Busanski Dubočac j4 177
Buşayrā d6 139
Busca b5 196
Buschberg △ h1 177
Busdorf c4 158
Buševec h4 177
Bush e1 165
Busha j1 201
Bushbush c4 226
Būshehr, Iran n7 137
Būshehr, Būshehr, Iran n7 137
Bushēngcaka f3 135
Bushenyi f4 225
Bushnell h5 259
Busigny b4 159
Busilmin l6 97
Bušince h3 171
Businga d3 224
Busira c4 224
Bus'k n6 169
Buskerud c2 156
Busko-Zdrój j5 169
Busobuso h5 97
Busovača c3 200
Buşrá al Ḩarīrī e4 138
Buşrā ash Shām e4 138
Bussang c3 184
Busselton b13 87
Busseri e2 225
Busseto e4 196
Bussière-Badil c3 186
Bussi sul Tirino c2 198
Bussum d2 159
Bustamante,
Nuevo León, Mex. j4 273
Bustamante,
Tamaulipas, Mex. e2 275
Bustamante, Bahía ◄ c5 295
Bustard Head ► d4 85
Buštěhrad c1 170
Bustillos, Lago ○ g2 297
Bustinza g2 297
Busto Arsizio c4 196
Busuanga, Phil. b4 100
Busuanga, Phil. b4 100
Busu-Djanoa d3 224
Bušuiha f2 150
Büsum b4 158
But b3 196
Buta d3 224
Butajira b2 226
Butak a6 129
Butana c5 130
Buta Ranquil c4 296
Butare e4 225
Butaritari H 75
Bute c4 164
Butea h2 201
Bute Giarti b3 226
Bute Inlet ◄ e6 248
Butembo e3 225
Buteni l5 171
Butha-Buthe h4 235
Buthidaung n9 125
Butka k4 147
Butler, Georgia, U.S.A. g3 259
Butler, Indiana, U.S.A. d5 254
Butler, Kentucky, U.S.A. d6 254
Butler,
Pennsylvania, U.S.A. g5 254
Butlers Bridge d2 165
Butner g7 254
Buton m7 99
Butor, Selat m7 99
Bütow f5 158
Butrimonys p1 169
Butryny j2 169
Bütschwil d2 196
Buttahatchee e2 258
Butte g3 262
Butte Creek b2 264
Buttelstedt g1 175
Buttenheim g4 175
Butterwick f2 162
Butterworth, Malay. b3 101
Butterworth, R.S.A. h6 235
Buttes, Sierra △ c2 264
Buttevant c4 165
Butt of Lewis ► b1 164
Buttonwillow d6 265
Buttstädt e1 175
Butty Head ► e13 87
Butuan e6 100
Butuan Bay ◄ e6 100
Buturlino h4 151
Buturlinovka f2 148
Butwal f6 135
Butzbach g3 174
Buuhoodle d2 226
Buulobarde d3 226
Buur Gaabo c4 226
Buurhabaka c3 226
Buvika c5 154
Buxar j7 125
Buxerolles c2 186
Buxtehude c5 158
Buxton, U.K. e3 162
Buxton,
North Carolina, U.S.A. m2 259
Buxton,
North Dakota, U.S.A. e7 250
Buxy a4 184
Buyant f2 112
Buyant-Ovoo d3 112
Buyant-Uhaa f3 112
Buyo c4 222
Buyo, Barrage de c4 222
Buyo, Lac de ○ c4 222
Buyuan Jiang c7 104
Büyükada b2 208
Büyük Ağrı Dağı △ f5 148
Büyükçekmece j5 201
Büyükkarıştıran h5 201
Büyükmenderes b4 208
Buzachi, Poluostrov ► d5 120
Buzançais d2 186
Buzancy c5 159
Buzău, Rom. h3 201
Buzău, Buzău, Rom. h3 201
Buze c1 106
Búzi, Moz. e3 233
Búzi, Sofala, Moz. e2 233
Buziaş e3 200
Buzica k3 171
Bužim h4 177
Buzuluk, Russ. Fed. f2 149
Buzuluk, Orenburgskaja
Oblast', Russ. Fed. j1 149
Buzzards Bay,
Massachusetts, U.S.A. ◄ k3 257
Bwagaoia l1 80
Byahoml' n5 157
Byala, Ruse, Bul. g4 201
Byala, Varna, Bul. h4 201
Byala Reka f1 210
Byala Slatina f4 201
Byal Izvor f1 210
Byalynichy c1 148
Byam Martin Island j1 242
Byarezina, Bela. m5 157
Byaroza n3 169
Byarozawka p2 169
Bychawa l4 169
Byczyna g4 168
Bydalen d5 154
Bydgoszcz g2 168
Byelaazyorsk p3 169
Byelaye, Vozyera ○ n2 169
Byel'ki m5 157
Byerazino, Minskaya
Voblasts', Bela. c1 148
Byerazino, Vitsyebskaya
Voblasts', Bela. n5 157
Byers b4 260
Byershty n2 169
Byeshankovichy c1 148
Byesville f6 254
Byfield, Aust. d3 84
Byfield, U.K. e4 163
Byfield National Park ☆ d3 84
Bygdeå h4 154
Bygdeträsket ○ h4 154
Bygdin c2 156
Bygland b3 156
Byglandsfjorden ○ b3 156
Byhleguhre k4 173
Bykhaw c1 148
Bykle b3 156
Bykleheiane b3 156
Bykovo g2 149
Bylas h9 263
Bylderup-Bov c4 158
Bylot Island p1 243
Byng Inlet f3 254
Bynum g2 262
Byramgore Reef ○ b6 126
Byrkjelo b2 156
Byrknesøy a2 156
Byrock h11 81
Byron,
Georgia, U.S.A. h3 259
Byron, Illinois, U.S.A. b4 254
Byron, Cape ► e6 85
Byron, Isla a5 295
Byrranga, Gory k2 119
Byrum d1 158
Byšice c1 170
Byske h4 154
Byskeälven g4 154
Bystřice, Ostravský kraj,
Czech Rep. g2 171
Bystřice, Středočeský kraj,
Czech Rep. c2 170
Bystřice nad Pernštejnem e2 170
Bystřice pod Hostýnem f2 171
Bystrinskij Golec,
Gora △ e1 112
Bystryj Istok v1 121
Bystrytsya m6 169
Bystrzyca Kłodzka e5 168
Bytča g2 171
Bytnica d3 168
Bytom g5 168
Bytoš' c5 150
Bytów f1 168
Byumba f4 225
Byurgyutli q2 137
Byuzmeyin s2 137
Byxelkrok g4 156
Bzenec j1 177
Bzura h3 169

C

Caacupé f5 293
Čaadajevka h5 151
Caaguazú, Para. f5 293
Caaguazú,
Caaguazú, Para. f5 293
Caaguazú,
Cordillera de f5 293
Caála b1 232
Caapiranga e4 285
Caapucú f5 293
Caarapó a5 290
Caatinga f2 291
Caazapá, Para. f5 293
Caazapá, Caazapá, Para. f5 293
Cabaad, Raas ► d2 226
Cabacera Nueva f5 275
Cabaiguán e3 266
Cabaliana, Lago ○ e4 285
Cabaliros, Pic de △ b6 187
Caballas b2 292
Caballococha c4 284
Caballo Reservoir ○ b5 261
Cabana, Ancash, Peru b1 292
Cabana, Ayacucho, Peru c2 292
Cabanac-et-Villagrains b4 186
Cabanaconde c3 292
Cabañaquinta e1 190
Cabanas c7 191
Cabañas △ b7 193
Cabanatuan c3 100
Cabanes e4 193
Cabang Tiga c3 101
Cabanillas c2 192
Cabano h5 253
Cabaraya, Cerro △ d3 292
Cabdul Qaadir c1 226
Cabe c2 190
Cabeceira Rio Manso a1 290
Cabeceiras e1 291
Cabeceiras de Basto c3 190
Cabeço de Vide c5 191
Cabedelo f3 288
Cabella Ligure d5 196
Cabestrada g5 275
Cabeza del Buey, Arg. c4 295
Cabeza del Buey, Spain e6 191
Cabeza de
Manzaneda △ c2 190
Cabeza de Vaca,
Punta ► c5 292
Cabeza Lagarto,
Punta ► b1 292
Cabezamesada a5 193
Cabezarados f6 191
Cabezarrubias del Puerto f6 191
Cabezas e3 293
Cabezas Rubias c7 191
Cabezo △ d5 193
Cabezo de Morés △ c3 192
Cabezón de la Sal f1 190
Cabezuela del Valle e4 190
Cabildo, Arg. g5 297
Cabildo, Chile b2 296
Cabimas c1 284
Cabinda, Ang. b5 224
Cabinda, Cabinda, Ang. b5 224
Cabinet Mountain
Wilderness ☆ k7 249
Cabingan c8 100
Čabiny k2 171
Cabo Blanco c5 295
Cabo Cruz f5 266
Cabo de Palos d7 193
Cabo de Santo Agostinho f3 288
Cabo Frio g5 291
Cabo Ledo b5 224
Cabollera, Peña △ g3 190
Cabonga, Réservoir q7 251
Cabool c1 258
Caboolture l9 81
Cabo Orange,
Parque Nacional de ☆ g3 285
Cabo Pantoja b4 284
Cabo Raso c4 295
Caborca g10 263
Cabo Rojo A 270
Cabot Strait n5 253
Cabra, Spain f7 191
Cabra,
Andalucía, Spain f7 191
Cabra del Santo Cristo a7 193
Cabral j5 271
Cabral, Serra do f2 291
Cabras, Italy Aa3 198
Cabras, Mex. d3 274
Cabras de Guadalupe d3 274
Cäbrayıl l2 137
Cabred e1 294
Cabrejas, Sierra de b3 192
Cabrela b6 191
Cabrera, Dom. Rep. k5 271
Cabrera, Spain g5 193
Cabrera, Sierra de la d2 190
Cabrero a4 296
Cabriel c5 193
Cabril, Embalse del b5 190
Cabrillas, Spain c4 192
Cabrillas,
Castilla y León, Spain d4 190
Cabrobó e3 288
Cabruta d2 284
Cabugao c2 100
Cabulauan c5 100
Cabullona j10 263
Cabutunan Point ► d1 100
Cacabelos d2 190
Caçador b7 289
Cacahuatepec e5 275
Čačak e4 200
Cacalutla d5 274
Cacao h3 285
Cacao, Isla c4 284
Caçapava f5 291
Caçapava do Sul f2 294
Caçapon b5 256
Caçarelhos d3 190
Cáceres k7 277
Cacbán c4 274
Caccamo c7 199
Caccia, Capo ► Aa2 198
Caccuri f5 199
Cacém a6 191
Cáceres, Braz. f3 293
Cáceres, Spain d5 191
Cáceres,
Extremadura, Spain d5 191
Cáceres, Embalse de ○ d5 191
Cachal d2 292
Cachari h4 297
Cache d2 258
Cache Creek a3 264
Cache Mountain △ h2 247
Cache Peak,
California, U.S.A. △ e6 265
Cache Peak,
Idaho, U.S.A. △ f4 262
Cacheu a3 222
Cacheuta c2 296
Cachi d5 292
Cachimbo b3 288
Cachimbo, Serra do b3 288
Cachimo d4 224
Cachi, Nevados de △ d4 292
Cachingues b1 232
Cáchira c2 284
Cachoeira, Bahia, Braz. e4 288
Cachoeira, Mato Grosso
do Sul, Braz. c3 290
Cachoeira Alta c3 290
Cachoeira de Goiás c2 290
Cachoeira do Arari c2 288
Cachoeira do Sul f2 294
Cachoeiras de Macacu g5 291
Cachoeiro de Itapemirim h4 291
Cachopo c7 191
Cachos, Punta de ► b1 294
Cachuela Esperanza d2 292
Cachuma, Lake ○ d7 265
Cacín, Spain g7 191
Cacín,
Andalucía, Spain g7 191
Čačinci j4 177
Cacine a3 222
Caciporé f3 285
Caciporé, Cabo ► g5 285
Cacolo c6 224
Caconda b1 232
Cacongo b5 224
Cactus Peak △ g4 264
Caçu c3 290
Cacuaco b5 224
Cacuiuvar a2 232
Cacula a1 232
Caculé d4 289
Caçununga b2 290
Cacuso c5 224
Cadale d3 226
Cadalso de los Vidrios f4 190
Cadaval a5 191
Čadca g2 171
Cadcadde, Raas ► d1 226
Caddo a2 258
Caddo Lake ○ c3 258
Cadelbosco di Sopra e5 196
Cadell Creek e7 80
Cadenberge c5 158
Cadenet b7 185
Cadereyta,
Nuevo León, Mex. j5 273
Cadereyta,
Querétaro, Mex. e3 275
Cadibarrawirracanna,
Lake ○ b10 81
Cadig Mountains d4 100
Cadillac, Can. p7 249
Cadillac, Fr. b4 186
Cadillac, U.S.A. d3 254
Cadiz d5 100
Cádiz, Spain e8 191
Cádiz, Andalucía, Spain d8 191
Cadiz, Kentucky, U.S.A. f1 258
Cadiz, Ohio, U.S.A. f5 254
Cádiz, Bahía de ◄ d8 191
Cádiz, Golfo de ◄ d8 191
Cadlao b5 100
Cadore ♦ g3 196
Cadours d5 187
Cadoux c12 87
Cadreita c2 192
Cadwell h3 259
Caen e3 182
Caen, Plaine de e3 182
Caernarfon b3 162
Caernarfon Bay ◄ b3 162
Caerphilly, Wales, U.K. c5 163
Caerphilly, Wales, U.K. c5 163
Caeté g3 291
Caeté, Baía do ◄ c2 288
Caetité d4 288
Cafayate d5 292
Cafelândia d4 290
Cafuini f3 285
Cagayan, Phil. c6 100
Cagayan, Phil. c2 100
Cagayan de Oro e6 100
Cagayan Islands c6 100
Çağış a3 208
Cagli g6 197
Cagliari Ab3 198
Cagnano Varano e3 198
Cagnes-sur-Mer d7 185
Čagoda c2 150
Caguán c3 284
Caguas A 270
Cahaba f3 258
Cahama a2 232
Cahersiveen a5 165
Cahir d4 165
Cahora Bassa,
Barragem de e2 233
Cahora Bassa,
Lago de ○ e2 232
Cahore Point ► e4 165
Cahors d4 187
Cahuapanas b5 284
Cahuinari c4 284
Cahuita, Punta ► f6 277
Cahul j3 201
Caia, Moz. f2 233
Caia, Port c5 191
Caia, Barragem do c5 191
Caiabis, Serra dos f2 293
Caianda d6 224
Caiapó c2 290
Caiapônia c2 290
Caiapó, Serra do c2 290
Caibarién e3 266
Cai Bâu, Đao d1 102
Caiçara d4 284
Caicara, Bolívar, Ven. d2 284
Caicara, Monagas, Ven. e2 285
Caicó e3 288
Caicos Islands j4 271
Caidian d4 106
Caiguna g13 87
Caihua b4 106
Cailloma c3 292
Caimanes b1 296
Caiman Point ► b3 100
Caimbambo a1 232
Caimodorro △ c4 192
Căineni g3 201
Cai Nước g11 103
Caipe d4 292
Caird Coast c2 298
Cairndow d3 164
Cairngorm Mountains e2 164
Cairn Mountain △ f3 246
Cairnryan c5 164
Cairns g4 80
Cairnsmore of
Carsphairn △ d4 164
Cairnsmore of Fleet △ d4 164
Cairo, El Qâhira, Egypt c6 136
Cairo, Monte △ c3 198
Cairo Montenotte c5 197
Caistor f3 162
Caitou a1 232
Caiundo b2 232
Caiwarro a6 85
Caiza d4 292
Caizhai f1 111
Caizi Hu ○ e4 111
Cajabamba b1 292
Cajamarca, Peru b5 284
Cajamarca, Cajamarca,
Peru b1 292
Cajambre, Isla b3 284
Cajapió d2 288
Cajarc d4 187
Cajari c2 288
Cajatambo b2 292
Cajati d6 290
Cajazeiras e3 288
Cajidiocan d4 100
Čajkovskij h4 147
Čajniče d4 200
Cajón a5 296
Cajones, Cayos f2 277
Cajon Pass f7 265
Cajón, Represa el e7 276
Cajuata d3 292
Caju, Ilha do d2 288
Cajuru e4 290
Cajutuba, Ilha c2 288
Čajvana g2 201
Čaka g3 171
Čakajovce g3 171
Čakovec h3 177
Cala, R.S.A. g5 235
Cala, Spain d7 191
Calabar f5 223
Calabozo d2 284
Calabozo,
Ensenada de ◄ c1 284
Calabria f5 199
Calabria, Parco
Nazionale della ☆ f5 199
Calaburra, Punta de ► f8 191
Calaceite e3 192
Calacuccia A 185
Cala d'Oliva Aa1 198
Cala, Embalse de ○ d7 191
Calaf f3 192
Calafat f4 201
Calafate b6 295
Calafell f3 192
Cala Figuera, Cap de ► g5 193
Calafindeşti h2 201
Calagua d4 272
Calagua Islands d3 100
Calahonda g8 191
Calahorra c2 192
Calai b2 232
Calais g2 183
Calakmul ♦ p8 273
Calalaste, Cerro △ d5 292
Calalin Channel D 74
Calalzo di Cadore g3 196
Calama, Braz. e1 293
Calama, Chile d4 292
Calamar, Bolívar, Col. k5 277
Calamar, Guaviare, Col. c3 284
Calamarca d3 292
Calamian Group b5 100
Calamocha c4 192
Calamonte d6 191
Călan f3 201
Calanaque e4 285
Calañas d7 191
Calanda d4 192
Calanda, Embalse de ○ d4 192
Calandagan c5 100
Calandula c5 224
Calang b13 103
Calangianus Ab2 198
Calanscio Sand Sea b2 218
Calapan c4 100
Cala Rajada h5 193
Calar Alta △ b7 193
Călăraşi, Mol. j2 201
Călăraşi, Rom. h3 201
Călăraşi, Călăraşi, Rom. h3 201
Calascibetta d7 199
Calasetta Aa3 198
Calasparra c6 193
Calatafimi b7 199
Calatañazor b3 192
Cala Tarida f6 193
Calatayud c3 192
Calatorao c3 192
Calatrava, Campo de ♦ g6 191
Calau j4 173
Calauag d4 100
Cala Vadella f6 193
Calaveras b3 264
Calavite, Cape ► c4 100
Calavite Passage c4 100
Calawit c4 100
Calayan c1 100
Calbayog e4 100
Calbiga e5 100
Calbuco b4 274
Calca c2 292
Calcanhar, Ponta do ► e3 288
Calcasieu c4 258
Calcasieu Lake ○ c5 258
Calceta a4 284
Calchaqui d1 294
Calçoene g3 285
Calcutta,
West Bengal, India l8 125
Căldăraru g3 201
Caldaro sulla Strada
del Vino f3 196
Caldas b2 284
Caldas da Rainha a5 191
Caldas de Reis b2 190
Caldas de Vizela b3 190
Caldas Novas d2 290
Caldearenas d2 192
Caldeirão e1 293
Caldeirão, Serra de b7 191
Calden e4 172
Caldera c5 292
Calderdale d3 162
Caldereros, Sierra de c4 192
Calderón c2 276
Caldervale h8 81
Caldes de Montbui g3 192
Caldicot d5 163
Çaldıran j3 209
Caldwell, Idaho, U.S.A. e4 262
Caldwell, Ohio, U.S.A. f6 254
Caldwell, Texas, U.S.A. a4 258
Caldwell, Isla A 286
Caledon, Leso. g5 235
Caledon, R.S.A. c7 234
Caledonia c2 256
Calella g3 192
Calen j6 80
Calenzana A 185
Calera f3 258
Calera y Chozas e5 191
Caleruega g3 190
Caleta Blanco
Encalada ◄ c4 292
Caleta Bonifacio ► a5 296
Caleta del Sebo Af1 189
Caleta el Cobre c4 292
Caleta Josefina c6 295
Caleta Lobos c4 292
Caleta Morritos b1 296
Caleta Pabellón de Pica c4 292
Caleta Teniente b1 296
Caletones b3 296
Caleufú, Arg. b3 296
Caleufú, La Pampa, Arg. e3 297
Caleufú, Neuquén, Arg. b6 296
Calexico f9 263
Calf of Man ► b2 162
Calgary k6 249
Calheta B 189
Calhoun, Alabama, U.S.A. f3 258
Calhoun, Georgia, U.S.A. g2 259
Calhoun City e3 258
Calhoun Falls h2 259
Cali b3 284
Calicoan e5 100
Calicut d7 126
Caliente f7 263
Caliente Creek e6 265
California e8 263
California Aqueduct e7 265
California, Golfo de ◄ c6 241
California Hot Springs e6 265
Calihualá e5 275
Călilabad m2 137
Calilegua e4 293
Călimăneşti g3 201
Calingasta c1 296
Calipan f4 275
Calipatria f9 263
Calistoga a3 264
Calitri e4 198
Calitzdorp d6 234
Calizzano c5 197
Callabonna Creek e10 81
Callabonna, Lake ○ d10 81
Callac b4 182
Callaghan, Mount △ g2 264
Callahan j4 259
Callan, Ire. d4 165
Callan, U.K. e2 165
Callander d3 164
Callang c2 100
Callanish b1 164
Callantsoog c2 159
Callao b2 292
Callas c7 185
Calles e2 275
Calling Lake ○ l4 249
Callington b6 163
Calliope k8 80
Callosa d'En Sarrià d6 193
Callosa de Segura d6 193
Čal'mny-Varre r3 155
Calmucó c4 296
Calnali e3 275
Calne d5 163
Calobre g6 277
Calolziocorte d4 196
Calonda d5 224
Calonge h3 192
Caloosahatchee j6 259
Calotmul q7 273
Caloundra l9 81
Calpe e6 193
Calpine c2 264
Calpulalpan e3 275
Calpulálpan e4 275
Calstock b6 163
Caltabellotta c7 199
Caltagirone d7 199
Caltanissetta,
Sicilia, Italy d7 199
Caltavuturo c7 199
Çaltılıbük b3 208
Caltojar b3 192
Caltra c3 165
Caluanga c5 224
Calucinga c6 224
Caluire-et-Cuire a5 185
Calulo b5 224
Calumbo b5 224
Calumet g7 250
Calumet City c5 254
Calunda d6 224
Calunga b2 232
Caluquembe a1 232
Calusa c6 100
Caluula e1 226
Caluula, Raas ► e1 226
Caluya c5 100
Calvados e3 182
Calvão b4 190
Calvello e4 198
Calver e3 162
Calvert, Aust. c4 80
Calvert, U.S.A. a4 258
Calvert Hills c4 80
Calvert Island c5 248
Calvert Range f9 87
Calvi A 185
Calvià g5 193
Calvillo c3 274
Calvi, Monte △ e6 197
Calvin a2 258
Calvinia c5 234
Calvitero △ e4 190
Calvo, Monte △ e3 198
Calvörde g3 173
Calvos c3 190
Calw d2 174
Calwa d5 264
Calzada de Calatrava g6 191
Calzada de Valdunciel e3 190
Calzadilla d4 190
Cam g4 163
Camabatela c5 224
Camacã j1 291
Camaçari e4 288
Camache Reservoir c3 264
Camacho h5 273
Camacuio a1 232
Camacupa c6 224
Camaguán d2 284
Camagüey f4 266
Camagüey,
Archipiélago de e3 266
Camah, Gunung △ b3 101
Camaiore e6 197
Camaiú f5 285
Camaleão, Ilha c2 288
Camamu e4 288
Camanã c3 292
Camana c3 292
Camananaú e4 285
Camanongue d6 224
Camapuã b3 290
Camaquã f2 294
Camar l4 171
Camará e4 285
Câmara de Lobos B 189
Camaraipi b2 288
Camarão d3 284
Camararé f2 293
Camarat, Cap ► c7 185
Camarena c4 193
Camarès e5 187
Camaret-sur-Mer a4 182
Camargo, Bol. d4 292
Camargo, Mex. k4 273
Camargo,
Parque Natural ☆ k4 273
Camargue ♦ a7 185
Camargue, Parc Naturel
Régional de ☆ a7 185
Camarico b3 296
Camarillas d4 192
Camarillas, Embalse de ○ c6 193
Camariñas a1 190
Camarón g2 274
Camarón, Cabo ► e3 276
Camarones c4 295
Camarones, Bahía ◄ c4 295
Camas d7 191
Camas Creek h3 262
Ca Mau g11 103
Camaxilo c5 224
Cambaceres g3 297
Cambados b2 190
Cambara f3 293
Cambará c5 290
Cambé c5 290
Camberley f5 163
Cambodia h7 93

CAMBODIA

THE KINGDOM OF CAMBODIA
Area 181,035km² (69,898sq miles)
Capital Phnom Penh
Organizations ASEAN
Population 13,810,000
Pop. growth (%) 2.7
Life expectancy 54 (m); 58 (f)
Languages Khmer
Literacy 70.1%
Currency riel (US $1 = 3990 riel)
GDP (US million $) 3410
GDP per head ($US) 246

Cambo-les-Bains a5 187
Cambongo b6 224
Camborne a6 163
Cambre de Baixo b4 190
Cambrai b4 159

Cambre → Carondelet 319

Cambre b1 190
Cambremer f3 183
Cambria b6 265
Cambridge, Can. f4 254
Cambridge, Jam. B 270
Cambridge, N.Z. e2 76
Cambridge, U.K. g4 163
Cambridge, Maryland, U.S.A. d6 256
Cambridge, Massachusetts, U.S.A. j2 257
Cambridge, Minnesota, U.S.A. e2 260
Cambridge, New York, U.S.A. g1 257
Cambridge, Ohio, U.S.A. f5 254
Cambridge Bay h2 242
Cambridge Gulf j4 86
Cambridgeshire g4 163
Cambrils f3 192
Cambuí e5 291
Cambulo d5 224
Cambundi-Catembo c6 224
Cambuquira f4 291
Camburg g1 175
Cambutal, Cerro g7 277
Camden, Aust. g2 83
Camden, U.K. h3 162
Camden, Alabama, U.S.A. f4 258
Camden, Arkansas, U.S.A. c3 258
Camden, Delaware, U.S.A. e5 256
Camden, New Jersey, U.S.A. e5 256
Camden, New York, U.S.A. j4 255
Camden, South Carolina, U.S.A. j2 259
Camden Bay h1 247
Camden, Isla b6 295
Cameia d6 224
Cameia, Parque Nacional da d6 224
Camelford b6 163
Camenca j1 201
Camerino h6 197
Camerles e4 192
Cameron, Louisiana, U.S.A. c5 258
Cameron, Missouri, U.S.A. e4 260
Cameron, South Carolina, U.S.A. j3 259
Cameron, Texas, U.S.A. a4 258
Cameron, West Virginia, U.S.A. f6 254
Cameron Highlands b3 101
Cameron Hills j2 248
Cameron Island j1 242
Cameron Mountains a7 77
Cameron Peak b3 260
Cameroon d4 217

CAMEROON

THE REPUBLIC OF CAMEROON
Area 475,442km² (183,569sq miles)
Capital Yaoundé
Organizations COMM, OIC, CEEAC
Population 15,730,000
Pop. growth (%) 2.4
Life expectancy 49 (m); 50 (f)
Languages English, French, many local languages
Literacy 74.6%
Currency CFA franc (US $1 = 534.95 CFA franc)
GDP (US million $) 9187
GDP per head ($US) 584

Camerota e4 198
Cameroun, Mont a3 224
Camet j4 297
Cametá, Amazonas, Braz. e1 293
Cametá, Pará, Braz. c2 288
Camfield k5 86
Camiguin, Phil. d1 100
Camiguin, Phil. e6 100
Camiling c3 100
Camilla g4 259
Caminha b3 190
Camino c3 264
Caminomorisco d4 190
Caminreal c4 192
Camiranga c2 288
Camiri e4 293
Camisea, Peru c2 292
Camisea, Cusco, Peru c2 292
Camissombo d5 224
Cammarata c7 199
Camocim d2 288
Camogli d5 197
Camooweal d5 80
Camooweal Caves National Park d6 80
Camopi, Braz. g3 285
Camopi, Fr. Gu. f3 285
Camorta a11 127
Camotes Sea e5 100
Camotlán de Miraflores b4 274
Camowen d2 165
Campagna e4 198
Campagnac f4 187
Campagnano di Roma g7 197
Campagne-lès-Hesdin g2 183
Campamento d3 276
Campan c5 187
Campana, Arg. h3 297
Campana, Italy f5 199
Campana, Mex. h4 272
Campana, Ur. j3 297
Campana, Isla a5 295
Campanario b3 296
Campanário, Mato Grosso do Sul, Braz. a5 290
Campanário, Minas Gerais, Braz. h3 291
Campanario e6 191
Campania d3 198
Camparredondo, Embalse de f2 190
Campaspe b2 84
Campaspero f3 190
Campbell, R.S.A. e4 234
Campbell, California, U.S.A. b4 264
Campbell, Missouri, U.S.A. d1 258
Campbell, Cape e4 77
Campbell Island C 77
Campbell, Mount k7 86
Campbell Plateau k9 301
Campbell River e6 248
Campbells Bay h3 255
Campbellsburg d6 254
Campbellton, Can. j5 253
Campbellton, U.S.A. g4 259
Campbelltown k13 81
Campbell Town Ab2 83
Campbeltown c4 164
Campdevànol g2 192
Campeche, Mex. o8 273
Campeche, Campeche, Mex. p8 273
Campeche, Bahía de n8 273
Campello d6 193
Câmpeni f2 201
Camperdown f15 81
Campestre e4 291
Camp Hill d4 256
Câmpia Turzii f2 201
Campi Bisenzio f6 197
Campiglia Marittima e6 197
Campilhas b7 191
Campilhas, Barragem de b7 191
Campillo de Alto Buey c5 193
Campillo de Llerena e6 191
Campillos f7 191
Câmpina g3 201
Campiña e7 191
Campinaçu c4 288
Campina da Lagoa b6 290
Campina Grande e3 288
Campina Grande do Sul d6 290
Campinas e5 290
Campina Verde d3 290
Campi Salentina h4 198
Campitello A 185
Campli c2 198
Camplong m10 99
Campo, Cam. f5 223
Campo, Moz. f2 233
Campo, Spain e2 192
Campoalegre b3 284
Campo Alegre de Lourdes d3 288
Campobasso, Italy d3 198
Campobasso, Molise, Italy d3 198
Campobello di Licata c7 199
Campobello di Mazara b7 199
Campo Belo f4 291
Campo da Feira b1 190
Campodarsego f4 196
Campo de Caso e1 190
Campo de Criptana a5 193
Campo de Diauarum b4 288
Campo del Cielo d1 294
Campo de San Pedro g3 190
Campodolcino d3 196
Campo do Tenente d6 290
Campo Erê b7 289
Campo Esperanza f4 293
Campofelice di Roccella c7 199
Campo Florido d3 290
Campoformido h3 196
Campo Formoso d4 288
Campofrío d7 191
Campo Gallo e5 293
Campo Grande, Amazonas, Braz. f1 293
Campo Grande, Mato Grosso do Sul, Braz. a4 290
Campo Lameiro b2 190
Campolândia c2 290
Campo Largo d6 290
Campo Ligure c5 196
Campo Maior, Braz. d2 288
Campo Maior, Port c5 191
Campomarino, Molise, Italy e3 198
Campomarino, Puglia, Italy g4 198
Campomoro, Punta di A 185
Campo Mourão b6 290
Campo Novo b7 289
Campo Nuevo g5 275
Campora San Giovanni f5 199
Camporeale c7 199
Campo, Réserve de b3 224
Camporrobles c5 193
Campos Altos e3 291
Campos Belos c4 288
Campos, Canal de f2 190
Campos del Puerto h5 193
Campos de Palmas b7 289
Campos do Jordão f5 291
Campos dos Goitacazes h4 291
Campo Serio c4 284
Campos Gerais f4 291
Campos Novos Paulista d5 290
Campos Sales d3 288
Campos, Tierra de f2 190
Campotéjar g7 191
Campotosto, Lago di h7 197
Campo Troco d3 284
Campo Tures f3 196
Camprodon g2 192
Campsie Fells d4 164
Campti c4 258
Campton h1 259
Câmpulung g3 201
Câmpulung Moldovenesc g2 201
Campuya, Peru c4 284
Campuya, Loreto, Peru c4 284
Camp Verde h8 263
Cam Ranh j10 103
Camrose l5 249
Camuñas g5 191
Camzinka, Respublika Mordovija, Russ. Fed. h4 151
Camzinka, Ul'janovskaja Oblast', Russ. Fed. j4 151
Çan a2 208
Caña k3 171
Canaan, Can. k5 253
Canaan, Trin. E 271
Canaan, Connecticut, U.S.A. g2 257
Canabrava f2 291
Canada d2 240

CANADA

CANADA
Area 9,958,319km² (3,844,928sq miles)
Capital Ottawa
Organizations COMM, G8, IADB, NAFTA, NATO, OECD
Population 31,410,000
Pop. growth (%) 0.8
Life expectancy 75 (m); 81 (f)
Languages English, French
Literacy 99%
Currency Canadian dollar (US $1 = 1.31 Canadian dollar)
GDP (US million $) 730,100
GDP per head ($US) 23,244

Canada Basin hh2 299
Cañada de Gómez g2 297
Cañada Honda c1 296
Cañada Nieto h2 297
Cañada Rosquín g2 297
Cañada Seca f3 297
Cañada Vellida d4 192
Canadian, U.S.A. c5 261
Canadian, Oklahoma, U.S.A. a2 258
Cañadón de las Vacas c6 295
Cañadón Grande, Sierra c4 295
Canaima, Parque Nacional e2 285
Canajoharie f2 256
Çanakkale, Tur. a2 208
Çanakkale, Çanakkale, Tur. b4 148
Çanakkale Boğazı a2 208
Canal 11 h4 297
Canal 12 h4 297
Canal 9 h4 297
Canale b5 196
Canalejas d3 296
Canals, Arg. f2 297
Canals, Spain d6 193
Canal Winchester e6 254
Cañamares, Spain b3 192
Cañamares, Spain b6 193
Cañamares, Castilla - La Mancha, Spain b4 192
Canamari d2 292
Cañamero e5 191
Canandaigua c2 256
Canandaigua Lake c2 256
Cananea h10 263
Cananéia e6 290
Canapiare, Cerro d3 284
Canápolis d3 290
Cañar, Ec. b4 284
Cañar, Cañar, Ec. b4 284
Canarana b4 288
Canárias, Ilha das d2 288
Canarias, Islas A 189
Canarreos, Archipiélago de los d3 266
Canary Basin h7 302
Canary Islands (Spain) A 189
Canasayab p8 273
Canaseraga c2 256
Canas, Isla de g7 277
Canastota e1 256
Canastra, Serra da, Braz. d1 290
Canastra, Serra da, Braz. e3 291
Canatlán g5 272
Cañaveral d5 191
Canaveral, Cape j5 259
Canaveral National Seashore j5 259
Cañaveras b4 192
Canavese b4 196
Canavieiras j1 291
Cañazas g6 277
Canazei f3 196
Canbelego h11 81
Canberra j13 81
Canby, California, U.S.A. c5 262
Canby, Minnesota, U.S.A. d2 260
Cancale d4 182
Cancarix c6 193
Cance a5 185
Canchas c5 292
Canche g2 183
Canchyuaya, Cerros de c5 284
Cancias d2 192
Cancon c4 186
Cancún r7 273
Candarave c3 292
Çandarlı a3 208
Çandarlı Körfezi a3 208
Candás e1 190
Candasnos d3 192
Candé d5 182
Candeias, Braz. e1 293
Candeias, Minas Gerais, Braz. f4 291
Candela, Italy e3 198
Candela, Mex. j4 273
Candelaria, Salta, Arg. d5 292
Candelaria, Arg. e2 296
Candelaria, Hond. c3 276
Candelaria, Campeche, Mex. b1 276
Candelaria, Mex. f2 272
Candelaria, Ven. d2 284
Candelaria Loxicha f6 275
Candelaria, Punta b1 190
Candelaro e3 198
Candeleda e4 190
Cândido de Abreu c6 290
Cândido Mendes c2 288
Cândido Sales h1 291
Çandır d2 208
Candle d2 246
Candle Lake q5 249
Candlewood, Lake g3 257
Cando d6 250
Candon c2 100
Candon Point c2 100
Candor, New York, U.S.A. d2 256
Candor, North Carolina, U.S.A. k2 259
Candor, Punta d8 191
Caneima, Isla e2 285
Canela Alta b1 296
Canela Baja b1 296
Canelli c5 196
Canelones, Ur. k3 297
Canelones, Canelones, Ur. j3 297
Canelos b4 284
Canena g6 191
Canet de Mar g3 192
Cañete, Chile a4 296
Cañete, Spain c4 193
Cañete de las Torres f7 191
Canet, Étang de f6 187
Caney, Kansas, U.S.A. a1 258
Caney, Kansas, U.S.A. b1 258
Canfranc-Estación d2 192
Cangalha e2 291
Cangallo, Arg. h4 297
Cangallo, Peru c2 292
Cangamba b1 232
Cangandala c5 224
Cangandala, Parque Nacional de c5 224
Cangas b2 190
Cangas del Narcea d1 190
Cangas de Onís e1 190
Cangombe c1 232
Cangonga c6 224
Cangshan f2 111
Canguaretama e3 288
Canguçu b2 294
Canguenjo, Serra c6 224
Cangumbe c6 224
Cangwu h7 104
Cangzhou j6 113
Canha, Port b6 191
Canha, Setúbal, Port b6 191
Caniapiscau r4 243
Caniapiscau, Lac g1 252
Caniçada, Barragem da b3 190
Canicatti c7 199
Canicattini Bagni e7 199
Canigao Channel e5 100
Canigou, Pic du e6 187
Caniles b7 193
Canillá b3 276
Canillo d6 187
Canim Lake g6 248
Canindé, Braz. d3 288
Canindé, Ceará, Braz. e2 288
Canindé, Pará, Braz. c2 288
Canindeyú f4 293
Canino f7 197
Canisteo, New York, U.S.A. c2 256
Canisteo, New York, U.S.A. c2 256
Canister Falls f2 285
Canisy d3 182
Cañitas de Felipe Pescador c2 274
Cañizal e3 190
Cañizares b4 192
Canjáyar b7 193
Çankırı, Tur. d2 208
Çankırı, Çankırı, Tur. d2 208
Cankuzo f4 225
Canlaon d5 100
Canna, Aust. b11 87
Canna, U.K. b2 164
Cannanore d7 126
Cannanore Islands c7 126
Canne j6 183
Canner c1 184
Cannes d7 185
Canneto e6 197
Cannich d2 164
Canning Hill c11 87
Cannington c5 163
Cannobio c3 196
Cannock d4 162
Cannonball b3 260
Cannon Ball c3 250
Cannonsville Reservoir e2 256
Cannonvale j6 80
Cann River j14 81
Canoa a4 284
Caño Araguao e2 285
Canoas b7 289
Canõas, Rio das b7 289
Caño Cocuinita e2 285
Caño Colorado d3 284
Canoeiros f3 291
Canoe Lake n4 249
Canoinhas b7 289
Canolo f6 199
Caño Macareo e2 285
Caño Manamo e2 285
Caño Mariusa e2 285
Canonbie f4 164
Canon City b4 260
Cañón del Río Blanco, Parque Nacional f4 275
Cañón del Sumidero, Parque Nacional h5 275
Canonniers, Pointe aux C 231
Canoochia j4 259
Canopus e12 81
Canora b5 250
Caño Riecito d2 284
Canosa di Puglia f3 198
Canot, Pointe C 271
Canova Beach j5 259
Canowindra j12 81
Can Picafort h5 193
Canredondo b4 192
Cansado a4 220
Cansahcab q7 273
Canso m6 253
Canso, Cape m6 253
Canta b2 292
Cantabria, Spain a1 192
Cantabria, Spain g1 190
Cantábrica, Cordillera e1 190
Cantagalo f4 285
Cantal e3 186
Cantalapiedra e3 190
Cantalejo g3 190
Cantalpino e3 190
Cantanhede b4 190
Cantantal d2 296
Cantaura e2 285
Canteleu g3 183
Canterbury, Can. j6 253
Canterbury, N.Z. c5 77
Canterbury, U.K. h5 163
Canterbury Bight d6 77
Canterbury Plains c5 77
Canterno, Lago di h8 197
Cân Thơ g10 103
Cantiano g6 197
Cantilan e6 100
Cantillana e7 191
Cantimpalos f3 190
Canto do Buriti d3 288
Canton, Guangdong, China j7 105
Canton, China j7 105
Canton, Georgia, U.S.A. g2 259
Canton, Illinois, U.S.A. a5 254
Canton, Mississippi, U.S.A. d3 258
Canton, New York, U.S.A. j3 255
Canton, North Carolina, U.S.A. h2 259
Canton, Ohio, U.S.A. f5 254
Canton, Pennsylvania, U.S.A. d3 256
Canton, Texas, U.S.A. b3 258
Canton Lake d4 261
Cantonment f4 258
Cantoria b7 193
Cantù d4 196
Cantwell g3 247
Canudos e3 288
Cañuelas h3 297
Canumã, Amazonas, Braz. f4 285
Canumã, Amazonas, Braz. e5 285
Canunda National Park b3 82
Canutama e1 293
Canutillo g4 272
Canvastown d4 77
Canvey Island g5 163
Cany-Barville f3 183
Cânyoles d6 193
Canyon, Can. k3 247
Canyon, U.S.A. c5 261
Canyondam b1 264
Canyon de Chelly National Monument j7 263
Canyon Ferry Lake h2 262
Canyonlands National Park j6 263
Canyonville b4 262
Cany, Ozero r1 121
Canzar d5 224
Cao Bằng f7 104
Cao'e g5 111
Caohekou m5 113
Caojian d3 102
Caombo c5 224
Cao Nguyên Đắc Lắc j9 103
Caorle g4 196
Caoshi n4 113
Caota g5 111
Caoxian d2 106
Cap c8 100
Capaccio e4 198
Capacciotti, Lago di e3 198
Capaci c6 199
Capaia d5 224
Capajevsk k5 151
Capalbio f7 197
Capalulu, Selat n5 99
Capana d4 284
Capanaparo d2 284
Capanema, Pará, Braz. c2 288
Capanema, Paraná, Braz. b6 290
Capanne di Marcarolo, Parco Naturale delle c5 196
Capanne, Monte e7 197
Capão Bonito d6 290
Capão Seco a4 290
Caparaó, Serra do g4 291
Capari b1 210
Caparica a6 191
Caparo c2 284
Caparro, Cerro d3 284
Caparroso c2 192
Capas c3 100
Capatárida c1 284
Cap-aux-Meules m5 253
Capay a3 264
Capbreton a5 187
Cap-Chat j4 253
Cap-de-la-Madeleine f5 252
Capdenac-Gare e4 186
Capdepera h5 193
Cape b2 84
Cape Arid National Park f13 87
Cape Basin l13 302
Cape Breton Island m5 253
Cape Canaveral j5 259
Cape Coast d4 222
Cape Cod Bay k3 257
Cape Cod National Seashore l3 256
Cape Coral j6 259
Cape Cross Seal Nature Reserve a3 232
Cape Dorset p3 243
Cape Elizabeth g7 252
Cape Fear k2 259
Cape Girardeau e1 258
Cape Hatteras National Seashore m2 259
Cape Horn c7 295
Cape Krusenstern National Monument c2 246
Capela b3 290
Capel Curig c3 162
Cape Le Grand National Park f13 87
Capelinha g2 291
Capella j7 80
Cape Lookout National Seashore l2 259
Capel St Mary h4 163
Cape May f6 256
Cape May Court House f5 256
Cape Melville National Park g3 80
Capenda-Camulemba c5 224
Capendu e5 187
Cape of Good Hope Nature Reserve c7 234
Cape Palmerston National Park c2 84
Cape Range National Park a8 87
Cape Romain National Wildlife Refuge k3 259
Capestang f5 187
Capesterre, Guad. C 271
Capestrano c2 198
Cape Tormentine l5 253
Cape Town c6 234
Cape Upstart National Park b1 84
Cape Verde h8 302

CAPE VERDE

THE REPUBLIC OF CAPE VERDE
Area 4033km² (1557sq miles)
Capital Praia
Organizations ECOWAS
Population 450,000
Pop. growth (%) 2.3
Life expectancy 64 (m); 71 (f)
Languages Portuguese, Creole
Literacy 76.5%
Currency Cape Verde escudo (US $1 = 108.95 Cape Verde escudo)
GDP (US million $) 639
GDP per head ($US) 1420

Cape Verde Basin g8 302
Cape Verde Plain h7 302
Cape Vincent h3 255
Cape Yakataga j3 247
Cape York Peninsula f2 80
Cap Ferret a4 186
Cap-Haïtien h5 271
Capibara d3 284
Capilla del Sauce k2 297
Capilla e6 191
Capilla de Guadalupe c3 274
Capilla del Señor h3 297
Capim, Braz. c2 288
Capim, Pará, Braz. c2 288
Capinha c4 190
Capinópolis d3 290
Capinota d3 292
Capistrello h8 197
Capitán Arturo Prat (Chile) ll1 298
Capitán Bermudez g2 297
Capitán Pastene a5 296
Capitán Sarmiento h3 297
Capitão Enéas g2 291
Capitão Leônidas Marques b6 290
Capitari e1 293
Capitola b5 264
Capitol Hill A 74
Capitol Reef National Park h7 263
Capivara, Represa c5 290
Capivari e4 288
Capixaba d4 288
Capizzi d7 199
Čaplje h5 177
Capljina g1 198
Cap Llitzet f2 192
Cap Lopez, Baie du a4 224
Caplygin e5 150
Capoche e1 233
Capodimonte f7 197
Capo di Ponte e3 196
Capo d'Orlando d6 199
Capoeira f5 285
Capolo b6 224
Capoterra Aa3 198
Cappadocia h7 197
Cappahayden r5 253
Cappeln (Oldenburg) d3 172
Cap, Pointe du J 271
Cappoquin d4 165
Capraia Isola d6 197
Capraia, Isola di d6 197
Caprara, Punta Aa1 198
Capri d4 198
Capricorn, Cape d3 84
Capricorn Channel e3 84
Capricorn Group e3 84
Capricorn Range c8 87
Capri, Isola di d4 198
Caprivi c2 232
Caprivi Strip c2 232
Cap Rock Escarpment c5 261
Captain's Flat j13 81
Captieux b4 187
Capua d3 198
Capuava e6 290
Capucapu f4 285
Capu di Senetosa A 185
Capulhuac e4 275
Capulín d3 274
Capuna b2 232
Caputh h3 173
Capvern-les-Bains c5 187
Caqueta c3 284
Caquetá c4 284
Cáqueza c3 284
Carabaña a4 192
Carabao c4 100
Carabelas g3 297
Carabobo d2 284
Caracal g3 201
Caracarai e3 285
Caracas d1 284
Carache, Ilha de a3 222
Caracol, Belize c2 276
Caracol, Mato Grosso do Sul, Braz. f4 293
Caracol, Piauí, Braz. d3 288
Caracol, Rondônia, Braz. e1 293
Caracoles, Punta h7 277
Caracollo d3 292
Caracuaro d4 274
Caracuel de Calatrava f6 191
Caraga f7 100
Caragabal e1 83
Caraguatá e2 294
Caraguatatuba f5 291
Carahue a5 296
Caraí h2 291
Caraiva j2 291
Carajari b3 288
Carajás b3 288
Carajás, Serra dos c3 288
Caramanico Terme d2 198
Caramat k6 251
Caramel b7 193
Caramoan Peninsula d4 100
Carampangue a4 296
Caramulo, Serra do b4 190
Caranavi d3 292
Carancho e4 296
Carandaí g4 291
Carandaiti e4 293
Carandazal f3 293
Caranga d1 190
Carangola g4 291
Caranguejeira b5 191
Caransebeş f3 201
Carantec b4 182
Carapajó c2 288
Cara Paraná c4 284
Carapeguá f5 293
Carapo e2 285
Caraquet k5 253
Caráquez a4 284
Carare c2 284
Caraşova e3 200
Caraş-Severin f3 201
Caratasca f3 277
Caratinga g3 291
Carat, Tanjung c6 98
Carauari d4 284
Caraúbas e3 288
Caravaca de la Cruz c6 193
Caravaggio d4 196
Caravela, Ilha a3 222
Caravelas j2 291
Caraveli c3 292
Caravelle, Presqu'île de la J 271
Carazinho b7 289
Carazo d5 276
Carbajales de Alba e3 190
Carballo b1 190
Carberry d6 250
Carbo h2 297
Carbó h11 263
Carbon-Blanc b4 186
Carbondale e3 256
Carboneras c8 193
Carboneras de Guadazaón c5 193
Carbonero El Mayor f3 190
Carboneros g6 191
Carbonia Aa3 198
Carbonin g3 196
Carbonita g2 291
Carbonne d5 187
Carcaboso d4 190
Carcaixent d5 193
Carcajou n2 247
Carcaliu j3 201
Carcans a3 186
Carcar d5 100
Cárcar c2 192
Carcaraña g2 297
Carcare c5 197
Carcassonne e5 187
Carcastillo c2 192
Cárcer d5 193
Carchi b3 284
Carcoar j12 81
Carcross l3 247
Cardal j3 297
Cardamom Range f9 103
Cardeña f6 191
Cardenal Cagliero f6 297
Cárdenas, Cuba d3 266
Cárdenas, San Luis Potosí, Mex. e3 275
Cárdenas, Tabasco, Mex. h4 275
Cardenete c5 193
Cardeto e6 199
Cardiel, Lago b5 295
Cardiff, Wales, U.K. c5 163
Cardiff, Wales, U.K. c5 163
Cardigan b4 163
Cardigan Bay b4 163
Cardington e5 254
Cardón Ae2 189
Cardona, Spain f3 192
Cardona, Ur. j2 297
Cardonal e3 275
Cardón, Cerro c4 272
Cardoner f3 192
Cardoso d4 290
Cardoso, Ilha do e6 290
Cardrona b6 77
Cardston l7 249
Cardwell, Aust. h5 80
Cardwell, U.S.A. d1 258
Careaçu f5 291
Careen Lake n3 249
Carega, Cima f4 196
Carei l4 171
Careiro f4 285
Careiro do Castanho e4 285
Carén, Coquimbo, Chile b2 294
Carén, Coquimbo, Chile b1 296
Carencro c4 258
Carentan d3 182
Cares f1 190
Carey Downs b9 87
Carey, Lake f11 87
Cargenbridge e4 164
Cargèse A 185
Cargill e3 164
Carhaix-Plouguer b4 182
Carhuáz b1 292
Carhué f4 297
Caria c4 190
Cariacica h4 291
Cariamanga b4 284
Cariango c6 224
Cariati f5 199
Caribbean Sea C8 302
Cariboo Mountains k2 249
Caribou, Can. n3 247
Caribou, U.S.A. h5 253
Caribou Lake j5 251
Carichic f4 272
Carigara e5 100
Carigara Bay e5 100
Carignan d5 159
Carignano b5 196
Cariñena c3 192
Carinhanha, Braz. c4 289
Carinhanha, Bahia, Braz. d4 289
Carini c6 199
Cariño c1 190
Caripare d4 288
Caripaya c3 284
Caripe e1 285
Caripito e1 285
Cariris Novos, Serra dos d3 288
Caris e2 285
Caritianas e1 293
Čarkajuvom h2 146
Carlentini e7 199
Carlet d5 193
Carleton e4 254
Carleton, Mount j5 253
Carleton Place h3 255
Carletonville g3 235
Cârlibaba g2 201
Carlin e5 262
Carlisle, U.K. f5 164
Carlisle, Arkansas, U.S.A. d2 258
Carlisle, Indiana, U.S.A. c6 254
Carlisle, Pennsylvania, U.S.A. c4 256
Carlisle Island b5 246
Carlisle Lakes h11 87
Carlit, Pic d6 187
Carl Junction b1 258
Carloforte Aa3 198
Carlopoli f5 199
Carlópolis d5 290
Carlos A. Carrillo g4 275
Carlos A. Madrazo h5 275
Carlos Ameghino, Istmo d4 295
Carlos Casares g3 297
Carlos Chagas h2 291
Carlos, Isla b6 295
Carlos Reyles j2 297
Carlos Salas g3 297
Carlos Tejedor f3 297
Carlow, Ire. e4 165
Carlow, Carlow, Ire. e4 165
Carloway b1 164
Carlsbad, California, U.S.A. f8 265
Carlsbad, New Mexico, U.S.A. b5 261
Carlsbad, Texas, U.S.A. c6 261
Carlsbad Caverns National Park b2 261
Carlsberg Ridge c5 300
Carlton Hills f5 235
Carluke e4 164
Carlux d4 186
Carlyle, Can. b6 250
Carlyle, U.S.A. b6 254
Carlyle Lake b6 254
Carmacks k3 247
Carmagnola b5 196
Carman d6 250
Carmanville q4 253
Carmarthen b5 163
Carmarthen Bay b5 163
Carmarthenshire b5 163
Carmaux e4 187
Carmel, Indiana, U.S.A. c6 254
Carmel, New York, U.S.A. g3 257
Carmel-by-the-Sea b5 264
Carmel Head b3 162
Carmel Highlands b5 265
Carmelita b2 276
Carmel, Mount b5 264
Carmelo h2 297
Carmel Valley b5 265
Carmen, Arg. g2 297
Carmen, Col. k6 277
Carmen, Mex. f2 272
Carmen, Mex. j5 273
Carmen, Phil. e6 100
Carmen, U.S.A. h10 263
Carmen, Ur. j2 297
Carmen Alto d4 292
Carmen de Areco h3 297
Carmen del Paraná f5 293
Carmen de Patagones f6 297
Cármenes e2 190
Carmensa d3 296
Carmi b6 254
Carmichael b3 264
Carmila j6 80
Carmo g4 291
Carmo da Cachoeira f4 291
Carmo de Minas f5 291
Carmo do Paranaíba e3 291
Carmona, C.R. e6 276
Carmona, Spain e7 191
Carmópolis de Minas f4 291
Carnac b5 182
Carnarvon, Aust. a9 87
Carnarvon, R.S.A. e5 234
Carnarvonleegte d5 234
Carnarvon National Park c4 84
Carnarvon Range, Queensland, Aust. c4 84
Carnarvon Range, Western Australia, Aust. e9 87
Carndonagh d1 165
Carnduff c6 250
Carnedd Llywelyn c3 162
Carnegie f9 87
Carnegie, Lake f10 87
Carnero, Punta del e8 191
Carnew e4 165
Carnforth d2 162
Car Nicobar n8 127
Carnlough b5 164
Carno c4 163
Carnot c3 224
Carnota a2 190
Carnot, Cape b13 81
Carnoustie f3 164
Carnsore Point e4 165
Carnwath n2 247
Carola Cay l5 80
Carol City j7 259
Carolei f5 199
Carolina, Arg. d2 296
Carolina, Braz. c3 288
Carolina, P.R. A 270
Carolina, R.S.A. j3 235
Carolina Beach l2 259
Caroline Island H 75
Caroline Islands G 74
Caroline Peak a6 77
Caroline Range h5 86
Carolusberg b4 234
Carondelet b3 284

320 Caroní → Cernavodă

Caroní e2 285
Carora c1 284
Carovigno g4 198
Carp h3 255
Carpaneto Piacentino d5 196
Carpathian Mountains b2 148
Carpații Meridionali g3 201
Carpegna g6 197
Carpentaria, Gulf of d3 80
Carpentersville b4 254
Carpentiría c1 296
Carpentras b6 185
Carpi e5 196
Carpignano Salentino c2 198
Carpina, Braz. e3 288
Carpina, Italy g6 197
Cărpineni j2 201
Cărpiniș j6 171
Carpino e3 198
Carpinone d3 198
Carpintería d7 265
Carpio, Spain e3 190
Carpio, U.S.A. c6 250
Carp Lake Provincial Park f4 248
Carquefou d5 182
Carradale East c4 164
Carraipía c1 284
Carra, Lough b3 165
Carranza, Cabo a3 296
Carrao e2 285
Carrapateira b7 191
Carrapichana c4 190
Carrara e5 197
Carrascosa del Campo b4 193
Carrascoy c7 193
Carrathool g13 81
Carratraca f8 191
Carrazedo de Montenegro c3 190
Carrbridge e2 164
Carregado b5 191
Carregal do Sal c4 190
Carreira b1 190
Carreiro, Punta a1 190
Carreña f1 190
Carrero, Cerro c4 296
Carreta Quemada j3 297
Carreteira c2 190
Carrick d4 164
Carrickfergus, England, U.K. b1 165
Carrickfergus, Northern Ireland, U.K. c5 164
Carrickmacross e3 165
Carrick-on-Shannon c3 165
Carrick-on-Suir d4 165
Carrier Mills e1 258
Carrieton d12 81
Carrigaline c5 165
Carrigallen d3 165
Carrigart d1 165
Carril h3 297
Carrillo h4 272
Carrillo Puerto b1 276
Carrilobo f1 297
Carrington d7 250
Carrington Point c7 265
Carrion f2 190
Carrión de Calatrava g5 191
Carrión de los Condes f2 190
Carrizal f2 272
Carrizal Bajo b1 294
Carrizales g2 297
Carrizo Colorado c3 274
Carrizo de la Ribera e2 190
Carrizos k5 273
Carrizosa a6 193
Carrizo Springs k3 273
Carrizozo b5 261
Carroll, Aust. d7 85
Carroll, U.S.A. e3 260
Carrollton, Georgia, U.S.A. g3 259
Carrollton, Mississippi, U.S.A. e3 258
Carrollton, Missouri, U.S.A. e4 260
Carrollton, Texas, U.S.A. a3 258
Carrolltown b4 256
Carron, Aust. e4 80
Carron, Scotland, U.K. d2 164
Carron, Scotland, U.K. d3 164
Carronbridge e4 164
Carro Quemado e4 296
Carros d7 185
Carrot r5 249
Carrot River b4 250
Carrouges e4 182
Carrowmore Lake b2 165
Carruthersville e1 258
Carryduff f2 165
Carry-le-Rouet b7 185
Çarşamba f2 209
Carsoli h7 197
Carson h4 86
Carson City d2 264
Carson Lake e2 264
Carstairs e4 164
Carswell Lake n2 249
Cartagena, Chile b2 296
Cartagena, Col. k5 277
Cartagena, Spain d7 193
Cartago, C.R. f6 277
Cartago, C.R. f6 277
Cartago, Col. b3 284
Cartago, U.S.A. e5 265
Cártama f8 191
Cartaxo b5 191
Cartaya c7 191
Cartaya, Cap c7 185
Carteret d3 182
Carteret, Cap de d3 182
Cartersville g2 259
Carterton, N.Z. e4 77
Carterton, U.K. e5 163
Carthage, Mississippi, U.S.A. e3 258
Carthage, Missouri, U.S.A. b1 258
Carthage, Tennessee, U.S.A. g1 259
Carthage, Texas, U.S.A. b3 258
Cartier Island f3 86
Cartoceto g6 197
Cartwright, Manitoba, Can. d6 250
Cartwright, Newfoundland, Can. p2 253
Caruachi e2 285
Caruaru e3 288
Carucedo d2 190
Carúpano e1 285
Carutapera c2 288
Carvalho b2 288
Carviçais d3 190
Carvin a4 159
Carvoeiro, Braz. e4 285
Carvoeiro, Port b7 191
Carvoeiro, Cabo a5 191
Carwell b4 84
Cary, Mississippi, U.S.A. d3 258
Cary, North Carolina, U.S.A. k2 259
Čaryš u2 121
Čaryškoe u2 121
Caryville g1 259
Casabermeja f8 191
Casabindo, Cerro de d4 292
Casablanca, Chile b2 296
Casablanca, Mor. c2 220
Casabona f5 199
Casa Branca, Braz. e4 290
Casa Branca, Port c6 191
Casacalenda d3 198
Casa de Janos e2 272
Casa del Campesino e2 275
Casa de Piedra d5 296
Casa de Piedra, Embalse d5 296
Casagiove d3 198
Casa Grande h9 263
Casa l'Abate h4 198
Casalarreina b2 192
Casalbordino d3 198
Casalbuttano ed Uniti d4 196
Casalegno g2 297
Casale Monferrato c4 196
Casalins h4 297
Casalmaggiore e5 196
Casalnuovo Monterotaro e3 198
Casalpusterlengo d4 196
Casalvecchio di Puglia e3 198
Casamance a3 222
Casamassima f4 198
Casanare, Col. c2 284
Casanare, Col. c2 284
Casarano h4 198
Casar de Cáceres d5 191
Casares d5 276
Casas e2 275
Casas Bajas c4 193
Casas de Don Pedro e5 191
Casas de Fernando Alonso b5 193
Casas de Juan Núñez c5 193
Casas del Puerto c6 193
Casas Grandes, Mex. f2 272
Casas Grandes, Chihuahua, Mex. f2 272
Casas-Ibáñez c5 193
Casasimarro b5 193
Casas Novas de Mares c6 191
Casatejada e5 191
Casavieja f4 190
Casbas f4 297
Casca b7 289
Cascada de Bassaseachic, Parque Nacional e3 272
Cascade, N.Z. b6 77
Cascade, U.S.A. h2 262
Cascade Point b6 77
Cascade Range b4 241
Cascade Reservoir f3 262
Cascais a6 191
Cascajal a5 284
Cascal, Paso del e5 276
Cascante c3 192
Cascapédia j4 253
Cascavel, Ceará, Braz. e2 288
Cascavel, Paraná, Braz. b6 290
Cascia h7 197
Casciana Terme e6 197
Cascina e6 197
Cáseda c2 192
Casekow k2 173
Caselle Torinese b4 196
Case Perrone f4 198
Caserta, Italy d3 198
Caserta, Campania, Italy d3 198
Casey (Aust.) s1 298
Casey Bay k1 298
Cashel, Galway, Ire. b3 165
Cashel, Ire. d4 165
Cashel, Zimb. e2 233
Cashiers h2 259
Casibare c3 284
Casigua, Falcón, Ven. c1 284
Casigua, Zulia, Ven. c2 284
Casiguran d2 100
Casiguran Sound d3 100
Casilda g2 297
Casillas del Ángel Af2 189
Casimcea j3 201
Casimiro Castillo b4 274
Casimiro de Abreu g5 291
Casina e5 196
Casino l10 81
Casinos d5 193
Casiquiare, Canal d3 284
Casita h10 263
Čáslav d2 170
Casma b1 292
Casoio d2 190
Casole d'Elsa f6 197
Casoli d2 198
Caspe d3 192
Casper b3 260
Casperia g7 197
Caspian Lowland h3 149
Caspian Sea h4 149
Cassà de la Selva g3 192
Cassacatiza e1 233
Cassai d6 224
Cassamba c1 232
Cassano allo Ionio f5 198
Cassano delle Murge f4 198
Cassano Spinola c5 196
Cassara e2 293
Cassel a4 159
Casselton e7 250
Cássia e4 291
Cassiar c2 248
Cassiar Mountains m4 247
Cassibile e8 199
Cassilândia c3 290
Cassinga b2 232
Cassino c3 198
Cassis b7 185
Cass Lake f7 250
Cassley d1 164
Cassoalala b5 224
Cassongue c6 224
Cassville c1 258
Častá f3 170
Castagna, Punta di a A 185
Castagnaro f4 196
Castagneto Carducci e6 197
Castagnole Monferrato c5 196
Castaic Lake e7 265
Castalia e5 254
Castalla d6 193
Castanet-Tolosan d5 187
Castanhal, Amazonas, Braz. e1 293
Castanhal, Pará, Braz. c2 288
Castanheira c4 190
Castanheira de Pêra b4 190
Castanheiro d4 284
Castanho e1 293
Castanho, Lago e4 285
Castaño c2 294
Castaño Nuevo c1 296
Castaños j4 273
Castaño Viejo c2 294
Castasegna d3 196
Casteggio d4 196
Castejón c2 192
Castejón de Monegros d3 192
Castejón de Sos e2 192
Castejón de Valdejasa d3 192
Castèl Baronia e3 198
Castelbuono d7 199
Casteldaccia c6 199
Castèl d'Ario e4 196
Casteldelfino b5 196
Castèl del Piano f7 197
Castèl del Rio f5 197
Castèl di Lama c2 198
Castèl di Lucio d7 199
Castèl di Sangro d3 198
Castelfidardo c1 198
Castelfiorentino e6 197
Castelfranco Emilia f5 196
Castelfranco in Miscano e3 198
Castelfranco Veneto f4 196
Castèl Gandolfo g8 197
Castèl Goffredo e4 196
Casteljaloux c4 187
Castellabate d4 198
Castell'Alfero c5 196
Castellammare del Golfo b6 199
Castellammare di Stabia d4 198
Castellamonte b4 196
Castellana Grotte g4 198
Castellane c7 185
Castellaneta f4 198
Castellaneta Marina f4 198
Castellar de la Frontera e8 191
Castellar de la Muela c4 192
Castellar de Santiago a6 193
Castell'Arquato d5 196
Castell'Azzara f7 197
Castellazzo Bormida c5 196
Castelldans e3 192
Castell de Cabres e4 192
Castelldefels f3 192
Castelleone d4 196
Castellfollit de la Roca g2 192
Castelli, Buenos Aires, Arg. j4 297
Castelli, Chaco, Arg. e5 293
Castellina in Chianti f6 197
Castellnou de Bassella f2 192
Castelló de Farfanya e3 192
Castelló de la Plana d5 193
Castelló d'Empúries h2 192
Castelló de Rugat d6 193
Castellón De La Plana d4 193
Castellote d4 192
Castello Tesino f3 196
Castelluccio dei Sauri e3 198
Castelluccio Inferiore e4 198
Castell'Umberto d6 199
Castelluzzo b6 199
Castèl Madama g8 197
Castelmagno b5 197
Castelmassa f4 196
Castelmauro d3 198
Castelnau-Barbarens c5 187
Castelnaudary d5 187
Castelnau-de-Médoc b3 186
Castelnau-de-Montmiral d5 187
Castelnau-Magnoac c5 187
Castelnau-Montratier d4 187
Castelnau-Rivière-Basse b5 187
Castelnovo ne'Monti e5 197
Castelnuovo Don Bosco b4 196
Castelo h4 291
Castelo Bom d4 190
Castelo Branco, Port c4 190
Castelo Branco, Bragança, Port d3 190
Castelo Branco, Castelo Branco, Port c5 191
Castelo de Bode, Barragem do b5 191
Castelo de Paiva b3 190
Castelo de Vide c5 191
Castelo do Piauí d3 288
Castelplanio h6 197
Castelrotto f3 196
Castèl San Giovanni d4 196
Castèl San Pietro Terme f5 197
Castelsardo Aa2 198
Castelsarrasin d4 187
Castelseras d4 192
Casteltermini c7 199
Castelvetrano b7 199
Castèl Volturno c3 198
Casterton e14 81
Castets a5 187
Castiadas Ab3 198
Castiello de Jaca d2 192
Castifao A 185
Castiglioncello e6 197
Castiglione del Lago g6 197
Castiglione della Pescaia e7 197
Castiglione della Stiviere e4 196
Castiglione Messer Marino d3 198
Castiglion Fiorentino f6 197
Castilblanco e5 191
Castilblanco de los Arroyos e7 191
Castilho c4 290
Castilla, Chile b1 294
Castilla, Peru a5 284
Castilla, Canal de f2 190
Castilla - La Mancha b5 193
Castilla y León f3 190
Castillejar b7 193
Castillejo de Martin Viejo d4 190
Castillo, Canal del a5 295
Castillo, Cerro del c2 296
Castillo de Bayuela f4 190
Castillo de Garcimuñoz b5 193
Castillo de Locubín g7 191
Castillo de Teayo f3 275
Castillon-en-Couserans d6 187
Castillon-la-Bataille b4 186
Castillonnès c4 186
Castillo, Pampa del c5 295
Castillos, Rocha, Ur. f2 294
Castillos, Soriano, Ur. j2 297
Castione della Presolana e4 196
Castiòns di Strada h4 196
Castlebar b3 165
Castlebay a3 164
Castlebellingham e3 165
Castleberry f4 258
Castleblayney e2 165
Castle Cary e5 163
Castlecomer d4 165
Castle Creek e2 256
Castle Douglas e5 164
Castlefinn d2 165
Castleford e3 162
Castlegar j7 248
Castleisland b4 165
Castlemaine, Aust. g14 81
Castlemaine, Ire. b4 165
Castlemartyr c5 165
Castle Mountain, Can. k6 249
Castle Mountain, Alaska, U.S.A. l2 247
Castle Mountain, California, U.S.A. c6 264
Castlepoint f4 76
Castlepollard d3 165
Castlerea c3 165
Castlereagh, Aust. c7 85
Castlereagh, U.K. b1 165
Castle Rock, Colorado, U.S.A. b4 260
Castle Rock, Washington, U.S.A. b2 262
Castleton f2 162
Castletown, Isle of Man, U.K. b2 162
Castletown, Scotland, U.K. e1 164
Castletown Bere b5 165
Castletownroche c4 165
Castlewellan f2 165
Častoozerskoe l5 147
Castor b7 254
Castor Creek c3 258
Castrejón de la Peña f2 190
Castrejón, Embalse de f5 190
Castres e5 187
Castricum c2 159
Castries, Languedoc-Roussillon, Fr. f5 187
Castries, Fr. f5 187
Castries, St Luc. J 271
Castrignano del Capo c3 199
Castril, Spain b7 193
Castril, Andalucía, Spain b7 193
Castrillo de la Reina a3 192
Castrillo de la Vega g3 190
Castro, Braz. d6 290
Castro, Chile b4 294
Castro, Italy c2 198
Castro, Spain a1 190
Castro Alves e4 288
Castrobarto g1 190
Castro Caldelas c2 190
Castrocaro Terme f5 197
Castrocontrigo d2 190
Castro Daire c4 190
Castro del Río f7 191
Castro de Rei c1 190
Castro, Embalse de d3 190
Castrofilippo c7 199
Castrojeriz f2 190
Castro Laboreiro b2 190
Castro Marim c7 191
Castromonte e3 190
Castronuevo e3 190
Castronuño e3 190
Castronuovo di Sicilia c7 199
Castropol c1 190
Castrop-Rauxel f3 159
Castro, Punta do a2 190
Castroreale e6 199
Castro-Urdiales a1 192
Castro Verde b7 191
Castroverde c1 190
Castroverde de Campos e3 190
Castrovillari f5 198
Castrovirreyna b2 292
Castuera e6 191
Casummit Lake g5 250
Caswell Sound a6 77
Čat h3 209
Catabola c6 224
Catacamas e3 276
Catacaos a5 284
Catacocha b4 284
Cataguases g4 291
Catahoula Lake c4 258
Cataiñgan d4 100
Çatak j4 209
Catalão d3 290
Çatalca j5 201
Catalina r4 253
Catalina Point C 74
Catalina, Punta c6 295
Cataluña f3 192
Çatalzeytin e2 208
Catamaran Ab3 83
Catamarca, Arg. c1 294
Catamarca, Catamarca, Arg. c1 294
Catamayo a4 284
Catanauan d4 100
Catandica e2 233
Catanduanes e4 100
Catanduva d4 290
Catanduvas b6 290
Catania, Sicilia, Italy d7 199
Catania, Sicilia, Italy e7 199
Catania, Golfo di e7 199
Catán Lil b5 296
Catanzaro, Italy f6 199
Catanzaro, Calabria, Italy f6 199
Catanzaro Marina f6 199
Cataqueamã e2 293
Catarina, Braz. e3 288
Catarina, U.S.A. k3 273
Catarino Rodriguez j5 273
Catarman e4 100
Catarroja d5 193
Catastrophe, Cape b13 81
Catatumbo c2 284
Catavi d3 292
Catawba j2 259
Cataxa e2 233
Catazajá a2 276
Cat Ba, Đao h5 102
Catbalogan e5 100
Cat Cays k7 259
Cateel f7 100
Cateel Bay f7 100
Catemaco g4 275
Catembe k3 235
Catemu b2 296
Catenanuova d7 199
Caterham f5 163
Catete b5 224
Cathcart g6 235
Cathedral City e9 263
Cathedral Rock National Park d7 85
Catherines Peak B 266
Cathlamet b2 262
Catillo b4 296
Catió a3 222
Catisimiña e3 285
Cat Island, Bah. g2 266
Cat Island, U.S.A. e4 258
Cat Lake g5 250
Catolé do Rocha e3 288
Caton d2 162
Catonsville d5 256
Catorce d2 274
Catoute d2 190
Catria, Monte g6 197
Catriel d4 296
Catriló f4 297
Catrimani, Braz. e3 285
Catrimani, Roraima, Braz. e3 285
Catshill d4 163
Catskill g2 257
Cattenom e5 159
Catterick e2 162
Cattolica g6 197
Cattolica Eraclea c7 199
Catuane k3 235
Catumbela a1 232
Catur f1 233
Caturiá, Ilha d4 284
Catus d4 186
Cauaburi d3 284
Căuaș l4 171
Cauaxi c2 288
Cauayan d6 100
Caubvick, Mount s4 243
Cauca, Col. b3 284
Cauca, Col. b2 284
Caucaia e2 288
Caucasia k7 277
Caucete c1 296
Cauchari, Salar de d4 292
Cauchon Lake e3 250
Caudau c4 186
Caudebec-en-Caux f3 183
Caudete d6 193
Caudiel d5 193
Caudry b4 159
Cauit Point f6 100
Caulnes c4 182
Caulonia f6 199
Caumont-l'Éventé e3 182
Caunes-Minervois e5 187
Caungula c5 224
Caupolican d2 292
Cauquenes a3 296
Caura e2 285
Caurés e4 285
Cauro A 185
Causapscal j4 253
Căușeni j2 201
Caussade d4 187
Cautário e2 293
Cauterets b6 187
Caution, Cape d6 248
Cauto f4 266
Caux, Pays de f3 183
Cava de'Tirreni d4 198
Cávado b3 190
Cavaglià c4 196
Cavaillon b7 185
Cavalaire-sur-Mer c7 185
Cavalcante, Goiás, Braz. e4 288
Cavalcante, Rondônia, Braz. e1 293
Cavaleiro b7 191
Cavalese f3 196
Cavalier e6 250
Cavalleria, Cap de A 193
Cavalli Islands d1 76
Cavallo, Île A 185
Cavalluccio, Punta d4 198
Cavally c4 222
Cavan, Ire. d3 165
Cavan, Cavan, Ire. d3 165
Cavanagh f2 297
Čavan'ga r3 155
Cavarzere g4 196
Cave c6 77
Cave City d1 258
Cave del Predil h3 196
Caveira g2 291
Cavenagh Range j10 87
Cavendish f14 81
Cavernoso, Serra do c6 290
Cave Run Lake e6 254
Cave Spring g2 259
Caviana, Ilha c1 288
Cavili c6 100
Cavite c3 100
Cavnic f2 201
Cavour b5 196
Cavtat h2 198
Çavuşçu c3 208
Cawndilla Lake b1 82
Caxambu f4 291
Caxias, Amazonas, Braz. c4 284
Caxias, Maranhão, Braz. d2 288
Caxias do Sul b7 289
Caxito b5 224
Çay c3 208
Cayambe b3 284
Cayambe, Volcán b3 284
Cayapas b3 284
Cayastá g1 297
Çaycuma d2 208
Çayeli h2 209
Cayenne, Fr. Gu. g3 285
Cayenne, Cayenne, Fr. Gu. g3 285
Cayetano j1 297
Cayeux-sur-Mer g2 183
Cayey A 270
Çayhan e4 208
Çayırhan c2 208
Caylus d4 187
Cayman Islands (U.K.) f4 241
Caynabo d2 226
Cayo c2 276
Cayon F 271
Cayres f4 186
Cayucos c6 265
Cayuga Lake d2 256
Cay Verde g4 266
Cazage d6 224
Cazalegas f4 190
Cazalegas, Embalse de f4 190
Cazalla de la Sierra e7 191
Cazals d4 186
Căzănești h3 201
Caza Pava e1 294
Cazaubon b5 187
Cazaux et de Sanguinet, Étang de a4 187
Cazê h4 135
Cazenovia e2 256
Cazères d5 187
Cazin g5 177
Čažma h4 177
Cazombo d6 224
Cazones f3 275
Cazorla b7 193
Ččikskoe Vodohranilišče e3 148
Cea, Spain e2 190
Cea, Castilla y León, Spain e2 190
Ceará e2 288
Ceará Mirim e3 288
Ceaucé e4 182
Cebaco, Isla g7 277
Ceballos g4 272
Čebarkul' k5 147
Cebes, Cabo d1 190
Čeboksary j3 151
Cebolla f5 191
Cebollar c1 294
Cebollatí f2 294
Cebollera b2 192
Ceboruco, Cerro b4 274
Ceboruco, Volcán b3 274
Čebovce h3 171
Čebsara e2 150
Cebu, Phil. d5 100
Cebu, Phil. d5 100
Ceccano h8 197
Cece g5 171
Čečenskaja Respublika g4 149
Čechtice d2 170
Cecil h4 259
Cecil Plains k9 81
Cecil Rhodes, Mount e9 87
Cecina, Italy e6 197
Cecina, Toscana, Italy e6 197
Ceclavín d5 191
Cedar, Michigan, U.S.A. e3 260
Cedar, Nebraska, U.S.A. d3 260
Cedar, North Dakota, U.S.A. b3 260
Cedar Bluff Reservoir d4 260
Cedar City g7 263
Cedar Creek Reservoir a3 258
Cedar Falls e3 260
Cedar Grove e5 264
Cedar Hill f1 258
Cedar Key h5 259
Cedar Lake c4 250
Cedar Rapids f3 260
Cedar Springs, Can. e4 254
Cedar Springs, U.S.A. d4 254
Cedartown g2 259
Cedar Vale a1 258
Cedarville, R.S.A. h5 235
Cedarville, U.S.A. d3 254
Cedegolo e3 196
Cedeira b1 190
Cedeño d4 276
Cederberg c6 234
Cedillo, Embalse de c5 191
Cedral, Quintana Roo, Mex. r7 273
Cedral, San Luis Potosí, Mex. d2 274
Cedrillas d4 192
Cedro e3 288
Cedros, Hond. d3 276
Cedros, Sonora, Mex. e4 272
Cedros, Zacatecas, Mex. j5 273
Cedros, Isla b3 272
Ceduna a12 81
Cedynia c3 168
Cée a2 190
Ceek d2 226
Ceel Afweyn d2 226
Ceelbuur d3 226
Ceeldheere d3 226
Ceel Gaal, Bari, Som. e1 226
Ceel Gaal, Woqooyi Galbeed, Som. c1 226
Ceerigaabo d1 226
Cefalù d6 199
Cega f3 190
Cegar Perah b3 101
Ceggia g4 196
Cegléd h4 171
Ceglédbercel h4 171
Ceglie Messapica g4 198
Cehegín c6 193
Čeheng e6 104
Čehov d4 150
Ceibas h2 297
Ceinos de Campos e2 190
Čejč h1 177
Čejkov k3 171
Čekalin d4 150
Çekerek e2 208
Ceków Kolonia g4 168
Čekšino f2 150
Čelákovice c1 170
Celano c2 198
Celanova c2 190
Celaque, Parque Nacional c3 276
Celaya d3 274
Celbridge e3 165
Célé d4 186
Celebes Sea l3 99
Celemín, Embalse de e8 191
Celendín b1 292
Celinac Donji j5 177
Celinnoe v1 121
Celinnyj h2 120
Čeljabinsk k5 147
Čeljabinskaja Oblast' k5 147
Celje g3 177
Cella c4 192
Celldömölk f4 170
Celle f3 172
Celles-sur-Belle b2 186
Cellettes g5 183
Cellina g3 196
Cellino San Marco g4 198
Čelopeci b1 210
Celorico da Beira c4 190
Celorico de Basto c3 190
Celtic Sea d5 165
Celtic Shelf k4 302
Cemaru, Gunung h4 99
Cembra f3 196
Čemerno d4 200
Cemilbey e2 208
Çemişgezek g3 209
Cemmaes c4 162
Cempi, Teluk k9 99
Čemšeniška planina f3 177
Cenajo, Embalse del c6 193
Cenderawasih, Teluk k6 97
Cendras a6 184
Cenei e3 200
Cenepa b4 284
Cenicero b2 192
Ceno d5 196
Cenon b4 186
Cenote Azul b2 276
Centelles g3 192
Centenario c5 296
Centenário do Sul c5 290
Centenary e2 233
Centennial Wash g9 263
Center, North Dakota, U.S.A. c7 250
Center, Texas, U.S.A. b4 258
Centerburg e5 254
Center Hill Lake g2 259
Center Moriches h4 257
Center Point f3 258
Center Valley e4 256
Centerville, Alabama, U.S.A. f3 258
Centerville, Pennsylvania, U.S.A. g5 254
Centerville, Texas, U.S.A. b4 258
Cento f5 196
Central, Bots. g1 235
Central, Braz. d4 288
Central, Chile c4 292
Central, Kenya b4 226
Central, Mal. a6 231
Central, Nepal g6 135
Central, Para. f5 293
Central, Sri L. A 127
Central, U.S.A. a5 261
Central, Zam. d1 233
Central African Republic e4 217

CENTRAL AFRICAN REPUBLIC

THE CENTRAL AFRICAN REPUBLIC
Area 622,984km^2 (240,535sq miles)
Capital Bangui
Organizations FZ, CEEAC
Population 3,820,000
Pop. growth (%) 1.6
Life expectancy 42 (m); 46 (f)
Languages French, Sango
Literacy 51.1%
Currency CFA franc (US $1 = 534.95 CFA franc)
GDP (US million $) 1028
GDP per head ($US) 269

Central Brahui Range c6 129
Central Bridge f2 257
Central City, Illinois, U.S.A. b6 254
Central City, Kentucky, U.S.A. f1 258
Central City, Nebraska, U.S.A. d3 260
Central City, Pennsylvania, U.S.A. b4 256
Central, Cordillera, Bol. d3 292
Central, Cordillera, Col. b3 284
Central, Cordillera, Dom. Rep. j5 271
Central, Cordillera, P.R. A 266
Central, Cordillera, Pan. g6 277
Central, Cordillera, Phil. c2 100
Central de Minas h3 291
Central Falls j3 257
Centralia b2 262
Central Island National Park b3 226
Central Islip g4 257
Central Kalahari Game Reserve e1 234
Central Makran Range b7 129
Central, Massif f3 186
Central Mount Stuart a6 80
Central Mount Wedge k8 86
Central'nyj l2 151
Central Pacific Basin l5 301
Central Patricia h5 250
Central Plateau Conservation Area Ab2 83
Central Range h4 235
Central Siberian Plateau l3 119
Central Village j3 257
Centre, Cam. b2 224
Centre, Fr. g5 183
Centre, U.S.A. g2 259
Centre, Canal du, Bel. b4 159
Centre, Canal du, Fr. k6 183
Centre Island a7 77
Centreville, Maryland, U.S.A. d5 256
Centreville, Virginia, U.S.A. c6 256
Centurion h2 235
Centuripe d7 199
Century f4 258
Cenur c4 101
Cenxi h7 104
Céou d4 186
Cepagatti d2 198
Čepeckij l2 151
Ceprano c3 198
Cepu f8 98
Ceranów l3 169
Cérans-Foulletourte f5 183
Ceraso e4 198
Cerbatana, Sierra de la d2 284
Cerbère f6 187
Cerbère, Cap f6 187
Cercal b7 191
Cercal, Serra do b7 191
Čerčany c2 170
Cercedo b2 190
Cercy-la-Tour f2 186
Cerda c7 199
Čerdakly k4 151
Cerdanyola del Vallès g3 192
Cerdon h5 183
Čerdyn' j3 147
Cère d4 186
Cerea f4 196
Cereales f4 297
Cereceda, Embalse de g2 190
Cered h3 171
Ceredigion c4 163
Ceregnano f4 196
Čereha n4 157
Čeremhovo k2 151
Čeremuhovo k3 147
Cérences d4 182
Čerepanovo j4 118
Čerepovec d2 150
Ceres, Arg. d1 294
Ceres, Braz. d1 290
Ceres, Italy b4 196
Ceres, R.S.A. c6 234
Ceres, U.S.A. c4 264
Ceresole, Lago di b4 196
Ceresole Reale b4 196
Céreste b7 185
Céret e6 187
Cereté k6 277
Čerevkovo f3 146
Cerezo de Abajo g3 190
Cergy h3 183
Cerignola e3 198
Çerikli d3 208
Cerillos b2 296
Cérilly e2 186
Cerisiers j4 183
Cerizay e6 182
Cerk f4 177
Çerkeş d2 208
Čerkesovskij f2 149
Čerkessk f3 149
Çerkezköy j5 201
Cerknica f4 177
Čerkutino e3 150
Cerkwica d1 168
Čermasan j1 149
Cermei k5 171
Çermik g3 209
Čermoz j4 147
Čern' d5 150
Cerna, Cro. d3 200
Cerna, Rom. j3 201
Cernache do Bonjardim b5 191
Cernadilla, Embalse de d2 190
Černaja j1 147
Černaja Holunica l2 151
Cernavodă j3 201

CHAD
THE REPUBLIC OF CHAD
Area 1,284,000km² (495,800sq miles)
Capital N'Djamena
Organizations FZ, OIC, CEEAC
Population 8,350,000
Pop. growth (%) 3.4
Life expectancy 43 (m); 46 (f)
Languages French, Arabic, many local languages
Literacy 47.5%
Currency CFA franc (US $1 = 570.96 CFA franc)
GDP (US million $) 1860
GDP per head ($US) 222

CHILE

THE REPUBLIC OF CHILE
Area 756,626km² (292,135sq miles)
Capital Santiago
Organizations IADB, SELA, LAIA
Population 15,590,000
Pop. growth (%) 1.2
Life expectancy 72 (m); 78 (f)
Languages Spanish
Literacy 96.2%
Currency Chilean peso (US $1 = 598.55 Chilean peso)
GDP (US million $) 62,200
GDP per head ($US) 3989

CHINA

THE PEOPLE'S REPUBLIC OF CHINA
Area 9,571,300km² (3,695,500sq miles)
Capital Beijing
Organizations APEC
Population 1,302,090,000
Pop. growth (%) 0.8
Life expectancy 67 (m); 72 (f)
Languages Northern Chinese (Mandarin) and others
Literacy 87%
Currency yuan, renminbi (US $1 = 8.27 yuan, renminbi)
GDP (US million $) 1,259,400
GDP per head ($US) 967

324 Conhelo → Crossville

Conhelo e4 296
Cónico, Cerro b4 295
Conie g4 183
Conil de la Frontera d8 191
Conills, Illa des f5 193
Conimbla National Park f1 83
Conisbrough e3 162
Coniston, Can. f2 254
Coniston, U.K. c2 162
Coniston Water c2 162
Conkal q7 273
Conlara e2 296
Conlie e4 182
Conliège b4 184
Connaux a6 185
Connecticut, U.S.A. h3 257
Connecticut, Connecticut, U.S.A. h3 257
Connel c3 164
Connell d2 262
Connellsville a4 256
Connemara, Aust. f8 80
Connemara, Ire. b3 165
Connemara National Park b3 165
Conner, Mount k9 87
Connerré f4 183
Conn, Lough b3 165
Connors Range c2 84
Cononaco, Ec. b4 284
Cononaco, Pastaza, Ec. b4 284
Conques e4 186
Conques-sur-Orbiel e5 187
Conquista, Bol. d2 292
Conquista, Braz. e3 290
Conquista, Spain f6 191
Conrad h1 262
Conroe b4 258
Consata d3 292
Conscripto Bernardi h1 297
Consdorf e5 159
Consejo c1 276
Conselheiro Lafaiete g4 291
Conselheiro Pena h3 291
Conselice f5 196
Consell g5 193
Consett e2 162
Consistorio b2 190
Consolación del Sur c3 266
Côn Sơn h11 103
Con, Sông g6 102
Constância b5 191
Constancia h2 297
Constância dos Baetas e1 293
Constanța, Rom. j3 201
Constanța, Constanța, Rom. j3 201
Constantí f3 192
Constantim d3 190
Constantina e7 191
Constantine f1 221
Constantine, Cape e4 246
Constanzana f4 190
Constitución, Chile a3 296
Constitución, Ur. j1 297
Consuegra g5 191
Consuelo, Aust. c4 84
Consuelo, Braz. e2 293
Consul j1 262
Contagem f3 291
Contamana b1 292
Contarina g4 196
Contas d4 288
Contenda d6 290
Contes d7 185
Contessa Entellina c7 199
Conthey b3 196
Contis-Plage a4 187
Contoocook j2 257
Contrada d4 198
Contralmirante Cordero c5 296
Contratacion c2 284
Contreras, Embalse de c5 193
Contreras, Isla a6 295
Contreras, Islas g7 277
Contres g5 183
Contrexéville b2 184
Contria f3 291
Controne e4 198
Contulmo a5 296
Contursi Terme e4 198
Contwoyto Lake g2 242
Conty h3 183
Convención c2 284
Convento Viejo b3 296
Conversano g4 198
Conway, R.S.A. f5 235
Conway, Arkansas, U.S.A. c2 258
Conway, Missouri, U.S.A. c1 258
Conway, New Hampshire, U.S.A. g7 252
Conway, South Carolina, U.S.A. k3 259
Conway, Cape c2 84
Conway National Park c2 84
Conwy, Wales, U.K. c3 162
Conwy, Wales, U.K. c3 162
Conwy, Wales, U.K. c3 162
Conwy Bay b4 162
Coober Pedy b10 81
Coogoon c5 85
Cook, Aust. k12 87
Cook, U.S.A. g7 250
Cook (Aoraki), Mount c5 77
Cook, Bahía de b7 295
Cook, Cape d6 248
Cooke, Mount c13 87
Cookes Peak b5 261
Cookhouse f6 235
Cook Ice Shelf IH w1 298
Cook Inlet g3 247
Cook Islands (New Zealand) j4 73
Cooksburg f2 257
Cook's Harbour q3 253
Cookstown, England, U.K. b2 165
Cookstown, Northern Ireland, U.K. e2 165
Cook Strait e4 77
Cooktown g3 80
Coolabah h11 81
Cooladdi g9 81
Coolah c7 85
Coolangatta e6 85
Coolarda c11 87
Coolgardie e12 87
Coolidge, Arizona, U.S.A. h9 263
Coolidge, Georgia, U.S.A. h4 259
Cooloola National Park e5 84
Cooma j14 81
Coombe Bissett e5 163
Coonabarabran j11 81
Coonalpyn d13 81
Coonamble j11 81
Coonana f12 87
Coon Creek b3 264
Coongan d7 86
Coongoola g9 81
Coonoor e7 126
Cooper b3 258
Cooper Creek d9 81
Cooper, Mount h10 87
Cooper Mountain, Can. j6 248
Cooper Mountain, U.S.A. g3 247
Cooper's Town l6 259
Cooperstown, New York, U.S.A. f2 256
Cooperstown, North Dakota, U.S.A. d7 250
Coopersville d4 254
Coor-de-Wandy b9 87
Coorong National Park a3 82
Coorong, The a3 82
Coorow c11 87
Cooroy l9 81
Coosa f3 258
Coos Bay a4 262
Cootamundra j13 81
Cootehill d2 165
Cooyar k9 81
Copahue, Volcán b4 296
Copainalá h5 275
Copala e5 275
Copalillo e4 275
Copalita f6 275
Copal Urcu c4 284
Copán c3 276
Copan b1 258
Copanello f6 199
Copán Ruinas c3 276
Cope c4 260
Cope, Cabo c7 193
Copenhagen, København (City District), Den. f3 158
Copere e3 293
Copertino h4 198
Copetonas g5 297
Copeton Reservoir d6 85
Copiapo b1 294
Copiapó c5 292
Copiapo, Volcán d5 292
Coplay e4 256
Copley d11 81
Coporaque c2 292
Coporolo a1 232
Copparo f5 196
Coppename f2 285
Copper h3 247
Copperas Cove a4 258
Copperbelt d1 233
Copper Center h3 247
Copper Cliff f2 254
Copperfield g5 80
Copper Harbor k7 251
Coppermine g2 242
Coppermine Point l7 251
Copperton e4 234
Copplestone c6 163
Copșa Mică g2 201
Coqên g4 135
Coquiarachi j10 263
Coquille a4 262
Coquimatlán c4 274
Coquimbo, Coquimbo, Chile b1 294
Coquimbo, Cuarta Región, Región IV, Chile b1 296
Corabia g4 201
Coração de Jesus f2 291
Coracora c3 292
Coral m5 251
Coral Bay a6 100
Coral Gables j7 259
Coral Harbour n3 243
Coral Sea j6 300
Coral Sea Basin j6 300
Coral Sea Islands Territory (Australia) j2 79
Corangamite, Lake c4 82
Coranzuli d4 292
Corato f3 198
Coray b4 182
Corbalán d4 192
Corbara, Lago di g7 197
Corbeil-Essonnes h4 183
Corbeiro, Cap a4 220
Corbélia b6 290
Corbeny b5 159
Corbett g3 297
Corbie h3 183
Corbières, Fr. e6 187
Corbières, Switz. b3 196
Corbigny f1 186
Corbones e7 191
Corbridge d2 162
Corbu j3 201
Corby f4 163
Corçà h3 192
Corchiano g7 197
Corcieux c2 184
Córcoles b5 193
Corcoran d5 265
Corcovado b4 295
Corcovado, Golfo de b4 295
Corcovado, Parque Nacional f6 277
Corcovado, Volcán b4 295
Corcubión a2 190
Corcubión, Ría de a2 190
Cordeiro g5 291
Cordele h4 259
Cordes d4 187
Cordilheiras, Serra das c3 288
Cordillera f4 293
Cordillera de los Picachos, Parque Nacional c3 284
Cordilleras Range d5 100
Cordillo Downs e9 81
Cordisburgo f3 291
Córdoba, Arg. f2 297
Córdoba, Córdoba, Arg. e1 297
Córdoba, Arg. c6 296
Córdoba, Col. b2 284
Córdoba, Durango, Mex. h4 272
Córdoba, Mex. f4 275
Córdoba, Spain f7 191
Córdoba, Andalucía, Spain f7 191
Córdoba, Sierra de f7 191
Cordobés e2 294
Cordobilla, Embalse de f7 191
Cordova, Peru b2 292
Cordova, U.S.A. h3 247
Cordova Bay l5 247
Coreaú d2 288
Corella c2 192
Corfe Castle d6 163
Corfinio c2 198
Corfu a3 210
Corguinho a3 290
Cori g8 197
Coria d5 191
Coribe d4 288
Coricudgy g1 83
Corigliano Calabro f5 198
Corinaldo h6 197
Coringa Islands k4 80
Corinna Aa2 83
Corinne q6 249
Corinth, Kentucky, U.S.A. d6 254
Corinth, Mississippi, U.S.A. e2 258
Corinto, Braz. f3 291
Corinto, Nic. d4 276
Coripe e8 191
Corisco a3 224
Corisco, Baie de a3 224
Corixa Grande f3 293
Corjeuți h1 201
Cork, Ire. c4 165
Cork, Cork, Ire. c5 165
Corlay b4 182
Corleone c7 199
Corleto Perticara f4 198
Çorlu h5 201
Cormatin a4 184
Cormeilles f3 183
Cormons h4 196
Cormorant c3 250
Cormorant Provincial Forest c3 250
Cornago b2 192
Cornelia, R.S.A. h3 235
Cornelia, U.S.A. h2 259
Cornélio Procópio c5 290
Corneliskondre f2 285
Cornelius j2 259
Cornellà de Llobregat g3 192
Cornellana d1 190
Corner Brook p4 253
Corner Inlet e4 83
Corneros c7 193
Cornersville f2 258
Cornești j2 201
Cornetto f3 196
Corni h2 201
Corniglio e5 197
Corning, Arkansas, U.S.A. d1 258
Corning, California, U.S.A. a2 264
Corning, New York, U.S.A. c2 256
Cornish a3 84
Corno Bianco b4 196
Corno dei Tre Signori e3 196
Corno di Campo e3 196
Corno, Monte c2 198
Cornouaille a5 182
Cornuda g4 196
Cornwall, Can. j3 255
Cornwall, U.K. b6 163
Cornwall, Cape a6 163
Cornwallis Island l1 243
Corny Point c13 81
Coroaci g3 291
Coroatá d2 288
Corocoro d3 292
Corocoro, Isla e2 285
Corofin b4 165
Coroglen e2 76
Coro, Golfete de c1 284
Coroico, Bol. d3 292
Coroico, La Paz, Bol. d3 292
Coromandel, Braz. e3 290
Coromandel, N.Z. e2 76
Coromandel Coast g6 126
Coromandel Peninsula e2 76
Coromandel Range e2 76
Coron, Phil. c5 100
Coron, Phil. c4 100
Corona f8 265
Coronado, Port b3 190
Coronado, U.S.A. f9 265
Coronado, Bahía de f6 276
Coronado Bay c7 100
Coronados, Golfo de los b4 295
Coronation Gulf g2 242
Coronation Island l5 247
Coronation Islands g4 86
Coron Bay c5 100
Coronda g1 297
Coronel a4 296
Coronel Alzogaray e2 296
Coronel Bogada g2 297
Coronel Brandsen h3 297
Coronel Dorrego g5 297
Coronel Fabriciano g3 291
Coronel Falcón g5 297
Coronel Francisco Sosa e6 296
Coronel Juliá y Echarrán e5 297
Coronel Moldes e2 296
Coronel Murta g2 291
Coronel Oviedo f5 293
Coronel Ponce a1 290
Coronel Portillo b4 284
Coronel Pringles g4 297
Coronel Rodolfo Bunge g4 297
Coronel Sapucaia f4 293
Coronel Suárez g4 297
Coronel Vidal j4 297
Coronel Vivida b6 290
Coroneo d3 274
Coroni E 271
Coronie f2 285
Çorovodë e5 200
Corowa h13 81
Corozal, Belize c1 276
Corozal, Belize c1 276
Corozal, Col. k6 277
Corozal, Mex. e3 275
Corozo Pando d2 284
Corpach c3 164
Corpen Aike c5 295
Corps b6 185
Corpus Christi a6 258
Corpus Christi, Lake d6 261
Corque d3 292
Corquín c3 276
Corral a5 296
Corral Chico d6 296
Corral de Almaguer a5 193
Corral de Bustos f2 297
Corral de Isaac d1 296
Corralejo Af2 189
Corrales, Mex. g5 272
Corrales, Spain e3 190
Corrales de Rábago d3 274
Corral Nuevo g4 275
Corral-Rubio c6 193
Corrandibby Range b9 87
Corraun Peninsula b3 165
Corre Caballo b2 274
Correggio e5 196
Córrego do Ouro c2 290
Córrego Novo g3 291
Corrente, Braz. d4 288
Corrente, Piauí, Braz. c4 288
Correntes, Braz. a2 290
Correntes, Mato Grosso, Braz. a2 290
Correntina d4 288
Corrèze, Fr. d3 186
Corrèze, Limousin, Fr. d3 186
Corrèze, Limousin, Fr. d3 186
Corrib, Lough b3 165
Corridonia c1 198
Corrientes, Arg. e1 294
Corrientes, Arg. e1 294
Corrientes, Arg. f5 293
Corrientes, Peru b4 284
Corrientes, Cabo, Arg. j5 297
Corrientes, Cabo, Col. b2 284
Corrientes, Cabo, Cuba b4 266
Corrigan b4 258
Corrigin c13 87
Corriverton f2 285
Corry g5 254
Corryong h14 81
Corse A 185
Corse, Cap A 185
Corse-du-Sud A 185
Corserine d4 164
Corsham d5 163
Corsicana a3 258
Corsico d4 196
Cortazar d3 274
Corte A 185
Corte de Peleas d6 191
Cortegada b2 190
Cortegana d7 191
Cortemilia c5 196
Corteolona d4 196
Cortes de Aragón d4 192
Cortes de Baza b7 193
Cortez a4 261
Cortiella e3 192
Cortijo de Arriba f5 191
Cortijos Nuevos b6 193
Cortina Creek a2 264
Cortina d'Ampezzo g3 196
Cortland, New York, U.S.A. d2 256
Cortland, Ohio, U.S.A. f5 254
Cortona f6 197
Corubal b3 222
Coruche b6 191
Çoruh h2 209
Çorum, Tur. e2 208
Çorum, Çorum, Tur. e2 208
Corumbá, Braz. d2 290
Corumbá, Mato Grosso do Sul, Braz. f3 293
Corumbá de Goiás d1 290
Corumbaíba d3 290
Corumbaú, Ponta j2 291
Corumiquara, Ponta e2 288
Coruña, Ría da b1 190
Corund g2 201
Coruripe e4 288
Corvallis b3 262
Corvara in Badia f3 196
Corvera c7 193
Corvette, Lac de la r4 251
Corvo A 220
Corwen c4 162
Corwin, Cape c4 246
Corydon f1 258
Coryville b3 256
Cosa c4 192
Cosalá f5 272
Cosamaloapan g4 275
Coscaya d3 292
Coscerno, Monte g7 197
Coscomatepec f4 275
Coscurita b3 192
Cosenza, Italy f5 199
Cosenza, Calabria, Italy f5 199
Coshocton f5 254
Cosigüina, Volcán d4 276
Cosío c2 274
Coslada g4 190
Cosmolédo Atoll d5 231
Cosmópolis e5 290
Cosne-Cours-sur-Loire h5 183
Cosne-d'Allier e2 186
Cosoleacaque g5 275
Coso Peak f5 265
Cospita a1 274
Cosquín e1 297
Cossato c4 196
Cossé-le-Vivien e5 182
Cosson g5 183
Cossonay a3 196
Costa d3 288
Costa Almeria b8 193
Costa Bela a6 191
Costa Blanca e6 193
Costa Brava f7 187
Costa da Galé b6 191
Costa da Prata a4 190
Costa de la Luz d8 191
Costa del Azahar e4 193
Costa del Silencio Ac2 189
Costa del Sol f8 191
Costa de Mosquitos f4 277
Costa do Algarve b8 191
Costa do Estoril a6 191
Costa Dorada f4 192
Costa do Sol a6 191
Costa Dourada a7 191
Costa Grande g2 297
Costa Marques e2 293
Costa Mesa f8 265
Costa Rica f7 241

COSTA RICA

THE REPUBLIC OF COSTA RICA
Area 51,100km^2
(19,730sq miles)
Capital San José
Organizations ACS, CACM, IADB, SELA
Population 4,090,000
Pop. growth (%) 1.5
Life expectancy 74 (m); 78 (f)
Languages Spanish
Literacy 96%
Currency Costa Rican colón
(US $1 = 417.23 Costa Rican colón)
GDP (US million $) 16,368
GDP per head ($US) 4001

Costa Rica, Braz. b3 290
Costa Rica, Mex. f5 272
Costa Teguise Af2 189
Costa Verde d1 190
Cost Cállda c7 193
Coșteiu k6 171
Costelloe b3 165
Costești, Mol. j2 201
Costești, Argeș, Rom. g3 201
Costești, Vaslui, Rom. h2 201
Costigan Lake q3 249
Costigliole d'Asti c5 196
Cosumes b3 264
Coswig, Sachsen, Ger. j1 175
Coswig, Sachsen-Anhalt, Ger. h4 173
Cotabambas c2 292
Cotabato e7 100
Cotacachi, Cerro b3 284
Cotacajes d3 292
Cotagaita d4 292
Cotahuasi c3 292
Cotati a3 264
Cotaxé h3 291
Cotaxtla f4 275
Coteaux g5 266
Côte Champenoise j4 183
Côte d'Argent a5 187
Côte d'Azur d7 185
Côte des Bars k4 183
Côte d'Ivoire b4 217

CÔTE D'IVOIRE

THE REPUBLIC OF CÔTE D'IVOIRE
Area 322,462km^2
(124,503sq miles)
Capital Yamoussoukro
Organizations ECOWAS, OIC
Population 16,370,000
Pop. growth (%) 2.1
Life expectancy 47 (m); 48 (f)
Languages French, many local languages
Literacy 51.7%
Currency CFA franc
(US $1 = 534.95 CFA franc)
GDP (US million $) 10,226
GDP per head ($US) 624

Côte d'Or a3 184
Côte-d'Or k5 183
Cotegipe d4 288
Cote, Mount m4 247
Cotentin d3 182
Côtes-d'Armor b4 182
Côtes de Meuse b1 184
Côte Vermeille f6 187
Cothi b5 163
Cotiella e2 192
Cotignac c7 185
Cotija c4 274
Cotillo Ae2 189
Cotinga e3 285
Cotiujeni j2 201
Cotnari h2 201
Cotonou e4 223
Cotopaxi b4 284
Cotopaxi, Volcán b4 284
Cotronei f5 199
Cotswold Hills e5 163
Cottanello g7 197
Cottbus k4 173
Cotteliar f6 126
Cottian Alps b5 196
Cottica g3 285
Cottingham f3 162
Cottondale g4 259
Cotton Plant d2 258
Cottonwood, California, U.S.A. b5 262
Cottonwood, Kansas, U.S.A. d4 260
Cottonwood Creek a1 264
Cottonwood Wash h8 263
Cotuí j5 271
Cotuit k3 257
Cotulla k3 273
Coțușca h1 201
Coubre, Pointe de la a3 186
Couches a4 184
Couço b6 191
Coucy-le-Château-Auffrique b5 159
Coudekerque-Branche a3 159
Coudersport b3 256
Coudres, Île aux g5 252
Coüedic, Cape de c14 81
Couëron d5 182
Couesnon d4 182
Couhé c2 186
Couiza e6 187
Coulanges-la-Vineuse j5 183
Coulanges-sur-Yonne j5 183
Coulans-sur-Gée f4 183
Coulee City d2 262
Coulman Island y2 298
Coulmier-le-Sec a3 184
Coulogne g2 183
Coulomby g2 183
Coulommiers j4 183
Coulon b7 185
Coulonge q7 251
Coulonges-sur-l'Autize b2 186
Coul Point b4 164
Coulterville, California, U.S.A. c4 264
Coulterville, Illinois, U.S.A. b6 254
Council Bluffs e3 260
Counva-Tabaquite-Talparo 271 271
Coupar Angus e3 164
Couptrain e4 182
Coura b3 190
Courcelles c4 159
Cour-Cheverny g5 183
Courcité e4 182
Courçon b2 186
Courgenay b2 196
Cournon-d'Auvergne f3 186
Couronne, Cap a7 185
Courpière f3 186
Courrejolles Point C 77
Coursan f5 187
Courseulles-sur-Mer e3 182
Cours-la-Ville a4 184
Courson-les-Carrières j5 183
Courtalain g4 183
Courtelary b2 196
Courtenay, Can. e7 248
Courtenay, Fr. j4 183
Courthézon a6 185
Courtisols a2 184
Courtland f2 258
Courtomer f4 183
Court-St-Etienne c4 159
Courville-sur-Eure g4 183
Couserans d6 187
Coushatta c3 258
Cousin k5 183
Couso, Punta de b2 190
Coussegrey k5 183
Coussey b2 184
Coustouges e6 187
Coutances d3 182
Couterne e4 182
Couto de Magalhães de Minas g3 291
Coutras b3 186
Coutts h1 262
Couvin c4 159
Couze c4 186
Couzeix d3 186
Cova da Serpe, Sierra da c1 190
Covadonga, Isla a5 295
Covaleda b3 192
Covarrubias g2 190
Covasna, Rom. h3 201
Covasna, Covasna, Rom. h3 201
Covè e4 223
Cove c2 164
Covello h4 297
Cove Mountains c5 256
Covendo d3 292
Coventry, England, U.K. h2 162
Coventry, England, U.K. e4 163
Cover e2 162
Covered Wells g9 263
Covilhã c4 190
Covington, Georgia, U.S.A. h3 259
Covington, Kentucky, U.S.A. d6 254
Covington, Virginia, U.S.A. f7 254
Cowal, Lake e1 83
Cowan, Lake f12 87
Cowansville f6 252
Cowcowing Lakes c12 87
Cowdenbeath e3 164
Cowell c12 81
Cowen f6 254
Cowes, Aust. g15 81
Cowes, U.K. e6 163
Cow Head p4 253
Cowichan Bay b1 262
Cowichan Lake e7 248
Cowley g9 81
Cowlitz b2 262
Cowpasture a6 256
Cowpens j2 259
Cowra j12 81
Cox, Aust. b3 80
Cox, Fr. d5 187
Cox, Spain d6 193
Coxilha de Santana e2 294
Coxilha Grande b7 289
Coxim, Braz. a3 290
Coxim, Mato Grosso do Sul, Braz. a3 290
Cox's Bazar m9 125
Coxwold e2 162
Coya b3 296
Coyah b4 222
Coy Aike c6 295
Coyote Creek b4 264
Coyotillos d3 274
Coyotitán a2 274
Coyuca de Benitez d5 274
Coyuca de Catalán d4 274
Coyutla f3 275
Cozes b3 186
Cozhê h3 135
Cozia, Vârful g3 201
Cozumel r7 273
Craboon j12 81
Crab Orchard National Wildlife Refuge f4 260
Cracow k8 81
Cradle Mountain Ab2 83
Cradle Mountain Lake St Clair National Park Aa2 83
Cradock, Aust. d11 81
Cradock, R.S.A. f6 235
Cradock Channel e2 76
Craig, Alaska, U.S.A. a4 248
Craig, Colorado, U.S.A. b3 260
Craigavon, England, U.K. b1 165
Craigavon, Northern Ireland, U.K. e2 165
Craigellachie e2 164
Craigieburn Forest Park c5 77
Craigmont e2 262
Craignure c3 164
Craik a5 250
Crail f3 164
Crailsheim c2 174
Craiova f3 201
Cramant j4 183
Cranberry Lake, New Jersey, U.S.A. f4 256
Cranberry Lake, New York, U.S.A. j3 255
Cranbourne g15 81
Cranbrook, Aust. c14 87
Cranbrook, Can. k7 249
Cranbrook, U.K. g5 163
Crandon b3 254
Crane c6 261
Crane Lake n6 249
Cranfield Point f2 165
Cranston j3 257
Craolândia c3 288
Craon e5 182
Craonne b5 159
Craponne-sur-Arzon f3 186
Crasna l4 171
Crasnoe j2 201
Crater Lake National Park b4 262
Craters of the Moon National Monument g4 262
Crateús d3 288
Crato, Braz. e3 288
Crato, Port c5 191
Crau a7 185
Craughwell c3 165
Cravant j5 183
Craven Arms d4 163
Cravinhos e4 290
Cravo Norte c2 284
Cravo Sur c3 284
Crawford c3 260
Crawfordjohn e4 164
Crawford Point b5 100
Crawfordsville, Arkansas, U.S.A. d2 258
Crawfordsville, Indiana, U.S.A. c5 254
Crawfordville, Florida, U.S.A. g4 259
Crawfordville, Georgia, U.S.A. h3 259
Crawley f5 163
Crazy Mountains h2 262
Creagorry a2 164
Creal Springs e1 258
Crean Lake p4 249
Crecy h2 235
Crécy-en-Ponthieu g2 183
Crécy-la-Chapelle h4 183
Crécy-sur-Serre b5 159
Credenhill d4 163
Crediton c6 163
Cree q2 249
Creel f4 272
Cree Lake p3 249
Creetown d5 164
Cregganbaun b3 165
Creglingen f3 174
Creighton c3 250
Creil h3 183
Crema d4 196
Crémenes e2 190
Crémieu b5 185
Cremlingen f3 173
Cremona, Italy d4 196
Cremona, Lombardia, Italy e4 196
Créon b4 186
Crepori f5 285
Crépy b5 159
Crépy-en-Valois h3 183
Cres, Cro. f5 177
Cres, Primorje - Gorski Kotar, Cro. f5 177
Cresaptown b5 256
Crescent c4 262
Crescent City a5 262
Crescent Group e2 96
Crescentino c4 196
Crescent Junction j6 263
Crescent Lake National Wildlife Refuge c3 260
Crespo g2 297
Crespos f4 190
Cressensac d3 186
Cresson b4 256
Cresswell Downs b4 80
Cressy c4 82
Crest b6 185
Crestline f7 265
Creston, Can. e1 262
Creston, California, U.S.A. c6 265
Creston, Iowa, U.S.A. e3 260
Creston, Wyoming, U.S.A. b3 260
Crestview, California, U.S.A. e4 264
Crestview, Florida, U.S.A. f4 258
Creswick f14 81
Creta Forata, Monte g3 196
Cretas e4 192
Crete e7 211
Créteil h4 183
Crete, Sea of e7 210
Creuse, Fr. d2 186
Creuse, Limousin, Fr. e2 186
Creußen f3 175
Creuzburg d1 174
Crevalcore f5 196
Crèvecœur-le-Grand h3 183
Crevillente, Spain d6 193
Crevillente, Valencia, Spain d6 193
Crevoladossola c3 196
Crewe d3 162
Crewkerne d6 163
Crianlarich d3 164
Criccieth b4 162
Criciúma c7 289
Crick e4 163
Crickhowell c5 163
Cricklade e5 163
Crieff e3 164
Criel-sur-Mer g2 183
Criffell e5 164
Crikvenica f4 177
Crillon, Mount k4 247
Crimmitschau h2 175
Crimond g2 164
Crinan c3 164
Criquetot-l'Esneval f3 183
Crișan j3 201
Crisfield j7 255
Crissolo b5 196
Cristalândia c4 288
Cristalina e2 290
Cristianópolis d2 290
Cristina f5 291
Cristino Castro d3 288
Cristóbal, Pan. h6 277
Cristóbal, Spain e4 190
Cristóbal Colón, Pico c1 284
Cristóbal, Punta A 286
Cristuru Secuiesc g2 201
Criuleni j2 201
Crivitz, Ger. e5 158
Crivitz, U.S.A. b3 254
Crixás, Braz. c4 288
Crixás, Goiás, Braz. c4 289
Crixás Açu c4 289
Crna b2 210
Crna Gora d4 200
Crni Vrh f3 201
Črni vrh g3 177
Črnomelj g4 177
Croagh Patrick b3 165
Croajingolong National Park f3 83
Croatia h5 144

CROATIA

THE REPUBLIC OF CROATIA
Area 56,610km^2
(21,857sq miles)
Capital Zagreb
Organizations CE, EBRD
Population 4,440,000
Pop. growth (%) -0.6
Life expectancy 69 (m); 77 (f)
Languages Serbo-Croat
Literacy 98.5%
Currency kuna
(US $1 = 6.27 kuna)
GDP (US million $) 22,856
GDP per head ($US) 5147

Croce di Serra, Monte b2 198
Croce, Monte f3 196
Crocker, Banjaran h2 99
Crocker Island l2 86
Crocketford e4 164
Crockett b4 258
Crocq e3 186
Croda Rossa g3 196
Crodo c3 196
Croeira, Serra do c3 288
Crofton f1 258
Croglin d2 162
Croisette, Cap b7 185
Croisic, Pointe de c5 182
Croisilles a4 159
Croix-Rousse b4 196
Crolles b5 185
Cromarty d2 164
Cromberg c2 264
Crombie, Mount k10 87
Cromer h4 162
Cromford e3 162
Cromwell b6 77
Cronce f3 186
Crooked c3 262
Crooked Creek e3 246
Crooked Island g3 266
Crooked Island Passage g3 266
Crooked River b4 250
Crookston e7 250
Crookstown c5 165
Crookwell j13 81
Croom c4 165
Cropalati f5 198
Cropani f6 199
Crosbie f3 80
Crosby, U.K. c3 162
Crosby, Minnesota, U.S.A. g7 250
Crosby, North Dakota, U.S.A. b6 250
Cross f4 223
Cross City h5 259
Cross Fell d2 162
Crossgar f2 165
Cross Harbour l7 259
Cross Inn b4 163
Cross Lake, Manitoba, Can. e3 250
Cross Lake, Manitoba, Can. e3 250
Crossley, Mount d5 77
Crossmaglen e2 165
Crossmolina b2 165
Cross River f4 223
Cross River National Park f4 223
Cross Sound k4 247
Cross Village d3 254
Crossville, Illinois, U.S.A. b6 254

Crossville → Dapiak, Mount 325

Crossville, Tennessee, U.S.A. g2 259
Crossways d5 163
Crosswind Lake h3 247
Croston d3 162
Croswell e4 254
Crothersville d6 254
Crotone, Italy f5 199
Crotone, Calabria, Italy g5 199
Crotto g4 297
Crouch g5 163
Croutelle c2 186
Crouy b5 159
Crowborough g5 163
Crowdy Bay National Park e7 85
Crowl a8 85
Crowley c4 258
Crowley, Lake e4 264
Crown Point, Indiana, U.S.A. c5 254
Crown Point, New York, U.S.A. k4 255
Crown Prince Frederik Island m1 243
Crown Prince Olav Coast k1 298
Crown Princess Martha Coast e2 298
Crows Nest e5 85
Crowsnest Pass k7 249
Croydon, Aust. f5 80
Croydon, U.K. h4 162
Crozet Plateau b8 300
Crozon a4 182
Cruas a6 185
Crucea g2 201
Crucero c2 292
Cruces d2 274
Cruces, Paso de las c3 284
Cruden Bay g2 164
Cruger d3 258
Cruillas k5 273
Crulai f4 183
Crumlin e2 165
Crummock Water c2 162
Cruseilles c4 185
Crusheen c4 165
Crusnes b1 184
Cruz e2 285
Cruz Alta, Arg. g2 297
Cruz Alta, Braz. b7 289
Cruz de Garibay c4 274
Cruz del Eje d2 294
Cruzeiro f5 291
Cruzeiro do Oeste b5 290
Cruzeiro do Sul c1 292
Cruz Grande e5 275
Crvenka d3 200
Crymych b5 163
Crysdale, Mount f4 248
Crystal City, Can. d6 250
Crystal City, Missouri, U.S.A. a6 254
Crystal City, Texas, U.S.A. k3 273
Crystal Falls b2 254
Crystal Lake b4 254
Crystal River h5 259
Crystal Springs d4 258
Csabacsűd j5 171
Csákánydoroszló e5 170
Csákberény g4 171
Csákvár g4 171
Csanádapáca j5 171
Csanádpalota j5 171
Császártöltés h5 171
Csátalja g5 171
Csávoly h5 171
Csengele h5 171
Csenger l4 171
Csengőd h5 171
Cserkeszőlő j5 171
Csernely j3 171
Csesztreg e5 170
Csikéria h5 171
Csókakő g4 171
Csokonyavisonta f5 170
Csongrád, Hung. j5 171
Csongrád, Csongrád, Hung. j5 171
Csorna f4 170
Csorvás j5 171
Csurgó f5 170
Cua d2 190
Cuadrada, Sierra c4 295
Cuadro Berregas c3 296
Cuajinicuilapa e5 275
Cualedro c3 190
Cuamato b2 232
Cuamba f1 233
Cuando c2 232
Cuando Cubango b2 232
Cuangar b2 232
Cuango, Ang. c5 224
Cuango, Cuando Cubango, Ang. b1 232
Cuango, L unda Norte, Ang. c5 224
Cuango, Uige, Ang. c5 224
Cuanza c5 224
Cuanza Norte b5 224
Cuanza Sul c6 224
Cuaro e2 294
Cuaró e2 294
Cuarte de Huerva d3 192
Cuarto f2 297
Cuatir b2 232
Cuatro Ciénegas h4 273
Cuatro Ojos e3 293
Cuatro Vientos e2 296
Cuauhtémoc, Chihuahua, Mex. f3 272
Cuauhtémoc, Colima, Mex. c4 274
Cuautitlán b4 274
Cuautla e4 275
Cuautlán Izcalli e4 275
Cuayuca e4 275
Cuba, Port c6 191
Cuba, Alabama, U.S.A. e3 258
Cuba, New Mexico, U.S.A. b4 261
Cuba, U.S.A. b2 256
Cuba f6 241

CUBA

THE REPUBLIC OF CUBA
Area 110,860km^2 (42,803sq miles)
Capital Havana
Organizations ACS, SELA, LAIA
Population 11,270,000
Pop. growth (%) 0.3
Life expectancy 74 (m); 78 (f)
Languages Spanish
Literacy 97%
Currency Cuban peso (US $1 = 21.00 Cuban peso)
GDP (US million $) 26,052
GDP per head ($US) 2311

Cubagua, Isla e1 284
Cubal, Ang. b6 224
Cubal, Benguela, Ang. a1 232
Cubanea f6 297
Cubango b2 232
Cubara c2 284
Cubatão e5 291
Cubells e3 192
Cub Hills q4 249
Cubia d1 190
Cubillas g7 191
Cubillas, Embalse de g7 191
Cubillo g2 190
Cubo de Bureba a2 192
Çubuk d2 208
Cubulco b3 276
Cuc f3 285
Cucao b4 295
Cucao, Bahía de b4 295
Cucharas f3 275
Cuchi, Ang. b1 232
Cuchi, Cuando Cubango, Ang. b1 232
Cuchilla de Peralta j2 297
Cuchillo-Có e5 296
Cuchivero d2 284
Cuckfield f5 163
Cuckmere g6 163
Čučkovo f4 150
Cucuí d3 284
Cucumbi c6 224
Cucurpe h10 263
Cucurrupí b3 284
Cúcuta c2 284
Cudahy c4 254
Cuddalore f7 126
Cuddapah f5 126
Cuddeback Lake f6 265
Cuddebackville f3 256
Cudillero d1 190
Čudovo a2 150
Cudworth, Can. a4 250
Cudworth, U.K. e3 162
Cue c10 87
Cuebe b2 232
Cueio c2 232
Cuelei b2 232
Cuéllar f3 190
Cuemaní c3 284
Cuemba c6 224
Cuenca, Ec. b4 284
Cuenca, Phil. c4 100
Cuenca, Spain b5 193
Cuenca, Castilla-La Mancha, Spain b4 193
Cuencamé h5 272
Cuenca, Serranía de c4 192
Cuerámaro d3 274
Cuerda del Pozo, Embalse de la b3 192
Cuernavaca e4 275
Cuero a5 258
Cuers c7 185
Cuerva f5 191
Cuervos f9 263
Cuesta Pass c6 265
Cuetzalán f3 275
Cuevas e4 192
Cuevas del Becerro e8 191
Cuevas del Campo b7 193
Cuevas de Vinromá e4 192
Cuevo e4 293
Čufarovo j4 151
Cugir f3 201
Cuglieri Aa2 198
Cugnaux d5 187
Cugo c5 224
Cuhloma g2 151
Cuiabá f3 293
Cuicatlan f5 275
Cuichapa g5 275
Cuijk d3 159
Cuilapa b3 276
Cuilapan f5 275
Cuillin Hills b2 164
Cuillin Sound b2 164
Cuilo c5 224
Cuiluan q2 113
Cuimba b5 224
Cuio a1 232
Cuiseaux b4 184
Cuisery a4 184
Cuitláhuac f4 275
Cuito b2 232
Cuito Cuanavale b2 232
Cuitzeo d4 274
Cuitzeo, Laguna de d4 274
Cuiuni e4 285
Cuixtla f5 275
Cukai c3 101
Čukockij Avtonomnyj Okrug s3 119
Čukockij, Mys u3 119
Čukockij Poluostrov u3 119
Çukurca j4 209
Culai Shan e1 111
Culan e2 186
Culardoch e2 164
Culasi d5 100
Culbertson, Montana, U.S.A. q7 249
Culbertson, Nebraska, U.S.A. c3 260
Culcairn h13 81
Culdaff d1 165
Cul de Sac Bay J 271
Culebras b1 292
Culebra, Sierra de la d3 190
Culemborg d3 159
Culgoa, Aust. b6 85
Culgoa, Victoria, Aust. c2 82
Culiacán f5 272
Culion, Phil. b5 100
Culion, Phil. b5 100
Čulkovo g4 151
Culla d4 192
Cullar b7 193
Cúllar-Baza b7 193
Cullen f2 164
Cullenagh b4 165
Cullen Point e1 80
Cullera d5 193
Cullman f2 258
Cullompton c6 163
Cully a3 196
Culmstock c6 163
Culo de Perro, Punta a8 193
Culoz b5 185
Culpaulin f11 81
Culpeper c6 256
Culpepper, Isla A 286
Culrain d2 164
Culter Fell e4 164
Culuene b4 288
Culver City e8 265
Culverden d5 77
Culver, Point g13 87
Čulym j4 118
Cumã, Baía do d2 288
Cumaná e1 285
Cumanacoa e1 285
Cumaovasi a3 208
Cumare, Cerro c3 284
Cumbal, Nevado de b3 284
Cumberland, Kentucky, U.S.A. h1 259
Cumberland, Kentucky, U.S.A. d7 254
Cumberland, Maryland, U.S.A. b5 256
Cumberland, Virginia, U.S.A. g7 254
Cumberland House b4 250
Cumberland Islands c2 84
Cumberland Lake r4 249
Cumberland, Lake d7 254
Cumberland Plateau g2 259
Cumberland Sound r2 243
Cumbernauld e4 164
Cumbre Alta f5 191
Cumbre Negro b4 295
Cumbres de Majalca, Parque Nacional f3 272
Cumbres de Monterey, Parque Nacional k5 273
Cumbres Mayores d6 191
Cumbria d2 162
Cumbrian Mountains c2 162
Cumbum f5 126
Cuminá f4 285
Cuminapanema a1 288
Cumlosen g2 173
Cummins b13 81
Cumnock d4 164
Cumpas j10 263
Cumpeo b3 296
Cumuripa e3 272
Cumuruxatiba j2 291
Čumyš u1 121
Čuna k4 119
Cunani g3 285
Cuñaré c3 284
Cunco a5 296
Cunderdin c12 87
Cundinamarca c2 284
Cunén b3 276
Cunene, Ang. b2 232
Cunene, Ang. a2 232
Cuneo, Italy b5 196
Cuneo, Piemonte, Italy b5 197
Cung Sơn j9 103
Çüngüş g3 209
Cunha f5 291
Cunhinga, Ang. c6 224
Cunhinga, Bié, Ang. b1 232
Čunja l3 119
Cunlhat f3 186
Cunnamulla g10 81
Cunshamayo b1 292
Cuorgnè b4 196
Cuoyang e2 111
Cuozhen e4 111
Čupa p3 155
Cupar, Can. a5 250
Cupar, U.K. e3 164
Cupica b2 284
Cupica, Golfo de Gu b2 284
Cupra Marittima c1 198
Ćuprija e4 200
Cupula, Pico d5 272
Cuquio c3 274
Curaçá c5 284
Curaça e5 285
Curaçá e3 288
Curaçao d1 284
Curacautín b5 296
Curacaví b2 296
Curacó e5 296
Curahuara de Carangas e3 292
Cura Malal f4 297
Curamalahue a4 296
Curanja c2 292
Curapaligüe f3 297
Čurapča p3 119
Curaray c4 284
Curarrehue b5 296
Curarú f3 297
Curatabaca e2 285
Curaumilla, Punta b2 296
Curaya e1 294
Curbaradó j7 277
Cure j5 183
Curepipe C 231
Curepto a3 296
Curiapo e2 285
Curicó b3 296
Curicó, Lago e6 296
Curicuriari, Serra d4 284
Curieuriari d4 284
Curimata d4 288
Curiñanco a5 296
Curiplaya c3 284
Curitiba d6 290
Curitibanos b7 289
Curiuaú e4 285
Curiúva c6 290
Curlew d1 262
Curlewis d7 85
Curoca a2 232
Curone d5 196
Čurov j2 151
Curraghchase Forest Park c4 165
Curragh, The e3 165
Currais Novos e3 288
Curral das Freiras B 189
Curral de Dentro h1 291
Curralinho c2 288
Currawilla e8 81
Currawinya National Park a6 85
Current, Bah. l7 259
Current, U.S.A. d1 258
Currie c4 82
Currituck h7 255
Currockbilly, Mount g2 83
Curry g3 246
Curtea de Argeş g3 201
Curtici k5 171
Curtina j2 297
Curtis c3 258
Curtis Channel e4 84
Curtis Island d3 84
Curuá, Braz. b3 288
Curuá, Pará, Braz. g4 285
Curuá do Sul b2 288
Curuaés b3 288
Curuaí f4 285
Curuai, Lago Grande do f4 285
Curuá, Ilha b1 288
Curuapanema b2 288
Curuá Una b2 288
Curuçá c2 288
Čurug e3 200
Curumu d2 288
Curup b6 98
Curupira e4 285
Curupira, Serra e3 285
Curuquete d1 292
Cururú e3 293
Cururu f1 293
Cururu Açu f1 293
Cururupu d2 288
Curutú, Cerro e3 285
Curuzú Cuatiá e1 294
Curvelo f3 291
Curza, Punta di A 185
Cusco, Peru c2 292
Cusco, Cusco, Peru c2 292
Cushabatay b5 284
Cushendall b4 164
Cushendun b4 164
Cushing a2 258
Cusiana c3 284
Čusovaja j4 147
Čusovoj j4 146
Cussac-Fort-Médoc b3 186
Cusset f2 186
Cusseta g3 259
Custer, Montana, U.S.A. b2 260
Custer, South Dakota, U.S.A. c3 260
Custines c2 184
Cut Bank g1 262
Cut Bank Creek g1 262
Cutervo, Parque Nacional b1 292
Cuthbert g4 259
Cutlerville d4 254
Cut Off d5 258
Cutral-Co c5 296
Cutro f5 199
Cutrofiano h5 198
Cuttack j9 125
Cuturi e2 285
Cutzamala de Pinzón d4 274
Čuvarlej j4 151
Čuvašskaja Respublika j4 151
Cuvelai b2 232
Cuvette c4 224
Cuvette Ouest b3 224
Cuvier, Cape a9 87
Cuxac-d'Aude e5 187
Cuxhaven b5 158
Cuya c3 292
Cuyahoga Falls f5 254
Cuyama c6 265
Cuyapo c3 100
Cuyo, Phil. c5 100
Cuyo, Phil. c5 100
Cuyo East Passage c5 100
Cuyo Islands c5 100
Cuyo West Passage c5 100
Cuyuní e2 285
Cuyuni-Mazaruni f2 285
Cuyutlán b4 274
Cuzco b1 292
Cuzna f6 191
Cwmbran c5 163
Cyangugu e4 225
Cybinka c3 168
Cyców m4 169
Cygnet Ab3 83
Cynthiana d6 254
Cynwyl Elfed b5 163
Cyp-Navolok p2 155
Cypress c4 258
Cypress Hills n7 249
Cyprus a5 92

CYPRUS

THE REPUBLIC OF CYPRUS
Area 9251km^2 (3572sq miles)
Capital Nicosia
Organizations COMM, EBRD
Population 710,000
Pop. growth (%) 1.1
Life expectancy 75 (m); 80 (f)
Languages Greek, Turkish
Literacy 97.6%
Currency Cyprus pound (US $1 = 0.47 Cyprus pound)
GDP (US million $) 10,186
GDP per head ($US) 14,346

Cyrenaica b2 218
Cyrene b1 218
Czaplinek e2 168
Czarna Białostocka m2 169
Czarna Dąbrówka f1 168
Czarna Woda g2 168
Czarne e2 168
Czarnków e3 168
Czarny Dunajec h6 169
Czchów j6 169
Czech Republic h5 144

CZECH REPUBLIC

THE CZECH REPUBLIC
Area 78,864km^2 (30,450sq miles)
Capital Prague
Organizations CE, CEFTA, EBRD, NATO, OECD
Population 10,224,000
Pop. growth (%) -0.1
Life expectancy 70 (m); 77 (f)
Languages Czech, German and others
Literacy 99%
Currency Czech koruna (US $1 = 26.19 Czech koruna)
GDP (US million $) 72,500
GDP per head ($US) 7091

Czekarzewice k4 169
Czempiń e3 168
Czeremcha m3 169
Czerna Wielka d4 168
Czernica f4 168
Czerniejewo f3 168
Czersk f2 168
Czerwieńsk d3 168
Czerwin k3 169
Czerwionka-Leszczyny g5 168
Częstochowa h5 169
Człopa e2 168
Człuchów f2 168
Czorneboh k4 175
Czyżew-Osada l3 169

D

Da'an n3 113
Daanbantayan d5 100
Daan Viljoen Game Park b1 234
Dåasen f2 156
Daba d4 130
Dabajuro c1 284
Dabakala d4 222
Daban Shan a7 112
Dabas h4 171
Daba Shan g2 104
Dabat e5 219
Dabatou b3 222
Dabeiba j7 277
Dabeibu e5 111
Dabeji c8 129
Dabel e5 158
Dabhoi f9 129
Dabhol c4 126
Dąbie, Lubuskie, Pol. d3 168
Dąbie, Wielkopolskie, Pol. g3 168
Dabie Shan d4 106
Ḍab'ī, Wādī aḍ e5 139
Dablana g8 129
Dabo d2 184
Dabola b3 222
Dabong c3 101
Dabou d4 222
Daboya d4 222
Dabra f7 124
Dąbroszyn c3 168
Dąbrowa Białostocka m2 169
Dąbrowa Chełmińska g2 168
Dąbrowa Górnicza h5 169
Dąbrowa Tarnowska j5 169
Dabs Nur m3 113
Dăbuleni g4 201
Dacarbudhug c2 226
Dachang f3 111
Dachau e2 175
Dachechang a6 112
Dachepalle f4 126
Dačice d2 170
Dad g4 171
Dadaj, Jezioro j2 169
Dadanawa f3 285
Daday d2 208
Daddato f5 219
Dade City h5 259
Dadès, Oued c2 220
Dadeville g3 259
Dadhar c6 129
Dadianji e3 111
Dadou d5 187
Dadra and Nagar Haveli c2 126
Dadu c7 129
Dadu He d4 104
Dadukou e4 111
Da Dung h10 103
Daedalus Reef e2 219
Daet d3 100
Dafang e5 104
Dafeng g3 111
Dafla Hills n6 125
Dafnes b4 210
Dafni, Dytiki Ellas, Grc. c5 211
Dafni, Kentriki Makedonia, Grc. e2 210
Dafni, Peloponnisos, Grc. c6 211
Dafnoudi, Akra a4 210
Dafoe a5 250
Dafu f5 111
Dág g4 171
Dag g9 129
Daga Medo c2 226
Dagana a2 222
Dagang g4 111
Dagcanglhamo d1 104
Dagda m4 157
Dagebüll b4 158
Dagestan, Respublika g4 149
Dagg Sound a6 77
Dağkızılca a3 208
Daglet Lagrouba f2 221
Daglung k5 135
Dagnino, Isla a6 295
Dagshai c4 130
Dagu j6 113
Dagua l6 97
Daguan d5 104
Dagu He g1 111
Daguokui Shan q3 113
Dagupan c2 100
Dagur p1 125
Dagwin c6 102
Dagzê m5 125
Dagzê Co h4 135
Dagzhuka j5 135
Dahab e7 136
Dahaneh-ye Ghowri d3 128
Dahanu c3 126
Daheiding Shan q1 113
Dahei He f5 112
Dahei Shan n4 113
Dahezhen s2 113
Dahina c5 130
Da Hinggan Ling l3 113
Dahin, Ḥarrāt ad f4 218
Dahlak Archipelago f4 219
Dahlak Marine National Park f4 219
Dahle j4 173
Dahlem e4 159
Dahlen j4 173
Dahlenburg f2 173
Dahlia d2 232
Dahme, Ger. j4 173
Dahme, Brandenburg, Ger. j4 173
Dahme, Schleswig-Holstein, Ger. e4 158
Dahm, Ramlat g4 219
Dahn e2 174
Dahod g9 129
Dahongliutan d2 130
Dahongqi m5 113
Dähre f3 173
Dahūk j4 209
Dahushan m5 113
Daibu f4 111
Daicheng j6 113
Daigo j3 115
Dai Hai g5 112
Daik c5 98
Daik-u c7 102
Dā'il e4 138
Dailamin Sum h3 112
Dailekh e5 130
Daimanji-san e4 114
Daimiel g5 191
Daimonia c6 211
Daingerfield b3 258
Dainichiga-take g4 115
Dainkog a2 104
Daintree National Park A 84
Daiquiri g5 266
Daira Din Panah e5 128
Daireaux g4 297
Dairût c8 136
Dai-sen e4 114
Daisen-Oki National Park e3 114
Daishan h4 111
Daixian g6 112
Dajal e6 129
Dajarra d6 80
Dajin Chuan d3 104
Dajindian c2 106
Dajing c7 112
Dajt d5 200
Da Juh p1 125
Daka d4 222
Dakar a3 222
Dakelangsi j5 135
Dakeng k5 105
Dakengkou j6 105
Daketa Shet' c2 226
Dakhin Shahbazpur Island m8 125
Dakhlet Nouâdhibou, Maurit. a4 220
Dakhlet Nouâdhibou, Maurit. a4 220
Dakingari e3 223
Đak Nghe j8 103
Dakoank n9 127
Dakor f9 129
Dakoro, Burkina c3 222
Dakoro, Niger f3 223
Dakota City d3 260
Dakou c2 106
Đakovica e4 200
Đakovo d3 200
Dakuang g1 111
Dákura f3 277
Dakwa e3 225
Dala d6 224
Dalaas b2 176
Dalaba b3 222
Dalai Nur j4 113
Dālaki n7 137
Dalamamiao g5 112
Dalaman b4 208
Dalandzadgad c4 112
Dalane b3 156
Dalanganem Islands c5 100
Dalaoba u7 121
Dalarna f2 156
Dalarö h3 157
Dalat f3 98
Đa Lat j10 103
Dalauda g9 129
Dalay b4 112
Dalbandin b6 129
Dalbeattie e5 164
Dalbosjön e3 156
Dalby, Aust. k9 81
Dalby, Fyn, Den. d3 158
Dalby, Den. f3 158
Dalby, Swe. e5 156
Dalbyover d2 158
Dalcahue b4 294
Dale, Hordaland, Nor. a2 156
Dale, Sogn og Fjordane, Nor. a2 156
Dale City c6 256
Dale Hollow Lake d7 254
Dalen b3 156
Daleszyce j5 169
Dalet a6 102
Daletme n9 125
Dalfsen e2 159
Dalgaranger, Mount c11 87
Dalhart c4 261
Dalholen c1 156
Dalhousie, Can. j4 253
Dalhousie, India c3 130
Dalhousie, Cape m1 247
Dali, Shaanxi, China b2 106
Dali, Yunnan, China e3 102
Dalian l6 113
Daliang Shan d4 104
Dalías b8 193
Dali He a1 106
Daliji e3 111
Dalin m4 113
Daling He k5 113
Daliyat el Karmil d4 138
Daliyuan e3 111
Dalizi p5 113
Dalj d3 200
Dalkeith e4 164
Dalkola k7 125
Dal Lake b2 130
Dallas, Georgia, U.S.A. g3 259
Dallas, North Carolina, U.S.A. j2 259
Dallas, Pennsylvania, U.S.A. e3 256
Dallas, Texas, U.S.A. a3 258
Dallastown d5 256
Dall Island l5 247
Dall Lake d3 246
Dall, Mount f3 246
Dallol Bosso e2 223
Dallol Foga e3 223
Dall Villaby c2 158
Dalmacio Vélez Sarsfield f2 297
Dalmally d3 164
Dalmatia d4 256
Dalmatovo k4 147
Dalmellington d4 164
Dalmine d4 196
Dal'nee Konstantinovo h4 151
Dal'negorsk k4 94
Dal'nerechensk s3 113
Dal'nie Zelency r2 155
Daloa c4 222
Dalou Shan f4 104
Dalrymple, Lake b2 84
Dalrymple, Mount c2 85
Dalsjöfors e4 156
Dals Långed e3 156
Daltenganj j7 125
Dalton, R.S.A. j4 235
Dalton, Georgia, U.S.A. g2 259
Dalton, Massachusetts, U.S.A. g2 257
Dalton-in-Furness c2 162
Dalua c4 165
Daludalu b5 101
Daluo Shan j7 105
Dalupiri c1 100
Dalvík A 152
Dalwallinu c12 87
Dalwhinnie d3 164
Daly k4 86
Daly City a4 264
Dalyokiya m5 157
Daly Waters a4 80
Dam d3 288
Dāmā e4 138
Damachava m4 169
Damagaram Takaya f3 223
Damagum g3 223
Damalisques de Leshwe d1 233
Daman c9 124
Daman and Diu b2 126
Damanava p3 169
Dāmaneh n5 137
Damanhûr c6 136
Damaq m4 137
Damaqun Shan h5 112
Damar f9 100
Damara c3 224
Damaraland b1 234
Damasak g3 223
Damascus, Dimashq (City), Syria e3 138
Damascus, Syria e3 138
Damascus, Arkansas, U.S.A. c2 258
Damascus, Maryland, U.S.A. c5 256
Damascus, Pennsylvania, U.S.A. e3 256
Damascus, Virginia, U.S.A. j1 259
Damasi c3 210
Damaskinia b2 210
Damasławek f3 168
Damaturu g3 223
Damauli g6 135
Damazan c4 187
Damba c5 224
Dambach-la-Ville d2 184
Dambai e4 223
Dambatta f3 223
Damboa g3 223
Dâmbovița g3 201
Dambulla g9 126
Damdy k2 120
Dameleivières c2 184
Dame Marie g5 266
Damghan q3 137
Daming d1 106
Daming Shan g7 104
Dāmiyā d4 139
Dammai c8 100
Dammarie g4 183
Dammarie-les-Lys h4 183
Dammartin-en-Goële h3 183
Dammastock c3 196
Damme d3 172
Damoh f8 124
Damongo d4 222
Damour d3 138
Dampelas, Tanjung k4 99
Dampier c7 86
Dampier Archipelago c7 86
Dampier Land f5 86
Dampierre b3 184
Dampierre-sur-Linotte c3 184
Dampierre-sur-Salon b3 184
Dampit g9 98
Dam Qu n3 125
Damville g4 183
Damvillers d5 159
Damxung m4 125
Dan g7 254
Dănă d6 139
Dana f5 135
Dañador a6 193
Dana, Mount d4 264
Danané c4 222
Đa Năng j7 102
Danao e5 100
Dana Point f8 265
Danata q2 137
Danba c3 104
Danbazhai a1 106
Danbury, Connecticut, U.S.A. g3 257
Danbury, North Carolina, U.S.A. f7 254
Dancheng d3 106
Dandaragan b12 87
Dande, Ang. b5 224
Dande, Eth. b3 226
Dandel'dhura e5 130
Dandeli d5 126
Dandenong g14 81
Dande Safari Area e2 233
Dandong n5 113
Dandot f4 128
Dandridge h1 259
Dane d3 162
Danеți g4 201
Danfeng b3 106
Danforth j6 253
Dangan Liedao k8 105
Dangbizhen r3 113
Dangchang e1 104
Dange c5 224
Danger Point c7 234
Dangé-St-Romain f6 183
Danggali Conservation Park b1 82
Danghara d1 128
Dangila e5 219
Dangori p6 125
Dangqên m4 125
Dangriga c2 276
Dangshan e2 106
Dangtu f4 111
Dan-Gulbi f3 223
Dangur, Eth. e5 219
Dangur, Eth. e4 219
Dangur, Benishangul, Eth. e5 219
Dangyang b4 106
Daniel Donovan d2 296
Daniel, Serra a4 288
Daniel's Harbour p3 253
Daniëlskuil e4 234
Danielson j3 257
Danielsville h2 259
Danilov f2 150
Danilovka n1 121
Danilovskaja Vozvyšennost' f2 150
Daning, Guangxi Zhuangzu Zizhiqu, China h6 104
Daning, Shanxi, China b1 106
Dänischenhagen d4 158
Dänizkänarı h4 149
Danjiangkou b3 106
Danjiangkou Shuiku b3 106
Danjo-guntō c5 114
Danjoutin c3 184
Dankhar d3 130
Dankov e5 150
Dankova, Pik r7 121
Danlí d3 276
Danling d3 104
Dannemarie d3 184
Dannemora g2 157
Dannenberg (Elbe) g2 173
Dannenwalde j2 173
Dannevirke f4 76
Dannewerk c4 158
Dannhauser j4 235
Dano d3 222
Dañoso, Cabo c5 295
Dan Sai e7 102
Danson Bay b7 102
Dansville c2 256
Danta, Gujarat, India f8 129
Danta, Rajasthan, India b6 130
Dantewara g3 126
Dantu f3 111
Danube e1 176
Danumparai h4 99
Danvers k2 257
Danville, California, U.S.A. b4 264
Danville, Georgia, U.S.A. h3 259
Danville, Illinois, U.S.A. c5 254
Danville, Kentucky, U.S.A. g1 259
Danville, Pennsylvania, U.S.A. d4 256
Danville, Virginia, U.S.A. g7 254
Danyang f4 111
Danzhou g9 104
Dao c5 100
Dão c5 190
Daocheng c4 104
Daodou'ao h4 111
Daoshiping b4 106
Daotanghe a7 112
Daotian f1 111
Daotou g1 111
Daoukro d4 222
Daoxian h6 104
Daozhen f4 104
Dapa f6 100
Dapaong e3 223
Daphabum c2 102
Daphne f4 258
Dapiak, Mount d6 100

DENMARK

THE KINGDOM OF DENMARK
Area 43,094km^2 (16,639sq miles)
Capital Copenhagen
Organizations CE, EBRD, EU, NATO, OECD
Population 5,350,000
Pop. growth (%) 0.3
Life expectancy 73 (m); 78 (f)
Languages Danish
Literacy 99%
Currency Danish Krone (US $1 = 6.06 Danish Krone)
GDP (US million $) 179,800
GDP per head ($US) 33,607

DJIBOUTI

THE REPUBLIC OF DJIBOUTI
Area 23,200km² (8,958sq miles)
Capital Djibouti
Organizations COMESA, LAS, OIC
Population 690,000
Pop. growth (%) 4.1
Life expectancy 44 (m); 47 (f)
Languages Arabic, French
Literacy 67.9%
Currency Djibouti franc (US $1 = 175 Djibouti franc)
GDP (US million $) 587
GDP per head ($US) 850

EAST TIMOR

THE DEMOCRATIC REPUBLIC OF EAST TIMOR
Area 14,874km² (5,741sq miles)
Capital Dili
Organizations n/a
Population 884,000
Pop. growth (%) 1.7
Life expectancy 46 (m); 48 (f)
Languages Portuguese, Tetum, Bahasa Indonesia
Literacy 48%
Currency US dollar
GDP (US million $) 403
GDP per head ($US) 455

Ecker → Elyria 329

Ecker b5 295
Eckernförde c4 158
Eckernförder Bucht f1 172
Eckerö h2 157
Éclaron-Braucourt-Ste-Livière a2 184
Écommoy f5 183
Ecoporanga h3 291
Écos g3 183
Écouen h3 183
Écrins, Parc National des c6 185
Ecuador c3 282

ECUADOR

THE REPUBLIC OF ECUADOR
Area 272,045km² (105,037sq miles)
Capital Quito
Organizations Andean Comm, IADB, SELA, LAIA
Population 12,156,608
Pop. growth (%) 1.7
Life expectancy 67 (m); 72 (f)
Languages Spanish, Quechua, other local languages
Literacy 92.4%
Currency US dollar
GDP (US million $) 20,800
GDP per head ($US) 1711

Ecuandureo c3 273
Écueillé g5 183
Écury-sur-Coole a2 184
Ed, Erit. f5 219
Ed, Swe. d3 156
Edam d2 159
Eday f1 164
Ed Da'ein c5 218
Ed Dair, Jebel d5 218
Ed Damazin d5 218
Ed Damer d4 218
Ed Debba d4 218
Eddrachillis Bay c1 164
Ed Dueim d5 218
Eddystone Point Ac2 82
Eddyville, Kentucky, U.S.A. e1 258
Eddyville, New York, U.S.A. f3 257
Ede, Neth. d2 159
Ede, Nig. e4 223
Edéa g5 223
Edéia d2 290
Edelény j3 171
Edemissen f3 172
Eden, Aust. j14 81
Eden, England, U.K. d2 162
Eden, U.K. c5 164
Eden, Mississippi, U.S.A. d3 258
Eden, Texas, U.S.A. d6 261
Edenbridge g5 163
Edenburg f4 235
Edendale, N.Z. b7 77
Edendale, R.S.A. j4 235
Edenderry d3 165
Eden, Mount C 77
Eden, Tanjung p8 99
Edenton h7 255
Edenville g3 235
Eder d4 172
Edermünde f1 174
Edesheim g3 174
Edessa c2 210
Edevik d5 154
Edewecht c2 172
Edgar, Mount e7 86
Edgar Ranges f6 86
Edgartown k3 257
Edgecumbe f2 76
Edgeley d7 250
Edgemont c3 260
Edgeøya c2 118
Edgeroi j11 81
Edgewater j5 259
Edgewood, Illinois, U.S.A. b6 254
Edgewood, Maryland, U.S.A. d5 256
Edgeworthstown d3 165
Edievale b6 77
Edinboro f5 254
Edinburg, Indiana, U.S.A. d6 254
Edinburg, Mississippi, U.S.A. e3 258
Edinburg, North Dakota, U.S.A. e6 250
Edinburg, Texas, U.S.A. k4 273
Edinburg, Virginia, U.S.A. b6 256
Edinburgh, Scotland, U.K. f3 164
Edinburgh, Scotland, U.K. e4 164
Edincik a2 208
Edineţ h1 201
Edirne, Tur. a2 208
Edirne, Edirne, Tur. h5 201
Edison g4 259
Edisto j3 259
Edith Cavell, Mount h5 248
Edith, Mount h2 262
Edjeleh f3 221
Édjérir e2 223
Edjudina f11 87
Edlitz h2 177
Edmond a2 258
Edmonds b2 262
Edmonton, Aust. g4 80
Edmonton, Can. l5 249
Edmore d6 250
Edmund Kennedy National Park A 84
Edmund Lake g3 250
Edmundston h5 253
Edna a5 258
Edna Bay a4 248
Edo f4 223
Edolo e3 196
Edremit a3 208
Edroso d3 190
Edrovo b3 150
Edsbro h3 157
Edsbruk g3 156
Edsbyn f2 156
Edson j5 249
Eduardo Castex e3 297
Eduni, Mount n2 247
Edward d2 82
Edward, Lake e4 225
Edward, Mount k8 87
Edwards d3 258
Edward's Creek b10 81
Edwards Plateau c6 261
Edward VIII Bay m1 298
Edward VII Peninsula cc2 298
Edzell f3 164
Edziza, Mount, Can. b3 248
Edziza, Mount, U.S.A. m4 247
Edzouga b4 224
Eek d3 246
Eeklo b3 159
Eel a2 264
Eem d2 159
Eenzamheidpan d3 234
Eerbeek e2 159
Éfaté F 74
Eferding f1 177
Effingham b6 254
Efimovskij c2 150
Eflâni d2 208
Efpali b4 210
Efrata d5 139
Efremov e5 150
Efringen-Kirchen d3 174
Efxeinoupoli c3 210
Eg f1 112
Ega b2 192
Egana h4 297
Egan Range f6 263
Egebæk b3 158
Egegik e4 246
Egeln g4 173
Egenolf Lake d1 250
Egense d2 158
Eger j4 171
Egerbakta j4 171
Egeria Point c10 98
Egernsund c4 158
Egersund b3 156
Egerton, Mount c9 87
Egestorf f2 172
Egg a2 176
Eggebek c4 158
Eggedøla c2 156
Eggegebirge d4 172
Eggenburg g1 177
Eggenfelden d1 176
Eggenstein-Leopoldshafen c5 174
Eggesin k2 173
Egg Harbor City f5 256
Eggingen d3 174
Egg Island Point e5 256
Eggiwil b3 196
Egg Lake q4 249
Egglham e1 176
Eggolsheim d5 175
Eggum d2 154
Eghezée c4 159
Egholm e3 158
Egilsstaðir A 152
Eginbah d7 86
Egindy q2 121
Eğirdir c4 208
Eğirdir Gölü c3 208
Egkomi b1 138
Egletons e3 186
Eglinton d1 165
Eglinton Island f1 242
Eglukalns m5 151
Eglwys Fach c4 163
Egmont, Cape d3 76
Egmont National Park e3 76
Egna f3 196
Egor'evsk e4 150
Egorlyk f3 148
Egremont c2 162
Égreville h4 183
Eğrigöz Dağı b3 208
Egsmark d2 158
Egtved c3 158
Egua d2 284
Éguas c4 288
Éguilles b7 185
Éguzon-Chantôme d2 186
Egyek j4 171
Egyházaskozár g5 171
Egyházasrádóc e4 170
Egypt e2 216

EGYPT

THE ARAB REPUBLIC OF EGYPT
Area 997,739km² (385,229sq miles)
Capital Cairo
Organizations COMESA, LAS, OAPEC, OIC
Population 70,510,000
Pop. growth (%) 1.8
Life expectancy 64 (m); 68 (f)
Languages Arabic, English, French
Literacy 57.7%
Currency Egyptian pound (US $1 = 6.16 Egyptian pound)
GDP (US million $) 77,504
GDP per head ($US) 1099

Ehime e5 114
Ehingen g3 175
Ehingen (Donau) f3 174
Ehle h3 173
Ehmej d2 138
Ehra-Lessien f3 173
Ehrenberg Range k8 87
Ehrenhausen g3 177
Ehrwald b2 176
Ehu e5 111
Eiao K 75
Eibar b1 192
Eibelstadt f3 174
Eibenstock h2 175
Eibergen e2 159
Eibiswald g3 177
Eibsee f5 175
Eichenbarleben g3 173
Eichendorf d1 176
Eichenzell e2 174
Eichgraben g1 177
Eichstätt f3 175
Eichwalde j3 173
Eide a5 154
Eider e1 172
Eidfjord b2 156
Eidsdal b1 156
Eidsvåg b5 154
Eidsvold k8 81
Eidsvoll d2 156
Eifel b3 174
Eigerøya a3 156
Eigg b3 164
Eight Degree Channel c9 126
Eights Coast hh2 298
Eighty Mile Beach e6 86
Eijsden d4 159
Eikesdalsvatnet b5 154
'Eilabun d4 138
Eildon d3 82
Eildon, Lake e3 83
Eildon State Park d3 82
Eilean nan Each b3 164
Eilenburg h4 173
Eilerts de Haan Gebergte f3 285
Eilerts de Haan, Natuurreservaat f3 285
Eilsleben g3 173
Eimke f3 172
Eina d2 156
Einasleigh, Queensland, Aust. g5 80
Einasleigh, Queensland, Aust. f4 80
Einbeck e4 172
Eindhoven d3 159
Einsiedeln c2 196
Ein Yahav d6 139
Eirunepé d1 292
Eisberg e4 172
Eiseb b3 232
Eisenach g2 174
Eisenberg d3 175
Eisenberg (Pfalz) f2 174
Eisenerz f2 177
Eisenerzer Alpen f2 177
Eisenhüttenstadt k3 173
Eisenstadt h2 177
Eisenwurzen f2 177
Eisfeld e2 175
Eišiškės n1 169
Eisleben Lutherstadt g4 173
Eiterfeld e2 174
Eivissa, Spain f6 193
Eivissa, Islas Baleares, Spain f6 193
Eja b3 190
Ejby, Fyn, Den. c3 158
Ejby, Roskilde, Den. e3 158
Ejea de los Caballeros c2 192
Ejeda Aa3 233
Ejido c2 284
Ejido El Guaje h3 272
Ejmiatsin k2 209
Ejsk e3 148
Ejstrupholm c3 158
Ejulve d4 192
Ejura d4 222
Ejutla f5 275
Ekaterinburg k4 147
Ekenäs k3 157
Ekenäskärgårds nationalpark k3 157
Eket f5 223
Eketahuna e4 76
Ekibastuz q2 121
Ekimoviči b4 150
Ekiti f4 223
Eklingji f8 129
Ekö g4 156
Ekoli d4 224
Ekoln g3 156
Ekouamou c3 224
Eksjö f4 156
Eksteenfontein b4 234
Ekuk e4 246
Ekuku d4 224
Ekwan m4 251
Ekwok e4 246
Ela c6 102
El Abanico b4 296
El Abiodh Sidi Cheikh e2 221
Elabuga l4 151
Elafonisos c6 211
Elafonisou, Steno c6 211
El Aguaje c4 274
El Aïn e2 138
Elaiochori e2 210
El 'Aiyat c7 136
El 'Alamein c1 218
El Alamito e2 275
El Alamo e10 263
El Alcihuatl b4 274
El Algar d7 193
El Alia f2 221
El Alquián b8 193
El Alto a4 284
El 'Amirîya c1 218
Elan', Sverdlovskaja Oblast', Russ. Fed. k4 147
Elan', Volgogradskaja Oblast', Russ. Fed. f2 149
Elands h2 235
El Arahal e7 191
El Arco c3 272
El Aricha d2 220
El 'Arîsh b5 139
Elasa g7 211
El Ashmûnein c8 136
Elassona c3 210
El Astillero g1 190
Elat c7 139
El 'Aûf a4 220
Elati, Dytiki Makedonia, Grc. b3 210
Elati, Ionioi Nisoi, Grc. a4 210
Elati, Thessalia, Grc. b3 210
Elatia c4 210
Elat'ma f4 150
Elato G 74
Elatochori c2 210
Elaur k5 151
Elazığ, Tur. g3 209
Elazığ, Elazığ, Tur. g3 209
El Badâri c8 136
El Bahsas d2 138
Elba, Isola d' e7 197
El Balata d4 139
El Ballâh d6 136
El Balyana c8 136
El'ban k2 94
El Banco c2 284
El Barranco e2 275
El Barril c2 274
El Barun d5 218
Elbasan e5 200
Elbașı e3 208
El Bauga d4 218
El Baúl d2 284
El Bayadh e2 221
Elbe e2 172
Elbe-Havel-Kanal g3 173
'Elb el Fçâl c4 220
Elberta c3 254
Elbert, Mount b4 260
Elberton h2 259
Elbe-Seitenkanal f3 173
Elbeuf g3 183
El Bierzo d2 190
El Billete, Cerro d4 274
Elbingerode (Harz) f4 173
Elbląg h1 169
Elbląski, Kanał h2 169
El Bluff f4 277
El Bodón d4 190
El Boldo a3 296
El Bolsón b4 294
El Bonillo b6 193
El Bordo c2 274
El Borma f2 221
El Bozal d2 274
El Brasil j4 273
El'brus f4 149
El Buheyrat e2 225
El Bullaque f5 191
Elburg d2 159
El Burgo f8 191
El Burgo de Ebro d3 192
El Burgo de Osma a3 192
El Burgo Ranero e2 190
El Burj c5 139
El Burrito c2 274
El Cabaco d4 190
El Cabo de Gata b8 193
El Cain c4 294
El Cajon g9 265
El Callao e2 285
El Camaineiro, Laguna c2 274
El Campo a5 258
El Caño j3 297
El Canton c2 284
El Capitan d4 264
El Capitan Mountain b5 261
El Carmen, Beni, Bol. e2 293
El Carmen, Bol. f3 293
El Carmen, Chile b4 296
El Carmen, Ec. b4 284
El Carmen, Ven. d3 284
El Caroche d5 193
El Carpio, Embalse de f7 191
El Carrizal d5 274
El Casco g5 272
El Castellar d3 192
El Castillo de las Guardas d7 191
El Cebú, Cerro h6 275
El Ceibal b2 276
El Centenillo g6 191
El Centro f9 263
El Cerro e3 293
El Cerro de Andévalo d7 191
El Chaparro d2 285
El Chapulín e2 275
El Charco f3 272
Elche d6 193
Elche de la Sierra b6 193
El Chichón g5 275
El Chichonal h5 275
El Chico, Parque Nacional e3 275
El Chilicote g3 272
Elchingen e4 174
Elcho Island c1 80
Elciego b2 192
El Cocuy, Parque Nacional c2 284
El Colomo b4 274
El Coronil e7 191
El Coyol g6 275
El Coyolito g5 275
El Cozén g10 263
El Cubo de Don Sancho d4 190
El Cubo de Tierra del Vino e3 190
El Cuervo d8 191
El Cuyo r7 273
Elda d6 193
El Dab'a c1 218
El Dátil g11 263
Elde h2 173
Elderwood d5 265
El Diamante h3 272
El Difícil c2 284
El'dikan p3 119
Eldingen f3 172
El Divisadero b4 274
El Diviso b3 284
El Divisorio g5 297
El Doctor f10 263
Eldon e4 260
El Dorado, Arg. g3 297
Eldorado, Arg. g5 293
Eldorado, Mato Grosso do Sul, Braz. a5 290
Eldorado, São Paulo, Braz. d6 290
El Dorado, Col. c3 284
El Dorado, Mex. f5 272
El Dorado, Arkansas, U.S.A. c3 258
Eldorado, Illinois, U.S.A. e1 258
El Dorado, Kansas, U.S.A. a1 258
Eldorado, Texas, U.S.A. c6 261
El Dorado, Ven. e2 285
Eldoret b3 226
Eldred, New York, U.S.A. f3 256
Eldred, Pennsylvania, U.S.A. b3 256
Eldridge, Mount j2 247
El Durazno e4 296
Eleanor f6 254
Elec e1 148
Eleckij l2 147
Electric Peak h3 262
Elefsina d4 210
Eleftheres e2 210
Eleftheroupoli e2 210
Eleja k4 157
El Ejido b8 193
Elektrėnai n1 169
Elektrostal' e4 150
Elena g4 201
Elena, Lago b5 295
El Encanto c4 284
El Encino e2 275
Elenskij c5 150
Eleodoro Lobos d2 296
El Epazote d2 274
Elephant Butte Reservoir b5 261
Elephant Island mm1 298
Elephant Point m9 125
Éléphants de Kaniama, Réserve des e5 225
Éléphants de Sakania, Réserve Partielle aux e6 225
Eleshnitsa f5 201
Eleşkirt j3 209
El Espinar f4 190
El Estor c3 276
El Eucaliptus j1 297
El Eulma f1 221
Eleuthera l7 259
Eleven Point d1 258
El Faiyûm c7 136
El Fașayil d4 139
El Fasher c5 218
El Fashn c7 136
El Fawwâr d5 139
Elfershausen f3 174
Elfin Cove k4 247
El Fluvià g2 192
El Francolí f3 192
El Fud c2 226
El Fuerte e4 272
El Funduq d4 139
Elgå d1 156
El Gaià f3 192
El Gallo d3 274
El Gancho a3 276
El Geneina b5 218
El Geteina d5 218
El Gezira d5 218
El Ghalla, Wadi C5 218
El Ghandouriyé d3 138
Elgin, U.K. e2 164
Elgin, U.S.A. c7 250
El'ginskij q3 119
El Gîza c7 136
El'gjaj m3 119
El Gogorrón, Parque Nacional d3 274
Elgoibar b1 192
El Goléa e2 221
El Golfo de Santa Clara f10 263
Elgon, Mount f3 225
Elgoras, Gora n2 155
El Grado e2 192
El Grullo, Jalisco, Mex. b4 274
El Grullo, Tamaulipas, Mex. k5 273
El Guanal h5 275
El Guante g2 272
El Hadjar f1 221
Elham h5 163
El Hamma f2 221
El Hammâm c1 218
El Ḥammâmi b4 220
El Hank d3 220
El Hasira d5 218
El Hato del Volcán f6 277
El Hawâmdîya c7 136
El Heiz c2 218
El Herrumblar c5 193
El Hierro Aa3 189
El Higo e3 275
El Hilla c5 218
El Homr e3 221
El Hoyo de Pinares f4 190
El Huecu b4 296
Eli 'Al d4 138
Elias Garcia d5 224
Elias Piña j5 271
Elie de Beaumont c5 77
Elifaz d7 139
Elika c6 211
Elikonas c4 210
Elila, D.R.C. e4 225
Elila, Maniema, D.R.C. e4 225
Elim d2 246
El Infiernillo d4 274
Elingampangu d4 224
Elin Pelin f4 201
Elipa d4 224
Eliseu Martins d3 288
Elista g3 149
Elizabeth, Aust. d13 81
Elizabeth, Illinois, U.S.A. a4 254
Elizabeth, New Jersey, U.S.A. f4 257
Elizabeth, West Virginia, U.S.A. f6 254
Elizabeth, Bahía A 286
Elizabeth Bay a3 234
Elizabeth City h7 255
Elizabeth Islands k3 257
Elizabeth, Mount h5 86
Elizabeth Point a3 234
Elizabethton h1 259
Elizabethtown, North Carolina, U.S.A. k2 259
Elizabethtown, Pennsylvania, U.S.A. d4 256
Elizabethville d4 256
Elizabeth, Volcán c5 295
Elizarovo h2 151
Elizavety, Mys l2 94
Elizondo c1 192
El Jacuixtle b2 274
El Jadida c2 220
El Jaralito g4 272
Eljas d4 190
El Jazmin e3 275
El Jebelein d5 218
El Jem g1 221
El Jicaral d4 276
El Jicaro d4 276
El Jilguero d5 274
El Juile g5 275
Ełk l2 169
Elk, Maryland, U.S.A. f6 254
Elk, Tennessee, U.S.A. f2 258
El Kab d4 218
El Kamlin d4 218
Elk City d5 261
Elk Creek a2 264
El Kelaâ des Srarhna c2 220
l Kerē c2 226
Elk Garden a5 256
Elk Grove b3 264
El Khandaq d4 218
El Khârga c9 136
El Kharrûba b5 139
Elkhart, Indiana, U.S.A. d5 254
Elkhart, Texas, U.S.A. b4 258
El Khnâchîch d4 220
Elkhorn, Can. c6 250
Elkhorn, Nebraska, U.S.A. d3 260
Elkhorn, Wisconsin, U.S.A. b4 254
Elkhorn City e7 254
Elkhovo h4 201
Elkin f7 254
Elkins g6 254
Elkins Park e4 256
Elk Island National Park l5 249
Elkland c3 256
Elk Mountain b3 260
Elko, Can. f1 262
Elko, U.S.A. f5 262
Elk Rapids d3 254
Elk River e2 260
Elkton, Kentucky, U.S.A. f1 258
Elkton, Maryland, U.S.A. e5 256
Elkton, Virginia, U.S.A. b6 256
El Kûbri a6 139
El Kuntilla c7 139
Elkville e1 258
El Lagowa c5 218
Ellamar h3 247
Elland e3 162
El Laurel g1 297
Ellaville g3 259
Ellé b4 182
Ellef Ringnes Island j1 242
l Lêh b3 226
Ellenabad g6 129
Ellendale d2 260
Ellen, Mount h6 263
Ellen Peak d14 87
Ellensburg c2 262
Ellenville f3 257
El León, Cerro b1 274
Ellerbe k2 259
Ellery, Mount f3 83
Ellesmere d4 162
Ellesmere Island n1 243
Ellesmere, Lake d5 77
Ellesmere Port d3 162
Ellicott City d5 256
Ellicottville b2 256
Ellidshøj c2 158
Ellijay g2 259
El Limón, Guerrero, Mex. d4 274
El Limón, Nayarit, Mex. b2 274
El Limón, Tamaulipas, Mex. e2 275
Elling d1 158
Ellington, U.K. e1 162
Ellington, U.S.A. a2 256
Elliot, Aust. a4 80
Elliot, R.S.A. g5 235
Elliotdale h5 235
Elliot Lake e2 254
Elliot, Mount A 84
el Liri, Jebel f1 224
Ellisras g1 235
Elliston, Aust. b12 81
Elliston, U.S.A. g2 262
Ellisville e4 258
El Llano d3 274
El Llobregat f3 192
Ellmau d2 176
Ellon f2 164
El Losar del Barco e4 190
Ellrich f4 173
Ellsworth h6 253
Ellsworth Land kk2 298
Ellwangen e2 174
El Macao k5 271
El Madroño e3 275
El Maestrazgo d4 192
El Mahalla el Kubra c6 136
El Mahârîq c9 136
El Mahia d4 220
El Maitén b4 294
El Majd c5 139
El Malpais National Monument a5 261
El Manaqil d5 218
El Mango d3 284
El Manguito h6 275
El Mannsour d3 220
El Mansûra c6 136
El Manteco e2 285
El Marâgha c8 136
El Mastranto d3 274
El Matarîya, Daqahlîya, Egypt d6 136
El Matarîya, El Qâhira, Egypt c6 136
El Mazâr b5 139
Elm City l2 259
El Médano d5 272
El Meghaïer f2 221
El Melón b2 296
Elmen b2 176
Elmer e5 256
El Mezquite c2 274
Elmhurst c5 254
El Milagro de Guadalupe d2 274
El Milia f1 221
Elmina d4 222
El Mina d2 138
El Minya, El Faiyûm, Egypt c7 136
El Minya, El Minya, Egypt c7 136
Elmira d2 256
El Mirador b3 274
El Mirage Lake f7 265
Elmira Heights d2 256
El Misti c3 292
Elmo f2 262
El Molar g4 190
El Molinillo f5 191
El Molino e3 275
El Moral, Mex. j3 273
El Moral, Spain b7 193
El Morro e2 296
Elmshorn c5 158
Elmswell g4 163
El Mughâzi c5 139
El Muglad c5 218
El Mugrón c6 193
Elmvale g3 254
Elmwood b5 254
El Naranjo e2 275
Elne e6 187
Elnesvågen a5 154
El Nevado, Cerro c3 284
El Nido b5 100
El Nihuel c3 296
El'niki g4 151
El Niybo b3 226
El'nja b4 150
Elnora c6 254
El Obeid d4 218
El Ocote, Parque Natural h5 275
El Ocotito e5 275
El Odre d4 296
El Oro, Ec. b4 284
El Oro, Coahuila, Mex. h4 272
El Oro, México, Mex. d4 274
Elorrio b1 192
Elortondo g2 297
Elorz c2 192
Elorza d2 284
Elos d7 211
El Oso f4 190
Előszállás g5 171
Elot c7 139
Elota a2 274
El Oued f2 221
Eloxochitlán e3 275
Eloy h9 263
Éloyes c2 184
El Palmar e2 285
El Palmito g5 272
El Pao, Bolívar, Ven. e2 285
El Pao, Cojedes, Ven. d2 284
El Papayo d5 274
El Paraiso, Hond. d4 276
El Paraíso, Mex. g5 275
El Paso, Iraq Ab2 189
El Paso, U.S.A. f2 272
El Paso Peak f6 265
El Pedernoso b5 193
El Pedroso e7 191
El Peñasco d2 274
El Peñón, Arg. d5 292
El Peñón, Chile b2 296
El Peregrino f3 297
El Perelló, Cataluña, Spain e4 192
El Perelló, Valencia, Spain d5 193
Elphin c3 165
El Picacho c3 276
El Picazo b5 193
El Pilar e1 285
El Piñal e3 275
El Pinalón, Cerro c3 276
El Piñero e3 190
El Pingo h1 297
El Pintado e4 293
El Plomo, Nevado c2 296
El Pluma b5 295
El Pobo d4 192
El Pobo de Dueñas c4 192
El Pocito e3 293
El Pont d'Armentera f3 192
El Port d5 193
El Portal d4 264
El Port de la Selva h2 192
El Porvenir, Col. c3 284
El Porvenir, Mex. g2 272
El Porvenir, Pan. h6 277
El Prat de Llobregat g3 192
El Progreso, Guat. b2 276
El Progreso, Guat. b3 276
El Provencio b5 193
El Pueblito h2 297
El Puente, Bol. d4 292
El Puente, Nic. d4 276
El Puente de Arzobispo e5 191
El Puerto de Santa María d8 191
El Qalamoun d2 138
El Qantara d6 136
El Qasr c2 218
El Quebrachal e5 293
El Quelital d2 274
Elqui b2 294
El Quisco b2 296
El Qurna d9 136
El Quseima c6 139
El Qûsiya c8 136
El Ranchito c4 274
El Real j6 277
El Recuenco b4 192
El Refugio d3 274
El Regocijo b2 274
El Remate b2 276
El Reno a2 258
El Retamo d2 296
El Retorno d2 274
El Rey, Parque Nacional e4 293
El Ridisîya Bahari d9 136
El Río d7 265
El Robledo f5 191
El Rocío d7 191
El Rom d3 138
El Ronquillo d7 191
El Rosario b2 276
Elroy a4 254
El Royo b3 192
El Rubio f7 191
El Rucio c2 274
Elsa, Can. l3 247
Elsa, Italy e6 197
El Saff c7 136
El Sahuaro g10 263
El Salado, Arg. c5 295
El Salado, Mex. j5 273
El Sâlhîya d6 136
El Salobral c6 193
El Salto, Durango, Mex. b2 274
El Salto, Jalisco, Mex. c3 274
El Salvador f7 241

EL SALVADOR

THE REPUBLIC OF EL SALVADOR
Area 21,041km² (8124sq miles)
Capital San Salvador
Organizations ACS, CACM, IADB, SELA
Population 6,420,000
Pop. growth (%) 1.9
Life expectancy 67 (m); 73 (f)
Languages Spanish
Literacy 80.1%
Currency US dollar (and colon) (US $1 = 8.75 US dollar)
GDP (US million $) 14,300
GDP per head ($US) 2227

El Salvador, Chile d5 292
El Salvador, Jalisco, Mex. c3 274
El Salvador, Mex. j5 273
El Salvador, Phil. e6 100
El Samán de Apure d2 284
El Sauce d4 276
El Saucejo e7 191
El Sauz, Chihuahua, Mex. f3 272
El Sauz, Nayarit, Mex. b3 274
El Sauzal e10 263
Elsbethen e2 176
Elsdorf c5 158
El Seibo k5 271
Elsenborn e4 159
Elsen Nur n2 125
Elsenz d3 174
El Serrat d6 187
Elsfleth d2 172
El Shallûfa a6 139
El Shatt a7 139
El Simbillâwein c6 136
Elsinore, California, U.S.A. f8 265
Elsinore, Utah, U.S.A. g6 263
Elsnigk h4 173
El Socorro, Coahuila, Mex. h4 273
El Socorro, Sonora, Mex. g10 263
El Sosneado c3 296
Elsterwerda j4 173
El Sueco f3 272
El Suweis a7 139
El Tabo b2 296
El Tajín f3 275
El Tama, Parque Nacional c2 284
Eltanin Fracture Zone p9 301
El Tecolote, Cerro d4 274
El Tejar g3 297
El Teleno d2 190
El Temascal k5 273
El Temblador e2 285
El Tepozteco, Parque Nacional e4 275
El Ter g2 192
Eltham e3 76
El Thamad c7 139
El Tiemblo f4 190
El Tigre, Mex. j10 263
El Tigre, Ven. e2 285
El Tigre, Parque Nacional b2 276
Eltmann d2 175
El Toboso b5 193
El Tocuyo d2 284
El'ton g2 149
El'ton, Ozero g2 149
El Toro b4 296
El Totumo c1 284
El Trébol g2 297
El Treinta e5 275
El Tren g10 263
El Trigo h3 297
El Triunfo, Arg. g3 297
El Triunfo, Baja California Sur, Mex. d6 272
El Triunfo, Tabasco, Mex. b2 276
El Triunfo, Cerro a3 276
El Tuito b3 274
El Tumbalejo d7 191
El Tunal e5 293
El Tuparro, Parque Nacional d2 284
El Tûr d7 136
El Turbio b6 295
El Turbón e2 192
Eltville d4 174
El Uqşur d9 136
Eluru g4 126
Elva m3 157
El Valle g6 277
El Vallecillo e3 272
Elvas c6 191
Elvebakken j2 155
El Veladero, Parque Nacional e5 275
Elven c5 182
El Venado b3 274
El Vendrell f3 192
El Verde Chico f1 275
Elverum d2 156
El Vicario, Embalse de f5 191
El Viejo, Col. c2 284
El Viejo, Nic. d4 276
El Vigía c2 284
El Vigía, Cerro b3 274
El Villar de Arnedo b2 192
Elvira c5 284
El Viso f6 191
El Viso del Alcor e7 191
El Volcán, Arg. d2 296
El Volcán, Chile b2 296
El Wak c3 226
El Wasta c7 136
El Wuz d5 218
Elx d6 193
Ely, U.K. g4 163
Ely, Minnesota, U.S.A. h7 250
Ely, Nevada, U.S.A. f6 262
El Yagual d2 284
Elyaqim d4 138
Elyria e5 254

EQUATORIAL GUINEA

THE REPUBLIC OF EQUATORIAL GUINEA
Area 28,051km²
(10,830sq miles)
Capital Malabo
Organizations FZ, CEEAC
Population 480,000
Pop. growth (%) 2.5
Life expectancy 48 (m); 51 (f)
Languages Spanish, Fang, many local languages
Literacy 85.7%
Currency CFA franc
(US $1 = 534.95 CFA franc)
GDP (US million $) 2492
GDP per head ($US) 5191

ERITREA

THE STATE OF ERITREA
Area 121,144km²
(46,774sq miles)
Capital Asmara
Organizations COMESA
Population 3,990,000
Pop. growth (%) 2.7
Life expectancy 50 (m); 53 (f)
Languages Arabic, Tigre, English
Literacy 58.6%
Currency nakfa
(US $1 = 9.60 nakfa)
GDP (US million $) 732
GDP per head ($US) 183

ESTONIA

THE REPUBLIC OF ESTONIA
Area 45,227km²
(17,462sq miles)
Capital Tallinn
Organizations CE, EBRD
Population 1,377,000
Pop. growth (%) -1.4
Life expectancy 64 (m); 75 (f)
Languages Estonian, Russian
Literacy 99.8%
Currency kroon
(US $1 = 12.76 kroon)
GDP (US million $) 6339
GDP per head ($US) 4603

ETHIOPIA

THE FEDERAL DEMOCRATIC REPUBLIC OF ETHIOPIA
Area 1,133,380km²
(437,600sq miles)
Capital Addis Ababa
Organizations COMESA
Population 67,220,000
Pop. growth (%) 2
Life expectancy 43 (m); 45 (f)
Languages Amharic, English, many local languages
Literacy 42.8%
Currency birr (US $1 = 8.55 birr)
GDP (US million $) 5700
GDP per head ($US) 84

Evergern → Fischamend Markt 331

Evergem b3 159
Everglades City j7 259
Everglades National Park ★ j7 259
Evergreen f4 258
Everöd f5 156
Evesham, Aust. f7 80
Evesham, U.K. e4 163
Evesham, Vale of e4 163
Évian-les-Bains c4 184
Evijärvi, Fin. ○ j5 155
Evijärvi, Länsi-Suomi, Fin. j5 155
Evinos b4 210
Evisa A 185
Evje b3 156
Evolène b3 196
Évora, Port c6 191
Évora, Évora, Port c6 191
Évora-Monte c6 191
Evosmo c2 210
Evowghli k2 137
Évran d4 182
Èvre d5 182
Évrecy e3 182
Evrejskaja Avtonomnaja Oblast' j3 94
Évreux g3 183
Évron e4 182
Evropos c2 210
Evros g1 210
Evrostina c4 210
Evrotas c5 211
Évry h4 183
Evrychou a1 138
Evzonoi c1 210
Ewan Lake ○ h3 247
Ewaso Ngiro b3 226
Ewen j7 251
Ewing f4 256
Ewing Island mm1 298
Ewirgol w6 121
Ewo b4 224
Exaltación d2 292
Examilia c5 211
Excelsior g4 235
Excelsior Mountain ▵ d3 264
Excelsior Springs e4 260
Excideuil d3 186
Excursion Inlet l4 247
Exe c6 163
Executive Committee Range ee2 298
Exeter, U.K. c6 163
Exeter, California, U.S.A. d5 265
Exeter, New Hampshire, U.S.A. k2 257
Exminster c6 163
Exmoor c5 163
Exmoor National Park ☆ c5 163
Exmore j7 255
Exmouth, Aust. b7 86
Exmouth, U.K. c6 163
Exmouth Gulf ◄ b8 87
Exmouth, Mount ▵ c7 85
Exochi d1 210
Expedition National Park ☆ c4 84
Expedition Range c4 84
Exploits p4 253
Extoraz e3 275
Extremadura e5 191
Extrême-Nord b1 224
Extremo b3 190
Exuma Cays f2 266
Eyach d4 174
Eyangu d4 224
Eyasi, Lake ○ f4 225
Eydehavn c3 156
Eye h4 163
Eyemouth f4 164
Eygues b6 185
Eyguières b7 185
Eygurande e3 186
Eyjafjallajökull IC A 152
Eyjafjörður ◄ A 152
Eyl d2 226
Eylar Mountain ▵ b4 264
Eymet c4 186
Eymoutiers d3 186
Eyragues a7 185
Eyrarbakki A 152
Eyre b4 186
Eyre (North), Lake ○ c10 81
Eyre (South), Lake ○ c10 81
Eyrecourt c3 165
Eyre Creek d8 81
Eyre Mountains b6 77
Eyre Peninsula ► b12 81
Eyre, Seno ◄ b5 295
Eyrieux a6 185
Eystrup e3 172
Eysturo B 152
Eyumojok f4 223
Eyvānaki p4 137
Ezakheni j4 235
Ezcaray b2 192
Ezequiel Ramos Mexía, Embalse ⊙ c5 296
Ezere k4 157
Ezernieki m4 157
Ezhou d4 106
Ezine b5 148
Ezinepazar f2 209
Ezuz c6 139
Ežva g3 146

F

Faadhippolhu Atoll ○ c10 126
Faafxadhuun c3 226
Faaite K 75
Fabens f2 272
Fåberg d2 156
Faber Lake ○ e3 242
Fabero d2 190
Fabianki h3 169
Fábiánsebestyén j5 171
Fåborg d3 158
Fabrègues, Languedoc-Roussillon, Fr. f5 187
Fabriano g6 197
Fábricas de San Juan de Alcaraz b6 193
Fabrizia f6 199
Facatativá c3 284
Facheng g1 111
Fachi g2 223
Facinas e8 191
Facing Island d3 84
Facpi Point ► C 74
Factoryville e3 256
Facundo b5 295
Fada b4 218
Fada-Ngourma e3 223
Fadd g5 171
Faddoi f2 225
Fadli ♦ g5 219
Fadnoun, Plateau du f3 221
Fænø ○ c3 158
Faenza f5 197
Færdesmyra Naturreservat ☆ m2 155
Faeto e3 198
Fafa c2 224
Fafanlap j6 97
Fafen Shet' c2 226
Faga e3 223
Făgăraș g3 201
Fågelsjön ○ e4 154
Fagernes c2 156
Fagerroskölen ▵ f2 156
Fagersta f3 156
Făget l6 171
Faggeta, Monte la ▵ f5 197
Faggo f3 223
Fagnano Castello f5 198
Fagnano, Lago ○ c6 295
Fagnières a2 184
Faguibine, Lac d2 222
Fagurhólsmýri A 152
Fagwir f2 225
Fahan d1 165
Fahl, Oued el e2 221
Fahraj q6 137
Faial A 220
Faicchio d3 198
Faido c3 196
Faioa, Île L 75
Fairbanks, Alaska, U.S.A. h2 247
Fairbanks, Louisiana, U.S.A. c3 258
Fair Bluff k2 259
Fairborn d6 254
Fairbury, Illinois, U.S.A. b5 254
Fairbury, Nebraska, U.S.A. d3 260
Fairchance g6 254
Fairfax, U.S.A. k6 257
Fairfax, Virginia, U.S.A. c6 256
Fairfield, California, U.S.A. a3 264
Fairfield, Idaho, U.S.A. f4 262
Fairfield, Illinois, U.S.A. b6 254
Fairfield, Montana, U.S.A. h2 262
Fairfield, Ohio, U.S.A. d6 254
Fairfield, Texas, U.S.A. a4 258
Fairhaven k3 257
Fair Haven k4 255
Fair Head ► e1 165
Fairhope f4 258
Fairie Queen a5 100
Fair Isle A 164
Fairland b1 258
Fairlie c6 77
Fairmont, Minnesota, U.S.A. e3 260
Fairmont, West Virginia, U.S.A. f6 254
Fairmount g2 259
Fairplay b4 260
Fairview, Aust. g3 80
Fairview, Oklahoma, U.S.A. d4 261
Fairview, Utah, U.S.A. h6 262
Fairview Peak ▵ e4 264
Fairview Valley e2 264
Fairweather, Mount ▵ k4 247
Fais G 74
Faisalabad f5 128
Faither, The ► A 164
Faizabad, Afg. b2 128
Faizabad, India h6 124
Fajardo A 270
Fajr, Wādī e2 219
Fajsławice l4 169
Fakahina K 75
Fakaofo H 75
Fakarava K 75
Fakehé e2 138
Fakel m3 151
Fakenham g4 162
Fåker e5 154
Fakfak j6 97
Fakhrabad p6 137
Fakiragram m6 125
Fakse f3 158
Fakse Bugt ◄ f3 158
Fakse Ladeplads f3 158
Faku m4 113
Falaba b4 222
Falagountou e3 223
Falaise e4 182
Falaise de Tiguidit f2 223
Falam a4 102
Falavarjan n5 137
Falcade f3 196
Falcarragh c1 165
Fălciu j2 201
Falcoeira, Cabo ► a2 190
Falco, Monte ▵ f6 197
Falcón c1 284
Falconara d7 199
Falconara Marittima h6 197
Falcone e6 199
Falcone, Punta ► Ab1 198
Falcon Island J 75
Falcon Lake ○ d7 261
Falda del Carmen e1 297
Faldsled d3 158
Falémé b3 222
Falenki l2 151
Falerna f5 199
Fălești h2 201
Falfurrias k4 273
Falită e2 138
Falkenberg, Ger. j4 173
Falkenberg, Swe. f2 158
Falkenhagen h2 173
Falkensee j3 173
Falkenstein, Bayern, Ger. h3 175
Falkenstein, Sachsen, Ger. h2 175
Falkirk, Scotland, U.K. f3 164
Falkirk, Scotland, U.K. e4 164
Falkland Escarpment e14 302
Falkland Islands (U.K.) e6 295
Falkland Sound e6 295
Falkonera d6 211
Falköping e3 156
Falkville f2 258
Fall b1 258
Fallbrook f8 265
Falleron d6 182
Fällfors h4 154
Fallingbostel e3 172
Fallon e2 264
Fallos, Canal b5 295
Fall River, Kansas, U.S.A. b1 258
Fall River, Massachusetts, U.S.A. j3 257
Fall River Pass b3 260
Falls Church k6 257
Falls City e3 260
Falls Creek b3 256
Falmey e3 223
Falmouth, Antig. D 271
Falmouth, Jam. B 270
Falmouth, U.K. a6 163
Falmouth, Kentucky, U.S.A. d6 254
Falmouth, Massachusetts, U.S.A. k3 257
Falmouth, Virginia, U.S.A. c6 256
Falmouth Bay ◄ a6 163
Falsa Chipana, Punta ► c4 292
False Bay ◄ c7 234
False Bay Park ☆ k3 235
False Pass d5 246
Falset e3 192
Falso Azufre, Nevado ▵ d5 292
Falso, Cabo ► f3 277
Falso Cabo de Hornos ► c7 295
Falster d4 158
Fălticeni h2 201
Falun f2 156
Famagusta, Cyp. b1 138
Famagusta, Famagusta, Cyp. b1 138
Famagusta Bay ► c1 138
Famatina c1 294
Famatina, Sierra de c1 294
Fambono c4 224
Fameck e5 159
Famenin m4 137
Famenne ♦ d4 159
Family Lake ○ f5 250
Famphøgdene ▵ d2 156
Fana c3 222
Fanad Head ► d1 165
Fånån e4 154
Fanandrana Ab2 233
Fanari f2 210
Fanari, Akra ► Aa1 211
Fanbyklacken ▵ g1 156
Fanchang f4 111
Fancun c1 106
Fandriana Ab3 233
Fane e3 165
Fanes Sennes Braies, Parco Naturale ☆ f3 196
Fang d6 102
Fangak f2 225
Fangatau K 75
Fangataufa K 75
Fangcheng c3 106
Fangchenggang g8 104
Fangcun e2 111
Fangdou Shan a4 106
Fango A 185
Fangö g3 156
Fangshan b1 106
Fangxian b3 106
Fangyüan n7 105
Fangzheng q3 113
Fangzi f1 111
Fanjeaux e5 187
Fannrem b5 154
Fanø b3 158
Fano h6 197
Fanø Bugt ◄ b3 158
Fanshan e4 111
Fanshi g6 112
Fan Si Pan ▵ f4 102
Fanxian d2 106
Fanxiang d2 106
Fanzhen e1 111
Faqqū'a d4 139
Faraba b3 222
Faradje e3 225
Farafangana Ab3 233
Farafenni a3 222
Farāgheh p6 137
Farāh, Afg. a4 128
Farāh, Farāh, Afg. a4 128
Farah c6 130
Farahalana Ac1 233
Farah Rūd a4 128
Faraïya d2 138
Farakhulm d3 128
Farallon de Medinilla A 74
Farallon de Pajaros ▲ A 74
Farallones de Cali, Parque Nacional ☆ b3 284
Faranah b3 222
Faranshat b2 130
Faraoani h2 201
Farap a1 128
Farasān, Jazā'ir f4 219
Fara San Martino d2 198
Faratsiho Ab2 233
Faraulep G 74
Fårberget g4 154
Fardella f4 198
Fardes a7 193
Farébersviller c1 184
Fareham e6 163
Fårevejle e3 158
Fårevejle Stationsby e3 158
Farewell f3 246
Farewell, Cape ► d4 77
Farewell Spit ► d4 77
Farfa g7 197
Färgelanda e3 156
Fargo e7 250
Faribault e2 260
Faridabad c5 130
Faridkot b4 130
Faridpur, Bang. l8 125
Faridpur, India d5 130
Färigh, Wādī al b1 218
Farilhões a5 191
Faringdon e5 163
Farington d3 162
Farinha c3 288
Farish l7 120
Färjestaden g4 156
Farkadhon c3 210
Farkhato d2 128
Farkhor d2 128
Farkwa b5 227
Farmahin m4 137
Farmakonisi Ab1 211
Farmer City b5 254
Farmer Island n1 251
Farmersburg c6 254
Farmersville, California, U.S.A. d5 265
Farmersville, Illinois, U.S.A. b6 254
Farmington, Maine, U.S.A. g6 252
Farmington, Missouri, U.S.A. d1 258
Farmington, Montana, U.S.A. g2 262
Farmington, New Mexico, U.S.A. a4 261
Farmington, Utah, U.S.A. h5 262
Far Mountain ▵ e5 248
Farmville g7 254
Farnā g3 171
Farnborough f5 163
Färnebofjärdens nationalpark ☆ g2 156
Farnese f7 197
Farnham e5 163
Farnham, Mount ▵ j6 249
Farnstädt g4 173
Farnworth d3 162
Faro, Arg. g5 297
Faro, Braz. f4 285
Faro, Cam. b2 224
Faro, Port c7 191
Faro, Spain c2 190
Fårö h3 157
Faroe Islands B 152
Faroe Islands (Denmark) k3 302
Faroma, Monte ▵ b4 196
Faro, Punta ► c1 284
Faro, Réserve du ☆ b2 224
Faro, Serra do c2 190
Fårösund h4 157
Farquhar Group e6 231
Farrandsville c3 256
Farrar d2 164
Farrars Creek e8 80
Farrāshband p7 137
Farrelones b2 296
Farrukhabad d6 130
Farrukhnagar c5 130
Fārs p7 137
Farsakh q5 137
Farsala c3 210
Farsaliotis c3 210
Fārsī a4 128
Farsø c2 158
Farson j4 262
Farsund b3 156
Fartak, Ra's ► h4 219
Fărtănești h3 201
Fartura, Serra da b7 289
Fārūj g9 120
Fårup c2 158
Fårvang c2 158
Farwell, Michigan, U.S.A. d4 254
Farwell, Texas, U.S.A. c5 261
Far Western e5 130
Fāryāb, Afg. b2 128
Fāryāb, Hormozgan, Iran r8 137
Fāryāb, Kermān, Iran r7 137
Fasā p7 137
Fasano g4 198
Fasnia Ac2 189
Faßberg f3 172
Fassūta d3 138
Fastiv c2 148
Fastivets' c2 148
Fataki f3 225
Fatala b3 222
Fatehabad d5 130
Fatehganj West d5 130
Fatehgarh d6 130
Fatehgarh Sahib c4 130
Fatehnagar g8 129
Fatehpur, Rajasthan, India b6 130
Fatehpur, India g7 124
Fatehpur, Pak. e5 128
Fatehpur Sikri c6 130
Fatḥābād q7 137
Fatick a3 222
Fati, Lac d2 222
Fátima b5 191
Fátima do Sul a5 290
Fatua, Pointe ► L 75
Fatu Hiva K 75
Fatu Huku K 75
Fatumanini, Passe ◄ L 75
Fatundu c4 224
Fatwa j7 125
Faucogney-et-la-Mer c3 184
Faugères f5 187
Faulenrost f5 158
Faulquemont c1 184
Faune Conkouati, Réserve de ☆ b4 224
Faune d'Ansongo-Ménaka, Réserve Partielle de ☆ e2 223
Faune de la Bahr Salamat, Réserve de ☆ d5 218
Faune de l'Abou-Telfân, Réserve de ☆ a5 218
Faune de la Lékoli-Pandaka, Réserve de ☆ b3 224
Faune de la Ouandja-Vakaga, Réserve de ☆ d2 224
Faune de l'Aouk-Aoakole, Réserve de ☆ d2 224
Faune de la Yata-Ngaya, Réserve de ☆ d2 224
Faune de Tamou, Réserve Totale de ☆ e3 223
Faune de Zémongo, Réserve de ☆ e2 225
Faune du Ferlo-Nord, Réserve de ☆ b2 222
Faune du Ferlo-Sud, Réserve de ☆ b3 222
Faune du Gribingui-Bamingui, Réserve de ☆ c2 224
Faune du Koukourou-Bamingui, Réserve de ☆ d2 224
Faune du Ndiael, Réserve de ☆ a2 222
Faune du N'Zo, Réserve de ☆ c4 222
Faune du Ouadi Rimé-Ouadi Achim, Réserve de ☆ a5 218
Faune du Popenguine, Réserve de ☆ a3 222
Faunique Ashuapmushuan, Réserve ☆ f4 252
Faunique de la Vérendrye, Réserve ☆ q7 251
Faunique de l'Île d'Anticosti, Réserve ☆ l4 253
Faunique de Mastigouche, Réserve ☆ f5 252
Faunique de Matane, Réserve ☆ j4 253
Faunique de Papineau-Labelle, Réserve ☆ e5 252
Faunique de Portneuf, Réserve ☆ g5 253
Faunique de Rimouski, Réserve ☆ j5 253
Faunique de Sept-Îles-Port-Cartier, Réserve ☆ j3 253
Faunique des Laurentides, Réserve ☆ g5 252
Faunique du St-Maurice, Réserve ☆ f5 252
Faunique Rouge-Matawin, Réserve ☆ e5 252
Fauquembergues h2 183
Făurei h3 201
Fauresmith f4 235
Fauske e3 154
Faustino M. Parera h2 297
Fauville-en-Caux f3 183
Favara, Italy c7 199
Favara, Spain d5 193
Favàritx, Cap de ► A 193
Faverges c5 185
Faverney c3 184
Faversham g5 163
Favignana b7 199
Favignana, Isola b7 199
Faw'arah d4 138
Fawn j3 251
Fawwārah j8 137
Faxaflói ◄ A 152
Faxälven f5 154
Faya a4 218
Fayd j8 137
Fayence c7 185
Fayette, Alabama, U.S.A. f3 258
Fayette, Ohio, U.S.A. d5 254
Fayetteville, Arkansas, U.S.A. b1 258
Fayetteville, Georgia, U.S.A. g3 259
Fayetteville, New York, U.S.A. e1 256
Fayetteville, North Carolina, U.S.A. k2 259
Fayetteville, Pennsylvania, U.S.A. c5 256
Fayetteville, West Virginia, U.S.A. f6 254
Fāyid d6 136
Fayl-la-Forêt b3 184
Fayón e3 192
Fay-sur-Lignon a6 185
Fayu G 74
Fazao e4 223
Fazao Malfakassa, Parc National de ☆ e4 223
Fazilka g5 128
Fazilpur e6 129
Fazrān, Jabal ▵ g2 219
Fdérik b4 220
Feale b4 165
Fear, Cape ► l3 259
Feather b3 264
Featherston e4 77
Featherstop, Mount ▵ e3 83
Fécamp f3 183
Fecht d2 184
Federacija Bosna i Hercegovina c4 200
Federación, Arg. j1 297
Federación, Ur. j2 297
Federal h1 297
Federal Capital Territory f4 223
Federalsburg e6 256
Federated States of Micronesia e2 72
Federsee ○ e4 174
Fedorovka, Kostanayskaya Oblast', Kaz. k5 147
Fedorovka, Pavlodarskaya Oblast', Kaz. r1 121
Fedorovskij n3 147
Fehérgyarmat l4 171
Fehmarn g1 173
Fehmarnsund f1 173
Fehrbellin h3 173
Fehring h3 177
Feia, Lagoa ○ h5 291
Feicheng e1 111
Feidong e4 111
Feiheji d3 106
Feijó c1 292
Feilding e4 76
Feira de Santana e4 288
Feira do Monte c1 190
Feistritz g2 177
Feiteira c7 191
Feixi e4 111
Feixian e2 111
Feixiang d1 111
Fejaj, Chott el ⊙ f2 221
Fejér g4 171
Fejø e4 158
Feke e4 208
Felanitx h5 193
Felcsút g4 171
Feldbach g3 177
Feldberg ▵ d5 174
Feldkirch a2 176
Feldkirchen bei Graz g2 177
Feldkirchen in Kärnten f3 177
Feldkirchen-Westerham c4 175
Feldru g2 201
Felgueiras b3 190
Feliciano e2 294
Felipe C. Puerto q8 273
Felipe Carrillo Puerto c4 274
Félix b8 193
Felixburg e2 233
Felixdorf h2 177
Felixlândia f3 291
Felixstowe h5 163
Felixton j4 235
Felizzano c5 196
Fella h3 196
Felletin e3 186
Fellingsbro f3 156
Felnac k5 171
Felsberg f1 174
Felsenthal National Wildlife Refuge ☆ c3 258
Felsőlajos h4 171
Felsőnyék g5 171
Felsőpakony h4 171
Felsőszentiván h5 171
Felsőzsolca j3 171
Felsted c4 158
Feltre f3 196
Feltwell g4 163
Fema, Monte ▵ h7 197
Femeas c4 288
Femer Bælt e4 158
Femø e4 158
Femunden ○ d1 156
Femundsenden d2 156
Femundsmarka Nasjonalpark ☆ e1 156
Fena Valley Reservoir ⊙ C 74
Fenestrelle b4 196
Fénétrange d2 184
Fengari ▵ f2 210
Fengcheng, Jiangxi, China k4 105
Fengcheng, Liaoning, China n5 113
Fengcheng, Shanghai, China g4 111
Fengdu f4 104
Fenggang f5 104
Fenghua g5 111
Fengjia g1 111
Fengjie a4 106
Fengjing g4 111
Fengkou c4 106
Fengnan k6 113
Fengning j5 113
Fengqiao g5 111
Fengqing d3 102
Fengqiu d2 106
Fengrun k6 113
Fengshan f6 104
Fengshuba Shuiku ⊙ k6 105
Fengtai e3 111
Fengxian, Jiangsu, China e2 111
Fengxian, Shaanxi, China f2 104
Fengxian, Shanghai, China g4 111
Fengyang e3 111
Fengzhen g5 112
Fen He ► f6 112
Fenhe Shuiku ⊙ b1 106
Feni m8 125
Feniak Lake ○ e1 246
Fenimore Pass Ad1 247
Fenis b4 196
Fennimore a4 254
Fenny m8 125
Fenoarivo Atsinanana Ab2 233
Fenoarivo Be Ab2 233
Feno, Capo di, Corse, Fr. ► A 185
Fenouillet ♦ e6 187
Fenshui f2 111
Fensmark e3 158
Fens, The ♦ g4 162
Fenxi b1 106
Fenyang b1 106
Fenyi k5 105
Feodosiya d3 148
Feragen ○ d1 156
Ferbane d3 165
Fer, Cap de ► f1 221
Ferdinand c6 254
Ferdinandea f6 199
Ferdinandshof j2 173
Ferdows s5 137
Fère-Champenoise j4 183
Fère-en-Tardenois j3 183
Feren ○ c5 154
Ferentillo g7 197
Ferentino h8 197
Feres g2 210
Férez c6 193
Fergana n7 121
Fergana Too Tizmegi q7 121
Ferganskaya Oblast' n7 121
Fergus f4 254
Fergus Falls e7 250
Ferguson a6 254
Fériana f2 221
Feria, Sierra de d6 191
Ferkessédougou c4 222
Ferla d7 199
Ferlach f3 177
Ferland j5 251
Ferlo, Vallée du a2 222
Fermanagh b2 165
Fermignano g6 197
Fermo c1 198
Fermont j2 253
Fermoselle d3 190
Fermoy c4 165
Fernáncaballero g5 191
Fernandina Beach j4 259
Fernandina, Embalse de la ⊙ g6 191
Fernandina, Isla A 286
Fernando de Magallanes, Parque Nacional ☆ b6 295
Fernando de Noronha ★ g3 282
Fernandópolis c4 290
Fernán Núñez f7 191
Fernão Dias f2 291
Ferndown e6 163
Fernhill Heath d4 163
Fernley d2 264
Fernpass b2 176
Ferns e4 165
Fernwood e2 262
Ferrals-les-Corbières e5 187
Ferrandina f4 198
Ferrara, Italy f5 196
Ferrara, Emilia-Romagna, Italy f5 196
Ferrarese f5 196
Ferrazzano d3 198
Ferré g3 297
Ferre, Cap ► J 271
Ferreira c1 190
Ferreira do Alentejo b6 191
Ferreira do Zêzere b5 191
Ferreiros b4 290
Ferreñafe b1 292
Ferreras de Abajo d3 190
Ferreruela de Huerva c3 192
Ferrette d3 184
Ferreyra e1 297
Ferriday d4 258
Ferriere d5 196
Ferrières h4 183
Ferris a3 258
Ferro, Capo ► Ab1 198
Ferrol b1 190
Ferron h6 262
Ferros g3 291
Ferrutx, Cap ► g5 193
Ferryhill e2 162
Feršampenuaz j5 147
Fertő-Hanság ☆ c2 200
Fertőszentmiklós e4 170
Fervenza, Embalse da ⊙ a2 190
Ferzikovo d4 150
Fès d2 220
Feshi c5 224
Fété Bowé b3 222
Fetești h3 201
Fethaland, Point of ► A 164
Fethard d4 165
Fethiye b4 208
Fethiye Körfezi ◄ b4 208
Fetisovo j4 149
Fetlar A 164
Fetsund d3 156
Fettercairn f3 164
Feucht e4 175
Feuchtwangen c2 174
Feurs a5 184
Fevik c3 156
Fevzipaşa f4 209
Feyzābād e2 128
Feyzābād q6 137
Ffestiniog c4 162
Fiambala c1 294
Fiambalá c1 294
Fiamignano h7 197
Fian d3 222
Fianarantsoa, Madag. Ab3 233
Fianarantsoa, Fianarantsoa, Madag. Ab3 233
Fianga c2 224
Fiano Romano g7 197
Fiché b2 226
Fichtelgebirge, Ger. g2 175
Fichtelgebirge, Ger. ▵ h2 175
Ficksburg g4 235
Ficulle g7 197
Fidalgo d3 288
Fidenza e5 196
Fieberbrunn d2 176
Fiegni, Monte ▵ h6 197
Fieni g3 201
Fier, Alb. k6 200
Fier, Fr. c5 185
Fiera di Primiero f3 196
Fiesch c3 196
Fife f3 164
Fife Lake d3 254
Fife Ness ► f3 164
Figarella A 185
Figari A 185
Figeac e4 186
Figeholm g4 156
Figueira da Foz b4 190
Figueira de Castelo Rodrigo d4 190
Figueirão b3 290
Figueres g2 192
Figueroa b4 295
Figueroles d4 193
Figuig d2 220
Figuil g4 223
Fiji g4 73

FIJI

THE REPUBLIC OF FIJI ISLANDS
Area 18,376km^2 (7095sq miles)
Capital Suva, on Viti Levu
Organizations COMM, SPC, PIF
Population 830,000
Pop. growth (%) 1.4
Life expectancy 66 (m); 70 (f)
Languages Fijian, Hindi, English
Literacy 93.7%
Currency Fiji dollar (US $1 = 1.74 Fiji dollar)
GDP (US million $) 1463
GDP per head ($US) 1762

Fik' c2 226
Fika g3 223
Filabres, Sierra de los b7 193
Filabusi d3 233
Filadelfia, C.R. e5 276
Filadelfia, Italy f6 199
Filadelfia, Para. e4 293
Filaki g1 210
Fil'akovo h3 171
Filamana c3 222
Filchner Ice Shelf IH a2 298
Filettino h8 197
Filey f2 162
Filiași f3 201
Filiates a3 210
Filiatra b5 211
Filicudi Porto d6 199
Filingué e3 223
Filiouri f1 210
Filipów l1 169
Filippiada a3 210
Filipstad f3 156
Filisur d3 196
Fillan b5 154
Fillmore, California, U.S.A. e7 265
Fillmore, Utah, U.S.A. g6 263
Fillyra f1 210
Filo de los Caballos e5 275
Filomeno Mata f3 275
Filotas b2 210
Filoti f5 211
Filottrano h6 197
Fils e4 174
Filton d5 163
Filtu c2 226
Finale d6 199
Finale Emilia f5 196
Finale Ligure c5 197
Fiñana b7 193
Fina, Réserve de ☆ c3 222
Fincastle g7 254
Findhorn e2 164
Findik h4 209
Findlay e5 254
Finedon f4 163
Finese, Monte ▵ f4 198
Fingal, Aust. Ac2 83
Fingal, U.S.A. e7 250
Finger Lakes ○ d2 256
Fingoè e2 233
Finhan d5 187
Finiels, Sommet de ▵ f4 187
Finike c4 208
Finike Körfezi ◄ c4 208
Finistère a4 182
Finisterre, Embalse de ⊙ g5 191
Finke a8 80
Finke Gorge National Park ☆ l9 87
Finke, Mount ▵ b11 81
Finland k2 145

FINLAND

THE REPUBLIC OF FINLAND
Area 338,144km^2 (130,558sq miles)
Capital Helsinki
Organizations CE, EBRD, EU, OECD
Population 5,200,000
Pop. growth (%) 0.2
Life expectancy 73 (m); 80 (f)
Languages Finnish, Swedish, Lapp
Literacy 99%
Currency euro (US $1 = 0.81 euro)
GDP (US million $) 134,900
GDP per head ($US) 25,942

Finland, Gulf of ◄ l3 157
Finlay d3 248
Finlay, Mount ▵ e3 248
Finley, Aust. g13 81
Finley, U.S.A. e7 250
Finn d2 165
Finna c2 156
Finnfjordvatnet ○ g2 154
Finnigan, Mount ▵ g3 80
Finniss, Cape ► b12 81
Finnmark l1 155
Finn Mountain ▵ e3 246
Finnskogen e2 156
Finnsnes f2 154
Finowfurt j3 173
Finse b2 156
Finskiy Zaliv ◄ m2 157
Finspång f3 156
Finsteraarhorn ▵ c3 196
Finsterwalde j4 173
Fintona d2 165
Fintown c2 165
Fiora f7 197
Fiordland National Park ☆ a6 77
Fiorenzuola d'Arda d5 196
Fiori, Campo dei ▵ c4 196
Fırat g3 209
Firebaugh c5 264
Firenze, Italy f6 197
Firenze, Toscana, Italy f6 197
Firenzuola f5 197
Firiña e3 285
Firlej l4 169
Firmat g2 297
Firmi e4 186
Firminópolis c2 290
Firminy a5 185
Firovo b3 150
Firoza e6 129
Firozabad d6 130
Firozpur, Haryana, India c6 130
Firozpur, Punjab, India g5 128
Firth of Clyde ◄ d4 164
Firth of Forth ◄ f3 164
Firth of Lorn ◄ c3 164
Firth of Tay ◄ e3 164
Firth of Thames ◄ e2 76
Fīrūzābād p7 137
Fīrūzeh r3 137
Fīrūzkūh p4 137
Firyuza s3 137
Fiscal d2 192
Fischamend Markt h1 177

332 Fischbach → Fröndenberg

Fischbach f5 159
Fischen im Allgäu g4 174
Fish, Nam. ≈ b3 234
Fish, R.S.A. ≈ d5 234
Fisher d2 258
Fisher Bay ◄ v1 298
Fishers Island ▭ j3 257
Fishguard b5 163
Fishing Branch Game Reserve ☆ k2 247
Fishing Creek d6 256
Fishing Lake ○ f4 250
Fish Lake Valley ≈ e4 264
Fiskå a1 156
Fiskardo a4 210
Fiskebäckskil d3 156
Fismes b5 159
Fisterra a2 190
Fisterra, Cabo ► a2 190
Fitchburg j2 257
Fitero c2 192
Fito, Mount △ M 75
Fitri, Lac ○ a5 218
Fitzcarrald c2 292
Fitzgerald, Can. m2 249
Fitzgerald, U.S.A. h4 259
Fitzgerald Bay ◄ a1 82
Fitzgerald River National Park ☆ d14 87
Fitz Hugh Sound ═ d6 248
Fitzmaurice ≈ k4 86
Fitz Roy c5 295
Fitzroy, Queensland, Aust. ≈ k7 80
Fitzroy, Western Australia, Aust. ≈ g5 86
Fitz Roy, Cerro △ b5 295
Fitzroy Crossing g6 86
Fitzwilliam Island ▭ b6 252
Fitzwilliam Strait ═ f1 242
Fiuggi h8 197
Fiumefreddo Bruzio f5 199
Fiumefreddo di Sicilia e7 199
Fiume Nicà, Punta ► g5 199
Fiumicino g8 197
Fium'Orbo ≈ A 185
Fivemiletown d2 165
Five Points c5 265
Fivizzano e5 197
Fizi e4 225
Fjällåsen h3 154
Fjällbacka d3 156
Fjällfjällen △ e4 154
Fjällsjöälven ≈ f5 154
Fjätan ≈ e2 156
Fjellbu f2 154
Fjellerup d2 158
Fjerritslev c1 158
Fjugesta f3 156
Fkih Ben Salah c2 220
Fladså ≈ b3 158
Flagler Beach j5 259
Flagstaff, R.S.A. h5 235
Flagstaff, U.S.A. h8 263
Flagstaff Lake ○ l3 255
Flaherty Island ▭ n3 251
Flakstad f2 154
Flåm b2 156
Flămânzi h2 201
Flambeau ≈ a3 254
Flamborough f2 162
Flamborough Head ► g2 162
Flamicell ≈ e2 192
Fläming ♦ h3 173
Flaming Gorge Reservoir ○ j5 262
Flampouro d2 210
Flanders ♦ b3 159
Flandre ♦ h2 183
Flandria c4 224
Flåren ○ f4 156
Flåsjön, Swe. ○ d5 154
Flåsjön, Swe. ○ e4 154
Flat, Can. ≈ n3 247
Flat, U.S.A. e3 246
Flateyri A 152
Flathead Lake ○ f2 262
Flatonia a5 258
Flattery, Cape, Aust. ► g3 80
Flattery, Cape, U.S.A. ► e7 248
Flåvatnet ○ c3 156
Flavigny-sur-Moselle c2 184
Flaxenpass ═ B2 176
Flaxman Island ▭ h1 247
Flaxton b6 250
Flechtingen g3 173
Flechtinger Höhenzug ☆ g3 173
Fleckeby c4 158
Flecken Zechlin h2 173
Fleesensee ○ h2 173
Fleetmark g3 173
Fleetwood, U.K. c3 162
Fleetwood, U.S.A. e4 256
Flekkefjord b3 156
Flémalle d4 159
Flemington f4 256
Flemish Cap ═ p5 302
Flen, Jönköping, Swe. ○ f4 156
Flen, Södermanland, Swe. g3 156
Flensborg Fjord ─ c4 158
Flensburg c4 158
Flenskampen △ d1 156
Flers e4 182
Flesko, Tanjung ► n4 99
Fletcher h2 259
Fletcher Peninsula ► jj2 298
Fleurance c5 187
Fleur de Lys p3 253
Fleur-de-May, Lac ○ k2 253
Fleuré c2 186
Fleurier a3 196
Fleurus c4 159
Fleury-les-Aubrais g5 183
Fleves ≈ d5 210
Flevoland ▣ d2 159
Flieden f2 174
Flimby e5 164
Flims d3 196
Flinders, Queensland, Aust. ≈ a2 84
Flinders, Victoria, Aust. d4 82
Flinders Chase National Park ☆ c13 81
Flinders Group ▭ g2 80
Flinders Island, South Australia, Aust. ▭ b12 81
Flinders Island, Tasmania, Aust. ▭ Ab1 83
Flinders Ranges ▣ a1 82
Flinders Ranges National Park ☆ d11 81
Flinders Reefs ○ j4 80
Flin Flon c3 250
Flint, U.K. c3 162
Flint, Georgia, U.S.A. ≈ g4 259
Flint, Michigan, U.S.A. e4 254
Flintbek d4 158
Flint Island ▭ H 75
Flintshire ▣ c3 162
Flintstone b5 256
Flippin c1 258
Flisa e2 156
Flitwick f4 163
Flix e3 192
Flixecourt h2 183
Flize c5 159
Floby e3 156
Floda e4 156
Flogny-la-Chapelle j5 183
Floh d4 174
Flöha, Ger. ≈ j5 173
Flöha, Sachsen, Ger. j2 175
Flood Range ▣ pp2 298
Floodwood g7 250
Flora, Illinois, U.S.A. b6 254
Flora, Mississippi, U.S.A. d3 258
Florac f4 187
Florala f4 258
Floral City h5 259
Flora, Mount △ c7 86
Florange e5 159
Flora Passage ═ A 84
Flora Reef ○ h4 80
Floraville d5 80
Flor de Punga c5 284
Florence, Italy f6 197
Florence, Alabama, U.S.A. f2 258
Florence, Arizona, U.S.A. h9 263
Florence, Kansas, U.S.A. d4 260
Florence, South Carolina, U.S.A. k2 259
Florence, Wisconsin, U.S.A. b3 254
Florence Court Forest Park ☆ d2 165
Florencia, Arg. e1 294
Florencia, Col. b3 284
Florennes c4 159
Florensac f5 187
Florentino Ameghino c4 295
Florentino Ameghino, Embalse ○ c4 295
Florenville d5 159
Flores, Arg. ≈ h3 297
Flores, Arm. ▭ A 220
Flores, Braz. d3 288
Flores, Guat. c2 276
Flores, Indon. ▭ l9 99
Flores, Ur. ▣ j2 297
Florescência d1 292
Flores de Goiás c4 289
Flores Island ▭ d7 248
Flores Sea ▭ k8 99
Floresta, Braz. e3 288
Floresta, Italy d7 199
Florestal de Munducurânia, Reserva ☆ f5 285
Florestal Gorotiré, Reserva ☆ g1 293
Floresta Nacional do Tapajós ☆ g4 285
Floreşti j2 201
Floresville k3 273
Floriada b3 210
Floriano d3 288
Floriano Peixoto d1 292
Florianópolis c7 289
Florida, Bol. e3 293
Florida, Chile a4 296
Florida, Cuba e4 266
Florida, U.S.A. ▣ h5 259
Florida, U.S.A. f3 257
Florida, Ur. ▣ j2 297
Florida, Florida, Ur. j3 297
Florida Bay ◄ j7 259
Florida Keys ▭ j7 259
Florida Negra c5 295
Flórida Paulista c4 290
Floridia e7 199
Florina b2 210
Florinas Aa2 198
Florínia c5 290
Florissant a6 254
Florø a2 156
Flossenbürg h3 175
Flotta ▭ g1 164
Flouda, Akra ► g6 211
Flour Lake ○ l2 253
Floydada c5 261
Fluchthorn △ b3 176
Flüelapass ═ d3 196
Flüelen c3 196
Fluessen ○ d2 159
Fluk h6 97
Flúmen ≈ d2 192
Flumet c5 185
Fluminimaggiore Aa3 198
Flyndersø ○ b2 158
Foa ▭ J 75
Foam Lake b5 250
Fobello c4 196
Foča d4 200
Foça a3 208
Focce dell'Adige ◄ g4 196
Fochabers e2 164
Focinho do Cabo, Braz. ▭ d6 289
Focinho do Cabo, Braz. ═ h5 291
Fockbek c4 158
Focşani h3 201
Fodé d2 224
Fodnanuten △ b2 156
Foelsche ≈ c4 80
Fogang j7 105
Fog Bay ◄ k3 86
Foggâret el Arab e3 221
Foggâret ez Zoûa e3 221
Foggia, Italy ▣ c3 198
Foggia, Puglia, Italy e3 198
Fogi p6 99
Foglia ≈ g6 197
Fogo, Can. g4 253
Fogo, Cape V. ▭ A 222
Fogo Island ▭ g4 253
Fogolawa f3 223
Fogolevo m6 121
Fohnsdorf f2 177
Föhr ▭ d1 172
Fóia △ b7 191
Foiano della Chiana f6 197
Foinaven △ d1 164
Foini a2 138
Foinikountas b6 211
Foix, Fr. ♦ d6 187
Foix, Fr. d6 187
Foix, Spain ≈ f3 192
Fojnica c4 200
Fokino c5 150
Fokku e3 223
Földeák j5 171
Foldereid d4 154
Földes k4 171
Folegandros, Grc. ▭ e5 211
Folegandros, Notio Aigaio, Grc. e6 211
Foley f4 258
Foleyet e1 254
Foley Island ▭ p2 243
Folgaria f4 196
Foligno g7 197
Folkestone h5 163
Folkingham f4 162
Folla ≈ d1 156
Follafoss c5 154
Folldal d1 156
Follina g4 196
Föllinge e5 154
Follonica e7 197
Follonica, Golfo di ◄ e7 197
Folson b3 264
Fominskoe g2 151
Fonda f2 257
Fond-du-Lac p2 249
Fond du Lac b4 254
Fondevila b3 190
Fondi c3 198
Fondón b8 193
Fonfría, Aragón, Spain c3 192
Fonfría, Castilla y León, Spain d3 190
Fonni Ab2 198
Fonseca c1 284
Fonseca, Golfo de ◄ d4 276
Fontaine, Franche-Comté, Fr. c3 184
Fontaine, Rhône-Alpes, Fr. b5 185
Fontainebleau h4 183
Fontaine-Française b3 184
Fontaine Lake ○ p2 249
Fontaine-le-Dun f3 183
Fontaine-lès-Dijon b3 184
Fontaine-lès-Luxeuil c3 184
Fontaine-l'Évêque c4 159
Fontana f7 265
Fontana, Lago ○ b4 295
Fontanarejo f5 191
Fontanellato e5 196
Fontanigorda d5 196
Fontanosas f6 191
Fontas ≈ g2 248
Fonte Boa d4 284
Fonte do Pau-d'Agua f2 293
Fontellas c2 192
Fontenay-le-Comte e6 182
Fontenay-Trésigny h4 183
Fonteneau, Lac ○ m3 253
Fontevraud-l'Abbaye f5 183
Fontgombault c2 186
Fonti, Cima △ f4 196
Fontiveros f4 190
Fontoy d5 159
Fontur ► A 152
Fonualei ▭ J 75
Fonyód f5 171
Fonz e2 192
Fonzaso f3 196
Foping g2 104
Foppolo d3 196
Fora ≈ c5 154
Foraker, Mount △ g2 247
Forano g7 197
Forat q4 137
Forata, Embalse de ○ d5 193
Forbach, Fr. c1 184
Forbach, Ger. d3 174
Forbes j12 81
Forbesganj k6 125
Forbes, Mount △ j5 248
Forcall d4 192
Forcalquier b7 185
Forcarei b2 190
Forchheim d4 175
Ford ≈ c2 254
Ford, Cape ► j3 86
Ford City, California, U.S.A. d6 265
Ford City, Pennsylvania, U.S.A. a4 256
Førde, Hordaland, Nor. a3 156
Førde, Sogn og Fjordane, Nor. a2 156
Fordongianus Aa3 198
Fords Bridge g10 81
Fordville e6 250
Fordyce c3 258
Forécariah b4 222
Foreland Point ► c5 163
Forenza e4 198
Foresight Mountain △ d5 248
Forest, Can. f4 254
Forest, U.S.A. e3 258
Forest City, North Carolina, U.S.A. j2 259
Forest City, Pennsylvania, U.S.A. e3 256
Forest Hill a4 84
Foresthill c2 264
Forestier Peninsula ► Ac3 83
Forest of Atholl ♦ e3 164
Forest of Bowland ☆ d3 162
Forest of Dean ♦ d5 163
Forestville, Can. h4 252
Forestville, U.S.A. a3 264
Forêt d'Orient, Parc Naturel Régional de la ☆ k4 183
Forez, Monts du ▣ f3 186
Forez, Plaine du ─ a5 185
Forfar f3 164
Forges-les-Eaux g3 183
Forio c4 198
Forked Deer ≈ e2 258
Fork, Lake ○ h5 262
Forks a2 262
Forksville d3 256
Forlev e3 158
Forli g5 197
Forli-Cesena ▣ g5 197
Forlimpopoli g5 197
Formazza c3 196
Formby c3 162
Formentera ▭ f6 193
Formentor, Cap de ► g5 193
Formerie g3 183
Formia c3 198
Formiche, Punta della ► d8 199
Formiga f4 291
Formigine e5 196
Formiguères e6 187
Formofoss d4 154
Formosa, Arg. ▣ f4 293
Formosa, Arg. f5 293
Formosa, Braz. e1 290
Formosa do Rio Preto c4 288
Formosa, Serra ▣ a4 288
Formoso, Braz. ≈ c4 288
Formoso, Braz. ≈ d4 288
Formoso, Mato Grosso do Sul, Braz. b4 290
Formoso, Tocantins, Braz. c4 288
Fornelli Aa1 198
Fornes f2 154
Forni Avoltri g3 196
Forni di Sopra g3 196
Forno di Zoldo g3 196
Fornos d3 190
Fornos de Algodres c4 190
Fornovo di Taro e5 196
Forolshogna △ c5 154
Foros do Arrão b5 191
Forráskút h5 171
Forres e2 164
Forrest j12 87
Forrest Lake ○ n3 249
Forrest Lakes ○ j11 87
Forró k3 171
Forsayth f5 80
Forsbacka g2 156
Forsby l2 157
Forserum f4 156
Forssa k2 157
Forst k4 173
Forster l12 81
Forsyth, Georgia, U.S.A. h3 259
Forsyth, Missouri, U.S.A. c1 258
Forsyth, Montana, U.S.A. b2 260
Forsyth Range ▣ f7 80
Fort Abbas f6 129
Fort Albany m4 251
Fortaleza, Pando, Bol. d1 292
Fortaleza, Bol. d2 292
Fortaleza, Braz. e2 288
Fortaleza de Santa Teresa f2 294
Fortanete d4 192
Fort Ashby b5 256
Fort Atkinson b4 254
Fort Augustus d2 164
Fort Beaufort g6 235
Fort Benton h2 262
Fort Bidwell c5 262
Fort Bragg b6 262
Fort Bridger h5 262
Fort Chipewyan m2 249
Fort Cobb Reservoir ○ d5 261
Fort Collins b3 260
Fort-Coulonge h3 255
Fort Davis, Alabama, U.S.A. g3 259
Fort Davis, Texas, U.S.A. h2 272
Fort-de-France J 271
Fort Deposit f3 258
Fort Dodge e3 260
Fort Duchesne j5 262
Forteau p3 253
Forte Veneza b3 288
Fortezza f3 196
Fort Fairfield j5 253
Fort Frances g6 250
Fort Gibson b2 258
Fort Gibson Lake ○ b2 258
Fort Good Hope m2 247
Forth ≈ d3 164
Fort Hall g4 262
Fort Hancock g2 272
Fortin f4 275
Fortín Aroma e4 293
Fortín Ávalos Sánchez e4 293
Fortín Boquerón f4 293
Fortín Capitán Demattei e4 293
Fortín Carlos Antonio López f4 293
Fortín Coronel Eugenio Garay e4 293
Fortín Galpón f3 293
Fortín General Caballero f4 293
Fortín General Díaz e4 293
Fortín General Mendoza e4 293
Fortín Hernandarías e4 293
Fortín Infante Rivarola e4 293
Fortín Juan de Zalazar f4 293
Fortín Lagerenza e4 293
Fortín Lavalle e5 293
Fortín Leonardo Britos e4 293
Fortín Leonida Escobar e4 293
Fortín Linares e4 293
Fortín Madrejón f4 293
Fortín May Alberto Gardel e4 293
Fortín Nueva Asunción e4 293
Fortín Olavarría f3 297
Fortín Pilcomayo e4 293
Fortín Presidente Ayala f4 293
Fortín Ravelo e3 293
Fortín Suárez Arana e3 293
Fortín Teniente Juan Echauri López e4 293
Fortín Teniente Mountania f4 293
Fortín Teniente Primero H. Mendoza f3 293
Fortín Teniente Rojas Silva e4 293
Fortín Uno e5 296
Fort Kent h5 253
Fort Klamath c4 262
Fort Lauderdale j6 259
Fort Liard f1 248
Fort Liberté j5 271
Fort Lockhart e4 128
Fort Loudon c5 256
Fort Macleod l7 249
Fort Madison f3 260
Fort-Mahon-Plage g2 183
Fort McMurray m3 249
Fort McPherson l2 247
Fort Meade j6 259
Fort Meyers Beach j6 259
Fort Morgan c3 260
Fort Munro e6 129
Fort Myers j6 259
Fort Nelson, British Columbia, Can. f2 248
Fort Nelson, British Columbia, Can. ≈ f2 248
Fort Ogden j6 259
Fort Payne g2 259
Fort Peck p7 249
Fort Pierce j6 259
Fort Pierre c2 260
Fort Plain f2 256
Fort Portal f3 225
Fort Providence f3 242
Fort Qu'Appelle r6 249
Fort Resolution g3 242
Fort Rixon d2 233
Fortrose, N.Z. b7 77
Fortrose, U.K. d2 164
Fort Scott b1 258
Fort Severn k2 251
Fort-Shevchenko h3 149
Fort Simpson e3 242
Fort Smith, Can. l1 249
Fort Smith, U.S.A. b2 258
Fort St James e4 248
Fort St John g3 248
Fort Stockton h2 273
Fort Sumner b5 261
Fort Thomas j9 263
Fortuna, Spain c6 193
Fortuna, California, U.S.A. a5 262
Fortuna, North Dakota, U.S.A. r7 249
Fortune q5 253
Fortune Bay ◄ q5 253
Fortune Harbour q4 253
Fort Vermilion j2 249
Fort Walton Beach f4 258
Fort Wayne d5 254
Fort White h5 259
Fort William c3 164
Fort Worth a3 258
Forty Fours, The ▭ A 77
Fortymile ≈ j2 247
Fort Yukon h2 247
Forūr, Jazireh-ye ▭ q8 137
Forvik d4 154
Forza d'Agrò e7 199
Fos c6 187
Fosforescente, Bahía ◄ A 266
Foshan j7 105
Foskvallen c5 154
Fosna ♦ c5 154
Fosnavåg a1 156
Foso d4 222
Fossacesia d2 198
Fossano b5 196
Fossil Downs g6 86
Fossombrone g6 197
Fosston f7 250
Fos-sur-Mer a7 185
Foster h15 81
Fosterdale f3 256
Foster Lakes ○ q3 249
Foster, Mount △ l4 247
Fosters f3 258
Fostoria e5 254
Fót h4 171
Foucarmont g3 183
Fouesnant a5 182
Foug b2 184
Fougamou b4 224
Fougères d4 182
Fouke c3 258
Foula ▭ A 164
Foulabala c3 222
Foulain b2 184
Foul Bay ◄ e2 219
Foulenzem f6 223
Foul Island ▭ a6 102
Foulness Point ► h5 163
Foul Point ► A 127
Foulwind, Cape ► c4 77
Foumban g4 223
Foumbot g4 223
Foum Zguid c2 220
Foundiougne a3 222
Fountain g4 259
Fountain Hill e4 256
Fountain Inn h2 259
Fouras a3 186
Fourchambault f1 186
Fourchu m6 253
Fouriesburg h4 235
Fourmies c4 159
Fourna b3 210
Fournels f4 186
Fournier, Cape ► A 77
Fournier, Lac ○ k3 253
Fournoi, Grc. ▭ Ab1 211
Fournoi, Voreio Aigaio, Grc. Ab1 210
Four Oaks k2 259
Fours f2 186
Fourzol d3 138
Fouta Djallon ♦ b3 222
Foveaux Strait ═ a7 77
Fowler, California, U.S.A. d5 264
Fowler, Colorado, U.S.A. b4 260
Fowler, Indiana, U.S.A. c5 254
Fowlers Bay ▣ l13 87
Fox, Can. ≈ f3 250
Fox, Alaska, U.S.A. h2 247
Fox, Illinois, U.S.A. ≈ b5 254
Foxas b1 190
Fox Creek, Aust. ≈ b3 84
Fox Creek, U.S.A. g1 259
Foxe Basin ~ p2 243
Foxe Channel ═ p3 243
Fox Glacier c5 77
Fox Lake Hills b4 254
Fox Mountain △ l3 247
Foxton e4 76
Foxton Beach e4 76
Foxworth e4 258
Foyle ≈ d2 165
Foyle, Lough ◄ d1 165
Foynes b4 165
Foz c1 190
Foz de Gregório c1 292
Foz do Copeá e4 285
Foz do Cunene a2 232
Foz do Iguaçu a6 290
Foz do Jamari e1 293
Foz do Jutaí d4 284
Foz do Mamoriá d4 284
Foz do Riosinho c1 292
Foz Giraldo c5 191
Frabosa Soprana b5 197
Frącki m2 169
Frackville d4 256
Frades de la Sierra e4 190
Fraga, Arg. e2 296
Fraga, Spain e3 192
Fragagnano f4 198
Fraile Muerto f2 294
Fraize d2 184
Fram Basin ~ h3 299
Frameries b4 159
Framingham j2 257
Framlev d2 158
Frammersbach g3 174
Frampol l5 169
Franca e4 290
Francavilla al Mare d2 198
Francavilla di Sicilia e7 199
Francavilla Fontana g4 198
Francavilla in Sinni f4 198
France e5 144

FRANCE

THE FRENCH REPUBLIC
Area 543,965km² (210,026sq miles)
Capital Paris
Organizations CE, EBRD, EU, G8, NATO, OECD, SPC
Population 59,470,000
Pop. growth (%) 0.3
Life expectancy 74 (m); 82 (f)
Languages French, Breton, Basque
Literacy 95%
Currency euro (US $1 = 0.81 euro)
GDP (US million $) 1,433,000
GDP per head ($US) 24,096

Frances, Aust. e14 81
Frances, Can. ≈ m3 247
Francescas c4 187
Frances Lake ○ m3 247
Francés, Punta ► c4 266
Francés Viejo, Cabo ► k5 267
Franceville b4 224
Franche-Comté ▣ c3 184
Francia j2 297
Francis Case, Lake ○ d3 260
Francisco de Orellana c4 284
Francisco I. Madero, Chiapas, Mex. h5 275
Francisco I. Madero, Coahuila, Mex. h5 272
Francisco I. Madero, Durango, Mex. g5 272
Francisco I. Madero, Nayarit, Mex. b3 274
Francisco Meeks h4 297
Francisco Sá g2 291
Francisco Zarco e9 263
Francistown d3 232
Franco da Rocha e5 291
Francofonte d7 199
Francois p5 253
François Lake ○ d5 248
Francois Peron National Park ☆ a9 87
Francorchamps d4 159
Francs Peak △ j4 262
Frane f2 221
Franeker d1 159
Frangy b4 185
Frankenberg j2 175
Frankenberg (Eder) g1 174
Frankenburg am Hausruck e1 176
Frankenheim f2 174
Frankenmarkt e2 176
Frankenmuth e4 254
Frankenthal f2 174
Frankenwald, Ger. ▣ g2 175
Frankenwald, Ger. ☆ g2 175
Frankfield B 270
Frankfort, R.S.A. h3 235
Frankfort, Indiana, U.S.A. c5 254
Frankfort, Kentucky, U.S.A. d6 254
Frankfort, Michigan, U.S.A. c3 254
Frankfurt am Main d2 174
Frankfurt an der Oder k3 173
Frank Hann National Park ☆ e13 87
Fränkische Alb ▣ g3 175
Fränkische Rezat ≈ f3 175
Fränkische Saale ≈ e2 174
Fränkische Schweiz ▣ g3 175
Fränkische Schweiz Veldensteiner Forst ☆ g2 175
Frankland, Cape ► Ab1 83
Franklin, R.S.A. h5 235
Franklin, Arizona, U.S.A. j9 263
Franklin, Georgia, U.S.A. g3 259
Franklin, Idaho, U.S.A. h4 262
Franklin, Louisiana, U.S.A. d5 258
Franklin, Massachusetts, U.S.A. j2 257
Franklin, New Jersey, U.S.A. f3 256
Franklin, North Carolina, U.S.A. h2 259
Franklin, Ohio, U.S.A. d6 254
Franklin, Pennsylvania, U.S.A. g5 254
Franklin, Texas, U.S.A. a4 258
Franklin, Virginia, U.S.A. h7 255
Franklin, West Virginia, U.S.A. a6 256
Franklin Bay ◄ n1 247
Franklin D. Roosevelt Lake ○ d1 262
Franklin-Gordon National Park ☆ Aa3 83
Franklin Grove b5 254
Franklin Harbor ► c12 81
Franklin Island ▭ y2 298
Franklin Mountains ▣ n2 247
Franklin, Point ► e1 246
Franklin Sound ═ Ab2 83
Franklinton d4 258
Franklinville b2 256
Frankston, Aust. d4 82
Frankston, U.S.A. b3 258
Frånsta g1 156
Františkovy Lázně a1 170
Franz Josef Glacier c5 77
Franz Josef Land ▭ e2 118
Franz Joseph Land ▭ n2 299
Frascati g8 197
Frascineto f5 198
Fraser ≈ g7 248
Fraserburg d5 234
Fraserburgh f2 164
Fraserdale m6 251
Fraser Island ♦ e4 84
Fraser Island National Park ☆ e4 84
Fraser, Mount △ d9 87
Fraser National Park ☆ d3 82
Fraser Plateau ▣ f5 248
Fraser Range, Western Australia, Aust. ▣ f12 87
Frasertown f3 76
Frasnes-lez-Buissenal b4 159
Frassinoro e5 197
Fratel c5 191
Fratta ≈ f4 196
Frauenfeld c2 196
Frauenkirchen h2 177
Frauenstein j2 175
Fray Bentos h2 297
Fray Luis Beltrán, Río Negro, Arg. e5 296
Fray Luis Beltrán, Santa Fé, Arg. g2 297
Fray Marcos k3 297
Frayssinet-le-Gélat d4 186
Frazee f7 250
Frazier Mountain △ e7 265
Frecăţei j3 201
Frechen e4 159
Frechilla f2 190
Frech, Mont △ f5 187
Fredensborg f3 158
Frederica e5 256
Fredericia c3 158
Frederick, Maryland, U.S.A. c5 256
Frederick, Oklahoma, U.S.A. d5 261
Frederick House ≈ n6 251
Frederick House Lake ○ n6 251
Fredericksburg, U.S.A. ▣ k7 257
Fredericksburg, Texas, U.S.A. k2 273
Fredericksburg, Virginia, U.S.A. c6 256
Frederick Sound ═ l4 247
Fredericktown d1 258
Frederick Willem IV Vallen ─ f3 285
Fredericton j6 253
Fredericton Junction j6 253
Frederiks c2 158
Frederiksberg, Den. ▣ e2 158
Frederiksberg, Frederiksberg, Den. f3 158
Frederiksberg, Vestsjælland, Den. e3 158
Frederiksborg ▣ f3 158
Frederikshavn d1 158
Frederikssund f3 158
Frederiksværk f3 158
Fredersdorf j3 173
Fredonia a2 256
Fredrika g4 154
Fredriksberg f2 156
Fredrikstad d3 156
Freehold f4 257
Freeland e3 256
Freeling Heights △ d11 81
Freeling, Mount △ a7 80
Freel Peak △ d3 264
Freels, Cape ► q43 253
Freeman, California, U.S.A. f6 265
Freeman, South Dakota, U.S.A. d3 260
Freemount c4 165
Freeport, Illinois, U.S.A. b4 254
Freeport, Maine, U.S.A. g7 252
Freeport, New York, U.S.A. g4 257
Freeport, Texas, U.S.A. b5 258
Freeport City k6 259
Freer k4 273
Free State ▣ g3 235
Freetown b4 222
Frégate, Lac de la ○ r4 251
Fregenal de la Sierra d6 191
Fréhel, Cap ► c4 182
Freiberg, Sachsen, Ger. j2 175
Freiburg, Ger. ▣ d5 174
Freiburg, Baden-Württemberg, Ger. d3 174
Freiburg (Elbe) c5 158
Freienstein c4 174
Frei Gonzaga h2 291
Frei Inocêncio h3 291
Freilassing d2 176
Freire a5 296
Freirina b1 294
Freisen f5 159
Freising d2 175
Freistadt f1 177
Freital j2 175
Freixedas c4 190
Freixo b3 190
Freixo de Espada à Cinta d3 190
Frejlev c1 158
Fréjus c7 185
Fremantle b13 87
Fremdingen g4 174
Fremont, California, U.S.A. b4 264
Fremont, Nebraska, U.S.A. d3 260
Fremont, Ohio, U.S.A. e5 254
Fremont, Utah, U.S.A. ≈ h6 263
Fremont Valley ≈ e6 265
Frenchburg h1 259
French Camp b4 264
French Creek ≈ f5 254
French Guiana (France) ▢ e2 282
French Island ▭ d4 82
French Lick c6 254
Frenchman, Montana, U.S.A. ≈ p7 249
Frenchman, Nevada, U.S.A. e2 264
Frenchman's Cap △ Aa3 83
Frenchpark c3 165
French Pass d4 76
French Polynesia (France) ▢ l5 73
Frenda e1 221
Frenštát pod Radhoštěm g2 171
Freren f2 159
Fresach e3 176
Fresco, Braz. ≈ b3 288
Fresco, C.I. c4 222
Fresnay-sur-Sarthe f4 183
Fresnes-en-Woëvre b1 184
Fresne-St-Mamès b3 184
Fresnillo c2 274
Fresno, Mex. d3 274
Fresno, California, U.S.A. ≈ d4 264
Fresno, California, U.S.A. d5 264
Fresno Alhándiga e4 190
Fresno de la Ribera e3 190
Fresno Reservoir ○ j1 262
Fresnoy-Folny g3 183
Fressel, Lac ○ r3 251
Fretigney-et-Velloreille b3 184
Freudenberg f4 174
Freudenstadt c2 174
Frévent h2 183
Frewena b5 80
Frewsburg a2 256
Freyburg (Unstrut) e1 175
Freycinet National Park ☆ Ac3 83
Freycinet Peninsula ► Ac3 83
Freyming-Merlebach c1 184
Freyre f1 297
Freystadt d4 175
Freyung e1 176
Fria b3 222
Fria, Cape ► a2 232
Friant d5 264
Friant-Kern Canal ─ d6 265
Frias c1 294
Fribourg b3 196
Frick c2 196
Fričovce j2 171
Friday Harbor b1 262
Fridaythorpe f2 162
Fridtjof Nansen, Mount △ aa3 298
Friedberg, Aus. h2 177
Friedberg, Ger. c4 175
Friedberg (Hessen) e2 174
Friedeburg c2 172
Friedens b4 256
Friedewald e2 174
Friedland, Brandenburg, Ger. k3 173
Friedland, Mecklenburg-Vorpommern, Ger. j2 173
Friedland, Niedersachsen, Ger. e4 172
Friedrichroda c3 175
Friedrichsdorf f2 174
Friedrichshafen d2 174
Friedrichskoog b4 158
Friedrichsruhe e5 158
Friedrichstadt c4 158
Friedrichswalde j2 173
Friemar d3 175
Friendship b2 256
Friesach f3 177
Friesack h3 173
Friesenheim c3 174
Friesland ▣ d1 159
Friesoythe c2 172
Frihetsli g2 154
Friitala j2 157
Frillesås f1 158
Frinton-on-Sea h5 163
Frio ≈ d6 261
Frio, Cabo ► g6 287
Friockheim f3 164
Friol c1 190
Frisco City f4 258
Fristad e4 156
Fritsla e4 156
Fritzlar f1 174
Friuli - Venezia Giulia ▣ g3 196
Friville-Escarbotin g2 183
Frizington c2 162
Frjanovo e3 150
Frjazino e4 150
Froan ▭ b5 154
Frobisher Bay ◄ r3 243
Frobisher Lake ○ n3 249
Frodisia a1 138
Frohavet ◄ b5 154
Frohburg k1 175
Frohnberg △ e3 174
Frohnleiten g2 177
Froissy h3 183
Frolišči g3 151
Frolovo f2 149
Frombork h1 169
Frome, Aust. ≈ d10 81
Frome, England, U.K. ≈ d6 163
Frome, England, U.K. d5 163
Frome, Lake ○ e11 81
Fromentières j4 183
Fromentine c6 182
Frómista f2 190
Fröndenberg c4 172

Fronhausen → Gedaref 333

Fronhausen f4 174
Fronsac b4 186
Fronteira c5 191
Fronteiras d3 288
Frontenac b1 258
Frontenard b4 184
Frontenay-Rohan-Rohan b2 186
Frontenhausen h4 175
Frontera, Iraq Aa3 189
Frontera, Coahuila, Mex. j4 273
Frontera, Tabasco, Mex. a1 276
Frontera Echeverría b2 276
Frontera Hidalgo a3 276
Fronteras, Guat. c3 276
Fronteras, Mex. j10 263
Frontignan f5 187
Fronton d5 187
Front Royal b6 256
Frosinone, Italy h8 197
Frosinone, Lazio, Italy h8 197
Frösö e5 154
Frosolone d3 198
Frosta c5 154
Frostburg b5 256
Frouard c2 184
Frouseira, Punta b1 190
Frövi f3 156
Frøya b5 154
Frøyfjorden b5 154
Frøyhavet b5 154
Fruges h2 183
Fruita a4 260
Fruitdale e4 258
Fruitland e6 256
Fruitvale e1 262
Frunze, Batken, Kyrg. n7 121
Frunze, Bishkek, Kyrg. q6 121
Frunzivka j2 201
Fruska Gora d3 200
Frutigen b3 196
Frutuoso e2 293
Fry Ab3 210
Frya c2 156
Frýdek-Místek g2 171
Frýdlant d1 170
Frýdlant nad Ostravicí g2 171
Fryeburg g6 252
Fryšták f2 171
Frysztak k6 169
Fuan e5 154
Fucecchio e6 197
Fuchang c4 106
Fucheng e1 106
Fuchū e4 114
Fuchun Jiang f5 111
Fuding n5 105
Fuego, Tierra del c6 295
Fuencaliente, Iraq Ab2 189
Fuencaliente, Spain f6 191
Fuendejalón c3 192
Fuengirola f8 191
Fuenlabrada g4 190
Fuenmayor b2 192
Fuensalida f4 190
Fuensanta c7 193
Fuensanta,
Embalse de la b6 193
Fuente-Álamo c6 193
Fuente Álamo c7 193
Fuentecambrón a3 192
Fuentecén g3 190
Fuente de Cantos d6 191
Fuente del Arco e6 191
Fuente de Piedra f7 191
Fuente de Piedra,
Laguna de f7 191
Fuente el Fresno g5 191
Fuenteguinaldo d4 190
Fuentelcésped g3 190
Fuentelespino de Haro b5 193
Fuente Obejuna e6 191
Fuentepinilla b3 192
Fuenterodos d3 192
Fuentesaúco e3 190
Fuentes de Ayódar d4 193
Fuentes de Ebro d3 192
Fuentes de Jiloca c3 192
Fuentes de León d6 191
Fuentes de Oñoro d4 190
Fuentespalda e4 192
Fuentestrún c3 192
Fuentidueña g3 190
Fu'er He p4 113
Fuerte, Isla b2 284
Fuerte Olimpo f4 293
Fuerteventura Af2 189
Fuga c1 100
Fuga'uvea, Passe L 75
Fügen c2 176
Fuglafjell b2 156
Fuglebjerg e3 158
Fugloy B 152
Fugløya h1 154
Fugong d2 102
Fugou, Henan, China d3 106
Fugou, Henan, China d2 106
Fuhai w4 121
Fuhne h4 173
Fuhse f3 172
Fuji, China d2 106
Fuji, Japan h4 115
Fujian l6 104
Fu Jiang h3 104
Fujieda h4 115
Fujin r2 113
Fujioka h3 115
Fuji-san h4 115
Fujisawa h4 115
Fujiyoshida h4 115
Fukagawa Ac2 114
Fukang w5 121
Fukuchiyama f4 115
Fukue-jima c5 114
Fukui, Japan g4 115
Fukui, Fukui, Japan g3 115
Fukuoka, Japan d5 114
Fukuoka, Fukuoka, Japan r9 113
Fukuroi g4 115
Fukushima, Japan j3 115
Fukushima,
Fukushima, Japan j3 115
Fukushima,
Hokkaidō, Japan Ab3 114
Fulacunda a3 222
Fulaga E 74
Fulan e2 156
Fulbourn g4 163
Fulda, Ger. e4 172
Fulda, Hessen, Ger. f4 174
Fule e6 104
Fuliang e5 111
Fuliji e3 111
Fuling f4 104
Fullerton Point D 271
Fulnek f2 171
Fülöpháza h5 171
Fülöpszállás h5 171
Fulpmes c2 176
Fulton, Arg. h4 297
Fulton, Arkansas, U.S.A. c3 258
Fulton, Missouri, U.S.A. f4 260
Fulton, New York, U.S.A. h4 255
Fultondale f3 258
Fumane k2 235
Fumay c5 159
Fumel c4 187
Funafuti N 75
Funan d3 111
Funäsdalen e1 156
Funchal B 189
Fundación c1 284
Fundão, Braz. h3 291
Fundão, Port c4 190
Fundición e4 272
Fundulea h3 201
Funhalouro l1 235
Funing, Jiangsu, China f3 111
Funing, Yunnan, China e7 104
Funiu Shan b3 106
Funnel Creek c3 84
Funsi d3 222
Funtua f3 223
Fuping h6 112
Fuqing m6 105
Fuqū' d5 139
Fur b2 158
Furancungo e1 233
Furano Ac2 114
Fureidis c4 138
Furesø f3 158
Furfooz,
Parc Naturel de c4 159
Fürgun, Küh-e r7 137
Furmanov f3 150
Furnas, Represa f4 291
Furneaux Group Ac1 83
Fürstenau c3 172
Fürstenberg j2 173
Fürstenberg (Lichtenfels) f1 173
Fürstenfeld h2 177
Fürstenfeldbruck d3 175
Fürstenwalde k3 173
Fürstenzell e1 176
Furta k4 171
Furtei Aa3 198
Fürth, Bayern, Ger. f5 175
Fürth, Hessen, Ger. f3 174
Furth im Wald h3 175
Furtwangen e2 174
Furudal f2 156
Furukawa j2 115
Furusund h3 157
Fusagasugá c3 284
Fuscaldo f5 199
Fushan, Jiangsu, China c4 111
Fushan, Shandong, China g1 111
Fushan, Shanxi, China b2 106
Fushun, Liaoning, China m5 113
Fushun, Sichuan, China e4 104
Fusine in Valromana h3 196
Fusong p4 113
Füssen g5 175
Fussing Sø c2 158
Fustiñana c2 192
Futago-san d5 114
Futaleufú b4 295
Futrikelv g2 154
Futrono a6 296
Futtsu h4 115
Futuna F 74
Futuna, Île L 75
Futun Xi l5 105
Fuwayriţ n8 137
Fuxian a2 106
Fuxian Hu d6 104
Fuxin, Liaoning, China l4 113
Fuyang, Anhui, China d3 106
Fuyang, Zhejiang, China f4 111
Fuyang He d1 106
Fuying Dao n5 105
Fuyu, Heilongjiang, China n2 113
Fuyu, Jilin, China p3 113
Füzesabony j4 171
Füzesgyarmat k4 171
Fuzhou m5 105
Fuzhoucheng l6 113
Fuzhuang f2 111
Fuzhuangyi e0 111
Füzuli g5 149
Fylde d3 162
Fyn, Den. d3 158
Fyn, Den. d3 158
Fyne d3 164
Fyne, Loch c3 164
Fyns Hoved d3 158
Fyresvatn c3 156
Fyteies b4 210
Fyti a2 138
Fyvie f2 164

G

Gaalkacyo d2 226
Ga'ash c4 139
Gabarret c5 187
Gabas b5 187
Gabbs f3 264
Gabbs Valley Range e3 264
Gabčíkovo f4 171
Gabela b6 224
Gabès g2 221
Gabès, Golfe de g2 221
Gabicce Mare g6 197
Gabilan Range b5 264
Gąbin h3 169
Gabino Barreda f4 275
Gablitz h1 177
Gabon d5 217

GABON

THE GABONESE REPUBLIC
Area 267,667km² (103,347sq miles)
Capital Libreville
Organizations FZ, OIC, CEEAC
Population 1,310,000
Pop. growth (%) 5.2
Life expectancy 51 (m); 53 (f)
Languages French, Fang, Bantu dialects
Literacy 63.2%
Currency CFA franc (US $1 = 534.95 CFA franc)
GDP (US million $) 4136
GDP per head ($US) 3157

Gáborján k4 171
Gaborone f2 235
Gaboto g2 297
Gabriel Vera d3 292
Gabriel y Galán,
Embalse de d4 190
Gabriel Zamora c4 274
Gabrnik g3 177
Gabrovnitsa f4 201
Gabrovo, Bul. g4 201
Gabrovo, Gabrovo, Bul. g4 201
Gabú b3 222
Gabuli f5 219
Gaby b4 196
Gacé f4 183
Gachsārān n6 137
Gacka g5 177
Gacko d4 200
Gada f3 223
Gâda f1 156
Gădăbäy g4 149
Gadag d5 126
Gadarwara f8 124
Gadchiroli g9 124
Gäddede e4 154
Gadebusch e5 158
Gadhada e9 129
Gadhap c8 129
Gadhka d9 129
Gadhra b9 124
Gadoni Ab3 198
Gádor b8 193
Gádor, Sierra de b8 193
Gadot d3 138
Gadra, Balochistan, Pak. c7 129
Gadra, Sindh, Pak. e8 129
Gadsden, Alabama, U.S.A. f2 258
Gadsden, Arizona, U.S.A. f9 263
Gadwal e4 126
Gadyn a1 128
Gadzi c3 224
Găeşti g3 201
Gaeta c3 198
Gaeta, Golfo di h8 197
Gafanha da Nazaré b4 190
Gaferut G 74
Gáfete c5 191
Gafsa f2 221
Gagal c2 224
Gagarin, Russ. Fed. c4 150
Gagarin, Uzb. m7 121
Gagere f3 223
Gaggenau f4 174
Gaggi e7 199
Gaggio Montano e5 197
Gagil-Tamil G 74
Gagino h4 151
Gagliano Castelferrato d7 199
Gagliano del Capo c3 199
Gagnoa c4 222
Gagra f4 148
Gaiab c3 234
Găiceana h2 201
Gaigalava m4 157
Gail, Aus. e3 176
Gail, U.S.A. c5 261
Gaildorf d4 174
Gaillac d5 187
Gaillon g3 183
Gailtaler Alpen e3 176
Gaimersheim e4 175
Gainesville, Florida, U.S.A. h5 259
Gainesville, Missouri, U.S.A. c1 258
Gainesville, Texas, U.S.A. a3 258
Gainsborough f3 162
Gairdner d14 87
Gairdner, Lake c12 81
Gair Loch c2 164
Gairloch c2 164
Gairo Ab3 198
Gaithersburg c5 256
Gaizhou m5 113
Gaiziņkalns l4 157
Gaj k2 149
Gajah Hutan, Bukit b2 101
Gajanejos b4 192
Gajar b7 129
Gajary e3 170
Gaji g3 223
Gajny h3 147
Gajutino e2 150
Gakarosa e3 234
Gakem f4 223
Gakona h3 247
Gakona Junction h3 247
Gakuch a1 130
Gala j5 135
Galaasiya b1 128
Gaładuś, Jezioro k5 157
Galambok f5 170
Galan c5 187
Galana b4 226
Galán, Cerro d5 292
Galang q3 137
Galang Besar d5 101
Galangue b1 232
Galanta f3 171
Galápagos, Islas, Ec. A 286
Galápagos, Islas, Ec. A 286
Galaroza d7 191
Galashiels f4 164
Galata h4 201
Galata, Nos j4 201
Galatas d5 211
Galatea f3 76
Galateia c1 138
Galaţi, Rom. h3 201
Galaţi, Galaţi, Rom. j3 201
Galatina h4 198
Galatini b2 210
Galatista d2 210
Galatone h4 198
Gala Water f4 164
Galax f7 254
Galaxidi c4 210
Galbraith e4 80
Gáldar Ad2 189
Galdhøpiggen c2 156
Galeana, Chihuahua, Mex. f2 272
Galeana, Nuevo León, Mex. j5 273
Galeh Dār p8 137
Galela h5 97
Galena, Alaska, U.S.A. e2 246
Galena, Illinois, U.S.A. a3 254
Galenbecker See j2 173
Galera, Spain b7 193
Galera, Andalucía, Spain b7 193
Galera, Punta, Chile a5 296
Galera, Punta, Ec. a3 284
Galera, Punta, Mex. f6 275
Galera, Punta de la b1 284
Galeras b3 284
Galéria A 185
Galéria, Golfe de A 185
Galesburg a5 254
Galeshewe f4 234
Galeton c3 256
Galey b4 165
Galgamácsa h4 171
Galguduud d2 226
Gália d5 290
Galiakot g9 129
Galiano Island b1 262
Galibier, Col du c5 185
Galič g2 151
Galicea Mare f3 201
Galicia c2 190
Galičica e5 200
Galičskaja
Vozvyšennost' f2 150
Galicy g3 151
Galilee, Lake a3 84
Galiléia h3 291
Galim Tignère g4 223
Galinakopf a2 176
Galina Point B 266
Galinda d3 274
Galiñeiro b2 190
Galiniporni c1 138
Galion e5 254
Galissonnière, Lac la l3 253
Galište Ezero b1 210
Galisteo d5 191
Galiwinku b2 80
Galkino k5 147
Gallabat e5 219
Gallarate c4 196
Gallardon g4 183
Gallatin h3 262
Galle g9 126
Gállego d2 192
Gallegón b7 193
Gallego Rise q6 301
Gallegos b6 295
Gallegos, Cabo a5 295
Gallegos de Solmirón e4 190
Galley Head c5 165
Galliate c4 196
Gallinas, Punta c1 284
Gallio f4 196
Gallipoli h4 198
Gallipolis e6 254
Gallipuén, Embalse de d4 192
Gällivare h3 154
Gallneukirchen f1 177
Gallo c4 192
Gällö e5 154
Gallocanta, Laguna de c4 192
Gallo, Lago di e3 196
Galloway, Mount B 77
Gallup a5 261
Gallur c3 192
Gallyaaral l7 121
Gal Oya A 127
Gal Shiikh d1 226
Gålsjön g5 154
Galston d4 164
Galt b3 264
Galtat Zemmour b3 220
Galtee Mountains c4 164
Galtelli Ab2 198
Galten, Den. c2 158
Galten, Swe. g3 156
Galtür b3 176
Galula b3 231
Galvarino a5 296
Galve de Sorbe a3 192
Galveias b5 191
Galveston b5 258
Galveston Bay b5 258
Galvez g2 297
Gálvez f5 191
Galvsjön g2 156
Galwa e5 130
Galway, Ire. c3 165
Galway, Galway, Ire. b3 165
Galway Bay b3 165
Gâm g4 102
Gama d2 290
Gamaches g3 183
Gamagōri g4 115
Gamaliel g1 259
Gamarra c2 284
Gamás f5 171
Gamawa g3 223
Gamay e4 297
Gamba, China j5 135
Gamba, Gabon a4 224
Gambaga d3 222
Gambang c4 101
Gambara e4 196
Gambarie e6 199
Gambēla, Eth. a2 226
Gambēla,
Gambēla, Eth. f2 225
Gambēla
National Park a2 226
Gambell b3 246
Gambettola g5 197
Gambia a3 222
Gambia Plain g8 302
Gambia, The a3 217

GAMBIA, The

THE REPUBLIC OF THE GAMBIA
Area 11,295km² (4361sq miles)
Capital Banjul
Organizations COMM, ECOWAS, OIC
Population 1,390,000
Pop. growth (%) 3.3
Life expectancy 44 (m); 46 (f)
Languages English, Mandinka, Fula Wolof, other local languages
Literacy 40.1%
Currency dalasi (US $1 = 30 dalasi)
GDP (US million $) 324
GDP per head ($US) 233

Gambier, Îles K 75
Gambier Islands c13 81
Gambo d3 224
Gambolò c4 196
Gamboma c4 224
Gamboola f4 80
Gamboula c3 224
Gambuta, Gunung m4 99
Gaming g2 177
Gamka Mountain
Reserve d6 234
Gamkapoort Nature
Reserve d6 234
Gamleby g4 156
Gamlitz g3 177
Gammertingen g4 174
Gammon Ranges
National Park d11 81
Gammtratten g5 154
Ga-Modjadji j1 235
Gamoep c5 234
Gamova, Mys r4 113
Gampaha g9 126
Gamud b3 226
Gan b5 187
Ganado j8 263
Gananoque h3 255
Ganaur c5 130
Ganäveh n7 137
Gäncä g4 149
Ganda a1 232
Gandadiwata, Bukit k6 99
Gandajika d5 224
Gándara, Galicia, Spain b1 190
Gandarbal b2 130
Gandari Mountain d6 129
Gandava c6 129
Gander,
Newfoundland, Can. q4 253
Gander, Newfoundland
and Labrador, Can. q4 253
Ganderkesee d2 172
Gander Lake q4 253
Gandesa e3 192
Gandhidham e9 129
Gandhinagar f9 129
Gandhi Sagar g8 129
Gandía d6 193
Gandino d4 196
Gandi, Wadi b5 218
Gand-i-Zureh a6 129
Gandomān n6 137
Gandrange e5 159
Gandrup d1 158
Gandu e4 288
Gandvik m1 155
Ganga, Bang. l7 125
Ganga, Sri L. A 127
Gangala Na Bodia e3 225
Gangán c4 295
Ganganagar f6 129
Gangán, Pampa de c4 295
Gangapur,
Rajasthan, India e6 124
Gangapur,
Rajasthan, India g8 129
Gangara f3 223
Ganga Sera e8 129
Gangaw b4 102
Gangawati e5 126
Gangaw Range c3 102
Gangca a7 112
Gangdhar g9 129
Gangdisê Shan f4 135
Ganges l7 125
Ganges f5 187
Ganges,
Mouths of the Aa2 123
Gangi d7 199
Gangkofen h4 175
Gangkou f4 111
Gangoh c5 130
Gangotri Group d4 130
Gangrampur l7 125
Gangrar g8 129
Gangtok j6 135
Gangu e1 104
Gangwa d4 224
Gangziyao d1 106
Gan He n1 113
Gani h6 97
Ganjam j3 127
Gan Jiang k5 105
Ganjing b2 106
Ganjur Sum h3 112
Ganlin g5 111
Ganluo d4 104
Gannan m2 113
Gannat f2 186
Gannett Peak j4 262
Ganora g9 129
Ganpu g4 111
Ganquan a1 106
Gansbaai c7 234
Gänsehals c2 174
Gänserndorf h1 177
Gansu b7 112
Ganta c4 222
Gantamaa c3 226
Gantang c7 112
Gantheaume Point e5 86
Gant'iadi f4 148
Gantt f4 258
Gan Yavne c5 139
Ganye g4 223
Ganyesa f3 234
Ganyu f2 111
Ganyushkino h3 149
Ganzhou k6 105
Ganzi f3 225
Ganzlin f5 158
Gao, Mali e2 223
Gao, Gao, Mali d2 222
Gao'an k4 105
Gaocheng d0 111
Gaochun f4 111
Gaogou f2 111
Gaojiayan b4 106
Gaolan b7 112
Gaoligong Shan b6 104
Gaoling a2 106
Gaomi f1 111
Gaoping, Hubei, China c2 106
Gaoping, Shanxi, China c2 106
Gaoqian d1 106
Gaoqing e1 111
Gaotang e1 111
Gaotouyao e6 112
Gaoua d3 222
Gaoual b3 222
Gaoxian e4 104
Gaoya f1 111
Gaoyang h6 112
Gaoyi d1 106
Gaoyou f3 111
Gaoyou Hu f3 111
Gaozhou h8 104
Gap c6 185
Gapan c3 100
Gapeau b7 185
Gapuwiyak b2 80
Gaqoi f5 135
Gar a7 129
Gara h5 171
Garabekevyul b1 128
Garacad d2 226
Garachiné h6 277
Garachiné, Punta h6 277
Garadag d2 226
Garagoa c2 284
Garaguso f4 198
Garah c6 85
Garalo c3 222
Gara, Lough c2 165
Garam d1 200
Garamba e3 225
Garamba,
Parc National de la e3 225
Garang b4 101
Garanhuns e3 288
Garapu b4 288
Garapuava e2 291
Garar, Plaine de b5 218
Garba d2 224
Garbahaarey c3 226
Garba Tula b3 226
Garbayuela f5 191
Garbów l4 169
Garbsen e3 172
Garça d5 290
Garças, Rio das b1 290
Garching an der Alz d1 176
Garching bei München e4 175
Garcia e3 192
García, Cerro c3 274
Garcia de la Cadena c3 274
Garcias b4 290
Garcia Sola,
Embalse de e5 191
Garcinarro b4 193
Garco j3 135
Gard, Fr. a7 185
Gard, Languedoc-
Roussillon, Fr. a6 185
Garda e4 196
Gardabani g4 149
Gârda de Sus l5 171
Garda, Lago di e4 196
Gardan Divāl d3 128
Gardanne b7 185
Garde, Cap de f1 221
Gardeja g2 168
Gardelegen g3 173
Garden City, Kansas, U.S.A. c4 261
Garden City, Texas, U.S.A. c6 261
Garden Lakes g2 259
Garden Plain a1 258
Gardermoen d2 156
Gardey h4 297
Gardez d4 128
Gardiki b4 210
Gardiner h6 252
Gardiner, Mount l8 86
Gardiner Range j6 86
Gardiners Bay h3 257
Gardiners Island h3 257
Garding b4 158
Gardner j2 257
Gardner, Isla A 286
Gardnerville d3 264
Gardno, Jezioro e2 168
Gardon de St Jean f4 187
Gardone Val Trompia e4 196
Gárdony g4 171
Gardsjøen m2 155
Gardsjönås f4 154
Garein b4 187
Garelochhead d3 164
Gareloi Island Ac2 247
Garešnica h4 177
Garessio c5 197
Garet El Djenoun f3 221
Gare Tigre g3 285
Garforth e3 162
Gargalianoi b5 211
Gargáligas e5 191
Gargallo d4 192
Gargan, Mont d3 186
Gargano,
Parco Nazionale del e3 198
Gargantua, Cape l7 251
Gargellen a3 176
Gargilesse-Dampierre d2 186
Gargnano e4 196
Gargrave d3 162
Garhdiwala b4 130
Garhi g9 129
Garhi Ikhtiar Khan e6 129
Garhi Khairo c6 129
Garhmuktesar d5 130
Garhshankar c4 130
Garhwa h7 125
Gari k4 147
Gariau j6 97
Garibaldi b7 289
Garibaldi, Mount f7 248
Gariep Dam Nature
Reserve f5 235
Garies b5 234
Garigliano b4 198
Garissa b4 226
Garkida g3 223
Garland f4 258
Garlasco c4 196
Garliava m1 169
Gârliciu j3 201
Garlieston d5 164
Garlin b5 187
Garmab b4 128
Garmdasht m6 137
Garmeh r3 137
Garmi m2 137
Garmisch-Partenkirchen g5 175
Garmsar p4 137
Garmushki a5 128
Garnett e4 260
Garnish q5 253
Garnpung Lake c1 82
Garona e2 192
Garonne b4 186
Garonne,
Canal latéral à la c4 187
Garoowe d2 226
Garoth g8 129
Garoua g4 223
Garoua Boulai b2 224
Garou, Lac d2 222
Garpenberg g2 156
Garpkölen f2 156
Garrafe de Torio e2 190
Garray b3 192
Garré f4 297
Garrel d3 172
Garrett d5 254
Garrigues a7 185
Garrison, U.K. c2 165
Garrison,
Montana, U.S.A. g2 262
Garrison,
North Dakota, U.S.A. c7 250
Garrison, Texas, U.S.A. b4 258
Garro b4 275
Garron Point,
Northern Ireland, U.K. c4 164
Garron Point, Northern
Ireland, U.K. f1 165
Garrovillas d5 191
Garrucha c7 193
Garruk b6 129
Garrygala r2 137
Garry Island l1 247
Garry Lake g2 242
Garry, Loch d3 164
Gars am Kamp g1 177
Garsdale Head d2 162
Garsen c4 226
Garsila b5 218
Garstang d3 162
Gartempe c2 186
Garthmyl c4 163
Gartow g2 173
Gärtringen d4 174
Gartz k2 173
Garut d8 98
Garvão b7 191
Garve d2 164
Garvie Mountains b6 77
Garwolin k4 169
Garwood a5 258
Gary c5 254
Garyarsa e4 130
Gary City b3 258
Garyi b3 104
Garyū-zan e4 114
Garz j1 173
Garza d1 294
Garza García j5 273
Gar Zangbo e3 130
Garzê b3 104
Garzón b3 284
Gasa j6 135
Gascogne c5 187
Gascoyne b9 87
Gascoyne Junction b9 87
Gascoyne, Mount c9 87
Gashaka g4 223
Gashaka Gumti National
Park g4 223
Gasherbrum I c2 130
Gash Setit Wildlife
Reserve e4 219
Gashua g3 223
Gasim j6 97
Gaskačokka f3 154
Gasny g3 183
Gaspar, Selat d6 98
Gaspé k4 253
Gaspé, Baie de k4 253
Gaspé, Cap k4 253
Gaspé, Péninsule de m3 253
Gaspoltshofen e1 176
Gassan j2 115
Gassane a3 222
Gassaway f6 254
Gasset, Embalse de g5 191
Gassino Torinese b4 196
Gassol g4 223
Gastonia j2 259
Gaston, Lake l1 259
Gastouni b5 211
Gastre c4 294
Gata d4 190
Gata, Cabo de b8 193
Gata, Cape b2 138
Gata de Gorgos e6 193
Gătaia e3 200
Gata, Sierra de d4 190
Gatčina a2 150
Gate City h1 259
Gatehouse of Fleet d5 164
Gateshead,
England, U.K. h1 162
Gateshead, England, U.K. e2 162
Gateshead Island j1 242
Gates of the Arctic
National Park and
Preserve f2 246
Gatesville a4 258
Gatico c4 292
Gâtinais h4 183
Gâtine f5 183
Gatineau, Québec, Can. r7 251
Gatineau, Québec, Can. j3 255
Gatlinburg h2 259
Gato f6 191
Gátova d5 193
Gattendorf h1 177
Gatteo a Mare g5 197
Gattinara c4 196
Gatton l9 81
Gatún h6 277
Gatún, Lago g6 277
Gatvand m5 137
Gau E 74
Gau-Algesheim g5 174
Gaúcha do Norte b4 288
Gauchy b5 159
Gaucín e8 191
Gaudalteba,
Embalse de e8 191
Gaud-i-Zirreh a5 128
Gauer Lake e2 250
Gauja, Lat. l4 157
Gauja, Lith p1 169
Gaujas nacionālais
parks l4 157
Gaujiena m4 157
Gaula c5 154
Gaurella g8 124
Gauripur l6 125
Gauri Sankar h5 135
Gause a4 258
Gausta c3 156
Gauteng h3 235
Gauting f2 175
Gautizalema d3 192
Gautsjøen c1 156
Gauzan b3 128
Gavà g3 192
Gavarnie b6 187
Gaväter a4 122
Gavdopoula e8 211
Gavdos e8 211
Gave d'Arrens b6 187
Gave d'Aspe b5 187
Gave d'Oloron b5 187
Gave d'Ossau b5 187
Gavi c5 196
Gavião, Braz. d4 289
Gavião, Port c5 191
Gaviotas f5 297
Gavirate c4 196
Gävle g2 156
Gävleborg g2 156
Gavlfjorden e2 154
Gavnø e3 158
Gavoi Ab2 198
Gavorrano e7 197
Gavray d4 182
Gavrilov-Jam e3 150
Gavrilov Posad f3 150
Gavrio e5 211
Gavrolimni b4 210
Gawachab b3 234
Gawai c2 102
Gawana d4 130
Gaweinstal h1 177
Gawilgarh Hills e9 124
Gawler d13 81
Gawler Ranges b12 81
Gåxsjön e5 154
Gaxun Nur a4 112
Gaya, India j7 125
Gaya, Nig. f3 223
Gaya, Niger e3 223
Gayam h8 99
Gayéri e3 223
Gaylord d3 254
Gayndah k8 81
Gaytaninovo d1 210
Gaz r8 137
Gaza, Gaza c5 139
Gaza, Moz. k1 235
Gaza c5 139
Gaz-Achak h7 120
Gazalkent m7 121
Gazan c6 129
Gazandzhyk q2 137
Gazawa g3 223
Gazi d3 224
Gaziantep, Tur. f4 209
Gaziantep, Gaziantep, Tur. f4 209
Gazimuro-Ononskij
Hrebet g1 112
Gazipaşa d4 208
Gazit d4 138
Gazli j7 120
Gazoros d1 210
Gazzuolo e4 196
Gbaaka c4 222
Gbadolite d3 224
Gbangbatok b4 222
Gbarnga c4 222
Gbatala c4 222
Gbely f3 170
Gboko f4 223
Gbwado d3 224
Gdańsk g1 168
Gdańsk, Gulf of h1 169
Gdov m3 157
Gdów j6 169
Gdynia g1 168
Gealldruig Mhòr c1 164
Geamăna j2 201
Gearhart Mountain c2 262
Geaune b5 187
Gêba b3 222
Gebesee f1 175
Gebre Guracha b2 226
Gech'a b2 226
Gedaref, Al Qaḍārif,
Sudan e5 219

GEORGIA
THE REPUBLIC OF GEORGIA
Area 69,700km²
(26,911sq miles)
Capital Tbilisi
Organizations CE, CIS, EBRD
Population 5,180,000
Pop. growth (%) -0.1
Life expectancy 68 (m); 76 (f)
Languages Georgian
Literacy 99%
Currency lari (US $1 = 2.19 lari)
GDP (US million $) 3300
GDP per head ($US) 637

GERMANY
THE FEDERAL REPUBLIC OF GERMANY
Area 356,974km²
(137,828sq miles)
Capital Berlin
Organizations CE, EBRD, EU, G8, NATO, OECD
Population 82,490,000
Pop. growth (%) 0.1
Life expectancy 74 (m); 80 (f)
Languages German
Literacy 99%
Currency euro
(US $1 = 0.81 euro)
GDP (US million $) 1,993,000
GDP per head ($US) 24,160

GHANA
THE REPUBLIC OF GHANA
Area 238,537km²
(92,100sq miles)
Capital Accra
Organizations COMM, ECOWAS
Population 20,470,000
Pop. growth (%) 2.3
Life expectancy 55 (m); 57 (f)
Languages English, many local languages
Literacy 74.9%
Currency cedi
(US $1 = 8809 cedi)
GDP (US million $) 5907
GDP per head ($US) 288

Gol → Greensboro 335

Gol c2 156
Gola, Cro. j3 177
Gola, India e5 130
Gołąb k4 169
Golaghat n6 125
Golak e4 176
Gołańcz f3 168
Golbāf r7 137
Golbahār d3 128
Gölbaşı f4 209
Golbey c2 184
Gölcük a3 208
Golčův Jeníkov d2 170
Golczewo c2 168
Gold c3 256
Gołdap l1 169
Gołdapa k5 157
Gold Beach a4 262
Goldberg f5 158
Gold Bridge f6 248
Gold Coast, Aust. l10 81
Gold Coast, Ghana e4 223
Gold Creek g3 247
Goldeck e3 176
Golden j6 249
Golden Bay d4 77
Golden City b1 258
Goldene Aue f4 173
Golden Gate Highlands
National Park h4 235
Golden Hinde e7 248
Golden Meadow d5 258
Goldenstedt d3 172
Golden Throne c2 130
Golden Vale c4 164
Goldfield f4 264
Gold Mountain f4 264
Goldpan Peak f3 246
Gold Rock g6 250
Goldsand Lake c2 250
Goldsboro,
Maryland, U.S.A. e5 256
Goldsboro,
North Carolina, U.S.A. l2 259
Goldsworthy d7 86
Goldthwaite d6 261
Goldvein c6 256
Göle j2 209
Goleen b5 165
Golegã b5 191
Goleniów c2 168
Golestān, Afg. a4 128
Golestān, Iran q3 137
Goleta d7 265
Goleta Point d7 265
Golfito f6 277
Golfo Aranci Ab2 198
Gol, Herlen, China j1 113
Goli, Cro. f5 177
Goli, Cro. f4 177
Goliad a5 258
Golicyno h5 151
Golina g3 168
Gölköy f2 209
Göllers Bach h1 177
Gollin j2 173
Gollmitz j2 173
Gölmarmara a3 208
Golmberg j3 173
Golmud p1 125
Golmud He p1 125
Golo, Fr. A 185
Golo, Phil. c4 100
Golodnaja Guba,
Ozero h2 147
Golondrina d1 294
Golongosso e2 225
Golovin d2 246
Golovinščino h5 151
Goloviţa, Lacul j3 201
Golpāyegān n5 137
Gölpazarı c2 208
Golpejas e4 190
Gölsen g1 177
Golspie e2 164
Golßen j4 173
Golte f3 177
Göltzsch h2 175
Golub-Dobrzyń h2 169
Golubovka q1 121
Golungo Alto b5 224
Goluzino f2 150
Golyama Syutkya g5 201
Golyama Zhelyazna g4 201
Golyam Persenk g5 201
Gołymin Ośrodek j3 169
Golyšmanovo m4 147
Golzow h3 173
Goma e4 225
Goma Hanu c2 130
Gomang Co j4 135
Gómara b3 192
Gomati, Grc. d2 210
Gomati, India e6 130
Gombari e3 225
Gombe, Nig. g3 223
Gombe, Nig. g3 223
Gombe, Tan. f4 225
Gombe Stream
National Park e4 225
Gombi g3 223
Gomecello e3 190
Gómez Farías e2 275
Gómez Palacio h5 272
Gómez Rendón a4 284
Gomishān p3 137
Gommern g3 173
Gomo g3 135
Gomo Co g3 135
Gonaives h5 271
Gonarezhou
National Park e3 233
Gonâve, Île de la h5 266
Gonbad-e Kavus q3 137
Goncelin b5 185
Gonda f6 135
Gondal e10 129
Gondar c4 284
Gonder e5 219
Gondey c2 224
Gondia g9 124
Gondola e2 233
Gondomar, Port b3 190
Gondomar, Spain b2 190
Gondrecourt-le-Château b2 184
Gondreville b2 184
Gönen d3 138
Gönen a2 208
Gonfaron c7 185
Gonfreville-l'Orcher f3 183
Gong'an c4 106
Gongbo'gyamda n5 125
Gongchangling m5 113
Gongcheng h6 104
Gonggar m5 125
Gongga Shan d4 104
Gonghe a7 112
Gonghui h5 112
Gongliu u6 121
Gongogi e4 289
Gongola g3 223
Gongolgon h11 81
Gongoué f6 223
Gongshan d2 102
Gongwang Shan d5 104
Gongxian e4 104
Gongyi c2 106
Gongzhuling n4 113
Goñi j2 297
Goniądz l2 169
Goniri g3 223
Gonjo b3 104
Gonnesa Aa3 198
Gonnoi c3 210
Gonnosfanadiga Aa3 198
Gonnosnò Aa3 198
Gonohe j1 115
Gönyű f4 171
Gonzaga e5 196
Gonzáles e2 275
Gonzales,
California, U.S.A. b5 264
Gonzales, Texas, U.S.A. a5 258
González, Canal b6 295
González Moreno f3 297
González Ortega c2 274
Gonzalo Vásquez h6 277
Goochland h7 255
Goodeve b5 250
Good Hope f2 235
Goodhope Bay d2 246
Good Hope, Cape of c7 234
Good Hope Mountain e6 248
Gooding f4 262
Goodland c4 260
Goodman,
Mississippi, U.S.A. e3 258
Goodman, Wisconsin, U.S.A. b3 254
Goodnews Bay d4 246
Goodooga h10 81
Goodrich,
North Dakota, U.S.A. c7 250
Goodrich, Texas, U.S.A. b4 258
Goole f3 162
Goolgowi g13 81
Goombalie g10 81
Goomeri e5 85
Goonda e2 233
Goondiwindi k10 81
Goongarrie, Lake e11 87
Goongarrie National
Park e12 87
Goonhavern a6 163
Goonyella h6 80
Goorly, Lake c11 87
Goose, Can. m2 253
Goose, U.S.A. d2 260
Goose Creek,
Idaho/Nevada, U.S.A. g5 262
Goose Creek,
South Carolina, U.S.A. j3 259
Goose Green e6 295
Goose Lake c5 262
Gooty e5 126
Gopalganj j6 125
Gopeng b3 101
Gopeshwar d4 130
Gopło, Jezioro g3 168
Göppingen d4 174
Gor a7 193
Góra, Dolnośląskie, Pol. e4 168
Góra, Mazowieckie, Pol. j3 169
Goragorskij g4 149
Góra Kalwaria k4 169
Gorakhpur h6 125
Goražde d4 200
Gorbačevo d5 150
Gorbea a5 296
Görbeháza k4 171
Gorbitsa Atxak b1 192
Gorchs h3 297
Görcsöny g6 171
Gorčuha g3 151
Gorczański Park
Narodowy h6 169
Gorda Cay l6 259
Gördalen e2 156
Gorda, Pico A 220
Gorda, Ponta d2 288
Gorda, Punta, Chile c3 292
Gorda, Punta, Nic. f3 277
Gordeevka a5 150
Gordes b7 185
Gördes b3 208
Gordil d2 224
Gørding b3 158
Gordo f3 258
Gordon, Aust. Aa3 83
Gordon, U.S.A. b3 259
Gordon Downs j6 86
Gordon, Isla c6 295
Gordon, Lake Ab3 83
Gordon Lake m33 249
Gordonsville b6 256
Gordonvale g4 80
Goré c2 224
Gorē b2 226
Gore, N.Z. b7 77
Gore, U.S.A. b5 256
Gore Bay e3 254
Gorebridge e4 164
Gorelki d4 150
Goreloe f5 150
Gorenja vas f3 177
Gorenjska f3 177
Gore Point f4 247
Goreville e1 258
Gorey, Chad c3 182
Gorey, Ire. e4 165
Gorgān q3 137
Gorge National Park,
Isla c4 84
Gorge Range,
Queensland, Aust. A 84
Gorge Range, Western
Australia, Aust. d7 86
Gorges b3 234
Görgeteg f5 170
Gorgol b2 222
Gorgona, Isla b3 284
Gorgona, Isola di d6 197
Gorgonzola d4 196
Gorgora e5 219
Gorgoram g3 223
Gorgos e6 193
Gorham g6 252
Gori k2 209
Goričko h3 177
Goricy d3 150
Gorinchem c3 159
Gorino g5 196
Goris g5 149
Goriška e3 176
Gorizia, Italy h4 196
Gorizia, Friuli - Venezia
Giulia, Italy h4 196
Gorj f3 201
Gorjačij Ključ e3 148
Gorjanci g4 177
Gorka e3 150
Gorkhā g6 135
Gorki l2 147
Gor'kiy, Nižegorodskaja
Oblast', Russ. Fed. g3 151
Gor'koe, Ozero t1 121
Gørlev e3 158
Gorlice k6 169
Görlitz h1 175
Gorlovo e5 150
Gormaz b3 192
Gorna Oryakhovitsa g4 201
Gorni Dŭbnik g4 201
Gornja Gračenica h4 177
Gornjak t2 121
Gornja Radgona g3 177
Gornje Jelenje f4 177
Gornje Vratno h3 177
Gornji Grad f3 177
Gornji Milanovac e3 200
Gornji Vakuf c4 200
Gorno-Altajsk v2 121
Gornopravdinsk m3 147
Gornotrakiyska Nizina g4 201
Gornozavodsk j4 147
Gornye Klyuchi s3 113
Gornyj m3 147
Goroch'an b2 226
Gorodec g3 151
Gorodišče h5 151
Gorohovec g3 151
Goroke e14 81
Gorom Gorom d3 222
Gorong, Kepulauan j6 97
Gorongosa, Moz. e2 233
Gorongosa, Sofala, Moz. e2 233
Gorongosa,
Parque Nacional de d2 233
Gorontalo m4 99
Gorostiaga h3 297
Goroubi e3 223
Gorouol e3 223
Górowo Iławeckie j1 169
Gorron e4 182
Gorščečnoe e2 148
Gorseinon b5 163
Gorski Kotar f4 177
Gort c3 165
Gortahork c1 165
Gortin Glen Forest Park d2 165
Gorumna Island b3 165
Gorutuba g1 291
Görviksjön e5 154
Gorzanak a4 128
Gorzano, Monte h7 197
Górzke h3 173
Gorzkowice h4 169
Górzno h2 169
Gorzów Śląski g4 168
Gorzów Wielkopolski d3 168
Górzyn c4 168
Gorzyń d3 168
Gosaldo f3 196
Gosau e2 176
Gosberton h4 162
Gösche d2 172
Gościno d1 168
Gose f4 115
Gosen h3 115
Gősfai Hegy h3 177
Gosford k12 81
Gosford Forest Park e2 165
Gosforth c2 162
Goshanak b7 129
Goshen, California, U.S.A. d5 265
Goshen, Connecticut, U.S.A. g3 257
Goshen, Kentucky, U.S.A. d6 254
Goshen,
Massachusetts, U.S.A. h2 257
Goshen, New York, U.S.A. f3 257
Goshogawara j1 115
Gosjokka k2 155
Goslar f4 172
Gosławskie, Jezioro g3 168
Goślice h3 169
Gosport e6 163
Gossas a3 222
Gossau d2 196
Gossi d2 222
Gossinga e2 225
Gößnitz h2 175
Gostivar e5 200
Göstling an der Ybbs f2 177
Gostycyn f2 168
Gostyń f4 168
Gostynin h3 169
Gota c2 226
Götaälven e3 156
Göta Kanal g3 156
Göteborg e1 158
Gotenba h4 115
Götene e3 156
Goteşti j2 201
Gotha d5 175
Gothem h4 157
Gothenburg, Swe. e1 158
Gothenburg, U.S.A. c3 260
Gothèye e3 223
Gotland, Swe. h4 157
Gotland, Gotland, Swe. h4 157
Gotse Delchev d1 210
Gotska Sandön h3 157
Götsu e4 114
Gottero, Monte d5 196
Göttingen e4 172
Gottmadingen g3 174
Gott Peak f6 248
Götzis a2 176
Gouarec b4 182
Goubangzi l5 113
Gouda c2 159
Goudge c3 296
Goudiri b3 222
Goudoumaria g3 223
Goudra f3 297
Gouéké c4 222
Gouesnou a4 182
Gouet c4 182
Gougane Barra
Forest Park b5 165
Goûgaram f2 223
Gough Fracture Zone j14 302
Gouin, Réservoir r6 251
Goul e4 186
Goulbin Kaba f3 223
Goulburn, New South
Wales, Aust. j13 81
Goulburn, New South
Wales, Aust. d8 85
Goulburn, Victoria, Aust. e3 83
Goulburn Islands a1 80
Goulburn River
National Park d8 85
Gould d3 258
Gould City d2 254
Gould, Mount c9 87
Goulia c4 222
Goumbou c3 222
Goumenissa c2 210
Gouna g4 223
Gounda g4 224
Goundam d2 222
Goundi c2 224
Gounou-Gaya c2 224
Gourcy d3 222
Gourdon d4 186
Gouré g3 223
Gourin b4 182
Gouripur m7 125
Gourits d7 234
Gourma-Rharous d2 222
Gournay-en-Bray g3 183
Gouro a4 218
Gourock Range f2 83
Goussainville h3 183
Gõuta e4 154
Gouvêa g3 291
Gouveia c4 190
Gouverneur j3 255
Gouzon e2 186
Govan a5 250
Govedartsi f4 201
Govenlock n7 249
Gove Peninsula c2 80
Governador Valadares h3 291
Governor Generoso f7 100
Governor's Harbour l7 259
Govi-Altay d3 182
Govĭ Altayn Nuruu b4 112
Govind Ballash Pant
Sagar h7 124
Govindgarh c6 130
Govurdak c2 128
Gowal d3 128
Gowanda b2 256
Gowan Range a4 84
Gowārān b6 129
Gowd-e Aḥmar q6 137
Gowienica k2 173
Gowmal Kalay d4 128
Gowna, Lough d3 165
Gowy d3 162
Goya e1 294
Goyave C 271
Göyçay g4 149
Goyder b2 80
Goyena f4 297
Göynük, Bingöl, Tur. h3 209
Göynük, Bolu, Tur. c2 208
Goyoum b2 224
Goyō-zan j2 115
Göytäpä m2 137
Gözareh a3 128
Goz-Beïda b5 218
Gözd k4 169
Gozdnica d4 168
Gözene g3 209
Gozha Co e2 130
Goz Regeb e4 219
Graaf-Reinet f6 234
Graafwater c6 234
Grabo c5 222
Grabovac g1 198
Grabow, Ger. h1 173
Grabow, Mecklenburg-
Vorpommern, Ger. e5 158
Grabowiec m5 169
Grabów nad Prosną g4 168
Gračac b3 200
Gračanica d3 200
Graçay g5 183
Gracefield h2 255
Grâce-Hollogne d4 159
Grace, Lake d13 87
Grachi s2 121
Graciano Sánchez e2 275
Gracias c3 276
Graciosa A 220
Graciosa, Isla Af1 189
Gradačac d3 200
Gradara g6 197
Gradaús b3 288
Gradaús, Serra dos b3 288
Gradec h4 177
Gradefes e2 190
Gradignan b4 186
Gradištea b3 201
Grado, Italy h4 196
Grado, Spain d1 190
Grado Bravo,
Serra do c3 288
Gradoli f7 197
Grady d2 258
Grad Zagreb h4 177
Græsted f2 158
Grafenau e1 176
Gräfenberg g4 175
Gräfenhainichen h4 173
Grafenrode e2 175
Grafham Water f4 163
Grafing bei München e2 175
Gräfjell c2 156
Grafton, Aust. l10 81
Grafton,
Massachusetts, U.S.A. j2 257
Grafton,
North Dakota, U.S.A. e6 250
Grafton, Cape A 84
Grafton, Islas b6 295
Grafton Passage A 84
Graham d5 261
Graham Island a5 248
Graham Land l11 298
Graham, Mount j9 263
Grahamstown g6 235
Graiguenamanagh e4 165
Grain g5 163
Grain Coast b4 222
Graissessac f5 187
Grajagan h9 99
Grajaú, Braz. c3 288
Grajaú, Maranhão, Braz. c3 288
Grajewo l2 169
Gråkampen d2 156
Gram c3 158
Gramastettan f1 177
Gramat d4 186
Grambling c3 258
Grambow k2 173
Grammendorf h1 173
Grammichele d7 199
Grammos a2 210
Grampian b4 256
Grampian Mountains e3 164
Grampians
National Park c3 82
Grampians, The c3 82
Gramsh e5 200
Gramzow k2 173
Grana b5 196
Granaatboskolk c5 234
Granada, Col. c3 284
Granada, Nic. e5 276
Granada, Nic. e5 276
Granada, Spain g8 191
Granada, Spain g7 191
Granada, U.S.A. c4 260
Granadilla de Abona Ac2 189
Gran Altiplanicie Central c5 295
Granån f1 156
Granard d3 165
Gran Bajo San Julián c5 295
Gran Bajo c5 295
Gran Bajo Salitroso d5 296
Granbury a3 258
Granby, Can. f6 252
Granby, U.S.A. h3 257
Gran Canaria Ad3 189
Gran Chaco e4 293
Grand, Fr. b2 184
Grand, Missouri, U.S.A. e4 260
Grand,
South Dakota, U.S.A. b3 260
Grandas d1 190
Grand Bahama l6 259
Grand Ballon d3 184
Grand Bank q5 253
Grand Banks of
Newfoundland e5 302
Grand-Bassam d4 222
Grand Bay, Can. j6 253
Grand Bay, U.S.A. e4 258
Grand Beach e5 250
Grand Bend f4 254
Grand Bérard c6 185
Grand-Bérébi c5 222
Grand Blanc e4 254
Grand Bourg C 271
Grand Bruit n5 253
Grand Caille Point J 271
Grandcamp-Maisy d3 182
Grand Canal c3 165
Grand Cane c3 258
Grand Canyon,
Arizona, U.S.A. g7 263
Grand Canyon,
Arizona, U.S.A. g7 263
Grand Canyon du
Verdon c7 185
Grand Canyon National
Park g7 263
Grand Cess c5 222
Grand-Champ c5 182
Grand Chenier c5 258
Grand Combin d5 185
Grand Coulee d2 262
Grand-Couronne g3 183
Grand Cul de Sac Marin C 271
Grande, Arg. c6 295
Grande, Arg. c4 296
Grande, Bol. e3 293
Grande, Braz. d4 288
Grande, Braz. f4 291
Grande, Braz. b2 224
Grande, Peru b2 292
Grande, Spain g6 191
Grande, Spain d5 193
Grande, Bahía c6 295
Grande, Cayo d1 284
Grande, Cerro, Mex. f5 275
Grande Cerro c3 274
Grande de Moa, Cabo g4 266
Grande de Tierra del
Fuego, Isla c6 295
Grande-Entree m5 253
Grande, Île b4 182
Grande, Ilha, Braz. b2 288
Grande, Ilha, Braz. f5 291
Grande Inferior,
Cuchilla j2 297
Grande, Isola b7 199
Grande, Lago, Braz. b2 288
Grande, Lago, Braz. b8 288
Grande Leyre b4 187
Grande Prairie h4 248
Grande, Punta c5 292
Grand Erg de Bilma g2 223
Grand Erg Occidental e2 221
Grand Erg Oriental f2 221
Grande Rise, Rio g13 302
Grande Rivière de la
Baleine q3 251
Grande Rochère b4 196
Grande Ronde e3 262
Grande, Salar d4 292
Grande, Salina d4 296
Grande Saudre h5 183
Grande, Serra, Braz. e3 285
Grande, Serra, Braz. e1 293
Grandes Jorasses a4 196
Grandes, Salinas d4 292
Grande-Synthe a3 159
Grande-Terre C 271
Grande Tête de l'Obiou b6 185
Grande Tournalin b4 196
Grand Falls,
New Brunswick, Can. j5 253
Grand Falls,
Newfoundland, Can. q4 253
Grand Forks, Can. d1 262
Grand Forks, U.S.A. e7 250
Grand-Fougeray d5 182
Grand Gabizos b6 187
Grand Gosier j5 271
Grand Haven c4 254
Grandin, Lac f3 242
Grand Island d3 260
Grand Isle d5 258
Grand Junction a4 260
Grand Lac Germain j3 253
Grand-Lahou d4 222
Grand Lake,
New Brunswick, Can. m2 253
Grand Lake, Newfoundland
and Labrador, Can. j6 253
Grand Lake, Newfoundland
and Labrador, Can. p4 253
Grand Lake,
Louisiana, U.S.A. c5 258
Grand Lake,
Louisiana, U.S.A. d5 258
Grand Lay e6 182
Grand Ledge d4 254
Grand-Lieu, Lac de d5 182
Grand Maine d6 182
Grand Manan Island j6 253
Grand Marais,
Michigan, U.S.A. l7 251
Grand Marais,
Minnesota, U.S.A. h7 250
Grand-Mère f5 252
Grand Morin j4 183
Grândola b6 191
Grândola, Serra de b6 191
Grand Passage F 74
Grand Pic de
Rochebrune c6 185
Grand Portage j7 251
Grand Prairie a3 258
Grandpré c5 159
Grand Rapids, Can. d4 250
Grand Rapids,
Michigan, U.S.A. d4 254
Grand Rapids,
Minnesota, U.S.A. g7 250
Grand Récif de Cook F 74
Grand Récif du Sud F 74
Grand Rhône a7 185
Grandrieu f4 186
Grand Santi g3 285
Grand Teton h4 262
Grand Teton National
Park h4 262
Grand Tower e1 258
Grand Turk j4 271
Grandview, Can. c5 250
Grandview, U.S.A. d2 262
Grand View h7 250
Grandvilliers g3 183
Grañén d3 192
Graneros b3 296
Granfjället e2 156
Grangärde f2 156
Grangemouth e3 164
Granger, Texas, U.S.A. a4 258
Granger,
Washington, U.S.A. c2 262
Granger, Wyoming, U.S.A. j5 262
Grängesberg f2 156
Grănicești h2 201
Granite City a6 254
Granite Falls e2 260
Granite Lake p4 253
Granite Mountain d2 246
Granite Peak,
Montana, U.S.A. j3 262
Granite Peak,
Utah, U.S.A. g5 262
Granites, The k7 86
Graniteville j3 259
Granitola, Capo b7 199
Granja d2 288
Granja de Moreruela e3 190
Granja de Torrehermosa e6 191
Gran Laguna Salada c4 295
Gran Morelos f3 272
Grann e3 156
Gränna f3 156
Granö g4 154
Granollers g3 192
Granowo e3 168
Gran Pajonal c2 292
Gran Pánfilo Natera c2 274
Gran Paradiso b4 196
Gran Paradiso,
Parco Nazionale del b4 196
Gran Pilastro f3 196
Gran Sasso d'Italia c2 198
Gran Sasso e Monti della
Laga, Parco
Nazionale del h7 197
Gransee j2 173
Gransjön f4 154
Gransö g3 156
Gran Tarajal Ae2 189
Grantham f4 162
Grant, Mount, Aust. f11 87
Grant, Mount,
Nevada, U.S.A. e3 264
Grant, Mount,
Nevada, U.S.A. f2 264
Grantown-on-Spey e2 164
Grant Range g5 86
Grants b5 261
Grantshouse f4 164
Grants Pass b4 262
Granville, Fr. d4 182
Granville, U.S.A. c6 250
Granville Lake c2 250
Granvin b2 156
Grão Mogol g2 291
Grapevine Peak f5 264
Grappa, Monte f4 196
Grapska k5 177
Graskop j2 235
Gräsö h2 157
Grasonville d6 256
Grassano f4 198
Grassau d2 176
Grasse c7 185
Grassflat b3 256
Grassington d2 162
Grasslands National
Park p7 249
Grass Patch e13 87
Grassrange a2 260
Grassridgedam f5 235
Grass River Provincial
Park c3 250
Grass Valley b2 264
Grassy d5 82
Gråsten c4 158
Grästorp e3 156
Gratallops e3 192
Gratkorn g2 177
Gratwein g2 177
Graulhet d5 187
Graus e2 192
Grávalos b2 192
Gravata e3 288
Gravataí b7 289
Gravdal d2 154
Gravedona d3 196
Gravelbourg p7 249
Gravelines h2 183
Gravellona Toce c4 196
Gravenhurst g3 254
Gravens c3 158
Grave Peak f2 262
Grave, Pointe de a3 186
Graves b4 186
Gravesend, Aust. k10 81
Gravesend, U.K. g5 163
Gravfjorden d4 154
Gravia c4 210
Gravigny g3 183
Gravina f4 198
Gravina in Puglia f4 198
Gravona A 185
Gray, Fr. b3 184
Gray, Georgia, U.S.A. h3 259
Gray, Kentucky, U.S.A. g1 259
Grayback Mountain,
Alaska, U.S.A. f4 246
Grayback Mountain,
Oregon, U.S.A. b4 262
Grayling, Alaska, U.S.A. d3 246
Grayling, Michigan, U.S.A. d3 254
Grays g5 163
Grays Harbor a2 262
Grays Lake h4 262
Grayson e6 254
Graz g2 177
Grazalema e8 191
Grdelica f4 201
Greåker d3 156
Great B 266
Great Abaco l6 259
Great Australian
Bight j13 87
Great Bahama Bank e2 266
Great Barrier Island e2 76
Great Barrier Reef h7 300
Great Barrier Reef
Marine Park
(Cairns Section) A 84
Great Barrier Reef
Marine Park
(Capricorn Section) d2 84
Great Barrier Reef
Marine Park
(Central Section) j5 80
Great Barrier Reef
Marine Park
(Far North Section) f2 80
Great Barrington g2 257
Great Basalt Wall
National Park a1 84
Great Basin e6 262
Great Basin National
Park f6 263
Great Bay f5 257
Great Bear n2 247
Great Bear Lake f2 242
Great Bend d4 260
Great Blasket I. a4 165
Great Coco Island n5 127
Great Dismal Swamp
National Wildlife
Refuge l1 259
Great Dunmow g5 163
Great Egg Harbor f5 257
Greater Antilles g7 241
Greater St Lucia Wetland
Park k3 235
Great Exuma f3 266
Great Fall e2 285
Great Falls,
Montana, U.S.A. h2 262
Great Falls,
South Carolina, U.S.A. j2 259
Great Fish g6 235
Great Fish Point g6 235
Great Gandak j6 125
Great Guana Cay l6 259
Great Harbour Cay k7 259
Great Harbour Deep p3 253
Great Haywood e4 162
Great Inagua h4 266
Great Island c5 165
Great Karoo d5 234
Great Kei h6 235
Great Keppel Island d3 84
Great Lake Ab2 83
Great Malvern d4 163
Great Meadows f4 256
Great Mercury Island e2 76
Great Namaqualand b3 234
Great Nicobar p9 127
Great Ormes Head c3 162
Great Ouse g4 163
Great Oyster Bay Ac3 83
Great Palm Island A 84
Great Peconic Bay h4 257
Great Pedro Bluff B 266
Great Plains c3 260
Great Quittacas Pond k3 257
Great Rhos c4 163
Great Rift Valley f5 225
Great Sacandaga Lake j4 255
Great Sale Cay k6 259
Great Salt Lake g5 262
Great Salt Lake Desert g5 262
Great Salt Plains Lake d4 261
Great Sand Hills n6 249
Great Sand Sea c2 218
Great Sandy Desert g6 86
Great Scarcies b4 222
Great Sea Reef E 74
Great Shelford g4 163
Great Sitkin Island Ac1 247
Great Slave Lake g3 242
Great Smoky
Mountains h2 259
Great Smoky Mountains
National Park h2 259
Great Snow Mountain e3 248
Great Stour g5 163
Great Torrington b6 163
Great Victoria Desert h11 87
Great Victoria Desert
Conservation Park j11 87
Great Victoria Desert
Nature Reserve j11 87
Great Wall g5 112
Great Wall (China) u1 298
Great Wass Island j6 253
Great Yarmouth h4 163
Grebbestad d3 156
Grebenhain g3 174
Grebenstein e4 172
Grębków k3 169
Greccio g7 197
Greco, Monte c3 198
Greding d3 175
Gredos, Sierra de e4 190
Gredstedbro b3 158
Greec c6 295
Greece, U.S.A. h4 255
Greece j7 145

GREECE

THE HELLENIC REPUBLIC
Area 131,957km^2
(50,949sq miles)
Capital Athens
Organizations CE, EBRD, EU, NATO, OECD
Population 10,970,000
Pop. growth (%) 0.3
Life expectancy 75 (m); 80 (f)
Languages Greek
Literacy 97.5%
Currency euro
(US $1 = 0.83 euro)
GDP (US million $) 130,700
GDP per head ($US) 11,914

Greeley b3 260
Green, Kentucky, U.S.A. d7 254
Green,
North Dakota, U.S.A. b3 260
Green, Utah, U.S.A. h6 263
Greenacres d6 265
Green Bay,
Wisconsin, U.S.A. c3 254
Green Bay,
Wisconsin, U.S.A. b3 254
Greenbelt d5 256
Greenbrier c2 258
Greenbush e6 250
Greenbushes c13 87
Green Cape g3 83
Greencastle, Ire. e1 165
Greencastle, Indiana, U.S.A. c6 254
Greencastle,
Pennsylvania, U.S.A. c5 256
Green Cove Springs j5 259
Greene e2 256
Greeneville h1 259
Greenfield,
California, U.S.A. b5 265
Greenfield, Illinois, U.S.A. a6 254
Greenfield,
Massachusetts, U.S.A. h2 257
Green Forest c1 258
Green Head b12 87
Green Island, Aust. A 84
Green Island, Jam. B 270
Greenisland c5 164
Green Island Bay b5 100
Greenland b2 258
Greenland (Denmark) h1 240
Greenland Basin k2 302
Greenland Sea k2 302
Green Lane Reservoir e4 256
Greenlaw f4 164
Green Lowther e4 164
Greenock d4 164
Greenodd c2 162
Greenore Point e4 165
Greenough, Western
Australia, Aust. b11 87
Greenough, Western
Australia, Aust. b11 87
Greenough, Mount j1 247
Greenport h3 257
Green River, P.N.G. l6 97
Green River, Utah, U.S.A. h6 263
Green River,
Wyoming, U.S.A. j5 262
Greensboro, Florida, U.S.A. g4 259

336 Greensboro → Gunung Ayer

Greensboro, Georgia, U.S.A. h3 259
Greensboro, Maryland, U.S.A. e6 256
Greensboro, North Carolina, U.S.A. g7 254
Greensburg, Indiana, U.S.A. d6 254
Greensburg, Kansas, U.S.A. d4 261
Greensburg, Pennsylvania, U.S.A. a4 256
Green Swamp k2 259
Greentown d5 254
Greenup, Illinois, U.S.A. b6 254
Greenup, Kentucky, U.S.A. e6 254
Greenvale g5 80
Green Valley h10 263
Greenville, Lib. c4 222
Greenville, Alabama, U.S.A. f4 258
Greenville, California, U.S.A. c1 264
Greenville, Florida, U.S.A. h4 259
Greenville, Georgia, U.S.A. g3 259
Greenville, Maine, U.S.A. h6 252
Greenville, Mississippi, U.S.A. d3 258
Greenville, Missouri, U.S.A. d1 258
Greenville, New Hampshire, U.S.A. j2 257
Greenville, New York, U.S.A. f2 257
Greenville, North Carolina, U.S.A. l2 259
Greenville, Ohio, U.S.A. d5 254
Greenville, Pennsylvania, U.S.A. f5 254
Greenville, South Carolina, U.S.A. h2 259
Greenville, Texas, U.S.A. a3 258
Greenwater Provincial Park r5 249
Greenwich, England, U.K. h3 162
Greenwich, U.K. f5 163
Greenwich, Connecticut, U.S.A. g3 257
Greenwich, New York, U.S.A. k4 255
Greenwich, Ohio, U.S.A. e5 254
Greenwood, Can. d1 262
Greenwood, Indiana, U.S.A. c6 254
Greenwood, Mississippi, U.S.A. d3 258
Greenwood, South Carolina, U.S.A. h2 259
Greenwood Lake f3 257
Greenwood, Lake j2 259
Greers Ferry Lake c2 258
Greese e4 165
Gregório c1 292
Gregory, Aust. d5 80
Gregory, Michigan, U.S.A. d4 254
Gregory, South Dakota, U.S.A. d3 260
Gregory, Texas, U.S.A. a6 258
Gregory Downs d5 80
Gregory, Lake h6 86
Gregory National Park k5 86
Gregory Range, Queensland, Aust. f5 80
Gregory Range, Western Australia, Aust. e7 86
Greian Head a2 164
Greifenburg e3 176
Greifensee c2 196
Greiffenberg j2 173
Greifswald j1 173
Greifswalder Bodden j1 173
Grein f1 177
Greiz h2 175
Greko, Cape c2 138
Gremiha d1 146
Gremjačinsk j4 147
Grenå d2 158
Grenada, U.S.A. e3 258
Grenada h6 241

GRENADA

GRENADA
Area 344km² (133sq miles)
Capital St George's
Organizations ACS, CARICOM, COMM, SELA, OECS
Population 101,000
Pop. growth (%) 0.2
Life expectancy 71 (m); 71 (f)
Languages English, French patois
Literacy 90%
Currency East Caribbean dollar (US $1 = 2.67 East Caribbean dollar)
GDP (US million $) 333
GDP per head ($US) 3297

Grenada Lake e3 258
Grenade d5 187
Grenade-sur-l'Adour b5 187
Grenchen b2 196
Grenen d1 158
Grenfell, Aust. j12 81
Grenfell, Can. b5 250
Grenoble b5 185
Grenville G 271
Grenville, Cape f1 80
Grenville Channel c5 248
Gréoux-les-Bains b7 185
Greshag b7 129
Greshak c7 129
Gresik g8 98
Gressåmoen Nasjonalpark d4 154
Gresse b5 185
Grésy-sur-Aix b5 185
Grésy-sur-Isère c5 185
Greta e2 162
Gretna e5 164
Greußen g1 175
Greve in Chianti f6 197
Grevelingen c3 159
Greven, Mecklenburg-Vorpommern, Ger. d5 158
Greven, Nordrhein-Westfalen, Ger. c3 172
Grevena b2 210
Grevenbroich e3 159
Grevenmacher e5 159
Grevesmühlen e5 158
Grevinge e3 158
Grey, Can. p5 253
Grey, N.Z. c5 77
Greyabbey f2 165
Greybull, Wyoming, U.S.A. a22 260
Greybull, Wyoming, U.S.A. a2 260
Grey, Cape c2 80
Grey Hunter Peak l3 247
Grey Islands q3 253
Greylingstad h3 235
Greymouth c5 77
Grey's Plains b9 87
Greytown, N.Z. e4 77
Greytown, R.S.A. j4 235
Grez-Doiceau c4 159
Grez-en-Bouère e5 182
Gribanovskij f2 148
Gribingui c2 224
Gridley b2 264
Griegos c4 192
Griesheim d3 174
Grieskirchen e1 176
Griffen f3 177
Griffin, Can. b6 250
Griffin, U.S.A. g3 259
Griffith h13 81
Griffiths Point e1 242
Grigiškės p1 169
Grignan a6 185
Grignols b4 187
Grigny a5 185
Grigoriopol j2 201
Grijalva h5 275
Grimaldi f5 199
Grimari d2 224
Grimaud c7 185
Grim, Cape Aa2 83
Griminis Point a2 164
Grimma j1 175
Grimmen j1 173
Grimming e2 176
Grimsby f3 162
Grímsey A 152
Grímsstaðir A 152
Grimstad c3 156
Grindaheim c2 156
Grindelwald c3 196
Grindsted b3 158
Grindstone Creek a2 264
Grindul Chituc c3 148
Grinnell e3 260
Grinnell Peninsula l1 243
Grințieș g2 201
Grintovec f3 177
Grío c3 192
Griou, Puy e3 186
Griqualand East h5 235
Griqualand West e4 234
Griquatown e4 234
Grisik b6 98
Gris Nez, Cap g2 183
Grisolles d5 187
Grisslehamn h2 157
Gritley B 164
Grjazi e1 148
Grjaznoe e4 150
Grjazovec f2 150
Grmeč h5 177
Groais Island q3 253
Gröbenzell e3 175
Grobiņa j4 157
Groblersdal h2 235
Groblershoop e4 234
Gröbming e2 176
Gröbzig g4 173
Gröde-Appelland d1 172
Gródek m2 169
Gröditz j4 173
Grodków f5 168
Grodzisk Mazowiecki j3 169
Grodzisk Wielkopolski e3 168
Groen, R.S.A. b5 234
Groen, Northern Cape, R.S.A. e5 234
Groenlo e2 159
Groesbeck a4 258
Groesbeek d3 159
Groitzsch j1 175
Groix b5 182
Groix, Île de b5 182
Grójec j4 169
Gromadka d4 168
Grömitz d4 158
Gromnik j6 169
Gromo d4 196
Gronau (Westfalen) f2 159
Grönfjället e4 154
Grong d4 154
Grong Grong e2 83
Gröningen g4 173
Groningen, Neth. e1 159
Groningen, Neth. e1 159
Groningen, Sur. f2 285
Grønsund f4 158
Grontjornan c5 154
Groot-Aarpan d3 234
Groot Berg c6 234
Grootdraaidam h3 235
Grootdrink d4 234
Grootebroek d2 159
Groote Eylandt c2 80
Grootfontein b2 232
Groot-Grannapan f4 235
Groot Karas Berg c3 234
Groot Laagte c3 232
Groot Letaba j1 235
Groot Marico g2 235
Grootmis b4 234
Grootpan g2 235
Grootrivierhoogte e6 234
Groot Swartberge e6 234
Grootvaalgraspan c3 234
Grootvlei h3 235
Grootvloer d5 234
Groot Winterberg, R.S.A. g6 235
Groot Winterberg, R.S.A. g6 235
Gropello Cairoli c4 196
Gropeni h3 201
Gros Cap d3 254
Grosio e3 196
Gros Islet J 271
Grosne a4 184
Gros Piton J 271
Grossa, Punta f5 193
Großarl e2 176
Große Aue d3 172
Große Enz d4 174
Große Laaber h4 175
Große Lauter e4 174
Großenaspe c5 158
Großengottern d1 175
Großenhain j1 175
Großenkneten d3 172
Großenlüder e3 174
Groß-Enzersdorf h1 177
Großer Lauter a1 176
Grosse Pointe C 271
Großer Arber j3 175
Großer Beerberg f5 173
Großer Bösenstein f2 177
Großer Buchstein f2 177
Großer Eyberg c3 174
Großer Gleichberg f2 175
Großer Jasmunder Bodden j1 173
Großer Lauter a1 176
Grosser Löffler c2 176
Großer Müggelsee j3 173
Großer Osser j3 175
Großer Plöner See f1 172
Großer Priel f2 177
Großer Rachel j3 175
Großer Selchower See k3 173
Grosser Speikkofel e3 176
Großer Speikkogel f3 177
Großer Waldstein g2 175
Großes Meer c2 172
Großes Wiesbachhorn d2 176
Grosseto, Italy f7 197
Grosseto, Toscana, Italy f7 197
Groß-Gerau d3 174
Groß-Gerungs f1 177
Groß Glienicke j3 173
Groß Grönau d5 158
Grossgrunden h5 154
Groß-Hesepe f2 159
Groß Köris j3 173
Groß Leine k3 173
Groß Leuthen k3 173
Groß Mohrdorf h1 173
Groß Oesingen f3 172
Großostheim d5 174
Großpetersdorf h2 177
Groß Plasten h2 173
Großräschen k4 173
Großrudestedt d1 175
Groß Sankt Florian g3 177
Groß Schönebeck j3 173
Groß Schwülper (Schwülper) f3 172
Groß-Siegharts g1 177
Gross Ums c1 234
Groß-Umstadt e2 174
Großvenediger d2 176
Grostenquin c2 184
Grosvener, Lake f4 246
Grosvenor Mountains x3 298
Groswater Bay p1 253
Grotåa e1 156
Grote Nete c3 159
Groton, Connecticut, U.S.A. h3 257
Groton, Massachusetts, U.S.A. j2 257
Groton, New York, U.S.A. d2 256
Grøtøy g1 154
Grøtsundet g2 154
Grottaferrata g8 197
Grottaglie g4 198
Grottaminarda e3 198
Grottammare c2 198
Grotte c7 199
Grotteria f6 199
Grottoes b6 256
Grouard Mission j4 249
Grouin, Pointe du d4 182
Groundhog m6 251
Grouw d1 159
Grove b1 258
Grove City, Ohio, U.S.A. e6 254
Grove City, Pennsylvania, U.S.A. f5 254
Grove Hill f4 258
Groveland j5 259
Grövelsjön e1 156
Grove Mountains p2 298
Grover Beach c6 265
Groves c5 258
Groveton, New Hampshire, U.S.A. g6 252
Groveton, Texas, U.S.A. b4 258
Grovfjord f2 154
Grovlån e2 156
Groznyj g4 149
Grubišno Polje j4 177
Gruczno g2 168
Grudusk j2 169
Grudziądz g2 168
Gruesa, Punta c4 292
Gruetli-Laager g2 259
Grugliasco b4 196
Gruinard Bay b2 164
Gruissan f5 187
Grumăzești h2 201
Grumento Nova e4 198
Grums e3 156
Grünau, Aus. e2 176
Grünau, Nam. c3 234
Grünberg f2 174
Grünburg f2 177
Grundagssätern e1 156
Grundfors e4 154
Grundorner b2 234
Grundsel h4 154
Grundsjön g1 156
Grundsund d3 156
Gruñidora d1 274
Grunow k3 173
Grünsfeld d3 174
Grünstadt g4 174
Gruyère, Lac de la b3 196
Gruyères b3 196
Gruzdžiai k4 157
Grycken g2 156
Gryfice d2 168
Gryfino c2 168
Gryfów Śląski d4 168
Gryllefjord f2 154
Gryt g3 156
Grytdalen b5 154
Grythyttan f3 156
Grytøya f2 154
Grzmiąca e2 168
Grzymiszew g3 168
Gschütt, Pass e2 176
Gschwend f4 174
Gstaad b3 196
Gua j8 125
Guà f4 196
Guabito f6 277
Guacamayita b2 274
Guacanayabo, Golfo de f4 266
Guacharía c2 284
Guachipas d5 292
Guaçu a5 290
Guaçuí h4 291
Guadahortuna, Spain a7 193
Guadahortuna, Andalucía, Spain g7 191
Guadaira e7 191
Guadairilla e7 191
Guadajira d6 191
Guadajoz f7 191
Guadalajara, Mex. c3 274
Guadalajara, Spain b4 192
Guadalajara, Castilla - La Mancha, Spain a4 192
Guadalaviar c4 192
Guadalbullón g7 191
Guadalcacín, Embalse de e8 191
Guadalcanal e6 191
Guadalcázar f7 191
Guadalefra e6 191
Guadalén a6 193
Guadalén, Embalse del g6 191
Guadalentín c7 193
Guadales d3 296
Guadalest, Embalse de d6 193
Guadalete e8 191
Guadalhorce f8 191
Guadalhorce, Embalse de f7 191
Guadalimar a6 193
Guadalmellato, Embalse de f6 191
Guadalmena b6 193
Guadalmena, Embalse del b6 193
Guadalmez, Spain f6 191
Guadalmez, Castilla-La Mancha, Spain f6 191
Guadalope d3 192
Guadalquivir d7 191
Guadalupe, Braz. d3 288
Guadalupe, Nuevo León, Mex. j5 273
Guadalupe, Puebla, Mex. f4 275
Guadalupe, Mex. c2 274
Guadalupe, Peru b1 292
Guadalupe, Spain e5 191
Guadalupe, Arizona, U.S.A. h9 263
Guadalupe, California, U.S.A. c7 265
Guadalupe, Texas, U.S.A. a5 258
Guadalupe Aguilera g5 272
Guadalupe Bravos f2 272
Guadalupe Mountains National Park b6 261
Guadalupe, Sierra de e5 191
Guadalupe Victoria g5 272
Guadalupe y Calvo f4 272
Guadamajud b4 192
Guadamatilla e6 191
Guadamez e6 191
Guadarrama, Spain f4 190
Guadarrama, Ven. d2 284
Guadarrama, Sierra de g3 190
Guadazaón c5 193
Guadeloupe (France) h7 241
Guadeloupe Passage C 271
Guadiamar d7 191
Guadiana c7 191
Guadiana, Bahía de b3 266
Guadiana Menor a7 193
Guadiaro e8 191
Guadiato e6 191
Guadiela b4 192
Guadiervas f4 190
Guadix a7 193
Guafo, Golfo de b4 295
Guafo, Isla b4 295
Guagua c3 100
Guaiçuí f2 291
Guaicuras f4 293
Guaillabamba b3 284
Guaimaca d3 276
Guáimaro f4 266
Guaina e2 285
Guainía, Col. d3 284
Guainía, Col. d3 284
Guaiquinima, Cerro e2 285
Guaíra, Paraná, Braz. a6 290
Guaíra, São Paulo, Braz. d4 290
Guairá f5 293
Guairaçá b5 290
Guaitecas, Islas b4 295
Guajaba, Cayo f4 266
Guajará Mirim d2 292
Guajaratuba e5 285
Guajarraã d1 292
Guajiniquil d3 276
Guajira c1 284
Guajira, Península de la c1 284
Gualaceo b4 284
Gualaco d3 276
Gualán c3 276
Gualaquiza b4 284
Gualdo Tadino g6 197
Gualeguay, Arg. h1 297
Gualeguay, Entre Ríos, Arg. h2 297
Gualeguaychu h2 297
Gualicho, Salina e6 296
Gualjaina b4 295
Guallatiri d3 292
Gualleco b3 296
Gualterio c2 274
Guam (U.S.A.) d1 72
Guamá c2 288
Guamblin, Isla b4 295
Guamini f4 297
Guampí, Sierra de d2 284
Guamúchil e5 272
Guamués b3 284
Gua Musang b3 101
Gu'an j6 113
Guanabacoa c3 266
Guanabara c2 292
Guanacaste e5 276
Guanacaste, Cordillera de e5 276
Guanacaste, Parque Nacional e5 276
Guanacevi g5 272
Guanaco, Cerro f4 297
Guanahacabibes, Península de b3 266
Guanaja e2 276
Guanajibo A 266
Guanajuato, Mex. d3 274
Guanajuato, Guanajuato, Mex. d3 274
Guanambi d4 289
Guaname d2 274
Guañape, Islas de b1 292
Guanare d2 284
Guanare Viejo d2 284
Guanarito, Ven. d2 284
Guanarito, Portuguesa, Ven. d2 284
Guanay d3 292
Guanay, Sierra d2 284
Guancheng, Shandong, China d2 106
Guancheng, Zhejiang, China g4 111
Guandacol c1 294
Guandaokou b2 106
Guandiankou b4 106
Guandiping b5 106
Guandi Shan b1 106
Guandu j6 105
Guane b3 266
Guang'an f3 104
Guangang e5 111
Guangchang l5 105
Guangde f4 111
Guangdong j6 104
Guangfeng m4 105
Guanghe d1 104
Guangling h6 112
Guangmao Shan c5 104
Guangming Ding f4 111
Guangnan e6 104
Guangping d1 106
Guangrao f1 111
Guangshan d4 106
Guangshui, Hubei, China c4 106
Guangxi Zhuangzu Zizhiqu g6 104
Guangyuan e2 104
Guangze l5 105
Guangzong d1 106
Guanhães g3 291
Guan He f2 111
Guanhe Kou f2 111
Guanhu f2 111
Guánica A 270
Guanipa e2 285
Guanling e6 104
Guanmian Shan a4 106
Guannan f2 111
Guanpo b3 106
Guanqiao e2 111
Guanshui n5 113
Guanta e1 285
Guantánamo g4 266
Guantanamo Bay g5 266
Guantao d1 106
Guanting e4 111
Guanxian d1 106
Guanyinsi b4 106
Guanyun f2 111
Guapé f4 291
Guapí b3 284
Guapiara d6 290
Guápiles f5 277
Guapo Bay E 271
Guaporé, Bol. e2 293
Guaporé, Braz. b7 289
Guaqui d3 292
Guará e4 290
Guarabira e3 288
Guaranda b4 284
Guarani g4 291
Guaraniaçu b6 290
Guarantã d4 290
Guarapari h4 291
Guarapuava c6 290
Guaraqueçaba d6 290
Guararapes c4 290
Guaratinga j2 291
Guaratinguetá f5 291
Guaratuba d6 290
Guaratuba, Baía de c7 289
Guarayos, Bol. e2 293
Guarayos, La Paz, Bol. d2 292
Guar Chempedak b3 101
Guarcino h8 197
Guarda, Port c4 190
Guarda, Guarda, Port c4 190
Guardal b7 193
Guardamar del Segura d6 193
Guardatinajas d2 284
Guardavalle f6 199
Guardia Escolta d1 294
Guardiagrele d2 198
Guardialfiera, Lago di d3 198
Guardián, Cabo c5 295
Guardia Perticara f4 198
Guardia Piemontese f5 199
Guardia Sanframondi d3 198
Guardiola de Berguedà f2 192
Guardo f2 190
Guareña, Spain e3 190
Guareña, Extremadura, Spain d6 191
Guarga d2 192
Guariba e1 293
Guárico, Ven. d2 284
Guárico, Ven. d2 284
Guárico, Embalse del d2 284
Guarico, Punta g4 266
Guarita c3 276
Guarrizas g6 191
Guarrojo c3 284
Guarromán g6 191
Guarujá e5 291
Guarulhos e5 291
Guasacavi d3 284
Guasacavi, Cerro d3 284
Guasare c1 284
Guasave e5 272
Guasdualito c2 284
Guasipati e2 285
Guastalla e5 196
Guatemala e7 241

GUATEMALA

THE REPUBLIC OF GUATEMALA
Area 108,889km² (42,042sq miles)
Capital Guatemala City
Organizations ACS, CACM, IADB, SELA
Population 11,990,000
Pop. growth (%) 3.8
Life expectancy 61 (m); 67 (f)
Languages Spanish, many local languages
Literacy 70.5%
Currency quetzal and US dollar (US $1 = 8.04 quetzal)
GDP (US million $) 23,800
GDP per head ($US) 1984

Guatemala, Guat. b3 276
Guatemala Basin r5 301
Guatimozin f2 297
Guatire d1 284
Guatope, Parque Nacional d2 284
Guatrache f4 297
Guatrochi c4 294
Guatuaro Point E 271
Guaviare, Col. c3 284
Guaviare, Col. c3 284
Guaxupé e4 291
Guayabal c3 284
Guayabero c3 284
Guayaguas, Sierra da d1 296
Guayaguayare E 271
Guayalejo e2 275
Guayama A 270
Guayaneco, Archipiélago a5 295
Guayapo d3 284
Guayaquil b4 284
Guayaquil, Golfo de a4 284
Guayaramerín d2 292
Guayas a4 284
Guayatayoc, Lago de d4 292
Guaycuru e1 294
Guaymas d4 272
Guaynabo A 270
Guayquiraró e2 294
Guazacapán b3 276
Guazhou f3 111
Guba e5 219
Gubadag k4 149
Gubaha j4 147
Gubat e4 100
Gubbio g6 197
Gubei d4 111
Guben k4 173
Gubin c4 168
Gubio g3 223
Gubkin e2 148
Gubkinskij n2 147
Gucheng, Hebei, China d1 106
Gucheng, Hubei, China b3 106
Gucheng, Shanxi, China b2 106
Gudalur e8 126
Gudar, Sierra de d4 192
Gudaut'a f4 148
Gudavac h5 177
Gudenå c3 158
Gudermes g4 149
Guderup c4 158
Gudha g7 129
Gudhjem f5 156
Gudivada g4 126
Gudme d3 158
Gudong He q4 113
Gudou Shan j7 105
Gudow d5 158
Gudri b7 129
Güdül d2 208
Gudum b2 158
Gudur f5 126
Gudvangen b2 156
Guebwiller d3 184
Guéckédou b4 222
Guedes, Lago do d4 284
Güejar c3 284
Guélengdeng h3 223
Guelma f1 221
Guelmine b3 220
Guelph f4 254
Guémar f2 221
Guémené-Penfao d5 182
Guémené-sur-Scorff b4 182
Guémez e2 275
Guéné e3 223
Guenguel b5 295
Guer c5 182
Guéra a5 218
Güera d2 285
Guéra, Massif du a5 218
Guérande c5 182
Guerara e2 221
Guercif d2 220
Guerende b3 218
Guéret d2 186
Guérigny f1 186
Guérin-Kouka e4 223
Guerneville a3 264
Guernsey, Chad c3 182
Guernsey, U.S.A. b3 260
Guernsey (U.K.) e7 161
Guérou b2 222
Guerrah Et-Tarf f1 221
Guerrero, Arg. j3 297
Guerrero, Mex. d5 274
Guerrero, Mex. k4 273
Guerrero, Spain d5 191
Guerrero Negro b4 272
Guerreys, Pic de c6 187
Guerri de la Sal f2 192
Guerzim d3 220
Güesa c2 192
Gueugnon a4 184
Gueydan c4 258
Guéyo c4 222
Guga b2 226
Gugē b2 226
Gugera f5 128
Gugh A 163
Guglieri d2 294
Guglionesi d3 198
Gugu b2 226
Guguan A 74
Guhakolak, Tanjung c8 98
Guhe e4 111
Guía de Isora Ac2 189
Guiana d2 190
Guiana Basin e9 302
Guiana Highlands e2 285
Guibéroua c4 222
Guichen d5 182
Guichen Bay a3 82
Guichi e4 111
Guichicovi g5 275
Guichón j2 297
Guidan-Roumji f3 223
Guidari c2 224
Guide a8 112
Guidel b5 182
Guider g4 223
Guidiguis b1 224
Guidimaka b2 222
Guiding f5 104
Guidong j6 105
Guidonia-Montecelio g8 197
Guienagati g5 275
Guier, Lac de a2 222
Guiers b5 185
Guietsou b4 224
Guigang g7 104
Guiglia e5 197
Guiglo c4 222
Guignes h4 183
Gui Jiang h6 104
Guiji Shan g5 111
Guijo de Granadilla d4 190
Guijuelo e4 190
Guil c6 185
Guildford f5 163
Guilherand a6 185
Guilin h6 104
Guillaumes c6 185
Guillestre c6 185
Guilvinec a5 182
Güímar Ac2 189
Guimarães, Braz. d2 288
Guimarães, Port b3 190
Guimaras d5 100
Guimaras Strait d5 100
Guimeng Ding e2 111
Guin f3 258
Guinagourou e4 223
Guinan c1 104
Guinda a3 264
Guindulman e6 100
Guinea a3 217

GUINEA

THE REPUBLIC OF GUINEA
Area 245,857km² (94,926sq miles)
Capital Conakry
Organizations ECOWAS, IDB, OIC
Population 8,360,000
Pop. growth (%) 2.9
Life expectancy 46 (m); 47 (f)
Languages French, Soussou, Manika, other local languages
Literacy 42.3%
Currency Guinean franc (US $1 = 2005 Guinean franc)
GDP (US million $) 3373
GDP per head ($US) 403

Guinea Basin k9 302
Guinea-Bissau a3 217

GUINEA-BISSAU

THE REPUBLIC OF GUINEA-BISSAU
Area 36,125km² (13,948sq miles)
Capital Bissau
Organizations ECOWAS, FZ, IDB, OIC
Population 1,450,000
Pop. growth (%) 1.1
Life expectancy 42 (m); 45 (f)
Languages Portuguese, Creole
Literacy 38.5%
Currency CFA franc (US $1 = 534.95 CFA franc)
GDP (US million $) 231
GDP per head ($US) 159

Guinea, Gulf of l9 302
Güines c3 266
Guînes g2 183
Guines, Lac m2 253
Guingamp b4 182
Guinguinéo a3 222
Guintinua d3 100
Guiones, Punta e6 276
Guipavas a4 182
Guiping h7 104
Guipúzcoa b1 192
Güira de Melena c3 266
Guiratinga b2 290
Guiri c1 224
Güiria e1 285
Guir, Oued d2 220
Guisanbourg g3 285
Guisane c6 185
Guisborough e2 162
Guiscard b5 159
Guise b5 159
Guissona f3 192
Guitiriz c1 190
Guîtres b3 186
Guitri c4 222
Guiuan e5 100
Guivi l2 155
Guiyang, Guizhou, China f5 104
Guiyang, Hunan, China j6 105
Guizhou f5 104
Gujan-Mestras a4 186
Gujarat f9 129
Gujar Khan f4 128
Gujba g3 223
Gujranwala b3 130
Gujrat b3 130
Gula c4 130
Gulabgarh c3 130
Gulabie k4 149
Gulang b7 112
Gulaothi c5 130
Gulargambone j11 81
Gul'bakhor m7 121
Gulbarga e4 126
Gulbene m4 157
Gülchö p7 121
Guldborg e4 158
Guldborg Sund e4 158
Gülek e4 208
Gülek Boğazı e4 208
Gulf Hammock h5 259
Gulfport e4 258
Gulf Shores f4 258
Gulf, The b4 300
Gulgong j12 81
Gulian g2 94
Guling d5 106
Gulistan, Pak. c5 128
Gulistan, Uzb. m7 121
Gülitz g2 173
Guliya Shan m1 113
Guljajevskie Koški, Ostrova j1 147
Gul Kach d5 128
Gulkana h3 247
Gull j6 251
Gullbrandstorp f2 158
Gull Lake n6 249
Gullspång f3 156
Güllük a4 208
Güllük Körfezi Ac1 211
Gulmarg b2 130
Gülnar d4 208
Gülper See h3 173
Gülpınar g3 210
Gulrip'shi h1 209
Gülşehir e3 208
Gul'shat q4 121
Gulsvik c2 156
Gulu f3 225
Gülübovo g4 201
Gulwe b5 227
Gulyantsi g4 201
Gumare c2 232
Gumbax, Raas e1 226
Gumbaz d5 128
Gumbiri f3 225
Gumbiro b6 227
Gumdag q2 137
Gumel f3 223
Gumgarhi f5 135
Gumiel de Hizán g3 190
Gumla j8 125
Gummersbach f3 159
Gümüşhane, Tur. g2 209
Gümüşhane, Gümüşhane, Tur. g2 209
Guna e7 124
Guna Terara e5 219
Gunbar g13 81
Güncang p5 125
Gundagai j13 81
Gundelfingen g4 174
Gundelfingen an der Donau e3 174
Gundelsheim f3 174
Gundji d3 224
Gündoğdu a2 208
Gündoğmuş d4 208
Gungu c5 224
Gunib g4 149
Gunisao Lake f4 250
Gunjur a3 222
Gunma h3 115
Gunmi f3 223
Gunnarn f4 154
Gunnaur d5 130
Gunnawarra g4 80
Gunnebo g4 156
Gunnedah k11 81
Gunnison, Colorado, U.S.A. a4 260
Gunnison, Utah, U.S.A. h6 262
Gunpowder Creek d5 80
Günsang f4 135
Guntakal e5 126
Güntersberge f4 173
Guntersville Lake g2 259
Guntramsdorf h1 177
Guntur g4 126
Gununa d4 80
Gunungapi p8 99
Gunung Ayer f3 98

Gunungsugih c7 98
Gunungtua a5 101
Gunupur h3 127
Günyüzü c3 208
Günzburg e4 174
Gunzenhausen d5 175
Guochengyi c7 112
Guodao c1 106
Guodian c2 106
Guo He, China d3 106
Guo He, Henan, China d2 106
Guojiaba b4 106
Guojiadian g1 111
Guojiaqiao e5 111
Guojiatun j5 113
Guojiazhuang g1 111
Guoyang e3 111
Gupi e2 111
Gupis a1 130
Gura Caliţei h3 201
Gura Galbenei j2 201
Gurahonţ l5 171
Gura Humorului g2 201
Gurais b2 130
Gurara f4 223
Gura Teghii h3 201
Gurban Hudag a6 112
Gurban Obo g4 112
Gurbantünggüt Shamo w5 121
Gürbe b3 196
Gurdaspur b3 130
Gurdon c3 258
Gur'evsk j1 169
Gurgaon c5 130
Gurgei, Jebel b5 218
Gurgueia d3 288
Gurha e8 129
Guri, Embalse de e2 285
Gurig National Park l2 86
Gurinhatã d3 290
Gurk f3 177
Gurktaler Alpen e3 176
Gurlen h7 120
Guro e2 233
Gürpinar j3 209
Gursahaiganj d6 130
Guru j5 135
Gurué f2 233
Gurun b3 101
Gürün f3 209
Gurupá g4 285
Gurupi, Braz. c2 288
Gurupi, Tocantins, Braz. c4 288
Gurupi, Cabo c2 288
Guru Sikhar f8 129
Guruve e2 233
Gurvan Sayan Uul b4 112
Gurz b4 128
Gusau f3 223
Gušće h4 177
Güsen g3 173
Gusev l1 169
Gusevskij f4 150
Gushan m6 113
Gushgy a3 128
Gushi d3 106
Gushiegu d4 222
Gushikawa B 115
Gus'-Hrustal'nyj f4 150
Gusinoozersk d2 94
Guspini Aa3 198
Güssing h2 177
Gussola e4 196
Gustavia C 271
Gustavo Diaz Ordaz g5 275
Gustavo Sotelo g10 263
Güsten g4 173
Gustine b4 264
Güstrow f5 158
Gusum g3 156
Gus'-Železnyj f4 150
Gutang p5 125
Gutau f1 177
Gutenstein g2 177
Gütersloh d4 172
Guthrie, Oklahoma, U.S.A. a2 258
Guthrie, Texas, U.S.A. c5 261
Gutian m5 105
Gutian Shuiku m5 105
Gutiérrez e3 293
Gutiérrez Zamora f3 275
Gutorfölde e5 170
Gutsuo h5 135
Gutu e2 233
Gutulia Nasjonalpark e2 156
Guwahati m6 125
Guwêr j4 209
Guxhagen c1 174
Guxian b1 106
Guyana e2 282

GUYANA

THE COOPERATIVE REPUBLIC OF GUYANA
Area 214,969km^2
(83,000sq miles)
Capital Georgetown
Organizations ACS, CARICOM, COMM, IADB, OIC, SELA
Population 763,000
Pop. growth (%) 0.5
Life expectancy 59 (m); 67 (f)
Languages English, Hindi, Urdu, Amerindian dialects
Literacy 98.8%
Currency Guyana dollar (US $1 = 179 Guyana dollar)
GDP (US million $) 747
GDP per head ($US) 979

Guyang, Henan, China d2 106
Guyang, Nei Mongol Zizhiqu, China f5 112
Guye k6 183
Guyenne c4 187
Guy Fawkes River National Park e7 85
Guymon c4 261
Güyom p7 137
Guyra k11 81
Guysborough m6 253
Guyu d3 233
Guyuan, Hebei, China h5 112
Guyuan, Ningxia Huizu Zizhiqu, China d8 112
Guzar c1 128
Güzelbahçe a3 208
Güzeldere j4 209
Güzelhisar Barajı a3 208
Guzhen e3 111
Guzmán f2 272
Guzmán, Lago de f2 272
Gvardejsk k1 169
Gwa b7 102
Gwabegar c7 85
Gwadabawa f3 223
Gwadar a8 129
Gwadar West Bay a8 129
Gwadu e3 223
Gwaii Haanas National Park Reserve b5 248
Gwaldam d4 130
Gwalior, Madhya Pradesh, India f6 124
Gwalior, Madhya Pradesh, India g8 129
Gwanda d3 233
Gwane e3 225
Gwarzo f3 223
Gwash b6 129
Gwatar Bay a8 129
Gwawele e3 225
Gwayi d2 233
Gwda e2 168
Gweebarra Bay c2 165
Gweedore c1 165
Gweensalia b2 165
Gweru, Zimb. d2 233
Gweru, Midlands, Zimb. d2 233
Gweta d3 232
Gwinner e7 250
Gwoza g3 223
Gwydir c6 85
Gwynedd c4 162
Gy b3 184
Gyablung n4 125
Gyaca n5 125
Gyál h4 171
Gyali Ac2 211
Gyangnyi Caka h2 135
Gyangrang g4 135
Gyangzê j5 135
Gyaring Co j4 135
Gyaring Hu q2 125
Gyaros, Grc. e5 211
Gyaros, Notio Aigaio, Grc. e5 211
Gyaur d8 120
Gydanskij Poluostrov h2 118
Gyêmdong n5 125
Gyhum e2 172
Gyimda n4 125
Gyirong g5 135
Gyldenløveshøj e3 158
Gylling d3 158
Gympie l9 81
Gyobingauk b6 102
Gyomaendrőd j5 171
Gyömrő h4 171
Gyöngyös h4 171
Gyöngyöspata h4 171
Gyöngyössolymos h4 171
Győr f4 171
Győrköny g5 171
Győr-Moson-Sopron f4 170
Győrtelek l4 171
Győrújbarát f4 171
Győrzámoly f4 171
Gypsumville d5 250
Gytheio c6 211
Gyumri j2 209
Gyungcang d3 130
Gyúró g4 171
Gyzylarbat r2 137
Gyzyletrek q3 137
Gzy j3 169

H

H. Bouchard f3 297
Haacht c4 159
Haag f1 177
Haag am Hausruck e1 176
Haag in Oberbayern h4 175
Haaksbergen e2 159
Ha'ano J 75
Ha'apai Group J 75
Haapajärvi, Fin. l5 155
Haapajärvi, Oulu, Fin. k5 155
Haapamäki l1 157
Haapaselkä, Fin. n1 157
Haapaselkä, Fin. n2 157
Haapavesi k4 155
Haapsalu k3 157
Haar c2 175
Haardt c3 174
Haaren d2 172
Haarlem, Neth. c2 159
Haarlem, R.S.A. e6 234
Haarstrang c2 173
Haast, N.Z. b5 77
Haast, West Coast, N.Z. b5 77
Haast Pass b6 77
Hab c7 129
Habahe w3 121
Habarane g8 126
Habar Cirir d3 226
Habariha h2 147
Habarovo k1 147
Habarovskij Kraj k2 94
Habartov a1 170
Habary s1 121
Habaswein b3 226
Ḩabawnāh, Wādī f4 219
Habay-la-Neuve d5 159
Ḩabbān g5 219
Habbouch d3 138
Hab Chauki c8 129
Habbah ash Shaykh, Ḩarrāt f4 219
Habicht c2 176
Habiganj m7 125
Habirag h4 112
Habo f4 156
Haboro Ab1 114
Habovka h2 171
Habsheim d3 184
Hacha b4 284
Hachado, Paso de b5 296
Hachenburg d2 174
Hachijō-jima h5 115
Hachimori h1 115
Hachinohe j1 115
Hachiōji h4 115
Hacıbektaş e3 208
Hacinas a3 192
Hacı Zeynalabdin h4 149
Hackås e5 154
Hackensack f4 257
Hacketstown e4 165
Hackettstown f4 256
Hackleburg f2 258
Hack, Mount d11 81
Hackney h3 162
Haco c6 224
Hacufera e3 233
Ḩadabat al Jilf al Kabīr c3 218
Hadamar g3 174
Ḩadan, Ḩarrat g3 219
Hadano h4 115
Ḩadbaram d3 138
Hadārba, Rās e3 219
HaDarom c6 139
Hadayang n1 113
Haddad, Ouadi a5 218
Haddenham g4 163
Haddington f4 164
Hadejia, Nig. f3 223
Hadejia, Jigawa, Nig. g3 223
Hadera c4 139
Haderslev c3 158
Haderup b2 158
Hadim d4 208
Hadjer Momou b4 218
Hadleigh g4 163
Hadley Bay h1 242
Hadong p8 113
Ha Đông g5 102
Ḩaḑramawt g4 219
Hadseløy e2 154
Hadsten d2 158
Hadsund d2 158
Hadyach d2 148
Hadyžensk e3 148
Haedo, Cuchilla de j1 297
Haeju n6 113
Haenam p8 113
Ḩafar al Bāţin k7 136
Hafik f3 209
Hafirat al'Aydā g8 136
Ḩafir at Taḩtā e3 138
Hafizabad a3 130
Haflong n7 125
Hafnarfjörður A 152
Haft Gel m6 137
Haftvān p8 137
Hafursfjörður A 152
Hag Abdullah d5 218
Haga-Haga h6 235
Hagari e5 126
Hagelberg h3 173
Hagemeister Island d4 246
Hagen f3 159
Hagen, Mount l7 97
Hagenow e5 158
Hagenwerder k1 175
Hägere Hiywet b2 226
Hägere Selam b2 226
Hagerman f4 262
Hagerstown, Indiana, U.S.A. d6 254
Hagerstown, Maryland, U.S.A. c5 256
Hagetmau b5 187
Hagfors e2 156
Haggin, Mount g2 262
Ha Giang e7 104
Ha Giao, Sông j8 103
Hagley d4 163
Hagondange c1 184
Hag's Head b4 165
Hague, Cap de la d3 182
Haguenau d2 184
Hahira h4 259
Hahle f4 172
Hahnbach d2 175
Hahnstätten d2 174
Hai b4 227
Hai'an g3 111
Haib c4 234
Haicheng m5 113
Haidenaab h3 175
Haidershofen f1 177
Hai Dương h5 102
Haifa, Ḩefa, Isr. c4 138
Haifeng k7 105
Haig h12 87
Haiger f4 174
Hai He j6 113
Hai, Ko a2 101
Haikou h8 104
Ḩā'il, Sau. Ar f2 219
Ḩā'il, Ḩā'il, Sau. Ar h8 136
Hailakandi n7 125
Hailar k1 113
Hailar He k1 113
Hailey f4 262
Haileybury g2 254
Haileymandi c5 130
Hailin q3 113
Hailing Dao h8 104
Hailong n4 113
Hailsham g6 163
Hailun p2 113
Hailuoto, Fin. k4 155
Hailuoto, Oulu, Fin. k4 155
Haimen, Guangdong, China l7 105
Haimen, Jiangsu, China g4 111
Haimi p6 105
Hainan, Hainan, China g9 104
Hainan, Hai-nan, China g9 104
Hainaut, Bel. b4 159
Hainaut, Fr. j2 183
Haindi b4 222
Haines l4 247
Haines City j5 259
Haines Junction k3 247
Hainfeld g1 177
Hainich f4 172
Hainichen j2 175
Hainich, Nationalpark f4 172
Haining g4 111
Hainleite f4 173
Hai Phong h5 102
Hairag a7 112
Hairhan Namag b5 112
Haiskinselkä l4 155
Haitan Dao m6 105
Haiti g7 241

HAITI

THE REPUBLIC OF HAITI
Area 27,750km^2
(10,714sq miles)
Capital Port-au-Prince
Organizations ACS, CARICOM, IADB, SELA
Population 8,220,000
Pop. growth (%) 1.8
Life expectancy 49 (m); 55 (f)
Languages French, Creole
Literacy 52.9%
Currency gourde (US $1 = 41.25 gourde)
GDP (US million $) 3181
GDP per head ($US) 386

Haitou g9 104
Haiwee Reservoirs f5 265
Haixing e0 106
Haiya e4 219
Haiyan, Qinghai, China a7 112
Haiyan, Zhejiang, China g4 111
Haiyang g1 111
Haiyuan c7 112
Haizhou f2 111
Haizhou Wan f2 111
Håja f2 154
Hajdú-Bihar k4 171
Hajdúböszörmény k4 171
Hajdúhadház k4 171
Hajdúnánás k4 171
Hajdúsámson k4 171
Hajdúszoboszló k4 171
Hajdúszovát k4 171
Haji c6 129
Hajiki-zaki h2 115
Ḩajjah f4 219
Ḩājjīābād, Fārs, Iran q7 137
Ḩājjīābād, Golestān, Iran q3 137
Ḩājjīābād, Hormozgan, Iran q7 137
Hajmáskér g4 171
Hajnáčka h3 171
Hajnówka m3 169
Hajo m6 125
Hájske f3 171
Hajuu-Us d2 112
Haka a4 102
Ḩakamā d4 138
Hakansson, Monts e5 225
Hakasija, Respublika k4 118
Hakefjord d4 156
Hakelhuincul, Altiplanicie de c6 296
Hakepa, Mount A 77
Hakkâri k4 209
Hakkâri j4 209
Hakken-zan f4 115
Hako-dake Ac1 114
Hakodate Ab3 114
Hakos Mountains b1 234
Hakseenpan d3 234
Hakui g3 115
Haku-san g3 115
Haku-san National Park g3 115
Hala d8 129
Ḩalab f4 209
Halabja k4 137
Halachó p7 273
Halahai n3 113
Halahora de Sus h1 201
Halaib e3 219
Halalo L 75
Halat d2 138
Ḩālat 'Ammār f7 136
Hălăuceşti h2 201
Ḩalāwah d4 139
Halba e2 138
Halberstadt g4 173
Halbrite b6 250
Halbyeitsa m5 157
Halcombe e4 76
Halcon, Mount c4 100
Halcottsville f2 256
Halcyon Drift h5 235
Halden d3 156
Haldensleben g3 173
Haldi k8 125
Haldibari l6 125
Hald Sø c2 158
Haldwani d5 130
Hale, Arg. g4 297
Hale, Aust. b8 80
Hāleh p8 137
Hale, Mount c10 87
Halenkov g2 171
Halesowen d4 163
Halesworth h4 163
Half Assini d4 222
Halfeti f4 209
Halfing d2 176
Halfmoon Bay b7 77
Halfway, Can. f3 248
Halfway, U.S.A. c5 256
Halgån e2 156
Halhgol k2 113
Ḩalḩūl d5 139
Haliburton Highlands c6 253
Halifax, Aust. h5 80
Halifax, Can. l6 253
Halifax, U.K. e3 162
Halifax, North Carolina, U.S.A. h7 255
Halifax, Pennsylvania, U.S.A. d4 256
Halifax, Virginia, U.S.A. g7 254
Halifax Bay A 84
Halifax, Mount A 84
Halilulik n9 99
Halimun, Gunung d8 98
Halimun National Park, Gunung d8 98
Ḩalī, Wādī f4 219
Haljala m3 157
Halkett, Cape f1 246
Halkirk e1 164
Hälla f5 154
Halladale e1 164
Ḩallamish d4 139
Halland e4 156
Hallands Väderö e4 156
Hällbymagasinet f5 154
Halle, Bel. c4 159
Halle, Ger. g4 173
Halle (Saale) g4 173
Halle (Westfalen) d3 172
Hällefors f3 156
Hälleforsnäs g3 156
Hallein e2 176
Hällekis e3 156
Hallen e5 154
Hallencourt g3 183
Hallertau g4 175
Hallettsville a5 258
Halley (U.K.) b2 298
Halliday b7 250
Halligen d1 172
Hallingdal c2 156
Hallingdalselva c2 156
Hall in Tirol c2 176
Hall Island a3 246
Hall Islands G 74
Hällnäs g4 154
Hallock e6 250
Hallsberg f3 156
Halls Creek f6 86
Hallstadt c3 175
Hallstahammar g3 156
Hallstatt e2 176
Hallstavik h2 157
Hallstead e3 256
Hallsville b3 258
Hallum d1 159
Hallviken e5 154
Hallwiler See c2 196
Halmahera h5 97
Halmahera Sea h6 97
Halmaj k3 171
Hal'mer-Ju l2 147
Halmstad e4 156
Halnefjorden c2 156
Halol f9 129
Haloze g3 177
Hals d2 158
Halsnøy a3 156
Halsskov d3 158
Halstad e7 250
Halstead g5 163
Halstenbek c5 158
Halsua k5 155
Haltern f3 159
Halton h2 162
Haltunchén p8 273
Haltwhistle d2 162
Ḩālūl h2 219
Halura l10 99
Halvad e9 129
Halver f3 159
Halwell c6 163
Halych n6 169
Haly, Mount d5 85
Ham, Chad c1 224
Ham, Fr. b5 159
Ham, Leb. e3 138
Hamada e4 114
Ḩamāda El Ḩaricha d4 220
Hamadān, Iran m4 137
Hamadān, Hamadān, Iran m4 137
Ḩamādat Murzuq g3 221
Hamaguir d2 220
Ḩamāh, Syria f5 209
Ḩamāh, Ḩamāh, Syria e1 138
Hamakita g4 115
Hamamatsu g4 115
Hamar d2 156
Hamarøy e2 154
Ḩamar, Wādī al g3 219
Ḩāmāt d2 138
Hamatonbetsu Ac1 114
Hambach d1 184
Hambantota g9 126
Hambühren e3 172
Hamburg, Ger. f2 172
Hamburg, Ger. c5 158
Hamburg, R.S.A. g6 235
Hamburg, Arkansas, U.S.A. d3 258
Hamburg, New Jersey, U.S.A. f3 256
Hamburg, Pennsylvania, U.S.A. e4 256
Hamburgisches Wattenmeer, Nationalpark d2 172
Hamburgsund d3 156
Hambye d4 182
Hamden, Connecticut, U.S.A. h3 257
Hamden, New York, U.S.A. e2 256
Hamdibey a3 208
Hamdorf c4 158
Hämeenkangas k2 157
Hämeenlinna l2 157
Hamel e3 172
Hamelin b10 87
Hameln e3 172
HaMerkaz c4 138
Hamer Koke b2 226
Hamersley Range c8 87
Hamert, Nationaal Park de e3 159
Hamgyŏng-sanmaek q5 113
Hamhŭng p6 113
Hami a4 94
Ḩamīd m6 137
Hamid d3 218
Hamidiye h5 201
Hamilton, Queensland, Aust. e7 80
Hamilton, Queensland, Aust. e7 80
Hamilton, South Australia, Aust. b9 81
Hamilton, Aust. f14 81
Hamilton, Can. g4 254
Hamilton, U.K. d4 164
Hamilton, Alabama, U.S.A. f3 258
Hamilton, Alaska, U.S.A. d3 246
Hamilton, Georgia, U.S.A. g3 259
Hamilton, Kansas, U.S.A. a1 258
Hamilton, New York, U.S.A. e2 256
Hamilton, Ohio, U.S.A. d6 254
Hamilton, Texas, U.S.A. d6 261
Hamilton City a2 264
Hamilton Inlet n2 253
Hamilton, Mount, Alaska, U.S.A. e3 246
Hamilton, Mount, California, U.S.A. b4 264
Hamilton Sound q4 253
Hamim, Wādī al b1 218
Hamina m2 157
Hamirpur, Himachal Pradesh, India c4 130
Hamirpur, Uttar Pradesh, India g7 124
Ḩāmir, Wādī al f1 219
Hamju p6 113
Hamlin, Pennsylvania, U.S.A. e3 256
Hamlin, Texas, U.S.A. c5 261
Hamm c4 172
Hammada du Drâa c3 220
Hammādat Tingharat g3 221
Ḩammām al 'Alīl j4 209
Ḩammāmāt Mā'in d5 139
Hammamet, Golfe de g1 221
Hammam-Lif g1 221
Hammāna d3 138
Hammarsjön f5 156
Hammarstrand f5 154
Hamme, Bel. c3 159
Hamme, Ger. d2 172
Hammel c2 158
Hammelburg e2 174
Hammelspring j2 173
Hamme-Mille c4 159
Hamme-Oste-Kanal d2 172
Hammerdal e5 154
Hammerfest j1 155
Hammersmith & Fulham h3 162
Hammerum c2 158
Hamminkeln e3 159
Hammond, Louisiana, U.S.A. d4 258
Hammond, Montana, U.S.A. b2 260
Hammonton f5 256
Hamna n1 155
Hamningberg n1 155
Hamont d3 159
Hampden, Can. p4 253
Hampden, N.Z. c6 77
Hampden Sydney g7 254
Håmpjåkk h3 154
Hamp'yŏng p8 113
Hampshire e5 163
Hampshire Downs e5 163
Hampstead, Maryland, U.S.A. d5 256
Hampstead, North Carolina, U.S.A. l2 259
Hampton, Can. k6 253
Hampton, New Hampshire, U.S.A. k2 257
Hampton, New Jersey, U.S.A. f4 256
Hampton, Tennessee, U.S.A. h1 259
Hampton, Virginia, U.S.A. h7 255
Hampton Bays h4 257
Hampton Tableland h12 87
Hamra f2 156
Ḩamra d4 139
Ḩamrah, Jabal al c7 139
Hamra nationalpark f2 156
Hamra, Ouadi b5 218
Hamrat esh Sheikh c5 218
Hamrin, Jabal k5 209
Hams Fork h5 262
Hamstreet g5 163
Ham-sur-Heure c4 159
Hamuku k6 97
Hamun-i-Lora b6 129
Hamun-i-Mashkel a6 129
Hamur j3 209
Hamyong p8 113
Hana Ac2 263
Hånådalstind b1 156
Hanahai d1 234
Ḩanak f9 137
Hanamaki j2 115
Hanang g4 225
Hanau f4 174
Hanchary p2 169
Hancheng b2 106
Hanchuan c4 106
Hancock, Maryland, U.S.A. b5 256
Hancock, Michigan, U.S.A. j7 251
Hancock, New York, U.S.A. e3 256
Hancock, Wisconsin, U.S.A. b3 254
Handan d1 111
Handeni b5 227
Handewitt c4 158
Handlová g3 171
Handsworth b6 250
Handyga p3 119
Hanerau-Hademarschen c4 158
Hanestad d2 156
Hanford d5 265
Han-gang p7 113
Hangkouping f5 111
Hångstaörn f1 156
Hangu, Pak. e4 128
Hangu, Rom. h2 201
Hanguang j6 105
Hangzhou g4 111
Hangzhou Wan g4 111
Hani h3 209
Ḩanīdh m8 137
Hanino d4 150
Hanji d2 111
Han Jiang l6 105
Hanjiang, Fujian, China m6 105
Hanjiang, Jiangsu, China f3 111
Hanjiaoshui c7 112
Hankasalem as. m1 157
Hankasalmi m1 157
Hankensbüttel f3 173
Hankey f6 234
Han Knežica h4 177
Hanko k3 157
Hankou d4 106
Hanle d3 130
Hanmer Forest Park d5 77
Hanmer Springs d5 77
Hann h5 86
Hanna m6 249
Hannaford d7 250
Hannah d6 250
Hannah Bay n5 251
Hannibal f4 260
Hann, Mount g4 86
Hannover, Ger. e3 172
Hannover, Niedersachsen, Ger. e3 172
Hannoversch Münden e4 172
Hannut d4 159
Hanö f5 156
Hanöbukten f5 156
Ha Nôi g5 102
Hanover, Can. f3 254
Hanover, Jam. B 266
Hanover, R.S.A. f5 234
Hanover, Pennsylvania, U.S.A. d5 256
Hanover, Virginia, U.S.A. h7 255
Hanover, Isla b6 295
Hanøy e2 154
Hanshan f4 111
Han Shui c4 106
Hansi c5 130
Hans Merensky Nature Reserve j1 235
Hansnes g2 154
Hanson a6 80
Hanstholm b1 158
Han Sum k3 113
Han-sur-Nied c2 184
Hanting f1 111
Hantsavichy b1 148
Hanty-Mansijsk m3 147
Hanty-Mansijskij Avtonomnyj Okrug m3 147
Hanumana h7 124
Hanumangarh g6 129
Hanušovce nad Topľou k2 171
Hanušovice e1 170
Hanuy Gol a2 112
Hanwood e2 83
Hanyang d4 106
Hanyin a3 106
Hanyuan d4 104
Hanzhong f2 104
Hanzhuang e2 111
Hao K 75
Haogou e3 111
Haora l8 125
Haouch Barada e2 138
Haouch Moussa d3 138
Haoud el Hamra f2 221
Haouza b3 220
Haozikou c4 106
Haparanda k4 155
Haparanda skärgård nationalpark j4 155
Hapch'ŏn q8 113
Hapoli n6 125
Häppälä m1 157
Happisburgh h4 162
Happy Valley - Goose Bay m2 253
Haptok p7 113
Hapur c5 130
Haputale g9 126
Ḩaql c7 139
Haqrayot d4 138
Hara Alol c1 226
Harabali g3 149
Ḩaradh g3 219
Haradok c1 148
Harads h3 154
Haraiki K 75
Haramachi j3 115
Haramukh b2 130
Hårån f4 156
Harappa Road f5 128
Harare e2 233
Harāt q6 137
Harat Island e4 219
Har-Ayrag e3 112
Haraza, Jebel d4 218
Haraz-Djombo a5 218
Haraz-Mangueigne d1 224
Harb e3 219
Harbatpur c4 130
Harbel b4 222
Harbin p3 113
Harbonnières h3 183
Harboør b2 158
Harbor Beach e4 254
Harbour Breton q5 253
Harbour Grace r5 253
Harburg (Schwaben) e3 175
Hårby d3 158
Harda e8 124
Hardangervidda b2 156
Hardangervidda Nasjonalpark b2 156
Hardap, Nam. b2 234
Hardap, Nam. b2 234
Hardap, Hardap, Nam. b2 234
Hardap Dam b2 234
Hardeeville j3 259
Hardegarijp d1 159
Hardelot-Plage g2 183
Hardenberg e2 159
Harden, Bukit h2 99
Harderwijk d2 159
Hardeveld c5 234
Hardey c8 87
Hardheim d4 174
Harding h5 235
Hardinxveld-Giessendam c3 159
Hardwick f6 252
Hardwicke Bay c13 81
Hardy d1 258
Hardy, Peninsula c7 295
Hare Bay q4 253
Harefjorden e3 156
Hareid b1 156
Hare, Mount k2 247
Haren (Ems) f2 159
Härer, Eth. c2 226
Härer, Eth. c2 226
Härer Wildlife Sanctuary c2 226
Harfleur f3 183
Hargant k1 113
Hargele c2 226
Hargeysa c2 226
Harghita g2 201
Harghita-Mădăraş, Vârful g2 201
Harhal Dağları h3 209
Harhatan d6 112
Haría Af1 189
Haribomo, Lac d2 222
Haridwar d5 130
Harihar d5 126
Harihari c5 77
Harij e9 129
Hari kurk k3 157
Ḩārim f4 209
Harima-nada f4 114
Harim, Jabal al q8 137
Haringey h3 162
Haringvliet c3 159
Haripur f4 128
Harisal e9 124
Ḩarjab, Wādī f4 219
Härjån e2 156
Harjavalta k2 157
Harkakötöny h5 171
Hårkan e5 154
Harkány g6 171
Harlan, Iowa, U.S.A. e3 260
Harlan, Kentucky, U.S.A. h1 259
Harlan County Lake d3 260
Hârlău h2 201
Harlech b4 162
Harlem n7 249
Harleston h4 163
Hårlev f3 158
Harlingen, Neth. d1 159
Harlingen, U.S.A. a6 258
Harlinger Land c2 172
Harlovka r2 155
Harlow g5 163
Harlowton j2 262
Harman a6 256
Harmånger g2 156
Harmelen c2 159
Harmil f4 219
Harmsdorf d5 158
Harnai c5 128
Harnauli e4 128
Harnes a4 159
Harney Basin d4 262
Harney Lake d4 262
Härnön h1 157
Härnösand g1 157
Har Nuden j1 113
Har Nur l3 113
Haro b2 192
Haroldswick A 164
Haroué c2 184
Harovsk f2 150
Harper c5 222
Harper Lake f6 265
Harper, Mount, Alaska, U.S.A. j2 247
Harper, Mount, Alaska, U.S.A. k2 247
Harpers Ferry c5 256
Harpersfield f2 256
Harpstedt d3 172
Harquahala Mountains g9 263
Ḩarrān al 'Awāmid e3 138
Harrand e6 129
Harricanaw p5 251
Harridslev d2 158
Harrietsham g5 163
Harrington e6 256
Harris a2 164
Harrisburg, Illinois, U.S.A. e1 258
Harrisburg, Pennsylvania, U.S.A. d4 256
Harris, Lake, Aust. b11 81
Harris, Lake, U.S.A. j5 259
Harrislee c4 158
Harrismith, Aust. c13 87
Harrismith, R.S.A. h4 235
Harris, Mount j9 87
Harrison, Arkansas, U.S.A. c1 258
Harrison, Michigan, U.S.A. d3 254
Harrison Bay g1 247
Harrisonburg, U.S.A. k6 257
Harrisonburg, Virginia, U.S.A. b6 256
Harrison, Cape p1 253
Harrison Lake f7 248
Harrisonville e4 260
Harriston d4 258
Harrisville, Michigan, U.S.A. e3 254
Harrisville, New York, U.S.A. j3 255
Harrodsburg g1 259
Harrogate e3 162
Harrow h2 162
Harrowsmith h3 255
Harry S. Truman Reservoir e4 260
Har Sai Shan a1 104
Harsefeld c5 158
Harsin l4 137
Harşit g2 209
Hârşova h3 201
Harstad f2 154
Harsvik c4 154
Harsyssel b2 158
Hart, Can. k2 247
Hart, U.S.A. c4 254
Hartao m4 113
Hartbees d4 234
Hartbeespoort g2 235
Hartberg g2 177
Hartenholm d5 158
Hartford, Alabama, U.S.A. g4 259
Hartford, Connecticut, U.S.A. h3 257
Hartford, South Dakota, U.S.A. d3 260
Hartha d1 175
Hartkirchen e1 176

Hirado → Hudson 339

Hirado q9 113
Hirado-shima c5 114
Hirakata f4 115
Hirakud Reservoir h9 125
Hiram f5 254
Hiraman b4 226
Hirara B 115
Hirata e4 114
Hiré-Watta c4 222
Hiroo Ac2 114
Hirosaki j1 115
Hiroshima, Japan e4 114
Hiroshima, Hiroshima, Japan e4 114
Hirschaid f2 175
Hirschau g3 175
Hirschberg, Ger. g5 175
Hirschberg, Thüringen, Ger. g3 175
Hirschfelde k2 175
Hirsholmene LH d1 158
Hirsingue d3 184
Hirson c5 159
Hirtshals c1 158
Hisai g4 115
Hisar b5 130
Hisarönü d2 208
Hisbān d5 139
Hislaviči b4 150
Hisor d1 128
Hispur Glacier b1 130
Hisyah e2 138
Hit j5 137
Hita a4 192
Hitachi j3 115
Hitachi-ōta j3 115
Hitchin f5 163
Hitchinbrook Island National Park A 84
Hitra b5 154
Hittarp f2 158
Hitzacker g2 173
Hiu F 74
Hiuchiga-take h3 115
Hiuchi-nada e4 114
Hiva Oa K 75
Hiwannee e4 258
Hixson g2 259
Hizan j3 209
Hjällerup d1 158
Hjälmaren f3 156
Hjalmar Lake h3 242
Hjelm d2 158
Hjelm Bugt f4 158
Hjelmeland b3 156
Hjelmsøya Naturreservat k1 155
Hjelset a5 154
Hjerkinn c1 156
Hjerm b2 158
Hjo f3 156
Hjordkær c3 158
Hjørring d1 158
Hjortø d4 158
Hjuvik e1 158
Hkok d5 102
Hkring Bum c2 102
Hlabisa j4 235
Hlaing b7 102
Hlane Royal National Park j3 235
Hlatikulu j3 235
Hlegu c7 102
Hliník nad Hronom g3 171
Hlinsko d2 170
Hlm f5 177
Hlobyne d2 148
Hlohovec f3 171
Hlotse h4 235
Hlubočky f2 170
Hluboká nad Vltavou c2 170
Hlučín g2 171
Hluhluwe k4 235
Hluhluwe Game Reserve k4 235
Hluk j1 177
Hlukhiv d2 148
Hlyboka g1 201
Hlybokaye m5 157
Hlynyany n6 169
Hniezdné j2 171
Hnivan' j1 201
Hnojník g2 171
Hnúšťa h3 171
Ho e4 223
Hòa Binh g5 102
Hoachanas c1 234
Hoan f2 156
Hoanib a2 232
Hoarusib a2 232
Hoaseb Store c1 234
Hobart, Aust. Ab3 83
Hobart, U.S.A. d5 261
Hobbs c5 261
Hobbs Coast pp2 298
Hobe Sound j6 259
Hobhouse g4 235
Hobo b3 284
Hoboksar v4 121
Hobro c2 158
Hobson j2 262
Hobyo d2 226
Hochandochtla Mountain e2 246
Höchberg f2 174
Hochbira f1 177
Hochfeind e2 176
Hochfeld b3 232
Hochfelden d2 184
Hochfläche d4 172
Hochgolling e2 176
Hochharz, Nationalpark f4 173
Höchheim f3 174
Hô Chi Minh h10 103
Hochobir f3 177
Hochschwab, Aus. g2 177
Hochschwab, Aus. g2 177
Höchstadt an der Aisch c2 175
Hochtannbergpass b2 176
Hochtaunus d2 174
Hochtor f2 177
Hochunnutz c2 176
Hochwang d3 196
Hockenheim g2 174
Hod c2 222
Hodal c6 130
Hodalen d1 156
Hô Dâu Tiêng h10 102
Hodda e1 226
Hodder d3 162
Hoddesdon f5 163
Hodenhagen e3 172
Hodge c3 258
Hodgenville g1 259
Hodgson e5 250
Hod HaSharon c4 139
Hodh Ech Chargui c2 222
Hodh El Gharbi c2 222
Hódmezővásárhely j5 171
Hodna, Chott el e1 221
Hodnet d4 162
Hodonice h1 177
Hodonín j1 177
Hodzana g2 247
Hœdic, Île de c5 182
Hoedspruit j2 235
Hoek van Holland c3 159
Hoensbroek d4 159
Hoeryŏng q4 113
Hoeyang p6 113
Hof d3 175
Hoffman's Cay l7 259
Hofheim am Taunus g2 174
Hofheim in Unterfranken d2 175
Hofmeyr f5 235
Höfn, Austurland, Ice. A 152
Höfn, Vesturland, Ice. A 152
Hofors g2 156
Hofrat en Nahas d2 224
Hofsjökull A 152
Högån e5 154
Höganäs f2 158
Hogan Group e4 83
Hogansville g3 259
Hoganthulla Creek b4 84
Hogarth, Mount c6 80
Hogback Mountain c3 260
Hoge Vaart d2 159
Hoge Veluwe, Nationaal Park de d2 159
Hoggar, Parc National du e4 221
Høg-Gia d1 156
Høgkjølen-Bakkjølen b5 154
Högsby g4 156
Høgste Breakulen b2 156
Hogsty Reef h4 266
Hőgyész g5 171
Hoh a2 262
Hohe Leier e3 176
Hohe Leiten e3 176
Hohenau e1 176
Hohenau an der March h1 177
Hohenbucko j4 173
Hohenems a2 176
Hohenlockstedt c5 158
Hohennauen h3 173
Hohensaaten k3 173
Hohenstein-Ernstthal h2 175
Hohenwald f2 258
Hohen Wangelin f5 158
Hohenwartetalsperre g2 175
Hohenwestedt c4 158
Hoher Dachstein e2 176
Hoher Göll j5 175
Hoher Rhön f2 174
Hoher Ifen b2 176
Hoher Vogelsberg, Naturpark e2 174
Hohe Sonnblick h5 174
Hohe Tauern d2 176
Hohe Tauern, Nationalpark d2 176
Hohhot f5 112
Hohlovo d2 150
Hohn e1 158
Hohne f3 172
Hohoe e4 223
Hoholitna f3 246
Hoh Sai Hu n2 125
Hohwachter Bucht f1 173
Hoh Xil Shan j2 135
Hội An j8 102
Hoima f3 225
Hoisdorf d5 158
Hội Xuân g5 102
Hojai n7 125
Højby, Fyn, Den. d3 158
Højby, Vestsjælland, Den. e3 158
Hojdype, Gora l2 147
Højer b4 158
Höjo e5 114
Højslev c2 158
Højslev Stationsby c2 158
Hok d5 102
Hokes Bluff g3 259
Hokianga Harbour d1 76
Hokitika c5 77
Hokkaidō, Japan Ac2 114
Hokkaidō, Hokkaidō, Japan Ac2 114
Hokksund c3 156
Hokmābād r3 137
Hokota j3 115
Hoktemberyan k2 209
Hol f2 156
Hola b4 226
Holanda e2 293
Hola Prystan' d3 148
Holasovice f2 171
Holbæk, Århus, Den. d2 158
Holbæk, Vestsjælland, Den. e3 158
Holbeach g4 162
Holberg c6 248
Holborne Island c1 84
Holbrook, Aust. h13 81
Holbrook, U.S.A. h8 263
Holden, Nor. c4 154
Holden, U.K. d3 162
Holden, U.S.A. g6 262
Holdenville a2 258
Holder h5 259
Holderness f3 162
Holdich c5 295
Holdorf d3 172
Holdrege d3 260
Hole in the Wall l7 259
Holešov f2 171
Holetown H 271
Holguera d5 192
Holguín f4 266
Holič f3 170
Holice e1 170
Holitna e3 246
Höljan e2 156
Höljes e1 156
Hollabrunn h1 177
Holladay h5 262
Holland, Can. d6 250
Holland, Michigan, U.S.A. c4 254
Holland, New York, U.S.A. b2 256
Holland, Texas, U.S.A. a4 258
Hollandale d3 258
Holland-on-Sea h5 163
Hollandstoun B 164
Hollenstein an der Ybbs f2 177
Hollfeld f2 175
Hollick-Kenyon Plateau hh2 298
Hollidaysburg b4 256
Hollis d5 261
Hollister b5 264
Holly Hill j3 259
Holly Springs e2 258
Hollywood j7 259
Holm, Nor. d4 154
Holm, Russ. Fed. a3 150
Holman f1 242
Hólmavík A 152
Holme b3 158
Holme-Olstrup e3 158
Holme-on-Spalding-Moor f3 162
Holmes Chapel d3 162
Holmes Reef h4 80
Holmestrand d3 156
Holmfirth e3 162
Holmöarna naturreservat h5 154
Holmön h5 154
Holmsjö, Västerbotten, Swe. g4 154
Holmsjö, Västernorrland, Swe. f5 154
Holmsjön, Swe. f5 154
Holmsjön, Swe. f1 156
Holmsland Klit b3 158
Holmsund h5 154
Holm-Žirkovskij b4 150
Holoby p4 169
Holon c4 139
Holoog b3 234
Holovanivs'k k1 201
Holovets'ko l6 169
Holroyd f3 80
Holsnøy a2 156
Holstebro b2 158
Holsted b3 158
Holston e7 254
Holsworthy b6 163
Holt, U.K. h4 162
Holt, Alabama, U.S.A. f3 258
Holt, Michigan, U.S.A. d4 254
Holtemme g4 173
Holton e4 260
Holtoson b1 112
Holtville f9 263
Holtwood d5 256
Holuj f3 150
Holuwon k6 97
Holwerd d1 159
Holycross d4 165
Holy Cross e3 246
Holy Cross, Mount of the b4 260
Holyhead b3 162
Holyhead Bay b3 162
Holy Island, Scotland, U.K. c4 164
Holy Island, Wales, U.K. b3 162
Holyoke, Colorado, U.S.A. c3 260
Holyoke, Massachusetts, U.S.A. h2 257
Holywood c5 164
Holzdorf j4 173
Holzhausen an der Haide d4 174
Holzkirchen c3 175
Holzminden e4 172
Holzthaleben f4 173
Holzwickede c4 172
Homa Bay a4 226
Homalin b3 102
Homathko e6 248
Homberg (Efze) e1 174
Homberg (Ohm) e1 174
Homboři d2 222
Hombourg-Haut c1 184
Hombre Muerto, Salar del d5 292
Homburg e3 174
Homécourt b1 184
Home Hill h5 80
Homeland Park h2 259
Homem b3 190
Homer, Alaska, U.S.A. g4 246
Homer, Georgia, U.S.A. h2 259
Homer, Louisiana, U.S.A. c3 258
Homer, New York, U.S.A. d2 256
Homer City a4 256
Homerville h4 259
Homestead, Aust. g6 80
Homestead, U.S.A. j7 259
Homewood f3 258
Hommelstø d4 154
Hommersåk a3 156
Homnabad e4 126
Homocea h2 201
Homoine l1 235
Homutovo e1 148
Homyel' c1 148
Homyel'skaya Voblasts' c1 148
Honavar d5 126
Honbetsu Ac2 114
Hon Chông g10 103
Hon Chuối g11 103
Honda c2 284
Honda Bay b6 100
Hondarribia c1 192
Hondeklipbaai b5 234
Hondo, Belize p8 273
Hondo, U.S.A. k3 273
Hondón de las Nieves d6 193
Honduras f7 241

HONDURAS

THE REPUBLIC OF HONDURAS
Area 112,088km^2 (43,277sq miles)
Capital Tegucigalpa
Organizations ACS, CACM, IADB, SELA
Population 6,780,000
Pop. growth (%) 3
Life expectancy 63 (m); 68 (f)
Languages Spanish
Literacy 76.8%
Currency lempira (US $1 = 17.72 lempira)
GDP (US million $) 6606
GDP per head ($US) 974

Honduras, Cabo de d2 276
Honduras, Gulf of c2 276
Honea Path h2 259
Hønefoss d2 156
Honesdale e3 256
Honey e3 275
Honey Grove b3 258
Honey Lake c5 262
Honeymoon Bay a1 262
Honey, Mount C 77
Honeyville g5 262
Honfleur f3 183
Høng e3 158
Hong'an d4 106
Hongch'ŏn p7 113
Hông Gai f8 104
Honggou e1 111
Hong He d3 106
Honghe f4 102
Honghu c5 106
Honghuatao b4 106
Hongjiang g5 104
Hong Kong, Hong Kong, China k7 105
Hong Kong, Hong Kong Special Administrative Region, Xianggang Tebie Xingzhengqu, China k7 105
Hongliu He a1 106
Hongliuyuan b6 112
Hong, Mouths of the h5 104
Hông Ngự g10 103
Hongor, China g3 112
Hongor, Mong. g3 112
Hongshan e1 111
Hongshansi c6 112
Hongshi p4 113
Hongshui He f6 104
Hongsŏng p7 113
Hông, Sông g5 102
Hongtong b1 106
Honguedo, Détroit d' k4 253
Hongwŏn p5 113
Hongxing m3 113
Hongze f3 111
Hongze Hu f3 111
Honikulu, Passe L 75
Honiton c6 163
Honjō j2 115
Hon Khoai g11 103
Honkilahti k2 157
Hon Mat h6 104
Hon Mê h6 104
Honnali d5 126
Hon Ne h6 104
Honnet Nature Reserve j1 235
Hönö e1 158
Honolulu Ac2 263
Honrubia b5 193
Honrubia de la Cuesta g3 190
Honshū g4 115
Hontianske Nemce g3 171
Hontoria de la Cantera g2 190
Hontoria del Pinar a3 192
Hon Tre j9 103
Honuu q3 119
Hood b3 264
Hood, Mount c3 262
Hood Point d14 87
Hoodsport b2 262
Hooge, Ger. d1 172
Hooge, Schleswig-Holstein, Ger. b4 158
Hoogeveen e2 159
Hoogezand-Sappemeer e1 159
Hoogstede e2 159
Hoogstraten c3 159
Hook f5 163
Hooker c4 261
Hook Head e4 165
Hook Island c2 84
Hook Point e4 84
Hook Reef c1 84
Hoonah l4 247
Hooper Bay c3 246
Hooper Island d6 256
Hoople e6 250
Hoopstad f3 235
Höör e5 156
Hoorn, Friesland, Neth. d1 159
Hoorn, Noord-Holland, Neth. d2 159
Hoorn, Îles de H 75
Hoosick g2 257
Hooversville b4 256
Höövör a3 112
Hopa h2 209
Hopatcong f4 256
Hopatcong, Lake f4 256
Hope, Can. c1 262
Hope, N.Z. d5 77
Hope, Alaska, U.S.A. g3 247
Hope, Arkansas, U.S.A. c3 258
Hope, Indiana, U.S.A. d6 254
Hope Bay B 270
Hopedale, Can. s4 243
Hopedale, Illinois, U.S.A. b5 254
Hopedale, Massachusetts, U.S.A. j2 257
Hopefield c6 234
Hope, Lake e13 87
Hopelchén q8 273
Hope Mountains l2 253
Hope, Point c1 246
Hoper f2 149
Hopes Advance, Cap r3 243
Hopetoun, Victoria, Aust. f13 81
Hopetoun, Western Australia, Aust. e13 87
Hopetown f4 234
Hope Valley j3 257
Hopewell h7 255
Hopewell Islands p1 251
Hopewell Junction g3 257
Hopfgarten im Brixental d2 176
Hopin c3 102
Hopkins c3 82
Hopkins, Lake j9 87
Hopland b6 263
Hopseidet l1 155
Hopsten c3 172
Hoptrup c3 158
Hoque a1 232
Hoquiam b2 262
Hor, China c1 104
Hor, Russ. Fed. k3 94
Hora Califo c2 226
Horadiz l2 137
Horasan j2 209
Horažďovice b2 170
Horb am Neckar g4 174
Horbelev f4 158
Hörby e5 156
Horcajo de los Montes f5 191
Horcajo de Santiago b5 193
Horcasitas g3 272
Horcón b2 296
Horconcitos f3 275
Hordaland a2 156
Horden e2 162
Horejver l2 147
Horeke d1 76
Horezu f3 201
Horgen c2 196
Hörh Uul c4 112
Hořice d1 170
Horinger f5 112
Horiult a3 112
Horka k4 173
Hořka j2 171
Horki c1 148
Horley f5 163
Horlick Mountains gg3 298
Horlivka e2 148
Hormigueros A 270
Hormozgan r8 137
Hormoz, Kūh-e q8 137
Hormūd-e Bāgh q8 137
Hormūd-e Mīr Khūnd q8 137
Hormuz, Strait of q8 137
Horn, Aus. g1 177
Horn, Ice. A 152
Hornachos d6 191
Hornachuelos e7 191
Hornån g5 154
Horná Súča f3 171
Hornavan f3 154
Horná Ves g3 171
Hornbæk f2 158
Hornbeck c4 258
Hornberg d2 174
Hornbrook b5 262
Hornburg f3 173
Horncastle f3 162
Horndal g2 156
Horneburg c5 158
Hörnefors g5 154
Hornell c2 256
Hornepayne l6 251
Hornfiskrøn e1 158
Horn Head d1 165
Horní Bečva g2 171
Horní Benešov f2 171
Horní Bříza b2 170
Horní Cerekev d2 170
Hornillos e4 272
Horní Maršov d1 170
Hornindal b2 156
Hørning d2 158
Horní Planá f1 177
Hornisgrinde d4 174
Horn Island a4 258
Horní Slavkov a1 170
Horní Suchá g2 171
Hornos b6 193
Hornos, Cabo de c7 295
Hornos, Parque Nacional de c7 295
Hornoy-le-Bourg g3 183
Hornsea f3 162
Hornslet d2 158
Horns, The A 77
Hornsyld c3 158
Hornum c2 158
Hörnum b4 158
Horný Tisovník h3 171
Horodenka g1 201
Horodok, Khmel'nyts'ka Oblast', Ukr. h1 201
Horodok, L'vivs'ka Oblast', Ukr. m6 169
Horokhiv n5 169
Horoměřice c1 170
Horonobe Ab1 114
Horošee s1 121
Horo Shan v6 121
Horoshiri-dake Ac2 114
Hořovice b2 170
Horqin Shadi l4 113
Horqueta f4 293
Horred f1 158
Horrocks b11 87
Horru m4 125
Horse Cave g1 259
Horse Creek b3 260
Horsehead Lake d2 260
Horseheads d2 256
Horse Islands q3 253
Hörsel f5 173
Horsens c3 158
Horsens Fjord d3 158
Horsham, Aust. f14 81
Horsham, U.K. f5 163
Hørsholm f3 158
Horslunde e4 158
Horšovský Týn a2 170
Horspath e5 163
Horst, Ger. e2 174
Horst, Neth. e3 159
Horst (Holstein) c5 158
Hörstel c3 172
Horstmar f2 159
Horsunlu b4 208
Horten d3 156
Hortensia g3 297
Hortezuela b3 192
Hortigüela g2 190
Hortobágy k4 171
Hortobágyi k4 171
Horton d2 242
Hortonville b3 254
Hørup hav c4 158
Hørve e3 158
Horw c2 196
Horwood Lake m7 251
Hosa'ina b2 226
Hösbach e2 174
Hosdurga e6 126
Hose, Pegunungan g3 98
Hoševtovo g3 149
Hoseynābād l4 137
Hoseyniyeh m6 137
Hoseyniyeh-ye Khodā Dād m5 137
Hosford g4 259
Hoshab a7 129
Hoshangabad e8 124
Hoshiarpur b4 130
Hōshōōt b1 112
Hosingen e4 159
Hospet e5 126
Hospital c4 165
Hospital de Orbigo e2 190
Hosseger a5 187
Hosséré Vokre b2 224
Hosston c3 258
Hosszúpályi k4 171
Hosszúpereszteg f4 170
Hosta e4 148
Hostalric g3 192
Hoste, Isla c7 295
Hostěradice h1 177
Hostinné d1 170
Hošťka c1 170
Hotagen e5 154
Hotaka g3 115
Hotan e1 130
Hotan He t8 121
Hotazel e3 234
Hô Thac Ba g4 102
Hotham, Cape k3 86
Hotham, Mount e3 83
Hoti j6 97
Hoting f4 154
Hotong Qagan Nur e6 112
Hô Tri An h10 102
Hot Springs, Arkansas, U.S.A. c2 258
Hot Springs, Montana, U.S.A. f2 262
Hot Springs, South Dakota, U.S.A. c3 260
Hottah Lake f3 242
Hotte, Massif de la h5 266
Hottentots Bay, Nam. a3 234
Hottentots Bay, Karas, Nam. a3 234
Hottentots Point a3 234
Hotton d4 159
Hotynec c5 150
Hotzenwald d5 174
Hou d1 158
Houat, Île d' c5 182
Houayxay e5 102
Houdan g4 183
Houeillès c4 187
Houffalize d4 159
Houghton, Michigan, U.S.A. j7 251
Houghton, New York, U.S.A. b2 256
Houghton Lake d3 254
Houghton le Spring e2 162
Houlton j5 253
Houma, China b2 106
Houma, U.S.A. d5 258
Houmt Souk g2 221
Houndé d3 222
Hounslow h3 162
Hourtin a3 186
Hourtin et de Carcans, Étang d' a3 186
Housatonic, Connecticut, U.S.A. g3 257
Housatonic, Massachusetts, U.S.A. g2 257
Houston, Mississippi, U.S.A. e3 258
Houston, Missouri, U.S.A. d1 258
Houston, Texas, U.S.A. b5 258
Hout h1 235
Hout Bay c7 234
Houten d2 159
Houthalen d3 159
Houtman Abrolhos a11 87
Houxia w6 121
Houzhen f1 111
Hov d3 158
Hova f3 156
Hovd, Mong. a3 94
Hovd, Övörhangay, Mong. b3 112
Hovd, Hovd, Mong. k5 118
Hovd Gol k5 118
Hove f6 163
Hövelhof d4 172
Hoven b3 158
Hover b2 158
Hoveyzeh m6 137
Hověží g2 171
Hovmantorp f4 156
Hövsgöl, Mong. a1 112
Hövsgöl, Dornogovĭ, Mong. e4 112
Hövsgöl Nuur c2 94
Hövüün b4 112
Howakil Island f4 219
Howa, Ouadi b4 218
Howard, Kansas, U.S.A. a1 258
Howard, Pennsylvania, U.S.A. c3 256
Howard Island b2 80
Howar, Wadi c4 218
Howden f3 162
Howe d5 254
Howe, Cape g3 83
Howell e4 254
Howes c2 260
Howes Valley g1 83
Howick j4 235
Howitt, Mount MP e3 83
Howland Island (U.S.A.) h2 73
Howth e3 165
Howz-e Panj r6 137
Howz i-Mian i-Tak q5 137
Hoxie d1 258
Höxter e4 172
Hoxtolgay w4 121
Hoy g1 164
Hoya e3 172
Høyanger b2 156
Hoyerswerda k4 173
Høylandet d4 154
Hoym g4 173
Hoyos d4 190
Hoyos del Espino e4 190
Höytiäinen m5 155
Hozat g3 209
Hozgarganta e8 191
Hozha m2 169
Hrabyně g2 171
Hradec Králové d1 170
Hrádek nad Nisou c1 170
Hradište g3 171
Hradište pod Vrátnom f3 171
Hranice, Karlovarský kraj, Czech Rep. a1 170
Hranice, Olomoucký kraj, Czech Rep. f2 171
Hranovnica j3 171
Hrastnik g3 177
Hrawzhyshki p1 169
Hrazdan g4 149
Hrebinka d2 148
Hriňová h3 171
Hrochot' h3 171
Hrodna m2 169
Hrodzyenskaya Voblasts' b1 148
Hronov e1 170
Hronovce g3 171
Hrotovice e2 170
Hroznová Lhota j1 177
Hrubieszów m5 169
Hrubý Jeseník f1 170
Hrušovany nad Jevišovkou h1 177
Hrvačani j5 177
Hrvatska Dubica h4 177
Hrvatska Kostajnica h4 177
Hrynyava g2 201
Hsenwi c4 102
Hsi-hseng c5 102
Hsilo n7 105
Hsinchu n6 105
Hsinchuang n6 105
Hsintien n6 105
Hsipaw c4 102
Hsiyüp'ing Yü m7 105
Hsüeh Shan n6 105
Hua'an l6 105
Huab a3 232
Huacaibamba b1 292
Huacaraje g2 293
Huacaya e4 293
Huachamacari, Cerro d3 284
Huachi, Bol. e2 293
Huachi, China e7 112
Huachinera j10 263
Huachipato a4 296
Huacho b2 292
Huachón b2 292
Huachongji f2 111
Huachuan r2 113
Huaco c2 294
Huacrachuco b1 292
Huacullani d3 292
Huade g5 112
Huadian p4 113
Huagaruancha b2 292
Hua Hin d9 103
Huahine K 75
Huai'an, Hebei, China h5 112
Huai'an, Jiangsu, China f3 111
Huaibei e3 111
Huaibin d3 106
Huaidezhen n4 113
Huai Had National Park g7 102
Huai He e3 111
Huaiji j7 105
Huailillas b1 292
Huailin e4 111
Huai Luang f7 102
Huainan e3 111
Huaining e4 106
Huairen g6 112
Huairou j5 113
Huaiyang d3 106
Huaiyin, Jiangsu, China f3 111
Huaiyuan e3 111
Huaji d3 106
Huajialing e1 104
Huajicori b2 274
Huajimic b3 274
Huajuápan de León f5 275
Huaki p8 99
Hualahuises k5 273
Hualapai Peak g8 263
Hualfín d5 292
Hualien n6 105
Hualla c2 292
Huallaga b1 292
Hualong b7 112
Hualpin a5 296
Hualqui a4 296
Huamachuco b1 292
Huamani b2 292
Huamanrazo b2 292
Huamantla f4 275
Huambo, Ang. b1 232
Huambo, Huambo, Ang. b1 232
Huamuxtitlán e5 275
Huanan r2 113
Huancache, Sierra c4 295
Huancapi c2 292
Huancavelica, Peru b2 292
Huancavelica, Huancavelica, Peru b2 292
Huancayo b2 292
Huancheng e1 111
Huanchilla f2 297
Huangbizhuang Shuiku h6 112
Huangcheng a7 112
Huangchuan d3 106
Huang Hai g3 300
Huang He d2 106
Huanghe Kou f1 111
Huanghetan p2 125
Huanghua, Hebei, China j6 113
Huanghua, Hubei, China b4 106
Huangji c3 106
Huangjiajian g3 111
Huangjinbu l4 105
Huangkou e2 111
Huangling a2 106
Huanglong a2 106
Huanglongtan b3 106
Huangmao Jian m5 105
Huangmei d4 106
Huangnihe p4 113
Huangpi d4 106
Huangqi m5 105
Huangqiao g3 111
Huangqi Hai g5 112
Huangshan f5 111
Huangshanguan g1 111
Huangshi d4 106
Huang Shui b7 112
Huangtu Gaoyuan e7 112
Huanguelén g4 297
Huangwan g4 111
Huangxian g1 111
Huangyan n4 105
Huangyuan a7 112
Huangze g5 111
Huangzhou d4 106
Huaning f3 102
Huan Jiang d7 112
Huanjiang g6 104
Huanjintepec e5 275
Huanren n5 113
Huanta c2 292
Huantai f1 111
Huantan c4 106
Huánuco, Peru b1 292
Huánuco, Huánuco, Peru b1 292
Huanuhuanu c3 292
Huanusco c3 274
Huanxian d7 112
Huanzo, Cordillera de c2 292
Huap'ing Yü n6 105
Huaquechula e4 275
Huar d3 292
Huaral b2 292
Huaráz b1 292
Huaren Chenque b5 296
Huari b1 292
Huariaca b2 292
Huarmey b2 292
Huarochirí b2 292
Huaron b2 292
Huarong c5 106
Huásabas j11 263
Huasaga b4 284
Huascarán, Nevado de b1 292
Huascarán, Parque Nacional b1 292
Huasco, Chile b1 294
Huasco, Atacama, Chile b1 294
Hua Shan b2 106
Huatabampo e4 272
Huating f1 104
Huatong l5 113
Huatusco, Mex. f4 275
Huatusco, Veracruz, Mex. f4 275
Huauchinango e3 275
Huauru, Islas de b2 292
Huautla f4 275
Huaxian, Guangdong, China j7 105
Huaxian, Henan, China d2 106
Huaxian, Shaanxi, China a2 106
Huayacocotla e3 275
Huayang e4 111
Huayhuash, Cordillera b2 292
Huayin b2 106
Huaylas b1 292
Huaynamota b3 274
Huayuan g4 104
Huayuankou c2 106
Huazhou h8 104
Huazi m5 113
Huazolotitlán f5 275
Hubbard Lake, Michigan, U.S.A. e3 254
Hubbard Lake, Michigan, U.S.A. e3 254
Hubbard, Mount k3 247
Hubei c4 106
Hubli d5 126
Hubová h2 171
Hucal e4 297
Huch'ang p5 113
Hückelhoven e3 159
Hückeswagen f3 159
Hucknall e3 162
Hucqueliers g2 183
Huddersfield e3 162
Hude (Oldenburg) d2 172
Huder l1 113
Hudiksvall g2 156
Hudson, U.S.A. g2 257
Hudson, Florida, U.S.A. h5 259
Hudson, Massachusetts, U.S.A. j2 257
Hudson, New Hampshire, U.S.A. j2 257
Hudson, New York, U.S.A. k6 257
Hudson, New York, U.S.A. g2 257

340 Hudson → Indi

Hudson, North Carolina, U.S.A. j2 259
Hudson, Ohio, U.S.A. f5 254
Hudson Bay, Can. b3 302
Hudson Bay, Saskatchewan, Can. b4 250
Hudson, Cerro b5 295
Hudson Falls k4 255
Hudson, Lake b1 258
Hudson Mountains hh2 298
Hudson's Hope g3 248
Hudson Strait c3 302
Huê h7 102
Huebra d4 190
Huecha c3 192
Huechucuicui, Punta b4 295
Huedin f2 201
Huehuetán a3 276
Huehuetenango b3 276
Huehuetlán e4 275
Huehueto, Cerro g5 272
Hueicoya a6 296
Huejotzingo e4 275
Huejúcar c2 274
Huejuquilla c2 274
Huejutla e3 275
Huélago a7 193
Huelgoat b4 182
Huelma g7 191
Huelva, Spain d7 191
Huelva, Spain d7 191
Huelva, Andalucía, Spain d7 191
Huelves b4 193
Huentelauquén b1 296
Huépac h11 263
Huepil b4 296
Hueque d1 284
Huequén a4 296
Huequi, Volcán b4 295
Huércal-Overa c7 193
Huérguina c4 193
Huérmeces g2 190
Huerta del Marquesada c4 193
Huerta del Rey a3 192
Huerta de Valdecarábanos g5 191
Huertas, Cabo de las d6 193
Huerta, Sierra de la d1 296
Huertecillas d1 274
Huesa a7 193
Huesca, Spain d2 192
Huesca, Aragón, Spain d2 192
Huéscar, Spain b7 193
Huéscar, Andalucía, Spain b7 193
Huétamo d4 274
Huete b4 193
Huétor-Tájar f7 191
Huétor-Vega g7 191
Hueva Toltén a5 296
Hueycantenango e5 275
Hueyotlipan e4 275
Huezna e7 191
Huezna, Embalse de e7 191
Hüfingen c4 174
Huftarøy a2 156
Hugh a8 80
Hughenden g6 80
Hughes, Arg. g2 297
Hughes, Alaska, U.S.A. f2 246
Hughes, Arkansas, U.S.A. d2 258
Hughesville, Maryland, U.S.A. d6 256
Hughesville, Pennsylvania, U.S.A. d3 256
Hughson c4 264
Hugh Town A 162
Hugo b2 258
Hugo Lake b2 258
Hugoton c4 261
Huguan c1 106
Huhucunya d3 284
Huhudi f3 234
Huhus n5 155
Hui'anpu d7 112
Huiarau Range f3 76
Huib-Hoch Plateau b3 234
Huichang k6 105
Huichapán e3 275
Huicholes, Sierra de los b2 274
Huich'ŏn p5 113
Huicun e3 111
Huidong d5 104
Huifa He p4 113
Huiguozhen c2 106
Huihe k1 113
Huiji He d2 106
Huikoujie e5 111
Huíla b1 232
Huila b3 284
Huilai l7 105
Huila, Nevado de d1 284
Huíla, Planalto de b2 232
Huili, Shandong, China g1 111
Huili, Sichuan, China d5 104
Huimangaro d4 274
Huimanguillo h5 275
Huimilpan d3 274
Huimin e1 111
Huinahuaca d4 292
Huinan, Jilin, China p4 113
Huinca Renancó e3 297
Huining e1 104
Huishui f5 104
Huisne f4 183
Huissen d3 159
Huiten Nur n2 125
Huiting e2 106
Huitong g5 104
Huitupan a2 276
Huitzila c3 274
Huitzo f5 275
Huitzuco e4 275
Huixian, Gansu, China f2 104
Huixian, Henan, China c2 106
Huixtla a3 276
Huize d5 104
Huizen d2 159
Huizhou k7 105
Huji c4 106
Hujirt c2 112
Hukawng Valley c2 102
Hukkelvatna c5 154
Hukou e5 111
Hukuntsi d1 234
Hulahula j1 247
Hulan p3 113
Hulan Ergi m2 113
Hulan He p2 113
Ḥulayfah h8 136
Hulimsunt k3 147
Hulin s3 113
Hulín f2 170
Hull j3 255
Hüllhorst d3 172
Hullo k3 157
Hulst c3 159
Hultsfred f4 156
Huludao l5 113
Hulu He a1 106
Hulun Nur j1 113
Hulu Yam Baharu b4 101
Hulyaypole e3 148
Huma h2 94
Humacao A 270
Humaita d2 292
Humaitá, Braz. e1 293
Humaitá, Para. f5 293
Humanes de Mohernando a4 192
Humansdorp f7 234
Humansville c1 258
Humay b2 292
Humaya f5 272
Ḥumayrah e2 138
Humbe a2 232
Humber, Mouth of The f3 162
Humberstone d4 292
Humberto de Campos d2 288
Humbe, Serra do b1 232
Humble d4 158
Humboldt, Arg. g1 297
Humboldt, Can. q5 249
Humboldt, Arizona, U.S.A. g8 263
Humboldt, Nevada, U.S.A. d5 262
Humboldt, Tennessee, U.S.A. e2 258
Humboldt Lake e1 264
Hume e5 264
Humeburn g9 81
Hu Men j7 105
Humenné k3 171
Hume Reservoir e2 83
Humlebæk f3 158
Humos, Cabo a3 296
Humpata a2 232
Humphrey d2 284
Humphreys, Mount e4 264
Humphreys Peak h8 263
Humpolec d2 170
Humppila k2 157
Hün h3 221
Húnaflói A 152
Hunan b5 106
Hunchun r4 113
Huncovce j2 171
Hundeluft h4 173
Hundested e3 158
Hundewali f5 128
Hundorp c2 156
Hundstein d2 176
Hunedoara, Rom. f3 201
Hunedoara, Hunedoara, Rom. f3 201
Hünfeld f4 174
Hungary h5 144

HUNGARY

THE REPUBLIC OF HUNGARY
Area 93,030km² (35,919sq miles)
Capital Budapest
Organizations CE, CEFTA, EBRD, NATO, OECD
Population 10,160,000
Pop. growth (%) -0.4
Life expectancy 66 (m); 75 (f)
Languages Hungarian
Literacy 99.4%
Currency forint (US $1 = 215.13 forint)
GDP (US million $) 64,300
GDP per head ($US) 6328

Hungen f4 174
Hungerford, Aust. g10 81
Hungerford, U.K. e5 163
Hungerford, U.S.A. a5 258
Hŭnghae q7 113
Hŭngnam p6 113
Hungry Horse f1 262
Hungry Horse Reservoir g2 262
Hưng Yên h5 102
Hun He n4 113
Hunissout Pan c5 234
Hunn g3 156
Hunnebostrand d3 156
Huns Mountains b3 234
Hunsrück c3 174
Hunstanton g4 162
Hunta m6 251
Hunte d2 172
Hunter, Arg. g3 297
Hunter, Aust. d8 85
Hunter, U.S.A. e7 250
Hunter Island, Aust. Aa2 83
Hunter Island, Can. c6 248
Hunter Islands Aa2 83
Hunter Mountains a6 77
Hunters d1 262
Hunters Hills, The c6 77
Hunterville e3 76
Huntingburg c6 254
Huntingdon, U.K. f4 163
Huntingdon, Pennsylvania, U.S.A. c4 256
Huntingdon, Tennessee, U.S.A. e1 258
Huntington, Indiana, U.S.A. d5 254
Huntington, Massachusetts, U.S.A. h2 257
Huntington, New York, U.S.A. g4 257
Huntington, Texas, U.S.A. b4 258
Huntington, Utah, U.S.A. h6 262
Huntington, West Virginia, U.S.A. e6 254
Huntington Beach e8 265
Huntington Station g4 257
Huntly, N.Z. e2 76
Huntly, U.K. f2 164
Hunt Mountain b2 260
Huntsville, Can. g3 254
Huntsville, Alabama, U.S.A. f2 258
Huntsville, Arkansas, U.S.A. c1 258
Huntsville, Texas, U.S.A. b4 258
Hunucmá q7 273
Hunyuan g6 112
Hunza, Jam.Kash. b1 130
Hunza, Jam.Kash. b1 130
Hunza, Pak. b1 130
Hunze e1 159
Huocheng t5 121
Huojia c2 106
Huolongmen n1 113
Hương Khê g6 102
Huonville Ab3 83
Huoqiu e3 111
Huoshan e4 111
Huozhou b1 106
Ḥūr r6 137
Ḥuraydin, Wādī c6 139
Hurayımilā l9 137
Hurbanovo g4 171
Hurdalssjøen d2 156
Hurd, Cape b6 252
Hurdiyo e1 226
Hure l4 113
Hure Jadgai d5 112
Hüremt b1 112
Hurepoix h4 183
Hurghada d8 136
Huriel e2 186
Hurley h7 250
Hurlford d4 164
Hurlock e6 256
Hurmagai b6 129
Huron, California, U.S.A. c5 265
Huron, Ohio, U.S.A. e5 254
Huron, South Dakota, U.S.A. d2 260
Huron Beach d3 254
Hurones, Embalse de los e8 191
Huron, Lake e3 254
Hurricane g7 263
Hursley e5 163
Hurtado, Chile b2 294
Hurtado, Coquimbo, Chile b2 294
Hürth e4 159
Hurunui d5 77
Hurup b2 158
Husain Nika d5 128
Húsavík B 152
Húsavík A 152
Hushcha m4 169
Huşi j2 201
Husinec b2 170
Huskvarna f4 156
Huslia e2 246
Husøy a2 156
Hussainabad j7 125
Hustopeče h1 177
Husum, Ger. c4 158
Husum, Swe. g5 154
Husyatyn h1 201
Hutag b1 112
Hütak r6 137
Hutan Melintang b4 101
Hutanopan a5 101
Hutchinson, R.S.A. e5 234
Hutchinson, U.S.A. d4 260
Hutou s3 113
Huttah Kulkyne National Park c2 82
Hüttau e2 176
Hüttenberg f3 177
Hutthurm e1 176
Hüttlingen f2 174
Huttoft g3 162
Hutton, Mount c4 85
Hutton Range f9 87
Huttwil b2 196
Hutubi w5 121
Hutun e1 111
Hutuo He g6 112
Huwan d4 106
Ḥuwāra d4 139
Huwaytat e2 219
Huxi k5 105
Huxian a2 106
Huxiang d2 111
Huxley, Mount, Aust. h6 86
Huxley, Mount, N.Z. b6 77
Huy d4 159
Hüzgān m6 137
Huzhen n4 105
Huzhou g4 111
Huzhu a7 112
Hvalynsk h1 149
Hvannadalshnúkur A 152
Hvar f1 198
Hvardiys'ke d3 148
Hvastoviči c5 150
Hveragerði A 152
Hvidbjerg b2 158
Hvide Sande b3 158
Hvitá A 152
Hvizdets' g1 201
Hvojnaja c2 150
Hvolsvöllur A 152
Hvorslev c2 158
Hwach'ŏn p6 113
Hwadae q5 113
Hwange d2 232
Hwange National Park d2 232
Hwangju n6 113
Hwasun p8 113
Hwayang q8 113
Hwedza e2 233
Hyannis, Massachusetts, U.S.A. k3 257
Hyannis, Nebraska, U.S.A. c3 260
Hyannis Port k3 257
Hyargas Nuur k5 118
Hybe h2 171
Hydaburg a4 248
Hyde c6 77
Hyden, Aust. d13 87
Hyden, U.S.A. h1 259
Hyde Park g3 257
Hyder b4 248
Hyderabad, India f4 126
Hyderabad, Pak. d8 129
Hyères c7 185
Hyères, Îles d' c8 185
Hyermanavichy m5 157
Hyesan q5 113
Hyland m3 247
Hyland, Mount e7 85
Hyllekrog e4 158
Hyltebruk e4 156
Hyndman b5 256
Hyndman Peak f4 262
Hynish Bay b3 164
Hyōgo b4 114
Hyōno-sen f4 114
Hyrynjärvi m4 155
Hyrynsalmi m4 155
Hythe, England, U.K. e6 163
Hythe, England, U.K. h5 163
Hyvinkää l2 157

I

Ia A Dun j9 103
Iacanga d4 290
Iaciara c4 289
Iaco d2 292
Iacobeni g2 201
Iacri c4 290
Iaçu d4 288
Iaeger f7 254
Iakora Ab3 233
Ialomiţa, Rom. h3 201
Ialomiţa, Rom. h3 201
Ianca h3 201
Iancu Jianu g3 201
Iapu g3 291
Iarauarune, Serra e3 285
Iargara j2 201
Iaşi, Rom. h2 201
Iaşi, Iaşi, Rom. h2 201
Iba b3 100
Ibadan e4 223
Ibagué b3 284
Ibaiti c5 290
Ibañeta, Puerto de c1 192
Ibáñez b5 295
Ibara e4 114
Ibaraki j3 115
Ibarra b3 284
Ibarreta f5 293
Ibb f5 219
Ibba, Sudan e2 225
Ibba, Western Equatoria, Sudan e3 225
Ibbenbüren c3 172
'Ibbin d4 139
Ibdeqqene e2 223
Ibdes c3 192
Ibeas de Juarros g2 190
Ibembo d3 224
Ibenga c3 224
Iberia, Loreto, Peru c5 284
Iberia, Madre de Dios, Peru d2 292
Ibertioga g4 291
Ibestad f2 154
Ibeto f3 223
Ibi, Indon. c13 103
Ibi, Nig. f4 223
Ibi, Spain d6 193
Ibiá e3 291
Ibiapaba, Serra da d2 288
Ibias d2 190
Ibicaraí e4 289
Ibicuí, Braz. e1 294
Ibicuí, Rio Grande do Sul, Braz. e1 294
Ibie a6 185
Ibimirim e3 288
Ibiporã c5 290
Ibirá d4 290
Ibiraçu h3 291
Ibiranhém h2 291
Ibitiara d4 288
Ibitinga d4 290
Ibitzbach h1 173
Ibiúna e5 290
Ibiza f6 193
Ibiza f6 193
Iblei, Monti d7 199
Ibonga e4 225
Ibonma j6 97
Ibotirama d4 288
Iboundji, Mont b4 224
Ibrā' f6 116
Ibra, Wadi b5 218
Ibresi j4 151
İbriktepe h5 201
Ibros g7 191
Ibshawāi c7 136
Ibstock e4 162
Ibu h5 97
Ibuhos c1 100
Içá d4 284
Ica, Peru b2 292
Ica, Ica, Peru b2 292
Icabaru e3 285
Icabarú e3 285
Icacos Point E 271
Içana, Braz. d3 284
Içana, Amazonas, Braz. d3 284
Icaraí e2 288
Icaraíma b5 290
Icatu d2 288
İçel, Tur. e4 208
İçel, İçel, Tur. e4 208
Iceland a1 144

ICELAND

THE REPUBLIC OF ICELAND
Area 103,000km² (39,769sq miles)
Capital Reykjavik
Organizations CE, EBRD, EFTA, NATO, OECD
Population 290,000
Pop. growth (%) 1.1
Life expectancy 76 (m); 81 (f)
Languages Icelandic
Literacy 99%
Currency Icelandic krona (US $1 = 73.2 Icelandic krona)
GDP (US million $) 8800
GDP per head ($US) 30,344

Iceland Basin h3 302
Icelandic Plateau v1 299
Icem d4 290
Ichalkaranji d4 126
Ichchapuram j3 127
Ichenhausen g5 174
Ichilo e3 293
Ichinomiya g4 115
Ichinoseki j2 115
Ichnya d2 148
Ichoa d3 292
Ich'ŏn, N. Korea p6 113
Ich'ŏn, S. Kor. p7 113
Ichtegem b3 159
Ichtershausen d3 175
Ichuña c3 292
Ickesburg c4 256
Icó e3 288
Icoca c5 224
Iconha h4 291
Icy Bay j4 247
Icy Cape d1 246
Icy Strait l4 247
Idabel b3 258
Idah f4 223
Idaho f3 262
Idaho Falls g3 262
Idalia National Park g8 84
Idalion b1 138
Ida, Mount, Grc. e7 211
Ida, Mount, Jam. B 266
Idanha-a-Nova c5 191
Idanha, Barragem da c5 190
Idar f9 129
Idar-Oberstein f5 159
Idd el Chanam b5 218
Idelès f4 221
Idestrup e4 158
Idfu d9 136
Idhān Awbārī g3 221
Idice f5 196
Ididole c2 226
Idiofa c4 224
Iditarod e3 246
Idkerberget f2 156
Idku c6 136
Idle f3 162
Idlib, Syria f5 209
Idlib, Idlib, Syria f5 209
Idnā c5 139
Idodi b5 227
Idom b2 158
Idre e2 156
Idrija f3 177
Idro e4 196
Idro, Lago d' e4 196
Idstein c2 174
Idutywa h6 235
Iecava, Lat. l4 157
Iecava, Bauska, Lat. l4 157
Iepê c5 290
Ieper a4 159
Ieperlee a3 159
Ierapetra f7 211
Ierax, Akra d6 211
Ierissos d2 210
Ierissou, Kolpos d2 210
Iernut g2 201
Iešjohka k2 155
Ifaistos f1 210
Ifakara b5 227
Ifalik G 74
'Ifāl, Wādī e2 219
Ifanadiana Ab3 233
Ife e4 223
Iferouâne f5 221
Iffezheim c4 174
Iffley e5 80
Ifon f4 223
Ifould Lake k12 87
Ifrane c2 220
Igal f5 171
Igalula f5 225
Igan f3 98
Iganga f3 225
Igara Paraná c4 284
Igarapava e4 290
Igarape Açú c2 288
Igarapé Grande d2 288
Igarapé Miri c2 288
Igaratá e5 291
Igarité d4 288
Igarka j3 118
Igatpuri c3 126
Igbeti e4 223
Igbor f4 223
Iğdır, Tur. j3 209
Iğdır, Iğdır, Tur. k3 209
Igel'veem b2 246
Iggensbach e1 176
Iggesund g2 156
Igikpak, Mount f2 246
Igiugig f4 246
Iglas c6 130
Iglesia c2 294
Iglesias Aa3 198
Igli d2 220
Iglino j5 147
Igloolik n2 243
Ignace h6 250
Ignacio Allende h5 272
Ignacio de la Llave g4 275
Ignacio Zaragosa f3 272
Ignacio Zaragoza, Chiapas, Mex. a2 276
Ignacio Zaragoza, Tamaulipas, Mex. e2 275
Ignacio Zaragoza, Zacatecas, Mex. c2 274
Ignalina m5 157
İğneada h5 201
İğneada Burnu b2 208
Igney c2 184
Ignon k5 183
Igoma a5 231
Igombe f4 225
Igoumenitsa a3 210
Igra m3 151
Igrim l3 147
Iguaçu d6 290
Iguaçu Falls a6 290
Iguaçu, Parque Nacional do b6 290
Iguaí d4 289
Iguaje, Mesa de c3 284
Iguala e4 275
Igualada f3 192
Igualtepec e5 275
Iguana, Isla g7 277
Iguape e6 290
Iguaraçu c5 290
Iguarapé f4 291
Iguatemi, Braz. a5 290
Iguatemi, Mato Grosso do Sul, Braz. a5 290
Iguatu e3 288
Iguéla a4 224
Iguéla, Lagune a4 224
Igueña d2 190
Iguetti, Sebkhet c3 220
Iguidi, Erg c3 220
Igunga a4 231
Iharaña Ab1 233
Iharosberény f5 170
Ihavandhippolhu Atoll c9 126
Ih Bogd Uul a3 112
Ihbulag d4 112
Iherir f3 221
Ihhayrhan c2 112
Ihiala f4 223
Ihirène, Oued e4 221
Iholdy a5 187
Ihosy Ab3 233
Ihotry, Farihy Ab2 233
Ihringen f4 174
Ihsuuj d1 112
Ih Tal m4 113
Ii k4 155
Iida g4 115
Iide-san h3 115
Iijärvi, Fin. l4 155
Iijärvi, Fin. m4 155
Iijoki l4 155
Iisalmi l5 155
Iisvesi, Fin. l5 155
Iisvesi, Itä-Suomi, Fin. l5 155
Iivaara m4 155
Iivantiira m4 155
Iiyama h3 115
Ijara c4 226
Ijebu-Ode e4 223
Ijevan g4 149
IJlst d1 159
IJmuiden c2 159
IJssel e2 159
IJsselmeer d2 159
Ijuí, Braz. b7 289
Ijuí, Rio Grande do Sul, Braz. b7 289
Ijuw B 74
IJzendijke b3 159
IJzer a3 159
Ikaalinen k2 157
Ikali d4 224
Ikamatua c5 77
Ikanda-Nord d4 224
Ikara f3 223
Ikare f4 223
Ikari c4 224
Ikaria h5 211
Ikast c2 158
Ikawhenua Range f3 76
Ikeda, Hokkaidō, Japan Ac2 114
Ikeda, Tokushima, Japan e4 114
Ikeja e4 223
Ikela d4 224
Ikelemba c3 224
Ikervár e4 170
Ikhtiman f4 201
Ikhutseng f4 234
Iki c5 114
Ikire e4 223
Ikom f4 223
Ikopa Ab2 233
Ikorodu e4 223
Ikosi e4 225
Ikot Ekpene f4 223
Ikoy b4 224
Ikpikpuk f1 246
Ikungu a5 231
Ikuno f4 114
Ila, D.R.C. d4 224
Ila, Nig. e4 223
Ilaferh, Oued e4 221
Ilaga k6 97
Ilagala e5 225
Ilagan c2 100
Ilaisamis b3 226
Ilajanjärvi n5 155
Ilak Island Ac2 247
Īlām, Iran l5 137
Īlām, Īlām, Iran l5 137
Ilam k6 125
Ilan n6 105
Ilanana Ab3 233
Ilaniyya d4 138
Ilanz d3 196
Ilava g3 171
Iława h2 169
Ilazārān, Kūh-e r7 137
İlbir Dağı Ac1 211
Il Bogd Uul a3 112
Ilchester d6 163
Ildefonso, Islas c7 295
Ile t6 121
Île-à-la-Crosse p4 249
Île-à-la-Crosse, Lac p4 249
Île-à-Vache h5 266
Ilebo d4 224
Île-de-France h4 183
Ilek j2 149
Ilen b5 165
Ileret b3 226
Ilesa e4 223
Îles Lavezzi, Réserve Naturelle des A 185
Îles Wallis et Futuna, Îles Wallis-et-Futuna h4 73
Ilet' k3 151
Ileza g1 151
Ilfeld f4 173
Ilford, Can. f2 250
Ilford, U.K. g5 163
Ilfov h3 201
Ilfracombe, Aust. g7 80
Ilfracombe, U.K. b5 163
Ilgaz d2 208
Ilgaz Dağları d2 208
Ilgın c3 208
Ilhabela f5 291
Ilha Grande d4 285
Ilha Grande, Baía da f5 291
Ilha Grande, Represa b5 290
Ilha Solteira, Represa c4 290
Ílhavo b4 190
Ilhéu do Bugio B 189
Ilhéus e4 289
Ilhéus Secos A 222
Ilia l6 171
Iliamna f4 246
Iliamna Lake f4 246
Ili Boleng m9 99
Iliç g3 209
Ilıca a3 208
Il'ich m7 121
Iligan e6 100
Iligan Bay e6 100
Iligan Point d1 100
Ilig, Raas d2 226
Il'inka v2 121
Il'inskij, Permskaja Oblast', Russ. Fed. h4 147
Il'inskij, Respublika Karelija, Russ. Fed. b1 150
Il'inskoe, Jaroslavskaja Oblast', Russ. Fed. e3 150
Il'inskoe, Kostromskaja Oblast', Russ. Fed. h2 151
Il'inskoe, Orlovskaja Oblast', Russ. Fed. c5 150
Iliomar p9 99
Ilion e1 256
Ilirska Bistrica f4 177
Ilkeston e4 162
Ilkley e3 162
Ill d2 184
'Illān d4 139
Illana Bay d7 100
Illapel b1 296
Illar b8 193
Illas Cíes b2 190
Illbillee, Mount l10 87
Ille d4 182
Ille-et-Vilaine d4 182
Illéla f3 223
Iller f4 174
Illertissen c3 174
Ille-sur-Têt e6 187
Illichivs'k k2 201
Illiers-Combray g4 183
Illimani, Nevado de d3 292
Illingen f5 159
Illinka k2 201
Illinois f3 260
Illintsi j1 201
Illiopolis b6 254
Illizi f3 221
Illkirch-Graffenstaden d2 184
Illora g7 191
Illueca c3 192
Illzach d3 184
Ilm g4 173
Ilmajoki j5 155
Ilma, Lake h11 87
Il'matsalu m3 157
Ilmenau, Ger. f2 172
Ilmenau, Thüringen, Ger. f2 175
Il'men', Ozero a2 150
Ilminster d6 163
Il'nytsya f1 201
Ilo c3 292
Ilobu e4 223
Iloca a3 296
Iloilo d5 100
Iloilo Strait d5 100
Ilomantsi n5 155
Ilorin e4 223
Ilova h4 177
Ilovlja, Russ. Fed. g2 149
Ilovlja, Volgogradskaja Oblast', Russ. Fed. f2 149
Iłowa d4 168
Iłowo Osada j2 169
Ilse f4 173
Ilsede f3 172
Ilsenburg (Harz) f4 173
Ilshofen e3 174
Ilu d3 224
Ilūkste m5 157
Ilulissat u2 243
Ilushi f4 223
Il'ya m5 157
Ilyç j3 147
Ilz, Aus. g2 177
Ilz, Ger. j4 175
Iłża k4 169
Imabari e4 114
Imabū f4 285
Imaichi h3 115
Imala f5 272
Imām al Ḥamzah k6 137
Imam-baba a2 128
İmamoğlu e4 208
Iman, Sierra del a7 289
Imari q9 113
Imata c3 292
Imataca, Serranía de e2 285
Imatra n2 157
Imavere l3 157
Imazu g4 115
Imbabura b3 284
Imbaimadai e2 285
Imbituba c7 289
Imbituva c6 290
imeni 26 Bakinskikh Komissarov q2 137
imeni Babuškina g2 151
imeni C. A. Niyazova a2 128
imeni Kerbabayeva h9 120
imeni Kuybysheva a2 128
imeni M. I. Kalinina h3 151
imeni Matrosova q3 119
imeni Stepana Razina h4 151
imeni Željabova d2 150
Imerimandroso Ab2 233
Imese c3 224
Imgyckoe Boloto m4 147
Imi c2 226
Imi-n-Tanoute c2 220
Imirhou, Oued f3 221
İmişli h5 149
Imit a1 130
Imja-do n8 113
Imlay d5 262
Imlay City e4 254
Imlili a4 220
Immenstadt g4 174
Immingham f3 162
Immokalee j6 259
Imn-Lor, Ozero n3 147
Imo, Nig. f4 223
Imo, Nig. f4 223
Imola f5 197
Imotski g1 198
Impendle h4 235
Imperatriz c3 288
Imperia, Italy b6 197
Imperia, Liguria, Italy c6 197
Imperial, Can. a5 250
Imperial, Peru b2 292
Imperial, California, U.S.A. f9 263
Imperial, Nebraska, U.S.A. c3 260
Imperial Beach e9 263
Imperial de Aragón, Canal c3 192
Imperial Valley f9 263
Impfondo c3 224
Imphal n7 125
Imphy f2 186
Impruneta f6 197
İmralı Adası b2 208
İmroz f2 210
Imsil p8 113
Imst b2 176
Imtān e4 139
Imuris h10 263
Imuruan Bay b5 100
Imuruk Basin c2 246
Ina, Japan g4 115
Ina, Pol. l2 173
Ina, U.S.A. b6 254
Inácio Martins c6 290
Inagauan b6 100
Inagh, Lough b3 165
Inahuaya b1 292
Inajá e3 288
Inaja, Serra do b3 288
Inambari, Peru c2 292
Inambari, Madre de Dios, Peru d2 292
In Aménas f3 221
In Amguel f4 221
Inangahua Junction c4 77
Inanwatan j6 97
Inari, Itä-Suomi, Fin. n5 155
Inari, Lappi, Fin. l2 155
Inarijärvi l2 155
Inarijoki k2 155
Inauini d1 292
In Belbel e3 221
Inca g5 193
Inca de Oro d5 292
Incahuasi, Nevado c1 294
İnce Burnu a2 208
İnce Burun e1 208
İncekum Burnu e4 208
Inch b4 165
Inchbare f3 164
Inchiri a4 220
Inchnadamph c1 164
Inch'ŏn p7 113
Incinillas g2 190
İncirliova a4 208
Incisa in Val d'Arno f6 197
Incline Village d2 264
Incomati k2 235
Inčoun b2 246
Incudine, Monte A 185
Indaiá f3 291
Indaiatuba e5 290
Indalsälven e5 154
Indaparapeo d4 274
India Silasĕ e5 219
Indaw, Sagaing, Myan. b4 102
Indaw, Shan, Myan. c5 102
Indawgyi, Lake c3 102
Inde b5 172
Indé g5 272
Independence, California, U.S.A. e5 264
Independence, Iowa, U.S.A. f3 260
Independence, Kansas, U.S.A. b1 258
Independence, Kentucky, U.S.A. d6 254
Independence, Louisiana, U.S.A. d4 258
Independence, Minnesota, U.S.A. g7 250
Independence, Missouri, U.S.A. e4 260
Independence Mountains e5 262
Independencia, Bol. d3 292
Independencia, Mex. f3 275
Independencia, Bahía de b2 292
Independenţa, Constanţa, Rom. j4 201
Independenţa, Galaţi, Rom. h3 201
Inderacha b2 226
Inderborskiy h2 149
Inder, Ozero d3 120
Indi e4 126

INDIA

THE REPUBLIC OF INDIA
Area 3,287,263km² (1,269,219sq miles)
Capital New Delhi
Organizations COMM, SAARC
Population 1,033,000,000
Pop. growth (%) 2.3
Life expectancy 62 (m); 62 (f)
Languages Hindi, English, many local languages
Literacy 59.5%
Currency rupee
(US $1 = 45.52 rupee)
GDP (US million $) 496,800
GDP per head ($US) 480

INDONESIA

THE REPUBLIC OF INDONESIA
Area 1,919,317km² (741,053sq miles)
Capital Jakarta
Organizations APEC, ASEAN, IDB, OPEC, OIC
Population 217,130,000
Pop. growth (%) 1.4
Life expectancy 63 (m); 67 (f)
Languages Bahasa Indonesia (a form of Malay), many local languages
Literacy 88.4%
Currency rupiah
(US $1 = 8475 rupiah)
GDP (US million $) 180,000
GDP per head ($US) 828

IRAN

THE ISLAMIC REPUBLIC OF IRAN
Area 1,648,000km² (636,296sq miles)
Capital Tehran
Organizations ECO, IDB, OIC, OPEC
Population 65,540,000
Pop. growth (%) 1.2
Life expectancy 67 (m); 68 (f)
Languages Farsi (Iranian), Turkic, other local languages
Literacy 79.1%
Currency Iranian rial
(US $1 = 8325 Iranian rial)
GDP (US million $) 114,375
GDP per head ($US) 1745

IRAQ

THE REPUBLIC OF IRAQ
Area 438,317km² (169,235sq miles)
Capital Baghdad
Organizations CAEU, IDB, LAS, OAPEC, OIC, OPEC
Population 24,510,000
Pop. growth (%) 2.1
Life expectancy 57 (m); 60 (f)
Languages Arabic, Kurdish, Turkoman
Literacy 40.4%
Currency Iraqi dinar
(US $1 = 0.31 Iraqi dinar)
GDP (US million $) 25,898
GDP per head ($US) 1056

IRELAND

THE REPUBLIC OF IRELAND
Area 70,285km² (27,137sq miles)
Capital Dublin
Organizations CE, EBRD, EU, OECD
Population 3,920,000
Pop. growth (%) 0.6
Life expectancy 73 (m); 78 (f)
Languages Irish, English
Literacy 99%
Currency euro
(US $1 = 0.81 euro)
GDP (US million $) 118,600
GDP per head ($US) 30,255

ISRAEL

THE STATE OF ISRAEL
Area 21,946km² (8473sq miles)
Capital Jerusalem
Organizations EBRD
Population 6,580,000
Pop. growth (%) 2.2
Life expectancy 76 (m); 80 (f)
Languages Hebrew, Arabic, many European languages
Literacy 95.6%
Currency shekel
(US $1 = 4.39 shekel)
GDP (US million $) 100,800
GDP per head ($US) 15,319

ITALY

THE ITALIAN REPUBLIC
Area 301,323km² (116,341sq miles)
Capital Rome
Organizations CE, EBRD, EU, G8, NATO, OECD
Population 57,480,000
Pop. growth (%) 0.1
Life expectancy 75 (m); 81 (f)
Languages Italian, German, French and other languages
Literacy 98.6%
Currency euro
(US $1 = 0.81 euro)
GDP (US million $) 1,184,000
GDP per head ($US) 20,598

342 Ivot → Jiayue

Ivot c5 150
Ivrea b4 196
Ivrindi a3 208
Ivris Ugheltekhili g4 149
Ivry-la-Bataille g4 183
Ivujivik p3 243
Ivvavik National Park k1 247
Iwai h3 115
Iwaizumi j2 115
Iwaki j3 115
Iwaki-san j1 115
Iwakuni e4 114
Iwamizawa Ab2 114
Iwan h3 99
Iwanai Ab2 114
Iwasaki h1 115
Iwasuge-yama h3 115
Iwata g4 115
Iwate, Japan j2 115
Iwate, Iwate, Japan j2 115
Iwate-san j2 115
Iwo e4 223
Iwŏn q5 113
Iwonicz Zdrój k6 169
Iwye p2 169
Ixaltepec g5 275
Ixcamilpa e4 275
Ixcateopan e4 275
Ixhuatán g5 275
Ixhuatlán, Veracruz, Mex. e3 275
Ixhuatlán, Veracruz, Mex. f4 275
Iximas d2 292
Ixmiquilpán e3 275
Ixopo j5 235
Ixtacamaxtitlán f4 275
Ixtacomitán h5 275
Ixtapa, Guerrero, Mex. d5 274
Ixtapa, Jalisco, Mex. b3 274
Ixtapan de la Sal e4 275
Ixtapa, Punta c5 274
Ixtlahuaca e4 275
Ixtlahuacán c4 274
Ixtlán, Michoacán, Mex. c3 274
Ixtlán, Nayarit, Mex. b3 274
Ixtlán, Oaxaca, Mex. f5 275
Ixworth g4 163
Iya i9 99
Iyo-nada e5 114
Izabal c3 276
Izabal, Lago de c3 276
Izalde a1 192
Izamal q7 273
Izari-dake Ab2 114
Izazi b5 227
Izberbaš g4 149
Izbica m5 169
Izbica Kujawska g3 168
Izeda d3 190
Izegem b4 159
Izeh m6 137
Izernore b4 184
Iževsk m3 151
Iževskoe f4 150
Ižma, Russ. Fed. h2 147
Ižma, Respublika Komi, Russ. Fed. h2 147
Izmayil j3 201
İzmir, Tur. a3 208
İzmir, İzmir, Tur. a3 208
İzmir Körfezi a3 208
İzmit Körfezi b2 208
Iznajar, Embalse de f7 191
Iznalloz g7 191
İznik Gölü b2 208
Iznoski c4 150
Izola e4 176
Izozog Bajo e3 293
Izra' e4 138
Izsák h5 171
Iztaccíhuatl-Popocatépetl, Parque Nacional e4 275
Iztaccíhuatl, Volcán e4 275
Iztapa b4 276
Iztochni Rodopi g5 201
Izúcar de Matamoros e4 275
Izu-hantō h4 115
Izuhara q8 113
Izumi, Ōsaka, Japan f4 115
Izumi, Miyagi, Japan j2 115
Izumisano f4 115
Izumo e4 114
Izu-shotō h5 115
Izu Trench h4 300
Izvestkovyj r1 113
Izvoarele, Giurgiu, Rom. g3 201
Izvoarele, Prahova, Rom. h3 201
Izvor, Mac. a1 210
Izvor, Mac. b1 210
Izvoru g3 201
Izyaslav b2 148
Izyndy k3 149
Izyum e2 148

J

J. Redmond Reservoir e4 260
Jääsjärvi m2 157
Jabā d3 138
Jabalanac f5 177
Jabal as Sirāj d3 128
Jabaliya c5 139
Jabalón a6 193
Jabalpur f8 124
Jabalquinto g6 191
Jabbār l6 137
Jabbeke b3 159
Jabiru a2 80
Jablah d1 138
Jablanac, Rt f4 177
Jablanica c4 200
Jablonec nad Nisou d1 170
Jablonica f3 170
Jabłonka h6 169
Jabłonna l4 169
Jablonné v Podještědí c1 170
Jablonovyj Hrebet e2 94
Jabłonowo Pomorskie h2 169
Jablůnka f2 171
Jablunkov g2 171
Jaboatão f3 288
Jaboticabal d4 290
Jaboticatubas g3 291
Jabron a6 185
Jabung, Tanjung c5 98
Jaburu e5 285
Jabuti f4 285
Jabwot D 74
Jaca d2 192
Jacala e3 275
Jacaltenango b3 276
Jacaré, Braz. d4 288
Jacaré, Mato Grosso, Braz. b4 288
Jacaré, Rondônia, Braz. e2 293
Jacareacanga f5 285
Jacareí e5 291
Jacaretinga f1 293
Jacarezinho d5 290
Jáchal c2 294
Jáchymov a1 170
Jaciara a1 290
Jacinto h2 291
Jacinto Arauz f5 297
Jaciparaná, Braz. e1 293
Jaciparaná, Rondônia, Braz. e1 293
Jackfish Lake n5 249
Jackhead Harbour e5 250
Jack Lee, Lake c3 258
Jackman g6 252
Jackpot f5 262
Jacksboro, Tennessee, U.S.A. g1 259
Jacksboro, Texas, U.S.A. d5 261
Jackson, Aust. j9 81
Jackson, Alabama, U.S.A. f4 258
Jackson, California, U.S.A. c3 264
Jackson, Georgia, U.S.A. h3 259
Jackson, Kentucky, U.S.A. h1 259
Jackson, Michigan, U.S.A. d4 254
Jackson, Minnesota, U.S.A. e3 260
Jackson, Mississippi, U.S.A. d3 258
Jackson, North Carolina, U.S.A. h7 255
Jackson, Ohio, U.S.A. e6 254
Jackson, Tennessee, U.S.A. e2 258
Jackson, Wyoming, U.S.A. h4 262
Jackson Bay b5 77
Jackson Head b5 77
Jackson Lake h3 262
Jackson's Arm p4 253
Jacksonville, Alabama, U.S.A. g3 259
Jacksonville, Arkansas, U.S.A. c2 258
Jacksonville, Florida, U.S.A. j4 259
Jacksonville, Illinois, U.S.A. a6 254
Jacksonville, North Carolina, U.S.A. l2 259
Jacksonville Beach j4 259
Jacmel h5 271
Jacobabad d6 129
Jacobina d4 288
Jacobsdal f4 234
Jacona c4 274
Jacques-Cartier, Détroit de k3 253
Jacques Cartier, Mont k4 253
Jacquet River j5 253
Jacuí e4 291
Jacuípe d4 288
Jacumba e9 263
Jacundá b2 288
Jacunda c2 288
Jacupemba h3 291
Jacupiranga e6 290
Jacura d1 284
Jacurici e4 288
Jadcherla f4 126
Jaddil e4 138
Jaddi, Ras a8 129
Jade d2 172
Jadebusen d2 172
Jadovnik c3 200
Jädraån g2 156
Jadraque b4 192
Jadrin j4 151
Jādū g2 221
Jægerspris e3 158
Jaén b5 284
Jaen c3 100
Jaén, Spain g7 191
Jaén, Andalucia, Spain g7 191
Jaén b6 193
Jæren a3 156
Ja'farābād, Ardabīl, Iran m2 137
Ja'farābād, Khorāsan, Iran g9 120
Jaffa, Tel Aviv, Isr. c4 139
Jaffa, Cape a3 82
Jaffna f8 126
Jaffna Peninsula A 127
Jaffrey h2 257
Jagadhri c4 130
Jägala l3 157
Jagalur e5 126
Jagdalak d3 128
Jagdalpur h3 126
Jagdispur j7 125
Jagersfontein f4 235
Jaggang d3 130
Jaggayyapeta g4 126
Jaghin r8 137
Jäglitz h3 173
Jagodina e4 200
Jagodnoe q3 119
Jagodnyj l4 147
Jagraon b4 130
Jagst e3 174
Jagstzell f5 174
Jagtial f3 126
Jaguapitã c5 290
Jaguarão, Braz. f2 294
Jaguarão, Ur. f2 294
Jaguarari d4 288
Jaguaretama e3 288
Jaguari, Braz. b7 289
Jaguari, Rio Grande do Sul, Braz. f1 294
Jaguariaíva d6 290
Jaguaribe, Braz. d3 288
Jaguaribe, Ceará, Braz. e3 288
Jaguaripe e4 288
Jaguaruana e2 288
Jague c1 294
Jagüé c1 294
Jagüey Grande d3 266
Jahanabad j7 125
Jahān Dāgh b9 120
Jahangirabad d5 130
Jahazpur g8 129
Jahdāniyah, Wādī al e7 139
Jahleel, Point k2 86
Jahodná f3 171
Jahrom p7 137
Jahtur, Ozero l4 147
Jahun f3 223
Jaicós d3 288
Jaidé d3 138
Jaijon Doaba c4 130
Jailolo h5 97
Jaiña d3 292
Jainca b8 112
Jaintiapur n7 125
Jaipur g7 129
Jaipurhat l7 125
Jaisalmer e7 129
Jaitaran g7 129
Jaitgarh f9 124
Jaiyūs d4 139
Jajarkot f5 135
Jajarm r3 137
Jajce c3 200
Jajpur k9 125
Jajva j4 147
Jakabszállás h5 171
Jakar m6 125
Jakarta d8 98
Jakhan d9 129
Jakharrah b2 218
Jakin c5 128
Jakkalsberg b4 234
Jäkkvik f3 154
Jakliat b5 130
Jaklovce k3 171
Jakobstad j5 155
Jakovlevo e2 148
Jakškur-Bod'ja m3 151
Jakubany j2 171
Jakutsk n3 119
Jal c5 261
Jala b3 274
Jalacingo f4 275
Jalājil k9 137
Jalālābād e3 128
Jalalabad, Punjab, India g5 128
Jalalabad, Uttar Pradesh, India c5 130
Jalalabad, Uttar Pradesh, India d6 130
Jalal-Abad, Jalal-Abad Oblast, Kyrg. p7 121
Jalal-Abad, Jalal-Abad, Kyrg. p7 121
Jalalpur h6 124
Jalam g3 223
Jalance c5 193
Jalandhar b4 130
Jalapa, Guat. c3 276
Jalapa, Mex. a2 276
Jalapa, Nic. d4 276
Jalapa de Díaz f4 275
Jalapa del Marqués g5 275
Jalapa Enríquez f4 275
Jalapur b3 130
Jalapur Pirwala e6 129
Jalasjärvi j5 155
Jalaun f6 124
Jalawlā' k4 137
Jalcocotán b3 274
Jalcomulco f4 275
Jaldak c5 128
Jaldhaka l6 125
Jaldrug e4 126
Jales c4 290
Jalesar d6 130
Jaleshwar k9 125
Jalgaon g10 129
Jalibah l6 137
Jaligny-sur-Besbre f2 186
Jalingo g4 223
Jalisco, Mex. b3 274
Jalisco, Nayarit, Mex. b3 274
Jallābi r8 137
Jalna d3 126
Jālo a7 129
Jalón c3 192
Jalor f8 129
Jalostotitlán c3 274
Jalpa, Guanajuato, Mex. d3 274
Jalpa, Zacatecas, Mex. c3 274
Jalpaiguri l6 125
Jalpan e3 275
Jalpatagua b3 276
Jaltenango de la Paz a3 276
Jaltepec g5 275
Jaltipan g5 275
Jaltocán e3 275
Jālū b2 218
Jālūd d4 139
Jaluit D 74
Jalutorovsk l4 147
Jamaame c3 226
Jamaica g7 241

JAMAICA

JAMAICA
Area 10,991km² (4244sq miles)
Capital Kingston
Organizations ACS, CARICOM, COMM, IADB, SELA
Population 2,630,000
Pop. growth (%) 0.9
Life expectancy 72 (m); 76 (f)
Languages English, local patois
Literacy 88%
Currency Jamaican dollar (US $1 = 59.88 Jamaican dollar)
GDP (US million $) 7952
GDP per head ($US) 3023

Jamaica Bay g4 257
Jamaica Channel g5 266
Jama Jamot c8 129
Jamalo-Neneckij Avtonomnyj Okrug n2 147
Jamalpur, Bang. l7 125
Jamalpur, India k7 125
Jamanxim f5 285
Jamari e1 293
Jamašurma k4 151
Jambi, Indon. b5 98
Jambi, Jambi, Indon. b5 98
Jambin k8 80
Jambirno g4 151
Jambo f7 129
Jamboaye c13 103
Jambongan j1 99
Jambuair, Tanjung c13 103
Jamburg n2 147
Jambusar f9 129
James, Missouri, U.S.A. c1 258
James, South Dakota, U.S.A. d3 260
James, Virginia, U.S.A. g7 254
Jamesabad d8 129
James Bay n3 251
James Cistern l7 259
James Craik f2 297
James, Isla b5 295
James Peak b6 77
James Ranges a8 80
James Ross Island mm1 298
Jamestown, Aust. d12 81
Jamestown, R.S.A. g5 235
Jamestown, California, U.S.A. c4 264
Jamestown, Kentucky, U.S.A. g1 259
Jamestown, New York, U.S.A. a2 256
Jamestown, North Carolina, U.S.A. k2 259
Jamestown, North Dakota, U.S.A. d7 250
Jamgort l2 147
Jamiltepec f5 275
Jamkhed c3 126
Jammā'īn d4 139
Jammerbugten c1 158
Jammerland Bugt e3 158
Jammu b3 130
Jammu and Kashmir (India/Pakistan) e5 92
Jamnagar e9 129
Jamni f5 124
Jamno, Jezioro e1 168
Jampang Kulon d8 98
Jampur e6 129
Jämsä l2 157
Jam Sahib d7 129
Jämsänkoski l2 157
Jamshedpur k8 125
Jamtari g4 223
Jämtland e5 154
Jamui k7 125
Jamuna, Bang. l7 125
Jamuna, India n6 125
Jamunkira j9 125
Jamuz d2 190
Jana p3 119
Janaale c3 226
Janakpur j6 125
Janaúba g1 291
Janaucú, Ilha b1 288
Janaul h4 147
Jand f4 128
Jandaia c2 290
Jandaia do Sul c5 290
Jandaq q4 137
Jandia Ae2 189
Jandiala, India b4 130
Jandiala, Pak. b4 130
Jandía Playa Ae2 189
Jandiatuba d4 284
Jandola e4 128
Jandongi d3 224
Jandowae d5 85
Jándula g6 191
Jándula, Embalse del g6 191
Jandulilla a7 193
Janeiro c4 288
Janeiro, Rio de h4 291
Janesville, California, U.S.A. c1 264
Janesville, Wisconsin, U.S.A. b4 254
Jangamo l2 235
Jangaon f4 126
Jangi d4 130
Jangipur l7 125
Jangngai Ri h3 135
Jang, Tanjung c5 98
Jäni Beyglū l2 137
Jänickendorf j3 173
Jani Khel e4 128
Janiópolis b6 290
Janis"jarvi, Ozero b3 146
Janja d3 200
Janjina g2 198
Jänkälä l3 155
Jan Kempdorp f3 234
Jánkmajtis l4 171
Jan Mayen k2 302
Jan Mayen (Norway) v2 299
Jan Mayen Ridge u1 299
Jannatābād n4 137
Janos e2 272
Jánoshalma h5 171
Jánosháza f4 170
Jánoshida j4 171
Jánossomorja f4 170
Janovice nad Úhlavou b2 170
Janów h5 169
Janowiec Wielkopolski f3 168
Janów Lubelski l5 169
Janowo j2 169
Janów Podlaski m3 169
Jansath c5 130
Jansenville f6 234
Jantarnyj h1 169
Januária f1 291
Janville g3 183
Janzar a8 129
Janzé d5 182
Jaora g9 129
Japan l5 93

JAPAN

JAPAN
Area 377,750km² (145,850sq miles)
Capital Tokyo
Organizations APEC, EBRD, G8, OECD
Population 127,480,000
Pop. growth (%) 0.4
Life expectancy 77 (m); 83 (f)
Languages Japanese
Literacy 99%
Currency yen (US $1 = 107.75 yen)
GDP (US million $) 3,933,000
GDP per head ($US) 30,851

Japan, Sea of g3 300
Japan Trench h3 300
Japog g7 129
Japón d3 276
Jäppilä m1 157
Japsand d1 172
Japtiksale n1 147
Japurá d4 284
Japvo Mount b3 102
Jaqué h7 277
Jar m2 151
Jaraba c3 192
Jarabacoa j5 271
Jarābulus g4 209
Jaraczewo f4 168
Jarafuel c5 193
Jaraguá d1 290
Jaraguá do Sul c7 289
Jaraguari a4 290
Jaraicejo e5 191
Jaraíz de la Vera e4 190
Jarājir e2 138
Jaral de Berrios d3 274
Jaral del Progreso d3 274
Jarama a4 192
Jarandilla de la Vera e4 190
Jaransk j3 151
Jarash, Jordan l4 139
Jarash, Jarash, Jordan d4 139
Jarauçu b2 288
Järbo g2 156
Jarcevo b4 150
Jardim, Ceará, Braz. e3 288
Jardim, Mato Grosso do Sul, Braz. f4 293
Jardín b6 193
Jardine River National Park f1 80
Jardines de la Reina, Archipiélago de los e4 266
Jardinópolis e4 290
Jarega h3 147
Jarensk g3 146
Jargalant, Arhangay, Mong. a2 112
Jargalant, Dornod, Mong. h2 112
Jargalthaan e2 112
Jårgastak k2 155
Jargeau h5 183
Jari b1 288
Jaridih Bazar k8 125
Jari, Lago e5 285
Jarkovo l4 147
Jarmah g3 221
Jarmen j2 173
Järna, Dalarna, Swe. f2 156
Järna, Stockholm, Swe. g3 157
Jarnac b3 186
Järnblasten g2 156
Järnlunden f3 156
Järnsjön e3 156
Jarny b1 184
Jarocin f4 168
Jaroměř d1 170
Jaroměřice nad Rokytnou d2 170
Jaroslavl' e3 150
Jaroslavskaja Oblast' e3 150
Jarosław l5 169
Järpen d5 154
Jarplund-Weding c4 158
Jarrettsville d5 256
Jarrillas f6 297
Jarroto Pervoe, Ozero m1 147
Jarroto Vtoroe, Ozero m1 147
Jar-Sale m2 147
Jartai c6 112
Jartai Yanchi c6 112
Jarú, Braz. e2 293
Jarú, Rondônia, Braz. e2 293
Järva-Jaani l3 157
Järvakandi l3 157
Järvenpää l2 157
Jarville-la-Malgrange c2 184
Jarvis Island (U.S.A.) j3 73
Järvsö g2 156
Järvsöklacken f2 156
Jary l1 147
Jašalta f3 149
Jasašnaja Tašla k5 151
Jaša Tomić e3 200
Jashpurnagar j8 125
Jasień d4 168
Jasieniec j4 169
Jasikan e4 223
Jasin c4 101
Jāsk r9 137
Jāsk-e Kohneh r9 137
Jaśliska k6 169
Jasło k6 169
Jašlūnai p1 169
Jasnogorsk d4 150
Jasnyj k2 149
Jasol f8 129
Jason Islands d6 295
Jason Peninsula mm1 298
Jasov j3 171
Jásová g4 171
Jasper, Can. h5 248
Jasper, Alabama, U.S.A. f3 258
Jasper, Arkansas, U.S.A. c1 258
Jasper, Florida, U.S.A. h4 259
Jasper, Missouri, U.S.A. b1 258
Jasper, New York, U.S.A. c2 256
Jasper, Tennessee, U.S.A. g2 259
Jasper, Texas, U.S.A. c4 258
Jasper National Park j5 248
Jasrana d6 130
Jasrasar f7 129
Jaşşān k5 137
Jastarnia g1 168
Jastrebarsko g4 177
Jastrowie e2 168
Jastrzębia k4 169
Jastrzębie-Zdrój g6 168
Jaswantpura f8 129
Jászapáti j4 171
Jászárokszállás h4 171
Jászberény h4 171
Jászkisér j4 171
Jász-Nagykun-Szolnok j4 171
Jászszentandrás j4 171
Jászszentlászló h5 171
Jataí c2 290
Jatapu f4 285
Jateí a5 290
Jath d4 126
Jati d8 129
Jatibarang e8 98
Jatiwangi e8 98
Jatobá b4 288
Jatoi e6 129
Jat Poti b5 128
Jatuarana e1 293
Jatusana c5 130
Jatznick j2 173
Jaú, Braz. e4 285
Jaú, São Paulo, Braz. d5 290
Jauaperi e4 285
Jauari, Serra b2 288
Jaua Sarisariñama, Parque Nacional e3 285
Jauco g4 266
Jauja b2 292
Jaumave e2 275
Jaun b3 196
Jaunay a2 186
Jaunay-Clan c2 186
Jaungulbene m4 157
Jaunjelgava l4 157
Jaunpiebalga m4 157
Jaunpils k4 157
Jaunpur h7 124
Jauntsarats c2 192
Jaupaci c2 290
Jaú, Parque Nacional do e4 285
Jaur e5 187
Jaurakkajärvi l4 155
Jauregui h3 297
Jauru, Braz. f3 293
Jauru, Mato Grosso do Sul, Braz. a3 290
Jausiers c6 185
Java e9 98
Javadi Hills f6 126
Javaés, Serra dos c4 288
Javalambre, Sierra de c4 193
Javand b3 128
Javari c4 284
Javarthushuu g1 112
Javas g4 151
Java Sea, Indon. f7 98
Java Sea, Indon. f6 300
Java Trench f6 300
Jávea e6 193
Jävenitz g3 173
Javier, Isla b5 295
Javorník f1 170
Javorník g3 177
Jävre h4 154
Javron-les-Chapelles e4 182
Jawa e9 98
Jawa Barat d8 98
Jawad g8 129
Jawala Mukhi c4 130
Jawa Tengah e8 98
Jawa Timur g8 98
Jawbān Bayk f4 209
Jawf, Wādī al f4 219
Jawhar, India c3 126
Jawhar, Som. d3 226
Jawor e4 168
Jawor Solecki k4 169
Jaworzno h5 169
Jaworzyna Śląska e5 168
Jay b1 258
Jayacatlán f5 275
Jayakwadi Sagar d3 126
Jayanca b1 292
Jaya, Puncak k6 97
Jayapura l6 97
Jaynagar k6 125
Jaypur h3 126
Jayrūd e3 138
Jaz h4 151
Jazirah Doberai j6 97
Jazīrat al Hamrā q9 137
Jazminal j5 273
Jazykovo j4 151
Jbaa d3 138
Jbail d2 138
Jdaidet Ghazir d2 138
Jdiriya b3 220
Jeanerette d5 258
Jebba e4 223
Jebba Dam e4 223
Jebba Reservoir e4 223
Jebel e3 200
Jebel Abyad Plateau c4 218
Jebel, Bahr el, Sudan f2 225
Jebel, Bahr el, Sudan f3 225
Jebel Chambi, Parc National du f1 221
Jeberos b5 284
Jebjerg c2 158
Jebri b7 129
Jedburgh f4 164
Jeddore Lake q4 253
Jedlanka l4 169
Jedlicze k6 169
Jedlińsk k4 169
Jedlnia-Letnisko k4 169
Jędrzejów j5 169
Jédula e8 191
Jedwabne l2 169
Jedwabno j2 169
Jeesiö l3 155
Jeesiöjoki l3 155
Jeetze g2 173
Jefferson, Montana, U.S.A. g3 262
Jefferson, New York, U.S.A. f2 256
Jefferson, North Carolina, U.S.A. j1 259
Jefferson, Ohio, U.S.A. f5 254
Jefferson, Texas, U.S.A. b3 258
Jefferson, Wisconsin, U.S.A. b4 254
Jefferson City, Missouri, U.S.A. e4 260
Jefferson City, Tennessee, U.S.A. h1 259
Jefferson, Mount, Nevada, U.S.A. g3 264
Jefferson, Mount, Oregon, U.S.A. c3 262
Jeffersonton c6 256
Jeffersontown d6 254
Jeffrey's Bay f7 234
Jega e3 223
Jegindø b2 158
Jegun c5 187
Jeinemeni, Cerro b5 295
Jejuí Guazú f4 293
Jēkabpils l4 157
Jelcz-Laskowice f4 168
Jeldēsa c2 226
Jelenec g3 171
Jelenia Góra d5 168
Jelgava k4 157
Jeli b3 101
Jelka f3 171
Jellico g1 259
Jellicoe k6 251
Jelling c3 158
Jelow Gir l5 137
Jels c3 158
Jelšane f4 177
Jelsi d3 198
Jemaja c3 98
Jemaluang c4 101
Jember g9 98
Jementah c4 101
Jemeppe c4 159
Jemgum f1 159
Jeminay, Xinjiang Uygur Zizhiqu, China v4 121
Jemma, Bauchi, Nig. f3 223
Jemma, Kaduna, Nig. f4 223
Jemnice g1 177
Jemo D 74
Jempang, Danau j5 99
Jena, Ger. f3 175
Jena, U.S.A. c4 258
Jenbach c2 176
Jendouba f1 221
Jeneč c1 170
Jengegietje e4 154
Jengish Chokusu t7 121
Jeniang b3 101
Jenikowo d2 168
Jenin d4 139
Jenipapo e5 285
Jenise j3 118
Jenjarom b4 101
Jenkins h1 259
Jenkintown e4 256
Jenks b1 258
Jennersdorf h3 177
Jennings, U.S.A. c4 258
Jennings, Antig. D 271
Jenolan Caves k12 81
Jensen Beach j6 259
Jens Munk Island n2 243
Jepara f8 98
Jeparit f14 81
Jeppo j5 155
Jequié d4 288
Jequitaí f2 291
Jequitinhonha, Braz. j1 291
Jequitinhonha, Minas Gerais, Braz. h2 291
Jerada d2 220
Jerantut c4 101
Jerba, Île de g2 221
Jerbar f2 225
Jerécuaro d3 274
Jérémie g5 266
Jeremoabo e4 288
Jereweh j9 99
Jerez c2 274
Jerez de la Frontera d8 191
Jerez de los Caballeros d6 191
Jérica d5 193
Jericho, Aust. h7 80
Jericho, W.B. d5 139
Jerid, Chott el f2 221
Jerijeh, Tanjung f3 98
Jerilderie g13 81
Jerisjärvi k3 155
Jermyn e3 256
Jerome b4 256
Jerónimo d4 274
Jeronimo Norte g1 297
Jerramungup d13 87
Jerruck d8 129
Jersey c3 182
Jersey (U.K.) e7 161
Jersey City f4 257
Jersey Shore c3 256
Jerte, Spain e4 190
Jerte, Extremadura, Spain e4 190
Jertih c3 101
Jerumenha d3 288
Jerusalem d5 139
Jervis Bay, Jervis Bay Territory, Aust. k13 81
Jervis Bay, Jervis Bay Territory, Aust. g2 83
Jervis Bay Territory g2 83
Jerzmanowice h5 169
Jerzu Ab3 198
Jesenice, Středočeský kraj, Czech Rep. b1 170
Jesenice, Czech Rep. c2 170
Jesenice, Slvn. f3 177
Jeseník f1 170
Jesenské j3 171
Jeserig h3 173
Jesi h6 197
Jesolo g4 196
Jessen h4 173
Jessheim d2 156
Jeßnitz h4 173
Jessore l8 125
Jestetten g2 174
Jesús Carranza g5 275
Jesus de Otoro d3 276
Jesús María, Arg. e1 297
Jesús María, Aguascalientes, Mex. c3 274
Jesús María, Chiapas, Mex. g5 275
Jesus Maria b2 274
Jesús María Garza h5 275
Jeta, Ilha de a3 222
Jetmore d4 260
Jeumont c4 159
Jevenstedt c4 158
Jever c2 172
Jevíčko e2 170
Jevišovice h1 177
Jevnaker d2 156
Jewar c5 130
Jewett, Illinois, U.S.A. b6 254
Jewett, Texas, U.S.A. a4 258
Jewett City j3 257
Jezerane g4 177
Jeżewo l2 169
Jeżewo Stare g2 168
Jeziorak, Jezioro h2 169
Jeziorany j2 169
Jeziorsko, Jezioro g4 168
Jeżów h4 169
Jeżowe l5 169
Jezzine d3 138
Jhabua g9 129
Jha Jha k7 125
Jhajhar c5 130
Jhajjar c5 130
Jhajju f7 129
Jhal c6 129
Jhalakati m8 125
Jhalawar e7 124
Jhal Jhao b7 129
Jhang f5 128
Jhanjharpur k6 125
Jhansi f7 124
Jharda g9 129
Jharkhand j8 125
Jharsuguda j9 125
Jhatpat d6 129
Jhelum, India f4 128
Jhelum, Pak. a3 130
Jhimpir d8 129
Jhinjhuvada e9 129
Jhiri c6 130
Jhok Bodo e5 128
Jhudo d8 129
Jhumritilaiya j7 125
Jhund e9 129
Jhunjhunun b5 130
Jiading g4 111
Jiahe j6 105
Jiahezhai e2 111
Jialing Jiang f3 104
Jialu He d2 106
Jiamusi r2 113
Ji'an, Jiangxi, China k5 105
Ji'an, Jilin, China p5 113
Jianchang, Liaoning, China k5 113
Jianchang, Liaoning, China n5 113
Jianchuan d2 102
Jiande f5 111
Jiang'an e4 104
Jiangba f3 111
Jiangcheng e4 102
Jiange e3 104
Jiangjiapo g1 111
Jiangjin f4 104
Jiangjunmu d1 106
Jiangkou, Guizhou, China g5 104
Jiangkou, Hubei, China b4 106
Jiangkou, Shaanxi, China f2 104
Jiangle l5 105
Jiangling c4 106
Jiangmen j7 105
Jiangning f4 111
Jiangshan, Zhejiang, China m4 105
Jiangshan, Zhejiang, China g5 111
Jiangshui c1 106
Jiangsu f3 111
Jiangtaibu c8 112
Jiangwan f5 111
Jiangxi k5 104
Jiangxia d4 106
Jiangxian b2 106
Jiangxigou a7 112
Jiangyan g3 111
Jiangyin g4 111
Jiangyong h6 104
Jiangyou e3 104
Jiangyu f1 111
Jianhe g5 104
Jianhu f3 111
Jianli c5 106
Jianning l5 105
Jian'ou m5 105
Jianping, Liaoning, China k5 113
Jianqiao e1 106
Jianshi a4 106
Jianshui f4 102
Jianshui Hu f2 135
Jianyang, Fujian, China m5 105
Jianyang, Sichuan, China e3 104
Jiaocheng c1 106
Jiaohe p4 113
Jiaokou b1 106
Jiaolai He, Nei Mongol Zizhiqu, China l4 113
Jiaolai He, Shandong, China f1 111
Jiaonan f2 111
Jiaotan e5 111
Jiaotou h5 111
Jiaoxie g3 111
Jiaozhou g1 111
Jiaozhou Wan g1 111
Jiaozuo c2 106
Jiapu f4 111
Jiashan g4 111
Jiashi r8 121
Jiawang e2 111
Jiaxian, Henan, China c3 106
Jiaxian, Shaanxi, China b1 106
Jiaxiang e2 111
Jiaxing g4 111
Jiayin r1 113
Jiayu c5 106
Jiayue f1 111

KENYA
THE REPUBLIC OF KENYA
Area 580,367km² (224,081sq miles)
Capital Nairobi
Organizations COMESA, COMM
Population 31,540,000
Pop. growth (%) 0.1
Life expectancy 51 (m); 53 (f)
Languages Kiswahili, English, Kikuyu, Luo
Literacy 85.1%
Currency Kenya shilling
(US $1 = 75.8 Kenya shilling)
GDP (US million $) 10,316
GDP per head ($US) 327

L

Langgapayung a5 101
Langgar n5 125
Langgöns d3 174
Langhirano e5 196
Langholm f4 164
Langjan Nature Reserve ☆ h1 235
Langjökull ▲ A 152
Langkawi ▭ a2 101
Langkesi, Kepulauan ▭ n7 99
Lang Kha Toek, Khao ▲ a1 101
Langkon j1 99
Langley b1 262
Langlo ≈ a4 84
Langlo Crossing g9 81
Langlois a4 262
Långnås g2 156
Langnau b3 196
Langogne f4 186
Langoiran b4 186
Langon b4 186
Langøya ▭ e2 154
Langphu ▲ h5 135
Langping b4 106
Langqên Zangbo ≈ e4 130
Langreo e1 191
Langres b3 184
Langres, Plateau de ⌒ b3 184
Långrösten ○ f2 156
Langruth d5 250
Langsa c13 103
Langsa, Teluk ◄ d13 103
Långselån ≈ e4 154
Långsele f5 154
Lang Shan ▲ d5 112
Langshan d5 112
Långshyttan g2 156
Långsjöblik ▲ e2 156
Långsjön ○ g2 156
Langslett h2 154
Lang Sơn f8 104
Langtang, Nepal g5 135
Langtang, Nig. f4 223
Langtang National Park ☆ j5 125
Langting n7 125
Langtou n5 113
Langtoutun l2 113
Langtry j3 273
Langue de Barbarie, Parc National de la ☆ a2 222
Languedoc ♦ e5 187
Languedoc-Roussillon ▣ e6 187
Langueyú h4 297
Languidic b5 182
Langui Langui ▲ j1 99
Languiñeo c4 295
Langundu, Tanjung ► k9 99
Langvatne ○ m2 155
Langvatnet, Nor. ○ c1 156
Langwedel e3 172
Langweid am Lech e4 175
Langxi f4 111
Langya Shan, Hebei, China ▲ h6 112
Langya Shan, Shandong, China ▲ f2 111
Langzhong f3 104
Lanigan a5 250
Lanín, Parque Nacional ☆ b5 296
Lanín, Volcán ▲ b5 296
Lanjak, Bukit ▲ f4 98
Lankao d2 106
Lānkāran m2 137
Lanlacuni Bajo c2 292
Lanmeur b4 182
Lannach g3 177
Lannavaara h2 154
Lannemezan c5 187
Lannemezan, Plateau de ⌒ c5 187
Lanngazhoinkang e4 130
Lannilis a4 182
Lannion b4 182
Lannion, Baie de ◄ b4 182
Lano L 75
La Noria, Bol. e3 293
La Noria, Mex. a2 274
Lanouaille d3 186
Lanping d2 102
Lansdowne d5 130
Lansdowne House k4 251
L'Anse j7 251
L'Anse-aux-Meadows National Historic Park ★ q3 253
Lans-en-Vercors b5 185
Lansford e4 256
Lanshan j6 105
Lansing, Can. ≈ l2 247
Lansing, U.S.A. d4 254
Länsi-Suomi ▣ k1 157
Lansjärv j3 155
Lanškie, Jezioro ○ j2 169
Lanškroun e2 170
Lanslebourg-Mont-Cenis c5 185
Lans, Montagne de ▲ b5 185
Lanta d5 187
Lantadilla f2 190
Lanta, Ko ▭ a2 101
Lantau Island ▭ j7 105
Lanterne ≈ c3 184
Lantian a2 106
La Nucía d6 193
Lanūf, Ra's ► a1 218
Lanús h3 297
Lanusei Ab3 198
Lanuza f6 100
Lanuza Bay ◄ f6 100
Lanvallay c4 182
Lanvollon c4 182
Lanxi, Heilongjiang, China p2 113
Lanxi, Hubei, China d4 106
Lanxi, Zhejiang, China m4 105
Lanya f2 225
Lanyi He ≈ f6 112
Lan Yü ▭ n7 105
Lanz g2 173
Lanzahita f4 190
Lanzarote ▭ Af2 189
Lanžhot h1 177
Lanzhou b7 112
Lanzijing m3 113
Lanzo Torinese b4 196
Laoag c1 100
Laoang e4 100
Laobie Shan ▲ b7 104
La Obispalia ♦ b5 193
Lao Cai f4 102
Laofengkou u4 121
Laoha He ≈ k5 113
Laohekou b3 106
Laohutun l6 113
Laois ▣ d4 165
Laoling p5 113
La Oliva Af2 189
Laon b5 159
Laonnois ♦ j3 183
Laons g4 183
La Orotava Ac2 189
La Oroya b2 292
Laos h7 93

LAOS

THE LAO PEOPLE'S DEMOCRATIC REPUBLIC
Area 236,800km² (91,400sq miles)
Capital Vientiane
Organizations ASEAN
Population 5,500,000
Pop. growth (%) 2.2
Life expectancy 51 (m); 53 (f)
Languages Lao (Laotian), French, many local languages
Literacy 67.3%
Currency new kip (US $1 = 7882 new kip)
GDP (US million $) 1749
GDP per head ($US) 318

Lao Shan ▲ g1 111
Laoshan g1 111
Laoshan Wan ◄ g1 111
Lao Thu, Cu ▭ j10 103
Laotougou q4 113
Lao Xanh, Cu ▭ j9 103
Laoximiao a5 112
Laoye Ling, Heilongjiang/Jilin, China ▲ p4 113
Laoye Ling, Heilongjiang/Jilin, China ▲ q3 113
Lapa d6 290
Lapac ▭ c8 100
La Paca c7 193
La Pacaudière f2 186
Lapachito f5 293
Lapai f4 223
La Paila h5 273
Lapalisse f2 186
La Palma, Chile b3 296
La Palma, El Sal. c3 276
La Palma, Guat. c2 276
La Palma, Iraq ▭ Ab2 189
La Palma, Pan. h6 277
La Palme e6 187
La Paloma f2 294
La Pampa ▣ e4 296
La Panza Range ▲ c6 265
La Paragua e2 285
Laparan ▭ b8 100
La Parejas g2 297
La Parilla b2 274
La Parra d6 191
La Parra de Las Vegas b5 193
Lapas b4 210
Lapathos b1 138
La Paya, Parque Nacional ☆ c3 284
La Paz, Córdoba, Arg. e2 296
La Paz, Entre Ríos, Arg. e2 294
La Paz, Arg. d2 296
La Paz, Bol. ▣ d2 292
La Paz, Bol. d2 292
La Paz, Hond. d3 276
La Paz, Mex. d5 272
La Paz, Nic. d4 276
La Paz, Ur. j3 297
La Paz, Ven. c1 284
La Paz, Bahía ◄ d5 272
La Pedrera d4 284
La Pelada d4 294
La Peña, Tamaulipas, Mex. e2 275
La Peña, Mex. g5 275
La Peña, Pan. g6 277
La Perla g3 272
La Pesca f2 275
La Petite-Pierre d2 184
Lapford c6 163
La Picada g1 297
La Piedad c3 274
La Piedra b2 276
La Piña ≈ e2 285
Lapinig e4 100
Lapinjärvi m2 157
La Pintada g6 277
Lapithos b1 138
Laplace d4 258
Lap Lae e7 102
Laplandija p2 155
Laplandskij Zapovednik ☆ b2 146
La Plant c2 260
La Plata, Arg. j3 297
La Plata, U.S.A. d6 256
La Playa e1 296
La Playa de Mogán Ad3 189
La Playosa f2 297
Lapleau e3 186
Laplume c4 187
La Pobla de Lillet f2 192
La Pobla de Segur e2 192
La Pola de Gordón e2 190
La Poma d4 292
Lapominka e2 146
La Ponderosa c2 276
La Porte c5 254
Laporte d3 256
La Portellada e4 192
La Portera c5 193
Laposo, Bukit ▲ k7 99
Lapotkova k4 147
Lapoutroie d2 184
La Poyata c3 284
La Poza Grande c5 272
Lappajärvi, Fin. ○ f5 155
Lappajärvi, Länsi-Suomi, Fin. j5 155
Lappe f3 156
Lappeenranta n2 157
Lappfjärd j1 157
Lappi, Fin. ▣ l3 155
Lappi, Länsi-Suomi, Fin. j2 157
La Presa g2 275
Laprida g4 297
La Primavera g4 297
La Proveda de Soria b2 192
La Pryor k3 273
Lâpseki a2 208
Laptev Sea ≈ n2 119
Lapua j5 155
Lapuanjoki ≈ j5 155
La Puebla de Almoradiel a5 193
La Puebla de Cazalla e7 191
La Puebla de los Infantes e7 191
La Puebla del Rio d7 191
La Puebla de Montalbán f5 191
La Puebla de Valdavia f2 190
La Puebla de Valverde d4 193
La Puerta, Córdoba, Arg. d2 294
La Puerta, Arg. c1 294
La Puerta, Ven. c2 284
La Puerta de Segura b6 193
Lapu-Lapu d5 100
La Punilla e2 296
La Purísima c4 272
Lăpuş g2 201
Lapwai e2 262
Łapy l3 169
La Quiaca d4 292
L'Aquila, Italy ▣ c2 198
L'Aquila, Abruzzo, Italy h7 197
L'Aquila ▣ h7 197
Lār q8 137
Lara ▣ d1 284
Larabanga d4 222
Laracha b1 190
Larache c1 220
Laragne-Montéglin b6 185
La Rambla f7 191
Laramie, Wyoming, U.S.A. ≈ b3 260
Laramie, Wyoming, U.S.A. b3 260
Laramie Mountains ▲ b3 260
Laranjal f4 285
Laranjal Paulista e5 290
Laranjeiras e4 288
Laranjeiras do Sul b6 290
Larantuka m9 99
La Raygat ♦ b4 220
Larba e1 221
L'Arbresle a5 185
Lärbro h4 157
Larceveau-Arros-Cibits a5 187
Larche d3 186
Lardaro e4 196
l'Ardenne, Plateau de ⌒ d5 159
L'Ardoise m6 253
Lardos Ad2 211
Lardosa c5 191
Laredo, Spain g1 190
Laredo, U.S.A. k4 273
La Reforma, Arg. d4 296
La Reforma, Chiapas, Mex. b2 276
La Reforma, Oaxaca, Mex. f5 275
La Reforma, Veracruz, Mex. f3 275
La Réole b4 186
Lares A 270
La Restinga Ab3 189
Larga h1 201
Largentière a6 185
L'Argentière-la-Bessée c6 185
Largo h6 259
Largo, Cayo ▭ d4 266
Largs d4 164
Lāri l2 137
L'Ariana g1 221
Lariang, Indon. ≈ k5 99
Lariang, Sulawesi Selatan, Indon. k5 99
La Rica h3 297
La Ricamarie a5 185
Larimore e6 250
Larino d3 198
La Rioja, Arg. ▣ d1 296
La Rioja, Arg. c1 294
La Rioja, Spain ▣ b2 192
Larisa c3 210
Larkana d7 129
Lark Harbour n4 253
Lar Koh ▲ a4 128
l'Arli, Réserve Partielle de ☆ e3 223
Larmor-Plage b5 182
Larnaca ▣ b2 138
Larnaca Bay ► b2 138
Larnaka b2 138
Larne, England, U.K. ▣ b2 165
Larne, Northern Ireland, U.K. c5 164
Larned d4 260
La Robla e2 190
La Roca de la Sierra d5 191
La Roche-Bernard c5 182
La Roche-Canillac d3 186
La Roche-Chalais c3 186
La Roche-de-Rame c6 185
La Roche-Derrien b4 182
La Roche-des-Arnauds b6 185
La Roche-en-Ardenne d4 159
La Rochefoucauld c3 186
La Roche-Guyon g3 183
La Rochelle a2 186
La Roche-Posay c2 186
La Roche-sur-Yon d6 182
La Rochette c5 185
La Roda b5 193
La Roda de Andalucía f7 191
La Romana k5 271
La Ronge q4 249
Laroquebrou e4 186
La Roquebrussanne b7 185
Laroque-Timbaut c4 187
La Rosita j3 273
Larraga c2 192
Larrainzar a2 276
Larrau b5 187
Larrey Point ► d6 86
Larrimah a3 80
Larroque h2 297
Larsen Bay f4 246
Larseng g2 154
Larsen Ice Shelf ⌒ l1 298
Larsnes a1 156
La Rubia d2 294
La Rumorosa e9 263
Laruns b6 187
Larvik d3 156
Larzac, Causse du ♦ f5 187
La Sabana, Arg. e1 294
La Sabana, Col. d3 284
Las Adjuntas, Presa de ○ e1 275
Lasah b3 101
Las Albercas d2 274
La Sal Junction j6 263
Lasalle f4 187
La Salle, Italy b4 196
La Salle, U.S.A. b5 254
La Salvetat-sur-Agout e5 187
Las Arenas f1 190
Las Armas j4 297
La Sarre g1 254
Las Asequias e2 297
La Sauceda d3 274
Las Aves, Islas ▭ d1 284
La Savina f6 193
Las Avispas, Arg. d1 294
Las Avispas, Mex. d3 272
Las Bandurrias g2 297
Las Bonitas d2 284
Las Breñas e5 293
Lásby c2 158
Las Cabezas de San Juan e8 191
Las Cabras, Chile b3 296
Las Cabras, Mex. b2 274
Las Cañas, Chile a3 296
Las Cañas, Ur. h2 297
Las Casas d5 193
Las Casuarinas c1 296
Las Catitas c2 296
Las Cebollas b1 274
Las Chacras e2 296
Las Chapas c4 295
Las Choapas g5 275
Las Colorados b2 296
Las Conchas, Bol. f3 293
Las Conchas, Guat. c3 276
Las Cruces, Baja California Sur, Mex. d5 272
Las Cruces, Mex. f3 272
Las Cruces, U.S.A. b5 261
Las Crucitas e2 275
Lascuarre e2 192
Las Delicias b3 276
La Sénia e4 192
La Serena, Chile b1 294
La Serena, Spain ♦ e6 191
Las Esperanças j4 273
Las Estancias, Sierra de ▲ b7 193
La Seyne-sur-Mer b7 185
Las Flores, Buenos Aires, Arg. h4 297
Las Flores, Arg. e4 293
Las Flores, Mex. f2 275
Las Flores, Cerro ▲ g5 275
Las Galenas b1 296
Las Garzas b3 296
Las Golas h2 297
Las Guacamayas c4 274
Las Heras c2 296
Las Herreras g5 272
Las Higueras e2 297
Lashio c4 102
Lashkar Gāh b5 128
Las Horquetas b5 295
Las Hortensias a5 296
La Sila ○ f5 199
La Silveta ▲ b6 295
Łasin h2 169
Lasinja g4 177
Las Isletas e2 296
Läsjerd p4 137
Las Jicamas d3 274
Las Juntas, Arg. c3 296
Las Juntas, Chile c1 294
Las Juntas, Mex. d4 274
Las Junturas f1 297
Łask h4 169
Łaskarzew k4 169
Laško g3 177
Las Lajas b5 296
Las Lajitas d2 284
Las Lavaderos e2 275
Las Leñas b3 296
Las Lomas a4 284
Las Lomitas e4 293
Lašma f4 150
Las Majadas b4 192
Las Malvinas c3 296
Las Maravillas h5 275
Las Margaritas b2 276
Las Marismas ⌒ d7 191
Las Martinetas c5 295
Las Menas b7 193
Las Mercedes d2 284
Las Mesteñas g3 272
Las Minas e1 285
Las Minas, Cerro de ▲ c3 276
Las Minas, Sierra de ▲ c3 276
Las Molles c3 296
Las Negras c8 193
Las Nieves g4 272
Las Nopaleras, Cerro ▲ f5 272
La Solana a6 193
Lasolo, Teluk ◄ m6 99
Las Omañas ♦ d2 190
La Sombra d5 274
La Souterraine d2 186
Las Ovejas b4 296
Las Palmas, Arg. f5 293
Las Palmas, Mex. c2 274
Las Palmas, Pan. g6 277
Las Palmas de Gran Canaria Ad2 189
Las Palomas, Serranía de ▲ b2 284
Las Paredes c3 296
Las Pedroñeras b5 193
Las Pedrosas d2 192
Las Perdices f2 297
Las Petas, Bol. ≈ f3 293
Las Petas, Santa Cruz, Bol. f3 293
La Spezia, Italy ▣ d5 196
La Spezia, Liguria, Italy d5 197
Las Piedras j3 297
Las Pipinas j3 297
Las Planchas e3 276
Las Plumas c4 295
Laspur f2 128
Las Quebradas c3 276
Las Rosas g2 297
Las Rozas de Madrid g4 190
Lassance f2 291
Lassay-les-Châteaux e4 182
Lassen Peak ▲ c5 262
Lassen Volcanic National Park ☆ c5 262
Lasseube b5 187
Lassigny a5 159
Laßnitz ≈ g3 177
Las Tablas, Chile b2 296
Las Tablas, Mex. e2 275
Las Tablas, Pan. g7 277
l'Astarac, Barrage de ⌒ c5 187
Lastarria, Volcán ▲ d5 292
Las Termas e5 293
Last Mountain Lake ○ q6 249
Las Torres de Cotillas c6 193
Las Tórtolas, Cerro ▲ b1 294
Lastoursville b4 224
Lastovo f2 198
Lastra g4 297
Las Tres Vírgenes, Volcán ▲ c4 272
Las Trincheras e2 285
Lastrup c3 172
Lastukoski m5 155
Las Tunas f4 266
La Suze-sur-Sarthe f5 183
Las Vacas b1 296
Las Vacas, Col. d2 284
Las Varas, Chihuahua, Mex. e3 272
Las Varas, Chihuahua, Mex. g3 272
Las Varas, Mex. b3 274
Las Varas, Ven. d2 284
Las Varillas f1 297
Las Vegas, Mex. b1 274
Las Vegas, Nevada, U.S.A. f7 263
Las Vegas, New Mexico, U.S.A. b5 261
Las Veguillas e4 190
Las Ventas de San Julián e4 190
Las Vertientes e2 296
Las Viajas, Isla de ▭ b2 292
Las Vigas de Ramirez f4 275
Las Yaras c3 292
Las Yeguas, Sierra de ▲ f7 191
Łaszczów m5 169
La Tabatière n3 253
Latacunga b4 284
Latady Island ▭ kk1 298
La Tagua c4 284
Latakia e5 208
Latalata ▭ p5 99
La Tapona d2 274
Lätäseno ≈ j2 155
Late ▭ J 75
Latehar j8 125
Latemar ▲ f3 196
Laterza f4 198
La Teste a4 186
La Tetilla, Cerro ▲ b3 274
Latgales augstiene ♦ m4 157
Latham c11 87
Lathen f2 159
Latheron e1 164
Lathi e7 129
Latiano g4 198
Lātīdān q8 137
Latina, Italy ▣ h8 197
Latina, Lazio, Italy b3 198
La Tinaja f4 275
Latisana h4 196
La Toma e2 296
Laton d5 265
La Torre de Cabdella e2 192
La Tortuga, Isla ▭ d1 284
Latouche Island ▭ g3 247
Latouche Treville, Cape ► e6 86
La Tour-du-Pin b5 185
Latowicz k3 169
La Tranca d2 296
La Tranche-sur-Mer d6 182
Látrány f5 171
La Tremblade a3 186
La Trimouille d2 186
La Trinidad, Nic. d4 276
La Trinidad, Phil. c2 100
La Trinitaria a2 276
La Trinité, Fr. d7 185
La Trinité, Mart. J 271
La Trinité-Porhoët c4 182
Latrobe, Aust. Ab2 83
Latrobe, U.S.A. a4 256
Latronico f4 198
Latronquière e4 186
La Troya ≈ c1 294
Latrun c5 139
Latsia b1 138
Lattes, Languedoc-Roussillon, Fr. f5 187
La Tuque f5 252
Latur e3 126
Latvia k3 145

LATVIA

THE REPUBLIC OF LATVIA
Area 64,589km² (24,938sq miles)
Capital Riga
Organizations CE, EBRD
Population 2,340,000
Pop. growth (%) -0.1
Life expectancy 63 (m); 75 (f)
Languages Latvian, Russian
Literacy 99.8%
Currency lats (US $1 = 0.54 lats)
GDP (US million $) 8052
GDP per head ($US) 3441

Lau, Nig. g4 223
Lau, Sudan f2 225
Laubach d5 174
Lauca ≈ d3 292
Lauca, Parque Nacional ☆ d3 292
Laucha ≈ h4 173
Lauchert ≈ e4 174
Lauchhammer j4 173
Lauchringen e3 174
Lauda-Königshofen g3 174
Lauder A 164
Lauderdale e3 258
Lauenbrück e2 172
Lauenburg (Elbe) d5 158
Lauer ≈ f2 174
Lauf an der Pegnitz d5 175
Laufen, Ger. d2 176
Laufen, Switz. b2 196
Laufenberg c2 196
Laufenburg (Baden) f3 174
Lauffen am Neckar d4 174
Lauge Koch Kyst ♦ t1 243
Laugharne b5 163
Laughlen, Mount ▲ b7 80
Laughlin Peak ▲ b4 260
Lauingen (Donau) f4 174
Laukaa l1 157
Laukøya ▭ h1 154
Laukuva k5 157
Laukvik m1 155
Laun d10 103
Launceston, Aust. Ab2 83
Launceston, U.K. b6 163
Laune ≈ b4 165
Launglon Bok Islands ▭ c9 103
La Unidad h6 275
La Unión, Bol. e3 293
La Unión, Chile a6 296
La Union b3 284
La Unión, El Sal. d4 276
La Unión, Hond. d3 276
La Unión, Coahuila, Mex. h3 273
La Unión, Mex. d5 274
La Unión, Huánuco, Peru b1 292
La Unión, Peru a5 284
La Unión, Spain d7 193
Launois-sur-Vence c5 159
Laupheim e2 174
Laur c3 100
Laura g3 80
La Urbana d2 284
Laureana di Borrello f6 199
Laurel, Delaware, U.S.A. e6 256
Laurel, Mississippi, U.S.A. e4 258
Laurel, Montana, U.S.A. a2 260
Laureldale e4 256
Laureles f5 293
Laurel Hill ▲ a4 256
Laurencekirk f3 164
Laurens h2 259
Laurenzana e4 198
Lauria e4 198
Lauricocha, Lago ○ b2 292
Lau Ridge ≈ l7 301
Laurier d5 250
Laurière d2 186
Laurinburg k2 259
Laurino e4 198
Laurium j7 251
Lauro d4 198
Lausanne a3 196
Laußnitz k1 175
Laut, Indon. ▭ e2 98
Laut, Indon. ▭ e5 98
Laut, Indon. ▭ h6 99
Lauta k4 173
Lautaro a5 296
Lautaro, Cerro ▲ b5 295
Lautem p9 99
Lautenbach d3 184
Lauter ≈ d3 174
Lauterbourg e2 184
Lauterbrunnen b3 196
Lauterecken c3 174
Lautersbach (Hessen) e2 174
Laut Kecil, Kepulauan ▭ j7 99
Lautoka E 74
Lautrec e5 187
Laut, Selat ═ h6 99
Laut Taka Bonerate National Park ☆ l8 99
Lauttawar, Danau ○ c13 103
Lauvsnes c4 154
Lauvuskylä m5 155
Lauwersmeer ○ e1 159
Lauzès d4 186
Lauzun c4 186
Lava ≈ j5 157
Lava Beds National Monument ☆ c5 262
Lavaca ≈ a5 258
Lavagna d5 197
Lava Hot Springs g4 262
Laval, Can. k3 255
Laval, Fr. e4 182
La Vale b5 256
La Valette-du-Var b7 185
Lavalle c2 296
Lavalleja ▣ f2 294
Lavamünd f3 177
Lävän p8 137
Lavandeira, Punta ► b1 190
Lava, Nosy ▭ Ab1 233
Lavansa ≈ f2 192
Lavant ≈ f2 177
Lavapié, Punta ► a4 296
Lävar n7 137
Lavara g1 210
Lavardac c4 187
Lavassaare l3 157
Lavaur d5 187
La Vecilla e2 190
La Vega, Dom. Rep. j5 271
La Vega, Mex. c3 274
Lavelanet d6 187
Lavello e3 198
Lavenham g4 163
Laveno c4 196
La Venta d3 276
La Ventosa b4 193
La Venturosa d2 284
La Vera ≈ e4 190
La Verde e3 296
Lavernock Point ► c5 163
La Verpillière b5 185
Laverton f11 87
Lavezzi, Îles ▭ A 185
Lavia k2 157
La Víbora h4 272
La Victoria, Mex. b2 276
La Victoria, Ven. d1 284
La Villa e7 197
La Villa de Don Fadrique a5 193
La Villedieu-du-Clain c2 186
Lavillette k5 253
Lavin e2 275
La Viña, Arg. d5 292
La Viña, Peru b1 292
Lavina j2 262
Lavinio-Lido di Enea b3 198
La Violeta g2 297
Lavit c5 187
La Viticola f5 297
La Vôge ♦ c2 184
Lavonia h2 259
Lavoriškės p1 169
Lavos b4 190
La Voulte-sur-Rhône a6 185
Lavoûte-Chilhac f3 186
Lavras f4 291
Lavre, Port ≈ b6 191
Lavre, Évora, Port b6 191
Lavrio e5 211
Lavumisa j3 235
Lavushi-Manda National Park ☆ f6 225
Lawa, India g7 129
Lawa, Lib. ≈ c4 222
Lawa, Pak. e4 128
Lawa, Sur. ≈ f3 285
Lawagamau ≈ p5 251
Lawas h2 99
Lawdar g5 219
Lawele m7 99
Lawin b3 101
Lawit, Gunung, Indon. ▲ g4 98
Lawit, Gunung, Malay. ▲ c3 101
Lawn Hill d5 80
Lawn Hill Creek ≈ d5 80
Lawn Hill National Park ☆ d5 80
Lawqah j7 137
Lawra d3 222
Lawrence, N.Z. b6 77
Lawrence, Indiana, U.S.A. c6 254
Lawrence, Kansas, U.S.A. e4 260
Lawrence, Massachusetts, U.S.A. j2 257
Lawrenceville, Illinois, U.S.A. c6 254
Lawrenceville, New Jersey, U.S.A. f4 256
Lawrenceville, Pennsylvania, U.S.A. c3 256
Lawrenceville, Virginia, U.S.A. h7 255
Lawrence Wells, Mount ▲ d10 87
Lawton, North Dakota, U.S.A. d6 250
Lawton, Oklahoma, U.S.A. d5 261
Lawz, Jabal al ▲ e2 219
Laxå f3 156
Laxe a1 190
Laxey b2 162
Laxo c2 164
Laxsjö e5 154
Laxsjön ○ f3 156
Lay ≈ a2 186
Layang Layang c5 101
La Yarada c3 292
Layar, Tanjung ► j7 99
Layeni h7 97
La Yesa d5 193
La Yesca b3 274
Layon ≈ e5 182
l'Ayrolle, Étang de ○ f5 187
Layton h5 262
Laytonville b6 262
Laza c2 190
La Zacatosa, Picacho ▲ e6 272
Lazagurría b2 192
La Zanja f4 297
Lázaro Cárdenas, Baja California Norte, Mex. f10 263
Lázaro Cárdenas, Chiapas, Mex. h5 275
Lázaro Cárdenas, Michoacán, Mex. c5 274
Lazcano f2 294
Lazdijai m1 169
Lazio ▣ b3 198
Lázně Bohdaneč d1 170
Lázně Kynžvart a1 170
Lazo, Arg. h2 297
Lazo, Russ. Fed. p3 119
Lazzarino h4 297
Lazzaro, Monte ▲ d5 196
Leach f9 103
Lead c2 260
Leadburn e4 164
Leadenham f3 162
Leader n6 249
Leader Water ≈ f4 164
Leadville b4 260
Leaf ≈ e4 258
League City b5 258
Leake, Mount ▲ h5 86
Leakey k3 273
Leales d5 292
Lealman h6 259
Leamington e4 254
Leamington Spa, Royal e4 163
Le'an k5 105
Leandra h3 235
Leandro N. Alem g3 297
Leanja Ab2 233
Learmonth b8 86
Leatherhead f5 163
Leavenworth, Kansas, U.S.A. e4 260
Leavenworth, Washington, U.S.A. c2 262
Leavitt Peak ▲ d3 264
Łeba f1 168
Lebach e5 159
Lebak e7 100
Lebamba b4 224
Lebanon, Indiana, U.S.A. c5 254
Lebanon a5 92

LEBANON

THE LEBANESE REPUBLIC
Area 104,523km² (40,360sq miles)
Capital Beirut
Organizations IDB, LAS, OIC
Population 3,600,000
Pop. growth (%) 1.8
Life expectancy 71 (m); 74 (f)
Languages Arabic, French, Kurdish, Armenian
Literacy 87.4%
Currency Lebanese pound (US $1 = 1515 Lebanese pound)
GDP (US million $) 17,941
GDP per head ($US) 4983

Lebanon, Kansas, U.S.A. d4 260
Lebanon, Missouri, U.S.A. c1 258
Lebanon, New Hampshire, U.S.A. k4 255
Lebanon, New Jersey, U.S.A. f4 256
Lebanon, Ohio, U.S.A. d6 254
Lebanon, Pennsylvania, U.S.A. d4 256
Lebanon, Virginia,U.S.A. h1 259
Lebanon Junction g1 259
Lebap h7 120
Lebapskaya Oblast' ▣ j8 120
Le Barp b4 186
Le Beausset b7 185
Lebec e7 265
Lebedevka l4 147
Lebedjan' e5 150
Lebedyn d2 148
Lebel-sur-Quévillon d4 252
Lebesby l1 155
Le Biot c4 184
Lebjaž'e, Kirovskaja Oblast', Russ. Fed. k3 151
Lebjaž'e, Kurganskaja Oblast', Russ. Fed. l5 147
Le Blanc d2 186
Le Bleymard f4 187
Lebnitsa ≈ d1 210
Lebo d3 224
Le Bois-d'Oingt a5 185
Lebombo Mountains ▲ k3 235
Lębork f1 168
Le Boulou e6 187
Le Bourg-d'Oisans c5 185
Le Bourget-du-Lac b5 185
Le Bourgneuf-la-Forêt e4 182
Lebowakgomo h2 235
Lebrija d8 191
Łebsko, Jezioro ○ f1 168
Lebu a4 296
Le Bugue c4 186
Lebus k3 173
Lebusa j4 173
Leça da Palmeira b3 190
Le Cannet d7 185
Le Cateau-Cambrésis b4 159
Le Catelet b4 159
Lecce, Italy ▣ h4 198
Lecce, Puglia, Italy h4 198
Lecco, Italy ▣ d4 196
Lecco, Lombardia, Italy d4 196
Lecco, Lago di ○ d4 196
Lécera d3 192
Lech, Aus. ≈ b2 176
Lech, Aus. b2 176
Lechaina b5 211
Le Chambon-Feugerolles a5 185
Le Chambon-sur-Lignon a5 185
Lechang j6 105
Le Chasseron ▲ a3 196
Le Château-d'Oléron a3 186
Le Châtelard c5 185
Le Châtelet e2 186
Le Châtelet-en-Brie h4 183
Le Chesne c5 159
Le Cheylard a6 185
Lechința g2 201
Lechlade e5 163
Lechovo b2 210
Lechtaler Alpen ▲ b2 176
Leciñena d3 192
Leck b4 158
Lecompte c4 258
Le Conquet a4 182
Le Coteau a4 184
Le Creusot a4 184
Lecrin g8 191
Le Croisic c5 182
Le Crotoy g2 183
Lectoure c5 187
Łęczna l4 169
Łęczyca h3 169
Łęczyce f1 168
Ledaig c3 164
Ledaña c5 193
Ledanca b4 192
Ledang, Gunung ▲ c4 101
Ledava ≈ h3 177
Ledbury d4 163
Lède ≈ c4 187
Ledeč nad Sázavou d2 170
Ledenice f1 177
Ledesma e3 190
Lédignan a7 184
Ledigos f2 190
Lédiguié d3 222
Ledkovo g2 147
Ledmore c1 164
Lednica, Jezioro ○ f3 168
Lednice h1 177

LESOTHO

THE KINGDOM OF LESOTHO
Area 30,355km² (11,720sq miles)
Capital Maseru
Organizations COMM, SADC
Population 1,800,000
Pop. growth (%) 1.9
Life expectancy 50 (m); 51 (f)
Languages English, Sesotho
Literacy 84.8%
Currency loti, plural maloti (US $1 = 6.38 maloti)
GDP (US million $) 731
GDP per head ($US) 406

LIBERIA

THE REPUBLIC OF LIBERIA
Area 97,754km² (37,743sq miles)
Capital Monrovia
Organizations ECOWAS
Population 3,240,000
Pop. growth (%) 1.4
Life expectancy 47 (m); 49 (f)
Languages English, many local languages and dialects
Literacy 57%
Currency Liberian dollar (and US dollar) (US $1 = 1.00 Liberian dollar)
GDP (US million $) 571
GDP per head ($US) 176

LIBYA

THE GREAT SOCIALIST PEOPLE'S LIBYAN ARAB JAMAHIRIYA
Area 1,775,500km² (685,524sq miles)
Capital Tripoli
Organizations IDB, LAS, OPEC, OIC
Population 5,450,000
Pop. growth (%) 1.9
Life expectancy 68 (m); 72 (f)
Languages Arabic, English, Italian
Literacy 82.5%
Currency Libyan dinar (US $1 = 1.26 Libyan dinar)
GDP (US million $) 13,249
GDP per head ($US) 2431

LIECHTENSTEIN

THE PRINCIPALITY OF LIECHTENSTEIN
Area 160km² (62sq miles)
Capital Vaduz
Organizations CE, EBRD, EFTA
Population 33,000
Pop. growth (%) 0
Life expectancy 66 (m); 73 (f)
Languages German, (Alemannic dialect)
Literacy 95%
Currency Swiss franc (US $1 = 1.26 Swiss franc)
GDP (US million $) 1315
GDP per head ($US) 39,848

LITHUANIA
THE REPUBLIC OF LITHUANIA
Area 65,300km² (25,212sq miles)
Capital Vilnius
Organizations CE, EBRD
Population 3,488,000
Pop. growth (%) -0.1
Life expectancy 66 (m); 76 (f)
Languages Lithuanian, Russian, Polish, Yiddish
Literacy 99.6%
Currency litas, (plural litai) (US $1 = 2.81 litai)
GDP (US million $) 13,964
GDP per head ($US) 4003

354 Lunel-Viel → Main-Donau-Kanal

Lunel-Viel, Languedoc-Roussillon, Fr. a7 184
Lünen f3 159
Lunenburg, Can. k6 253
Lunenburg, U.S.A. g7 254
Lunestedt b5 158
Lunéville f4 184
Lunga c2 211
Lunga d1 232
Lungdo f3 135
Lungern c3 196
Lunggar f4 135
Lungi b4 222
Lunglei n8 125
Lungmu Co e2 130
Lungo, Lago g7 197
Lungro f5 198
Lungwebungu c1 232
Luni, India e8 129
Luni, India f7 129
Luning e3 264
Lunino h5 151
Luninyets b1 148
L'Union d5 187
Lunkaransar f6 129
Lunkha f6 129
Lunkho f2 128
Lunna n2 169
Lünne f2 159
Lunow k3 173
Lunsar b4 222
Lunsemfwa d1 233
Lunyuk j9 99
Lunzenau h2 175
Luobei r2 113
Luochanghe e4 111
Luocheng g6 104
Luochuan a2 106
Luoding h7 104
Luodžio ežeras m5 157
Luogosanto Ab1 198
Luo He a5 106
Luohe d3 106
Luo He a2 106
Luo Jiang h7 104
Luokou e1 111
Luoma Hu f2 111
Luonan b2 106
Luoning b2 106
Luonselkä l3 155
Luoping e6 104
Luopmosjávrrit l2 155
Luoshan d3 106
Luoshe g4 111
Luotian d4 106
Luoto j5 155
Luoxiao Shan j5 105
Luoyang c2 106
Luoyuan m5 105
Luozi b4 224
Lupane d2 233
Lupanshui e5 104
Łupawa f1 168
Lupe c6 191
Lupeni f3 201
Luperón j5 271
Lupfen d4 174
Lupilichi b6 227
Lupire b1 232
Łupków l6 169
Lupon f7 100
Luppa h4 173
Luqiao, Anhui, China e3 111
Luqiao, Shandong, China f1 111
Luqiao, Zhejiang, China n4 105
Luqu d1 104
Luquan d0 106
Luque f7 191
Lūrā Shīrīn k3 137
Luray b6 256
Lurcy-Lévis e2 186
Lure c3 184
Lureco b6 231
Luremo c5 224
Lures e5 200
Lurgainn, Loch c1 164
Lurgan e2 165
Luri A 185
Luribay d3 292
Lurín b2 292
Lurio b6 231
Lúrio c6 227
Lury-sur-Arnon h5 183
Lusahunga f4 225
Lusaka, D.R.C. e5 225
Lusaka, Zam. d2 233
Lusaka, Lusaka, Zam. d2 233
Lusambo d4 224
Lusanga c4 224
Lusangi e4 225
Luseland n5 249
Lusenga Plain National Park e5 225
Lusengo c3 224
Luserna San Giovanni b5 196
Lushan, Henan, China c3 106
Lushan, Sichuan, China d3 104
Lushi b2 106
Lush, Mount h5 86
Lushnjë d5 200
Lushoto b4 227
Lushui d3 102
Lüshun l6 113
Lüsi g3 111
Lusi f8 98
Lusignan c2 186
Lusigny-sur-Barse a2 184
Lusika e4 225
Lusikisiki h5 235
Lusk b3 260
Lus-la-Croix-Haute b6 185
Lussac b4 186
Lussac-les-Châteaux c2 186
Lussac-les-Églises d2 186
Lussan a6 185
Lüßberg f3 172
Lussvale h9 81
Lustenau a2 176
Luster b2 156
Lutago f3 196
Lü Tao n7 105
Lutécia c5 290
Lutembo c1 232
Luterskie, Jezioro j1 169
Luthersburg b3 256
Lutherstadt Wittenberg h4 173
Lutiba e4 225
Lutín f2 170
Lütingyi e4 111
Lütjenburg d4 158
Luton, England, U.K. h2 162
Luton, England, U.K. f5 163
Lutong g2 98
Lutou c3 106
Lutry j1 169
Łutselk'e g3 242
Lutshi e4 225
Luts'k b2 148
Lutter am Barenberge f4 172
Lutterworth e4 163
Lutuai c1 232
Lututów g4 168
Lutz h5 259
Lützow e5 158
Lützow-Holm Bay j1 298
Lutzputs d4 234
Lutzville c5 234
Luumäen kk m2 157
Luuq c3 226
Luusua l3 155
Luve j3 235
Luverne, Alabama, U.S.A. f4 258
Luverne, Minnesota, U.S.A. d3 260
Luvua e5 225
Luvuei c1 232
Luvuvhu j1 235
Luwegu g5 225
Luwero f3 225
Luwingu e6 225
Luwuk m5 99
Luxembourg f5 144

LUXEMBOURG

THE GRAND DUCHY OF LUXEMBOURG
Area 2587km² (999sq miles)
Capital Luxembourg
Organizations CE, EBRD, EU, NATO, OECD
Population 441,000
Pop. growth (%) 1.5
Life expectancy 73 (m); 80 (f)
Languages Letzeburgish (German-Moselle-Frankish dialect), French, German
Literacy 99%
Currency euro (US $1 = 0.81 euro)
GDP (US million $) 21,200
GDP per head ($US) 48,072

Luxembourg, Bel. d5 159
Luxembourg, Lux. e5 159
Luxeuil-les-Bains c3 184
Luxey b4 187
Luxi, Yunnan, China d3 102
Luxi, Yunnan, China d6 104
Luxikegongba h4 135
Luxolweni f5 235
Luxor, Qena, Egypt d9 136
Luxor, Qena, Egypt d2 218
Luxora e2 258
Luy b5 187
Luyamba e4 225
Lüyangyi l5 113
Luya Shan f6 112
Luy de Béarn b5 187
Luyi d3 106
Luynes f5 183
Luz f3 291
Luza, Russ. Fed. j1 151
Luza, Kirovskaya Oblast', Russ. Fed. j1 151
Luzarches h3 183
Luzech d4 187
Luzhou e4 104
Luziânia e2 290
Luzilândia d2 288
Luzino g1 168
Luz, Isla b5 295
Lužnice c2 170
Luzon c3 100
Luzy f2 186
Luzzi f5 199
L'viv n6 169
L'vovskij d4 150
Lwówek e3 168
Lwówek Śląski d4 168
Lyall, Mount, Can. k7 249
Lyall, Mount, N.Z. a6 77
Lyal'mikar c2 128
Lyangar l7 120
Lyaskovets g4 201
Lyasnaya, Bela. m3 169
Lyasnaya, Brestskaya Voblasts', Bela. p3 169
Lybster e1 164
Lycia b4 208
Lyckovo b3 150
Lycksele g4 154
Lydd g6 163
Lydenburg j2 235
Lydford b6 163
Lydney d5 163
Lydum b3 158
Lyel'chytsy c2 148
Lyell Brown, Mount k8 87
Lyell Island b5 248
Lyell, Mount d4 264
Lyepyel' c1 148
Lyford a6 258
Lygnern e4 156
Lygourio d5 211
Lykens d4 256
Lykodimo b6 211
Lykofos g1 210
Lykoporia c4 210
Lykso f3 234
Lyman h5 262
Lymans'ke j2 201
Lyme Bay d6 163
Lyme Regis d6 163
Lymington e6 163
Lympstone c6 163
Łyna j1 169
Lynch h1 259
Lynchburg, South Carolina, U.S.A. j2 259
Lynchburg, Virginia, U.S.A. g7 254
Lynches j2 259
Lynd g4 80
Lynden b1 262
Lyndhurst, Aust. d11 81
Lyndhurst, U.K. e6 163
Lyndoch a2 82
Lyndon, Western Australia, Aust. b8 87
Lyne d1 162
Lyngdal b3 156
Lyngen h2 154
Lyngna b3 156
Lyngør c3 156
Lyngseidet h2 154
Lynmouth c5 163
Lynn, Alabama, U.S.A. f2 258
Lynn, Indiana, U.S.A. d5 254
Lynn Canal l4 247
Lynndyl g6 262
Lynn Haven g4 259
Lynn Lake c2 250
Lynton c5 163
Lyntupy m5 157
Lynx Lake h3 242
Lyø d3 158
Lyon, Fr. a5 185
Lyon, U.K. d3 164
Lyonnais, Monts du a5 185
Lyons, Aust. a11 81
Lyons, Indiana, U.S.A. c6 254
Lyons, New York, U.S.A. d1 256
Lyons-la-Forêt g3 183
Lyracrumpane b4 165
Lyrkeia c5 211
Lys, Fr. h2 183
Lys, Italy b4 196
Lysá nad Labem c1 170
Lysá pod Makytou g2 171
Lysekammen b3 156
Lysekil d3 156
Lysi b1 138
Lysimachia, Limni b4 210
Lyskovo h3 151
Łysomice g2 168
Lysøysund b5 154
Lystrup d2 158
Lys'va j4 147
Lysychans'k e2 148
Lytham St Anne's c3 162
Lythrodontas b2 138
Lytkarino d4 150
Lyttelton d5 77
Lyuban' c1 148
Lyubashivka k2 201
Lyubeshiv p4 169
Lyubimets h5 201
Lyubishchytsy p3 169
Lyubotyn d2 148
Lyulyakovo h4 201
Lža n4 157

M

M.A.B., Réserve d6 224
M'banza Congo b5 224
M'Clintock f2 250
M'Daourouch f1 221
M'Saken g1 221
M'Sila e1 221
M'zab, Oued a5 221
Ma d4 102
Ma Sekatok j3 99
Ma, Sông g5 102
Ma'alé Efrayim d4 139
Ma'an g5 223
Ma'anshan f4 111
Ma'on d5 139
Ma'rib g4 219
Ma'ād d4 138
Ma'agan d4 138
Maakalla j4 155
Ma'alé Gamla d4 138
Maalhosmadulu Atoll c10 126
Ma'alot-Tarshiḥa d3 138
Maam b3 165
Maamba d2 232
Ma'an, Jordan e6 139
Ma'an, Ma'an, Jordan d6 139
Maaninka l5 155
Maaninkavaara m3 155
Maanselkä m5 155
Maanyt, Bulgan, Mong. b1 112
Maanyt, Töv, Mong. d2 112
Maap G 74
Maaraké d3 138
Maardu l3 157
Maarianvaara m5 155
Ma'arrat an Nu'mān f5 209
Maas, Ire. c2 165
Maas, Neth. d3 159
Maasbracht d3 159
Maaseik d3 159
Maasin e5 100
Maasmechelen d4 159
Maassluis c3 159
Maasstroom h1 235
Maastricht d4 159
Maatsuyker Group Ab3 83
Maaza Plateau d2 218
Maba, China f3 111
Maba, Indon. h5 97
Maba, Ouadi b4 218
Mababe Depression c2 232
Mabalacat c3 100
Mabalane k1 235
Mabana e3 225
Mabanda b4 224
Mabank a3 258
Mabaruma q10 271
Mabbu'im c5 139
Mabel Creek b10 81
Mabel Lake h6 248
Mabesi, Lake b4 222
Mabi c2 106
Mabian d4 104
Mablethorpe g3 162
Mableton g3 259
Mably a4 184
Mabote l1 235
Mabou m5 253
Mabrūk h3 221
Mabuasehube Game Reserve e2 234
Mabutsane e2 234
Mac. Robertson Land n2 298
Macá, Monte b5 295
Macachín f4 297
Macacos, Ilha dos b2 288
Macadam Plains c9 87
Macaé h5 291
Macael b7 193
Macaíba e3 288
Macajalar Bay e6 100
Macajuba d4 288
Macalister e3 83
Macaloge b6 227
MacAlpine Lake j2 242
Macandze k1 235
Mação c5 191
Macapá, Amapá, Braz. g3 285
Macapá, Amazonas, Braz. d1 292
Macará, Col. b4 284
Macará, Ec. b4 284
Macaracas g7 277
Macarani h1 291
Macarena, Cordillera c3 284
Macas b4 284
Maçãs d3 190
Macau, Braz. e3 288
Macau, China j7 105
Macau, Macau Special Administrative Region, Macao, China j7 105
Macaúba b4 288
Macaúbas d4 288
Macayari c3 284
Macbride Head e6 295
Maccaretane k2 235
Macclenny h4 259
Macclesfield d3 162
Macdiarmid g6 251
Macdonald, Lake j8 87
Macdonnell Ranges l8 87
MacDowell Lake g4 250
Macduff f2 164
Maceda c2 190
Macedo j4 297
Macedo de Cavaleiros d3 190
Macedon d3 82
Macedonia j6 145

MACEDONIA

THE FORMER YUGOSLAV REPUBLIC OF MACEDONIA
Area 25,713km² (9928sq miles)
Capital Skopje
Organizations CE, EBRD
Population 2,050,000
Pop. growth (%) -1.5
Life expectancy 70 (m); 74 (f)
Languages Macedonian, Albanian, Serbo-Croat
Literacy 93%
Currency Macedonian denar (US $1 = 50.01 Macedonian denar)
GDP (US million $) 3813
GDP per head ($US) 1860

Maceió e3 288
Maceira b5 191
Macenta c4 222
Macerata, Italy h6 197
Macerata c1 198
Macesta e4 148
Macfarlane, Lake b12 81
Macgillycuddy's Reeks b5 164
Mach c6 129
Machacalis h2 291
Machacamarca d3 292
Machachi b4 284
Machadinho e1 293
Machadinho, Ilha c2 288
Machado f4 291
Machadodorp j2 235
Machaila k1 235
Machakos b4 226
Machala b4 284
Machali b3 296
Machanao, Mount C 74
Machang, China f2 111
Machang, Malay. c3 101
Machanga e3 233
Machar Marshes f2 225
Macharetí e4 293
Machault c5 159
Machecoul d6 182
Machelen c4 159
Macheng d4 106
Macherla f4 126
Machern h4 173
Machesna Mountain c6 265
Machghara d3 138
Machhiwara c4 130
Machhlishahr h7 124
Machias j6 253
Machico B 189
Machilipatnam g4 126
Machinga f3 233
Machiques c1 284
Machnaqa d2 138
Machov e1 170
Machupo e2 293
Machynlleth c4 163
Macia k2 235
Maciejowice k4 169
Maciel g2 297
Mâcin j3 201
Macintyre Brook d6 85
Maçka g2 209
Mackay g6 80
Mackay, Lake j8 86
Mackenzie, Aust. c5 84
Mackenzie, Can. m2 247
Mackenzie Bay, Anguilla n1 298
Mackenzie Bay, Can. k1 247
Mackenzie Delta l1 247
Mackenzie King Island g1 242
Mackenzie Mountains m2 247
Mackinac Island d3 254
Mackinaw City d3 254
Mackintosh Range g10 87
Macksville l11 81
Mackunda Creek e7 80
Maclean l10 81
Maclear h5 235
Macleay e7 85
MacLeod, Lake b9 87
Macmillan l3 247
Macocola c5 224
Macolo c5 224
Macomb a5 254
Macomer Aa2 198
Macomia c6 227
Mâcon a4 184
Macon, Georgia, U.S.A. h3 259
Macon, Illinois, U.S.A. b6 254
Macon, Mississippi, U.S.A. e3 258
Macondo c1 232
Mâconnais a4 184
Macosquin e1 165
Macotera e4 190
Macoun Lake r3 249
Macovane f3 233
Macquarie, New South Wales, Aust. b7 85
Macquarie, Tasmania, Aust. Ab2 83
Macquarie Harbour Aa3 83
Macquarie Marshes b7 85
Macquarie Marshes Nature Reserve b7 85
Macquarie Mountain f1 83
Macquarie, Lake g1 83
Macroom c5 165
Mactún b2 276
Macú d3 284
Macuelizo c3 276
Macugnaga b4 196
Macuiltepec a1 276
Macuiltianguis f5 275
Macuira, Parque Nacional c1 284
Macuje c3 284
Macuma b4 284
Macururé e3 288
Macusani c2 292
Macuspana a2 276
Macuzari, Presa e4 272
Mād k3 171
Mad a1 264
Mada f4 223
Madā'in Şāliḥ f8 136
Mādabā, Jordan d5 139
Mādabā d5 139
Madadeni j3 235
Madagan b6 129
Madagascar g7 217

MADAGASCAR

THE REPUBLIC OF MADAGASCAR
Area 587,041km² (226,658sq miles)
Capital Antananarivo
Organizations COMESA
Population 16,920,000
Pop. growth (%) 2.7
Life expectancy 50 (m); 52 (f)
Languages Malagasy, French, Hova, other local languages
Literacy 68.9%
Currency Malagasy franc (US $1 = 5910 Malagasy franc)
GDP (US million $) 4900
GDP per head ($US) 289

Madagascar Basin b7 300
Madagascar Plateau a8 300
Madakasira e6 126
Madalena e2 288
Madama g4 221
Madan e1 210
Madanapalle f6 126
Madang e5 111
Mădăraș k5 171
Madaripur m8 125
Madau g2 137
Madaula c5 130
Madawaska, Can. d6 252
Madawaska, U.S.A. h5 253
Madaya c4 102
Maḍāyā e3 138
Maddaloni d3 198
Made c3 159
Madeira, Arm. a2 220
Madeira, Braz. e1 293
Madeira (Portugal) B 189
Madeirinha e1 293
Madeleine, Îles de la l5 253
Madeleine, Monts de la f3 186
Madeleine-Centre k4 253
Madeley, England, U.K. d4 162
Madeline Island f2 260
Maden g3 209
Madeniyet s4 121
Madera, Mex. e3 272
Madera, Spain b6 193
Madera, California, U.S.A. c5 264
Madera, Pennsylvania, U.S.A. b4 256
Madera Peak d4 264
Maderano f3 190
Madererspitze b2 176
Madgaon c5 126
Madhepura k7 125
Madhira g4 126
Madhkūr, Bi'r al a6 139
Madhopur b3 130
Madhubani k6 125
Madhupur k7 125
Madhya Pradesh f8 124
Madian g1 111
Madibira a5 227
Madibogo f3 235
Madidi d2 292
Madikeri d6 126
Madill a2 258
Madimba, Ang. b5 224
Madimba, D.R.C. c5 224
Madinani c4 222
Madingo b4 224
Madingo-Kayes b4 224
Madingou b4 224
Madingrin c2 224
Madirovalo Ab2 233
Madison, Florida, U.S.A. h4 259
Madison, Georgia, U.S.A. h3 259
Madison, Indiana, U.S.A. d6 254
Madison, Maine, U.S.A. h6 252
Madison, Minnesota, U.S.A. d2 260
Madison, Montana, U.S.A. h3 262
Madison, Nebraska, U.S.A. d3 260
Madison, Ohio, U.S.A. f5 254
Madison, South Dakota, U.S.A. d3 260
Madison, Virginia, U.S.A. b6 256
Madison, West Virginia, U.S.A. f6 254
Madison, Wisconsin, U.S.A. b4 254
Madisonville, Louisiana, U.S.A. d4 258
Madisonville, Tennessee, U.S.A. g2 259
Madisonville, Texas, U.S.A. b4 258
Madita l10 99
Madiun f8 98
Madiyi l3 247
Madjingo c2 224
Madley, Mount f9 87
Mado Gashi b3 226
Madoc h3 255
Madocsa g5 171
Madoi b1 104
Madon c2 184
Madona m4 157
Madonna di Campiglio e3 196
Madpura e8 129
Madras g6 126
Madre de Deus de Minas f4 291
Madre de Dios, Peru c2 292
Madre de Dios, Peru d2 292
Madre de Dios, Isla a6 295
Madre del Sur, Sierra e7 241
Madre Mountains, Sierra d7 265
Madre Occidental, Sierra d6 241
Madre, Laguna, Mex. L5 273
Madre, Laguna, U.S.A. a6 258
Madre, Sierra d2 100
Madrès, Pic de e6 187
Madrid, Phil. e6 100
Madrid, Spain g4 190
Madrid, Spain g4 190
Madrid, U.S.A. g4 259
Madridejos, Phil. d5 100
Madridejos, Spain g5 191
Madrigal de las Altas Torres f3 190
Madrigalejo e5 191
Madrisahorn e3 196
Madriz d4 276
Madrona, Sierra f6 191
Madroñera e5 191
Madrūsah g4 221
Madu l8 99
Madua m7 125
Maducang c5 100
Madugula h4 126
Madura h8 87
Madura, Indon. g8 98
Madura, Selat g8 98
Madurai f8 126
Madwas g7 124
Madyan f3 128
Madyo a5 227
Madžalis g4 149
Madzharovo g5 201
Madziwadzido d2 233
Mae Hong Son c6 102
Mae Li d6 102
Mae Nam Chi g8 102
Mae Nam Khong g6 102
Mae Nam Mun f8 102
Mae Nam Nan e6 102
Mae Nam Pa Sak e7 102
Mae Nam Pattani b2 101
Mae Nam Sai Buri b2 101
Mae Nam Songkhram f7 102
Mae Nam Tha Pi a1 101
Mae Nam Wang d7 102
Mae Ping National Park d7 102
Mae Ramat d7 102
Mae Rim d6 102
Mae Sariang c6 102
Mae Sot d7 102
Mae Wong National Park d8 102
Mae Yom National Park e6 102
Maebashi h3 115
Maelang m4 99
Maël-Carhaix b4 182
Maella e3 192
Maenclochog b5 163
Maengsan p6 113
Maep'o q7 113
Măeriște l4 171
Maestra, Sierra f4 266
Maestre de Campo c4 100
Maestro, Canale f7 197
Maevatanana Ab2 233
Maéwo F 74
Mafa h5 97
Mafa'a, Pointe L 75
Mafeteng g4 235
Maffin k6 97
Mafia Channel g5 225
Mafia Island g5 225
Mafikeng f2 235
Mafil a5 296
Mafinga b5 227
Mafou b4 222
Mafra a6 191
Magadan r4 119
Magadanskaja Oblast' r3 119
Magadi b4 226
Magadi, Lake b4 226
Magalia b2 264
Magaliesberg g2 235
Magallanes d4 100
Magallanes y Antártica Chilena b6 295
Magallanes, Estrecho de b6 295
Magallón c3 192
Magalluf g5 193
Magaña b3 192
Magangue k6 277
Măgara d4 208
Magaria f3 223
Magas g4 149
Magat c2 100
Magaz f3 190
Magazine Mountain c2 258
Magbakele d3 224
Magburaka b4 222
Magdagachi h2 94
Magdalena, Arg. j3 297
Magdalena, Bol. e2 293
Magdalena, Col. c1 284
Magdalena, Col. c2 284
Magdalena, Mex. d2 272
Magdalena, Baja California Sur, Mex. c4 272
Magdalena, Sonora, Mex. h10 263
Magdalena Cuayucatepec f4 275
Magdaline, Gunung j2 99
Magdeburg, Ger. g3 173
Magdeburg g3 173
Magé g5 291
Magee, Island f2 165
Magelang f8 98
Magén c5 139
Magenta c4 196
Magenta, Lake d13 87
Magerøya k1 155
Magescq a5 187
Maggia, Switz. c3 196
Maggia c3 196
Maggiolo f2 297
Maggiorasca, Monte d5 196
Maggotty B 270
Maghāgha c7 136
Maghama b2 222
Maghār d4 138
Maghārah, Jabal b6 139
Maghdouche d3 138
Maghera e2 165
Magherafelt, England, U.K. b2 165
Magherafelt e2 165
Maghnia d2 220
Maghor a3 128
Maghull d3 162
Mágina g7 191
Magione g6 197
Măgireşti h2 201
Magiscatzin e2 275
Maglaj d3 200
Magliano de'Marsi h7 197
Magliano in Toscana f7 197
Magliano Sabina g7 197
Maglie c2 198
Magna Grande e7 199
Magnac-Laval d2 186
Magnetic Island A 84
Magnières c2 184
Magnitogorsk j5 147
Magnolia, Arkansas, U.S.A. c3 258
Magnolia, Mississippi, U.S.A. d4 258
Magnor e3 156
Magnuszew k4 169
Magny-en-Vexin g3 183
Mago, Fiji E 74
Mago l2 94
Mago National Park b2 226
Magoé e2 233
Magog f6 252
Magori f9 129
Magoula c5 211
Magoye d2 233
Magozal f3 275
Magpie, Ontario, Can. l6 251
Magpie, Québec, Can. k3 253
Magpie, Lac k3 253
Magre d5 193
Magruder Mountain f4 264
Magrur d5 218
Magrur, Wadi c4 218
Magta' Lahjar b2 222
Magu f4 225
Maguan g4 102
Magude k2 235
Magudu j3 235
Magueyal h4 273
Magumeri g3 223
Magurski Park Narodowy k6 169
Magwe, Magway, Myan. b5 102
Magwe, Myan. b5 102
Magwe, Sudan f3 225
Magweggana c2 232
Magyarbánhegyes j5 171
Magyarból g6 171
Magyarszék g5 171
Magyichaung n9 125
Maha Sarakham f7 102
Mahābād k3 137
Mahaban c6 130
Mahabe Ab2 233
Mahabharat Range g6 135
Mahabo, Toliara, Madag. Aa3 233
Mahabo, Toliara, Madag. Ab3 233
Mahačkala g4 149
Mahad c3 126
Mahaddayweyne d3 226
Mahadeo Hills f8 124
Mahaffey b4 256
Mahagi f3 225
Mahagi Port f3 225
Mahaica-Berbice f2 285
Mahajan f6 129
Mahajanga, Madag. Ab2 233
Mahajanga Ab2 233
Mahajjah e4 138
Mahakam j5 99
Mahalapye g1 235
Mahale Mountains National Park f5 225
Mahalevona Ab2 233
Mahallāt n5 137
Maham c5 130
Māhān r6 137
Mahanadi j9 125
Mahanoro Ab2 233
Maharajganj j6 125
Maharashtra d3 126
Mahārish, Ra's e2 219
Maharivo Aa3 233
Mahasamund h9 124
Mahatsinjo, Fianarantsoa, Madag. Ab3 233
Mahatsinjo, Mahajanga, Madag. Ab2 233
Maḥaṭṭat Abū Ţarafah d7 139
Maḥaṭṭat 'Amrāwah d7 139
Maḥaṭṭat Ḑab'ah e5 139
Mahavavy Ab2 233
Mahavelona Ab2 233
Mahaweli Ganga A 127
Mahbub c5 218
Mahbubabad g4 126
Mahbubnagar e4 126
Mahd adh Dhahab f3 219
Mahdia, Alg. e1 221
Mahdia, Guy. f2 285
Mahdia, Tun. g1 221
Mahé A 226
Mahendragarh c5 130
Mahendragiri j3 124
Mahenge b5 227
Maheno c6 77
Mahesana f9 129
Maheshwar g9 129
Mahi f9 129
Mahia Peninsula f3 76
Mahide d3 190
Mahilyow c1 148
Mahilyowskaya Voblasts' c1 148
Mahina b3 222
Mahinerangi, Lake b6 77
Māhīş d4 139
Mahiya d3 130
Mahlabatini j3 235
Mahlaing b5 102
Mahlangasi j3 235
Mahlangatsha j3 235
Mahlberg c4 174
Mahlébourg C 231
Mahlsdorf g3 173
Maḥmūd-e 'Erāqī d3 128
Mahmudia j3 201
Mahnevo k4 147
Mahnomen f7 250
Mahoba f7 124
Mahomet b5 254
Mahón A 195
Mahongo Game Park c2 232
Mahony Lake n2 247
Mahora c5 193
Mahou d3 222
Mahrès g2 221
Mahuta, Nig. e3 223
Mahuta, Tan. b6 227
Mahuva e10 129
Mahya Dağı h5 201
Mahyār n5 137
Maia b3 190
Maiana H 75
Maiao K 75
Maibang n7 125
Maicasagi q5 251
Maicasagi, Lac q6 251
Maiche c3 184
Maichen g8 104
Maici e5 285
Maicuru b1 288
Maiden Creek e4 256
Maiden Newton d6 163
Maidenhead f5 163
Maidi h5 97
Maidstone g5 163
Maiduguri g3 223
Maiella, Parco Nazionale della d3 198
Maienfeld d2 196
Maierato f6 199
Maieru g2 201
Maigmó d6 193
Maignelay-Montigny h3 183
Maigualida, Sierra d2 285
Maigue c4 165
Maihar g7 124
Maihara g4 115
Maikala Range g8 124
Maiko e4 225
Maiko, Parc National de la e4 225
Maikoor j7 97
Mailan Hill h8 125
Mailani e5 130
Maïlao h3 223
Maillezais b2 186
Mailly-le-Camp k4 183
Mailly-Maillet a4 159
Mailsi f6 129
Main, Can. p4 253
Main, Ger. e3 174
Main, U.K. e2 165
Mā'īn d5 139
Main Channel b6 252
Main Range National Park e6 85
Mainaguri l6 125
Mainalo c5 211
Mainburg g4 175
Mai-Ndombe, Lac c4 224
Main-Donau-Kanal g3 175

Maindong → Mantes-la-Jolie 355

Maindong g4 135
Maine, Fr. ≈ e5 182
Maine, U.S.A. [1] h6 255
Mainé Hanari, Cerro △ c4 284
Maine, Gulf of ◄ m4 255
Maine-et-Loire [2] e5 182
Maïné-Soroa g3 223
Maingkwan c2 102
Mainhardt e3 174
Mainit e6 100
Mainit, Lake ○ e6 100
Mainland, Scotland, U.K. ▭ A 164
Mainland, Scotland, U.K. ▭ B 164
Mainleus g2 175
Mainling p5 125
Mainoru ≈ b2 80
Mainpuri d6 130
Mainsat e2 186
Maintenon g4 183
Maintirano Aa2 233
Mainua l4 155
Mainvilliers g4 183
Mainyaung b4 102
Mainz d2 174
Maio ▭ A 222
Maiolati Spontini h6 197
Maior ≈ b5 191
Maiori d4 198
Maipo ≈ c3 296
Maipú, Buenos Aires, Arg. j4 297
Maipú, Arg. c2 296
Maipú, Chile b2 296
Maipú, Volcán △ c3 296
Maipures d2 284
Maipuri Landing f3 285
Maiquetía d1 284
Maiquinique h1 291
Maira ≈ b5 196
Mairi d4 288
Mairiporã e5 291
Mairipotaba d2 290
Mairos △ c3 190
Maïrouba d2 138
Maisach g4 175
Maishi j4 105
Maiskhal Island ▭ m9 125
Maisons-Laffitte h4 183
Maitencillo b1 296
Maitland, New South Wales, Aust. k12 81
Maitland, South Australia, Aust. c13 81
Maitland, Mount △ d9 87
Maitri (India) ▪ f2 298
Maiwang c4 106
Maiyu, Mount △ j5 86
Maíz, Isla del ▭ f4 277
Maizar d4 128
Maizhokunggar m5 125
Maizières-lès-Metz c1 184
Maizières-lè-Vic c2 184
Maizuru f4 115
Maja ≈ p4 119
Maja Jezercë △ d4 200
Majačnyj j1 149
Majadahonda g4 190
Majalgaon e3 126
Majari ≈ e3 285
Majd el Kurūm d4 138
Majdal Shams d3 138
Majdel Silim d3 138
Majene k6 99
Majī b2 226
Majia He ≈ e1 111
Majiang, Guangxi Zhuangzu Zizhiqu, China h7 104
Majiang, Guizhou, China f5 104
Majitha b4 130
Majja p3 119
Majkop f3 148
Majkor h4 147
Majma v1 121
Majna, Respublika Hakasija, Russ. Fed. k4 118
Majna, Ul'janovskaja Oblast', Russ. Fed. j4 151
Majoma d2 274
Major, Puig △ f5 193
Majorca ▭ g5 193
Majuriã e1 293
Majuro ▭ D 74
Majuro Lagoon ▭ D 74
Maka b3 222
Makabana b4 224
Makaha Ab2 263
Makak g5 223
Makale k6 99
Makalu △ h6 135
Makalu Barun National Park ☆ k6 125
Makamba e4 225
Makanchi u4 121
Makanya b4 227
Makar'e k2 151
Makar'ev g3 151
Makarewa b7 77
Makari g3 223
Makarov l3 94
Makarove l3 171
Makarska g1 198
Makarwal e4 128
Makassar k7 99
Makassar, Sulawesi Selatan, Indon. k7 99
Makassar Strait ═ k5 99
Makat j3 149
Makatini Flats k3 235
Makaw c2 102
Makbon j6 97
Makeni b4 222
Makere f4 225
Makete a5 231
Makgadikgadi d3 232
Makgadikgadi Pans National Park ☆ c3 232
Makhad e4 128
Makhfar al Ḩammām g5 209
Makhmal h9 120
Makhmūr j5 209
Maki j6 97
Makikihi c6 77
Makin ▭ H 75
Makindu b4 226
Makinsk n1 121
Makinson Inlet ◄ p1 243
Makiv h1 201
Makiyivka e2 148
Makkabim d5 139
Makkah, Sau. Ar [1] f3 219
Makkah e3 219
Makkoshotyka k3 171
Makljenovac k5 177
Makó j5 171
Makoa, Serra ⛰ f3 285
Makogai ▭ E 74
Makoka e4 225
Makokou b3 224
Makonde Plateau g6 225
Makongolosi a5 231
Makopong e2 234
Makoro e3 225
Makotipoko c4 224
Makoua c4 224
Makov g2 171
Makovnik △ g4 177
Maków Mazowiecki k3 169
Maków Podhalański h6 169
Mąkowarsko f2 168
Makra ▭ f6 211
Makrakomi c4 210
Makran ♦ a7 129
Makrana g7 129
Makrany n4 169
Makri ▭ a4 210
Makrochori c2 210
Makronisi, Grc. ▭ e5 211
Makronisi, Grc. ▭ g5 211
Makrychori c3 210
Makrygialos, Kentriki Makedonia, Grc. c2 210
Makrygialos, Kriti, Grc. f7 211
Maksatiha c3 150
Maksotag a6 129
Maktau b4 227
Mākū k3 209
Makumbako a5 227
Makumbi d5 224
Makunguwiro b6 227
Makurazaki d6 114
Makurdi f4 223
Makushin Volcano ▲ c5 246
Makutu Mountains ⛰ f6 225
Makuungo c3 226
Makuyuni b4 227
Makwassie f3 235
Mal l6 125
Mal Abrigo j3 297
Mal Kazanje △ a3 210
Mal'čevskaja f2 148
Mal'kavichy b1 148
Mala, Peru ≈ b2 292
Mala, Lima, Peru b2 292
Malá g7 191
Malå g4 154
Mala Bilozerka d3 148
Mala Divytsya d2 148
Malá Fatra ☆ g2 171
Mała Ina ≈ l2 173
Mala Kapela ⛰ g5 177
Mala Subotica e5 170
Mala Vyska c2 148
Mała Wełna ≈ f3 168
Mala, Punta ► g7 277
Malabang e7 100
Malabar Coast d7 126
Malabo f5 223
Malabuñgan a6 100
Malacacheta g2 291
Malacca, Strait of ═ b4 101
Malacky f3 170
Malad City g4 262
Maladzyechna m5 157
Málaga, Spain [2] f8 191
Málaga f8 191
Malaga, California, U.S.A. d5 264
Malaga, New Jersey, U.S.A. e5 256
Malaga, New Mexico, U.S.A. b5 261
Malagarasi, Bur. ≈ f4 225
Malagarasi f5 225
Malagon ≈ c7 191
Malagón g5 191
Malaḩ e4 138
Malahar l9 99
Mălăieşti j2 201
Malaimbandy Ab3 233
Malaja Cil'na j4 151
Malaja Pera h2 147
Malaja Višera b2 150
Malaka △ k9 99
Malakal f2 225
Malakand e3 128
Malakhera c6 130
Malakheti e5 130
Malakoff a3 258
Malakula ▭ F 74
Malakwal f4 128
Malalbergo f5 196
Malalhue a5 296
Malali f2 285
Malamala l6 99
Malån ≈ g4 154
Malan, Ras ► b8 129
Malanda d3 224
Malandar, Punta de ► d8 191
Malandrino c4 210
Malang g8 98
Malangali a5 227
Malangwa j6 125
Malanje, Ang. [1] c5 224
Malanje c5 224
Malanville e3 223
Malanzán c2 294
Mälaren ○ g3 156
Malargüe, Arg. ≈ c3 296
Malargüe, Mendoza, Arg. c3 296
Malari d4 130
Malaripo g3 285
Malartic g1 254
Malaryta n4 169
Malasoro, Teluk ◄ k7 99
Malaspina c4 295
Malaspina Glacier j4 247
Malatayur, Tanjung ► g6 98
Malatya, Tur. [1] f3 209
Malatya g3 209
Malaucène b6 185
Malaunay g3 183
Malaut g5 128
Malavate g3 285
Malāvī l5 137
Malawali ▭ j1 99
Malawi f6 217

MALAWI

THE REPUBLIC OF MALAWI
Area 118,484km² (45,747sq miles)
Capital Lilongwe
Organizations COMESA, COMM, SADC
Population 11,870,000
Pop. growth (%) 2
Life expectancy 40 (m); 40 (f)
Languages English, Chichewa, other local languages
Literacy 62.7%
Currency Malawian kwacha (US $1 = 106.05 Malawian kwacha)
GDP (US million $) 1860
GDP per head ($US) 156

Malawiya e4 219
Malax h5 154
Malay Sary r5 121
Malaya Byerastavitsa m2 169
Malaybalay e6 100
Malāyer m4 137
Malaysia h8 93

MALAYSIA

THE FEDERATION OF MALAYSIA
Area 329,758km² (127,320sq miles)
Capital Kuala Lumpur
Organizations APEC, ASEAN, COMM, IDB, OIC
Population 23,970,000
Pop. growth (%) 2.1
Life expectancy 69 (m); 74 (f)
Languages Bahasa Malaysia, English Chinese, Tamil, Iban
Literacy 88.9%
Currency ringgit (US $1 = 3.80 ringgit)
GDP (US million $) 94,380
GDP per head ($US) 3937

Malaysia, Semenanjung ► b3 98
Malazgirt j3 209
Malbarco, Lago ○ b4 296
Malbon e6 80
Malbork h1 169
Malborn e5 159
Malbrán d1 294
Malbuisson c4 184
Malcata, Serra de ⛰ c4 190
Malcesine e4 196
Malchin f5 158
Malchiner See ○ h2 173
Malchow f5 158
Malcolm e11 87
Malcolm's Point ► b3 164
Malcov k2 171
Malczyce e4 168
Maldegem b3 159
Malden Bridge g2 257
Malden Island ▭ H 75
Maldives e8 92

MALDIVES

THE REPUBLIC OF MALDIVES
Area 298km² (115sq miles)
Capital Malé
Organizations COMM, IDB, OIC, SAARC
Population 310,000
Pop. growth (%) 3.2
Life expectancy 66 (m); 64 (f)
Languages Divehi (Maldivian, related to Sinhala)
Literacy 97.4%
Currency rufiyaa (US $1 = 12.8 rufiyaa)
GDP (US million $) 274
GDP per head ($US) 883

Maldon g5 163
Maldonado, Ur. [1] f2 294
Maldonado, Maldonado, Ur. f2 294
Maldonado, Punta ► e5 275
Małdyty h2 169
Malè e3 196
Male c4 102
Malé Karpaty ⛰ f3 170
Maleas, Akra ► d6 211
Malegaon d9 124
Malela e4 225
Malele c5 224
Malema f1 233
Malemba Nkulu e5 225
Maleme d7 211
Malemort-sur-Corrèze d3 186
Malente d4 158
Maler Kotla b4 130
Males f7 211
Malesherbes h4 183
Malesina d4 210
Mālestān c4 128
Malestroit c5 182
Maletto d7 199
Malevka e5 150
Malfa d6 199
Malgobek g4 149
Malgrat de Mar g3 192
Malha c4 218
Malhada d4 289
Malham l9 137
Malhargarh g8 129
Malheur ≈ e4 262
Malheur Lake ○ d4 262
Mali b3 216

MALI

THE REPUBLIC OF MALI
Area 1,240,192km² (478,841sq miles)
Capital Bamako
Organizations ECOWAS, OIC
Population 12,620,000
Pop. growth (%) 2.1
Life expectancy 49 (m); 51 (f)
Languages French and 12 other official languages
Literacy 27.9%
Currency CFA franc (US $1 = 534.95 CFA franc)
GDP (US million $) 3272
GDP per head ($US) 259

Mali, D.R.C. e4 225
Mali, Gui. b3 222
Mali Hka ≈ c2 102
Mali Kyun ▭ d9 103
Mali Rajinac △ g5 177
Malia f7 211
Malian He ≈ d8 112
Maliana n9 99
Malibu e7 265
Malicorne-sur-Sarthe e5 182
Maligay Bay ═ d7 100
Māliḩ, Bi'r al ⌄ c6 139
Māliḩī, Bi'r al ⌄ b6 139
Malik Naro △ a6 129
Malikdin d4 128
Maliku m5 99
Malili l6 99
Målilla f4 156
Malim Nawar b3 101
Malimba, Monts ⛰ e5 225
Malin Beg c2 165
Malin Head ► d1 165
Malinavka p3 169
Malindang, Mount △ d6 100
Malindi c4 227
Malindi Marine National Park ☆ c4 226
Malinga b4 224
Målingen ○ f2 156
Mălini h2 201
Malino k7 99
Malino, Gunung △ l4 99
Malinovka f5 150
Malinovoe Ozero s2 121
Malinyi b5 227
Maliq e5 200
Malita e7 100
Malitbog e5 100
Maliwun d10 103
Maliya e9 129
Malka Mari National Park ☆ b3 226
Malkangiri g3 126
Malkapur e9 124
Malkara h5 201
Małkinia Górna l3 169
Malkiyya d3 138
Malko Tŭrnovo h5 201
Mallacoota Inlet ◄ f3 83
Mallaig c3 164
Mallala d13 81
Mallasvesi ○ l2 157
Mallawi c8 136
Mallee Cliffs National Park ☆ c2 82
Mallén c3 192
Mallersdorf h4 175
Mallery Lake ○ k3 242
Malles Venosta e3 196
Mallet c6 290
Malling d2 158
Mallnitz e3 176
Mallorca ▭ g5 193
Mallow c4 165
Malm c4 154
Malmbäck f4 156
Malmberget h3 154
Malmédy e4 159
Malmesbury, R.S.A. c6 234
Malmesbury, U.K. d5 163
Malmö e5 156
Malmslätt f3 156
Malmyž l3 151
Malnate c4 196
Malo, Indon. ▭ f8 100
Malo, Veneto, Italy f4 196
Malo, Vanuatu ▭ F 74
Maloca, Amazonas, Braz. e4 285
Maloca, Pará, Braz. f3 285
Maloca Salamaim e2 293
Maloe Borisovo d2 150
Maloelap ▭ D 74
Malojaroslavec d4 150
Malolos c3 100
Malolotja Nature Reserve ☆ j3 235
Malombe, Lake ○ b6 231
Małomice d4 168
Malone, Florida, U.S.A. g4 259
Malone, New York, U.S.A. j3 255
Malonga d6 224
Malonje △ f5 225
Malonty c3 170
Małopolskie [1] j6 169
Malo-Starygino j2 151
Malošujka d3 146
Malott d1 262
Malounta b1 138
Måløy a2 156
Malozemel'skaja Tundra h1 147
Malpartida d4 190
Malpartida de Cáceres d5 191
Malpartida de Plasencia d5 191
Malpaso, Iraq △ Aa3 189
Malpaso, Mex. c2 274
Malpica b1 190
Malpica do Tejo c5 191
Malprabha ≈ d5 126
Malpura g7 129
Malsch d4 174
Malše ≈ c3 171
Målsnes g2 154
Malta g7 144

MALTA

THE REPUBLIC OF MALTA
Area 316km² (122sq miles)
Capital Valletta
Organizations CE, EBRD
Population 395,000
Pop. growth (%) 1.1
Life expectancy 75 (m); 80 (f)
Languages Maltese, English, Italian
Literacy 92.8%
Currency Maltese lira (US $1 = 0.35 Maltese lira)
GDP (US million $) 3616

Malta m4 157
Malta, Lat. ≈ m4 157
Malta, U.S.A. p7 249
Maltahöhe b2 234
Malterdingen c4 174
Maltion luonnonpuisto ☆ m3 155
Malton f2 162
Maluenda c3 192
Maluku [1] h6 97
Maluku, Kepulauan ▭ p5 99
Ma'lūlā e3 138
Malumfashi f3 223
Malung e2 156
Malungen ○ g1 156
Maluti Mountains ⛰ h4 235
Maluwe d4 222
Malvan c4 126
Malveira a6 191
Malvern c2 258
Malvern Link d4 163
Malvik c5 154
Malwal f2 225
Mały Płock l2 169
Malý Šariš k2 171
Malyj, Ostrov ▭ m2 157
Malykaj m3 119
Malyn c2 148
Malyy Uzen' ≈ g2 149
Mamadyš l4 151
Mamanuca-i-Cake Group ▭ E 74
Mamaranui d1 76
Mamarrosa b4 190
Mamasa k6 99
Mambai c4 289
Mambajao e6 100
Mambasa e3 225
Mambéré-Kadéï [1] c3 224
Mambi k6 99
Mambili ≈ c3 224
Mamborê b6 290
Mambrui c4 227
Mamburao c4 100
Mamers f4 183
Mamfé f4 223
Mamiá e4 285
Mamiá, Lago ○ e4 285
Mamili National Park ☆ c2 232
Mamiña d4 292
Mamirolle c3 184
Mamison Pass, Geor. ═ f4 149
Mamison Pass, Russ. Fed. △ f4 148
Mamlyutka m5 147
Mammari b1 138
Mammoth h9 263
Mammoth Cave National Park ★ c7 254
Mammoth Lakes e4 264
Mamonal k5 277
Mamonovo h1 169
Mamontovo, Altajskij Kraj, Russ. Fed. t1 121
Mamontovo, Hantj-Mansijskij Avtonomnjj Okrug, Russ. Fed. n3 147
Mamoré ≈ d2 292
Mamori d4 284
Mamori, Lago ○ e4 285
Mamoriá d1 292
Mamou b3 222
Mampikony Ab2 233
Mampoko c3 224
Mampong d4 222
Mamry, Jezioro ○ k1 169
Mamuju k6 99
Mamuno d1 234
Mamykovo l4 151
Man, C.I. c4 222
Man, India ≈ d4 126
Man, Jam.Kash. d3 130
Man Jiang ≈ p4 113
Man Na c4 102
Man Si c3 102
Mana, Fr. Gu. ≈ f3 285
Mana, Fr. Gu. g2 285
Mana d4 130
Maňa g3 171
Mana Bárbara c2 284
Mana Maroka National Park ☆ g4 235
Mana Pass ═ d4 130
Mana Pools National Park ★ d2 233
Manabí [1] b4 284
Manacacías ≈ c3 284
Manacapuru e4 285
Manacapuru, Lago Grande de ○ e4 285
Manacor h5 193
Manado n4 99
Manadotua ▭ n4 99
Managua, Nic. [1] d4 276
Managua, Nic. d4 276
Managua, Lago de ○ d4 276
Manakara Ab3 233
Manali c3 130
Manambaho ≈ Aa2 233
Manambovo ≈ Ab3 233
Manamelkudi f7 126
Manamoc ▭ c5 100
Mananantañana ≈ Ab3 233
Mananara, Fianarantsoa, Madag. ≈ Ab2 233
Mananara, Mahajanga/Toamasina, Madag. ≈ Ab3 233
Mananara Avaratra Ab2 233
Mananara, Parc National de ☆ Ab2 233
Manangatang c2 82
Manangoora c4 80
Mananjary Ab3 233
Manankoliva Ab3 233
Manankoro c3 222
Manantali, Lac de ○ b3 222
Manantavadi e7 126
Manantenina Ab3 233
Manapire ≈ d2 284
Manapouri a6 77
Manapouri, Lake ○ a6 77
Manapparai f7 126
Manarantsandry Ab2 233
Manas w5 121
Manas, India ≈ m6 125
Manas He ≈ v5 121
Manas Hu ○ w5 121
Manas, Gora △ n6 121
Manasa g8 129
Manaslu △ g5 135
Manasquan f4 257
Manassas c6 256
Manassas Park, U.S.A. [2] k6 257
Manassas Park, Virginia, U.S.A. c6 256
Manatang n9 99
Manatí A 270
Manatuto n9 99
Manaus e4 285
Manavgat c4 208
Manawar g9 129
Manawashei b5 218
Manawatu ≈ f4 76
Manawatu-Wanganui [1] e3 76
Manay f7 100
Manbij f4 209
Mancelona d3 254
Mancelos b3 190
Mancha Real g7 191
Manche [2] d4 182
Mancheng h6 112
Manchester, Jam. [1] B 266
Manchester, England, U.K. [2] h1 162
Manchester d3 162
Manchester, Connecticut, U.S.A. h3 257
Manchester, Georgia, U.S.A. g3 259
Manchester, Kentucky, U.S.A. h1 259
Manchester, Maryland, U.S.A. d5 256
Manchester, Massachusetts, U.S.A. k2 257
Manchester, New Hampshire, U.S.A. j2 257
Manchester, Ohio, U.S.A. e6 254
Manchester, Vermont, U.S.A. k4 255
Manchhar Lake ○ c7 129
Manching g4 175
Manchioneal B 270
Manchita d6 191
Manciano f7 197
Manciet c5 187
Mancis c4 101
Mand a7 129
Manda f5 225
Manda Island ▭ c4 226
Manda, Jebel △ d2 224
Mandabe Aa3 233
Mandaguaçu b5 290
Mandaguari c5 290
Mandal, Gujarat, India e9 129
Mandal, India g8 129
Mandal, Mong. d1 112
Mandal, Nor. b3 156
Mandala, Puncak △ l6 97
Mandalay c5 102
Mandalay, Mandale, Myan. [1] b5 102
Mandalgarh g8 129
Mandalgovĭ d3 112
Mandalī k5 137
Mandalt Sum g3 112
Mandalya Körfezi ◄ a4 208
Mandan c7 250
Mandanici e6 199
Mandaon d4 100
Mandar, Teluk ◄ k6 99
Mandara Mountains ⛰ g3 223
Mandas Ab3 198
Mandatoriccio f5 199
Mandav Hills ⛰ e9 129
Mandawa b5 130
Mandayona b4 192
Mandelieu-la-Napoule c7 185
Mandello del Lario d4 196
Mandera c3 226
Manderscheid e4 159
Mandeville, Jam. B 270
Mandeville b6 77
Mandha e7 129
Mandhan c5 130
Mandheera c2 226
Mandi c4 130
Mandi Angin, Gunung △ c3 101
Mandi Bahauddin a3 130
Mandi Burewala f5 128
Mandiakui d3 222
Mandiana c3 222
Mandié e2 233
Mandili ▭ e5 210
Mandimba f1 233
Mandingues, Monts ⛰ c3 222
Mandioli ▭ p5 99
Mandioré, Lagoa ○ f3 293
Mandirituba d6 290
Mandjé, Lac ○ b4 224
Mandji b4 224
Mandla g8 124
Mandleshwar g9 129
Mandø ▭ b3 158
Mandor f7 129
Mandora e6 86
Mandoro Ab2 233
Mandouri e3 223
Mandra, Grc. d4 210
Mandra, Pak. f4 128
Mandraki Ac2 211
Mandrare ≈ Ab3 233
Mandres b1 138
Mandriko Ac2 211
Mandritsara Ab2 233
Mandrosonoro Ab3 233
Mandsaur g8 129
Mandu g9 129
Mandul ▭ j3 99
Mandurah b13 87
Manduria g4 198
Mandvi d9 129
Mandya e6 126
Manek Urai c3 101
Manell Point ► C 74
Manendragarh h8 124
Maner ≈ f3 126
Manerbio e4 196
Mănești g3 201
Manětín b2 170
Manevychi p4 169
Manfalût c8 136
Manfjellet △ c2 156
Manfredonia e3 198
Manfredonia, Golfo di ◄ f3 198
Manga, Braz. d4 289
Manga d3 222
Mangabeiras, Serra das ⛰ c3 288
Mangai c4 224
Mangalagiri g4 126
Mangaldai n6 125
Mangalia j4 201
Mangalmé a5 218
Mangalore d6 126
Mangalpur d3 128
Mangalvedha d4 126
Mangamuka d1 76
Mangan j6 135
Mangapet g3 126
Mangarang f9 100
Mangaratiba f5 291
Mangareva ▭ K 75
Mangatawhiri e2 76
Mangaung g4 235
Mangaweka, N.Z. △ f3 76
Mangaweka e3 76
Mangawhai e2 76
Mangembe e4 225
Mangere Island ▭ A 77
Mangerivola, Réserve de ☆ Ab2 233
Mangfall ≈ g5 175
Manggawitu j6 97
Mangham d3 258
Mangistauskaya Oblast' [1] d5 120
Mangit h6 120
Mangkalihat, Tanjung ► k4 99
Mangla a3 130
Manglares, Punta ► b1 284
Manglaur c5 130
Mangnai n3 117
Mangochi f1 233
Mangodara d4 222
Mangoky, Toliara, Madag. ≈ Aa3 233
Mangoky, Toliara, Madag. ≈ Ab3 233
Mangole ▭ n5 99
Mangole, Selat ▭ n5 99
Mangonui d1 76
Mangoro ≈ Ab2 233
Mangotsfield d5 163
Mangral e10 129
Mangrove Cay ▭ k6 259
Mangualde c4 190
Manguari d4 284
Manguchar c6 129
Mangueigne b5 218
Mangueira, Lago ○ f2 294
Mangueirinha b6 290
Manguéni, Plateau du g4 221
Mangui g2 94
Manguinha, Pontal do ► e4 288
Mangulile d3 276
Mangunça, Ilha ▭ d2 288
Mangupung ▭ p2 99
Mangut g1 112
Mangyshlak, Poluostrov ► d6 120
Mangystau h4 149
Manhairu c5 130
Manhattan d4 260
Manhattan Beach e8 265
Manhay d4 159
Manhica k2 235
Manhuaçu, Braz. ≈ h3 291
Manhuaçu, Minas Gerais, Braz. g4 291
Manhumirim h4 291
Mani, Col. c3 284
Mani, Grc. ► c6 211
Mani g1 210
Mania ≈ Ab2 233
Maniace d7 199
Maniago g3 196
Maniamba e1 233
Manic Trois, Réservoir ⊙ h3 253
Manica, Moz. [1] e2 233
Manica e2 233
Manicaland [1] e2 233
Manicoré, Braz. ≈ e5 285
Manicoré, Amazonas, Braz. e5 285
Manicouagan ≈ h4 253
Manicouagan, Réservoir ⊙ h3 252
Maniema [1] e4 225
Manīfah m8 137
Manifold, Cape ► d3 85
Maniganggo b3 104
Manihari k7 125
Manihi ▭ K 75
Manihiki ▭ H 75
Maniitsoq u2 243
Manika, Plateau de la e5 225
Manikganj m8 125
Manila c3 100
Manila Bay ◄ c3 100
Manilaid ▭ l3 157
Manilla k11 81
Manilva e8 191
Manimbaya, Tanjung ► k5 99
Maningoza, Réserve de ☆ Aa2 233
Maningrida b2 80
Manipur, India [1] a3 102
Manipur, India ≈ a3 102
Manisa, Tur. [1] b3 208
Manisa a3 208
Manises d5 193
Manissauá Missu ≈ b4 288
Manistee, Michigan, U.S.A. ≈ d3 254
Manistee, Michigan, U.S.A. c3 254
Manistique c3 254
Manito Lake ○ n5 249
Manitoba [1] e2 250
Manitoba, Lake ○ d5 250
Manitou, Manitoba, Can. d6 250
Manitou, Québec, Can. ≈ k3 253
Manitou Islands ▭ c3 254
Manitou, Lake ○ b6 252
Manitoulin Island ▭ a6 252
Manitowaning f3 254
Manitowoc c3 254
Maniwaki j2 255
Manizales b2 284
Manjā d5 139
Manja Aa3 233
Manjacaze k2 235
Manjak Ab2 233
Manjeri e7 126
Manjhand d8 129
Manjiang p5 113
Manjil m3 137
Manjimup c14 87
Manjirenji Recreational Park ☆ e3 233
Manjo f5 223
Manjra ≈ e3 126
Mank g1 177
Mankato e2 260
Mankera e5 128
Mankim g4 223
Mankono c4 222
Mankulam g8 126
Manley Hot Springs g2 246
Manlleu g3 192
Manmad d9 124
Mann ≈ a2 80
Mann Ranges ⛰ j10 87
Mann, Mount △ j9 87
Manna b7 98
Mannahill d12 81
Mannar f8 126
Mannar, Gulf of ◄ A 127
Mannargudi f7 126
Manndalen ≈ h2 154
Manneru ≈ f5 126
Mannheim d3 174
Manning, Aust. ≈ d7 85
Manning, U.S.A. b7 250
Manning, Cape ► H 75
Mannington f6 254
Manningtree h5 163
Männlifluh △ b3 196
Mannu, Capo ► Aa2 198
Mano, Lib. ≈ b4 222
Mano b4 222
Mano River b4 222
Manoa d1 292
Manoharpur c6 130
Manokotak e4 246
Manokwari j6 97
Manol ≈ g2 192
Manombo ≈ Ab2 233
Manombo Atsimo Aa3 233
Manombo, Réserve de ☆ Ab3 233
Manomet k3 257
Manompana Ab2 233
Manong b3 101
Manongarivo, Réserve de ☆ Ab1 233
Manono e5 225
Manoppello d2 198
Manor, Can. b6 250
Manor, U.S.A. a4 258
Manorbier b5 163
Manorhamilton c2 165
Manoron d10 103
Manosque b7 185
Manouane, Québec, Can. ≈ g4 252
Manouane, Québec, Can. j2 255
Manouane, Lac ○ g3 252
Manp'o p5 113
Manpur g9 129
Manra ▭ H 75
Manresa f3 192
Mansa, India f9 129
Mansa, India b5 130
Mansa, Zam. e6 225
Mansa Konko a3 222
Mansabá a3 222
Mansalay Bay ◄ c4 100
Manschnow k3 173
Mansehra f3 128
Mansel Island ▭ n3 243
Mansfield, Aust. h14 81
Mansfield, U.K. e3 162
Mansfield, Arkansas, U.S.A. b2 258
Mansfield, Georgia, U.S.A. h3 259
Mansfield, Louisiana, U.S.A. c3 258
Mansfield, Missouri, U.S.A. c1 258
Mansfield, Ohio, U.S.A. e5 254
Mansfield, Pennsylvania, U.S.A. c3 256
Mansfield, Texas, U.S.A. a3 258
Mansfield Woodhouse e3 162
Manshīyat Banī Ḩasan e4 139
Mansidão d4 288
Mansilla b2 192
Mansilla de las Mulas e2 190
Mansle c3 186
Mansôa, Gui.-B. ≈ a3 222
Mansôa a3 222
Manson c2 262
Manson Creek e4 248
Mansoura d3 138
Mansuela h6 97
Mansura c4 258
Mansurlu e4 208
Manta a4 284
Mantalingajan, Mount △ a6 100
Mantamados g3 210
Mantantale d4 224
Mantaro ≈ b2 292
Mantasoa, Farihy ○ Ab2 233
Manteca b4 264
Mantecal d2 284
Manteigas c4 190
Mantena h3 291
Manteo m2 259
Mantes-la-Jolie g4 183

356 Mantet, Réserve Naturelle de → Maswe Game Reserve

Mantet, Réserve Naturelle de ☆ e6 187
Manthani f3 126
Manthelan f5 183
Manti h6 262
Mantin b4 101
Mantiqueira, Serra da f5 291
Manto d3 276
Manton d3 254
Mantos Blancos c4 292
Mantoudi d4 210
Mantova, Italy e4 196
Mantova e4 196
Mäntsälä l2 157
Mänttä l1 157
Mantuan Downs h8 80
Manturovo h2 151
Mäntyharju m2 157
Mäntyjärvi l3 155
Mäntyluoto j2 157
Manú c2 292
Manú, Parque Nacional ★ c2 292
Manua Islands M 75
Manuae K 75
Manuel e2 275
Manuel Alves c4 288
Manuel Alves Grande c3 288
Manuel Correia e2 293
Manuel J. Cobo j3 297
Manuel M. Diéguez c4 274
Manuel Ocampo g2 297
Manuel Ribas c6 290
Manuel Rodríguez, Isla b6 295
Manuel Urbano d1 292
Manuel Vitorino d4 289
Manuelzinho b3 288
Manuhangi K 75
Manui m6 99
Manūjān r8 137
Manuk Manka c8 100
Manukan d6 100
Manukau e2 76
Manukau Harbour ◄ e2 76
Manunda a1 82
Manupari d2 292
Manurimi d2 292
Manuripe d2 292
Manuripi d2 292
Manurú f4 285
Manutuke f3 76
Manvel e6 250
Manvi e5 126
Manville, New Jersey, U.S.A. f4 256
Manville, Rhode Island, U.S.A. j3 257
Many c4 258
Many Island Lake ○ n6 249
Many Peaks, Mount △ d14 87
Manyame e2 233
Manyana f2 235
Manyara, Lake ○ g4 225
Manyč-Gudilo, Ozero ○ f3 149
Manyeleti Game Reserve ☆ j2 235
Manyoni a5 227
Manzai e4 128
Manzanal, Puerto del d2 190
Manzanares a5 193
Manzanares el Real g4 190
Manzanera d4 193
Manzanilla Point ► E 271
Manzanillo, Cuba f4 266
Manzanillo, Mex. b4 274
Manzano d3 274
Manzanza e5 225
Manzariyeh n4 137
Manzat e3 186
Manzhouli j1 113
Manziana g7 197
Manzini j3 235
Mao, Chad h3 223
Mao, Dom. Rep. j5 271
Maoba a4 106
Maocifan c4 106
Maodianzi n5 113
Maoji c3 106
Maojiachuan d7 112
Maoke, Pegunungan k6 97
Maokeng g3 235
Maolin f4 111
Maomao Shan △ b7 112
Maoming h8 104
Maoniushan q1 125
Maosipu c5 106
Maotanchang e4 106
Maotou Shan △ c6 104
Mapai j1 235
Mapam Yumco ○ e4 130
Mapane l5 99
Mapanza d2 232
Mapastepec a3 276
Mapi k7 97
Mapia, Kepulauan j5 97
Mapimí h5 272
Mapin b7 100
Mapinhane l1 235
Mapire e2 285
Mapireme g3 285
Mapiri, Bol. d2 292
Mapiri, La Paz, Bol. d3 292
Mapirpán c3 284
Maple, Iowa, U.S.A. e3 260
Maple, North Dakota, U.S.A. d2 260
Maple Creek n7 249
Mapoon e1 80
Mapoon Aboriginal Reserve ♦ f2 80
Mapor c4 98
Mapoteng g4 235
Mapuca c5 126
Mapuera f4 285
Mapulanguene k2 235
Mapumulo j4 235
Mapunda d5 224
Mapungubwe Cultural Landscape ♦ h1 235
Maputo, Moz. k2 235
Maputo, Moz. k3 235
Maputo k2 235
Maputo, Baía de ◄ k3 235
Maqar an Na'am h5 136
Maqên Kangri △ b1 104
Maqnā e7 136
Maqteïr b4 220
Maquan He f4 135
Maqueda b4 190
Maqueda Channel e4 100
Maquela do Zombo c5 224
Maquinchao c4 294
Maquinista Levet d2 296
Maquoketa, Iowa, U.S.A. f3 260
Maquoketa, Iowa, U.S.A. a4 254
Mār c2 156
Mar, Pak. b8 129
Mar b3 190
Mar Chiquita j4 297
Mar Chiquita, Lago ○ d2 294
Mar de Ajó j4 297
Mar del Plata j4 297
Mar Menor ◄ d7 193
Mar Muerto, Laguna, Mex. ○ g5 275
Mar Muerto, Laguna, Mex. ○ g5 275
Mar, Serra do, Braz. f5 291
Mar, Serra do, Braz. g5 291
Mar''ina Horka, Minskaya Voblasts', Bela. c1 148
Mar''ina Horka, Minskaya Voblasts', Bela. c1 148
Mara, Guy. f2 285
Mara, India p5 125
Mara, India h8 124
Mara, R.S.A. h1 235
Mara, Tan. f4 225
Mara Rosa c4 288
Maraã d4 284
Marabá c3 288
Marabahan h6 99
Marabatua j7 99
Marabitanas d3 284
Maracá, Ilha de b1 288
Maracaí c5 290
Maracaibo c1 284
Maracaibo, Lago de ○ c2 284
Maracaju a4 290
Maracaju, Serra de a4 290
Maracanã c2 288
Maracanaquará, Planalto b2 288
Maracás d4 288
Maracay d1 284
Marachkova n5 157
Marādah a2 218
Maradi, Niger f3 223
Maradi f3 223
Maradin d4 128
Maragateria ♦ d2 190
Marāgheh l3 137
Maragogi e3 288
Maragondon c3 100
Marah k9 137
Marahoué c4 222
Marahra d6 130
Marahuaca, Cerro △ d3 284
Marais des Cygnes e4 260
Marais Poitevin, Val de Sèvre et Vendée, Parc Naturel Régional du ☆ b2 186
Marajó, Baía de ◄ c2 288
Marajó, Ilha de c2 288
Marakei H 75
Marakele National Park ☆ g2 235
Maralal b3 226
Maralal National Sanctuary ☆ b3 226
Maraldy r1 121
Maraldy, Ozero ○ r1 121
Marali c2 224
Maralinga k12 87
Marambio (Arg.) ▪ mm1 298
Marampit p2 99
Maramureș f2 201
Maran, Malay. c4 101
Maran, Pak. △ b6 129
Marana h9 263
Maranchón b3 192
Marand k2 137
Maranello e5 196
Marang, Malay. c3 101
Marang, Myan. d10 103
Maranguape e2 288
Maranhão, Braz. c3 288
Maranhão, Braz. c5 289
Maranhão, Barragem do c5 191
Marano di Napoli d4 198
Marano, Laguna di ○ h4 196
Maranoa c5 85
Marañón b4 284
Marans b2 186
Maraoué, Parc National de la ☆ c4 222
Marapanim c2 288
Marape f2 293
Marari d5 284
Marasende k7 99
Mărășești h3 201
Mărașu h3 201
Maratea e5 198
Marateca b5 191
Marathia, Akra ► e2 211
Marathokampos Ab1 210
Marathon, Can. k6 251
Marathon, New York, U.S.A. d2 256
Marathon, Texas, U.S.A. h2 272
Marathon, Wisconsin, U.S.A. b3 254
Marathonas d4 210
Maratua k3 99
Maraú e4 289
Marauá d4 284
Marauiá d3 285
Maravatio d4 274
Marawi e6 100
Marāyā f4 219
Maraye-en-Othe j4 183
Marayes d1 296
Mārāzā h4 149
Marazion a6 163
Marbach b3 196
Marbach am Neckar e4 174
Marbella f8 191
Marble Bar d7 86
Marble Canyon h7 263
Marble Hall h2 235
Marblehead k2 257
Marbul Pass b3 130
Marburg j5 235
Marburg an der Lahn d2 174
Marca b2 292
Marca, Ponta do ► a2 232
Marcala c3 276
Marcali f5 170
Marcapata c2 292
Marcaria e4 196
Marcelino d4 284
Marcellus d4 254
March g4 163
Marcha e4 163
Marchamalo a4 192
Marchant Hill △ a1 82
Marchaux c3 184
Marche, Fr. ♦ d2 186
Marche, Italy c1 198
Marche, Plateaux de la d2 186
Marche-en-Famenne d4 159
Marchegg h1 177
Marchena e7 191
Marchena, Isla A 286
Marchenoir g5 183
Marcheprime b4 186
Marchihue b3 296
Marchinbar Island c1 80
Marchtrenk f1 177
Marciac c5 187
Marciana e7 197
Marcigny a4 184
Marcillac-la-Croisille e3 186
Marcillat-en-Combraille e2 186
Marcilly-le-Hayer j4 183
Marcinkonys n1 169
Marck g2 183
Marckolsheim d2 184
Marco de Canaveses b3 190
Marcona b3 292
Marcopeet Islands p2 251
Marcos Juárez f2 297
Marcos Paz h3 297
Marcq-en-Barœul b4 159
Marcus Baker △ h3 247
Marcy, Mount △ k3 255
Mardan f3 128
Mardiān c2 128
Mardie b7 86
Mardin h4 209
Mardın h4 209
Mardzad b3 112
Mare a5 185
Maré F 74
Mare de Déu del Toro △ A 193
Marebbe f3 196
Marechal Cândido Rondon a6 290
Maree, Loch ○ c2 164
Mareeba g4 80
Maremma ♦ f7 197
Maremma, Parco Naturale della ☆ f7 197
Marennes a3 186
Maret Islands g4 86
Marettimo b7 199
Marettimo, Isola b7 199
Mareuil c3 186
Mareuil-sur-Arnon e2 186
Mareuil-sur-Lay-Dissais d6 182
Marevo b3 150
Marey-sur-Tille b3 184
Marfa g2 272
Margam Ri g3 135
Margaree Harbour m5 253
Margaret, South Australia, Aust. c10 81
Margaret, Western Australia, Aust. h6 86
Margaret Lake ○ k2 249
Margaret River b13 87
Margaretville f2 256
Margarita d1 294
Margarita, Isla de e1 285
Margate, R.S.A. j5 235
Margate, U.K. h5 163
Margate City f5 256
Mărgău l5 171
Margecany j3 171
Margeride, Monts de la f4 186
Margherita p6 125
Margherita di Savoia f3 198
Margherita Peak △ e3 225
Marghita l4 171
Margilan n7 121
Margina l6 171
Marginea g2 201
Margo, Dasht-i a5 128
Margonin f3 168
Margosatubig d7 100
Marguerittes a7 185
Margut d5 159
Margyang k5 135
Marha m3 119
Marḥab e4 139
Marhaj Khalil l5 137
Marhañ k2 171
Marhanets' f3 148
Marhinote k1 297
Marhoum d2 220
Mari, Cyp. b2 138
Mari, P.N.G. l7 97
Maria, Fr. Poly. K 75
Maria, Fr. Poly. K 75
María b7 193
María Cleofas, Isla a3 274
Maria Elena d4 292
Maria Grande h4 297
Maria Island, Northern Territory, Aust. b3 80
Maria Island, Tasmania, Aust. Ac3 83
Maria Lankowitz g2 177
Maria Lombardo de Casso g5 275
Maria Luggau d3 176
Maria Luisa g1 297
Maria Magdalena, Isla a3 274
Maria National Park ☆ Ab3 83
Maria Saal f3 177
María Teresa g3 297
Maria van Diemen, Cape ► d1 76
Mariager c2 158
Mariager Fjord d2 158
Mariala National Park ☆ a4 84
Marialva c4 190
Marian j6 80
Mariana g4 291
Mariana Trench h5 300
Mariani p6 125
Marianna g4 259
Mariannelund f4 156
Mariano Loza e1 294
Mariano Moreno b5 296
Mariano Unzué g4 297
Mariánské Lázně a2 170
Mariapiri, Mesa de d3 284
Mariápolis c4 290
Marias c1 262
Mariato, Punta ► g7 277
Mariazell g2 177
Maribo e4 158
Maribor g3 177
Maricá g5 291
Maricopa, Arizona, U.S.A. g9 263
Maricopa, California, U.S.A. d6 265
Maricunga, Salar de d5 292
Maridi, Sudan e2 225
Maridi e3 225
Marié d4 284
Marie Byrd Land ♦ ff2 298
Mariec k3 151
Mariefred g3 156
Marie-Galante C 271
Mariehamn h2 157
Mariembero d4 288
Marienbourg c4 159
Marienberg j2 175
Marienhafe f1 159
Mariental b2 234
Marienville a3 256
Mariestad e3 156
Marieta d2 284
Marietta, Georgia, U.S.A. g3 259
Marietta, Ohio, U.S.A. f6 254
Marietta, Oklahoma, U.S.A. a3 258
Mariga f3 223
Marigliano d4 198
Marignane b7 185
Marigny d3 182
Marigot, Dom. p7 271
Marigot, Guad. C 271
Mariinsk j4 118
Mariinskij Posad j3 151
Mariinskoe h1 120
Marij El, Respublika k3 151
Marijampolė m1 169
Marikostinovo d1 210
Marília d5 290
Marillana d8 86
Mariluz b6 290
Marimba c5 224
Marín, Mex. j5 273
Marín b2 190
Marina b5 264
Marina di Camerota e4 198
Marina di Campo e7 197
Marina di Castagneto Donoratico e6 197
Marina di Ginosa f4 198
Marina di Gioiosa Ionica f6 199
Marina di Grosseto e7 197
Marina di Leuca c3 199
Marina di Novaglie c3 199
Marina di Pulsano g4 198
Marina di Ragusa d8 199
Marina di Ravenna g5 196
Marina Romea g5 196
Marinduque c4 100
Marine City e4 254
Marinella b7 199
Marineo c7 199
Marinette c3 254
Maringá c5 290
Maringa d3 224
Maringué e2 233
Maringues f3 186
Marinha das Ondas b4 190
Marinha Grande b5 191
Marinhas b3 190
Marinjab n4 137
Marion, Alabama, U.S.A. f3 258
Marion, Indiana, U.S.A. d5 254
Marion, Kentucky, U.S.A. e1 258
Marion, Mississippi, U.S.A. e3 258
Marion, North Carolina, U.S.A. h2 259
Marion, Ohio, U.S.A. e5 254
Marion, South Carolina, U.S.A. k2 259
Marion Downs d7 80
Marion Junction f3 258
Marion Lake ○ d4 260
Marion Reef l5 80
Marion, Lake ○ j3 259
Marionville c1 258
Mariovo ♦ b1 210
Maripasoula g3 285
Mariposa, California, U.S.A. c4 264
Mariposa, California, U.S.A. d4 264
Mariquita c2 284
Marisa l4 99
Mariscal Estigarribia e4 293
Mariscala e5 275
Mărișelu g2 201
Marite j2 235
Maritime Alps c6 185
Maritsa, Bul. g4 201
Maritsa Ad2 211
Mariupol' e3 148
Mariusa, Isla e2 285
Marivān l4 137
Marjaliza g5 191
Märjamaa l3 157
Marjayoûn d3 138
Mark c3 159
Mark Twain Lake ○ f4 260
Märkä e5 139
Markā h5 139
Marka c3 226
Markaba d3 138
Markakol', Ozero ○ w3 121
Markala c3 222
Markam b4 104
Markapur f5 126
Markaryd e4 156
Markazī m4 137
Markdorf e5 174
Markelsdorfer Huk ► g1 173
Marken d2 159
Markermeer SE d2 159
Market Deeping f4 162
Market Drayton d4 162
Market Harborough f4 163
Market Rasen f3 162
Market Warsop e3 162
Market Weighton f3 162
Markgraben g3 173
Markham, Mount △ x3 298
Markhamet p7 121
Marki k3 169
Markinch e3 164
Märkisch Buchholz j3 173
Markit r8 121
Markitta h3 154
Markkleeberg j1 175
Markleeville d3 264
Markleysburg a5 256
Marklohe e3 172
Markneukirchen h2 175
Markog Qu c2 104
Markopoulo d5 211
Markounda c2 224
Markovac Našički k4 177
Markovo, Ivanovskaja Oblast', Russ. Fed. f3 150
Markovo, Krasnojarskij Kraj, Russ. Fed. j3 118
Markoye e3 223
Marks g2 149
Marks, U.S.A. d2 258
Marksuhl f2 174
Marksville c4 258
Markt Bibart f3 174
Markt Erlbach f3 175
Markt Sankt Florian f1 177
Markt Sankt Martin h2 177
Marktheidenfeld e3 174
Marktleugast g2 175
Marktoberdorf f5 175
Marktrodach f2 175
Marl f3 159
Marlboro g3 257
Marlborough, Aust. j7 80
Marlborough, N.Z. d4 77
Marlborough, U.K. e5 163
Marlborough, Massachusetts, U.S.A. j2 257
Marlborough, New Hampshire, U.S.A. h2 257
Marle b5 159
Marlenheim d2 184
Marlera, Rt ► f5 177
Marlieux b4 184
Marlin a4 258
Marlinton f6 254
Marlo j14 81
Marlow f4 158
Marlow, U.S.A. a2 258
Marly b4 159
Marmaduke d1 258
Marmagao c5 126
Marmagne b4 184
Marmande c4 186
Marmara c4 210
Marmara Denizi ◄ b2 208
Marmara Gölü ○ b3 208
Marmaraereğlisi h5 201
Marmari e4 210
Marmaris b4 208
Marmaro g4 210
Marmarth c2 260
Marmelos e5 285
Marmen ○ g2 156
Marmet f6 254
Marmion Lake ○ h6 250
Marmion, Lake ○ e11 87
Mármol a2 274
Marmolada △ f3 196
Marmolejo f6 191
Marmot Bay ◄ f4 246
Marmoutier d2 184
Marnay b3 184
Marnaz c4 184
Marne, Fr. j4 183
Marne, Fr. k3 183
Marne c5 158
Marne à la Saône, Canal de la b3 184
Marne au Rhin, Canal de la c2 184
Marne-la-Vallée h4 183
Marneuli g4 149
Maro c2 224
Maroantsetra Ab2 233
Marofandilia Aa3 233
Marokau K 75
Marokopa e3 76
Marol, Jam.Kash. c2 130
Marol, Pak. f6 129
Marolambo Ab3 233
Maroldsweisach f2 175
Maromandia Ac2 233
Maromica k2 151
Maromme g3 183
Maromokotro △ Ab1 233
Marondera e2 233
Maroni f3 285
Maronne e3 186
Maroochydore l9 81
Maroon Peak △ b4 260
Maroona c3 82
Maros, Hung. j5 170
Maros k7 99
Maroseranana Ab2 233
Maroslele j5 171
Marostica, Veneto, Italy f4 196
Marostica, Veneto, Italy f4 196
Marostica, Veneto, Italy f4 196
Marot b6 130
Marotandrano Ab2 233
Marotiri K 75
Marotolana Ab1 233
Maroua g3 223
Marouini f3 285
Marova e4 285
Marovato, Antsirañana, Madag. Ab1 233
Marovato, Toliara, Madag. Ab4 233
Marovoay Ab2 233
Marowali l5 99
Marowijne, Sur. g2 285
Marowijne, Sur. g2 285
Marpingen f5 159
Marpissa f5 211
Marqādah h5 209
Marquard g4 235
Marquelia e5 275
Marquês de Valença g5 291
Marquesas Fracture Zone p6 301
Marquette k7 251
Marquez a4 258
Marquinho b6 290
Marquion b4 159
Marquis, Cap ► J 271
Marquise g2 183
Marquises, Îles K 75
Marra b7 85
Marra Marra National Park ☆ g1 83
Marra Plateau b5 218
Marra, Jebel △ b5 218
Marracuene k2 235
Marradi f5 197
Marrāk f4 219
Marrakech c2 220
Marrangua, Lagoa ○ l2 235
Marrawah Aa2 83
Marrecas, Serra das d3 288
Marree d10 81
Marrero d5 258
Marromeu f2 233
Marromeu, Reserva de ☆ f2 233
Marrupa b6 227
Mars e3 186
Mars Hill, Maine, U.S.A. j5 253
Mars Hill, North Carolina, U.S.A. h2 259
Marsa al Burayqah a1 218
Marsa Alam e9 136
Marsa 'Igli e9 136
Marsa Matrūḥ c1 218
Marsa Tundaba e9 136
Marsabit b3 226
Marsabit National Reserve ☆ b3 226
Marsac-en-Livradois f3 186
Marsaglia d5 196
Marsala b7 199
Marsanne a6 185
Marsassoum a3 222
Marsberg d4 172
Marsciano g7 197
Marsden h12 81
Marsden Point e1 76
Marsdiep c2 159
Marseillan f5 187
Marseille b7 185
Marseille-en-Beauvaisis g3 183
Marsella d2 292
Marsfjället △ e4 154
Marsh Harbour l6 259
Marsh Island d5 258
Marsh Lake ○ l3 247
Marsh Point ► g2 250
Marshall, Aust. c7 80
Marshall, Lib. b4 222
Marshall, Alaska, U.S.A. d3 246
Marshall, California, U.S.A. a3 264
Marshall, Minnesota, U.S.A. e2 260
Marshall, Missouri, U.S.A. e4 260
Marshall, Texas, U.S.A. b3 258
Marshall, Virginia, U.S.A. c6 256
Marshall Bay ◄ Ab1 83
Marshall Islands g1 73

MARSHALL ISLANDS

THE REPUBLIC OF THE MARSHALL ISLANDS
Area 180km² (70sq miles)
Capital Delap-Uliga-Djarrit
Organizations SPC, PIF
Population 57,000
Pop. growth (%) 3
Life expectancy 64 (m); 68 (f)
Languages English, Marshallese, Japanese
Literacy 91%
Currency US dollar
GDP (US million $) 91
GDP per head ($US) 1596

Marshalls Creek e3 256
Marshalltown e3 260
Marshfield, Missouri, U.S.A. c1 258
Marshfield, Wisconsin, U.S.A. a3 254
Marshūn m3 137
Marsico Nuovo e4 198
Marsjaty k3 147
Marson a2 184
Märsta g3 157
Marstal d4 158
Marstal Bugt ◄ d4 158
Marston e5 163
Marstrand d4 156
Marsyangdi g5 135
Marta f7 197
Martaban c7 102
Martaban, Gulf of ◄ c7 102
Martanai Besar j1 99
Martano c2 198
Martano, Monte △ b2 198
Martap g4 223
Martapura, Kalimantan Selatan, Indon. h6 99
Martapura, Sumatera Selatan, Indon. c7 98
Marte g3 223
Marte R. Gómez, Presa j4 273
Martel d4 186
Martelange d5 159
Martellago g4 196
Mártély j5 171
Martfeld e3 172
Martfű j4 171
Martha's Vineyard k3 257
Marthon c3 186
Martí f4 266
Martigné-Briand e5 182
Martigné-Ferchaud d5 182
Martigné-sur-Mayenne e4 182
Martigny b3 196
Martigny-les-Bains b2 184
Martim Longo c7 191
Martin g2 171
Martin d3 192
Martin, Michigan, U.S.A. d4 254
Martin, North Dakota, U.S.A. c7 250
Martin, South Dakota, U.S.A. c3 260
Martin Chico h3 297
Martin Colman h4 297
Martín de Loyola d3 296
Martín de Yeltes d4 190
Martín del Río d4 192
Martín García, Isla h3 297
Martín Gonzalo, Embalse de ⊙ f6 191
Martín Muñoz de las Posadas f3 190
Martin Peninsula ► ff2 298
Martin Point ► j1 247
Martin, Lake ○ g3 259
Martina Franca g4 198
Martinborough e4 77
Martinet f2 192
Martinez f3 275
Martinez, California, U.S.A. a3 264
Martinez, Georgia, U.S.A. h3 259
Martinganga b5 191
Martinho Campos f3 291
Martinique (France) h6 241
Martinique Passage p7 271
Martinniemi k4 155
Martino d4 210
Martinópolis c5 290
Martins Ferry f5 254
Martinsburg, Pennsylvania, U.S.A. b4 256
Martinsburg, West Virginia, U.S.A. c5 256
Martinsville, Illinois, U.S.A. c6 254
Martinsville, Indiana, U.S.A. c6 254
Martinsville, Virginia, U.S.A. g7 254
Martis Aa2 198
Martonvásár g4 171
Martorell f3 192
Martos g7 191
Martre, Lac la ○ f3 242
Martres-Tolosane d5 187
Martti m3 155
Martuk k2 149
Martuni g4 149
Maruchak a3 128
Marudi h2 99
Marudu, Teluk ◄ j1 99
Maruf c5 128
Marugame e4 114
Maruia d5 77
Maruim e4 288
Marukhis Ugheltekhili △ f4 148
Maruko h3 115
Marulan f2 83
Marull f1 297
Marūn m6 137
Maruoka g3 115
Marusthali MR ♦ f7 129
Marutea, Fr. Poly. K 75
Marutea, Fr. Poly. K 75
Maruwa Hills f2 225
Marv Dasht p7 137
Marvão c5 191
Marvast q6 137
Marvata c4 274
Marvejols f4 186
Marvell d2 258
Marville d5 159
Marvine, Mount △ h6 263
Marwar Junction f8 129
Mary, Northern Territory, Aust. k3 86
Mary, Queensland, Aust. e5 84
Mary, Aust. h6 86
Mary, Turk. h9 120
Mary Kathleen e6 80
Mary, Puy △ e3 186
Mary's Harbour q2 253
Maryborough, Queensland, Aust. l8 81
Maryborough, Victoria, Aust. f14 81
Marydale e4 234
Maryfield c6 250
Maryland d6 256
Marypark e2 164
Maryport e5 164
Marys Igloo c2 246
Marystown q5 253
Marysvale g6 263
Marysville, Can. j6 253
Marysville, California, U.S.A. b2 264
Marysville, Kansas, U.S.A. d4 260
Marysville, Ohio, U.S.A. e5 254
Marysville, Pennsylvania, U.S.A. d4 256
Marysville, Washington, U.S.A. b1 262
Maryvale A 84
Maryville, Missouri, U.S.A. e3 260
Maryville, Tennessee, U.S.A. h2 259
Maryyskaya Oblast' j9 120
Marzabotto f5 197
Marzagão d2 290
Marzahna h3 173
Marzahne h3 173
Marzamemi e8 199
Marzo, Cabo ► b2 284
Mas de las Matas d4 192
Masachapa d5 276
Masada ★ d5 139
Mas'adah d3 138
Masagua b3 276
Masai c5 101
Masai Mara National Reserve ☆ b4 226
Masai Steppe g4 225
Masaka f4 225
Masalembu Besar h7 99
Masalembu Kecil h7 99
Masallı m2 137
Masamba, Indon. △ l6 99
Masamba l6 99
Masan q8 113
Masāqif f4 219
Masari, Cyp. b1 138
Masari, Grc. Ad2 211
Masasi b6 227
Masatepe d5 276
Masavi e3 293
Masaya, Nic. e4 276
Masaya, Nic. d5 276
Masaya, Volcán △ d5 276
Masbate, Phil. d4 100
Masbate d4 100
Mascalucia e7 199
Mascara e1 221
Mascarene Basin b6 300
Mascareños f3 275
Mascasin d1 296
Mascota b3 274
Mascote j1 291
Masegoso de Tajuña b4 192
Masela h7 97
Maseno a3 226
Masepe m6 99
Maseru g4 235
Masevaux c3 184
Mash'abbé Sade c5 139
Mashābih e2 219
Mashai h4 235
Masham e2 162
Mashan g7 104
Mashang e1 111
Mashava e3 233
Mash'en c5 139
Masherbrum △ c2 130
Mashhad g9 120
Mashike Ab2 114
Mashket a1 129
Mashki Chah a6 129
Mashonaland Central e2 233
Mashonaland East e2 233
Mashonaland West d2 233
Masi j2 155
Masiáca e4 272
Masibambane g5 235
Masilo g4 235
Masi-Manimba c4 224
Masindi f3 225
Masinga Reservoir ⊙ b4 226
Masinloc b3 100
Masis k2 209
Masisea c1 292
Masisi e4 225
Masjed Soleymān m6 137
Masjid Tanah c4 101
Mask, Lough ○ b3 165
Maskail c2 276
Maskan, Raas ► c1 226
Maskanah g4 209
Masku k2 157
Masljanskij m5 147
Masloc k5 171
Maslti b6 129
Masma c1 190
Masoala, Tanjona ► Ac2 233
Masoarivo Aa2 233
Masohi h6 97
Masoller k1 297
Mason, Michigan, U.S.A. d4 254
Mason, Texas, U.S.A. d6 261
Mason Bay ◄ a7 77
Mason City e3 260
Masoni n5 99
Masonville e2 256
Maspalomas Ad3 189
Masqat f6 116
Massa e5 197
Massa Lubrense d4 198
Massa Marittimo e6 197
Massa Martana g7 197
Massa-Carrara d5 196
Massachusetts h2 257
Massaciuccoli, Lago di ○ e4 176
Massafra g4 198
Massaguet h3 223
Massakory h3 223
Massamagrell d5 193
Massambará e1 294
Massan e4 128
Massana b4 224
Massangena e3 233
Massango c5 224
Massangulo f1 233
Massaroca d3 288
Massarosa e6 197
Massat d6 187
Massava k3 147
Massawa e4 219
Massay g5 183
Massena j3 255
Massenya h3 223
Masset a4 248
Masset Inlet ◄ a5 248
Masseube c5 187
Massiac f3 186
Massiaru l4 157
Massibi d6 224
Massigui c3 222
Massillon f5 254
Massina c3 222
Massinga l1 235
Massingir k1 235
Massingir, Barragem de k1 235
Massintonto j2 235
Masson Island q1 298
Massu'a d4 139
Mastallone, Parco Naturale ☆ c4 196
Masterton e4 76
Mastic Point k7 259
Mastichari Ac2 211
Masticho, Akra ► f4 210
Mastuj f2 128
Mastung c6 129
Masty n2 169
Masua Aa3 198
Masuika d5 225
Masuleh m3 137
Māsvik g2 154
Masvingo, Zimb. e3 233
Masvingo e3 233
Maswe a4 231
Maswe Game Reserve ☆ f4 225

Maşyāf → Mendez-Nunez 357

Maşyāf e1 138
Masyevichy m4 169
Maszewo d2 168
Mat c6 130
Mata Amarilla b5 295
Mata Bia, Gunung △ p9 99
Mata Grande e3 288
Mata Negra e2 285
Matā'utu L 75
Matā'utu, Baie de ◄ L 75
Matabaan d2 226
Matabeleland North ⊡ d2 233
Matabeleland South ⊡ d3 233
Matachel ≈ e6 191
Matachic f3 272
Matacuni ≈ e3 285
Matadi b5 224
Matagalpa, Nic. ⊡ e4 276
Matagalpa, Nic. e4 276
Matagami d4 252
Matagami, Lac ○ q6 251
Matagorda b5 258
Matagorda Island ▭ a5 258
Mataiva ▭ K 75
Matak, Indon. ▭ d3 98
Matak q3 121
Matakana, Aust. g12 81
Matakana, N.Z. e2 76
Matala, Ang. b1 232
Matala, Grc. e8 211
Matala', Pointe ► L 75
Matalascañas d7 191
Matale g9 126
Matalebreras b3 192
Matallana, Embalse de ⊙ a3 192
Matam b2 222
Matamata e2 76
Matamey f3 223
Matamoras f3 256
Matamoros, Campeche, Mex. b1 276
Matamoros, Chihuahua, Mex. g4 272
Matamoros, Coahuila, Mex. h5 272
Matamoros, Oaxaca, Mex. g5 275
Matamoros, Tamaulipas, Mex. a7 258
Matana, Danau ○ l6 99
Matanal Point ► c8 100
Matanayet ech Choumar d3 138
Matancilla b1 296
Matandu ≈ g5 225
Matane j4 253
Matang g3 111
Matanui e4 128
Matanzas d3 266
Matanzilla, Pampa de la — c4 296
Matão d4 290
Matão, Serra do ▣ b3 288
Mataojo j1 297
Matapalo, Cabo ► f6 277
Matapédia j5 253
Matapédia, Lac ○ j4 253
Mataporquera f2 190
Matapozuelos f3 190
Matapu, Pointe ► L 75
Mataquescuintla b3 276
Mataquito ≈ b3 296
Matará d1 294
Matara g10 126
Mataragka b4 210
Mataram j9 99
Mataranka a3 80
Matarape, Teluk ◄ m6 99
Matarinao Bay ◄ e5 100
Mataró g3 192
Matarombea ≈ l6 99
Matarraña ≈ e3 192
Matas Blancas Ae2 189
Matasiri ▭ h7 99
Matatiele h5 235
Mataura, N.Z. ≈ b7 77
Mataura b7 77
Mataveni ≈ d3 284
Matawai f3 76
Matawaia d1 76
Matawin ≈ f5 252
Matay s5 121
Maṯbakh, Ra's al ► h2 219
Mategua e2 293
Matehuala d2 274
Matelândia b6 290
Matelica h6 197
Matemanga b6 227
Matera, Italy ⊡ f4 198
Matera f4 198
Mátészalka l4 171
Matetsi d2 232
Mateur f1 221
Mateus Leme f3 291
Matha b3 186
Mathaji e7 129
Mathay c3 184
Matheson f1 254
Matheson Island e5 250
Mathias b6 256
Mathis a5 258
Mathoura d2 82
Mathura c6 130
Mati f7 100
Matia ≈ b4 226
Matiacoali e3 223
Matian c1 106
Matiari d8 129
Matias Barbosa g4 291
Matias Cardoso d4 289
Matias Romero g5 275
Matignon c4 182
Matina f5 277
Matinenda Lake ○ m7 251
Matinhos d6 290
Matino h4 198
Matjiesfontein d6 234
Matlabas, R.S.A. ≈ g1 235
Matlabas g2 235
Matli d8 129
Matlock e3 162
Matmata g2 221
Mato ≈ d1 285
Mato Grosso, Braz. ⊡ b4 288
Mato Grosso, Mato Grosso, Braz. f3 293
Mato Grosso do Sul ⊡ b4 290
Mato Verde g1 291
Mato, Cerro △ d2 284
Matobo National Park ☆ d3 233
Matogrossense, Pantanal — f3 293
Matola k2 235
Matos ≈ d2 292
Matosinhos b3 190
Matou, Hebei, China d1 106
Matou, Hebei, China e1 111
Matou, Jiangxi, China d5 106
Matou, Shandong, China f2 111
Matouji d2 106
Matour a4 184
Matozinhos f3 291
Mātra △ h4 171
Maṭraḥ f6 116
Mátramindszent h4 171
Mátraszele h3 171
Matrei am Brenner c2 176
Matroosberg △ c6 234
Matru b4 222
Matsap e4 234
Matsena g3 223
Matsiatra ≈ Ab3 233
Matsu Tao ▭ n5 105
Matsue e4 114
Matsumae Ab3 114
Matsumoto g3 115
Matsusaka g4 115
Matsuyama e5 114
Mattagami ≈ n6 251
Mattaldi e3 297
Mattamuskeet, Lake ○ l2 259
Mattawa g2 254
Mattawamkeag h6 253
Matterhorn, Italy △ b4 196
Matterhorn, U.S.A. △ f5 262
Mattersburg h2 177
Matthew Town h4 266
Matthews Peak △ b3 226
Matthews Ridge e2 285
Mattice m6 251
Mattig ≈ e1 176
Mattighofen e1 176
Mattinata f3 198
Mattituck h4 257
Mattō g3 115
Mattoon b6 254
Matu f3 98
Matucana b2 292
Matugama g9 126
Matuku ▭ E 74
Matumbo b1 232
Ma'tuq d5 218
Matureivavoa ▭ K 75
Maturín e2 285
Maturuca e3 285
Matusadona National Park ☆ d2 233
Matute △ b3 192
Matutuang ▭ n2 99
Matveev Kurgan e3 148
Matveev, Ostrov ▭ j1 147
Matveevo g2 151
Matwabeng g4 235
Matxitxako, Cabo ► b1 192
Mau Aimma g7 124
Mau Rampur f7 124
Maúa b6 227
Maubeuge b4 159
Maubin b7 102
Maubourguet c5 187
Mauchline d4 164
Maud b3 258
Maud, Point ► a8 87
Maudaha g7 124
Maude d2 82
Mauern f1 175
Maués, Braz. ≈ f4 285
Maués, Amazonas, Braz. f4 285
Maug Islands ▭ A 74
Mauganj g7 124
Maughold b2 162
Mauguio, Languedoc-Roussillon, Fr. a7 184
Mauguio, Étang de ○ a7 185
Maui ▭ Ad2 263
Maulde ≈ d3 186
Mauldin h2 259
Maule, Chile ≈ b3 296
Maule, Maule, Chile b3 296
Maule, Región VII, Chile ⊡ b3 296
Maule, Lago del ○ b4 296
Mauléon e6 182
Mauléon-Licharre b5 187
Maumaupaki △ e2 76
Maumee e5 254
Maumee Bay ◄ e5 254
Maumere m9 99
Maun c2 232
Maun Game Sanctuary ☆ c3 232
Mauna Kea △ A 263
Mauna Loa △ A 263
Maunath Bhanjan h7 125
Maunatlala g1 235
Maungahaumi △ f3 76
Maungapohatu △ f3 76
Maungatapere e1 76
Maungaturoto e2 76
Maungdaw n9 125
Maungmagan Islands ▭ c8 103
Maungmagon d8 103
Maunoir, Lac ○ e2 242
Maupihaa ▭ K 75
Maupiti ▭ K 75
Maure-de-Bretagne d5 182
Maurepas, Lake ○ d4 258
Maures, Massif des ▣ c7 185
Mauri ≈ d3 292
Mauriac e3 186
Maurice e5 256
Maurice, Lake ○ k11 87
Maurienne ♦ c5 185
Mauritania a3 216

MAURITANIA

THE ISLAMIC REPUBLIC OF MAURITANIA
Area 1,030,700km² (397,950sq miles)
Capital Nouakchott
Organizations ECOWAS, LAS, OIC
Population 2,810,000
Pop. growth (%) 2.8
Life expectancy 48 (m); 52 (f)
Languages Arabic, French, many local languages
Literacy 41.7%
Currency ouguiya (US $1 = 263.11 ouguiya)
GDP (US million $) 913
GDP per head ($US) 324

Mauritius h7 217

MAURITIUS

THE REPUBLIC OF MAURITIUS
Area 2040km² (788sq miles)
Capital Port Louis
Organizations COMESA, COMM, SADC
Population 1,210,000
Pop. growth (%) 2.8
Life expectancy 66 (m); 74 (f)
Languages English, Creole, other local languages
Literacy 85.6%
Currency Mauritian rupee (US $1 = 26.5 Mauritian rupee)
GDP (US million $) 4871
GDP per head ($US) 4025

Mauron c4 182
Maurs e4 186
Maury e6 187
Mausdale d4 256
Mauterndorf e2 176
Mauthausen f1 177
Mauvezin c5 187
Mauzé-sur-le-Mignon b2 186
Mava e3 225
Mavago b6 227
Mavanza l1 235
Mavengue b2 232
Mavinga c2 232
Mavita e2 233
Mavra ▭ g5 211
Mavrokklisi g1 210
Mavrommati b3 210
Mavropetra, Akra ► f6 211
Mavros, Akra ► f6 211
Mavrothalassa d2 210
Mavrovo ☆ e5 200
Mavrovouni, Grc. ▣ c3 210
Mavrovouni c2 210
Mavuzi ≈ e2 233
Maw Taung △ d10 103
Mawa, Bukit △ g4 98
Mawai c5 101
Māwān, Khashm △ g3 219
Mawanga c5 224
Mawasangka m7 99
Mawchi c6 102
Mawhun c3 102
Mawkmai c5 102
Mawlaik b4 102
Mawphlang m7 125
Mawqaq h8 136
Mawson (Aust.) ■ m1 298
Max c7 250
Maxán c1 294
Maxcanú q7 273
Maxhamish Lake ○ f2 248
Maxial a5 191
Máximo Paz g2 297
Maxineni h3 201
Maxixe l1 235
Maxmo j5 155
Maxton e2 254
Maxwell a2 264
Maxwelton f6 80
May ≈ g5 86
May Pen B 270
May Point, Cape ► f6 256
Maya c2 224
Maya, Indon. ▭ e5 98
Maya Mountains ▣ c2 276
Mayaguana ▭ h3 266
Mayaguana Passage ═ h3 266
Mayagüez A 270
Mayahi f3 223
Mayakovskiy, Qullai △ e2 128
Mayakum m6 121
Mayama b4 224
Mayamba c4 224
Mayamey q3 137
Mayang g5 104
Mayaro Bay ◄ E 271
Maya-san △ h2 115
Maybole d4 164
Maych'ew e5 219
Maydā Shahr d3 128
Maydena Ab3 83
Maydh d1 226
Mayen f4 159
Mayenne, Fr. ≈ e5 182
Mayenne e4 182
Mayenne, Pays de la Loire, Fr. ⊡ e4 182
Mayer g8 263
Mayet f5 183
Mayfield, N.Z. c5 77
Mayfield, U.K. g5 163
Mayflower c2 258
Mayhan b2 112
Mayhill b5 261
Mayi He ≈ q3 113
Maykain q2 121
Maykamys r4 121
Maykhura d1 128
Mayluu-Suu p7 121
Maymak n6 121
Maymyo c4 102
Mayne ≈ e7 80
Mayni d4 126
Maynooth e3 165
Mayo, Arg. ≈ b5 295
Mayo, Can. l3 247
Mayo, Ire. ⊡ b2 165
Mayo, Mex. ≈ e4 272
Mayo Alim g4 223
Mayo Bay ◄ f7 100
Mayo Daga g4 223
Mayo Darlé g4 223
Mayo Lake ○ l3 247
Mayo-Belwa g4 223
Mayodan g7 254
Mayo-Kébbi ⊡ b2 224
Mayoko b4 224
Mayon △ d4 100
Mayor, Spain ≈ b2 192
Mayor, Spain ≈ b4 193
Mayor Buratovich f5 297
Mayor Island ▭ f2 76
Mayor Pablo Lagerenza e3 293
Mayor, Cabo ► g1 190
Mayor, Isla ▭ d7 191
Mayorga e2 190
Mayotte (France) ❑ g6 217
Mayraira Point ► c1 100
Mayrhofen c2 176
Mays Landing f5 256
Mayskoye s2 121
Maysville p3 249
Maysville l2 259
Maytiguid ▭ b5 100
Mayu ▭ p4 99
Mayum La △ f4 135
Mayumba b4 224
Mayuram f7 126
Mayville a2 256
Maywood c3 260
Maza, Arg. f4 297
Máza, Hung. g5 171
Maza, Russ. Fed. d2 150
Mazabuka d2 233
Mazagão g4 285
Mazagón d7 191
Mazamet e5 187
Mazamitla c4 274
Mazán, Peru ≈ c4 284
Mazán, Loreto, Peru c4 284
Māzandarān ⊡ e9 120
Mazapil j5 273
Mazar c1 130
Mazār d5 139
Mazara del Vallo b7 199
Mazara, Val di ≈ b7 199
Mazār-e Sharif c2 128
Mazarete b4 192
Mazarrón c7 193
Mazarrón, Golfo de ◄ c7 193
Mazaruni ≈ e2 285
Mazatán d3 272
Mazatenango b3 276
Mazatlán a2 274
Mazatzal Peak △ h8 263
Mažeikiai r8 137
Mazeikiai h6 235
Mažeikiai k4 157
Mazères d5 187
Mazhan f1 111
Mazières-en-Gâtine b2 186
Mazirbe k4 157
Mazkeret Batya c5 139
Mazocahui h11 263
Mazocruz d3 292
Mazomora b5 227
Mazotos b2 138
Mazowe ≈ e2 233
Mazowieckie ⊡ j3 169
Mazra'a d4 138
Mazra'at Bayt Jinn d3 138
Mazraat Chouf d3 138
Mazraat Kfardibiane d3 138
Mazsalaca l4 157
Māzū m5 137
Mazunga d3 233
Mazyr c1 148
Mazzarino d7 199
Mazzarrone d7 199
Mazzuva d3 138
Mbabane j3 235
Mbacké a3 222
Mbaéré ≈ c3 224
Mbahiakro d4 222
Mbaïki c3 224
Mbakaou, Lac de ○ b2 224
Mbala f5 225
Mbalabala d3 233
Mbalam b3 224
Mbale a3 226
Mbalmayo g5 223
Mbamba Bay a6 227
Mbandaka c4 224
Mbang b3 224
Mbanga f5 223
Mbanza-Ngungu b5 224
Mbarara f4 225
Mbari ≈ d2 224
Mbata c3 224
Mbati f6 225
Mbatto d4 222
Mbé, Cam. g4 223
Mbé, Congo c4 224
Mbé, Gabon ≈ b3 224
Mbembesi d2 233
Mbemkuru ≈ g5 225
Mbengwi g4 223
Mbenqué c3 222
Mberengwa d3 233
Mbereshi e5 225
Mbeya, Tan. ⊡ f5 225
Mbeya a5 231
Mbi ≈ c3 224
Mbigou b4 224
Mbilapé a4 224
Mbinda b4 224
Mbinga b6 227
Mbini, Eq. Gui. ≈ g5 223
Mbini f5 223
Mbizi e3 233
Mboki e2 225
Mbomo b3 224
Mbomou, C.A.R. ⊡ d3 224
Mbomou, C.A.R. ≈ d3 224
Mboro a2 222
Mbotou d2 224
Mbouda g4 223
Mbour a3 222
Mbout b2 222
Mbozi a5 231
Mbrès c2 224
Mbuji-Mayi d5 224
Mbulu b4 227
Mburucuyá e1 294
Mbuye f4 225
Mbuyuni b5 227
McAdam j6 253
McAdoo e4 256
McAlester b2 258
McAlevys Fort c4 256
McAlister △ f2 83
McAllen k4 273
McArthur, Aust. ≈ c4 80
McArthur, U.S.A. e6 254
McArthur Wildlife Sanctuary ☆ l3 247
McBee j2 259
McCall Creek d4 258
McCamey h2 273
McCammon g4 262
McCarthy j3 247
McCauley Island ▭ b5 248
McClellanville k3 259
McClintock Channel ═ j1 242
McClintock Range ▣ h6 86
McCloud b5 262
McClure c4 256
McClure Strait ═ f1 242
McClure, Lake ○ c4 264
McClusky c7 250
McComb, Mississippi, U.S.A. d4 258
McComb, Ohio, U.S.A. e5 254
McConaughy, Lake ○ c3 260
McConnellsburg c5 256
McCook c3 260
McCormick h3 259
McCreary d5 250
McDavid f4 258
McDermitt e5 262
McDonald Peak △ g2 262
McDouall Range ▣ b5 80
McDougall's Bay ◄ b4 234
McEnsk d5 150
McEwen f1 258
McFarland, California, U.S.A. d6 265
McFarland, Wisconsin, U.S.A. b4 254
McFarlane ≈ n2 249
McFarlane, Mount △ b5 77
McGehee d3 258
McGill f6 262
McGrath f3 246
McGraw d2 256
McGregor, Can. ≈ g4 248
McGregor c6 234
McGregor, U.S.A. a4 258
McGregor Range ▣ f9 81
McGregor, Lake ○ l6 249
McGuire, Mount △ f3 262
Mcherrah ♦ d3 220
Mchinga b5 227
Mchinji e1 233
McInnes Lake ○ g4 250
McIntosh e4 258
McKean ▭ H 75
McKenzie, Alabama, U.S.A. f4 258
McKenzie, Oregon, U.S.A. ≈ b3 262
McKerrow, Lake ○ a6 77
McKinlay, Queensland, Aust. ≈ e6 80
McKinlay e6 80
McKinley, Mount △ g2 247
McKinleyville a5 262
McKinney a5 258
McKittrick d6 265
McKittrick Summit △ d6 265
McLain e4 258
McLaughlin c2 260
McLean b5 254
McLeod ≈ k5 249
McLoughlin, Mount △ b4 262
McMurdo (U.S.A.) ■ x2 298
McMurdo Sound ◄ x2 298
McNeil c3 258
McPherson d4 260
McPherson Range ▣ e6 85
McQuesten ≈ k3 247
McRae d2 258
McVeytown c4 256
McVille d7 250
McWilliams f4 258
Mdandu a5 227
Mdantsane g6 235
Mdennah ♦ d4 220
Meacham a4 250
Meadie, Loch ○ d1 164
Meadow Lake Provincial Park ☆ n4 249
Meadow Valley Wash ≈ f7 263
Meadowview j1 259
Meadville, Mississippi, U.S.A. d4 258
Meadville, Pennsylvania, U.S.A. f5 254
Meaford f3 254
Meaken-dake △ Ad2 114
Meal Fuar-mhonaidh △ d2 164
Mealasta Island ▭ a1 164
Mealhada b4 190
Meall Dubh △ d2 164
Mealy Mountains ▣ n2 253
Meana Sardo Ab3 198
Meandarra j9 81
Meander River j2 248
Meares ▭ n2 99
Mearim ≈ c3 288
Mease ≈ e4 162
Meath ⊡ e3 165
Meaux h4 183
Mebo, Gunung △ j6 97
Mebridege ≈ b5 224
Mebulu, Tanjung ► h9 99
Mecatán b3 274
Mecaya ≈ b3 284
Mecca, Makkah, Sau. Ar b6 116
Mecca, Makkah, Sau. Ar e3 219
Mechanicsburg, Ohio, U.S.A. e5 254
Mechanicsburg, Pennsylvania, U.S.A. c4 256
Mechanicsville, Maryland, U.S.A. d6 256
Mechanicsville, Virginia, U.S.A. h7 255
Mechanicville g2 257
Mechára c2 226
Mechelen c3 159
Mecheria d2 220
Mechernich e4 159
Mechiméré h3 223
Mechita g3 297
Mechongue h5 297
Mecidiye a3 208
Mecimgen a2 246
Mecina-Bombarón a8 193
Mecitözü e2 208
Meckenbeuren c2 174
Meckenheim f4 159
Mecklenburger Bucht ◄ g1 173
Mecklenburgische Seenplatte ♦ h2 173
Mecklenburg-Vorpommern ⊡ h2 173
Meco a4 192
Meconta b6 227
Mecsek △ d2 200
Mecubúri, Moz. ≈ b6 231
Mecubúri b6 227
Mecúfi c6 227
Mecula b6 227
Med'aa e3 138
Meda c4 190
Medak f3 126
Medan d14 103
Medang ▭ j9 99
Medano e1 296
Médanos, Buenos Aires, Arg. f5 297
Médanos, Entre Ríos, Arg. h2 297
Médanos de Coro, Parque Nacional ☆ d1 284
Médanos, Istmo de IT d1 284
Medanosa, Punta ► c5 295
Medaryville c5 254
Medawachchiya g8 126
Medchal f4 126
Mede c4 196
Médéa e1 221
Medebach f1 174
Medeiros Neto h2 291
Medel, Piz △ c3 196
Medelim c4 190
Medellín, Col. b2 284
Medellín, Spain e6 191
Medemblik d2 159
Meden ≈ e3 162
Medenine g2 221
Medenychi m6 169
Mederdra a2 222
Medford, Oregon, U.S.A. b4 262
Medford, Wisconsin, U.S.A. a3 254
Medfra f3 246
Medgidia j3 201
Medgyesbodzás j5 171
Medgyesegyháza k5 171
Media e5 256
Media Luna d3 296
Media Naranja, Punta de la ► c8 193
Mediana d3 192
Medianeira a6 290
Medias g2 201
Medicina f5 197
Medicine Bow b3 260
Medicine Bow Mountains ▣ b3 260
Medicine Bow Peak △ b3 260
Medicine Hat m6 249
Medicine Lake ○ b1 260
Medicine Lodge d4 261
Medina, Braz. h2 291
Medina, Col. c3 284
Medina, Al Madinah, Sau. Ar b6 116
Medina, Sau. Ar e3 219
Medina, North Dakota, U.S.A. d7 250
Medina, Ohio, U.S.A. f5 254
Medina de las Torres d6 191
Medina de Rioseco e3 190
Medina del Campo f3 190
Medina Gounas b3 222
Médina Sabakh a3 222
Medinaceli b3 192
Medina-Sidonia e8 191
Medininkai p1 169
Medinipur k8 125
Mediterranean Sea SE m6 302
Medje e3 225
Medjerda, Monts de la ▣ f1 221
Medle h4 154
Mednogorsk s4 149
Mednyj, Ostrov ▭ s4 119
Médoc ♦ b3 186
Mêdog p5 125
Medora b7 250
Médouneu g5 223
Medousa f1 210
Medrano c2 296
Médréac c4 182
Međumurje, Cro. ⊡ h3 177
Međumurje, Cro. ♦ h3 177
Meduna ≈ g4 196
Medveđa e4 200
Medvedevo j3 151
Medvedica ≈ f2 149
Medvedok l3 151
Medvėgalio kalnis △ k5 157
Medvež'egorsk q5 155
Medway, England, U.K. ⊡ g5 163
Medway, England, U.K. ≈ g5 163
Medyka l6 169
Medyn' c4 150
Medzev j3 171
Medzilaborce k2 171
Meeberrie b10 87
Meekatharra d10 87
Meeks Bay c2 264
Meelpaeg Reservoir ⊙ p4 253
Meerbusch e3 159
Meerkerk c3 159
Meersburg f2 174
Meerut c5 130
Meeteetse a2 260
Meeuwen d3 159
Mēga b3 226
Mega j6 97
Mega Escarpment ▣ b3 226
Megala Kalyvia b3 210
Megali Panagia d2 210
Megalo c2 226
Megalo Chorio, Notio Aigaio, Grc. Ab1 210
Megalo Chorio, Notio Aigaio, Grc. Ac2 211
Megalochori b3 210
Megalopoli c5 211
Meganisi ▭ a4 210
Mégantic, Lac ○ g6 252
Megara d4 210
Megève c5 185
Megezez △ b2 226
Meghalaya ⊡ m7 125
Meghasani △ k9 125
Meghna ≈ m8 125
Meghri l2 137
Megiddo d4 138
Megion h3 118
Megisti ▭ b4 208
Megyaszó k3 171
Mehaïguène, Oued ≈ e2 221
Mehar c7 129
Meharry, Mount △ d8 87
Mehedinți ⊡ f3 201
Meherpur l8 125
Mehetia ▭ k1 259
Mehetia ▭ K 75
Mehidpur g9 129
Mehikoorma m3 157
Méhkerék k5 171
Mehmadabad f9 129
Mehndawal h6 125
Meḥola d4 139
Mehonskoe l4 147
Mehrābān l2 137
Mehrān, Iran ≈ q8 137
Mehrān, Iran q8 137
Mehrān, Iraq l5 137
Mehren e4 159
Mehriz q6 137
Mehtar Lām e3 128
Mehuin a5 296
Mehun-sur-Yèvre h5 183
Mei Jiang ≈ k5 105
Meia Meia b5 227
Meia Ponte ≈ d2 290
Meicheng f5 111
Meichuan d4 106
Meidrim b5 163
Meiganga b2 224
Meighen Island ▭ j1 242
Meigs g4 259
Meijel d3 159
Meijendel ☆ c2 159
Meikeng k6 105
Meikle Says Law △ f4 164
Meiktila b5 102
Meilen c2 196
Meilhan-sur-Garonne c4 186
Meimoa c4 190
Meina c4 196
Meine f3 173
Meinersen f3 172
Meiningen f3 174
Meira c1 190
Meira, Serra de ▣ c1 190
Meiringen c3 196
Meisenheim e4 174
Meishan, Sichuan, China d3 104
Meishan, Zhejiang, China f4 111
Meishan Shuiku ⊙ d4 106
Meiss ej Jabal d3 138
Meiße ≈ e3 172
Meißen h1 175
Meitan f5 104
Meitingen f4 175
Meixi, Heilongjiang, China q2 113
Meixi, Zhejiang, China f4 111
Meizhou l6 105
Méjan, Sommet de △ a6 185
Méjean, Causse ♦ f4 187
Mejicana △ c1 294
Mejillones c4 292
Mejillones del Sur, Bahía de ◄ c4 292
Mejit ▭ D 74
Mejrup b2 158
Mek'elē e5 219
Mékambo b3 224
Mekerrhane, Sebkha ⊙ e3 221
Mékhé a2 222
Mekhtar d5 128
Meknès c2 220
Mekong ≈ g9 103
Mekong ≈ a3 104
Mekong, Mouths of the — h11 102
Mekongga, Teluk ◄ l7 99
Mekoryuk c3 246
Mel g3 196
Mel, Ilha do ▭ d6 290
Mel'nikovo n2 157
Mela c3 101
Méla, Mont △ d2 224
Melaka, Malacca, Malay. ⊡ c4 101
Melala ≈ b7 231
Melalo, Tanjung ► c5 98
Melampes e7 211
Melanau, Gunung △ je3 98
Melanesian Basin — k5 301
Melanthi b2 210
Melaut ≈ j2 99
Melawi ≈ g5 98
Melbourn g4 163
Melbourne, Aust. g14 81
Melbourne, U.S.A. j5 259
Melbu e2 154
Melby A 164
Melchor de Mencos c2 276
Melchor Ocampo j5 273
Melchor, Isla ▭ b5 295
Meldal b5 154
Meldino h3 146
Meldola g5 197
Meldrum Bay e3 254
Mele c5 197
Mele, Capo ► c6 197
Melegnano d4 196
Melehovo f3 150
Melendiz Dağı △ e3 208
Melendugno c2 198
Melenki f4 150
Meleuz j1 149
Mélfi a5 218
Melfi e4 198
Melfort q5 249
Melgaço b2 288
Melgar de Fernamental f2 190
Melgar de Tera d3 190
Melhus c5 154
Melide b2 190
Melides b6 191
Meligalas b5 211
Meliki c2 210
Melilis ▭ m5 99
Melilla, Norf. I. d1 220
Melilla (Spain) ❑ b1 216
Melilli e7 199
Melimoyu, Monte △ b4 295
Melincué g2 297
Melintang, Danau ○ h5 99
Melipeuco b5 296
Melipilla b2 296
Melissa, Grc. e1 210
Melissa, Italy g5 199
Melita c6 250
Meliti b2 210
Melito di Porto Salvo e7 199
Melitopol' d3 148
Melivoia c3 210
Melk g1 177
Melka Guba b3 226
Melkbospunt ► b4 234
Melkbosstrand c6 234
Melkfjellet △ e3 154
Meliksham d5 163
Mella ≈ e4 196
Mellakoski k3 155
Mellanfryken ○ e3 156
Mellansel g5 154
Mellansjö f1 156
Mellansjön ○ f1 156
Melle, Fr. b2 186
Melle, Ger. d3 172
Mellendorf (Wedemark) e3 172
Mellerud e3 156
Mellizo Sur, Cerro △ b5 295
Mellrichstadt e3 174
Mellum ▭ c3 163
Mellum ▭ d2 172
Melmerby d2 162
Melmoth j4 235
Mělník c1 170
Melo, Arg. f3 297
Melo, Ur. f2 294
Meloco b6 227
Melolo l9 99
Mêlong f4 223
Meløysund d3 154
Melozitna ≈ f2 246
Melres b3 190
Melrhir, Chott ⊙ f2 221
Melrose A 164
Mels a2 176
Melsungen d1 174
Meltaus k3 155
Meltausjoki ≈ k3 155
Meltingvatnet ○ c5 154
Melton Mowbray f4 162
Meluan f4 98
Meluco b6 227
Melun h4 183
Melur f7 126
Melut d5 218
Melvaig c2 164
Melvern, Lake ○ e4 260
Melvich e1 164
Melville b5 250
Melville Island, Aust. ▭ k2 86
Melville Island, Can. ▭ g1 242
Melville Peninsula ► m2 243
Melville, Cape, Aust. ► g3 80
Melville, Cape, Phil. ► a7 100
Melville, Lake ○ n2 253
Melvin, Lough ○ c2 165
Mélykút h5 171
Melzo d4 196
Mēmar Co ○ f2 135
Memba c6 227
Memboro k9 99
Membrío c5 191
Memel h3 235
Mēmele ≈ l4 157
Memmelsdorf f5 175
Memmingen c2 174
Mempawah e4 98
Memphis, Egypt ★ d2 218
Memphis, Tennessee, U.S.A. d2 258
Memphis, Texas, U.S.A. c5 261
Memphrémagog, Lac ○ f6 252
Memsie f2 164
Memuro-dake △ Ac2 114
Mena, Eth. b2 226
Mena, Indon. n9 99
Mena, U.S.A. b2 258
Mena, Ukr. d2 148
Menabe ♦ Aa3 233
Menafra j2 297
Menaggio d3 196
Menai Bridge b3 162
Ménaka e2 223
Menang B 74
Menang Point ► B 74
Menanga n5 99
Menapod, Gunung △ a7 100
Menarandra ≈ Aa3 233
Menard d6 261
Menars g5 183
Menasalbas f5 191
Menasha b3 254
Menat e2 186
Mencué c6 296
Mendana Fracture Zone ═ r6 301
Mendawai g6 98
Mende f4 186
Mendebo Mountains ▣ b2 226
Mendefera e5 219
Mendeleevsk m4 151
Mendeleyev Ridge ═ mm3 299
Menden (Sauerland) c4 172
Mendenhall e4 258
Mendenhall Glacier — l4 247
Mendenhall, Cape ► c4 246
Mendenitsa c4 210
Méndez, Tamaulipas, Mex. k5 273
Méndez, Veracruz, Mex. e2 275
Mendez-Nuñez c3 100

358 Mendī → Minnesota

Mendī g2 225
Mendig f4 159
Mendip Hills d5 163
Mendocino Fracture Zone m3 301
Mendota, California, U.S.A. c5 264
Mendota, Illinois, U.S.A. b5 254
Mendota Canal, Delta — b4 264
Mendoza, Arg. c3 296
Mendoza, Arg. c2 296
Mendoza, Arg. c2 296
Mendoza, Bol. d3 292
Mendoza, Ur. j3 297
Mends, Lake e13 87
Mene de Mauroa c1 284
Mene Grande c2 284
Ménéac c4 182
Menegosa, Monte d5 196
Menemen a3 208
Menen b4 159
Menesjärvi l2 155
Menez Hom a4 182
Menfi b7 199
Meng b2 224
Meng Shan f2 111
Mengalum h1 99
Mengban e4 102
Mengcheng e3 111
Mengcun e0 111
Mengen, Ger. e2 174
Mengen, Tur. d2 208
Menggala c7 98
Menghai e5 102
Mengibar g7 191
Mengisor, Ozero m5 147
Mengjin c2 106
Mengkarak c4 101
Mengkofen h4 175
Mengkoka, Gunung l6 99
Mengkuang c4 101
Mengla e5 102
Menglian d4 102
Mengong g5 223
Mengshan h6 104
Mengtuan f1 111
Mengyin e2 111
Mengzhou c2 106
Mengzi f4 102
Menidi b3 210
Ménigoute b2 186
Menihek j1 253
Menihek Lakes j1 253
Menindee f12 81
Menindee Lake c1 82
Meningie d13 81
Ménistouc, Lac j2 253
Menna e5 219
Mennecy h4 183
Mennetou-sur-Cher g5 183
Menominee c3 254
Menomonee Falls b4 254
Menongue b1 232
Menor, Isla d7 191
Menorca A 193
Menorca, Cap A 193
Menouarar d2 220
Mens b6 185
Mensalong j3 99
Menslage c3 172
Mentana g7 197
Mentapok j2 99
Mentarang j3 99
Mentasta Lake j3 247
Mentasta Mountains j3 247
Mentawai, Kepulauan b6 96
Mentawai, Selat b6 96
Mentaya g5 98
Mentekab c4 101
Menteroda e1 175
Mentok c6 98
Mentolat, Monte b4 295
Menton d7 185
Mentone c6 261
Mentor f5 254
Mentrida f4 190
Mentuba g5 98
Menukung g5 98
Menunu l4 99
Menyapa, Gunung j4 99
Menyuan a7 112
Menza e1 112
Menzel Bourguiba f1 221
Menzelinsk m4 151
Menzies e11 87
Menzies, Mount m2 298
Meobbaai a2 234
Méobecq d2 186
Meolo g4 196
Meoqui g3 272
Meponda e1 233
Meppel e2 159
Meppen f2 159
Mequinenza e3 192
Mequinenza, Embalse de e3 192
Mequon c4 254
Mer g5 183
Mer d'Iroise SE a4 182
Mera g3 151
Merah j4 99
Merak d7 98
Meråker c5 154
Meramangye, Lake k11 87
Merano f3 196
Merapuh b3 101
Merari, Serra e3 285
Merate d4 196
Meratswe f1 234
Merauke l7 97
Merbau c5 101
Merbein f13 81
Merbes-le-Château c4 159
Mercatino Conca g6 197
Mercato San Severino d4 198
Mercato Saraceno g6 197
Merced c4 264
Merced del Potrero f5 275
Mercedario, Cerro b1 296
Mercedes, Buenos Aires, Arg. h3 297
Mercedes, Corrientes, Arg. e1 294
Mercedes, Arg. e2 296
Mercedes, Ur. h2 297
Merceditas b1 294
Mercer h7 250
Mercersburg c5 256
Mercerville f4 256
Mercês, Acre, Braz. d1 292
Mercês, Minas Gerais, Braz. g4 291
Merchtem c4 159
Mercier d2 292
Mercœur d3 186
Mercogliano d4 198
Mercury Islands e2 76
Mercy, Cape s3 243
Merdja Zerga, Réserve de c2 220
Merdrignac c4 182
Mere d5 163
Mere Lava F 74
Meredith d3 82
Meredith, Cape d6 295
Meredith, Lake c5 261
Mereeg d3 226
Merefa e2 148
Merenberg c2 174
Mereni j2 201
Merenkurkku h5 154
Mergozzo c4 196
Mergui b4 103
Mergui Archipelago c10 103
Meriç, Grc. g1 210
Meriç h5 201
Merichas e5 211
Mericourt a4 159
Mérida, Mex. q7 273
Mérida, Spain d6 191
Mérida, Ven. c2 284
Mérida, Mérida, Ven. c2 284
Mérida, Cordillera de c2 284
Meriden h3 257
Meridian, Georgia, U.S.A. j4 259
Meridian, Idaho, U.S.A. e4 262
Meridian, Mississippi, U.S.A. e3 258
Meridiano f3 297
Meridianville f2 258
Mèridja d2 220
Mérignac b4 186
Merigold d3 258
Merijärvi k4 155
Merikarvia j2 157
Merimbula j14 81
Merinda j6 80
Mering f3 175
Meringa g3 223
Meringur e13 81
Merino Jarpa b5 295
Merinos j2 297
Merirumã g3 285
Merivale b4 84
Merkel c5 261
Merkendorf f4 175
Merkinė n1 169
Merksplas c3 159
Merkys l5 157
Merlimau c4 101
Merlo e2 296
Merluna e2 80
Mernye f5 171
Mero b1 190
Meron d4 138
Merowe d4 218
Mêrqung Co g4 135
Merredin d12 87
Merrick d4 164
Merrill, Oregon, U.S.A. c4 262
Merrill, Wisconsin, U.S.A. b3 254
Merriman e5 234
Merriman, U.S.A. c3 260
Merriott d6 163
Merritt g6 248
Merritt Island j5 259
Merrygoen j11 81
Mersa Fatma f5 219
Mersch e5 159
Merse f6 197
Merseburg (Saale) g4 173
Mersey d3 162
Mersin e4 208
Mersing c4 101
Mers-les-Bains g2 183
Mērsrags k4 157
Merta g7 129
Merta Road f7 129
Merthyr Tydfil, Wales, U.K. h2 162
Merthyr Tydfil c5 163
Merti b3 226
Mértola c7 191
Mértola, Serra de c7 191
Merton h3 162
Merton Glacier v1 298
Méru h3 183
Meru, Kenya b3 226
Meru, Tan. g4 225
Meru Betiri National Park g9 98
Meru National Park b3 226
Merui a6 129
Mervans b4 184
Merweville d6 234
Méry-sur-Seine j4 183
Merzifon e2 208
Merzig e5 159
Mesa g3 235
Meša k4 151
Mesa, Spain c3 192
Mesa, U.S.A. h9 263
Mesa Bolívar c2 284
Mesa Geitonia b2 138
Mesa Verde National Park b4 261
Mesabi Range e2 260
Mesagne g4 198
Mesanagros Ac2 211
Mesão Frio c3 190
Mesaoria Plain b1 138
Meschede d4 172
Meščovsk c4 150
Meselefors f4 154
Meseta de Montemayor c4 295
Meseta del Cerro Jáua e3 285
Mesfinto e5 219
Mesgouez Lake r5 251
Meshekli h7 120
Meshkān s3 137
Meshra'er Req e2 225
Mesick d3 254
Mesimeri d2 210
Meski d2 220
Meškuičiai k4 157
Meslay-du-Maine e5 182
Mesocco d4 196
Mesochora b3 210
Mesochori Ac3 211
Mesola g5 196
Mesolongi b4 210
Mesón do Vento b1 190
Mesopotamia b2 210
Mesopotamia, Iraq j4 136
Mesopotamo a3 210
Mesoraca f5 199
Mesquita g3 291
Mesquite a3 258
Messaad e2 221
Messac d5 182
Messalo b6 231
Messaména b3 224
Messancy d5 159
Messaoud, Oued d3 220
Meßdorf g3 173
Messier, Canal b5 295
Messina, Sicilia, Italy d7 199
Messina e6 199
Messina Nature Reserve j1 235
Messini c5 211
Messiniakos Kolpos c6 211
Meßkirch d2 174
Meßstetten d2 174
Messum Mountains a3 232
Mesta, Bul. d1 210
Mesta f4 210
Mestanza f6 191
Městec Králové d1 170
Meston, Akra f4 210
Mestre g4 196
Mesudiye f2 209
Mesuji c6 98
Mesumba g5 225
Mesvres a4 184
Mesvrin k6 183
Mesza Peak m4 247
Meszah Peak b2 248
Meta, Col. c3 284
Meta, Col. d2 284
Metagkitsi d2 210
Metairie d5 258
Metaline e1 262
Metallostroj a2 150
Metamora b5 254
Metán d5 292
Metangula e1 233
Metapan c3 276
Metar c5 139
Metarica f1 233
Metauro h6 197
Metaxades g1 210
Metelen f2 159
Metema e5 219
Meteor Creek c4 84
Meteora b3 210
Methana d5 211
Metheringham f3 162
Methoni b6 211
Methuen j2 257
Methuen, Mount g4 86
Methven c5 77
Methwin, Mount e9 87
Metileo f3 297
Metković g1 198
Metlakatla b4 248
Metlaltoyuca f3 275
Metlaoui f2 221
Metlatonoc e5 275
Metlika g4 177
Metlili Chaamba e2 221
Metlili, Oued e2 221
Metnitz f3 177
Metochi, Dytiki Ellas, Grc. b4 210
Metochi, Peloponnisos, Grc. c5 211
Metoro b6 227
Metro c7 98
Metropolis e1 258
Metsäkylä m4 155
Metsovo b3 210
Mettendorf e5 159
Metter h3 259
Mettet c4 159
Mettlach e5 159
Mettmann e3 159
Mettur e7 126
Metu b2 226
Metuchen f4 257
Metz c1 184
Metzervisse e5 159
Metzingen c2 174
Metzquititlán e3 275
Meu c4 182
Meudt g2 174
Meulaboh c13 103
Meulan g3 183
Meulebeke b4 159
Meung-sur-Loire g5 183
Meursault a4 184
Meurthe c2 184
Meurthe-et-Moselle c2 184
Meuse, Bel. k3 183
Meuse, Fr. b1 184
Meuselwitz j1 175
Meuzac d3 186
Meuzin b3 184
Mevasseret Ẓiyyon d5 139
Mexcala e5 275
Mexcaltitán b3 274
Mexiana, Ilha c1 288
Mexicali f9 263
México, Mex. e4 275
México, Distrito Federal, Mex. e4 275
Mexico, U.S.A. f4 260
Mexico d6 241

MEXICO

THE UNITED MEXICAN STATES
Area 1,958,201km^2 (756,066sq miles)
Capital Mexico City
Organizations ACS, IADB, LAIA, NAFTA, OECD, SELA
Population 103,230,000
Pop. growth (%) 1.6
Life expectancy 69 (m); 75 (f)
Languages Spanish, many local languages
Literacy 92%
Currency Mexican peso (US $1 = 11.23 Mexican peso)
GDP (US million $) 637,200
GDP per head ($US) 6172

Mexico Basin r4 301
Mexico Beach g5 259
Mexico, Gulf of r4 301
Meximieux b5 185
Mexquitic d2 274
Meybod p5 137
Meyenburg f5 158
Meyers Chuck a4 248
Meyersdale a5 256
Meyerton h3 235
Meylan b5 185
Meymac e3 186
Meymaneh b3 128
Meymeh n5 137
Meyo Centre g5 223
Meyrargues b7 185
Meyrueis f4 187
Meyssac d3 186
Mezadot Yehuda d5 139
Mezcala e5 275
Mezcalapa, Mex. h5 275
Mezcalapa, Tabasco, Mex. h5 275
Meždurečenskij l4 147
Mèze f5 187
Mézel c7 185
Mezen', Russ. Fed. f2 146
Mezen' f2 146
Mézenc, Mont e5 181
Mezenskaja Guba e2 146
Mežica f3 177
Mézidon-Canon e3 182
Mézières-en-Brenne d2 186
Mézières-sur-Issoire c2 186
Mezimĕstí e1 170
Mézin c4 187
Mezio c4 190
Mezőberény k5 171
Mezőcsát j4 171
Mezőcsokonya f5 171
Mezőfalva g5 171
Mezőhegyes j5 171
Mezőkeresztes j4 171
Mezőkovácsháza j5 171
Mezőkövesd j4 171
Mezőörs f4 171
Mezőszilas g5 171
Mezőtárkány j4 171
Mezőtúr j5 171
Mežozernyj j5 147
Mezquita de Jarque d4 192
Mezquital, Mex. b2 274
Mezquital, Durango, Mex. b2 274
Mezquital del Oro c3 274
Mezquitic c2 274
Mezzana e3 196
Mezzano f3 196
Mezzojuso c7 199
Mezzola, Lago di d3 196
Mezzolombardo f3 196
Mfou g5 223
Mfuwe e1 233
Mgbidi f4 223
Mglin b5 150
Mhangura e2 233
Mhasvad d4 126
Mhlosheni j3 235
Mhlume j3 235
Mhow g9 129
Mi n9 125
Mi He f1 111
Mī'ēso c2 226
Mia Milia b1 138
Miacatlan e4 275
Miączyn m5 169
Miahuatlán f5 275
Miajadas e5 191
Mialet c3 186
Miamérè c2 224
Miami, Florida, U.S.A. j7 259
Miami, Oklahoma, U.S.A. b1 258
Miami Beach j7 259
Miami Canal j6 259
Miamisburg d6 254
Mian Chanmun f5 128
Mian Kalai e3 128
Mian Kaleh Shebh-e Jazireh-ye d9 120
Miānābād r3 137
Mianaz a7 129
Miancaowan b1 104
Miancheng c4 106
Mianchi b2 106
Miāndasht r3 137
Miandowāb l3 137
Miandrivazo Ab2 233
Mianduhe l1 113
Miāneh l3 137
Miangas p2 99
Miani, India b4 130
Miani, India d4 130
Miani, Pak. f4 128
Miani Hor c8 129
Mianjoi b4 128
Mianmian Shan c5 104
Mianning d4 104
Mianwali e4 128
Mianxian f2 104
Mianyang e3 104
Mianzhu e3 104
Miao Dao g1 111
Miao'ergou u5 121
Miaodao Liedao g1 111
Miaoli n6 105
Miaoshan e1 111
Miaotan b3 106
Miaotou f2 111
Miarinarivo, Antananarivo, Madag. Ab2 233
Miarinarivo, Toamasina, Madag. Ab2 233
Miass, Russ. Fed. l5 149
Miass k5 147
Miasteczko Krajeńskie f2 168
Miastko e1 168
Mica j2 235
Mica, Cerro de c4 292
Micaela Cascallares g5 297
Micang Shan f2 104
Micanopy h5 259
Micaune f2 233
Michalovce k3 171
Michelago f2 83
Michelau in Oberfranken e3 175
Micheldorf in Oberösterreich f2 177
Michelson, Mount h1 247
Michelstadt g5 174
Michendorf j3 173
Miches k5 271
Michigan d3 254
Michigan City c5 254
Michigan, Lake c4 254
Michihuao c6 296
Michika g3 223
Michipicoten Bay l7 251
Michipicoten Island l7 251
Michipicoten River l7 251
Michoacán d4 274
Michów l4 169
Mico e4 276
Micos e2 275
Micoud J 271
Micronesia e2 73

MICRONESIA

THE FEDERATED STATES OF MICRONESIA
Area 700km^2 (270sq miles)
Capital Palikir on Pohnpei
Organizations ESCAP, SPC, PIF
Population 126,000
Pop. growth (%) 1.8
Life expectancy 69 (m); 74 (f)
Languages English, Trukese, Pohnpeian
Literacy n/a
Currency US dollar
GDP (US million $) 259
GDP per head ($US) 2,055

Micula l4 171
Mičurinsk f5 150
Mid Western f5 135
Midai d3 98
Midale b6 250
Mid-Atlantic Ridge f6 302
Middelburg, Neth. b3 159
Middelburg, Eastern Cape, R.S.A. f5 235
Middelburg, R.S.A. h2 235
Middelfart c3 158
Middelharnis c3 159
Middelpos d5 234
Middle Alkali Lake c5 262
Middle America Trench r5 301
Middle Andaman n6 127
Middle Caicos j4 271
Middle Fork, Alaska, U.S.A. h2 247
Middle Fork, California, U.S.A. c3 264
Middle Fork American c3 264
Middle Fork Feather b2 264
Middle Loup c3 260
Middle Ridge Wildlife Reserve q4 253
Middle Yuba c2 264
Middleboro k3 257
Middleburg, Pennsylvania, U.S.A. c4 256
Middleburg, Virginia, U.S.A. c6 256
Middleburgh f2 257
Middlebury k3 255
Middlefield f5 254
Middlemarch c6 77
Middlemarsh d6 163
Middlemount c3 84
Middleport e6 254
Middlesboro h1 259
Middlesbrough, England, U.K. h1 162
Middlesbrough e2 162
Middlesex c2 276
Middleton, Aust. e7 80
Middleton, Can. k6 253
Middleton, R.S.A. f6 235
Middleton, U.K. g4 162
Middleton Island h4 247
Middleton-on-the-Wolds f3 162
Middletown, U.K. e2 165
Middletown, California, U.S.A. a3 264
Middletown, Connecticut, U.S.A. h3 257
Middletown, Delaware, U.S.A. e5 256
Middletown, Maryland, U.S.A. c5 256
Middletown, New Jersey, U.S.A. f4 257
Middletown, New York, U.S.A. f3 257
Middletown, Ohio, U.S.A. d6 254
Middletown, Pennsylvania, U.S.A. d4 256
Middletown, Rhode Island, U.S.A. j3 257
Middletown, Virginia, U.S.A. b5 256
Midelt d2 220
Midhurst f6 163
Midi d'Ossau, Pic du b6 187
Midi de Bigorre, Pic du c6 187
Midi, Canal du e5 187
Mid-Indian Basin d6 300
Mid-Indian Ridge c7 300
Midi-Pyrénées d5 187
Midland, Can. g3 254
Midland, Michigan, U.S.A. d4 254
Midland, Texas, U.S.A. c5 261
Midlands d2 233
Midleton c5 165
Midlothian f3 164
Midlum b5 158
Midongy Atsimo Ab3 233
Midou b5 187
Midouze b5 187
Mid-Pacific Mountains k4 301
Midsayap e7 100
Midsund a5 154
Midu e3 102
Midville h3 259
Midway g3 259
Midway Islands (U.S.A.) b5 12
Midway Park l2 259
Midwest b3 260
Midwest City a2 258
Midyat h4 209
Midzhur f4 201
Mie g4 115
Miechów j5 169
Miedwie, Jezioro d2 168
Międzybórz f4 168
Międzychód d3 168
Międzylesie e5 168
Międzyrzec Podlaski l4 169
Międzyrzecz d3 168
Międzyzdroje c2 168
Miejsce Piastowe k6 169
Miejska Górka e4 168
Miélan c5 187
Mielec k5 169
Mielno e1 168
Miembwe b5 227
Mieminger Gebirge b2 176
Mien c1 156
Miena Ab2 83
Mienhua Yü p6 105
Mier y Noriaga d2 274
Mierasjärvi l2 155
Miercurea-Ciuc g2 201
Mieres e1 190
Mieron j2 155
Mieroszów e5 168
Mierzawa j5 169
Mierzeja Helska h5 157
Miesbach e3 175
Mieste g3 173
Mieszkowice c3 168
Mifflinburg c4 256
Mifflintown c4 256
Migang Shan c8 112
Migdal Ha'Emeq d4 138
Migdol f3 235
Migennes j5 183
Migliarino f5 196
Migliarino-San Rossore-Massaciuccoli, Parco Naturale di e6 197
Miglionica f4 198
Mignone f7 197
Miguel Alemán f4 275
Miguel Alemán, Presa f4 275
Miguel Alves d2 288
Miguel Auza h5 272
Miguel Calmon d4 288
Miguel de la Borda g6 277
Miguel Esteban a5 193
Miguel Hidalgo e2 275
Miguel Hidalgo, Presa e4 272
Miguel Riglos f4 297
Miguelete j3 297
Migyaunglaung d8 103
Mihăileşti g3 201
Mihajlov e4 150
Mihajlovka f2 149
Mihajlovskij s2 121
Mihajlovskoe h3 151
Mihaliççık c3 208
Mihama f4 115
Mihara e4 114
Mihara-yama h4 115
Miharu j3 115
Mihnevo d4 150
Mi'ilyā d3 138
Mijas f8 191
Mijdrecht c2 159
Mijoux c4 184
Mikado e3 254
Mikasa Ab2 114
Mikepércs k4 171
Mikhalishki m5 157
Mikhaylovka r1 121
Mikhaylovo f4 201
Mikhmoret c4 139
Mikitänjärvi m4 155
Mikkeli m2 157
Mikkwa k3 249
Miklavž g3 177
Mikołajki k2 169
Mikołów g5 168
Mikra Volvi d2 210
Mikro Dereio g1 210
Mikstat f4 168
Mikuláš d2 170
Mikulčice j1 177
Mikulkin, Mys f2 146
Mikulov h1 177
Mikulovice f1 170
Mikumi b5 227
Mikumi National Park g5 225
Mikun' g3 146
Mikuni g3 115
Mikuni-sanmyaku h3 115
Mikura-jima h5 115
Mila f1 221
Milaca e2 260
Miladhunmadulu Atoll c9 126
Milagres e3 288
Milagro, Arg. e1 296
Milagro, Ec. b4 284
Milagro c2 192
Milak d5 130
Milan, Italy d4 196
Milan, U.S.A. e4 254
Milando c5 224
Milang d13 81
Milano, Italy d4 196
Milano, U.S.A. a4 258
Milanoa Ab1 233
Milanów l4 169
Milaş g2 201
Milas a4 208
Milatos f7 211
Milavidy p3 169
Milazzo e6 199
Milazzo, Capo di e6 199
Milbank d2 260
Mildenhall g4 163
Mildred d3 256
Mildura f13 81
Mile d6 104
Milē Serdo Reserve c1 226
Milena c7 199
Milepa b6 227
Miles k9 81
Miles City b2 260
Milesburg c4 256
Mileto f6 199
Miletto, Monte c3 198
Mileura c10 87
Milevsko c2 170
Milfontes b7 191
Milford, Ire. d1 165
Milford, U.K. f5 163
Milford, Connecticut, U.S.A. g3 257
Milford, Delaware, U.S.A. e6 256
Milford, Massachusetts, U.S.A. j2 257
Milford, New Hampshire, U.S.A. j2 257
Milford, New Jersey, U.S.A. e4 256
Milford, Pennsylvania, U.S.A. f3 256
Milford, Utah, U.S.A. g6 263
Milford Haven a5 163
Milford Lake d4 260
Milford Sound a6 77
Milgarra e5 80
Milgoo, Mount d11 87
Milgun d9 87
Milhão d3 190
Milhaud a7 185
Mili D 74
Milibangalala, Ponta k3 235
Milicz f4 168
Milies d3 210
Milín c2 170
Miling c12 87
Milis Aa2 198
Militello in Val di Catania d7 199
Miljana g3 177
Milk b1 260
Milk River g1 262
Milk, Wadi el c4 218
Milki k2 169
Mill Creek g6 254
Mill Hall c3 256
Mill Island g1 298
Millaa Millaa g4 80
Millares b5 193
Millárs d4 193
Millau f4 187
Millboro g7 254
Millbrae a4 264
Millbrook b6 163
Millbrook, U.S.A. g3 257
Mille Lacs e2 260
Mille Lacs, Lac des h6 250
Milledgeville h3 259
Millennium Island H 75
Miller d2 260
Miller Mountain e3 264
Miller, Mount j3 247
Millerovo f2 148
Millers Flat b6 77
Millersburg, Michigan, U.S.A. d3 254
Millersburg, Ohio, U.S.A. f5 254
Millersburg, Pennsylvania, U.S.A. d4 256
Millersville d5 256
Millerton g3 257
Millerton Lake d4 264
Milleur Point c4 164
Millevaches e3 186
Millheim c4 256
Millicent e14 81
Milligan f4 258
Millinocket h6 253
Millíri, Cerro d4 292
Millisle c5 164
Millmerran k9 81
Millom c2 162
Millport d4 164
Millsboro e6 256
Millstream-Chichester National Park c7 86
Millstreet b4 165
Millthorpe f1 83
Milltown, Montana, U.S.A. g2 262
Milltown, New Jersey, U.S.A. f4 257
Milltown Malbay b4 165
Millungera e5 80
Millville, New Jersey, U.S.A. e5 256
Millville, Pennsylvania, U.S.A. d3 256
Millwood Lake c3 258
Milly Milly c10 87
Milly-la-Forêt h4 183
Milmarcos c3 192
Milmersdorf j2 173
Milnthorpe d2 162
Milo c4 222
Milo e7 199
Milomlyn h2 169
Milos e6 211
Milos, Notio Aigaio, Grc. e6 211
Miloslavskoe e5 150
Miłosław f3 168
Milove f2 148
Milparinka e10 81
Milpitas b4 264
Milroy c4 256
Miltenberg e3 174
Milton, N.Z. b7 77
Milton, Delaware, U.S.A. e6 256
Milton, Florida, U.S.A. f4 258
Milton, North Dakota, U.S.A. d6 250
Milton, Pennsylvania, U.S.A. d3 256
Milton, Vermont, U.S.A. k3 255
Milton, Wisconsin, U.S.A. b4 254
Milton Abbot b6 163
Milton Keynes, England, U.K. f4 163
Milton Keynes f4 163
Milton-Freewater d3 262
Miltzow j1 173
Milwaukee c4 254
Milybulabk q3 121
Mim d4 222
Mimbelly c3 224
Mimizan a4 187
Mimoň c1 170
Mimongo b4 224
Mimosa Rocks National Park g3 83
Mimoso do Sul h4 291
Mimuro-yama f4 114
Min Jiang, China m5 105
Min Jiang, Sichuan, China e4 104
Min Shan d2 104
Mina, Mex. j4 273
Mina, U.S.A. e3 264
Mina Bazar d5 128
Mina Clavero e1 296
Mina Jebel Ali q9 137
Mina, Nevado c3 292
Mīnā' Sa'ūd m7 137
Mīnāb r8 137
Minaçu c4 288
Minahasa, Semenanjung m3 99
Minaki f6 250
Minami Alps National Park h4 115
Minas, Indon. b5 101
Minas, Ur. e2 294
Minas Channel k6 253
Minas de Corrales e2 294
Minas de Matahambre c3 266
Minas de Riotinto d7 191
Minas Gerais f3 291
Minas Novas g2 291
Minateda c6 193
Minatitlán, Colima, Mex. b4 274
Minatitlán, Veracruz, Mex. g4 275
Minaya b5 193
Minbu b5 102
Minbya n9 125
Minch, The c1 164
Mincha b1 296
Minchinabad f5 128
Minchinmávida b4 295
Minchumina, Lake f3 246
Mincivan l2 137
Minco a2 258
Mindanao, Phil. e7 100
Mindanao, Phil. e7 100
Minde b5 191
Mindel f4 174
Mindelheim f2 174
Mindelo A 222
Minden d3 172
Minden, Louisiana, U.S.A. c3 258
Minden, Nevada, U.S.A. d3 264
Minden City e4 254
Mindenmines b1 258
Mindif g3 223
Mindiptana l7 97
Mindon b6 102
Mindona Lake c1 82
Mindoro c3 100
Mindoro Strait c4 100
Mindouli b4 224
Mindszent j5 171
Minduri f4 291
Mine Centre g6 250
Mine Head d5 165
Minehead c5 163
Mineiros b2 290
Mineola b3 258
Miner k2 247
Mineral del Monte e3 275
Mineral del Refugio d3 274
Mineral Point a4 254
Mineral Wells d5 261
Mineral'ne Vody f3 149
Minerales de la Pampa e5 296
Minerbio f5 196
Minerva f5 254
Minervino Murge f3 198
Minfeng f1 135
Minga e6 225
Mingäçevir g4 149
Mingäçevir Su Anbarı g4 149
Mingala d2 224
Mingan k3 253
Mingan, Îles de l3 253
Mingary e12 81
Mingbulak j6 120
Mingela h5 80
Mingenew b11 87
Minger j2 201
Minggang d3 106
Mingguang f3 111
Mingin b4 102
Mingin Range b3 102
Ming-Kush q7 121
Minglanilla c5 193
Mingorría f4 190
Mingoyo b6 227
Mingshui n2 113
Mingteke b1 130
Mingũri c6 227
Minhe b7 112
Minhla, Magwe, Myan. b6 102
Minhla, Pegu, Myan. b7 102
Minho B 266
Miničevo f4 201
Minico, Parco del e4 196
Minicoy c8 126
Minigwal, Lake f11 87
Minilla, Embalse de la d7 191
Minilya b8 87
Minilya, Western Australia, Aust. b8 87
Miñimiñe d3 292
Minin e3 138
Mininco a4 296
Mininian c3 222
Miniota c5 250
Minipi Lake m2 253
Miniss Lake h5 250
Ministra, Sierra b3 192
Ministro Remos Mexía d6 296
Minitonas c4 250
Minjar j5 147
Minlaton c13 81
Minle a6 112
Minna f4 223
Minneapolis e2 260
Minnedosa d5 250
Minnesota, U.S.A. e2 260

Minnesota, Minnesota, U.S.A. e2 260
Minnewaukan d6 250
Minnie Creek b8 87
Minnipa b12 81
Minnitaki Lake h6 250
Mino g4 115
Miño b3 190
Minobu h4 115
Minocqua b3 254
Minonk b5 254
Minorca A 193
Minot c6 250
Minqin b6 112
Minqing m5 105
Minquan d2 106
Minsk b1 148
Mińsk Mazowiecki k3 169
Minskaya Voblasts' b1 148
Minta b3 224
Mintaka Pass b1 130
Mintlaw g2 164
Minto, Manitoba, Can. c6 250
Minto, Can. j5 253
Minto, U.S.A. g2 247
Minto Inlet f1 242
Minto Reef G 74
Minto, Lac r1 251
Mintom b3 224
Minturn b4 260
Minturno c3 198
Minucciano e5 197
Minudasht q3 137
Minûf c6 136
Minusinsk k4 118
Minutang q5 125
Minvoul b3 224
Minxian e1 104
Mionica e3 200
Miquan w6 121
Miquelon p5 253
Miquihuana e2 275
Mir Bacheh Kowt d3 128
Mira, Col. b3 284
Mira, Italy g4 196
Mira, Port b7 191
Mira, Port b4 190
Mira, Spain c5 193
Mira, Spain c5 193
Mira Pampa f3 297
Mirabel d5 191
Mirabela f2 291
Mirabel-aux-Baronnies b6 185
Miracema g4 291
Miracema do Tocantins c3 288
Miradero, Cerro a2 276
Mirador b5 290
Mirador, Parque Nacional de c3 288
Mirador, Punta b4 295
Miradouro g4 291
Miradoux c5 187
Miraflores, Boyaca, Col. c2 284
Miraflores, Col. c3 284
Miraflores, Mex. e6 272
Miraflores de la Sierra g4 190
Mirah, Wādī al h6 136
Miraí g4 291
Miraj d4 126
Miralta g2 291
Miramar, Buenos Aires, Arg. j5 297
Miramar, Córdoba, Arg. f1 297
Miramar, Lago o9 273
Miramare g5 197
Miramas b7 185
Mirambeau b3 186
Mirambel d4 192
Miramichi Bay k5 253
Miraña c4 284
Miranda, Arg. h4 297
Miranda, Braz. f4 293
Miranda, Braz. f4 293
Miranda, Ven. d1 284
Miranda de Ebro b2 192
Miranda do Corvo b4 190
Miranda do Douro d3 190
Mirande c5 187
Mirandela c3 190
Mirandillas c3 274
Mirandola f5 196
Mirano g4 196
Mirante do Paranapanema c5 290
Mirante, Serra do c5 290
Mirapinima e4 285
Miras e5 200
Miraspur c5 130
Mirassol d4 290
Miravalles d2 190
Miravci c1 210
Mirbāţ e7 116
Mircze m5 169
Mirë e5 182
Mirebalais h5 271
Mirebeau, Bourgogne, Fr. b3 184
Mirebeau, Poitou-Charentes, Fr. f6 183
Mirecourt c2 184
Miren e4 176
Mirepoix d5 187
Mirgarh f6 129
Miri h2 99
Miri, Pak. a6 129
Miri Hills b2 102
Miria f3 223
Miriam Vale d4 84
Mirim, Lagoa f2 294
Mirim, Lagoa do c7 289
Mirimire d1 284
Mirimiri j6 97
Miriñay e1 294
Mirjäveh a4 122
Mirna, Cro. e5 176
Mirna, Slvn. g4 177
Mirny (Rus. Fed.) q1 298
Mirnyj, Respublika Saha (Jakutija), Russ. Fed. m3 119
Mirnyj, Samarskaja Oblast', Russ. Fed. l5 151
Mirond Lake r4 249
Miroslav h1 177
Mirosławiec e2 168
Mirovice c2 170
Mirow h2 173
Mirpur a3 130
Mirpur Batoro d8 129
Mirpur Khas d8 129
Mirpur Sakro c8 129
Mirsk d5 168
Mirtna h6 80
Mirto Crosia f5 198
Mirtoö Pelagos SE d6 211
Miryang q8 113
Mirzawal f6 129
Misa l4 157
Misaki f4 115
Misantla f4 275
Misaw Lake r2 249
Misawa j1 115
Miscou Island k5 253
Misfaq b5 139
Misgar b1 130
Mishan r3 113
Mishawaka c5 254
Misheguk Mountain d1 246
Mishima h4 115
Mi-shima d4 114
Mishlah, Khashm g3 219
Mishmi Hills c1 102
Misilmeri c6 199
Misiones, Arg. f1 294
Misiones, Para. f5 293
Misiones, Sierra de f1 294
Miskah j9 137
Miske h5 171
Miškino k5 147
Miskitos, Cayos f3 277
Miskolc j3 171
Mislinja g3 177
Mišnjak f5 177
Misoöl j6 97
Mişrātah h2 221
Missanello f4 198
Missinaibi n5 251
Missinaibi Lake m6 251
Mission, South Dakota, U.S.A. c3 260
Mission, Texas, U.S.A. k4 273
Mission Viejo f8 265
Missisa Lake l4 251
Missisicabi p5 251
Missisagi m7 251
Mississauga g4 254
Mississippi, Can. de6 252
Mississippi, U.S.A. e3 258
Mississippi, U.S.A. d3 258
Missoula g2 262
Missour d2 220
Missouri, U.S.A. e4 260
Missouri, Missouri, U.S.A. f4 260
Missouri Valley e3 260
Mistake Creek j5 86
Mistake Creek, Queensland, Aust. b3 84
Mistassibi f4 252
Mistassini f4 252
Mistegna g3 210
Mistelbach h1 177
Misterbianco e7 199
Misteriosa Bank f1 277
Misterton f3 162
Mistinibi, Lac f3 252
Mistissini f3 252
Mistretta d7 199
Mistros d4 210
Misty Fiords National Monument Wilderness m5 247
Misty Lake s2 249
Misurina g3 196
Mišvan' h2 147
Mît Ghamr c6 136
Mita Hills Dam d1 233
Mita, Punta de b3 274
Mitaraca g3 285
Mitchell, New South Wales, Aust. e6 85
Mitchell, Queensland, Aust. A 84
Mitchell, Aust. h9 81
Mitchell, Aust. e3 83
Mitchell, Indiana, U.S.A. c6 254
Mitchell, South Dakota, U.S.A. d3 260
Mitchell and Alice Rivers National Park f3 80
Mitchell Point j2 86
Mitchell Range b2 80
Mitchell, Lake A 84
Mitchell, Mount h2 259
Mitchelstown c4 165
Mitha Tiwano f4 128
Mithankot e6 129
Mithapur d9 129
Mithi d8 129
Mithrau d7 129
Mithymna g3 210
Mititai g4 76
Mitkof Island l4 247
Mitla, Mex. f5 275
Mitla, Oaxaca, Mex. f5 275
Mito j3 115
Mitole b5 227
Mitre e4 77
Mitre Island H 75
Mitre Peak a6 77
Mitre, Península c6 295
Mitrofania Island e5 246
Mitropoli b3 210
Mitrousi d1 210
Mitsinjo Ab2 233
Mitsio, Nosy Ab1 233
Mitsukaidō h3 115
Mitsuke h3 115
Mitta Mitta h14 81
Mittagong g2 83
Mittelberg, Tirol, Aus. b3 176
Mittelberg, Vorarlberg, Aus. b2 176
Mittelfranken f3 175
Mittelland b3 196
Mittellandkanal g3 173
Mittelradde c3 172
Mittenwald d2 175
Mittenwalde j2 173
Mittersill d2 176
Mitterteich h3 175
Mittweida h2 175
Mitú c3 284
Mitumba, Monts e4 225
Mituva k5 157
Mitwaba e5 225
Mitzic b3 224
Mi-Wuk Village c3 264
Mixteco e5 275
Mixtlán b3 274
Miyagi j2 115
Miyāh, Wādī al g5 209
Miyake-jima h5 115
Miyako g2 115
Miyakonojō d6 114
Miyaly j2 149
Miyani d10 129
Miyanojō d6 114
Miyazaki, Japan d5 114
Miyazaki d6 114
Miyazu f4 115
Miyi d5 104
Miyoshi e4 114
Miyun j5 113
Mizan Teferī b2 226
Mizāni c4 128
Mizdah g2 221
Mizen Head, Ire. b5 165
Mizen Head, Ire. f4 165
Mizhevichy p3 169
Mizhhir"ya f1 201
Mizhi h1 106
Miziara b2 138
Mizil h3 201
Miziya f4 201
Mizoram n8 125
Mizpe Ramon c6 139
Mizpe Shalēm d5 139
Mizpe Yeriḥo d5 139
Mizque d3 292
Mizunami g4 115
Mizusawa j2 115
Mjaksa e2 150
Mjällån f5 154
Mjällom g5 154
Mjatlevo c4 150
Mjaundža q3 119
Mjölby f3 156
Mjøndalen d3 156
Mjörn e4 156
Mjøsa d2 156
Mkata b5 227
Mkoani b5 227
Mkokotoni b5 227
Mkomazi b4 227
Mkushi d1 233
Mkuze k3 235
Mkuzi Game Reserve k3 235
Mladá Boleslav c1 170
Mladé Buky d1 170
Mladenovac e3 200
Mława j2 169
Mljet, Cro. c4 200
Mlungisi g5 235
Młynary h1 169
Młynarze k3 169
Mmabatho f2 235
Mmamabula g1 235
Mmathethe f2 235
Mncwasa Point h6 235
Mnichovice c2 170
Mnichovo Hradiště c1 170
Mniów j4 169
Mníšek nad Hnilcom j3 171
Mníšek pod Brdy c2 170
Mo e4 223
Mo i Rana e3 154
Moa, Braz. c5 284
Moa, Indon. p9 99
Moa, S. L. b4 222
Moab j6 263
Moabi b4 224
Moala j8 74
Moamba k2 235
Moanda b4 224
Moate d3 165
Moatize e2 233
Moba e5 225
Mobārakābād p7 137
Mobārakeh n5 137
Mobaye d3 224
Mobayi-Mbongo d3 224
Mobeka c3 224
Moberly e4 260
Mobile e4 258
Mobile Point e4 258
Mobo d4 100
Mobridge c2 260
Mobwasa d3 224
Môc Châu g5 102
Moča g4 171
Moçajuba c2 288
Moçambicano, Planalto b6 231
Moçambique c7 227
Moçambique, Ilha de c7 231
Mocanal Ab3 189
Mocapra d2 284
Moçarria b5 191
Moce E 74
Mocejón g5 191
Močenok f3 171
Mocha, Isla a5 296
Mochales c3 192
Mochicahui e5 272
Mochudi g2 235
Mocidade, Serra da e3 285
Mocimboa da Praia c6 227
Mocimboa do Rovuma b6 227
Mociu g2 201
Möckeln f3 156
Mockfjärd f2 156
Mockrehna h4 173
Mocksville j2 259
Moclín g7 191
Mocoa b3 284
Mococa e4 291
Mocoduene l1 235
Mocorito f5 272
Mocra j2 201
Moctezuma, Mex. e3 275
Moctezuma, Chihuahua, Mex. f2 272
Moctezuma, San Luis Potosí, Mex. d2 274
Moctezuma, Sonora, Mex. j11 263
Mocuba f2 233
Modane c5 185
Modasa f9 129
Modder f4 235
Model Town g5 128
Modena, Italy e5 196
Modena e5 196
Moder d2 184
Modestino Pizarro e3 296
Modesto c4 264
Modesto Méndez c3 276
Modica d8 199
Modigliana f5 197
Modimolle h2 235
Modinagar c5 130
Mödling h1 177
Modot e2 112
Modowi j6 97
Modra f3 170
Modrany g4 171
Modriča d3 200
Modřice e2 170
Mödringberg f3 177
Modriště b1 210
Modrý Kameň h3 171
Modugno f3 198
Moe h15 81
Moehau e2 76
Moëlan-sur-Mer b5 182
Moelv d2 156
Moen g2 154
Moengo g2 285
Moenkopi h7 263
Moenkopi Wash h7 263
Moeraki Point c6 77
Moerbeke b3 159
Moerewa e1 76
Moerkesung g4 135
Moers e3 159
Moervaart b3 159
Moesa d3 196
Moffat e4 164
Mofreita d3 190
Moga b4 130
Mogadishu d3 226
Mogadishu, Banaadir, Som. d3 226
Mogadouro d3 190
Mogadouro, Serra de d3 190
Mogalakwena h1 235
Mogalo c3 224
Mogán Ad3 189
Mogapi g1 235
Mogapinyana g1 235
Mogeltønder c3 102
Mogenstrup b4 158
Mögglingen e3 158
Mogielnica e2 174
Mogielnica j4 169
Mogi-Guaçu e5 291
Mogilno f3 168
Mogi-Mirim e5 291
Mogincual c7 227
Mogiquiçaba j2 291
Mogliano Veneto g4 196
Mogocha f2 94
Mogogh f2 225
Mogoi j6 97
Mogok c4 102
Mogoro Aa3 198
Mogoșești-Siret h2 201
Mograt Island d2 218
Mogroum h3 223
Moguer d7 191
Moguqi m2 113
Mogyoród h4 171
Mohács g6 171
Mohaka f3 76
Mohale's Hoek g5 235
Mohall c6 250
Mohammadia e1 221
Mohan c4 130
Mohanganj m7 125
Mohave, Lake f8 261
Mohawk, U.S.A. f2 256
Mohawk, Michigan, U.S.A. j7 251
Moheda f4 156
Mohegan Lake g3 257
Mohelnice e2 170
Mohembo c2 232
Mohican, Cape c3 246
Möhkö n5 155
Möhne d3 172
Mohns Ridge u2 299
Mohnyin c3 102
Moho d3 292
Mohora h4 171
Mohoro b5 227
Mohovoe d5 150
Mohsogolloh n3 119
Mohyliv Podil's'kyy h1 201
Moi b3 156
Moià g3 192
Moimenta da Beira c4 190
Moincêr e4 130
Moinda m5 125
Moine d5 182
Moinești h2 201
Moira e2 165
Moirans b5 185
Moirans-en-Montagne b4 184
Moires e7 211
Mõisaküla l3 157
Moisdon-la-Rivière d5 182
Moisés Ville d2 294
Moisie j3 253
Moissac d4 187
Moissala c2 224
Moita A 191
Moita a6 191
Moitaco e2 285
Moixent d6 193
Mojácar c7 193
Mojados f3 190
Mojave, California, U.S.A. e6 265
Mojave, California, U.S.A. f6 265
Mojave Desert f6 265
Moji das Cruzes e5 291
Mojiang e4 102
Moji-Guaçu e5 290
Mojo, Bol. d4 292
Mojo, Eth. b2 226
Mojocoya e3 293
Mojokerto g8 98
Mojones, Cerro d5 292
Moju, Braz. c2 288
Moju, Pará, Braz. c2 288
Mōka j3 115
Mokama j7 125
Mokaria d3 224
Mokau, N.Z. e3 76
Mokau e3 76
Mokéko c3 224
Mokhotlong h4 235
Mokhino g1 221
Mokohinau Islands e1 76
Mokokchung p6 125
Mokolo, Cam. g3 223
Mokolo, D.R.C. c3 224
Mokolo, R.S.A. g1 235
Mokolo Dam Nature Reserve g2 235
Mokopane h2 235
Mokp'o p8 113
Mokre, Jezioro k2 169
Mokša g4 151
Mokšan h5 151
Möksy k5 155
Mokwa f4 223
Mol d3 159
Mol Len b3 102
Mola di Bari g3 198
Moladava p3 169
Molango e3 275
Molanosa a3 250
Molaoi c6 211
Molares c3 190
Molatón c5 193
Mold c3 162
Moldary s2 121
Moldava nad Bodvou j3 171
Molde a5 154
Moldjord e3 154
Moldova k5 145

MOLDOVA

THE REPUBLIC OF MOLDOVA
Area 33,700km^2 (13,010sq miles)
Capital Chisinau
Organizations BSEC, CE, CIS, EBRD
Population 4,270,000
Pop. growth (%) 0.5
Life expectancy 62 (m); 70 (f)
Languages Moldovan (Romanian), Russian
Literacy 99.1%
Currency Moldovan leu (US $1 = 12.87 Moldovan leu)
GDP (US million $) 1566
GDP per head ($US) 366

Moldova Nouă e3 200
Moldoveanu, Vârful g3 201
Moldovița g2 201
Møldrup c2 158
Mole National Park d4 222
Moledet d4 138
Molen h3 235
Molenbeek-St-Jean c4 159
Molène, Île de a4 182
Molepolole f2 235
Molėtai l5 157
Molfetta f3 198
Molfsee d4 158
Molières d4 187
Molina, Arg. c2 296
Molina, Chile b3 296
Molina de Aragón c4 192
Molina de Segura c6 193
Moline a5 254
Molinella f5 196
Molinges b4 184
Molino Doll g2 297
Molinos d5 292
Molinos de Matachel, Embalse de los e6 191
Molins de Rei g3 192
Moliro f5 225
Molise d3 198
Moliterno e4 198
Molkom e3 156
Mölle f2 158
Møllebjerg c3 158
Möllenbeck j2 173
Mollendo c3 292
Möllenhagen h2 173
Mollerussa e3 192
Mollet del Vallès g3 192
Molln f2 177
Mölln d5 158
Molló g2 192
Mölltorp d3 156
Mölnlycke f1 158
Molocue b7 231
Molodezhnaya (Rus. Fed.) k1 298
Molodizhne d3 148
Molodogvardeyskoye m5 147
Molodoj Tud b3 150
Molokai Ac2 263
Molokai Fracture Zone n4 301
Molokovo d2 150
Moloma k2 151
Molong j12 81
Molopo e2 234
Moloporivier f2 234
Molos c4 210
Moloundou c3 224
Molovata j2 201
Molowaie d5 224
Molsheim d2 184
Molson Lake e3 250
Molteno g5 235
Molucca Sea SE n4 99
Molumbo f2 233
Molveno e3 196
Molveno, Lago di e3 196
Moma, D.R.C. d4 224
Moma, Moz. f2 233
Momax c3 274
Mombaça e3 288
Mombasa b4 227
Mombeltrán e4 190
Mombenzélé c3 224
Mombjerge b2 158
Momboyo c4 224
Mömbris e4 174
Mombuca, Serra da b3 290
Mombuey d2 190
Momchilgrad f1 210
Momed f4 219
Momence c5 254
Momi e4 225
Momignies c4 159
Momling e3 174
Momo c4 196
Momotombo, Volcán d4 276
Mompog Passage d4 100
Mompono d3 224
Mompós c2 284
Momskij Hrebet q3 119
Møn f4 158
Mon, Myan. c7 102
Mon c6 102
Mona Quimbundo c5 224
Mona, Isla l5 267
Mona, Punta de la g8 191
Monacia-d'Aullène A 185
Monaco f6 145

MONACO

THE PRINCIPALITY OF MONACO
Area 2km^2 (1sq mile)
Capital Monaco
Organizations
Population 34,000
Pop. growth (%) 0
Life expectancy 78 (m); 78 (f)
Languages French, Monegasque, Italian, English
Literacy 99%
Currency euro (US $1 = 0.81 euro)
GDP (US million $) 847
GDP per head ($US) 24,911

Monaco Plain h6 302
Monadhliath Mountains d2 164
Monagas e2 285
Monaghan, Ire. e2 165
Monaghan e2 165
Monahans c6 261
Monango d7 250
Monapo c6 227
Monaragala g9 126
Monarch Mountain e6 248
Monarch Pass b4 260
Monasterace f6 199
Monasterevan d3 165
Monastir, Italy Ab3 198
Monastir, Tun. g1 221
Monastiraki a4 210
Monastyrščina a4 150
Monastyrys'ka p6 169
Monastyryshche j1 201
Monatélé g5 223
Monbazillac c4 186
Monbetsu, Hokkaidō, Japan Ac1 114
Monbetsu, Hokkaidō, Japan Ac2 114
Monboré b2 224
Moncalieri b4 196
Moncalvo c4 196
Moncalvo, Spain d2 190
Monção b2 190
Moncarapacho c7 191
Mončegorsk p3 155
Mönchengladbach e3 159
Mönchhof h2 177
Monchique b7 191
Monchique, Serra de b7 191
Moncks Corner j3 259
Monclar-de-Quercy d5 187
Monclova, Campeche, Mex. b1 276
Monclova, Coahuila, Mex. j4 273
Moncontour c4 182
Moncouche, Lac g4 252
Moncoutant e6 182
Moncton k5 253
Mondai g5 293
Mondavio g6 197
Monday a6 290
Mondego c5 190
Mondego, Cabo b4 190
Mondéjar a4 192
Mondello c6 199
Mondeville e3 182
Mondimbi d3 224
Mondjamboli d3 224
Mondjuku d4 224
Mondlo j3 235
Mondo h3 223
Mondolfo h6 197
Mondombe d4 224
Mondoñedo c1 190
Mondoubleau f5 183
Mondovi b5 197
Mondragon a6 185
Mondragón b1 192
Mondragone c3 198
Mondsee e2 176
Mondúver d5 193
Moneague B 270
Moneglia d5 197
Monegrillo d3 192
Monegros, Canal de d3 192
Monein b5 187
Monemvasia d6 211
Monessen g5 254
Monesterio d6 191
Monestier-de-Clermont b6 185
Monestiés e4 187
Monêteau j5 183
Monett c1 258
Monette d2 258
Moneygall d4 165
Monfalcone h4 196
Monflanquin c4 186
Monforte d3 284
Monfort, Col. c5 187
Monfort, Fr. c5 191
Monforte, Port c5 191
Monforte, Spain c2 190
Monforte d'Alba b5 196
Monforte da Beira c5 191
Monfortinho d4 190
Monfurado, Serra de b6 191
Mong Hai d5 102
Mong Hpayak d5 102
Mong Hsat d5 102
Mong Hsu d5 102
Mong Kung c5 102
Mong Ma d5 102
Mong Mir c4 102
Mong Nai c5 102
Mong Nawng d5 102
Mong Pan d5 102
Mong Si d4 102
Mong Yai d4 102
Mong Yang d5 102
Mong Yawng e5 102
Monga d3 224
Mongaguá e6 291
Mongala d3 224
Mongar m6 125
Mongers Lake c11 87
Mongge j6 97
Monggon Qulu k1 113
Monggŭmp'o-ri n6 113
Monghidoro f5 197
Mongo a5 218
Mongo, S. L. b4 222
Mongolia h4 93

MONGOLIA

MONGOLIA
Area 1,566,500km^2 (604,829sq miles)
Capital Ulan Bator
Organizations ADB
Population 2,560,000
Pop. growth (%) 2.5
Life expectancy 59 (m); 63 (f)
Languages Khalkha Mongolian, Kazakh
Literacy 98.6%
Currency tugrik (US $1 = 1126 tugrik)
GDP (US million $) 970
GDP per head ($US) 378

Mongomo b3 224
Mongona, Mount h4 86
Mongonu g3 223
Mongora f3 128
Mongororo b5 218
Mongoumba c3 224
Mongrove, Punta c5 274
Mongu c2 232
Monguelfo g3 196
Mönh Hayrhan Uul n1 117
Monheim e4 175
Moni b2 138
Monigotes d2 294
Moniquirá c2 284
Möniste m4 157
Monistrol-sur-Loire a5 184
Monitor Range g3 264
Moñitos j6 277
Monjolos f3 291
Monkey Bay f1 233
Monkey River Town c2 276
Mońki l2 169
Monkira e8 80
Monkoto d4 224
Monleón d4 192
Monmouth d5 163
Monmouth, U.S.A. a5 254
Monmouth Mountain f6 248
Monmouthshire d5 163
Monnaie f5 183
Monnow d5 163
Mono e4 223
Mono Lake e4 264
Mono, Punta del f5 277
Monolithos Ac2 211
Monomoy Island l3 257
Monon c5 254
Monona b4 254
Monopoli g4 198
Monor h4 171
Monorgahela f6 254
Monou b4 218
Monóvar d6 193
Monowai, Lake a6 77
Monpazier c4 186
Monreal, Spain b5 193
Monreal c2 192
Monreal del Campo c4 192
Monreale c6 199
Monroe, Georgia, U.S.A. h3 259
Monroe, Louisiana, U.S.A. c3 258
Monroe, Michigan, U.S.A. e5 254
Monroe, New York, U.S.A. f3 257
Monroe, Washington, U.S.A. c2 262
Monroe Lake c6 254
Monroeton d3 256
Monroeville g5 254
Monrovia b4 222
Monroy d5 191
Monroyo d4 192
Mons, Bel. b4 159
Mons, Fr. c7 185
Møns Klint f4 158
Monsalvo j4 297
Monsarás, Ponta de j3 288
Monschau e4 159
Monségur c4 186
Monselice f4 196
Monsols a4 184
Monson h6 252
Mönsterås g4 156
Monsummano Terme e6 197
Mont Alto c5 256
Mont Cenis, Col du c5 185
Mont Fouari, Réserve du b4 224
Mont Peko, Parc National du c4 222
Mont Sangbé, Parc National du c4 222
Montabaur g2 174
Montafon a2 176
Montagnac f5 187
Montagnana f4 196
Montagne b4 186
Montagne d'Ambre, Parc National de la Ab1 233
Montagne de Reims, Parc Naturel Régional de la k3 183
Montagnes Noires b4 182
Montagrier c3 186
Montagu d6 234
Montague c4 254
Montague Island h4 247
Montague Range d10 87
Montague, Isla b2 272
Montaigu d6 182
Montaigu-de-Quercy d4 187
Montaigut e2 186
Montaigut-sur-Save d5 187
Montalbán d4 192
Montalbano Elicona e6 199
Montalbano Jonico f4 198
Montalbo b5 193
Montalcino f6 197
Montalegre c3 190
Montalieu-Vercieu b5 185
Montalto e6 199
Montalto di Castro f7 197
Montalto Uffugo f5 199
Montalvão c5 191
Montalvo, Ec. b4 284
Montalvo, Port. b5 191
Montamarta e3 190
Montana, Bul. f4 201
Montana, Bul. f4 201
Montana, Switz. b3 196
Montana, U.S.A. d2 262
Montana, Alaska, U.S.A. g3 246
Montaña de Comayagua, Parque Nacional d3 276
Montaña de Covadonga, Parque Nacional de la e1 190
Montaña de Cusuco, Parque Nacional c3 276
Montaña de Yoro d3 276
Montánchez, Spain d5 191
Montánchez d5 191
Montanejos d4 193
Montaner b5 187
Montanha h3 291
Montano Antilia e4 198
Montargil b5 191
Montargil, Barragem de b5 191
Montargis h5 183
Montastruc-la-Conseillère d5 187
Montataire h3 183
Montauban d4 187
Montauk j3 257
Montauk Point j3 257
Montbard a3 184
Montbarrey b3 184
Montbazens e4 187
Montbazon f5 183
Montbéliard c3 184
Montblanc f3 192
Montbozon c3 184
Montbrison a5 184
Montbron c3 186
Montceau-les-Mines a4 184
Montcenis a4 184
Montchanin a4 184
Montclair f4 257
Montcornet c5 159
Montcuq d4 187
Mont-de-Marsan b5 187
Montdidier h3 183
Mont-Dore e3 186
Monte Águila a4 296
Monte Alegre g4 285
Monte Alegre de Goiás c4 288
Monte Alegre de Minas d3 290
Monte Aprazível d4 290
Monte Azul d5 289
Monte Azul Paulista d4 290
Monte Buey f2 297
Monte Carmelo e3 290
Monte Caseros e2 294
Monte Comán d3 296
Monte Corno, Parco Naturale f3 196
Monte Cristi j5 271
Monte Cristo, Arg. f1 297
Monte Cristo, Bol. e2 293
Monte da Pedra c5 191
Monte da Rocha, Barragem do b7 191
Monte das Flores c6 191
Monte Dinero c6 295
Monte do Trigo c6 191
Monte Dourado g4 285
Monte Escobedo c2 274
Monte Falterona, Campigna e delle Foreste Casentinesi, Parco Nazionale del Ab2 198
Monte Figo, Serra de c7 191
Monte Grande h3 297
Monte Hermoso g5 297
Monte León c6 295
Monte Líbano, Col. k6 277
Monte Líbano, Mex. b2 276
Monte Maíz f2 297
Monte Novo, Barragem do c6 191
Monte Patria b2 294
Monte Quemado e5 293
Monte Real b5 191
Monte Redondo b5 191
Monte Romano f7 197
Monte San Savino f6 197
Monte San Vito h6 197
Monte Sant'Angelo e3 198
Monte Santo de Minas e4 291
Monte Santu, Capo di Ab2 198
Monte Vera g1 297
Monte Vista b4 261
Monte, Lago del f4 297
Monteagle g2 259
Monteagudo e3 293
Montealegre de las Vicarías b3 192
Montealegre del Castillo c6 193
Montebello e7 199
Montebello Islands b7 86
Montebelluna g4 196
Montebourg d3 182
Monte-Carlo b6 197
Montecastrilli g7 197
Montecatini Terme e6 197
Montecchio Emilia e5 196
Montecchio Maggiore, Veneto, Italy f4 196

MOROCCO

THE KINGDOM OF MOROCCO

Area 710,850km²
(274,461sq miles)
Capital Rabat
Organizations IDB, LAS, OIC
Population 29,630,000
Pop. growth (%) 1.9
Life expectancy 64 (m); 68 (f)
Languages Arabic, Berber, Spanish, French
Literacy 51.7%
Currency Moroccan dirham
(US $1 = 8.97 Moroccan dirham)
GDP (US million $) 40,045
GDP per head ($US) 1351

Moyynkum → Nagarzê 361

Moyynkum, Zhambylskaya Oblast', Kaz. p5 121
Moyynkum, Peski, Karagandinskaya Oblast', Kaz. l4 121
Moyynkum, Peski, Yuzhnyy Kazakhstan/ Zhambylskaya Oblast', Kaz. n5 121
Moyynty p4 121
Možajsk d4 150
Mozambique f7 217

MOZAMBIQUE

THE REPUBLIC OF MOZAMBIQUE
Area 799,380km² (308,641sq miles)
Capital Maputo
Organizations COMM, SADC, OIC
Population 18,540,000
Pop. growth (%) 1.9
Life expectancy 39 (m); 41 (f)
Languages Portuguese, many local languages
Literacy 47.8%
Currency metical (US $1 = 23352 metical)
GDP (US million $) 2810
GDP per head ($US) 151

Mozambique Channel c7 227
Mozambique Plateau a8 300
Mozárbez e4 190
Mozarlândia b4 289
Mozdok g4 149
Mozdūrān h9 120
Možga m3 151
Mozirske Planine f3 177
Mozitan e4 111
Mozogo-Gokoro, Parc National de g3 223
Mpaathutlwa Pan e2 234
Mpal a2 222
Mpala e5 225
Mpama c4 224
Mpanda f5 225
Mpandamatenga d2 232
Mpé b4 224
Mpessoba c3 222
Mpigi f3 225
Mpika f6 225
Mpoko c2 224
Mporokoso f5 225
Mpouya c4 224
Mpui f5 225
Mpulungu f5 225
Mpumalanga, Eastern Transvaal, R.S.A. j3 235
Mpumalanga j4 235
Mpwapwa b5 227
Mqanduli h5 235
Mrągowo k2 169
Mrakovo k1 149
Mrežičko b1 210
Mrežnica g4 177
Mrkonjić-Grad c3 200
Mrkopalj f4 177
Mrocza f2 168
Mroczno h2 169
Msambweni b4 227
Msata b5 227
Mšeno c1 170
Mšinskaja n3 157
Msta b2 150
Mstera f3 150
Mstsislaw a4 150
Mszana Dolna j6 169
Mszczonów j4 169
Mt'at'ushet'is Nakrdzali g4 149
Mtakuja f5 225
Mtelo b3 226
Mtorwi f5 225
Mts'khet'a g4 149
Mtubatuba k4 235
Mtunzini j4 235
Mtwara, Tan. g6 225
Mtwara c6 227
Mu, Myan. b4 102
Mu, Port b7 191
Mu Ko Chang National Park f10 103
Mu Us Shamo e6 112
Mu'tah d5 139
Muaguide b6 227
Mualama f2 233
Muan p8 113
Muana c2 288
Muanda b5 224
Muang Hinboun g7 102
Muang Kao f6 102
Muang Không g8 103
Muang Khôngxédôn g8 102
Muang Khoua f5 102
Muang Kirirath a1 101
Muang Ngoy f5 102
Muang Nong h7 102
Muang Ou Nua e4 102
Muang Pakbeng e6 102
Muang Phalan g7 102
Muang Phiang e6 102
Muang Sing e5 102
Muang Soum f6 102
Muang Souy f6 102
Muang Thadua e6 102
Muang Va f5 102
Muang Xay f5 102
Muang Xon f5 102
Muangai b1 232
Muanza e2 233
Muar, Malay. c4 101
Muar c4 101
Muaraancalong j4 99
Muaraatap j4 99
Muarabeliti b6 98
Muarabungo b5 98
Muaradua c7 98
Muaraenim b6 98
Muarainu h5 99
Muarakaman j5 99
Muaralesan j4 99
Muararupit b6 98
Muaras Reef k4 99
Muarasipongi a5 101
Muarasoma a5 101
Muaratebo b5 98
Muaratembesi b5 98
Muarateweh h5 99
Muarawahau j4 99
Muari p5 99
Mu'āwīya d4 138
Muazzam g5 128
Mubarakpur h6 125
Mubarek b1 128
Mubende f3 225
Mubi g3 223
Mūbiş d4 139
Mubur d3 98
Mucaba, Serra c5 224
Mucajá f4 285
Mucajaí, Serra do e3 285
Mucanha e2 233
Muccan e7 86
Much f4 159
Much Pai Khel e4 128
Muchinga Escarpment e1 233
Muchiri e3 293
Muchot, Puntan A 74
Muchówka j6 169
Muchuan d4 104
Mücka k4 173
Muckadilla j9 81
Muco c3 284
Mucojo c6 227
Muconda d6 224
Mucope a2 232
Mucsi-hegy k3 177
Múcsony j3 171
Mucubela f2 233
Mucuim e5 285
Mucumbura e2 233
Mucunambiba, Ilha d2 288
Mucupia f2 233
Mucur e3 208
Mucura e4 285
Mucuri, Braz. j3 291
Mucuri, Bahia, Braz. j3 291
Mucurici h3 291
Mucuripe d4 284
Mucuripe, Ponta de e2 288
Mud Lake f4 264
Mudabidri d6 126
Mudan Ling q4 113
Mudanjiang q3 113
Mudayrah l7 137
Muddus nationalpark h3 154
Muddy Boggy Creek a2 258
Muddy Gap Pass b3 260
Müden (Aller) f3 172
Mudgee j12 81
Mudki b4 130
Mudon c7 102
Mudu g4 111
Mudug d2 226
Mudukani b4 227
Mudumu National Park c2 232
Mudurnu c2 208
Muecate b6 227
Mueda b6 227
Muel c3 192
Muela de Arés d4 192
Muelas del Pan e3 190
Muen d2 156
Muenster a3 258
Muezerskij p5 155
Mufu Shan d5 106
Mufulira d1 233
Mufumbwe d1 232
Mugaguadavic Lake j6 253
Muğan Düzü b8 120
Mugang d5 106
Mugardos b1 190
Mugarripug h3 135
Muge, Port b5 191
Muge b5 191
Mugeba f2 233
Mügeln j1 175
Muggar Kangri h3 135
Muggia h4 196
Mughal Kot d5 128
Mughal Sarai h7 125
Mūghār p5 137
Mughayrā' f7 136
Mughayyir as Sarḩān e4 139
Mughsu e1 128
Mugila, Monts e5 225
Muğla, Tur. b4 208
Muğla b4 208
Müglitz j5 173
Mugodzharskoye k2 149
Mugodzhary, Gory g3 120
Mugron b5 187
Mugu Karnali f5 135
Muguia b6 227
Mugutira j6 97
Mugxung p3 125
Muhagiriya c5 218
Muhala e5 225
Muhammad Ashraf d7 129
Muhammad Qol e3 219
Muḩammad, Ra's d2 218
Muhashsham, Wādī c7 139
Muḩayy d6 139
Muheza b5 227
Mühlacker d4 174
Mühlbach j2 173
Mühlberg j4 173
Mühldorf am Inn d1 176
Mühlen f2 177
Mühlenbeck j3 173
Mühlhausen (Thüringen) d1 174
Mühlheim d2 174
Mühltroff g2 175
Muhola k5 155
Muhos k4 155
Muḩradah e1 138
Muhri c6 129
Muhtolovo g4 151
Muhu k3 157
Muhulu e4 225
Muhuwesi g6 225
Mui b2 226
Mui Ba Lang An j8 102
Mui Ca Mau g11 103
Mui Dinh j10 103
Mui Độc h7 102
Mui Kê j10 103
Mui Nây j9 103
Mui Ron h6 102
Muidumbe b6 227
Muié c1 232
Muine Bheag e4 165
Muir of Ord d2 164
Muirdrum f3 164
Muirkirk d4 164
Muisne b3 284
Muite b6 227
Muji s9 121
Muju p7 113
Mujuí Joboti g4 285
Muk, Ko a2 101
Mukacheve l3 171
Mukah, Malay. g3 98
Mukah g3 98
Mukandgarh b6 130
Mükangsar h5 135
Mukařov c2 170
Mukawa Ab2 114
Mu-kawa Ac2 114
Mukāwir d5 139
Mukdahan g7 102
Mukerian b4 130
Mukhayyamī Ramdān e3 138
Mukhmās d5 139
Mukinbudin d12 87
Mukomuko a6 98
Mukono f3 225
Mukry b2 128
Mukteswar d5 130
Muktinath f5 135
Muktsar g5 128
Mukuku e6 225
Mukur, Atyraū Oblysy, Kaz. j3 149
Mukur, Vostochnyy Kazakhstan, Kaz. t2 121
Mukutawa e4 250
Mul'da k2 147
Mula, Spain c7 193
Mula c6 193
Mulaly s5 121
Mulan q3 113
Mulana c4 130
Mulanay d4 100
Mulanje f2 233
Mulanje, Mount b7 231
Mulatos e3 272
Mula-tupo j6 277
Mulatupo Sasardi j6 277
Mulayḩ d5 139
Mulayḩah e3 138
Mulayjah m8 137
Mulbekh c2 130
Mulben e2 164
Mulberry, Arkansas, U.S.A. b2 258
Mulberry, Florida, U.S.A. j6 259
Mulchatna e3 246
Mulchén a4 296
Muldraugh g1 259
Mule Creek b3 260
Muleba f4 225
Mulegé d4 272
Mules l9 99
Muleshoe c5 261
Mulevala f2 233
Mulgathing b11 81
Mulhacén a7 193
Mulhall a1 258
Mülheim an der Ruhr e3 159
Mulhouse d3 184
Muli, China c5 104
Muli, India e9 129
Mulia k6 97
Mulila e9 129
Muling He r3 113
Mulinu'u, Cape M 75
Mull c3 164
Mulla Ali m3 137
Mullaghareirk Mts b4 164
Mullaghmore e2 165
Mullaittivu g8 126
Mullan f2 262
Mullengudgery h11 81
Muller b7 80
Muller, Pegunungan g4 98
Mullet, The a2 165
Mullewa b11 87
Müllheim c5 174
Mullica f5 256
Mulligan d8 80
Mullinavat d4 165
Mullingar d3 165
Mullion a6 163
Mullovka k4 151
Müllrose k3 173
Mullsjö e4 156
Mullumbimby l10 81
Mullutu laht k3 157
Mulobezi d2 232
Mulongo e5 225
Mulrany b3 165
Mulsanne f5 183
Multai f9 124
Multan e5 128
Multia l1 157
Multien h3 183
Mulu, Gunung h2 99
Mulumbe, Monts e5 225
Mulungushi Dam d1 233
Mulurulu Lake c1 82
Mulym'ja, Russ. Fed. l3 147
Mulym'ja l3 147
Mum Nok, Laem a2 101
Muma d3 224
Mumbeji c1 232
Mumbles Head c5 163
Mumbondo b6 224
Mumbué b1 232
Mumbwa d1 232
Mume e5 225
Mumra g3 149
Mun'gyŏng q7 113
Muna, Indon. m7 99
Muna, Mex. q7 273
Muna, Russ. Fed. m2 119
Munabao e8 129
Muñana e4 190
Munayly j3 149
Munch'ŏn p6 113
Münchberg g2 175
Müncheberg k3 173
München g4 175
Munchique, Cerro b3 284
Munchique, Parque Nacional b3 284
Muncho Lake Provincial Park d2 248
Münchwilen d2 196
Muncie d5 254
Muncy d3 256
Munda e5 128
Mundaka b1 192
Mundawar c6 130
Mundel Lake A 127
Mundemba f5 223
Munderfing e1 176
Munderkingen c2 174
Mundesley h4 162
Mundjura Creek e5 80
Mundo c6 193
Mundo Novo d4 288
Mundra d9 129
Mundrabilla h12 87
Mundubbera k8 81
Mundwa f7 129
Munebrega c3 192
Munera b5 193
Muneru g4 126
Munfordville g1 259
Mungallala b5 85
Mungallala Creek b5 85
Mungana g4 80
Mungaoli f7 124
Mungári e2 233
Mungaroona Range Nature Reserve d7 86
Mungbere e3 225
Mungeli g8 124
Munger k7 125
Mungeranie d10 81
Mungguresak, Tanjung e4 98
Mungia b1 192
Mungindi j10 81
Mungla l8 125
Mungo c6 224
Mungo National Park c1 82
Mungo, Lake c1 82
Mungwi f6 225
Munhamade f2 233
Munhango b1 232
Munhino a1 232
Muni, Río g5 223
Munich g4 175
Muñico e4 190
Muniesa d3 192
Munilla b2 192
Munim d2 288
Munising k7 251
Muniz Freire h4 291
Munjpur e9 129
Munkebo d3 158
Munkedal d3 156
Munkfors e3 156
Munkhafaḑ al Qaţţārah c1 218
Munku-Sardyk, Gora b2 94
Munlochy d2 164
Münnerstadt f2 174
Munning Point A 77
Muñoz Gamero, Península de b6 295
Munro, Mount Ac2 83
Munsan p7 113
Munse m7 99
Münsingen, Ger. e4 174
Münsingen, Switz. b3 196
Munster d2 184
Münster, Ger. c4 172
Münster, Hessen, Ger. d3 174
Münster, Niedersachsen, Ger. f3 172
Münster, Ger. c4 172
Münster, Switz. c3 196
Münsterland c4 172
Muntadgin d12 87
Munte k4 99
Munyati d2 233
Münzkirchen e1 176
Muojärvi m4 155
Muonio j3 155
Muonioälven j3 155
Mupa b2 232
Mupa, Parque Nacional da b2 232
Mupfure d2 233
Muping g1 111
Muqaddam d4 218
Muqeibila d4 138
Muquem c4 289
Muqui h4 291
Mur g3 177
Mura h3 177
Muradal, Serra do c5 190
Muradiye, Manisa, Tur. a3 208
Muradiye, Van, Tur. j3 209
Murakami h2 115
Murakeresztúr e5 170
Murallón, Cerro b5 295
Muramvya e4 225
Muráň j3 171
Muranga b4 226
Muraši k2 151
Muraszemenye e5 170
Murat e3 186
Murat, Tur. h3 209
Murat Dağı b3 208
Muratlı h5 201
Murato A 185
Murat-sur-Vèbre e5 187
Murau f2 177
Muravera Ab3 198
Muravlenko n3 147
Murayama j2 115
Murayr, Jazīrat e3 219
Muraysah, Ra's al c1 218
Murça c3 190
Murchante c2 192
Murcheh Khvort n5 137
Murchin j2 173
Murchison, Aust. b10 87
Murchison, Aust. g14 81
Murchison, N.Z. d4 77
Murchison Falls National Park f3 225
Murchison Range b6 80
Murchison, Mount, Aust. c10 87
Murchison, Mount, N.Z. c5 77
Murcia, Spain c7 193
Murcia c7 193
Murcielagos Bay e6 100
Murczyn f3 168
Mur-de-Barrez e4 186
Mûr-de-Bretagne c4 182
Murdo c3 260
Mureck g3 177
Mürefte h5 201
Murehwa e2 233
Mures c6 191
Mureş g2 201
Mureşul l6 171
Muret d5 187
Murfjället e4 154
Murfreesboro, Arkansas, U.S.A. c2 258
Murfreesboro, North Carolina, U.S.A. h7 255
Murfreesboro, Tennessee, U.S.A. f2 258
Murg d4 174
Murgap, Turk. a2 128
Murgap, Maryyskaya Oblast', Turk. h9 120
Murgap, Maryyskaya Oblast', Turk. a2 128
Murgeni j2 201
Murgha Kibzai d5 128
Murgha Mehterzai c5 128
Murghab, Afg. a3 128
Murghab, Afg. b3 128
Murghob, Taj. f1 128
Murghob g1 128
Murgia b2 192
Murgon k9 81
Murgoo c10 87
Muri, China a7 112
Muri, India j8 125
Mūrī r3 137
Muriaé g4 291
Murias de Paredes d2 190
Murid c6 129
Muriege d5 224
Murih, Pulau e3 98
Murilo G 74
Murinda c4 130
Müritz Seenpark h2 173
Müritz, Nationalpark j2 173
Muriwai f3 76
Murkong Selek p6 125
Murmansk p2 155
Murmanskaja Oblast' c1 146
Murmanskij Bereg d1 146
Murmino f4 150
Murnau am Staffelsee e4 175
Muro, Fr. A 185
Muro, Spain f5 193
Muro, Spain h5 193
Muro de Alcoy d6 193
Muro Lucano e4 198
Muro, Capo di A 185
Murol e3 186
Murom g4 151
Murongo f4 225
Muroran Ab2 114
Muros a2 190
Muros e Noia, Ría de a2 190
Muroto f5 114
Muroto-zaki f5 114
Murovani Kurylivtsi h1 201
Murowana Goślina f3 168
Murphy h2 259
Murphys c3 264
Murr e4 174
Murra Murra h10 81
Murrah g3 219
Murray, Aust. e2 83
Murray, Aust. c13 87
Murray, Can. g4 248
Murray, U.S.A. e1 258
Murray Bridge d13 81
Murray Downs b6 80
Murray Fracture Zone n3 301
Murray Harbour l5 253
Murray Range j9 87
Murray Sunset National Park b2 82
Murray, Lake j2 259
Murray, Mount m3 247
Murraysburg e5 234
Murrayville e13 81
Murrayville, U.S.A. a6 254
Murree f4 128
Murrhardt g5 174
Murrí b2 284
Murringo j13 81
Murrumbidgee e2 83
Murrumburrah j13 81
Murrupula f2 233
Murrurundi k11 81
Mursan c6 130
Murska Sobota h3 177
Mursko Središće h3 177
Mūrt a7 129
Murtajapur e9 124
Murtas a8 193
Murten b3 196
Murtoa c3 82
Murtosa b4 190
Murtovaara m4 155
Muru c1 292
Murud c3 126
Murud, Gunung h3 99
Murung h4 99
Muruntau k7 120
Murupara f3 76
Mururoa K 75
Muruti, Ilha b2 288
Murviel-lès-Béziers f5 187
Murwara g8 124
Murwillumbah l10 81
Murygino k2 151
Mürz g2 177
Murzechirla h8 120
Mürzsteg g2 177
Murzūq g3 221
Murzynowo d3 168
Mürzzuschlag g2 177
Muş, Tur. h3 209
Muş h3 209
Musa c3 224
Mūsa l4 157
Musa Āli Terara f5 219
Musa Khel Bazar d5 128
Musa Qala b4 128
Musabani k8 125
Musadi d4 224
Musala, Bul. f4 201
Musala, Indon. d15 103
Musan q4 113
Musandam Peninsula r8 137
Muscat f6 116
Muscatine f3 260
Musè l5 157
Muse f5 225
Musgrave f3 80
Musgrave Ranges k10 87
Musgrave, Mount c5 77
Mūshakī d4 128
Mushāsh Ḩadraj e5 139
Mushaytī, Jabal al c7 139
Mushayyish, Wādī al e6 139
Mushenge d4 224
Mushie c4 224
Mushin e4 223
Mushkaf c6 129
Musholm e3 158
Musholm Bugt e3 158
Musi f4 126
Musina j1 235
Muskah f4 219
Muskeget Channel k3 257
Muskegon c4 254
Muskingum f6 254
Muskogee b2 258
Muskoka, Lake c6 252
Muskwa f2 248
Muslimbagh c5 128
Musmar e4 219
Musoma a4 226
Musquanousse, Lac m3 253
Musquaro, Lac m3 253
Musquodoboit Harbour l6 253
Mussara, Serra de la e3 192
Musselburgh e4 164
Musselshell j2 262
Mussende c6 224
Musserra b5 224
Mussidan c3 186
Mussolo c5 224
Mussomeli c7 199
Mussoorie d4 130
Mussy-sur-Seine a3 184
Mustafabad d6 130
Mustafakemalpaşa b2 208
Mustahīl c2 226
Müstair e3 196
Mustamaa m2 157
Mustang f5 135
Mustau, Gora v4 121
Musters d6 296
Musters, Lago c5 295
Mustjala k3 157
Mustla l3 157
Mustvee m3 157
Musu l6 97
Musu-dan q5 113
Muswellbrook k12 81
Muszaki j2 169
Muszyna j6 169
Mut, Egypt c2 218
Mut, Tur. d4 208
Mutá, Ponta do e4 288
Mutanda d1 232
Mutarara f2 233
Mutare e2 233
Muthallath al 'Āriḑah d4 139
Muthallath al Mişrī d4 139
Muthill e3 164
Muting l7 97
Mutirikwi Recreational Park e3 233
Mutis b2 284
Mutis, Gunung n9 99
Mutné h2 171
Mutoko e2 233
Mutorashanga e2 233
Mutoto d5 224
Mutshatsha d6 224
Mutsu Ab3 114
Muttaburra g7 80
Muttekopf b2 176
Muttenz b2 196
Mutterstadt e4 174
Mutton Bay n3 253
Muttonbird Islands a7 77
Muttukuru g5 126
Mutuali f1 233
Mutum, Braz. d5 284
Mutum, Minas Gerais, Braz. h3 291
Mutum Biyu g4 223
Mutumparaná e1 293
Mutunópolis c4 288
Mutur g8 126
Mutusjärvi l2 155
Mutzig d2 184
Muuratjärvi l1 157
Muurola k3 155
Muxaluando b5 224
Muxía a1 190
Muxima b5 224
Muyinga f4 225
Muynak k4 149
Muyumba e5 225
Muyuping b4 106
Muz Tag h1 135
Muzaffarabad a2 130
Muzaffargarh e5 128
Muzaffarnagar c5 130
Muzaffarpur j6 125
Muzambinho e4 291
Muzat He t7 121
Muzhen e4 111
Muži l2 147
Muzidian d4 106
Muzillac c5 182
Muzon, Cape l5 247
Múzquiz j4 273
Muztag e1 130
Muztagata g1 128
Mvadi b3 224
Mvangan b3 224
Mvolo e2 225
Mvomero b5 227
Mvoung b3 224
Mvouti b4 224
Mvuma e2 233
Mwabvi Game Reserve b7 231
Mwali Aa1 233
Mwami d2 233
Mwanza, D.R.C. e5 225
Mwanza, Tan. f4 225
Mwanza, Tan. f4 225
Mwea National Reserve b4 226
Mweelrea b3 165
Mweka d4 224
Mwenda e6 225
Mwene-Ditu d5 224
Mwenezi, Zimb. e3 233
Mwenezi e3 233
Mwenga e4 225
Mwereni b4 227
Mweru Wantipa, Lake e5 225
Mweru, Lake e5 225
Mwilambwe d5 224
Mwimba d5 224
Mwingi b4 226
Mwinilunga d6 224
Mwokil G 74
My Tho h10 103
Mya, Oued e3 221
Myadzyel m5 157
Myaing b5 102
Myajlar e7 129
Myall Lake e8 85
Myall Lakes National Park e8 85
Myanaung b6 102
Myanmar g6 93

MYANMAR (BURMA)

THE UNION OF MYANMAR
Area 676,553km² (261,218sq miles)
Capital Yangon (Rangoon)
Organizations ASEAN
Population 48,850,000
Pop. growth (%) 0.4
Life expectancy 53 (m); 58 (f)
Languages Myanmar (Burmese) and other local languages
Literacy 85.6%
Currency kyat (US $1 = 6.42 kyat)
GDP (US million $) 4755
GDP per head ($US) 97

Myaungmya b7 102
Mybster e1 164
Mycanae c5 210
Myedna m4 169
Myerstown d4 256
Myingyan b5 102
Myinmoletkat d9 103
Myitkyina c3 102
Myittha b4 102
Myjava f3 171
Mykhaylivka d3 148
Myki e1 210
Mykines B 152
Myklebostad e3 154
Mykolayiv, L'vivs'ka Oblast', Ukr. m6 169
Mykolayiv, Mykolayivs'ka Oblast', Ukr. d3 148
Mykolayivka k2 201
Mykolayivka-Novorosiys'ka j2 201
Mykolo-Hulak d3 148
Mykonos f5 211
Mykonos, Notio Aigaio, Grc. f5 211
Myla, Russ. Fed. g2 146
Myla g2 147
Myllykoski m2 157
Myllymäki k5 155
Myloi c5 211
Mylopotamos c6 211
Mylor Bridge a6 163
Mymensingh m7 125
Mynäjoki k2 157
Mynämäki k2 157
Mynaral p5 121
Mynfontein e5 234
Mynydd Preseli b5 163
Myohaung n9 125
Myŏngch'ŏn q5 113
Myŏnggan q5 113
Myory m5 157
Mýrdalsjökull A 152
Myre e2 154
Myrheden h4 154
Myrhorod d2 148
Myrina f3 210
Myrlandshaugen f2 154
Myronivka c2 148
Myrskylä l2 157
Myrtle Beach k3 259
Myrtle Point a4 262
Myrtleford e3 83
Myrtos f7 211
Myrtou b1 138
Myrvike e5 154
Myrzakent m7 121
Mysen d3 156
Myskelsjön e1 156
Myškin e3 150
Myślenice h6 169
Myśliborskie, Jezioro c2 168
Myślibórz c3 168
Myślice h2 169
Mysłowice h5 169
Mysore e6 126
Mystic j3 257
Mystras c5 210
Myszków h5 169
Myszyniec k2 169
Myt g3 151
Mytilinioi Ab1 210
Mytišči d4 150
Mýtna h3 171
Mýto b2 170
Myton h5 262
Myzove n4 169
Mže a2 170
Mziha b5 227
Mzimba a6 231
Mzingwani d3 233
Mzuzu a6 231

N

N'dalatando b5 224
N'gangula b6 224
N'gungo, Cuanza Sul, Ang. c6 224
N'gungo, Cuanza Sul, Ang. b6 224
N'harea c6 224
N'zeto b5 224
Na Noi e6 102
Na Thawi b2 101
Na Yong a2 101
Na'am e2 225
Naab h3 175
Naala h3 223
Naalehu Ad3 263
Naam e2 225
Naama d2 220
Naamankajärvi m4 155
Naantali k2 157
Naarden d2 159
Naas e3 165
Näätämöjoki m2 155
Näätänmaa n1 157
Nababeep b4 234
Nabarangapur h3 126
Nabari g4 115
Nabas d5 100
Nabatîyé d3 138
Nabatiyet et Tahta d3 138
Nabb d6 254
Nabberu, Lake e9 87
Nabburg h3 175
Nabéré, Réserve Partielle de d3 222
Naberera b4 227
Naberežne Čelny m4 151
Nabesna j3 247
Nabeul g1 221
Nabha, India c4 130
Nabha, Leb. e2 138
Nabi Chit e3 138
Nabi Rachadé e3 138
Nabi Sbat e3 138
Nabire k6 97
Nāblus d4 139
Nabolo d3 222
Naboomspruit h2 235
Nabq e7 136
Nacajuca h4 275
Nacala c6 227
Nacaltepec f5 275
Nacaome d4 276
Nacaroa b6 227
Načeradec c2 170
Nacha n1 169
Nachikatsuura f5 115
Nachingwea b6 227
Nachna e7 129
Náchod e1 170
Nachuge n7 127
Nacimiento, Chile a4 296
Nacimiento, Spain b7 193
Nacimiento b7 193
Nacional de Cortes de la Frontera, Reserva e8 191
Nacional Pacaya Samiria, Reserva c4 284
Naco j10 263
Nacogdoches b4 258
Nacori Chico j11 263
Nacozari de García j10 263
Nacuñan d3 296
Nadarzyce e2 168
Nadbai c6 130
Nadder e5 163
Nadezhdinka k5 147
Nadgee Nature Reserve f3 83
Nadiad f9 129
Nădlac j5 171
Nadol f8 129
Nador d1 220
Nador, Col du d2 220
Nádudvar k4 171
Naduri E 74
Nadūshan p5 137
Nadvirna g1 201
Nadvoicy q5 155
Nadym n2 147
Naenwa g8 129
Nærbø a3 156
Næsbyhoved Broby d3 158
Næstved e3 158
Nafada g3 223
Näfels d2 196
Nafpaktos b4 210
Nafplio c5 211
Naft Shahr k4 137
Naft-e Safīd m6 137
Nafūd ad Daḩl g3 219
Nafūd as Surrah f3 219
Nafūsah, Jabal g2 221
Nafy j9 137
Nag' Hammâdi d8 136
Nag, Co m4 125
Nag's Head F 271
Naga d4 100
Naga Hills b2 102
Nagagami l6 251
Nagahama, Ehime, Japan e5 114
Nagahama, Shiga, Japan g4 115
Nagai j2 115
Nagai Island d5 246
Nagal d5 130
Nagaland b2 102
Nagano, Japan g3 115
Nagano h3 115
Nagaoka h3 115
Nagaokakyō f4 115
Nagaon n6 125
Nagapattinam f7 126
Nagar c6 130
Nagar Parkar e8 129
Nagari Hills f6 126
Nagarjuna Sagar Reservoir f4 126
Nagarote d4 276
Nagarzê k5 135

Nagasaki c5 114
Nagaur f7 129
Nagavali h3 127
Nagda g9 129
Nagercoil e8 126
Nagha Kalat b7 129
Nagichot f3 225
Nagina d5 130
Nagineh r4 137
Nagłowice j5 169
Nagold, Ger. d4 174
Nagold e4 174
Nagor'e e3 150
Nagorsk l2 151
Nago-Torbole e4 196
Nagoya g4 115
Nagpur f9 124
Nagqu n4 125
Nagrota c3 130
Nagua k5 271
Naguabo A 270
Nagyatád f5 170
Nagybajom f5 171
Nagybaracska g5 171
Nagyberény g5 171
Nagyberki g5 171
Nagydorog g5 171
Nagyhalász k3 171
Nagyigmánd g4 171
Nagykálló k4 171
Nagykanizsa e5 170
Nagykapornak e5 170
Nagykáta h4 171
Nagykereki k4 171
Nagykónyi g5 171
Nagykőrös h4 171
Nagylak j5 171
Nagynyárád g6 171
Nagyoroszi h4 171
Nagyszénás j5 171
Nagyszokoly g5 171
Nagyvázsony f5 171
Naha B 115
Nahal Shittim d6 139
Nahan c4 130
Nahang a7 129
Nahanni National Park d3 242
Naharāyim d4 138
Nahariyya d3 138
Naharros b4 193
Nahāvand m4 137
Nahe c3 174
Nahhālīn d5 139
Nahlé e2 138
Nahna c4 130
Nahoï, Cap F 74
Nahon g5 183
Nahr Ibrahim d2 138
Nahuala b3 276
Nahuatzen d4 274
Nahuel Mapá d3 296
Nahuel Niyeu d6 296
Nahuel Rucá j4 297
Nahuelbuta, Parque Nacional a4 296
Nāhūg a7 129
Nahunta j4 259
Nai Ga c2 102
Naibabad c2 128
Naic c3 100
Naica g4 272
Naicó e4 297
Naidăş e3 200
Naikliu m9 99
Naila d4 175
Nailloux d5 187
Nailsea d5 163
Nailsworth d5 163
Nailung n5 125
Na'ima d5 218
Nain s4 243
Nā'īn p5 137
Nainital d5 130
Nainpur g8 124
Naintré f6 183
Naiopué f2 233
Nairai E 74
Nairn, Scotland, U.K. d2 164
Nairn e2 164
Nairn, Mount c9 87
Nairobi, Kenya b4 226
Nairobi b4 226
Nairobi National Park b4 226
Naissaar l3 157
Naitaba E 74
Naivasha b4 226
Naivasha, Lake b4 226
Naizishan p4 113
Najac d4 187
Najafābād n5 137
Najd f3 219
Nájera b2 192
Najerilla b2 192
Najibabad d5 130
Nájima d5 192
Najin r4 113
Najmah n8 137
Najrān g4 219
Najrān, Wādī f4 219
Najsten''jarvi c3 146
Naju p8 113
Naka b2 101
Nakadōri-shima c5 114
Nakajō h2 115
Nakambé d3 222
Nakaminato j3 115
Nakamura e5 114
Nakano h3 115
Nakasato Ab3 114
Nakashibetsu Ad2 114
Nakasongola f3 225
Nakatsugawa g4 115
Nakfa e4 219
Nakfa Wildlife Reserve e4 219
Nakhl b7 139
Nakhl-e Taqī p8 137
Nakhodka s4 113
Nakhola n6 125
Nakhon Nayok e8 103
Nakhon Pathom e9 103
Nakhon Phanom g7 102
Nakhon Ratchasima f8 103
Nakhon Sawan e8 102
Nakhon Si Thammarat a1 101
Nakhon Thai e7 102
Nakhtarana d9 129
Nakina k5 251
Nakło nad Notecią f2 168
Naknek e4 246
Nakodar b4 130
Nakonde a5 231
Nakop d4 234
Nakskov e4 158
Näkten e5 154
Naktong-gang q8 113
Nakuru b4 226
Nal, Pak. b7 129
Nal c7 129
Nal'čik f4 149
Nalagach c4 130
Näläntöjärvi l5 155
Nalayh d2 112
Nalázi k2 235
Nalbari m6 125
Nalbaugh National park f3 83
Naldera c4 130
Näldsjön e5 154
Naldurg e4 126
Nałęczów l4 169
Nalerigu d3 222
Nalgonda f4 126
Nalhati k7 125
Naliya d9 129
Nallamala Hills f5 126
Nallıhan c2 208
Nalolo c2 232
Nalón e1 190
Nālūt g2 221
Nalžovské Hory b2 170
Nam Beng e5 102
Năm Căn g11 103
Nam Co m4 125
Nam Đinh h5 102
Nam Hka d5 102
Nam Hsin d5 102
Nam Khan f6 102
Nam Lik f6 102
Nam Loi e5 102
Nam Mae Ing e6 102
Nam Mae Kok d5 102
Nam Mae Yuam e6 102
Nam Na d7 104
Nam Nao National Park e7 102
Nam Ngum f6 102
Nam Ngum Reservoir f6 102
Nam Ou f5 102
Nam Pang d4 102
Nam Pat e7 102
Nam Phong f7 102
Nam Pilu c5 102
Nam Sam g6 102
Nam Tamai c2 102
Nam Teng d5 102
Nam Tha e5 102
Nam Tok d8 103
Nam Yi Tu c4 102
Nama G 74
Namacu E 74
Namacunde b2 232
Namacurra f2 233
Namadgi National Park f2 83
Namahadi h3 235
Namak, Daryācheh-ye n4 137
Namakgale j1 235
Nāmakī q6 137
Namakkal f7 126
Namanga b4 227
Namangan n7 121
Namanganskaya Oblast' n7 121
Namanyere f5 225
Namapa b6 227
Namaqua National Park b5 234
Namaqualand b4 234
Namarrói f2 233
Namber j6 97
Nambour l9 81
Nambroca g5 191
Nambucca Heads l11 81
Nambung National Park b12 87
Namco m4 125
Namcy n3 119
Namdalseid c4 154
Nāmdō h3 157
Namerikawa g3 115
Náměšť nad Oslavou e2 170
Námestovo h2 171
Nametil b7 227
Namew Lake r4 249
Namhae p8 113
Namhkam c4 102
Namhsan c4 102
Nami b2 101
Namib Desert a2 234
Namibe, Ang. a2 232
Namibe a2 232
Namibe, Reserva de a2 232
Namibia d2 217

NAMIBIA

THE REPUBLIC OF NAMIBIA
Area 824,292km² (318,261sq miles)
Capital Windhoek
Organizations COMESA, COMM, SADC
Population 1,960,000
Pop. growth (%) 2.7
Life expectancy 45 (m); 45 (f)
Languages English, Afrikaans, German, local languages
Literacy 84%
Currency Namibian dollar (US $1 = 6.38 Namibian dollar)
GDP (US million $) 2849
GDP per head ($US) 1453

Namibia Plain l12 302
Namib-Naukluft Game Park a2 234
Namidobe f2 233
Namie j3 115
Namies c4 234
Namin m2 137
Namioka j1 115
Namjagbarwa Feng p5 125
Namlan c4 102
Namlang c4 102
Namlea p6 99
Namling j5 135
Nammijärvi m2 155
Namoi c7 85
Namoluk G 74
Namonuito G 74
Namorik D 74
Namoya e4 225
Namp'o n6 113
Namp'yŏng p8 113
Nampa, Nepal e4 130
Nampa, U.S.A. e4 262
Nampala c2 222
Nampula, Moz. b7 231
Nampula b7 227
Namrole p6 99
Namsang c5 102
Namsos c4 154
Namsskogan d4 154
Namtok Chattakan National Park e7 102
Namtok Mae Surin National Park d6 102
Namtu c4 102
Namu D 74
Namuka-i-lau E 74
Namuli, Monte b7 231
Namuno b6 227
Namur, Bel. c4 159
Namur c4 159
Namutoni b2 232
Namwala d2 232
Namwŏn p8 113
Namysłów f4 168
Nan e6 102
Nan Ling h6 104
Nan'an m6 105
Nan'ao Dao l7 105
Nana, C.A.R. c2 224
Nana f8 129
Nana Bakassa c2 224
Nana Barya c2 224
Nana-Grébizi c2 224
Nanaimo f7 248
Nanam q5 113
Nana-Mambéré c2 224
Nanamib Plateau b2 234
Nanao g3 115
Nanay c4 284
Nanbu f3 104
Nancagua b3 296
Nancha q2 113
Nanchang k4 105
Nancheng l5 105
Nanchital g4 275
Nanchong f3 104
Nanchuan f4 104
Ñancorainza e4 293
Nancowry n9 127
Nancun, Anhui, China e4 111
Nancun, Henan, China c2 106
Nancun, Shandong, China g1 111
Nancy c2 184
Nanda Kot e4 130
Nanded e3 126
Nandewar Range d7 85
Nandigama g4 126
Nanding He b7 104
Nandu f4 111
Nandu Jiang h9 104
Nandurbar g10 129
Nandyal f5 126
Nănești h3 201
Nanfen m5 113
Nanfeng l5 105
Nang n5 125
Nang Eboko b3 224
Nang Parbat b2 130
Nangade b6 227
Nangah Dedai f5 98
Nangahembaloh g4 98
Nangahkemangai g5 98
Nangahmau f5 98
Nangahpinoh f5 98
Nangahsuruk g4 98
Nangahtempuai g4 98
Nangalala b2 80
Nangalao c5 100
Nangar National Park f1 83
Nangarhār e3 128
Nangatayap f5 98
Nangin d10 103
Nangis j4 183
Nangnim p5 113
Nangnim-sanmaek p5 113
Nangong d1 106
Nangqên q3 125
Nanguan c1 106
Nangulangwa b5 227
Nanhe d1 106
Nanhua e3 102
Nanhui g4 111
Nani d4 128
Nanjangud e6 126
Nanji Shan n5 105
Nanjian e3 102
Nanjiang f2 104
Nanjing f3 111
Nanjing Jiang b7 104
Nankang k6 105
Nankoku e5 114
Nanle d1 106
Nanlei He c7 104
Nanling f4 111
Nanlinqiao d5 106
Nanliu Jiang g7 104
Nanluji d2 111
Nannine d10 87
Nanning g7 104
Nanniwan a1 106
Nannup b13 87
Naños, Isla b6 295
Nanpan Jiang f6 104
Nanpara e6 130
Nanpi e0 106
Nanpiao l5 113
Nanping, Fujian, China m5 105
Nanping, Hubei, China c5 106
Nanpu Xi m5 105
Nanqiao c4 106
Nanri Dao m6 105
Nansa f1 190
Nansei-shotō B 115
Nansen Basin n3 299
Nansen Bordillera m3 299
Nansio f4 225
Nans-les-Pins b7 185
Nant f4 187
Nant Bran c4 163
Nant'ou n7 105
Nantais g8 129
Nanterre h4 183
Nantes d5 182
Nanteuil-le-Haudouin h3 183
Nanthi Kadal A 127
Nantiat b7 98
Nantiat d2 186
Nanticoke, Can. f4 254
Nanticoke, Maryland, U.S.A. e6 256
Nanticoke, Maryland, U.S.A. e6 256
Nanticoke, Pennsylvania, U.S.A. d3 256
Nantong g4 111
Nantua b4 184
Nantucket k3 257
Nantucket Island l3 257
Nantucket Sound k3 257
Nantulo b6 227
Nantwich d3 162
Nanty Glo b4 256
Nanumanga N 75
Nanumea N 75
Nanuque h2 291
Nanusa, Kepulauan p2 99
Nanushuk g1 247
Nanutarra Roadhouse b8 86
Nanwang e2 111
Nanxi, Anhui, China d4 106
Nanxi, Sichuan, China e4 104
Nanxian c5 106
Nanxiong k6 105
Nanxun g4 111
Nanyandang Shan n5 105
Nanyang c3 106
Nanyang Hu e2 111
Nanyuki b4 226
Nanzamu n5 113
Nanzhang b4 106
Nanzhao c3 106
Nanzhaoji d3 106
Nanzhiqiu d1 106
Nao e3 128
Nao, Cabo de la e6 193
Naococane, Lac g2 252
Naogaon l7 125
Naokot d8 129
Naoli He s2 113
Naolinco f4 275
Naong, Bukit g3 98
Naoshera b3 130
Naousa, Kentriki Makedonia, Grc. c2 210
Naousa, Notio Aigaio, Grc. f5 211
Naozhou Dao h8 104
Napa, California, U.S.A. a3 264
Napa, California, U.S.A. a3 264
Napa Valley a3 264
Napaimiut e3 246
Napajedla f2 171
Napakiak d3 246
Napaktulik Lake g2 242
Napaleofú h4 297
Napanee h3 255
Napanwainami k6 97
Napasar f7 129
Napaskiak d3 246
Naperville b5 254
Napf b2 196
Napido k6 97
Napier, N.Z. f3 76
Napier, R.S.A. c7 234
Napinka c6 250
Napiwoda j2 169
Naples d4 198
Naples, Italy d4 198
Naples, Florida, U.S.A. j6 259
Naples, New York, U.S.A. c2 256
Napo e7 104
Napo, Ec. b4 284
Napo, Ec. c4 284
Napoli d4 198
Napoli, Passo di f6 199
Naposta f5 297
Napuka K 75
Naqadeh k3 137
Nar'jan-Mar h2 147
Nara, India d9 129
Nara, Japan f4 115
Nara, Japan f4 115
Nara, Mali c2 222
Narach, Bela. m5 157
Narach m5 157
Naracoorte e14 81
Naradhan e1 83
Naraina g7 129
Narainpur g3 126
Naranbulag g1 112
Narang e3 128
Naranjal, Ec. b4 284
Naranjal, Ec. b4 284
Naranjal, Peru b5 284
Naranjito A 270
Naranjo e5 272
Naranjos f3 275
Naraq n5 137
Narasannapeta j3 127
Narasapatnam, Point g4 126
Narasapur g4 126
Narasaraopet g4 126
Narasun g1 112
Narat v6 121
Narat Shan u6 121
Narathiwat b2 101
Narayanganj m8 125
Narayangaon d3 126
Narayangarh g8 129
Narayanpet e4 126
Narayanpur c6 130
Narayangarh c4 130
Narberth b5 163
Narbonne f5 187
Narbonne-Plage f5 187
Narborough g4 162
Narcao Aa3 198
Narcea d1 190
Narcondam Island p6 127
Nardin q3 137
Nardò h4 198
Nare g1 297
Narembeen d13 87
Narendranagar d4 130
Nares Plain d7 302
Nares Strait bb2 299
Narew, Pol. k3 169
Narew m3 169
Närhilä l5 155
Nari c6 129
Narib b2 234
Narie, Jezioro j2 169
Nariga, Punta de b1 190
Narin d2 128
Narin Gol n1 125
Narince g4 209
Nariño b3 284
Narkanda c4 130
Narkatiaganj g6 135
Narken j3 155
Narki d6 130
Narmada f10 129
Narnaul c5 130
Narni g7 197
Naro, Fiji E 74
Naro, Italy c7 199
Narodnaja, Gora k2 147
Národní park České Švýcar c1 170
Národní park Podyjí d3 170
Naro-Fominsk d4 150
Narok b4 226
Narol m5 169
Narovčat g5 151
Narowlya c2 148
Närpes j1 157
Närpes å j1 157
Narrabri j11 81
Narragansett j3 257
Narran b6 85
Narran Lake b6 85
Narrandera h13 81
Narrogin c13 87
Narromine j12 81
Narrow Hills Provincial Park q5 249
Narrows, The F 271
Narryer, Mount c10 87
Narsaq v3 243
Närsen f2 156
Narsimhapur f8 124
Narsingdi m8 125
Narsinghgarh e8 124
Narsipatnam h4 126
Nart, China h4 112
Nart, Mong. c1 112
Narta h4 177
Nartkala f4 149
Nartuby c7 185
Naruje c3 284
Naruszewo j3 169
Naruto f4 114
Narva m3 157
Narva Bay m3 157
Narva Reservoir n3 157
Narvacan c2 100
Narvik f2 154
Narwana c5 130
Narwiański Park Krajobrazowy l2 169
Narwietooma l8 87
Narymskiy Khrebet v3 121
Naryn, Kyrg. q7 121
Naryn, Kyrg. q7 121
Naryn, Kyrg. q7 121
Naryn, Uzb. p7 121
Narynkol t6 121
Naryškino c5 150
Nås f2 156
Nåsåker f5 154
Năsăud g2 201
Nasavrky d2 170
Näsberg f2 156
Nasbinals f4 186
Naschel e2 296
Naseby c6 77
Nashik c9 124
Nashū, Wādī an g3 221
Nashua j2 257
Nashville, Michigan, U.S.A. d4 254
Nashville, Tennessee, U.S.A. f1 258
Nashwauk g7 250
Nasia d3 222
Našib e4 139
Našice k4 177
Nasielsk j3 169
Näsijärvi k2 157
Nasir, Pak. d6 129
Nasir, Sudan f2 225
Nāşir, Buhayrat d3 218
Nasirabad, India g7 129
Nasirabad, Pak. d6 129
Näskånselkä l3 155
Naso d6 199
Nasolot National Reserve b3 226
Nasondoye e6 225
Nasr c6 136
Naşrābād n4 137
Nasral Khan e4 128
Naşrīān-e Pā'īn l5 137
Nass m5 247
Nassarawa, Nig. f4 223
Nassarawa f4 223
Nassau, Bah. l7 259
Nassau, Cook Is. H 75
Nassau, U.S.A. g2 257
Nassau, Naturpark c2 174
Nassereith b2 176
Nassian d4 222
Nässjö f4 156
Nastapoca r2 251
Nastapoka Islands q2 251
Nasu-dake h3 115
Nasugbu c3 100
Nasva a3 150
Nata, Bots. d3 232
Nata, Bots. d3 232
Nata, Tan. a4 226
Nataboti p6 99
Natagaima b3 284
Natal, Amazonas, Braz. e1 293
Natal, Rio Grande do Norte, Braz. e3 288
Natal Basin a7 301
Națanz n5 137
Natashquan, Newfoundland and Labrador/Québec, Can. m3 253
Natashquan, Québec, Can. m3 253
Natchez d4 258
Natchitoches c4 258
Natewa Bay E 74
Nathalia g14 81
Nathana b4 130
Nathdwara f8 129
Nati, Punta A 193
Natillas j5 273
Natimuk e14 81
National City f9 265
National West Coast Tourist Recreation Area a1 234
Natitingou e3 223
Natividade, Rio de Janeiro, Braz. h4 291
Natividade, Tocantins, Braz. c4 288
Natkyizin c8 103
Natl d5 139
Nátora e3 272
Natron, Lake g4 225
Nattai National Park g2 83
Nattaung c6 102
Nattavaara h3 154
Natuna Besar e2 98
Natuna, Kepulauan d3 98
Natural do Estuário do Sado, Reserva b6 191
Natural Integral de Muniellos, Reserva d1 190
Natural Integral do Luando, Reserva c6 224
Naturaliste Channel a9 87
Naturaliste, Cape b13 87
Naturno e3 196
Nau Hissar c5 128
Naucelle e4 187
Nauchas b1 234
Nauders b3 176
Nauen h3 173
Naufragados, Ponta dos c7 289
Naugatuck g3 257
Naujamiestis l5 157
Naujan c4 100
Naujoji Akmenė k4 157
Naukh f7 129
Naukluft b2 234
Naulavaara m5 155
Naulila a2 232
Naumburg (Hessen) f1 174
Naumburg (Saale) g1 175
Naundorf j2 175
Naungpale c6 102
Na'ūr d5 139
Nauroz Kalat b6 129
Naurskaja g4 149
Nauru f3 73

NAURU

THE REPUBLIC OF NAURU
Area 21km² (8sq miles)
Capital Yaren is main town
Organizations COMM, SPC, PIF
Population 13,000
Pop. growth (%) 0.5
Life expectancy 56 (m); 63 (f)
Languages Nauruan, English
Literacy 99%
Currency Australian dollar (US $1 = 1.34 Australian dollar)
GDP (US million $) 94
GDP per head ($US) 7230

Naushahro Firoz d7 129
Naushara d7 129
Nauški d1 112
Naustdal a2 156
Nauta c4 284
Naute Dam c3 234
Nautla f3 275
Nauzad b4 128
Nava j3 273
Nava de la Asunción f3 190
Nava del Rey e3 190
Navachica g8 191
Navaconcejo e4 190
Navadwip l8 125
Navafria g3 190
Navahermosa f5 191
Navahrudak p2 169
Navajo Lake b4 261
Naval, Phil. e5 100
Naval, Spain e2 192
Navalcaballo b3 192
Navalcán, Embalse de e4 190
Navalcarnero f4 190
Navalero b3 192
Navalmanzano f3 190
Navalmoral f4 190
Navalmoral de la Mata e5 191
Navalonguilla e4 190
Navalosa f4 190
Navalperal de Pinares f4 190
Navalpino f5 191
Navaluenga f4 190
Navalvillar de Pela e5 191
Navan e3 165
Navapolatsk c1 148
Navarcles f3 192
Navardún c2 192
Navarin, Mys u3 119
Navarn g1 156
Navarra c2 192
Navarrenx b5 187
Navarrés d5 193
Navarrete b2 192
Navarro, Arg. h3 297
Navarro, Peru b1 292
Navàs f3 192
Navas de San Juan a6 193
Navas del Madroño d5 191
Navascués c2 192
Navašino g4 151
Navasota, Texas, U.S.A. a4 258
Navasota, Texas, U.S.A. a4 258
Navassa Island (U.S.A.) g5 266
Navatalgordo f4 190
Navayel'nya p2 169
Nave, Italy e4 196
Nave, Port b7 191
Nave de Haver d4 190
Navelli c2 198
Navenne c3 184
Naver d1 164
Navès f3 192
Navezuelas e5 191
Navia, Arg. d3 296
Navia, Spain c2 190
Navia d1 190
Navia, Ría de d1 190
Navibandar d10 129
Navidad, Chile b2 296
Navidad, U.S.A. a5 258
Navidad Bank k4 271
Naviraí a5 290
Naviti E 74
Naviz p4 169
Navlakhi e9 129
Navlja d1 148
Năvodari j3 201
Navoi k7 120
Navoiyskaya Oblast' k6 120
Navojoa e4 272
Navolato f5 272
Navsari f10 129
Navua E 74
Nawa g7 129
Nawá e4 138
Nawabganj, Bang. l7 125
Nawabganj, Uttar Pradesh, India g6 124
Nawabganj, Uttar Pradesh, India d5 130
Nawabshah d7 129
Nawada j7 125
Nawagai e3 128
Nāwah c4 128
Nawakot e6 129
Nawalgarh b6 130
Nawan Kot e5 128
Nawanshahr c4 130
Nawashahr f3 128
Nawāşīf, Ḩarrāt LF f3 219
Nawnghkio c4 102
Nawojowa j6 169
Naxçıvan k2 137
Naxi e4 104
Naxos f5 211
Naxos, Notio Aigaio, Grc. f5 211
Näy Band, Küh-e r5 137
Naya b3 284
Nayagarh j9 125
Nayak c3 128
Nayar b2 274
Nayarit b2 274
Nayau E 74
Nayong e5 104
Nayoro Ac1 114
Nayudupeta f6 126
Nayyāl, Wādī e2 219
Nazaré d3 284
Nazaré, Amapá Braz. g3 285
Nazaré, Pará, Braz. b3 288
Nazaré, Port. a5 191
Nazareno h5 272
Nazareth d4 138
Nazário d2 290
Nazarovka f4 150
Nazas, Mex. g5 272
Nazas, Durango, Mex. g5 272
Nazca c2 292
Nazca Ridge s7 301
Naze B 115
Naze, The h5 163
Nazerat 'Illit d4 138
Nazija a2 150
Nāzik k2 137
Nazik Gölü j3 209
Nazilli b4 208
Nazimabad c8 129
Nazir Hat m8 125
Nazira p6 125
Nazko e5 248
Nāzlū k3 137
Nazran' g4 149
Nazrēt b2 226
Nazwá f6 116
Nazyvajevsk m5 147
Nchelenge e5 225
Ncue g5 223
Ndali e4 223
Ndanda m10 99
Ndao d2 224
Ndarassa f4 223
Ndeji c2 224
Ndélé b3 224
Ndélélé d2 224
Ndendé b4 224
Ndikiniméki g5 223
Ndindi b4 224
Ndjamena h3 223
Ndji d2 224
Ndjim b3 224
Ndjolé b4 224
Ndogo, Lagune b4 224
Ndola d1 233
Ndougou a4 224
Ndumu Game Reserve k3 235
Nduye e3 225
Né b3 186
Nea Alikarnassos f7 211
Nea Anchialos c3 210
Nea Apollonia d2 210
Nea Artaki d4 210
Nea Dimmata a1 138
Nea Epidavros d5 211
Nea Fokaia d2 210
Nea Ionia c3 210
Nea Kallikrateia d2 210
Nea Karvali e2 210
Nea Kerdylia d2 210
Nea Liosia d4 210
Nea Madytos d2 210
Nea Makri d4 210
Nea Michaniona c2 210
Nea Moudania d2 210
Nea Peramos, Anatoliki Makedonia kai Thraki, Grc. e2 210
Nea Peramos, Attiki, Grc. d4 210
Nea Poteidaia d2 210
Nea Roda d2 210
Nea Styra e4 210
Nea Tirynthа c5 211
Nea Vyssa g1 210
Nea Zichni d1 210
Neabul Creek b5 85
Neagh, Lough e2 165
Neale Junction Nature Reserve h11 87
Neale, Lake k9 87
Neales c10 81
Neamț h2 201
Neapoli, Dytiki Makedonia, Grc. b2 210
Neapoli, Kriti, Grc. f7 211
Neapoli, Peloponnisos, Grc. d6 211
Near Islands Aa1 247
Neath, Wales, U.K. c5 163
Neath c5 163
Neath Port Talbot c5 163
Nebaj b3 276
Nebbi f3 225
Nebbio A 185
Nebbou d3 222
Nebel, Ger. h2 173
Nebel b4 158
Nebelhorn f5 174
Nebesnaya, Gora t6 121
Nebine Creek b5 85
Neblina, Pico da d3 284
Nebljusi g5 177
Nebo j6 80
Nebolči b2 150
Nebra (Unstrut) b3 175
Nebraska d3 260
Nebraska City e3 260
Nebrodi, Monti d7 199
Nečajevka h5 151
Nechayane c3 148
Neche e6 250
Neches b4 258
Nechí c2 284
Nechisar National Park b2 226
Nechite a7 195
Neckar e3 174
Neckarsteinach g2 174
Neckarsulm d3 174
Neckartal-Odenwald, Naturpark e3 174
Neckartenzlingen e3 174
Necochea h5 297
Necoclí j6 277
Nécy e4 182
Nedas b5 211
Neddemin j2 173
Neded f3 171
Nedéley a4 218
Nedelino f1 210
Nedelišće h3 177
Neder Vindinge e3 158
Nedhams point H 271
Nedoboyivtsi h1 201
Nedong m5 125
Nedożery-Brezany g3 171
Nedre Soppero h2 154
Nedre Tokke c3 156
Nedrow d2 256
Nedstrand a3 156
Needham Market h4 163
Needles f8 263
Needles, The e6 163
Needmore b5 256
Ñeembucú f5 293
Neenah b3 254
Neepawa d5 250
Neerpelt d3 159
Nefedovo n4 147
Nefta f2 221
Neftçala m2 137
Neftegujansk n3 147
Neftekamsk h4 147
Negage c5 224
Négala c3 222
Negār r7 137
Negara, Bali, Indon. h9 99
Negara, Kalimantan Selatan, Indon. h6 99
Negaunee k7 251
Negēlē, Oromia, Eth. b2 226
Negēlē, Oromia, Eth. b2 226
Negeri Sembilan c4 101
Negev Desert c6 139
Negla f4 293
Negola a1 232
Negomane b6 227
Negombo f9 126
Negotin f3 201
Negra, Cordillera b1 292
Negra, Peña d2 190
Negra, Punta, Peru a5 284
Negra, Punta, Spain a8 193
Negra, Serra g3 291
Negrais, Cape a7 102
Negrar e4 196
Negratín, Embalse de b7 193
Negre, Pic f2 192
Negredo b3 192
Negreira b2 190
Negreiros d3 292
Negrepelisse d4 187
Negrești h2 201
Negrești-Oaș f2 201
Negrete a4 296
Negrete, Cabo d7 193
Negri h2 201
Negril B 270
Négrine f2 221
Negritos a4 284
Negro, Arg. e1 294
Negro, Arg. e5 297
Negro, Para. f4 293
Negro, Som. e4 285
Negro Spain d2 190
Negro Ur. j2 297
Negro Muerto e5 296
Negro, Rio, Arg. d5 296

NEPAL

THE KINGDOM OF NEPAL
Area 147,181km² (56,827sq miles)
Capital Kathmandu
Organizations ADB, SAARC
Population 24,610,000
Pop. growth (%) 2.1
Life expectancy 57 (m); 57 (f)
Languages Nepali, Maithir, Bhojpuri
Literacy 45.1%
Currency Nepalese rupee (US $1 = 73 Nepalese rupee)
GDP (US million $) 5480
GDP per head ($US) 222

NETHERLANDS

THE KINGDOM OF THE NETHERLANDS
Area 33,939km² (13,104sq miles)
Capital Amsterdam
Organizations CE, EBRD, EU, NATO, OECD
Population 16,140,000
Pop. growth (%) 0.4
Life expectancy 75 (m); 80 (f)
Languages Dutch
Literacy 99%
Currency euro (US $1 = 0.81 euro)
GDP (US million $) 452,000
GDP per head ($US) 28,004

NEW ZEALAND

NEW ZEALAND
Area 270,534km² (104,454sq miles)
Capital Wellington
Organizations APEC, COMM, OECD, SPC, PIF
Population 3,850,000
Pop. growth (%) 0.9
Life expectancy 74 (m); 79 (f)
Languages English, Maori language
Literacy 99%
Currency NZ dollar (US $1 = 1.54 NZ dollar)
GDP (US million $) 57,241
GDP per head ($US) 14,867

NICARAGUA

THE REPUBLIC OF NICARAGUA
Area 120,254km² (46,430sq miles)
Capital Managua
Organizations ACS, CACM, IADB, SELA
Population 5,340,000
Pop. growth (%) 2
Life expectancy 65 (m); 70 (f)
Languages Spanish, English
Literacy 67.5%
Currency gold cordoba (US $1 = 15.38 gold cordoba)
GDP (US million $) 2500
GDP per head ($US) 468

NIGER

THE REPUBLIC OF NIGER
Area 1,267,000km² (489,191sq miles)
Capital Niamey
Organizations ECOWAS, IDB, OIC
Population 11,540,000
Pop. growth (%) 2.9
Life expectancy 44 (m); 44 (f)
Languages French, many local languages
Literacy 17.6%
Currency CFA franc (US $1 = 534.95 CFA franc)
GDP (US million $) 2170
GDP per head ($US) 188

NIGERIA

THE FEDERAL REPUBLIC OF NIGERIA
Area 923,768km² (356,669sq miles)
Capital Abuja
Organizations COMM, ECOWAS, OIC
Population 120,910,000
Pop. growth (%) 2.7
Life expectancy 51 (m); 51 (f)
Languages English, Hausa, Yoruba, Ibo
Literacy 68.1%
Currency naira (US $1 = 137.25 naira)
GDP (US million $) 40,700
GDP per head ($US) 336

Nikolajevsk g2 149
Nikolayevsk-na-Amure l2 94
Nikolsdorf d3 176
Nikopol g4 201
Nikopol' d3 148
Nikopoli a3 210
Nikouria f6 211
Niksar f2 209
Nikšić d4 200
Nikumaroro H 75
Nikunau H 75
Nikuran c5 130
Nila f4 128
Nilakka l5 155
Nilanga e3 126
Nilaveli g8 126
Nile, Afr. d2 218
Nile, Sudan d4 218
Nilgiri Hills e7 126
Ni'līn d5 139
Nilka u6 121
Nilópolis g5 291
Nilsiä m5 155
Niltepec g5 275
Nimach g8 129
Nimaj g7 129
Nimba Mountains c4 222
Nimbahera g8 129
Nîmes a7 185
Nimka Thana b6 130
Nimmitabel j14 81
Nimos Ac2 211
Nimpkish d6 248
Nīmrūz a5 128
Nims b3 174
Nimu c2 130
Nimule f3 225
Nimule National Park f3 225
Ninda c1 232
Nindigully j10 81
Nine Degree Channel c8 126
Nine Mile Lake f11 81
Ninety Mile Beach, Aust. e4 83
Ninety Mile Beach, N.Z. d1 76
Ninetyeast Ridge d6 300
Ninfas, Punta d4 295
Ninfield g6 163
Ning'an q3 113
Ningaloo Marine Park a8 87
Ningbo g5 111
Ningcheng k5 113
Ningde m5 105
Ningdu k5 105
Ningerum l7 97
Ningguo f4 111
Ninghai g5 111
Ningi f3 223
Ninging p5 125
Ningjin, Hebei, China d1 106
Ningjin, Shandong, China e1 111
Ningjing Shan b3 104
Ninglang c5 104
Ningling d2 106
Ningming f7 104
Ningnan d5 104
Ningshan g2 104
Ningwu g6 112
Ningxia Huizu Zizhiqu c7 112
Ningxian f1 104
Ningxiang j4 105
Ningyang e2 111
Ningyuan h6 104
Ninh Binh h5 102
Ninh Hoa j9 103
Ninhue a4 296
Ninilchik g3 246
Ninove c4 159
Nioaque f4 293
Niobrara c3 260
Nioka f3 225
Nioki c4 224
Nioko p6 125
Niokolo Koba, Parc National du b3 222
Niono c3 222
Nioro c2 222
Nioro du Rip a3 222
Niort b2 186
Nipani d4 126
Ñipas a4 296
Nipawin q5 249
Nipigon, Ontario, Can. j6 251
Nipigon, Ontario, Can. j6 251
Nipigon Bay j6 251
Nipigon, Lake j6 251
Nipishish Lake m1 253
Nipissing, Lake p7 251
Nipomo c6 265
Nipper's Harbour q4 253
Niquelândia c4 289
Niquen b4 296
Niquero f4 266
Nir, Ardabīl, Iran l2 137
Nir, Yazd, Iran q6 137
Nira d3 126
Nireguao b5 295
Nirivilo a3 296
Nirmal f3 126
Nirmal Range e3 126
Nirmali k6 125
Niš e4 200
Nisa, Port c5 191
Nisa c5 191
Nişāb k7 137
Nišava f4 201
Niscemi d7 199
Nishio g4 115
Nishiwaki f4 114
Nísia Floresta e3 288
Niskanselkä l4 155
Nisko l5 169
Nisling k3 247
Nisporeni j2 201
Nisqually b2 262
Nissan e4 156
Nisser c3 156
Nissum Bredning b2 158
Nissum Fjord b2 158
Nisswa f7 250
Nister c5 172
Nisutlin l3 247
Nisyros Ac2 211
Nītaure l4 157
Nitchequon g2 252
Niterói g5 291
Niti Pass d4 130
Nitmiluk National Park l4 86
Nitra, Slvk. g3 171
Nitra g3 171
Nitrianske Pravno g3 171
Nitriansky kraj g3 171
Nitro f6 254
Nitry j5 183
Nittedal d2 156
Niue (New Zealand) j4 73
Niulakita H 75
Niulan Jiang d5 104
Niumaowu n5 113
Niur, Pulau b5 98
Niutao N 75
Niutoushan f4 111
Niuxintai m5 113
Niuzhuang m5 113
Nivå f3 158
Nivala k5 155
Nive, Aust. b4 84
Nive, Fr. a5 187
Nive Downs h8 81
Nivelles c4 159
Nivernais j5 183
Nivernais, Canal du j5 183
Nivillers h3 183
Nivnice j1 177
Nivskij p3 155
Niwai g7 129
Nixa c1 258
Nixon d2 264
Niya He t9 121
Niyut, Gunung e4 98
Niž Ufalej k5 147
Nizam Sagar e3 126
Nizamabad f3 126
Nižbor c2 170
Nižegorodskaja Oblast' h3 151
Nizh Aydere r2 137
Nizhneangarsk d1 94
Nizhniye Kayrakty p3 121
Nizhyn c2 148
Nizip f4 209
Nízke Tatry h3 171
Nizki Island Aa1 247
Nižnejansk p2 119
Nižnekamsk l4 151
Nižnevartovsk h3 118
Nižnie Narykary l3 147
Nižnie Sergi j4 147
Nižnij Enangsk j2 151
Nižnij Lomov g5 151
Nižnij Odes h3 146
Nižnij Škaft h5 151
Nižnij Tagil j4 147
Nižnij Takanyš l4 151
Nižnjaja Eljuzan' j5 151
Nižnjaja Peša f2 147
Nižnjaja Salda k4 147
Nižnjaja Suetka s1 121
Nižnjaja Tunguska k3 118
Nižnjaja Tura j4 146
Nizy-le-Comte c5 159
Nizza Monferrato c5 196
Nizzané Sinay c6 139
Nizzanim c5 139
Njagan' l3 147
Njaksimvol' k3 147
Njandoma e3 146
Njandomskij Vozvyšennost' f1 150
Njarðvík A 152
Njašabož h2 147
Njazidja Aa1 233
Njinjo b5 227
Njoko c2 232
Njombe, Tan. f5 225
Njombe a5 227
Njuja m3 119
Njuksenica h1 151
Njumis g2 154
Njurba m3 119
Njurundabommen g1 156
Nkambe g4 223
Nkandla j4 235
Nkasi f5 225
Nkawkaw d4 222
Nkayi d2 233
Nkhata Bay a6 231
Nkhotakota e1 233
Nkhotakota Game Reserve a6 231
Nkolabona b3 224
Nkomi, Lagune a4 224
Nkomo j1 235
Nkondwe f5 225
Nkongsamba f5 223
Nkoranza d4 222
Nkoteng g5 223
Nkundi f5 225
Nkurenkuru b2 232
Nkusi f3 225
Nkwalini j4 235
Nkwenkwezi g6 235
Nmai Hka d2 102
Nnewi f4 223
No Mans Land k3 257
Noailles h3 183
Noain c2 192
Noakhali m8 125
Noalejo g7 191
Noamundi j8 125
Noasca b4 196
Noatak, Alaska, U.S.A. d2 246
Noatak, Alaska, U.S.A. d2 246
Noatak National Preserve e1 246
Noble b6 254
Noblesville c5 254
Noboribetsu Ab2 114
Nobres f2 293
Nocé f4 183
Noce e3 196
Nocera Inferiore d4 198
Nocera Terinese f5 199
Nocera Umbra g6 197
Noceto e5 196
Nochistlán c3 274
Nochixtlán f5 275
Noci g4 198
Nočia l5 157
Nockatunga f9 81
Nockberge, Nationalpark e3 176
Nodales, Bahía de los c5 295
Nods c3 184
Noenieput d3 234
Noetinger f2 297
Nogales, Mex. h10 263
Nogales d6 191
Nogales, U.S.A. h10 263
Nogara f4 196
Nogaro b5 187
Nogat h1 169
Nogent b2 184
Nogent-le-Roi g4 183
Nogent-le-Rotrou f4 183
Nogent-sur-Oise h3 183
Nogent-sur-Seine j4 183
Nogent-sur-Vernisson h5 183
Noginsk, Evenkijskij Avtonomnjj Okrug, Russ. Fed. k3 118
Noginsk, Moskovskaja Oblast', Russ. Fed. e4 150
Nogliki l2 94
Nogo d4 84
Nogoa b4 84
Nōgōhaku-san g4 115
Nogoya h2 297
Nogoyá h2 297
Nógrád h4 171
Nogueira, Serra de d3 190
Noguera c4 192
Noguera Pallaresa f2 192
Noguera Ribagorçana e2 192
Nohain j5 183
Nohar b5 130
Nohèdes, Réserve Naturelle de e6 187
Noheji j1 115
Nohfelden f5 159
Nohjhil c6 130
Noia b2 190
Noida c5 130
Noidans-lès-Vesoul c3 184
Noir, Causse f4 187
Noir, Isla b6 295
Noirétable f3 186
Noirmoutier, Île de c6 182
Noirmoutier-en-l'Île c5 182
Nojabr'sk n3 147
Nojima-zaki h4 115
Nok Kundi a6 129
Nokesville c6 256
Nokha f7 129
Nokhbur a8 129
Nokhur r2 137
Nokia k2 157
Nokomis a5 250
Nokomis Lake r3 249
Nokou g3 223
Nokoué, Lac e4 223
Nokrek Peak m7 125
Nola, C.A.R. c3 224
Nola, Italy d4 198
Nolay a4 184
Noli, Capo di c5 197
Nolinsk k3 151
Nombre de Dios b2 274
Nome c2 246
Nome, Cape c2 246
Nomeny c2 184
Nomexy c2 184
Nomgon c4 112
Nomhon q1 125
Nomin Gol m1 113
Nomonde g5 235
Nomo-zaki c5 114
Nomtsas b2 234
Nomuka J 75
Nomuka Group J 75
Nomwin G 74
Nomža g2 151
Nonancourt g4 183
Nonant-le-Pin f4 183
Nondalton f4 246
Nondweni j4 235
None b5 196
Nonette h3 183
Nông Hèt g6 102
Nong Khai f7 102
Nong'an n3 113
Nongoma j3 235
Nongpoh m7 125
Nongstoin m7 125
Nonnweiler e5 159
Nonoai b7 289
Nonoava f4 272
Nonouti H 75
Nonquén a4 296
Nonsan p7 113
Nonthaburi e9 103
Nontron c3 186
Nonvianuk Lake f4 246
Nonza A 185
Nonzwakazi f5 234
Nooitgedacht Dam Nature Reserve j2 235
Noojee e3 83
Nookawarra c10 87
Noonan b6 250
Noondie, Lake d11 87
Noorama Creek b6 85
Noordbergum e1 159
Noordbeveland b3 159
Noord-Brabant d3 159
Noord-Holland c2 159
Noordhollands Duinreservaat c2 159
Noordoewer b4 234
Noordoost Polder PO d2 159
Noordpunt d1 284
Noordwijk-Binnen c2 159
Noormarkku j2 157
Noorvik d2 246
Noosa Heads e5 85
Nootka Island d7 248
Nootka Sound d7 248
Nopala f5 275
Nopaltepec f4 275
Noqueves d1 296
Nóqui b5 224
Nora f3 156
Nørager c2 158
Norak d1 128
Norala e7 100
Noranda g1 254
Norberg f2 156
Norberto de la Riestra h3 297
Norcia h7 197
Nord, Cam. b2 224
Nord, Fr. j2 183
Nord, U.S.A. b2 264
Nord - Pas-de-Calais h2 183
Nord, Canal du j2 183
Nord, Pointe Aa1 233
Nordaustlandet d2 118
Nordborg c3 158
Nordbotn j2 155
Nordby, Århus, Den. d3 158
Nordby, Ribe, Den. b3 158
Norden f1 159
Nordenham b5 158
Norder Hever d1 172
Norderland c2 172
Norderney, Ger. c2 172
Norderney f1 159
Norderstedt c5 158
Nordfjordeid a2 156
Nordfold e3 154
Nordfriesische Inseln d1 172
Nordfriesland d1 172
Nord-Fugløy Naturreservat h1 154
Nordhastedt c4 158
Nordhausen f4 173
Nordholz b5 158
Nordhorn f2 159
Nordjylland c2 158
Nordkapp l1 155
Nord-Kivu e4 225
Nordkjosbotn g2 154
Nord-Kvaløy g1 154
Nordkynhalvøya l1 155
Nordland e3 154
Nordli d4 154
Nördlicher Oberpfälzer Wald h3 175
Nördlingen d3 174
Nordmaling g5 154
Nordman e1 262
Nordmarsch-Langeness d1 172
Nord-Mesna d2 156
Nord-Ostsee-Kanal e1 172
Nord-Ouest b2 224
Nord-Pas-de-Calais, Parc Naturel Régional du g2 183
Nordpfälzer Bergland c3 174
Nordre Rønner d1 158
Nordrhein-Westfalen c4 172
Nordsjö g2 156
Nordstemmen e3 172
Nordstrand d1 172
Nord-Trøndelag c4 154
Norðurland eystra A 152
Norðurland vestra A 152
Nordvik g2 298
Nordvika b5 154
Nordwalde f2 159
Nore, Ire. d4 165
Nore. Swe. g2 156
Noreikiškės m1 169
Noresund c2 156
Norfolk, U.K. g4 162
Norfolk, Nebraska, U.S.A. d3 260
Norfolk, Virginia, U.S.A. h7 255
Norfolk Island(Australia) f5 73
Norfolk Ridge k7 301
Norfork Lake c1 258
Norg e1 159
Norheimsund b2 156
Nori n2 147
Noria d4 292
Noria de Ángeles d2 274
Norikura-dake g3 115
Noril'sk j3 118
Norma g8 197
Norma Co j3 135
Normal, Alabama, U.S.A. f2 258
Normal, Illinois, U.S.A. b5 254
Norman, Aust. e5 80
Norman, U.S.A. a2 258
Norman Wells n2 247
Norman, Lake j2 259
Normanby, Aust. g3 80
Normanby e3 76
Normanby Range d3 84
Normandia f3 285
Normandie, Collines de e4 182
Normanton e4 80
Norogachic f4 272
Noroy-le-Bourg c3 184
Norquay b5 250
Norquín b4 296
Ñorquinco b4 294
Norra Barken f2 156
Norra Dellen g2 156
Norra Kvarken h5 154
Norra Ljusterö h3 157
Norråker e4 154
Norrälven f2 156
Norrbo g2 156
Norrbotten g3 154
Nørre Åby c3 158
Nørre Alslev e4 158
Nørre Broby d3 158
Nørre Halne c1 158
Nørre Lyndelse d3 158
Nørre Nebel b3 158
Nørre Snede c3 158
Nørre Vejrup b3 158
Norrent-Fontes a4 159
Nørresundby c1 158
Norrfjärden h4 154
Norris Arm q4 253
Norris City e1 258
Norris Lake h1 259
Norristown e4 256
Norrköping g3 156
Norrmogen f3 156
Norrsundet g2 156
Norrtälje h3 157
Nors b1 158
Nors Sø b1 158
Norseman e13 87
Norsewood f4 76
Norsjø c3 156
Norsjö g4 154
Norsup F 74
Norte de Santander c2 284
Norte, Cabo c1 288
Norte, Canal do b1 288
Norte, Cerro b5 295
Norte, Punta, Arg. c6 295
Norte, Punta, Arg. d4 295
Norte, Punta, Arg. j4 297
Norte, Punta, Chile b4 295
Norte, Rio Grande do e3 288
Norte, Serra do f2 293
Nortelândia f2 293
Nörten-Hardenberg e4 172
North j3 259
North Adams g2 257
North American Basin d5 302
North Andaman n6 127
North Atlanta g3 259
North Attleboro j3 257
North Australian Basin f6 300
North Ayrshire d4 164
North Balabac Strait a6 100
North Battleford n5 249
North Bay g2 254
North Belcher Islands p2 251
North Bend, Oregon, U.S.A. a4 262
North Bend, Pennsylvania, U.S.A. c3 256
North Bennington g2 257
North Berwick f3 164
North Bosque a4 258
North Bourke g11 81
North Caicos j4 271
North Cape, Can. l5 253
North Cape, N.Z. d1 76
North Cape, N.Z. B 77
North Cape, U.S.A. a5 246
North Caribou Lake h4 250
North Carolina k2 259
North Cascades National Park c1 262
North Catasauqua e4 256
North Central A 127
North Channel, Can. a5 252
North Channel, U.K. c4 164
North Charleston k3 259
North Chicago c4 254
North Collins b2 256
North Conway g6 252
North Cowichan b1 262
North Creek k4 255
North Crossett d3 258
North Dakota c2 260
North Dell b1 164
North Dorset Downs d6 163
North Downs e5 163
North East, Bots. d3 232
North East, U.S.A. e5 256
North East Lincolnshire h1 162
North End Point g2 266
North Esk f3 164
North Fiji Basin k7 301
North Foreland h5 163
North Fork, Alaska, U.S.A. f3 246
North Fork, California, U.S.A. c3 264
North Fork, California, U.S.A. d5 264
North Fork, California, U.S.A. d4 264
North Fork, Missouri, U.S.A. c1 258
North Fork American c3 264
North Fork Grand b3 260
North Fort Myers j6 259
North French n5 251
North Gawahati m6 125
North Grafton j2 257
North Grosvenor Dale j3 257
North Haven h3 257
North Head d2 76
North Highlands b3 264
North Horr b3 226
North Island, N.Z. e2 76
North Island, Phil. d1 100
North Islet c6 100
North Kitui National Reserve b4 226
North Knife Lake e1 250
North Korea k4 93

NORTH KOREA

THE DEMOCRATIC PEOPLE'S REPUBLIC OF KOREA
Area 120,538km² (46,540sq miles)
Capital P'yongyang
Organizations
Population 22,540,000
Pop. growth (%) 1.8
Life expectancy 60 (m); 66 (f)
Languages Korean
Literacy 99%
Currency won (US $1 = 2.20 won)
GDP (US million $) 4396
GDP per head ($US) 195

North Lakhimpur p6 125
North Lanarkshire f3 164
North Las Vegas f7 263
North Lincolnshire f3 162
North Little Rock c2 258
North Loup c3 260
North Luangwa National Park f6 225
North Maalhosmadulu Atoll c10 126
North Mam Peak b4 260
North Miami j7 259
North Mountain d3 256
North Nahanni n3 247
North Negril Point B 266
North New River Canal j6 259
North Palisade e4 264
North Platte, Nebraska, U.S.A. c3 260
North Platte, Nebraska, U.S.A. c3 260
North Point, Aust. b12 87
North Point, Barb. H 271
North Point, Sey. A 226
North Providence j3 257
North Reef Island n6 127
North Rim g7 263
North Ronaldsay B 164
North Santiam b3 262
North Saskatchewan m5 249
North Sea SE l4 302
North Sentinel Island m7 127
North Shoal Lake e5 250
North Shoshone Peak f2 264
North Simlipal National Park k9 125
North Somercotes g3 162
North Somerset d5 163
North Sound b3 165
North Spirit Lake g4 250
North Stradbroke Island e5 85
North Sunderland g4 164
North Sydney m5 253
North Taranaki Bight e3 76
North Tarrytown g3 257
North Terre Haute c6 254
North Thompson h5 248
North Thoresby f3 162
North Twin Island n4 251
North Twin Lake p4 253
North Tyne d1 162
North Tyneside h1 162
North Ubian c7 100
North Ugie f2 164
North Uist a2 164
North Umpqua b4 262
North Vancouver b1 262
North Verde b5 100
North Vernon d6 254
North Wabasca Lake k3 249
North Walsham h4 162
North West f3 235
North West Cape, Aust. a7 86
North West Cape, N.Z. C 77
North West Frontier f3 128
North West River m2 253
North Western A 127
North York g4 254
North York Moors f2 162
North Yorkshire e2 162
North Yuba c2 264
North Zulch a4 258
North, Cape m5 253
Northallerton e2 162
Northam, Aust. c12 87
Northam, R.S.A. g2 235
Northam, U.K. b5 163
Northampton, Aust. b11 87
Northampton, U.K. f4 163
Northampton, Massachusetts, U.S.A. h2 257
Northampton, Pennsylvania, U.S.A. e4 256
Northamptonshire f4 163
Northcliffe c14 87
Northeast Cape b3 246
Northeast Point h4 266
Northeast Providence Channel l7 259
North-Eastern c3 226
Northeim e4 172
Northern, Mal. a6 231
Northern, Sri L. A 127
Northern, Sudan d4 218
Northern, Zam. f6 225
Northern Areas b1 130
Northern Bahr el Ghazal e2 225
Northern Cape d4 234
Northern Darfur c4 218
Northern Indian Lake e2 250
Northern Ireland c4 144
Northern Kordofan c4 218
Northern Light Lake h6 250
Northern Mariana Islands (U.S.A.) d1 72
Northern Range E 271
Northern Territory k6 86
Northfield h2 257
Northgate b6 250
Northland d1 76
Northleach e5 163
Northome f7 250
Northport, Alabama, U.S.A. f3 258
Northport, Michigan, U.S.A. d3 254
Northport, Washington, U.S.A. e1 262
Northumberland, U.K. d1 162
Northumberland, U.S.A. d4 256
Northumberland Isles d2 85
Northumberland National Park d1 162
Northumberland Strait l5 253
Northway Junction j3 247
Northwest Atlantic Mid-Ocean Canyon f4 302
Northwest Cape b3 246
Northwest Gander q4 253
Northwest Pacific Basin j3 300
Northwest Providence Channel k6 259
Northwest Territories f3 242
North-Western c1 232
Northwich d3 162
Northwind Plain ll2 299
Norton, Can. k6 253
Norton, U.K. f2 162
Norton, Kansas, U.S.A. d4 260
Norton, U.S.A. h1 259
Norton, Zimb. e2 233
Norton Bay d2 246
Norton Shores c4 254
Norton Sound d3 246
Nortorf c4 158
Nort-sur-Erdre d5 182
Norumbega g3 297
Norwalk, Connecticut, U.S.A. g3 257
Norwalk, Ohio, U.S.A. e5 254
Norway, Maine, U.S.A. g6 252
Norway, U.S.A. c3 254
Norway f2 144

NORWAY

THE KINGDOM OF NORWAY
Area 323,877km² (125,050sq miles)
Capital Oslo
Organizations CE, EBRD, EFTA, NATO, OECD
Population 4,540,000
Pop. growth (%) 0.5
Life expectancy 75 (m); 81 (f)
Languages Norwegian (Bokmal and Nynorsk or neo-Norwegian), Lapp
Literacy 99%
Currency Norwegian krone (US $1 = 6.67 Norwegian krone)
GDP (US million $) 191,700
GDP per head ($US) 42,224

Norway Bay j1 242
Norway House e4 250
Norwegian Sea SE l3 302
Norwich h4 162
Norwich, Connecticut, U.S.A. h3 257
Norwich, Kansas, U.S.A. a1 258
Norwich, New York, U.S.A. e2 256
Norwich, New York, U.S.A. e2 256
Norwood, Massachusetts, U.S.A. j2 257
Norwood, North Carolina, U.S.A. j2 259
Norwood, Ohio, U.S.A. d6 254
Norzagaray c3 100
Nosapu-misaki Ad2 114
Nose, Pico c6 295
Noshappu-misaki Ab1 114
Noshiro j1 115
Nosivka c2 148
Noskivtsi h1 201
Nosop d2 234
Nosovaja h1 147
Noss Head f1 164
Nossa Senhora da Glória c1 292
Nossa Senhora do Livramento f3 293
Nossebro e3 156
Nossen k1 175
Nossob c2 234
Nossombougou c3 222
Nosy Mangabe, Réserve de Ab2 233
Nosy Varika Ab3 233
Noszlop f4 170
Nota m2 155
Notaresco c2 198
Notasulga g3 259
Noteć e2 168
Notia c1 210
Nőtincs h4 171
Notio Aigaio f6 211
Notios Evvoïkos Kolpos d4 210
Noto e8 199
Noto, Golfo di e8 199
Notodden c3 156
Noto-hantō g3 115
Notransko-kraška f4 177
Notre Dame Bay q4 253
Notre Dame, Monts j4 253
Notre-Dame-de-Gravenchon f3 183
Notsé e4 223
Nottawasaga Bay b6 252
Nottaway p5 251
Nottingham, England, U.K. h2 162
Nottingham e4 162
Nottingham Island p3 243
Nottingham Road j4 235
Nottinghamshire e3 162
Nottoway, Virginia, U.S.A. h7 255
Nottoway, Virginia, U.S.A. g7 254
Nottuln f3 159
Notukeu Creek p7 249
Nouâdhibou a4 220
Nouâdhibou, Râs a4 220
Nouakchott a2 222
Nouâmghâr a5 220
Nouan-le-Fuzelier h5 183
Nouans-les-Fontaines g5 183
Nouméa F 74
Noun b3 224
Nouna d3 222
Noup Head B 164
Noupoort f5 234
Nousu m3 155
Nouvelle j4 253
Nouvelle Calédonie f4 73
Nouvion g2 183
Nouzonville c5 159
Nov m7 121
Nova e5 170
Nova, Lith k5 157
Nova Almeida h4 291
Nova Alvorada a4 290
Nova América c5 289
Nova Andradina b5 290
Nova Astrakhan' e2 148
Nova Aurora d3 290
Nová Baňa g3 171
Nová Bystrica h2 171
Nová Bystřice g1 177
Nova Caipemba b5 224
Nova Cantu b6 290
Nova Cruz e3 288
Nová Dubnica g3 171
Nova Era g3 291
Nova Esperança b5 290
Nova Friburgo g5 291
Nova Gorica e4 176
Nova Gradiška j4 177
Nova Granada d4 290
Nova Iguaçu g5 291
Nova Kakhovka d3 148
Nova Levante f3 196
Nova Lima g3 291
Nova Londrina b5 290
Nova Mambone f3 233
Nova Nabúri f2 233
Nova Odesa c3 148
Nová Paka d1 170
Nova Paraiso e3 285
Nova Pilão Arcado d3 288
Nova Ponte e3 290
Nova Ponte, Represa e3 290
Nova Remanso d3 288
Nova Resende e4 291
Nova Russas d2 288
Nova Santa Rosa b6 290
Nova Scotia k6 253
Nova Serrana f3 291
Nova Siri f4 198
Nova Soure e4 288
Nova Topola j4 177
Nova Ushytsya h1 201
Nova Vandúzi e2 233
Nova Varoš d4 200
Nova Vas f4 177
Nova Venécia h3 291
Nová Ves I d1 170
Nova Viçosa j2 291
Nova Vida, Amazonas, Braz. d4 284
Nova Vida, Rondônia, Braz. e2 293
Nova Xavantino b4 289
Nova Zagora h4 201
Novaci f3 201
Novafeltria g6 197
Novaja Ladoga b1 150
Novaja Ljalja k4 147
Novaja Majna k4 151
Novaja Malykla k4 151
Novaja Sahča l4 151
Novaja Sibir', Ostrov r2 119
Novaja Zemlja f2 118
Novajidrány k3 171
Novaki g4 177
Nováky g3 171
Novallas c3 192
Novalukoml' c1 148
Novara, Italy c4 196
Novara c4 196
Novate Mezzola d3 196
Novato a3 264
Novaya Kazanka h2 149
Nove Gorki f3 150
Nové Hrady f1 177
Nové Město nad Metuj e1 170
Nové Mesto nad Váhom f3 171
Nové Strašecí b1 170
Nove Turdaki h5 151
Nové Zámky g4 171
Novelda d6 193
Novellara e5 196
Noves a7 185
Novgorodskaja Oblast' b2 150
Novhorodka d2 148
Novhorod-Sivers'kyy d2 148
Novi Bečej e3 200
Novi Chervyshcha p4 169
Novi di Modena e5 196
Novi Dojran c1 210
Novi Iskŭr f4 201
Novi Ligure c5 196
Novi Marof h3 177
Novi Pazar, Bul. h4 201
Novi Pazar, Serbia/Mont. e4 200
Novi Sad d3 200
Novi Vinodolski f4 177
Novičiha t1 121
Novigrad e4 176
Novigrad Podravski h3 177
Novillero b2 274
Novion-Porcien c5 159
Novki f3 150
Novlenskoe e2 150
Novljanka f4 150
Novo b2 288
Novo Airão e4 285
Novo Aripuanã e5 285
Novo Beograd e3 200
Novo Cruzeiro h2 291
Novo Delchevo d1 210
Novo Hamburgo b7 289
Novo Horizonte d4 290
Novo Marapi d4 284
Novo Mesto g4 177
Novo Olinda do Norte f4 285
Novo Oriente d3 288
Novo Parnarama d3 288
Novo Selo c1 210
Novo Virje f5 170
Novo, Lago b1 288
Novoaleksandrovsk f3 148
Novoaltajsk u1 121
Novoanninskij f2 149
Novoarkhanhel's'k k1 201
Novoazovs'k e3 148
Novoberezovka m4 147
Novobod, Taj. d1 128
Novobod, Taj. e1 128
Novočeboksarsk j3 151
Novočerkassk f3 148
Novodmitrievka g4 151
Novodnistrovs'k h1 201
Novodolinka p2 121
Novodugino c4 150
Novodvinsk e2 146
Novoe Dubovoe e1 148
Novoegor'evskoe t2 121
Novoenisejsk k4 118
Novohradské Hory c3 170
Novohrad-Volyns'kyy b2 148
Novokaolinovyj k1 149
Novokubansk f3 148
Novokujbyševsk k5 151
Novokuzneck w1 121
Novolazarevskaya (Rus. Fed.) g1 298
Novoleuškovskaja e3 148
Novomarkovka p2 121
Novomičurinsk e4 150
Novomihajlovskij e3 148
Novomoskovs'k d2 148
Novomoskovsk e4 150
Novomyrhorod c2 148
Novonikolajevskij f2 149
Novonikolayevka n6 121
Novooleksiyivka d3 148
Novoorsk k2 149
Novopavlivka k2 201
Novopokrovka, Kostanayskaya Oblast', Kaz. l5 147
Novopokrovka, Severnyy Kazakhstan, Kaz. l5 147
Novopokrovka, Vostochnyy Kazakhstan, Kaz. t2 121
Novopokrovskaja f3 148
Novorossijsk e3 148
Novorozsosh e2 148

Novorybinka → Olderdalen 365

Novorybinka n2 121
Novošahtinsk e3 148
Novoselki g4 151
Novoselytsya h1 201
Novosergievka j1 149
Novosibirsk j4 118
Novosibirskaja Oblast' s1 121
Novosibirskie Ostrova q2 119
Novosibirskoe Vodohranilišče j4 118
Novosil' e1 148
Novospasskoe j5 151
Novostroevo k1 169
Novot' h2 171
Novotroick k2 149
Novotroickoe h4 151
Novotroyits'ke d3 148
Novoural'sk k2 149
Novouzensk h2 149
Novovolyns'k n5 169
Novovoronež e2 148
Novovorontsovka d3 148
Novovoznesenovka s6 121
Novoyavorivs'ke m6 169
Novozavidovskij d3 150
Novožilovskaja g2 147
Novozybkov c1 148
Novska h4 177
Nový Bor c1 170
Nový Bydžov d1 170
Novy Dvor n3 169
Nový Jičín f2 171
Novyj Belyj Jar k5 151
Novyj Bor h2 147
Novyj Kajak l2 119
Novyj Oskol e2 148
Novyj Port n1 147
Novyj Tor'jal k3 151
Novyj Urengoj h3 118
Novyy Buh d3 148
Novyy Rozdil n6 169
Novyy Urgal j2 94
Novyya Kruki m5 157
Now q6 137
Now Dezh n4 137
Now Gombad p5 137
Now Kharegan q3 137
Now Shahr n3 137
Nowa Dęba k5 169
Nowa Karczma g1 168
Nowa Ruda e5 168
Nowa Sarzyna l5 169
Nowa Sól d4 168
Nowa Wieś Ełcka l2 169
Nowata b1 258
Nowdi m3 137
Nowe g2 168
Nowe Miasteczko d4 168
Nowe Miasto nad Pilicą j4 169
Nowe Miasto nad Wartą f3 168
Nowe Skalmierzyce f4 168
Nowe Warpno c2 168
Nowen Hill b5 165
Nowgong f7 124
Nowogard d2 168
Nowogród k2 169
Nowogród Bobrzański d4 168
Nowogrodziec d4 168
Nowra k13 81
Nowshahr m2 137
Nowshera f3 128
Nowy Dwór f2 168
Nowy Dwór Gdański h1 169
Nowy Dwór Mazowiecki j3 169
Nowy Korczyn j5 169
Nowy Sącz j6 169
Nowy Staw h1 169
Nowy Targ j6 169
Nowy Tomyśl e3 168
Nowy Wiśnicz j6 169
Nowy Żmigród k6 169
Noxen d3 256
Noxubee National Wildlife Refuge e3 258
Noya a3 224
Noyant f5 183
Noyelles-sur-Mer g2 183
Noyers j5 183
Noyers-sur-Jabron b6 185
Noyes Island l5 247
Noyil e7 126
Noyon a5 159
Nožaj-Jurt g4 149
Nozay d5 182
Nozeroy c4 184
Nqamakwe g6 235
Nqutu j4 235
Nsa c4 224
Nsambi c4 224
Nsanje f2 233
Nsawam d4 222
Nsoko j3 235
Nsombo e6 225
Nsondia c4 224
Nsuatre d4 222
Nsukka f4 223
Ntandembele c4 224
Ntcheu e1 233
Ntchisi e1 233
Ntem b3 224
Ntomba, Lac c4 224
Ntoum f5 223
Ntui g5 223
Ntungamo f4 225
Ntwetwe Pan d3 232
Ntywenka h5 235
Nu Jiang d2 102
Nu Shan b5 104
Nuaillé-d'Aunis b2 186
Nuangan n4 99
Nuapara h9 124
Nuasjärvi m4 155
Nuba, Lake d3 218
Ñuble b4 296
Nubledo e1 190
Nubu E 74
Nucet l5 171
Nüden f4 112
Nudo de Zempoaltépetl g5 275
Nueces a6 258
Nu'eima d5 139
Nueltin Lake k3 242
Nuenen d3 159
Nueno d2 192
Nuestra Señora del Pilar f6 193
Nueuray b4 284
Nueva f1 190
Nueva Alejandría c5 284
Nueva California c2 296
Nueva Concepción, El Sal. c3 276
Nueva Concepción, Guat. b3 276
Nueva Constitución d3 296
Nueva Escocia e2 296
Nueva Esparta e1 285
Nueva Florida d2 284
Nueva Galia e3 296
Nueva Germania f4 293
Nueva Gerona c4 266
Nueva Harberton c6 295
Nueva Helvecia j3 297
Nueva Imperial a5 296
Nueva Italia de Ruiz c4 274
Nueva Loja b3 284
Nueva Lubecka b4 295
Nueva Ocotepeque c3 276
Nueva Palmira h2 297
Nueva Polonia e2 275
Nueva Rosita j4 273
Nueva San Salvador c4 276
Nueva Santa Rosa b3 276
Nueva Segovia d4 276
Nueva Trinidad c3 276
Nueva Venecia b3 276
Nueva Villa de Padilla e1 275
Nueva, Isla c7 295
Nuevitas f4 266
Nuevo Berlín j2 297
Nuevo Campechito a1 276
Nuevo Casas Grandes f2 272
Nuevo Ideal g5 272
Nuevo Laredo k4 273
Nuevo León k4 273
Nuevo Montecristo b2 276
Nuevo Pilares b2 274
Nuevo Valle de Moreno d3 274
Nuevo, Golfo d4 295
Nuevo-Morelos e2 275
Nuga Nuga, Lake d3 84
Nugaal, Som. d2 226
Nugaal, Som. d2 226
Nugget Point b7 77
Nuh c5 130
Nuhaka f3 76
Nui N 75
Nui Ti On h8 102
Nuits-St-Georges a3 184
Nujiang q4 125
Nuka Island g4 247
Nuku L 75
Nuku Hiva K 75
Nuku'alofa J 75
Nukuatea L 75
Nukufetau N 75
Nukulaelae N 75
Nukuloa L 75
Nukunono H 75
Nukus k4 149
Nukutapu L 75
Nukutavaké K 75
Nukuteatea L 75
Nukutepipi K 75
Nulato e2 246
Nules d5 193
Nullagine e7 86
Nullarbor k12 87
Nullarbor National Park j12 87
Nullarbor Plain h12 87
Nullarbor Regional Reserve k12 87
Nulvi Aa2 198
Num h6 135
Numalla, Lake a6 85
Numan g4 223
Nu'mān e2 219
Numata h3 115
Numatinna e2 225
Numazu h4 115
Numbulwar b3 80
Numedal c3 156
Numfoor j6 97
Numgi n2 147
Numin He n2 113
Nummijärvi k1 157
Numto m3 147
Numurkah g14 81
Nunapitchuk d3 246
Nunasvaara j2 155
Nunavut l2 243
Nünchritz h1 175
Nunda, D.R.C. e4 225
Nunda, U.S.A. c2 256
Nuneaton e4 163
Nungarin d12 87
Nungatta National Park f3 83
Nungesser Lake g5 250
Nungnain Sum k3 113
Nunjamo b2 246
Nunkun c2 130
Nuñoa c2 292
Nuñomoral d4 190
Nunsdorf j3 173
Nunukan j3 99
Nuorajärvi n5 155
Nuorgam l1 155
Nuoro Ab2 198
Nuort Saulo f3 154
Nuqayy, Jabal a3 218
Nuqrah h9 136
Nuqruş, Jabal d3 218
Nuquí b2 284
Nur, Iran p3 137
Nur l3 169
Nur Dağları f4 209
Nur Gal e3 128
Nur Gama c6 129
Nura n2 121
Nūrābād n6 137
Nurallao Ab3 198
Nuraminis Ab3 198
Nurata k7 120
Nuratau, Khrebet l7 120
Nūrestān e3 128
Nuri e3 272
Nuria, Altiplanicie de e2 285
Nuria, Monte h7 197
Nuriootpa d13 81
Nurla c2 130
Nurlat l4 151
Nurlaty k4 151
Nurmahal b4 130
Nurmes m5 155
Nurmijärvi l2 157
Nurmo j5 155
Nürnberg g3 175
Nurpur, India b3 130
Nurpur, India d5 130
Nurpur, Pak. e5 128
Nurri, Mount b7 85
Nursery a5 258
Nursfjellet d4 154
Nürtingen f4 174
Nusa Tenggara Barat j9 99
Nusa Tenggara Timur l9 99
Nusaybin h4 209
Nuşayriyah, Jabal an e1 138
Nuşeirāt c5 139
Nuşfalău l4 171
Nushagak e4 246
Nushagak Peninsula e4 246
Nushki c6 129
Nutrioso j9 263
Nuttal d6 129
Nutwood Downs b3 80
Nuuk u3 243
Nuupas l3 155
Nuwakot f5 135
Nuwara Eliya g9 126
Nuweiba el Muzeina e7 136
Nuwerus c5 234
Nuweveldberge d6 234
Nuxco d5 274
Nuyakuk Lake e4 246
Nuyts Archipelago Conservation Park a12 81
Nuyts, Point c14 87
Nuytsland Nature Reserve g13 87
Nuzvid g4 126
Nwanedi Nature Reserve j1 235
Nxai Pan National Park c2 232
Nxaunxau c2 232
Ny Nørup c3 158
Nyabessan g5 223
Nyabing d13 87
Nyac e3 246
Nyack g3 257
Nyadire e2 233
Nyah West f13 81
Nyahua a5 231
Nyahururu b3 226
Nyainqêntanglha Feng m4 125
Nyainqêntanglha Shan n4 125
Nyainrong n3 125
Nyakanazi f4 225
Nyåker g5 154
Nyakhachava p3 169
Nyala b5 218
Nyalam h5 135
Nyamandhlovu d2 233
Nyamlell e2 225
Nyamtumbo b6 227
Nyanding f2 225
Nyang Qu n5 125
Nyanga, Congo b4 224
Nyanga, Gabon b4 224
Nyanga, Gabon b4 224
Nyanga, Zimb. e2 233
Nyanga National Park e2 233
Nyanga, Réserve de la b4 224
Nyankpala d4 222
Nyanza, Kenya a4 226
Nyanza e4 225
Nyanza-Lac e4 225
Nyapa, Gunung j4 99
Nyapongeth f2 225
Nyársapát h4 171
Nyasa, Lake f6 225
Nyathi d2 233
Nyaunglebin c7 102
Nyazura e2 233
Nybergsund e2 156
Nyborg, Den. d3 158
Nyborg, Nor. m1 155
Nyborg Fjord d3 158
Nybro f4 156
Nyby h5 154
Nyda n2 147
Nyékládháza j4 171
Nyêmo k5 135
Nyeri b4 226
Nyerol f2 225
Nygčigen, Mys a2 246
Nyika National Park f6 225
Nyima h4 135
Nyimba e1 233
Nyingchi p5 125
Nyírád f4 170
Nyíradony k4 171
Nyírbéltek l4 171
Nyírbogát l4 171
Nyírbogdány k3 171
Nyíregyháza k4 171
Nyírgelse k4 171
Nyírmada l3 171
Nyírmihálydi k4 171
Nyírtelek k3 171
Nyiru, Mount b3 226
Nyitra d1 200
Nykarleby j5 155
Nykøbing e4 158
Nykøbing Mors b2 158
Nykøbing Sjælland e3 158
Nyköping g3 156
Nykroppa f3 156
Nyksund e2 154
Nyland f5 154
Nylsvley h2 235
Nymagee e6 85
Nymboida e6 85
Nymboida National Park e6 85
Nymburk d1 170
Nymindegab b3 158
Nynäshamn g3 157
Nyngan h11 81
Nyoman m2 169
Nyon a3 196
Nyonni Ri h5 135
Nyons b6 185
Nyord f3 158
Nýřany b2 170
Nyrob j3 147
Nýrsko b2 170
Nysa f5 168
Nysa Kłodzka 5e 168
Nysa Łużycka c4 168
Nysockensjön e3 156
Nysted e4 158
Nytva h4 147
Nyūdō-zaki h1 115
Nyúl f4 171
Nyunzu e5 225
Nyūzen g3 115
Nyzhankovychi l6 169
Nyzhn'ohirs'kyy d3 148
Nyzhni Vorota f1 201
Nyzhniy Bystryy f1 201
Nzambi b4 224
Nzébéla c4 222
Nzega f4 225
Nzérékoré c4 222
Nzhelele Dam h1 235
Nzi d4 222
Nzilo, Lac e6 225
Nzingu e4 225
Nzo c4 222
Nzoia a3 226
Nzwani Aa1 233

O

O Barco d2 190
O Bolo c2 190
O Cádabo c2 190
O Carballiño b2 190
O Castelo b2 190
O Castro b2 190
O Corgo c2 190
O Grove b2 190
O Seixo b3 190
O'Brien b4 262
O'Fallon b2 260
O'Grady, Lake c12 87
O'Higgins, Antofagasta, Chile c4 292
O'Higgins, Región VI, Chile b3 296
O'Higgins, Cerro b5 295
O'Higgins, Lago b5 295
O'Leary k5 253
O'Neill d3 260
Oahe, Lake c2 260
Oahu Ac2 263
Oak Bay b1 262
Oak Bluffs k3 257
Oak Hill, Florida, U.S.A. j5 259
Oak Hill, West Virginia, U.S.A. f7 254
Oak Knolls c7 265
Oak Lake, Manitoba, Can. c6 250
Oak Lake, Manitoba, Can. c6 250
Oak Park, Illinois, U.S.A. c5 254
Oak Park, Michigan, U.S.A. d4 254
Oak Point d5 250
Oak Ridge g1 259
Oak View d7 265
Oakboro j2 259
Oakdale, California, U.S.A. c4 264
Oakdale, Connecticut, U.S.A. h3 257
Oakdale, Louisiana, U.S.A. c4 258
Oakdale, New York, U.S.A. g4 257
Oakengates d4 162
Oakes d7 250
Oakey k9 81
Oakfield b4 254
Oakham f4 162
Oakhurst d4 264
Oakland, California, U.S.A. a4 264
Oakland, Maryland, U.S.A. a5 256
Oakland, Mississippi, U.S.A. e2 258
Oakland, Nebraska, U.S.A. d3 260
Oakley c4 260
Oaktown c6 254
Oakura d3 76
Oakville g3 257
Oakwood, Ohio, U.S.A. d5 254
Oakwood, Texas, U.S.A. b4 258
Oamaru c6 77
Oasis f4 264
Oatlands Ab3 83
Oaxaca, Mex. f5 275
Oaxaca, Oaxaca, Mex. f5 275
Ob' l3 147
Ob'jačevo k1 151
Oba l6 251
Obaa k7 97
Obala g5 223
Obalno-kraška e4 176
Obama f4 115
Oban, Nig. f4 223
Oban, U.K. c3 164
Obanazawa j2 115
Obanbori Norak d1 128
Obarenes, Montes a2 192
Obbola h5 154
Obdach f2 177
Obeliai l5 157
Obelisk b6 77
Ober Engadin d3 196
Oberammergau g5 175
Oberasbach f3 175
Oberau g5 175
Oberaula e2 174
Oberbayern g5 175
Oberderdingen d3 174
Oberdrauburg d3 176
Obere Donau d4 174
Oberegg d2 196
Oberfranken g2 175
Ober-Grafendorf g1 177
Obergünzburg f5 174
Obergurgl c3 176
Oberhausen e3 159
Oberjochpass b2 176
Oberkirch d4 174
Oberlausitz k4 173
Oberlin, Kansas, U.S.A. c4 260
Oberlin, Louisiana, U.S.A. c4 258
Obermoschel c3 174
Obernai d2 184
Obernberg am Inn e1 176
Oberndorf am Neckar d4 174
Obernkirchen e3 172
Obernzell e1 176
Obero b3 276
Oberösterreich e2 176
Oberpfalz h3 175
Oberpfälzer Wald h3 175
Oberpullendorf h2 177
Obersinn e2 174
Oberstaufen f5 174
Oberstdorf f5 174
Oberthal f5 159
Oberthulba e2 174
Obertilliach d3 176
Obertraubling h4 175
Obertshausen d2 174
Obertyn g1 201
Oberueckersee j2 173
Obervellach e3 176
Oberviechtach h3 175
Oberwälder Land e4 172
Oberwart h2 177
Oberweißbach g2 175
Oberwölz f2 177
Obi f4 223
Obi, Kepulauan p5 99
Óbidos, Braz. f4 285
Óbidos a5 191
Obigarm d1 128
Obihiro Ac2 114
Obing d1 176
Obion, Tennessee, U.S.A. b7 254
Obion, Tennessee, U.S.A. e1 258
Obira Ab1 114
Obispos c2 284
Objat d3 186
Öblarn e2 176
Oblivskaja f2 149
Obluč'e r1 113
Obninsk d4 150
Obo, C.A.R. e2 225
Obo, China a7 112
Obobogorap d3 234
Obock f5 219
Obojan' e2 148
Obokote e4 225
Oborin k3 171
Oborniki e3 168
Oborniki Śląskie e4 168
Obouya c4 224
Obozerskij e3 146
Obra h7 124
Obra, Pol. d3 168
Obrage e1 294
Obregón, Presa e4 272
Obrenovac e3 200
Obrov f4 177
Obrovac b3 200
Obruk d3 208
Obry, Kanał e4 168
Obrzycko e3 168
Obšarovka k5 151
Obščij Syrt j2 149
Observatorio, Isla d6 295
Obskaja Guba n1 147
Obsza l5 169
Obuasi d4 222
Obudu f4 223
Obukhiv c2 148
Obva h4 147
Ocala h5 259
Ocamo e3 285
Ocampo, Chihuahua, Mex. e3 272
Ocampo, Coahuila, Mex. h4 273
Ocampo, Guanajuato, Mex. d3 274
Ocampo, Tamaulipas, Mex. e2 275
Ocaña, Col. c2 284
Ocaña, Peru c2 292
Ocaña, Spain g5 191
Occhiobello f5 196
Occidental, Cordillera, Col. b3 284
Occidental, Cordillera, Peru b2 292
Occoquan c6 256
Ocean Cape j4 247
Ocean Cay k7 259
Ocean City, Maryland, U.S.A. e6 256
Ocean City, New Jersey, U.S.A. f5 256
Ocean Falls d5 248
Ocean Park a2 262
Ocean Springs e4 258
Oceano c6 265
Oceanographer Fracture Zone g6 302
Oceanside, California, U.S.A. f8 265
Oceanside, New York, U.S.A. g4 257
Oceanville f5 257
Ocejón a3 192
Očer h4 146
Och'amch'ire h1 209
Ochakiv c3 148
Ochiishi-misaki Ad2 114
Ochil Hills e3 164
Ochlocknee g4 259
Ochlockonee g4 259
Ocho Rios B 270
Ochodnica g2 171
Ochsenfurt f3 174
Ochsenhausen e4 174
Ochthonia e4 210
Ochthonia, Akra e4 210
Ochtrup f2 159
Ocilla h4 259
Ockelbo g2 156
Öckerö e1 158
Ockholm b4 158
Ocmulgee h3 259
Ocna Sibiului g3 201
Ocnița h1 201
Ocolașul Mare, Vârful h2 201
Ocoña, Peru c3 292
Ocoña, Arequipa, Peru c3 292
Oconee h3 259
Oconee, Lake h3 259
Oconto c3 254
Ocoroni e5 272
Ocos a3 276
Ocosingo a2 276
Ocotal d4 276
Ocotepec f5 275
Ocotlán, Jalisco, Mex. c3 274
Ocotlán, Oaxaca, Mex. f5 275
Ocozocoautla h5 275
Ocracoke m2 259
Ocreza b5 190
Öcsa h4 171
Octeville c5 182
Ocú g7 277
Ocuilan de Arteaga e4 275
Ocumare del Tuy d1 284
Ocurí d3 292
Oda d4 222
Öda e4 114
Oda, Jebel e3 219
Ódáðahraun LF A 152
Ódaejin q5 113
Ódate j1 115
Odawara h4 115
Odda b2 156
Odder d3 158
Odearce c6 191
Odeceixe b7 191
Odei e2 250
Odeleite, Port c7 191
Odeleite c7 191
Odell b5 254
Odelouca b7 191
Odem a6 258
Odemira b7 191
Ödemiş a3 208
Odendaalsrus g3 235
Odense d3 158
Odense Fjord d3 158
Odenwald e3 174
Oderberg k3 173
Oderbruch k3 173
Oderbucht j1 173
Oder-Havel-Kanal j3 173
Oder-Spree-Kanal k3 173
Oderzo g4 196
Odesa k2 201
Ödeshog f3 156
Odessa c6 261
Odet b4 182
Odiáxere b7 191
Odiel d7 191
Odienné c4 222
Odiham f5 163
Odincovo d4 150
Odivelas, Port b6 191
Odivelas, Beja, Port b6 191
Odivelas, Lisboa, Port a6 191
Odivelas, Barragem de b6 191
Odobeşti h3 201
Odoev d5 150
Odolanów f4 168
Odon e3 182
Odŏngk g10 103
Odoorn e2 159
Odorheiu Secuiesc g2 201
Odou b2 138
Odra, Ger. c2 168
Odra, Spain f2 190
Odry f2 171
Odrzywół j4 169
Ødsted c3 158
Odum h4 259
Odžaci d3 200
Odzala, Parc National d' b3 224
Odzi, Zimb. e2 233
Odzi e2 233
Oebisfelde f3 173
Oeiras, Braz. d3 288
Oeiras, Port c7 191
Oeiras a6 191
Oelde d4 172
Oelemari f3 285
Oelrichs c3 260
Oelsnitz, Sachsen, Ger. h2 175
Oelsnitz, Sachsen, Ger. h2 175
Oelwein f3 260
Oenpelli a2 80
Oensingen b2 196
Oeste, Canal a6 295
Oetz b2 176
Oeversee c4 158
Ofanto f3 198
Ofaqim c5 139
Offa e4 223
Offaly e3 165
Offenbach d2 174
Offenburg c4 174
Offerdal e5 154
Officer Creek, The l10 87
Offranville g3 183
Ofidoussa g6 211
Ofiki e4 223
Ofu M 75
Ōfunato j2 115
Oga, Indon. h4 99
Oga h2 115
Ogachi j2 115
Ogadēn d2 226
Oga-hantō h2 115
Ōgaki g4 115
Ogallala c3 260
Ogan c6 98
Ogarevka d5 150
Ogbomoso e4 223
Ogden, Iowa, U.S.A. e3 260
Ogden, Utah, U.S.A. h5 262
Ogden, Mount, Can. a2 248
Ogden, Mount, U.S.A. l4 247
Ogdensburg j3 255
Ogea Levu E 74
Ogeechee h3 259
Oggiono d4 196
Oghi f3 128
Oghna f8 129
Ogi h3 115
Ogies h3 235
Ogilvie k2 247
Ogilvie Mountains k2 247
Oglala Pass Aa2 247
Oglesby b5 254
Oglethorpe g3 259
Oglethorpe, Mount g2 259
Ogliastro Cilento e4 198
Oglio e4 196
Ogliuga Island Ac2 247
Ogluhino m5 147
Ogmore j7 80
Ognon c3 184
Ogoamas, Gunung l5 99
Ogoja f4 223
Ogoki, Ontario, Can. k5 251
Ogoki, Ontario, Can. l5 251
Ogoki Lake k5 251
Ogooué b4 224
Ogooué-Ivindo b3 224
Ogooué-Lolo b4 224
Ogooué-Maritime a4 224
Ogosta f4 201
Ogou e4 223
Ogre, Lat. l4 157
Ogre l4 157
Ogrodniki k3 169
Ogrodzieniec h5 169
Ogulin g4 177
Ogun, Nig. e4 223
Ogun, Nig. e4 223
Ogurchinskiy, Ostrov d8 120
Oğuz g4 149
Ohad c5 139
Ohaeawai d1 76
Ohafia f4 223
Ohakune e3 76
Ohanes b7 193
Ohanet f3 221
Ohangwena b2 232
Ohansk h4 147
Ōhata Ab3 114
Ohau, Lake b6 77
Ohaupo e2 76
Ohio, U.S.A. e5 254
Ohio, Ohio/West Virginia, U.S.A. d6 254
Ohioville f3 257
Ohrdruf f2 175
Ohře h2 175
Ohre g3 173
Ohrid a1 210
Ohrid, Lake e5 200
Ohrigstad j2 235
Ohrigstad Dam Nature Reserve j2 235
Öhringen d5 174
Ohvat b3 150
Oi Qu b4 104
Oia f6 211
Oiā b4 190
Oiapoque g3 285
Oiba c2 284
Oich d2 164
Oignies a4 159
Oijärvi k4 155
Oildale d6 265
Oimbra c3 190
Oion b2 192
Oisans c5 185
Oise, Fr. h3 183
Oise, Picardie, Fr. h3 183
Oiseaux du Djoudj, Parc National des a2 222
Oisemont g3 183
Oisterwijk d3 159
Oita d5 114
Oiti c4 210
Oityo c6 211
Oiuru a3 218
Öja h4 157
Ojai d7 265
Öjän e5 154
Ojcowski Park Narodowy h5 169
Öje e2 156
Ojeda e3 297
Ojén f8 191
Öjen g1 156
Ojinaga g3 272
Ojitlán f4 275
Ojiya h3 115
Ojo de Agua, Arg. e1 296
Ojo de Agua, Mex. d3 274
Ojo de Laguna f3 272
Ojocaliente c2 274
Ojos del Salado, Nevado d5 292
Ojrzeń j3 169
Oju f4 223
Ojuelos de Jalisco d3 274
Öjungen, Stora f2 156
Oka f4 123
Oka, Russ. Fed. g4 151
Okaba k7 97
Okahandja b3 232
Okahukura e3 76
Okaihau d1 76
Okaka e4 223
Okanagan Lake h7 248
Okanogan, U.S.A. d1 262
Okanogan, Washington, U.S.A. d1 262
Okanogan Range c1 262
Okány k5 171
Okapi, Parc National de la e3 225
Okara f5 128
Okarche a2 258
Okarem q2 137
Okasise b3 232
Okaukuejo b2 232
Okavango, Afr. c2 232
Okavango, Nam. b2 232
Okavango Delta c2 232
Okawville b6 254
Okaya h3 115
Okayama, Japan e4 114
Okayama e4 114
Okazaki g4 115
Okch'ŏn p7 113
Okeechobee, Lake j6 259
Okefenokee National Wildlife Refuge and Wilderness h4 259
Okehampton b6 163
Oke-Iho e4 223
Okemah a2 258
Okene f4 223
Oker f3 172
Okha, India d9 129
Okha, Russ. Fed. l2 94
Okhaldhunga h6 135
Okhimath d4 130
Okhotsk q4 119
Okhotsk Basin h2 300
Okhotsk, Sea of q4 119
Okhotskoye More q4 119
Okhtyrka d2 148
Okiep b4 234
Okinawa, Okinawa, Japan B 115
Okinawa B 115
Okinawa-shotō B 115
Okino-shima d4 114
Oki-shotō e3 114
Okitipupa e4 223
Okkan b7 102
Okku p8 113
Oklahoma d5 261
Oklahoma City a2 258
Oklawaha j5 259
Oklee f7 250
Okmulgee b2 258
Oko, Wadi e3 219
Okola g5 223
Okolona, Kentucky, U.S.A. d6 254
Okolona, Mississippi, U.S.A. e2 258
Okombache b3 232
Okondja b4 224
Okonek e2 168
Okoppe Ac1 114
Ököritófülpös l4 171
Okoyo c4 224
Okpety, Gora t4 121
Okrühle k2 171
Oksapmin l7 97
Oksbøl b3 158
Øksfjord j1 155
Oksibil l6 97
Oksovskij d3 146
Oksskolten e3 154
Okta c2 156
Oktjabr'sk k5 151
Oktjabr'skij, Čitinskaja Oblast', Russ. Fed. k1 113
Oktjabr'skij, Arhangel'skaja Oblast', Russ. Fed. g1 151
Oktjabr'skij, Kostromskaja Oblast', Russ. Fed. h2 151
Oktjabr'skij, Nižegorodskaja Oblast', Russ. Fed. h3 151
Oktjabr'skij, Respublika Baškortostan, Russ. Fed. m4 151
Oktjabr'skij, Rjazanskaja Oblast', Russ. Fed. e5 150
Oktjabr'skij, Rjazanskaja Oblast', Russ. Fed. e4 150
Oktjabr'skij, Sverdlovskaja Oblast', Russ. Fed. j4 147
Oktjabr'skij, Ul'janovskaja Oblast', Russ. Fed. j5 151
Oktjabr'skij, Vladimirskaja Oblast', Russ. Fed. g3 151
Oktjabr'skij, Volgogradskaja Oblast', Russ. Fed. f3 149
Oktjabr'skoe, Čeljabinskaja Oblast', Russ. Fed. k5 147
Oktjabr'skoe, Hantj-Mansijskij Avtonomnij Okrug, Russ. Fed. l3 147
Oktjabr'skoe, Orenburgskaja Oblast', Russ. Fed. j1 149
Oktjabr'skoj Revoljucii, Ostrov k2 118
Oktumkum, Peski d7 120
Oktwin c6 102
Oktyabr'skiy j1 120
Oktyabr'skoye k1 120
Oktyah'sk k4 149
Okučani j4 177
Okulovka b2 150
Okushiri Aa2 114
Okushiri-tō Aa2 114
Okuta e4 223
Okwa e1 234
Ol'hovatka e2 148
Ol'hovka k4 147
Ol'oinka l5 147
Ola c2 258
Olaeta f2 297
Olague c2 192
Olancha e5 265
Olancha Peak e5 265
Olanchito d3 276
Öland g4 156
Olanta k3 259
Olar j3 259
Olargues e5 187
Olary e12 81
Olary, South Australia, Aust. b1 82
Olascoaga g3 297
Olathe e4 260
Olavarría g4 297
Oława f5 168
Olbernhau j2 175
Olbersdorf k2 175
Olbia Ab2 198
Olching g4 175
Olcott g4 254
Old Bahama Channel e3 266
Old Bastar g3 126
Old Cork c7 80
Old Crow, Can. k2 247
Old Crow, U.S.A. j1 247
Old Fields b5 256
Old Forge e3 256
Old Harbor f4 246
Old Harbour B 270
Old Head of Kinsale c5 165
Old Man of Coniston, The c2 162
Old Oyo National Park e4 223
Old Perlican r5 253
Old Road D 271
Old Road Town F 271
Old Saybrook h3 257
Old Town h6 253
Old Wives Lake p6 249
Old Womans Point B 266
Oldcastle d3 165
Oldenbrok b5 158
Oldenburg c2 172
Oldenburg in Holstein d4 158
Oldenswort b4 158
Oldenzaal e2 159
Olderdalen h2 154

366 Oldham → Otnes

Oldham, England, U.K. h1 162
Oldham d3 162
Oldmeldrum f2 164
Olds k6 249
Öldziyt, Arhangay, Mong. a1 112
Öldziyt, Dornogovĭ, Mong. e3 112
Olean b2 256
Olecko l1 169
Oleggio c4 196
Oleiros c5 191
Olekma g1 94
Olekminsk n3 119
Oleksandrivka, Kirovohrads'ka Oblast', Ukr. d2 148
Oleksandrivka, Mykolayivs'ka Oblast', Ukr. c3 148
Oleksandriya d2 148
Olema f2 147
Olema, U.S.A. a3 264
Olen c3 159
Ølen a3 156
Olenegorsk p2 155
Olenek, Russ. Fed. n2 119
Olenek m3 119
Olenekskij Zaliv n2 119
Olenica q3 155
Olenino b3 150
Olenivka e3 148
Olenti q1 121
Oléron, Île d' a3 186
Oles'ko n6 169
Olesa de Montserrat f3 192
Oleśnica f4 168
Olesno g5 168
Olet Tongo j9 99
Oletta A 185
Olette e6 187
Olevs'k b2 148
Olga, Lac q6 251
Olga, Mount k9 87
Ølgod b3 158
Olhão c7 191
Olhava k4 155
Olhos d'Agua g2 291
Oliana f2 192
Oliena Ab2 198
Oliete d3 192
Olifants, Moz. j1 235
Olifants, Nam. c2 234
Olifants, Western Cape, R.S.A. c6 234
Olifantshoek e3 234
Olifantsrivierberge c6 234
Olimar Grande f2 294
Olimarao G 74
Olimpia d4 290
Olinalá e5 275
Olinda f3 288
Olinga f2 233
Olingdal f2 156
Olite c2 192
Oliva, Arg. f2 297
Oliva d6 193
Oliva de la Frontera d6 191
Oliva de Mérida d6 191
Oliva, Cordillera de c1 294
Olivares de Júcar b5 193
Olive Branch e2 258
Olive Hill e6 254
Olivebridge f3 257
Olivehurst b2 264
Oliveira f4 291
Oliveira de Azeméis b4 190
Oliveira de Frades b4 190
Oliveira do Bairro b4 190
Oliveira do Hospital c4 190
Oliveira dos Brejinhos d4 288
Olivenza, Port c6 191
Olivenza c6 191
Oliver d1 262
Oliver Lake r3 249
Oliveros g2 297
Olivet g5 183
Olivet, U.S.A. d4 254
Olivia e2 260
Olivine Range b6 77
Olivone c3 196
Öljaren g3 156
Oljutorskij, Mys t4 119
Oljuvatnet b2 156
Olkkajärvi l3 155
Olkusz h5 169
Olla c4 258
Ollachea c2 292
Ollagüe d4 292
Ollagüe, Volcán d4 292
Ollen c4 156
Ollerton e3 162
Ollerup d3 158
Olliergues f3 186
Ollioules b7 185
Ollita, Cordillera de b1 296
Ollitas b1 296
Ollombo c4 224
Ollon a3 196
Olmedilla de Roa g3 190
Olmedo, Italy Aa2 198
Olmedo, Spain f3 190
Olmeto A 185
Olmos, Arg. f2 297
Olmos, Peru b5 284
Olmos de Ojeda f2 190
Olney f4 163
Olney, Illinois, U.S.A. b6 254
Olney, Maryland, U.S.A. c5 256
Olney, Montana, U.S.A. f1 262
Olocau d5 193
Olofström f4 156
Olomane m3 253
Olomouc f2 170
Olomoucký kraj f2 170
Olonec b1 150
Olongapo c3 100
Olongliko h5 99
Olonne-sur-Mer d6 182
Olonzac e5 187
Oloron-Ste-Marie b5 187
Olosega M 75
Olost g3 192
Olot g2 192
Olovi a1 170
Olovyannaya f2 94
Olpe c1 174
Olperer c2 176
Olršov f2 171
Olsa f2 177
Olsberg d4 172
Olshammar f3 156
Olst e2 159
Ølstykke f3 158
Olszewo-Borki k2 169
Olsztyn j2 169
Olsztynek j2 169
Olt, Rom. g3 201
Olt, Rom. g3 201
Olta c2 294
Olte, Sierra de c4 295
Olten b2 196
Olteniţa h3 201
Oltina h3 201
Oltu h2 209
Olula del Rio b7 193
Olutanga c8 100
Ölvega c3 192
Olvera e8 191
Olvera, Embalse de a6 193
Olympia b2 262
Olympic National Park b2 262
Olympos, Grc. c2 210
Olympos, Grc. d4 210
Olympos Ac3 211
Olympus, Mount b2 262
Olynthos d2 210
Olyphant e3 256
Om Hajêr e5 219
Om' q1 121
Oma f3 135
Oma Ab3 114
Oma f2 146
Omachi g3 115
Omae-zaki h4 115
Ōmagari j2 115
Omagh, England, U.K. b2 165
Omagh d2 165
Omaguas c4 284
Omaha, Nebraska, U.S.A. e3 260
Omaha, Texas, U.S.A. b3 258
Omaheke c1 234
Omak h7 248
Omalos d7 211
Oman c6 92

OMAN

THE SULTANATE OF OMAN
Area 309,500km²
(119,500sq miles)
Capital Muscat
Organizations CCASG, IDB, LAS, OIC
Population 2,770,000
Pop. growth (%) 2.3
Life expectancy 69 (m); 72 (f)
Languages Arabic, English
Literacy 75.8%
Currency Omani rial
(US $1 = 0.38 Omani rial)
GDP (US million $) 20,237
GDP per head ($US) 7305

Oman, Gulf of c4 300
Omapere, Lake d1 76
Omarama b6 77
Omarkot e6 129
Omaruru b3 232
Omas b2 292
Omatako b3 232
Omate c3 292
Omaweneno e2 234
Oma-zaki j1 115
Ombai, Selat n9 99
Ombella-Mpoko c2 224
Omboué a4 224
Ombrone f7 197
Ombu h4 135
Ombúes de Lavalle j2 297
Omdurman d4 218
Omealca f4 275
Omegna c4 196
Omeo h14 81
'Omer c5 139
Ömerköy b3 208
Omessa A 185
Ometepec e5 275
Omidiyeh m6 137
Omineca Mountains n4 247
Omiš f1 198
Omišalj f4 177
Omitara b1 234
Omitlán e5 275
Ōmiya j3 115
Ommaney, Cape l4 247
Omme b3 158
Ommen e2 159
Ömnögovĭ c4 112
Omø e3 158
Omo National Park b2 226
Omo Wenz b2 226
Omoku f4 223
Omoloj p3 119
Omono-gawa j2 115
Omskaja Oblast' m5 147
Ōmū Ac1 114
O-mu d4 102
Omu, Vârful g3 201
Omulew k2 169
Omulew, Jezioro j2 169
Omurtag h4 201
Omusati b2 232
Omutinskoe l4 147
Omutninsk m2 151
Oña g2 190
Onagawa j2 115
Onalaska f3 260
Onaman Lake k5 251
Onang k6 99
Onangué, Lac b4 224
Onaping Lake n7 251
Onarga b5 254
Onatchiway, Lac g4 252
Oñati b1 192
Onavas e3 272
Onaway d3 254
Oncala, Puerto de b3 192
Oncativo f1 297
Onchan b2 162
Oncócua a2 232
Onda d5 193
Ondangwa b2 232
Ondara e6 193
Ondarroa b1 192
Ondjiva b2 232
Ondo, Nig. f4 223
Ondo e4 223
Ondor Had l3 113
Ondor Mod c5 112
Ondor Sum g4 112
Öndörhaan f2 112
Öndörhushuu g1 112
One d1 234
One, Nor. a2 156
Oneata E 74
Onega, Russ. Fed. e1 150
Onega d3 146
Oneida, New York, U.S.A. j4 255
Oneida, Tennessee, U.S.A. g1 259
Oneida Lake j4 255
Onekotan, Ostrov r5 119
Oneonta, Alabama, U.S.A. f3 258
Oneonta, New York, U.S.A. e2 256
Oneroa e2 76
Oneşti h2 201
Onet-le-Château e4 187
Onezhskoe Ozero c1 150
Onežskaja Guba d2 146
Ong h9 125
Onga b4 224
Ongandjera b2 232
Ongers e2 234
Ongerup d13 87
Ongi, Övörhangay, Mong. b2 112
Ongi, Dundgovĭ, Mong. b3 112
Ongjin n7 113
Ongole g5 126
Ongon b2 112
Ongudaj w2 121
Oni j1 209
Onich c3 164
Onil d6 193
Onilahy Aa3 233
Onistagane, Lac g3 252
Onitsha f4 223
Onjati Mountain b1 234
Onkamo p1 157
Onkamojärvi m3 155
Onkivesi l5 155
Ono E 74
Ōno g4 115
Ono, Japan f4 114
Ono, U.S.A. d4 256
Onomichi e4 114
Onon f1 112
Onon, Russ. Fed. g1 112
Onon Gol f1 112
Onotoa H 75
Ons, Illa de b2 190
Onseepkans c4 234
Onsella c2 192
Önskasjön g5 154
Onslow b7 86
Onslow Bay l2 259
Onsŏng q4 113
Ontake-san g4 115
Ontario, Can. k5 251
Ontario, California, U.S.A. f7 265
Ontario, Oregon, U.S.A. e3 262
Ontario, Lake h4 255
Ontiñena e3 192
Ontinyent d6 193
Ontojärvi m4 155
Ontonagon j7 251
Ontong Java Rise j5 300
Ontur c6 193
Onverwacht f2 285
Onyx e6 265
Onzain g5 183
Onzonilla e2 190
Oodnadatta b9 81
Oodweyne d2 226
Ooldea k12 87
Ooldea Range k12 87
Oologah Lake b1 258
Oorindi e6 80
Oostburg c4 254
Oostende a3 159
Oosterhout c3 159
Oosterschelde b3 159
Oosterwolde e2 159
Oostkamp b3 159
Oost-Souburg b3 159
Oostvaardersplassen d2 159
Oost-Vlaanderen b4 159
Oostvleteren a4 159
Oost-Vlieland d1 159
Ootmarsum e2 159
Ootsa Lake d5 248
Opal h5 273
Opala d4 224
Opalenica e3 168
Opari f3 225
Oparino k2 151
Opasatika, Ontario, Can. m6 251
Opasatika, Ontario, Can. m6 251
Opasatika Lake m6 251
Opasquia g4 250
Opasquia Provincial Park g4 250
Opataca, Lac r5 251
Opatija f4 177
Opatovice nad Labem d1 170
Opatów k5 169
Opatówek g4 168
Opatowiec j5 169
Opava f2 171
Opel c3 174
Opelika g3 259
Opelousas c4 258
Open Door h3 297
Opeongo Lake c6 252
Opglabbeek d3 159
Opheim p7 249
Ophir, Alaska, U.S.A. e3 246
Ophir, Oregon, U.S.A. a4 262
Ophir, Gunung b5 96
Opienge e3 225
Opihi c6 77
Opinaca q4 251
Opinaca, Réservoir q4 251
Opinnagau m3 251
Opiscotéo, Lac j2 253
Opobo f5 223
Opočno e1 170
Opoco d3 292
Opocopa, Lac j2 253
Opoczno j4 169
Opodepe h11 263
Opole f5 168
Opole Lubelskie k4 169
Opolskie f5 168
Opononi d1 76
Oporets' f1 201
Opotiki f3 76
Opp f4 258
Oppach j1 175
Oppdal c1 156
Oppenau d4 174
Oppenheim d3 174
Oppido Lucano e4 198
Oppido Mamertina e6 199
Oppland c2 156
Opportunity, Montana, U.S.A. g2 262
Opportunity, Washington, U.S.A. e2 262
Optaşi-Măgura g3 201
Opua e1 76
Opunake d3 76
Ópusztaszer j5 171
Opuwo a2 232
Oquitoa h10 263
Or 'Aqiva c4 138
Or Yehuda c4 139
Ora, Cyp. b2 138
Ora, Italy f3 196
Øra h1 154
Oracle h9 263
Orada c6 191
Oradea k4 171
Oradour-sur-Glane d3 186
Oradour-sur-Vayres c3 186
Öræfajökull A 152
Orahovica j4 177
Orai f7 124
Orain b4 184
Oraiokastro c2 210
Oraison b7 185
Orajärvi l3 155
Oran, Alg. d1 220
Oran, U.S.A. e1 258
Orán e4 293
Örån g4 154
Ŏrang q5 113
Orange, Aust. j12 81
Orange, Fr. a6 185
Orange, Nam. b4 234
Orange, California, U.S.A. f8 265
Orange, Connecticut, U.S.A. g3 257
Orange, Massachusetts, U.S.A. h2 257
Orange, Texas, U.S.A. c4 258
Orange, Virginia, U.S.A. b6 256
Orange City j5 259
Orange Cove d5 264
Orange Lake h5 259
Orange Walk, Belize c1 276
Orange Walk, Belize c1 276
Orange, Cabo g3 285
Orangeburg j3 259
Orangeville f4 254
Orango, Ilha de a3 222
Orani, Italy Ab2 198
Orani, Phil. c3 100
Oranienburg j3 173
Oranje Gebergte g3 285
Oranjefontein g1 235
Oranjemund b4 234
Oranjestad, Aruba j8 271
Oranjestad, Neth. Ant. n6 271
Oranjeville h3 235
Oranmore c3 165
Orapa d3 232
Oraque d7 191
Orari c5 77
Oras e4 100
Oras Bay e4 100
Orašac g2 198
Orăştie f3 201
Orativ j1 201
Oravais j5 155
Oravská Polhora h2 171
Oravský Podzámok h2 171
Orawia a7 77
Orb f5 187
Orba Co e2 130
Orbacém b3 190
Ørbæk d3 158
Orbassano b4 196
Orbe a3 196
Orbec f3 183
Orbetello f7 197
Orbetello, Laguna di f7 197
Orbieu e5 187
Orbisonia c4 256
Orbost j14 81
Örbyhus g2 157
Orcadas (Arg.) a1 298
Orcera b6 193
Orchies b4 159
Orchila, Isla d1 284
Orchowo g3 168
Orcia f7 197
Orcières c6 185
Orco b4 196
Orcotuna b2 292
Ord j4 86
Ord River Nature Reserve j4 86
Ord, Mount g5 86
Orda j4 147
Ordbend a2 264
Orderville g7 263
Ordes b1 190
Ordesa - Monte Perdido, Parque Nacional e2 192
Ordizia b1 192
Ordoñez f2 297
Ordrup Næs e3 158
Ordu, Tur. f2 209
Ordu f2 209
Ordubad l2 137
Orduña a2 192
Ordway c4 260
Ordzhonikidze h1 120
Ore e4 223
Orea c4 192
Öreälven g5 154
Öreälven f2 156
Orebić g2 198
Örebro, Swe. f3 156
Örebro f3 156
Örefjärden h5 154
Öregcsertő h5 171
Öreg-Futóné k2 177
Öreglak f5 171
Oregon, U.S.A. c4 262
Oregon, Ohio, U.S.A. e5 254
Öregrund h2 157
Öregrundsgrepen h2 157
Orehoved e4 158
Orehovo f2 150
Orehovo-Zuevo e4 150
Oreini d1 210
Orel b1 210
Orellana b1 292
Orellana de la Sierra e5 191
Orellana, Embalse de e5 191
Orem h5 262
Ören a4 208
Orenburg j2 149
Orenburgskaja Oblast' j1 149
Orense, Arg. h5 297
Orense c2 190
Orense, Galicia, Spain c2 190
Oreoi d4 210
Orepuki a7 77
Öreskilsälven g3 156
Orestiada g1 210
Orestimba Creek b4 264
Öresund e5 156
Oreti b6 77
Orewa e2 76
Orford Ab3 83
Orford Ness h4 163
Organ Pipe Cactus National Monument g9 263
Organabo g2 285
Organyà f2 192
Orgaz g5 191
Orge h4 183
Orgelet b4 184
Orgères-en-Beauce g4 183
Orgiano f4 196
Orgiva g8 191
Orgon b7 185
Orgosolo Ab2 198
Orgūn d4 128
Orhanlar a3 208
Orhei j2 201
Orhon c1 112
Orhon Gol c1 112
Orhontuul c1 112
Orhy, Pic d' b6 175
Oria, Italy g4 198
Oria, Spain b7 193
Oria, País Vasco, Spain b1 192
Oriči k2 151
Orick a5 262
Oriental f4 275
Oriental, Cordillera, Bol. d3 292
Oriental, Cordillera, Col. c3 284
Oriental, Cordillera, Peru c2 292
Orientale e3 225
Oriente, Arg. g5 297
Oriente, Braz. e1 293
Origny-Ste-Benoîte b5 159
Orihuela d6 193
Orihuela del Tremedal c4 192
Orikhiv d3 148
Orillia g3 254
Orimattila l2 157
Orinase-gawa j1 115
Orinoco e2 285
Orinoco Delta e2 285
Orio b1 192
Oriola c6 191
Oriolo f4 198
Orion a5 254
Oripää k2 157
Oriskany j4 255
Orissa j9 125
Orissaare k3 157
Oristano Aa3 198
Óriszentpéter e5 170
Orituco d2 284
Orivesi, Fin. n1 157
Orivesi l2 157
Oriximiná f4 285
Orizaba f4 275
Orizaba, Pico de f4 275
Orizatlán e3 275
Orizona d2 290
Ørje d3 156
Orkanger b5 154
Orke d4 172
Örkelljunga e4 156
Örkény h4 171
Orkla b5 154
Orkney g3 235
Orkney, U.K. B 164
Orkney Islands f1 164
Orla, Ger. g5 173
Orla, Pol. e4 168
Orla, U.S.A. c6 261
Orlamünde g2 175
Orland a2 264
Orlândia e4 290
Orlando j5 259
Orleaes c7 289
Orléanais g4 183
Orléans g5 183
Orleans, Massachusetts, U.S.A. l3 257
Orleans, Vermont, U.S.A. f6 252
Orléans, Canal d' h5 183
Orléans, Île d' g5 252
Orlen f3 156
Orlice d1 171
Orlické Hory e1 170
Orljava j4 177
Orlov k2 151
Orlov Gaj h2 149
Orlová g2 171
Orlovskaja Oblast' e1 148
Orlovskij f3 149
Ormara b8 129
Ormara, Ras b8 129
Örménykút j5 171
Ormesby St Margaret h4 162
Ormideia b2 138
Ormoc e5 100
Ormond Beach j5 259
Ormos e5 211
Ormos Agiou Nikolaou d6 211
Ormos Almyrou e7 211
Ormos Mesara e7 211
Ormos Panormou f5 211
Ormož h3 177
Ormsjön f4 154
Ormskirk d3 162
Ormylia d2 210
Ornach c7 129
Ornain a2 184
Ornans c3 184
Orne, Fr. f4 183
Orne, Basse-Normandie, Fr. f4 183
Ørnes d3 154
Orneta j1 169
Ornö h3 157
Örnsköldsvik g5 154
Orø e3 158
Oro, Mex. g5 272
Oro p5 113
Oro Grande f7 265
Oro, Lac d2 222
Orobayaya e2 293
Orobo, Serra do d4 288
Orocó e3 288
Orocué c3 284
Orodara d3 222
Orofino e2 262
Orog Nuur a3 112
Orogrande b5 261
Oroluk G 74
Oromia b2 226
Oromocto j6 253
Oromocto Lake j6 253
Oron, Isr. d6 139
Oron, Nig. f5 223
Orona H 75
Oron-la-Ville a3 196
Oronoque, Guy. f3 285
Oronoque, East Berbice - Corentyne, Guy. f3 285
Oronsay b3 164
Oropa b4 196
Orope c2 284
Oropeo d4 274
Oropesa e4 193
Oropesa, Cabo de e4 193
Oropuche E 271
Oroquieta d6 100
Orós e3 288
Orós, Açude e3 288
Orosei Ab2 198
Orosei, Golfo di Ab2 198
Orosháza j5 171
Oroszlány g4 171
Orote Peninsula C 74
Oroville b2 264
Orpheus Island A 84
Orpierre b6 185
Orqohan l1 113
Orquideas, Parque Nacional las b2 284
Orrefors f4 156
Orrin d2 164
Orrkjølen d2 156
Orroroo d12 81
Orrville f5 254
Orsa f2 156
Orsasjön f2 156
Őrségi c2 200
Orsha c1 148
Orsiera-Rocciavrè, Parco Naturale b4 196
Orsières b3 196
Orsjön g2 156
Orsk k2 149
Ørslev e3 158
Orşova f3 201
Ørsted d2 158
Orta Nova e3 198
Ortakent a4 208
Ortaklar a4 208
Orte g7 197
Ortega b3 284
Ortegal, Cabo c1 190
Orteguaza b3 284
Ortenberg e2 174
Ortenburg e1 176
Orthez b5 187
Ortho d2 292
Ortholmen e1 156
Orthovouni b3 210
Ortiga e6 191
Ortigueira, Braz. c6 290
Ortigueira c1 190
Ortisei f3 196
Ortiz d3 272
Ortíz d2 284
Ortoire E 271
Ortolo A 185
Ortona d2 198
Ortonville d2 260
Ortrand j4 173
Örträsk g4 154
Ortueri Aa2 198
Örtze f3 172
Ørum, Århus, Den. d2 158
Ørum, Viborg, Den. c2 158
Orūmīyeh k3 137
Oruro, Bol. d3 292
Oruro, Oruro, Bol. d3 292
Orusco a4 192
Orust d3 156
Orūzgān c4 128
Orvalho c4 190
Orvault d5 182
Orvieto g7 197
Orvinio g7 197
Orwell h4 163
Orxon Gol j1 113
Orynyn h1 201
Orz k3 169
Orzinuovi d4 196
Orzola Af1 189
Orzyc k2 169
Orzysz k2 169
Os d1 156
Oša m4 157
Osa h4 147
Osa de Vega b5 193
Osa, Península de f6 277
Ōsaka, Japan f4 115
Ōsaka f4 115
Osakarovka p2 121
Osan p7 113
Osaro, Monte e5 196
Osasco e5 291
Osburn f2 262
Øsby c3 158
Osby e4 156
Oscar g3 285
Oscar Range g5 86
Osceola, Arkansas, U.S.A. d2 258
Osceola, Iowa, U.S.A. e3 260
Osceola Mills b4 256
Oschatz j1 175
Oschersleben (Bode) g3 173
Oschiri Ab2 198
Oscoda e3 254
Osečina d3 200
Osen c4 154
Osensjøen d2 156
Osera d3 192
Osetr e4 150
Ōse-zaki c5 114
Osh p7 121
Osh p7 121
Oshakati b2 232
Oshamanbe Ab2 114
Oshana b2 232
Oshawa g4 254
Oshika-hantō j2 115
Oshikango b2 232
Oshikoto b2 232
Oshikuku b2 232
Ō-shima, Japan Aa3 114
Ō-shima, Japan h4 115
Oshkosh, Nebraska, U.S.A. c3 260
Oshkosh, Wisconsin, U.S.A. b3 254
Oshnovīyeh k3 137
Oshogbo e4 223
Oshwe c4 224
Osieck k4 169
Osieczna, Pomorskie, Pol. g2 168
Osieczna, Wielkopolskie, Pol. e4 168
Osiek k5 169
Osiek, Jezioro d3 168
Osielsko g2 168
Osijek d3 200
Osijek-Baranja k4 177
Osilo Aa2 198
Osima l6 97
Osimo c1 198
Osinniki w1 121
Osipaonica e3 200
Osire b3 232
Osiyan f7 129
Osizweni j3 235
Osjaków g4 168
Osječenica c3 200
Oskaloosa e3 260
Oskarshamn g4 156
Oskarström e4 156
Oskava f2 170
Oskol d2 148
Oskořínek d1 170
Oslava e2 170
Oslo, Nor. d3 156
Oslo d3 156
Oslob d6 100
Oslobip l7 97
Osmanabad e3 126
Osmancık e2 208
Osmaniye, Tur. f4 209
Osmaniye f4 209
Osmankajärvi l4 155
Ošmar'ja k3 147
Ösmo g3 157
Osmussaar k3 157
Osnabrück d3 172
Osnaburgh House h5 250
Ośno Lubuskie c3 168
Oso e4 225
Osoblaha f1 171
Osogovska Planina f5 201
Osoppo h3 196
Osor, Cro. f5 177
Osor f5 177
Osor, Rt f5 177
Osório b7 289
Osorno, Chile a6 296
Osorno f2 190
Osorno, Volcán b4 294
Osoyoos d1 262
Osøyri a2 156
Ospino d2 284
Ospitaletto e4 196
Osprey Reef h2 80
Osrednjeslovenska f3 177
Oss d3 159
Ossa c3 210
Ossa de Montiel b6 193
Ossa, Mount Ab2 83
Ossa, Serra de c6 191
Osse, Fr. c5 187
Osse, Nig. f4 223
Osseo f2 260
Ossi Aa2 198
Ossineke e3 254
Ossining g3 257
Ossipee g7 252
Ossokmanuan Lake k2 253
Ossu h7 97
Oštarije g4 177
Ostaškov b3 150
Ostbevern c3 172
Østbirk c3 158
Østby e2 156
Oste e2 172
Osted e3 158
Ostellato f5 196
Osten c5 158
Ostende j4 297
Ostenfeld (Husum) c4 158
Oster b4 150
Øster Agger b2 158
Øster Hurup d2 158
Øster Vrå d1 158
Osterburken e3 174
Österbybruk g2 157
Österbymo f4 156
Østerdalen d2 156
Østerdalen Naturreservat e3 154
Östergotland f3 156
Osterhever b4 158
Osterhofen e1 176
Osterholz-Scharmbeck d2 172
Østerild b1 158
Osternig e3 176
Osterode am Harz f4 172
Östersund e5 154
Östervåla g2 156
Osterwieck f4 173
Ostfildern e4 174
Østfold d3 156
Ostfriesische Inseln c2 172
Ostfriesland c2 172
Östhammar h2 157
Osthofen d3 174
Ostiano e4 196
Ostiglia f4 196
Östliche Chiemgauer Alpen h5 175
Östliche Karwendelspitze c2 176
Östmark e2 156
Ostpeene h2 173
Ostra h6 197
Östra Kvarken h5 154
Östra Lägern f4 156
Östra Nedsjön e4 156
Ostrach, Ger. e5 174
Ostrach e5 174
Ostrava g2 171
Ostravský kraj g2 171
Ostrhauderfehn c2 172
Ostróda h2 169
Ostrogožsk e2 148
Ostrołęka k2 169
Ostroměř d1 170
Ostroróg e3 168
Ostrov, Czech Rep. a1 170
Ostrov, Rom. h3 201
Ostrov, Rom. j3 201
Ostrov, Russ. Fed. n4 157
Ostrów Lubelski l4 169
Ostrów Mazowiecka k3 169
Ostrów Wielkopolski f4 168
Ostrowice d2 168
Ostrowiec Świętokrzyski k5 169
Ostrožac g5 177
Ostrožská Nová Ves f2 170
Ostryj, Mys j5 157
Ostrzeszów f4 168
Ostseebad Binz j1 173
Ostseebad Boltenhagen e5 158
Ostseebad Göhren j1 173
Ostseebad Kühlungsborn e4 158
Ostseebad Prerow am Darß f4 158
Ostseebad Sellin j1 173
Ostseebad Wustrow f4 158
Ostuacán h5 275
Ostula c4 274
Ostuni g4 198
Osum a2 210
Osŭm g4 201
Ōsumi-hantō d6 114
Ōsumi-shotō B 115
Osun e4 223
Osuna e7 191
Osvaldo Cruz c4 290
Oswego, New York, U.S.A. h4 255
Oswego, New York, U.S.A. h4 255
Oswestry c4 162
Oświęcim h5 169
Osyka d4 258
Ōta h3 115
Ota b5 191
Otaci h1 201
Otago b6 77
Otago Peninsula c6 77
Ōtaki j4 115
Otaki e4 76
Otakwa k6 97
Otanmäki l4 155
Otar q6 121
Otare, Cerro c3 284
Otaru Ab2 114
Otatara b7 77
Otatitlán f4 275
Otautau a7 77
Otava, Czech Rep. b2 171
Otava m2 157
Otavalo b3 284
Otavi b2 232
Ōtawara j3 115
Otchinjau a2 232
Otego e2 256
Oteiza c2 192
Oţelu Roşu f3 201
Otematata c6 77
Otepää m3 157
Oteren g2 154
Otermajärvi l4 155
Otero de Bodas d3 190
Otero de Herreros f4 190
Oteševo a2 210
Otgon Tenger Uul p1 117
Othe, Forêt d' j4 183
Othe, Pays d' j4 183
Othrys c3 210
Oti, Ghana e4 223
Oti k5 99
Otinapa b1 274
Otira c5 77
Otis g2 257
Otis Reservoir h2 257
Otisco Lake d2 256
Otish, Monts g2 253
Otívar g8 191
Otjihavana b1 234
Otjikondo b2 232
Otjinene b3 232
Otjiwarongo b3 232
Otjosondu b3 232
Otjozondjupa b2 232
Otmuchów f5 168
Otnes d2 156

Otočac → Panarukan 367

Otočac g5 177
Otofuke Ac2 114
Otonga e1 76
Otoque, Isla h6 277
Otoro, Jebel d5 218
Otorohanga e3 76
Otoskwin j5 251
Otpan, Gora c5 120
Otra b3 156
Otradinskij d5 150
Otradnaja f3 148
Otradnoe a2 150
Otradnoe, Ozero p2 157
Otradnyj l5 151
Otranto c2 198
Otricoli g7 197
Otrokovice f2 171
Otrøy a5 154
Ōtsu f4 115
Ōtsuchi j2 115
Otta c2 156
Ottadalen b2 156
Ottana Ab2 198
Ottawa, Ontario, Can. j3 255
Ottawa, Can. p7 251
Ottawa, Illinois, U.S.A. b5 254
Ottawa, Kansas, U.S.A. e4 260
Ottawa, Ohio, U.S.A. d5 254
Ottenby g4 156
Ottendorf-Okrilla h1 175
Ottenschlag g1 177
Ottensheim f1 177
Otter Lake q4 249
Otter Rapids m5 251
Otter Tail Lake e2 260
Otterburn d1 162
Otterndorf b5 158
Ottersberg e2 172
Otterup d3 158
Öttevény f4 171
Ottnaren g2 156
Ottobeuren f5 174
Ottobrunn g4 175
Öttömös h5 171
Ottosdal f3 235
Ottoshoop f2 235
Ottsjön d5 154
Ottumwa e3 260
Ottweiler f5 159
Otukpa f4 223
Otukpo f4 223
Otumba e4 275
Otway National Park c4 82
Otway Range c4 82
Otway, Cape c4 82
Otwock k3 169
Otyń d4 168
Otyniya g1 201
Ötztaler Ache b2 176
Ötztaler Alpen f1 177
Ouachita c3 258
Ouachita Mountains b2 258
Ouachita, Lake c2 258
Ouadâne b4 220
Ouadda d2 224
Ouaddaï b5 218
Ouâdi et Tourkmane e2 138
Ouagadougou d3 222
Ouahigouya d3 222
Ouaka, C.A.R. d2 224
Ouaka, C.A.R. d2 224
Oualâta c2 222
Oualâta, Ḍhar c2 222
Oualé e3 223
Ouallam e3 223
Ouallene e4 221
Ouanary g3 285
Ouanda-Djailé d2 224
Ouandago c2 224
Ouandja, Haute-Kotto, C.A.R. d2 224
Ouandja, Vakaga, C.A.R. d2 224
Ouando e2 225
Ouango d3 224
Ouangolodougou c4 222
Ouaqui, Fr. Gu. f3 285
Ouaqui, St-Laurent-du-Maroni, Fr. Gu. g3 285
Ouara d2 224
Ouarâne c4 220
Ouargaye e3 223
Ouargla f2 221
Ouarkziz, Jbel c3 220
Ouarville g4 183
Ouarzazate c2 220
Oubergpas f6 234
Ouche b3 184
Ouche, Pays d' f4 183
Ouchikou c5 106
Oucques g5 183
Oud-Beijerland c3 159
Ouddorp b3 159
Oude Rijn c2 159
Oudenaarde b4 159
Oudenbosch c3 159
Oudon e5 182
Oudtshoorn e6 234
Oued Zem c2 220
Ouéléssébougou c3 222
Ouémé e4 223
Ouen, Île F 74
Ouessa d3 222
Ouessant, Île d' a4 182
Ouésso c3 224
Ouest b2 224
Ouezzane c2 220
Oughterard b3 165
Ouguela c5 191
Ouham, C.A.R. c2 224
Ouham, C.A.R. c2 224
Ouham Pendé c2 224
Ouidah e4 223
Ouinardene d2 222
Ouiriego e4 272
Ouistreham e3 182
Oujda d2 220
Oujeft b5 220
Oulad Teïma b2 220
Oulainen k4 155
Oulangan kansallispuisto m3 155
Oulankajoki m3 155
Oulchy-le-Château j3 183
Ould Yenjé b2 222
Oulder e4 159
Oulé c4 222
Ouled Djellal f2 221
Ouled Farès e1 221
Oullins a5 185
Oulou, Bahr d1 224
Oulu k4 155
Oulujärvi l4 155
Oulujoki l4 155
Oulunsalo k4 155
Oulx a4 196
Oum Dba, Sabkhat b3 220
Oum el Bouaghi f1 221
Oum er Rbia, Oued c2 220
Oum Hadjer, Ouadi b4 218
Oum-Chalouba b4 218
Oumé c4 222
Oum-Hadjer a5 218
Oumm eḍ Ḍroûs Guebli, Sebkhet b4 220
Oumm eḍ Ḍroûs Telli, Sebkha b4 220
Ounara c2 220
Ounasjoki k2 155
Oundle f4 163
Ounianga Kébir b4 218
Ounianga Sérir b4 218
Oupeye d4 159
Ouranopoli d2 210
Ource k5 183
Ourcq j3 183
Ouré Kaba b3 222
Ourém c2 288
Ourense c2 190
Ouricurí d3 288
Ourinhos d5 290
Ourique b7 191
Ouro, Braz. c3 288
Ouro, Spain c1 190
Ouro Branco g4 291
Ouro Fino e5 291
Ouro Preto g4 291
Ouro, Ponta do k3 235
Ourol c1 190
Ourthe d4 159
Ous k4 147
Ouse, England, U.K. f3 162
Ouse, England, U.K. g6 163
Oust, Fr. c5 182
Oust d6 187
Out Skerries A 164
Outamba Kilimi National Park b4 222
Outardes h3 252
Outardes Quatre, Réservoir h3 252
Outarville h4 183
Outat Oulad el Haj d2 220
Outeniekwaberge e6 234
Outer Hebrides b2 164
Outer Island f2 260
Outer Santa Barbara Channel e8 265
Outjo b3 232
Outlook p6 249
Outokumpu m5 155
Outomuro c2 190
Outpost Mountain g1 247
Outreau g2 183
Ouvéa F 74
Ouvèze b6 185
Ouyanghai Shuiku j6 105
Ouyen f13 81
Ouzel f5 163
Ouzinkie f4 246
Ouzouer-le-Marché g5 183
Ouzouer-sur-Loire h5 183
Ovace, Punta d' A 185
Ovacık g3 209
Ovacık Burnu d4 208
Ovada c5 196
Ovakent b3 208
Oval c3 256
Ovalau E 74
Ovalle b2 294
Ovan b3 224
Ovar b4 190
Oveja e2 296
Ovejas k6 277
Ovejería d3 296
Ovelgönne b5 158
Oveng b3 224
Ovens e3 83
Over Hornbæk c2 158
Over Jerstal c3 158
Over Wallop e5 163
Overath f4 159
Overhalla c4 154
Overijse c4 159
Overijssel e2 159
Överkalix j3 155
Overlander Roadhouse b10 87
Övermark h5 154
Overo, Volcán c3 296
Overton b3 258
Övertorneå j3 155
Överum g4 156
Överuman e3 154
Ovesca c3 196
Ovid d2 256
Ovidiopol' k2 201
Ovidiu j3 201
Oviedo e1 190
Ovindoli c2 198
Oviši j4 157
Oviston Nature Reserve f5 235
Ovodda Ab2 198
Ovoot g3 112
Övörhangay b3 112
Øvre Anarjokka Nasjonalpark k2 155
Øvre Årdal b2 156
Øvre Dividal Nasjonalpark g2 154
Øvre Fiplingvatnet d4 154
Øvre Forra c5 154
Övre Fryken e2 156
Övre Gla e3 156
Øvre Pasvik Nasjonalpark m2 155
Øvre Rendal d2 156
Ovruch c2 148
Övt b2 112
Ovtrup b3 158
Owaka b7 77
Owando c4 224
Owani j1 115
Owasco Lake d2 256
Owase g4 115
Owasso b1 258
Owatonna e2 260
Owbeh a3 128
Owego d2 256
Owel, Lough d3 165
Owen Falls Dam f3 225
Owen River d4 77
Owen Sound f3 254
Owen, Mount d4 77
Owendo f5 223
Owenmore b2 165
Owenreagh d2 165
Owens e4 264
Owens Lake f5 264
Owensboro f1 258
Owensville c6 254
Owerri f4 223
Owhango e3 76
Owikeno Lake d6 248
Owingsville e6 254
Owl Creek a3 260
Owo f4 223
Owosso d4 254
Owyhee e4 262
Öxarfjörður A 152
Oxbow b6 250
Oxeia b4 210
Oxelösund g3 156
Oxford, Can. l6 253
Oxford, N.Z. d5 77
Oxford, U.K. e5 163
Oxford, Alabama, U.S.A. g3 259
Oxford, Maryland, U.S.A. d6 256
Oxford, Massachusetts, U.S.A. j2 257
Oxford, Mississippi, U.S.A. e2 258
Oxford, New York, U.S.A. e2 256
Oxford, North Carolina, U.S.A. g7 254
Oxford, Ohio, U.S.A. d6 254
Oxford, Pennsylvania, U.S.A. e5 256
Oxford House f3 250
Oxford Lake e3 250
Oxfordshire e5 163
Oxkutzcab q7 273
Oxley Wild Rivers National Park e7 85
Oxleys Peak d7 85
Oxnard d7 265
Oxylithos e4 210
Oyabe g3 115
Oyama h3 115
Oyambre, Cabo de f1 190
Oyapock f3 285
Oyem b3 224
Oye-Plage h2 183
Øyeren d3 156
Øyjord e3 154
Oykel d2 164
Oyo, Congo c4 224
Oyo, Nig. e4 223
Oyo, Nig. e4 223
Oyón b2 292
Oyonnax b4 184
Oyster Rocks c5 126
Oy-Tal q7 121
Oyten e2 172
Oytograk e1 130
Özalp k3 209
Ozamiz d6 100
Ozanne g4 183
Ozark g4 259
Ozark Plateau c1 258
Ozarks, Lake of the e4 260
Ożarów k5 169
Ózd j3 171
Ožďany h3 171
Ožena k6 169
Ozera Segiz f5 120
Ozerel'e e4 150
Ozerki u1 121
Ozerne p4 169
Ozernoe, Orenburgskaja Oblast', Russ. Fed. h2 149
Ozernoe, Tjumenskaja Oblast', Russ. Fed. m4 147
Ozernoye k5 147
Ozernyj, Orenburgskaja Oblast', Russ. Fed. h2 120
Ozernyj, Smolenskaja Oblast', Russ. Fed. b4 150
Ozeros, Limni b4 210
Ozersk l1 169
Ozery e4 150
Özgön p7 121
Ozieri Ab2 198
Ozimek g5 168
Ozinki h2 149
Ozona j2 273
Ozorków h4 169
Özu e5 114
Ozuluama f3 275
Ozumba de Alzate e4 275
Ozurget'i j2 209

P

P''yatykhatky d2 148
P'abal-li q5 113
P'engchia Yü p6 105
P'enghu Ch'üntao m7 105
P'enghu Tao m7 105
P'ingtung n7 105
P'jana h4 151
P'och'ŏn p7 113
P'ohang q7 113
P'ot'i h1 209
P'skhus Nakrdzali f4 148
P'ungsan q5 113
P'yŏngch'ang q7 113
P'yŏnggang p6 113
P'yŏnghae q7 113
P'yŏngnamjin p5 113
P'yŏngsong n6 113
P'yŏngt'aek p7 113
P'yŏngwŏn n6 113
P'yŏngyang n6 113
På d3 222
Pääjärvi k5 155
Paama F 74
Paamiut v3 243
Pa-an c7 102
Paar g4 175
Paarl c6 234
Paatari l2 155
Pab Range c8 129
Pabeilón de Arteaga c2 274
Pabianice h4 169
Pabillonis Aa3 198
Pablo f2 262
Pablo Acosta h4 297
Pabna l7 125
Pabradė l5 157
Pacaás Novos, Parque Nacional e2 293
Pacaás, Serra dos e2 293
Pacaembu c4 290
Pacahuaras d2 292
Pacajaí, Ilha Grande do b2 288
Pacajus e2 288
Pacaltsdorp e7 234
Pacaraima, Serra e3 285
Pacarán b2 292
Pacasmayo b1 292
Pacatuba e2 288
Pacaya c5 284
Pace f4 258
Paceco b7 199
Pachaco c1 296
Pachaimalai Hills f7 126
Pachaug Pond j3 257
Pacheco, Chihuahua, Mex. e2 272
Pacheco, Zacatecas, Mex. c1 274
Pacheco, Isla b6 295
Pachia f6 211
Pachía c3 292
Pachia Ammos f7 211
Pachino e8 199
Pachitea c1 292
Pachiza b1 292
Pachmarhi f8 124
Pachna a2 138
Pachni e1 210
Pachpadra f8 129
Pachpadra Salt Depot f8 129
Pachpahar g8 129
Pachuca e3 275
Paciano g6 197
Pacific Grove b5 264
Pacific Ocean p6 301
Pacific Rim National Park e7 248
Pacifica a4 264
Pacific-Antarctic Ridge l10 301
Pačiha f3 146
Pacijan e5 100
Pácin k3 171
Pacitan f9 98
Pack f3 177
Packsattel f3 177
Pacos de Ferreira b3 190
Pacov c2 170
Pacoval g4 285
Pacsa f5 170
Pacy-sur-Eure g3 183
Paczków f5 168
Padada e7 100
Padalere m6 99
Padamarang l7 99
Padamo d3 285
Padampur f6 129
Padana d9 129
Padang b4 98
Padang Besar b2 101
Padang Endau c4 101
Padang Tengku b3 101
Padangtikar, Indon. e5 98
Padangtikar e5 98
Padany p5 155
Padarosk n3 169
Padas h2 99
Padasjoki l2 157
Padauiri e3 285
Padborg c4 158
Padcaya e4 293
Paddle Prairie j2 248
Paddock Wood g5 163
Padeabesar m6 99
Paden City f6 254
Paderborn d4 172
Paderborner d4 172
Paderne b2 190
Padeșu, Vârful f3 201
Padilla e3 293
Padina h3 201
Padjelanta nationalpark f3 154
Padova, Italy f4 196
Padova f4 196
Padrão, Ponta b5 224
Padre Island a6 258
Padre Island National Seashore a6 258
Padre Paraíso h2 291
Padria Aa2 198
Padro, Monte A 185
Padrón b2 190
Padrone, Cape g6 235
Padru Ab2 198
Padstow b6 163
Padsvillye m5 157
Paducah, Kentucky, U.S.A. e1 258
Paducah, Texas, U.S.A. c5 261
Padul g7 191
Padula e4 198
Paduli d3 198
Padum c3 130
Paegam q5 113
Paengnyŏng-do n7 113
Paeroa e2 76
Paesana b5 196
Paese g4 196
Paete c3 100
Páez b3 284
Pafos a2 138
Pafuri j1 235
Pag, Cro. b3 200
Pag b3 200
Paga Conta g4 285
Pagadenbaru d8 98
Pagadian d7 100
Pagai Selatan a6 98
Pagan b5 102
Pagan, N. Mar. Is. A 74
Paganella f3 196
Paganico f7 197
Pagaralam b7 98
Pagatan, Kalimantan Selatan, Indon. h6 99
Pagatan, Kalimantan Tengah, Indon. g6 98
Page, Arizona, U.S.A. h7 263
Page, North Dakota, U.S.A. e7 250
Page, Mount g5 86
Pagėgiai j5 157
Pageland j2 259
Pagerdewa c6 98
Paget Cay k5 80
Pagiriai p1 169
Paglia f7 197
Pago Bay C 74
Pagoh c4 101
Pagosa Springs b4 261
Pagouda e4 223
Pagri j6 135
Paguyaman m4 99
Pagwachuan l6 251
Pagwi l6 97
Pahang, Malay. c4 101
Pahang, Malay. c4 101
Pahari c6 130
Paharpur e4 128
Pahauman e4 98
Pahi c3 101
Pahia Point a7 77
Pahiatua e4 76
Pahlgam b2 130
Pahokee j6 259
Pahomovo d4 150
Pahranichny m2 169
Paiaguás f3 293
Paicines b5 264
Paide l3 157
Paige a4 258
Paignton c6 163
Paihia e1 76
Paiján b1 292
Päijänne l2 157
Päijänteen kansallispuisto l2 157
Paiko c2 210
Paikū Co g5 135
Pail c4 130
Pailahueque a5 296
Pailhès d5 187
Pailin f9 103
Paillaco a6 296
Pailolo Channel Ac2 263
Paimbœuf c5 182
Paimio k2 157
Paimpol b4 182
Paimpont c4 182
Painan a5 98
Paine b2 296
Paine, Cerro b6 295
Paineiras f3 291
Painesdale j7 251
Pains f4 291
Painswick d5 163
Paint Lake d3 250
Paint Lake Provincial Recreation Park d3 250
Painted Desert h8 263
Painted Post c2 256
Paintersville c4 256
Paintsville e7 254
Paipa c2 284
Pairi h9 124
País Vasco b1 192
Paisley d4 164
Paisley, U.S.A. c4 262
Paita a5 284
Paitan, Teluk j1 99
Paithan d3 126
Paitou g5 111
Paiva c5 190
Paixban b2 276
Paizhou c4 106
Pajala j3 155
Pajan a4 284
Pajapán g4 275
Pájara Ae2 189
Pajarito c2 284
Pajarón c5 193
Pajęczno g4 168
Pajer, Gora l2 147
Pajeú e3 288
Paj-Hoj, Hrebet k1 147
Pak Phanang b1 101
Pak Phayun b2 101
Pak Thong Chai f8 103
Páka e5 170
Pakaraima Mountains e2 285
Pakch'ŏn n6 113
Pakhtaabad p7 121
Pakistan d6 92

PAKISTAN

THE ISLAMIC REPUBLIC OF PAKISTAN
Area 796,095km² (307,374sq miles)
Capital Islamabad
Organizations COMM, ECO, IDB, OIC, SAARC
Population 149,910,000
Pop. growth (%) 1.1
Life expectancy 59 (m); 58 (f)
Languages Urdu, Punjabi, Pushto, Sindhi, Saraiki, English
Literacy 45.7%
Currency Pakistani rupee (US $1 = 57.44 Pakistani rupee)
GDP (US million $) 62,300
GDP per head ($US) 415

Pakkat d14 103
Paklenica, Cro. b3 200
Pakokku b5 102
Pakość g3 168
Pakoskie, Jezioro f3 168
Pakotai d1 76
Pakowki Lake m7 249
Pakowki Lake Game Bird Sanctuary m7 249
Pakpattan f5 128
Pakra h4 177
Pakrac j4 177
Pakruojis k5 157
Paks g5 171
Paktiā d4 128
Paktīkā d4 128
Paku, Tanjung d6 98
Pakue l6 99
Pakwash Lake g5 250
Pakxan f6 102
Pakxé g8 102
Pal'co c5 150
Pal'janovo l3 147
Pal'vart b1 128
Pala, Chad b2 224
Pala, Myan. d9 103
Palabuhanratu d8 98
Palacios d2 292
Palacios de Sanabria d2 190
Palacios del Sil d2 190
Palaciosrubios e3 190
Paladru, Lac de b5 185
Palafrugell h3 192
Palagiano g4 198
Palagonia d7 199
Palaia e6 197
Palaia Epidavros d5 211
Palaia Fokaia d5 211
Palaichori b2 138
Palaikastro Ab3 210
Palaio Trikeri d3 210
Palaiochora d7 211
Palaiochori b2 210
Palaiopoli e5 211
Palaiopyrgos b3 210
Palairos a4 210
Palaiseau h4 183
Palakollu g4 126
Palam Pur c3 130
Palamakoloi e1 234
Palamas c3 210
Palamós h3 192
Palamuse m3 157
Palamut a3 208
Palana, India f7 129
Palana, Russ. Fed. r4 119
Palanan d2 100
Palanan Point d2 100
Palancia d5 193
Palanga j5 157
Palanges, Montagne des e4 187
Palangkaraya g6 98
Palani e7 126
Palanpur f8 129
Palanquinos e2 190
Palanro k7 99
Palantak b7 129
Palapag e4 100
Palapye g1 235
Palar f6 126
Palárikovo g3 171
Palas de Rei c2 190
Palasa l4 99
Palasbari m6 125
Palatka j5 259
Palau c2 72

PALAU

THE REPUBLIC OF PALAU
Area 508km² (196sq miles)
Capital Koror
Organizations SPC, PIF
Population 20,000
Pop. growth (%) 2.1
Life expectancy 60 (m); 63 (f)
Languages Palauan, English
Literacy n/a
Currency US dollar
GDP (US million $) 109
GDP per head ($US) 5450

Palau Ab1 198
Palau Trench j4 97
Palaui d1 100
Palauig b3 100
Palauig Point b3 100
Palauk d9 103
Palausekopong, Tanjung d7 98
Palavas-les-Flots, Languedoc-Roussillon, Fr f5 187
Palaw d9 103
Palawan b6 100
Palawan Passage b5 100
Palayan c3 100
Palayankottai e8 126
Palazzo San Gervasio f4 198
Palazzo, Punta A 185
Palazzolo Acreide d7 199
Palazzolo sull'Oglio d4 196
Paldiski l3 157
Paleleh l4 99
Palembang c6 98
Palemón Huergo g3 297
Palena, Chile b4 295
Palena, Aisén, Chile b4 295
Palena, Chile b4 295
Palena, Italy d3 198
Palena, Lago b4 295
Palencia, Spain f2 190
Palencia f2 190
Palenque, Mex. o9 273
Palenque, Chiapas, Mex. a2 276
Palermo, Sicilia, Italy c7 199
Palermo c6 199
Paleśnica j6 169
Palestine, Arkansas, U.S.A. d2 258
Palestine, Texas, U.S.A. b4 258
Palestrina g8 197
Paletwa n9 125
Palezgir d5 128
Palghar c3 126
Palghat e7 126
Palgrave Point a3 232
Palgrave, Mount b8 87
Pálháza k3 171
Palhoça c7 289
Pali, Chhattisgarh, India h8 124
Pali, Rajasthan, India f8 129
Paliat h8 99
Palik n5 157
Palikir G 74
Palimbang e7 100
Palinges a4 184
Palinuro e4 198
Palinuro, Capo e5 198
Paliouri d3 210
Paliouri, Akra d3 210
Paliouria b3 210
Palisade a4 260
Palisades h4 262
Paliseul d5 159
Palitana e10 129
Palivere k3 157
Paliyad e9 129
Palizada a1 276
Paljakan luonnonpuisto m4 155
Palk Bay A 127
Palk Strait A 127
Pälkäne l2 157
Pälkänevesi l2 157
Palkino n4 157
Palkohda h3 127
Palkonda Range f6 126
Palladio f1 210
Pallagorio f5 199
Pallapalla c2 292
Pallarés d6 191
Pallas Green c4 165
Pallas ja Ounastunturin kansallispuisto j2 155
Pallasjärvi k3 155
Pallaskenry c4 165
Pallasovka g2 149
Pallavaram g6 126
Pallinup d14 87
Pallisa f3 225
Palliser Bay e4 77
Palliser, Cape e4 77
Pallu g6 129
Palluau d6 182
Palm Bay j5 259
Palm Beach j6 259
Palm Desert e9 263
Palm Springs e9 263
Palma, Braz. g4 288
Palma, Moz. c6 227
Palma, Port b6 191
Palma Campania d4 198
Palma de Mallorca g5 193
Palma del Río e7 191
Palma di Montechiaro c7 199
Palma Nova g5 193
Palma Pegada d2 274
Palma Sola f4 275
Palma Soriano g4 266
Palma, Badia de g5 193
Palmaces, Embalse de b3 192
Palmaiola, Isola b9 197
Palmanova h4 196
Palmar c1 284
Palmar Chico d4 274
Palmar Sur f6 277
Palmar, Punta del f2 294
Palmares, Acre, Braz. d2 292
Palmares, Pernambuco, Braz. e3 288
Palmarito c2 284
Palmas, Paraná, Braz. b7 289
Palmas, Tocantins, Braz. c4 288
Palmas, Cape c4 222
Palmdale e7 265
Palmeira c6 290
Palmeira das Missões b7 289
Palmeira dos Índios e3 288
Palmeirais d3 288
Palmeiras de Goiás d2 290
Palmeirinhas, Ponta das b5 224
Palmer, Northern Territory, Aust. a8 80
Palmer, Aust. f3 80
Palmer, Alaska, U.S.A. g3 247
Palmer, Massachusetts, U.S.A. h2 257
Palmer, Texas, U.S.A. a3 258
Palmer (U.S.A.) ll1 298
Palmer Land ll2 298
Palmers Crossing e4 258
Palmerston c6 77
Palmerston North e4 76
Palmerston, Cape c2 84
Palmerton e4 256
Palmerville g3 80
Palmetto d4 258
Palmetto Point, Antig. D 271
Palmetto Point, Bah. l7 259
Palmi e6 199
Palmillas e2 275
Palmira, Arg. c2 296
Palmira, Col. b3 284
Palmital, Paraná, Braz. b6 290
Palmital, São Paulo, Braz. c5 290
Palmitas j2 297
Palmito del Verde, Isla b2 274
Palmyra, New York, U.S.A. c1 256
Palmyra, Pennsylvania, U.S.A. d4 256
Palmyra, Virginia, U.S.A. g7 254
Palmyra Atoll (U.S.A.) j2 73
Palmyras Point k2 127
Palni Hills e7 126
Palo e5 100
Palo, Spain g5 191
Palo Alto, Aguascalientes, Mex. c3 274
Palo Alto, Mex. e1 275
Palo Alto, U.S.A. a4 264
Palo Blanco, Arg. d5 292
Palo Blanco, Mex. j4 273
Palo de las Letras j7 277
Palo del Colle f3 198
Palo Santo f5 293
Palo Verde, Parque Nacional e5 276
Palo, Étang de A 185
Palodeia b2 138
Paloh, Johor, Malay. c4 101
Paloh, Sarawak, Malay. f3 98
Paloich d5 218
Palojärvi j2 155
Palojoensuu j2 155
Palojoki j2 155
Palokki m5 155
Palomani d2 292
Palomares g5 275
Palomares del Río d7 191
Palomas d6 191
Palombara Sabina g7 197
Palomera, Sierra c4 192
Palomilas d6 191
Palomitas d4 292
Paloncha g4 126
Palopo l6 99
Palos de la Frontera d7 191
Palos, Cabo de d7 193
Palosi f3 128
Palotina b6 290
Palotunturi l3 155
Palouse e2 262
Palovesi l2 157
Palpa, Ica, Peru b2 292
Palpa, Lima, Peru b2 292
Palparara e8 80
Palpetu, Tanjung n6 99
Palquico b2 296
Pals h3 192
Pålsboda f3 156
Pålsbufjorden c2 156
Paltâive h2 154
Paltamo l4 155
Paltaselkä l4 155
Palu, Indon. l9 99
Palu, Indon. k5 99
Palu, Indon. k5 99
Palu, Tur. g3 209
Paluan c4 100
Paluan Bay c4 100
Palung National Park, Gunung f5 98
Paluzza h3 196
Palwal c5 130
Palyatskishki p1 169
Pama c3 224
Pama, Réserve Partielle de e3 223
Pamanukan d8 98
Pamar c4 284
Pamban Channel A 127
Pamekasan g8 98
Pameungpeuk d8 98
Pamgarh h9 124
Pamiers d5 187
Pamir f1 128
Pamlico l2 259
Pamlico Sound l2 259
Pampa, Chile c4 292
Pampa, U.S.A. c5 261
Pampa Chica c5 295
Pampa de Infierno e5 293
Pampa Grande e3 293
Pampachiri c2 292
Pampana b4 222
Pampanua l7 99
Pampas, Arg. f3 297
Pampas, Peru c2 292
Pampelonne e4 187
Pamphylia c4 208
Pampilhosa da Serra c4 190
Pamplona, Col. c2 284
Pamplona d6 100
Pampow e5 158
Pamukan, Teluk j6 99
Pamukova c2 208
Pamzal d2 130
Pan de Azúcar c5 292
Pan, Tierra del e3 190
Pan'an n4 105
Pana, Gabon b4 224
Pana, U.S.A. b6 254
Panabá q7 273
Panabo e7 100
Panabutan Bay c7 100
Panaca f7 263
Panacea g4 259
Panachaïko b4 210
Panache, Lake n7 251
Panadura f9 126
Panagia, Anatoliki Makedonia kai Thraki, Grc. e2 210
Panagia, Voreio Aigaio, Grc. f3 210
Panagtaran Point b6 100
Panagyurishte g4 201
Panaitan c8 98
Panaitoliko b4 210
Panajevsk m2 147
Panaji c5 126
Panama f7 241

PANAMA

THE REPUBLIC OF PANAMA
Area 75,517km² (29,157sq miles)
Capital Panama City
Organizations ACS, Andean Comm, CACM, IADB, SELA
Population 3,060,000
Pop. growth (%) 1.3
Life expectancy 72 (m); 76 (f)
Languages Spanish
Literacy 92.5%
Currency balboa and US dollar (US $1 = 1.00 balboa)
GDP (US million $) 10,499
GDP per head ($US) 3431

Panamá h6 277
Panamá h6 277
Panama, U.S.A. b2 258
Panama Basin s5 301
Panama Canal h6 277
Panama City g4 259
Panamá, Bahía de h6 277
Panamá, Golfo de h7 277
Panamint Range f5 264
Panamint Springs f5 265
Panamint Valley f5 265
Panamuk c2 130
Pananim, Ilha e4 285
Panao b1 292
Panaon e6 100
Panar k7 125
Panarea, Isola d6 199
Panarik e3 98
Panarukan g8 98

PAPUA NEW GUINEA

THE INDEPENDENT STATE OF PAPUA NEW GUINEA

Area 462,840km² (178,704sq miles)
Capital Port Moresby
Organizations APEC, COMM, SPC, PIF
Population 5,590,000
Pop. growth (%) 2.2
Life expectancy 54 (m); 56 (f)
Languages Pidgin, English, Motu, many local languages
Literacy 66%
Currency kina (US $1 = 3.29 kina)
GDP (US million $) 2771
GDP per head ($US) 495

PARAGUAY

THE REPUBLIC OF PARAGUAY

Area 406,752km² (157,048sq miles)
Capital Asunción
Organizations IADB, MERCOSUR, SELA, LAIA
Population 5,740,000
Pop. growth (%) 2.2
Life expectancy 67 (m); 72 (f)
Languages Spanish, Guarani
Literacy 93.9%
Currency guarani (US $1 = 6025 guarani)
GDP (US million $) 5525
GDP per head ($US) 962

Peixe, Braz. c5 290
Peixe, Tocantins, Braz. c4 288
Peixes f2 293
Peixian e2 111
Peixoto de Azevedo, Braz. b4 288
Peixoto de Azevedo, Mato Grosso, Braz. b4 288
Pejantan d4 98
Pekabata k6 99
Pekalongan e8 98
Pekan c4 101
Pekan Jabi c4 101
Pekanbaru b5 101
Peking j6 113
Pela c4 222
Pelabuhan Kelang b4 101
Pelabuhan Sandakan ◄ k2 99
Pelada, Pampa c5 295
Pelado △ c5 193
Pelahatchie e3 258
Pelaihari h6 99
Pelalawan b4 98
Pelapis e5 98
Pelarco b3 296
Pelariga b5 191
Pelasgia c4 210
Pelat, Mont △ c6 185
Pelawanbesar j4 99
Pelczyce d2 168
Pelechuco d2 292
Pelee Island b7 252
Pelee Point ► b7 252
Pelée, Montagne △ J 271
Peleng m5 99
Peleng, Selat m5 99
Peleta c5 211
Pelham h2 257
Pelhřimov d2 170
Pelican k4 247
Pelican Lake, Can. ○ c4 250
Pelican Lake, U.S.A. ○ e1 260
Pelican Lake, Wisconsin, U.S.A. b3 254
Pelican Narrows b3 250
Pelican Rapids c4 250
Pelinia h2 201
Pelister ☆ b2 210
Pelja-Hovanskaja h4 151
Pelkosenniemi l3 155
Pell City f3 258
Pella c4 234
Pellaro e6 199
Pellegrini f4 297
Pellegrini, Lago ○ d5 296
Pellegrino Parmense d5 196
Pellegrue c4 186
Pellesmäki l5 155
Pellevoisin g6 183
Pellice b5 196
Pellizzano e3 196
Pello, Fin. j3 155
Pello, Swe. j3 155
Pelluhue a3 296
Pellworm d1 172
Pelly, Saskatchewan, Can. c5 250
Pelly, Yukon Territory, Can. l3 247
Pelly Crossing k3 247
Pelly Island l1 247
Pelly Mountains l3 247
Pelokang k8 99
Peloponnisos c5 211
Peloritani, Monti e6 199
Pelotas f2 294
Pelotas, Rio das b7 289
Pelova, Rt ► f4 177
Pelplin g2 168
Pelvoux, Massif du c6 185
Pelvoux, Mont △ c6 185
Pelymskij Tuman, Ozero ○ k3 147
Pemadumcook Lake ○ m3 255
Pemalang e8 98
Pemangkat e4 98
Pemarung, Pulau j5 99
Pematangsiantar d14 103
Pemba, Moz. c6 227
Pemba, Zam. d2 232
Pemba Channel ◄ g5 225
Pemba Island g5 225
Pemba North h4 225
Pemba South h4 225
Pemba, Baía de ◄ c6 231
Pemberton b14 87
Pembina, Can. k5 249
Pembina, U.S.A. e6 250
Pembina, U.S.A. d6 250
Pembroke, Can. h3 255
Pembroke, U.K. b5 163
Pembroke, Maine, U.S.A. j6 253
Pembroke, North Carolina, U.S.A. k2 259
Pembroke Dock b5 163
Pembroke Pines j7 259
Pembroke, Cape ► e6 295
Pembrokeshire b5 163
Pembrokeshire Coast National Park ☆ a5 163
Pembuanghulu g6 98
Pemuco a4 296
Pena Barrosa d4 292
Peña Blanca b1 296
Peña Blanca, Montañas △ b3 276
Peña de Francia, Sierra de la d4 190
Peña del Águila, Embalse de la ⊙ d5 191
Peña Nevada, Cerro △ e2 275
Peñacerrada b2 192
Penacova b4 190
Peñafiel b3 190
Peñafiel f3 190
Peñaflor e7 191
Peñaflor de Hornija f3 190
Penal Debe 271 271
Peñalara △ g4 190
Peñalba d3 192
Peñalsordo e6 191
Penalva do Castelo c4 190
Penamacor c4 190
Penamiller e3 275
Penampang j2 99
Peñaranda de Bracamonte e4 190
Peñaranda de Duero g3 190
Peñarroya △ d4 192
Peñarroya, Embalse de ⊙ a5 193
Peñarroya-Pueblonuevo e6 191
Peñarrubia b6 193
Penarth c5 163
Peñas Blancas, Arg. d4 296
Peñas Blancas, Nic. e5 276
Peñas de San Pedro c6 193
Peñas, Cabo ► c6 295
Peñas, Cabo de ► e1 190
Penas, Golfo de ◄ b5 295
Peñas, Punta ► e1 284
Pench f9 124
Pencheng d1 106
Pěnčín d1 170
Pend Oreille e1 262
Pendang b3 101
Pendé c2 224
Pendembu, Eastern, S. L. b4 222
Pendembu, Northern, S. L. b4 222
Pender Bay ◄ f5 86
Pendilhe c4 190
Pendjari, Parc National de la ☆ e3 223
Pendle Hill △ d3 162
Pendleton, Indiana, U.S.A. d6 254
Pendleton, Oregon, U.S.A. d3 262
Pendopo b6 98
Penebangan e5 98
Peneda Gerês, Parque Nacional da ☆ b3 190
Penedono c4 190
Penela b4 190
Pénessoulou e4 223
Penetanguishene g3 254
Penfield b3 256
Penganga f3 126
Penge, D.R.C. d5 224
Penge, R.S.A. j2 235
Penggong f4 111
Penghu m6 105
Pengiki e4 98
Pengkalan Hulu b3 101
Penglai g1 111
Pengshui g4 104
Penguin Ab2 83
Pengxi e3 104
Pengze e5 111
Pengzhou d3 104
Penhir, Pointe de ► a4 182
Penhoek Pass △ g5 235
Penibética, Cordillera b7 193
Peniche a5 191
Penicuik e4 164
Penida h9 99
Peninsula, Parry ► n1 247
Peñíscola e4 192
Penitente, Serra do c3 288
Penjamo d3 274
Pênjwin k4 137
Penkridge d4 162
Penmarch a5 182
Penmarch, Pointe de ► a5 182
Penn Forest Reservoir ⊙ e4 256
Penn Hills g5 254
Penn Valley b2 264
Penn Yan c2 256
Penna, Punta della ► d2 198
Pennabilli g6 197
Penne c2 198
Penne-d'Agenais c4 187
Penner e5 126
Penneshaw c13 81
Pennines d2 162
Pennino, Monte △ g6 197
Penns Creek c4 256
Pennsboro f6 254
Pennsville e5 256
Pennsylvania h5 255
Peno b3 150
Penobscot m3 255
Penola e14 81
Peñón Blanco g5 272
Peñón de Ifach ► e6 193
Penong l12 87
Penonomé g6 277
Penrhyn H 75
Penrhyn Mawr ► b3 162
Penrhyndeudraeth b4 162
Penrith, Aust. k12 81
Penrith, U.K. d2 162
Penryn a6 163
Pensacola f4 258
Pensacola Bay ◄ f4 258
Pensacola Mountains mm3 298
Pensamiento e2 293
Pensiangan j2 99
Pensilva b6 163
Pentageia a1 138
Pentalofo b4 210
Pentalofos b2 210
Pentecost Island F 74
Pentecôte j3 253
Penthièvre c4 182
Pentire Point ► b6 163
Pentland g6 80
Pentland Firth e1 164
Pentland Hills e4 164
Pentraeth b3 162
Penttilänvaara m4 155
Penukonda e5 126
Penunjuk, Tanjung ► c3 101
Penwegon c6 102
Penygadair △ c4 162
Pen-y-Ghent △ d2 162
Penza h5 151
Penzance a6 163
Penzberg g5 175
Penzenskaja Oblast' g1 149
Penžinskij Hrebet s3 119
Peoples Creek n7 249
Peoria, Arizona, U.S.A. g9 263
Peoria, Illinois, U.S.A. b5 254
Pepacton Reservoir ⊙ f2 256
Pepe Nuñéz j1 297
Pepel b4 222
Pepiri Guaçú b7 289
Peplos g2 210
Pěqin d5 200
Pequi f3 291
Pequot Lakes f7 250
Pér f4 171
Pera b1 138
Pera Chorion b1 138
Pera Head ► e2 80
Perachora c4 210
Perä-Hyyppä k1 157
Perai b3 101
Peraia b2 210
Peraitepuy e3 285
Perak, Malay. b3 101
Perak, Malay. a3 101
Perak, Malay. b3 101
Peralejos c4 192
Peralejos de las Truchas c4 192
Perales del Alfambra d4 192
Perales del Puerto d4 190
Peralta, Arg. g5 297
Peralta, Spain c2 192
Peraltilla d2 192
Peralveche b4 192
Perama, Attiki, Grc. d5 211
Perama, Ipeiros, Grc. a3 210
Perambalur f7 126
Perämeren kansallispuisto ☆ k4 155
Perä-Posio l3 155
Perarolo di Cadore g3 196
Peräseinäjoki j5 155
Percé k4 253
Perche, Collines du f4 183
Perchtoldsdorf h1 177
Percival Lakes g7 86
Percy d4 182
Percy Fyfe Nature Reserve ☆ h2 235
Percy Isles d2 84
Perdasdefogu Ab3 198
Perdices h2 297
Perdida c3 288
Perdido, Arg. c4 295
Perdido, Braz. f4 293
Perdido, Monte △ e2 192
Perdiguère, Pic △ e2 192
Perdika a3 210
Perdikkar b2 210
Perdizes e3 290
Perdões f4 291
Perdu, Lac ○ g3 252
Peredo d3 190
Peregrebnoe l3 147
Peregu Mare j5 171
Perehins'ke g1 201
Perehoda a2 150
Pereira b3 284
Pereira Barreto c4 290
Pereira, Braz. e3 288
Pereiro c7 191
Pereiro de Aguiar c2 190
Perejiles c3 192
Perelešinskij f2 148
Peremyshlyany n6 169
Peremyšl' d4 150
Perenjori c11 87
Pereruela e3 190
Pereslavl'-Zalesskij e3 150
Pereslavskij Nacional'nyj Park ☆ e3 150
Peresypkino Pervoe g5 151
Pereval Akbaytal f1 128
Pereval Tagarkaty f2 128
Pereyaslav-Khmel'nyts'kyy c2 148
Pérez g2 297
Perfugas Aa2 198
Perg f1 177
Pergamino g2 297
Pergine Valsugana f3 196
Pergola g6 197
Perham f7 250
Perhentian Besar, Pulau c3 101
Perho k5 155
Perhonjoki j5 155
Periam j5 171
Peribán de Ramos c4 274
Péribonca, Québec, Can. g5 252
Péribonca, Québec, Can. f4 252
Péribonca, Lac ○ g3 252
Pericos, Nayarit, Mex. b2 274
Pericos, Sinaloa, Mex. f5 272
Peridot h9 263
Perieni h2 201
Périers d3 182
Périgord ♦ c4 186
Périgord Blanc ♦ c4 186
Périgord Noir ♦ c4 186
Perigoso, Canal e2 288
Périgueux c3 186
Perijá, Parque Nacional ☆ c2 293
Perijá, Sierra de c1 284
Perilla de Castro e3 190
Peringat c3 101
Periquito, Serra do e3 288
Peristasi c2 210
Peristera e3 210
Peristerio d4 210
Peristerona, Famagusta, Cyp. b1 138
Peristerona, Nicosia, Cyp. b1 138
Periteasca, Lacul ○ j3 201
Periteasca-Gura Portiţei j3 201
Perithorio d1 210
Perito Moreno b5 295
Perito Moreno, Parque Nacional ☆ b5 295
Perivar e8 126
Perivoli a3 210
Periyakulam e7 126
Periyar Lake ○ e8 126
Perkasie e4 256
Perkat, Tanjung ► c5 98
Perkins a2 258
Perkivtsi h1 201
Perl e5 159
Perlas, Archipiélago de las h6 277
Perlas, Laguna de ○ f4 277
Perlas, Punta de ► f4 277
Perleberg g2 173
Perlez e3 200
Perlis b2 101
Perly k1 169
Perm' j4 147
Permas h2 151
Permatang Bendahari b3 101
Permisi h4 151
Permskaja Oblast' j4 147
Pernambuco e3 288
Pernambuco Plain h10 302
Pernarec b2 170
Pernat, Rt ► f4 177
Pernegg an der Mur g2 177
Pernes b5 191
Pernes-les-Fontaines b7 185
Perni e1 210
Pernik, Bul. f4 201
Pernik f4 201
Perniö k2 157
Pernitz g2 177
Pero d4 196
Perolândia b2 290
Peron, Cape ► a9 87
Peron, Point ► b13 87
Péronnas b4 184
Péronne a5 159
Perosa Argentina b5 196
Perote f4 275
Pérouges b5 185
Perpendicular, Point ► g2 83
Perpignan e6 187
Perquenco a5 296
Perrault Falls g5 250
Perrecy-les-Forges a4 184
Perrigny b4 184
Perrine j7 259
Perris f8 265
Perris, Lake ○ f8 265
Perro, Punta del ► d8 191
Perros-Guirec b4 182
Perry, Florida, U.S.A. h4 259
Perry, Georgia, U.S.A. h3 259
Perry, Oklahoma, U.S.A. a1 258
Perry, Utah, U.S.A. g5 262
Perrysburg e5 254
Perryton c4 261
Perryville, Alaska, U.S.A. e5 246
Perryville, Kentucky, U.S.A. g1 259
Perryville, Maryland, U.S.A. d5 256
Persberg f3 156
Persenbeug g1 177
Persfjorden n1 155
Perstorp e4 156
Pertek g3 209
Perth, Aust. b12 87
Perth, Can. h3 255
Perth, U.K. e3 164
Perth & Kinross d3 164
Perth Amboy f4 257
Perth Basin f7 300
Perth-Andover j5 253
Perthes a2 184
Perthois ♦ k4 183
Perthus, Col du e6 187
Pertouli b3 210
Pertuis b7 185
Pertuis Breton a2 186
Pertuis d'Antioche a2 186
Pertusa d2 192
Pertusato, Capo ► A 185
Peru c4 282

PERU

THE REPUBLIC OF PERU
Area 1,285,216km²
(496,225sq miles)
Capital Lima
Organizations APEC, IADB, Andean Comm, SELA, LAIA
Population 26,750,000
Pop. growth (%) 1.5
Life expectancy 66 (m); 70 (f)
Languages Spanish, Quechua, Aymara
Literacy 90.9%
Currency new sol
(US $1 = 3.47 new sol)
GDP (US million $) 55,700
GDP per head ($US) 2082

Perú, Arg. e4 297
Perú, Bol. d2 292
Peru, Indiana, U.S.A. c5 254
Peru, U.S.A. k3 255
Peru Basin s7 301
Peruc b1 170
Peru-Chile Trench t7 301
Perugia, Italy g6 197
Perugia g6 197
Perugorría e1 294
Peruíbe e6 291
Perušić g5 177
Pervelos, Akra ► e5 211
Pervenchères f4 183
Pervomajsk g4 151
Pervomajskij, Orenburgskaja Oblast', Russ. Fed. j2 149
Pervomajskij, Smolenskaja Oblast', Russ. Fed. b4 150
Pervomajskij, Tambovskaja Oblast', Russ. Fed. f5 150
Pervomajskij, Tul'skaja Oblast', Russ. Fed. d4 150
Pervomay q6 121
Pervomays'k, Luhans'ka Oblast', Ukr. e2 148
Pervomays'k, Mykolayivs'ka Oblast', Ukr. k1 201
Pervomays'ke d3 148
Pervomays'kyy e2 148
Pervomayskiy u2 121
Pervoural'sk j4 147
Peša f2 146
Pesaguan f5 98
Pesaro g6 197
Pesaro E Urbino g6 197
Pescada, Ponta da ► b1 288
Pescadero c5 295
Pescadores, Punta ► c3 292
Pesčanokopskoe f3 148
Pesčanyj, Mys ► c6 120
Pescara, Italy c2 198
Pescara, Italy d2 198
Pescara d2 198
Pescasseroli c3 198
Peschici f3 198
Pescia e6 197
Pescina c2 198
Pesco Sannita d3 198
Pescolanciano d3 198
Pescopagano e4 198
Pescopennataro d3 198
Peseux a3 196
Peshawar e3 128
Peshkopi e5 200
Peshtera g4 201
Peshtigo, Wisconsin, U.S.A. b3 254
Peshtigo, Wisconsin, U.S.A. c3 254
Pesjakov, Ostrov j1 147
Peski, Kaz. l5 147
Peski, Turk. a1 128
Peskovka m2 151
Pesmes b3 184
Pesnica g3 177
Peso da Régua c3 190
Pesočnja f4 150
Pesočnoe e2 150
Pespire d4 276
Pesqueira, Braz. e3 288
Pesqueira, Mex. h11 263
Pesquera de Duero f3 190
Pessac b4 186
Pest h4 171
Pestovo c2 150
Pestravka h1 149
Petacalco, Bahía de ◄ c5 274
Petah Tiqwa c4 139
Petäjävesi l1 157
Petal e4 258
Petalas b4 210
Petalida, Akra ► f6 211
Petalidi b6 211
Petaling Jaya b4 101
Petalioi e4 210
Petalion, Kolpos ◄ e5 210
Petaluma a3 264
Pétange d5 159
Petaquillas j6 99
Petare d1 284
Petas b3 210
Petatlán d5 274
Petauke e1 233
Petawawa h3 255
Petén Itzá, Lago ○ c2 276
Petenwell Lake ○ a3 254
Peter Pond Lake ○ n3 249
Peterborough, South Australia, Aust. d12 81
Peterborough, Victoria, Aust. f15 81
Peterborough, Can. g3 254
Peterborough, England, U.K. f4 163
Peterborough, U.K. f4 163
Peterborough, U.S.A. j2 257
Peterculter f2 164
Peterhead g2 164
Peterlee e2 162
Petermann Ranges j9 87
Peteroa, Volcán △ b3 296
Peters Mine f2 285
Petersberg e2 174
Petersburg, Alaska, U.S.A. m4 247
Petersburg, Virginia, U.S.A. h7 255
Petersburg, West Virginia, U.S.A. a6 256
Petersen mountain △ d2 264
Petersfield f5 163
Petershagen, Brandenburg, Ger. j3 173
Petershagen, Brandenburg, Ger. k3 173
Petershagen, Nordrhein-Westfalen, Ger. d3 172
Petersham h2 257
Petershausen g4 175
Pétervására j3 171
Petilia Policastro f5 199
Pétionville h5 271
Petit Lac Manicouagan ○ j3 253
Petit Lay d6 182
Petit Maine d6 182
Petit Mécatina n3 253
Petit Mécatina, Île du n3 253
Petit Morin j4 183
Petit Rhône a7 185
Petit Saut Dam g2 285
Petit St-Bernard, Col du △ c5 185
Petite-Bourg C 271
Petite Creuse d2 186
Petite Leyre b4 187
Petite Rivière de la Baleine r3 251
Petite Saulde h5 183
Petite Terre, Îles de la C 271
Petit-Goâve h5 271
Petit-Loango, Réserve de ☆ a4 224
Petitot g2 248
Petkeljärven kansallispuisto ☆ n5 155
Petkula l3 155
Petlad f9 129
Petlalcingo f4 275
Petlawad g9 129
Peto q7 273
Petőfiszállás h5 171
Petorca b2 296
Petoskey d3 254
Petra, Grc. g3 210
Petra, Jordan ♦ d6 139
Petra, Spain h5 193
Petra Velikogo, Zaliv ► s4 113
Petralia-Soprana d7 199
Petrana b2 210
Petrer d6 193
Petreto-Bicchisano A 185
Petrich d1 210
Petrified Forest National Park ☆ j8 263
Petrila f3 201
Petrinja h4 177
Petrivka, Luhans'ka Oblast', Ukr. e2 148
Petrivka, Odes'ka Oblast', Ukr. k2 201
Petro, Cerro de △ c1 294
Petrochori b4 210
Petrokhanski Prokhod △ f4 201
Pétrola c6 193
Petrolândia e3 288
Petrolina, Amazonas, Braz. d4 284
Petrolina, Pernambuco, Braz. d3 288
Petrolina de Goiás d2 290
Petron, Limni ○ e5 200
Petronà f5 199
Petropavlovka t5 121
Petropavlovsk m5 147
Petropavlovsk-Kamčackij r4 119
Petrópolis g5 291
Petroşani f3 201
Petroussa e1 210
Petrov Val g2 149
Petrova Gora, Cro. ☆ b5 200
Petrovac e3 200
Petrovice c2 170
Petrovice u Karvine g2 171
Petrovka m5 147
Petrovsk g1 149
Petrovskij f3 150
Petrovskoe e3 150
Petrovsk-Zabaykal'skiy d2 94
Petrozavodsk c3 146
Petru Rareş g2 201
Petrus Steyn h3 235
Petrusburg f4 235
Petruşeni h2 201
Petrusville f5 234
Petřvald g2 171
Petsana h3 235
Pettigo d2 165
Pettneu am Arlberg b2 176
Pettis a5 258
Pettorano sul Gizio c2 198
Petuhovo f5 147
Petuški e4 150
Petworth f6 163
Petzeck △ d3 176
Peuerbach e1 176
Peuetsagu, Gunung △ c13 103
Peumo b3 296
Peurasuvanto l3 155
Peurauere ○ f3 154
Peureula c13 103
Pevek a1 298
Pevensey Levels g6 163
Peveragno b5 197
Pewsey e5 163
Pêxung n3 125
Peyne f5 187
Peyrano g2 297
Peyrat-le-Château d3 186
Peyrehorade a5 187
Peyreleau f4 187
Peyrolles-en-Provence b7 185
Peyruis b6 185
Peza f2 166
Pézenas f5 187
Pezinok f3 170
Pezu e4 128
Pfaffenhausen f4 174
Pfaffenhofen an der Ilm g4 175
Pfaffensattel △ g2 177
Pfälzer Wald, Ger. c3 174
Pfälzer Wald, Ger. ☆ c3 174
Pfalzgrafenweiler d4 174
Pfarrkirchen d1 176
Pfitzner, Mount △ b7 80
Pforzheim d4 174
Pfreimd, Ger. h3 175
Pfreimd h3 175
Pfronten f5 175
Pfullendorf e5 174
Pfullingen e4 174
Pfunds b3 176
Pfungstadt d3 174
Pfyn c2 196
Phagwara b4 130
Phalaborwa j1 235
Phalia a3 130
Phalodi f7 129
Phalsbourg d2 184
Phalsund e7 129
Phaltan d4 126
Phalut Peak △ j6 135
Phan d6 102
Phan Rang j10 103
Phan Thiêt j10 103
Phanat Nikhom e9 103
Phangan, Ko e11 103
Phangnga a1 101
Phanom Thuan d8 103
Phaplu h6 135
Pharr k4 273
Phat Diêm h5 102
Phatthalung b2 101
Phayao d6 102
Phelps c2 256
Phelps Lake, Can. ○ r2 249
Phelps Lake, U.S.A. ○ l2 259
Phenix City g3 259
Phet Buri d9 103
Phetchabun e7 102
Phichai e7 102
Phichit e7 102
Phil Campbell f2 258
Philadelphia, Mississippi, U.S.A. e3 258
Philadelphia, Pennsylvania, U.S.A. e5 256
Philadelphia, Tennessee, U.S.A. g2 259
Philip c2 260
Philip Smith Mountains h1 247
Philippeville c4 159
Philippi f6 254
Philippine Basin g5 300
Philippine Sea SE g4 300
Philippine Trench g5 300
Philippines k7 93

PHILIPPINES

THE REPUBLIC OF THE PHILIPPINES
Area 300,000km²
(115,831sq miles)
Capital Manila
Organizations APEC, ASEAN
Population 79,500,000
Pop. growth (%) 2
Life expectancy 66 (m); 70 (f)
Languages Filipino (based on Tagalog), English, many other local languages
Literacy 95.6%
Currency Philippine peso
(US $1 = 55.44 Philippine peso)
GDP (US million $) 75,900
GDP per head ($US) 954

Philippolis f5 235
Philippsburg d3 174
Philipsburg, Neth. Ant. n5 271
Philipsburg, Montana, U.S.A. g2 262
Philipsburg, Pennsylvania, U.S.A. b4 256
Philipstown f5 234
Phillaur b4 130
Phillip Island d4 82
Phillipsburg, Kansas, U.S.A. d4 260
Phillipsburg, New Jersey, U.S.A. e4 256
Phillipston a4 256
Philmont g2 257
Philo b5 254
Phiritona g3 235
Phitsanulok e7 102
Phnum Aôral △ g9 103
Phnum Pénh g10 103
Phnum Tumpôr △ f9 103
Pho, Laem ► b2 101
Phoenicia f2 257
Phoenix, Arizona, U.S.A. g9 263
Phoenix, Oregon, U.S.A. b4 262
Phoenix Islands H 75
Phon Phisai f6 102
Phong Thô f4 102
Phôngsali f5 102
Phong Thô c2 170
Phoques Bay ◄ c4 82
Photaksur c2 130
Phou Bia △ f6 102
Phou Houie Moc △ f5 102
Phou Sam Sao f5 102
Phou Sao △ f6 102
Phou Sao △ f6 102
Phou Set △ h8 102
Phouphieng Bolovens h8 102
Phra Saeng a1 101
Phrae e6 102
Phu Lôc h7 102
Phu Luang National Park ☆ e7 102
Phu Ly g5 102
Phu Miang △ e7 102
Phu Phac Mo △ g5 102
Phu Phan National Park ☆ f7 102
Phu Quôc g10 103
Phu Quôc, Đao f11 103
Phu Tho g5 102
Phuchong-Nayoi National Park ☆ g8 103
Phuduhudu c3 232
Phuentsholing l6 125
Phuket a2 101
Phulbani j9 125
Phulera g7 129
Phulji c7 129
Phumĭ Chhuk g10 103
Phumĭ Kâmpóng Trach g10 103
Phumĭ Kâmpóng Trâlach g9 103
Phumĭ Kaôh Kert g9 103
Phumĭ Kaôh Kŏng f10 103
Phumĭ Prêk Kak g9 103
Phumĭ Puŏk Chăs f9 103
Phumĭ Sâmraông f8 103
Phumĭ Thalabârĭvăt g9 103
Phumĭ Toêng g9 103
Phung Hiêp g11 103
Phươc Long g11 103
Phuthaditjhaba h4 235
Pi He e4 111
Piaca c3 288
Piacatu c4 290
Piacenza, Italy d5 196
Piacenza d4 196
Piacouadie, Lac ○ g3 252
Piadena e4 196
Piai, Tanjung ► c5 101
Piamonte g2 297
Pian c6 85
Piana A 185
Piana degli Albanesi c7 199
Piana del Fucino c3 198
Piancastagnaio f7 197
Pianella d2 198
Piano del Voglio f5 197
Pianoro f5 197
Pianosa e7 197
Pianosa, Isola e7 197
Pianotolli-Caldarello A 185
Piansano f7 197
Pias c6 191
Piaseczno k3 169
Piasek c3 168
Piaski l4 169
Piassabussu e4 288
Piastów j3 169
Piatã d4 288
Piątek h3 169
Piatra h4 201
Piatra Neamţ h2 201
Piatra Olt g3 201
Piaui d3 288
Piauí, Serra de d3 288
Piave g4 196
Piawaning c12 87
Piaxtla b1 274
Piazza al Serchio e5 197
Piazza Armerina d7 199
Piazza Brembana d4 196
Piazzatorre d4 196
Piazzola sul Brenta, Veneto, Italy f4 196
Pibor f2 225
Pibor Post f2 225
Pic k6 251
Pic d'Ivohibe, Réserve de ☆ Ab3 233
Pica d4 292
Picacho h9 263
Picachos b2 274
Picachos, Cerro dos △ b3 272
Pičajevo g5 151
Picaracho △ c5 193
Picardie, Fr. h3 183
Picardie, Fr. ♦ g3 183
Picassent d5 193
Picayune e4 258
Picco della Croce △ f3 196
Picerno e4 198
Pich p8 273
Picha c2 292
Pícháchic f3 272
Pichanal e4 293
Picheng f3 111
Picher b1 258
Pichi Ciego c2 296
Pichi Mahuida e5 296
Pichi Trafui b6 296
Pichidanguí b2 296
Pichilemu a3 296
Pichilingue d5 272
Pichincha b3 284
Pichirropulli a6 296
Pichucalco h5 275
Pickens h2 259
Pickering f2 162
Pickering, Vale of f2 162
Pickford d2 254
Pickle Crow h5 250
Pickle Lake h5 250
Pico Arm. A 220
Pico Arm. △ A 220
Pico Bonito, Parque Nacional ☆ d3 276
Pico da Neblina, Parque Nacional do ☆ d3 284
Pico de Orizaba, Parque Nacional ☆ f4 275
Pico de Tancítaro, Parque Nacional ☆ c4 274
Pico Truncado c5 295
Picos d3 288
Picos de Europa e1 190
Picos, Punta dos ► b3 190
Picota b1 292
Picquigny h3 183
Picton, Aust. g2 83
Picton, N.Z. e4 77
Picton, Isla c7 295
Picton, Mount △ Ab3 83
Pictou l6 253
Pictured Rocks National Lakeshore ☆ c2 254
Picuí e3 288
Picún Leufú, Neuquén, Arg. c5 296
Picún Leufú, Arg. c5 296
Pidarak a8 129
Pidhaytsi p6 169
Pidhorodna k1 201
Pidinga l12 87
Pidurutalagala △ A 127
Pie de Palo, Sierra d1 296
Piechowice d5 168
Piecki k2 169
Piedade e5 290
Piedade, Ponta da ► b7 191
Piedicorte-di-Gaggio A 185
Piedicroce A 185
Piediluco, Lago di ○ g7 197
Piedimonte Matese d3 198
Piedmont, Alabama, U.S.A. g3 259
Piedmont, South Carolina, U.S.A. h2 259
Piedra c3 192
Piedra Aguda, Embalse de ⊙ c6 191
Piedra Blanca j5 273
Piedra de Águila b6 296
Piedra de Águila, Embalse ⊙ c6 296
Piedra de Cucuy △ d3 284
Piedra Sola j2 297
Piedrabuena f5 191
Piedrafita de Babia d2 190
Piedrahita e4 190
Piedralaves f4 190
Piedras Albas d5 191
Piedras Blancas e1 190
Piedras Blancas Point ► b6 265
Piedras Negras, Guat. b2 276
Piedras Negras, Coahuila, Mex. j3 273
Piedras Negras, Veracruz, Mex. f4 275
Piedras Point ► b5 100
Piedras, Embalse de ⊙ c7 191
Piedras, Punta, Arg. ► j3 297
Piedras, Punta, Trin. ► E 271
Piedras, Rio de las d2 292
Piedritas f3 297
Piégut-Pluviers c3 186
Piekary Śląskie g5 168
Pieksämäen mlk m1 157
Pieksämäki m1 157
Pielach g2 177
Pielavesi, Fin. ○ l5 155
Pielavesi l5 155
Pielinen ○ m5 155
Pieljekaise nationalpark ☆ f3 154
Piemonte b4 196
Pienaarsrivier h2 235
Pieniężno j1 169
Pieniński Park Narodowy ☆ j6 169
Pieńsk d4 168
Pienza f7 197
Pierce Lake ○ g3 250
Pieres h5 297
Pieria ♦ c2 210
Pierowall B 164
Pierre c2 260
Pierre Bayou c4 258
Pierre-Buffière d3 186
Pierre-de-Bresse b4 184
Pierrefitte-sur-Aire b2 184
Pierrefitte-sur-Sauldre h5 183
Pierrefonds i5 159
Pierrefontaine-les-Varans c3 184
Pierrefort e4 186
Pierrelatte a6 185
Pierreville E 271
Pierry j3 183
Pierson j5 259
Piešťany f3 171
Pieszyce e5 168
Piet Retief j3 235
Pietermaritzburg j4 235

POLAND

THE REPUBLIC OF POLAND
Area 312,685km²
(120,728sq miles)
Capital Warsaw
Organizations CE, CEFTA,
EBRD, NATO, OECD
Population 38,620,000
Pop. growth (%) 0.3
Life expectancy 68 (m); 77 (f)
Languages Polish, German
Literacy 99.8%
Currency złoty
(US $1 = 3.8 złoty)
GDP (US million $) 184,000
GDP per head ($US) 4764

Poleski Park → Prattsville 371

Poleski Park Krajobrazowy ☆ m4 169
Polessk k1 169
Polevskoj k4 147
Polewali k6 99
Polgár k4 171
Polgárdi g4 171
Põlgyo p8 113
Poli, Cam. g4 223
Poli, Shandong, China f2 111
Poli, Shandong, China f2 111
Polia f6 199
Poliangting e4 106
Police c2 168
Polichnitos g3 210
Polička e2 170
Policoro f4 198
Policzna k4 169
Polientes g2 190
Polignano a Mare g4 198
Poligny b4 184
Polillo ▭ c3 100
Polillo Islands ▭ d3 100
Polillo Strait ═ c3 100
Polis a1 138
Polis'ke c2 148
Polistena f6 199
Polizzi Generosa d7 199
Poljarne Zori p3 155
Poljarnyj p2 155
Poljarnyj Ural ⊡ l2 147
Polk g5 254
Polla e4 198
Pollachi e7 126
Pölläkkä n1 157
Pöllau g2 177
Pöllauberg g2 177
Polle e4 172
Pollença h5 193
Pollença, Badia de ◄ f5 193
Pollina d7 199
Polling g5 175
Pollino, Monte △ f5 198
Pollino, Parco Nazionale del ☆ f5 198
Polloc Harbour ◄ d7 100
Pollock c4 258
Pollos e3 190
Pollux △ b6 77
Polmak l1 155
Polminhac e4 186
Polmont e4 164
Polná d2 170
Polnovat l3 147
Polo, Fin. m4 155
Polo, U.S.A. b5 254
Polohy e3 148
Polokwane h1 235
Polom l2 151
Polomka h3 171
Polomoloc e7 100
Polonnaruwa g9 126
Polonne b2 148
Polotnjanyj Zavod c4 150
Polovinnoe l5 147
Polovragi f3 201
Polpaico b2 296
Polperro b6 163
Pöls, Aus. ≈ f2 177
Pöls f2 177
Polskava ≈ g3 177
Polski Trŭmbesh g4 201
Polson f2 262
Poltár h3 171
Poltava d2 148
Poltavka m5 147
Põltsamaa, Est. ≈ l3 157
Põltsamaa l3 157
Poludino m5 147
Polunočnoe k3 147
Põlva m3 157
Polvaredos c2 296
Polvijärvi m5 155
Polvoxal b1 276
Polyaigos ▭ e6 211
Polyana l3 171
Polyantho f1 210
Polygyros d2 210
Polyiagou-Folegandrou, Steno ═ e6 211
Polykastano b2 210
Polykastro c2 210
Pom k6 97
Pomabamba b1 292
Pomarance e6 197
Pomarez b5 187
Pomarkku k2 157
Pomáz h4 171
Pomba ≈ g4 291
Pombal, Pará, Braz. b2 288
Pombal, Braz. e3 288
Pombal, Bragança, Port c3 190
Pombal, Leiria, Port b5 191
Pombo ≈ b4 290
Pomègues, Île ▭ b7 185
Pomene l1 235
Pomeroon-Supenaam ⊡ f2 285
Pomeroy, R.S.A. j4 235
Pomeroy, U.K. e2 165
Pomeroy, U.S.A. e2 262
Pomezia g8 197
Pomichna c2 148
Pommard a3 184
Pommersche Bucht ◄ f1 167
Pomokaira ♦ k3 155
Pomona, Belize c2 276
Pomona, Nam. a3 234
Pomona, U.S.A. f7 265
Pomona Reservoir ○ e4 260
Pomono e5 296
Pomorie h4 201
Pomorska, Zatoka ◄ c1 168
Pomorskie ⊡ f1 168
Pomorskij Proliv ═ g1 146
Pomos a1 138
Pomozdino h3 147
Pompano Beach j6 259
Pompei d4 198
Pompéia c5 290
Pompeu f3 291
Pompey c2 184
Pompton Lakes f3 257
Pompué ≈ e2 233
Pomurska ⊡ h3 177
Ponazyrevo j2 151
Ponca City a1 258
Ponce A 270
Ponce de Leon Bay ◄ j7 259
Poncha Springs b4 260
Ponchatoula d4 258
Poncheville, Lac ○ q5 251
Poncin b4 184
Poncitlán c3 274
Pond Creek a1 258
Pond Inlet p1 243
Pond, Island ○ p4 253
Pondicherry, India ⊡ g7 126
Pondicherry f7 126
Pondoland ♦ h5 235
Poneloya d4 276
Ponferrada d2 190
Pong Tamale d4 222
Pongara, Pointe ► a3 224
Pongaroa f4 76
Pongau ≈ h1 177
Pongdong p8 113
Ponghwa q7 113
Pongo ≈ e2 225
Pongo de Manseriche ≈ b4 284
Pongola ≈ j3 235
Pongolapoort Dam ⊸ j3 235
Poniatowa l4 169
Poniec e4 168
Poniki, Gunung △ m4 99
Ponindilisa, Tanjung ► l5 99
Ponnaivar ≈ f6 126
Ponnani d7 126
Ponneri g6 126
Ponnyadaung Range ⊡ b4 102
Ponomarevka h5 147
Ponornytsya d2 148
Ponorogo f8 98
Pons b3 186
Ponsacco e6 197
Ponsul ≈ b5 190
Pont de Suert e2 192
Ponta de Pedras c2 288
Ponta Delgada, Arm. B 189
Ponta Delgada, Arm. A 220
Ponta do Pargo B 189
Ponta do Sol B 189
Ponta dos Índios g3 285
Ponta Grossa c6 290
Ponta Porã f4 293
Pontacq b5 187
Pontailler-sur-Saône b3 184
Pontal ≈ d3 288
Pontal do Ipiranga j3 291
Pontal do Sul d6 290
Pontalina d2 290
Pont-à-Mousson c2 184
Pontant g4 297
Pontão c3 288
Pontardawe c5 163
Pontarion d3 186
Pontarlier c4 184
Pontassieve f6 197
Pontaubault d4 182
Pont-Audemer f3 183
Pontaumur e3 186
Pont-Aven b5 182
Pont-Canavese b4 196
Pontcharra c5 185
Pontchartrain, Lake ○ d4 258
Pontchâteau c5 182
Pont-Croix a4 182
Pont-d'Ain b4 184
Pont-d'Ouilly e4 183
Pont-de-Chéruy b5 185
Pont-de-Roide c3 184
Pont-de-Salars e4 187
Pont-de-Vaux a4 184
Pont-de-Veyle a4 184
Pont-du-Château f3 186
Ponte b3 190
Ponte Alta do Norte c4 288
Ponte Branca b2 290
Ponte Caldelas b2 190
Ponte da Barca b3 190
Ponte de Lima b3 190
Ponte de Pedra, Mato Grosso, Braz. a2 290
Ponte de Pedra, Mato Grosso, Braz. f2 293
Ponte de Sor b5 191
Ponte dell'Olio d5 196
Ponte di Piave g4 196
Ponte do Rio Verde b3 290
Ponte Firme e3 291
Ponte Nova g4 291
Ponte Vedra Beach j4 259
Ponteareas b2 190
Pontebba h3 196
Ponte-Ceso b1 190
Pontecorvo c3 198
Pontedera e6 197
Pontedeume b1 190
Pontefract e3 162
Ponteland e1 162
Pontelandolfo d3 198
Ponte-Leccia A 185
Pont-en-Royans b5 185
Pontenure d4 196
Pontenx-les-Forges a4 187
Ponterwyd c4 163
Pontes-e-Lacerda f3 293
Pontevedra, Spain ⊡ b2 190
Pontevedra b2 190
Pontevedra, Ría de ◄ b2 190
Pont-Évêque a5 185
Pontfaverger-Moronvilliers c5 159
Pontgibaud e3 186
Pont-Hébert d3 182
Pontiac e4 254
Pontian Kechil c5 101
Pontianak e5 98
Pontigny j5 183
Pontinia c3 198
Pontivy c4 182
Pont-l'Abbé a5 182
Pont-l'Évêque f3 183
Pont-les-Moulins c3 184
Pontlevoy g5 183
Pontoetoe f3 285
Pontoise h3 183
Ponton ≈ f12 87
Pontón, Puerto del ═ e1 190
Pontonnyj a2 150
Pontorson d4 182
Pontotoc e2 258
Pontremoli d5 197
Pontresina d3 196
Pontrieux b4 182
Ponts f3 192
Pont-Scorff b5 182
Pont-Ste-Maxence h3 183
Pont-St-Esprit a6 185
Pont-St-Martin b4 196
Pont-sur-Yonne j4 183
Pontvallain f5 183
Pontypool c5 163
Pontypridd c5 163
Ponza b4 198
Ponza, Isola di ▭ g9 197
Ponziane, Isole ▭ g9 197
Ponzone c5 196
Poochera b12 81
Pool ⊡ c4 224
Poola h5 154
Poole, England, U.K. ⊡ h2 162
Poole e6 163
Poole Bay ◄ e6 163
Pooler j3 259
Poolewe c2 164
Pooncarie f12 81
Poondarrie, Mount △ c10 87
Poopelloe, Lake ○ g11 81
Poopó d3 292
Poopó, Lago de ○ d3 292
Poor Knights Islands ▭ e1 76
Popa Mountain △ b5 102
Popa, Isla ▭ f6 277
Popayán b3 284
Pope e2 258
Poperinge a4 159
Popes Creek d6 256
Popești-Leordeni h3 201
Popilta Lake ○ b1 82
Poplar, Can. ≈ e4 250
Poplar, Montana, U.S.A. ≈ b1 260
Poplar, Montana, U.S.A. q7 249
Poplar, Wisconsin, U.S.A. h7 250
Poplar Bluff d1 258
Poplar Hill f4 250
Poplarville e4 258
Popocatépetl, Volcán △ e4 275
Popof Island ▭ e5 246
Popoh f9 98
Popokabaka c5 224
Popoli c2 198
Popovača h4 177
Popovka d2 150
Popovo h4 201
Poppberg △ g3 175
Poppi f6 197
Poprad j2 171
Popricani h2 201
Pŏptong p6 113
Poptún c2 276
Pópulo c3 190
Populonia e7 197
Poquis, Nevado de △ d4 292
Poquoson h7 255
Por Chaman a4 128
Porangahau f4 76
Porangatu c4 288
Porazava n3 169
Porbandar d10 129
Porce ≈ c2 284
Porcher Island ▭ b5 248
Porcien ♦ k3 183
Porciúncula g4 291
Porco d3 292
Porcsalma l4 171
Porcuna f7 191
Porcupine ≈ j2 247
Porcupine Creek, Aust. ≈ a2 84
Porcupine Creek, U.S.A. ≈ p7 249
Porcupine Dome △ h2 247
Porcupine Gorge National Park ☆ a2 84
Porcupine Hills ⊡ r5 249
Porcupine Mountains △ f2 260
Porcupine Provincial Forest ☆ r5 249
Porcupine, Cape ► p1 253
Pordenone, Italy ⊡ g3 196
Pordenone g4 196
Pordic c4 182
Pore c2 284
Poręba k3 169
Poreč e4 176
Poreč'e d2 150
Poreč'e-Rybnoe e3 150
Porecatu c5 290
Poreckoe j4 151
Porez l3 151
Pórfido, Punta ► c4 295
Porgera l7 97
Porhov n4 157
Pori j2 157
Porirua e4 77
Poriyya d4 138
Porkkala l3 157
Porlamar e1 285
Porlezza d3 196
Porlock c5 163
Porma ≈ e2 190
Porma, Embalse de ⊙ e2 190
Pormpuraaw e3 80
Pörnbach g4 175
Pornic c5 182
Poro ▭ e5 100
Poro, Monte △ e6 199
Porog j3 147
Poroluoto ▭ j5 155
Poros, Grc. ▭ d5 211
Poros, Attiki, Grc. d5 211
Poros, Ionioi Nisoi, Grc. a4 210
Poroshkove l3 171
Porosozero p5 155
Poroszló j4 171
Porovesi ○ l5 155
Porožsk h3 147
Porpoise Bay ◄ t1 298
Porquerolles, Île de ▭ c8 185
Porrentruy b2 196
Porreres h5 193
Porretta Terme e5 197
Porriño b2 190
Porsangen ⊸ k1 155
Porsangerhalvøya ► k1 155
Porsgrunn c3 156
Porsuk ≈ c3 208
Port Adelaide a2 82
Port Alberni e7 248
Port Albert h15 81
Port Alexander l4 247
Port Alfred g6 235
Port Alice d6 248
Port Allegany b3 256
Port Allen d4 258
Port Alma k7 80
Port Alsworth f3 246
Port Angeles b1 262
Port Antonio B 270
Port Arthur, Aust. Ab3 83
Port Arthur, U.S.A. c5 258
Port Askaig b4 164
Port Augusta c12 81
Port Austin e3 254
Port Barre d4 258
Port Beaufort d7 234
Port Bell d3 225
Port Blair n7 127
Port Blandford q4 253
Port Broughton c12 81
Port Campbell f15 81
Port Campbell National Park ☆ c4 82
Port Canning l8 125
Port Carbon d4 256
Port Chalmers c6 77
Port Charles e2 76
Port Charlotte h6 259
Port Chester g4 257
Port Clements a5 248
Port Clinton e5 254
Port d'Andratx g5 193
Port d'Envalira ═ d6 187
Port Davey ◄ Aa3 83
Port de Pollença h5 193
Port de Sóller g5 193
Port de Venasque ═ c6 187
Port Dickson b4 101
Port Douglas g4 80
Port Edward j5 235
Port Edwards b3 254
Port Elgin, New Brunswick, Can. k5 253
Port Elgin, Ontario, Can. f3 254
Port Elizabeth f6 235
Port Ellen b4 164
Port Erin b2 162
Port Eynon b5 163
Port Fairy f15 81
Port Fitzroy e2 76
Port Gamble b2 262
Port Germein d12 81
Port Gibson d4 258
Port Glasgow d4 164
Port Glaud A 226
Port Graham g4 246
Port Harcourt f5 223
Port Hawkesbury m6 253
Port Hedland d7 86
Port Heiden e4 246
Port Henry k3 255
Port Hood m5 253
Port Hope Simpson p2 253
Port Hueneme d7 265
Port Huron e4 254
Port Isabel a6 258
Port Jackson ◄ g1 83
Port Jefferson Station g4 257
Port Jervis f3 256
Port Kaiser B 270
Port Kaituma q11 271
Port Kembla k13 81
Port Lavaca a5 258
Port Lincoln b13 81
Port Lions f4 246
Port Logan d5 164
Port Loko b4 222
Port Louis, Guad. C 271
Port Louis, Maur. C 231
Port MacDonnell b4 82
Port Macquarie l11 81
Port Maria B 270
Port McNeill d6 248
Port Moller d5 246
Port Morant B 270
Port Mouton k7 253
Port Neches c5 258
Port Neill c13 81
Port Nelson g3 266
Port Ness b1 164
Port Noarlunga a2 82
Port Nolloth b4 234
Port Norris e5 256
Port of Spain E 271
Port Orange j5 259
Port Pegasus ◄ a7 77
Port Penn e5 256
Port Phillip Bay ◄ d4 82
Port Pirie d12 81
Port Renfrew a1 262
Port Rexton r4 253
Port Royal, Jam. B 270
Port Royal, Pennsylvania, U.S.A. c4 256
Port Royal, Virginia, U.S.A. c6 256
Port Royal Sound ═ j3 259
Port Said, Būr Sa'īd, Egypt d6 136
Port Salvador e6 295
Port Sanilac e4 254
Port Saunders p3 253
Port Shepstone j5 235
Port Simpson b4 248
Port St Joe g5 259
Port St Johns h5 235
Port St Lucie City j6 259
Port Stephens, Aust. ◄ e8 85
Port Stephens, Falk. Is d6 295
Port Sudan e4 219
Port Sulphur e5 258
Port Talbot c5 163
Port Tambang ◄ d3 100
Port Townsend b1 262
Port Trevorton d4 256
Port Vila F 74
Port Vincent a2 82
Port Vladimir p2 155
Port Wakefield d13 81
Port Washington c4 254
Port Weld b3 101
Port Welshpool e4 83
Port William d5 164
Port Wing h7 250
Portachuelo e3 293
Portacloy b2 165
Portada Covunco b5 296
Portadown e2 165
Portaferry f2 165
Portage, Pennsylvania, U.S.A. b4 256
Portage, Wisconsin, U.S.A. b4 254
Portage la Prairie d6 250
Portageville e1 258
Portal, Georgia, U.S.A. j3 259
Portal, North Dakota, U.S.A. b6 250
Portalegre, Port ⊡ c5 191
Portalegre c5 191
Portales c5 261
Porta-Piment g5 266
Portaria d2 210
Portarlington d3 165
Portas, Embalse das ⊙ c2 190
Port-au-Port Bay ◄ n4 253
Port-au-Prince h5 271
Portavogie f2 165
Portbail d3 182
Portbou h2 192
Port-Cartier j3 253
Port-Cros, Île de ▭ c8 185
Port-Cros, Parc National de ☆ c7 185
Port-de-Bouc a7 185
Port-de-Paix h5 271
Porteira f4 285
Porteirinha g1 291
Portel, Braz. b2 288
Portel, Port. c6 191
Portelândia b2 290
Portena f1 297
Port-en-Bessin-Huppain e3 182
Porteño ≈ e1 294
Porter Lake ○ p3 249
Porterville, R.S.A. c6 234
Porterville, California, U.S.A. d5 265
Porterville, Mississippi, U.S.A. e3 258
Portes-lès-Valence a6 185
Portfjellet △ d4 154
Port-Gentil a4 224
Porthcawl c5 163
Porthmadog b4 162
Porthmos Zakynthou ═ a5 210
Porticcio A 185
Port-Iliç m2 137
Portilla de la Reina f1 190
Portillo, Chile b2 296
Portillo, Spain f3 190
Portillon, Col du ═ c6 187
Portimão b7 191
Portinatx f5 193
Portinho da Arrábida b6 191
Port-Joinville c6 182
Portknockie f2 164
Portland, Aust. e15 81
Portland, Jam. ⊡ B 266
Portland, N.Z. e1 76
Portland, Arkansas, U.S.A. d3 258
Portland, Indiana, U.S.A. d5 254
Portland, Maine, U.S.A. g7 252
Portland, Michigan, U.S.A. d4 254
Portland, North Dakota, U.S.A. e7 250
Portland, Oregon, U.S.A. b3 262
Portland, Tennessee, U.S.A. f1 258
Portland, Texas, U.S.A. a6 258
Portland Bay ◄ b4 82
Portland Bight ◄ B 266
Portland Canal ═ b4 248
Portland Island ► f3 76
Portland Point ► B 266
Port-la-Nouvelle f5 187
Portlaoise d3 165
Portlaw d4 165
Port-Louis b5 182
Portmahomack e2 164
Portman d7 193
Portmarnock e3 165
Portmore B 270
Portnacroish c3 164
Portnaguran b1 164
Portnahaven b4 164
Port-Navalo c5 182
Portneuf, Can. ≈ h3 252
Portneuf, U.S.A. ≈ g4 262
Portneuf-sur-Mer h4 252
Porto, Braz. d2 288
Porto, Fr. A 185
Porto, Port ⊡ b3 190
Porto, Port b3 190
Porto Acre d1 292
Porto Alegre, Amazonas, Braz. d1 292
Porto Alegre, Mato Grosso do Sul, Braz. b4 290
Porto Alegre, Braz. b2 288
Porto Alegre, S. Tom./P. f5 223
Porto Alencastro c3 290
Porto Amarante e2 293
Porto Amazonas d6 290
Porto Amboim b6 224
Porto Artur a4 288
Porto Azzurro e7 197
Porto Belo c7 289
Porto Camargo b5 290
Porto Cavlo e3 288
Porto Cervo Ab1 198
Porto Cesareo g4 198
Porto Colom h5 193
Porto Covo da Bandeira b7 191
Porto Cristo h5 193
Porto da Cruz B 189
Porto da Folha e3 288
Porto da Lontra b2 288
Porto de Lagos b7 191
Porto de Meinacos b4 288
Porto de Mós b5 191
Porto de Moz g4 285
Porto de Piedrafita ═ c2 190
Porto de Santa Cruz h1 291
Porto do Barka b3 288
Porto do Barqueiro c1 190
Porto do Massacas e2 293
Porto do Son a2 190
Porto dos Gaúchos Óbidos f2 293
Porto Empedocle c7 199
Porto Ercole f7 197
Porto Esperança f3 293
Porto Esperidião f3 293
Porto Estrêla f3 293
Porto Feliz e5 290
Porto Ferreira e4 290
Porto Firme g4 291
Porto Franco c3 288
Porto Garibaldi g5 196
Porto Grande g3 285
Porto Guareí b5 290
Porto Inglês A 222
Porto Jofre f3 293
Porto Levante, Sicilia, Italy d6 199
Porto Levante, Veneto, Italy g4 196
Porto Luceno b7 289
Porto Mauá b7 289
Porto Mendes a6 290
Porto Moniz B 189
Porto Murtinho f4 293
Porto Nacional c4 288
Porto Petra h5 193
Porto Primavera b5 290
Porto Primavera, Represa ⊙ b4 290
Porto Rafti e5 211
Porto Recanati c1 198
Porto Rico b5 224
Porto San Giorgio c1 198
Porto San Paolo Ab2 198
Porto Sant'Elpidio c1 198
Porto Santana g4 285
Porto Santo B 189
Porto Santo Stefano f7 197
Porto Santo, Ilha de ▭ B 189
Porto São José b5 290
Porto Seguro j2 291
Porto Tolle g5 196
Porto Torres Aa2 198
Porto Triunfo e2 293
Porto União b7 289
Porto Velho e1 293
Porto Wälter c1 292
Porto, Golfe de ◄ A 185
Portobelo h6 277
Portobelo, Parque Nacional ☆ h6 277
Portocheli d5 211
Portodemouros, Embalse de ⊙ b2 190
Portoferraio e7 197
Portofino d5 197
Portogruaro g4 196
Portola c2 264
Portomaggiore f5 196
Portomarín c2 190
Porto-Novo e4 223
Portopalo di Capo Passero e8 199
Portoscuso Aa3 198
Porto-Vecchio A 185
Porto-Vecchio, Golfe de ◄ A 185
Portovenere d5 197
Portoviejo a4 284
Portpatrick c5 164
Portrane e3 165
Portree b2 164
Portrush e1 165
Pörtschach am Wörther See f3 177
Portsmouth, Dom. p7 271
Portsmouth, England, U.K. ⊡ h2 162
Portsmouth, U.K. e6 163
Portsmouth, New Hampshire, U.S.A. k1 257
Portsmouth, Ohio, U.S.A. e6 254
Portsmouth, Rhode Island, U.S.A. j3 257
Portsmouth, Virginia, U.S.A. h7 255
Portsoy f2 164
Port-Ste-Marie c4 187
Portstewart e1 165
Port-St-Louis-du-Rhône a7 185
Portugal c7 144

PORTUGAL

THE PORTUGUESE REPUBLIC
Area 92,270km^2 (35,626sq miles)
Capital Lisbon
Organizations CE, EBRD, EU, NATO, OECD
Population 10,050,000
Pop. growth (%) 0.1
Life expectancy 71 (m); 78 (f)
Languages Portuguese
Literacy 93.3%
Currency euro (US $1 = 0.81 euro)
GDP (US million $) 121,500
GDP per head ($US) 12,089

Portugal Cove South r5 253
Portugalete a1 192
Portuguesa, Ven. ⊡ d2 284
Portuguesa, Ven. ≈ d2 284
Portumna c3 165
Portumna Forest Park ☆ c3 165
Port-Vendres f6 187
Portville b2 256
Porus B 270
Porvenir, Arg. f3 297
Porvenir, Pando, Bol. d2 292
Porvenir, Bol. e2 293
Porvenir, Chile b6 295
Porvenir, Ur. j2 297
Porvoo l2 157
Porvoonjoki ≈ l2 157
Porzuna f5 191
Posada, Italy Ab2 198
Posada, Spain e1 190
Posadas, Arg. f5 293
Posadas e7 191
Posavina ♦ j4 177
Posavsko Hribovje ♦ g3 177
Poschiavo e3 196
Pose, Mount △ d2 264
Pošehon'e e2 150
Poseidonia e5 211
Poselki j5 151
Posen e3 254
Posets △ e2 192
Posht-e Badam q5 137
Posio m3 155
Positano d4 198
Poso l5 99
Poso, Danau ○ l5 99
Poso, Teluk ◄ l5 99
Posof j2 209
Posŏng p8 113
Posorja a4 284
Pospeliha t1 121
Possagno f4 196
Posse c4 288
Possel c2 224
Possession Island ▭ a3 234
Pößneck g2 175
Post c5 261
Post Falls e2 262
Post Weygand e4 221
Poşta Câlnău h3 201
Posta Piana e3 198
Postiglione e4 198
Postmasburg e4 234
Postojna f4 177
Postoloprty b1 170
Postomino e1 168
Postville n1 253
Pot Mountain △ f2 262
Pota l9 99
Pótam d4 272
Potamia c6 211
Potamoi e1 210
Potamos c6 211
Potaro ≈ f2 285
Potaro-Siparuni ⊡ f3 285
Potash City d5 139
Potchefstroom g3 235
Potcoava g3 201
Poté h2 291
Poteau b2 258
Potęgowo f1 168
Potenza, Italy ⊡ e4 198
Potenza, Italy ≈ h6 197
Potenza e4 198
Potenza Picena c1 198
Poteriteri, Lake ○ a7 77
Potes f1 190
Potfontein f5 234
Poth k3 273
Potidania c4 210
Potigny e4 182
Potikal g3 126
Potiraguá j1 291
Potiskum g3 223
Potlatch e2 262
Potnarvin F 74
Poto d2 292
Potomac, Maryland, U.S.A. c5 256
Potomac, Maryland/Virginia, U.S.A. ≈ d6 256
Potomana, Gunung △ n9 99
Potosí, Bol. ⊡ d4 292
Potosí, Potosí, Bol. d3 292
Pototan d5 100
Potou c2 106
Potrerillos, Chile d5 292
Potrerillos, Hond. d3 276
Potrerilos c2 296
Potrero del Llano, Chihuahua, Mex. g3 272
Potrero del Llano, Veracruz, Mex. f3 275
Potrero Largo g5 275
Pötschenhöhe △ e2 176
Potsdam, Ger. j3 173
Potsdam, U.S.A. j3 255
Potsdamer Havelseengebiet ☆ h3 173
Potštát f2 171
Pott, Île ▭ F 74
Pottangi h3 127
Pottendorf h2 177
Pottenstein g3 175
Potters Bar f5 163
Pottstown e4 256
Pottsville d4 256
Pottuvil g9 126
Potwar ♦ f4 128
Potworów j4 169
Pouancé d5 182
Pouch Cove r5 253
Poughkeepsie g3 257
Pougues-les-Eaux f1 186
Pouilly-en-Auxois a3 184
Pouilly-sous-Charlieu a4 184
Pouilly-sur-Loire e1 186
Poulin de Courval, Lac ○ g4 252
Poulithra c5 211
Poŭn p7 113
Pound h1 259
Pounta, Akra ► e4 210
Pourri, Mont △ c5 185
Pourtalé g4 297
Pouso Alegre f5 291
Pouso Alto b2 290
Pouthisat f9 103
Pouto e2 76
Pouxeux c2 184
Pouy-de-Touges d5 187
Pouzauges e6 182
Povenec q5 155
Poverty Bay ◄ f3 76
Poviglio e5 196
Povlen △ d3 200
Póvoa de Lanhoso b3 190
Póvoa de São Miguel c6 191
Póvoa de Varzim b3 190
Póvoa, Barragem da ⊸ c5 191
Povoação j3 291
Povolžskij k5 151
Povorino f2 149
Povorotnyj, Mys ► s4 113
Povors'k p4 169
Povrly c1 170
Poway f9 265
Powder, Montana, U.S.A. ≈ b2 260
Powder, Oregon, U.S.A. ≈ e3 262
Powder River b3 260
Powell a2 260
Powell Point ► l7 259
Powell River e7 248
Powell, Lake ○ h7 261
Powers c3 254
Powers Lake b6 250
Powhatan h7 255
Powidzkie, Jezioro ○ f3 168
Pownal g2 257
Powys ⊡ c4 163
Poxoréu a1 290
Poyang Hu ○ l4 105
Poyatos b4 192
Poygan, Lake ○ f2 260
Poynette b4 254
Poyntz Pass e2 165
Poyo, Cerro △ b7 193
Pöyrisjoki ≈ k2 155
Poysdorf h1 177
Poza de la Sal g2 190
Poza Rica f3 275
Pozanti e4 208
Požarevac e3 200
Požega, Cro. j4 177
Požega, Serbia/Mont. e4 200
Požega-Slavonija ⊡ j4 177
Požeška Gora ⊡ j4 177
Pozezdrze k1 169
Poznań e3 168
Pozo Alcón b7 193
Pozo Betbeder e5 293
Pozo Cañada c6 193
Pozo Colorado f4 293
Pozo de los Ramos, Embalse de ⊙ a3 192
Pozo del Molle f2 297
Pozo del Tigre e4 293
Pozo Hondo e5 293
Pozo Negro Af2 189
Pozo Nuevo d3 272
Pozo San Martin d1 294
Pozoamargo b5 193
Pozoblanco f6 191
Pozohondo c6 193
Pozo-Lorente c5 193
Pozos, Punta ► c5 295
Pozuelo b6 193
Pozuelo de Alarcón g4 190
Pozuelo de Zarzón d4 190
Pozuelo del Páramo e2 190
Požva j4 147
Pozzallo d8 199
Pozzomaggiore Aa2 198
Pozzuoli d4 198
Pra ≈ d4 222
Prabumulih c6 98
Prabuty h2 169
Pracana, Barragem de ⊸ c5 191
Prachatice c2 170
Prachi ≈ k9 125
Prachin Buri e8 103
Prachuap Khiri Khan d10 103
Prada, Embalse de ⊙ c2 190
Praděd △ f1 170
Pradelles f4 186
Prádena g3 190
Pradera b3 284
Prades e5 187
Pradillo b2 192
Prado j2 291
Prado del Rey e8 191
Prado Flood Control Basin ⊸ f8 265
Pradoluengo a2 192
Pradópolis d4 290
Prads-Haute-Bléone c6 185
Præstø f3 158
Pragersko g3 177
Prägraten d2 176
Prague, Czech Rep. c1 170
Prague, U.S.A. a2 258
Praha ⊡ c1 170
Prahecq b2 186
Prahova ⊡ g3 201
Praia a Mare e5 198
Praia da Tocha b4 190
Praia de Leste d6 290
Praia de Mira b4 190
Praia do Bilene k2 235
Praia Grande e6 291
Praia Rica f2 293
Prainha, Amazonas, Braz. e1 293
Prainha, Pará, Braz. g4 285
Prairie g6 80
Prairie du Chien f3 260
Prakhon Chai f8 103
Pram ≈ e1 176
Pram, Khao △ a1 101
Pramanta b3 210
Pran Buri d9 103
Prang e3 128
Prangli ▭ l3 157
Pranhita ≈ f3 126
Prankerhöhe △ f2 177
Prapat d14 103
Praslin Bay ◄ J 271
Prasonisi, Akra ► Ad3 211
Prastion b1 138
Praszka g4 168
Prat de Comte e4 192
Prata, Braz. ≈ b3 290
Prata, Braz. ≈ d3 290
Prata, Minas Gerais, Braz. d3 290
Pratabnagar d4 130
Pratapgarh g8 129
Pratinha e3 291
Prato, Italy ⊡ f6 197
Prato f6 197
Prato allo Stelvio e3 196
Pratola Peligna c2 198
Prats de Lluçanès g3 192
Prats-de-Mollo-la-Preste e6 187
Pratt d4 261
Prättigau ≈ d3 196
Prattsburg c2 256
Prattsville f2 257

Qambar → Rapid City 373

Qambar d7 129
Qamdo q4 125
Qamea E 74
Qaminis a1 218
Qamruddin Karez d5 128
Qamşar n5 137
Qana d3 138
Qanāt as Suways a5 139
Qanawāt e4 138
Qandala d1 226
Qangdin Sum h4 112
Qangzê d4 130
Qapan q3 137
Qapqal t6 121
Qaqortoq v3 243
Qar Goliis d2 226
Qara c2 218
Qara Tarai b3 128
Qaraaoun d3 138
Qārah, Sau. Ar h7 136
Qārah, Syria e2 138
Qarah Bāgh, Ghaznī, Afg. d4 128
Qarah Bāgh, Kābul, Afg. d3 128
Qarak r8 121
Qarārat an Nā'ikah a2 218
Qardho d2 226
Qareh Chāy n4 137
Qarhan p1 125
Qarokŭl f1 128
Qarqan He m3 117
Qarqi t7 121
Qārqi q3 137
Qarqin c2 128
Qartaba d2 138
Qaryat al Ulyā l8 137
Qasamī r5 137
Qāsemābād, Khorāsan, Iran g9 120
Qāsemābād, Khorāsan, Iran r4 137
Qasigiannguit u2 243
Qāsim e4 138
Qaşr al Azraq e5 139
Qaşr al Ḩallābāt e4 139
Qaşr al Kharānah e5 139
Qaşr al Khubbāz j5 137
Qaşr aş Şabiyah m7 137
Qasr Farafra c2 218
Qasr Khiyār g2 221
Qaşr Larocu g3 221
Qaţanā e3 138
Qatar c6 92

QATAR

THE STATE OF QATAR
Area 11,437km² (4416sq miles)
Capital Doha
Organizations CCASG, IDB, LAS, OAPEC, OIC, OPEC
Population 600,000
Pop. growth (%) -0.3
Life expectancy 68 (m); 70 (f)
Languages Arabic, English
Literacy 82.5%
Currency Qatar riyal (US $1 = 3.64 Qatar riyal)
GDP (US million $) 17,566
GDP per head ($US) 29,276

Qatif c5 139
Qatlish r3 137
Qatorkŭhi Zarafshon d1 128
Qaţrūyeh q7 137
Qattara Depression c1 218
Qaţţinah, Buḩayrat f5 209
Qavāmābād r6 137
Qax g4 149
Qāyen f4 116
Qayroqqum m7 121
Qayū n5 125
Qayyārah j5 209
Qazangödağ k2 137
Qazax g4 149
Qazi Ahmad d7 129
Qazımämmäd h4 149
Qazrin d4 138
Qazvīn, Iran b9 120
Qazvīn m3 137
Qeh a4 112
Qelelevu E 74
Qelin Ul h3 112
Qena d8 136
Qeqertarsuaq u2 243
Qeshet d4 138
Qeshlāq l4 137
Qeshm r8 137
Qetura d7 139
Qeydār m3 137
Qezi'ot c6 139
Qi He d2 106
Qian He f1 104
Qian Shan m5 113
Qian'an, Hebei, China k6 113
Qian'an, Jilin, China n3 113
Qiangwei He f2 111
Qianjiang, Chongqing, China a5 106
Qianjiang, Hubei, China c4 106
Qianjietou f2 111
Qianjin s2 113
Qiankou d1 106
Qianning c3 104
Qianqihao m3 113
Qianshan e4 111
Qianshanlaoba v5 121
Qianxi, Guizhou, China f5 104
Qianxi, Hebei, China k5 113
Qiaojia d5 104
Qiaotou h1 111
Qibā' k8 137
Qichun d4 106
Qidaogou p5 113
Qidong, Hunan, China j5 105
Qidong, Jiangsu, China g4 111
Qidu e4 111
Qiemo f2 122
Qihe e1 111
Qijiang f4 104
Qila Abdullah c5 128
Qila Ladgasht a7 129
Qila Saifullah d5 128
Qilaotu Shan l5 113
Qilian a6 112
Qilian Shan, Gansu/Qinghai, China p3 117
Qilihe l5 113
Qiman Tag m1 125
Qimen e5 111
Qin He c2 106
Qin Ling a3 106
Qinā, Wādī d2 218
Qing Jiang a4 106
Qing'an p2 113
Qingcheng e1 111
Qingchengzi m5 113
Qingchuan e2 104
Qingdao g1 111
Qingfeng, Henan, China d2 106
Qingfeng, Hubei, China b3 106
Qinggang p2 113
Qingguandu b5 106
Qinghai p3 117
Qinghai Hu a7 112
Qinghe, Hebei, China d1 106
Qinghe, Jilin, China n5 113
Qinghecheng n5 113
Qinghemen l5 113
Qinghezhen e1 111
Qingjian b1 106
Qinglong, Guizhou, China e6 104
Qinglong, Hebei, China k5 113
Qinglong He k5 113
Qingpu g4 111
Qingshan, Anhui, China e4 111
Qingshan, Hubei, China d4 106
Qingshen d4 104
Qingshizui a7 112
Qingshui f1 104
Qingshuihe f6 112
Qingshuihezi t5 121
Qingshuilang Shan b5 104
Qingtaiping b4 106
Qingtang j6 105
Qingtongxia d6 112
Qingtuo f2 111
Qingyang, Anhui, China e4 111
Qingyang, Gansu, China d7 112
Qingyuan, Guangdong, China j7 105
Qingyuan, Liaoning, China n4 113
Qingyuan, Zhejiang, China m5 105
Qingyun e1 111
Qingzang Gaoyuan h3 135
Qingzhen f5 104
Qingzhou b4 106
Qinhuangdao k6 113
Qinshui c2 106
Qintong g3 111
Qinxian c1 106
Qinyang c2 106
Qinyuan c1 106
Qinzhou g8 104
Qionglai d3 104
Qionglai Shan d3 104
Qiongzhong g9 104
Qiongzhou Haixia h8 104
Qiqihar m2 113
Qir p7 137
Qira e1 130
Qiryat Ata d4 138
Qiryat Bialik d4 138
Qiryat Gat c5 139
Qiryat Mal'akhi c5 139
Qiryat Motzkin d4 138
Qiryat Shemona d3 138
Qiryat Tiv'on d4 138
Qiryat Yam d4 138
Qishn h4 219
Qishuyan g4 111
Qitaihe r3 113
Qiubei e6 104
Qiucun g5 111
Qiumuzhuang m5 113
Qiuxian d1 106
Qixia g1 111
Qixian, Henan, China d2 106
Qixian, Shanxi, China c1 106
Qixianji e3 111
Qixing He r2 113
Qiyang h5 104
Qiying d7 112
Qizhou d4 106
Qizhou Liedao h9 104
Qizilrabot g2 128
Qlaiaa d3 138
Qojūr l3 137
Qolleh-ye Damāvand p3 137
Qom n4 137
Qomsheh n5 137
Qonaqkänd h4 149
Qong Muztag f2 135
Qonggyai m5 125
Qongj e5 112
Qooriga Neegro d2 226
Qornet es Saouda e2 138
Qorveh l4 137
Qoryale d2 226
Qosh Tepe j4 209
Qoţbābād, Fārs, Iran p7 137
Qoţbābād, Hormozgan, Iran r8 137
Qoţūr k3 209
Qotūr Chai k2 137
Qoubaiyat e2 138
Qu Jiang f3 104
Qu'Appelle r6 249
Quabbin Reservoir h2 257
Quadra Island e6 248
Quadros, Lago dos b7 289
Quaidabad e4 128
Quairading c13 87
Quakenbrück c3 172
Quakertown e4 256
Qualake d4 224
Qualay'ah, Ra's al h2 219
Qualicum Beach a1 262
Quambone h11 81
Quamby e6 80
Quân Đao Nam Du g11 103
Quan He d3 106
Quanah d5 261
Quanaru, Ilha e4 285
Quanbao Shan b2 106
Quang Ngai j8 102
Quanjiao f3 111
Quankou d5 106
Quanyang p4 113
Quanzhou, Fujian, China m6 105
Quanzhou, Guangxi Zhuangzu Zizhiqu, China h6 104
Quaraí, Braz. e2 294
Quaraí, Rio Grande do Sul, Braz. e2 294
Quarenta c6 224
Quarré-les-Tombes f1 186
Quarryville d5 256
Quarteira b7 191
Quarto, Lago di g6 177
Quartu Sant'Elena Ab3 198
Quartzsite f9 263
Quatá c5 290
Quatretonda d6 193
Quba h4 149
Quchan g9 120
Queanbeyan j13 81
Québec, Can. f3 252
Québec, Québec, Can. g5 252
Quebeck g2 259
Quebra Anzol e3 291
Quebracho j2 297
Quebrada del Toro, Parque Nacional de la d1 284
Quebradillas A 270
Quechultenango e5 275
Quedal, Cabo b4 294
Quedas e2 233
Quedas do Iguaçu b6 290
Quedlinburg g4 173
Queen Bess, Mount e6 248
Queen Charlotte a5 248
Queen Charlotte Bay d6 295
Queen Charlotte Islands a5 248
Queen Charlotte Sound c6 248
Queen Charlotte Strait d6 248
Queen Elizabeth Islands l1 243
Queen Elizabeth Range v3 298
Queen Fabiola Mountains j2 298
Queen Mary Coast r1 298
Queen Mary Land q2 298
Queen Maud Land f2 298
Queen Victoria Spring Nature Reserve f12 87
Queens k6 257
Queens Channel j4 86
Queenscliff g15 81
Queensland f7 80
Queenstown, Aust. Aa3 83
Queenstown, N.Z. b6 77
Queenstown, R.S.A. g5 235
Queenstown, U.S.A. d6 256
Queguay Grande j2 297
Quehué e4 297
Queich d3 174
Queijo, Cabo a1 192
Queimada e1 293
Queimada, Ilha b2 288
Queimadas e4 288
Queiroz c4 290
Queixada, Isla b4 295
Quela c5 224
Quelimane f2 233
Quelite a2 274
Quella a4 296
Quellón b4 295
Quelo b5 224
Queluz f5 291
Quemada g3 190
Quemada Grande, Ilha c6 289
Quembo c1 232
Quemú-Quemú f4 297
Quenamari, Nevado de c2 292
Quend g2 183
Queniborough e4 162
Quequén h5 297
Quequén Grande h5 297
Queralbs g2 192
Quercy d4 187
Querência b4 288
Querência do Norte b5 290
Querendaro d4 274
Querétaro, Mex. e3 275
Querétaro, Querétaro, Mex. d3 274
Querfurt g4 173
Quérigut e6 187
Quero a5 193
Querobabi h10 263
Querol f3 192
Querpon b5 284
Quesada a7 193
Queshan d3 106
Quesnel, British Columbia, Can. f5 248
Quesnel, British Columbia, Can. f5 248
Quesnel Lake g5 248
Quessoy c4 182
Questembert c5 182
Quetena de Lípez d4 292
Quetta c5 128
Quettehou d3 182
Quetzalapa, Guerrero, Mex. e4 275
Quetzalapa, Hidalgo, Mex. e3 275
Queuco b4 296
Queulat, Parque Nacional b4 295
Queule a5 296
Quevedo b4 284
Quéven b5 182
Queyras, Parc Naturel Régional du c6 185
Quezaltenango b3 276
Quezaltepeque, El Sal. c4 276
Quezaltepeque, Guat. c3 276
Quezon, Phil. b6 100
Quezon, Phil. d5 100
Quezon City c3 100
Qufu e2 111
Qui Châu g6 102
Qui Nhơn j9 103
Quibala b6 224
Quibaxe b5 224
Quibdó b2 284
Quiberon b5 182
Quiberon, Baie de b5 182
Quiberon, Presqu'île de b5 182
Quibor d2 284
Quiçama, Parque Nacional do b5 224
Quickborn c5 158
Quiculungo c5 224
Quidico a5 296
Quiévrain b4 159
Quihuhu c5 224
Quilá f5 272
Quilaco a4 296
Quilalí d4 276
Quilca c3 292
Quilco g4 297
Quilenda b6 224
Quilengues a1 232
Quilimarí b2 296
Quilino d2 294
Quill Lake a4 250
Quillabamba c2 292
Quill Lakes q6 249
Quillacollo d3 292
Quillaicillo b1 296
Quillan e6 187
Quillén, Lago b5 296
Quillón a4 296
Quillota b2 296
Quilmes h3 297
Quilmes, Sierra del c1 294
Quilon e8 126
Quilpie g9 81
Quilpué b2 296
Quilua f2 233
Quimbango c6 224
Quimbele c5 224
Quimbonge c5 224
Quimichis b2 274
Quimilí d1 294
Quimome e3 293
Quimper a5 182
Quimperlé b5 182
Quinabucasan Point d3 100
Quinault b2 262
Quince Mil c2 292
Quincinetto b4 196
Quincy, California, U.S.A. c2 264
Quincy, Illinois, U.S.A. f4 260
Quincy, Massachusetts, U.S.A. j2 257
Quincy, Washington, U.S.A. d2 262
Quindio b3 284
Quines e2 296
Quinéville d3 182
Quinga c7 227
Quinguimo b2 296
Quinhagak d4 246
Quinhámel a3 222
Quiñihual g4 297
Quiniluban c5 100
Quinn e5 262
Quiñones d2 292
Quinson c7 185
Quinta b3 296
Quinta de Tilcoco b3 296
Quintana c5 290
Quintana de la Serena e6 191
Quintana del Castillo d2 190
Quintana del Pino g2 190
Quintana del Puente f2 190
Quintana Redonda b3 192
Quintana Roo p8 273
Quintana-Martín Galíndez a2 192
Quintanapalla g2 190
Quintanar de la Orden a5 193
Quintanar de la Sierra a3 192
Quintanar del Rey c5 193
Quintanilha d3 190
Quintanilla de Onésimo f3 190
Quintay b2 296
Quintero b2 296
Quintin c4 182
Quinto, Arg. e3 296
Quinto d3 192
Quinxo, Monte do b3 190
Quinzano d'Oglio e4 196
Quinzau b5 224
Quionga c6 227
Quiotepec f5 275
Quipapá e3 288
Quipar c6 193
Quipungo a1 232
Quiquive d3 292
Quirihue a4 296
Quirima c6 224
Quirimba, Ilha c6 231
Quirimbo b6 224
Quirindi d7 85
Quirinópolis c3 290
Quiroga, Arg. g3 297
Quiroga, Bol. d3 292
Quiroga, Mex. d4 274
Quiroga, Spain c2 190
Quiroga, Lago b5 295
Quiroz b4 284
Quiruelas de Vidriales e2 190
Quisiro c1 284
Quissac f5 187
Quissamã h5 291
Quissanga c6 227
Quissico l2 235
Quissico, Lagoa l2 235
Quita Sueño Bank g3 277
Quitapa c6 224
Quiterajo c6 227
Quitman, Georgia, U.S.A. h4 259
Quitman, Mississippi, U.S.A. e3 258
Quito b4 284
Quitovac g10 263
Quixadá e2 288
Quixeramobim e3 288
Qujiang, Guangdong, China j6 105
Qujiang, Jiangxi, China k4 105
Qujing d6 104
Qulin Gol m2 113
Qulūsana c7 136
Qumar He n2 125
Qumbu h5 235
Qunayyin, Sabkhat al b1 218
Qungtag h4 135
Quntamari m3 135
Quoich l3 243
Quoin Point c7 234
Quonochontaug j3 257
Quorn d12 81
Quoxo f1 234
Qurayqirah d6 139
Qurayyah, Wādī c6 139
Qŭrghonteppa d2 128
Qus d9 136
Qusar h4 149
Quseir e8 136
Qūshchī k3 137
Qusum, Xizang Zizhiqu, China n5 125
Qusum, Xizang Zizhiqu, China d3 130
Qutū' Island f4 219
Quwan c3 106
Quwu Shan c7 112
Quxian f3 104
Qüxü m5 113
Quyang h6 112
Quzhou, Hebei, China d1 106
Quzhou, Zhejiang, China m4 105
Qvareli g4 149

R

R. L. Harris Reservoir g3 259
Ra's al Khaymah q9 137
Ra's al Mish āb m7 137
Ra's an Naqb d6 139
Raab g3 177
Raabs an der Thaya g1 177
Raahe k4 155
Rääkkylä n1 157
Raalte e2 159
Raamsdonksveer c3 159
Ra'anana c4 139
Raas h8 99
Raasay b2 164
Raasiku l3 157
Raate m4 155
Rab f5 177
Rába f4 170
Raba k9 99
Raba, Pol. j6 169
Rabaale d2 226
Rábade c1 190
Rābāgani l5 171
Rabak d5 218
Rabang e3 130
Rabastens d5 187
Rabastens-de-Bigorre c5 187
Rabat, Malta g1 221
Rabat, Mor. c2 220
Rabbi f5 197
Rabbit d2 248
Rabčice h2 171
Rabi E 74
Rabida, Isla A 286
Rabinal b3 276
Rabka Zdrój h6 169
Rabnabad Islands m9 125
Rabnitz Bach g2 177
Rábor r7 137
Rabotki h3 151
Rabt Sbayta b4 220
Rabyānah, Ramlat b2 218
Racale h5 198
Racalmás g4 171
Racalmuto c7 199
Racconigi b5 196
Raccoon Cay g3 266
Race Point k2 257
Raceland d5 258
Rach Gia g11 103
Racha Yai, Ko a2 101
Rachaïya d3 138
Rachaïya el Foukhar d3 138
Rachal k4 273
Rachidiyé d3 138
Raciąż j3 169
Racibórz g5 168
Racine c4 254
Răciu g2 201
Ráckeve g4 171
Racoş g2 201
Racoviţa h3 201
Raczki l2 157
Radal a5 296
Radama, Nosy Ab1 233
Radashkovichy m5 157
Rădăuţi g2 201
Raddusa d7 199
Rade d3 156
Radeberg k1 175
Radebeul h1 175
Radeburg k1 175
Radeče g3 177
Radekhiv n5 169
Radenthein e3 176
Radevormwald f3 159
Radhanpur e9 129
Radicondoli f6 197
Radisson d2 252
Radium h2 275
Radlinski, Mount gg3 298
Radlje ob Dravi g3 177
Radnevo g4 201
Radnice b2 170
Rădoaia j2 201
Radolfzell d5 174
Radom, Pol. k4 169
Radom, Sudan d2 224
Radom National Park d2 224
Radomir f4 201
Radomka k4 169
Radomsko h4 169
Radomyšl b2 170
Radomyśl Wielki k5 169
Radošina f3 171
Radošovce f3 170
Radoszyce j4 169
Radoviš f5 201
Radovljica f3 177
Radowo Małe d2 168
Radøy a2 156
Radožda a1 210
Radstadt e2 176
Radstock d5 16
Răducăneni h2 201
Radun' n1 169
Radužnyj k2 151
Radvanice e1 170
Radviliškis k5 157
Raḑwá, Jabal e3 219
Radymno l6 169
Radyvyliv b2 148
Radzanów j3 169
Radziejów g3 168
Radziłów l2 169
Radzovce h3 171
Radzymin k3 169
Radzyń Chełminski g2 168
Radzyń Podlaski l4 169
Rae Bareli g6 124
Rae Lakes f3 242
Rae Strait l2 243
Raeford k2 259
Raeren e4 159
Raesfeld e3 159
Raeside, Lake f11 87
Raetihi e3 76
Rāf e2 219
Rafael a4 296
Rafael J. Garcia f4 275
Rafael Obligado g3 297
Rafaela g1 297
Rafaï d3 224
Raffadali c7 199
Rafḩā' j7 136
Rafiaḩ c5 139
Rafiaḩ Yam c5 139
Rafili e2 225
Rafina e4 210
Rafsanjān q6 137
Raft g4 262
Raga e2 225
Ragag b5 218
Ragang, Mount e7 100
Ragay Gulf d4 100
Rågelin h2 173
Ragged Island g3 266
Ragged, Mount f13 87
Raghwān, Wādī g4 219
Raglan, N.Z. e2 76
Raglan, U.K. d5 163
Rago Nasjonalpark e3 154
Ragösen h3 173
Raguhn h4 173
Ragusa, Sicilia, Italy d8 199
Ragusa d8 199
Raguva l5 157
Raha, India n6 125
Raha, Indon. m7 99
Rahad e5 219
Rahad d5 218
Rahad Canal e5 218
Rahad el Berdi b5 218
Rāḩah, Jabal ar a7 139
Rahat c5 139
Rahaţ, Ḩarrat LF f3 219
Rahden d3 172
Rahimatpur d4 126
Rahimyar Khan e6 129
Rahin c3 184
Rahjerd n4 137
Raḩmah d7 139
Rahole National Reserve b3 226
Rahotu d3 76
Rahué b5 296
Rahue b4 296
Rahuri d3 126
Raiatea K 75
Raices h1 297
Raichur e4 126
Raiford h4 259
Raiganj l7 125
Raigarh h9 125
Raijua l10 99
Raikot b4 130
Raikuu n1 157
Rain f4 175
Rainbow Beach e4 84
Rainelle f7 254
Rainier National Park, Mount c2 262
Rainier, Mount c2 262
Rainis f8 100
Rainy, Can. e1 260
Rainy, U.S.A. e1 260
Rainy Lake g6 250
Rainy River f6 250
Raipur, Chhattisgarh, India g9 124
Raipur, Rajasthan, India g7 129
Raipur, Rajasthan, India g8 129
Rairangpur k8 125
Raisar c6 130
Raisduottarhaldi h2 154
Raisinghnagar f6 129
Raistakka m3 155
Raïte e3 138
Raith j6 251
Raivavae K 75
Raiwind g5 128
Raj Mahal g8 129
Raj Nandgaon g9 124
Raja g8 98
Rajabasa, Gunung c7 98
Rajahmundry g4 126
Raja-Jooseppi m2 155
Rajaldesar g6 129
Rajamäki l2 157
Rajampet f5 126
Rajang g4 98
Rajanpur e6 129
Rajapalaiyam e8 126
Rajapur c4 126
Rajasthan f7 129
Rajauli j7 125
Rajbiraj k6 125
Rajčihinsk q1 113
Rájec e2 170
Rajec g2 171
Rajgarh, Himachal Pradesh, India c4 130
Rajgarh, Madhya Pradesh, India e7 124
Rajgarh, Rajasthan, India b5 130
Rajgarh, Rajasthan, India c6 130
Rajgarh, Uttaranchal, India d4 130
Rajghat e5 128
Rajgród l2 169
Rajgrodzkie, Jezioro l2 169
Rajhrad e2 170
Rajhradice e2 170
Rājib d4 139
Rajim g9 124
Rajka f3 170
Rajkot e9 129
Rajmahal k7 125
Rajmahal Hills k7 125
Rajouri b3 130
Rajpipla f10 129
Rajpura c4 130
Rajsamand f8 129
Rajshahi, Bang. l7 125
Rajshahi l7 125
Rajula e10 129
Raka g5 135
Rakahanga H 75
Rakai f4 225
Rakaia c5 77
Rakaposhi b1 130
Rakhab Dev f8 129
Rakhiv g1 201
Rakhni d5 128
Rakhshan b7 129
Rakiraki E 74
Rakit e7 98
Rakke m3 157
Rakkestad d3 156
Rakmanovskie Klyuchi w3 121
Rakoniewice e3 168
Rakops c3 232
Rakovica g5 177
Rakovitsa f4 201
Rakovník b1 170
Rakovski g4 201
Rakša f5 150
Råkvåg c5 154
Rakvere m3 157
Raleigh, Can. q3 253
Raleigh, U.S.A. k2 259
Raleighvallen Voltsberg, Natuurreservaat f3 285
Ralik Chain D 74
Ralingen e5 159
Ralla k7 99
Ralston d3 256
Rama d4 138
Rama, Nic. e4 276
Ramacca d7 199
Ramaceto, Monte d5 196
Ramaditas d4 292
Ramales de la Victoria g1 190
Ramalho, Serra do d4 288
Ramallah d5 139
Ramallo g2 297
Ramanagaram e6 126
Ramanathapuram f8 126
Ramanuj Ganj h8 125
Ramas, Cape c5 126
Ramat Gan c4 139
Ramat HaSharon c4 139
Ramat Magshimim d4 138
Ramat Yishay d4 138
Ramatlabama f2 235
Rambervillers c2 184
Rambhapur g9 129
Rambla del Moro c6 193
Rambouillet g4 183
Ramechhap h6 135
Ramena Ab1 233
Ramerupt a2 184
Rameshwar e5 130
Rameški d3 150
Ramesvaram f8 126
Ramgarh, Bang. m8 125
Ramgarh, Jharkhand, India j8 125
Ramgarh, Rajasthan, India e7 129
Ramgarh, Rajasthan, India b5 130
Ramgarh, Rajasthan, India c5 130
Ramgarh, Rajasthan, India b6 130
Ramghat d5 130
Rāmhormoz m6 137
Ramirás c2 190
Ramírez, Isla a6 295
Ramis Shet' c2 226
Ramla c5 139
Ramm, Jabal d7 139
Ramme b2 158
Ramnulotsi g3 235
Ramnabergnuten b2 156
Ramnagar, Madhya Pradesh, India g7 124
Ramnagar, Uttar Pradesh, India h7 125
Ramnagar, Uttar Pradesh, India d5 130
Ramnagar, Uttaranchal, India d5 130
Ramnagar, Jam.Kash. b3 130
Ramnäs g3 156
Râmnicu Sărat h3 201
Râmnicu Vâlcea g3 201
Ramo c2 226
Ramón Corona c1 274
Ramón Lista c5 295
Ramón M. Castro c5 296
Ramón Santamarina h5 297
Ramona g8 265
Ramonville-St-Agne d5 187
Ramos, Arg. e4 293
Ramos, Mex. g5 272
Ramos Arizpe j5 273
Ramot d4 138
Ramot Naftali d3 138
Ramotswa f2 235
Rampart g2 246
Ramparts m2 247
Rampside c2 162
Rampur, Himachal Pradesh, India c4 130
Rampur, Uttar Pradesh, India c5 130
Rampur, Uttar Pradesh, India d5 130
Rampura g8 129
Ramree Island a6 102
Ramsele, Västerbotten, Swe. g4 154
Ramsele, Västernorrland, Swe. f5 154
Ramsey, England, U.K. f4 163
Ramsey, Isle of Man, U.K. b2 162
Ramsey, U.S.A. b6 254
Ramsey Lake m7 251
Ramsgate h5 163
Rāmshir m6 137
Ramsing b1 102
Ramsjö f1 156
Ramsloh (Saterland) c2 172
Ramsøyfjorden b5 154
Ramstein-Miesenbach e5 174
Ramtek f9 124
Ramu n9 125
Ramundberget d5 154
Ramusio, Lac l1 253
Ramygala l5 157
Ramzaj h5 151
Råna f2 154
Rana Pratap Sagar g8 129
Rana, Cerro d3 284
Ranaghat l8 125
Ranapur g9 129
Ranasar e8 129
Ranau j2 99
Ranau, Danau b7 98
Rancagua b3 296
Rance, Fr. c4 182
Rancharia c5 290
Rancheria b1 248
Ranchi j8 125
Rancho Cordova b3 264
Rancho Cucamonga f7 265
Rancho de Caçados Tapiúnas f2 293
Rancho Grande c2 274
Rancho Nuevo f2 275
Ranchos h3 297
Ranco, Lago a6 296
Randallstown d5 256
Randalstown e2 165
Randan f2 186
Randazzo d7 199
Randers d2 158
Randers Fjord d2 158
Randijaure g3 154
Randleman k2 259
Randolph b2 256
Randow k2 173
Randowaya k6 97
Randsfjorden d2 156
Randsjö e1 156
Randsverk c2 156
Råneå j4 155
Råneälven h3 154
Ranemsletta c4 154
Ranérou b2 222
Rânes e4 182
Ranfurly c6 77
Rangae b2 101
Rangamati n8 125
Rangapara North n6 125
Rangasa, Tanjung k6 99
Rangatira Island A 77
Rangaunu Bay d1 76
Range, Selwyn e6 80
Rangedalen c5 154
Rangeley g6 252
Rangeley Lake l3 255
Rangia Patharughat m6 125
Rangiora d5 77
Rangiroa K 75
Rangitikei e3 76
Rangkasbitung d8 98
Rangkūl g1 128
Rangoon c7 102
Rangoon, Yangôn, Myan. c7 102
Rangpur, Bang. l7 125
Rangpur, Pak. e5 128
Rangsang b4 98
Rangsdorf j3 173
Rani f8 129
Rania b5 130
Ranibennur d5 126
Ranijula Peak h8 125
Ranikhet d5 130
Ranipur, India d5 130
Ranipur, Pak. d7 129
Raniwara f8 129
Ranken c6 80
Rankin Inlet l3 242
Rankin Pass g2 235
Rankin's Springs h12 81
Rankūs e3 138
Rankweil a2 176
Rann of Kachchh d9 129
Rannes k8 80
Ränninvaara l4 155
Rannoch Moor d3 164
Rano f3 223
Ranobe Aa2 233
Ranohira Ab3 233
Ranomafana, Parc National de Ab3 233
Ranomatana Ab3 233
Ranomena Ab3 233
Ranong d11 103
Ranot b2 101
Ranpur e9 129
Ranquil del Norte c4 296
Ranrkan d5 128
Ransiki j6 97
Rantad b4 101
Rantasalmi n1 157
Rantau h6 99
Rantau, Riau, Indon. b4 98
Rantau Panjang b2 101
Rantaukampar b5 101
Rantaupanjang, Kalimantan Tengah, Indon. g5 98
Rantaupanjang, Kalimantan Timur, Indon. j3 99
Rantauprapat a4 101
Rantaupulut g5 98
Rantemario, Gunung l6 99
Rantepao k6 99
Rantsila k4 155
Rantzausminde d3 158
Ranua l4 155
Ranue a6 296
Ranum c2 158
Rãnya k3 137
Ranyah, Wādī f3 219
Raohe s2 113
Raon-l'Étape c2 184
Raoping l7 105
Raoyang h6 112
Rapa K 75
Rapallo d5 197
Rapar e9 129
Rapel, Chile b2 296
Rapel, O'Higgins, Chile b2 296
Raper, Cabo a5 295
Raphoe d2 165
Rapid Bay d13 81
Rapid City, Can. c5 250

374 Rapid City → Rio Bananal

Rapid City, U.S.A. c2 260
Rapid River c3 254
Rapidan c6 256
Răpina m3 157
Rapirrân d2 292
Rapla l3 157
Rapolla e4 198
Raposa b5 191
Rapotín e2 170
Rappahannock c6 256
Rappang k6 99
Rappbodetalstausee f4 173
Rapsani c3 210
Rapti f6 135
Rapulo d2 292
Rapur d9 129
Raritan Bay f4 257
Raroia K 75
Raron b3 196
Ras g7 129
Râs el Aâssi e2 138
Ras el Ma d2 220
Râs el Mâ d2 222
Ras el Naqb c7 139
Ras en Nabi Younès d3 138
Râs Ghârib d7 136
Ra's Matârimah a7 139
Râs Matarma a7 139
Ras Tannūrah n8 137
Rasa b4 101
Rasa, Phil. b6 100
Rasa, Punta d4 294
Rascafría g4 190
Raşcov j2 201
Raseiniai k5 157
Rashaant d3 112
Rashad d5 218
Rashîd c6 136
Rashid Qala c5 128
Rasht m3 137
Rasines g1 190
Rasivaara n1 157
Råsjö f1 156
Räsk a4 122
Raška e4 200
Raskam r9 121
Raskoh b6 129
Raslavice k2 171
Rasmi g8 129
Râşnov g3 201
Raso A 222
Raso da Catarina e3 288
Raso, Cabo c4 295
Rason Lake g11 87
Rasony c1 148
Rasovo f4 201
Raspenava d1 170
Rasquera e3 192
Rasra h7 125
Rass Ajdir g2 221
Rasskazovo f1 148
Rasšua, Ostrov r5 119
Răstăţno h2 154
Rastatt d4 174
Råsted c2 158
Rastegai'sa l1 155
Rastenfeld g1 177
Rastkogel c2 176
Råstojaure h2 154
Rasueros e3 190
Rasul a3 130
Rasulnagar a3 130
Råsvalen f3 156
Raszków f4 168
Rat Buri d9 103
Rat Island Aa2 247
Rat Islands Aa2 247
Rat Lake d2 250
Ratak Chain D 74
Ratan h5 154
Ratangarh, Madhya Pradesh, India g8 129
Ratangarh, Rajasthan, India g6 129
Rätansbyn f1 156
Ratekau d5 158
Rath f7 124
Rath Nath c8 129
Rathangan e3 165
Rathbun Lake e3 260
Rathcormack c4 165
Rathdowney d4 165
Rathdrum e4 165
Rathedaung n9 125
Rathenow h3 173
Rathfriland e2 165
Rathkeale c4 165
Rathlin Island e1 165
Rathluirc c4 165
Rathmore b4 165
Rathwell d6 250
Rätikon b3 176
Ratingen e3 159
Ratitovec f3 177
Ratiya b5 130
Ratlam g9 129
Ratmanova, Ostrov b2 246
Ratnagiri c4 126
Ratnapura g9 126
Ratne n4 169
Rato Dero d7 129
Raton b4 261
Ratonneau, Île b7 185
Ratten g2 177
Rattosjärvi k3 155
Rattray Head g2 164
Rättvik f2 156
Ratz, Mount, Can. a3 248
Ratz, Mount, U.S.A. l4 247
Ratzeburg d5 158
Ratzeburger See f2 173
Rätzlingen g3 173
Raub b4 101
Raubling d2 176
Rauch h4 297
Rauco b3 296
Raudales de Malpaso h5 275
Raudanjoki l3 155
Raudanvesi l5 155
Raudhatain l7 137
Raudna l3 157
Raufarhöfn A 152
Raufoss d2 156
Raukumara Range f2 76
Raúl Leoni, Represa e2 285
Raul Soares g4 291
Rauma j2 157
Raumati e4 76
Rauna l4 157
Raundalselvi b2 156
Raupeljan b2 246
Raurimu e3 76
Rauris d2 176
Raurkela j8 125
Rausu Ad1 114
Raut, Monte g3 196
Rautalampi l5 155
Rautavaara m5 155
Rautavesi k2 157
Ravahere K 75
Ravänsar l4 137
Ravanusa c7 199
Rävar r6 137
Rava-Rus'ka m5 169
Ravasd f4 171
Ravča g1 198
Ravello d4 198
Ravels c3 159
Ravelsbach g1 177
Ravena g2 257
Ravenglass c2 162
Ravenna, Italy g5 196
Ravenna g5 197
Ravenoville d3 182
Ravensbourne Creek a4 84
Ravensburg e5 174
Ravenshoe g4 80
Ravensthorpe e13 87
Ravenswood h6 80
Ravi f5 128
Ravna Gora j4 177
Ravnina, Maryyskaya Oblast', Turk. a2 128
Ravnina, Maryyskaya Oblast', Turk. a1 128
Ravnina Dar'yalyktakyr k5 120
Ravshan k4 149
Rawa Aopa Watumohai National Park l7 99
Rawa Mazowiecka j4 169
Rāwah h5 209
Rawaki H 75
Rawala Kot a3 130
Rawalpindi f4 128
Rawāndiz k3 137
Rawang b4 101
Rawas b6 98
Rawatsar g6 129
Rawi, Ko a2 101
Rawicz e4 168
Rawka j4 169
Rawlinna g12 87
Rawlins b3 260
Rawlinson Range h9 87
Rawlinson, Mount h9 87
Rawson, Buenos Aires, Arg. g3 297
Rawson, Chubut, Arg. c4 295
Rawson Mountains x3 298
Rawu q5 125
Raxaul j6 125
Raxón, Cerro c3 276
Raxrujá b3 276
Ray b6 250
Ray, Cape n5 253
Raya f3 277
Raya, Bukit, Kalimantan Barat, Indon. g5 98
Raya, Bukit, Kalimantan Barat/Kalimantan Tengah, Indon. f5 98
Rayachoti f5 126
Rayadurg e5 126
Rayagada h3 127
Rayak e3 138
Rayen r7 137
Rayleigh g5 163
Raymond b2 262
Raymond Terrace k12 81
Raymondville a6 258
Raymore a5 250
Rayón, San Luis Potosí, Mex. e3 275
Rayón, Sonora, Mex. h11 263
Rayones j5 273
Rayong e9 103
Raystown Lake b4 256
Rayville d3 258
Raz, Pointe du a4 182
Razam h3 127
Razan m4 137
Razani e4 128
Ražanj e4 200
Razboj j4 177
Razdol d1 210
Razeh m5 137
Razgrad, Bul. h4 201
Razgrad h4 201
Razlog f5 201
Razmak d4 128
Rāznas m4 157
Ráztočno g3 171
Ré, Île de a2 186
Rea Brook d4 163
Rea, Lough c3 165
Reading, England, U.K. h2 162
Reading f5 163
Reading, Michigan, U.S.A. d5 254
Reading, Ohio, U.S.A. d6 254
Reading, Pennsylvania, U.S.A. e4 256
Real e4 288
Real Audiencia h4 297
Real de Padre d3 296
Realeza b6 290
Realicó e3 297
Réalmont e5 187
Reao K 75
Reardan e2 262
Reata j4 273
Reay e1 164
Rebaa f2 221
Rebbenesøy g1 154
Rebecca, Lake f12 87
Rébénacq b5 187
Rébenty e6 187
Rebollosa de Jadraque b3 192
Reboly n5 155
Rebordelo c3 190
Rebouças c6 290
Rebriha u1 121
Rebun Ab1 114
Rebun-tō Ab1 114
Recalde g4 297
Recanati c1 198
Recaş k6 171
Recco d5 197
Recey-sur-Ource a3 184
Recherche Archipelago Nature Reserve f14 87
Rechnitz h2 177
Recht e4 159
Rechytsa c1 148
Récif des Français F 74
Recife f3 288
Recife, Cape f7 235
Recinto b4 296
Recke c3 172
Recklinghausen f3 159
Recknitz h1 173
Rečnoj k2 151
Recoaro Terme f4 196
Reconquista e1 294
Recreio, Mato Grosso, Braz. f1 293
Recreio, Minas Gerais, Braz. g4 291
Recreo, Catamarca, Arg. c1 294
Recreo, Santa Fé, Arg. g1 297
Recsk j4 171
Rector d1 258
Recz d2 168
Reczno h4 169
Red, Can. e6 250
Red, U.S.A. c4 258
Red Bank, California, U.S.A. a1 264
Red Bank, New Jersey, U.S.A. f4 257
Red Bay p3 253
Red Bluff, Aust. d9 87
Red Bluff, U.S.A. a1 264
Red Cliffs f13 81
Red Cloud d3 260
Red Deer, Alberta, Can. l5 249
Red Deer, Alberta/Saskatchewan, Can. l6 249
Red Deer Lake s5 249
Red Devil e3 246
Red Hill e4 256
Red Hills d4 261
Red Hook g3 257
Red Idol Gorge j5 135
Red Indian Lake p4 253
Red Lake, Ontario, Can. g5 250
Red Lake, Can. g5 250
Red Lake, Minnesota, U.S.A. e1 260
Red Lake, Minnesota, U.S.A. f7 250
Red Lion d5 256
Red Lodge j3 262
Red Mountain f6 265
Red Oak e3 260
Red Peak g2 262
Red Rock, British Columbia, Can. f5 248
Red Rock, Can. j6 251
Red Rock, U.S.A. g3 262
Red Sea e3 219
Red Sucker Lake g3 250
Red Wine m2 253
Red Wing e2 260
Reda g1 168
Redang c3 101
Redange d5 159
Redberry Lake p5 249
Redbridge h2 162
Redcar e2 162
Redcar & Cleveland h1 162
Redcliff d2 233
Redcliffe l9 81
Redcliffe, Mount e11 87
Reddersburg g4 235
Redding b5 262
Redditch e4 163
Redefin e5 158
Redelinghuys c6 234
Redenção, Pará, Braz. b3 288
Redenção, Piauí, Braz. d3 288
Redeyef f2 221
Redfield d2 260
Redhill, Aust. d12 81
Redhill, U.K. f5 163
Rédics e5 170
Redkey d5 254
Redkino d3 150
Redlands e7 265
Redmond, Utah, U.S.A. h6 262
Redmond, Washington, U.S.A. b2 262
Rednitz g3 175
Redon c5 182
Redonda Island e6 248
Redondela b2 190
Redondo c6 191
Redondo Beach e8 265
Redruth a6 163
Redstone n2 247
Redvale a4 260
Redvers c6 250
Redwood City a4 264
Redwood Falls e2 260
Redwood National Park b5 262
Redwood Valley b5 262
Ree, Lough c3 165
Reed City d4 254
Reed Lake c3 250
Reedley d5 264
Reedsville c4 256
Reedy Creek a3 84
Reefton c5 77
Rees e3 159
Refahiye g3 209
Reform e3 258
Reforma, Chiapas, Mex. h5 275
Reforma, Oaxaca, Mex. g5 275
Refugio a5 258
Rega l1 173
Regaditos d5 274
Regalbuto d7 199
Regallo d3 192
Regen, Ger. h3 175
Regen e1 176
Regência j3 291
Regensburg h3 175
Regenstauf h3 175
Regent b7 250
Regente Feijó c5 290
Reggane e3 221
Regge e2 159
Reggello f6 197
Reggio di Calabria e6 199
Reggio di Calibria f6 199
Reggio Nell Emilia e5 196
Reggio nell'Emilia e5 196
Reggiolo e5 196
Reghin g2 201
Regi b4 128
Regina q6 249
Régina g3 285
Regina Beach a5 250
Registan b5 128
Registro e6 290
Regozero n4 155
Regstrup e3 158
Reguengo b2 190
Reguengos de Monsaraz c6 191
Regunungan Barisan a6 98
Rehau h2 175
Rehburg (Rehburg-Loccum) e3 172
Rehden d3 172
Rehlingen-Siersburg e5 159
Rehna e5 158
Rehoboth b1 234
Rehoboth Bay e6 256
Rehoboth Beach e6 256
Rehon d5 159
Rehovot c5 139
Rehra d5 130
Reiche Ebrach f3 175
Reicheia d6 211
Reichenau e5 174
Reichenau an der Rax g2 177
Reichenbach h2 175
Reichenbach (Oberlausitz) j1 175
Reichenfels f3 177
Reichenspitze d2 176
Reichertshausen g4 175
Reichertshofen g4 175
Reichraming f2 177
Reichshoffen d2 184
Reid j12 87
Reiden b2 196
Reidsville, Georgia, U.S.A. h3 259
Reidsville, North Carolina, U.S.A. g7 254
Reigate f5 163
Reillanne b7 185
Reillo c5 193
Re'im c5 139
Reims k3 183
Reina e6 191
Reina Adelaida, Archipiélago de la b6 295
Reinach, Aargau, Switz. c2 196
Reinach, Basellandschaft, Switz. b2 196
Reinbek d5 158
Reindeer Island e4 250
Reindeer Lake r3 249
Reine d3 154
Reinfeld (Holstein) d5 158
Reinga, Cape d1 76
Reinheim d3 174
Reinosa f2 190
Reinøy g2 154
Reinøya Naturreservat k1 155
Reins a4 185
Reinsfjellet a5 154
Reinsnosi b3 156
Reiphólsfjöll A 152
Reisa Nasjonalpark j2 155
Reisaelva h2 154
Reisbach h4 175
Reisjärvi k5 155
Reisterstown d5 256
Reitano d7 199
Reitz h3 235
Reivilo f3 234
Rejmyre f3 156
Rejowiec Fabryczny m4 169
Rejsby b3 158
Reka e5 170
Rékaréka K 75
Rekavice j5 177
Reken f3 159
Rekgwash c6 129
Reksjåeggi c2 156
Rėkyvos ežeras k5 157
Reliance h3 242
Religione, Punta d8 199
Relizane e1 221
Rellano g4 272
Relleu d6 193
Rellingen c5 158
Remada g2 221
Remagen f4 159
Rémalard f4 183
Remarkable, Mount c12 81
Rembang f8 98
Rembau c4 101
Remboutsadika f2 210
Remecó f4 297
Remedios, Punta c4 276
Remel el Abiod f2 221
Remels (Uplengen) c2 172
Remer g7 250
Remeskylä l5 155
Remich e5 159
Rémilly c1 184
Remington c6 256
Rémire g3 285
Remiremont c2 184
Remmel Mountain g7 248
Remolinos c3 192
Remoulins a7 185
Rempang d5 101
Rems e4 174
Remscheid f3 159
Rémuzat b6 185
Ren He a4 106
Rena, Nor. d2 156
Rena, Spain e5 191
Renaico a4 296
Renazé d5 182
Renca e2 296
Rencēni l4 157
Rench d4 174
Rencontre East q5 253
Rencun c1 106
Rend Lake b6 254
Renda k4 157
Rendsburg c4 158
Renedo g1 190
Renedo de la Vega f2 190
René-Levasseur, Île h3 252
Renens a3 196
Renews r5 253
Renfeng e1 111
Renfrew h3 255
Renfrewshire f3 164
Rengat b5 98
Renggam c5 101
Rengit c5 101
Rengo b3 296
Rengsdorf f4 159
Renheji d4 106
Renhua j6 105
Renhuai f5 104
Reni j3 201
Renick f7 254
Renko l2 157
Renmark e13 81
Renmin n2 113
Renner Springs a5 80
Rennerod d2 174
Rennes d4 182
Rennesøy a3 156
Rennie f6 250
Renningen d4 174
Rennweg e2 176
Reno, Italy g5 196
Reno, U.S.A. d2 264
Renòn f3 196
Renovo c3 256
Renqiu j6 113
Rensjön g2 154
Rensselaer, Indiana, U.S.A. c5 254
Rensselaer, New York, U.S.A. g2 257
Rentería c1 192
Rentina b3 210
Renton b2 262
Renuka c4 130
Renukut h7 125
Renwez c5 159
Renxian d1 106
Réo d3 222
Reo l9 99
Repartimento, Braz. d5 284
Repartimento, Amazonas, Braz. f4 285
Repembe e3 233
Repetek a1 128
Repki l3 169
Repojoki k2 155
Repolka n3 157
Reporoa f3 76
Reposaari j2 157
Reppenstedt f2 172
Republic, Missouri, U.S.A. c1 258
Republic, Washington, U.S.A. d1 262
Republican d4 260
Republika Srpska d4 200
Repulse Bay, Aust. c2 84
Repulse Bay, Can. m2 243
Repvåg k1 155
Requejada, Embalse de f2 190
Requena, Peru c5 284
Requena, Spain c5 193
Requinoa b3 296
Réquista e4 187
Reriutaba d2 288
Reşadıye j3 209
Reşadiye f2 209
Reşadiye Yarımadası a4 208
Resag, Gunung c7 98
Resen b1 210
Resenbro c2 158
Resende, Braz. f5 291
Resende c3 190
Reserva c6 290
Reshetylivka d2 148
Reshi b5 106
Resia, Lago di e3 196
Resistencia f5 293
Reşiţa e3 200
Resko d2 168
Resko Przymorskie, Jezioro d1 168
Resolute dd2 298
Resolute Bay l1 242
Resolution Island, Can. s3 243
Resolution Island, N.Z. a6 77
Resolven c5 163
Resort, Loch b1 164
Resplendor h3 291
Resskinskaja n3 147
Ressons-sur-Matz h3 183
Restigouche j5 253
Restinga Seca f1 294
Reston c6 250
Resuttano d7 199
Reszel k1 169
Retalhuleu b3 276
Retamito c2 296
Retaxo c5 191
Retem, Oued er e2 221
Retén Atalaya b2 296
Retén Llico a3 296
Retenue de la Lufira, Lac de e6 225
Retenue de Nangbéto e4 223
Retezat, Parcul Naţional f3 201
Retford f3 162
Rethel c5 159
Rethem (Aller) e3 172
Rethymno e7 211
Retiers d5 182
Retín d6 191
Retiro b4 296
Retortillo, Embalse de e7 191
Retournac a5 184
Rétság h4 171
Retuerta c3 192
Retz g1 177
Retz, Pays de d6 182
Reuden h3 173
Reuilly e1 186
Reumen a5 296
Reunión a4 296
Réunion B 231
Réunion (France) h7 217
Reus f3 192
Reusam, Pulau c14 103
Reusel d3 159
Reuss c3 196
Reuterstadt Stavenhagen h2 173
Reutlingen e4 174
Reutte b2 176
Reuver e3 159
Revda q3 155
Revel e5 187
Revellata, Pointe de la A 185
Revelstoke h6 248
Reventadero e2 275
Reventazón a5 284
Revermont b4 184
Révfülöp f5 171
Rèvia b6 227
Reviga h3 201
Revigny-sur-Ornain a2 184
Revilla del Campo g2 190
Revillagigedo Island l4 247
Revillagigedo, Islas d8 272
Revin c5 159
Revivim c5 139
Řevnice c2 170
Řevničov b1 170
Revolcadores b6 193
Revolyutsiya, Qullai f1 128
Revsbotn k1 155
Revsnes f2 154
Revsundssjön e5 154
Revúboè e2 233
Revúca j3 171
Rewa g7 124
Rewal d1 168
Rewari c5 130
Rex, Mount kk2 298
Rexton, Can. k5 253
Rexton, U.S.A. d2 254
Rey Bouba b2 224
Rey, Isla del h6 277
Reyes d2 292
Reyes Peak d7 265
Reyes, Point b7 263
Reykjahlíð A 152
Reykjanes A 152
Reykjanes Basin g3 302
Reykjanes Ridge h3 302
Reykjanestá A 152
Reykjavík, Ice. A 152
Reykjavík A 152
Reyno d1 258
Reynolds e7 250
Reynolds Range l8 86
Reynosa k4 273
Reyssouze b4 184
Rež, Russ. Fed. k4 147
Rež k4 147
Rezé d5 182
Rēzekne m4 157
Rezina j2 201
Rezinjski vrh f4 177
Rezovo j5 201
Rezvānshahr m3 137
Rezzato e4 196
Rharbi, Oued el e2 221
Rhayader c4 163
Rheda-Wiedenbrück d4 172
Rhede e3 159
Rhede (Ems) f1 159
Rheidol c4 163
Rhein, Can. b5 250
Rhein, Ger. e3 159
Rheinau c4 174
Rheinbach e4 159
Rheinberg e3 159
Rheine f2 159
Rheinfelden b2 196
Rheinhessen-Pfalz c3 174
Rheinland-Pfalz c3 174
Rheinsberg h2 173
Rheinstetten d4 174
Rhein-Taunus, Naturpark d2 174
Rheinwaldhorn d3 196
Rhein-Westerwald, Naturpark c2 174
Rhin d4 174
Rhinau d2 184
Rhine e3 159
Rhinebeck g3 257
Rhinelander b3 254
Rhinluch h3 173
Rhino Camp f3 225
Rhinow h3 173
Rhir, Cap b2 220
Rhisnes c4 159
Rho d4 196
Rhode Island j3 257
Rhodes Ad2 211
Rhodes Peak f2 262
Rhondda Cynon Taff c5 163
Rhône, Fr. a7 185
Rhône, Fr. a5 185
Rhône au Rhin, Canal du d2 184
Rhône-Alpes b5 185
Rhosllanerchrugog c3 162
Rhoufi f1 221
Rhuddlan c3 162
Rhue e3 186
Rhume f4 172
Rhuys, Presqu'île de c5 182
Rhyl c3 162
Rhynie f2 164
Ria de Aveiro b4 190
Riaba f5 223
Riace f6 199
Riachão c3 288
Riachão das Neves d4 288
Riacho de Santana d4 288
Riacho dos Machados g1 291
Riaguas g3 190
Riaillé d5 182
Rial b2 190
Rialma d1 290
Rialp f2 192
Riangnom e2 225
Riaño f2 190
Riaño, Embalse de f2 190
Rianópolis d1 290
Rians b7 185
Riansáres a5 193
Rianxo b2 190
Rias Altas a1 190
Rias Bajas a2 190
Riasi b3 130
Riau b4 98
Riau, Kepulauan c4 98
Riaza, Spain g3 190
Riaza g3 190
Riba de Saelices b4 192
Ribadavia b2 190
Ribadelago d2 190
Ribadeo c1 190
Ribadesella e1 190
Riba-roja, Pantà de e3 192
Ribas do Rio Pardo b4 290
Ribat d2 128
Ribatejo b5 191
Ribáuè b6 227
Ribble d3 162
Ribe, Den. b3 158
Ribe, Den. b3 158
Ribe b3 158
Ribeauvillé d2 184
Ribécourt-Dreslincourt a5 159
Ribeira, Braz. d6 290
Ribeira, Braz. d6 290
Ribeira, Port b3 190
Ribeira de Pena c3 190
Ribeirão Branco d6 290
Ribeirão das Neves f3 291
Ribeirão do Pinhal c5 290
Ribeirão Preto e4 290
Ribemont b5 159
Ribera c7 199
Ribera del Fresno d6 191
Ribérac c3 186
Ribes de Freser g2 192
Ribesalbes d4 193
Ribiers b6 185
Ribnica f4 177
Ribnitz-Damgarten f4 158
Ribnovo f5 201
Ribnyak Jezero h5 177
Rica Aventura d4 292
Ricadi e6 199
Říčany c2 170
Ricardo Flores Magón f3 272
Riccal f2 162
Riccia d3 198
Riccione g5 197
Rice a3 258
Rice Lake, Can. c6 253
Rice Lake, U.S.A. f2 260
Rich Square h7 255
Richan g5 250
Richard Toll a2 222
Richards b4 258
Richards Bay k4 235
Richards Inlet z3 298
Richardson, Can. m2 249
Richardson, U.S.A. a3 258
Richardson Mountains, Can. l2 247
Richardson Mountains, N.Z. b6 77
Richardson Peak c2 276
Richardton b7 250
Richelieu f5 183
Richer e6 250
Richfield, Idaho, U.S.A. f4 262
Richfield, Pennsylvania, U.S.A. c4 256
Richfield, Utah, U.S.A. g6 263
Richfield Springs f2 256
Richford, New York, U.S.A. d2 256
Richford, Vermont, U.S.A. f6 252
Richhill e2 165
Richland, Georgia, U.S.A. g3 259
Richland, Texas, U.S.A. a4 258
Richland, Washington, U.S.A. d2 262
Richland Center a4 254
Richlands f7 254
Richmond, Aust. k12 81
Richmond, Queensland, Aust. f6 80
Richmond, Aust. Ab3 83
Richmond, British Columbia, Can. b1 262
Richmond, Can. f6 252
Richmond, N.Z. d4 77
Richmond, R.S.A. j4 235
Richmond, R.S.A. e5 234
Richmond, U.K. e2 162
Richmond, Indiana, U.S.A. d6 254
Richmond, Kentucky, U.S.A. g1 259
Richmond, New York, U.S.A. k6 257
Richmond, Utah, U.S.A. h5 262
Richmond, Vermont, U.S.A. k3 255
Richmond, Virginia, U.S.A. h7 255
Richmond Heights j7 259
Richmond Hill g4 254
Richmond Range, Aust. e6 85
Richmond Range, N.Z. d4 77
Richmond, Mount d4 77
Richmond-Upon-Thames h3 162
Richmondville f2 256
Richtersveld National Park b4 234
Rickleån h4 154
Rickling d4 158
Ricla c3 192
Rico (U.S.A.), Puerto h7 241
Rico Trench, Puerto d7 302
Ricobayo, Embalse de e3 190
Riddes b3 196
Riddlesburg b4 256
Rideau e6 252
Rideau Lakes d6 252
Ridge l5 251
Ridgecrest f6 265
Ridgefield g3 257
Ridgeland j3 259
Ridgetown f4 254
Ridgway b3 256
Riding Mountain National Park c5 250
Ridingan, Bukit c7 98
Riebeek Wes c6 234
Riebeek-Oos g6 235
Riecito d1 284
Ried im Innkreis e1 176
Riedbergerhorn f5 174
Riedenburg g4 175
Riedlingen e4 174
Riegelsberg e5 159
Riegersburg g2 177
Riello e2 190
Rienza g3 196
Rieponlahti l5 155
Riesa j4 173
Riesco, Isla b6 295
Rieseby c4 158
Riesi d7 199
Rieste d3 172
Riestedt g4 173
Riet f4 235
Riet se Vloer d5 234
Rietavas j5 157
Rietberg d4 172
Rietbron e6 234
Rieti, Italy h7 197
Rieti g7 197
Rietkuil h3 235
Rietschen k4 173
Rietvlei j4 235
Rieumes d5 187
Rieupeyroux e4 187
Rieux d5 187
Rieux-Minervois e5 187
Riez c7 185
Rifaina e4 290
Rifstangi A 152
Rift Valley b3 226
Rīga l4 157
Riga, Gulf of k4 157
Rigacikun f3 223
Rigain Pünco h3 135
Rigaio c3 210
Rigby h4 262
Rignac e4 187
Rignano Flaminio g7 197
Rigolet n1 253
Rig-Rig g3 223
Riḩāb e4 139
Rihand h8 124
Riihimäki l2 157
Riisitunturin kansallispuisto m3 155
Riito f9 263
Rijau f3 223
Riječki Zaliv f4 177
Rijeka f4 177
Rijen c3 159
Rijl al Khallah a6 139
Rijssen e2 159
Rikā, Wādī ar f3 219
Rikkavesi m5 155
Riksgränsen g2 154
Rikuzen-takata j2 115
Rila f4 201
Rileyville b6 256
Rillieux-la-Pape a5 185
Rillito h9 263
Rillo d4 192
Rilly-la-Montagne k3 183
Rima f3 223
Rimatara K 75
Rimau, Pulau c6 98
Rimavská Sobota j3 171
Rimbo h3 157
Rimersburg a3 256
Rimetea f2 201
Rimforsa f3 156
Rimini, Italy g6 197
Rimini g5 197
Rimogne c5 159
Rimont d6 187
Rimouski h4 253
Rimpar e3 174
Rimsdale, Loch d1 164
Rinbung j5 135
Rinca k9 99
Rincão d4 290
Rinchnach e1 176
Rincon j3 259
Rincón de Cololó j2 297
Rincón de la Victoria f8 191
Rincón de la Vieja e5 276
Rincón de la Vieja, Parque Nacional e5 276
Rincón de los Sauces c4 296
Rincón de Palacio j2 297
Rincón de Romos c2 274
Rincón de Tamayo d3 274
Rincón del Atuel c3 296
Rincón del Pino j3 297
Rincón, Cerro del d4 292
Rinconada, Arg. d4 292
Rinconada, Mex. f4 275
Rinconada, Sierra de la f5 191
Rinda j4 157
Rindal b5 154
Rineia f5 211
Rinella d6 199
Ring Co j2 135
Ringarooma Ab2 83
Ringarooma Bay Ab2 83
Ringas b6 130
Ringaskiddy c5 165
Ringe d3 158
Ringebu d2 156
Ringelspitz d3 196
Ringim f3 223
Ringkøbing, Den. b2 158
Ringkøbing b2 158
Ringkøbing Fjord b3 158
Ringmer g6 163
Ringsön g3 156
Ringsted e3 158
Ringvassøy g2 154
Ringwood e6 163
Riñihue a5 296
Riñinahué a6 296
Rinjani National Park, Gunung j9 99
Rinjani, Gunung j9 99
Rinns of Galloway c5 164
Rinns Point b4 164
Rinópolis c4 290
Rinøyvåg e2 154
Rinteln e3 172
Rio b4 210
Rio Alegre f3 293
Rio Azul c6 290
Rio Bananal h3 291

Rouxville g5 235
Rouy f1 186
Rouyn g1 254
Rovaniemi k3 155
Rovasenda c4 196
Rovato e4 196
Rovereto f4 196
Roversi d1 294
Roverud e2 156
Roviano g7 197
Rovigo, Italy f4 196
Rovigo f4 196
Rovinari f3 201
Rovinj e4 176
Rovinka f3 170
Rovnoe g2 149
Rovubu National Park f4 225
Rów c3 168
Rowena j10 81
Rowland k2 259
Rowlands Gill e2 162
Rowley Island p2 243
Rowley Shoals d5 86
Roxa, Ilha a3 222
Roxas, Phil. d5 100
Roxas, Phil. b5 100
Roxas, Phil. c4 100
Roxas, Phil. d6 100
Roxas, Phil. c2 100
Roxboro g7 254
Roxborough Downs d7 80
Roxburgh b6 77
Roxen f3 156
Roxie d4 258
Roxo b7 191
Roxo, Barragem do c7 191
Roxo, Cabo a3 222
Roy,
New Mexico, U.S.A. b5 261
Roy, Utah, U.S.A. g5 262
Roy Hill d8 86
Royal Canal d3 165
Royal Chitwan National
Park j6 125
Royal Natal National
Park h4 235
Royal National Park g2 83
Royal Oak,
Maryland, U.S.A. d6 256
Royal Oak,
Michigan, U.S.A. e4 254
Royan a3 186
Royat f3 186
Roye a5 159
Royère-de-Vassivière d3 186
Røyrvik d4 154
Royston f4 163
Royston, U.S.A. h2 259
Rožaje e4 200
Różan k3 169
Rozavlea g2 201
Rozay-en-Brie h4 183
Rožďalovice d1 170
Roždestveno,
Jaroslavskaja Oblast',
Russ. Fed. d3 150
Roždestveno,
Tverskaja Oblast',
Russ. Fed. d3 150
Rozdil'na k2 201
Rozdol'ne d3 148
Rozel c3 182
Rozhdestvenka n2 121
Rozhniv g1 201
Rozivka e3 148
Rożki l3 151
Rožňava j3 171
Rožnov pod
Radhoštěm g2 171
Rożnów j6 169
Rożnowskie,
Jezioro j6 169
Rozoga k2 169
Rozogi k2 169
Rozoy-sur-Serre c5 159
Roztoczański Park
Narodowy l5 169
Roztoka Wielka j6 169
Roztoky, Středočeský
kraj, Czech Rep. b1 170
Roztoky, Středočeský
kraj, Czech Rep. c1 170
Rozveh n5 137
Rozzano d4 196
Rrëshen d5 200
Rrogozhinë d5 200
Rtiščevo f1 149
Ru b1 190
Rua c4 190
Rua, Tanjung k9 137
Ruabon c4 162
Ruacana a2 232
Ruaha National Park f5 225
Ruahine Forest Park e3 76
Ruahine Range f3 76
Ruakaka e1 76
Ruanda a6 227
Ruang n3 99
Ruapehu, Mount e3 76
Ruapuke Island b7 77
Ruatangata e1 76
Ruatapu c5 77
Ruatoria g2 76
Rub' al Khālī g4 219
Rubano, Veneto, Italy f4 196
Rubayo g1 190
Rubbestadneset a3 156
Rubcovsk t2 121
Rubelita g2 291
Rubén Figueroa d5 274
Rubena g2 190
Rubeshibe Ac2 114
Rubha Ardvule a2 164
Rubha nan Leacan b4 164
Rubi, D.R.C. e3 225
Rubi e3 225
Rubiácea c4 290
Rubielos de Mora d4 193
Rubim h2 291
Rubinéia c4 290
Rubizhne e2 148
Rubondo
National Park f4 225
Ruby,
Alaska, U.S.A. f2 246
Ruby,
New York, U.S.A. g2 257
Ruby Dome f5 262
Rubyvale b3 84
Rucanelo e4 296
Rucăr g3 201
Rucava j4 157
Rucheng j6 105
Ruciane-Nida k2 169
Ruckersville b6 256
Ruda g5 168
Ruda Maleniecka j4 169
Ruda Śląska g5 168
Rudall River
National Park f8 86
Rudarpur h6 125
Rudbar a5 128
Rūdbār m3 137
Rūd-e Kor p6 137
Rūd-e Mand p7 137
Rudersdorf h2 177
Rüdersdorf Berlin j3 173
Rüdesheim c3 174
Rudice h5 177
Rūd-i-Shur r6 137
Rūdiškės n1 169
Rudkøbing d4 158
Rudná c1 170
Rudna e4 168
Rudne m6 169
Rudnichnyy s5 121
Rudničnyj, Kirovskaja
Oblast', Russ. Fed. m2 151
Rudničnyj, Sverdlovskaja
Oblast', Russ. Fed. k4 147
Rudnik nad Sanem l5 169
Rudniki g4 168
Rudnja c1 148
Rudnytsya j1 201
Rudnyy j1 120
Rudo d4 200
Rudolfo Iselin c3 296
Rudolfov f1 177
Rudolstadt g2 175
Rudong,
Guangdong, China h8 104
Rudong,
Jiangsu, China g3 111
Rudovka g5 151
Rudozem e1 210
Rudraprayag d4 130
Rudrón g2 190
Ruds Vedby e3 158
Rūdsar n3 137
Rudyard,
Michigan, U.S.A. d2 254
Rudyard,
Montana, U.S.A. h1 262
Rue g2 183
Ruecas e5 191
Rueda f3 190
Rueda de Jalón c3 192
Ruelle-sur-Touvre c3 186
Ruenya e2 233
Rufa'a d5 218
Ruffano c3 199
Ruffec c2 186
Ruffieu b4 185
Ruffieux b5 185
Rufiji g5 225
Rufino f3 297
Rufisque a3 222
Rufunsa d2 233
Rugāji m4 157
Rugao g3 111
Rugby, U.K. e4 163
Rugby, U.S.A. c6 250
Rugeley e4 162
Rugged Mountain d6 248
Rugles f4 183
Ruhengeri e4 225
Ruhla f2 174
Ruhland j4 173
Ruhnu k4 157
Ruhpolding d2 176
Ruhr b4 172
Ruhudji g5 225
Rui'an n5 105
Ruichang d5 106
Ruicheng b2 106
Ruidera b6 193
Ruidoso b5 261
Ruijin k6 105
Ruinas Aa3 198
Ruinen e2 159
Ruipa b5 227
Ruiz b3 274
Ruiz Cortines e2 275
Ruiz, Nevado del b2 284
Rujaylah, Ḩarrat ar f5 136
Rūjiena l4 157
Ruk d7 129
Rukanpur f6 129
Rukatunturi m3 155
Ruki c4 224
Rukungiri e4 225
Rukuwa n7 99
Rukwa f5 225
Rukwa, Lake f5 225
Rūl Ḑadnah r9 137
Rulbo f2 156
Ruleville d3 258
Rulhieres, Cape h3 86
Rum e4 170
Rum, U.K. b2 164
Rum, U.S.A. e2 260
Rum Cay g3 266
Rum Jungle k3 86
Ruma d3 200
Ruma National Park a4 225
Rumāh l9 137
Rumahtinggih l7 97
Rumayn f4 219
Rumbalara b8 81
Rumbek e2 225
Rumblar,
Embalse del g6 191
Rumburk c1 170
Rumford g6 252
Rumia g1 168
Rumigny c5 159
Rumilly b5 185
Rummukkala n1 157
Rumney c5 163
Rumoi Ab2 114
Rumonge e4 225
Rumont b2 184
Rumphi a6 231
Rumst c3 159
Rumula g4 80
Rumuruti b3 226
Runan d3 106
Runanga c5 77
Runaway, Cape f2 76
Runcorn d3 162
Runcu f3 201
Runde a1 156
Runde, Zimb. e3 233
Rundēni m4 157
Rundenigale
Reservoir A 127
Rundhaug g2 154
Rundu b2 232
Rundvik g5 154
Rungu e3 225
Rungwa, Tan. f5 225
Rungwa,
Rukwa, Tan. f5 225
Rungwa,
Singida, Tan. a5 231
Rungwa
Game Reserve f5 225
Runheji e3 111
Rūnīz-e Bālā p7 137
Runkauksen
luonnonpuisto k3 155
Runkel d2 174
Runmarö h3 157
Runn f2 156
Runton Range f8 87
Ruokolahti n2 157
Ruoms a6 185
Ruoqiang f2 122
Ruotsalainen l2 157
Ruovesi, Fin. l2 157
Ruovesi l2 157
Ruoxi d5 106
Rupa n6 125
Rupanyup f14 81
Rupat a4 98
Rupea g2 201
Rupert, Can. p5 251
Rupert, U.S.A. f7 254
Rupert Bay p5 251
Rupert Coast cc2 298
Rupnagar g7 129
Ruponda b6 227
Rupshu d3 130
Rupt-sur-Moselle c3 184
Rupununi f3 285
Rur b5 172
Rural Retreat f7 254
Rurrenabaque d2 292
Rurutu K 75
Rus b5 193
Rusape e2 233
Ruscova g2 201
Ruse, Bul. g4 201
Ruse g4 201
Rusenski Lom h4 201
Rusenski Lom,
Naroden Park h4 201
Rusețu h3 201
Ruševo j4 177
Rush e3 165
Rushan g1 111
Rushankou g1 111
Rushden f4 163
Rushinga e2 233
Rushon e1 128
Rushui He d8 112
Rushville,
Illinois, U.S.A. a5 254
Rushville,
Indiana, U.S.A. d6 254
Rushville,
Nebraska, U.S.A. c3 260
Rusinowo e2 168
Rusk b4 258
Ruskele g4 154
Rusken f4 156
Ruskin b5 185
Ruskington f3 162
Rusnė j5 157
Rušonu ezers m4 157
Russas e2 288
Rußbach h1 177
Russell, Can. c5 250
Russell, N.Z. e1 76
Russell, Kansas, U.S.A. d4 260
Russell,
Pennsylvania, U.S.A. a3 256
Russell Island k1 242
Russell Lake, Northwest
Territories, Can. q3 249
Russell Lake,
Saskatchewan, Can. c2 250
Russell Range f13 87
Russell Springs g1 259
Russellville, Alabama, U.S.A. f2 258
Russellville, Arkansas, U.S.A. c2 258
Russelsheim d2 174
Russfjärden e5 154
Russi g5 197
Russian a3 264
Russian Federation g2 93

RUSSIA

THE RUSSIAN FEDERATION
Area 17,075,400km² (6,592,850sq miles)
Capital Moscow
Organizations BSEC, CE, CIS, EBRD, G8, APEC
Population 144,080,000
Pop. growth (%) -0.2
Life expectancy 60 (m); 72 (f)
Languages Russian, Tatar, Yakut, Chuvash, Bashkir and others
Literacy 99.6%
Currency Russian rouble (US $1 = 29.4 Russian rouble)
GDP (US million $) 343,000
GDP per head ($US) 2380

Russian Mission d3 246
Russkaja-Poljana p1 121
Russkij Zavorot,
Poluostrov h1 147
Russkij, Ostrov s4 113
Rust h2 177
Rust'avi g4 149
Rustburg g7 254
Rustenburg g2 235
Rustenburg Nature
Reserve g2 235
Ruston c3 258
Ruszów d4 168
Rutana e4 225
Rute f7 191
Ruteng l9 99
Rutenga e3 233
Rüthen d4 172
Rutherfordton j2 259
Ruthin c3 162
Rüti c2 196
Ruti Dam e2 233
Rutigliano g3 198
Rutino e4 198
Rutka j3 151
Rutka Tartak l1 169
Rutki-Kossaki l2 169
Rutland, U.K. f4 163
Rutland, U.S.A. k4 255
Rutland Island n7 127
Rutland Plains e3 80
Rutland Water f4 162
Rutledge h1 259
Rutog n5 125
Rutög d3 130
Rutshuru e4 225
Rutter f2 254
Rutul g4 149
Ruukki k4 155
Ruunaanjärvi n5 155
Ruurlo e2 159
Ruuvaoja m3 155
Ruvaslahti m5 155
Ruvo di Puglia f3 198
Ruvuma, Moz. g6 225
Ruvuma, Tan. g6 225
Ruwaydah k9 137
Ruwer b3 174
Ruya e2 233
Ruyang c2 106
Ruynes-en-Margeride f3 186
Ruza d4 150
Ruzajevka h4 151
Ruzayevka l1 120
Ruzhany n3 169
Ruzhou c2 106
Ružomberok h2 171
Ruzsa h5 171
Rwanda e5 217

RWANDA

THE RWANDESE REPUBLIC
Area 26,338km² (10,169sq miles)
Capital Kigali
Organizations COMESA, CEEAC
Population 8,270,000
Pop. growth (%) 8
Life expectancy 38 (m); 40 (f)
Languages French, English, Kinyarwanda, Kiswahili
Literacy 70.4%
Currency Rwandan franc (US $1 = 556.55 Rwandan franc)
GDP (US million $) 1800
GDP per head ($US) 217

Rwenzori Mountains
National Park e3 225
Ry c2 158
Ryå c1 158
Ryābād q3 137
Ryan a2 258
Ryan, Loch d5 164
Rybach'ye t4 121
Rybačij j5 157
Rybinsk e2 150
Rybinskoe
Vodohranilišče e2 150
Rybkino g4 151
Rybnaja Vataga l3 151
Rybnik g5 168
Rybno k2 169
Rybnoe e4 150
Ryboły m3 169
Rychliki h2 169
Rychnov nad Kněžnou e1 170
Rychtal f4 168
Rychwał g3 168
Ryck j1 173
Ryd f4 156
Rydaholm f4 156
Ryde e6 163
Rydet f1 158
Rydułtowy g5 168
Rydzyna e4 168
Rye, England, U.K. e2 162
Rye, U.K. g6 163
Rye, U.S.A. g4 257
Rye Bay g6 163
Rye Beach k2 257
Rye Patch Reservoir d5 262
Ryegate j2 262
Ryes e3 182
Ryfylke a3 156
Rygge d3 156
Rygnestad b3 156
Ryiwegaise e4 154
Rykhta b1 201
Ryki k4 169
Rylstone j12 81
Rymań d2 168
Rymanów k6 169
Rýmařov f2 170
Ryn k2 169
Ryn-Peski b4 120
Ryökäsvesi m2 157
Ryomgård d2 158
Ryōtsu h2 115
Rypin h2 169
Ryslinge d3 158
Rytel f2 168
Rytterknægten A 158
Ryūgasaki j4 115
Ryukyu Islands B 115
Ryukyu Trench g4 300
Ržaksa f1 149
Ržanovo a1 210
Rzeczyca j4 169
Rzepin c3 168
Rzesznikowo d2 168
Rzeszów l5 169
Ržev c3 150

S

S'Arenal g5 193
S'Espalmador f6 193
S'Espardell f6 193
Sa Cabaneta g5 193
Sa Conillera f5 193
Sa Creu, Punta de f6 193
Sa Đec g10 103
Sa Dragonera g5 193
Sa Huynh j8 103
Sa Keo e9 103
Sa Mola, Cap de g5 193
Sa Pobla h5 193
Sa'gya h5 135
Sa'indezh l3 137
Sa'ābād r4 137
Saacow c3 226
Sa'ad c5 139
Sa'ādah al Barşā' e7 139
Sa'ādatābād, Fārs, Iran p6 137
Sääksjärvi k2 157
Saal an der Donau g4 175
Saalach h5 175
Saalbach d3 174
Saalbach-Hinterglemm d2 176
Saale g4 173
Saales d2 184
Saalfeld g2 175
Saalfelden am Steinernen
Meer d2 176
Saana h2 154
Saâne c5 185
Saane b3 196
Saanen b3 196
Saanijärvi k5 155
Saar b3 174
Saarbrücken b2 174
Saarburg e5 159
Sääre k4 157
Saaremaa k3 157
Saarenkylä k3 155
Saar-Hunsrück,
Naturpark b4 174
Saarijärvi k5 155
Saariselkä l2 155
Saarland b3 174
Saarlouis e5 159
Saas Fee b3 196
Saatlı h5 149
Saavedra f4 297
Sab'atayn, Ramlat as g4 219
Saba e2 219
Saba'a a6 139
Šabac d3 200
Sabadell g3 192
Sabae g4 115
Sabah j2 99
Sabak b4 101
Sabak, Cape Aa1 247
Sabalana k8 99
Sabalana, Kepulauan j8 99
Sabalgarh e6 124
Sabamagrande d4 276
Saban d2 284
Sabana de Barriolo k5 271
Sabana de la Mar k5 271
Sabana Grande A 270
Sabana, Archipiélago de d3 266
Sabanalarga k5 277
Sabancuy b1 276
Sabaneta j5 271
Sabaneta, Puntan A 74
Sabang, Aceh, Indon. b13 103
Sabang, Irian Jaya, Indon. k6 97
Sabang, Sulawesi
Selatan, Indon. l6 99
Sabang, Sulawesi
Tengah, Indon. k4 99
Sabanilla a2 276
Sabano c4 284
Şabanözü d2 208
Săbăoani h2 201
Sabará g3 291
Sabaragamuwa A 127
Sabari g3 126
Sabaru k8 99
Sabastiya d4 139
Sabathu c4 130
Sabaudia c3 198
Sabaya d3 292
Şabāyā Island f4 219
Sabbionetta e5 196
Şabbūrah e3 138
Saberania k6 97
Sabero e2 190
Şabḩā e4 139
Sabhā g3 221
Sabhrai d9 129
Sabie, Moz. k2 235
Sabie, Moz. k2 235
Sabie, R.S.A. j2 235
Sabile k4 157
Sabina e6 254
Sabinal f2 272
Sabinal, Cayo f4 266
Sabiñánigo d2 192
Sabinar, Punta a8 193
Sabinar, Punta del b8 193
Sabinas, Mex. j4 273
Sabinas, Coahuila, Mex. j4 273
Sabinas Hidalgo j4 273
Sabine Lake c5 258
Sabine National Wildlife
Refuge e6 261
Sabini, Monti g7 197
Sabinópolis g3 291
Sabinosa Aa3 189
Sabinov k2 171
Sabiote a6 193
Sabirabad h4 149
Sabiwa d3 233
Sablayan c4 100
Sable Island n7 253
Sable Island, Cape ki7 253
Sable, Cape, Can. k7 253
Sable, Cape, U.S.A. j7 259
Sable, Lac du j1 253
Sablé-sur-Sarthe e5 182
Sablon, Pointe du a7 185
Sabnie l3 169
Saboeiro e3 288
Sabon Kafi f3 223
Sabou d3 222
Sabrātah g2 221
Sabres b4 187
Sabrina Coast t1 298
Sabro d2 158
Sabrosa c3 190
Sabtang c1 100
Sabugal c4 190
Şabulu l5 99
Şabury j2 151
Şabyā f4 219
Sabzevār r3 137
Sacaca d3 292
Săcălaz k6 171
Sacandica c5 224
Sacanta f1 297
Sacco c3 198
Sacecorbo b4 192
Sacedón b4 192
Săcel g2 201
Săcele, Brașov, Rom. g3 201
Săcele,
Constanța, Rom. j3 201
Săceni g3 201
Saceruela f6 191
Sach Pass c3 130
Sachanga c6 224
Sachigo h3 250
Sachigo Lake h4 250
Sachs Harbour, Can. n1 247
Sachsen j4 173
Sachsen-Anhalt g4 173
Sächsische Schweiz,
Nationalpark k5 173
Şacile g4 196
Šack f4 150
Sackets Harbor h4 255
Saco, Maine, U.S.A. g7 252
Saco, Montana, U.S.A. p7 249
Sacol c8 100
Sacramento, Braz. e3 290
Sacramento,
California, U.S.A. b3 264
Sacramento,
California, U.S.A. b3 264
Sacramento Mountains b5 261
Sacramento Valley b2 264
Sacratif, Cabo g8 191
Săcueni l4 171
Sad Istragh f2 128
Sada, R.S.A. g6 235
Sada, Spain b1 190
Sádaba c2 192
Sadabad d6 130
Sa'dābād n7 137
Şadad e2 138
Şa'dah f4 219
Sadang k6 99
Sadao b2 101
Sadd as Sulṭānī e5 139
Sadd Qādisīyah j5 209
Sadda e4 128
Saddat al Hindiyah k5 137
Saddle Peak n6 127
Saddleback Mesa c5 261
Sadêng p4 125
Sadhaura c4 130
Sadi g2 225
Sadiola b3 222
Sadiqabad e6 129
Sadiya p6 125
Sad-Kharv r3 137
Sado e2 219
Sadoga-shima h2 115
Sadon k1 209
Sadovoe g3 149
Sadra f9 129
Sadri f8 129
Şadrino j2 151
Şadrinsk k4 147
Sadská c1 170
Sadulshahar g6 129
Sadût c5 139
Sädvaluspen f3 154
Sæby d1 158
Saelices b5 193
Saelices de la Sal b4 192
Saelices de Mayorga e2 190
Saerbeck c3 172
Særslev d3 158
Saeul d5 159
Safakulevo k5 147
Safara c6 191
Safed Koh e3 128
Saffānīyah, Ra's as g2 219
Säffle e3 156
Safford j9 263
Saffron Walden g4 163
Safi c2 220
Safiabad r3 137
Safid m3 137
Safid Dasht m5 137
Safidon c5 130
Safiras, Serra das h3 291
Şāfītā e2 138
Safonovo b4 150
Safranbolu d2 208
Safwān l6 137
Sag Harbor h4 257
Saga, China g5 135
Saga, Japan d5 114
Saga, Kaz. k2 120
Sagaba d6 224
Sagae j2 115
Sagaing, Myan. b4 102
Sagaing b5 102
Sagamihara h4 115
Sagami-nada h4 115
Sagami-wan h4 115
Sagamore,
Massachusetts, U.S.A. k3 257
Sagamore,
Pennsylvania, U.S.A. a4 256
Sagamoso c2 284
Sagamu e4 223
Saganthit Kyun d9 103
Sagar, Karnataka, India d5 126
Sagar, Madhya Pradesh,
India f8 124
Sagar Island l9 125
Sagard j1 173
Sagarejo g4 149
Sagarmatha
National Park k6 125
Sagavanirktok g1 247
Sage Creek h1 262
Sagelvvatnet g2 154
Sagfjorden e3 154
Saggat f3 154
Saghand q5 137
Saghar a4 128
Saghbine d3 138
Sagiada a3 210
Sagileru f5 126
Saginaw e4 254
Sagiz j2 149
Sagleipie c4 222
Sagone A 185
Sagone, Golfe de A 185
Sagra b7 193
Sagrada Familia b3 296
Sagres b7 191
Sagthale g9 129
Sagu m9 99
Sagua de Tánamo g4 266
Sagua la Grande d3 266
Saguache b4 260
Saguaro National Park h9 263
Saguenay g5 252
Sagunto d5 193
Ságvár g5 171
Sagwara g9 129
Sagyndyk, Mys c6 120
Sagyz d3 120
Saha (Jakutija),
Respublika n3 119
Saḩāb e5 139
Sahabab d5 130
Saḩābah, Jabal b6 139
Sahagún, Col. k6 277
Sahagún, Mex. e4 275
Sahagún e2 190
Sahalin l2 94
Sahalinskaja Oblast' l2 94
Saham d4 138
Saham al Jawlān d4 138
Sahand, Kūh-e l3 137
Sahara, Afr. e2 223
Sahara g8 129
Sahara Well f7 86
Saharanpur c5 130
Saharsa k7 125
Sahaswan d5 130
Şahbuz k2 137
Sahel,
Réserve Partielle du d3 222
Sahibganj k7 125
Şahin h5 201
Sahiwal, Punjab, Pak. f5 128
Sahl al Maţrān g8 136
Şahnāyā e3 138
Şahneh l4 137
Šahovskaja c3 150
Šahty f3 148
Sahuaripa e3 272
Sahuayo c3 274
Šahun'ja j3 151
Šahy g3 171
Sahyadriparvat Range e9 124
Sai h7 124
Sai Buri b2 101
Sai Dao Tai, Khao e9 103
Sai Island d3 218
Saïda, Alg. e2 221
Saïda, Leb. d3 138
Sa'īdī a7 129
Saidpur, Bang. l7 125
Saidpur, India h7 125
Saidu f3 128
Saignes e3 186
Saignon b7 185
Saigō e3 114
Saigon h10 103
Saiha n8 125
Saihan Toroi a5 112
Saijō e5 114
Saikai National Park c5 114
Saikanosy Masoala Ac2 233
Saillans b6 185
Sailolof j6 97
Saima n5 113
Saimaa n2 157
Saimaankanava n2 157
Saimbeyli f3 209
Sain Alto c2 274
Sainsoubou b3 222
Sains-Richaumont b5 159
Saint b7 254
St Abb's Head f4 164
Sainte Agathe e6 250
Saintes b3 186
Saintes, Îles des C 271
St Agnes A 163
St Albans k3 255
St Aldhelm's Head d6 163
St-Alexandre h5 252
St-Alexis-des-Monts f5 252
Saint-André C 231
St Andrew, Barb. H 271
St Andrew, Jam. B 266
St Andrews, Can. j6 253
St Andrews, U.S.A. k3 259
St Andrew Sound j4 259
St-Angel e3 186
St Ann B 266
St Ann's Bay B 270
St-Anselme g5 252
St Anthony q3 253
St-Antoine k5 253
Sainte Anne e6 250
Sainte Anne, Lac k5 249
St-Augustin n3 253
St Augustine j5 259
St Austell Bay b6 163
St-Ay g5 183
St-Aygulf c7 185
St Barbe p3 253
St-Barthélemy-d'Anjou e5 182
St-Barthélemy n6 267
St-Barthélemy, Pic de d6 187
St Bathans, Mount b6 77
St-Bauzille-de-Putois f5 187
St-Béat c6 187
St-Beauzély e4 187
St Bees Head c2 162
St-Benin-d'Azy f1 186
Saint-Benoît C 231
St-Benoît-du-Sault d2 186
St-Béron b5 185
St-Blaise a2 196
St-Blin-Semilly b2 184
St-Bonnet-de-Joux a4 184
St-Bonnet-en-Champsaur c6 185
St Brendan's r4 253
St-Brevin-les-Pins c5 182
St-Brice-en-Coglès d4 182
St Bride's Bay a5 163
St-Brieuc c4 182
St-Brieuc, Baie de c4 182
St-Broing-les-Moines a3 184
St-Calais f5 183
St-Cannat b7 185
St-Cast-le-Guildo c4 182
St Catharines g4 254
St Catherine B 266
St Catherine, Mount p8 271
St Catherine Reserve d2 218
St Catherine's Point e6 163
St-Céré d4 186
St-Cernin e3 186
St-Chamarand d4 186
St-Chamas b7 185
St-Chamond a5 185
St-Chaptes a7 185
St Charles, Illinois, U.S.A. b5 254
St Charles,
Maryland, U.S.A. d6 256
St Charles, Michigan, U.S.A. d4 254
St Charles, Missouri, U.S.A. a6 254
St-Chély-d'Apcher f4 186
St-Chély-d'Aubrac e4 186
St-Chinian e5 187
St Christoffelberg d1 284
St-Christol-lès-Alès a6 184
St-Christophe-en-Bazelle g5 183
St-Ciers-sur-Gironde b3 186
St Clair, Michigan, U.S.A. e4 254
St Clair,
Pennsylvania, U.S.A. d4 256
St Clair, Lake a7 252
St Clair Shores e4 254
St-Clair-sur-Epte g3 183
St-Clair-sur-l'Elle d3 182
St Clairsville f5 254
St-Clar c5 187
St-Claud c3 186
St-Claude b4 184
St Cloud, Florida, U.S.A. j5 259
St Cloud,
Minnesota, U.S.A. e2 260
St-Cosme-en-Vairais f4 183
St Croix Falls e2 260
St Croix e2 260
St-Cyprien d4 186
St-Cyr-l'École h4 183
St-Cyr-sur-Loire f5 183
St David, Arizona, U.S.A. h10 263
St David, Illinois, U.S.A. a5 254
St David's Head a5 163
Saint-Denis C 231
St-Denis, Île-de-France, Fr. h4 183
St-Denis, Languedoc-
Roussillon, Fr. e5 187
St-Denis-de-l'Hôtel h5 183
St-Denis-d'Orques e4 182
St-Denis-en-Bugey b5 185
St-Denis-sur-Sarthon e4 182
St-Dié c2 184
St-Dizier a2 184
St-Donat-sur-l'Herbasse a5 185
St-Doulchard e1 186
Ste-Agathe-des-Monts j2 255
Ste-Alvère c4 186
Ste-Anne-d'Auray c5 182
Ste-Anne-de-Beaupré g5 252
Ste-Anne-du-Lac j2 255
Ste-Anne, Lac h3 253
Ste-Catherine, Pointe a4 224
Ste-Croix, Can. g5 252
Ste-Croix, Switz. a3 196
Ste-Croix, Lac de c7 185
Steelport j2 235
Ste-Engrâce b5 187
Ste-Félicité j4 253
Ste-Foy g5 252
Ste-Foy-la-Grande c4 186
Ste-Foy-Tarentaise c5 185
Ste-Geneviève-sur-Argence e4 186
Ste-Hélène b4 186
Ste-Hermine d6 182
Ste-Julienne k3 255
St Elias, Cape h4 247
St Elias Mountains k3 247
St Élie g3 285
St Elizabeth B 266
Ste-Lucie-de-Tallano A 185
Ste-Marguerite j3 253
Ste-Marie J 271
Ste-Marie-aux-Mines d2 184
Ste-Maure-de-Touraine f5 183
Ste-Maxime c7 185
Ste-Menehould a1 184
Ste-Mère-Église d3 182
Ste-Rose C 271
Ste-Savine k4 183
Ste-Sévère-sur-Indre e2 186
Ste-Sigolène a5 185
Stes-Maries-de-la-Mer a7 185
Ste-Suzanne e4 182
Ste-Thorette e1 186
St-Étienne a5 185
St-Étienne-de-Baïgorry a5 187
St-Étienne-de-St-Geoirs b5 185
St-Étienne-de-Tinée c6 185
St-Étienne-du-Rouvray g3 183
St-Étienne-en-Dévoluy b6 185
St-Étienne-les-Orgues b6 185
Ste-Tulle b7 185
St-Eustache k3 255
St Eustatius n6 267
St-Fargeau j5 183

St-Félicien → Samro, Ozero 377

St-Félicien, Can. f4 252
St-Félicien, Fr. a5 185
Saintfield f2 1
St-Firmin c6 185
St-Florent A 185
St-Florent, Golfe de A 185
St-Florentin j4 183
St-Florent-le-Vieil d5 182
St-Florent-sur-Cher e2 186
St Floris, Parc National d2 224
St-Flour f3 186
St-Fons a5 185
St Francesville d4 258
St Francis c4 260
St Francis, Cape, Can. q5 253
St Francis, Cape, R.S.A. f7 234
St Francis Isles a12 81
St Francis d2 258
St-François C 271
St-François, Lac g6 252
St-François f6 252
St-Fulgent d6 182
St-Gabriel f5 252
St-Gabriel-de-Rimouski h4 253
St-Galmier a5 185
St-Gaudens c5 187
St-Gaultier d2 186
St-Gein b5 187
St-Gély-du-Fesc, Languedoc-Roussillon, Fr. f5 187
St-Geniez-d'Olt e4 187
St-Genis-de-Saintonge b3 186
St-Genis-Laval a5 185
St-Genis-Pouilly c4 184
St-Genix-sur-Guiers b5 185
St-Geoire-en-Valdaine b5 185
St George, Can. j6 253
St George, South Carolina, U.S.A. j3 259
St George, Utah, U.S.A. g7 263
St George Head g2 83
St George Island, U.S.A. g5 259
St George Island, Alaska, U.S.A b4 246
St-Georges, Can. g5 252
St-Georges, Fr. c2 184
St-Georges, Fr. Gu. g3 285
St George's G 271
St George's Bay, Newfoundland and Labrador, Can. m6 253
St George's Bay, Nova Scotia, Can. n4 253
St George's Cay d2 276
St George's Channel f4 165
St-Georges-de-Didonne b3 186
St-Georges-lès-Baillargeaux c2 186
St-Georges-sur-Loire e5 182
St-Geours-de-Maremne a5 187
St-Germain-de-la-Coudre f4 183
St-Germain-des-Fossés f2 186
St-Germain-du-Bois b4 184
St-Germain-du-Puy e1 186
St-Germain-du-Teil f4 187
St-Germain-en-Laye h4 183
St-Germain-Lembron f3 186
St-Germain-les-Belles d3 186
St-Germain-l'Herm f3 186
St-Germain-sur-Ay d3 182
St-Gervais-d'Auvergne e2 186
St-Gervais-sur-Mare f5 187
St-Géry d4 187
St-Gildas-des-Bois c5 182
St-Gildas, Pointe de c5 182
St-Gilles a7 185
St-Gilles-Croix-de-Vie d6 182
St-Girons d6 187
St-Girons-Plage a5 187
St Govan's Head b5 163
St-Guénolé a5 182
St-Haon-le-Châtel f2 186
St Helena (U.K.) b6 217
St Helena Bay c6 234
St Helena Fracture Zone j11 302
St Helena, Mount a3 264
St Helens h1 162
St Helens, Mount b2 262
St Helens Point Ac2 83
St-Hilaire e5 187
St-Hilaire-de-Riez d6 182
St-Hilaire-de-Villefranche b3 186
St-Hilaire-du-Harcouët d4 182
St-Hilaire-Fontaine f2 186
St-Hippolyte c3 184
St-Hippolyte-du-Fort f5 187
Sainthiya k8 125
St-Honoré-les-Bains f2 186
St-Hubert d4 159
St-Hyacinthe f6 252
St Ignace d3 254
St Ignace Island k6 251
St Ignatius f3 285
St-Imier a2 196
St Ives Bay a6 163
St-Jacques-de-la-Lande d4 182
St-James d4 182
St James, Michigan, U.S.A. d3 254
St James, U.S.A. g4 257
St James, Jam. B 266
St James, Cape b6 248
St Jean g2 285
St Jean Baptiste e6 250
St-Jean-Brévelay c5 182
St-Jean-d'Angély b3 186
St-Jean-d'Assé f4 183
St-Jean-de-Bournay b5 185
St-Jean-de-Braye g5 183
St-Jean-de-la-Ruelle g5 183
St-Jean-de-Losne b3 184
St-Jean-de-Luz a5 187
St-Jean-de-Maurienne c5 185
St-Jean-de-Monts c6 182
St-Jean, Lac f4 252
St-Jean-Pied-de-Port a5 187
St-Jean-Poutge c5 187
St-Jean k3 253
St-Jean-sur-Richelieu k3 255
St-Jérôme j3 255
St-Joachim c5 182
St Joe e2 262
Saint John j6 253
St John Bay p3 253
St John, Cape q4 253
St John Island p3 253
St John, Lib. c4 222
St John, U.S.A. j6 253
St John's, Antig. D 271
St John's, Can. r5 253
St John's, Mont. n6 271
St Johns, Arizona, U.S.A. j8 263
St Johns, Michigan, U.S.A. d4 254
St Johnsbury f6 252
St John's Point f2 165
St Johns j5 259
St Johnsville f1 256
St-Joseph J 271
St Joseph, Louisiana, U.S.A. d4 258
St Joseph, Missouri, U.S.A. e4 260
St-Joseph-de-Beauce g5 262
St Joseph Island a6 258
St Joseph, Lake h5 250
St Joseph d5 254
St-Jouin-Bruneval f3 183
Saint-Joseph C 231
St Jovité j2 255
St-Juéry e5 187
St-Julien-Chapteuil a5 184
St-Julien-de-Concelles d5 182
St-Julien-de-Vouvantes d5 182
St-Julien-du-Sault j4 183
St-Julien-en-Born a4 187
St-Julien-en-Genevois c4 184
St-Julien-l'Ars c2 186
St-Junien c3 186
St-Just-en-Chaussée h3 183
St-Just-en-Chevalet f3 186
St-Justin b5 187
St-Just-St-Rambert a5 185
St Kitts and Nevis h6 241

ST KITTS & NEVIS

THE FEDERATION OF ST KITTS AND NEVIS
Area 261km² (101sq miles)
Capital Basseterre
Organizations ACS, CARICOM, COMM, OECS
Population 40,000
Pop. growth (%) -2.7
Life expectancy 67 (m); 70 (f)
Languages English
Literacy 97.3%
Currency East Caribbean dollar (US $1 = 2.67 East Caribbean dollar)
GDP (US million $) 264
GDP per head ($US) 6600

St-Laurent-Blangy a4 159
St-Laurent-de-la-Salanque e6 187
St-Laurent-du-Maroni, St-Laurent-du-Maroni, Fr. Gu. g2 285
St-Laurent-du-Maroni, Fr. Gu. g3 285
St-Laurent-du-Pont b5 185
St-Laurent-en-Caux f3 183
St-Laurent-en-Grandvaux b4 184
St-Laurent-sur-Sèvre e6 182
St Lawrence, Newfoundland, Can. q5 253
St Lawrence, Québec, Can. h4 253
St Lawrence, Cape m5 253
St Lawrence, Gulf of m4 253
St Lawrence Island b3 246
St Lawrence Seaway e6 252
St Lazare c5 250
St-Léger-sur-Dheune a4 184
St-Léonard j5 253
St Leonard d6 256
St-Léonard-de-Noblat d3 186
St Lewis p2 253
St Louis, Can. a4 250
Saint Louis, Maur. C 231
St-Louis, Fr. d3 184
St-Louis, Guad. C 271
St-Louis, Sen. a2 222
St Louis, Michigan, U.S.A. d4 254
St Louis, Missouri, U.S.A. a6 254
St-Louis-de-Kent k5 253
St-Louis du Nord h5 271
St-Loup-Lamairé e6 182
St-Loup-sur-Semouse c3 184
St Lucia h6 241

ST LUCIA

ST LUCIA
Area 616km² (238sq miles)
Capital Castries
Organizations ACS, CARICOM, COMM, OECS
Population 160,000
Pop. growth (%) 1.7
Life expectancy 70 (m); 75 (f)
Languages English, French
Literacy 81.5%
Currency East Caribbean dollar (US $1 = 2.67 East Caribbean dollar)
GDP (US million $) 609
GDP per head ($US) 3806

St Lucia Channel J 271
St Lucia Game Reserve k4 235
St Lucia, Lake k3 235
St Lucia Park k4 235
St Lucie Canal j6 259
St-Lunaire c4 182
St-Lys d5 187
St-Macaire b4 186
St-Macaire-en-Mauges e5 182
St Magnus Bay A 164
St-Maixent-l'École b2 186
St-Malo c4 182
St-Malo, Golfe de c4 182
St-Mandrier-sur-Mer b7 185
St Marc h5 271
St-Marc, Canal de h5 266
St-Marcel a4 184
St-Marcellin b5 185
St Marcel, Mont g3 285
St-Marcouf, Îles d3 182
St Maries e2 262
St Marks g4 259
St-Mars-la-Jaille d5 182
St-Martin-Boulogne g2 183
St Martin, Cap J 271
St-Martin, Cape b6 234
St-Martin-d'Auxigny h5 183
St-Martin-de-Belleville c5 185
St-Martin-de-Crau a7 185
St-Martin-de-Londres f5 187
St-Martin-d'Entraunes c6 185
St-Martin-de-Ré a2 186
St-Martin-d'Hères b5 185
St-Martin-en-Bresse b4 184
St Martin n5 267
St Martin, Lake d5 250
St Martin's A 163
St Martin's Island n9 125
St-Martin-Vésubie d6 185
St-Martory c5 187
St Mary B 266
St Mary j7 249
St Mary Peak d11 81
St Mary Reservoir l7 249
St Mary's A 163
St Mary's, Can. r5 253
St Mary's, U.S.A. d3 246
St Marys, Ohio, U.S.A. d5 254
St Marys, Pennsylvania, U.S.A. b3 256
St Marys, West Virginia, U.S.A. f6 254
St Mary's Bay r5 253
St Mary's, Cape q5 253
St Marys City d6 256
St-Mathieu c3 186
St-Mathieu, Pointe de a4 182
St Matthew Island a3 246
St Matthews j3 259
St-Maur-des-Fossés h4 183
St-Maurice a3 196
St Maurice f5 252
St-Max c2 184
St-Maximin-la-Ste-Baume b7 185
St-Médard-en-Jalles b4 186
St-Méen-le-Grand c4 182
St-Menges c5 159
St Michael d3 246
St Michaels d6 256
St Michael's Bay q2 253
St-Michel-de-Maurienne c5 185
St-Michel, Montagne a4 182
St-Michel-sur-Meurthe c2 184
St-Mihiel b2 184
St-Nazaire c5 182
St-Nicolas-de-la-Grave d4 187
St-Nicolas-de-Port c2 184
St-Nicolas-de-Redon c5 182
St-Nicolas-du-Pélem b4 182
St-Oedenrode d3 159
St-Omer h2 183
St-Pacôme h5 252
St-Pair-sur-Mer d4 182
St-Palais a5 187
St-Pamphile h5 252
St-Pardoux-la-Rivière c3 186
St-Paterne f4 183
St-Paterne-Racan f5 183
Saint Paul C 231
St Paul, Can m5 249
St-Paul, Fr. c6 185
St Paul, Minnesota, U.S.A. e2 260
St Paul, Nebraska, U.S.A. d3 260
St-Paul-Cap-de-Joux d5 187
St Paul, Cape e4 223
St-Paul-de-Fenouillet e6 187
St Paul Fracture Zone h9 302
St Paul Island b4 246
St-Paul-lès-Dax a5 187
St Paul, Lib. b4 222
St Paul's, St K./N. F 271
St Pauls, North carolina, U.S.A. k2 259
St-Paul-Trois-Châteaux a6 185
St-Péray a6 185
St Peter's m6 253
St Peters l5 253
St Petersburg h6 259
St-Philbert-de-Grand-Lieu d5 182
Saint-Pierre C 231
St-Pierre, Mart. J 271
St-Pierre, Sey. e5 231
St Pierre-Jolys e6 250
St-Pierre, Lac f5 252
St Pierre and Miquelon (France) j4 241
St-Pierre-de-Chignac c3 186
St-Pierre-de-la-Fage f5 187
St-Pierre-des-Champs e5 187
St-Pierre-des-Corps f5 183
St-Pierre-d'Oléron a3 186
St-Pierre-Église d3 182
St-Pierre-en-Port f3 183
St-Pierre et Miquelon j4 241
St-Pierre-le-Moûtier f2 186
St-Pierre-sur-Dives e3 182
St-Pierreville a6 185
St-Plancard c5 187
St-Pois d4 182
St-Poix d5 182
St-Pol-de-Léon b4 182
St-Pol-sur-Ternoise h2 183
St-Pompont d4 186
St-Pons-de-Thomières e5 187
St-Porchaire b3 186
St-Pourçain-sur-Sioule f2 186
St-Priest a5 185
St-Priest-de-Champs e3 186
St-Quentin b5 159
St-Quentin, Canal de j3 183
St-Rambert-d'Albon a5 185
Středočeský kraj c2 170
St Regis f2 262
Střela j2 175
St-Rémy-de-Provence a7 185
St-Rémy-sur-Durolle f3 186
St-Renan a4 182
St-Révérien f1 186
St-Riquier g2 183
St-Romain-le-Puy a5 184
St-Rome-de-Cernon e4 187
St-Rome-de-Tarn e4 187
Sainte Rose du Lac d5 250
St-Saëns g3 183
St-Saturnin-lès-Apt b7 185
St-Saulge f1 186
St-Sauveur, Bretagne, Fr. a4 182
St-Sauveur, Franche-Comté, Fr. c3 184
St-Sauveur-en-Puisaye j5 183
St-Sauveur-Lendelin d3 182
St-Sauveur-le-Vicomte d3 182
St-Sauveur-sur-Tinée d6 185
St-Savin, Aquitaine, Fr. b3 186
St-Savin, Poitou-Charentes, Fr. c2 186
St-Savinien b3 186
St Sebastian Bay d7 234
St-Sébastien-sur-Loire d5 182
St-Seine-l'Abbaye a3 184
St-Sernin-sur-Rance e5 187
St-Sever b5 187
St Shotts r5 253
St Siméon h5 252
St-Simon b5 159
St Simons Island j5 259
St Stephen, Can. j6 253
St Stephen, U.S.A. k3 259
St-Sulpice-les-Champs e3 186
St-Sulpice-les-Feuilles d2 186
St-Sulpice-sur-Lèze d5 187
St-Sylvestre-sur-Lot c4 187
St-Symphorien b4 187
St-Symphorien-de-Lay a5 184
St Thomas, Can. f4 254
St Thomas, U.S.A. e6 250
St Thomas, Jam. B 266
St-Tite f5 252
St-Tite-des-Caps g5 252
Saintonge b3 186
St-Trivier-de-Courtes b4 184
St-Trojan-les-Bains a3 186
St-Tropez c7 185
St-Tropez, Cap de c7 185
St-Vaast-la-Hougue d3 182
St-Valérien j4 183
St-Valery-en-Caux f3 183
St-Valery-sur-Somme g2 183
St-Vallier, Bourgogne, Fr. a4 184
St-Vallier, Rhône-Alpes, Fr. a5 185
St-Vallier-de-Thiey c7 185
St-Varent e6 182
St-Vaury d2 186
St-Véran c6 185
St-Vincent b4 196
St Vincent e6 250
St Vincent and the Grenadines h6 241

ST VINCENT & THE GRENADINES

ST VINCENT AND THE GRENADINES
Area 389km² (150sq miles)
Capital Kingstown
Organizations ACS, CARICOM, COMM, OECS
Population 120,000
Pop. growth (%) 0.9
Life expectancy 72 (m); 72 (f)
Languages English
Literacy 82%
Currency East Caribbean dollar (US $1 = 2.67 East Caribbean dollar)
GDP (US million $) 300
GDP per head ($US) 2500

St Vincent, Cape Aa3 83
St-Vincent-de-Tyrosse a5 187
St Vincent, Gulf a2 82
St-Vincent, Mont a4 184
St Vincent Passage J 271
St-Vit b3 184
St-Vith e4 159
St-Vivien-de-Médoc a3 186
St-Yan a4 184
St-Yorre f2 186
St-Yrieix-la-Perche d3 186
St-Zacharie b7 185
Saipal e5 130
Saipan A 74
Saipan Channel A 74
Saiqi m5 105
Saira f2 297
Saison l8 99
Saissac e5 187
Saitama h3 115
Saiwa Swamp National Park b4 226
Saiyidwala f5 128
Sajam j6 97
Šajgino j3 151
Sājir k9 137
Sajno, Jezioro m2 169
Sajó j3 170
Sajókeresztúr j3 171
Sajószentpéter j3 171
Sajzi p5 137
Sak d4 234
Saka b2 226
Saka Kalat b7 129
Sakai, Fukui, Japan g3 115
Sakai, Ibaraki, Japan h3 115
Sakaide e4 114
Sakaiminato e4 114
Sakākah h7 137
Sakakawea, Lake c2 260
Sakala j8 99
Sakami, Québec, Can. r4 251
Sakami, Québec, Can. e2 252
Sakami Lake g4 251
Sakar, Bul. h5 201
Sakar a1 128
Sakaraha Aa3 233
Sakar-Chaga h9 120
Sakarya, Tur. c2 208
Sakarya, Tur. c2 208
Sakarya c2 208
Sakassou c4 222
Sakata h2 115
Sakawa e5 114
Sakchu n5 113
Saken Seyfullin p3 121
Sakesar f4 128
Sakété e4 223
Sakhi f6 129
Sakhi Sarwar e6 129
Sakhnin d4 138
Sakhnovshchyna d2 148
Sakhra g9 120
Sakht-Sar n3 137
Şäki g4 149
Saki e4 223
Šakiai k5 157
Sakishima-shotō B 115
Sakkā d5 139
Sakon Nakhon g7 102
Sakpiegu d4 222
Sakrand d7 129
Sakrivier d5 234
Saksaul'skiy h4 120
Saksħaug c5 154
Sakskøbing e4 158
Saku h3 115
Sakura-jima d6 114
Saky d3 148
Säkylä k2 157
Sal, Cape. V. A 222
Sal, Russ. Fed. f3 148
Sal, Cayo de d1 284
Sal, Point c7 265
Sal, Punta d3 276
Sal'sk f3 148
Šal'a f3 171
Sala g3 156
Sala Consilina e4 198
Sala, Ouadi b4 218
Salaberry-de-Valleyfield j3 255
Salaca l4 157
Sălacea l4 171
Salacgriva l4 157
Salada de la Mata, Laguna d6 193
Salada de Torrevieja, Laguna dd7 193
Salada, Bahía b1 294
Salada, Lago j4 297
Salada, Laguna b1 272
Saladas e1 294
Saladillo, Arg. d2 294
Saladillo, Arg. f2 297
Saladillo, Buenos Aires, Arg. h3 297
Saladillo, San Luis, Arg. e2 296
Salado, Arg. d1 294
Salado, Arg. e1 294
Salado, Arg. d3 296
Salado, Arg. h3 297
Salado, Cuba f4 266
Salado, Ec. b4 284
Salado, Mex. k4 273
Salado, Mex. d2 274
Salado, Andalucía, Spain d8 191
Salado, Andalucía, Spain e8 191
Salado, Andalucía, Spain f7 191
Saladou c3 222
Salaga d4 222
Sālah e4 138
Salahuddin k4 209
Sālaj f2 201
Salajwe f1 234
Salak b4 101
Salakas m5 157
Šalakuša e3 146
Salal h3 223
Salala b4 222
Salāla e3 219
Şalālah e7 116
Salamá, Guat. b3 276
Salamá, Hond. d3 276
Salamanca, Chile b1 296
Salamanca, Mex. d3 274
Salamanca, Spain e4 190
Salamanca e4 190
Salamanca, U.S.A. b2 256
Salamanga k3 235
Salamanperän luonnonpuisto k5 155
Salamat b5 218
Salamat, Bahr c2 224
Salāmatābād l4 137
Salamban h6 99
Salamina d5 210
Salamiyah f5 209
Salandra f4 198
Salanga, Isla a4 284
Salantai j4 157
Salar f7 191
Salar de Pocitos d4 292
Sălard l4 171
Salardu e2 192
Salari b7 129
Salas d1 190
Salas de los Infantes a2 192
Salas, Embalse de c3 190
Salaspils l4 157
Salat d5 187
Salatiga f8 98
Salavan h8 102
Salavat h5 147
Salaverry b1 292
Salawati j6 97
Salaya e6 100
Salaya d9 129
Salayar l8 99
Salayar, Selat l7 99
Salazar, Arg. f4 297
Salazar, Spain c2 192
Salbertrand a4 196
Salbris h5 183
Salcantay, Cerro c2 292
Salcedo j5 271
Salcha h2 247
Šalčia l5 157
Salčiile h3 201
Šalčininkai p1 169
Sălcioara h3 201
Salcombe c6 163
Salda Gölü b4 208
Saldana b3 284
Saldaña f2 190
Saldanha b6 234
Saldanha Bay b6 234
Saldungaray g5 297
Saldura e3 196
Saldus k4 157
Sale, Aust. h15 81
Sale, U.K. d3 162
Sale Creek g2 259
Salea f5 99
Saleh, Teluk j9 99
Şāleḩābād m4 137
Salehard l2 147
Salekhard f7 126
Salem, India g6 235
Salem, R.S.A. g6 235
Salem, Arkansas, U.S.A. d1 258
Salem, Illinois, U.S.A. b6 254
Salem, Indiana, U.S.A. c6 254
Salem, Kentucky, U.S.A. e1 258
Salem, Massachusetts, U.S.A. k2 257
Salem, Missouri, U.S.A. d1 258
Salem, New Hampshire, U.S.A. j2 257
Salem, New Jersey, U.S.A. e5 256
Salem, Ohio, U.S.A. f5 254
Salem, Oregon, U.S.A. b3 262
Salem, West Virginia, U.S.A. f6 254
Salemal m2 147
Salemi b7 199
Salen f4 156
Sälen e2 156
Salen g3 297
Salernes c7 185
Salerno, Italy e4 198
Salerno d4 198
Salerno, Golfo di d4 198
Salers e3 186
Sales Oliveira e4 290
Sales Point h5 163
Salesópolis f5 291
Salevā l5 155
Salford, England, U.K. h1 162
Salford d3 162
Salgada d3 162
Salgado e4 288
Salgótarján h3 171
Salgueiro, Braz. e3 288
Salgueiro c5 191
Salguero f3 297
Sali d3 220
Šali g4 149
Šali k4 151
Salibabu p3 99
Salies-de-Béarn b5 187
Salignac-Eyvignes d4 186
Salihli b3 208
Salihorsk b1 148
Salima e1 233
Salimbatu j3 99
Salime, Embalse de d1 190
Salimi d5 224
Salimo b6 227
Salina, Kansas, U.S.A. d4 260
Salina, Utah, U.S.A. h6 263
Salina Cruz g5 275
Salina Point g3 266
Salina, Isola d6 199
Salinas, Braz. g2 291
Salinas, Ec. a4 284
Salinas, San Luis Potosí, Mex. d2 274
Salinas, Mex. g4 275
Salinas e1 190
Salinas, U.S.A. b5 264
Salinas c6 265
Salinas de Garci Mendoza d3 292
Salinas de Sín e2 192
Salinas del Manzano c4 193
Salinas o Lachay, Punta de b2 292
Salinas Peak b5 261
Salinas, Ponta das a1 232
Salinas, Sierra de b5 264
Salin-de-Giraud a7 185
Salindres a6 184
Saline, Arkansas, U.S.A. c3 258
Saline, Kansas, U.S.A. c4 260
Saline Bay E 271
Salines, Point G 271
Salines, Pointe des J 271
Salingyi b5 102
Salinópolis c2 288
Salins-les-Bains b4 184
Salir b7 191
Salisbury, Aust. d13 81
Salisbury, U.K. e5 163
Salisbury, Maryland, U.S.A. e6 256
Salisbury, North Carolina, U.S.A. j2 259
Salisbury, Pennsylvania, U.S.A. a5 256
Salisbury Island p3 243
Salisbury Plain e5 163
Săliște f3 201
Salitral de Carrera c2 274
Salitral de la Perra d4 296
Salitre d4 288
Šalja j4 147
Şalkhad e4 139
Salla m3 155
Sallanches c5 185
Sallent f3 192
Salles-Curan e4 187
Salles-sur-l'Hers d5 187
Salling c2 158
Salliqueló f4 297
Sallisaw b2 258
Sallom e4 219
Salluit p3 243
Sallyana f5 135
Salm b3 174
Salmās k2 137
Salme k3 157
Salmi a1 150
Salmo e1 262
Salmon e1 262
Salmon Arm h6 248
Salmon Falls Creek f4 262
Salmon River Mountains f3 262
Salmon-Priest Wilderness j7 248
Salmoral e4 190
Salmtal e5 159
Salo, C.A.R. c3 224
Salo, Fin k2 157
Salò e4 196
Salobreña g8 191
Saloinen k4 155
Salome g9 263
Salomon, Cap J 271
Salon b3 184
Salon-de-Provence b7 185
Salonga d4 224
Salonga Nord, Parc National de la d4 224
Salonga Sud, Parc National de la d4 224
Salonta k5 171
Salor d5 191
Salor, Embalse de d5 191
Salorino c5 191
Salou, Cap de f3 192
Saloum a3 222
Salovci h3 177
Salpausselkä m2 157
Salsacate e1 296
Salsadella e4 192
Salsbruket c4 154
Salses-le-Château e6 187
Salsomaggiore Terme d5 196
Salsvatnet c4 154
Salt, R.S.A. e6 234
Salt, Spain g3 192
Salt, Arizona, U.S.A. h9 263
Salt, Missouri, U.S.A. f4 260
Salt, Wyoming, U.S.A. f4 262
Salt Flat g2 272
Salt Fork Arkansas a1 258
Salt Lake City h5 262
Salt Lake, The f11 81
Salt Wells e2 264
Salta, Arg. e4 293
Salta, Salta, Arg. d4 292
Saltaim, Ozero m4 147
Saltash b6 163
Saltbæk Vig h9 103
Saltcoats, Can. b5 250
Saltcoats d4 164
Saltee Islands e4 165
Saltfjellet Svartisen Nasjonalpark e3 154
Saltholm f3 158
Saltillo, Mex. j5 273
Saltillo, U.S.A. e2 258
Salto, Arg. g3 297
Salto, Braz. e5 290
Salto, Port. c3 190
Salto, Ur. j1 297
Salto, Salto, Ur. j1 297
Salto c2 198
Salto da Divisa j2 291
Salto de Agua, Chiapas, Mex. a2 276
Salto de Agua, San Luis Potosí, Mex. e2 275
Salto del Ángel (980m) e2 285
Salto del Guairá a6 290
Salto Grande, Arg. g2 297
Salto Grande, Braz. d5 290
Salto Grande, Mex. a1 274
Salto Grande, Embalse de j1 297
Salto Osório, Represa b6 290
Salto, Lago del h7 197
Saltode Las Rosas c3 296
Salton City f9 263
Salton Sea f9 263
Saltpond d4 222
Saltykovo g1 149
Saluda, South Carolina, U.S.A. h2 259
Saluda, South Carolina, U.S.A. j3 259
Saluda, Virginia, U.S.A. h7 255
Salue Timpaus, Selat m5 99
Saluebesar m5 99
Salumbar g8 129
Salur h3 127
Salussola c4 196
Saluzzo b5 196
Salvacañete c4 193
Salvada c7 191
Salvador, Arg. e1 296
Salvador, Braz. e4 288
Salvador Mazza e4 293
Salvador, Lake d5 258
Salvagnac d5 187
Salvaleón d6 191
Salvaterra c2 288
Salvaterra de Magos b5 191
Salvatierra, Mex. d3 274
Salvatierra, Spain b1 192
Salviac d4 186
Salvora, Illa de a2 190
Salween d5 102
Salyan h5 149
Salyersville e7 254
Salym m3 147
Salza, Aus. f2 177
Salza, Ger. g4 173
Salzach e2 176
Salzbergen f2 159
Salzbrunn b2 234
Salzburg, Aus. e2 176
Salzburg e2 176
Salzgitter f3 172
Salzhausen f2 172
Salzhemmendorf e3 172
Salzkammergut e2 176
Salzkotten d4 172
Salzmünde g4 173
Salzwedel g3 173
Salzweg e1 176
Sam, Gabon b3 224
Sam, India e7 129
Sam Rayburn Reservoir b4 258
Sâm Sơn g6 102
Sama c3 292
Samadet b5 187
Samai f8 129
Samaipata e3 293
Samak, Tanjung d5 98
Samal e7 100
Samalanga c13 103
Samalayuca f2 272
Samales Group c7 100
Samalga Pass b5 246
Samalkha c5 130
Samalkot h4 126
Samalût c7 136
Samaná k5 271
Samana c4 130
Samana Cay h3 266
Samaná, Cabo k5 267
Samandağı e4 208
Samangān c3 128
Samangwa d4 224
Samani Ac2 114
Samaniego b3 284
Samannûd c6 136
Samaqua f4 252
Samar d7 139
Samar, Phil. e5 100
Samar Sea SE e5 100
Samara, Russ. Fed. j1 149
Samara l5 151
Samaria d4 139
Samariapo d2 284
Samarinda b2 210
Samarinda j5 99
Samarkand c1 128
Samarkandskaya Oblast' l8 120
Samarqand, Qullai d1 128
Sāmarrā' j5 209
Samarskaja Oblast' k5 151
Samarskoe e3 148
Samarskoye u3 121
Samary j4 147
Samary n4 169
Samasata e6 129
Samassi Aa3 198
Samatan c5 187
Samate j6 97
Samaúma e1 293
Şamaxı h4 149
Samba, D.R.C. d3 224
Samba, D.R.C. e4 225
Samba, Indon. g5 98
Samba, Indon. b3 130
Samba, Jam.Kash. b3 130
Samba Cajú c5 224
Sambailo b3 222
Sambaliung k4 99
Sambalpur h9 125
Sambapolulu, Gunung l7 99
Sambar, Tanjung f6 98
Sambas e4 98
Sambava Ac1 233
Sambhal d5 130
Sambhar g7 129
Sambiase f6 199
Sambir m6 169
Sambit k4 99
Sambito d3 288
Sambo, Ang. b1 232
Sambo, Indon. k6 99
Samboal f3 190
Samboja j5 99
Sambor h9 103
Samborombón, Bahía j3 297
Sambre j2 183
Sambú h7 277
Sambuca di Sicilia c7 199
Samburu National Reserve b3 226
Samch'ŏk q7 113
Samdi Dag k4 209
Same b4 227
Samedan d3 196
Samer g2 183
Sames e1 190
Şamfya e6 225
Şamhal g4 149
Sami, Grc. a4 210
Sami, India e9 129
Sami, Pak. a7 129
Samirah j8 137
Samiriia c5 284
Samjiyŏn q5 113
Samka c5 102
Şamkir g4 149
Samma a3 208
Sammū' d5 139
Samnangjin q8 113
Samnū g3 221
Samo b1 190
Samoa h4 73

SAMOA

THE INDEPENDENT STATE OF SAMOA
Area 2831km² (1093sq miles)
Capital Apia, on Upolu
Organizations COMM, SPC, PIF
Population 180,000
Pop. growth (%) 0.5
Life expectancy 65 (m); 72 (f)
Languages Samoan, English
Literacy 98.7%
Currency tala (Samoan dollar) (US $1 = 2.81 tala)
GDP (US million $) 245
GDP per head ($US) 1361

Samobor g4 177
Samod b6 130
Samoded e3 146
Samoëns c4 184
Samokov f4 201
Samorín f3 170
Samos, Notio Aigaio, Grc. Ab1 211
Samos Ab1 210
Samosir d14 103
Samothraki f2 210
Samothraki, Anatoliki Makedonia kai Thraki, Grc. f2 210
Sampacho e2 296
Sampaga k6 99
Sampang g8 98
Sampatiki, Akra d6 211
Sampeyre b5 196
Sampit g6 98
Sampit, Teluk g6 98
Sampla c5 130
Sampolawa m7 99
Sampwe e5 225
Samrala c4 130
Samro, Ozero n3 157

SAN MARINO

THE REPUBLIC OF SAN MARINO
Area 61km² (24sq miles)
Capital San Marino
Organizations CE
Population 30,000
Pop. growth (%) 1.5
Life expectancy 73 (m); 79 (f)
Languages Italian
Literacy 98.4%
Currency euro
(US $1 = 0.81 euro)
GDP (US million $) 478
GDP per head ($US) 15,933

Sangu → Saravan 379

Sangu ≈ n9 125
Sangū'īyeh r7 137
Sangue ≈ f2 293
Sangüesa c2 192
Sanguinet a4 187
Sangutane ≈ k1 235
Sangwŏn p6 113
Sangzhi b5 106
Sanhe j6 113
Sanhezhen e4 111
Sanhûr c7 136
Sanibel Island ▭ h6 259
Sañicó b6 296
Sanin-kaigan National Park ☆ f4 114
Sanislău l4 171
Sanitz f4 158
Sanjai ≈ j8 125
Sanjawi d5 128
Sanjbod m3 137
Sanje b5 227
Sanjeli f9 129
Sanjiang g6 104
Sanjie g5 111
Sanjō h3 115
Sankanbiaiwa ▲ b4 222
Sankarani ≈ c3 222
Sankasya d6 130
Sankeshwar d4 126
Sankh ≈ j8 125
Sankhu b5 130
Sankra, Rajasthan, India e7 129
Sankra, Uttar Pradesh, India d5 130
Sankt Aegyd am Neuwalde g2 177
Sankt Andrä f3 177
Sankt Andreasberg f4 173
Sankt Anton am Arlberg b2 176
Sankt Augustin f4 159
Sankt Gallen d2 196
Sankt Georgen d4 174
Sankt Georgen am Walde f1 177
Sankt Georgen im Lavanttal f3 177
Sankt Gilgen e2 176
Sankt Goar c2 174
Sankt Ingbert f5 159
Sankt Jakob im Rosental f3 177
Sankt Johann am Tauern f2 177
Sankt Johann im Pongau e2 176
Sankt Johann im Walde d3 176
Sankt Johann in Tirol d2 176
Sankt Kanzian am Klopeiner See f3 177
Sankt Leonhard am Forst g1 177
Sankt Margarethen c5 158
Sankt Margarethen im Burgenland h2 177
Sankt Michael im Lungau e2 176
Sankt Michael in Obersteiermark g2 177
Sankt Michaelisdonn c5 158
Sankt Moritz d3 196
Sankt Niklaus b3 196
Sankt Paul im Lavanttal f3 177
Sankt Peter am Kammersberg f2 177
Sankt Peter am Ottersbach g3 177
Sankt Peter-Ording b4 158
Sankt Pölten g1 177
Sankt Stefan im Gailtal e3 176
Sankt Valentin f1 177
Sankt Veit an der Glan f3 177
Sankt Wendel f5 159
Sankt-Peterburg a2 150
Sankuru ≈ d4 224
Sanligang c4 106
Şanlıurfa, Tur. ▣ g4 209
Şanlıurfa g4 209
Sanlong g3 111
Sanlúcar de Barrameda d8 191
Sanlúcar de Guadiana c7 191
Sanlúcar la Mayor d7 191
Sanluri Aa3 198
Sanmen Wan ◄ n4 105
Sanmenxia b2 106
Sanming l5 105
Sannazzaro de'Burgondi c4 196
Sanni c6 129
Sannicandro Garganico e3 198
Sannicola h4 198
San-Nicolao A 185
Sânnicolau Mare j5 171
Sannieshof f3 235
Sanniquellie c4 222
Sanniriya d4 139
Sannohe j1 115
Sano h3 115
Sanok l6 169
San-Pédro c5 222
Sânpetru Mare j5 171
Sanpu e2 111
Sanqaçal h4 149
Sanquhar e4 164
Sanquianga, Parque Nacional ☆ b3 284
Sans Toucher ▲ C 226
Sansalé b3 222
Sansanding c3 222
Sansanné-Mango e3 223
Sansepolcro g6 197
Sansha n5 105
Sanski Most h5 177
Sansol b2 192
Sanson e4 130
Sant Agustí de Lluçanès g2 192
Sant Benet ▲ g3 192
Sant Boi de Llobregat g3 192
Sant Carles de la Ràpita e4 192
Sant Celoni g3 192
Sant Feliu de Guíxols h3 192
Sant Feliu de Pallerols g2 192
Sant Feliu Sasserra g3 192
Sant Hilari Sacalm g3 192
Sant Joan de les Abadesses g2 192
Sant Jordi, Golf de ◄ e4 192
Sant Julià de Lòria d6 187
Sant Llorenç de Morunys f2 192
Sant Llorenç del Munt, Parc Natural de ☆ g3 192
Sant Mateu e4 192
Sant Miquel f5 193
Sant Pere de Ribes f3 192
Sant Quirze de Besora g2 192
Sant Sadurní d'Anoia f3 192
Sant Salvador, Puig de ▲ f5 193
Sant Vincenç de Castellet f3 192
Sant'Agata de'Goti d3 198
Sant'Agata del Bianco f6 199
Sant'Agata di Esaro e5 198
Sant'Agata di Militello d6 199
Sant'Anastasia d4 198
Sant'Andrea Apostolo dello Ionio f6 199
Sant'Andrea Frius Ab3 198
Sant'Angelo a Fasanella e4 198
Sant'Angelo dei Lombardi e4 198
Sant'Angelo di Brolo d6 199
Sant'Angelo in Lizzola g6 197
Sant'Angelo Lodigiano d4 196
Sant'Anna Arresi Aa3 198
Sant'Anna, Ilha de ▭ h5 291
Sant'Antioco Aa3 198
Sant'Antonio di Santadi Aa3 198
Sant'Arcangelo f4 198
Sant'Elia a Pianisi d3 198
Sant'Elpidio a Mare c1 198
Sant'Eufemia d'Aspromonte e6 199
Sant'Onofrio f6 199
Santa, Peru ≈ b1 292
Santa, Ancash, Peru b1 292
Santa Adélia d4 290
Santa Amalia d5 191
Santa Amelia c2 276
Santa Ana, Arg. d5 292
Santa Ana, La Paz, Bol. d3 292
Santa Ana, Bol. f3 293
Santa Ana, El Sal. c3 276
Santa Ana, Guat. c2 276
Santa Ana, México, Mex. e4 275
Santa Ana, Nuevo León, Mex. d1 274
Santa Ana, Mex. h10 263
Santa Ana, Spain c6 193
Santa Ana, California, U.S.A. ≈ f8 265
Santa Ana, U.S.A. f8 265
Santa Ana, Ven. ≈ c2 284
Santa Ana de Yacuma d2 292
Santa Ana Mountains ▣ f8 265
Santa Anita, Arg. h2 297
Santa Anita, Baja California Sur, Mex. e6 272
Santa Anita, Jalisco, Mex. c3 274
Santa Anna d6 261
Santa Bárbara, Braz. f3 293
Santa Bárbara, Chile a4 296
Santa Bárbara, Hond. c3 276
Santa Bárbara, Chihuahua, Mex. g4 272
Santa Bárbara, Mex. c3 274
Santa Bárbara, Spain ▲ b7 193
Santa Bárbara, Spain ▲ c6 193
Santa Bàrbara e4 192
Santa Barbara d7 265
Santa Bárbara, Amazonas, Ven. d3 284
Santa Bárbara, Barinas, Ven. c2 284
Santa Barbara Channel ═ c7 265
Santa Bárbara d'Oeste e5 290
Santa Bárbara de Casa c7 191
Santa Bárbara do Sul b7 289
Santa Barbara Island ▭ d8 265
Santa Bárbara, Ilha ▭ e5 288
Santa Bárbara, Parque Nacional ☆ c3 276
Santa Bárbara, Serra de ▲ A 220
Santa Bárbara, Serra de ▣ b4 290
Santa Bernardina j2 297
Santa Catalina, Arg. e2 297
Santa Catalina, Chile d5 292
Santa Catalina, Col. k5 277
Santa Catalina, Pan. g6 277
Santa Catalina, Ven. e2 285
Santa Catalina de Armada b1 190
Santa Catalina Island ▭ e8 265
Santa Catalina, Gulf of ◄ f8 264
Santa Catarina, Braz. ▣ b7 289
Santa Catarina, Baja California Norte, Mex. f11 263
Santa Catarina, Nuevo León, Mex. j5 273
Santa Catarina, San Luis Potosí, Mex. e3 275
Santa Catarina, Ilha de ▭ c7 289
Santa Caterina di Pittinuri Aa2 198
Santa Caterina Juquila f5 275
Santa Caterina Villarmosa d7 199
Santa Cesarea Terme c2 198
Santa Cilia de Jaca d2 192
Santa Clara, Chile a4 296
Santa Clara, Col. d4 284
Santa Clara, Cuba e3 266
Santa Clara, Mex. f3 272
Santa Clara, California, U.S.A. ≈ d7 265
Santa Clara, California, U.S.A. b4 264
Santa Clara, Utah, U.S.A. g7 263
Santa Clara de Buena Vista g1 297
Santa Clara de Louredo c7 191
Santa Clara de Saguier g1 297
Santa Clara, Barragem de ⊸ b7 191
Santa Clara, Isla ▭ a4 284
Santa Clara-a-Velha b7 191
Santa Clarita e7 265
Santa Clotilde c4 284
Santa Coloma de Farners g3 192
Santa Coloma de Gramanet g3 192
Santa Coloma de Queralt f3 192
Santa Colomba de Somoza d2 190
Santa Comba Dão b4 190
Santa Comba de Rossas d3 190
Santa Croce Camerina d8 199
Santa Croce sull'Arno e6 197
Santa Croce, Capo ► e7 199
Santa Cruz, Arg. ▣ c5 295
Santa Cruz, Arg. ≈ b6 295
Santa Cruz, Arm. B 189
Santa Cruz, Bol. ▣ e3 293
Santa Cruz, Bol. e3 293
Santa Cruz, Espírito Santo, Braz. h3 291
Santa Cruz, Pará, Braz. g4 285
Santa Cruz, Braz. c2 288
Santa Cruz, C.R. e5 276
Santa Cruz, Chile b3 296
Santa Cruz, Nayarit, Mex. b3 274
Santa Cruz, Mex. h10 263
Santa Cruz, Peru b5 284
Santa Cruz, Phil. c2 100
Santa Cruz, Phil. c3 100
Santa Cruz, Phil. b3 100
Santa Cruz, Port a5 191
Santa Cruz, Spain ▲ c3 192
Santa Cruz, U.S.A. ≈ h9 263
Santa Cruz, California, U.S.A. a5 264
Santa Cruz Barillas b3 276
Santa Cruz Cabrália j2 291
Santa Cruz Channel ═ d8 265
Santa Cruz das Palmeiras e4 290
Santa Cruz de Goiás d2 290
Santa Cruz de la Palma Ab2 189
Santa Cruz de la Sierra e5 191
Santa Cruz de la Zarza a5 193
Santa Cruz de las Flores c3 274
Santa Cruz de Moya c5 193
Santa Cruz de Mudela g6 191
Santa Cruz de Tenerife Ac2 189
Santa Cruz de Yojoa d3 276
Santa Cruz del Quiché b3 276
Santa Cruz del Retamar f4 190
Santa Cruz del Sur f4 266
Santa Cruz do Rio Pardo d5 290
Santa Cruz do Sul b7 289
Santa Cruz Huatulco f6 275
Santa Cruz Island ▭ d7 265
Santa Cruz Mountains ▣ a4 264
Santa Cruz, Isla ▭ A 286
Santa Cruz, Puerto ◄ c6 295
Santa Domenica Talao e5 198
Santa Domenica Vittoria d7 199
Santa Efigênia de Minas g3 291
Santa Elena, Buenos Aires, Arg. g4 297
Santa Elena, Arg. h1 297
Santa Elena, Bol. e4 293
Santa Elena, Peru c5 284
Santa Elena, Ven. e3 285
Santa Elena, Cabo ► e5 276
Santa Elena, Punta ► a4 284
Santa Eleonora f3 297
Santa Eufemia, Arg. f2 297
Santa Eufemia f6 191
Santa Eufemia, Golfo di ◄ f6 199
Santa Eugenia b2 190
Santa Eulalia, Guat. b3 276
Santa Eulalia, Mex. j3 273
Santa Eulália c5 191
Santa Eulalia c4 192
Santa Eulalia del Río f6 193
Santa Fe ▣ g1 297
Santa Fé, Arg. g1 297
Santa Fé, Pan. g6 277
Santa Fe, Spain g7 191
Santa Fe, U.S.A. b5 261
Santa Fé de Minas f2 291
Santa Fé do Sul c4 290
Santa Fé, Isla ▭ A 286
Santa Filomena c3 288
Santa Gertrudis g4 272
Santa Giusta Aa3 198
Santa Helena, Maranhão, Braz. c2 288
Santa Helena, Paraná, Braz. a6 290
Santa Helena de Goiás c2 290
Santa Inês, Bahia, Braz. e4 288
Santa Inês, Maranhão, Braz. c2 288
Santa Ines f5 275
Santa Inés, Isla ▭ b6 295
Santa Isabel, La Pampa, Arg. d4 296
Santa Isabel, Arg. g2 297
Santa Isabel, Bol. d4 292
Santa Isabel, Braz. e2 293
Santa Isabel, P.R. A 270
Santa Isabel de Sihuas c3 292
Santa Isabel do Ivaí b5 290
Santa Isabel, Ilha Grande de ▭ d2 288
Santa Juana a4 296
Santa Juliana e3 290
Santa Liestra y San Quílez e2 192
Santa Luce e6 197
Santa Lucia, Arg. ≈ e1 294
Santa Lucía, Arg. g2 297
Santa Lucía, Chile c4 292
Santa Lucía, Ec. b4 284
Santa Lucía, Guat. b3 276
Santa Lucía ≈ k3 297
Santa Lucía, Ur. j3 297
Santa Lucia de la Sierra b2 274
Santa Lucia del Mela e6 199
Santa Lucia Range ▣ b6 265
Santa Luisa g4 297
Santa Luísa, Serra de ▣ a3 290
Santa Luiza, Serra de ▣ c4 288
Santa Luzia, Maranhão, Braz. c2 288
Santa Luzia, Braz. e3 288
Santa Luzia, Cape. V. ▭ A 222
Santa Luzia, Barragem de ⊸ c4 190
Santa Magdalena f3 297
Santa Magdalena de Pulpis e4 192
Santa Magdalena, Isla ▭ d5 272
Santa Mare h2 201
Santa Margarida de Montbui f3 192
Santa Margarida do Sádão b6 191
Santa Margarita, Arg. d1 294
Santa Margarita, Spain h5 193
Santa Margarita, California, U.S.A. ≈ f8 265
Santa Margarita, California, U.S.A. c6 265
Santa Margherita di Belice c7 199
Santa Margherita Ligure d5 197
Santa Maria, Arm. ▭ A 220
Santa Maria, Bol. e3 293
Santa Maria, Braz. ≈ f2 294
Santa Maria, Amazonas, Braz. f4 285
Santa Maria, Amazonas, Braz. e4 285
Santa Maria, Pará, Braz. g4 285
Santa Maria, Rio Grande do Sul, Braz. f1 294
Santa Maria, Mex. ≈ f3 272
Santa María, Mex. ≈ d3 274
Santa María, Campeche, Mex. b1 276
Santa María, Mex. b1 276
Santa María, Pan. ≈ g6 277
Santa María, Spain ≈ d7 191
Santa María, Spain d2 192
Santa Maria, Arizona, U.S.A. ≈ g8 263
Santa Maria, California, U.S.A. c7 265
Santa Maria d2 284
Santa Maria Ajoloapan e4 275
Santa Maria Capua Vetere d3 198
Santa Maria da Boa Vista e3 288
Santa Maria da Feira b4 190
Santa Maria da Vitória d4 288
Santa Maria das Barreiras c3 288
Santa María de Guadalupe e2 275
Santa María de Huazamota b2 274
Santa María de Huertas b3 192
Santa María de Ipire d2 284
Santa Maria de Nieva c7 193
Santa Maria del Campo g2 190
Santa María del Campo Rus b5 193
Santa Maria del Cedro e5 198
Santa María del Monte f4 275
Santa María del Oro g5 272
Santa María del Oro b3 274
Santa María del Páramo e2 190
Santa Maria del Refugio d2 274
Santa María del Río d3 274
Santa Maria di Castellabate d4 198
Santa Maria do Salto h2 291
Santa Maria do Suaçuí g3 291
Santa Maria Ecatepec g5 275
Santa Maria Huatulco f6 275
Santa Maria Island ▭ F 74
Santa María Ixcatlán f5 275
Santa María Jajalpa e4 275
Santa Maria la Real de Nieva f3 190
Santa Maria Maggiore c3 196
Santa Maria Navarrese Ab3 198
Santa María Tlalixtac f5 275
Santa María Zaniza f5 275
Santa María Zoquitlán f5 275
Santa Maria, Cabo de, Moz. ► k2 235
Santa Maria, Cabo de, Port ► c8 191
Santa María, Cayo ▭ e3 266
Santa María, Isla, Chile ▭ a4 296
Santa María, Isla, Ec. ▭ A 286
Santa Maria, Punta ► b2 292
Santa María, Volcán ▲ b3 276
Santa Marina Salina d6 199
Santa Marinella f7 197
Santa Marta, Col. c1 284
Santa Marta, Castilla - La Mancha, Spain b5 193
Santa Marta, Extremadura, Spain d6 191
Santa Marta de Penaguião c3 190
Santa Marta de Tormes e4 190
Santa Marta Grande, Cabo de ► c7 288
Santa Marta, Cabo de ► a1 232
Santa Marta, Cerro ▲ g4 275
Santa Monica e7 265
Santa Monica Mountains ▣ e7 265
Santa Monica, Pico ▲ c4 272
Santa Ninfa b7 199
Santa Olalla f4 190
Santa Ollala del Cala d7 191
Santa Panagia, Capo ► e7 199
Santa Paula d7 265
Santa Pola d6 193
Santa Pola, Cabo de ► d6 193
Santa Quitéria d2 288
Santa Regina f3 297
Santa Rita, Mato Grosso, Braz. f1 293
Santa Rita, Braz. f3 288
Santa Rita, Col. c3 284
Santa Rita, Hond. d3 276
Santa Rita, Coahuila, Mex. j4 273
Santa Rita, Mex. d1 274
Santa Rita, U.S.A. g1 262
Santa Rita, Guárico, Ven. d2 284
Santa Rita, Zulia, Ven. c1 284
Santa Rita de Cassia d4 288
Santa Rita do Araguaia b2 290
Santa Rita do Pardo b4 290
Santa Rita do Sapucaí f5 291
Santa Rita do Weil d4 284
Santa Rosa, Corrientes, Arg. e1 294
Santa Rosa, La Pampa, Arg. e4 297
Santa Rosa, Mendoza, Arg. c2 296
Santa Rosa, Río Negro, Arg. d6 296
Santa Rosa, Arg. d4 292
Santa Rosa, Bol. d2 292
Santa Rosa, Acre, Braz. c1 292
Santa Rosa, Braz. b7 289
Santa Rosa, Col. d3 284
Santa Rosa, Ec. b4 284
Santa Rosa, Michoacán, Mex. d4 274
Santa Rosa, Nuevo León, Mex. d1 274
Santa Rosa, San Luis Potosí, Mex. e3 275
Santa Rosa, Mex. f1 275
Santa Rosa, Para. f5 293
Santa Rosa, Loreto, Peru c4 284
Santa Rosa, Peru c2 292
Santa Rosa, California, U.S.A. a3 264
Santa Rosa, U.S.A. b5 261
Santa Rosa, Ur. j3 297
Santa Rosa, Amazonas, Ven. d3 284
Santa Rosa, Apure, Ven. d2 284
Santa Rosa Beach f4 258
Santa Rosa de Copán c3 276
Santa Rosa de la Roca e3 293
Santa Rosa de Osos b2 284
Santa Rosa de Vigo d2 292
Santa Rosa de Viterbo e4 290
Santa Rosa del Conlara e2 296
Santa Rosa del Palmar e3 293
Santa Rosa del Río Primero f1 297
Santa Rosa Island, California, U.S.A. ▭ c8 265
Santa Rosa Island, Florida, U.S.A. ▭ f4 258
Santa Rosa Jauregui d3 274
Santa Rosa Range ▣ e5 262
Santa Rosa, Mount ▲ C 74
Santa Rosalía c4 272
Santa Severina f5 199
Santa Sofia, Italy f6 197
Santa Sofia, Port b6 191
Santa Susana b6 191
Santa Susana Mountains ▣ e7 265
Santa Sylvina d1 294
Santa Teresa, Arg. g2 297
Santa Teresa, Aust. b8 80
Santa Teresa, Braz. ≈ c4 288
Santa Teresa, Braz. h3 291
Santa Teresa, Nayarit, Mex. b2 274
Santa Teresa, Tamaulipas, Mex. a7 258
Santa Teresa di Gallura Ab1 198
Santa Teresa di Riva e7 199
Santa Teresa, Embalse de ◎ e4 190
Santa Teresita j4 297
Santa Terezinha b4 288
Santa Vitória c3 290
Santa Vitória do Ameixial c6 191
Santa Vitória do Palmar f2 294
Santa Ynez ≈ c7 265
Santa Ynez Mountains ▣ d7 265
Santa, Isla ▭ b1 292
Santadi Aa3 198
Santaella f7 191
Santafé de Bogotá ▣ c3 284
Santai, Sichuan, China e3 104
Santai, Xinjiang Uygur Zizhiqu, China t5 121
Santalpur e9 129
Santa-Manza, Golfe de ◄ A 185
Santa-Maria-di-Lota A 185
Santa-Maria-Siché A 185
Santan j5 99
Santana, Arm. B 189
Santana, Belize c2 276
Santana, Amazonas, Braz. d3 284
Santana, Bahia, Braz. d4 288
Sântana k5 171
Santana da Boa Vista f2 294
Santana da Serra b7 191
Santana do Acarau d2 288
Santana do Araguaia b3 288
Santana do Livramento e2 294
Santana, Ilha ▭ d2 288
Santander, Col. ▣ c2 284
Santander, Col. b3 284
Santander g1 190
Santanyí h5 193
Santaquin h6 262
Santarcangelo di Romagna g5 197
Santarém, Braz. g4 285
Santarém, Port ▣ b5 191
Santarém b5 191
Santaren Channel ═ e3 266
Šantarskie Ostrova ▭ k1 94
Santee, California, U.S.A. g9 265
Santee, South Carolina, U.S.A. ≈ k3 259
Santeramo in Colle f4 198
Santerre ♦ h3 183
Santhià c4 196
Santiago, Braz. f1 294
Santiago, Región Metropolitana, Chile ▣ b2 296
Santiago, Chile b2 296
Santiago, Dom. Rep. j5 271
Santiago, Ec. ≈ b3 284
Santiago, Baja California Sur, Mex. e6 272
Santiago, Colima, Mex. b4 274
Santiago, Mex. j5 273
Santiago, Pan. g6 277
Santiago, Para. f5 293
Santiago, Peru ≈ b4 284
Santiago, Peru b2 292
Santiago, Phil c2 100
Santiago Astata g5 275
Santiago de Alcántara c5 191
Santiago de Calatrava f7 191
Santiago de Cao b1 292
Santiago de Compostela b2 190
Santiago de Cuba g4 266
Santiago de la Espada b6 193
Santiago de la Peña f3 275
Santiago de la Ribera d7 193
Santiago de Mendez b4 284
Santiago de Paguaras d2 292
Santiago del Estero, Arg. ▣ d1 294
Santiago del Estero, Santiago del Estero, Arg. d1 294
Santiago del Teide Ac2 189
Santiago do Cacém b6 191
Santiago do Escoural b6 191
Santiago Ixcuintla b3 274
Santiago Ixtayutla f5 275
Santiago Juxtlahuaca e5 275
Santiago Minas f5 275
Santiago Mitlatengo f5 275
Santiago Papasquiaro g5 272
Santiago Peak ▲ f8 265
Santiago Temple f1 297
Santiago Tutla g5 275
Santiago Tuxtla g4 275
Santiago Vazquez j3 297
Santiago, Cabo ► a6 295
Santiago, Cerro ▲ g6 277
Santiago, Rio Grande de ≈ b3 274
Santiago, Sierra de ▣ f3 293
Santiaguillo, Laguna de ○ g5 272
Santibáñez de la Sierra e4 190
Santibáñez de Vidriales d2 190
Santiki, Tanjung ► l4 99
Santillana f1 190
Santillana, Embalse de ◎ g4 190
Santiponce d7 191
Säntis ▲ d2 196
Santisteban del Puerto a6 193
Santiuste de San Juan Bautista f3 190
Santo Aleixo c6 191
Santo Amaro e4 288
Santo Amaro de Campos h4 291
Santo André, Braz. e5 291
Santo André, Port. b6 191
Santo Angelo b7 289
Santo Antão ▭ A 222
Santo Antão ≈ f1 291
Santo Antônio, Braz. ≈ g3 291
Santo Antônio, Amazonas, Braz. e4 285
Santo Antônio, Maranhão, Braz. c3 288
Santo Antônio, Rio Grande do Norte, Braz. e3 288
Santo António, S. Tom./P. f5 223
Santo Antônio da Barra c2 290
Santo Antônio da Cachoeira g4 285
Santo Antônio da Platina c5 290
Santo Antônio de Jesus e4 288
Santo Antônio de Pádua g4 291
Santo Antônio do Amparo f4 291
Santo Antônio do Içá d4 284
Santo Antônio do Jacinto h2 291
Santo Antônio do Rio Verde e2 290
Santo Antônio, Cabo ► e4 288
Santo Antônio, Ponta ► e5 289
Santo Antônio, Ponta de ► f3 288
Santo Corazón f3 293
Santo Croce, Lago di ○ g3 196
Santo Domingo, Arg. j4 297
Santo Domingo, Chile b2 296
Santo Domingo, Dom. Rep. k5 271
Santo Domingo, Guat. c3 276
Santo Domingo, Mex. ≈ f4 275
Santo Domingo, Baja California Norte, Mex. b3 272
Santo Domingo, Baja California Sur, Mex. d5 272
Santo Domingo, Oaxaca, Mex. g5 275
Santo Domingo, Mex. d2 274
Santo Domingo, Nic. e4 276
Santo Domingo, Peru d2 292
Santo Domingo de la Calzada b2 192
Santo Domingo de los Colorados b4 284
Santo Domingo de Morelos f6 275
Santo Domingo Ozolotepec f5 275
Santo Domingo Petapa g5 275
Santo Domingo Tehuantepec g5 275
Santo Eduardo h4 291
Santo Estêvão b6 191
Santo Estevo, Embalse de ◎ c2 190
Santo Hipólito f3 291
Santo Inácio c5 290
Santo Stefano d'Aveto d5 196
Santo Stefano di Camastra d6 199
Santo Stefano di Magra d5 196
Santo Tirso b3 190
Santo Tomás, Baja California Norte, Mex. e10 263
Santo Tomás, Mex. f3 272
Santo Tomás, Nic. d4 276
Santo Tomás, Peru ≈ c2 292
Santo Tomás, Cusco, Peru c2 292
Santo Tomé, Corrientes, Arg. e1 294
Santo Tomé, Arg. g1 297
Santo Tomé a6 193
Santolea, Embalse de ◎ d4 192
Santoña g1 190
Santong He ≈ p4 113
Santo-Pietro-di-Tenda A 185
Santos e5 291
Santos Dumont g4 291
Santos Mercado d1 292
Santos Plateau ≈ f12 302
Santos, Sierra de los ▣ e6 191
Santovenia e3 190
Santrampur f9 129
Santu Lussurgiu Aa2 198
Santurtzi a1 192
Sānūr d4 139
Sanvignes-les-Mines a4 184
Sanwer g9 129
Sanxenxo b2 190
Sanxing g4 111
Sanya j6 102
Sanyang c4 106
Sanyati ≈ d2 233
Sanyuan a2 106
Sanyuanpu n4 113
Sanza e4 198
Sanza Pombo c5 224
Sanzhuang f2 111
São Barnabé b7 191
São Bartolomeu c5 191
São Bartolomeu de Messines b7 191
São Benedito, Braz. ≈ f1 293
São Benedito, Ceará, Braz. d2 288
São Bento, Amazonas, Braz. d1 292
São Bento, Maranhão, Braz. d2 288
São Bento, Roraima, Braz. e3 285
São Bento do Amparo c6 290
São Bento do Norte e3 288
São Bernardo d2 288
São Bernardo do Campo e5 291
São Borja e1 294
São Brás c7 191
São Brás de Alportel c7 191
São Carlos, Rondônia, Braz. e1 293
São Carlos, São Paulo, Braz. e5 290
São Cristóvão, Port ≈ b6 191
São Cristóvão b6 191
São Desidério, Braz. ≈ d4 288
São Desidério, Bahia, Braz. d4 288
São Domingos, Braz. c4 288
São Domingos b7 191
São Domingos do Norte h3 291
São Domingos, Serra de ▣ c4 288
São Felipe, Serra de ▣ g1 291
São Félix, Bahia, Braz. e4 288
São Félix, Mato Grosso, Braz. b4 288
São Félix da Marinha b3 190
São Félix do Xingu b3 288
São Fidélis h4 291
São Francisco, Braz. ≈ e3 288
São Francisco, Acre, Braz. d2 292
São Francisco, Amazonas, Braz. e5 285
São Francisco, Minas Gerais, Braz. f1 291
São Francisco de Assis e1 294
São Francisco de Goiás d1 290
São Francisco de Paula b7 289
São Francisco de Sales d3 290
São Francisco do Sul c7 289
São Gabriel f2 294
São Gabriel da Palha h3 291
São Geraldo b6 191
São Gonçalo g5 291
São Gonçalo do Abaeté f3 291
São Gotardo f3 291
São Jerônimo da Serra c5 290
São Jerônimo, Serra de ▣ a2 290
São João d4 284
São João da Aliança c4 289
São João da Barra h4 291
São João da Boa Vista e4 291
São João da Madeira b4 190
São João da Pesqueira c3 190
São João da Ponte f1 291
São João das Duas Pontas c4 290
São João de Meriti g5 291
São João del Rei f4 291
São João do Araguaia c3 288
São João do Caiuá b5 290
São João do Campo b4 190
São João do Cariri e3 288
São João do Paraíso g1 291
São João do Piauí d3 288
São João do Triunfo c6 290
São João dos Caldeireiros c7 191
São João dos Patos d3 288
São João Evangelista g3 291
São João Nepomuceno g4 291
São João, Ilhas de ▭ d2 288
São João, Serra de ▣ e1 293
São Joaquim, Amazonas, Braz. d3 284
São Joaquim, Santa Catarina, Braz. c7 289
São Jorge ▭ A 220
São Jorge do Limpopo k1 235
São José, Amazonas, Braz. d4 284
São José, Santa Catarina, Braz. c7 289
São José da Serra a1 290
São José de Piranhas e3 288
São José do Anauá e3 285
São José do Belmonte e3 288
São José do Divino h3 291
São José do Egito e3 288
São José do Jacurí g3 291
São José do Peixe d3 288
São José do Rio Pardo e4 291
São José do Rio Preto d4 290
São José dos Campos f5 291
São José dos Dourados ≈ c4 290
São José dos Pinhais d6 290
São José, Baía de ◄ d2 288
São Leopoldo b7 289
São Lourenço, Braz. ≈ a2 290
São Lourenço, Mato Grosso, Braz. a2 290
São Lourenço, Minas Gerais, Braz. f5 291
São Lourenço, Pantanal de ⊸ f3 293
São Luís, Braz. d2 288
São Luís, Port. b7 191
São Luís de Montes Belos c2 290
São Luís do Paraitinga f5 291
São Luís do Quitunde e3 288
São Luís do Tapajós f4 285
São Luís, Ilha de ▭ d2 288
São Manços c6 191
São Manuel d5 290
São Marceline d3 284
São Marcos ≈ e2 290
São Marcos da Serra b7 191
São Marcos, Baía de ◄ d2 288
São Martinho f5 285
São Martinho da Cortiça b4 190
São Martinho das Amoreiras b7 191
São Martinho do Porto a5 191
São Mateus j3 291
São Mateus do Sul c6 290
São Matias c6 191
São Miguel ▭ A 220
São Miguel Arcanjo e5 290
São Miguel de Machede c6 191
São Miguel do Araguaia b4 288
São Miguel do Iguaçu a6 290
São Miguel do Outeiro b4 190
São Miguel do Tapuio d3 288
São Nicolau ▭ A 222
São Paulo, Braz. ▣ d5 290
São Paulo, São Paulo, Braz. e5 291
São Paulo de Olivença d4 284
São Pedro, Braz. ≈ e3 288
São Pedro, Amazonas, Braz. f4 285
São Pedro, Mato Grosso do Sul, Braz. c3 290
São Pedro, Rondônia, Braz. e1 293
São Pedro, São Paulo, Braz. e5 290
São Pedro da Aldeia g5 291
São Pedro da Cadeira a5 191
São Pedro da Torre b3 190
São Pedro de Solis c7 191
São Pedro do Desterro d1 292
São Pedro do Ivaí c5 290
São Pedro do Sul, Braz. f1 294
São Pedro do Sul, Port. b4 190
São Raimundo das Mangabeiras c3 288
São Raimundo Nonato d3 288
São Romão, Amazonas, Braz. d5 284
São Romão, Minas Gerais, Braz. f2 291
São Roque e5 290
São Roque de Minas e4 291
São Roque, Cabo de ► e3 288
São Sebastião, Amazonas, Braz. c1 292
São Sebastião, Pará, Braz. b3 288
São Sebastião, Rondônia, Braz. e1 293
São Sebastião, São Paulo, Braz. f5 291
São Sebastião da Amoreira c5 290
São Sebastião da Boa Vista c2 288
São Sebastião do Paraíso e4 291
São Sebastião dos Poções d4 289
São Sebastião, Ilha de ▭ f5 291
São Simão, Mato Grosso do Sul, Braz. f4 293
São Simão, Minas Gerais, Braz. c3 290
São Simão, Barragem de ⊸ c3 290
São Teotónio b7 191
São Tiago, Braz. f4 291
São Tiago, Cape. V. ▭ A 222
São Tomé, S. Tom./P. ▭ f5 223
São Tomé f5 223
São Tomé and Príncipe c4 217

SÃO TOMÉ & PRÍNCIPE

THE DEMOCRATIC REPUBLIC OF SÃO TOMÉ AND PRÍNCIPE
Area 1,001km^2 (387sq miles)
Capital São Tomé
Organizations CEEAC
Population 150,000
Pop. growth (%) 2.1
Life expectancy 67 (m); 67 (f)
Languages Portuguese, many local dialects
Literacy 25%
Currency dobra (US $1 = 8700 dobra)
GDP (US million $) 44
GDP per head ($US) 293

São Tomé, Cabo de ► h5 291
São Tomé, Pico de ▲ f5 223
São Vicente, Arm. B 189
São Vicente, Braz. e5 291
São Vicente, Cape. V. ▭ A 222
São Vicente, Port c3 190
São Vicente Ferrer d2 288
São Vicente, Cabo de ► a7 191
Saona, Isla ► k5 267
Saône ≈ b3 184
Saône-et-Loire ▣ a4 184
Saorge d7 185
Sao-Siu h5 97
Saou b6 185
Saoura, Oued ≈ d3 220
Sapanca Gölü ○ c2 208
Saparua h6 97
Sape, Selat ═ k9 99
Sapele f4 223
Sapes f1 210
Şaphane Dağı ▲ c3 208
Sapientza ▭ b6 211
Sapo National Park ☆ c4 222
Sapo, Serranía del ▣ h7 277
Saponara e6 199
Sapopema c5 290
Sapotskin m2 169
Sapožok f5 150
Sappho a1 262
Sapporo Ab2 114
Sapri e4 198
Sapucaia f4 285
Sapudi ▭ h8 99
Sapulpa a2 258
Sapulut j2 99
Saqqez l3 137
Sar Dasht k3 137
Sar Kūh a7 129
Sar'ja h2 151
Sarā l3 137
Sara Buri e8 103
Sara Peak ▲ f4 223
Sarāb l3 137
Saraca, Lago ○ f4 285
Sarafand d3 138
Sarahan c4 130
Sarai c4 128
Sarai Sidhu f5 128
Saraikela j8 125
Saraipali h9 125
Säräisniemi l4 155
Sarajevo d4 200
Sarakhs h9 120
Sarakiniko, Akra ► d4 210
Saraktaš k2 149
Saraland e4 258
Sarama a2 138
Saramacca, Sur. ▣ f2 285
Saramacca, Sur. ≈ f3 285
Saramati ▲ b3 102
Sarameriza b4 284
Saramon c5 187
Saran g5 183
Saran, Gunung ▲ f5 98
Saran' p3 121
Saranac Lake j3 255
Sarānd k4 171
Saranda a5 227
Sarandi, Paraná, Braz. c5 290
Sarandi, Rio Grande do Sul, Braz. b7 289
Sarandí de Navarro j2 297
Sarandí del Yí e2 294
Sarandí Grande j2 297
Saranga j3 151
Sarangani ▭ e8 100
Sarangani Bay ◄ e8 100
Sarangani Islands ▭ e8 100
Sarangani Strait ═ e8 100
Sarangarh h9 125
Sarangpur e8 124
Saransk h4 151
Sarantaporo c2 210
Sarantaporos ≈ a2 210
Saraphi d6 102
Sarapul h4 147
Sarare ≈ c2 284
Sarasota h6 259
Sarat, Ḩarrat as LF f4 219
Sarata j2 201
Saratoga b3 260
Saratoga Springs, New York, U.S.A. g1 257
Saratok f4 98
Saratov g2 149
Saratovskaja Oblast' ▣ g2 149
Saravan a7 129

380 Sarawak → Selatpanjang

Sarawak g3 98
Saray h5 201
Saraya, Gui. b3 222
Saraya, Sen. b3 222
Sarayönü d3 208
Sărbeni g3 201
Sarbhāng m6 125
Sárbogárd g5 171
Sarca e4 196
Sarcelles h4 183
Sarcham m3 137
Sarčino t1 121
Sarco b1 294
Sarcoxie b1 258
Sarda e5 130
Sardão, Cabo b7 191
Sardara Aa3 198
Sardarpur g9 129
Sardarshahr g6 129
Sardasht, Khūzestān, Iran m5 137
Sardasht, Khūzestān, Iran n6 137
Sardegna, Italy A 198
Sardegna,
Sardegna, Italy Ab2 198
Sardhana c5 130
Sardinata c2 284
Sardindida Plain c3 226
Sardine Peak c2 264
Sardinia, C.R. e5 276
Sardinia b4 210
Sardinia, Italy Ab2 198
Sardis Lake e2 258
Sardoal b5 191
Sar-e Pol, Afg. c3 128
Sar-e Pol b2 128
Sare Yazd g6 137
Sarege k8 99
Sareks nationalpark f3 154
Sarektjåkkå f3 154
Sarempaka, Gunung h5 99
Sargans d7 196
Sargasso Sea SE d7 302
Sargentu Loros c4 284
Sarghaya e3 138
Sargodha f4 128
Sarh c2 224
Sarho, Jbel c2 220
Sari p3 137
Sar-i Pīrān k4 209
Sāri Qamish q3 137
Saria Ac3 211
Sar-i-Bum c3 128
Sáric h10 263
Sarichashma d2 128
Sarichioi j3 201
Sari-d'Orcino A 185
Saridu, Lago d3 284
Sariegos e2 190
Sarigan A 74
Sarigh Jilganang Kol d2 130
Sarıgöl b3 208
Sarıkamış j2 209
Sarikei f3 98
Sarıköy a2 208
Sarina j6 80
Sariñena d3 192
Sar-i-Pul c3 128
Sarir Tibesti a3 218
Šarišské Michal'any k2 171
Sarita a6 258
Sariwŏn n6 113
Sarıyar Barajı c2 208
Sarız f3 209
Sarjankylä k4 155
Sark c3 182
Sarkad k5 171
Sarkand s5 121
Sarkari Tala e7 129
Sárkeresztes g4 171
Sárkeresztúr g5 171
Şarkikaraağaç c3 208
Şarkışla f3 209
Şarköy h5 201
Sarlat-la-Canéda d4 186
Sarles d6 250
Sarliac-sur-l'Isle c3 186
Sarlyk j1 149
Sarmalan b4 128
Şărmăşag l4 171
Sărmașu g2 201
Sármellék f5 170
Sarmi k6 97
Sarmiento c5 295
Sarmiento, Canal b6 295
Sarmiento, Lago b6 295
Sarmiento, Monte b6 295
Särna e2 156
Sarnadas do Ródão c5 191
Sarnaki l3 169
Sarnano h6 197
Sarneh l5 137
Sarnen c3 196
Sarnia e4 254
Sarnıç d3 208
Sarnico d4 196
Sarno d4 198
Särnstugan e2 156
Sarny b2 148
Särö e1 158
Saroako l6 99
Sarolangun b6 98
Saroma-ko Ad1 114
Saronikos Kolpos d5 210
Saronno d4 196
Saros Körfezi a2 208
Sárospatak k3 171
Sarotra f8 129
Šarova g4 151
Šarovce g3 171
Sarowbi d3 128
Sarpa, Ozero g3 149
Sarpsborg d3 156
Sarracín g2 190
Sarral f3 192
Sarralbe d2 184
Sarre d2 184
Sarre Blanche d2 184
Sarrebourg d2 184
Sarreguemines d1 184
Sarre-Union d1 184
Sarria c2 190
Sarrià de Ter g2 192
Sarrión d4 193
Sarro c3 222
Sarroca de Lleida e3 192
Sarroch Ab3 198
Sarród e4 170
Sarrola-Carcopino A 185
Sarsina g6 197
Sarssonne e3 186
Sarstedt e3 172
Sárszentágota g5 171
Sárszentlőrinc g5 171
Sartanahu e7 129
Sarteano f7 197
Sartène A 185
Sarthe, Fr. e5 182
Sarthe,
  Pays de la Loire, Fr. f5 183
Sartilly d4 182
Sartų ežeras l5 157
Sartyn'ja k3 147
Saruhanlı a3 208
Sarule Ab2 198
Sarumasa-yama e4 114
Saruna c7 129
Sarupsar f6 129
Şarur g5 149
Sarvābād l4 137
Sárvár e4 170
Sarvestān p7 137
Sarvisé d2 192
Sarwar g7 129
Sary Yazikskoye
  Vodokhranilishche a2 128
Saryagach m7 121
Sarybasat h4 120
Sary-Bulak p7 121
Sarykamyshskoye Ozero f7 120
Sarykemer n6 121
Sarykiyak q2 121
Sarykol Range g1 128
Sarylah q3 119
Sarymoyyn, Ozero k2 120
Saryozek s5 121
Saryshagan p4 121
Sarysu l4 121
Sary-Tash f1 128
Saryter, Gora r6 121
Saryyesik-Atyrau,
  Peski r5 121
Saryzhaz s6 121
Sarzana d5 197
Sarzeau c5 182
Sarzhal s3 121
Sasa d3 138
Sa'sa' e3 138
Sasabeneh c2 226
Sasar, Tanjung k9 99
Sasaram j7 125
Sásd g5 171
Saskatchewan q4 249
Saskatoon p5 249
Saskylah m2 119
Saslaya e4 276
Saslaya, Parque Nacional e4 276
Sasmik, Cape Ac2 247
Sasolburg g3 235
Sasovo f4 150
Sass Town c5 222
Sassandra, C.I. c4 222
Sassandra c5 222
Sassari Aa2 198
Saßbach g3 177
Sassello c5 197
Sassenage b5 185
Sassenberg d4 172
Sassetta e6 197
Sassnitz j1 173
Sasso della Paglia d3 196
Sasso di Castro f5 197
Sasso Lungo f3 196
Sasso Marconi f5 197
Sassocorvaro g6 197
Sassoferrato g6 197
Sassuolo e5 196
Sástago d3 192
Šaštín-Stráže f3 170
Sastobe n6 121
Sastre g1 297
Sasykkol', Ozero t4 121
Satadougou b3 222
Šatalovo b4 150
Sata-misaki d6 114
Satão c4 190
Satara, India d4 126
Satara, R.S.A. j2 235
Satawal G 74
Satawan G 74
Satellite Beach j5 259
Satengar, Kepulauan j8 99
Sätenäs f2 156
Satevó f4 272
Satilla h4 259
Satipo c2 292
Satka j5 147
Satkania n9 125
Satkhira l8 125
Šatki h4 151
Satmala Range f3 126
Satna g7 124
Šatoj g4 149
Sátoraljaújhely k3 171
Satorina g5 177
Satovcha d1 210
Satow e5 158
Satpayev l3 121
Satpura Range g10 129
Satriano di Lucania e4 198
Šatrovo l4 147
Sattahip e9 103
Sattanen l3 155
Satti c2 130
Sattley c2 264
Satu Mare, Rom. f2 201
Satu Mare l4 171
Saţun b2 101
Šatura e4 150
Saturnino M. Laspiur f1 297
Sau, Pantà de g3 192
Saualpe f3 177
Saúca b3 192
Saucats b4 186
Sauce e2 294
Sauce Blanco e6 297
Sauce de Luna h1 297
Saucedo j1 297
Saucelle, Embalse de d3 190
Saucier e4 258
Saucillo g3 272
Sauda b3 156
Saudakent m6 121
Sauðárkrókur A 152
Saudi Arabia b6 92

SAUDI ARABIA

THE KINGDOM OF SAUDI ARABIA
Area 2,240,000km^2 (864,869sq miles)
Capital Riyadh
Organizations CCASG, IDB, LAS, OAPEC, OIC, OPEC
Population 22,000,000
Pop. growth (%) 3.5
Life expectancy 69 (m); 72 (f)
Languages Arabic
Literacy 78.7%
Currency Saudi riyal (US $1 = 3.75 Saudi riyal)
GDP (US million $) 185,632
GDP per head ($US) 8437

Saudron b2 184
Sauer d2 184
Sauerlach g5 175
Sauerland d4 172
Sauêruiná f2 293
Saugatuck c4 254
Saugues f4 186
Saujil c1 294
Saujon b3 186
Sauk Center e2 260
Saukonkylä j5 155
Saukville c4 254
Saul g3 285
Sauldre g5 183
Saulgrub g5 175
Saulieu a3 184
Saulkrasti l4 157
Saulnois c2 184
Sault b6 185
Sault Sainte Marie, Can. d2 254
Sault Sainte Marie, U.S.A. d2 254
Sault-de-Navailles b5 187
Saulx, Fr. b2 184
Saulx c3 184
Saulzais-le-Potier e2 186
Sauma, Pointe L 75
Saumalkol' m5 147
Saumarez Reef l6 80
Saumur e5 182
Saunders Island d6 295
Saunders, Mount k3 86
Saundersfoot b5 163
Saung a1 101
Sauquoit e1 256
Saur, Khrebet v4 121
Saurat d6 187
Saurimo d5 224
Sauris g3 196
Sausalito a4 264
Sausapor j6 97
Saussy a3 184
Sautar c6 224
Sauteurs G 271
Sautso Kraftverk j2 155
Sauve f5 187
Sauveterre-de-Béarn b5 187
Sauveterre-de-Guyenne b4 186
Sauvo k2 157
Sauvolles, Lac f2 252
Sauxillanges f3 186
Sauzal, Maule, Chile a3 296
Sauzal, O'Higgins, Chile b3 296
Sauzé-Vaussais c2 186
Sauzon b5 182
Sava j4 177
Savá d3 276
Sava g4 198
Savai'i M 75
Savai'i, Cape M 75
Savalou e4 223
Savanna a4 254
Savannah, Georgia, U.S.A. j3 259
Savannah,
  South Carolina, U.S.A. j3 259
Savannah Sound l7 259
Savannakhét g7 102
Savanna-la-Mar B 270
Savant Lake,
  Ontario, Can. h5 250
Savant Lake, Ontario, Can. h5 250
Savanur d5 126
Sävar h5 154
Sävarån h5 154
Săvârșin l5 171
Savaștepe a3 208
Savè e4 223
Save, Fr. c5 187
Save, Moz. e3 233
Sāveh n4 137
Savelugu d4 222
Savenay d5 182
Săveni h2 201
Saverdun d5 187
Saveretik f3 285
Saverne d2 184
Saviaho m5 155
Savigliano b5 196
Savignac-les-Églises c3 186
Savignano Irpino e3 198
Savigné-l'Évêque f4 183
Savigny-lès-Beaune a3 184
Savigny-sur-Braye f5 183
Savigny-sur-Orge h4 183
Savines-le-Lac c6 185
Săvinești h2 201
Savinja f3 177
Savinjska g3 177
Savinobor j3 147
Savinskij e3 146
Savitaipale m2 157
Savli f9 129
Šavnik d4 200
Savognin d3 196
Savoie c5 185
Savona, Can. g6 248
Savona, Italy c5 197
Savona c5 197
Savonlinna n2 157
Savonranta n1 157
Savoonga b3 246
Savran' k1 201
Şavşat j2 209
Sävsjö f4 156
Savu m10 99
Savudrija e4 176
Savudrija, Rt e4 176
Savukoski m3 155
Savur h4 209
Savusavu E 74
Savusavu Bay E 74
Savuti c2 232
Sawahlunto a5 98
Sawai k6 97
Sawai Madhopur e7 124
Sawai, Gunung e8 98
Sawan h5 99
Sawankhalok d7 102
Sawar g8 129
Sawara j4 115
Sawasaki-bana h3 115
Sawatch Range b4 260
Sawbridgeworth g5 163
Sawdā', Jabal as g3 221
Sawin m4 169
Sawla d4 222
Sawmills d2 233
Sawston g4 163
Sawtell e7 85
Sawtooth Peak e6 265
Sawtry f4 163
Sawu l10 99
Sawu Sea SE l9 99
Sawyer c6 250
Sax d6 193
Saxān e4 154
Saxilby f3 162
Saxmundham h4 163
Saxnäs e4 154
Saxon b3 196
Saxton b4 256
Say, Mali d3 222
Say, Niger e3 223
Şāyā d1 138
Sayago d3 190
Sayak r4 121
Sayama h4 115
Sayanna-la-Mar B 270
Sayat a1 128
Sayatón b4 192
Sayaxché b2 276
Saybrook b5 254
Sayda j2 175
Şaydnāyā e3 138
Saye b3 186
Sāyen q6 137
Sayghān c3 128
Sayḩūt h4 219
Sayla e9 129
Säynätsalo l1 157
Saynshand f3 112
Sayram Hu t5 121
Sayramskiy, Pik n6 121
Sayre, Oklahoma, U.S.A. d5 261
Sayre, Pennsylvania, U.S.A. d3 256
Sayreville f4 257
Sayula, Jalisco, Mex. c4 274
Sayula, Veracruz, Mex. g5 275
Sayula, Laguna de c4 274
Say'ūn g4 219
Say-Utes j3 149
Sayward e6 248
Sázava, Czech Rep. d2 170
Sázava c2 170
Sazin a2 130
Sažino j4 147
Sazonovo c2 150
Sbaa d3 220
Sbeitla f1 221
Scaddan e13 87
Scaër b4 182
Scafa d2 198
Scafell Pike c2 162
Scalasaig b3 164
Scalby f2 162
Scalea e5 198
Scaletta Zanclea e6 199
Scammon b1 258
Scammon Bay c3 246
Scandale f5 199
Scandiano e5 196
Scanlon g7 250
Scanno c3 198
Scano di Montiferro Aa2 198
Scansano f7 197
Scânteia h3 201
Scanzano Jonico f4 198
Scapa Flow g1 164
Scarborough, Can. g4 254
Scarborough, Trin. E 271
Scarborough, U.K. f2 162
Scarborough Shoal a3 100
Scardovari g5 196
Scargill d5 77
Scarinish b3 164
Scario e4 198
Scarpe h2 183
Scarperia f6 197
Scarriff c4 165
Scarsdale g3 257
Scartaglen b4 165
Scaterie Island n5 253
Scauri a8 199
Scavaig, Loch b2 164
Ščekino d4 150
Ščel'jajur h2 147
Ščetinskoe e2 150
Scey-sur-Saône-et-St-Albin b3 184
Schaalbeke h2 173
Schaale f2 173
Schaalsee f2 173
Schaffhausen c2 196
Schafflund c4 158
Schafstädt g4 173
Schagen c2 159
Schalkau g2 175
Schallstadt c5 174
Schapen f2 159
Scharbeutz d4 158
Schärding e1 176
Scharfreiter c2 176
Scharhörn d1 172
Scharmützelsee k3 173
Scharnitz c2 176
Scharnitzpass c2 176
Scharrel (Oldenburg) c2 172
Scharteberg b2 174
Schebheim f3 174
Scheer e4 174
Scheeßel e2 172
Schefferville j1 253
Scheggino g7 197
Scheibbs g2 177
Scheifling f2 177
Schelde b4 159
Schell Creek Range f6 263
Schellerten f3 172
Schellsburg b4 256
Schenectady g2 257
Schenefeld c5 158
Schermbeck e3 159
Scherpenheuvel c4 159
Schertz k3 273
Scheßlitz g3 175
Schesaplana e5 174
Schiedam c3 159
Schiehallion d3 164
Schierling h4 175
Schiermonnikoog e1 159
Schiermonnikoog
  Nationaal Park e1 159
Schiers d3 196
Schiffdorf b5 158
Schilde c3 159
Schilde, Ger. g2 173
Schilpario e3 196
Schiltach d4 174
Schiltigheim d2 184
Schimatari d4 210
Schio, Veneto, Italy f4 196
Schipkau j4 173
Schirmeck d2 184
Schitu Duca h2 201
Schiza b6 211
Schkölen g1 175
Schlabendorf j4 173
Schladen f3 173
Schladming e2 176
Schlei e1 172
Schleiden e4 159
Schleife k4 173
Schleitheim c2 196
Schleiz g2 175
Schleswig c4 158
Schleswig-Holstein e1 172
Schleswig-Holsteinisches
  Wattenmeer,
  Nationalpark d1 172
Schleusingen f2 175
Schliersee g5 175
Schlitz e2 174
Schloss Holte-Stukenbrock d4 172
Schlosswil b3 196
Schlotheim d1 175
Schluchsee, Ger. d5 174
Schluchsee d5 174
Schlüchtern e2 174
Schlüsselfeld f3 175
Schmalfeld c5 158
Schmalfelder Au f2 172
Schmallenberg c1 174
Schmelz e5 159
Schmidmühlen g3 175
Schmidtsdrif f4 234
Schmittenhöhe d2 176
Schmölln,
  Brandenburg, Ger. k2 173
Schmölln, Thüringen, Ger. h2 175
Schmutter f4 175
Schneeberg h2 175
Schneidlingen g4 173
Schneverdingen e2 172
Schoberpass f2 177
Schœlcher J 271
Schoenberg e4 159
Schoharie f2 257
Schoinoussa f6 211
Schombee f5 235
Schönau am Königssee d2 176
Schönberg d5 158
Schönberg (Holstein) d4 158
Schönbuch d4 174
Schönbuch, Naturpark d4 174
Schönebeck h2 173
Schöneiche Berlin j3 173
Schönermark j2 173
Schongau f5 175
Schönhausen h3 173
Schöningen f3 173
Schönkirchen d4 158
Schöntal e3 174
Schönwalde j4 173
Schönwalde am
  Bungsberg d4 158
Schoonhoven c3 159
Schopfheim c5 174
Schöpfl g1 177
Schorfheide HE j3 173
Schorndorf e4 174
Schortens c2 172
Schotten e2 174
Schouten Island Ac3 83
Schrader d3 256
Schramberg d4 174
Schrankogel c2 176
Schreiber k6 251
Schrems g1 177
Schriesheim d3 174
Schrobenhausen g4 175
Schrozberg e3 174
Schruns a2 176
Schübelbach c2 196
Schuby c4 158
Schulenburg a5 258
Schull b5 165
Schultz Lake k3 242
Schulzendorf k3 173
Schulzendorf bei Eichwalde j3 173
Schüpfheim c3 196
Schurz e3 264
Schussen e5 174
Schutter c4 174
Schutterwald c4 174
Schüttorf f2 159
Schuylkill e4 256
Schuylkill Haven d4 256
Schwaan f5 158
Schwabach g3 175
Schwaben f4 175
Schwäbisch Gmünd e4 174
Schwäbisch Hall e3 174
Schwäbische Alb e3 174
Schwäbisch-Fränkischer
  Wald, Naturpark e4 174
Schwabmünchen f4 175
Schwaförden d3 172
Schwaigern e3 174
Schwalm e5 172
Schwalmstadt-
  Ziegenhain e2 174
Schwanden d2 196
Schwandorf h3 175
Schwanebeck g4 173
Schwanenstadt e1 176
Schwaner,
  Pegunungan g5 98
Schwanewede d2 172
Schwangau f5 175
Schwansen f1 172
Schwarmstedt e3 172
Schwartau f1 173
Schwarz h2 173
Schwarzach im Pongau e2 176
Schwarze Elster j4 173
Schwarze Laber g3 175
Schwarzenbek d5 158
Schwarzenberg h2 175
Schwarzenburg b3 196
Schwarzenfeld h3 175
Schwarzenstein f2 196
Schwarzer Mann b2 174
Schwarzhorn c3 196
Schwarzrand b2 234
Schwarzwald d4 174
Schwaz c2 176
Schwechat h1 177
Schwedeneck d4 158
Schwedt an der Oder k3 173
Schwegenheim d3 174
Schweich e5 159
Schweinfurt f2 174
Schweinrich h2 173
Schweizer-Reneke f3 235
Schwelm f3 159
Schwenningen b1 174
Schwepnitz j4 173
Schwerin e5 158
Schweriner See f2 173
Schwertberg f1 177
Schwerte f3 159
Schwetzingen d3 174
Schwielochsee k3 173
Schwinge j1 173
Schwyz c2 196
Sciacca c7 199
Scicli d8 199
Scie g3 183
Sciez c4 184
Ščigry e2 148
Sciliar,
  Parco Naturale dello f3 196
Scilla e6 199
Ścinawa e4 168
Ścinawka e5 168
Scionzier c4 184
Sciota e4 256
Scioto e6 254
Scipio g6 262
Scituate k2 257
Scituate Reservoir j3 257
Scleddau b5 163
Scobey q7 249
Scoglia d'Africa e7 197
Scoglitti d8 199
Scole h4 163
Scone k12 81
Scooba e3 258
Scopello c4 196
Scordia d7 199
Scorff b5 182
Scornicești g3 201
Scorzè g4 196
Scotia g2 257
Scotia Ridge e15 302
Scotia Sea SE g15 302
Scotland d3 144
Scotlandville d4 258
Scott City c4 260
Scott Island c5 248
Scott Lake p2 249
Scott Reef f4 86
Scott, Cape c6 248
Scott, Mount,
  Oklahoma, U.S.A. a3 258
Scott, Mount,
  Oregon, U.S.A. b4 262
Scottburgh j5 235
Scottdale a4 256
Scotter f3 162
Scottish Borders e4 164
Scottsbluff c3 260
Scottsboro f2 258
Scottsburg d6 254
Scottsdale Ab2 83
Scottsdale, U.S.A. h9 263
Scottville c4 254
Scotty's Junction f4 264
Scourie c1 164
Scrabster e1 164
Scranton,
  North Dakota, U.S.A. b7 250
Scranton,
  Pennsylvania, U.S.A. e3 256
Scremerston g4 164
Screven h4 259
Scrivia c5 196
Ščuč'e, Russ. Fed. m2 147
Ščuč'e, Kurganskaja
  Oblast', Russ. Fed. k5 147
Ščuč'e Ozero j4 147
Scugog, Lake c6 252
Scunthorpe f3 162
Scuol e3 196
Scurrival Point a2 164
Sea Isle City f5 256
Sea Lake f13 81
Sea Lion Islands e6 295
Sea of Galilee d4 138
Sea, Solomon SE j6 300
Seabrook, Lake e12 87
Seaford, U.K. g6 163
Seaford, U.S.A. e6 256
Seaforth, Aust. j6 80
Seaforth, Can. f4 254
Seahorse Bank a5 100
Seal e1 250
Seal Bay d2 298
Seal Cove p4 253
Seal Lake m1 253
Seal, Cape e7 234
Seale g3 259
Sealevel l2 259
Sealga, Loch na c2 164
Seara b3 190
Searchlight f8 263
Searcy d2 258
Searles f6 265
Searles Lake f6 265
Sears d4 256
Seascale c2 162
Seaside, California, U.S.A. b5 264
Seaside, Oregon, U.S.A. b3 262
Seaside Park f5 257
Seattle b2 262
Seaview Range A 84
Seaward Kaikoura Range d5 77
Seba l10 99
Sebaco d4 276
Sebago Lake l4 255
Sebakwe Dam e2 233
Šebalino v2 121
Sebangan, Teluk g6 98
Sebangka c4 98
Sebastián Vizcaino,
  Bahía b3 272
Sebastopol, Aust. c3 82
Sebastopol, U.S.A. a3 264
Sebatik k2 99
Sebauh g3 98
Sebayan, Bukit f5 98
Sebba e3 223
Sebdou d2 220
Sébé b4 224
Sebeka f7 250
Šebekino e2 148
Sébékoro c3 222
Seben c2 208
Sebeş f3 201
Sebesi c7 98
Sebewaing e4 254
Sebež n4 157
Şebinkarahisar g2 209
Sebiş l5 171
Sebka de Tindouf c3 220
Seblat, Gunung b6 98
Sebnitz k2 175
Sebou, Oued c2 220
Sebree f1 258
Sebring j6 259
Sebuku, Indon. j6 99
Sebuku, Indon. j2 99
Sebuku, Teluk j3 99
Seč d2 170
Seca, Pampa e3 296
Secas, Islas f7 277
Sečenovo h4 151
Sechura a5 284
Sechura, Bahía de a5 284
Sechura, Desierto de a5 284
Seckach e3 174
Seckau f2 177
Seclin b4 159
Seco e4 192
Second Mountain d4 256
Secondigny e6 182
Sečovce k3 171
Secretary Island a6 77
Secunda h3 235
Secunderabad f4 126
Sécure d3 292
Secusigiu j5 171
Seda, Lat. l4 157
Seda, Lith k4 157
Seda, Port c5 191
Sedalia e4 260
Sedam e4 126
Sedan c5 159
Sedan, U.S.A. a1 258
Sedanka Island c5 246
Sedano g2 190
Sedbergh d2 162
Seddon e4 77
Seddonville c4 77
Sedé Avraham c5 139
Sedé Boqer c6 139
Sedeh p6 137
Seden d3 158
Séderon b6 185
Sederot c5 139
Sédhiou a3 222
Sedico g3 196
Sedilo Aa2 198
Sedini Aa2 198
Sedlčany c2 170
Sedlec Prčice c2 170
Sedlice b2 170
Sedlyshche p4 169
Šedok f3 148
Sedom d5 139
Sedro-Woolley b1 262
Seduka c5 101
Šeduva k5 157
Sędziszów j5 169
Sędziszów Małopolski k5 169
See b2 176
Sée d4 182
Seebad Heringsdorf k2 173
Seeberg f3 177
Seeboden e3 176
Seedorf d5 158
Seefeld (Stadland) b5 158
Seefeld in Tirol c2 176
Seeg f5 175
Seehausen,
  Brandenburg, Ger. j2 173
Seehausen, Sachsen-
  Anhalt, Ger. g3 173
Seehausen (Altmark) g3 173
Seeheim b3 234
Seeheim-Jugenheim d3 174
Seeis b1 234
Seekirchen am Wallersee e2 176
Seekoegat e6 234
Seelow k3 173
Seelze e3 172
Seemade d2 226
Seerücken c2 196
Sées f4 183
Seesen f4 172
Seeshaupt g5 175
Seeve f2 172
Seevetal d5 158
Seewalchen am Attersee e2 176
Seewiesen g2 177
Séez c5 185
Seez d2 196
Sefadu b4 222
Sefare g1 235
Seferihisar a3 208
Sefid, Kūh-e m5 137
Sefrou d2 220
Sefton, N.Z. d5 77
Sefton, U.K. c3 162
Sefton, Mount b5 77
Segag c2 226
Ségala, Fr. e4 187
Ségala b3 222
Segama b8 100
Segamat c4 101
Şegarcea f3 201
Ségbana e3 223
Sege j6 97
Segesd f5 170
Seget j6 97
Segeža q5 155
Seghnān e2 128
Segiz l5 120
Segl, Lago da d3 196
Segni h8 197
Segonzac b3 186
Segorbe d5 193
Ségou, Mali c3 222
Ségou c3 222
Segovia, Col. c2 284
Segovia, Spain f3 190
Segovia f4 190
Segozerskoe, Ozero c3 146
Segré e5 182
Segre e3 192
Ségrie f3 183
Seguam Island a5 246
Seguam Pass a5 246
Séguédine g4 221
Séguéla, C.I. c4 222
Séguéla, Mali c3 222
Séguélon c4 222
Seguí g2 297
Seguin a5 258
Segula Island Ab1 247
Segundo f1 297
Segura d5 191
Segura, Spain d6 193
Segura de la Sierra b6 193
Segura de León d6 191
Segura de los Baños d4 192
Segurilla f4 190
Sehithwa c3 232
Sehlabathebe
  National Park h5 235
Sehnde e3 172
Seho n6 99
Sehore e8 124
Sehwan c7 129
Seia c4 190
Seiche d4 182
Seiches-sur-le-Loir e5 182
Seiersberg g2 177
Seierstad c4 154
Seifhennersdorf k2 175
Seignelay j5 183
Seignelégier a2 196
Seikpyu b5 102
Seiland j1 155
Seilhac d3 186
Seiling d4 261
Seillans c7 185
Seille, Fr. b4 184
Seille, Fr. c2 184
Sein, Île de a4 182
Seinäjärvi k1 157
Seinäjoki, Fin. j5 155
Seinäjoki j5 155
Seine f3 183
Seine, Baie de d3 182
Seine, Val de j4 183
Seine-et-Marne j4 183
Seine-Maritime f3 183
Seine-St-Denis b3 182
Seini f2 201
Seipinang h5 99
Seira e2 192
Seissan c5 187
Seitenstetten f1 177
Seitovka h3 149
Seitsemisen
  kansallispuisto k2 157
Seival f2 294
Seix d6 187
Seixal B 189
Seixe b7 191
Sejerby e3 158
Sejerø e3 158
Sejerø Bugt e3 158
Sejka w2 121
Sejny m1 169
Sekadau f4 98
Sekanak, Teluk c5 98
Sekatak Bengara j3 99
Sekayu b6 98
Seke a4 231
Sekenke a4 231
Seki g4 115
Sekicau, Gunung c7 98
Sekinchan b4 101
Sekoma e2 234
Sekondi d5 222
Šeksna e2 150
Sel'co c5 150
Sela Dingay b2 226
Šelaboliha u1 121
Selagan a6 98
Šelagskij, Mys t2 119
Selah c2 262
Selama b3 101
Selangor c3 101
Selargius Ab3 198
Selatan, Tanjung h7 99
Selatpanjang c5 101

Selawik → Shepard Island 381

Selawik d2 246
Selawik e2 246
Selb h2 175
Selbekken b5 154
Selbitz, Ger. g2 175
Selbitz g2 175
Selbu c5 154
Selbusjøen a7 100
Selby, U.K. e3 162
Selby, U.S.A. c2 260
Selbyville e6 256
Selçuk a4 208
Seldovia g4 246
Sele e4 198
Selebi-Phikwe d3 233
Selegu g5 225
Selemdža j2 94
Selenge, D.R.C. c4 224
Selenge, Mong. d1 112
Selenge, Mong. a1 112
Selenge Mörön c1 112
Selenicë d5 200
Selero e1 210
Sélestat d2 184
Seletinskoye p1 121
Seleuș k5 171
Seleznevo n2 157
Selfoss A 152
Selfridge c2 260
Seli b4 222
Sélibabi b2 222
Seligenstadt d2 174
Seliger, Ozero b3 150
Seligman c1 258
Šelihova, Zaliv r4 119
Selimiye a4 208
Sélingué, Lac de c3 222
Selinous c4 210
Selinsgrove d4 256
Selišče b3 150
Seliu d6 98
Seližarovo b3 150
Selje a1 156
Seljord c3 156
Selke g4 173
Selkirk, Can. e5 250
Selkirk, U.K. f4 164
Selkirk Mountains e1 262
Sellano g7 197
Sellasia c5 211
Sellers k2 259
Sellersburg d6 254
Selles-sur-Cher g5 183
Sellia e7 211
Sellia Marina f6 199
Sellières b4 184
Sellrain c2 176
Sells h10 263
Sellye f6 171
Selm f3 159
Selma, Alabama, U.S.A. f3 258
Selma, California, U.S.A. d5 264
Selma, North Carolina, U.S.A. k2 259
Selmo d2 190
Selmsdorf d5 158
Selommes g5 183
Šelon' n4 157
Selong j9 99
Selongey b3 184
Sélouma b3 222
Selous Game Reserve g5 225
Selsey f6 163
Selsingen c5 158
Selters (Westerwald) c2 174
Selty m3 151
Seltz e2 184
Seluan d2 98
Sélune e4 182
Selva g4 198
Selva Obscura a5 296
Selvagens, Ilhas a2 220
Selvänä k3 137
Selviria c4 290
Selway f2 262
Selwyn Mountain, m3 247
Selyatyn g2 201
Selz d3 174
Selzthal f2 177
Sem Tripa b2 288
Seman d5 200
Semanggol b3 101
Semangka, Teluk c7 98
Semarang f8 98
Sematan e4 98
Semau m10 99
Semayang, Danau j5 99
Sembadel f3 186
Sembakung j3 99
Sembé b3 224
Semblançay f5 183
Şemdinli k3 137
Séméac c5 187
Semeliškės n1 169
Semendua c4 224
Semenivka d1 148
Semenov h3 151
Semenovskoe e2 150
Semenyih b4 101
Semidi Islands e4 246
Semigorodnjaja f2 150
Semillero b3 276
Semiluki e2 148
Semily d1 170
Seminara e6 199
Seminary e4 258
Semine b4 184
Seminoe Reservoir b3 260
Seminole, Oklahoma, U.S.A. a2 258
Seminole, Texas, U.S.A. c5 261
Seminole, Lake g4 259
Seminskij Hrebet v2 121
Semiozernoye k1 120
Semipalatinsk t2 121
Semipolka l5 147
Semirara c5 100
Semirara Islands c5 100
Semirom n6 137
Semisopochnoi Island Ac1 247
Semitau f4 98
Semiyarka s2 121
Semizbuga q2 121
Semlevo b4 150
Semliki f3 225
Semmedaban, Hrebet p3 119
Semmenstedt f3 173
Semmering g2 177
Semnān, Iran q4 137
Semnān p4 137
Sêmnyi a7 112
Semois d5 159
Semonkong h4 235
Sempach c2 196
Sempacher See c2 196
Semporna b8 100
Šempu g9 98
Šemša k3 171
Semur-en-Auxois a3 184
Semur-en-Brionnais a4 184
Šemurša j4 151
Semypolky c2 148
Semža f2 147
Sen'kina g2 146
Sena, Bol. d2 292
Seňa, Slvk. k3 171
Sena, Spain d3 192
Sena Madureira d1 292
Senador Canedo d2 290
Senador Pompeu e3 288
Senai c5 101
Senaja a7 100
Senaki j1 209
Senales e3 196
Senanayake Samudra A 127
Senanga c2 232
Sénas b7 185
Senatobia e2 258
Sendai, Kagoshima, Japan d6 114
Sendai, Miyagi, Japan j2 115
Senden, Bayern, Ger. f4 174
Senden, Nordrhein-Westfalen, Ger. f3 159
Sendenhorst c4 172
Sendim d3 190
Sêndo p4 125
Sene d4 222
Senebui, Tanjung b4 101
Senec f3 170
Seneca Falls d2 256
Seneca Lake d2 256
Seneca Rocks a6 256
Sénégal b2 222
Senegal a3 217

SENEGAL

THE REPUBLIC OF SENEGAL
Area 196,722km² (75,955sq miles)
Capital Dakar
Organizations ECOWAS, OIC
Population 9,860,000
Pop. growth (%) 2.7
Life expectancy 50 (m); 54 (f)
Languages French, many local languages
Literacy 40.2%
Currency CFA franc (US $1 = 534.95 CFA franc)
GDP (US million $) 5345
GDP per head ($US) 542

Seneghe Aa2 198
Senekal g4 235
Seney l7 251
Senez c7 185
Senftenberg j4 173
Senga Hill f5 225
Sengar f6 124
Sengata j4 99
Sengejskij, Ostrov g1 146
Sengerema f4 225
Sengés d6 290
Senggarang c5 101
Sênggê Zangbo e3 130
Senggi l6 97
Senguerr b5 295
Sengwa d2 233
Senhor do Bonfim d4 288
Senhora do Rosário c5 191
Senica f3 170
Senigallia h6 197
Senillosa c5 296
Senir d3 138
Senis Aa3 198
Senise f4 198
Senj f5 177
Senja f2 154
Şenkaya j2 209
Senko c4 222
Senkobo d2 232
Šenku c2 130
Šenkursk e3 146
Šenkvice f3 170
Senlin Shan r4 113
Senlis h3 183
Senmonorom h9 103
Sennar d5 218
Sennar, Sinnār, Sudan d5 218
Sennar Dam d5 218
Sennariolo Aa2 198
Sennecey-le-Grand a4 184
Senneterre h1 255
Sennoj g1 149
Sennori Aa2 198
Sennybridge c5 163
Senoia g3 259
Sénonais j4 183
Senonches g4 183
Senones c2 184
Senorbì Ab3 198
Senouire f3 186
Senožeče f4 177
Senqu h5 235
Sens j4 183
Sens-de-Bretagne d4 182
Sensuntepeque c4 276
Senta j6 171
Šentala k4 151
Senthal d5 130
Šentilj g3 177
Sentinel g9 263
Sentinel Peak g4 248
Sentinel Range jj2 298
Sentispac b3 274
Šentjur pri Celju g3 177
Sento Sé d3 288
Sentrum g2 235
Şenyurt h4 209
Seonath g9 124
Seoni f8 124
Seoni-Malwa e8 124
Seoul p7 113
Seoul, Sŏul-t'ŭkpyŏlsi, S. Kor. p7 113
Séoune c4 187
Sep'o p6 113
Sepanjang h8 99
Separation Point d4 77
Sepasu j4 99
Sepatini d1 292
Sepetiba, Baía de g5 291
Sepinang k4 99
Sepino d3 198
Sępólno Krajeńskie g2 168
Sepopol k1 169
Sepotuba f3 293
Seppa n6 125
Şepreuş k5 171
Septèmes-les-Vallons b7 185
Septfonds d4 187
Sept-Îles j3 253
Sepúlveda g3 190
Sepupa c2 232
Sequals g3 196
Sequeira j1 297
Sequillo f2 190
Sequim b1 262
Sequoia National Park e5 264
Serafimovič f2 149
Seraing d4 159
Seram h6 97
Seram Sea SE h6 97
Serami k6 97
Séran b5 185
Serang d8 98
Serapi, Gunung e4 98
Serasan e3 98
Serasan, Selat e3 98
Seravezza e6 197
Seraya e3 98
Serbia e3 200
Serbia and Montenegro j6 145

SERBIA & MONTENEGRO

STATE COMMUNITY OF SERBIA AND MONTENEGRO
Area 102,173km² (39,449sq miles)
Capital Belgrade
Organizations
Population 10,540,000
Pop. growth (%) 0.1
Life expectancy 69 (m); 74 (f)
Languages Serbo-Croat (Cyrillic script)
Literacy 89%
Currency Dinar (Kosovo: euro & dinar, Montenegro: euro) (US $1 = 55.70 Dinar)
GDP (US million $) 13,698
GDP per head ($US) 1299

Sêrbug Co j3 135
Serchio e6 197
Serdán g3 272
Serdang, Kedah, Malay. b3 101
Serdang, Selangor, Malay. b4 101
Serdce-Kamen', Mys b2 246
Serdo f5 219
Serdobsk g1 149
Serebrjane Prudy e4 150
Serebryansk u3 121
Sered' f3 170
Sereda f3 150
Seredejskij c4 150
Seredyne l3 171
Seredžius k5 157
Şereflikoçhisar d3 208
Seregélyes g4 171
Seregno d4 196
Serein k5 183
Seremban b4 101
Serena, Embalse de la e6 191
Serengeti National Park f4 225
Serengeti Plains b4 231
Serenje e1 233
Sereno c3 288
Sérent c5 182
Serere f3 225
Sereža g4 151
Serfaus b2 176
Serfopoula e5 211
Sergač k4 151
Sergeja Kirova, Ostrova k2 118
Sergelen, Dornod, Mong. h1 112
Sergelen, Sühbaatar, Mong. f2 112
Sergen h5 201
Sergeyevka, Akmolinskaya Oblast', Kaz. m2 121
Sergeyevka, Severnyy Kazakhstan, Kaz. l5 147
Sergiev Posad e3 150
Sergino l3 147
Sergipe e4 288
Serhiyivka, Odes'ka Oblast', Ukr. k2 201
Seria h2 99
Serian f4 98
Seribudolok d14 103
Sérifontaine g3 183
Serifos e5 211
Serifos, Notio Aigaio, Grc. e5 211
Serifou, Steno e5 211
Sérignan f5 187
Serik c4 208
Serikkembelo h6 97
Seringa, Serra da b3 288
Serino d4 198
Serir Nerastro b3 218
Serkaly l3 147
Serkhiv p4 169
Serkout f4 221
Sermaises h4 183
Sermano A 185
Sermide f5 196
Sermoneta h8 197
Sernancelhe c4 190
Sernovodsk l5 151
Serock k3 169
Serodino g2 297
Serón b7 193
Serón de Nájima b3 183
Serones, Embalse de f4 190
Seronga c2 232
Serós e3 192
Serov k4 147
Serowe g1 235
Serpa c7 191
Serpa, Ilha de f4 285
Serpent's Mouth E 271
Serpentine b13 87
Serpentine Lakes j11 87
Serpis d6 193
Serpneve j2 201
Serpovoe f5 150
Serpuhov d4 150
Serquigny f3 183
Serra, Braz. h4 291
Serra d5 193
Serra da Bocaina, Parque Nacional da f5 291
Serra da Bodoquena, Parque Nacional da f4 293
Serra da Canastra, Parque Nacional da e4 291
Serra da Capivara, Parque Nacional da d3 288
Serra da Estrela, Parque Natural da c4 190
Serra da Mesa, Represa c4 289
Serra das Araras c1 291
Serra de Outes b2 190
Serra de'Conti h6 197
Serra do Divisor, Parque Nacional da c1 292
Serra do Navio g3 285
Serra do Salitre e3 291
Serra dos Aimorés h2 291
Serra Riccò c5 196
Serra San Bruno f6 199
Serra Talhada e3 288
Serracapriola e3 198
Serradifalco c7 199
Serra-di-Ferro A 185
Serramanna Aa3 198
Serramazzoni e5 197
Serrana e4 290
Serrana Bank g3 277
Serranía de la Neblina, Parque Nacional d3 284
Serranilla Bank h3 277
Serrano f3 297
Serranópolis b3 290
Serras de Aire e Candeeiros, Parque Natural das b5 191
Serrat de les Pedres g3 192
Serravalle Scrivia c5 196
Serre, Fr. j3 183
Serre e4 198
Serre, Massif de la b3 184
Serrenti Aa3 198
Serre-Ponçon, Lac de c6 185
Serres, Fr. b6 185
Serres, Grc. d1 210
Serrezuela c2 294
Serri Ab3 198
Serrières a5 185
Serrinha e4 288
Serrita e3 288
Sêrro g3 291
Serrota e4 190
Serrucho b4 295
Sertã b5 191
Sertânia e3 288
Sertanópolis c5 290
Sertãozinho e4 290
Sertolovo a1 150
Sertung c8 98
Séru c2 226
Serui k6 97
Serule d3 232
Seruna f6 129
Serutu e5 98
Seruyan g6 98
Servia c2 210
Serviana e3 192
Servigliano c1 198
Servol e4 192
Servoz c5 185
Serwaru h7 97
Sêrxü b2 104
Ses Salines, Cap de g5 193
Sesa d3 192
Sešan b2 246
Sesayap, Indon. j3 99
Sesayap j3 99
Sese Islands f4 225
Seseganaga Lake j5 251
Sesepe h6 97
Sesfontein a2 232
Seshachalam Hills e5 126
Sesheke c2 232
Sesia c4 196
Sesimbra a6 191
Seskarö j4 155
Seskilo Ac2 211
Šešma l4 151
Sesma b2 192
Sessa c1 198
Sessa Aurunca c3 198
Šessaya f2 154
Šestakovo l2 151
Sestao b1 192
Sestino g6 197
Sesto al Reghena g4 196
Sesto Calende c4 196
Sesto Fiorentino f6 197
Sesto San Giovanni d4 196
Sestola e5 197
Sestri Levante d5 197
Sestriere a5 196
Sestroreck n2 157
Sestu Ab3 198
Šešupė m1 169
Šešuvis k5 157
Sesvete h4 177
Set e3 192
Šeta l5 157
Setana Aa2 114
Sète f5 187
Sete Barras e6 290
Sete Lagoas f3 291
Šetekšna l5 157
Setenil e8 191
Setermoen g2 154
Setesdal b3 156
Seti f6 135
Sétif f1 221
Setil Misanimkeh l7 97
Setit e5 219
Seto g4 115
Seto-naikai SE e4 115
Seto-naikai National Park e4 114
Settat c2 220
Setté Cama a4 224
Settimo Torinese b4 196
Settle d2 162
Settlers h2 235
Setúbal, Port b6 191
Setúbal b6 191
Setúbal, Baía de a6 191
Setubinha g2 291
Seudre b3 186
Seugne b3 186
Seui Ab3 198
Seul, Lac g5 250
Seulimeum b13 103
Seulles e3 182
Seulo Ab3 198
Seurre b3 184
Sevan g4 149
Sevana Lich g4 149
Sévaré d3 222
Sevaruyo d3 292
Sevastopol' d3 148
Seven Stones A 163
Sevenoaks g5 163
Sever do Vouga b4 190
Sévérac-le-Château f4 187
Severin h4 177
Severino Ribeiro e2 294
Severn, Aust. d6 85
Severn, Can. j3 251
Severn e3 234
Severn, U.K. d5 163
Severn Lake h4 250
Severna Park d5 256
Severnaja j1 151
Severnaja Dvina e3 146
Severnaja Osetija-Alanija, Respublika f4 149
Severnaja Zemlja l1 119
Severnyj, Moskovskaja Oblast', Russ. Fed. d3 150
Severnyj, Respublika Komi, Russ. Fed. l2 147
Severnyj Anjujskij Hrebet s3 119
Severnyj Berezovyj, Ostrov n2 157
Severnyj Kommunar h4 147
Severnyj Ural j3 147
Severnyy Chink Ustyurta f4 120
Severnyy Kazakhstan m1 121
Severobaykal'sk d1 94
Severodvinsk d2 146
Severo-Enisejskij k3 119
Severomorsk p2 155
Severoonežsk d3 146
Severo-Osetinskij Zapovednik g4 149
Severo-Sibirskaja Nizmennost' l2 119
Severoural'sk j3 147
Severskaja e3 148
Seveso d4 196
Ševětín c2 170
Sevettijärvi m2 155
Sevier g7 263
Sevier Desert g6 262
Sevier Lake g6 261
Sevierville h2 259
Sevilla, Spain e7 191
Sevilla e7 191
Seville e7 191
Sevilleja de la Jara f5 191
Sevingé j4 297
Sevlievo g4 201
Sevnica g3 177
Sèvre Nantaise d5 182
Sévrier c5 185
Sevron b4 184
Sevsk d1 148
Sewa b4 222
Sewani b5 130
Seward, Alaska, U.S.A. g3 247
Seward, Nebraska, U.S.A. d3 260
Seward Peninsula c2 246
Sewell b3 296
Sexan f2 156
Sextin g4 272
Seybaplaya p8 273
Seychelles h5 217

SEYCHELLES

THE REPUBLIC OF SEYCHELLES
Area 454km² (176sq miles)
Capital Victoria, on Mahé
Organizations COMESA, COMM, SADC
Population 81,000
Pop. growth (%) 1.3
Life expectancy 65 (m); 74 (f)
Languages Creole, English, French
Literacy 85%
Currency Seychelles rupee (US $1 = 5.5 Seychelles rupee)
GDP (US million $) 700
GDP per head ($US) 8641

Seyches c4 186
Seydi a1 128
Seydişehir c4 208
Seyðisfjörður A 152
Seye d3 182
Seyfe Gölü e3 208
Seyhan e3 209
Seyitgazi c3 208
Seym d2 148
Seymour, Aust. g14 81
Seymour, R.S.A. g6 235
Seymour, Connecticut, U.S.A. g3 257
Seymour, Indiana, U.S.A. d6 254
Seymour, Missouri, U.S.A. d1 258
Seymour, Texas, U.S.A. d5 261
Seymour Inlet d6 248
Seymour Range a8 80
Seymour, Isla A 286
Seymourville d4 258
Seyne c6 185
Seynod c5 185
Seyssel b5 185
Seysses d5 187
Seyyedābād d3 128
Sežana e4 176
Sézanne j4 183
Sezela j5 235
Sezimovo Ústí c2 170
Sezze c3 198
Sfaka Aa3 210
Sfakia e7 211
Sfaktiria b6 211
Sfântu Gheorghe g3 201
Sfax g2 221
Sfikia, Limni c2 210
Sgurr Alasdair b2 164
Sgurr Dhomhnuill c3 164
Sgurr Mòr c2 164
Sha He d1 106
Sha Xi l1 113
Sha'al d3 138
Shaanxi a2 106
Shaban c6 129
Shabeellaha Dhexe d3 226
Shabeellaha Hoose c3 226
Shabestar k2 137
Shabla j4 201
Shabla, Nos j4 201
Shabogamo Lake j2 253
Shabunda e4 225
Shabwah g4 219
Shache r8 121
Shackleton Ice Shelf r1 298
Shackleton Range b3 298
Shadadkot c7 129
Shadaogou a5 106
Shādegān m6 137
Shadihar c6 129
Shādkām p6 137
Shady Grove h4 259
Sha'fat Ibn Jād d7 139
Shafi'abad r3 137
Shafirkan k7 120
Shafter d6 265
Shaftesbury d5 163
Shag c6 77
Shagan, Kaz. f4 120
Shagan, Kaz. s2 121
Shageluk e3 246
Shaglyteniz, Ozero m5 147
Shagyrlyk k4 149
Shah Alam b4 101
Shah Bilawal c8 129
Shah Fuladi c3 128
Shah Hussain f5 128
Shah Ismail b6 129
Shah Jehan c4 128
Shah Umar b6 129
Shahabad, Haryana, India c4 130
Shahabad, Karnataka, India e4 126
Shahabad, Uttar Pradesh, India e6 130
Shahada g10 129
Shahana a7 129
Shahapur d5 126
Shahbā' e4 138
Shahbandar c8 129
Shahbaz Kalat b7 129
Shahbeg c8 129
Shahdād r6 137
Shahdadpur d8 129
Shahdara c5 130
Shahdol g8 124
Shahdura g5 128
Shahe, Hebei, China d1 106
Shahe, Jiangsu, China f2 111
Shahe, Shandong, China f1 111
Shahgarh d7 129
Shahjahanpur, Rajasthan, India c6 130
Shahjahanpur, Uttar Pradesh, India d6 130
Shahpur, India e4 126
Shahpur, Pak. d6 129
Shahpur, Punjab, Pak. f4 128
Shahpur, Sindh, Pak. d7 129
Shahpura, Rajasthan, India g8 129
Shahpura, Rajasthan, India c6 130
Shahr Rey n4 137
Shahr Sultan e6 129
Shahrabad Kord r3 137
Shahrak b3 128
Shahrān f4 219
Shahr-e Bābak q6 137
Shahr-e Kord n5 137
Shahrig c5 128
Shahr-i-Safa c5 128
Shahriston d1 128
Shahrtuz d2 128
Shahu c4 106
Shaiai c4 130
Shaighalu d5 128
Shaikh Husain b6 129
Sha'irah, Jabal c7 139
Shajapur e8 124
Shajianzi n5 113
Shakar Bolāghī l3 137
Shakaskraal j4 235
Shakawe c2 232
Shaker Heights f5 254
Shakhrikhan p7 121
Shakhrisabz c1 128
Shakhs, Ras f5 219
Shakhtinsk p3 121
Shākir f4 219
Shakopee e2 260
Shakotan-hantō Ab2 114
Shakotan-misaki Ab2 114
Shaktoolik d2 246
Shala Häyk' b2 226
Shālamzār n5 137
Shalday s2 121
Shalginskiy n4 121
Shaling m5 113
Shalkar, India d4 130
Shalkar, Kaz. k3 149
Shalkar, Ozero c2 120
Shallotte k3 259
Shallow Bay k1 247
Shaluli Shan c3 104
Shaluni q5 125
Shama f5 225
Shamalzā'i c5 128
Shamattawa g2 250
Shambār m5 137
Shambe f2 225
Shambe National Park f2 225
Shambu b2 226
Shambuanda d5 224
Shamgarh g8 129
Shamil r8 137
Shamli c5 130
Shamokin d4 256
Shamrock, Florida, U.S.A. h5 259
Shamrock, Texas, U.S.A. c5 261
Shamva e2 233
Shan d5 102
Shan, Daiyun, China m6 105
Shan, Daiyun, Fujian, China m6 105
Shandan a6 112
Shandiz g9 120
Shandong f1 111
Shandong Bandao g1 111
Shandrūkh k5 137
Shang Chu j5 135
Shangani, Zimb. d2 233
Shangani d2 233
Shangbahe d4 106
Shangcai d3 106
Shangcheng d4 106
Shangchengzen n4 113
Shangchuan Dao j8 105
Shangdu g5 112
Shangfu k4 105
Shanggang g3 111
Shangganling q2 113
Shanghai, China g4 111
Shanghai g4 111
Shanghe e1 111
Shanghekou n5 113
Shangjin b3 106
Shangkuli l1 113
Shanglian m5 105
Shangnan b3 106
Shangombo c2 232
Shangpai d2 106
Shangqiu l4 105
Shangrao l4 105
Shangshiqiao d4 106
Shangshui d3 106
Shangsi g7 104
Shangxinhe f4 111
Shangyi f5 112
Shangyou Shuiku 121
Shangyu g4 111
Shangzhi p3 113
Shangzhou a3 106
Shanhetun p3 113
Shani, Nig. g3 223
Shani, W.B. d5 139
Shanklin e6 163
Shankou g8 104
Shanli e5 111
Shannon, Ire. d2 165
Shannon, N.Z. e4 76
Shannon, R.S.A. g4 235
Shannon, U.S.A. e2 258
Shannon National Park c14 87
Shannon, Mouth of the b4 164
Shanpo d4 106
Shansonggang p4 113
Shantipur l8 125
Shantou l7 105
Shanwei k7 105
Shanxi c1 106
Shanxian e2 111
Shanyang a3 106
Shanyin g6 112
Shaoguan j6 105
Shaowu l5 105
Shaoxing g4 111
Shaoyang, Hunan, China h5 104
Shaoyang, Hunan, China h5 104
Shap d2 162
Shapinsay f1 164
Shaqq el Giefer, Wadi c4 218
Shaqq el Khadir c5 218
Shaqqā e4 138
Shaqrā' k9 137
Shar t3 121
Sharafa c5 218
Sharan Jogizai d5 128
Sharashova n3 169
Shardara l7 121
Shardi b2 130
Shargun' c1 128
Sharhorod j1 201
Sharhulsan c3 112
Shari Ad2 114
Shārī, Buḥayrat j5 209
Shari-dake Ad2 114
Shark Bay a9 87
Shark Fin Bay b5 100
Shark Reef h3 80
Sharka-leb La m5 125
Sharkawshchyna m5 157
Sharlouk q2 137
Sharm el Sheikh e8 136
Sharmah e7 136
Sharon, Connecticut, U.S.A. g3 257
Sharon, Massachusetts, U.S.A. j2 257
Sharon, Pennsylvania, U.S.A. f5 254
Sharpe Lake g3 250
Sharpsburg c5 256
Sharqī, Jabal ash e3 138
Sharwayn, Ra's h4 219
Shashe d3 233
Shashemenē b2 226
Shashubay q4 121
Shasta b5 262
Shasta Lake b5 262
Shasta, Mount b5 262
Shaṭanā d4 139
Shāṭi', Wādī ash g3 221
Shatrana c5 130
Shats'k, Ukr. a2 148
Shats'k m4 169
Shatuji d2 106
Shaul'der m6 121
Shaunavon n7 249
Shaw, Arg. h4 297
Shaw, Aust. d7 86
Shaw, U.S.A. d3 258
Shawan v5 121
Shawangunk Mountains f3 257
Shawano b3 254
Shawbury d4 162
Shawinigan f5 252
Shawmariyah, Jabal ash f5 209
Shawnee a2 258
Shawneetown e1 258
Shawo d4 106
Shaxi g4 111
Shaxian f5 105
Shay Gap e7 86
Shayan, China c3 106
Shayan, Kaz. m6 121
Shayang c4 106
Shaybārā e2 219
Shaykh Jūwī l5 137
Shaykh Miskīn e4 138
Shaykh Sa'd l5 137
Shayzar e1 138
Shāzand m5 137
Shazud f2 128
Shchara n2 169
Shcherbakty s1 121
Shcholkine d3 148
Shchors c2 148
Shchuchinsk n1 121
Shchuchyn n2 169
Shchyrets' m6 169
Shea f3 285
Sheberghān b2 128
Sheboygan c4 254
Shebshi Mountains g4 223
Shediac k5 253
Shedin Peak, Can. d4 248
Shedin Peak, U.S.A. n5 247
Sheelin, Lough d3 165
Sheenjek j2 247
Sheep Mountain b4 260
Sheepmoor j3 235
Sheerness g5 163
Sheet Harbour l6 253
Shefar'am d4 138
Shefer d4 138
Sheffield, N.Z. d5 77
Sheffield, England, U.K. e3 162
Sheffield, U.K. e3 162
Sheffield, Alabama, U.S.A. f2 258
Sheffield, Illinois, U.S.A. b5 254
Sheffield, Massachusetts, U.S.A. g2 257
Sheffield, Pennsylvania, U.S.A. a3 256
Sheffield Lake p4 253
Shefford f4 163
Shegah b5 128
Shehong e3 104
Shehy Mts b5 164
Sheikh Budin e4 128
Shekhawati b6 130
Shekhupura g5 128
Shekou d4 106
Shela n4 125
Shelburn c6 254
Shelburne k7 253
Shelburne Bay f1 80
Shelburne Falls h2 257
Shelby, Michigan, U.S.A. c4 254
Shelby, Montana, U.S.A. m7 249
Shelby, North Carolina, U.S.A. j2 259
Shelbyville, Illinois, U.S.A. b6 254
Shelbyville, Indiana, U.S.A. d6 254
Shelbyville, Lake f4 260
Sheldon, R.S.A. f6 235
Sheldon, U.S.A. b1 258
Sheldon Point c3 246
Shelikof Strait f4 246
Shellbrook p5 249
Shelley g4 262
Shellharbour k13 81
Shelter Point b7 77
Shelton, Connecticut, U.S.A. g3 257
Shelton, Washington, U.S.A. b2 262
Shemankar f4 223
Shemonaikha t2 121
Shemya Island Aa1 247
Shen Khan Bandar d2 128
Shenandoah, Iowa, U.S.A. e3 260
Shenandoah, Pennsylvania, U.S.A. d4 256
Shenandoah, Virginia, U.S.A. b6 256
Shenandoah National Park b6 256
Shenbertal h3 120
Shenchi g6 112
Shendam f4 223
Shendi d4 218
Shenge b4 222
Shengel'di m7 121
Shengel'dy h5 120
Shengena g4 225
Shengli Daban w6 121
Shengping n2 113
Shengsi h4 111
Shengsi Liedao h4 111
Shengze g4 111
Shengzhou g5 111
Shenhou c2 106
Shenjing j8 105
Shennong Ding b4 106
Shennongjia b4 106
Shenqiu d3 106
Shenqiucheng d3 106
Shenshu q2 113
Shenton, Mount f10 87
Shenxian d1 106
Shenyang m5 113
Shenze d0 106
Shenzhen k7 105
Shenzhou d1 106
Sheoganj f8 129
Sheopur e7 124
Shepard Island pp2 298

382 Shepetivka → Sittang

Shepetivka b2 148
Shepherd b4 258
Shepherd Islands F 74
Shepparton g14 81
Shepton Mallet d5 163
Sheqi c3 106
Sheqiao d3 106
Sher Khan Qala c6 129
Sherabad c2 128
Sherborne d6 163
Sherbro Island b4 222
Sherbrooke, Nova Scotia, Can. m6 253
Sherbrooke, Québec, Can. g6 252
Sherburne e2 256
Shercock e3 165
Sherdoyak u3 121
Shereiq d4 218
Shergarh f7 129
Sherghati j7 125
Sheridan, Texas, U.S.A. a5 258
Sheridan, Wyoming, U.S.A. b2 260
Sheringa b12 81
Sheringham h4 162
Sherman, Mississippi, U.S.A. e2 258
Sherman, New York, U.S.A. a2 256
Sherman, Texas, U.S.A. a3 258
Sherman Mills h6 253
Sherman Mountain f5 262
Sherman Reservoir d3 260
Sherpur m7 125
Sherridon c3 250
Shertally e8 126
's-Hertogenbosch d3 159
Sherwood, Arkansas, U.S.A. c2 258
Sherwood, Tennessee, U.S.A. g2 259
Sherwood Ranch g1 235
Sheshea c1 292
Sheshegwaning e3 254
Sheshtamad r3 137
Shethanei Lake c1 250
Shetland A 164
Shetpe j3 149
Shevaroy Hills f7 126
Shevchenko h4 149
Shevchenko, Zaliv h4 120
Shewa Gimira b2 226
Shexian, Anhui, China f5 111
Shexian, Hebei, China c1 106
Shexiang e1 111
Sheyang, Jiangsu, China g3 111
Sheyang, Jiangsu, China f3 111
Sheyenne, North Dakota, U.S.A. c3 260
Sheyenne, North Dakota, U.S.A. d7 250
Shi'erdaogou p5 113
Shiant Islands b2 164
Shibām, Yemen g4 219
Shibām g4 219
Shibata h3 115
Shibecha Ad2 114
Shibetsu, Hokkaidō, Japan Ad2 114
Shibetsu, Hokkaidō, Japan Ac1 114
Shibh Jazīrat Sīnā' d2 218
Shibīn el Kôm c6 136
Shibing g5 104
Shibogama Lake k4 251
Shibu f1 111
Shicheng l5 105
Shickshinny d3 256
Shicun e3 111
Shidao h1 111
Shidao Wan h1 111
Shiderti q2 121
Shido f4 114
Shiel Bridge c2 164
Shiel, Loch c3 164
Shieldaig c2 164
Shifang l6 105
Shiga g4 115
Shigang g3 111
Shiguai c1 106
Shihezi w5 121
Shihuajie b3 106
Shiikh d2 226
Shijiazhuang d0 106
Shijiu Hu f4 111
Shikabe Ab2 114
Shikarpur, India d5 126
Shikarpur, India c5 130
Shikarpur, Pak. d7 129
Shikengkong j6 105
Shikohabad d6 130
Shikoku-sanchi e5 115
Shikotsu-Tōya National Park Ab2 114
Shilianghe Shuiku f2 111
Shiliguri l6 125
Shilipu c4 106
Shilla d3 130
Shillelagh e4 165
Shillington e4 256
Shillong m7 125
Shilong j7 105
Shilou b1 106
Shimamoto f4 115
Shimane e4 114
Shimanovsk h2 94
Shimba Hills National Reserve b4 231
Shimbiris d1 226
Shimen b5 106
Shimian d4 104
Shimizu, Hokkaidō, Japan Ac2 114
Shimizu, Shizuoka, Japan h4 115
Shimla c4 130
Shimoda h4 115
Shimodate h3 115
Shimoga d6 126
Shimokita-hantō j1 114
Shimoni b4 227
Shimonoseki r9 113
Shimsha e6 126
Shimshal b1 130
Shin Narai Thana c5 128
Shindand a4 128
Shiner a5 258
Shingbwiyang c2 102
Shinghar d5 128
Shinghshal Pass b1 130
Shinglehouse b3 256
Shingozha t4 121
Shingū g5 115
Shingwedzi, R.S.A. j1 235
Shingwedzi j1 235
Shinjō j2 115
Shinkai Hills d4 128
Shinkay c5 128
Shinminato g3 115
Shinnecock Bay h4 257
Shinpokh e3 128
Shintoku Ac2 114
Shinyanga, Tan. f4 225
Shinyanga a4 231
Shiogama j2 115
Shiokawa B 114
Shiono-misaki f5 115
Shioya-zaki j3 115
Ship Chan Cay l7 259
Ship Cove q5 253
Shipai e4 111
Shipdham g4 162
Shiping f4 102
Shipka Prokhod g4 201
Shipley e3 162
Shippensburg c4 256
Shippenville a3 256
Shiprock a4 261
Shipston on Stour e4 163
Shipton e2 162
Shipton-under-Wychwood e5 163
Shiqian g5 104
Shiqiao f4 111
Shiqqat al Kharitah g4 219
Shiquan g2 104
Shirābād m2 137
Shirakami-misaki Ab3 114
Shirakawa j3 115
Shirane-san, Japan h3 115
Shirane-san, Japan h4 115
Shiranuka Ad2 114
Shiraoi Ab2 114
Shirase Coast bb2 298
Shirāz p7 137
Shirbīn c6 136
Shire b7 231
Shireet g3 112
Shiren p5 113
Shiretoko National Park Ad1 114
Shiretoko-misaki Ad1 114
Shireza b7 129
Shirin m7 121
Shirin Tagāb b2 128
Shirinab c6 129
Shiriya-zaki j1 115
Shirkala f4 120
Shiroishi j3 115
Shirone h3 115
Shirpur g10 129
Shirvān r3 137
Shishaldin Volcano d5 246
Shishang l5 105
Shishmaref c2 246
Shishmaref Inlet c2 246
Shishou c5 106
Shitai e4 111
Shitang h6 104
Shitouzui d4 106
Shiumenzi m6 113
Shiv e7 129
Shivpuri e7 124
Shiwa Ngandu f6 225
Shiwan a1 106
Shiyan b3 106
Shiyiwei g4 111
Shizhu n4 105
Shizipu f4 111
Shizugawa j2 115
Shizuishan d6 112
Shizukuishi j2 115
Shizunai Ac2 114
Shizuoka, Japan h4 115
Shizuoka h4 115
Shkhara f4 149
Shklo m6 169
Shklow c1 148
Shklyn' p5 169
Shkodër d4 200
Shlapan' p4 169
Shoal Lake c5 250
Shoals c6 254
Shoalwater Bay d3 84
Shōbara e4 114
Shoghlābād g9 120
Shoh d2 128
Shokanbetsu-dake Ab2 114
Sholaksay k2 120
Shollakorgan m6 121
Shomishkol' k3 149
Shongar m6 125
Shoptykol' q2 121
Shor c3 130
Shor Barsa-Kel'mes f6 120
Shor Tepe c2 128
Shoran c6 129
Shoranur e7 126
Shorap b8 129
Shorapur e4 126
Shorewood e4 254
Shorkot f5 128
Shorkozakhly, Solonchak e7 120
Shortandy n2 121
Shortsville c2 256
Shoshone f4 262
Shoshone Lake h3 262
Shoshone Mountains f3 264
Shoshong g1 235
Shoshoni a3 260
Shostka d2 148
Shouchang f5 111
Shouguang f1 111
Shouning m5 105
Shouxian e3 111
Shouyang c1 106
Shouyang Shan a3 106
Show Low h8 263
Showak e5 219
Shpola c2 148
Shpykiv j1 201
Shreveport c3 258
Shrewsbury d4 162
Shrewsbury, U.S.A. j2 257
Shri Mohangarh e7 129
Shrivenham e5 163
Shropshire d4 163
Shrule b3 165
Shu p6 121
Shu He f2 111
Shu'aiba l6 137
Shuajingsi d2 104
Shuangbai e3 102
Shuangcheng p3 113
Shuangfeng j5 105
Shuangfu d3 111
Shuanggou, Hubei, China c3 106
Shuanggou, Jiangsu, China e2 111
Shuanghe, Hubei, China c4 106
Shuanghe, Hubei, China c4 106
Shuanghedagang r1 113
Shuangliao m4 113
Shuangpai h6 104
Shuangyang n4 113
Shuangyashan n2 113
Shuangzhidian f2 111
Shubarkuduk k2 149
Shubarshi k2 149
Shubrā el Kheima c6 136
Shubuta e4 258
Shucheng e4 111
Shucushuyacu b5 284
Shufu g1 128
Shuhedun e4 111
Shuiji m5 105
Shuikouguan f7 104
Shuikoushan j5 105
Shuiquanzi a6 112
Shuituo He c4 104
Shuiye d1 106
Shuizhai e1 111
Shujaabad e6 129
Shulan p3 113
Shumagin Islands e5 246
Shumanay k4 149
Shumarinai-ko Ac1 114
Shumba d2 232
Shumen, Bul. h4 201
Shumen h4 201
Shunak, Gora p4 121
Shūnat Nimrīn d5 139
Shunchang l5 105
Shunde j7 105
Shungnak e2 246
Shuozhou g6 112
Shupiyan b3 130
Shuqrah g5 219
Shuqualak e3 258
Shūr p7 137
Shūr Āb, Iran q6 137
Shūr Āb n4 137
Shūrāb, Chahār Maḩall va Bakhtiār, Iran n5 137
Shūrāb, Khorāsan, Iran r5 137
Shūrāb, Yazd, Iran q5 137
Shurchi c2 128
Shureghestan p5 137
Shūrjestān p6 137
Shurugwi e2 233
Shūsh m5 137
Shūshat al Maghārah b6 139
Shushtar m5 137
Shuswap Lake h6 248
Shuyak Island f4 246
Shuyang f2 111
Shuzhang c2 106
Shwebandaw b6 102
Shwebo b4 102
Shwegun c7 102
Shwegyin c7 102
Shweli c4 102
Shwenyaung c5 102
Shweudaung c4 102
Shyganak n5 121
Shygys Konyrat q4 121
Shymkent m6 121
Shyok, India c2 130
Shyok d2 130
Shyroke d3 148
Shyryayeve k2 201
Si Lanna National Park d6 102
Si Racha e9 103
Si'an f4 111
Sia b2 138
Siabu a5 101
Siachen Glacier c2 130
Siagne c7 185
Siah Chashmeh k3 209
Siāh Kūh a5 128
Siahan Range b7 129
Siahgird c2 128
Siak Sri Inderapura c5 101
Sialkot b3 130
Sianów e1 168
Siantan d3 98
Siapa d3 284
Siargao f6 100
Siasconset l3 257
Siasi, Phil. c8 100
Siasi c8 100
Siaškotan, Ostrov r5 119
Siatista d2 201
Siaton d6 100
Siau n3 99
Šiauliai k5 157
Sib a7 129
Sib f6 116
Sibaj k1 149
Sibari f5 198
Sibay c5 100
Sibayi, Lake k3 235
Sibbo l2 157
Šibenik b4 200
Siberut b6 96
Siberut, Selat b6 96
Sibi c6 129
Sibidiri l7 97
Sibigo b14 103
Sibiloi National Park b3 226
Sibirskij m3 147
Sibiti b4 224
Sibiu, Rom. g3 201
Sibiu g3 201
Sibley d4 258
Sibó, Ilha do d4 288
Siboa l4 99
Sibolga d15 103
Siborongborong d14 103
Sibsagar p6 125
Sibsey g3 162
Sibu f3 98
Sibuco d7 100
Sibuco Bay c7 100
Sibuguey d7 100
Sibuguey Bay c7 100
Sibut c2 224
Sibutu b8 100
Sibutu Passage b8 100
Sibuyan d4 100
Sibuyan Sea SE d4 100
Sibuyu Forest Reserve d2 232
Sicapoo c2 100
Sicayari, Mesa de c4 284
Siccus d11 81
Sichon a1 101
Sichuan d3 104
Sichuan Pendi e4 104
Sicié, Cap b7 185
Sicilia d7 198
Sicilian Channel b7 199
Sicily Island d4 258
Sicuani c2 292
Siculiana c7 199
Šid d3 200
Sidangoli h5 97
Sidaogou p5 113
Sidaouet f2 223
Siddeburen e1 159
Siddhapur f9 129
Siddipet f3 126
Sidenreng, Danau k6 99
Sidéradougou d3 222
Siderno f6 199
Sideros, Akra g7 211
Sidhai f5 128
Sidhi g7 124
Sidhpura d6 130
Sidi Ali e1 221
Sidi Barrani c1 218
Sidi Bel Abbès d1 220
Sidi Bennour c2 220
Sidi Bouzid f1 221
Sidi El Hani, Sebkhet de g1 221
Sidi Ifni b3 220
Sidi Kacem c2 220
Sidi Khaled e2 221
Sidi Okba f2 221
Sidi Toui, Parc National g2 221
Sidikalang d14 103
Sidikila c3 222
Sidirokastro, Kentriki Makedonia, Grc. d1 210
Sidirokastro, Peloponnisos, Grc. b5 211
Sidi-Smaïl c2 220
Sidlaw Hills e3 164
Sidley, Mount ee2 298
Sidmouth c6 163
Sidnaw j7 251
Sidney, Can. b1 262
Sidney, Montana, U.S.A. b2 260
Sidney, Nebraska, U.S.A. c3 260
Sidney, New York, U.S.A. e2 256
Sidney, Ohio, U.S.A. d5 254
Sidney Lanier, Lake h2 259
Sido c3 222
Sidoan l4 99
Sidoarjo g8 98
Sidon d3 258
Sidrolândia a4 290
Sidzhak n7 121
Siebe j2 155
Siebejokka j2 155
Siebenlehn b2 175
Siedlce l3 169
Siedliszcze m4 169
Sieg c5 172
Siegburg f4 159
Siegen d2 174
Siegendorf im Burgenland h2 177
Sielkentjakke e4 154
Siemianowice Śląskie h5 169
Siemiatycze l3 169
Siemień l4 169
Siĕmpang h8 103
Siĕmréab f9 103
Siena, Italy f6 197
Siena f6 197
Sieniawa l5 169
Sienne d4 182
Sieradz g4 168
Sieraków e3 168
Sierakówek h3 169
Sierakowice f1 168
Sierck-les-Bains e5 159
Sierentz d3 184
Sierning f1 177
Sierpc h3 169
Sierra Blanca g2 272
Sierra Chica g4 297
Sierra City c2 264
Sierra Colorada d6 296
Sierra de Fuentes d5 191
Sierra de Luna d2 192
Sierra de Yeguas f7 191
Sierra Grande c4 294
Sierra Leone a4 217

SIERRA LEONE

THE REPUBLIC OF SIERRA LEONE
Area 71,740km² (27,699sq miles)
Capital Freetown
Organizations COMM, ECOWAS, OIC
Population 4,760,000
Pop. growth (%) 2.5
Life expectancy 36 (m); 38 (f)
Languages English, Krio (Creole), other local languages
Literacy 31.4%
Currency leone (US $1 = 2450 leone)
GDP (US million $) 723
GDP per head ($US) 151

Sierra Mojada h4 272
Sierra Morena h5 275
Sierra Nevada de Santa Marta, Parque Nacional c1 284
Sierra Nevada, Parque Nacional c2 284
Sierra Vista h10 263
Sierra, Punta c4 295
Sierras Bayas g4 297
Sierras de Córdoba d2 296
Sierraville c2 264
Sierre b3 196
Sierre naturreservat h3 154
Siesta h6 259
Sievi k5 155
Siewierz h5 169
Sifang g1 111
Sifang Ling f7 104
Sifangtai p2 113
Sifié c4 222
Sifnos e5 211
Sifnou, Steno e5 211
Sifton c5 250
Sigatoka E 74
Sigean f5 187
Sighetu Marmației f2 201
Sighișoara g2 201
Sigillo g6 197
Sigli b13 103
Siglufjörður A 152
Sigma d5 100
Sigmaringen e4 174
Signa f6 197
Signal de Botrange e4 159
Signal de Vaudémont c2 184
Signal du Viviers e5 182
Signalberg h3 175
Signy-l'Abbaye c5 159
Signy-le-Petit c5 159
Sigogne b3 186
Sigri f3 210
Sigri, Akra f3 210
Sigtuna g3 157
Siguatepeque d3 276
Sigüenza b3 192
Siguer d6 187
Sigües c2 192
Siguiri c3 222
Sigulda l4 157
Sigurd h6 263
Sihany g1 149
Sihelné h2 171
Sihhoya j2 235
Sihlsee c2 196
Sihong f3 111
Sihora g8 124
Sihuas b1 292
Sihui j7 105
Siikajoki, Fin. k4 155
Siikajoki k4 155
Siilinjärvi l5 155
Siirt, Tur. j4 209
Siirt h4 209
Sijawal d7 129
Sijunjung a5 98
Sik b3 101
Sika d9 129
Sikandarabad c5 130
Sikandra c6 130
Sikandra Rao d6 130
Sikanni Chief f3 248
Sikar b6 130
Sikaram d3 128
Sikasso, Mali c3 222
Sikasso c3 222
Sikaw c4 102
Sikea d2 210
Sikeli l7 99
Sikhote-Alin' k3 94
Sikinos, Grc. f6 211
Sikinos f6 211
Sikkim j6 135
Siklós g6 171
Siko p4 99
Sikuati j1 99
Šil c2 190
Šil'da k2 149
Silacayoapan e5 275
Silago e5 100
Silalė k5 157
Silam, Gunung k2 99
Silandro e3 196
Silantek, Gunung f4 98
Silanus Aa2 198
Silao d3 274
Silas e4 258
Silat edh Dhahr d4 139
Silay d5 100
Silba b3 200
Silchar n7 125
Sile g4 196
Šilega f2 147
Silenrieux c4 159
Siler City k2 259
Sileru g3 126
Siles b6 193
Silet e4 221
Sileti p1 121
Siletiteniz, Ozero p1 121
Silfiac b4 182
Silgarhi e5 130
Silghat n6 125
Siliana f1 221
Siliau b4 101
Silifke d4 208
Siligo Aa2 198
Silikatnyj k3 151
Siling Co j4 135
Siliqua Aa3 198
Silisili, Mount M 75
Siliștea g3 201
Siliștea Nouă g3 201
Silistra, Bul. h4 201
Silistra h3 201
Silivri j5 201
Siljan f2 156
Siljansnäs f2 156
Šilka f2 94
Silkeborg c2 158
Sill c2 176
Silla d5 193
Sillajhuay d3 292
Sillamäe m3 157
Sillaro f5 196
Sille d4 208
Silleda b2 190
Silleiro, Cabo b2 190
Sillé-le-Guillaume e4 182
Sillery k3 183
Sillian d3 176
Sillon de Talbert b4 182
Silloth e5 164
Siloam Springs b1 258
Silong j5 135
Šilovo f5 150
Sils g3 192
Silsbee b4 258
Silsby Lake f3 250
Siltaharju l3 155
Siltepec a3 276
Siluas e4 98
Siluko f4 223
Silūp a8 129
Šilutė j5 157
Silva Jardim g5 291
Silvan h3 209
Silvânia d2 290
Silvaplana d3 196
Silvassa c9 124
Silveiras b6 191
Silver Bank k4 271
Silver Bay h7 250
Silver City a5 261
Silver Islet j6 251
Silver Lake c4 262
Silver Peak Range f4 264
Silver Spring d6 256
Silverdale e2 76
Silverdalen f4 156
Silverthrone Mountain e6 248
Silvertip Mountain g7 248
Silverton c6 163
Silves, Braz. f4 285
Silves b7 191
Silvi d2 198
Silvia b3 284
Silvituc b1 276
Silvrettahorn b3 176
Silwād d5 139
Silz b2 176
Sim j5 147
Simancas f3 190
Şimand k5 171
Simantra d2 210
Simao e4 102
Simão Dias e4 288
Simara d4 100
Simaraña e3 285
Simard, Lac q7 251
Simat de la Valdigna d5 193
Simau l4 99
Simayr f4 219
Simba d3 224
Simbach d1 176
Simbach am Inn e1 176
Simbario f6 199
Simcoe f4 254
Simcoe, Lake c6 252
Simdega j8 125
Simen g4 111
Simen Mountain National Park e5 219
Simēn Mountains e5 219
Simeria f3 201
Simeulue c14 103
Simferopol' d3 148
Simga g9 124
Simi Valley e7 264
Simikot e5 130
Similaun e3 196
Simitli f5 201
Simla b4 260
Şimleu Silvaniei l4 171
Simmerath e4 159
Simmern (Hunsrück) f5 159
Simmesport d4 258
Simnas m1 169
Simo k4 155
Simojärvi l3 155
Simojoki l4 155
Simon h5 273
Simon's Town c7 234
Simontornya g5 171
Simoom Sound d6 248
Simopoulo b5 211
Simos b4 210
Simpang, Indon. c5 98
Simpang, Malay. b3 101
Simpang Empat, Perak, Malay. b4 101
Simpang Empat, Perlis, Malay. b2 101
Simpang Mangayau, Tanjung j1 99
Simpelejärvi n2 157
Simplício Mendes d3 288
Simplon c3 196
Simpson b5 295
Simpson Desert c8 80
Simpson Desert National Park d8 80
Simpson Hill h10 87
Simpson Lake n1 247
Simpson Park Mountains g2 264
Simpson Peak, Can. b2 248
Simpson Peak, U.S.A. m4 247
Simpson, Isla b5 295
Simpsonville d5 256
Simrishamn f5 156
Šimsk a2 150
Simskardet d4 154
Simunjan f4 98
Simunul b8 100
Simušir, Ostrov r5 119
Sin'gye p6 113
Sina d3 126
Sina Dhaqa d2 226
Sinabang c14 103
Sinabelkirchen g2 177
Sinabung d14 103
Sinai Peninsula b7 139
Sinai, Mount G 271
Sinaia g3 201
Sinaloa f5 272
Sinalunga f6 197
Sinamaica c1 284
Sinan g5 104
Sinanju n6 113
Sinara k4 147
Sinarcas c5 193
Sināwin g2 221
Sinbo c3 102
Sincan f3 209
Sincé k6 277
Sincelejo k6 277
Sinch'ang q5 113
Sinch'ŏn n6 113
Sinclair, Lake h3 259
Sinclair's Bay e1 164
Sind f5 124
Sind Sagar Doab e5 128
Sindal d1 158
Sindañgan d6 100
Sindangan Bay d6 100
Sindangbarang d8 98
Sindara b4 224
Sindari e8 129
Sindeh, Teluk l9 99
Sindelfingen d4 174
Sindgi e4 126
Sindh d8 129
Sindi l3 157
Sindia Aa2 198
Sindihui f5 275
Sindırgı b3 208
Sindkhed e3 126
Sindor g3 147
Sindos c2 210
Sindphana d3 126
Sindri k8 125
Sine, Vallée du a3 222
Sinegor'e l2 151
Sinekçi a2 208
Sinekli j5 201
Sinello d2 198
Sinendé e3 223
Sines b7 191
Sines, Cabo de b7 191
Sinettä k3 155
Sineu h5 193
Sinezerki c5 150
Sinfra c4 222
Sing Buri e8 103
Singa d5 218
Singahi e5 130
Singapore c5 101
Singapore h8 93

SINGAPORE

THE REPUBLIC OF SINGAPORE
Area 646km² (250sq miles)
Capital Singapore
Organizations ASEAN, COMM
Population 4,131,000
Pop. growth (%) 2.6
Life expectancy 74 (m); 79 (f)
Languages Malay, Chinese (Mandarin), Tamil, English
Literacy 93.1%
Currency Singapore dollar (US $1 = 1.71 Singapore dollar)
GDP (US million $) 88,300
GDP per head ($US) 21,374

Singaraja h9 99
Singen d5 174
Singerei j2 201
Singhana b5 130
Singida, Tan. f5 225
Singida a4 227
Singkaling Hkamti b3 102
Singkang l7 99
Singkawang e4 98
Singkep c5 98
Singkil c14 103
Singleton k12 81
Singleton, Mount, Northern Territory, Aust. k7 86
Singleton, Mount, Western Australia, Aust. c11 87
Singoli g8 129
Singou, Réserve Totale du e3 223
Singuilucan e4 275
Singureni g3 201
Sinhŭng p5 113
Sinij-Šihan h2 120
Siniloan c3 100
Sinio, Gunung k5 99
Siniscola Ab2 198
Sinj c4 200
Sinjai l7 99
Sinjaja n4 157
Sinjār h4 209
Sinjār, Jabal h4 209
Sinjil d4 139
Sinkat e4 219
Sinlabajos f3 190
Sinn, Ger. e2 174
Sinn d2 174
Sinnai Ab3 198
Sinnamary g2 285
Sinnar d3 126
Sinnemahoning b3 256
Sinnes b3 156
Sinni f4 198
Sinnūris c7 136
Sinop, Braz. a4 288
Sinop, Tur. e2 208
Sinop e1 208
Sinoquipe h10 263
Sinp'a p5 113
Sinp'o q5 113
Sinp'yŏng p6 113
Sinsheim d3 174
Sint'aein p8 113
Sintang f4 98
Şinteu l4 171
Sint-Niklaas c3 159
Sintok b2 101
Sinton a5 258
Sintra a6 191
Sint-Truiden d4 159
Sinú b2 284
Sinŭiju n5 113
Sinujiif d2 226
Sinzig f4 159
Sinzing h4 175
Sió e3 192
Siocon d7 100
Siófok g5 171
Sioma c2 232
Sioma Ngwezi National Park c2 232
Sion b3 196
Sioulet f2 186
Sioux Center d3 260
Sioux City d3 260
Sioux Falls d3 260
Sioux Lookout h5 250
Sioux Narrows f6 250
Sipacate b4 276
Sipalay d6 100
Sipaliwini, Sur. f3 285
Sipaliwini, Sur. f3 285
Sipaliwini, Natuurreservaat f3 285
Sipang, Tanjung f4 98
Sipapo d3 284
Siparia, Trinidad, Trin. 271 271
Siparia, Trinidad, Trin. E 271
Šipicyno j1 151
Siping n4 113
Sipitang h2 99
Sipiwesk e3 250
Sipiwesk Lake e3 250
Siple Coast cc3 298
Siple, Mount ee2 298
Šipote h2 201
Sipotina j2 201
Šipovo c3 200
Sipsey f3 258
Šipunovo u1 121
Siputeh b3 101
Siqueira Campos d5 290
Siquia e4 276
Siquijor, Phil. d6 100
Siquijor d6 100
Siquisique d1 284
Sir d8 129
Şir Abū Nu'āyr q9 137
Sir Alexander, Mount g5 248
Sīr ed Danniyé e2 138
Sir Edward Pellew Group c3 80
Sir Joseph Banks Group c13 81
Sir Sandford, Mount j6 248
Sir Thomas, Mount j10 87
Sir Wilfrid Laurier, Mount h5 248
Sira, India e6 126
Sira, Nor. b3 156
Sira, Nor. b3 156
Siracusa, Sicilia, Italy e7 199
Siracusa e7 199
Sirajganj l7 125
Şiran g2 209
Sirba e3 223
Sirdalsvatn b3 156
Sirē b2 226
Sirekude b4 222
Sireniki a2 246
Siret h2 201
Sirevåg a3 156
Şirfah d5 139
Sirha k6 125
Sirhind c4 130
Siri Kit Dam e7 102
Şiria k5 171
Sirik r8 137
Sirik, Tanjung f3 98
Sirjān q7 137
Sirkka k3 155
Sirkön f4 156
Sirmaur c4 130
Sirmione e4 196
Şırnak, Tur. j4 209
Şırnak j4 209
Sirohi f8 129
Sironj e7 124
Sirpur f3 126
Sirrayn Island f4 219
Sirretta Peak e6 265
Sirrī, Jazīreh-ye q9 137
Sirsa b5 130
Sirsi, Karnataka, India d5 126
Sirsi, Uttar Pradesh, India d5 130
Siruela e6 191
Siruguppa e5 126
Sirupa e3 272
Sirvan j3 209
Širvenos ežeras l4 157
Širvintos l5 157
Sisak h4 177
Sisaket g8 102
Sisak-Moslavina h4 177
Sisante b5 193
Sishen e3 234
Sishilijie l4 105
Sishuang Liedao n5 105
Sishui, Henan, China c2 106
Sishui, Shandong, China e2 111
Sisian g5 149
Sisimiut u2 243
Sisipuk Lake s4 249
Sisogúichic f4 272
Sisŏphŏn f9 103
Sisquoc d7 265
Sissach b2 196
Sissano l6 97
Sisseton d2 260
Sissili d3 222
Sissonne b5 159
Sissonville f6 254
Sistān a5 128
Sistan, Daryācheh-ye a1 128
Sistema Central f4 190
Sister Bay c3 254
Sisteron b6 185
Sisters, The A 77
Sistersville f6 254
Sisto h8 197
Sitamarhi j6 125
Sitamau g9 129
Sitampiky Ab2 233
Sitapur e6 130
Sitarganj d5 130
Siteia Ab3 210
Siteki j3 235
Sitges f3 192
Sithonia d2 210
Sitiawan b3 101
Sitidgi Lake l1 247
Sítio da Abadia c4 289
Sítio do Mato d4 288
Sitka l4 247
Sitkalidak Island f4 246
Sitkinak Island f4 246
Sitkinak Strait f4 246
Sitpur e6 129
Sitrah h2 219
Sittang c6 102

Sittard d4 159
Sittensen c5 158
Sittingbourne g5 163
Sittwe n9 125
Situbondo h8 99
Siumpu m7 99
Siuna e4 276
Siuri k8 125
Siuruanjoki l4 155
Sivaganga f8 126
Sivakasi e8 126
Sivas, Tur. f3 209
Sivas f3 209
Sivasamudram Island e6 126
Sivé b2 222
Siverek g4 209
Siverga, Ozero m1 121
Siverskij a2 150
Sivin' h4 151
Sivomaskinskij k2 147
Sivrice g3 209
Sivrihisar c3 208
Sivry-sur-Meuse d5 159
Siwa, Egypt c2 218
Siwa, Indon. l6 99
Sīwah, Wāḥāt c2 218
Siwalik Range d5 130
Siwan, Bihar, India j6 125
Siwan, Haryana, India c5 130
Siwana f8 129
Six Cross Roads H 271
Six-Fours-les-Plages b7 185
Sixian e3 111
Sixmilecross d2 165
Siyabuswa h2 235
Şiyāghah d5 139
Siyana d5 130
Siyang f3 111
Siyäzän h4 149
Siyitang e5 112
Siyom p5 125
Sīyunī p5 137
Sizandro a5 191
Sizhan p1 113
Sizjabsk h2 146
Sizun a4 182
Sjælland e3 158
Sjællands Odde e3 158
Sjamozero, Ozero c3 146
Sjamža f1 150
Sjas'troj b1 150
Sjaunja naturreservat g3 154
Sjava j2 151
Sjenica e4 200
Sjöbo e5 156
Sjöfallets nationalpark,
Stora f3 154
Sjøholt b1 156
Sjørup c2 158
Sjoutnäset e4 154
Sjøvegan f2 154
Sjulsåsen e4 154
Sjun h5 147
Sjunejsale m2 147
Skadarsko Jezero,
Serbia/Mont. d4 200
Skadarsko Jezero,
Serbia/Mont. d4 200
Skadovs'k d3 148
Skælsør e3 158
Skærbæk b3 158
Skævinge f3 158
Skaftárós A 152
Skaftung j1 157
Skagastolstindane b2 156
Skagen d1 158
Skagern f3 156
Skagerrak c1 158
Skaget c2 156
Skagit c1 262
Skagit Mountain g7 248
Skagul Island Ac2 247
Skagway l4 247
Skaidi k1 155
Skaidiškės p1 169
Skaistkalne l4 157
Skal'nyj j4 147
Skala, Notio Aigaio, Grc. Ab1 210
Skala, Peloponnisos, Grc. c6 211
Skala Eresou f3 210
Skala Marion e2 210
Skala Oropou d4 210
Skaland f2 154
Skala-Podil's'ka h1 201
Skalbmierz j5 169
Skälderviken e4 156
Skalica f3 170
Skalino f2 150
Skalité g2 171
Skallingen b3 158
Skalmodal e4 154
Skaloti e1 210
Skals, Den. c2 158
Skals c2 158
Skalten a5 154
Skanderborg c2 158
Skåne e4 156
Skaneateles d2 256
Skaneateles Lake d2 256
Skånevik a3 156
Skänninge f3 156
Skansholm f4 154
Skansnäs f4 154
Skantzoura e3 210
Skara e3 156
Skärblacka f3 156
Skardu b2 130
Skärgårdshavets
nationalpark j3 157
Skärhamn d4 156
Skarnes d2 156
Skarø d3 158
Skarsfjord g2 154
Skarstind c1 156
Skarszewy g1 168
Skårup d3 158
Skaryszew k4 169
Skarżysko-Kamienna j4 169
Skaudvilė k5 157
Skaulen b3 156
Skawa h6 169
Skawina h6 169
Skaymat a4 220
Skeena d3 248
Skeena Mountains m4 247
Skegness g3 162
Skei b2 156
Skeleton Coast Game
Park a2 232
Skellefteå h4 154
Skellefteälven g4 154
Skelleftebukten h3 154
Skelleftehamn h4 154
Skelton d2 162
Skerries e3 165
Ski d3 156
Skiathos, Grc. d3 210
Skiathos d3 210
Skiatook a1 258
Skibbereen b5 165
Skibby e3 158
Skibotn h2 154
Skibotndalen h2 154
Skidal' n2 169
Skiddaw c2 162
Skidegate Mission b5 248
Skidmore a5 258
Skien c3 156
Skierniewice j4 169
Skikda f1 221
Skillingaryd f4 156
Skinari, Akra a5 210
Skio c3 130
Skipskjølen m1 155
Skipton, Aust. f14 81
Skipton, U.K. d3 162
Skive c2 158
Skjálfandafljót A 152
Skjeberg d3 156
Skjellbreid d4 154
Skjern, Den. b3 158
Skjern, Den. b3 158
Skjern, Nor. c4 154
Skjervøy h1 154
Skjolden b2 156
Skjombotn f2 154
Sklithro c3 210
Skobeleva, Pik f1 128
Skoczów g6 168
Skodborg c3 158
Skodje b1 156
Škofja Loka f3 177
Skofljica f4 177
Skoganvarre k2 155
Skogerøya m2 155
Skoghall e3 156
Skogsfjordvatnet g1 154
Skoki f3 168
Skokie c4 254
Skole m6 169
Skoltenes e2 154
Skopelos, Grc. d3 210
Skopelos, Thessalia, Grc. d3 210
Skopelos,
Voreio Aigaio, Grc. g3 210
Skopin e5 150
Skopje e5 200
Skórcz g2 168
Skorodum m4 147
Skorpa a2 156
Skørping c2 158
Skorstad c4 154
Skorvhögarna f1 156
Skorzęcińskie, Jezioro g3 168
Skotterud e3 156
Skoutari,
Kentriki Makedonia, Grc. d1 210
Skoutari, Peloponnisos, Grc. c6 211
Skoutaros g3 210
Skövde e3 156
Skovlund b3 158
Skovorodino g2 94
Skra c1 210
Skreia d2 156
Skridulaupen b2 156
Skrīveri l4 157
Škrlatica e3 176
Skrofa, Akra b4 210
Skrova e2 154
Skrudaliena m5 157
Skrunda k4 157
Skruv f4 156
Skudeneshavn a3 156
Skukum, Mount l3 247
Skuleskogens
nationalpark g5 154
Skull Valley g8 263
Skulpfonteinpunt b5 234
Skulsk g3 168
Skultorp e3 156
Skultuna g3 156
Skunk f3 260
Skuodas j4 157
Skurup e5 156
Skuteč d2 170
Skutskär g2 156
Skutvik e2 154
Skúvoy B 152
Skvyra c2 1486
Skwentna, Alaska, U.S.A. g3 246
Skwentna,
Alaska, U.S.A. f3 24
Skwierzyna d3 168
Skydra c2 210
Skye b2 164
Skylloura b1 138
Skyring, Península b5 295
Skyring, Seno b5 295
Skyros e4 210
Skyros, Sterea Ellas, Grc. e4 210
Slabodka m5 157
Sládkovičovo f3 171
Sladkovo m5 147
Slættaratindur B 152
Slagelse e3 158
Slagnäs g4 154
Slamet, Gunung e8 98
Slancy n3 157
Slanec k3 171
Slaney e4 165
Slangerup f3 158
Slănic g3 201
Slănic Moldova h2 201
Slano g2 198
Slaný c1 170
Šlapanice e2 170
Slapjuma kalns m4 157
Slapovi Krke b4 200
Śląskie h5 169
Slaterville Springs d2 256
Slatina, Cro. j4 177
Slatina, Rom. g3 201
Slatiňany d2 170
Slatington e4 256
Slatinski Drenovac j4 177
Slave g3 242
Slave Coast e4 223
Slavgorod s1 121
Slavičín f2 171
Slavjansk-na-Kubani e3 148
Slavkino j5 151
Slavkov f2 171
Slavkov u Brna e2 170
Slavkoviči n4 157
Slavnik e4 176
Slavonice g1 177
Slavonija j4 177
Slavonski Brod k4 177
Slavonski Brod -
Posavina j4 177
Slavošovce j3 171
Slavsk j5 157
Slavsko Polje g4 177
Slavuta b2 148
Slavutych c2 148
Slavyanovo g4 201
Sława e4 168
Sławatycze m4 169
Slawharad c1 148
Sławno e1 168
Sławoborze d2 168
Sławskie, Jezioro d4 168
Slea f4 162
Slea Head a4 165
Sleaford f3 162
Sleaford Bay b13 81
Sleat, Point of b2 164
Sled Lake p4 249
Sledge Island c2 246
Sledmere f2 162
Sleeper Islands p2 251
Sleetmute e3 246
Sleights f2 162
Sleman f8 98
Slepcovskaja g4 149
Ślesin, Kujawsko-
Pomorskie, Pol. f2 168
Ślesin, Wielkopolskie, Pol. g3 168
Sletterhage d2 158
Sliač h3 171
Slide Mountain f2 257
Slidell e4 258
Slidre c2 156
Šlienava n1 169
Slierogaise e3 154
Slieve Bloom Mts d3 164
Slieve Gamph c2 164
Slieve Gullion Forest
Park e2 165
Slieve League c2 165
Slieve Mish Mts b4 164
Slieve Snaght d1 165
Slieveardagh Hills d4 164
Slievekimalta c4 165
Slievenamon d4 165
Sligachan b2 164
Sligo, Ire. c2 165
Sligo, Ire. c2 165
Sligo, U.S.A. a3 256
Sligo Bay c2 165
Slim b4 101
Slim River b4 101
Slinge e2 159
Šlissel'burg a2 150
Slite h4 157
Sliven, Bul. h4 201
Sliven h4 201
Slivo Pole h4 201
Śliwice g2 168
Sljeme g4 177
Sloan f8 263
Slobidka j2 201
Slobodskoj l2 151
Slobozia, Mol. j2 201
Slobozia, Rom. h3 201
Slobozia Bradului h3 201
Slocum Mountain f6 265
Słomniki j5 169
Slonim p2 169
Słońsk c3 168
Slotermeer d2 159
Slottet e2 156
Slough, England, U.K. h2 162
Slough f5 163
Slov''yans'k e2 148
Slovakia h5 144

SLOVAKIA

THE SLOVAK REPUBLIC
Area 49,036km² (18,933sq miles)
Capital Bratislava
Organizations CE, CEFTA, EBRD
Population 5,380,000
Pop. growth (%) 0.4
Life expectancy 68 (m); 76 (f)
Languages Slovak, Hungarian, Czech and others
Literacy 93%
Currency Slovak koruna (US $1 = 33.57 Slovak koruna)
GDP (US million $) 23,784
GDP per head ($US) 4420

Slovenia g5 144

SLOVENIA

THE REPUBLIC OF SLOVENIA
Area 20,253km² (7820sq miles)
Capital Ljubljana
Organizations CE, CEFTA, EBRD
Population 1,990,000
Pop. growth (%) -0.1
Life expectancy 71 (m); 78 (f)
Languages Slovene, Hungarian, Italian
Literacy 99.7%
Currency tolar (US $1 = 193.04 tolar)
GDP (US million $) 19,563
GDP per head ($US) 9830

Slovenj Gradec g3 177
Slovenska Bistrica g3 177
Slovenská Ľupča h3 171
Slovenská Ves j2 171
Slovenske Gorice g3 177
Slovenský raj j3 171
Sløvra e2 154
Słowiński Park
Narodowy f1 168
Słubice, Lubuskie, Pol. c3 168
Słubice, Mazowieckie, Pol. h3 169
Sluch b2 148
Sludka k2 151
Sluis b3 159
Slunj g4 177
Słupca f3 168
Słupia j4 169
Słupno h3 169
Słupsk f1 168
Slušovice f2 171
Slutsk b1 148
Slyne Head a3 165
Slyudyanka c2 94
Smackover c3 258
Smådalsvatni c2 156
Smagne b2 186
Smålandsfarvandet e3 158
Smålandsstenar e4 156
Smalininkai k5 157
Small Point m4 255
Smallwood Reservoir k1 253
Smalyanitsa n3 169
Smalyavichy n5 157
Smarhon' m5 157
Smeaton a4 250
Smederevo e3 200
Smederevska Palanka e3 200
Smedjebacken f2 156
Smeeni h3 201
Smethport b3 256
Smethwick e4 163
Śmigiel e3 168
Smila c2 148
Smilde e2 159
Smiltene l4 157
Smiřice d1 170
Smirnovo m5 147
Smith, Arg. g3 297
Smith, U.S.A. h2 262
Smith Arm e2 242
Smith Bay f1 246
Smith Mountain Lake g7 254
Smithers d4 248
Smithfield g5 235
Smithland e1 258
Smiths Falls h3 255
Smiths Grove f1 258
Smiths Station g3 259
Smithsburg c5 256
Smithton Aa2 83
Smithtown g4 257
Smithville, Georgia, U.S.A. g4 259
Smithville, Texas, U.S.A. a4 258
Smögen d3 156
Smoky h4 248
Smoky Bay a12 81
Smoky Cape e7 85
Smoky Hill c4 260
Smoky Hills d4 260
Smøla b5 154
Smolenice f3 170
Smolensk b4 150
Smolenskaja Oblast' b4 150
Smolník j3 171
Smolyan, Bul. g5 201
Smolyan e1 210
Smooth Rock Falls m6 251
Smoothstone Lake p4 249
Smotrych h1 201
Smyków j4 169
Smyrna, Tur. a3 208
Smyrna, Delaware, U.S.A. e5 256
Smyrna, Georgia, U.S.A. g3 259
Smyrna, Tennessee, U.S.A. f2 258
Smyth, Canal b6 295
Snaefell b2 162
Snæfell A 152
Snag j3 247
Snaith e3 162
Snake, Can. l2 247
Snake, Nebraska, U.S.A. c3 260
Snake,
Washington, U.S.A. d2 262
Snake Island e4 83
Snake River Plain g4 262
Snaptun d3 158
Snare Lake p2 249
Snåsa d4 154
Snedsted b2 158
Sneek d1 159
Sneekermeer d1 159
Sneem b5 165
Sneeuberge f5 234
Snegamook Lake m1 253
Snejbjerg b2 158
Snelling c4 264
Snells Beach e2 76
Snettisham g4 162
Sneum b3 158
Snežnik f4 177
Snežnogorsk j3 118
Śniadowo k2 169
Śniardwy, Jezioro k2 169
Snihurivka d3 148
Snina l3 171
Snizhne e2 148
Snizort, Loch b2 164
Snjoheii b3 156
Snøfjell b5 154
Snoghøj c3 158
Snohomish b2 262
Snønuten b3 156
Snoqualmie Pass c2 262
Snow Hill l2 259
Snow Lake c3 250
Snow Mountain a2 264
Snowcrest Mountain j7 249
Snowdon b3 162
Snowdonia National
Park b3 162
Snowdoun f3 258
Snowtown d12 81
Snowy f3 83
Snowy Mountain j4 255
Snowy Mountains f3 83
Snug Corner h3 266
Snuŏl h9 103
Snyatyn g1 201
Snyder, Oklahoma, U.S.A. d5 261
Snyder, Texas, U.S.A. c5 261
Soahany Aa2 233
Soajo b3 190
Soaker, Mount a6 77
Soalala Ab2 233
Soalara Aa3 233
Soalhães b3 190
Soanierana-Ivongo Ab2 233
Soan-kundo p8 113
Soap Lake d2 262
Soata c2 284
Soave f4 196
Soavina Ab3 233
Soavinandriana Ab2 233
Sobaek-sanmaek p8 113
Sobat f2 225
Soběslav c2 170
Sobo-san d5 114
Sobotín f1 170
Sobotište f3 170
Sobótka, Dolnośląskie, Pol. e5 168
Sobótka,
Wielkopolskie, Pol. f4 168
Sobradinho e1 290
Sobradinho,
Barragem de d3 288
Sobrado, Bahia, Braz. d3 288
Sobrado, Braz. b3 288
Sobrado b2 190
Sobral d2 288
Sobrance l3 171
Sobraon b4 130
Sobrarbe e2 192
Sobreira Formosa c5 191
Søby d4 158
Soc Trăng h11 103
Soča e3 176
Soca k3 297
Sŏch'ŏn p7 113
Sochaczew j3 169
Sochaux c3 184
Sochocin j3 169
Sochos d2 210
Soči e4 148
Société, Archipel de la K 75
Society Hill k2 259
Socodor k5 171
Socompa d4 292
Socompa, Volcán d4 292
Socorro, Braz. e5 291
Socorro, Col. c2 284
Socorro, U.S.A. b5 261
Socorro, Isla d8 272
Socota b1 292
Socovos c6 193
Socuéllamos b5 193
Soda Lake d6 265
Soda Plains d2 130
Soda Springs h4 262
Sodankylä l3 155
Soddy-Daisy g2 259
Söderfors g2 156
Söderhamn g2 156
Söderköping g3 156
Södermanland g3 156
Södertälje g3 157
Sodiri c5 218
Sodo b2 226
Södra Barken f2 156
Södra Dellen g2 156
Södra Vi f4 156
Sodražica b3 200
Sodwana Bay National
Park k3 235
Soë n9 99
Soekmekaar h1 235
Soela väin k3 157
Soest, Ger. d4 172
Soest, Neth. d2 159
Soeste c3 172
Soetdoring Nature
Reserve f4 235
Sofades c3 210
Sofala, Beira, Moz. e2 233
Sofala e3 233
Sofala, Baía de e3 233
Sofiko d5 211
Sofiya, Bul. f4 201
Sofiya f4 201
Sofiya-Grad f4 201
Søften d2 158
Sog n4 125
Sogamoso c2 284
Sögel f2 159
Sogn og Fjordane b2 156
Søgne b3 156
Sogo Nur a4 112
Sogod e5 100
Sogod Bay e5 100
Sogom m3 147
Söğüt c2 208
Söğütalan b2 208
Sohâg c8 136
Sohagpur f8 124
Soham g4 163
Sohawa f4 128
Sohm Plain e6 302
Sohna c5 130
Sohrag a7 129
Sohren f5 159
Sohŭksan-do n8 113
Søhundehavn f3 158
Sŏhŭng p6 113
Soignies c4 159
Şoimi l5 171
Soini k5 155
Soisberg e5 172
Soissons b5 159
Soitue d3 296
Sõja e4 114
Sojat f8 129
Sojat Road f8 129
Sojitra f9 129
Šojna f2 146
Sojoton Point d6 100
Söjtör e5 170
Sok l4 151
Sokal' n5 169
Sokch'o q6 113
Söke a4 208
Sokele d5 224
Sokhumi h1 209
Sokna c2 156
Soknedal c5 154
Sokodé e4 223
Sokol f2 150
Sokolivka, Cherkas'ka
Oblast', Ukr. k1 201
Sokolivka, Khmel'nyts'ka
Oblast', Ukr. h1 201
Sokółka m2 169
Sokolo c3 222
Sokolohirne d3 148
Sokolov a1 170
Sokolovka m5 147
Sokołów Małopolski l5 169
Sokołow Podlaski l3 169
Sokoły l3 169
Sokone a3 222
Sokoto, Nig. f3 223
Sokoto, Nig. e3 223
Sokoto f3 223
Sokyryany h1 201
Sol de Julio d1 294
Sol'cy a2 150
Sol'-Ileck j2 149
Sol'vyčegodsk j1 151
Sola, Arg. h2 297
Sola, D.R.C. e5 225
Sola, Nor. a3 156
Soła h6 169
Solan c4 130
Solana de los Barros d6 191
Solana del Pino f6 191
Solander Island a7 77
Solanet h4 297
Solano c2 100
Solano, Ven. d3 284
Solano, Bahía c5 295
Solapur d4 126
Solarino e7 199
Solberg f5 154
Solbergfjorden f2 154
Solbjerg d2 158
Solbjerg Sø d2 158
Solca g2 201
Soldado Bartra b4 284
Soldados, Cerro b4 284
Sölden c3 176
Soldeu d6 187
Soldotna g3 246
Solec Kujawski g2 168
Soledad, Arg. d2 294
Soledad, Col. k5 277
Soledad, U.S.A. b5 265
Soledad, Ven. e2 285
Soledad de Doblado f4 275
Soledad Diez Gutierrez d2 274
Soledade d1 292
Sølendet c5 154
Solenoe, Ozero m5 147
Sølensjøen d2 156
Solent, The e6 163
Solenzara A 185
Solesino f4 196
Solesmes b4 159
Soleto h4 198
Solfjellsjøen d3 154
Solginskij f1 150
Solhan h3 209
Soliera e5 196
Solihull, England, U.K. h2 162
Solihull e4 163
Solikamsk j4 147
Solingen f3 159
Solis d4 274
Solita b3 284
Solitaire a1 234
Solivella f3 192
Sölkpass k5 174
Söll d2 176
Sollefteå f5 154
Sollentuna g3 157
Sóller g5 193
Søllested e4 158
Söllichau h4 173
Solliès-Pont c7 185
Solling e4 172
Solms d2 174
Solnečnogorsk d3 150
Solnice e1 170
Solnut b2 156
Solo, Indon. f8 98
Solo, Indon. l6 99
Solofra d4 198
Sologne g5 183
Solok a5 98
Sololá b3 276
Solomon Islands n9 93

SOLOMON ISLANDS

SOLOMON ISLANDS
Area 27,556km² (10,639sq miles)
Capital Honiara, on Guadalcanal
Organizations COMM, SPC, PIF
Population 463,000
Pop. growth (%) 3.4
Life expectancy 66 (m); 68 (f)
Languages English, Melanesian, Pidgin, other local languages
Literacy 60%
Currency SI dollar (US $1 = 7.49 SI dollar)
GDP (US million $) 264
GDP per head ($US) 570

Solomon d4 260
Solomons d6 256
Solon l2 113
Solon Springs h7 250
Solonchakovyye Vpadiny
Unguz h8 120
Solonešnoe v2 121
Solor m9 99
Solor, Kepulauan m9 99
Solosancho f4 190
Sološnica f3 170
Solothurn b2 196
Solotvyn g1 201
Solov'evsk h1 112
Solov'yevsk g2 94
Soloveckie Ostrova d2 146
Solre-le-Château c4 159
Solsona f3 192
Solt h5 171
Soltānābād, Khorāsan, Iran s3 137
Soltānābād, Tehrān, Iran n4 137
Soltān-e Bakva a4 128
Solţanqolī l5 137
Soltau e3 172
Soltvadkert h5 171
Solutré-Pouilly a4 184
Solva a5 163
Solvang c7 265
Solvay d1 256
Sölvesborg f4 156
Solway Firth e5 164
Solwezi d1 232
Sōma j3 115
Soma a3 208
Somain b4 159
Somali c2 226
Somali Basin b5 300
Somalia g4 217

SOMALIA

THE SOMALI DEMOCRATIC REPUBLIC
Area 637,657km² (246,201sq miles)
Capital Mogadishu
Organizations LAS, OIC
Population 9,480,000
Pop. growth (%) 3.3
Life expectancy 45 (m); 48 (f)
Languages Somali, Arabic, English, Italian
Literacy 24.1%
Currency Somali shilling (US $1 = 2620.00 Somali shilling)
GDP (US million $) 4300
GDP per head ($US) 453

Somanga b5 227
Somanya d4 222
Sombang, Gunung j3 99
Sombernon a3 184
Sombo d5 224
Sombor h6 171
Sombrerete c2 274
Sombrero c6 295
Sombrero Channel n9 127
Sombrio, Lago do c7 289
Somdari f8 129
Someren d3 159
Somero k2 157
Sõmerpalu m4 157
Somers Point f5 256
Somerset, Aust. Aa2 83
Somerset, U.K. d5 163
Somerset, Kentucky, U.S.A. g1 259
Somerset,
Massachusetts, U.S.A. j3 257
Somerset,
Pennsylvania, U.S.A. a5 256
Somerset East f6 235
Somerset Island l1 243
Somerset West c7 234
Somerset, Lake e5 85
Somerton d5 163
Somerville,
New Jersey, U.S.A. f4 256
Somerville,
Tennessee, U.S.A. e2 258
Somerville, Texas, U.S.A. a4 258
Somerville Reservoir a4 258
Somes, Point A 77
Someshwar d5 130
Someydeh l5 137
Somianka k3 169
Somiedo,
Parque Natural de d1 190
Somma Lombardo c4 196
Sommariva del Bosco b5 196
Sommarøy f2 154
Sommatino c7 199
Somme, Fr. g2 183
Somme, Fr. j6 183
Somme, Picardie, Fr. h3 183
Somme, Baie de la g2 183
Somme, Canal de la h3 183
Sommen f3 156
Sommepy-Tahure a1 184
Sömmerda e1 175
Sommersted c3 158
Somme-Soude k4 183
Sommesous k4 183
Sommet, Lac du h2 252
Sommières a7 184
Sommières-du-Clain c2 186
Somnath b9 124
Somogy f5 171
Somogyapáti f5 171
Somogyjád f5 171
Somogyvár f5 171
Somotillo d4 276
Somoto d4 276
Sompion luonnonpuisto l2 155
Sompolno g3 168
Somport, Col du b6 187
Son, India g8 124
Son d3 156
Sơn Ha j8 102
Sơn La f5 102
Son Servera h5 193
Sơn Tây g5 102
Soná g7 277
Sonai n6 125
Sonaly n3 121
Sonamura m8 125
Sonapur h9 125
Sonar f5 124
Soncillo g2 190
Soncino d4 196
Sondalo e3 196
Sønder Balling b2 158
Sønder Bjert c3 158
Sønder Dråby b2 158
Sønder Felding b3 158
Sønder Nissum b2 158
Sønder Omme b3 158
Sønderborg c4 158
Sønderjylland c3 158
Sondershausen f4 173
Sondersø f3 158
Søndersø d3 158
Sønderup c2 158
Sondrio, Italy d3 196
Sondrio d3 196
Song, Gabon g5 223
Song, Nig. g4 223
Sông Cau j9 103
Song Ling l5 113
Song Shan c2 106
Songa h6 97
Songbu d4 106
Sŏngch'ŏn p6 113
Songcun, Shandong, China g1 111
Songcun, Zhejiang, China f5 111
Songe c3 156
Songea b6 227
Songeons g3 183
Songevatnet b3 156
Songhua Jiang r2 113
Songhuajiang n3 113
Songhwa n6 113
Sŏnghwan p7 113
Songjiang g4 111
Songjianghe p4 113
Songjŏng p8 113
Sŏngju q8 113
Songkan f4 104
Songkhla b2 101
Songköl q7 121
Songming d6 104
Sŏngnam p7 113
Songnim n6 113
Songo, Ang. b5 224
Songo, Moz. e2 233
Songpan d2 104
Songsak m7 125
Sŏngsan p9 113
Songshu m6 113
Songshuzhen p5 113
Songt'an p7 113
Songtao g4 104
Šonguj p2 155
Songxi m5 105
Songxian c2 106
Songyan c1 106
Songzi b4 106
Sonhat h8 124
Sonipat c5 130
Sonkajärvi l5 155
Sonkovo d3 150
Sonmiani c8 129
Sonmiani Bay c8 129
Sonneberg g2 175
Sonnewalde j4 173
Sonnino c3 198
Sono, Braz. c4 288
Sono, Braz. f2 291
Sonobe f4 115
Sonoita g10 263
Sonoma a3 264
Sonoma Mountains a3 264
Sonora, Mex. d3 272
Sonora, Mex. d3 272
Sonora, California, U.S.A. c4 264
Sonora, Texas, U.S.A. j2 273
Sonprayag d4 130
Sonqor l4 137
Sŏnsan q7 113
Sonseca g5 191
Sonsón b2 284
Sonsonate c4 276
Sonstraal e3 234
Sonthofen f5 174
Sontra j1 174
Soorts-Hossegor a5 187
Sop Prap d7 102
Sopas j1 297
Sopeira e2 192
Sopka Kronockaja s4 119
Sopka Šiveluč s4 119
Sopot, Bul. g4 201
Sopot, Pol. g1 168
Sopron e4 170
Sopur b2 130
Soputan, Gunung n4 99
Sor e5 187
Sôr c5 191
Sor c1 190
Sor Kaydak d5 120
Sor Kondinskij m3 147
Sor Mertvyy Kultuk d5 120
Sorada j3 127
Söråker g1 157
Sorano f7 197
Sorapis g3 196
Soras c2 292
Sorata d3 292
Sorbarden b1 156
Sorbas b7 193
Sorbe a3 192
Sørbymagle e3 158
Sore b4 187
Sorel f5 252
Sorell Ab3 83
Sorell Lake Ab3 83
Soresina d4 196
Sørfjord d3 154
Sørfolda e3 154
Sorge e1 172
Sorgono Ab2 198
Sorgues, Fr. e5 187
Sorgues a6 185
Sorgun e3 208
Soria, Spain b3 192
Soria b3 192
Soriano, Ur. j2 297
Soriano, Soriano, Ur. h2 297
Soriano Calabro f6 199
Soriano nel Cimino g7 197
Sorihuela del Gaudalimar a6 193
Sorikmarapi a5 101
Sorinj, Rt f5 177
Sorkheh p4 137
Sørkjosen h2 154
Sørland d3 154
Sørli d4 154
Sør-Mesna d2 156
Sormitz g2 175

Sormonne k3 183
Sornac e3 186
Sorne b2 196
Sorø e3 158
Soroca j1 201
Sorocaba e5 290
Soročinsk j1 149
Sorokino v1 121
Sorol G 74
Soron d6 130
Sorondiweri k6 97
Sorong j6 97
Soroni Ac2 211
Sororó c3 288
Sororoca e3 285
Soroti f3 225
Sørøya j1 155
Sørøysundet j1 155
Sorraia b6 191
Sørreisa g2 154
Sorrento, Aust. g15 81
Sorrento, Italy d4 198
Sorrento, U.S.A. d4 258
Sorris Sorris a3 232
Sorsakoski m1 157
Sorsatunturi m3 155
Sorsavesi m1 157
Sorsele f4 154
Sorso Aa2 198
Sorsogon e4 100
Sørstraumen h2 154
Sort f2 192
Sortavala b3 146
Sortino e7 199
Sortland e2 154
Sør-Trøndelag c5 154
Sørungen c5 154
Sörup c4 158
Sørvær h1 154
Sørvågen d3 154
Sorvilán a8 193
Sorviži k3 151
Sos c4 187
Sos del Rey Católico c2 192
Sos'va, Russ. Fed. k3 147
Sos'va, Sverdlovskaja Oblast', Russ. Fed. k4 147
Sŏsan p7 113
Sosandra c2 210
Söse f4 172
Sosedka g5 151
Sosedno n3 157
Sosenskij c4 150
Soshanguve h2 235
Sosna e1 148
Sosneado c3 296
Sosnivka n5 169
Sosnogorsk h3 147
Sosnovec q4 155
Sosnovka, Kaz. s2 121
Sosnovka, Kaliningradskaja Oblast', Russ. Fed. k1 169
Sosnovka, Kirovskaja Oblast', Russ. Fed. l3 151
Sosnovka, Penzenskaja Oblast', Russ. Fed. f1 149
Sosnovka, Russ. Fed. f5 150
Sosnovo a1 150
Sosnovoborsk j5 151
Sosnovo-Ozerskoye e2 94
Sosnovskoe g4 151
Sosnovyj Bor n3 157
Sosnowiec h5 169
Sospel d7 185
Sostis f1 210
Sosyka e3 148
Sota e3 223
Sotara, Volcán b3 284
Soteapan g4 275
Sotillo e6 191
Sotillo de la Adrada f4 190
Sotira b1 138
Sotkamo m4 155
Soto, Arg. d2 294
Soto, Spain d1 190
Soto de Ribera e1 190
Soto del Real g4 190
Soto La Marina, Mex. e2 275
Soto la Marina, Tamaulipas, Mex. e2 275
Sotonera, Embalse de d2 192
Sotopalacios g2 190
Sotouboua e4 223
Sotresgudo f2 190
Sotrondio e1 190
Sotta A 185
Sottern f3 156
Sotteville-lès-Rouen g3 183
Sottomarina g4 196
Sottrum e2 172
Sotuélamos b5 193
Sotuta q7 273
Souain-Perthes-lès-Hurlus a1 184
Soual e5 187
Souanké b3 224
Soubré c4 222
Soudan c6 80
Souderton e4 256
Souesmes h5 183
Soufflenheim d2 184
Soufli g1 210
Soufrière, Guad. C 271
Soufrière, St Luc. J 271
Souguéta b3 222
Sougueur e1 221
Souillac d4 186
Souilly b1 184
Souk Ahras f1 221
Souk el Arbaâ du Rharb c2 220
Soulac-sur-Mer a3 186
Soulatgé e6 187
Souli c5 211
Soulles d3 182
Soultzeren d2 184
Soultzmatt d3 184
Soumagne d4 159
Soumoulou b5 187
Sound Island n6 127
Sound of Bute c4 164
Sound of Harris a2 164
Sound of Jura c4 164
Sound of Monach a2 164
Sound of Raasay b2 164
Sound of Sleat c2 164
Souni a2 138
Sounou d3 222
Souppes-sur-Loing h4 183
Souprosse b5 187
Soûr d3 138
Sour Lake b4 258
Sourdeval e4 182
Soure, Braz. c2 288
Soure b4 190
Souris, Manitoba, Can. c6 250
Souris, Prince Edward Island, Can. l5 253
Sournia e6 187
Sous, Oued c2 220
Sousa, Braz. e3 288
Sousa, Port b3 190
Sousceyrac e4 186
Sousel c6 191
Sousse g1 221
Souss-Massa, Parc National c3 220
Soustons a5 187
South A 127
South Africa e8 217

SOUTH AFRICA

THE REPUBLIC OF SOUTH AFRICA
Area 1,219,080km² (470,689sq miles)
Capital Pretoria (& Cape Town & Bloemfontein)
Organizations COMM, SADC
Population 45,450,000
Pop. growth (%) 1.9
Life expectancy 53 (m); 59 (f)
Languages Afrikaans, English, and nine African languages
Literacy 86.4%
Currency rand (US $1 = 6.38 rand)
GDP (US million $) 102,635
GDP per head ($US) 2258

South Alligator l3 86
South Andaman n7 127
South Australia l11 87
South Australian Basin g8 301
South Australian Plain h8 300
South Ayrshire d4 164
South Baldy b5 261
South Baymouth e3 254
South Bend c5 254
South Benfleet g5 163
South Bight f3 266
South Boston g7 254
South Branch n5 253
South Branch Potomac a5 256
South Carolina j2 259
South Charleston f6 254
South China Basin f4 300
South China Sea f5 300
South Dakota c2 260
South Dartmouth k3 257
South Dorset Downs d6 163
South Downs f6 163
South East f2 235
South East Cape Ab3 83
South East Isles f14 87
South East Point e4 83
South Esk e3 164
South Esk Tableland h7 86
South Fiji Basin k7 301
South Fork, Alaska, U.S.A. f3 246
South Fork, Colorado, U.S.A. b4 261
South Fork, Pennsylvania, U.S.A. b4 256
South Fork American c3 264
South Fork Grand b3 260
South Fork Moreau b3 260
South Fork South Branch a6 256
South Fulton e1 258
South Georgia (U.K.) g8 283
South Georgia and South Sandwich Islands (U.K.) g8 283
South Gloucestershire d5 163
South Hadley h2 257
South Hatia Island m8 125
South Haven, Kansas, U.S.A. a1 258
South Haven, Michigan, U.S.A. c4 254
South Head, N.Z. e2 76
South Head e2 76
South Hill g7 254
South Honshu Ridge f1 97
South Horr b3 226
South Houston b5 258
South Indian Basin f9 300
South Indian Lake d2 250
South Island c5 77
South Island National Park b3 226
South Islet, N.Z. B 77
South Islet, Phil. b6 100
South Kitui National Reserve b4 226
South Korea k5 93

SOUTH KOREA

THE REPUBLIC OF KOREA
Area 99,392km² (38,375sq miles)
Capital Seoul
Organizations APEC, EBRD
Population 47,640,000
Pop. growth (%) 1
Life expectancy 70 (m); 78 (f)
Languages Korean
Literacy 98.1%
Currency won (US $1 = 1185.05 won)
GDP (US million $) 470,600
GDP per head ($US) 9878

South Lake Tahoe c3 264
South Lanarkshire e4 164
South Loup d3 260
South Luangwa National Park e1 233
South Mills h7 255
South Molton c5 163
South Moose Lake c4 250
South Mountains c4 256
South Nahanni d3 242
South Naknek e4 246
South Negril Point B 266
South Orkney Islands a1 298
South Plainfield f4 257
South Platte c3 260
South Point, Bah. g3 266
South Point, Barb. H 271
South Point, U.S.A. c8 265
South Pole a3 298
South River, Can. g3 254
South River, U.S.A. f4 257
South Ronaldsay f1 164
South Rukuru f6 225
South Sand Bluff j5 235
South Sandwich Islands (U.K.) g8 283
South Sandwich Trench h15 302
South Saskatchewan n6 249
South Seal d1 249
South Shetland Islands mm1 298
South Shields e2 161
South Sound b3 165
South Taranaki Bight e3 76
South Tons g7 124
South Tucson h9 263
South Turkana Nature Reserve b3 226
South Twin Island n4 251
South Twin Lake q4 253
South Tyne d2 162
South Tyneside f2 162
South Uist a2 164
South Umpqua b4 262
South Ventana Cone b5 265
South Victoria Hill m7 259
South Wellesley Islands d4 80
South West Cape, Aust. Aa3 83
South West Cape, N.Z. a7 77
South West Island e4 83
South West National Park Ab3 83
South Wootton g4 162
South Yarmouth k3 257
South Yuba c2 264
Southam e4 163
Southampton, England, U.K. h2 162
Southampton, U.K. e6 163
Southampton, U.S.A. h4 257
Southampton Island m3 243
Southampton, Cape n3 243
Southbank e4 248
Southbridge d5 77
Southbridge, U.S.A. h2 257
Southeast Cape b3 246
Southeast Indian Ridge e9 300
Southeast Pacific Basin q10 301
Southeast Point h4 266
Southend, England, U.K. g5 163
Southend, U.K. c4 164
Southend-on-Sea g5 163
Southern, Eth. b2 226
Southern, Mal. b7 231
Southern, Zam. d2 232
Southern Alps c5 77
Southern Cross d12 87
Southern Darfur c5 218
Southern Indian Lake d2 250
Southern Kordofan d5 218
Southern Lueti c2 232
Southern National Park e2 231
Southern Ocean d10 300
Southern Pines k2 259
Southern Uplands e4 164
Southery g4 163
Southey a5 250
Southfield e4 254
Southfields f3 257
Southgate e4 254
Southington h3 257
Southland a6 77
Southminster g5 163
Southport, Queensland, Aust. e5 85
Southport, Tasmania, Aust. Ab3 83
Southport, U.K. c3 162
Southport, New York, U.S.A. d2 256
Southport, North Carolina, U.S.A. k3 259
Southwark h3 162
Southwest Cape a3 246
Southwest Conservation Area Aa2 83
Southwest Indian Ridge b8 300
Southwest Miramichi j5 253
Southwest Pacific Basin m8 301
South-West Point H 75
Southwest Rock h2 277
Southwold h4 163
Southwood National Park c5 85
Souto, Guarda, Port d4 190
Souto, Viana do Castelo, Port b3 190
Soutpan, Nam. c1 234
Soutpan, Free State, R.S.A. g4 235
Soutpan, Gauteng, R.S.A. h2 235
Soutpansberg j1 235
Souvigny f2 186
Sovata g2 201
Soveckaja, Krasnodarskij Kraj, Russ. Fed. f3 148
Soveckaja, Stavropol'skij Kraj, Russ. Fed. g3 149
Soveckij, Hantj-Mansijskij Avtonomnjj Okrug, Russ. Fed. k3 147
Soveckij, Leningradskaja Oblast', Russ. Fed. n2 157
Soveckij, Respublika Komi, Russ. Fed. l2 147
Soveckij, Respublika Marij El, Russ. Fed. k3 151
Soven e3 296
Soverato f6 199
Sovereign Mountain g3 247
Soveria Mannelli f5 199
Sovet d1 128
Sovetsk, Kaliningradskaja Oblast', Russ. Fed. j5 157
Sovetsk, Kirovskaja Oblast', Russ. Fed. k3 151
Sovetskaya Gavan' l3 94
Søvik b1 156
Sovpol'e e2 147
Sovyets'kyy d3 148
Sowa Pan d3 232
Sowerby e2 162
Soweto g3 235
Soyaló h5 275
Sōya-misaki Ac1 114
Soyaux c3 186
Soyo b5 224
Soyons a6 185
Soyopa e3 272
Sozh c1 148
Sozimskij m2 151
Sozopol h4 201
Spa d4 159
Spadafora e6 199
Spaichingen d4 174
Spain d7 144

SPAIN

THE KINGDOM OF SPAIN
Area 504,782km² (194,897sq miles)
Capital Madrid
Organizations CE, EBRD, EU, NATO, OECD
Population 40,980,000
Pop. growth (%) 0.1
Life expectancy 74 (m); 81 (f)
Languages Castilian Spanish, others
Literacy 97.9%
Currency euro (US $1 = 0.81 euro)
GDP (US million $) 648,800
GDP per head ($US) 15,832

Spalding f4 162
Span Head c5 163
Spangenberg e1 174
Spanish, Ontario, Can. n7 251
Spanish, Ontario, Can. e2 254
Spanish Fork h5 262
Spanish Point, Antig. D 271
Spanish Point b4 165
Spanish Town B 270
Spanish Wells l7 259
Spargaio, Monte b6 199
Sparanise d3 198
Sparks, Georgia, U.S.A. h4 259
Sparks, Nevada, U.S.A. d2 264
Sparlingville e4 254
Sparreholm g3 156
Sparta, Georgia, U.S.A. h3 259
Sparta, Kentucky, U.S.A. d6 254
Sparta, New Jersey, U.S.A. f3 256
Sparta, North Carolina, U.S.A. f7 254
Sparta, Tennessee, U.S.A. g2 259
Sparta, Wisconsin, U.S.A. f3 260
Spartanburg j2 259
Sparti c5 211
Spartivento, Capo f7 199
Sparto b4 210
Spas-Demensk c4 150
Spas-Klepiki f4 150
Spassk-Dal'niy s3 113
Spasskij j5 147
Spasskoye m1 121
Spata d5 211
Spatha, Akra d7 211
Spathi, Akra, Grc. c6 211
Spathi, Akra, Attiki, Grc. d5 211
Spatsizi Plateau Wilderness Provincial Park m4 247
Spean Bridge d3 164
Spearfish c2 260
Spearman c4 261
Speedway c6 254
Speedwell Island e6 295
Speer d2 196
Speichersdorf g3 175
Speichersee g4 175
Speightstown H 271
Speikkogel g2 177
Speke Gulf f4 225
Spelle f2 159
Spello g7 197
Spencer, Indiana, U.S.A. c6 254
Spencer, Iowa, U.S.A. e3 260
Spencer, Massachusetts, U.S.A. j2 257
Spencer, New York, U.S.A. d2 256
Spencer, North Carolina, U.S.A. j2 259
Spencer, West Virginia, U.S.A. f6 254
Spencer Bay b2 234
Spencer Gulf c12 81
Spencer Range j4 86
Spencer, Cape, Aust. c13 81
Spencer, Cape, U.S.A. k4 247
Spencer, Point c2 246
Spennymoor e2 162
Spenser Mountains d5 77
Spentrup d2 158
Spercheios c4 210
Sperillen c2 156
Sperlinga d7 199
Sperlonga c3 198
Spermezeu g2 201
Sperrin Mountains d2 164
Sperryville b6 256
Spessart e2 173
Spetses, Grc. d5 211
Spetses d5 211
Spetsopoula d5 211
Spey d2 164
Speyer d3 174
Spezand c6 129
Spezzano Albanese f5 198
Spezzano della Sila f5 199
Spiczyn l4 169
Spiegelau e1 176
Spiekeroog c2 172
Spiez b3 196
Spijkenisse c3 159
Spili e7 211
Spilia a2 138
Spilimbergo g3 196
Spilsby g3 162
Spīn Būldak c5 128
Spinazzola f4 198
Spincourt d5 159
Špindlerův Mlýn d1 170
Spintangi d6 129
Spinwam e4 128
Spioenkopdam h4 235
Spiro b2 258
Spišská Belá j2 171
Spišská Nová Ves j3 171
Spišská Stará Ves j2 171
Spišské Vlachy j3 171
Spišský Hrušov j3 171
Spit Point d7 86
Spitak k2 209
Spital am Pyhrn f2 177
Spitsbergen m2 302
Spitsbergen Bank r2 299
Spittal an der Drau e3 176
Spittal of Glenshee e3 164
Spitz g1 177
Spitzbergen b2 118
Spitzkofel d3 176
Spitzmeilen d2 196
Spjald b2 158
Spjelkavik b1 156
Split c4 200
Split Lake f2 250
Splügen d3 196
Spodakhy j1 201
Spodnjeposavska g4 177
Spodsbjerg d4 158
Spokane, Washington, U.S.A. e2 262
Spokane, Washington, U.S.A. e2 262
Spoleto g7 197
Spong g9 103
Spoon a5 254
Spooner f2 260
Sporawskaye, Vozyera p3 169
Spornitz e5 158
Spot Bay h1 277
Spotswood f4 257
Spotsylvania c6 256
Spotted Horse b2 260
Sprague c4 262
Spranger, Mount g5 248
Spratly Islands e3 96
Spratly Islands (disputed) e3 96
Spree j3 173
Spreewald, Ger. k4 173
Spreewald, Ger. k4 173
Spremberg k4 173
Spresiano g4 196
Sprimont d4 159
Spring City g2 259
Spring Creek, Aust. c5 80
Spring Creek d4 77
Spring Creek, U.S.A. c3 260
Spring Garden f2 285
Spring Glen, New York, U.S.A. f3 257
Spring Glen, Pennsylvania, U.S.A. d4 256
Spring Glen, Utah, U.S.A. h6 262
Spring Green a4 254
Spring Hill f2 258
Spring Hope k2 259
Spring Lake Heights f4 257
Spring Mountains f7 263
Spring Valley, California, U.S.A. g9 265
Spring Valley, New York, U.S.A. f3 257
Springbok b4 234
Springdale, Can. q4 253
Springdale, U.S.A. b1 258
Springe e3 172
Springer b4 261
Springerville j8 263
Springfield c5 77
Springfield, Colorado, U.S.A. c4 261
Springfield, Florida, U.S.A. g4 259
Springfield, Georgia, U.S.A. j3 259
Springfield, Illinois, U.S.A. b6 254
Springfield, Massachusetts, U.S.A. h2 257
Springfield, Massachusetts, U.S.A. h2 257
Springfield, Minnesota, U.S.A. e2 260
Springfield, Missouri, U.S.A. c1 258
Springfield, Ohio, U.S.A. e6 254
Springfield, Tennessee, U.S.A. f1 258
Springfield, Vermont, U.S.A. k4 255
Springfield, West Virginia, U.S.A. b5 256
Springfontein f5 235
Springhill k6 253
Springholm e4 164
Springs Junction d5 77
Springsure j8 80
Springvale e7 80
Springville, Alabama, U.S.A. f3 258
Springville, California, U.S.A. e5 265
Springville, New York, U.S.A. b2 256
Springville, Pennsylvania, U.S.A. e3 256
Springville, Utah, U.S.A. h5 262
Sprockhövel f3 159
Sprogø e3 158
Spruce Brook n4 253
Spruce Knob a6 256
Spruce Mountain f5 262
Spruce Pine h2 259
Spui c3 159
Spurn Head g3 162
Spurr, Mount f3 246
Spychowo k2 169
Spytihněv f2 171
Squamish, British Columbia, Can. f6 248
Squamish, British Columbia, Can. f7 248
Square Islands q2 253
Squaw Harbor d5 246
Squillace f6 199
Squillace, Golfo di f6 199
Squinzano h4 198
Squires, Mount h10 87
Squirrel d2 246
Sragen f8 98
Srbac j4 177
Srbija e3 200
Srbobran d3 200
Srbovac e4 200
Srê Âmběl f10 103
Sre Khtum h9 103
Sredets h4 201
Sredinnyj Hrebet r4 119
Sredna Gora g4 201
Srednee Kujto, Ozero c2 146
Srednekolymsk r3 119
Sredne-Russkaja Vozvyšennost' d5 150
Sredne-Sibirskoe Ploskogor'e l3 119
Srednij Ural j4 147
Srednja Vrata, Kanal f4 177
Srednogorie g4 201
Śrem f3 168
Sremska Mitrovica d3 200
Sremski Karlovci d3 200
Sretensk f2 94
Sri Aman f4 98
Sri Govindpur b4 130
Sri Jayewardenepura Kotte f9 126
Sri Kalahasti f6 126
Sri Lanka f8 92

SRI LANKA

THE DEMOCRATIC SOCIALIST REPUBLIC OF SRI LANKA
Area 65,610km² (25,332sq miles)
Capital Colombo (& Sri Jayewardenepura Kotte)
Organizations COMM, SAARD
Population 16,864,687
Pop. growth (%) 1.3
Life expectancy 69 (m); 74 (f)
Languages Sinhala, Tamil, English
Literacy 92.3%
Currency Sri Lanka rupee (US $1 = 96.64 Sri Lanka rupee)
GDP (US million $) 16,257
GDP per head ($US) 963

Sri Madhopur b6 130
Sri Pada A 127
Srikakulam j3 127
Srinagar, Jammu and Kashmir (Indian section), India b2 130
Srinagar, Uttaranchal, India d4 130
Srirangam f7 126
Srivardhan c3 126
Środa Śląska e4 168
Środa Wielkopolska f3 168
Srpska Crnja e3 200
St Agnes a6 163
St Albans f5 163
St Andrews f3 164
St Anne c3 182
St Arnaud, Aust. f14 81
St Arnaud, N.Z. d4 77
St Asaph c3 162
St Athan c5 163
St Austell b6 163
St Bees c2 162
St Brelade c3 182
St Clears b5 163
St Clement c3 182
St Columb Major b6 163
St David's a5 163
St Endellion b6 163
St Faith's j5 235
St Gennys b6 163
St George j10 81
St Helens, Aust. Ac2 83
St Helens, U.K. d3 162
St Helier c3 182
St Ives, England, U.K. f4 163
St Ives, England, U.K. a6 163
St John's Town of Dalry d4 164
St Keverne a6 163
St Lawrence j7 80
St Lucia Estuary k4 235
St Margaret's at Cliffe h5 163
St Margaret's Hope B 164
St Mary in the Marsh g6 163
St Mary's Bay g5 163
St Marys Ac2 83
St Mawes a6 163
St Neots f4 163
St Peter c3 182
St Peter Port c3 182
St Sampson c3 182
Staaten f4 80
Staaten River National Park f4 80
Staatsburg g3 257
Staatz h1 177
Stabbursdalen Nasjonalpark k1 155
Staberhuk g1 173
Staby b2 158
Stachy b2 170
Stade c5 158
Stadil Fjord b2 158
Stadlandet a1 156
Stadl-Paura e1 176
Stadskanaal, Neth. e2 159
Stadskanaal e2 159
Stadtallendorf e2 174
Stadtbergen f4 175
Stadthagen e3 172
Stadtilm g2 175
Stadtkyll e4 159
Stadtlauringen f2 174
Stadtlohn e3 159
Stadtoldendorf e4 172
Stadtroda g2 175
Stäfa c2 196
Staffelberg g2 175
Staffelsee g5 175
Staffin b2 164
Staffora d5 196
Stafford, U.K. d4 162
Stafford, U.S.A. c6 256
Stafford Springs h3 257
Staffordshire d3 162
St-Affrique e5 187
Stagen j6 99
St-Agrève a5 185
Stahlstown a4 256
Staicele l4 157
St-Aignan g5 183
Stainach f2 177
Staines f5 163
Stainforth e3 162
Stainz g3 177
Staìti f7 199
Stakčín l3 171
Stakhanov e2 148
Stalać e4 200
Stalden b3 196
Stalham h4 162
Stalheim b2 156
Stalin, Mount e2 248
Stalingrad g2 149
Stalingrad, Volgogradskaja Oblast', Russ. Fed. g2 149
Ställdalen f3 156
Stallhofen g2 177
Stalowa Wola l5 169
Stâlpu h3 201
St-Amand-en-Puisaye j5 183
St-Amand-les-Eaux b4 159
St-Amand-Longpré g5 183
St-Amand-Montrond e2 186
St-Amans f4 186
St-Amant-de-Boixe c3 186
St-Amant-Roche-Savine f3 186
St-Amant-Tallende f3 186
St-Amarin d3 184
Stamboliyski g4 201
St-Ambroix a6 184
Stamford f4 162
Stamford, Connecticut, U.S.A. g3 257
Stamford, New York, U.S.A. f2 256
Stamford, Texas, U.S.A. d5 261
Stamford, Vermont, U.S.A. g2 257
Stamford Bridge f3 162
Stammham g4 175
St-Amour b4 184
Stampede Reservoir c2 264
Stamping Ground d6 254
Stampriet c2 234
Stamsund d2 154
Stanardsville b6 256
Stanberry e3 260
Stancija Skuratovo d5 150
Standerton h3 235
Standish e4 254
St-André-de-Cubzac b4 186
St-André-de-l'Eure g4 183
St-André-les-Alpes c7 185
Stănești g3 201
Stanfield h9 263
Stanford, R.S.A. c7 234
Stanford, Kentucky, U.S.A. g1 259
Stanford, Montana, U.S.A. h2 262
Stanford-le-Hope g5 163
Stånga h4 157
Stångån f4 156
Stange d2 156
Stanger j4 235
Stanhope d2 162
Stănilești j2 201
Stanin l4 169
Stanisławów k3 169
Staňkov b2 170
Stankovany h2 171
Stanley, Aust. Aa2 83
Stanley, Falk. Is e6 295
Stanley, U.K. e2 162
Stanley, North Dakota, U.S.A. b6 250
Stanley, Virginia, U.S.A. b6 256
Stanley, Mount, Northern Territory, Aust. k8 86
Stanley, Mount, Tasmania, Aust. c5 82
Stann Creek, Belize c2 276
Stann Creek, Belize c2 276
Stannington e1 162
Stanos b4 210
Stanovoe Nagor'e m4 119
Stanovoj Hrebet h1 94
Stans c3 196
Stansmore Range j7 86
St-Anthème f3 186
Stanthorpe k10 81
Stanton, U.K. e2 258
Stanton, U.S.A. g4 163
St-Antonin-Noble-Val d4 187
Stantsiya Elektrii Varzob d1 128
Stanwix f5 164
Stanychno-Luhans'ke e2 148
Stanz im Mürztal g2 177
Stanzach b2 176
Staphorst e2 159
Staples f7 250
Stapleton, Alabama, U.S.A. f4 258
Stapleton, Nebraska, U.S.A. c3 260
Stąporków j4 169
Star, Aust. A 84
Star, Mississippi, U.S.A. d3 258
Star, North Carolina, U.S.A. k2 259
Star Keys A 77
Star Peak d5 262
Stara Błotnica j4 169
Stara Gradina j4 177
Stara Kiszewa g2 168
Stara Łubianka e2 168
Stará Ľubovňa j2 171
Stara Novalja f5 177
Stara Pazova e3 200
Stara Planina g4 201
Stará Turá f3 171
Stara Ushytsya h1 201
Stará Ves nad Ondřejnicí g2 171
Stara Vyzhivka n4 169
Stara Zagora, Bul. g4 201
Stara Zagora g4 201
Starachowice k4 169
Staraja Majna k4 151
Staraja Russa a3 150
Staraja Sahča k4 151
Staravina b1 210
Starbuck e6 250
Starbuck Island H 75
Starchiojd h3 201
Starcross c6 163
Stare Czarnowo c2 168
Staré Město e1 170
Stare Miasto g3 168
Stare Selo n6 169
Stargard Szczeciński d2 168
Stari Majdan h5 177
Starica c3 150
Starigrad, Lika-Senj, Cro. f5 177
Starigrad, Split-Dalmacija, Cro. f1 198
Starke h5 259
Starkville e3 258
Starnberg g5 175
Starnberger See g5 175
St-Arnoult-en-Yvelines g4 183
Staro Oryakhovo h4 201
Staroalejskoe u2 121
Starobil's'k e2 148
Starodub d1 148
Staroe f2 150
Staroe Šajgovo h4 151
Staroe Šajmurzino j4 151
Starogard Gdański g2 168
Starojur'evo f5 150
Starokostyantyniv b2 148
Starominskaja e3 148
Starosel g4 201
Starosiedle c4 168
Starotimoškino j5 151
Start Bay c6 163
Start Point c6 163
Starup c3 158
Stary Kisielin d4 168
Starý Kolín d1 170
Stary Lubotyń k3 169
Starý Plzenec b2 170
Stary Sącz j6 169
Starý Smokovec j2 171
Staryj Katyš l4 147
Staryj Nadym n2 147
Staryj Oskol e2 148
Staryj Studenec k4 151
Staryy Chortoryys'k p4 169
Staryy Sambir l6 169
St-Astier c3 186
Staszów k5 169
State College c4 256
State Line e4 258
Statenville h4 259
Statesboro j3 259
Statesville j2 259
Station No. 6 d3 218
St-Auban c7 185
St-Aubin b3 184
St-Aubin-d'Aubigné d4 182
St-Aubin-du-Cormier d4 182
St-Aubin-sur-Aire b2 184
Stauchitz h1 175
Staufen c5 174
Staufenberg d2 174
Staufersberg f4 175
St-Aulaye c3 186
Staunton k6 257
Staunton a6 256
Stavanger a3 156
St-Avé c5 182
Stave Lake f7 248
Staveley d2 162
Stavelot d4 159
Stavern d3 156
Stavertsi g4 201
Stavkove k2 201
St-Avold c1 184
Stavoren d2 159
Stavreshoved d3 158
Stavropol' f3 148
Stavropol'skaja Vozvyšennost' f3 149
Stavropol'skij Kraj f3 149
Stavropolka l1 120
Stavros, Cyp. a1 138
Stavros, Grc. d2 210
Stavros, Akra, Kriti, Grc. e7 211
Stavros, Akra, Notio Aigaio, Grc. f5 211
Stavroupoli e1 210
Stavsnäs h3 157
Stavtrup d2 158
Staw c3 168
Stawell f6 80
Stawell f14 81
Stawiguda j2 169
Stawiski l2 169
Stawiszyn g4 168
Steamboat Springs b3 260
Stębark j2 169
Stebbins d3 246
Steccato f6 199
Steckborn c2 196
Steele d7 250
Steele Island mm2 298
Steelton d4 256
Steenkampsberge MR j2 235
Steens Mountain d4 262
Steenvoorde a4 159
Steenwijk e2 159
Steep Point a10 87
Steeping g3 162
Steeple Jason d6 295
Ștefan Vodă h3 201
Stefanoviki c3 210
Stefansson Island h1 242
Steffen, Cerro b4 295
Stege f4 158
Stege Bugt f4 158
Stege Nor f4 158
Stegersbach h2 177
Steggerda e2 159
St-Égrève b5 185
Stehekin c1 262
Ștei l5 171
Steiermark g2 177
Steigerwald f3 174

Stein b2 196
Steinach g2 175
Steinach am Brenner c2 176
Steinau an der Straße e2 174
Steinbach e6 250
Steinbach am Wald g2 175
Steinbourg d2 184
Steindorf am Ossiacher See f3 177
Steine e2 154
Steinen c5 174
Steinfeld e3 176
Steinfeld (Oldenburg) d3 172
Steinfurt f2 159
Steinfurter Aa ≈ c3 172
Steingaden f5 175
Steinhagen, Mecklenburg-Vorpommern, Ger. h1 173
Steinhagen, Nordrhein-Westfalen, Ger. d3 172
Steinhausen b3 232
Steinhuder Meer ○ d3 172
Steinkjer c4 154
Steinkopf △ d2 174
Steinkopf b4 234
Steinsdorf k3 173
Stella f3 234
Stella, Monte della △ e4 198
Stellarton l6 253
Stelle d5 158
Stellenbosch c6 234
Steller, Mount △ j3 247
Stello, Monte △ A 185
St-Éloy-les-Mines e2 186
Stelvio, Parco Nazionale dello ☆ e3 196
Stenay d5 159
Stenbjerg b2 158
Stendal g3 173
Stende k4 157
Stenderup c3 158
Steneto, Naroden Park ☆ g4 200
Steni Dirfios d4 210
Stenico e3 196
Stenlille e3 158
Stenløse f3 158
Steno c5 211
Steno, Akra ► e5 211
Stensele f4 154
Stenshuvuds nationalpark ☆ f5 156
Stenstorp e3 156
Stenstrup d3 158
Stensved f4 158
Stenudden f3 154
Stenungsund d3 156
Stenzharychi n5 169
Step' Chardara l7 121
Step' Karnabchul' b1 128
Step' Zhusandala q5 121
Stepancevo f3 150
Stepanci b1 210
Stepenitz ≈ g2 173
Stephen e6 250
Stephens c3 258
Stephens City b5 256
Stephens Creek e11 81
Stephens Island ▭ b4 248
Stephens Lake ○ f2 250
Stephens Passage ═ l4 247
Stephens, Cape ► d4 77
Stephenson c3 254
Stephenson, Mount △ ll1 298
Stephenville, Can. n4 253
Stephenville, U.S.A. d5 261
Stepnica c2 168
Stepnoe g3 149
Stepnogorsk p1 121
Stepnyak n1 121
Stepovak Bay ◄ e5 246
Sterdyń-Osada l3 169
Sterea Ellas ⊡ d4 210
Sterkfontein Dam ⊸ h4 235
Sterkspruit g5 235
Sterkstroom g5 235
Sterławki Wielkie k1 169
Sterling, R.S.A. d5 234
Sterling, Alaska, U.S.A. g3 246
Sterling, Colorado, U.S.A. c3 260
Sterling, Michigan, U.S.A. d3 254
Sterling, North Dakota, U.S.A. c7 250
Sterling City c6 261
Sterlington c3 258
Sterlitamak h5 147
Sterna g1 210
Sternberg e5 158
Šternberk f2 170
Sternes e7 211
Stes-Maries-de-la-Mer a7 185
Stęszew e3 168
Štěti c1 170
Stettiner Haff ◄ k2 173
Steubenville f5 254
Stevenage f5 163
Stevens Point b3 254
Stevens Village g2 247
Stevenson g2 259
Stevenson Entrance ═ f4 246
Stevenson Lake ○ e3 250
Stevns Klint f3 158
Stevnstrup c2 158
Stewart, British Columbia, Can. c4 248
Stewart, Yukon Territory, Can. ≈ k3 247
Stewart Island ▭ b7 77
Stewart, Cape ► b1 80
Stewart, Isla ▭ b6 295
Stewarton d4 164
Stewartstown d5 256
Stewiacke l6 253
Steyerberg e3 172
Steyning f6 163
Steynrus g3 235
Steynsburg f5 235
Steyr f1 177
Steyregg f1 177
Steytlerville f6 234
Stężyca f1 168
Stia f6 197
Stibb Cross b6 163
Stickney g3 162
Stiens d1 159
Stigliano f4 198
Stigtomta g3 156
Stikine ≈ b3 248
Stilbaai, R.S.A. ◄ d7 234
Stilbaai d7 234
Stilfontein g3 235
Stili, Akra ► e6 211
Stilling c2 158
Stillwater, Minnesota, U.S.A. e2 260
Stillwater, Montana, U.S.A. ≈ j3 262
Stillwater, Oklahoma, U.S.A. a1 258
Stillwater Range ⊠ e2 264
Stilo f6 199
Stilwell b2 258
Stintino Aa2 198
Štip f5 201
Stipanov Grič △ g5 177
Stiring-Wendel c1 184
Stirling, Aust. a6 80
Stirling, Aust. d13 81
Stirling, Scotland, U.K. ⊡ d3 164
Stirling, U.K. e3 164
Stirling Creek ≈ j5 86
Stirling Range National Park ☆ d14 87
Stirrat e7 254
Stizzon ≈ f4 196
Stjernøya IS j1 155
Stjørdalselva ≈ c5 154
Stjørdalshalsen c5 154
Stjørnfjorden ⊸ b5 154
Stochov b1 170
Stocka g2 156
Stockach e5 174
Stockbridge e5 163
Stockbridge, U.S.A. g3 259
Stockdale a5 258
Stockelsdorf d5 158
Stockerau h1 177
Stockheim g2 175
Stockholm, Swe. ⊡ h3 157
Stockholm, Swe. h3 157
Stockholm, U.S.A. f3 256
Stockhorn △ b3 196
Stockport, England, U.K. ⊡ h2 162
Stockport d3 162
Stocksbridge e3 162
Stockstadt am Rhein d3 174
Stockton, California, U.S.A. b4 264
Stockton, Illinois, U.S.A. a4 254
Stockton, Kansas, U.S.A. d4 260
Stockton Lake ○ c1 258
Stockton-on-Tees, England, U.K. ⊡ h1 162
Stockton-on-Tees e2 162
Stockyard Gully Nature Reserve ☆ b12 87
Stoczek Łukowski k4 169
Stod b2 170
Stoddard h1 257
Stöde g1 156
Stödesjön g1 156
Stodolišče b4 150
Stœng Trêng g9 103
Stoer, Point of ► c1 164
Stoholm c2 158
Stokenchurch f5 163
Stoke-on-Trent, England, U.K. ⊡ h2 162
Stoke-on-Trent d4 162
Stokes National Park ☆ e13 87
Stokes Point ► d5 82
Stokes Range ⊠ k4 86
Stokes, Cerro △ b6 295
Stokes, Isla ▭ b4 295
Stokes, Mount △ e4 77
Stokesley e2 162
Stokhid ≈ p4 169
Stokkvågen d3 154
Stokmarknes e2 154
Stol △ e3 176
Stolac g1 198
Stolberg (Harz) Kurort f4 173
Stolberg (Rheinland) e4 159
Stolczno f2 168
Stolin b2 148
Stollberg h2 175
Stöllet e2 156
Stolniceni j2 201
Stolno g2 168
Stolpen h2 175
Stølsnostind b2 156
Stolzenau e3 172
Stomio c3 210
Ston g2 198
Stone d4 162
Stone Harbor f5 256
Stone Mountain Provincial Park ☆ n4 247
Stone Ridge f3 257
Stonehaven f3 164
Stonehenge f8 80
Stonehouse e4 164
Stoneville g7 254
Stonewall, Can. e5 250
Stonewall, U.S.A. c3 258
Stonewall Mountain △ f4 264
Stoney Point f2 164
Stonglandseidet f2 154
Stonington b6 254
Stony Brook g4 257
Stony Creek ≈ a2 264
Stony Lake ○ d1 250
Stony Point, Michigan, U.S.A. e5 254
Stony Point, North Carolina, U.S.A. j2 259
Stony Rapids q2 249
Stony River e3 246
Stonyford a2 264
Stopnica j5 169
Stör e2 172
Stor Kallberget △ e2 156
Storå f3 156
Stora ≈ b2 158
Stora Dímun B 152
Storån ≈ e5 154
Storavan ○ g4 154
Storbäcken e2 156
Storbekkfjellet △ d2 156
Storbo f2 156
Storby h2 157
Stord ▭ a3 156
Stordal b1 156
Store Bælt ═ d3 158
Store Darum b3 158
Store Heddinge f3 158
Store Jukleeggi △ c2 156
Store Korssjøen ○ d1 156
Store Majavatnet ○ d4 154
Store Merløse e3 158
Store Molvik m1 155
Store Moss nationalpark ☆ f4 156
Store Namsvatnet ○ d4 154
Store Øljusjøen ○ c2 156
Store Skorøya ▭ g1 154
Store Sotra ▭ a2 156
Storejen ○ f2 156
Storelv j1 155
Støren c5 154
Storfjärden ○ g2 156
Storfjellet △ d5 154
Storfjordbotn l1 155
Storfloa ○ d4 154
Storfors f3 156
Storforshei e3 154
Storgalten Naturreservat ☆ j1 155
Storgryta ≈ d2 156
Storhøa △ d2 156
Storje e4 176
Storjola e4 154
Storjord e3 154
Storjorm ○ e3 154
Storjuktan ○ f4 154
Storkälen ○ e5 154
Storkow j3 173
Stor-Laxsjön ○ f5 154
Storlia Naturreservat ☆ e3 154
Storlien d5 154
Storm Bay ◄ Ab3 83
Storm Lake e3 260
Stormberg g5 235
Stormberge ⊠ g5 235
Stornes f2 154
Storneshamn h2 154
Stor-Nien ○ g2 156
Stornoway b1 164
Storo e4 196
Storodden b5 154
Storoževsk h3 147
Storozhynets' g1 201
Storr, The △ b2 164
Storrensjön ○ d5 154
Storrs h3 257
Storseleby f4 154
Storsjøen, Nor. ○ d1 156
Storsjøen, Nor. ○ d2 156
Storsjön, Swe. ○ d5 154
Storsjön, Swe. ○ e5 154
Storsjön, Swe. ○ f5 154
Storsjön, Swe. ○ f2 156
Storsjön, Swe. ○ g2 156
Storskarhø △ c1 156
Storslett h2 154
Storsteinnes g2 154
Storstrøm ⊡ f3 158
Stor-Svartliden △ g4 154
Storteinelk ≈ d1 159
Storuman, Swe. ○ f4 154
Storuman f4 154
Stor-Valsjön ○ f1 156
Storvik g2 156
Storvindeln ○ f4 154
Storvollen d1 158
Storvreta g3 157
Stoughton, Can. b6 250
Stoughton, U.S.A. j2 257
Stoŭng, Stœng g9 103
Stour, England, U.K. ≈ d1 163
Stour, England, U.K. ≈ e4 163
Stour, England, U.K. ≈ h5 163
Stourbridge d4 163
Stourport-on-Severn d4 163
Stout Lake ○ f4 250
Støvring c2 158
Stow f5 254
Stowbtsy b1 148
Stowmarket g4 163
Stow-on-the-Wold e5 163
Stoyaniv n5 169
Stra g4 196
Straach h4 173
Strabane, England, U.K. ⊡ b2 165
Strabane d2 165
Strachan k4 164
Strączno e2 168
Stradbally d3 165
Stradella d4 196
Straelen e3 159
Strahan Aa3 83
Straitsatjåkkå △ e3 154
Straits of Florida ═ k7 259
Strakonice b2 170
Straldzha h4 201
Stralsund j1 173
Stráňavy g2 171
Strand c7 234
Stranda b1 156
Strandås Naturreservat ☆ e3 154
Strandavatnet ○ b2 156
Strandby d1 158
Strandhill c2 165
Strangers Cay ▭ l6 259
Strangford Lough ◄ e2 165
Strängnäs g3 156
Strangways Range ⊠ b7 80
Strání j1 177
Stranorlar d2 165
Stranraer c5 164
St-Raphaël c7 185
Strasatti b7 199
Strasbourg, Can. a5 250
Strasbourg, Fr. d2 184
Strasburg, Ger. j2 173
Strasburg, North Dakota, U.S.A. c7 250
Strasburg, Ohio, U.S.A. f5 254
Strasburg, Virginia, U.S.A. b6 256
Strășeni j2 201
Strassa f3 156
Strasshof an der Norbahn h1 177
Straßwalchen e2 176
Stratford, Aust. h14 81
Stratford, Can. f4 254
Stratford, N.Z. e3 76
Stratford, California, U.S.A. d5 265
Stratford, Connecticut, U.S.A. g3 257
Stratford, Oklahoma, U.S.A. a2 258
Stratford, Texas, U.S.A. c4 261
Stratford-upon-Avon e4 163
Strath Earn ≈ d3 164
Strathalbyn d13 81
Strathaven d4 164
Strathbeg, Loch of ○ g2 164
Strathgordon Ab3 83
Strathmore, U.K. ≈ d1 164
Strathmore, U.S.A. d5 265
Strathpeffer d2 164
Strathspey ≈ e2 164
Strathy Point ► d1 164
Stratoni d2 210
Stratoniki d2 210
Stratos b4 210
Stratton b6 163
Stratton, U.S.A. g6 252
Straubing h4 175
Straume e2 154
Straumen, Nordland, Nor. e3 154
Straumen, Nord-Trøndelag, Nor. c5 154
Straumnes ► A 152
Straupitz k4 173
Strausberg j3 173
Straußfurt f1 175
Strausstown d4 256
Strawberry Mountain △ d3 262
Strawberry Reservoir ○ h5 262
Stráž nad Nežárkou c2 170
Strážnice j1 177
Strážný e1 176
Strážske k3 171
Streaky Bay b12 81
Streaky Bay, South Australia, Aust. ◄ b12 81
Streator b5 254
Strečno g2 171
Streedagh Point ► c2 165
Street d5 163
Streeter d7 250
Streetman a4 258
Strehaia f3 201
Strehla j4 173
Strejeşti, Lacul ○ g3 201
Strel'na ≈ d2 146
Střelice e2 170
Strelley d7 86
Strem ≈ h2 177
Strenči l4 157
Stresa c4 196
Stretton e4 162
Streu ≈ f2 174
Streymoy ▭ B 152
Streževoj h3 118
Strib c3 158
Striberg f3 156
Stříbro a2 170
Strichen f2 164
Strimonas ≈ d2 210
Striži k2 151
Strobel, Lago ○ b5 295
Strobl e2 176
Strøby Egede f3 158
Stroeder f6 297
Strofades ▭ b5 211
Strofylia d4 210
Ströhen d3 172
Strokestown c3 165
Stromberg-Heuchelberg, Naturpark ☆ e3 174
Stromboli, Isola ▭ e6 199
Stromeferry c2 164
Stromness B 164
Stromsburg d3 260
Strömsnäsbruk e4 156
Strömstad d3 156
Strömsund e5 154
Strong c3 258
Strongoli g5 199
Stronie Śląskie e5 168
Stronsay ▭ f1 164
Stronsdorf h1 177
Strontian c3 164
Stropkov k2 171
Stroud, Aust. k12 81
Stroud, U.K. d5 163
Stroud, U.S.A. a2 258
Stroudsburg e4 256
Stroumpi a2 138
Strovija b1 210
Strovolos b1 138
Strub, Pass △ d2 176
Strücklingen (Saterland) c2 172
Struer b2 158
Struga a1 210
Strugi-Krasne n3 157
Strule ≈ d2 165
Struma ≈ d1 210
Strumeshnitsa ≈ d1 210
Strumica, Mac. ≈ c1 210
Strumica c1 210
Strunino e3 150
Struthers f5 254
Strużec h4 177
Stryama ≈ g4 201
Strydenburg e4 234
Strydpoort f3 235
Stryker f1 262
Stryków h4 169
Strymoniko d1 210
Stryn b2 156
Strynø ▭ d4 158
Strynsvatnet ○ b2 156
Stryukove k2 201
Stryy, Ukr. ≈ m6 169
Stryy m6 169
Strzegom e5 168
Strzegowo j3 169
Strzelce h3 169
Strzelce Krajeńskie d3 168
Strzelce Opolskie g5 168
Strzelce Wielkie h4 169
Strzelecki Creek ≈ e10 81
Strzelecki, Mount △ a6 80
Strzelecki Peak △ Ac2 83
Strzelin f5 168
Strzelno g3 168
Strzyżów k6 169
Stuart, Aust. ≈ d5 84
Stuart, Florida, U.S.A. j6 259
Stuart, Virginia, U.S.A. f7 254
Stuart Bluff Range ⊠ k8 86
Stuart Island ▭ d3 246
Stuart Lake ○ e4 248
Stuart Range ⊠ b10 81
Stuart Town f1 83
Stubaier Alpen ⊠ c2 176
Stubbæk c4 158
Stubbington e6 163
Stubenberg g2 177
Studénka g2 171
Studholme Junction c6 77
Studienka f3 170
Studsvik g3 156
Study Butte h3 272
Stuhr d2 172
Stuie d5 248
Stull Lake ○ g3 250
Stulpicani g2 201
Stump Lake ○ d2 260
Stuorajávri ○ j2 155
Stupava f3 170
Stupino e4 150
Stura ≈ c4 196
Stura di Demonte ≈ b5 196
Stura di Lanzo ≈ b4 196
Sturbridge h2 257
Sturge Island ▭ x1 298
Sturgeon ≈ n7 251
Sturgeon Bay, Can. ◄ e4 250
Sturgeon Bay, U.S.A. c3 254
Sturgeon Falls g2 254
Sturgeon Lake ○ h5 250
Sturgis, Michigan, U.S.A. d5 254
Sturgis, South Dakota, U.S.A. c2 260
Sturkö ▭ f4 156
Sturminster Newton d6 163
Štúrovo g4 171
Sturt Creek ≈ j6 86
Sturt National Park ☆ e10 81
Sturt Plain ⊸ l5 86
Sturt Stony Desert ≈ e10 81
Sturt, Mount △ e10 81
Stutterheim g6 235
Stuttgart e4 174
Stuttgart ⊡ e4 174
Stuttgart, U.S.A. d2 258
Stykkishólmur A 152
Stylida c4 210
Stymfalia, Limni ○ c5 210
Styr ≈ p4 169
Styra e4 210
Suai e9 99
Suaita c2 284
Suakin e4 219
Suan p6 113
Suana d5 224
Suances f1 190
Suapure Chivapuri ≈ d2 284
Suaqui Grande e3 272
Suara, Mount △ e4 219
Suardi d2 294
Suárez, Col. ≈ c2 284
Suárez, Cauca, Col. b3 284
Suata d2 285
Subačius l5 157
Suban Point ► d4 100
Subang d8 98
Subansiri ≈ p6 125
Subarnarekha ≈ k8 125
Subāshī m4 137
Subasio, Monte △ g6 197
Subate l4 157
Subay ♦ g2 219
Subbiano f6 197
Subcetate g2 201
Subi Besar ▭ e3 98
Subi Kecil ▭ e3 98
Subiaco h8 197
Subkowy g1 168
Subotica h5 171
Subucle △ f5 219
Subugo △ b4 226
Sučany g2 171
Suc-au-May △ d3 186
Suceava, Rom. ⊡ g2 201
Suceava h2 201
Sucha Beskidzka h2 171
Suchá Hora h2 171
Suchan ≈ s4 113
Suchdol nad Lužnicí f1 177
Suchedniów j4 169
Suchet, Mont △ a3 196
Suchil c2 274
Suchixtepec f5 275
Suchowola m2 169
Sucio ≈ b2 284
Suck ≈ c3 165
Suckow e5 158
Sucre, Bol. d3 292
Sucre, Col. ⊡ c2 284
Sucre, Ven. ⊡ e1 285
Sucuaro d3 284
Sucumbíos ⊡ b3 284
Sucunduri ≈ f5 285
Sućuraj g1 198
Sucuriú ≈ b4 290
Sud ⊡ b3 232
Sud Ouest, Pointe ► C 231
Sud, Pointe ► Aa1 233
Sud, Pointe du ► A 226
Sudaj g2 151
Sudak d3 148
Sudan e3 217

SUDAN

THE REPUBLIC OF SUDAN
Area 2,505,813km^2 (967,500sq miles)
Capital Khartoum
Organizations COMESA, LAS, OIC
Population 32,470,000
Pop. growth (%) 0.1
Life expectancy 53 (m); 56 (f)
Languages Arabic, English and local languages
Literacy 61%
Currency Sudanese dinar (US $1 = 259.85 Sudanese dinar)
GDP (US million $) 13,589
GDP per head ($US) 418

Sudbury, Can. f2 254
Sudbury g4 163
Sudd ⊠ f2 225
Suddie f2 285
Sude ≈ g2 173
Süderhastedt c4 158
Süderlügum b4 158
Süderoog ▭ b1 172
Sudety ⊠ d1 170
Südfall ▭ d1 172
Sudimir c5 150
Sudislavl' e2 150
Sud-Kivu ⊡ e4 225
Südlohn e3 159
Süd-Nord-Kanal ⊸ c3 172
Sudogda f4 150
Sudomskie Vysoty ♦ n4 157
Sud-Ouest ⊡ a2 224
Sudova Vyshnya m6 169
Sudr a7 139
Südradde ≈ c3 172
Suðurland ⊡ A 152
Suðuroy ▭ B 152
Sudža d2 148
Sue ≈ e2 225
Sueca d5 193
Süedinenie g4 201
Suelli Ab3 198
Suez, El Suweis, Egypt a7 139
Suez, El Suweis, Egypt d2 218
Suez Canal ⊸ a5 139
Suez, Gulf of ◄ d7 136
Suffolk, U.K. ⊡ h4 163
Suffolk, U.S.A. h7 255
Süfiān k2 137
Sugana, Val ≈ f3 196
Sugar Land b5 258
Sugar Notch e3 256
Sugarbush Hill △ f2 260
Sugarcreek g5 254
Sugarloaf Point ► e8 85
Sugbuhan Point ► f5 100
Sugi ▭ b4 98
Šugozero c2 150
Sugun r8 121
Sugur l3 147
Sugut ≈ j1 99
Suguta ≈ b3 226
Suha Krajina ♦ f4 177
Suhait b1 218
Suhaia g4 201
Şuhār c6 112
Suhaymī, Wādī as ≈ f6 116
Sühbaatar, Mong. ⊡ b7 139
Sühbaatar g2 112
Suheli Par ▭ d1 112
Suhi vrh △ c7 126
Suhiniči f4 177
Suhl c4 150
Suhlendorf f2 175
Suhobezvodnoe f3 173
Suhoborka h3 151
Suhodol'skij k2 151
Suhodol'skoe, Ozero ○ e5 150
Suhoj n2 157
Suhoj Log f3 148
Suhona ≈ k4 147
Suhopolje f2 150
Suhum j4 177
Şuhut d4 222
Sui c3 208
Sui Vehar d6 129
Sui, Laem ► e6 129
Suiá Missur ≈ a1 101
Suibin b4 288
Suichuan r2 113
Suide k5 105
Suifen He ≈ b1 106
Suigam r3 113
Suihua e8 129
Suijiang p2 113
Suileng d4 104
Suining, Hunan, China p2 113
Suining, Jiangsu, China h5 104
Suining, Sichuan, China e3 111
Suininki ○ e3 104
Suipacha m3 155
Suiping h3 297
Suippe ≈ d3 106
Suippes k3 183
Suir ≈ a1 184
Suisun City d4 165
Suixi, Anhui, China a3 264
Suixi, Guangdong, China e3 111
Suixian h8 104
Suiyang, Guizhou, China d2 106
Suiyang, Henan, China f5 104
Suizhong d2 106
Suizhou l5 113
Suj c4 106
Šuja d4 112
Sujangarh f3 150
Sujanpur, Himachal Pradesh, India g7 129
Sujanpur, Punjab, India c4 130
Sujawal b3 130
Šujskoe d8 129
Sukabumi f2 150
Sukadana, Kalimantan Barat, Indon. d8 98
Sukadana, Lampung, Indon. e5 98
Sukadana, Teluk ◄ c7 98
Sukagawa e5 98
Sukaramai j3 115
Sukau f6 98
Sukchŏn b8 100
Sukeva n6 113
Sukha Reka ≈ l5 155
Sukhothai h4 201
Sukkozero d7 102
Sukkur p5 155
Sukma d7 129
Süknah g3 126
Sukon, Ko ▭ h3 221
Süköśd a2 101
Sukses g5 171
Suksun b3 232
Sukumo j4 147
Sul, Canal do ⊸ e5 114
Sul, Pantanal ⊸ c2 288
Sul, Rio Grande do ⊡ f3 293
Sula, Nor. ▭ b7 289
Sula, Russ. Fed. ≈ a2 156
Sula Sgeir ▭ g2 146
Sula, Kepulauan ▭ c1 164
Sulabesi ▭ n6 99
Sulaco p6 99
Sulaiman Range ⊠ d3 276
Sulak d6 129
Sülär g4 149
Sulat n6 137
Sulawesi ▭ e5 100
Sulawesi Selatan ⊡ l5 99
Sulawesi Tengah ⊡ k6 99
Sulawesi Tenggara ⊡ l5 99
Sulawesi Utara ⊡ l6 99
Sulaymān Beg n4 99
Sulby k4 136
Suldrup b2 162
Sule Skerry ▭ c2 158
Sule Stack ▭ d1 164
Sulechów d1 164
Sulęcin d3 168
Sulęcin Szlachecki d3 168
Sulęczyno k3 169
Suledeh f1 168
Suleja, Nig. n3 137
Suleja, Russ. Fed. f4 223
Sulejów j5 147
Sulejówek h4 169
Sulejowskie, Jezioro ○ k3 169
Suleman, Teluk ◄ h4 169
Süleymanlı k4 99
Sulia f4 209
Sulima e4 225
Sulina b4 222
Sulingen j3 201
Suliskongen △ d3 172
Sulitjelma f3 154
Sulkava f3 154
Sułkowice n2 157
Sullana h6 169
Sullane ≈ a4 284
Sulligent b5 165
Sullivan Lake ○ e3 258
Sully-sur-Loire l5 249
Sulm ≈ h5 183
Šulma g3 177
Sulmierzyce d2 150
Sulmona f4 168
Sulphur, Louisiana, U.S.A. c2 198
Sulphur, Oklahoma, U.S.A. c4 258
Sulphur, Texas, U.S.A. ≈ a2 258
Sulphur Springs b3 258
Sultan b3 258
Sultana b1 218
Sultanhanı d5 264
Sultanhisar d3 208
Sultaniça b4 208
Sultanpur, Punjab, India g2 210
Sultanpur, Uttar Pradesh, India b4 130
Sultansandzharskoye h6 124
Vodokhranilishche ⊙ h7 120
Sulu Archipelago ▭ l2 99
Sulu Sea ⊸ b6 100
Suluan ▭ f5 100
Sülüklü d3 208
Sülüktü d1 128
Sululta b2 226
Suluntah b1 218
Sulüq b1 218
Suluru g6 126
Sulz am Neckar d4 174
Sulzbach e3 174
Sulzbach an der Murr e3 174
Sulzbach/Saar f5 159
Sulzbach-Rosenberg g3 175
Sulzberger Bay ◄ bb2 298
Sumaco, Volcán △ b4 284
Sumäil f6 116
Sumalata m4 99
Sumampa d1 294
Sumangat, Tanjung ► a7 100
Sumapaz, Parque Nacional ☆ c3 284
Sumatera ▭ b5 98
Sumatera Barat ⊡ a5 98
Sumatera Selatan ⊡ b6 98
Sumatera Utara ⊡ a4 101
Šumava e1 293
Šumava ☆ b2 170
Sumba ▭ B 152
Sumba, Indon. ▭ l9 99
Sumba, Île ▭ c3 224
Sumba, Selat ═ k9 99
Sumbawa ▭ k9 99
Sumbawabesar j9 99
Sumbawanga f5 225
Sumbay c3 292
Sumbe b6 224
Sumbing, Gunung △ a6 98
Sumbu f5 225
Sumbu National Park ☆ f5 225
Sumburgh A 164
Sumburgh Head ► A 164
Sumbuya b4 222
Sumdo d2 130
Sumdum, Mount △ l4 247
Sumé e3 288
Sumedang d8 98
Sume'eh Sarā m3 137
Sümeg f5 170
Sumeih e2 225
Sumenep g8 98
Šumerlja j4 151
Sumerpur f8 129
Sumiainen l5 155
Šumiha k5 147
Sümiyn Bulag h1 112
Sumiyō B 115
Šumjači b5 150
Sumki l5 147
Sumkino m4 147
Summanen ○ l1 157
Summël j9 209
Summer Beaver j4 251
Summer Island ▭ c3 254
Summer Isles ▭ c1 164
Summerside l5 253
Summersville f6 254
Summerton j3 259
Summerville, Georgia, U.S.A. g2 259
Summerville, South Carolina, U.S.A. j3 259
Summit g3 247
Summit Lake ○ h3 247
Summit Mountain △ e6 262
Summit Peak △ b4 261
Sumnal d2 130
Sumner d5 77
Sumner Strait ═ l4 247
Sumner, Lake ○ d5 77
Sumon-dake △ h3 115
Sumoto f4 114
Sumpangbinangae k7 99
Šumperk e2 170
Sumprabum c2 102
Sumqayıt h4 149
Sumrahu e7 129
Sumsar n7 121
Sumskij Posad q4 155
Šumšu, Ostrov ▭ r4 119
Sumter j3 259
Sumur c2 130
Sumy d2 148
Sumzom q5 125
Sun ≈ g2 262
Sun City, R.S.A. g2 235
Sun City, Arizona, U.S.A. g9 263
Sun City, California, U.S.A. f8 265
Sun Kosi ≈ h6 135
Sun Prairie b4 254
Suna l3 151
Sunagawa Ab2 114
Sunam b4 130
Sunamganj m7 125
Sunan n6 113
Sunbilla c1 192
Sunbright g1 259
Sunbury, Aust. g14 81
Sunbury, North Carolina, U.S.A. h7 255
Sunbury, Ohio, U.S.A. e5 254
Sunbury, Pennsylvania, U.S.A. d4 256
Sunch'ang p8 113
Sunch'ŏn, N. Korea n6 113
Sunch'ŏn, S. Kor. p8 113
Sunchales g1 297
Suncho Corral d1 294
Suncun e2 111
Sund d2 154
Sunda Shelf ≈ f5 300
Sunda, Selat ═ c8 98
Sundance b2 260
Sundarbans ♦ l9 125
Sundarbans National Park ☆ l9 125
Sundargarh j8 125
Sundarnagar c4 130
Sundblad f3 297
Sunde, Hordaland, Nor. a3 156
Sunde, Sør-Trøndelag, Nor. b5 154
Sunderland, England, U.K. ⊡ h1 162
Sunderland e2 162
Sundern (Sauerland) d4 172
Sundgau ♦ d3 184
Sündiken Dağları ⊠ c3 208
Sundown National Park ☆ d6 85
Sunds c2 158
Sundsvall g1 156
Sundukli, Peski ≈ k8 120
Sundvatnet ○ m2 155
Sunga b4 227
Sungai Bayor b3 101
Sungai Besar b4 101
Sungai Lembing c4 101
Sungai Mati c4 101
Sungai Siput b3 101
Sungaiapit c5 101
Sungaiguntung b4 98
Sungaikabung c5 101
Sungaipenuh a6 98
Sungaipinyuh e4 98
Sungei Petani b3 101
Sungeng e1 111
Sungguminasa k7 99
Sunggho n6 113
Sungju p8 113
Sungkai b4 101
Sungu c4 224
Sungurlu e2 208
Suni Aa2 198
Šunija ≈ k5 157
Suning h6 112
Sunipani, Nevado de △ c2 292
Sunja, Cro. ≈ h4 177
Sunja h4 177
Sunkar, Gora △ q5 121
Sunkosh Chhu ≈ j6 135
Sunndalen ≈ b5 154
Sunndalsøra b5 154
Sunne e3 156
Sunnersta f5 154
Sunni ≈ e2 225
Sunnyside f5 253
Sunnyvale a4 264
Sunrise j6 259
Sunset Beach Ab2 263
Sunshine g14 81
Suntar m3 119
Suntar Hajata, Hrebet ⊠ q3 119
Suntrana g3 247
Suntsar a8 129
Suntuanji e3 111
Sunwu p1 113
Sunyani d4 222
Suojarvi c3 146
Suolahti k5 155
Suolijärvi ○ m4 155
Suolisjärvi ○ m2 155
Suomussalmi m4 155
Suō-nada ◄ d5 114
Suonenjoki l5 155
Suontee, Fin. ○ m2 157
Suontee m1 157
Suontienselkä ○ l5 155
Suorva g3 154
Suoshi b5 106
Supa d5 126
Supamo ≈ e2 285
Superfosfatnyy c1 128

Superior, Arizona, U.S.A. h9 263
Superior, Laguna g5 275
Superior, Lake c2 254
Superiore, Lago e4 196
Superior, Montana, U.S.A. f2 262
Superior, Nebraska, U.S.A. d3 260
Superior, Wisconsin, U.S.A. g7 250
Supetar f1 198
Suphan Buri e8 103
Süphan Dağı j3 209
Suphellenipa b2 156
Supino h8 197
Suplacu de Barcău l4 171
Suprasl m2 169
Sup'sa j2 209
Supur l4 171
Sūq ash Shuyūkh l6 137
Suqian f3 111
Şūr f6 116
Sur, Point b6 265
Sura, Russ. Fed. j4 151
Sura h5 151
Şura Mare g3 201
Şura Mică g3 201
Şuraabad h4 149
Surab c6 129
Surabaya g8 98
Surahammar g3 156
Surai b6 129
Surajgarh b5 130
Surakarta f8 98
Suramana k5 99
Suran b4 184
Şūrān e1 138
Surany g3 171
Surára e4 285
Surat, Aust. j9 81
Surat, India f10 129
Surat Thani a1 101
Suratgarh f6 129
Suraž l3 169
Surаž b5 150
Surazh c1 148
Surbiton h7 80
Sürdäsh k4 137
Surdila-Greci h3 201
Surduc f2 201
Surdulica f4 201
Süre e5 159
Surendranagar e9 129
Suretka f6 277
Surf City f5 257
Surgères b2 186
Surgut n3 147
Surhuisterveen e1 159
Süria f3 192
Suriapet f4 126
Surigao e6 100
Surigao Strait e5 100
Surimena c3 284
Surin f8 103
Suriname e2 282

SURINAME

THE REPUBLIC OF SURINAME
Area 163,265km^2 (63,037sq miles)
Capital Paramaribo
Organizations ACS, CARICOM, IADB, OIC, SELA
Population 430,000
Pop. growth (%) 0.4
Life expectancy 67 (m); 72 (f)
Languages Dutch, Hindi, Javanese, Sranang Tongo, Chinese, English
Literacy 93%
Currency Surinam guilder (US $1 = 2515 Surinam guilder)
GDP (US million $) 789
GDP per head ($US) 1834

Suriname, Sur. g2 285
Suring b3 254
Surinsk k5 151
Suripá, Ven. c2 284
Suripá, Barinas, Ven. d2 284
Surir c6 130
Suriyān p6 137
Surkhābād p4 137
Surkhandar'inskaya Oblast' c1 128
Surkhandar'ya c2 128
Surkhduz b5 128
Surkhet e5 130
Surkhob e1 128
Surma l3 151
Surman g2 221
Surmaq p6 137
Surmelin j4 183
Sürmene h2 209
Surnadalsøra b5 154
Surnevo g4 201
Surnujärvi m2 155
Surovatiha g4 151
Surovikino f2 149
Surprise Lake l4 247
Surpura f7 129
Surrazala c5 191
Surrey f5 163
Sursee c2 196
Sursk h5 151
Surskoe j4 151
Surt h2 221
Surtainville d3 182
Surte e4 156
Surtsey A 152
Sürü r8 137
Surubiú c2 288
Sürüç g4 209
Surud, Raas g5 219
Suruga-wan h4 115
Surulangun b6 98
Surup f7 100
Surwold f2 159
Sury-le-Comtal a5 184
Suryškarskij Sor, Ozero l2 147
Suryškary l2 147
Suşa g5 149
Susä e3 158
Susa b4 196
Susaki e5 114
Süsangerd m6 137
Susanino f2 150
Susanville c5 262
Susch e3 196
Susegana g4 196
Suşehri g2 209
Süsel d4 158
Sushitsa g4 201
Sushui He b2 106
Sušice b2 170
Susiec m5 169
Susitna g3 246
Susitna Lake h3 247
Suškodom f2 150
Susleni j2 201
Suslonger k3 151
Suso a2 101
Susong e4 111
Susono h4 115
Susquehanna, Pennsylvania, U.S.A. e3 256
Susquehanna, Pennsylvania, U.S.A. d3 256
Susquehanna, Pennsylvania, U.S.A. d5 256
Susques d4 292
Süßen e4 174
Sussex, Can. k6 253
Sussex, New Jersey, U.S.A. f3 256
Sussex, Virginia, U.S.A. h7 255
Susteren d3 159
Susticacán c2 274
Susua l6 99
Susuman q3 119
Susunu j6 97
Susupi A 74
Susupu h5 97
Susurluk b3 208
Susuzmüsellim h5 201
Šušvė k5 157
Susz h2 169
Sutak c3 130
Sutherland d6 234
Sutherland, U.S.A. c3 260
Sutherland Range g9 87
Sutherlin b4 262
Sutjeska d4 200
Sutlej c4 130
Sutter b2 264
Sutter Buttes b2 264
Sutter Creek c3 264
Sutton, Can. l3 251
Sutton, U.K. h3 162
Sutton, Alaska, U.S.A. g3 247
Sutton, West Virginia, U.S.A. f6 254
Sutton Bridge g4 162
Sutton Coldfield e4 163
Sutton in Ashfield e3 162
Sutton on Trent f3 162
Suttor b2 84
Suttsu Ab2 114
Sutwik Island e4 246
Suugant d3 112
Suure-Jaani l3 157
Suur-Pakri k3 157
Suva E 74
Suvainiškis l4 157
Suvanto l3 155
Suvasvesi m5 155
Suvero, Capo f6 199
Suvodol b1 210
Suvorov, Mol. j3 201
Suvorov, Russ. Fed. d4 150
Suvorove j3 201
Suwa h3 115
Suwakong h5 99
Suwałki l1 169
Suwannaphum f8 102
Suwannee h5 259
Suwaran, Gunung j4 99
Suwarrow H 75
Suwayliḥ d4 139
Suwaymah d5 139
Suwŏn p7 113
Suyangshan e2 111
Suykbulak t3 121
Suyo a4 284
Suz, Mys d7 120
Suzak m5 121
Suzdal' f3 150
Suzemka d1 148
Suzhou, Anhui, China e3 111
Suzhou, Jiangsu, China g4 111
Suzu g3 115
Suzuka g4 115
Suzu-misaki g3 115
Suzun u1 121
Suzzara e5 196
Svabensverk f2 156
Svæholtklubben Naturreservat l1 155
Svågan g2 156
Svalbard s3 299
Svalbard (Norway) b2 118
Svalenik h4 201
Svalöv e5 156
Svalyava l3 171
Svaneke f5 156
Svängsta f4 156
Svaningssjön e4 154
Svanskog e3 156
Svappavaara l3 155
Svärdsjö f2 156
Svarta l2 157
Svartå f3 156
Svartälven f2 156
Svartån, Swe. e3 156
Svartån, Swe. g3 156
Svartåmoen b5 154
Svartlögafjärden h3 157
Svartnes e3 154
Svatobořice-Mistřín j1 177
Svatove e2 148
Svätuše k3 171
Svätý Jur f3 170
Svätý Peter g4 171
Svay Chek f9 103
Svay Riĕng g10 103
Svebølle e3 158
Svedala e5 156
Svėdasai l5 157
Sveg f1 156
Svegsjön f1 156
Sveindal b3 156
Svejbæk c2 158
Svěkšna j5 157
Svelgen a2 156
Svellingen b5 154
Svelvik d3 156
Sven' c5 150
Švenčionėliai l5 157
Švenčionys m5 157
Svendborg d3 158
Svenstavik e5 154
Svenstrup, Nordjylland, Den. c2 158
Svenstrup, Sønderjylland, Den. c3 158
Svenstrup, Vestsjælland, Den. e3 158
Sventes ezers m5 157
Šventoji, Lith l5 157
Šventoji j4 157
Sverdlovsk e2 148
Sverdlovskaja Oblast' k4 147
Sverdrup Channel k1 242
Švėtė k4 157
Sveti Damjan, Rt f5 177
Sveti Grgur f5 177
Sveti Nikole e5 200
Světlá Hora f1 170
Světlá nad Sázavou d2 170
Svetlaya k3 94
Svetlogorsk, Kaliningradskaja Oblast', Russ. Fed. j5 157
Svetlogorsk, Krasnojarskij Kraj, Russ. Fed. j3 118
Svetlograd f3 149
Svetlyj, Kaliningradskaja Oblast', Russ. Fed. j1 169
Svetlyj, Orenburgskaja Oblast', Russ. Fed. h2 120
Svetogorsk n2 157
Švica g5 177
Svicha n6 169
Svidník k2 171
Švihov b2 170
Svilaja c4 200
Svilajnac e3 200
Svilengrad h5 201
Svinecea Mare, Vârful f3 201
Svinesund d3 156
Svinia k2 171
Svinninge, Vestsjælland, Den. e3 158
Svinoy B 152
Svintsovy Rudnik c2 128
Svir m5 157
Svir' b1 150
Svir'stroj b1 150
Svishtov g4 201
Svislach n2 169
Svit j2 171
Svitava e2 170
Svitávka e2 170
Svitavy e2 170
Svitlovods'k d2 148
Svjatoslavka f2 149
Svoboda k1 169
Svobodnyy h2 94
Svodín g4 171
Svoge f4 201
Svolvær e2 154
Svorkmo b5 154
Svratka e2 170
Svrčinovec g2 171
Svrljiške Planine f4 201
Svullrya e2 156
Svyetlahorsk c1 148
Swabi f3 128
Swadlincote e4 162
Swaffham g4 162
Swain Reefs l7 80
Swains Island H 75
Swainsboro h3 259
Swakop b1 234
Swakopmund a1 234
Swale e2 162
Swale, The g5 163
Swan, Aust. c12 87
Swan, Can. r6 249
Swan Hill f13 81
Swan Islands f2 277
Swan Lake, Can. c4 250
Swan Lake, U.S.A. e2 260
Swan Lake, Montana, U.S.A. g2 262
Swan Reach d13 81
Swan River c4 250
Swanage e6 163
Swanley g5 163
Swanlinbar d2 165
Swanquarter National Wildlife Refuge l2 259
Swansea, New South Wales, Aust. g1 83
Swansea, Aust. Ac3 83
Swansea, Wales, U.K. b5 163
Swansea, U.K. c5 163
Swansea, U.S.A. j3 259
Swansea Bay c5 163
Swanton k3 255
Swarożyn g1 168
Swartberg h5 235
Swartkops f6 235
Swartput se Pan c3 234
Swartruggens g2 235
Swartz Creek e4 254
Swarzędz f3 168
Swat Kohistan f3 128
Sway e6 163
Swaziland f7 217

SWAZILAND

THE KINGDOM OF SWAZILAND
Area 17,363km^2 (6704sq miles)
Capital Mbabane
Organizations COMESA, COMM, SADC
Population 1,070,000
Pop. growth (%) 1.9
Life expectancy 49 (m); 52 (f)
Languages English, siSwati
Literacy 81.6%
Currency lilangeni, plural emalangeni (US $1 = 6.38 emalangeni)
GDP (US million $) 1350
GDP per head ($US) 1261

Sweden g2 144

SWEDEN

THE KINGDOM OF SWEDEN
Area 449,964km^2 (173,732sq miles)
Capital Stockholm
Organizations CE, EBRD, EU, OECD
Population 8,880,000
Pop. growth (%) 0.1
Life expectancy 76 (m); 81 (f)
Languages Swedish, Finnish, Lapp
Literacy 99%
Currency Swedish krona (US $1 = 7.31 Swedish krona)
GDP (US million $) 235,100
GDP per head ($US) 26,475

Sweet Briar g7 254
Sweetwater, Tennessee, U.S.A. g2 259
Sweetwater, Texas, U.S.A. c5 261
Sweetwater, Wyoming, U.S.A. a3 260
Swellendam d7 234
Świątki g2 169
Świdnica, Dolnośląskie, Pol. e5 168
Świdnica, Lubuskie, Pol. d4 168
Świdnik l4 169
Świdwin d2 168
Świebodzice e5 168
Świebodzin d3 168
Świecie g2 168
Świerzawa d4 168
Świerże m4 169
Świerzenko e1 168
Świerzno c2 168
Świętokrzyskie j5 169
Swift Current p6 249
Swiftcurrent Creek p6 249
Swifton d2 258
Swilly, Lough d1 164
Swindon, England, U.K. h2 162
Swindon e5 163
Swinford c3 165
Świnoujście c2 168
Swinton e3 162
Switzerland f5 144

SWITZERLAND

THE SWISS CONFEDERATION
Area 41,284km^2 (15,940sq miles)
Capital Bern
Organizations CE, EBRD, EFTA, OECD
Population 7,290,000
Pop. growth (%) 0.3
Life expectancy 75 (m); 81 (f)
Languages German, French, Italian, and other languages
Literacy 99%
Currency Swiss franc (US $1 = 1.26 Swiss franc)
GDP (US million $) 272,700
GDP per head ($US) 37,407

Swords e3 165
Sycamore, Georgia, U.S.A. h4 259
Sycamore, Ohio, U.S.A. e5 254
Syčevka c4 150
Syčevo d4 150
Syców f4 168
Sydney k12 81
Sydney, Can. m5 253
Sydney Lake f5 250
Sydney Mines m5 253
Syeverodonets'k e2 148
Syke d3 172
Sykea c6 211
Sykesville b3 256
Syki d3 210
Sykia c3 210
Sykkylven b1 156
Sykouri c3 210
Syktyvkar g3 146
Sylacauga f3 258
Sylhet, Bang. m7 125
Sylhet m7 125
Syloga e3 147
Sylt d1 172
Syltefjorden n1 155
Sylvania, Georgia, U.S.A. j3 259
Sylvania, Ohio, U.S.A. e5 254
Sylvester h4 259
Sylvia, Mount e3 248
Symi, Grc. Ac2 211
Symi Ac2 211
Syndicate d4 100
Synel'nykove d2 148
Syngyrli, Mys d7 120
Synhovd c2 156
Synja j2 147
Synnfjell c2 156
Synnott, Mount g5 86
Synsiä m1 157
Syowa (Japan) j1 298
Syracuse, Kansas, U.S.A. c4 260
Syracuse, New York, U.S.A. d1 256
Syrdar'inskaya Oblast' m7 121
Syrdar'ya, As./C. Is. l5 120
Syrdar'ya m7 121
Syre d1 164
Syria a5 92

SYRIA

THE SYRIAN ARAB REPUBLIC
Area 185,180km^2 (71,498sq miles)
Capital Damascus
Organizations CAEU, IDB, LAS, OAPEC, OIC
Population 17,131,000
Pop. growth (%) 2.7
Life expectancy 69 (m); 71 (f)
Languages Arabic, Kurdish
Literacy 76.9%
Currency Syrian pound (US $1 = 48.51 Syrian pound)
GDP (US million $) 20,299
GDP per head ($US) 1184

Syriam c7 102
Syrian Desert g5 136
Syrkovoe, Ozero l3 147
Syrna Ab2 211
Syros e5 211
Syrsan g4 156
Sysenvatnet b2 156
Sysmä, Fin. n5 155
Sysmä, Fin. m1 157
Sysmä l2 157
Sysola l1 151
Syssleback e2 156
Sytkivtsi j1 201
Sytomino m3 147
Syvota a3 210
Syvsten d1 158
Syzran' k5 151
Szabadhidvég g5 171
Szabadkígyós k5 171
Szabadszállás h5 171
Szabolcsbáka l3 171
Szabolcs-Szatmár-Bereg k4 171
Szakály g5 171
Szakes g5 171
Szalánta g6 171
Szalkszentmárton h5 171
Szalonna j3 171
Szamocin f2 168
Szamosszeg l3 171
Szamotuły e3 168
Szany f4 170
Szarvas j5 171
Szászberek j4 171
Szatymaz j5 171
Szazhalombatta g4 171
Szczawnica j6 169
Szczebrzeszyn l5 169
Szczecin c2 168
Szczecinek e2 168
Szczeciński, Zalew c2 168
Szczekociny h5 169
Szczerców h4 169
Szczucin k5 169
Szczuczyn l2 169
Szczurkowo j1 169
Szczyrk h6 169
Szczytna e5 168
Szczytno j2 169
Szczytno, Jezioro f2 168
Szécsény h3 171
Szederkény g5 171
Szeged j5 171
Szeghalom k4 171
Székely k3 171
Székesfehérvár g4 171
Székkutas j5 171
Szekszárd g5 171
Szendehely h4 171
Szendrő j3 171
Szentendre h4 171
Szentes j5 171
Szentgotthárd e5 170
Szentlászló f5 171
Szentmártonkáta h4 171
Szentőrinc f5 171
Szepetnek e5 170
Szerencs k3 171
Szerep k4 171
Szeska Góra k5 157
Szestno k2 169
Szigetcsép g4 171
Szigetszentmiklós h4 171
Szigetvár f5 171
Szigliget f5 170
Szikszó j3 171
Szil f4 170
Szirmabesenyő j3 171
Szklarska Poręba d5 168
Szkwa k2 169
Szlichtyngowa e4 168
Szob g4 171
Szolnok j4 171
Szőlősgyörök f5 171
Szombathely e4 170
Szomód g4 171
Szprotawa d4 168
Szstum h2 169
Sztutowo h1 169
Szubin f2 168
Szurdokpüspöki h4 171
Szydłowiec j4 169
Szynkielów g4 168
Szypliszki m1 169

T

T'aean p7 113
T'aebaek-sanmaek q6 113
T'aepaek q7 113
T'aet'an n6 113
T'aichung n6 105
T'ainan n7 105
T'aipei n6 105
T'aitung n7 105
T'ana Häyk' e5 219
T'bilisi g4 149
T'elavi g4 149
T'oejo p6 113
T'ongch'ŏn p6 113
T'unghsiao n6 105
Ta Khli e8 102
Ta Loung San f5 102
Ta'erwan c4 106
Taabo, Lac de c4 222
Taal, Lake c4 100
Taalabaya d3 138
Tab g5 171
Tabaco d4 100
Tabago Hills c5 218
Tābah j8 137
Tabajara e1 293
Tabala f5 272
Tabanan h9 99
Tabanera de Cerrato f2 190
Tabang j4 99
Tabankulu h5 235
Ţabaqah g5 209
Ţabaqat Faḥl d4 139
Tábara d3 190
Tabarja d2 138
Ţabas r5 137
Tabasco, Mex. n8 273
Tabasco, Zacatecas, Mex. c3 274
Tabāsin r6 137
Tabatinga d4 284
Tabatinga, Serra e3 285
Tabatinga, Serra da d4 288
Tabayin b4 102
Tabelbala d3 220
Taber l7 249
Taberg f4 156
Tabernas b7 193
Tabi b5 224
Tabia Tsaka g4 135
Tabili e3 225
Tabir b5 98
Tabiteuea H 75
Tablas d4 100
Tablas de Daimiel, Parque Nacional de las g5 191
Tablas Strait c4 100
Tablas, Cabo b1 296
Tablazo, Bahía de c1 284
Table Bay c6 234
Table Cape f3 76
Table Point b3 100
Table Rock Reservoir c1 258
Tabligbo e4 223
Tablillas f6 191
Taboada c2 190
Taboca e4 285
Taboga, Isla h6 277
Tábor c2 170
Tabor City k2 259
Tabora, Tan. f5 225
Tabora f5 225
Tabory l4 147
Taboshar m7 121
Tabossi h1 297
Tabou c5 222
Tabrīz l2 137
Tábua b4 190
Tabuaeran H 75
Tabuenca c3 192
Tabūk, Sau. Ar. e2 219
Tabulga f7 136
Tabulam l10 81
Tabuny s1 121
Tabwémasana, Mount F 74
Täby h3 157
Tacaipu, Serra b2 288
Tacalé g3 285
Tacámbaro d4 274
Tacaná, Volcán de k10 273
Tacarcuna, Cerro b2 284
Tacarigua, Laguna de d1 284
Tacheng u4 121
Tacherting d1 176
Tachikawa h4 115
Táchira c2 284
Tachov a2 170
Taciuã, Lago e4 285
Tacloban e5 100
Tacna, Col. c4 284
Tacna, Peru c3 292
Tacna, Peru c3 292
Tacna, U.S.A. g9 263
Taco Pozo e5 293
Tacoma b2 262
Tacora, Volcán d3 292
Tactic b3 276
Tacuarembó, Ur. k2 297
Tacuarembó, Tacuarembó, Ur. k1 297
Tacuari g3 297
Tacuarí f2 294
Tacupeto e3 272
Tacuru a5 290
Tacutu e3 285
Tadcaster e3 162
Tademaït, Plateau du e3 221
Tadjeraout, Oued e4 221
Tadjmout e3 221
Tadjoura f5 219
Tadjoura, Golfe de f5 219
Tadjrouna e2 221
Tadley e5 163
Tadmur g5 209
Tadó b2 284
Tadotsu e4
114Tadoussac h4 252
Tadpatri e5 126
Tadrart g4 221
Taech'ŏng-do n7 113
Taedŏk p8 113
Taegu q8 113
Taegwan n5 113
Taehŭksan-kundo n8 113
Taejŏn p7 113
Tælavåg a2 156
Taenga K 75
Taf b5 163
Tafalla c2 192
Ţafas e4 138
Tafelberg f3 285
Tafelberg, Natuurreservaat f3 285
Tafi Viejo d5 292
Tafiré c4 222
Tafraoute c3 220
Tafresh m4 137
Taft, Iran q6 137
Taft, U.S.A. d6 265
Taga g2 192
Tagab c4 128
Tagab d4 218
Tagagawik e2 246
Tagaj j4 151
Taganrog e3 148
Taganrog, Gulf of e3 148
Tagant b2 222
Tagaranna k3 157
Tagbilaran d6 100
Taggia b6 197
Taghit d2 220
Taghmon e4 165
Tagish Lake l4 247
Tagliacozzo h7 197
Tagliamento g3 196
Taglio di Po g4 196
Tagoloan e6 100
Tagomago f5 193
Tagsjön, Stora f5 154
Tagta k4 149
Tagtabazar a3 128
Taguatinga, Minas Gerais, Braz. d1 290
Taguatinga, Tocantins, Braz. c4 288
Taguatinga, Serra c4 288
Tagudin c2 100
Tagula l1 80
Tagum e7 100
Tah, Sabkhat b3 220
Tahaa K 75
Tahaetkun Mountain h6 248
Tahal b7 193
Tahan, Gunung c3 101
Tahanaoute c2 220
Tahanea K 75
Tahat, Mont f4 221
Tahdzibichén q7 273
Tahe g2 94
Taheke d1 76
Ţāherī p8 137
Tahiti K 75
Tahkuna nina LH 157
Tahlequah b2 258
Tahoe City c2 264
Tahoe, Lake c2 264
Tahoka c5 261
Tahoua, Niger f2 223
Tahoua f3 223
Tahrūd, Iran r7 137
Tahrūd r7 137
Tahta c8 136
Tahtali Dağ c4 208
Tahtsa Peak d5 248
Tahuamanú, Bol. d2 292
Tahuamanú, Peru d2 292
Tahuata K 75
Tahulandang n3 99
Tahuna e9 100
Taï c4 222
Tai Hu g4 111
Tai Rom Yen National Park a1 101
Tai, Parc National de c4 222
Tai'an, Liaoning, China m5 113
Tai'an, Shandong, China e1 111
Tai'erzhuang e2 111
Taibai f1 104
Taibai Shan, Shaanxi, China f2 104
Taibai Shan, Shanxi, China h6 112
Taibilla b6 193
Taibique Ab3 189
Taibus Qi g4 111
Taicang g4 115
Taieri c6 77
Taigu c1 106
Taihang Shan, China c1 106
Taihang Shan, Hebei, China h6 112
Taihape e3 76
Taihe, Anhui, China d3 111
Taihe, Jiangxi, China k5 105
Taihe, Shandong, China f1 111
Taihu e4 106
Taijiang g5 104
Taikang d2 106
Taiki Ac2 114
Taikkyi b7 102
Tailai m2 113
Tailako n9 99
Tailem Bend d13 81
Taim f2 294
Taimani a4 128
Tain d2 164
Tainaro, Akra c6 211
Tainhas b7 289
Tain-l'Hermitage a5 185
Taiobeiras g1 291
Taipa, Indon. l5 99
Taipa, N.Z. d1 76
Taiping, China c3 106
Taiping, Malay. b3 101
Taiping Ling l2 113
Taipingchuan m3 113
Taipingpu a6 112
Taipingshao n5 113
Taipu e3 288
Taipudia p6 125
Taiqian d2 106
Tairua e2 76
Tais b7 98
Taisha e4 114
Taishan j7 105
Taishun m5 105
Taitaitanopo a6 98
Taitao, Peninsula de b5 295
Taitao, Punta a5 295
Taiti b3 226
Taivalkoski m4 155
Taivaskero j2 155
Taiwan k6 93

TAIWAN

THE REPUBLIC OF CHINA
Area 36,000km^2 (13,900sq miles)
Capital T'aipei
Organizations APEC
Population 22,092,387
Pop. growth (%) 1.2
Life expectancy 72 (m); 78 (f)
Languages Northern Chinese (Mandarin), Taiwanese
Literacy 93.7%
Currency New Taiwan dollar (US $1 = 34.02 New Taiwan dollar)
GDP (US million $) 278,200
GDP per head ($US) 12,592

Taiwan Strait m6 105
Taixing g3 111
Taiyiba, W.B. d5 139
Taiyiba, W.B. c4 139
Taiyuan c1 106
Taiyue Shan c1 106
Taizhao n4 125
Taizhou f3 111
Taizhou Liedao p4 105
Taizhou Wan n4 105
Ta'izz f5 219
Tajal d7 129
Tajamulco, Volcán de b3 276
Tajarḥi g4 221
Tajbola p2 155
Taj-e Malekī n7 137
Tajem, Gunung e6 98
Tajga j4 118
Tajgonos, Mys r3 119
Tajgonos, Poluostrov s3 119
Tajikistan e5 92

TAJIKISTAN

THE REPUBLIC OF TAJIKISTAN
Area 143,100km^2 (55,251sq miles)
Capital Dushanbe
Organizations CIS, EBRD, ECO, OIC
Population 6,430,000
Pop. growth (%) 1.4
Life expectancy 64 (m); 70 (f)
Languages Tajik (Arabic script), Russian
Literacy 99.4%
Currency somoni (US $1 = 2.78 somoni)
GDP (US million $) 1090
GDP per head ($US) 169

Tajima h3 115
Tajimi g4 115
Tajitos g10 263
Tajlakova n4 147
Tajmyr, Ozero l2 119
Tajmyr, Poluostrov l2 119
Tajmyrskij (Dolgano-Neneckij) Avtonomnyj Okrug j2 118
Tajuña b4 192
Tak d7 102
Tak Bai b2 101
Taka D 74
Taka'Bonerate, Kepulauan l8 99
Takāb l3 137
Takabba c3 226
Takácsi f4 170
Takahagi j3 115
Takahama f4 115
Takahashi e4 114
Takahata j2 115
Takahe, Mount ff2 298
Takaka d4 76
Takalaou c1 224
Takalous, Oued f4 221
Takama f2 285
Takamaka A 226
Takamatsu f4 114
Takanosu j1 115
Takaoka g3 115
Takapau f4 76
Takapuna e2 76
Takaroa K 75
Takasaki h3 115
Takatokwane f2 234
Takatshwaane d1 234
Takatshwaane Pan d1 234
Takatsuki f4 115
Takatsuki-yama e5 114
Takatu f3 285
Takaungu b4 227
Takayama g3 115
Takefu g4 115
Takehara e4 114
Takengon c13 103
Takeo f3 156
Takestān m3 137
Takēv g10 103
Takfon d1 128
Takhar d2 128
Takhatgarh f8 129
Takht Apān, Kūh-e m5 137
Takhta Pul Post b5 128
Takhtabrod l1 121
Takhtakupyr h6 120
Takhteh p7 137
Takht-i-Sulaiman e5 128
Takht-i-Suleiman cp 120
Takikawa Ab2 114
Takingeun h6 99
Takitimu Mountains a6 77
Takla Lake d4 248
Taklax h5 154
Taklimakan Shamo e2 122
Takob d1 128
Takoradi d5 222
Takotna e3 246
Takpa Shiri n5 125
Taku a2 248
Takua Pa a1 101
Takua Thung a1 101
Takum f4 223
Tal g9 129
Tal Shaḥar c5 139
Tal'menka u1 121
Tal'ne k1 201
Tal'yanky k1 201
Tala, Mex. c3 274
Tala, Ur. k3 297
Tala Norte f1 297
Talacasto c1 296
Talachyn c1 148
Talagang f4 128
Talagante b2 296
Talaiassa, Serra f6 193
Talaimannar f8 126
Talaja f10 129
Talakan s1 113
Talamanca, Cordillera de f6 277

Talamone → Tech 387

Talamone f7 197
Talandža r1 113
Talang, Gunung a5 98
Talangbatu c7 98
Talangbetutu c6 98
Talant b3 184
Talara a4 284
Talar-i-Band b8 129
Talas p6 121
Talas, Kaz. n6 121
Talas, Kyrg. p6 121
Talas Ala-Too n6 121
Talaškino b4 150
Talaud, Kepulauan p3 99
Talavera de la Reina f5 191
Talawakale g9 126
Talawanta e5 80
Talawgyi c3 102
Talayan e7 100
Talayuela e5 191
Talayuelas c5 193
Talayuelo b5 193
Talbisah e2 138
Talbot Inlet p1 243
Talbot Lake d3 250
Talbot, Mount h10 87
Talbotton g3 259
Talbragar c8 85
Talca b3 296
Talca, Punta b2 296
Talcahuala d6 296
Talcahuano a4 296
Talcamávida a4 296
Talcher j9 125
Taldom d3 150
Taldyk k4 149
Taldykorgan s5 121
Taldy-Suu s6 121
Talea de Castro f5 275
Taleex d2 226
Talent b4 262
Talgar r6 121
Talgar, Pik r6 121
Talhadas b4 190
Tali Post f2 225
Taliabu n5 99
Taliard c6 185
Talibon e5 100
Talica, Russ. Fed. l2 151
Talica, Kostromskaja Oblast', Russ. Fed. j2 151
Talicy g3 151
Taliesin c4 163
Táliga c6 191
Talihina b2 258
Talikota e4 126
Talikud e7 100
Talimardzhan b1 128
Tal-i-Mir Ghazi d3 128
Taliparamba d6 126
Talisay d5 100
Talisayan, Indon. k4 99
Talisayan, Phil. e6 100
Talisei n4 99
Talita e2 296
Taliwang j9 99
Talkeetna g3 246
Talkkunapää m2 155
Tall 'Afar j4 209
Tall Baydar h4 209
Tall Kalakh e2 138
Tall Kayf j4 209
Tall Kūjik j4 209
Tall Shihāb d4 138
Tall 'Uwaynāt j4 209
Talla f6 197
Talla Talla Seghir Island e4 219
Tallacootra, Lake l12 87
Talladale c2 164
Talladega f3 258
Tallaght e3 165
Tallahassee g4 259
Tallahatchie d2 258
Tallangatta h14 81
Tallaringa Conservation Park a10 81
Tällberg f2 156
Tallering Peak b10 87
Tallinn l3 157
Tallinna laht l3 157
Tallow c4 165
Tallulah d3 258
Tallūza d4 139
Tällvattnet, Stora g5 154
Tălmaciu g3 201
Talmaz j2 201
Talmiã f3 285
Talmont-St-Hilaire d6 182
Talod f9 129
Taloda g10 129
Talodi d5 218
Talofofo Bay C 74
Talong n6 125
Tāloqān d2 128
Talovaja f2 148
Taloyoak l2 242
Talpa b3 274
Talsi k4 157
Taltal c5 292
Taltson g3 242
Talu p4 125
Taludaa m4 99
Talvera f3 196
Talvik j1 155
Talwood j10 81
Talyawalka c1 82
Tam Ky j8 102
Tama e3 260
Tama Wildlife Reserve b2 226
Tamajón a3 192
Tamale d4 222
Tamalung g5 98
Tamames d4 190
Taman Negara National Park c3 101
Tamana, Col. b2 284
Tamana, Kir. H 75
Tamana, Mount E 271
Tamanar c2 220
Tamanco c5 284
Tamangueyú h5 297
Tamanhint g3 221
Tamanrasset f4 221
Tamanrasset, Oued e4 221
Tamanthi b3 102
Tamapatz e3 275
Tamaqua e4 256
Tamar b6 163
Tamarike l7 97
Tamarite de Litera e3 192
Tămășeni h2 201
Tamási g5 171
Tamași h2 201
Tamasopo e3 275
Tamaulipas k5 273
Tamaulipas, Sierra de e2 275
Tamaya c1 292
Tamazula, Durango, Mex. f5 272
Tamazula, Jalisco, Mex. c4 274
Tamazulápam f5 275
Tamazunchale e3 275
Tambach b3 226
Tambach-Dietharz f2 175
Tambacounda b3 222
Tambalongang l8 99
Tambangsawah b6 98
Tambaqui e5 285
Tambara e2 233
Tambau e4 290
Tambaur e6 130
Tambawel e3 223
Tambelan Besar d4 98
Tambelan, Kepulauan d4 98
Tambellup c14 87
Tamberías c1 296
Tamberu g8 98
Tambillos, Nevados de los c1 294
Tambisan b8 100
Tambo b4 84
Tambo, Aust. e3 83
Tambo, Peru c3 292
Tambo Grande a4 284
Tambobamba c2 292
Tambohorano Aa2 233
Tambopata d2 292
Tambor g5 272
Tambora, Gunung j9 99
Tambores j1 297
Tamboril d2 288
Tamboritha e3 83
Tamboryacu c4 284
Tamboura e2 225
Tambov f1 148
Tambovka, Amurskaja Oblast', Russ. Fed. q1 113
Tambovka, Astrahanskaja Oblast', Russ. Fed. g3 149
Tambovskaja Oblast' f1 148
Tambre b2 190
Tambu, Teluk k4 99
Tambunan j2 99
Tambura e2 225
Tâmchekkeț b2 222
Tamdybulak k7 120
Tamdytau, Gory k7 120
Tame c2 284
Tâmega c3 190
Tamel Aike b5 295
Tamelos, Akra e5 211
Tameside h1 162
Tamghas f5 135
Tamgué, Massif du b3 222
Tamiahua f3 275
Tamiahua, Laguna de f3 275
Tamiami Canal j7 259
Tamiang c13 103
Tamil Nadu f7 126
Tamirin Gol a2 112
Tâmîya c7 136
Tamlelt, Plaine de d2 220
Tammela n4 155
Tammio m2 157
Tämnaren g2 156
Támoga c1 190
Tampa h6 259
Tampa Bay h6 259
Tampacán e3 275
Tampamolón e3 275
Tampang c7 98
Tampere k2 157
Tampico, Mex. f2 275
Tampico, U.S.A. b5 254
Tampico el Alto f2 275
Tampin c4 101
Tampo m7 99
Tampoc f3 285
Tampoketsa d'Analamaitso, Réserve de Ab2 233
Tamra d4 138
Tamsag Muchang b5 112
Tamsagbulag j2 113
Tamsalu m3 157
Tamshiyacu c4 284
Tamsweg e2 176
Tamu b3 102
Tamuín e2 275
Tamulté de las Sabanas a1 276
Tamurejo f6 191
Tamworth, Aust. k11 81
Tamworth, U.K. e4 162
Tamyang p8 113
Tan r3 121
Tân An h10 103
Tan Emellel f3 221
Tana b4 226
Tana Bru m1 155
Tanabe f5 115
Tanabi d4 290
Tanacross j3 247
Tanafjorden m1 155
Tanaga Island Ac1 247
Tanaga Pass Ac2 247
Tanaga Volcano Ac2 247
Tanagura j3 115
Tanah Merah c3 101
Tanah Rata b3 101
Tanah, Tanjung e8 98
Tanahgrogot j5 99
Tanahjampea l8 99
Tanahmasa b6 96
Tanahmerah, Irian Jaya, Indon. l7 97
Tanahmerah, Kalimantan Timur, Indon. j3 99
Tanahputih b5 101
Tanak, Cape b5 246
Tanakeke k7 99
Tanakpur e5 130
Tanambung k6 99
Tanami Desert k6 86
Tanana, Alaska, U.S.A. g2 247
Tanana, Alaska, U.S.A. f2 246
Tanandava Aa3 233
Tanaro b5 196
Tanat c4 162
Tanauan e5 100
Tanbar e8 81
Tanbu, Jiangxi, China k4 105
Tanbu, Shandong, China f2 111
Tancarville f3 183
Tanch'ŏn q5 113
Tancheng f2 111
Tancitaro c4 274
Tancítaro, Cerro de c4 274
Tanda, C.I. d4 222
Tanda, India b4 130
Tanda, Uttar Pradesh, India h6 124
Tanda, Uttar Pradesh, India d5 130
Tanda, Lac d2 222
Tandag f6 100
Țăndărei h3 201
Tandaué b2 232
Tandek a7 100
Tandi c3 130
Tandil h4 297
Tandil, Sierra del h4 297
Tandjilé c2 224
Tando Adam d8 129
Tando Alahyar d8 129
Tando Bago d8 129
Tando Muhammad Khan d8 129
Tandou Lake b1 82
Tandövarn e2 156
Tandragee e2 165
Tandubatu c8 100
Tandula g9 124
Tandur e4 126
Tanduri c6 129
Tanen Taunggyi d6 102
Taneytown c5 256
Tanezrouft, Alg. d4 220
Tanezrouft, Alg. d4 220
Tang He c3 106
Tanga, Tan. g5 225
Tanga b5 227
Tangaehe e2 76
Tangalla g9 126
Tangamandapio c4 274
Tangancícuaro de Arista c4 274
Tanganyika, Lake e5 225
Tangar q3 137
Tangaray c2 224
Tangcun, Shandong, China e2 111
Tangcun, Zhejiang, China f5 111
Tange Sø c2 158
Tangeli q3 137
Tanger, Ger. c1 173
Tanger c1 220
Tangerang d8 98
Tangerhütte g3 173
Tangermünde g3 173
Tanggo m4 125
Tanggu j6 113
Tanggula Shan, Qinghai/Xizang, China m3 125
Tanggula Shan, Qinghai/Xizang, China j3 135
Tanggula Shankou m3 125
Tanggulashan n2 125
Tanghe c3 106
Tangi e3 128
Tangier c1 220
Tangipahoa d4 258
Tangjiawan f4 111
Tangkak c4 101
Tangkelemboko, Gunung l6 99
Tangkittebak, Gunung c7 98
Tangkou f4 111
Tangmai p4 125
Tangorin a2 84
Tangqi g4 111
Tangra Yumco h4 135
Tangse b13 103
Tangshan k6 113
Tangte c3 102
Tangtou f2 111
Tangub, Phil. d5 100
Tangub, Phil. d6 100
Tanguieta e3 223
Tangwang He q2 113
Tangwanghe q1 113
Tangxianzhen c4 106
Tang-yan d4 102
Tangyan He g4 104
Tangyin d2 106
Tangyuan q2 113
Tangyung Tso h4 135
Tanhaçu d4 288
Tanhua l3 155
Taniantaweng Shan p4 125
Tanimbar, Kepulauan j7 97
Taninges c4 184
Tanisapata j6 97
Taniwel h6 97
Tanjay d6 100
Tanjung, Jambi, Indon. b5 98
Tanjung, Kalimantan Selatan, Indon. h6 99
Tanjung Dawai b3 101
Tanjung Malim b4 101
Tanjung Sepat b4 101
Tanjungbalai, Riau, Indon. c5 101
Tanjungbalai, Sumatera Utara, Indon. a4 101
Tanjungbaliha p6 99
Tanjungbatu, Kalimantan Timur, Indon. k3 99
Tanjungbatu, Riau, Indon. c5 101
Tanjungbuayabuaya, Pulau k4 99
Tanjunggaru j6 99
Tanjungpandan d6 98
Tanjungpinang d5 101
Tanjungpura d14 103
Tanjungraja c6 98
Tanjungredeb j3 99
Tanjungsaleh e5 98
Tanjungsatai e5 98
Tanjungselor j3 99
Tank e4 128
Tankara e9 129
Tankse d2 130
Tankwa-Karoo National Park c6 234
Tanlacut e3 275
Tanlajas e3 275
Tann d1 176
Tanna F 74
Tännäs e1 156
Tannay f1 186
Tänndalen e1 156
Tanner f2 258
Tanner, Mount h7 248
Tannersville e3 256
Tannfjell d2 156
Tannheim b2 176
Tannila k4 155
Tannis Bugt d1 158
Tannourine el Faouqa e3 138
Tannum Sands d3 84
Tannu-Ola, Hrebet k4 118
Tano d4 222
Tañon Strait d6 100
Tanot e7 129
Tanout f3 223
Tanquian e3 275
Tansen f6 135
Tanshui n6 105
Tansyk s4 121
Tanta c6 136
Tan-Tan b3 220
Tantou f5 111
Tantoyuca e3 275
Tantu m2 113
Tantura c4 138
Tanuku g4 126
Tanumshede d3 156
Tanvald d1 170
Tanwakka, Sabkhat b4 220
Tanyang q7 113
Tanyi f2 111
Tanzania f5 217

TANZANIA

THE UNITED REPUBLIC OF TANZANIA
Area 945,087km^2 (364,900sq miles)
Capital Dodoma
Organizations COMM, SADC
Population 34,569,232
Pop. growth (%) 3.1
Life expectancy 50 (m); 52 (f)
Languages Swahili, English, many local languages
Literacy 78.1%
Currency Tanzanian shilling (US \$1 = 1061.98 Tanzanian shilling)
GDP (US million \$) 9134
GDP per head (\$US) 264

Tao He b8 112
Tao, Ko d10 103
Tao'er He l2 113
Taochuan h6 104
Taocun g1 111
Taole d6 112
Taolin, Hunan, China c5 106
Taolin, Shandong, China f2 111
Taonan m3 113
Taongi D 74
Taormina e7 199
Taoru c5 130
Taoudenni d4 220
Taounate d2 220
Taourirt d2 220
Taouz d2 220
Taoxing c1 106
Taoyuan h4 104
Taozhuang e2 111
Tap l4 147
Tapa l3 157
Tapaan Passage c8 100
Tapachula a3 276
Tapaga, Cape M 75
Tapah b3 101
Tapajós a2 288
Tapaktuan c14 103
Tapalpa c4 274
Tapalqué g4 297
Tapan a6 98
Tapanahoni f3 285
Tapanatepec g5 275
Tapanuli, Teluk d15 103
Tapará, Ilha Grande do b2 288
Tapara, Serra do b2 288
Tapauá, Braz. d5 284
Tapauá, Amazonas, Braz. e5 285
Tapawera d4 77
Tapera, Rio Grande do Sul, Braz. b7 289
Tapera, Braz. e4 285
Tapera, Chile b4 295
Taperoá e4 288
Tapeta c4 222
Tapi f10 129
Tapi Aike b6 295
Tapiche c5 284
Tapijulapa a2 276
Tápióság h4 171
Tápiószecső h4 171
Tápiószele h4 171
Tapira, Minas Gerais, Braz. e3 291
Tapira, Paraná, Braz. b5 290
Tapiracanga d4 288
Tapiraí e5 290
Tapirapé b4 288
Tapirapecó, Sierra e3 285
Tapirapuã f2 293
Tapis, Gunung c3 101
Tapisuelas e4 272
Táplánszentkereszt e4 170
Tapoa e3 223
Tapolca f5 170
Tappahannock h7 255
Tappal c5 130
Tapuaenuku d4 77
Tapul c8 100
Tapul Group c8 100
Tapulonanjing a5 101
Tapun b6 102
Tapung b5 101
Tapurú e4 285
Tapurucuara d4 285
Taqar f5 219
Ṭaqṭaq k4 137
Taquara b7 289
Taquaral, Serra do a1 290
Taquari, Braz. a3 290
Taquari, Mato Grosso, Braz. b1 290
Taquari, Pantanal do f3 293
Taquari, Serra do b3 290
Taquaritinga d4 290
Taquarituba d5 290
Taquimilán b4 296
Tar c4 165
Tar Ahmad Rind e8 129
Tar, Lago b5 295
Tara, Aust. k9 81
Tara, Phil. c4 100
Taraba, Nig. g4 223
Taraba, Nig. g4 223
Tarabaí c5 290
Ṭarābulus g2 221
Taraclia, Căușeni, Mol. j2 201
Taraclia, Cahul, Mol. j3 201
Taraco d3 292
Taracua d3 284
Taradale f3 76
Taraghin g3 221
Tarago j13 81
Taraíra d4 284
Tarajalejo Ae2 189
Tarakan, Indon. j3 99
Tarakan j3 99
Taraklı c2 208
Tarama-jima B 114
Taran, Mys h5 157
Tarana f1 83
Taranagar b5 130
Taranaki e3 76
Taranaki, Mount e3 76
Tarancón a4 193
Taranga Hill f9 129
Tarangire National Park g4 225
Tarankol', Ozero m5 147
Taranovskoye j1 120
Taransay a2 164
Taranto, Italy g4 198
Taranto g4 198
Taranto, Golfo di g4 198
Tarapacá, Chile d3 292
Tarapacá, Col. d4 284
Tarapoto b1 292
Tarare a5 185
Tarariras e3 297
Tararua Forest Park e4 77
Tararua Range e4 77
Tarascon a7 185
Tarascon-sur-Ariège d6 187
Tarashany h1 201
Tarashcha c2 148
Tarasht r5 137
Tarasovo f2 147
Tarasovskij f2 148
Tarat f3 221
Tarata, Bol. d3 292
Tarata, Peru c3 292
Tarauacá, Braz. c1 292
Tarauacá, Acre, Braz. c1 292
Taravo A 185
Tarawa H 75
Tarawera f3 76
Tarawera, Lake f3 76
Tarawera, Mount f3 76
Taraz n6 121
Tarazona c3 192
Tarazona de la Mancha c5 193
Tarbagatay t4 121
Tarbagatay, Hrebet MR j5 118
Tarbagatay, Khrebet u4 121
Tarbat Ness e2 164
Tárbena d6 193
Tarbert, Ire. b4 165
Tarbert, Scotland, U.K. c4 164
Tarbert, Scotland, U.K. b2 164
Tarbes c5 187
Tarbet d3 164
Tarboro l2 259
Tarcento h3 196
Tarcoola b11 81
Tarcoon h11 81
Tarcutta e2 83
Tarczyn j4 169
Tard d4 182
Tardajos g2 190
Tardelcuende b3 192
Tardenois j3 183
Tardes e2 186
Tardets-Sorholus b5 187
Tardienta d3 192
Tardoire c3 186
Taree l11 81
Tareifing d5 218
Tärendö j3 155
Tarengo d3 274
Tarentaise c5 185
Taretán d4 274
Ṭarfā, Ra's aț f4 219
Ṭarfā', Wādī aț d2 218
Ṭarfāwī, Bi'r aț b2 218
Tarfaya b3 220
Targhee Pass h3 262
Targon b4 186
Târgoviște g3 201
Târgu Bujor h3 201
Târgu Cărbunești f3 201
Târgu Frumos h2 201
Târgu Jiu f3 201
Târgu Lăpuș f2 201
Târgu Mureș g2 201
Târgu Neamț h2 201
Târgu Ocna h2 201
Târgu Secuiesc h2 201
Targyn u3 121
Tarhūnah g2 221
Tari l7 97
Tarian Gol e6 112
Tarib, Wādī f4 219
Tarifa e8 191
Tarifa, Punta de e8 191
Tarigtig Point d2 100
Tarija, Bol. e4 293
Tarija, Tarija, Bol. e4 293
Tarim He u7 121
Tarim Pendi e2 122
Tarime a4 226
Tarimoro d3 274
Tarin Kowt b4 128
Taringuiti e4 293
Tarján g4 171
Tarka f6 235
Tarka, Vallée de f3 223
Tarkastad g6 235
Tarkio e3 260
Tarko-Sale h3 118
Tarkwa d4 222
Tarlac, Phil. c3 100
Tarlac c3 100
Tarlo River National Park f2 83
Tarłów k4 169
Tarm b3 158
Tarma, Junín, Peru b2 292
Tarma, Loreto, Peru c4 284
Tarmstedt e2 172
Tarn, Fr. d4 187
Tarn, Midi-Pyrénées, Fr. e5 187
Tarna, Puerto de e1 190
Tärnaby e4 154
Tarnalelesz j3 171
Târnăveni g2 201
Tarnawa Duża l5 169
Tarnaszadány j4 171
Tarn-et-Garonne d4 187
Tärnö f4 156
Tarnobrzeg k5 169
Tarnogród l5 169
Tarnos a5 187
Tarnów j5 169
Tarnowskie Góry g5 168
Tärnsjö g2 156
Tärnvik e3 154
Taro d5 196
Tarō j2 115
Taro Co f4 135
Tarod f9 129
Ṭārom q7 137
Taroom j8 81
Tarouca c4 190
Taroudannt c2 220
Tarp, Den. b3 158
Tarp, Ger. c4 158
Tarpa l3 171
Tarpon Springs h5 259
Tarporley d3 162
Tarpum Bay l7 259
Tarq n5 137
Tarquinia f7 197
Tarquinia Lido f7 197
Tarqūmiya d5 139
Tarragona, Spain e3 192
Tarragona f3 192
Tårrajaur g3 154
Tarraleah Ab3 83
Tarran Hills b8 85
Tarras b6 77
Tàrrega f3 192
Tårs d1 158
Tarsia f5 198
Tarso Ahon a3 218
Tarso Emissi a3 218
Tarso Kobour a3 218
Tarsus e4 208
Tartagal, Salta, Arg. e4 293
Tartagal, Santa Fé, Arg. e1 294
Tärtär g4 149
Tartas b5 187
Tartu m3 157
Ṭarṭūs, Syria e5 209
Ṭarṭūs d2 138
Tarumirim h3 291
Tarumizu d6 114
Tarumovka g3 149
Tarusa d4 150
Tārūt n8 137
Tarutao, Ko a2 101
Tarutung d14 103
Tarutyne j2 201
Tarva b5 154
Tarvefjorden b5 154
Tarvisio h3 196
Tarvo e3 293
Tarz r6 137
Tasaral p4 121
Tasāwah g3 221
Tasbuget k5 120
Taseko Mountain f6 248
Tašelka k5 151
Tasgaon d4 126
Tashir k2 209
Tashiyi c5 106
Tashk, Daryācheh-ye p7 137
Tashkent m7 121
Tashkentskaya Oblast' m7 121
Tashkepri a2 128
Tash-Kömür p7 121
Tasik Air Pedu b2 101
Tasik Chenderoh b3 101
Tasik Dampar c4 101
Tasik Kenyir c3 101
Tasik Temengor b2 101
Tasikmalaya e8 98
Tasil d4 138
Tåsinge d4 158
Tåsjö e4 154
Tåsjön e4 154
Tasker g2 223
Taskesken t4 121
Taşköprü e2 208
Tas-Kystaby, Hrebet a2 94
Taşlıçay j3 209
Tasman d4 77
Tasman Basin j9 300
Tasman Bay d4 77
Tasman Fracture Zone h9 300
Tasman Head Ab3 83
Tasman Mountains d4 77
Tasman Peninsula Ac3 83
Tasman Plateau h9 300
Tasman Sea j9 300
Tasman, Mount c5 77
Tasmania A 83
Tășnad l4 171
Tașova f2 209
Tassara f2 223
Tassili du Hoggar f4 221
Tassili n'Ajjer f3 221
Tassili N'Ajjer, Parc National de f3 221
Tassiné e3 223
Tassin-la-Demi-Lune a5 185
Taștagol w1 121
Tastiota d3 272
Tåstrup f3 158
Tasty m5 121
Tasty-Taldy l2 120
Tata, Hung. g4 171
Tata, Mor. c3 220
Tata Mailau, Gunung n9 99
Tataba m5 99
Tatabánya g4 171
Tataháza h5 171
Tatahuicapan g4 275
Tatakoto K 75
Tataltepec f5 275
Tataouine g2 221
Tatarlar h5 201
Tatarpur c6 130
Tatarsk h4 118
Tatarskij Proliv l3 94
Tatarskij Sajman j5 151
Tatarstan, Respublika l4 151
Tătăruși h2 201
Tatau g3 98
Tataurovo k3 151
Tatawa k6 97
Tate, Aust. g4 80
Tate, U.S.A. g2 259
Tateyama h4 115
Tate-yama g3 115
Tathlina Lake f3 242
Tathlīth, Wādī f4 219
Tati g3 233
Tatiščevo g2 149
Tatitlek h3 247
Tatlatui Provincial Park n4 247
Tatnam, Cape h2 250
Tatranský j2 171
Tatry d1 200
Tatrzański Park Narodowy j6 169
Tatsuno g4 115
Tatta c8 129
Tatti p6 121
Tatuí e5 290
Tatuk Mountain e5 248
Tatula l4 157
Tatum c5 261
Tatvan j3 209
Tau, Am.Sam. M 75
Tau a3 156
Tau Tso j3 135
Taua d3 288
Tauapeçaçu e4 285
Tauariã e5 285
Taubaté f5 291
Taube h4 173
Tauber e3 174
Tauberbischofsheim e3 174
Taucha h4 173
Tauchik h3 149
Tauer k4 173
Tauere K 75
Taufkirchen g4 175
Taufkirchen (Vils) h4 175
Taufstein e2 174
Tauhoa e2 76
Tauini f3 285
Taukum, Peski q5 121
Taulov c3 158
Taumarunui e3 76
Taumaturgo c1 292
Taunay f4 293
Taung f3 234
Taungdwingyi b5 102
Taunggyi c5 102
Taungnyo Range c8 102
Taunqup b6 102
Taunsa e5 128
Taunsa Barrage e5 128
Taunton, U.K. c5 163
Taunton, U.S.A. j3 257
Taunus d2 174
Taupeka Point A 77
Tauplitz f2 177
Taupo f3 76
Taupo, Lake e3 76
Taurach e2 176
Tauragė k5 157
Tauramena c3 284
Tauranga f2 76
Taureau, Réservoir e5 252
Taurianova f6 199
Taurikura e1 76
Taurion d3 186
Taurisano h5 198
Tauroa Point d1 76
Taurova n4 147
Tauste c3 192
Taute d3 182
Tauves e3 186
Tavagnacco h3 196
Tavaklı g3 210
Tavares j5 259
Tavaux b3 184
Tavda l4 147
Taveiro b4 190
Taverna f5 199
Tavernes c7 185
Tavernes de la Valldigna d5 193
Taverny h3 183
Taveta b4 227
Taveuni E 74
Tavgetos c5 211
Taviano h5 198
Tavignano A 185
Tavildara e1 128
Tavira c7 191
Tavira, Ilha de c7 191
Tavistock b6 163
Tavolzhan r1 121
Távora c3 190
Tavoy d8 103
Tavoy Point c9 103
Tavricheskoye u2 121
Tavropou, Limni b3 210
Tavuki E 74
Tavullia g6 197
Tavvaätno h2 154
Taw c5 163
Tawa e4 77
Tawai, Bukit j2 99
Tawakoni, Lake a3 258
Tawas City e3 254
Tawau j2 99
Tawau, Teluk a8 100
Tawe c5 163
Tawitawi b8 100
Tawu n7 105
Taxco e4 275
Taxenbach d2 176
Taxisco b3 276
Taxkorgan b2 128
Tay, Can. l3 247
Tay, U.K. e3 164
Tây Ninh h10 103
Tay, Lake e13 87
Tay, Loch d3 164
Tayabamba b1 292
Tayabas Bay c4 100
Tayan f5 98
Tayandu, Kepulauan j7 97
Tayeeglow c3 226
Tayirove k2 201
Taylor, Colorado, U.S.A. b4 260
Taylor, Nebraska, U.S.A. d3 260
Taylor, Pennsylvania, U.S.A. e3 256
Taylor, Texas, U.S.A. a4 258
Taylor, Mount, N.Z. c5 77
Taylor, Mount, U.S.A. b5 261
Taymā' g8 136
Taymouth j5 253
Taynuilt c3 164
Tayoltita b1 274
Tayport f3 164
Ṭayr, Jabal aț LH f4 219
Taysoygan, Peski d3 120
Taytay, Phil. b5 100
Taytay, Phil. c3 100
Taytay Bay b5 100
Tayu f8 98
Tayynsha m5 147
Taz j3 118
Taza d2 220
Tāza Khurmātū k5 209
Tazeh Kand g5 149
Tazenakht c2 220
Tazewell, Tennessee, U.S.A. h1 259
Tazewell, Virginia, U.S.A. f7 254
Tazin n1 249
Tazin Lake n2 249
Tāzirbū b2 218
Tázlár h5 171
Tazlău h2 201
Tazlina h3 247
Tazlina Lake h3 247
Tazoukert d4 220
Tazovskaja Guba n1 147
Tazovskij Poluostrov n1 147
Tazrouk f4 221
Tchabal Gangdaba b2 224
Tchabal Mbabo b2 224
Tchamba e4 223
Tchaourou e4 223
Tchetti e4 223
Tchibanga b4 224
Tchindjenje a1 232
Tchin-Tabaradene f2 223
Tcholliré b2 224
Tchula d3 258
Tczew g1 168
Te Anau a6 77
Te Anau, Lake a6 77
Te Araroa g2 76
Te Aroha e2 76
Te Awamutu e3 76
Te Hana e2 76
Te Kaha f2 76
Te Kao d1 76
Te Kauwhata e2 76
Te Kopuru d2 76
Te Kuiti e3 76
Te Paki d1 76
Te Puke f2 76
Te Teko f3 76
Te Waewae Bay a7 77
Te Wharau e4 77
Teacapán b2 274
Teague a4 258
Teangue c2 164
Teano d3 198
Teano Range c9 87
Teapa h5 275
Tearaght Island a4 165
Teba, Indon. k6 97
Teba, Spain f8 191
Tebay d2 162
Tebedu f4 98
Teberau c5 101
Teberda f4 148
Teberdinskij Zapovednik f4 148
Tébessa f1 221
Tebicuary, Para. f5 293
Tebicuary, Ñeembucú, Para. f5 293
Tebingtinggi, Sumatera Selatan, Indon. b6 98
Tebingtinggi, Sumatera Utara, Indon. d14 103
Tebnine d3 138
Tebo a5 98
Téboursouk f1 221
Tebulos Mt'a g4 149
Teča k5 147
Tecalitlán c4 274
Tecamac e4 275
Tecamachalco f4 275
Tecamachalco Nogales f4 275
Tecate e9 263
Tech e6 187

388 Techiman → Tierra Colorada

Techiman d4 222
Techirghiol j3 201
Tecka, Arg. b4 295
Tecka, Chubut, Arg. b4 295
Tecklenburger Land c3 172
Tecocomulca e4 275
Tecoh q7 273
Tecolotlán b3 274
Tecolutilla h4 275
Tecolutla f3 275
Tecomán c4 274
Tecomatlán e4 275
Tecoripa e3 272
Técpan d5 274
Tecuala b2 274
Tecuán, Jalisco, Mex. b3 274
Tecuán, Jalisco, Mex. b4 274
Tecuci h3 201
Tecumseh a2 258
Ted c3 226
Tedzani Falls a7 231
Tedzhenstroy h9 120
Teec Nos Pos j7 263
Teeth, The b6 100
Tefé, Braz. d4 284
Tefé, Amazonas, Braz. e4 285
Tefé, Lago e4 285
Tefeli f7 211
Tegal e8 98
Tegernsee g5 175
Teggiano e4 198
Tegina f3 223
Téglás k4 171
Teglio e3 196
Tégua F 74
Tegucigalpa d3 276
Teguidda-n-Tessoumt f2 223
Teguise Af1 189
Tehachapi e6 265
Tehachapi Mountains e7 265
Tehachapi Pass e6 265
Téhini d4 222
Tehrān, Iran n4 137
Tehrān n4 137
Tehri d4 130
Tehuacán f4 275
Tehuantepec g5 275
Tehuantepec, Golfo de m10 273
Tehuantepec, Istmo de IT g5 275
Tehuitzingo e4 275
Tehuixtepec e5 275
Teichl f2 177
Teide, Pico del Ac2 189
Teifi b4 163
Teignmouth c6 163
Teillay d5 182
Teisendorf d2 176
Teith d3 164
Teitipac f5 275
Teiuş f2 201
Teixeira e3 288
Teixeira de Freitas j2 291
Teixeira Soares c6 290
Teixeiras g4 291
Teixeiro b1 190
Teixoso c4 190
Teja c3 190
Tejado b3 192
Tejakula h9 99
Tejar f4 275
Tejeda Ad3 189
Tejeda y Almijara,
Sierra de g8 191
Tejkovo f3 150
Tejo b5 191
Tejon Pass e7 265
Tejupan, Punta c4 274
Tejupilco d4 274
Tekapo, Lake c5 77
Tekax q7 273
Teke m6 121
Teke, Ozero p1 121
Tekeli s5 121
Tekes, China t6 121
Tekes, Kaz. t6 121
Tekes He t6 121
Tekezē Wenz e5 219
Tekiliktag e1 130
Tekirdağ, Tur. a2 208
Tekirdağ h5 201
Tekkali j3 127
Tekman h3 209
Teknaf n9 125
Tekokota K 75
Tekom q7 273
Tekonsha d4 254
Tekouiat, Oued e4 221
Tekovské Lužany g3 171
Teku m5 99
Tekun g3 151
Tel h9 125
Tel Aviv c4 139
Tel Mond c4 139
Tel'č'e d5 150
Tel'pos-Iz, Gora j2 147
Tela d3 276
Télagh d2 220
Telaki l3 169
Telan d5 101
Télataï e2 223
Telč d2 170
Telchac Puerto q7 273
Telciu g2 201
Telde Ad3 189
Tele d3 224
Télé, Lac d2 222
Teleckoe, Ozero w2 121
Telefomin l7 97
Telegapulang g6 98
Telegino h5 151
Telegraph Creek b3 248
Telekgerendás j5 171
Telêmaco Borba c6 290
Telemark c3 156
Telembi b3 284
Telén e4 296
Teleneşti j2 201
Teleorman, Rom. g3 201
Teleorman, Rom. g4 201
Telerhteba, Djebel f4 221
Teles Pires f1 293
Telescope Peak f5 265
Telescope Point G 271
Telese d3 198
Telford d4 162
Telford and Wrekin d4 162
Telfs c2 176
Telgárt j3 171
Telgte c4 172
Telica d4 276
Telida f3 246
Télimélé b3 222
Telixtlahuaca f5 275
Teljo, Jebel c5 218
Telkwa d4 248
Tell City f1 258
Teller c2 246
Tellicherry d7 126
Tellin d4 159
Tellingstedt c4 158
Tellodar k2 201
Telloh l6 137
Telões c3 190
Telok Datok b4 101
Teloloapán e4 275
Telpani e5 130
Telsen c4 294
Telšiai k5 157
Telti Ab2 198
Teluk Anson b3 101
Telukbatang e5 98
Telukkuantan a5 98
Teluknaga d8 98
Telukpakedai e5 98
Tema e4 223
Temacapulín c3 274
Temagami Lake p7 251
Temaju e4 98
Temangan c3 101
Temanggung f8 98
Temapache f3 275
Temascal f4 275
Temascaltepec de
González d4 274
Tematangi K 75
Temax q7 273
Temba h2 235
Tembagapura k6 97
Tembe Elephant Park k3 235
Tembesi b6 98
Tembilahan b5 98
Tembisa h3 235
Tembleque g5 191
Temblor Range d6 265
Tembo Aluma c5 224
Tembuland h5 235
Teme d4 163
Temecula f8 265
Temelli d3 208
Temeni c4 210
Téméra d2 222
Temerin d3 200
Temerluh c4 101
Teminabuan j6 97
Temir k2 149
Temirlanovka m6 121
Temirtau p2 121
Témiscamie, Lac f3 252
Témiscaming g2 254
Témiscamingue, Lac q7r 251
Temiyang c4 98
Temjasovo k1 149
Temkino c4 150
Temma Aa2 83
Temnikov g4 151
Temósachic f3 272
Tempe h9 263
Tempe, Danau k7 99
Tempio Pausania Ab2 198
Temple a4 258
Temple Bay f2 80
Temple Dera d6 129
Temple Sowerby d2 162
Templemore d4 165
Templer Bank a5 100
Templeton d6 80
Templin j2 173
Tempoal, Mex. e3 275
Tempoal, Veracruz, Mex. e3 275
Tempué b1 232
Temrjuk e3 148
Temrjukskij Zaliv e3 148
Temse c3 159
Temuco a5 296
Temuka c6 77
Ten Degree Channel n8 127
Ten Mile Lake p3 253
Ten Sleep b2 260
Ten Thousand Islands j7 259
Ten'guševo g4 151
Tena b4 284
Tenabo, Mount e5 262
Tenacatita b4 274
Ténado d3 222
Tenaha b4 258
Tenakee Springs l4 247
Tenali g4 126
Tenamaxtlán b3 274
Tenancingo e4 275
Tenango, México, Mex. e4 275
Tenango, Oaxaca, Mex. g5 275
Tenarunga K 75
Tenasserim, Myan. d9 102
Tenasserim, Myan. d9 103
Tenasserim d9 103
Tenay b5 185
Tenbury Wells d4 163
Tenby b5 163
Tenby Bay e2 254
Tence a5 185
Tencia, Campo c3 196
Tendaho f5 219
Tende d6 185
Tende, Col de d6 185
Tendelti d5 218
Te-n-Dghâmcha,
Sebkhet a2 222
Tendō j2 115
Tendrara d2 220
Tendre, Mont a3 196
Tendürek Dağı j3 209
Tené c5 139
Ténenkou d3 222
Tenente Marques f2 293
Tenenys j5 157
Ténéré f2 223
Ténéré du Tafassâsset g4 221
Ténéré, Erg du g2 223
Tenerife Ac2 189
Ténès e1 221
Tengah, Kepulauan j8 99
Tengchong d3 102
Tengen d5 174
Tenggarong j5 99
Tengger Shamo c6 112
Tenggul c3 101
Tengiz, Ozero m2 121
Tengqiao j6 102
Tengréla c3 222
Tengxian h7 104
Tengzhou e2 111
Teniente Enciso, Parque
Nacional e4 293
Teniente General E. Frías e6 297
Teniente Origone f5 297
Teningen c4 174
Te-n-Ioubrar, Sebkhet a2 222
Tenixtepec f3 275
Teniz, Ozero l5 147
Tenk j4 171
Tenka Pta f4 177
Tenkasi e8 126
Tenke e6 225
Tenkeli q2 119
Tenkodogo d3 222
Tennant Creek b5 80
Tennengebirge e2 176
Tennessee, U.S.A. f2 258
Tennessee, U.S.A. c7 254
Tennessee National
Wildlife Refuge e2 258
Tennessee Pass b4 260
Tenneville d4 159
Tennevoll f2 154
Tenniöjoki m3 155
Teno, Chile b3 296
Teno, Maule, Chile b3 296
Tenochtitlán f4 275
Tenojoki l2 155
Tenom h2 99
Tenosique b2 276
Tenryū g4 115
Tensift, Oued c2 220
Tenteno l5 99
Tenterfield l10 81
Tentolomatinan, Gunung l4 99
Tenu d6 182
Teocaltiche c3 274
Teocelo f4 275
Teocuitatlán de Corona c3 274
Teodelina g3 297
Teodoro Beltrán a2 274
Teodoro Sampaio b5 290
Teodoro Schmidt a5 296
Teófilo Otoni h2 291
Teomabal c7 100
Teonthar g7 124
Teopisca a2 276
Teora e4 198
Teotihuacan e4 275
Teotitlán f4 275
Teotitlán del Valle f5 275
Tepa h7 97
Tepache j11 263
Tepalcatepec, Mex. c4 274
Tepalcatepec,
Michoacán, Mex. c4 274
Tepalcingo e4 275
Tepasto k3 155
Tepatepec e3 275
Tepatitlán c3 274
Tepeaca f4 275
Tepeapulco e4 275
Tepechitlán c3 274
Tepeguajes f2 275
Tepehuaje a1 274
Tepehuanes g5 272
Tepeji e4 275
Tepelmeme de Morelos f5 275
Tepequem, Serra e3 285
Tepetates d3 274
Tepetengo c2 274
Tepetixtla d5 274
Tepetzintla f3 275
Tepexi de Rodríguez f4 275
Tepeyahualco f4 275
Tëpi b2 226
Tepianlangsat j4 99
Tepic b3 274
Teplá, Czech Rep. h2 175
Teplá a2 170
Teplice b1 170
Teplička j3 171
Teplička nad Váhom g2 171
Teploe, Lipeckaja Oblast',
Russ. Fed. e5 150
Teploe, Tul'skaja Oblast',
Russ. Fed. d5 150
Teplogorka m1 151
Teploozersk r1 113
Teposcolula f5 275
Tepoto K 75
Tepoztlan e4 275
Tepuxtepec d4 274
Teqoa' d5 139
Tequila c3 274
Tequisistlán g5 275
Tequisquiapán e3 275
Tequixquitla f4 275
Tequixtépec f4 275
Ter Apel f2 159
Tera a2 138
Téra e3 223
Tera, Port c6 191
Tera, Spain e3 190
Teraina H 75
Teram Kangri c2 130
Teramo, Italy c2 198
Teramo c2 198
Teranum b4 101
Teras b4 101
Teratani d6 129
Teratyn m5 169
Terbuny e1 148
Tercan h3 209
Terceira A 220
Terchová h2 171
Tereben' c5 150
Terebeşti l4 171
Terebovlja b2 148
Teregova f3 201
Terek, Russ. Fed. g4 149
Terek g4 149
Térékolé b2 222
Terek-Say n7 121
Terektinskij Hrebet v2 121
Terekty, Karagandinskaya
Oblast', Kaz. m3 121
Terekty, Vostochnyy
Kazakhstan, Kaz. v3 121
Teremia Mare j6 171
Teren'ga k5 151
Terena c6 191
Terengganu, Malay. c3 101
Terengganu, Trengganu,
Malay. c3 101
Terenos a4 290
Terenozek k5 120
Terensaj k2 149
Terentang e5 98
Terentang, Pulau j5 99
Terepaima,
Parque Nacional d2 284
Teresa Cristina c6 290
Teresina d3 288
Teresina de Goiás c4 288
Teresita d3 284
Tereška g1 149
Teresópolis g5 291
Terespol m3 169
Teressa Island n8 127
Teresva f1 201
Terezín c1 170
Terezinha g3 285
Terezino Polje j4 177
Terges c7 191
Tergnier b5 159
Tergola f4 196
Teriang c4 101
Teriberka q2 155
Terisakkan l2 121
Térlicko g2 171
Terlizzi f3 198
Terma, Ras f5 219
Termas de Chillán b4 296
Termas de Flaco b3 296
Termas de Pemehue b5 296
Termas de Socos b2 294
Termas de Tolhuaca b5 296
Termas de Villavicencio c2 296
Termas del Arapey j1 297
Terme f2 209
Terme Luigiane e5 199
Terme, Cap de e3 199
Termens e3 192
Termez c2 128
Termini Imerese c7 199
Termini Imerese, Golfo di c6 199
Terminillo, Monte g7 197
Termit-Kaoboul g2 223
Termoli d3 198
Tern d4 162
Ternate h5 97
Ternberg f2 177
Terndrup d2 158
Terneuzen b3 159
Terni, Italy g7 197
Terni g7 197
Ternin k6 183
Ternitz h2 177
Ternivka j1 201
Ternois h2 183
Ternoise h2 183
Ternopil' b2 148
Terolak b4 101
Teror Ad2 189
Terovou a3 210
Terpenija, Mys l3 94
Terra Alta a5 256
Terra Bella d6 265
Terra Boa b5 290
Terra Branca g2 291
Terra Firma e2 234
Terra Preta f5 285
Terra Rica b5 290
Terra Roxa a6 290
Terrace c4 248
Terrace Bay k6 251
Terraces, The e11 87
Terracina c3 198
Terrades g1 192
Terråk d4 154
Terral a3 254
Terralba Aa3 198
Terranova da Sibari f5 198
Terranova di Pollino f5 198
Terranuova Bracciolini f6 197
Terras do Bouro b3 190
Terrasini c6 199
Terrassa g3 192
Terrasson-la-Villedieu d3 186
Terrazas f3 272
Terre de Bas C 271
Terre de Haut C 271
Terre Haute c6 254
Terre Plaine k5 183
Terrebonne Bay d5 258
Terrell a3 258
Terrenate f4 275
Terrenceville q5 253
Terrero f3 272
Terriente c4 192
Territoire de Belfort c3 184
Território indígena
Waimiri-Atroari e4 285
Terrugem c6 191
Terry, Mississippi, U.S.A. d3 258
Terry, Montana, U.S.A. b2 260
Tersa f2 149
Terschelling d1 159
Terskey Ala-Too r7 121
Tertenia Ab3 198
Tertius d1 172
Teruel, Spain d4 192
Teruel c4 192
Terung b3 101
Terutao National Park a2 101
Tervajoki j5 155
Tervakoski l2 157
Tervel h4 201
Tervo l5 155
Tervola k3 155
Terwara e8 129
Teša, Russ. Fed. g4 151
Teša g4 151
Tešanj g5 177
Tesaret, Oued e3 221
Teseney e4 219
Teshekpuk Lake f1 246
Teshikaga Ad2 114
Teshio Ab1 114
Teshio-dake Ac1 114
Teshio-gawa Ab1 114
Tesia e4 272
Tesimo f3 196
Tesistán c3 274
Teslić j5 177
Teslin,
Yukon Territory, Can. a1 248
Teslin,
Yukon Territory, Can. b2 248
Teslin Lake l3 247
Tesouro b2 290
Tesovo-Netyl'skij a2 150
Tessalit e4 221
Tessaoua f3 223
Tessin f4 158
Tessy-sur-Vire d4 182
Test e5 163
Testa dell'Acqua d8 199
Testeboån g2 156
Testeiro, Montes do b2 190
Tët e6 187
Têt f4 171
Tetachuck Lake e5 248
Tetas, Punta c4 292
Tetbury d5 163
Tété d2 224
Tete, Moz. e2 233
Tete e2 233
Tête-à-la-Baleine n3 253
Tetela d5 274
Tetela de Ocampo f4 275
Tetela de Volcán e4 275
Teteriv c2 148
Teterow f5 158
Teteven g4 201
Tetica de Bacares b7 193
Tetillas c2 274
Tetiyiv c2 148
Tetjuši k4 151
Tetlin j3 247
Tetlin Junction j3 247
Tetlin Lake j3 247
Teton h2 262
Tétouan c1 220
Tetovo e4 200
Tetpur e10 129
Tetrino d2 146
Tettnang e5 174
Teublitz h3 175
Teuchi c6 114
Teuco e4 293
Teufels Moor e2 172
Teufelsbach b1 234
Teul de González Ortega c3 274
Teulada Aa4 198
Teulon e5 250
Teunom, Indon. b13 103
Teunom b13 103
Teupasenti d3 276
Teupitz j3 173
Teuri-tō Ab1 114
Teustepe e4 276
Teutoburger Wald d4 172
Teutschenthal g4 173
Teuva j1 157
Tevere g7 197
Teverone g7 197
Teverya d4 138
Teviot f4 164
Teviotdale f4 164
Teviothead f4 164
Tewane g1 235
Tewantin l9 81
Teweh h5 99
Tewkesbury d5 163
Tewli n3 169
Têwo d1 104
Texada Island e7 248
Texarkana, Arkansas, U.S.A. b3 258
Texarkana, Texas, U.S.A. b3 258
Texas k10 81
Texas, U.S.A. d5 261
Texas City b5 258
Texcoco e4 275
Texel c1 159
Texhoma c4 261
Texistepec g5 275
Texmelucan e4 275
Texoma, Lake a3 258
Teyateyaneng g4 235
Teyvareh b4 128
Teza f3 150
Teziutlán f4 275
Tezoatlán f5 275
Tezonapa f4 275
Tezontehuitz, Volcán a2 276
Tezontepec e3 275
Tezpur n6 125
Tezu q6 125
Tfaritiy b3 220
Tha Li e7 102
Tha Sala a1 101
Thab Lan National Park f8 103
Thaba Nchu g4 235
Thaba Putsoa, Leso. g4 235
Thaba Putsoa, Leso. g4 235
Thabana-Ntlenyana h4 235
Thaba-Tseka h4 235
Thabaung b7 102
Thabazimbi g2 235
Thabong g3 235
Thādiq k9 137
Thagyettaw d9 103
Thai Binh h5 102
Thai Muang d11 103
Thai Nguyên g5 102
Thailand h7 93

THAILAND

THE KINGDOM OF THAILAND
Area 513,115km² (198,115sq miles)
Capital Bangkok
Organizations APEC, ASEAN
Population 63,480,000
Pop. growth (%) 1.3
Life expectancy 66 (m); 72 (f)
Languages Thai, Chinese, Malay
Literacy 96%
Currency baht (US $1 = 39.64 baht)
GDP (US million $) 120,200
GDP per head ($US) 1893

Thailand, Gulf of e5 300
Thaj m8 137
Thakèk g7 102
Thakurdwara d5 130
Thakurmunda k9 125
Thal e4 128
Thal Desert e5 128
Thala f1 221
Thalang d11 103
Thale (Harz) g4 173
Thale Luang b2 101
Thale Noi b2 101
Thalfang e5 159
Thalgau e2 176
Thalheim h2 175
Thallon j10 81
Thalmässing g3 175
Thalo b6 129
Thamaga f2 235
Thamar, Jabal g5 219
Thame, England, U.K. f5 163
Thame f5 163
Thames e2 76
Thames, U.K. g5 163
Thamesville f4 254
Than Uyen f5 102
Thana Ghazi c6 130
Thana Kasba e7 124
Thanbyuzayat c8 102
Thandaung c6 102
Thandla g9 129
Thane c3 126
Thanesar c5 130
Thăng Bình j8 102
Thangadh e9 129
Thangoo f6 86
Thangool d4 84
Thangra d3 130
Thanh Hoa g6 102
Thanjavur f7 126
Thann d3 184
Thannhausen f4 174
Thano Bula Khan c8 129
Thaoge c2 232
Thaon-les-Vosges c2 184
Thap Put a1 101
Thar Desert e7 129
Thara e9 129
Tharabwin d9 103
Tharad e8 129
Tharali d4 130
Tharandt j2 175
Thargomindah f9 81
Tharrawaddy b7 102
Tharrawaw b7 102
Tharsis c7 191
Tharthār, Buḩayrat ath j5 209
Tharthār, Wādī ath j5 209
Tharwa f2 83
Thasos e2 210
Thasos, Anatoliki
Makedonia kai
Thraki, Grc. e2 210
Thatcher j9 263
Thaton c7 102
Thau, Bassin de f5 187
Thaungdut b3 102
Thaungyin d7 102
Thaxted g5 163
Thayawthadangyi Kyun c9 103
Thayer, Kansas, U.S.A. b1 258
Thayer, Missouri, U.S.A. d1 258
Thayetchaung d9 103
Thayetmyo b6 102
Thayngen c2 196
Thazi c5 102
The Bluff l7 259
The Crane H 271
The Dalles c3 262
The Entrance g1 83
the Farallones, Gulf of a4 264
The Hague c2 159
The Key a6 77
The Lynd Junction g5 80
The Mumbles c5 163
The Pas c4 250
The Rock h13 81
The Twins b11 81
The Valley n5 271
The Woodlands b4 258
Thebes d2 218
Thedford c3 260
Theinkun d10 103
Theix c5 182
Thelle g3 183
Them c2 158
Themar f2 175
Thénezay e6 182
Theniet El Had e1 221
Thenon d3 186
Theo, Mount k7 86
Theodore k8 80
Theodore, Can. b5 250
Theodore, U.S.A. e4 258
Theodore Roosevelt e1 293
Theodore Roosevelt Lake h9 261
Theodore Roosevelt
National Park c2 260
Theologos e2 210
Théols h6 183
Thérain h3 183
Theresa Creek b3 84
Therma f2 210
Thermaïkos Kolpos c2 210
Thermisia d5 211
Thermo b4 210
Thermopolis a3 260
Thermopyles c4 210
Thespies d4 210
Thesprotiko a3 210
Thessalia c3 210
Thessalon e2 254
Thessaloniki c2 210
Thet g4 163
Thetford g4 163
Thetford Mines g5 252
Thethit d4 200
Theunissen g4 235
Thevenard a12 81
Thevenard Island b7 86
Thèze b5 187
Thiaucourt-Regniéville b2 184
Thibaudeau f2 250
Thiberville f3 183
Thibodaux d5 258
Thiéblemont-Farémont a2 184
Thief River Falls e6 250
Thiel Mountains hh3 298
Thielsen, Mount b4 262
Thiendorf b2 175
Thiene, Veneto, Italy f4 196
Thiérache j3 183
Thierrens a3 196
Thiers f3 186
Thierville-sur-Meuse b1 184
Thiès a3 222
Thießow j1 173
Thiézac e3 186
Thika b4 226
Thiladhunmathee Atoll c9 126
Thilogne b2 222
Thimbu Chhu j6 135
Thimphu j6 135
Thio F 74
Thionville e5 159
Thira, Grc. f6 211
Thira f6 211
Thirasia f6 211
Thirlmere c2 162
Thironne g4 183
Thirrach c4 130
Thirsk e2 162
Thisted b2 158
Thistle Island c13 81
Thiu Khao Phanom
Dong Rak g8 103
Thiva d4 210
Thiviers c3 186
Thizy a4 185
Thô Chu, Đao f11 103
Thoen d7 102
Thohoyandou j1 235
Thoirette b4 184
Thoissey a4 184
Tholen c3 159
Tholey f5 159
Tholon j5 183
Thomas a5 256
Thomas Hill Reservoir ee4 260
Thomasboro b5 254
Thomaston,
Connecticut, U.S.A. g3 257
Thomastown d4 165
Thomasville,
Alabama, U.S.A. f4 258
Thomasville,
Georgia, U.S.A. h4 259
Thomes Creek a2 264
Thompson,
British Columbia, Can. g6 248
Thompson, Can. e3 250
Thompson,
Missouri, U.S.A. e3 260
Thompson,
Pennsylvania, U.S.A. e3 256
Thompson Falls f2 262
Thompson Peak b5 261
Thomson, Aust. a3 84
Thomson, U.S.A. h3 259
Thondhe c3 130
Thônes c5 185
Thonon-les-Bains c4 184
Thorame-Haute c6 185
Thoré e5 187
Thörl g2 177
Þorlákshöfn A 163
Thornbury d5 163
Thorndale h1 235
Thorne f3 162
Thorney f4 162
Thornhill e4 164
Thornton c3 258
Thornton Dale f2 162
Thorpeness h4 163
Thorsager d2 158
Thorshavnheiane j2 298
Thorsø c2 158
Thouarcé e5 182
Thouars e6 182
Thouet e5 182
Thouin, Cape c7 86
Thourotte a5 159
Thousand Oaks e7 265
Thrakiko Pelagos f2 210
Thrapston f4 163
Three Hummock
Island Aa2 83
Three Kings Islands d1 76
Three Lakes b3 254
Three Oaks c5 254
Three Points, Cape d5 222
Three Rivers,
California, U.S.A. e5 265
Three Rivers,
Texas, U.S.A. k3 273
Three Sisters e5 234
Three Sisters, U.S.A. c3 262
Three Springs b11 87
Throckmorton d5 261
Throssel Range e7 86
Throssell, Lake g10 87
Thrushton National
Park b5 85
Thu Dâu Môt h10 103
Thueyts a6 184
Thuin c4 159
Thuir e6 187
Thul d6 129
Thule aa2 298
Thuli, Zimb. d3 233
Thuli d3 233
Thuli Safari Area d3 233
Thumbs, The c5 77
Thun b3 196
Thunda f8 81
Thundelarra c11 87
Thunder Bay,
Ontario, Can. j6 251
Thunder Bay, Can. j6 251
Thunder Bay, U.S.A. e3 254
Thunder Creek q6 249
Thunder Knoll g2 277
Thunderbolt j3 259
Thuner See b3 196
Thung Salaeng Luang
National Park e7 102
Thung Song a1 101
Thung Wa a2 101
Thur, Fr. d3 184
Thur, Switz. c2 196
Thuret f3 186
Thüringen a2 176
Thüringen, Ger. f4 173
Thüringer Becken f4 173
Thüringer Wald, Ger. f5 173
Thürkow f5 158
Thurles d4 165
Thurmont c5 256
Thurn, Pass d2 176
Thurnau g2 175
Thurø d3 158
Thurrock g5 163
Thursby e5 164
Thurso, Scotland, U.K. e1 164
Thurso e1 164
Thurston Island hh2 298
Thury-Harcourt e4 182
Thusis d3 196
Thy b2 158
Thyamis a3 210
Thyborøn b2 158
Thylungra f9 81
Thymaina Ab1 211
Thymerais g4 183
Thymiana g4 210
Thyregod c3 158
Ti Tree a7 80
Tiāb r8 137
Tian'e f6 104
Tianchang f3 111
Tiandong f7 104
Tianfanjie e5 111
Tiângol Lougguéré b2 222
Tianguá d2 288
Tiânguél Bôri b3 222
Tianguistengo e3 275
Tianheng Dao g2 111
Tianjin j6 113
Tianjin, Tientsin,
China j6 113
Tianjun p3 117
Tianlin f6 104
Tianmen c4 106
Tianmu Shan f4 111
Tianqiaoling g4 113
Tianquan d3 104
Tianshifu n5 113
Tianshui e1 104
Tianshuihai d2 130
Tiantai n4 105
Tiantaiyong j4 113
Tianwangsi f4 111
Tianyang f7 104
Tianzhen h5 112
Tianzhu,
Gansu, China b7 112
Tianzhu,
Guizhou, China g5 104
Tianzhuangtai m5 113
Tiaret e1 221
Tiaro l8 81
Tiassalé d4 222
Tibagi, Braz. c5 290
Tibagi, Paraná, Braz. c6 290
Tibal, Wādī h5 136
Tibaná c2 284
Tibati g4 223
Tibba e6 129
Tibé, Pic de c4 222
Tiber Reservoir h1 262
Tiberias, Lake d4 138
Tibesti a3 218
Tibet j4 135
Tibi, India g6 129
Tibi, Spain d6 193
Tibi, Embalse de d6 193
Tiboku Falls f2 285
Tibooburra f10 81
Tibrikot f5 135
Tibro f3 156
Tiburón, Cabo b2 284
Tiburón, Isla c3 272
Ticao d4 100
Tichît c2 222
Tîchît, Dhar c2 222
Tichla b4 220
Ticino c4 196
Tickhill e3 162
Ţicleni f3 201
Ticonderoga k4 255
Ticul q7 273
Tidaholm e3 156
Tidan e3 156
Tiddim a4 102
Tidhkâr f4 219
Tidikelt, Plaine du e3 221
Tidioute a3 256
Tidjikja b2 222
Tidsit, Sabkhet b4 220
Tidworth e5 163
Tie Plant e3 258
Tiébissou c4 222
Tiechang p5 113
Tiefencastel d3 196
Tiefensee j3 173
Tiel, Neth. d3 159
Tiel, Sen. a3 222
Tieli p2 113
Tieling m4 113
Tielongtan d2 130
Tielt b4 159
Tiémé c4 222
Tien Shan s7 121
Tiên Yên f8 104
Tienen c4 159
Tiengen d5 174
Tiercé e5 182
Tierga c3 192
Tierp g2 157
Tierra Amarilla b4 261
Tierra Blanca, Mex. f4 275
Tierra Blanca, Peru b1 292
Tierra Colorada e5 275

Tierra del Fuego, Parque Nacional → Torrente del Cinca 389

Tierra del Fuego, Parque Nacional c6 295
Tierrablanca d3 274
Tierralta j6 277
Tierranueva d3 274
Tieshan d4 106
Tiétar, Valle de f4 190
Tietê, Braz. c4 290
Tietê, São Paulo, Braz. e5 290
Tieyon a9 81
Tifore p4 99
Tifton h4 259
Tifu p6 99
Tiga, Malay. h2 99
Tiga, New Cal. F 74
Tigalda Island c5 246
Tigănești g4 201
Tigani, Akra c6 211
Tigapuluh, Pegunungan b5 98
Tigen h3 149
Tighina j2 201
Tigiretskiy Khrebet u2 121
Tignale e4 196
Tignère g4 223
Tignes c5 185
Tignish k5 253
Tigray e5 219
Tigre, Ec. c4 284
Tigre, Ven. e2 285
Tigre, Cerro del e2 275
Tigris l5 137
Tiguent a2 222
Tigui a4 218
Tigy h5 183
Tigzerte, Oued c3 220
Tih, Jabal at b7 139
Tihāmah f4 219
Tihany f5 171
Tihmenevo e2 150
Tihonova Pustyn' d4 150
Tihoreck f3 148
Tihosuco q7 273
Tihtozero n4 155
Tihuatlán f3 275
Tihvin b2 150
Tiilikkajärven kansallispuisto l5 155
Tijara c6 130
Tijesno b4 200
Tiji g2 221
Tijola b7 193
Tijuana e9 263
Tijucas c7 289
Tijucas do Sul d6 290
Tijucas, Baia de c7 289
Tijuco d3 290
Tikal c2 276
Tikal, Parque Nacional c2 276
Tikamgarh f7 124
Tikéi K 75
Tikem c2 224
Tikhvinskaja Grjada c2 150
Tikitiki g2 76
Tikokino f3 76
Tikopia H 75
Tikrit j5 209
Tikse c2 130
Tikšeozero, Ozero c2 146
Tiksi, n2 119
Tikveš Ezero b1 210
Tilaiya Reservoir j7 125
Tilama b2 296
Tilavar q3 137
Tilbooroo g9 81
Tilburg d3 159
Tilbury g5 163
Til-Châtel b3 184
Tilden k3 273
Tileagd l4 171
Tilghman d6 256
Tilh b5 187
Tilhar d6 130
Tilia, Oued e3 221
Tilin b5 102
Tilisarao e2 296
Tillabéri, Niger e3 223
Tillabéri e3 223
Tillanchong Island n8 127
Tillberga g3 156
Tille b3 184
Tillia e2 223
Tillicoultry e3 164
Tillsonburg f4 254
Tiloa e2 223
Tilomonte d4 292
Tilos Ac2 211
Tilpa g11 81
Tilrhemt e2 221
Tilt e3 164
Tiltil b2 296
Tilton c5 254
Tilu, Bukit l5 99
Tim b2 158
Tima c8 136
Timanskij Krjaž g2 146
Timar j3 209
Timare k6 97
Timaru c6 77
Timaševsk e3 148
Timau h3 196
Timbaúba e3 288
Timbebas (Parque Nacional de Abrolhos), Recife das e5 289
Timbebas, Recife das e5 289
Timbedgha c2 222
Timber Creek k4 86
Timberville b6 256
Timbiqui b3 284
Timbo, Gui. d6 126
Timbo, Lib. c4 222
Timboon f15 81
Timbué, Ponta b7 231
Timbuktu d2 222
Timbuktu, Tombouctou, Mali d2 222
Timbun Mata k2 99
Timétrine, Mali d2 222
Timétrine d5 220
Timi a2 138
Timia f2 223
Timiaouine e4 221
Timimoun e3 221
Timirist, Râs a2 222
Timirjazevo j5 157
Timiryazev l5 147
Timiryazevo l5 147
Timiș, Rom. e3 201
Timiș, Rom. f3 201
Timișoara k6 171
Ti-m-Meghsoi f4 221
Timmendorfer Strand d5 158
Timmernabben g4 156
Timmins f1 254
Timms Hill f2 260
Timohino d2 150
Timon d3 288
Timonium d5 256
Timor Sea g6 300
Timote f3 297
Timóteo g3 291
Timoudi d3 220
Timpaus n5 99
Timpson b4 258
Timrå g1 156
Tims Ford Lake f2 258
Timur m6 121
Tin Alkoum g4 221
Tin Amzi, Oued f4 221
Tin, Ra's at b1 218
Tinaca Point e8 100
Tinaco d2 284
Tinaga d3 100
Tinajo Af1 189
Tinaquillo d2 284
Tinca k5 171
Tinchebray e4 182
Tindila c3 222
Tindivanam f6 126
Tindouf c3 220
Tinée d6 185
Tineo d1 190
Tinerhir c2 220
Ti-n-Essako e2 223
Tinfouchy c3 220
Ting Jiang l6 105
Tinggi d4 101
Tinggi Madi, Dataran g4 98
Tinggi Usun Apau, Dataran h3 99
Tingi Mountains b4 222
Tingkawk Sakan c2 102
Tinglev c4 158
Tingo Maria b1 292
Tingri, Xizang Zizhiqu, China h5 135
Tingsryd f4 156
Tingstäde h4 157
Tingüindin c4 274
Tinguiririca b3 296
Tingvoll b5 154
Tingxia g5 111
Tinharé, Ilha de e4 288
Tinian A 74
Tinjil c8 98
Tinkisso c3 222
Tinne c3 156
Tinnoset c3 156
Tinnsjø c3 156
Tinoco f1 297
Tinogasta c1 294
Tinompo l4 99
Tinos f5 211
Tinos, Notio Aigaio, Grc. f5 211
Tiñoso, Cabo c7 193
Tinrhert, Plateau du f3 221
Tinsukia p6 125
Tintagel b6 163
Tintâne b2 222
Ti-n-Tarabine, Oued f4 221
Tinténiac d4 182
Tintina e5 293
Tintinara e13 81
Tinto, Spain d7 191
Tinto, U.K. e4 164
Tinui f4 76
Ti-n-Zaouâtene e5 221
Tioga c3 256
Tioga Pass d4 264
Tioman d4 101
Tione e4 196
Tione di Trento e3 196
Tionesta a3 256
Tionesta Lake a3 256
Tioughnioga d2 256
Tip Top Hill k6 251
Tipasa e1 221
Tipitapa d4 276
Tipova j2 201
Tipperary, Ire. d4 165
Tipperary c4 165
Tipperne-Værnengene b3 158
Tiptala Bhanjyang k6 125
Tipton d5 265
Tipton, Mount f8 263
Tiptur e6 126
Tipuani d3 292
Tiquicheo d4 274
Tiquié d3 284
Tiquisate b3 276
Tira c4 139
Tiracambu, Serra do c2 288
Tirahart, Oued e4 221
Tirān n5 137
Tirana d5 200
Tirana, Tiranë, Alb. d5 200
Tirano e3 196
Tirari Desert d9 81
Tiraspol j2 201
Tirat Karmel c4 138
Tirau e2 76
Tiraz Mountains b3 234
Tire a3 208
Tiree b3 164
Tirgo b2 192
Tiri, Jam.Kash. d3 130
Tiri, Pak. c6 129
Tirich Mir e2 128
Tiriez b6 193
Tiriolo f6 199
Tiripetio d4 274
Tiris Zemmour c4 220
Tirljanskij j5 147
Tirna e4 126
Tirnova h1 201
Tirol b2 176
Tiroler Ache h5 175
Tirón a2 192
Tiros f3 291
Tiroungoulou d2 224
Tirschenreuth h3 175
Tirteafuera f6 193
Tirthahalli d6 126
Tirúa a5 296
Tirua Point e3 76
Tirua, Punta a5 296
Tiruchchendur f8 126
Tiruchchirappalli f7 126
Tiruchengodu e7 126
Tirukkoyilur f7 126
Tirunelveli e8 126
Tiruntán b1 292
Tirupati f6 126
Tiruppattur f6 126
Tiruppur e7 126
Tirutturaippundi f7 126
Tiruvannamalai f6 126
Tiruvottiyur g6 126
Tiryns c5 210
Tirza m3 157
Tisa j6 171
Tisaren f3 156
Tisău h3 201
Tisdale q5 249
Tishomingo a2 258
Tisiyah e4 139
Tisjön e2 156
Tiskilwa b5 254
Tisnaren f3 156
Tišnov e2 170
Tisovec h3 171
Tissamaharama g9 126
Tissemsilt e1 221
Tissø e3 158
Tista l6 125
Tistrup Stationsby b3 158
Tisvilde f2 158
Tisza j4 170
Tiszaalpár h5 171
Tiszabecs l3 171
Tiszabezdéd l3 171
Tiszacsege k4 171
Tiszaföldvár j5 171
Tiszafüred j4 171
Tiszakécske j5 171
Tiszakerecseny l3 171
Tiszalök k3 171
Tiszanána j4 171
Tiszaörs j4 171
Tiszasüly j4 171
Tiszatenyő j4 171
Tiszaújváros k4 171
Tiszavasvári k4 171
Tit, Adrar, Alg. e3 221
Tit, Tamanrasset, Alg. f4 221
Titabar p6 125
Titaf d3 220
Titaguas c5 193
Titao d3 222
Titarisios c3 210
Tit-Ary n2 119
Titel e3 200
Tithwal a2 130
Titicaca, Lago d3 292
Titisee d5 174
Titlagarh h9 125
Titlis c3 196
Tito e4 198
Titov Drvar c3 200
Titova Korenica g5 177
Titovka n2 155
Titovo g5 151
Titran b5 154
Tittling e1 176
Tittmoning d1 176
Titu g3 201
Titumate j6 277
Titusville j5 259
Tiumpan Head b1 164
Tiurana f3 192
Tivari f7 129
Tiveden nationalpark f3 156
Tiverton c6 163
Tiverton, U.S.A. j3 257
Tivissa e3 192
Tivoli g8 197
Tiwal, Wadi b5 218
Tiworo, Selat m7 99
Tixcalpupu q7 273
Tixkokob q7 273
Tixtla e5 275
Tizayuca e4 275
Tizi Ouzou e1 221
Tizimín q7 273
Tiznados d2 284
Tiznap He r9 121
Tiznit c3 220
Tjæreborg b3 158
Tjagun v1 121
Tjaktjajaure g3 154
Tjåmotis g3 154
Tjaneni j2 235
Tjavelkjaure g3 154
Tjeggelvas f3 154
Tjeldøya e2 154
Tjeukemeer d2 159
Tjörn d3 156
Tjøtta d4 154
Tjrma s1 113
Tjul'kino j4 147
Tjuli m3 147
Tjuljači l4 151
Tjumen' l4 147
Tjumencevo t1 121
Tjumenskaja Oblast' m4 147
Tjung n3 119
Tjuva-Guba p2 155
Tlachichila c3 274
Tlachichilo e3 275
Tlacoapa e5 275
Tlacolula f5 275
Tlacolulita g5 275
Tlacotalpán g4 275
Tlacotenco e4 275
Tlacotepec e5 275
Tlacotepec, Cerro d5 274
Tlacuilotepec e3 275
Tlahualilo h4 272
Tlahuapan e4 275
Tlajomulco c3 274
Tlalchapa d4 274
Tlalchichuca f4 275
Tlalixcoyan f4 275
Tlalixtaquilla e5 275
Tlalmanalco e4 275
Tlalnepantla e4 275
Tlalpujahua d4 274
Tlaltenango de Sánchez Román c3 274
Tlaltizapan e4 275
Tlancualpican e4 275
Tlapa e5 275
Tlapacoyan f4 275
Tlapehuala d4 274
Tlaquepaque c3 274
Tlaquilpa f4 275
Tlaxcala, Mex. e4 275
Tlaxcala, Tlaxcala, Mex. e4 275
Tlaxco e4 275
Tlaxcoapán e3 275
Tlaxiaco f5 275
Tlemcen d2 220
Tlhakgameng f3 234
Tljarata g4 149
Tlokweng f2 235
Tlučná b2 170
Tlumach g1 201
Tlumačov f2 171
Tluszcz k3 169
Tmassah h3 221
Tmeïmîchât b4 220
Toa g4 266
Toad River e2 248
Toamasina, Madag. Ab2 233
Toamasina Ab2 233
Toano, Italy e5 197
Toano, U.S.A. h7 255
Toau K 75
Toay e4 297
Toba, China q4 125
Toba, Japan e4 115
Toba and Kakar Ranges d5 128
Toba Gargaji f6 129
Toba Inlet e6 248
Toba Tek Singh f5 128
Toba, Danau d14 103
Tobago E 271
Tobakoni Point b4 222
Tobarra c6 193
Tobas d1 294
Tobelo h5 97
Tobermorey c7 80
Tobermory, Aust. f9 81
Tobermory, Can. f3 254
Tobermory, U.K. b3 164
Tobetsu Ab2 114
Tobias Barreto e4 288
Tobin Lake r5 249
Tobin, Lake h7 86
Tobin, Mount e5 262
Tobique j5 253
Tobi-shima h2 115
Toboali d6 98
Tobol, Kaz. l4 147
Tobol j1 120
Tobol'sk m4 147
Toboso d5 100
Tobseda h1 146
Tobyhanna e3 256
Tobyš g2 146
Tocache Nuevo b1 292
Tocantínia c3 288
Tocantinópolis c3 288
Tocantins, Braz. c4 288
Tocantins, Braz. c2 288
Toccoa h2 259
Tocha b4 190
Tochigi, Japan h3 115
Tochigi h3 115
Tochimizolco e4 275
Tochio h3 115
Tochni b2 138
Töcksfors d3 156
Toco, Chile d4 292
Toco, Trin. E 271
Tocoa d3 276
Toconao d4 292
Tocopilla c4 292
Tocorpuri, Cerros de d4 292
Tocumwal g13 81
Tocuyo d1 284
Tod, Mount h6 248
Toda Bhim e6 124
Toda Rai Singh g7 129
Todalsfjellet b5 154
Todd, Arg. g3 297
Todd, Aust. b8 80
Todgarh f8 129
Todi g7 197
Tödi c3 196
Todmorden d3 162
Todog u5 121
Todoga-saki k2 115
Todos os Santos, Baía de e4 288
Todos Santos, Bol. d3 292
Todos Santos, Mex. d6 272
Todtmoos c5 174
Todtnau c5 174
Toekornstig Stuwmeer f3 285
Toén c2 190
Toetoes Bay b7 77
Töfsingdalens nationalpark e1 156
Toft A 164
Toftan f2 156
Tofte d3 156
Tofterup b3 158
Toftlund c3 158
Tofua J 75
Toga F 74
Togbo c2 224
Togdheer d2 226
Toggenburg d2 196
Togiak d4 246
Togiak Bay d4 246
Togian l5 99
Togian, Kepulauan m5 99
Töging am Inn d1 176
Togo c4 217

TOGO

THE TOGOLESE REPUBLIC
Area 56,785km² (21,925sq miles)
Capital Lomé
Organizations ECOWAS, FZ, OIC
Population 4,800,000
Pop. growth (%) 2.3
Life expectancy 50 (m); 52 (f)
Languages French, Kabiye, Ewe, other local languages
Literacy 60.9%
Currency CFA franc (US $1 = 534.95 CFA franc)
GDP (US million $) 1463
GDP per head ($US) 304

Togtoh f5 112
Togton He m2 125
Toguçin j4 118
Togul v1 121
Toguz h4 120
Tohana b5 130
Tohenbatu g4 98
Tohmajärvi, Fin. n1 157
Tohmajärvi p1 157
Toholampi k5 155
Tohom c5 112
Töhöm e3 112
Toijala k2 157
Toi-misaki d6 114
Toineke n10 99
Toisvesi k1 157
Toivala l5 155
Toiyabe Range f3 264
Tojaci b1 210
Tojikobod e1 128
Tōjō e4 114
Tok, Russ. Fed. j1 149
Tok, U.S.A. j3 247
Tokachi-gawa Ac2 114
Tōkai g4 115
Tokai b2 101
Tokaj k3 171
Tokala, Gunung f5 99
Tōkamachi h3 115
Tokanui b7 77
Tokar e4 219
Tokara-rettō B 115
Tokarevka, Kaz. p2 121
Tokarevka, Russ. Fed. f2 148
Tokat, Tur. f2 209
Tokat f2 209
Tokatoka d2 76
Tŏkch'ŏn p6 113
Tŏkchŏk-to n7 113
Tokelau H 75
Tokelau (New Zealand) h3 73
Tokmak d3 148
Tokmok q6 121
Tokomaru Bay g3 76
Tokoro-gawa Ac2 114
Tokorozawa h4 115
Tokounou c4 222
Toksook Bay c3 246
Toktogul p7 121
Toktogul Suu Saktagychy p7 121
Tokty u5 121
Tokū J 75
Tokunoshima B 115
Tokushima, Japan f5 114
Tokushima f4 114
Tōkyō, Japan h4 115
Tōkyō h4 115
Tōkyō-wan h4 115
Tokyrau q4 121
Tokzār c3 128
Tol'jatti k5 151
Tolaga Bay g3 76
Tōlañaro Ab4 233
Tolar, Cerro d5 292
Tolastadh a'Chaolais b1 164
Tolastadh Ùr b1 164
Tolé g6 277
Tole Bi p6 121
Toledo, Belize c2 276
Toledo, Belize c2 276
Toledo, Amazonas, Braz. c5 284
Toledo, Braz. b6 290
Toledo, Chile c5 292
Toledo, Spain f4 190
Toledo f5 191
Toledo, U.S.A. e5 254
Toledo Bend Reservoir c4 258
Toledo, Montes de f5 191
Tolentino h6 197
Toles Gebirge e2 176
Tolga d1 156
Tolhuaca, Parque Nacional b5 296
Toli u5 121
Toliara, Madag. Ab3 233
Toliara Aa3 233
Tolima b3 284
Tolimán, Jalisco, Mex. c4 274
Tolimán, Querétaro, Mex. e3 275
Tolitoli l4 99
Tolitoli, Teluk l4 99
Tolkmicko h1 169
Tolland h3 257
Tollarp e5 156
Tollense j2 173
Tollesbury g5 163
Tolleshunt D'Arcy g5 163
Tollhouse d4 264
Tølløse e3 158
Tolmačevo n3 157
Tolmezzo h3 196
Tolmin e3 176
Tolna, Hung. g5 171
Tolna g5 171
Tolo, D.R.C. c4 224
Tolo, Grc. c5 211
Toloa Creek d3 276
Tolono b6 254
Tolosa b1 192
Tolovana g2 247
Tolox f8 191
Tolsan-do p8 113
Tolsmaville e3 254
Tolstoj, Mys r4 119
Toltén, Chile a5 296
Toltén, Araucanía, Chile a5 296
Tolú k6 277
Toluca e4 275
Tolva e2 192
Tolve f4 198
Tolybay j2 120
Tolzac c4 187
Tom Burke g1 235
Tom Price c8 86
Tom' j4 118
Toma d3 222
Tomah a4 254
Tomahawk d4 246
Tomahawk Coastal Reserve Ab2 83
Tomakomai Ab2 114
Tomales a3 264
Tomamae Ab1 114
Tomanivi E 74
Tomar, Braz. e4 285
Tomar b5 191
Tomaros a3 210
Tomarza e3 208
Tomás Gomensoro e2 294
Tomas, Isla c7 295
Tomashpil' j1 201
Tomášov f3 170
Tomášovce h3 171
Tomaszów Lubelski m5 169
Tomaszów Mazowiecki j4 169
Tomatlán b4 274
Tomave d4 292
Tomazina d5 290
Tombador, Serra do, Braz. d4 288
Tombador, Serra do, Braz. f2 293
Tomball b4 258
Tombigbee e3 258
Tombila, Gunung m5 99
Tombo, Punta c4 295
Tomboa Point f6 100
Tomboco b5 224
Tombos g4 291
Tombouctou d2 222
Tombstone h10 263
Tombstone Mountain k2 247
Tombua a2 232
Tomé a4 296
Tome l1 235
Tomea m7 99
Tomelilla e5 156
Tomelloso a5 193
Tomenaryk l6 120
Tomi c2 224
Tominé b3 222
Tomine, Embalse de c3 284
Tomingley j12 81
Tomini, Teluk l5 99
Tominian d3 222
Tomintoul e2 164
Tomislavgrad c4 200
Tomiyama h4 115
Tomkinson Ranges j10 87
Tommerup d3 158
Tommerup Stationsby d3 158
Tommot n4 119
Tomo, Col. d2 284
Tomo, Guainía, Col. d3 284
Tomóchic f3 272
Tomortei g5 112
Tompa h5 171
Tompira l6 99
Tompo k5 99
Tomra b1 156
Toms Place e4 264
Toms River f5 257
Tomsk j4 118
Tomskaja Oblast' j4 118
Tomtabacken f4 156
Tomtor, Respublika Saha (Jakutija), Russ. Fed. q3 119
Tomtor, Respublika Saha (Jakutija), Russ. Fed. p3 119
Tomuraushi-yama Ac2 114
Tona g3 192
Tonalá h5 275
Tonala c3 274
Tonalá, Oaxaca, Mex. f5 275
Tonalá, Veracruz, Mex. g4 275
Tonalapa de Rio e4 275
Tonantins d4 284
Tonara Ab2 198
Tonasket d1 262
Tonate g2 285
Tonaya c4 274
Tonbridge g5 163
Tondano n4 99
Tondela b4 190
Tønder b4 158
Tondi f8 126
Tone c6 163
Tonezza del Cimone f4 196
Tonga h4 73

TONGA

THE KINGDOM OF TONGA
Area 748km² (289sq miles)
Capital Nuku'alofa
Organizations COMM, SPC, PIF
Population 101,000
Pop. growth (%) 0.8
Life expectancy 66 (m); 70 (f)
Languages Tongan, English
Literacy 93%
Currency pa'anga (Tongan dollar) (US $1 = 2.06 pa'anga)
GDP (US million $) 130
GDP per head ($US) 1287

Tong'an m6 105
Tonga, Cam. g5 223
Tonga, Sudan f2 225
Tonga Plateau d2 232
Tonga Ridge l7 301
Tonga Trench l7 301
Tongaat j4 235
Tongariro e3 76
Tongariro National Park e3 76
Tongatapu J 75
Tongatapu Group J 75
Tongbai c3 106
Tongbai Shan c3 106
Tongcheng e4 111
Tongchenghe b4 106
Tongchuan a2 106
Tongdao g5 104
Tongde c1 104
Tongduch'ŏn p7 113
Tongeren d4 159
Tonggu Zui h9 104
Tongguan, Hunan, China j4 105
Tongguan, Shaanxi, China b2 106
Tonghae q7 113
Tonghai f3 102
Tonghe q3 113
Tonghua, Jilin, China n5 113
Tonghua, Jilin, China n5 113
Tongjiang, Heilongjiang, China s2 113
Tongjiang, Sichuan, China f3 104
Tongjosŏn-man q6 113
Tongken He p2 113
Tongking, Gulf of h6 102
Tongli g4 111
Tongliang f4 104
Tongliao m4 113
Tongling, Anhui, China e4 111
Tonglu f5 111
Tongnae q8 113
Tongnan e3 104
Tongo Lake f11 81
Tongoa F 74
Tongobory Aa3 233
Tongoy b2 294
Tongquil d7 100
Tongren, Guizhou, China g5 104
Tongren, Qinghai, China c1 104
Tongshan, Hubei, China d5 106
Tongshan, Jiangsu, China e2 111
Tongta d5 102
Tongtian He p2 125
Tongue d1 164
Tongue, U.S.A. b2 260
Tongwei e1 104
Tongxiang g4 111
Tongxin c7 112
Tongxu d2 106
Tongyanghe e4 111
Tongyu, Jilin, China m3 113
Tongyu, Shanxi, China c1 106
Tongyuanpu m5 113
Tongzhou j6 113
Tongzi f4 104
Tonica b5 254
Tónichi e3 272
Tonila c4 274
Tonj, Sudan e2 225
Tonj e2 225
Tonk g7 129
Tonkābon m3 137
Tonkawa a1 258
Tonkino j3 151
Tônlé Kông h9 103
Tônlé Sab g9 103
Tônlé San h9 103
Tônlé Srêpok h9 103
Tonnay-Boutonne b3 186
Tonnay-Charente b3 186
Tonneins c4 187
Tonnerre j5 183
Tonnerrois k5 183
Tönning b4 158
Tōno j2 115
Tonopah f3 264
Tonoshō f4 114
Tonosí g7 277
Tons c4 130
Tonšajevo j3 151
Tonšalovo d2 150
Tønsberg d3 156
Tonstad b3 156
Tontal, Sierra c1 296
Tonyrefail c5 163
Toobeah j10 81
Toobli c4 222
Tooele g5 262
Toolik g1 247
Toolonga Nature Reserve b10 87
Tooma f2 83
Toomebridge e2 165
Toompine g9 81
Toorberg f6 234
Tootsi l3 157
Toowoomba k9 81
Tooxin e1 226
Top d3 128
Top Springs k5 86
Topalapa del Sur e4 275
Topalki d2 150
Topana g3 201
Topares b7 193
Topčiha u1 121
Topeka e4 260
Topia f5 272
Topinabee d3 254
Topki j4 118
Topko, Gora k1 94
Toplița g2 201
Töplitz h3 173
Topocalma, Punta a3 296
Topolčani b1 210
Topoľčany g3 171
Topoľníky f4 171
Topolobampo e5 272
Topolog j3 201
Topolovățu Mare k6 171
Topoloveni g3 201
Topolovgrad h4 201
Topozero, Ozero b2 146
Toppenish c2 262
Topsham c6 163
Topuni e2 76
Tor f2 225
Tor Baldak c5 128
Tor Bay c6 163
Tor Vaianica g8 197
Tor'kovskoe Vodohranilišče g3 151
Torà f3 192
Toral de los Vados d2 190
Torasovej, Ostrov l1 147
Torata c3 292
Torbalı a3 208
Torbat-e Heydarīyeh f3 116
Torbat-e Jām g3 116
Torbay h2 162
Torbeevo g4 151
Torbert, Mount f3 246
Torcal de Antequera f8 191
Torcello g4 196
Torchyn p5 169
Tordera g3 192
Tordesillas e3 190
Tordesilos c4 192
Tordino c2 198
Töre j4 155
Töreboda f3 156
Torekov f2 158
Torella del Sannio d3 198
Torellano d6 193
Torelló g2 192
Toreno d2 190
Toreo m6 99
Torez e2 148
Torfaen h2 162
Torfou d5 182
Torgau h4 173
Torgelow j2 173
Torgiano g6 197
Torgun g2 149
Torhamn f4 156
Torhout b3 159
Torigni-sur-Vire e3 182
Torija a4 192
Torino, Italy b4 196
Torino b4 196
Torit f3 225
Torkamān l3 137
Torkhan e4 128
Torkoviči a2 150
Torla d2 192
Tormes e3 190
Tormón c4 193
Tormosin f2 149
Tornado Mountain k7 249
Tornajuelos b7 193
Tornal'a j3 171
Tornby c1 158
Torne f3 162
Torneälven j3 155
Tornesch c5 158
Torneträsk, Swe. g2 154
Torneträsk g2 154
Tornio k4 155
Torno d4 196
Tornquist f5 297
Tornyospálca l3 171
Toro, Nig. f3 223
Toro, Spain e3 190
Torö g3 157
Toro, Cerro del c1 294
Toro, Lago del b6 295
Toro, Punta b2 296
Torobuku m7 99
Torodi e3 223
Törökbálint g4 171
Törökszentmiklós j4 171
Toronto g4 254
Toropec a3 150
Tororo a3 226
Toros Dağları a4 208
Torpè Ab2 198
Torpo c2 156
Torquato Severo f2 294
Torquay c6 163
Torquemada f2 190
Torralba Aa2 198
Torralba de Oropesa e5 191
Torrance e8 265
Torrão b6 191
Torre c4 190
Torre Annunziata d4 198
Torre Canne g4 198
Torre de Abraham, Embalse de la f5 191
Torre de Cadí f2 192
Torre de Dona Chama c3 190
Torre de Juan Abad a6 193
Torre de Moncorvo c3 190
Torre de'Passeri c2 198
Torre del Águila, Embalse de la e7 191
Torre del Bierzo d2 190
Torre del Burgo a4 192
Torre del Campo g7 191
Torre del Greco d4 198
Torre del Mar f8 191
Torre Mileto e3 198
Torre Nuovo Scalo d6 197
Torre Orsaia e4 198
Torre Pellice b5 196
Torre San Giovanni h5 198
Torre Santa Susanna g4 198
Torre-Alhaquime e8 191
Torrebaja c4 193
Torreblanca e4 193
Torrecaballeros f4 190
Torrecampo f6 191
Torre-Cardela a7 193
Torrecerredo f1 190
Torrecilla f8 191
Torrecilla en Cameros b2 192
Torredembarra f3 192
Torredonjimeno g7 191
Torrejón de Ardoz g4 190
Torrejón del Rey a4 192
Torrejón el Rubio e5 191
Torrejoncillo d5 191
Torrejoncillo del Rey b4 193
Torrejón-Tajo, Embalse de e5 191
Torrejón-Tiétar, Embalse de e5 190
Torrelacarcel c4 192
Torrelaguna g4 190
Torrelapaja c3 192
Torrelavega f1 190
Torrelodones g4 190
Torremaggiore e3 198
Torremegía d6 191
Torremocha d5 191
Torremocha de Jiloca c4 192
Torremolinos f8 191
Torrens Creek, Queensland, Aust. a2 84
Torrens Creek g6 80
Torrens, Lake c11 81
Torrent, Arg. e1 294
Torrent d5 193
Torrente del Cinca e3 192

Torrenueva a6 193
Torreón h5 272
Torre-Pacheco d7 193
Torreperogil a6 193
Torres, Braz. c7 289
Torres, Mex. d3 272
Torres, Spain g7 191
Torres del Paine, Parque Nacional b6 295
Torres Islands F 74
Torres Novas b5 191
Torres Strait l7 97
Torres Vedras a5 191
Torres, Cabo e1 190
Torreta, Sierra f6 193
Torrevieja d7 193
Torri del Benaco e4 196
Torricella g4 198
Torridge b6 163
Torridon c2 164
Torriglia d5 196
Torrijas d4 193
Torrijo del Campo c4 192
Torrijos f5 191
Torring c3 158
Torringen g1 156
Torrington, Connecticut, U.S.A. g3 257
Torrington, Wyoming, U.S.A. b3 260
Torrita di Siena f7 197
Torroal b6 191
Torroella de Montgrí h2 192
Torrön d5 154
Torronsuon kansallispuisto k2 157
Torrox g8 191
Torrox, Punta de g8 191
Torsa Chhu j6 135
Torsås g4 156
Torsborg d5 154
Torsby e2 156
Torshälla g3 156
Tórshavn B 152
Torsminde b2 158
Torsö e3 156
Torsvåg g1 154
Torsvatnet b1 156
Torteval c3 182
Tortkuduk q2 121
Tortola, Isla e2 285
Tórtoles de Esgueva f3 190
Tortoli Ab3 198
Tortona c5 196
Tortora e5 198
Tortoreto c2 198
Tortorici d6 199
Tortosa e4 192
Tortuera c4 192
Tortuga, Isla A 286
Tortuga, Laguna e2 275
Tortugas g2 297
Tortuguero, Parque Nacional f5 277
Tortum h2 209
Torūd g4 137
Torul g2 209
Toruń g2 168
Torup e4 156
Tõrva l3 157
Torvizcón a8 193
Torvløysa b1 156
Torvsjö f4 154
Tory Island c1 165
Tory Sound c1 164
Toržok c3 150
Torzym d3 168
Tosa e5 114
Tosa, Cima e3 196
Tosashimizu e5 114
Tosbotn d4 154
Tosca e2 234
Toscana e6 197
Toscano, Arcipelago e7 197
Toscolano-Maderno e4 196
Tosham b5 130
Tōshima-yama j1 115
Tosno a2 150
Toson Hu q1 125
Tossa g3 192
Tossal de l'Orri f2 192
Tossal de la Baltasana f3 192
Tossal de Suró f3 192
Tostado d1 294
Tōstamaa k3 157
Tostedt c5 158
Tosto, Cabo a1 190
Tosya g2 208
Toszek g5 168
Tot'ma g2 151
Tota, Lago c2 284
Totak b3 156
Totana c7 193
Totapola A 127
Totatiche c3 274
Toteng c3 232
Totenkopf c4 174
Tõtes g3 183
Tótkomlós j5 171
Totnes c6 163
Totness f2 285
Totolapan f5 275
Totolapilla g5 275
Tototepec f4 275
Totomica g2 151
Totonicapán b3 276
Totontepec g5 275
Totoral, Arg. d1 296
Totoral, Chile b1 294
Totoralejos d1 294
Totoras g2 297
Totota c4 222
Tototlán c3 274
Totoya E 74
Totson Mountain e2 246
Tottenham h12 81
Totton e6 163
Tottori, Japan e4 114
Tottori f4 114
Totutla f4 275
Tótvázsony f4 171
Touba, C.I. c4 222
Touba, Sen. a3 222
Toubkal, Jbel c2 220
Toubkal, Parc National c2 220
Touboro c2 224
Touch b5 187
Touchet d2 262
Toucy j5 183
Toudaohu c6 112
Tougan d3 222
Touggourt f2 221
Tougouri d3 222
Tougué b3 222
Touil b2 222
Toukoto c3 222
Toul b2 184
Toulépleu c4 222
Touliu n7 105
Toulnustouc j3 253
Toulon b7 185
Toulon-sur-Arroux a4 184
Toulouges e6 187
Toulouse d5 187
Toumodi c4 222
Toungo g4 223
Toungoo c6 102
Touques, Fr. f3 183
Touques f3 183
Toura, Monts c4 222
Touraine f5 183
Touraine, Val de f5 183
Toural b2 190
Tourba h3 223
Tourcoing b4 159
Touriñán, Cabo a1 190
Tourkovigla, Akra, Grc. a4 210
Tourkovigla, Akra, Grc. d6 211
Tourlaville d3 182
Tournai b4 159
Tournavista c1 292
Tournay c5 187
Tourndo, Oued g4 221
Tournon-d'Agenais c4 187
Tournon-St-Martin c2 186
Tournon-sur-Rhône a5 185
Tournus a4 184
Touros e3 288
Tourouvre f4 183
Tourrette-Levens d7 185
Tours f5 183
Tourteron c5 159
Toury g4 183
Tous, Embalse de d5 193
Toussiana d3 222
Toussidé, Pic a3 218
Toussoro, Mont d2 224
Toutalga c6 191
Touwsrivier d6 234
Toužim a1 170
Töv c2 112
Tovačov f2 170
Tovar c2 284
Tovarkovo c4 150
Tovarkovskij e5 150
Tove e4 163
Tovuz g4 149
Tow Law e2 162
Towada-Hachimantai National Park j1 115
Towada-ko j1 115
Towai e1 76
Towakaima f2 285
Towanda d3 256
Towari l7 99
Towcester f4 163
Tower g7 250
Tower City d4 256
Tower Hamlets h3 162
Tower Peak d3 264
Towerhill Creek a2 84
Towner c6 250
Townsend, Massachusetts, U.S.A. j2 257
Townsend, Montana, U.S.A. h2 262
Townsend, Mount f3 83
Townsends Inlet f5 256
Townshend Island d3 84
Townsville h5 80
Towori, Teluk l6 99
Towot f2 225
Towr Kham e3 128
Towraghondi a3 128
Towson d5 256
Towuti, Danau l6 99
Toxkan He s7 121
Toy e1 264
Toyah h2 272
Tōya-ko Ab2 114
Toyama, Japan g3 115
Toyama g3 115
Toyama-wan g3 115
Toyang p8 113
Toykut n4 169
Toymskardlia d4 154
Toyohashi g4 115
Toyokawa g4 115
Toyooka f4 114
Toyoshina g3 115
Toyota g4 115
Toyotomi Ab1 114
Töysä j5 155
Toytepa m7 121
Tozeur f2 221
Tozi, Mount g2 247
Tozitna g2 247
Tqibuli j1 209
Tqvarch'eli h1 209
Tra Ban h5 104
Tra Vinh h11 103
Trabanca d3 190
Trabazos d3 190
Traben-Trarbach f5 159
Trabia c7 199
Trablous d2 138
Trabzon, Tur. g2 209
Trabzon g2 209
Trachi c5 210
Trachila, Akra c6 211
Trachili e4 210
Tracino b8 199
Tracy, Can. f5 252
Tracy, U.S.A. e2 260
Tradewater c7 254
Trafalgar, Cabo d8 191
Trafford h1 162
Traful b6 296
Tragacete c4 192
Traian g4 201
Traid c4 192
Traiguén, Chile b5 295
Traiguén, Araucania, Chile a5 296
Traiguera e4 192
Trail e1 262
Traipu e3 288
Trairí e3 288
Trairi e2 288
Traisen g1 177
Traiskirchen h1 177
Traismauer g1 177
Traitsching h3 175
Trajano de Morais g5 291
Trakai, Lith l5 157
Trakai n1 169
Trakt g3 147
Tralee b4 165
Tralee Bay b4 165
Tramacastilla c4 192
Tramán Tepuí e2 285
Tramazzo f5 197
Tramonti di Sopra g3 196
Tramore d4 165
Tramuntana, Serra de f5 193
Tranås f3 156
Tranbjerg d2 158
Trancas d5 292
Tranco de Beas, Embalse del b6 193
Trancoso, Braz. j2 291
Trancoso c4 190
Tranebjerg d3 158
Tranemo e4 156
Trang a2 101
Trangan j7 97
Trangie h12 81
Trängslet e2 156
Traní f3 198
Tranoroa Ab3 233
Tranquera, Embalse de la c3 192
Tranqueras k1 297
Tranquilla b2 296
Transantarctic Mountains w2 298
Transcona e6 250
Trans-en-Provence c7 185
Transfiguracion e4 275
Transtrand e2 156
Trapani, Sicilia, Italy b7 199
Trapani b6 199
Trapiche d2 296
Trappenkamp d4 158
Trapper Peak f3 262
Trappes h4 183
Traralgon h15 81
Trarza b2 222
Trasacco c3 198
Trashigang m6 125
Trasimeno, Lago b1 198
Träslövsläge f1 158
Trasmiras c2 190
Trasobares c3 192
Trás-os-Montes e Alto Douro c3 190
Trasvase Tajo-Segura, Canal de — b5 193
Trasvase, Canal de — b5 193
Trat f9 103
Traun f1 177
Traun, Ger. h5 175
Traunreut d2 176
Traunstein d2 176
Trave f2 173
Travellers Lake c1 82
Traver d5 265
Travers, Mount d4 77
Traverse City d3 254
Travesía Puntana d3 296
Travessão h4 291
Travis, Lake a4 258
Travnik c3 200
Travo A 185
Trawangan j9 99
Trayning c12 87
Trbovlje g3 177
Trbuk k5 171
Trebatice f3 171
Trebatsch k3 173
Trebbia d5 196
Trebbin j3 173
Trebebvić d4 200
Trebel h2 173
Třebenice b1 170
Trèbes e5 187
Trèbeurden b4 182
Třebíč d2 170
Trebinje d4 200
Trebisacce f5 198
Trebišov k3 171
Trebnje g4 177
Trebolares f3 297
Třeboň f1 177
Trebsen j1 175
Trebujena d8 191
Trecate c4 196
Trecchina e4 198
Trecenta f4 196
Treene e1 172
Treffort-Cuisiat b4 184
Treffurt d1 174
Tregaron c4 163
Trégastel b4 182
Tregosse Islets and Reefs k4 80
Treguaco a4 296
Tréguier b4 182
Trégunc b5 182
Treia, Ger. c4 158
Treia, Italy h6 197
Treignac d3 186
Treinta y Tres, Ur. f2 294
Treinta y Tres, Treinta y Tres, Ur. f2 294
Treis f4 159
Trelawney B 266
Trelde Næs c3 158
Trelew c4 295
Trelleborg e5 156
Trélon c4 159
Tremadog Bay b4 162
Tremblant, Mont e5 252
Trembleur Lake e4 248
Tremelo c4 159
Tremiti, Isole e2 198
Tremont d4 256
Tremonton g5 262
Třemošná b2 170
Tremp e2 192
Trenche f4 252
Trenčianska Teplá g3 171
Trenčianska Turná g3 171
Trenčianske Jastrabie g3 171
Trenčiansky kraj g3 171
Trenčín g3 171
Trendelburg e4 172
Trenel e3 297
Trêng f9 103
Trenggalek f9 98
Trenque Lauquén f3 297
Trensacq b4 187
Trent f3 162
Trentino - Alto Adige f3 196
Trento, Italy e3 196
Trento f3 196
Trenton, Can. h3 255
Trenton, Florida, U.S.A. h5 259
Trenton, Georgia, U.S.A. g2 259
Trenton, Kentucky, U.S.A. f1 258
Trenton, Missouri, U.S.A. e3 260
Trenton, New Jersey, U.S.A. f4 256
Trenton, North Carolina, U.S.A. l2 259
Treppeln k3 173
Trepuzzi h4 198
Tres Algarrobas f3 297
Tres Arboles j2 297
Tres Arroyos g5 297
Três Bicos c6 290
Tres Bocas, Arg. h2 297
Tres Bocas, Ur. j2 297
Tres Cerros c5 295
Três Corações f4 291
Tres Cruces, Arg. d4 292
Tres Cruces, Chile b1 294
Tres Cruces, Cerro a3 276
Tres Cruces, Nevados c1 294
Tres Esquinas, Col. b3 284
Tres Esquinas, Ur. j3 297
Três Irmãos, Represa c4 290
Tres Isletas e5 293
Três Lagoas b4 290
Tres Lagos c5 295
Tres Lomas f4 297
Tres Marias f3 291
Três Marias, Represa f3 291
Tres Matas d2 284
Tres Montes, Golfo b5 295
Tres Montes, Península b5 295
Tres Palos e5 275
Tres Picachos, Sierra f3 272
Tres Picos, Arg. b4 295
Tres Picos, Arg. f5 297
Tres Picos, Mex. h6 275
Tres Picos, Cerro, Arg. g5 297
Tres Picos, Cerro, Mex. f5 275
Tres Piedras b4 261
Três Pontas f4 291
Tres Porteñas c2 296
Tres Puentes b1 294
Tres Puntas, Cabo c5 295
Tres Ranchos e3 290
Três Rios g5 291
Tres Sargentos h3 297
Três Unidos d1 292
Tres Valles f4 275
Tresana d5 197
Tresco A 163
Trescore Balneario d4 196
Tresigallo f5 196
Tresjuncos b5 193
Treska b1 210
Tresnuraghes Aa2 198
Trespaderne g2 190
Třešť d2 170
Trets b7 185
Tretten d2 156
Treuchtlingen f4 175
Treuen h2 175
Treuenbrietzen h3 173
Trevelín b4 295
Trevi g7 197
Trévières e3 182
Treviglio d4 196
Treviño b2 192
Treviso, Italy g4 196
Treviso g4 196
Trevorton d4 256
Trévoux a5 185
Trezanos Pinto g1 297
Trézelles f2 186
Trezevant e2 258
Trgovište f4 201
Trhové Sviny f1 177
Triabunna Ab2 211
Triaize Ab3 83
Triangle d6 182
Triangle, The c6 256
Trianta d2 102
Tribal Areas Ad2 211
Tribulation, Gunung d4 128
Tricarico j2 99
Tricase f4 198
Tricesimo c3 199
Trichardtsdal h3 196
Trichonida, Limni j2 235
Trichur b4 210
Tricot e7 126
Trida h3 183
Trieben g12 81
Trier, Ger. f2 177
Trier b2 174
Trieste, Italy e5 159
Trieste h4 196
Trieste, Gulf of h4 196
Trie-sur-Baïse e4 176
Trieux c5 187
Triftern b4 182
Triggiano e1 176
Triglav f3 198
Trigno e3 176
Trigrad d3 198
Triguerros e1 210
Trikala d7 191
Trikalitikos c4 183
Trikeri, Grc. b3 210
Trikeri c5 210
Trikeri, Akra d5 211
Trikomon d3 210
Trikora, Puncak d6 211
Trilby b1 138
Trill k6 97
Trillick h5 259
Triloknath f3 297
Trilport c3 130
Trim h4 183
Trincheras e3 165
Trincomalee h10 263
Trindade, Braz. g8 126
Trindade, Beja, Port d2 290
Trindade, Bragança, Port c7 191
Trinec c3 190
Tring g2 171
Tringia f5 163
Trinidad, Bol. b3 210
Trinidad, Cuba e2 293
Trinidad, Mex. e4 266
Trinidad, Trin. E 271
Trinidad, Colorado, U.S.A. b4 261
Trinidad, U.S.A. a3 258
Trinidad, Ur. j2 297
Trinidad and Tobago h6 241

TRINIDAD & TOBAGO

THE REPUBLIC OF TRINIDAD AND TOBAGO
Area 5128km² (1980sq miles)
Capital Port of Spain, on Trinidad
Organizations ACS, CARICOM, COMM, IADB, SELA
Population 1,280,000
Pop. growth (%) 1.2
Life expectancy 71 (m); 76 (f)
Languages English, French, Spanish, Indi, Chinese
Literacy 98.6%
Currency Trinidad and Tobago dollar (US $1 = 6.15 Trinidad and Tobago dollar)
GDP (US million $) 9000
GDP per head ($US) 7031

Trinidad, Golfo a5 295
Trinidad, Isla g5 297
Trinità d'Agultu Aa2 198
Trinitapoli f3 198
Trinity, California, U.S.A. b5 262
Trinity, Texas, U.S.A. b4 258
Trinity Bay, Aust. A 84
Trinity Bay, Can. r4 253
Trinity Islands f4 246
Trino c4 196
Trins c2 176
Trionto, Capo f5 199
Triora b6 197
Tripa c14 103
Tripiti, Akra b5 210
Tripkau g2 173
Tripoli c5 211
Tripoli, Ash Shamāl, Leb. d2 138
Tripoli, Leb. e5 208
Tripoli, Libya g2 221
Tripolitania g2 221
Tripotama b5 211
Triptis g2 175
Tripunittura e8 126
Tripura m8 125
Trisanna b3 176
Trischen d1 172
Tristan da Cunha Fracture Zone j13 302
Tristenspitze e3 176
Trisul d4 130
Trittau d5 158
Triunfo, Pernambuco, Braz. e3 288
Triunfo, Braz. e2 293
Triunfo, Hond. d4 276
Trivandrum e8 126
Trivento d3 198
Trivero c4 196
Trnava, Czech Rep. f2 171
Trnava, Slvk. f3 171
Trnavá Hora g3 171
Trnavský kraj f3 171
Troarn e3 182
Trochtelfingen e4 174
Troekurovo, Lipeckaja Oblast', Russ. Fed. e5 150
Troense d3 158
Trofa b3 190
Trofaiach f2 177
Trofali, Akra a3 210
Trofors d4 154
Trogir d3 200
Trogkofel e3 176
Troia e3 198
Tróia b6 191
Troica, Russ. Fed. m3 147
Troica, Rjazanskaja Oblast', Russ. Fed. f4 150
Troick, Čeljabinskaja Oblast', Russ. Fed. k5 147
Troick, Respublika Mordovija, Russ. Fed. g4 151
Troickij Sungur j5 151
Troickoe, Altajskij Kraj, Russ. Fed. v1 121
Troickoe, Orenburgskaja Oblast', Russ. Fed. m5 151
Troickoe, Respublika Kalmjkija - Halm'g-Tangč, Russ. Fed. g3 149
Troicko-Pečorsk j3 147
Troina d7 199
Trois Fourches, Cap des d1 220
Trois Seigneurs, Pic des d6 187
Trois-Cornes, Puy des d2 186
Troisdorf f4 159
Trois-Pistoles h4 252
Trois-Rivières, Can. f5 252
Trois-Rivières, Guad. C 271
Troizina c4 210
Trollhättan e3 156
Tromba Grande, Cabo e4 289
Trombetas f4 285
Tromen, Volcán b4 296
Tromie d2 164
Trompsburg f5 235
Troms g2 154
Tromsa d2 156
Tromsdalen g2 154
Tromsø g2 154
Tromvik g2 154
Trona f6 265
Troncoso c2 274
Trondheim c5 154
Trondheimsfjorden c5 154
Trones d4 154
Trongsa m6 125
Tronville-en-Barrois b2 184
Tronzano Vercellese c4 196
Troo f5 183
Troödos a2 138
Troödos, Mount a2 138
Troon d4 164
Tropea e6 199
Tropeiros, Serra dos c5 289
Tropojë e4 200
Troš h2 147
Trosa g3 157
Troškūnai l5 157
Trosna d1 148
Trossin h4 173
Trossingen d4 174
Trostan e1 165
Trostberg d1 176
Trostyanets', Sums'ka Oblast', Ukr. d2 148
Trostyanets', Vinnyts'ka Oblast', Ukr. j1 201
Troulloi b1 138
Troup Head f2 164
Trout Creek f2 262
Trout Lake, British Columbia, Can. e3 242
Trout Lake, Ontario, Can. g5 250
Trout Run c3 256
Troutville g7 254
Troviscal b5 191
Trovolhue a5 296
Trowbridge d5 163
Trowutta Aa2 83
Troy, Alabama, U.S.A. g4 259
Troy, Montana, U.S.A. f1 262
Troy, New Hampshire, U.S.A. h2 257
Troy, New York, U.S.A. g2 257
Troy, Ohio, U.S.A. d5 254
Troy, Pennsylvania, U.S.A. d3 256
Troy, Tennessee, U.S.A. e1 258
Troy, Texas, U.S.A. a4 258
Troy Peak f6 263
Troyan g4 201
Troyanka k1 201
Troyes k4 183
Troyits'ke k2 201
Trpanj g1 198
Trpejca a2 210
Tršice f2 170
Trstená h2 171
Trstenik e4 200
Trstín f3 170
Truandó b2 284
Trubčevsk d1 148
Trubia, Spain d1 190
Trubia e1 190
Truchas d2 190
Truckee, California, U.S.A. c2 264
Truckee, California, U.S.A. c2 264
Trudfront g3 149
Truer Range k8 86
Trujillanos d6 191
Trujillo, Hond. e3 276
Trujillo, Peru b2 292
Trujillo e5 191
Trujillo, Ven. c2 284
Trujillo, Trujillo, Ven. c2 284
Trujillo Alto A 270
Trulben c3 174
Trumann d2 258
Trumansburg d2 256
Trumbull g3 257
Trumbull, Mount g7 263
Trumon c14 103
Trün f4 201
Trun f4 183
Trundle h12 81
Truro, Can. l6 253
Truro, U.K. a6 163
Trusan, Malay. h2 99
Trusan h2 99
Trușeşti h2 201
Truskavets' m6 169
Trustrup d2 158
Truth or Consequences b5 261
Trutnov d1 170
Truyère f4 186
Truženik c2 150
Tryavna g4 201
Trybukhivtsi g1 201
Trygona b3 210
Tryon h2 259
Trypimeni b1 138
Trypiti, Akra e7 211
Trysil e2 156
Tryškiai k4 157
Trzcianka, Mazowieckie, Pol. k3 169
Trzcianka, Wielkopolskie, Pol. e2 168
Trzciel d3 168
Trzebiatów d1 168
Trzebiechów d3 168
Trzebiel c4 168
Trzebież c2 168
Trzebinia h5 169
Trzebnica f4 168
Trzeciewiec g2 168
Trzemeszno f3 168
Tržič f3 177
Trzrcińsko Zdrój c3 168
Ts'khinvali j1 209
Tsada a2 138
Tsagaan Ovoo g1 112
Tsagaannuur k2 113
Tsaka La d3 130
Tsakartsianos a4 210
Tsalenjikha j1 209
Tsama I b4 224
Tsao c3 232
Tsaramandroso Ab2 233
Tsaratanana Ab2 233
Tsaratanana, Massif du Ab1 233
Tsaratanana, Réserve de Ab1 233
Tsarevo h4 201
Tsarimir g4 201
Tsaris Mountains b2 234
Tsavo East National Park b4 226
Tsebrykove k2 201
Tsengel a1 112
Tses c2 234
Tsetseng e1 234
Tsetserleg a2 112
Tsévié e4 223
Tshabong e3 234
Tshako d5 224
Tshane d2 234
Tshela b4 224
Tshesebe d3 233
Tshibwika d5 224
Tshikapa, D.R.C. d5 224
Tshikapa d5 224
Tshilenge d5 224
Tshimbo e5 225
Tshimbulu d5 224
Tshinsenda d1 233
Tshitanzu d5 224
Tshitupa d5 224
Tshiumbe d5 224
Tshofa e5 225
Tsholotsho d2 233
Tshootsha d1 234
Tshopo e3 225
Tshumbiri c4 224
Tsiigehtchic l2 247
Tsimanampetsotsa, Réserve de Aa3 233
Tsineng e3 234
Tsinjomay Ab2 233
Tsintsabis b2 232
Tsiombe Ab4 233
Tsiroanomandidy Ab2 233
Tsitsikamma Forest and Coastal National Park f6 234
Tsitsutl Peak e5 248
Tsnori g4 149
Tsolo h5 235
Tsomo g6 235
Tsotili b2 210
Tsoulou, Réserve de b4 224
Tsqaltubo j1 209
Tsubame h3 115
Tsubata g3 115
Tsuchiura j3 115
Tsugarū-kaikyō j1 115
Tsul-Ulaan c2 112
Tsumeb b2 232
Tsumis Park b1 234
Tsumkwe c2 232
Tsuru h4 115
Tsuruga g4 115
Tsurugi g3 115
Tsurugi-san f5 114
Tsuruoka h2 115
Tsushima c4 114
Tsuyama f4 114
Tswaane d1 234
Tsyelyakhany p3 169
Tua c4 224
Tua, Port c3 190
Tuakau e2 76
Tual j7 97
Tuam c3 165
Tuamarina d4 77
Tuamoto Ridge n7 301
Tuamotu, Archipel des K 75
Tuân Giao f5 102
Tuanfeng d4 106
Tuangku c14 103
Tuapeka Mouth b7 77
Tuapí f3 277
Tuapse e3 148
Tuatapere a7 77
Tuath, Loch a' b1 164
Tūbā d4 138
Tubac h10 263
Tuban g8 98
Tubarão c7 289
Tūbās d4 139
Tubau g3 98
Tubbataha Reefs b6 100
Tubbercurry c2 165
Tubigan c7 100
Tubilla del Agua g2 190
Tübingen, Ger. e4 174
Tübingen e4 174
Tubize c4 159
Tubmanburg b4 222
Tubod d6 100
Tubruq b1 218
Tubuai K 75
Tubutama h10 263
Tuc de les Carants e2 192
Tucacas d1 284
Tucandera e4 285
Tucannon e2 262
Tucano e4 288
Tucapel b4 296
Tucapel, Punta a4 296
Tucavaca, Bol. f3 293
Tucavaca, Santa Cruz, Bol. f3 293
Tuchan e6 187
Tucheng b4 111
Tuchheim h3 173
Tuchola f2 168
Tuchomie f1 168
Tuchów k6 169
Tuckanarra d10 87
Tuckerman d2 258
Tuckerton f5 257
Tučkovo d4 150
Tucson h9 263
Tucuco c2 284
Tucumán c1 294
Tucumcari c5 261
Tucunuco c2 294
Tucuparé f5 285
Tucupita e2 285
Tucuruí e2 288
Tucuruí, Represa c2 288
Tuczna m4 169
Tuczno e2 168
Tudeà e3 158
Tudela c2 192
Tudela de Duero f3 190
Tudor Vladimirescu h3 201
Tudora h2 201
Tudu m3 157
Tudweiliog b4 162
Tuela c3 190
Tueré b2 288
Tuerto e2 190
Tufayh m8 136
Tuffé f4 183
Tugalovo m4 147
Tugela j4 235
Tugela Ferry j4 235
Tugidak Island f4 246
Tuglung n4 125
Tugnug Point e5 100
Tuguegarao c2 100
Tugulym l4 147
Tugwi e3 233
Tugyl v4 121
Tuhai He e1 111
Tuhemberua c15 103
Tui b2 190
Tuichi d2 292
Tuilianpui n8 125
Tuineje Ae2 189
Tuira j6 277
Tujmazy h5 147
Tukan j5 147
Tukangbesi, Kepulauan n7 99
Tukarak Island p2 251
Tukayel d2 226
Tukche f5 135
Tukhavichy p3 169
Tukhtamish g2 128
Tukituki f3 76
Tükrah b1 218
Tuktoyaktuk, Can. l1 247
Tuktut Nogait National Park e2 242
Tukums k4 157
Tukung, Bukit f5 98
Tukuyu a5 231
Tul'chyn j1 201
Tul'skaja Oblast' d5 150
Tul'skoye q1 121
Tula, Italy Aa2 198
Tula, Hidalgo, Mex. e3 275
Tula, Mex. e2 275
Tula, Russ. Fed. d4 150
Tulagt Ar Gol m1 125
Tulahuén b1 296
Tulak a4 128
Tulancingo e3 275
Tulangbawang c7 98
Tulare d5 265
Tulare Lake Bed d5 265
Tularosa b5 261
Tulasi h3 126
Tulbagh c6 234
Tulcán b3 284
Tulcea, Rom. j3 201
Tulcea j3 201
Tulčík k2 171
Tulcingo e4 275
Tule Mod f3 113
Tulehu h6 97
Tulette a6 185
Tulgheş g2 201
Tulia c5 261
Tulik Volcano b5 247
Tuliszków g3 168
Tulit'a n2 247
Tulkarm d4 139
Tulla c4 165
Tullahoma f2 258
Tullamore d3 165
Tulle d3 186
Tullebølle d4 158
Tullibigeal h12 81
Tullins b5 185
Tulln h1 177
Tullos c4 258
Tullow e4 165
Tully, Queensland, Aust. A 84
Tully h4 80
Tully, U.S.A. d2 256
Tully Falls A 84
Tulnici h3 201
Tulpan j3 147
Tulppio m3 155
Tulsa b1 258
Tulsequah a2 248
Tulsipur f5 135
Tulsk c3 165
Tuluá b3 284
Tuluceşti j3 201
Tuluksak d3 246
Tulum, Mex. p7 273
Tulum, Quintana Roo, Mex. r7 273
Tulumayo b2 292
Tulun c2 94
Tulungagung f9 98
Tulu-Tuloi, Serra e3 285
Tuma, Nic. e4 276
Tuma f5 150
Tumaco b3 284
Tumaco, Rada de b3 284
Tumain m3 125
Tuman, Ozero l4 147
Tumannyj q2 155
Tumanovo c4 150
Tumatumari f2 285
Tumba, D.R.C. d4 224
Tumba, Swe. g3 157
Tumba, Lac c4 224
Tumbalá a2 276
Tumbangmiri g5 98
Tumbangsamba g5 98
Tumbao e7 100
Tumbarumba j13 81
Tumbes, Peru a4 284
Tumbes, Tumbes, Peru a4 284

Tumbiscatio c4 274
Tumby Bay c13 81
Tumen, Jilin, China q4 113
Tumen, Shaanxi, China b3 106
Tumen Jiang q4 113
Tumenzi b7 112
Tumeremo e2 285
Tumereng e2 285
Tumindao b8 100
Tumiritinga h3 291
Tumkur e6 126
Tummel e3 164
Tumon Bay C 74
Tump a7 129
Tumpah h5 99
Tumpat c2 101
Tumputiga, Gunung m5 99
Tumshuk c1 128
Tumu d3 222
Tumucumaque, Serra g3 285
Tumudibandh h3 127
Tumuja d5 191
Tumupasa d2 292
Tumusla d4 292
Tumut j13 81
Tumut, New South Wales, Aust. f2 83
Tumwater b2 262
Tumxuk t7 121
Tuna e9 129
Tuna Bay d7 100
Tunapuna E 271
Tunari d3 292
Tunas de Zaza e4 266
Tunbridge Wells, Royal g5 163
Tunceli, Tur. g3 209
Tunceli g3 209
Tundla d6 130
Tundun-Wada f3 223
Tunduru b6 227
Tundzha h4 201
Tunga f4 223
Tungabhadra e5 126
Tungabhadra Reservoir d5 126
Tungaru f1 225
Tungawan d7 100
Tungku b8 100
Tungla e4 276
Tungsten m3 247
Tungue, Baía de c6 231
Tungun, Bukit g4 98
Tungurahua b4 284
Tuni h4 126
Tunica d2 258
Tunis g1 221
Tunis, Golfe de g1 221
Tunisia c1 216

TUNISIA

THE TUNISIAN REPUBLIC
Area 163,610km^2
(63,170sq miles)
Capital Tunis
Organizations COMM, LAS, NAM, OIC
Population 9,780,000
Pop. growth (%) 1.1
Life expectancy 68 (m); 70 (f)
Languages Arabic, Berber, French
Literacy 74.2%
Currency Tunisian dinar
(US $1 = 1.23 Tunisian dinar)
GDP (US million $) 21,272
GDP per head ($US) 2175

Tunja c2 284
Tunjang b2 101
Tunkás q7 273
Tunkhannock e3 256
Tunkhannock Creek e3 256
Tunki e4 276
Tunliu c1 106
Tunna d1 156
Tunnsjøen d4 154
Tunø d3 158
Tunošna f3 150
Tunstall h4 163
Tuntou e1 111
Tuntutuliak d3 246
Tununak c3 246
Tunuyán, Arg. d2 296
Tunuyán, Mendoza, Arg. c2 296
Tunzi d2 106
Tuo He e3 111
Tuo Jiang e4 104
Tuoheji e3 106
Tuoji Dao g1 111
Tuolumne, California, U.S.A. c4 264
Tuolumne, California, U.S.A. c4 264
Tuomioja k4 155
Tuoniang Jiang e6 104
Tüp s6 121
Tupã c4 290
Tupaciguara d3 290
Tupai K 75
Tupana e4 285
Tupanaóca e4 285
Tupanciretã b7 289
Tuparro d3 284
Tupelo e2 258
Tupi Paulista c4 290
Tupinambarama, Ilha f4 285
Tupiza d4 292
Tuplice c4 168
Tupper Lake j3 255
Tuptugur, Ozero k1 120
Tupungato c2 296
Tupungato, Cerro c2 296
Tuqiao e4 111
Tuquan l3 113
Túquerres b3 284
Tur''ye m6 169
Tura, India m7 125
Tura, Russ. Fed. l3 119
Turabah, Hā'īl, Sau. Ar j7 136
Turabah, Makkah, Sau. Ar f3 219
Turagua, Serranía e2 285
Turakina e4 76
Turan Lowland j6 120
Turangi e3 76
Turano g7 197
Turano, Lago di h7 197
Turar Ryskulov n6 121
Turawa g5 168
Turayf g6 136
Turbaco k5 277
Turbat a7 129
Turbenthal c2 196
Turbo j6 277
Turčianske Teplice g3 171
Turco d3 292
Turda f2 201
Turdine a5 185
Turégano f3 190
Tūreh m4 137
Tureia K 75
Turek g3 168
Turenki l2 157
Turgay, Kaz. j3 120
Turgay, Akmolinskaya Oblast', Kaz. p2 121
Turgay, Kostanayskaya Oblast', Kaz. j3 120
Turgayskaya Dolina k2 120
Turgayskaya Stolovaya Strana LA j2 120
Turgeon p6 251
Turgojak k5 147
Tŭrgovishte, Bul. h4 201
Tŭrgovishte h4 201
Turgut, Konya, Tur. c3 208
Turgut, Muğla, Tur. b4 208
Turgutlu a3 208
Turhal f2 209
Türi l3 157
Turi g4 198
Turia d5 193
Turiaçu, Braz. c2 288
Turiaçu, Maranhão, Braz. c2 288
Turiaçu, Baía de c2 288
Turiamo d1 284
Turiapo d2 292
Turie g2 171
Turin b4 196
Turinsk k4 147
Turinskaja-Sloboda l4 147
Turís d5 193
Turiya n4 169
Turiys'k n4 169
Turka m6 169
Turkana, Lake b3 226
Turkestan m6 121
Turkestan Range d1 128
Túrkeve j4 171
Turkey a5 92

TURKEY

THE REPUBLIC OF TURKEY
Area 779,452km^2
(300,948sq miles)
Capital Ankara
Organizations CE, EBRD, ECO, IDB, NATO, OECD, OIC
Population 69,630,000
Pop. growth (%) 1.2
Life expectancy 66 (m); 71 (f)
Languages Turkish, Kurdish
Literacy 86.5%
Currency Turkish lira
(US $1 = 1440000 Turkish lira)
GDP (US million $) 181,700
GDP per head ($US) 2609

Turkey, U.S.A. f3 260
Turkey Creek j5 86
Türkheim f4 175
Turki f2 149
Türkmen Dağı c3 208
Turkmenabat a1 128
Turkmenbashi j4 149
Turkmengala a2 128
Turkmenistan c5 92

TURKMENISTAN

TURKMENISTAN
Area 488,100km^2
(188,456sq miles)
Capital Ashgabat
Organizations CIS, EBRD, ECO, OIC
Population 4,835,000
Pop. growth (%) -0.7
Life expectancy 62 (m); 68 (f)
Languages Turkmen (Latin-based script), Russian, Uzbek, Kazakh
Literacy 98%
Currency Turkmen manat
(US $1 = 5200 Turkmen manat)
GDP (US million $) 7300
GDP per head ($US) 1509

Turkmenkarakul' a3 128
Turkmenskiy Zaliv d8 120
Türkoğlu f4 209
Turks and Caicos Islands (U.K.) g7 241
Turks Islands j4 271
Turku k2 157
Turkwel b3 226
Turleque g5 191
Turley b1 258
Turlock c4 264
Turmalina g2 291
Turmantas m5 157
Turmus, Wādī at f2 219
Turňa nad Bodvou j3 171
Turnaco, Rada de b3 284
Turnagain, Cape f4 76
Turneffe Islands d2 276
Turner, Mount c8 87
Turnhout c3 159
Türnitz g2 177
Turnor Lake n3 249
Turnov d1 170
Turnu Măgurele g4 201
Turobin l5 169
Turočak w1 121
Turon f1 83
Turovec f2 150
Turów l4 169
Turquino, Pic f4 266
Turrach e3 176
Turrell d2 258
Turri Aa3 198
Turrialba f6 277
Turriers c6 185
Turriff f2 164
Turs'kyy Kanal n4 169
Tursāq k5 137
Tursi f4 198
Tursunckij Tuman, Ozero l3 147
Turtkul' h7 120
Turtle Flambeau Flowage b2 254
Turtle Islands, Phil. k1 99
Turtle Islands, S. L. b4 222
Turtle Lake n5 249
Turugart Pass q7 121
Turuhansk j3 118
Turvelândia c2 290
Turvo, Braz. c2 290
Turvo, Braz. d4 290
Turvo, Braz. d5 290
Turvo, Paraná, Braz. c6 290
Turynka n5 169
Turzovka g2 171
Ţūs g9 120
Tús b6 193
Tusa d7 199
Tuscaloosa f3 258
Tuscaloosa, Lake f3 258
Tuscania f7 197
Tuscarawas f5 254
Tuscarora Mountains c4 256
Tuscola, Illinois, U.S.A. b6 254
Tuscola, Texas, U.S.A. d5 261
Tuscumbia f2 258
Tuse e3 158
Tushchybas, Zaliv g5 120
Tuskegee g3 259
Tussey Mountains c4 256
Tussøya f2 154
Tustna b5 154
Tuszyn h4 169
Tutajev e3 150
Tutak j3 209
Tutia Khel e4 128
Tuticorin f8 126
Tutoh h3 99
Tutong h2 99
Tutrakan h3 201
Tuttle d7 250
Tuttle Creek Reservoir d4 260
Tuttlingen d5 174
Tutuala h7 97
Tutubu f5 225
Tutuila M 75
Tutume d3 232
Tütüncü a2 208
Tutunendo b2 284
Tutupaca, Volcán d3 292
Tututalak Mountain d2 246
Tututepec f5 275
Tutwiler d2 258
Tutzing g5 175
Tuul Gol c1 112
Tuun-bong q5 113
Tuusjärvi, Fin. m1 157
Tuusjärvi m5 155
Tuvalu g3 73

TUVALU

TUVALU
Area 26km^2 (10sq miles)
Capital Fongafale, on Funafuti atoll
Organizations COMM, SPC, PIF
Population 10,000
Pop. growth (%) 0
Life expectancy 62 (m); 65 (f)
Languages Tuvaluan, English
Literacy 95%
Currency Australian dollar
(US $1 = 1.34 Australian dollar)
GDP (US million $) 9
GDP per head ($US) 900

Tuvuka E 74
Tuwau j4 99
Tuwayq, Jabal, Sau. Ar g2 219
Tuwayq, Jabal, Sau. Ar g3 219
Tuxcacuesco c4 274
Tuxer Gebirge g1 177
Tuxford f3 162
Tuxpan, Mex. f3 275
Tuxpan, Jalisco, Mex. c4 274
Tuxpan, Nayarit, Mex. b3 274
Tuxpan, Veracruz, Mex. f3 275
Tuxtla Chico a3 276
Tuxtla Gutiérrez h5 275
Tuy Hoa j9 103
Tuya Lake b2 248
Tuyên Quang g5 102
Tūysarkān m4 137
Tuyuk s6 121
Tuz Gölü d3 208
Tuz Khurmātū k4 137
Tuža j3 151
Tuzla, Bos. d3 200
Tuzla, Rom. j3 201
Tuzla, Çanakkale, Tur. g3 210
Tuzla, Tur. e4 208
Tuzla Gölü a2 208
Tuzsér l3 171
Tuzugu a3 218
Tvååker f1 158
Tvärån h4 154
Tvåråsen e2 156
Tvedestrand c3 156
Tver' c3 150
Tverrådalskyrkja b2 156
Tverrlimyran c4 154
Tverskaja Oblast' c3 150
Tversted d1 158
Tvis b2 158
Tvrdošovce g3 171
Tvŭrditsa g4 201
Twardogóra f4 168
Twee Rivier c2 234
Twee Rivieren d3 234
Tweed f4 164
Tweede Exloërmond e2 159
Tweedmouth f4 164
Tweeling h3 235
Tweespruit g4 235
Twente e2 159
Twentynine Palms e8 263
Tweya c4 224
Twilight b2 234
Twin Falls, Can. k2 253
Twin Falls, U.S.A. f4 262
Twin Hills d4 246
Twin Lakes h4 259
Twin Peak c2 264
Twin Peaks c14 87
Twins Creek d10 81
Twisp c1 262
Twist f2 159
Twiste e4 172
Twistringen d3 172
Twitchen Reservoir c6 265
Twizel c6 77
Two Harbors h7 250
Two Rivers c3 254
Twofold Bay g3 83
Twyford e5 163
Ty Ty h4 259
Tyachiv f1 201
Tychówko e2 168
Tychowo e2 168
Tychy g5 168
Tyczyn l6 169
Tydal c5 154
Tygda h2 94
Tyin c2 156
Tykhero g1 210
Tykocin l2 169
Tyler b3 258
Tylertown d4 258
Tylösand f2 158
Tylstrup c1 158
Tympaki e7 211
Týn nad Vltavou c2 170
Tynda g1 94
Tyndrum d3 164
Tyne f4 164
Týnec nad Labem d1 170
Týnec nad Sázavou c2 170
Tynset d1 156
Tyonek g3 246
Tyräjärvi m4 155
Tyrawa Wołoska l6 169
Tyrifjorden d2 156
Tyringe e4 156
Tyrma r1 113
Tyrnävä k4 155
Tyrnavos c3 210
Tyrnjauz f4 149
Tyrone, New Mexico, U.S.A. a5 261
Tyrone, Pennsylvania, U.S.A. b4 256
Tyrrell, Lake c2 82
Tyrrhenian Sea e8 197
Tyshkivka k1 201
Tysmenytsya g1 201
Tysnesøy a2 156
Tysse a2 156
Tyssedal b2 156
Tystrup Sø e3 158
Tyszowce m5 169
Tythøa c1 156
Tytuvėnai k5 157
Tyub-Karagan, Mys b5 120
Tyulen'i Ostrova b5 120
Tyuyamuyunskoye Vodokhranilishche h7 120
Tyva, Respublika b2 94
Tyvriv j1 201
Tywa k2 173
Tywi c5 163
Tywyn b4 163
Tzaneen j1 235
Tzermiado f7 211
Tzucacab q7 273
Tzummarum d1 159

U

Ua Huka K 75
Ua Pu K 75
Uaboe B 74
Uacauyén e3 285
Uainambi d3 284
Uamanda c2 232
Uara d4 284
Uari f1 293
Uarini d4 285
Uaruma d3 284
Uatumã f4 285
Uauá e3 288
Uauaris e3 285
Uaupés, Braz. d3 284
Uaupés, Amazonas, Braz. d4 284
Uaxactún c2 276
Ubá g4 291
Uba u2 121
Übach-Palenberg e4 159
Ubaí f2 291
Ubaporanga g3 291
Ubate c2 284
Ubatuba f5 291
Ubauro d6 129
Ubaye c6 185
Ubayyiḍ, Wādī al h6 136
Ubby e3 158
Ube r9 113
Úbeda g6 191
Uberaba e3 290
Uberaba, Lagoa f3 293
Uberlândia d3 290
Überlingen e3 174
Überlinger See e5 174
Ubiña, Peña e1 190
Ubiratã b6 290
Ubolratna Dam f7 102
Ubombo k3 235
Ubon Ratchathani g8 102
Ubondo e4 225
Ubrique e8 191
Ubstadt-Weiher d3 174
Ubundu e4 225
Ucacha f2 297
Učaly j5 147
Ucar g4 149
Ucayali, Peru c2 292
Ucayali, Peru c5 284
Uceda g4 190
Ucero a3 192
Uch, Balochistan, Pak. d6 129
Uch, Punjab, Pak. e6 129
Uch-Adzhi a1 128
Ūchān n3 137
Ucharal t4 121
Uchi Lake g5 250
Uchiura-wan Ab2 114
Uchiza b1 292
Uchkuduk j6 120
Uchkyay c2 128
Uchsay k4 149
Uchte, Ger. g3 173
Uchte d3 172
Ucieza f2 190
Ucker j2 173
Ückeritz k1 173
Uckermark j2 173
Uckfield g6 163
Ucon h4 262
Ucross b2 260
Uda Walawe Reservoir A 127
Udačnyj m3 119
Udagamandalam e7 126
Udaipur, Rajasthan, India b6 130
Udaipur, Tripura, India m8 125
Udaipur Garhi k6 125
Udalguri n6 125
Udanti h9 124
Udaquilla h4 297
Udavské k3 171
Uday d2 148
Udayagiri f5 126
Udbina b3 200
Uddeholm e2 156
Uddevalla d3 156
Uden d3 159
Udero Lal d8 129
Udgir e3 126
Udhampur b3 130
Udhruḥ d6 139
Udimskij h1 151
Udine, Italy h3 196
Udine h3 196
Udintsey Fracture Zone n9 301
Udit f7 129
Udmurckaja Respublika m3 151
Udomlja c3 150
Udon Thani f7 102
Udskaja Guba k1 94
Udumalaippettai e7 126
Udupi d6 126
Udyl', Ozero k2 94
Udzungwa Mountains National Park g5 225
Uëbonti l5 99
Ueckermünde k2 173
Ueda h3 115
Uekuli l5 99
Uel'kal' u3 118
Uele d3 224
Uelen b2 246
Uelsen e2 159
Uelzen f3 173
Ueno g4 115
Uenohara h4 115
Uere e3 225
Uetersen c5 158
Uettingen e3 174
Uetze f3 172
Ufa, Russ. Fed. j5 147
Ufa h5 147
Uffenheim f3 174
Uffing am Staffelsee g5 175
Ufra j4 149
Ugab a3 232
Ugak Bay f4 246
Ugāle k4 157
Ugalla f5 225
Ugalla River Game Reserve f5 225
Uganda f4 217

UGANDA

THE REPUBLIC OF UGANDA
Area 241,139km^2
(93,104sq miles)
Capital Kampala
Organizations COMESA, COMM, OIC
Population 24,750,000
Pop. growth (%) 2.9
Life expectancy 41 (m); 42 (f)
Languages English, Luganda, other local languages
Literacy 69.8%
Currency new shilling
(US $1 = 1942.5 new shilling)
GDP (US million $) 5860
GDP per head ($US) 236

Ugarteche c2 296
Ugashik e4 246
Uge c4 158
Ugento h5 198
Ugerløse e3 158
Uggerby d1 158
Ughelli f4 223
Ugie h5 235
Ugíjar a8 193
Ugine c5 185
Uglegorsk l3 94
Uglič e3 150
Ugljan b3 200
Uglovka b2 150
Uglovskoe t2 121
Ugol'noe q3 119
Ugra c4 150
Uğurlu f2 210
Ugut n3 147
Uharte-Arakil c2 192
Uherské Hradiště f2 170
Uherský Brod f2 171
Uhingen e4 174
Úhlava b2 170
Uhldingen e5 174
Uhlenhorst b1 234
Uhniv m5 169
Uhrichsville f5 254
Uhta h3 147
Uhyst k4 173
Uibaí d4 288
Uig b2 164
Uíge, Ang. c5 224
Uíge c5 224
Ŭijŏngbu p7 113
Ŭiju n5 113
Uil d3 120
Uimaharju n5 155
Uinskoe j4 147
Uinta j5 262
Uinta Mountains h5 262
Ŭiryŏng q8 113
Uis Mine a3 232
Ŭisŏng q7 113
Uitenhage f6 235
Uithuizen e1 159
Uithuizermeeden e1 159
Ujae D 74
Ujelang G 74
Újezd u Brna e2 170
Újfehértó k4 171
Ujhani d6 130
Uji-guntō c6 114
Ujiji e4 225
Ujjain g9 129
Újkér e4 170
Ujohbilang h4 99
Ujście e2 168
Ujście Warty, Park Narodowy c3 168
Ujskoe k5 147
Újszász j4 171
Újszentiván j5 171
Újszentmargita k4 171
Ujung Kulon National Park c8 98
Ujung Raja c14 103
Ujung Tamiang d13 103
Ukal Sagar f10 129
Ukara Island f4 225
Ukata f3 223
Ukerewe Island f4 225
Ukhahlamba Drakensberg Park h4 235
Ukhrul p7 125
Ukiah, California, U.S.A. b6 262
Ukiah, Oregon, U.S.A. d3 262
Ukleja l2 173
Ukmergė l5 157
Ukraine l5 145

UKRAINE

UKRAINE
Area 603,700km^2
(233,090sq miles)
Capital Kiev
Organizations BSEC, CE, CIS, EBRD
Population 48,900,000
Pop. growth (%) -0.6
Life expectancy 62 (m); 73 (f)
Languages Ukrainian (Cyrillic script), Russian, Romanian, Hungarian, Polish
Literacy 99.7%
Currency hryvnya
(US $1 = 5.34 hryvnya)
GDP (US million $) 41,200
GDP per head ($US) 842

Ukrainka, Vostochnyy Kazakhstan, Kaz. u2 121
Ukrainka, Vostochnyy Kazakhstan, Kaz. u3 121
Ukrina j5 177
Uksjanskoe k5 147
Uku b6 224
Uku-jima c5 114
Ukuma b1 232
Ukwi d1 234
Ukwi Pan d1 234
UL Bend National Wildlife Refuge a2 260
Ul'ba u2 121
Ul'gili l2 121
Ul'janiha d2 150
Ul'janovo, Kaliningradskaja Oblast', Russ. Fed. l1 169
Ul'janovo, Kalužcskaja Oblast', Russ. Fed. c5 150
Ul'janovsk k4 151
Ul'janovskaja Oblast' j5 151
Ul'kayak j3 120
Ul'ken Sulutar q6 121
Ul'ken-Karoy, Ozero n2 121
Ul't-Jagun n3 147
Ul'yanovka k1 201
Ul'yanovo m7 121
Ul'yanovskiy p2 121
Ūla n2 169
Ula b4 208
Ula Tirso Aa2 198
Ulaan Nuur b3 112
Ulaanbaatar, Mong. d2 112
Ulaanbaatar d2 112
Ulaan-Ereg e2 112
Ulaanhudag c2 112
Ulaan-Uul f3 112
Ulak Island Ac2 247
Ulan f1 83
Ulan Bator d2 112
Ulan Buh Shamo d6 112
Ulan Erge g3 149
Ulan Tohoi a5 112
Ulan Ul Hu k2 135
Ulanbel' n5 121
Ulan-Hol g3 149
Ulanhot m2 113
Ulanów l5 169
Ulansuhai Nur e5 112
Ulan-Ude d2 94
Ulapes d1 296
Ulapes, Sierra d1 296
Ulaş f3 209
Ulastai w6 121
Ulaya b5 227
Ulbjerg c2 158
Ulchin q7 113
Ulcinj d5 200
Ulco f4 234
Uldum c3 158
Uldz, Mong. h1 112
Uldz f1 112
Ulefoss c3 156
Ulei F 74
Uleila del Campo b7 193
Ulen e7 250
Ulëz d5 200
Ulfborg b2 158
Ulft e3 159
Ulgain Gol k3 113
Ulhasnagar c3 126
Uliaga Island b5 246
Uliastay b3 94
Ulič l3 171
Ulindi e4 225
Ulita c1 146
Ulithi G 74
Uljuan tekojärvi l4 155
Ulla b2 190
Ulladulla k13 81
Ullapool c2 164
Ullared f1 158
Ullatti h3 154
Ullava j5 155
Ullavanjärvi k5 155
Ulldecona e4 192
Ulldemolins e3 192
Ullerslev d3 158
Üllés h5 171
Ullibarri, Embalse de b2 192
Ullin e1 258
Ullmer, Mount jj2 298
Ulloma d3 292
Ullsfjorden g2 154
Ullswater d2 162
Ullŭng-do r7 113
Ŭllyul n6 113
Ulm e4 174
Ulm, U.S.A. h2 262
Ulmarra l10 81
Ulme b5 191
Ulmen e4 159
Ulmeni, Călăraşi, Rom. h3 201
Ulmeni, Maramureş, Rom. f2 201
Ulongue e1 233
Uloya h2 154
Ulricehamn e4 156
Ulrichsberg e1 176
Ulsan q8 113
Ulsberg b5 154
Ulsta A 164
Ulsted d1 158
Ulsteinvik a1 156
Ulster d3 256
Ulster Canal d2 165
Ulstrup, Vestsjælland, Den. d3 158
Ulstrup, Viborg, Den. c2 158
Ulsvåg e2 154
Ultima f13 81
Ultzama c2 192
Ulu n3 99
Ulu Kali, Gunung b4 101
Ulu Soh, Gunung b3 101
Ulúa c3 276
Ulubat Gölü b2 208
Uluborlu c3 208
Uludağ b2 208
Ulukışla e4 208
Ulundi j4 235
Ulungur He m1 117
Ulungur Hu w4 121
Uluṟu k9 87
Uluṟu-Kata Tjuṯa National Park k9 87
Ulverston c2 162
Ulverstone Ab2 83
Ulvinsalon luonnonpuisto n5 155
Ulvsjön g1 156
Ulysses c4 261
Ulytau l3 121
Ulytau, Gory l3 121
Uly-Zhylanshyk k3 120
Umag e4 176
Umala d3 292
Umán q7 273
Uman' k1 201
Umarao b6 129
Umaria g8 124
Umarkhed e3 126
Umarkot, India h3 126
Umarkot, Pak. d8 129
Umatilla d3 262
Umayan e6 100
Umba q3 155
Umbai c4 101
Umbakumba c2 80
Umbelasha d2 224
Umbele m6 99
Umbertide g6 197
Umbria b2 198
Umbriatico f5 199
Umeå h5 154
Umeälven g4 154
Umera h6 97
Umet g4 151
Umfolozi j4 235
Umfolozi Game Reserve j4 235
Umfors e4 154
Umfreville Lake f5 250
Umirzak h4 149
Umkomaas j5 235
Umlazi j4 235
Umm al Qaywayn q9 137
Umm ar Raşāş d5 139
Umm at Qalbān h8 136
Umm Bāb n9 137
Umm Bāţinah d3 138
Umm Bel c5 218
Umm el Fahm d4 138
Umm Farud a2 218
Umm Ḩamāţ d5 139
Umm Ḩarb f8 136
Umm Keddada c5 218
Umm Khushayb, Jabal a6 139
Umm Lajj f9 136
Umm Qaşr l6 137
Umm Qays d4 138
Umm Ruwaba d5 218
Umm Sa'ad c1 218
Umm Sa'īd, Bi'r b7 139
Umm Saggat, Wadi b4 218
Umm Sa'id n9 137
Umm Saiyala d5 218
Umm Şalāl 'Alī n9 137
Umm Walad e4 138
Ummanz j1 173
Umnak Island b5 246
Umnak Pass c5 246
Umnäs f4 154
Umpilua b6 227
Umpqua b4 262
Umpulo b1 232
Umred f9 124
Umreth f9 129
Ŭmsŏng p7 113
Umtamvuna Nature Reserve j5 235
Umtata h5 235
Umtentweni j5 235
Umuahia f4 223
Umuarama b5 290
Umurbey a2 208
Umurlu a4 208
Umzimkulu h5 235
Umzinto j5 235
Una, Bos. h5 177
Una, Braz. e3 288
Una, Braz. e5 289
Una, India c4 130
Uña c4 193
Una, Mount d5 77
'Unāb, Wādī al e6 139
Unadilla e2 256
Unaí e2 291
Unalakleet d3 246
Unalaska c5 246
Unalaska Island c5 246
Unalga Island Ac2 247
Unango f1 233
Unare, Laguna de d1 285
Unari, Fin. k3 155
Unari k3 155
Unauna l5 99
'Unayzah, Jordan d6 139
'Unayzah, Sau. Ar j8 137
Unchaulia e6 130
Uncompahgre Plateau a4 260
Undara National Park g5 80
Unden f3 156
Underberg h4 235
Underbool e13 81
Undersåker d5 154
Underwood c7 250
Undløse e3 158
Undu, Tanjung l10 99
Undur j6 97
Undva nina j3 157
Uneča d1 148
Uneiuxi d4 284
Unga Island d5 246
Ungarie h12 81
Ungava Bay r4 243
Ungava, Péninsule d' q3 243
Ungheni, Mol. h2 201
Ungheni, Rom. g2 201
Ungurași g2 201
Ungwana Bay c4 226
Unhais da Serra c4 190
Uni l3 151
União, Acre, Braz. c1 292
União, Minas Gerais, Braz. c3 290
União, Piauí, Braz. d2 288
União da Vitória b7 289
União do Marará e4 285
União dos Palmares e3 288
Uniara g7 129
Unicoi h1 259
Uničov f2 170
Uniejów g4 168
Unieux a5 185
Unije f5 177
Unilla c3 284
Unimak Pass c5 246
Unini, Braz. e4 285
Unini, Peru c2 292
Unión, Arg. e3 296
Unión, Para. f4 293
Union, New Jersey, U.S.A. f4 257
Union, South Carolina, U.S.A. j2 259
Union, West Virginia, U.S.A. f7 254
Union Bridge c5 256
Union Camp c2 276
Union City, California, U.S.A. a4 264
Union City, Georgia, U.S.A. g3 259
Union City, Michigan, U.S.A. d4 254
Union City, Tennessee, U.S.A. e1 258
Unión de Tula b4 274
Unión Hidalgo g5 275
Unión Juárez a3 276
Union Springs g3 259
Union Valley Reservoir c3 264
Uniondale e6 234
Uniontown g6 254
Unionville, Michigan, U.S.A. e4 254
Unionville, Pennsylvania, U.S.A. c4 256
Unionville, Virginia, U.S.A. c6 256
United a4 256
United Arab Emirates c6 92

UNITED ARAB EMIRATES

THE UNITED ARAB EMIRATES
Area 77,700km^2
(30,000sq miles)
Capital Abu Dhabi
Organizations CAEU, CCASG, IDB, LAS, OAPEC, OIC, OPEC
Population 2,940,000
Pop. growth (%) 5.9
Life expectancy 73 (m); 77 (f)
Languages Arabic, English
Literacy 77.8%
Currency UAE dirham
(US $1 = 3.67 UAE dirham)
GDP (US million $) 67,382
GDP per head ($US) 22,919

United Kingdom d3 144

UNITED KINGDOM

THE UNITED KINGDOM OF GREAT BRITAIN AND NORTHERN IRELAND
Area 241,752km² (93,341sq miles)
Capital London
Organizations CE, COMM, EBRD, EU, G8, NATO, OECD, SPC
Population 59,756,000
Pop. growth (%) 0.3
Life expectancy 74 (m); 79 (f)
Languages English, Welsh
Literacy 99%
Currency pound sterling (US $1 = 0.57 pound sterling)
GDP (US million $) 1,545,000
GDP per head ($US) 25,855

United States of America d5 241

UNITED STATES

THE UNITED STATES OF AMERICA
Area 9,809,155km² (3,787,319sq miles)
Capital Washington D.C.
Organizations G8, IADB, NAFTA, NATO, OECD, SPC
Population 291,040,000
Pop. growth (%) 1.3
Life expectancy 73 (m); 79 (f)
Languages English, Spanish
Literacy 95%
Currency US dollar
GDP (US million $) 10,456,000
GDP per head ($US) 35,926

Uniti g5 196
Unity n5 249
University City a6 254
Unjha f9 129
Unkel f4 159
Unken d2 176
Unkurda j5 147
Unna c4 172
Unnao g6 124
Unnukka m1 157
Uno, Ilha de a3 222
Ünp'a n6 113
Unquillo e1 297
Unsan n5 113
Ŭnsan p6 113
Unst A 164
Unstrut f1 175
Unțeni h2 201
Unter Engadin e3 196
Unter Inn Thal g1 177
Unteres Odertal, Nationalpark k2 173
Unterfranken f2 174
Unterhaching g4 175
Untermaßfeld f2 174
Unterschleißheim g4 175
Untersteinach g2 175
Unterueckersee j2 173
Unterweißenbach f1 177
Unturán, Sierra de e3 285
Unža h2 151
Unzen-Amakusa National Park d5 114
Unzen-dake d5 114
Uozu g3 115
Upano b4 284
Upata e2 285
Upavon e5 163
Upemba, Lac e5 225
Upemba, Parc National de l' e5 225
Upernaviarsuk v3 243
Upernavik t1 243
Upi e7 100
Upía c3 284
Úpice e1 170
Upington d4 234
Upleta e10 129
Upnuk Lake e3 246
Upolu M 75
Uporovo l4 147
Upper Alkali Lake c5 262
Upper Arlington e5 254
Upper Arrow Lake h6 248
Upper Blackville k5 253
Upper Demerara - Berbice f2 285
Upper Humber p4 253
Upper Iowa f3 260
Upper Kalskag d3 246
Upper Klamath Lake b4 262
Upper Lake a2 264
Upper Liard c1 248
Upper Lough Erne d2 165
Upper Marlboro d6 256
Upper Nile f2 225
Upper Red Lake e1 260
Upper Salmon Reservoir p4 253
Upper Takaka d4 77
Upper Takutu - Upper Essequibo f3 285
Upper Ugashik Lake e4 246
Uppingham f4 163
Upplands-Väsby g3 157
Uppsala, Swe. h2 157
Uppsala g3 157
Upright, Cape b3 246
Upsala h6 250
Upshi c3 130
Upstart Bay b1 84
Upstart, Cape b1 85
Upton g1 259
Upton upon Severn d4 163
'Uqlat aş Şuqūr j9 137
Ura e4 138
Urabá, Golfo de b2 284
Ūrāf r6 137
Urahoro Ac2 114
Uraiújfalu e4 170
Uraj l3 147
Urakawa Ac2 114
Ural, Aust. e1 83
Ural, Kaz. k1 149
Ural Mountains j3 147
Ural'sk h2 149
Ural'skij Hrebet j3 147
Uralla k11 81
Urambo f5 225
Urana h13 81
Urana, Lake e2 83
Urandangi d6 80
Urandi d4 289
Uranium City n2 249
Uraricoera, Braz. e3 285
Uraricoera, Roraima, Braz. e3 285
Uras Aa3 198
Uraucaima, Serra e3 285
Urawa h4 115
Uray'irah m9 137
'Urayq Sāqān g2 219
Urbana c1 258
Urbania g6 197
Urbano Santos d2 288
Urbel g2 190
Urbino g6 197
Urbino, Étang d' A 185
Urbión b2 192
Určice f2 170
Urcos c2 292
Urd Tamir Gol a2 112
Urda, Kaz. g2 149
Urda, Spain g5 191
Urdampolleta g4 297
Urdax-Urdazuli c1 192
Urdinarrain h2 297
Urdoma g3 146
Urdos b6 187
Urdzhar t4 121
Ure e2 162
Urelik a2 246
Uren' h3 151
Urengoj h3 118
Urenui e3 76
Urépararapa F 74
Urepel a5 187
Ures h11 263
Urewera National Park f3 76
Urga h4 151
Urgench h7 120
Ürgüp e3 208
Urgut c1 128
Urho v4 121
Urho Kekkosen kansallispuisto l2 155
Uri b2 130
Uriah, Mount c4 77
Uribante c2 284
Uribe, Canal b6 295
Uriburu f4 297
Urie f2 164
Urim c5 139
Uripitijuata, Cerro c4 274
Urique f4 272
Uri-Rotstock c3 196
Uritskiy l5 147
Urituyacu b4 284
Urjala k2 157
Urjupinsk f2 149
Urk d2 159
Urla a3 208
Urlați h3 201
Urlingford d4 165
Urluk d1 112
Urman j5 147
'Urmān e4 138
Urmary j4 151
Urmetan d1 128
Urmi s1 113
Urola b1 192
Ürön h4 171
Uromi f4 223
Uroševac e4 200
Ūroteppa d1 128
Urretxu b1 192
Urroz c2 192
Urru Co h4 135
Urrunaga, Embalse de b2 192
Úrsulo Galván e2 275
Ursulo Galván f4 275
Urt, Fr. a5 187
Urt, Mong. a4 112
Urt Moron n1 125
Uruáchic e4 272
Uruaçu c4 289
Uruana d1 290
Uruapan, Baja California Norte, Mex. e10 263
Uruapan, Michoacán, Mex. c4 274
Urubamba, Peru c2 292
Urubamba, Cusco, Peru c2 292
Urubu f4 285
Urucara f4 285
Urucu e4 285
Uruçuí d3 288
Uruçuí Preto d3 288
Uruçuí, Serra do d3 288
Urucuia, Braz. f2 291
Urucuia, Minas Gerais, Braz. f2 291
Urucum f3 293
Urucuricaia, Ilha b2 288
Urucurituba f4 285
Uruguai b7 289
Urugua-í, Embalse b7 289
Uruguaiana e1 294
Uruguay e6 283

URUGUAY

THE ORIENTAL REPUBLIC OF URUGUAY
Area 176,215km² (68,037sq miles)
Capital Montevideo
Organizations IADB, MERCOSUR, SELA, LAIA
Population 3,361,000
Pop. growth (%) 0.6
Life expectancy 70 (m); 78 (f)
Languages Spanish
Literacy 97.8%
Currency Uruguayan peso (US $1 = 29.21 Uruguayan peso)
GDP (US million $) 11,824
GDP per head ($US) 3518

Uruguay, Arg. h2 297
Ürümqi w6 121
Urunga l11 81
Uruno Point C 74
Urup f3 148
Urup, Ostrov r5 119
Ururi e3 198
Urussu m4 151
Urutaí, Ilha b2 288
Uruti e3 76
Uruwira f5 225
Uryl' w3 121
Urzędów l5 169
Urziceni, Ialomița, Rom. h3 201
Urziceni, Satu Mare, Rom. l4 171
Urzulei Ab2 198
Uržum l3 151
Usa, Russ. Fed. j2 147
Usa, Russ. Fed. k5 151
Usada c8 100
Usagre d6 191
Uşak, Tur. b3 208
Uşak b3 208
Usakos b3 232
Usambara Mountains g4 225
Usborne, Mount e6 295
Ušće e4 200
Usčerp'e c1 148
Uscio d5 197
Usedom, Ger. k2 173
Usedom j2 173
Usellus Aa3 198
Ushanovo u3 121
Usharal n6 121
Ushayqir k9 137
Ushtobe r5 121
Ushuaia c6 295
Usi n5 113
Usina b3 288
Usingen d2 174
Usini Aa2 198
Usinsk j2 147
Usk, Wales, U.K. d5 163
Usk, U.K. d5 163
Usk, U.S.A. e1 262
Uskedal a3 156
Uslar e4 172
Usman' e1 148
Usmas ezers k4 157
Usmat c1 128
Uso e5 191
Usogorsk g3 146
Usoke f5 225
Usol'e k5 151
Usol'ye-Sibirskoye c2 94
Usov f2 170
Uspallata c2 296
Uspen'e g2 151
Uspenka r1 121
Uspenskiy p3 121
Ussassai Ab3 198
Usseglio b4 196
Ussel e3 186
Usses b4 185
Usson-du-Poitou c2 186
Usson-en-Forez f3 186
Ussuri s2 113
Ussurijsk r4 113
Ust'-Bagarjak k4 147
Ust'-Barguzin d2 94
Ust'-Cil'ma h2 147
Ust'-Džeguta f3 148
Ust'e, Russ. Fed. e3 150
Ust'e, Tambovskaja Oblast', Russ. Fed. f5 150
Ust'e, Vologodskaja Oblast', Russ. Fed. e2 150
Ust'e, Vologodskaja Oblast', Russ. Fed. g2 151
Ust'-Ilimsk c1 94
Ust'-Ilimskij
Vodohranilišče l4 119
Ust'-Ilja g1 112
Ust'-Ilyč j3 147
Ust'ja h1 151
Ust'-Kalmanka u1 121
Ust'-Kamenogorsk u3 121
Ust'-Kan v2 121
Ust'-Kara l1 147
Ust'-Kišert' j4 147
Ust'-Koksa v2 121
Ust'-Kujga p2 119
Ust'-Kulom h3 147
Ust'-Kut d1 94
Ust'-Labinsk e3 148
Ust'Išim m4 147
Ust'-Luga n3 157
Ust'-Lyža j2 147
Ust'-Maja p3 119
Ust'-Man'ja k3 147
Ust'-Nera q3 119
Ust'-Olenek m2 119
Ust'-Omčug q3 119
Ust'-Ordynskij Burjackij Avtonomnyj Okrug c2 94
Ust'-Ordynskiy c2 94
Ust'-Pinega e2 146
Ust'-Šonoša f1 150
Ust'-Ulagan w2 121
Ust'-Uls j3 147
Ust'-Unja j3 147
Ust'-Usa j2 147
Ust'-Voja j2 147
Usta h3 151
Usta Muhammad d6 129
Ustaoset c2 156
Ustaritz a5 187
Ústecký kraj b1 170
Úštěk c1 170
Uster c2 196
Ustevatn b2 156
Ústí nad Labem c1 170
Ústí nad Orlicí e2 170
Ustjuckoe c3 150
Ustjužna d2 150
Ustka e1 168
Ustovo e1 210
Ustrem, Bul. h4 201
Ustrem, Russ. Fed. l2 147
Ustroń g6 168
Ustronie Morskie d1 168
Ustrzyki Dolne l6 169
Ustyluh n5 169
Ustyurt Plateau e5 120
Usu v5 121
Usulután c4 276
Usumacinta o9 273
Usurbil b1 192
Uszód g5 171
Uta k6 97
Utah h6 262
Utah Lake h5 262
Utajärvi l4 155
Utashinai Ac2 114
'Utaybah e3 138
Utayyiq m8 137
Utcubamba b5 284
Utebo d3 192
Utembo c2 232
Utena b3 264
Uterlai e8 129
Utete b5 227
Uthai Thani e8 102
Uthal c8 129
Utiariti f2 293
Utica, Michigan, U.S.A. e4 254
Utica, New York, U.S.A. j4 255
Utiel c5 193
Utikuma Lake k4 249
Utila d2 276
Utinga d4 288
Utladalen b2 156
Utlängan f4 156
Utö h3 157
Utopia b7 80
Utracán e4 297
Utrecht, Neth. d2 159
Utrecht, Neth. d2 159
Utrecht, R.S.A. j3 235
Utrera e7 191
Utrik D 74
Utrillas d4 192
Utroja m4 157
Utsjoki l2 155
Utskor e2 154
Utsunomiya h3 115
Utta g3 149
Uttar Pradesh d6 130
Uttaradit e7 102
Uttaranchal d4 130
Uttarkashi d4 130
Uttendorf d2 176
Utterån g5 154
Utting am Ammersee g4 175
Uttoxeter e4 162
Utu Magalua L 75
Utuado A 270
Utubulak w4 121
Utukok d1 246
Utva d2 120
Uulu l3 157
Uurainen, Fin. m1 157
Uurainen k5 155
Uusikaupunki j2 157
Uutapi a2 232
Uva, Col. c3 284
Uva m3 151
Uva, Sri L. A 127
Uvåg e2 154
Uval Karabaur f6 120
Uval Muzbel' e6 120
Uvalda h3 259
Uvalde k3 273
Úvaly c1 170
Uvarovka c4 150
Uvarovo f2 149
Uvat m4 147
Uvdal c2 156
Uvea, Île L 75
Úvecik g3 210
Uvel'ka k5 147
Uvel'skij k5 147
Uvinza f5 225
Uvira e4 225
Uvongo j5 235
Uvs a3 94
Uvs Nuur k4 118
Uwajima e5 114
'Uwaynāt Wannīn g3 221
'Uwayriḍ, Ḥarrat al LF e2 219
Uweinat, Jebel c3 218
Uwi d4 98
Uxbridge j2 257
Uxin Ju e6 112
Uxmal p7 273
Uxpanapa g5 275
Uy k5 147
Uyaly h5 120
Üydzin d3 112
Uyo f4 223
Uyu Chaung b3 102
Uyuk n6 121
Uyun m9 137
'Uyûn Mûsa a7 139
Uyuni, Salar de d4 292
Uza g1 149
Užava j4 157
'Uzaym, Nahr al k5 209
Uzbekistan d4 92

UZBEKISTAN

THE REPUBLIC OF UZBEKISTAN
Area 447,400km² (172,740sq miles)
Capital Tashkent
Organizations CIS, EBRD, ECO, OIC
Population 25,370,000
Pop. growth (%) 1.3
Life expectancy 65 (m); 71 (f)
Languages Uzbek (Latin script), Russian, Kazakh
Literacy 99.3%
Currency som (US $1 = 977.06 som)
GDP (US million $) 7877
GDP per head ($US) 310

Uzdin e3 200
Uzel c4 182
Uzerche d3 186
Uzès a6 185
Uzh c2 148
Uzhhorod l3 171
Uzhok l3 171
Užice d4 200
Uzlovaja e5 150
Uzmyony m5 157
Uzola g3 151
Uzun d1 128
Uzunagach, Almatinskaya Oblast', Kaz. r6 121
Uzunbulak v5 121
Uzunköprü h5 201
Uzunkuyu a3 208
Uževntis k5 157
Uzynkair h5 120

V

V. J. José Perez d3 292
Va d2 224
Vaajakoski l1 157
Vaal f4 234
Vaal Dam h3 235
Vaala l4 155
Vaalajärvi k3 155
Vaalbos National Park f4 234
Vaals e4 159
Vaalwater h2 235
Vaasa h5 154
Vaassen d2 159
Vabalninkas l5 157
Vabkent k7 120
Vabre e5 187
Vác h4 171
Vacaria b7 289
Vacaria, Campo da b7 289
Vacaria, Serra a4 290
Vacaville b3 264
Vaccarès, Étang de a7 185
Vacha f2 174
Váchartyán h4 171
Vacoas C 231
Vad, Russ. Fed. g5 151
Vad h4 151
Vada c3 126
Vadakste k4 157
Vădăstrița g4 201
Väddö h3 157
Vadehavet b3 158
Vādeni h3 201
Vadheim a2 156
Vadi c5 126
Vadinsk g5 151
Vadnagar f9 129
Vado Ligure c5 197
Vado, Embalse del a4 192
Vadodara f9 129
Vadsø m1 155
Vadstena f3 156
Vadu Crișului l5 171
Vadu Moților l5 171
Vadum c1 158
Vaduz e2 174
Væggerløse e4 158
Været b5 154
Værøy c3 154
Vaga e3 146
Vagaj m4 147
Vågåmo c2 156
Vaganski Vrh b3 200
Vagar B 152
Vaggatem m2 155
Vaggeryd f4 156
Vaglio Basilicata e4 198
Vagos b4 190
Vågsele g4 154
Våh g2 171
Vähäkyrö j5 155
Vahanga K 75
Vahhābī r7 137
Vahitahi K 75
Vahtan j3 151
Vaiaku N 75
Vaiano f6 197
Vaiden e3 258
Vaigai f8 126
Vaiges e4 182
Vaihingen an der Enz d4 174
Vaijapur d3 126
Väike-Maarja m3 157
Väike-Pakri k3 157
Vailala L 75
Vailly-sur-Aisne b5 159
Vailly-sur-Sauldre h5 183
Vaiņode j4 157
Vainosjärvi m2 155
Vaippar f8 126
Vairaatea K 75
Vairano Scalo d3 198
Vaire c6 185
Vairowal b4 130
Vaison-la-Romaine b6 185
Vaitupu N 75
Vaja l4 171
Vajszló f6 171
Vajta g5 171
Vajukosken allas l3 155
Vakaga, C.A.R. d2 224
Vakaga, C.A.R. d2 224
Vakhsh, Taj. d1 128
Vakhsh d2 128
Vaksdal a2 156
Val del Ticino, Parco della c4 196
Val Marie p7 249
Val'tevo f2 147
Valachchenai g9 126
Vålådalen d5 154
Vålådalen naturreservat d5 154
Valadouro c1 190
Valamaz m3 151
Vålån d5 154
Valandovo c1 210
Valareña c2 192
Valašská Bystřice g2 171
Valašská Polanka f2 171
Valašské Klobouky g2 171
Valašské Meziříčí f2 171
Vålberg e3 156
Valbo g2 156
Valbona d4 193
Valbondione e3 196
Valbonnais b6 185
Valbornedo, Embalse de b2 192
Vâlcănești g3 201
Vâlcea g3 201
Valcheta d6 296
Valcuerna e3 192
Val-d'Isère c5 185
Val-d'Izé d4 182
Val-d'Oise h3 183
Val-d'Or h1 255
Valdagno f4 196
Valdahon c3 184
Valdaj, Novgorodskaja Oblast', Russ. Fed. b3 150
Valdaj, Respublika Karelija, Russ. Fed. q5 155
Valdajskaja Vozvyšennost' b3 150
Valdavia f2 190
Valdeazogues f6 191
Valdecaballeros e5 191
Valdecañas, Embalse de e5 190
Valdecarros e4 190
Valdecilla g1 190
Valdecuenca c4 192
Valdefuentes d5 191
Valdeganga c5 193
Valdelamusa d7 191
Valdelinares d4 192
Valdemanco del Esteras f6 191
Val-de-Marne b3 182
Valdemārpils k4 157
Valdemarsvik g3 156
Valdemeca c4 193
Valdemedé d6 191
Valdemembra c5 193
Val-de-Meuse b2 184
Valdense j3 297
Valdeobispo, Embalse de d4 190
Valdeolivas b4 192
Valdepeñas g6 191
Valdepeñas de Jaén g7 191
Valderaduey e3 190
Valderas g3 183
Valderice b6 199
Valderiès e4 187
Valderrobres e4 192
Valdés g3 297
Valdés, Península d4 295
Val-des-Bois j3 255
Valdetorres e5 191
Valdevimbre e2 190
Valdez h3 247
Valdice d1 170
Valdisotto e3 196
Valdivia, Chile a5 296
Valdivia, Col. k7 277
Valdobbiadene f4 196
Valdoie c3 184
Valdosa g3 190
Valdosta h4 259
Valdres c2 156
Valdunquillo e2 190
Vale, Chad c3 182
Vale, Geor. j2 209
Vale de Açor, Beja, Port c7 191
Vale de Açor, P ortalegre, Port c5 191
Vale de Cambra b4 190
Vale de Cavalos b5 191
Vale de Espinho d4 190
Vale de Estrela c4 190
Vale de Gaio, Barragem de b6 191
Vale de Prazeres c4 190
Vale de Reis b6 191
Vale do Peso c5 191
Vale Verde j2 291
Valea Ciorii h3 201
Valea lui Mihai l4 171
Valea Lungă, Alba, Rom. g2 201
Valea Lungă, Dâmbovița, Rom. g3 201
Valeggio sul Mincio e4 196
Valença, Braz. e4 288
Valença b2 190
Valença do Piauí d3 288
Valençay g5 183
Valence, Midi-Pyrénées, Fr. c4 187
Valence, Rhône-Alpes, Fr. a6 185
Valence-d'Albigeois e4 187
Valence-sur-Baïse c5 187
Valencia, Comunidad Valenciana, Spain d5 193
Valencia d5 193
Valencia, Ven. d1 284
Valencia de Alcántara c5 191
Valencia de Don Juan e2 190
Valencia de las Torres d6 191
Valencia del Ventoso d6 191
Valencia Island a5 165
Valencia, Golfo de d5 193
Valenciennes b4 159
Vălenii de Munte h3 201
Valensole b7 185
Valensole, Plateau de c7 185
Valente Díaz y La Loma f4 275
Valentigney c3 184
Valentim, Serra do d3 288
Valentine, Nebraska, U.S.A. c3 260
Valentine, Texas, U.S.A. g2 272
Valentine National Wildlife Refuge c3 260
Valenza c4 196
Valenzuela, Phil. c3 100
Valenzuela, Spain f7 191
Valenzuela, Isla a6 295
Våler d2 156
Valera c2 284
Valera de Arriba b5 193
Valerio f4 272
Vales Mortos c7 191
Valfabbrica g6 197
Valga m4 157
Valgejõgi l3 157
Valgorge a6 184
Valgrisenche b4 196
Valguarnera Caropepe d7 199
Valhelhas c4 190
Valiente, Península g6 277
Valier, Mont d6 187
Valikhanovo n1 121
Valimi c4 210
Valinco, Golfe de A 185
Valinhos e5 291
Valira f2 192
Valjevo d3 200
Valjunquera e4 192
Valka m4 157
Valkeakoski l2 157
Valkenswaard d3 159
Valkininkai n1 169
Valky d2 148
Valkyrie Dome j2 298
Vall d'Alba d4 193
Vall de Uxó d5 193
Valladolid, Mex. q7 273
Valladolid, Spain f3 190
Valladolid f3 190
Vallage b2 184
Vällaj l4 171
Vallard, Lac h2 252
Vallata e3 198
Valldal b1 156
Valldemossa g5 193
Valle, Col. b3 284
Valle, Lat. l4 157
Valle, Spain f1 190
Valle Cura, Río de c1 294
Valle Daza e4 296
Valle de Banderas b3 274
Valle de Bravo d4 274
Valle de Guadalupe c3 274
Valle de la Pascua d2 284
Valle de Matamoros d6 191
Valle de Olivos f4 272
Valle de Rosario f4 272
Valle de Santiago d3 274
Valle de Zaragoza g4 272
Valle Grande, Arg. d4 292
Valle Grande, Bol. e3 293
Valle Hermoso, Arg. e1 297
Valle Hermoso, Mex. a7 258
Valle Lambro, Parco della d4 196
Valle Nacional f5 275
Vallecillos k4 273
Vallecito d1 296
Vallecitos, Guerrero, Mex. d5 274
Vallecitos, Nuevo León, Mex. d1 274
Valledolmo c7 199
Valledoria Aa2 198
Valledupar c1 284
Vallehermoso Ab2 189
Vallejo, Mex. d2 274
Vallejo, U.S.A. a3 264
Vallelunga Pratameno c7 199
Vallenar b1 294
Vallendar c2 174
Valleraugue f4 187
Vallermosa Aa3 198
Vallet d5 182
Valletta g1 221
Valley, Can. c5 250
Valley, U.K. b3 162
Valley, U.S.A. e1 262
Valley City d7 250
Valley Forge e4 256
Valley Head, Alabama, U.S.A. g2 259
Valley Head, West Virginia, U.S.A. f6 254
Valley Mills a4 258
Valley Springs c3 264
Valley Station d6 254
Valley View, Pennsylvania, U.S.A. d4 256
Valley View, Texas, U.S.A. a3 258
Valleyview j4 248
Valfogona de Riucorb f3 192
Valli di Comacchio g5 196
Valliant b2 258
Vallmoll f3 192
Vallo della Lucania e4 198
Valloire c5 185
Vallombrosa f6 197
Vallon de St-Imier b2 196
Vallon-Pont-d'Arc a6 185
Vallorbe a3 196
Valls f3 192
Valmayor, Embalse de g4 190
Valmiera l4 157
Valmojado f4 190
Valmont f3 183
Valmontone g8 197
Valmy a1 184
Valnera g1 190
Valognes d3 182
Valois h3 183
Valongo b3 190
Válor b8 193
Valoria la Buena f3 190
Valozhyn m5 157
Valpaços c3 190
Valpalmas d2 192
Valparai e7 126
Valparaíso, Braz. c4 290
Valparaíso, Región V, Aconcagua, Chile b2 296
Valparaíso, Chile b2 296
Valparaíso, Mex. c2 274
Valparaíso, Florida, U.S.A. f4 258
Valparaíso, Indiana, U.S.A. c5 254
Valparaíso, Embalse de d3 190
Valpovo d3 200
Valras-Plage f5 187
Valréas a6 185
Valsad c9 124
Valseca f3 190
Valsequillo, Iraq Ad3 189
Valsequillo, Spain e6 191
Valserine b4 184
Valsinni f4 198
Valsjöbyn e4 154
Vals-les-Bains a6 185
Valspan f3 234
Valstagna f4 196
Valtero d1 210
Valtice h1 177
Valtiendas g3 190
Valtierra c2 192
Valtimo m5 155
Valtou b3 210
Valtournenche b4 196
Valujki e2 148
Valverde Ab3 189
Valverde de Júcar b5 193
Valverde de Leganés d6 191
Valverde de Llerena e6 191
Valverde del Camino d7 191
Valverde del Fresno d4 190
Valvestino, Lago di e4 196
Valvika e3 154
Valyasy n4 157
Vama, Satu Mare, Rom. f1 201
Vama, Suceava, Rom. g2 201
Vâmân f2 156
Vamberk e1 170
Vamdrup c3 158
Vâmhus f2 156
Vamizi, Ilha c6 231
Vammala k2 157
Vammen c2 158
Vamos e7 211
Vámosmikola g4 171
Vámospércs k4 171
Vámosújfalu k3 171
Vamvakofyto d1 210
Van, Tur. j3 209
Van j3 209
Van Buren, Arkansas, U.S.A. b2 258
Van Buren, Maine, U.S.A. j5 253
Van Buren, Missouri, U.S.A. d1 258
Van Diemen Gulf k2 86
Van Diemen, Cape, Northern Territory, Aust. k2 86
Van Diemen, Cape, Queensland, Aust. e4 80
Van Etten d2 256
Van Gölü j3 209
Van Harinxmakanaal d1 159
Van Horn g2 272
Van Reenen h4 235
Van Rees, Pegunungan k6 97
Van Truer Tableland f10 87
Van Wert d5 254
Van Wyksdorp d6 234
Van Zylsrus e3 234
Vanadzor k2 209
Vanajavesi l2 157
Vanån e2 156
Vânători j3 201
Vanavana K 75
Vanavara l3 119
Vana-Vigala l3 157
Vanceburg e6 254
Vancouver f7 248
Vancouver Island e7 248
Vancouver, Cape, Aust. d14 87
Vancouver, Cape, U.S.A. c3 246
Vancouver, Isla b6 295
Vancouver, Mount k3 247
Vandalia, Illinois, U.S.A. b6 254
Vandalia, Ohio, U.S.A. d6 254
Vandekerckhove Lake s3 249
Vandellós e3 192
Vandeloos Bay A 127
Vandenesse-en-Auxois a3 184
Vanderbijlpark g3 235
Vanderhoof e4 248
Vanderkloof Dam f5 234
Vanderlin Island c3 80
Vandet Sø b2 158
Vandœvre-lès-Nancy c2 184
Vandoies f3 196
Vändra l3 157
Vandry f5 252
Vandžiogala k5 157
Vänern e3 156
Vänersborg e3 156
Vang, Mount ll2 298
Vanga b4 227
Vangaindrano Ab3 233
Vangsmjøsi c2 156
Vangsnes b2 156
Vangsvik f2 154
Vanier j3 255
Vanil Noir b3 196
Vanimo l6 97
Vanino l3 94
Vanivilasa Sagara e6 126
Vaniyambadi f6 126
Vanj e1 128
Vänjaurbäck g4 154
Vânju Mare f3 201
Vankavesi l2 157
Vankleek Hill j3 255
Vanlay k4 183
Vanna g1 154
Vännäs g5 154
Vännäsberget j3 155
Vannavalen g1 154
Vannes c5 182
Vännskär LH h4 154
Vanoise, Massif de la c5 185
Vanoise, Parc National de la c5 185
Vanrhynsdorp c5 234
Vanrook e4 80
Vansant e7 254
Vansbro f2 156
Vansittart Island n2 243
Vansjø d3 156
Vanstadensrus g4 235
Vantaa l2 157
Vanua Balavu E 74
Vanua Lava F 74
Vanua Levu E 74
Vanua Levu Barrier Reef E 74
Vanua Vatu E 74
Vanuatu f4 73

VANUATU

THE REPUBLIC OF VANUATU
Area 12,190km² (4707sq miles)
Capital Port Vila
Organizations COMM, SPC, PIF
Population 210,000
Pop. growth (%) 2.5
Life expectancy 66 (m); 69 (f)
Languages Bislama, English, French, many local languages
Literacy 53%
Currency vatu (US $1 = 112.39 vatu)
GDP (US million $) 219
GDP per head ($US) 1042

Vanwyksvlei, R.S.A. e5 234
Vanwyksvlei d5 234
Vanzevat l2 147
Vao, Embalse de c2 190
Vaour d4 187
Vapnyarka j1 201

VATICAN CITY

THE VATICAN CITY STATE
Area 0.44km² (0.17sq miles)
Capital Vatican City
Organizations
Population 1000
Pop. growth (%) n/a
Life expectancy n/a
Languages Italian, Latin
Literacy 100%
Currency euro
(US $1 = 0.81 euro)
GDP (US million $) 19
GDP per head ($US) 19,000

VENEZUELA

THE BOLIVARIAN REPUBLIC OF VENEZUELA
Area 912,050km² (352,144sq miles)
Capital Caracas
Organizations ACS, Andean Comm, IADB, OPEC, SELA, LAIA
Population 25,230,000
Pop. growth (%) 2
Life expectancy 69 (m); 75 (f)
Languages Spanish
Literacy 93.4%
Currency bolivar
(US $1 = 2802.27 bolivar)
GDP (US million $) 84,600
GDP per head ($US) 3353

VIETNAM

THE SOCIALIST REPUBLIC OF VIETNAM
Area 331,114km² (127,844sq miles)
Capital Hanoi
Organizations ASEAN, APEC
Population 79,730,000
Pop. growth (%) 1.4
Life expectancy 65 (m); 69 (f)
Languages Vietnamese
Literacy 93%
Currency đong
(US $1 = 15,637 đong)
GDP (US million $) 33,800
GDP per head ($US) 423

396 Wellington → Wolmaransstad

Wellington, Colorado, U.S.A. b3 260
Wellington, Kansas, U.S.A. a1 258
Wellington, Nevada, U.S.A. d3 264
Wellington, Texas, U.S.A. c5 261
Wellington, Utah, U.S.A. h6 262
Wellington, Isla ▭ b5 295
Wellington, Lake ○ e4 83
Wells, U.K. d5 163
Wells, U.S.A. f5 262
Wells Gray Provincial Park ☆ h5 248
Wells, Lake ○ f10 87
Wellsboro c3 256
Wellsburg f5 254
Wellsford e2 76
Wells-next-the-Sea g4 162
Wellsville, New York, U.S.A. c2 256
Wellsville, Ohio, U.S.A. f5 254
Wellsville, Utah, U.S.A. h5 262
Wellton f9 263
Welney g4 163
Wels f1 177
Welschbillig e5 159
Welse ≈ j2 173
Welsford j6 253
Welshpool c4 162
Welsickendorf j4 173
Welwyn Garden City f5 163
Welzow k4 173
Wem d4 162
Wema d4 224
Wembere ≈ f4 225
Wembesi h4 235
Wemding f4 175
Wemel Shet' ≈ c2 226
Wemindji c2 252
Wemyss Bay d4 164
Wemyss Bight l7 259
Wenamu ≈ e2 285
Wenatchee c2 262
Wenatchee Mountains ▲ c2 262
Wenchi d4 222
Wench'it Shet' ≈ b1 226
Wendelstein, Ger. △ h5 175
Wendelstein g3 175
Wenden c2 174
Wendeng h1 111
Wendesi j6 97
Wendisch Rietz k3 173
Wendland ♦ g2 173
Wendo b2 226
Wéndou Mbôrou b3 222
Wendover f5 262
Weng'an f5 104
Wenge d3 224
Wengshui b4 104
Wenling n4 105
Wenlock ≈ f2 80
Wenman, Isla ▭ A 286
Wennigsen (Deister) e3 172
Wenning ≈ d2 162
Wenns b2 176
Wenona e6 256
Wenqu b3 106
Wenquan, Chongqing, China a4 106
Wenquan, Qinghai, China b1 104
Wenquan, Xinjiang Uygur Zizhiqu, China t5 121
Wenquanzhen d5 106
Wenshan e7 104
Wenshang e2 111
Wenshui, Guizhou, China f4 104
Wenshui, Shanxi, China c1 106
Wensu t7 121
Wensum ≈ h4 162
Went ≈ e3 162
Wentworth e13 81
Wenut j6 97
Wenxi b2 106
Wenxian, Gansu, China e2 104
Wenxian, Henan, China c2 106
Wenyu He ≈ b1 106
Wenzenbach h5 175
Wenzhou n5 105
Wenzlow h3 173
Wenzu e1 111
Weobley d4 163
Wepener g4 235
Werbellin j3 173
Werben (Elbe) g3 173
Werbkowice m5 169
Werbomont d4 159
Werda e2 234
Werdau h2 175
Werdër d2 226
Werder h3 173
Werdohl h1 174
Werfen e2 176
Weri j6 97
Werinama j6 97
Werl c4 172
Werlte c3 172
Wermsdorf j1 175
Wern ≈ e3 174
Wernau e4 174
Wernberg e3 176
Werne c4 172
Werneck f3 174
Werneuchen j3 173
Wernigerode f4 173
Werra ≈ e4 172
Werris Creek k11 81
Werse ≈ c4 172
Wertach ≈ f5 175
Wertheim e3 174
Wertingen f4 175
Werwaru h7 97
Weschnitz ≈ d3 174
Wesel e3 159
Wesenberg h2 173
Wesendorf f3 173
Weser, Ger. ◄ d2 172
Weser, Ger. ≈ e3 172
Weserbergland ▲ e3 172
Weser-Ems ▣ d3 172
Wesergebirge ▲ e3 172
Weskan c4 260
Weslaco a6 258
Wesleyville f4 254
Wessel Islands ▭ c1 80
Wessel, Cape ► c1 80
Wesselburen b4 158
Wesseling e4 159
Wesselsbron g3 235
Wesselsvlei e3 234
Wessington Springs d2 260
West, Mississippi, U.S.A. e3 258
West, Texas, U.S.A. a4 258
West Allis b4 254
West Andover j2 257
West Baines ≈ j4 86
West Bank ▭ d4 139
West Bay, Cay. Is. g1 277
West Bay, U.S.A. ◄ g4 259
West Bend b4 254
West Bengal ▣ k8 125
West Berkshire ▣ e5 163
West Boylston j2 257
West Branch d3 254
West Branch Susquehanna ≈ b3 256
West Bromwich e4 163
West Burra ▭ A 164
West Cape ► a7 77
West Caroline Basin ⌣ h5 300
West Chester e5 256
West Coast ▣ c5 77
West Coast National Park ☆ c6 234
West Dover h2 257
West Dunbartonshire ▣ f3 164
West End, Bah. k6 259
West End, U.S.A. k2 259
West End Point ► k6 259
West European Basin ⌣ j5 302
West Fargo e7 250
West Fayu ▭ G 74
West Grand Lake ○ n3 255
West Hamlin e6 254
West Hartford h3 257
West Haven h3 257
West Hazleton e4 256
West Helena d2 258
West Ice Shelf ⸺ p1 298
West Island, Aust. ▭ c3 80
West Island, India ▭ n6 127
West Jordan h5 262
West Kingston j3 257
West Lafayette c5 254
West Liberty e7 254
West Lothian ▣ f3 164
West Lunga National Park ☆ c1 232
West MacDonnell National Park ☆ a7 80
West Mariana Basin ⌣ h4 300
West Memphis d2 258
West Mifflin g5 254
West Monroe c3 258
West Nicholson d3 233
West Palm Beach j6 259
West Paterson f4 257
West Plains d1 258
West Point, Aust. ► Aa2 83
West Point, Alaska, U.S.A. △ h2 247
West Point, California, U.S.A. ► d7 265
West Point, California, U.S.A. c3 264
West Point, Georgia, U.S.A. g3 259
West Point, Kentucky, U.S.A. g1 259
West Point, Mississippi, U.S.A. e3 258
West Point, New York, U.S.A. g3 257
West Point, Virginia, U.S.A. h7 255
West Point Lake ○ g3 259
West Road ≈ e5 248
West Sacramento b3 264
West Sister Island ▭ Ab1 83
West Springfield h2 257
West Sussex ▣ f6 163
West Townshend h1 257
West Unity d5 254
West Valley City h5 262
West Vancouver b1 262
West Virginia ▣ f6 254
West Walker ≈ d3 264
West Warwick j3 257
West Winfield e2 256
West Wyalong h12 81
West Wycombe f5 163
West York d5 256
Westall, Point ► a12 81
Westbrook g7 252
Westbrookville f3 256
Westbury, Aust. Ab2 83
Westbury, U.K. d5 163
Westby f3 260
Westend f6 265
Wester Ross ♦ c2 164
Westerburg c2 174
Westerholt f1 159
Westerland b4 158
Westerlo c3 159
Westerly j3 257
Western, Aust. ≈ f7 80
Western, Kenya ▣ a3 226
Western, Nepal ▣ f5 135
Western, Sri L. ▣ A 127
Western, Zam. ▣ c2 232
Western Australia ▣ e9 87
Western Bahr el Ghazal ▣ e2 225
Western Cape ▣ e6 234
Western Darfur ▣ b5 218
Western Equatoria ▣ e2 225
Western Ghats ▲ c4 126
Western Isles ▣ b1 164
Western Kordofan ▣ c5 218
Western Port ◄ d4 82
Western Rocks ▭ A 163
Western Sahara a2 217
Westerschelde ◄ b3 159
Westerstede c2 172
Westerstetten e4 174
Westerville e5 254
Westerwald ♦ d2 174
Westfield, Indiana, U.S.A. c5 254
Westfield, Massachusetts, U.S.A. h2 257
Westfield, New York, U.S.A. a2 256
Westfield, Pennsylvania, U.S.A. c3 256
Westfield, Wisconsin, U.S.A. b4 254
Westgat ═ e1 159
Westgate h9 81
Westhampton h4 257
Westhausen f4 174
Westhill f2 164
Westhoek Natuurreservaat ☆ a3 159
Westhoff a5 258
Westhope c6 250
Westkapelle b3 159
Westlake c4 258
Westland f7 80
Westland National Park ☆ b5 77
Westmar c5 85
Westmeath ▣ d3 165
Westminster d5 256
Westmont b4 256
Westmoreland, Aust. d4 80
Westmoreland, U.S.A. f1 258
Westmorland ▣ B 266
Weston, Malay. h2 99
Weston, U.K. d6 163
Weston, U.S.A. f6 254
Westonaria g3 235
Weston-super-Mare d5 163
Westover e6 256
Westport, Ire. b3 165
Westport, N.Z. c4 77
Westport, Connecticut, U.S.A. g3 257
Westport, Indiana, U.S.A. d6 254
Westport, Washington, U.S.A. a2 262
Westport Quay b3 165
Westray ▭ B 164
Westrich ♦ c3 174
West-Terschelling d1 159
Westtown f3 256
Westville, Can. l6 253
Westville, U.S.A. b2 258
West-Vlaanderen ▣ a4 159
Westward Ho! b5 163
Westwood k7 80
Westwood, Can. b5 250
Westwood, U.S.A. c1 264
Wetar ▭ p8 99
Wetar, Selat ═ p9 99
Wetaskiwin l5 249
Wete b5 227
Wethersfield h3 257
Wetter ≈ d2 174
Wetter (Hessen) d2 174
Wetter (Ruhr) f3 159
Wetterau ♦ d2 174
Wetteren b3 159
Wettin g4 173
Wettingen c2 196
Wetzlar d2 174
Wewahitchka g4 259
Wexford, Ire. ▣ e4 165
Wexford e4 165
Wexford Bay ◄ e4 165
Wexford Harbour ◄ e4 165
Weyauwega b3 254
Weybridge f5 163
Weyburn r7 249
Weyer Markt f2 177
Weyhausen f3 173
Weyhe d3 172
Weymouth, Can. k6 253
Weymouth, U.K. d6 163
Weymouth, U.S.A. k2 257
Weymouth, Cape ► f2 80
Whakatane, N.Z. ≈ f3 76
Whakatane f2 76
Whalan Creek ≈ c6 85
Whale Cay ▭ k7 259
Whalley d3 162
Whalsay ▭ A 164
Whangamata e2 76
Whanganui National Park ☆ e3 76
Whangaparaoa e2 76
Whangara g3 76
Whangarei e1 76
Whangaruru Harbour ◄ e1 76
Whapmagoostui m3 251
Wharfe ≈ e3 162
Wharton a5 258
Wharton Basin ⌣ e7 300
Wharton Lake ○ g3 242
Wharton, Mount △ x3 298
Whataroa c5 77
Whatley f4 258
Whauphill d5 164
Wheatland, California, U.S.A. b2 264
Wheatland, Wyoming, U.S.A. b3 260
Wheatley e4 254
Wheaton b5 254
Wheaton-Glenmont c5 256
Wheddon Cross c5 163
Wheeler e2 258
Wheeler Lake ○ f2 258
Wheeler Peak, California, U.S.A. △ d3 264
Wheeler Peak, Nevada, U.S.A. △ f6 263
Wheeler Peak, New Mexico, U.S.A. △ b4 261
Wheeling f5 254
Wheelwright g2 297
Whernside △ d2 162
Whidbey, Point ► b13 81
Whiddon Down c6 163
Whim Creek c7 86
Whinham, Mount △ k9 87
Whirinaki Forest Park ☆ f3 76
Whiskey Jack Lake ○ s2 249
Whitakers h7 255
Whitburn e4 164
Whitby f2 162
Whitchurch, England, U.K. d4 162
Whitchurch, England, U.K. e5 163
Whitcombe, Mount △ c5 77
White, Can. ≈ k3 247
White, Can. ≈ l6 251
White, Arkansas, U.S.A. ≈ d2 258
White, Colorado, U.S.A. ≈ b3 260
White, Indiana, U.S.A. ≈ c6 254
White, Wisconsin, U.S.A. ≈ a2 254
White Bay ◄ p3 253
White Bluff f1 258
White Castle d4 258
White Coomb △ e4 164
White Earth ≈ r7 249
White Fox a4 250
White Haven e3 256
White Hill △ m5 253
White Horse, Vale of ≈ e5 163
White House f1 258
White Island, Anguilla ▭ k1 298
White Island, Can. ▭ m2 243
White Island, N.Z. ▭ f2 76
White Lake, Ontario, Can. ○ l6 251
White Lake, Can. ○ d6 252
White Lake, U.S.A. ○ c5 258
White Mills e3 256
White Mountain d2 246
White Mountain Peak △ e4 264
White Mountains ▲ e4 264
White Mountains National Park ☆ a2 84
White Nile ▣ d5 218
White Nile Dam ⸺ d4 218
White Nossob ≈ c1 234
White Pigeon d5 254
White Plains g3 257
White River l6 251
White River Junction k4 255
White River National Wildlife Refuge ☆ d2 258
White Rock b1 262
White Sands National Monument ☆ b2 261
White Springs h4 259
White Sulphur Springs h2 262
White, Lake ○ j7 86
Whiteadder Water ≈ f4 164
Whitecoomb △ b6 77
Whitecourt k4 249
Whitefish f1 262
Whitefish Lake ○ e3 246
Whitehall B 164
Whitehaven c2 162
Whitehead c5 164
Whitehorse l3 247
Whitemark Ac2 83
Whitemouth Lake ○ f6 250
Whiten Head ► d1 164
Whitesail Lake ○ d5 248
Whitesand ≈ r6 249
Whitesboro a3 258
Whiteside, Canal ═ b6 295
Whitesville f1 258
Whiteville e2 258
Whitewater, Indiana, U.S.A. ≈ d6 254
Whitewater, Wisconsin, U.S.A. b4 254
Whitewater Baldy △ a5 261
Whitewater Lake ○ j5 251
Whitewood, Aust. f6 80
Whitewood, Can. b5 250
Whitewright a3 258
Whitfield h5 163
Whitford Point ► b5 163
Whithorn, Jam. B 270
Whithorn d5 164
Whitianga e2 76
Whiting b3 254
Whiting Bay c4 164
Whitinsville j2 257
Whitley City g1 259
Whitman k2 257
Whitmire j2 259
Whitmore Mountains ▲ gg3 298
Whitney g3 254
Whitney Point e2 256
Whitney, Mount △ e5 264
Whitstable h5 163
Whitsand Bay ◄ b6 163
Whitsunday Group ▭ c2 84
Whitsunday Island ▭ c2 84
Whitsunday Island National Park ☆ c2 84
Whitsunday Passage ═ c2 84
Whittier, Alaska, U.S.A. g3 247
Whittier, California, U.S.A. e8 265
Whittington Range ▲ a5 80
Whittlesea g6 235
Whittlesey f4 163
Whitton h13 81
Whitwell g2 259
Whyalla c12 81
Whycocomagh m6 253
Wiang Kosai National Park ☆ d7 102
Wiang Pa Pao d6 102
Wiang Sa e6 102
Wiarton f3 254
Wiasi d3 222
Wia-Wia, Natuurreservaat ☆ g2 285
Wiawso d4 222
Wiązów f5 168
Wichita, Kansas, U.S.A. a1 258
Wichita, Texas, U.S.A. ≈ d5 261
Wichita Falls d5 261
Wichita Mountains ▲ d5 261
Wichita Mountains National Wildlife Refuge ☆ d5 261
Wick, England, U.K. d5 163
Wick, Scotland, U.K. ≈ e1 164
Wick, Scotland, U.K. e1 164
Wickenburg g9 263
Wickenrode (Helsa) f1 174
Wickepin c13 87
Wickham, Northern Territory, Aust. ≈ k5 86
Wickham, Aust. c7 86
Wickham, U.K. e6 163
Wickham Market h4 163
Wickham, Cape ► c4 82
Wickham, Mount △ j5 86
Wickliffe e1 258
Wicklow, Ire. ▣ e3 165
Wicklow e4 165
Wicklow Head ► f4 165
Wicklow Mountains ▲ e3 164
Wicklow Mts National Park ☆ e3 165
Wicko f1 168
Wicko, Jezioro ○ e1 168
Widawa g4 168
Widawka ≈ h4 169
Wide Bay ◄ e4 84
Widgeegoara ≈ b6 85
Widgiemooltha e12 87
Widnes d3 162
Wi-do ▭ p8 113
Więcbork f2 168
Wieczno, Jezioro ○ g2 168
Wied ≈ c5 172
Wiefelstede b5 158
Wiehengebirge ▲ d3 172
Wiehl f4 159
Wiek j1 173
Wielbark j2 169
Wieleń e3 168
Wieleńskie, Jezioro ○ e4 168
Wielgomłyny h4 169
Wielichowo e3 168
Wieliczka j6 169
Wielimie, Jezioro ○ e2 168
Wielkie Oczy m5 169
Wielkie Partęczyny, Jezioro ○ h2 169
Wielkie, Jezioro ○ d3 168
Wielkopolskie ▣ f3 168
Wielopole Skrzyńskie k6 169
Wieluń g4 168
Wien ▣ h1 177
Wiener Neudorf h1 177
Wiener Neustadt h2 177
Wieprz ≈ l4 169
Wierden e2 159
Wieren f3 173
Wieruszów g4 168
Wierzbica k4 169
Wierzbięcin d2 168
Wierzchowo e2 168
Wierzchowo, Jezioro ○ e2 168
Wies g3 177
Wiesau h3 175
Wiesbaden d2 174
Wieselburg g1 177
Wiesent ≈ g3 175
Wiesentheid f3 174
Wiesloch d3 174
Wiesmoor c2 172
Wietmarschen f2 159
Wietze e3 172
Wietzen e3 172
Wietzendorf e3 172
Wieżyca △ g1 168
Wigan, England, U.K. ▣ d3 162
Wigan d3 162
Wiggins e4 258
Wighi, Ramlat al ≈ a3 218
Wigierski Park Narodowy ☆ m1 169
Wigmore d4 163
Wigry, Jezioro ○ m2 169
Wigston e4 163
Wigton e5 164
Wigtown d5 164
Wigtown Bay ◄ d5 164
Wijchen d3 159
Wijk bij Duurstede d3 159
Wik'ro e5 219
Wil d2 196
Wilamowice h6 169
Wilbur d2 262
Wilcannia f11 81
Wilcox b3 256
Wilczęta h1 169
Wild Coast ♦ h5 235
Wild Horse Hill △ c3 260
Wild Rice ≈ d2 260
Wildalpen f2 177
Wildberg h3 173
Wildcat Hill Wilderness Area ☆ r5 249
Wildcat Peak △ g2 264
Wildeck-Obersuhl f2 174
Wilderness e6 234
Wilderness, U.S.A. c6 256
Wilderness National Lakes Area ☆ e6 234
Wildersville e2 258
Wildervank e1 159
Wildeshausen d3 172
Wildhay ≈ j5 248
Wildhorn △ b3 196
Wildon g3 177
Wildspitze △ b3 176
Wildwood f6 256
Wiley Ford b5 256
Wilga k4 169
Wilge, R.S.A. ≈ h2 235
Wilge, Free State, R.S.A. ≈ h3 235
Wilhelmina Gebergte ▲ f3 285
Wilhelmsburg g1 177
Wilhelmshaven b5 158
Wilhelmstal b3 232
Wilkau-Haßlau h2 175
Wilkes Coast u1 298
Wilkes Land ♦ t2 298
Wilkes-Barre e3 256
Wilkesboro j1 259
Wilkinson Lakes ○ a10 81
Wilkołaz l4 169
Wilków k4 169
Wilkowo d3 168
Will, Mount, Can. △ c3 248
Will, Mount, U.S.A. △ m4 247
Willamette ≈ b3 262
Willandra Billabong ≈ d1 82
Willandra National Park ★ d1 82
Willapa Bay ◄ a2 262
Willard, Mex. d3 272
Willard, Missouri, U.S.A. c1 258
Willard, Utah, U.S.A. g5 262
Willards e6 256
Willcox j9 263
Willebadessen e4 172
Willem Pretorius Game Reserve ☆ g4 235
Willemstad c3 159
Willemstad, Neth. Ant. k8 271
Willeroo k4 86
Willet e2 256
William Creek c10 81
William Lake ○ d3 250
William, Mount, Victoria, Aust. △ c3 82
William, Mount, Western Australia, Aust. △ b13 87
Williams c13 87
Williams, U.S.A. a2 264
Williams Island ▭ k7 259
Williams Lake f5 248
Williamsburg, Kentucky, U.S.A. g1 259
Williamsburg, Pennsylvania, U.S.A. b4 256
Williamsburg, Virginia, U.S.A. h7 255
Williamson e7 254
Williamsport, Indiana, U.S.A. c5 254
Williamsport, Pennsylvania, U.S.A. c3 256
Williamston l2 259
Williamstown g2 257
Williamsville b6 254
Willich e3 159
Willimantic h3 257
Willingboro f4 256
Willington g4 163
Willis b4 258
Willis Group ▭ j4 80
Willisau c2 196
Williston, R.S.A. d5 234
Williston, Florida, U.S.A. h5 259
Williston, North Dakota, U.S.A. r7 249
Williston, South Carolina, U.S.A. j3 259
Williston Lake ○ e3 248
Willisville e1 258
Williton c5 163
Willits b6 262
Willmar e2 260
Willmore Wilderness Provincial Park ☆ h5 248
Willow, Can. ≈ f5 248
Willow, U.S.A. g3 247
Willow Bunch q7 249
Willow City c6 250
Willow Creek, California, U.S.A. b5 262
Willow Creek, Oregon, U.S.A. ≈ a2 264
Willow Hill c4 256
Willow Reservoir ○ a3 254
Willow Springs d1 258
Willowmore e6 234
Willowra l7 86
Willows a2 264
Willowvale h6 235
Wills Creek ≈ d7 80
Wills, Lake ○ j7 86
Willshire d5 254
Willunga d13 81
Wilmer a3 258
Wilmington d12 81
Wilmington, Illinois, U.S.A. b5 254
Wilmington, North Carolina, U.S.A. l2 259
Wilmington, Ohio, U.S.A. e6 254
Wilmington, Vermont, U.S.A. h2 257
Wilmington Manor e5 256
Wilmot d3 258
Wilmslow d3 162
Wilnsdorf d2 174
Wilpena ≈ d11 81
Wilsdruff h1 175
Wilseder Berg △ e2 172
Wilson, Queensland, Aust. ≈ f9 81
Wilson, Aust. ≈ h5 86
Wilson, Kansas, U.S.A. d4 260
Wilson, North Carolina, U.S.A. l2 259
Wilson, Oklahoma, U.S.A. a2 258
Wilson Lake ○ f2 258
Wilson, Cape ► n2 243
Wilson, Mount, Colorado, U.S.A. △ b4 260
Wilson, Mount, Oregon, U.S.A. △ c3 262
Wilson's Promontory ► e4 83
Wilson's Promontory National Park ☆ e4 83
Wiltersdorf h1 177
Wilthen j1 175
Wilton e5 163
Wilton, New Hampshire, U.S.A. j2 257
Wilton, North Dakota, U.S.A. c7 250
Wiltshire ▣ e5 163
Wiltz d5 159
Wiluna e10 87
Wimbleball Lake ○ c5 163
Wimbledon d7 250
Wimborne Minster d6 163
Wimereux g2 183
Wimmera ≈ c3 82
Wimmis b3 196
Winbin ≈ a5 85
Winburg g4 235
Wincanton d5 163
Winchelsea, Aust. c4 82
Winchelsea, U.K. g6 163
Winchendon h2 257
Winchester, Can. j3 255
Winchester, N.Z. c6 77
Winchester, U.K. e5 163
Winchester, Indiana, U.S.A. d5 254
Winchester, Kentucky, U.S.A. g1 259
Winchester, New Hampshire, U.S.A. h2 257
Winchester, Virginia, U.S.A. b5 256
Wind, Can. ≈ l2 247
Wind, U.S.A. ≈ j4 262
Wind Cave National Park ☆ c3 260
Wind Mountain △ b5 261
Wind River Range ▲ j4 262
Windber b4 256
Windermere, England, U.K. ○ d2 162
Windermere d2 162
Windhoek b1 234
Windischeschenbach h3 175
Windischgarsten f2 177
Windlestraw Law △ f4 164
Windom e3 260
Windorah f8 81
Windrush ≈ e5 163
Windsbach f3 175
Windsor, Aust. k12 81
Windsor, Newfoundland, Can. q4 253
Windsor, Nova Scotia, Can. k6 253
Windsor, Can. e4 254
Windsor, U.K. f5 163
Windsor, California, U.S.A. a3 264
Windsor, Connecticut, U.S.A. h3 257
Windsor, North Carolina, U.S.A. h7 255
Windsor, Vermont, U.S.A. k4 255
Windsor and Maidenhead ▣ h2 162
Windsor Dam ⸺ h2 257
Windsor Locks h3 257
Windsorton f4 234
Windward Islands, Cape. V. ▭ q8 271
Windward Islands, N.Z. ▭ B 77
Windward Passage ═ h5 266
Winefred Lake ○ m4 249
Winfield, Alabama, U.S.A. f3 258
Winfield, Kansas, U.S.A. a1 258
Wing c7 250
Wingate j2 259
Wingate Mountains ▲ k4 86
Wingham l11 81
Wingham, Can. f4 254
Wingo e1 258
Wini n9 99
Winifred j2 262
Winifred, Lake ○ f8 87
Winifreda e4 297
Winisk, Ontario, Can. ≈ k3 251
Winisk, Ontario, Can. l3 251
Winisk Lake ○ k4 251
Winisk River Provincial Park ☆ k4 251
Winkana c8 102
Winkelpos g3 235
Winkleigh c6 163
Winklern d3 176
Winnalls Ridge ▲ k9 87
Winneba d4 222
Winnebago, Lake ○ b4 254
Winnecke Creek ≈ k6 86
Winnemucca e5 262
Winnemucca Lake ○ d1 264
Winnenden e4 174
Winner d3 260
Winnfield c4 258
Winnibigoshish, Lake ○ e2 260
Winnie b5 258
Winning b8 87
Winningen g4 173
Winnipeg, Manitoba, Can. e6 250
Winnipeg, Manitoba/Ontario, Can. ≈ e5 250
Winnipeg, Lake, Can. ○ d4 250
Winnipeg, Lake, Manitoba, Can. ○ d4 250
Winnipegosis d5 250
Winnipesaukee, Lake ○ l4 255
Winnsboro, Louisiana, U.S.A. d3 258
Winnsboro, South Carolina, U.S.A. j2 259
Winnsboro, Texas, U.S.A. b3 258
Winona, Michigan, U.S.A. j7 251
Winona, Minnesota, U.S.A. f2 260
Winona, Mississippi, U.S.A. e3 258
Winona, Missouri, U.S.A. d1 258
Winooski k3 255
Winschoten f1 159
Winscombe d5 163
Winsen (Aller) e3 172
Winsen (Luhe) d5 158
Winsford d3 162
Wińsko e4 168
Winslow h8 263
Winsted, Connecticut, U.S.A. g3 257
Winston-Salem f7 254
Winsum e1 159
Winter Garden j5 259
Winter Harbor h6 253
Winter Haven j5 259
Winter Park j5 259
Winterberg j1 174
Winterbourne Abbas d6 163
Winterlingen e4 174
Winterport h6 253
Winters, California, U.S.A. b3 264
Winters, Texas, U.S.A. d6 261
Winterstown d5 256
Winterswijk e3 159
Winterthur c2 196
Winterton r5 253
Winthrop c1 262
Winton, Aust. f7 80
Winton, N.Z. b7 77
Winton, U.S.A. h7 255
Wintzenheim d2 184
Wipper, Ger. ≈ f4 173
Wipper, Ger. ≈ g4 173
Wipperfürth f3 159
Wippra Kurort g4 173
Wirmaf j6 97
Wirral ► c3 162
Wirraminna c11 81
Wirrulla b12 81
Wisbech g4 162
Wischhafen c5 158
Wisconsin, U.S.A. ▣ f2 260
Wisconsin, Wisconsin, U.S.A. ≈ a4 254
Wisconsin Dells b4 254
Wisconsin Rapids b3 254
Wiseman g2 246
Wishart b5 250
Wishaw e4 164
Wisil Dabarow d2 226
Wiske ≈ e2 162
Wiskitki j3 169
Wisła, Pol. ≈ h5 157
Wisła, Pol. ≈ g1 168
Wisła g6 168
Wiślany, Zalew ◄ h1 169
Wisłok ≈ l5 169
Wisłoka ≈ k6 169
Wismar e5 158
Wismarbucht ◄ g2 173
Wisner d4 258
Wiśniew l3 169
Wiśniewo j2 169
Wissant g2 183
Wissembourg d1 184
Wissen c2 174
Wissenkerke b3 159
Wister b2 258
Wisznia ≈ m6 169
Wisznia Mała f4 168
Wisznice m4 169
Witbank h2 235
Witbooisvlei c2 234
Witdraai d3 234
Witham, England, U.K. ≈ f3 162
Witham g5 163
Witheridge c6 163
Withernsea g3 162
Witherspoon, Mount △ h3 247
Witjira National Park ☆ b9 81
Witkowo f3 168
Witless Bay r5 253
Witley f5 163
Witney e5 163
Witnica c3 168
Wittdün b4 158
Witteberg, Eastern Cape, R.S.A. ▲ d6 234
Witteberg, Eastern Cape, R.S.A. ▲ g5 235
Witteberg, Free State, R.S.A. ▲ h4 235
Wittelsheim d3 184
Witten f3 159
Wittenberg b3 254
Wittenberge g3 173
Wittenburg e5 158
Wittenhagen j1 173
Wittenheim d3 184
Wittenoom d8 86
Wittensee ○ e1 172
Wittingen f3 173
Wittlich e5 159
Wittmund c2 172
Wittow ► j1 173
Wittstock h2 173
Witu c4 226
Witvlei c1 234
Witwatersrand ▲ g3 235
Witzenhausen e4 172
Wivenhoe, Lake ○ e5 85
Wiwon p5 113
Wiżajny l1 169
Wizna l2 169
Wkra ≈ j3 169
Władysławowo g1 168
Wleń d4 168
Włocławek h3 169
Włodawa m4 169
Włoszczowa h5 169
Wlotza's Baken a1 234
Woburn j2 257
Wodonga h14 81
Wodzisław Śląski g5 168
Woerden c2 159
Wœrth d2 184
Wohko ≈ e2 225
Wohlen c2 196
Wohlthat Mountains ▲ f2 298
Wohra ≈ d5 172
Woippy c1 184
Wojcieszów d5 168
Wójcin g3 168
Wojnicz j6 169
Wojnowo f2 168
Wokam ▭ k7 97
Woken He ≈ r3 113
Wokha p6 125
Woking f5 163
Wokingham, Aust. ≈ f6 80
Wokingham, England, U.K. ▣ h2 162
Wokingham f5 163
Woko National Park ☆ d7 85
Wola Uhruska m4 169
Wolanów j4 169
Wolbórz h4 169
Wolbrom h5 169
Wolcott, Indiana, U.S.A. c5 254
Wolcott, New York, U.S.A. h4 255
Wołczyn g4 168
Wold Newton f2 162
Woldegk j2 173
Woldendorp f1 159
Woleai ▭ G 74
Woleu-Ntem ▣ b3 224
Wolf, Can. ≈ l3 247
Wolf, Tennessee, U.S.A. ≈ e2 258
Wolf, Wisconsin, U.S.A. ≈ b3 254
Wolf Creek, Montana, U.S.A. g2 262
Wolf Creek, Oklahoma, U.S.A. ≈ c4 261
Wolf Creek Pass ═ b4 261
Wolf Lake ○ m3 247
Wolf Mountain △ e2 246
Wolf Point q7 249
Wolf, Volcán △ A 286
Wolfegg e5 174
Wolfen h4 173
Wolfenbüttel f3 173
Wolfenschiessen c3 196
Wolfhagen e4 172
Wolfratshausen g5 175
Wolfsberg f3 177
Wolfsburg f3 173
Wolfstein c3 174
Wolgast j1 173
Wolhusen c2 196
Wolin c2 168
Wolkersdorf h1 177
Wollaston, Islas ▭ c7 295
Wollbach f2 174
Wollemi National Park ☆ d8 85
Wollerau c2 196
Wolletzee ○ j2 173
Wollongong k13 81
Wolmaransstad f3 235

398 Yawatahama → Ždírec nad Doubravou

Yawatahama e5 114
Yawatongguz He f1 135
Yawatongguzlangar u9 121
Yaxchilan b2 276
Yaxley f4 163
Yazd, Iran p6 137
Yazd q6 137
Yazd-e Khväst p6 137
Yazıhan g3 209
Yazoo d3 258
Yazoo City d3 258
Yazovir Kamchiya h4 201
Yazovir Ticha h4 201
Ybbs f2 177
Ybbs an der Donau g1 177
Ybbsitz f2 177
Ybycuí f5 293
Yding Skovhøj c3 158
Ydra, Grc. d5 211
Ydra d5 211
Ydras, Kolpos d5 211
Ydstebøhamn a3 156
Ye c8 102
Ye Kyun a6 102
Yea d3 82
Yealmpton c6 163
Yebbi-Bou a3 218
Yebbi-Souma a3 218
Yecheng r9 121
Yecla c6 193
Yécora e3 272
Yecuautla f4 275
Yedashe c6 102
Yedi Burun Başı b4 208
Yedseram g3 223
Yedy m5 157
Yeelanna b13 81
Yeghegnadzor g5 149
Yegindybulak r3 121
Yeguas f6 191
Yeguas, Embalse del f6 191
Yégué e4 223
Yehud c4 139
Yei, Sudan f2 225
Yei f3 225
Yeji, China d4 111
Yeji, Ghana d4 222
Yekokora d3 224
Yekumbe d4 224
Yel'sk c2 148
Yelarbon k10 81
Yelbarsli h8 120
Yelcho b4 295
Yelcho, Lago b4 295
Yélimané b2 222
Yell A 164
Yell Sound A 164
Yellabina Regional Reserve l12 87
Yellandu g4 126
Yellapur d5 126
Yellow f2 260
Yellow Mountain b8 85
Yellow River d2 106
Yellow Sea g3 300
Yellowdine d12 87
Yellowhead Pass h5 248
Yellowknife g3 242
Yellowstone b2 260
Yellowstone Lake h3 262
Yellowstone National Park h3 262
Yeloten a2 128
Yeltes d4 190
Yelucá e3 276
Yemaotai m4 113
Yemassee j3 259
Yemen b7 92

YEMEN

THE REPUBLIC OF YEMEN
Area 536,869km^2 (207,286sq miles)
Capital San'a
Organizations CAEU, IDB, LAS, OIC
Population 19,500,000
Pop. growth (%) 2.5
Life expectancy 58 (m); 60 (f)
Languages Arabic
Literacy 50.3%
Currency Yemeni rial (US $1 = 178 Yemeni rial)
GDP (US million $) 9407
GDP per head ($US) 482

Yen b3 224
Yên Bai g5 102
Yenagoa f5 223
Yenakiyeve e2 148
Yenangyaung b5 102
Yenanma b6 102
Yenbekshi m7 121
Yendi d4 222
Yénéganou b4 224
Yengan c5 102
Yenge d4 224
Yengejeh l3 137
Yengema b4 222
Yengisar r8 121
Yengo c3 224
Yengo National Park g1 83
Yenice, Çanakkale, Tur. a3 208
Yenice, Bursa, Tur. b3 208
Yeniceoba d3 208
Yenifoça a3 208
Yeniköy a3 208
Yenne b5 185
Yenshui n7 105
Yentna g3 247
Yeo Lake g10 87
Yeo Lake Nature Reserve g11 87
Yeola d9 124
Yeovil d6 163
Yepachi e3 272
Yeppoon k7 80
Yerbabuena d2 274
Yerbent k5 149
Yerementau, Gory p2 121
Yerevan g4 149
Yereymentau p2 121
Yerington d3 264
Yerkesik b4 208
Yerköy e3 208
Yerla d4 126
Yerlisu h5 201
Yermo, Mex. g4 272
Yermo, U.S.A. g7 265
Yerofey Pavlovich g2 94
Yeroham c6 139
Yerre g4 183
Yerupaja b2 292
Yerushalayim c5 139
Yerville f3 183
Yes Tor c6 163
Yesa c2 192
Yesa, Embalse de c2 192
Yesagyo b5 102
Yesan p7 113
Yesil' l2 120
Yeşilhisar e3 208
Yeşilırmak f2 209
Yeso h1 297
Yeste b6 193
Yesud HaMa'ala d3 138
Yetman k10 81
Yeu b4 102
Yeu, Île d' c6 182
Yevlax g4 149
Yevpatoriya d3 148
Yèvre h5 183
Yevul c5 139
Yexian c3 106
Yeygen'yevka r6 121
Yeyik f1 135
Ygos-St-Saturnin b5 187
Ygrande e2 186
Yguazú f5 293
Yi j2 297
Yi He, Henan, China c2 106
Yi He, Shandong, China f2 111
Yi Shan, Shandong, China f1 111
Yi'an n2 113
Yi'ong Zangbo p4 125
Yibā, Wādī f4 219
Yibin e4 104
Yibug Caka h3 135
Yichang, Hubei, China b4 106
Yicheng, Hubei, China b4 106
Yicheng, Hubei, China c4 106
Yicheng, Shandong, China e2 111
Yicheng, Shanxi, China b2 106
Yichuan, Henan, China c2 106
Yichuan, Shaanxi, China b2 106
Yichun, Heilongjiang, China q2 113
Yichun, Jiangxi, China k5 105
Yidun b3 104
Yifeng k4 105
Yijiangzhen f4 111
Yijun a2 106
Yilaha n1 113
Yilan q2 113
Yıldızeli f3 209
Yıldızlı Dağı c4 208
Yilehuli Shan, China m1 113
Yilehuli Shan, Heilongjiang/Nei Mongol Zizhiqu, China n1 113
Yiliang, Yunnan, China e5 104
Yiliang, Yunnan, China d6 104
Yiling n2 113
Yilong Hu d7 104
Yimen, Anhui, China e3 106
Yimen, Yunnan, China f3 102
Yimianpo q3 113
Yimin He k1 113
Yin Shan e5 112
Yinan f2 111
Yinbaing c7 102
Yinchuan d6 112
Yincun d1 106
Yindarlgooda, Lake f12 87
Yindian c3 106
Ying He d3 106
Yingcheng c4 106
Yingchengzi n4 113
Yingde j6 105
Yinggehai j6 102
Yinghe e3 106
Yingkou m5 113
Yingpanshui c7 112
Yingshan, Hubei, China d4 106
Yingshan, Sichuan, China f3 104
Yingshang e3 111
Yingtan l4 105
Yining t6 121
Yinjiahui e4 111
Yinjiang, Guizhou, China g5 104
Yinjiang, Zhejiang, China g5 111
Yinkengxu k5 105
Yinma He n3 113
Yinmabin b4 102
Yinnyein c7 102
Yipinglang e3 102
Yirga Alem b2 226
Yirga Ch'efē b2 226
Yirkā d4 138
Yirol f2 225
Yirrkala c2 80
Yirshi k2 113
Yishui f2 111
Yitong n4 113
Yitong He n3 113
Yiwu e5 102
Yixian, Anhui, China e5 106
Yixian, Liaoning, China l5 113
Yixing f4 111
Yixun He j5 113
Yiyang, Henan, China c2 106
Yiyang, Hunan, China j4 105
Yiyang, Jiangxi, China l4 105
Yiyuan f1 111
Yizhang j6 105
Yizheng f3 111
Yizre'el d4 138
Ylä-Keitele k5 155
Ylakiai j4 157
Yläne k2 157
Ylihärmä j5 155
Yli-Ii k4 155
Yli-Kärppä k4 155
Yliki, Limni d4 210
Ylikiiminki l4 155
Yli-Kitka m3 155
Ylistaro j5 155
Ylitornio j3 155
Ylivieska k4 155
Ylöjärvi k2 157
Yngaren g3 156
Ynykčanskij p3 119
Yoakum a5 258
Yobe g3 223
Yobetsu-dake Ab2 114
Yoboki f5 219
Yŏch'ŏn p8 113
Yogan, Cerro b6 295
Yogana f5 275
Yoğuntaş h5 201
Yogyakarta, Indon. f9 98
Yogyakarta f8 98
Yohmor d3 138
Yoho National Park j6 249
Yoichi Ab2 114
Yojoa, Lago de d3 276
Yŏju p7 113
Yokadouma c3 224
Yōkaichi g4 115
Yokawa f4 115
Yokkaichi g4 115
Yoko g4 223
Yokohama h4 115
Yokolo d4 224
Yokosuka h4 115
Yokote j2 115
Yokotsu-dake Ab3 114
Yol c3 130
Yola g4 223
Yolaina, Cordillera de e5 277
Yolla Bolly Middle Eel Wilderness a1 264
Yolo b3 264
Yolombo d4 224
Yolotepec f5 275
Yolox f5 275
Yoloxóchitl e5 275
Yoluk r7 273
Yŏmju n6 113
Yomou c4 222
Yomuka k7 97
Yon a2 186
Yonago e4 114
Yonaguni-jima p6 105
Yŏnan p7 113
Yonatan d4 138
Yŏnch'ŏn p6 113
Yoneshiro-gawa j1 115
Yonezawa j3 115
Yong Peng c4 101
Yong'an, Fujian, China l6 105
Yong'an, Shandong, China f1 111
Yŏng-am p8 113
Yŏngch'ŏn q8 113
Yongchang, Gansu, China a6 112
Yongchang, Xizang Zizhiqu, China j4 135
Yongcheng e3 111
Yongchuan e4 104
Yongde d3 102
Yongdeng b7 112
Yongding l6 105
Yŏngdŏk q7 113
Yŏngdong p7 113
Yongfeng k5 105
Yongfengqu w6 121
Yŏnggwang p8 113
Yonghe b1 106
Yŏnghŭng p6 113
Yŏngil-man q7 113
Yongji, Jilin, China p4 113
Yongji, Shanxi, China b2 106
Yongjin Qu c1 106
Yongjing b8 112
Yŏngju q7 113
Yongkang n4 105
Yongnian d1 111
Yongning g7 104
Yongping d3 102
Yongqing j6 113
Yongren c5 104
Yongshan d4 104
Yongsheng c5 104
Yongshou g1 104
Yongwol q7 113
Yŏngwon p6 113
Yongxing j5 105
Yongxiu k4 105
Yŏngyang q7 113
Yongzhou h5 104
Yŏnhwa-san p5 113
Yonkers g4 257
Yonne, Fr. j4 183
Yonne, Bourgogne, Fr. j5 183
Yŏngbyŏn n6 113
Yopal c2 284
Yopurga r8 121
Yoqne'am 'Illit d4 138
Yoquivo f4 272
Yordu b3 130
Yoricostio d4 274
Yorito d3 276
York, Aust. c12 87
York, England, U.K. e3 162
York, U.K. e3 162
York, Alabama, U.S.A. e3 258
York, Nebraska, U.S.A. d3 260
York, North Dakota, U.S.A. d6 250
York, Pennsylvania, U.S.A. d5 256
York, South Carolina, U.S.A. j2 259
York Downs f2 80
York Landing e2 250
York Springs c4 256
York, Cape f1 80
York, Vale of e2 162
Yorke Peninsula a2 82
Yorketown c13 81
Yorkshire Dales National Park d2 162
Yorkshire Wolds f2 162
Yorkton b5 250
Yorktown h7 255
Yoro d3 276
Yŏrŏŏ Gol d1 112
Yorosso d3 222
Yos Sudarso l7 97
Yosemite National Park d4 264
Yosemite Village d4 264
Yoshida e5 114
Yoshino-gawa f4 114
Yoshino-Kumano National Park g5 115
Yŏsu p8 113
Yotvata d7 139
You Jiang f7 104
You Shui h4 104
Youghal d5 165
Youghiogheny River Lake a5 256
Youkounkoun b3 222
Youlin f1 111
Young, Aust j13 81
Young, Can. a5 250
Young, U.S.A. h8 263
Young, Ur. j2 297
Young Island x1 298
Young, Cape A 77
Younghusband Peninsula a2 82
Youngstown, Florida, U.S.A. g4 259
Youngstown, Ohio, U.S.A. f5 254
Youngsville, North Carolina, U.S.A. g7 254
Youngsville, Pennsylvania, U.S.A. a3 256
Younine e2 138
Yountville a3 264
Youssoufia c2 220
Youvarou d2 222
Youxian j5 105
Youyang g4 104
Youyi r2 113
Youyi Feng w3 121
Yovon d1 128
Yowah a5 85
Yowereena Hill e9 87
Yozgat, Tur. e3 208
Yozgat e3 208
Ypané f4 293
Ypati c4 210
Ypé-Jhú f4 293
Yport f3 183
Yppäri k4 155
Ypsilanti e4 254
Ypsous c5 211
Yreka b5 262
Ysbyty Ystwyth c4 163
Yser h2 183
Ysper g1 177
Yssingeaux a5 184
Ystad e5 156
Ystrad, Wales, U.K. c3 162
Ystrad c5 163
Ystradgynlais c5 163
Ystwyth c4 163
Ysyk-Köl, Kyrg. r6 121
Ysyk-Köl, Kyrg. s6 121
Ythan f2 164
Ytre Samlen b2 156
Ytterhogdal f1 156
Ytyk-Kjuel' p3 119
Yu He g5 112
Yu Jiang g7 104
Yü Shan MP n7 105
Yu'alliq, Jabal b6 139
Yuan Jiang, Hunan, China h4 104
Yuan Jiang, Yunnan, China d7 104
Yuan'an b4 106
Yuanbao Shan g6 104
Yuanling h4 104
Yuanmou c6 104
Yuanping g6 112
Yuanqu b2 106
Yuanquzhan b2 106
Yuanshi d1 106
Yuantan e4 111
Yuantou d1 106
Yuanyang c2 106
Yuba b2 264
Yuba City b2 264
Yūbari Ab2 114
Yubdo b2 226
Yūbetsu Ac1 114
Yubileynyy t3 121
Yucaipa f7 265
Yucatán, Mex. p7 273
Yucatán, Mex. p8 273
Yucatan Basin b7 302
Yucca f8 263
Yucca Valley e8 263
Yucheng, Henan, China d2 106
Yucheng, Shandong, China e1 111
Yucheng, Shandong, China e2 111
Yudu k6 105
Yuecheng d1 106
Yuechi f3 104
Yuekou c4 106
Yueliang Pao m3 113
Yuendumu k8 86
Yueqing n4 105
Yueshan e4 111
Yuexi e4 111
Yueyang c5 106
Yugan l4 105
Yuhang g4 111
Yuhangzhen f4 111
Yuhuang Ding e1 111
Yukanbey a3 208
Yukarısarıkaya e3 208
Yuki c4 224
Yūki h3 115
Yukon, Can. d3 246
Yukon, U.S.A. a2 258
Yukon Territory b2 242
Yukon-Charley Rivers National Preserve j2 247
Yüksekova k4 209
Yulara k9 87
Yule d7 86
Yuli g4 223
Yüli n7 105
Yulin, Hainan, China j6 102
Yulin, Shaanxi, China e6 112
Yulong Xueshan c5 104
Yuma f9 263
Yuma, Bahía de k5 267
Yumbel a4 296
Yumbi, Bandundu, D.R.C. c4 224
Yumbi, Maniema, D.R.C. e4 225
Yumbo b3 284
Yumenzhen b4 94
Yumin u4 121
Yun Ling b5 104
Yun Shui c4 106
Yuna b11 87
Yuna, Dom. Rep. k5 271
Yunak c3 208
Yunan h7 104
Yunaska Island b5 246
Yunchara b4 292
Yuncheng, Shandong, China d2 106
Yuncheng, Shanxi, China b2 106
Yuncler g4 190
Yuncos g4 190
Yundamindera f11 87
Yung La j5 135
Yungang g5 112
Yungay, Antofagasta, Chile d4 292
Yungay, Biobío, Chile a4 296
Yungui Gaoyuan d6 104
Yunlong d3 102
Yunmeng c3 106
Yunnan c6 104
Yunquera de Henares a4 192
Yunta d12 81
Yunwu Shan h7 104
Yunxi b3 106
Yunxian, Hubei, China b3 106
Yunxian, Yunnan, China e3 102
Yunxiao l7 105
Yunyang, Chongqing, China a4 106
Yunyang, Henan, China c3 106
Yuping g5 104
Yuqian f4 111
Yuqing f5 104
Yura, Bol. d4 292
Yura, Potosí, Bol. d4 292
Yuracyacu b5 284
Yuratsishki p1 169
Yuraygir National Park e6 85
Yurba Co h2 135
Yurécuaro c3 274
Yurimaguas b5 284
Yuriria d3 274
Yuruari e2 285
Yürük h5 201
Yurungkax He d1 130
Yuscarán d4 276
Yushan m4 105
Yushan Liedao p4 105
Yushe c1 106
Yushu, Jilin, China p3 113
Yushu, Qinghai, China q3 125
Yusufeli h2 209
Yutai e2 111
Yutian, Hebei, China j6 113
Yutian, Xinjiang Uygur Zizhiqu, China e1 130
Yuting e5 111
Yutuyaco f4 297
Yuty f5 293
Yutz e5 159
Yuwang d7 112
Yuxi f3 102
Yuxiakou b4 106
Yuxian, Hebei, China h6 112
Yuxian, Shanxi, China c1 106
Yuxikou f4 111
Yuyangguan b4 106
Yuyao g4 111
Yuza h2 115
Yuzawa j2 115
Yuzhno-Sakhalinsk l3 94
Yuzhnoukrayinsk c3 148
Yuzhnyy Altay, Khrebet w3 121
Yuzhnyy Kazakhstan m6 121
Yuzhong c8 112
Yuzhou c2 106
Yuzkuduk g6 120
Yvel c4 182
Yvelines g4 183
Yverdon a3 196
Yvetot f3 183
Yvignac c4 182
Yvoire c4 184
Yvonand a3 196
Ywamun b5 102
Yxningen g3 156
Yxnö g3 156
Yylanly k4 149
Yzerfonteinpunt b6 234
Yzeure f2 186

Z

Za Qu p3 125
Za, Oued d2 220
Za'gya Zangbo k3 135
Zaachila f5 275
Zaamin f1 128
Zaandam c2 159
Zāb al Kabīr, Nahr az j4 209
Zāb aş Şaghīr, Nahr az j5 209
Zabābida d4 139
Zabajkal'sk j1 113
Zabarjad, Jazirat e3 219
Zabia e3 225
Zabid, Yemen f5 219
Zabīd, Wādī f5 219
Ząbki k3 169
Ząbkowice Śląskie e5 168
Žabljak d4 200
Zabłudów m2 169
Žabno, Cro. h4 177
Žabno, Pol. j5 169
Zabok g3 177
Žabokreky g2 171
Zābol, Afg. c4 128
Zābol a3 122
Zāboli a4 122
Zabolotiv g1 201
Zabolottya n4 169
Zabor'e c2 150
Žabowo d2 168
Zăbrani k5 171
Zabré d3 222
Zábřeh e2 170
Zabrze g5 168
Zabuzhzhya m4 169
Zabzugu e4 223
Zacapa c3 276
Zacapoaxtla f4 275
Zacapu d4 274
Zacapuato d4 274
Zacatal b1 276
Zacatecas, Mex. h6 272
Zacatecas, Zacatecas, Mex. c2 274
Zacatecoluca c4 276
Zacatelco e4 275
Zacatepec, Morelos, Mex. e4 275
Zacatepec, Oaxaca, Mex. f5 275
Zacatepec, Oaxaca, Mex. g5 275
Zacatlán f4 275
Zacharo b5 211
Zachodniopomorskie d2 168
Zacoalco c3 274
Zacualpán e4 275
Zacualpan, Nayarit, Mex. b3 274
Zacualpan, Veracruz, Mex. e3 275
Zacualtipán e3 275
Zadar b3 200
Zadetkale Kyun c11 103
Zadoi p3 125
Zadorra b2 192
Zadovka j5 151
Za'farāna d7 136
Zafarwal b3 130
Zafferana Etnea e7 199
Zafora Ab2 211
Zafra d6 191
Zafririm c5 139
Zag c3 220
Žaga e3 176
Żagań d4 168
Žagarė k4 157
Zagazig c6 136
Zāgheh n4 137
Zāgheh-ye Bālā l4 137
Zaghouan g1 221
Zaglavak f4 201
Zagon h3 201
Zagora, Grc. d3 210
Zagora, Mor. c2 220
Zagorje g3 177
Zagórów f3 168
Zagórz l6 169
Zagra f7 191
Zagrazhden g5 201
Zagreb, Cro. g4 177
Zagreb g4 177
Žagubica e3 200
Zahara e8 191
Zahara - El Gastor, Embalse de e8 191
Zaharovo e4 150
Zāhedān p7 137
Zahidabad d3 128
Zahinos d6 191
Zahlé d3 138
Zahna h4 173
Záhony l3 171
Záhorská Ves e3 170
Zahrebetnoe r2 155
Zahrez Chergui f1 221
Zahrez Rharbi e1 221
Zaida, Laguna de c3 192
Zaidín e3 192
Zaindeh p5 137
Zair k4 149
Zaire b5 224
Zaj l4 151
Zaječar f4 201
Zaka e3 233
Zakamensk b1 112
Zakhmet a2 128
Zākhō j4 209
Zaki, Kūh-e k3 209
Zakiyah e3 138
Zaklików l5 169
Zakopane h6 169
Zakouma a5 218
Zakouma, Parc National de a5 218
Zakroczym j3 169
Zakros g7 211
Zakrzewo g3 168
Zakupne h1 201
Zákupy c1 170
Zakwaski, Mount g6 248
Zakynthos b5 211
Zakynthos, Ionioi Nisoi, Grc. a5 210
Zal'vyanka n2 169
Zala b5 224
Zala, Hung. e5 170
Zalaapáti f5 170
Zalaegerszeg e5 170
Zalai-domsag e5 170
Zalakomár f5 170
Zalalövő e5 170
Zalamea de la Serena e6 191
Zalamea la Real d7 191
Zalanga g3 223
Zalantun m2 113
Zalaszántó f5 170
Zalaszentgrót f5 170
Zalaszentiván e5 170
Zalaszentmihály e5 170
Zalău f2 201
Załazy k4 169
Žalec g3 177
Zalegošč' d5 150
Zales'e, Kaliningradskaja Oblast', Russ. Fed. k1 169
Zales'e, Vologodskaja Oblast', Russ. Fed. d2 150
Zalesovo v1 121
Zalewo h2 169
Zalim f3 219
Zalingei b5 218
Zalishchyky g1 201
Zalissya g1 201
Zallāf, Wādī az g3 221
Zalmā, Jabal az e2 219
Zalno f2 168
Zaltan g2 221
Zaltan, Jabal a2 219
Zaltbommel d3 159
Zaluč'e a3 150
Zalukhiv n4 169
Zalun b7 102
Zama Lake h2 248
Zamanti f3 209
Zambales Mountains c3 100
Zamberk e1 170
Zambeze e2 233
Zambezi c1 232
Zambezi Escarpment d2 232
Zambezi National Park d2 232
Zambézia b7 231
Zambia e6 217

ZAMBIA

THE REPUBLIC OF ZAMBIA
Area 752,614km^2 (290,586sq miles)
Capital Lusaka
Organizations COMESA, COMM, SADC
Population 10,700,000
Pop. growth (%) 5
Life expectancy 40 (m); 40 (f)
Languages English, Nyanja, Bemba, Tonga, Lozi, Lunda, Luvale
Literacy 80.7%
Currency Zambian kwacha (US $1 = 4610 Zambian kwacha)
GDP (US million $) 3776
GDP per head ($US) 352

Zamboanga d7 100
Zamboanga Peninsula d7 100
Zamboanguita d6 100
Zambrana b2 192
Zambrano, Col. k6 277
Zambrano, Hond. d3 276
Zambrów l3 169
Zambue e2 233
Zambujeira do Mar b7 191
Zamfara, Nig. f3 223
Zamfara, Nig. f3 223
Zamora, Ec. b4 284
Zamora, Ec. b4 284
Zamora, Spain e3 190
Zamora, Spain e3 190
Zamora, U.S.A. b3 264
Zamora de Hidalgo c4 274
Zamora-Chinchipe b4a 284
Zamość k2 169
Zams b2 176
Zamuro, Punta d1 284
Zamzam, Wādī g2 221
Zanaga b4 224
Zanatepec g5 275
Záncara b5 193
Zanda d4 130
Zandamela l2 235
Zanderij f2 285
Zandhoven c3 159
Žandov c1 170
Zandvoort c2 159
Zanesville e6 254
Zangasso c3 222
Zangilan l2 137
Zangla c3 130
Zanhuang d1 106
Zani d6 129
Zanjān, Iran b9 120
Zanjān m3 137
Zanjitas d2 296
Zanskar c3 130
Zanskar Mountains c3 130
Zanthus f12 87
Zantiébougou c3 222
Zanzibar b5 227
Zanzibar Channel g5 225
Zanzibar Island g5 225
Zanzibar North g5 225
Zanzibar South g5 225
Zanzibar West g5 225
Zaoqiang d1 106
Zaorejas b4 192
Zaoshi, Hubei, China c4 106
Zaoshi, Hunan, China b5 106
Zaouatallaz f4 221
Zaoxi f4 111
Zaoyang c3 106
Zaoyangzhan c3 106
Zaō-zan j2 115
Zaozer'e e3 150
Zaozernyy n1 121
Zaozhuang e2 111
Zap, Tur. j4 209
Zap, U.S.A. c7 250
Zapadna Morava e4 200
Zapadnaja Dvina b3 150
Zapadnaja Lica n2 155
Zapadnaya Dvina b3 150
Zapadni Rodopi g5 201
Zapadnyj Berezovyj, Ostrov n2 157
Zapadnyj Kil'din q2 155
Zapadnyj Sajan a2 94
Zapadnyy Alamedin, Pik q6 121
Zapadnyy Chink Ustyurta, Kaz. d5 120
Zapadnyy Chink Ustyurta, Kaz. e6 120
Zapadnyy Kazakhstan c3 120
Zapala b5 296
Zapaleri, Cerro d4 292
Zapallar b2 296
Zapałów l5 169
Zapardiel f3 190
Zapata, Arg. c2 296
Zapata, U.S.A. k4 273
Zapata, Península de d3 266
Zapatoca c2 284
Zapatón d5 191
Zapiga d3 292
Zăpodeni h2 201
Zapol'e d2 150
Zapoljarnyj, Russ. Fed. k2 147
Zapoljarnyj, Murmanskaja Oblast', Russ. Fed. n2 155
Zapopan c3 274
Zaporizhzhya d3 148
Zapotiltic c4 274
Zapotitlán, Jalisco, Mex. c4 274
Zapotitlán, Puebla, Mex. f4 275
Zapotitlán Salinas f4 275
Zapotlanejo c3 274
Zappeio c3 210
Zapponeta e3 198
Zaprešić g4 177
Zaprudnja d3 150
Zaprudy n3 169
Zapug e3 130
Zaqatala g4 149
Zaqqui a2 218
Zara f3 209
Zarafshan k7 120
Zarafshon d1 128
Zaragoza, Col. k7 277
Zaragoza, Chihuahua, Mex. f2 272
Zaragoza, Coahuila, Mex. j3 273
Zaragoza, Nuevo León, Mex. e2 275
Zaragoza, Mex. f4 275
Zaragoza d3 192
Zaragozana d4 192
Zarajsk e4 150
Zarand, Kermān, Iran r6 137
Zarand, Markazi, Iran n4 137
Zarang d4 130
Zaranikh Reserve d1 218
Zaranj a3 122
Zarasai m5 157
Zaratán f3 190
Zárate h3 297
Zarautz b1 192
Zaraza d2 285
Zarbdar m7 121
Zarcilla de Ramos c7 193
Zard b6 129
Zārdab g4 149
Zardak s4 137
Zarečensk n3 155
Zarechka p3 169
Zarečka f3 147
Zarečnyj l3 151
Zāreh m4 137
Zarembo Island l4 247
Zarghat h8 137
Zarghūn Shahr d4 128
Zari c3 128
Zaria f3 223
Zarichne b2 148
Zarīneh Rūd l3 137
Zarinsk v1 121
Žarki h5 169
Zarkos c3 210
Zarmardan a4 128
Zărnești g3 201
Žarnovica g3 171
Żarnów j4 169
Żarnowieckie, Jezioro f1 168
Zaros e7 211
Žarošice e2 170
Zarow j2 173
Żarów e5 168
Zarqān p7 137
Zarra c5 193
Zarubino b2 150
Żary d4 168
Zarza la Mayor d5 191
Zarzaïtine f3 221
Zarzal b3 284
Zarzis g2 221
Zas b1 190
Zasa l4 157
Zasavska f3 177
Zašeek p3 155
Zashchita u3 121
Žaškov h2 171
Zaslawye m5 157
Zásmuky d2 170
Zastražišće f1 198
Zastron g5 235
Žataj n3 119
Žatec b1 170
Zaterečnyj g3 149
Zatobol'sk k5 147
Zatoka k2 201
Zator h6 169
Zaturtsi n5 169
Zatyshshya j2 201
Zauche h3 173
Zaunguzskiye Karakumy g7 120
Zautla f4 275
Zav'jalovo t1 121
Zavalia g3 297
Zavalla, Arg. g2 297
Zavalla, U.S.A. b4 258
Zavallya k1 201
Zavareh p5 137
Zavattarello b5 196
Závažná Poruba h2 171
Zave e2 233
Zavidoviči d3 200
Zavitinsk q1 113
Zavodoukovsk l4 147
Zavodouspenskoe l4 147
Zavods'ke g1 201
Zavolžsk g1 151
Závora, Ponta l2 235
Zawa a7 112
Zawadzkie g5 168
Zawgyi c5 102
Zawichost k5 169
Zawidów d4 168
Zawiercie h5 169
Zawilah h3 221
Zāwiyat Masūs b1 218
Zawr, Ra's az g2 219
Zaya h1 177
Zaysan v4 121
Zaysan, Ozero v4 121
Zayü q5 125
Zazafotsy Ab3 233
Zažina h4 177
Zazir, Oued f4 221
Zbąszyń d3 168
Zbąszynek d3 168
Zbąszyńskie, Jezioro d3 168
Zbiroh b2 170
Zblewo g2 168
Zboriv p6 169
Zborov k2 171
Zbraslavice d2 170
Zbůch b2 170
Zbuczyn Poduchowny l3 169
Ždamirovo j4 151
Žďár nad Sázavou d2 170
Ždiar j2 171
Ždice b2 170
Ždírec nad Doubravou d2 170

ACKNOWLEDGEMENTS

1 Still Pictures/S Rocha/UNEP
2-3 Mount Everest, Nepal/www.impactphotos.com/Yann Arthus-Bertrand
8-9 Cappadocia, Turkey/www.impactphotos.com/ Yann Arthus-Bertrand
10-11 © RD/European Map Graphics Ltd
11 TL © RD/Geo-Innovations
16-17 © RD/Mirashade, senior designer Matt Gould
18 © RD/Mirashade, senior designer Matt Gould
19 TL Science Photo Library/Bernhard Edmaier **21 TL** www.osf.uk.com/Doug Allan **21-22 T** Science Photo Library/NASA **22 TC** Science Photo Library/Michael Marten **BR** Ardea, London/J-M La Roque
23 © RD/Mirashade, senior designer Matt Gould (*4 globes*) © RD/Trevor Bounford
24 (*cormorant*) Science Photo Library/Mark Deeble & Victoria Stone (*crab*) Woodfall Wild Images/Michael Leach (*whale*) Ardea, London/Francois Gohier (*seal*) Science Photo Library/Doug Allan (*tiger shark*) Nature Picture Library/Jeff Rotman **TR** © RD/Mirashade, senior designer Matt Gould (*cod*) Nature Picture Library/Doug Allan (*flying fish*) www.osf.uk.com/Richard Herrmann (*seahorse*) Woodfall Wild Images/Lawson Wood (*squid*) Nature Picture Library/Jeff Rotman (*diatoms*) NHPA/M I Walker **BL** © RD/European Map Graphics Ltd (*smoker vent*) Science Photo Library/Dr Ken MacDonald **24-25** (*cross-section*) © RD/Geo-Innovations (*background*) © RD/Geo-Innovations (*jellyfish*) Ardea, London/Ken Lucas **25** (*globes*) © RD/European Map Graphics Ltd (*starfish*) Nature Picture Library/Jurgen Freund (*tube worms*) Science Photo Library/P Obendrauf (*kelp*) Science Photo Library/Gregory Ochocki (*nudibranch*) Ardea, London/Ken Lucas (*clam*) Nature Picture Library/Jurgen Freund (*angler fish*) Nature Picture Library/David Shale (*hatchet fish*) Nature Picture Library/David Shale (*background*) © RD/Encompass Graphics Ltd
26 L © RD/Mirashade, senior designer Matt Gould **TR** Still Pictures/Gene Rhoden (*hurricane damage*) Panos Pictures/Marc French (*bush fire*) Panos Pictures/Dean Sewell **26-27** (*background*) Still Pictures/Kent Wood **C** © RD/European Map Graphics Ltd
27 TC © RD/Grundy & Northedge (*water temperature*) © RD/Encompass Graphics Ltd **TR** © RD/European Map Graphics Ltd **CR** Science Photo Library/Sam Ogden **BL** Science Photo Library/Fred K Smith **BC** Network Photographers/Mike Goldwater
28 TL Nature Picture Library/Jeff Foott **TR** Still Pictures/Jan-Peter Lahall **CR** Nature Picture Library/Jurgen Freund (*rain forest*) © RD/Jurgen Ziewe (*desert*) © RD/Jurgen Ziewe/Raymond Turvey **B** NHPA/Laurie Campbell **28-29** © RD/European Map Graphics Ltd **29 TL** Woodfall Wild Images/Nigel Hicks **TR** NHPA/Bryan & Cherry Alexander (*tur*) NHPA/Michael Leach (*panda*) Nature Picture Library/Lynn Stone (*tarsier*) NHPA/Daniel Heuclin (*lion*) Bruce Coleman Ltd/Hans Reinhard (*moringa trees*) Ardea, London/Peter Steyn (*orang utan*) Nature Picture Library/Anup Shah (*Great Barrier Reef*) © RD/Jurgen Ziewe (*whale*) Ardea, London/Francois Gohier (*Tasmanian devil*) Nature Picture Library/John Cancalosi
30 T Woodfall Wild Images/Tom Murphy (*eagle*) NHPA/John Shaw (*prairie dogs*) NHPA/Rich Kirchner **BL** Science Photo Library/© 1995, Worldsat International and J Knighton **30-31** (*desert*) NHPA/John Shaw **31** (*bear*) NHPA/John Shaw (*caribou*) Bryan & Cherry Alexander (*wolf*) Ardea, London/Francois Gohier **BR** Nature Picture Library/Jeff Foott (*coyote*) www.osf.uk.com/Mark Hamblin (*lizard*) Ardea, London/Francois Gohier
32 TL Science Photo Library/© 1995 Worldsat International and J Knighton (*macaws*) Nature Picture Library (*capybaras*) Ardea, London (*hoatzin*) Ardea, London/M. Watson (*frog*) NHPA/James Carmichael Jr (*dolphin*) www.osf.uk.com/Norbert Wu (*piranhas*) Nature Picture Library/Hugh Maynard **32-33 T** Nature Picture Library **B** NHPA/Martin Wendler **33** (*ocelot*) Ardea, London (*iguana*) NHPA/Kevin Schafer (*sea lion*) www.osf.uk.com/Tui de Roi (*giant tortoises*) Ardea, London/D. Parer & E Parer-Cook (*crocodile*) Ardea, London/M.Watson (*rainforest*) © RD/Jurgen Ziewe
34 TL NHPA/Vicente Garcia Canseco **TC** Nature Picture Library/Jose B Ruiz **TR** NHPA/Vicente Garcia Canseco **BL** NHPA/John Buckingham (*dolphin*) Nature Picture Library/Tom Walmsley **34-35** (*woodland*) Ardea, London/Bob Gibbons (*mountains*) Woodfall Wild Images/Andreas Leeman **35** (*ptarmigan*) Woodfall Wild Images/Mark Hamblin (*ibex*) Bruce Coleman Ltd/Dr Eckart Pott (*owl*) Bruce Coleman Ltd/Roine Magnusson (*bear*) Ardea, London/S Meyes (*lynx*) www.osf.uk.com/Konrad Wothe (*wolf*) Ardea, London/Jean-Paul Ferrero BR Science Photo Library/© 1995, Worldsat International and J Knighton
36 (*tree*) NHPA/Hellio & Van Ingen (*hedgehog*) NHPA/Daniel Heuclin (*hyena*) NHPA/Anthony Bannister (*cheetah*) www.osf.uk.com/Daniel Cox (*map*) Science Photo Library/© 1995 Worldsat International and J Knighton (*wildebeeste*) Ardea, London/Joanna Van Gruisen (*desert oasis*) © RD/Jurgen Ziewe/Raymond Turvey **36-37** (*camel caravan*) Mauritania/www.impactphotos.com/Yann Arthus-Bertrand **37 T** Ardea, London/Peter Steyn (*gecko*) NHPA/Nick Garbutt (*lemur*) Nature Picture Library/Peter Oxford (*gorilla*) Ardea, London/Adrian Warren (*stork*) Woodfall Wild Images/Mike Lane (*hippo*) Nature Picture Library/Peter Scoones (*Okavango*) Ardea, London/Peter Steyn
38 (*ghats*) Frans Lanting **TR** NHPA/Nick Garbutt **CR** Ardea, London/P Morris **CL** www.osf.uk.com/Mary Plage (*slow loris*) Nature Picture Library/Anup Shah (*panda*) Nature Picture Library/Lynn Stone (*Siberia*) Bryan & Cherry Alexander (*musk oxen*) Ardea, London/Francois Gohier (*snowy owl*) NHPA/Hellio & Van Ingen **39 TC** Science Photo Library/© 1995, Worldsat International and J Knighton (*tiger*) www.osf.uk.com/Mike Powles (*jungle*) NHPA/Martin Harvey (*rafflesia*) Bruce Coleman Ltd/Alain Compost (*orang utan*) Nature Picture Library/Anup Shah
40 TL Science Photo Library/© 1995, Worldsat International and J Knighton (*koala*) NHPA/John Shaw (*wombat*) Nature Picture Library/Dave Watts **BL** Bruce Coleman Ltd/Gerald S Cubitt (*takahe*) Nature Picture Library/Albert Aanensen (*kiwi*) NHPA/ANT Photo Library (*gecko*) Bruce Coleman Ltd/Gerald S Cubitt **40-41** (*kangaroos*) www.osf.uk.com/Adrienne T Gibson/AA (*reef*) NHPA/ANT Photo Library (*whale*) Ardea, London/Francois Gohier
41 TC © RD/Jurgen Ziewe **CL** Bruce Coleman Ltd/Pacific Stock **C** www.osf.uk.com/David Fleetham **CR** www.osf.uk.com/Howard Hall (*penguins*) NHPA/John Shaw (*seal*) Ardea, London/Geoff Trinder
42-43 (*village*) Still Pictures/Sean Sprague **43 BC** Still Pictures/Shehzad Noorani **BL** Panos Pictures/Jon Spaull
44 TR Still Pictures/Jim Wark **44-45 T** The German Space Agency/NASA/DLR **C** Still Pictures/NRSC **B** Getty Images Ltd/Taxi **45 TL** Science Photo Library/Space Imaging Europe
46 TR Still Pictures/Jochen Tack **46-47** (*background*) Digital Vision (*maps*) © RD/Grundy & Northedge **47 BR** © RD/Axos Design
48 TL Science Photo Library/George Haling **CL** Panos Pictures/Bill Stephenson **CR** Science Photo Library/Philippe Plailly/Eurelios (*gauchos*) Network Photographers/Christopher Pillitz **CR** Panos Pictures/Jeremy Hartley **BC** Nike **48-49 T** Network Photographers/Rainer Drexel (*map*) © RD **49 TR** Still Pictures/Julio Etchart **CL** Science Photo Library/Carl Schmidt-Luchs **CR** Panos Pictures/Chris Sattlberger
50 TL Panos Pictures/Mark McEvoy **C** Still Pictures/Ron Giling **CR** Science Photo Library/Pat & Tom Leeson **50-51** (*background: tractor in field, Montana, USA*) www.impactphotos.com/Yann Arthus-Bertrand © RD/Grundy & Northedge
52-53 (*background*) Digital Vision **53 T** © RD/Axos Design
54-55, 56-57, 58-59, 60-61, 62-63, 64-65 © RD/Grundy & Northedge
70-71 (*graphics*) © RD/Grundy & Northedge (*population map*) © RD/Axos Design **71 TR** (*landuse map*) © RD/European Map Graphics Ltd (1) Science Photo Library/CNES, Distribution Spot Image (*Australia*) Science Photo Library/© 1995, Worldsat International and J Knighton (2) Science Photo Library/NASA (3) Science Photo Library/Bernhard Edmaier
88-89 © RD/Geo-Innovations
90 (*Asia*) Science Photo Library/© 1995, Worldsat International and J Knighton (1) Science Photo Library/NASA (2) Science Photo Library/Earth Satellite Corporation (3) www.osf.uk.com/NASA
90-91 (*graphics*) © RD/Grundy & Northedge (*population map*) © RD/Axos Design **91 CR** (*landuse map*) © RD/European Map Graphics Ltd
107-110 © RD/Geo-Innovations **108 TR** © RD/Encompass Graphics Ltd **110 T** © RD/European Map Graphics Ltd **TR** Panos Pictures/Chris Stowers **CR** © RD/Encompass Graphics Ltd **B** © RD/European Map Graphics Ltd
131 BL © RD/Encompass Graphics Ltd **131-134** © RD/Geo-Innovations
133-134 B © RD/Mirashade
140-141 © RD/Geo-Innovations
142 (1) © RD/NASA (*Europe*) Science Photo Library/© 1995, Worldsat International and J Knighton (2) Science Photo Library/Geospace (3) Science Photo Library/CNES, 1998 Distribution Spot Image **142-143** (*population map*) © RD/Axos Design (*graphics*) © RD/Grundy & Northedge **143 TR** (*landuse map*) © RD/European Map Graphics Ltd
203 B © RD/Encompass Graphics Ltd **203-206** © RD/Geo-Innovations Ltd
212-213 © RD/Geo-Innovations
214 (*population map*) © RD/Axos Design **214-215** (*graphics*) © RD/Grundy & Northedge **215** (1) © RD/NASA (*Africa*) Science Photo Library/© 1995, Worldsat International and J Knighton (2) Science Photo Library/Earth Satellite Corporation (3) Science Photo Library/Bernhard Edmaier (*landuse map*) © RD/European Map Graphics Ltd
227-230 © RD/Geo-Innovations **230 R** Science Photo Library/Earth Satellite Corporation
236-237 © RD/Geo-Innovations
238 (*population map*) © RD/Axos Design **238-239** (*graphics*) © RD/Grundy & Northedge **239** (2) Science Photo Library/Earth Satellite Corporation (1) Science Photo Library/Earth Satellite Corporation (*N America*) Science Photo Library/© 1995 Worldsat International and J Knighton (3) Science Photo Library/NASA **BR** (*landuse map*) © RD/European Map Graphics Ltd
267-270 © RD/Geo-Innovations **270 T** © RD/European Map Graphics Ltd **CR** © RD/Encompass Graphics Ltd **B** © RD/European Map Graphics Ltd
278-279 © RD/Geo-Innovations
280 (*S America*) Science Photo Library/© 1995 Worldsat International and J Knighton (2) Science Photo Library/Earth Satellite Corporation (1) Science Photo Library/CNES, 1986 Distribution Spot Image (3) Science Photo Library/NASA **BL** (*landuse map*) © RD/European Map Graphics Ltd **280-281** (*graphics*) © RD/Grundy & Northedge **281** (*population map*) © RD/Axos Design
Cover Geo-Innovations

STATISTICAL SOURCES

The statistical information contained in this book was obtained from the following organizations and reference works.

Organizations

British Petroleum • The Carnegie Institute • Conservation International • The Flag Institute • The Home Office • International Telecommunication Union • North American Space Agency (NASA) • Population Reference Bureau • Telegeography Research Group – PriMetrica Inc • United Nations Children's Fund (UNICEF) • United Nations Development Plan (UNDP) • United Nations Environment Programme (UNEP) • United Nations Food and Agriculture Organization (FAO) • United Nations Statistics Division • United States Census Bureau • The World Bank • World Health Organization (WHO) • World Tourism Organization

Books and Internet sources

The Cambridge Factfinder, Cambridge University Press • *Chambers Book of Facts*, Chambers • *The CIA Factbook* (www.cia.gov/cia/publications/factbook) • *Encyclopaedia Britannica* • *Guide to Economic Indicators*, The Economist • *Guinness Book of Records* • *Pocket Asia in Figures*, The Economist • *Pocket Europe in Figures*, The Economist • *Pocket World in Figures*, The Economist • *Financial Times World Desk Reference*, Dorling Kindersley • *The Statesman's Yearbook*, Palgrave Macmillan • *Times Comprehensive Atlas*, Times Books • *Top Ten of Everything*, Dorling Kindersley • *UN Demographic Yearbook*, United Nations • *UN Population & Vital Statistics Report 2003*, United Nations

The Reader's Digest World Atlas was edited and designed by The Reader's Digest Association Limited, London

First edition Copyright © 2004
The Reader's Digest Association Limited
11 Westferry Circus, Canary Wharf,
London E14 4HE
www.readersdigest.co.uk

Reprinted with amendments 2004

We are committed both to the quality of our products and the service we provide to our customers. We value your comments so please feel free to contact us on **08705 113366** or via our web site at **www.readersdigest.co.uk.**

If you have any comments or suggestions about the content of our books you can contact us at **gbeditorial@readersdigest.co.uk**

Copyright © 2004 by The Reader's Digest Association, Inc.
Copyright © 2004 by The Reader's Digest Association (Canada) Ltd

Copyright © 2004 Reader's Digest (Australia) Pty Limited
Copyright © 2004 Reader's Digest (New Zealand) Limited

Copyright © 2004 Reader's Digest Association Far East Limited
Philippines Copyright © 2004 Reader's Digest Association Far East Limited

Published by Heritage Publishers (Pty) Limited, representing the Reader's Digest Association in Southern Africa. 10 Mill Street, Newlands, 7700, South Africa

All rights reserved. No part of this book may be reproduced, stored in a retrieval system, or transmitted in any form or by any means, electronic, electrostatic, magnetic tape, mechanical, photocopying, recording or otherwise, without permission in writing from the publishers.

© Reader's Digest, The Digest and the Pegasus logo are registered trademarks of The Reader's Digest Association, Inc, of Pleasantville, New York, USA

Origination Colour Systems Ltd
Printing and binding DeAgostini, Italy

PROJECT TEAM
Editor Lisa Thomas
Art Editor Louise Turpin
Senior Designer Austin Taylor
Writer Elizabeth Wyse
Editors Caroline Boucher, Cécile Landau, Marion Moisy
Cartographic Editor Alison Ewington MA Dip.Cart, MA FRGS
Consultants Joan Candy BSc, Jonathan Elphick BSc FZD, Dr Douglas Palmer BSc PhD, Heather Couper BSc DLitt DSc FInstP CPhys FRAS, Nigel Henbest BSc MSc FRAS
Picture Researcher Julie MacMahon
Proofreaders Barry Gage, Rosemary Wighton

UK EDITORIAL TEAM
Editorial Director Cortina Butler
Art Director Nick Clark
Executive Editor Julian Browne
Managing Editor Alastair Holmes
Picture Resource Manager Martin Smith
Pre-press Account Manager Penny Grose

GLOBAL EDITORIAL TEAM
Vice-President and Global Editor-in-Chief Iain Parsons
Deputy Global Editor Chris Walton
Global Design Consultant Tony Cobb
Editor-in-Chief (France) Gérard Chenuet
Senior Editor (Germany) Stefan Kuballa
Art and Art Research Director (Germany) Rudi Schmidt

CARTOGRAPHY
Maps and digital map database European Map Graphics Limited
Production Managers Alan Horsfield, Nigel Wright
Editorial Consultant Craig Asquith
Editorial team Alan Horsfield, Jennifer Skelley, John Watkins
Production team Nigel Wright, Angela Wilson, Amber Banks, Nathan Tidy, Tom Brown, Melissa Pye, Doug Hibbit, Tony Fox, Ian West
Indexing Tony Fox
Traditional relief shading Gizi Map, Budapest
Digital relief mapping Alan Collinson, Geo Innovations

OTHER ILLUSTRATIONS AND MAPS
Axos Ltd, Encompass Graphics, Grundy & Northedge, Jurgen Ziewe, Mirashade

Digital studio Ian Atkinson

Concept code UK1727/G
Book code 400-097-02
ISBN 0 276 42724 6
Oracle 250008306H.00.24

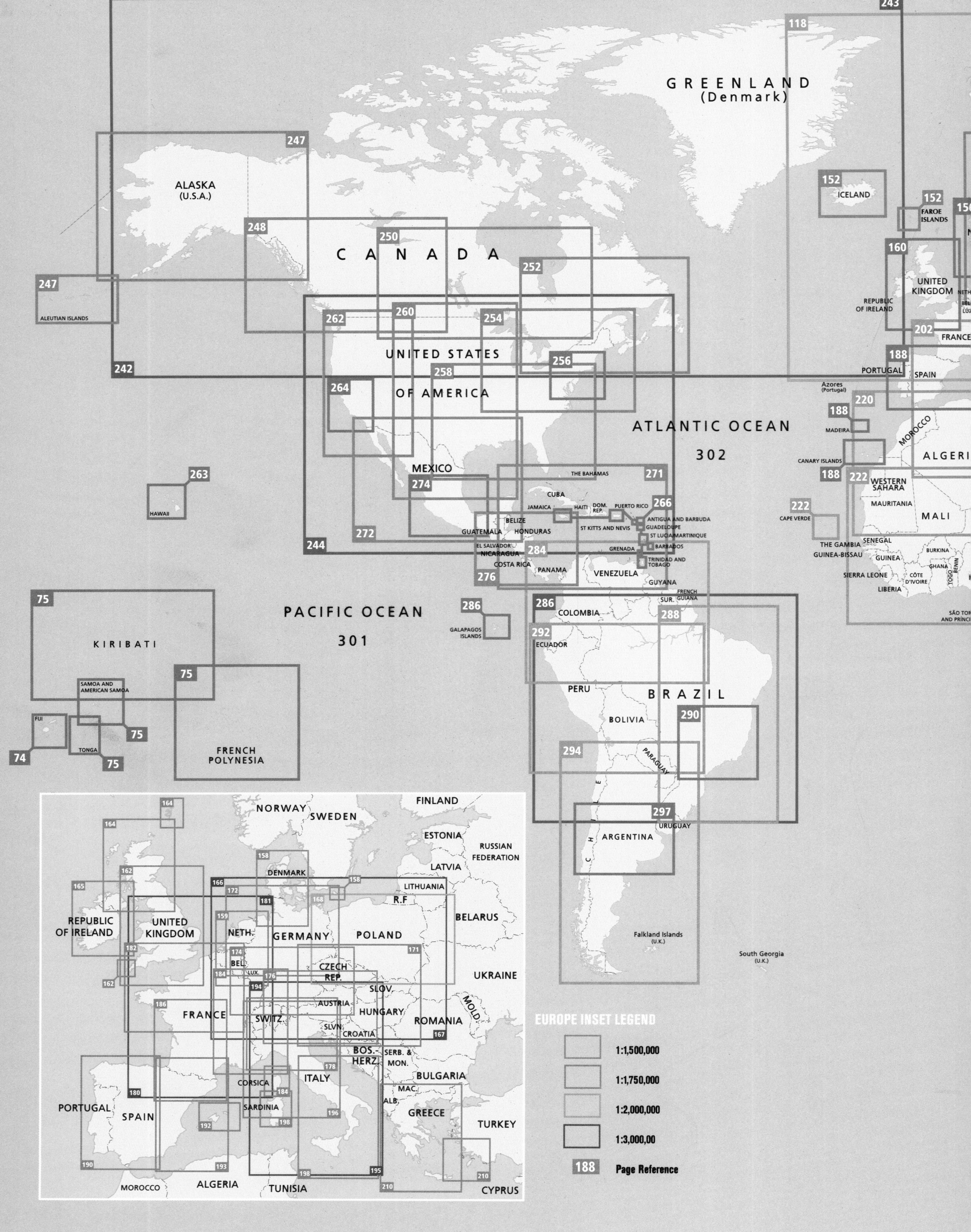

GREENLAND
(Denmark)
243
118
247
ALASKA
(U.S.A.)
248
250
CANADA
252
247
ALEUTIAN ISLANDS
242
262
260
254
UNITED STATES
258
OF AMERICA
256
264
ATLANTIC OCEAN
302
152
ICELAND
152
FAROE ISLANDS
160
UNITED KINGDOM
REPUBLIC OF IRELAND
202
FRANCE
188
PORTUGAL
SPAIN
Azores (Portugal)
220
188
MADEIRA
MOROCCO
ALGERI
CANARY ISLANDS
188
222
WESTERN SAHARA
MAURITANIA
MALI
222
CAPE VERDE
THE GAMBIA
GUINEA-BISSAU
SENEGAL
GUINEA
BURKINA
GHANA
TOGO
BENIN
SIERRA LEONE
CÔTE D'IVOIRE
LIBERIA
SÃO TOM AND PRÍNCI
263
HAWAII
MEXICO
274
272
244
THE BAHAMAS
271
CUBA
JAMAICA
HAITI
DOM. REP.
PUERTO RICO
266
ANTIGUA AND BARBUDA
GUADELOUPE
ST KITTS AND NEVIS
ST LUCIA
MARTINIQUE
BARBADOS
GRENADA
TRINIDAD AND TOBAGO
BELIZE
GUATEMALA
HONDURAS
EL SALVADOR
NICARAGUA
284
COSTA RICA
PANAMA
276
VENEZUELA
GUYANA
FRENCH GUIANA
SUR.
PACIFIC OCEAN
301
286
GALAPAGOS ISLANDS
286
COLOMBIA
288
292
ECUADOR
PERU
BRAZIL
BOLIVIA
290
294
PARAGUAY
297
URUGUAY
CHILE
ARGENTINA
Falkland Islands (U.K.)
South Georgia (U.K.)
75
KIRIBATI
75
SAMOA AND AMERICAN SAMOA
FIJI
74
TONGA
75
75
FRENCH POLYNESIA
NORWAY
SWEDEN
FINLAND
164
164
ESTONIA
RUSSIAN FEDERATION
158
LATVIA
DENMARK
162
165
166
172
158
LITHUANIA
181
R.F
168
BELARUS
REPUBLIC OF IRELAND
UNITED KINGDOM
159
NETH.
GERMANY
POLAND
182
174
171
BEL.
CZECH REP.
UKRAINE
162
184
LUX.
176
194
SLOV.
186
AUSTRIA
MOLD.
FRANCE
SWITZ.
HUNGARY
ROMANIA
SLVN.
CROATIA
167
BOS.-HERZ.
SERB. & MON.
178
CORSICA
ITALY
BULGARIA
180
184
MAC.
ALB.
PORTUGAL
SARDINIA
GREECE
SPAIN
192
198
196
TURKEY
190
193
198
195
210
210
MOROCCO
ALGERIA
TUNISIA
CYPRUS
EUROPE INSET LEGEND
1:1,500,000
1:1,750,000
1:2,000,000
1:3,000,00
188
Page Reference